# LINUX COMPLETE

## Command Reference

Compiled by J. Purcell

**Red Hat Software, Inc.**

201 West 103rd Street
Indianapolis, Indiana 46290

For more information on the Linux operating system and
Red Hat Software, Inc., check http://www.redhat.com.

International Standard Book Number: 0-672-31104-6

Library of Congress Catalog Card Number: 97-66202

2000  99              4  3

Interpretation of the printing code: the rightmost double-digit number is the year of the book's printing; the rightmost single-digit, the number of the book's printing. For example, a printing code of 97-1 shows that the first printing of the book occurred in 1997.

Composed in AGaramond and MCPdigital by Macmillan Computer Publishing

Printed in the United States of America

**TRADEMARKS**

| | |
|---:|:---|
| **President** | Richard K. Swadley |
| **Publisher and Director of Acquisitions** | Jordan Gold |
| **Director of Product Development** | Dean Miller |
| **Managing Editor** | Kitty Wilson Jarrett |
| **Indexing Manager** | Johnna L. VanHoose |
| **Director of Marketing** | Kelli S. Spencer |
| **Associate Product Marketing Manager** | Jennifer Pock |
| **Marketing Coordinator** | Linda Beckwith |

**Acquisitions Editor**
Grace M. Buechlein

**Development Editor**
Brian Proffitt

**Software Development Specialist**
Patricia J. Brooks

**Production Editor**
Kitty Wilson Jarrett
Kate Shoup Welsh

**Copy Editors**
Kimberly K. Hannel
Carolyn Linn
Kristine Simmons

**Indexer**
Christine L. Nelsen

**Technical Reviewer**
Bill Ball

**Editorial Coordinators**
Mandie Rowell
Katie Wise

**Technical Edit Coordinator**
Lynette Quinn

**Editorial Assistants**
Carol Ackerman
Andi Richter
Rhonda Tinch-Mize
Karen Williams

**Cover Designer**
Karen Ruggles

**Book Designer**
Ann Jones

**Copy Writer**
David Reichwein

**Production Team Supervisor**
Beth Lewis

**Production Team**
Erin Danielson, Bryan Flores,
DiMonique Ford, Julie Geeting,
Kay Hoskin, Christy M. Lemasters,
Tony McDonald, Darlena Murray,
Julie Searls, Sossity Smith

# Overview

## Part I User Commands

## Part   II   System Calls

## Part     III     Library Functions

## Part    IX    Kernel Reference Guide

# Tell Us What You Think!

As a reader, you are the most important critic of and commentator on our books. We value your opinion and want to know what we're doing right, what we could do better, what areas you'd like to see us publish in, and any other words of wisdom you're willing to pass our way. You can help us make strong books that meet your needs and give you the computer guidance you require.

Do you have access to the World Wide Web? Then check out our site at http://www.mcp.com.

> **NOTE**
>
> If you have a technical question about this book, call the technical support line at 317-581-3833 or e-mail support@mcp.com.

As the team leader of the group that created this book, I welcome your comments. You can fax, e-mail, or write me directly to let me know what you did or didn't like about this book—as well as what we can do to make our books stronger. Here's the information:

Fax:      317-581-4669

E-mail:   opsys_mgr@sams.mcp.com

Mail:     Dean Miller
          Comments Department
          Sams Publishing
          201 W. 103rd Street
          Indianapolis, IN 46290

# Copyright

exit(2), access(2), alarm(2), close(2), dup(2), fcntl(2), link(2), mkdir(2), mknod(2), open(2), read(2), rename(2), rmdir(2), symlink(2), write(2) copyright © 1992 Drew Eckhardt; 1993 Michael Haardt, Ian Jackson.

unlink(2), remove(3) copyright © 1992 Drew Eckhardt; 1993 Ian Jackson.

chdir(2), chmod(2), chown(2), chroot(2), clone(2), execve(2), fork(2), getrlimit(2), gettimeofday(2), kill(2), nice(2), pause(2), pipe(2), reboot(2), setup(2), stime(2), swapon(2), sync(2), time(2), times(2), umask(2), uname(2), uselib(2), utime(2) copyright © 1992 Drew Eckhardt (drew@cs.colorado.edu), March 28, 1992.

mprotect(2) copyright © 1995 Michael Shields (shields@tembel.org).

select(2) copyright © 1992 Drew Eckhardt, copyright © 1995 Michael Shields.

acct(2), brk(2), intro(2), ioperm(2), phys(2), ptrace(2), setsid(2), termios(2), ascii(7), crypt(3), environ(5), ftime(3), ftw(3), group(5), hd(4), intro(1), intro(3), intro(4), intro(5), intro(6), intro(7), intro(8), isatty(3), issue(5), longjmp(3), mem(4), motd(5), nologin(5), null(4), passwd(5), ram(4), securetty(5), setjmp(3), shells(5), termcap(7), tty(4), ttys(4), ttytype(5), utmp(5), lp(4), perror(3) copyright © 1993, 1994, 1995 Michael Haardt.

bind(2), connect(2), flock(2), fsync(2), getdomainname(2), getdtablesize(2), getgid(2), getgroups(2), gethostid(2), gethostname(2), getpagesize(2), getpid(2), getuid(2), idle(2), iopl(2), profil(2), recv(2), sigvec(2), undocumented(2), vhangup(2), vm86(2), acosh(3), getdiren-tries(3), ctrlaltdel(8), dmesg(8), fdformat(8), fdisk(8), fsck.minix(8), ipcrm(8), ipcs(8), sync(8), sd(4), clear(1), clock(8), domainname(1), mkfs.minix(8), mkswap(8), passwd(1), rdev(8), reset(1), setfdprm(8), setserial(8), shutdown(8), kbdrate(8), update state(8), chkdupexe(1), cytune(8) copyright 1992, 1993, 1994, 1995 Rickard E. Faith (faith@cs.unc.edu).

getdents(2), llseek(2), readdir(2), syslog(2), console.4 copyright 1994, 1995 Andries Brouwer (aeb@cwi.nl).

mount(2) copyright 1993 Rickard E. Faith (faith@cs.unc.edu), copyright 1994 Andries E. Brouwer (aeb@cwi.nl).

adjtimex(2), bdflush(2), ipc(2), modify ldt(2), obsolete(2), socketcall(2), unimplemented(2) copyright © 1995 Michael Chastain (mec@shell.portal.com).

accept(2), getpeername(2), listen(2), lseek(2), getpriority(2), getsockname(2), getsockopt(2), ioctl(2), killpg(2), mmap(2), readlink(2), send(2), setpgid(2), setregid(2), setreuid(2), shut-down(2), sigblock(2), sigpause(2), socket(2), socketpair(2), statfs(2),truncate(2), alloca(3), fclose(3), ferror(3), fflush(3), fread(3), fseek(3), getpass(3), mailaddr(7), popen(3), printf(3), scanf(3), setbuf(3), stdarg(3), stdio(3), banner(6), cal(1), col(1), colcrt(1), colrm(1), column(1), fstab(5), getoptprog(1), logger(1), look(1), lpc(8), lpd(8), lpq(1), lpr(1), lprm(1), lptest(1), mesg(1), mount(8), pac(8), ping(8), syslog.conf(5), syslogd(8), tsort(8), vipw(1), write(1), vi(1), rev(1), biff(1), tset(1), w(1), aliases(5), ftp(1), ftpd(8), inetd(8), newaliases(1), rcp(1), resolver(5), rexecd(8), rlogin(1), routed(8), rpc.rusersd(8), rpc.rwalld(8), rsh(1), rshd(8), rup(1), rusers(1), rwall(1), rwho(1), rwhod(8), sendmail(8), sliplogin(8), talk(1), talkd(8), telnet(1), telnetd(8), tftp(1), tftpd(8), timed(8), timedc(8), traceroute(8) copyright © 1980, 1983, 1985, 1989, 1990, 1991, 1992 The Regents of the University of California. All rights reserved.

getitimer(2) copyright 1993 by Darren Senn (sinster@scintilla.santa-clara.ca.us).

modules(2), ksyms(1), insmod(1), lsmod(1), rmmod(1) copyright © 1994, 1995 Bjorn Ekwall (bj0rn@blox.se).

msgctl(2), msgget(2), msgop(2), semctl(2), semget(2), semop(2), ftok(3), ipc(5) copyright 1993 Giorgio Ciucci (giorgio@crcc.it).

setgid(2), setuid(2), realpath(3) copyright © 1994, Graeme W. Wilford.

# Part I:
# User Commands

# Introduction

This section introduces and describes user commands.

## AUTHORS

Look at the header of the manual page for the author(s) and copyright conditions. Note that these can be different from page to page.

# addftinfo

addftinfo—Add information to troff font files for use with groff

## SYNOPSIS

addftinfo [ -paramvalue... ] res *unitwidth font*

## DESCRIPTION

addftinfo reads a troff font file and adds some additional font-metric information that is used by the groff system. The font file with the information added is written on the standard output. The information added is guessed using some parametric information about the font and assumptions about the traditional troff names for characters. The main information added is the heights and depths of characters. The res and unitwidth arguments should be the same as the corresponding parameters in the DESC file; font is the name of the file describing the font; if font ends with I, the font will be assumed to be italic.

## OPTIONS

Each of the f options changes one of the parameters that is used to derive the heights and depths. Like the existing quantities in the font file, each value is in inches/res for a font whose point size is unitwidth. param must be one of the following:

| | |
|---|---|
| x-height | The height of lowercase letters without ascenders such as x |
| fig-height | The height of figures (digits) |
| asc-height | The height of characters with ascenders, such as b, d, or l |
| body-height | The height of characters such as parentheses |
| cap-height | The height of uppercase letters such as A |
| comma-depth | The depth of a comma |
| desc-depth | The depth of characters with descenders, such as p, q, or y |
| body-depth | The depth of characters such as parentheses |

addftinfo makes no attempt to use the specified parameters to guess the unspecified parameters. If a parameter is not specified, the default will be used. The defaults are chosen to have the reasonable values for a Times font.

## SEE ALSO

font(5) groff_font(5), groff(1), groff_char(7)

*Groff Version 1.09, 6 August 1992*

# afmtodit

afmtodit—Create font files for use with groff -Tps

## SYNOPSIS

afmtodit [ -ns ][-d*desc_file* ][-e*enc_file* ][-i*n* ][-a*n* ] *afm_file map_file font*

## DESCRIPTION

afmtodit creates a font file for use with groff and grops. afmtodit is written in Perl; you must have Perl version 3 installed in order to run afmtodit. afm_file is the AFM (Adobe Font Metric) file for the font. map_file is a file that says which groff character names map onto each PostScript character name; this file should contain a sequence of lines of the form:

*ps_char groff_char*

where ps_char is the PostScript name of the character and groff_char is the groff name of the character (as used in the groff font file.) The same ps_char can occur multiple times in the file; each groff_char must occur, at most, once. font is the groff name of the font. If a PostScript character is in the encoding to be used for the font but is not mentioned in map_file, then afmtodit will put it in the groff font file as an unnamed character, which can be accessed by the \N escape sequence in troff. The groff_font file will be output to a file called font.

If there is a downloadable font file for the font, it may be listed in the file /usr/lib/groff/font/devps/download; see grops(1).

If the -i option is used, afmtodit will automatically generate an italic correction, a left italic correction, and a subscript correction for each character (the significance of these parameters is explained in groff_font(5)); these parameters may be specified for individual characters by adding to the afm_file lines of the form:

```
italicCorrectionps charn
leftItalicCorrectionps charn
subscriptCorrectionps charn
```

where ps_char is the PostScript name of the character, and n is the desired value of the corresponding parameter in thousandths of an em. These parameters are normally needed only for italic (or oblique) fonts.

## OPTIONS

| | |
|---|---|
| -n | Don't output a ligatures command for this font. Use this with constant-width fonts. |
| -s | The font is special. The effect of this option is to add the special command to the font file. |
| -d*desc_file* | The device description file is *desc_file* rather than the default DESC. |
| -e*enc_file* | The PostScript font should be reencoded to use the encoding described in *enc_file*. The format of *enc_file* is described in grops(1). |
| -a*n* | Use *n* as the slant parameter in the font file; this is used by groff in the positioning of accents. By default, afmtodit uses the negative of the ItalicAngle specified in the *afm_file*; with true italic fonts, it is sometimes desirable to use a slant that is less than this. If you find that characters from an italic font have accents placed too far to the right over them, then use the -a option to give the font a smaller slant. |
| -i*n* | Generate an italic correction for each character so that the character's width plus the character's italic correction is equal to n thousandths of an em plus the amount by which the right edge of the character's bounding is to the right of the character's origin. If this would result in a negative italic correction, use a zero italic correction instead. |
| | Also generate a subscript correction equal to the product of the tangent of the slant of the font and four-fifths of the x-height of the font. If this would result in a subscript correction greater than the italic correction, use a subscript correction equal to the italic correction instead. |
| | Also generate a left italic correction for each character equal to n thousandths of an em plus the amount by which the left edge of the character's bounding box is to the left of the character's origin. The left italic correction may be negative. |
| | This option is normally needed only with italic (or oblique) fonts. The font files distributed with groff were created using an option of -i50 for italic fonts. |

## FILES

| | |
|---|---|
| /usr/lib/groff/font/devps/DESC | Device description file |
| /usr/lib/groff/font/devps/*F* | Font description file for font *F* |
| /usr/lib/groff/font/devps/download | List of downloadable fonts |

/usr/lib/groff/font/devps/text.enc          Encoding used for text fonts

/usr/lib/groff/font/devps/generate/textmap  Standard mapping

## SEE ALSO

groff(1), grops(1), groff_font(5), perl(1)

*Groff Version 1.09, 14 February 1994*

# ansi2knr

ansi2knr—Convert ANSI C to Kernighan & Ritchie C

## SYNOPSIS

ansi2knr *input_file output_file*

## DESCRIPTION

If no *output_file* is supplied, output goes to stdout. There are no error messages.

ansi2knr recognizes functions by seeing a nonkeyword identifier at the left margin, followed by a left parenthesis, with a right parenthesis as the last character on the line. It will recognize a multiline header if the last character on each line but the last is a left parenthesis or comma. These algorithms ignore whitespace and comments, except that the function name must be the first thing on the line.

The following constructs will confuse it:

■ Any other construct that starts at the left margin and follows the above syntax (such as a macro or function call)
■ Macros that tinker with the syntax of the function header

*31 December 1990*

# anytopnm

anytopnm—Attempt to convert an unknown type of image file to a portable anymap

## SYNOPSIS

anytopnm *file*

## DESCRIPTION

anytopnm uses the file program, possibly augmented by the magic numbers file included with PBMPLUS, to try to figure out what type of image file it is. If that fails (very few image formats have magic numbers), looks at the filename extension. If that fails, punt.

The type of the output file depends on the input file.

## SEE ALSO

pnmfile(1), pnm(5), file(1)

## BUGS

It's a script. Scripts are not portable to non-UNIX environments.

## AUTHOR

Copyright © 1991 by Jef Poskanzer

*27 July 1990*

# appres

appres—List X application resource database

## SYNOPSIS

appres [[*class* [*instance*]] [-1] [*toolkitoptions*]

## DESCRIPTION

The appres program prints the resources seen by an application (or subhierarchy of an application) with the specified class and instance names. It can be used to determine which resources a particular program will load. For example,

% appres XTerm

will list the resources that any xterm program will load. If no application class is specified, the class -AppResTest- is used.

To match a particular instance name, specify an instance name explicitly after the class name, or use the normal Xt toolkit option. For example,

% appres XTerm myxterm

or

% appres XTerm -name myxterm

To list resources that match a subhierarchy of an application, specify hierarchical class and instance names. The number of class and instance components must be equal, and the instance name should not be specified with a toolkit option. For example,

% appres Xman.TopLevelShell.Form xman.topBox.form

will list the resources of widgets of xman topBox hierarchy. To list just the resources matching a specific level in the hierarchy, use the -1 option. For example,

% appres XTerm.VT100 xterm.vt100 -1

will list the resources matching the xterm vt100 widget.

## SEE ALSO

X(1), xrdb(1), listres(1)

## AUTHOR

Jim Fulton (MIT X Consortium)

*X Version 11 Release 6*


# ar

ar—Create, modify, and extract from archives

## SYNOPSIS

ar [ - ] dmpqrtx[abcilosuvV] [ *membername* ] *archive files* ...

## DESCRIPTION

The GNU ar program creates, modifies, and extracts from archives. An archive is a single file holding a collection of other files in a structure that makes it possible to retrieve the original individual files (called members of the archive).

The original files' contents, mode (permissions), timestamp, owner, and group are preserved in the archive, and may be reconstituted on extraction.

GNU ar can maintain archives whose members have names of any length; however, depending on how ar is configured on your system, a limit on member-name length may be imposed (for compatibility with archive formats maintained with other tools). If it exists, the limit is often 15 characters (typical of formats related to a.out) or 16 characters (typical of formats related to coff).

ar is considered a binary utility because archives of this sort are most often used as libraries holding commonly needed subroutines.

ar will create an index to the symbols defined in relocatable object modules in the archive when you specify the modifier s. Once created, this index is updated in the archive whenever ar makes a change to its contents (save for the q update operation). An archive with such an index speeds up linking to the library, and allows routines in the library to call each other without regard to their placement in the archive.

You may use nm -s or nm —print-armap to list this index table. If an archive lacks the table, another form of ar called ranlib can be used to add just the table.

ar insists on at least two arguments to execute: one keyletter specifying the operation (optionally accompanied by other keyletters specifying modifiers ), and the archive name to act on.

Most operations can also accept further files arguments, specifying particular files to operate on.

## OPTIONS

GNU ar allows you to mix the operation code p and modifier flags mod in any order, within the first command-line argument.

If you wish, you may begin the first command-line argument with a dash.

The p keyletter specifies what operation to execute; it may be any of the following, but you must specify only one of them:

d
Delete modules from the archive. Specify the names of modules to be deleted as files ; the archive is untouched if you specify no files to delete.

If you specify the v modifier, ar will list each module as it is deleted.

m
Use this operation to move members in an archive.

The ordering of members in an archive can make a difference in how programs are linked using the library if a symbol is defined in more than one member.

If no modifiers are used with m, any members you name in the files arguments are moved to the end of the archive; you can use the a, b, or i modifiers to move them to a specified place instead.

p
Print the specified members of the archive to the standard output file. If the v modifier is specified, show the membername before copying its contents to standard output.

If you specify no files, all the files in the archive are printed.

q
Quick append; add files to the end of archive without checking for replacement.

The modifiers a, b, and i do not affect this operation; new members are always placed at the end of the archive.

The modifier v makes ar list each file as it is appended.

Since the point of this operation is speed, the archive's symbol table index is not updated, even if it already existed; you can use ar s or ranlib explicitly to update the symbol table index.

r
Insert files into archive (with replacement). This operation differs from q in that any previously existing members are deleted if their names match those being added.

If one of the files named in files doesn't exist, ar displays an error message and leaves undisturbed any existing members of the archive matching that name.

By default, new members are added at the end of the file, but you may use one of the modifiers a, b, or i to request placement relative to some existing member.

The modifier v used with this operation elicits a line of output for each file inserted, along with one of the letters a or r to indicate whether the file was appended (no old member deleted) or replaced.

t    Display a table listing the contents of archive, or those of the files listed in files that are present in the archive. Normally, only the membername is shown; if you also want to see the modes (permissions), timestamp, owner, group, and size, you can request that by also specifying the v modifier.

If you do not specify any files, all files in the archive are listed.

If there is more than one file with the same name (say, fie) in an archive (say, b.a), ar t b.a fie will list only the first instance; to see them all, you must ask for a complete listing—in our example, ar t b.a.

x    Extract members (named files) from the archive. You can use the v modifier with this operation to request that ar list each name as it extracts it.

If you do not specify any files, all files in the archive are extracted.

A number of modifiers (mod) may immediately follow the p keyletter, to specify variations on an operation's behavior, as follows:

a    Add new files after an existing member of the archive. If you use the modifier a, the name of an existing archive member must be present as the membername argument, before the archive specification.

b    Add new files before an existing member of the archive. If you use the modifier b, the name of an existing archive member must be present as the membername argument, before the archive specification (same as i).

c    Create the archive. The specified archive is always created if it didn't exist when you request an update. But a warning is issued unless you specify in advance that you expect to create it by using this modifier.

i    Insert new files before an existing member of the archive. If you use the modifier i, the name of an existing archive member must be present as the membername argument, before the archive specification. (same as b).

l    This modifier is accepted but not used.

o    Preserve the original dates of members when extracting them. If you do not specify this modifier, files extracted from the archive will be stamped with the time of extraction.

s    Write an object-file index into the archive, or update an existing one, even if no other change is made to the archive. You may use this modifier flag either with any operation, or alone. Running ar s on an archive is equivalent to running ranlib on it.

u    Normally, ar r... inserts all files listed into the archive. If you would like to insert only those of the files you list that are newer than existing members of the same names, use this modifier. The u modifier is allowed only for the operation r (replace). In particular, the combination qu is not allowed, since checking the timestamps would lose any speed advantage from the operation q.

v    This modifier requests the verbose version of an operation. Many operations display additional information, such as filenames processed, when the modifier v is appended.

V    This modifier shows the version number of ar.

## SEE ALSO

binutils entry in info; *The GNU Binary Utilities*, Roland H. Pesch (October 1991); nm(1), anlib(1)

## COPYING

# arch

arch—Print architecture

## SYNOPSIS

arch

## DESCRIPTION

arch displays machine architecture type.

## SEE ALSO

uname(1), uname(2)

*Debian GNU/Linux, 15 January 1994*

# GNU as

GNU as—The portable GNU assembler

## SYNOPSIS .

as [ -a ¦ -al ¦ -as ][-D ][-f ][-I *path* ][-K ][-L ][-o *objfile* ][-R ][-v ][-w ][--\¦\
*files* ...]

i960-only options:

[ -ACA¦ -ACA A ¦ -ACB ¦ -ACC¦ -AKA¦ -AKB ¦ -AKC¦ -AMC][-b ][-no-relax ]

m680x0-only options:

[ -l ][-mc68000¦ -mc68010¦ -mc68020]

## DESCRIPTION

GNU as is really a family of assemblers. If you use (or have used) the GNU assembler on one architecture, you should find a fairly similar environment when you use it on another architecture. Each version has much in common with the others, including object file formats, most assembler directives (often called pseudo-ops) and assembler syntax.

For information on the syntax and pseudo-ops used by GNU as, see as entry in info (or the manual *Using as: The GNU Assembler*).

as is primarily intended to assemble the output of the GNU C compiler gcc for use by the linker ld. Nevertheless, we've tried to make as assemble correctly everything that the native assembler would. This doesn't mean as always uses the same syntax as another assembler for the same architecture; for example, we know of several incompatible versions of 680x0 assembly language syntax.

Each time you run as, it assembles exactly one source program. The source program is made up of one or more files. (The standard input is also a file.)

If as is given no filenames, it attempts to read one input file from the as standard input, which is normally your terminal. You may have to type Ctrl-D to tell as there is no more program to assemble. Use -- if you need to explicitly name the standard input file in your command line.

as may write warnings and error messages to the standard error file (usually your terminal). This should not happen when as is run automatically by a compiler. Warnings report an assumption made so that as could keep assembling a flawed program; errors report a grave problem that stops the assembly.

## OPTIONS

| | |
|---|---|
| -al-all-as | Turn on assembly listings; -al, listing only, -as, symbols only, -a, everything. |
| -D | This option is accepted only for script compatibility with calls to other assemblers; it has no effect on as. |
| -f | "Fast"–skip preprocessing (assume source is compiler output). |
| -I\\*path* | Add path to the search list for .include directives. |
| -K | Issue warnings when difference tables altered for long displacements. |
| -L | Keep (in symbol table) local symbols, starting with L. |
| -o\\*objfile* | Name the object-file output from as. |
| -R | Fold data section into text section. |
| -v | Announce as version. |
| -W | Suppress warning messages. |
| --\¦\*files*... | Source files to assemble, or standard input (--). |
| -A*var* | (When configured for Intel 960.) Specify which variant of the 960 architecture is the target. |
| -b | (When configured for Intel 960.) Add code to collect statistics about branches taken. |
| -no-relax | (When configured for Intel 960.) Do not alter compare-and-branch instructions for long displacements; error if necessary. |
| -l | (When configured for Motorola 68000.) Shorten references to undefined symbols to one word instead of two. |
| -mc68000¦-mc68010¦-mc68020 | (When configured for Motorola 68000.) Specify which processor in the 68000 family is the target (default 68020). |

Options may be in any order, and may be before, after, or between filenames. The order of filenames is significant.

The double hyphens command (−) by itself names the standard input file explicitly, as one of the files for as to assemble.

Except for --, any command line argument that begins with a hyphen (-) is an option. Each option changes the behavior of as. No option changes the way another option works. An option is a hyphen followed by one or more letters; the case of the letter is important. All options are optional.

The -o option expects exactly one filename to follow. The filename may either immediately follow the option's letter (compatible with older assemblers) or it may be the next command argument (GNU standard).

These two command lines are equivalent:

```
as -o my-object-file.o mumble.s

as -omy-object-file.o mumble.s
```

## SEE ALSO

as entry in info; *Using as: The GNU Assembler*, gcc(1), ld(1).

## COPYING

# asciitopgm

asciitopgm—Convert ASCII graphics into a portable graymap

## SYNOPSIS

asciitopgm [-d divisor] *height width* [*asciifile*]

## DESCRIPTION

Reads ASCII data as input. Produces a portable graymap with pixel values that are an approximation of the brightness of the ASCII characters, assuming black-on-white printing. In other words, a capital *M* is very dark, a period is very light, and a space is white. Input lines that are fewer than *width* characters are automatically padded with spaces.

The divisor argument is a floating-point number by which the output pixels are divided; the default value is 1.0. This can be used to adjust the brightness of the graymap; for example, if the image is too dim, reduce the divisor.

In keeping with (I believe) FORTRAN line-printer conventions, input lines beginning with a + (plus) character are assumed to overstrike the previous line, allowing a larger range of gray values.

This tool contradicts the message in the pbmtoascii manual: "Note that there is no asciitopbm tool—this transformation is one-way."

## BUGS

The table of ASCII-to-gray values is subject to interpretation, and, of course, depends on the typeface intended for the input.

## SEE ALSO

pbmtoascii(1), pgm(5)

## AUTHOR

Wilson H. Bent, Jr. (whb@usc.edu)

*26 December 1994*


# atktopbm

atktopbm—Convert Andrew Toolkit raster object to portable bitmap

## SYNOPSIS

atktopbm [*atkfile*]

## DESCRIPTION

atktopbm reads an Andrew Toolkit raster object as input and produces a portable bitmap as output.

## SEE ALSO

pbmtoatk(1), pbm(5)

## AUTHOR

Copyright © 1991 by Bill Janssen

*26 September 1991*

# bash

bash—GNU Bourne–again shell

## SYNOPSIS

bash [*options*] [*file*]

## DESCRIPTION

bash is an sh–compatible command language interpreter that executes commands read from the standard input or from a file. bash also incorporates useful features from the Korn and C shells (ksh and csh).

bash is ultimately intended to be a conformant implementation of the IEEE POSIX Shell and Tools specification (IEEE Working Group 10032).

## OPTIONS

In addition to the single–character shell options documented in the description of the set built-in command, bash interprets the following flags when it is invoked:

| | |
|---|---|
| -c *string* | If the -c flag is present, then commands are read from *string*. If there are arguments after the string, they are assigned to the positional parameters, starting with $0. |
| -i | If the -i flag is present, the shell is interactive. |
| -s | If the -s flag is present, or if no arguments remain after option processing, then commands are read from the standard input. This option allows the positional parameters to be set when invoking an interactive shell. |
| - | A single - signals the end of options and disables further option processing. Any arguments after the - are treated as filenames and arguments. An argument of — is equivalent to an argument of -. |

bash also interprets a number of multicharacter options. To be recognized, these options must appear on the command line before the single–character options.

| | |
|---|---|
| -norc | Do not read and execute the personal initialization file ˜/.bashrc if the shell is interactive. This option is on by default if the shell is invoked as sh. |
| -noprofile | Do not read either the system–wide startup file /etc/profile or any of the personal initialization files ˜/.bash_profile, ˜/.bash_login, or ˜/.profile. By default, bash normally reads these files when it is invoked as a login shell. (See the "Invocation" section, later in this manual page.) |
| -rcfile *file* | Execute commands from file instead of the standard personal initialization file ˜/.bashrc, if the shell is interactive. (See "Invocation.") |
| -version | Show the version number of this instance of bash when starting. |
| -quiet | Do not be verbose when starting up (do not show the shell version or any other information). This is the default. |
| -login | Make bash act as if it had been invoked as a login shell. |
| -nobraceexpansion | Do not perform curly brace expansion. (See "Brace Expansion," later in this manual page.) |
| -nolineediting | Do not use the GNU readline library to read command lines if interactive. |
| -posix | Change the behavior of bash where the default operation differs from the POSIX 1003.2 standard to match the standard. |

## ARGUMENTS

If arguments remain after option processing, and neither the -c nor the -s option has been supplied, the first argument is assumed to be the name of a file containing shell commands. If bash is invoked in this fashion, is set to the name of the file, and the positional parameters are set to the remaining arguments. bash reads and executes commands from this file, then exits. bash's exit status is the exit status of the last command executed in the script.

## DEFINITIONS

| | |
|---|---|
| blank | A space or tab. |
| word | A sequence of characters considered as a single unit by the shell. Also known as a token. |
| name | A word consisting only of alphanumeric characters and underscores and beginning with an alphabetic character or an underscore. Also referred to as an identifier. |
| meta character | A character that, when unquoted, separates words. One of the following:<br>    &#124;, &, ;, (, ), <, >, space, tab |
| control operator | A token that performs a control function. It is one of the following symbols:<br>    &#124;&#124;, &, &&, ;, ;;, (, ), &#124;, \<newline\> |

## RESERVED WORDS

Reserved words are words that have a special meaning to the shell. The following words are recognized as reserved when unquoted and either the first word of a simple command (see "Shell Grammar," next) or the third word of a case or for command:

```
! case  do done elif else esac fi for function if in select then until while { }
```

## SHELL GRAMMAR

### SIMPLE COMMANDS

A *simple command* is a sequence of optional variable assignments followed by words and redirections separated by blank and terminated by a control operator. The first word specifies the command to be executed. The remaining words are passed as arguments to the invoked command.

The return value of a simple command is its exit status, or `128+n` if the command is terminated by signal `n`.

### PIPELINES

A *pipeline* is a sequence of one or more commands separated by the character &#124;. The format for a pipeline is

```
[!]command [ ¦ command2 ... ]
```

The standard output of command is connected to the standard input of `command2`. This connection is performed before any redirections specified by the command. (See the "Redirection" section, later in this manual page.)

If the reserved word `!` precedes a pipeline, the exit status of that pipeline is the logical `NOT` of the exit status of the last command. Otherwise, the status of the pipeline is the exit status of the last command. The shell waits for all commands in the pipeline to terminate before returning a value.

Each command in a pipeline is executed as a separate process (that is, in a subshell).

### LISTS

A *list* is a sequence of one or more pipelines separated by one of these operators: ;, &, &&, or ¦¦, and terminated by one of these: ;, &, or \<newline\>.

Of these list operators, && and ¦¦ have equal precedence, followed by ; and &, which have equal precedence.

If a command is terminated by the control operator &, the shell executes the command in the background in a subshell. The shell does not wait for the command to finish, and the return status is `0`. Commands separated by a ; are executed sequentially; the shell waits for each command to terminate in turn. The return status is the exit status of the last command executed.

The control operators && and ¦¦ denote `AND` lists and `OR` lists, respectively. An `AND` list has the form:

```
command && command2
```

`command2` is executed if, and only if, command returns an exit status of Zero.

An OR list has the form

```
command command2
```

*command2* is executed if, and only if, command returns a non–zero exit status. The return status of AND and OR lists is the exit status of the last command executed in the list.

## COMPOUND COMMANDS

A *compound command* is one of the following:

```
(list)
```

list is executed in a subshell. Variable assignments and built-in commands that affect the shell's environment do not remain in effect after the command completes. The return status is the exit status of list.

```
{ list; }
```

*list* is simply executed in the current shell environment. This is known as a group command. The return status is the exit status of *list*.

```
for name [ in word;] do list ; done
```

The list of words following in is expanded, generating a list of items. The variable name is set to each element of this list in turn, and list is executed each time. If the in word is omitted, the for command executes *list* once for each positional parameter that is set. (See "Parameters," later in this manual page.)

```
select name [ in word;] do list ; done
```

The list of words following in is expanded, generating a list of items. The set of expanded words is printed on the standard error, each preceded by a number. If the in word is omitted, the positional parameters are printed. (See "Parameters.") The PS3 prompt is then displayed and a line read from the standard input. If the line consists of the number corresponding to one of the displayed words, then the value of name is set to that word. If the line is empty, the words and prompt are displayed again. If EOF is read, the command completes. Any other value read causes name to be set to null. The line read is saved in the variable REPLY. The list is executed after each selection until a break or return command is executed. The exit status of select is the exit status of the last command executed in list, or zero if no commands were executed.

```
case word in [ pattern [ ¦ pattern ]
```

A case command first expands *word*, and tries to match it against each *pattern* in turn, using the same matching rules as for pathname expansion. (See "Pathname Expansion," later in this manual page.) When a match is found, the corresponding list is executed. After the first match, no subsequent matches are attempted. The exit status is zero if no patterns are matches. Otherwise, it is the exit status of the last command executed in *list*.

```
if list then list [ elif list then list ] ... [ else list ] fi
```

The if list is executed. If its exit status is zero, the then list is executed. Otherwise, each elif list is executed in turn, and if its exit status is zero, the corresponding then list is executed and the command completes. Otherwise, the else list is executed, if present. The exit status is the exit status of the last command executed, or zero if no condition tested True.

```
while list do list done
```

```
until list do list done
```

The while command continuously executes the do list as long as the last command in *list* returns an exit status of zero. The until command is identical to the while command, except that the test is negated; the do list is executed as long as the last command in *list* returns a non–zero exit status. The exit status of the while and until commands is the exit status of the last do *list* command executed, or zero if none was executed.

```
[ function ] name () { list; }
```

This defines a function named *name*. The body of the function is the list of commands between { and }. This list is executed whenever *name* is specified as the name of a simple command. The exit status of a function is the exit status of the last command executed in the body. (See "Functions," later in this manual page.)

## COMMENTS

In a noninteractive shell, or an interactive shell in which the `-o interactive-comments` option to the set builtin is enabled, a word beginning with # causes that word and all remaining characters on that line to be ignored. An interactive shell without the `-o interactive-comments` option enabled does not allow comments.

## QUOTING

Quoting is used to remove the special meaning of certain characters or words to the shell. Quoting can be used to disable special treatment for special characters, to prevent reserved words from being recognized as such, and to prevent parameter expansion.

Each of the meta characters listed earlier under "Definitions" has special meaning to the shell and must be quoted if it is to represent itself. There are three quoting mechanisms: the escape character, single quotes, and double quotes.

A nonquoted backslash (\) is the escape character. It preserves the literal value of the next character that follows, with the exception of `<newline>`. If a `\<newline>` pair appears, and the backslash is not quoted, the `\<newline>` is treated as a line continuation; that is, it is effectively ignored.

Enclosing characters in single quotes preserves the literal value of each character within the quotes. A single quote may not occur between single quotes, even when preceded by a backslash.

Enclosing characters in double quotes preserves the literal value of all characters within the quotes, with the exception of $, ', and \. The characters $ and ' retain their special meaning within double quotes. The backslash retains its special meaning only when followed by one of the following characters: $, ', ", \, or `<newline>`. A double quote may be quoted within double quotes by preceding it with a backslash.

The special parameters * and @ have special meaning when in double quotes. (See "Parameters," next.)

## PARAMETERS

A *parameter* is an entity that stores values, somewhat like a variable in a conventional programming language. It can be a name, a number, or one of the special characters listed under "Special Parameters," following. For the shell's purposes, a variable is a parameter denoted by a name.

A parameter is set if it has been assigned a value. The null string is a valid value. Once a variable is set, it may be unset only by using the unset built-in command. (See "Shell Built-in Commands," later in this manual page.)

A variable may be assigned to by a statement of the form:

`name=[value]`

If *value* is not given, the variable is assigned the null string. All values undergo tilde expansion, parameter and variable expansion, command substitution, arithmetic expansion, and quote removal. If the variable has its -i attribute set (see `declare` in "Shell Built-in Commands") then *value* is subject to arithmetic expansion even if the `$[...]` syntax does not appear. Word splitting is not performed, with the exception of `"$@"`, as explained under "Special Parameters." Pathname expansion is not performed.

## POSITIONAL PARAMETERS

A *positional parameter* is a parameter denoted by one or more digits, other than the single digit 0. Positional parameters are assigned from the shell's arguments when it is invoked, and may be reassigned using the set built-in command. Positional parameters may not be assigned to with assignment statements. The positional parameters are temporarily replaced when a shell function is executed. (See "Functions," later in this manual page.)

When a positional parameter consisting of more than a single digit is expanded, it must be enclosed in braces. (See "Expansion," later in this manual page.)

## SPECIAL PARAMETERS

The shell treats several parameters specially. These parameters may only be referenced; assignment to them is not allowed.

| | |
|---|---|
| * | Expands to the positional parameters, starting from one. When the expansion occurs within double quotes, it expands to a single word with the value of each parameter separated by the first character of the IFS special variable. That is, "$*" is equivalent to "$1c$2c...", where c is the first character of the value of the IFS variable. If IFS is null or unset, the parameters are separated by spaces. |
| @ | Expands to the positional parameters, starting from one. When the expansion occurs within double quotes, each parameter expands as a separate word. That is, "$@" is equivalent to "$1" "$2" .... When there are no positional parameters, "$@" and $@ expand to nothing (in other words, they are removed). |
| # | Expands to the number of positional parameters in decimal. |
| ? | Expands to the status of the most recently executed foreground pipeline. |
| - | Expands to the current option flags as specified upon invocation, by the set built-in command, or those set by the shell itself (such as the -i flag). |
| $ | Expands to the process ID of the shell. In a () subshell, it expands to the process ID of the current shell, not the subshell. |
| ! | Expands to the process ID of the most recently executed background (asynchronous) command. |
| 0 | Expands to the name of the shell or shell script. This is set at shell initialization. If bash is invoked with a file of commands, is set to the name of that file. If bash is started with the -c option, then is set to the first argument after the string to be executed, if one is present. Otherwise, it is set to the pathname used to invoke bash, as given by argument zero. |
| _ | Expands to the last argument to the previous command, after expansion. Also set to the full pathname of each command executed and placed in the environment exported to that command. |

## SHELL VARIABLES

The following variables are set by the shell:

| | |
|---|---|
| PPID | The process ID of the shell's parent. |
| PWD | The current working directory as set by the cd command. |
| OLDPWD | The previous working directory as set by the cd command. |
| REPLY | Set to the line of input read by the read built-in command when no arguments are supplied. |
| UID | Expands to the user ID of the current user, initialized at shell startup. |
| EUID | Expands to the effective user ID of the current user, initialized at shell startup. |
| BASH | Expands to the full pathname used to invoke this instance of bash. |
| BASH_VERSION | Expands to the version number of this instance of bash. |
| SHLVL | Incremented by one each time an instance of bash is started. |
| RANDOM | Each time this parameter is referenced, a random integer is generated. The sequence of random numbers may be initialized by assigning a value to RANDOM. If RANDOM is unset, it loses its special properties, even if it is subsequently reset. |
| SECONDS | Each time this parameter is referenced, the number of seconds since shell invocation is returned. If a value is assigned to SECONDS, the value returned upon subsequent references is the number of seconds since the assignment plus the value assigned. If SECONDS is unset, it loses its special properties, even if it is subsequently reset. |
| LINENO | Each time this parameter is referenced, the shell substitutes a decimal number representing the current sequential line number (starting with 1) within a script or function. When not in a script or function, the value substituted is not guaranteed to be meaningful. When in a function, the value is not the number of the source line that the command appears on (that information has been lost by the time the function is executed), but is an approximation of the number of simple commands executed in the current function. If LINENO is unset, it loses its special properties, even if it is subsequently reset. |

| | |
|---|---|
| HISTCMD | The history number, or index in the history list, of the current command. If HISTCMD is unset, it loses its special properties, even if it is subsequently reset. |
| OPTARG | The value of the last option argument processed by the getopts built-in command. (See "Shell Built-in Commands," later in this manual page). |
| OPTIND | The index of the next argument to be processed by the getopts built-in command. (See "Shell Built-in Commands.") |
| HOSTTYPE | Automatically set to a string that uniquely describes the type of machine on which bash is executing. The default is system-dependent. |
| OSTYPE | Automatically set to a string that describes the operating system on which bash is executing. The default is system-dependent. |

The following variables are used by the shell. In some cases, bash assigns a default value to a variable; these cases are noted in the following list:

| | |
|---|---|
| IFS | The internal field separator that is used for word splitting after expansion and to split lines into words with the read built-in command. The default value is <space><tab><newline>. |
| PATH | The search path for commands. It is a colon-separated list of directories in which the shell looks for commands. (See "Command Execution," later in this manual page). The default path is system–dependent, and is set by the administrator who installs bash. A common value is /usr/gnu/bin:/usr/local/bin:/usr/ucb:/bin:/usr/bin:. |
| HOME | The home directory of the current user; the default argument for the cd built-in command. |
| CDPATH | The search path for the cd command. This is a colon-separated list of directories in which the shell looks for destination directories specified by the cd command. A sample value is .:¯:/usr. |
| ENV | If this parameter is set when bash is executing a shell script, its value is interpreted as a filename containing commands to initialize the shell, as in .bashrc. The value of ENV is subjected to parameter expansion, command substitution, and arithmetic expansion before being interpreted as a pathname. PATH is not used to search for the resultant pathname. |
| MAIL | If this parameter is set to a filename and the MAILPATH variable is not set, bash informs the user of the arrival of mail in the specified file. |
| MAILCHECK | Specifies how often (in seconds) bash checks for mail. The default is 60 seconds. When it is time to check for mail, the shell does so before prompting. If this variable is unset, the shell disables mail checking. |
| MAILPATH | A colon-separated list of pathnames to be checked for mail. The message to be printed may be specified by separating the pathname from the message with a question mark (?). $_ stands for the name of the current mailfile. |
| | Example: |
| | ```
MAILPATH\
='/usr/spool/mail/bfox?"You have
mail":¯/shell-mail?"$_has mail!"'
``` |
| | bash supplies a default value for this variable, but the location of the user mail files that it uses is system-dependent (for example, /usr/spool/mail/$USER). |
| MAIL_WARNING | If set, and a file that bash is checking for mail has been accessed since the last time it was checked, the message "The mail in mail-file has been read" is printed. |
| PS1 | The value of this parameter is expanded (see "Prompting," later in this manual page) and used as the primary prompt string. The default value is bash\$. |
| PS2 | The value of this parameter is expanded and used as the secondary prompt string. The default is >. |
```

| | |
|---|---|
| PS3 | The value of this parameter is used as the prompt for the select command. (See "Shell Grammar," earlier in this manual page.) |
| PS4 | The value of this parameter is expanded and the value is printed before each command bash displays during an execution trace. The first character of PS4 is replicated multiple times, as necessary, to indicate multiple levels of indirection. The default is +. |
| HISTSIZE | The number of commands to remember in the command history, (See "History," later in this manual page.) The default value is 500. |
| HISTFILE | The name of the file in which command history is saved. (See "History.") The default value is ~/.bash_history. If unset, the command history is not saved when an interactive shell exits. |
| HISTFILESIZE | The maximum number of lines contained in the history file. When this variable is assigned a value, the history file is truncated, if necessary, to contain no more than that number of lines. The default value is 500. |
| OPTERR | If set to the value 1, bash displays error messages generated by the getopts built-in command. (See "Shell Built-in Commands."). OPTERR is initialized to 1 each time the shell is invoked or a shell script is executed. |
| PROMPT_COMMAND | If set, the value is executed as a command prior to issuing each primary prompt. |
| IGNOREEOF | Controls the action of the shell on receipt of an EOF character as the sole input. If set, the value is the number of consecutive EOF characters typed as the first characters on an input line before bash exits. If the variable exists but does not have a numeric value, or has no value, the default value is 10. If it does not exist, EOF signifies the end of input to the shell. This is only in effect for interactive shells. |
| TMOUT | If set to a value greater than zero, the value is interpreted as the number of seconds to wait for input after issuing the primary prompt. bash terminates after waiting for that number of seconds if input does not arrive. |
| FCEDIT | The default editor for the fc built-in command. |
| FIGNORE | A colon-separated list of suffixes to ignore when performing filename completion. (See "Readline," later in this manual page.) A filename whose suffix matches one of the entries in FIGNORE is excluded from the list of matched filenames. A sample value is .o:~. |
| INPUTRC | The filename for the readline startup file, overriding the default of ~/.inputrc. (See "Readline.") |
| notify | If set, bash reports terminated background jobs immediately, rather than waiting until before printing the next primary prompt. (See also the -b option to the set built-in command.) |
| history_control HISTCONTROL | If set to a value of ignorespace, lines that begin with a space character are not entered on the history list. If set to a value of ignoredups, lines matching the last history line are not entered. A value of ignoreboth combines the two options. If unset, or if set to any other value than the preceding, all lines read by the parser are saved on the history list. |
| command_oriented_history | If set, bash attempts to save all lines of a multiple–line command in the same history entry. This allows easy reediting of multiline commands. |
| glob_dot_filenames | If set, bash includes filenames beginning with a period (.) in the results of pathname expansion. |
| allow-null_glob_expansion | If set, bash allows pathname patterns which match no files (see "Pathname Expansion") to expand to a null string, rather than themselves. |
| histchars | The two or three characters that control history expansion and tokenization. (See "History Expansion," later in this manual page.) The first character is the history expansion character; that is, the character that signals the start of a history expansion, |

normally !. The second character is the quick substitution character, which is used as shorthand for rerunning the previous command entered, substituting one string for another in the command. The default is ^. The optional third character is the character that signifies that the remainder of the line is a comment, when found as the first character of a word, normally #. The history comment character causes history substitution to be skipped for the remaining words on the line. It does not necessarily cause the shell parser to treat the rest of the line as a comment.

nolinks
: If set, the shell does not follow symbolic links when executing commands that change the current working directory. It uses the physical directory structure instead. By default, bash follows the logical chain of directories when performing commands that change the current directory, such as cd. See also the description of the -P option to the set builtin ("Shell Built-in Commands").

hostname_completion_file HOSTFILE
: Contains the name of a file in the same format as /etc/hosts that should be read when the shell needs to complete a hostname. The file may be changed interactively; the next time hostname completion is attempted bash adds the contents of the new file to the already existing database.

noclobber
: If set, bash does not overwrite an existing file with the >, >&, and <> redirection operators. This variable may be overridden when creating output files by using the redirection operator >¦ instead of >. (See also the -C option to the set built-in command.)

auto_resume
: This variable controls how the shell interacts with the user and job control. If this variable is set, single word simple commands without redirections are treated as candidates for resumption of an existing stopped job. There is no ambiguity allowed; if there is more than one job beginning with the string typed, the job most recently accessed is selected. The name of a stopped job, in this context, is the command line used to start it. If set to the value exact, the string supplied must match the name of a stopped job exactly; if set to substring, the string supplied needs to match a substring of the name of a stopped job. The substring value provides functionality analogous to the %? job ID. (See "Job Control," later in this manual page.) If set to any other value, the supplied string must be a prefix of a stopped job's name; this provides functionality analogous to the % job id.

no_exit_on_failed_exec
: If this variable exists, a noninteractive shell will not exit if it cannot execute the file specified in the exec built-in command. An interactive shell does not exit if exec fails.

cdable_vars
: If this is set, an argument to the cd built-in command that is not a directory is assumed to be the name of a variable whose value is the directory to change to.

## EXPANSION

Expansion is performed on the command line after it has been split into words. There are seven kinds of expansion performed: brace expansion, tilde expansion, parameter and variable expansion, command substitution, arithmetic expansion, word splitting, and pathname expansion.

The order of expansions is as follows: brace expansion, tilde expansion, parameter, variable, command, and arithmetic substitution (done in a left–to–right fashion), word splitting, and pathname expansion.

On systems that can support it, there is an additional expansion available: process substitution.

Only brace expansion, word splitting, and pathname expansion can change the number of words of the expansion; other expansions expand a single word to a single word. The single exception to this is the expansion of "$@", as explained earlier. (See "Parameters.")

## BRACE EXPANSION

*Brace expansion* is a mechanism by which arbitrary strings may be generated. This mechanism is similar to pathname expansion, but the filenames generated need not exist. Patterns to be brace expanded take the form of an optional preamble, followed by a series of comma-separated strings between a pair of braces, followed by an optional postamble. The preamble is prepended to each string contained within the braces, and the postamble is then appended to each resulting string, expanding left to right.

Brace expansions may be nested. The results of each expanded string are not sorted; left to right order is preserved. For example, a{d,c,b}e expands into ade ace abe.

Brace expansion is performed before any other expansions, and any characters special to other expansions are preserved in the result. It is strictly textual. bash does not apply any syntactic interpretation to the context of the expansion or the text between the braces.

A correctly formed brace expansion must contain unquoted opening and closing braces, and at least one unquoted comma. Any incorrectly formed brace expansion is left unchanged.

This construct is typically used as shorthand when the common prefix of the strings to be generated is longer than in the preceding example, such as

mkdir /usr/local/src/bash/{old,new,dist,bugs}

or

chown root /usr/{ucb/{ex,edit},lib/{ex?.?*,how_ex}}

Brace expansion introduces a slight incompatibility with traditional versions of sh, the Bourne shell. sh does not treat opening or closing braces specially when they appear as part of a word, and preserves them in the output. bash removes braces from words as a consequence of brace expansion. For example, a word entered to sh as file{1,2} appears identically in the output. The same word is output as file1 file2 after expansion by bash. If strict compatibility with sh is desired, start bash with the –nobraceexpansion flag (see "Options," earlier in this manual page) or disable brace expansion with the +o braceexpand option to the set command. (See "Shell Built-in Commands.")

## TILDE EXPANSION

If a word begins with a tilde character (˜), all of the characters preceding the first slash (or all characters, if there is no slash) are treated as a possible login name. If this login name is the null string, the tilde is replaced with the value of the parameter HOME. If HOME is unset, the home directory of the user executing the shell is substituted instead.

If a + follows the tilde, the value of PWD replaces the tilde and + If a - follows, the value of OLDPWD is substituted. If the value following the tilde is a valid login name, the tilde and login name are replaced with the home directory associated with that name. If the name is invalid, or the tilde expansion fails, the word is unchanged.

Each variable assignment is checked for unquoted instances of tildes following a : or =. In these cases, tilde substitution is also performed. Consequently, one may use pathnames with tildes in assignments to PATH, MAILPATH, and CDPATH, and the shell assigns the expanded value.

## PARAMETER EXPANSION

The $ character introduces parameter expansion, command substitution, or arithmetic expansion. The parameter name or symbol to be expanded may be enclosed in braces, which are optional but serve to protect the variable to be expanded from characters immediately following it which could be interpreted as part of the name.

${*parameter*}   The value of *parameter* is substituted. The braces are required when *parameter* is a positional parameter with more than one digit, or when *parameter* is followed by a character that is not to be interpreted as part of its name.

In each of the following cases, *word* is subject to tilde expansion, parameter expansion, command substitution, and arithmetic expansion. bash tests for a parameter that is unset or null; omitting the colon results in a test only for a parameter that is unset.

| | |
|---|---|
| ${parameter:-word} | Use default values. If *parameter* is unset or null, the expansion of *word* is substituted. Otherwise, the value of *parameter* is substituted. |
| ${parameter:=word} | Assign default values. If *parameter* is unset or null, the expansion of *word* is assigned to parameter. The value of *parameter* is then substituted. Positional parameters and special parameters may not be assigned to in this way. |
| ${parameter:?word} | Display Error if null or unset. If *parameter* is null or unset, the expansion of *word* (or a message to that effect if *word* is not present) is written to the standard error and the shell, if it is not interactive, exits. Otherwise, the value of *parameter* is substituted. |
| ${parameter:+word} | Use Alternate Value. If *parameter* is null or unset, nothing is substituted; otherwise, the expansion of *word* is substituted. |
| ${#parameter} | The length in characters of the value of *parameter* is substituted. If parameter is * or @, the length substituted is the length of * expanded within double quotes. |
| ${parameter#word} ${parameter##word} | The *word* is expanded to produce a pattern just as in pathname expansion. If the pattern matches the beginning of the value of *parameter*, then the expansion is the value of *parameter* with the shortest matching pattern deleted (the # case) or the longest matching pattern deleted (the ## case). |
| ${parameter%word} ${parameter%%word} | The *word* is expanded to produce a pattern just as in pathname expansion. If the pattern matches a trailing portion of the value of *parameter*, then the expansion is the value of *parameter* with the shortest matching pattern deleted (the % case) or the longest matching pattern deleted (the %% case). |

## COMMAND SUBSTITUTION

Command substitution allows the output of a command to replace the command name.

There are two forms:

$(*command* )

or

'*command*'

performs the expansion by executing *command* and replacing the command substitution with the standard output of the command, with any trailing newlines deleted.

When the old–style backquote form of substitution is used, backslash retains its literal meaning except when followed by $, ', or \. When using the $(*command*) form, all characters between the parentheses make up the command; none are treated specially.

Command substitutions may be nested. To nest when using the old form, escape the inner backquotes with backslashes.

If the substitution appears within double quotes, word splitting and pathname expansion are not performed on the results.

## ARITHMETIC EXPANSION

Arithmetic expansion allows the evaluation of an arithmetic expression and the substitution of the result. There are two formats for arithmetic expansion:

$[expression]
$((expression))

The expression is treated as if it were within double quotes, but a double quote inside the braces or parentheses is not treated specially. All tokens in the expression undergo parameter expansion, command substitution, and quote removal. Arithmetic substitutions may be nested.

The evaluation is performed according to the rules listed under "Arithmetic Evaluation," later in this section. If *expression* is invalid, bash prints a message indicating failure and no substitution occurs.

## PROCESS SUBSTITUTION

Process substitution is supported on systems that support named pipes (FIFOs) or the /dev/fd method of naming open files. It takes the form of <(*list*) or >(*list*). The process list is run with its input or output connected to a FIFO or some file in /

dev/fd. The name of this file is passed as an argument to the current command as the result of the expansion. If the >(*list*) form is used, writing to the file will provide input for list. If the <(*list*) form is used, the file passed as an argument should be read to obtain the output of list.

On systems that support it, process substitution is performed simultaneously with parameter and variable expansion, command substitution, and arithmetic expansion.

## WORD SPLITTING

The shell scans the results of parameter expansion, command substitution, and arithmetic expansion that did not occur within double quotes for word splitting.

The shell treats each character of IFS as a delimiter, and splits the results of the other expansions into words on these characters. If the value of IFS is exactly <space><tab><newline>, the default, then any sequence of IFS characters serves to delimit words. If IFS has a value other than the default, then sequences of the whitespace characters space and tab are ignored at the beginning and end of the word, as long as the whitespace character is in the value of IFS (an IFS whitespace character). Any character in IFS that is not IFS whitespace, along with any adjacent IFS whitespace characters, delimits a field. A sequence of IFS whitespace characters is also treated as a delimiter. If the value of IFS is null, no word splitting occurs. IFS cannot be unset.

Explicit null arguments ("" or '') are retained. Implicit null arguments, resulting from the expansion of parameters that have no values, are removed.

Note that if no expansion occurs, no splitting is performed.

## PATHNAME EXPANSION

After word splitting, unless the -f option has been set, bash scans each word for the characters *, ?, and [. If one of these characters appears, then the word is regarded as a pattern and replaced with an alphabetically sorted list of pathnames matching the pattern. If no matching pathnames are found, and the shell variable allow_null_glob_expansion is unset, the word is left unchanged. If the variable is set, and no matches are found, the word is removed. When a pattern is used for pathname generation, the character (.) at the start of a name or immediately following a slash must be matched explicitly, unless the shell variable glob_dot_filenames is set. The slash character must always be matched explicitly. In other cases, the (.) character is not treated specially.

The special pattern characters have the following meanings:

| | |
|---|---|
| * | Matches any string, including the null string. |
| ? | Matches any single character. |
| [...] | Matches any one of the enclosed characters. A pair of characters separated by a minus sign denotes a range; any character lexically between those two characters, inclusive, is matched. If the first character following the [ is a ! or a ^, then any character not enclosed is matched. A - or ] may be matched by including it as the first or last character in the set. |

## QUOTE REMOVAL

After the preceding expansions, all unquoted occurrences of the characters \, ', and " are removed.

## REDIRECTION

Before a command is executed, its input and output may be redirected using a special notation interpreted by the shell. Redirection may also be used to open and close files for the current shell execution environment. The following redirection operators may precede or appear anywhere within a simple command or may follow a command. Redirections are processed in the order they appear, from left to right.

In the following descriptions, if the file descriptor number is omitted, and the first character of the redirection operator is <, the redirection refers to the standard input (file descriptor 0). If the first character of the redirection operator is >, the redirection refers to the standard output (file descriptor 1).

The word that follows the redirection operator in the following descriptions is subjected to brace expansion, tilde expansion, parameter expansion, command substitution, arithmetic expansion, quote removal, and pathname expansion. If it expands to more than one word, bash reports an error.

Note that the order of redirections is significant. For example, the command:

`ls > dirlist 2>&1`

directs both standard output and standard error to the file *dirlist*, while the command

`ls 2>&1 > dirlist`

directs only the standard output to file *dirlist*, because the standard error was duplicated as standard output before the standard output was redirected to dirlist.

## REDIRECTING INPUT

Redirection of input causes the file whose name results from the expansion of word to be opened for reading on file descriptor *n*, or the standard input (file descriptor 0) if *n* is not specified.

The general format for redirecting input is

`[n]<word`

## REDIRECTING OUTPUT

Redirection of output causes the file whose name results from the expansion of word to be opened for writing on file descriptor n, or the standard output (file descriptor 1) if n is not specified. If the file does not exist, it is created; if it does exist it is truncated to zero size.

The general format for redirecting output is

`[n]>word`

If the redirection operator is >¦, then the value of the -C option to the set built-in command is not tested, and file creation is attempted. (See also the description of noclobber under "Shell Variables," earlier in this manual page.)

## APPENDING REDIRECTED OUTPUT

Redirection of output in this fashion causes the file whose name results from the expansion of word to be opened for appending on file descriptor *n*, or the standard output (file descriptor 1) if *n* is not specified. If the file does not exist, it is created.

The general format for appending output is

`[n]>>word`

## REDIRECTING STANDARD OUTPUT AND STANDARD ERROR

bash allows both the standard output (file descriptor 1) and the standard error output (file descriptor 2) to be redirected to the file whose name is the expansion of word with this construct.

There are two formats for redirecting standard output and standard error:

`&>word`

and

`>&word`

Of the two forms, the first is preferred. This is semantically equivalent to

`>word 2>&1`

## HERE-DOCUMENTS

This type of redirection instructs the shell to read input from the current source until a line containing only word (with no trailing blanks) is seen. All of the lines read up to that point are then used as the standard input for a command.

The format of here-documents is as follows:

`<<[-]word here-document delimiter`

No parameter expansion, command substitution, pathname expansion, or arithmetic expansion is performed on *word*. If any characters in *word* are quoted, the *delimiter* is the result of quote removal on *word*, and the lines in the *here-document* are not expanded. Otherwise, all lines of the *here-document* are subjected to parameter expansion, command substitution, and arithmetic expansion. In the latter case, the pair `\<newline>` is ignored, and `\` must be used to quote the characters `\`, `$`, and `'`.

If the redirection operator is `<<-`, then all leading tab characters are stripped from input lines and the line containing delimiter. This allows here-documents within shell scripts to be indented in a natural fashion.

## DUPLICATING FILE DESCRIPTORS

The redirection operator:

`[n]<&word`

is used to duplicate input file descriptors. If *word* expands to one or more digits, the file descriptor denoted by *n* is made to be a copy of that file descriptor. If word evaluates to -, file descriptor *n* is closed. If *n* is not specified, the standard input (file descriptor 0) is used.

The operator:

`[n]>&word`

is used similarly to duplicate output file descriptors. If *n* is not specified, the standard output (file descriptor 1) is used. As a special case, if *n* is omitted, and word does not expand to one or more digits, the standard output and standard error are redirected as described previously.

## OPENING FILE DESCRIPTORS FOR READING AND WRITING

The redirection operator:

`[n]<>word`

causes the file whose name is the expansion of word to be opened for both reading and writing on file descriptor *n*, or as the standard input and standard output if *n* is not specified. If the file does not exist, it is created.

# FUNCTIONS

A shell function, defined as described above under "Shell Grammar," stores a series of commands for later execution. Functions are executed in the context of the current shell; no new process is created to interpret them (contrast this with the execution of a shell script). When a function is executed, the arguments to the function become the positional parameters during its execution. The special parameter `#` is updated to reflect the change. Positional parameter 0 is unchanged.

Variables local to the function may be declared with the `local` built-in command. Ordinarily, variables and their values are shared between the function and its caller.

If the built-in command `return` is executed in a function, the function completes and execution resumes with the next command after the function call. When a function completes, the values of the positional parameters and the special parameter `#` are restored to the values they had prior to function execution.

Function names may be listed with the `-f` option to the `declare` or `typeset` built-in commands. Functions may be exported so that subshells automatically have them defined with the `-f` option to the `export` builtin.

Functions may be recursive. No limit is imposed on the number of recursive calls.

# ALIASES

The shell maintains a list of aliases that may be set and unset with the `alias` and `unalias` built-in commands. (See "Shell Built-in Commands."). The first word of each command, if unquoted, is checked to see if it has an alias. If so, that word is replaced by the text of the alias. The alias name and the replacement text may contain any valid shell input, including the meta characters listed above, with the exception that the alias name may not contain `=`. The first word of the replacement text is tested for aliases, but a word that is identical to an alias being expanded is not expanded a second time. This means that one may alias ls to ls -F, for instance, and bash does not try to recursively expand the replacement text. If the last character of the alias value is a blank, then the next command word following the alias is also checked for alias expansion.

Aliases are created and listed with the alias command, and removed with the unalias command.

There is no mechanism for using arguments in the replacement text, as in csh. If arguments are needed, a shell function should be used.

Aliases are not expanded when the shell is not interactive.

The rules concerning the definition and use of aliases are somewhat confusing. bash always reads at least one complete line of input before executing any of the commands on that line. Aliases are expanded when a command is read, not when it is executed. Therefore, an alias definition appearing on the same line as another command does not take effect until the next line of input is read. This means that the commands following the alias definition on that line are not affected by the new alias. This behavior is also an issue when functions are executed. Aliases are expanded when the function definition is read, not when the function is executed, because a function definition is itself a compound command. As a consequence, aliases defined in a function are not available until after that function is executed. To be safe, always put alias definitions on a separate line, and do not use alias in compound commands.

Note that for almost every purpose, aliases are superseded by shell functions.

## JOB CONTROL

Job control refers to the ability to selectively stop (suspend) the execution of processes and continue (resume) their execution at a later point. A user typically employs this facility via an interactive interface supplied jointly by the system's terminal driver and bash.

The shell associates a job with each pipeline. It keeps a table of currently executing jobs, which may be listed with the jobs command. When bash starts a job asynchronously (in the background), it prints a line that looks like this:

[1] 25647

indicating that this job is job number 1 and that the process ID of the last process in the pipeline associated with this job is 25647. All of the processes in a single pipeline are members of the same job. bash uses the job abstraction as the basis for job control.

To facilitate the implementation of the user interface to job control, the system maintains the notion of a current terminal process group ID. Members of this process group (processes whose process group ID is equal to the current terminal process group ID) receive keyboard-generated signals such as SIGINT. These processes are said to be in the foreground. Background processes are those whose process group ID differs from the terminal's; such processes are immune to keyboard-generated signals. Only foreground processes are allowed to read from or write to the terminal. Background processes that attempt to read from (write to) the terminal are sent a SIGTTIN (SIGTTOU) signal by the terminal driver, which, unless caught, suspends the process.

If the operating system on which bash is running supports job control, bash allows you to use it. Typing the suspend character (typically ^Z, Control-Z) while a process is running causes that process to be stopped and returns you to bash. Typing the delayed suspend character (typically ^Y, Control-Y) causes the process to be stopped when it attempts to read input from the terminal, and control to be returned to bash. You may then manipulate the state of this job, using the bg command to continue it in the background, the fg command to continue it in the foreground, or the kill command to kill it. A Ctrl+Z takes effect immediately, and has the additional side effect of causing pending output and typeahead to be discarded.

There are a number of ways to refer to a job in the shell. The character % introduces a job name. Job number *n* may be referred to as %*n*. A job may also be referred to using a prefix of the name used to start it, or using a substring that appears in its command line. For example, %ce refers to a stopped ce job. If a prefix matches more than one job, bash reports an error. Using %?ce, on the other hand, refers to any job containing the string ce in its command line. If the substring matches more than one job, bash reports an error. The symbols %% and %+ refer to the shell's notion of the current job, which is the last job stopped while it was in the foreground. The previous job may be referenced using %-.In output pertaining to jobs (for example, the output of the jobs command), the current job is always flagged with a +, and the previous job with a -.

Simply naming a job can be used to bring it into the foreground: %1 is a synonym for fg %1, bringing job 1 from the background into the foreground. Similarly, %1 & resumes job 1 in the background, equivalent to bg %1.

The shell learns immediately whenever a job changes state. Normally, bash waits until it is about to print a prompt before reporting changes in a job's status so as to not interrupt any other output. If the -b option to the set built-in command is set, bash reports such changes immediately. (See also the description of the notify variable in "Shell Variables," earlier in this manual page.)

If you attempt to exit bash while jobs are stopped, the shell prints a message warning you. You may then use the jobs command to inspect their status. If you do this, or try to exit again immediately, you are not warned again, and the stopped jobs are terminated.

## SIGNALS

When bash is interactive, it ignores SIGTERM (so that kill 0 does not kill an interactive shell), and SIGINT is caught and handled (so that the wait built-in is interruptible). In all cases, bash ignores SIGQUIT. If job control is in effect, bash ignores SIGTTIN, SIGTTOU, and SIGTSTP.

Synchronous jobs started by bash have signals set to the values inherited by the shell from its parent. When job control is not in effect, background jobs (jobs started with &) ignore SIGINT and SIGQUIT. Commands run as a result of command substitution ignore the keyboard-generated job control signals SIGTTIN, SIGTTOU, and SIGTSTP.

## COMMAND EXECUTION

After a command has been split into words, if it results in a simple command and an optional list of arguments, the following actions are taken.

If the command name contains no slashes, the shell attempts to locate it. If there exists a shell function by that name, that function is invoked as described earlier in "Functions." If the name does not match a function, the shell searches for it in the list of shell builtins. If a match is found, that builtin is invoked.

If the name is neither a shell function nor a builtin, and contains no slashes, bash searches each element of the PATH for a directory containing an executable file by that name. If the search is unsuccessful, the shell prints an error message and returns a nonzero exit status.

If the search is successful, or if the command name contains one or more slashes, the shell executes the named program. Argument 0 is set to the name given, and the remaining arguments to the command are set to the arguments given, if any.

If this execution fails because the file is not in executable format, and the file is not a directory, it is assumed to be a shell script, a file containing shell commands. A subshell is spawned to execute it. This subshell reinitializes itself, so that the effect is as if a new shell had been invoked to handle the script, with the exception that the locations of commands remembered by the parent (see hash under "Shell Built-in Commands") are retained by the child.

If the program is a file beginning with #!, the remainder of the first line specifies an interpreter for the program. The shell executes the specified interpreter on operating systems that do not handle this executable format themselves. The arguments to the interpreter consist of a single optional argument following the interpreter name on the first line of the program, followed by the name of the program, followed by the command arguments, if any.

## ENVIRONMENT

When a program is invoked, it is given an array of strings called the environment. This is a list of name/value pairs, of the form name=value.

The shell allows you to manipulate the environment in several ways. On invocation, the shell scans its own environment and creates a parameter for each name found, automatically marking it for export to child processes. Executed commands inherit the environment. The export and declare -x commands allow parameters and functions to be added to and deleted from the environment. If the value of a parameter in the environment is modified, the new value becomes part of the environment, replacing the old. The environment inherited by any executed command consists of the shell's initial environment, whose values may be modified in the shell, less any pairs removed by the unset command, plus any additions via the export and declare -x commands.

The environment for any simple command or function may be augmented temporarily by prefixing it with parameter assignments, as described earlier in "Parameters." These assignment statements affect only the environment seen by that command.

If the -k flag is set (see the set built-in command), then all parameter assignments are placed in the environment for a command, not just those that precede the command name.

When bash invokes an external command, the variable is set to the full path name of the command and passed to that command in its environment.

## EXIT STATUS

For the purposes of the shell, a command which exits with a zero exit status has succeeded. An exit status of zero indicates success. A non–zero exit status indicates failure. When a command terminates on a fatal signal, bash uses the value of 128+signal as the exit status.

If a command is not found, the child process created to execute it returns a status of 127. If a command is found but is not executable, the return status is 126.

bash itself returns the exit status of the last command executed, unless a syntax error occurs, in which case it exits with a non–zero value. (See also the exit built-in command.)

## PROMPTING

When executing interactively, bash displays the primary prompt PS1 when it is ready to read a command, and the secondary prompt PS2 when it needs more input to complete a command. bash allows these prompt strings to be customized by inserting a number of backslash-escaped special characters that are decoded as follows:

| | |
|---|---|
| \t | The current time in *HH:MM:SS* format |
| \d | The date in "Weekday Month Date" format (for example, "Tue May 26") |
| \n | Newline |
| \s | The name of the shell, the basename of $0 (the portion following the final slash) |
| \w | The current working directory |
| \W | The basename of the current working directory |
| \u | The username of the current user |
| \h | The hostname |
| \# | The command number of this command |
| \! | The history number of this command |
| \$ | If the effective UID is 0, a #, otherwise a $ |
| \nnn | The character corresponding to the octal number nnn |
| \\ | A backslash |
| \[ | Begin a sequence of nonprinting characters, which could be used to embed a terminal control sequence into the prompt |
| \] | End a sequence of nonprinting characters |

The command number and the history number are usually different: the history number of a command is its position in the history list, which may include commands restored from the history file (see "History," later in this manual page), while the command number is the position in the sequence of commands executed during the current shell session. After the string is decoded, it is expanded via parameter expansion, command substitution, arithmetic expansion, and word splitting.

# READLINE

This is the library that handles reading input when using an interactive shell, unless the -nolineediting option is given. By default, the line editing commands are similar to those of emacs. A vi-style line editing interface is also available.

In this section, the emacs-style notation is used to denote keystrokes. Control keys are denoted by C-*key*; for example, C-n means Ctrl–N. Similarly, meta keys are denoted by M-*key*, so M-x means Meta-X. (On keyboards without a meta key, M-x means Esc-X; that is, press the Escape key, then the X key. This makes ESC the meta prefix. The combination M-C-x means Esc–Control-x, or press the Escape key then hold the Control key while pressing the X key.)

The default key-bindings may be changed with a /.inputrc file. The value of the shell variable INPUTRC, if set, is used instead of ˜/.inputrc. Other programs that use this library may add their own commands and bindings.

For example, placing

M-Control-u: *universal-argument*

or

C-Meta-u: *universal-argument*

into the /.inputrc would make M-C-u execute the readline command universal–argument.The following symbolic character names are recognized: RUBOUT, DEL, ESC, LFD, NEWLINE, RET, RETURN, SPC, SPACE, and TAB. In addition to command names, readline allows keys to be bound to a string that is inserted when the key is pressed (a macro).

Readline is customized by putting commands in an initialization file. The name of this file is taken from the value of the INPUTRC variable. If that variable is unset, the default is ˜/.inputrc. When a program that uses the readline library starts up, the init file is read, and the key bindings and variables are set. There are only a few basic constructs allowed in the readline init file. Blank lines are ignored. Lines beginning with a # are comments. Lines beginning with a $ indicate conditional constructs. Other lines denote key bindings and variable settings.

The syntax for controlling key bindings in the ˜/.inputrc file is simple. All that is required is the name of the command or the text of a macro and a key sequence to which it should be bound. The name may be specified in one of two ways: as a symbolic key name, possibly with Meta- or Control- prefixes, or as a key sequence. When using the form *keyname:function-name* or *macro*, *keyname* is the name of a key spelled out in English. For example,

```
Control-u: universal-argument
Meta-Rubout: backward-kill-word
Control-o: ">&output"
```

In the preceding example, C-u is bound to the function universal-argument, M-DEL is bound to the function backward-kill-word,and C-o is bound to run the macro expressed on the righthand side (that is, to insert the text >&output into the line).

In the second form, "*keyseq*":*function-name* or *macro*, *keyseq* differs from *keyname* in that strings denoting an entire key sequence may be specified by placing the sequence within double quotes. Some GNU emacs-style key escapes can be used, as in the following example:

```
"\C-u": universal-argument
"\C-x\C-r": re-read-init-file
"\e[11˜": "Function Key 1"
```

In this example, C-u is again bound to the function universal-argument. C-x C-r is bound to the function re-read-init-file, and ESC[11˜ is bound to insert the text Function Key 1. The full set of escape sequences is

| | |
|---|---|
| \C- | Control prefix |
| \M- | Meta prefix |
| \e | An escape character |
| \\ | Backslash |
| \" | Literal " |
| \' | Literal ' |

When entering the text of a macro, single or double quotes should be used to indicate a macro definition. Unquoted text is assumed to be a function name. Backslash will quote any character in the macro text, including " and '.

bash allows the current readline key bindings to be displayed or modified with the bind built-in command. The editing mode may be switched during interactive use by using the -o option to the set built-in command. (See "Shell Built-in Commands.")

Readline has variables that can be used to further customize its behavior. A variable may be set in the inputrc file with a statement of the form:

set variable-name value

Except where noted, readline variables can take the values On or Off. The variables and their default values are as follows:

| | |
|---|---|
| horizontal-scroll-mode (Off) | When set to On, makes readline use a single line for display, scrolling the input horizontally on a single screen line when it becomes longer than the screen width rather than wrapping to a new line. |
| editing-mode (emacs) | Controls whether readline begins with a set of key bindings similar to emacs or vi. editing-mode can be set to either emacs or vi. |
| mark-modified-lines (Off) | If set to On, history lines that have been modified are displayed with a preceding asterisk (*). |
| bell-style (audible) | Controls what happens when readline wants to ring the terminal bell. If set to none, readline never rings the bell. If set to visible, readline uses a visible bell if one is available. If set to audible, readline attempts to ring the terminal's bell. |
| comment-begin ("#") | The string that is inserted in vi mode when the vi-comment command is executed. |
| meta-flag (Off) | If set to On, readline will enable eight-bit input (that is, it will not strip the high bit from the characters it reads), regardless of what the terminal claims it can support. |
| convert-meta (On) | If set to On, readline will convert characters with the eighth bit set to an ASCII key sequence by stripping the eighth bit and prepending an escape character (in effect, using escape as the meta prefix). |
| output-meta (Off) | If set to On, readline will display characters with the eighth bit set directly rather than as a meta-prefixed escape sequence. |
| completion-query-items (100) | This determines when the user is queried about viewing the number of possible completions generated by the possible-completions command. It may be set to any integer value greater than or equal to zero. If the number of possible completions is greater than or equal to the value of this variable, the user is asked whether or not he wishes to view them; otherwise, they are simply listed on the terminal. |
| keymap (emacs) | Set the current readline keymap. The set of legal keymap names is emacs, emacs-standard, emacs-meta, emacs-ctlx, vi, vi-move, vi-command, and vi-insert. vi is equivalent to vi-command; emacs is equivalent to emacs-standard. The default value is emacs; the value of editing-mode also affects the default keymap. |
| show-all-if-ambiguous (Off) | This alters the default behavior of the completion functions. If set to On, words which have more than one possible completion cause the matches to be listed immediately instead of ringing the bell. |
| expand-tilde (Off) | If set to On, tilde expansion is performed when readline attempts word completion. |

Readline implements a facility similar in spirit to the conditional compilation features of the C preprocessor that allows key bindings and variable settings to be performed as the result of tests. There are three parser directives used.

| | |
|---|---|
| $if | The $if construct allows bindings to be made based on the editing mode, the terminal being used, or the application using readline. The text of the test extends to the end of the line; no characters are required to isolate it. |

| mode | The `mode=` form of the `$if` directive is used to test whether `readline` is in emacs or vi mode. This may be used in conjunction with the set keymap command, for instance, to set bindings in the `emacs-standard` and `emacs-ctlx` keymaps only if `readline` is starting out in emacs mode. |
|---|---|
| term | The `term=` form may be used to include terminal-specific key bindings, perhaps to bind the key sequences output by the terminal's function keys. The word on the right side of the - is tested against the full name of the terminal and the portion of the terminal name before the first -. This allows `sun` to match both `sun` and `sun-cmd`, for instance. |
| application | The application construct is used to include `application-specific` settings. Each program using the `readline` library sets the application name, and an initialization file can test for a particular value. This could be used to bind key sequences to functions useful for a specific program. For instance, the following command adds a key sequence that quotes the current or previous word in bash: |

```
$if Bash
# Quote the current or previous word
"\C-xq": "\eb\"\ef\""
$endif
```

| $endif | This command, as shown in the preceding example, terminates an `$if` command. |
|---|---|
| $else | Commands in this branch of the `$if` directive are executed if the test fails. |

`readline` commands may be given numeric arguments, which normally act as a repeat count. Sometimes, however, it is the sign of the argument that is significant. Passing a negative argument to a command that acts in the forward direction (such as `kill-line`) causes that command to act in a backward direction. Commands whose behavior with arguments deviates from this are noted.

When a command is described as killing text, the text deleted is saved for possible future retrieval (yanking). The killed text is saved in a kill–ring. Consecutive kills cause the text to be accumulated into one unit, which can be yanked all at once. Commands that do not kill text separate the chunks of text on the kill–ring.

The following is a list of the names of the commands and the default key sequences to which they are bound.

### Commands for Moving

| | |
|---|---|
| beginning-of-line (C-a) | Move to the start of the current line. |
| end-of-line (C-e) | Move to the end of the line. |
| forward-char (C-f) | Move forward a character. |
| backward-char (C-b) | Move back a character. |
| forward-word (M-f) | Move forward to the end of the next word. Words are composed of alphanumeric characters (letters and digits). |
| backward-word (M-b) | Move back to the start of this, or the previous, word. Words are composed of alphanumeric characters (letters and digits). |
| clear-screen (C-l) | Clear the screen leaving the current line at the top of the screen. With an argument, refresh the current line without clearing the screen. |
| redraw-current-line | Refresh the current line. By default, this is unbound. |

## Commands for Manipulating the History

| | |
|---|---|
| `accept-line (Newline, Return)` | Accept the line regardless of where the cursor is. If this line is non–empty, add it to the history list according to the state of the HIST-CONTROL variable. If the line is a modified history line, then restore the history line to its original state. |
| `previous-history (C-p)` | Fetch the previous command from the history list, moving back in the list. |
| `next-history (C-n)` | Fetch the next command from the history list, moving forward in the list. |
| `beginning-of-history (M-<)` | Move to the first line in the history. |
| `end-of-history (M->)` | Move to the end of the input history, that is, the line currently being entered. |
| `reverse-search-history (C-r)` | Search backward starting at the current line and moving "up" through the history as necessary. This is an incremental search. |
| `forward-search-history (C-s)` | Search forward starting at the current line and moving "down" through the history as necessary. This is an incremental search. |
| `non-incremental-reverse-search-history (M-p)` | Search backward through the history, starting at the current line using a non–incremental search for a string supplied by the user. |
| `non-incremental-forward-search-history (M-n)` | Search forward through the history using a nonincremental search for a string supplied by the user. |
| `history-search-forward` | Search forward through the history for the string of characters between the start of the current line and the current point. This is a nonincremental search. By default, this command is unbound. |
| `history-search-backward` | Search backward through the history for the string of characters between the start of the current line and the current point. This is a nonincremental search. By default, this command is unbound. |
| `yank-nth-arg (M-C-y)` | Insert the first argument to the previous command (usually the second word on the previous line) at point (the current cursor position). With an argument $n$, insert the $n$th word from the previous command (the words in the previous command begin with word 0). A negative argument inserts the nth word from the end of the previous command. |
| `yank-last-arg (M-., M-_)` | Insert the last argument to the previous command (the last word on the previous line). With an argument, behave exactly like @codefyank-nth-argg. |
| `shell-expand-line (M-C-e)` | Expand the line the way the shell does when it reads it. This performs alias and history expansion as well as all of the shell word expansions. See "History Expansion," later in this manual page, for a description of history expansion. |
| `history-expand-line (M-^)` | Perform history expansion on the current line. See "History Expansion." |
| `insert-last-argument (M-., M-_)` | A synonym for yank-last-arg. |
| `operate-and-get-next (C-o)` | Accept the current line for execution and fetch the next line relative to the current line from the history for editing. Any argument is ignored. |

## Commands for Changing Text

| | |
|---|---|
| `delete-char (C-d)` | Delete the character under the cursor. If point is at the beginning of the line, there are no characters in the line, and the last character typed was not C-d, then return EOF. |
| `backward-delete-char (Rubout)` | Delete the character behind the cursor. When given a numeric argument, save the deleted text on the kill–ring. |
| `quoted-insert (C-q, C-v)` | Add the next character that you type to the line verbatim. This is how to insert characters like C-q, for example. |
| `tab-insert (C-v Tab)` | Insert a tab character. |
| `self-insert (a, b, A, 1, !, ...)` | Insert the character typed. |

| | |
|---|---|
| transpose-chars (C-t) | Drag the character before point forward over the character at point. Point moves forward as well. If point is at the end of the line, then transpose the two characters before point. Negative arguments don't work. |
| transpose-words (M-t) | Drag the word behind the cursor past the word in front of the cursor, moving the cursor over that word as well. |
| upcase-word (M-u) | Uppercase the current (or following) word. With a negative argument, do the previous word, but do not move point. |
| downcase-word (M-l) | Lowercase the current (or following) word. With a negative argument, do the previous word, but do not move point. |
| capitalize-word (M-c) | Capitalize the current (or following) word. With a negative argument, do the previous word, but do not move point. |

## *Killing and Yanking*

| | |
|---|---|
| kill-line (C-k) | Kill the text from the current cursor position to the end of the line. |
| backward-kill-line (C-x C-Rubout) | Kill backward to the beginning of the line. |
| UNIX-line-discard (C-u) | Kill backward from point to the beginning of the line. |
| kill-whole-line | Kill all characters on the current line, no matter where the cursor is. By default, this is unbound. |
| kill-word (M-d) | Kill from the cursor to the end of the current word, or if between words, to the end of the next word. Word boundaries are the same as those used by forward-word. |
| backward-kill-word (M-Rubout) | Kill the word behind the cursor. Word boundaries are the same as those used by backward-word. |
| UNIX-word-rubout (C-w) | Kill the word behind the cursor, using whitespace as a word boundary. The word boundaries are different from backward-kill-word. |
| delete-horizontal-space | Delete all spaces and tabs around point. By default, this is unbound. |
| yank (C-y) | Yank the top of the kill ring into the buffer at the cursor. |
| yank-pop (M-y) | Rotate the kill–ring, and yank the new top. Only works following yank or yank-pop. |

## *Numeric Arguments*

| | |
|---|---|
| digit-argument (M-0, M-1, ..., M—) | Add this digit to the argument already accumulating, or start a new argument. M— starts a negative argument. |
| universal-argument | Each time this is executed, the argument count is multiplied by four. The argument count is initially one, so executing this function the first time makes the argument count four. By default, this is not bound to a key. |

## *Completing*

| | |
|---|---|
| complete (TAB) | Attempt to perform completion on the text before point. Bash attempts completion treating the text as a variable (if the text begins with $), username (if the text begins with ˉ), hostname (if the text begins with @), or command (including aliases and functions) in turn. If none of these produces a match, filename completion is attempted. |
| possible-completions (M-?) | List the possible completions of the text before point. |
| insert-completions | Insert all completions of the text before point that would have been generated by possible-completions. By default, this is not bound to a key. |
| complete-filename (M-/) | Attempt filename completion on the text before point. |

*continues*

*Completing*

| | |
|---|---|
| possible-filename-completions (C-x /) | List the possible completions of the text before point, treating it as a filename. |
| complete-username (M-˜) | Attempt completion on the text before point, treating it as a username. |
| possible-username-completions (C-x ˜) | List the possible completions of the text before point, treating it as a username. |
| comploto-variable (M-$) | Attempt completion on the text before point, treating it as a shell variable. |
| possible-variable-completions (C-x $) | List the possible completions of the text before point, treating it as a shell variable. |
| complete-hostname (M-@) | Attempt completion on the text before point, treating it as a hostname. |
| possible-hostname-completions (C-x @) | List the possible completions of the text before point, treating it as a hostname. |
| complete-command (M-!) | Attempt completion on the text before point, treating it as a command name. Command completion attempts to match the text against aliases, reserved words, shell functions, builtins, and finally executable filenames, in that order. |
| possible-command-completions (C-x !) | List the possible completions of the text before point, treating it as a command name. |
| dynamic-complete-history (M-TAB) | Attempt completion on the text before point, comparing the text against lines from the history list for possible completion matches. |
| complete-into-braces (M-{) | Perform filename completion and return the list of possible completions enclosed within braces so the list is available to the shell. (See "Brace Expansion," earlier in this manual page.) |

*Keyboard Macros*

| | |
|---|---|
| start-kbd-macro (C-x () | Begin saving the characters typed into the current keyboard macro. |
| end-kbd-macro (C-x )) | Stop saving the characters typed into the current keyboard macro and save the definition. |
| call-last-kbd-macro (C-x e) | Re-execute the last keyboard macro defined, by making the characters in the macro appear as if typed at the keyboard. |

*Miscellaneous*

| | |
|---|---|
| re-read-init-file (C-x C-r) | Read in the contents of your init file, and incorporate any bindings or variable assignments found there. |
| abort (C-g) | Abort the current editing command and ring the terminal's bell (subject to the setting of bell–style). |
| do-uppercase-version (M-a, M-b, ...) | Run the command that is bound to the corresponding uppercase character. |
| prefix-meta (ESC) | Metafy the next character typed. ESC-f is equivalent to Meta–f. |
| undo (C-_, C-x C-u) | Incremental undo, separately remembered for each line. |
| revert-line (M-r) | Undo all changes made to this line. This is like typing the undo command enough times to return the line to its initial state. |
| tilde-expand (M-˜) | Perform tilde expansion on the current word. |
| dump-functions | Print all of the functions and their key bindings to the readline output stream. If a numeric argument is supplied, the output is formatted in such a way that it can be made part of an inputrc file. |
| display-shell-version (C-x C-v) | Display version information about the current instance of bash. |
| emacs-editing-mode (C-e) | When in vi editing mode, this causes a switch to emacs editing mode. |

## HISTORY

When interactive, the shell provides access to the command history, the list of commands previously typed. The text of the last HISTSIZE commands (default 500) is saved in a history list. The shell stores each command in the history list prior to parameter and variable expansion (see "Expansion," earlier in this manual page) but after history expansion is performed, subject to the values of the shell variables command_oriented_history and HISTCONTROL. On startup, the history is initialized from the file named by the variable HISTFILE (default ˜/.bash_history). HISTFILE is truncated, if necessary, to contain no more than HISTFILESIZE lines. The built-in command fc (see Shell Built-in Commands, later in this manual page) may be used to list or edit and re-execute a portion of the history list. The history builtin can be used to display the history list and manipulate the history file. When using the command-line editing, search commands are available in each editing mode that provide access to the history list. When an interactive shell exits, the last HISTSIZE lines are copied from the history list to HISTFILE. If HISTFILE is unset, or if the history file is unwritable, the history is not saved.

## HISTORY EXPANSION

The shell supports a history expansion feature that is similar to the history expansion in csh. This section describes what syntax features are available. This feature is enabled by default for interactive shells, and can be disabled using the H option to the set built-in command. (See "Shell Built-in Commands," later in this manual page.) Noninteractive shells do not perform history expansion.

History expansion is performed immediately after a complete line is read, before the shell breaks it into words. It takes place in two parts. The first is to determine which line from the previous history to use during substitution. The second is to select portions of that line for inclusion into the current one. The line selected from the previous history is the event, and the portions of that line that are acted upon are words. The line is broken into words in the same fashion as when reading input, so that several meta character–separated words surrounded by quotes are considered as one word. Only the backslash (\) and single quotes can quote the history escape character, which is ! by default.

The shell allows control of the various characters used by the history expansion mechanism. (See the description of histchars under "Shell Variables," earlier in this manual page.)

## EVENT DESIGNATORS

An event designator is a reference to a command line entry in the history list.

| | |
|---|---|
| ! | Start a history substitution, except when followed by a blank, newline, =, or (. |
| !! | Refer to the previous command. This is a synonym for !-1. |
| !n | Refer to command line *n*. |
| !-n | Refer to the current command line minus *n*. |
| !string | Refer to the most recent command starting with *string*. |
| !?string[?] | Refer to the most recent command containing *string*. |
| ^string1^string2^ | Quick substitution. Repeat the last command, replacing *string1* with *string2*. Equivalent to !!:s/ *string1*/*string2*/. (See "Modifiers," later in this manual page.) |
| !# | The entire command line typed so far. |

## WORD DESIGNATORS

A colon (:) separates the event specification from the word designator. It can be omitted if the word designator begins with a ^, $, *, or %. Words are numbered from the beginning of the line, with the first word being denoted by a 0 (zero).

| | |
|---|---|
| 0 (zero) | The zeroth word. For the shell, this is the command word. |
| n | The *n*th word. |
| ^ | The first argument. That is, word 1. |
| $ | The last argument. |
| % | The word matched by the most recent ?string? search. |
| x-y | A range of words; -y abbreviates 0-y. |
| * | All of the words but the zeroth. This is a synonym for 1-$. It is not an error to use * if there is just one word in the event; the empty string is returned in that case. |
| x* | Abbreviates x-$. |
| x- | Abbreviates x-$ like x*, but omits the last word. |

## MODIFIERS

After the optional word designator, you can add a sequence of one or more of the following modifiers, each preceded by a :

| | |
|---|---|
| h | Remove a trailing pathname component, leaving only the head. |
| r | Remove a trailing suffix of the form .*xxx*, leaving the basename. |
| e | Remove all but the trailing suffix. |
| t | Remove all leading pathname components, leaving the tail. |
| p | Print the new command but do not execute it. |
| q | Quote the substituted words, escaping further substitutions. |
| x | Quote the substituted words as with q, but break into words at blanks and newlines. |
| s/old/new/ | Substitute *new* for the first occurrence of *old* in the event line. Any delimiter can be used in place of /. The final delimiter is optional if it is the last character of the event line. The delimiter may be quoted in old and new with a single backslash. If & appears in *new*, it is replaced by *old*. A single backslash will quote the &. |
| & | Repeat the previous substitution. |
| g | Cause changes to be applied over the entire event line. This is used in conjunction with :s (for example, :gs/old/new/) or :&. If used with :s, any delimiter can be used in place of /, and the final delimiter is optional if it is the last character of the event line. |

## ARITHMETIC EVALUATION

The shell allows arithmetic expressions to be evaluated, under certain circumstances. (See the let built-in command and "Arithmetic Expansion.") Evaluation is done in long integers with no check for overflow, though division by 0 is trapped and flagged as an error. The following list of operators is grouped into levels of equal-precedence operators. The levels are listed in order of decreasing precedence.

| | |
|---|---|
| - + | Unary minus and plus |
| ! ~ | Logical and bitwise negation |
| * / % | Multiplication, division, remainder |
| + - | Addition, subtraction |
| << >> | Left and right bitwise shifts |
| <= >= <> | Comparison |
| == != | Equality and inequality |
| & | Bitwise AND |
| ^ | Bitwise exclusive OR |
| ¦ | Bitwise OR |
| && | Logical AND |
| ¦¦ | Logical OR |
| = *= /= %= += -= <<= >>=&=^=¦= | Assignment |

Shell variables are allowed as operands; parameter expansion is performed before the expression is evaluated. The value of a parameter is coerced to a long integer within an expression. A shell variable need not have its integer attribute turned on to be used in an expression.

Constants with a leading 0 are interpreted as octal numbers. A leading 0x or 0X denotes hexadecimal. Otherwise, numbers take the form [*base#*]*n*, where base is a decimal number between 2 and 36 representing the arithmetic base, and *n* is a number in that base. If *base* is omitted, then base 10 is used.

Operators are evaluated in order of precedence. Subexpressions in parentheses are evaluated first and may override the precedence rules.

# SHELL BUILT-IN COMMANDS

: [*arguments*]

No effect; the command does nothing beyond expanding arguments and performing any specified redirections. A zero exit code is returned.

. *filename* [*arguments*]
source *filename* [*arguments*]

Read and execute commands from `filename` in the current shell environment and return the exit status of the last command executed from `filename`. If `filename` does not contain a slash, pathnames in PATH are used to find the directory containing filename. The file searched for in PATH need not be executable. The current directory is searched if no file is found in PATH. If any arguments are supplied, they become the positional parameters when `file` is executed. Otherwise, the positional parameters are unchanged. The return status is the status of the last command exited within the script (0 if no commands are executed), and False if filename is not found.

alias [*name*[=*value*] ...]

alias with no arguments prints the list of aliases in the form *name=value* on standard output. When arguments are supplied, an alias is defined for each name whose value is given. A trailing space in value causes the next word to be checked for alias substitution when the alias is expanded. For each name in the argument list for which no value is supplied, the name and value of the alias is printed. alias returns True unless a name is given for which no alias has been defined.

bg [*jobspec*]

Place *jobspec* in the background, as if it had been started with &. If *jobspec* is not present, the shell's notion of the current job is used. bg jobspec returns 0 unless run when job control is disabled or, when run with job control enabled, if jobspec was not found or started without job control.

bind [-m *keymap*][-lvd][-q *name*]
bind [-m *keymap*] -f *filename*
bind [-m *keymap*]
*keyseq:function-name*

Display current readline key and function bindings, or bind a key sequence to a readline function or macro. The binding syntax accepted is identical to that of .inputrc, but each binding must be passed as a separate argument; for example, "\C-x\C-r": re-read-init-file. Options, if supplied, have the following meanings:

| | |
|---|---|
| –m *keymap* | Use *keymap* as the keymap to be affected by the subsequent bindings. Acceptable *keymap* names are emacs, emacs-standard, emacs-meta, emacs-ctlx, vi, vi-move, vi-command, and vi-insert. vi is equivalent to vi-command; emacs is equivalent to emacs-standard. |
| –l | List the names of all readline functions. |
| –v | List current function names and bindings. |
| –d | Dump function names and bindings in such a way that they can be reread. |
| –f *filename* | Read key bindings from filename. |
| –q *function* | Query about which keys invoke the named function. |

The return value is 0 unless an unrecognized option is given or an error occurred.

break [*n*]

Exit from within a for, while, or until loop. If *n* is specified, break *n* levels. *n* must be 1. If *n* is greater than the number of enclosing loops, all enclosing loops are exited. The return value is 0 unless the shell is not executing a loop when break is executed.

builtin *shell-builtin* [*arguments*]

Execute the specified shell builtin, passing it arguments, and return its exit status. This is useful when you wish to define a function whose name is the same as a shell builtin, but need the functionality of the builtin within the function itself. The cd builtin is commonly redefined this way. The return status is False if *shell-builtin* is not a shell builtin command.

cd [*dir*]

Change the current directory to *dir*. The variable HOME is the default *dir*. The variable CDPATH defines the search path for the directory containing *dir*. Alternative directory names are separated by a colon (:). A null directory name in CDPATH is the same as the current directory, that is, (.). If *dir* begins with a slash (/), then CDPATH is not used. An argument of - is equivalent to $OLDPWD. The return value is True if the directory was successfully changed; False otherwise.

**command [-pVv] *command* [*arg* ...]**

Run command with args suppressing the normal shell function lookup. Only built-in commands or commands found in the PATH are executed. If the -p option is given, the search for *command* is performed using a default value for PATH that is guaranteed to find all of the standard utilities. If either the -V or -v option is supplied, a description of *command* is printed. The -v option causes a single word indicating the command or pathname used to invoke command to be printed; the -V option produces a more verbose description. An argument of —disables option checking for the rest of the arguments. If the -V or -v option is supplied, the exit status is 0 if *command* was found, and 1 if not. If neither option is supplied and an error occurred or *command* cannot be found, the exit status is 127. Otherwise, the exit status of the command builtin is the exit status of *command*.

**continue [*n*]**

Resume the next iteration of the enclosing for, while, or until loop. If *n* is specified, resume at the nth enclosing loop. *n* must be 1. If *n* is greater than the number of enclosing loops, the last enclosing loop (the top–level loop) is resumed. The return value is 0 unless the shell is not executing a loop when continue is executed.

**declare [-frxi][*name*[=*value*]]**
**typeset [-frxi][*name*[=*value*]]**

Declare variables and/or give them attributes. If no names are given, then display the values of variables instead. The options can be used to restrict output to variables with the specified attribute.

| | |
|---|---|
| -f | Use function names only. |
| -r | Make names read-only. These names cannot then be assigned values by subsequent assignment statements. |
| -x | Mark names for export to subsequent commands via the environment. |
| -i | The variable is treated as an integer; arithmetic evaluation (see "Arithmetic Evaluation") is performed when the variable is assigned a value. |

Using + instead of - turns off the attribute instead. When used in a function, makes names local, as with the local command. The return value is 0 unless an illegal option is encountered, an attempt is made to define a function using "-f foo=bar", one of the names is not a legal shell variable name, an attempt is made to turn off read-only status for a read-only variable, or an attempt is made to display a nonexistent function with -f.

**dirs [-l][+/-*n*]**

Display the list of currently remembered directories. Directories are added to the list with the pushd command; the popd command moves back up through the list.

| | |
|---|---|
| +*n* | Displays the nth entry counting from the left of the list shown by dirs when invoked without options, starting with zero. |
| -*n* | Displays the nth entry counting from the right of the list shown by dirs when invoked without options, starting with zero. |
| -l | Produces a longer listing; the default listing format uses a tilde to denote the home directory. |

The return value is 0 unless an illegal option is supplied or n indexes beyond the end of the directory stack.

**echo [-neE][*arg* ...]**

Output the args, separated by spaces. The return status is always 0. If -*n* is specified, the trailing newline is suppressed. If the -e option is given, interpretation of the following backslash-escaped characters is enabled. The -E option disables the interpretation of these escape characters, even on systems where they are interpreted by default.

| | |
|---|---|
| \a | Alert (bell) |
| \b | Backspace |
| \c | Suppress trailing newline |
| \f | Form feed |
| \n | Newline |
| \r | Carriage return |
| \t | Horizontal tab |
| \v | Vertical tab |
| \\ | Backslash |
| \nnn | The character whose ASCII code is nnn (octal) |

**enable [-n][-all][name ...]**

Enable and disable builtin shell commands. This allows the execution of a disk command that has the same name as a shell builtin without specifying a full pathname. If -n is used, each name is disabled; otherwise, names are enabled. For example, to use the test binary found via the PATH instead of the shell builtin version, type enable -n test. If no arguments are given, a list of all enabled shell builtins is printed. If only -n is supplied, a list of all disabled builtins is printed. If only -all is supplied, the list printed includes all builtins, with an indication of whether or not each is enabled. enable accepts -a as a synonym for -all. The return value is 0 unless a name is not a shell builtin.

**eval [arg ...]**

The args are read and concatenated together into a single command. This command is then read and executed by the shell, and its exit status is returned as the value of the eval command. If there are no args, or only null arguments, eval returns True.

**exec [[-] command [arguments]]**

If command is specified, it replaces the shell. No new process is created. The arguments become the arguments to command. If the first argument is -, the shell places a dash in the zeroth arg passed to command. This is what login does. If the file cannot be executed for some reason, a noninteractive shell exits, unless the shell variable no_exit_on_failed_exec exists, in which case it returns failure. An interactive shell returns failure if the file cannot be executed. If command is not specified, any redirections take effect in the current shell, and the return status is 0.

**exit [n]**

Cause the shell to exit with a status of n. If n is omitted, the exit status is that of the last command executed. A trap on exit is executed before the shell terminates.

**export [-nf][name[=word]] ...**
**export -p**

The supplied names are marked for automatic export to the environment of subsequently executed commands. If the -f option is given, the names refer to functions. If no names are given, or if the -p option is supplied, a list of all names that are exported in this shell is printed. The -n option causes the export property to be removed from the named variables. An argument of — disables option checking for the rest of the arguments. export returns an exit status of 0 unless an illegal option is encountered, one of the names is not a legal shell variable name, or -f is supplied with a name that is not a function.

**fc [-e ename][-nlr][first][last]**
**fc -s [pat=rep][cmd]**

Fix command. In the first form, a range of commands from first to last is selected from the history list. first and last may be specified as a string (to locate the last command beginning with that string) or as a number (an index into the history list, where a negative number is used as an offset from the current command number). If last is not specified, it is set to the current command for listing (so that fc -1 -10 prints the last 10 commands) and to first otherwise. If first is not specified, it is set to the previous command for editing and -16 for listing.

The -n flag suppresses the command numbers when listing. The -r flag reverses the order of the commands. If the -l flag is given, the commands are listed on standard output. Otherwise, the editor given by ename is invoked on a file containing those commands. If ename is not given, the value of the FCEDIT variable is used, and the value of EDITOR if FCEDIT is not set. If neither variable is set, vi is used. When editing is complete, the edited commands are echoed and executed.

In the second form, *command* is reexecuted after each instance of *pat* is replaced by *rep*. A useful alias to use with this is r=fc -s, so that typing r cc runs the last command beginning with cc and typing r reexecutes the last command.

If the first form is used, the return value is 0 unless an illegal option is encountered or *first* or *last* specify history lines out of range. If the -e option is supplied, the return value is the value of the last command executed or failure if an error occurs with the temporary file of commands. If the second form is used, the return status is that of the command reexecuted, unless cmd does not specify a valid history line, in which case fc returns failure.

**fg [*jobspec*]**

Place *jobspec* in the foreground, and make it the current job. If *jobspec* is not present, the shell's notion of the current job is used. The return value is that of the command placed into the foreground, or failure if run when job control is disabled or, when run with job control enabled, if *jobspec* does not specify a valid job or *jobspec* specifies a job that was started without job control.

**getopts *optstring* name [*args*]**

getopts is used by shell procedures to parse positional parameters. *optstring* contains the option letters to be recognized; if a letter is followed by a colon, the option is expected to have an argument, which should be separated from it by whitespace. Each time it is invoked, getopts places the next option in the shell variable name, initializing *name* if it does not exist, and the index of the next argument to be processed into the variable OPTIND. OPTIND is initialized to 1 each time the shell or a shell script is invoked. When an option requires an argument, getopts places that argument into the variable OPTARG. The shell does not reset OPTIND automatically; it must be manually reset between multiple calls to getopts within the same shell invocation if a new set of parameters is to be used.

getopts can report errors in two ways. If the first character of *optstring* is a colon, silent error reporting is used. In normal operation, diagnostic messages are printed when illegal options or missing option arguments are encountered. If the variable OPTERR is set to 0, no error message will be displayed, even if the first character of *optstring* is not a colon.

If an illegal option is seen, getopts places a question mark (?) into *name* and, if not silent, prints an error message and unsets OPTARG. If getopts is silent, the option character found is placed in OP-TARG and no diagnostic message is printed.

If a required argument is not found, and getopts is not silent, a question mark (?) is placed in *name*, OPTARG is unset, and a diagnostic message is printed. If getopts is silent, then a colon (:) is placed in *name* and OPTARG is set to the option character found.

getopts normally parses the positional parameters, but if more arguments are given in args, getopts parses those instead. getopts returns True if an option, specified or unspecified, is found. It returns False if the end of options is encountered or an error occurs.

**hash [-r][*name*]**

For each *name*, the full pathname of the command is determined and remembered. The -r option causes the shell to forget all remembered locations. If no arguments are given, information about remembered commands is printed. An argument of — disables option checking for the rest of the arguments. The return status is True unless a name is not found or an illegal option is supplied.

**help [*pattern*]**

Display helpful information about built-in commands. If *pattern* is specified, help gives detailed help on all commands matching pattern; otherwise, a list of the builtins is printed. The return status is 0 unless no command matches pattern.

| | |
|---|---|
| `history [n]`<br>`history -rwan [filename]` | With no options, display the command history list with line numbers. Lines listed with a * have been modified. An argument of *n* lists only the *last n* lines. If a nonoption argument is supplied, it is used as the name of the history file; if not, the value of HISTFILE is used. Options, if supplied, have the following meanings: |

| | |
|---|---|
| -a | Append the "new" history lines (history lines entered since the beginning of the current bash session) to the history file. |
| -n | Read the history lines not already read from the history file into the current history list. These are lines appended to the history file since the beginning of the current bash session. |
| -r | Read the contents of the history file and use them as the current history. |
| w- | Write the current history to the history file, overwriting the history file's contents. |

The return value is 0 unless an illegal option is encountered or an error occurs while reading or writing the history file.

| | |
|---|---|
| `jobs [-lnp][jobspec ... ]`<br>`jobs -x command [ args ... ]` | The first form lists the active jobs. The -l option lists process IDs in addition to the normal information; the -p option lists only the process ID of the job's process group leader. The -n option displays only jobs that have changed status since last notified. If *jobspec* is given, output is restricted to information about that job. The return status is 0 unless an illegal option is encountered or an illegal *jobspec* is supplied. |

If the -x option is supplied, jobs replaces any *jobspec* found in *command* or *args* with the corresponding process group ID, and executes *command*, passing it *args*, returning its exit status.

| | |
|---|---|
| `kill [-s sigspec ¦ -sigspec]`<br>`[pid ¦ jobspec] ...`<br>`kill -l [signum]` | Send the signal named by sigspec to the processes named by *pid* or *jobspec*. *sigspec* is either a signal name such as SIGKILL or a signal number. If *sigspec* is a signal name, the name is not case sensitive and may be given with or without the SIG prefix. If sigspec is not present, then SIGTERM is assumed. An argument of -l lists the signal names. If any arguments are supplied when -l is given, the names of the specified signals are listed, and the return status is 0. An argument of — disables option checking for the rest of the arguments. kill returns True if at least one signal was successfully sent, or False if an error occurs or an illegal option is encountered. |

| | |
|---|---|
| `let arg [arg ...]` | Each *arg* is an arithmetic expression to be evaluated. (See "Arithmetic Evaluation.") If the last *arg* evaluates to 0, let returns 1; 0 is returned otherwise. |

| | |
|---|---|
| `local [name[=value] ...]` | For each argument, create a local variable named *name*, and assign it *value*. When local is used within a function, it causes the variable name to have a visible scope restricted to that function and its children. With no operands, local writes a list of local variables to the standard output. It is an error to use local when not within a function. The return status is 0 unless local is used outside a function, or an illegal name is supplied. |

| | |
|---|---|
| `logout` | Exit a login shell. |
| `popd [+/-n]` | Removes entries from the directory stack. With no arguments, removes the top directory from the stack, and performs a cd to the new top directory. |

| | |
|---|---|
| +n | Removes the nth entry counting from the left of the list shown by dirs, starting with zero. For example, popd +0 removes the first directory, popd +1 the second. |
| -n | Removes the nth entry counting from the right of the list shown by dirs, starting with zero. For example, popd -0 removes the last directory, popd -1 the next to last. |

If the popd command is successful, a dirs is performed as well, and the return status is 0. popd returns False if an illegal option is encountered, the directory stack is empty, a nonexistent directory stack entry is specified, or the directory change fails.

pushd [*dir*] pushd +/-*n*     Adds a directory to the top of the directory stack, or rotates the stack, making the new top of the stack the current working directory. With no arguments, exchanges the top two directories and returns 0, unless the directory stack is empty.

| | |
|---|---|
| +*n* | Rotates the stack so that the nth directory (counting from the left of the list shown by dirs) is at the top. |
| -*n* | Rotates the stack so that the nth directory (counting from the right) is at the top. |
| *dir* | Adds *dir* to the directory stack at the top, making it the new current working directory. |

If the pushd command is successful, a dirs is performed as well. If the first form is used, pushd returns 0 unless the cd to *dir* fails. With the second form, pushd returns 0 unless the directory stack is empty, a nonexistent directory stack element is specified, or the directory change to the specified new current directory fails.

pwd     Print the absolute pathname of the current working directory. The path printed contains no symbolic links if the -P option to the set builtin command is set. (See also the description of nolinks under "Shell Variables," earlier in this manual page.) The return status is 0 unless an error occurs while reading the pathname of the current directory.

read [-r][*name* ...]     One line is read from the standard input, and the first word is assigned to the first name, the second word to the second name, and so on, with leftover words assigned to the last name. Only the characters in IFS are recognized as word delimiters. If no names are supplied, the line read is assigned to the variable REPLY. The return code is zero, unless end-of-file is encountered. If the -r option is given, a backslash-newline pair is not ignored, and the backslash is considered to be part of the line.

readonly [-f][*name* ...]  
readonly -p     The given names are marked readonly and the values of these names may not be changed by subsequent assignment. If the -f option is supplied, the functions corresponding to the names are so marked. If no arguments are given, or if the -p option is supplied, a list of all readonly names is printed. An argument of — disables option checking for the rest of the arguments. The return status is 0 unless an illegal option is encountered, one of the names is not a legal shell variable name, or -f is supplied with a name that is not a function.

return [*n*]     Causes a function to exit with the return value specified by *n*. If *n* is omitted, the return status is that of the last command executed in the function body. If used outside a function, but during execution of a script by the . (source) command, it causes the shell to stop executing that script and return either *n* or the exit status of the last command executed within the script as the exit status of the script. If used outside a function and not during execution of a script by (. , the return status is False.

set [ —abefhkmnptuvxldCHP]  
[-o option][*arg* ...]

| | |
|---|---|
| -a | Automatically mark variables that are modified or created for export to the environment of subsequent commands. |
| -b | Cause the status of terminated background jobs to be reported immediately, rather than before the next primary prompt. (Also see notify under "Shell Variables.") |
| -e | Exit immediately if a simple command (see "Shell Grammar," earlier in this manual page) exits with a non–zero status. The shell does not exit if the command that fails is part of an until |

or while loop, part of an if statement, part of a && or ¦¦ list, or if the command's return value is being inverted via !.

-f        Disable pathname expansion.

-h        Locate and remember function commands as functions are defined. Function commands are normally looked up when the function is executed.

-k        All keyword arguments are placed in the environment for a command, not just those that precede the command name.

-m        Monitor mode. Job control is enabled. This flag is on by default for interactive shells on systems that support it. (See "Job Control," earlier in this manual page.) Background processes run in a separate process group and a line containing their exit status is printed upon their completion.

-n        Read commands but do not execute them. This may be used to check a shell script for syntax errors. This is ignored for interactive shells.

-o *option-name*    The *option-name* can be one of the following:

allexport—Same as -a.

braceexpand—The shell performs brace expansion. (See "Brace Expansion," earlier in this manual page.) This is on by default.

emacs—Use an emacs-style command line editing interface. This is enabled by default when the shell is interactive, unless the shell is started with the -nolineediting option.

errexit—Same as -e.

histexpand—Same as -H.

ignoreeof—The effect is as if the shell command 'IGNOREEOF=10' had been executed. (See "Shell Variables.")

interactive-comments—Allow a word beginning with # to cause that word and all remaining characters on that line to be ignored in an interactive shell. (See "Comments," earlier in this manual page.)

monitor—Same as -m.

noclobber—Same as -C.

noexec—Same as -n.

noglob—Same as -f.

nohash—Same as -d.

notify—Same as -b.

nounset—Same as -u.

physical—Same as -P.

posix—Change the behavior of bash where the default operation differs from the POSIX 1003.2 standard to match the standard.

privileged—Same as -p.

verbose—Same as -v.

vi—Use a vi-style command line editing interface.

xtrace—Same as -x.

If no *option-name* is supplied, the values of the current options are printed.

-p          Turn on privileged mode. In this mode, the $ENV file is not processed, and shell functions are not inherited from the environment. This is enabled automatically on startup if the effective user (group) ID is not equal to the real user (group) ID. Turning this option off causes the effective user and group IDs to be set to the real user and group IDs.

-t          Exit after reading and executing one command.

-u          Treat unset variables as an error when performing parameter expansion. If expansion is attempted on an unset variable, the shell prints an error message, and, if not interactive, exits with a non–zero status.

-v          Print shell input lines as they are read.

-x          After expanding each simple command, bash displays the expanded value of PS4, followed by the command and its expanded arguments.

-l          Save and restore the binding of name in a for name [in word] command. (See "Shell Grammar," earlier in this manual page.)

-d          Disable the hashing of commands that are looked up for execution. Normally, commands are remembered in a hash table, and once found, do not have to be looked up again.

-C          The effect is as if the shell command noclobber= had been executed. (See "Shell Variables.")

-H          Enable ! style history substitution. This flag is on by default when the shell is interactive.

-P          If set, do not follow symbolic links when performing commands such as cd that change the current directory. The physical directory is used instead.

—           If no arguments follow this flag, then the positional parameters are unset. Otherwise, the positional parameters are set to the args, even if some of them begin with a -.

-           Signal the end of options, cause all remaining args to be assigned to the positional parameters. The -x and -v options are turned off. If there are no args, the positional parameters remain unchanged.

            The flags are off by default unless otherwise noted. Using + rather than - causes these flags to be turned off. The flags can also be specified as options to an invocation of the shell. The current set of flags may be found in $-. After the option arguments are processed, the remaining n args are treated as values for the positional parameters and are assigned, in order, to $1, $2, ... $n. If no options or args are supplied, all shell variables are printed. The return status is always True unless an illegal option is encountered.

shift [n]          The positional parameters from n+1 ... are renamed to .... Parameters represented by the numbers $# down to $#-n+1 are unset. If n is 0, no parameters are changed. If n is not given, it is assumed to be 1. n must be a non-negative number less than or equal to $#. If n is greater than $#, the positional parameters are not changed. The return status is greater than 0 if n is greater than or less than 0; otherwise 0.

suspend [-f]          Suspend the execution of this shell until it receives a SIG-CONT signal. The -f option says not to complain if this is a login shell; just suspend anyway. The return status is

0 unless the shell is a login shell and -f is not supplied, or if job control is not enabled.

**test expr[expr]**

Return a status of 0 (True) or 1 (False) depending on the evaluation of the conditional expression expr. Expressions may be unary or binary. Unary expressions are often used to examine the status of a file. There are string operators and numeric comparison operators as well. Each operator and operand must be a separate argument. If file is of the form /dev/fd/n, then file descriptor n is checked.

-b *file*— True if *file* exists and is block special.

-c *file*—True if *file* exists and is character special.

-d *file*—True if *file* exists and is a directory.

-e *file*—True if *file* exists.

-f *file*—True if *file* exists and is a regular file.

-g *file*—True if *file* exists and is set-group-id.

-k *file*—True if *file* has its "sticky" bit set.

-L *file*—True if *file* exists and is a symbolic link.

-p *file*—True if *file* exists and is a named pipe.

-r *file*—True if *file* exists and is readable.

-s *file*—True if *file* exists and has a size greater than zero.

-S *file*—True if *file* exists and is a socket.

-t *fd*—True if *fd* is opened on a terminal.

-u *file*—True if *file* exists and its set-user-id bit is set.

-w *file*—True if *file* exists and is writable.

-x *file*—True if *file* exists and is executable.

-O *file*—True if *file* exists and is owned by the effective user ID.

-G *file*—True if *file* exists and is owned by the effective group ID.

*file1* -nt *file2*—True if *file1* is newer (according to modification date) than *file2*.

*file1* -ot *file2*—True if *file1* is older than *file2*.

*file1* -ef *file*—True if *file1* and *file2* have the same device and inode numbers.

-z *string*—True if the length of *string* is zero.

-n *string*—True if the length of *string* is non–zero.

*string1* = *string2*—True if the strings are equal.

*string1* != *string2*—True if the strings are not equal.

! *expr*—True if *expr* is False.

*expr1* -a *expr2*—True if both *expr1* AND *expr2* are True.

*expr1* -o *expr2*—True if either *expr1* OR *expr2* is True.

*arg1* OP *arg2* OP is one of -eq, -ne, -lt, -le, -gt, or -ge. These arithmetic binary operators return True if *arg1* is equal, not-equal, less-than, less-than-or-equal, greater-than, or greater-than-or-equal than *arg2*, respectively. *Arg1* and *arg2* may be positive integers, negative integers, or the special expression -l *string*, which evaluates to the length of *string*.

**times**

Print the accumulated user and system times for the shell and for processes run from the shell. The return status is 0.

**trap [-l][*arg*][*sigspec*]**

The command *arg* is to be read and executed when the shell receives signal(s) *sigspec*. If *arg* is absent or –, all specified signals are reset to their original values (the values they had upon entrance to the shell). If *arg* is the null string, this signal is ignored by the shell and by the commands it invokes. *sigspec* is either a signal name defined in <signal.h>, or a signal number. If *sigspec* is EXIT (0), the command *arg* is executed on exit from the shell. With no arguments, trap prints the list of commands associated with each signal number. The -1 option causes the shell to print a list of signal names and their corresponding numbers. An argument of − disables option checking for the rest of the arguments. Signals ignored upon entry to the shell cannot be trapped or reset. Trapped signals are reset to their original values in a child process when it is created. The return status is False if either the trap name or number is invalid; otherwise, trap returns True.

`type [-all][-type ¦ -path] name [name ...]`

With no options, indicate how each name would be interpreted if used as a command name. If the -type flag is used, type prints a phrase that is one of alias, keyword, function, builtin, or file if *name* is an alias, shell reserved word, function, builtin, or disk file, respectively. If the name is not found, then nothing is printed, and an exit status of False is returned. If the -path flag is used, type either returns the name of the disk file that would be executed if *name* were specified as a command name, or nothing if -type would not return file. If a command is hashed, -path prints the hashed value, not necessarily the file that appears first in PATH. If the -all flag is used, type prints all of the places that contain an executable named *name*. This includes aliases and functions, if and only if the -path flag is not also used. The table of hashed commands is not consulted when using -all. type accepts -a, -t, and -p in place of -all, -type, and -path, respectively. An argument of − disables option checking for the rest of the arguments. type returns True if any of the arguments are found, False if none are found.

`ulimit [-SHacdfmstpnuv [limit]]`

ulimit provides control over the resources available to the shell and to processes started by it, on systems that allow such control. The value of limit can be a number in the unit specified for the resource, or the value unlimited. The H and S options specify that the hard or soft limit is set for the given resource. A hard limit cannot be increased once it is set; a soft limit may be increased up to the value of the hard limit. If neither H nor S is specified, the command applies to the soft limit. If limit is omitted, the current value of the soft limit of the resource is printed, unless the H option is given. When more than one resource is specified, the limit name and unit is printed before the value. Other options are interpreted as follows:

| | |
|---|---|
| -a | All current limits are reported. |
| -c | The maximum size of core files created. |
| -d | The maximum size of a process's data segment. |
| -f | The maximum size of files created by the shell. |
| -m | The maximum resident set size. |
| -s | The maximum stack size. |
| -t | The maximum amount of cpu time in seconds. |
| -p | The pipe size in 512-byte blocks. (This may not be set.) |
| -n | The maximum number of open file descriptors. (Most systems do not allow this value to be set, only displayed.) |
| -u | The maximum number of processes available to a single user. |
| -v | The maximum amount of virtual memory available to the shell. |

An argument of − disables option checking for the rest of the arguments. If limit is given, it is the new value of the specified resource (the -a option is display only). If no option is given, then -f is assumed. Values are in 1024-byte increments, except for -t, which is in seconds; -p, which is in units of 512-byte blocks; and -n and -u, which are unscaled values. The return status is 0 unless an illegal option is encountered, a non-numeric argument other than unlimited is supplied as limit, or an error occurs while setting a new limit.

umask [-S][*mode*]

The user file-creation mask is set to *mode*. If *mode* begins with a digit, it is interpreted as an octal number; otherwise, it is interpreted as a symbolic mode mask similar to that accepted by chmod(1). If mode is omitted, or if the -S option is supplied, the current value of the mask is printed. The -S option causes the mask to be printed in symbolic form; the default output is an octal number. An argument of − disables option checking for the rest of the arguments. The return status is 0 if the mode was successfully changed or if no *mode* argument was supplied, and False otherwise.

unalias [-a][*name* ...]

Remove names from the list of defined aliases. If -a is supplied, all alias definitions are removed. The return value is True unless a supplied name is not a defined alias.

unset [-fv][*name* ...]

For each name, remove the corresponding variable or, given the -f option, function. An argument of − disables option checking for the rest of the arguments. Note that PATH, IFS, PPID, PS1, PS2, UID, and EUID cannot be unset. If any of RANDOM, SECONDS, LINENO, or HISTCMD are unset, they lose their special properties, even if they are subsequently reset. The exit status is True unless a name does not exist or is non-unsettable.

wait [*n*]

Wait for the specified process and return its termination status. *n* may be a process ID or a job specification; if a job spec is given, all processes in that job's pipeline are waited for. If *n* is not given, all currently active child processes are waited for, and the return status is zero. If *n* specifies a nonexistent process or job, the return status is 127. Otherwise, the return status is the exit status of the last process or job waited for.

## INVOCATION

A *login shell* is one whose first character of argument zero is a -, or one started with the -login flag.

An *interactive shell* is one whose standard input and output are both connected to terminals (as determined by isatty(3)), or one started with the -i option. PS1 is set and includes i if bash is interactive, allowing a shell script or a startup file to test this state.

```
Login shells:
On login (subject to the −noprofile option):
if /etc/profile exists, source it.
if ˜/.bash_profile exists, source it,
else if ˜/.bash_login exists, source it,
else if ˜/.profile exists, source it.
On exit:
if ˜/.bash_logout exists, source it.
Non-login interactive shells:
On startup (subject to the −norc and −rcfile options):
if ˜/.bashrc exists, source it.
Non-interactive shells:
On startup:
if the environment variable ENV is non-null, expand
it and source the file it names, as if the command
if [ "$ENV" ]; then . $ENV; fi
had been executed, but do not use PATH to search
for the pathname. When not started in Posix mode, bash
looks for BASH_ENV before ENV.
```

If Bash is invoked as sh, it tries to mimic the behavior of sh as closely as possible. For a login shell, it attempts to source only / etc/profile and ˜/.profile, in that order. The -noprofile option may still be used to disable this behavior. A shell invoked as sh does not attempt to source any other startup files.

When bash is started in posix mode, as with the -posix command line option, it follows the POSIX standard for startup files. In this mode, the ENV variable is expanded and that file sourced; no other startup files are read.

## SEE ALSO

*Bash Features*, Brian Fox and Chet Ramey

*The Gnu Readline Library*, Brian Fox and Chet Ramey

*The Gnu History Library*, Brian Fox and Chet Ramey

*A System V Compatible Implementation of 4.2BSD Job Control*, David Lennert

*Portable Operating System Interface (POSIX) Part 2: Shell and Utilities*, IEEE

sh(1), ksh(1), csh(1), emacs(1), vi(1) readline(3)

## FILES

| | |
|---|---|
| /bin/bash | The bash executable |
| /etc/profile | The systemwide initialization file, executed for login shells |
| /.bash_profile | The personal initialization file, executed for login shells |
| /.bashrc | The individual per-interactive-shell startup file |
| /.inputrc | Individual readline initialization file |

## AUTHORS

Brian Fox (Free Software Foundation; primary author; bfox@ai.MIT.Edu), Chet Ramey (Case Western Reserve University; chet@ins.CWRU.Edu)

## COPYRIGHT

Copyright © 1989, 1991 by the Free Software Foundation, Inc.

## BUG REPORTS

If you find a bug in bash, you should report it. But first, you should make sure that it really is a bug, and that it appears in the latest version of bash that you have.

Once you have determined that a bug actually exists, mail a bug report to bash–maintainers@prep.ai.MIT.Edu. If you have a fix, you are welcome to mail that as well! Suggestions and "philosophical" bug reports may be mailed to bug-bash@prep.ai.MIT.Edu or posted to the Usenet newsgroup gnu.bash.bug.

ALL bug reports should include the following:

The version number of bash

The hardware and operating system

The compiler used to compile

A description of the bug behavior

A short script or "recipe" that exercises the bug

Comments and bug reports concerning this manual page should be directed to chet@ins.cwru.edu.

## BUGS

It's too big and too slow.

There are some subtle differences between bash and traditional versions of sh, mostly because of the POSIX specification.

Aliases are confusing in some uses.

# bdftopcf

bdftopcf—Convert X font from Bitmap Distribution Format to Portable Compiled Format

## SYNOPSIS

bdftopcf [ -p*n* ][-u*n* ][-m ][-l ][-M ][-L ][-t ][-i ][-o *outputfile* ] fontfile.bdf

## DESCRIPTION

bdftopcf is a font compiler for the X server and font server. Fonts in Portable Compiled Format can be read by any architecture, although the file is structured to allow one particular architecture to read them directly without reformatting. This allows fast reading on the appropriate machine, but the files are still portable (but read more slowly) on other machines.

## OPTIONS

| | |
|---|---|
| -p*n* | Sets the font glyph padding. Each glyph in the font will have each scanline padded in to a multiple of *n* bytes, where *n* is 1, 2, 4, or 8. |
| -u*n* | Sets the font scanline unit. When the font bit order is different from the font byte order, the scanline unit *n* describes what unit of data (in bytes) are to be swapped; the unit i can be 1, 2, or 4 bytes. |
| -m | Sets the font bit order to MSB (most significant bit) first. Bits for each glyph will be placed in this order; that is, the leftmost bit on the screen will be in the highest valued bit in each unit. |
| -l | Sets the font bit order to LSB (least significant bit) first. The leftmost bit on the screen will be in the lowest valued bit in each unit. |
| -M | Sets the font byte order to MSB first. All multibyte data in the file (metrics, bitmaps, and everything else) will be written most significant byte first. |
| -L | Sets the font byte order to LSB first. All multibyte data in the file (metrics, bitmaps, and everything else) will be written least significant byte first. |
| -t | When this option is specified, bdftopcf will convert fonts into terminal fonts when possible. A *terminal font* has each glyph image padded to the same size; the X server can usually render these types of fonts more quickly. |
| -i | This option inhibits the normal computation of ink metrics. When a font has glyph images that do not fill the bitmap image (that is, the "on" pixels don't extend to the edges of the metrics), bdftopcf computes the actual ink metrics and places them in the PCF file; the -t option inhibits this behavior. |
| -o *output-file-name* | By default bdftopcf writes the PCF file to standard output; this option gives the name of a file to be used instead. |

## SEE ALSO

x(1)

## AUTHOR

Keith Packard, MIT X Consortium

*X Version 11 Release 6*

# beforelight

beforelight—Screen saver

## SYNOPSIS

beforelight [ -*toolkitoption* ... ]

## DESCRIPTION

The `beforelight` program is a sample implementation of a screen saver for X servers supporting the `MIT-SCREEN-SAVER` extension.

## AUTHORS

Keith Packard (MIT X Consortium)

*X Version 11 Release 6*

# biff

biff—Be notified if mail arrives and who it is from

## SYNOPSIS

`biff [ny]`

## DESCRIPTION

`biff` informs the system whether you want to be notified when mail arrives during the current terminal session.

Options supported by `biff`:

| | |
|---|---|
| n | Disables notification |
| y | Enables notification |

When mail notification is enabled, the header and first few lines of the message will be printed on your screen whenever mail arrives. A

`biff y`

command is often included in the file `.login` or `.profile` to be executed at each login.

Biff operates asynchronously. For synchronous notification use the `MAIL` variable of `sh(1)` or the mail variable of `csh(1)`.

## SEE ALSO

`csh(1)`, `mail(1)`, `sh(1)`, `comsat(8)`

## HISTORY

The `biff` command appeared in BSD 4.0.

*BSD 4, 14 March 1991*

# bioradtopgm

bioradtopgm—Convert a Biorad confocal file into a portable graymap

## SYNOPSIS

`bioradtopgm [-image#][imagedata]`

## DESCRIPTION

Reads a Biorad confocal file as input. Produces a portable graymap as output. If the resulting image is upside down, run it through `pnmflip -tb`.

## OPTIONS

-image#  A Biorad image file may contain more than one image. With this flag, you can specify which image to extract (only one at a time). The first image in the file has number zero. If no image number is supplied, only information about the image size and the number of images in the input is printed out. No output is produced.

## BUGS

A Biorad image may be in word format. If PbmPlus is not compiled with the BIGGRAYS flag, word files cannot be converted. See the makefile.

## SEE ALSO

pgm(5), pnmflip(1)

## AUTHORS

Copyright © 1993 by Oliver Trepte

*28 June 1993*

# bitmap, bmtoa, atobm

bitmap, bmtoa, atobm—Bitmap editor and converter utilities for the X Window System

## SYNOPSIS

bitmap [ *-options* ...][*filename* ][*basename* ]

bmtoa [ *-chars* ...][*filename* ]

atobm [ *-chars cc* ][-name *variable* ][-xhot *number* ][-yhot *number* ][*filename* ]

## DESCRIPTION

The bitmap program is a rudimentary tool for creating or editing rectangular images made up of 1s and 0s. Bitmaps are used in X for defining clipping regions, cursor shapes, icon shapes, and tile and stipple patterns.

The bmtoa and atobm filters convert bitmap files (FILE FORMAT) to and from ASCII strings. They are most commonly used to quickly print out bitmaps and to generate versions for including in text.

## COMMAND-LINE OPTIONS

Bitmap supports the standard X Toolkit command-line arguments; see X(1). The following additional arguments are supported as well:

| | |
|---|---|
| -size *WIDTHxHEIGHT* | Specifies size of the grid in squares. |
| -sw *dimension* | Specifies the width of squares in pixels. |
| -sh *dimension* | Specifies the height of squares in pixels. |
| -gt *dimension* | Grid tolerance. If the square dimensions fall below the specified value, grid will be automatically turned off. |
| -grid, +grid | Turns on or off the grid lines. |
| -axes, +axes | Turns on or off the major axes. |
| -dashed, +dashed | Turns on or off dashing for the frame and grid lines. |
| -stippled, +stippled | Turns on or off stippling of highlighted squares. |

| | |
|---|---|
| `-proportional, +proportional` | Turns proportional mode on or off. If proportional mode is on, square width is equal to square height. If proportional mode is off, bitmap will use the smaller square dimension, if they were initially different. |
| `-dashes filename` | Specifies the bitmap to be used as a stipple for dashing. |
| `-stipple filename` | Specifies the bitmap to be used as a stipple for highlighting. |
| `-hl color` | Specifies the color used for highlighting. |
| `-fr color` | Specifies the color used for the frame and grid lines. |
| `filename` | Specifies the bitmap to be initially loaded into the program. If the file does not exist, bitmap will assume it is a new file. |
| `basename` | Specifies the basename to be used in the C code output file. If it is different than the basename in the working file, bitmap will change it when saving the file. |

`bmtoa` accepts the following option:

| | |
|---|---|
| `-chars cc` | This option specifies the pair of characters to use in the string version of the bitmap. The first character is used for 0 bits and the second character is used for 1 bits. The default is to use dashes (-) for 0s and number signs (#) for 1s. |

`atobm` accepts the following options:

| | |
|---|---|
| `-chars cc` | This option specifies the pair of characters to use when converting string bitmaps into arrays of numbers. The first character represents a 0 bit and the second character represents a 1 bit. The default is to use dashes (-) for 0s and number signs (#) for 1s. |
| `-name variable` | This option specifies the variable name to be used when writing out the bitmap file. The default is to use the basename of the filename command-line argument or leave it blank if the standard input is read. |
| `-xhot number` | This option specifies the X coordinate of the hot spot. Only positive values are allowed. By default, no hot spot information is included. |
| `-yhot number` | This option specifies the Y coordinate of the hot spot. Only positive values are allowed. By default, no hot spot information is included. |

## USAGE

bitmap displays grid in which each square represents a single bit in the picture being edited. Actual size of the bitmap image, as it would appear normally and inverted, can be obtained by pressing Meta-I. You are free to move the image pop-up out of the way to continue editing. Pressing the left mouse button in the pop-up window or Meta-I again will remove the real size bitmap image.

If the bitmap is to be used for defining a cursor, one of the squares in the images may be designated as the hot spot. This determines where the cursor is actually pointing. For cursors with sharp tips (such as arrows or fingers), this is usually at the end of the tip; for symmetric cursors (such as crosses or bulls-eyes), this is usually at the center.

Bitmaps are stored as small C code fragments suitable for including in applications. They provide an array of bits as well as symbolic constants giving the width, height, and hot spot (if specified) that may be used in creating cursors, icons, and tiles.

## EDITING

To edit a bitmap image, simply click on one of the buttons with drawing commands (Point, Curve, Line, Rectangle, and so on) and move the pointer into the bitmap grid window. Press one of the buttons on your mouse and the appropriate action will take place. You can either set, clear, or invert the grid squares. Setting a grid square corresponds to setting a bit in the bitmap image to 1. Clearing a grid square corresponds to setting a bit in the bitmap image to 0. Inverting a grid square corresponds to changing a bit in the bitmap image from 0 to 1 or 1 to 0, depending what its previous state was. The default behavior of mouse buttons is as follows:

```
MouseButton1 Set
MouseButton2 Invert
MouseButton3 Clear
MouseButton4 Clear
MouseButton5 Clear
```

This default behavior can be changed by setting the button function resources. Here is an example:

```
bitmap*button1Function: Set
bitmap*button2Function: Clear
bitmap*button3Function: Invert
etc.
```

The button function applies to all drawing commands, including copying, moving and pasting, flood filling, and setting the hot spot.

## DRAWING COMMANDS

Here is the list of drawing commands accessible through the buttons at the left side of the application's window. Some commands can be aborted by pressing A inside the bitmap window, allowing the user to select different guiding points where applicable.

| | |
|---|---|
| Clear | This command clears all bits in the bitmap image. The grid squares will be set to the background color. Pressing C inside the bitmap window has the same effect. |
| Set | This command sets all bits in the bitmap image. The grid squares will be set to the foreground color. Pressing S inside the bitmap window has the same effect. |
| Invert | This command inverts all bits in the bitmap image. The grid squares will be inverted appropriately. Pressing I inside the bitmap window has the same effect. |
| Mark | This command is used to mark an area of the grid by dragging out a rectangular shape in the highlighting color. After the area is marked, it can be operated on by a number of commands (see Up, Down, Left, Right, Rotate, Flip, Cut, and so on). Only one marked area can be present at any time. If you attempt to mark another area, the old mark will vanish. The same effect can be achieved by pressing Shift-MouseButton1 and dragging out a rectangle in the grid window. Pressing Shift-MouseButton2 will mark the entire grid area. |
| Unmark | This command will cause the marked area to vanish. The same effect can be achieved by pressing Shift-MouseButton3. |
| Copy | This command is used to copy an area of the grid from one location to another. If there is no marked grid area displayed, Copy behaves just like Mark. Once there is a marked grid area displayed in the highlighting color, this command has two alternative behaviors. If you click a mouse button inside the marked area, you will be able to drag the rectangle that represents the marked area to the desired location. After you release the mouse button, the area will be copied. If you click outside the marked area, Copy will assume that you wish to mark a different region of the bitmap image, thus it will behave like Mark again. |
| Move | This command is used to move an area of the grid from one location to another. Its behavior resembles the behavior of Copy command, except that the marked area will be moved instead of copied. |
| Flip Horizontally | This command will flip the bitmap image with respect to the horizontal axes. If a marked area of the grid is highlighted, it will operate only inside the marked area. Pressing H inside the bitmap window has the same effect. |
| Up | This command moves the bitmap image one pixel up. If a marked area of the grid is highlighted, it will operate only inside the marked area. Pressing UpArrow inside the bitmap window has the same effect. |

| | |
|---|---|
| Flip Vertically | This command will flip the bitmap image with respect to the vertical axes. If a marked area of the grid is highlighted, it will operate only inside the marked area. Pressing V inside the bitmap window has the same effect. |
| Left | This command moves the bitmap image one pixel to the left. If a marked area of the grid is highlighted, it will operate only inside the marked area. Pressing LeftArrow inside the bitmap window has the same effect. |
| Fold | This command will fold the bitmap image so that the opposite corners become adjacent. This is useful when creating bitmap images for tiling. Pressing F inside the bitmap window has the same effect. |
| Right | This command moves the bitmap image one pixel to the right. If a marked area of the grid is highlighted, it will operate only inside the marked area. Pressing the right arrow inside the bitmap window has the same effect. |
| Rotate Left | This command rotates the bitmap image 90 degrees to the left (counter clockwise.) If a marked area of the grid is highlighted, it will operate only inside the marked area. Pressing L inside the bitmap window has the same effect. |
| Down | This command moves the bitmap image one pixel down. If a marked area of the grid is highlighted, it will operate only inside the marked area. Pressing the down arrow inside the bitmap window has the same effect. |
| Rotate Right | This command rotates the bitmap image 90 degrees to the right (clockwise.) If a marked area of the grid is highlighted, it will operate only inside the marked area. Pressing R inside the bitmap window has the same effect. |
| Point | This command will change the grid squares underneath the mouse pointer if a mouse button is being pressed down. If you drag the mouse button continuously, the line may not be continuous, depending on the speed of your system and frequency of mouse motion events. |
| Curve | This command will change the grid squares underneath the mouse pointer if a mouse button is being pressed down. If you drag the mouse button continuously, it will make sure that the line is continuous. If your system is slow or bitmap receives very few mouse motion events, it might behave quite strangely. |
| Line | This command will change the grid squares in a line between two squares. Once you press a mouse button in the grid window, bitmap will highlight the line from the square where the mouse button was initially pressed to the square where the mouse pointer is located. By releasing the mouse button, you will cause the change to take effect, and the highlighted line will disappear. |
| Rectangle | This command will change the grid squares in a rectangle between two squares. Once you press a mouse button in the grid window, bitmap will highlight the rectangle from the square where the mouse button was initially pressed to the square where the mouse pointer is located. By releasing the mouse button you will cause the change to take effect, and the highlighted rectangle will disappear. |
| Filled Rectangle | This command is identical to Rectangle, except at the end the rectangle will be filled rather than outlined. |
| Circle | This command will change the grid squares in a circle between two squares. Once you press a mouse button in the grid window, bitmap will highlight the circle from the square where the mouse button was initially pressed to the square where the mouse pointer is located. By releasing the mouse button you will cause the change to take effect, and the highlighted circle will disappear. |
| Filled Circle | This command is identical to Circle, except at the end the circle will be filled rather than outlined. |
| Flood Fill | This command will flood fill the connected area underneath the mouse pointer when you click on the desired square. Diagonally adjacent squares are not considered to be connected. |

| Set Hot Spot | This command designates one square in the grid as the hot spot if this bitmap image is to be used for defining a cursor. Pressing a mouse button in the desired square will cause a diamond shape to be displayed. |
| Clear Hot Spot | This command removes any designated hot spot from the bitmap image. |
| Undo | This command will undo the last executed command. It has depth one, that is, pressing Undo after Undo will undo itself. |

## FILE MENU

The File menu commands can be accessed by pressing the File button and selecting the appropriate menu entry, or by pressing the Ctrl key with another key. These commands deal with files and global bitmap parameters, such as size, basename, filename, and so forth.

| New | This command will clear the editing area and prompt for the name of the new file to be edited. It will not load in the new file. |
| Load | This command is used to load a new bitmap file into the bitmap editor. If the current image has not been saved, user will be asked whether to save or ignore the changes. The editor can edit only one file at a time. If you need interactive editing, run a number of editors and use the cut and paste mechanism as described later in this section. (See "Cut and Paste.") |
| Insert | This command is used to insert a bitmap file into the image being currently edited. After being prompted for the filename, click inside the grid window and drag the outlined rectangle to the location where you want to insert the new file. |
| Save | This command will save the bitmap image. It will not prompt for the filename unless it is said to be \<none>. If you leave the filename undesignated or –, the output will be piped to stdout. |
| Save As | This command will save the bitmap image after prompting for a new filename. It should be used if you want to change the filename. |
| Resize | This command is used to resize the editing area to the new number of pixels. The size should be entered in the width| height format. The information in the image being edited will not be lost unless the new size is smaller that the current image size. The editor was not designed to edit huge files. |
| Rescale | This command is used to rescale the editing area to the new width and height. The size should be entered in the width| height format. It will not do antialiasing and information will be lost if you rescale to the smaller sizes. Feel free to add you own algorithms for better rescaling. |
| Filename | This command is used to change the filename without changing the basename nor saving the file. If you specify – for a filename, the output will be piped to stdout. |
| Basename | This command is used to change the basename, if a different one from the specified filename is desired. |
| Quit | This command will terminate the bitmap application. If the file was not saved, user will be prompted and asked whether to save the image or not. Quit is preferred over killing the process. |

## EDIT MENU

The Edit menu commands can be accessed by pressing the Edit button and selecting the appropriate menu entry, or by pressing Meta key with another key. These commands deal with editing facilities such as grid, axes, zooming, cut and paste, and so on.

| Image | This command will display the image being edited and its inverse in its actual size in a separate window. The window can be moved away to continue with editing. Pressing the left mouse button in the image window will cause it to disappear from the screen. |

| | |
|---|---|
| Grid | This command controls the grid in the editing area. If the grid spacing is below the value specified by `gridTolerance resource` (8 by default), the grid will be automatically turned off. It can be enforced by explicitly activating this command. |
| Dashed | This command controls the stipple for drawing the grid lines. The stipple specified by dashes resource can be turned on or off by activating this command. |
| Axes | This command controls the highlighting of the main axes of the image being edited. The actual lines are not part of the image. They are provided to aid user when constructing symmetrical images, or whenever having the main axes highlighted helps your editing. |
| Stippled | This command controls the stippling of the highlighted areas of the bitmap image. The stipple specified by stipple resource can be turned on or off by activating this command. |
| Proportional | This command controls the proportional mode. If the proportional mode is on, width and height of all image squares are forced to be equal, regardless of the proportions of the bitmap window. |
| Zoom | This command controls the zoom mode. If there is a marked area of the image already displayed, bitmap will automatically zoom into it. Otherwise, the user will have to highlight an area to be edited in the zoom mode and bitmap will automatically switch into it. You can use all the editing commands and other utilities in the zoom mode. When you zoom out, undo command will undo the whole zoom session. |
| Cut | This commands cuts the contents of the highlighted image area into the internal cut and paste buffer. |
| Copy | This command copies the contents of the highlighted image area into the internal cut and paste buffer. |
| Paste | This command will check if there are any other bitmap applications with a highlighted image area, or if there is something in the internal cut and paste buffer and copy it to the image. To place the copied image, click in the editing window and drag the outlined image to the position where you want to place i, and then release the button. |

## CUT AND PASTE

Bitmap supports two cut and paste mechanisms; the internal cut and paste and the global X selection cut and paste. The internal cut and paste is used when executing copy and move drawing commands and also cut and copy commands from the Edit menu. The global X selection cut and paste is used whenever there is a highlighted area of a bitmap image displayed anywhere on the screen. To copy a part of image from another bitmap editor, simply highlight the desired area by using the Mark command or pressing the shift key and dragging the area with the left mouse button. When the selected area becomes highlighted, any other applications (such as xterm) that use primary selection will discard their selection values and unhighlight the appropriate information. Now, use the Paste command from the Edit menu or control mouse button to copy the selected part of image into another (or the same) bitmap application. If you attempt to do this without a visible highlighted image area, the bitmap will fall back to the internal cut and paste buffer and paste whatever was stored there at the moment.

## WIDGETS

Following is the widget structure of the bitmap application. The widget class name is given first, followed by the widget instance name. All widgets except the bitmap widget are from the standard Athena widget set.

```
Bitmap bitmap
TransientShell image
Box box
Label normalImage
Label invertedImage
TransientShell input
```

```
Dialog dialog
Command okay
Command cancel
TransientShell error
Dialog dialog
Command abort
Command retry
TransientShell qsave
Dialog dialog
Command yes
Command no
Command cancel
Paned parent
Form formy
MenuButton fileButton
SimpleMenu fileMenu
SmeBSB new
SmeBSB load
SmeBSB insert
SmeBSB save
SmeBSB saveAs
SmeBSB resize
SmeBSB rescale
SmeBSB filename
SmeBSB basename
SmeLine line
SmeBSB quit
MenuButton editButton
SimpleMenu editMenu
SmeBSB image
SmeBSB grid
SmeBSB dashed
SmeBSB axes
SmeBSB stippled
SmeBSB proportional
SmeBSB zoom
SmeLine line
SmeBSB cut
SmeBSB copy
SmeBSB paste
Label status
Pane pane
Bitmap bitmap
Form form
Command clear
Command set
Command invert
Toggle mark
Command unmark
Toggle copy
Toggle move
Command flipHoriz
Command up
Command flipVert
Command left
Command fold
Command right
Command rotateLeft
Command down
Command rotateRight
```

```
Toggle point
Toggle curve
Toggle line
Toggle rectangle
Toggle filledRectangle
Toggle circle
Toggle fillcdCircle
Toggle floodFill
Toggle setHotSpot
Command clearHotSpot
Command undo
```

## COLORS

If you would like bitmap to be viewable in color, include the following in the `#ifdef COLOR` section of the file you read with xrdb:

`*customization: -color`

This will cause bitmap to pick up the colors in the app-defaults color customization file:

`<XRoot>/lib/X11/app-defaults/Bitmap-color`

where `<XRoot>` refers to the root of the X11 install tree.

## BITMAP WIDGET

Bitmap widget is a standalone widget for editing raster images. It is not designed to edit large images, although it may be used in that purpose as well. It can be freely incorporated with other applications and used as a standard editing tool. The following are the resources provided by the bitmap widget:

| | |
|---|---|
| Header file | `Bitmap.h` |
| Class | `bitmapWidgetClass` |
| Class Name | `Bitmap` |
| Superclass | `Bitmap` |

All the Simple Widget resources plus…

| Name | Class | Type | Default Value |
|---|---|---|---|
| foreground | Foreground | Pixel | XtDefaultForeground |
| highlight | Highlight | Pixel | XtDefaultForeground |
| framing | Framing | Pixel | XtDefaultForeground |
| gridTolerance | GridTolerance | Dimension | 8 |
| size | Size | String | 32x32 |
| dashed | Dashed | Boolean | True |
| grid | Grid | Boolean | True |
| stippled | Stippled | Boolean | True |
| proportional | Proportional | Boolean | True |
| axes | Axes | Boolean | False |
| squareWidth | SquareWidth | Dimension | 16 |
| squareHeight | SquareHeight | Dimension | 16 |
| margin | Margin | Dimension | 16 |
| xHot | XHot | Position | NotSet (−1) |
| yHot | YHot | Position | NotSet (−1) |
| button1Function | Button1Function | DrawingFunction | Set |

| Name | Class | Type | Default Value |
|------|-------|------|---------------|
| button2Function | Button2Function | DrawingFunction | Invert |
| button3Function | Button3Function | DrawingFunction | Clear |
| button4Function | Button4Function | DrawingFunction | Invert |
| button5Function | Button5Function | DrawingFunction | Invert |
| filename | Filename | String | None ("") |
| basename | Basename | String | None ("") |

## AUTHOR

Davor Matic (MIT X Consortium)

*X Version 11 Release 6*

# bmptoppm

bmptoppm—Convert a BMP file into a portable pixmap

## SYNOPSIS

bmptoppm [bmpfile]

## DESCRIPTION

bmptoppm reads a Microsoft Windows or OS/2 BMP file as input and produces a portable pixmap as output.

## SEE ALSO

ppmtobmp(1), ppm(5)

## AUTHOR

Copyright © 1992 by David W. Sanderson

*26 October 1992*

# brushtopbm

brushtopbm—Convert a doodle brush file into a portable bitmap

## SYNOPSIS

brushtopbm [*brushfile*]

## DESCRIPTION

brushtopbm reads a Xerox doodle brush file as input and produces a portable bitmap as output.

Note that there is currently no pbmtobrush tool.

## SEE ALSO

pbm(5)

## AUTHOR

Copyright © 1988 by Jef Poskanzer

*28 August 1988*

# cal

cal—Displays a calendar

## SYNOPSIS

cal [-jy] [*month* [*year*]]

## DESCRIPTION

cal displays a simple calendar. If arguments are not specified, the current month is displayed. The options are as follows:

| | |
|---|---|
| -j | Display Julian dates (days one-based, numbered from January 1) |
| -y | Display a calendar for the current year |

A single parameter specifies the year (1–9999) to be displayed; note the year must be fully specified:

cal 89

will not display a calendar for 1989. Two parameters denote the month (1–12) and year. If no parameters are specified, the current month's calendar is displayed.

A year starts on Jan 1.

The Gregorian Reformation is assumed to have occurred in 1752 on the 3rd of September. By this time, most countries had recognized the reformation (although a few did not recognize it until the early 1900s.) Ten days following that date were eliminated by the reformation, so the calendar for that month is a bit unusual.

## HISTORY

A cal command appeared in version 6 AT&T UNIX

*6 June 1993*

# cat

cat—Concatenate files and print on the standard output

## SYNOPSIS

cat [-benstuvAET] [−number] [−number-nonblank] [−squeeze-blank]

[−show-nonprinting] [−show-ends] [−show-tabs] [−show-all]

[−help] [−version] [*file...*]

## DESCRIPTION

This manual page documents the GNU version of cat. cat writes the contents of each given file, or the standard input if none are given or when a file named - is given, to the standard output.

## OPTIONS

| | |
|---|---|
| -b, −number-nonblank | Number all nonblank output lines, starting with 1. |
| -e | Equivalent to −vE. |
| -n, −number | Number all output lines, starting with 1. |
| -s, −squeeze-blank | Replace multiple adjacent blank lines with a single blank line. |
| -t | Equivalent to -vT. |
| -u | Ignored; for UNIX compatibility. |

| | |
|---|---|
| -v, —show-nonprinting | Display control characters except for LFD and TAB using ^ notation and precede characters that have the high bit set with M-. |
| -A, —show-all | Equivalent to -vET. |
| -E, —show-ends | Display a $ after the end of each line. |
| -T, —show-tabs | Display tab characters as ^I. |
| —help | Print a usage message and exit with a nonzero status. |
| —version | Print version information on standard output then exit. |

*GNU Text Utilities*

# chattr

chattr—Change file attributes on a Linux second extended file system

## SYNOPSIS

chattr [ -RV ][-v version ] [ mode ] *files...*

## DESCRIPTION

chattr changes the files attributes on an second extended file system. The format of a symbolic mode is +-=[Sacdisu].

The operator + causes the selected attributes to be added to the existing attributes of the files; - causes them to be removed; and = causes them to be the only attributes that the files have. The letters Sacdisu select the new attributes for the files: synchronous updates (S), append only (a), compressed ($\chi$), immutable(i), nodump (d), securedeletion (s), and undeletable (u).

## OPTIONS

| | |
|---|---|
| -R | Recursively change attributes of directories and their contents. |
| -V | Verbosely describe changed attributes. |
| -v version | Set the file's version. |

## ATTRIBUTES

A file with the a attribute set can only be open in append mode for writing.

A file with the c attribute set is automatically compressed on the disk by the kernel. A read from this file returns uncompressed data. A write to this file compresses data before storing them on the disk.

A file with the d attribute set is not candidate for backup when the dump(8) program is run.

A file with the i attribute cannot be modified: it cannot be deleted or renamed, no link can be created to this file and no data can be written to the file. Only the superuser can set or clear this attribute.

When a file with the s attribute set is deleted, its blocks are zeroed and written back to the disk.

When a file with the u attribute set is modified, the changes are written synchronously on the disk; this is equivalent to the syn' mount option applied to a subset of the files.

When a file with the u attribute set is deleted, its contents is saved. This allows the user to ask for its undeletion.

## AUTHOR

chattr has been written by Remy Card, <card@masi.ibp.fr>, the developer and maintainer of the ext2 fs.

## BUGS AND LIMITATIONS

As of ext2 fs 0.5a, the c and u attributes are not honored by the kernel code.

These attributes will be implemented in a future ext2 fs version.

## AVAILABILITY

chattr is available for anonymous ftp from ftp.ibp.fr and tsx-11.mit.edu in /pub/linux/packages/ext2fs.

## SEE ALSO

lsattr(1)

*Version 0.5b, November 1994*

# chfn

chfn—Change your finger information

## SYNOPSIS

chfn [ -f *full-name* ][-o *office*][-p *office-phone* ] [ -h *home-phone* ] [ -u ] [ -v ]
[*username* ]

## DESCRIPTION

chfn is used to change your finger information. This information is stored in the /etc/passwd file, and is displayed by the finger program. The Linux finger command will display four pieces of information that can be changed by chfn: your real name, your work room and phone, and your home phone.

## COMMAND LINE

Any of the four pieces of information can be specified on the command line. If no information is given on the command line, chfn enters interactive mode.

## INTERACTIVE MODE

In interactive mode, chfn will prompt for each field. At a prompt, you can enter the new information, or just press return to leave the field unchanged. Enter the keyword none to make the field blank.

## OPTIONS

| | |
|---|---|
| -f, —full-name | Specify your real name. |
| -o, —office | Specify your office room number. |
| -p, —office-phone | Specify your office phone number. |
| -h, —home-phone | Specify your home phone number. |
| -u, —help | Print a usage message and exit. |
| -v, —version | Print version information and exit. |

## SEE ALSO

finger(1), passwd(5)

## AUTHOR

Salvatore Valente (<svalente@mit.edu>)

*chfn, October 13 1994*

# chgrp

chgrp—Change the group ownership of files

## SYNOPSIS

chgrp [-Rcfv] [—recursive] [—changes] [—silent] [—quiet] [—verbose] [—help]
[—version] *group file...*

## DESCRIPTION

This manual page documents the GNU version of chgrp. chgrp changes the group ownership of each given file to the named group, which can be either a group name or a numeric group ID.

## OPTIONS

| | |
|---|---|
| -c, —changes | Verbosely describe only files whose ownership actually changes. |
| -f, —silent, —quiet | Do not print error messages about files whose ownership cannot be changed. |
| -v, —verbose | Verbosely describe ownership changes. |
| -R, —recursive | Recursively change ownership of directories and their contents. |
| —help | Print a usage message on standard output and exit successfully. |
| —version | Print version information on standard output, then exit successfully. |

*GNU File Utilities*

# chkdupexe

chkdupexe—Find duplicate executables

## SYNOPSIS

chkdupexe

## DESCRIPTION

chkdupexe will scan many standard directories that hold executable, and report duplicates.

## AUTHOR

Nicolai Langfeldt

## BUGS

Requires GNU ls(1).

Search paths that point to the same directory will cause many bogus duplicates to be found. You might want to edit the script to eliminate some paths that are equivalent on your machine.

*11 March 1995*

# chmod

chmod—Change the access permissions of files

## SYNOPSIS

chmod [-Rcfv] [—recursive] [—changes] [—silent] [—quiet] [—verbose] [—help]
[—version] *mode file...*

## DESCRIPTION

This manual page documents the GNU version of chmod. chmod changes the permissions of each given file according to mode, which can be either a symbolic representation of changes to make, or an octal number representing the bit pattern for the new permissions.

The format of a symbolic mode is [ugoa...][[+-=][rwxXstugo...]...][,...]. Multiple symbolic operations can be given, separated by commas.

A combination of the letters ugoa controls which users' access to the file will be changed: the user who owns it (u), other users in the file's group (g), other users not in the file's group (o), or all users (a). If none of these are given, the effect is as if a were given, but bits that are set in the umask are not affected.

The operator + causes the permissions selected to be added to the existing permissions of each file; - causes them to be removed; and = causes them to be the only permissions that the file has.

The letters rwxXstugo select the new permissions for the affected users: read (r), write (w), execute (or access for directories) (x), execute only if the file is a directory or already has execute permission for some user (X), set user or group ID on execution (s), save program text on swap device (t), the permissions that the user who owns the file currently has for it (u), the permissions that other users in the file's group have for it (g), and the permissions that other users not in the file's group have for it (o).

A numeric mode is from one to four octal digits (0–7), derived by adding up the bits with values 4, 2, and 1. Any omitted digits are assumed to be leading zeros. The first digit selects the set user ID (4) and set group ID (2) and save text image (1) attributes. The second digit selects permissions for the user who owns the file: read (4), write (2), and execute (1); the third selects permissions for other users in the file's group, with the same values; and the fourth for other users not in the file's group, with the same values.

chmod never changes the permissions of symbolic links; the chmod system call cannot change their permissions. This is not a problem since the permissions of symbolic links are never used. However, for each symbolic link listed on the command line, chmod changes the permissions of the pointed-to file. In contrast, chmod ignores symbolic links encountered during recursive directory traversals.

## OPTIONS

| | |
|---|---|
| -c, —changes | Verbosely describe only files whose permissions actually change. |
| -f, —silent, —quiet | Do not print error messages about files whose permissions cannot be changed. |
| -v, —verbose | Verbosely describe changed permissions. |
| -R, —recursive | Recursively change permissions of directories and their contents. |
| —help | Print a usage message on standard output and exit successfully. |
| —version | Print version information on standard output, then exit successfully. |

*GNU File Utilities*

# chown

chown—Change the user and group ownership of files

## SYNOPSIS

chown [-Rcfv] [—recursive] [—changes] [—help] [—version] [—silent] [—quiet]
[—verbose] [*user*][:.][*group*] *file*...

## DESCRIPTION

This manual page documents the GNU version of chown. chown changes the user and/or group ownership of each given file, according to its first nonoption argument, which is interpreted as follows. If only a username (or numeric user ID) is given, that user is made the owner of each given file, and the files' group is not changed. If the username is followed by a colon or dot and a group name (or numeric group ID), with no spaces between them, the group ownership of the files is changed as well. If a colon or dot but no group name follows the username, that user is made the owner of the files and the group of the files is changed to that user's login group. If the colon or dot and group are given, but the username is omitted, only the group of the files is changed; in this case, chown performs the same function as chgrp.

## OPTIONS

| | |
|---|---|
| -c, —changes | Verbosely describe only files whose ownership actually changes. |
| -f, —silent, —quiet | Do not print error messages about files whose ownership cannot be changed. |
| -v, —verbose | Verbosely describe ownership changes. |
| -R, —recursive | Recursively change ownership of directories and their contents. |
| —help | Print a usage message on standard output and exit successfully. |
| —version | Print version information on standard output then exit successfully. |

*GNU File Utilities*

# chsh

chsh—Change your login shell

## SYNOPSIS

chsh [ -s shell ] [ -l ] [ -u ] [ -v ] [ *username* ]

## DESCRIPTION

chsh is used to change your login shell. If a shell is not given on the command line, chsh prompts for one.

## VALID SHELLS

chsh will accept the full pathname of any executable file on the system. However, it will issue a warning if the shell is not listed in the /etc/shells file.

## OPTIONS

| | |
|---|---|
| -s, —shell | Specify your login shell. |
| -l, —list-shells | Print the list of shells listed in /etc/shells and exit. |
| -u, —help | Print a usage message and exit. |
| -v, —version | Print version information and exit. |

## SEE ALSO

login(1), passwd(5), shells(5)

## AUTHOR

Salvatore Valente (<svalente@mit.edu>)

*chsh, 13 October 1994*

# ci

ci—Check in RCS revisions

## SYNOPSIS

ci [*options*] *file* ...

## DESCRIPTION

ci stores new revisions into RCS files. Each pathname matching an RCS suffix is taken to be an RCS file. All others are assumed to be working files containing new revisions. ci deposits the contents of each working file into the corresponding RCS file. If only a working file is given, ci tries to find the corresponding RCS file in an RCS subdirectory and then in the working file's directory. (For more details, see "File Naming," later in this manual page.)

For ci to work, the caller's login must be on the access list, unless the access list is empty or the caller is the superuser or the owner of the file. To append a new revision to an existing branch, the tip revision on that branch must be locked by the caller. Otherwise, only a new branch can be created. This restriction is not enforced for the owner of the file if non-strict locking is used; see rcs(1). A lock held by someone else can be broken with the rcs command.

Unless the -f option is given, ci checks whether the revision to be deposited differs from the preceding one. If not, instead of creating a new revision ci reverts to the preceding one. To revert, ordinary ci removes the working file and any lock; ci –l keeps and ci -u removes any lock, and then they both generate a new working file much as if co -l or co -u had been applied to the preceding revision. When reverting, any -n and -s options apply to the preceding revision.

For each revision deposited, ci prompts for a log message. The log message should summarize the change and must be terminated by end-of-file or by a line containing . by itself. If several files are checked in, ci asks whether to reuse the previous log message. If the standard input is not a terminal, ci suppresses the prompt and uses the same log message for all files. (See also -m.)

If the RCS file does not exist, ci creates it and deposits the contents of the working file as the initial revision (default number: 1.1). The access list is initialized to empty. Instead of the log message, ci requests descriptive text (See -t.)

The number rev of the deposited revision can be given by any of the options -f, -i, -I, -j, -k, -l, -M, -q, -r, or -u. rev can be symbolic, numeric, or mixed. Symbolic names in rev must already be defined; see the -n and -N options for assigning names during checkin. If rev is $, ci determines the revision number from keyword values in the working file.

If rev begins with a period, then the default branch (normally the trunk) is prepended to it. If rev is a branch number followed by a period, then the latest revision on that branch is used.

If rev is a revision number, it must be higher than the latest one on the branch to which rev belongs, or must start a new branch.

If rev is a branch rather than a revision number, the new revision is appended to that branch. The level number is obtained by incrementing the tip revision number of that branch. If rev indicates a nonexistent branch, that branch is created with the initial revision numbered rev.1.

If rev is omitted, ci tries to derive the new revision number from the caller's last lock. If the caller has locked the tip revision of a branch, the new revision is appended to that branch. The new revision number is obtained by incrementing the tip revision number. If the caller locked a nontip revision, a new branch is started at that revision by incrementing the highest branch number at that revision. The default initial branch and level numbers are 1.

If rev is omitted and the caller has no lock, but owns the file and locking is not set to strict, then the revision is appended to the default branch. (Normally the trunk; see the -b option of rcs(1).)

Exception: On the trunk, revisions can be appended to the end, but not inserted.

# OPTIONS

| | |
|---|---|
| -r*rev* | Check in revision *rev*. |
| -r | The bare -r option (without any revision) has an unusual meaning in ci. With other RCS commands, a bare -r option specifies the most recent revision on the default branch, but with ci, a bare -r option reestablishes the default behavior of releasing a lock and removing the working file, and is used to override any default -l or -u options established by shell aliases or scripts. |
| -l[*rev*] | Works like -r, except it performs an additional co -l for the deposited revision. Thus, the deposited revision is immediately checked out again and locked. This is useful for saving a revision although one wants to continue editing it after the checkin. |
| -u[*rev*] | Works like -l, except that the deposited revision is not locked. This lets one read the working file immediately after checkin. |

The -l, bare -r, and -u options are mutually exclusive and silently override each other. For example, ci -u -r is equivalent to ci -r because bare -r overrides -u.

| | |
|---|---|
| -f[*rev*] | Forces a deposit; the new revision is deposited even it is not different from the preceding one. |
| -k[*rev*] | Searches the working file for keyword values to determine its revision number, creation date, state, and author—see co(1)—and assigns these values to the deposited revision, rather than computing them locally. It also generates a default login message noting the login of the caller and the actual checkin date. This option is useful for software distribution. A revision that is sent to several sites should be checked in with the -k option at these sites to preserve the original number, date, author, and state. The extracted keyword values and the default log message can be overridden with the options -d, -m, -s, -w, and any option that carries a revision number. |
| -q[*rev*] | Quiet mode; diagnostic output is not printed. A revision that is not different from the preceding one is not deposited, unless -f is given. |
| -i[*rev*] | Initial checkin; report an error if the RCS file already exists. This avoids race conditions in certain applications. |
| -j[*rev*] | Just check in and do not initialize; report an error if the RCS file does not already exist. |
| -I[*rev*] | Interactive mode; the user is prompted and questioned even if the standard input is not a terminal. |
| -d[*date*] | Uses date for the checkin date and time. The date is specified in free format as explained in co(1). This is useful for lying about the checkin date, and for -k if no date is available. If date is empty, the working file's time of last modification is used. |
| -M[*rev*] | Set the modification time on any new working file to be the date of the retrieved revision. For example, ci -d -M -u f does not alter f's modification time, even if f's contents change due to keyword substitution. Use this option with care; it can confuse make(1). |
| -m*msg* | Uses the string *msg* as the log message for all revisions checked in. By convention, log messages that start with # are comments and are ignored by programs like GNU emacs's vc package. Also, log messages that start with clumpname (followed by whitespace) are meant to be clumped together if possible, even if they are associated with different files; the clumpname label is used only for clumping, and is not considered to be part of the log message itself. |
| -n*name* | Assigns the symbolic name to the number of the checked-in revision. ci prints an error message if that name is already assigned to another number. |
| -N*name* | Same as -n, except that it overrides a previous assignment of name. |
| -s*state* | Sets the state of the checked-in revision to the identifier state. The default state is Exp. |
| -t*file* | Writes descriptive text from the contents of the named file into the RCS file, deleting the existing text. The file cannot begin with -. |
| -t-*string* | Write descriptive text from the string into the RCS file, deleting the existing text. |

The –t option, in both its forms, has effect only during an initial checkin; it is silently ignored otherwise.

During the initial checkin, if -t is not given, ci obtains the text from standard input, terminated by end-of-file or by a line containing a dot (.) by itself. The user is prompted for the text if interaction is possible; see -I.

For backwards compatibility with older versions of RCS, a bare -t option is ignored.

-T
Set the RCS file's modification time to the new revision's time if the former precedes the latter and there is a new revision; preserve the RCS file's modification time otherwise. If you have locked a revision, ci usually updates the RCS file's modification time to the current time, because the lock is stored in the RCS file and removing the lock requires changing the RCS file. This can create an RCS file newer than the working file in one of two ways: first, ci -M can create a working file with a date before the current time; second, when reverting to the previous revision the RCS file can change while the working file remains unchanged. These two cases can cause excessive recompilation caused by a make(1) dependency of the working file on the RCS file. The -T option inhibits this recompilation by lying about the RCS file's date. Use this option with care; it can suppress recompilation even when a checkin of one working file should affect another working file associated with the same RCS file. For example, suppose the RCS file's time is 01:00, the (changed) working file's time is 02:00, some other copy of the working file has a time of 03:00, and the current time is 04:00. Then ci –d –T sets the RCS file's time to 02:00 instead of the usual 04:00; this causes make(1) to think (incorrectly) that the other copy is newer than the RCS file.

-w*login*
Uses login for the author field of the deposited revision. Useful for lying about the author, and for -k if no author is available.

-V
Print RCS's version number.

-V*n*
Emulate RCS version *n*. See co(1) for details.

-x*suffixes*
Specifies the suffixes for RCS files. A nonempty suffix matches any pathname ending in the suffix. An empty suffix matches any pathname of the form RCS/path or path1/RCS/path2. The -x option can specify a list of suffixes separated by /. For example, -x,v/ specifies two suffixes: ,v and the empty suffix. If two or more suffixes are specified, they are tried in order when looking for an RCS file; the first one that works is used for that file. If no RCS file is found but an RCS file can be created, the suffixes are tried in order to determine the new RCS file's name. The default for suffixes is installation-dependent; normally it is ,v/ for hosts like UNIX that permit commas in filenames, and is empty (that is, just the empty suffix) for other hosts.

-z*zone*
Specifies the date output format in keyword substitution, and specifies the default time zone for date in the -d*date* option. The zone should be empty, a numeric UTC offset, or the special string LT for local time. The default is an empty zone, which uses the traditional RCS format of UTC without any time-zone indication and with slashes separating the parts of the date; otherwise, times are output in ISO 8601 format with time zone indication. For example, if local time is January 11, 1990, 8 p.m. Pacific Standard Time, eight hours west of UTC, then the time is output as follows:

| Option | Time Output |
| --- | --- |
| –z | 1990/01/12 04:00:00 (default) |
| –zLT | 1990-01-11 20:00:00-08 |
| –z+05:30 | 1990-01-12 09:30:00+05:30 |

The -z option does not affect dates stored in RCS files, which are always UTC.

## FILE NAMING

Pairs of RCS files and working files can be specified in three ways. (See also "Examples," next.)

1.  Both the RCS file and the working file are given. The RCS pathname is of the form path1/workfileX and the working pathname is of the form path2/workfile where path1/ and path2/ are (possibly different or empty) paths, workfile is a filename, and X is an RCS suffix. If X is empty, path1/ must start with RCS/ or must contain /RCS/.
2.  Only the RCS file is given. Then the working file is created in the current directory and its name is derived from the name of the RCS file by removing path1/ and the suffix X.

3. Only the working file is given. Then ci considers each RCS suffix X in turn, looking for an RCS file of the form path2/ RCS/workfileX or (if the former is not found and X is nonempty) path2/workfileX.

If the RCS file is specified without a path in one of the first two preceding scenarios, ci looks for the RCS file first in the directory ./RCS and then in the current directory.

ci reports an error if an attempt to open an RCS file fails for an unusual reason, even if the RCS file's pathname is just one of several possibilities. For example, to suppress use of RCS commands in a directory d, create a regular file named d/RCS so that casual attempts to use RCS commands in d fail because d/RCS is not a directory.

## EXAMPLES

Suppose ,v is an RCS suffix and the current directory contains a subdirectory RCS with an RCS file io.c,v. Then each of the following commands checks in a copy of io.c into RCS/io.c,v as the latest revision, removing io.c:

```
ci io.c; ci RCS/io.c,v; ci io.c,v;
ci io.c RCS/io.c,v; ci io.c io.c,v;
ci RCS/io.c,v io.c; ci io.c,v io.c;
```

Suppose instead that the empty suffix is an RCS suffix and the current directory contains a subdirectory RCS with an RCS file io.c. Then each of the following commands checks in a new revision:

```
ci io.c; ci RCS/io.c;
ci io.c RCS/io.c;
ci RCS/io.c io.c;
```

## FILE MODES

An RCS file created by ci inherits the read and execute permissions from the working file. If the RCS file exists already, ci preserves its read and execute permissions. ci always turns off all write permissions of RCS files.

## FILES

Temporary files are created in the directory containing the working file, and also in the temporary directory. (See TMPDIR under "Environment.") A semaphore file or files are created in the directory containing the RCS file. With a nonempty suffix, the semaphore names begin with the first character of the suffix; therefore, do not specify an suffix whose first character could be that of a working filename. With an empty suffix, the semaphore names end with an underscore (_), so working filenames should not end in _. ci never changes an RCS or working file. Normally, ci unlinks the file and creates a new one; but instead of breaking a chain of one or more symbolic links to an RCS file, it unlinks the destination file instead. Therefore, ci breaks any hard or symbolic links to any working file it changes; and hard links to RCS files are ineffective, but symbolic links to RCS files are preserved.

The effective user must be able to search and write the directory containing the RCS file. Normally, the real user must be able to read the RCS and working files and to search and write the directory containing the working file; however, some older hosts cannot easily switch between real and effective users, so on these hosts the effective user is used for all accesses. The effective user is the same as the real user unless your copies of ci and co have setuid privileges. These privileges yield extra security if the effective user owns all RCS files and directories, and if only the effective user can write RCS directories.

Users can control access to RCS files by setting the permissions of the directory containing the files; only users with write access to the directory can use RCS commands to change its RCS files. For example, in hosts that allow a user to belong to several groups, one can make a group's RCS directories writable to that group only. This approach suffices for informal projects, but it means that any group member can arbitrarily change the group's RCS files, and can even remove them entirely. Hence, more formal projects sometimes distinguish between an RCS administrator, who can change the RCS files at will, and other project members, who can check in new revisions but cannot otherwise change the RCS files.

## setuid USE

To prevent anybody but their RCS administrator from deleting revisions, a set of users can employ setuid privileges as follows:

■ Check that the host supports RCS setuid use. Consult a trustworthy expert if there are any doubts. It is best if the setuid system calls works as described in POSIX 1003.1a Draft 5, because RCS can switch back and forth easily between real and effective users, even if the real user is root. If not, the second best is if the setuid system call supports saved setuid (the {_POSIX_SAVED_IDS} behavior of POSIX 1003.1-1990); this fails only if the real or effective user is root. If RCS detects any failure in setuid, it quits immediately.

■ Choose a user A to serve as RCS administrator for the set of users. Only A can invoke the rcs command on the users' RCS files. A should not be root or any other user with special powers. Mutually suspicious sets of users should use different administrators.

■ Choose a pathname B to be a directory of files to be executed by the users.

■ Have A set up B to contain copies of ci and co that are setuid to A by copying the commands from their standard installation directory D as follows:
mkdir B cp D/c[io] B chmod go-w,u+s B/c[io]

■ Have each user prepend B to his/her path as follows:
PATH=B:$PATH; export PATH # ordinary shell
set path=(B $path) # C shell

■ Have A create each RCS directory R with write access only to A as follows:
mkdir R chmod go-w R

■ If you want to let only certain users read the RCS files, put the users into a group G, and have A further protect the RCS directory as follows:
chgrp G Rchmod g-w,o-rwx R

■ Have A copy old RCS files (if any) into R, to ensure that A owns them.

■ An RCS file's access list limits who can check in and lock revisions. The default access list is empty, which grants checkin access to anyone who can read the RCS file. If you want limit checkin access, have A invoke rcs -a on the file; see rcs(1). In particular, rcs -e -aA limits access to just A.

■ Have A initialize any new RCS files with rcs -i before initial checkin, adding the -a option if you want to limit checkin access.

■ Give setuid privileges only to ci, co, and rcsclean; do not give them to rcs or to any other command.

■ Do not use other setuid commands to invoke RCS commands; setuid is trickier than you think!

## ENVIRONMENT

RCSINIT    Options prepended to the argument list, separated by spaces. A backslash escapes spaces within an option. The RCSINIT options are prepended to the argument lists of most RCS commands. Useful RCSINIT options include -q, -V, -x, and -z.

TMPDIR     Name of the temporary directory. If not set, the environment variables TMP and TEMPs0 are inspected instead and the first value found is taken; if none of them are set, a host-dependent default is used, typically /tmp.

## DIAGNOSTICS

For each revision, ci prints the RCS file, the working file, and the number of both the deposited and the preceding revision. The exit status is zero if and only if all operations were successful.

## IDENTIFICATION

Author: Walter F. Tichy.

Manual page revision: 5.17; Release date 16 June 1995

Copyright © 1982, 1988, 1989 Walter F. Tichy

Copyright © 1990, 1991, 1992, 1993, 1994, 1995 Paul Eggert

## SEE ALSO

co(1), emacs(1), ident(1), make(1), rcs(1), rcsclean(1), rcsdiff(1), rcsintro(1), rcsmerge(1), rlog(1), setuid(2), rcsfile(5)

Walter F. Tichy, "RCS—A System for Version Control," *Software Practice & Experience* 15, 7 (July 1985), 637–654.

*GNU, 16 June 1995*

# cidentd

cidentd—identd server

## SYNOPSIS

cidentd [-usqvnah] [-f file] [-l file] [-t seconds]

## DESCRIPTION

cidentd gives authentication information.

cidentd is an RFC 1314- and 931-compliant identd daemon. It accepts connections on a port (113 default) and answers queries for port owner of a connection. command;

cidentd normally terminates when the remote command does. The options are as follows:

-u          Turns on the use of the .authlie file in the user's home directory to give the requesting system whatever information the user provides. This file is overridden by the -a option and the system file the format is as follows:

| mynameis | name-to-be-given | # give this userid |
| hideme | | # hide user id |
| host-ip | name-to-be-given | # userid for them |
| host-ip | no-info | # hide you to them |

host-ip can be an ip in dot notation or a name. The file is set so that whatever comes last is what they get.

-s          Closes the connection after a single query.

-q          Quits the daemon after 1 connection (default in 1.0b).

-v          Turns on verbose logging to the syslogs.

-n          Makes cident act like the old school identd with nothing special.

-a          Enables the /etc/cident.users file for options, which overrides the user files if -u is specified. The format is as follows:

| username | name-to-send | # send this for username |
| username | | # must send there username |
| all | name-to-send | # send for every query |
| all | no-info | # send nothing every query |
| host-ip | name-to-send | # send to that host |
| host-ip | no-info | # send nothing to them |

host-ip can be an ip in dot notation or a name. The file is set so that whatever comes last is what they get.

-h          Displays the help list to the screen you might not want to do this from some terminal types.

-f          Sets the file to find the ports and ids of connections. Use this to specify a file other than /proc/net/tcp.

-l          Used to specify a file other than /etc/cident.users must be used with the -a option unless you like redundancy.

-t          Sets the time out of a connection in seconds. This does not work in this version to cidentd.

If no arguments are specified, the program just runs as normal, almost like the -n.

cidentd -t 30 -a sets timer to 30 seconds and tells it to look at .authlie files.

## FILES

    /etc/cidentd.users
    $(HOME)/ authlie

## SEE ALSO

    identd(1)

## BUGS

None that I know of.

*Linux/FreeBSD, May 1996*

# cksum

cksum—Checksum and count the bytes in a file

## SYNOPSIS

    cksum [—help] [—version] [file...]

## DESCRIPTION

This manual page documents the GNU version of cksum. cksum computes a cyclic redundancy check (CRC) for each named file, or the standard input if none are given or when a file named - is given. It prints the CRC for each file along with the number of bytes in the file, and the filename unless no arguments were given.

cksum is typically used to make sure that files transferred by unreliable means (such as netnews) have not been corrupted. This is accomplished by comparing the cksum output for the received files with the cksum output for the original files. The CRC algorithm is specified by the POSIX.2 standard. It is not compatible with the BSD or System V sum programs; it is more robust.

Available options are

| —help | Print a usage message and exit with a nonzero status. |
| —version | Print version information on standard output then exit. |

*GNU Text Utilities*

# clear

clear—Clear terminal screen

## SYNOPSIS

    clear

## DESCRIPTION

clear calls tput(1) with the clear argument. This causes tput to attempt to clear the screen, checking the data in /etc/termcap (for the GNU or BSD tput) or in the terminfo database (for the ncurses tput) and sending the appropriate sequence to the terminal. This command can be redirected to clear the screen of some other terminal.

## SEE ALSO

reset(1), stty(1), tput(1)

## AUTHOR

Rik Faith (faith@cs.unc.edu)

*Linux 0.99, 10 October 1993*

# cmuwmtopbm

cmuwmtopbm—Convert a CMU window manager bitmap into a portable bitmap

## SYNOPSIS

cmuwmtopbm [cmuwmfile]

## DESCRIPTION

Reads a CMU window manager bitmap as input. Produces a portable bitmap as output.

## SEE ALSO

pbmtocmuwm(1), pbm(5)

## AUTHOR

Copyright © 1989 by Jef Poskanzer

*15 April 1989*

# co

co—Check out RCS revisions

## SYNOPSIS

co [options] file ...

## DESCRIPTION

co retrieves a revision from each RCS file and stores it into the corresponding working file.

Pathnames matching an RCS suffix denote RCS files; all others denote working files. Names are paired as explained in ci(1).

Revisions of an RCS file can be checked out locked or unlocked. Locking a revision prevents overlapping updates. A revision checked out for reading or processing (for example, compiling) need not be locked. A revision checked out for editing and later checkin must normally be locked. Checkout with locking fails if the revision to be checked out is currently locked by another user. (A lock can be broken with rcs(1).) Checkout with locking also requires the caller to be on the access list of the RCS file, unless he is the owner of the file or the superuser, or the access list is empty. Checkout without locking is not subject to access list restrictions, and is not affected by the presence of locks.

A revision is selected by options for revision or branch number, checkin date/time, author, or state. When the selection options are applied in combination, co retrieves the latest revision that satisfies all of them. If none of the selection options is specified, co retrieves the latest revision on the default branch, normally the trunk; see the -b option of rcs(1). A revision or branch number can be attached to any of the options -f, -I, -l, -M, -p, -q, -r, or -u. The options -d (date), -s (state), and -w (author) retrieve from a single branch, the selected branch (which is specified by -f or -u), or the default branch.

A co command applied to an RCS file with no revisions creates a zero-length working file. co always performs keyword substitution.

## OPTIONS

-r[*rev*]    Retrieves the latest revision whose number is less than or equal to *rev*. If *rev* indicates a branch rather than a revision, the latest revision on that branch is retrieved. If *rev* is omitted, the latest revision on the default branch is retrieved; see the -b option of rcs(1). If *rev* is $, co determines the revision number from keyword values in the working file. Otherwise, a revision is composed of one or more numeric or symbolic fields separated by periods. If *rev* begins with a period, then the default branch (normally the trunk) is prepended to it. If *rev* is a branch number followed by a period, then the latest revision on that branch is used. The numeric equivalent of a symbolic field is specified with the -n option of the commands ci(1) and rcs(1).

-l[*rev*]    Same as -r, except that it also locks the retrieved revision for the caller.

-u[*rev*]    Same as -r, except that it unlocks the retrieved revision if it was locked by the caller. If *rev* is omitted, -u retrieves the revision locked by the caller, if there is one; otherwise, it retrieves the latest revision on the default branch.

-f[*rev*]    Forces the overwriting of the working file; useful in connection with -q. (See also "File Modes," later in this manual page.)

-kkv    Generate keyword strings using the default form, for example, $Revision: 5.13 $ for the Revision keyword. A locker's name is inserted in the value of the Header, Id, and Locker keyword strings only as a file is being locked, that is, by ci -l and co -l. This is the default.

-kkvl    Like -kkv, except that a locker's name is always inserted if the given revision is currently locked.

-kk    Generate only keyword names in keyword strings; omit their values. (See "Keyword Substitution," later in this manual page.) For example, for the Revision keyword, generate the string $Revision$ instead of $Revision: 5.13 $. This option is useful to ignore differences due to keyword substitution when comparing different revisions of a file. Log messages are inserted after $Log$ keywords even if -kk is specified, since this tends to be more useful when merging changes.

-ko    Generate the old keyword string, present in the working file just before it was checked in. For example, for the Revision keyword, generate the string $Revision: 1.1 $ instead of $Revision: 5.13 $ if that is how the string appeared when the file was checked in. This can be useful for file formats that cannot tolerate any changes to substrings that happen to take the form of keyword strings.

-kb    Generate a binary image of the old keyword string. This acts like -ko, except it performs all working file input and output in binary mode. This makes little difference on POSIX and UNIX hosts, but on DOS-like hosts one should use rcs -i -kb to initialize an RCS file normally refuses to merge files when -kb is in effect.

-kv    Generate only keyword values for keyword strings. For example, for the Revision keyword, generate the string 5.13 instead of $Revision: 5.13 $. This can help generate files in programming languages where it is hard to strip keyword delimiters like $Revision: $ from a string. However, further keyword substitution cannot be performed once the keyword names are removed, so this option should be used with care. Because of this danger of losing keywords, this option cannot be combined with -l, and the owner write permission of the working file is turned off; to edit the file later, check it out again without -kv.

-p[*rev*]    Prints the retrieved revision on the standard output rather than storing it in the working file. This option is useful when co is part of a pipe.

-q[*rev*]    Quiet mode; diagnostics are not printed.

-I[*rev*]    Interactive mode; the user is prompted and questioned even if the standard input is not a terminal.

-d*date*    Retrieves the latest revision on the selected branch whose checkin date/time is less than or equal to date. The date and time can be given in free format. The time zone LT stands for local time; other common time zone names are understood. For example, the following dates are equivalent if local time is January 11, 1990, 8 p.m. Pacific Standard Time, eight hours west of Coordinated Universal Time (UTC):

> 8:00 PM lt
> 4:00 AM, Jan. 12, 1990              Default is UTC

| | |
|---|---|
| 1990-01-12 04:00:00+00 | ISO 8601 (UTC) |
| 1990-01-11 20:00:00–08 | ISO 8601 (local time) |
| 1990/01/12 04:00:00 | Traditional RCS format |
| Thu Jan 11 20:00:00 1990 LT | Output of ctime(3) + LT |
| Thu Jan 11 20:00:00 PST 1990 | Output of date(1) |
| Fri Jan 12 04:00:00 GMT 1990 | |
| Thu, 11 Jan 1990 20:00:00 –0800 | Internet RFC 822 |
| 12-January-1990, 04:00 WET | |

Most fields in the date and time can be defaulted. The default time zone is normally UTC, but this can be overridden by the -z option. The other defaults are determined in the order year, month, day, hour, minute, and second (most to least significant). At least one of these fields must be provided. For omitted fields that are of higher significance than the highest provided field, the time zone's current values are assumed. For all other omitted fields, the lowest possible values are assumed. For example, without -z, the date 20, 10:30 defaults to 10:30:00 UTC of the 20th of the UTC time zone's current month and year. The date/time must be quoted if it contains spaces.

-M[*rev*]    Sets the modification time on the new working file to be the date of the retrieved revision. Use this option with care; it can confuse make(1).

-s*state*    Retrieves the latest revision on the selected branch whose state is set to state.

-T    Preserves the modification time on the RCS file even if the RCS file changes because a lock is added or removed. This option can suppress extensive recompilation caused by a make(1) dependency of some other copy of the working file on the RCS file. Use this option with care; it can suppress recompilation even when it is needed, in other words, when the change of lock would mean a change to keyword strings in the other working file.

-w[*login*]    Retrieves the latest revision on the selected branch that was checked in by the user with login name *login*. If the argument *login* is omitted, the caller's login is assumed.

-j*joinlist*    Generates a new revision which is the join of the revisions on *joinlist*. This option is largely made obsolete by rcsmerge(1), but is retained for backwards compatibility.

The *joinlist* is a comma-separated list of pairs of the form *rev2*:*rev3*, where *rev2* and *rev3* are (symbolic or numeric) revision numbers. For the initial such pair, *rev1* denotes the revision selected by the options -f, -w. For all other pairs, *rev1* denotes the revision generated by the previous pair. (Thus, the output of one join becomes the input to the next.)

For each pair, co joins revisions *rev1* and *rev3* with respect to *rev2*. This means that all changes that transform *rev2* into *rev1* are applied to a copy of *rev3*. This is particularly useful if *rev1* and *rev3* are the ends of two branches that have *rev2* as a common ancestor. If *rev1*<*rev2*<*rev3* on the same branch, joining generates a new revision which is like *rev3*, but with all changes that lead from *rev1* to *rev2* undone. If changes from *rev2* to *rev1* overlap with changes from *rev2* to *rev3*, co reports overlaps as described in merge(1).

For the initial pair, *rev2* can be omitted. The default is the common ancestor. If any of the arguments indicate branches, the latest revisions on those branches are assumed. The options -l and -u lock or unlock *rev1*.

-V    Prints RCS's version number.

-V*n*    Emulates RCS version *n*, where *n* can be 3, 4, or 5. This can be useful when interchanging RCS files with others who are running older versions of RCS. To see which version of RCS your correspondents are running, have them invoke rcs -V; this works with newer versions of RCS. If it doesn't work, have them invoke rlog on an RCS file; if none of the first few lines of output contain the string branch:, it is version 3; if the dates' years have just two digits, it is version 4; otherwise, it is version 5. An RCS file generated while emulating version 3 loses its default branch. An RCS revision generated while emulating version 4 or earlier has a timestamp that is off by up to 13 hours. A revision extracted while emulating version 4 or earlier contains abbreviated dates of the form yy/mm/dd and can also contain different whitespace and line prefixes in the substitution for $Log$.

| | |
|---|---|
| `-xsuffixes` | Uses suffixes to characterize RCS files. See `ci(1)` for details. |
| `-zzone` | Specifies the date output format in keyword substitution, and specifies the default time zone for date in the `-ddate` option. The *zone* should be empty, a numeric UTC offset, or the special string LT for local time. The default is an empty zone, which uses the traditional RCS format of UTC without any time zone indication and with slashes separating the parts of the date; otherwise, times are output in ISO 8601 format with time zone indication. For example, if local time is January 11, 1990, 8 p.m. Pacific Standard Time, eight hours west of UTC, then the time is output as follows: |

| Option | Time Output |
|---|---|
| `-z` | `1990/01/12 04:00:00` (default) |
| `-zLT` | `1990-01-11 20:00:00-08` |
| `-z+05:30` | `1990-01-12 09:30:00+05:30` |

The `-z` option does not affect dates stored in RCS files, which are always UTC.

## KEYWORD SUBSTITUTION

Strings of the form $ *keyword* $ and $ *keyword* : ... $ embedded in the text are replaced with strings of the form $ *keyword* : *value* $, where *keyword* and *value* are pairs in the following list. Keywords can be embedded in literal strings or comments to identify a revision.

Initially, the user enters strings of the form `$keyword$`. On checkout, `co` replaces these strings with strings of the form `$keyword : value$`. If a revision containing strings of the latter form is checked back in, the *value* fields will be replaced during the next checkout. Thus, the keyword values are automatically updated on checkout. This automatic substitution can be modified by the `-k` options.

Keywords and their corresponding values:

| | |
|---|---|
| `$Author$` | The login name of the user who checked in the revision. |
| `$Date$` | The date and time the revision was checked in. With `-zzone`, a numeric time zone offset is appended; otherwise, the date is UTC. |
| `$Header$` | A standard header containing the full pathname of the RCS file, the revision number, the date and time, the author, the state, and the locker (if locked). With `-zzone`, a numeric time zone offset is appended to the date; otherwise, the date is UTC. |
| `$Id$` | Same as `$Header$`, except that the RCS filename is without a path. |
| `$Locker$` | The login name of the user who locked the revision (empty if not locked). |
| `$Log$` | The log message supplied during checkin, preceded by a header containing the RCS filename, the revision number, the author, and the date and time. With `-zzone` a numeric time zone offset is appended; otherwise, the date is UTC. Existing log messages are not replaced. Instead, the new log message is inserted after `$Log: ... $`. This is useful for accumulating a complete change log in a source file. |

Each inserted line is prefixed by the string that prefixes the `$Log$` line. For example, if the `$Log$` line is `// $Log: tan.cc $`, RCS prefixes each line of the log with `//`. This is useful for languages with comments that go to the end of the line. The convention for other languages is to use a `*` prefix inside a multiline comment. For example, the initial log comment of a C program conventionally is of the following form:

```
/*
 * $Log$
 */
```

For backwards compatibility with older versions of RCS, if the log prefix is `/*` or `(*` surrounded by optional whitespace, inserted log lines contain a space instead of `/` or `(`; however, this usage is obsolescent and should not be relied on.

| | |
|---|---|
| `$Name$` | The symbolic name used to check out the revision, if any. For example, `co -r Joe` generates `$Name: Joe $`. Plain `co` generates just `$Name: $`. |

| | |
|---|---|
| `$RCSfile$` | The name of the RCS file without a path. |
| `$Revision$` | The revision number assigned to the revision. |
| `$Source$` | The full pathname of the RCS file. |
| `$State$` | The state assigned to the revision with the -s option of rcs(1) or ci(1). |

The following characters in keyword values are represented by escape sequences to keep keyword strings well-formed.

| *Character* | *Escape Sequence* |
|---|---|
| tab | `\t` |
| newline | `\n` |
| space | `\040` |
| $ | `\044` |
| \ | `\\` |

## FILE MODES

The working file inherits the read and execute permissions from the RCS file. In addition, the owner write permission is turned on, unless -kv is set or the file is checked out unlocked and locking is set to strict; see rcs(1).

If a file with the name of the working file exists already and has write permission, co aborts the checkout, asking beforehand if possible. If the existing working file is not writable or -f is given, the working file is deleted without asking.

## FILES

co accesses files much as ci(1) does, except that it does not need to read the working file unless a revision number of $ is specified.

## ENVIRONMENT

`RCSINIT`    Options prepended to the argument list, separated by spaces. See ci(1) for details.

## DIAGNOSTICS

The RCS pathname, the working pathname, and the revision number retrieved are written to the diagnostic output. The exit status is zero if and only if all operations were successful.

## IDENTIFICATION

Author: Walter F. Tichy.

Manual Page Revision: 5.13; Release Date: 1995/06/01.

Copyright © 1982, 1988, 1989 Walter F. Tichy.

Copyright © 1990, 1991, 1992, 1993, 1994, 1995 Paul Eggert.

## SEE ALSO

rcsintro(1), ci(1), ctime(3), date(1), ident(1), make(1), rcs(1), rcsclean(1), rcsdiff(1), rc-smerge(1), rlog(1), rcsfile(5)

Walter F. Tichy, "RCS—A System for Version Control," *Software Practice & Experience* 15, 7 (July 1985), 637-654.

## LIMITS

Links to the RCS and working files are not preserved.

There is no way to selectively suppress the expansion of keywords, except by writing them differently. In nroff and troff, this is done by embedding the null-character \& into the keyword.

# col

col—Filter reverse line feeds from input

## SYNOPSIS

col [-bfx] [-l *num*]

## DESCRIPTION

col filters out reverse (and half-reverse) line feeds so the output is in the correct order with only forward and half-forward line feeds, and replaces whitespace characters with tabs where possible. This can be useful in processing the output of nroff(1) and tbl(1). col reads from standard input and writes to standard output.

The options are as follows:

-b              Do not output any backspaces, printing only the last character written to each column position.

-f              Forward half-line feeds are permitted (fine mode). Normally characters printed on a half-line boundary are printed on the following line.

-x              Output multiple spaces instead of tabs.

-l*num*         Buffer at least *num* lines in memory. By default, 128 lines are buffered.

The control sequences for carriage motion that col understands and their decimal values are listed in the following table:

| *Control Sequence* | *Decimal Value* |
| --- | --- |
| Esc+7 | Reverse line feed (escape then 7) |
| Esc+8 | Half-reverse line feed (escape then 8) |
| Esc+9 | Half-forward line feed (escape then 9) |
| Backspace | Moves back one column (8); ignored in the first column |
| Carriage return | (13) |
| Newline | Forward line feed (10); also does carriage return |
| Shift in | Shift to normal character set (15) |
| Shift out | Shift to alternate character set (14) |
| Space | Moves forward one column (32) |
| Tab | Moves forward to next tab stop (9) |
| Vertical tab | Reverse line feed (11) |

All unrecognized control characters and escape sequences are discarded.

col keeps track of the character set as characters are read and makes sure the character set is correct when they are output.

If the input attempts to back up to the last flushed line, col will display a warning message.

## SEE ALSO

expand(1), nroff(1), tbl(1)

## HISTORY

A col command appeared in version 6 AT&T UNIX.

*17 June 1991*

# colcrt

colcrt—Filter nroff output for CRT previewing

## SYNOPSIS

colcrt [-] [-2] [*file* ...]

## DESCRIPTION

colcrt provides virtual half-line and reverse-line feed sequences for terminals without such capability, and on which overstriking is destructive. Half-line characters and underlining (changed to dashing -) are placed on new lines in between the normal output lines.

Available options:

-             Suppress all underlining. This option is especially useful for previewing all boxed tables from tbl(1).

-2          Causes all half-lines to be printed, effectively double spacing the output. Normally, a minimal space output format is used which will suppress empty lines. The program never suppresses two consecutive empty lines, however. The -2 option is useful for sending output to the line printer when the output contains superscripts and subscripts that would otherwise be invisible.

## EXAMPLES

A typical use of colcrt would be

tbl exum2.n ¦ nroff -ms ¦ colcrt - ¦ more

## SEE ALSO

nroff(1), troff(1), col(1), more(1), ul(1)

## BUGS

Should fold underlines onto blanks even with the - option so that a true underline character would show.

Can't back up more than 102 lines.

General overstriking is lost; as a special case ¦ overstruck with ' ' or underline becomes +. Lines are trimmed to 132 characters.

Some provision should be made for processing superscripts and subscripts in documents that are already double-spaced.

## HISTORY

The colcrt command appeared in BSD 3.0.

*BSD 3, 30 June 1993*

# colrm

colrm—Remove columns from a file

## SYNOPSIS

colrm [*startcol* [*endcol*]]

## DESCRIPTION

colrm removes selected columns from a file. Input is taken from standard input. Output is sent to standard output.

If called with one parameter, the columns of each line will be removed starting with the specified column. If called with two parameters, the columns from the first column to the last column will be removed.

Column numbering starts with column 1.

## SEE ALSO

awk(1), column(1), expand(1), paste(1)

## HISTORY

The colrm command appeared in BSD 3.0.

# column

column—Columnate lists

## SYNOPSIS

column [-tx] [-ccolumns] [-ssep] [...file]

## DESCRIPTION

The column utility formats its input into multiple columns. Rows are filled before columns. Input is taken from file operands, or, by default, from the standard input. Empty lines are ignored.

The options are as follows:

| | |
|---|---|
| -c | Output is formatted for a display columns wide. |
| -s | Specify a set of characters to be used to delimit columns for the -t option. |
| -t | Determine the number of columns the input contains and create a table. Columns are delimited with whitespace, by default, or with the characters supplied using the -s option. Useful for pretty-printing displays. |
| -x | Fill columns before filling rows. |

Column exits 0 on success, >0 if an error occurred.

## ENVIRONMENT

The environment variable COLUMNS is used to determine the size of the screen if no other information is available.

## EXAMPLES

(printf "PERM LINKS OWNER SIZE MONTH DAY HH:MM/YEAR NAME"; ls -l j sed 1d) j column -t

## SEE ALSO

colrm(1), ls(1), paste(1), sort(1)

## HISTORY

The column command appeared in BSD 4.3 Reno.

# comm

comm—Compare two sorted files line by line

## SYNOPSIS

comm [-123] [—help] [—version] *file1 file2*

## DESCRIPTION

This manual page documents the GNU version of comm. comm prints lines that are common, and lines that are unique, to two input files. The two files must be sorted before comm can be used. The filename - means the standard input.

With no options, comm produces three column output. Column one contains lines unique to *file1*, column two contains lines unique to *file2*, and column three contains lines common to both files.

## OPTIONS

The options -1, -2, and -3 suppress printing of the corresponding columns.

—help            Print a usage message and exit with a nonzero status.

—version         Print version information on standard output then exit.

*GNU Text Utilities*

# convdate

convdate—Convert time/date strings and numbers

## SYNOPSIS

convdate [ -c ][-n ][-s ] *arg*...

## DESCRIPTION

convdate translates the date/time strings specified as arguments on its command line, outputting the results one to a line.

If the -s flag is used, then each argument is taken as a date string to be parsed by parse-date(3) and is output as a string formatted by ctime(3). This is the default.

If the -n flag is used, then each argument is converted the same way but is output as a time t; see time(2).

If the -c flag is used, then each argument is taken to be a time t and is output in ctime format.

Here's an example:

```
% convdate 'feb 10 10am'
Sun Feb 10 10:00:00 1991

% convdate 12pm 5/4/90
Fri Dec 13 00:00:00 1991
Fri May 4 00:00:00 1990

% convdate -n 'feb 10 10am' '12pm 5/4/90'
666198000
641880000
% convdate -c 666198000
Sun Feb 10 10:00:00 1991
```

## HISTORY

Written by Rich $alz (rsalz@uunet.uu.net).

## SEE ALSO

parsedate(3)

# cp

cp—Copy files

## SYNOPSIS

```
cp [options] source dest
cp [options] source... dircotory
```

Options:

```
[-abdfilprsuvxPR] [-S backup-suffix] [-V fnumbered,existing,simpleg] [—backup]
[—no-dereference] [—force] [—interactive] [—one-file-system] [—preserve]
[—recursive][—update] [—verbose] [—suffix=backup-suffix]
[—version-control=fnumbered,existing,simpleg] [—archive] [—parents] [—link]
[—symbolic-link] [—help] [—version]
```

## DESCRIPTION

This manual page documents the GNU version of cp. If the last argument names an existing directory, cp copies each other given file into a file with the same name in that directory. Otherwise, if only two files are given, it copies the first onto the second. It is an error if the last argument is not a directory and more than two files are given. By default, it does not copy directories.

## OPTIONS

| | |
|---|---|
| -a, —archive | Preserve as much as possible of the structure and attributes of the original files in the copy. The same as -dpR. |
| -b, —backup | Make backups of files that are about to be overwritten or removed. |
| -d, —no-dereference | Copy symbolic links as symbolic links rather than copying the files that they point to, and preserve hard link relationships between source files in the copies. |
| -f, —force | Remove existing destination files. |
| -i, —interactive | Prompt whether to overwrite existing regular destination files. |
| -l, —link | Make hard links instead of copies of nondirectories. |
| -P, —parents | Form the name of each destination file by appending to the target directory a slash and the specified name of the source file. The last argument given to cp must be the name of an existing directory. For example, the command cp —parents a/b/c existing_dir copies the file a/b/c to existing_dir/a/b/c, creating any missing intermediate directories. |
| -p, —preserve | Preserve the original files' owner, group, permissions, and timestamps. |
| -r | Copy directories recursively, copying all nondirectories as if they were regular files. |
| -s, —symbolic-link | Make symbolic links instead of copies of nondirectories. All source filenames must be absolute (starting with /) unless the destination files are in the current directory. This option produces an error message on systems that do not support symbolic links. |
| -u, —update | Do not copy a nondirectory that has an existing destination with the same or newer modification time. |
| -v, —verbose | Print the name of each file before copying it. |
| -x, —one-file-system | Skip subdirectories that are on different filesystems from the one that the copy started on. |
| -R, —recursive | Copy directories recursively. |
| —help | Print a usage message on standard output and exit successfully. |
| —version | Print version information on standard output then exit successfully. |
| -S, —suffix backup-suffix | The suffix used for making simple backup files can be set with the SIMPLE_BACKUP_SUFFIX environment variable, which can be overridden by this option. If neither of those is given, the default is -, as it is in emacs. |

-V, —version-control
{numbered,existing,simple}

The type of backups made can be set with the VERSION_CONTROL environment variable, which can be overridden by this option. If VERSION_CONTROL is not set and this option is not given, the default backup type is existing. The value of the VERSION_CONTROL environment variable and the argument to this option are like the GNU emacs version- control variable; they also recognize synonyms that are more descriptive. The valid values are (unique abbreviations are accepted) the following:

| | |
|---|---|
| t or numbered | Always make numbered backups |
| nil or existing | Make numbered backups of files that already have them, simple backups of the others |
| never or simple | Always make simple backups |

# cccp, cpp

cccp, cpp—The GNU C-compatible compiler preprocessor

## SYNOPSIS

```
cccp    [-$][-A predicate [( value )]] [ -C ][-D name [ = definition ]]
        [-dD][-dM][-I\ directory ][-H ][-I- ][-imacros file ][-
        include file ][-idirafter dir ][-iprefix prefix ][-iwithprefix dir ]
        [ -lang-c][-lang-c++][-lang-objc ][-lang-objc++ ][-lint ][-
        M[-MG ]] [ -MM[-MG ]] [ -MD file ][-MMD file ][-nostdinc ]
        [ -nostdinc++][-P][-pedantic ][-pedantic-errors ][-traditional ]
        [ -trigraphs ][-U name ][-undef ][-Wtrigraphs ][-Wcomment ]
        [ -Wall ][-Wtraditional ]
        [ infile ¦- ][ outfile ¦- ]
```

## DESCRIPTION

The C preprocessor is a macro processor that is used automatically by the C compiler to transform your program before actual compilation. It is called a macro processor because it allows you to define macros, which are brief abbreviations for longer constructs.

The C preprocessor provides four separate facilities that you can use as you see fit:

- Inclusion of header files. These are files of declarations that can be substituted into your program.
- Macro expansion. You can define macros, which are abbreviations for arbitrary fragments of C code, and then the C preprocessor will replace the macros with their definitions throughout the program.
- Conditional compilation. Using special preprocessing directives, you can include or exclude parts of the program according to various conditions.
- Line control. If you use a program to combine or rearrange source files into an intermediate file which is then compiled, you can use line control to inform the compiler of where each source line originally came from.

C preprocessors vary in some details. For a full explanation of the GNU C preprocessor, see the info file cpp.info, or the manual *The C Preprocessor*. Both of these are built from the same documentation source file, cpp.texinfo. The GNU C preprocessor provides a superset of the features of ANSI Standard C.

ANSI Standard C requires the rejection of many harmless constructs commonly used by today's C programs. Such incompatibility would be inconvenient for users, so the GNU C preprocessor is configured to accept these constructs by default. Strictly speaking, to get ANSI Standard C, you must use the options -trigraphs, -undef, and -pedantic, but in practice the consequences of having strict ANSI Standard C make it undesirable to do this.

When you use the C preprocessor, you will usually not have to invoke it explicitly: the C compiler will do so automatically. However, the preprocessor is sometimes useful individually.

When you call the preprocessor individually, either name (cpp or cccp) will do; they are completely synonymous.

The C preprocessor expects two filenames as arguments, `infile` and `outfile`. The preprocessor reads `infile` together with any other files it specifies with `#include`. All the output generated by the combined input files is written in `outfile`. Either `infile` or `outfile` may be -, which as `infile` means to read from standard input and as `outfile` means to write to standard output. Also, if `outfile` or both filenames are omitted, the standard output and standard input are used for the omitted filenames.

## OPTIONS

Here is a table of command options accepted by the C preprocessor. These options can also be given when compiling a C program; they are passed along automatically to the preprocessor when it is invoked by the compiler.

| | |
|---|---|
| -P | Inhibit generation of # lines with line-number information in the output from the preprocessor. This might be useful when running the preprocessor on something that is not C code and will be sent to a program which might be confused by the # lines. |
| -C | Do not discard comments: pass them through to the output file. Comments appearing in arguments of a macro call will be copied to the output before the expansion of the macro call. |
| -traditional | Try to imitate the behavior of old-fashioned C, as opposed to ANSI C. |
| -trigraphs | Process ANSI standard trigraph sequences. These are three-character sequences, all starting with ??, that are defined by ANSI C to stand for single characters. For example, ??/ stands for \, so ??/n is a character constant for a newline. Strictly speaking, the GNU C preprocessor does not support all programs in ANSI Standard C unless -trigraphs is used, but if you ever notice the difference, it will be with relief. You don't want to know any more about trigraphs. |
| —pedantic | Issue warnings required by the ANSI C standard in certain cases such as when text other than a comment follows #else or #endif. |
| -pedantic-errors | Like -pedantic, except that errors are produced rather than warnings. |
| —Wtrigraphs | Warn if any trigraphs are encountered (assuming they are enabled). |
| —Wcomment —Wcomments | Warn whenever a comment-start sequence /* appears in a comment. (Both forms have the same effect.) |
| —Wall | Requests both -Wtrigraphs and -Wcomment (but not -Wtraditional). |
| —Wtraditional | Warn about certain constructs that behave differently in traditional and ANSI C. |
| -I directory | Add the directory *directory* to the end of the list of directories to be searched for header files. This can be used to override a system header file, substituting your own version, since these directories are searched before the system header file directories. If you use more than one -I option, the directories are scanned in left-to-right order; the standard system directories come after. |
| -I- | Any directories specified with -I options before the -I- option are searched only for the case of #include " file "; they are not searched for #include < file >. If additional directories are specified with -I options after the -I-, these directories are searched for all #include directives. In addition, the -I- option inhibits the use of the current directory as the first search directory for #include " file ". Therefore, the current directory is searched only if it is requested explicitly with -I followed by a period (.). Specifying both -I- and -I. allows you to control precisely which directories are searched before the current one and which are searched after. |
| -nostdinc | Do not search the standard system directories for header files. Only the directories you have specified with -I options (and the current directory, if appropriate) are searched. |
| -nostdinc++ | Do not search for header files in the C++-specific standard directories, but do still search the other standard directories. (This option is used when building libg++.) |
| -D name | Predefine *name* as a macro, with definition 1. |
| -D name=definition | Predefine name as a macro, with definition *definition*. There are no restrictions on the contents of definition, but if you are invoking the preprocessor from a shell or shell-like program, you may need to use the shell's quoting syntax to protect characters such as spaces that have a meaning in the shell syntax. If you use more than one -D for the same name, the rightmost definition takes effect. |

| | |
|---|---|
| -U *name* | Do not predefine *name*. If both -U and -D are specified for one name, the -U beats the -D and the name is not predefined. |
| -undef | Do not predefine any nonstandard macros. |
| -A *name*(value) | Assert (in the same way as the #assert directive) the predicate name with tokenlist value . Remember to escape or quote the parentheses on shell command lines. You can use -A- to disable all predefined assertions; it also undefines all predefined macros. |
| -dM | Instead of outputting the result of preprocessing, output a list of #define directives for all the macros defined during the execution of the preprocessor, including predefined macros. This gives you a way of finding out what is predefined in your version of the preprocessor; assuming you have no file foo.h, the command |
| | touch foo.h; cpp -dM foo.h |
| | will show the values of any predefined macros. |
| -dD | Like -dM except in two respects: it does not include the predefined macros, and it outputs both the #define directives and the result of preprocessing. Both kinds of output go to the standard output file. |
| -M[-MG] | Instead of outputting the result of preprocessing, output a rule suitable for make describing the dependencies of the main source file. The preprocessor outputs one make rule containing the object filename for that source file, a colon, and the names of all the included files. If there are many included files then the rule is split into several lines using \\ (newline). |
| | -MG says to treat missing header files as generated files and assume they live in the same directory as the source file. It must be specified in addition to -M. |
| | This feature is used in automatic updating of makefiles. |
| -MM[-MG] | Like -M but mention only the files included with #include " file ". System header files included with #include < file > are omitted. |
| -MD*file* | Like -M but the dependency information is written to file. This is in addition to compiling the file as specified. -MD does not inhibit ordinary compilation the way -M does. |
| | When invoking gcc, do not specify the file argument. gcc will create filenames made by replacing .c with .d at the end of the input filenames. |
| | In Mach, you can use the utility md to merge multiple files into a single dependency file suitable for using with the make command. |
| -MMD*file* | Like -M except mention only user header files, not system header files. |
| -H | Print the name of each header file used, in addition to other normal activities. |
| -imacros *file* | Process file as input, discarding the resulting output, before processing the regular input file. Because the output generated from file is discarded, the only effect of -imacros file is to make the macros defined in file available for use in the main input. The preprocessor evaluates any -D and -U options on the command line before processing –imacros file. |
| -include *file* | Process file as input, and include all the resulting output, before processing the regular input file. |
| -idirafter *dir* | Add the directory dir to the second include path. The directories on the second include path are searched when a header file is not found in any of the directories in the main include path (the one that -I adds to). |
| -iprefix *prefix* | Specify prefix as the prefix for subsequent -iwithprefix options. |
| -iwithprefix *dir* | Add a directory to the second include path. The directory's name is made by concatenating prefix and dir, where prefix was specified previously with -iprefix. |
| -lang-c<br>-lang-c++<br>-lang-objc<br>-lang-objc++ | Specify the source language. -lang-c++ makes the preprocessor handle C++ comment syntax, and includes extra default include directories for C++, and -lang-objc enables the Objective C #import directive. -lang-c explicitly turns off both of these extensions, and -lang-objc++ enables both. These options are generated by the compiler driver gcc, but not passed from the gcc command line. |
| -lint | Look for commands to the program checker lint embedded in comments, and emit them preceded by #pragma lint. For example, the comment /* NOTREACHED */ becomes #pragma lint NOTREACHED.<br>This option is available only when you call cpp directly; gcc will not pass it from its command line. |

-$         Forbid the use of $ in identifiers. This is required for ANSI conformance. gcc automatically supplies this option to the preprocessor if you specify -ansi, but gcc doesn't recognize the -$ option itself; to use it without the other effects of -ansi, you must call the preprocessor directly.

## SEE ALSO

cpp entry in info; *The C Preprocessor*, Richard M. Stallman.

gcc(1); gcc entry in info; *Using and Porting GNU CC* (for version 2.0), Richard M. Stallman.

## COPYING

Copyright © 1991, 1992, 1993 Free Software Foundation, Inc. Permission is granted to make and distribute verbatim copies of this manual provided the copyright notice and this permission notice are preserved on all copies.

Permission is granted to copy and distribute modified versions of this manual under the conditions for verbatim copying, provided that the entire resulting derived work is distributed under the terms of a permission notice identical to this one.

Permission is granted to copy and distribute translations of this manual into another language, under the above conditions for modified versions, except that this permission notice may be included in translations approved by the Free Software Foundation instead of in the original English.

*GNU Tools, 30 April 1993*

# crontab

crontab—Manipulate per-user crontabs (Dillon's Cron)

## SYNOPSIS

| | |
|---|---|
| crontab file [-u *user*] | Replace crontab from file |
| crontab - [-u *user*] | Replace crontab from stdin |
| crontab -l [*user*] | List crontab for *user* |
| crontab -e [*user*] | Edit crontab for *user* |
| crontab -d [*user*] | Delete crontab for *user* |
| crontab -c *dir* | Specify crontab directory |

## DESCRIPTION

crontab manipulates the crontab for a particular user. Only the superuser may specify a different user and/or crontab directory. Generally, the -e option is used to edit your crontab. crontab will use /usr/bin/vi or the editor specified by your VISUAL environment variable to edit the crontab.

Unlike other crond/crontabs, this crontab does not try to do everything under the sun. Frankly, a shell script is much more able to manipulate the environment than cron, and I see no particular reason to use the user's shell (from his password entry) to run cron commands when this requires special casing of nonuser crontabs, such as those for UUCP. When a crontab command is run, this crontab runs it with /bin/sh and sets up only three environment variables: USER, HOME, and SHELL.

crond automatically detects changes in the time. Reverse-indexed time changes less then an hour old will NOT rerun crontab commands already issued in the recovered period. Forward-indexed changes less then an hour into the future will issue missed commands exactly once. Changes greater then an hour into the past or future cause crond to resynchronize and not issue missed commands. No attempt will be made to issue commands lost due to a reboot, and commands are not reissued if the previously issued command is still running. For example, if you have a crontab command sleep 70 that you wish to run once a minute, cron will only be able to issue the command once every two minutes. If you do not like this feature, you can run your commands in the background with an &.

The `crontab` format is roughly similar to that used by `vixiecron`, but without complex features. Individual fields may contain a time, a time range, a time range with a skip factor, a symbolic range for the day of week and month in year, and additional subranges delimited with commas. Blank lines in the `crontab` or lines that begin with a hash (#) are ignored. If you specify both a day in the month and a day of week, the result is effectively ORd; the `crontab` entry will be run on the specified day of week and on the specified day in the month.

```
# MIN HOUR DAY MONTH DAYOFWEEK COMMAND
# at 6:10 a.m. every day
10 6 ***date

# every two hours at the top of the hour
0 */2 ***date

# every two hours from 11p.m. to 7a.m., and at 8a.m.
0 23-7/2,8 ***date

# at 11:00 a.m. on the 4th and on every mon, tue, wed
0 11 4 * mon-wed date

# 4:00 a.m. on january 1st
0 4 1 jan *date

# once an hour, all output appended to log file
0 4 1 jan *date>>/var/log/messages 2>&1
```

The command portion of the line is run with /bin/sh -c <command>, and may therefore contain any valid Bourne shell command. A common practice is to run your command with exec to keep the process table uncluttered. It is also common to redirect output to a log file. If you do not, and the command generates output on stdout or stderr, the result will be mailed to the user in question. If you use this mechanism for special users, such as UUCP, you may want to create an alias for the user to direct the mail to someone else, such as root or postmaster.

Internally, this `cron` uses a quick indexing system to reduce CPU overhead when looking for commands to execute. Several hundred `crontabs` with several thousand entries can be handled without using noticeable CPU resources.

## BUGS

Ought to be able to have several `crontab` files for any given user, as an organizational tool.

## AUTHOR

Matthew Dillon (`dillon@apollo.west.oic.com`)

*1 May 1994*

# csplit

`csplit`—Split a file into sections determined by context lines

## SYNOPSIS

```
csplit [-sqkz] [-f prefix] [-b suffix] [-n digits] [—prefix=prefix]
[—suffix-format=suffix] [—digits=digits] [—quiet] [—silent]
[—keep-files] [—elide-empty-files] [—help] [—version]
file pattern...
```

## DESCRIPTION

This manual page documents the GNU version of `csplit`. `csplit` creates zero or more output files containing sections of the given input file, or the standard input if the name - is given. By default, `csplit` prints the number of bytes written to each output file after it has been created.

The contents of the output files are determined by the pattern arguments. An error occurs if a pattern argument refers to a nonexistent line of the input file, such as if no remaining line matches a given regular expression. After all the given patterns have been matched, any remaining output is copied into one last output file. The types of pattern arguments are

line
: Create an output file containing the current line up to (but not including) line line (a positive integer) of the input file. If followed by a repeat count, also create an output file containing the next line lines of the input file once for each repeat.

/regexp/[offset]
: Create an output file containing the current line up to (but not including) the next line of the input file that contains a match for regexp. The optional offset is a + or - followed by a positive integer. If it is given, the input up to the matching line plus or minus offset is put into the output file, and the line after that begins the next section of input.

%regexp%[offset]
: Like the previous type, except that it does not create an output file, so that section of the input file is effectively ignored.

{repeat-count}
: Repeat the previous pattern repeat-count (a positive integer) additional times. An asterisk may be given in place of the (integer) repeat count, in which case the preceding pattern is repeated as many times as necessary until the input is exhausted.

The output filenames consist of a prefix followed by a suffix. By default, the suffix is merely an ascending linear sequence of two-digit decimal numbers starting with 00 and ranging up to 99; however, this default may be overridden by either the —digits option or by the —suffix-format option. (See "Options," next.) In any case, concatenating the output files in sorted order by filename produces the original input file, in order. The default output filename prefix is xx.

By default, if csplit encounters an error or receives a hangup, interrupt, quit, or terminate signal, it removes any output files that it has created so far before it exits.

## OPTIONS

-f, —prefix=*prefix*
: Use *prefix* as the output filename prefix string.

-b, —suffix-format=*suffix*
: Use *suffix* as the output filename suffix string. When this option is specified, the suffix string must include exactly one printf(3) style conversion specification (such as %d, possibly including format specification flags, a field width, a precision specifications, or all of these kinds of modifiers). The conversion specification must be suitable for converting a binary integer argument to readable form. Thus, only d, i, u, o, x, and X format specifiers are allowed. The entire suffix string is given (with the current output file number) to sprintf(3) to form the filename suffixes for each of the individual output files in turn. Note that when this option is used, the —digits option is ignored.

-n, —digits=*digits*
: Use output filenames containing numbers that are *digits* digits long instead of the default 2.

-k, —keep-files
: Do not remove output files when errors are encountered.

-z, —elide-empty-files
: Suppress the generation of zero-length output files. (In cases where the section delimiters of the input file are supposed to mark the first lines of each of the sections, the first output file will generally be a zero-length file unless you use this option.) Note that the output file sequence numbers will always run consecutively, starting from 0, even in cases where zero-length output sections are suppressed due to the use of this option.

-s, -q, —silent, —quiet
: Do not print counts of output file sizes.

—help
: Print a usage message and exit with a nonzero status.

—version
: Print version information on standard output, then exit.

# ctags

ctags—Generates tags and (optionally) refs files

## SYNOPSIS

ctags [-BSstvraT] *filenames...*

## DESCRIPTION

ctags generates the tags and refs files from a group of C source files. The tags file is used by the elvis :tag command, control-] command, and -t option. The refs file is sometimes used by the ref(1) program.

Each C source file is scanned for #define statements and global function definitions. The name of the macro or function becomes the name of a tag. For each tag, a line is added to the tags file that contains the following:

- The name of the tag
- A tab character
- The name of the file containing the tag
- A tab character
- A way to find the particular line within the file

The *filenames* list will typically be the names of all C source files in the current directory, like this:

$ ctags -stv *.[ch]

## OPTIONS

| | |
|---|---|
| -B | Normally, ctags encloses regular expressions in slashes (/regexp/), which causes elvis to search from the top of the file. The -B flag causes ctags to enclose the regular expressions in question marks (?regexp?) so elvis will search backward from the bottom of the file. This rarely matters. |
| -t | Include typedefs. A tag will be generated for each user-defined type. Also tags will be generated for struct and enum names. Types are considered to be global if they are defined in a header file, and static if they are defined in a C source file. |
| -v | Include variable declarations. A tag will be generated for each variable, except for those that are declared inside the body of a function. |
| -s | Include static tags. ctags will normally put global tags in the tags file, and silently ignore the static tags. This flag causes both global and static tags to be added. The name of a static tag is generated by prefixing the name of the declared item with the name of the file where it is defined, with a colon in between. For example, static foo(){} in bar.c results in a tag named bar.c:foo. |
| -S | Include static tags, but make them look like global tags. Most tags-aware programs don't like the filename:tagname tags produced by the -s flag, so -S was added as an alternative. If elvis and ref are the only programs that read the tags file, then you don't need -S; otherwise, you do. |
| -r | This causes ctags to generate both tags and refs. Without -r, it would only generate tags. |
| -a | Append to tags, and maybe refs. Normally, ctags overwrites these files each time it is invoked. This flag is useful when you have too many files in the current directory for you to list them on a single command line; it allows you to split the arguments among several invocations. |
| -T | This flag isn't available on all systems. UNIX has it, but most others don't. The -T flag prevents ctags from generating a tags file. This is useful when you want to generate a refs without changing tags. |

## FILES

| | |
|---|---|
| tags | A cross-reference that lists each tag name, the name of the source file that contains it, and a way to locate a particular line in the source file. |
| refs | The refs file contains the definitions for each tag in the tags file, and very little else. This file can be useful, for example, when licensing restrictions prevent you from making the source code to the standard C library readable by everybody, but you still want everybody to know what arguments the library functions need. |

## BUGS

ctags is sensitive to indenting and line breaks. Consequently, it might not discover all of the tags in a file that is formatted in an unusual way.

## SEE ALSO

elvis(1), refo(1)

## AUTHOR

Steve Kirkendall (kirkenda@cs.pdx.edu)

# CU

cu—Call up another system

## SYNOPSIS

cu [ options ] [ system ¦ phone ¦ "*dir*" ]

## DESCRIPTION

The cu command is used to call up another system and act as a dial in terminal. It can also do simple file transfers with no error checking.

cu takes a single argument, besides the options. If the argument is the string *dir*, cu will make a direct connection to the port. This may only be used by users with write access to the port, as it permits reprogramming the modem.

Otherwise, if the argument begins with a digit, it is taken to be a phone number to call. Otherwise, it is taken to be the name of a system to call. The -z or —system option may be used to name a system beginning with a digit, and the -c or —phone option may be used to name a phone number that does not begin with a digit.

cu locates a port to use in the UUCP configuration files. If a simple system name is given, it will select a port appropriate for that system. The -p, —port, -l, —line, -s, and —speed options may be used to control the port selection.

When a connection is made to the remote system, cu forks into two processes. One reads from the port and writes to the terminal, while the other reads from the terminal and writes to the port.

cu provides several commands that may be used during the conversation. The commands all begin with an escape character, initially ˜ (tilde). The escape character is only recognized at the beginning of a line. To send an escape character to the remote system at the start of a line, it must be entered twice. All commands are either a single character or a word beginning with % (percent sign).

cu recognizes the following commands:

| | |
|---|---|
| ˜. | Terminate the conversation. |
| ˜! *command* | Run *command* in a shell. If command is empty, starts up a shell. |
| ˜$ *command* | Run *command*, sending the standard output to the remote system. |
| ˜¦ *command* | Run *command*, taking the standard input from the remote system. |
| ˜+ *command* | Run *command*, taking the standard input from the remote system and sending the standard output to the remote system. |
| ˜#, ˜%break | Send a break signal, if possible. |
| ˜c *directory*, ˜%cd *directory* | Change the local directory. |
| ˜> *file* | Send a file to the remote system. This just dumps the file over the communication line. It is assumed that the remote system is expecting it. |
| ˜< | Receive a file from the remote system. This prompts for the local filename and for the remote command to execute to begin the file transfer. It continues accepting data until the contents of the eofread variable are seen. |

| | |
|---|---|
| ˜p from to, ˜%put from to | Send a file to a remote UNIX system. This runs the appropriate commands on the remote system. |
| ˜t from to, ˜%take from to | Retrieve a file from a remote UNIX system. This runs the appropriate commands on the remote system. |
| ˜s variable value | Set a cu variable to the given *value*. If *value* is not given, the variable is set to True. |
| ˜! variable | Set a cu variable to False. |
| ˜z | Suspend the cu session. This is only supported on some systems. On systems for which ^Z may be used to suspend a job, ˜˜z will also suspend the session. |
| ˜%nostop | Turn off XON/XOFF handling. |
| ˜%stop | Turn on XON/XOFF handling. |
| ˜v | List all the variables and their values. |
| ˜? | List all commands. |
| | cu also supports several variables. They may be listed with the ˜v command, and set with the ˜s or ˜! commands. |
| escape | The escape character. Initially ˜ (tilde). |
| delay | If this variable is True, cu will delay for a second after recognizing the escape character before printing the name of the local system. The default is True. |
| eol | The list of characters which are considered to finish a line. The escape character is only recognized after one of these is seen. The default is carriage return, ^U, ^C, ^O, ^D, ^S, ^Q, ^R. |
| binary | Whether to transfer binary data when sending a file. If this is False, then newlines in the file being sent are converted to carriage returns. The default is False. |
| binary-prefix | A string used before sending a binary character in a file transfer, if the binary variable is True. The default is ^Z. |
| echo-check | Whether to check file transfers by examining what the remote system echoes back. This probably doesn't work very well. The default is False. |
| echonl | The character to look for after sending each line in a file. The default is carriage return. |
| timeout | The timeout to use, in seconds, when looking for a character, either when doing echo checking or when looking for the echonl character. The default is 30. |
| kill | The character to use to delete a line if the echo check fails. The default is ^U. |
| resend | The number of times to resend a line if the echo check continues to fail. The default is 10. |
| eofwrite | The string to write after sending a file with the ˜> command. The default is ^D. |
| eofread | The string to look for when receiving a file with the ˜< command. The default is $, which is intended to be a typical shell prompt. |
| verbose | Whether to print accumulated information during a file transfer. The default is True. |

## OPTIONS

The following options may be given to cu:

| | |
|---|---|
| -e, —parity=even | Use even parity. |
| -o, —parity=odd | Use odd parity. |
| —parity=none | Use no parity. No parity is also used if both -e and -o are given. |
| -h, —halfduplex | Echo characters locally (half-duplex mode). |
| -z system, —system system | The system to call. |
| -c phone-number, —phone phone-number | The phone number to call. |
| -p port, —port port | Name the port to use. |
| -a port | Equivalent to —port *port*. |
| -l line, —line line | Name the line to use by giving a device name. This may be used to dial out on ports that are not listed in the UUCP configuration files. Write access to the device is required. |

| | |
|---|---|
| -s *speed*, —speed *speed* | The speed (baud rate) to use. |
| -# | Where # is a number, equivalent to —speed #. |
| -n, —prompt | Prompt for the phone number to use. |
| -d | Enter debugging mode. Equivalent to -debug all. |
| -x *type*, —debug *type* | Turn on particular debugging types. The following types are recognized: abnormal, chat, handshake, uucpproto, proto, port, config, spooldir, execute, incoming, outgoing. Only abnormal, chat, handshake, port, config, incoming and outgoing are meaningful for cu. Multiple types may be given, separated by commas, and the —debug option may appear multiple times. A number may also be given, which will turn on that many types from the foregoing list; for example, —debug 2 is equivalent to —debug abnormal,chat. —debug all may be used to turn on all debugging options. |
| -I *file*, —config *file* | Set configuration file to use. This option may not be available, depending upon how cu was compiled. |
| -v, —version | Report version information and exit. |
| —help | Print a help message and exit. |

## BUGS

This program does not work very well.

## FILES

The filename may be changed at compilation time, so this is only an approximation. Configuration file:

/usr/lib/uucp/config

## AUTHOR

Ian Lance Taylor (ian@airs.com)

*Taylor UUCP 1.05*


# cut

cut—Remove sections from each line of files

## SYNOPSIS

cut {-b *byte-list*, —bytes=*byte-list*} [-n] [—help] [—version] [*file*...]

cut {-c *character-list*, —characters=*character-list*} [—help] [—version] [*file*...]

cut {-f *field-list*, —fields=*field-list*} [-d *delim*] [-s] [—delimiter=*delim*]
[—only-delimited] [—help] [—version] [*file*...]

## DESCRIPTION

This manual page documents the GNU version of cut. cut prints sections of each line of each input file, or the standard input if no files are given. A filename of - means standard input. The sections to be printed are selected by the options.

## OPTIONS

The *byte-list*, *character-list*, and *field-list* options are one or more numbers or ranges (two numbers separated by a dash) separated by commas. The first byte, character, and field are numbered 1. Incomplete ranges may be given: -m means 1-m; n- means n through end of line or last field.

| | |
|---|---|
| -b, —bytes *byte-list* | Print only the bytes in positions listed in *byte-list*. Tabs and backspaces are treated like any other character; they take up one byte. |
| -c, —characters *character-list* | Print only characters in positions listed in *character-list*. The same as -b for now, but internationalization will change that. Tabs and backspaces are treated like any other character; they take up one character. |
| -f, —fields *field-list* | Print only the fields listed in *field-list*. Fields are separated by TAB by default. |
| -d, —delimiter *delim* | For -f, fields are separated by the first character in *delim* instead of by TAB. |
| -n | Do not split multibyte characters (no-op for now). |
| -s, —only-delimited | For -f, do not print lines that do not contain the field separator character. |
| —help | Print a usage message and exit with a nonzero status. |
| —version | Print version information on standard output then exit. |

*GNU Text Utilities*

# CVS

cvs—Concurrent Versions System

## SYNOPSIS

cvs [ cvs_options ] cvs-command [ command_options ][command_args ]

## DESCRIPTION

cvs is a front end to the rcs(1) revision control system, which extends the notion of revision control from a collection of files in a single directory to a hierarchical collection of directories consisting of revision controlled files. These directories and files can be combined together to form a software release. cvs provides the functions necessary to manage these software releases and to control the concurrent editing of source files among multiple software developers.

cvs keeps a single copy of the master sources. This copy is called the source *repository*; it contains all the information to permit extracting previous software releases at any time based on either a symbolic revision tag, or a date in the past.

## ESSENTIAL COMMANDS

cvs provides a rich variety of commands (cvs_command in the Synopsis), each of which often has a wealth of options, to satisfy the many needs of source management in distributed environments. However, you don't have to master every detail to do useful work with cvs; in fact, five commands are sufficient to use (and contribute to) the source repository.

| | |
|---|---|
| cvs checkout *modules...* | A necessary preliminary for most cvs work: creates your private copy of the source for modules (named collections of source; you can also use a path relative to the source repository here). You can work with this copy without interfering with others' work. At least one subdirectory level is always created. |
| cvs update | Execute this command from within your private source directory when you wish to update your copies of source files from changes that other developers have made to the source in the repository. |
| cvs add *file...* | Use this command to enroll new files in cvs records of your working directory. The files will be added to the repository the next time you run cvs commit. Note: You should use the cvs import command to bootstrap new sources into the source repository. cvs add is only used for new files to an already checked-out module. |
| cvs remove *file...* | Use this command (after erasing any files listed) to declare that you wish to eliminate files from the repository. The removal does not affect others until you run cvs commit. |
| cvs commit *file...* | Use this command when you wish to "publish" your changes to other developers, by incorporating them in the source repository. |

## OPTIONS

The cvs command line can include cvs_options, which apply to the overall cvs program; a cvs_command, which specifies a particular action on the source repository; and command_options and command_arguments to fully specify what the cvs_command will do.

### WARNING

You must be careful of precisely where you place options relative to the cvs_command. The same option can mean different things depending on whether it is in the cvs_options position (to the left of a cvs command) or in the command_options position (to the right of a cvs command).

There are only two situations where you may omit cvs_command: cvs -H or cvs -help elicits a list of available commands, and cvs -v or cvs -version displays version information on cvs itself.

## CVS OPTIONS

As of release 1.6, cvs supports GNU style long options as well as short options. Only a few long options are currently supported; these are listed in brackets after the short options whose functions they duplicate.

Use these options to control the overall cvs program:

| | |
|---|---|
| -H [-help] | Display usage information about the specified cvs command (but do not actually execute the command). If you don't specify a command name, cvs -H displays a summary of all the commands available. |
| -Q | Causes the command to be really quiet; the command will generate output only for serious problems. |
| -q | Causes the command to be somewhat quiet; informational messages, such as reports of recursion through subdirectories, are suppressed. |
| -b *bindir* | Use *bindir* as the directory where RCS programs are located. Overrides the setting of the RCSBIN environment variable. This value should be specified as an absolute pathname. |
| -d *CVS_root_directory* | Use *CVS_root_directory* as the root directory pathname of the master RCS source repository. Overrides the setting of the CVS-ROOT environment variable. This value should be specified as an absolute pathname. |
| -e *editor* | Use *editor* to enter revision log information. Overrides the setting of the CVSEDITOR and the EDITOR environment variables. |
| -f | Do not read the cvs startup file (˜/.cvsrc). |
| -l | Do not log the cvs_command in the command history (but execute it anyway). See the description of the history command for information on command history. |
| -n | Do not change any files. Attempt to execute the cvs_command, but only to issue reports; do not remove, update, or merge any existing files, or create any new files. |
| -t | Trace program execution; display messages showing the steps of cvs activity. Particularly useful with -n to explore the potential impact of an unfamiliar command. |
| -r | Makes new working files read-only. Same effect as if the CVS-READ environment variable is set. |
| -v [-version] | Displays version and copyright information for cvs. |
| -w | Makes new working files read-write (default). Overrides the setting of the CVSREAD environment variable. |
| -z *compression-level* | When transferring files across the network use gzip with compression level *compression-level* to compress and decompress data as it is transferred. Requires the presence of the GNU gzip program in the current search path at both ends of the link. |

## USAGE

Except when requesting general help with cvs -H, you must specify a cvs_command to cvs to select a specific release control function to perform. Each cvs command accepts its own collection of options and arguments. However, many options are available across several commands. You can display a usage summary for each command by specifying the -H option with the command.

## CVS STARTUP FILE

Normally, when cvs starts up, it reads the .cvsrc file from the home directory of the user reading it. This startup procedure can be turned off with the -f flag.

The .cvsrc file lists cvs commands with a list of arguments, one command per line. For example, the following line in .cvsrc:

```
diff -c
```

will mean that the cvs diff command will always be passed the -c option in addition to any other options that are specified in the command line (in this case, it will have the effect of producing context sensitive diffs for all executions of cvs diff ).

## CVS COMMAND SUMMARY

Here are brief descriptions of all the cvs commands:

| | |
|---|---|
| add | Add a new file or directory to the repository, pending a cvs commit on the same file. Can only be done from within sources created by a previous cvs checkout invocation. Use cvs import to place whole new hierarchies of sources under cvs control. (Does not directly affect repository; changes working directory.) |
| admin | Execute RCS control functions on the source repository. (Changes repository directly; uses working directory without changing it.) |
| checkout | Make a working directory of source files for editing. (Creates or changes working directory.) |
| commit | Apply to the source repository changes, additions, and deletions from your working directory. (Changes repository.) |
| diff | Show differences between files in working directory and source repository, or between two revisions in source repository. (Does not change either repository or working directory.) |
| export | Prepare copies of a set of source files for shipment off site. Differs from cvs checkout in that no cvs administrative directories are created (and therefore cvs commit cannot be executed from a directory prepared with cvs export), and a symbolic tag must be specified. (Does not change repository; creates directory similar to working directories). |
| history | Show reports on cvs commands that you or others have executed on a particular file or directory in the source repository. (Does not change repository or working directory.) History logs are kept only if enabled by creation of the $CVSROOT/CVSROOT/history file; see cvs(5). |
| import | Incorporate a set of updates from off-site into the source repository, as a "vendor branch." (Changes repository.) |
| log | Display RCS log information. (Does not change repository or working directory.) |
| rdiff | Prepare a collection of diffs as a patch file between two releases in the repository. (Does not change repository or working directory.) |
| release | Cancel a cvs checkout, abandoning any changes. (Can delete working directory; no effect on repository.) |
| remove | Remove files from the source repository, pending a cvs commit on the same files. (Does not directly affect repository; changes working directory.) |
| rtag | Explicitly specify a symbolic tag for particular revisions of files in the source repository. See also cvs tag. (Changes repository directly; does not require or affect working directory.) |
| status | Show current status of files: latest version, version in working directory, whether working version has been edited and, optionally, symbolic tags in the RCS file. (Does not change repository or working directory.) |

tag                 Specify a symbolic tag for files in the repository. By default, tags the revisions that were last synchro-
                    nized with your working directory. (Changes repository directly; uses working directory without
                    changing it.)

update              Bring your working directory up to date with changes from the repository. Merges are performed
                    automatically when possible; a warning is issued if manual resolution is required for conflicting
                    changes. (Changes working directory; does not change repository.)

## COMMON COMMAND OPTIONS

This section describes the command_options that are available across several cvs commands. Not all commands support all of these options; each option is only supported for commands where it makes sense. However, when a command has one of these options you can count on the same meaning for the option as in other commands. (Other command options, which are listed with the individual commands, may have different meanings from one cvs command to another.)

### WARNING

The history command is an exception; it supports many options that conflict even with these standard options.

-D *date*           Use the most recent revision no later than date_spec (a single argument, date description specifying a
                    date in the past). A wide variety of date formats are supported by the underlying RCS facilities, similar
                    to those described in co(1), but not exactly the same. The date_spec is interpreted as being in the local
                    time zone, unless a specific time zone is specified. The specification is "sticky" when you use it to make
                    a private copy of a source file; that is, when you get a working file using -D, cvs records the date you
                    specified, so that further updates in the same directory will use the same date (unless you explicitly
                    override it; see the description of the update command). -D is available with the checkout, diff, history,
                    export, rdiff, rtag, and update commands. Examples of valid date specifications include the following:

                        1 month ago
                        2 hours ago
                        400000 seconds ago
                        last year
                        last Monday
                        yesterday
                        a fortnight ago
                        3/31/92 10:00:07 PST
                        January 23, 1987 10:05pm
                        22:00 GMT

-f                  When you specify a particular date or tag to cvs commands, they normally ignore files that do not
                    contain the tag (or did not exist on the date) that you specified. Use the -f option if you want files
                    retrieved even when there is no match for the tag or date. (The most recent version is used in this
                    situation.) -f is available with these commands: checkout, export, rdiff, rtag, and update.

-H                  Help; describe the options available for this command. This is the only option supported for all cvs
                    commands.

-k *kflag*          Alter the default RCS processing of keywords; all the -k options described in co(1) are available. The -k
                    option is available with the add, checkout, diff, export, rdiff, and update commands. Your *kflag*
                    specification is "sticky" when you use it to create a private copy of a source file; that is, when you use
                    this option with the checkout or update commands, cvs associates your selected *kflag* with the file, and
                    continues to use it with future update commands on the same file until you specify otherwise.

                    Some of the more useful *kflags* are –ko and –kb (for binary files, only compatible with RCS version 5.7
                    or later), and –kv, which is useful for an export where you wish to retain keyword information after an
                    import at some other site.

-l          Local; run only in current working directory, rather than recurring through subdirectories. Available with the following commands: `checkout`, `commit`, `diff`, `export`, `remove`, `rdiff`, `rtag`, `status`, `tag`, and `update`.

**WARNING**

This is not the same as the overall cvs -l option, which you can specify to the left of a cvs command.

-n          Do not run any `checkout`/`commit`/`tag`/`update` program. (A program can be specified to run on each of these activities, in the modules database; this option bypasses it.) Available with the `checkout`, `commit`, `export`, and `rtag` commands.

**WARNING**

This is not the same as the overall cvs -n option, which you can specify to the left of a cvs command.

-P          Prune (remove) directories that are empty after being updated, on checkout, or update. Normally, an empty directory (one that is void of revision-controlled files) is left alone. Specifying -P will cause these directories to be silently removed from your checked-out sources. This does not remove the directory from the repository, only from your checked out copy. Note that this option is implied by the -r or -D options of `checkout` and `export`.

-p          Pipe the files retrieved from the repository to standard output, rather than writing them in the current directory. Available with the `checkout` and `update` commands.

-r tag     Use the revision specified by the tag argument instead of the default head revision. As well as arbitrary tags defined with the tag or rtag command, two special tags are always available: HEAD refers to the most recent version available in the repository, and BASE refers to the revision you last checked out into the current working directory. The tag specification is "sticky" when you use this option with cvs checkout or cvs update to make your own copy of a file: cvs remembers the tag and continues to use it on future update commands, until you specify otherwise. tag can be either a symbolic or numeric tag, in RCS fashion. Specifying the -q global option along with the -r command option is often useful, to suppress the warning messages when the RCS file does not contain the specified tag. -r is available with the `checkout`, `commit`, `diff`, `history`, `export`, `rdiff`, `rtag`, and `update` commands.

**WARNING**

This is not the same as the overall cvs -r option, which you can specify to the left of a cvs command.

## CVS COMMANDS

Here (finally) are details on all the cvs commands and the options each accepts. The summary lines at the top of each command's description highlight three kinds of things:

| | |
|---|---|
| Command Options and Arguments | Special options are described in detail; common command options may appear only in the summary line. |
| Working Directory, or Repository? | Some cvs commands require a working directory to operate; some require a repository. Also, some commands change the repository, some change the working directory, and some change nothing. |
| Synonyms | Many commands have synonyms, which you may find easier to remember (or type) than the principal name. |

■ add [-k *kflag*][-m '*message*'] *files...*

| | |
|---|---|
| Requires: | Repository, working directory |
| Changes: | Working directory |
| Synonym: | new |

Use the add command to create a new file or directory in the RCS source repository. The files or directories specified with add must already exist in the current directory (which must have been created with the checkout command). To add a whole new directory hierarchy to the source repository (for example, files received from a third-party vendor), use the cvs import command instead.

If the argument to cvs add refers to an immediate subdirectory, the directory is created at the correct place in the RCS source repository, and the necessary cvs administration files are created in your working directory. If the directory already exists in the source repository, cvs add still creates the administration files in your version of the directory. This allows you to use cvs add to add a particular directory to your private sources even if someone else created that directory after your checkout of the sources. You can do the following:

```
example% mkdir new_directory
example% cvs add new_directory
example% cvs update new_directory
```

An alternate approach using cvs update might be:

```
example% cvs update -d new_directory
```

(To add any available new directories to your working directory, it's probably simpler to use cvs checkout or cvs update -d.)

The added files are not placed in the RCS source repository until you use cvs commit to make the change permanent. Doing a cvs add on a file that was removed with the cvs remove command will resurrect the file, if no cvs commit command intervened.

You will have the opportunity to specify a logging message, as usual, when you use cvs commit to make the new file permanent. If you'd like to have another logging message associated with just creation of the file (for example, to describe the file's purpose), you can specify it with the -m *message* option to the add command.

The -k *kflag* option specifies the default way that this file will be checked out. The *kflag* argument is stored in the RCS file and can be changed with cvs admin. Specifying -ko is useful for checking in binaries that shouldn't have the RCS id strings expanded.

■ admin [*rcs-options*] *files...*

| | |
|---|---|
| Requires: | Repository, working directory |
| Changes: | Repository |
| Synonym: | rcs |

This is the cvs interface to assorted administrative RCS facilities, documented in rcs(1). cvs admin simply passes all its options and arguments to the rcs command; it does no filtering or other processing. This command does work recursively, however, so extreme care should be used.

■ checkout [options] *modules...*

| | |
|---|---|
| Requires: | Repository |
| Changes: | Working directory |
| Synonyms: | co, get |

Make a working directory containing copies of the source files specified by modules. You must execute cvs checkout before using most of the other cvs commands, since most of them operate on your working directory.

*modules* are either symbolic names [themselves defined as the module modules in the source repository; see cvs(5)] for some collection of source directories and files, or paths to directories or files in the repository.

Depending on the modules you specify, checkout may recursively create directories and populate them with the appropriate source files. You can then edit these source files at any time (regardless of whether other software developers are editing their own copies of the sources); update them to include new changes applied by others to the source repository; or commit your work as a permanent change to the RCS repository.

Note that `checkout` is used to create directories. The top-level directory created is always added to the directory where `checkout` is invoked, and usually has the same name as the specified module. In the case of a module alias, the created subdirectory may have a different name, but you can be sure that it will be a subdirectory, and that `checkout` will show the relative path leading to each file as it is extracted into your private work area (unless you specify the -Q global option).

Running `cvs checkout` on a directory that was already built by a prior `checkout` is also permitted, and has the same effect as specifying the -d option to the `update` command described later.

The options permitted with `cvs checkout` include the standard command options -P, -f, -k kflag, -l, -n, -p, -r tag, and -D date. In addition to those, you can use several special command options with `checkout`, as detailed in the following paragraphs.

Use the -A option to reset any sticky tags, dates, or -k options. (If you get a working file using one of the -r, -D, or -k options, `cvs` remembers the corresponding tag, date, or kflag and continues using it on future updates; use the -A option to make `cvs` forget these specifications, and retrieve the head version of the file).

The -j branch option merges the changes made between the resulting revision and the revision that it is based on (for example, if the tag refers to a branch, `cvs` will merge all changes made in that branch into your working file).

With two -j options, `cvs` will merge in the changes between the two respective revisions. This can be used to "remove" a certain delta from your working file.

In addition, each -j option can contain on optional date specification which, when used with branches, can limit the chosen revision to one within a specific date. An optional date is specified by adding a colon (:) to the tag. An example might be what `cvs import` tells you to do when you have just imported sources that have conflicts with local changes:

```
example% cvs checkout -jTAG:yesterday -jTAG module
```

Use the -N option with -d *dir* to avoid shortening module paths in your working directory. (Normally, `cvs` shortens paths as much as possible when you specify an explicit target directory.)

Use the -c option to copy the module file, sorted, to the standard output, instead of creating or modifying any files or directories in your working directory.

Use the -d *dir* option to create a directory called *dir* for the working files, instead of using the module name. Unless you also use -N, the paths created under `dir` will be as short as possible.

Use the -s option to display per-module status information stored with the -s option within the modules file.

■ commit [-lnR][-m 'log_message' ¦ -f file][-r revision][*files...*]

| | |
|---|---|
| Requires: | Working directory, repository |
| Changes: | Repository |
| Synonym: | ci |

Use `cvs commit` when you want to incorporate changes from your working source files into the general source repository.

If you don't specify particular files to commit, all of the files in your working current directory are examined. `commit` is careful to change in the repository only those files that you have really changed. By default (or if you explicitly specify the -r option), files in subdirectories are also examined and committed if they have changed; you can use the -l option to limit `commit` to the current directory only. Sometimes you may want to force a file to be committed even though it is unchanged; this is achieved with the -f flag, which also has the effect of disabling recursion (you can turn it back on with -R, of course).

`commit` verifies that the selected files are up-to-date with the current revisions in the source repository; it will notify you, and exit without committing, if any of the specified files must be made current first with `cvs update`. `commit` does not call the `update` command for you, but rather leaves that for you to do when the time is right.

When all is well, an editor is invoked to allow you to enter a log message that will be written to one or more logging programs and placed in the RCS source repository file. You can instead specify the log message on the command line with the -m option, thus suppressing the editor invocation, or use the -F option to specify that the argument file contains the log message.

The -r option can be used to commit to a particular symbolic or numeric revision within the RCS file. For example, to bring all your files up to the RCS revision 3.0 (including those that haven't changed), you might use

```
example% cvs commit -r3.0
```

cvs will only allow you to commit to a revision that is on the main trunk (a revision with a single dot). However, you can also commit to a branch revision (one that has an even number of dots) with the -r option. To create a branch revision, one typically use the -b option of the rtag or tag commands. Then, either checkout or update can be used to base your sources on the newly created branch. From that point on, all commit changes made within these working sources will be automatically added to a branch revision, thereby not perturbing mainline development in any way. For example, if you had to create a patch to the 1.2 version of the product, even though the 2.0 version is already under development, you might use this:

```
example% cvs rtag -b -rFCS1_2 FCS1_2 Patch product_module
example% cvs checkout -rFCS1_2_Patch product module
example% cd product module
[[ hack away ]]
example% cvs commit
```

Say you have been working on some extremely experimental software, based on whatever revision you happened to checkout last week. If others in your group would like to work on this software with you, but without disturbing mainline development, you could commit your change to a new branch. Others can then check out your experimental stuff and utilize the full benefit of cvs conflict resolution. The scenario might look like this:

```
example% cvs tag -b EXPR1
example% cvs update -rEXPR1
[[ hack away ]]
example% cvs commit
```

Others would simply do cvs checkout -rEXPR1 *whatever_module* to work with you on the experimental change.

■    diff [-kl][*rcsdiff_options*][[-r *rev1* ¦ -D *date1*][-r *rev2* ¦ -D *date2*]] [*files*...]
        Requires:          Working directory, repository
        Changes:          Nothing

You can compare your working files with revisions in the source repository, with the cvs diff command. If you don't specify a particular revision, your files are compared with the revisions they were based on. You can also use the standard cvs command option -r to specify a particular revision to compare your files with. Finally, if you use -r twice, you can see differences between two revisions in the repository. You can also specify -D options to diff against a revision in the past. The -r and -D options can be mixed together with at most two options ever specified.

See rcsdiff(1) for a list of other accepted options.

If you don't specify any files, diff will display differences for all those files in the current directory (and its subdirectories, unless you use the standard option -l) that differ from the corresponding revision in the source repository (that is, files that you have changed), or that differ from the revision specified.

■    export [-f lNnQq] -r *rev* ¦ -D *date* [-d *dir*][-k *kflag*] *module*...
        Requires:          Repository
        Changes:          Current directory

This command is a variant of cvs checkout; use it when you want a copy of the source for *module* without the cvs administrative directories. For example, you might use cvs export to prepare source for shipment off-site. This command requires that you specify a date or tag (with -D or -r), so that you can count on reproducing the source you ship to others.

The only nonstandard options are -d *dir* (write the source into directory *dir*) and -N (don't shorten module paths). These have the same meanings as the same options in cvs checkout.

The -kv option is useful when export is used. This causes any RCS keywords to be expanded such that an import done at some other site will not lose the keyword revision information. Other *kflag* options may be used with cvs export and are described in co(1).

■ history [*-report*][*-flags*][*-options args*][*files...*]
    Requires:          The file $CVSROOT/CVSROOT/history
    Changes:           Nothing

cvs keeps a history file that tracks each use of the checkout, commit, rtag, update, and release commands. You can use cvs history to display this information in various formats.

## WARNING

cvs history uses -f, -l, -n, and -p in ways that conflict with the descriptions in "Common Command Options," earlier in this manual page.

Several options (shown as [*-report*] in the preceding bulleted code line) control what kind of report is generated:

-c                    Report on each time commit was used (that is, each time the repository was modified).

-m *module*           Report on a particular module. (You can meaningfully use -m more than once on the command line.)

-o                    Report on checked-out modules.

-T                    Report on all tags.

-x *type*             Extract a particular set of record types X from the cvs history. The types are indicated by single letters, which you may specify in combination. Certain commands have a single record type: check-out (type O), release (type F), and rtag (type T). One of four record types may result from an update: W, when the working copy of a file is deleted during update (because it was gone from the repository); U, when a working file was copied from the repository; G, when a merge was necessary and it succeeded; and C, when a merge was necessary but collisions were detected (requiring manual merging). Finally, one of three record types results from commit: M, when a file was modified; A, when a file is first added; and R, when a file is removed.

-e                    Everything (all record types); equivalent to specifying -xMACFROGWUT.

-z *zone*             Use time zone *zone* when outputting history records. The zone name LT stands for local time; numeric offsets stand for hours and minutes ahead of UTC. For example, +0530 stands for 5 hours and 30 minutes ahead of (that is, east of) UTC.

The options shown as *-flags* constrain the report without requiring option arguments:

-a                    Show data for all users. (The default is to show data only for the user executing cvs history.)

-l                    Show last modification only.

-w                    Show only the records for modifications done from the same working directory where cvs history is executing.

The options shown as *-options args* constrain the report based on an argument:

-b *str*              Show data back to a record containing the string *str* in either the module name, the filename, or the repository path.

-D *date*             Show data since *date*.

-p *repository*       Show data for a particular source repository (you can specify several -p options on the same command line).

-r *rev*              Show records referring to revisions since the revision or tag named *rev* appears in individual RCS files. Each RCS file is searched for the revision or tag.

-t *tag*              Show records since tag *tag* was last added to the history file. This differs from the -r flag in that it reads only the history file, not the RCS files, and is much faster.

-u *name*             Show records for username.

- `import [-options]` *`repository vendortag releasetag ...`*

  | | |
  |---|---|
  | Requires: | Repository, source distribution directory |
  | Changes: | Repository |

Use `cvs import` to incorporate an entire source distribution from an outside source (for example, a source vendor) into your source repository directory. You can use this command both for initial creation of a repository, and for wholesale updates to the module form the outside source.

The `repository` argument gives a directory name (or a path to a directory) under the CVS root directory for repositories; if the directory did not exist, `import` creates it.

When you use `import` for updates to source that has been modified in your source repository (since a prior `import`), it will notify you of any files that conflict in the two branches of development; use `cvs checkout -j` to reconcile the differences, as `import` instructs you to do.

By default, certain filenames are ignored during `cvs import`: names associated with CVS administration, or with other common source control systems; common names for patch files, object files, archive files, and editor backup files; and other names that are usually artifacts of assorted utilities. Currently, the default list of ignored files includes files matching these names:

```
RCSLOG RCS SCCS
CVS* cvslog.*
tags TAGS
.make.state .nse_depinfo
~ #* .#* ,
.old *.bak *.BAK *.orig *.rej .del-*
.a *.o *.so *.Z *.elc *.ln core
```

The outside source is saved in a first-level RCS branch, by default 1.1.1. Updates are leaves of this branch; for example, files from the first imported collection of source will be revision 1.1.1.1, then files from the first imported update will be revision 1.1.1.2, and so on.

At least three arguments are required. *`repository`* is needed to identify the collection of source. *`vendortag`* is a tag for the entire branch (for example, for 1.1.1). You must also specify at least one *`releasetag`* to identify the files at the leaves created each time you execute `cvs import`.

One of the standard `cvs` command options is available: `-m` *`message`*. If you do not specify a logging message with `-m`, your editor is invoked (as with `commit`) to allow you to enter one.

There are three additional special options.

Use `-d` to specify that each file's time of last modification should be used for the checkin date and time.

Use `-b` *`branch`* to specify a first-level branch other than 1.1.1.

Use `-I` *`name`* to specify filenames that should be ignored during import. You can use this option repeatedly. To avoid ignoring any files at all (even those ignored by default), specify `-I !`.

- `log [-l]` *`rlog-options`* `[`*`files...`*`]`

  | | |
  |---|---|
  | Requires: | Repository, working directory |
  | Changes: | Nothing |
  | Synonym: | `rlog` |

Display log information for *`files`*. `cvs log` calls the RCS utility `rlog`; all the options described in `rlog(1)` are available. Among the more useful `rlog` options are `-h` to display only the header (including tag definitions, but omitting most of the full log); `-r` to select logs on particular revisions or ranges of revisions; and `-d` to select particular dates or date ranges. See `rlog(1)` for full explanations. This command is recursive by default, unless the `-l` option is specified.

- `rdiff [-flags][-V vn][-r t¦-D d [-r t2¦-D d2]] modules...`

  | | |
  |---|---|
  | Requires: | Repository |
  | Changes: | Nothing |
  | Synonym: | `patch` |

Builds a Larry Wall format `patch(1)` file between two releases that can be fed directly into the `patch` program to bring an old release up-to-date with the new release. (This is one of the few `cvs` commands that operates directly from the repository and doesn't require a prior checkout.) The `diff` output is sent to the standard output device. You can specify (using the standard `-r` and `-D` options) any combination of one or two revisions or dates. If only one revision or date is specified, the `patch` file reflects differences between that revision or date and the current head revisions in the RCS file.

Note that if the software release affected is contained in more than one directory, then it may be necessary to specify the -p option to the `patch` command when patching the old sources, so that `patch` is able to find the files that are located in other directories.

If you use the option -V *vn*, RCS keywords are expanded according to the rules current in RCS version *vn* (the expansion format changed with RCS version 5).

The standard option *flags* -f and -1 are available with this command. There are also several special options *flags*.

If you use the -s option, no `patch` output is produced. Instead, a summary of the changed or added files between the two releases is sent to the standard output device. This is useful for finding out, for example, which files have changed between two dates or revisions.

If you use the -t option, a `diff` of the top two revisions is sent to the standard output device. This is most useful for seeing what the last change to a file was.

If you use the -u option, the `patch` output uses the newer `unidiff` format for context `diff`s.

You can use -c to explicitly specify the diff -c form of context `diff`s (which is the default), if you like.

- `release [-dQq] modules...`

  | | |
  |---|---|
  | Requires: | Working directory |
  | Changes: | Working directory, history log |

This command is meant to safely cancel the effect of `cvs checkout`. Since `cvs` doesn't lock files, it isn't strictly necessary to use this command. You can always simply delete your working directory, if you like; but you risk losing changes you may have forgotten, and you leave no trace in the `cvs history` file that you've abandoned your checkout.

Use `cvs release` to avoid these problems. This command checks that no uncommitted changes are present; that you are executing it from immediately above, or inside, a `cvs` working directory; and that the repository recorded for your files is the same as the repository defined in the module database.

If all these conditions are true, `cvs release` leaves a record of its execution (attesting to your intentionally abandoning your checkout) in the `cvs history` log.

You can use the -d flag to request that your working copies of the source files be deleted if the `release` succeeds.

- `remove [-lR][files...]`

  | | |
  |---|---|
  | Requires: | Working directory |
  | Changes: | Working directory |
  | Synonyms: | `rm, delete` |

Use this command to declare that you wish to remove files from the source repository. Like most `cvs` commands, `cvs remove` works on files in your working directory, not directly on the repository. As a safeguard, it also requires that you first erase the specified files from your working directory.

The files are not actually removed until you apply your changes to the repository with `commit`; at that point, the corresponding RCS files in the source repository are moved into the `Attic` directory (also within the source repository).

This command is recursive by default, scheduling all physically removed files that it finds for removal by the next commit. Use the -1 option to avoid this recursion, or just specify that actual files that you wish remove to consider.

■ rtag [-f alnRQq][-b][-d][-r *tag* ¦ -D *date*] *symbolic_tag modules*...

| Requires: | Repository |
|---|---|
| Changes: | Repository |
| Synonym: | rfreeze |

You can use this command to assign symbolic tags to particular, explicitly specified source versions in the repository. cvs rtag works directly on the repository contents (and requires no prior checkout). Use cvs tag instead, to base the selection of versions to tag on the contents of your working directory.

In general, tags (often the symbolic names of software distributions) should not be removed, but the -d option is available as a means to remove completely obsolete symbolic names if necessary (as might be the case for an Alpha release, say).

cvs rtag will not move a tag that already exists. With the -F option, however, cvs rtag will relocate any instance of symbolic_tag that already exists on that file to the new repository versions. Without the -F option, attempting to use cvs rtag to apply a tag that already exists on that file will produce an error message.

The -b option makes the tag a *branch* tag, allowing concurrent, isolated development. This is most useful for creating a patch to a previously released software distribution.

You can use the standard -r and -D options to tag only those files that already contain a certain tag. This method would be used to rename a tag: tag only the files identified by the old tag, then delete the old tag, leaving the new tag on exactly the same files as the old tag.

rtag executes recursively by default, tagging all subdirectories of modules you specify in the argument. You can restrict its operation to top-level directories with the standard -1 option; or you can explicitly request recursion with -R.

The modules database can specify a program to execute whenever a tag is specified; a typical use is to send electronic mail to a group of interested parties. If you want to bypass that program, use the standard -n option.

Use the -a option to have rtag look in the Attic for removed files that contain the specified tag. The tag is removed from these files, which makes it convenient to reuse a symbolic tag as development continues (and files get removed from the upcoming distribution).

■ status [-lRqQ][-v][*files* ...]

| Requires: | Working directory, repository |
|---|---|
| Changes: | Nothing |

Display a brief report on the current status of files with respect to the source repository, including any sticky tags, dates, or -k options. (Sticky options will restrict how cvs update operates until you reset them; see the description of cvs update -A....

You can also use this command to anticipate the potential impact of a cvs update on your working source directory. If you do not specify any files explicitly, reports are shown for all files that cvs has placed in your working directory. You can limit the scope of this search to the current directory itself (not its subdirectories) with the standard -1 option flag; or you can explicitly request recursive status reports with the -R option.

The -v option causes the symbolic tags for the RCS file to be displayed as well.

■ tag [-lQqR][-F][-b][-d][-r *tag* ¦ -D *date*][-f] symbolic_tag [*files* ...]

| Requires: | Working directory, repository |
|---|---|
| Changes: | Repository |
| Synonym: | freeze |

Use this command to assign symbolic tags to the nearest repository versions to your working sources. The tags are applied immediately to the repository, as with rtag. One use for tags is to record a "snapshot" of the current sources when the software freeze date of a project arrives. As bugs are fixed after the freeze date, only those changed sources that are to be part of the release need be retagged.

The symbolic tags are meant to permanently record which revisions of which files were used in creating a software distribution. The checkout, export, and update commands allow you to extract an exact copy of a tagged release at any time in the future, regardless of whether files have been changed, added, or removed since the release was tagged.

You can use the standard -r and -D options to tag only those files that already contain a certain tag. This method would be used to rename a tag: tag only the files identified by the old tag, then delete the old tag, leaving the new tag on exactly the same files as the old tag.

Specifying the -f flag in addition to the -r or -D flags will tag those files named on the command line even if they do not contain the old tag or did not exist on the specified date.

By default (without a -r or -D flag), the versions to be tagged are supplied implicitly by the cvs records of your working files' history rather than applied explicitly.

If you use cvs tag -d symbolic tag..., the symbolic tag you specify is deleted instead of being added.

## WARNING

Be very certain of your ground before you delete a tag; doing this effectively discards some historical information, which may later turn out to have been valuable.

cvs tag will not move a tag that already exists. With the -F option, however, cvs tag will relocate any instance of symbolic tag that already exists on that file to the new repository versions. Without the -F option, attempting to use cvs tag to apply a tag that already exists on that file will produce an error message.

The -b option makes the tag a branch tag, allowing concurrent, isolated development. This is most useful for creating a patch to a previously released software distribution.

Normally, tag executes recursively through subdirectories; you can prevent this by using the standard -1 option, or specify the recursion explicitly by using -R.

- update [-Adf lPpQqR][-d][-r *tag*¦-D *date*] *files*...
  Requires:           Repository, working directory
  Changes:            Working directory

After you've run checkout to create your private copy of source from the common repository, other developers will continue changing the central source. From time to time, when it is convenient in your development process, you can use the update command from within your working directory to reconcile your work with any revisions applied to the source repository since your last checkout or update.

update keeps you informed of its progress by printing a line for each file, prefaced with one of the characters U, A, R, M, C, or ? to indicate the status of the file:

| | |
|---|---|
| U *file* | The file was brought up-to-date with respect to the repository. This is done for any file that exists in the repository but not in your source, and for files that you haven't changed but are not the most recent versions available in the repository. |
| A *file* | The file has been added to your private copy of the sources, and will be added to the RCS source repository when you run cvs commit on the file. This is a reminder to you that the file needs to be committed. |
| R *file* | The file has been removed from your private copy of the sources, and will be removed from the RCS source repository when you run cvs commit on the file. This is a reminder to you that the file needs to be committed. |
| M *file* | The file is modified in your working directory. M can indicate one of two states for a file you're working on: either there were no modifications to the same file in the repository, so that your file remains as you last saw it; or there were modifications in the repository as well as in your copy, but they were merged successfully, without conflict, in your working directory. |

C *file*  A conflict was detected while trying to merge your changes to *file* with changes from the source repository. *file* (the copy in your working directory) is now the output of the rcsmerge(1) command on the two versions; an unmodified copy of your file is also in your working directory, with the name .#*file*.*version*, where *version* is the RCS revision that your modified file started from. (Note that some systems automatically purge files that begin with .# if they have not been accessed for a few days. If you intend to keep a copy of your original file, it is a very good idea to rename it.)

? *file*  *file* is in your working directory, but does not correspond to anything in the source repository, and is not in the list of files for cvs to ignore; see the description of the -I option.

Use the -A option to reset any sticky tags, dates, or -k options. (If you get a working copy of a file by using one of the -r, -D, or -k options, cvs remembers the corresponding tag, date, or kflag and continues using it on future updates; use the -A option to make cvs forget these specifications, and retrieve the head version of the file).

The -jbranch option merges the changes made between the resulting revision and the revision that it is based on. (For example, if the tag refers to a branch, cvs will merge all changes made in that branch into your working file.)

With two -j options, cvs will merge in the changes between the two respective revisions. This can be used to "remove" a certain delta from your working file. For example, if the file foo.c is based on revision 1.6 and I want to remove the changes made between 1.3 and 1.5, I might do this:

```
example% cvs update -j1.5 -j1.3 foo.c # note the order...
```

In addition, each -j option can contain on optional date specification which, when used with branches, can limit the chosen revision to one within a specific date. An optional date is specified by adding a colon (:) to the tag:

```
-jSymbolic Tag:Date Specifier
```

Use the -d option to create any directories that exist in the repository if they're missing from the working directory. (Normally, update acts only on directories and files that were already enrolled in your working directory.) This is useful for updating directories that were created in the repository since the initial checkout; but it has an unfortunate side effect. If you deliberately avoided certain directories in the repository when you created your working directory (either through use of a module name or by listing explicitly the files and directories you wanted on the command line), then updating with -d will create those directories, which may not be what you want.

Use -I *name* to ignore files whose names match *name* (in your working directory) during the update. You can specify -I more than once on the command line to specify several files to ignore. By default, update ignores files whose names match any of the following:

```
RCSLOG RCS SCCS
CVS* cvslog.*
tags TAGS
.make.state .nse_depinfo
˜ #* .#* ,
.old *.bak *.BAK *.orig *.rej .del-*
.a *.o *.so *.Z *.elc *.ln core
```

Use -I! to avoid ignoring any files at all.

The standard cvs command options -f, -k, -l, -P, -p, and -r are also available with update.

## FILES

For more detailed information on cvs supporting files, see cvs(5).

Files in home directories:

.cvsrc  The cvs initialization file. Lines in this file can be used to specify default options for each cvs command. For example, the line diff -c will ensure that cvs diff is always passed the -c option in addition to any other options passed on the command line.

.cvswrappers  Specifies wrappers to be used in addition to those specified in the CVSROOT/cvswrappers file in the repository.

Files in working directories:

| | |
|---|---|
| CVS | A directory of cvs administrative files. Do not delete. |
| CVS/Entries | List and status of files in your working directory. |
| CVS/Entries.Backup | A backup of CVS/Entries. |
| CVS/Entries.Static | Flag: do not add more entries on cvs update. |
| CVS/Root | Pathname to the repository (CVSROOT) location at the time of checkout. This file is used instead of the CVSROOT environment variable if the environment variable is not set. A warning message will be issued when the contents of this file and the CVSROOT environment variable differ. The file may be overridden by the presence of the CVS_IGNORE_REMOTE_ROOT environment variable. |
| CVS/Repository | Pathname to the corresponding directory in the source repository. |
| CVS/Tag | Contains the per-directory sticky tag or date information. This file is created/updated when you specify -r or -D to the checkout or update commands, and no files are specified. |
| CVS/Checkin.prog | Name of program to run on cvs commit. |
| CVS/Update.prog | Name of program to run on cvs update. |

Files in source repositories:

| | |
|---|---|
| $CVSROOT/CVSROOT | Directory of global administrative files for repository. |
| CVSROOT/commitinfo,v | Records programs for filtering cvs commit requests. |
| CVSROOT/cvswrappers,v | Records cvs wrapper commands to be used when checking files into and out of the repository. Wrappers allow the file or directory to be processed on the way in and out of CVS. The intended uses are many; one possible use would be to reformat a C file before the file is checked in, so all of the code in the repository looks the same. |
| CVSROOT/editinfo,v | Records programs for editing/validating cvs commit log entries. |
| CVSROOT/history | Log file of cvs transactions. |
| CVSROOT/loginfo,v | Records programs for piping cvs commit log entries. |
| CVSROOT/modules,v | Definitions for modules in this repository. |
| CVSROOT/rcsinfo,v | Records pathnames to templates used during a cvs commit operation. |
| CVSROOT/taginfo,v | Records programs for validating/logging cvs tag and cvs rtag operations. |
| MODULE/Attic | Directory for removed source files. |
| #cvs.lock | A lock directory created by cvs when doing sensitive changes to the RCS source repository. |
| #cvs.tfl.pid | Temporary lock file for repository. |
| #cvs.rfl.pid | A read lock. |
| #cvs.wfl.pid | A write lock. |

## ENVIRONMENT VARIABLES

| | |
|---|---|
| CVSROOT | Should contain the full pathname to the root of the cvs source repository (where the RCS files are kept). This information must be available to cvs for most commands to execute; if CVSROOT is not set, or if you wish to override it for one invocation, you can supply it on the command line: cvs -d cvsroot cvs command.... You may not need to set CVSROOT if your cvs binary has the right path compiled in; use cvs -v to display all compiled-in paths. |
| CVSREAD | If this is set, checkout and update will try hard to make the files in your working directory read-only. When this is not set, the default behavior is to permit modification of your working files. |
| RCSBIN | Specifies the full pathname where to find RCS programs, such as co(1) and ci(1). If not set, a compiled-in value is used; see the display from cvs -v. |
| CVSEDITOR | Specifies the program to use for recording log messages during commit. If not set, the EDITOR environment variable is used instead. If EDITOR is not set either, the default is /usr/ucb/vi. |
| CVS_IGNORE_REMOTE_ROOT | If this variable is set, then cvs will ignore all references to remote repositories in the CVS/Root file. |

| | |
|---|---|
| CVS_RSH | cvs uses the contents of this variable to determine the name of the remote shell command to use when starting a cvs server. If this variable is not set then rsh is used. |
| CVS_SERVER | cvs uses the contents of this variable to determine the name of the cvs server command. If this variable is not set then cvs is used. |
| CVSWRAPPERS | This variable is used by the cvswrappers script to determine the name of the wrapper file, in addition to the wrappers defaults contained in the repository (CVSROOT/cvswrappers) and the user's home directory (˜/.cvswrappers). |

## AUTHORS

| | |
|---|---|
| Dick Grune | Original author of the cvs shell script version posted to comp.sources.unix in the volume 6 release of December, 1986. Credited with much of the cvs conflict resolution algorithms. |
| Brian Berliner | Coder and designer of the cvs program itself in April, 1989, based on the original work done by Dick. |
| Jeff Polk | Helped Brian with the design of the cvs module and vendor branch support and author of the checkin(1) shell script (the ancestor of cvs import). |

## SEE ALSO

ci(1), co(1), cvs(5), cvsbug(8), diff(1), grep(1), patch(1), rcs(1), rcsdiff(1), rcsmerge(1), rlogbug(8)

*13 March 1996*

# date

date—Show and set date and time

## SYNOPSIS

date [ -u ][-c ][-n ][-d *dsttype* ] [ -t *minutes-west* ] [ -a [+¦-]*sss.fff* ][+*format* ][
[*yyyy*]*mmddhhmm*[*yy*][.*ss*]]

## DESCRIPTION

Date without arguments writes the date and time to the standard output in the form:

Wed Mar 8 14:54:40 EST 1989

with EST replaced by the local time zone's abbreviation (or by the abbreviation for the time zone specified in the TZ environment variable if set). The exact output format depends on the locale.

If a command-line argument starts with a plus sign (+), the rest of the argument is used as a format that controls what appears in the output. In the format, when a percent sign (%) appears, it and the character after it are not output, but rather identify part of the date or time to be output in a particular way (or identify a special character to output):

| Argument | Sample output | Explanation |
|---|---|---|
| %a | Wed | Abbreviated weekday name* |
| %A | Wednesday | Full weekday name* |
| %b | Mar | Abbreviated month name* |
| %B | March | Full month name* |
| %c | Wed Mar 08 14:54:40 1989 | Date and time* |
| %C | 19 | Century |
| %d | 08 | Day of month (always two digits) |
| %D | 03/08/89 | Month/day/year (eight characters) |

| Argument | Sample output | Explanation |
| --- | --- | --- |
| %e | 8 | Day of month (leading zero blanked) |
| %h | Mar | Abbreviated month name* |
| %H | 14 | 24-hour-clock hour (two digits) |
| %I | 02 | 12-hour-clock hour (two digits) |
| %j | 067 | Julian day number (three digits) |
| %k | 2 | 12-hour-clock hour (leading zero blanked) |
| %l | 14 | 24-hour-clock hour (leading zero blanked) |
| %m | 03 | Month number (two digits) |
| %M | 54 | Minute (two digits) |
| %n | nn | Newline character |
| %p | PM | AM/PM designation |
| %r | 02:54:40 PM | Hour:minute:second AM/PM designation |
| %R | 14:54 | Hour:minute |
| %S | 40 | Second (two digits) |
| %t | nt | Tab character |
| %T | 14:54:40 | Hour:minute:second |
| %U | 10 | Sunday-based week number (two digits) |
| %w | 3 | Day number (one digit, Sunday is 0) |
| %W | 10 | Monday-based week number (two digits) |
| %x | 03/08/89 | Date* |
| %X | 14:54:40 | Time* |
| %y | 89 | Last two digits of year |
| %Y | 1989 | Year in full |
| %Z | EST | Time zone abbreviation |
| %+ | Wed Mar 8 14:54:40 EST 1989 | Default output format* |

* The exact output depends on the locale.

If a character other than one of those shown in the preceding table appears after a percent sign in the format, that following character is output. All other characters in the format are copied unchanged to the output; a newline character is always added at the end of the output.

In Sunday-based week numbering, the first Sunday of the year begins week 1; days preceding it are part of week 0. In Monday-based week numbering, the first Monday of the year begins week 1.

To set the date, use a command-line argument with one of the following forms:

| | |
| --- | --- |
| 1454 | 24-hour-clock hours (first two digits) and minutes |
| 081454 | Month day (first two digits), hours, and minutes |
| 03081454 | Month (two digits, January is 01), month day, hours, minutes |
| 8903081454 | Year, month, month day, hours, minutes |
| 0308145489 | Month, month day, hours, minutes, year (on System V-compatible systems) |
| 030814541989 | Month, month day, hours, minutes, four-digit year |
| 198903081454 | Four-digit year, month, month day, hours, minutes |

If the century, year, month, or month day is not given, the current value is used. Any of the preceding forms may be followed by a period and two digits that give the seconds part of the new time; if no seconds are given, zero is assumed.

These options are available:

| | |
|---|---|
| -u or -c | Use GMT when setting and showing the date and time. |
| -n | Do not notify other networked systems of the time change. |
| -d *dsttype* | Set the kernel-stored Daylight Saving Time type to the given value. (The kernel-stored DST type is used mostly by "old" binaries.) |
| -t *minutes-west* | Set the kernel-stored "minutes west of GMT" value to the one given on the command line. (The kernel-stored DST type is used mostly by "old" binaries.) |
| -a *adjustment* | Change the time forward (or backward) by the number of seconds (and fractions thereof) specified in the adjustment argument. Either the seconds part or the fractions part of the argument (but not both) may be omitted. On BSD-based systems, the adjustment is made by changing the rate at which time advances; on System-V–based systems, the adjustment is made by changing the time. |

## FILES

| | |
|---|---|
| /usr/lib/locale/L/LC TIME | Description of time locale L |
| /usr/local/etc/zoneinfo | Time zone information directory |
| /usr/local/etc/zoneinfo/localtime | Local time zone file |
| /usr/local/etc/zoneinfo/posixrules | Used with POSIX-style TZs |
| /usr/local/etc/zoneinfo/GMT | For UTC leap seconds |

If /usr/local/etc/zoneinfo/GMT is absent, UTC leap seconds are loaded from /usr/local/etc/zoneinfo/posixrules.

# dd

dd—Convert a file while copying it (data dumper)

## SYNOPSIS

dd [—help] [—version] [if=*file*] [of=*file*] [ibs=*bytes*] [obs=*bytes*] [bs=*bytes*]
[cbs=*bytes*] [skip=*blocks*] [seek=*blocks*] [count=*blocks*] [conv={ascii,
ebcdic, ibm, block, unblock, lcase, ucase, swab, noerror, notrunc, sync}]

## DESCRIPTION

This manual page documents the GNU version of dd. dd copies a file (from the standard input to the standard output, by default) with a user-selectable blocksize, while optionally performing conversions on it.

## OPTIONS

Numbers can be followed by a multiplier:

b=512, c=1, k=1024, w=2, xm=number m

These options are available:

| | |
|---|---|
| —help | Print a usage message on standard output and exit successfully. |
| —version | Print version information on standard output then exit successfully. |
| if=*file* | Read from file instead of the standard input. |
| of=*file* | Write to file instead of the standard output. Unless conv=notrunc is given, truncate file to the size specified by seek= (0 bytes if seek= is not given). |
| ibs=*bytes* | Read *bytes* bytes at a time. |
| obs=*bytes* | Write *bytes* bytes at a time. |
| bs=*bytes* | Read and write *bytes* bytes at a time. Override ibs and obs. |

| | |
|---|---|
| cbs=*bytes* | Convert *bytes* bytes at a time. |
| skip=*blocks* | Skip *blocks* ibs-sized blocks at start of input. |
| seek=*blocks* | Skip *blocks* obs-sized blocks at start of output. |
| count=*blocks* | Copy only *blocks* ibs-sized input blocks. |
| conv=*conversion*[,*conversion*...] | Convert the file as specified by the conversion arguments. |

Conversions:

| | |
|---|---|
| ascii | Convert EBCDIC to ASCII. |
| ebcdic | Convert ASCII to EBCDIC. |
| ibm | Convert ASCII to alternate EBCDIC. |
| block | Pad newline-terminated records to size of cbs, replacing newline with trailing spaces. |
| unblock | Replace trailing spaces in cbs-sized block with newline. |
| lcase | Change uppercase characters to lowercase. |
| ucase | Change lowercase characters to uppercase. |
| swab | Swap every pair of input bytes. Unlike the UNIX dd, this works when an odd number of bytes are read. If the input file contains an odd number of bytes, the last byte is simply copied (since there is nothing to swap it with). |
| noerror | Continue after read errors. |
| notrunc | Do not truncate the output file. |
| sync | Pad every input block to size of ibs with trailing NULLs. |

*GNU File Utilities*

# depmod, modprobe

depmod, modprobe—Handle loadable modules automatically

## SYNOPSIS

```
depmod [-a]
depmod module1.o module2.o ...

modprobe module.o [symbol=value ...]
modprobe -t tag pattern
modprobe -a -t tag pattern modprobe -l [ -t tag ] pattern
modprobe -r module
modprobe -c
```

## DESCRIPTION

These utilities are intended to make a Linux modular kernel manageable for all users, administrators, and distribution maintainers.

depmod creates a makefile-like dependency file, based on the symbols it finds in the set of modules mentioned on the command line (or in a default place). This dependency file can later be used by modprobe to automatically load the relevant module(s).

modprobe is used to load a set of modules—either a single module, a stack of dependent modules, or all modules that are marked with a specified tag.

modprobe will automatically load all base modules needed in a module stack, as described by the dependency file modules.dep. If the loading of one of these modules fails, the whole current stack of modules will be unloaded (by rmmod) automatically.

modprobe has two ways of loading modules. One way (the probe mode) will try to load a module out of a list (defined by pattern). It stops loading as soon as one module load successfully. This can be used to autoload one Ethernet driver out of a list, for example. The other way is to load all modules from a list. This can be used to load some modules at boot time.

With the option -r, modprobe will automatically unload a stack of modules, similar to the way rmmod -r does.

Option -l combined with option -t lists all available modules of a certain type. An enhanced mount command could use the command:

```
modprobe -l -t fs
```

to get the list of all file system drivers available and on request load the proper one. So, the mount command could become more generic as well. (The kerneld solves this without changing the mount utility.)

Option -c will print all configuration (default + configuration file).

The normal use of depmod is to include the line /sbin/depmod -a in one of the rc-files in /etc/rc.d, so that the correct module dependencies will be available immediately after booting the system.

Option -d puts depmod in debug mode. It outputs all commands it is issuing.

Option -e outputs the list of unresolved symbol for each module, Normally, depmod only outputs the list of unloadable modules.

Option -v outputs the list of all processed modules.

Modules may be located at different place in the filesystem, but there will always be some need to override this, especially for module developers. We expect some official standard will emerge, defined by the FSSTND. Until that time, you might as well use this suggested directory structure.

## CONFIGURATION

The behavior of depmod and modprobe can be adjusted by the (optional) configuration file /etc/conf.modules.

The configuration file consists of a set of lines. All empty lines, and all text on a line after a #, will be ignored. Lines may be continued by ending the line with a \. The remaining lines should all conform to one of the following formats:

```
keep
parameter=value
options module symbol=value ...
alias module real_name
pre-install module command ...
install module command ...
post-install module command ...
pre-remove module command ...
remove module command ...
post-remove module command ...
parameter=value options module symbol=value ... alias module real_name
```

All values in the parameter lines will be processed by a shell, which means that shell tricks like wildcards and commands enclosed in backquotes can be used:

```
path[misc]=/lib/modules/1.1.5?/misc
path[net]=/lib/modules/`uname -r`/net
```

Parameters may be repeated multiple times.

These are the legal parameters:

| | |
|---|---|
| depfile=DEPFILE_PATH | This is the path to the dependency file that will be created by depmod and used by modprobe. |
| path=SOME_PATH | The path parameter specifies a directory to search for the modules. |
| path[tag]=SOME_PATH | The path parameter can carry an optional tag. This tells us a little more about the purpose of the modules in this directory and allows some automated operations by modprobe. The tag is appended to the path keyword enclosed in square brackets. If the tag is missing, the tag misc is assumed. One very useful tag is boot, which can be used to mark all modules that should be loaded at boot time. |

If the configuration file /etc/conf.modules is missing, or if any parameter is not overridden, the following defaults are assumed:

```
depfile=/lib/modules/'uname -r'/modules.dep
path[boot]=/lib/modules/boot

path[fs]=/lib/modules/'uname -r'/fs
path[misc]=/lib/modules/'uname -r'/misc
path[net]=/lib/modules/'uname -r'/net
path[scsi]=/lib/modules/'uname -r'/scsi

path[fs]=/lib/modules/default/fs
path[misc]=/lib/modules/default/misc
path[net]=/lib/modules/default/net
path[scsi]=/lib/modules/default/scsi

path[fs]=/lib/modules/fs
path[misc]=/lib/modules/misc
path[net]=/lib/modules/net
path[scsi]=/lib/modules/scsi
```

All option lines specify the default options that are needed for a module, as in

```
modprobe de620 bnc=1
```

These options will be overridden by any options given on the modprobe command line.

The alias lines can be used to give alias names to modules. A line in /etc/conf.modules that looks like this:

```
alias iso9660 isofs
```

makes it possible to write modprobe iso9660, although there is no such module available.

## STRATEGY

The idea is that modprobe will look first at the directory containing modules compiled for the current release of the kernel. If the module is not found there, modprobe will look in the directory containing modules for a default release.

When you install a new Linux, the modules should be moved to a directory related to the release (and version) of the kernel you are installing. Then you should do a symlink from this directory to the default directory.

Each time you compile a new kernel, the command make modules_install will create a new directory, but won't change the default.

When you get a module unrelated to the kernel distribution, you should place it in one of the version-independent directories under /lib/modules.

This is the default strategy, which can be overridden in /etc/conf.modules.

## EXAMPLES

| | |
|---|---|
| modprobe -t net | Load one of the modules that are stored in the directory tagged net. Each module is tried until one succeeds. (Default: /lib/modules/net). |
| modprobe -a -t boot | All modules that are stored in the directory tagged boot will be loaded. (Default: /lib/modules/boot). |
| modprobe slip.o | This will attempt to load the module slhc.o if it was not previously loaded, since the slip module needs the functionality in the slhc module. This dependency will be described in the file modules.dep that was created automatically by depmod. |
| modprobe -r slip.o | Will unload slip.o. It will also unload slhc.o automatically, unless it is used by some other module as well (such as ppp.o). |

## FILES

```
/etc/conf.modules
/lib/modules/*/modules.dep
/lib/modules/*
```

## SEE ALSO

lsmod(1), kerneld(8), ksyms(1), modules(2)

## REQUIRED UTILITIES

insmod(1), nm(1) rmmod(1)

## NOTES

The pattern supplied to modprobe will often be escaped to ensure that it is evaluated in the proper context.

## AUTHOR

Jacques Gelinas (jack@solucorp.qc.ca), Bjorn Ekwall (bj0rn@blox.se)

## BUGS

Naah...

*Linux, 14 May 1995*

# df

df—Summarize free disk space

## SYNOPSIS

df [-aikPv] [-t *fstype*] [-x *fstype*] [—all] [—inodes] [—type=*fstype*]
[—exclude-type=*fstype*] [—kilobytes] [—portability] [—print-type]
[—help] [—version] [filename...]

## DESCRIPTION

This manual page documents the GNU version of df. df displays the amount of disk space available on the filesystem containing each filename argument. If no filename is given, the space available on all currently mounted filesystems is shown. Disk space is shown in 1K blocks by default, unless the environment variable POSIXLY_CORRECT is set, in which case 512-byte blocks are used.

If an argument is the absolute filename of a disk device node containing a mounted filesystem, df shows the space available on that filesystem rather than on the filesystem containing the device node (which is always the root filesystem). This version of df cannot show the space available on unmounted filesystems, because on most kinds of systems doing so requires very nonportable, intimate knowledge of filesystem structures.

## OPTIONS

-a, —all
Include in the listing filesystems that have 0 blocks, which are omitted by default. Such filesystems are typically special-purpose pseudo-filesystems, such as automounter entries. On some systems, filesystems of type ignore or auto are also omitted by default and included in the listing by this option.

-i, —inodes
List inode usage information instead of block usage. An inode (short for "index node") is a special kind of disk block that contains information about a file, such as its owner, permissions, timestamps, and location on the disk.

-k, —kilobytes
Print sizes in 1K blocks instead of 512-byte blocks. This overrides the environment variable POSIXLY_CORRECT.

-P, —portability
Use the POSIX output format. This is like the default format except that the information about each filesystem is always printed on exactly one line; a mount device is never put on a line by itself. This means that if the mount device name is more than 20 characters long (as for some network mounts), the columns are misaligned.

| -T, —print-type | Print a type string for each filesystem. Any such printed filesystem type name may be used as an argument to either of the —type= or —exclude-type= options. |
|---|---|
| -t, —type=*fstype* | Limit the listing to filesystems of type *fstype*. Multiple filesystem types can be shown by giving multiple -t options. By default, all filesystem types are listed. |
| -x, —exclude-type=*fstype* | Limit the listing to filesystems not of type fstype. Multiple filesystem types can be eliminated by giving multiple -x options. By default, all filesystem types are listed. |
| -v | Ignored; for compatibility with System V versions of df. |
| —help | Print a usage message on standard output and exit successfully. |
| —version | Print version information on standard output then exit successfully. |

*GNU File Utilities*

# dig

dig—Send domain name query packets to name servers

## SYNOPSIS

dig [@*server*] *domain* [<*query-type*>][<*query-class*>][+<*query-option*>][-<*dig-option*>]
[%*comment*]

## DESCRIPTION

dig (domain information groper) is a flexible command-line tool that can be used to gather information from the Domain Name System servers. dig has two modes: simple interactive mode that makes a single query, and batch that executes a query for each in a list of several query lines. All query options are accessible from the command line.

The usual simple use of dig takes the form:

dig @*server* *domain* *query-type* *query-class*

where

| *server* | May be either a domain name or a dot-notation Internet address. If this optional field is omitted, dig will attempt to use the default name server for your machine. |
|---|---|

### NOTE

If a domain name is specified, this will be resolved using the domain name system resolver (BIND). If your system does not support DNS, you may have to specify a dot-notation address. Alternatively, if there is a server at your disposal somewhere, all that is required is that /etc/resolv.conf be present and indicate where the default name servers reside, so that server itself can be resolved. See resolver(5) for information on /etc/resolv.conf.

### WARNING

Changing /etc/resolv.conf will affect the standard resolver library and potentially several programs that use it.) As an option, the user may set the environment variable LOCALRES to name a file which is to be used instead of /etc/resolv.conf (LOCALRES is specific to the dig resolver and not referenced by the standard resolver). If the LOCALRES variable is not set or the file is not readable, then /etc/resolv.conf will be used.

| *domain* | The domain name for which you are requesting information. See "Options" [-x] for a convenient way to specify inverse address query. |
|---|---|

query-type    The type of information (DNS query type) that you are requesting. If omitted, the default is a (T_A = address). The following types are recognized:

| Type | Example | Description |
|---|---|---|
| a | T_A | Network address |
| any | T_ANY | All/any information about specified domain |
| mx | T_MX | Mail exchanger for the domain |
| ns | T_NS | Name servers |
| soa | T_SOA | Zone of authority record |
| hinfo | T_HINFO | Host information |
| axfr | T_AXFR | Zone transfer (must ask an authoritative server) |
| txt | T_TXT | Arbitrary number of strings |

(See RFC 1035 for the complete list.)

query-class    The network class requested in the query. If omitted, the default is in (C_IN = Internet). The following classes are recognized:

| | | |
|---|---|---|
| in | C_IN | Internet class domain |
| any | C_ANY | All/any class information |

(See RFC 1035 for the complete list.)

## NOTE

any can be used to specify a class and/or a type of query. dig will parse the first occurrence of any to mean query-type = T_ANY.

To specify query-class = C_ANY you must either specify any twice, or set query-class using -c option. (See "Other Options," next.)

## OTHER OPTIONS

%ignored-comment    % is used to include an argument that is simply not parsed. This may be useful if running dig in batch mode. Instead of resolving every @server-domain-name in a list of queries, you can avoid the overhead of doing so, and still have the domain name on the command line as a reference. Example:

dig @128.9.0.32 %venera.isi.edu mx isi.edu

-<dig option>    - is used to specify an option that affects the operation of dig. The following options are currently available (although not guaranteed to be useful):

-x dot-notation-address    Convenient form to specify inverse address mapping. Instead of

dig 32.0.9.128.in-addr.arpa

one can simply use

dig -x 128.9.0.32

-f file    File for dig batch mode. The file contains a list of query specifications (dig command lines) which are to be executed successively. Lines beginning with ;, #, or \n are ignored. Other options may still appear on the command line, and will be in effect for each batch query.

-T time    Time in seconds between start of successive queries when running in batch mode. Can be used to keep two or more batch dig commands running roughly in sync. Default is zero.

| | |
|---|---|
| -p *port* | Port number. Query a name server listening to a nonstandard port number. Default is 53. |
| -P[*ping-string*] | After query returns, execute a ping(8) command for response time comparison. This rather unelegantly makes a call to the shell. The last three lines of statistics is printed for the command: |
| | ping –s server_name 56 3 |
| | If the optional ping string is present, it replaces ping -s in the shell command. |
| -t *query-type* | Specify type of query. May specify either an integer value to be included in the type field or use the abbreviated mnemonic as discussed earlier (mx = T_MX). |
| -c *query-class* | Specify class of query. May specify either an integer value to be included in the class field or use the abbreviated mnemonic as discussed earlier (in = C_IN). |
| -envsav | This flag specifies that the dig environment (defaults, print options, and so on), after all of the arguments are parsed, should be saved to a file to become the default environment. Useful if you do not like the standard set of defaults and do not desire to include a large number of options each time dig is used. The environment consists of resolver state variable flags, timeout, and retries as well as the flags detailing dig output (see below). If the shell environment variable LOCALDEF is set to the name of a file, this is where the default dig environment is saved. If not, the file DiG.env is created in the current working directory. |

## NOTE

LOCALDEF is specific to the dig resolver, and will not affect operation of the standard resolver library.

| | |
|---|---|
| | Each time dig is executed, it looks for ./DiG.env or the file specified by the shell environment variable LOCALDEF. If such file exists and is readable, then the environment is restored from this file before any arguments are parsed. |
| -envset | This flag only affects batch query runs. When -envset is specified on a line in a dig batch file, the dig environment after the arguments are parsed, becomes the default environment for the duration of the batch file, or until the next line which specifies -envset. |
| -[no]stick | This flag only affects batch query runs. It specifies that the dig environment (as read initially or set by -envset switch) is to be restored before each query (line) in a dig batch file. The default -nostick means that the dig environment does not stick, hence options specified on a single line in a dig batch file will remain in effect for subsequent lines (that is, they are not restored to the sticky default). |
| +<*query option*> | + is used to specify an option to be changed in the query packet or to change dig output specifics. Many of these are the same parameters accepted by nslookup(8). If an option requires a parameter, the form is as follows: |
| | +*keyword*[=*value*] |
| | Most keywords can be abbreviated. Parsing of the + options is very simplistic—a value must not be separated from its keyword by whitespace. The following keywords are currently available: |

| Keyword Abbreviation | Meaning (Default) |
|---|---|
| [no]debug (deb) | Turn on/off debugging mode [deb] |
| [no]d2 | Turn on/off extra debugging mode [nod2] |
| [no]recurse (rec) | Use/don't use recursive lookup [rec] |
| retry=# (ret) | Set number of retries to # [4] |

*continues*

| *Keyword Abbreviation* | *Meaning (Default)* |
|---|---|
| time=# (ti) | Set timeout length to # seconds [4] |
| [no]ko | Keep open option (implies vc) [noko] |
| [no]vc | Use/don't use virtual circuit [novc] |
| [no]defname (def) | Use/don't use default domain name [def] |
| [no]search (sea) | Use/don't use domain search list [sea] |
| domain=NAME (do) | Set default domain name to NAME |
| [no]ignore (i) | Ignore/don't ignore trunc. errors [noi] |
| [no]primary (pr) | Use/don't use primary server [nopr] |
| [no]aaonly (aa) | Authoritative query only flag [noaa] |
| [no]sort (sor) | Sort resource records [nosor] |
| [no]cmd | Echo parsed arguments [cmd] |
| [no]stats (st) | Print query statistics [st] |
| [no]Header (H) | Print basic header [H] |
| [no]header (he) | Print header flags [he] |
| [no]ttlid (tt) | Print TTLs [tt] |
| [no]cl | Print class info [nocl] |
| [no]qr | Print outgoing query [noqr] |
| [no]reply (rep) | Print reply [rep] |
| [no]ques (qu) | Print question section [qu] |
| [no]answer (an) | Print answer section [an] |
| [no]author (au) | Print authoritative section [au] |
| [no]addit (ad) | Print additional section [ad] |
| pfdef | Set to default print flags |
| pfmin | Set to minimal default print flags |
| pfset=# | Set print flags to # (# can be hex/octal/decimal) |
| pfand=# | Bitwise and print flags with # |
| pfor=# | Bitwise or print flags with # |

The retry and time options affect the retransmission strategy used by resolver library when sending datagram queries. The algorithm is as follows:

```
August 30, 1990
for i = 0 to retry - 1
for j = 1 to num_servers
send_query
wait((time * (2**i)) / num_servers)
end
end
```

Note that dig always uses a value of 1 for num_servers.

## DETAILS

dig once required a slightly modified version of the BIND resolver (3) library. BIND's resolver has (as of BIND 4.9) been augmented to work properly with dig. Essentially, dig is a straightforward (albeit not pretty) effort of parsing arguments and setting appropriate parameters. dig uses resolver routines res_init(), res_mkquery(), res_send() as well as accessing _res structure.

## FILES

`/etc/resolv.conf`                    Initial domain name and name server addresses

## ENVIRONMENT

`LOCALRES` file to use in place of `/etc/resolv.conf`

`LOCALDEF` default environment file

## AUTHOR

Steve Hotz (`hotz@isi.edu`)

## ACKNOWLEDGMENTS

`dig` uses functions from `nslookup`(8) authored by Andrew Cherenson.

## BUGS

`dig` has a serious case of "creeping featurism," the result of considering several potential uses during its development. It would probably benefit from a rigorous diet. Similarly, the print flags and granularity of the items they specify make evident their rather ad hoc genesis.

`dig` does not consistently exit nicely (with appropriate status) when a problem occurs somewhere in the resolver (Most of the common exit cases are handled.) This is particularly annoying when running in batch mode. If it exits abnormally (and is not caught), the entire batch aborts; when such an event is trapped, `dig` simply continues with the next query.

## SEE ALSO

`named`(8), `resolver`(3), `resolver`(5), `nslookup`(8)

*30 August 1990*

# dnsquery

dnsquery—Query domain name servers using resolver

## SYNOPSIS

`dnsquery [-n `*nameserver*`] [-t `*type*`] [-c `*class*`] [-r `*retry*`] [-p `*retry*` period]`
`[-d] [-s] [-v] `*host*

## DESCRIPTION

The `dnsquery` program is a general interface to nameservers via `BIND` resolver library calls. The program supports queries to the nameserver with an opcode of `QUERY`. This program is intended to be a replacement or supplement to programs like `nstest`, `nsquery`, and `nslookup`. All arguments except for `host` and `ns` are treated without case-sensitivity.

## OPTIONS

`-n`           The nameserver to be used in the query. Nameservers can appear as either Internet addresses of the form *w.x.y.z* or can appear as domain names. (default: as specified in `/etc/resolv.conf`)

`-t`           The type of resource record of interest. Types include:

|  |  |
|---|---|
| A | Address |
| NS | Nameserver |
| CNAME | Canonical name |
| PTR | Domain name pointer |
| SOA | Start of authority |

| | |
|---|---|
| WKS | Well-known service |
| HINFO | Host information |
| MINFO | Mailbox information |
| MX | Mail exchange |
| RP | Responsible person |
| MG | Mail group member |
| AFSDB | DCE or AFS server |
| ANY | Wildcard |

## NOTE

Any case may be used (the default is ANY)

-c         The class of resource records of interest. Classes include the following:

| | |
|---|---|
| IN | Internet |
| HS | Hesiod |
| CHAOS | Chaos |
| ANY | Wildcard |

## NOTE

Any case may be used (the default is IN).

| | |
|---|---|
| -r | The number of times to retry if the nameserver is not responding. (default: 4) |
| -p | Period to wait before timing out. (default: RES_TIMEOUT) options field. (default: any answer) |
| -d | Turn on debugging. This sets the RES_DEBUG bit of the resolver's options field. (default: no debugging) |
| -s | Use a stream rather than a packet. This uses a TCP stream connection with the nameserver rather than a UDP datagram. This sets the RES_USEVC bit of the resolver's options field. (default: UDP) |
| -v | Synonym for the s flag. |
| host | The name of the host (or domain) of interest. |

## FILES

| | |
|---|---|
| /etc/resolv.conf | To get the default ns and search lists. |
| <arpa/nameser.h> | List of usable RR types and classes |
| <resolv.h> | List of resolver flags |

## SEE ALSO

nslookup(8), nstest(1), nsquery(1), named(8), resolver(5)

## DIAGNOSTICS

If the resolver fails to answer the query and debugging has not been turned on, dnsquery will simply print a message like this:

Query failed (rc = 1) : Unknown host

The value of the return code is supplied by h_errno.

## BUGS

Queries of a class other than IN can have interesting results since ordinarily a nameserver only has a list of root nameservers for class IN resource records.

Query uses a call to inet_addr() to determine if the argument for the -n option is a valid Internet address. Unfortunately, inet_addr() seems to cause a segmentation fault with some (bad) addresses (for example, 1.2.3.4.5).

## AUTHOR

Bryan Beecher

*10 March 1990*

# domainname

domainname—Set or print domain of current host

## SYNOPSIS

domainname [ *name* ]

## DESCRIPTION

domainname prints the domain name of the current host, from the getdomainname(3) library call. If an argument is present and the effective UID is 0, domainname changes the name of the host, with the setdomainname(2) system call. This is usually done at boot time in the /etc/rc.local script.

## FILES

/etc/rc.local

## SEE ALSO

getdomainname(3), setdomainname(2), uname(1), uname(2)

## AUTHOR

Lars Wirzenius by substituting in hostname.c

*Linux 0.98, 26 December 1992*

# dsplit

dsplit—Split a large file into pieces

## SYNOPSIS

dsplit [ -size *nnn* ][*input_file* [ *output_base* ]]

## DESCRIPTION

dsplit splits binary files into smaller chunks so that they may be placed on floppy disks.

## OPTIONS

| | |
|---|---|
| -size *nnn* | Specifies the size of each output file, in bytes. The default is 1457000, which is enough to will a 1.44MB floppy disk. |
| *input_file* | Specifies the name of the file to split up. A - indicates standard input. The default is standard input. |

| | |
|---|---|
| *output_base* | Specifies the name of the output files to be written. `dsplit` will append `000`, `001`, `...`, to the *output_base*. The default is `dsplit`. |

## AUTHOR'S NOTES

Submitted by: David Arnstein (`arnstein@netcom.com`)

Posting number: Volume 40, Issue 51

Archive name: `dsplit/part01`

Environment: MS-DOS, UNIX

Here is a portable binary file splitting program. It reads a binary file and splits it into pieces. I use this program to put large binary files on floppy disks. For this reason, the default size of the output files is 1,457,000 bytes, which just about fills up a 1.44MB floppy disk.

Unlike other binary split programs I have seen, `dsplit` does not `malloc` a huge block of memory. `dsplit` is suitable for use under MS-DOS and other primitive operating systems.

(The program came from `gatekeeper.dec.com:/pub/usenet/comp.sources.misc/volume40/dsplit`).

*Linux 1.1, 5 July 1994*

# du

du—Summarize disk usage

## SYNOPSIS

```
du [-abcklsxDLS] [−all] [−total] [−count-links] [−summarize] [−bytes]
[−kilobytes] [−one-file-system] [−separate-dirs] [−dereference]
[−dereference-args] [−help] [−-version] [filename...]
```

## DESCRIPTION

This manual page documents the GNU version of `du`. `du` displays the amount of disk space used by each argument and for each subdirectory of directory arguments. The space is measured in 1K blocks by default, unless the environment variable `POSIXLY_CORRECT` is set, in which case 512-byte blocks are used.

## OPTIONS

| | |
|---|---|
| `-a, −all` | Display counts for all files, not just directories. |
| `-b, −bytes` | Print sizes in bytes. |
| `-c, −total` | Write a grand total of all of the arguments after all arguments have been processed. This can be used to find out the disk usage of a directory, with some files excluded. |
| `-k, −kilobytes` | Print sizes in kilobytes. This overrides the environment variable `POSIXLY_CORRECT`. |
| `-l, −count-links` | Count the size of all files, even if they have appeared already in another hard link. |
| `-s, −summarize` | Display only a total for each argument. |
| `-x, −one-file-system` | Skip directories that are on different filesystems from the one that the argument being processed is on. |
| `-D, −dereference-args` | Dereference symbolic links that are command-line arguments. Does not affect other symbolic links. This is helpful for finding out the disk usage of directories like `/usr/tmp` where they are symbolic links. |
| `-L, −dereference` | Dereference symbolic links (show the disk space used by the file or directory that the link points to instead of the space used by the link). |
| `-S, −separate-dirs` | Count the size of each directory separately, not including the sizes of subdirectories. |
| `−help` | Print a usage message on standard output and exit successfully. |
| `−version` | Print version information on standard output, then exit successfully. |

## BUGS

On BSD systems, du reports sizes that are half the correct values for files that are NFS-mounted from HP-UX systems. On HP-UX systems, it reports sizes that are twice the correct values for files that are NFS-mounted from BSD systems. This is due to a flaw in HP-UX; it also affects the HP-UX du program.

*GNU File Utilities*

# editres

editres—A dynamic resource editor for X Toolkit applications

## SYNTAX

editres [ *-toolkitoption* ... ]

## OPTIONS

editres accepts all of the standard X Toolkit command-line options (see X(1)). The order of the command-line options is not important.

## DESCRIPTION

editres is a tool that allows users and application developers to view the full widget hierarchy of any X Toolkit application that speaks the editres protocol. In addition, editres will help the user construct resource specifications, allow the user to apply the resource to the application and view the results dynamically. Once the user is happy with a resource specification, editres will append the resource string to the user's X Resources file.

## USING editres

editres provides a window consisting of the following four areas:

| | |
|---|---|
| Menu Bar | A set of pop-up menus that allow you full access to editres's features. |
| Panner | The panner provides a more intuitive way to scroll the application tree display. |
| Message Area | Displays information to the user about the action that editres expects. |
| Application Widget Tree | This area is used to display the selected application's widget tree. |

To begin an editres session, select the Get Widget Tree menu item from the Command menu. This will change the pointer cursor to crosshair. You should now select the application you wish look at by clicking on any of its windows. If this application understands the editres protocol, editres will display the application's widget tree in its tree window. If the application does not understand the editres protocol, editres will inform you of this fact in the message area after a few seconds delay.

After you have a widget tree, you may select any of the other menu options. The effect of each of these is described in "Commands," next.

## COMMANDS

| | |
|---|---|
| Get Widget Tree | Allows the user to click on any application that speaks the editres protocol and receive its widget tree. |
| Refresh Current Widget Tree | editres only knows about the widgets that exist at the present time. Many applications create and destroy widgets on the fly. Selecting this menu item will cause editres to ask the application to resend its widget tree, thus updating its information to the new state of the application. |
| | For example, xman only creates the widgets for its topbox when it starts up. None of the widgets for the manual page window are created until the user actually clicks on the Manual Page button. If you retrieved xman's widget tree before the manual page is active, you may wish to refresh the widget tree after the manual page has been displayed. This will allow you to also edit the manual page's resources. |

| Dump Widget Tree to a File | When documenting applications it is often useful to be able to dump the entire application widget tree to an ASCII file. This file can then be included in the manual page. When this menu item is selected, a pop-up dialog is activated. Type the name of the file in this dialog, and either select Okay, or type a carriage-return. editres will dump the widget tree to this file. To cancel the file dialog, select the Cancel button. |
|---|---|
| Show Resource Box | This command will pop up a resource box for the current application. This resource box (described in detail later in this section) will allow the user to see exactly which resources can be set for the widget that is currently selected in the widget tree display. Only one widget may be currently selected; if greater or fewer are selected, editres will refuse to pop up the resource box and put an error message in the Message Area. |
| Set Resource | This command will pop up a simple dialog box for setting an arbitrary resource on all selected widgets. You must type in the resource name, as well as the value. You can use the Tab key to switch between the resource name field and the resource value field. |
| Quit | Exits editres. |

## TREE COMMANDS

The Tree menu contains several commands that enable operations to be performed on the widget tree.

| Select Widget in Client | This menu item allows you to select any widget in the application; editres will then highlight the corresponding element the widget tree display. After this menu item is selected, the pointer cursor will again turn to a crosshair, and you must click any pointer button in the widget you wish to have displayed. Since some widgets are fully obscured by their children, it is not possible to get to every widget this way, but this mechanism does give very useful feedback between the elements in the widget tree and those in the actual application. |
|---|---|
| Select All, Unselect All, Invert All | These functions allow the user to select, unselect, or invert all widgets in the widget tree. |
| Select Children, Select Parents | These functions select the immediate parent or children of each of the currently selected widgets. |
| Select Descendants, Select Ancestors | These functions select all parents or children of each of the currently selected widgets. This is a recursive search. |
| Show Widget Names, Show Class Names, Show Widget Windows | When the tree widget is initially displayed, the labels of each widget in the tree correspond to the widget names. These functions will cause the label of all widgets in the tree to be changed to show the class name, IDs, or window associated with each widget in the application. The widget IDs, and windows are shown as hex numbers. |
| | In addition, there are keyboard accelerators for each of the Tree operations. If the input focus is over an individual widget in the tree, then that operation will only affect that widget. If the input focus is in the Tree background, it will have exactly the same effect as the corresponding menu item. |
| | The translation entries shown may be applied to any widget in the application. If that widget is a child of the Tree widget, then it will only affect that widget; otherwise, it will have the same effect as the commands in the Tree menu. |
| Flash Active Widgets | This command is the inverse of the Select Widget in Client command; it will show the user each widget that is currently selected in the widget tree by flashing the corresponding widget in the application numFlashes (three by default) times in the flash-Color. |

| Key | Option | Translation Entry |
|---|---|---|
| space | Unselect | Select(nothing) |
| w | Select | Select(widget) |
| s | Select | Select(all) |
| i | Invert | Select(invert) |

| Key | Option | Translation Entry |
|---|---|---|
| c | Select | Children Select(children) |
| d | Select Descendants | Select(descendants) |
| p | Select Parent | Select(parent) |
| a | Select Ancestors | Select(ancestors) |
| N | Show Widget Names | Relabel(name) |
| C | Show Class Names | Relabel(class) |
| I | Show Widget IDs | Relabel(id) |
| W | Show Widget Windows | Relabel(window) |
| T | Toggle Widget/Class Name | Relabel(toggle) |

Clicking button 1 on a widget adds it to the set of selected widgets. Clicking button 2 on a widget deselects all other widgets and then selects just that widget. Clicking button 3 on a widget toggles its label between the widget's instance name the widget's class name.

## USING THE RESOURCE BOX

The resource box contains five different areas. Each of the areas, as they appear on the screen from top to bottom, are discussed in the following list:

The Resource Line

This area at the top of the resource box shows the current resource name exactly as it would appear if you were to save it to a file or apply it.

The Widget Names and Classes

This area enables you to select exactly which widgets this resource will apply to. The area contains four lines; the first contains the name of the selected widget and all its ancestors, and the more restrictive dot (.) separator. The second line contains less specific class names of each widget, as well as the less restrictive star (*) separator. The third line contains a set of special buttons called Any Widget that will generalize this level to match any widget. The last line contains a set of special buttons called Any Widget Chain that will turn the single level into something that matches zero or more levels.

The initial state of this area is the most restrictive, using the resource names and the dot separator. By selecting the other buttons in this area, you can ease the restrictions to allow more and more widgets to match the specification. The extreme case is to select all the Any Widget Chain buttons, which will match every widget in the application. As you select different buttons, the tree display will update to show you exactly which widgets will be affected by the current resource specification.

Normal and Constraint Resources

The next area allows you to select the name of the normal or constraint resources you wish to set. Some widgets may not have constraint resources, so that area will not appear.

Resource Value

This next area allows you to enter the resource value. This value should be entered exactly as you would type a line into your resource file. Thus, it should contain no unescaped newlines. There are a few special character sequences for this file:

| | |
|---|---|
| \n- | This will be replaced with a newline. |
| \###- | Where # is any octal digit. This will be replaced with a single byte that contains this sequence interpreted as an octal number. For example, a value containing a NULL byte can be stored by specifying \000. |
| \<new-line>- | This will compress to nothing. |
| \\- | This will compress to a single backslash. |

Command Area

This area contains several command buttons, described in the following list:

The Set Save File button allows the user to modify file that the resources will be saved to. This button will bring up a dialog box that will ask you for a filename; after the filename has been entered, either hit carriage-return or click on the Okay button. To pop down the dialog box without changing the save file, click the Cancel button.

The Save button will append the resource line already described to the end of the current save file. If no save file has been set, the Set Save File dialog box will be popped up to prompt the user for a filename.

The Apply button attempts to perform a XtSetValues call on all widgets that match the resource line described earlier. The value specified is applied directly to all matching widgets. This behavior is an attempt to give a dynamic feel to the resource editor. Since this feature allows users to put an application in states it may not be willing to handle, a hook has been provided to allow specific applications to block these SetValues requests. (See "Blocking editres Requests," following).

Unfortunately, due to design constraints imposed on the widgets by the X Toolkit and the Resource Manager, trying to coerce an inherently static system into dynamic behavior can cause strange results. There is no guarantee that the results of an apply will be the same as what will happen when you save the value and restart the application. This functionality is provided to try to give you a rough feel for what your changes will accomplish, and the results obtained should be considered suspect at best. Having said that, this is one of the neatest features of editres, and I strongly suggest that you play with it, and see what it can do.

The Save and Apply button combines the Save and Apply actions described earlier into one button.

The Popdown Resource Box button will remove the resource box from the display.

## BLOCKING editres REQUESTS

The editres protocol has been built into the Athena Widget set. This allows all applications that are linked against Xaw to be able to speak to the resource editor. Although this provides great flexibility, and is a useful tool, it can quite easily be abused. It is therefore possible for any Xaw application to specify a value for the editresBlock resource to keep editres from divulging information about its internals, or to disable the SetValues part of the protocol.

editresBlock (Class Editresblock) specifies which type of blocking this application wishes to impose on the editres protocol.

The accepted values are as follows:

all             Block all requests.

setValues       Block all SetValues requests. As this is the only editres request that actually modifies the application, this is in effect stating that the application is read-only.

none            Allow all editres requests.

Remember that these resources are set on any Xaw application, not editres. They allow individual applications to keep all or some of the requests editres makes from ever succeeding. Of course, editres is also an Xaw application, so it may also be viewed and modified by editres (rather recursive, I know); these commands can be blocked by setting the editresBlock resource on editres itself.

## RESOURCES

For editres, the available application resources are as follows:

numFlashes (Class NumFlashes) specifies the number of times the widgets in the application will be flashed when the Show Active Widgets command in invoked.

flashTime (Class FlashTime) specifies the mount of time between the flashes described in the preceding entry.

flashColor (Class flashColor) specifies the color used to flash application widgets. A bright color should be used that will immediately draw your attention to the area being flashed, such as red or yellow.

saveResourcesFile (Class SaveResourcesFile) is the file the resource line will be append to when the Save button activated in the resource box.

## WIDGETS

In order to specify resources, it is useful to know the hierarchy of the widgets that compose editres. In the following notation, indentation indicates hierarchical structure. The widget class name is given first, followed by the widget instance name.

```
Editres editres
     Paned paned
          Box box
                    MenuButton commands
                         SimpleMenu menu
                         SmeBSB sendTree
                         SmeBSB refreshTree
                         SmeBSB dumpTreeToFile
                         SmeLine line SmeBSB getResourceList
                         SmeLine line
                         SmeBSB quit
                    MenuButton treeCommands
                         SimpleMenuumenu
                         SmeBSB showClientWidget
                         SmeBSB selectAll
                         SmeBSB unselectAll
                         SmeBSB invertAll
                         SmeLine line
                         SmeBSB selectChildren
                         SmeBSB selectParent
                         SmeBSB selectDescendants
                         SmeBSB selectAncestors
                         SmeLine line
                         SmeBSB showWidgetNames
                         SmeBSB showClassNames
                         SmeBSB showWidgetIDs
                         SmeBSB showWidgetWindows
                         SmeLine line
                         SmeBSB flashActiveWidgets
               Paned hPane
                    Panner panner
                    Label userMessage
                    Grip grip
               Porthole porthole
                    Tree tree
                         Toggle <name of widget in application>
                              .
                              .
                              .
                         TransientShell resourceBox
                         Paned pane
                         Label resourceLabel
                         Form namesAndClasses
                         Toggle dot
                         Toggle star
                         Toggle any
                         Toggle name
```

```
              Toggle class
              .
              .
              .
              Label namesLabel
              List namesList
              Label constraintLabel
              List constraintList
              Form valueForm
              Label valueLabel
              Text valueText
              Box commandBox
              Command setFile
              Command save
              Command apply
              Command saveAndApply
              Command cancel
              Grip grip
       Grip grip
```

## ENVIRONMENT

DISPLAY              To get the default host and display number

XENVIRONMENT     To get the name of a resource file that overrides the global resources stored in the RESOURCE_MANAGER
                 property.

## FILES

`<XRoot>/lib/X11/app-defaults/Editres` specifies required resources.

## SEE ALSO

X(1), xrdb(1), Athena Widget Set

## RESTRICTIONS

This is a prototype. There are lots of nifty features I would love to add, but I hope this will give you some ideas about what a
resource editor can do.

## AUTHOR

Chris D. Peterson (formerly MIT X Consortium)

X Version 11 Release 6

# elvis, ex, vi, view, input

elvis, ex, vi, view, input—The editor

## SYNOPSIS

`elvis [flags][+cmd][files...]`

## DESCRIPTION

elvis is a text editor that emulates vi/ex.

On systems which pass the program name as an argument, such as UNIX and Minix, you may also install elvis under the
names ex, vi, view, and input. These extra names would normally be links to elvis; see the ln shell command.

When elvis is invoked as vi, it behaves exactly as though it was invoked as elvis. However, if you invoke elvis as view, then the readonly option is set as though you had given it the -R flag. If you invoke elvis as ex, then elvis will start up in the colon command mode instead of the visual command mode, as though you had given it the -e flag. If you invoke elvis as input or edit, then elvis will start up in input mode, as though the -i flag was given.

## OPTIONS

| | |
|---|---|
| -r | To the real vi, this flag means that a previous edit should be recovered. elvis, though, has a separate program, called elvrec(1), for recovering files. When you invoke elvis with -r, elvis will tell you to run elvrec. |
| -R | This sets the readonly option, so you won't accidentally overwrite a file. |
| -s | This sets the safer option, which disables many potentially harmful commands. It has not been rigorously proven to be absolutely secure, however. |
| -t tag | This causes elvis to start editing at the given tag. |
| -m [file] | elvis will search through *file* for something that looks like an error message from a compiler. It will then begin editing the source file that caused the error, with the cursor sitting on the line where the error was detected. If you don't explicitly name a file, then errlist is assumed. |
| -e | elvis will start up in colon command mode. |
| -v | elvis will start up in visual command mode. |
| -i | elvis will start up in input mode. |
| -w winsize | Sets the window option's value to winsize. |
| +command or -c command | If you use the +command parameter, then after the first file is loaded, command is executed as an EX command. A typical example would be elvis +237 foo, which would cause elvis to start editing foo and then move directly to line 237. The -c command variant was added for UNIX SysV compatibility. |

## FILES

| | |
|---|---|
| /tmp/elv* | During editing, elvis stores text in a temporary file. For UNIX, this file will usually be stored in the /tmp directory, and the first three characters will be elv. For other systems, the temporary files may be stored someplace else; see the version-specific section of the documentation. |
| tags | This is the database used by the :tags command and the -t option. It is usually created by the ctags(1) program. |
| .exrc or elvis.rc | On UNIX-like systems, a file called .exrc in your home directory is executed as a series of ex commands. A file by the same name may be executed in the current directory, too. On non-UNIX systems, .exrc is usually an invalid filename; there, the initialization file is called elvis.rc instead. |

## ENVIRONMENT

| | |
|---|---|
| TERM | This is the name of your terminal's entry in the termcap or terminfo database. The list of legal values varies from one system to another. |
| TERMCAP | Optional. If your system uses termcap, and the TERMCAP variable is unset, then elvis will read your terminal's definition from /etc/termcap. If TERMCAP is set to the full pathname of a file (starting with a /) then elvis will look in the named file instead of /etc/termcap. If TERMCAP is set to a value which doesn't start with a /, then its value is assumed to be the full termcap entry for your terminal. |
| TERMINFO | Optional. If your system uses terminfo, and the TERMINFO variable is unset, then elvis will read your terminal's definition from the database in the /usr/lib/terminfo database. If TERMINFO is set, then its value is used as the database name to use instead of /usr/lib/terminfo. |
| LINES, COLUMNS | Optional. These variables, if set, will override the screen size values given in the termcap/terminfo for your terminal. On windowing systems such as X, elvis has other ways of determining the screen size, so you should probably leave these variables unset. |
| EXINIT | Optional. This variable can hold EX commands which will be executed instead of the .exrc file in your home directory. |

| | |
|---|---|
| SHELL | Optional. The SHELL variable sets the default value for the shell option, which determines which shell program is used to perform wildcard expansion in filenames, and also which is used to execute filters or external programs. The default value on UNIX systems is /bin/sh. |
| | Note: Under MS-DOS, this variable is called COMSPEC instead of SHELL. |
| HOME | This variable should be set to the name of your home directory. elvis looks for its initialization file there; if HOME is unset, then the initialization file will not be executed. |
| TAGPATH | Optional. This variable is used by the ref program, which is invoked by the shift-K, control-], and :tag commands. See ref for more information. |
| TMP, TEMP | These optional environment variables are only used in non-UNIX versions of elvis. They allow you to supply a directory name to be used for storing temporary files. |

## SEE ALSO

ctags(1), ref(1), elvprsv(1), elvrec(1)

*Elvis—A Clone of Vi/Ex*, the complete elvis documentation.

## BUGS

There is no Lisp support. Certain other features are missing, too.

Auto-indent mode is not quite compatible with the real vi. Among other things, 0^D and ^^D don't do what you might expect.

Long lines are displayed differently. The real vi wraps long lines onto multiple rows of the screen, but elvis scrolls sideways.

## AUTHOR

Steve Kirkendall (kirkenda@cs.pdx.edu)

Many other people have worked to port elvis to various operating systems. To see who deserves credit, run the :version command from within elvis, or look in the system-specific section of the complete documentation.

# elvprsv

elvprsv—Preserve the modified version of a file after a crash

## SYNOPSIS

```
elvprsv ["-why elvis died"] /tmp/filename...
elvprsv -R /tmp/filename...
```

## DESCRIPTION

elvprsv preserves your edited text after elvis dies. The text can be recovered later, via the elvprsv program.

For UNIX-like systems, you should never need to run this program from the command line. It is run automatically when elvis is about to die, and it should be run (via /etc/rc) when the computer is booted. THAT'S ALL!

For non-UNIX systems such as MS-DOS or VMS, you can either use elvprsv the same way as under UNIX systems (by running it from your AUTOEXEC.BAT file), or you can run it separately with the -R flag to recover the files in one step.

If you're editing a file when elvis dies (due to a bug, system crash, power failure, and so on), then elvprsv will preserve the most recent version of your text. The preserved text is stored in a special directory; it does not overwrite your text file automatically. (If the preservation directory hasn't been set up correctly, then elvprsv will simply send you a mail message describing how to manually run elvprsv.)

elvprsv will send mail to any user whose work it preserves, if your operating system normally supports mail.

## FILES

| | |
|---|---|
| /tmp/elv* | The temporary file that elvis was using when it died. |
| /usr/preserve/p* | The text that is preserved by elvprsv. |
| /usr/preserve/Index | A text file which lists the names of all preserved files, and the names of the /usr/preserve/p* files that contain their preserved text. |

## BUGS

Due to the permissions on the /usr/preserve directory, on UNIX systems elvprsv must be run as superuser. This is accomplished by making the elvprsv executable be owned by root and turning on its "set user id" bit.

If you're editing a nameless buffer when elvis dies, then elvprsv will pretend that the file was named foo.

## AUTHOR

Steve Kirkendall (kirkenda@cs.pdx.edu)

# elvrec

elvrec— Recover the modified version of a file after a crash

## SYNOPSIS

elvrec [*preservedfile* [*newfile*]]

## DESCRIPTION

If you're editing a file when elvis dies, the system crashes, or power fails, the most recent version of your text will be preserved. The preserved text is stored in a special directory; it does not overwrite your text file automatically.

The elvrec program locates the preserved version of a given file, and writes it over the top of your text file—or to a new file, if you prefer. The recovered file will have nearly all of your changes.

To see a list of all recoverable files, run elvrec with no arguments.

> **NOTE**
>
> If you haven't set up a directory for file preservation, you'll have to manually run the elvprsv program instead of elvrec.

## FILES

| | |
|---|---|
| /usr/preserve/p* | The text that was preserved when elvis died. |
| /usr/preserve/Index | A text file that lists the names of all preserved files, and the names of the /usr/preserve/p* files that contain their preserved text. |

## BUGS

elvrec is very picky about filenames. You must tell it to recover the file using exactly the same pathname as when you were editing it. The simplest way to do this is to go into the same directory that you were editing, and invoke elvrec with the same filename as elvis. If that doesn't work, then try running elvrec with no arguments, to see exactly which pathname it is using for the desired file.

Due to the permissions on the /usr/preserve directory, on UNIX systems elvrec must be run as superuser. This is accomplished by making the elvrec executable be owned by root and setting its "set user id" bit.

If you're editing a nameless buffer when elvis dies, then elvrec will pretend that the file was named foo.

## AUTHOR

Steve Kirkendall (kirkenda@cs.pdx.edu)

# emacs

emacs—GNU project emacs

## SYNOPSIS

emacs [ command-line switches ] [ *files ...* ]

## DESCRIPTION

GNU emacs is a version of emacs, written by the author of the original (PDP-10) emacs, Richard Stallman.

The primary documentation of GNU emacs is in the *GNU Emacs Manual,* which you can read online using info, a subsystem of emacs. Please look there for complete and up-to-date documentation. This man page is updated only when someone volunteers to do so; the emacs maintainers' priority goal is to minimize the amount of time this man page takes away from other more useful projects.

The user functionality of GNU emacs encompasses everything other emacs editors do, and it is easily extensible since its editing commands are written in Lisp.

emacs has an extensive interactive help facility, but the facility assumes that you know how to manipulate emacs windows and buffers. Ctrl+h (backspace or Ctrl+h) enters the Help facility. Help Tutorial (Ctrl+h t) requests an interactive tutorial that can teach beginners the fundamentals of emacs in a few minutes. Help Apropos (Ctrl+h a) helps you find a command given its functionality, Help Character (Ctrl+h c) describes a given character's effect, and Help Function (Ctrl+h f) describes a given Lisp function specified by name.

emacs's Undo can undo several steps of modification to your buffers, so it is easy to recover from editing mistakes.

GNU emacs's many special packages handle mail reading (RMail) and sending (Mail), outline editing (Outline), compiling (Compile), running subshells within emacs windows (Shell), running a Lisp read-eval-print loop (Lisp-Interaction-Mode), and automated psychotherapy (Doctor).

There is an extensive reference manual, but users of other emacses should have little trouble adapting even without a copy. Users new to emacs will be able to use basic features fairly rapidly by studying the tutorial and using the self-documentation features.

## OPTIONS

The following options are of general interest:

| | |
|---|---|
| *file* | Edit *file.* |
| *+number* | Go to the line specified by *number* (do not insert a space between the + sign and the number). |
| -q | Do not load an init file. |
| -u *user* | Load user's init file. |
| -t *file* | Use specified file as the terminal instead of using stdin/stdout. This must be the first argument specified in the command line. |

The following options are Lisp-oriented (these options are processed in the order encountered):

| | |
|---|---|
| -f *function* | Execute the Lisp function *function.* |
| -l *file* | Load the Lisp code in the file *file.* |

The following options are useful when running emacs as a batch editor:

| | |
|---|---|
| -batch | Edit in batch mode. The editor will send messages to stdout. This option must be the first in the argument list. You must use -l and -f options to specify files to execute and functions to call. |
| -kill | Exit emacs while in batch mode. |

## USING emacs WITH X

emacs has been tailored to work well with the X Window System. If you run emacs from under X windows, it will create its own X window to display in. You will probably want to start the editor as a background process so that you can continue using your original window.

emacs can be started with the following X switches:

| | |
|---|---|
| -rn *name* | Specifies the program name which should be used when looking up defaults in the user's X resources. This must be the first option specified in the command line. |
| -name *name* | Specifies the name that should be assigned to the emacs window. |
| -r | Display the emacs window in reverse video. |
| -i | Use the "kitchen sink" bitmap icon when iconifying the emacs window. |
| —font *font*, -fn *font* | Set the emacs window's font to that specified by font. You will find the various X fonts in the /usr/lib/X11/fonts directory. Note that emacs will only accept fixed width fonts. Under the X11 Release 4 font-naming conventions, any font with the value m or c in the eleventh field of the font name is a fixed width font. Furthermore, fonts whose name are of the form width×height are generally fixed width, as is the font fixed. See xlsfonts(1) for more information. |
| | When you specify a font, be sure to put a space between the switch and the font name. |
| -b *pixels* | Set the emacs window's border width to the number of pixels specified by pixels. Defaults to one pixel on each side of the window. |
| -ib *pixels* | Set the window's internal border width to the number of pixels specified by *pixels*. Defaults to one pixel of padding on each side of the window. |
| -geometry *geometry* | Set the emacs window's width, height, and position as specified. The *geometry* specification is in the standard uformat; see X(1) for more information. The width and height are specified in characters; the default is 80 by 24. |
| -fg *color* | On color displays, sets the color of the text. See the file /usr/lib/X11/rgb.txt for a list of valid color names. |
| -bg *color* | On color displays, sets the color of the window's background. |
| -bd *color* | On color displays, sets the color of the window's border. |
| -cr *color* | On color displays, sets the color of the window's text cursor. |
| -ms *color* | On color displays, sets the color of the window's mouse cursor. |
| -d *displayname*, -display *displayname* | Create the emacs window on the display specified by *displayname*. Must be the first option specified in the command line. |
| -nw | Tells emacs not to use its special interface to X. If you use this switch when invoking emacs from an xterm(1) window, display is done in that window. This must be the first option specified in the command line. |

You can set X default values for your emacs windows in your Xresources file; see xrdb(1). Use the following format:

emacs.*keyword*:*value*

where *value* specifies the default value of *keyword*. emacs lets you set default values for the following keywords:

| | |
|---|---|
| font (class Font) | Sets the window's text font. |
| reverseVideo (class ReverseVideo) | If reverseVideo's value is set to on, the window will be displayed in reverse video. |
| bitmapIcon (class BitmapIcon) | If bitmapIcon's value is set to on, the window will iconify into the "kitchen sink." |
| borderWidth (class BorderWidth) | Sets the window's border width in pixels. |
| internalBorder (class BorderWidth) | Sets the window's internal border width in pixels. |
| foreground (class Foreground) | For color displays, sets the window's text color. |
| background (class Background) | For color displays, sets the window's background color. |
| borderColor (class BorderColor) | For color displays, sets the color of the window's border. |

| cursorColor (class Foreground) | For color displays, sets the color of the window's text cursor. |
| pointerColor (class Foreground) | For color displays, sets the color of the window's mouse cursor. |
| geometry (class Geometry) | Sets the geometry of the emacs window. |
| title (class Title) | Sets the title of the emacs window. |
| iconName (class Title) | Sets the icon name for the emacs window icon. |

If you try to set color values while using a black-and-white display, the window's characteristics will default as follows: The foreground color will be set to black, the background color will be set to white, the border color will be set to gray, and the text and mouse cursors will be set to black.

## USING THE MOUSE

The following lists the mouse button bindings for the emacs window under X11.

| Mouse Button | Function |
| --- | --- |
| left | Set point. |
| middle | Paste text. |
| right | Cut text into X cut buffer. |
| Shift+middle | Cut text into X cut buffer. |
| Shift+right | Paste text. |
| Ctrl+middle | Cut text into X cut buffer and kill it. |
| Ctrl+right | Select this window, then split it into two windows. Same as typing Ctrl+x 2. |
| Ctrl+Shift+left | X buffer menu; hold the buttons and keys down, wait for menu to appear, select buffer, and release. Move mouse out of menu and release to cancel. |
| Ctrl+Shift+middle | X help menu; pop up index card menu for emacs help. |
| Ctrl+Shift+right | Select window with mouse, and delete all other windows. Same as typing Ctrl+x 1. |

## MANUALS

You can order printed copies of the *GNU Emacs Manual* from the Free Software Foundation, which develops GNU software. See the file ORDERS for ordering information.

Your local emacs maintainer might also have copies available. As with all software and publications from FSF, everyone is permitted to make and distribute copies of the emacs manual. The TeX source to the manual is also included in the emacs source distribution.

## FILES

| /usr/local/info | Files for the info documentation browser (a subsystem of emacs) to refer to. Currently not much of UNIX is documented here, but the complete text of the emacs reference manual is included in a convenient tree structured form. |
| /usr/local/lib/emacs/$VERSION/src | C source files and object files. |
| /usr/local/lib/emacs/$VERSION/lisp | Lisp source files and compiled files that define most editing commands. Some are preloaded; others are autoloaded from this directory when used. |
| /usr/local/lib/emacs/$VERSION/etc | Various programs that are used with GNU emacs, and some files of information. |
| /usr/local/lib/emacs/$VERSION/etc/DOC.* | Contains the documentation strings for the Lisp primitives and preloaded Lisp functions of GNU emacs. They are stored here to reduce the size of emacs proper. |

| | |
|---|---|
| `/usr/local/lib/emacs/$VERSION/etc/DIFF` | Discusses GNU emacs versus Twenex emacs. |
| `/usr/local/lib/emacs/$VERSION/etc/CCADIFF` | Discusses GNU emacs versus CCA emacs. |
| `/usr/local/lib/emacs/$VERSION/etc/GOSDIFF` | Discusses GNU emacs versus Gosling emacs. |
| `/usr/local/lib/emacs/$VERSION/etc/SERVICE` | Lists people offering various services to assist users of GNU emacs, including education, troubleshooting, porting, and customization. |
| | These files also have information useful to anyone wanting to write programs in the emacs Lisp extension language, which has not yet been fully documented. |
| `/usr/local/lib/emacs/lock` | Holds lock files that are made for all files being modified in emacs, to prevent simultaneous modification of one file by two users. |
| `/usr/local/lib/emacs/$VERSION/$ARCHITECTURE/cpp` | The GNU cpp, needed for building emacs on certain versions of UNIX where the standard cpp cannot handle long names for macros. |
| `/usr/lib/X11/rgb.txt` | List of valid X color names. |

## BUGS

There is a mailing list, `bug-gnu-emacs@prep.ai.mit.edu` on the Internet (`ucbvax!prep.ai.mit.edu!bug-gnu-emacs` on UUCPnet), for reporting emacs bugs and fixes. But before reporting something as a bug, please try to be sure that it really is a bug, not a misunderstanding or a deliberate feature. We ask you to read the section "Reporting emacs Bugs" near the end of the reference manual (or info system) for hints on how and when to report bugs. Also, include the version number of the emacs you are running in every bug report that you send in.

Do not expect a personal answer to a bug report. The purpose of reporting bugs is to get them fixed for everyone in the next release, if possible. For personal assistance, look in the SERVICE file for a list of people who offer it.

Please do not send anything but bug reports to this mailing list. Send requests to be added to mailing lists to the special list `info-gnu-emacs-request@prep.ai.mit.edu` (or the corresponding UUCP address). For more information about emacs mailing lists, see the file `/usr/local/emacs/etc/MAILINGLISTS`. Bugs tend actually to be fixed if they can be isolated, so it is in your interest to report them in such a way that they can be easily reproduced.

One bug that I know about: Shell will not work with programs running in Raw mode on some UNIX versions.

## UNRESTRICTIONS

emacs is free; anyone may redistribute copies of emacs to anyone under the terms stated in the emacs General Public License, a copy of which accompanies each copy of emacs and which also appears in the reference manual.

Copies of emacs may sometimes be received packaged with distributions of UNIX systems, but it is never included in the scope of any license covering those systems. Such inclusion violates the terms on which distribution is permitted. In fact, the primary purpose of the General Public License is to prohibit anyone from attaching any other restrictions to redistribution of emacs.

Richard Stallman encourages you to improve and extend emacs, and urges that you contribute your extensions to the GNU library. Eventually GNU (GNU's Not UNIX) will be a complete replacement for Berkeley UNIX. Everyone will be free to use, copy, study, and change the GNU system.

## SEE ALSO

X(1), xlsfonts(1), xterm(1), xrdb(1)

## AUTHORS

emacs was written by Richard Stallman and the Free Software Foundation. Joachim Martillo and Robert Krawitz added the X features.

19 April 1994

# emacstool

emacstool—Run emacs under Sun windows with function key and mouse support.

## SYNOPSIS

emacstool [{window_args} {-rc run_command_path} args ... ]

## TYPICAL USAGE

In ~/.suntools or ~/.rootmenu, include a line like this:

"Emacstool" emacstool -WI emacs.icon -f emacstool-init

## DESCRIPTION

emacstool creates a SunView frame and a tty subwindow within which mouse events and function keys are translated to ASCII sequences that emacs can parse. The translated input events are sent to the process running in the tty subwindow, which is typically GNU emacs. emacstool thereby allows GNU emacs users to make full use of the mouse and function keys. GNU emacs can be loaded with functions to interpret the mouse and function-key events to make a truly fine screen-oriented editor for the Sun Workstation.

### NOTE

GNU emacs has a special interface to the X Window System as well. The X Window System has many technical advantages, it is an industry standard, and it is also free software. The Free Software Foundation urges you to try X Windows, and distributes a free copy of X on emacs distribution tapes.

Function keys are translated to a sequence of the form ^X*[a-o][lrt]. The last character is l, r, or t, corresponding to whether the key is among the Left, Right, or Top function keys. The third character indicates which button of the group was pressed. Thus, the function key in the lower-right corner will transmit the sequence ^X*or. In addition, the [lrt] is affected by the Control, Meta, and Shift keys. Unshifted Ctrl keys will be nonalphabetic: C-l is [,], C-r is [2], C-t is [4].

Mouse buttons are encoded as ^X^@([124] x y)\n. ^X^@ is the standard GNU emacs mouse event prefix; it is followed by a list indicating the button pressed and the character row and column of the point in the window where the mouse cursor is, and followed by a newline character. In GNU emacs, the ^X^@ dispatches to a mouse event handler which then reads the following list.

## OPTIONS

emacstool supports all the standard window arguments, including font and icon specifiers.

By default, emacstool runs the program emacs in the created subwindow. The value of the environment variable EMACSTOOL can be used to override this if your version of emacs is not accessible on your search path by the name emacs. In addition, the run command can be set by the pathname following the last occurrence of the -rc flag. This is convenient for using emacstool to run on remote machines.

All other command-line arguments not used by the window system are passed as arguments to the program that runs in the emacstool window.

For example,

local% (emacstool -rc rlogin remote -8 &)&

will create an emacstool window logged in to a machine named remote. If emacs is run from this window, emacstool will encode mouse and function keys, and send them to rlogin. If emacs is run from this shell on the remote machine, it will see the mouse and function keys properly. However, since the remote host does not have access to the screen, the cursor cannot be changed, menus will not appear, and the selection buffer (STUFF) is limited.

## USING WITH GNU emacs

The GNU emacs files `lisp/term/sun.el`, `lisp/sun-mouse.el`, `lisp/sun-fns.el`, and `src/sunfns.c` provide emacs support for the emacstool and function keys. emacstool will automatically set the TERM environment variable to be sun and unset the environment variable TERMCAP. That is, these variables will not be inherited from the shell that starts emacstool. Since the terminal type is SUN (that is, the environment variable TERM is set to SUN), emacs will automatically load the file `lisp/term/sun`. This, in turn, will ensure that `sun-mouse.el` is autoloaded when any mouse events are detected. It is suggested that `sun-mouse` and `sun-fns` be loaded in your `site-init.el` file, so that they will always be loaded when running on a Sun workstation.

In addition, emacstool sets the environment variable IN_EMACSTOOL = "t". Lisp code in your ˜/.emacs can use (getenv "IN_EMACSTOOL") to determine whether to do emacstool-specific initialization. Sun.el uses this to automatically call emacstool-init if (getenv "IN_EMACSTOOL") is defined.

The file `src/sunfns.c` defines several useful functions for emacs on the Sun. Among these are procedures to pop up SunView menus, put and get from the SunView STUFF buffer, and a procedure for changing the cursor icon. If you want to define or edit cursor icons, there is a rudimentary mouse-driven icon editor in the file `lisp/sun-cursors.el`. Try invoking (sc:edit-cursor).

## BUGS

It takes a few milliseconds to create a menu before it pops up.

## ENVIRONMENT VARIABLES

EMACSTOOL, IN_EMACSTOOL, TERM, TERMCAP

## FILES

emacs

## SEE ALSO

emacs(1), .../etc/SUN-SUPPORT, .../lisp/term/sun.el

# etags

etags—Generate tag file for emacs

ctags—Generate tag file for vi·

## SYNOPSIS

```
etags [ -aCDSVH] [ -i file ][-o tagfile ]
[ --c++ ] [ --no-defines] [ --ignore-indentation ] [ --help ] [ --version ]
[ --include=file ] [ --output=tagfile ] [ --append ] file ...

ctags [ -aCdSVH] [ -BtTuvwx ] [ -o tagfile ]
[ --c++ ] [ --defines ] [ --ignore-indentation ]
[ --backward-search] [ --forward-search ] [ --typedefs ] [ --typedefs-and-c++]
[ --no-warn ] [ --cxref ] [ --help ] [ --version ]
[ --output=tagfile ] [ --append ] [ --update ] file ...
```

## DESCRIPTION

The etags program is used to create a tag table file, in a format understood by emacs(1); the ctags program is used to create a similar table in a format understood by vi(1) . Both forms of the program understand the syntax of C, FORTRAN, Pascal, LaTeX, Scheme, emacs Lisp/Common Lisp, and most assembler–like syntaxes. Both forms read the files specified on the command line, and write a tag table (defaults: TAGS for etags, tags for ctags) in the current working directory. The programs recognize the language used in an input file based on its filename and contents; there are no switches for specifying the language.

## OPTIONS

Some options make sense only for the vi-style tag files produced by ctags; etags does not recognize them. The programs accept unambiguous abbreviations for long option names.

| | |
|---|---|
| -a, --append | Append to existing tag file. (For vi-format tag files, see also --update.) |
| -B, --backward-search | Tag files written in the format expected by vi contain regular expression search instructions; the -B option writes them using the delimiter ?, to search backwards through files. The default is to use the delimiter / to search forwards through files. Only ctags accepts this option. |
| -C, --c++ | Treat files with .c and .h extensions as C++ code, not C code. Files with .C, .H, .cxx, .hxx, or .cc extensions are always assumed to be C++ code. |
| -d, --defines | Create tag entries for C preprocessor definitions, too. This is the default behavior for etags, so this option is only accepted by ctags. |
| -D, --no-defines | Do not create tag entries for C preprocessor definitions. This may make the tags file much smaller if many header files are tagged. This is the default behavior for ctags, so this option is only accepted by etags. |
| -i file, --include=*file* | Include a note in tag file indicating that, when searching for a tag, one should also consult the tags file *file* after checking the current file. Only etags accepts this option. |
| -o tagfile, --output=*tagfile* | Explicit name of file for tag table; overrides default TAGS or tags. (But ignored with -v or -x.) |
| -S, --ignore-indentation | Don't rely on indentation as much as we normally do. Currently, this means not to assume that a closing brace in the first column is the final brace of a function or structure definition in C and C++. |
| -t, --typedefs | Record typedefs in C code as tags. Since this is the default behavior of etags, only ctags accepts this option. |
| -T, --typedefs-and-c++ | Generate tag entries for typedefs, struct, enum, and union tags, and C++ member functions. Since this is the default behavior of etags, only ctags accepts this option. |
| -u, --update | Update tag entries for files specified on command line, leaving tag entries for other files in place. Currently, this is implemented by deleting the existing entries for the given files and then rewriting the new entries at the end of the tags file. It is often faster to simply rebuild the entire tag file than to use this. Only ctags accepts this option. |
| -v, --vgrind | Instead of generating a tag file, write index (in vgrind format) to standard output. Only ctags accepts this option. |
| -w, --no-warn | Suppress warning messages about duplicate entries. The etags program does not check for duplicate entries, so this option is not allowed with it. |
| -x, --cxref | Instead of generating a tag file, write a cross-reference (in cxref format) to standard output. Only ctags accepts this option. |
| -H, --help | Print usage information. |
| -V, --version | Print the current version of the program (same as the version of the emacs etags is shipped with). |

## SEE ALSO

emacs entry in info; *GNU Emacs Manual*, Richard Stallman.

cxref(1), emacs(1), vgrind(1), vi(1).

## COPYING

Permission is granted to copy and distribute translations of this manual into another language, under the above conditions for modified versions, except that this permission notice may be included in translations approved by the Free Software Foundation instead of in the original English.

GNU Tools, 19 April 1994

# expand

expand—Convert tabs to spaces

## SYNOPSIS

```
expand [-tab1[,tab2[,...]]] [-t tab1[,tab2[,...]]] [-i] [—tabs=tab1[,tab2[,...]]]
[--initial] [--help] [--version] [file...]
```

## DESCRIPTION

This manual page documents the GNU version of expand. expand writes the contents of each given file, or the standard input if none are given or when a file named - is given, to the standard output, with tab characters converted to the appropriate number of spaces. By default, expand converts all tabs to spaces. It preserves backspace characters in the output; they decrement the column count for tab calculations. The default action is equivalent to -8 (set tabs every 8 columns).

## OPTIONS

| | |
|---|---|
| -, -t, --tabs tab1[,tab2[,...]] | If only one tab stop is given, set the tabs tab1 spaces apart instead of the default 8. Otherwise, set the tabs at columns tab1, tab2, and so forth (numbered from 0) and replace any tabs beyond the tab stops given with single spaces. If the tab-stops are specified with the -t or --tabs option, they can be separated by blanks as well as by commas. |
| -i, --initial | Only convert initial tabs (those that precede all nonspace or tab characters) on each line to spaces. |
| --help | Print a usage message and exit with a nonzero status. |
| --version | Print version information on standard output then exit. |

GNU Text Utilities

# find

find—Search for files in a directory hierarchy

## SYNOPSIS

```
find [path...] [expression]
```

## DESCRIPTION

This manual page documents the GNU version of find. find searches the directory tree rooted at each given filename by evaluating the given expression from left to right, according to the rules of precedence (see "Operators," later in this manual page), until the outcome is known (the left side is False for AND operations, True for OR), at which point find moves on to the next filename.

The first argument that begins with -, (, ), ,, or ! is taken to be the beginning of the expression; any arguments before it are paths to search, and any arguments after it are the rest of the expression. If no paths are given, the current directory is used. If no expression is given, the expression -print is used.

find exits with status 0 if all files are processed successfully, greater than 0 if errors occur.

## EXPRESSIONS

The expression is made up of options (which affect overall operation rather than the processing of a specific file, and always return True), tests (which return a True or False value), and actions (which have side effects and return a True or False value), all separated by operators. -and is assumed where the operator is omitted. If the expression contains no actions other than -prune, -print is performed on all files for which the expression is true.

## OPTIONS

All options always return True. They always take effect, rather than being processed only when their place in the expression is reached. Therefore, for clarity, it is best to place them at the beginning of the expression.

| | |
|---|---|
| -daystart | Measure times (for -amin, -atime, -cmin, -ctime, -mmin, and -mtime) from the beginning of today rather than from 24 hours ago. |
| -depth | Process each directory's contents before the directory itself. |
| -follow | Dereference symbolic links. Implies -noleaf. |
| -help, —help | Print a summary of the command-line usage of find and exit. |
| -maxdepth *levels* | Descend at most *levels* (a nonnegative integer) levels of directories below the command-line arguments. -maxdepth 0 means only apply the tests and actions to the command-line arguments. |
| -mindepth *levels* | Do not apply any tests or actions at levels less than *levels* (a nonnegative integer). -mindepth 1 means process all files except the command-line arguments. |
| -mount | Don't descend directories on other filesystems. An alternate name for -xdev, for compatibility with some other versions of find. |
| -noleaf | Do not optimize by assuming that directories contain two fewer subdirectories than their hard link count. This option is needed when searching filesystems that do not follow the UNIX directory-link convention, such as CD-ROM or MS-DOS filesystems or AFS volume mount points. Each directory on a normal UNIX filesystem has at least 2 hard links: its name and its . entry. Additionally, its subdirectories (if any) each have a .. entry linked to that directory. When find is examining a directory, after it has statted two fewer subdirectories than the directory's link count, it knows that the rest of the entries in the directory are nondirectories (leaf files in the directory tree). If only the files' names need to be examined, there is no need to stat them; this gives a significant increase in search speed. |
| -version, —version | Print the find version number and exit. |
| -xdev | Don't descend directories on other filesystems. |

## TESTS

Numeric arguments can be specified as

| | |
|---|---|
| +*n* | Greater than *n*. |
| -*n* | Less than *n*. |
| *n* | Exactly *n*. |
| -amin *n* | File was last accessed *n* minutes ago. |
| -anewer *file* | File was last accessed more recently than *file* was modified. -anewer is affected by -follow only if -follow comes before -anewer on the command line. |
| -atime *n* | File was last accessed *n*\*24 hours ago. |
| -cmin *n* | File's status was last changed *n* minutes ago. |
| -cnewer *file* | File's status was last changed more recently than file was modified. -cnewer is affected by -follow only if -follow comes before -cnewer on the command line. |
| -ctime *n* | File's status was last changed *n*\*24 hours ago. |
| -empty | File is empty and is either a regular file or a directory. |
| -false | Always false. |

| | |
|---|---|
| -fstype *type* | File is on a filesystem of type *type*. The valid filesystem types vary among different versions of UNIX; an incomplete list of filesystem types that are accepted on some version of UNIX or another is: ufs, 4.2, 4.3, nfs, tmp, mfs, S51K, S52K. You can use -printf with the %F directive to see the types of your filesystems. |
| -gid *n* | File's numeric group ID is *n*. |
| -group *gname* | File belongs to group *gname* (numeric group ID allowed). |
| -ilname *pattern* | Like -lname, but the match is case-insensitive. |
| -iname *pattern* | Like -name, but the match is case-insensitive. For example, the patterns fo* and F?? match the filenames Foo, FOO, foo, fOo, and so on. |
| -inum *n* | File has inode number *n*. |
| -ipath *pattern* | Like -path, but the match is case-insensitive. |
| -iregex *pattern* | Like -regex, but the match is case-insensitive. |
| -links *n* | File has *n* links. |
| -lname *pattern* | File is a symbolic link whose contents match shell pattern *pattern*. The meta characters do not treat / or . specially. |
| -mmin *n* | File's data was last modified *n* minutes ago. |
| -mtime *n* | File's data was last modified *n*\*24 hours ago. |
| -name *pattern* | Base of filename (the path with the leading directories removed) matches shell pattern *pattern*. The meta characters (*, ?, and []) do not match a . at the start of the base name. To ignore a directory and the files under it, use -prune; see an example in the description of -path. |
| -newer *file* | File was modified more recently than file. -newer is affected by -follow only if -follow comes before -newer on the command line. |
| -nouser | No user corresponds to file's numeric user ID. |
| -nogroup | No group corresponds to file's numeric group ID. |
| -path *pattern* | Filename matches shell pattern *pattern*. The meta characters do not treat / or . specially; so, for example, <br><br>find . –path './sr*sc' <br><br>will print an entry for a directory called ./src/misc (if one exists). To ignore a whole directory tree, use -prune rather than checking every file in the tree. For example, to skip the directory src/emacs and all files and directories under it, and print the names of the other files found, do something like this: <br><br>find . –path './src/emacs' -prune -o -print |
| -perm *mode* | File's permission bits are exactly mode (octal or symbolic). Symbolic modes use mode 0 as a point of departure. |
| -perm -*mode* | All of the permission bits mode are set for the file. |
| -perm +*mode* | Any of the permission bits mode are set for the file. |
| -regex *pattern* | Filename matches regular expression pattern. This is a match on the whole path, not a search. For example, to match a file named ./fubar3, you can use the regular expression .\*bar. or .\*b.\*3, but not b.\*r3. |
| -size *n*[bckw] | File uses n units of space. The units are 512-byte blocks by default or if b follows *n*, bytes if c follows *n*, kilobytes if k follows *n*, or 2-byte words if w follows *n*. The size does not count indirect blocks, but it does count blocks in sparse files that are not actually allocated. |
| -true | Always true. |
| -type *c* | File is of type c. Possible types: |

       b    Block (buffered) special

       c    Character (unbuffered) special

       d    Directory

       p    Named pipe (FIFO)

|   | f | Regular file l symbolic link |
|---|---|---|
|   | s | Socket |

| -uid *n* | File's numeric user ID is *n*. |
|---|---|
| -used *n* | File was last accessed *n* days after its status was last changed. |
| -user *uname* | File is owned by user *uname* (numeric user ID allowed). |
| -xtype *c* | The same as -type unless the file is a symbolic link. For symbolic links: if -follow has not been given, True if the file is a link to a file of type *c*; if -follow has been given, True if *c* is 1. In other words, for symbolic links, -xtype checks the type of the file that -type does not check. |

## ACTIONS

| -exec *command*; | Execute *command*; True if 0 status is returned. All following arguments to find are taken to be arguments to the command until an argument consisting of ; is encountered. The string {} is replaced by the current filename being processed everywhere it occurs in the arguments to the command, not just in arguments where it is alone, as in some versions of find. Both of these constructions might need to be escaped (with a \) nor quoted to protect them from expansion by the shell. The command is executed in the starting directory. |
|---|---|
| -fls *file* | True; like -ls but write to *file* like -fprint. |
| -fprint *file* | True; print the full filename into file *file*. If *file* does not exist when find is run, it is created; if it does exist, it is truncated. The filenames /dev/stdout and /dev/stderr are handled specially; they refer to the standard output and standard error output, respectively. |
| -fprint0 *file* | True; like -print0 but write to file like -fprint. |
| -fprintf *file format* | True; like -printf but write to file like -fprint. |
| -ok *command*; | Like -exec but ask the user first (on the standard input); if the response does not start with y or Y, do not run the command, and return False. |
| -print | True; print the full filename on the standard output, followed by a newline. |
| -print0 | True; print the full filename on the standard output, followed by a null character. This allows filenames that contain newlines to be correctly interpreted by programs that process the find output. |
| -printf *format* | True; print format on the standard output, interpreting n escapes and % directives. Field widths and precisions can be specified as with the printf C function. Unlike -print, -printf does not add a newline at the end of the string. The escapes and directives are as follows: |

|   | \a | Alarm bell |
|---|---|---|
|   | \b | Backspace |
|   | \c | Stop printing from this format immediately and flush the output |
|   | \f | Form feed |
|   | \n | Newline |
|   | \r | Carriage return |
|   | \t | Horizontal tab |
|   | \v | Vertical tab |
|   | \\ | A literal backslash ('\') |

A \ character followed by any other character is treated as an ordinary character, so they both are printed:

|   | %% | A literal percent sign. |
|---|---|---|
|   | %a | File's last access time in the format returned by the C ctime function. |
|   | %Ak | File's last access time in the format specified by k, which is either @ or a directive for the C strftime function. The possible values for k are listed below; some of them might not be available on all systems, due to differences in strftime between systems. |

@ seconds since Jan. 1, 1970, 00:00 GMT.

*Time fields:*

| | |
|---|---|
| H | Hour (00..23) |
| I | Hour (01..12) |
| k | Hour (0..23) |
| l | Hour (1..12) |
| M | Minute (00..59) |
| p | Locale's a.m. or p.m. |
| r | Time, 12-hour (hh:mm:ss [AP]M) |
| u | Second (00..61) |
| T | Time, 24-hour (hh:mm:ss) |
| X | Locale's time representation (H:M:S) |
| Z | Time zone (for example, EDT), or nothing if no time zone is determinable |

*Date fields:*

| | |
|---|---|
| a | Locale's abbreviated weekday name (Sun..Sat) |
| A | Locale's full weekday name, variable length (Sunday..Saturday) |
| b | Locale's abbreviated month name (Jan..Dec) |
| B | Locale's full month name, variable length (January.. December) |
| c | Locale's date and time (Sat Nov 04 12:02:33 EST 1989) |
| d | Day of month (01..31) |
| D | Date (mm/dd/yy) |
| h | Same as b |
| j | Day of year (001..366) |
| m | Month (01..12) |
| U | Week number of year with Sunday as first day of week (00..53) |
| w | Day of week (0..6) |
| W | Week number of year with Monday as first day of week (00..53) |
| x | Locale's date representation (mm/dd/yy) |
| y | Last two digits of year (00..99) |
| Y | Year (1970...) |

%b   File's size in 512-byte blocks (rounded up).

%c   File's last status change time in the format returned by the C ctime function.

%Ck   File's last status change time in the format specified by k, which is the same as for %A.

%d   File's depth in the directory tree; 0 means the file is a command-line argument.

%f   File's name with any leading directories removed (only the last element).

%F   Type of the filesystem the file is on; this value can be used for -fstype.

%g   File's group name, or numeric group ID if the group has no name.

%G   File's numeric group ID.

%h   Leading directories of file's name (all but the last element).

%H   Command-line argument under which file was found.

%i   File's inode number (in decimal).

%k   File's size in 1K blocks (rounded up).

%l   Object of symbolic link (empty string if file is not a symbolic link).

| | |
|---|---|
| %m | File's permission bits (in octal). |
| %n | Number of hard links to file. |
| %p | File's name. |
| %P | File's name with the name of the command-line argument under which it was found removed. |
| %s | File's size in bytes. |
| %t | File's last modification time in the format returned by the C ctime function. |
| %Tk | File's last modification time in the format specified by k, which is the same as for %A. |
| %u | File's username, or numeric user ID if the user has no name. |
| %U | File's numeric user ID. |
| | A % character followed by any other character is discarded (but the other character is printed). |
| -prune | If -depth is not given, True; do not descend the current directory. |
| | If -depth is given, False; no effect. |
| -ls | True; list current file in ls -dils format on standard output. The block counts are of 1K blocks, unless the environment variable POSIXLY_CORRECT is set, in which case 512- byte blocks are used. |

## OPERATORS

Listed in order of decreasing precedence:

| | |
|---|---|
| ( *expr* ) | Force precedence. |
| ! *expr* | True if expr is false. |
| -not *expr* | Same as ! *expr*. |
| *expr1 expr2* | And (implied); *expr2* is not evaluated if *expr1* is false. |
| *expr1* -a *expr2* | Same as *expr1 expr2*. |
| *expr1* -and *expr2* | Same as *expr1 expr2*. |
| *expr1* -o *expr2* | Or; *expr2* is not evaluated if *expr1* is true. |
| *expr1* -or *expr2* | Same as *expr1* -o *expr2*. |
| *expr1, expr2* | List; both *expr1* and *expr2* are always evaluated. The value of *expr1* is discarded; the value of the list is the value of *expr2*. |

## SEE ALSO

locate(1L), locatedb(5L), updatedb(1L), xargs(1L) Finding Files (online in info, or printed)

GNU File Utilities

# fitstopnm

fitstopnm—Convert a FITS file into a portable anymap

## SYNOPSIS

fitstopnm [-image N][-noraw][-scanmax][-printmax][-min f][-max f][*FITSfile*]

## DESCRIPTION

Reads a FITS file as input. Produces a portable pixmap if the FITS file consists of 3 image planes (NAXIS = 3 and NAXIS3 = 3), a portable graymap if the FITS file consists of 2 image planes (NAXIS = 2), or whenever the -image flag is specified. The results may need to be flipped top for bottom; if so, just pipe the output through pnmflip -tb.

## OPTIONS

The -image option is for FITS files with three axes. The assumption is that the third axis is for multiple images, and this option lets you select which one you want.

Flags -min and -max can be used to override the min and max values as read from the FITS header or the image data if no DATAMIN and DATAMAX keywords are found. Flag -scanmax can be used to force the program to scan the data even when DATAMIN and DATAMAX are found in the header. If -printmax is specified, the program will just print the min and max values and quit. Flag -noraw can be used to force the program to produce an ASCII portable anymap.

The program will tell what kind of anymap is writing. All flags can be abbreviated to their shortest unique prefix.

## REFERENCES

FITS stands for Flexible Image Transport System. A full description can be found in *Astronomy & Astrophysics Supplement Series 44* (1981), page 363.

## SEE ALSO

pnmtofits(1), pgm(5), pnmflip(1)

## AUTHOR

Copyright © 1989 by Jef Poskanzer, with modifications by Daniel Briggs (dbriggs@nrao.edu) and Alberto Accomazzi (alberto@cfa.harvard.edu)

20 September 1989

# fmt

fmt—Adjust line-length for paragraphs of text

## SYNOPSIS

fmt [-*width*][*files*]...

## DESCRIPTION

fmt is a simple text formatter. It inserts or deletes newlines, as necessary, to make all lines in a paragraph be approximately the same width. It preserves indentation and word spacing.

The default line width is 72 characters. You can override this with the -width flag. If you don't name any files on the command line, then fmt will read from stdin.

It is typically used from within vi to adjust the line breaks in a single paragraph. To do this, move the cursor to the top of the paragraph, type !gfmt, and press Return.

## AUTHOR

Steve Kirkendall (kirkenda@cs.pdx.edu)

# fold

fold—Wrap each input line to fit in specified width

## SYNOPSIS

fold [-bs] [-w *width*] [—bytes] [—spaces] [—width=*width*] [—help]
[—version] [*file*...]

## DESCRIPTION

This manual page documents the GNU version of fold. fold prints the specified files, or the standard input when no files are given or the filename - is encountered, on the standard output. It breaks long lines into multiple shorter lines by inserting a newline at column 80. It counts screen columns, so tab characters usually take more than one column, backspace characters decrease the column count, and carriage return characters set the column count back to zero.

## OPTIONS

| | |
|---|---|
| -b, —bytes | Count bytes rather than columns, so that tabs, backspaces, and carriage returns are each counted as taking up one column, just like other characters. |
| -s, —spaces | Break at word boundaries. If the line contains any blanks, the line is broken after the last blank that falls within the maximum line length. If there are no blanks, the line is broken at the maximum line length, as usual. |
| -w, —width *width* | Use a maximum line length of width columns instead of 80. |
| —help | Print a usage message and exit with a nonzero status. |
| —version | Print version information on standard output then exit. |

GNU Text Utilities

# free

free—Display amount of free and used memory in the system

## SYNOPSIS

free [-b ¦ -k ¦ -m] [-o] [-s *delay*] [-t]

## DESCRIPTION

free displays the total amount of free and used physical and swap memory in the system, as well as the shared memory and buffers used by the kernel.

## OPTIONS

The -b switch displays the amount of memory in bytes; the -k switch (set by default) displays it in kilobytes; the -m switch displays it in megabytes.

The -t switch displays a line containing the totals.

The -o switch disables the display of a "buffer adjusted" line. Unless specified free subtracts/adds buffer memory from/to the used/free memory reports (respectively!).

The -s switch activates continuous polling delay seconds apart. You may actually specify any floating point number for delay, usleep(3) is used for microsecond resolution delay times.

## FILES

| | |
|---|---|
| /proc/meminfo | Memory information |

## SEE ALSO

ps(1), top(1)

## AUTHORS

Brian Edmonds

Cohesive Systems, 20 March 1993

# fsinfo

`fsinfo`—X font server information utility

## SYNOPSIS

`fsinfo [-server servername]`

## DESCRIPTION

`fsinfo` is a utility for displaying information about an X font server. It is used to examine the capabilities of a server, the predefined values for various parameters used in communicating between clients and the server, and the font catalogues and alternate servers that are available.

## EXAMPLE

The following is a sample produced by `fsinfo`.

```
name of server: hansen:7100
version number: 1
vendor string: Font Server Prototype
vendor release number: 17
maximum request size: 16384 longwords (65536 bytes)
number of catalogues: 1
all
Number of alternate servers: 2
#0 hansen:7101
#1 hansen:7102
number of extensions: 0
```

## ENVIRONMENT

`FONTSERVER`               To get the default fontserver

## SEE ALSO

`xfs`(1), `fslsfonts`(1)

## AUTHOR

Dave Lemke (Network Computing Devices, Inc.)

X Version 11 Release 6

# fslsfonts

`fslsfonts`—List fonts served by X font server

## SYNOPSIS

`fslsfonts [-options ...] [-fn pattern]`

## DESCRIPTION

`fslsfonts` lists the fonts that match the given pattern. The wildcard character * may be used to match any sequence of characters (including none), and ? to match any single character. If no pattern is given, * is assumed.

The * and ? characters must be quoted to prevent them from being expanded by the shell.

## OPTIONS

`-server host:port`       This option specifies the X font server to contact.

`-l`                       Lists some attributes of the font on one line in addition to its name.

| | |
|---|---|
| -ll | Lists font properties in addition to -l output. |
| -lll | Supported for compatibility with xlsfonts, but output is the same as for -ll. |
| -m | This option indicates that long listings should also print the minimum and maximum bounds of each font. |
| -C | This option indicates that listings should use multiple columns. This is the same as -n 0. |
| -1 | This option indicates that listings should use a single column. This is the same as -n 1. |
| -w *width* | This option specifies the width in characters that should be used in figuring out how many columns to print. The default is 79. |
| -n *columns* | This option specifies the number of columns to use in displaying the output. The default is 0, which will attempt to fit as many columns of font names into the number of character specified by -w width. |
| -u | This option indicates that the output should be left unsorted. |

## SEE ALSO

xfs(1), showfont(1), xlsfonts(1)

## ENVIRONMENT

| | |
|---|---|
| FONTSERVER | To get the default host and port to use |

## BUGS

Doing fslsfonts -l can tie up your server for a very long time. This is really a bug with single-threaded nonpreemptable servers, not with this program.

## AUTHOR

Dave Lemke (Network Computing Devices, Inc.)

X Version 11 Release 6 1

# fstobdf

fstobdf—Generate BDF font from X font server

## SYNOPSIS

fstobdf [ -server *server* ] -fn *fontname*

## DESCRIPTION

The fstobdf program reads a font from a font server and prints a BDF file on the standard output that may be used to recreate the font. This is useful in testing servers, debugging font metrics, and reproducing lost BDF files.

## OPTIONS

| | |
|---|---|
| -server *servername* | This option specifies the server from which the font should be read. |
| -fn *fontname* | This option specifies the font for which a BDF file should be generated. |

## ENVIRONMENT

| | |
|---|---|
| FONTSERVER | Default server to use |

## SEE ALSO

xfs(1), bdftopcf(1), fslsfonts(1)

## AUTHOR

Olaf Brandt (Network Computing Devices), Dave Lemke (Network Computing Devices), Jim Fulton (MIT X Consortium)

X Version 11 Release 6

# fstopgm

`fstopgm`—Convert a Usenix FaceSaver file into a portable graymap

## SYNOPSIS

`fstopgm [fsfile]`

## DESCRIPTION

Reads a Usenix FaceSaver file as input. Produces a portable graymap as output.

FaceSaver files sometimes have rectangular pixels. Although `fstopgm` won't rescale them into square pixels for you, it will give you the precise pnmscale command that will do the job. Because of this, reading a FaceSaver image is a two-step process. First you do

`fstopgm > /dev/null`

This will tell you whether you need to use pnmscale. Then use one of the following pipelines:

```
fstopgm ¦ pgmnorm
fstopgm ¦ pnmscale -whatever ¦ pgmnorm
```

To go to PBM, you want something more like one of these:

```
fstopgm ¦ pnmenlarge 3 ¦ pgmnorm ¦ pgmtopbm
fstopgm ¦ pnmenlarge 3 ¦ pnmscale <whatever> ¦ pgmnorm ¦ pgmtopbm
```

You want to enlarge when going to a bitmap because otherwise you lose information; but enlarging by more than 3 does not look good.

FaceSaver is a registered trademark of Metron Computerware Ltd. of Oakland, CA.

## SEE ALSO

pgmtofs(1), pgm(5), pgmnorm(1), pnmenlarge(1), pnmscale(1), pgmtopbm(1)

## AUTHOR

Copyright © 1989 by Jef Poskanzer

6 April 1989

# ftp

`ftp`—ARPAnet file transfer program

## SYNOPSIS

`ftp [-v] [-d] [-i] [-n] [-g] [host]`

## DESCRIPTION

`ftp` is the user interface to the ARPAnet standard File Transfer Protocol. The program allows a user to transfer files to and from a remote network site.

Options may be specified at the command line, or to the command interpreter.

| | |
|---|---|
| -v | Verbose option forces ftp to show all responses from the remote server, as well as report on data transfer statistics. |
| -n | Restrains ftp from attempting auto-login upon initial connection. If auto-login is enabled, ftp will check the (see below) file in the user's home directory for an entry describing an account on the remote machine. If no entry exists, ftp will prompt for the remote machine login name (default is the user identity on the local machine), and, if necessary, prompt for a password and an account with which to login. |
| -i | Turns off interactive prompting during multiple file transfers. |
| -d | Enables debugging. |
| -g | Disables filename globbing. |

The client host with which ftp is to communicate may be specified on the command line. If this is done, ftp will immediately attempt to establish a connection to an FTP server on that host; otherwise, ftp will enter its command interpreter and await instructions from the user. When ftp is awaiting commands from the user, the prompt

ftp>

is provided to the user. The following commands are recognized by ftp :

| | |
|---|---|
| ! [command] [args] | Invoke an interactive shell on the local machine. If there are arguments, the first is taken to be a command to execute directly, with the rest of the arguments as its arguments. |
| $ macro-name [args] | Execute the macro macro-name that was defined with the macdef command. Arguments are passed to the macro unglobbed. |
| account [passwd] | Supply a supplemental password required by a remote system for access to resources once a login has been successfully completed. If no argument is included, the user will be prompted for an account password in a nonechoing input mode. |
| append local-file [remote-file] | Append a local file to a file on the remote machine. If remote-file is left unspecified, the local filename is used in naming the remote file after being altered by any ntrans or nmap setting. File transfer uses the current settings for type, format, mode, and structure. |
| ascii | Set the file transfer type to network ASCII. This is the default type. |
| bell | Arrange that a bell be sounded after each file transfer command is completed. |
| binary | Set the file transfer type to support binary image transfer. |
| bye | Terminate the FTP session with the remote server and exit ftp. An end of file will also terminate the session and exit. |
| case | Toggle remote computer filename case mapping during mget commands. When case is on (default is off), remote computer filenames with all letters in upper case are written in the local directory with the letters mapped to lowercase. |
| cd remote-directory | Change the working directory on the remote machine to remote-directory. |
| cdup | Change the remote machine working directory to the parent of the current remote machine working directory. |
| chmod mode file-name | Change the permission modes of the file file-name on the remote system to mode. |
| close | Terminate the FTP session with the remote server, and return to the command interpreter. Any defined macros are erased. |
| cr | Toggle carriage return stripping during ASCII type file retrieval. Records are denoted by a carriage return/linefeed sequence during ASCII type file transfer. When cr is on (the default), carriage returns are stripped from this sequence to conform with the UNIX single linefeed record delimiter. Records on non-UNIX remote systems may contain single linefeeds; when an ASCII type transfer is made, these linefeeds may be distinguished from a record delimiter only when cr is off. |
| delete remote-file | Delete the file remote-file on the remote machine. |

| | |
|---|---|
| debug [*debug-value*] | Toggle debugging mode. If an optional *debug-value* is specified, it is used to set the debugging level. When debugging is on, ftp prints each command sent to the remote machine, preceded by the string —>. |
| dir [*remote-directory*] [*local-file*] | Print a listing of the directory contents in the directory, *remote-directory*, and, optionally, placing the output in *local-file*. If interactive prompting is on, ftp will prompt the user to verify that the last argument is indeed the target local file for receiving dir output. If no directory is specified, the current working directory on the remote machine is used. If no local file is specified, or *local-file* is -, output comes to the terminal. |
| disconnect | A synonym for close. |
| form *format* | Set the file transfer form to *format*. The default *format* is file. |
| get *remote-file* [*local-file*] | Retrieve the *remote-file* and store it on the local machine. If the local filename is not specified, it is given the same name it has on the remote machine, subject to alteration by the current case, ntrans, and nmap settings. The current settings for type, form, mode, and structure are used while transferring the file. |
| glob | Toggle filename expansion for mdelete, mget, and mput. If globbing is turned off with glob, the filename arguments are taken literally and not expanded. Globbing for mput is done as in csh 1. For mdelete and mget, each remote filename is expanded separately on the remote machine and the lists are not merged. Expansion of a directory name is likely to be different from expansion of the name of an ordinary file: the exact result depends on the foreign operating system and FTP server, and can be previewed by doing mls remote-files Note: mget and mput are not meant to transfer entire directory subtrees of files. That can be done by transferring a tar 1 archive of the subtree (in binary mode). |
| hash | Toggle hash-sign (#) printing for each data block transferred. The size of a data block is 1024 bytes. |
| help [*command*] | Print an informative message about the meaning of *command*. If no argument is given, ftp prints a list of the known commands. |
| idle [*seconds*] | Set the inactivity timer on the remote server to *seconds* seconds. If *seconds* is omitted, the current inactivity timer is printed. |
| lcd [*directory*] | Change the working directory on the local machine. If no directory is specified, the user's home directory is used. |
| ls [*remote-directory*] [*local-file*] | Print a listing of the contents of a directory on the remote machine. The listing includes any system-dependent information that the server chooses to include; for example, most systems will produce output from the command ls 1. (See also nlist.) If *remote-directory* is left unspecified, the current working directory is used. If interactive prompting is on, ftp will prompt the user to verify that the last argument is indeed the target local file for receiving ls output. If no local file is specified, or if *local-file* is -, the output is sent to the terminal. |
| macdef *macro-name* | Define a macro. Subsequent lines are stored as the macro *macro-name*; a null line (consecutive newline characters in a file or carriage returns from the terminal) terminates macro input mode. There is a limit of 16 macros and 4096 total characters in all defined macros. Macros remain defined until a close command is executed. The macro processor interprets $ and \ as special characters. A $ followed by a number (or numbers) is replaced by the corresponding argument on the macro invocation command line. A $ followed by an i signals that macro processor that the executing macro is to be looped. On the first pass $i is replaced by the first argument on the macro invocation command line, on the second pass it is replaced by the second argument, and so on. A \ followed by any character is replaced by that character. Use the \to prevent special treatment of the $. |
| mdelete [*remote-files*] | Delete the *remote-files* on the remote machine. |

**mdir** *remote-files local-file*

Like dir, except multiple remote files may be specified. If interactive prompting is on, ftp will prompt the user to verify that the last argument is indeed the target local file for receiving mdir output.

**mget** *remote-files*

Expand the *remote-files* on the remote machine and do a get for each filename thus produced. See glob for details on the filename expansion. Resulting filenames will then be processed according to case, ntrans, and nmap settings. Files are transferred into the local working directory, which can be changed with lcd directory ; new local directories can be created with !mkdir directory.

**mkdir** *directory-name*

Make a directory on the remote machine.

**mls** *remote-files local-file*

Like nlist, except multiple remote files may be specified, and the local-file must be specified. If interactive prompting is on, ftp will prompt the user to verify that the last argument is indeed the target local file for receiving mls output.

**mode** [*mode-name*]

Set the file transfer mode to *mode-name*. The default mode is stream mode.

**modtime** *file-name*

Show the last modification time of the file on the remote machine.

**mput** *local-files*

Expand wildcards in the list of local files given as arguments and do a put for each file in the resulting list. See glob for details of filename expansion. Resulting filenames will then be processed according to ntrans and nmap settings.

**newer** *file-name*

Get the file only if the modification time of the remote file is more recent that the file on the current system. If the file does not exist on the current system, the remote file is considered newer. Otherwise, this command is identical to get.

**nlist** [*remote-directory*]
[*local-file*]

Print a list of the files in a directory on the remote machine. If *remote-directory* is left unspecified, the current working directory is used. If interactive prompting is on, ftp will prompt the user to verify that the last argument is indeed the target local file for receiving nlist output. If no local file is specified, or if *local-file* is -, the output is sent to the terminal.

**nmap** [*inpattern*] *outpattern*

Set or unset the filename mapping mechanism. If no arguments are specified, the filename mapping mechanism is unset. If arguments are specified, remote filenames are mapped during mput commands and put commands issued without a specified remote target filename. If arguments are specified, local filenames are mapped during mget commands and get commands issued without a specified local target filename. This command is useful when connecting to a non-UNIX remote computer with different file naming conventions or practices. The mapping follows the pattern set by inpattern and outpattern. Inpattern is a template for incoming filenames (which may have already been processed according to the ntrans and case settings). Variable templating is accomplished by including the sequences $1, $2,..., $9 in inpattern. Use \ to prevent this special treatment of the $ character. All other characters are treated literally, and are used to determine the nmap inpattern variable values. For example, given inpattern $1.$2 and the remote filename mydata.data, $1 would have the value mydata, and $2 would have the value "data". The outpattern determines the resulting mapped filename. The sequences $1, $2,...., $9 are replaced by any value resulting from the inpattern template. The sequence $0 is replaced by the original filename. Additionally, the sequence *seq1, seq2* is replaced by *seq1* if *seq1* is not a null string; otherwise, it is replaced by seq2. For example, the command nmap $1.$2.$3 [$1,$2].[$2,file] would yield the output filename myfile.data for input filenames my-file. data and myfile.data.old, myfile.file for the input filename my-file, and myfile.myfile for the input filename .myfile. Spaces may be included in outpattern, as in the example: nmap $1 sed "s/ *$//" > $1. Use the \ character to prevent special treatment of the $, [, [, and , characters.

**ntrans** [*inchars*] [*outchars*]

Set or unset the filename character translation mechanism. If no arguments are specified, the filename character translation mechanism is unset. If arguments are specified, characters in remote filenames are translated during mput commands and put commands issued without a specified remote target filename. If arguments are specified, characters in local filenames are translated during mget commands and get commands issued without a specified local target filename. This command is useful when connecting to a non-UNIX remote computer with different file naming conventions or practices. Characters in a filename matching a character in *inchars* are replaced with the corresponding character in *outchars*. If the character's position in *inchars* is longer than the length of *outchars*, the character is deleted from the filename.

**open** *host* [*port*]

Establish a connection to the specified host FTP server. An optional port number may be supplied, in which case, ftp will attempt to contact an FTP server at that port. If the auto-login option is on (default), ftp will also attempt to automatically log the user in to the FTP server (see below).

**prompt**

Toggle interactive prompting. Interactive prompting occurs during multiple file transfers to allow the user to selectively retrieve or store files. If prompting is turned off (default is on), any mget or mput will transfer all files, and any mdelete will delete all files.

**proxy** *ftp-command*

Execute an ftp command on a secondary control connection. This command allows simultaneous connection to two remote FTP servers for transferring files between the two servers. The first proxy command should be an open, to establish the secondary control connection. Enter the command "proxy ?" to see other ftp commands executable on the secondary connection. The following commands behave differently when prefaced by proxy :, open will not define new macros during the auto-login process, close will not erase existing macro definitions, get and mget transfer files from the host on the primary control connection to the host on the secondary control connection, and put, mput, and append transfer files from the host on the secondary control connection to the host on the primary control connection. Third-party file transfers depend upon support of the FTP protocol PASV command by the server on the secondary control connection.

**put** *local-file* [*remote-file*]

Store a local file on the remote machine. If *remote-file* is left unspecified, the local filename is used after processing according to any ntrans or nmap settings in naming the remote file. File transfer uses the current settings for type, format, mode, and structure.

**pwd**

Print the name of the current working directory on the remote machine.

**quit**

A synonym for bye.

**quote** *arg1 arg2...*

The arguments specified are sent, verbatim, to the remote FTP server.

**recv** *remote-file* [*local-file*]

A synonym for get.

**reget** *remote-file* [*local-file*]

Reget acts like get, except that if *local-file* exists and is smaller than *remote-file*, *local-file* is presumed to be a partially transferred copy of *remote-file* and the transfer is continued from the apparent point of failure. This command is useful when transferring very large files over networks that are prone to dropping connections.

**remotehelp** [*command-name*]

Request help from the remote FTP server. If a *command-name* is specified, it is supplied to the server as well.

**remotestatus** [*file-name*]

With no arguments, show status of remote machine. If *file-name* is specified, show status of *file-name* on remote machine.

**rename** [*from*] [*to*]

Rename the file from on the remote machine, to the file *to*.

**reset**

Clear reply queue. This command resynchronizes command/reply sequencing with the remote FTP server. Resynchronization may be necessary following a violation of the FTP protocol by the remote server.

**restart** *marker*

Restart the immediately following get or put at the indicated marker. On UNIX systems, *marker* is usually a byte offset into the file.

| | |
|---|---|
| rmdir *directory-name* | Delete a directory on the remote machine. |
| runique | Toggle storing of files on the local system with unique filenames. If a file already exists with a name equal to the target local filename for a get or mget command, a .1 is appended to the name. If the resulting name matches another existing file, a .2 is appended to the original name. If this process continues up to .99, an error message is printed, and the transfer does not take place. The generated unique filename will be reported. Note that runique will not affect local files generated from a shell command. The default value is off. |
| send *local-file* [*remote-file*] | A synonym for put. |
| sendport | Toggle the use of PORT commands. By default, ftp will attempt to use a PORT command when establishing a connection for each data transfer. The use of PORT commands can prevent delays when performing multiple file transfers. If the PORT command fails, ftp will use the default data port. When the use of PORT commands is disabled, no attempt will be made to use PORT commands for each data transfer. This is useful for certain FTP implementations which do ignore PORT commands but, incorrectly, indicate they've been accepted. |
| site *arg1 arg2...* | The arguments specified are sent, verbatim, to the remote FTP server as a SITE command. |
| size *file-name* | Return size of file-name on remote machine. |
| status | Show the current status of ftp. |
| struct [*struct-name*] | Set the file transfer structure to *struct-name*. By default stream structure is used. |
| sunique | Toggle storing of files on remote machine under unique filenames. Remote FTP server must support ftp protocol STOU command for successful completion. The remote server will report unique name. Default value is off. |
| system | Show the type of operating system running on the remote machine. |
| tenex | Set the file transfer type to that needed to talk to TENEX machines. |
| trace | Toggle packet tracing. |
| type [*type-name*] | Set the file transfer type to *type-name*. If no type is specified, the current type is printed. The default type is network ASCII. |
| umask [*newmask*] | Set the default umask on the remote server to *newmask*. If *newmask* is omitted, the current umask is printed. |
| user *user-name* [*password*] [*account*] | Identify yourself to the remote FTP server. If the password is not specified and the server requires it, ftp will prompt the user for it (after disabling local echo). If an account field is not specified, and the FTP server requires it, the user will be prompted for it. If an account field is specified, an account command will be relayed to the remote server after the login sequence is completed if the remote server did not require it for logging in. Unless ftp is invoked with auto-login disabled, this process is done automatically on initial connection to the FTP server. |
| verbose | Toggle verbose mode. In verbose mode, all responses from the FTP server are displayed to the user. In addition, if verbose is on, when a file transfer completes, statistics regarding the efficiency of the transfer are reported. By default, verbose is on. |
| ? [*command*] | A synonym for help. |

Command arguments which have embedded spaces may be quoted with quotation marks (").

## ABORTING A FILE TRANSFER

To abort a file transfer, use the terminal interrupt key (usually Ctrl-C). Sending transfers will be immediately halted. Receiving transfers will be halted by sending an FTP protocol ABOR command to the remote server, and discarding any further data received. The speed at which this is accomplished depends upon the remote server's support for ABOR processing.

If the remote server does not support the ABOR command, an ftp> prompt will not appear until the remote server has completed sending the requested file.

The terminal interrupt key sequence will be ignored when ftp has completed any local processing and is awaiting a reply from the remote server. A long delay in this mode may result from the ABOR processing described earlier in this section, or from unexpected behavior by the remote server, including violations of the FTP protocol. If the delay results from unexpected remote server behavior, the local ftp program must be killed by hand.

## FILE NAMING CONVENTIONS

Files specified as arguments to ftp commands are processed according to the following rules:

If the filename - is specified, the stdin (for reading) or stdout (for writing) is used.

If the first character of the filename is *j*, the remainder of the argument is interpreted as a shell command. ftp then forks a shell, using popen 3 with the argument supplied, and reads (writes) from the stdout (stdin). If the shell command includes spaces, the argument must be quoted; for example, ls -lt. A particularly useful example of this mechanism is: dir more.

Failing the preceding checks, if "globbing" is enabled, local filenames are expanded according to the rules used in the csh 1; c.f. the glob command. If the ftp command expects a single local file (for example, put), only the first filename generated by the "globbing" operation is used.

For mget commands and get commands with unspecified local filenames, the local filename is the remote filename, which may be altered by a case, ntrans, or nmap setting. The resulting filename may then be altered if runique is on.

For mput commands and put commands with unspecified remote filenames, the remote filename is the local filename, which may be altered by an ntrans or nmap setting. The resulting filename may then be altered by the remote server if sunique is on.

## FILE TRANSFER PARAMETERS

The FTP specification specifies many parameters that may affect a file transfer. The type may be one of ASCII, image (binary), ebcdic, and local byte size (for PDP Ns -10s and PDP Ns -20s mostly). ftp supports the ASCII and image types of file transfer, plus local byte size 8 for tenex mode transfers.

ftp supports only the default values for the remaining file transfer parameters: mode, form, and struct.

## THE .netrc FILE

The file contains login and initialization information used by the auto-login process. It resides in the user's home directory. The following tokens are recognized; they may be separated by spaces, tabs, or newlines:

| | |
|---|---|
| machine *name* | Identify a remote machine name. The auto-login process searches the file for a machine token that matches the remote machine specified on the ftp command line or as an open command argument. When a match is made, the subsequent tokens are processed, stopping when the end of file is reached or another machine or a default token is encountered. |
| default | This is the same as machine name except that default matches any name. There can be only one default token, and it must be after all machine tokens. This is normally used as *default login anonymous password user@site*, thereby giving the user automatic anonymous ftp login to machines not specified. This can be overridden by using the -n flag to disable auto-login. |
| login *name* | Identify a user on the remote machine. If this token is present, the auto-login process will initiate a login using the specified name. |
| password *string* | Supply a password. If this token is present, the auto-login process will supply the specified string if the remote server requires a password as part of the login process. Note that if this token is present in the file for any user other than anonymous, ftp will abort the auto-login process if the is readable by anyone besides the user. |
| account *string* | Supply an additional account password. If this token is present, the auto-login process will supply the specified string if the remote server requires an additional account password, or the auto-login process will initiate an ACCT command if it does not. |

macdef *name*                    Define a macro. This token functions like the ftp macdef command functions. A macro is defined
                                 with the specified name; its contents begin with the next line and continue until a null line
                                 (consecutive newline characters) is encountered. If a macro named init is defined, it is automati-
                                 cally executed as the last step in the auto-login process.

## ENVIRONMENT

ftp utilizes the following environment variables:

HOME                     For default location of a file, if one exists
SHELL                    For default shell

## SEE ALSO

ftpd(8)

## HISTORY

The ftp command appeared in BSD 4.2.

## BUGS

Correct execution of many commands depends upon proper behavior by the remote server.

An error in the treatment of carriage returns in the BSD 4.2 ASCII-mode transfer code has been corrected. This correction
may result in incorrect transfers of binary files to and from BSD 4.2 servers using the ASCII type. Avoid this problem by
using the binary image type.

BSD 4.2, 30 July 1991

# fuser

fuser—Identify processes using files

## SYNOPSIS

```
fuser [-a¦-s][-signal][-kmuv] filename ... [-][-signal][-kmuv] filename ...
fuser [-l]
```

## DESCRIPTION

fuser displays the PIDs of processes using the specified files or file systems. In the default display mode, each filename is
followed by a letter denoting the type of access:

c                        Current directory.
e                        Executable being run.
f                        Open file. f is omitted in default display mode.
r                        Root directory.
m                        mmap'ed file or shared library.

fuser returns a nonzero return code if none of the specified files is accessed or in case of a fatal error. If at least one access has
been found, fuser returns zero.

## OPTIONS

-a                       Show all files specified on the command line. By default, only files that are accessed by at least one process
                         are shown.
-k                       Kill processes accessing the file. Unless changed with -signal, SIGKILL is sent. A fuser process never kills
                         itself, but may kill other fuser processes.

| u | List all known signal names. |
|---|---|
| -m | *filename* specifies a file on a mounted file system or a block device that is mounted. All processes accessing files on that file system are listed. If a directory file is specified, it is automatically changed to `filename/.` to use any file system that might be mounted on that directory. |
| -s | Silent operation. -a, -u, and -v are ignored in this mode. |
| -signal | Use the specified signal instead of SIGKILL when killing processes. Signals can be specified either by name (for example, -HUP) or by number (for example, -1). |
| -u | Append the username of the process owner to each PID. |
| -v | Verbose mode. Processes are shown in a ps-like style. The fields PID, USER, and COMMAND are similar to ps. ACCESS shows how the process accesses the file. |
| - | Reset all options and set the signal back to SIGKILL. |

## FILES

/proc      Location of the proc file system

## EXAMPLES

`fuser -km /home` kills all processes accessing the file system `/home` in any way.

In this example:

`if fuser -s /dev/ttyS1; then :; else something`

`fi` invokes something if no other process is using `/dev/ttyS1`.

## RESTRICTIONS

Processes accessing the same file or filesystem several times in the same way are only shown once.

## AUTHOR

Werner Almesberger (`<almesber@di.epfl.ch>U`)

## SEE ALSO

kill(1), killall(1), ps(1), kill(2)

Linux, 11 October 1994

# g++

g++ – GNU project C++ Compiler

## SYNOPSIS

g++ [ *option* ¦ *filename* ]. ..

## DESCRIPTION

The C and C++ compilers are integrated; g++ is a script to call gcc with options to recognize C++. gcc processes input files through one or more of four stages: preprocessing, compilation, assembly, and linking. This man page contains full descriptions for only C++ specific aspects of the compiler, though it also contains summaries of some general-purpose options. For a fuller explanation of the compiler, see gcc(1).

C++ source files use one of the suffixes .C, .cc, .cxx, .cpp, or .c++; preprocessed C++ files use the suffix .ii.

## OPTIONS

There are many command-line options, including options to control details of optimization, warnings, and code generation, which are common to both gcc and g++. For full information on all options, see gcc(1).

Options must be separate: -dr is quite different from -d -r.

Most -f and -W options have two contrary forms: -fname and -fno-name (or —Wname and -Wno-name). Only the nondefault forms are shown here.

| | |
|---|---|
| -c | Compile or assemble the source files, but do not link. The compiler output is an object file corresponding to each source file. |
| -Dmacro | Define macro *macro* with the string 1 as its definition. |
| -Dmacro=defn | Define macro macro as defn. |
| -E | Stop after the preprocessing stage; do not run the compiler proper. The output is preprocessed source code, which is sent to the standard output. |
| -fall-virtual | Treat all possible member functions as virtual, implicitly. All member functions (except for constructor functions and new or delete member operators) are treated as virtual functions of the class where they appear. |

This does not mean that all calls to these member functions will be made through the internal table of virtual functions. Under some circumstances, the compiler can determine that a call to a given virtual function can be made directly; in these cases the calls are direct in any case.

| | |
|---|---|
| -fdollars-in-identifiers | Permit the use of $ in identifiers. Traditional C allowed the character $ to form part of identifiers; by default, GNU C also allows this. However, ANSI C forbids $ in identifiers, and GNU C++ also forbids it by default on most platforms (though on some platforms it's enabled by default for GNU C++ as well). |
| -felide-constructors | Use this option to instruct the compiler to be smarter about when it can elide constructors. Without this flag, GNU C++ and cfront both generate effectively the same code for |

```
A foo ();

A x (foo ()); // x initialized by 'foo ()', no ctor called

A y = foo (); // call to 'foo ()' heads to temporary, // y is initial-
ized from the temporary.
```

Note the difference. With this flag, GNU C++ initializes y directly from the call to foo() without going through a temporary.

| | |
|---|---|
| -fenum-int-equiv | Normally GNU C++ allows conversion of enum to int, but not the other way around. Use this option if you want GNU C++ to allow conversion of int to enum as well. |
| -fexternal-templates | Produce smaller code for template declarations, by generating only a single copy of each template function where it is defined. To use this option successfully, you must also mark all files that use templates with either #pragma implementation (the definition) or #pragma interface (declarations). |

When your code is compiled with -fexternal-templates, all template instantiations are external. You must arrange for all necessary instantiations to appear in the implementation file; you can do this with a typedef that references each instantiation needed. Conversely, when you compile using the default option -fno- external-templates, all template instantiations are explicitly internal.

| | |
|---|---|
| -fno-gnu-linker | Do not output global initializations (such as C++ constructors and destructors) in the form used by the GNU linker (on systems where the GNU linker is the standard method of handling them). Use this option when you want to use a non-GNU linker, which also requires using the collect2 program to make sure the system linker includes constructors and destructors. (collect2 is included in the GNU CC distribution.) For systems which must use collect2, the compiler driver gcc is configured to do this automatically. |
| -fmemoize-lookups -fsave-memorized | These flags are used to get the compiler to compile programs faster using heuristics. They are not on by default since they are only effective about half the time. The other half of the time programs compile more slowly (and take more memory). |

The first time the compiler must build a call to a member function (or reference to a data member), it must (1) determine whether the class implements member functions of that name; (2) resolve which member function to call (which involves figuring out what sorts of type conversions need to be made); and (3) check the visibility of the member function to the caller. All of this adds up to slower compilation. Normally, the second time a call is made to that member function (or reference to that data member), it must go through the same lengthy process again. This means that code like this:

```
cout << "This " << p << "has"<< n << " legs.\n";
```

makes six passes through all three steps. By using a software cache, a "hit" significantly reduces this cost. Unfortunately, using the cache introduces another layer of mechanisms which must be implemented, and so incurs its own overhead. -fmemorize- lookups enables the software cache.

Because access privileges (visibility) to members and member functions may differ from one function context to the next, g++ may need to flush the cache. With the -fmemoize-lookups flag, the cache is flushed after every function that is compiled. The -fsave-memorized flag enables the same software cache, but when the compiler determines that the context of the last function compiled would yield the same access privileges of the next function to compile, it preserves the cache. This is most helpful when defining many member functions for the same class: with the exception of member functions which are friends of other classes, each member function has exactly the same access privileges as every other, and the cache need not be flushed.

-fno-default-inline

Do not make member functions inline by default merely because they are defined inside the class scope. Otherwise, when you specify -0, member functions defined inside class scope are compiled inline by default; that is, you don't need to add inline in front of the member function name.

-fno-strict-prototype

Consider the declaration int foo;(). In C++, this means that the function foo takes no arguments. In ANSI C, this is declared int foo(void);. With the flag -fno-strict-prototype, declaring functions with no arguments is equivalent to declaring its argument list to be untyped, that is, int foo(); is equivalent to saying int foo (...);.-fnonnull-objects. Normally, GNU C++ makes conservative assumptions about objects reached through references. For example, the compiler must check that a is not null in code like the following:

```
obj &a = g ();
```

```
a.f (2);
```

Checking that references of this sort have non-null values requires extra code, however, and it is unnecessary for many programs. You can use -fnonnull-objects to omit the checks for null, if your program doesn't require the default checking.

-fhandle-signatures-
fno-handle-signatures

These options control the recognition of the signature and sigof constructs for specifying abstract types. By default, these constructs are not recognized.

-fthis-is-variable

The incorporation of user-defined free store management into C++ has made assignment to this an anachronism. Therefore, by default GNU C++ treats the type of this in a member function of class X to be X *const. In other words, it is illegal to assign to this within a class member function. However, for backwards compatibility, you can invoke the old behavior by using -fthis-is-variable.

-g

Produce debugging information in the operating system's native format (for DBX or SDB or DWARF). GDB also can work with this debugging information. On most systems that use DBX format, -g enables use of extra debugging information that only GDB can use.

Unlike most other C compilers, GNU CC allows you to use -g with -0. The shortcuts taken by optimized code may occasionally produce surprising results: some variables you declared may not exist at all; flow of control may briefly move where you did not expect it; some statements may not be executed because they compute constant results or their values were already at hand; some statements may execute in different places because they were moved out of loops.

Nevertheless, it proves possible to debug optimized output. This makes it reasonable to use the optimizer for programs that might have bugs.

| | |
|---|---|
| `-Idir` | Append directory *dir* to the list of directories searched for include files. |
| `-Ldir` | Add directory *dir* to the list of directories to be searched for -l. |
| `-llibrary` | Use the library named *library* when linking. (C++ programs often require -lg++ for successful linking.) |
| `-nostdinc` | Do not search the standard system directories for header files. Only the directories you have specified with -I options (and the current directory, if appropriate) are searched. |
| `-nostdinc++` | Do not search for header files in the standard directories specific to C++, but do still search the other standard directories. (This option is used when building libg++.) |
| `-O` | Optimize. Optimizing compilation takes somewhat more time, and a lot more memory for a large function. |
| `-o file` | Place output in file *file*. |
| `-S` | Stop after the stage of compilation proper; do not assemble. The output is an assembler code file for each nonassembler input file specified. |
| `-traditional` | Attempt to support some aspects of traditional C compilers. Specifically, for both C and C++ programs: |

In the preprocessor, comments convert to nothing at all, rather than to a space. This allows traditional token concatenation.

In the preprocessor, macro arguments are recognized within string constants in a macro definition (and their values are stringified, though without additional quote marks, when they appear in such a context). The preprocessor always considers a string constant to end at a newline.

The preprocessor does not predefine the macro STDC when you use -traditional, but still predefines GNUC (since the GNU extensions indicated by GNUC are not affected by -traditional). If you need to write header files that work differently depending on whether -traditional is in use, by testing both of these predefined macros you can distinguish four situations: GNU C, traditional GNU C, other ANSI C compilers, and other old C compilers.

In the preprocessor, comments convert to nothing at all, rather than to a space. This allows traditional token concatenation.

String "constants" are not necessarily constant; they are stored in writable space, and identical looking constants are allocated separately. For C++ programs only (not C), -traditional has one additional effect: assignment to this is permitted. This is the same as the effect of -fthis-is-variable.

| | |
|---|---|
| `-Umacro` | Undefine macro *macro*. |
| `-Wall` | Issue warnings for conditions that pertain to usage that we recommend avoiding and that we believe is easy to avoid, even in conjunction with macros. |
| `-Wenum-clash` | Warn when converting between different enumeration types. |
| `-Woverloaded-virtual` | In a derived class, the definitions of virtual functions must match the type signature of a virtual function declared in the base class. Use this option to request warnings when a derived class declares a function that may be an erroneous attempt to define a virtual function; that is, warn when a function with the same name as a virtual function in the base class, but with a type signature that doesn't match any virtual functions from the base class. |

| | |
|---|---|
| -Wtemplate-debugging | When using templates in a C++ program, warn if debugging is not yet fully available. |
| -w | Inhibit all warning messages. |
| +eN | Control how virtual function definitions are used, in a fashion compatible with cfront 1.x. |

## PRAGMAS

Two #pragma directives are supported for GNU C++, to permit using the same header file for two purposes: as a definition of interfaces to a given object class, and as the full definition of the contents of that object class.

| | |
|---|---|
| #pragma interface | Use this directive in header files that define object classes, to save space in most of the object files that use those classes. Normally, local copies of certain information (backup copies of inline member functions, debugging information, and the internal tables that implement virtual functions) must be kept in each object file that includes class definitions. You can use this pragma to avoid such duplication. When a header file containing #pragma interface is included in a compilation, this auxiliary information will not be generated (unless the main input source file itself uses #pragma implementation). Instead, the object files will contain references to be resolved at link time. |
| #pragma implementation<br>#pragma implementation !objects.h! | Use this pragma in a main input file, when you want full output from included header files to be generated (and made globally visible). The included header file, in turn, should use #pragma interface. Backup copies of inline member functions, debugging information, and the internal tables used to implement virtual functions are all generated in implementation files. |
| | If you use #pragma implementation with no argument, it applies to an include file with the same basename as your source file; for example, in allclass.cc, #pragma implementation by itself is equivalent to #pragma implementation "allclass.h". Use the string argument if you want a single implementation file to include code from multiple header files. |
| | There is no way to split up the contents of a single header file into multiple implementation files. |

## FILES

| | |
|---|---|
| file.h | C header (preprocessor) file |
| file.i | Preprocessed C source |
| file file.C | C++ source file |
| file.cc | C++ source file |
| file.cxx | C++ source file |
| file.s | Assembly language file |
| file.o | Object file |
| a.out | Link edited output |
| TMPDIR/cc | Temporary files |
| LIBDIR/cpp | Preprocessor |
| LIBDIR/cc1plus | Compiler |
| LIBDIR/collect | Linker front end needed on some machines |
| LIBDIR/libgcc.a | GCC subroutine library |
| /lib/crt[01n].o | Start-up routine |
| LIBDIR/ccrt0 | Additional start-up routine for C++ |
| /lib/libc.a | Standard C library; see intro(3) |

| | |
|---|---|
| /usr/include | Standard directory for #include files |
| LIBDIR/include | Standard gcc directory for #include files |
| LIBDIR/g++-include | Additional g++ directory for #include |

LIBDIR is usually /usr/local/lib/machine/version.

TMPDIR comes from the environment variable TMPDIR (default /usr/tmp if available, else /tmp).

## SEE ALSO

gcc(1), cpp(1), as(1), ld(1), gdb(1), adb(1), dbx(1), sdb(1), gcc, cpp, as, ld, and gdb entries in info.

*Using and Porting GNU CC* (for version 2.0), Richard M. Stallman; *The C Preprocessor*, Richard M. Stallman; *Debugging with GDB: the GNU Source-Level Debugger*, Richard M. Stallman and Roland H. Pesch; *Using as: the GNU Assembler*, Dean Elsner, Jay Fenlason and friends; *gld: the GNU linker*, Steve Chamberlain and Roland Pesch.

## BUGS

For instructions on how to report bugs, see the GCC manual.

## COPYING

Copyright © 1991, 1992, 1993 Free Software Foundation, Inc. Permission is granted to make and distribute verbatim copies of this manual provided the copyright notice and this permission notice are preserved on all copies.

Permission is granted to copy and distribute modified versions of this manual under the conditions for verbatim copying, provided that the entire resulting derived work is distributed under the terms of a permission notice identical to this one.

Permission is granted to copy and distribute translations of this manual into another language, under the above conditions for modified versions, except that this permission notice may be included in translations approved by the Free Software Foundation instead of in the original English.

## AUTHORS

See the GNU CC Manual for the contributors to GNU CC.

GNU Tools, 30 April 1993

# g3topbm

g3topbm—Convert a Group 3 fax file into a portable bitmap

## SYNOPSIS

g3topbm [-kludge][-reversebits][-stretch][*g3file*]

## DESCRIPTION

Reads a Group 3 fax file as input. Produces a portable bitmap as output.

## OPTIONS

| | |
|---|---|
| -kludge | Tells g3topbm to ignore the first few lines of the file; sometimes fax files have some junk at the beginning. |
| -reversebits | Tells g3topbm to interpret bits least-significant first, instead of the default most-significant first. Apparently, some fax modems do it one way and others do it the other way. If you get a whole bunch of "bad code word" messages, try using this flag. |
| -stretch | Tells g3topbm to stretch the image vertically by duplicating each row. This is for the low-quality transmission mode. |

All flags can be abbreviated to their shortest unique prefix.

## REFERENCES

The standard for Group 3 fax is defined in CCITT Recommendation T.4.

## BUGS

Probably.

## SEE ALSO

pbmtog3(1), pbm(5)

## AUTHOR

Copyright © 1989 by Paul Haeberli (paul@manray.sgi.com)

2 October 1989

# gawk

gawk—Pattern scanning and processing language

## SYNOPSIS

```
gawk [ POSIX or GNU style options ] -f program-file [ -- ] file ...
gawk [ POSIX or GNU style options ] [ -- ] program-text file ...
```

## DESCRIPTION

gawk is the GNU Project's implementation of the awk programming language. It conforms to the definition of the language in the 1003.2 Command Language and Utilities Standard. This version in turn is based on the description in *The AWK Programming Language*, by Aho, Kernighan, and Weinberger, with the additional features defined in the System V Release 4 version of awk. gawk also provides some GNU-specific extensions.

The command line consists of options to gawk itself, the awk program text (if not supplied via the -f or —file options), and values to be made available in the ARGC and ARGV predefined awk variables.

## OPTIONS

gawk options may be either the traditional one-letter options, or the GNU-style long options. Traditional style options start with a single -, while GNU long options start with --. GNU-style long options are provided for both GNU-specific features and for mandated features. Other implementations of the awk language are likely to only accept the traditional one-letter options.

Following the standard, gawk-specific options are supplied via arguments to the -W option. Multiple -W options may be supplied, or multiple arguments may be supplied together if they are separated by commas, or enclosed in quotes and separated by whitespace. Case is ignored in arguments to the -W option. Each -W option has a corresponding GNU-style long option, as detailed below. Arguments to GNU-style long options are either joined with the option by an = sign, with no intervening spaces, or they may be provided in the next command-line argument.

gawk accepts the following options:

| | |
|---|---|
| -F *fs*, --field-separator=*fs* | Use *fs* for the input field separator (the value of the FS-predefined variable). |
| -v *var=val*, --assign=*var=val* | Assign the value *val*, to the variable *var*, before execution of the program begins. Such variable values are available to the BEGIN block of an awk program. |
| -f *program-file*, --file=*program-file* | Read the awk program source from the file *program-file*, instead of from the first command-line argument. Multiple -f (or --file) options may be used. |
| -mf=*NNN*, -mr=*NNN* | Set various memory limits to the value *NNN*. The f flag sets the maximum number of fields, and the r flag sets the maximum record size. These two flags and the -m option are from the AT&T Bell Labs research version of awk. They are ignored by gawk, since gawk has no predefined limits. |

| | |
|---|---|
| -W compat, --compat | Run in compatibility mode. In compatibility mode, gawk behaves identically to awk; none of the GNU-specific extensions are recognized. See "GNU Extensions," later in this manual page, for more information. |
| -W copyleft, -W copyright, --copyleft, --copyright | Print the short version of the GNU copyright information message on the error output. |
| -W help, -W usage --help, --usage | Print a relatively short summary of the available options on the error output. Per the GNU Coding Standards, these options cause an immediate, successful exit. |
| -W lint, --lint | Provide warnings about constructs that are dubious or nonportable to other awk implementations. |
| -W posix, --posix | This turns on compatibility mode, with the following additional restrictions:\x escape sequences are not recognized. |
| | The synonym func for the keyword function is not recognized. |
| | The operators ** and **= cannot be used in place of ^ and ^=. |
| -W source=*program-text*, --source=*program-text* | Use *program-text* as awk program source code. This option allows the easy intermixing of library functions (used via the -f and --file options) with source code entered on the command line. It is intended primarily for medium to large awk programs used in shell scripts. |
| | The -W source= form of this option uses the rest of the command-line argument for *program-text*; no other options to -W will be recognized in the same argument. |
| -W version, --version | Print version information for this particular copy of gawk on the error output. This is useful mainly for knowing if the current copy of gawk on your system is up-to-date with respect to whatever the Free Software Foundation is distributing. Per the GNU Coding Standards, these options cause an immediate, successful exit. |
| -- | Signal the end of options. This is useful to allow further arguments to the awk program itself to start with a -. This is mainly for consistency with the argument-parsing convention used by most other programs. |

In compatibility mode, any other options are flagged as illegal, but are otherwise ignored. In normal operation, as long as program text has been supplied, unknown options are passed on to the awk program in the ARGV array for processing. This is particularly useful for running awk programs via the #! executable interpreter mechanism.

## awk PROGRAM EXECUTION

An awk program consists of a sequence of pattern-action statements and optional function definitions:

```
pattern { action statements }
function name(parameter list) { statements }
```

gawk first reads the program source from the program-file(s) if specified, from arguments to -W source=, or from the first nonoption argument on the command line. The -f and -W source= options may be used multiple times on the command line. gawk will read the program text as if all the program-files and command-line source texts had been concatenated together. This is useful for building libraries of awk functions, without having to include them in each new awk program that uses them. It also provides the ability to mix library functions with command-line programs.

The environment variable AWKPATH specifies a search path to use when finding source files named with the -f option. If this variable does not exist, the default path is .:/usr/lib/awk:/usr/local/lib/awk.

If a filename given to the -f option contains a / character, no path search is performed.

gawk executes awk programs in the following order. First, all variable assignments specified via the -v option are performed. Next, gawk compiles the program into an internal form. Then, gawk executes the code in the BEGIN block(s) (if any), and then proceeds to read each file named in the ARGV array. If there are no files named on the command line, gawk reads the standard input.

If a filename on the command line has the form *var=val*, it is treated as a variable assignment. The variable *var* will be assigned the value *val*. (This happens after any BEGIN block(s) have been run.) Command-line variable assignment is most useful for dynamically assigning values to the variables awk uses to control how input is broken into fields and records. It is also useful for controlling state if multiple passes are needed over a single data file.

If the value of a particular element of ARGV is empty (""), gawk skips over it.

For each line in the input, gawk tests to see if it matches any *pattern* in the awk program. For each pattern that the line matches, the associated *action* is executed. The patterns are tested in the order they occur in the program.

Finally, after all the input is exhausted, gawk executes the code in the END block(s) (if any).

## VARIABLES AND FIELDS

awk variables are dynamic; they come into existence when they are first used. Their values are either floating-point numbers or strings, or both, depending upon how they are used. awk also has one-dimensional arrays; arrays with multiple dimensions may be simulated. Several predefined variables are set as a program runs; these will be described as needed and summarized in the "Built-In Variables" subsection.

## FIELDS

As each input line is read, gawk splits the line into fields, using the value of the FS variable as the field separator. If FS is a single character, fields are separated by that character. Otherwise, FS is expected to be a full regular expression. In the special case that FS is a single blank, fields are separated by runs of blanks or tabs. Note that the value of IGNORECASE (see the following) will also affect how fields are split when FS is a regular expression.

If the FIELDWIDTHS variable is set to a space separated list of numbers, each field is expected to have fixed width, and gawk will split up the record using the specified widths. The value of FS is ignored. Assigning a new value to FS overrides the use of FIELDWIDTHS, and restores the default behavior.

Each field in the input line may be referenced by its position, $1, $2, and so on. $0 is the whole line. The value of a field may be assigned to as well. Fields need not be referenced by constants:

```
n =5
print $n
```

prints the fifth field in the input line. The variable NF is set to the total number of fields in the input line.

References to nonexistent fields (that is, fields after $NF) produce the null-string. However, assigning to a nonexistent field (for example, $(NF+2) = 5) will increase the value of NF, create any intervening fields with the null string as their value, and cause the value of $0 to be recomputed, with the fields being separated by the value of OFS. References to negative-numbered fields cause a fatal error.

## BUILT-IN VARIABLES

awk's built-in variables are the following:

| | |
|---|---|
| ARGC | The number of command-line arguments (does not include options to gawk, or the program source). |
| ARGIND | The index in ARGV of the current file being processed. |
| ARGV | Array of command-line arguments. The array is indexed from 0 to ARGC - 1. Dynamically changing the contents of ARGV can control the files used for data. |
| CONVFMT | The conversion format for numbers, "%.6g", by default. |
| ENVIRON | An array containing the values of the current environment. The array is indexed by the environment variables, each element being the value of that variable (for example, ENVIRON["HOME"] might be /u/arnold). Changing this array does not affect the environment seen by programs which gawk spawns via redirection or the system() function. (This may change in a future version of gawk.) |
| ERRNO | If a system error occurs either doing a redirection for getline, during a read for getline, or during a close(), then ERRNO will contain a string describing the error. |
| FIELDWIDTHS | A whitespace-separated list of fieldwidths. When set, gawk parses the input into fields of fixed width, instead of using the value of the FS variable as the field separator. The fixed field width facility is still experimental; expect the semantics to change as gawk evolves over time. |

FILENAME                The name of the current input file. If no files are specified on the command line, the value of FILENAME is -. However, FILENAME is undefined inside the BEGIN block.

FNR                     The input record number in the current input file.

FS                      The input field separator, a blank by default.

IGNORECASE              Controls the case-sensitivity of all regular expression operations. If IGNORECASE has a nonzero value, then pattern matching in rules, field splitting with FS, regular expression matching with ~ and !~, and the gsub( ), index( ), match( ), split( ),and sub( ) predefined functions will all ignore case when doing regular expression operations. Thus, if IGNORECASE is not equal to zero, /aB/ matches all of the strings ab, aB, Ab, and AB. As with all awk variables, the initial value of IGNORECASE is zero, so all regular expression operations are normally case-sensitive.

NF                      The number of fields in the current input record.

NR                      The total number of input records seen so far.

OFMT                    The output format for numbers, "%.6g", by default.

OFS                     The output field separator, a blank by default.

ORS                     The output record separator, by default a newline.

RS                      The input record separator, by default a newline. RS is exceptional in that only the first character of its string value is used for separating records. (This will probably change in a future release of gawk.) If RS is set to the null string, then records are separated by blank lines. When RS is set to the null string, then the newline character always acts as a field separator, in addition to whatever value FS may have.

RSTART                  The index of the first character matched by match(); 0 if no match.

RLENGTH                 The length of the string matched by match(); -1 if no match.

SUBSEP                  The character used to separate multiple subscripts in array elements, by default n034.

## ARRAYS

Arrays are subscripted with an expression between square brackets. If the expression is an expression list (*expr*, *expr* ...) then the array subscript is a string consisting of the concatenation of the (string) value of each expression, separated by the value of the SUBSEP variable. This facility is used to simulate multiply dimensioned arrays. For example,

```
i = "A" ; j = "B" ; k = "C"
x[i, j, k] = "hello, world\n"
```

assigns the string hello, world\n to the element of the array x which is indexed by the string "A\034B\034C". All arrays in awk are associative, that is indexed by string values.

The special operator in may be used in an if or while statement to see if an array has an index consisting of a particular value:

```
if (val in array)
print array[val]
```

If the array has multiple subscripts, use (i,j)in array.

The in construct may also be used in a for loop to iterate over all the elements of an array.

An element may be deleted from an array using the delete statement. The delete statement may also be used to delete the entire contents of an array.

## VARIABLE TYPING AND CONVERSION

Variables and fields may be floating-point numbers, or strings, or both. How the value of a variable is interpreted depends upon its context. If used in a numeric expression, it will be treated as a number; if used as a string, it will be treated as a string.

To force a variable to be treated as a number, add 0 to it; to force it to be treated as a string, concatenate it with the null string.

When a string must be converted to a number, the conversion is accomplished using atof(3). A number is converted to a string by using the value of CONVFMT as a format string for sprintf(3), with the numeric value of the variable as the argument. However, even though all numbers in awk are floating-point, integral values are *always* converted as integers. Thus, given this:

```
CONVFMT = "%2.2f"
a =12
b =a""
```

the variable b has a string value of 12 and not 12.00.

gawk performs comparisons as follows: If two variables are numeric, they are compared numerically. If one value is numeric and the other has a string value that is a "numeric string," then comparisons are also done numerically. Otherwise, the numeric value is converted to a string and a string comparison is performed. Two strings are compared, of course, as strings. According to the standard, even if two strings are numeric strings, a numeric comparison is performed. However, this is clearly incorrect, and gawk does not do this.

Uninitialized variables have the numeric value 0 and the string value " " (the null, or empty, string).

## PATTERNS AND ACTIONS

awk is a line-oriented language. The pattern comes first, and then the action. Action statements are enclosed in and .BR. Either the pattern may be missing, or the action may be missing, but, of course, not both. If the pattern is missing, the action will be executed for every single line of input. A missing action is equivalent to

```
{ print }
```

which prints the entire line.

Comments begin with the # character, and continue until the end of the line. Blank lines may be used to separate statements. Normally, a statement ends with a newline, however, this is not the case for lines ending in a ,, {, ?, :, &&, or ¦¦. Lines ending in do or else also have their statements automatically continued on the following line. In other cases, a line can be continued by ending it with a \, in which case the newline will be ignored.

Multiple statements may be put on one line by separating them with a semicolon. This applies to both the statements within the action part of a pattern-action pair (the usual case), and to the pattern-action statements themselves.

## PATTERNS

awk patterns may be one of the following:

```
BEGIN
END
/regular expression/
relational expression
pattern && pattern
pattern jj pattern
pattern ? pattern : pattern
(pattern)
! pattern
pattern1, pattern2
```

BEGIN and END are two special kinds of patterns that are not tested against the input. The action parts of all BEGIN patterns are merged as if all the statements had been written in a single BEGIN block. They are executed before any of the input is read. Similarly, all the END blocks are merged, and executed when all the input is exhausted (or when an exit statement is executed). BEGIN and END patterns cannot be combined with other patterns in pattern expressions. BEGIN and END patterns cannot have missing action parts.

For /regular expression/ patterns, the associated statement is executed for each input line that matches the regular expression. Regular expressions are the same as those in egrep(1), and are summarized as follows:

A *relational expression* may use any of the operators defined later in the section on actions. These generally test whether certain fields match certain regular expressions.

The &&, ¦¦, and ! operators are logical AND, logical OR, and logical NOT, respectively, as in C. They do short-circuit evaluation, also as in C, and are used for combining more primitive pattern expressions. As in most languages, parentheses may be used to change the order of evaluation.

The ?: operator is like the same operator in C. If the first pattern is true, then the pattern used for testing is the second pattern; otherwise, it is the third. Only one of the second and third patterns is evaluated.

The *pattern1*, *pattern2* form of an expression is called a *range pattern*. It matches all input records starting with a line that matches *pattern1*, and continuing until a record that matches *pattern2*, inclusive. It does not combine with any other sort of pattern expression.

## REGULAR EXPRESSIONS

Regular expressions are the extended kind found in egrep. They are composed of characters as follows:

| | |
|---|---|
| c | Matches the non-meta-character c. |
| \c | Matches the literal character c. |
| . | Matches any character except newline. |
| ^ | Matches the beginning of a line or a string. |
| $ | Matches the end of a line or a string. |
| [abc...] | Character class, matches any of the characters abc.... |
| [^abc...] | Negated character class, matches any character except abc... and newline. |
| r1¦r2 | Alternation: matches either *r1* or *r2*. |
| r1r2 | Concatenation: matches *r1*, and then *r2*. |
| r+ | Matches one or more *r*s. |
| r* | Matches zero or more *r*s. |
| r? | Matches zero or one *r*s. |
| (r) | Grouping: matches *r*. |

The escape sequences that are valid in string constants are also legal in regular expressions.

## ACTIONS

Action statements are enclosed in braces, { and }. Action statements consist of the usual assignment, conditional, and looping statements found in most languages. The operators, control statements, and input/output statements available are patterned after those in C.

## OPERATORS

The operators in awk, in order of increasing precedence, are

| | |
|---|---|
| =+=-= <br> *= /= %= ^= | Assignment. Both absolute assignment (*var* = *value*) and operator-assignment (the other forms) are supported. |
| ?: | The C conditional expression. This has the form *expr1* ? *expr2* : *expr3* .If *expr1* is true, the value of the expression is *expr2*; otherwise, it is *expr3*. Only one of *expr2* and *expr3* is evaluated. |
| ¦¦ | Logical OR. |
| && | Logical AND. |
| ~ !~ | Regular expression match, negated match. NOTE: Do not use a constant regular expression (/foo/) to the left of a ~ or !~. Only use one on the right side. The expression /foo/ ~ *exp* has the same meaning as (($0 ~ /foo/) ~ *exp*). This is usually *not* what was intended. |
| < >, <=>= | The regular relational operators. |
| blank | String concatenation. |
| +- | Addition and subtraction. |

| | |
|---|---|
| `*/%` | Multiplication, division, and modulus. |
| `+-!` | Unary plus, unary minus, and logical negation. |
| `^` | Exponentiation (`**` may also be used, and `**=` for the assignment operator). |
| `++ --` | Increment and decrement, both prefix and postfix. |
| `$` | Field reference. |

## CONTROL STATEMENTS

The control statements are as follows:

```
if (condition) statement [ else statement ]
while (condition) statement
do statement while (condition)
for (expr1; expr2; expr3) statement
for (var in array) statementbreak
 continue
 delete array[index]
delete array
exit [ expression ]
{ statements }
```

## I/O STATEMENTS

The input/output statements are as follows:

| | |
|---|---|
| `close(filename)` | Close file (or pipe, see paragraph following this list). |
| `getline` | Set `$0` from next input record; set NF, NR, FNR. |
| `getline <file` | Set `$0` from next record of `file`; set NF. |
| `getline var` | Set `var` from next input record; set NF, FNR. |
| `getline var <file` | Set `var` from next record of `file`. |
| `next` | Stop processing the current input record. The next input record is read and processing starts over with the first pattern in the awk program. If the end of the input data is reached, the END block(s), if any, are executed. |
| `next file` | Stop processing the current input file. The next input record read comes from the next input file. FILENAME is updated, FNR is reset to 1, and processing starts over with the first pattern in the awk program. If the end of the input data is reached, the END block(s), if any, are executed. |
| `print` | Prints the current record. |
| `print expr-list` | Prints expressions. Each expression is separated by the value of the OFS variable. The output record is terminated with the value of the ORS variable. |
| `print expr-list >file` | Prints expressions on `file`. Each expression is separated by the value of the OFS variable. The output record is terminated with the value of the ORS variable. |
| `printf fmt, expr-list` | Format and print. |
| `printf fmt, expr-list >file` | Format and print on `file`. |
| `system(cmd-line)` | Execute the command `cmd-line`, and return the exit status. (This may not be available on -POSIX systems.) |

Other input/output redirections are also allowed. For print and printf, `>>file` appends output to the `file`, while `¦ command` writes on a pipe. In a similar fashion, `command ¦ getline` pipes into `getline`. The `getline` command will return 0 on end of file, and -1 on an error.

## THE printf STATEMENT

The awk versions of the printf statement and sprintf() function accept the following conversion specification formats:

| | |
|---|---|
| `%c` | An ASCII character. If the argument used for %c is numeric, it is treated as a character and printed. Otherwise, the argument is assumed to be a string, and the only first character of that string is printed. |

| | |
|---|---|
| %d | A decimal number (the integer part). |
| %i | Just like %d. |
| %e | A floating-point number of the form [-]d.ddddddE[+-]dd. |
| %f | A floating-point number of the form [-]ddd.dddddd. |
| %g | Use e or f conversion, whichever is shorter, with nonsignificant zeros suppressed. |
| %o | An unsigned octal number (again, an integer). |
| %s | A character string. |
| %x | An unsigned hexadecimal number (an integer). |
| %X | Like %x, but using ABCDEF instead of abcdef. |
| %% | A single % character; no argument is converted. |

There are optional, additional parameters that may lie between the % and the control letter:

| | |
|---|---|
| - | The expression should be left-justified within its field. |
| width | The field should be padded to this width. If the number has a leading zero, then the field will be padded with zeros. Otherwise, it is padded with blanks. This applies even to the nonnumeric output formats. |
| .prec | A number indicating the maximum width of strings or digits to the right of the decimal point. |

The dynamic *width* and *prec* capabilities of the C printf() routines are supported. A * in place of either the *width* or *prec* specifications will cause their values to be taken from the argument list to printf or sprintf().

## SPECIAL FILENAMES

When doing I/O redirection from either print or printf into a file, or via getline from a file, gawk recognizes certain special filenames internally. These filenames allow access to open file descriptors inherited from gawk's parent process (usually the shell). Other special filenames provide access information about the running gawk process. The filenames are

| | |
|---|---|
| /dev/pid | Reading this file returns the process ID of the current process, in decimal, terminated with a newline. |
| /dev/ppid | Reading this file returns the parent process ID of the current process, in decimal, terminated with a newline. |
| /dev/pgrpid | Reading this file returns the process group ID of the current process, in decimal, terminated with a newline. |
| /dev/user | Reading this file returns a single record terminated with a newline. The fields are separated with blanks. $1 is the value of the getuid(2) system call, $2 is the value of the geteuid(2) system call, $3 is the value of the getgid(2) system call, and $4 is the value of the getegid( 2) system call. If there are any additional fields, they are the group IDs returned by getgroups(2). Multiple groups may not be supported on all systems. |
| /dev/stdin | The standard input. |
| /dev/stdout | The standard output. |
| /dev/stderr | The standard error output. |
| /dev/fd/n | The file associated with the open file descriptor *n*. |

These are particularly useful for error messages. For example, you could use

```
print "You blew it!" > "/dev/stderr"
```

whereas you would otherwise have to use

```
print "You blew it!" j "cat 1>&2"
```

These filenames may also be used on the command line to name data files.

## NUMERIC FUNCTIONS

awk has the following predefined arithmetic functions:

| | |
|---|---|
| atan2(y, x) | Returns the arctangent of *y/x* in radians. |
| cos(expr) | Returns the cosine in radians. |

| | |
|---|---|
| exp(*expr*) | The exponential function. |
| int(*expr*) | Truncates to integer. |
| log(*expr*) | The natural logarithm function. |
| rand() | Returns a random number between 0 and 1. |
| sin(*expr*) | Returns the sine in radians. |
| sqrt(*expr*) | The square root function. |
| srand(*expr*) | Use *expr* as a new seed for the random number generator. If no *expr* is provided, the time of day will be used. The return value is the previous seed for the random number generator. |

## STRING FUNCTIONS

awk has the following predefined string functions:

| | |
|---|---|
| gsub(*r*, *s*, *t*) | For each substring matching the regular expression *r* in the string *t*, substitute the string *s*, and return the number of substitutions. If *t* is not supplied, use $0. |
| index(*s*, *t*) | Returns the index of the string *t* in the string *s*,or 0 if *t* is not present. |
| length(*s*) | Returns the length of the string *s*, or the length of $0 if *s* is not supplied. |
| match(*s*, *r*) | Returns the position in *s* where the regular expression *r* occurs, or 0 if *u* is not present, and sets the values of RSTART and RLENGTH. |
| split(*s*, *a*, *r*) | Splits the string *s* into the array *a* on the regular expression *r*, and returns the number of fields. If *r* is omitted, FS is used instead. The array *a* is cleared first. |
| sprintf(*fmt*, *expr-list*) | Prints *expr-list* according to *fmt*, and returns the resulting string. |
| sub(*r*, *s*, *t*) | Just like gsub(), but only the first matching substring is replaced. |
| substr(*s*, *i*, *n*) | Returns the *n*-character substring of *s* starting at *i*. If *n* is omitted, the rest of *s* is used. |
| tolower(*str*) | Returns a copy of the string *str*, with all the uppercase characters in *str* translated to their corresponding lowercase counterparts. Nonalphabetic characters are left unchanged. |
| toupper(*str*) | Returns a copy of the string *str*, with all the lowercase characters in *str* translated to their corresponding uppercase counterparts. Nonalphabetic characters are left unchanged. |

## TIME FUNCTIONS

Since one of the primary uses of awk programs is processing log files that contain time stamp information, gawk provides the following two functions for obtaining time stamps and formatting them.

| | |
|---|---|
| systime() | Returns the current time of day as the number of seconds since the Epoch (Midnight UTC, January 1, 1970 on systems). |
| strftime(*format*, *timestamp*) | Formats *timestamp* according to the specification in *format*. The *timestamp* should be of the same form as returned by systime(). If *timestamp* is missing, the current time of day is used. See the specification for the strftime() function in C for the format conversions that are guaranteed to be available. A public-domain version of strftime(3) and a man page for it are shipped with gawk; if that version was used to build gawk, then all of the conversions described in that man page are available to gawk. |

## STRING CONSTANTS

String constants in awk are sequences of characters enclosed between double quotes ("). Within strings, certain *escape sequences* are recognized, as in C. These are

| | |
|---|---|
| \\ | A literal backslash. |
| \a | The "alert" character; usually the ASCII BEL character. |
| \b | Backspace. |
| \f | Formfeed. |
| \n | Newline. |

| \r | Carriage return. |
|---|---|
| \t | Horizontal tab. |
| \v | Vertical tab. |
| \xhex digits | The character represented by the string of hexadecimal digits following the \x. As in C, all following hexadecimal digits are considered part of the escape sequence. (This feature should tell us something about language design by committee.) For example, "\x1B" is the ASCII ESC (escape) character. |
| \ddd | The character represented by the 1-, 2-, or 3-digit sequence of octal digits. For example, "\033" is the ASCII ESC (escape) character. |
| \c | The literal character c. |

The escape sequences may also be used inside constant regular expressions (for example, /[\\\t\f\n\r\v]/ matches whitespace characters).

## FUNCTIONS

Functions in awk are defined as follows:

```
function name(parameter list) { statements }
```

Functions are executed when called from within the action parts of regular pattern-action statements. Actual parameters supplied in the function call are used to instantiate the formal parameters declared in the function. Arrays are passed by reference, other variables are passed by value.

Functions were not originally part of the awk language, so the provision for local variables is rather clumsy: They are declared as extra parameters in the parameter list. The convention is to separate local variables from real parameters by extra spaces in the parameter list. For example

```
function f(p, q, a, b) { # a & b are local
..... }
/abc/ { ... ; f(1, 2) ; ... }
```

The left parenthesis in a function call is required to immediately follow the function name, without any intervening whitespace. This is to avoid a syntactic ambiguity with the concatenation operator. This restriction does not apply to the built-in functions listed earlier.

Functions may call each other and may be recursive. Function parameters used as local variables are initialized to the null string and the number zero upon function invocation.

The word func may be used in place of function.

## EXAMPLES

Print and sort the login names of all users:

```
BEGIN { FS = ":" }
{ print $1 j "sort" }
```

Count lines in a file:

```
{ nlines++ }
END { print nlines }
```

Precede each line by its number in the file:

```
{ print FNR, $0 }
```

Concatenate and line number (a variation on a theme):

```
{ print NR, $0 }
```

## SEE ALSO

egrep(1), getpid(2), getppid(2), getpgrp(2), getuid(2), geteuid(2), getgid(2), getegid(2), get-groups(2)

*The AWK Programming Language*, Alfred V. Aho, Brian W. Kernighan, Peter J. Weinberger, Addison-Wesley, 1988. ISBN 0-201-07981-X.

*The GAWK Manual*, Edition 0.15, published by the Free Software Foundation, 1993.

## POSIX COMPATIBILITY

A primary goal for gawk is compatibility with the standard, as well as with the latest version of awk. To this end, gawk incorporates the following user-visible features that are not described in the awk book, but are part of awk in System V Release 4, and are in the standard.

The -v option for assigning variables before program execution starts is new. The book indicates that command-line variable assignment happens when awk would otherwise open the argument as a file, which is after the BEGIN block is executed. However, in earlier implementations, when such an assignment appeared before any filenames, the assignment would happen *before* the BEGIN block was run. Applications came to depend on this "feature." When awk was changed to match its documentation, this option was added to accommodate applications that depended upon the old behavior. (This feature was agreed on by both the AT&T and GNU developers.)

The -W option for implementation-specific features is from the standard.

When processing arguments, gawk uses the special option -- to signal the end of arguments. In compatibility mode, it will warn about, but otherwise ignore, undefined options. In normal operation, such arguments are passed on to the awk program for it to process.

The awk book does not define the return value of srand(). The System V Release 4 version of awk (and the standard) has it return the seed it was using, to allow keeping track of random number sequences. Therefore, srand() in gawk also returns its current seed.

Other new features are: the use of multiple -f options (from MKS awk); the ENVIRON array; the \a, and \v escape sequences (done originally in gawk and fed back into AT&T's version); the tolower() and toupper() built-in functions (from AT&T); and the C conversion specifications in printf (done first in AT&T's version).

## GNU EXTENSIONS

gawk has some extensions to awk. They are described in this section. All the extensions described here can be disabled by invoking gawk with the -W compat option.

The following features of gawk are not available in awk:

The \x escape sequence.

The systime() and strftime() functions.

The special filenames available for I/O redirection are not recognized.

The ARGIND and ERRNO variables are not special.

The IGNORECASE variable and its side effects.

The FIELDWIDTHS variable and fixed width field splitting.

No path search is performed for files named via the -f option. Therefore, the AWKPATH environment variable is not special.

The use of next file to abandon processing of the current input file.

The use of delete *array* to delete the entire contents of an array.

The awk book does not define the return value of the close() function. gawk's close() returns the value from fclose(3), or pclose(3), when closing a file or pipe, respectively.

When gawk is invoked with the -W compat option, if the fs argument to the -F option is t, then FS will be set to the tab character. Since this is a rather ugly special case, it is not the default behavior. This behavior also does not occur if -Wposix has been specified.

## HISTORICAL FEATURES

There are two features of historical awk implementations that gawk supports. First, it is possible to call the length() built-in function not only with no argument, but even without parentheses! Thus, this:

```
a = length
```

is the same as either of these:

```
a = length()
a = length($0)
```

This feature is marked as "deprecated" in the standard, and gawk will issue a warning about its use if -W lint is specified on the command line.

The other feature is the use of either the continue or the break statements outside the body of a while, for, or do loop. Traditional awk implementations have treated such usage as equivalent to the next statement. gawk will support this usage if -W compat has been specified.

## ENVIRONMENT VARIABLES

If POSIXLY_CORRECT exists in the environment, then gawk behaves exactly as if − ·posix had been specified on the command line. If − ·lint has been specified, gawk will issue a warning message to this effect.

## BUGS

The -F option is not necessary given the command-line variable assignment feature; it remains only for backwards compatibility.

If your system actually has support for /dev/fd and the associated /dev/stdin, /dev/stdout, and /dev/stderr files, you may get different output from gawk than you would get on a system without those files. When gawk interprets these files internally, it synchronizes output to the standard output with output to /dev/stdout, while on a system with those files, the output is actually to different open files. Caveat emptor.

## VERSION INFORMATION

This man page documents gawk, version 2.15.

Starting with the 2.15 version of gawk, the -c, -V, -C, -D, -a, and -e options of the 2.11 version are no longer recognized. This fact will not even be documented in the manual page for the next major version.

## AUTHORS

The original version of awk was designed and implemented by Alfred Aho, Peter Weinberger, and Brian Kernighan of AT&T Bell Labs. Brian Kernighan continues to maintain and enhance it.

Paul Rubin and Jay Fenlason, of the Free Software Foundation, wrote gawk, to be compatible with the original version of awk distributed in the seventh edition. John Woods contributed a number of bug fixes. David Trueman, with contributions from Arnold Robbins, made gawk compatible with the new version of awk. Arnold Robbins is the current maintainer.

The initial DOS port was done by Conrad Kwok and Scott Garfinkle. Scott Deifik is the current DOS maintainer. Pat Rankin did the port to VMS, and Michal Jaegermann did the port to the Atari ST. The port to OS/2 was done by Kai Uwe Rommel, with contributions and help from Darrel Hankerson.

## BUG REPORTS

If you find a bug in gawk, please send electronic mail to

bug-gnu-utils@prep.ai.mit.edu,

with a copy to arnold@gnu.ai.mit.edu. Please include your operating system and its revision, the version of gawk, what C compiler you used to compile it, and a test program and data that are as small as possible for reproducing the problem.

Before sending a bug report, please do two things. First, verify that you have the latest version of gawk. Many bugs (usually subtle ones) are fixed at each release, and if yours is out of date, the problem may already have been solved. Second, please read this man page and the reference manual carefully to be sure that what you think is a bug really is, instead of just a quirk in the language.

## ACKNOWLEDGMENTS

Brian Kernighan of Bell Labs provided valuable assistance during testing and debugging.

We thank him.

*Free Software Foundation, 24 November 1994*

# gcal

gcal—Displays month/year calendar sheets, eternal holiday lists for Julian and Gregorian years, and fixed date warning lists—all in a variety of ways.

## SYNOPSIS

gcal [[ *Option...* ][*%Date* ][*@File...* ]] [ *Command* ]

## DESCRIPTION

gcal is a program similar the standard calendar programs BSD-'cal' and calendar.

gcal displays Gregorian calendars, Julian calendars (before September 1752).

If gcal is started without any options or commands, a calendar of the current month is displayed.

If the calendar of a definite year is wanted, the year must be fully specified. For example, gcal 94 displays a year calendar of the year 94, not of the year 1994.

If two arguments are given in the *command* part, the first argument denotes the month and the second argument denotes the year. In case any illegal commands are given running gcal, the program will use internal defaults.

The Gregorian Reformation is assumed to have occurred in 1752 on the 3rd of September. Ten days following that date were eliminated by the reformation, so the calendar for that month is a bit unusual.

## MORE PROGRAM INFORMATION

You get more program information if you start gcal as follows:

```
gcal -h gcal -? gcal –help
resp.,
gcal -hh gcal -?? gcal –long-help[=ARG]j[=?] gcal –usage[=ARG]j[=?]
```

A hypertext file gcal.info containing detailed online information should be available, which you can inspect using your GNU Infobrowser.

## COPYRIGHT

gcal copyright © 1994, 1995, 1996 by Thomas Esken. This software doesn't claim completeness, correctness, or usability. On principle, I will not be liable for any damages or losses (implicit or explicit), which result from using or handling my software. If you use this software, you agree without any exception to this agreement, which binds you legally.

gcal is free software and distributed under the terms of the GNU General Public License; published by the Free Software Foundation; version 2 or (at your option) any later version.

Any suggestions, improvements, extensions, bug reports, donations, proposals for contract work, and so forth are welcome! If you like this tool, I'd appreciate a postcard from you!

```
Enjoy it =8^)
```

## AUTHOR

Thomas Esken (esken@uni-muenster.de)

Im Hagenfeld 84

D-48147 Muenster; Germany

Phone : +49 251 232585

## SEE ALSO

cal(1), calendar(1)

*16 July 1996*

# gcc, g++

gcc, g++ – GNU project C and C++ Compiler (v2.7)

## SYNOPSIS

```
gcc [ option j filename ]. . .
g++ [ option j filename ]...
```

## WARNING

The information in this man page is an extract from the full documentation of the GNU C compiler and is limited to the meaning of the options.

This man page is not kept up-to-date except when volunteers want to maintain it. If you find a discrepancy between the man page and the software, please check the info file, which is the authoritative documentation.

If we find that the things in this man page that are out of date cause significant confusion or complaints, we will stop distributing the man page. The alternative, updating the man page when we update the info file, is impossible because the rest of the work of maintaining GNU CC leaves us no time for that. The GNU project regards man pages as obsolete and should not let them take time away from other things.

For complete and current documentation, refer to the info file gcc or the manual *Using and Porting GNU CC* (for version 2.0). Both are made from the Texinfo source file gcc.texinfo.

## DESCRIPTION

The C and C++ compilers are integrated. Both process input files through one or more of four stages: preprocessing, compilation, assembly, and linking. Source filename suffixes identify the source language, but which name you use for the compiler governs default assumptions:

| | |
|---|---|
| gcc | Assumes preprocessed (.i) files are C and assumes C-style linking. |
| g++ | Assumes preprocessed (.i) files are C++ and assumes C++-style linking. |

Suffixes of source filenames indicate the language and kind of processing to be done:

| | |
|---|---|
| .c | C source; preprocess, compile, assemble |
| .C | C++ source; preprocess, compile, assemble |
| .cc | C++ source; preprocess, compile, assemble |
| .cxx | C++ source; preprocess, compile, assemble |
| .m | Objective-C source; preprocess, compile, assemble |
| .i | Preprocessed C; compile, assemble |
| .ii | Preprocessed C++; compile, assemble |
| .s | Assembler source; assemble |

| .S | Assembler source; preprocess, assemble |
| .h | Preprocessor file; not usually named on command line |

Files with other suffixes are passed to the linker. Common cases include

```
.o Object file
.a Archive file
```

Linking is always the last stage unless you use one of the -c, -S, or -E options to avoid it (or unless compilation errors stop the whole process). For the link stage, all .o files corresponding to source files, -1 libraries, unrecognized filenames (including named .o object files, and .a archives) are passed to the linker in command-line order.

## OPTIONS

Options must be separate: -dr is quite different from -d -r.

Most -f and -W options have two contrary forms: -fname and -fno-name (or -Wname and -Wno-name). Only the nondefault forms are shown here.

Here is a summary of all the options, grouped by type. Explanations are in the following sections.

### Overall Options

```
-c -S -E -o file -pipe -v -x language
```

### Language Options

| | | |
|---|---|---|
| -ansi | -fall-virtual | -fcond-mismatch |
| -fdollars-in-identifiers | -fenum-int-equiv | -fexternal-templates |
| -fno-asm | -fno-builtin | -fno-strict-prototype |
| -fsigned-bitfields | -fsigned-char | -fthis-is-variable |
| -funsigned-bitfields | -funsigned-char | -fwritable-strings |
| -traditional | -traditional-cpp | -trigraphs |

### Warning Options

| | | |
|---|---|---|
| -fsyntax-only | -pedantic | -pedantic-errors |
| -w -W -Wall | -Waggregate-return | -Wcast-align |
| -Wcast-qual | -Wchar-subscript | -Wcomment |
| -Wconversion | -Wenum-clash | -Werror |
| -Wformat | -Wid-clash-len | -Wimplicit |
| -Winline | -Wmissing-prototypes | -Wmissing-declarations |
| -Wnested-externs | -Wno-import | -Wparentheses |
| -Wpointer-arith | -Wredundant-decls | -Wreturn-type |
| -Wshadow | -Wstrict-prototypes | -Wswitch |
| -Wtemplate-debugging | -Wtraditional | -Wtrigraphs |
| -Wuninitialized | -Wunused | -Wwrite-strings |

### Debugging Options

```
-a -dletters -fpretend-float -g -glevel -gcoff -gxcoff -gxcoff+ -gdwarf -gdwarf+ -gstabs -gstabs+ -ggdb -p -pg -save- temps -print-file-name=library -print-libgcc-file-name - print-prog-name=program
```

### Optimization Options

| | | |
|---|---|---|
| -fcaller-saves | -fcse-follow-jumps | -fcse-skip-blocks |
| -fdelayed-branch | -felide-constructors | -fexpensive-optimizations |
| -ffast-math | -ffloat-store | -fforce-addr |
| -fforce-mem | -finline-functions | -fkeep-inline-functions |

```
-fmemorize-lookups          -fno-default-inline       -fno-defer-pop
-fno-function-cse           -fno-inline               -fno-peephole
-fomit-frame-pointer        -frerun-cse-after-loop    -fschedule-insns
-fschedule-insns2           -fstrength-reduce         -fthread-jumps
-funroll-all-loops          -funroll-loops            -O -O2
```

### Preprocessor Options

-A*assertion* -C -dD -dM -dN -D*macro*[=*defn*]-E -H- idirafter *dir* -include *file* -imacros *file* -iprefix *file* -iwithprefix *dir* -M -MD -MM -MMD -nostdinc -P -U*macro* -undef

### Assembler Option

-Wa,*option*

### Linker Options

-l*library* -nostartfiles -nostdlib -static -shared -symbolic -Xlinker*option* -Wl,*option* -u *symbol*

### Directory Options

-B*prefix* -I*dir* -I- -L*dir*

### Target Options

-b machine -V *version*

### Configuration-Dependent Options

#### *M680x0 Options*

-m68000-m68020 -m68020-40-m68030-m68040-m68881 -mbitfield -mc68000 -mc68020 -mfpa -mnobitfield -mrtd -mshort -msoft-float

#### *VAX Options*

-mg -mgnu -munix

#### *SPARC Options*

-mepilogue -mfpu -mhard-float -mno-fpu -mno-epilogue -msoft-float -msparclite -mv8 -msupersparc -mcypress

#### *Convex Options*

-margcount -mc1 -mc2 -mnoargcount

#### *AMD29K Options*

-m29000-m29050 -mbw -mdw -mkernel-registers -mlarge -mnbw -mnodw -msmall -mstack-check -muser-registers

#### *M88K Options*

```
-m88000 -m88100 -m88110      -mbig-pic
-mcheck-zero-division        -mhandle-large-shift
-midentify-revision          -mno-check-zero-division
-mno-ocs-debug-info          -mno-ocs-frame-position
-mno-optimize-arg-area       -mno-serialize-volatile
-mno-underscores             -mocs-debug-info
-mocs-frame-position         -moptimize-arg-area
-mserialize-volatile         -mshort-data-num
-msvr3 -msvr4                -mtrap-large-shift
-muse-div-instruction        -mversion-03.00
-mwarn-passed-structs
```

### RS6000 Options

```
-mfp-in-toc -mno-fop-in-toc
```

### RT Options

```
-mcall-lib-mul            -mfp-arg-in-fpregs        -mfp-arg-in-gregs
-mfull-fp-blocks          -mhc-struct-return        -min-line-mul
-mminimum-fp-blocks                                 -mnohc-struct-return
```

### MIPS Options

```
-mcpu=cpu type -mips2 -mips3                    -mint64 -mlong64
-mlonglong128                   -mmips-as      -mgas          -mrnames
-mno-rnames                     -mgpopt        -mno-gpopt     -mstats
-mno-stats -mmemcpy -mno-memcpy -mno-mips-tfile
-mmips-tfile                    -msoft-float   -mhard-float   -mabicalls
-mno-abicalls -mhalf-pic -mno-half-pic -G num -nocpp
```

### i386 Options

```
-m486 -mno-486 -msoft-float -mno-fp-ret-in-387
```

### HPPA Options

```
-mpa-risc-1-0 -mpa-risc-1-1 -mkernel -mshared-libs - mno-shared-libs -mlong-calls -mdisable-fpregs -mdisable-indexing -mtrailing-colon
```

### i960 Options

```
-mcpu-type
-mnumerics                -msoft-float              -mleaf-procedures
-mno-leaf-procedures      -mtail-call               -mno-tail-call
-mcomplex-addr            -mno-complex-addr         -mcode-align
-mno-code-align           -mic-compat               -mic2.0-compat
-mic3.0-compat            -masm-compat              -mintel-asm
-mstrict-align            -mno-strict-align         -mold-align
-mno-old-align
```

### DEC Alpha Options

```
-mfp-regs -mno fp-regs -mno-soft-float -msoft-float
```

### System V Options

```
-G -Qy -Qn -YP,paths -Ym,dir
```

### Code-Generation Options

```
-fcall-saved-reg -fcall-used-
reg -ffixed-reg -finhibit-
size-directive -fnonnull-
objects -fno-common -fno-ident
-fno-gnu-linker -fpcc-struct-
return -fpic -fPIC -freg-
struct- return -fshared-data -
fshort-enums -fshort-double -
fvolatile -fvolatile-global -
fverbose-asm
```

## OVERALL OPTIONS

-x *language*     Specify explicitly the *language* for the following input files (rather than choosing a default based on the filename suffix). This option applies to all following input files until the next -x option. Possible values of *language* are c, objective-c, c-header, c++, cpp-output, assembler, and assembler-with-cpp.

-x none     Turn off any specification of a language, so that subsequent files are handled according to their filename suffixes (as they are if -x has not been used at all).

If you want only some of the four stages (preprocess, compile, assemble, link), you can use -x (or filename suffixes) to tell gcc where to start, and one of the options -c, -S, or -E to say where gcc is to stop. Note that some combinations (for example, -x cpp-output -E) instruct gcc to do nothing at all.

-c     Compile or assemble the source files, but do not link. The compiler output is an object file corresponding to each source file.

By default, gcc makes the object filename for a source file by replacing the suffix .c, .i, .s, and so on, with .o. Use -o to select another name.

gcc ignores any unrecognized input files (those that do not require compilation or assembly) with the -c option.

-S     Stop after the stage of compilation proper; do not assemble. The output is an assembler code file for each nonassembler input file specified.

By default, gcc makes the assembler filename for a source file by replacing the suffix .c, .i, and so on, with .s. Use -o to select another name.

gcc ignores any input files that don't require compilation.

-E     Stop after the preprocessing stage; do not run the compiler proper. The output is preprocessed source code, which is sent to the standard output.

gcc ignores input files that don't require preprocessing.

-o *file*     Place output in file *file*. This applies regardless to whatever sort of output gcc is producing, whether it be an executable file, an object file, an assembler file, or preprocessed C code.

Since only one output file can be specified, it does not make sense to use -o when compiling more than one input file, unless you are producing an executable file as output.

If you do not specify -o, the default is to put an executable file in a.out, the object file for *source.suffix* in *source.o*, its assembler file in *source.s*, and all preprocessed C source on standard output.

-v     Print (on standard error output) the commands executed to run the stages of compilation. Also print the version number of the compiler driver program and of the preprocessor and the compiler proper.

-pipe     Use pipes rather than temporary files for communication between the various stages of compilation. This fails to work on some systems where the assembler cannot read from a pipe; but the GNU assembler has no trouble.

## LANGUAGE OPTIONS

The following options control the dialect of C that the compiler accepts:

-ansi     Support all ANSI standard C programs.

This turns off certain features of GNU C that are incompatible with ANSI C, such as the asm, inline, and typeof keywords, and predefined macros such as unix and vax that identify the type of system you are using. It also enables the undesirable and rarely used ANSI trigraph feature, and disallows $ as part of identifiers. The alternate keywords __asm__, __extension__, __inline__, and __typeof__ continue to work despite -ansi. You would not want to use them in an ANSI C program, of course, but it is useful to put them in header files that might be included in compilations done with -ansi. Alternate predefined macros such as __unix__ and __vax__ are also available, with or without -ansi.

The -ansi option does not cause non-ANSI programs to be rejected gratuitously. For that, -pedantic is required in addition to -ansi.

The preprocessor predefines a macro __STRICT_ANSI__ when you use the -ansi option. Some header files may notice this macro and refrain from declaring certain functions or defining certain macros that the ANSI standard doesn't call for; this is to avoid interfering with any programs that might use these names for other things.

-fno-asm
Do not recognize asm, inline, or typeof as a keyword. These words may then be used as identifiers. You can use __asm__, __inline__, and __typeof__ instead. -ansi implies -fno-asm.

-fno-builtin
Don't recognize built-in functions that do not begin with two leading underscores. Currently, the functions affected include _exit, abort, abs, alloca, cos, exit, fabs, labs, memcmp, memcpy, sin, sqrt, strcmp, strcpy, and strlen.

The -ansi option prevents alloca and _exit from being built-in functions.

-fno-strict-prototype
Treat a function declaration with no arguments, such as int foo();, as C would treat it—as saying nothing about the number of arguments or their types (C++ only). Normally, such a declaration in C++ means that the function foo takes no arguments.

-trigraphs
Support ANSI C trigraphs. The -ansi option implies -trigraphs.

-traditional
Attempt to support some aspects of traditional C compilers. For details, see the *GNU C Manual*; the duplicate list here has been deleted so that we won't get complaints when it is out of date.

But one note about C++ programs only (not C). -traditional has one additional effect for C++: assignment to this is permitted. This is the same as the effect of -fthis-is-variable.

-traditional-cpp
Attempt to support some aspects of traditional C preprocessors. This includes the items that specifically mention the preprocessor previously, but none of the other effects of -traditional.

-fdollars-in-identifiers
Permit the use of $ in identifiers (C++ only). You can also use -fno-dollars-in-identifiers to explicitly prohibit use of $. (GNU C++ allows $ by default on some target systems but not others.)

-fenum-int-equiv
Permit implicit conversion of int to enumeration types (C++ only). Normally GNU C++ allows conversion of enum to int, but not the other way around.

-fexternal-templates
Produce smaller code for template declarations, by generating only a single copy of each template function where it is defined (C++ only). To use this option successfully, you must also mark all files that use templates with either #pragma implementation (the definition) or #pragma interface (declarations).

When your code is compiled with -fexternal-templates, all template instantiations are external. You must arrange for all necessary instantiations to appear in the implementation file; you can do this with a typedef that references each instantiation needed. Conversely, when you compile using the default option -fno-external-templates, all template instantiations are explicitly internal.

-fall-virtual
Treat all possible member functions as virtual, implicitly. All member functions (except for constructor functions and new or delete member operators) are treated as virtual functions of the class where they appear. This does not mean that all calls to these member functions will be made through the internal table of virtual functions. Under some circumstances, the compiler can determine that a call to a given virtual function can be made directly; in these cases, the calls are direct in any case.

-fcond-mismatch
Allow conditional expressions with mismatched types in the second and third arguments. The value of such an expression is void.

-fthis-is-variable
Permit assignment to this (C++ only). The incorporation of user-defined free store management into C++ has made assignment to this an anachronism. Therefore, by default it is invalid to assign to this within a class member function. However, for backwards compatibility, you can make it valid with -fthis-is-variable.

-funsigned-char
Let the type char be unsigned, like unsigned char.

Each kind of machine has a default for what char should be. It is either like unsigned char by default or like signed char by default.

Ideally, a portable program should always use signed char or unsigned char when it depends on the signedness of an object. But many programs have been written to use plain char and expect it to be signed, or expect it to be unsigned, depending on the machines they were written for. This option, and its inverse, lets you make such a program work with the opposite default.

The type char is always a distinct type from each of signed char and unsigned char, even though its behavior is always just like one of those two.

-fsigned-char

Let the type char be signed, like signed char.

Note that this is equivalent to -fno-unsigned-char, which is the negative form of -funsigned-char. Likewise, -fno-signed-char is equivalent to -funsigned-char.

-fsigned-bitfields
-funsigned-bitfields

These options control whether a bitfield is signed or unsigned, when declared with no explicit or unsigned qualifier.

-fno-signed-bitfields

By default, such a bitfield is signed, because this is consistent: The basic integer types such as int

-fno-unsigned-bitfields

signed are signed types.

However, when you specify -traditional, bitfields are all unsigned no matter what.

-fwritable-strings

Store string constants in the writable data segment and don't uniquize them. This is for compatibility with old programs which assume they can write into string constants. -traditional also has this effect.

Writing into string constants is a very bad idea; constants should be constant.

## PREPROCESSOR OPTIONS

These options control the C preprocessor, which is run on each C source file before actual compilation.

If you use the -E option, gcc does nothing except preprocessing. Some of these options make sense only together with -E because they cause the preprocessor output to be unsuitable for actual compilation.

-include *file*

Process *file* as input before processing the regular input file. In effect, the contents of *file* are compiled first. Any -D and -U options on the command line are always processed before -include *file*, regardless of the order in which they are written. All the -include and -imacros options are processed in the order in which they are written.

-imacros *file*

Process *file* as input, discarding the resulting output, before processing the regular input file. Because the output generated from *file* is discarded, the only effect of -imacros *file* is to make the macros defined in *file* available for use in the main input. The preprocessor evaluates any -D and -U options on the command line before processing -imacros *file*, regardless of the order in which they are written. All the -include and -imacros options are processed in the order in which they are written.

-idirafter *dir*

Add the directory *dir* to the second include path. The directories on the second include path are searched when a header file is not found in any of the directories in the main include path (the one that -I adds to).

-iprefix *prefix*

Specify *prefix* as the prefix for subsequent -iwithprefix options.

-iwithprefix *dir*

Add a directory to the second include path. The directory's name is made by concatenating *prefix* and *dir,* where *prefix* was specified previously with -iprefix.

-nostdinc

Do not search the standard system directories for header files. Only the directories you have specified with -I options (and the current directory, if appropriate) are searched.

By using both -nostdinc and -I-, you can limit the include file search file to only those directories you specify explicitly.

-nostdinc++

Do not search for header files in the C++–specific standard directories, but do still search the other standard directories. (This option is used when building libg++.)

-undef

Do not predefine any nonstandard macros (including architecture flags).

-E

Run only the C preprocessor. Preprocess all the C source files specified and output the results to standard output or to the specified output file.

-C

Tell the preprocessor not to discard comments. Used with the -E option.

| | |
|---|---|
| -P | Tell the preprocessor not to generate #line commands. Used with the -E option. |
| -M [-MG] | Tell the preprocessor to output a rule suitable for make describing the dependencies of each object file. For each source file, the preprocessor outputs one make -rule whose target is the object filename for that source file and whose dependencies are all the files that have been included with #include. This rule may be a single line or may be continued with \-newline if it is long. The list of rules is printed on standard output instead of the preprocessed C program. -M implies -E. |
| | -MG says to treat missing header files as generated files and assume they live in the same directory as the source file. It must be specified in addition to -M. |
| -MM [-MG] | Like -M but the output mentions only the user header files included with #include " *file* ". System header files included with #include < *file* > are omitted. |
| -MD | Like -M but the dependency information is written to files with names made by replacing .o with .d at the end of the output filenames. This is in addition to compiling the file as specified; -MD does not inhibit ordinary compilation the way -M does. |
| | The Mach utility md can be used to merge the .d files into a single dependency file suitable for using with the make command. |
| -MMD | Like -MD except mention only user header files, not system header files. |
| -H | Print the name of each header file used, in addition to other normal activities. |
| -Aquestion(answer) | Assert the answer *answer* for *question,* in case it is tested with a preprocessor conditional such as #if #question(answer). -A- disables the standard assertions that normally describe the target machine. |
| -Aquestion ( answer ) | Assert the answer *answer* for *question,* in case it is tested with a preprocessor conditional such as #if # question ( answer ). -A-disables the standard assertions that normally describe the target machine. |
| -Dmacro | Define macro *macro* with the string 1 as its definition. |
| -Dmacro=defn | Define macro *macro* as *defn*. All instances of -D on the command line are processed before any -U options. |
| -Umacro | Undefine macro *macro*. -U options are evaluated after all -D options, but before any -include and -imacros options. |
| -dM | Tell the preprocessor to output only a list of the macro definitions that are in effect at the end of preprocessing. Used with the -E option. |
| -dD | Tell the preprocessor to pass all macro definitions into the output, in their proper sequence in the rest of the output. |
| -dN | Like -dD except that the macro arguments and contents are omitted. Only #define *name* is included in the output. |

## ASSEMBLER OPTION

| | |
|---|---|
| -Wa,option | Pass *option* as an option to the assembler. If *option* contains commas, it is split into multiple options at the commas. |

## LINKER OPTIONS

These options come into play when the compiler links object files into an executable output file. They are meaningless if the compiler is not doing a link step.

| | |
|---|---|
| object-file-name | A filename that does not end in a special recognized suffix is considered to name an object file or library. (Object files are distinguished from libraries by the linker according to the file contents.) If gcc does a link step, these object files are used as input to the linker. |
| -llibrary | Use the library named *library* when linking. |
| | The linker searches a standard list of directories for the library, which is actually a file named lib *library*.a. The linker then uses this file as if it had been specified precisely by name. |

The directories searched include several standard system directories plus any that you specify with -L.

Normally, the files found this way are library files—archive files whose members are object files. The linker handles an archive file by scanning through it for members that define symbols that have so far been referenced but not defined. However, if the linker finds an ordinary object file rather than a library, the object file is linked in the usual fashion. The only difference between using an -l option and specifying a filename is that -l surrounds *library* with lib and .a and searches several directories.

| | |
|---|---|
| -lobjc | You need this special case of the -l option in order to link an Objective C program. |
| -nostartfiles | Do not use the standard system startup files when linking. The standard libraries are used normally. |
| -nostdlib | Don't use the standard system libraries and startup files when linking. Only the files you specify will be passed to the linker. |
| -static | On systems that support dynamic linking, this prevents linking with the shared libraries. On other systems, this option has no effect. |
| -shared | Produce a shared object which can then be linked with other objects to form an executable. Only a few systems support this option. |
| -symbolic | Bind references to global symbols when building a shared object. Warn about any unresolved references (unless overridden by the link editor option -Xlinker -z -Xlinker defs). Only a few systems support this option. |
| -Xlinker option | Pass option as an option to the linker. You can use this to supply system-specific linker options which GNU CC does not know how to recognize. |
| | If you want to pass an option that takes an argument, you must use -Xlinker twice: once for the option and once for the argument. For example, to pass -assert definitions, you must write -Xlinker -assert -Xlinker definitions. It does not work to write -Xlinker "-assert definitions", because this passes the entire string as a single argument, which is not what the linker expects. |
| -Wl,option | Pass option as an option to the linker. If option contains commas, it is split into multiple options at the commas. |
| -u symbol | Pretend the symbol symbol is undefined, to force linking of library modules to define it. You can use -u multiple times with different symbols to force loading of additional library modules. |

## DIRECTORY OPTIONS

These options specify directories to search for header files, for libraries, and for parts of the compiler:

| | |
|---|---|
| -Idir | Append directory dir to the list of directories searched for include files. |
| -I- | Any directories you specify with -I options before the -I- option are searched only for the case of #include "file"; they are not searched for #include <file>. |
| | If additional directories are specified with -I options after the -I-, these directories are searched for all #include directives. (Ordinarily *all* -I directories are used this way.) |
| | In addition, the -I- option inhibits the use of the current directory (where the current input file came from) as the first search directory for #include " file ". There is no way to override this effect of -I-. With -I. you can specify searching the directory that was current when the compiler was invoked. That is not exactly the same as what the preprocessor does by default, but it is often satisfactory. |
| | -I- does not inhibit the use of the standard system directories for header files. Thus, -I- and -nostdinc are independent. |
| -Ldir | Add directory dir to the list of directories to be searched for -l. |
| -Bprefix | This option specifies where to find the executables, libraries, and data files of the compiler itself. |
| | The compiler driver program runs one or more of the subprograms cpp, cc1 (or, for C++, cc1plus), as, and ld. It tries prefix as a prefix for each program it tries to run, both with and without *machine* / *version* /. |

For each subprogram to be run, the compiler driver first tries the -B prefix, if any. If that name is not found, or if -B was not specified, the driver tries two standard prefixes, which are /usr/lib/gcc/ and /usr/local/lib/gcc-lib/. If neither of those results in a filename that is found, the compiler driver searches for the unmodified program name, using the directories specified in your PATH environment variable.

The runtime support file libgcc.a is also searched for using the -B prefix, if needed. If it is not found there, the two standard prefixes (preceding paragraph) are tried, and that is all. The file is left out of the link if it is not found by those means. Most of the time, on most machines, libgcc.a is not actually necessary.

You can get a similar result from the environment variable GCC_EXEC_PREFIX; if it is defined, its value is used as a prefix in the same way. If both the -B option and the GCC_EXEC_PREFIX variable are present, the -B option is used first and the environment variable value second.

# WARNING OPTIONS

Warnings are diagnostic messages that report constructions that are not inherently erroneous but are risky or suggest there may have been an error.

These options control the amount and kinds of warnings produced by GNU CC:

| | |
|---|---|
| -fsyntax-only | Check the code for syntax errors, but don't emit any output. |
| -w | Inhibit all warning messages. |
| -Wno-import | Inhibit warning messages about the use of #import. |
| -pedantic | Issue all the warnings demanded by strict ANSI standard C; reject all programs that use forbidden extensions. |

Valid ANSI standard C programs should compile properly with or without this option (though a rare few will require -ansi). However, without this option, certain GNU extensions and traditional C features are supported as well. With this option, they are rejected. There is no reason to use this option; it exists only to satisfy pedants.

-pedantic does not cause warning messages for use of the alternate keywords whose names begin and end with '__'. Pedantic warnings are also disabled in the expression that follows extension. However, only system header files should use these escape routes; application programs should avoid them.

| | |
|---|---|
| -pedantic-errors | Like -pedantic, except that errors are produced rather than warnings. |
| -W | Print extra warning messages for these events: |

A nonvolatile automatic variable might be changed by a call to longjmp. These warnings are possible only in optimizing compilation. The compiler sees only the calls to setjmp. It cannot know where longjmp will be called; in fact, a signal handler could call it at any point in the code. As a result, you may get a warning even when there is in fact no problem because longjmp cannot in fact be called at the place which would cause a problem.

A function can return either with or without a value. (Falling off the end of the function body is considered returning without a value.) For example, this function would evoke such a warning:

```
foo (a)
{
if (a > 0)
return a;
}
```

Spurious warnings can occur because GNU CC does not realize that certain functions (including abort and longjmp) will never return.

An expression-statement or the left side of a comma expression contains no side effects. To suppress the warning, cast the unused expression to void. For example, an expression such as x[i,j] will cause a warning, but x[(void)i,j] will not.

An unsigned value is compared against zero with > or <=.

| | |
|---|---|
| `-Wimplicit` | Warn whenever a function or parameter is implicitly declared. |
| `-Wreturn-type` | Warn whenever a function is defined with a return-type that defaults to int. Also warn about any return statement with no return-value in a function whose return-type is not void. |
| `-Wunused` | Warn whenever a local variable is unused aside from its declaration, whenever a function is declared static but never defined, and whenever a statement computes a result that is explicitly not used. |
| `-Wswitch` | Warn whenever a switch statement has an index of enumeral type and lacks a case for one or more of the named codes of that enumeration. (The presence of a default label prevents this warning.) case labels outside the enumeration range also provoke warnings when this option is used. |
| `-Wcomment` | Warn whenever a comment-start sequence / appears in a comment. |
| `-Wtrigraphs` | Warn if any trigraphs are encountered (assuming they are enabled). |
| `-Wformat` | Check calls to printf and scanf, and so on, to make sure that the arguments supplied have types appropriate to the format string specified. |
| `-Wchar-subscripts` | Warn if an array subscript has type char. This is a common cause of error, as programmers often forget that this type is signed on some machines. |
| `-Wuninitialized` | An automatic variable is used without first being initialized. |

These warnings are possible only in optimizing compilation, because they require data flow information that is computed only when optimizing. If you don't specify -0, you simply won't get these warnings.

These warnings occur only for variables that are candidates for register allocation. Therefore, they do not occur for a variable that is declared volatile, or whose address is taken, or whose size is other than 1, 2, 4, or 8 bytes. Also, they do not occur for structures, unions, or arrays, even when they are in registers.

Note that there may be no warning about a variable that is used only to compute a value that itself is never used, because such computations may be deleted by data flow analysis before the warnings are printed.

These warnings are made optional because GNU CC is not smart enough to see all the reasons why the code might be correct despite appearing to have an error. Here is one example of how this can happen:

```
{
int x;
switch (y)
{
case 1: x = 1;
break;
case 2: x = 4;
break;
case 3: x = 5;
}
foo (x);
}
```

If the value of y is always 1, 2, or 3, then x is always initialized, but GNU CC doesn't know this. Here is another common case:

```
{
int save_y;
if (change_y) save_y =y,y =new_y;
...
if (change_y)y =save_y;
}
```

This has no bug because save_y is used only if it is set.

Some spurious warnings can be avoided if you declare as volatile all the functions you use that never return.

| | |
|---|---|
| -Wparentheses | Warn if parentheses are omitted in certain contexts. |
| -Wtemplate-debugging | When using templates in a C++ program, warn if debugging is not yet fully available (C++ only). |
| -Wall | All of the preceding -W options combined. These are all the options that pertain to usage that we recommend avoiding and that we believe is easy to avoid, even in conjunction with macros. |

The remaining -W... options are not implied by -Wall because they warn about constructions that we consider reasonable to use, on occasion, in clean programs.

| | |
|---|---|
| -Wtraditional | Warn about certain constructs that behave differently in traditional and ANSI C: |
| | Macro arguments occurring within string constants in the macro body. These would substitute the argument in traditional C, but are part of the constant in ANSI C. |
| | A function declared external in one block and then used after the end of the block. |
| | A switch statement has an operand of type long. |
| -Wshadow | Warn whenever a local variable shadows another local variable. |
| -Wid-clash-*len* | Warn whenever two distinct identifiers match in the first *len* characters. This may help you prepare a program that will compile with certain obsolete, brain-damaged compilers. |
| -Wpointer-arith | Warn about anything that depends on the size of a function type or of void. GNU C assigns these types a size of 1, for convenience in calculations with void pointers and pointers to functions. |
| -Wcast-qual | Warn whenever a pointer is cast so as to remove a type qualifier from the target type. For example, warn if a const char is cast to an ordinary char. |
| -Wcast-align | Warn whenever a pointer is cast such that the required alignment of the target is increased. For example, warn if a char is cast to an int on machines where integers can only be accessed at two- or four-byte boundaries. |
| -Wwrite-strings | Give string constants the type const char[ *length* ] so that copying the address of one into a non-const char pointer will get a warning. These warnings will help you find at compile time code that can try to write into a string constant, but only if you have been very careful about using const in declarations and prototypes. Otherwise, it will just be a nuisance; this is why we did not make -Wall request these warnings. |
| -Wconversion | Warn if a prototype causes a type conversion that is different from what would happen to the same argument in the absence of a prototype. This includes conversions of fixed point to floating and vice versa, and conversions changing the width or signedness of a fixed point argument except when the same as the default promotion. |
| -Waggregate-return | Warn if any functions that return structures or unions are defined or called. (In languages where you can return an array, this also elicits a warning.) |
| -Wstrict-prototypes | Warn if a function is declared or defined without specifying the argument types. (An old-style function definition is permitted without a warning if preceded by a declaration which specifies the argument types.) |
| -Wmissing-prototypes | Warn if a global function is defined without a previous prototype declaration. This warning is issued even if the definition itself provides a prototype. The aim is to detect global functions that fail to be declared in header files. |
| -Wmissing-declarations | Warn if a global function is defined without a previous declaration. Do so even if the definition itself provides a prototype. Use this option to detect global functions that are not declared in header files. |
| -Wredundant-decls | Warn if anything is declared more than once in the same scope, even in cases where multiple declaration is valid and changes nothing. |
| -Wnested-externs | Warn if an extern declaration is encountered within an function. |
| -Wenum-clash | Warn about conversion between different enumeration types (C++ only). |
| -Woverloaded-virtual | (C++ only.) In a derived class, the definitions of virtual functions must match the type signature of a virtual function declared in the base class. Use this option to request warnings when a derived class declares a function that may be an erroneous attempt to define a virtual function; |

that is, warn when there is a function with the same name as a virtual function in the base class, but with a type signature that doesn't match any virtual functions from the base class.

-Winline                Warn if a function cannot be inlined, and either it was declared as inline, or else the `-finline-functions` option was given.

-Werror                 Treat warnings as errors; abort compilation after any warning.

## DEBUGGING OPTIONS

GNU CC has various special options that are used for debugging either your program or gcc:

-g                      Produce debugging information in the operating system's native format (stabs, COFF, XCOFF, or DWARF). GDB (the GNU debugger) can work with this debugging information.

On most systems that use stabs format, -g enables use of extra debugging information that only GDB can use; this extra information makes debugging work better in GDB but will probably make other debuggers crash or refuse to read the program. If you want to control for certain whether to generate the extra information, use -gstabs, -gstabs, -gxcoff+, -gxcoff, -gdwarf+, or -gdwarf.

Unlike most other C compilers, GNU CC allows you to use -g with -O. The shortcuts taken by optimized code may occasionally produce surprising results: Some variables you declared may not exist at all; flow of control may briefly move where you did not expect it; some statements may not be executed because they compute constant results or their values were already at hand; some statements may execute in different places because they were moved out of loops.

Nevertheless, it proves possible to debug optimized output. This makes it reasonable to use the optimizer for programs that might have bugs.

The following options are useful when GNU CC is generated with the capability for more than one debugging format.

-ggdb                   Produce debugging information in the native format (if that is supported), including GDB extensions if at all possible.

-gstabs                 Produce debugging information in stabs format (if that is supported), without GDB extensions. This is the format used by DBX on most BSD systems.

-gstabs+                Produce debugging information in stabs format (if that is supported), using GNU extensions understood only by the GNU debugger (GDB). The use of these extensions is likely to make other debuggers crash or refuse to read the program.

-gcoff                  Produce debugging information in COFF format (if that is supported). This is the format used by SDB on most System V systems prior to System V Release 4.

-gxcoff                 Produce debugging information in XCOFF format (if that is supported). This is the format used by the DBX debugger on IBM RS/6000 systems.

-gxcoff+                Produce debugging information in XCOFF format (if that is supported), using GNU extensions understood only by the GNU debugger (GDB). The use of these extensions is likely to make other debuggers crash or refuse to read the program.

-gdwarf                 Produce debugging information in DWARF format (if that is supported). This is the format used by SDB on most System V Release 4 systems.

-gdwarf+                Produce debugging information in DWARF format (if that is supported), using GNU extensions understood only by the GNU debugger (GDB). The use of these extensions is likely to make other debuggers crash or refuse to read the program.

```
-glevel
-ggdblevel
-gstabslevel
-gcofflevel -gxcofflevel
```

-gdwarf*level*          Request debugging information and also use *level* to specify how much information. The default level is 2.

Level 1 produces minimal information, enough for making backtraces in parts of the program that you don't plan to debug. This includes descriptions of functions and external variables, but no information about local variables and no line numbers.

Level 3 includes extra information, such as all the macro definitions present in the program. Some debuggers support macro expansion when you use -g3.

| | |
|---|---|
| -p | Generate extra code to write profile information suitable for the analysis program prof. |
| -pg | Generate extra code to write profile information suitable for the analysis program gprof. |
| -a | Generate extra code to write profile information for basic blocks, which will record the number of times each basic block is executed. This data could be analyzed by a program like tcov. Note, however, that the format of the data is not what tcov expects. Eventually, GNU gprof should be extended to process this data. |
| -d*letters* | Says to make debugging dumps during compilation at times specified by *letters*. This is used for debugging the compiler. The filenames for most of the dumps are made by appending a word to the source filename (for example, foo.c.rtl or foo.c.jump). |
| -dM | Dump all macro definitions at the end of preprocessing, and write no output. |
| -dN | Dump all macro names, at the end of preprocessing. |
| -dD | Dump all macro definitions at the end of preprocessing, in addition to normal output. |
| -dy | Dump debugging information during parsing, to standard error. |
| -dr | Dump after RTL generation, to *file*.rtl. |
| -dx | Just generate RTL for a function instead of compiling it. Usually used with r. |
| -dj | Dump after first jump optimization, to *file* .jump. |
| -ds | Dump after CSE (including the jump optimization that sometimes follows CSE), to *file* .cse. |
| -dL | Dump after loop optimization, to *file* .loop. |
| -dt | Dump after the second CSE pass (including the jump optimization that sometimes follows CSE), to *file* .cse2. |
| -df | Dump after flow analysis, to *file* .flow. |
| -dc | Dump after instruction combination, to *file* .combine. |
| -dS | Dump after the first instruction scheduling pass, to *file* .sched. |
| -dl | Dump after local register allocation, to *file* .lreg. |
| -dg | Dump after global register allocation, to *file* .greg. |
| -dR | Dump after the second instruction scheduling pass, to *file* .sched2. |
| -dJ | Dump after last jump optimization, to *file* .jump2. |
| -dd | Dump after delayed branch scheduling, to *file* .dbr. |
| -dk | Dump after conversion from registers to stack, to *file* .stack. |
| -da | Produce all the dumps listed previously. |
| -dm | Print statistics on memory usage, at the end of the run, to standard error. |
| -dp | Annotate the assembler output with a comment indicating which pattern and alternative was used. |
| -fpretend-float | When running a cross-compiler, pretend that the target machine uses the same floating-point format as the host machine. This causes incorrect output of the actual floating constants, but the actual instruction sequence will probably be the same as GNU CC would make when running on the target machine. |
| -save-temps | Store the usual temporary intermediate files permanently; place them in the current directory and name them based on the source file. Thus, compiling foo.c with -c -save-temps would produce files foo.cpp and foo.s, as well as foo.o. |
| -print-file-name=*library* | Print the full absolute name of the library file *library* would be used when linking, and do not do anything else. With this option, GNU CC does not compile or link anything; it just prints the filename. |
| -print-libgcc-file-name | Same as —print-file-name=libgcc.a. |
| -print-prog-name=*program* | Like -print-file-name, but searches for a program such as cpp. |

## OPTIMIZATION OPTIONS

These options control various sorts of optimizations:

| | |
|---|---|
| -O, -O1 | Optimize. Optimizing compilation takes somewhat more time, and a lot more memory for a large function. |

Without -O, the compiler's goal is to reduce the cost of compilation and to make debugging produce the expected results. Statements are independent: If you stop the program with a breakpoint between statements, you can then assign a new value to any variable or change the program counter to any other statement in the function and get exactly the results you would expect from the source code.

Without -O, only variables declared register are allocated in registers. The resulting compiled code is a little worse than produced by PCC without -O.

With -O, the compiler tries to reduce code size and execution time.

When you specify -O, the two options -fthread-jumps and -fdefer-pop are turned on. On machines that have delay slots, the -fdelayed-branch option is turned on. For those machines that can support debugging even without a frame pointer, the -fomit-frame-pointer option is turned on. On some machines other flags may also be turned on.

| | |
|---|---|
| -O2 | Optimize even more. Nearly all supported optimizations that do not involve a space-speed tradeoff are performed. Loop unrolling and function inlining are not done, for example. As compared to -O, this option increases both compilation time and the performance of the generated code. |
| -O3 | Optimize yet more. This turns on everything -O2 does, along with also turning on -finline-functions. |
| -O0 | Do not optimize. |

If you use multiple -O options, with or without level numbers, the last such option is the one that is effective.

Options of the form -f *flag* specify machine-independent flags. Most flags have both positive and negative forms; the negative form of -ffoo would be -fno-foo. The following list shows only one form—the one which is not the default. You can figure out the other form by either removing no- or adding it.

| | |
|---|---|
| -ffloat-store | Do not store floating-point variables in registers. This prevents undesirable excess precision on machines such as the 68000 where the floating registers (of the 68881) keep more precision than a double is supposed to have. |

For most programs, the excess precision does only good, but a few programs rely on the precise definition of IEEE floating point. Use -ffloat-store for such programs.

| | |
|---|---|
| -fmemorize-lookups<br>-fsave-memorized | Use heuristics to compile faster (C++ only). These heuristics are not enabled by default, since they are only effective for certain input files. Other input files compile more slowly. |

The first time the compiler must build a call to a member function (or reference to a data member), it must (1) determine whether the class implements member functions of that name; (2) resolve which member function to call (which involves figuring out what sorts of type conversions need to be made); and (3) check the visibility of the member function to the caller. All of this adds up to slower compilation. Normally, the second time a call is made to that member function (or reference to that data member), it must go through the same lengthy process again. This means that code like this:

```
cout << "This " << p << "has"<< \ << " legs.\n"
```

makes six passes through all three steps. By using a software cache, a hit significantly reduces this cost. Unfortunately, using the cache introduces another layer of mechanisms which must be implemented, and so incurs its own overhead. -fmemorize- lookups enables the software cache.

Because access privileges (visibility) to members and member functions may differ from one function context to the next, g++ may need to flush the cache. With the -fmemorize-lookups flag, the cache is flushed after every function that is compiled. The -fsave-memorized flag enables the same software cache, but when the compiler determines that the context of the last function compiled would yield the same access privileges of the next function to compile, it preserves the cache. This is most helpful when defining many member functions for the same class: with the exception of member functions which are friends of other classes, each member function has exactly the same access privileges as every other, and the cache need not be flushed.

-fno-default-inline

Don't make member functions inline by default merely because they are defined inside the class scope (C++ only).

-fno-defer-pop

Always pop the arguments to each function call as soon as that function returns. For machines which must pop arguments after a function call, the compiler normally lets arguments accumulate on the stack for several function calls and pops them all at once.

-fforce-mem

Force memory operands to be copied into registers before doing arithmetic on them. This may produce better code by making all memory references potential common subexpressions. When they are not common subexpressions, instruction combination should eliminate the separate register-load. I am interested in hearing about the difference this makes.

-fforce-addr

Force memory address constants to be copied into registers before doing arithmetic on them. This may produce better code just as -fforce-mem may. I am interested in hearing about the difference this makes.

-fomit-frame-pointer

Don't keep the frame pointer in a register for functions that don't need one. This avoids the instructions to save, set up and restore frame pointers; it also makes an extra register available in many functions. It also makes debugging impossible on most machines.

On some machines, such as the VAX, this flag has no effect because the standard calling sequence automatically handles the frame pointer and nothing is saved by pretending it doesn't exist. The machine-description macro FRAME_POINTER_REQUIRED controls whether a target machine supports this flag.

-finline-functions

Integrate all simple functions into their callers. The compiler heuristically decides which functions are simple enough to be worth integrating in this way.

If all calls to a given function are integrated, and the function is declared static, then gcc normally does not output the function as assembler code in its own right.

-fcaller-saves

Enable values to be allocated in registers that will be clobbered by function calls, by emitting extra instructions to save and restore the registers around such calls. Such allocation is done only when it seems to result in better code than would otherwise be produced.

This option is enabled by default on certain machines, usually those which have no call preserved registers to use instead.

-fkeep-inline-functions

Even if all calls to a given function are integrated, and the function is declared static, nevertheless output a separate runtime callable version of the function.

-fno-function-cse

Do not put function addresses in registers; make each instruction that calls a constant function contain the function's address explicitly.

This option results in less efficient code, but some strange hacks that alter the assembler output may be confused by the optimizations performed when this option is not used.

-fno-peephole

Disable any machine-specific peephole optimizations.

-ffast-math

This option allows gcc to violate some ANSI or IEEE specifications in the interest of optimizing code for speed. For example, it allows the compiler to assume arguments to the sqrt function are nonnegative numbers.

This option should never be turned on by any -O option because it can result in incorrect output for programs which depend on an exact implementation of IEEE or ANSI rules/ specifications for math functions.

The following options control specific optimizations. The -O2 option turns on all of these optimizations except -funroll-loops and -funroll-all-loops.

The -O option usually turns on the -fthread-jumps and -fdelayed-branch options, but specific machines may change the default optimizations.

You can use the following flags in the rare cases when fine-tuning of optimizations to be performed is desired:

| | |
|---|---|
| `-fstrength-reduce` | Perform the optimizations of loop strength reduction and elimination of iteration variables. |
| `-fthread-jumps` | Perform optimizations where we check to see if a jump branches to a location where another comparison subsumed by the first is found. If so, the first branch is redirected to either the destination of the second branch or a point immediately following it, depending on whether the condition is known to be true or false. |
| `-funroll-loops` | Perform the optimization of loop unrolling. This is only done for loops whose number of iterations can be determined at compile time or runtime. |
| `-funroll-all-loops` | Perform the optimization of loop unrolling. This is done for all loops. This usually makes programs run more slowly. |
| `-fcse-follow-jumps` | In common subexpression elimination, scan through jump instructions when the target of the jump is not reached by any other path. For example, when CSE encounters an `if` statement with an `else` clause, CSE will follow the jump when the condition tested is false. |
| `-fcse-skip-blocks` | This is similar to `-fcse-follow-jumps`, but causes CSE to follow jumps which conditionally skip over blocks. When CSE encounters a simple `if` statement with no `else` clause, `-fcse-skip-blocks` causes CSE to follow the jump around the body of the `if`. |
| `-frerun-cse-after-loop` | Rerun common subexpression elimination after loop optimizations has been performed. |
| `-felide-constructors` | Elide constructors when this seems plausible (C++ only). With this flag, GNU C++ initializes y directly from the call to `foo` without going through a temporary in the following code: A foo (); A y = foo (); Without this option, GNU C++ first initializes y by calling the appropriate constructor for type A; then assigns the result of `foo` to a temporary; and, finally, replaces the initial value of y with the temporary. The default behavior (`-fno-elide-constructors`) is specified by the draft ANSI C++ standard. If your program's constructors have side effects, using `-felide-constructors` can make your program act differently, since some constructor calls may be omitted. |
| `-fexpensive-optimizations` | Perform a number of minor optimizations that are relatively expensive. |
| `-fdelayed-branch` | If supported for the target machine, attempt to reorder instructions to exploit instruction slots available after delayed branch instructions. |
| `-fschedule-insns` | If supported for the target machine, attempt to reorder instructions to eliminate execution stalls due to required data being unavailable. This helps machines that have slow floating point or memory load instructions by allowing other instructions to be issued until the result of the load or floating point instruction is required. |
| `-fschedule-insns2` | Similar to `-fschedule-insns`, but requests an additional pass of instruction scheduling after register allocation has been done. This is especially useful on machines with a relatively small number of registers and where memory load instructions take more than one cycle. |

## TARGET OPTIONS

By default, GNU CC compiles code for the same type of machine that you are using.

However, it can also be installed as a cross-compiler, to compile for some other type of machine. In fact, several different configurations of GNU CC, for different target machines, can be installed side by side. Then you specify which one to use with the -b option.

In addition, older and newer versions of GNU CC can be installed side by side. One of them (probably the newest) will be the default, but you may sometimes want to use another.

| | |
|---|---|
| `-b` *machine* | The argument *machine* specifies the target machine for compilation. This is useful when you have installed GNU CC as a cross-compiler. The value to use for *machine* is the same as was specified as the machine type when configuring GNU CC as a cross-compiler. For example, if a cross-compiler was configured with `configure` |

i386v, meaning to compile for an 80386 running System V, then you would specify -b i386v to run that cross compiler.

When you do not specify -b, it normally means to compile for the same type of machine that you are using.

-V version  The argument *version* specifies which version of GNU CC to run. This is useful when multiple versions are installed. For example, *version* might be 2.0, meaning to run GNU CC version 2.0.

The default version, when you do not specify -V, is controlled by the way GNU CC is installed. Normally, it will be a version that is recommended for general use.

## MACHINE-DEPENDENT OPTIONS

Each of the target machine types can have its own special options, starting with -m, to choose among various hardware models or configurations—for example, 68010 versus 68020, floating coprocessor or none. A single installed version of the compiler can compile for any model or configuration, according to the options specified.

Some configurations of the compiler also support additional special options, usually for command-line compatibility with other compilers on the same platform.

These are the -m options defined for the 68000 series:

-m68000  
-mc68000  Generate output for a 68000. This is the default when the compiler is configured for 68000-based systems.

-m68020  
-mc68020  Generate output for a 68020 (rather than a 68000). This is the default when the compiler is configured for 68020-based systems.

-m68881  Generate output containing 68881 instructions for floating point. This is the default for most 68020-based systems unless -nfp was specified when the compiler was configured.

-m68030  Generate output for a 68030. This is the default when the compiler is configured for 68030-based systems.

-m68040  Generate output for a 68040. This is the default when the compiler is configured for 68040-based systems.

-m68020-40  Generate output for a 68040, without using any of the new instructions. This results in code which can run relatively efficiently on either a 68020/68881 or a 68030 or a 68040.

-mfpa  Generate output containing Sun FPA instructions for floating point.

-msoft-float  Generate output containing library calls for floating point.

## WARNING

The requisite libraries are not part of GNU CC. Normally, the facilities of the machine's usual C compiler are used, but this can't be done directly in cross-compilation. You must make your own arrangements to provide suitable library functions for cross-compilation.

-mshort  Consider type int to be 16 bits wide, like short int.

-mnobitfield  Do not use the bit-field instructions. -m68000 implies -mnobitfield.

-mbitfield  Do use the bit-field instructions. -m68020 implies -mbitfield. This is the default if you use the unmodified sources.

-mrtd  Use a different function-calling convention, in which functions that take a fixed number of arguments return with the rtd instruction, which pops their arguments while returning. This saves one instruction in the caller since there is no need to pop the arguments there.

This calling convention is incompatible with the one normally used on UNIX, so you cannot use it if you need to call libraries compiled with the UNIX compiler.

Also, you must provide function prototypes for all functions that take variable numbers of arguments (including `printf` ); otherwise, incorrect code will be generated for calls to those functions.

In addition, seriously incorrect code will result if you call a function with too many arguments. (Normally, extra arguments are harmlessly ignored.)

The `rtd` instruction is supported by the 68010 and 68020 processors, but not by the 68000.

These -m options are defined for the VAX:

| | |
|---|---|
| -munix | Do not output certain jump instructions (`aobleq` and so on) that the UNIX assembler for the VAX cannot handle across long ranges. |
| -mgnu | Do output those jump instructions, on the assumption that you will assemble with the GNU assembler. |
| -mg | Output code for g-format floating-point numbers instead of d-format. |

These -m switches are supported on the SPARC:

| | |
|---|---|
| -mfpu<br>-mhard-float | Generate output containing floating-point instructions. This is the default. |
| -mno-fpu<br>-msoft-float | Generate output containing library calls for floating point. |

## WARNING

There is no GNU floating-point library for SPARC. Normally, the facilities of the machine's usual C compiler are used, but this cannot be done directly in cross-compilation. You must make your own arrangements to provide suitable library functions for cross-compilation.

| | |
|---|---|
| -msoft-float | Changes the calling convention in the output file; therefore, it is only useful if you compile *all* of a program with this option. |
| -mno-epilogue<br>-mepilogue | With -mepilogue (the default), the compiler always emits code for function exit at the end of each function. Any function exit in the middle of the function (such as a return statement in C) will generate a jump to the exit code at the end of the function. With -mno-epilogue, the compiler tries to emit exit code inline at every function exit. |
| -mno-v8<br>-mv8<br>msparclite | These three options select variations on the SPARC architecture. By default (unless specifically configured for the Fujitsu SPARClite), gcc generates code for the v7 variant of the SPARC architecture. |
| | -mv8 will give you SPARC v8 code. The only difference from v7 code is that the compiler emits the integer multiply and integer divide instructions that exist in SPARC v8 but not in SPARC v7. |
| | -msparclite will give you SPARClite code. This adds the integer multiply, integer divide step and scan (`ffs`) instructions that exist in SPARClite but not in SPARC v7. |
| -mcypress<br>-msupersparc | These two options select the processor for which the code is optimized. |
| | With -mcypress (the default), the compiler optimizes code for the Cypress CY7C602 chip, as used in the SparcStation and SparcServer 3xx series. This is also appropriate for the older SparcStation 1, 2, IPX, and so on. |
| | With -msupersparc the compiler optimizes code for the SuperSparc cpu, as used in the SparcStation 10, 1000, and 2000 series. This flag also enables use of the full SPARC v8 instruction set. |

These –m options are defined for the Convex:

| | |
|---|---|
| -mc1 | Generate output for a C1. This is the default when the compiler is configured for a C1. |
| -mc2 | Generate output for a C2. This is the default when the compiler is configured for a C2. |

-margcount      Generate code which puts an argument count in the word preceding each argument list. Some nonportable Convex and VAX programs need this word. (Debuggers don't, except for functions with variable-length argument lists; this information is in the symbol table.)

-mnoargcount      Omit the argument count word. This is the default if you use the unmodified sources.

These −m options are defined for the AMD Am29000:

-mdw      Generate code that assumes the DW bit is set, that is, that byte and half-word operations are directly supported by the hardware. This is the default.

-mnodw      Generate code that assumes the DW bit is not set.

-mbw      Generate code that assumes the system supports byte and halfword write operations. This is the default.

-mnbw      Generate code that assumes the systems does not support byte and halfword write operations. This implies -mnodw.

-msmall      Use a small memory model that assumes that all function addresses are either within a single 256KB segment or at an absolute address of less than 256K. This allows the call instruction to be used instead of a const, consth, calli sequence.

-mlarge      Do not assume that the call instruction can be used; this is the default.

-m29050      Generate code for the Am29050.

-m29000      Generate code for the Am29000. This is the default.

-mkernel-registers      Generate references to registers gr64–gr95 instead of gr96–gr127. This option can be used when compiling kernel code that wants a set of global registers disjoint from that used by user-mode code.

     Note that when this option is used, register names in -f flags must use the normal, user-mode, names.

-muser-registers      Use the normal set of global registers, gr96–gr127. This is the default.

-mstack-check      Insert a call to msp check after each stack adjustment. This is often used for kernel code.

These -m options are defined for Motorola 88K architectures:

-m88000      Generate code that works well on both the m88100 and the m88110.

-m88100      Generate code that works best for the m88100, but that also runs on the m88110.

-m88110      Generate code that works best for the m88110, and may not run on the m88100.

-midentify-revision      Include an ident directive in the assembler output recording the source filename, compiler name and version, timestamp, and compilation flags used.

-mno-underscores      In assembler output, emit symbol names without adding an underscore character at the beginning of each name. The default is to use an underscore as prefix on each name.

-mcheck-zero-division
-mno-check-zero-division      Early models of the 88K architecture had problems with division by zero; in particular, many of them didn't trap. Use these options to avoid including (or to include explicitly) additional code to detect division by zero and signal an exception. All gcc configurations for the 88K use -mcheck-zero-division by default.

-mocs-debug-info
-mno-ocs-debug-info      Include (or omit) additional debugging information (about registers used in each stack frame) as specified in the 88Open Object Compatibility Standard, OCS. This extra information is not needed by GDB. The default for DG/UX, SVr4, and Delta 88 SVr3.2 is to include this information; other 88K configurations omit this information by default.

-mocs-frame-position
-mno-ocs-frame-position      Force (or do not require) register values to be stored in a particular place in stack frames, as specified in OCS. The DG/UX, Delta88 SVr3.2, and BCS configurations use -mocs-frame-position; other 88K configurations have the default -mno-ocs- frame-position.

-moptimize-arg-area
-mno-optimize-arg-area      Control how to store function arguments in stack frames. -moptimize-arg-area saves space, but may break some debuggers (not GDB). -mno-optimize-arg-area conforms better to standards. By default gcc does not optimize the argument area.

| | |
|---|---|
| -mshort-data-*num* | Generate smaller data references by making them relative to r0, which allows loading a value using a single instruction (rather than the usual two). You control which data references are affected by specifying *num* with this option. For example, if you specify -mshort-data-512, then the data references affected are those involving displacements of less than 512 bytes. -mshort-data-*num* is not effective for *num* greater than 64K. |
| -mserialize-volatile<br>-mno-serialize-volatile | Do, or do not, generate code to guarantee sequential consistency of volatile memory references. GNU CC always guarantees consistency by default, for the preferred processor submodel. How this is done depends on the submodel. |

The m88100 processor does not reorder memory references and so always provides sequential consistency. If you use -m88100, GNU CC does not generate any special instructions for sequential consistency.

The order of memory references made by the m88110 processor does not always match the order of the instructions requesting those references. In particular, a load instruction may execute before a preceding store instruction. Such reordering violates sequential consistency of volatile memory references, when there are multiple processors. When you use -m88000 or -m88110, GNU CC generates special instructions when appropriate, to force execution in the proper order.

The extra code generated to guarantee consistency may affect the performance of your application. If you know that you can safely forgo this guarantee, you may use the option -mno-serialize-volatile.

If you use the -m88100 option but require sequential consistency when running on the m88110 processor, you should use -mserialize-volatile.

| | |
|---|---|
| -msvr4, -msvr3 | Turn on (-msvr4) or off (-msvr3) compiler extensions related to System V release 4 (SVr4). This controls the following: |

Which variant of the assembler syntax to emit (which you can select independently using -mversion-03.00).

-msvr4 makes the C preprocessor recognize #pragma weak.

-msvr4 makes gcc issue additional declaration directives used in SVr4.

-msvr3 is the default for all m88K configurations except the SVr4 configuration.

| | |
|---|---|
| -mtrap-large-shift<br>-mhandle-large-shift | Include code to detect bit-shifts of more than 31 bits; respectively, trap such shifts or emit code to handle them properly. By default, gcc makes no special provision for large bit shifts. |
| -muse-div-instruction | Very early models of the 88K architecture didn't have a divide instruction, so gcc avoids that instruction by default. Use this option to specify that it's safe to use the divide instruction. |
| -mversion-03.00 | In the DG/UX configuration, there are two flavors of SVr4. This option modifies -msvr4 to select whether the hybrid-COFF or real-ELF flavor is used. All other configurations ignore this option. |
| -mwarn-passed-structs | Warn when a function passes a struct as an argument or result. Structure-passing conventions have changed during the evolution of the C language, and are often the source of portability problems. By default, gcc issues no such warning. |

These options are defined for the IBM RS6000:

| | |
|---|---|
| -mfp-in-toc<br>-mno-fp-in-toc | Control whether or not floating-point constants go in the table of contents (TOC), a table of all global variable and function addresses. By default gcc puts floating-point constants there; if the TOC overflows, -mno-fp-in-toc will reduce the size of the TOC, which may avoid the overflow. |

These -m options are defined for the IBM RT PC:

| | |
|---|---|
| -min-line-mul | Use an inline code sequence for integer multiplies. This is the default. |
| -mcall-lib-mul | Call lmul$$ for integer multiples. |
| -mfull-fp-blocks | Generate full-size floating-point data blocks, including the minimum amount of scratch space recommended by IBM. This is the default. |

| | |
|---|---|
| -mminimum-fp-blocks | Do not include extra scratch space in floating-point data blocks. This results in smaller code, but slower execution, since scratch space must be allocated dynamically. |
| -mfp-arg-in-fpregs | Use a calling sequence incompatible with the IBM calling convention in which floating-point arguments are passed in floating-point registers. Note that varargs.h and stdargs.h will not work with floating-point operands if this option is specified. |
| -mfp-arg-in-gregs | Use the normal calling convention for floating-point arguments. This is the default. |
| -mhc-struct-return | Return structures of more than one word in memory, rather than in a register. This provides compatibility with the MetaWare HighC (hc) compiler. Use -fpcc-struct-return for compatibility with the Portable C Compiler (PCC). |
| -mnohc-struct-return | Return some structures of more than one word in registers, when convenient. This is the default. For compatibility with the IBM-supplied compilers, use either -fpcc-struct-return or -mhc-struct-return. |

These -m options are defined for the MIPS family of computers:

| | |
|---|---|
| -mcpu=*cpu-type* | Assume the defaults for the machine type *cpu-type* when scheduling instructions. The default *cpu-type* is default, which picks the longest cycles times for any of the machines, in order that the code run at reasonable rates on all MIPS CPUs. Other choices for *cpu-type* are r2000, r3000, r4000,and r6000. While picking a specific *cpu-type* will schedule things appropriately for that particular chip, the compiler will not generate any code that does not meet level 1 of the MIPS ISA (instruction set architecture) with-out the -mips2 or -mips3 switches being used. |
| -mips2 | Issue instructions from level 2 of the MIPS ISA (branch likely, square root instructions). The -mcpu=r4000 or -mcpu=r6000 switch must be used in conjunction with -mips2. |
| -mips3 | Issue instructions from level 3 of the MIPS ISA (64-bit instructions). The -mcpu=r4000 switch must be used in conjunction with -mips2. |
| -mint64, -mlong64 -mlonglong128 | These options don't work at present. |
| -mmips-as | Generate code for the MIPS assembler, and invoke mips-tfile to add normal debug information. This is the default for all platforms except for the OSF/1 reference platform, using the OSF/rose object format. If any of the -ggdb, -gstabs, or -gstabs+ switches are used, the mips-tfile program will encapsulate the stabs within MIPS ECOFF. |
| -mgas | Generate code for the GNU assembler. This is the default on the OSF/1 reference platform, using the OSF/rose object format. |
| -mrnames, -mno-rnames | The -mrnames switch says to output code using the MIPS software names for the registers, instead of the hardware names (for example, a0 instead of $4). The GNU assembler does not support the -mrnames switch, and the MIPS assembler will be instructed to run the MIPS C preprocessor over the source file. The -mno-rnames switch is default. |
| -mgpopt, -mno-gpopt | The -mgpopt switch says to write all of the data declarations before the instructions in the text section, to all the MIPS assembler to generate one-word memory references instead of using two words for short global or static data items. This is on by default if optimization is selected. |
| -mstats, -mno-stats | For each noninline function processed, the -mstats switch causes the compiler to emit one line to the standard error file to print statistics about the program (number of registers saved, stack size, and so on). |
| -mmemcpy, -mno-memcpy | The -mmemcpy switch makes all block moves call the appropriate string function (memcpy or bcopy) instead of possibly generating inline code. |
| -mmips-tfile -mno-mips-tfile | The -mno-mips-tfile switch causes the compiler to not post-process the object file with the mips-tfile program, after the MIPS assembler has generated it to add debug support. If mips-tfile is not run, then no local variables will be available to the debugger. In addition, stage2 and stage3 objects will have the temporary filenames passed to the assembler embedded in the object file, which means the objects will not compare the same. |
| -msoft-float | Generate output containing library calls for floating point. |

### WARNING

The requisite libraries are not part of GNU CC. Normally, the facilities of the machine's usual C compiler are used, but this can't be done directly in cross-compilation. You must make your own arrangements to provide suitable library functions for cross-compilation.

| | |
|---|---|
| -mhard-float | Generate output containing floating point instructions. This is the default if you use the unmodified sources. |
| -mfp64 | Assume that the FR bit in the status word is on, and that there are 32 64-bit floating-point registers, instead of 32 32-bit floating-point registers. You must also specify the -mcpu=r4000 and -mips3 switches. |
| -mfp32 | Assume that there are 32 32-bit floating-point registers. This is the default. |
| -mabicalls<br>-mno-abicalls | Emit (or do not emit) the .abicalls, .cpload, and .cprestore pseudo operations that some System V.4 ports use for position-independent code. |
| -mhalf-pic<br>-mno-half-pic | The -mhalf-pic switch says to put pointers to extern references into the data section and load them up, rather than put the references in the text section. This option does not work at present. |
| -G*num* | Put global and static items less than or equal to *num* bytes into the small data or bss sections instead of the normal data or bss section. This allows the assembler to emit one-word memory reference instructions based on the global pointer (gp or $28), instead of the normal two words used. By default, *num* is 8 when the MIPS assembler is used, and 0 when the GNU assembler is used. The -G*num* switch is also passed to the assembler and linker. All modules should be compiled with the same -G*num* value. |
| -nocpp | Tell the MIPS assembler to not run its preprocessor over user assembler files (with an .s suffix) when assembling them. |

These -m options are defined for the Intel 80386 family of computers:

| | |
|---|---|
| -m486, -mno-486 | Control whether or not code is optimized for a 486 instead of a 386. Code generated for a 486 will run on a 386 and vice versa. |
| -msoft-float | Generate output containing library calls for floating point. |

### WARNING

The requisite libraries are not part of GNU CC. Normally, the facilities of the machine's usual C compiler are used, but this can't be done directly in cross-compilation. You must make your own arrangements to provide suitable library functions for cross-compilation.

| | |
|---|---|
| | On machines where a function returns floating point results in the 80387 register stack, some floating-point opcodes may be emitted even if -msoft-float is used. |
| -mno-fp-ret-in-387 | Do not use the FPU registers for return values of functions. |
| | The usual calling convention has functions return values of types float and double in an FPU register, even if there is no FPU. The idea is that the operating system should emulate an FPU. |
| | The option -mno-fp-ret-in-387 causes such values to be returned in ordinary CPU registers instead. |

These -m options are defined for the HPPA family of computers:

| | |
|---|---|
| -mpa-risc-1-0 | Generate code for a PA 1.0 processor. |
| -mpa-risc-1-1 | Generate code for a PA 1.1 processor. |

| | |
|---|---|
| -mkernel | Generate code which is suitable for use in kernels. Specifically, avoid add instructions in which one of the arguments is the DP register; generate addil instructions instead. This avoids a rather serious bug in the HP-UX linker. |
| -mshared-libs | Generate code that can be linked against HP-UX shared libraries. This option is not fully functioning yet, and is not on by default for any PA target. Using this option can cause incorrect code to be generated by the compiler. |
| -mno-shared-libs | Don't generate code that will be linked against shared libraries. This is the default for all PA targets. |
| -mlong-calls | Generate code which allows calls to functions greater than 256K away from the caller when the caller and callee are in the same source file. Do not turn this option on unless code refuses to link with branch out of range errors from the linker. |
| -mdisable-fpregs | Prevent floating-point registers from being used in any manner. This is necessary for compiling kernels that perform lazy context switching of floating-point registers. If you use this option and attempt to perform floating-point operations, the compiler will abort. |
| -mdisable-indexing | Prevent the compiler from using indexing address modes. This avoids some rather obscure problems when compiling MIG-generated code under MACH. |
| -mtrailing-colon | Add a colon to the end of label definitions (for ELF assemblers). |

These -m options are defined for the Intel 80960 family of computers:

| | |
|---|---|
| -m*cpu-type* | Assume the defaults for the machine type *cpu-type* for instruction and addressing-mode availability and alignment. The default *cpu-type* is kb; other choices are ka, mc, ca, cf, sa, and sb. |
| -mnumerics<br>-msoft-float | The -mnumerics option indicates that the processor does support floating-point instructions. The -msoft-float option indicates that floating-point support should not be assumed. |
| -mleaf-procedures<br>-mno-leaf-procedures | Do (or do not) attempt to alter leaf procedures to be callable with the *bal* instruction as well as *call*. This will result in more efficient code for explicit calls when the *bal* instruction can be substituted by the assembler or linker, but less efficient code in other cases, such as calls via function pointers, or using a linker that doesn't support this optimization. |
| -mtail-call<br>-mno-tail-call | Do (or do not) make additional attempts (beyond those of the machine-independent portions of the compiler) to optimize tail-recursive calls into branches. You may not want to do this because the detection of cases where this is not valid is not totally complete. The default is -mno-tail-call. |
| -mcomplex-addr<br>-mno-complex-addr | Assume (or do not assume) that the use of a complex addressing mode is a win on this implementation of the i960. Complex addressing modes may not be worthwhile on the K-series, but they definitely are on the C-series. The default is currently -mcomplex-addr for all processors except the CB and CC. |
| -mcode-align<br>-mno-code-align | Align code to 8-byte boundaries for faster fetching (or don't bother). Currently turned on by default for C-series implementations only. |
| -mic-compat<br>-mic2.0-compat<br>-mic3.0-compat | Enable compatibility with iC960 v2.0 or v3.0. |
| -masm-compat<br>-mintel-asm | Enable compatibility with the iC960 assembler. |
| -mstrict-align<br>-mno-strict-align | Do not permit (do permit) unaligned accesses. |
| -mold-align | Enable structure-alignment compatibility with Intel's gcc release version 1.3 (based on gcc 1.37). Currently this is buggy in that #pragma align 1 is always assumed as well, and cannot be turned off. |

These -m options are defined for the DEC Alpha implementations:

-mno-soft-float
-msoft-float

Use (do not use) the hardware floating-point instructions for floating-point operations. When -msoft-float is specified, functions in libgcc1.c will be used to perform floating-point operations. Unless they are replaced by routines that emulate the floating-point operations, or compiled in such a way as to call such emulations routines, these routines will issue floating-point operations. If you are compiling for an Alpha without floating-point operations, you must ensure that the library is built so as not to call them.

Note that Alpha implementations without floating-point operations are required to have floating-point registers.

-mfp-reg, -mno-fp-regs

Generate code that uses (does not use) the floating-point register set. -mno-fp-regs implies -msoft-float. If the floating-point register set is not used, floating-point operands are passed in integer registers as if they were integers and floating-point results are passed in $0 instead of $f0. This is a nonstandard calling sequence, so any function with a floating-point argument or return value called by code compiled with -mno-fp-regs must also be compiled with that option.

A typical use of this option is building a kernel that does not use, and hence need not save and restore, any floating-point registers.

These additional options are available on System V Release 4 for compatibility with other compilers on those systems:

-G

On SVr4 systems, gcc accepts the option -G (and passes it to the system linker), for compatibility with other compilers. However, we suggest you use -symbolic or -shared as appropriate, instead of supplying linker options on the gcc command line.

-Qy

Identify the versions of each tool used by the compiler, in an .ident assembler directive in the output.

-Qn

Refrain from adding .ident directives to the output file (this is the default).

-YP,*dirs*

Search the directories *dirs,* and no others, for libraries specified with -l. You can separate directory entries in *dirs* from one another with colons.

-Ym,*dir*

Look in the directory *dir* to find the M4 preprocessor. The assembler uses this option.

## CODE GENERATION OPTIONS

These machine-independent options control the interface conventions used in code generation.

Most of them begin with -f. These options have both positive and negative forms; the negative form of -ffoo would be -fno-foo. In the following table, only one of the forms is listed—the one which is not the default. You can figure out the other form by either removing no- or adding it.

-fnonnull-objects

Assume that objects reached through references are not null (C++ only).

Normally, GNU C++ makes conservative assumptions about objects reached through references. For example, the compiler must check that a is not null in code like the following:

obj &a = g (); a.f (2);

Checking that references of this sort have nonnull values requires extra code, however, and it is unnecessary for many programs. You can use -fnonnull-objects to omit the checks for null, if your program doesn't require checking.

-fpcc-struct-return

Use the same convention for returning struct and union values that is used by the usual C compiler on your system. This convention is less efficient for small structures, and on many machines it fails to be reentrant; but it has the advantage of allowing intercallability between gcc-compiled code and pcc-compiled code.

-freg-struct-return

Use the convention that struct and union values are returned in registers when possible. This is more efficient for small structures than -fpcc-struct-return.

If you specify neither -fpcc-struct-return nor -freg-struct-return, GNU CC defaults to whichever convention is standard for the target. If there is no standard convention, GNU CC defaults to -fpcc-struct-return.

| | |
|---|---|
| -fshort-enums | Allocate to an enum type only as many bytes as it needs for the declared range of possible values. Specifically, the enum type will be equivalent to the smallest integer type that has enough room. |
| -fshort-double | Use the same size for double as for float. |
| -fshared-data | Requests that the data and non-const variables of this compilation be shared data rather than private data. The distinction makes sense only on certain operating systems, where shared data is shared between processes running the same program, while private data exists in one copy per process. |
| -fno-common | Allocate even uninitialized global variables in the bss section of the object file, rather than generating them as common blocks. This has the effect that if the same variable is declared (without extern) in two different compilations, you will get an error when you link them. The only reason this might be useful is if you want to verify that the program will work on other systems which always work this way. |
| -fno-ident | Ignore the #ident directive. |
| -fno-gnu-linker | Do not output global initializations (such as C++ constructors and destructors) in the form used by the GNU linker (on systems where the GNU linker is the standard method of handling them). Use this option when you want to use a non-GNU linker, which also requires using the collect2 program to make sure the system linker includes constructors and destructors. (collect2 is included in the GNU CC distribution.) For systems that *must* use collect2, the compiler driver gcc is configured to do this automatically. |
| -finhibit-size-directive | Don't output a .size assembler directive, or anything else that would cause trouble if the function is split in the middle, and the two halves are placed at locations far apart in memory. This option is used when compiling crtstuff.c; you should not need to use it for anything else. |
| -fverbose-asm | Put extra commentary information in the generated assembly code to make it more readable. This option is generally only of use to those who actually need to read the generated assembly code (perhaps while debugging the compiler itself). |
| -fvolatile | Consider all memory references through pointers to be volatile. |
| -fvolatile-global | Consider all memory references to extern and global data items to be volatile. |
| -fpic | If supported for the target machines, generate position-independent code, suitable for use in a shared library. |
| -fPIC | If supported for the target machine, emit position-independent code, suitable for dynamic linking, even if branches need large displacements. |
| -ffixed-*reg* | Treat the register named *reg* as a fixed register; generated code should never refer to it (except perhaps as a stack pointer, frame pointer, or in some other fixed role). |
| | *reg* must be the name of a register. The register names accepted are machine-specific and are defined in the REGISTER_NAMES macro in the machine description macro file. |
| | This flag does not have a negative form, because it specifies a three-way choice. |
| -fcall-used-*reg* | Treat the register named *reg* as an allocable register that is clobbered by function calls. It may be allocated for temporaries or variables that do not live across a call. Functions compiled this way will not save and restore the register *reg*. |
| | Use of this flag for a register that has a fixed pervasive role in the machine's execution model, such as the stack pointer or frame pointer, will produce disastrous results. |
| | This flag does not have a negative form, because it specifies a three-way choice. |
| -fcall-saved-*reg* | Treat the register named *reg* as an allocable register saved by functions. It may be allocated even for temporaries or variables that live across a call. Functions compiled this way will save and restore the register *reg* if they use it. |
| | Use of this flag for a register that has a fixed pervasive role in the machine's execution model, such as the stack pointer or frame pointer, will produce disastrous results. |
| | A different sort of disaster will result from the use of this flag for a register in which function values may be returned. |
| | This flag does not have a negative form, because it specifies a three-way choice. |

## PRAGMAS

Two #pragma directives are supported for GNU C++ to permit using the same header file for two purposes: as a definition of interfaces to a given object class, and as the full definition of the contents of that object class.

| | |
|---|---|
| #pragma interface | (C++ only.) Use this directive in header files that define object classes, to save space in most of the object files that use those classes. Normally, local copies of certain information (backup copies of inline member functions, debugging information, and the internal tables that implement virtual functions) must be kept in each object file that includes class definitions. You can use this pragma to avoid such duplication. When a header file containing #pragma interface is included in a compilation, this auxiliary information will not be generated (unless the main input source file itself uses #pragma implementation). Instead, the object files will contain references to be resolved at link time. |
| #pragma implementation<br>#pragma implementation<br>"objects.h" | (C++ only.) Use this pragma in a main input file, when you want full output from included header files to be generated (and made globally visible). The included header file, in turn, should use #pragma interface. Backup copies of inline member functions, debugging information, and the internal tables used to implement virtual functions are all generated in implementation files. |
| | If you use #pragma implementation with no argument, it applies to an include file with the same basename as your source file; for example, in allclass.cc, #pragma implementation by itself is equivalent to #pragma i-plementation "allclass.h". Use the string argument if you want a single implementation file to include code from multiple header files. |
| | There is no way to split up the contents of a single header file into multiple implementation files. |

## FILES

| | |
|---|---|
| file.c | C source file |
| file.h | C header (preprocessor) file |
| file.i | Preprocessed C source file |
| file.C | C++ source file |
| file.cc | C++ source file |
| file.cxx | C++ source file |
| file.m | Objective-C source file |
| file.s | Assembly language file |
| file.o | Object file |
| a.out | Link edited output |
| *TMPDIR*/cc | Temporary files |
| *LIBDIR*/cpp | Preprocessor |
| *LIBDIR*/cc1 | Compiler for C |
| *LIBDIR*/cc1plus | Compiler for C++ |
| *LIBDIR*/collect | Linker front end needed on some machines |
| *LIBDIR*/libgcc.a | gcc subroutine library |
| /lib/crt[01n].o | Startup routine |
| *LIBDIR*/ccrt0 | Additional startup routine for C++ |
| /lib/libc.a | Standard C library; see intro(3) |
| /usr/include | Standard directory for #include files |
| *LIBDIR*/include | Standard gcc directory for #include files |
| *LIBDIR*/g++-include | Additional g++ directory for #include |

*LIBDIR* is usually /usr/local/lib/*machine*/*version*.

*TMPDIR* comes from the environment variable TMPDIR (default /usr/tmp if available; otherwise, /tmp.).

## SEE ALSO

cpp(1), as(1), ld(1), gdb(1), adb(1), dbx(1), sdb(1)

gcc, cpp, as, ld, and gdb entries in info.

*Using and Porting GNU CC* (for version 2.0), Richard M. Stallman; *The C Preprocessor*, Richard M. Stallman; *Debugging with GDB: the GNU Source-Level Debugger*, Richard M. Stallman and Roland H. Pesch; *Using as: the GNU Assembler*, Dean Elsner, Jay Fenlason & friends; *ld: the GNU Linker*, Steve Chamberlain and Roland Pesch.

## BUGS

For instructions on reporting bugs, see the GCC manual.

## COPYING

Copyright 1991, 1992, 1993 Free Software Foundation, Inc.

Permission is granted to make and distribute verbatim copies of this manual provided the copyright notice and this permission notice are preserved on all copies.

Permission is granted to copy and distribute modified versions of this manual under the conditions for verbatim copying, provided that the entire resulting derived work is distributed under the terms of a permission notice identical to this one.

Permission is granted to copy and distribute translations of this manual into another language, under the preceding conditions for modified versions, except that this permission notice may be included in translations approved by the Free Software Foundation instead of in the original English.

## AUTHORS

See the GNU CC manual for the contributors to GNU CC.

*GNU Tools, 13 October 1993*

# gemtopbm

gemtopbm—Convert a GEM IMG file into a portable bitmap

## SYNOPSIS

gemtopbm [-d] [ gemfile ]

## DESCRIPTION

Reads a GEM IMG file as input. Reads from stdin if input file is omitted. Produces a portable bitmap as output.

## OPTIONS

-d              Produce output describing the contents of the IMG file.

## BUGS

Does not support files containing more than one plane.

## SEE ALSO

pbmtogem(1), pbm(5)

## AUTHOR

Copyright© 1988 Diomidis D. Spinellis (dds@cc.ic.ac.uk).

*11 July 1992*

# geqn

geqn—Format equations for troff

## SYNOPSIS

geqn [ -rvCNN ][ dcc ][-T*name* ][-M*dir* ][-fF ][-s*n* ][-p*n* ][-m*n* ][*files* ... ]

## DESCRIPTION

This manual page describes the GNU version of eqn, which is part of the groff document formatting system. eqn compiles descriptions of equations embedded within troff input files into commands that are understood by troff. Normally, it should be invoked using the -e option of groff. The syntax is quite compatible with UNIX eqn. The output of GNU eqn cannot be processed with UNIX troff; it must be processed with GNU troff. If no files are given on the command line, the standard input will be read. A filename of - will cause the standard input to be read.

eqn searches for the file eqnrc using the path .:/usr/lib/groff/tmac:/usr/lib/tmac. If it exists, eqn will process it before the other input files. The -R option prevents this.

GNU eqn does not provide the functionality of neqn: it does not support low-resolution, typewriter-like devices (although it may work adequately for very simple input).

## OPTIONS

| | |
|---|---|
| -C | Recognize .EQ and .EN even when followed by a character other than space or newline. |
| -N | Don't allow newlines within delimiters. This option allows eqn to recover better from missing closing delimiters. |
| -v | Print the version number. |
| -r | Only one size reduction. |
| -m*n* | The minimum point-size is *n*. eqn will not reduce the size of subscripts or superscripts to a smaller size than *n*. |
| -T*name* | The output is for device *name*. The only effect of this is to define a macro *name* with a value of 1. Typically, eqnrc will use this to provide definitions appropriate for the output device. The default output device is ps. |
| -M*dir* | Search *dir* for eqnrc before the default directories. |
| -R | Don't load eqnrc. |
| -fF | This is equivalent to a gfontF command. |
| -s*n* | This is equivalent to a gsize*n* command. This option is deprecated. eqn will normally set equations at whatever the current pointsize is when the equation is encountered. |
| -p*n* | This says that subscripts and superscripts should be *n* points smaller than the surrounding text. This option is deprecated. Normally, eqn makes sets subscripts and superscripts at 70 percent of the size of the surrounding text. |

## USAGE

Only the differences between GNU eqn and UNIX eqn are described here.

Most of the new features of GNU eqn are based on TeX. There are some references to the differences between TeX and GNU eqn as follows; these may safely be ignored if you do not know TeX.

## AUTOMATIC SPACING

eqn gives each component of an equation a type, and adjusts the spacing between components using that type. Possible types are

| | |
|---|---|
| ordinary | An ordinary character such as 1 or x |
| operator | A large operator such as ; |
| binary | A binary operator such as + |
| relation | A relation such as = |

| | |
|---|---|
| opening | An opening bracket such as ( |
| closing | A closing bracket such as ) |
| punctuation | A punctuation character such as , |
| inner | A subformula contained within brackets |
| suppress | Spacing that suppresses automatic spacing adjustment |

Components of an equation get a type in one of two ways:

**type** *e* *t* e — This yields an equation component that contains *e* but that has type *t*, where *t* is one of the types mentioned previously. For example, times is defined as

```
type "binary" \(mu
```

The name of the type doesn't have to be quoted, but quoting protects from macro expansion.

**chartype** *t* *text* — Unquoted groups of characters are split up into individual characters, and the type of each character is looked up; this changes the type that is stored for each character; it says that the characters in *text* from now on have type *t*. For example

```
chartype "punctuation" .,;:
```

would make the characters .,;: have type punctuation whenever they subsequently appeared in an equation. The type *t* can also be letter or digit; in these cases, chartype changes the font type of the characters. See the "Fonts" section, later in this manual page.

## NEW PRIMITIVES

*e1* **smallover** *e2* — This is similar to over; smallover reduces the size of *e1* and *e2*; it also puts less vertical space between *e1* or *e2* and the fraction bar. The over primitive corresponds to the \over primitive in display styles; smallover corresponds to \over in nondisplay styles.

**vcenter** *e* — This vertically centers *e* about the math axis. The math axis is the vertical position about which characters such as + and - are centered; also it is the vertical position used for the bar of fractions. For example, sum is defined as

{ type "operator" vcenter size +5 \(*S }

*e1* **accent** *e2* — This sets *e2* as an accent over *e1*. *e2* is assumed to be at the correct height for a lowercase letter; *e2* will be moved down according if *e1* is taller or shorter than a lowercase letter. For example, hat is defined as

accent { "^" }

dotdot, dot, tilde, vec, and dyad are also defined using the accent primitive.

*e1* **uaccent** *e2* — This sets *e2* as an accent under *e1*. *e2* is assumed to be at the correct height for a character without a descender; *e2* will be moved down if *e1* has a descender. utilde is predefined using uaccent as a tilde accent below the baseline.

**split** *text* — This has the same effect as simply text, but text is not subject to macro expansion because it is quoted; text will be split up and the spacing between individual characters will be adjusted.

**nosplit** *text* — This has the same effect as text, but because *text* is not quoted it will be subject to macro expansion; *text* will not be split up and the spacing between individual characters will not be adjusted.

*e* **opprime** — This is a variant of prime that acts as an operator on e.It produces a different result from prime in a case such as Aopprimesub1: With opprime the 1 will be tucked under the prime as a subscript to the A (as is conventional in mathematical typesetting), whereas with prime the 1 will be a subscript to the prime character. The precedence of opprime is the same as that of bar and under, which is higher than that of everything except accent and uaccent. In unquoted text, a ' that is not the first character will be treated like opprime.

**special** *text* *e* — This constructs a new object from *e* using a gtroff(1) macro named *text*. When the macro is called, the string 0s will contain the output for *e*, and the number registers 0w, 0h, 0d, 0skern and 0skew will contain the width, height, depth, subscript kern, and skew of *e*. (The *subscript kern* of an object says how much a subscript on that object should be tucked in; the *skew* of an object says how far to the right of the center of the object an accent over the object should be placed.) The macro must modify 0s so that it will output the desired result with its origin at the current point, and increase the current horizontal position by the width of the object. The number registers must also be modified so that they correspond to the result.

For example, suppose you wanted a construct that cancels an expression by drawing a diagonal line through it:

```
.EQ
define cancel 'special Ca'
.EN
.de Ca
.ds 0c \Z'\\*(0s'\v'\\n(0du'\D'l \\n(0wu -\\n(0hu-\\n(0du'\v'\\n(0hu'
..
```

Then you could cancel an expression $U$ with `cancel e`.

Here's a more complicated construct that draws a box around an expression:

```
.EQ
define box 'special Bx'
.EN
.de Bx
.ds 0s \Z'\h'1n'\\*(0s\
\Z'\v'\\n(0du+1n'\D'l \\n(0wu+2n 0'\D'l 0 -\\n(0hu-\\n(0du-2n'\
\D'l -\\n(0wu-2n 0'\D'l 0 \\n(0hu+\\n(0du+2n"\h'\\n(0wu+2n'
.nr 0w +2n
.nr 0d +1n
.nr 0h +1n
..
```

## CUSTOMIZATION

The appearance of equations is controlled by a large number of parameters. These can be set using the `set` command.

`set`*pn*    This sets parameter *p* to value *n*; *n* is an integer. For example

            `set x_height 45`

            says that eqn should assume an x height of 0.45 ems.

Possible parameters are as follows. Values are in units of hundredths of an em unless otherwise stated. These descriptions are intended to be expository rather than definitive.

`minimum_size`    eqn will not set anything at a smaller point size than this. The value is in points.

`fat_offset`    The `fat` primitive emboldens an equation by overprinting two copies of the equation horizontally offset by this amount.

`over_hang`    A fraction bar will be longer by twice this amount than the maximum of the widths of the numerator and denominator; in other words, it will overhang the numerator and denominator by at least this amount.

`accent_width`    When bar or under is applied to a single character, the line will be this long. Normally, bar or under produces a line whose length is the width of the object to which it applies; in the case of a single character, this tends to produce a line that looks too long.

`delimiter_factor`    Extensible delimiters produced with the left and right primitives will have a combined height and depth of at least this many thousandths of twice the maximum amount by which the subequation that the delimiters enclose extends away from the axis.

`delimiter_shortfall`    Extensible delimiters produced with the left and right primitives will have a combined height and depth not less than the difference of twice the maximum amount by which the subequation that the delimiters enclose extends away from the axis and this amount.

`null_delimiter_space`    This much horizontal space is inserted on each side of a fraction.

`script_space`    The width of subscripts and superscripts is increased by this amount.

`thin_space`    This amount of space is automatically inserted after punctuation characters.

`medium_space`    This amount of space is automatically inserted on either side of binary operators.

`thick_space`    This amount of space is automatically inserted on either side of relations.

| | |
|---|---|
| x_height | The height of lowercase letters without ascenders such as *x*. |
| axis_height | The height above the baseline of the center of characters such as + and -. It is important that this value be correct for the font you are using. |
| default_rule_thickness | This should set to the thickness of the \(ru character, or the thickness of horizontal lines produced with the \D escape sequence. |
| num1 | The over command will shift up the numerator by at least this amount. |
| num2 | The smallover command will shift up the numerator by at least this amount. |
| denom1 | The over command will shift down the denominator by at least this amount. |
| denom2 | The smallover command will shift down the denominator by at least this amount. |
| sup1 | Normally superscripts will be shifted up by at least this amount. |
| sup2 | Superscripts within superscripts or upper limits or numerators of smallover fractions will be shifted up by at least this amount. This is usually less than sup1. |
| sup3 | Superscripts within denominators or square roots or subscripts or lower limits will be shifted up by at least this amount. This is usually less than sup2. |
| sub1 | Subscripts will normally be shifted down by at least this amount. |
| sub2 | When there is both a subscript and a superscript, the subscript will be shifted down by at least this amount. |
| sup_drop | The baseline of a superscript will be no more than this amount below the top of the object on which the superscript is set. |
| sub_drop | The baseline of a subscript will be at least this much below the bottom of the object on which the subscript is set. |
| big_op_spacing1 | The baseline of an upper limit will be at least this much above the top of the object on which the limit is set. |
| big_op_spacing2 | The baseline of a lower limit will be at least this much below the bottom of the object on which the limit is set. |
| big_op_spacing3 | The bottom of an upper limit will be at least this much above the top of the object on which the limit is set. |
| big_op_spacing4 | The top of a lower limit will be at least this much below the bottom of the object on which the limit is set. |
| big_op_spacing5 | This much vertical space will be added above and below limits. |
| baseline_sep | The baselines of the rows in a pile or matrix will normally be this far apart. In most cases, this should be equal to the sum of num1 and denom1. |
| shift_down | The midpoint between the top baseline and the bottom baseline in a matrix or pile will be shifted down by this much from the axis. In most cases, this should be equal to axis_height. |
| column_sep | This much space will be added between columns in a matrix. |
| matrix_side_sep | This much space will be added at each side of a matrix. |
| draw_lines | If this is nonzero, lines will be drawn using the \D escape sequence, rather than with the \l escape sequence and the \(ru character. |
| body_height | The amount by which the height of the equation exceeds this will be added as extra space before the line containing the equation (using \x.) The default value is 85. |
| body_depth | The amount by which the depth of the equation exceeds this will be added as extra space after the line containing the equation (using \x.) The default value is 35. |
| nroff | If this is nonzero, then ndefine will behave like define and tdefine will be ignored; otherwise, tdefine will behave like define and ndefine will be ignored. The default value is 0. (This is typically changed to 1 by the eqnrc file for the ascii and latin1 devices.) |

A more precise description of the role of many of these parameters can be found in Appendix H of *The TeXbook*.

## MACROS

Macros can take arguments. In a macro body, $ *n* where *n* is between 1 and 9, will be replaced by the *n*th argument if the macro is called with arguments; if there are fewer than *n* arguments, it will be replaced by nothing. A word containing a left parenthesis where the part of the word before the left parenthesis has been defined using the `define` command will be recognized as a macro call with arguments; characters following the left parenthesis up to a matching right parenthesis will be treated as comma-separated arguments; commas inside nested parentheses do not terminate an argument.

| | |
|---|---|
| `sdefinenameXanythingX` | This is like the `define` command, but *name* will not be recognized if called with arguments. |
| `includefile` | Include the contents of *file*. Lines of *file* beginning with `.EQ` or `.EN` will be ignored. |
| `ifdefnameXanythingX` | If *name* has been defined by `define` (or has been automatically defined because *name* is the output device), process *anything*; otherwise ignore *anything*. |
| | *X* can be any character not appearing in *anything*. |

## FONTS

eqn normally uses at least two fonts to set an equation: an italic font for letters, and a Roman font for everything else. The existing `gfont` command changes the font that is used as the italic font. By default this is `I`. The font that is used as the Roman font can be changed by using the new `grfont` command.

`grfontf`                Set the Roman font to *f*.

The italic primitive uses the current italic font set by `gfont`; the Roman primitive uses the current Roman font set by `grfont`. There is also a new `gbfont` command, which changes the font used by the bold primitive. If you only use the Roman, italic, and bold primitives to change fonts within an equation, you can change all the fonts used by your equations just by using `gfont`, `grfont`, and `gbfont` commands.

You can control which characters are treated as letters (and therefore set in italic) by using the `chartype` command described earlier. A type of letter will cause a character to be set in italic type. A type of digit will cause a character to be set in Roman type.

## FILES

`/usr/lib/groff/tmac/eqnrc`   Initialization file

## BUGS

Inline equations will be set at the `pointsize` that is current at the beginning of the input line.

## SEE ALSO

`groff`(1), `gtroff`(1), `groff_font`(5), *The TeX*book

# getlist

getlist—Get a list from an NNTP server

## SYNOPSIS

`getlist [ -h host ][list [ pattern [ types ]]]`

## DESCRIPTION

The `getlist` program obtains a list from an NNTP server and sends it to standard output.

The list may be one of active, active.times, distributions, or newsgroups. These values request the active(5), active.times, /news/lib/distributions, or /news/lib/newsgroups files, respectively.

If the `-h` flag is used, then the program connects to the server on the specified host. The default is to connect to the server specified in the `inn.conf`(5) file.

If the *list* parameter is active, then the pattern and types parameters may be used to limit the output. When pattern is used, only active lines with groups that match according to wildmat(3) are printed. When *types* is also given, only active lines that have a fourth field starting with a character found in *types* are printed.

For example, the following command will obtain the one-line descriptions of all newsgroups found on UUNET:

```
getlist -h news.uu.net newsgroups
```

The following line lists all groups where local postings are permitted, moderated, or aliased:

```
getlist active '*' ym=
```

Note that the listing files other than the active file is a common extension to the NNTP protocol and may not be available on all servers.

## HISTORY

Written by Landon Curt Noll (<chongo@toad.com>) for InterNetNews.

## SEE ALSO

active(5), nnrpd(8), wildmat(3)

# getopt

getopt—Parse command options

## SYNOPSIS

```
set - 'getopt optstring $*'
```

## DESCRIPTION

getopt is used to break up options in command lines for easy parsing by shell procedures, and to check for legal options. optstring is a string of recognized option letters; see getopt(3). If a letter is followed by a colon, the option is expected to have an argument that may or may not be separated from it by whitespace. The special option − - is used to delimit the end of the options. getopt will place − - in the arguments at the end of the options, or recognize it if used explicitly. The shell arguments ($1 $2 ...) are reset so that each option is preceded by a - and in its own shell argument; each option argument is also in its own shell argument.

## EXAMPLE

The following code fragment shows how one might process the arguments for a command that can take the options a and b, and the option o, which requires an argument:

```
set — 'getopt abo: $*'
        if test $? != 0
        then
                echo 'Usage: ...'
                exit 2
        fi
        for i
        do
                case "$i"
                in
                        -a¦-b)
                                flag=$i; shift;;
                        -o)
                                oarg=$2; shift; shift;;
                        --)
                                shift; break;;
                esac
        done
```

This code will accept any of the following as equivalent:

```
cmd -aoarg file file
cmd -a -o arg file file
cmd -oarg -a file file
cmd -a -oarg -- file file
```

## SEE ALSO

sh(1), getopt(3)

## DIAGNOSTICS

getopt prints an error message on the standard error output when it encounters an option letter not included in optstring.

## HISTORY

Written by Henry Spencer, working from a Bell Labs manual page. Behavior believed identical to the Bell version.

## BUGS

Whatever getopt(3) has.

Arguments containing whitespace or embedded shell meta characters generally will not survive intact; this looks easy to fix but isn't.

The error message for an invalid option is identified as coming from getopt rather than from the shell procedure containing the invocation of getopt; this, again, is hard to fix.

The precise best way to use the set command to set the arguments without disrupting the value(s) of shell options varies from one shell version to another.

*21 June 1993*

# giftopnm

giftopnm—Convert a GIF file into a portable anymap

## SYNOPSIS

giftopnm [-verbose][-comments][-image *N*][*GIFfile*]

## DESCRIPTION

Reads a GIF file for input, and outputs portable anymap.

## OPTIONS

| | |
|---|---|
| -verbose | Produces verbose output about the GIF file input. |
| -comments | Only outputs GIF89 comment fields. |
| -image | Outputs the specified GIF image from the input GIF archive (where *N* is 1, 2, 20 . . .). Normally, there is only one image per file, so this option is not needed. |

All flags can be abbreviated to their shortest unique prefix.

## BUGS

This does not correctly handle the Plain Text Extension of the GIF89 standard, since I did not have any example input files containing them.

## SEE ALSO

ppmtogif(1), ppm(5)

## AUTHOR

Copyright © 1993 by David Koblas (koblas@netcom.com)

*29 September 1993*

# gindxbib

gindxbib—Make inverted index for bibliographic databases

## SYNOPSIS

gindxbib [-vw] [-c *file*] [-d *dir*] [-f *file*] [-h n] [-i *string*]
[-k n] [-l n] [-n n] [-o *file*] [-t n] [*filename* ...]

## DESCRIPTION

gindxbib makes an inverted index for the bibliographic databases in *filename*... for use with grefer(1), glookbib(1), and lkbib(1). The index will be named *filename*.i; the index is written to a temporary file which is then renamed to this. If no filenames are given on the command line because the -f option has been used, and no -o option is given, the index will be named Ind.i.

Bibliographic databases are divided into records by blank lines. Within a record, each fields starts with a % character at the beginning of a line. Fields have a one-letter name that follows the % character.

The values set by the -c, -n, -l, and -t options are stored in the index; when the index is searched, keys will be discarded and truncated in a manner appropriate to these options; the original keys will be used for verifying that any record found using the index actually contains the keys. This means that a user of an index need not know whether these options were used in the creation of the index, provided that not all the keys to be searched for would have been discarded during indexing and that the user supplies at least the part of each key that would have remained after being truncated during indexing. The value set by the -i option is also stored in the index and will be used in verifying records found using the index.

## OPTIONS

| | |
|---|---|
| -v | Print the version number. |
| -w | Index whole files. Each file is a separate record. |
| -c*file* | Read the list of common words from *file* instead of /usr/lib/groff/eign. |
| -d*dir* | Use *dir* as the pathname of the current working directory to store in the index, instead of the path printed by pwd(1). Usually *dir* will be a symbolic link that points to the directory printed by pwd(1). |
| -f*file* | Read the files to be indexed from *file*. If *file* is -, files will be read from the standard input. The -f option can be given at most once. |
| -i*string* | Don't index the contents of fields whose names are in *string*. Initially, *string* is XYZ. |
| -h*n* | Use the first prime greater than or equal to *n* for the size of the hash table. Larger values of *n* will usually make searching faster, but will make the index larger and gindxbib use more memory. Initially, *n* is 997. |
| -k*n* | Use at most *n* keys per input record. Initially, *n* is 100. |
| -l*n* | Discard keys that are shorter than *n*. Initially, *n* is 3. |
| -n*n* | Discard the *n* most common words. Initially, *n* is 100. |
| -o*basename* | The index should be named *basename*.i. |
| -t*n* | Truncate keys to *n*. Initially, *n* is 6. |

## FILES

| | |
|---|---|
| `filename.i` | Index |
| `Ind.i` | Default index name |
| `/usr/lib/groff/eign` | List of common words |
| `indxbibXXXXXX` | Temporary file |

## SEE ALSO

grefer(1), lkbib(1), glookbib(1)

*Groff Version 1.09, 16 April 1993*

# glookbib

glookbib—Search bibliographic databases

## SYNOPSIS

glookbib [ -v ][-i*string* ][-t*n* ] *filename* ...

## DESCRIPTION

glookbib prints a prompt on the standard error (unless the standard input is not a terminal), reads from the standard input a line containing a set of keywords, searches the bibliographic databases *filename* ... for references containing those keywords, prints any references found on the standard output, and repeats this process until the end of input. For each database *filename* to be searched, if an index *filename*.i created by gindxbib(1) exists, then it will be searched instead; each index can cover multiple databases.

## OPTIONS

| | |
|---|---|
| -v | Print the version number. |
| -i*string* | When searching files for which no index exists, ignore the contents of fields whose names are in *string*. |
| -t*n* | Only require the first *n* characters of keys to be given. Initially, *n* is 6. |

## FILE

| | |
|---|---|
| `filename.i` | Index files |

## SEE ALSO

grefer(1), lkbib(1), gindxbib(1)

# gnroff

gnroff—Emulate nroff command with groff

## SYNOPSIS

gnroff [ -h ][-i ][-m*name* ][-n*num* ][-o*list* ][-r*cn* ][-T*name* ][*file*...]

## DESCRIPTION

The gnroff script emulates the nroff command using groff. The -T option with an argument other than ascii and latin1 will be ignored. The -h option is equivalent to the grotty -h option. The -i, -n, -m, -o, and -r options have the effect described in gtroff(1). In addition, gnroff silently ignores options of -e, -q, or -s.

## SEE ALSO

groff(1), gtroff(1), grotty(1)

*Groff Version 1.09, 17 May 1993*

# gouldtoppm

gouldtoppm—Convert Gould scanner file into a portable pixmap

## SYNOPSIS

gouldtoppm[*gouldfile*]

## DESCRIPTION

Reads a file produced by the Gould scanner as input. Produces a portable pixmap as output.

## SEE ALSO

ppm(5)

## AUTHOR

Copyright© 1990 by Stephen Paul Lesniewski

*20 May 1990*

# gpic

gpic—Compile pictures for troff or TeX

## SYNOPSIS

gpic [ -nvC ][*filename ... ] gpic -t [ -cvzC ][*filename ... ]

## DESCRIPTION

This manual page describes the GNU version of pic, which is part of the groff document formatting system. pic compiles descriptions of pictures embedded within troff or TeX input files into commands that are understood by TeX or troff. Each picture starts with a line beginning with .PS and ends with a line beginning with .PE. Anything outside of .PS and .PE is passed through without change.

It is the user's responsibility to provide appropriate definitions of the PS and PE macros. When the macro package being used does not supply such definitions (for example, old versions of -ms), appropriate definitions can be obtained with -mpic: These will center each picture.

## OPTIONS

Options that do not take arguments may be grouped behind a single -. The special option -- can be used to mark the end of the options. A filename of - refers to the standard input.

-C        Recognize .PS and .PE even when followed by a character other than space or newline.

-n        Don't use the groff extensions to the troff drawing commands. You should use this if you are using a postprocessor that doesn't support these extensions. The extensions are described in groff_out(5). The -n option also causes pic not to use zero-length lines to draw dots in troff mode.

-t        TeX mode.

-c        Be more compatible with tpic. Implies -t. Lines beginning with n are not passed through transparently. Lines beginning with . are passed through with the initial . changed to \. A line beginning with .ps is given special treatment: It takes an optional integer argument specifying the line thickness (pen size) in milli-inches; a missing argument restores the previous line thickness; the default line thickness is 8 milli-inches. The line thickness thus specified takes effect only when a nonnegative line thickness has not been specified by use of the thickness attribute or by setting the linethick variable.

-v          Print the version number.

-z          In TeX mode draw dots using zero-length lines.

The following options supported by other versions of pic are ignored:

-D          Draw all lines using the \D escape sequence. pic always does this.

-Tdev       Generate output for the troff device *dev*. This is unnecessary because the troff output generated by pic is device-independent.

## USAGE

This section describes only the differences between GNU pic and the original version of pic. Many of these differences also apply to newer versions of UNIX pic.

### mode

mode is enabled by the -t option. In mode, pic will define a vbox called ngraph for each picture. You must yourself print that vbox using, for example, the command:

\centerline{\box\graph}

Actually, since the vbox has a height of zero, this will produce slightly more vertical space above the picture than below it, the line

\centerline{\raise 1em\box\graph}

would avoid this.

You must use a driver that supports the tpic specials, version 2.

Lines beginning with \are passed through transparently; a % is added to the end of the line to avoid unwanted spaces. You can safely use this feature to change fonts or to change the value of \baselineskip. Anything else may well produce undesirable results; use at your own risk. Lines beginning with a period are not given any special treatment.

## COMMANDS

| | |
|---|---|
| for *variable* = *expr1* to *expr2*<br>by [*]*expr3* do X *body* X<br>[Set *variable* to *expr1* | While the value of *variable* is less than or equal to *expr2*, do *body* and increment *variable* by *expr3*; if by is not given, increment *variable* by 1. If *expr3* is prefixed by * then *variable* will instead be multiplied by *expr3*. X can be any character not occurring in *body*. |
| if *expr* then X *if-true* X<br>[else Y *if-false* Y] | Evaluate *expr*; if it is nonzero, do *if-true*; otherwise, do *if-false*. *u* can be any character not occurring in *if-true*. Y can be any character not occurring in *if-false*. |
| print *arg* ... | Concatenate the arguments and print as a line on stderr. Each *arg* must be an expression, a position, or text. This is useful for debugging. |
| command *arg* ... | Concatenate the arguments and pass them through as a line to troff or TeX. Each *arg* must be an expression, a position, or text. This has a similar effect to a line beginning with . or \, but allows the values of variables to be passed through. |
| sh X *command* X | Pass *command* to a shell. X can be any character not occurring in *command*. |
| copy "*filename*" | Include *filename* at this point in the file. |
| copy ["*filename*"] thru X *body* X<br>[until "*word*"]<br>copy ["*filename*"] thru *macro*<br>[until "*word*"] | This construct does *body* once for each line of *filename*; the line is split into blank-delimited words, and occurrences of $ *i* in *body*, for *i* between 1 and 9, are replaced by the *i*-th word of the line. If *filename* is not given, lines are taken from the current input up to .PE. If an until clause is specified, lines will be read only until a line the first word of which is *word*; that line will then be discarded. X can be any character not occurring in *body*. For example, |

```
.PS
copy thru % circle at ($1,$2) % until "END"
1 2
3 4
5 6
END
box
.PE
```

is equivalent to

```
.PS
circle at (1,2)
circle at (3,4)
circle at (5,6)
box
.PE
```

The commands to be performed for each line can also be taken from a macro defined earlier by giving the name of the macro as the argument to thru.

reset *variable1*, *variable2* ...    Reset predefined variables *variable1*, *variable2* ... to their default values. If no arguments are given, reset all predefined variables to their default values. Note that assigning a value to scale also causes all predefined variables that control dimensions to be reset to their default values times the new value of scale.

plot *expr* ["*text*"]    This is a text object which is constructed by using as a format string for *text* sprintf with an argument of *expr*. If *text* is omitted, a format string of %g is used. Attributes can be specified in the same way as for a normal text object. Be very careful that you specify an appropriate format string; pic does only very limited checking of the string. This is deprecated in favor of sprintf.

*variable*:=*expr*    This is similar to = except *variable* must already be defined, and the value of *variable* will be changed only in the innermost block in which it is defined. (By contrast, = defines the variable in the current block if it is not already defined there, and then changes the value in the current block.)

Arguments of the form

XanythingX

are also allowed to be of the form:

anything

In this case, anything can contain balanced occurrences of and .BR. Strings may contain X or imbalanced occurrences of and .BR.

## EXPRESSIONS

The syntax for expressions has been significantly extended:

```
x^y (exponentiation)
sin(x)
cos(x)
atan2(y,x)
log(x) (base 10)
exp(x) (base 10, ie 10'-.4m'x'.4m')
sqrt(x)
int(x)
rand() (return a random number between 0 and 1)
rand(x) (return a random number between 1 and x; deprecated)
max(e1,e2)
min(e1,e2)
!e
```

```
e1 && e2
e1 ¦¦ e2
e1 == e2
e1 != e2
e1 >= e2
e1 > e2
e1 <= e2
e1 < e2
"str1"=="str2"
"str1"!="str2"
```

String comparison expressions must be parenthesized in some contexts to avoid ambiguity.

## OTHER CHANGES

A bare expression, expr, is acceptable as an attribute; it is equivalent to `dir expr`, where `dir` is the current direction. For example

```
line 2i
```

means draw a line 2 inches long in the current direction.

The maximum width and height of the picture are taken from the variables maxpswid and maxpsht. Initially, these have values 8.5 and 11.

Scientific notation is allowed for numbers. For example

```
x = 5e-2
```

Text attributes can be compounded. For example

```
"foo" above ljust
```

is legal.

There is no limit to the depth to which blocks can be examined. For example

```
[A: [B: [C: box ]]] with .A.B.C.sw at 1,2
circle at last [].A.B.C
```

is acceptable.

Arcs now have compass points determined by the circle of which the arc is a part.

Circles and arcs can be dotted or dashed. In mode, splines can be dotted or dashed.

Boxes can have rounded corners. The rad attribute specifies the radius of the quarter-circles at each corner. If no rad or diam attribute is given, a radius of boxrad is used. Initially, boxrad has a value of 0. A box with rounded corners can be dotted or dashed.

The .PS line can have a second argument specifying a maximum height for the picture. If the width of zero is specified, the width will be ignored in computing the scaling factor for the picture. Note that GNU pic will always scale a picture by the same amount vertically as horizontally. This is different from the DWB 2.0 pic, which may scale a picture by a different amount vertically than horizontally if a height is specified.

Each text object has an invisible box associated with it. The compass points of a text object are determined by this box. The implicit motion associated with the object is also determined by this box. The dimensions of this box are taken from the width and height attributes; if the width attribute is not supplied, then the width will be taken to be textwid; if the height attribute is not supplied, then the height will be taken to be the number of text strings associated with the object times textht. Initially textwid and textht have a value of 0.

In places where a quoted text string can be used, an expression of the form:

```
sprintf(format,arg,...)
```

can also be used; this will produce the arguments formatted according to `format`, which should be a string as described in `printf(3)`, appropriate for the number of arguments supplied, using only the `e`, `f`, `g`, or `%` format characters.

The thickness of the lines used to draw objects is controlled by the `linethick` variable. This gives the thickness of lines in points. A negative value means use the default thickness: in output mode, this means use a thickness of 8 milli-inches; in output mode with the `-c` option, this means use the line thickness specified by `.ps` lines; in `troff` output mode, this means use a thickness proportional to the `point size`. A zero value means draw the thinnest possible line supported by the output device. Initially, it has a value of `-1`. There is also a `thick[ness]` attribute. For example,

```
circle thickness 1.5
```

would draw a circle using a line with a thickness of 1.5 points. The thickness of lines is not affected by the value of the `scale` variable, nor by the width or height given in the `.PS` line.

Boxes (including boxes with rounded corners), circles, and ellipses can be filled by giving then an attribute of `fill[ed]`. This takes an optional argument of an expression with a value between `0` and `1`; `0` will fill it with white, `1` with black, values in between with a proportionally gray shade. A value greater than `1` can also be used: this means fill with the shade of gray that is currently being used for text and lines. Normally this will be black, but output devices may provide a mechanism for changing this. Without an argument, then the value of the variable `fillval` will be used. Initially, this has a value of `0.5`. The invisible attribute does not affect the filling of objects. Any text associated with a filled object will be added after the object has been filled, so that the text will not be obscured by the filling.

Arrowheads will be drawn as solid triangles if the variable `arrowhead` is nonzero and either mode is enabled or the `-x` option has been given. Initially, `arrowhead` has a value of `1`.

The `troff` output of `pic` is device-independent. The `-T` option is therefore redundant. All numbers are taken to be in inches; numbers are never interpreted to be in `troff` machine units.

Objects can have an `aligned` attribute. This will only work when the postprocessor is `grops`. Any text associated with an object having the `aligned` attribute will be rotated about the center of the object so that it is aligned in the direction from the start point to the end point of the object. Note that this attribute will have no effect for objects whose start and end points are coincident.

In places where *nth* is allowed, *expr*`'th` is also allowed. Note that `'th` is a single token: no space is allowed between the `'` and the `th`. For example,

```
fori =1 to 4 do{
line from 'i'th box.nw to 'i+1'th box.se
}
```

## FILE

`/usr/lib/groff/tmac/tmac.pic`     Sample definitions of the PS and PE macros.

## SEE ALSO

`gtroff(1)`, `groff_out(5)`, `tex(1)`

TPIC: PIC for AT&T Bell Laboratories, Computing Science Technical Report No. 116, *PIC—A Graphics Language for Typesetting.* (This can be obtained by sending an e-mail message to `netlib@research.att.com` with a body of "send 116 from research/cstr.")

## BUGS

Input characters that are illegal for `groff` (those with ASCII code 0 or between 013 and 037 octal or between 0200 and 0237 octal) are rejected even in mode.

The interpretation of `fillval` is incompatible with the `pic` in 10th edition UNIX, which interprets `0` as black and `1` as white.

# gprof

gprof—Display call graph profile data

## SYNOPSIS

gprof [ -abcsz ] [ -ej-E *namo* ] [-fj-F *name* ][-k *fromname toname* ] [ *objfile* [ *gmon.out* ]]

## DESCRIPTION

gprof produces an execution profile of C, Pascal, or Fortran77 programs. The effect of called routines is incorporated in the profile of each caller. The profile data is taken from the call graph profile file (gmon.out default), which is created by programs that are compiled with the -pg option of cc(1), pc(1),and f77(1). The -pg option also links in versions of the library routines that are compiled for profiling. gprof reads the given object file (the default is a.out) and establishes the relation between its symbol table and the call graph profile from gmon.out. If more than one profile file is specified, the gprof output shows the sum of the profile information in the given profile files.

gprof calculates the amount of time spent in each routine. Next, these times are propagated along the edges of the call graph. Cycles are discovered, and calls into a cycle are made to share the time of the cycle. The first listing shows the functions sorted according to the time they represent, including the time of their call graph descendants. Below each function entry is shown its (direct) call graph children, and how their times are propagated to this function. A similar display above the function shows how this function's time and the time of its descendants is propagated to its (direct) call graph parents.

Cycles are also shown, with an entry for the cycle as a whole and a listing of the members of the cycle and their contributions to the time and call counts of the cycle.

Second, a flat profile is given, similar to that provided by prof(1). This listing gives the total execution times, the call counts, the time in milliseconds, the call spent in the routine itself, and the time in milliseconds the call spent in the routine itself, including its descendants.

Finally, an index of the function names is provided.

## OPTIONS

The following options are available:

| | |
|---|---|
| -a | Suppresses the printing of statically declared functions. If this option is given, all relevant information about the static function (for example, time samples, calls to other functions, calls from other functions) belongs to the function loaded just before the static function in the objfile file. |
| -b | Suppresses the printing of a description of each field in the profile. |
| -c | The static call graph of the program is discovered by a heuristic that examines the text space of the object file. Static-only parents or children are shown with call counts of 0. |
| -e *name* | Suppresses the printing of the graph profile entry for routine *name* and all its descendants (unless they have other ancestors that aren't suppressed). More than one -e option may be given. Only one *name* may be given with each -e option. |
| -E *name* | Suppresses the printing of the graph profile entry for routine *name* (and its descendants) as -e, previously and also excludes the time spent in *name* (and its descendants) from the total and percentage time computations. (For example, -E mcount -E mcleanup is the default.) |
| -f *name* | Prints the graph profile entry of only the specified routine *name* and its descendants. More than one -f option may be given. Only one *name* may be given with each -f option. |
| -F *name* | Prints the graph profile entry of only the routine *name* and its descendants (as -f, previously) and also uses only the times of the printed routines in total time and percentage computations. More than one -F option may be given. Only one *name* may be given with each -F option. The -F option overrides the -E option. |
| -k *fromname toname* | Will delete any arcs from routine *fromname* to routine *toname*. This can be used to break undesired cycles. More than one -k option may be given. Only one pair of routine names may be given with each -k option. |

| -s | A profile file gmon.sum is produced that represents the sum of the profile information in all the specified profile files. This summary profile file may be given to later executions of gprof (probably also with an -s) to accumulate profile data across several runs of an objfile file. |
| -v | Prints the version number for gprof, and then exits. |
| -z | Displays routines that have zero usage (as shown by call counts and accumulated time). This is useful with the -c option for discovering which routines were never called. |

## FILES

| a.out | The name list and text space |
| gmon.out | Dynamic call graph and profile |
| gmon.sum | Summarized dynamic call graph and profile |

## SEE ALSO

monitor(3), profil(2), cc(1), prof(1)

"An Execution Profiler for Modular Programs," by S. Graham, P. Kessler, M. McKusick; *Software—Practice and Experience*, Vol. 13, pp. 671-685, 1983.

"gprof: A Call Graph Execution Profiler," by S. Graham, P. Kessler, M. McKusick; *Proceedings of the SIGPLAN '82 Symposium on Compiler Construction*, SIGPLAN Notices, Vol. 17, No 6, pp. 120-126, June 1982.

## HISTORY

gprof appeared in 4.2 BSD.

## BUGS

The granularity of the sampling is shown, but remains statistical at best. We assume that the time for each execution of a function can be expressed by the total time for the function divided by the number of times the function is called. Thus, the time propagated along the call graph arcs to the function's parents is directly proportional to the number of times that arc is traversed.

Parents that are not themselves profiled will have the time of their profiled children propagated to them, but they will appear to be spontaneously invoked in the call graph listing, and will not have their time propagated further. Similarly, signal catchers, even though profiled, will appear to be spontaneous (although for more obscure reasons). Any profiled children of signal catchers should have their times propagated properly, unless the signal catcher was invoked during the execution of the profiling routine, in which case all is lost.

The profiled program must call exit(2) or return normally for the profiling information to be saved in the gmon.out file.

*29 January 1993*

# grefer

grefer—Preprocess bibliographic references for groff

## SYNOPSIS

grefer [-benvCPRS] [-a n] [-c fields] [-f n] [-i fields] [-k field] [-l m,n] [-p filename] [-s fields] [-t n] [-B field.macro] [filename...]

## DESCRIPTION

This file documents the GNU version of refer, which is part of the groff document formatting system. refer copies the contents of *filename*... to the standard output, except that lines between .[ and .] are interpreted as citations, and lines between .R1 and .R2 are interpreted as commands about how citations are to be processed.

Each citation specifies a reference. The citation can specify a reference that is contained in a bibliographic database by giving a set of keywords that only that reference contains. Alternatively, it can specify a reference by supplying a database record in the citation. A combination of these alternatives is also possible.

For each citation, refer can produce a mark in the text. This mark consists of some label that can be separated from the text and from other labels in various ways. For each reference, it also outputs groff commands that can be used by a macro package to produce a formatted reference for each citation. The output of refer must therefore be processed using a suitable macro package. The -ms and -me macros are both suitable. The commands to format a citation's reference can be output immediately after the citation, or the references may be accumulated, and the commands output at some later point. If the references are accumulated, then multiple citations of the same reference will produce a single formatted reference.

The interpretation of lines between .R1 and .R2 as commands is a new feature of GNU refer. Documents making use of this feature can still be processed by UNIX refer just by adding the lines:

```
.de R1
.ig R2
..
```

to the beginning of the document. This will cause troff to ignore everything between .R1 and .R2. The effect of some commands can also be achieved by options. These options are supported mainly for compatibility with UNIX refer. It is usually more convenient to use commands.

refer generates .lf lines so that filenames and line numbers in messages produced by commands that read refer output will be correct; it also interprets lines beginning with .lf so that filenames and line numbers in the messages and .lf lines that it produces will be accurate even if the input has been preprocessed by a command such as gsoelim(1).

## OPTIONS

Most options are equivalent to commands (for a description of these commands, see "Commands," later in this manual page):

| | |
|---|---|
| -b | no-label-in-text; no-label-in-reference |
| -e | accumulate |
| -n | no-default-database |
| -C | compatible |
| -P | move-punctuation |
| -S | label "(A.n¦Q) ', ' (D.y¦D)"; bracket-label " (" ) "; " |
| -a*n* | reverse A*n* |
| -c*fields* | capitalize *fields* |
| -f*n* | label %*n* |
| -i*fields* | search-ignore *fields* |
| -k | label L%a |
| -k*field* | label *field*%a |
| -l | label A.nD.y%a |
| -l*m* | label A.n+*m*D.y%a |
| -l,*n* | label A.nD.y-*n*%a |
| -l*m*,*n* | label A.n+*m*D.y-*n*%a |
| -p*filename* | database *filename* |
| -s*spec* | sort *spec* |
| -t*n* | search-truncate *n* |

These options are equivalent to the following commands with the addition that the filenames specified on the command line are processed as if they were arguments to the bibliography command instead of in the normal way:

| | |
|---|---|
| -B | Annotate X AP; no-label-in-reference |
| -B*field.macro* | Annotate *field macro*; no-label-in-reference |

The following options have no equivalent commands:

| | |
|---|---|
| -v | Print the version number |
| -R | Don't recognize lines beginning with .R1/.R2 |

## USAGE

### BIBLIOGRAPHIC DATABASES

The bibliographic database is a text file consisting of records separated by one or more blank lines. Within each record, fields start with a % at the beginning of a line. Each field has a one-character name that immediately follows the %. It is best to use only uppercase and lowercase letters for the names of fields. The name of the field should be followed by exactly one space, and then by the contents of the field. Empty fields are ignored. The conventional meaning of each field is as follows:

| | |
|---|---|
| A | The name of an author. If the name contains a title such as Jr. at the end, it should be separated from the last name by a comma. There can be multiple occurrences of the A field. The order is significant. It is a good idea always to supply an A field or a Q field. |
| B | For an article that is part of a book, the title of the book. |
| C | The place (city) of publication. |
| D | The date of publication. The year should be specified in full. If the month is specified, the name rather than the number of the month should be used, but only the first three letters are required. It is a good idea always to supply a D field; if the date is unknown, a value such as in press or unknown can be used. |
| E | For an article that is part of a book, the name of an editor of the book. Where the work has editors and no authors, the names of the editors should be given as A fields (ed) or (eds) should be appended to the last author. |
| G | U.S. government ordering number. |
| I | The publisher (issuer). |
| J | For an article in a journal, the name of the journal. |
| K | Keywords to be used for searching. |
| L | Label. |
| N | Journal issue number. |
| O | Other information. This is usually printed at the end of the reference. |
| P | Page number. A range of pages can be specified as $m$-$n$. |
| Q | The name of the author, if the author is not a person. This will only be used if there are no A fields. There can only be one Q field. |
| R | Technical report number. |
| S | Series name. |
| T | Title. For an article in a book or journal, this should be the title of the article. |
| V | Volume number of the journal or book. |
| X | Annotation. |

For all fields except A and E, if there is more than one occurrence of a particular field in a record, only the last such field will be used.

If accent strings are used, they should follow the character to be accented. This means that the AM macro must be used with the -ms macros. Accent strings should not be quoted: use one \ rather than two.

### CITATIONS

The format of a citation is

```
.[opening-text
flags keywords
fields
.]closing-text
```

The *opening-text*, *closing-text,* and *flags* components are optional. Only one of the *keywords* and *fields* components need be specified.

The *keywords* component says to search the bibliographic databases for a reference that contains all the words in *keywords*. It is an error if more than one reference if found.

The *fields* components specifies additional fields to replace or supplement those specified in the reference. When references are being accumulated and the *keywords* component is nonempty, then additional fields should be specified only on the first occasion that a particular reference is cited, and will apply to all citations of that reference.

The *opening-text* and *closing-text* component specifies strings to be used to bracket the label instead of the strings specified in the bracket-label command. If either of these components is nonempty, the strings specified in the bracket-label command will not be used; this behavior can be altered using the [ and ] flags. Note that leading and trailing spaces are significant for these components.

The *flags* component is a list of nonalphanumeric characters, each of which modifies the treatment of this particular citation. UNIX refer will treat these flags as part of the keywords and so will ignore them because they are nonalphanumeric. The following flags are currently recognized:

| | |
|---|---|
| # | This says to use the label specified by the short-label command, instead of that specified by the label command. If no short label has been specified, the normal label will be used. Typically, the short label is used with author-date labels and consists of only the date and possibly a disambiguating letter; the # is supposed to be suggestive of a numeric type of label. |
| [ | Precede *opening-text* with the first string specified in the bracket-label command. |
| ] | Follow *closing-text* with the second string specified in the bracket-label command. |

One advantage of using the [ and ] flags rather than including the brackets in *opening-text* and *closing-text* is that you can change the style of bracket used in the document just by changing the bracket-label command. Another advantage is that sorting and merging of citations will not necessarily be inhibited if the flags are used.

If a label is to be inserted into the text, it will be attached to the line preceding the .[ line. If there is no such line, then an extra line will be inserted before the .[ line and a warning will be given.

There is no special notation for making a citation to multiple references. Just use a sequence of citations, one for each reference. Don't put anything between the citations. The labels for all the citations will be attached to the line preceding the first citation. The labels may also be sorted or merged. (See the description of the <> label expression, and of the sort-adjacent- labels and abbreviate-label-ranges command.) A label will not be merged if its citation has a nonempty *opening-text* or *closing-text*. However, the labels for a citation using the ] flag and without any *closing-text* immediately followed by a citation using the [ flag and without any *opening-text* may be sorted and merged even though the first citation's *opening-text* or the second citation's *closing-text* is nonempty. (If you want to prevent this, just make the first citation's *closing-text* \&.)

## COMMANDS

Commands are contained between lines starting with .R1 and .R2. Recognition of these lines can be prevented by the -R option. When an .R1 line is recognized, any accumulated references are flushed out. Neither .R1 nor .R2 lines, nor anything between them, is output.

Commands are separated by newlines or semicolons. # introduces a comment that extends to the end of the line (but does not conceal the newline). Each command is broken up into words. Words are separated by spaces or tabs. A word that begins with an open quote (") extends to the next close quote (") that is not followed by another open quote ("). If there is no such open quote (") the word extends to the end of the line. Pairs of open quotes (") in a word beginning with collapse to a single open quote ("). Neither # nor ; is recognized inside open quotes ("). A line can be continued by ending it with \; this works everywhere except after a #.

Each command *name* that is marked with * has an associated negative command no-*name* that undoes the effect of *name*. For example, the no-sort command specifies that references should not be sorted. The negative commands take no arguments.

In the following description, each argument must be a single word; `field` is used for a single uppercase or lowercase letter naming a field; `fields` is used for a sequence of such letters; *m* and *n* are used for a nonnegative numbers; `string` is used for an arbitrary string; `filename` is used for the name of a file.

| | |
|---|---|
| abbreviate*`fields`string1 `string2`string3`string4` | Abbreviate the first names of `fields`. An initial letter will be separated from another initial letter by `string1`, from the last name by `string2`, and from anything else (such as a von or de) by `string3`. These default to a period followed by a space. In a hyphenated first name, the initial of the first part of the name will be separated from the hyphen by `string4`; this defaults to a period. No attempt is made to handle any ambiguities that might result from abbreviation. Names are abbreviated before sorting and before label construction. |
| abbreviate-label-ranges*`string` | Three or more adjacent labels that refer to consecutive references will be abbreviated to a label consisting of the first label, followed by `string`, followed by the last label. This is mainly useful with numeric labels. If `string` is omitted it defaults to -. |
| accumulate* | Accumulate references instead of writing out each reference as it is encountered. Accumulated references will be written out whenever a reference of the form:<br><br>.[<br>$LIST$<br>.]<br><br>is encountered, after all input files have been processed, and whenever an .R1 line is recognized. |
| annotate*`field`string | `field` is an annotation; print it at the end of the reference as a paragraph preceded by the line<br><br>.string<br><br>If macro is omitted, it will default to AP; if `field` is also omitted, it will default to X. Only one `field` can be an annotation. |
| articles`string` ... `string` ... | These are definite or indefinite articles, and should be ignored at the beginning of T fields when sorting. Initially, *the*, *a*, and *an* are recognized as articles. |
| bibliography`filename` ... | Write out all the references contained in the bibliographic databases `filename` ... |
| bracket-label`string` `1`string2`string3` | In the text, bracket each label with `string1` and `string2`. An occurrence of `string2` immediately followed by `string1` will be turned into `string3`. The default behavior is bracket-label \*([. \*(.] ", " |
| capitalize`fields` | Convert `fields` to caps and small caps. |
| compatible* | Recognize .R1 and .R2 even when followed by a character other than space or newline. |
| database`filename`... | Search the bibliographic databases `filename`... For each `filename` if an index `filename`.i created by gindxbib(1) exists, then it will be searched instead; each index can cover multiple databases. |
| date-as-label*`string` | `string` is a label expression that specifies a string with which to replace the D field after constructing the label. See "Label Expressions," later in this manual page, for a description of label expressions. This command is useful if you do not want explicit labels in the reference list, but instead want to handle any necessary disambiguation by qualifying the date in some way. The label used in the text would typically be some combination of the author and date. In most cases, you should also use the no-label-in-reference command. For example,<br><br>date-as-label D.+yD.y%a*D.-y<br><br>would attach a disambiguating letter to the year part of the D field in the reference. |
| default-database* | The default database should be searched. This is the default behavior, so the negative version of this command is more useful. refer determines whether the default database should be searched on the first occasion that it needs to do a search. Thus, a no-default-database command must be given before then, in order to be effective. |

| | |
|---|---|
| discard*`fields` | When the reference is read, `fields` should be discarded; no string definitions for `fields` will be output. Initially, `fields` are XYZ. |
| et-al*`stringmn` | Control use of et al in the evaluation of @ expressions in `label` expressions. If the number of authors needed to make the author sequence unambiguous is *u* and the total number of authors is *t*, then the last *t - u* authors will be replaced by `string`, provided that *t - u* is not less than *m* and *t* is not less than *n*. The default behavior is et-al " et al" 2 3. |
| include`filename` | Include `filename` and interpret the contents as commands. |
| join-authors`string1` `string2`string3` | This says how authors should be joined together. When there are exactly two authors, they will be joined with `string1`. When there are more than two authors, all but the last two will be joined with `string2`, and the last two authors will be joined with `string3`. If `string3` is omitted, it will default to `string1`; if `string2` is also omitted, it will also default to `string1`. For example, join-authors " and " ", " ", and " will restore the default method for joining authors. |
| label-in-reference* | When outputting the reference, define the string [F to be the reference's label. This is the default behavior; so the negative version of this command is more useful. |
| label-in-text* | For each reference, output a label in the text. The label will be separated from the surrounding text as described in the bracket-label command. This is the default behavior; so the negative version of this command is more useful. |
| label`string` | `string` is a label expression describing how to label each reference. |
| separate-label-second-parts `string` | When merging two-part labels, separate the second part of the second label from the first label with `string`. See the description of the <> label expression. |
| move-punctuation* | In the text, move any punctuation at the end of line past the label. It is usually a good idea to give this command unless you are using superscripted numbers as labels. |
| reverse*`string` | Reverse the fields whose names are in `string`. Each field name can be followed by a number that says how many such fields should be reversed. If no number is given for a field, all such fields will be reversed. |
| search-ignore*`fields` | While searching for keys in databases for which no index exists, ignore the contents of `fields`. Initially, fields XYZ are ignored. |
| search-truncate*`n` | Only require the first *n* characters of keys to be given. In effect, when searching for a given key, words in the database are truncated to the maximum of *n* and the length of the key. Initially, *n* is 6. |
| short-label*`string` | `string` is a label expression that specifies an alternative (usually shorter) style of label. This is used when the # flag is given in the citation. When using author-date style labels, the identity of the author or authors is sometimes clear from the context, and so it may be desirable to omit the author or authors from the label. The short-label command will typically be used to specify a label containing just a date and possibly a disambiguating letter. |
| sort*`string` | Sort references according to string. References will automatically be accumulated. `string` should be a list of field names, each followed by a number, indicating how many fields with the name should be used for sorting. + can be used to indicate that all the fields with the name should be used. Also, . can be used to indicate the references should be sorted using the (tentative) label. (The "Label Expressions" subsection describes the concept of a tentative label.) |
| sort-adjacent-labels* | Sort labels that are adjacent in the text according to their position in the reference list. This command should usually be given if the abbreviate-label-ranges command has been given, or if the label expression contains a <> expression. This will have no effect unless references are being accumulated. |

## LABEL EXPRESSIONS

Label expressions can be evaluated both normally and tentatively. The result of normal evaluation is used for output. The result of tentative evaluation, called the tentative label, is used to gather the information that normal evaluation needs to disambiguate the label. Label expressions specified by the date-as-label and short-label commands are not evaluated tentatively. Normal and tentative evaluation are the same for all types of expression other than @, *, and % expressions. The following description applies to normal evaluation, except where otherwise specified.

| | |
|---|---|
| field, field *n* | The *n*th part of field. If *n* is omitted, it defaults to 1. |
| 'string' | The characters in *string* literally. |
| @ | All the authors joined as specified by the join-authors command. The whole of each author's name will be used. However, if the references are sorted by author (that is the sort specification starts with A+), then authors' last names will be used instead, provided that this does not introduce ambiguity, and also an initial subsequence of the authors may be used instead of all the authors, again provided that this does not introduce ambiguity. The use of only the last name for the *i*-th author of some reference is considered to be ambiguous if there is some other reference, such that the first i - 1 authors of the references are the same, the *i*-th authors are not the same, but the *i*-th authors' last names are the same. A proper initial subsequence of the sequence of authors for some reference is considered to be ambiguous if there is a reference with some other sequence of authors that also has that subsequence as a proper initial subsequence. When an initial subsequence of authors is used, the remaining authors are replaced by the string specified by the et-al command; this command may also specify additional requirements that must be met before an initial subsequence can be used. @ tentatively evaluates to a canonical representation of the authors, such that authors that compare equally for sorting purpose will have the same representation. |
| %n, %a, %A, %i, %I | The serial number of the reference formatted according to the character following the %. The serial number of a reference is 1 plus the number of earlier references with same tentative label as this reference. These expressions tentatively evaluate to an empty string. |
| expr* | If there is another reference with the same tentative label as this reference, then *expr*; otherwise, an empty string. It tentatively evaluates to an empty string. |
| expr+n, expr-n | The first (+) or last (-) n uppercase or lowercase letters or digits of *expr*. troff special characters (such as \('a) count as a single letter. Accent strings are retained but do not count toward the total. |
| expr.l | *expr* converted to lowercase. |
| expr.u | *expr* converted to uppercase. |
| expr.c | *expr* converted to caps and small caps. |
| expr.r | *expr* reversed so that the last name is first. |
| expr.a | *expr* with first names abbreviated. Note that fields specified in the abbreviate command are abbreviated before any labels are evaluated. Thus .a is useful only when you want a field to be abbreviated in a label but not in a reference. |
| expr.y | The year part of *expr*. |
| expr.+y | The part of *expr* before the year, or the whole of *expr* if it does not contain a year. |
| expr.-y | The part of *expr* after the year, or an empty string if *expr* does not contain a year. |
| expr.n | The last name part of *expr*. |
| expr1expr2 | *expr1* except that if the last character of *expr1* is - then it will be replaced by *expr2*. |
| expr1 expr2 | The concatenation of *expr1* and *expr2*. |
| expr1¦expr2 | If *expr1* is nonempty, then *expr1*; otherwise, *expr2*. |
| expr1&expr2 | If *expr1* is nonempty, then *expr2*; otherwise, an empty string. |
| expr1?expr2:expr3 | If *expr1* is nonempty, then *expr2*; otherwise, *expr3*. |
| <expr> | The label is in two parts, which are separated by *expr*. Two adjacent two-part labels that have the same first part will be merged by appending the second part of the second label onto the first label separated by the string specified in the separate-label-second-parts command (initially, a comma followed by a |

space); the resulting label will also be a two-part label with the same first part as before merging, and so additional labels can be merged into it. Note that it is permissible for the first part to be empty; this may be desirable for expressions used in the short-label command.

(*expr*)          The same as *expr*. Used for grouping.

The preceding expressions are listed in order of precedence (highest first); & and ¦ have the same precedence.

## MACRO INTERFACE

Each reference starts with a call to the macro ]-. The string [F will be defined to be the label for this reference, unless the no-label-in-reference command has been given. There then follows a series of string definitions, one for each field: string [X corresponds to field X. The number register [P is set to 1 if the P field contains a range of pages. The [T, [A, and [O number registers are set to 1 according as the T, A, and O fields end with one of the characters .?!. The [E number register will be set to 1 if the [E string contains more than one name. The reference is followed by a call to the ][ macro. The first argument to this macro gives a number representing the type of the reference. If a reference contains a J field, it will be classified as type 1; otherwise, if it contains a B field, it will be type 3; otherwise, if it contains a G or R field it will be type 4, otherwise if it contains an I field, it will be type 2; otherwise, it will be type 0. The second argument is a symbolic name for the type: other, journal-article, book, article-in-book, or tech-report. Groups of references that have been accumulated or are produced by the bibliography command are preceded by a call to the ]< macro and followed by a call to the ]> macro.

## FILES

/usr/dict/papers/Ind          Default database

*file*.i Index files

## SEE ALSO

gindxbib(1), glookbib(1), lkbib(1)

## BUGS

In label expressions, <> expressions are ignored inside .char expressions.

*Groff Version 1.09*

# grep, egrep, fgrep

grep, egrep, fgrep—Print lines matching a pattern

## SYNOPSIS

grep [ -[[AB]]*num* ][-[CEFGVBchilnsvwx]][-e ] *pattern* j -f*file* ][*files...* ]

## DESCRIPTION

grep searches the named input *files* (or standard input if no files are named, or the filename - is given) for lines containing a match to the given *pattern*. By default, grep prints the matching lines.

There are three major variants of grep, controlled by the following options:

-G          Interpret *pattern* as a basic regular expression (see the list following this one). This is the default.

-E          Interpret *pattern* as an extended regular expression.

-F          Interpret *pattern* as a list of fixed strings, separated by newlines, any of which is to be matched.

In addition, two variant programs, egrep and fgrep, are available. egrep is similar (but not identical) to grepn-E, and is compatible with the historical UNIX egrep. Fgrep is the same as grepn-F.

All variants of grep understand the following options:

| | |
|---|---|
| -*num* | Matches will be printed with *num* lines of leading and trailing context. However, grep will never print any given line more than once. |
| -A *num* | Print *num* lines of trailing context after matching lines. |
| -B *num* | Print *num* lines of leading context before matching lines. |
| -C | Equivalent to -2. |
| -V | Print the version number of grep to standard error. This version number should be included in all bug reports. |
| -b | Print the byte offset within the input file before each line of output. |
| -c | Suppress normal output; instead print a count of matching lines for each input file. With the -v option, count nonmatching lines. |
| -e *pattern* | Use *pattern* as the pattern; useful to protect patterns beginning with -. |
| -f *file* | Obtain the pattern from *file*. |
| -h | Suppress the prefixing of filenames on output when multiple files are searched. |
| -i | Ignore case distinctions in both the *pattern* and the input files. |
| -L | Suppress normal output; instead print the name of each input file from which no output would normally have been printed. |
| -l | Suppress normal output; instead print the name of each input file from which output would normally have been printed. |
| -n | Prefix each line of output with the line number within its input file. |
| -q | Quiet; suppress normal output. |
| -s | Suppress error messages about nonexistent or unreadable files. |
| -v | Invert the sense of matching, to select nonmatching lines. |
| -w | Select only those lines containing matches that form whole words. The test is that the matching substring must either be at the beginning of the line, or preceded by a nonword constituent character. Similarly, it must be either at the end of the line or followed by a nonword-constituent character. Word-constituent characters are letters, digits, and the underscore. |
| -x | Select only those matches that exactly match the whole line. |

## REGULAR EXPRESSIONS

A regular expression is a pattern that describes a set of strings. Regular expressions are constructed analogously to arithmetic expressions, by using various operators to combine smaller expressions.

grep understands two different versions of regular expression syntax: *basic* and *extended*. In GNU\grep, there is no difference in available functionality using either syntax. In other implementations, basic regular expressions are less powerful. The following description applies to extended regular expressions; differences for basic regular expressions are summarized afterwards.

The fundamental building blocks are the regular expressions that match a single character. Most characters, including all letters and digits, are regular expressions that match themselves. Any meta character with special meaning may be quoted by preceding it with a backslash.

A list of characters enclosed by [ and ] matches any single character in that list; if the first character of the list is the caret (ˆ) then it matches any character *not* in the list. For example, the regular expression [0123456789] matches any single digit. A range of ASCII characters may be specified by giving the first and last characters, separated by a hyphen. Finally, certain named classes of characters are predefined. Their names are self-explanatory, and they are [:alnum:], [:alpha:], [:cntrl:], [:digit:], [:graph:], [:lower:], [:print:], [:punct:], [:space:], [:upper:], and [:xdigit:]. For example, [[:alnum:]] means [0-9A-Za- z], except the latter form is dependent upon the ASCII character encoding, whereas the former is portable. (Note that the brackets in these class names are part of the symbolic names, and must be included in addition to the brackets delimiting the bracket list.) Most meta characters lose their special meaning inside lists. To include a literal ], place it first in the list. Similarly, to include a literal ˆ, place it anywhere but first. Finally, to include a literal --, place it last.

The period matches any single character. The symbol \w is a synonym for [[:alnum:]] and \W is a synonym for [ˆ[:alnum]].

The caret and the dollar sign are meta characters that respectively match the empty string at the beginning and end of a line. The symbols \< and \>, respectively, match the empty string at the beginning and end of a word. The symbol \b matches the empty string at the edge of a word, and \B matches the empty string provided it's *not* at the edge of a word.

A regular expression matching a single character may be followed by one of several repetition operators:

| | |
|---|---|
| ? | The preceding item is optional and matched at most once. |
| * | The preceding item will be matched zero or more times. |
| + | The preceding item will be matched one or more times. |
| *n* | The preceding item is matched exactly *n* times. |
| *n,* | The preceding item is matched *n* or more times. |
| *,m* | The preceding item is optional and is matched at most *m* times. |
| *n,m* | The preceding item is matched at least *n* times, but not more than *m* times. |

Two regular expressions may be concatenated; the resulting regular expression matches any string formed by concatenating two substrings that respectively match the concatenated subexpressions.

Two regular expressions may be joined by the infix operator |; the resulting regular expression matches any string matching either subexpression.

Repetition takes precedence over concatenation, which in turn takes precedence over alternation. A whole subexpression may be enclosed in parentheses to override these precedence rules.

The back reference \n, where *n* is a single digit, matches the substring previously matched by the *n*th parenthesized subexpression of the regular expression.

In basic regular expressions, the meta characters |, (, and ) lose their special meaning; instead use the backslashed versions \?, \+, \f, \j, \(, and \).

In egrep, the meta character { loses its special meaning; instead use \{.

## DIAGNOSTICS

Normally, exit status is 0 if matches were found, and 1 if no matches were found. (The .B -v option inverts the sense of the exit status.) Exit status is 2 if there were syntax errors in the pattern, inaccessible input files, or other system errors.

## BUGS

E-mail bug reports to bug-gnu-utils@prep.ai.mit.edu. Be sure to include the word grep somewhere in the "Subject:" field.

Large repetition counts in the m ,n construct may cause grep to use lots of memory. In addition, certain other obscure regular expressions require exponential time and space, and may cause grep to run out of memory.

Back references are very slow, and may require exponential time.

*GNU Project, 10 September 1992*

# grephistory

grephistory—Display filenames from Usenet history file

## SYNOPSIS

grephistory [ -f *filename* ][-e ][-n ][-q ][-l ][-i ][-s ][*messageid* ]

## DESCRIPTION

grephistory queries the dbz(3) index into the history(5) file for an article having a specified Message ID.

If messageid cannot be found in the database, the program prints "Not found" and exits with a nonzero status. If messageid is in the database, the program prints the pathname and exits successfully. If no pathname exists, the program will print /dev/

`null` and exit successfully. This can happen when an article has been canceled, or if it has been expired but its history is still retained. This is default behavior, which can be obtained by using the -n flag.

If the -q flag is used, then no message is displayed. The program will still exit with the appropriate exit status. If the -e flag is used, then *grephistory* will only print the filename of an existing article.

If the -l flag is used, then the entire line from the history file will be displayed.

If the -i flag is used, then *grephistory* will read a list of Message-IDs on standard input, one per line. Leading and trailing whitespace is ignored, as are any malformed lines. It will print on standard output those Message-IDs that are not found in the history database. This flag is used in processing ihave control messages.

If the -s flag is used, then *grephistory* will read a similar list from its standard input. It will print on standard output a list of filenames for each article that is still available. This flag is used in processing sendme control messages.

To specify a different value for the history file and database, use the -f flag.

## HISTORY

Written by Rich $alz (`rsalz@uunet.uu.net`) for InterNetNews.

## SEE ALSO

dbz(3), history(5)

# grodvi

grodvi—Convert groff output to TeX dvi format

## SYNOPSIS

grodvi [ -dv ][-w*n* ][-F*dir* ][*files ...* ]

## DESCRIPTION

grodvi is a driver for groff that produces dvi format. Normally, it should be run by groff-Tdvi. This will run gtroff-Tdvi; it will also input the macros /usr/lib/groff/tmac/tmac.dvi; if the input is being preprocessed with geqn, it will also input /usr/lib/groff/font/devdvi/eqnchar.

The dvi file generated by grodvi can be printed by any correctly written dvi driver. The troff drawing primitives are implemented using the tpic version 2 specials. If the driver does not support these, the \D commands will not produce any output.

There is an additional drawing command available:

\D'R*dhdv*'        Draw a rule (solid black rectangle), with one corner at the current position, and the diagonally opposite corner at the current position +(*dh,dv*). Afterwards, the current position will be at the opposite corner. This produces a rule in the dvi file and so can be printed even with a driver that does not support the tpic specials, unlike the other \D commands.

The groff command \X'*anything*' is translated into the same command in the dvi file as would be produced by \special{ anything } in TeX; *anything* may not contain a newline.

Font files for grodvi can be created from tfm files using tfmtodit(1). The font description file should contain the following additional commands:

internalname name        The name of the tfm file (without the .tfm extension) is *name*.
checksum *n*             The checksum in the tfm file is *n*.
designsize *n*          The designsize in the tfm file is *n*.

These are automatically generated by tfmtodit.

In troff, the \N escape sequence can be used to access characters by their position in the corresponding tfm file; all characters in the tfm file can be accessed this way.

## OPTIONS

| | |
|---|---|
| -d | Do not use tpic specials to implement drawing commands. Horizontal and vertical lines will be implemented by rules. Other drawing commands will be ignored |
| -v | Print the version number. |
| -w*n* | Set the default line thickness to *n* thousandths of an em. |
| -F*dir* | Search directory *dir*/devdvi for font and device description files. |

## FILES

| | |
|---|---|
| /usr/lib/groff/font/devdvi/DESC | Device description file |
| /usr/lib/groff/font/devdvi/ F | Font description file for font *F* |
| /usr/lib/groff/tmac/tmac.dvi | Macros for use with grodvi |

## BUGS

dvi files produced by grodvi use a different resolution (57,816 units per inch) than those produced by TeX. Incorrectly written drivers that assume the resolution used by TeX, rather than using the resolution specified in the dvi file, will not work with grodvi.

When using the -d option with boxed tables, vertical and horizontal lines can sometimes protrude by one pixel. This is a consequence of the way TeX requires that the heights and widths of rules be rounded.

## SEE ALSO

tfmtodit(1), groff(1), gtroff(1), geqn(1), groff_out(5), groff_font(5), groff_char(7)

*Groff Version 1.09 14*

# groff

groff—Front end for the groff document formatting system

## SYNOPSIS

groff [ -tpeszaivhblCENRVXZ][-w*name* ][-W*name* ][-m*name* ][-F*dir* ][-T*dev* ] [ -ff*am* ][-M*dir* ][-dcs ][-rcn ][-n*num* ] [-o*list* ][-P*arg* ][*files* ... ]

## DESCRIPTION

groff is a front-end to the groff document formatting system. Normally, it runs the gtroff program and a postprocessor appropriate for the selected device. Available devices are

| | |
|---|---|
| ps | For PostScript printers and previewers |
| dvi | For TeX dvi format |
| X75 | For a 75 dpi X11 previewer |
| X100 | For a 100dpi X11 previewer |
| ascii | For typewriter-like devices |
| latin1 | For typewriter-like devices using the ISO Latin-1 character set. |

The postprocessor to be used for a device is specified by the postpro command in the device description file. This can be overridden with the -X option.

The default device is ps. It can optionally preprocess with any of gpic, geqn, gtbl, grefer, or gsoelim.

Options without an argument can be grouped behind a single -. A filename of - denotes the standard input.

The grog command can be used to guess the correct groff command to use to format a file.

## OPTIONS

| | |
|---|---|
| -h | Print a help message. |
| -e | Preprocess with geqn. |
| -t | Preprocess with gtbl. |
| -p | Preprocess with gpic. |
| -s | Preprocess with gsoelim. |
| -R | Preprocess with grefer. No mechanism is provided for passing arguments to grefer because most grefer options have equivalent commands that can be included in the file. See grefer(1) for more details. |
| -v | Make programs run by groff print out their version number. |
| -V | Print the pipeline on stdout instead of executing it. |
| -z | Suppress output from gtroff. Only error messages will be printed. |
| -Z | Do not postprocess the output of gtroff. Normally, groff will automatically run the appropriate postprocessor. |
| -Parg | Pass *arg* to the postprocessor. Each argument should be passed with a separate -P option. Note that groff does not prepend - to *arg* before passing it to the postprocessor. |
| -l | Send the output to a printer. The command used for this is specified by the print command in the device description file. |
| -Larg | Pass *arg* to the spooler. Each argument should be passed with a separate -L option. Note that groff does not prepend - to *arg* before passing it to the postprocessor. |
| -Tdev | Prepare output for device *dev*. The default device is ps. |
| -X | Preview with gxditview instead of using the usual postprocessor. This is unlikely to produce good results except with -Tps. |
| -N | Don't allow newlines with eqn delimiters. This is the same as the -N option in geqn. |

The options -a, -b, -i, -C, -E, -w*name*, -W*name*, -m*name*, -o*list*, -d*cs*, -r*cn*, -F*dir*, -M*dir*, -f*fam*, *and* -n*num* are described in gtroff(1).

## ENVIRONMENT

| | |
|---|---|
| GROFF_COMMAND_PREFIX | If this is sct *X*, then groff will run *X*troff instead of gtroff. This also applies to tbl, pic, eqn, refer, and soelim. It does not apply to grops, grodvi, grotty, and gxditview. |
| GROFF_TMAC_PATH | A colon-separated list of directories in which to search for macro files. |
| GROFF_TYPESETTER | Default device. |
| GROFF_FONT_PATH | A colon-separated list of directories in which to search for the dev*name* directory. |
| PATH | The search path for commands executed by groff. |
| GROFF_TMPDIR | The directory in which temporary files will be created. If this is not set and TMPDIR is set, temporary files will be created in that directory. Otherwise, temporary files will be created in /tmp. The grops(1) and grefer(1) commands can create temporary files. |

## FILES

| | |
|---|---|
| /usr/lib/groff/font/dev*name*/DESC | Device description file for device *name*. |
| /usr/lib/groff/font/dev*name*/F | Font file for font *F* of device *name*. |

## AUTHOR

James Clark (jjc@jclark.com)

## BUGS

Report bugs to bug-groff@prep.ai.mit.edu. Include a complete, self-contained example that will allow the bug to be reproduced, and say which version of groff you are using.

## COPYRIGHT

Copyright 1989, 1990, 1991, 1992 Free Software Foundation, Inc.

groff is free software; you can redistribute it or modify it under the terms of the GNU General Public License as published by the Free Software Foundation; either version 2, or (at your option) any later version.

groff is distributed in the hope that it will be useful, but without any warranty; without even the implied warranty of merchantability or fitness for a particular purpose. See the GNU General Public License for more details.

You should have received a copy of the GNU General Public License along with groff; see the file COPYING. If not, write to the Free Software Foundation, 675 Mass Ave, Cambridge, MA 02139, USA.

## AVAILABILITY

The most recent released version of groff is always available for anonymous ftp from prep.ai.mit.edu (18.71.0.38) in the directory pub/gnu.

## SEE ALSO

grog(1), gtroff(1), gtbl(1), gpic(1), geqn(1), gsoelim(1), grefer(1), grops(1), grodvi(1), grotty(1), gxditview(1), groff_font(5), grof_out(5), groff_ms(7), groff_me(7), groff_char(7)

*Groff Version 1.09, 29 October 1992*

# grog

grog—Guess options for groff command

## SYNOPSIS

grog [ -*option* ...][*files* ... ]

## DESCRIPTION

grog reads *files* and guesses which of the groff(1) options -e, -man, -me, -mm, -ms, -p, -s, and -t are required for printing *files*, and prints the groff command including those options on the standard output. A filename of - is taken to refer to the standard input. If no files are specified, the standard input will be read. Any specified options will be included in the printed command. No space is allowed between options and their arguments. For example,

'grog -Tdvi paper.ms'

will guess the appropriate command to print paper.ms and then run it after adding the -Tdvi option.

## SEE ALSO

doctype(1), groff(1), gtroff(1), gtbl(1), gpic(1), geqn(1), gsoelim(1)

*Groff Version 1.09 14*

# grops

grops—PostScript driver for groff

## SYNOPSIS

grops [ -glv ][-b*n* ][-c*n* ][-w*n* ][-F*dir* ][*files* ... ]

## DESCRIPTION

grops translates the output of GNU troff to PostScript. Normally, grops should be invoked by using the groff command with a -Tps option. If no files are given, grops will read the standard input. A filename of - will also cause grops to read the standard input. PostScript output is written to the standard output. When grops is run by groff, options can be passed to grops by using the groff -P option.

## OPTIONS

-b*n*    Work around broken spoolers and previewers. Normally grops produces output that conforms the Document Structuring Conventions version 3.0. Unfortunately, some spoolers and previewers can't handle such output. The value of *n* controls what grops does to its output acceptable to such programs. A value of 0 will cause grops not to employ any workarounds. Add 1 if no %%BeginDocumentSetup and %%EndDocumentSetup comments should be generated; this is needed for early versions of TranScript that get confused by anything between the %%EndProlog comment and the first %%Page comment. Add 2 if lines in included files beginning with %! should be stripped out; this is needed for Sun's pageview previewer. Add 4 if %%Page, %%Trailer, and %%EndProlog comments should be stripped out of included files; this is needed for spoolers that don't understand the %%BeginDocument and %%EndDocument comments. Add 8 if the first line of the PostScript output should be %!PS-Adobe-2.0 rather than %!PS-Adobe-3.0; this is needed when using Sun's Newsprint with a printer that requires page reversal. The default value can be specified by a broken*n* command in the DESC file. Otherwise, the default value is 0.

-c*n*    Print *n* copies of each page.

-g    Guess the page length. This generates PostScript code that guesses the page length. The guess will be correct only if the imageable area is vertically centered on the page. This option allows you to generate documents that can be printed both on letter (8.5×11) paper and on A4 paper without change.

-l    Print the document in landscape format.

-F*dir*    Search the directory *dir*/dev*name* for font and device description files; *name* is the name of the device, usually ps.

-w*n*    Lines should be drawn using a thickness of *n* thousandths of an em.

-v    Print the version number.

## USAGE

There are styles called R, I, B, and BI mounted at font positions 1 to 4. The fonts are grouped into families A, BM, C, H, HN, N, P, and T having members in each of these styles:

| | |
|---|---|
| AR | AvantGarde-Book |
| AI | AvantGarde-BookOblique |
| AB | AvantGarde-Demi |
| ABI | AvantGarde-DemiOblique |
| BMR | Bookman-Light |
| BMI | Bookman-LightItalic |
| BMB | Bookman-Demi |
| BMBI | Bookman-DemiItalic |
| CR | Courier |
| CI | Courier-Oblique |
| CB | Courier-Bold |
| CBI | Courier-BoldOblique |
| HR | Helvetica |
| HI | Helvetica-Oblique |
| HB | Helvetica-Bold |
| HBI | Helvetica-BoldOblique |
| HNR | Helvetica-Narrow |
| HNI | Helvetica-Narrow-Oblique |

| HNB | Helvetica-Narrow-Bold |
| HNBI | Helvetica-Narrow-BoldOblique |
| NR | NewCenturySchlbk-Roman |
| NI | NewCenturySchlbk-Italic |
| NB | NewCenturySchlbk-Bold |
| NBI | NewCenturySchlbk-BoldItalic |
| PR | Palatino-Roman |
| PI | Palatino-Italic |
| PB | Palatino-Bold |
| PBI | Palatino-BoldItalic |
| TR | Times-Roman |
| TI | Times-Italic |
| TB | Times-Bold |
| TBI | Times-BoldItalic |

There is also the following font which is not a member of a family:

| ZCMI | ZapfChancery-MediumItalic |

There are also some special fonts called SS and S. Zapf Dingbats is available as ZD and a reversed version of ZapfDingbats (with symbols pointing in the opposite direction) is available as ZDR; most characters in these fonts are unnamed and must be accessed using \N.

grops understands various X commands produced using the \X escape sequence; grops will only interpret commands that begin with a ps: tag.

`\X'ps:exec`*`code`*`'`    This executes the arbitrary PostScript commands in code. The PostScript currentpoint will be set to the position of the \nX command before executing code. The origin will be at the top left corner of the page, and y coordinates will increase down the page. A procedure u will be defined that converts groff units to the coordinate system in effect. For example,

```
\X'ps: exec \nx u 0 rlineto stroke'
```

will draw a horizontal line one inch long. code may make changes to the graphics state, but any changes will persist only to the end of the page. A dictionary containing the definitions specified by def and mdef will be on top of the dictionary stack. If your code adds definitions to this dictionary, you should allocate space for them using \X'ps*mdefn*'. Any definitions will persist only until the end of the page. If you use the \Y escape sequence with an argument that names a macro, code can extend over multiple lines. For example,

```
.nr x 1i
.de y
ps: exec
\nx u 0 rlineto
stroke
..
\Yy
```

is another way to draw a horizontal line one inch long.

`\X'ps:`*`filename`*`'`    This is the same as the exec command except that the PostScript code is read from file *name*.

`\X'ps:def`*`code`*`'`    Place a PostScript definition contained in code in the prologue. There should be at most one definition per \X command. Long definitions can be split over several \X commands; all the code arguments are simply joined together separated by newlines. The definitions are placed in a dictionary which is automatically pushed on the dictionary stack when an exec command is executed. If you use the \Y escape sequence with an argument that names a macro, code can extend over multiple lines.

| | |
|---|---|
| `\X'ps:mdefncode'` | Like def, except that code may contain up to *n* definitions. grops needs to know how many definitions code contains so that it can create an appropriately sized PostScript dictionary to contain them. |
| `\X'ps:importfile llxllyurxurywidth [height]'` | Import a PostScript graphic from file. The arguments llx, lly, urx, and ury give the bounding box of the graphic in the default PostScript coordinate system; they should all be integers; llx and lly are the x and y coordinates of the lower-left corner of the graphic; urx and ury are the x and y coordinates of the upper-right corner of the graphic; *width* and *height* are integers that give the desired width and height in groff units of the graphic. The graphic will be scaled so that it has this width and height and translated so that the lower-left corner of the graphic is located at the position associated with \X command. If the height argument is omitted, it will be scaled uniformly in the x and y directions so that it has the specified width. Note that the contents of the \X command are not interpreted by troff; so vertical space for the graphic is not automatically added, and the width and height arguments are not allowed to have attached scaling indicators. If the PostScript file complies with the Adobe Document Structuring Conventions and contains a %%BoundingBox comment, then the bounding box can be automatically extracted from within groff by using the sy request to run the psbb command. |

The -mps macros (which are automatically loaded when grops is run by the groff command) include a PSPIC macro that allows a picture to be easily imported. This has the format:

```
.PSPIC file [ -L j -R j -I n ][width [ height ]]
```

*file* is the name of the file containing the illustration; *width* and *height* give the desired width and height of the graphic. The *width* and *height* arguments may have scaling indicators attached; the default scaling indicator is i. This macro will scale the graphic uniformly in the x and y directions so that it is no more than *width* wide and *height* high. By default, the graphic will be horizontally centered. The -L and -R cause the graphic to be left-aligned and right-aligned, respectively. The -I option causes the graphic to be indented by *n*.

| | |
|---|---|
| `\X'ps: invis', \X'ps: endinvis'` | No output will be generated for text and drawing commands that are bracketed with these \X commands. These commands are intended for use when output from troff will be previewed before being processed with grops; if the previewer is unable to display certain characters or other constructs, then other substitute characters or constructs can be used for previewing by bracketing them with these \X commands. |

For example, gxditview is not able to display a proper \(em character because the standard X11 fonts do not provide it; this problem can be overcome by executing the following request:

```
.char \(em \X'ps: invis'\
\Z'\v'-.25m'\h'.05m'\D'l .9m 0'\h'.05m"\
\X'ps: endinvis'\(em
```

In this case, gxditview will be unable to display the \(em character and will draw the line, whereas grops will print the \(em character and ignore the line.

The input to grops must be in the format output by gtroff(1). This is described in groff_out(1). In addition, the device and font description files for the device used must meet certain requirements. The device and font description files supplied for ps device meet all these requirements. afmtodit(1) can be used to create font files from AFM files. The resolution must be an integer multiple of 72 times the sizescale. The ps device uses a resolution of 72000 and a sizescale of 1000. The device description file should contain a command:

```
paperlengthn
```

which says that output should be generated that is suitable for printing on a page whose length is *n* machine units. Each font description file must contain a command:

```
internalnamepsname
```

which says that the PostScript name of the font is *psname*. It may also contain a command:

```
encodingenc file
```

which says that the PostScript font should be reencoded using the encoding described in `enc_file`; this file should consist of a sequence of lines of the form:

`pschar code`

where *pschar* is the PostScript name of the character, and `code` is its position in the encoding expressed as a decimal integer. The code for each character given in the font file must correspond to the code for the character in encoding file, or to the code in the default encoding for the font if the PostScript font is not to be reencoded. This code can be used with the `\N` escape sequence in troff to select the character, even if the character does not have a groff name. Every character in the font file must exist in the PostScript font, and the widths given in the font file must match the widths used in the PostScript font. grops will assume that a character with a groff name of space is blank (makes no marks on the page); it can make use of such a character to generate more efficient and compact PostScript output.

grops can automatically include the downloadable fonts necessary to print the document. Any downloadable fonts which should, when required, be included by grops must be listed in the file `/usr/lib/groff/font/devps/download`; this should consist of lines of the form:

`font filename`

where *font* is the PostScript name of the font, and `filename` is the name of the file containing the font; lines beginning with `#` and blank lines are ignored; fields may be separated by tabs or spaces; `filename` will be searched for using the same mechanism that is used for groff font metric files. The download file itself will also be searched for using this mechanism.

If the file containing a downloadable font or imported document conforms to the Adobe Document Structuring Conventions, then grops will interpret any comments in the files sufficiently to ensure that its own output is conforming. It will also supply any needed font resources that are listed in the download file as well as any needed file resources. It is also able to handle interresource dependencies. For example, suppose that you have a downloadable font called Garamond, and also a downloadable font called Garamond-Outline that depends on Garamond (typically, it would be defined to copy Garamond's font dictionary, and change the PaintType), then it is necessary for Garamond to appear before Garamond-Outline in the PostScript document. grops will handle this automatically provided that the downloadable font file for Garamond-Outline indicates its dependence on Garamond by means of the Document Structuring Conventions, for example by beginning with the following lines:

```
%!PS-Adobe-3.0 Resource-Font
%%DocumentNeededResources: font Garamond
%%EndComments
%%IncludeResource: font Garamond
```

In this case, both Garamond and Garamond-Outline would need to be listed in the download file. A downloadable font should not include its own name in a `%%DocumentSuppliedResources` comment.

grops will not interpret `%%DocumentFonts` comments.

The `%%DocumentNeededResources`, `%%DocumentSuppliedResources`, `%%IncludeResource`, `%%BeginResource`, and `%%EndResource` comments (or possibly the old `%%DocumentNeededFonts`, `%%DocumentSuppliedFonts`, `%%IncludeFont`, `%%BeginFont`, and `%%EndFont` comments) should be used.

## FILES

| | |
|---|---|
| `/usr/lib/groff/font/devps/DESC` | Device description file |
| `/usr/lib/groff/font/devps/F` | Font description file for font *F* |
| `/usr/lib/groff/font/devps/download` | List of downloadable fonts. |
| `/usr/lib/groff/font/devps/text.enc` | Encoding used for text fonts |
| `/usr/lib/groff/tmac/tmac.ps` | Macros for use with grops; automatically loaded by troffrc |
| `/usr/lib/groff/tmac/tmac.pspic` | Definition of PSPIC macro, automatically loaded by tmac.ps |
| `/usr/lib/groff/tmac/tmac.psold` | Macros to disable use of characters not present in older PostScript printers; automatically loaded by tmac.ps |
| `/usr/lib/groff/tmac/tmac.psnew` | Macros to undo the effect of tmac.psold |
| `/tmp/gropsXXXXXX` | Temporary file |

## SEE ALSO

afmtodit(1), groff(1), gtroff(1), psbb(1), groff_out(5), groff_font(5), groff_char(7)

*Groff Version 1.09, 14 February 1995*

# grotty

grotty —groff driver for typewriter-like devices

## SYNOPSIS

grotty [ -hfbuodBUv ][-F*dir* ][*files ... ]

## DESCRIPTION

grotty translates the output of GNU troff into a form suitable for typewriter-like devices. Normally, grotty should invoked by using the groff command with a -Tascii or -Tlatin1 option. If no files are given, grotty will read the standard input. A filename of - will also cause grotty to read the standard input. Output is written to the standard output.

Normally, grotty prints a bold character *c* using the sequence 'c BACKSPACE c' and an italic character *c* by the sequence '_BACKSPACE c'. These sequences can be displayed on a terminal by piping through ul(1). Pagers such as more(1) or less(1) are also able to display these sequences. Use either -B or -U when piping into less(1); use -b when piping into more(1). There is no need to filter the output through col(1) since grotty never outputs reverse line feeds.

The font description file may contain a command:

internalname*n*

where *n* is a decimal integer. If the 01 bit in *n* is set, then the font will be treated as an italic font; if the 02 bit is set, then it will be treated as a bold font. The code field in the font description field gives the code that will be used to output the character. This code can also be used in the \N escape sequence in troff.

## OPTIONS

| | |
|---|---|
| -F*dir* | Search the directory *dir*/dev*name* for font and device description files; *name* is the name of the device, usually ascii or latin1. |
| -h | Use horizontal tabs in the output. Tabs are assumed to be set every 8 columns. |
| -f | Use form feeds in the output. A form feed will be output at the end of each page that has no output on its last line. |
| -b | Suppress the use of overstriking for bold characters. |
| -u | Suppress the use of underlining for italic characters. |
| -B | Use only overstriking for bold-italic characters. |
| -U | Use only underlining for bold-italic characters. |
| -o | Suppress overstriking (other than for bold or underlined characters). |
| -d | Ignore all \D commands. Without this, grotty will render \D'l ...' commands that have at least one zero argument (and so are either horizontal or vertical) using -, ¦, and + characters. |
| -v | Print the version number. |

## FILES

| | |
|---|---|
| /usr/lib/groff/font/devascii/DESC | Device description file for ascii device. |
| /usr/lib/groff/font/devascii/F | Font description file for font F of ascii device. |
| /usr/lib/groff/font/devlatin1/DESC | Device description file for latin1 device. |
| /usr/lib/groff/font/devlatin1/F | Font description file for font F of latin1 device. |
| /usr/lib/groff/tmac/tmac.tty | Macros for use with grotty. |
| /usr/lib/groff/tmac/tmac.tty-char | Additional kludgy character definitions for use with grotty. |

## BUGS

grotty is intended only for simple documents.

There is no support for fractional horizontal or vertical motions.

There is no support for \D commands other than horizontal and vertical lines.

Characters above the first line (that is, with a vertical position of 0) cannot be printed.

## SEE ALSO

groff(1), gtroff(1), groff_out(5), groff_font(5), groff_char(7), ul(1), more(1), less(1)

*Groff Version1.09, 14 February 1995*

# gsoelim

gsoelim—Interpret .so requests in groff input

## SYNOPSIS

gsoelim [ -Cv ][*files ...* ]

## DESCRIPTION

gsoelim reads *files* and replaces lines of the form

.sofile

by the contents of *file*. It is useful if files included with so need to be preprocessed. Normally, gsoelim should be invoked
with the -s option of groff.

## OPTIONS

-C        Recognize .so even when followed by a character other than space or newline

-v        Print the version number

## SEE ALSO

groff(1)

*Groff Version1.09, 15 September 1992*

# gtbl

gtbl—Format tables for troff

## SYNOPSIS

gtbl [ -Cv ][*files ...* ]

## DESCRIPTION

This manual page describes the GNU version of tbl, which is part of the groff document formatting system. tbl compiles
descriptions of tables embedded within troff input files into commands that are understood by troff. Normally, it should
be invoked using the -t option of groff. It is highly compatible with UNIX tbl. The output generated by GNU tbl cannot
be processed with UNIX troff; it must be processed with GNU troff. If no files are given on the command line, the
standard input will be read. A filename of - will cause the standard input to be read.

## OPTIONS

-C        Recognize .TS and .TE even when followed by a character other than space or newline

-v        Print the version number

## USAGE

Only the differences between GNU tbl and UNIX tbl are described here.

Normally, tbl attempts to prevent undesirable breaks in the table by using diversions. This can sometimes interact badly with macro packages' own use of diversions, when footnotes, for example, are used. The nokeep option tells tbl not to try to prevent breaks in this way.

The decimalpoint option specifies the character to be recognized as the decimal point character in place of the default period. It takes an argument in parentheses, which must be a single character, as for the tab option.

The f format modifier can be followed by an arbitrary length font name in parentheses.

There is a d format modifier that means that a vertically spanning entry should be aligned at the bottom of its range.

There is no limit on the number of columns in a table, nor any limit on the number of text blocks. All the lines of a table are considered in deciding column widths, not just the first 200. Table continuation (.T&) lines are not restricted to the first 200 lines.

Numeric and alphabetic items may appear in the same column.

Numeric and alphabetic items may span horizontally.

tbl uses register, string, macro and diversion names beginning with 3. When using tbl, you should avoid using any names beginning with a 3.

## BUGS

You should use .TSH/.TH in conjunction with a supporting macro package for *all* multipage boxed tables. If there is no header that you want to appear at the top of each page of the table, place the .TH line immediately after the format section. Do not enclose a multipage table within keep/release macros, or divert it in any other way.

A text block within a table must be able to fit on one page.

The bp request cannot be used to force a page-break in a multipage table. Instead, define BP as follows:

```
.de BP
.ie '\\n(.z" .bp \\$1
.el \!.BP \\$1
..
```

and use BP instead of bp.

## SEE ALSO

groff(1), gtroff(1)

*Groff Version 1.09, 1 April 1993*

# gtroff

gtroff—Format documents

## SYNOPSIS

gtroff [-abivzCER] [-w *name*] [-W *name*] [-d cs] [-f *fam*] [-m *name*] [-n *num*] [-o *list*] [-r cn] [-T *name*] [-F *dir*] [-M *dir*] [*nfiles...*n]

## DESCRIPTION

This manual page describes the GNU version of troff, which is part of the groff document formatting system. It is highly compatible with UNIX troff. Usually, it should be invoked using the groff command, which will also run preprocessors and postprocessors in the appropriate order and with the appropriate options.

## OPTIONS

| | |
|---|---|
| -a | Generate an ASCII approximation of the typeset output. |
| -b | Print a backtrace with each warning or error message. This backtrace should help track down the cause of the error. The line numbers given in the backtrace may not always correct: troff's idea of line numbers gets confused by as or am requests. |
| -i | Read the standard input after all the named input files have been processed. |
| -v | Print the version number. |
| -wname | Enable warning *name*. Available warnings are described in the "Warnings" subsection as follows. Multiple -w options are allowed. |
| -Wname | Inhibit warning *name*. Multiple -W options are allowed. |
| -E | Inhibit all error messages. |
| -z | Suppress formatted output. |
| -C | Enable compatibility mode. |
| -dcs, -dname=s | Define *c* or *name* to be a string *s*; *c* must be a one-letter name. |
| -ffam | Use *fam* as the default font family. |
| -mname | Read in the file tmac.*name*. Normally, this will be searched for in /usr/lib/groff/tmac. |
| -R | Don't load troffrc. |
| -nnum | Number the first page *num*. |
| -olist | Output only pages in *list*, which is a comma-separated list of page ranges; *n* means print page *n*, *m-n* means print every page between *m* and *n*, *-n* means print every page up to *n*, *n-* means print every page from *n*. Troff will exit after printing the last page in the list. |
| -rcn, -rname=n | Set number register *c* or *name* to *n*; *c* must be a one-character name; *n* can be any troff numeric expression. |
| -Tname | Prepare output for device *name*, rather than the default ps. |
| -Fdir | Search *dir* for subdirectories devname (*name* is the name of the device) for the DESC file and font files before the normal /usr/lib/groff/font. |
| -Mdir | Search directory *dir* for macro files before the normal /usr/lib/groff/tmac. |

## USAGE

Only the features not in UNIX troff are described here.

## LONG NAMES

The names of number registers, fonts, strings/macros/diversions, special characters can be of any length. In escape sequences, where you can use (*xx* for a two-character name, you can use [*xxx*] for a name of arbitrary length:

| | |
|---|---|
| \[*xxx*] | Print the special character called *xxx*. |
| \f[*xxx*] | Set font *xxx*. |
| \*[*xxx*] | Interpolate string *xxx*. |
| \n[*xxx*] | Interpolate number register *xxx*. |

## FRACTIONAL POINT SIZES

A scaled point is equal to 1/sizescale points, where sizescale is specified in the DESC file (1 by default.) There is a new scale indicator z that has the effect of multiplying by sizescale. Requests and escape sequences in troff interpret arguments that represent a point size as being in units of scaled points, but they evaluate each such argument using a default scale indicator of z. Arguments treated in this way are the argument to the ps request, the third argument to the cs request, the second and fourth arguments to the tkf request, the argument to the \H escape sequence, and those variants of the \s escape sequence that take a numeric expression as their argument.

For example, suppose sizescale is 1,000; then a scaled point will be equivalent to a millipoint; the request .ps 10.25 is equivalent to .ps 10.25z, and so sets the point size to 10,250 scaled points, which is equal to 10.25 points.

The number register \n(.s returns the point size in points as decimal fraction. There is also a new number register \n[.ps] that returns the point size in scaled points.

It would make no sense to use the z scale indicator in a numeric expression whose default scale indicator was neither u nor z, and so troff disallows this. Similarly, it would make no sense to use a scaling indicator other than z or u in a numeric expression whose default scale indicator was z, and so troff disallows this as well.

There is also new scale indicator s that multiplies by the number of units in a scaled point. So, for example, \n[.ps]s is equal to 1m. Be sure not to confuse the s and z scale indicators.

## NUMERIC EXPRESSIONS

Spaces are permitted in a number expression within parentheses.

M indicates a scale of hundredths of an em.

| | |
|---|---|
| e1>?e2 | The maximum of e1 and e2. |
| e1<?e2 | The minimum of e1 and e2. |
| (c;e) | Evaluate e using c as the default scaling indicator. If c is missing, ignore scaling indicators in the evaluation of e. |

## NEW ESCAPE SEQUENCES

| | |
|---|---|
| \A'anything' | This expands to 1 or 0 according to whether *anything* is or is not acceptable as the name of a string, macro, diversion, number register, environment, or font. It will return 0 if *anything* is empty. This is useful if you want to look up user input in some sort of associative table. |
| \C'xxx' | Typeset character named *xxx*. Normally it is more convenient to use \[*xxx*]. But \C has the advantage that it is compatible with recent versions of UNIX and is available in compatibility mode. |
| \E | This is equivalent to an escape character, but it's not interpreted in copy mode. For example, strings to start and end superscripting could be defined like this: |

```
.ds { \v'-.3m'\s'\En[.s]*6u/10u'
.ds } \s0\v'.3m'
```

The use of \E ensures that these definitions will work even if \*f gets interpreted in copy-mode (for example, by being used in a macro argument).

| | |
|---|---|
| \N'n' | Typeset the character with code *n* in the current font. *n* can be any integer. Most devices only have characters with codes between 0 and 255. If the current font does not contain a character with that code, special fonts will *not* be searched. The \N escape sequence can be conveniently used on conjunction with the char request: |

```
.char \[phone] \f(ZDnN'37'
```

The code of each character is given in the fourth column in the font description file after the charset command. It is possible to include unnamed characters in the font description file by using a name of —; the \N escape sequence is the only way to use these.

| | |
|---|---|
| \R'namen' | This has the same effect as .nrnamen |
| \s(nn | Set the point size to nn points; nn must be exactly two digits. |
| \s[n], \s'n' | Set the point size to n scaled points; n is a numeric expression with a default scale indicator of z. |
| \Vx\V(xx \V[xxx] | Interpolate the contents of the environment variable *xxx*, as returned by getenv(3). \V is interpreted in copy-mode. |

| | |
|---|---|
| \Yx\Y(xx  \Y[xxx] | This is approximately equivalent to \X'\*[xxx]'. However, the contents of the string or macro *xxx* are not interpreted; also, it is permitted for *xxx* to have been defined as a macro and thus contain newlines (it is not permitted for the argument to \X to contain newlines). The inclusion of newlines requires an extension to the UNIX troff output format and will confuse drivers that do not know about this extension. |
| \Z'anything' | Print anything and then restore the horizontal and vertical position; *anything* may not contain tabs or leaders. |
| \$0 | The name by which the current macro was invoked. The als request can make a macro have more than one name. |
| \$* | In a macro, the concatenation of all the arguments separated by spaces. |
| \$@ | In a macro, the concatenation of all the arguments with each surrounded by double quotes, and separated by spaces. |
| \$( nn, \$[ nnn ] | In a macro, this gives the *nn*th or *nnn*th argument. Macros can have an unlimited number of arguments. |
| \?anything\? | When used in a diversion, this will transparently embed *anything* in the diversion. *anything* is read in copy mode. When the diversion is reread, *anything* will be interpreted. *anything* may not contain newlines; use \! if you want to embed newlines in a diversion. The escape sequence \? is also recognized in copy mode and turned into a single internal code; it is this code that terminates *anything*. Thus |

```
.nr x 1
.nf
.di d
\?\\?\\\?\\\\\\\nx\\\\?\\?\\?\?
.di
.nr x 2
.di e
.d
.di
.nr x 3
.di f
.e
.di
.nr x 4
.f
```

| | |
|---|---|
| | will print 4. |
| \/ | This increases the width of the preceding character so that the spacing between that character and the following character will be correct if the following character is a Roman character. For example, if an italic *f* is immediately followed by a Roman right parenthesis, then in many fonts the top right portion of the *f* will overlap the top left of the right parenthesis, producing *f)*, which is ugly. Inserting \/ produces and avoids this problem. It is a good idea to use this escape sequence whenever an italic character is immediately followed by a Roman character without any intervening space. |
| \, | This modifies the spacing of the following character so that the spacing between that character and the preceding character will correct if the preceding character is a Roman character. For example, inserting \, between the parenthesis and the *f* changes to (*f* It is a good idea to use this escape sequence whenever a Roman character is immediately followed by an italic character without any intervening space. |
| \) | Like \& except that it behaves like a character declared with the cflags request to be transparent for the purposes of end-of-sentence recognition. |
| \~ | This produces an unbreakable space that stretches like a normal interword space when a line is adjusted. |
| \# | Everything up to and including the next newline is ignored. This is interpreted in copy mode. This is like \% except that \% does not ignore the terminating newline. |

## NEW REQUESTS

.aln*xxyy*

Create an alias *xx* for number register object named *yy*. The new name and the old name will be exactly equivalent. If *yy* is undefined, a warning of type reg will be generated, and the request will be ignored.

.als*xxyy*

Create an alias *xx* for request, string, macro, or diversion object named *yy*. The new name and the old name will be exactly equivalent (it is similar to a hard rather than a soft link). If *yy* is undefined, a warning of type mac will be generated, and the request will be ignored. The de, am, di, da, ds, and as requests only create a new object if the name of the macro, diversion, or string diversion is currently undefined or if it is defined to be a request; normally, they modify the value of an existing object.

.asciify*xx*

This request only exists in order to make it possible to make certain gross hacks work with GNU troff. It unformats the diversion *xx* in such a way that ASCII characters that were formatted and diverted into *xx* will be treated like ordinary input characters when *xx* is reread. For example, this:

```
.tr @.
.di x
@nr\n\1
.br
.di
.tr @@
.asciify x
.x
```

will set register n to 1.

.backtrace

Print a backtrace of the input stack on stderr.

.break

Break out of a while loop. See also the while and continue requests. Be sure not to confuse this with the br request.

.cflags*nc1c2*...

Characters *c1*, *c2*, ... have properties determined by *n*, which is ORed from the following.

1

The character ends sentences. (Initially, characters .?! have this property.)

2

Lines can be broken before the character (initially, no characters have this property); a line will not be broken at a character with this property unless the characters on each side both have nonzero hyphenation codes.

4

Lines can be broken after the character (initially, characters -\(hy\(em have this property); a line will not be broken at a character with this property unless the characters on each side both have nonzero hyphenation codes.

8

The character overlaps horizontally (initially, characters \(ul\(rn\(ru have this property).

16

The character overlaps vertically (initially, character \(br has this property).

32

An end-of-sentence character followed by any number of characters with this property will be treated as the end of a sentence if followed by a newline or two spaces; in other words, the character is transparent for the purposes of end-of-sentence recognition; this is the same as having a zero space factor in TeX (initially, characters ')]*\(dg\(rq have this property).

.char*cstring*

Define character *c* to be *string*. Every time character *c* needs to be printed, *string* will be processed in a temporary environment and the result will be wrapped up into a single object. Compatibility mode will be turned off and the escape character will be set to \ while *string* is being processed. Any emboldening, constant spacing, or track kerning will be applied to this object rather than to individual characters in *string*. A character defined by this request can be used just like a normal character provided by the output device. In particular, other characters can be translated to it with the tr request; it can be made the leader character by the lc request; repeated patterns can be drawn with the character by using the \l and \L escape sequences; words containing the character can be hyphenated correctly, if the hcode request is used to give the character a hyphenation code. There is a special antirecursion feature: Use of character within the character's definition will be handled like normal characters not defined with char. A character definition can be removed with the rchar request.

| | |
|---|---|
| .chop*xx* | Chop the last character off macro, string, or diversion *xx*. This is useful for removing the newline from the end of diversions that are to be interpolated as strings. |
| .close*stream* | Close the stream named *stream*; *stream* will no longer be an acceptable argument to the write request. See the open request. |
| .continue | Finish the current iteration of a while loop. See also the while and break requests. |
| .cp*n* | If *n* is nonzero or missing, enable compatibility mode; otherwise, disable it. In compatibility mode, long names are not recognized, and the incompatibilities caused by long names do not arise. |
| .do*xxx* | Interpret .*xxx* with compatibility mode disabled. For example, .do fam T would have the same effect as .fam T except that it would work even if compatibility mode had been enabled. Note that the previous compatibility mode is restored before any files sourced by *xxx* are interpreted. |
| .fam*xx* | Set the current font family to *xx*. The current font family is part of the current environment. See the description of the sty request for more information on font families. |
| .fspecial*fs1s2* ... | When the current font is *f*, fonts *s1*, *s2*, ... will be special; that is, they will searched for characters not in the current font. Any fonts specified in the special request will be searched after fonts specified in the fspecial request. |
| .ftr*fg* | Translate font *f* to *g*. Whenever a font named *f* is referred to in \f escape sequence, or in the ft, ul, bd, cs, tkf, special, fspecial, fp, or sty requests, font *g* will be used. If *g* is missing, or equal to *f*, then font *f* will not be translated. |
| .hcode*c1code1c2code2*... | Set the hyphenation code of character *c1* to *code1* and that of *c2* to *code2*. A hyphenation code must be a single input character (not a special character) other than a digit or a space. Initially, each lowercase letter has a hyphenation code, which is itself, and each uppercase letter has a hyphenation code which is the lowercase version of itself. See also the hpf request. |
| .hla*lang* | Set the current hyphenation language to *lang*. Hyphenation exceptions specified with the hw request and hyphenation patterns specified with the hpf request are both associated with the current hyphenation language. The hla request is usually invoked by the troffrc file. |
| .hlm*n* | Set the maximum number of consecutive hyphenated lines to *n*. If *n* is negative, there is no maximum. The default value is -1. This value is associated with the current environment. Only lines output from an environment count towards the maximum associated with that environment. Hyphens resulting from \% are counted; explicit hyphens are not. |
| .hpf*file* | Read hyphenation patterns from *file*; this will be searched for in the same way that tmac.*name* is searched for when the -m*name* option is specified. It should have the same format as the argument to the \patterns primitive in TeX; the letters appearing in this file are interpreted as hyphenation codes. A % character in the patterns file introduces a comment that continues to the end of the line. The set of hyphenation patterns is associated with the current language set by the hla request. The hpf request is usually invoked by the troffrc file. |
| .hym*n* | Set the *hyphenation* margin to *n*: when the current adjustment mode is not b, the line will not be hyphenated if the line is no more than *n* short. The default hyphenation margin is 0. The default scaling indicator for this request is m. The hyphenation margin is associated with the current environment. The current hyphenation margin is available in the \n[.hym] register. |
| .hys*n* | Set the *hyphenation* space to *n*: when the current adjustment mode is b, don't hyphenate the line if the line can be justified by adding no more than *n* extra space to each word space. The default hyphenation space is 0. The default scaling indicator for this request is m. The hyphenation space is associated with the current environment. The current hyphenation space is available in the \n[.hys] register. |
| .kern*n* | If *n* is nonzero or missing, enable pairwise kerning; otherwise, disable it. |
| .mso*file* | The same as the so request except that *file* is searched for in the same way that tmac.*name* is searched for when the -m*name* option is specified. |
| .nroff | Make the n built-in condition true and the t built-in condition false. This can be reversed using the troff request. |
| .open*streamfilename* | Open *filename* for writing and associate the stream named *stream* with it. See also the close and write requests. |

| | |
|---|---|
| .open*astreamfilename* | Like open, but if `filename` exists, append to it instead of truncating it. |
| .pnr | Print the names and contents of all currently defined number registers on stderr. |
| .pso*command* | This behaves like the so request except that input comes from the standard output of `command`. |
| .ptr | Print the names and positions of all traps (not including input line traps and diversion traps) on stderr. Empty slots in the page trap list are printed as well, because they can affect the priority of subsequently planted traps. |
| .rchar*c1c2...* | Remove the definitions of characters *c1*, *c2*, ... This undoes the effect of a char request. |
| .rj, .rj*n* | Right justify the next *n* input lines. Without an argument, right justify the next input line. The number of lines to be right justified is available in the `\n[.rj]` register. This implicitly does `.ce0`. The ce request implicitly does `.rj0`. |
| .rnn*xxyy* | Rename number register *xx* to *yy*. |
| .shc*c* | Set the soft hyphen character to c. If c is omitted, the soft hyphen character will be set to the default `\(hy`. The soft hyphen character is the character that will be inserted when a word is hyphenated at a line break. If the soft hyphen character does not exist in the font of the character immediately preceding a potential break point, then the line will not be broken at that point. Neither definitions (specified with the char request) nor translations (specified with the tr request) are considered when finding the soft hyphen character. |
| .shift*n* | In a macro, shift the arguments by *n* positions: argument *i* becomes argument *i-n*; arguments 1 to *n* will no longer be available. If *n* is missing, arguments will be shifted by 1. Shifting by negative amounts is currently undefined. |
| .special*s1s2...* | Fonts *s1*, *s2* are special and will be searched for characters not in the current font. |
| .sty*nf* | Associate style *f* with font position *n*. A font position can be associated either with a font or with a style. The current font is the index of a font position and so is also either a font or a style. When it is a style, the font that is actually used is the font the name of which is the concatenation of the name of the current family and the name of the current style. For example, if the current font is 1 and font position 1 is associated with style R and the current font family is T, then font TR will be used. If the current font is not a style, then the current family is ignored. When the requests cs, bd, tkf, uf, or fspecial are applied to a style, then they will instead be applied to the member of the current family corresponding to that style. The default family can be set with the -f option. The styles command in the DESC file controls which font positions (if any) are initially associated with styles rather than fonts. |
| .tkf*fs1n1s2n2* | Enable track kerning for font *f*. When the current font is *f*, the width of every character will be increased by an amount between *n1* and *n2*; when the current point size is less than or equal to *s1*, the width will be increased by *n1*; when it is greater than or equal to *s2*, the width will be increased by *n2*; when the point size is greater than or equal to *s1* and less than or equal to *s2*, the increase in width is a linear function of the point size. |
| .trf*filename* | Transparently output the contents of file `filename`. Each line is output as it would be were it preceded by `\!`; however, the lines are not subject to copy-mode interpretation. If the file does not end with a newline, then a newline will be added. For example, you can define a macro *x* containing the contents of file *f*, using |

```
.dix
.trff
.di
```

Unlike with the cf request, the file cannot contain characters such as NUL that are not legal troff input characters.

| | |
|---|---|
| .trnt *abcd* | This is the same as the tr request except that the translations do not apply to text that is transparently throughput into a diversion with `\!`. For example, |

```
.tr ab
.di x
\!.tm a
```

```
.di
.x
```

will print b; if trnt is used instead of tr, it will print a.

.troff

Make the n built-in condition false, and the t built-in condition true. This undoes the effect of the nroff request.

.vpt*n*

Enable vertical position traps if *n* is nonzero, disable them otherwise. Vertical position traps are traps set by the wh or dt requests. Traps set by the it request are not vertical position traps. The parameter that controls whether vertical position traps are enabled is global. Initially, vertical position traps are enabled.

.warn*n*

Control warnings. *n* is the sum of the numbers associated with each warning that is to be enabled; all other warnings will be disabled. The number associated with each warning is listed in the "Warnings" subsection. For example, .warn 0 will disable all warnings, and .warn 1 will disable all warnings except that about missing characters. If *n* is not given, all warnings will be enabled.

.while*c**anything*

While condition *c* is true, accept *anything* as input; *c* can be any condition acceptable to an if request; *anything* can comprise multiple lines if the first line starts with \{ and the last line ends with \}. See also the break and continue requests.

.writestream*stream**anything*

Write *anything* to the stream named *stream*. *stream* must previously have been the subject of an open request. *anything* is read in copy mode; a leading will be stripped.

# EXTENDED REQUESTS

.cf*filename*

When used in a diversion, this will embed in the diversion an object which, when reread, will cause the contents of *filename* to be transparently copied through to the output. In UNIX troff, the contents of *filename* are immediately copied through to the output regardless of whether there is a current diversion; this behavior is so anomalous that it must be considered a bug.

.ev*xx*

If *xx* is not a number, this will switch to a named environment called *xx*. The environment should be popped with a matching ev request without any arguments, just as for numbered environments. There is no limit on the number of named environments; they will be created the first time that they are referenced.

.fp*nf1f2*

The fp request has an optional third argument. This argument gives the external name of the font, which is used for finding the font description file. The second argument gives the internal name of the font, which is used to refer to the font in troff after it has been mounted. If there is no third argument, then the internal name will be used as the external name. This feature allows you to use fonts with long names in compatibility mode.

.ss*mn*

When two arguments are given to the ss request, the second argument gives the sentence space size. If the second argument is not given, the sentence space size will be the same as the word space size. Like the word space size, the sentence space is in units of one twelfth of the spacewidth parameter for the current font. Initially, both the word space size and the sentence space size are 12. The sentence space size is used in two circumstances: If the end of a sentence occurs at the end of a line in fill mode, then both an interword space and a sentence space will be added; if two spaces follow the end of a sentence in the middle of a line, then the second space will be a sentence space. Note that the behavior of UNIX troff will be exactly that exhibited by GNU troff if a second argument is never given to the ss request. In GNU troff, as in UNIX troff, you should always follow a sentence with either a newline or two spaces.

.ta*n1n2...nnTr1r2...rn*

Set tabs at positions *n1, n2,...,nn* and then set tabs at *nn+r1, nn+r2,...., nn+rn* and then at *nn+rn+r1, nn+rn+r2,..., nn+rn+rn*, and so on. For example, .ta T .5i will set tabs every half an inch.

| | |
|---|---|
| \n[.fam] | The current font family. This is a string-valued register. |
| \n[.fp] | The number of the next free font position. |
| \n[.g] | Always 1. Macros should use this to determine whether they are running under GNU troff. |
| \n[.hla] | The current hyphenation language as set by the hla request. |
| \n[.hlc] | The number of immediately preceding consecutive hyphenated lines. |
| \n[.hlm] | The maximum allowed number of consecutive hyphenated lines, as set by the hlm request. |
| \n[.hy] | The current hyphenation flags (as set by the hy request.) |
| \n[.hym] | The current hyphenation margin (as set by the hym request.) |
| \n[.hys] | The current hyphenation space (as set by the hys request.) |
| \n[.in] | The indent that applies to the current output line. |
| \n[.kern] | 1 if pairwise kerning is enabled, 0 otherwise. |
| \n[.lg] | The current ligature mode (as set by the lg request.) |
| \n[.ll] | The line length that applies to the current output line. |
| \n[.lt] | The title length as set by the lt request. |
| \n[.ne] | The amount of space that was needed in the last ne request that caused a trap to be sprung. Useful in conjunction with the \n[.trunc] register. |
| \n[.pn] | The number of the next page: either the value set by a pn request, or the number of the current page plus 1. |
| \n[.ps] | The current pointsize in scaled points. |
| \n[.psr] | The last requested pointsize in scaled points. |
| \n[.rj] | The number of lines to be right-justified as set by the rj request. |
| \n[.sr] | The last requested pointsize in points as a decimal fraction. This is a string-valued register. |
| \n[.tabs] | A string representation of the current tab settings suitable for use as an argument to the ta request. |
| \n[.trunc] | The amount of vertical space truncated by the most recently sprung vertical position trap, or, if the trap was sprung by an ne request, minus the amount of vertical motion produced by the ne request. In other words, at the point a trap is sprung, it represents the difference of what the vertical position would have been but for the trap, and what the vertical position actually is. Useful in conjunction with the \n[.ne] register. |
| \n[.ss] \n[.sss] | These give the values of the parameters set by the first and second arguments of the ss request. |
| \n[.vpt] | 1 if vertical position traps are enabled, 0 otherwise. |
| \n[.warn] | The sum of the numbers associated with each of the currently enabled warnings. The number associated with each warning is listed in the "Warnings" subsection. |
| \n(.x | The major version number. For example, if the version number is 1.03 then \n(.x will contain 1. |
| \n(.y | The minor version number. For example, if the version number is 1.03 then \n(.y will contain 03. |

The following registers are set by the \w escape sequence:

\n[rst]

\n[rsb]          Like the st and sb registers, but takes account of the heights and depths of characters.

\n[ssc]          The amount of horizontal space (possibly negative) that should be added to the last character before a subscript.

\n[skw]          How far to right of the center of the last character in the \w argument, the center of an accent from a roman font should be placed over that character.

The following read/write number registers are available:

\n[systat]       The return value of the system() function executed by the last sy request.

\n[slimit]       If greater than 0, the maximum number of objects on the input stack. If less than or equal to 0, there is no limit on the number of objects on the input stack. With no limit, recursion can continue until virtual memory is exhausted.

## MISCELLANEOUS

Fonts not listed in the DESC file are automatically mounted on the next available font position when they are referenced. If a font is to be mounted explicitly with the fp request on an unused font position, it should be mounted on the first unused font position, which can be found in the \n[.fp] register; although troff does not enforce this strictly, it will not allow a font to be mounted at a position whose number is much greater than that of any currently used position.

Interpolating a string does not hide existing macro arguments. Thus in a macro, a more efficient way of doing

.xx\\$@

is

\\*[xx]\\

If the font description file contains pairwise kerning information, characters from that font will be kerned. Kerning between two characters can be inhibited by placing a \& between them.

In a string comparison in a condition, characters that appear at different input levels to the first delimiter character will not be recognized as the second or third delimiters. This applies also to the tl request. In a \w escape sequence, a character that appears at a different input level to the starting delimiter character will not be recognized as the closing delimiter character. When decoding a macro argument that is delimited by double quotes, a character that appears at a different input level to the starting delimiter character will not be recognized as the closing delimiter character. The implementation of \$@ ensures that the double quotes surrounding an argument will appear the same input level, which will be different to the input level of the argument itself. In a long escape name ] will not be recognized as a closing delimiter except when it occurs at the same input level as the opening ]. In compatibility mode, no attention is paid to the input level.

There are some new types of condition:

.ifr*xxx*        True if there is a number register named *xxx*.

.ifd*xxx*        True if there is a string, macro, diversion, or request named *xxx*.

.ifc*ch*         True if there is a character *ch* available; *ch* is either an ASCII character or a special character \(xx or \[xxx]; the condition will also be true if *ch* has been defined by the char request.

## WARNINGS

The warnings that can be given by troff are divided into the following categories. The name associated with each warning is used by the -w and -W options; the number is used by the warn request, and by the .warn register.

char1            Nonexistent characters. This is enabled by default.

number2          Invalid numeric expressions. This is enabled by default.

break4           In fill mode, lines which could not be broken so that their length was less than the line length. This is enabled by default.

delim8           Missing or mismatched closing delimiters.

| | |
|---|---|
| el16 | Use of the el request with no matching ie request. |
| scale32 | Meaningless scaling indicators. |
| range64 | Out of range arguments. |
| syntax128 | Dubious syntax in numeric expressions. |
| di256 | Use of di or da without an argument when there is no current diversion. |
| mac512 | Use of undefined strings, macros, and diversions. When an undefined string, macro, or diversion is used, that string is automatically defined as empty. So, in most cases, at most one warning will be given for each name. |
| reg1024 | Use of undefined number registers. When an undefined number register is used, that register is automatically defined to have a value of 0. A definition is automatically made with a value of 0. So, in most cases, at most one warning will be given for use of a particular name. |
| tab2048 | Inappropriate use of a tab character. Either use of a tab character where a number was expected, or use of tab character in an unquoted macro argument. |
| right-brace4096 | Use of \g where a number was expected. |
| missing8192 | Requests that are missing nonoptional arguments. |
| input16384 | Illegal input characters. |
| escape32768 | Unrecognized escape sequences. When an unrecognized escape sequence is encountered, the escape character is ignored. |
| space65536 | Missing space between a request or macro and its argument. This warning will be given when an undefined name longer than two characters is encountered, and the first two characters of the name make a defined name. The request or macro will not be invoked. When this warning is given, no macro is automatically defined. This is enabled by default. This warning will never occur in compatibility mode. |
| font131072 | Nonexistent fonts. This is enabled by default. |
| ig262144 | Illegal escapes in text ignored with the ig request. These are conditions that are errors when they do not occur in ignored text. |

There are also names that can be used to refer to groups of warnings:

| | |
|---|---|
| all | All warnings except di, mac, and reg. It is intended that this covers all warnings that are useful with traditional macro packages. |
| w | All warnings. |

## INCOMPATIBILITIES

Long names cause some incompatibilities. UNIX troff will interpret

.dsabcd

as defining a string ab with contents cd. Normally, GNU troff will interpret this as a call of a macro named dsabcd. Also UNIX troff will interpret \*[ or \n[ as references to a string or number register called [. In GNU troff, however, this will normally be interpreted as the start of a long name. In compatibility mode GNU troff will interpret these things in the traditional way. In compatibility mode, however, long names are not recognized. Compatibility mode can be turned on with the -C command-line option, and turned on or off with the cp request. The number register \n(.C is 1 if compatibility mode is on, 0 otherwise.

GNU troff does not allow the use of the escape sequences in names of strings, macros, diversions, number registers, fonts, or environments; UNIX troff does. The \A escape sequence may be helpful in avoiding use of these escape sequences in names.

Fractional point sizes cause one noteworthy incompatibility. In UNIX troff the ps request ignores scale indicators and so

.ps 10u

will set the pointsize to 10 points, whereas in GNU troff it will set the pointsize to 10 scaled points.

In GNU troff there is a fundamental difference between unformatted, input characters, and formatted, output characters. Everything that affects how an output character will be output is stored with the character; after an output character has been constructed, it is unaffected by any subsequent requests that are executed, including bd, cs, tkf, tr, or fp requests. Normally output characters are constructed from input characters at the moment immediately before the character is added to the current output line. Macros, diversions, and strings are all, in fact, the same type of object; they contain lists of input characters and output characters in any combination. An output character does not behave like an input character for the purposes of macro processing; it does not inherit any of the special properties that the input character from which it was constructed might have had. For example, this:

```
.di x
\\\\
.br
.di
.x
```

will print \\ in GNU troff; each pair of input \s is turned into one output \ and the resulting output \s are not interpreted as escape characters when they are reread. UNIX troff would interpret them as escape characters when they were reread and would end up printing one \. The correct way to obtain a printable \ is to use the \e escape sequence: this will always print a single instance of the current escape character, regardless of whether or not it is used in a diversion; it will also work in both GNU troff and UNIX troff. If you wish for some reason to store in a diversion an escape sequence that will be interpreted when the diversion is reread, you can either use the traditional \! transparent output facility, or, if this is unsuitable, the new \? escape sequence.

## ENVIRONMENT

| | |
|---|---|
| GROFF_TMAC_PATH | A colon-separated list of directories in which to search for macro files. |
| GROFF_TYPESETTER | Default device. |
| GROFF_FONT_PATH | A colon-separated list of directories in which to search for the devname directory. troff will search in directories given in the -F option before these, and in standard directories (:/usr/lib/groff/font, :/usr/lib/font, and :/usr/lib/font) after these. |

## FILES

| | |
|---|---|
| /usr/lib/groff/font/devname/DESC | |
| /usr/lib/groff/tmac/troffrc | Initialization file |
| /usr/lib/groff/tmac/tmac.name | Macro files |
| /usr/lib/groff/font/devname/DESC | Device description file for device name |
| /usr/lib/groff/font/devname/F | Font file for font F of device name |

## SEE ALSO

groff(1) gtbl(1), gpic(1), geqn(1), grops(1), grodvi(1), grotty(1), groff_font(5), groff_out(5), groff_char(7)

*Groff Version 1.09, 14 February 1994*

# gzip, gunzip, zcatgzip, gunzip, zcat

gzip, gunzip, zcatgzip, gunzip, zcat—Compress or expand files

## SYNOPSIS

```
gzip [ -acdfhlLnNrtvV19 ][-Ssuffix] [ name ... ]
gunzip [ -acfhlLnNrtvV ][-Ssuffix] [ name ... ]
zcat [ -fhLV ][name ... ]
```

## DESCRIPTION

gzip reduces the size of the named files using Lempel-Ziv coding (LZ77). Whenever possible, each file is replaced by one with the extension .gz, while keeping the same ownership modes, access, and modification times. (The default extension is -gz for VMS, z for MS-DOS, OS/2 FAT, Windows NT FAT and Atari.) If no files are specified, or if a filename is -, the standard input is compressed to the standard output. gzip will only attempt to compress regular files. In particular, it will ignore symbolic links.

If the compressed filename is too long for its filesystem, gzip truncates it. gzip attempts to truncate only the parts of the filename longer than three characters. (A part is delimited by dots.) If the name consists of small parts only, the longest parts are truncated. For example, if filenames are limited to 14 characters, gzip.msdos.exe is compressed to gzi.msd.exe.gz. Names are not truncated on systems that do not have a limit on filename length.

By default, gzip keeps the original filename and timestamp in the compressed file. These are used when decompressing the file with the -N option. This is useful when the compressed filename was truncated or when the time stamp was not preserved after a file transfer.

Compressed files can be restored to their original form using gzip -d or gunzip or zcat. If the original name saved in the compressed file is not suitable for its filesystem, a new name is constructed from the original one to make it legal.

gunzip takes a list of files on its command line and replaces each file whose name ends with .gz, -gz, .z, -z, z, or .Z and which begins with the correct magic number with an uncompressed file without the original extension. gunzip also recognizes the special extensions .tgz and .taz as shorthands for .tar.gz and .tar.Z respectively. When compressing, gzip uses the .tgz extension if necessary instead of truncating a file with a .tar extension.

gunzip can currently decompress files created by gzip, zip, compress, compress -H, or pack. The detection of the input format is automatic. When using the first two formats, gunzip checks a 32-bit CRC. For pack, gunzip checks the uncompressed length. The standard compress format was not designed to allow consistency checks. However, gunzip is sometimes able to detect a bad .Z file. If you get an error when uncompressing a .Z file, do not assume that the .Z file is correct simply because the standard uncompress does not complain. This generally means that the standard uncompress does not check its input, and happily generates garbage output. The SCO compress -H format (1zh compression method) does not include a CRC but also allows some consistency checks.

Files created by zip can be uncompressed by gzip only if they have a single member compressed with the deflation method. This feature is only intended to help conversion of tar.zip files to the tar.gz format. To extract zip files with several members, use unzip instead of gunzip.

zcat is identical to gunzip -c. (On some systems, zcat may be installed as gzcat to preserve the original link to compress.) zcat uncompresses either a list of files on the command line or its standard input and writes the uncompressed data on standard output. zcat will uncompress files that have the correct magic number whether they have a .gz suffix or not.

gzip uses the Lempel-Ziv algorithm used in zip and PKZIP. The amount of compression obtained depends on the size of the input and the distribution of common substrings. Typically, text such as source code or English is reduced by 60 to 70 percent. Compression is generally much better than that achieved by LZW (as used in compress), Huffman coding (as used in pack), or adaptive Huffman coding (compact).

Compression is always performed, even if the compressed file is slightly larger than the original. The worst case expansion is a few bytes for the gzip file header, plus 5 bytes every 32KB block, or an expansion ratio of 0.015 percent for large files. Note that the actual number of used disk blocks almost never increases. gzip preserves the mode, ownership, and timestamps of files when compressing or decompressing.

## OPTIONS

| | |
|---|---|
| -a -ascii | ASCII text mode: convert end-of-lines using local conventions. This option is supported only on some non-UNIX systems. For MS-DOS, CR LF is converted to LF when compressing, and LF is converted to CR LF when decompressing. |
| -c -stdout -to-stdout | Write output on standard output; keep original files unchanged. If there are several input files, the output consists of a sequence of independently compressed members. To obtain better compression, concatenate all input files before compressing them. |

| | |
|---|---|
| -d -decompress -uncompress | Decompress. |
| -f -force | Force compression or decompression even if the file has multiple links or the corresponding file already exists, or if the compressed data is read from or written to a terminal. If the input data is not in a format recognized by gzip, and if the option -stdout is also given, copy the input data without change to the standard output; let zcat behave as cat. If -f is not given, and when not running in the background, gzip prompts to verify whether an existing file should be overwritten. |
| -h -help | Display a help screen and quit. |
| -l -list | For each compressed file, list the following fields: compressed size (size of the compressed file), uncompressed size (size of the uncompressed file), ratio (compression ratio—0.0% if unknown), uncompressed name (name of the uncompressed file). The uncompressed size is given as -1 for files not in gzip format, such as compressed .Z files. To get the uncompressed size for such a file, you can use: |

```
zcat file.Z ¦ wc -c
```

In combination with the -verbose option, the following fields are also displayed: method (compression method), crc (the 32-bit CRC of the uncompressed data), date & time (timestamp for the uncompressed file). The compression methods currently supported are deflate, compress, lzh (SCO compress -H) and pack. The crc is given as ffffffff for a file not in gzip format.

With -name, the uncompressed name, date and time are those stored within the compressed file if present.

With -verbose, the size totals and compression ratio for all files is also displayed, unless some sizes are unknown. With -quiet, the title and totals lines are not displayed.

| | |
|---|---|
| -L -license | Display the gzip license and quit. |
| -n -no-name | When compressing, do not save the original filename and timestamp by default. (The original name is always saved if the name had to be truncated.) When decompressing, do not restore the original filename if present (remove only the gzip suffix from the compressed filename) and do not restore the original timestamp if present (copy it from the compressed file). This option is the default when decompressing. |
| -N -name | When compressing, always save the original filename and timestamp; this is the default. When decompressing, restore the original filename and timestamp if present. This option is useful on systems that have a limit on filename length or when the timestamp has been lost after a file transfer. |
| -q -quiet | Suppress all warnings. |
| -r -recursive | Travel the directory structure recursively. If any of the filenames specified on the command line are directories, gzip will descend into the directory and compress all the files it finds there (or decompress them in the case of gunzip). |
| -S .suf -suffix .suf | Use suffix .suf instead of .gz. Any suffix can be given, but suffixes other than .z and .gz should be avoided to avoid confusion when files are transferred to other systems. A null suffix forces gunzip to try decompression on all given files regardless of suffix, as in the following: |

```
gunzip -S "" * (*.* for MS-DOS)
```

Previous versions of gzip used the .z suffix. This was changed to avoid a conflict with pack(1).

| | |
|---|---|
| -t -test | Test. Check the compressed file integrity. |
| -v -verbose | Verbose. Display the name and percentage reduction for each file compressed or decompressed. |
| -V -version | Version. Display the version number and compilation options, then quit. |
| -# -fast -best | Regulate the speed of compression using the specified digit #, where -1 or --fast indicates the fastest compression method (less compression) and -9 or --best indicates the slowest compression method (best compression). The default compression level is -6 (that is, biased towards high compression at expense of speed). |

## ADVANCED USAGE

Multiple compressed files can be concatenated. In this case, gunzip will extract all members at once. For example,

```
gzip -c file1 >foo.gz gzip -c file2>>> foo.gz
```

Then

```
gunzip -c foo
```

is equivalent to

```
cat file1 file2
```

In case of damage to one member of a .gz file, other members can still be recovered (if the damaged member is removed). However, you can get better compression by compressing all members at once.

```
cat file1 file2 ¦ gzip > foo.gz
```

compresses better than

```
gzip -c file1 file2 >foo.gz
```

If you want to recompress concatenated files to get better compression, use

```
gzip -cd old.gz ¦ gzip > new.gz
```

If a compressed file consists of several members, the uncompressed size and CRC reported by the -list option applies to the last member only. If you need the uncompressed size for all members, you can use

```
gzip -cd file.gz ¦ wc -c
```

If you wish to create a single archive file with multiple members so that members can later be extracted independently, use an archiver such as tar or zip. GNU tar supports the -z option to invoke gzip transparently. gzip is designed as a complement to tar, not as a replacement.

## ENVIRONMENT

The environment variable GZIP can hold a set of default options for gzip. These options are interpreted first and can be overwritten by explicit command-line parameters. For example,

For sh: GZIP="-8v –name"

Export GZIP for csh: setenv GZIP "-8v –name"

For MS-DOS: set GZIP=-8v –name

On Vax/VMS, the name of the environment variable is GZIP_OPT, to avoid a conflict with the symbol set for invocation of the program.

## SEE ALSO

znew(1), zcmp(1), zmore(1), zforce(1), gzexe(1), zip(1), unzip(1), compress(1), pack(1), compact(1)

## DIAGNOSTICS

Exit status is normally 0; if an error occurs, exit status is 1. If a warning occurs, exit status is 2.

Usage: gzip [-cdfhlLnNrtvV19] [-S suffix] [file ...]

Invalid options were specified on the command line.

file: not in gzip format

The file specified to gunzip has not been compressed.

file: Corrupt input. Use zcat to recover some data.

The compressed file has been damaged. The data up to the point of failure can be recovered using

```
zcat file > recover
```

`file: compressed with `*`xx`*` bits, can only handle `*`yy`*` bits`

`file` was compressed (using LZW) by a program that could deal with more bits than the decompress code on this machine. Recompress the file with `gzip`, which compresses better and uses less memory.

`file: already has .gz suffix--no change`

The file is assumed to be already compressed. Rename the file and try again.

`file already exists; do you wish to overwrite (y or n)?`

Respond y if you want the output file to be replaced; n if not.

`gunzip: corrupt input`

A SIGSEGV violation was detected, which usually means that the input file has been corrupted.

`xx.x%`

Percentage of the input saved by compression. (Relevant only for –v and –l.)

`- not a regular file or directory: ignored`

When the input file is not a regular file or directory, (such as a symbolic link, socket, FIFO, device file), it is left unaltered.

`- has `*`xx`*` other links: unchanged`

The input file has links; it is left unchanged. See ln(1) for more information.

Use the `-f` flag to force compression of files that are multiply linked.

## CAVEATS

When writing compressed data to a tape, it is generally necessary to pad the output with zeroes up to a block boundary. When the data is read and the whole block is passed to `gunzip` for decompression, `gunzip` detects that there is extra trailing garbage after the compressed data and emits a warning by default. You have to use the `-quiet` option to suppress the warning. This option can be set in the `GZIP` environment variable as in the following:

```
for sh: GZIP="-q" tar -xfz -block-compress /dev/rst0 for csh:
(setenv GZIP -q; tar -xfz -block-compr /dev/rst0
```

In the preceding example, `gzip` is invoked implicitly by the `-z` option of GNU tar. Make sure that the same block size (`-b` option of tar) is used for reading and writing compressed data on tapes. (This example assumes you are using the GNU version of tar.)

## BUGS

The `-list` option reports incorrect sizes if they exceed two gigabytes. The `-list` option reports sizes as `-1` and `crc` as `ffffffff` if the compressed file is on a nonseekable media.

In some rare cases, the `-best` option gives worse compression than the default compression level (-6). On some highly redundant files, `compress` compresses better than `gzip`.

*Local*

# gzexe

`gzexe`—Compress executable files in place

## SYNOPSIS

`gzexe [ name ... ]`

## DESCRIPTION

The gzexe utility enables you to compress executables in place and have them automatically uncompress and execute when you run them (at a penalty in performance). For example if you execute gzexe /bin/cat, it will create the following two files:

```
-r-xr-xr-x 1 root bin 9644 Feb 11 11:16 /bin/cat
-r-xr-xr-x 1 bin bin 24576 Nov 23 13:21 /bin/cat˜
```

/bin/cat˜ is the original file and /bin/cat is the self-uncompressing executable file. You can remove /bin/cat˜ when you are sure that /bin/cat works properly.

This utility is most useful on systems with very small disks.

## OPTIONS

-d          Decompress the given executables instead of compressing them

## SEE ALSO

gzip(1), znew(1), zmore(1), zcmp(1), zforce(1)

## CAVEATS

The compressed executable is a shell script. This may create some security holes. In particular, the compressed executable relies on the PATH environment variable to find gzip and some other utilities (tail, chmod, ln, sleep).

## BUGS

gzexe attempts to retain the original file attributes on the compressed executable, but you may have to fix them manually in some cases, using chmod or chown.

# head

head—Output the first part of files

## SYNOPSIS

```
head [-c N[bkm]] [-n N] [-qv] [--bytes=N[bkm]] [--lines=N] [--quiet] [--silent]
[--verbose] [--help] [--version] [file...]

head [-Nbcklmqv] [file...]
```

## DESCRIPTION

This manual page documents the GNU version of head. head prints the first part (10 lines by default) of each given file; it reads from standard input if no files are given or when a filename of - is encountered. If more than one file is given, it prints a header consisting of the file's name enclosed in ==> and <== before the output for each file.

## OPTIONS

head accepts two option formats: the new one, in which numbers are arguments to the option letters; and the old one, in which the number precedes any option letters.

-c N, --bytes N         Print first N bytes. N is a nonzero integer, optionally followed by one of the following characters to specify a different unit.

b  512-byte blocks.

k  1-kilobyte blocks.

m  1-megabyte blocks.

-l, -n N, --lines N     Print first N lines.

-q, --quiet, --silent   Never print filename headers.

| -v, --verbose | Always print filename headers. |
| --help | Print a usage message and exit with a nonzero status. |
| --version | Print version information on standard output, then exit. |

# hexdump

hexdump—ASCII, decimal, hexadecimal, octal dump

## SYNOPSIS

hexdump [-bcdovx] [-e format_string] [-f format_file] [-n length] [-s skip] [file ...]

## DESCRIPTION

The hexdump utility is a filter that displays the specified files, or the standard input, if no files are specified, in a user-specified format.

The options are as follows:

| | |
|---|---|
| -b | One-byte octal display. Display the input offset in hexadecimal, followed by sixteen space-separated, three-column, zero-filled bytes of input data, in octal, per line. |
| -c | One-byte character display. Display the input offset in hexadecimal, followed by sixteen space-separated, three-column, space-filled, characters of input data per line. |
| -d | Two-byte decimal display. Display the input offset in hexadecimal, followed by eight space-separated, five-column, zero-filled, two-byte units of input data, in unsigned decimal, per line. |
| -e format_string | Specify a format string to be used for displaying data. |
| -f format_file | Specify a file that contains one or more newline separated format strings. Empty lines and lines whose first nonblank character is a hash mark (#) are ignored. |
| -n length | Interpret only length bytes of input. |
| -o | Two-byte octal display. Display the input offset in hexadecimal, followed by eight space-separated, six-column, zero-filled, two-byte quantities of input data, in octal, per line. |
| -s offset | Skip offset bytes from the beginning of the input. By default, offset is interpreted as a decimal number. With a leading 0x or 0X, offset is interpreted as a hexadecimal number; otherwise, with a leading 0, offset is interpreted as an octal number. Appending the character b, k, or m to offset causes it to be interpreted as a multiple of 512, 1024, or 1048576, respectively. |
| -v | The -v option causes hexdump to display all input data. Without the -v option, any number of groups of output lines, which would be identical to the immediately preceding group of output lines (except for the input offsets), are replaced with a line comprised of a single asterisk. |
| -x | Two-byte hexadecimal display. Display the input offset in hexadecimal, followed by eight, space-separated, four-column, zero-filled, two-byte quantities of input data, in hexadecimal, per line. |

For each input file, hexdump sequentially copies the input to standard output, transforming the data according to the format strings specified by the -e and -f options, in the order that they were specified.

## FORMATS

A format string contains any number of format units, separated by whitespace. A format unit contains up to three items: an iteration count, a byte count, and a format.

The iteration count is an optional positive integer, which defaults to one. Each format is applied iteration count times.

The byte count is an optional positive integer. If specified, it defines the number of bytes to be interpreted by each iteration of the format.

If an iteration count and/or a byte count is specified, a single slash must be placed after the iteration count and/or before the byte count to disambiguate them. Any whitespace before or after the slash is ignored.

The format is required and must be surrounded by double quote (" ") marks. It is interpreted as an fprintf-style format string (see fprintf(3)) with the following exceptions:

- An asterisk (*) may not be used as a field width or precision.
- A byte count or field precision is required for each s conversion character (unlike the fprintf(3) default, which prints the entire string if the precision is unspecified).
- The conversion characters h, l, n, p, and q are not supported.
- The single-character escape sequences described in the C standard are supported:

| | |
|---|---|
| NUL | \0 |
| Alert character | \a |
| Backspace | \b |
| Form-feed | \f |
| Newline | \n |
| Carriage return | \r |
| Tab | \t |
| Vertical tab | \v |

hexdump also supports the following additional conversion strings:

a[dox]  Display the input offset, cumulative across input files, of the next byte to be displayed. The appended characters d, o, and x specify the display base as decimal, octal, or hexadecimal respectively.

A[dox]  Identical to the a conversion string except that it is only performed once, when all of the input data has been processed.

c  Output characters in the default character set. Nonprinting characters are displayed in three-character, zero-padded octal, except for those representable by standard escape notation (see preceding list), which are displayed as two-character strings.

p  Output characters in the default character set. Nonprinting characters are displayed as a single period.

u  Output U.S. ASCII characters, with the exception that control characters are displayed using the lowercase names in the following mini-table. Characters greater than 0xff, hexadecimal, are displayed as hexadecimal strings.

| | | | | | |
|---|---|---|---|---|---|
| 000 nul | 001 soh | 002 stx | 003 etx | 004 eot | 005 enq |
| 006 ack | 007 bel | 008 bs | 009 ht | 00A lf | 00B vt |
| 00C ff | 00D cr | 00E so | 00F si | 010 dle | 011 dc1 |
| 012 dc2 | 013 dc3 | 014 dc4 | 015 nak | 016 syn | 017 etb |
| 018 can | 019 em | 01A sub | 01B esc | 01C fs | 01D gs |
| 01E rs | 01F us | 0FF del | | | |

The default and supported byte counts for the conversion characters are as follows:

| | |
|---|---|
| %_c, %_p, %_u, %c | One-byte counts only. |
| %d, %i, %o, %u, %X, %x | Four-byte default; one-, two-, and four-byte counts supported. |
| %E, %e, %f, %G, %g | Eight-byte default, four-byte counts supported. |

The amount of data interpreted by each format string is the sum of the data required by each format unit, which is the iteration count times the byte count, or the iteration count times the number of bytes required by the format if the byte count is not specified.

The input is manipulated in *blocks*; a block is defined as the largest amount of data specified by any format string. Format strings interpreting less than an input block's worth of data, whose last format unit both interprets some number of bytes and does not have a specified iteration count, have the iteration count incremented until the entire input block has been processed or there is not enough data remaining in the block to satisfy the format string.

If, either as a result of user specification or hexdump modifying the iteration count as described, an iteration count is greater than one, no trailing whitespace characters are output during the last iteration.

It is an error to specify a byte count as well as multiple conversion characters or strings unless all but one of the conversion characters or strings is a or A. If, as a result of the specification of the -n option or end-of-file being reached, input data only partially satisfies a format string, the input block is zero-padded sufficiently to display all available data (that is, any format units overlapping the end of data will display some number of the zero bytes).

Further output by such format strings is replaced by an equivalent number of spaces. An equivalent number of spaces is defined as the number of spaces output by an s conversion character with the same field width and precision as the original conversion character or conversion string but with any +, " ", # conversion flag characters removed, and referencing a NULL string.

If no format strings are specified, the default display is equivalent to specifying the -x option.

hexdump exits 0 on success and >0 if an error occurred.

## EXAMPLES

Display the input in perusal format:

```
"%06.6_ao " 12/1 "%3_u "
"\t\t" "%_p "
"\n"
```

Implement the -x option:

```
"%07.7_Ax\n"
"%07.7_ax " 8/2 "%04x " "\n"
```

## SEE ALSO

adb(1)

*18 April 1994*

# hipstopgm

hipstopgm—Convert a HIPS file into a portable graymap

## SYNOPSIS

hipstopgm [hipsfile]

## DESCRIPTION

Hipstopgm reads a HIPS file as input and produces a portable graymap as output.

If the HIPS file contains more than one frame in sequence, hipstopgm will concatenate all the frames vertically.

HIPS is a format developed at the Human Information Processing Laboratory, NYU.

## SEE ALSO

pgm(5)

## AUTHOR

Copyright © 1989 by Jef Poskanzer

*24 August 1989*

# host

host—Look up hostnames using domain server

## SYNOPSIS

host [-l] [-v] [-w] [-r] [-d] [-t querytype] [-a] host [ server ]

## DESCRIPTION

host looks for information about Internet hosts. It gets this information from a set of interconnected servers that are spread across the country. By default, it simply converts between hostnames and Internet addresses. However with the -t or -a options, it can be used to find all of the information about this host that is maintained by the domain server.

The arguments can be either hostnames or host numbers. The program first attempts to interpret them as host numbers. If this fails, it will treat them as hostnames. A host number consists of first decimal numbers separated by dots, for example, 128.6.4.194. A hostname consists of names separated by dots, for example, topaz.rutgers.edu. Unless the name ends in a dot, the local domain is automatically tacked on the end. Thus, a Rutgers user can say "host topaz", and it will actually look up topaz.rutgers.edu. If this fails, the name is tried unchanged (in this case, topaz). This same convention is used for mail and other network utilities. The actual suffix to tack on the end is obtained by looking at the results of a hostname call, and using everything starting at the first dot. (Following is a description of how to customize the hostname lookup.)

The first argument is the hostname you want to look up. If this is a number, an *inverse query* is done; that is, the domain system looks in a separate set of databases used to convert numbers to names.

The second argument is optional. It allows you to specify a particular server to query. If you don't specify this argument, the default server (normally the local machine) is used.

If a name is specified, you may see output of three different kinds. Here is an example that shows all of them:

```
% host sun4
sun4.rutgers.edu is a nickname for ATHOS.RUTGERS.EDU
ATHOS.RUTGERS.EDU has address 128.6.5.46
ATHOS.RUTGERS.EDU has address 128.6.4.4
ATHOS.RUTGERS.EDU mail is handled by ARAMIS.RUTGERS.EDU
```

The user has typed the command host sun4. The first line indicates that the name sun4.rutgers.edu is actually a nickname. The official hostname is ATHOS.RUTGERS.EDU. The next two lines show the address. If a system has more than one network interface, there will be a separate address for each. The last line indicates that ATHOS.RUTGERS.EDU does not receive its own mail. Mail for it is taken by ARAMIS.RUTGERS.EDU. There may be more than one such line, as some systems have more than one other system that will handle mail for them. Technically, every system that can receive mail is supposed to have an entry of this kind. If the system receives its own mail, there should be an entry the mentions the system itself, for example "XXX mail is handled by XXX." However many systems that receive their own mail do not bother to mention that fact. If a system has a "mail is handled by" entry, but no address, this indicates that it is not really part of the Internet, but a system that is on the network will forward mail to it. Systems on Usenet, bitnet, and a number of other networks have entries of this kind.

There are a number of options that can be used before the hostname. Most of these options are meaningful only to the staff who have to maintain the domain database.

The option -w causes host to wait forever for a response. Normally it will time out after around a minute.

The option -v causes printout to be in a verbose format. This is the official domain master file format, which is documented in the man page for named. Without this option, output still follows this format in general terms, but some attempt is made to make it more intelligible to normal users. Without -v, a, mx, and cname records are written out as has address, mail is handled by, and is a nickname for, and TTL and class fields are not shown.

The option -r causes recursion to be turned off in the request. This means that the name server will return only data it has in its own database. It will not ask other servers for more information.

The option -d turns on debugging. Network transactions are shown in detail.

The option -t allows you to specify a particular type of information to be looked up. The arguments are defined in the man page for named. Currently supported types are a, ns, md, mf, cname, soa, mb, mg, mr, null, wks, ptr, hinfo, minfo, mx, uinfo, uid, gid, unspec, and the wildcard, which may be written as either any or *. Types must be given in lowercase. Note that the default is to look first for a, and then mx, except that if the verbose option is turned on, the default is only a.

The option -a (for "all") is equivalent to -v -t any.

The option -l causes a listing of a complete domain. For example,

```
host -l rutgers.edu
```

will give a listing of all hosts in the rutgers.edu domain. The -t option is used to filter what information is presented, as you would expect. The default is address information, which also include PTR and NS records. The command host:

```
-l -v -t any rutgers.edu
```

will give a complete download of the zone data for rutgers.edu, in the official master file format. (However the SOA record is listed twice, for arcane reasons.)

### NOTE

-l is implemented by doing a complete zone transfer and then filtering out the information you have asked for. This command should be used only if it is absolutely necessary.

## CUSTOMIZING HOSTNAME LOOKUP

In general, if the name supplied by the user does not have any dots in it, a default domain is appended to the end. This domain can be defined in /etc/resolv.conf, but is normally derived by taking the local hostname after its first dot. The user can override this, and specify a different default domain, using the environment variable LOCALDOMAIN. In addition, the user can supply his own abbreviations for hostnames. They should be in a file consisting of one line per abbreviation. Each line contains an abbreviation, a space, and then the full hostname. This file must be pointed to by an environment variable HOSTALIASES, which is the name of the file.

## SEE ALSO

named(8)

## BUGS

Unexpected effects can happen when you type a name that is not part of the local domain. Please always keep in mind that the local domain name is tacked onto the end of every name, unless it ends in a dot. Only if this fails is the name used unchanged.

The -l option only tries the first name server listed for the domain that you have requested. If this server is dead, you may need to specify a server manually. For example, to get a listing of foo.edu, you could try host -t ns foo.edu to get a list of all the name servers for foo.edu, and then try host -l foo.edu xxx for all xxx on the list of name servers, until you find one that works.

# hostid

hostid—Set or print system's host ID.

## SYNTAX

hostid [-v] [ *decimal-id* ]

## DESCRIPTION

The hostid command prints the current host ID number in hexadecimal and both decimal and hexadecimal in parenthesis if the -v option is given. This numeric value is expected to be unique across all hosts and is normally set to resemble the host's Internet address.

Only the superuser can set the hostid by giving an argument. This value is stored in the file /etc/hostid and need only be performed once.

## AUTHOR

hostid is written by Mitch D'Souza (m.dsouza@mrc-apu.cam.ac.uk).

## SEE ALSO

gethostid(2), sethostid(2)

# hostname

hostname—Show or set the system's hostname

dnsdomainname--Show the system's domain name

## SYNOPSIS

```
hostname [-d][--domain][-Ffilename] [--filefilename] [-f][--fqdn][-h][--help]
[--long][-s][--short][-v][--version][name]
dnsdomainname
```

## DESCRIPTION

hostname is the program that is used to either set the hostname or display the current host or domain name of the system. This name is used by many of the networking programs to identify the machine.

When called without any arguments, the program displays the current name as set by the hostname command. You can change the output format to display always the short or the long hostname (FQDN). When called with arguments, the program will set the value of the hostname to the value specified. This usually is done only once, at system startup time, by the /etc/rc.d/rc.inet1 configuration script.

Note that only the superuser can change the hostname.

If the program was called as dnsdomainname, it will show the domain name server (DNS) domain name. You can't change the DNS domain name with dnsdomainname. (See the following subsection.)

## OPTIONS

| | |
|---|---|
| -d, --domain | Display the name of the DNS domain. Don't use the com-mand domainname to get the DNS domain name because it will show the NIS domain name and not the DNS domain name. |
| -F, --file filename | Read the hostname from the specified file. Comments (lines starting with a #) are ignored. |
| -f, --fqdn, --long | Display the FQDN (fully-qualified domain name). An FQDN consists of a short hostname and the DNS domain name. Unless you are using bind or NIS for host lookups, you can change the FQDN and the DNS domain name (which is part of the FQDN) in the /etc/hosts file. |
| -h, --help | Print a usage message on standard output and exit successfully. |
| -s, --short | Display the short hostname. |
| -v, --version | Print version information on standard output and exit successfully. |

## FILES

/etc/hosts

## AUTHOR

Peter Tobias, (tobias@server.et-inf.fho-emden.de)

*Linux, 28 July 1994*

# hpcdtoppm v0.3

hpcdtoppm v0.3—Convert a Photo-CD file into a portable pixmap

## SYNOPSIS

hpcdtoppm [options] pcd-file [ppm-file]

## DESCRIPTION

hpcdtoppm reads a Photo-CD image file or overview file, and outputs a portable pixmap. Image files you can find on the Photo-CD in photo_cd/images are named as imgnnnn.pcd, where nnnn is a 4-digit-number. The Overview file is at photo_cd/overview.pcd. If there is no ppm-file given, output will be printed to stdout. hpcdtoppm stands for "Hadmut's pcdtoppm" to make it distinguishable in case someone else is building the same thing and calling it pcdtoppm.

## OPTIONS

| | |
|---|---|
| -i | Give some information from the fileheader to stderr. It works only for image files. (It is not working correctly, just printing some strings.) |
| -s | Apply simple sharpness-operator on the luma channel. |
| -d | Do not show the complete image, but only the decompressed difference. It works only on the 4Base and the 16Base resolution. It does not have any deeper sense, but it was simple to implement and it shows what causes different sizes of image files. |
| -r | Rotate the picture clockwise for portraits. |
| -l | Rotate the picture counter-clockwise for portraits. |
| -a | Try to find out the image orientation. This doesn't work for overview files yet. It is very experimental and depends on one byte. Please tell me if it doesn't work. |
| -x | Overskip mode. Works on Base/16, Base/4, Base, and 4Base. In Photo-CD images, the luma channel is stored in full resolution, the two chroma channels are stored in half resolution only and have to be interpolated. In the Overskip mode, the chroma channels of the next higher resolution are taken instead of interpolating. To see the difference, generate one ppm with and one ppm without this flag. Use pnmarith to generate the difference image of these two images. Call ppmhist for this difference or show it with xv (push the HistEq button in the color editor). |
| -1 ¦ -Base/16 ¦ -128x192 | Extract the Base/16 size picture (size 128×192 pixels). Note that you can only give one size option. |
| -2 ¦ -Base/4 ¦ -256x384 | Extract the Base/4 size picture. |
| -3 ¦ -Base ¦ -512x768 | Extract the Base size picture. |
| -4 ¦ -4Base ¦ -1024x1536 | Extract the 4Base size picture. |
| -5 ¦ -16Base ¦ -2048x3072 | Extract the 16Base size picture. |
| -0 ¦ -Overview ¦ -O | Extract all pictures from an Overview file. A ppm filename must be given. If the given name is foo, the files are named foonnnn, where nnnn is a 4-digit number. They are stored in Base/16 format, so they are extracted in this format. |
| -ycc | Suppress the ycc to rgb conversion. This is experimental only. You can use this and apply ppmtorgb3 on the file. Then you will get three pgm files, one luma and two chroma files. |

## BUGS

I still don't have enough information about the Photo-CD to take care of all data structures. The information I have is quite vague and this program was developed by staring at the hexdumps and using the famous trial-and-error-method. :-) If anything doesn't work, please send me a report and perhaps you could try to find out why it doesn't work.

## SEE ALSO

ppm(5), ppmquant(1), ppmtopgm(1), ppmhist(1), pnmarith(1), ppmtorgb3(1), xv(1)

## AUTHOR

Copyright© 1992 by Hadmut Danisch (danisch@ira.uka.de). Permission to use and distribute this software and its documentation for noncommercial use and without fee is hereby granted, provided that the preceding copyright notice appear in all copies and that both that copyright notice and this permission notice appear in supporting documentation. This software may not be sold in any way. This software is not public domain.

*28 November 1992*

# httpd

httpd—Apache Hypertext Transfer Protocol server

## SYNOPSIS

httpd [ -vX? ][-d *serverroot* ][-f *config* ]

## DESCRIPTION

httpd is the Apache Hypertext Transfer Protocol (HTTP) server process. The server may be invoked by the Internet daemon inetd(1M) each time a connection to the HTTP service is made, or alternatively it may run as a daemon.

## OPTIONS

| | |
|---|---|
| -d *serverroot* | Set the initial value for the ServerRoot variable to serverroot. This can be overridden by the ServerRoot command in the configuration file. The default is /usr/local/etc/httpd. |
| -f *config* | Execute the commands in the file *config* on startup. If *config* does not begin with a /, then it is taken to be a path relative to the ServerRoot. The default is conf/httpd.conf. |
| -X | Run in single-process mode, for internal debugging purposes only; the daemon does not detach from the terminal or fork any children. Do not use this mode to provide ordinary Web service. |
| -v | Print the version of httpd, and then exit. |
| -? | Print a list of the httpd options, and then exit. |

## FILES

/usr/local/etc/httpd/conf/httpd.conf
/usr/local/etc/httpd/conf/srm.conf
/usr/local/etc/httpd/conf/access.conf
/usr/local/etc/httpd/conf/mime.types
/usr/local/etc/httpd/logs/error_log
/usr/local/etc/httpd/logs/access_log
/usr/local/etc/httpd/logs/httpd.pid

## SEE ALSO

inetd(1m)

Documentation for the Apache HTTP server is available from http://www.apache.org.

*October 1995*

# icontopbm

icontopbm—Convert a Sun icon into a portable bitmap

## SYNOPSIS

icontopbm [iconfile]

## DESCRIPTION

icontopbm reads a Sun icon as input and produces a portable bitmap as output.

## SEE ALSO

pbmtoicon(1), pbm(5)

## AUTHOR

Copyright© 1988 by Jef Poskanzer

*31 August 1988*


# ident

ident—Identify RCS keyword strings in files

## SYNOPSIS

ident [ -q ][-V ][*file ... * ]

## DESCRIPTION

ident searches for all instances of the pattern $ keyword : text $ in the named files or, if no files are named, the standard input.

These patterns are normally inserted automatically by the RCS command co(1), but can also be inserted manually. The option -q suppresses the warning given if there are no patterns in a file. The option -V prints ident's version number.

ident works on text files as well as object files and dumps. For example, if the C program in f.c contains

```
#include <stdio.h>
static char const rcsid[] =
"$Id: f.c,v 5.4 1993/11/09 17:40 eggert Exp $";
int main() { return printf("%s\n", rcsid) == EOF; }
```

and f.c is compiled into f.o, then the command

```
ident f.c f.o
```

will output

```
f.c:
$Id: f.c,v 5.4 1993/11/09 17:40 eggert Exp $
f.o:
$Id: f.c,v 5.4 1993/11/09 17:40 eggert Exp $
```

If a C program defines a string like the rcsid but does not use it, lint(1) may complain, and some C compilers will optimize away the string. The most reliable solution is to have the program use the rcsid string, as shown in the example.

ident finds all instances of the $ keyword : text $ pattern, even if keyword is not actually an RCS-supported keyword. This gives you information about nonstandard keywords like $XConsortium$.

## KEYWORDS

Here is the list of keywords currently maintained by co(1). All times are given in Coordinated Universal Time (UTC, sometimes called GMT by default), but if the files were checked out with co's -zzone option, times are given with a numeric time zone indication appended.

| | |
|---|---|
| `$Author$` | The login name of the user who checked in the revision. |
| `$Date$` | The date and time the revision was checked in. |
| `$Header$` | A standard header containing the full pathname of the RCS file, the revision number, the date and time, the author, the state, and the locker (if locked). |
| `$Id$` | Same as `$Header$`, except that the RCS filename is without a path. |
| `$Locker$` | The login name of the user who locked the revision (empty if not locked). |
| `$Log$` | The log message supplied during checkin. For ident's purposes, this is equivalent to `$RCSfile$`. |
| `$Name$` | The symbolic name used to check out the revision, if any. |
| `$RCSfile$` | The name of the RCS file without a path. |
| `$Revision$` | The revision number assigned to the revision. |
| `$Source$` | The full pathname of the RCS file. |
| `$State$` | The state assigned to the revision with the -s option of rcs(1) or ci(1). |

co(1) represents the following characters in keyword values by escape sequences to keep keyword strings well formed.

| *Character* | *Escape Sequence* |
|---|---|
| Tab | `\t` |
| Newline | `\n` |
| Space | `\040` |
| $ | `\044` |
| \ | `\\` |

## IDENTIFICATION

Author: Walter F. Tichy

Manual Page Revision: 5.4; Release date September 11, 1993.

Copyright© 1982, 1988, 1989 Walter F. Tichy. Copyright© 1990, 1992, 1993 Paul Eggert.

## SEE ALSO

ci(1), co(1), rcs(1), rcsdiff(1), rcsintro(1), rcsmerge(1), rlog(1), rcsfile(5)

Walter F. Tichy, *RCS—A System for Version Control, Software–Practice & Experience* 15, 7 (July 1985), 637–654.

*GNU, 9 November 1993*

# ilbmtoppm

ilbmtoppm—Convert an ILBM file into a portable pixmap

## SYNOPSIS

ilbmtoppm [-verbose][-ignore<chunkID>] [-isham¦-isehb][-adjustcolors][ILBMfile]

## DESCRIPTION

ilbmtoppm reads an IFF ILBM file as input and produces a portable pixmap as output. Supported ILBM types are Normal ILBMs with 1–16 planes.

Amiga Extra Halfbrite (EHB)

Amiga HAM with 3–16 planes

24-bit

Multiplatte (normal or HAM) pictures

Colormap (BMHD and CMAP chunk only, nPlanes = 0)

Unofficial direct color; 1–16 planes for each color component.

| | |
|---|---|
| Chunks used: | BMHD, CMAP, CAMG (only HAM and EHB flags used), PCHG, BODY unofficial DCOL chunk to identify direct color ILBM |
| Chunks ignored: | GRAB, DEST, SPRT, CRNG, CCRT, CLUT, DPPV, DRNG, EPSF |
| Other chunks (ignored but displayed in verbose mode): | NAME, AUTH, (d), ANNO, DPI |

Unknown chunks are skipped.

## OPTIONS

| | |
|---|---|
| -verbose | Give some information about the ILBM file. |
| -ignore <chunkID> | Skip a chunk. <chunkID> is the 4-letter IFF chunk identifier of the chunk to be skipped. |
| -isham ¦ -isehb | Treat the input file as a HAM or Extra Halfbrite picture, even if these flags or not set in the CAMG chunk (or if there is no CAMG chunk). |
| -adjustcolors | If all colors in the CMAP have a value of less then 16, ilbmtoppm assumes a 4-bit colormap and gives a warning. With this option, the colormap is scaled to 8 bits. |

## BUGS

The multipalette PCHG BigLineChanges and Huffman decompression code are untested.

## REFERENCES

*Amiga ROM Kernel Reference Manual—Devices* (3rd Ed.). Addison Wesley, ISBN 0-201-56775-X.

## SEE ALSO

ppm(5), ppmtoilbm(1)

## AUTHORS

Copyright© 1989 by Jef Poskanzer.

Modified October 1993 by Ingo Wilken (Ingo.Wilken@informatik.uni-oldenburg.de)

*4 October 1993*

# imake

imake—C preprocessor interface to the make utility

## SYNOPSIS

imake [ -D*define* ][-I*dir* ][-T*template* ][-f *filename* ][-C *filename* ][-s *filename* ]
[-e ][-v ]

## DESCRIPTION

imake is used to generate Makefiles from a template, a set of cpp macro functions, and a per-directory input file called an Imakefile. This allows machine dependencies (such as compiler options, alternate command names, and special make rules) to be kept separate from the descriptions of the various items to be built.

## OPTIONS

The following command-line options may be passed to imake:

-D*define*         This option is passed directly to cpp. It is typically used to set directory-specific variables. For example, the X Window System uses this flag to set TOPDIR to the name of the directory containing the top of the core distribution and CURDIR to the name of the current directory, relative to the top.

-I*directory*      This option is passed directly to cpp. It is typically used to indicate the directory in which the imake template and configuration files may be found.

-T*template*       This option specifies the name of the master template file (which is usually located in the directory specified with -I) used by cpp. The default is Imake.tmpl.

-f *filename*      This option specifies the name of the per-directory input file. The default is Imakefile.

-C *filename*      This option specifies the name of the .c file that is constructed in the current directory. The default is Imakefile.c.

-s *filename*      This option specifies the name of the make description file to be generated but make should not be invoked. If the filename is a hyphen (-), the output is written to stdout. The default is to generate, but not execute, a Makefile.

-e                 This option indicates the imake should execute the generated Makefile. The default is to leave this to the user.

-v                 This option indicates that imake should print the cpp command line that it is using to generate the Makefile.

## HOW IT WORKS

Imake invokes cpp with any -I or -D flags passed on the command line and passes the name of a file containing the following three lines:

```
#define IMAKE_TEMPLATE "Imake.tmpl"
#define INCLUDE_IMAKEFILE <Imakefile>
#include IMAKE_TEMPLATE
```

where Imake.tmpl and Imakefile may be overridden by the -T and -f command options, respectively.

The IMAKE_TEMPLATE typically reads in a file containing machine-dependent parameters (specified as cpp symbols), a site-specific parameters file, a file defining variables, a file containing cpp macro functions for generating make rules, and finally the Imakefile (specified by INCLUDE_IMAKEFILE) in the current directory. The Imakefile uses the macro functions to indicate what targets should be built; imake takes care of generating the appropriate rules.

Imake configuration files contain two types of variables, imake variables and make variables. The imake variables are interpreted by cpp when imake is run. By convention they are mixed case. The make variables are written into the Makefile for later interpretation by make. By convention make variables are uppercase.

The rules file (usually named Imake.rules in the configuration directory) contains a variety of cpp macro functions that are configured according to the current platform. Imake replaces any occurrences of the string @@ with a newline to allow macros that generate more than one line of make rules. For example, when called with program_target(foo, foo1.o foo2.o), the macro:

```
#define program_target(program, objlist) @@\
program: objlist @@\
$(CC) -o $@ objlist $(LDFLAGS)
```

will expand to

```
foo: foo1.o foo2.o
$(CC) -o $@ foo1.o foo2.o $(LDFLAGS)
```

imake also replaces any occurrences of the word XCOMM with the character # to permit placing comments in the Makefile without causing invalid directive errors from the preprocessor.

Some complex imake macros require generated make variables local to each invocation of the macro, often because their value depends on parameters passed to the macro. Such variables can be created by using an imake variable of the form XVARdef*n*, where *n* is a single digit. A unique make variable will be substituted. Later occurrences of the variable XVARuse*n* will be replaced by the variable created by the corresponding XVARdef*n*.

On systems whose cpp reduces multiple tabs and spaces to a single space, imake attempts to put back any necessary tabs (make is very picky about the difference between tabs and spaces). For this reason, colons (:) in command lines must be preceded by a backslash (\).

## USE WITH THE X WINDOW SYSTEM

The X Window System uses imake extensively, for both full builds within the source tree and external software. As mentioned earlier, two special variables, TOPDIR and CURDIR, are set to make referencing files using relative pathnames easier. For example, the following command is generated automatically to build the Makefile in the directory lib/X/ (relative to the top of the sources):

```
% ../../../config/imake -I../../../config \
-DTOPDIR=../../../. -DCURDIR=./lib/X
```

When building X programs outside the source tree, a special symbol UseInstalled is defined and TOPDIR and CURDIR are omitted. If the configuration files have been properly installed, the script xmkmf(1) may be used.

## INPUT FILES

Here is a summary of the files read by imake as used by X. The indentation shows which files include which other files.

```
Imake.tmpl generic variables
site.def site-specific, BeforeVendorCF defined
.cf machine-specific
Lib.rules shared library rules
site.def site-specific, AfterVendorCF defined
Imake.rules rules
Project.tmpl X-specific variables
Lib.tmpl shared library variables
Imakefile
Library.tmpl library rules
Server.tmpl server rules
Threads.tmpl multi-threaded rules
```

Note that site.def is included twice, once before the *.cf file and once after. Although most site customizations should be specified after the *.cf file, some, such as the choice of compiler, need to be specified before, because other variable settings may depend on them.

The first time site.def is included, the variable BeforeVendorCF is defined, and the second time, the variable AfterVendorCF is defined. All code in site.def should be inside a #ifdef for one of these symbols.

## FILES

| | |
|---|---|
| Imakefile.c | Temporary input file for cpp |
| /tmp/Imf.XXXXXX | Temporary Makefile for -s |
| /tmp/IIf.XXXXXX | Temporary Imakefile if specified Imakefile uses # comments |
| /lib/cpp | Default C preprocessor |

## SEE ALSO

make(1), xmkmf(1)

S. I. Feldman, *Make—A Program for Maintaining Computer Programs.*

## ENVIRONMENT VARIABLES

The following environment variables may be set; however, their use is not recommended as they introduce dependencies that are not readily apparent when `imake` is run.

IMAKEINCLUDE       If defined, this should be a valid include argument for the C preprocessor. Example:

`-I/usr/include/local`

Actually, any valid `cpp` argument will work here.

IMAKECPP          If defined, this should be a valid path to a preprocessor program. Example:

`/usr/local/cpp`

By default, `imake` will use `/lib/cpp`.

IMAKEMAKE         If defined, this should be a valid path to a make program, such as

`/usr/local/make`

By default, `imake` will use whatever `make` program is found using execvp(3). This variable is only used if the `-e` option is specified.

## AUTHORS

Todd Brunhoff, Tektronix and MIT Project Athena

Jim Fulton, MIT X Consortium

*X Version 11 Release 6*

# imgtoppm

`imgtoppm`—Convert an `Img-whatnot` file into a portable pixmap

## SYNOPSIS

`imgtoppm [imgfile]`

## DESCRIPTION

`imgtoppm` reads an `Img-whatnot` file as input and produces a portable pixmap as output. The `Img-whatnot` toolkit is available for FTP on `venera.isi.edu`, along with numerous images in this format.

## SEE ALSO

ppm(5)

## AUTHOR

Based on a simple conversion program posted to `comp.graphics` by Ed Falk.

Copyright© 1989 by Jef Poskanzer.

*5 September 1989*

# inews

`inews`—Send a Usenet article to the local news server for distribution

## SYNOPSIS

`inews [ -h ][-D ][-O ][-R ][-S ][header_flags ][input ]`

## DESCRIPTION

Inews reads a Usenet news article (perhaps with headers) from the named file or standard input if no file is given. It adds some headers and performs some consistency checks. If the article does not meet these checks (for example, too much quoting of old articles, or posting to nonexistent newsgroups), then the article is rejected. If it passes the checks, inews sends the article to the local news server as specified in the inn.conf(5) file for distribution.

In the standard mode of operation, the input consists of the article headers, a blank line, and the message body. For compatibility with older software, the -h flag must be used. If there are no headers in the message, then this flag may be omitted.

Several headers may be specified on the command line, shown in the synopsis above as header flags. Each of these flags takes a single parameter; if the value is more than one word (for example, almost all Subject lines) then quotes must be used to prevent the shell from splitting it into multiple words. The options, and their equivalent headers, are as follows:

| | |
|---|---|
| a | Approved |
| c | Control |
| d | Distribution |
| e | Expires |
| f | From |
| w | Followup-To |
| n | Newsgroups |
| r | Reply-To |
| t | Subject |
| F | References |
| o | Organization |
| x | Path prefix |

The Path header is built according to the following rules. If the —x flag is used, then its value will be the start of the header. Any other host will see the site in the header, and therefore not offer the article to that site. If the pathhost configuration parameter is specified in the inn.conf(5) file, then it will be added to the Path. Otherwise, if the server configuration parameter is specified, then the full domain name of the local host will be added to the Path. The Path will always end not-for-mail.

The default Organization header will be provided if none is present in the article or if the -o flag is not used. To prevent adding the default, use the -O flag.

As a debugging aide, if the -D flag is used, the consistency checks will be performed, and the article will be sent to the standard output, rather then sent to the server.

For compatibility with C News, inews accepts, but ignores, the -A, -V, and -W flags. The C News -N flag is treated as the -D flag.

If a file named .signature exists in the user's home directory, inews will try to append it to the end of the article. If the file cannot be read, or if it is too long (for example, more than four lines or one standard I/O buffer), or if some other problem occurs, then the article will not be posted. To suppress this action, use the -S flag.

If the -R flag is used then inews will reject any attempts to post control messages.

If an unapproved posting is made to a moderated newsgroup, inews will try to mail the article to the moderator for posting. It uses the moderators(5) file to determine the mailing address. If no address is found, it will use the inn.conf file to determine a "last-chance" host to try.

If the NNTP server needs to authenticate the client, inews will use the NNTPsendpass-word(3) routine to authenticate itself. In order to do this, the program will need read access to the passwd.nntp(5) file. This is typically done by having the file group-readable and making inews run setgid to that group.

Inews exits with a zero status if the article was successfully posted or mailed, or with a nonzero status if the article could not be delivered.

Since inews will spool its input if the server is unavailable, it is usually necessary to run rnews(1) with the -U flag on a regular basis, usually out of cron(8).

## HISTORY

Written by Rich $alz (rsalz@uunet.uu.net) for *InterNetNews*.

## SEE ALSO

moderators(5), inn.conf(5). rnews(1)

# info

info—GNU's hypertext system

## SYNOPSIS

info [ --option-name option-value ] enu-item...

## DESCRIPTION

The GNU project has a hypertext system called info that allows the same source file to be either printed as a paper manual, or viewed using info. It is possible to use the info program from inside Emacs, or to use the standalone version described here. This manual page gives a brief summary of its capabilities.

## OPTIONS

| | |
|---|---|
| --directory *directory-path* | Add *directory-path* to the list of directory paths searched when info needs to find a file. You may issue --directory multiple times. Alternatively, you may specify a value for the environment variable INFOPATH; if --directory is not given, the value of INFOPATH is used. The value of INFOPATH is a colon-separated list of directory names. If you do not supply either INFOPATH or *-directory-path*, info uses a default path. |
| -f *filename* | Specify a particular info file to visit. By default, info visits the file dir; if you use this option, info will start with (FILENAME)Top as the first file and node. |
| -n *nodename* | Specify a particular node to visit in the initial file that info loads. This is especially useful in conjunction with --file. You may specify --node multiple times. |
| -o *file* | Direct output to file instead of starting an interactive info session. |
| -h | Produce a relatively brief description of the available info options. |
| --version | Print the version information of info and exit. |
| menu-item | info treats its remaining arguments as the names of menu items. The first argument is a menu item in the initial node visited, while the second argument is a menu item in the first argument's node. You can easily move to the node of your choice by specifying the menu names that describe the path to that node. For example, info emacs buffers first selects the menu item emacs in the node (dir)Top, and then selects the menu item buffers in the node (emacs)Top. |

## COMMANDS

In info, the following commands are available:

| | |
|---|---|
| h | Invoke the info tutorial. |
| ? | Get a short summary of info commands. |
| h | Select the info node from the main directory; this is much more complete than just using ?. |
| Ctrl-g | Abort whatever you are doing. |
| Ctrl-l | Redraw the screen. |

Selecting other nodes:

| | |
|---|---|
| n | Move to the next node of this node. |
| p | Move to the previous node of this node. |
| u | Move to this node's up node. |
| m | Pick a menu item specified by name. Picking a menu item causes another node to be selected. You do not need to type a complete nodename; if you type a few letters and then a space or tab, info will try to fill in the rest of the nodename. If you ask for further completion without typing any more characters, you'll be given a list of possibilities; you can also get the list with ?. If you type a few characters and then hit Enter, info will try to do a completion, and if it is ambiguous, use the first possibility. |
| f | Follow a cross reference. You are asked for the name of the reference, using command completion as for m. |
| l | Move to the last node you were at. |

Moving within a node:

| | |
|---|---|
| Space | Scroll forward a page. |
| DEL | Scroll backward a page. |
| b | Go to the beginning of this node. |

Advanced commands:

| | |
|---|---|
| q | Quit info. |
| 1 | Pick first item in node's menu. |
| 2 — 5 | Pick second to fifth item in node's menu. |
| g | Move to node specified by name. You may include a filename as well, as (FILENAME)NODENAME. |
| s | Search through this info file for a specified string, and select the node in which the next occurrence is found. |
| M-x print-node | Pipe the contents of the current node through the command in the environment variable INFO_PRINT_COMMAND. If the variable does not exist, the node is simply piped to lpr. |

## ENVIRONMENT

| | |
|---|---|
| INFOPATH | A colon-separated list of directories to search for info files. Used if --directory is not given. |
| INFO_PRINT_COMMAND | The command used for printing. |

## SEE ALSO

emacs(1)

## AUTHOR

Brian Fox, Free Software Foundation (bfox@ai.mit.edu)

## MANUAL AUTHOR

Robert Lupton (rhl@astro.princeton.edu); updated by Robert J. Chassell (bob@gnu.ai.mit.edu).

*7 December 1990*


# innconfval

innconfval—Get an *InterNetNews* configuration parameter

## SYNOPSIS

innconfval [ -f ][*parameter...* ]

## DESCRIPTION

Innconfval prints the values of the parameters specified on the command line. Values are retrieved from the inn.conf(5) file and are described there.

Values are retrieved by using the GetConfigValue routine, or GetFileConfigValue if the -f flag is used. Both are described in libinn(3).

## HISTORY

Written by Rich $alz (rsalz@uunet.uu.net) for *InterNetNews.*

## SEE ALSO

libinn(3), inn.conf(5)

# insmod

insmod—Install loadable modules (aout and ELF format)

## SYNOPSIS

insmod [ -fkmsxv ] [ -o internal_name ] object_file [ symbol=value ... ]

## DESCRIPTION

insmod installs a loadable module in the kernel.

insmod tries to load a module into the kernel, and resolves all symbols from the exported kernel symbols, with version information, if available. The module will get its name by removing the .o extension from the basename of the object file. If the .o extension is omitted, insmod will attempt to locate the module in some common default directories. If the environment contains the variable MODPATH, where all directories are separated with :, insmod will look in these directories for the module, in the specified order.

It is possible to load unversioned modules in a versioned kernel, and all combinations of these.

It is also possible to load ELF modules into an a.out kernel, and all combinations of these.

It is possible to stack modules, that is, let one module use a previously loaded module. All modules that are referenced are updated with this reference. This ensures that a module can't be unloaded if there is another module that refers to it.

It is possible to change integer values in the module when loading it. This makes it possible to tune the module.

The options are as follows:

| | |
|---|---|
| -f | The -f option tries to load the module even if the kernel or symbol versions differs from the version expected by the module. A warning will be issued if the module is locked to a specific kernel version that differs from the current version. |
| -k | This option should really only be used by modprobe, to indicate that the module insertion was requested by kerneld. All modules inserted using this option will be subject to autoremoval by the kerneld utility if they have been unused for more that a minute. (The usage count is zero and no modules depend on this module.) If the kernel is not kerneld-aware, the module will be rejected by the kernel. Just load it without the -k option, and all should be well. |
| -m | The -m option will make insmod output a load map, that will make it easier to debug your modules after a kernel panic, thanks to Derek Atkins (warlord@MIT.EDU). |
| -o | The -o option allows the module to be named to an explicit name instead of having a name derived from the name of the object file. Note that this option can also be placed after the module name, so that the syntax of insmod looks more similar to ld. |

symbol=value[,*value*] ...     The values of all integer or character pointer symbols in the module can be changed at load-time by naming a symbol and giving the new value(s). If the symbol is defined as an array of integers or character pointers, the elements in the array can be initialized by giving the values separated by commas. Specific array entries can be skipped by omitting the value, as in symbol=*value1*,,*value2*. Each integer value can be given as a decimal, octal, or hexadecimal value: 17, 021, or 0x11. If the first character in the given value is nonnumeric, the value is interpreted as a string. The symbol is assumed to be a character pointer, which will be initialized to point to the string. Extra space in the module will be allocated for the string itself. Note the syntax: no spaces are allowed around the = or , signs!

-s     With this option, insmod will produce debugging information and error messages using the syslog facility. (Also used by kerneld, if you have installed it.)

-v     If you want verbose information from the loading, select this option.

-x     The no-export flag, which will inhibit the default insmod behavior—inserting all the module's external symbols into the kernel symbol table. Note that the kernel will still update the references that the module makes to previously loaded modules.

## SEE ALSO

rmmod(1), modprobe(1), depmod(1), lsmod(1), ksyms(1), modules(2), genksyms(8)

## HISTORY

The module support was first conceived by Anonymous (as far as I know). Linux version by Bas Laarhoven (bas@vimec.nl). 0.99.14 version by Jon Tombs (jon@gtex02.us.es). Extended by Bjorn Ekwall (bj0rn@blox.se). ELF help from Eric Youngdale (eric@aib.com).

## BUGS

insmod relies on the "fact" that symbols, for which one wants to change the value, are defined as integers or character pointers, and that sizeof(int) == sizeof(char *).

*Linux, 14 May 1995*

# install

install—Copy files and set their attributes; GNU file installer

## SYNOPSIS

```
install [options] [-s] [--strip] source dest
install [options] [-s] [--strip] source... directory
install [options] [-d,--directory] directory...
```

Options:

```
[-c] [-g group] [-m mode] [-o owner] [--group=group] [--mode=mode]
[--owner=owner] [--help] [--version]
```

## DESCRIPTION

This manual page documents the GNU version of install. install copies files and sets their permission modes and, if possible, their owner and group. Used similarly to cp; typically used in Makefiles to copy programs into their destination directories. It can also be used to create the destination directories and any leading directories, and to set the final directory's modes. It refuses to copy files onto themselves.

## OPTIONS

| | |
|---|---|
| -c | Ignored; for compatibility with old UNIX versions of install. |
| -d, --directory | Create each given directory and its leading directories, if they do not already exist. Set the owner, group, and mode as given on the command line or to the defaults. Also gives any leading directories that are created those attributes. This is different from the SunOS 4.x install, which gives directories that it creates the default attributes. |
| -g, --group *group* | Set the group ownership of the installed file or directory to the group ID of *group* (default is process's current group). *group* may also be a numeric group ID. |
| -m, --mode *mode* | Set the permission mode for the installed file or directory to *mode*, which can be either an octal number, or a symbolic mode as in chmod, with 0 as the point of departure. The default mode is 0755. |
| -o, --owner *owner* | If run as root, set the ownership of the installed file to the user ID of *owner* (default is root). *owner* may also be a numeric user ID. |
| -s, --strip | Strip the symbol tables from installed programs. |
| --help | Print a usage message on standard output and exit successfully. |
| --version | Print version information on standard output and exit successfully. |

*GNU File Utilities*

# installit

installit—File/directory installation tool

## SYNOPSIS

installit [ -o *owner* ][-g *group* ][-O *owner* ][-G *group* ][-m *mode* ][-b *backup* ]
[-s ][-t ] source destination

## DESCRIPTION

installit puts a copy of source into the specified destination.

If *source* is a period, then *destination* is taken to be the name of a directory that should be created. Otherwise, *source* is taken to name an existing file and *destination* may be either a file or directory; it is interpreted according to the same rules as cp(1).

If *destination* names a preexisting file, it will be removed before the copy is done. To make a backup copy, use the –b flag; the existing file will be renamed to have the specified extension. If *source* and *destination* are the same string, or if the two files are identical, then no copying is done, and only the -o, -g, -m, and -s flags are processed. In this case, the modification time on the *destination* will be updated using touch(1) unless the -n (don't touch) flag is used.

After the *destination* has been created, it is possible to set the owner, group, and mode that it should have. This is done by using the -o, -g, and -m flags, respectively. The -O and -G flags set the owner and group only if installit is being run by root, as determined by whoami(1). To strip(1) an installed executable, use the -s flag.

Note that installit uses no special privileges to copy files from one place to another.

## BUGS AND LIMITATIONS

Flags cannot be combined.

The chown(8) command must exist in either the /etc or /usr/etc directory or the user's PATH.

The whoami command must exist in the /usr/ucb directory or the user's PATH.

## HISTORY

Written by Rich $alz (rsalz@uunet.uu.net) for *InterNetNews.*

# ispell, buildhash, munchlist, findaffix, tryaffix, icombine, ijoin

ispell, buildhash, munchlist, findaffix, tryaffix, icombine, ijoin--Interactive spelling checking

## SYNOPSIS

```
ispell [common-flags][-M¦-N][-Lcontext] [-V] files
ispell [common-flags] -l
ispell [common-flags][-f file] [-s]-a¦ -A
ispell [-d file][-w chars] -c
ispell [-d file][-w chars] -e[e]
ispell [-d file] -D
ispell -v[v]

common-flags:[-t][-n][-b][-x][-B][-C][-P][-m][-S][-d file][-p file][-w chars]
[-W n][-T type]

buildhash [-s] dict-file affix-file hash-file
buildhash -s count affix-file munchlist [-l aff-file][-c conv-file]
[-T suffix][-s hash-file] [-D][-v][-w chars][files] findaffix [-p¦-s][-f][-c]
[-m min][-M max][-e elim][-t tabchar][-l low][files]

tryaffix [-p¦-s] [-c] expanded-file affix[+addition]

icombine [-T type][aff-file]

ijoin [-s¦-u] join-options file1 file2
```

## DESCRIPTION

ispell is fashioned after the spell program from ITS (called ispell on Twenex systems.) The most common usage is ispell filename. In this case, ispell will display each word which does not appear in the dictionary at the top of the screen and allow you to change it. If there are "near misses" in the dictionary (words that differ by only a single letter, a missing or extra letter, a pair of transposed letters, or a missing space or hyphen), then they are also displayed on following lines. As well as near misses, ispell may display other guesses at ways to make the word from a known root, with each guess preceded by question marks. Finally, the line containing the word and the previous line are printed at the bottom of the screen. If your terminal can display in reverse video, the word itself is highlighted. You have the option of replacing the word completely or choosing one of the suggested words. Commands are single characters as follows (case is ignored):

| | |
|---|---|
| R | Replace the misspelled word completely. |
| Space | Accept the word this time only. |
| A | Accept the word for the rest of this ispell session. |
| I | Accept the word, capitalized as it is in the file, and update private dictionary. |
| U | Accept the word, and add an uncapitalized (actually, all lowercase) version to the private dictionary. |
| 0-*n* | Replace with one of the suggested words. |
| L | Look up words in system dictionary (controlled by the WORDS compilation option). |
| X | Write the rest of this file, ignoring misspellings, and start next file. |
| Q | Exit immediately and leave the file unchanged. |
| ! | Shell escape. |

| `^L` | Redraw screen. |
|---|---|
| `^Z` | Suspend `ispell`. |
| `?` | Give help screen. |

If the `-M` switch is specified, a one-line mini-menu at the bottom of the screen will summarize these options. Conversely, the `-N` switch may be used to suppress the mini-menu. (The mini-menu is displayed by default if `ispell` was compiled with the `MINIMENU` option, but these two switches will always override the default.)

If the `-L` flag is given, the specified number is used as the number of lines of context to be shown at the bottom of the screen. (The default is to calculate the amount of context as a certain percentage of the screen size.) The amount of context is subject to a system-imposed limit.

If the `-V` flag is given, characters that are not in the 7-bit ANSI printable character set will always be displayed in the style of `cat -v`, even if `ispell` thinks that these characters are legal ISO Latin-1 on your system. This is useful when working with older terminals. Without this switch, `ispell` will display 8-bit characters as is if they have been defined as string characters for the chosen file type.

Besides the `-l`, `-a`, and `-A` options, Normal mode accepts the following common flags on the command line:

| `-t` | The input file is in TeX or LaTeX format. |
|---|---|
| `-n` | The input file is in `nroff/troff` format. |
| `-b` | Create a backup file by appending `.bak` to the name of the input file. |
| `-x` | Don't create a backup file. |
| `-B` | Report run-together words with missing blanks as spelling errors. |
| `-C` | Consider run-together words as legal compounds. |
| `-P` | Don't generate extra root/affix combinations. |
| `-m` | Make possible root/affix combinations that aren't in the dictionary. |
| `-S` | Sort the list of guesses by probable correctness. |
| `-d` *file* | Specify an alternate dictionary file. For example, use `-d deutsch` to choose a German dictionary in a German installation. |
| `-p` *file* | Specify an alternate personal dictionary. |
| `-w` *chars* | Specify additional characters that can be part of a word. |
| `-W` *n* | Specify length of words that are always legal. |
| `-T` *type* | Assume a given formatter type for all files. |

The `-n` and `-t` options select whether `ispell` runs in `nroff/troff` (`-n`) or TeX/LaTeX (`-t`) input mode. (The default is controlled by the `DEFTEXFLAG` installation option.) TeX/LaTeX mode is also automatically selected if an input file has the extension `.tex`, unless overridden by the `-n` switch. In TeX/LaTeX mode, whenever a backslash (`\`) is found, `ispell` skips to the next whitespace or TeX/LaTeX delimiter. Certain commands contain arguments that should not be checked, such as labels and reference keys found in the `\cite` command, because they contain arbitrary, nonword arguments. Spell checking is also suppressed when in math mode. Thus, for example, given

`\chapter {This is a Ckapter} \cite{SCH86}`

`ispell` will find "Ckapter" but not "SCH." The `-t` option does not recognize the TeX comment character `%`, so comments are also spell checked. It also assumes correct LaTeX syntax. Arguments to infrequently used commands and some optional arguments are sometimes checked unnecessarily. The bibliography will not be checked if `ispell` was compiled with `IGNOREBIB` defined. Otherwise, the bibliography will be checked but the reference key will not.

References for the `tib`(1) bibliography system (text between a `[.` or `<.` and `.]` or `.>`) will always be ignored in TeX/LaTeX mode.

The `-b` and `-x` options control whether `ispell` leaves a backup (`.bak`) file for each input file.

The `.bak` file contains the precorrected text. If there are file opening/writing errors, the `.bak` file may be left for recovery purposes even with the `-x` option. The default for this option is controlled by the `DEFNOBACKUPFLAG` installation option.

The -B and -C options control how ispell handles run-together words, such as *notthe* for *not the*. If -B is specified, such words will be considered errors, and ispell will list variations with an inserted blank or hyphen as possible replacements. If -C is specified, run-together words will be considered to be legal compounds, so long as both components are in the dictionary, and each component is at least as long as a language-dependent minimum (three characters, by default). This is useful for languages such as German and Norwegian, where many compound words are formed by concatenation. (Note that compounds formed from three or more root words will still be considered errors). The default for this option is language-dependent; in a multilingual installation, the default may vary depending on which dictionary you choose.

The -P and -m options control when ispell automatically generates suggested root/affix combinations for possible addition to your personal dictionary. (These are the entries in the "guess" list that are preceded by question marks.) If -P is specified, such guesses are displayed only if ispell cannot generate any possibilities that match the current dictionary. If -m is specified, such guesses are always displayed. This can be useful if the dictionary has a limited word list, or a word list with few suffixes. However, you should be careful when using this option, as it can generate guesses that produce illegal words. The default for this option is controlled by the dictionary file used.

The -S option suppresses ispell's normal behavior of sorting the list of possible replacement words. Some people may prefer this, since it somewhat enhances the probability that the correct word will be low-numbered.

The -d option is used to specify an alternate hashed dictionary file, other than the default. If the filename does not contain a /, the library directory for the default dictionary file is prefixed; thus, to use a dictionary in the local directory -d ./xxx.hash must be used. This is useful to allow dictionaries for alternate languages. Unlike previous versions of ispell, a dictionary of /dev/null is illegal because the dictionary contains the affix table. If you need an effectively empty dictionary, create a one-entry list with an unlikely string (for example, "qqqqq").

The -p option is used to specify an alternate personal dictionary file. If the filename does not begin with /, $HOME is prefixed. Also, the shell variable WORDLIST may be set, which renames the personal dictionary in the same manner. The command line overrides any WORDLIST setting. If neither the -p switch nor the WORDLIST environment variable is given, ispell will search for a personal dictionary in both the current directory and $HOME, creating one in $HOME if none is found. The preferred name is constructed by appending .ispell to the base name of the hash file. For example, if you use the English dictionary, your personal dictionary would be named .ispell_english. However, if the file .ispell_words exists, it will be used as the personal dictionary regardless of the language hash file chosen. This feature is included primarily for backwards compatibility.

If the -p option is not specified, ispell will look for personal dictionaries in both the current directory and the home directory. If dictionaries exist in both places, they will be merged. When words are added to the personal dictionary, they will be written to the current directory if a dictionary already existed in that place; otherwise, they will be written to the dictionary in the home directory.

The -w option may be used to specify characters other than alphabetics that may also appear in words. For instance, -w "&" will allow "AT&T" to be picked up. Underscores are useful in many technical documents. There is an admittedly crude provision in this option for 8-bit international characters. Nonprinting characters may be specified in the usual way by inserting a backslash followed by the octal character code, for example, \014 for a form feed. Alternatively, if n appears in the character string, the (up to) three characters following are a decimal code, 0–255, for the character. For example, to include bells and form feeds in your words (an admittedly silly thing to do, but aren't most pedagogical examples):

```
n007n012
```

Numeric digits other than the three following n are simply numeric characters. Use of n does not conflict with anything because actual alphabetics have no meaning; alphabetics are already accepted. ispell will typically be used with input from a file, meaning that preserving parity for possible 8-bit characters from the input text is okay. If you specify the -1 option, and actually type text from the terminal, this may create problems if your stty settings preserve parity.

The -W option may be used to change the length of words that ispell always accepts as legal. Normally, ispell will accept all one-character words as legal, which is equivalent to specifying -W 1. (The default for this switch is actually controlled by the MINWORD installation option, so it may vary at your installation.) If you want all words to be checked against the dictionary, regardless of length, you might want to specify -W 0. On the other hand, if your document specifies to accept all words of three letters or less, then regardless of the setting of this option, ispell will only generate words that are in the dictionary as suggested replacements for words; this prevents the list from becoming too long. Obviously, this option can be very dangerous, since short misspellings may be missed. If you use this option a lot, you should probably make a last pass without it before you publish your document, to protect yourself against errors.

The -T option is used to specify a default formatter type for use in generating string characters. This switch overrides the default type determined from the filename. The type argument may be either one of the unique names defined in the language affix file (such as nroff) or a file suffix including the dot (for example, .tex). If no -T option appears and no type can be determined from the filename, the default string character type declared in the language affix file will be used.

The -l or list option to ispell is used to produce a list of misspelled words from the standard input.

The -a option is intended to be used from other programs through a pipe. In this mode, ispell prints a one-line version identification message, and then begins reading lines of input. For each input line, a single line is written to the standard output for each word checked for spelling on the line. If the word was found in the main dictionary, or your personal dictionary, then the line contains only a *. If the word was found through affix removal, then the line contains a +, a space, and the root word. If the word was found through compound formation (concatenation of two words, controlled by the -C option), then the line contains only a -.

If the word is not in the dictionary, but there are near misses, then the line contains an &, a space, the misspelled word, a space, the number of near misses, the number of characters between the beginning of the line and the beginning of the misspelled word, a colon, another space, and a list of the near misses separated by commas and spaces. Following the near misses (and identified only by the count of near misses), if the word could be formed by adding (illegal) affixes to a known root, is a list of suggested derivations, again separated by commas and spaces. If there are no near misses at all, the line format is the same, except that the & is replaced by ? (and the near-miss count is always zero). The suggested derivations following the near misses are in the form:

```
[prefix+] root [-prefix] [-suffix] [+suffix]
```

(for example, "re+fry-y+ies" to get "refries") where each optional pfx and sfx is a string. Also, each near miss or guess is capitalized the same as the input word unless such capitalization is illegal; in the latter case each near miss is capitalized correctly according to the dictionary.

Finally, if the word does not appear in the dictionary, and there are no near misses, then the line contains a #, a space, the misspelled word, a space, and the character offset from the beginning of the line. Each sentence of text input is terminated with an additional blank line, indicating that ispell has completed processing the input line.

These output lines can be summarized as follows:

| | |
|---|---|
| OK: | * |
| Root: | + <root> |
| Compound: | - |
| Miss: | & <original><count><offset>: <miss>, <miss>, ..., <guess>, ... |
| Guess: | ? <original> 0 <offset>: <guess>, <guess>, ... |
| None: | # <original> <offset> |

For example, a dummy dictionary containing the words *fray, Frey, fry,* and *refried* might produce the following response to the command echo 'frqy refries ¦ ispell -a -m -d ./test.hash:

```
(#) International Ispell Version 3.0.05 (beta), 08/10/91
& frqy 3 0: fray, Frey, fry
& refries 1 5: refried, re+fry-y+ies
```

This mode is also suitable for interactive use when you want to figure out the spelling of a single word.

The -A option works just like -a, except that if a line begins with the string "&Include File&", the rest of the line is taken as the name of a file to read for further words. Input returns to the original file when the include file is exhausted. Inclusion may be nested up to five deep. The key string may be changed with the environment variable INCLUDE_STRING (the ampersands, if any, must be included).

When in the -a mode, ispell will also accept lines of single words prefixed with any of the following: *, &, @, +, -, ˜, #, !, %, or ˆ. A line starting with * tells ispell to insert the word into the user's dictionary (similar to the I command). A line starting with & tells ispell to insert an all-lowercase version of the word into the user's dictionary (similar to the U command). A line starting with @ causes ispell to accept this word in the future (similar to the A command). A line starting with +, followed immediately by tex or nroff, will cause ispell to parse future input according the syntax of that formatter. A line consisting solely of a + will place ispell in TeX/LaTeX mode (similar to the -t option) and - returns ispell to nroff/troff mode (but these commands are obsolete). However, string character type is not changed, the ˜ command must be used to do this. A line starting with ˜ causes ispell to set internal parameters (in particular, the default string character type) based on the filename given in the rest of the line. (A file suffix is sufficient, but the period must be included. Instead of a filename or suffix, a unique name, as listed in the language affix file, may be specified.) However, the formatter parsing is not changed; the + command must be used to change the formatter. A line prefixed with # will cause the personal dictionary to be saved. A line prefixed with ! will turn on terse mode (explained later in this subsection), and a line prefixed with % will return ispell to normal (non-terse) mode. Any input following the prefix characters +, -, #, !, or % is ignored, as is any input following the filename on a ˜ line. To allow spell checking of lines beginning with these characters, a line starting with ˆ has that character removed before it is passed to the spell checking code. It is recommended that programmatic interfaces prefix every data line with an up arrow to protect themselves against future changes in ispell.

To summarize these:

| | |
|---|---|
| * | Add to personal dictionary |
| @ | Accept word, but leave out of dictionary |
| # | Save current personal dictionary |
| ˜ | Set parameters based on filename |
| + | Enter TeX mode |
| - | Exit TeX mode |
| ! | Enter terse mode |
| % | Exit terse mode |
| ˆ | Spell check rest of line |

In terse mode, ispell will not print lines beginning with *, +, or -, all of which indicate correct words. This significantly improves running speed when the driving program is going to ignore correct words anyway.

The -s option is only valid in conjunction with the -a or -A options, and only on BSD-derived systems. If specified, ispell will stop itself with a SIGTSTP signal after each line of input. It will not read more input until it receives a SIGCONT signal. This may be useful for handshaking with certain text editors.

The -f option is only valid in conjunction with the -a or -A options. If -f is specified, ispell will write its results to the given file, rather than to standard output.

The -v option causes ispell to print its current version identification on the standard output and exit. If the switch is doubled, ispell will also print the options that it was compiled with.

The -c, -e[1-4], and -D options of ispell are primarily intended for use by the munchlist shell script. The -c switch causes a list of words to be read from the standard input. For each word, a list of possible root words and affixes will be written to the standard output. Some of the root words will be illegal and must be filtered from the output by other means; the munchlist script does this. As an example, the command

```
echo BOTHER ¦ ispell -c
```

produces

```
BOTHER BOTHE/R BOTH/R
```

The -e switch is the reverse of -c; it expands affix flags to produce a list of words. For example, the command

```
echo BOTH/R ¦ ispell -e
```

produces

```
BOTH BOTHER
```

An optional expansion level can also be specified. A level of 1 (-e1) is the same as -e alone. A level of 2 causes the original root/affix combination to be prepended to the line:

```
BOTH/R BOTH BOTHER
```

A level of 3 causes multiple lines to be output, one for each generated word, with the original root/affix combination followed by the word it creates:

```
BOTH/R BOTH
BOTH/R BOTHER
```

A level of 4 causes a floating-point number to be appended to each of the level 3 lines, giving the ratio between the length of the root and the total length of all generated words including the root:

```
BOTH/R BOTH 2.500000
BOTH/R BOTHER 2.500000
```

Finally, the -D flag causes the affix tables from the dictionary file to be dumped to standard output.

Unless your system administrator has suppressed the feature to save space, ispell is aware of the correct capitalizations of words in the dictionary and in your personal dictionary. As well as recognizing words that must be capitalized (such as *George*) and words that must be all capitals (such as *NASA*), it can also handle words with unusual capitalization (for example, *IT-Corp* or *TeX*). If a word is capitalized incorrectly, the list of possibilities will include all acceptable capitalizations. (More than one capitalization may be acceptable; for example, my dictionary lists both *ITCorp* and *ITcorp*.)

Normally, this feature will not cause you surprises, but there is one circumstance you need to be aware of. If you use I to add a word to your dictionary that is at the beginning of a sentence (for example, the first word of this paragraph if *normally* were not in the dictionary), it will be marked as "capitalization required." A subsequent usage of this word without capitalization will be considered a misspelling by ispell, and it will suggest the capitalized version. You must then compare the actual spellings by eye, and then type I to add the uncapitalized variant to your personal dictionary. You can avoid this problem by using U to add the original word, rather than I.

The rules for capitalization are as follows:

1.  Any word may appear in all capitals, as in headings.
2.  Any word that is in the dictionary in all lowercase form may appear either in lowercase or capitalized (as at the beginning of a sentence).
3.  Any word that has unusual capitalization (that is, it contains both cases and there is an uppercase character besides the first) must appear exactly as in the dictionary, except as permitted by rule 1. If the word is acceptable in all lowercase, it must appear thus in a dictionary entry.

## buildhash

The buildhash program builds hashed dictionary files for later use by ispell. The raw word list (with affix flags) is given in dict-file, and the affix flags are defined by affix-file. The hashed output is written to hash-file. The formats of the two input files are described in ispell(4). The -s (silent) option suppresses the usual status messages that are written to the standard error device.

## munchlist

The munchlist shell script is used to reduce the size of dictionary files, primarily personal dictionary files. It is also capable of combining dictionaries from various sources. The given files are read (standard input if no arguments are given), reduced to a minimal set of roots and affixes that will match the same list of words, and written to standard output.

Input for munchlist contains of raw words (such as those from your personal dictionary files) or root and affix combinations (probably generated in earlier munchlist runs). Each word or root/affix combination must be on a separate line.

The -D (debug) option leaves temporary files around under standard names instead of deleting them, so that the script can be debugged. Warning: This option can eat up an enormous amount of temporary file space.

The -v (verbose) option causes progress messages to be reported to stderr so you won't get nervous that munchlist has hung.

If the -s (strip) option is specified, words that are in the specified hash-file are removed from the word list. This can be useful with personal dictionaries.

The -l can be used to specify an alternate affix-file for munching dictionaries in languages other than English.

The -c option can be used to convert dictionaries that were built with an older affix file, without risk of accidentally introducing unintended affix combinations into the dictionary.

The -T option allows dictionaries to be converted to a canonical string-character format. The suffix specified is looked up in the affix file (-l switch) to determine the string-character format used for the input file; the output always uses the canonical string-character format. For example, a dictionary collected from TeX source files might be converted to canonical format by specifying -T tex.

The -w option is passed on to ispell.

## findaffix

The findaffix shell script is an aid to writers of new language descriptions in choosing affixes. The given dictionary files (standard input if none are given) are examined for possible prefixes (-p switch) or suffixes (-s switch, the default). Each commonly occurring affix is presented along with a count of the number of times it appears and an estimate of the number of bytes that would be saved in a dictionary hash file if it were added to the language table. Only affixes that generate legal roots (found in the original input) are listed.

If the -c option is not given, the output lines are in the following format:

strip/add/count/bytes

where strip is the string that should be stripped from a root word before adding the affix, add is the affix to be added, count is a count of the number of times that this strip/add combination appears, and bytes is an estimate of the number of bytes that might be saved in the raw dictionary file if this combination is added to the affix file. The field separator in the output will be the tab character specified by the -t switch; the default is a slash (/).

If the -c (clean output) option is given, the appearance of the output is made visually cleaner (but harder to post process) by changing it to

-strip+add<tab>count<tab>bytes

where strip, add, count, and bytes are as before, and <tab> represents the ASCII tab character.

The method used to generate possible affixes will also generate longer affixes which have common headers or trailers. For example, the two words *moth* and *mother* will generate not only the obvious substitution +er but also -h+her and -th+ther (and possibly even longer ones, depending on the value of min). To prevent cluttering the output with such affixes, any affix pair that shares a common header (or, for prefixes, trailer) string longer than elim characters (default 1) will be suppressed. You may want to set elim to a value greater than 1 if your language has string characters; usually, the need for this parameter will become obvious when you examine the output of your findaffix run.

Normally, the affixes are sorted according to the estimate of bytes saved. The -f switch may be used to cause the affixes to be sorted by frequency of appearance.

To save output file space, affixes which occur fewer than 10 times are eliminated; this limit may be changed with the -l switch. The -M switch specifies a maximum affix length (default 8). Affixes longer than this will not be reported. (This saves on temporary disk space and makes the script run faster.)

Affixes which generate stems shorter than three characters are suppressed. (A stem is the word after the strip string has been removed, and before the add string has been added.) This reduces both the running time and the size of the output file. This limit may be changed with the -m switch. The minimum stem length should only be set to 1 if you have a lot of free time and disk space (in the range of many days and hundreds of megabytes).

The findaffix script requires a nonblank field-separator character for internal use. Normally, this character is a slash (/), but if the slash appears as a character in the input word list, a different character can be specified with the -t switch.

ispell dictionaries should be expanded before being fed to findaffix; in addition, characters that are not in the English alphabet (if any) should be translated to lowercase.

## tryaffix

The `tryaffix` shell script is used to estimate the effectiveness of a proposed prefix (`-p` switch) or suffix (`-s` switch, the default) with a given `expanded-file`. Only one affix can be tried with each execution of `tryaffix`, although multiple arguments can be used to describe varying forms of the same affix flag (for example, the `D` flag for English can add either `D` or `ED` depending on whether a trailing `E` is already present). Each word in the expanded dictionary that ends (or begins) with the chosen suffix (or prefix) has that suffix (prefix) removed; the dictionary is then searched for root words that match the stripped word. Normally, all matching roots are written to standard output, but if the `-c` (count) flag is given, only a statistical summary of the results is written. The statistics given are a count of words the affix potentially applies to and an estimate of the number of dictionary bytes that a flag using the affix would save. The estimate will be high if the flag generates words that are currently generated by other affix flags (for example, in English, bathers can be generated by either `bath/X` or `bather/S`). The dictionary file, `expanded-file`, must already be expanded (using the `-e` switch of `ispell`) and sorted, and things will usually work best if uppercase has been folded to lower with `tr`.

The `affix` arguments are things to be stripped from the dictionary file to produce trial roots: for English, `con` (prefix) and `ing` (suffix) are examples. The `addition` parts of the argument are letters that would have been stripped off the root before adding the affix. For example, in English the affix `ing` normally strips `e` for words ending in that letter (for example, `like` becomes `liking`), so we might run

```
tryaffix ing ing+e
```

to cover both cases.

All of the shell scripts contain documentation as commentary at the beginning; sometimes these comments contain useful information beyond the scope of this manual page.

It is possible to install `ispell` in such a way as to only support ASCII range text if desired.

## icombine

The `icombine` program is a helper for `munchlist`. It reads a list of words in dictionary format (roots plus flags) from the standard input, and produces a reduced list of standard output that combines common roots found on adjacent entries. Identical roots that have differing flags will have their flags combined, and roots that have differing capitalizations will be combined in a way that only preserves important capitalization information. The optional `aff-file` specifies a language file that defines the character sets used and the meanings of the various flags. The `-T` switch can be used to select among alternative string character types by giving a dummy suffix that can be found in an `altstringtype` statement.

## ijoin

The `ijoin` program is a reimplementation of `join(1)`, which handles long lines and 8-bit characters correctly. The `-s` switch specifies that the `sort(1)` program used to prepare the input to `ijoin` uses signed comparisons on 8-bit characters; the `-u` switch specifies that `sort(1)` uses unsigned comparisons. All other options and behaviors of `join(1)` are duplicated as exactly as possible based on the manual page, except that `ijoin` will not handle newline as a field separator. See the `join(1)` manual page for more information.

## ENVIRONMENT

| | |
|---|---|
| `DICTIONARY` | Default dictionary to use if no `-d` flag is given |
| `WORDLIST` | Personal dictionary filename |
| `INCLUDE_STRING` | Code for file inclusion under the `-A` option |
| `TMPDIR` | Directory used for some of `munchlist`'s temporary files |

## FILES

| | |
|---|---|
| `!!LIBDIR!!/!!DEFHASH!!` | Hashed dictionary (may be found in some other local directory, depending on the system) |
| `!!LIBDIR!!/!!DEFLANG!!` | Affix-definition file for `munchlist` |
| `/usr/dict/web2` or `/usr/dict/words` | For the Lookup function (depending on the `WORDS` compilation option) |
| | User's private dictionary |
| `.ispell_hashfile` | Directory-specific private dictionary |

## SEE ALSO

spell(1), egrep(1), look(1), join(1), sort(1), sq(1L), tib(1L), ispell(4L), english(4L)

## BUGS

It takes several to many seconds for ispell to read in the hash table, depending on size.

When all options are enabled, ispell may take several seconds to generate all the guesses at corrections for a misspelled word; on slower machines this time is long enough to be annoying.

The hash table is stored as a quarter-megabyte (or larger) array, so a PDP-11 or 286 version does not seem likely.

Ispell should understand more troff syntax, and deal more intelligently with contractions.

Although small personal dictionaries are sorted before they are written out, the order of capitalizations of the same word is somewhat random.

When the -x flag is specified, ispell will unlink any existing BAK file.

There are too many flags, and many of them have non-mnemonic names.

munchlist does not deal very gracefully with dictionaries that contain nonword characters. Such characters ought to be deleted from the dictionary with a warning message. findaffix and munchlist require tremendous amounts of temporary file space for large dictionaries. They do respect the TMPDIR environment variable, so this space can be redirected. However, a lot of the temporary space needed is for sorting, so TMPDIR is only a partial help on systems with an uncooperative sort(1). (*Cooperative* is defined as accepting the undocumented -T switch). At its peak usage, munchlist takes 10 to 40 times the original dictionary's size in kilobytes. (The larger ratio is for dictionaries that already have heavy affix use, such as the one distributed with ispell). munchlist is also very slow; munching a normal-sized dictionary (15KB roots, 45KB expanded words) takes around an hour on a small workstation. (Most of this time is spent in sort(1), and munchlist can run much faster on machines that have a more modern sort that makes better use of the memory available to it.) findaffix is even worse; the smallest English dictionary cannot be processed with this script in a mere 50KB of free space, and even after specifying switches to reduce the temporary space required, the script will run for more than 24 hours on a small workstation.

## AUTHORS

Pace Willisson (pace@mit-vax), 1983, based on the PDP-10 assembly version. That version was written by R. E. Gorin in 1971, and later revised by W. E. Matson (1974) and W. B. Ackerman (1978). Collected, revised, and enhanced for the Usenet by Walt Buehring, 1987. Table-driven multilingual version by Geoff Kuenning, 1987–88. Large dictionaries provided by Bob Devine (vianet!devine). A complete list of contributors is too large to list here, but is distributed with the ispell sources in the file Contributors.

## VERSION

The version of ispell described by this manual page is International Ispell version 3.1.00, October 8, 1993.

# join

join—Join lines of two files on a common field

## SYNOPSIS

```
join [-a 1¦2] [-v 1¦2] [-e empty-string] [-o field-list...] [-t char]
[-j[1¦2] field] [-1 field] [-2 field] file1 file2
join {--help,--version}
```

## DESCRIPTION

This manual page documents the GNU version of join. join prints to the standard output a line for each pair of input lines, one each from *file1* and *file2*, that have identical join fields. Either filename (but not both) can be -, meaning the standard input. *file1* and *file2* should be already sorted in increasing order (not numerically) on the join fields; unless the -t option is given, they should be sorted ignoring blanks at the start of the line, as sort does when given the -b option.

The defaults are the following: The join field is the first field in each line; fields in the input are separated by one or more blanks, with leading blanks on the line ignored; fields in the output are separated by a space; each output line consists of the join field, the remaining fields from *file1*, then the remaining fields from *file2*.

## OPTIONS

| | |
|---|---|
| -a file-number | Print a line for each unpairable linc in file file-number (either 1 or 2), in addition to the normal output. |
| -e string | Replace empty output fields (those that are missing in the input) with string. |
| -1, -j1 field | Join on field field (a positive integer) of file 1. |
| -2, -j2 field | Join on field field (a positive integer) of file 2. |
| -j field | Equivalent to -1 field -2 field. |
| -o field-list... | Construct each output line according to the format in field-list. Each element in field-list consists of a file number (either 1 or 2), a period, and a field number (a positive integer). The elements in the list are separated by commas or blanks. Multiple field-list arguments can be given after a single -o option; the values of all lists given with -o are concatenated together. |
| -t char | Use character char as the input and output field separator. |
| -v file-number | Print a line for each unpairable line in file file-number (either 1 or 2), instead of the normal output. |

In addition, when GNU join is invoked with exactly one argument, the following options are recognized:

| | |
|---|---|
| --help | Print a usage message on standard output and exit successfully. |
| --version | Print version information on standard output, then exit successfully. |

*GNU Text Utilities*

# kill

kill—Terminate a process

## SYNOPSIS

```
kill [ -s signal ¦ -p ] [-a]pid ...
kill -l [ signal ]
```

## DESCRIPTION

kill sends the specified signal to the specified process. If no signal is specified, the TERM signal is sent. The TERM signal will kill processes that do not catch this signal. For other processes, if may be necessary to use the KILL(9) signal because this signal cannot be caught.

Most modern shells have a built-in kill function.

## OPTIONS

| | |
|---|---|
| pid ... | Specify the list of processes that kill should signal. Each pid can be a process ID, or a process name. |
| -s | Specify the signal to send. The signal may be given as a signal name or number. |
| -p | Specify that kill should only print the process ID (pid) of the named process, and should not send it a signal. |
| -l | Print a list of signal names. These are found in /usr/include/linux/signal.h. |

## SEE ALSO

bash(1), tcsh(1), kill(2), sigvec(2)

## AUTHOR

Taken from BSD 4.4. The ability to translate process names to process ids was added by Salvatore Valente (`<svalente@mit.edu>`).

# killall

killall—Kill processes by name

## SYNOPSIS

```
killall [-iv][-signal] name ...
killall [-l]
```

## DESCRIPTION

killall sends a signal to all processes running any of the specified commands. If no signal name is specified, SIGTERM is sent.

Signals can be specified either by name (for example, -HUP) or by number (for example, -1). Signal 0 (check if a process exists) can only be specified by number.

If the command name contains a slash (/), processes executing that particular file will be selected for killing, independent of their name.

killall returns a nonzero return code if no process has been killed for any of the listed commands. If at least one process has been killed for each command, killall returns zero.

A killall process never kills itself (but may kill other killall processes).

## OPTIONS

-i          Interactively ask for confirmation of killing.

-l          List all known signal names.

-v          Report if the signal was successfully sent.

## FILES

/proc   Location of the proc filesystem

## KNOWN BUGS

Killing by file only works for executables that are kept open during execution; that is, impure executables can't be killed this way.

## AUTHOR

Werner Almesberger (`almesber@di.epfl.ch`)

## SEE ALSO

kill(1), fuser(1), ps(1), kill(2)

# ksyms

ksyms—Shows the exported kernel symbols

## SYNOPSIS

```
ksyms [-a][-h][-m]
```

## DESCRIPTION

ksyms shows information about all exported kernel symbols. The format is

*address name [defining module]*

The describing header can be turned off with the option -h.

Normally, only the symbols defined by the loaded modules are shown, but with the option -a, all exported symbols can be seen.

The information can also be seen in /proc/ksyms. A shell-script version ksyms.sh can be used to get the information from /proc/ksyms instead, but this program gets the symbol information directly from the kernel with a system call.

With the option -m (stands for memory map), you can also see the starting address and the size of the allocated memory for every loaded module.

## SEE ALSO

insmod(1), modprobe(1), depmod(1), rmmod(1), lsmod(1), modules(2)

## HISTORY

The ksyms command was first conceived by Bjorn Ekwall (bj0rn@blox.se). The -m option was inspired by David Hinds (dhinds@allegro.stanford.edu)

## BUGS

Ksyms might have some, but they are well hidden....

*Linux, 14 May 1995*

# last

last—Indicate last logins by user or terminal

## SYNOPSIS

last [-*number*][-f *filename*][-t *tty*][-h *hostname*][-i *address*][-l][-y][*name*...]

## DESCRIPTION

Last looks back in the wtmp file, which records all logins and logouts for information about a user, a teletype, or any group of users and teletypes. Arguments specify names of users or teletypes of interest. If multiple arguments are given, the information that applies to any of the arguments is printed. For example last root console would list all of root's sessions as well as all sessions on the console terminal. Last displays the sessions of the specified users and teletypes, most recent first, indicating the times at which the session began, the duration of the session, and the teletype that the session took place on. If the session is still continuing or was cut short by a reboot, last so indicates.

The pseudo-user reboot logs in at reboots of the system.

Last with no arguments displays a record of all logins and logouts, in reverse order.

If last is interrupted, it indicates how far the search has progressed in wtmp. If interrupted with a quit signal, last indicates how far the search has progressed so far, and the search continues.

## OPTIONS

| | |
|---|---|
| -*number* | Limit the number of entries displayed to that specified by *number*. |
| -f *filename* | Use *filename* as the name of the accounting file instead of /var/log/wtmp. |
| -h *hostname* | List only logins from *hostname*. |
| -i IP *address* | List only logins from IP *address*. |

| `-l` | List IP addresses of remote hosts instead of truncated hostnames. |
| `-t tty` | List only logins on *tty*. |
| `-y` | Also report year of dates. |

## FILES

| `/var/log/wtmp` | Login database |

*20 March 1992*

# lbxproxy

lbxproxy—LBX proxy server for the X Window system

## SYNOPSIS

lbxproxy [`:displaynumber`] [option ...]

## NOTE

This manual page is not definitive or "official." It is derived from information contained in the README file in the lbx source.

## DESCRIPTION

lbxproxy is the Low Bandwidth X pseudo-server. It runs on the remote side of low bandwidth, high-latency connections, such as serial lines and wide area networks. It accepts connections from X clients at the remote end and forwards them to an X server at the local end. The LBX protocol used for the low bandwidth connection includes compression and optimizations designed to make effective use of the bandwidth available. The current version of LBX is not a standard of the X Consortium, and will not be compatible with the final version. The current version should be treated as an "alpha" or "prototype" for people interested in experimenting with it.

## OPTIONS

lbxproxy accepts the following options:

| `:displaynumber` | lbxproxy runs as the given `displaynumber`, which by default is `0`. A value different from 0 should be used if the host running lbxproxy has a local X display. If multiple lbxproxy servers or other X servers are to run simultaneously on a host, each must have a unique display number. (See the "Display Names" section of the X(1) manual page to learn how to specify which display number clients should try to use.) |
| `-ac` | Disables host-based access control mechanisms. Enables access by any host, and permits any host to modify the access control list. Use with extreme caution. This option exists primarily for running test suites remotely. |
| `-display` `display-number` | Sets the name of the X server display that lbxproxy connects to. |
| `-help` | Prints a usage message. |
| `-I` | Causes all remaining command-line arguments to be ignored. |
| `-to seconds` | Sets default connection time-out in seconds. |

## NETWORK CONNECTIONS

lbxproxy supports client connections via most of the connection types supported by the X servers. (Refer to the Xserver(1) manual page and hardware-specific X server manual pages for details.) Note that in the current implementation some of the connections types have not been implemented correctly. This mostly applies to System V.

## EXAMPLES

To setup lbxproxy, start the X server as usual, and then start the proxy. The lbxproxy is a pseudo-server, so any clients that wish to use it need to adjust their DISPLAY. By default, the proxy will listen on <hostname>:1. This can be changed with the :displaynumber argument.

If the proxy is to be running on a host named sharedhost, connecting to an LBX-capable X server on a desktop machine named mydesktop, you could use the following command to start the proxy (which would be known as display sharedhost:7):

```
mydesktop% rlogin sharedhost
sharedhost% lbxproxy -display mydesktop:0 :7 &
sharedhost% xclient -display sharedhost:7
```

If you are running LBX over a TERM connection between mydesktop and sharedhost, try something like this:

```
mydesktop% trsh
sharedhost% tredir -r 6008 6000
sharedhost% lbxproxy -display sharedhost:8 :7 &
sharedhost% xclient -display sharedhost:7
```

## SEE ALSO

General information: X(1)

Server-specific man pages: Xserver(1), Xdec(1), XmacII(1), Xsun(1), Xnest(1), Xvfb(1), XF86_Accel(1), XF86_Mono(1), XF86_SVGA(1), XF86_VGA16(1), XFree86(1)

## AUTHORS

The LBX team includes Dave Lemke, Dale Tonogai, Keith Packard, Jim Fulton from NCD, and Chris Kanterjiev from Xerox.

*X Version 11 Release 6*

# ld

ld—The GNU linker

## SYNOPSIS

```
ld [ -o.I output ] .I objfile . . . .br .RB ["-A output ] objfile ...
[-A architecture ][-b\ input-format ][-Bstatic ][-c\ commandfile ]
[ -d¦-dc¦-dp ]
[ -defsym\ symbol = expression ][-e\ entry ][-F ][-F\ format ][-
format\ input-format ][-g ][-G size ][--help ][-i ][-l ar ][-
L searchdir ][-M][-Map mapfile ][-m emulation ][-n¦-N][-
noinhibit-exec ][-oformat\ output-format ][-R\ filename ][-relax ]
[ -r¦-Ur][-S ][-s ][-sort-common][-T\ commandfile ][-Ttext\
textorg ][-Tdata\ dataorg ][-Tbss\ bssorg ][-t ][-u\ sym ][-V ][-
v][--verbose ][--version ][-warn-common][-warn-once][-X ]
[ -x ]
```

## DESCRIPTION

ld combines a number of object and archive files, relocates their data, and ties up symbol references. Often the last step in building a new compiled program to run is a call to ld.

ld accepts Linker Command Language files to provide explicit and total control over the linking process. This man page does not describe the command language; see the ld entry in info, or the manual *Ld: The GNU Linker,* for full details on the command language and on other aspects of the GNU linker.

This version of ld uses the general-purpose BFD libraries to operate on object files. This allows ld to read, combine, and write object files in many different formats, for example, COFF or a.out. Different formats may be linked together to produce any available kind of object file. You can use objdump -i to get a list of formats supported on various architectures; see objdump(1).

Aside from its flexibility, the GNU linker is more helpful than other linkers in providing diagnostic information. Many linkers abandon execution immediately upon encountering an error; whenever possible, ld continues executing, allowing you to identify other errors (or, in some cases, to get an output file in spite of the error).

The GNU linker ld is meant to cover a broad range of situations, and to be as compatible as possible with other linkers. As a result, you have many choices to control its behavior through the command line, and through environment variables.

## OPTIONS

The plethora of command-line options may seem intimidating, but in actual practice few of them are used in any particular context. For instance, a frequent use of ld is to link standard UNIX object files on a standard, supported UNIX system. On such a system, this line links a file hello.o :

```
$ ld -o output /lib/crt0.o hello.o -lc
```

This tells ld to produce a file called output as the result of linking the file /lib/crt0.o with hello.o and the library libc.a, which will come from the standard search directories.

The command-line options to ld may be specified in any order, and may be repeated at will. For the most part, repeating an option with a different argument will either have no further effect or override prior occurrences (those further to the left on the command line) of an option.

The exceptions—which may meaningfully be used more than once—are -A, -b (or its synonym -format), -defsym, -L, -l, -R, and -u.

The list of object files to be linked together, shown as objfile, may follow, precede, or be mixed in with command-line options, except that an objfile argument may not be placed between an option flag and its argument.

Usually the linker is invoked with at least one object file, but other forms of binary input files can also be specified with -l, -R, and the script command language. If no binary input files at all are specified, the linker does not produce any output, and issues the message No input files.

Option arguments must either follow the option letter without intervening whitespace or be given as separate arguments immediately following the option that requires them.

-Aarchitecture              In the current release of ld, this option is useful only for the Intel 960 family of architectures. In that ld configuration, the architecture argument is one of the two-letter names identifying members of the 960 family; the option specifies the desired output target and warns of any incompatible instructions in the input files. It also modifies the linker's search strategy for archive libraries to support the use of libraries specific to each particular architecture, by including in the search loop names suffixed with the string identifying the architecture.

For example, if your ld command line included -ACA as well as -ltry, the linker would look (in its built-in search paths, and in any paths you specify with -L) for a library with the names

try

libtry.a

tryca

libtryca.a

The first two possibilities would be considered in any event; the last two are due to the use of -ACA.

Future releases of ld may support similar functionality for other architecture families.

You can meaningfully use -A more than once on a command line, if an architecture family allows combination of target architectures; each use will add another pair of name variants to search for when -1 specifies a library.

**-b** *input-format*

Specify the binary format for input object files that follow this option on the command line. You don't usually need to specify this, as ld is configured to expect as a default input format the most usual format on each machine. *input-format* is a text string, the name of a particular format supported by the BFD libraries.

**-format** *input-format*

has the same effect, as does the script command TARGET.

You may want to use this option if you are linking files with an unusual binary format. You can also use -b to switch formats explicitly (when linking object files of different formats), by including

**-b** *input-format*

before each group of object files in a particular format.

The default format is taken from the environment variable GNUTARGET. You can also define the input format from a script, using the command TARGET.

**-Bstatic**

This flag is accepted for command-line compatibility with the SunOS linker, but has no effect on ld.

**-c** *commandfile*

Directs ld to read link commands from the file commandfile. These commands will completely override ld's default link format (rather than adding to it); commandfile must specify everything necessary to describe the target format.

You may also include a script of link commands directly in the command line by bracketing it between { and } characters.

**-d, -dc, -dp**

These three options are equivalent; multiple forms are supported for compatibility with other linkers. Use any of them to make ld assign space to common symbols even if a relocatable output file is specified (-r). The script command FORCE_COMMON_ALLOCATION has the same effect.

**-defsym** *symbol= expression*

Create a global symbol in the output file, containing the absolute address given by *expression*. You may use this option as many times as necessary to define multiple symbols in the command line. A limited form of arithmetic is supported for the *expression* in this context; you may give a hexadecimal constant or the name of an existing symbol, or use + and - to add or subtract hexadecimal constants or symbols. If you need more elaborate expressions, consider using the linker command language from a script.

**-e** *entry*

Use *entry* as the explicit symbol for beginning execution of your program, rather than the default entry point.

**-F, -F***format*

Some older linkers used this option throughout a compilation toolchain for specifying object-file format for both input and output object files. ld's mechanisms (the -b or -format options for input files, the TARGET command in linker scripts for output files, the GNUTARGET environment variable) are more flexible, but it accepts (and ignores) the -F option flag for compatibility with scripts written to call the old linker.

**-format** *input-format*

Synonym for -b *input-format*.

**-g**

Accepted, but ignored; provided for compatibility with other tools.

**-G** *size*

Set the maximum size of objects to be optimized using the GP register to *size* under MIPS ECOFF. Ignored for other object file formats.

**--help**

Print a summary of the command-line options on the standard output and exit. This option and --version begin with two hyphens instead of one for compatibility with other GNU programs. The other options start with only one hyphen for compatibility with other linkers.

**-i**

Perform an incremental link (same as option -r).

| | |
|---|---|
| `-lar` | Add an archive file *ar* to the list of files to link. This option may be used any number of times. `ld` will search its path list for occurrences of `lib` *ar* `.a` for every *ar* specified. |
| `-Lsearchdir` | This command adds path *searchdir* to the list of paths that `ld` will search for archive libraries. You may use this option any number of times. |
| | The default set of paths searched (without being specified with `-L`) depends on what emulation mode `ld` is using, and in some cases also on how it was configured. The paths can also be specified in a link script with the `SEARCH_DIR` command. |
| `-M` | Print (to the standard output file) a link map—diagnostic in-formation about where symbols are mapped by `ld`, and information on global common storage allocation. |
| `-Map mapfile` | Print to the file `mapfile` a link map—diagnostic information about where symbols are mapped by `ld`, and information on global common storage allocation. |
| `-m emulation` | Emulate the `emulation` linker. You can list the available emulations with the `--verbose` option. This option overrides the compiled-in default, which is the system for which you configured `ld`. |
| `-N` | Specifies readable and writable `text` and `data` sections. If the output format supports UNIX-style magic numbers, the output is marked as `OMAGIC`. |
| | When you use the `-N` option, the linker does not page-align the data segment. |
| `-n` | Sets the text segment to be read-only, and `NMAGIC` is written if possible. |
| `-noinhibit-exec` | Normally, the linker will not produce an output file if it encounters errors during the link process. With this flag, you can specify that you wish the output file retained even after nonfatal errors. |
| `-o output output` | `output` is a name for the program produced by `ld`; if this option is not specified, the name `a.out` is used by default. The script command `OUTPUT` can also specify the output filename. |
| `-oformat output-format` | Specify the binary format for the output object file. You don't usually need to specify this, as `ld` is configured to produce as a default output format the most usual format on each machine. `output-format` is a text string, the name of a particular format supported by the BFD libraries. The script command `OUTPUT_FORMAT` can also specify the output format, but this option overrides it. |
| `-R filename file` | Read symbol names and their addresses from `filename`, but do not relocate it or include it in the output. This allows your output file to refer symbolically to absolute locations of memory defined in other programs. |
| `-relax` | An option with machine-dependent effects. Currently this option is only supported on the H8/300. |
| | On some platforms, use this option to perform global optimizations that become possible when the linker resolves addressing in your program, such as relaxing address modes and synthesizing new instructions in the output object file. |
| | On platforms where this is not supported, `-relax` is accepted, but has no effect. |
| `-r` | Generates relocatable output, that is, an output file that can in turn serve as input to `ld`. This is often called *partial linking*. As a side effect, in environments that support standard UNIX magic numbers, this option also sets the output file's magic number to `OMAGIC`. If this option is not specified, an absolute file is produced. When linking C++ programs, this option will not resolve references to constructors; `-Ur` is an alternative. |
| | This option does the same as `-i`. |
| `-S` | Omits debugger symbol information (but not all symbols) from the output file. |
| `-s` | Omits all symbol information from the output file. |
| `-sort-common` | Normally, when `ld` places the global common symbols in the appropriate output sections, it sorts them by size. First come all the one-byte symbols, then all the two bytes, then all the four bytes, and then everything else. This is to prevent gaps between symbols due to alignment constraints. This option disables that sorting. |

| | |
|---|---|
| -Tbss *org*, -Tdata *org*, -Ttext *org* | Use *org* as the starting address for—respectively—the bss, data, or the text segment of the output file. textorg must be a hexadecimal integer. |
| -T *commandfile*, -Tcommandfile | Equivalent to -c *commandfile*; supported for compatibility with other tools. |
| -t | Prints names of input files as ld processes them. |
| -u *sym* | Forces *sym* to be entered in the output file as an undefined symbol. This may, for example, trigger linking of additional modules from standard libraries. -u may be repeated with different option arguments to enter additional undefined symbols. |
| -Ur | For anything other than C++ programs, this option is equivalent to -r : it generates relocatable output, that is, an output file that can in turn serve as input to ld. When linking C++ programs, -Ur will resolve references to constructors, unlike -r. |
| --verbose | Display the version number for ld and list the supported emulations. Display which input files can and can not be opened. |
| -v, -V | Display the version number for ld. |
| --version | Display the version number for ld and exit. |
| -warn-common | Warn when a common symbol is combined with another common symbol or with a symbol definition. UNIX linkers allow this somewhat sloppy practice, but linkers on some other operating systems do not. This option allows you to find potential problems from combining global symbols. |
| -warn-once | Only warn once for each undefined symbol, rather than once per module that refers to it. |
| -X | If -s or -S is also specified, delete only local symbols beginning with L. |
| -x | If -s or -S is also specified, delete all local symbols, not just those beginning with L. |

## ENVIRONMENT

You can change the behavior of ld with the environment variable GNUTARGET.

GNUTARGET determines the input-file object format if you don't use -b (or its synonym -format). Its value should be one of the BFD names for an input format. If there is no GNUTARGET in the environment, ld uses the natural format of the host. If GNUTAR-GET is set to default, then BFD attempts to discover the input format by examining binary input files; this method often succeeds, but there are potential ambiguities, since there is no method of ensuring that the magic number used to flag object-file formats is unique. However, the configuration procedure for BFD on each system places the conventional format for that system first in the search-list, so ambiguities are resolved in favor of convention.

## SEE ALSO

objdump(1); ld and binutils entries in info

*Ld: The GNU Linker*, Steve Chamberlain and Roland Pesch; *The GNU Binary Utilities*, Roland H. Pesch.

## COPYING

Copyright © 1991, 1992 Free Software Foundation, Inc.

Permission is granted to make and distribute verbatim copies of this manual provided the copyright notice and this permission notice are preserved on all copies.

Permission is granted to copy and distribute modified versions of this manual under the conditions for verbatim copying, provided that the entire resulting derived work is distributed under the terms of a permission notice identical to this one.

Permission is granted to copy and distribute translations of this manual into another language, under the above conditions for modified versions, except that this permission notice may be included in translations approved by the Free Software Foundation instead of in the original English.

*Cygnus support, 17 August 1992*

# lispmtopgm

lispmtopgm—Convert a Lisp Machine bitmap file into PGM format

## SYNOPSIS

lispmtopgm [*lispmfile*]

## DESCRIPTION

lispmtopgm reads a Lisp machine bitmap as input and produces a portable graymap as output.

This is the file format written by the tv:write-bit-array-file function on TI Explorer and Symbolics Lisp machines.

Multiplane bitmaps on Lisp machines are color; but the lispm image file format does not include a colormap, so it must be treated as a graymap instead. This is unfortunate.

## SEE ALSO

pgmtolispm(1), pgm(5)

## BUGS

The lispm bitmap file format is a bit quirky; Usually the image in the file has its width rounded up to the next higher multiple of 32, but not always. If the width is not a multiple of 32, we don't deal with it properly, but because of the lispm microcode, such arrays are probably not image data anyway.

Also, the lispm code for saving bitmaps has a bug, in that if you are writing a bitmap that is not mod32 across, the file may be up to seven bits too short. They round down instead of up, and we don't handle this bug gracefully.

No color.

## AUTHOR

Copyright© 1991 by Jamie Zawinski and Jef Poskanzer.

*6 March 1990*

# lkbib

lkbib—Search bibliographic databases

## SYNOPSIS

lkbib [ -v ][-i*fields* ][-p*filename* ][-t*n* ] *key* ...

## DESCRIPTION

lkbib searches bibliographic databases for references that contain the keys *key*... and prints any references found on the standard output. lkbib will search any databases given by -p options, and then a default database. The default database is taken from the REFER environment variable if it is set, otherwise it is

/usr/dict/papers/Ind.

For each database filename to be searched, if an index filename.i created by gindxbib(1) exists, then it will be searched instead; each index can cover multiple databases.

## OPTIONS

| | |
|---|---|
| -v | Print the version number. |
| -p*filename* | Search *filename*. Multiple -p options can be used. |
| -i*string* | When searching files for which no index exists, ignore the contents of fields whose names are in *string*. |
| -t*n* | Only require the first *n* characters of keys to be given. Initially *n* is 6. |

## ENVIRONMENT

REFER      Default database

## FILES

/usr/dict/papers/Ind      Default database to be used if the REFER environment variable is not set.

filename.i      Index files.

## SEE ALSO

grefer(1), glookbib(1), gindxbib(1)

*Groff Version 1.09, 6 August 1992*

# ln

ln—Make links between files

## SYNOPSIS

```
ln [options] source [dest]
ln [options] source... directory
```

Options:

```
[-bdfinsvF] [-S backup-suffix] [-V {numbered,existing,simple}]
[--version-control={numbered,existing,simple}] [--backup] [--directory]
[--force] [--interactive] [--no-dereference] [--symbolic] [--verbose]
[--suffix=backup-suffix] [--help] [--version]
```

## DESCRIPTION

This manual page documents the GNU version of ln. If the last argument names an existing directory, ln links each other given file into a file with the same name in that directory. If only one file is given, it links that file into the current directory. Otherwise, if only two files are given, it links the first onto the second. It is an error if the last argument is not a directory and more than two files are given. It makes hard links by default. By default, it does not remove existing files.

## OPTIONS

| | |
|---|---|
| -b, --backup | Make backups of files that are about to be removed. |
| -d, -F, --directory | Allow the superuser to make hard links to directories. |
| -f, --force | Remove existing destination files. |
| -i, --interactive | Prompt whether to remove existing destination files. |
| -n, --no-dereference | When the specified destination is a symbolic link to a directory, attempt to replace the symbolic link rather than dereferencing it to create a link in the directory to which it points. This option is most useful in conjunction with --force. |
| -s, --symbolic | Make symbolic links instead of hard links. This option produces an error message on systems that do not support symbolic links. |
| -v, --verbose | Print the name of each file before linking it. |
| --help | Print a usage message on standard output and exit successfully. |
| --version | Print version information on standard output then exit successfully. |
| -S, --suffix backup-suffix | The suffix used for making simple backup files can be set with the SIMPLE_BACKUP_SUFFIX environment variable, which can be overridden by this option. If neither of those is given, the default is ˜, as it is in Emacs. |

-V, --version-control    The type of backups made can be set with the VERSION_CONTROL environment variable, which
{numbered,existing,simple}  can be overridden by this option. If VERSION_CONTROL is not set and this option is not given,
the default backup type is existing. The value of the VERSION_CONTROL environment variable
and the argument to this option are like the GNU Emacs version-control variable; they
also recognize synonyms that are more descriptive. The valid values (unique abbreviations
are accepted) are the following:

| | |
|---|---|
| t or numbered | Always make numbered backups. |
| nil or existing | Make numbered backups of files that already have them, simple backups of the others. |
| never or simple | Always make simple backups. |

*GNU File Utilities*

# lndir

lndir—Create a shadow directory of symbolic links to another directory tree

## SYNOPSIS

lndir fromdir [todir]

## DESCRIPTION

lndir makes a shadow copy todir of a directory tree fromdir, except that the shadow is not populated with real files but
instead with symbolic links pointing at the real files in the fromdir directory tree. This is usually useful for maintaining
source code for different machine architectures. You create a shadow directory containing links to the real source which you
will have usually NFS mounted from a machine of a different architecture, and then recompile it. The object files will be in
the shadow directory, while the source files in the shadow directory are just symlinks to the real files.

This has the advantage that if you update the source, you need not propagate the change to the other architectures by hand
because all source in shadow directories are symlinks to the real thing: Just cd to the shadow directory and recompile away.

The todir argument is optional and defaults to the current directory. The fromdir argument may be relative (for example,
../src) and is relative to todir (not the current directory).

Note that RCS, SCCS, and CVS.adm directories are not shadowed.

If you add files, simply run lndir again. Deleting files is a more painful problem; the symlinks will just point into never-
neverland.

## BUGS

patch gets upset if it cannot change the files. You should never run patch from a shadow directory anyway.

You need to use something like this:

find todir -type l -print ¦ xargs rm

to clear out all files before you can relink (if fromdir moved, for instance). Something like this:

find . \! -type d -print

will find all files that are not directories.

*X Version 11 Release 6*

# locate

locate—List files in databases that match a pattern

## SYNOPSIS

locate [-d path] [--database=path] [--version] [--help] pattern...

## DESCRIPTION

This manual page documents the GNU version of locate. For each given pattern, locate searches one or more databases of filenames and displays the filenames that contain the pattern. Patterns can contain shell-style meta characters: *, ?, and []. The meta characters do not treat / or . specially. Therefore, a pattern foo*bar can match a filename that contains foo3/bar, and a pattern *duck* can match a filename that contains lake/.ducky. Patterns that contain meta characters should be quoted to protect them from expansion by the shell.

If a pattern is a plain string—it contains no meta characters—locate displays all filenames in the database that contain that string anywhere. If a pattern does contain meta characters, locate only displays filenames that match the pattern exactly. As a result, patterns that contain meta characters should usually begin with a * and will most often end with one as well. The exceptions are patterns that are intended to explicitly match the beginning or end of a filename.

The filename databases contain lists of files that were on the system when the databases were last updated. The system administrator can choose the filename of the default database, the frequency with which the databases are updated, and the directories for which they contain entries; see updatedb(1L).

## OPTIONS

| | |
|---|---|
| -d path, --database=path | Instead of searching the default filename database, search the filename databases in *path*, which is a colon-separated list of database filenames. You can also use the environment variable LOCATE_PATH to set the list of database files to search. The option overrides the environment variable if both are used. |
| | The filename database format changed starting with GNU find and locate version 4.0 to allow machines with different byte orderings to share the databases. This version of locate can automatically recognize and read databases produced for older versions of GNU locate or UNIX versions of locate or find. |
| --help | Print a summary of the options to locate and exit. |
| --version | Print the version number of locate and exit. |

## ENVIRONMENT

| | |
|---|---|
| LOCATE_PATH | Colon-separated list of databases to search |

## SEE ALSO

find(1L), locatedb(5L), updatedb(1L), xargs(1L), *Finding Files* (online in info, or printed)

# logger

logger—Make entries in the system log

## SYNOPSIS

logger [-is] [-f file] [-p pri] [-t tag] [message ...]

## DESCRIPTION

logger provides a shell command interface to the syslog(3) system log module.

## OPTIONS

-i          Log the process ID of the logger process with each line.

-s          Log the message to standard error, as well as the system log.

-f *file*   Log the specified file.

-p *pri*    Enter the message with the specified priority. The priority may be specified numerically or as a `facility.level` pair. For example, -p `local3.info` logs the message(s) as informational level in the local3 facility. The default is `user.notice`.

-t *tag*    Mark every line in the log with the specified tag.

*message*   Write the message to log; if not specified, and the -f flag is not provided, standard input is logged.

The `logger` utility exits `0` on success, and `>0` if an error occurs.

## EXAMPLE

logger system rebooted:

logger -p local0.notice -t HOSTIDM -f /dev/idmc

## SEE ALSO

syslog(3), syslogd(8)

## STANDARDS

The `logger` command is expected to be compatible with IEEE Std 1003.2 (POSIX).

*BSD 4.3, 6 June 1993*

# login

login—Sign on

## SYNOPSIS

login [ *name* ]
login -p
login -h *hostname*
login -f *name*

## DESCRIPTION

login is used when signing on to a system. It can also be used to switch from one user to another at any time. (Most modern shells have support for this feature built into them, however.)

If an argument is not given, login prompts for the username.

If the user is not root, and if /etc/nologin exists, the contents of this file are printed to the screen, and the login is terminated. This is typically used to prevent logins when the system is being taken down.

If the user is root, then the login must be occurring on a tty listed in /etc/securetty. Failures will be logged with the syslog facility.

After these conditions are checked, the password will be requested and checked (if a password is required for this username). Ten attempts are allowed before login dies, but after the first three, the response starts to get very slow. Login failures are reported via the syslog facility. This facility is also used to report any successful root logins.

If the file .hushlogin exists, then a quiet login is performed (this disables the checking of the checking of mail and the printing of the last login time and message of the day). Otherwise, if /var/log/lastlog exists, the last login time is printed (and the current login is recorded).

Random administrative things, such as setting the UID and GID of the tty, are performed. The TERM environment variable is preserved, if it exists; other environment variables are preserved if the -p option is used. Then the HOME, PATH, SHELL, TERM, MAIL, and LOGNAME environment variables are set. PATH defaults to /usr/local/bin:/bin:/usr/bin:. for normal users, and to /sbin:/bin:/usr/sbin:/usr/bin for root. Last, if this is not a quiet login, the message of the day is printed and the file with the user's name in /usr/spool/mail will be checked, and a message printed if it has nonzero length.

The user's shell is then started. If no shell is specified for the user in /etc/passwd, then /bin/sh is used. If there is no directory specified in /etc/passwd, then / is used. (The home directory is checked for the .hushlogin file described earlier.)

## OPTIONS

-p        Used by getty(8) to tell login not to destroy the environment.

-f        Used to skip a second login authentication. This specifically does not work for root, and does not appear to work well under Linux.

-h        Used by other servers (such as telnetd(8)) to pass the name of the remote host to login so that it may be placed in utmp and wtmp. Only the superuser may use this option.

## FILES

/var/run/utmp

/var/log/wtmp

/var/log/lastlog

/usr/spool/mail/*

/etc/motd

/etc/passwd

/etc/nologin

/etc/usertty

.hushlogin

## SEE ALSO

init(8), getty(8), mail(1), passwd(1), passwd(5), environ(7), shutdown(8)

## BUGS

Linux, unlike other Draconian operating systems, does not check quotas.

The undocumented BSD -r option is not supported. This may be required by some rlogind(8) programs.

## AUTHOR

Derived from BSD login 5.40 (May 9, 1989) by Michael Glad (glad@daimi.dk) for HP-UX Ported to Linux 0.12: Peter Orbaek (poe@daimi.aau.dk).

*Linux 0.99, 1 February 1993*

# look

look—Display lines beginning with a given string

## SYNOPSIS

look [-dfa] [-t termchar] string [file]

## DESCRIPTION

The look utility displays any lines in file that contain string as a prefix. As look performs a binary search, the lines in file must be sorted.

If file is not specified, the file /usr/dict/words is used, only alphanumeric characters are compared, and the case of alphabetic characters is ignored.

## OPTIONS

-d       Dictionary character set and order; that is, only alphanumeric characters are compared.

-f       Ignore the case of alphabetic characters.

-a       Use the alternate dictionary /usr/dict/web2.

-t       Specify a string termination character; that is, only the characters in string up to and including the first occurrence of termchar are compared.

The look utility exits 0 if one or more lines were found and displayed, 1 if no lines were found, and >1 if an error occurred.

## FILES

/usr/dict/words   The dictionary

/usr/dict/web2   The alternate dictionary

## SEE ALSO

grep(1), sort(1)

## COMPATIBILITY

The original manual page stated that tabs and blank characters participated in comparisons when the -d option was specified. This was incorrect and the current man page matches the historic implementation.

## HISTORY

look appeared in version 7 AT&T UNIX.

*14 June 1993*

# lpq

lpq—Spool queue examination program

## SYNOPSIS

lpq [-l] [-P printer] [job # ...] [user ...]

## DESCRIPTION

lpq examines the spooling area used by lpd(8) for printing files on the line printer, and reports the status of the specified jobs or all jobs associated with a user. lpq invoked without any arguments reports on any jobs currently in the queue.

## OPTIONS

-P       Specify a particular printer; otherwise the default line printer is used (or the value of the PRINTER variable in the environment). All other arguments supplied are interpreted as usernames or job numbers to filter out only those jobs of interest.

-l       Information about each of the files comprising the job entry is printed. Normally, only as much information as will fit on one line is displayed.

For each job submitted—in other words, each time lpr(1) is invoked—lpq reports the user's name, current rank in the queue, the names of files comprising the job, the job identifier (a number that may be supplied to lprm(1) for removing a specific job), and the total size in bytes. Job ordering is dependent on the algorithm used to scan the spooling directory and is supposed to be FIFO (First in First Out). Filenames comprising a job may be unavailable (when lpr(1) is used as a sink in a pipeline) in which case the file is indicated as (standard input).

If lpq warns that there is no daemon present (due to some malfunction, for example), the lpc(8) command can be used to restart the printer daemon.

## ENVIRONMENT

If the following environment variable exists, it is used by lpq:

PRINTER     Specifies an alternate default printer

## FILES

| | |
|---|---|
| /etc/printcap | To determine printer characteristics |
| /var/spool/* | The spooling directory, as determined from printcap |
| /var/spool/*/cf* | Control files specifying jobs |
| Pa/var/spool/*/lock | The lock file to obtain the currently active job |
| /usr/share/misc/termcap | For manipulating the screen for repeated display |

## SEE ALSO

lpr(1), lprm(1), lpc(8), lpd(8)

## HISTORY

lpq appeared in BSD 3.

## BUGS

Due to the dynamic nature of the information in the spooling directory, lpq may report unreliably. Output formatting is sensitive to the line length of the terminal; this can result in widely spaced columns.

## DIAGNOSTICS

Unable to open various files. The lock file is malformed. Garbage files when there is no daemon active, but files in the spooling directory.

*BSD 4.2, 9 May 1991*

# lpr

lpr—Offline print

## SYNOPSIS

```
lpr [-P printer] [-# num] [-C class] [-J job] [-T title] [-U user]
[-i [numcols]] [-1234 font] [-w num] [-cdfghlnmprstv] [name ...]
```

## DESCRIPTION

lpr uses a spooling daemon to print the named files when facilities become available. If no names appear, the standard input is assumed.

The following single-letter options are used to notify the line printer spooler that the files are not standard text files. The spooling daemon will use the appropriate filters to print the data accordingly.

-c      The files are assumed to contain data produced by cifplot(1).

-d      The files are assumed to contain data from TeX (DVI format from Stanford).

-f      Use a filter that interprets the first character of each line as a standard FORTRAN carriage control character.

-g      The files are assumed to contain standard plot data as produced by the plot routines. (See also plot for the filters used by the printer spooler.)

| | |
|---|---|
| -1 | Use a filter that allows control characters to be printed and suppresses page breaks. |
| -n | The files are assumed to contain data from ditroff (device independent troff). |
| -p | Use pr(1) to format the files (equivalent to print). |
| -t | The files are assumed to contain data from troff(1) (cat phototypesetter commands). |
| -v | The files are assumed to contain a raster image for devices like the Benson Varian. |

These options apply to the handling of the print job:

| | |
|---|---|
| -P | Force output to a specific printer. Normally, the default printer is used (site-dependent), or the value of the environment variable PRINTER is used. |
| -h | Suppress the printing of the burst page. |
| -m | Send mail upon completion. |
| -r | Remove the file upon completion of spooling or upon completion of printing (with the -s option). |
| -s | Use symbolic links. Usually, files are copied to the spool directory. The -s option will use symlink(2) to link data files rather than trying to copy them so large files can be printed. This means the files should not be modified or removed until they have been printed. |

The remaining options apply to copies, the page display, and headers:

| | |
|---|---|
| -# num | The quantity *num* is the number of copies desired of each file named. For example, |

    lpr -#3 foo.c bar.c more.c

would result in three copies of the file foo.c, followed by three copies of the file bar.c, and so on. On the other hand,

    cat foo.c bar.c more.c ¦ lpr -#3

will give three copies of the concatenation of the files. Often a site will disable this feature to encourage use of a photocopier instead.

| | |
|---|---|
| 1234 font | Specifies a font to be mounted on font position *i*. The daemon will construct a .railmag file referencing the font pathname. |
| -C Ar class | Job classification to use on the burst page. For example |

    lpr -C EECS foo.c

causes the system name—the name returned by hostname(1)—to be replaced on the burst page by EECS, and the file foo.c to be printed.

| | |
|---|---|
| -J Ar job | Job name to print on the burst page. Normally, the first file's name is used. |
| -T Ar title | Title name for pr(1), instead of the filename. |
| -U user | Username to print on the burst page, also for accounting purposes. This option is only honored if the real user ID is daemon (or that specified in the printcap file instead of daemon), and is intended for those instances where print filters wish to requeue jobs. |
| -i numcols | The output is indented. If the next argument is numeric numcols, it is used as the number of blanks to be printed before each line; otherwise, eight characters are printed. |
| -w Ns Ar num | Uses num as the page width for pr(1). |

## ENVIRONMENT

If the following environment variable exists, it is used by lpr:

PRINTER    Specifies an alternate default printer

## FILES

| | |
|---|---|
| etc/passwd | Personal identification. |
| /etc/printcap | Printer capabilities database. |
| /usr/sbin/lpd* | Line printer daemons. |
| /var/spool/output/* | Directories used for spooling. |

| | |
|---|---|
| `/var/spool/output/*/cf*` | Daemon control files. |
| `/var/spool/output/*/df*` | Data files specified in cf files. |
| `/var/spool/output/*/tf*` | Temporary copies of cf files. |

## SEE ALSO

lpq(1), lprm(1), pr(1), symlink(2), printcap(5), lpc(8), lpd(8)

## HISTORY

The lpr command appeared in BSD 3.

## DIAGNOSTICS

If you try to spool too large a file, it will be truncated. lpr will object to printing binary files. If a user other than root prints a file and spooling is disabled, lpr will print a message saying so and will not put jobs in the queue. If a connection to lpd(1) on the local machine cannot be made, lpr will say that the daemon cannot be started. Diagnostics may be printed in the daemon's log file regarding missing spool files by lpd(1).

## BUGS

Fonts for troff(1) and TeX reside on the host with the printer. It is currently not possible to use local font libraries.

*BSD 4, 24 July 1991*

# lprm

lprm—Remove jobs from the line printer spooling queue

## SYNOPSIS

lprm [-P printer] [- job # ...] [user ...]

## DESCRIPTION

lprm will remove a job, or jobs, from a printer's spool queue. Since the spooling directory is protected from users, using lprm is normally the only method by which a user may remove a job. The owner of a job is determined by the user's login name and hostname on the machine where the lpr(1) command was invoked.

Options and arguments:

| | |
|---|---|
| -P printer | Specify the queue associated with a specific printer; otherwise, the default printer is used. |
| - | If a single - is given, lprm will remove all jobs that a user owns. If the superuser employs this flag, the spool queue will be emptied entirely. |
| user | Causes lprm to attempt to remove any jobs queued belonging to that user (or users). This form of invoking lprm is useful only to the superuser. |
| job # | A user may dequeue an individual job by specifying its job number. This number may be obtained from the lpq(1) program. For example |

```
lpq - -l
1st:ken                              [job#013ucbarpa]
          (standard input)            100 bytes
lprm 13
```

If neither arguments nor options are given, lprm will delete the currently active job if it is owned by the user who invoked lprm.

lprm announces the names of any files it removes and is silent if there are no jobs in the queue that match the request list.

lprm will kill off an active daemon, if necessary, before removing any spooling files. If a daemon is killed, a new one is automatically restarted upon completion of file removals.

## ENVIRONMENT

If the following environment variable exists, it is utilized by lprm:

PRINTER    If the environment variable PRINTER exists, and a printer has not been specified with the -P option, the default printer is assumed from PRINTER.

## FILES

| | |
|---|---|
| /etc/printcap | Printer characteristics file |
| /var/spool/* | Spooling directories |
| /var/spool/*/lock | Lock file used to obtain the pid of the current daemon and the job number of the currently active job |

## SEE ALSO

lpr(1), lpq(1), lpd(8)

## DIAGNOSTICS

"Permission denied" if the user tries to remove files other than his own.

## BUGS

Because there are race conditions possible in the update of the lock file, the currently active job may be incorrectly identified.

## HISTORY

The lprm command appeared in BSD 3.0.

*BSD 4.2, 9 May 1991*


# lptest

lptest—Generate line printer ripple pattern

## SYNOPSIS

lptest [length] [count]

## DESCRIPTION

lptest writes the traditional "ripple test" pattern on standard output. In 96 lines, this pattern will print all 96 printable ASCII characters in each position. Although originally created to test printers, it is quite useful for testing terminals, driving terminal ports for debugging purposes, or any other task where a quick supply of random data is needed.

The length argument specifies the output line length if the default length of 79 is inappropriate.

The count argument specifies the number of output lines to be generated if the default count of 200 is inappropriate. Note that if count is to be specified, length must also be specified.

## HISTORY

lptest appeared in BSD 4.3.

*BSD 4.3, 9 May 1991*

# `ls, dir, vdir`

`ls, dir, vdir`—List contents of directories

## SYNOPSIS

`ls [-abcdfgiklmnpqrstuxABCFGLNQRSUX1] [-w cols] [-T cols] [-I pattern] [--all]`
`[--escape] [--directory] [--inode] [--kilobytes] [--numeric-uid-gid] [-no-group]`
`[--hide-control-chars] [--reverse] [--size] [--width=cols] [--tabsize-cols]`
`[--almost-all] [--ignore-backups] [--classify] [--file-type] [--full-time]`
`[--ignore=pattern] [--dereference] [--literal] [--quote-name] [--recursive]`
`[-- -sort={none, time, size, extension}] [--format={long, verbose, commas,`
`across, vertical, single-column}] [--time={atime, access, use, ctime, status}]`
`[--help] [--version] [name...]`

## DESCRIPTION

This manual page documents the GNU version of `ls`. `dir` and `vdir` are versions of `ls` with different default output formats. These programs list each given file or directory name. Directory contents are sorted alphabetically. For `ls`, files are by default listed in columns, sorted vertically, if the standard output is a terminal; otherwise, they are listed one per line. For `dir`, files are by default listed in columns, sorted vertically. For `vdir`, files are by default listed in long format.

## OPTIONS

| | |
|---|---|
| `-a, --all` | List all files in directories, including all files that start with a period (.). |
| `-b, --escape` | Quote nongraphic characters in filenames using alphabetic and octal backslash sequences like those used in C. |
| `-c, --time=ctime,`<br>`--time=status` | Sort directory contents according to the files' status change time instead of the modification time. If the long listing format is being used, print the status change time instead of the modification time. |
| `-d, --directory` | List directories like other files, rather than listing their contents. |
| `-f` | Do not sort directory contents; list them in whatever order they are stored on the disk. This is the same as enabling -a and -U and disabling -l, -s, and -t. |
| `--full-time` | List times in full, rather than using the standard abbreviation heuristics. |
| `-g` | Ignored; for UNIX compatibility. |
| `-i, --inode` | Print the index number of each file to the left of the filename. |
| `-k, --kilobytes` | If file sizes are being listed, print them in kilobytes. This overrides the environment variable POSIXLY_CORRECT. |
| `-l, --format=long,`<br>`--format=verbose` | In addition to the name of each file, print the file type, permissions, number of hard links, owner name, group name, size in bytes, and timestamp (the modification time unless other times are selected). For files with a time that is more than six months old or more than one hour into the future, the timestamp contains the year instead of the time of day. |
| `-m, --format=commas` | List files horizontally, with as many as will fit on each line, separated by commas. |
| `-n, --numeric-uid-gid` | List the numeric UID and GID instead of the names. |
| `-p` | Append a character to each filename indicating the file type. |
| `-q, --hide-control-chars` | Print question marks instead of nongraphic characters in filenames. |
| `-r, --reverse` | Sort directory contents in reverse order. |
| `-s, --size` | Print the size of each file in 1KB blocks to the left of the filename. If the environment variable POSIXLY_CORRECT is set, 512-byte blocks are used instead. |
| `-t, --sort=time` | Sort directory contents by timestamp instead of alphabetically, with the newest files listed first. |
| `-u, --time=atime,`<br>`--time=access,--time=use` | Sort directory contents according to the files' last access time instead of the modification time. If the long listing format is being used, print the last access time instead of the modification time. |

| | |
|---|---|
| `-x, --format=across,`<br>`--format=horizontal` | List the files in columns, sorted horizontally. |
| `-A, --almost-all` | List all files in directories, except for '.' and '..'. |
| `-B, --ignore-backups` | Do not list files that end with ˜, unless they are given on the command line. |
| `-C, --format=vertical` | List files in columns, sorted vertically. |
| `-F, --classify` | Append a character to each filename indicating the file type. For regular files that are executable, append a *. The file type indicators are / for directories, @ for symbolic links, ¦ for FIFOs, = for sockets, and nothing for regular files. |
| `-G, --no-group` | Inhibit display of group information in a long format directory listing. |
| `-L, --dereference` | List the files linked to by symbolic links instead of listing the contents of the links. |
| `-N, --literal` | Do not quote filenames. |
| `-Q, --quote-name` | Enclose filenames in double quotes and quote nongraphic characters as in C. |
| `-R, --recursive` | List the contents of all directories recursively. |
| `-S, --sort=size` | Sort directory contents by file size instead of alphabetically, with the largest files listed first. |
| `-U, --sort=none` | Do not sort directory contents; list them in whatever order they are stored on the disk. This option is not called -f because the UNIX ls -f option also enables -a and disables -l, -s, and -t. It seems useless and ugly to group those unrelated things together in one option. Because this option doesn't do that, it has a different name. |
| `-X, --sort=extension` | Sort directory contents alphabetically by file extension (characters after the last period); files with no extension are sorted first. |
| `-1, --format=single-column` | List one file per line. |
| `-w, --width cols` | Assume the screen is cols columns wide. The default is taken from the terminal driver if possible; otherwise, the environment variable COLUMNS is used if it is set; otherwise, the default is 80. |
| `-T, --tabsize cols` | Assume that each tab stop is cols columns wide. The default is 8. |
| `-I, --ignore pattern` | Do not list files whose names match the shell pattern pattern unless they are given on the command line. As in the shell, an initial period (.) in a filename does not match a wildcard at the start of pattern. |
| `--help` | Print a usage message on standard output and exit successfully. |
| `--version` | Print version information on standard output then exit successfully. |

## BUGS

On BSD systems, the -s option reports sizes that are half the correct values for files that are NFS-mounted from HP-UX systems. On HP-UX systems, it reports sizes that are twice the correct values for files that are NFS-mounted from BSD systems. This is due to a flaw in HP-UX; it also affects the HP-UX ls program.

*GNU File Utilities*

# lsattr

lsattr—List file attributes on a Linux second extended filesystem

## SYNOPSIS

lsattr [ -Radv ] [ *files...* ]

## DESCRIPTION

lsattr lists the files attributes on an second extended filesystem.

## OPTIONS

| | |
|---|---|
| -R | Recursively list attributes of directories and their contents. |
| -a | List all files in directories, including files that start with period (.). |
| -d | List directories like other files, rather than listing their contents. |
| -v | List the files version. |

## AUTHOR

lsattr has been written by Remy Card (card@masi.ibp.fr), the developer and maintainer of the ext2 fs.

## BUGS

There are none :-).

## AVAILABILITY

lsattr is available for anonymous FTP from ftp.ibp.fr and tsx-11.mit.edu in /pub/linux/packages/ext2fs.

## SEE ALSO

chattr(1)

*Version 0.5b, November 1994*

# lsmod

lsmod—show the loaded modules

## SYNOPSIS

lsmod

## DESCRIPTION

lsmod shows information about all loaded modules. The format is

name size [list of referring modules]

size is in 4Kb pages.

This information is a copy of the contents of /proc/modules.

## SEE ALSO

insmod(1), modprobe(1), depmod(1), rmmod(1), ksyms(1), modules(2)

## HISTORY

The module support was first conceived by Anonymous (as far as I know…). Linux version by Bas Laarhoven (bas@vimec.nl), 0.99.14 version by Jon Tombs (jon@gtex02.us.es), extended by Bjorn Ekwall (bj0rn@blox.se).

## BUGS

lsmod might have some, but they are well hidden.…

*Linux, 14 May 1995*

# lynx

lynx—A general-purpose distributed information browser for the World Wide Web

## SYNOPSIS

lynx [*options*] [*path or URL*]

Use lynx -help to display a complete list of current options.

## DESCRIPTION

lynx is a fully-featured World Wide Web (WWW) client for users running cursor-addressable, character-cell display devices (for example, vt100 terminals, vt100 emulators running on PCs or Macs, or any other "curses-oriented" display). It will display Hypertext Markup Language (HTML) documents containing links to files residing on the local system, as well as files residing on remote systems running Gopher, HTTP, FTP, WAIS, and NNTP servers. Current versions of lynx run on UNIX and VMS.

lynx can be used to access information on the World Wide Web, or to build information systems intended primarily for local access. For example, lynx has been used to build several Campus Wide Information Systems (CWIS). In addition, lynx can be used to build systems isolated within a single LAN.

## OPTIONS

At startup, lynx will load any local file or remote URL specified at the command line. For help with URLs, press ? or h while running lynx. Then follow the link titled "Help on URLs."

| | |
|---|---|
| - | If the only argument is -, then lynx expects to receive the arguments from stdin. This is to allow for the potentially very long command line that can be associated with the -get_data or -post_data arguments. (See entries for each later in this list.) |
| -anonymous | Used to specify the anonymous account. |
| -ascii | Disable kanji code translation when Japanese mode is on. |
| -auth=*ID:PASSWD* | Set authorization ID and password for protected documents at startup. |
| -book | Use the bookmark page as the startfile. The default or command line startfile is still set for the Main screen command, and will be used if the bookmark page is unavailable or blank. |
| -buried_news | Toggles scanning of news articles for buried references, and converts them to news links. Not recommended because e-mail addresses enclosed in angle brackets will be converted to false news links, and uuencoded messages can be trashed. |
| -cache=*NUMBER* | Set the NUMBER of documents cached in memory. The default is 10. |
| -case | Enable case-sensitive string searching. |
| -cfg=*FILENAME* | Specifies a lynx configuration file other than the default lynx.cfg. |
| -child | Exit on left-arrow in startfile, and disable save to disk. |
| -crawl | With -traversal, output each page to a file. With -dump, format output as with -traversal, but to stdout. |
| -display=*DISPLAY* | Set the display variable for X rexeced programs. |
| -dump | Dumps the formatted output of the default document or one specified on the command line to standard out. This can be used in the following way: lynx -dump http://www.w3.org/default.html. |
| -editor=*EDITOR* | Enable Edit mode using the specified EDITOR (vi, ed, emacs, and so on). |
| -emacskeys | Enable Emacs-like key movement. |
| -enable_scrollback | Toggle compatibility with comm programs' scrollback keys (may be incompatible with some packages). |
| -error_file=*FILE* | Define a file where lynx will report HTTP access codes. |
| -euc | Set kanji code to EUC when Japanese mode is on. |
| -fileversions | Include all versions of files in local VMS directory listings. |
| -force_html | Forces the first document to be interpreted as HTML. |

| | |
|---|---|
| -ftp | Disable FTP access. |
| -get_data | Send form data from stdin using GET method and dump results. |
| -head | Send a HEAD request for the mime headers. |
| -help | Print this lynx command syntax usage message. |
| -historical | Toggles use of > or -> as a terminator for comments. |
| -homepage=*URL* | Set home page separate from start page. |
| -image_links | Toggles inclusion of links for all images. |
| -index=*URL* | Set the default index file to the specified URL. |
| -jpn | Toggles Japanese character translations on or off. |
| -link=*UMBER* | Starting count for lnk#.dat files produced by -crawl. |
| -localhost | Disable URLs that point to remote hosts. |
| -locexec | Enable local program execution from local files only (if lynx was compiled with local execution enabled). |
| -mime_header | Prints the MIME header of a fetched document along with its source. |
| -minimal | Toggles minimal versus valid comment parsing. |
| -nobrowse | Disable directory browsing. |
| -noexec | Disable local program execution (default). |
| -nolist | Disable the link list feature in dumps. |
| -nolog | Disable mailing of error messages to document owners. |
| -noprint | Disable print functions. |
| -noredir | Prevents automatic redirection and prints a message with a link to the new URL. |
| -nostatus | Disable the retrieval status messages. |
| -number_links | Force numbering of links. |
| -post_data | Send form data from stdin using POST method and dump results. |
| -print | Enable print functions (default). |
| -pseudo_inlines | Toggles pseudo-ALTs for inlines with no ALT string. |
| -realm | Restricts access to URLs in the starting realm. |
| -reload | Flushes the cache on a proxy server (only the first document affected). |
| -restrictions=[option] [,option][,option]... | Allows a list of services to be disabled selectively. The following list is printed if no options are specified. |
| | all—Restricts all options. |
| | bookmark--Disallow changing the location of the bookmark file. |
| | bookmark_exec--Disallow execution links via the bookmark file. |
| | Change_exec_perms—Disallow changing the execute permission on files (but still allow it for directories) when local file management is enabled. |
| | default--Same as command-line option -anonymous. Disables default services for anonymous users. Currently set to all restricted except for the following: inside_telnet, outside_telnet, inside_news, inside_ftp, outside_ftp, inside_rlogin, outside_rlogin, jump, mail, and goto. Defaults are settable within userdefs.h. |
| | dired_support—Disallow local file management. |
| | disk_save—Disallow saving binary files to disk in the download menu. |
| | download--Disallow downloaders in the download menu. |
| | editor—Disallow editing. |
| | exec--Disable execution scripts. |
| | exec_frozen--Disallow the user from changing the local execution option. |
| | file_url--Disallow using goto to go to file: URLs. |
| | goto—Disable the g (goto) command. |

inside_ftp—Disallow FTPs for people coming from inside your domain. (utmp required for selectivity.)

inside_news—Disallow Usenet news posting for people coming from inside your domain. (utmp required for selectivity.)

inside_rlogin—Disallow rlogins for people coming from inside your domain. (utmp required for selectivity.)

inside_telnet --Disallow Telnets for people coming from inside your domain. (utmp required for selectivity.)

jump—Disable the j (jump) command.

mail --Disable mailing feature.

news_post --Disable Usenet news posting.

options_save --Disallow saving options in .lynxrc.

outside_ftp—Disallow FTPs for people coming from outside your domain. (utmp required for selectivity.)

outside_news—Disallow Usenet news posting for people coming from outside your domain. (utmp required for selectivity.)

outside_rlogin—Disallow rlogins for people coming from outside your domain. (utmp required for selectivity.)

outside_telnet—Disallow Telnets for people coming from outside your domain. (utmp required for selectivity.)

print—Disallow most print options.

shell—Disallow shell escapes and lynxexec or lynxprog goto's.

suspend --Disallow UNIX Ctrl+Z suspends with escape to shell.

telnet_port—Disallow specifying a port in Telnet goto's.

| | |
|---|---|
| -rlogin | Disable recognition of rlogin commands. |
| -selective | Require .www browsable files to browse directories. |
| -show_cursor | If enabled, the cursor will not be hidden in the right-hand corner but will instead be positioned at the start of the currently selected link. show_cursor is the default for systems without FANCY_CURSES capabilities, and the default configuration can be changed in userdefs.h. |
| -sjis | Set kanji code to Shift JIS when Japanese mode is on. |
| -source | Works the same as dump but outputs HTML source instead of formatted text. |
| -telnet | Disable recognition of Telnet commands. |
| -term=TERM | Tell lynx what terminal type to assume it's talking to. (This may be useful for remote execution when, for example, lynx connects to a remote TCP/IP port that starts a script that, in turn, starts another lynx process.) |
| -trace | Turns on WWW trace mode. |
| -traversal | Traverse all HTTP links derived from startfile. When used with -crawl, each link that begins with the same string as startfile is output to a file, intended for indexing. See CRAWL.announce for more information. |
| -underscore | Toggles use of _underline_format in dumps. |
| -validate | Accept only HTTP URLs (for validation). Complete security restrictions also are implemented. |
| -version | Print version information. |
| -vikeys | Enable vi-like key movement. |

## COMMANDS

- Use Up arrow and Down arrow to scroll through hypertext links.
- Right arrow or Return will follow a highlighted hypertext link.
- Left Arrow will retreat from a link.

- Type h or ? for online help and descriptions of keystroke commands.
- Type k for a complete list of the current keystroke command mappings.

## NOTES

This is the Lynx 2.5 Release for UN*X/VMS.

If you wish to contribute to the further development of lynx, subscribe to our mailing list. Send e-mail to majordomo@sig.net with "subscribe lynx-dev" as the only line in the body of your message.

Send bug reports, comments, and suggestions to lynx-dev@sig.net after subscribing.

Unsubscribe by sending e-mail to majordomo@sig.net with unsubscribe lynx-dev as the only line in the body of your message. Do not send the unsubscribe message to the lynx-dev list itself.

## ACKNOWLEDGMENTS

lynx has incorporated code from a variety of sources along the way. The earliest versions of lynx included code from Earl Fogel of Computing Services at the University of Saskatchewan, who implemented HYPERREZ in the UN*X environment. HYPERREZ was developed by Niel Larson of Think.com and served as the model for the early versions of lynx. Those versions also incorporated libraries from the UN*X Gopher clients developed at the University of Minnesota, and the later versions of lynx rely on the WWW client library code developed by Tim Berners-Lee and the WWW community. Also a special thanks to Foteos Macrides, who ported much of lynx to VMS and to everyone on the Net who has contributed to lynx's development either directly (through comments or bug reports) or indirectly (through inspiration and development of other systems).

## AUTHORS

Lou Montulli, Garrett Blythe, Craig Lavender, Michael Grobe, Charles Rezac
Academic Computing Services
University of Kansas
Lawrence, Kansas 66047

Foteos Macrides
Worcester Foundation
Shrewsbury, Massachusetts 01545

*Local*

# macptopbm

macptopbm—Convert a MacPaint file into a portable bitmap

## SYNOPSIS

macptopbm [-extraskip N][*macpfile*]

## DESCRIPTION

macptopbm reads a MacPaint file as input and produces a portable bitmap as output.

## OPTIONS

-extraskip    This flag is to get around a problem with some methods of transferring files from the Mac world to the UNIX world. Most of these methods leave the Mac files alone, but a few of them add the find-erinfo data onto the front of the UNIX file. This means an extra 128 bytes to skip over when reading the file. The symptom to watch for is that the resulting PBM file looks shifted to one side. If you get this, try -extraskip 128, and if that still doesn't look right, try another value.

All flags can be abbreviated to their shortest unique prefix.

## SEE ALSO

picttoppm(1), pbmtomacp(1), pbm(5)

## AUTHOR

Copyright © 1988 by Jef Poskanzer. The MacPaint-reading code is copyright © 1987 by Patrick J. Naughton (naughton@wind.sun.com).

*29 March 1989*

# make

make—GNU make utility to maintain groups of programs

## SYNOPSIS

make [ -f makefile ] [ option ] ... target ...

## WARNING

This man page is an extract of the documentation of GNU make. It is updated only occasionally because the GNU project does not use nroff. For complete, current documentation, refer to the info file make or the DVI file make.dvi, which are made from the texinfo source file make.texinfo.

## DESCRIPTION

The purpose of the make utility is to determine automatically which pieces of a large program need to be recompiled, and issue the commands to recompile them. This manual page describes the GNU implementation of make, which was written by Richard Stallman and Roland McGrath. Our examples show C programs because they are most common, but you can use make with any programming language whose compiler can be run with a shell command. In fact, make is not limited to programs. You can use it to describe any task where some files must be updated automatically from others whenever the others change.

To prepare to use make, you must write a file called the makefile that describes the relationships among files in your program and states the commands for updating each file. In a program, typically, the executable file is updated from object files, which are in turn made by compiling source files.

Once a suitable makefile exists, each time you change some source files, this simple shell command:

make

suffices to perform all necessary recompilations. The make program uses the makefile database and the last-modification times of the files to decide which of the files need to be updated. For each of those files, it issues the commands recorded in the database.

make executes commands in the makefile to update one or more target names, where name is typically a program. If no -f option is present, make will look for the makefiles GNU-makefile, makefile, and Makefile, in that order.

Normally you should call your makefile either makefile or Makefile. (We recommend Makefile because it appears prominently near the beginning of a directory listing, right near other important files such as README.) The first name checked, GNUmakefile, is not recommended for most makefiles. You should use this name if you have a makefile that is specific to GNU make, and will not be understood by other versions of make. If makefile is -, the standard input is read.

make updates a target if it depends on prerequisite files that have been modified since the target was last modified, or if the target does not exist.

## OPTIONS

| | |
|---|---|
| -b, -m | These options are ignored for compatibility with other versions of make. |
| -C *dir* | Change to directory *dir* before reading the makefiles or doing anything else. If multiple -C options are specified, each is interpreted relative to the previous one: -C / -C etc is equivalent to -C /etc. This is typically used with recursive invocations of make. |
| -d | Print debugging information in addition to normal processing. The debugging information says which files are being considered for remaking, which file times are being compared and with what results, which files actually need to be remade, which implicit rules are considered and which are applied—everything interesting about how make decides what to do. |
| -e | Give variables taken from the environment precedence over variables from makefiles. |
| -f *file* | Use *file* as a makefile. |
| -i | Ignore all errors in commands executed to remake files. |
| -I *dir* | Specifies a directory *dir* to search for included makefiles. If several -I options are used to specify several directories, the directories are searched in the order specified. Unlike the arguments to other flags of make, directories given with -I flags may come directly after the flag: -I*dir* is allowed, as well as -I *dir*. This syntax is allowed for compatibility with the C preprocessor's -I flag. |
| -j *jobs* | Specifies the number of jobs (commands) to run simultaneously. If there is more than one -j option, the last one is effective. If the -j option is given without an argument, make will not limit the number of jobs that can run simultaneously. |
| -k | Continue as much as possible after an error. Although the target that failed, and those that depend on it, cannot be remade, the other dependencies of these targets can be processed all the same. |
| -l, <br> -l *load* | Specifies that no new jobs (commands) should be started if there are other jobs running and the load average is at least *load* (a floating-point number). With no argument, removes a previous load limit. |
| -n | Print the commands that would be executed, but do not execute them. |
| -o *file* | Do not remake the file *file* even if it is older than its dependencies, and do not remake anything because of changes in *file*. Essentially, the file is treated as very old and its rules are ignored. |
| -p | Print the database (rules and variable values) that results from reading the makefiles; then execute as usual or as otherwise specified. This also prints the version information given by the -v switch (see below). To print the database without trying to remake any files, use make -p -f/dev/null. |
| -q | Question mode. Do not run any commands or print anything; just return an exit status that is zero if the specified targets are already up-to-date, nonzero otherwise. |
| -r | Eliminate use of the built-in implicit rules. Also clear out the default list of suffixes for suffix rules. |
| -s | Silent operation; do not print the commands as they are executed. |
| -S | Cancel the effect of the -k option. This is never necessary except in a recursive make where -k might be inherited from the top-level make via MAKEFLAGS or if you set -k in MAKEFLAGS in your environment. |
| -t | Touch files (mark them up-to-date without really changing them) instead of running their commands. This is used to pretend that the commands were done, in order to fool future invocations of make. |
| -v | Print the version of the make program plus a copyright, a list of authors, and a notice that there is no warranty. After this information is printed, processing continues normally. To get this information without doing anything else, use make -v -f/dev/null. |
| -w | Print a message containing the working directory before and after other processing. This may be useful for tracking down errors from complicated nests of recursive make commands. |
| -W *file* | Pretend that the target file has just been modified. When used with the -n flag, this shows you what would happen if you were to modify that file. Without -n, it is almost the same as running a touch command on the given file before running make, except that the modification time is changed only in the imagination of make. |

## SEE ALSO

/usr/local/doc/gnumake.dvi

*The GNU Make Manual*

## BUGS

See the chapter "Problems and Bugs" in *The GNU Make Manual*.

## AUTHOR

This manual page contributed by Dennis Morse of Stanford University. It has been reworked by Roland McGrath.

*GNU, ?? August 1989*

# makedepend

makedepend—Create dependencies in makefiles

## SYNOPSIS

```
makedepend [ -Dname=def ][-Dname ][-Iincludedir ][-Yincludedir ][-a ]
[-fmakefile ][-oobjsuffix ][-pobjprefix ][-sstring ][-wwidth ][-v ][-m ]
[--otheroptions -- ] sourcefile . . .
```

## DESCRIPTION

makedepend reads each *sourcefile* in sequence and parses it like a C-preprocessor, processing all #include, #define, #undef, #ifdef, #ifndef, #endif, #if and #else directives so that it can correctly tell which #include, directives would be used in a compilation. Any #include, directives can reference files having other #include directives, and parsing will occur in these files as well.

Every file that a source file includes, directly or indirectly, is what makedepend calls a *dependency*. These dependencies are then written to a makefile in such a way that make(1) will know which object files must be recompiled when a dependency has changed.

By default, makedepend places its output in the file named makefile if it exists; otherwise, Makefile. An alternate makefile may be specified with the -f option. It first searches the makefile for the line:

```
# DO NOT DELETE THIS LINE -- make depend depends on it.
```

or one provided with the -s option, as a delimiter for the dependency output. If it finds it, it will delete everything following this to the end of the makefile and put the output after this line. If it doesn't find it, the program will append the string to the end of the makefile and place the output following that. For each sourcefile appearing on the command line, makedepend puts lines in the makefile of the form:

```
sourcefile.o: dfile . . .
```

where sourcefile.o is the name from the command line with its suffix replaced with .o, and dfile is a dependency discovered in a #include directive while parsing *sourcefile* or one of the files it included.

## EXAMPLE

Normally, makedepend will be used in a makefile target so that typing makedepend will bring the dependencies up-to-date for the makefile. For example,

```
SRCS = file1.c file2.c . . .
CFLAGS = -O -DHACK -I../foobar -xyz
depend:
makedepend -- $(CFLAGS) -- $(SRCS)
```

## OPTIONS

makedepend will ignore any option that it does not understand so that you may use the same arguments that you would for cc(1).

| | |
|---|---|
| -Dname=def or<br>-Dname | Define. This places a definition for *name* in makedepend's symbol table. Without =def, the symbol becomes defined as 1. |

| | |
|---|---|
| -Iincludedir | Include directory. This option tells makedepend to prepend includedir to its list of directories to search when it encounters a #include directive. By default, makedepend only searches the standard include directories (usually /usr/include and possibly a compiler-dependent directory). |
| -Yincludedir | Replace all of the standard include directories with the single specified include directory; you can omit the includedir to simply prevent searching the standard include directories. |
| -a | Append the dependencies to the end of the file instead of replacing them. |
| -fmakefile | Filename. This allows you to specify an alternate makefile in which makedepend can place its output. |
| -oobjsuffix | Object file suffix. Some systems may have object files whose suffix is something other than .o. This option allows you to specify another suffix, such as .b with -o.b or :obj with -o:obj and so forth. |
| -pobjprefix | Object file prefix. The prefix is prepended to the name of the object file. This is usually used to designate a different directory for the object file. The default is the empty string. |
| -sstring | Starting string delimiter. This option permits you to specify a different string for makedepend to look for in the makefile. |
| -wwidth | Line width. Normally, makedepend will ensure that every output line that it writes will be no wider than 78 characters for the sake of readability. This option enables you to change this width. |
| -v | Verbose operation. This option causes makedepend to emit the list of files included by each input file on standard output. |
| -m | Warn about multiple inclusion. This option causes makedepend to produce a warning if any input file includes another file more than once. In previous versions of makedepend, this was the default behavior; the default has been changed to better match the behavior of the C compiler, which does not consider multiple inclusion to be an error. This option is provided for backwards compatibility, and to aid in debugging problems related to multiple inclusion. |
| -- options -- | If makedepend encounters a double hyphen (--) in the argument list, then any unrecognized argument following it will be silently ignored; a second double hyphen terminates this special treatment. In this way, makedepend can be made to safely ignore esoteric compiler arguments that might normally be found in a CFLAGS make macro. (See the preceding "Example" section.) All options that makedepend recognizes and that appear between the pair of double hyphens are processed normally. |

## ALGORITHM

The approach used in this program enables it to run an order of magnitude faster than any other dependency generator I have ever seen. Central to this performance are two assumptions: that all files compiled by a single makefile will be compiled with roughly the same -I and -D options; and that most files in a single directory will include largely the same files.

Given these assumptions, makedepend expects to be called once for each makefile, with all source files that are maintained by the makefile appearing on the command line. It parses each source and include file exactly once, maintaining an internal symbol table for each. Thus, the first file on the command line will take an amount of time proportional to the amount of time that a normal C preprocessor takes. But on subsequent files, if it encounters an include file that it has already parsed, it does not parse it again.

For example, imagine you are compiling two files, file1.c and file2.c; they both include the header file header.h, and the file header.h in turn includes the files def1.h and def2.h. When you run the command:

```
makedepend file1.c file2.c
```

makedepend will parse file1.c and consequently, header.h and then def1.h and def2.h. It then decides that the dependencies for this file are

```
file1.o: header.h def1.h def2.h
```

But when the program parses file2.c and discovers that it, too, includes header.h, it does not parse the file, but simply adds header.h, def1.h, and def2.h to the list of dependencies for file2.o.

## SEE ALSO

cc(1), make(1)

## BUGS

makedepend parses, but does not currently evaluate, the SVR4 #predicate(token-list) preprocessor expression; such expressions are simply assumed to be true. This may cause the wrong #include directives to be evaluated.

Imagine you are parsing two files, say file1.c and file2.c, and each includes the file def.h. The list of files that def.h includes might truly be different when def.h is included by file1.c than when it is included by file2.c. But when makedepend arrives at a list of dependencies for a file, it is cast in concrete.

## AUTHOR

Todd Brunhoff, Tektronix, Inc. and MIT Project Athena

*X Version 11 Release 6*

# makestrs

makestrs—Make string table C source and header(s)

## SYNOPSIS

makestrs [-f source] [-abioptions ...]

## DESCRIPTION

The makestrs command creates string table C source files and headers. If -f source is not specified, makestrs will read from stdin. The C source file is always written to stdout. makestrs creates one or more C header files as specified in the source file. The following options may be specified: -sparcabi, -intelabi, -functionabi, -arrayperabi, and -defaultabi.

-sparcabi is used on SPARC platforms conforming to the SPARC Compliance Definition, i.e., SVR4/Solaris.

-intelabi used on Intel platforms conforming to the System V Application Binary Interface (SVR4).

-earlyR6abi may be used in addition to -intelabi for situations where the vendor wishes to maintain binary compatibility between X11R6 public-patch 11 (and earlier) and X11R6 public-patch 12 (and later).

-functionabi generates a functional application binary interface to the string table. This mechanism imposes a severe performance penalty and it's recommended that you not use it.

-arrayperabi results in a separate array for each string. This is the default behavior if makestrs was compiled with -DARRAYPERSTR (it almost never is).

-defaultabi forces the generation of the "normal" string table even if makestrs was compiled with -DARRAYPERSTR. makestrs is almost never compiled with -DARRAYPERSTR, so this is the default behavior if no application binary interface (ABI) options are specified.

## SYNTAX

The syntax for string-list file is as follows (items in square brackets are optional):

```
#prefix <text>
#feature <text>
#externref <text>
#externdef [<text>]
[#ctempl <text>]
#file <filename>
#table <tablename>
[#htempl] <text>
...
<text>
[#table <tablename>
<text>
...
```

```
<text>
...
#table <tablename>
...]
[#file <filename>
...]
```

You may have one or more `#file` directives. Each `#file` may have one or more `#table` directives.

The `#prefix` directive determines the string that `makestr` will prefix to each definition.

The `#feature` directive determines the string that `makestr` will use for the feature-test macro, for example, X=STRINGDEFINES.

The `#externref` directive determines the string that `makestr` will use for the extern clause; typically this will be extern, but Motif wants it to be externalref.

The `#externdef` directive determines the string that `makestr` will use for the declaration; typically, this will be the null string, and Motif will use externaldef(_xmstrings).

The `#ctmpl` directive determines the name of the file used as a template for the C source file that is generated.

Each `#file <filename>` directive will result in a corresponding header file by that name containing the appropriate definitions as specified by command-line options. A single C source file containing the declarations for the definitions in all the headers will be printed to stdout.

The `#htmpl` directive determines the name of the file used as a template for the C header file that is generated.

Each `#table <tablename>` directive will be processed in accordance with the ABI. On most platforms, all tables will be catenated into a single table with the name of the first table for that file. To conform to the Intel ABI, separate tables will be generated with the names indicated.

The template files specified by the `#ctmpl` and `#htmpl` directives are processed by copying line for line from the template file to the appropriate output file. The line containing the string <<<STRING_TABLE_GOES_HERE>>> is not copied to the output file. The appropriate data is then copied to the output file and then the remainder of the template file is copied to the output file.

## BUGS

makestrs is not very forgiving of syntax errors. Sometimes you need a trailing space after # directives, other times they will mess you up. No warning messages are emitted.

## SEE ALSO

SPARC Compliance Definition 2.2, SPARC International Inc., 535 Middlefield Road, Suite 210, Menlo Park, CA 94025

*System V Application Binary Interface*, Third Edition, ISBN 0-13-100439-5, UNIX Press, PTR Prentice Hall, 113 Sylvan Avenue, Englewood Cliffs, NJ 07632

*System V Application Binary Interface*, Third Edition, Intel386 Architecture Processor Supplement, ISBN 0-13-104670-5, UNIX Press, PTR Prentice Hall, 113 Sylvan Avenue, Englewood Cliffs, NJ 07632

*System V Application Binary Interface*, Third Edition, SPARCArchitecture Processor Supplement, ISBN 0-13-104696-9, UNIX Press, PTR Prentice Hall, 113 Sylvan Avenue, Englewood Cliffs, NJ 07632

*X Version 11 Release 6*

# mattrib

mattrib—Change MS-DOS file attribute flags

## SYNOPSIS

```
mattrib [ -a¦+a ][-h¦+h ][-r¦+r ][-s¦+s ] msdosfile [ msdosfiles... ]
```

## DESCRIPTION

mattrib adds attribute flags to an MS-DOS file (with the + operator) or removes attribute flags (with the - operator).

mattrib allows the following command-line options:

a           Archive bit. Used by some backup programs to indicate a new file.

r           Read-only bit. Used to indicate a read-only file. Files with this bit set cannot be erased by DEL or modified.

s           System bit. Used by MS-DOS to indicate an operating system file.

h           Hidden bit. Used to make files hidden from DIR.

## SEE ALSO

mtools(1)

*Local*

# mbadblocks

mbadblocks—Scan an MS-DOS floppy and mark its unused bad blocks as bad.

## SYNOPSIS

mbadblocks drive:

## DESCRIPTION

mbadblocks scans an MS-DOS floppy for bad blocks. All unused bad blocks are marked as such in the FAT. This is intended to be used right after mformat. It is not intended to salvage bad disks.

## SEE ALSO

mtools(1)

## BUGS

This should (but doesn't :-( ) also try to salvage bad blocks that are in use by reading them repeatedly, and then mark them bad.

# mcd

mcd—Change MS-DOS directory

## SYNOPSIS

mcd [ msdosdirectory ]

## DESCRIPTION

Without arguments, mcd will report the current device and working directory. Otherwise, mcd changes the current device and current working directory relative to an MS-DOS filesystem.

The environmental variable MCWD may be used to locate the file where the device and current working directory information is stored. The default is $HOME/.mcwd. Information in this file is ignored if the file is more than six hours old.

MS-DOS subdirectory names are supported with either the / or \ separator. The use of the \ separator or wildcards will require the directory name to be enclosed in quotes to protect it from the shell.

mcd returns 0 on success or 1 on failure.

## SEE ALSO

mdir(1)

## BUGS

Unlike MS-DOS versions of CD, mcd can be used to change to another device.

It may be wise to remove old .mcwd files at logout.

*Local*

# mcookie

mcookie—Generate magic cookies for xauth

## SYNOPSIS

mcookie

## DESCRIPTION

mcookie generates a 128-bit random hexadecimal number for use with the X authority system. Typical usage:

xauth add :0 . 'mcookie'

## SEE ALSO

X(1), xauth(1)

*12 February 1995*

# mcopy

mcopy—Copy MS-DOS files to/from UNIX

## SYNOPSIS

mcopy [ -tnvmoOsSrRA ] *sourcefile targetfile*
mcopy [ -tnvmoOsSrRA ] *sourcefile* [ *sourcefiles...* ] *targetdirectory*
mcopy [ -tnvm ] *MSDOSsourcefile*

## DESCRIPTION

mcopy copies the specified file to the named file, or copies multiple files to the named directory. The source and target can be either MS-DOS or UNIX files.

The use of a drive letter designation on the MS-DOS files—a: for example—determines the direction of the transfer. A missing drive designation implies a UNIX file whose path starts in the current directory. If a source drive letter is specified with no attached filename (for example, mcopy a: .), all files are copied from that drive.

If only a single, MS-DOS source parameter is provided (for example, mcopy a:foo.exe), an implied destination of the current directory (.) is assumed.

A filename of - means standard input or standard output, depending on its position on the command line.

mcopy will allow the following command-line options:

| | |
|---|---|
| t | Text file transfer. mcopy will translate incoming carriage return/line feeds to line feeds. |
| n | No warning. mcopy will not warn the user when overwriting an existing file. |
| v | Verbose mode. |
| m | Preserve the file modification time. |

If the target file already exists, and the -n option is not in effect, mcopy asks whether to overwrite the file or to rename the new file. (See the mtools(1) man page for details.)

## SEE ALSO

mtools(1), mread(1), mwrite(1)

## BUGS

Unlike MS-DOS, the + operator (append) from MS-DOS is not supported.

*Local*

# md5sum

md5sum—Generate/check MD5 message digests

## SYNOPSIS

```
md5sum [-bv][-c [ file ]]
md5sum file ...
```

## DESCRIPTION

md5sum generates and checks MD5 message digests, as described in RFC-1321. The message digest produced can be thought of as a 128-bit "signature" of the input file. Typically, md5sum is used to verify the integrity of files made available for distribution via anonymous FTP (for example, announcements for new versions of irc(1) usually contain MD5 signatures). Message digests for a tree of files can be generated with a command similar to the following:

```
find . -type f -print ¦ xargs md5sum
```

The output of this command is suitable as input for the -c option.

## OPTIONS

-c [file]    Check message digests. Input is taken from stdin or from the specified file. The input should be in the same format as the output generated by md5sum.

-v    Verbose. Print filenames when checking.

-b    Read files in binary mode; otherwise, end-of-file conventions will be ignored.

## HISTORY

The md5sum program was written by Branko Lankester and may be freely distributed. The original source code is in the MIT PGP 2.6.2 distribution. Those concerned about the integrity of this version should obtain the original sources and compile their own version.

The underlying implementation of Ron Rivest's MD5 algorithm was written by Colin Plumb and is in the public domain. (Equivalent code is also available from RSA Data Security, Inc.)

## SEE ALSO

sum(1), cksum(1), pgp(1)

*Linux 1.0, 11 February 1995*

# mdel

mdel—Delete an MS-DOS file

## SYNOPSIS

```
mdel [ -v ] msdosfile [ msdosfiles... ]
```

## DESCRIPTION

mdel deletes a file on an MS-DOS filesystem.

mdel will allow the following command-line option:

v          Verbose mode. Echo the filenames as they are processed.

mdel will ask for verification prior to removing a read–only file.

## SEE ALSO

mtools(1)

*Local*

# mdeltree

mdeltree—Remove an MS-DOS directory tree

## SYNOPSIS

mdeltree [ -v ] *msdosdirectory* [ *msdosdirectories...* ]

## DESCRIPTION

mdeltree removes a directory and all the files and subdirectories it contains from an MS-DOS filesystem. mdeltree will allow the following command-line option:

v          Verbose mode. Displays each file or directory as it is removed.

An error occurs if the directory does not exist.

## SEE ALSO

mtools(1), mrd(1)

*Local*

# mdir

mdir—Display an MS-DOS directory

## SYNOPSIS

mdir [ -w ] *msdosdirectory*
mdir [ -w ][-a ] *msdosfile* [ *msdosfiles...* ]

## DESCRIPTION

mdir displays the contents of an MS-DOS directory.

mdir will allow the following command-line options:

w          Wide output. This option will print the filenames across the page without displaying the file size or creation date.
a          Also list hidden files.

An error occurs if a component of the path is not a directory.

## SEE ALSO

mtools(1)

*Local*

# merge

merge—Three-way file merge

## SYNOPSIS

```
merge [ options ] file1 file2 file3
```

## DESCRIPTION

merge incorporates all changes that lead from *file2* to *file3* into *file1*. The result ordinarily goes into *file1*. merge is useful for combining separate changes to an original. Suppose *file2* is the original, and both *file1* and *file3* are modifications of *file2*. Then merge combines both changes.

A conflict occurs if both *file1* and *file3* have changes in a common segment of lines. If a conflict is found, merge normally outputs a warning and brackets the conflict with <<<<<<< and >>>>>>> lines. A typical conflict will look like this:

```
<<<<<<< file A
lines in file A
=======
lines in file B
>>>>>>> file B
```

If there are conflicts, the user should edit the result and delete one of the alternatives.

## OPTIONS

-A       Output conflicts using the -A style of diff3(1), if supported by diff3. This merges all changes leading from file2 to file3 into file1, and generates the most verbose output.

-E, -e    These options specify conflict styles that generate less information than -A. See diff3(1) for details. The default is -E. With -e, merge does not warn about conflicts.

-L *label*    This option may be given up to three times, and specifies labels to be used in place of the corresponding filenames in conflict reports. That is, merge-Lx-L y -Lz a b c generates output that looks like it came from files x, y, and z instead of from files a, b, and c.

-p       Send results to standard output instead of overwriting file1.

-q       Quiet; do not warn about conflicts.

-V       Print RCS's version number.

## DIAGNOSTICS

Exit status is 0 for no conflicts, 1 for some conflicts, 2 for trouble.

## IDENTIFICATION

Author: Walter F. Tichy.
Manual Page Revision: 5.7; Release Date: 1995/06/01.
Copyright © 1982, 1988, 1989 Walter F. Tichy.
Copyright © 1990, 1991, 1992, 1993, 1994, 1995 Paul Eggert.

## SEE ALSO

diff3(1), diff(1), rcsmerge(1), co(1)

## BUGS

It normally does not make sense to merge binary files as if they were text, but merge tries to do it anyway.

# mesg

mesg—Display (do not display) messages from other users

## SYNOPSIS

mesg [n][y]

## DESCRIPTION

The mesg utility is invoked by a users to control write access others have to the terminal device associated with the standard error output. If write access is allowed, then programs such as talk(1) and write(1) may display messages on the terminal.

Traditionally, write access is allowed by default. However, as users become more conscious of various security risks, there is a trend to remove write access by default, at least for the primary login shell. To make sure your ttys are set the way you want them to be set, mesg should be executed in your login scripts.

Options available:

n         Disallows messages

y         Permits messages to be displayed

If no arguments are given, mesg displays the present message status to the standard error output.

The mesg utility exits with one of the following values:

\0        Messages are allowed.

\1        Messages are not allowed.

1         An error has occurred.

## FILES

/dev/[pt]ty[pq]?

## SEE ALSO

biff(1), talk(1), write(1), wall(1), login(1), xterm(1)

## HISTORY

A mesg command appeared in version 6 AT&T UNIX.

*Linux 1.2, 10 March 1995*

# mformat

mformat—Add an MS-DOS filesystem to a low-level formatted disk

## SYNOPSIS

mformat [ -t tracks ] [ -h heads ] [ -s sectors ] [ -l volume label ]
[ -S sizecode ] [ -2 sectors on track 0 ] [ -M software sector size ]
[ -a ][ -X ][ -C ][ -H hidden sectors ] drive:

## DESCRIPTION

mformat adds a minimal MS-DOS filesystem (boot sector, FAT, and root directory) to a disk that has already been formatted by a UNIX low-level format.

The follow options are supported: (The S, 2, 1, and M options may not exist if this copy of mtools has been compiled without the USE_2M option).

| | |
|---|---|
| t | The number of tracks (not cylinders). |
| h | The number of heads (sides). |
| s | The number of sectors per track. If the 2m option is given, number of 512-byte sector equivalents on generic tracks (that is, not head 0 track). If the 2m option is not given, number of physical sectors per track (which may be bigger than 512 bytes). |
| l | An optional volume label. |
| S | The sizecode. The size of the sector is 2 ^ (sizecode + 7). |
| 2 | 2m format. The parameter to this option describes the number of sectors on track 0, head 0. This option is recommended for sectors bigger than normal. |
| 1 | Don't use a 2m format, even if the current geometry of the disk is a 2m geometry. |
| M | Software sector size. This parameter describes the sector size in bytes used by the MS-DOS filesystem. By default it is the physical sector size. |
| a | If this option is given, an Atari-style serial number is generated. Ataris store their serial number in the OEM label. |
| X | Formats the disk as an Xdf disk. Xdf disks are used by OS/2. This format can hold 1756Kb, and is faster than the equivalent 2m formats. The disk has first to be low-level formatted using the xdfcopy utility included in the fdutils package. |
| C | Creates the disk image file to install the MS-DOS filesystem on it. Obviously, this is useless on physical devices such as floppies and hard disk partitions. |
| H | Number of hidden sectors. This parameter is useful for formatting hard disk partitions, which are not aligned on track boundaries (in other words, first head of first track doesn't belong to the partition, but contains a partition table). In that case the number of hidden sectors is in general the number of sectors per cylinder. This is untested. |
| n | Serial number. |

To format a disk at a density other than the default, you must supply (at least) those command-line parameters that are different from the default.

Mformat returns 0 on success or 1 on failure.

## SEE ALSO

mlabel(1)

## BUGS

Requires a low-level format utility from UNIX.

Doesn't detect (or record) bad block information.

*Local*

# mgrtopbm

mgrtopbm—Convert an MGR bitmap into a portable bitmap

## SYNOPSIS

mgrtopbm [*mgrfile*]

## DESCRIPTION

mgrtopbm reads an MGR bitmap as input and produces a portable bitmap as output.

## SEE ALSO

pbmtomgr(1), pbm(5)

## AUTHOR

Copyright © 1989 by Jef Poskanzer.

# mkdir

mkdir—Make directories

## SYNOPSIS

mkdir [-p] [-m mode] [--parents] [--mode=mode] [--help] [--version] dir...

## DESCRIPTION

This manual page documents the GNU version of mkdir. mkdir creates a directory with each given name. By default, the mode of created directories is 0777 minus the bits set in the umask.

## OPTIONS

| | |
|---|---|
| -m, --mode *mode* | Set the mode of created directories to *mode*, which is symbolic as in chmod and uses the default mode as the point of departure. |
| -p, --parents | Ensure that each given directory exists. Create any missing parent directories for each argument. Parent directories default to the umask modified by u+wx. Do not consider an argument directory that already exists to be an error. |
| --help | Print a usage message on standard output and exit successfully. |
| --version | Print version information on standard output then exit successfully. |

*GNU File Utilities*

# mkdirhier

mkdirhier—Make a directory hierarchy

## SYNOPSIS

mkdirhier *directory* ...

## DESCRIPTION

The mkdirhier command creates the specified directories. Unlike mkdir, if any of the parent directories of the specified directory do not exist, it creates them as well.

## SEE ALSO

mkdir(1)

*X Version 11 Release 6*

# mkfifo

mkfifo—Make FIFOs (named pipes)

## SYNOPSIS

mkfifo [-m mode] [--mode=mode] [--help] [--version] filename...

## DESCRIPTION

This manual page documents the GNU version of mkfifo. mkfifo creates a FIFO with each given name. By default, the mode of created FIFOs is 0666 minus the bits set in the umask.

## OPTIONS

-m, --mode *mode*    Set the mode of created FIFOs to *mode*, which is symbolic as in chmod and uses the default mode as the point of departure.

--help               Print a usage message on standard output and exit successfully.

--version            Print version information on standard output then exit successfully.

*GNU File Utilities*

# mkmanifest

mkmanifest—Create a shell script to restore UNIX filenames

## SYNOPSIS

mkmanifest [ *files* ]

## DESCRIPTION

mkmanifest creates a shell script that will aid in the restoration of UNIX filenames that got clobbered by the MS-DOS filename restrictions. MS-DOS filenames are restricted to eight-character names, three-character extensions, uppercase only, no device names, and no illegal characters.

The mkmanifest program is compatible with the methods used in pcomm, arc, and mtools to change perfectly good UNIX filenames to fit the MS-DOS restrictions.

## EXAMPLE

Say you want to copy the following UNIX files to an MS-DOS disk (using the mcopy command):

```
very_long_name
2.many.dots
illegal:
good.c
prn.dev
Capital
```

mcopy will convert the names to

```
very_lon
2xmany.dot
illegalx
good.c
xprn.dev
capital
```

The command:

```
mkmanifest very_long_name 2.many.dots illegal: good.c prn.dev Capital > manifest
```

would produce the following:

```
mv very_lon very_long_name
mv 2xmany.dot 2.many.dots
mv illegalx illegal:
mv xprn.dev prn.dev
mv capital Capital
```

Notice that good.c did not require any conversion, so it did not appear in the output.

Suppose I've copied these files from the disk to another UNIX system, and I now want the files back to their original names. If the file manifest (the output captured above) was sent along with those files, it could be used to convert the filenames.

## BUGS

The short names generated by mkmanifest follow the old convention (from mtools-2.0.7) and not the one from Windows 95 and mtools-3.0.

## SEE ALSO

arc(1), pcomm(1), mtools(1)

*Local*

# mknod

mknod—Make special files

## SYNOPSIS

```
mknod [options] filename {bcu} major minor
mknod [options] filename p
```

Options:

```
[-m mode] [--mode=mode] [--help] [--version]
```

## DESCRIPTION

This manual page documents the GNU version of mknod. mknod creates a FIFO, character special file, or block special file with the given filename. By default, the mode of created files is 0666 minus the bits set in the umask.

The argument after filename specifies the type of file to make:

p for a FIFO

b for a block (buffered) special file

c or u for a character (unbuffered) special file

When making a block or character special file, the major and minor device numbers must be given after the file type.

## OPTIONS

-m, --mode *mode*   Set the mode of created files to *mode*, which is symbolic as in chmod and uses the default mode as the point of departure.

--help   Print a usage message on standard output and exit successfully.

--version   Print version information on standard output then exit successfully.

*GNU File Utilities*

# mlabel

mlabel—Make an MS-DOS volume label

## SYNOPSIS

```
mlabel [ -v ] drive: [ new_label ]
```

## DESCRIPTION

mlabel displays the current volume label, if present. If *new_label* is not given, and if neither the c nor the s options are set, it prompts the user for a new volume label. To delete an existing volume label, press return at the prompt.

mlabel supports the following command-line option:

v          Verbose mode. Display the new volume label if the label supplied is invalid.

c          Clears an existing label, without prompting the user.

s          Shows the existing label, without prompting the user.

Reasonable care is taken to create a valid MS-DOS volume label. If an invalid label is specified, mlabel will change the label (and display the new label if the verbose mode is set).

Mlabel returns 0 on success or 1 on failure.

## SEE ALSO

mformat(1)

*Local*

# mmd

mmd—Make an MS-DOS subdirectory

## SYNOPSIS

mmd [ -voOsSrRA ] *msdosdirectory* [ *msdosdirectories...* ]

## DESCRIPTION

mmd makes a new directory on an MS-DOS filesystem.

mmd will allow the following command-line option:

v          Verbose mode. Display the new directory name as it is created.

An error occurs if the directory already exists.

## SEE ALSO

mtools(1), mrd(1),

*Local*

# mmount

mmount—Mount an MS-DOS disk

## SYNOPSIS

mmount msdosdrive [mountargs]

## DESCRIPTION

mmount reads the boot sector of an MS-DOS disk, configures the drive geometry, and finally mounts it, passing mountargs to mount. If no mount arguments are specified, the name of the device is used. If the disk is write-protected, it is automatically mounted read-only.

## SEE ALSO

mtools(1), mount(8)

# mmove

mmove   Move or rename an existing MS-DOS file or subdirectory

## SYNOPSIS

mmove [ -voOsSrRA ] *sourcefile targetfile*
mmove [ -voOsSrRA ] sourcefile [ sourcefiles... ] targetdirectory

## DESCRIPTION

mmove moves or renames an existing MS-DOS file or subdirectory.

mmove will allow the following command-line option:

v            Verbose mode. Display the new filename if the name supplied is invalid.

Additionally, it allows the clash-handling options described in the man page for mtools.

MS-DOS subdirectory names are supported with either the / or \ separator. The use of the \ separator or wildcards will require the names to be enclosed in quotes to protect them from the shell. Unlike the MS-DOS version of MOVE, mmove is able to move subdirectories.

## SEE ALSO

mren(1), mtools(1)

# more

more—File perusal filter for crt viewing

## SYNOPSIS

more [-dlfpcsu] [-num] [+/ pattern] [+ linenum]

## DESCRIPTION

more is a filter for paging through text one screenful at a time. This version is especially primitive. Users should realize that less(1) provides more(1) emulation and extensive enhancements.

## OPTIONS

Command-line options are described in the following list. Options are also taken from the environment variable MORE (make sure to precede them with a hyphen (-)) but command-line options will override them.

-num         This option specifies an integer that is the screen size (in lines).

-d           more will prompt the user with the message [Press space to continue, 'q' to quit.] and will display [Press 'h' for instructions.] instead of ringing the bell when an illegal key is pressed.

-l           more usually treats (form feed) as a special character, and will pause after any line that contains a form feed. The -l option will prevent this behavior.

-f           Causes more to count logical, rather than screen lines (that is, long lines are not folded).

-p           Do not scroll. Instead, clear the whole screen and then display the text.

-c           Do not scroll. Instead, paint each screen from the top, clearing the remainder of each line as it is displayed.

| | |
|---|---|
| -s | Squeeze multiple blank lines into one. |
| -u | Suppress underlining. |
| +/ | The +/ option specifies a string that will be searched for before each file is displayed. |
| +num | Start at line number. |

## COMMANDS

Interactive commands for more are based on vi(1). Some commands may be preceded by a decimal number, called k in the following descriptions. In the following descriptions, ˆX means control-X.

| | |
|---|---|
| h or ? | Help: display a summary of these commands. If you forget all the other commands, remember this one. |
| SPACE | Display next k lines of text. Defaults to current screen size. |
| z | Display next k lines of text. Defaults to current screen size. Argument becomes new default. |
| RETURN | Display next k lines of text. Defaults to 1. Argument becomes new default. |
| d or ˆD | Scroll k lines. Default is current scroll size, initially 11. Argument becomes new default. |
| q or Q INTERRUPT | Exit. |
| s | Skip forward k lines of text. Defaults to 1. |
| f | Skip forward k screenfuls of text. Defaults to 1. |
| b or ˆB | Skip backwards k screenfuls of text. Defaults to 1. |
| ' | Go to place where previous search started. |
| = | Display current line number. |
| /pattern | Search for kth occurrence of regular expression. Defaults to 1. |
| n | Search for kth occurrence of last r.e. Defaults to 1. |
| !<cmd> or :!<cmd> | Execute <cmd> in a subshell. |
| v | Start up /usr/bin/vi at current line. |
| ˆL | Redraw screen. |
| :n | Go to kth next file. Defaults to 1. |
| :p | Go to kth previous file. Defaults to 1. |
| Ic :f | Display current filename and line number. |
| . | Repeat previous command. |

## ENVIRONMENT

more utilizes the following environment variables, if they exist:

| | |
|---|---|
| MORE | This variable may be set with favored options to more. |
| SHELL | Current shell in use (normally set by the shell at login time). |
| TERM | Specifies terminal type, used by more to get the terminal characteristics necessary to manipulate the screen. |

## SEE ALSO

vi(1), less(1)

## AUTHORS

Eric Shienbrood, UC Berkeley. Modified by Geoff Peck, UCB to add underlining, single spacing. Modified by John Foderaro, UCB to add -c and MORE environment variable.

## HISTORY

The more command appeared in BSD 3.0. This man page documents more version 5.19 (Berkeley 29 June 1988), which is currently in use in the Linux community. Documentation was produced using several other versions of the man page, and extensive inspection of the source code.

*Linux 0.98, 25 December 1992*

# mrd

mrd—Remove an MS-DOS subdirectory

## SYNOPSIS

mrd [ -v ] msdosdirectory [ msdosdirectories... ]

## DESCRIPTION

mrd removes a directory from an MS-DOS filesystem. mmd will allow the following command-line option:

v          Verbose mode. Display the directory name as it is removed.

An error occurs if the directory does not exist or is not empty.

## SEE ALSO

mtools(1), mmd(1), mdeltree(1)

*Local*

# mread

mread—Read (copy) an MS-DOS file to UNIX

## SYNOPSIS

mread [ -tnvmoOsSrRA ] *msdosfile unixfile*

mread [ -tnvmoOsSrRA ] *msdosfile* [ *msdosfiles...* ] *unixdirectory*

## DESCRIPTION

This command is obsolete, and only supplied for backwards compatibility reasons with old scripts. Use mcopy instead.

## SEE ALSO

mcopy(1), mtype(1), mtools(1)

# mren

mren—Rename or move an existing MS-DOS file or subdirectory

## SYNOPSIS

mren [ -voOsSrRA ] *sourcefile targetfile*

mmove [ -voOsSrRA ] sourcefile [ sourcefiles... ] targetdirectory

## DESCRIPTION

mren renames an existing file on an MS-DOS filesystem.

Mren will allow the following command-line option:

voOsSrRA   Verbose mode. Display the new filename if the name supplied is invalid.

If the first syntax is used (only one sourcefile), and if the target name doesn't contain any slashes or colons, the file (or subdirectory) will be renamed in the same directory, instead of being moved to the current mcd directory as would be the case with mmove. Unlike the MS-DOS version of REN, mren can be used to rename directories.

## BUGS

Unlike the MS-DOS version of REN, mren can be used to rename directories.

## SEE ALSO

mcd(1)

*Local*

# mtest

mtest—Test the mtools configuration files

## SYNOPSIS

mtest

## DESCRIPTION

mtest reads the mtools configuration files and prints the cumulative configuration to stdout. The output can be used as a configuration file itself (although you might want to remove redundant clauses). You may use this program to convert old-style configuration files into new style configuration files.

## SEE ALSO

mtools(5)

*Local*

# mtools

mtools—A collection of tools for manipulating MS-DOS files

## SYNOPSIS

The mtools are

mattrib—Change MS-DOS file attribute flags

mbadblocks—Test a floppy disk, and mark the bad blocks in the FAT

mcd—Change MS-DOS directory

mcopy—Copy MS-DOS files to/from UNIX

mdel—Delete an MS-DOS file

mdir—Display an MS-DOS directory

mformat—Add an MS-DOS filesystem to a low-level formatted floppy disk

mlabel—Make an MS-DOS volume label

mmd—Make an MS-DOS subdirectory

mmount—Mount an MS-DOS disk

mrd—Remove an MS-DOS subdirectory

mmove—Move or rename an MS-DOS file or subdirectory

mren—Rename an existing MS-DOS file

mtype—Display contents of an MS-DOS file

mtest—Test and display the configuration

## DESCRIPTION

mtools is a public domain collection of programs to allow UNIX systems to read, write, and manipulate files on an MS-DOS filesystem (typically a floppy disk). Where reasonable, each program attempts to emulate the MS-DOS equivalent command. However, unnecessary restrictions and oddities of DOS are not emulated. For instance, it is possible to move subdirectories from one subdirectory to another.

MS-DOS filenames are optionally composed of a drive letter followed by a colon, a subdirectory, and a filename. Filenames without a drive letter refer to UNIX files. Subdirectory names can use either the / or \ separator. The use of the \ separator or wildcards will require the names to be enclosed in quotes to protect them from the shell. (Note: Wildcards in UNIX filenames should not be enclosed in quotes, because here users want the shell to expand them.)

## DIFFERENCES WITH MS-DOS

The regular expression "pattern matching" routines follow the UNIX-style rules. For example, * matches all MS-DOS files in lieu of *.*. The archive, hidden, read-only, and system attribute bits are ignored during pattern matching.

All options use the - (minus) flag, not / as you'd expect in MS-DOS.

Most mtools commands allow multiple filename parameters, which doesn't follow MS-DOS conventions, but which is more user friendly.

## WORKING DIRECTORY

The mcd command is used to establish the device and the current working directory (relative to the MS-DOS filesystem); otherwise, the default is assumed to be A:/. However, unlike MS-DOS, there is only one working directory, and not one per drive.

## VFAT-STYLE LONG FILENAMES

This version of mtools supports VFAT-style long filenames. If a UNIX filename is too long to fit in a short DOS name, it is stored as a VFAT long name, and a companion short name is generated. This short name is what you see when you examine the disk with a pre-7.0 version of DOS. The following table shows some examples of short names:

| UNIX Name | MS-DOS Name | Reason for the Change |
|---|---|---|
| thisisatest | THISISAT | Filename too long |
| alain.knaff | ALAIN.KNA | Extension too long |
| prn.txt | XRN.TXT | PRN is a device name |
| .abc | X.ABC | Null filename |
| hot+cold | HOTXCOLD | Illegal character |

The initial UNIX-style filename (whether long or short) is also called *primary* name, and the derived short name is also called *secondary* name.

Example:

mcopy /etc/motd a:Reallylongname

mtools creates a VFAT entry for Reallylongname, and uses REALLYLO as a short name. Reallylongname is the primary name, and REALLYLO is the secondary name.

In this example:

copy /etc/motd a:motd

motd fits into the DOS filename limits. mtools doesn't need to derivate another name. motd is the primary name, and there is no secondary name.

In a nutshell: The primary name is the long name, if one exists, or the short name if there is no long name.

## NAME CLASHES

When writing a file to disk, its long name (primary name) or short name may collide with an already existing file or directory. This may happen for all commands that create new directory entries: mcopy, mmd, mren, mmove, mwrite, and mread.

When a name clash happens, mtools asks you what it should do. It offers several choices:

overwrite        Overwrites the existing file. It is not possible to overwrite a directory with a file.

rename           Renames the newly created file. mtools will prompt for the new filename.

autorename       Renames the newly created file. mtools will chose a name by itself, without prompting.

skip             Gives up on this file, and moves on to the next (if any).

To choose an option, type its first letter at the prompt. If you use a lowercase letter, the option applies for this file only; if you use an uppercase letter, the option applies to all files.

You may also choose options (for all files) on the command line when invoking mtools:

-o        Overwrites primary names by default

-O        Overwrites secondary names by default

-r        Renames primary name by default

-R        Renames secondary name by default

-a        Autorenames primary name by default

-A        Autorenames secondary name by default

-s        Skips primary name by default

-S        Skips secondary name by default

-m        Asks user what to do with primary name

-M        Asks user what to do with secondary name

By default, the user is prompted if the primary name clashes, and the secondary name is autorenamed.

If a name clash occurs in a UNIX directory, mtools only asks whether to overwrite the file or to skip it.

## CASE SENSITIVITY OF THE VFAT FILESYSTEM

The VFAT filesystem is able to remember the case of the filenames. However, filenames that differ only in case are not allowed to coexist in the same directory. For example if you store a file called LongFileName on a VFAT filesystem, mdir will show this file as LongFileName, and not as Longfilename. However, if you then try to add LongFilename to the same directory, it will be refused, because case is ignored for clash checks.

The VFAT filesystem allows the storing of the case of a filename in the attribute byte, if all letters of the filename are the same case, and if all letters of the extension are the same case too. mtools uses this information when displaying the files, and also to generate the UNIX when mcopying to a UNIX directory. This may have unexpected results when applied to files written using a pre-7.0 version of DOS; indeed, these filenames map to all uppercase. This is different from the behavior of the old version of mtools, which used to generate lowercase UNIX filenames.

## XDF DISKS (LINUX ONLY)

Xdf is a high-capacity format supported by OS/2. It can hold 1,840KB per disc. That's not very high compared to the best 2m formats, but its main advantage is that it is fast: 600 milliseconds per track. That's faster than the good old 21 sector format, and almost as fast as the standard 18 sector format. In order to access these disks, set the use_xdf variable for the drive. See mtools(5) for details on how to do this. Fast Xdf access is only available for kernels more recent than 1.1.34.

### CAUTION

Attention distributors: If mtools is compiled on Linux, on a kernel more recent than 1.3.34, it won't run on an older kernel. However, if it has been compiled on an older kernel, it will still run on a newer kernel, except that Xdf access is slower. It is recommended that distribution authors only include mtools binaries compiled on kernels older than 1.3.34 until 2.0 comes out. When 2.0 is out, mtools binaries compiled on newer kernels may (and should) be distributed. mtools binaries compiled on kernels older than 1.3.34 won't run on any kernel 2.1 or later.

## EXIT CODES

All the mtools commands return 0 on success, 1 on utter failure, or 2 on partial failure. All the mtools commands perform a few sanity checks before going ahead, to make sure that the disk is indeed an MS-DOS disk (as opposed to, say, an ext2 or minix disk). These checks may reject partially corrupted disks, which might otherwise still be readable. To avoid these checks, set the MTOOLS_SKIP_CHECK environmental variable.

## SEE ALSO

mattrib(1), mbadblocks(1), mcd(1), mdel(1), mformat(1), mmove(1), mrd(1), mren(1), mtype(1), mcopy(1), mdir(1), mlabel(1), mmd(1), mmount(1)

## BUGS

An unfortunate side effect of not guessing the proper device (when multiple disk capacities are supported) is an occasional error message from the device driver. These can be safely ignored.

The fat checking code chokes on 1.72MB disks mformatted with pre-2.0.7 mtools. Set the environmental variable MTOOLS_FAT_COMPATIBILITY to bypass the fat checking.

The support for non-Linux OS variants has not been tested for a long time. It may contain bugs, or even not work at all.

*Local*

# mtvtoppm

mtvtoppm—Convert output from the MTV or PRT ray tracers into a portable pixmap

## SYNOPSIS

mtvtoppm [*mtvfile*]

## DESCRIPTION

mtvtoppm reads an input file from Mark Van De Wettering's MTV ray tracer and produces a portable pixmap as output.

The PRT ray tracer also produces this format.

## SEE ALSO

ppm(5)

## AUTHOR

Copyright © 1989 by Jef Poskanzer

*2 February 1989*

# mtype

mtype—Display contents of an MS-DOS file

## SYNOPSIS

mtype [ -ts ] *msdosfile* [ *msdosfiles...* ]

## DESCRIPTION

mtype displays the specified MS-DOS file on the screen.

mtype will allow the following command-line options:

t           Text file viewing. mtype will translate incoming carriage return/line feeds to line feeds.

s           Strip high bit. mtype will strip the high bit from the data.

MS-DOS subdirectory names are supported with either the / or \ separator. The use of the \ separator or wildcards will require the names to be enclosed in quotes to protect them from the shell.

The mcd command may be used to establish the device and the current working directory (relative to MS-DOS); otherwise, the default is A:/.

mtype returns 0 on success, 1 on utter failure, or 2 on partial failure.

## SEE ALSO

mcd(1), mread(1)

## BUGS

Allows multiple arguments, which does not follow the MS-DOS convention.

*Local*

# mv

mv—Rename files

## SYNOPSIS

```
mv [options] source dest
mv [options] source... directory
```

Options:

```
[-bfiuv] [-S backup-suffix] [-V {numbered,existing,simple}] [--backup] [--force]
[--interactive] [--update] [--verbose] [--suffix=backup-suffix]
[--version-control={numbered,existing,simple}] [--help] [--version]
```

## DESCRIPTION

This manual page documents the GNU version of mv. If the last argument names an existing directory, mv moves each other given file into a file with the same name in that directory. Otherwise, if only two files are given, it moves the first onto the second. It is an error if the last argument is not a directory and more than two files are given. It can move only regular files across filesystems. If a destination file is unwritable, the standard input is a tty, and the -f or --force option is not given, mv prompts the user for whether to overwrite the file. If the response does not begin with y or Y, the file is skipped.

## OPTIONS

| | |
|---|---|
| -b, --backup | Make backups of files that are about to be removed. |
| -f, --force | Remove existing destination files and never prompt the user. |
| -i, --interactive | Prompt whether to overwrite each destination file that already exists. If the response does not begin with y or Y, the file is skipped. |
| -u, --update | Do not move a nondirectory that has an existing destination with the same or newer modification time. |
| -v, --verbose | Print the name of each file before moving it. |
| --help | Print a usage message on standard output and exit successfully. |
| --version | Print version information on standard output, then exit successfully. |

| -S, --suffix backup-suffix | The suffix used for making simple backup files can be set with the SIMPLE_BACKUP_SUFFIX environment variable, which can be overridden by this option. If neither of those is given, the default is ˜, as it is in Emacs. |
|---|---|
| -V, --version-control {numbered,existing,simple} | The type of backups made can be set with the VERSION_CONTROL environment variable, which can be overridden by this option. If VERSION_CONTROL is not set and this option is not given, the default backup type is existing. The value of the VERSION_CONTROL environment variable and the argument to this option are like the GNU Emacs version-control variable; they also recognize synonyms that are more descriptive. |

The valid values are the following (unique abbreviations are accepted):

t or numbered--Always make numbered backups.

nil or existing--Make numbered backups of files that already have them, simple backups of the others.

never or simple—Always make simple backups.

*GNU File Utilities*

# mwrite

mwrite—Low-level write (copy) a UNIX file to MS-DOS

## SYNOPSIS

mwrite [ -tnvmoOsSrRA ] *unixfile msdosfile*

mwrite [ -tnvmoOsSrRA ] *unixfile* [ *unixfiles...* ] *msdosdirectory*

## DESCRIPTION

This command is obsolete and only supplied for backward compatibility reasons with old scripts. Use mcopy instead.

## SEE ALSO

mcopy(1), mtools(1)

*Local*

# namei

namei—Follow a pathname until a terminal point is found

## SYNOPSIS

namei [-mx] *pathname* [ *pathname ...* ]

## DESCRIPTION

namei uses its arguments as pathnames to any type of UNIX file (symlinks, files, directories, and so forth). namei then follows each pathname until a terminal point is found (a file, directory, char device, and so on). If it finds a symbolic link, the user shows the link, and starts following it, indenting the output to show the context.

This program is useful for finding too many levels of symbolic links problems.

For each line output, namei outputs the following characters to identify the file types found:

| f: | The pathname the user is currently trying to resolve |
|---|---|
| d | Directory |
| l | Symbolic link (both the link and its contents are output) |
| s | Socket |

| b | Block device |
|---|---|
| c | Character device |
| - | Regular file |
| ? | An error of some kind |

`Namei` prints an informative message when the maximum number of symbolic links this system can have has been exceeded.

## OPTIONS

-x    Show mount point directories with a `D` rather than a `d`.

-m    Show the mode bits of each file type in the style of `ls(1)`, for example, `rwxr-xr-x`.

## AUTHOR

Roger Southwick (`rogers@amadeus.wr.tek.com`)

## BUGS

To be discovered

## CAVEATS

`namei` will follow an infinite loop of symbolic links forever. To escape, use `SIGINT` (usually `^C`).

## SEE ALSO

`ls(1)`, `stat(1)`

*Local*

# newaliases

`newaliases`—Rebuild the database for the mail aliases file

## SYNOPSIS

`newaliases`

## DESCRIPTION

`newaliases` rebuilds the random access database for the mail aliases file. It must be run each time it is changed in order for the change to take effect.

## SEE ALSO

`aliases(5)`, `sendmail(8)`

## HISTORY

The `newaliases` command appeared in BSD 4.0.

*BSD 4, 30 July 1991*

# newgrp

`newgrp`—Log in to a new group

## SYNOPSIS

`newgrp [ group ]`

## DESCRIPTION

newgrp changes the group identification of its caller, analogously to login(1). The same person remains logged in, and the current directory is unchanged, but calculations of access permissions to files are performed with respect to the new group ID.

If no group is specified, the GID is changed to the login GID.

## FILES

```
/etc/group
/etc/passwd
```

## SEE ALSO

login(1), group(5)

*Linux 0.99, 9 October 1993*

# nl

nl—Number lines of files

## SYNOPSIS

```
nl [-h header-style] [-b body-style] [-f footer-style] [-p] [-d cc]
[-v start-number] [-i increment] [-l lines] [-s line-separator]
[-w line-no-width] [-n {ln,rn,rz}] [--header-numbering=style]
[--body-numbering=style] [--footer-numbering=style]
[--first-page=number] [--page-increment=number] [--no-renumber]
[--join-blank-lines=number] [--number-separator=string]
[--number-width=number] [--number-format={ln,rn,rz}]
[--section-delimiter=cc] [--help] [--version] [file...]
```

## DESCRIPTION

This manual page documents the GNU version of nl. nl copies each given file, or the standard input if none are given or when a file named - is given, to the standard output, with line numbers added to some or all of the lines.

nl considers its input to be composed of logical pages; by default, the line number is reset to 1 at the top of each logical page. nl treats all of the input files as a single document; it does not reset line numbers or logical pages between files.

A logical page consists of three sections: header, body, and footer. Any of the sections can be empty. Each can be numbered in a different style from the others.

The beginnings of the sections of logical pages are indicated in the input file by a line containing nothing except one of the following delimiter strings:

```
\:\:\: start of header
\:\: start of body
\: start of footer
```

The two characters from which these strings are made can be changed with an option (see the next subsection), but the pattern and length of each string cannot be changed.

The section delimiter strings are replaced by an empty line on output. Any text that comes before the first section delimiter string in the input file is considered to be part of a body section, so a file that does not contain any section delimiter strings is considered to consist of a single body section.

## OPTIONS

-h, --header-numbering=style    See --footer-numbering.

-b, --body-numbering=style    See --footer-numbering.

| | |
|---|---|
| -f, --footer-numbering=style | Select the numbering style for lines in the footer section of each logical page. When a line is not numbered, the current line number is not incremented, but the line number separator character is still prepended to the line. The styles are |

| | |
|---|---|
| a | Number all lines |
| t | Number only nonempty lines (default for body) |
| n | Number no lines (default for header and footer) |
| pregexp | Number only lines that contain a match for regexp |

| | |
|---|---|
| -p, --no-renumber | Do not reset the line number at the start of a logical page. |
| -v, --first-page=number | Set the initial line number on each logical page to number (default 1). |
| -i, --page-increment=number | Increment line numbers by number (default 1). |
| -l, --join-blank-lines=number | Consider number (default 1) consecutive empty lines to be one logical line for numbering, and only number the last one. Where fewer than number consecutive empty lines occur, do not number them. An empty line is one that contains no characters, not even spaces or tabs. |
| -s, --number-separator=string | Separate the line number from the text line in the output with string (default is a tab character). |
| -w, --number-width=number | Use number characters for line numbers (default 6). |
| -n, --number-format={ln,rn,rz} | Select the line numbering format: |

| | |
|---|---|
| ln | Left justified, no leading zeros |
| rn | Right justified, no leading zeros (default) |
| rz | Right justified, leading zeros |

| | |
|---|---|
| -d, --section-delimiter=cc | Set the two delimiter characters that indicate the beginnings of logical page sections; if only one is given, the second remains :. To enter \, use \\. |
| --help | Print a usage message and exit with a nonzero status. |
| --version | Print version information on standard output, then exit. |

*GNU Text Utilities*

# nlmconv

nlmconv—Convert object code into an NLM

## SYNOPSIS

nlmconv[ -Ibfdname¦--input-target=bfdname] [ -Obfdname¦
--output-target=bfdname ] [ -Theaderfile¦--header-file=headerfile ]
[ -V¦--version ][--help ] infile outfile

## DESCRIPTION

nlmconv converts the relocatable object file infile into the NetWare Loadable Module (NLM) outfile, optionally reading headerfile for NLM header information. For instructions on writing the NLM command file language used in header files, see *The NetWare Tool Maker Specification Manual,* available from Novell, Inc. nlmconv currently works with i386 object files in COFF, ELF, ora.out format, and with SPARC object files in ELF or a.out format. nlmconv uses the GNU binary file descriptor library to read infile.

## OPTIONS

| | |
|---|---|
| -I bfdname, --input-target=bfdname | Consider the source file's object format to be bfdname, rather than attempting to deduce it. |
| -O bfdname, --output-target=bfdname | Write the output file using the object format bfdname. nlmconv infers the output format based on the input format, for example, for an i386 input file the output format is nlm32-i386. |

| | |
|---|---|
| -T *headerfile*,<br>--header-file=*headerfile* | Reads *headerfile* for NLM header information. For instructions on writing the NLM command file language used in header files, see *The NetWare Tool Maker Specification Manual,* available from Novell, Inc. |
| -V, --version | Show the version number of nlmconv and exit. |
| -h, --help | Show a summary of the options to nlmconv and exit. |

## SEE ALSO

binutils entry in info; *The GNU Binary Utilities*, Roland H. Pesch (June 1993).

## COPYING

Copyright © 1993 Free Software Foundation, Inc. Permission is granted to make and distribute verbatim copies of this manual provided the copyright notice and this permission notice are preserved on all copies.

Permission is granted to copy and distribute modified versions of this manual under the conditions for verbatim copying, provided that the entire resulting derived work is distributed under the terms of a permission notice identical to this one.

Permission is granted to copy and distribute translations of this manual into another language, under the above conditions for modified versions, except that this permission notice may be included in translations approved by the Free Software Foundation instead of in the original English.

*Cygnus support, June 1993*

# nm

nm—List symbols from object files

## SYNOPSIS

```
nm [ -a¦--debug-syms][-g¦--extern-only ][-B ][-C¦--demangle ]
[-D¦--dynamic ][-s¦--print-armap][-o¦--print-file-name]
[-n¦--numeric-sort ][-p¦--no-sort ][-r¦--reverse-sort ][--size-sort ]
[ -u¦--undefined-only][--help ][--version ][-t radix¦--radix=radix ]
[ -P¦-portability ] [ -f format¦--format=format ][--target=bfdname ][ objfile ...]
```

## DESCRIPTION

GNU nm lists the symbols from object files *objfile*. If no object files are given as arguments, nm assumes a.out.

## OPTIONS

The long and short forms of options, shown here as alternatives, are equivalent.

| | |
|---|---|
| -A, -o<br>--print-file-name | Precede each symbol by the name of the input file where it was found, rather than identifying the input file once only before all of its symbols. |
| -a, --debug-syms | Display debugger-only symbols; normally these are not listed. |
| -B | The same as --format=bsd (for compatibility with the MIPS nm). |
| -C, --demangle | Decode (demangle) low-level symbol names into user-level names. Besides removing any initial underscore prepended by the system, this makes C++ function names readable. |
| -D, --dynamic | Display the dynamic symbols rather than the normal symbols. This is only meaningful for dynamic objects, such as certain types of shared libraries. |
| -f *format* | Use the output format *format*, which can be bsd, sysv, or posix. The default is bsd. Only the first character of format is significant; it can be either uppercase or lowercase. |
| -g, --extern-only | Display only external symbols. |
| -n, -v, --numeric-sort | Sort symbols numerically by their addresses, not alphabetically by their names. |

| | |
|---|---|
| -p, --no-sort | Don't bother to sort the symbols in any order; just print them in the order encountered. |
| -P, --portability | Use the POSIX.2 standard output format instead of the default format. Equivalent to -f posix. |
| -s, --print-armap | When listing symbols from archive members, include the index, a mapping (stored in the archive by ar or ranlib) of which modules contain definitions for what names. |
| -r, --reverse-sort | Reverse the sense of the sort (whether numeric or alphabetic); let the last come first. |
| --size-sort | Sort symbols by size. The size is computed as the difference between the value of the symbol and the value of the symbol with the next higher value. The size of the symbol is printed, rather than the value. |
| -t radix, --radix=radix | Use radix as the radix for printing the symbol values. It must be d for decimal, o for octal, or x for hexadecimal. |
| --target=bfdname | Specify an object code format other than your system's default format. See objdump(1) for information on listing available formats. |
| -u, --undefined-only | Display only undefined symbols (those external to each object file). |
| -V, --version | Show the version number of nm and exit. |
| --help | Show a summary of the options to nm and exit. |

## SEE ALSO

binutils entry in info; *The GNU Binary Utilities*, Roland H. Pesch (October 1991); ar(1), objdump(1), ranlib(1).

## COPYING

Copyright © 1991 Free Software Foundation, Inc. Permission is granted to make and distribute verbatim copies of this manual provided the copyright notice and this permission notice are preserved on all copies.

Permission is granted to copy and distribute modified versions of this manual under the conditions for verbatim copying, provided that the entire resulting derived work is distributed under the terms of a permission notice identical to this one.

Permission is granted to copy and distribute translations of this manual into another language, under the above conditions for modified versions, except that this permission notice may be included in translations approved by the Free Software Foundation instead of in the original English.

*Cygnus support, 5 November 1991*

# nntpget

nntpget—Get Usenet articles from a remote NNTP server

## SYNOPSIS

nntpget [ -d *dist* ][-f *file* ][-n *newsgroups* ][-t *timestring* ][-o ][-u *file* ][-v ] *host*

## DESCRIPTION

nntpget connects to the NNTP server at the specified *host* and retrieves articles from it. The articles are sent to standard output.

The —o flag may be used only if the command is executed on the host where the innd(8) server is running. If this flag is used, nntpget connects to the specified remote host to retrieve articles. Any article not present in the local history database is then fetched from the remote site and offered to the local server.

If the -v flag is used with the -o flag, then the Message-ID of each article will be sent to standard output as it is processed.

The list of article Message-IDs is normally read from standard input. If the -f flag is used, then a newnews command is used to retrieve all articles newer than the modification date of the specified *file*. The -u flag is the same except that if the transfer succeeded, the file will be updated with a statistics line, modifying its timestamp so that it can be used in later invocations. If the -t flag is used, then the specified *timestring* is used as the time and date parameter to the newnews command.

If either the -t or -f flags are used, then the -n flag may be used to specify a newsgroup list and the -d flag may be used to specify a distribution list. The default is * for all newsgroups, and no distribution list.

## BUGS

Truncates articles at 512 lines.

## HISTORY

Written by Rich $alz (rsalz@uunet.uu.net) for *InterNetNews*.

## SEE ALSO

innd(8)

# objcopy

objcopy—Copy and translate object files

## SYNOPSIS

```
objcopy [ -Fbfdname¦--target=bfdname ]
[ -Ibfdname¦ --input-target=bfdname ] [ -Obfdname¦
--output-target=bfdname ] [ -Rsectionname¦
--remove-section=sectionname ] [ -S¦ --strip-all ][-g¦
--strip-debug ][-x¦--discard-all ][-X¦
--discard-locals][-bbyte¦--byte=byte ] [ -iinterleave¦
--interleave=interleave ] [ -v¦--verbose][-V¦
--version ][--help ] infile [ outfile ]
```

## DESCRIPTION

The GNU objcopy utility copies the contents of an object file to another. objcopy uses the GNU BFD library to read and write the object files. It can write the destination object file in a format different from that of the source object file. The exact behavior of objcopy is controlled by command-line options.

objcopy creates temporary files to do its translations and deletes them afterward. objcopy uses BFD to do all its translation work; it knows about all the formats BFD knows about, and thus is able to recognize most formats without being told explicitly.

infile and outfile are the source and output files, respectively. If you do not specify outfile, objcopy creates a temporary file and destructively renames the result with the name of the input file.

## OPTIONS

| | |
|---|---|
| -I bfdname, --input-target=bfdname | Consider the source file's object format to be *bfdname*, rather than attempting to deduce it. |
| -O bfdname, --output-target=bfdname | Write the output file using the object format *bfdname*. |
| -F bfdname, --target=bfdname | Use *bfdname* as the object format for both the input and the output file; that is, simply transfer data from source to destination with no translation. |
| -R sectionname, --remove-section, =sectionname | Remove the named section from the file. This option may be given more than once. Note that using this option inappropriately may make the output file unusable. |
| -S, --strip-all | Do not copy relocation and symbol information from the source file. |
| -g, --strip-debug | Do not copy debugging symbols from the source file. |
| -x, --discard-all | Do not copy nonglobal symbols from the source file. |
| -X, --discard-locals | Do not copy compiler-generated local symbols. (These usually start with L or .). |

| | |
|---|---|
| -b *byte*, --byte=*byte* | Keep only every *byte* byte of the input file (header data is not affected). *byte* can be in the range from 0 to the interleave-1. This option is useful for creating files to program ROMs. It is typically used with an srec output target. |
| -i *interleave*, --interleave=*interleave* | Only copy one out of every interleave bytes. The one to copy is selected by the -b or --byte option. The default is 4. The interleave is ignored if neither -b nor --byte is given. |
| -v, --verbose | Verbose output: list all object files modified. In the case of archives, objcopy -V lists all members of the archive. |
| -V, --version | Show the version number of objcopy and exit. |
| --help | Show a summary of the options to objcopy and exit. |

## SEE ALSO

binutils entry in info; *The GNU Binary Utilities*, Roland H. Pesch (June 1993).

## COPYING

Copyright © 1993 Free Software Foundation, Inc. Permission is granted to make and distribute verbatim copies of this manual provided the copyright notice and this permission notice are preserved on all copies.

Permission is granted to copy and distribute modified versions of this manual under the conditions for verbatim copying, provided that the entire resulting derived work is distributed under the terms of a permission notice identical to this one.

Permission is granted to copy and distribute translations of this manual into another language, under the above conditions for modified versions, except that this permission notice may be included in translations approved by the Free Software Foundation instead of in the original English.

*Cygnus support, June 1993*

# objdump

objdump—Display information from object files.

## SYNOPSIS

objdump [ -a¦--archive-headers ][-b\ *bfdname* ¦ --target= *bfdname* ]
[ -d¦--disassemble][-D¦--disassemble-all ][-f¦--file-headers ]
[ -h¦--section-headers ¦ --headers ][-i¦--info ][-j\ *section*
¦ --section= *section* ][-l¦--line-numbers ][-m\ *machine* ¦ --
-architecture= *machine* ][-r¦--reloc ][-R¦--dynamic-reloc ]
[ -s¦--full-contents ][--stabs ][-t¦--syms ][-T¦--dynamic-
syms][-x¦--all-headers ][--version ][--help ] *objfile* ...

## DESCRIPTION

objdump displays information about one or more object files. The options control what particular information to display. This information is mostly useful to programmers who are working on the compilation tools, as opposed to programmers who just want their program to compile and work.

objfile... are the object files to be examined. When you specify archives, objdump shows information on each of the member object files.

## OPTIONS

Where long and short forms of an option are shown together, they are equivalent. At least one option besides -1 (--line-numbers) must be given.

| | |
|---|---|
| -a, --archive-headers | If any files from *objfile* are archives, display the archive header information (in a format similar to ls -1). Besides the information you could list with ar tv, objdump -a shows the object file format of each archive member. |

| | |
|---|---|
| -b *bfdname*,<br>--target=*bfdname* | Specify the object-code format for the object files to be *bfdname*. This may not be necessary; *objdump* can automatically recognize many formats. For example, objdump -b oasys -m vax -h fu.o displays summary information from the section headers (-h) of fu.o, which is explicitly identified (-m) as a Vax object file in the format produced by Oasys compilers. You can list the formats available with the -i option. |
| -d, --disassemble | Display the assembler mnemonics for the machine instructions from *objfile*. This option only disassembles those sections that are expected to contain instructions. |
| -D, --disassemble-all | Like -d, but disassemble the contents of all sections, not just those expected to contain instructions. |
| -f, --file-headers | Display summary information from the overall header of each file in *objfile*. |
| -h, --section-headers,<br>--headers | Display summary information from the section headers of the object file. |
| --help | Print a summary of the options to *objdump* and exit. |
| -i, --info | Display a list showing all architectures and object formats available for specification with -b or -m. |
| -j *name*, --section=*name* | Display information only for section name. |
| -l, --line-numbers | Label the display (using debugging information) with the filename and source line numbers corresponding to the object code shown. Only useful with -d or -D. |
| -m *machine*,<br>--architecture=*machine* | Specify the object files *objfile* are for architecture *machine*. You can list available architectures using the -i option. |
| -r, --reloc | Print the relocation entries of the file. If used with -d or -D, the relocations are printed interspersed with the disassembly. |
| -R, --dynamic-reloc | Print the dynamic relocation entries of the file. This is only meaningful for dynamic objects, such as certain types of shared libraries. |
| -s, --full-contents | Display the full contents of any sections requested. |
| --stabs | Display the contents of the .stab, .stab.index, and .stab.excl sections from an ELF file. This is only useful on systems (such as Solaris 2.0) in which .stab debugging symbol-table entries are carried in an ELF section. In most other file formats, debugging symbol-table entries are interleaved with linkage symbols, and are visible in the --syms output. |
| -t, --syms | Symbol table. Print the symbol table entries of the file. This is similar to the information provided by the nm program. |
| -T, --dynamic-syms | Dynamic symbol table. Print the dynamic symbol table entries of the file. This is only meaningful for dynamic objects, such as certain types of shared libraries. This is similar to the information provided by the nm program when given the -D (--dynamic) option. |
| --version | Print the version number of *objdump* and exit. |
| -x, --all-headers | Display all available header information, including the symbol table and relocation entries. Using -x is equivalent to specifying all of -a -f -h -r -t. |

## SEE ALSO

binutils entry in info; *The GNU Binary Utilities*, Roland H. Pesch (October 1991); nm(1).

## COPYING

# oclock

oclock—Round X clock

## SYNOPSIS

oclock [-option ... ]

## DESCRIPTION

oclock simply displays the current time on an analog display.

## OPTIONS

| | |
|---|---|
| -fg *color* | Choose a different color for both hands and the jewel on the clock |
| -bg *color* | Choose a different color for the background. |
| -jewel *color* | Choose a different color for the jewel on the clock. |
| -minute *color* | Choose a different color for the minute hand of the clock. |
| -hour *color* | Choose a different color for the hour hand of the clock. |
| -backing { WhenMapped Always NotUseful} | Select an appropriate level of backing store. |
| -geometry *geometry* | Define the initial window geometry; see X(1). |
| -display *display* | Specify the display to use; see X(1). |
| -bd *color* | Choose a different color for the window border. |
| -bw *width* | Choose a different width for the window border. As the Clock widget changes its border around quite a bit, this is most usefully set to zero. |
| -shape | Cause the clock to use the Shape extension to create an oval window. This is the default unless the shapeWindow resource is set to false. |
| -noshape | Cause the clock to not reshape itself and ancestors to exactly fit the outline of the clock. |
| -transparent | Cause the clock to consist only of the jewel, the hands, and the border. |

## COLORS

If you would like your clock to be viewable in color, include the following in the #ifdef COLOR section you read with xrdb:

*customization: -color

This will cause oclock to pick up the colors in the app-defaults color customization file: <XRoot>/lib/X11/app-defaults/ Clock-color. The default colors are

| | |
|---|---|
| Clock*Background | Gray |
| Clock*BorderColor | Light blue |
| Clock*hour | Yellow |
| Clock*jewel | Yellow |
| Clock*minute | Yellow |

## SEE ALSO

X(1), X Toolkit documentation

## AUTHOR

Keith Packard, MIT X Consortium

*X Version 11 Release 6*

# od

od—Dump files in octal and other formats

## SYNOPSIS

```
od [-abcdfhiloxv] [-s[bytes]] [-w[bytes]] [-A radix] [-j bytes] [-N bytes]
[-t type] [--skip-bytes=bytes] [--address-radix=radix] [--read-bytes=bytes]
[--format=type] [--output-duplicates] [--strings[=bytes]] [--width[=bytes]]
[--traditional] [--help] [--version] [file...]
```

## DESCRIPTION

This manual page documents the GNU version of od. od writes to the standard output the contents of the given files, or of the standard input if the name - is given. Each line of the output consists of the offset in the input file in the leftmost column of each line, followed by one or more columns of data from the file, in a format controlled by the options. By default, od prints the file offsets in octal and the file data as two-byte octal numbers.

## OPTIONS

| | |
|---|---|
| -A, --address-radix=*radix* | Select the base in which file offsets are printed. *radix* can be one of the following: |

| | |
|---|---|
| d | Decimal |
| o | Octal |
| x | Hexadecimal |
| n | None (do not print offsets) |

The default is octal.

| | |
|---|---|
| -j, --skip-bytes=*bytes* | Skip *bytes* input bytes before formatting and writing. If bytes begins with 0x or 0X, it is interpreted in hexadecimal; otherwise, if it begins with 0, in octal; otherwise, in decimal. Appending b multiplies it by 512, k by 1024, and m by 1048576. |
| -N, --read-bytes=*bytes* | Only output up to *bytes* bytes of each input file. Any prefixes and suffixes on *bytes* are interpreted as for the -j option. |
| -t, --format=*type* | Select the format in which to output the file data. *type* is a string of one or more of the following type indicator characters. If you include more than one type indicator character in a single *type* string or use this option more than once, od writes one copy of each output line using each of the data types that you specified, in the order that you specified. |

| | |
|---|---|
| a | Named character |
| c | ASCII character or backslash escape |
| d | Signed decimal |
| f | Floating point |
| o | Octal |
| u | Unsigned decimal |
| x | Hexadecimal |

Except for types a and c, you can specify the number of bytes to use in interpreting each number in the given data type by following the type indicator character with a decimal integer. Alternately, you can specify the size of one of the C compiler's built-in data types by following the type indicator character with one of the following characters. For integers (d, o, u, x):

| | |
|---|---|
| C | char |
| S | short |
| I | int |
| L | long |

For floating point (f):

| | |
|---|---|
| F | float |
| D | double |
| L | long double |

| | |
|---|---|
| -v, --output-duplicates | Output consecutive lines that are identical. By default, when two or more consecutive output lines would be equal, od outputs only the first line, and puts just an asterisk on the following line to indicate that identical lines have been elided. |
| -s, --strings[=bytes] | Instead of the normal output, output only string constants in the input, which are a run of at least bytes ASCII graphic (or formatting) characters, terminated by a NUL. If bytes is omitted, it defaults to 3. |
| -w, --width[=bytes] | The number of input bytes to format per output line. It must be a multiple of the least common multiple of the sizes associated with the specified output types. If bytes is omitted, it defaults to 32. If this option is not given, it defaults to 16. |
| --help | Print a usage message and exit with a nonzero status. |
| --version | Print version information on standard output, then exit. |

The next several options map the old, pre-POSIX format specification options to the corresponding POSIX format specs. GNU od accepts any combination of old- and new-style options. Format specification options accumulate.

| | |
|---|---|
| -a | Output as named characters. Equivalent to -t a. |
| -b | Output as octal bytes. Equivalent to -t oC. |
| -c | Output as ASCII characters or backslash escapes. Equivalent to -t c. |
| -d | Output as unsigned decimal shorts. Equivalent to -t u2. |
| -f | Output as floats. Equivalent to -t fF. |
| -h | Output as hexadecimal shorts. Equivalent to -t x2. |
| -i | Output as decimal shorts. Equivalent to -t d2. |
| -l | Output as decimal longs. Equivalent to -t d4. |
| -o | Output as octal shorts. Equivalent to -t o2. |
| -x | Output as hexadecimal shorts. Equivalent to -t x2. |
| --traditional | Recognize the pre-POSIX nonoption arguments that some older versions of od accepted. The following syntax: |

```
od --traditional [file] [[+]offset[.][b] [[+]label[.][b]]]
```

can be used to specify at most one file and optional arguments specifying an offset and a pseudo-start address, label. By default, offset is interpreted as an octal number specifying how many input bytes to skip before formatting and writing. The optional trailing decimal point forces the interpretation of offset as a decimal number. If no decimal is specified and the offset begins with 0x or 0x, it is interpreted as a hexadecimal number. If there is a trailing b, the number of bytes skipped will be offset multiplied by 512. The label argument is interpreted just like offset, but it specifies an initial pseudo-address. The pseudo addresses are displayed in parentheses following any normal address.

*GNU Text Utilities*

# passwd

passwd—Change password

## SYNOPSIS

passwd [ name ]

## DESCRIPTION

passwd changes the specified user's password. Only the superuser is allowed to change other users' passwords. If the user is not root, then the old password is prompted for and verified.

A new password is prompted for twice, to avoid typing mistakes. Unless the user is the superuser, the new password must have more than six characters, and must have either both uppercase and lowercase letters, or nonletters. Some passwords that are similar to the user's name are not allowed.

## FILES

```
/etc/passwd
/etc/shells
```

## SEE ALSO

chsh(1), chfn(1)

## BUGS

A password consisting of all digits is allowed.

No warnings are printed if the superuser chooses a poor password.

The -f and -s options are not supported.

## AUTHOR

Peter Orbaek (poe@daimi.aau.dk)

*Linux 1.0, 22 June 1994*

# paste

paste—Merge lines of files

## SYNOPSIS

```
paste [-s] [-d delim-list] [--serial] [--delimiters=delim-list] [--help]
[--version] [file...]
```

## DESCRIPTION

This manual page documents the GNU version of paste. paste prints lines consisting of sequentially corresponding lines of each given file, separated by tabs, terminated by a newline. If no files are given, the standard input is used. A filename of - means standard input.

## OPTIONS

| | |
|---|---|
| -s, --serial | Paste the lines of one file at a time rather than one line from each file. |
| -d, --delimiters delim-list | Consecutively use the characters in delim-list instead of TAB to separate merged lines. When delim-list is exhausted, start again at its beginning. |
| --help | Print a usage message and exit with a nonzero status. |
| --version | Print version information on standard output, then exit. |

*GNU Text Utilities*

# pbmclean

pbmclean—Flip isolated pixels in portable bitmap

## SYNOPSIS

pbmclean [-connect] [*pbmfile*]

## DESCRIPTION

pbmclean reads a portable bitmap as input and outputs a portable bitmap with every pixel that has less than connect identical neighbors inverted. pbmclean can be used to clean up "snow" on bitmap images.

## SEE ALSO

pbm(5)

## AUTHOR

Copyright © 1990 by Angus Duggan. Copyright © 1989 by Jef Poskanzer.

Permission to use, copy, modify, and distribute this software and its documentation for any purpose and without fee is hereby granted, provided that the above copyright notice appear in all copies and that both that copyright notice and this permission notice appear in supporting documentation. This software is provided "as is" without express or implied warranty.

# pbmfilters

pbmfilters—List of all programs in the PBMPlus package

## DESCRIPTION

| | |
|---|---|
| anytopnm | Attempt to convert an unknown type of image file to a portable anymap |
| asciitopgm | Convert ASCII graphics into a portable graymap |
| atktopbm | Convert Andrew Toolkit raster object to a portable bitmap |
| bioradtopgm | Convert a Biorad confocal file into a portable graymap |
| bmptoppm | Convert a BMP file into a portable pixmap |
| brushtopbm | Convert a doodle brush file into a portable bitmap |
| cmuwmtopbm | Convert a CMU window manager bitmap into a portable bitmap |
| fitstopnm | Convert a FITS file into a portable anymap |
| fstopgm | Convert a Usenix FaceSaver file into a portable graymap |
| g3topbm | Convert a Group 3 fax file into a portable bitmap |
| gemtopbm | Convert a GEM IMG file into a portable bitmap |
| giftopnm | Convert a GIF file into a portable anymap |
| gouldtoppm | Convert Gould scanner file into a portable pixmap |
| hipstopgm | Convert a HIPS file into a portable graymap |
| hpcdtoppm | Convert a Photo-CD file into a portable pixmap |
| icontopbm | Convert a Sun icon into a portable bitmap |
| ilbmtoppm | Convert an ILBM file into a portable pixmap |
| imgtoppm | Convert an IMG-whatnot file into a portable pixmap |
| lispmtopgm | Convert a Lisp machine bitmap file into PGM format |
| macptopbm | Convert a MacPaint file into a portable bitmap |
| mgrtopbm | Convert an MGR bitmap into a portable bitmap |
| mtvtoppm | Convert output from the MTV or PRT ray tracers into a portable pixmap |

| | |
|---|---|
| pbmclean | Flip isolated pixels in portable bitmap |
| pbmlife | Apply Conway's Rules of Life to a portable bitmap |
| pbmmake | Create a blank bitmap of a specified size |
| pbmmask | Create a mask bitmap from a regular bitmap |
| pbmpscale | Enlarge a portable bitmap with edge smoothing |
| pbmreduce | Read a portable bitmap and reduce it N times |
| pbmtext | Render text into a bitmap |
| pbmto10x | Convert a portable bitmap into Gemini 10X printer graphics |
| pbmto4425 | Display PBM images on an AT&T 4425 terminal |
| pbmtoascii | Convert a portable bitmap into ASCII graphics |
| pbmtoatk | Convert a portable bitmap to Andrew Toolkit raster object |
| pbmtobg | Convert a portable bitmap into BitGraph graphics |
| pbmtocmuwm | Convert a portable bitmap into a CMU window manager bitmap |
| pbmtoepsi | Convert a portable bitmap into an encapsulated PostScript |
| pbmtoepson | Convert a portable bitmap into Epson printer graphics |
| pbmtog3 | Convert a portable bitmap into a Group 3 fax file |
| pbmtogem | Convert a portable bitmap into a GEM IMG file |
| pbmtogo | Convert a portable bitmap into compressed GraphOn graphics |
| pbmtoicon | Convert a portable bitmap into a Sun icon |
| pbmtolj | Convert a portable bitmap into HP LaserJet format |
| pbmtoln03 | Convert portable bitmap to DEC LN03+ Sixel output |
| pbmtolps | Convert portable bitmap to PostScript |
| pbmtomacp | Convert a portable bitmap into a MacPaint file |
| pbmtomgr | Convert a portable bitmap into an MGR bitmap |
| pbmtopgm | Convert a portable bitmap to portable graymap by averaging areas |
| pbmtopi3 | Convert a portable bitmap into an Atari Degas .pi3 file |
| pbmtopk | Convert a portable bitmap into a packed (PK) format font |
| pbmtoplot | Convert a portable bitmap into a UNIX plot(5) file |
| pbmtoptx | Convert a portable bitmap into Printronix printer graphics |
| pbmtox10bm | Convert a portable bitmap into an X10 bitmap |
| pbmtoxbm | Convert a portable bitmap into an X11 bitmap |
| pbmtozinc | Convert a portable bitmap into a Zinc bitmap |
| pbmupc | Create a Universal Product Code bitmap |
| pcxtoppm | Convert a PCX file into a portable pixmap |
| pgmbentley | Bentleyize a portable graymap |
| pgmcrater | Create cratered terrain by fractal forgery |
| pgmedge | Edge-detect a portable graymap |
| pgmenhance | Edge-enhance a portable graymap |
| pgmhist | Print a histogram of the values in a portable graymap |
| pgmkernel | Generate a convolution kernel |
| pgmnoise | Create a graymap made up of white noise |
| pgmnorm | Normalize the contrast in a portable graymap |
| pgmoil | Turn a portable graymap into an oil painting |
| pgmramp | Generate a grayscale ramp |
| pgmtexture | Calculate textural features on a portable graymap |
| pgmtofs | Convert a portable graymap to Usenix FaceSaver format |

| | |
|---|---|
| pgmtolispm | Convert a portable graymap into Lisp machine format |
| pgmtopbm | Convert a portable graymap into a portable bitmap |
| pgmtoppm | Colorize a portable graymap into a portable pixmap |
| pgmtoybm | Convert a portable bitmap into a Bennet Yee "face" file |
| pi1toppm | Convert an Atari Degas PI1 into a portable pixmap |
| pi3topbm | Convert an Atari Degas PI3 file into a portable bitmap |
| picttoppm | Convert a Macintosh PICT file into a portable pixmap |
| pjtoppm | Convert an HP PaintJet file into a portable pixmap |
| pktopbm | Convert packed (PK) format font into portable bitmap(s) |
| pnmalias | Antialias a portable anymap |
| pnmarith | Perform arithmetic on two portable anymaps |
| pnmcat | Concatenate portable anymaps |
| pnmcomp | Composite two portable anymap files together |
| pnmconvol | General MxN convolution on a portable anymap |
| pnmcrop | Crop a portable anymap |
| pnmcut | Cut a rectangle out of a portable anymap |
| pnmdepth | Change the maxval in a portable anymap |
| pnmenlarge | Read a portable anymap and enlarge it N times |
| pnmfile | Describe a portable anymap |
| pnmflip | Perform one or more flip operations on a portable anymap |
| pnmgamma | Perform gamma correction on a portable anymap |
| pnmhistmap | Draw a histogram for a PGM or PPM file |
| pnmindex | Build a visual index of a bunch of anymaps |
| pnminvert | Invert a portable anymap |
| pnmmargin | Add a border to a portable anymap |
| pnmnlfilt | Nonlinear filters: smooth, alpha trim mean, optimal |
| pnmnoraw | Force a portable anymap into plain format |
| pnmpad | Add borders to portable anymap |
| pnmpaste | Paste a rectangle into a portable anymap |
| pnmrotate | Rotate a portable anymap by some angle |
| pnmscale | Scale a portable anymap |
| pnmshear | Shear a portable anymap by some angle |
| pnmsmooth | Smooth out an image |
| pnmtile | Replicate a portable anymap into a specified size |
| pnmtoddif | Convert a portable anymap to DDIF format |
| pnmtofits | Convert a portable anymap into FITS format |
| pnmtops | Convert portable anymap to PostScript |
| pnmtorast | Convert a portable pixmap into a Sun raster file |
| pnmtosgi | Convert a portable anymap to an SGI image file |
| pnmtosir | Convert a portable anymap into a Solitaire format |
| pnmtotiff | Convert a portable anymap into a TIFF file |
| pnmtoxwd | Convert a portable anymap into an X11 window dump |
| ppm3d | Convert two portable pixmap into a red/blue 3D glasses pixmap |
| ppmbrighten | Change an images Saturation and Value from an HSV map |
| ppmchange | Change all pixels of one color to another in a portable pixmap |
| ppmdim | Dim a portable pixmap down to total blackness |

| | |
|---|---|
| ppmdist | Simplistic grayscale assignment for machine generated, color images |
| ppmdither | Ordered dither for color images |
| ppmflash | Brighten a picture up to complete white-out |
| ppmforge | Fractal forgeries of clouds, planets, and starry skies |
| ppmhist | Print a histogram of a portable pixmap |
| ppmmake | Create a pixmap of a specified size and color |
| ppmmix | Blend together two portable pixmaps |
| ppmnorm | Normalize the contrast in a portable pixmap |
| ppmntsc | Make a portable pixmap look like it was taken from an American TV show |
| ppmpat | Make a pretty pixmap |
| ppmquant | Quantize the colors in a portable pixmap down to a specified number |
| ppmquantall | Run ppmquant on a bunch of files all at once, so they share a common colormap |
| ppmqvga | 8-plane quantization |
| ppmrelief | Run a Laplacian relief filter on a portable pixmap |
| ppmshift | Shift lines of a portable pixmap left or right by a random amount |
| ppmspread | Displace a portable pixmap's pixels by a random amount |
| ppmtoacad | Convert portable pixmap to AutoCAD database or slide |
| ppmtobmp | Convert a portable pixmap into a BMP file |
| ppmtogif | Convert a portable pixmap into a GIF file |
| ppmtoicr | Convert a portable pixmap into NCSA ICR format |
| ppmtoilbm | Convert a portable pixmap into an ILBM file |
| ppmtomap | Extract all colors from a portable pixmap |
| ppmtomitsu | Convert a portable pixmap to a Mitsubishi S340-10 file |
| ppmtopcx | Convert a portable pixmap into a PCX file |
| ppmtopgm | Convert a portable pixmap into a portable graymap |
| ppmtopi1 | Convert a portable pixmap into an Atari Degas PI1 file |
| ppmtopict | Convert a portable pixmap into a Macintosh PICT file |
| ppmtopj | Convert a portable pixmap to an HP PaintJet file |
| ppmtopjxl | Convert a portable pixmap into an HP PaintJet XL PCL file |
| ppmtopuzz | Convert a portable pixmap into an X11 "puzzle" file |
| ppmtorgb3 | Separate a portable pixmap into three portable graymaps |
| ppmtosixel | Convert a portable pixmap into DEC sixel format |
| ppmtotga | Convert portable pixmap into a TrueVision Targa file |
| ppmtouil | Convert a portable pixmap into a Motif UIL icon file |
| ppmtoxpm | Convert a portable pixmap into an X11 pixmap |
| ppmtoyuv | Convert a portable pixmap into an Abekas YUV file |
| ppmtoyuvsplit | Convert a portable pixmap into three subsampled raw YUV files |
| psidtopgm | Convert PostScript "image" data into a portable graymap |
| pstopnm | Convert a PostScript file into a portable anymap |
| qrttoppm | Convert output from the QRT ray tracer into a portable pixmap |
| rasttopnm | Convert a Sun raster file into a portable anymap |
| rawtopgm | Convert raw grayscale bytes into a portable graymap |
| rawtoppm | Convert raw RGB bytes into a portable pixmap |
| rgb3toppm | Combine three portable graymaps into one portable pixmap |
| sgitopnm | Convert an SGI image file into a portable anymap |
| sirtopnm | Convert a Solitaire file into a portable anymap |

| | |
|---|---|
| sldtoppm | Convert an AutoCAD slide file into a portable pixmap |
| spctoppm | Convert an Atari compressed Spectrum file into a portable pixmap |
| spottopgm | Convert SPOT satellite images to Portable Graymap format |
| sputoppm | Convert an Atari uncompressed Spectrum file into a portable pixmap |
| tgatoppm | Convert TrueVision Targa file into a portable pixmap |
| tifftopnm | Convert a TIFF file into a portable anymap |
| xbmtopbm | Convert an X11 or X10 bitmap into a portable bitmap |
| ximtoppm | Convert an XIM file into a portable pixmap |
| xpmtoppm | Convert an X11 pixmap into a portable pixmap |
| xvminitoppm | Convert an XV thumbnail picture to PPM |
| xwdtopnm | Convert an X11 or X10 window dump file into a portable anymap |
| ybmtopbm | Convert a Bennet Yee "face" file into a portable bitmap |
| yuvplittoppm | Convert a Y-, U- and V-file into a portable pixmap |
| yuvtoppm | Convert Abekas YUV bytes into a portable pixmap |
| zeisstopnm | Convert a Zeiss confocal file into a portable anymap |

## SEE ALSO

anytopnm(1), asciitopgm(1), atktopbm(1), bioradtopgm(1), bmptoppm(1), brushtopbm(1), cmuwmtopbm(1), fitstopnm(1), fstopgm(1), g3topbm(1), gemtopbm(1), giftopnm(1), gouldtoppm(1), hipstopgm(1), hpcdtoppm(1), icontopbm(1), ilbmtoppm(1), imgtoppm(1), lispmtopgm(1), macptopbm(1), mgrtopbm(1), mtvtoppm(1), pbmclean(1), pbmlife(1), pbmmake(1), pbmmask(1), pbmpscale(1), pbmreduce(1), pbmtext(1), pbmto10x(1), pbmto4425(1), pbmtoascii(1), pbmtoatk(1), pbmtobbnbg(1), pbmtocmuwm(1), pbmtoepsi(1), pbmtoepson(1), pbmtog3(1), pbmtogem(1), pbmtogo(1), pbmtoicon(1), pbmtolj(1), pbmtoln03(1), pbmtolps(1), pbmtomacp(1), pbmtomgr(1), pbmtopgm(1), pbmtopi3(1), pbmtopk(1), pbmtoplot(1), pbmtoptx(1), pbmtox10bm(1), pbmtoxbm(1), pbmtoybm(1), pbmtozinc(1), pbmupc(1), pcxtoppm(1), pgmbentley(1), pgmcrater(1), pgmedge(1), pgmenhance(1), pgmhist(1), pgmkernel(1), pgmnoise(1), pgmnorm(1), pgmoil(1), pgmramp(1), pgmtexture(1), pgmtofs(1), pgmtolispm(1), pgmtopbm(1), pgmtoppm(1), pi1toppm(1), pi3topbm(1), picttoppm(1), pjtoppm(1), pktopbm(1), pnmalias(1), pnmarith(1), pnmcat(1), pnmcomp(1), pnmconvol(1), pnmcrop(1), pnmcut(1), pnmdepth(1), pnmenlarge(1), pnmfile(1), pnmflip(1), pnmgamma(1), pnmhistmap(1), pnmindex(1), pnminvert(1), pnmmargin(1), pnmnlfilt(1), pnmnoraw(1), pnmpad(1), pnmpaste(1), pnmrotate(1), pnmscale(1), pnmshear(1), pnmsmooth(1), pnmtile(1), pnmtoddif(1), pnmtofits(1), pnmtops(1), pnmtorast(1), pnmtosgi(1), pnmtosir(1), pnmtotiff(1), pnmtoxwd(1), ppm3d(1), ppmbrighten(1), ppmchange(1), ppmdim(1), ppmdist(1), ppmdither(1), ppmflash(1), ppmforge(1), ppmhist(1), ppmmake(1), ppmmix(1), ppmnorm(1), ppmntsc(1), ppmpat(1), ppmquant(1), ppmquantall(1), ppmqvga(1), ppmrelief(1), ppmshift(1), ppmspread(1), ppmtoacad(1), ppmtobmp(1), ppmtogif(1), ppmtoicr(1), ppmtoilbm(1), ppmtomap(1), ppmtomitsu(1), ppmtopcx(1), ppmtopgm(1), ppmtopi1(1), ppmtopict(1), ppmtopj(1), ppmtopjxl(1), ppmtopuzz(1), ppmtorgb3(1), ppmtosixel(1), ppmtotga(1), ppmtouil(1), ppmtoxpm(1), ppmtoyuv(1), ppmtoyuvsplit(1), psidtopgm(1), pstopnm(1), qrttoppm(1), rasttopnm(1), rawtopgm(1), rawtoppm(1), rgb3toppm(1), sgitopnm(1), sirtopnm(1), sldtoppm(1), spctoppm(1), spottopgm(1), sputoppm(1), tgatoppm(1), tifftopnm(1), xbmtopbm(1), ximtoppm(1), xpmtoppm(1), xvminitoppm(1), xwdtopnm(1), nybmtopbm(1), yuvsplittoppm(1), yuvtoppm(1), zeisstopnm(1)

## AUTHORS

Many. See the individual manual pages.

# pbmlife

pbmlife—Apply Conway's Rules of Life to a portable bitmap

## SYNOPSIS

pbmlife [*pbmfile*]

## DESCRIPTION

pbmlife reads a portable bitmap as input, applies the Rules of Life to it for one generation, and produces a portable bitmap as output.

A white pixel in the image is interpreted as a live beastie, and a black pixel as an empty space.

## SEE ALSO

pbm(5)

## AUTHOR

Copyright © 1988, 1991 by Jef Poskanzer

*21 February 1991*

# pbmmake

pbmmake—Create a blank bitmap of a specified size

## SYNOPSIS

pbmmake [ -white¦-black¦-gray ] *width height*

## DESCRIPTION

pbmmake produces a portable bitmap of the specified width and height. The color defaults to white.

## OPTIONS

In addition to the usual -white and -black, this program implements -gray. This gives a simple 50 percent gray pattern with 1's and 0's alternating.

All flags can be abbreviated to their shortest unique prefix.

## SEE ALSO

pbm(5), ppmmake(1)

## AUTHOR

Copyright © 1989 by Jef Poskanzer

*22 February 1989*

# pbmmask

pbmmask—Create a mask bitmap from a regular bitmap

## SYNOPSIS

pbmmask [ -expand][*pbmfile*]

## DESCRIPTION

pbmmask reads a portable bitmap as input and creates a corresponding mask bitmap and writes it out.

The color to be interpreted as background is determined automatically. Regardless of which color is background, the mask will be white where the background is white and black where the figure is black.

This lets you do a masked paste like this, for objects with a black background:

```
pbmmask obj > objmask
pnmpaste < dest -and objmask <x><y>¦pnmpaste -or obj <x><y>
```

For objects with a white background, you can either invert them or add a step:

```
pbmmask obj > objmask
pnminvert objmask ¦ pnmpaste -and obj 0 0 > blackback
pnmpaste < dest -and objmask <x><y>¦pnmpaste -or blackback <x><y>
```

Note that this three-step version works for objects with black backgrounds, too, if you don't care about the wasted time.

You can also use masks with graymaps and pixmaps, using the pnmarith tool. For instance:

```
ppmtopgm obj.ppm ¦ pgmtopbm -threshold ¦ pbmmask > objmask.pbm
pnmarith -multiply dest.ppm objmask.pbm > t1.ppm
pnminvert objmask.pbm ¦ pnmarith -multiply obj.ppm - > t2.ppm
pnmarith -add t1.ppm t2.ppm
```

An interesting variation on this is to pipe the mask through the pnmsmooth script before using it. This makes the boundary between the two images less sharp.

## OPTIONS

-expand     Expands the mask by one pixel out from the image. This is useful if you want a little white border around your image. (A better solution might be to turn the pbmlife tool into a general cellular automaton tool...)

## SEE ALSO

pnmpaste(1), pnminvert(1), pbm(5), pnmarith(1), pnmsmooth(1)

## AUTHOR

Copyright © 1988 by Jef Poskanzer

*8 August 1989*

# pbmpscale

pbmpscale—Enlarge a portable bitmap with edge smoothing

## SYNOPSIS

pbmpscale N [ *pbmfile* ]

## DESCRIPTION

pbmpscale reads a portable bitmap as input and outputs a portable bitmap enlarged N times. Enlargement is done by pixel replication, with some additional smoothing of corners and edges.

## SEE ALSO

pnmenlarge(1), ppmscale(1), pbm(5)

## AUTHOR

Copyright © 1990 by Angus Duggan. Copyright © 1989 by Jef Poskanzer.

## NOTES

pbmpscale works best for enlargements of 2. Enlargements greater than 2 should be done by as many enlargements of 2 as possible, followed by an enlargement by the remaining factor.

# pbmreduce

pbmreduce—Read a portable bitmap and reduce it N times

## SYNOPSIS

pbmreduce [-floyd¦-fs¦-threshold ][-value *val*] N [*pbmfile*]

## DESCRIPTION

pbmreduce reads a portable bitmap as input, reduces it by a factor of *N*, and produces a portable bitmap as output.

pbmreduce duplicates a lot of the functionality of pgmtopbm; you could do something like pnmscale ¦ pgmtopbm, but pbmreduce is a lot faster.

pbmreduce can be used to "re-halftone" an image. Say you have a scanner that only produces black and white, not grayscale, and it does a terrible job of halftoning (most black-and-white scanners fit this description). One way to fix the halftoning is to scan at the highest possible resolution, say 300dpi, and then reduce by a factor of three or so using pbmreduce. You can even correct the brightness of an image, by using the -value flag.

## OPTIONS

By default, the halftoning after the reduction is done via boustrophedonic Floyd-Steinberg error diffusion; however, the -threshold flag can be used to specify simple thresholding. This gives better results when reducing line drawings.

The -value flag alters the thresholding value for all quantizations. It should be a real number between 0 and 1. Above 0.5 means darker images; below 0.5 means lighter.

All flags can be abbreviated to their shortest unique prefix.

## SEE ALSO

pnmenlarge(1), pnmscale(1), pgmtopbm(1), pbm(5)

## AUTHOR

Copyright © 1988 by Jef Poskanzer

*2 August 1989*

# pbmtext

pbmtext—Render text into a bitmap

## SYNOPSIS

pbmtext [-font *fontfile*][-builtin *fontname*][*text*]

## DESCRIPTION

pbmtext takes the specified text, either a single line from the command line or multiple lines from standard input, and renders it into a bitmap.

## OPTIONS

By default, pbmtext uses a built-in font called bdf (about a 10-point Times Roman font). You can use a fixed-width font by specifying -builtin fixed.

You can also specify your own font with the -font flag. The *fontfile* is either a BDF file from the X Window System or a PBM file.

If the `fontfile` is a PBM file, it is created in a very specific way. In your window system of choice, display the following text in the desired (fixed-width) font:

```
M ",/ˆ ['jpqy¦ M
/ !"#$%&'()*+ /
< ,-./01234567 <
> 89:;<=>?@ABC >
@ DEFGHIJKLMNO @
PQRSTUVWXYZ[
{ \]ˆ 'abcdefg {
} hijklmnopqrs }
¯ tuvwxyz{¦}¯¯
M ",/ˆ ['jpqy¦ M
```

Do a screen grab or window dump of that text, using for instance `xwd`, `xgrabsc`, or `screen-dump`. Convert the result into a PBM file. If necessary, use `pnmcut` to remove everything except the text. Finally, run it through `pnmcrop` to make sure the edges are right up against the text. `pbmtext` can figure out the sizes and spacings from that.

## SEE ALSO

pbm(5), pnmcut(1), pnmcrop(1)

## AUTHOR

Copyright© 1993 by Jef Poskanzer and George Phillips

*26 October 1993*


# pbmto10x

pbmto10x—Convert a portable bitmap into Gemini 10X printer graphics

## SYNOPSIS

pbmto10x [-h][*pbmfile*]

## DESCRIPTION

pbmto10x reads a portable bitmap as input and produces a file of Gemini 10X printer graphics as output. The 10X's printer codes are alleged to be similar to the Epson codes.

Note that there is no `10xtopbm` tool; this transformation is one-way.

## OPTIONS

The resolution is normally 60H by 72V. If the `-h` flag is specified, resolution is 120H by 144V. You may find it useful to rotate landscape images before printing.

## SEE ALSO

pbm(5)

## AUTHOR

Copyright © 1990 by Ken Yap1

*January 1990*

# pbmto4425

pbmto4425—Display PBM images on an AT&T 4425 terminal

## SYNOPSIS

pbmto4425 [*pbmfile*]

## DESCRIPTION

Pbmto4425 displays PBM format images on an AT&T 4425 ASCII terminal using that terminal's mosaic graphics character set. The program should also work with other VT100-like terminals with mosaic graphics character sets such as the C. Itoh CIT-101, but it has not yet been tested on terminals other than the 4425.

Pbmto4425 puts the terminal into 132-column mode to achieve the maximum resolution of the terminal. In this mode the terminal has a resolution of 264 columns by 69 rows. The pixels have an aspect ratio of 1:2.6; therefore, an image should be processed before being displayed in a manner such as this:

```
% pnmscale -xscale 2.6 pnmfile \
¦ pnmscale -xysize 264 69 \
¦ ppmtopgm \
¦ pgmtopbm \
¦ pbmto4425
```

## AUTHOR

Copyright © 1993 by Robert Perlberg

# pbmtoascii

pbmtoascii—Convert a portable bitmap into ASCII graphics

## SYNOPSIS

pbmtoascii [-1x2¦-2x4][*pbmfile*]

## DESCRIPTION

pbmtoascii reads a portable bitmap as input and produces a somewhat crude ASCII graphic as output.

Note that there is no asciitopbm tool; this transformation is one-way.

## OPTIONS

The -1x2 and -2x4 flags provide two alternate ways for the bits to get mapped to characters. With 1x2, the default, each character represents a group of 1 bit across by 2 bits down. With -2x4, each character represents 2 bits across by 4 bits down. With the 1x2 mode you can see the individual bits, so it's useful for previewing small bitmaps on a nongraphics terminal. The 2x4 mode lets you display larger bitmaps on a standard 80-column display, but it obscures bit-level details. 2x4 mode is also good for displaying graymaps. pnmscale -width 158 ¦ pgmnorm ¦ pgmtopbm -thresh should give good results.

## SEE ALSO

pbm(5)

## AUTHOR

Copyright © 1988, 1992 by Jef Poskanzer

*20 March 1992*

# pbmtoatk

pbmtoatk—Convert portable bitmap to Andrew Toolkit raster object

## SYNOPSIS

pbmtoatk [*pbmfile*]

## DESCRIPTION

pbmtoatk reads a portable bitmap as input and produces an Andrew Toolkit raster object as output.

## SEE ALSO

atktopbm(1), pbm(5)

## AUTHOR

Copyright © 1991 by Bill Janssen

*26 September 1991*

# pbmtobg

pbmtobg—Convert a portable bitmap into BitGraph graphics

## SYNOPSIS

pbmtobg [*rasterop*][*x y*]< *pbmfile*

## DESCRIPTION

pbmtobg reads a portable bitmap as input and produces BBN BitGraph terminal display pixel data (DPD) sequence as output.

The rasterop can be specified on the command line. If this is omitted, 3 (replace) will be used. A position in (x,y) coordinates can also be specified. If both are given, the rasterop comes first. The portable bitmap is always taken from the standard input.

Note that there is no bgtopbm tool.

## SEE ALSO

pbm(5)

## AUTHOR

Copyright © 1989 by Mike Parker

*16 May 1989*

# pbmtocmuwm

pbmtocmuwm—Convert a portable bitmap into a CMU window manager bitmap

## SYNOPSIS

pbmtocmuwm [*pbmfile*]

## DESCRIPTION

pbmtocmuwm reads a portable bitmap as input and produces a CMU window manager bitmap as output.

## SEE ALSO

cmuwmtopbm(1), pbm(5)

## AUTHOR

Copyright © 1989 by Jef Poskanzer

*15 April 1989*

# pbmtoepsi

pbmtoepsi—Convert a portable bitmap into an encapsulated PostScript-style preview bitmap

## SYNOPSIS

pbmtoepsi [-bbonly][*pbmfile*]

## DESCRIPTION

pbmtoepsi reads a portable bitmap as input and produces an encapsulated PostScript-style bitmap as output. The output is not a standalone PostScript file; it is only a preview bitmap, which can be included in an encapsulated PostScript file. Note that there is no epsitopbm tool; this transformation is one-way.

This utility is a part of the pstoepsi tool by Doug Crabill (dgc@cs.purdue.edu).

## OPTIONS

-bbonly    Only create a boundary box, don't fill it with the image.

## SEE ALSO

pbm(5), pnmtops(1), psidtopgm(1)

## AUTHOR

Copyright © 1988 by Jef Poskanzer, modified by Doug Crabill 1992

*1992*

# pbmtoepson

pbmtoepson—Convert a portable bitmap into Epson printer graphics

## SYNOPSIS

pbmtoepson [*pbmfile*]

## DESCRIPTION

pbmtoepson reads a portable bitmap as input and produces a file of Epson printer graphics as output.

Note that there is no epsontopbm tool; this transformation is one-way.

## SEE ALSO

pbm(5)

## AUTHOR

Copyright © 1991 by John Tiller (tiller@galois.msfc.nasa.gov) and Jef Poskanzer

*4 January 1991*

# pbmtog3

pbmtog3—Convert a portable bitmap into a Group 3 fax file

## SYNOPSIS

pbmtog3 [*pbmfile*]

## DESCRIPTION

pbmtog3 reads a portable bitmap as output and produces a Group 3 fax file as input.

## REFERENCES

The standard for Group 3 fax is defined in CCITT Recommendation T.4.

## BUGS

Probably.

## SEE ALSO

g3topbm(1), pbm(5)

## AUTHOR

Copyright © 1989 by Paul Haeberli (<paul@manray.sgi.com>)

*2 October 1989*

# pbmtogem

pbmtogem—Convert a portable bitmap into a GEM IMG file

## SYNOPSIS

pbmtogem [*pbmfile*]

## DESCRIPTION

pbmtogem reads a portable bitmap as input and produces a compressed GEM IMG file as output.

## BUGS

pbmtogem does not support compression of repeated lines.

## SEE ALSO

gemtopbm(1), pbm(5)

## AUTHORS

Copyright © 1988 by David Beckemeyer and Jef Poskanzer

*11 July 1992*

# pbmtogo

pbmtogo—Convert a portable bitmap into compressed GraphOn graphics

## SYNOPSIS

pbmtogo [*pbmfile*]

## DESCRIPTION

`pbmtogo` reads a portable bitmap as input and produces 2D compressed GraphOn graphics as output. Be sure to set up your GraphOn with the following modes: 8 bits/no parity; obeys no XON/XOFF; NULs are accepted. These are all on the Comm menu. Also, remember to turn off tty post processing. Note that there is no `gotopbm` tool.

## SEE ALSO

pbm(5)

## AUTHORS

Copyright © 1988, 1989 by Jef Poskanzer, Michael Haberler, and Bo Thide

*24 November 1989*

# pbmtoicon

pbmtoicon—Convert a portable bitmap into a Sun icon

## SYNOPSIS

pbmtoicon [*pbmfile*]

## DESCRIPTION

`pbmtoicon` reads a portable bitmap as input and produces a Sun icon as output.

## SEE ALSO

icontopbm(1), pbm(5)

## AUTHOR

Copyright © 1988 by Jef Poskanzer

*31 August 1988*

# pbmtolj

pbmtolj—Convert a portable bitmap into HP LaserJet format

## SYNOPSIS

pbmtolj [-resolution *N*][-float][-noreset][*pbmfile*]

## DESCRIPTION

`pbmtolj` reads a portable bitmap as input and produces HP LaserJet data as output.

Note that there is no `ljtopbm` tool.

## OPTIONS

| | |
|---|---|
| -resolution | Specifies the resolution of the output device, in dpi. Typical values are 75, 100, 150, 300. The default is 75. |
| -float | Suppresses positioning information. The default is to write the sequence ESC & 1 0 E to the output file. |
| -noreset | Prevents `pbmtolj` from writing the reset sequences to the beginning and end of the output file. |

All flags can be abbreviated to their shortest unique prefix.

## SEE ALSO

pbm(5)

## AUTHORS

Copyright © 1988 by Jef Poskanzer and Michael Haberler. `-float` and `-noreset` options added by Wim Lewis

*29 August 1988*

# pbmtoln03

pbmtoln03—Convert portable bitmap to DEC LN03+ Sixel output

## SYNOPSIS

`pbmtoln03 [-rltbf]` *pbmfile*

## DESCRIPTION

pbmtoln03 reads a portable bitmap as input and produces a DEC LN03+ Sixel output file.

## OPTIONS

-l *nn*     Use *nn* as value for left margin (default `0`).

-r *nn*     Use *nn* as value for right margin (default `2400`).

-t *nn*     Use *nn* as value for top margin (default `0`).

-b *nn*     Use *nn* as value for bottom margin (default `3400`).

-f *nn*     Use *nn* as value for form length (default `3400`).

## SEE ALSO

pbm(5)

## AUTHOR

Tim Cook, 26 February 1992

*7 May 1993*

# pbmtolps

pbmtolps—Convert a portable bitmap to PostScript

## SYNOPSIS

`pbmtolps [ -dpi n ] [` *pbmfile* `]`

## DESCRIPTION

pbmtolps reads a portable bitmap as input, and outputs PostScript. The output PostScript uses lines instead of the image operator to generate a (device-dependent) picture that will be imaged much faster.

The PostScript path length is constrained to be less that 1000 points so that no limits are overrun on the Apple Laserwriter and (presumably) no other printers.

## SEE ALSO

pgmtops(1), ppmtops(1), pbm(5)

## AUTHOR

George Phillips (<phillips@cs.ubc.ca>)

# pbmtomacp

pbmtomacp—Convert a portable bitmap into a MacPaint file

## SYNOPSIS

pbmtomacp [-l *left*][-r *right*][-b *bottom*][-t *top*][*pbmfile*]

## DESCRIPTION

pbmtomacp reads a portable bitmap as input. If no input file is given, standard input is assumed. Produces a MacPaint file as output.

The generated file is only the data fork of a picture. You will need a program such as mcvert to generate a Macbinary or a BinHex file that contains the necessary information to identify the file as a PNTG file to MacOS.

## OPTIONS

*Left*, *right*, *bottom*, and *top* let you define a square into the PBM file, which must be converted. Default is the whole file. If the file is too large for a MacPaint file, the bitmap is cut to fit from (*left*, *top*).

## BUGS

The source code contains comments in a language other than English.

## SEE ALSO

ppmtopict(1), macptopbm(1), pbm(5), mcvert(1)

## AUTHOR

Copyright © 1988 by Douwe van der Schaaf (...!mcvax!uvapsy!vdschaaf)

*31 August 1988*

# pbmtomgr

pbmtomgr—Convert a portable bitmap into an MGR bitmap

## SYNOPSIS

pbmtomgr [*pbmfile*]

## DESCRIPTION

pbmtomgr reads a portable bitmap as input and produces an MGR bitmap as output.

## SEE ALSO

mgrtopbm(1), pbm(5)

## AUTHOR

Copyright © 1989 by Jef Poskanzer

*24 January 1989*

# pbmtopgm

pbmtopgm—Convert portable bitmap to portable graymap by averaging areas

## SYNOPSIS

pbmtopgm <width><height> [*pbmfile*]

## DESCRIPTION

pbmtopgm reads a portable bitmap as input and outputs a portable graymap created by averaging the number of pixels within a sample area of width by height around each point. pbmtopgm is similar to a special case of ppmconvol. A ppmsmooth step may be needed after pbmtopgm.

pbmtopgm has the effect of antialiasing bitmaps that contain distinct line features.

## SEE ALSO

pbm(5)

## AUTHOR

Copyright © 1990 by Angus Duggan. Copyright © 1989 by Jef Poskanzer.

## NOTES

pbmtopgm works best with odd sample widths and heights.

# pbmtopi3

pbmtopi3—Convert a portable bitmap into an Atari Degas PI3 file

## SYNOPSIS

pbmtopi3 [pbmfile]

## DESCRIPTION

pbmtopi3 reads a portable bitmap as input and produces an Atari Degas PI3 file as output.

## SEE ALSO

pi3topbm(1), pbm(5), ppmtopi1(1), pi1toppm(1)

## AUTHOR

*Copyright © 1988 by David Beckemeyer (*bdt!david*) and Jef Poskanzer.*

*11 March 1990*

# pbmtopk

pbmtopk—Convert a portable bitmap into a packed (PK) format font

## SYNOPSIS

pbmtopk pkfile[.pk] tfmfile[.tfm] resolution [-s designsize] [-p num param...]
[-C cod-ingscheme] [-F family] [-f optfile] [-c num] [-W width] [-H height]
[-D depth] [-I ital] [-h horiz] [-v vert] [-x xoff] [-y yoff] [*pbmfile*]...

## DESCRIPTION

pbmtopk reads portable bitmaps as input and produces a packed (PK) font file and a TFM (TeX font metric) file as output. The resolution parameter indicates the resolution of the font, in dots per inch. If the filename - is used for any of the filenames, the standard input stream (or standard output, where appropriate) will be used.

## OPTIONS

| | |
|---|---|
| -s designsize | Sets the design size of the font, in TeX's points (72.27 points to the inch). The default design size is 1. The TFM parameters are given as multiples of the design size. |
| -p num param... | Sets the first num font parameters for the font. The first seven parameters are the slant, interword spacing, interword space stretchability, interword space shrinkability, x-height, quad width, and post-sentence extra space of the font. Math and symbol fonts may have more parameters; see *The TeXbook* for a list of these. Reasonable default values are chosen for parameters that are not specified. |
| -C codingscheme | Sets the coding scheme comment in the TFM file. |
| -F family | Sets the font family comment in the TFM file. |
| -f optfile | Reads the file optfile, which should contain a line of the form: |

```
filename xoff yoff horiz vert width height depth ital
```

The PBM files specified by the filename parameters are inserted consecutively in the font with the specified attributes. If any of the attributes are omitted, or replaced with *, a default value will be calculated from the size of the bitmap. The settings of the -W, -H, -D, -I, -h, -v, -x, and -y options do not affect characters created in this way. The character number can be changed by including a line starting with =, followed by the new number. Lines beginning with % or # are ignored.

| | |
|---|---|
| -c num | Sets the character number of the next bitmap encountered to num. |
| -W width | Sets the TFM width of the next character to width (in design size multiples). |
| -H height | Sets the TFM height of the next character to height (in design size multiples). |
| -D depth | Sets the TFM depth of the next character to depth (in design size multiples). |
| -I ital | Sets the italic correction of the next character to ital (in design size multiples). |
| -h horiz | Sets the horizontal escapement of the next character to horiz (in pixels). |
| -v vert | Sets the vertical escapement of the next character to vert (in pixels). |
| -x xoff | Sets the horizontal offset of the next character to xoff (in pixels). |
| -y yoff | Sets the vertical offset of the next character to yoff (in pixels, from the top row). |

## SEE ALSO

pktopbm(1), pbm(5)

## AUTHOR

Adapted from Tom Rokicki's pxtopk by Angus Duggan (ajcd@dcs.ed.ac.uk).

*6 August 1990*

# pbmtoplot

pbmtoplot—Convert a portable bitmap into a UNIX plot(5) file

## SYNOPSIS

pbmtoplot [*pbmfile*]

## DESCRIPTION

pbmtoplot reads a portable bitmap as input and produces a UNIX plot file.

Note that there is no plottopbm tool; this transformation is one way.

## SEE ALSO

pbm(5), plot(5)

## AUTHOR

Copyright © 1990 by Arthur David Olson.

*1 September 1990*

# pbmtoptx

pbmtoptx—Convert a portable bitmap into Printronix printer graphics

## SYNOPSIS

pbmtoptx [*pbmfile*]

## DESCRIPTION

pbmtoptx reads a portable bitmap as input and produces a file of Printronix printer graphics as output.

Note that there is no ptxtopbm tool; this transformation is one-way.

## SEE ALSO

pbm(5)

## AUTHOR

Copyright© 1988 by Jef Poskanzer

*31 August 1988*

# pbmtox10bm

pbmtox10bm—Convert a portable bitmap into an X10 bitmap

## SYNOPSIS

pbmtox10bm [*pbmfile*]

## DESCRIPTION

pbmtox10bm reads a portable bitmap as input and produces an X10 bitmap as output. This older format is maintained for compatibility.

Note that there is no x10bmtopbm tool because xbmtopbm can read both X11 and X10 bitmaps.

## SEE ALSO

pbmtoxbm(1), xbmtopbm(1), pbm(5)

## AUTHOR

Copyright© 1988 by Jef Poskanzer.

*31 August 1988*

# pbmtoxbm

pbmtoxbm—Convert a portable bitmap into an X11 bitmap

## SYNOPSIS

pbmtoxbm [*pbmfile*]

## DESCRIPTION

pbmtoxbm reads a portable bitmap as input and produces an X11 bitmap as output.

## SEE ALSO

pbmtox10bm(1), xbmtopbm(1), pbm(5)

## AUTHOR

Copyright © 1988 by Jef Poskanzer.

*31 August 1988*

# pgmtoybm

pgmtoybm—Convert a portable bitmap into a Bennet Yee "face" file

## SYNOPSIS

pbmtoybm [*pbmfile*]

## DESCRIPTION

pgmtoybm reads a portable bitmap as input and produces as output a file acceptable to the face and xbm programs by Bennet Yee (bsy+@cs.cmu.edu).

## SEE ALSO

ybmtopbm(1), pbm(5), face(1), face(5), xbm(1)

## AUTHORS

Copyright © 1991 by Jamie Zawinski and Jef Poskanzer.

*6 March 1990*

# pbmtozinc

pbmtozinc—Convert a portable bitmap into a Zinc bitmap

## SYNOPSIS

pbmtozinc [*pbmfile*]

## DESCRIPTION

pbmtozinc reads a portable bitmap as input and produces a bitmap in the format used by the Zinc Interface Library (ZIL) version 1.0 as output.

## SEE ALSO

pbm(5)

## AUTHORS

Copyright © 1988 by James Darrell McCauley (jdm5548@diamond.tamu.edu) and Jef Poskanzer.

*2 November 1990*

# pbmupc

pbmupc—Create a Universal Product Code bitmap

## SYNOPSIS

pbmupc [-s1¦-s2] type manufac product

## DESCRIPTION

pbmupc generates a Universal Product Code symbol. The three arguments are: a one-digit product type, a five-digit manufacturer code, and a five-digit product code. For example, 0 72890 00011 is the code for Heineken.

As presently configured, pbmupc produces a bitmap 230 bits wide and 175 bits high. The size can be altered by changing the defines at the beginning of the program, or by running the output through pnmenlarge or pnmscale.

## OPTIONS

The -s1 and -s2 flags select the style of UPC to generate. The default, -s1, looks more or less like this:

```
|||||||||||||||||
|||||||||||||||||
|||||||||||||||||
|||||||||||||||||
|||||||||||||||||
0¦¦12345¦¦67890¦¦5
```

The other style, -s2, puts the product type digit higher up, and doesn't display the checksum digit:

```
|||||||||||||||||
|||||||||||||||||
|||||||||||||||||
0¦¦¦¦¦¦¦¦¦¦¦¦¦¦¦¦
|||||||||||||||||
¦¦12345¦¦67890¦¦
```

## SEE ALSO

pbm(5)

## AUTHOR

Copyright © 1989 by Jef Poskanzer.

*14 March 1989*

# pcxtoppm

pcxtoppm—Convert a PCX file into a portable pixmap

## SYNOPSIS

pcxtoppm[pcxfile]

## DESCRIPTION

pcxtoppm reads a PCX file as input and produces a portable pixmap as output.

## SEE ALSO

ppmtopcx(1), ppm(5)

## AUTHOR

Copyright © 1990 by Michael Davidson.

*9 April 1990*

# pfbtops

pfbtops—Translate a PostScript font in PFB format to ASCII

## SYNOPSIS

pfbtops [ *pfb_file* ]

## DESCRIPTION

pfbtops translates a PostScript font in PFB format to ASCII. If pfb_file is omitted, the PFB file will be read from the standard input. The ASCII format PostScript font will be written on the standard output. PostScript fonts for MS-DOS are normally supplied in PFB format.

The resulting ASCII format PostScript font can be used with groff. It must first be listed in /usr/lib/groff/font/devps/download.

## SEE ALSO

grops(1)

*Groff Version 1.09, 6 August 1992*

# pgmbentley

pgmbentley—Bentleyize a portable graymap

## SYNOPSIS

pgmbentley [pgmfile]

## DESCRIPTION

pgmbentley reads a portable graymap as input, performs the Bentley Effect, and writes a portable graymap as output.

The Bentley Effect is described in *Beyond Photography* by Holzmann, Chapter 4, photo 4. It's a vertical smearing based on brightness.

## SEE ALSO

pgmoil(1), ppmrelief(1), pgm(5)

## AUTHOR

Copyright © 1990 by Wilson Bent (whb@hoh-2.att.com).

*11 January 1991*

# pgmcrater

pgmcrater—Create cratered terrain by fractal forgery

## SYNOPSIS

pgmcrater [ -number *n*][ -height¦ -ysize *s*][ -width¦ -xsize *s*][ -gamma *g*]

## DESCRIPTION

pgmcrater creates a portable graymap that mimics cratered terrain. The graymap is created by simulating the impact of a given number of craters with random position and size, then rendering the resulting terrain elevations based on a light source shining from one side of the screen. The size distribution of the craters is based on a power law that results in many more small craters than large ones. The number of craters of a given size varies as the reciprocal of the area as described on pages 31 and 32 of *The Science Of Fractal Images,* edited by H.O. Peitgen and D. Saupe (New York: Springer-Verlag, 1988). Cratered bodies in the solar system are observed to obey this relationship. The formula used to obtain crater radii governed by this law from a uniformly distributed pseudorandom sequence was developed by Rudy Rucker.

High resolution images with large numbers of craters often benefit from being piped through pnmsmooth. The averaging performed by this process eliminates some of the jagged pixels and lends a mellow "telescopic image" feel to the overall picture.

## OPTIONS

-number *n*  Causes *n* craters to be generated. If no -number specification is given, 50,000 craters will be generated. Don't expect to see them all! For every large crater, there are many, many more tiny ones that tend simply to erode the landscape. In general, the more craters you specify, the more realistic the result; ideally, you want the entire terrain to have been extensively turned over again and again by cratering. High-resolution images containing five to ten million craters are stunning but take quite a while to create.

-height *height*    Sets the height of the generated image to *height* pixels. The default height is 256 pixels.

-width *width*    Sets the width of the generated image to *width* pixels. The default width is 256 pixels.

-xsize *width*    Sets the width of the generated image to *width* pixels. The default width is 256 pixels.

-ysize *height*    Sets the height of the generated image to *height* pixels. The default height is 256 pixels.

-gamma *factor*    The specified factor is used to gamma correct the graymap in the same manner as performed by pnmgamma. The default value is 1.0, which results in a medium contrast image. Values larger than 1 lighten the image and reduce contrast, while values less than 1 darken the image, increasing contrast.

All flags can be abbreviated to their shortest unique prefix.

## BUGS

The -gamma option isn't really necessary because you can achieve the same effect by piping the output from pgmcrater through pnmgamma. However, pgmcrater performs an internal gamma map anyway in the process of rendering the elevation array into a graymap, so there's no additional overhead in allowing a user-specified gamma.

Real craters have two distinct morphologies. pgmcrater simulates only small craters, which are hemispherical in shape (regardless of the incidence angle of the impacting body, as long as the velocity is sufficiently high). Large craters, such as Copernicus and Tycho on the moon, have a "walled plain" shape with a cross-section more like:

```
/\/\
____/ \____  /\____/ \____
```

Larger craters should really use this profile, including the central peak, and totally obliterate the preexisting terrain.

## SEE ALSO

pgm(5), pnmgamma(1), pnmsmooth(1)

## AUTHOR

John Walker
Autodesk SA Avenue des Champs-Montants 14b
CH-2074 MARIN
Suisse/Schweiz/Svizzera/Svizra/Switzerland

Usenet:  kelvin@Autodesk.com
Fax:     038/33 88 15
Voice:   038/33 76 33

PLUGWARE! If you like this kind of stuff, you may also enjoy James Gleick's "Chaos—The Software" for MS-DOS, available for $59.95 from your local software store or directly from Autodesk, Inc., Attn: Science Series, 2320 Marinship Way, Sausalito, CA 94965, USA. Telephone: 800-688-2344 toll-free or, outside the U.S. (415) 332-2344 Ext 4886. Fax: 415-289-4718. "Chaos—The Software" includes a more comprehensive fractal forgery generator that creates three-dimensional landscapes as well as clouds and planets, plus five more modules that explore other aspects of Chaos. The user guide of more than 200 pages includes an introduction by James Gleick and detailed explanations by Rudy Rucker of the mathematics and algorithms used by each program.

*15 October 1991*

# pgmedge

pgmedge—Edge detect a portable graymap

## SYNOPSIS

pgmedge [pgmfile]

## DESCRIPTION

pgmedge reads a portable graymap as input, outlines the edges, and writes a portable graymap as output. Piping the result through pgmtopbm -threshold and playing with the threshold value will give a bitmap of the edges.

The edge detection technique used is to take the Pythagorean sum of two Sobel gradient operators at 90 degrees to each other. For more details see *Digital Image Processing* by Gonzalez and Wintz, Chapter 7.

## SEE ALSO

pgmenhance(1), pgmtopbm(1), pgm(5), pbm(5)

## AUTHOR

*4 February 1990*

# pgmenhance

pgmenhance—Edge enhance a portable graymap

## SYNOPSIS

pgmenhance [-N][pgmfile]

## DESCRIPTION

pgmenhance reads a portable graymap as input, enhances the edges, and writes a portable graymap as output.

The edge enhancing technique is taken from Philip R. Thompson's xim program, which took it from section 6 of *Digital Halftones by Dot Diffusion*, D. E. Knuth, *ACM Transaction on Graphics* Vol. 6, No. 4, October 1987, which in turn got it from two 1976 papers by J. F. Jarvis et. al.

## OPTIONS

The optional -N flag should be a digit from 1 to 9. 1 is the lowest level of enhancement, 9 is the highest; the default is 9.

## SEE ALSO

pgmedge(1), pgm(5), pbm(5)

## AUTHOR

Copyright © 1989 by Jef Poskanzer.

*13 January 1989*


# pgmhist

pgmhist—Print a histogram of the values in a portable graymap

## SYNOPSIS

pgmhist [*pgmfile*]

## DESCRIPTION

pgmhist reads a portable graymap as input and prints a histogram of the gray values.

## SEE ALSO

pgmnorm(1), pgm(5), ppmhist(1)

## AUTHOR

Copyright © 1989 by Jef Poskanzer

*28 February 1989*


# pgmkernel

pgmkernel—Generate a convolution kernel

## SYNOPSIS

pgmkernel [ –weight *w* ] *width* [ *height* ]

## DESCRIPTION

pgmkernel generates a portable graymap array of size *width* x *height* (or *width* x *width* if *height* is not specified) to be used as a convolution file by pnmconvol. The data in the convolution array K are computed according to the formula:

$$K(i,j) = \frac{1}{1+w\sqrt{(i\text{-width/2})^2 + (j\text{-height/2})^2}}$$

where *w* is a coefficient specified via the -weight flag, and *width* and *height* are the X and Y filter sizes.

The output PGM file is always written out in ASCII format.

## OPTIONS

The optional -weight flag should be a real number greater than -1. The default value is 6.0.

## BUGS

The computation time is proportional to width * height. This increases rapidly with the increase of the kernel size. A better approach could be to use a FFT in these cases.

## SEE ALSO

pnmconvol(1), pnmsmooth(1)

## AUTHOR

Alberto Accomazzi (alberto@cfa.harvard.edu)

*10 December 1992*

# pgmnoise

pgmnoise—Create a graymap made up of white noise

## SYNOPSIS

pgmnoise width height

## DESCRIPTION

pgmnoise creates a portable graymap that is made up of random pixels with gray values in the range of 0 to PGM_MAXMAXVAL (depends on the compilation, either 255 or 65535). The graymap has a size of width * height pixels.

## SEE ALSO

pgm(5)

## AUTHOR

Copyright © 1993 by Frank Neumann

*16 November 1993*

# pgmnorm

pgmnorm—Normalize the contrast in a portable graymap

## SYNOPSIS

pgmnorm[ -bpercent *N* ¦ -bvalue *N*][ -wpercent *N* ¦ -wvalue *N*][*pgmfile*]

## DESCRIPTION

pgmnorm reads a portable graymap as input; normalizes the contrast by forcing the lightest pixels to white, the darkest pixels to black, and linearly rescaling the ones in between; and produces a portable graymap as output.

## OPTIONS

By default, the darkest two percent of all pixels are mapped to black, and the lightest one percent are mapped to white. You can override these percentages by using the -bpercent and -wpercent flags, or you can specify the exact pixel values to be mapped by using the `-bvalue` and `-wvalue` flags. Appropriate numbers for the flags can be gotten from the `pgmhist` tool. If you just want to enhance the contrast, then choose values at elbows in the histogram; for example, if value `29` represents 3 percent of the image but value `30` represents 20 percent, choose `30` for `bvalue`. If you want to lighten the image, then set `bvalue` to `0` and just fiddle with `wvalue`; similarly, to darken the image, set `wvalue` to `maxval` and play with `bvalue`.

All flags can be abbreviated to their shortest unique prefix.

## SEE ALSO

pgmhist(1), ppmnorm(1), pgm(5)

## AUTHOR

Partially based on the `fbnorm` filter in Michael Mauldin's "Fuzzy Pixmap" package.

Copyright© 1989 by Jef Poskanzer.

*28 February 1989*

# pgmoil

pgmoil—Turn a portable graymap into an oil painting

## SYNOPSIS

pgmoil [ -n *N* ][*pgmfile*]

## DESCRIPTION

pgmoil reads a portable graymap as input, does an "oil transfer," and writes a portable graymap as output.

The oil transfer is described in *Beyond Photography* by Holzmann, Chapter 4, photo 7. It's a sort of localized smearing.

## OPTIONS

The optional `-n` flag controls the size of the area smeared. The default value is `3`.

## BUGS

Takes a long time to run.

## SEE ALSO

pgmbentley(1), ppmrelief(1), pgm(5)

## AUTHOR

Copyright© 1990 by Wilson Bent (`whb@hoh-2.att.com`).

*11 January 1991*

# pgmramp

pgmramp—Generate a grayscale ramp

## SYNOPSIS

pgmramp -lr¦-tb ¦ -rectangle¦-ellipse width height

## DESCRIPTION

pgmramp generates a graymap of the specified size containing a black-to-white ramp. These ramps are useful for multiplying with other images, using the `pnmarith` tool.

## OPTIONS

| | |
|---|---|
| `-lr` | A left to right ramp |
| `-tb` | A top to bottom ramp |
| `-rectangle` | A rectangular ramp |
| `-ellipse` | An elliptical ramp |

All flags can be abbreviated to their shortest unique prefix.

## SEE ALSO

`pnmarith(1)`, `pgm(5)`

## AUTHOR

Copyright © 1989 by Jef Poskanzer.

*24 November 1989*

# pgmtexture

`pgmtexture`—Calculate textural features on a portable graymap

## SYNOPSIS

`pgmtexture [-d d][pgmfile]`

## DESCRIPTION

`pgmtexture` reads a portable graymap as input. Calculates textural features based on spatial dependence matrices at 0, 45, 90, and 135 degrees for a distance `d` (default = `1`). Textural features include

| | |
|---|---|
| (1) | Angular Second Moment |
| (2) | Contrast |
| (3) | Correlation |
| (4) | Variance |
| (5) | Inverse Difference Moment |
| (6) | Sum Average |
| (7) | Sum Variance |
| (8) | Sum Entropy |
| (9) | Entropy |
| (10) | Difference Variance |
| (11) | Difference Entropy |
| (12, 13) | Information Measures of Correlation |
| (14) | Maximal Correlation Coefficient |

Algorithm taken from "Textural Features for Image Classification," *IEEE Transactions on Systems, Man, and Cybertinetics*, R.M. Haralick, K. Shanmugam, and I. Dinstein, 1973. SMC-3(6):610–621.

## BUGS

The program can run incredibly slowly for large images (larger than 64×64) and command-line options are limited. The method for finding the maximal correlation coefficient, which requires finding the second largest `eigenvalue` of a matrix Q, does not always converge.

## REFERENCES

*IEEE Transactions on Systems, Man, and Cybertinetics*, SMC-3(6):610–621.

## SEE ALSO

pgm(5), pnmcut(1)

## AUTHOR

Copyright © 1991 by Texas Agricultural Experiment Station, employer-for-hire of James Darrell McCauley.

*22 August 1991*

# pgmtofs

pgmtofs—Convert portable graymap to Usenix FaceSaver format

## SYNOPSIS

pgmtofs [*pgmfile*]

## DESCRIPTION

pgmtofs reads a portable graymap as input. Produces Usenix FaceSaver format as output.

FaceSaver is a registered trademark of Metron Computerware Ltd. of Oakland, CA.

## SEE ALSO

fstopgm(1), pgm(5)

## AUTHOR

Copyright© 1991 by Jef Poskanzer.

*18 May 1990*

# pgmtolispm

pgmtolispm—Convert a portable graymap into Lisp machine format

## SYNOPSIS

pgmtolispm [pgmfile]

## DESCRIPTION

pgmtolispm reads a portable graymap as input and produces a Lisp machine bitmap as output.

This is the file format read by the tv:read-bit-array-file function on TI Explorer and Symbolics Lisp machines.

Given a PGM (instead of a PBM), a multiplane image will be output. This is probably not useful unless you have a color Lisp machine.

Multiplane bitmaps on Lisp machines are color; but the lispm image file format does not include a colormap, so it must be treated as a graymap instead. This is unfortunate.

## SEE ALSO

lispmtopgm(1), pgm(5)

## BUGS

Output width is always rounded up to the nearest multiple of 32; this might not always be what you want, but it probably is (arrays that are not modulo 32 cannot be passed to the lispm BITBLT function, and thus cannot easily be displayed on the screen).

No color.

## AUTHOR

Copyright © 1991 by Jamie Zawinski and Jef Poskanzer.

*6 March 1990*

# pgmtopbm

pgmtopbm—Convert a portable graymap into a portable bitmap

## SYNOPSIS

```
pgmtopbm [-floyd¦-fs¦-threshold ¦-hilbert ¦-dither8¦-d8¦-cluster3
¦-c3¦-cluster4¦-c4 ¦-cluster8¦-c8][-value val][-clump size][pgmfile]
```

## DESCRIPTION

pgmtopbm reads a portable graymap as input and produces a portable bitmap as output.

Note that there is no pbmtopgm converter because any pgm program can read PBM files automagically.

## OPTIONS

The default quantization method is boustrophedonic Floyd-Steinberg error diffusion (-floyd or -fs). Also available are simple thresholding (-threshold); Bayer's ordered dither (-dither8) with a 16×16 matrix; and three different sizes of 45-degree clustered-dot dither (-cluster3, -cluster4, -cluster8). A space-filling curve halftoning method using the Hilbert curve is also available. (-hilbert).

Floyd-Steinberg will almost always give the best looking results; however, looking good is not always what you want. For instance, thresholding can be used in a pipeline with the pnmconvol tool, for tasks like edge and peak detection. And clustered-dot dithering gives a newspaper-like look, a useful special effect. The -value flag alters the thresholding value for Floyd-Steinberg and simple thresholding. It should be a real number between 0 and 1. Above 0.5 means darker images; below 0.5 means lighter.

The Hilbert curve method is useful for processing images before display on devices that do not render individual pixels distinctly (like laser printers). This dithering method can give better results than the dithering usually done by the laser printers themselves. The -clump flag alters the number of pixels in a clump. This is usually an integer between 2 and 100 (default 5). Smaller clump sizes smear the image less and are less grainy, but seem to loose some grayscale linearity. Typically, a PGM image will have to be scaled to fit on a laser printer page (2400 × 3000 pixels for an A4 300dpi page), and then dithered to a PBM image before being converted to a PostScript file. A printing pipeline might look something like this:

```
pnmscale -xysize 2400 3000 image.pgm ¦ pgmtopbm -hil ¦ pnmtops -scale 0.25 image.ps
```

All flags can be abbreviated to their shortest unique prefix.

## REFERENCES

The only reference you need for this stuff is *Digital Halftoning* by Robert Ulichney, MIT Press, ISBN 0-262-21009-6.

The Hilbert curve space filling method is taken from "Digital Halftoning with Space Filling Curves" by Luiz Velho, *Computer Graphics* Volume 25, Number 4, proceedings of SIGRAPH '91, page 81. ISBN 0-89791-436-8

## SEE ALSO

pbmreduce(1), pgm(5), pbm(5), pnmconvol(1), pnmscale(1), pnmtops(1)

## AUTHOR

Copyright © 1989 by Jef Poskanzer.

*26 July 1988*

# pgmtoppm

pgmtoppm—Colorize a portable graymap into a portable pixmap

## SYNOPSIS

```
pgmtoppm colorspec [pgmfile]
pgmtoppm colorspec1-colorspec2 [pgmfile]
pgmtoppm -map mapfile [pgmfile]
```

## DESCRIPTION

pgmtoppm reads a portable graymap as input, colorizes it by multiplying the gray values by specified color or colors, and produces a portable pixmap as output.

If only one color is specified, black in the PGM file stays black and white in the PGM file turns into the specified color in the PPM file. If two colors (separated by a hyphen) are specified, then black gets mapped to the first color and white gets mapped to the second.

The color can be specified in five ways:

- A name, assuming that a pointer to an X11-style color names file was compiled in.
- An X11-style hexadecimal specifier: rgb:r/g/b, where r, g, and b are each 1- to 4-digit hexadecimal numbers.
- An X11-style decimal specifier: rgbi:r/g/b, where r, g, and b are floating-point numbers between 0 and 1.
- For backwards compatibility, an old-X11-style hexadecimal number: #rgb, #rrggbb, #rrrgggbbb, or #rrrrggggbbbb.
- For backwards compatibility, a triplet of numbers separated by commas: r,g,b, where r, g, and b are floating-point numbers between 0 and 1. (This style was added before MIT came up with the similar rgbi style.)

Also, the -map flag lets you specify an entire colormap to be used. The mapfile is just a PPM file; it can be any shape, all that matters is the colors in it and their order. In this case, black gets mapped to the first color in the mapfile, and white gets mapped to the last.

## SEE ALSO

rgb3toppm(1), ppmtopgm(1), ppmtorgb3(1), ppm(5), pgm(5)

## AUTHOR

Copyright© 1991 by Jef Poskanzer.

*11 January 1991*

# pi1toppm

pi1toppm—Convert an Atari Degas PI1 into a portable pixmap

## SYNOPSIS

```
pi1toppm [pi1file]
```

## DESCRIPTION

pi1toppm reads an Atari Degas PI1 file as input and produces a portable pixmap as output.

## SEE ALSO

ppmtopi1(1), ppm(5), pi3topbm(1), pbmtopi3(1)

## AUTHORS

Copyright© 1991 by Steve Belczyk (seb3@gte.com) and Jef Poskanzer.

*19 July 1990*

# pi3topbm

pi3topbm—Convert an Atari Degas PI3 file into a portable bitmap

## SYNOPSIS

pi3topbm [*pi3file*]

## DESCRIPTION

pi3topbm reads an Atari Degas PI3 file as input. Produces a portable bitmap as output.

## SEE ALSO

pbmtopi3(1), pbm(5), pi1toppm(1), ppmtopi1(1)

## AUTHORS

Copyright© 1988 by David Beckemeyer (bdt!david) and Diomidis D. Spinellis.

*11 March 1990*

# picttoppm

picttoppm—Convert a Macintosh PICT file into a portable pixmap

## SYNOPSIS

picttoppm [-verbose][-fullres][-noheader][-quickdraw][-fontdir*file*] [*pictfile*]

## DESCRIPTION

picttoppm reads a PICT file (version 1 or 2) and outputs a portable pixmap. Useful as the first step in converting a scanned image to something that can be displayed on UNIX.

## OPTIONS

| | |
|---|---|
| -fontdir *file* | Make the list of BDF fonts in *file* available for use by pict-toppm when drawing text. For the format of the fontdir file, see the "fontdir File Format" subsection. |
| -fullres | Force any images in the PICT file to be output with at least their full resolution. A PICT file may indicate that a contained image is to be scaled down before output. This option forces images to retain their sizes and prevent information loss. Use of this option disables all PICT operations except images. |
| -noheader | Do not skip the 512-byte header that is present on all PICT files. This is useful when you have PICT data that was not stored in the data fork of a PICT file. |
| -quickdraw | Execute only pure quickdraw operations. In particular, turn off the interpretation of special PostScript printer operations. |
| -verbose | Turns on verbose mode, which prints a whole bunch of information that only picttoppm hackers really care about. |

## BUGS

The PICT file format is a general drawing format. picttoppm does not support all the drawing commands, but it does have full support for any image commands and reasonable support for line, rectangle, polygon, and text drawing. It is useful for converting scanned images and some drawing conversion.

Memory is used very liberally with at least six bytes needed for every pixel. Large bitmap PICT files will likely run your computer out of memory.

## `fontdir` FILE FORMAT

`picttoppm` has a built-in default font and your local installer probably provided adequate extra fonts. You can point `picttoppm` at more fonts that you specify in a font directory file. Each line in the file is either a comment line, which must begin with #, or font information. The font information consists of four whitespace separated fields. The first is the font number, the second is the font size in pixels, the third is the font style, and the fourth is the name of a BDF file containing the font. The BDF format is defined by the X Window System and is not described here.

The font number indicates the type face. Here is a list of known font numbers and their faces.

| | |
|---|---|
| 0 | Chicago |
| 1 | Application font |
| 2 | New York |
| 3 | Geneva |
| 4 | Monaco |
| 5 | Venice |
| 6 | London |
| 7 | Athens |
| 8 | San Francisco |
| 9 | Toronto |
| 11 | Cairo |
| 12 | Los Angeles |
| 20 | Times Roman |
| 21 | Helvetica |
| 22 | Courier |
| 23 | Symbol |
| 24 | Taliesin |

The font style indicates a variation on the font. Multiple variations may apply to a font and the font style is the sum of the variation numbers, which are

| | |
|---|---|
| 1 | Boldface |
| 2 | Italic |
| 4 | Underlined |
| 8 | Outlined |
| 16 | Shadow |
| 32 | Condensed |
| 64 | Extended |

Obviously, the font definitions are strongly related to the Macintosh. More font numbers and information about fonts can be found in Macintosh documentation.

## SEE ALSO

Inside Macintosh volumes 1 and 5, ppmtopict(1), ppm(5)

## AUTHOR

Copyright ©1993 George Phillips.

*29 November 1991*

# pjtoppm

pjtoppm—Convert an HP PaintJet file to a portable pixmap

## SYNOPSIS

pjtoppm [*paintjet*]

## DESCRIPTION

pjtoppm reads an HP PaintJet file as input and converts it into a portable pixmap. This was a quick hack to save some trees, and it only handles a small subset of the paintjet commands. In particular, it will only handle enough commands to convert most raster image files.

## REFERENCES

*HP PaintJet XL Color Graphics Printer User's Guide*

## SEE ALSO

ppmtopj(1)

## AUTHOR

Copyright© 1991 by Christos Zoulas.

*14 July 1991*

# pktopbm

pktopbm—Convert packed (PK) format font into portable bitmap(s)

## SYNOPSIS

pktopbm pkfile[.pk] [-c *num*] *pbmfile* ...

## DESCRIPTION

pktopbm reads a packed (PK) font file as input and produces portable bitmaps as output. If the filename "-" is used for any of the filenames, the standard input stream (or standard output where appropriate) will be used.

## OPTIONS

-c *num*    Sets the character number of the next bitmap written to *num*.

## SEE ALSO

pbmtopk(1), pbm(5)

## AUTHOR

Adapted from Tom Rokicki's pxtopk by Angus Duggan (ajcd@dcs.ed.ac.uk).

*6 August 1990*

# pnmalias

pnmalias—Antialias a portable anymap.

## SYNOPSIS

pnmalias [-bgcolor *color*][-fgcolor *color*][-bonly][-fonly][-balias][-falias]
[-weight *w*][*pnmfile*]

## DESCRIPTION

pnmalias reads a portable anymap as input and applies antialiasing to background and foreground pixels. If the input file is a portable bitmap, the output antialiased image is promoted to a graymap, and a message is printed informing the user of the change in format.

## OPTIONS

-bgcolor *colorb*,      Set the background color to *colorb*, and the foreground to color to *colorf*. Pixels with these values
-fgcolor *colorf*     will be antialiased. By default, the background color is taken to be black, and foreground color is assumed to be white. The colors can be specified in five ways:

- A name, assuming that a pointer to an X11-style color names file was compiled in.
- An X11-style hexadecimal specifier: rgb:r/g/b, where r, g, and b are each 1- to 4-digit hexadecimal numbers.
- An X11-style decimal specifier: rgbi:r/g/b, where r, g, and b are floating-point numbers between 0 and 1.
- For backwards compatibility, an old-X11-style hexadecimal number: #rgb, #rrggbb, #rrrgggbbb, or #rrrrggggbbbb.
- For backwards compatibility, a triplet of numbers separated by commas: r,g,b, where r, g, and b are floating-point numbers between 0 and 1. (This style was added before MIT came up with the similar rgbi style.)

Note that even when dealing with graymaps, background and foreground colors need to be specified in the fashion described in the preceding list. In this case, background and foreground pixel values are taken to be the value of the red component for the given color.

-bonly, -fonly     Apply antialiasing only to background (-bonly), or foreground (-fonly) pixels.

-balias, -falias     Apply antialiasing to all pixels surrounding background (-balias), or foreground (-falias) pixels. By default, antialiasing takes place only among neighboring background and foreground pixels.

-weight *w*     Use *w* as the central weight for the aliasing filter. *w* must be a real number in the range $0 < w < 1$. The lower the value of *w* is, the "blurrier" the output image is. The default is $w = 1/3$.

## SEE ALSO

pbmtext(1), pnmsmooth(1), pnm(5)

## AUTHOR

Copyright© 1992 by Alberto Accomazzi, Smithsonian Astrophysical Observatory.

*30 April 1992*

# pnmarith

pnmarith—Perform arithmetic on two portable anymaps

## SYNOPSIS

pnmarith -add¦-subtract¦-multiply¦-difference *pnmfile1 pnmfile2*

## DESCRIPTION

pnmarith reads two portable anymaps as input, performs the specified arithmetic operation, and produces a portable anymap as output. The two input anymaps must be the same width and height.

The arithmetic is performed between corresponding pixels in the two anymaps, as if maxval was 1.0, black was 0.0, with a linear scale in between. Results that fall outside of [0..1) are truncated.

The operator -difference calculates the absolute value of

pnmarith -subtract *pnmfile1 pnm-file2*

In other words, no truncation is done.

All flags can be abbreviated to their shortest unique prefix.

## SEE ALSO

pbmmask(1), pnmpaste(1), pnminvert(1), pnm(5)

## AUTHOR

Copyright© 1989, 1991 by Jef Poskanzer. Lightly modified by Marcel Wijkstra (wijkstra@fwi.uva.nl).

*26 August 1993*

# pnmcat

pnmcat—Concatenate portable anymaps

## SYNOPSIS

pnmcat [-white¦-black] -leftright¦-lr [-jtop¦-jbottom] *pnmfile* pnmfile ...
pnmcat [-white¦-black] -topbottom¦-tb [-jleft¦-jright] *pnmfile* pnmfile ...

## DESCRIPTION

pnmcat reads portable anymaps as input, concatenates them either left to right or top to bottom, and produces a portable anymap as output.

## OPTIONS

If the anymaps are not all the same height (left-right) or width (top-bottom), the smaller ones have to be justified with the largest. By default, they get centered, but you can specify one side or the other with one of the -j* flags. So, -topbottom -jleft would stack the anymaps on top of each other, flush with the left edge.

The -white and -black flags specify which color to use to fill in the extra space when doing this justification. If neither is specified, the program makes a guess.

All flags can be abbreviated to their shortest unique prefix.

## SEE ALSO

pnm(5)

## AUTHOR

Copyright© 1989 by Jef Poskanzer.

*12 March 1989*

# pnmcomp

pnmcomp—Composite two portable anymap files together

## SYNOPSIS

pnmcomp [-invert][-xoffN] [-yoffN] [-alphapgmfile] overlay [*pnm-input*][*pnm-output*]

## DESCRIPTION

pnmcomp reads in a portable anymap image and puts an overlay upon it, with optional alpha mask. The -alphapgmfile allows you to also add an alpha mask file to the compositing process; the range of max and min can be swapped by using the -invert option. The -xoff and -yoff arguments can be negative, allowing you to shift the overlay off the top corner of the screen.

## SEE ALSO

pnm(5)

## AUTHOR

Copyright© 1992 by David Koblas (koblas@mips.com).

*21 February 1989*

# pnmconvol

pnmconvol—General MxN convolution on a portable anymap

## SYNOPSIS

pnmconvol *convolutionfile* [*pnmfile*]

## DESCRIPTION

pnmconvol reads two portable anymaps as input, convolves the second using the first, and writes a portable anymap as output.

Convolution means replacing each pixel with a weighted average of the nearby pixels. The weights and the area to average are determined by the convolution matrix. The unsigned numbers in the convolution file are offset by -maxval/2 to make signed numbers, and then normalized, so the actual values in the convolution file are only relative.

Here is a sample convolution file; it does a simple average of the nine immediate neighbors, resulting in a smoothed image:

```
P2
3 3
18
10 10 10
10 10 10
10 10 10
```

To see how this works, do the offset mentioned in the preceding paragraph: $10 - 18/2$ gives 1. The possible range of values is from 0 to 18, and after the offset that's -9 to 9. The normalization step makes the range -1 to 1, and the values get scaled correspondingly so they become 1/9—exactly what you want. The equivalent matrix for 5×5 smoothing would have maxval 50 and be filled with 26.

The convolution file will usually be a graymap, so that the same convolution is applied to each color component. However, if you want to use a pixmap and do a different convolution to different colors, you can certainly do that.

## SEE ALSO

pnmsmooth(1), pnm(5)

## AUTHOR

Copyright© 1989, 1991 by Jef Poskanzer.

*13 January 1991*

# pnmcrop

pnmcrop—Crop a portable anymap

## SYNOPSIS

pnmcrop [-white¦-black][-left][-right][-top][-bottom][*pnmfile*]

## DESCRIPTION

pnmcrop reads a portable anymap as input, removes edges that are the background color, and produces a portable anymap as output.

## OPTIONS

By default, it makes a guess as to what the background color is. You can override the default with the -white and -black flags.

The options -left, -right, -top and -bottom restrict cropping to the sides specified. The default is to crop all sides of the image.

All flags can be abbreviated to their shortest unique prefix.

## SEE ALSO

pnmcut(1), pnm(5)

## AUTHOR

Copyright © 1989 by Jef Poskanzer.

*25 February 1989*


# pnmcut

pnmcut—Cut a rectangle out of a portable anymap

## SYNOPSIS

pnmcut *x* *y* width height [*pnmfile*]

## DESCRIPTION

pnmcut reads a portable anymap as input, extracts the specified rectangle, and produces a portable anymap as output. The *x* and *y* can be negative, in which case they are interpreted relative to the right and bottom of the anymap, respectively.

## SEE ALSO

pnm(5)

## AUTHOR

Copyright © 1989 by Jef Poskanzer.

*21 February 1989*


# pnmdepth

pnmdepth—Change the maxval in a portable anymap

## SYNOPSIS

pnmdepth newmaxval [pnmfile]

## DESCRIPTION

pnmdepth reads a portable anymap as input, scales all the pixel values, and writes out the image with the new maxval. Scaling the colors down to a smaller maxval will result in some loss of information.

Be careful of off-by-one errors when choosing the new maxval. For instance, if you want the color values to be five bits wide, use a maxval of 31, not 32.

## SEE ALSO

pnm(5), ppmquant(1), ppmdither(1)

## AUTHOR

Copyright © 1989, 1991 by Jef Poskanzer.

*12 January 1991*


# pnmenlarge

pnmenlarge—Read a portable anymap and enlarge it N times

## SYNOPSIS

pnmenlarge *N* [*pnmfile*]

## DESCRIPTION

pnmenlarge reads a portable anymap as input, replicates its pixels *N* times, and produces a portable anymap as output.

pnmenlarge can only enlarge by integer factors. The slower but more general pnmscale can enlarge or reduce by arbitrary factors, and pbmreduce can reduce by integer factors, but only for bitmaps.

If you enlarge by a factor of 3 or more, you should probably add a pnmsmooth step; otherwise, you can see the original pixels in the resulting image.

## SEE ALSO

pbmreduce(1), pnmscale(1), pnmsmooth(1), pnm(5)

## AUTHOR

Copyright © 1989 by Jef Poskanzer.

*26 February 1989*


# pnmfile

pnmfile—Describe a portable anymap

## SYNOPSIS

pnmfile [*pnmfile*] ...

## DESCRIPTION

pnmfile reads one or more portable anymaps as input and writes out short descriptions of the image type, size, and so on. This is mostly for use in shell scripts, so the format is not particularly pretty.

## SEE ALSO

pnm(5), file(1)

*9 January 1991*

# pnmflip

pnmflip—Perform one or more flip operations on a portable anymap

## SYNOPSIS

```
pnmflip [-leftright¦-lr][-topbottom¦-tb][-transpose¦-xy][-rotate90¦-r90¦-ccw ]
[-rotate270¦-r270¦-cw ][-rotate180¦-r180][pnmfile]
```

## DESCRIPTION

pnmflip reads a portable anymap as input, performs one or more flip operations in the order specified, and writes out a portable anymap.

## OPTIONS

The flip operations available are left for right (-leftright or -lr); top for bottom (-topbottom or -tb); and transposition (-transpose or -xy). In addition, some canned concatenations are available: -rotate90 or -ccw is equivalent to -transpose -topbottom; -rotate270 or -cw is equivalent to -transpose -leftright; and -rotate180 is equivalent to -leftright -topbottom.

All flags can be abbreviated to their shortest unique prefix.

## SEE ALSO

pnmrotate(1), pnm(5)

*25 July 1989*

# pnmgamma

pnmgamma—Perform gamma correction on a portable anymap

## SYNOPSIS

```
pnmgamma value [pnmfile]
pnmgamma redvalue greenvalue bluevalue [pnmfile]
```

## DESCRIPTION

pnmgamma reads a portable anymap as input, performs gamma correction, and produces a portable anymap as output.

The arguments specify what gamma value(s) to use. A value of 1.0 leaves the image alone, less than 1 darkens it, and greater than 1 lightens it.

## SEE ALSO

pnm(5)

*12 January 1991*

# pnmhistmap

pnmhistmap—Draw a histogram for a PGM or PPM file

## SYNOPSIS

pnmhistmap [-black][-white][-max N][-verbose][pnmfile]

## DESCRIPTION

pnmhistmap reads a portable anymap as input, although bitmap (PBM) input produces an error message and no image, and produces an image showing a histogram of the color (or gray) values in the input. A graymap (PGM) input produces a bitmap output. A pixmap (PPM) input produces pixmap output with three overlaid histograms: a red one for the red input, a green one for the green input, and a blue one for the blue input. The output is fixed in size: 256 pixels wide by 200 pixels high.

## OPTIONS

-black    Ignores the count of black pixels when scaling the histogram.

-white    Ignores the count of white pixels when scaling the histogram.

The -black and -white options, which can be used separately or together, are useful for images with a large percentage of pixels whose value is zero or 255, which can cause the remaining histogram data to become unreadably small. Note that, for pixmap inputs, these options apply to all colors; if, for example, the input has a large number of bright-red areas, you will probably want to use the -white option.

-max N    Force the scaling of the histogram to use $N$ as the largest-count value. This is useful for inputs with a large percentage of single-color pixels that are not black or white.

-verbose    Report the progress of making the histogram, including the largest-count value used to scale the output.

All flags can be abbreviated to their shortest unique prefix.

## BUGS

Assumes maxval is always 255. Images with a smaller maxval will only use the lower-value side of the histogram. This can be overcome either by piping the input through pnmdepth 255 or by cutting and scaling the lower-value side of the histogram. Neither is a particularly elegant solution.

Should allow the output size to be specified.

## SEE ALSO

pgmhist(1), ppmhist(1), pgm(5), ppm(5)

## AUTHOR

Wilson H. Bent, Jr. (whb@usc.edu).

*25 October 1993*

# pnmindex

pnmindex—Build a visual index of a bunch of anymaps

## SYNOPSIS

pnmindex [-size N][-across N][-colors N][-black] pnmfile ...

## DESCRIPTION

This script makes small versions of a bunch of anymaps, adds labels, and concatenates them together into a collage.

## OPTIONS

| | |
|---|---|
| `-size` | Controls how big each image becomes; the default is `100x100`. |
| `-across` | Controls how many images are in each row; the default is six. |
| `-colors` | Controls how many colors the final index gets quantized to, if quantization is necessary; the default is `256`. |
| `-black` | Controls the color of the padding between the images; normally it's white and the labels are black lettering on white background, but the `-black` flag reverses this. |

## SEE ALSO

pnmscale(1), pnmcat(1), pbmtext(1), ppmquant(1), pnm(5)

## BUGS

It's very slow.

It's a `csh` script. `csh` scripts are not portable to System V. Scripts in general are not portable to non-UNIX environments.

## AUTHOR

Copyright © 1991 by Jef Poskanzer.

*9 January 1991*

# pnminvert

pnminvert—Invert a portable anymap

## SYNOPSIS

pnminvert [*pnmfile*]

## DESCRIPTION

pnminvert reads a portable anymap as input, inverts it black for white, and produces a portable anymap as output.

## SEE ALSO

pnm(5)

## AUTHOR

Copyright © 1989 by Jef Poskanzer.

*8 August 1989*

# pnmmargin

pnmmargin—Add a border to a portable anymap

## SYNOPSIS

pnmmargin [-white¦-black¦-color *colorspec*] *size* [*pnmfile*]

## DESCRIPTION

pnmmargin reads a portable anymap as input, adds a border of the specified number of pixels, and produces a portable anymap as output.

## OPTIONS

You can specify the border color with the -white, -black, and -color flags. If no color is specified, the program makes a guess.

## SEE ALSO

pnm(5)

## BUGS

It's a script. Scripts are not portable to non-UNIX environments.

## AUTHOR

Copyright © 1991 by Jef Poskanzer.

*9 January 1991*


# pnmnlfilt

pnmnlfilt--Nonlinear filters: smooth, alpha trim mean, optimal estimation smoothing, edge enhancement.

## SYNOPSIS

pnmnlfilt alpha radius [*pnmfile*]

## DESCRIPTION

This is something of a Swiss army knife filter. It has three distinct operating modes. In all of the modes, each pixel in the image is examined and processed according to it and its surrounding pixels values. Rather than using the nine pixels in a 3×3 block, seven hexagonal area samples are taken, the size of the hexagons being controlled by the radius parameter. A radius value of 0.3333 means that the seven hexagons exactly fit into the center pixel (that is, there will be no filtering effect). A radius value of 1.0 means that the seven hexagons exactly fit a 3×3 pixel array.

### ALPHA-TRIMMED MEAN FILTER (0.0 < = alpha < = 0.5)

The value of the center pixel will be replaced by the mean of the seven hexagon values, but the seven values are sorted by size and the top and bottom alpha portion of the seven are excluded from the mean. This implies that an alpha value of 0.0 gives the same sort of output as a normal convolution (that is, averaging or smoothing filter), where radius will determine the "strength" of the filter. A good value to start from for subtle filtering is alpha = 0.0, radius = 0.55. For a more blatant effect, try alpha = 0.0 and radius = 1.0.

An alpha value of 0.5 will cause the median value of the seven hexagons to be used to replace the center pixel value. This sort of filter is good for eliminating "pop" or single pixel noise from an image without spreading the noise out or smudging features on the image. Judicious use of the radius parameter will fine-tune the filtering. Intermediate values of alpha give effects somewhere between smoothing and "pop" noise reduction. For subtle filtering, try starting with values of alpha = 0.4, radius = 0.6. For a more blatant effect, try alpha = 0.5, radius = 1.0.

### OPTIMAL ESTIMATION SMOOTHING. (1.0 < = alpha < = 2.0)

This type of filter applies a smoothing filter adaptively over the image. For each pixel, the variance of the surrounding hexagon values is calculated, and the amount of smoothing is made inversely proportional to it. The idea is that if the variance is small, then it is due to noise in the image, while if the variance is large, it is because of "wanted" image features. As usual, the radius parameter controls the effective radius, but it probably advisable to leave the radius between 0.8 and 1.0 for the variance calculation to be meaningful. The alpha parameter sets the noise threshold, over which less smoothing will be done. This means that small values of alpha will give the most subtle filtering effect, while large values will tend to smooth all parts of the image. You could start with values like alpha = 1.2, radius = 1.0 and try increasing or decreasing the alpha parameter to get the desired effect. This type of filter is best for filtering out dithering noise in both bitmap and color images.

## EDGE ENHANCEMENT. (`-0.1 > = alpha > = -0.9`)

This is the opposite type of filter to the smoothing filter. It enhances edges. The `alpha` parameter controls the amount of edge enhancement, from subtle (`-0.1`) to blatant (`-0.9`). The `radius` parameter controls the effective radius as usual, but useful values are between `0.5` and `0.9`. Try starting with values of `alpha = 0.3`, `radius = 0.8`.

## COMBINATION USE

The various modes of `pnmnlfilt` can be used one after the other to get the desired result. For instance to turn a monochrome dithered image into a grayscale image, you could try one or two passes of the smoothing filter, followed by a pass of the optimal estimation filter, then some subtle edge enhancement. Note that using edge enhancement is only likely to be useful after one of the nonlinear filters (alpha-trimmed mean or optimal estimation filter), as edge enhancement is the direct opposite of smoothing.

For reducing color quantization noise in images (that is, turning GIF files back into 24-bit files), you could try a pass of the optimal estimation filter (`alpha 1.2`, `radius 1.0`), a pass of the median filter (`alpha 0.5`, `radius 0.55`), and possibly a pass of the edge enhancement filter. Several passes of the optimal estimation filter with declining `alpha` values are more effective than a single pass with a large `alpha` value. As usual, there is a tradeoff between filtering effectiveness and loosing detail. Experimentation is encouraged.

## REFERENCES

The alpha-trimmed mean filter is based on the description in *IEEE CG&A*, May 1990, page 23, by Mark E. Lee and Richard A. Redner, and has been enhanced to allow continuous alpha adjustment.

The optimal estimation filter is taken from an article "Converting Dithered Images Back to Grayscale" by Allen Stenger, *Dr. Dobb's Journal*, November 1992, and this article references "Digital Image Enhancement and Noise Filtering by Use of Local Statistics" by Jong-Sen Lee, *IEEE Transactions on Pattern Analysis and Machine Intelligence*, March 1980.

The edge enhancement details are from `pgmenhance`(1), which is taken from Philip R. Thompson's `xim` program, which in turn took it from Section 6 of "Digital Halftones by Dot Diffusion" by D. E. Knuth, *ACM Transaction on Graphics* Vol. 6, No. 4, October 1987, which in turn got it from two 1976 papers by J. F. Jarvis et al.

## SEE ALSO

`pgmenhance`(1), `pnmconvol`(1), `pnm`(5)

## BUGS

Integers and tables may overflow if `PPM_MAXMAXVAL` is greater than `255`.

## AUTHOR

Graeme W. Gill (`graeme@labtam.oz.au`).

*5 February 1993*

# pnmnoraw

`pnmnoraw`—Force a portable anymap into plain format

## SYNOPSIS

`pnmnoraw [`*pnmfile*`]`

## DESCRIPTION

`pnmnoraw` reads a portable anymap as input and writes it out in plain (nonraw) format. This is fairly useless if you haven't defined the `PBMPLUS_RAWBITS` compile-time option.

## SEE ALSO

pnm(5)

## AUTHOR

Copyright © 1991 by Jef Poskanzer.

*8 January 1991*

# pnmpad

pnmpad—Add borders to portable anymap

## SYNOPSIS

pnmpad [-white¦-black] [-l#] [-r#] [-t#] [-b#] [*pnmfile*]

## DESCRIPTION

pnmpad reads a portable anymap as input and outputs a portable anymap with extra borders of the sizes specified. The color of the borders can be set to black or white (default black).

## SEE ALSO

pbmmake(1), pnmpaste(1), pbm(5)

## AUTHOR

Copyright © 1990 by Angus Duggan. Copyright © 1989 by Jef Poskanzer.

# pnmpaste

pnmpaste—Paste a rectangle into a portable anymap

## SYNOPSIS

pnmpaste [-replace¦-or¦-and ¦-xor] *frompnmfile x y* [*intopnmfile*]

## DESCRIPTION

pnmpaste reads two portable anymaps as input, inserts the first anymap into the second at the specified location, and produces a portable anymap the same size as the second as output. If the second anymap is not specified, it is read from stdin. The *x* and *y* can be negative, in which case they are interpreted relative to the right and bottom of the anymap, respectively.

This tool is most useful in combination with pnmcut. For instance, if you want to edit a small segment of a large image, and your image editor cannot edit the large image, you can cut out the segment you are interested in, edit it, and then paste it back in.

Another useful companion tool is pbmmask.

The optional flag specifies the operation to use when doing the paste. The default is -replace. The other logical operations are only allowed if both input images are bitmaps. These operations act as if white is TRUE and black is FALSE.

All flags can be abbreviated to their shortest unique prefix.

## SEE ALSO

pnmcut(1), pnminvert(1), pnmarith(1), pnm(5), pbmmask(1)

## AUTHOR

Copyright © 1989, 1991 by Jef Poskanzer.

*21 February 1991*

# pnmrotate

pnmrotate—Rotate a portable anymap by some angle

## SYNOPSIS

`pnmrotate [-noantialias] angle [pnmfile]`

## DESCRIPTION

pnmrotate reads a portable anymap as input, rotates it by the specified angle, and produces a portable anymap as output. If the input file is in color, the output will be, too; otherwise, it will be grayscale. The angle is in degrees (floating-point), measured counter-clockwise. It can be negative, but it should be between -90 and 90. Also, for rotations greater than 45 degrees you may get better results if you first use `pnmflip` to do a 90-degree rotation and then `pnmrotate` less than 45 degrees back the other direction.

The rotation algorithm is Alan Paeth's three-shear method. Each shear is implemented by looping over the source pixels and distributing fractions to each of the destination pixels. This has an antialiasing effect—it avoids jagged edges and similar artifacts. However, it also means that the original colors or gray levels in the image are modified. If you need to keep precisely the same set of colors, you can use the `-noantialias` flag. This does the shearing by moving pixels without changing their values. If you want antialiasing and don't care about the precise colors, but still need a limited *number* of colors, you can run the result through ppmquant.

All flags can be abbreviated to their shortest unique prefix.

## REFERENCES

"A Fast Algorithm for General Raster Rotation" by Alan Paeth, *Graphics Interface '86*, pages 77–81.

## SEE ALSO

pnmshear(1), pnmflip(1), pnm(5), ppmquant(1)

## AUTHOR

Copyright © 1989, 1991 by Jef Poskanzer.

*12 January 1991*

# pnmscale

pnmscale—Scale a portable anymap

## SYNOPSIS

```
pnmscale s [pnmfile]
pnmscale -xsize¦-width¦-ysize¦ -height s [pnmfile]
pnmscale -xscale¦-yscale s [pnmfile]
pnmscale -xscale¦-xsize¦-width s -yscale¦-ysize¦-height s [pnmfile]
pnmscale -xysize x y [pnmfile]
pnmscale –pixels n [pnmfile]
```

## DESCRIPTION

pnmscale reads a portable anymap as input, scales it by the specified factor or factors, and produces a portable anymap as output. If the input file is in color, the output will be, too; otherwise, it will be grayscale. You can both enlarge (scale factor > 1) and reduce (scale factor < 1).

You can specify one dimension as a pixel size, and the other dimension will be scaled correspondingly.

You can specify one dimension as a scale, and the other dimension will not be scaled.

You can specify different sizes or scales for each axis.

You can use the special -xysize flag, which fits the image into the specified size without changing the aspect ratio.

Or, you can use the -pixels flag, which fits the image into the specified number of pixels without changing the aspect ratio.

All flags can be abbreviated to their shortest unique prefix.

If you enlarge by a factor of three or more, you should probably add a pnmsmooth step; otherwise, you can see the original pixels in the resulting image.

## SEE ALSO

pbmreduce(1), pnmenlarge(1), pnmsmooth(1), pnm(5)

## AUTHOR

Copyright © 1989, 1991 by Jef Poskanzer.

*12 January 1991*

# pnmshear

pnmshear—Shear a portable anymap by some angle

## SYNOPSIS

pnmshear [-noantialias] *angle* [*pnmfile*]

## DESCRIPTION

pnmshear reads a portable anymap as input, shears it by the specified angle, and produces a portable anymap as output. If the input file is in color, the output will be too; otherwise, it will be grayscale. The angle is in degrees (floating-point), and measures this:

```
+----+ +----+
| | |\\
| OLD| |\NEW \
| | |an\\
+----+ |gle+----+
```

If the angle is negative, it shears the other way:

```
+----+ |-an+----+
| | |gl//
| OLD | |e/ NEW /
| | |//
+----+ +----+
```

The angle should not get too close to 90 or -90, or the resulting anymap will be unreasonably wide.

The shearing is implemented by looping over the source pixels and distributing fractions to each of the destination pixels. This has an antialiasing effect—it avoids jagged edges and similar artifacts. However, it also means that the original colors or gray levels in the image are modified. If you need to keep precisely the same set of colors, you can use the -noantialias flag.

This does the shearing by moving pixels without changing their values. If you want antialiasing and don't care about the precise colors, but still need a limited *number* of colors, you can run the result through ppmquant.

All flags can be abbreviated to their shortest unique prefix.

## SEE ALSO

pnmrotate(1), pnmflip(1), pnm(5), ppmquant(1)

## AUTHOR

Copyright © 1989, 1991 by Jef Poskanzer.

*12 January 1991*

# pnmsmooth

pnmsmooth—Smooth out an image

## SYNOPSIS

pnmsmooth [*pnmfile*]

## DESCRIPTION

pnmsmooth smooths out an image by replacing each pixel with the average of its nine immediate neighbors. It is implemented as a simple script using pnmconvol.

## SEE ALSO

pnmconvol(1), pnm(5)

## BUGS

It's a script. Scripts are not portable to non-UNIX environments.

## AUTHOR

Copyright © 1989, 1991 by Jef Poskanzer

*13 January 1991*

# pnmtile

pnmtile—Replicate a portable anymap into a specified size

## SYNOPSIS

pnmtile width height [*pnmfile*]

## DESCRIPTION

pnmtile reads a portable anymap as input, replicates it until it is the specified size, and produces a portable anymap as output.

## SEE ALSO

pnm(5)

## AUTHOR

Copyright © 1989 by Jef Poskanzer.

*13 May 1989*

# pnmtoddif

pnmtoddif—Convert a portable anymap to DDIF format

## SYNTAX

pnmtoddif pnmtoddif [-resolution x y] [pnmfile [ddiffile]]

## OPTIONS

resolution *x y*    The horizontal and vertical resolution of the output image in dots per inch. Defaults to 78dpi.

*pnmfile*           The filename for the image file in PNM format. If this argument is omitted, input is read from stdin.

*ddiffile*          The filename for the image file to be created in DDIF format. If this argument is omitted, the *ddiffile* is written to standard output. It can only specified if a *pnmfile* is also specified.

## DESCRIPTION

pnmtoddif takes a portable anymap from standard input and converts it into a DDIF image file on standard output or the specified DDIF file.

PBM format (bitmap) data is written as 1-bit DDIF, PGM format data (grayscale) as 8-bit grayscale DDIF, and PPM format data is written as 8,8,8-bit color DDIF. All DDIF image files are written as uncompressed. The data plane organization is interleaved by pixel.

In addition to the number of pixels in the width and height dimension, DDIF images also carry information about the size that the image should have, that is, the physical space that a pixel occupies. PBMPLUS images do not carry this information, hence it has to be externally supplied. The default of 78dpi has the beneficial property of not causing a resize on most Digital Equipment Corporation color monitors.

## AUTHOR

Burkhard Neidecker-Lutz
Digital Equipment Corporation, CEC Karlsruhe
neideck@nestvx.enet.dec.com

# pnmtofits

pnmtofits—Convert a portable anymap into FITS format

## SYNOPSIS

pnmtofits [-max f][-min f][*pnmfile*]

## DESCRIPTION

pnmtofits reads a portable anymap as input and produces a FITS (Flexible Image Transport System) file as output. The resolution of the output file is either 8 bits/pixel, or 16 bits/pixel, depending on the value of maxval in the input file. If the input file is a portable bitmap or a portable graymap, the output file consists of a single plane image (NAXIS = 2). If instead the input file is a portable pixmap, the output file will consist of a three-plane image (NAXIS = 3, NAXIS3 = 3). A full description of the FITS format can be found in *Astronomy & Astrophysics Supplement Series 44* (1981), page 363.

## OPTIONS

Flags -min and -max can be used to set DATAMAX, DATAMIN, BSCALE, and BZERO in the FITS header, but do not cause the data to be rescaled.

## SEE ALSO

fitstopnm(1), pgm(5)

## AUTHOR

Copyright © 1989 by Wilson H. Bent (whb@hoh-2.att.com), with modifications by Alberto Accomazzi (alberto@cfa.harvard.edu).

*5 December 1992*

# pnmtops

pnmtops—Convert portable anymap to PostScript

## SYNOPSIS

pnmtops [-scale s][-turn¦-noturn][-rle¦-runlength][-dpi n][-width n][-height n]
[-center¦-nocenter][*pnmfile*]

## DESCRIPTION

pnmtops reads a portable anymap as input and produces encapsulated PostScript as output.

If the input file is in color (PPM), a color PostScript file gets written. Some PostScript interpreters can't handle color PostScript. If you have one of these, you will need to run your image through ppmtopgm first.

Note that there is no pstopnm tool; this transformation is one-way, because a pstopnm tool would be a full-fledged PostScript interpreter, which is beyond the scope of this package. However, see the psidtopgm tool, which can read grayscale non-run-length PostScript image data. Also, if you're willing to install the fairly large GhostScript package, it comes with a pstoppm script.

## OPTIONS

The -scale flag controls the scale of the result. The default scale is 1, which on a 300dpi printer such as the Apple LaserWriter makes the output look about the same size as the input would if it was displayed on a typical 72dpi screen. To get one PNM pixel per 300dpi printer pixel, use -scale 0.25.

The -turn and -noturn flags control whether the image gets turned 90 degrees. Normally, if an image is wider than it is tall, it gets turned automatically to better fit the page. If the -turn flag is specified, it will be turned no matter what its shape; and if the -noturn flag is specified, it will not be turned no matter what its shape.

The -rle or -runlength flag specifies run-length compression. This may save time if the host-to-printer link is slow; but normally the printer's processing time dominates, so -rle makes things slower.

The -dpi flag lets you specify the dots per inch of your output device. The default is 300dpi. In theory PostScript is device-independent and you don't have to worry about this, but in practice its raster rendering can have unsightly bands if the device pixels and the image pixels aren't in sync.

The -width and -height flags let you specify the size of the page. The default is 8.5 inches by 11 inches.

With the -nocenter flag, the output is not centered on the page; it appears in the upper-left corner. This is useful for programs that can include PostScript files, but can't cope with pictures that are not positioned in the upper-left corner. The default is -center--the image is centered on the page.

All flags can be abbreviated to their shortest unique prefix.

## SEE ALSO

pnm(5), psidtopgm(1)

## AUTHOR

*Copyright © 1989, 1991 by Jef Poskanzer. Modified November 1993 by Wolfgang Stuerzlinger (wrzl@gup.uni-linz.ac.at).*

*26 October 1991*

# pnmtorast

pnmtorast—Convert a portable pixmap into a Sun raster file

## SYNOPSIS

pnmtorast [-standard¦-rle][*pnmfile*]

## DESCRIPTION

pnmtorast reads a portable pixmap as input and produces a Sun raster file as output.

Color values in Sun raster files are eight bits wide, so pnmtorast will automatically scale colors to have a maxval of 255. An extra pnmdepth step is not necessary.

## OPTIONS

The -standard flag forces the result to be in RT_STANDARD form; the -rle flag, RT_BYTE_ENCODED, which is smaller but, well, less standard. The default is -rle.

All flags can be abbreviated to their shortest unique prefix.

## SEE ALSO

rasttopnm(1), pnm(5)

## AUTHOR

Copyright © 1989, 1991 by Jef Poskanzer.

*12 January 1991*

# pnmtosgi

pnmtosgi—Convert a portable anymap to an SGI image file

## SYNOPSIS

pnmtosgi [-verbatim¦-rle][-imagename *Name*][pnmfile]

## DESCRIPTION

pnmtosgi reads a portable anymap as input and produces an SGI image file as output. The SGI image will be two-dimensional (one channel) for PBM and PGM input, and three-dimensional (three channels) for PPM.

## OPTIONS

| | |
|---|---|
| -verbatim | Write an uncompressed file. |
| -rle (default) | Write a compressed (run-length–encoded) file. |
| -imagename *name* | Write the string *name* into the imagename field of the header. The *name* string is limited to 79 characters. If no name is given, pnmtosgi writes no name into this field. |

## BUGS

Probably.

## REFERENCES

SGI image file format documentation (draft v0.95) by Paul Haeberli (paul@sgi.com). Available via FTP at sgi.com:graphics/ SGIIMAGESPEC.

## SEE ALSO

pnm(5), sgitopnm(1)

## AUTHOR

*Copyright © 1994 by Ingo Wilken (*Ingo.Wilken@informatik.uni-oldenburg.de*).*

*29 January 1994*

# pnmtosir

pnmtosir—Convert a portable anymap into a Solitaire format

## SYNOPSIS

pnmtosir [pnmfile]

## DESCRIPTION

pnmtosir reads a portable anymap as input and produces a Solitaire image recorder format.

pnmtosir produces an MGI TYPE 17 file for PBM and PGM files. For ppm, it writes an MGI TYPE 11 file.

## SEE ALSO

sirtopnm(1), pnm(5)

## AUTHOR

Copyright © 1991 by Marvin Landis.

*20 March 1991*

# pnmtotiff

pnmtotiff—Convert a portable anymap into a TIFF file

## SYNOPSIS

pnmtotiff [-none¦-packbits¦ -lzw¦-g3¦-g4][-2d][-fill][-predictor *n*]
[-msb2lsb¦-lsb2msb] [-rowsperstrip *n*][*pnmfile*]

## DESCRIPTION

pnmtotiff reads a portable anymap as input. Produces a TIFF file as output.

## OPTIONS

By default, pnmtotiff creates a TIFF file with LZW compression. This is your best bet most of the time. However, some TIFF readers can't deal with it. If you want to try another compression scheme or tweak some of the other even more obscure output options, there are a number of flags to play with.

The -none, -packbits, -lzw, -g3,and-g4 options are used to override the default and set the compression scheme used in creating the output file. The CCITT Group 3 and Group 4 compression algorithms can only be used with bilevel data. The -2d and -fill options are meaningful only with Group 3 compression: -2d requests two-dimensional encoding, while -fill requests that each encoded scanline be zero-filled to a byte boundary. The -predictor option is only meaningful with LZW compression: a predictor value of 2 causes each scanline of the output image to undergo horizontal differencing before it is encoded; a value of 1 forces each scanline to be encoded without differencing. By default, pnmtotiff creates a TIFF file with msb-to-lsb fill order. The -msb2lsb and -lsb2msb options are used to override the default and set the fill order used in creating the file. The -rowsperstrip option can be used to set the number of rows (scanlines) in each strip of data in the output file. By default, the output file has the number of rows per strip set to a value that will ensure each strip is no more than eight kilobytes long.

## BUGS

This program is not self-contained. To use it you must fetch the TIFF Software package listed in the OTHER.SYSTEMS file and configure PBMPLUS to use libtiff. See PBM-PLUS's Makefile for details on this configuration.

## SEE ALSO

tifftopnm(1), pnm(5)

## AUTHOR

Derived by Jef Poskanzer from ras2tiff.c, which is Copyright© 1990 by Sun Microsystems, Inc. Author: Patrick J. Naughton (naughton@wind.sun.com).

*13 January 1991*

# pnmtoxwd

pnmtoxwd—Convert a portable anymap into an X11 window dump

## SYNOPSIS

pnmtoxwd [-pseudodepth *n*][-directcolor][*pnmfile*]

## DESCRIPTION

pnmtoxwd reads a portable anymap as input and produces an X11 window dump as output. This window dump can be displayed using the xwud tool.

Normally, pnmtoxwd produces a StaticGray dump file for PBM and PGM files. For ppm, it writes a PseudoColor dump file if there are up to 256 colors in the input, and a DirectColor dump file otherwise. The -directcolor flag can be used to force a DirectColor dump. The -pseudodepth flag can be used to change the depth of PseudoColor dumps from the default of 8 bits/256 colors.

## SEE ALSO

xwdtopnm(1), pnm(5), xwud(1)

## AUTHOR

Copyright© 1989, 1991 by Jef Poskanzer.

*24 September 1991*

# ppm3d

ppm3d—Convert two portable pixmap into a red/blue 3D glasses pixmap

## SYNOPSIS

ppm3d *leftppmfile rightppmfile* [*horizontal_offset*]

## DESCRIPTION

ppm3d reads two portable pixmaps as input and produces a portable pixmap as output, with the images overlapping by horizontal_offset pixels in blue/red format.

horizontal_offset defaults to 30 pixels. Pixmaps *must* be the same size.

## SEE ALSO

ppm(5)

## AUTHOR

Copyright © 1993 by David K. Drum.

*2 November 1993*

# ppmbrighten

ppmbrighten—Change an image's saturation and value from an HSV map

## SYNOPSIS

ppmbrighten [-n] [-s <+- saturation>] [-v <+- value>] <ppmfile>

## DESCRIPTION

ppmbrighten reads a portable pixmap as input, converts the image from RGB space to HSV space, and changes the value by <+- value> as a percentage; the same with the saturation. Use

ppmbrighten -v 100

to add 100 percent to the value.

The n option normalizes the value to exist between 0 and 1 (normalized).

## SEE ALSO

pgmnorm(1), ppm(5)

## AUTHOR

Copyright© 1990 by Brian Moffet. Copyright© 1989 by Jef Poskanzer.

Permission to use, copy, modify, and distribute this software and its documentation for any purpose and without fee is hereby granted, provided that the above copyright notice appear in all copies and that both that copyright notice and this permission notice appear in supporting documentation. This software is provided "as is" without express or implied warranty.

## NOTES

This program does not change the number of colors.

*20 November 1990*

# ppmchange

ppmchange—Change all pixels of one color to another in a portable pixmap

## SYNOPSIS

ppmchange *oldcolor newcolor* [...] [*ppmfile*]

## DESCRIPTION

ppmchange reads a portable pixmap as input and changes all pixels of oldcolor to newcolor, leaving all others unchanged. Up to 256 colors may be replaced by specifying couples of colors on the command line.

The colors can be specified in five ways:

- A name, assuming that a pointer to an X11-style color names file was compiled in.
- An X11-style hexadecimal specifier: rgb:r/g/b, where r, g, and b are each 1- to 4-digit hexadecimal numbers.
- An X11-style decimal specifier: rgbi:r/g/b, where r, g, and b are floating-point numbers between 0 and 1.
- For backwards compatibility, an old-X11-style hexadecimal number: #rgb, #rrggbb, #rrrgggbbb, or #rrrrggggbbbb.
- For backwards compatibility, a triplet of numbers separated by commas: r,g,b, where r, g, and b are floating-point numbers between 0 and 1. (This style was added before MIT came up with the similar rgbi style.)

## SEE ALSO

pgmtoppm(1), ppm(5)

## AUTHOR

Wilson H. Bent, Jr. (whb@usc.edu), with modifications by Alberto Accomazzi (alberto@cfa.harvard.edu).

*3 December 1993*


# ppmdim

ppmdim—Dim a portable pixmap down to total blackness

## SYNOPSIS

ppmdim *dimfactor* [*ppmfile*]

## DESCRIPTION

ppmdim reads a portable pixmap as input and diminishes its brightness by the specified dimfactor down to total blackness. The *dimfactor* may be in the range from 0.0 (total blackness, deep night, nada, null, nothing) to 1.0 (original picture's brightness).

As pnmgamma does not do the brightness correction in the way I wanted it, I wrote this small program.

ppmdim is similar to ppmbrighten, but not exactly the same.

## SEE ALSO

ppm(5), ppmflash(1), pnmgamma(1), ppmbrighten(1)

## AUTHOR

Copyright© 1993 by Frank Neumann.

*16 November 1993*


# ppmdist

ppmdist—Simplistic grayscale assignment for machine-generated color images

## SYNOPSIS

ppmdist [-intensity¦-frequency][*ppmfile*]

## DESCRIPTION

ppmdist reads a portable pixmap as input and performs a simplistic grayscale assignment intended for use with grayscale or bitmap printers.

Often conversion from ppm to pgm will yield an image with contrast too low for good printer output. The program maximizes contrast between the gray levels' output.

A ppm input of n colors is read, and a pgm of n gray levels is written. The gray levels take on the values 0...n-1, while maxval takes on n-1.

The mapping from color to stepped grayscale can be performed in order of input pixel intensity, or input pixel frequency (number of repetitions).

## OPTIONS

| | |
|---|---|
| -frequency | Sort input colors by the number of times a color appears in the input, before mapping to evenly distributed gray levels of output. |
| -intensity | Sort input colors by their grayscale intensity, before mapping to evenly distributed gray levels of output. This is the default. |

## BUGS

Helpful only for images with a very small number of colors. Perhaps should have been an option to ppmtopgm(1).

## SEE ALSO

ppmtopgm(1), ppmhist(1), ppm(5)

## AUTHOR

Copyright© 1993 by Dan Stromberg.

*22 July 1992*

# ppmdither

ppmdither—Ordered dither for color images

## SYNOPSIS

ppmdither [-dim *dimension*][-red *shades*][-green *shades*][-blue *shades*][*ppmfile*]

## DESCRIPTION

ppmdither reads a portable pixmap as input, and applies dithering to it to reduce the number of colors used down to the specified number of shades for each primary. The default number of shades is red=5, green=9, blue=5, for a total of 225 colors. To convert the image to a binary RGB format suitable for color printers, use -red 2 -green 2 -blue 2. The maximum number of colors that can be used is 256 and can be computed as the product of the number of red, green, and blue shades.

## OPTIONS

| | |
|---|---|
| -dim *dimension* | The size of the dithering matrix. Must be a power of 2. |
| -red *shades* | The number of red shades to be used; minimum of 2. |
| -green *shades* | The number of green shades to be used; minimum of 2. |
| -blue *shades* | The number of blue shades to be used; minimum of 2. |

## SEE ALSO

pnmdepth(1), ppmquant(1), ppm(5)

## AUTHOR

Copyright© 1991 by Christos Zoulas.

*14 July 1991*

# ppmflash

ppmflash—Brighten a picture up to complete white-out

## SYNOPSIS

ppmflash *flashfactor* [*ppmfile*]

## DESCRIPTION

ppmflash reads a portable pixmap as input and increases its brightness by the specified *flashfactor* up to a total white-out image. The *flashfactor* may be in the range from 0.0 (original picture's brightness) to 1.0 (full white-out, The Second After).

As pnmgamma does not do the brightness correction in the way I wanted it, I wrote this small program.

This program is similar to ppmbrighten, but not exactly the same.

## SEE ALSO

ppm(5), ppmdim(1), pnmgamma(1), ppmbrighten(1)

## AUTHOR

Copyright© 1993 by Frank Neumann.

*16 November 1993*


# ppmforge

ppmforge—Fractal forgeries of clouds, planets, and starry skies

## SYNOPSIS

ppmforge [-clouds][-night][-dimension *dimen*][-hour *hour*][-inclination¦-tilt *angle*]
[-mesh *size*][-power *factor*][-glaciers *level*][-ice *level*][-saturation *sat*]
[-seed *seed*] [-stars *fraction*][-xsize¦-width *width*][-ysize¦-height *height*]

## DESCRIPTION

ppmforge generates three kinds of "random fractal forgeries," the term coined by Richard F. Voss of the IBM Thomas J. Watson Research Center for seemingly realistic pictures of natural objects generated by simple algorithms embodying randomness and fractal self-similarity. The techniques used by ppmforge are essentially those given by Voss, particularly the technique of spectral synthesis explained in more detail by Dietmar Saupe. (The "See Also" subsection provides more detailed information about these men's work.)

The program generates two varieties of pictures, planets and clouds, which are just different renderings of data generated in an identical manner, illustrating the unity of the fractal structure of these very different objects. A third type of picture, a starry sky, is synthesized directly from pseudorandom numbers.

The generation of planets or clouds begins with the preparation of an array of random data in the frequency domain. The size of this array, the *mesh size*, can be set with the -mesh option; the larger the mesh, the more realistic the pictures, but the calculation time and memory requirement increases as the square of the mesh size. The fractal dimension, which you can specify with the -dimension option, determines the roughness of the terrain on the planet or the scale of detail in the clouds. As the fractal dimension is increased, more high frequency components are added into the random mesh.

After the mesh is generated, an inverse two-dimensional Fourier transform is performed upon it. This converts the original random frequency domain data into spatial amplitudes. You scale the real components that result from the Fourier transform into numbers from 0 to 1 associated with each point on the mesh. You can further modify this number by applying a *power law scale* to it with the -power option. Unity scale leaves the numbers unmodified; a power scale of 0.5 takes the square root of the numbers in the mesh, while a power scale of 3 replaces the numbers in the mesh with their cubes. Power law scaling is best envisioned by thinking of the data as representing the elevation of terrain; powers less than one yield landscapes with vertical scarps that look like glacial-carved valleys; powers greater than one make fairy-castle spires (which require large mesh sizes and high resolution for best results).

After these calculations, you have an array of the specified size containing numbers that range from 0 to 1. The pixmaps are generated as follows:

Clouds      A color map is created that ranges from pure blue to white by increasing admixture (desaturation) of blue with white. Numbers less than 0.5 are colored blue, and numbers between 0.5 and 1.0 are colored with corresponding levels of white, with 1.0 being pure white.

Planet      The mesh is projected onto a sphere. Values less than 0.5 are treated as water and values between 0.5 and 1.0 as land. The water areas are colored based on the water depth; land, based on its elevation. The random depth data are used to create clouds over the oceans. An atmosphere approximately like the Earth's is simulated; its light absorption is calculated to create a blue cast around the limb of the planet. A function that rises from 0 to 1 based on latitude is modulated by the local elevation to generate polar ice caps—high altitude terrain carries glaciers farther from the pole. Based on the position of the star with respect to the observer, the apparent color of each pixel of the planet is calculated by ray-tracing from the star to the planet to the observer and applying a lighting model that sums ambient light and diffuse reflection (for most planets ambient light is zero, as their primary star is the only source of illumination). Additional random data are used to generate stars around the planet.

Night      A sequence of pseudorandom numbers is used to generate stars with a user-specified density.

Cloud pictures always contain 256 or fewer colors and may be displayed on most color-mapped devices without further processing. Planet pictures often contain tens of thousands of colors that must be compressed with ppmquant or ppmdither before encoding in a color-mapped format. If the display resolution is high enough, ppmdither generally produces better-looking planets. ppmquant tends to create discrete color bands, particularly in the oceans, which are unrealistic and distracting. The number of colors in starry sky pictures generated with the -night option depends on the value specified for -saturation. Small values limit the color temperature distribution of the stars and reduce the number of colors in the image. If the -saturation is set to 0, none of the stars will be colored and the resulting image will never contain more than 256 colors. Night sky pictures with many different star colors often look best when color-compressed by pnmdepth rather than ppmquant or ppmdither. Try newmaxval settings of 63, 31, or 15 with pnmdepth to reduce the number of colors in the picture to 256 or fewer.

## OPTIONS

-clouds      Generate clouds. A pixmap of fractal clouds is generated. Selecting clouds sets the default for fractal dimension to 2.15 and power scale factor to 0.75.

-dimension *dimen*      Sets the fractal dimension to the specified dimen, which may be any floating-point value between 0 and 3. Higher fractal dimensions create more "chaotic" images, which require higher resolution output and a larger FFT mesh size to look good. If no dimension is specified, 2.4 is used when generating planets and 2.15 for clouds.

-glaciers *level*      The floating-point level setting controls the extent to which terrain elevation causes ice to appear at lower latitudes. The default value of 0.75 makes the polar caps extend toward the equator across high terrain and forms glaciers in the highest mountains, as on Earth. Higher values make ice sheets that cover more and more of the land surface, simulating planets in the midst of an ice age. Lower values tend to be boring, resulting in unrealistic geometrically precise ice cap boundaries.

-hour *hour*      When generating a planet, hour is used as the hour angle at the central meridian. If you specify -hour 12, for example, the planet will be fully illuminated, corresponding to high noon at the longitude at the center of the screen. You can specify any floating-point value between 0 and 24 for hour, but values which place most of the planet in darkness (0 to 4 and 20 to 24) result in crescents which, while pretty, don't give you many illuminated pixels for the amount of computing that's required. If no -hour option is specified, a random hour angle is chosen, biased so that only 25 percent of the images generated will be crescents.

| | |
|---|---|
| -ice *level* | Sets the extent of the polar ice caps to the given floating-point level. The default level of 0.4 produces ice caps similar to those of the Earth. Smaller values reduce the amount of ice, while larger -ice settings create more prominent ice caps. Sufficiently large values, such as 100 or more, in conjunction with small settings for -glaciers (try 0.1) create "ice balls" like Europa. |
| -inclination\|-tilt *angle* | The inclination angle of the planet with regard to its primary star is set to angle, which can be any floating-point value from -90 to 90. The inclination angle can be thought of as specifying, in degrees, the "season" the planet is presently experiencing or, more precisely, the latitude at which the star transits the zenith at local noon. If 0, the planet is at equinox; the star is directly overhead at the equator. Positive values represent summer in the northern hemisphere, negative values summer in the southern hemisphere. The Earth's inclination angle, for example, is about 23.5 at the June solstice, 0 at the equinoxes in March and September, and -23.5 at the December solstice. If no inclination angle is specified, a random value between -21.6 and 21.6 degrees is chosen. |
| -mesh *size* | A mesh of size by size will be used for the fast Fourier transform (FFT). Note that memory requirements and computation speed increase as the square of size; if you double the mesh size, the program will use four times the memory and run four times as long. The default mesh is 256x256, which produces reasonably good looking pictures while using half a megabyte for the 256x256 array of single precision complex numbers required by the FFT. On machines with limited memory capacity, you may have to reduce the mesh size to avoid running out of RAM. Increasing the mesh size produces better looking pictures; the difference becomes particularly noticeable when generating high-resolution images with relatively high fractal dimensions (between 2.2 and 3). |
| -night | A starry sky is generated. The stars are created by the same algorithm used for the stars that surround planet pictures, but the output consists exclusively of stars. |
| -power *factor* | Sets the power factor used to scale elevations synthesized from the FFT to factor, which can be any floating-point number greater than zero. If no factor is specified, a default of 1.2 is used if a planet is being generated, or 0.75 if clouds are selected by the -clouds option. The result of the FFT image synthesis is an array of elevation values between 0 and 1. A nonunity power factor exponentiates each of these elevations to the specified power. For example, a power factor of 2 squares each value, while a power factor of 0.5 replaces each with its square root. (Note that exponentiating values between 0 and 1 yields values that remain within that range.) Power factors less than 1 emphasize large-scale elevation changes at the expense of small variations. Power factors greater than 1 increase the roughness of the terrain and, like high fractal dimensions, may require a larger FFT mesh size or higher screen resolution to look good. |
| -saturation *sat* | Controls the degree of color saturation of the stars that surround planet pictures and fill starry skies created with the -night option. The default value of 125 creates stars that resemble the sky as seen by the human eye from Earth's surface. Stars are dim; only the brightest activate the cones in the human retina, causing color to be perceived. Higher values of sat approximate the appearance of stars from Earth orbit, where better dark adaptation, absence of sky glow, and the concentration of light from a given star onto a smaller area of the retina thanks to the lack of atmospheric turbulence enhances the perception of color. Values greater than 250 create "science fiction" skies that, while pretty, don't occur in this universe. |
| | Thanks to the inverse square law combined with nature's love of mediocrity, there are many, many dim stars for every bright one. This population relationship is accurately reflected in the skies created by ppmforge. Dim, low mass stars live much longer than bright, massive stars; consequently there are many reddish stars for every blue giant. This relationship is preserved by ppmforge. You can reverse the proportion, simulating the sky as seen in a starburst galaxy, by specifying a negative sat value. |

| | |
|---|---|
| -seed *num* | Sets the seed for the random number generator to the integer *num*. The seed used to create each picture is displayed on standard output (unless suppressed with the -quiet option). Pictures generated with the same seed will be identical. If no -seed is specified, a random seed derived from the date and time will be chosen. Specifying an explicit seed allows you to re-render a picture you particularly like at a higher resolution or with different viewing parameters. |
| -stars *fraction* | Specifies the percentage of pixels, in tenths of a percent, that will appear as stars, either surrounding a planet or filling the entire frame if -night is specified. The default *fraction* is 100. |
| -xsize¦-width *width* | Sets the width of the generated image to *width* pixels. The default width is 256 pixels. Images must be at least as wide as they are high; if a width less than the height is specified, it will be increased to equal the height. If you must have a long, skinny pixmap, make a square one with ppmforge, then use pnmcut to extract a portion of the shape and size you require. |
| -ysize¦-height *height* | Sets the height of the generated image to *height* pixels. The default height is 256 pixels. If the height specified exceeds the width, the width will be increased to equal the height. |

All flags can be abbreviated to their shortest unique prefix.

## BUGS

The algorithms require the output pixmap to be at least as wide as it is high, and the width to be an even number of pixels. These constraints are enforced by increasing the size of the requested pixmap if necessary.

You may have to reduce the FFT mesh size on machines with 16-bit integers and segmented pointer architectures.

## SEE ALSO

pnmcut(1), pnmdepth(1), ppmdither(1), ppmquant(1), ppm(5)

"Random Fractal Forgeries" by Richard F. Voss, in *Fundamental Algorithms for Computer Graphics by* Earnshaw et al. Berlin: Springer-Verlag, 1985.

*The Science Of Fractal Images*, edited by H. O. Peitgen and D. Saupe. New York: Springer-Verlag, 1988.

## AUTHOR

John Walker
Autodesk SA
Avenue des Champs-Montants 14b
CH-2074 MARIN
Suisse/Schweiz/Svizzera/Svizra/Switzerland

| | |
|---|---|
| Usenet: | kelvin@Autodesk.com |
| Fax: | 038/33 88 15 |
| Voice: | 038/33 76 33 |

Permission to use, copy, modify, and distribute this software and its documentation for any purpose and without fee is hereby granted, without any conditions or restrictions. This software is provided "as is" without express or implied warranty.

PLUGWARE! If you like this kind of stuff, you may also enjoy James Gleick's "Chaos—The Software" for MS-DOS, available for $59.95 from your local software store or directly from Autodesk, Inc., Attn: Science Series, 2320 Marinship Way, Sausalito, CA 94965, USA. Telephone: 800-688-2344 toll-free or, outside the U.S. 415-332-2344 Ext 4886. Fax: 415-289-4718. "Chaos—The Software" includes a more comprehensive fractal forgery generator that creates three-dimensional landscapes as well as clouds and planets, plus five more modules that explore other aspects of Chaos. The user guide of more than 200 pages includes an introduction by James Gleick and detailed explanations by Rudy Rucker of the mathematics and algorithms used by each program.

*25 October 1991*

# ppmhist

ppmhist—Print a histogram of a portable pixmap

## SYNOPSIS

ppmhist [*ppmfile*]

## DESCRIPTION

ppmhist reads a portable pixmap as input and generates a histogram of the colors in the pixmap.

## SEE ALSO

ppm(5), pgmhist(1)

## AUTHOR

Copyright© 1989 by Jef Poskanzer.

*3 April 1989*

# ppmmake

ppmmake—Create a pixmap of a specified size and color

## SYNOPSIS

ppmmake *color width height*

## DESCRIPTION

ppmmake produces a portable pixmap of the specified color, width, and height.

The color can be specified in five ways:

- A name, assuming that a pointer to an X11-style color names file was compiled in.
- An X11-style hexadecimal specifier: rgb:r/g/b, where r, g, and b are each 1- to 4-digit hexadecimal numbers.
- An X11-style decimal specifier: rgbi:r/g/b, where r, g, and b are floating-point numbers between 0 and 1.
- For backwards compatibility, an old-X11-style hexadecimal number: #rgb, #rrggbb, #rrrgggbbb, or #rrrrggggbbbb.
- For backwards compatibility, a triplet of numbers separated by commas: r,g,b, where r, g, and b are floating-point numbers between 0 and 1. (This style was added before MIT came up with the similar rgbi style.)

## SEE ALSO

ppm(5), pbmmake(1)

## AUTHOR

Copyright© 1991 by Jef Poskanzer.

*24 September 1991*

# ppmmix

ppmmix—Blend together two portable pixmaps

## SYNOPSIS

ppmmix *fadefactor ppmfile1 ppmfile2*

## DESCRIPTION

ppmmix reads two portable pixmaps as input and mixes them together using the specified fade factor. The fade factor may be in the range from 0.0 (only *ppmfile1*'s image data) to 1.0 (only *ppmfile2*'s image data). Anything in between gains a smooth blend between the two images.

The two pixmaps must have the same size.

## SEE ALSO

ppm(5)

## AUTHOR

Copyright© 1993 by Frank Neumann.

*16 November 1993*

# ppmnorm

ppmnorm—Normalize the contrast in a portable pixmap

## SYNOPSIS

ppmnorm[-bpercent *N* ¦ -bvalue *N*][-wpercent *N* ¦ -wvalue *N*][*ppmfile*]

## DESCRIPTION

ppmnorm reads a portable pixmap as input; normalizes the contrast by forcing the lightest pixels to white, the darkest pixels to black, and linearly rescaling the ones in between; and produces a portable pixmap as output.

It works by computing the relative gray level of each pixel as with ppmtopgm, and uses those values to scale the RGB levels. Note that this is different from using pgmnorm on the individual red, green, and blue graymaps (as produced by ppmtorgb3) and recombining them.

## OPTIONS

By default, the darkest two percent of all pixels are mapped to black, and the lightest one percent are mapped to white. You can override these percentages by using the -bpercent and -wpercent flags, or you can specify the exact pixel values to be mapped by using the -bvalue and -wvalue flags. Appropriate numbers for the flags can be gotten from the ppmhist tool. If you just want to enhance the contrast, then choose values at elbows in the histogram; for example, if value 29 represents 3 percent of the image but value 30 represents 20 percent, choose 30 for bvalue. If you want to lighten the image, then set bvalue to 0 and just fiddle with wvalue; similarly, to darken the image, set wvalue to maxval and play with bvalue.

All flags can be abbreviated to their shortest unique prefix.

## SEE ALSO

pgmnorm(1), ppmhist(1), ppm(5)

## AUTHOR

Wilson H. Bent, Jr. (whb@usc.edu), heavily based on the pgmnorm filter by Jef Poskanzer.

*7 October 1993*

# ppmntsc

ppmntsc—Make a portable pixmap look like it is taken from an American TV show

## SYNOPSIS

ppmntsc *dimfactor* [*ppmfile*]

## DESCRIPTION

ppmntsc reads a portable pixmap as input and dims every other row of image data down by the specified dim factor. This factor may be in the range of 0.0 (the alternate lines are totally black) to 1.0 (original image).

This creates an effect similar to what I saw once in the video clip "You Could be Mine" by Guns'n' Roses. In the scene I'm talking about you can see John Connor on his motorbike, looking up from the water trench (?) he's standing in. While the camera pulls back, the image becomes "normal" by brightening up the alternate rows of it. I thought this would be an interesting effect to try in MPEG. I did not yet check this out, however. Try for yourself.

## SEE ALSO

ppm(5), ppmdim(1)

## AUTHOR

Copyright© 1993 by Frank Neumann.

*16 November 1993*

# ppmpat

ppmpat—Make a pretty pixmap

## SYNOPSIS

ppmpat -gingham2¦-g2¦-gingham3¦ -g3¦-madras¦-tartan¦ -poles¦-squig¦-camo¦
 -anticamo *width height*

## DESCRIPTION

ppmpat produces a portable pixmap of the specified width and height, with a pattern in it.

This program is mainly to demonstrate use of the ppmdraw routines, a simple but powerful drawing library. See the ppmdraw.h include file for more information on using these routines. Still, some of the patterns can be rather pretty. If you have a color workstation, something like ppmpat -squig 300 300 ¦ "ppmquant 128" should generate a nice background.

## OPTIONS

The different flags specify various different pattern types:

| | |
|---|---|
| -gingham2 | A gingham check pattern. Can be tiled. |
| -gingham3 | A slightly more complicated gingham. Can be tiled. |
| -madras | A madras plaid. Can be tiled. |
| -tartan | A tartan plaid. Can be tiled. |
| -poles | Color gradients centered on randomly placed poles. May need to be run through ppmquant. |
| -squig | Squiggly tubular pattern. Can be tiled. May need to be run through ppmquant. |
| -camo | Camouflage pattern. May need to be run through ppmquant. |
| -anticamo | Anticamouflage pattern; like -camo, but ultra-bright colors. May need to be run through ppmquant. |

All flags can be abbreviated to their shortest unique prefix.

## REFERENCES

Some of the patterns are from "Designer's Guide to Color 3" by Jeanne Allen.

## SEE ALSO

pnmtile(1), ppmquant(1), ppm(5)

# ppmquant

ppmquant—Quantize the colors in a portable pixmap down to a specified number

## SYNOPSIS

```
ppmquant [-floyd¦-fs] ncolors [ppmfile]
ppmquant [-floyd¦-fs] -map mapfile [ppmfile]
```

## DESCRIPTION

ppmquant reads a portable pixmap as input. It chooses ncolors colors to best represent the image, maps the existing colors to the new ones, and writes a portable pixmap as output.

The quantization method is Heckbert's "median cut."

Alternately, you can skip the color-choosing step by specifying your own set of colors with the -map flag. The mapfile is just a ppm file; it can be any shape, all that matters is the colors in it. For instance, to quantize down to the 8-color IBM TTL color set, you might use the following:

```
P3
8 1
255
0 0 0
255 0 0
0 255 0
0 0 255
255 255 0
255 0 255
0 255 255
255 255 255
```

If you want to quantize one pixmap to use the colors in another one, just use the second one as the mapfile. You don't have to reduce it down to only one pixel of each color, just use it as is.

The -floyd/-fs flag enables a Floyd-Steinberg error diffusion step. Floyd-Steinberg gives vastly better results on images where the unmodified quantization has banding or other artifacts, especially when going to a small number of colors such as the preceding IBM set. However, it does take substantially more CPU time, so the default is off.

All flags can be abbreviated to their shortest unique prefix.

## REFERENCES

"Color Image Quantization for Frame Buffer Display," by Paul Heckbert, SIGGRAPH '82 Proceedings, page 297.

## SEE ALSO

ppmquantall(1), pnmdepth(1), ppmdither(1), ppm(5)

# ppmquantall

ppmquantall—Run ppmquant on a bunch of files all at once, so they share a common colormap

## SYNOPSIS

ppmquantall *ncolors ppmfile* ...

## DESCRIPTION

ppmquantall takes a bunch of portable pixmap as input. It chooses *ncolors* colors to best represent all of the images, maps the existing colors to the new ones, and overwrites the input files with the new quantized versions.

Verbose explanation: Say you have a dozen pixmaps that you want to display on the screen all at the same time. Your screen can only display 256 different colors, but the pixmaps have a total of a thousand or so different colors. For a single pixmap, you solve this problem with ppmquant; this script solves it for multiple pixmaps. All it does is concatenate them together into one big pixmap, run ppmquant on that, and then split it up into little pixmaps again.

(Note that another way to solve this problem is to preselect a set of colors and then use ppmquant's -map option to separately quantize each pixmap to that set.)

## SEE ALSO

ppmquant(1), ppm(5)

## BUGS

It's a csh script. csh scripts are not portable to System V. Scripts in general are not portable to non-UNIX environments.

## AUTHOR

Copyright© 1991 by Jef Poskanzer.

*27 July 1990*

# ppmqvga

ppmqvga—8-plane quantization

## SYNOPSIS

ppmqvga [ options ] [ input file ]

## DESCRIPTION

ppmqvga quantizes PPM files to eight planes, with optional Floyd-Steinberg dithering. Input is a PPM file from the file named, or standard input if no file is provided.

## OPTIONS

| | |
|---|---|
| -d dither | Apply Floyd-Steinberg dithering to the data |
| -q quiet | Produces no progress reporting, and no terminal output unless an error occurs. |
| -v verbose | Produces additional output describing the number of colors found, and some information on the resulting mapping. May be repeated to generate loads of internal table output, but generally only useful once. |

## EXAMPLES

ppmqvga -d my_image.ppm ¦ ppmtogif >my_image.gif

tgatoppm zombie.tga ¦ ppmqvga ¦ ppmtotif > zombie.tif

## SEE ALSO

ppmquant

## DIAGNOSTICS

Error messages if problems; various levels of optional progress reporting.

## AUTHORS

Original by Lyle Rains (1rains@netcom.com) as ppmq256 and ppmq256fs combined; documented and enhanced by Bill Davidsen (davidsen@crd.ge.com).

## COPYRIGHT

Copyright© 1991, 1992 by Bill Davidsen, all rights reserved. The program and documentation may be freely distributed by anyone in source or binary format. Please clearly note any changes.

*Local*

# ppmrelief

ppmrelief—Run a Laplacian relief filter on a portable pixmap

## SYNOPSIS

ppmrelief [*ppmfile*]

## DESCRIPTION

ppmrelief reads a portable pixmap as input, does a Laplacian relief filter, and writes a portable pixmap as output.

The Laplacian relief filter is described in *Beyond Photography* by Holzmann, equation 3.19. It's a sort of edge-detection.

## SEE ALSO

pgmbentley(1), pgmoil(1), ppm(5)

## AUTHOR

Copyright© 1990 by Wilson Bent (whb@hoh-2.att.com).

*11 January 1991*

# ppmshift

ppmshift—Shift lines of a portable pixmap left or right by a random amount

## SYNOPSIS

ppmshift *shift* [*ppmfile*]

## DESCRIPTION

ppmshift reads a portable pixmap as input and shifts every row of image data to the left or right by a certain amount. The *shift* parameter determines by how many pixels a row is to be shifted at most.

Another one of those effects I intended to use for MPEG tests. Unfortunately, this program will not help me here—it creates patterns that are too random to be used for animations. Still, it might give interesting results on still images.

## EXAMPLE

Check this out: Save your favorite model's picture from something like `alt.binaries.pictures.supermodels` (okay, or from any other picture source), convert it to ppm, and process it like this, assuming the picture is 800×600 pixels:

1. Take the upper half and leave it like it is: `pnmcut 0 0 800 300 cs.ppm >upper.ppm`.
2. Take the lower half, flip it upside down, dim it, and distort it a little: `pnmcut 0 300 800 300 cs.ppm ¦ pnmflip -tb ¦ ppmdim 0.7 ¦ ppmshift 10 >lower.ppm`.
3. Concatenate the two pieces: `pnmcat -tb upper.ppm lower.ppm >newpic.ppm`.

The resulting picture looks like the image being reflected on a water surface with slight ripples.

## SEE ALSO

ppm(5), pnmcut(1), pnmflip(1), ppmdim(1), pnmcat(1)

## AUTHOR

Copyright© 1993 by Frank Neumann.

*16 November 1993*

# ppmspread

ppmspread—Displace a portable pixmap's pixels by a random amount

## SYNOPSIS

ppmspread *amount* [*ppmfile*]

## DESCRIPTION

ppmspread reads a portable pixmap as input and moves every pixel around a bit relative to its original position. `amount` determines by how many pixels a pixel is to be moved around at most.

Pictures processed with this filter will seem to be somewhat dissolved or unfocussed (although they appear more coarse than images processed by something like `pnmconvol`).

## SEE ALSO

ppm(5), pnmconvol(1)

## AUTHOR

Copyright© 1993 by Frank Neumann.

*16 November 1993*

# ppmtoacad

ppmtoacad—Convert portable pixmap to AutoCAD database or slide

## SYNOPSIS

ppmtoacad [-dxb][-poly][-background *colour*][-white][-aspect *ratio*][-8][*ppmfile*]

## DESCRIPTION

ppmtoacad reads a portable pixmap as input. Produces an AutoCAD slide file or binary database import (DXB) file as output. If no `ppmfile` is specified, input is read from standard input.

## OPTIONS

-dxb
: An AutoCAD binary database import (DXB) file is written. This file is read with the DXBIN command and, once loaded, becomes part of the AutoCAD geometrical database and can be viewed and edited like any other object. Each sequence of identical pixels becomes a separate object in the database; this can result in very large AutoCAD drawing files. However, if you want to trace over a bitmap, it lets you zoom and pan around the bitmap as you wish.

-poly
: If the -dxb option is not specified, the output of ppmtoacad is an AutoCAD slide file. Normally, each row of pixels is represented by an AutoCAD line entity. If -poly is selected, the pixels are rendered as filled polygons. If the slide is viewed on a display with higher resolution than the source pixmap, this will cause the pixels to expand instead of appearing as discrete lines against the screen background color. Regrettably, this representation yields slide files that occupy more disc space and take longer to display.

-background *color*
: Most AutoCAD display drivers can be configured to use any available color as the screen background. Some users prefer a black screen background, others white, while splinter groups advocate burnt ocher, tawny puce, and shocking gray. Discarding pixels whose closest AutoCAD color representation is equal to the background color can substantially reduce the size of the AutoCAD database or slide file needed to represent a bitmap. If no -background color is specified, the screen background color is assumed to be black. Any AutoCAD color number may be specified as the screen background; color numbers are assumed to specify the hues defined in the standard AutoCAD 256-color palette.

-white
: Because many AutoCAD users choose a white screen background, this option is provided as a short-cut. Specifying -white is identical in effect to -background 7.

-aspect *ratio*
: If the source pixmap had nonsquare pixels, the ratio of the pixel width to pixel height should be specified as ratio. The resulting slide or DXB file will be corrected so that pixels on the AutoCAD screen will be square. For example, to correct an image made for a 320×200 VGA/MCGA screen, specify -aspect 0.8333.

-8
: Restricts the colors in the output file to the eight RGB shades.

All flags can be abbreviated to their shortest unique prefix.

## BUGS

AutoCAD has a fixed palette of 256 colors, distributed along the hue, lightness, and saturation axes. Pixmaps that contain many nearly identical colors, or colors not closely approximated by AutoCAD's palette, may be poorly rendered.

ppmtoacad works best if the system displaying its output supports the full 256 color AutoCAD palette. Monochrome, 8-color, and 16-color configurations will produce less than optimal results.

When creating a DXB file or a slide file with the -poly option, ppmtoacad finds both vertical and horizontal runs of identical pixels and consolidates them into rectangular regions to reduce the size of the output file. This is effective for images with large areas of constant color, but it's no substitute for true raster to vector conversion. In particular, thin diagonal lines are not optimized at all by this process.

Output files can be huge.

## SEE ALSO

*AutoCAD Reference Manual*: "Slide File Format" and "Binary Drawing Interchange (DXB) Files"; ppm(5)

## AUTHOR

John Walker
Autodesk SA
Avenue des Champs-Montants 14b
CH-2074 MARIN
Suisse/Schweiz/Svizzera/Svizra/Switzerland

Usenet:    kelvin@Autodesk.com
Fax:       038/33 88 15
Voice:     038/33 76 33

Permission to use, copy, modify, and distribute this software and its documentation for any purpose and without fee is hereby granted, without any conditions or restrictions. This software is provided "as is" without express or implied warranty.

AutoCAD and Autodesk are registered trademarks of Autodesk, Inc.

*10 October 1991*

# ppmtobmp

ppmtobmp—Convert a portable pixmap into a BMP file

## SYNOPSIS

ppmtobmp [-windows][-os2][ppmfile]

## DESCRIPTION

ppmtobmp reads a portable pixmap as input and produces a Microsoft Windows or OS/2 BMP file as output.

## OPTIONS

-windows    Tells the program to produce a Microsoft Windows BMP file.

-os2        Tells the program to produce an OS/2 BMP file. (This is the default.)

All flags can be abbreviated to their shortest unique prefix.

## SEE ALSO

bmptoppm(1), ppm(5)

## AUTHOR

Copyright© 1992 by David W. Sanderson.

*26 October 1992*

# ppmtogif

ppmtogif—Convert a portable pixmap into a GIF file

## SYNOPSIS

ppmtogif [-interlace][-sort][-map mapfile][-transparent color][ppmfile]

## DESCRIPTION

ppmtogif reads a portable pixmap as input and produces a GIF file as output.

## OPTIONS

-interlace       Tells the program to produce an interlaced GIF file.

-sort            Produces a GIF file with a sorted colormap.

-map mapfile     Uses the colors found in the mapfile to create the colormap in the GIF file, instead of the colors from ppmfile. The mapfile can be any ppm file; all that matters is the colors in it. If the colors in ppmfile do not match those in mapfile, they are matched to a "best match." A (much) better result can be obtained by using the following filter in advance:

```
ppmquant -floyd -map mapfile
```

-transparent color      Mark the given color as transparent in the GIF file. The color is specified as in ppmmake(1). Note that this option outputs a GIF89a format file, which might not be understood by your software.

All flags can be abbreviated to their shortest unique prefix.

## SEE ALSO

giftoppm(1), ppmquant(1), ppm(5)

## AUTHOR

Based on GIFENCOD by David Rowley (mgardi@watdcsu.waterloo.edu). Lempel-Ziv compression based on compress.

Copyright© 1989 by Jef Poskanzer.

*30 June 1993*

# ppmtoicr

ppmtoicr—Convert a portable pixmap into NCSA ICR format

## SYNOPSIS

ppmtoicr [-windowname *name*][-expand *expand*][-display *display*][-rle][*ppmfile*]

## DESCRIPTION

ppmtoicr reads a portable pixmap file as input and produces an NCSA Telnet Interactive Color Raster graphic file as output. If ppmfile is not supplied, ppmtoicr will read from standard input.

Interactive Color Raster (ICR) is a protocol for displaying raster graphics on workstation screens. The protocol is implemented in NCSA Telnet for the Macintosh version 2.3. The ICR protocol shares characteristics of the Tektronix graphics terminal emulation protocol. For example, escape sequences are used to control the display.

ppmtoicr will output the appropriate sequences to create a window of the dimensions of the input pixmap, create a colormap of up to 256 colors on the display, then load the picture data into the window.

Note that there is no icrtoppm tool; this transformation is one-way.

## OPTIONS

-windowname*name*    Output will be displayed in *name*. (Default is to use ppm-file or "untitled" if standard input is read.)

-expand*expand*    Output will be expanded on display by factor *expand*. (For example, a value of 2 will cause four pixels to be displayed for every input pixel.)

-display*display*    Output will be displayed on screen numbered *display*.

-rle    Use run-length encoded format for display. (This will nearly always result in a quicker display, but may skew the colormap.)

## EXAMPLES

This displays a ppm file using the protocol:

```
ppmtoicr ppmfile
```

This will create a window named ppmfile on the display with the correct dimensions for ppmfile, create and download a colormap of up to 256 colors, and download the picture into the window. The same effect may be achieved by the following sequence:

```
ppmtoicr ppmfile > filename
cat filename
```

To display a GIF file using the protocol in a window titled after the input file, zoom the displayed image by a factor of 2, and run-length encode the data:

```
giftoppm giffile ¦ ppmtoicr -w giffile -r -e 2
```

## BUGS

The protocol uses frequent `fflush` calls to speed up display. If the output is saved to a file for later display via `cat`, drawing will be much slower. In either case, increasing the Blocksize limit on the display will speed up transmission substantially.

## SEE ALSO

ppm(5)

*NCSA Telnet for the Macintosh*, University of Illinois at Urbana-Champaign (1989)

## AUTHOR

Copyright© 1990 by Kanthan Pillay (`svpillay@Princeton.EDU`), Princeton University Computing and Information Technology.

*30 July 1990*

# ppmtoilbm

ppmtoilbm—Convert a portable pixmap into an ILBM file

## SYNOPSIS

```
ppmtoilbm [-maxplanes¦-mp N][-fixplanes¦-fp N][-ham6¦-ham8][-dcbits-dcplanesrgb]
[-normal¦-hamif¦-hamforce¦-24if¦-24force¦ -dcif¦-dcforce¦-cmaponly] [-ecs¦-aga]
[- compress¦-nocompress][-cmethod type][-mapppmfile] [-savemem][ppmfile]
```

## DESCRIPTION

ppmtoilbm reads a portable pixmap as input and produces an ILBM file as output. Supported ILBM types are the following:

Normal ILBMs with 1–16 planes

Amiga HAM with 3–16 planes

24-bit

Colormap (BMHD and CMAP chunk only, nPlanes = 0)

Unofficial direct color    1–16 planes for each color component

Chunks written:  BMHD, CMAP, CAMG (only for HAM), BODY (not for colormap files) unofficial DCOL chunk for direct color ILBM

## OPTIONS

Options marked with (*) can be prefixed with no, for example, -nohamif. All options can be abbreviated to their shortest unique prefix.

| | |
|---|---|
| -maxplanes ¦ -mp *n* | (default 5, minimum 1, maximum 16) Maximum planes to write in a normal ILBM. If the pixmap does not fit into *n* planes, ppmtoilbm writes a HAM file (if -hamif is used), a 24-bit file (if -24if is used), a direct color file (if -dcif is used). or aborts with an error. |
| -fixplanes ¦ -fp *n* | (min 1, max 16) If a normal ILBM is written, it will have exactly *n* planes. |
| -hambits ¦ -hamplanes *n* | (default 6, min 3, max 16) Select number of planes for HAM picture. The current Amiga hardware supports 6 and 8 planes, so for now you should only use this values. |

| | |
|---|---|
| -normal (default) | Turns off -hamif/-24if/-dcif, -hamforce/-24force/-dcforce and -cmaponly. Also sets compression type to byterun1. |
| -hamif (*), -24if (*), -dcif (*) | Write a HAM/24-bit/direct color file if the pixmap does not fit into maxplanes planes. |
| -hamforce (*), -24force (*), -dcforce (*) | Write a HAM/24-bit/direct color file. |
| -dcbits ¦ -dcplanes r g b | (default 5, min 1, max 16). Select number of bits for red, green, and blue in a direct color ILBM. |
| -ecs (default) | Shortcut for: -hamplanes 6 -maxplanes 5 |
| -aga | Shortcut for: -hamplanes 8 -maxplanes 8 |
| -ham6 | Shortcut for: -hamplanes 6 -hamforce |
| -ham8 | Shortcut for: -hamplanes 8 -hamforce |
| -compress (*) (default), -cmethod none¦byterun1 | Compress the BODY chunk. The default compression method is byterun1. Compression requires building the ILBM image in memory; turning compression off allows stream-writing of the image, but the resulting file will usually be 30 percent to 50 percent larger. Another alternative is the -savemem option; this will keep memory requirements for compression at a minimum, but is very slow. |
| -map *ppmfile* | Write a normal ILBM using the colors in *ppmfile* as the colormap. The colormap file also determines the number of planes; a -maxplanes or -fixplanes option is ignored. |
| -cmaponly | Write a colormap file: only BMHD and CMAP chunks, no BODY chunk, nPlanes = 0. |
| -savemem | See the -compress option. |

## BUGS

HAM pictures will always get a grayscale colormap; a real color selection algorithm might give better results. On the other hand, this allows row-by-row operation on HAM images, and all HAM images of the same depth (number of planes) share a common colormap, which is useful for building HAM animations.

## REFERENCES

Amiga ROM Kernel Reference Manual—Devices (Third Edition), Addison Wesley, ISBN 0-201-56775-X

## SEE ALSO

ppm(5), ilbmtoppm(1)

## AUTHORS

Copyright© 1989 by Jef Poskanzer; modified October 1993 by Ingo Wilken (Ingo.Wilken@informatik.uni-oldenburg.de).

*31 October 1993*

# ppmtomap

ppmtomap—Extract all colors from a portable pixmap

## SYNOPSIS

ppmtomap [-sort][-square][*ppmfile*]

## DESCRIPTION

ppmtomap reads a portable pixmap as input and produces a portable pixmap as output, representing a colormap of the input file. All *N* different colors found are put in an NX1 portable pixmap. This colormap file can be used as a mapfile for ppmquant or ppmtogif.

## OPTIONS

-sort       Produces a portable pixmap with the colors in some sorted order

-square    Produces a (more or less) square output file, instead of putting all colors on the top row

All flags can be abbreviated to their shortest unique prefix.

## WARNING

If you want to use the output file as a mapfile for ppmtogif, you first have to do a ppmquant 256 because ppmtomap is not limited to 256 colors (but to 65536).

## SEE ALSO

ppmtogif(1), ppmquant(1), ppm(5)

## AUTHOR

Marcel Wijkstra (wijkstra@fwi.uva.nl)

Copyright© 1989 by Jef Poskanzer.

*11 August 1993*

# ppmtomitsu

ppmtomitsu—Convert a portable pixmap to a Mitsubishi S340-10 file

## SYNOPSIS

ppmtomitsu [-sharpness *val*][-enlarge *val*][-media *string*][-copy *val*]
[-dpi300][-tiny] [*ppmfile*]

## DESCRIPTION

ppmtomitsu reads a portable pixmap as input and converts it into a format suitable to be printed by a Mitsubishi S340-10 printer, or any other Mitsubishi color sublimation printer.

The Mitsubishi S340-10 Color Sublimation printer supports 24-bit color. Images of the available sizes take so long to transfer that there is a fast method, employing a lookup table that ppmtomitsu will use if there is a maximum of 256 colors in the pixmap. ppmtomitsu will try to position your image to the center of the paper, and will rotate your image for you if xsize is larger than ysize. If your image is larger than the media allows, ppmtomitsu will quit with an error message. (We decided that the media were too expensive to have careless users produce misprints.) After data transmission has started, the job can't be stopped in a sane way without resetting the printer. The printer understands putting together images in the printer's memory; ppmtomitsu doesn't utilize this as pnmcat and so on provide the same functionality and let you view the result onscreen, too. The S340-10 is the lowest common denominator printer; for higher resolution printers, there's the dpi300 option. The other printers also support higher values for enlarge eg, but I don't think that's essential enough to warrant a change in the program.

| | |
|---|---|
| -sharpness 1-4 | Sharpness designation. Default is to use the current sharpness. |
| -enlarge 1-3 | Enlarge by a factor; default is 1 (no enlarge) |
| -media A, A4, AS, A4S | Designate the media you're using. Default is 1184 x 1350, which will fit on any media. A is 1216 x 1350, A4 is 1184 x 1452, AS is 1216 x 1650, and A4S is 1184 x 1754. A warning: If you specify a different media than the printer currently has, the printer will wait until you put in the correct media or switch it off. |
| -copy 1-9 | The number of copies to produce. Default is 1. |
| -dpi300 | Double the number of allowed pixels for a S3600-30 Printer in S340-10 compatibility mode. (The S3600-30 has 300dpi.) |

-tiny        Memory-safing, but always slow. The printer will get the data line-by-line in 24-bit. It's probably a good idea to use this if your machine starts paging a lot without this option.

## REFERENCES

Mitsubishi Sublimation Full Color Printer S340-10; Specifications of Parallel Interface LSP-F0232F

## SEE ALSO

ppmquant(1), pnmscale(1), ppm(5)

## BUGS

We didn't find any—yet. Besides, they're called features anyway :-) If you should find one, please e-mail me at the following address.

## AUTHOR

Copyright© 1992, 1993 by S. Petra Zeidler, MPIFR Bonn, Germany (spz@specklec.mpifr-bonn.mpg.de).

*29 January 1992*

# ppmtopcx

ppmtopcx—Convert a portable pixmap into a PCX file

## SYNOPSIS

ppmtopcx [*ppmfile*]

## DESCRIPTION

ppmtopcx reads a portable pixmap as input and produces a PCX file as output.

## SEE ALSO

pcxtoppm(1), ppm(5)

## AUTHOR

Copyright © 1990 by Michael Davidson.

*9 April 1990*

# ppmtopgm

ppmtopgm—Convert a portable pixmap into a portable graymap

## SYNOPSIS

ppmtopgm [*ppmfile*]

## DESCRIPTION

ppmtopgm reads a portable pixmap as input and produces a portable graymap as output. The quantization formula used is .299 r + .587 g + .114 b.

Note that although there is a pgmtoppm program, it is not necessary for simple conversions from pgm to ppm, because any ppm program can read pgm (and pbm ) files automagically. pgmtoppm is for colorizing a pgm file. Also, see ppmtorgb3 for a different way of converting color to gray.

## QUOTE

*Cold-hearted orb that rules the night*
*Removes the colors from our sight*
*Red is gray, and yellow white*
*But we decide which is right*
*And which is a quantization error.*

## SEE ALSO

pgmtoppm(1), ppmtorgb3(1), rgb3toppm(1), ppm(5), pgm(5)

## AUTHOR

Copyright© 1989 by Jef Poskanzer.

*23 December 1988*

# ppmtopi1

ppmtopi1—Convert a portable pixmap into an Atari Degas PI1 file

## SYNOPSIS

ppmtopi1 [*ppmfile*]

## DESCRIPTION

ppmtopi1 reads a portable pixmap as input and produces an Atari Degas PI1 file as output.

## SEE ALSO

pi1toppm(1), ppm(5), pbmtopi3(1), pi3topbm(1)

## AUTHOR

Copyright© 1991 by Steve Belczyk (seb3@gte.com) and Jef Poskanzer.

*19 July 1990*

# ppmtopict

ppmtopict—Convert a portable pixmap into a Macintosh PICT file

## SYNOPSIS

ppmtopict [*ppmfile*]

## DESCRIPTION

ppmtopict reads a portable pixmap as input and produces a Macintosh PICT file as output.

The generated file is only the data fork of a picture. You will need a program such as mcvert to generate a Macbinary or a BinHex file that contains the necessary information to identify the file as a PICT file to MacOS.

Even though PICT supports 2 and 4 bits per pixel, ppmtopict always generates an 8-bits-per-pixel file.

## BUGS

The picture size field is only correct if the output is to a file because writing into this field requires seeking backwards on a file. However, the PICT documentation seems to suggest that this field is not critical anyway because it is only the lower 16 bits of the picture size.

## SEE ALSO

picttoppm(1), ppm(5), mcvert(1)

## AUTHOR

Copyright© 1990 by Ken Yap (`ken@cs.rocester.edu`).

*15 April 1990*

# ppmtopj

ppmtopj—Convert a portable pixmap to an HP PaintJet file

## SYNOPSIS

```
ppmtopj [-gamma val][-xpos val][-ypos val][-back dark¦lite][-rle][-center]
[-render none¦snap¦bw¦dither¦diffuse¦monodither¦monodiffuse¦clusterdither¦
monoclusterdither][ppmfile]
```

## DESCRIPTION

ppmtopj reads a portable pixmap as input and converts it into a format suitable to be printed by an HP PaintJet printer.

For best results, the input file should be in 8-color RGB form; that is, it should have only the eight binary combinations of full-on and full-off primaries. You could get this by sending the input file through ppmquant -map with a mapfile such as

```
P3
8 1
255
0 0 0 2550 0 02550 0 0 255
255 255 0 255 0 255 0 255 255 255 255 255
```

Or else you could use ppmdither -red 2 -green 2 -blue 2.

## OPTIONS

| | |
|---|---|
| -rle | Run-length encode the image. (This can result in larger images.) |
| -back | Enhance the foreground by indicating if the background is light or dark compared to the foreground. |
| -render *alg* | Use an internal rendering algorithm (default dither). |
| -gamma *int* | Gamma correct the image using the integer parameter as a gamma (default 0). |
| -center | Center the image to an 8.5 by 11 page. |
| -xpos *pos* | Move by *pos* pixels in the x direction. |
| -ypos *pos* | Move by *pos* pixels in the y direction. |

## REFERENCES

*HP PaintJet XL Color Graphics Printer User's Guide*

## SEE ALSO

pnmdepth(1), ppmquant(1), ppmdither(1), ppm(5)

## BUGS

Most of the options have not been tested because of the price of the paper.

## AUTHOR

Copyright© 1991 by Christos Zoulas.

*13 July 1991*

# ppmtopjxl

ppmtopjxl—Convert a portable pixmap into an HP PaintJet XL PCL file

## SYNOPSIS

```
ppmtopjxl [-nopack] [-gamma <n> ] [-presentation] [-dark] [-diffuse]
[-cluster] [-dither] [-xshift <s> ] [-yshift <s> ] [-xshift <s> ] [-yshift <s> ]
[-xsize¦-width¦-xscale <s> ] [-ysize¦-height¦-yscale <s> ] [ppmfile]
```

## DESCRIPTION

ppmtopjxl reads a portable pixmap as input and produces a PCL file suitable for printing on an HP PaintJet XL printer as output.

The generated file is not suitable for printing on a normal PrintJet printer. The -nopack option generates a file that does not use the normal TIFF 4.0 compression method. This file might be printable on a normal PaintJet printer (not an XL).

The -gamma option sets the gamma correction for the image. The useful range for the PaintJet XL is approximately 0.6 to 1.5.

The rendering algorithm used for images can be altered with the -dither, -cluster, and -diffuse options. These options select ordered dithering, clustered ordered dithering, or error diffusion, respectively. The -dark option can be used to enhance images with a dark background when they are reduced in size. The -presentation option turns on presentation mode, in which two passes are made over the paper to increase ink density. This should be used only for images where quality is critical.

The image can be resized by setting the -xsize and -ysize options. The parameter to either of these options is interpreted as the number of dots to set the width or height to, but an optional dimension of pt (points), dp (decipoints), in (inches), or cm (centimeters) may be appended. If only one dimension is specified, the other will be scaled appropriately.

The options -width and -height are synonyms of -xsize and -ysize.

The -xscale and -yscale options can alternatively be used to scale the image by a simple factor.

The image can be shifted on the page by using the -xshift and -yshift options. These move the image the specified dimensions right and down.

## SEE ALSO

ppm(5)

## AUTHOR

Angus Duggan

*14 March 1991*

# ppmtopuzz

ppmtopuzz—Convert a portable pixmap into an X11 puzzle file

## SYNOPSIS

```
ppmtopuzz [ppmfile]
```

## DESCRIPTION

ppmtopuzz reads a portable pixmap as input and produces an X11 puzzle file as output. A puzzle file is for use with the puzzle program included with the X11 distribution; puzzle's -picture flag lets you specify an image file.

## SEE ALSO

ppm(5), puzzle(1)

## AUTHOR

Copyright© 1991 by Jef Poskanzer.

*22 August 1990*

# ppmtorgb3

ppmtorgb3—Separate a portable pixmap into three portable graymaps

## SYNOPSIS

ppmtorgb3 [*ppmfile*]

## DESCRIPTION

ppmtorgb3 reads a portable pixmap as input and writes three portable graymaps as output, one each for red, green, and blue.

The output filenames are constructed by taking the input filename, stripping off any extension, and appending .red, .grn, and .blu. For example, separating lenna.ppm would result in lenna.red, lenna.grn, and lenna.blu. If the input comes from stdin, the names are noname.red, noname.grn, and noname.blu.

## SEE ALSO

rgb3toppm(1), ppmtopgm(1), pgmtoppm(1), ppm(5), pgm(5)

## AUTHOR

Copyright© 1991 by Jef Poskanzer.

*10 January 1991*

# ppmtosixel

ppmtosixel—Convert a portable pixmap into DEC sixel format

## SYNOPSIS

ppmtosixel [-raw][-margin][*ppmfile*]

## DESCRIPTION

ppmtosixel reads a portable pixmap as input and produces sixel commands (SIX) as output. The output is formatted for color printing, for example, for a DEC LJ250 color inkjet printer.

If RGB values from the PPM file do not have maxval=100, the RGB values are rescaled. A printer control header and a color assignment table begin the SIX file. Image data is written in a compressed format by default. A printer control footer ends the image file.

## OPTIONS

-raw      If specified, each pixel will be explicitly described in the image file. If -raw is not specified, output will default to compressed format in which identical adjacent pixels are replaced by repeat pixel commands. A raw file is often an order of magnitude larger than a compressed file and prints much slower.

-margin   If -margin is not specified, the image will start at the left margin (of the window, paper, or whatever). If -margin is specified, a 1.5 inch left margin will offset the image.

## PRINTING

Generally, sixel files must reach the printer unfiltered. Use the `lpr -x` option or `cat filename > /dev/tty0?`.

## BUGS

Upon rescaling, truncation of the least significant bits of RGB values may result in poor color conversion. If the original PPM `maxval` was greater than 100, rescaling also reduces the image depth. While the actual RGB values from the `ppm` file are more or less retained, the color palette of the LJ250 may not match the colors on your screen. This seems to be a printer limitation.

## SEE ALSO

ppm(5)

## AUTHOR

Copyright© 1991 by Rick Vinci.

*26 April 1991*

# ppmtotga

ppmtotga—Convert portable pixmap into a TrueVision Targa file

## SYNOPSIS

ppmtotga [-mono¦-cmap¦-rgb][-norle][*ppmfile*]

## DESCRIPTION

ppmtotga reads a portable pixmap as input and produces a TrueVision Targa file as output.

## OPTIONS

-mono      Forces Targa file to be of type 8-bit monochrome. Input must be a portable bitmap or a portable graymap.

-cmap      Forces Targa file to be of type 24-bit colormapped. Input must be a portable bitmap, a portable graymap, or a portable pixmap containing no more than 256 distinct colors.

-rgb       Forces Targa file to be of type 24-bit unmapped color.

-norle     Disables run-length encoding, in case you have a Targa reader that can't read run-length encoded files.

All flags can be abbreviated to their shortest unique prefix. If no file type is specified, the most highly constained compatible type is used, where monochrome is more constained than colormapped, which is in turn more constained than unmapped.

## BUGS

Does not support all possible Targa file types. Should really be in `pnm`, not `ppm`.

## SEE ALSO

tgatoppm(1), ppm(5)

## AUTHOR

Copyright© 1989, 1991 by Mark Shand and Jef Poskanzer.

*28 October 1991*

# ppmtouil

ppmtouil—Convert a portable pixmap into a Motif UIL icon file

## SYNOPSIS

ppmtouil [-name *uilname*][*ppmfile*]

## DESCRIPTION

ppmtouil reads a portable pixmap as input and produces a Motif UIL icon file as output.

If the program was compiled with an rgb database specified, and an RGB value from the ppm input matches an RGB value from the database, then the corresponding color name mnemonic is printed in the UIL's colormap. If no rgb database was compiled in, or if the RGB values don't match, then the color will be printed with the #RGB, #RRGGBB, #RRRGGGBBB, or #RRRRGGGGBBBB hexadecimal format.

## OPTIONS

-name     Allows you to specify the prefix string that is printed in the resulting UIL output. If not specified, it will default to the filename (without extension) of the ppmfile argument. If -name is not specified and no ppmfile is specified (that is, piped input), the prefix string will default to the string "noname".

All flags can be abbreviated to their shortest unique prefix.

## SEE ALSO

ppm(5)

## AUTHOR

Converted by Jef Poskanzer from ppmtoxpm.c, which is copyright© 1990 by Mark W. Snitily.

*31 August 1990*

# ppmtoxpm

ppmtoxpm—Convert a portable pixmap into an X11 pixmap

## SYNOPSIS

ppmtoxpm [-name <xpmname>] [-rgb <rgb-textfile>][<*ppmfile*>]

## DESCRIPTION

ppmtoxpm reads a portable pixmap as input and produces an X11 pixmap (version 3) as output that can be loaded directly by the XPM library.

The -name option allows you to specify the prefix string which is printed in the resulting XPM output. If not specified, it will default to the filename (without extension) of the ppmfile argument. If -name is not specified and ppmfile is not specified (that is, piped input), the prefix string will default to the string "noname".

The -rgb option allows you to specify an X11 rgb text file for the lookup of color name mnemonics. This RGB text file is typically the /usr/lib/X11/rgb.txt of the MIT X11 distribution, but any file using the same format may be used. When specified and an RGB value from the ppm input matches an RGB value from the <rgb-textfile>, then the corresponding color name mnemonic is printed in the XPM's colormap. If -rgb is not specified, or if the RGB values don't match, then the color will be printed with the #RGB, #RRGGBB, #RRRGGGBBB, or #RRRRGGGGBBBB hexadecimal format.

All flags can be abbreviated to their shortest unique prefix.

For example, to convert the file dot (found in `/usr/include/X11/bitmaps`), from xbm to xpm, you could specify

```
xbmtopbm dot ¦ ppmtoxpm -name dot
```

or, with an `rgb` text file (in the local directory)

```
xbmtopbm dot ¦ ppmtoxpm -name dot -rgb rgb.txt
```

## BUGS

An option to match the closest (rather than exact) color name mnemonic from the `rgb` text would be a desirable enhancement.

Truncation of the least significant bits of an RGB value may result in nonexact matches when performing color name mnemonic lookups.

## SEE ALSO

ppm(5)

XPM Manual by Arnaud Le Hors (`lehors@mirsa.inria.fr`).

## AUTHOR

Copyright © 1990 by Mark W. Snitily. This tool was developed for Schlumberger Technologies, ATE Division, and with their permission is being made available to the public with the above copyright notice and permission notice.

Upgraded to XPM2 by Paul Breslaw, Mecasoft SA, Zurich, Switzerland (`paul@mecazh.uu.ch`); Thu, Nov 8, 16:01:17, 1990.

Upgraded to XPM version 3 by Arnaud le Hors (`lehors@mirsa.inria.fr`).

*9 April 1991*

# ppmtoyuv

ppmtoyuv—Convert a portable pixmap into an Abekas YUV file

## SYNOPSIS

```
ppmtoyuv [ppmfile]
```

## DESCRIPTION

ppmtoyuv reads a portable pixmap as input and produces an Abekas YUV file as output.

## SEE ALSO

yuvtoppm(1), ppm(5)

## AUTHOR

Marc Boucher (`<marc@PostImage.COM>`), based on Example Conversion Program, *A60/A64 Digital Video Interface Manual*, page 69. Copyright© 1991 by DHD Post Image Inc. Copyright© 1987 by Abekas Video Systems Inc.

*25 March 1991*

# ppmtoyuvsplit

ppmtoyuvsplit—Convert a portable pixmap into three subsampled raw YUV files

## SYNOPSIS

```
ppmtoyuvsplit basename [ppmfile]
```

## DESCRIPTION

ppmtoyuvsplit reads a portable pixmap as input and produces three raw files—basename.Y, basename.U, and basename.V—as output. These files are the subsampled raw YUV representation of the input pixmap, as required by the Stanford MPEG code. The subsampling is done by arithmetic mean of 4 pixels colors into one. The YUV values are scaled according to CCIR.601, as assumed by MPEG.

## SEE ALSO

mpeg(1), ppm(5)

## AUTHOR

Copyright© 1993 by Andre Beck (AndreBeck@IRS.Inf.TU-Dresden.de). Based on ppmtoyuv.c.

*9 September 1993*

# pr

pr—Convert text files for printing

## SYNOPSIS

pr [+PAGE] [-COLUMN] [-abcdfFmrtv] [-e[in-tab-char[in-tab-width]]] [-h header]
[-i[out-tab-char[out-tab-width]]] [-l page-length] [-n[number-separator[digits]]]
[-o left-margin] [-s[column-separator]] [-w page-width] [--help] [-- version] [file...]

## DESCRIPTION

This manual page documents the GNU version of pr. pr prints on the standard output a paginated and optionally multicolumn copy of the text files given on the command line, or of the standard input if no files are given or when the filename - is encountered. Form feeds in the input cause page breaks in the output.

## OPTIONS

| | |
|---|---|
| PAGE | Begin printing with page PAGE. |
| -COLUMN | Produce COLUMN-column output and print columns down. The column width is automatically decreased as COLUMN increases; unless you use the -w option to increase the page width as well, this option might cause some columns to be truncated. |
| -a | Print columns across rather than down. |
| -b | Balance columns on the last page. |
| -c | Print control characters using hat notation (for example, ^G); print other unprintable characters in octal backslash notation. |
| -d | Double-space the output. |
| -e[in-tab-char [in-tab-width]] | Expand tabs to spaces on input. Optional argument in-tab-char is the input tab character, default tab. Optional argument in-tab-width is the input tab character's width, default 8. |
| -F, -f | Use a form feed instead of newlines to separate output pages. |
| -h *header* | Replace the filename in the header with the string *header*. |
| --help | Print a usage message and exit with a nonzero status. |
| -i[out-tab-char [out-tab-width]] | Replace spaces with tabs on output. Optional argument out-tab-char is the output tab character, default tab. Optional argument out-tab-width is the output tab character's width, default 8. |
| -l *page-length* | Set the page length to *page-length* lines. The default is 66. If *page-length* is less than 10, the headers and footers are omitted, as if the -t option had been given. |
| -m | Print all files in parallel, one in each column. |

| | |
|---|---|
| -n[number-separator [digits]] | Precede each column with a line number; with parallel files, precede each line with a line number. Optional argument number-separator is the character to print after each number, default tab. Optional argument digits is the number of digits per line number, default 5. |
| -o left-margin | Offset each line with a margin left-margin spaces wide. The total page width is this offset plus the width set with the -w option. |
| -r | Do not print a warning message when an argument file cannot be opened. Failure to open a file still makes the exit status nonzero, however. |
| -s[column-separator] | Separate columns by the single character column-separator, default tab, instead of spaces. |
| -t | Do not print the 5-line header and the 5-line trailer that are normally on each page, and do not fill out the bottoms of pages (with blank lines or form feeds). |
| -v | Print unprintable characters in octal backslash notation. |
| --version | Print version information on standard output then exit. |
| -w page-width | Set the page width to page-width columns. The default is 72. |

*GNU Text Utilities*

# ps

ps—Report process status

## SYNOPSIS

ps [-][lujsvmaxScewhrnu][txx][O[+¦-]k1[[+¦-]k2...]] [pids]

There are also two long options:

--sortX[+¦-]key[,[+¦-]key[,...]]

--help

More long options are on the way...

## DESCRIPTION

ps gives a snapshot of the current processes. If you want a repetitive update of this status, use top. This man page documents the /proc-based version of ps, or tries to.

## COMMAND-LINE OPTIONS

Command-line arguments may optionally be preceded by a -, but there is no need for it. There are also some long options in GNU style; see the following subsection for those.

| | |
|---|---|
| l | Long format. |
| u | User format: gives username and start time. |
| j | Jobs format: pgid sid. |
| s | Signal format. |
| v | vm format. |
| m | Displays memory information (combine with p flag to get number of pages). |
| f | Forest family tree format for command line. |
| a | Show processes of other users too. |
| x | Show processes without controlling terminal. |
| S | Add child cpu time and page faults. |
| c | Command name from task struct. |
| e | Show environment after command line and +. |

| | |
|---|---|
| w | Wide output: don't truncate command lines to fit on one line. |
| h | No header. |
| r | Running procs only. |
| n | Numeric output for USER and WCHAN. |
| txx | Only procs with controlling tty xx; use for xx the same letters as shown in the TT field. The tty name must be given immediately after the option, with no intervening space, for example, ps -tv1. |
| O[+¦-]k1[,[+¦-]k2[,...]] | Order the process listing according to the multilevel sort specified by the sequence of short keys from SORT KEYS, k1, k2, .... Default order specifications exist for each of the various formats of ps. These are overridden by a user-specified ordering. The + is quite optional, merely reiterating the default direction on a key. - reverses direction only on the key it precedes. As with t and pids, the O option must be the last option in a single command argument, but specifications in successive arguments are catenated. |
| pids | List only the specified processes; they are comma-delimited. The list must be given immediately after the last option in a single command-line argument, with no intervening space, for example, ps -j1,4,5. Lists specified in subsequent arguments are catenated, for example, ps -11,23,4 5 6 will list all of the processes 1-6 in long format. |

## LONG COMMAND-LINE OPTIONS

These options are preceded by a double hyphen.

| | |
|---|---|
| --sortX[+¦-]key[, [+¦-]key[,...]] | Choose a multiletter key from the SORTKEYS section. X may be any convenient separator character. To be GNU-ish, use =. The + is really optional because default direction is increasing numerical or lexicographic order. Example:<br>ps -jax --sort=uid,-ppid,+pid |
| --help | Get a help message that summarizes the usage and gives a list of supported sort keys. This list may be more up-to-date than this man page. |

## SORT KEYS

Note that the values used in sorting are the internal values ps uses and *not* the "cooked" values used in some of the output format fields. If someone wants to volunteer to write special comparison functions for the cooked values,...;-)

| Short | Long | Description |
|---|---|---|
| c | cmd | Simple name of executable |
| C | cmdline | Full command line |
| f | flags | Flags as in long format F field |
| g | pgrp | Process group ID |
| G | tpgid | Controlling tty process group ID |
| j | cutime | Cumulative user time |
| J | cstime | Cumulative system time |
| k | utime | User time |
| K | stime | System time |
| m | min_flt | Number of minor page faults |
| M | maj_flt | Number of major page faults |
| n | cmin_flt | Cumulative minor page faults |
| N | cmaj_flt | Cumulative major page faults |
| o | session | Session ID |
| p | pid | Process ID |

*continues*

| Short | Long | Description |
|-------|------|-------------|
| P | ppid | Parent process ID |
| r | rss | Resident set size |
| R | resident | Resident pages |
| c | size | Memory size in kilobytes |
| s | share | Amount of shared pages |
| t | tty | The minor device number of tty |
| T | start_time | Time process was started |
| U | uid | User ID number |
| u | user | Username |
| v | vsize | Total VM size in bytes |
| y | priority | Kernel scheduling priority |

## FIELD DESCRIPTIONS

| | |
|---|---|
| PRI | This is the counter field in the task struct. It is the time in HZ of the process's possible time slice. |
| NI | Standard UNIX nice value; a positive value means less cpu time. |
| SIZE | Virtual image size; size of text+data+stack. |
| RSS | Resident set size; kilobytes of program in memory. |
| WCHAN | Name of the kernel function where the process is sleeping, with the sys stripped from the function name. If /boot/psdatabase does not exist, it is just a hex number instead. |
| STAT | Information about the status of the process. The first field is R for runnable, S for sleeping, D for uninterruptible sleep, T for stopped or traced, or Z for a zombie process. The second field contains W if the process has no resident pages. The third field is N if the process has a positive nice value (NI field). |
| TT | Controlling tty. |
| PAGEIN | Number of major page faults (page faults that cause pages to be read from disk, including pages read from the buffer cache). |
| TRS | Text resident size. |
| SWAP | Kilobytes (or pages if -p is used) on swap device. |
| SHARE | Shared memory. |

## UPDATING

This proc-based ps works by reading the files in the proc filesystem, mounted on /proc. This ps does not need to be suid kmem or have any privileges to run. *Do not give this ps any special permissions.*

You will need to update the /boot/psdatabase file by running /usr/sbin/psupdate to get meaningful information from the WCHAN field. This should be done every time you compile a new kernel.

## NOTES

The member used_math of task_struct is not shown, since crt0.s checks to see if math is present. This causes the math flag to be set for all processes, and so it is worthless.

Programs swapped out to disk will be shown without command-line arguments, and unless the c option is given, in parentheses.

%CPU shows the cputime/realtime percentage. It will not add up to 100 percent unless you are lucky. It is time used divided by the time the process has been running.

The SIZE and RSS fields don't count the page tables and the task struct of a proc; this is at least 12k of memory that is always resident. SIZE is the virtual size of the proc (code+data+stack).

## BUGS

tty names are hard-coded: virtual consoles are `v1`, `v2`,...; serial lines are `s0` and `s1`; pty's are `pp0`, `pp1` ... `pq0`, `pq1`, ....

## AUTHORS

`ps` was originally written by Branko Lankester (`lankeste@fwi.uva.nl`) Michael K. Johnson (`johnsonm@sunsite.unc.edu`) rewrote it significantly to use the `proc` filesystem, changing a few things in the process. Michael Shields (`mjshield@nyx.cs.du.edu`) added the `multiple-pids` feature. Charles Blake(`cblake@ucsd.edu`) added multilevel sorting and is the current maintainer of the `proc-ps` suite.

*Cohesive Systems, 27 July 1994*

# psbb

psbb—Extract bounding box from PostScript document

## SYNOPSIS

psbb *file*

## DESCRIPTION

psbb reads *file*, which should be a PostScript document conforming to the document structuring conventions and looks for a `%%BoundingBox` comment. If it finds one, it prints a line

`llx lly urx ury`

on the standard output and exits with zero status. If it doesn't find such a line or if the line is invalid, it prints a message and exits with nonzero status.

## SEE ALSO

grops(1)

*Groff Version 1.09, 6 August 1992*

# psidtopgm

psidtopgm—Convert PostScript image data into a portable graymap

## SYNOPSIS

psidtopgm width height bits/sample [*imagedata*]

## DESCRIPTION

psidtopgm reads the image data from a PostScript file as input and produces a portable graymap as output.

This is a very simple and limited program, and is here only because so many people have asked for it. To use it you have to manually extract the `readhexstring` data portion from your PostScript file, and then give the width, height, and bits/sample on the command line. Before you attempt this, you should at least read the description of the `image` operator in the *PostScript Language Reference Manual.*

It would probably not be too hard to write a script that uses this filter to read a specific variety of PostScript image, but the variation is too great to make a general-purpose reader. Unless, of course, you want to write a full-fledged PostScript interpreter...

## SEE ALSO

pnmtops(1), pgm(5)

## AUTHOR

Copyright© 1989 by Jef Poskanzer.

*2 August 1989*

# pstopnm

pstopnm—Convert a PostScript file into a portable anymap

## SYNOPSIS

pstopnm [-forceplain][-help][-llx s][-lly s][-landscape][-portrait][-nocrop]
[-pbm ¦-pgm ¦-ppm][-urx s][-ury s][-verbose][-xborder n][-xmax n][-xsize f]
[-yborder f][-ymax n][-ysize n] psfile[.ps]

## DESCRIPTION

pstopnm reads a PostScript file as input and produces portable anymap files as output. This program is just a useful shell script that runs GhostScript to render a PostScript into one or more pnm files. pstopnm will create as many files as the number of pages in the PostScript document. If the input file is named psfile.ps, the name of the files will be psfile001.ppm, psfile002.ppm, and so on.

The program maps a rectangular portion of the PostScript document into an image file according to the command-line options. The selected area will always be centered in the output file, and may have borders around it. The image area to be extracted from the PostScript file and rendered into a portable anymap is defined by four numbers, the lower-left corner and the upper-right corner x and y coordinates. These coordinates are usually specified by the BoundingBox comment in the PostScript file header, but they can be overridden by the user by specifying one or more of the following flags: -llx, -lly, -urx, and -ury. The presence and thickness of a border to be left around the image area is controlled by the use of the flags -xborder and -yborder. If BoundingBox parameters are not found, and image area coordinates are not specified on the command line, default values are used. Unless both output file width and height are specified via the -xsize and -ysize flags, the program will map the document into the output image by preserving its aspect ratio.

## OPTIONS

| | |
|---|---|
| —forceplain | Forces the output file to be a plain (in other words, not "raw") portable anymap. |
| -help | Prints the command syntax. |
| -llx *bx* | Selects *bx* as the lower left corner x coordinate (in inches). |
| -lly *by* | Selects *by* as the lower left corner y coordinate (in inches). |
| —landscape | Renders the image in landscape mode. |
| -portrait | Renders the image in portrait mode. |
| —nocrop | Does not crop the output image dimensions to match the PostScript image area dimensions. |
| -pbm -pgm -ppm | Selects the format of the output file. By default, all files are rendered as portable pixmaps (ppm format). |
| —urx *tx* | Selects *tx* as the upper-right corner x coordinate (in inches). |
| -ury *ty* | Selects *ty* as the upper-right corner y coordinate (in inches). |
| -verbose | Prints processing information to stdout. |
| -xborder *frac* | Specifies that the border width along the Y axis should be *frac* times the document width as specified by the bounding box comment in the PostScript file header. The default value is 0.1. |
| -xmax *xs* | Specifies that the maximum output image width should have a size less or equal to *xs* pixels (default: 612). |
| -xsize *xs* | Specifies that the output image width must be exactly *xs* pixels. |
| -yborder *frac* | Specifies that the border width along the X axis should be *frac* times the document width as specified by the bounding box comment in the PostScript file header. The default value is 0.1. |
| -ymax *ys* | Specifies that the maximum output image height should have a size less or equal to *ys* pixels (default: 792). |
| -ysize *ys* | Specifies that the output image height must be exactly *ys* pixels. |

## BUGS

The program will produce incorrect results with PostScript files that initialize the current transformation matrix. In these cases, page translation and rotation will not have any effect. To render these files, probably the best bet is to use the following flags:

```
pstopnm -xborder 0 -yborder 0 -portrait -nocrop file.ps
```

Additional flags may be needed if the document is supposed to be rendered on a medium different from letter-size paper.

## SEE ALSO

gs(l), pstofits(l)

## COPYRIGHT

Copyright© 1992 Smithsonian Astrophysical Observatory. PostScript is a trademark of Adobe Systems Inc.

## AUTHOR

Alberto Accomazzi, WIPL, Center for Astrophysics

*28 December 1992*

# pstree

pstree—Display a tree of processes

## SYNOPSIS

pstree [-a][-c][-h][-l][-p][-u][*pid¦user*]

## DESCRIPTION

pstree shows running processes as a tree. The tree is rooted at either pid or init if pid is omitted. If a username is specified, all process trees rooted at processes owned by that user are shown.

pstree visually merges identical branches by putting them in square brackets and prefixing them with the repetition count; for example,

```
init-¦-getty
     ¦-getty
     ¦-getty
     '-getty
```

becomes

```
init--4*[getty]
```

## OPTIONS

-a     Show command-line arguments. If the command line of a process is swapped out, that process is shown in parentheses. -a implicitly disables compaction.

-c     Disable compaction of identical subtrees. By default, subtrees are compacted whenever possible.

-h     Highlight the current process and its ancestors. This is a no-op if the terminal doesn't support highlighting or if neither the current process nor any of its ancestors are in the subtree being shown.

-l     Display long lines. By default, lines are truncated to the display width or 132 if output is sent to a non-tty or if the display width is unknown.

-p     Show pids. pids are shown as decimal numbers in parentheses after each process name. -p implicitly disables compaction.

-u     Show uid transitions. Whenever the uid of a process differs from the uid of its parent, the new uid is shown in parentheses after the process name.

## FILES

/proc   Location of the proc filesystem

## AUTHOR

Werner Almesberger (almesber@di.epfl.ch)

## SEE ALSO

ps(1), top(1)

*Linux, 11 October 1994*

# psupdate

psupdate—Update the ps database of kernel offsets

## SYNOPSIS

psupdate [system path]

## DESCRIPTION

psupdate updates the /boot/psdatabase file to correspond to the current kernel image system mapfile, /usr/src/linux/vmlinux by default.

## OPTIONS

If your system mapfile is not /usr/src/linux/vmlinux, you may give the name of an alternate mapfile on the command line.

## FILES

/boot/psdatabase
/usr/src/linux/vmlin

## SEE ALSO

ps(1), top(1), utmp(5)

## AUTHORS

Original code written by Branko Lankaster, horribly munged by Michael K. Johnson in a desperate effort to add /etc/psdatabase support to procps. Someday, it should be rewritten, and the support in ps for alternate namelists added. Anyone want to volunteer to be added to the "Authors" section?

*Cohesive Systems, 15 September 1993*

# qrttoppm

qrttoppm—Convert output from the QRT ray tracer into a portable pixmap

## SYNOPSIS

qrttoppm [*qrtfile*]

## DESCRIPTION

qrttoppm reads a QRT file as input and produces a portable pixmap as output.

## SEE ALSO

ppm(5)

## AUTHOR

Copyright© 1989 by Jef Poskanzer.

*25 August 1989*

# quota

quota—Display disk usage and limits

## SYNOPSIS

```
quota [ -guv ¦ q ]
quota [ -uv ¦ q ] user
quota [ -gv ¦ q ] group
```

## DESCRIPTION

quota  displays users' disk usage and limits. By default, only the user quotas are printed.

-g      Print group quotas for the group of which the user is a member. The optional -u flag is equivalent to the default.

-v      Will display quotas on filesystems where no storage is allocated.

-q      Print a more terse message, containing only information on filesystems where usage is over quota.

Specifying both -g  and -u  displays both the user quotas and the group quotas (for the user).

Only the superuser may use the -u  flag and the optional user  argument to view the limits of other users. Non-superusers can use the -g  flag and optional group  argument to view only the limits of groups of which they are members.

The -q  flag takes precedence over the -v  flag.

quota  reports the quotas of all the filesystems listed in /etc/fstab.  For filesystems that are NFS-mounted, a call to the rpc.rquotad  on the server machine is performed to get the information. If quota  exits with a nonzero status, one or more filesystems are over quota.

## FILES

quota.user      Located at the filesystem root with user quotas

quota.group      Located at the filesystem root with group quotas

/etc/fstab      To find filesystem names and locations

## SEE ALSO

quotactl(2), fstab(5), edquota(8), quotacheck(8), quotaon(8), repquota(8)

*8 January 1993*

# ranlib

ranlib—Generate index to archive

## SYNOPSIS

```
ranlib [ -v¦-V] archive
```

## DESCRIPTION

ranlib generates an index to the contents of an archive and stores it in the archive. The index lists each symbol defined by a member of an archive that is a relocatable object file.

You may use nm -s or nm --print-armap to list this index.

An archive with such an index speeds up linking to the library, and allows routines in the library to call each other without regard to their placement in the archive.

The GNU ranlib program is another form of GNU ar; running ranlib is completely equivalent to executing ar -s.

## OPTIONS

-v          Print the version number of ranlib and exit

## SEE ALSO

binutils entry in info; *The GNU Binary Utilities*, Roland H. Pesch (October 1991); ar(1); nm(1).

## COPYING

*Cygnus support, 5 November 1991*

# rasttopnm

rasttopnm—Convert a Sun raster file into a portable anymap

## SYNOPSIS

rasttopnm [*rastfile*]

## DESCRIPTION

rasttopnm reads a Sun raster file as input and produces a portable anymap as output. The type of the output file depends on the input file—if it's black and white, a pbm file is written; else if it's grayscale, a pgm file; else a ppm file. The program tells you which type it is writing.

## SEE ALSO

pnmtorast(1), pnm(5)

## AUTHOR

*Copyright © 1989, 1991 by Jef Poskanzer.*

*13 January 1991*

# rawtopgm

`rawtopgm`—Convert raw grayscale bytes into a portable graymap

## SYNOPSIS

`rawtopgm [-headerskip N][-rowskip N][-tb¦-topbottom][`*`width height`*`][`*`imagedata`*`]`

## DESCRIPTION

`rawtopgm` reads raw grayscale bytes as input and produces a portable graymap as output. The input file is just grayscale bytes. If you don't specify the width and height on the command line, the program will check the size of the image and try to make a quadratic image of it. It is an error to supply a non-quadratic image without specifying width and height. The `maxval` is assumed to be 255.

## OPTIONS

| | |
|---|---|
| `-headerskip` | If the file has a header, you can use this flag to skip over it. |
| `-rowskip` | If there is padding at the ends of the rows, you can skip it with this flag. Note that `rowskip` can be a real number. Amazingly, I once had an image with 0.376 bytes of padding per row. This turned out to be due to a file transfer problem, but I was still able to read the image. |
| `-tb -topbottom` | Flips the image upside down. The first pixel in a `pgm` file is in the lower-left corner of the image. For conversion from images with the first pixel in the upper-left corner (for example, the Molecular Dynamics and Leica confocal formats), this flips the image right. This is equivalent to `rawtopgm [file] ¦ pnmflip -tb`. |

## BUGS

If you don't specify the image width and height, the program will try to read the entire image to a memory buffer. If you get a message that states that you are out of memory, try to specify the width and height on the command line. Also, the `-tb` option consumes much memory.

## SEE ALSO

`pgm(5)`, `rawtoppm(1)`, `pnmflip(1)`

## AUTHORS

Copyright© 1989 by Jef Poskanzer; modified June 1993 by Oliver Trepte (`oliver@fysik4.kth.se`).

*15 June 1993*

# rawtoppm

`rawtoppm`—Convert raw RGB bytes into a portable pixmap

## SYNOPSIS

`rawtoppm[-headerskip N][-rowskip N][-rgb¦-rbg¦-grb ¦-gbr¦-brg¦-bgr ]`
`[-interpixel¦-interrow] `*`width height`*` [`*`imagedata`*`]`

## DESCRIPTION

`rawtoppm` reads raw RGB bytes as input and produces a portable pixmap as output. The input file is just RGB bytes. You have to specify the width and height on the command line because the program obviously can't get them from the file. The `maxval` is assumed to be 255. If the resulting image is upside down, run it through `pnmflip -tb`.

## OPTIONS

| | |
|---|---|
| `-headerskip` | If the file has a header, you can use this flag to skip over it. |
| `-rowskip` | If there is padding at the ends of the rows, you can skip it with this flag. |
| `-rgb -rbg -grb -gbr -brg -bgr` | These flags let you specify alternate color orders. The default is `-rgb`. |
| `-interpixel -interrow` | These flags let you specify how the colors are interleaved. The default is `-interpixel`, meaning interleaved by pixel. A byte of red, a byte of green, and a byte of blue, or whatever color order you specified. `-interrow` means interleaved by row—a row of red, a row of green, a row of blue, assuming standard RGB color order. An `-interplane` flag—all the red pixels, then all the green, then all the blue—would be an obvious extension, but is not implemented. You could get the same effect by splitting the file into three parts (perhaps using `dd`), turning each part into a PGM file with `rawtopgm`, and then combining them with `rgb3toppm`. |

## SEE ALSO

ppm(5), rawtopgm(1), rgb3toppm(1), pnmflip(1)

## AUTHOR

Copyright© 1991 by Jef Poskanzer.

*6 February 1991*

# rcp

rcp—Remote file copy

## SYNOPSIS

```
rcp [-px] [-k realm] file1 file2
rcp [-px] [-r] [-k Ar realm] file ... directory
```

## DESCRIPTION

rcp copies files between machines. Each file or directory argument is either a remote filename of the form `rname@rhost:path`, or a local filename (containing no : characters, or a / before any : characters).

| | |
|---|---|
| -r | If any of the source files are directories, rcp copies each subtree rooted at that name; in this case the destination must be a directory. |
| -p | Causes rcp to attempt to preserve (duplicate) in its copies the modification times and modes of the source files, ignoring the umask . By default, the mode and owner of `file2` are preserved if it already existed; otherwise, the mode of the source file modified by the `umask 2` on the destination host is used. |
| -k | Requests rcp to obtain tickets for the remote host in realm `realm` instead of the remote host's realm as determined by `krb_realmofhost 3`. |
| -x | Turns on DES encryption for all data passed by rcp. This may impact response time and CPU utilization, but provides increased security. |

If path is not a full pathname, it is interpreted relative to the `login` directory of the specified user `ruser` on `rhost`, or your current username if no other remote username is specified. A path on a remote host may be quoted (using \, ", or ') so that the meta characters are interpreted remotely.

rcp does not prompt for passwords; it performs remote execution via `rsh(1)`, and requires the same authorization.

rcp handles third-party copies, where neither source nor target files are on the current machine.

## SEE ALSO

cp(1), ftp(1), rsh(1), rlogin(1)

## HISTORY

The rcp command appeared in BSD 4.2 . The version of rcp described here has been reimplemented with Kerberos in BSD 4.3 Reno.

## BUGS

Doesn't detect all cases in which the target of a copy might be a file when only a directory should be legal.

Is confused by any output generated by commands in a or file on the remote host.

The destination username and hostname may have to be specified as rhost.rname when the destination machine is running the BSD 4.2 version of rcp.

*BSD 4.3r, 27 July 1991*

# rcs

rcs—Change RCS file attributes

## SYNOPSIS

rcs *options file* ...

## DESCRIPTION

rcs creates new RCS files or changes attributes of existing ones. An RCS file contains multiple revisions of text, an access list, a change log, descriptive text, and some control attributes. For rcs to work, the caller's login name must be on the access list—unless the access list is empty, the caller is the owner of the file or the superuser, or the -i option is present.

Pathnames matching an RCS suffix denote RCS files; all others denote working files. Names are paired as explained in ci(1). Revision numbers use the syntax described in ci(1).

## OPTIONS

| | |
|---|---|
| -i | Create and initialize a new RCS file, but do not deposit any revision. If the RCS file has no path prefix, try to place it first into the subdirectory ./RCS, and then into the current directory. If the RCS file already exists, print an error message. |
| -a*logins* | Append the login names appearing in the comma-separated list *logins* to the access list of the RCS file. |
| -A*oldfile* | Append the access list of *oldfile* to the access list of the RCS file. |
| -e[*logins*] | Erase the login names appearing in the comma-separated list *logins* from the access list of the RCS file. If *logins* is omitted, erase the entire access list. |
| -b[*rev*] | Set the default branch to *rev*.If *rev* is omitted, the default branch is reset to the (dynamically) highest branch on the trunk. |
| -c*string* | Set the comment leader to *string*. An initial ci,or an rcs -i without -c, guesses the comment leader from the suffix of the working filename. |

This option is obsolescent, since RCS normally uses the preceding $Log$ line's prefix when inserting log lines during checkout (see co(1)). However, older versions of RCS use the comment leader instead of the $Log$ line's prefix, so if you plan to access a file with both old and new versions of RCS, make sure its comment leader matches its $Log$ line prefix.

| | |
|---|---|
| -k*subst* | Set the default keyword substitution to *subst*. The effect of keyword substitution is described in co(1). Giving an explicit -k option to co, rcsdiff, and rcsmerge overrides this default. Beware rcs -kv, because -kv is incompatible with co -l. Use rcs -kkv to restore the normal default keyword substitution. |

| | |
|---|---|
| -l[rev] | Lock the revision with number *rev*. If a branch is given, lock the latest revision on that branch. If *rev* is omitted, lock the latest revision on the default branch. Locking prevents overlapping changes. If someone else already holds the lock, the lock is broken as with rcs -u. |
| -u[rev] | Unlock the revision with number *rev*. If a branch is given, unlock the latest revision on that branch. If *rev* is omitted, remove the latest lock held by the caller. Normally, only the locker of a revision can unlock it. Somebody else unlocking a revision breaks the lock. This causes a mail message to be sent to the original locker. The message contains a commentary solicited from the breaker. The commentary is terminated by end-of-file or by a line containing a period by itself. |
| -L | Set locking to strict. strict locking means that the owner of an RCS file is not exempt from locking for checkin. This option should be used for files that are shared. |
| -U | Set locking to non-strict. non-strict locking means that the owner of a file need not lock a revision for checkin. This option should *not* be used for files that are shared. Whether default locking is strict is determined by your system administrator, but it is normally strict. |
| -mrev:msg | Replace revision *rev*'s log message with *msg*. |
| -M | Do not send mail when breaking somebody else's lock. This option is not meant for casual use; it is meant for programs that warn users by other means, and invoke rcs -u only as a low-level lock-breaking operation. |
| -nname[:[rev]] | Associate the symbolic name *name* with the branch or revision *rev*. Delete the symbolic name if both : and *rev* are omitted; otherwise, print an error message if *name* is already associated with another number. If *rev* is symbolic, it is expanded before association. A *rev* consisting of a branch number followed by a period stands for the current latest revision in the branch. A : with an empty *rev* stands for the current latest revision on the default branch, normally the trunk. For example, rcs -nname: RCS/* associates *name* with the current latest revision of all the named RCS files; this contrasts with rcs -nname:$ RCS/*, which associates *name* with the revision numbers extracted from keyword strings in the corresponding working files. |
| -Nname[:[rev]] | Act like -n, except override any previous assignment of *name*. |
| -orange | Deletes ("outdates") the revisions given by range. A range consisting of a single revision number means that revision. A range consisting of a branch number means the latest revision on that branch. A range of the form *rev1:rev1* means revisions *rev1* to *rev2* on the same branch, :*rev* means from the beginning of the branch containing *rev* up to and including *rev*, and *rev*: means from revision *rev* to the end of the branch containing *rev*. None of the outdated revisions can have branches or locks. |
| -q | Run quietly; do not print diagnostics. |
| -I | Run interactively, even if the standard input is not a terminal. |
| -sstate[:rev] | Set the state attribute of the revision *rev* to *state*. If *rev* is a branch number, assume the latest revision on that branch. If *rev* is omitted, assume the latest revision on the default branch. Any identifier is acceptable for *state*. A useful set of states is Exp (for experimental), Stab (for stable), and Rel (for released). By default, ci(1) sets the state of a revision to Exp. |
| -t[file] | Write descriptive text from the contents of the named *file* into the RCS file, deleting the existing text. The *file* pathname cannot begin with -. If *file* is omitted, obtain the text from standard input, terminated by end-of-file or by a line containing a period by itself. Prompt for the text if interaction is possible; see -I. With -i, descriptive text is obtained even if -t is not given. |
| -t-string | Write descriptive text from the *string* into the RCS file, deleting the existing text. |
| -T | Preserve the modification time on the RCS file unless a revision is removed. This option can suppress extensive recompilation caused by a make(1) dependency of some copy of the working file on the RCS file. Use this option with care; it can suppress recompilation even when it is needed, that is, when a change to the RCS file would mean a change to keyword strings in the working file. |
| -V | Print RCS's version number. |
| -Vn | Emulate RCS version *n*. See co(1) for details. |
| -xsuffixes | Use *suffixes* to characterize RCS files. See ci(1) for details. |
| -zzone | Use *zone* as the default time zone. This option has no effect; it is present for compatibility with other RCS commands. |

At least one explicit option must be given, to ensure compatibility with future planned extensions to the rcs command.

## COMPATIBILITY

The -brev option generates an RCS file that cannot be parsed by RCS version 3 or earlier.

The -k*subst* options (except -kkv) generate an RCS file that cannot be parsed by RCS version 4 or earlier.

Use rcs -V*n* to make an RCS file acceptable to RCS version *n* by discarding information that would confuse version *n*.

RCS version 5.5 and earlier does not support the -x option, and requires a ,v suffix on an RCS pathname.

## FILES

rcs accesses files much as ci(1) does, except that it uses the effective user for all accesses, it does not write the working file or its directory, and it does not even read the working file unless a revision number of $ is specified.

## ENVIRONMENT

RCSINITf1[:*rev*]   Options prepended to the argument list, separated by spaces. See ci(1) for details.

## DIAGNOSTICS

The RCS pathname and the revisions outdated are written to the diagnostic output. The exit status is zero if and only if all operations were successful.

## IDENTIFICATION

Author: Walter F. Tichy.
Manual Page Revision: 5.13; Release Date: 1995/06/05.
Copyright 1982, 1988, 1989 Walter F. Tichy.
Copyright 1990, 1991, 1992, 1993, 1994, 1995 Paul Eggert.

## SEE ALSO

rcsintro(1), co(1), ci(1), ident(1), rcsclean(1), rcsdiff(1), rcsmerge(1), rlog(1), rcsfile(5)

"RCS—A System for Version Control" by Walter F. Tichy, Software Practice & Experience 15, 7 (July 1985), pages 637-654.

## BUGS

A catastrophe (for example, a system crash) can cause RCS to leave behind a semaphore file that causes later invocations of RCS to claim that the RCS file is in use. To fix this, remove the semaphore file. A semaphore file's name typically begins with a comma or ends with an underscore.

The separator for revision ranges in the -o option used to be - instead of :, but this leads to confusion when symbolic names contain -. For backwards compatibility, rcs -o still supports the old - separator, but it warns about this obsolete use.

Symbolic names need not refer to existing revisions or branches. For example, the -o option does not remove symbolic names for the outdated revisions; you must use -n to remove the names.

*GNU, 5 June 1995*

# rcsclean

rcsclean—Clean up working files

## SYNOPSIS

rcsclean [*options*][*file* ...]

## DESCRIPTION

rcsclean removes files that are not being worked on. rcsclean -u also unlocks and removes files that are being worked on but have not changed.

For each *file* given, rcsclean compares the working file and a revision in the corresponding RCS file. If it finds a difference, it does nothing. Otherwise, it first unlocks the revision if the -u option is given, and then removes the working file unless the working file is writable and the revision is locked. It logs its actions by outputting the corresponding rcs -u and rm -f commands on the standard output.

Files are paired as explained in ci(1). If no *file* is given, all working files in the current directory are cleaned. Pathnames matching an RCS suffix denote RCS files; all others denote working files.

The number of the revision to which the working file is compared may be attached to any of the options -n, -q, -r, or -u. If no revision number is specified, then if the -u option is given and the caller has one revision locked, rcsclean uses that revision; otherwise, rcsclean uses the latest revision on the default branch, normally the root.

rcsclean is useful for clean targets in makefiles. See also rcsdiff(1), which prints out the differences, and ci(1), which normally reverts to the previous revision if a file was not changed.

## OPTIONS

| | |
|---|---|
| -k*subst* | Use *subst*-style keyword substitution when retrieving the revision for comparison. See co(1) for details. |
| -n[*rev*] | Do not actually remove any files or unlock any revisions. Using this option will tell you what rcsclean would do without actually doing it. |
| --q[*rev*] | Do not log the actions taken on standard output. |
| --r[*rev*] | This option has no effect other than specifying the revision for comparison. |
| -T | Preserve the modification time on the RCS file even if the RCS file changes because a lock is removed. This option can suppress extensive recompilation caused by a make(1) dependency of some other copy of the working file on the RCS file. Use this option with care; it can suppress recompilation even when it is needed, that is, when the lock removal would mean a change to keyword strings in the other working file. |
| -u[*rev*] | Unlock the revision if it is locked and no difference is found. |
| -V | Print RCS's version number. |
| -V*n* | Emulate RCS version *n*. See co(1) for details. |
| -x*suffixes* | Use *suffixes* to characterize RCS files. See ci(1) for details. |
| -z*zone* | Use *zone* as the time zone for keyword substitution; see co(1) for details. |

## EXAMPLES

rcsclean *.c *.h removes all working files ending in .c or .h that were not changed since their checkout.

rcsclean removes all working files in the current directory that were not changed since their check-out.

## FILES

rcsclean accesses files much as ci(1) does.

## ENVIRONMENT

RCSINIT     Options prepended to the argument list, separated by spaces. A backslash escapes spaces within an option. The RCSINIT options are prepended to the argument lists of most rcs commands. Useful RCSINIT options include -q, -V, -x, and -z.

## DIAGNOSTICS

The exit status is zero if and only if all operations were successful. Missing working files and RCS files are silently ignored.

## IDENTIFICATION

Author: Walter F. Tichy.
Manual Page Revision: 1.12; Release Date: 1993/11/03.
Copyright© 1982, 1988, 1989 Walter F. Tichy.
Copyright© 1990, 1991, 1992, 1993 Paul Eggert.

## SEE ALSO

ci(1), co(1), ident(1), rcs(1), rcsdiff(1), rcsintro(1), rcsmerge(1), rlog(1), rcsfile(5)

"RCS—A System for Version Control" by Walter F. Tichy, Software Practice & Experience 15, 7 (July 1985), pages
637-654.

## BUGS

At least one `file` must be given in older UNIX versions that do not provide the needed directory scanning operations.

*GNU, 3 November 1993*

# rcsdiff

rcsdiff—Compare rcs revisions

## SYNOPSIS

rcsdiff [ -k*subst* ][-q ][-r*rev1* [ -r*rev2* ]][-T ][-V[*n*]][-x*suffixes* ][-z*zone* ]
[*diff* options ] *file* . . .

## DESCRIPTION

rcsdiff runs diff(1) to compare two revisions of each RCS file given.

Pathnames matching an RCS suffix denote RCS files; all others denote working files. Names are paired as explained in ci(1).

The option -q suppresses diagnostic output. Zero, one, or two revisions may be specified with -r. The option -k*subst* affects keyword substitution when extracting revisions, as described in co(1); for example, -kk -r1.1 -r1.2 ignores differences in keyword values when comparing revisions 1.1 and 1.2. To avoid excess output from locker name substitution, -kkvl is assumed if at most one revision option is given, no -k option is given, -kkv is the default keyword substitution, and the working file's mode would be produced by co -l. See co(1) for details about -T, -V, -x, and -z. Otherwise, all options of diff(1) that apply to regular files are accepted, with the same meaning as for diff.

If both *rev1* and *rev2* are omitted, rcsdiff compares the latest revision on the default branch (by default the trunk) with the contents of the corresponding working file. This is useful for determining what you changed since the last checkin.

If *rev1* is given, but *rev2* is omitted, rcsdiff compares revision *rev1* of the RCS file with the contents of the corresponding working file.

If both *rev1* and *rev2* are given, rcsdiff compares revisions *rev1* and *rev2* of the RCS file.

Both *rev1* and *rev2* may be given numerically or symbolically.

## EXAMPLE

The command

rcsdiff f.c

compares the latest revision on the default branch of the RCS file to the contents of the working file f.c.

## ENVIRONMENT

RCSINIT    Options prepended to the argument list, separated by spaces. See ci(1) for details.

## DIAGNOSTICS

Exit status is 0 for no differences during any comparison, 1 for some differences, 2 for trouble.

## IDENTIFICATION

Author: Walter F. Tichy.
Manual Page Revision: 5.5; Release Date: 1993/11/03.
Copyright© 1982, 1988, 1989 Walter F. Tichy.
Copyright© 1990, 1991, 1992, 1993 Paul Eggert.

## SEE ALSO

ci(1), co(1), diff(1), ident(1), rcs(1), rcsintro(1), rcsmerge(1), rlog(1)

"RCS—A System for Version Control" by Walter F. Tichy, Software Practice & Experience 15, 7 (July 1985), pages 637–654.

*GNU, 3 November 1993*

# rcsfreeze

rcsfreeze—Freeze a configuration of sources checked in under RCS

## SYNOPSIS

rcsfreeze [*name*]

## DESCRIPTION

rcsfreeze assigns a symbolic revision number to a set of RCS files that form a valid configuration.

The idea is to run rcsfreeze each time a new version is checked in. A unique symbolic name (C_number, where number is increased each time rcsfreeze is run) is then assigned to the most recent revision of each RCS file of the main trunk.

An optional *name* argument to rcsfreeze gives a symbolic name to the configuration. The unique identifier is still generated and is listed in the log file, but it will not appear as part of the symbolic revision name in the actual RCS files.

A log message is requested from the user for future reference.

The shell script works only on all RCS files at one time. All changed files must be checked in already. Run rcsclean(1) first and see whether any sources remain in the current directory.

## FILES

RCS/.rcsfreeze.ver     Version number
RCS/.rcsfreeze.log     Log messages, most recent first

## AUTHOR

Stephan V. Bechtolsheim

## SEE ALSO

co(1), rcs(1), rcsclean(1), rlog(1)

## BUGS

rcsfreeze does not check whether any sources are checked out and modified.

Although both source filenames and RCS filenames are accepted, they are not paired as usual with rcs commands.

Error checking is rudimentary.

rcsfreeze is just an optional example shell script, and should not be taken too seriously. See cvs for a more complete solution.

*GNU, 3 November 1990*

# rcsintro

rcsintro—Introduction to rcs commands

## DESCRIPTION

The Revision Control System (RCS) manages multiple revisions of files. RCS automates the storing, retrieval, logging, identification, and merging of revisions. RCS is useful for text that is revised frequently; for example programs, documentation, graphics, papers, and form letters.

The basic user interface is extremely simple. The novice only needs to learn two commands: ci(1) and co(1). ci, short for check in, deposits the contents of a file into an archival file called an RCS file. An RCS file contains all revisions of a particular file. co, short for check out, retrieves revisions from an RCS file.

## FUNCTIONS OF RCS

**Store and retrieve multiple revisions of text**. RCS saves all old revisions in a space-efficient way. Changes no longer destroy the original because the previous revisions remain accessible. Revisions can be retrieved according to ranges of revision numbers, symbolic names, dates, authors, and states.

**Maintain a complete history of changes**. RCS logs all changes automatically. Besides the text of each revision, RCS stores the author, the date and time of checkin, and a log message summarizing the change. The logging makes it easy to find out what happened to a module without having to compare source listings or having to track down colleagues.

**Resolve access conflicts**. When two or more programmers wish to modify the same revision, RCS alerts the programmers and prevents one modification from corrupting the other.

**Maintain a tree of revisions**. RCS can maintain separate lines of development for each module. It stores a tree structure that represents the ancestral relationships among revisions.

**Merge revisions and resolve conflicts**. Two separate lines of development of a module can be coalesced by merging. If the revisions to be merged affect the same sections of code, RCS alerts the user about the overlapping changes.

**Control releases and configurations**. Revisions can be assigned symbolic names and marked as released, stable, experimental, and so on. With these facilities, configurations of modules can be described simply and directly.

**Automatically identify each revision with name, revision number, creation time, author, and so on**. The identification is like a stamp that can be embedded at an appropriate place in the text of a revision. The identification makes it simple to determine which revisions of which modules make up a given configuration.

**Minimize secondary storage**. RCS needs little extra space for the revisions (only the differences). If intermediate revisions are deleted, the corresponding deltas are compressed accordingly.

## GETTING STARTED WITH RCS

Suppose you have a file f.c that you wish to put under control of RCS. If you have not already done so, make an RCS directory with the command:

mkdir RCS

Then invoke the check in command:

ci f.c

This command creates an RCS file in the RCS directory, stores f.c into it as revision 1.1, and deletes f.c. It also asks you for a description. The description should be a synopsis of the contents of the file. All later check in commands will ask you for a log entry, which should summarize the changes that you made.

Files in the RCS directory are called RCS files; the others are called working files. To get back the working file f.c in the previous example, use the check out command:

```
co f.c
```

This command extracts the latest revision from the RCS file and writes it into f.c. If you want to edit f.c, you must lock it as you check it out with the command:

```
co -l f.c
```

You can now edit f.c.

Suppose after some editing you want to know what changes that you have made. The command:

```
rcsdiff f.c
```

tells you the difference between the most recently checked-in version and the working file. You can check the file back in by invoking

```
ci f.c
```

This increments the revision number properly.

If ci complains with the message:

```
ci error: no lock set by your name
```

then you have tried to check in a file even though you did not lock it when you checked it out. Of course, it is too late now to do the checkout with locking, because another checkout would overwrite your modifications. Instead, invoke

```
rcs -l f.c
```

This command will lock the latest revision for you, unless somebody else got ahead of you already. In that case, you'll have to negotiate with that person.

Locking assures that you, and only you, can check in the next update, and avoids nasty problems if several people work on the same file. Even if a revision is locked, it can still be checked out for reading, compiling, and so on. All that locking prevents is a check-in by anybody but the locker.

If your RCS file is private—if you are the only person who is going to deposit revisions into it—strict locking is not needed and you can turn it off. If strict locking is turned off, the owner of the RCS file need not have a lock for checkin; all others still do. Turning strict locking off and on is done with the commands rcs -U f.c and rcs -L f.c. If you don't want to clutter your working directory with RCS files, create a subdirectory called RCS in your working directory, and move all your RCS files there. rcs commands will look first into that directory to find needed files. All the commands discussed here will still work, without any modification. (Actually, pairs of RCS and working files can be specified in three ways: both are given, only the working file is given, or only the RCS file is given. Both RCS and working files may have arbitrary path prefixes; rcs commands pair them up intelligently.)

To avoid the deletion of the working file during checkin (in case you want to continue editing or compiling), invoke

```
ci -l f.c or ci -u f.c
```

These commands check in f.c as usual, but perform an implicit checkout. The first form also locks the checked in revision, the second one doesn't. Thus, these options save you one checkout operation. The first form is useful if you want to continue editing, the second one if you just want to read the file. Both update the identification markers in your working file. (See the following subsection, "Automatic Identification.")

You can give ci the number you want assigned to a checked in revision. Assume all your revisions were numbered 1.1, 1.2, 1.3, etc., and you would like to start release 2. The command:

```
ci -r2 f.c or ci -r2.1 f.c
```

assigns the number 2.1 to the new revision. From then on, ci will number the subsequent revisions with 2.2, 2.3, and so on. The corresponding co commands:

```
co -r2 f.c
```

and

```
co -r2.1 f.c
```

retrieve the latest revision numbered 2.x and the revision 2.1, respectively. co without a revision number selects the latest revision on the trunk, that is, the highest revision with a number consisting of two fields. Numbers with more than two fields are needed for branches. For example, to start a branch at revision 1.3, invoke

```
ci -r1.3.1 f.c
```

This command starts a branch numbered 1 at revision 1.3, and assigns the number 1.3.1.1 to the new revision. For more information about branches, see rcsfile(5).

## AUTOMATIC IDENTIFICATION

RCS can put special strings for identification into your source and object code. To obtain such identification, place the marker:

```
$Id$
```

into your text, for instance inside a comment. RCS will replace this marker with a string of the form:

```
$Id: filename revision date time author state $
```

With such a marker on the first page of each module, you can always see with which revision you are working. RCS keeps the markers up-to-date automatically. To propagate the markers into your object code, simply put them into literal character strings. In C, this is done as follows:

```
static char rcsid[] = "$Id$";
```

The command ident extracts such markers from any file, even object code and dumps. Thus, ident lets you find out which revisions of which modules were used in a given program.

You may also find it useful to put the marker $Log$ into your text, inside a comment. This marker accumulates the log messages that are requested during checkin. Thus, you can maintain the complete history of your file directly inside it. There are several additional identification markers; see co(1) for details.

## IDENTIFICATION

Author: Walter F. Tichy.
Manual Page Revision: 5.3; Release Date: 1993/11/03.
Copyright© 1982, 1988, 1989 Walter F. Tichy.
Copyright© 1990, 1991, 1992, 1993 Paul Eggert.

## SEE ALSO

ci(1), co(1), ident(1), rcs(1), rcsdiff(1), rcsintro(1), rcsmerge(1), rlog(1)

"RCS—A System for Version Control" by Walter F. Tichy, Software Practice & Experience 15, 7 (July 1985), pages 637–654.

*GNU, 3 November 1993*

# rcsmerge

rcsmerge—Merge RCS revisions

## SYNOPSIS

```
rcsmerge [options] file
```

## DESCRIPTION

rcsmerge incorporates the changes between two revisions of an RCS file into the corresponding working file.

Pathnames matching an RCS suffix denote RCS files; all others denote working files. Names are paired as explained in ci(1).

At least one revision must be specified with one of the options described in the next subsection, usually -r. At most two revisions may be specified. If only one revision is specified, the latest revision on the default branch (normally the highest branch on the trunk) is assumed for the second revision. Revisions may be specified numerically or symbolically.

rcsmerge prints a warning if there are overlaps, and delimits the overlapping regions as explained in merge(1). The command is useful for incorporating changes into a checked-out revision.

## OPTIONS

| | |
|---|---|
| -A | Output conflicts using the -A style of diff3(1), if supported by diff3. This merges all changes leading from file2 to file3 into file1, and generates the most verbose output. |
| -E, -e | These options specify conflict styles that generate less information than -A. See diff3(1) for details. The default is -E. With -e, rcsmerge does not warn about conflicts. |
| -ksubst | Use *subst*-style keyword substitution. See co(1) for details. For example, -kk -r1.1 -r1.2 ignores differences in keyword values when merging the changes from 1.1 to 1.2. It normally does not make sense to merge binary files as if they were text, so rcsmerge refuses to merge files if -kb expansion is used. |
| -p[rev] | Send the result to standard output instead of overwriting the working file. |
| -q[rev] | Run quietly; do not print diagnostics. |
| -r[rev] | Merge with respect to revision *rev*. Here an empty *rev* stands for the latest revision on the default branch, normally the head. |
| -T | This option has no effect; it is present for compatibility with other rcs commands. |
| -V | Print RCS's version number. |
| -V*n* | Emulate RCS version *n*. See co(1) for details. |
| -xsuffixes | Use *suffixes* to characterize RCS files. See ci(1) for details. |
| -zzone | Use *zone* as the time zone for keyword substitution. See co(1) for details. |

## EXAMPLES

Suppose you have released revision 2.8 of f.c. Assume, furthermore, that after you complete an unreleased revision 3.4, you receive updates to release 2.8 from someone else. To combine the updates to 2.8 and your changes between 2.8 and 3.4, put the updates to 2.8 into file f.c and execute

```
rcsmerge -p -r2.8 -r3.4 f.c >f.merged.c
```

Then examine f.merged.c. Alternatively, if you want to save the updates to 2.8 in the RCS file, check them in as revision 2.8.1.1 and execute co -j:

```
ci -r2.8.1.1 f.c
co -r3.4 -j2.8:2.8.1.1 f.c
```

As another example, the following command undoes the changes between revision 2.4 and 2.8 in your currently checked out revision in f.c:

```
rcsmerge -r2.8 -r2.4 f.c
```

Note the order of the arguments, and that f.c will be overwritten.

## ENVIRONMENT

RCSINIT    Options prepended to the argument list, separated by spaces. See ci(1) for details.

## DIAGNOSTICS

Exit status is 0 for no overlaps, 1 for some overlaps, 2 for trouble.

## IDENTIFICATION

Author: Walter F. Tichy.
Manual Page Revision: 5.6; Release Date: 1995/06/01.
Copyright© 1982, 1988, 1989 Walter F. Tichy.
Copyright© 1990, 1991, 1992, 1993, 1994, 1995 Paul Eggert.

## SEE ALSO

ci(1), co(1), ident(1), merge(1), rcs(1), rcsdiff(1), rcsintro(1), rlog(1), rcsfile(5)

"RCS—A System for Version Control" by Walter F. Tichy, Software-Practice & Experience 15, 7 (July 1985), pages 637–654.

*GNU, 1 June 1995*

# rdist

rdist—Remote file distribution program

## SYNOPSIS

```
rdist [-nqbRhivwy] [-f distfile] [-d var=value] [-m host] [name ...]
rdist [-nqbRhivwy] -c name ... [login@host:dest]
```

## DESCRIPTION

rdist is a program to maintain identical copies of files over multiple hosts. It preserves the owner, group, mode, and mtime of files if possible and can update programs that are executing. rdist reads commands from distfile to direct the updating of files and/or directories.

Options specific to the first SYNOPSIS form:

| | |
|---|---|
| - | If distfile is -, the standard input is used. |
| -f distfile | Use the specified distfile. |

If either the -f or - option is not specified, the program looks first for distfile, then Distfile to use as the input. If no names are specified on the command line, rdist will update all of the files and directories listed in distfile. Otherwise, the argument is taken to be the name of a file to be updated or the label of a command to execute. If label and filenames conflict, it is assumed to be a label. These may be used together to update specific files using specific commands.

Options specific to the second SYNOPSIS form:

-c      Forces rdist to interpret the remaining arguments as a small distfile.

The equivalent distfile is as follows:

```
name ... -¿ login@ host install dest ;
```

Options common to both forms:

| | |
|---|---|
| -b | Binary comparison. Perform a binary comparison and update files if they differ rather than comparing dates and sizes. |
| -d var=value | Define var to have value. The -d option is used to define or override variable definitions in the distfile. value can be the empty string, one name, or a list of names surrounded by parentheses and separated by tabs and/or spaces. |
| -h | Follow symbolic links. Copy the file that the link points to rather than the link itself. |
| -i | Ignore unresolved links. rdist will normally try to maintain the link structure of files being transferred and warn the user if all the links cannot be found. |
| -m host | Limit which machines are to be updated. Multiple -m arguments can be given to limit updates to a subset of the hosts listed in the distfile. |

| | |
|---|---|
| -n | Print the commands without executing them. This option is useful for debugging `distfile`. |
| -q | Quiet mode. Files that are being modified are normally printed on standard output. The `-q` option suppresses this. |
| -R | Remove extraneous files. If a directory is being updated, any files that exist on the remote host that do not exist in the master directory are removed. This is useful for maintaining truly identical copies of directories. |
| -v | Verify that the files are up-to-date on all the hosts. Any files that are out-of-date will be displayed, but no files will be changed nor any mail sent. |
| -w | Whole mode. The whole filename is appended to the destination directory name. Normally, only the last component of a name is used when renaming files. This will preserve the directory structure of the files being copied instead of flattening the directory structure. For example, renaming a list of files such as `dir1/f1 dir2/f2` to `dir3` would create files `dir3/dir1/f1` and `dir3/dir2/f2` instead of `dir3/f1` and `dir3/f2`. |
| -y | Younger mode. Files are normally updated if their mtime and size (see `stat(2)`for more details) disagree. The `-y` option causes rdist not to update files that are younger than the master copy. This can be used to prevent newer copies on other hosts from being replaced. A warning message is printed for files that are newer than the master copy. |

distfile contains a sequence of entries that specify the files to be copied, the destination hosts, and what operations to perform to do the updating. Each entry has one of the following formats:

```
<variable name>'=' <name list>
[label:]<source list> '->' <destination list><command list>
[label:]<source list> '::' <time_stamp file><command list>
```

The first format is used for defining variables. The second format is used for distributing files to other hosts. The third format is used for making lists of files that have been changed since some given date. The source list specifies a list of files and/or directories on the local host that are to be used as the master copy for distribution. The destination list is the list of hosts to which these files are to be copied. Each file in the source list is added to a list of changes if the file is out-of-date on the host that is being updated (second format), or the file is newer than the timestamp file (third format).

Labels are optional. They are used to identify a command for partial updates.

Newlines, tabs, and blanks are only used as separators and are otherwise ignored. Comments begin with # and end with a newline.

Variables to be expanded begin with $ followed by one character or a name enclosed in curly braces (see the examples at the end).

The source and destination lists have the following format: `<name>` or `'(' <zero or more names separated by white-space> ')'`.

The shell meta characters [, ], {, }, *, and ? are recognized and expanded (on the local host only) in the same way as csh(1). They can be escaped with a backslash. The ˜ character is also expanded in the same way as csh(1) but is expanded separately on the local and destination hosts. When the -w option is used with a filename that begins with ˜, everything except the home directory is appended to the destination name. Filenames that do not begin with / or ˜ use the destination user's home directory as the root directory for the rest of the filename.

The command list consists of zero or more commands of the following format:

```
'install' <options> opt_dest_name ';'
'notify' <name list> ';'
'except' <name list> ';'
'except_pat' <pattern list> ';'
'special' <name list> string ';'
```

The install command is used to copy out-of-date files and/or directories. Each source file is copied to each host in the destination list. Directories are recursively copied in the same way. opt_dest_name is an optional parameter to rename files. If no install command appears in the command list or the destination name is not specified, the source filename is used.

Directories in the pathname will be created if they do not exist on the remote host. To help prevent disasters, a nonempty directory on a target host will never be replaced with a regular file or a symbolic link. However, under the -R option, a nonempty directory will be removed if the corresponding filename is completely absent on the master host. The options are -R, -h, -i, -v, -w, -y, and -b and have the same semantics as options on the command line except they only apply to the files in the source list. The login name used on the destination host is the same as the local host unless the destination name is of the format login@host.

The notify command is used to mail the list of files updated (and any errors that may have occurred) to the listed names. If no @ appears in the name, the destination host is appended to the name (for example, name1@host, name2@host).

The except command is used to update all of the files in the source list except for the files listed in name list . This is usually used to copy everything in a directory except certain files.

The except_pat command is like the except command except that pattern list is a list of regular expressions (see ed(1) for details). If one of the patterns matches some string within a filename, that file will be ignored. Note that because \ is a quote character, it must be doubled to become part of the regular expression. Variables are expanded in pattern list, but not shell file pattern-matching characters. To include a $, it must be escaped with \.

The special command is used to specify sh(1) commands that are to be executed on the remote host after the file in name list is updated or installed. If the name list is omitted, then the shell commands will be executed for every file updated or installed. The shell variable FILE is set to the current filename before executing the commands in string . string starts and ends with double quotes (") and can cross multiple lines in distfile . Multiple commands to the shell should be separated by a semicolon. Commands are executed in the user's home directory on the host being updated. The special command can be used to rebuild private databases, and so on after a program has been updated.

The following is a small example:

```
HOSTS = ( matisse root@arpa )

FILES = ( /bin /lib /usr/bin /usr/games
/usr/include/{*.h,{stand,sys,vax*,pascal,machine}/*.h
/usr/lib /usr/man/man? /usr/ucb /usr/local/rdist )

EXLIB = ( Mail.rc aliases aliases.dir aliases.pag crontab dshrc sendmail.cf
sendmail.fc sendmail.hf sendmail.st uucp vfont )

${FILES} -> ${HOSTS} install -R ; except /usr/lib/${EXLIB} ; except /usr/games/lib ;
special /usr/lib/sendmail "/usr/lib/sendmail -bz" ;

srcs: /usr/src/bin -> arpa except pat ( \\.o\$ /SCCS\$);

IMAGEN = (ips dviimp catdvi)

imagen: /usr/local/${IMAGEN} -> arpa install /usr/local/lib ; notify ralph ;

${FILES} :: stamp.cory notify root@cory ;
```

## FILES

distfile        Input command file

/tmp/rdist*     Temporary file for update lists

## SEE ALSO

sh(1), csh(1), stat(2)

## HISTORY

The rdist command appeared in BSD 4.3.

## DIAGNOSTICS

A complaint about mismatch of rdist version numbers may really stem from some problem with starting your shell; for example, you are in too many groups.

## BUGS

Source files must reside on the local host where rdist is executed.

There is no easy way to have a special command executed after all files in a directory have been updated.

Variable expansion only works for name lists; there should be a general macro facility.

rdist aborts on files that have a negative mtime (before Jan 1, 1970).

There should be a force option to allow replacement of nonempty directories by regular files or symlinks. A means of updating file modes and owners of otherwise identical files is also needed.

*BSD 4.3, 30 December 1993*

# reconfig

reconfig—Convert old Xconfig to new XF86Config

## SYNOPSIS

reconfig < Xconfig > XF86Config

## DESCRIPTION

The reconfig program converts the Xconfig file format used in XFree86 versions prior to 3.1 into the XF86Config format currently used. The XF86Config format contains more information than the Xconfig format, so manual editing is required after converting.

## SEE ALSO

XFree86(1), XF86Config(4/5), xf86config(1)

## AUTHOR

Gertjan Akkerman

## BUGS

Comment lines are stripped out when converting.

*XFree86 Version 3.1.1*

# ref

ref—Display a C function header

## SYNOPSIS

ref [-t] [-x] [-c *class*]... [-f *file*]... *tag*

## DESCRIPTION

ref quickly locates and displays the header of a function. To do this, ref looks in the tags file for the line that describes the function, and then scans the source file for the function. When it locates the function, it displays an introductory comment (if there is one), the function's declaration, and the declarations of all arguments.

## SEARCH METHOD

ref uses a fairly sophisticated tag look-up algorithm. If you supply a filename via -f file, then elvis first scans the tags file for a static tag from that file. This search is limited to the tags file in the current directory.

If you supply a class name via -c class, then elvis searches for a tag from that class. This search is not limited to the current directory; You can supply a list of directories in the environment variable TAGPATH, and ref will search through the tags file in each directory until it finds a tag in the desired class.

If that fails, ref will then try to look up an ordinary global tag. This search checks all of the directories listed in TAGPATH, too. If the tag being sought doesn't contain any colons, and you haven't given a -x flag, then any static tags in a tags file will be treated as global tags.

If you've given the -t flag, then ref will simply output the tag line that it found, and then exit. Without -t, though, ref will search for the tag line. It will try to open the source file, which should be in the same directory as the tags file where the tag was discovered. If the source file doesn't exist, or is unreadable, then ref will try to open a file called refs in that directory. Either way, ref will try to locate the tag, and display whatever it finds.

## INTERACTION WITH elvis

ref is used by the elvis shift-K command. If the cursor is located on a word such as *splat*, in the file foo.c, then elvis will invoke ref with the command ref -f foo.c splat.

If elvis has been compiled with the -DEXTERNAL_TAGS flag, then elvis will use ref to scan the tags files. This is slower than the built-in tag searching, but it allows elvis to access the more sophisticated tag lookup provided by ref. Other than that, external tags should act exactly like internal tags.

## OPTIONS

| | |
|---|---|
| -t | Output tag info, instead of the function header. |
| -f *file* | The tag might be a static function in file. You can use several -f flags to have ref consider static tags from more than one file. |
| -c *class* | The tag might be a member of class class. You can use several -c flags to have ref consider tags from more than one class. |

## FILES

| | |
|---|---|
| tags | List of function names and their locations, generated by ctags |
| refs | Function headers extracted from source files (optional) |

## ENVIRONMENT

| | |
|---|---|
| TAGPATH | List of directories to be searched. The elements in the list are separated by either semicolons (for MS-DOS, Atari TOS, and AmigaDos), or by colons (every other operating system). For each operating system, ref has a built-in default which is probably adequate. |

## NOTES

You might want to generate a `tags` file for the directory that contains the source code for standard C library on your system. If licensing restrictions prevent you from making the library source readable by everybody, then you can have `ctags` generate a `refs` file, and make `refs` readable by everybody.

If your system doesn't come with the library source code, then perhaps you can produce something workable from the `lint` libraries.

## SEE ALSO

elvis(1), ctags(1)

## AUTHOR

Steve Kirkendall (kirkenda@cs.pdx.edu)

# reset

reset—Reset the terminal

## SYNOPSIS

clear

## DESCRIPTION

reset calls `tput(1)` with the `clear`, `rmacs`, `rmm`, `rmul`, `rs1`, `rs2`, and `rs3` arguments. This causes `tput` to send appropriate reset strings to the terminal based on information in `/etc/termcap` (for the GNU or BSD `tput`) or in the `terminfo` database (for the `ncurses` `tput`). This sequence seems to be sufficient to reset the Linux VC's when they start printing "funny-looking" characters. For good measure, `stty(1)` is called with the `sane` argument in an attempt to get Cooked mode back.

## SEE ALSO

reset(1), stty(1), tput(1)

## AUTHOR

Rik Faith (faith@cs.unc.edu)

*Linux 0.99, 10 October 1993*

# resize

resize—Set TERMCAP and terminal settings to current xterm window size

## SYNOPSIS

resize [ -u ¦ -c ][-s [ *row col* ]]

## DESCRIPTION

resize prints a shell command for setting the TERM and TERMCAP environment variables to indicate the current size of xterm window from which the command is run. For this output to take effect, resize must either be evaluated as part of the command line (usually done with a shell alias or function) or else redirected to a file that can then be read in. From the C shell (usually known as /bin/csh), the following alias could be defined in the user's .cshrc:

% alias rs 'set noglob; eval 'resize''

After resizing the window, the user would type:

%rs

Users of versions of the Bourne shell (usually known as /bin/sh) that don't have command functions will need to send the output to a temporary file and the read it back in with the . command:

```
$ resize > /tmp/out
$ . /tmp/out
```

## OPTIONS

The following options may be used with resize:

| | |
|---|---|
| -u | This option indicates that Bourne shell commands should be generated even if the user's current shell isn't /bin/sh. |
| -c | This option indicates that C shell commands should be generated even if the user's current shell isn't /bin/csh. |
| -s [*rows columns*] | This option indicates that Sun console escape sequences will be used instead of the special xterm escape code. If *rows* and *columns* are given, resize will ask the xterm to resize itself. However, the window manager may choose to disallow the change. |

## FILES

| | |
|---|---|
| /etc/termcap | For the base termcap entry to modify |
| ˜/.cshrc | User's alias for the command |

## SEE ALSO

csh(1), tset(1), xterm(1)

## AUTHORS

Mark Vandevoorde (MIT-Athena), Edward Moy(Berkeley)
Copyright© 1984, 1985 by XConsortium
See X(1) for a complete copyright notice.

## BUGS

The -u or -c must appear to the left of -s if both are specified.

*X Version 11 Release 6*

# rev

rev—Reverse lines of a file

## SYNOPSIS

rev [*file*]

## DESCRIPTION

The rev utility copies the specified files to the standard output, reversing the order of characters in every line. If no files are specified, the standard input is read.

*21 March 1992*

# rgb3toppm

rgb3toppm—Combine three portable graymaps into one portable pixmap

## SYNOPSIS

`rgb3toppm`*redpgmfile greenpgmfile bluepgmfile*

## DESCRIPTION

`rgb3toppm` reads three portable graymaps as input and combines them and produces one portable pixmap as output.

## SEE ALSO

ppmtorgb3(1), pgmtoppm(1), ppmtopgm(1), ppm(5), pgm(5)

## AUTHOR

Copyright© 1991 by Jef Poskanzer.

*15 February 1990*

# rlog

`rlog`—Print log messages and other information about RCS files

## SYNOPSIS

`rlog` [ *options* ] *file* ...

## DESCRIPTION

`rlog` prints information about RCS files.

Pathnames matching an RCS suffix denote RCS files; all others denote working files. Names are paired as explained in ci(1).

`rlog` prints the following information for each RCS file: RCS pathname, working pathname, head (the number of the latest revision on the trunk), default branch, access list, locks, symbolic names, suffix, total number of revisions, number of revisions selected for printing, and descriptive text. This is followed by entries for the selected revisions in reverse chronological order for each branch. For each revision, `rlog` prints revision number, author, date/time, state, number of lines added/deleted (with respect to the previous revision), locker of the revision (if any), and log message. All times are displayed in Coordinated Universal Time (UTC) by default; this can be overridden with `-z`. Without options, `rlog` prints complete information. The options below restrict this output.

| | |
|---|---|
| `-L` | Ignore RCS files that have no locks set. This is convenient in combination with `-h`, `-l`, and `-R`. |
| `-R` | Print only the name of the RCS file. This is convenient for translating a working pathname into an RCS pathname. |
| `-h` | Print only the RCS pathname, working pathname, head, default branch, access list, locks, symbolic names, and suffix. |
| `-t` | Print the same as `-h`, plus the descriptive text. |
| `-N` | Do not print the symbolic names. |
| `-b` | Print information about the revisions on the default branch, normally the highest branch on the trunk. |
| `-d`*dates* | Print information about revisions with a checkin date/time in the ranges given by the semicolon-separated list of *dates*. A range of the form d1<d2 or d2>d1 selects the revisions that were deposited between d1 and d2 exclusive. A range of the form <d or d> selects all revisions earlier than d. A range of the form d< or >d selects all revisions dated later than d. If < or > is followed by =, then the ranges are inclusive, not exclusive. A range of the form d selects the single, latest revision dated d or earlier. The date/time strings d, d1, and d2 are in the free format explained in co(1). Quoting is normally necessary, especially for < and >. Note that the separator is a semicolon. |
| `-l`[*lockers*] | Print information about locked revisions only. In addition, if the comma-separated list *lockers* of login names is given, ignore all locks other than those held by the *lockers*. For example, `rlog -L -R -l`wft RCS/* prints the name of RCS files locked by the user `wft`. |

| | |
|---|---|
| -r[*revisions*] | Print information about revisions given in the comma-separated list *revisions* of revisions and ranges. A range rev1:rev2 means revisions rev1 to rev2 on the same branch, :rev means revisions from the beginning of the branch up to and including rev, and rev: means revisions starting with rev to the end of the branch containing rev. An argument that is a branch means all revisions on that branch. A range of branches means all revisions on the branches in that range. A branch followed by a . means the latest revision in that branch. A bare -r with no revisions means the latest revision on the default branch, normally the trunk. |
| -s*states* | Print information about revisions whose state attributes match one of the states given in the comma-separated list *states*. |
| -w[*logins*] | Print information about revisions checked in by users with login names appearing in the comma-separated list logins. If logins is omitted, the user's login is assumed. |
| -T | This option has no effect; it is present for compatibility with other rcs commands. |
| -V | Print the RCS version number. |
| -V*n* | Emulate RCS version *n* when generating logs. (See co(1) for more details.) |
| -x*suffixes* | Use *suffixes* to characterize RCS files. (See ci(1) for details.) |

rlog prints the intersection of the revisions selected with the options -d, -l, -s, and -w, intersected with the union of the revisions selected by -b and -r.

| | |
|---|---|
| -z*zone* | Specifies the date output format, and specifies the default time zone for date in the -d*dates* option. The *zone* should be empty, a numeric UTC offset, or the special string LT for local time. The default is an empty *zone*, which uses the traditional RCS format of UTC without any time zone indication and with slashes separating the parts of the date; otherwise, times are output in ISO 8601 format with time zone indication. For example, if local time is January 11, 1990, 8 p.m. Pacific Standard Time, eight hours west of UTC, then the time is output as follows: |

```
option    time output
------    ---- ------
-z        1990/01/12 04:00:00     (default)
-zLT      1990-01-11 20:00:00-08
-z+05:30  1990-01-12 09:30:00+05:30
```

## EXAMPLES

Here are four rlog commands:

```
rlog -L -R RCS/*
rlog -L -h RCS/*
rlog -L -l RCS/*
rlog RCS/*
```

The first command prints the names of all RCS files in the subdirectory RCS that have locks. The second command prints the headers of those files, and the third prints the headers plus the log messages of the locked revisions. The last command prints complete information.

## ENVIRONMENT

RCSINIT    Options prepended to the argument list, separated by spaces. (See ci(1) for details.)

## DIAGNOSTICS

The exit status is zero if and only if all operations were successful.

## IDENTIFICATION

Author: Walter F. Tichy
Manual Page Revision: 5.9; Release Date: 1995/06/16
Copyright© 1982, 1988, 1989 Walter F. Tichy
Copyright© 1990, 1991, 1992, 1993, 1994, 1995 Paul Eggert

## SEE ALSO

ci(1), co(1), ident(1), rcs(1), rcsdiff(1), rcsintro(1), rcsmerge(1), rcsfile(5)

"RCS-A System for Version Control" by Walter F. Tichy, *Software-Practice & Experience* 15, 7 (July 1985), pages 637–654.

## BUGS

The separator for revision ranges in the -r option used to be - instead of :, but this leads to confusion when symbolic names contain -. For backwards compatibility, rlog -r still supports the old - separator, but it warns about this obsolete use.

*GNU, 16 June 1995*

# rlog

rlogin—Remote login

## SYNOPSIS

rlogin [-8EKLdx] [-e char] [-k realm] [-l username] *host*

## DESCRIPTION

rlogin starts a terminal session on a remote host *host*.

rlogin first attempts to use the Kerberos authorization mechanism, described in the following subsection. If the remote host does not support Kerberos, the standard Berkeley authorization mechanism is used. The options are as follows:

-8    The -8 option allows an eight-bit input data path at all times; otherwise, parity bits are stripped except when the remote side's stop and start characters are other than ˆS/ˆQ.

-E    The -E option stops any character from being recognized as an escape character. When used with the -8 option, this provides a completely transparent connection.

-K    The -K option turns off all Kerberos authentication.

-L    The -L option allows the rlogin session to be run in litout mode.(See tty(4) for details).

-d    The -d option turns on socket debugging (see the setsockopt(2) man page) on the TCP sockets used for communication with the remote host.

-e    The -e option allows user specification of the escape character, which is the tilde (˜) by default. This specification may be as a literal character, or as an octal value in the form nnnn.

-k    The -k option requests rlogin to obtain tickets for the remote host in realm realm instead of the remote host's realm as determined by krb_realmofhost(3).

-x    The -x option turns on DES encryption for all data passed via the rlogin session. This may impact response time and CPU utilization, but provides increased security.

A line of the form <escape char> disconnects from the remote host. Similarly, the line <escape char>ˆZ will suspend the rlogin session, and <escape char><delayed-suspend char> suspends the send portion of the rlogin, but allows output from the remote system. By default, the tilde (˜) character is the escape character, and normally control -Y (ˆY) is the delayed-suspend character.

All echoing takes place at the remote site, so that (except for delays) the rlogin is transparent. Flow control via ˆS/ˆQ and flushing of input and output on interrupts is handled properly.

## KERBEROS AUTHENTICATION

Each user may have a private authorization list in the file in his or her home directory. Each line in this file should contain a Kerberos principal name of the form `principal.instance (@realm)`. If the originating user is authenticated to one of the principals named, access is granted to the account. The `principal accountname.(@localrealm)` is granted access if there is no file. Otherwise, a login and password will be prompted for on the remote machine as in `login(1)`. To avoid certain security problems, the file must be owned by the remote user.

If Kerberos authentication fails, a warning message is printed and the standard Berkeley `rlogin` is used instead.

## ENVIRONMENT

The following environment variable is utilized by `rlogin`:

TERM        Determines the user's terminal type

## SEE ALSO

rsh(1), kerberos(3), krb_sendauth(3), krb_realmofhost(3)

## HISTORY

The `rlogin` command appeared in BSD 4.2.

## BUGS

`rlogin` will be replaced by `telnet(1)` in the near future.

More of the environment should be propagated.

*BSD 4.2, 27 July 1991*

# rm

rm—Remove files

## SYNOPSIS

```
rm [-dfirvR] [--directory] [--force] [--interactive] [--recursive]
[--help] [--version] [--verbose] name...
```

## DESCRIPTION

This manual page documents the GNU version of `rm`. `rm` removes each specified file. By default, it does not remove directories. If a file is unwritable, the standard input is a `tty`, and the `-f` or `--force` option is not given, `rm` prompts the user for whether to remove the file. If the response does not begin with y or Y, the file is skipped.

GNU `rm`, like every program that uses the `getopt` function to parse its arguments, lets you use the `--` option to indicate that all following arguments are nonoptions. To remove a file called `-f` in the current directory, you could type either

rm -- -f

or

rm ./-f

The UNIX `rm` program's use of a single - for this purpose predates the development of the `getopt` standard syntax.

## OPTIONS

-d, --directory    Remove directories with `unlink` instead of `rmdir`, and don't require a directory to be empty before trying to unlink it. Only works for the superuser. Because unlinking a directory causes any files in the deleted directory to become unreferenced, it is wise to `fsck` the filesystem after doing this.

| -f, --force | Ignore nonexistent files and never prompt the user. |
| -i, --interactive | Prompt whether to remove each file. If the response does not begin with y or Y, the file is skipped. |
| -r, -R, --recursive | Remove the contents of directories recursively. |
| -v, --verbose | Print the name of each file before removing it. |
| --help | Print a usage message on standard output and exit successfully. |
| --version | Print version information on standard output, then exit successfully. |

*GNU File Utilities*

# rmdir

rmdir—Remove empty directories

## SYNOPSIS

**rmdir** [-p] [--parents] [--help] [--version] dir...

## DESCRIPTION

This manual page documents the GNU version of rmdir. rmdir removes each given empty directory. If any nonoption argument does not refer to an existing empty directory, it is an error.

## OPTIONS

| -p, --parents | Remove any parent directories that are explicitly mentioned in an argument, if they become empty after the argument file is removed. |
| --help | Print a usage message on standard output and exit successfully. |
| --version | Print version information on standard output, then exit successfully. |

*GNU File Utilities*

# rmmod

rmmod—Unload loadable modules

## SYNOPSIS

rmmod [ -r ] module ...

## DESCRIPTION

rmmod unloads loadable modules from the kernel.

rmmod tries to unload a set of modules from the kernel, with the restriction that they are not in use and that they are not referred to by other modules.

If more than one module is named on the command line, the modules will be removed in the given order. This supports unloading of stacked modules.

With the option -r, a recursive removal of modules will be attempted. This means that if a top module in a stack is named on the command line, all modules that are used by this module will be removed as well, if possible.

## SEE ALSO

insmod(1), lsmod(1), ksyms(1), modules(2)

## HISTORY

The module support was first conceived by Anonymous (as far as I know…). Linux version by Bas Laarhoven (bas@vimec.nl), 0.99.14 version by Jon Tombs (jon@gtex02.us.es), extended by Bjorn Ekwall (bj0rn@blox.se).

## BUGS

rmmod might have some, but they are well hidden.

*Linux, 14 May 1995*

# rnews

rnews—Receive news from a UUCP connection

## SYNOPSIS

rnews [ -h *host* ][ -v ][ -U ][ -S *master* ][ *input* ]

## DESCRIPTION

rnews reads messages sent by a downstream uucp newsfeed and sends them to the local InterNetNews server. The message is read from the specified input file, or standard input if no input is named.

If the -S flag is used, then rnews will connect to the specified host. If the flag is not used, it will try to connect to the server by opening a UNIX-domain stream connection. If that fails, it will try to open a TCP connection to the default remote server.

If the server is not available, the message is spooled into a new file created in the /var/spool/rnews directory. The -U flag may be used to send all spooled messages to the server when it becomes available again, and can be invoked regularly by cron(8).

When sent over uucp, Usenet articles are typically joined in a single batch to reduce the uucp overhead. Batches can also be compressed, to reduce the communication time. If a message does not start with a number sign (#) and an exclamation point, then the entire input is taken as a single news article. If it does start with those two characters, then the first line is read and interpreted as a batch command.

If the command is #! rnews *nnn*, where *nnn* is a number, then the next *nnn* bytes (starting with the next line) are read as a news article.

If the command is #! cunbatch, then the rest of input is fed to the compress(1) program with the -d flag to uncompress it, and the output of this pipe is read as input from rnews. This is for historical compatibility—there is no program named cunbatch. A compressed batch will start with a #! cunbatch line, then contain a series of articles separated by #! rnews *nnn* lines.

If the command is any other word, then rnews will try to execute a program with that name in the directory /news/bin/rnews. The batch will be fed into the program's standard input, and the standard output will be read back as input into rnews.

If rnews detects any problems with an article, such as a missing header or an unintelligible reply from the server, it will save a copy of the article in the /var/spool/rnews/bad directory. If the -v flag is used, it will print a notice of all such errors on the standard error, naming the input file (if known) and printing the first few characters of the input. Errors are always logged through syslog(3).

If the -h flag is given, or failing that, the environment variable UU_MACHINE is set, then rnews will log the Message-ID and host for each article offered to the server via syslog(3). Logging will only be done if the value is not an empty string.

## BUGS

rnews cannot process articles that have embedded \0s in them.

## HISTORY

Written by Rich $alz (rsalz@uunet.uu.net) for InterNetNews.

## SEE ALSO

innd(8).

# rpcgen

rpcgen—An RPC protocol compiler

## SYNOPSIS

```
rpcgen infile
rpcgen [-D name[= value]] [-T] [-K secs] infile
rpcgen -c¦-h¦-l¦-m¦-t [-o outfile] infile
rpcgen [-I] -s nettype [-o outfile] infile
rpcgen -n netid [-o outfile] infile
```

## DESCRIPTION

rpcgen is a tool that generates C code to implement an RPC protocol. The input to rpcgen is a language similar to C known as RPC language (Remote Procedure Call Language). rpcgen is normally used as in the first synopsis where it takes an input file and generates up to four output files. If the infile is named proto.x, then rpcgen will generate a header file in proto.h, xdr routines in proto_xdr.c, server-side stubs in proto_svc.c, and client-side stubs in proto_clnt.c.

With the -T option, it will also generate the RPC dispatch table in proto_tbl.i. With the -Sc option, it will also generate sample code that would illustrate how to use the remote procedures on the client side. This code would be created in proto_client.c. With the -Ss option, it will also generate a sample server code that would illustrate how to write the remote procedures. This code would be created in proto_server.c. The server created can be started both by the port monitors (for example, inetd or listen) or by itself. When it is started by a port monitor, it creates servers only for the transport for which the file descriptor 0 was passed. The name of the transport must be specified by setting up the environmental variable PM_TRANSPORT.

When the server generated by rpcgen is executed, it creates server handles for all the transports specified in NETPATH environment variable, or if it is unset, it creates server handles for all the visible transports from /etc/netconfig file. Note: the transports are chosen at runtime and not at compile time. When the server is self-started, it backgrounds itself by default. A special define symbol RPC_SVC_FG can be used to run the server process in the foreground. The second synopsis provides special features that allow for the creation of more sophisticated RPC servers. These features include support for user-provided #defines and RPC dispatch tables. The entries in the RPC dispatch table contain

- Pointers to the service routine corresponding to that procedure
- A pointer to the input and output arguments
- The size of these routines

A server can use the dispatch table to check authorization and then to execute the service routine; a client library may use it to deal with the details of storage management and xdr data conversion. The other three synopses shown in the preceding paragraph are used when one does not want to generate all the output files, but only a particular one. (Some examples of their usage is described in the "Example" subsection.) When rpcgen is executed with the -s option, it creates servers for that particular class of transports. When executed with the -n option, it creates a server for the transport specified by netid. If infile is not specified, rpcgen accepts the standard input. The C preprocessor, cc -E (see cc(1) for details), is run on the input file before it is actually interpreted by rpcgen. For each type of output file, rpcgen defines a special preprocessor symbol for use by the rpcgen programmer, as follows:

| | |
|---|---|
| `RPC_HDR` | Defined when compiling into header files |
| `RPC_XDR` | Defined when compiling into XDR routines |
| `RPC_SVC` | Defined when compiling into server-side stubs |
| `RPC_CLNT` | Defined when compiling into client-side stubs |
| `RPC_TBL` | Defined when compiling into RPC dispatch tables Any line beginning with `%` is passed directly into the output file, uninterpreted by rpcgen. For every data type referred to in `infile`, rpcgen assumes that there exists a routine with the string `xdr` prepended to the name of the data type. If this routine does not exist in the RPC/XDR library, it must be provided. Providing an undefined data type allows customization of XDR routines. The following options are available: |

| | |
|---|---|
| `-a` | Generate all the files including sample code for client and server side. |
| `-b` | This generates code for the SunOS4.1 style of rpc. It is for backwards compatibility. This is the default. |
| `-5` | This generates code for the SysVr4 style of rpc. It is used by the Transport Independent RPC that is in Svr4 systems. By default, rpcgen generates code for SunOS4.1 type of rpc. |
| `-c` | Compile into XDR routines. |
| `-C` | Generate code in ANSI C. This option also generates code that could be compiled with the C++ compiler. This is the default. |
| `-k` | Generate code in K&R C. The default is ANSI C. |
| `-Dname[=value]` | Define a symbol *name*. Equivalent to the `#define` directive in the source. If no *value* is given, *value* is defined as `1`. This option may be specified more than once. |
| `-h` | Compile into C data-definitions (a header file). `-T` option can be used in conjunction to produce a header file that supports RPC dispatch tables. |
| `-I` | Generate a service that can be started from inetd. The default is to generate a static service that handles transports selected with `-s`. Using `-I` allows starting a service by either method. |
| `-K secs` | By default, services created using rpcgen wait 120 seconds after servicing a request before exiting. That interval can be changed using the `-K` flag. To create a server that exits immediately upon servicing a request, `-K 0` can be used. To create a server that never exits, the appropriate argument is `-K -1`. |
| | When monitoring for a server, some port monitors, such as listen(1M), always spawn a new process in response to a service request. If it is known that a server will be used with such a monitor, the server should exit immediately on completion. For such servers, rpcgen should be used with `-K -1`. |
| `-l` | Compile into client-side stubs. |
| `-m` | Compile into server-side stubs, but do not generate a main routine. This option is useful for doing callback-routines and for users who need to write their own main routine to do initialization. |
| `-n netid` | Compile into server-side stubs for the transport specified by *netid*. There should be an entry for *netid* in the netconfig database. This option may be specified more than once, so as to compile a server that serves multiple transports. |
| `-N` | Use the newstyle of rpcgen. This allows procedures to have multiple arguments. It also uses the style of parameter passing that closely resembles C. So, when passing an argument to a remote procedure, you do not have to pass a pointer to the argument but the argument itself. This behavior is different from the old style of rpcgen-generated code. The new style is not the default case because of backwards compatibility. |
| `-o outfile` | Specify the name of the output file. If none is specified, standard output is used (`-c`, `-h`, `-l`, `-m`, `-n`, `-s`, `-sc`, `-ss`, and `-t` modes only). |

| | |
|---|---|
| -s *nettype* | Compile into server-side stubs for all the transports belonging to the class `nettype`. The supported classes are `netpath`, `visible`, `circuit_n`, `circuit_v`, `datagram_n`, `datagram_v`, `tcp`, and `udp`. See rpc(3N) for the meanings associated with these classes. This option may be specified more than once. Note: The transports are chosen at runtime and not at compile time. |
| -Sc | Generate sample code to show the use of remote procedure and how to bind to the server before calling the client-side stubs generated by rpcgen. |
| -Ss | Generate skeleton code for the remote procedures on the server side. You would need to fill in the actual code for the remote procedures. |
| -t | Compile into RPC dispatch table. |
| -T | Generate the code to support RPC dispatch tables. The options -c, -h, -l, -m, u, and -t are used exclusively to generate a particular type of file, while the options -D and -T are global and can be used with the other options. |

## NOTES

The RPC language does not support nesting of structures. As a workaround, structures can be declared at the top level, and their name used inside other structures in order to achieve the same effect. Name clashes can occur when using program definitions because the apparent scoping does not really apply. Most of these can be avoided by giving unique names for programs, versions, procedures, and types. The server code generated with the -n option refers to the transport indicated by netid and hence is very site-specific.

## EXAMPLE

The following example:

```
$ rpcgen -T prot.x
```

generates five files: `prot.h`, `prot_clnt.c`, `prot_svc.c`, `prot_xdr.c`, and `prot_tbl.i`.

This example:

```
$ rpcgen -h prot.x
```

sends the C data-definitions (header file) to the standard output.

To send the test version of the -DTEST, server-side stubs for all the transport belonging to the class `datagram_n` to standard output, use

```
$ rpcgen -s datagram_n -DTEST prot.x
```

To create the server-side stubs for the transport indicated by *netid* `tcp`, use

```
$ rpcgen -n tcp -o prot_svc.c prot.x
```

## SEE ALSO

cc(1).

# rsh

rsh—Remote shell

## SYNOPSIS

```
rsh [-Kdnx] [-k realm] [-l username] host command
```

## DESCRIPTION

rsh executes command on host.

rsh copies its standard input to the remote command, the standard output of the remote command to its standard output, and the standard error of the remote command to its standard error. Interrupt, quit, and terminate signals are propagated to the remote command; rsh normally terminates when the remote command does. The options are as follows:

-K        Turns off all Kerberos authentication.

-d        Using setsockopt(2), turns on socket debugging on the TCP sockets used for communication with the remote host.

-k        Causes rsh to obtain tickets for the remote host in realm instead of the remote host's realm as determined by krb_realmofhost(3).

-l        By default, the remote username is the same as the local username. The -l option allows the remote name to be specified. Kerberos authentication is used, and authorization is determined as in rlogin(1).

-n        The -n option redirects input from the special device. (See the "Bugs" section of this manual page.)

-x        The -x option turns on DES encryption for all data exchange. This may introduce a significant delay in response time.

If no command is specified, you will be logged in on the remote host using rlogin(1).

Shell metacharacters that are not quoted are interpreted on local machine, while quoted metacharacters are interpreted on the remote machine. For example, the command:

```
rsh otherhost cat remotefile >> localfile
```

appends the remote file remotefile to the local file localfile, while

```
rsh otherhost cat remotefile >> other remotefile
```

appends remotefile to other remotefile.

## FILES

/etc/hosts

## SEE ALSO

rlogin(1), kerberos(3), krb sendauth(3), krb_realmofhost(3)

## HISTORY

The rsh command appeared in BSD 4.2.

## BUGS

If you are using csh(1) and put a rsh in the background without redirecting its input away from the terminal, it will block even if no reads are posted by the remote command. If no input is desired you should redirect the input of rsh to using the -n option.

You cannot run an interactive command (rogue(6) or vi(1), for example) using rsh; use rlogin(1) instead.

Stop signals stop the local rsh process only; this is arguably wrong, but currently hard to fix for reasons too complicated to explain here.

*BSD 4.2, 24 July 1991*

# rstart

rstart—A sample implementation of a Remote Start client

## SYNOPSIS

rstart [-c *context*] [-g] [-l *username*] [-v] *hostname command args* ...

## DESCRIPTION

rstart is a simple implementation of a Remote Start client as defined in "A Flexible Remote Execution Protocol Based on rsh." It uses rsh as its underlying remote execution mechanism.

## OPTIONS

| | |
|---|---|
| -c context | This option specifies the context in which the command is to be run. A context specifies a general environment the program is to be run in. The details of this environment are host-specific; the intent is that the client need not know how the environment must be configured. If omitted, the context defaults to X. This should be suitable for running X programs from the host's "usual" X installation. |
| -g | Interprets command as a *generic command*, as discussed in the protocol document. This is intended to allow common applications to be invoked without knowing what they are called on the remote system. Currently, the only generic commands defined are Terminal, LoadMonitor, ListContexts, and ListGenericCommands. |
| -l username | This option is passed to the underlying rsh; it requests that the command be run as the specified user. |
| -v | This option requests that rstart be verbose in its operation. Without this option, rstart discards output from the remote's rstart helper, and directs the rstart helper to detach the program from the rsh connection used to start it. With this option, responses from the helper are displayed and the resulting program is not detached from the connection. |

## NOTES

This is a trivial implementation. Far more sophisticated implementations are possible and should be developed.

Error-handling is nonexistent. Without -v, error reports from the remote are discarded silently. With -v, error reports are displayed.

The $DISPLAY environment variable is passed. If it starts with a colon, the local hostname is prepended. The local domain name should be appended to unqualified hostnames, but isn't.

The $SESSION_MANAGER environment variable should be passed, but isn't.

X11 authority information is passed for the current display.

ICE authority information should be passed, but isn't. It isn't completely clear how rstart should select what ICE authority information to pass.

Even without -v, the sample rstart helper will leave a shell waiting for the program to complete. This causes no real harm and consumes relatively few resources, but if it is undesirable it can be avoided by explicitly specifying the exec command to the shell, for example, 0 rstart somehost exec xterm.

This is obviously dependent on the command interpreter being used on the remote system; the example given will work for the Bourne and C shells.

## SEE ALSO

rstartd(1), rsh(1), "A Flexible Remote Execution Protocol Based on rsh"

## AUTHOR

Jordan Brown, Quarterdeck Office Systems

*X Version 11 Release 6*

# rstartd

rstartd—A sample implementation of a Remote Start rsh helper

## SYNOPSIS

rstartd

rstartd.real [-c *configfilename*]

## DESCRIPTION

rstartd is an implementation of a Remote Start "helper" as defined in "A Flexible Remote Execution Protocol Based on rsh."

This document describes the peculiarities of rstartd and how it is configured.

## OPTIONS

-c *configfilename*    This option specifies the global configuration file that rstartd is to read. Normally, rstartd is a shell script that invokes rstartd.real with the -c switch, allowing local configuration of the location of the configuration file. If rstartd.real is started without the -c option, it reads <XRoot>/lib/X11/rstart/config, where <XRoot> refers to the root of the X11 install tree.

## INSTALLATION

It is critical to successful interoperation of the Remote Start protocol that rstartd be installed in a directory that is in the default search path, so that default rsh requests and the ilk will be able to find it.

## CONFIGURATION AND OPERATION

rstartd is by design highly configurable. One would like things like configuration file locations to be fixed, so that users and administrators can find them without searching, but reality is that no two vendors will agree on where things should go, and nobody thinks the original location is "right." Thus, rstartd allows the relocation of all of its files and directories.

rstartd has a hierarchy of configuration files that are executed in order when a request is made. They are global config, per-user ("local") config, global per-context config, per-user ("local") per-context config, config from request.

As you might guess from the presence of config from request, all of the config files are in the format of an rstart request. rstartd defines a few additional keywords with the INTERNAL- prefix for specifying its configuration.

rstartd starts by reading and executing the global config file. This file will normally specify the locations of the other configuration files and any system-wide defaults.

rstartd will then read the user's local config file, default name $HOME/.rstart.

rstartd will then start interpreting the request.

Presumably, one of the first lines in the request will be a CONTEXT line. The context name is converted to lowercase.

rstartd will read the global config file for that context, default name <XRoot>/lib/X11/rstart/contexts/<name>, if any.

It will then read the user's config file for that context, default name $HOME/.rstart.contexts/<name>, if any.

(If neither of these exists, rstartd aborts with a Failure message.)

rstartd will finish interpreting the request, and execute the program specified. This allows the system administrator and the user a large degree of control over the operation of rstartd. The administrator has final say, because the global config file doesn't need to specify a per-user config file. If it does, however, the user can override anything from the global file, and can even completely replace the global context config files.

The config files have a somewhat more flexible format than requests do; they are allowed to contain blank lines and lines beginning with # are comments and ignored. (#s in the middle of lines are data, not comment markers.)

Any commands run are provided a few useful pieces of information in environment variables. The exact names are configurable, but the supplied defaults are

| | |
|---|---|
| $RSTART_CONTEXT | The name of the context |
| $RSTART_GLOBAL_CONTEXTS | The global contexts directory |
| $RSTART_LOCAL_CONTEXTS | The local contexts directory |
| $RSTART_GLOBAL_COMMANDS | The global generic commands directory |
| $RSTART_LOCAL_COMMANDS | The local generic commands directory |

$RSTART_{GLOBAL,LOCAL}_CONTEXTS should contain one special file, @List, which contains a list of the contexts in that directory in the format specified for ListContexts. The supplied version of ListContexts will cat both the global and local copies of @List.

Generic commands are searched for in several places: (defaults)

| | |
|---|---|
| Per-user per-context directory | $HOME/.rstart.commands/<context> |
| Global per-context directory | <XRoot>/lib/X11/rstart/commands/<context> |
| Per-user all-contexts directory | $HOME/.rstart.commands |

Global all-contexts directory (<XRoot>/lib/X11/rstart/commands)

(Yes, this means you can't have an all-contexts generic command with the same name as a context. It didn't seem like a big deal.)

Each of these directories should have a file called @List that gives the names and descriptions of the commands in that directory in the format specified for ListGenericCommands.

## CONFIGURATION KEYWORDS

There are several special rstart keywords defined for rstartd configuration. Unless otherwise specified, there are no defaults; related features are disabled in this case.

Internal-Registries name...—Gives a space-separated list of MISC registries that this system understands. (Registries other than these are accepted but generate a warning.)

Internal-Local-Default relative_filename—Gives the name ($HOME relative) of the per-user config file.

INTERNAL-GLOBAL-CONTEXTS absolute_directory_name—Gives the name of the system-wide contexts directory.

INTERNAL-LOCAL-CONTEXTS relative_directory_name—Gives the name ($HOME relative) of the per-user contexts directory.

INTERNAL-GLOBAL-COMMANDS absolute_directory_name—Gives the name of the system-wide generic commands directory.

INTERNAL-LOCAL-COMMANDS relative_directory_name—Gives the name ($HOME relative) of the per-user generic commands directory.

INTERNAL-VARIABLE-PREFIX prefix—Gives the prefix for the configuration environment variables rstartd passes to its kids.

INTERNAL-AUTH-PROGRAM authscheme program argv[0] argv[1]...—Specifies the program to run to set up authentication for the specified authentication scheme. program argv[0] ... gives the program to run and its arguments, in the same form as the EXEC keyword.

INTERNAL-AUTH-INPUT authscheme—Specifies the data to be given to the authorization program as its standard input. Each argument is passed as a single line. $n, where n is a number, is replaced by the nth argument to the AUTH authscheme arg1 arg2 ... line.

INTERNAL-PRINT arbitrary text—Prints its arguments as a Debug message. Mostly for rstartd debugging, but could be used to debug config files.

## NOTES

When using the C shell, or any other shell that runs a script every time the shell is started, the script may be run several times. In the worst case, the script may be run three times: By rsh, to run rstartd; by rstartd, to run the specified command; by the command, such as xterm.

rstartd currently limits lines, both from config files and requests, to BUFSIZ bytes.

DETACH is implemented by redirecting file descriptors 0, 1, and 2 to /dev/null and forking before executing the program.

CMD is implemented by invoking $SHELL (default /bin/sh) with -c and the specified command as arguments.

POSIX-UMASK is implemented in the obvious way.

The authorization programs are run in the same context as the target program—same environment variables, path, and so on. Long term, this might be a problem.

In the X context, GENERIC-CMD Terminal runs xterm. In the OpenWindows context, GENERIC-CMD Terminal runs cmdtool.

In the X context, GENERIC-CMD LoadMonitor runs xload. In the OpenWindows context, GENERIC-CMD LoadMonitor runs perfmeter.

GENERIC-CMD ListContexts lists the contents of @List in both the system-wide and per-user contexts directories. It is available in all contexts.

GENERIC-CMD ListGenericCommands lists the contents of @List in the system-wide and per-user commands directories, including the per-context subdirectories for the current context. It is available in all contexts.

CONTEXT None is not implemented.

CONTEXT Default is really dull.

For installation ease, the contexts directory in the distribution contains a file @Aliases, which lists a context name and aliases for that context. This file is used to make symlinks in the contexts and commands directories.

All MISC values are passed unmodified as environment variables.

You can mistreat rstartd in any number of ways, resulting in anything from stupid behavior to core dumps. Other than by explicitly running programs, I don't think it can write or delete any files, but there's no guarantee of that. The important thing is that (a) it probably won't do anything REALLY stupid and (b) it runs with the user's permissions, so it can't do anything catastrophic.

@List files need not be complete; contexts or commands that are dull or which need not or should not be advertised need not be listed. In particular, per-user @List files should not list things that are in the system-wide @List files. In the future, perhaps ListContexts and ListGenericCommands will automatically suppress lines from the system-wide files when there are per-user replacements for those lines.

Error-handling is OK to weak. In particular, no attempt is made to properly report errors on the exec itself. (Perversely, exec errors could be reliably reported when detaching, but not when passing the stdin/out socket to the app.)

If compiled with -DODT1_DISPLAY_HACK, rstartd will work around a bug in SCO ODT version 1. (1.1?) (The bug is that the X clients are all compiled with a bad library that doesn't know how to look hostnames up using DNS. The fix is to look up a hostname in $DISPLAY and substitute an IP address.) This is a trivial example of an incompatibility that rstart can hide.

## SEE ALSO

rstart(1), rsh(1), "A Flexible Remote Execution Protocol Based on rsh"

## AUTHOR

Jordan Brown, Quarterdeck Office Systems

*X Version 11 Release 6*

# rup

rup—Remote status display

## SYNOPSIS

```
rup [-dhlt] [host ...]
```

## DESCRIPTION

rup displays a summary of the current system status of a particular host or all hosts on the local network. The output shows the current time of day, how long the system has been up, and the load averages. The load average numbers give the number of jobs in the run queue averaged over 1, 5 and 15 minutes.

The following options are available:

-d       For each host, report what its local time is. This is useful for checking time synchronization on a network.

-h       Sort the display alphabetically by hostname.

-l       Sort the display by load average.

-t       Sort the display by up time.

The rpc.rstatd(8) daemon must be running on the remote host for this command to work. rup uses an RPC protocol defined in /usr/include/rpcsvc/rstat.x.

## EXAMPLE

```
example% rup otherhost
otherhost up 6 days, 16:45, load average: 0.20, 0.23, 0.18
example%
```

## DIAGNOSTICS

rup: RPC: Program not registered—The rpc.rstatd(8) daemon has not been started on the remote host.

rup: RPC: Timed out—A communication error occurred. Either the network is excessively congested, or the rpc.rstatd(8) daemon has terminated on the remote host.

rup: RPC: Port mapper failure - RPC: Timed out—The remote host is not running the portmapper (see portmap(8) man page), and cannot accommodate any RPC-based services. The host may be down.

## SEE ALSO

ruptime(1), portmap(8), rpc.rstatd(8)

## HISTORY

The rup command appeared in SunOS.

*BSD 4.3, 7 June 1993*

# rusers

rusers—Output who is logged in to machines on local network

## SYNOPSIS

```
rusers [-al] [host ...]
```

## DESCRIPTION

The rusers command produces output similar to who, but for the list of hosts or all machines on the local network. For each host responding to the rusers query, the hostname with the names of the users currently logged on is printed on each line.

The `rusers` command will wait for one minute to catch late responders.

The following options are available:

-a        Print all machines responding even if no one is currently logged in.

-l        Print a long format listing. This includes the username, hostname, `tty` that the user is logged in to, the date and time the user logged in, the amount of time since the user typed on the keyboard, and the remote host the user logged in from (if applicable).

## DIAGNOSTICS

`rusers: RPC: Program not registered`—The `rpc.rusersd(8)` daemon has not been started on the remote host.

`rusers: RPC: Timed out`—A communication error occurred. Either the network is excessively congested, or the `rpc.rusersd(8)` daemon has terminated on the remote host.

`rusers: RPC: Port mapper failure - RPC: Timed out`—The remote host is not running the portmapper (see `portmap(8)` for more information), and cannot accommodate any RPC-based services. The host may be down.

## SEE ALSO

`rwho(1)`, `users(1)`, `who(1)`, `portmap(8)`, `rpc.rusersd(8)`

## HISTORY

The `rusers` command appeared in SunOS.

## BUGS

The sorting options are not implemented.

*BSD 4.2, 23 April 1991*

# rwall

rwall—Send a message to users logged on a host

## SYNOPSIS

`rwall host`

## DESCRIPTION

The `rwall` command sends a message to the users logged in to the specified host. The message to be sent can be typed in and terminated with `EOF` or it can be in a file.

## DIAGNOSTICS

`rwall: RPC: Program not registered`—The `rpc.rwalld(8)` daemon has not been started on the remote host.

`rwall: RPC: Timed out`—A communication error occurred. Either the network is excessively congested, or the `rpc.rwalld(8)` daemon has terminated on the remote host.

`rwall: RPC: Port mapper failure - RPC: Timed out`—The remote host is not running the portmapper, and cannot accommodate any RPC-based services. The host may be down.

## SEE ALSO

`wall(1)`, `portmap(8)`, `rpc.rwalld(8)`

## HISTORY

The `rwall` command appeared in SunOS.

*BSD 4.2, 23 April 1991*

# rwho

rwho—Output who is logged in on local machines

## SYNOPSIS

rwho -a

## DESCRIPTION

The rwho command produces output similar to who, but for all machines on the local network. If no report has been received from a machine for 11 minutes, then rwho assumes the machine is down, and does not report users last known to be logged in to that machine.

If a user hasn't typed to the system for a minute or more, then rwho reports this idle time. If a user hasn't typed to the system for an hour or more, then the user will be omitted from the output of rwho unless the -a flag is given.

## FILES

/var/rwho/whod.*        Information about other machines

## SEE ALSO

finger(1), rup(1), ruptime(1), rusers(1), who(1), rwhod(8)

## HISTORY

The rwho command appeared in BSD 4.3.

## BUGS

This is unwieldy when the number of machines on the local net is large.

*BSD 4.2, 23 April 1991*


# script

script—Make typescript of terminal session

## SYNOPSIS

script [-a] [*file*]

## DESCRIPTION

script makes a typescript of everything printed on your terminal. It is useful for students who need a hardcopy record of an interactive session as proof of an assignment, as the typescript file can be printed out later with lpr(1).

If the argument file is given, script saves all dialogue in file. If no filename is given, the typescript is saved in the file typescript.

Option:

-a        Append the output to file or typescript, retaining the prior contents

The script ends when the forked shell exits (a control-D to exit the Bourne shell, sh(1), and exit, logout, or control-d (if ignoreeof is not set) for the C-shell, csh(1)).

Certain interactive commands, such as vi(1), create garbage in the typescript file. Script works best with commands that do not manipulate the screen; the results are meant to emulate a hardcopy terminal.

## ENVIRONMENT

The following environment variable is utilized by script:

SHELL      If the variable SHELL exists, the shell forked by script will be that shell. If SHELL is not set, the Bourne shell is assumed. (Most shells set this variable automatically.)

## SEE ALSO

csh(1) (for the history mechanism)

## HISTORY

The script command appeared in BSD 3.0.

## BUGS

script places everything in the log file, including linefeeds and backspaces. This is not what the naive user expects.

*BSD 4, 27 July 1991*

# sed

sed—Stream-oriented editor

## SYNOPSIS

sed [ -hnV ][-e *script* ][-f *script-file* ][--help ][--quiet ][--silent ]
[--version][--expression=*script* ][--file=*script-file* ][*file* ... ]

## DESCRIPTION

sed reads the specified files or the standard input if no files are specified, makes editing changes according to a list of commands, and writes the results to the standard output.

## OPTIONS

| | |
|---|---|
| -h, --help | Print a usage message on standard output and exit successfully. |
| -n, --quiet, --silent | Suppress the default output. sed only displays lines explicitly specified for output with the p command or the p flag of the **s** command. The default behavior is to echo each line of input, after edits, to the standard output. |
| -V, --version | Print the version number on the standard output and exit successfully. |
| -e *script*, --expression=*script* | Append one or more commands specified in the string *script* to the list of commands. If there is just one -e option and no -f options, the -e flag may be omitted. |
| -f *script-file*, --file=*script-file* | Append the editing commands from *script-file* to the list of commands. |

Multiple -e and -f commands may be specified. Scripts are added to the list of commands to execute in the order specified, regardless of their origin.

## USAGE

### OPERATION

sed operates as follows:

Each line of input, not including its terminating newline character, is successively copied into a pattern space (a temporary buffer).

All editing commands whose addresses match that pattern space are sequentially applied to the pattern space.

When reaching the end of the command list, the pattern space is written to the standard output (except under -n) with an appended newline.

The pattern space is cleared and the process is repeated for each line in the input.

With sed, original input files remain unchanged because editing commands only modify a copy of the input.

Some sed commands use a hold space to save all or part of the pattern space for later retrieval.

## COMMAND SYNTAX

A sed script consists of commands with the general form:

`[address[,address]][!]command[arguments]`

Typically, there is only one command per line, but commands may also be concatenated on a single line by semicolons.

Whitespace characters may be inserted before the first address and the command portions of the script command.

## ADDRESSES

A sed command, as indicated, can specify zero, one, or two addresses. An address can be

A `line number`, represented in decimal. The internal line number count maintained by sed is cumulative across input files and is not reset for each input file.

A `pattern` that is a regular expression, represented by ncpatternc, where c is any character except backslash (\) or newline. In the address nxabcnxdefx, the second x stands for itself, so the regular expression is abcxdef. However, the preferred (and equivalent) method to construct a regular expression is to enclose the pattern in slashes—/pattern/. Additionally, \n can be used to match any newline in the pattern space, except for the final newline character.

A `$` character that addresses the last line of input.

GNU sed also implements a new type of address. The address has form $n \tilde{\ } m$, which matches any line where the line number modulo *m* is equal to *n* modulo *m*. If *m* is 0 or missing, then 1 is used in its place. This feature is not specified by POSIX.

The following rules apply to addressed commands:

A command line with no address selects each input line.

A command line with one address selects any line matching the address. Several commands accept only one address: =, a, i, r,and q.

A command line with two comma-separated addresses selects the first matching line and all following lines up to and including the line matching the second address. If the second address starts before or is the same line as the first address, then only the first line is selected.

An address followed by ! selects all lines that do not match the address.

## REGULAR EXPRESSIONS

Regular expressions are patterns used in selecting text. For example, the sed command

`/string/p`

prints all lines containing *string*.

In addition to specifying string literals, regular expressions can represent classes of strings. Strings thus represented are said to be matched by the corresponding regular expression. If it is possible for a regular expression to match several strings in a line, then the leftmost longest match is the one selected.

The following symbols are used in constructing search patterns:

|  |  |
|---|---|
|  | The null regular expression is equivalent to the last regular expression used. |
| c | Any character c not listed here—including {, }, ,, <, >, ¦, and +—matches itself. |
| \c | Any backslash-escaped character c, except for {, }, ,, <, >, ¦, and +, matches itself. |
| '-1n'. | Matches any single character except newline. |

| | |
|---|---|
| `[char-class]` | Matches any single character, other than newline, in `char-class`. To include a `]` in `char-class`, it must be the first character. A range of characters may be specified by separating the end characters of the range with a `-`, for example, `a-z` specifies the lowercase characters. The following literal expressions can also be used in `char-class` to specify sets of characters: |

`[:alnum:] [:cntrl:] [:lower:] [:space:]`

`[:alpha:] [:digit:] [:print:] [:upper:]`

`[:blank:] [:graph:] [:punct:] [:xdigit:]`

If `-` appears as the first or last character of `char-class`, then it matches itself. All other characters in `char-class` match themselves.

| | |
|---|---|
| `[^char-class]` | Matches any single character, other than newline, not in `char-class`. `char-class` is defined as in the preceding entry. |
| `^` | If `^` is the first character of a regular expression, then it anchors the regular expression to the beginning of a line. Otherwise, it matches itself. |
| `$` | If `$` is the last character of a regular expression, it anchors the regular expression to the end of a line. Otherwise, it matches itself. |
| `\<, \>` | Anchors the single-character regular expression or subexpression immediately following it to the beginning (`\<`) or ending (`\>`) of a word, that is, in ASCII, a maximal string of alphanumeric characters, including the underscore (`_`). |
| `\(re\)` | Defines a (possibly null) subexpression `re`. Subexpressions may be nested. A subsequent back reference of the form `'\n'`, where *n* is a number in the range 1–9, expands to the text matched by the nth subexpression. For example, the regular expression `\(a.c\)\1` matches the string `'abcabc'`, but not `'abcadc'`. Subexpressions are ordered relative to their left delimiter. |
| `*` | Matches the single-character regular expression or subexpression immediately preceding it zero or more times. If `*` is the first character of a regular expression or subexpression, then it matches itself. The `*` operator sometimes yields unexpected results. For example, the regular expression `b*` matches the beginning of the string `'abbb'` (as opposed to the substring `'bbb'`) because a null match is the only leftmost match. |
| `\+` | Matches the single character regular expression or subexpression immediately preceding it one or more times. |
| `\¦` | Matches the regular expression or subexpression specified before or after it. |
| `\{n,m\}` or `\{n,\}` or `\{n\}` | Matches the single-character regular expression or subexpression immediately preceding it at least *n* and at most *m* times. If *m* is omitted, then it matches at least *n* times. If the comma is also omitted, then it matches exactly *n* times. |
| `(\group\)` | Matches the enclosed group of regular expressions. |

The following characters only have special meaning when used in replacement patterns:

| | |
|---|---|
| `\` | Escape the following character. |
| `\n` | Matches the nth pattern previously saved by `\(` and `\)`, where *n* is a number from 0 to 9. Previously saved patterns are counted from the leftmost position on the line. |
| `&` | Prints the entire search pattern when used in a replacement string. |

## COMMENTS

If the first nonwhite character in a line is a `#`), sed treats that line as a comment, and ignores it. If, however, the first such line is of the form:

`#n`

sed runs as if the `-n` flag were specified.

## GROUPING COMMANDS

Braces ({, }) can be used to nest one address within another or to apply multiple commands to the same address:

```
[address][,address]{
command 1 command 2 ...
}
```

The opening { must end a line and the closing } must be on a line by itself.

## COMMANDS

The maximum number of permissible addresses for each command is indicated in parentheses in the following list.

An argument denoted text consists of one or more lines of text. If text is longer than one line in length, then any newline characters must be hidden by preceding them with a backslash (\).

An argument denoted read-filename or write-filename must terminate the command line and must be preceded by exactly one space. Each write-filename is created before processing begins.

| | |
|---|---|
| (0) | An empty command is ignored. |
| (0) #comment | The line is a comment and is ignored by sed. If, however, the first such line in a script is of the form #n, then sed behaves as if the -n flag had been specified. |
| (0) : *label* | Affix *label* to a line in the script for a transfer of control by b or t commands. |
| (1) = | Write the current line number on the standard output as a line. |
| (1)a\text | Append text following each line matched by the address on the standard output before reading the next input line. |
| (2) b *label* | Unconditionally transfer control to the : command bearing the *label*. If no *label* is specified, then branch to the end of the script; no more commands are executed on the current pattern space. |
| (2) c\text | Change the pattern space by replacing the selected pattern with *text*. When multiple lines are specified, all lines in the pattern space are replaced with a single copy of *text*. The end result is that the pattern space is deleted and no further editing commands can be applied to it. |
| (2) d | Delete the pattern space, preventing the line from being passed to the standard output, and start the next cycle. |
| (2) D | Delete the initial segment of the pattern space through the first newline and start the next cycle. |
| (2) g | Replace the contents of the pattern space by the contents of the hold space. |
| (2) G | Append a newline character followed by the contents of the hold space to the pattern space. |
| (2) h | Replace the contents of the hold space by the contents of the pattern space. |
| (2) H | Append a newline character followed by the contents of the pattern space to the hold space. |
| (1) i\text | Insert *text* by writing it to the standard output. |
| (2) l | Write the pattern space to standard output in a visually unambiguous form. Nonprinting characters are displayed as either three-digit octal values, preceded by a \, or as one of the following character constant escape sequences: |

| | |
|---|---|
| \\ | Backslash |
| \a | Alert |
| \b | Backspace |
| \f | Form-feed |
| \n | Newline |
| \r | Carriage-return |
| \t | Tab |
| \v | Vertical tab |

Long lines are folded, with the point of folding indicated by a backslash (\) and a newline character. The end of every line is marked with a $.

| | |
|---|---|
| (2) n | Copy the pattern space to the standard output. Replace the pattern space with the next line of input. |
| (2) N | Append the next line of input to the pattern space with an embedded newline. (The current line number changes.) |
| (2) p | Print the pattern space to the standard output. |
| (2) P | Copy the initial segment of the pattern space through the first newline to the standard output. |
| (1) q | Quit by transferring control to the end of the script and do not start a new cycle. The pattern space is still written to the standard output. |
| (2) r *read-filename* | Read the contents of *read-filename*. Place them on the output before reading the next input line. |
| (2) s/*regularexpression*/ *replacement*/flags | Substitute the *replacement* string for instances of the *regular expression* in the pattern space. Any character may be used instead of /. (For a fuller description, see the explanation of replacement patterns in the "Regular Expressions" section of this manual page.) flags is zero or more of: |

    n      Substitute for just the nth occurrence of the *regular expression*.

    g      Globally substitute for all nonoverlapping instances of the *regular expression* rather than just the first one.

    p      Print the pattern space if a replacement was made.

| | |
|---|---|
| w *write-filename* | Append the pattern space to *write-filename* if a replacement was made. |
| (2) t *label* | Branch to the : command bearing the *label* if any substitutions have been made since the most recent reading of an input line or execution of a t. If *label* is empty, branch to the end of the script. |
| (2) w *write-filename* | Append the pattern space to *write-filename*. |
| (2) x | Exchange the contents of the pattern and hold spaces. |
| (2) y/*string1*/*string2*/ | Replace all occurrences of characters in *string1* with the corresponding character in *string2*. The lengths of *string1* and *string2* must be equal. Any character other than ' ' or newline can be used instead of slash to delimit the strings. Within *string1* and *string2*, the delimiter itself can be used as a literal character if it is preceded by a backslash. |

## DIAGNOSTICS

Command only uses one address—A command that takes one address had two addresses specified.

Command doesn't take any addresses—A command that takes no addresses had an address specified.

Extra characters after command—A command had extra text after the end.

Unexpected End-of-file—The end of a script was reached before it should have been. This usually occurs when a command is started, but not finished.

No previous regular expression—A metacharacter calling for a previous regular expression before any regular expressions were used.

Missing command—An address was not followed by a command.

Unknown command—A command was not one of the ones recognized by sed.

Unexpected ','—A command had a spurious comma after an address.

Multiple '!'s—More than one ! (exclamation point) was used in a command.

Unexpected g—A g character was given in a command without a preceding f.

Unexpected f—An f character was given in a command without a following g.

} doesn't want any addresses—} should be alone on a line.

`: doesn't want any addresses`—The : command should not be preceded by an address.

`Unterminated s command`—The replacement field of the s command should be completed with a / character.

`Multiple p options to s command`—The p option was given more than once in an s command.

`Multiple g options to s command`—The g option was given more than once in an s command.

`Multiple number options to s command`—More than one number option was given to an s command.

`Unknown option to s`—An unknown option was used for the s command. Maybe you shouldn't do that.

`Strings for y command are different lengths`—There should be a one-to-one mapping between strings for the y command.

`Missing ' ' before filename`—There was no space between an r, w, or s///w command, and the filename specified for that command.

`Hopelessly evil compiled in limit on number of open file. re-compile sed.`—An attempt was made to open too many files, no matter how you look at it.

## SEE ALSO

awk(1), ed(1), grep(1), perl(1), regex(3)

## HISTORY

A sed command appeared in version 7 AT&T UNIX.

## STANDARDS

GNU sed is expected to be a superset of the IEEE Std1003.2 (POSIX) specification.

## CAVEATS

GNU sed uses the POSIX basic regular expression syntax. According to the standard, the meaning of some escape sequences is undefined in this syntax; notably \¦ and \+.

As in all GNU programs that use POSIX basic regular expressions, sed interprets these escape sequences as metacharacters. So, x\+ matches one or more occurrences of x. abc\¦def matches either abc or def.

This syntax may cause problems when running scripts written for other versions of sed. Some sed programs have been written with the assumption that \¦ and \+ match the literal characters ¦ and +. Such scripts must be modified by removing the spurious backslashes if they are to be used with GNU sed.

## BUGS

It has long been noted that GNU sed is much slower than other implementations. The current bottleneck is the way sed reads and writes data files. It should read large blocks at a time (or even map files, where that is supported). When possible, it should avoid copying its input from one place in memory to another. Patches to make it do those things are welcome!

*Version 2.05, December 1994*

# sessreg

sessreg—Manage utmp/wtmp entries for non-init clients

## SYNOPSIS

sessreg [-w *wtmp-file*] [-u *utmp-file*] [-l *line-name*] [-h *host-name*]
[-s *slot-number*] [-x *Xservers-file*] [-t *ttys-file*] [-a] [-d] *user-name*

## DESCRIPTION

sessreg is a simple program for managing utmp/wtmp entries for xdm sessions.

System V has a better interface to /etc/utmp than BSD; it dynamically allocates entries in the file instead of writing them at fixed positions indexed by position in /etc/ttys.

To manage BSD-style utmp files, sessreg has two strategies. In conjunction with xdm, the -x option counts the number of lines in /etc/ttys and then adds to that the number of the line in the Xservers file that specifies the display. The display name must be specified as the *line-name* using the -l option. This sum is used as the *slot-number* in /etc/utmp that this entry will be written at. In the more general case, the -s option specifies the *slot-number* directly. If for some strange reason your system uses a file other that /etc/ttys to manage init, the -t option can direct sessreg to look elsewhere for a count of terminal sessions.

Conversely, System V managers will never need to use these options (-x, -s, and -t). To make the program easier to document and explain, sessreg accepts the BSD-specific flags in the System V environment and ignores them.

BSD also has a *host-name* field in the utmp file that doesn't exist in System V. This option is also ignored by the System V version of sessreg.

## USAGE

In Xstartup, place a call like:

sessreg -a -l $DISPLAY -x /usr/X11R6/lib/xdm/Xservers $USER

and in Xreset:

sessreg -d -l $DISPLAY -x /usr/X11R6/lib/xdm/Xservers $USER

## OPTIONS

| | |
|---|---|
| -w *wtmp-file* | This specifies an alternate wtmp file, instead of /usr/adm/wtmp for BSD or /etc/wtmp for sysV. The special name none disables writing records to /usr/adm/wtmp. |
| -u *utmp-file* | This specifies an alternate utmp file, instead of /etc/utmp. The special name none disables writing records to /etc/utmp. |
| -l *line-name* | This describes the line name of the entry. For terminal sessions, this is the final pathname segment of the terminal device filename (for example, ttyd0). For X sessions, it should probably be the local display name given to the users session (for example, :0). If none is specified, the terminal name will be determined with ttyname(3) and stripped of leading components. |
| -h *host-name* | This is set for BSD hosts to indicate that the session was initiated from a remote host. In typical xdm usage, this options is not used. |
| -s *slot-number* | Each potential session has a unique slot number in BSD systems; most are identified by the position of the *line-name* in the /etc/ttys file. This option overrides the default position determined with ttys-lot(3). This option is inappropriate for use with xdm, the -x option is more useful. |
| -x *Xservers-file* | As X sessions are one-per-display, and each display is entered in this file, this options sets the *slot-number* to be the number of lines in the *ttys-file* plus the index into this file that the *line-name* is found. |
| -t *ttys-file* | This specifies an alternate file that the -x option will use to count the number of terminal sessions on a host. |
| -a | This session should be added to utmp/wtmp. |
| -d | This session should be deleted from utmp/wtmp. -a or -d must be specified. |

## SEE ALSO

xdm(1)

## AUTHOR

Keith Packard, MIT X Consortium

# setterm

setterm—Set terminal attributes

## SYNOPSIS

```
setterm [ -term terminal name ]

setterm [-reset ]

setterm [ -initialize ]

setterm [ -cursor [on¦off] ]

setterm [ -keyboard pc¦olivetti¦dutch¦extended ]

setterm [ -repeat [on¦off] ]

setterm [ -appcursorkeys [on¦off] ]

setterm [ -linewrap [on¦off] ] .

setterm [ -snow [on¦off] ]

setterm [ -softscroll [on¦off] ]

setterm [ -defaults ]

setterm [ -foreground black¦red¦green¦yellow¦blue¦magenta¦cyan¦white¦default ]

setterm [ -background black¦red¦green¦yellow¦blue¦magenta¦cyan¦white¦default ]

setterm [ -ulcolor black¦grey¦red¦green¦yellow¦blue¦magenta¦cyan¦white ]

setterm [ -ulcolor bright red¦green¦yellow¦blue¦magenta¦cyan¦white ]

setterm [ -hbcolor black¦grey¦red¦green¦yellow¦blue¦magenta¦cyan¦white ]

setterm [ -hbcolor bright red¦green¦yellow¦blue¦magenta¦cyan¦white ]

setterm [ -inversescreen [on¦off] ]

setterm [ -bold [on¦off] ]

setterm [ -half-bright [on¦off] ]

setterm [ -blink [on¦off] ]

setterm [ -reverse [on¦off] ]

setterm [ -underline [on¦off] ]

setterm [ -store ]

setterm [ -clear [ all¦rest ] ]

setterm [ -tabs [tab1 tab2 tab3 ... ] ] where (tabn = 1-160)

setterm [ -clrtabs [ tab1 tab2 tab3 ... ] where (tabn = 1-160)
```

```
setterm [ -regtabs [ 1-160 ]]

setterm [ -blank [ 0-60 ]]

setterm [ -dump [ 1-NR CONS ]]

setterm [ -append [ 1-NR CONS ]]

setterm [ -file dumpfilename ]

setterm [ -standout [ attr ]]
```

## DESCRIPTION

setterm writes to standard output a character string that will invoke the specified terminal capabilities. Where possible, / etc/termcap is consulted to find the string to use. Some options, however, do not correspond to a termcap(5) capability. In this case, if the terminal type is minix-vc or minix-vcam, the string that invokes the specified capabilities on the PC Minix virtual console driver is output. Options that are not implemented by the terminal are ignored.

## OPTIONS

Most options are self-explanatory. The less obvious options are as follows:

| | |
|---|---|
| -term | Can be used to override the TERM environment variable |
| -reset | Displays the terminal reset string, which typically resets the terminal to its power on state |
| -initialize | Displays the terminal initialization string, which typically sets the terminal's rendering options, and other attributes to the default values |
| -default | Sets the terminal's rendering options to the default values |
| -store | Stores the terminal's current rendering options as the default values |

*Linux 0.98, 25 December 1992*

## SEE ALSO

tput(1), stty(1), termcap(5), tty(4)

## BUGS

Differences between the Minix and Linux versions are not documented.

## AUTHORS

Gordon Irlam (gordoni@cs.ua.oz.au); adaptation to Linux by Peter MacDonald; enhancements by Mika Liljeberg (liljeber@cs.Helsinki.FI)

*Linux 0.98, 25 December 1992*

# sgitopnm

sgitopnm—Convert an SGI image file to a portable anymap

## SYNOPSIS

sgitopnm [-verbose][SGIfile]

## DESCRIPTION

Reads an SGI image file as input. Produces a PGM image for a two-dimensional (one-channel) input file, and a PPM image for a three-dimensional (three or more channels) input file.

## OPTIONS

-verbose  Give some information about the SGI image file

## BUGS

Probably

## REFERENCES

SGI Image File Format documentation (draft v0.95) by Paul Haeberli (paul@sgi.com). Available via ftp at sgi.com:graphics/SGIIMAGESPEC.

## SEE ALSO

pnm(5), pnmtosgi(1)

## AUTHOR

Copyright© 1994 by Ingo Wilken (Ingo.Wilken@informatik.uni-oldenburg.de).

*29 January 1994*

# shar

shar—Create shell archives

## SYNOPSIS

```
shar [ options ] file ...
shar -S [ options ]
```

## DESCRIPTION

shar creates shell archives (or shar files) that are in text format and can be mailed. These files may be unpacked later by executing them with /bin/sh. The resulting archive is sent to standard out unless the -o option is given. A wide range of features provide extensive flexibility in manufacturing shars and in specifying shar "smartness." Archives may be "vanilla" or comprehensive. This manual page reflects shar version 4.0.

## OPTIONS

Options have a one-letter version starting with - or a long version starting with --. The exceptions are --help and --version, which do not have short versions. Options can be given in any order. Some options depend on each other: The -o option is required if the -l or -L option is used.

The -n option is required if the -a option is used.

See -V in the following list.

These are the available options:

| | |
|---|---|
| --version | Print the version number of the program on standard output, then immediately exit. |
| --help | Print a help summary on standard output, then immediately exit. |
| -V, --vanilla-operation | Produce vanilla shars that rely only upon the existence of sed and echo in the unsharing environment. In addition, if test must also be supported if the -X option is used. The -V silently disables options offensive to the network cop (or brown shirt), but does warn you if it is specified with -B, -z, -Z, -p, or -M (any of which does or might require uudecode, gzip or compress in the unsharing environment). |

| | |
|---|---|
| -v, --no-verbose | Verbose OFF. disables the inclusion of comments to be output when the archive is unpacked. |
| -w, --no-character-count | Do NOT check with wc -c after unpack. The default is to check. |
| -n *name*, --archive-name=*name* | Name of archive to be included in the header of the shar files. (See the -a switch.) |
| -a, --net-headers | Allows automatic generation of headers: |

Submitted by: who@where

Archive-name: <name>/part##

The *<name>* must be given with the -n switch. If *name* includes a /, then / part isn't used. Thus -n xyzzy produces the following:

xyzzy/part01

xyzzy/part02

-n xyzzy/patch produces the following:

xyzzy/patch01

xyzzy/patch02

-n xyzzy/patch01. produces the following:

xyzzy/patch01.01

xyzzy/patch01.02

The who@where can be explicitly stated with the -s switch if the default isn't appropriate. who@where is essentially built as 'whoami'@'uname'.

| | |
|---|---|
| -s who@where, --submitter=who@where | Override automatically determined submitter name. |
| -x, --no-check-existing | Overwrite existing files without checking. If neither -x nor -X is specified, the unpack will check for and not overwrite existing files when unpacking the archive (unless -c is passed as a parameter to the script when unpacking). |
| -X, --query-user | Interactively overwrite existing files (Do not use for shars submitted to the Net.) |
| -B, --uuencode | Treat all files as binary; use uuencode prior to packing. This increases the size of the archive. The recipient must have uudecode in order to unpack. (Use of uuencode is not appreciated by many on the Net.) |
| -T, --text-files | Treat all files as text (default). |
| -z, --gzip | Use gzip and uuencode on all files prior to packing. The recipient must have uudecode and gzip (used with -d) in order to unpack. (Use of uuencode and gzip is not appreciated by many on the Net.) |
| -Z, --compress | Use compress and uuencode on all files prior to packing. The recipient must have uudecode and compress (used with -d) in order to unpack. (Use of uuencode and compress is not appreciated by many on the Net.) Option -C is synonymous to -z, but is being depreciated. |
| -m, --no-timestamp | Avoid generating touch commands to restore the file modification dates when unpacking files from the archive. |
| -p, --intermix-type | Allow positional parameter options. The options -B, -T, -z, and -Z may be embedded, and files to the right of the option will be processed in the specified mode. |
| -g X, --level-for-gzip=X | When doing compression, use -X as a parameter to gzip. The -g option turns on the -z option by default. |
| -b X, --bits-per-code=X | When doing compression, use -bX as a parameter to compress. The -B option turns on the -Z option by default. |

| | |
|---|---|
| -M, --mixed-uuencode | Mixed mode. Determine if the files are text or binary and archive correctly. Files found to be binary are uudecoded prior to packing. (Use of uuencode is not appreciated by many on the Net.) |
| -P, --no-piping | Use temporary files instead of pipes in the shar file. |
| -c, --cut-mark | Start the shar with a cut line. A line saying Cut here is placed at the start of each output file. |
| -f, --*basename* | Restore by filename only, rather than path. This option causes only filenames to be used, which is useful when building a shar from several directories, or another directory. Note that if a directory name is passed to shar, the substructure of that directory will be restored whether -f is specified or not. |
| -d *XXX*, --here-delimiter=*XXX* | Use *XXX* to delimit the files in the shar instead of SHAR_EOF. This is for those who want to personalize their shar files. |
| -F, --force-*prefix* | Forces the *prefix* character (normally X unless the parameter to the -d option starts with X) to be prepended to every line even if not required. This option may slightly increase the size of the archive, especially if -B or -Z is used. |
| -o *XXX* --output-prefix=*XXX* | Save the archive to files *XXX*.01 through *XXX*.*nn* instead of standard out. Must be used when the -l or the -L switches are used. |
| -l *XX* --whole-size-limit=*XX* | Limit the output file size to *XX*k bytes, but don't split input files. |
| -L *XX* --split-size-limit=*XX* | Limit output file size to *XX*k bytes and split files if necessary. The archives created with this option must be unpacked in correct order. |
| -S --stdin-file-list | Read list of files to be packed from the standard input rather than from the command line. Input must be in a form similar to that generated by the find command, one filename per line. This switch is especially useful when the command line will not hold the list of files to be packed. For example: |

```
find . -type f -print ¦ sort ¦ shar -S -Z -L50 -o /tmp/big
```

If -p is specified on the command line, then the options -B, -T, -z, and -Z may be included in the standard input (on a line separate from filenames). The maximum number of lines of standard input, filenames, and options may not exceed 1024.

## EXAMPLES

```
shar *.c > cprog.shar # all C prog sources
shar -v *.[ch] > cprog.shar # non-verbose, .c and .h files
shar -B -l28 -oarc.sh *.arc # all binary .arc files, into
# files arc.sh.01 thru arc.sh.NN
shar -f /lcl/src/u*.c > u.sh # use only the filenames
```

## WARNINGS

No chmod or touch is ever generated for directories created when unpacking. Thus, if a directory is given to shar, the protection and modification dates of corresponding unpacked directory may not match those of the original.

If a directory is passed to shar, it may be scanned more than once. Therefore, one should be careful not to change the directory while shar is running.

Be careful that the output file(s) are not included in the inputs or shar may loop until the disk fills up. Be particularly careful when a directory is passed to shar that the output files are not in that directory (or a subdirectory of that directory).

Use of the -B, -z, or -Z, and especially -M, may slow the archive process considerably, depending on the number of files.

Use of -X produces shars that will cause problems with many unshar procedures. Use this feature only for archives to be passed among agreeable parties. Certainly, -X is not for shell archives that are to be submitted to Usenet. Usage of -B, -z, or -Z in Net shars will cause you to be flamed off the earth. Not using -m or not using -F may also get you occasional complaints.

## SEE ALSO

unshar(1)

## DIAGNOSTICS

There are error messages for illegal or incompatible options; for nonregular, missing, or inaccessible files; or for (unlikely) memory allocation failure.

## AUTHORS

shar(3) is a derived work based on the efforts of the following: James Gosling at CMU (decvax!microsof!uw-beave!jim), Michael A. Thompson, Dalhousie University, Halifax, N.S., Canada, Bill Davidsen (davidsen@sixhub), Richard H. Gumpertz (rhg@CPS.COM), Colas Nahaboo (colas@avahi.inria.fr), Bill Aten (bill@netagw.com), Dennis Boylan (dennis%nanovx@gatech.edu), Warren Tucker (wht%n4hgf@gatech.edu), and other anonymous persons. Jan Djfrv (jhd@irfu.se) created the man pages.

*27 September 1990*

# shlock

shlock—Create lock files for use in shell scripts

## SYNOPSIS

shlock -p *pid* -f *name* [ -b ][ -u ][ -c ]

## DESCRIPTION

shlock tries to create a lock file named *name* and write the process ID *pid* into it. If the file already exists, shlock will read the process ID from the file and test to see if the process is currently running. If the process exists, then the file will not be created.

shlock exits with a zero status if it was able to create the lock file, or non-zero if the file refers to the currently active process.

Process IDs are normally read and written in ASCII. If the -b flag is used, then they will be written as a binary int. For compatibility with other systems, the -u flag is accepted as a synonym for -b because binary locks are used by many uucp packages.

The following example shows how shlock would be used within a shell script:

```
LOCK=/news/lib/LOCK.send
trap 'rm -f ${LOCK} ;exit1' 1 2 3 15
if shlock -p $$ -f ${LOCK} ; then
# Do appropriate work
else
echo Locked by 'cat ${LOCK}'
fi
```

If the -c flag is used, then shlock will not create a lock file, but will instead use the file to see if the lock is held by another program. If the lock is valid, the program will exit with a non-zero status; if the lock is not valid (that is, invoking shlock without the flag would have succeeded), then the program will exit with a zero status.

## HISTORY

Written by Rich $alz (rsalz@uunet.uu.net) after a description of HDB UUCP locking given by Peter Honeyman.

# showrgb

showrgb—Uncompile an RGB colorname database

## SYNOPSIS

showrgb [ *database* ]

## DESCRIPTION

The showrgb program reads an RGB colorname database compiled for use with the dbm database routines and converts it back to source form, printing the result to standard output. The default database is the one that X was built with, and may be overridden on the command line. Specify the database name without the .pag or .dir suffix.

## FILES

<XRoot>/lib/X11/rgb    Default database

*X Version 11 Release 6*

# shrinkfile

shrinkfile—Shrink a file on a line boundary

## SYNOPSIS

shrinkfile [ -s *size* ][-v ] *file...*

## DESCRIPTION

The shrinkfile program shrinks files to a given size, preserving the data at the end of the file. Truncation is performed on line boundaries, where a line is a series of bytes ending with a newline, \n. There is no line length restriction and files may contain any binary data.

Temporary files are created in the /tmp directory. The TMPDIR environment variable may be used to specify a different directory.

A newline will be added to any nonempty file that does not end with a newline. The maximum file size will not be exceeded by this addition.

By default, files are truncated to zero bytes. The -s flag may be used to change the maximum size. Because the program truncates only on line boundaries, the final size may be may be smaller then the specified maximum. The size parameter may end with a k, m, or g, indicating kilobyte (1024), megabyte (1048576) or gigabyte (1073741824) lengths. Uppercase letters are also allowed. The maximum file size is 2147483647 bytes.

If the -v flag is used, then shrinkfile will print a status line if a file was shrunk.

## HISTORY

Written by Landon Curt Noll (chongo@toad.com) and Rich $alz (rsalz@uunet.uu.net) for InterNetNews.

# sirtopnm

sirtopnm—Convert a Solitaire file into a portable anymap

## SYNOPSIS

sirtopnm [*sirfile*]

## DESCRIPTION

Reads a Solitaire Image Recorder file as input. Produces a portable anymap as output. The type of the output file depends on the input file; if it's an MGI TYPE 17 file, a pgm file is written. If it's an MGI TYPE 11 file, a ppm file is written. The program tells you which type it is writing.

## SEE ALSO

pnmtosir(1), pnm(5)

## AUTHOR

Copyright© 1991 by Marvin Landis.

*20 March 1991*

# size

size—List section sizes and total size

## SYNOPSIS

```
size [ -A ¦ -B ¦ --format=compatibility ][--help ]
[ -d ¦ -o ¦ -x ¦ --radix=number ]
[ --target=bfdname ][-V ¦ --version ] objfile ...
```

## DESCRIPTION

The GNU size utility lists the section sizes and the total size for each of the object files *objfile* in its argument list. By default, one line of output is generated for each object file or each module in an archive.

## OPTIONS

| | |
|---|---|
| -A, -B, --format compatibility | Using one of these options, you can choose whether the output from GNU size resembles output from System V size (using -A, or --format=sysv ), or Berkeley size (using -B or --format=berkeley). The default is the one-line format similar to Berkeley's. |
| --help | Show a summary of acceptable arguments and options. |
| -d, -o, -x, --radix number | Using one of these options, you can control whether the size of each section is given in decimal (-d, or --radix 10); octal (-o, or --radix 8); or hexadecimal (-x, or --radix 16). In --radix number, only the three values (8, 10, 16) are supported. The total size is always given in two radices: decimal and hexadecimal for -d or -x output, or octal and hexadecimal if you're using -o. |
| --target bfdname | You can specify a particular object-code format for objfile as *bfdname* . This may not be necessary; size can automatically recognize many formats. (See objdump(1) for information on listing available formats.) |
| -V, --version | Display version number information on size itself. |

## SEE ALSO

binutils entry in info; *The GNU Binary Utilities,* Roland H. Pesch (October 1991); ar(1), objdump(1)

## COPYING

Copyright© 1991 Free Software Foundation, Inc. Permission is granted to make and distribute verbatim copies of this manual, provided the copyright notice and this permission notice are preserved on all copies.

Permission is granted to copy and distribute modified versions of this manual under the conditions for verbatim copying, provided that the entire resulting derived work is distributed under the terms of a permission notice identical to this one.

Permission is granted to copy and distribute translations of this manual into another language, under the above conditions for modified versions, except that this permission notice may be included in translations approved by the Free Software Foundation instead of in the original English.

*Cygnus Support, 5 November 1991*

# sldtoppm

sldtoppm—Convert an AutoCAD slide file into a portable pixmap

## SYNOPSIS

sldtoppm [-adjust][-dir][-height¦-ysize s][-info][-lib¦-Lib *name*][-scale s]
[-verbose][-width¦-xsize s][*slidefile*]

## DESCRIPTION

sldtoppm reads an AutoCAD slide file and outputs a portable pixmap. If no slidefile is specified, input is read from standard input. The ppmdraw library is used to convert the vector and polygon information in the slide file to a pixmap; see the file ppmdraw.h for details on this package.

## OPTIONS

| | |
|---|---|
| -adjust | If the display on which the slide file was created had nonsquare pixels, when the slide is processed with sldtoppm and the -adjust option is not present, the following warning will appear: Warning - pixels on source screen were non-square. |
| | Specifying -adjust will correct image width to compensate. Specifying the -adjust option causes sldtoppm to scale the width of the image so that pixels in the resulting portable pixmap are square (and hence circles appear as true circles, not ellipses). The scaling is performed in the vector domain, before scan-converting the objects. The results are, therefore, superior in appearance to what you'd obtain were you to perform the equivalent scaling with pnmscale after the bitmap had been created. |
| -dir | The input is assumed to be an AutoCAD slide library file. A directory listing each slide in the library is printed on standard error. |
| -height *size* | Scales the image in the vector domain so it is *size* pixels in height. If no -width or -xsize option is specified, the width will be adjusted to preserve the pixel aspect ratio. |
| -info | Dump the slide file header on standard error, displaying the original screen size and aspect ratio among other information. |
| -lib *name* | Extracts the slide with the given *name* from the slide library given as input. The specified *name* is converted to uppercase. |
| -Lib *name* | Extracts the slide with the given *name* from the slide library given as input. The *name* is used exactly as specified; it is not converted to uppercase. |
| -scale s | Scales the image by factor s, which may be any floating-point value greater than zero. Scaling is done after aspect ratio adjustment, if any. Because scaling is performed in the vector domain, before rasterization, the results look much better than running the output of sldtoppm through pnmscale. |
| -verbose | Dumps the slide file header and lists every vector and polygon in the file on standard error. |
| -width *size* | Scales the image in the vector domain, so it is *size* pixels wide. If no -height or -ysize option is specified, the height will be adjusted to preserve the pixel aspect ratio. |
| -xsize *size* | Scales the image in the vector domain so it is *size* pixels wide. If no -height or -ysize option is specified, the height will be adjusted to preserve the pixel aspect ratio. |
| -ysize *size* | Scales the image in the vector domain so it is *size* pixels in height. If no -width or -xsize option is specified, the width will be adjusted to preserve the pixel aspect ratio. |

All flags can be abbreviated to their shortest unique prefix.

## BUGS

Only Level 2 slides are converted. Level 1 format has been obsolete since the advent of AutoCAD Release 9 in 1987 and was not portable across machine architectures.

Slide library items with names containing 8-bit (such as ISO) or 16-bit (Kanji, for example) characters may not be found when chosen with the -lib option unless sldtoppm has been built with character set conversion functions appropriate to the locale. You can always retrieve slides from libraries regardless of the character set by using the -Lib option and specifying the precise name of library member. Use the -dir option to list the slides in a library if you're unsure of the exact name.

## SEE ALSO

*AutoCAD Reference Manual:* "Slide File Format"; pnmscale(1), ppm(5)

## AUTHOR

John Walker
Autodesk SA
Avenue des Champs-Montants 14b
CH-2074 MARIN
Suisse/Schweiz/Svizzera/Svizra/Switzerland

Usenet:   kelvin@Autodesk.com
Fax:      038/33 88 15
Voice:    038/33 76 33

Permission to use, copy, modify, and distribute this software and its documentation for any purpose and without fee is hereby granted, without any conditions or restrictions. This software is provided "as is" without express or implied warranty.

AutoCAD and Autodesk are registered trademarks of Autodesk, Inc.

*10 October 1991*

# smproxy

smproxy—Session Manager Proxy

## SYNOPSIS

smproxy [-clientId *id*] [-restore *saveFile*]

## OPTIONS

-clientId *id*        Specifies the session ID used by smproxy in the previous session.
-restore saveFile     Specifies the file used by smproxy to save state in the previous session.

## DESCRIPTION

smproxy allows X applications that do not support X11R6 session management to participate in an X11R6 session.

In order for smproxy to act as a proxy for an X application, one of the following must be true:

■ The application maps a top-level window containing the WM_CLIENT_LEADER property. This property provides a pointer to the client leader window that contains the WM_CLASS, WM_NAME, WM_COMMAND, and WM_CLIENT_MACHINE properties.
or
■ The application maps a top-level window that does not contain the WM_CLIENT_LEADER property. However, this top-level window contains the WM_CLASS, WM_NAME, WM_COMMAND, and WM_CLIENT_MACHINE properties.

An application that supports the WM_SAVE_YOURSELF protocol will receive a WM_SAVE_YOURSELF client message each time the session manager issues a checkpoint or shutdown. This allows the application to save state. If an application does not support the WM_SAVE_YOURSELF protocol, then the proxy will provide enough information to the session manager to restart the application (using WM_COMMAND), but no state will be restored.

## SEE ALSO

xsm(1)

## AUTHOR

Ralph Mor, X Consortium

*X Version 11 Release 6*

# sort

sort—Sort lines of text files

## SYNOPSIS

```
sort [-cmus] [-t separator] [-o output-file] [-T tempdir] [-bdfiMnr]
[+POS1 [-POS2]] [-k POS1[,POS2]] [file...]
sort {--help,--version}
```

## DESCRIPTION

This manual page documents the GNU version of sort. sort sorts, merges, or compares all the lines from the given files, or the standard input if no files are given. A filename of - means standard input. By default, sort writes the results to the standard output.

sort has three modes of operation: sort (the default), merge, and check for sortedness. The following options change the operation mode:

-c       Check whether the given files are already sorted; if they are not all sorted, print an error message and exit with a status of 1.

-m       Merge the given files by sorting them as a group. Each input file should already be individually sorted. It always works to sort instead of merge; merging is provided because it is faster, in the case where it works.

A pair of lines is compared as follows: if any key fields have been specified, sort compares each pair of fields, in the order specified on the command line, according to the associated ordering options, until a difference is found or no fields are left.

If any of the global options Mbdfinr are given but no key fields are specified, sort compares the entire lines according to the global options.

Finally, as a last resort when all keys compare equal (or if no ordering options were specified at all), sort compares the lines byte by byte in machine collating sequence. The last resort comparison honors the -r global option. The -s (stable) option disables this last-resort comparison so that lines in which all fields compare equal are left in their original relative order. If no fields or global options are specified, -s has no effect.

GNU sort has no limits on input line length or restrictions on bytes allowed within lines. In addition, if the final byte of an input file is not a newline, GNU sort silently supplies one.

If the environment variable TMPDIR is set, sort uses it as the directory in which to put temporary files instead of the default, /tmp. The -T tempdir option is another way to select the directory for temporary files; it overrides the environment variable.

The following options affect the ordering of output lines. They may be specified globally or as part of a specific key field. If no key fields are specified, global options apply to comparison of entire lines; otherwise, the global options are inherited by key fields that do not specify any special options of their own.

-b          Ignore leading blanks when finding sort keys in each line.

-d          Sort in phone directory order; ignore all characters except letters, digits, and blanks when sorting.

-f          Fold lowercase characters into the equivalent uppercase characters when sorting so that, for example, b is sorted the same way B is.

-i          Ignore characters outside the ASCII range 040–0176 octal (inclusive) when sorting.

-M          An initial string, consisting of any amount of whitespace, followed by three letters abbreviating a month name, is folded to uppercase and compared in the order 'JAN' < 'FEB' < ... < 'DEC'. Invalid names compare low to valid names.

-n          Compare according to arithmetic value an initial numeric string consisting of optional whitespace, an optional - sign, and zero or more digits, optionally followed by a decimal point and zero or more digits.

-r          Reverse the result of comparison, so that lines with greater key values appear earlier in the output instead of later.

Other options are

-o *output-file*          Write output to *output-file* instead of to the standard output. If *output-file* is one of the input files, sort copies it to a temporary file before sorting and writing the output to *output-file*.

-t *separator*          Use character *separator* as the field separator when finding the sort keys in each line. By default, fields are separated by the empty string between a nonwhitespace character and a whitespace character. That is to say, given the input line foo bar, sort breaks it into fields foo and bar. The field separator is not considered to be part of either the field preceding or the field following it.

-u          For the default case or the -m option, only output the first of a sequence of lines that compare equal. For the -c option, check that no pair of consecutive lines compares equal.

+POS1 [ -POS2]          Specify a field within each line to use as a sorting key. The field consists of the portion of the line starting at POS1 and up to (but not including) POS2 (or to the end of the line if POS2 is not given). The fields and character positions are numbered starting with 0.

-k POS1[ ,POS2]          An alternate syntax for specifying sorting keys. The fields and character positions are numbered starting with 1.

A position has the form f.c, where f is the number of the field to use and c is the number of the first character from the beginning of the field (for +pos) or from the end of the previous field (for -pos). The .c part of a position may be omitted, in which case it is taken to be the first character in the field. If the -b option has been given, the .c part of a field specification is counted from the first nonblank character of the field (for +pos) or from the first nonblank character following the previous field (for -pos).

A +pos or -pos argument may also have any of the option letters Mbdfinr appended to it, in which case the global ordering options are not used for that particular field. The -b option may be independently attached to either or both of the +pos and -pos parts of a field specification, and if it is inherited from the global options, it will be attached to both. If a -n or -M option is used, thus implying a -b option, the -b option is taken to apply to both the +pos and the -pos parts of a key specification. Keys may span multiple fields.

In addition, when GNU join is invoked with exactly one argument, the following options are recognized:

--help          Print a usage message on standard output and exit successfully

--version          Print version information on standard output, then exit successfully

## COMPATIBILITY

Historical (BSD and System V) implementations of sort have differed in their interpretation of some options, particularly -b, -f, and -n. GNU sort follows the POSIX behavior, which is usually (but not always) like the System V behavior. According to POSIX, -n no longer implies -b. For consistency, -M has been changed in the same way. This may affect the meaning of character positions in field specifications in obscure cases. If this bites you, the fix is to add an explicit -b.

## BUGS

The different meaning of field numbers depending on whether -k is used is confusing. It's all POSIX's fault!

# spctoppm

spctoppm—Convert an Atari compressed Spectrum file into a portable pixmap

## SYNOPSIS

spctoppm [*spcfile*]

## DESCRIPTION

spctoppm reads an Atari compressed Spectrum file as input and produces a portable pixmap as output.

## SEE ALSO

sputoppm(1), ppm(5)

## AUTHOR

Copyright© 1991 by Steve Belczyk (seb3@gte.com) and Jef Poskanzer.

*19 July 1990*

# split

split—Split a file into pieces

## SYNOPSIS

split [-*lines*] [-l *lines*] [-b *bytes*[bkm]] [-C *bytes*[bkm]] [--lines=*lines*]
[--bytes=*bytes*[bkm]] [--line-bytes=*bytes*[bkm]] [--help] [--version]
[infile [outfile-prefix]]

## DESCRIPTION

This manual page documents the GNU version of split. split creates one or more output files (as many as necessary) containing consecutive sections of the infile, or the standard input if none is given or the name - is given. By default, split puts 1000 lines of the input file, or whatever is left if it is less than that, into each output file.

The output filenames consist of a prefix followed by a group of letters, chosen so that concatenating the output files in sorted order by filename produces the original input file, in order. The default output filename prefix is x. If the outfile-prefix argument is given, it is used as the output filename prefix instead.

## OPTIONS

| | |
|---|---|
| -*lines*, -l *lines*, --lines=*lines* | Put *lines* lines of the input file into each output file. |
| -b *bytes*[bkm], --bytes=*bytes*[bkm] | Put *bytes* bytes of the input file into each output file. *bytes* is a non-zero integer, optionally followed by one of the following characters to specify a different unit: |
| | b    512-byte blocks |
| | k    1-kilobyte blocks |
| | m    1-megabyte blocks |
| -C *bytes*[bkm], --line-bytes=*bytes*[bkm] | Put into each output file as many complete lines of the input file as is possible without exceeding *bytes* bytes. If a line that is longer than *bytes* bytes occurs, put *bytes* bytes of it into each output file until less than *bytes* bytes of the line are left, then continue normally. bytes has the same format as for the --bytes option. |

| `--help` | Print a usage message and exit with a non-zero status. |
| `--version` | Print version information on standard output then exit. |

*GNU Text Utilities*

# spottopgm

spottopgm—Convert SPOT satellite images to portable graymap format

## SYNTAX

spottopgm [-1¦2¦3] [*Firstcol Firstline Lastcol Lastline*] *inputfile*

## OPTIONS

| -1¦2¦3 | Extract the given color from the SPOT image. The colors are infrared, visible light, and ultra-violet, although I don't know which corresponds to which number. If the image is in color, this will be announced on standard error. The default color is 1. |
| *Firstcol Firstline Lastcol Lastline* | Extract the specified rectangle from the SPOT image. Most SPOT images are 3,000 lines long and 3,000 or more columns wide. Unfortunately, the SPOT format only gives the width and not the length. The width is printed on standard error. The default rectangle is the width of the input image by 3,000 lines. |

## DESCRIPTION

spottopgm converts the named `inputfile` into portable graymap format, defaulting to the first color and the whole SPOT image unless specified by the options.

## INSTALLATION

You must edit the source program and either define BIGENDIAN or LITTLEENDIAN, and fix the typedefs for uint32t, uint16t, and uint8t appropriately.

## BUGS

Currently, spottopgm doesn't determine the length of the input file; this would involve two passes over the input file. It defaults to 3,000 lines instead.

spottopgm could extract a three-color image (ppm), but I didn't feel like making the program more complicated than it is now. Besides, there is no one-to-one correspondence between red, green, blue, and infra-red, visible, and ultra-violet.

I've had only a limited number of SPOT images to play with, and therefore wouldn't guarantee that this will work on any other images.

## AUTHOR

Warren Toomey (wkt@csadfa.cs.adfa.oz.au)

## SEE ALSO

The rest of the pbmplus suite.

# sputoppm

sputoppm—Convert an Atari uncompressed Spectrum file into a portable pixmap

## SYNOPSIS

```
sputoppm [spufile]
```

## DESCRIPTION

sputoppm reads an Atari uncompressed Spectrum file as input and produces a portable pixmap as output.

## SEE ALSO

spctoppm(1), ppm(5)

## AUTHOR

Copyright© 1991 by Steve Belczyk (seb3@gte.com) and Jef Poskanzer.

*19 July 1990*

# sq

sq—Squeeze a sorted word list

unsq—Unsqueeze a sorted word list

## SYNOPSIS

```
sq < infile > outfile
unsq < infile > outfile
```

## DESCRIPTION

sq compresses a sorted list of words (a dictionary). For example,

```
sort /usr/dict/words ¦ sq ¦ compress > words.sq.Z
```

will compress dict by about a factor of 4.

unsq uncompresses the output of sq. For example,

```
compress -d < words.sq.Z ¦ unsq ¦ sort -f -o words
```

will uncompress a dictionary compressed with sq. The squeezing is achieved by eliminating common prefixes and replacing them with a single character that encodes the number of characters shared with the preceding word. The prefix size is encoded as a single printable character: 0–9 represent 0–9, A–Z represent 10–35, and a–z represent 36–61.

## AUTHOR

Mike Wexler

## SEE ALSO

compress(1), sort(1).

*Local*

# startx

startx—Initialize an X session

## SYNOPSIS

```
startx [[client ] options ..] [-- [ server ] options ... ]
```

## DESCRIPTION

**NOTE**

The startx script supplied with the X11 distribution is a sample designed more as a base for customization than as a finished product. Site administrators are urged to customize it for their site—and to update this manual page when they do.

The `startx` script is a front end to `xinit` that provides a somewhat nicer user interface for running a single session of the X Window System. It is typically run with no arguments.

To determine the client to run, `startx` first looks for a file called `.xinitrc` in the user's home directory. If that is not found, it uses the file `xinitrc` in the xinit library directory. If command-line client options are given, they override this behavior. To determine the server to run, `startx` first looks for a file called `.xserverrc` in the user's home directory. If that is not found, it uses the file `xserverrc` in the xinit library directory. If command-line server options are given, they override this behavior. Users rarely need to provide a `.xserverrc` file. (See the `xinit(1)` manual page for more details on the arguments.)

The `.xinitrc` is typically a shell script that starts many clients according to the user's preference. When this shell script exits, `startx` kills the server and performs any other session shutdown needed. Most of the clients started by `.xinitrc` should be run in the background. The last client should run in the foreground; when it exits, the session will exit. People often choose a session manager, window manager, or `xterm` as the "magic" client.

## EXAMPLE

Following is a sample `xinitrc` that starts several applications and leaves the window manager running as the "last" application. Assuming that the window manager has been configured properly, the user then chooses the Exit menu item to shut down X.

```
xrdb -load $HOME/.Xresources
xsetroot -solid gray &
xbiff -geometry -430+5 &
oclock -geometry 75x75-0-0 &
xload -geometry -80-0 &
xterm -geometry +0+60 -ls &
xterm -geometry +0-100 &
xconsole -geometry -0+0 -fn 5x7 &
exec twm
```

## ENVIRONMENT VARIABLES

DISPLAY    This variable gets set to the name of the display to which clients should connect. Note that this gets set, not read.

## FILES

| | |
|---|---|
| `$(HOME)/.xinitrc` | Client to run. Typically a shell script that runs many programs in the background. |
| `$(HOME)/.xserverrc` | Server to run. The default is X. |
| `<XRoot>/lib/X11/xinit/xinitrc` | Client to run if the user has no `.xinitrc` file. `<XRoot>` refers to the root of the X11 install tree. |
| `<XRoot>/lib/X11/xinit/xserverrc` | Client to run if the user has no `.xserverrc` file. This is only needed if the server needs special arguments or is not named. `<XRoot>` refers to the root of the X11 install tree. |

## SEE ALSO

`xinit(1)`

# strings

`strings`—Print the strings of printable characters in files

## SYNOPSIS

```
strings [ -a¦-¦--all ][-f¦--print-file-name][-o ][--help ][-v¦--version ]
[ -n min-len ¦-min-len ¦--bytes= min-len ][-t o,x,d ]
[ --target=bfdname ] ¦--radix= o,x,d ] file
```

## DESCRIPTION

For each `file` given, GNU `strings` prints the printable character sequences that are at least four characters long (or the number given with the options below) and are followed by a NUL or newline character. By default, it only prints the strings from the initialized data sections of object files; for other types of files, it prints the strings from the whole file.

`strings` is mainly useful for determining the contents of nontext files.

## OPTIONS

The long and short forms of options, shown here as alternatives, are equivalent.

| | |
|---|---|
| `-a, --all, -` | Do not scan only the initialized data section of object files; scan the whole files. |
| `-f, --print-file-name` | Print the name of the file before each string. |
| `--help` | Print a summary of the options to strings on the standard output and exit. |
| `-v, --version` | Print the version number of strings on the standard output and exit. |
| `-n min-len, -min-len, -bytes=min-len` | Print sequences of characters that are at least `min-len` characters long, instead of the default 4. |
| `-t o,x,d, --radix=o,x,d` | Print the offset within the file before each string. The single character argument specifies the radix of the offset—octal, hexadecimal, or decimal. |
| `--target=bfdname` | Specify an object code format other than your system's default format. (See objdump(1), for information on listing available formats.) |
| `-o` | Like -t o. |

## SEE ALSO

binutils entry in info; *The GNU Binary Utilities*, Roland H. Pesch (October 1991); ar(1), nm(1), objdump(1), ranlib(1).

## COPYING

*Cygnus Support, 25 June 1993*

# strip

strip—Discard symbols from object files.

## SYNOPSIS

```
strip [ -Fbfdname¦--target=bfdname ] [ -Ibfdname¦
--input-target=bfdname ] [ -Obfdname¦--output-target=bfdname ]
[-Rsectionname¦--remove-section=sectionname ] [ -s¦--strip-all ]
[-S¦-g¦--strip-debug ][-x¦--discard-all ][-X¦ discard-locals]
[-v¦--verbose ][-V¦--version ][-V¦--help ] objfile ...
```

## DESCRIPTION

GNU strip discards all symbols from the object files *objfile*. The list of object files may include archives. At least one object file must be given.

strip modifies the files named in its argument, rather than writing modified copies under different names.

## OPTIONS

| | |
|---|---|
| -F *bfdname*, --target=*bfdname* | Treat the original *objfile* as a file with the object code format *bfdname*, and rewrite it in the same format. |
| --help | Show a summary of the options to strip and exit. |
| -I *bfdnamefdname*", --input-target=*bfdname* | Treat the original *objfile* as a file with the object code format *bfdname*. |
| -O *bfdname*, --output-target=*bfdname* | Replace *objfile* with a file in the output format *bfdname*. |
| -R *sectionname*, --remove-section=*sectionname* | Remove the named section from the file. This option may be given more than once. Note that using this option inappropriately may make the object file unusable. |
| -s, --strip-all | Remove all symbols. |
| -S, -g, --strip-debug | Remove debugging symbols only. |
| -x, --discard-all | Remove nonglobal symbols. |
| -X, --discard-locals | Remove compiler-generated local symbols. (These usually start with L or a period. |
| -v, --verbose | Verbose output: list all object files modified. In the case of archives, strip -V lists all members of the archive. |
| -V, --version | Show the version number for strip and exit. |

## SEE ALSO

binutils entry in info; *The GNU Binary Utilities*, Roland H. Pesch (October 1991)

## COPYING

Copyright© 1991 Free Software Foundation, Inc. Permission is granted to make and distribute verbatim copies of this manual provided the copyright notice and this permission notice are preserved on all copies.

Permission is granted to copy and distribute modified versions of this manual under the conditions for verbatim copying, provided that the entire resulting derived work is distributed under the terms of a permission notice identical to this one.

Permission is granted to copy and distribute translations of this manual into another language, under the above conditions for modified versions, except that this permission notice may be included in translations approved by the Free Software Foundation instead of in the original English.

*Cygnus Support, 5 November 1991*

# subst

subst—Substitute definitions into file(s)

## SYNOPSIS

```
subst [ -e editor ] -f substitutions victim ...
```

## DESCRIPTION

subst makes substitutions into files, in a way that is suitable for customizing software to local conditions. Each *victim* file is altered according to the contents of the *substitutions* file.

The *substitutions* file contains one line per substitution. A line consists of two fields separated by one or more tabs. The first field is the name of the substitution, the second is the value. Neither should contain the character #, and use of text-editor metacharacters like & and \ is also unwise; the name in particular is best restricted to alphanumeric. A line starting with # is a comment and is ignored.

In the victim files, each line on which a substitution is to be made (a target line) must be preceded by a prototype line. The prototype line should be delimited in such a way that it will be taken as a comment by whatever program processes the file later. The prototype line must contain a prototype of the target line bracketed by =()< and >()=; everything else on the prototype line is ignored. subst extracts the prototype, changes all instances of substitution names bracketed by @< and >@ to their values, and then replaces the target line with the result.

Substitutions are done using the sed(1) editor, which must be found in either the /bin or /usr/bin directories. To specify a different executable, use the -e flag.

## EXAMPLE

If the *substitutions* file is

```
FIRST 111
SECOND 222
```

and the victim file is

```
x =2;
/* =()<y =@<FIRST>@+@<SECOND>@;>()= */
y =88 +99;
z =5;
```

then subst -f substitutions victim changes victim to

```
x =2;
/* =()<y =@<FIRST>@+@<SECOND>@;>()= */
y = 111 + 222;
z =5;
```

## FILES

| | |
|---|---|
| *victimdir*/substtmp.new | New version being built |
| *victimdir*/substtmp.old | Old version during renaming |

## SEE ALSO

sed(1)

## DIAGNOSTICS

Complains and halts if it is unable to create its temporary files or if they already exist.

## HISTORY

Written at University of Toronto by Henry Spencer.

Rich $alz added the -e flag July, 1991.

## BUGS

When creating a file to be substed, it's easy to forget to insert a dummy target line after a prototype line; if you forget, subst ends up deleting whichever line did in fact follow the prototype line.

*Local*

# sum

sum—Checksum and count the blocks in a file

## SYNOPSIS

sum [-rs] [--sysv] [--help] [--version] [*file...*]

## DESCRIPTION

This manual page documents the GNU version of sum. sum computes a 16-bit checksum for each named file, or the standard input if none are given or when a file named - is given. It prints the checksum for each file along with the number of blocks in the file (rounded up). By default, each corresponding filename is also printed if at least two arguments are specified. With the --sysv option, corresponding filenames are printed when there is at least one file argument. By default, the GNU sum computes checksums using an algorithm that is compatible with the BSD sum and prints file sizes in units of 1K blocks.

## OPTIONS

| | |
|---|---|
| -r | Use the default (BSD-compatible) algorithm. This option is included for compatibility with the System V sum. Unless the -s option was also given, it has no effect. |
| -s, --sysv | Compute checksums using an algorithm that is compatible with the one the System V sum uses by default and print file sizes in units of 512-byte blocks instead of 1K. |
| --help | Print a usage message and exit with a non-zero status. |
| --version | Print version information on standard output, then exit. |

*GNU Text Utilities*

# SuperProbe

SuperProbe—Probe for and identify installed video hardware

## SYNOPSIS

SuperProbe [-verbose] [-no16] [-excl *list*] [-mask10] [-order *list*] [-noprobe *list*] [-bios *base*]
[-no bios] [-no dac] [-no mem] [-info]

## DESCRIPTION

SuperProbe is a program that will attempt to determine the type of video hardware installed in an EISA/ISA/VLB-bus system by checking for known registers in various combinations at various locations (MicroChannel and PCI machines may not be fully supported; many work with the use of the -no_bios option.) This is an error-prone process, especially on UNIX (which usually has a lot more esoteric hardware installed than MS-DOS systems do), so SuperProbe may likely need help from the user.

SuperProbe runs on SVR3, SVR4, Linux, 386BSD/FreeBSD/NetBSD, Minix-386, and Mach. It should be trivial to extend it to work on any other UNIX-like operating system, and even non-UNIX operating systems. All of the operating system (OS) dependencies are isolated to a single file for each OS.

At this time, SuperProbe can identify MDA, Hercules, CGA, MCGA, EGA, VGA, and an entire horde of SVGA chipsets. (See the -info option under "Options.") It can also identify several HiColor/True-color RAMDACs in use on SVGA boards, and the amount of video memory installed (for many chipsets). It can identify 8514/A and some derivatives, but not XGA, or PGC (although the author intends to add those capabilities). Nor can it identify other esoteric video hardware (like Targa, TIGA, or Microfield boards).

## OPTIONS

| | |
|---|---|
| -verbose | SuperProbe will be verbose and provide lots of information as it does its work. |
| -no16 | SuperProbe will not attempt to use any ports that require 16-bit I/O address decoding. The original ISA bus only specified that I/O ports be decoded to 10 bits. Therefore, some old cards (including many 8-bit cards) will misdecode references to ports that use the upper 6 bits, and may get into funny states because they think that they are being addressed when they are not. It is recommended that this option be used initially if any 8-bit cards are present in the system. |
| -excl\*list* | SuperProbe will not attempt to access any I/O ports on the specified exclusion list. Some video cards use rather nonstandard I/O ports that may conflict with other cards installed in your system. By specifying to SuperProbe, a list of ports already in use, it will know that there cannot be any video cards that use those ports, and hence will not probe them (which could otherwise confuse your hardware). The exclusion list is specified as a comma-separated list of I/O ports or port ranges. A range is specified as *low-high*, and is inclusive. The ports can be specified in decimal, in octal (numbers begin with 0), or hexadecimal (numbers begin with 0x). |
| -mask10 | This option is used in combination with -excl. It tells SuperProbe that when comparing an I/O port under test against the exclusion list, the port address should be masked to 10 bits. This is important with older 8-bit cards that only do 10-bit decoding, and for some cheap 16-bit cards as well. This option is simply a less drastic form of the -no16 option. |
| -order\*list* | This option specifies which chipsets SuperProbe should test, and in which order. The list parameter is a comma-separated list of chipset names. This list overrides the built-in default testing order. To find the list of acceptable names, use the -info option described later in this list. Note that items displayed as "Standard video hardware" are not usable with the -order option. |
| -noprobe\*list* | This option specifies which chipsets SuperProbe should not test. The order of testing will either be the default order, or that specified with the -order option. The list parameter is a comma-separated list of chipset names. To find the list of acceptable names, use the -info option. Note that items displayed as "Standard video hardware" are not usable with the -noprobe option. |
| -bios\*base* | This option specifies the base address for the graphics-hardware BIOS. By default, SuperProbe will attempt to locate the BIOS base on its own (the normal address is 0xC0000). If it fails to correctly locate the BIOS (an error message will be printed if this occurs), the -bios option can be used to specify the base. |
| -no_bios | Disallow reading of the video BIOS and assume that an EGA or later (VGA, SVGA) board is present as the primary video hardware. |
| -no_dac | Skip probing for the RAMDAC type when an (S)VGA is identified. |
| -no_mem | Skip probing for the amount of installed video memory. |
| -info | SuperProbe will print out a listing of all the video hardware that it knows how to identify. |

## EXAMPLES

To run SuperProbe in its most basic and automated form, simply enter the following:

```
SuperProbe
```

> ## NOTE
>
> You may want to redirect stdout to a file when you run SuperProbe (especially if your OS does not support Virtual Terminals on the console).

However, if you have any 8-bit cards installed, you should initially run SuperProbe as

SuperProbe -verbose -no16

(the -verbose option is included so you can see what SuperProbe is skipping).

Finer granularity can be obtained with an exclusion list, for example,

SuperProbe -verbose -excl 0x200,0x220-0x230,0x250

will not test for any device that uses port 0x200, ports 0x220 through 0x230, inclusive, or port 0x250. If you have any 8-bit cards installed, you should add -mask10 to the list of options.

To restrict the search to Western Digital, Tseng, and Cirrus chipset, run SuperProbe as follows:

SuperProbe -order WD,Tseng,Cirrus

## BUGS

Probably a lot at this point. Please report any bugs or incorrect identifications to the author.

It is possible that SuperProbe can lock up your machine. Be sure to narrow the search by using the -no16, -excl, and -mask10 options provided to keep SuperProbe from conflicting with other installed hardware.

## SEE ALSO

The vgadoc3.zip documentation package by Finn Thoegersen, available in the MS-DOS archives of many FTP repositories.

*Programmer's Guide to the EGA and VGA Cards*, Second Edition, by Richard Ferraro.

## AUTHOR

David E. Wexelblat (dwex@xfree86.org) with help from David Dawes (dawes@xfree86.org) and the XFree86 development team.

*Version 2.2*

# tac

tac—Concatenate and print files in reverse

## SYNOPSIS

tac [-br] [-s separator] [--before] [--regex] [--separator=*separator*]
[--help] [--version] [*file...*]

## DESCRIPTION

This manual page documents the GNU version of tac. tac copies each given file, or the standard input if none are given or when a filename of - is encountered, to the standard output with the order of the records reversed. The records are separated by instances of a string, or a newline if none is given. By default, the separator string is attached to the end of the record that it follows in the file.

## OPTIONS

| | |
|---|---|
| -b, --before | The separator is attached to the beginning of the record that it precedes in the file. |
| -r, --regex | The separator is a regular expression. |
| -s *string*, --separator=*string* | Use *string* as the record separator. |
| --help | Print a usage message and exit with a non-zero status. |
| --version | Print version information on standard output, then exit. |

*GNU Text Utilities*

# tail

tail—Output the last part of files

## SYNOPSIS

```
tail [-c [+]N[bkm]] [-n [+]N] [-fqv] [--bytes=[+]N[bkm]] [--lines=[+]N]
[--follow] [--quiet] [--silent] [--verbose] [--help] [--version] [file...]

tail [{-,+}Nbcfklmqv] [file...]
```

## DESCRIPTION

This manual page documents the GNU version of tail. tail prints the last part (10 lines by default) of each given file; it reads from standard input if no files are given or when a filename of - is encountered. If more than one file is given, it prints a header consisting of the file's name enclosed in ==> and <== before the output for each file.

The GNU tail can output any amount of data, unlike the UNIX version, which uses a fixed size buffer. It has no -r option (print in reverse). Reversing a file is really a different job from printing the end of a file; the BSD tail can only reverse files that are at most as large as its buffer, which is typically 32KB. A reliable and more versatile way to reverse files is the GNU tac command.

## OPTIONS

tail accepts two option formats: the new one, in which numbers are arguments to the option letters, and the old one, in which a + or - and optional number precede any option letters.

If a number (*N*) starts with a +, tail begins printing with the *N*th item from the start of each file, instead of from the end.

| | |
|---|---|
| -c *N*, --bytes *N* | Tail by *N* bytes. *N* is a non-zero integer, optionally followed by one of the following characters to specify a different unit. |
| | b      512-byte blocks |
| | k      1-kilobyte blocks |
| | m      1-megabyte blocks |
| -f, --follow | Loop forever, trying to read more characters at the end of the file, on the assumption that the file is growing. Ignored if reading from a pipe. If more than one file is given, tail prints a header whenever it gets output from a different file, to indicate which file that output is from. |
| -l, -n *N*, --lines *N* | Tail by *N* lines. -1 is only recognized using the old option format. |
| -q, --quiet, --silent | Never print filename headers. |
| -v, --verbose | Always print filename headers. |
| --help | Print a usage message and exit with a non-zero status. |
| --version | Print version information on standard output then exit. |

*GNU Text Utilities*

# talk

talk—Talk to another user

## SYNOPSIS

talk *person* [*ttyname*]

## DESCRIPTION

talk is a visual communication program that copies lines from your terminal to that of another user.

The following options are available:

*person*    If you wish to talk to someone on your own machine, then person is just the person's login name. If you wish to talk to a user on another host, then person is of the form *user@host*.

*ttyname*   If you wish to talk to a user who is logged in more than once, the *ttyname* argument may be used to indicate the appropriate terminal name, where *ttyname* is of the form

*ttyxx*

When first called, talk sends the message Message from TalkDaemon@his_machine...:

```
talk: connection requested by your_name@your_machine
talk: respond with: talk your_name@your_machine
```

to the user you wish to talk to. At this point, the recipient of the message should reply by typing

**talk your_name@your_machine**

It doesn't matter from which machine the recipient replies, as long as his login name is the same. Once communication is established, the two parties may type simultaneously, with their output appearing in separate windows. Typing control-L ^ L-will cause the screen to be reprinted, while your erase, kill, and word kill characters will behave normally. To exit, just type your interrupt character; talk then moves the cursor to the bottom of the screen and restores the terminal to its previous state.

Permission to talk may be denied or granted by use of the mesg 1 command. At the outset, talking is allowed. Certain commands, in particular nroff 1 and pr 1, disallow messages in order to prevent messy output.

## FILES

/etc/hosts       To find the recipient's machine
/var/run/utmp    To find the recipient's tty

## SEE ALSO

mail(1), mesg(1), who(1), write(1)

## BUGS

The version of talk 1 released with BSD 4.3 uses a protocol that is incompatible with the protocol used in the version released with BSD 4.2.

## HISTORY

The talk command appeared in BSD 4.2.

*BSD 4.2, 22 April 1991*

# tcal

`tcal`—Runs the `gcal` program with the date of tomorrow's day

## SYNOPSIS

`tcal [ --help ¦ --version ] ¦ [ --shift=[+¦-]number ][Argument... ]`

## DESCRIPTION

`tcal` is a program that runs `gcal` with a date set one day ahead (equivalent to the `--shift=1` option). All given `arguments` are passed unmodified to the `gcal` program. If the `gcal` program shall be called with a date other than tomorrow's date, this desired date can be selected by using the `--shift=[+¦-]number` option, in which `[+¦-]number` is the number of days the desired date is distant from the actual date. The `--shift` option must be given before all other arguments, which are passed to the `gcal` program. An exit status of `0` means all processing is successfully done; any other value means an error has occurred.

## OPTIONS

| | |
|---|---|
| `--help` | Print a usage message listing all available options, then exit successfully. |
| `--version` | Print the version number, then exit successfully. |
| `--shift=[+¦-]number` | Define the displacement in `[+¦-]number` days the desired date is distant from the actual date. |

## ENVIRONMENT

`GCALPROG`       The `GCALPROG` environment variable contains the filename of the executable `gcal` program, which is used by `tcal` to call `gcal`. Takes precedence over the filename `gcal`, which is burned-in during the compilation step of `tcal`.

## COPYRIGHT

Copyright© 1995, 1996 by Thomas Esken. This software doesn't claim completeness, correctness, or usability. On principle, I will not be liable for any damages or losses (implicit or explicit), which result from using or handling my software. If you use this software, you agree without any exception to this agreement, which binds you *LEGALLY.*

`tcal` is free software and distributed under the terms of the GNU General Public License; published by the Free Software Foundation; version 2 or (at your option) any later version.

Any suggestions, improvements, extensions, bug reports, donations, proposals for contract work, and so forth are welcome! If you like this tool, I'd appreciate a postcard from you!

Enjoy it =8^)

## AUTHOR

Thomas Esken (`esken@uni-muenster.de`)
m Hagenfeld 84
D-48147 Muenster; Germany
Phone : +49 251 232585

## SEE ALSO

`gcal(1)`

*16 July 1996*

# telnet

telnet—User interface to the Telnet protocol

## SYNOPSIS

telnet [-d] [-a] [-n tracefile] [-e escapechar] [[-l user] host [port]]

## DESCRIPTION

The telnet command is used to communicate with another host using the Telnet protocol. If telnet is invoked without the host argument, it enters command mode, indicated by its prompt telnet>. In this mode, it accepts and executes the commands listed below. If it is invoked with arguments, it performs an open command with those arguments.

## OPTIONS

| | |
|---|---|
| -d | Sets the initial value of the debug toggle to True. |
| -a | Attempt automatic login. Currently, this sends the username via the USER variable of the ENVIRON option if supported by the remote system. The name used is that of the current user as returned by getlogin 2 if it agrees with the current user ID; otherwise, it is the name associated with the user ID. |
| -n tracefile | Opens tracefile for recording trace information. See the set tracefile command in the "Commands" section. |
| -l user | When connecting to the remote system, if the remote system understands the ENVIRON option, then user will be sent to the remote system as the value for the variable USER. This option implies the -a option. This option may also be used with the open command. |
| -e escape char | Sets the initial telnet escape character to escape char. If escape char is omitted, then there will be no escape character. |
| host | Indicates the official name, an alias, or the Internet address of a remote host. |
| port | Indicates a port number (address of an application). If a number is not specified, the default telnet port is used. |

Once a connection has been opened, telnet will attempt to enable the TELNETLINEMODE option. If this fails, then telnet will revert to one of two input modes—either character-at-a-time or old line-by-line, depending on what the remote system supports.

When LINEMODE is enabled, character processing is done on the local system, under the control of the remote system. When input editing or character echoing is to be disabled, the remote system will relay that information. The remote system will also relay changes to any special characters that happen on the remote system, so that they can take effect on the local system.

In character-at-a-time mode, most text typed is immediately sent to the remote host for processing.

In old line-by-line mode, all text is echoed locally, and (normally) only completed lines are sent to the remote host. The local echo character (initially ^E) may be used to turn off and on the local echo. (This would mostly be used to enter passwords without the password being echoed.)

If the LINEMODE option is enabled, or if the localchars toggle is True (the default for old line-by-line), the user's quit, intr, and flush characters are trapped locally, and sent as Telnet protocol sequences to the remote side. If LINEMODE has ever been enabled, then the user's susp and eof are also sent as Telnet protocol sequences, and quit is sent as a TELNET ABORT instead of BREAK There are options (see toggle autoflush and toggle autosynch in the following list) that cause this action to flush subsequent output terminal (until the remote host acknowledges the telnet sequence) and flush previous terminal input (in the case of quit and intr).

## COMMANDS

While connected to a remote host, telnet command mode may be entered by typing the telnet escape character (initially ^]). When in command mode, the normal terminal editing conventions are available.

The following telnet commands are available. Only enough of each command to uniquely identify it need be typed. (This is also true for arguments to the mode, set, toggle, unset, slc, environ, and display commands.)

| | |
|---|---|
| close | Close a telnet session and return to command mode. |
| display argument... | Displays all, or some, of the set and toggle values. |
| mode *type* | *type* is one of several options, depending on the state of the telnet session. The remote host is asked for permission to go into the requested mode. If the remote host is capable of entering that mode, the requested mode will be entered. The *type* options are |

|  |  |
|---|---|
| character | Disable the TELNET LINEMODE option, or, if the remote side does not understand the LINEMODE option, then enter character at a time mode. |
| line | Enable the TELNET LINEMODE option, or, if the remote side does not understand the LINEMODE option, then attempt to enter old-line-by-line mode. |
| isig -isig | Attempt to enable (disable) the TRAPSIG mode of the LINEMODE option. This requires that the LINEMODE option be enabled. |
| edit -edit | Attempt to enable (disable) the EDIT mode of the LINEMODE option. This requires that the LINEMODE option be enabled. |
| softtabs | Attempt to enable (disable) the SOFT_TAB mode of the LINEMODE option. This requires that -softtabs the LINEMODE option be enabled. |
| litecho -litecho | Attempt to enable (disable) the LIT_ECHO mode of the LINEMODE option. This requires that the LINEMODE option be enabled. |
| ? | Prints out help information for the mode command. |

| | |
|---|---|
| open host<br>user] [-port] | Open a connection to the named host. If no port number is specified, telnet will attempt to [-1 contact a Telnet server at the default port. The host specification may be either a hostname (see hosts(5)for more information) or an Internet address specified in the dot notation (see inet(3) for more information). The -1 option may be used to specify the username to be passed to the remote system via the ENVIRON option. When connecting to a nonstandard port, telnet omits any automatic initiation of telnet options. When the port number is preceded by a minus sign, the initial option negotiation is done. After establishing a connection, the file in the user's home directory is opened. Lines beginning with a # are comment lines. Blank lines are ignored. Lines that begin without whitespace are the start of a machine entry. The first thing on the line is the name of the machine that is being connected to. The rest of the line, and successive lines that begin with whitespace, are assumed to be telnet commands and are processed as if they had been typed in manually to the telnet command prompt. |
| quit | Close any open telnet session and exit telnet. An end-of-file (in command mode) will also close a session and exit. |
| send arguments | Sends one or more special character sequences to the remote host. The following are the arguments that may be specified (more than one argument may be specified at a time): |

| | |
|---|---|
| abort | Sends the TELNET ABORT (Abort Processes) sequence. |
| ao | Sends the TELNET AO (Abort Output) sequence, which should cause the remote system to flush all output from the remote system to the user's terminal. |
| ayt | Sends the TELNET AYT (Are You There) sequence, to which the remote system may or may not choose to respond. |
| brk | Sends the TELNET BRK (Break) sequence, which may have significance to the remote system. |

| | |
|---|---|
| ec | Sends the TELNET EC (Erase Character) sequence, which should cause the remote system to erase the last character entered. |
| el | Sends the TELNET EL (Erase Line) sequence, which should cause the remote system to erase the line currently being entered. |
| eof | Sends the TELNET EOF (End-of-File) sequence. |
| eor | Sends the TELNET EOR (End of Record) sequence. |
| escape | Sends the current telnet escape character (initially ^). |
| ga | Sends the TELNET GA (Go Ahead) sequence, which likely has no significance to the remote system. |
| getstatus | If the remote side supports the TELNET STATUS command, getstatus will send the subnegotiation to request that the server send its current option status. |
| ip | Sends the TELNET IP (Interrupt Process) sequence, which should cause the remote system to abort the currently running process. |
| nop | Sends the TELNET NOP (no operation) sequence. |
| susp | Sends the TELNET SUSP (suspend process) sequence. |
| synch | Sends the TELNET SYNCH sequence. This sequence causes the remote system to discard all previously typed (but not yet read) input. This sequence is sent as TCP urgent data (and may not work if the remote system is a BSD 4.2 system—if it doesn't work, a lowercase r may be echoed on the terminal). |
| ? | Prints out help information for the send command. |

**set argument value, unset argument value** The set command will set any one of a number of telnet variables to a specific value or to True. The special value off turns off the function associated with the variable; this is equivalent to using the unset command. The unset command will disable or set to False any of the specified functions. The values of variables may be interrogated with the display command. The variables that may be set or unset, but not toggled, are listed here. In addition, any of the variables for the toggle command may be explicitly set or unset using the set and unset commands.

| | |
|---|---|
| echo | This is the value (initially ^E) which, when in line-by-line mode, toggles between doing local echoing of entered characters (for normal processing), and suppressing echoing of entered characters (for entering, say, a password). |
| eof | If telnet is operating in LINEMODE or old line-by-line mode, entering this character as the first character on a line will cause this character to be sent to the remote system. The initial value of the eof character is taken to be the terminal's eof character. |
| erase | If telnet is in localchars mode (see toggle localchars, following), and if telnet is operating in character at a time mode, then when this character is typed, a TELNET EC sequence (see send ec, earlier in this man page) is sent to the remote system. The initial value for the erase character is taken to be the terminal's erase character. |
| escape | This is the telnet escape character (initially ^[) which causes entry into telnet command mode (when connected to a remote system). |
| flushoutput | If telnet is in localchars mode (see toggle localchars) and the flushoutput character is typed, a TELNET AO sequence is sent to the remote host. The initial value for the flush character is taken to be the terminal's flush character. |
| interrupt | If telnet is in localchars mode (see toggle localchars) and the interrupt character is typed, a TELNET IuP sequence is sent to the remote host. The initial value for the interrupt character is taken to be the terminal's intr character. |

| | |
|---|---|
| kill | If telnet is in localchars mode (see toggle localchars), and if telnet is operating in character at a time mode, then when this character is typed, a TELNET EL sequence is sent to the remote system. The initial value for the kill character is taken to be the terminal's kill character. |
| lnext | If telnet is operating in LINEMODE or old line-by-line mode, then this character is taken to be the terminal's lnext character. The initial value for the lnext character is taken to be the terminal's lnext character. |
| quit | If telnet is in localchars mode (see toggle localchars) and the quit character is typed, a TELNET BRK sequence is sent to the remote host. The initial value for the quit character is taken to be the terminal's quit character. |
| reprint | If telnet is operating in LINEMODE or old line-by-line mode, then this character is taken to be the terminal's reprint character. The initial value for the reprint character is taken to be the terminal's reprint character. |
| start | If the TELNETTOGGLE-FLOW-CONTROL option has been enabled, then this character is taken to be the terminal's start character. The initial value for the start character is taken to be the terminal's start character. |
| stop | If the TELNETTOGGLE-FLOW-CONTROL option has been enabled, then this character is taken to be the terminal's stop character. The initial value for the kill character is taken to be the terminal's stop character. |
| susp | If telnet is in localchars mode, or LINEMODE is enabled, and the suspend character is typed, a TELNET SUSP sequence is sent to the remote host. The initial value for the suspend character is taken to be the terminal's suspend character. |
| tracefile | This is the file to which the output, caused by netdata or option tracing being True, will be written. If it is set to -, then tracing information will be written to standard output (the default). |
| worderase | If telnet is operating in LINEMODE or old line-by-line mode, then this character is taken to be the terminal's worderase character. The initial value for the worderase character is taken to be the terminal's worderase character. |
| ? | Displays the set unset commands. |

**slc state**

The slc command (Set Local Characters) is used to set or change the state of the special characters when the TELNETLINEMODE option has been enabled. Special characters are characters that get mapped to telnet command sequences (like ip or quit) or line-editing characters (like erase and kill). By default, the local special characters are exported. The variables are

| | |
|---|---|
| export | Switch to the local defaults for the special characters. The local default characters are those of the local terminal at the time telnet was started. |
| import | Switch to the remote defaults for the special characters. The remote default characters are those of the remote system at the time when the telnet connection was established. |
| check | Verify the current settings for the current special characters. The remote side is requested to send all the current special character settings, and if there are any discrepancies with the local side, the local side will switch to the remote value. |
| ? | Prints out help information for the slc command. |

| environ arguments... | The environ command is used to manipulate the variables that may be sent through the TELNET ENVIRON option. The initial set of variables is taken from the users environment, with only the DISPLAY and PRINTER variables being exported by default. The USER variable is also exported if the -a or -l options are used. |
|---|---|

Valid arguments for the environ command are

| define *variable value* | Define the variable *variable* to have a value of *value*. Any variables defined by this command are automatically exported. The value may be enclosed in single or double quotes so that tabs and spaces may be included. |
|---|---|
| undefine *variable* | Remove *variable* from the list of environment variables. |
| export *variable* | Mark the variable *variable* to be exported to the remote side. |
| unexport *variable* | Mark the variable *variable* to not be exported unless explicitly asked for by the remote side. |
| list | List the current set of environment variables. Those marked with a * will be sent automatically; other variables will only be sent if explicitly requested. |
| ? | Prints out help information for the environ command. |

| toggle arguments... | Toggle (between True and False ) various flags that control how telnet responds to events. These flags may be set explicitly to True or False using the set and unset commands listed earlier. More than one argument may be specified. The state of these flags may be interrogated with the display command. Valid arguments are |
|---|---|

| autoflush | If autoflush and localchars are both True, then when the ao or quit characters are recognized (and transformed into telnet sequences; see set for details), telnet refuses to display any data on the user's terminal until the remote system acknowledges (via a TELNET TIMING MARK option) that it has processed those telnet sequences. The initial value for this toggle is True if the terminal user had not done an "stty noflsh"; otherwise, False. (See stty(1) for more details.) |
|---|---|
| autosynch | If autosynch and localchars are both True, then when either the intr or quit character is typed (see set for descriptions of the intr and quit characters), the resulting telnet sequence sent is followed by the TELNET SYNCH sequence. This procedure should cause the remote system to begin throwing away all previously typed input until both of the telnet sequences have been read and acted upon. The initial value of this toggle is False. |
| binary | Enable or disable the TELNET BINARY option on both input and output. |
| inbinary | Enable or disable the TELNET BINARY option on input. |
| outbinary | Enable or disable the TELNET BINARY option on output. |
| crlf | If this is True, then carriage returns will be sent as <CR><LF>. If this is False, then carriage returns will be sent as <CR><NUL>. The initial value for this toggle is False. |
| crmod | Toggle carriage return mode. When this mode is enabled, most carriage return characters received from the remote host will be mapped into a carriage return followed by a line feed. This mode does not affect those characters typed by the user, only those received from the remote host. This mode is not very useful unless the remote host only sends carriage return, but never line feed. The initial value for this toggle is False. |

| | | |
|---|---|---|
| | debug | Toggles socket level debugging (useful only to the super user). The initial value for this `toggle` is `False`. |
| | localchars | If this is `True`, then the `flush`, `interrupt`, `quit`, `erase`, and `kill` characters (see `set`) are recognized locally, and transformed into (hopefully) appropriate `telnet` control sequences (respectively `ao`, `ip`, `brk`, `ec`, and `el` ; see `send`). The initial value for this toggle is `True` in old line-by-line mode, and `False` in character at a time mode. When the `LINEMODE` option is enabled, the value of `localchars` is ignored, and assumed to always be `True`. If `LINEMODE` has ever been enabled, then `quit` is sent as `abort`, and `eof` and `suspend` are sent as `eof` and `susp`; see `send`. |
| | netdata | Toggles the display of all network data (in hexadecimal format). The initial value for this toggle is `False`. |
| | options | Toggles the display of some internal `telnet` protocol processing (having to do with `telnet` options). The initial value for this toggle is `False`. |
| | prettydump | When the `netdata` toggle is enabled, if `prettydump` is enabled, the output from the `netdata` command will be formatted in a more user-readable format. Spaces are put between each character in the output, and the beginning of any `telnet` escape sequence is preceded by an `*` to aid in locating them. |
| | ? | Displays the legal toggle commands. |
| z | | Suspend `telnet`. This command only works when the user is using the `csh`(1). |
| ! *command* | | Execute a single command in a subshell on the local system. If *command* is omitted, then an interactive subshell is invoked. |
| status | | Show the current status of `telnet`. This includes the peer one is connected to, as well as the current mode. |
| ? *command* | | Get help. With no arguments, `telnet` prints a help summary. If a command is specified, `telnet` will print the help information for just that command. |

## ENVIRONMENT

`telnet` uses at least the `HOME`, `SHELL`, `DISPLAY`, and `TERM` environment variables. Other environment variables may be propagated to the other side via the `TELNET ENVIRON` option.

## FILES

`~/.telnetrc`     User customized `telnet` startup values

## HISTORY

The `telnet` command appeared in BSD 4.2.

## NOTES

On some remote systems, `echo` has to be turned off manually when in old line-by-line mode.

In old line-by-line mode or `LINEMODE`, the terminal's `eof` character is only recognized (and sent to the remote system) when it is the first character on a line.

*BSD 4.2, 27 July 1991*

# tfmtodit

tfmtodit—Create font files for use with `groff -Tdvi`

## SYNOPSIS

`tfmtodit [ -sv ][-ggf file ][-kskewchar ] tfm file map file font`

## DESCRIPTION

tfmtodit creates a font file for use with `groff -Tdvi`. `tfm_file` is the name of the font metric file for the font. `map_file` is a file giving the `groff` names for characters in the font; this file should consist of a sequence of lines of the form:

`n c1c2 ...`

where *n* is a decimal integer giving the position of the character in the font, and `c1`, `c2,...` are the `groff` names of the character. If a character has no `groff` names but exists in the `tfm` file, then it will be put in the `groff` font file as an unnamed character. `font` is the name of the `groff` font file. The `groff` font file is written to `font`.

The `-s` option should be given if the font is special (a font is special if `troff` should search it whenever a character is not found in the current font.) If the font is special, it should be listed in the `fonts` command in the `DESC` file; if it is not special, there is no need to list it because `troff` can automatically mount it when it's first used.

To do a good job of math typesetting, `groff` requires font metric information not present in the `tfm` file. The reason for this is that has separate math italic fonts whereas `groff` uses normal italic fonts for math. The additional information required by `groff` is given by the two arguments to the `math_fit` macro in the Metafont programs for the Computer Modern fonts. In a text font (a font for which `math_fitting` is False), Metafont normally ignores these two arguments. Metafont can be made to put this information in the `gf` file by loading the following definition after `cmbase` when creating `cm.base`:

```
def ignore_math_fit(expr left_adjustment,right_adjustment) =
special "adjustment";
numspecial left_adjustment*16/designsize;
numspecial right_adjustment*16/designsize;
enddef;
```

The `gf` file created using this modified `cm.base` should be specified with the `-g` option. The `-g` option should not be given for a font for which `math_fitting` is true.

## OPTIONS

| | |
|---|---|
| `-v` | Print the version number. |
| `-s` | The font is special. The effect of this option is to add the `special` command to the font file. |
| `-kn` | The `skewchar` of this font is at position *n*. *n* should be an integer; it may be given in decimal, or with a leading `0` in octal, or with a leading `0x` in hexadecimal. The effect of this option is to ignore any kerns whose second component is the specified character. |
| `-ggf_file` | `gf_file` is a `gf` file produced by Metafont containing special and `num` special commands giving additional font metric information. |

## FILES

| | |
|---|---|
| `/usr/lib/groff/font/devdvi/DESC` | Device description file. |
| `/usr/lib/groff/font/devdvi/F` | Font description file for font *F*. |

## SEE ALSO

`groff(1)`, `grodvi(1)`, `groff_font(5)`

*Groff Version 1.09, 14 February 1994*

# tftp

tftp—Trivial file transfer program

## SYNOPSIS

tftp [*host*]

## DESCRIPTION

tftp is the user interface to the Internet TFTP (Trivial File Transfer Protocol), which allows users to transfer files to and from a remote machine. The remote host may be specified on the command line, in which case tftp uses *host* as the default host for future transfers. (See the connect command in the following section.)

## COMMANDS

Once tftp is running, it issues the prompt:

tftp>

and recognizes the following commands:

| | |
|---|---|
| ? *command-name* ... | Print help information. |
| ascii | Shorthand for "mode ascii" |
| binary | Shorthand for "mode binary" |
| connect host-name *port* | Set the *host* (and optionally *port* ) for transfers. Note that the TFTP protocol, unlike the FTP protocol, does not maintain connections between transfers; thus, the connect command does not actually create a connection, but merely remembers what host is to be used for transfers. You do not have to use the connect command; the remote host can be specified as part of the get or put commands. |
| get filename,<br>get remotename localname,<br>get file1 file2 ... *fileN* | Get a file or set of files from the specified sources. Source can be in one of two forms: a filename on the remote host, if the host has already been specified; or a string of the form hosts:filename to specify both a host and filename at the same time. If the latter form is used, the last hostname specified becomes the default for future transfers. |
| mode *transfer-mode* | Set the mode for transfers; *transfer-mode* may be ascii or binary. The default is ascii. |
| put *file*<br>put *localfile remotefile*<br>put *file1 file2* ...<br>*fileN remote-directory* | Put a file or set of files to the specified remote file or directory. The destination can be in one of two forms: a filename on the remote host, if the host has already been specified; or a string of the form hosts:filename to specify both a host and filename at the same time. If the latterform is used, the hostname specified becomes the default for future transfers. If the remote-directory form is used, the remote host is assumed to be a UNIX machine. |
| quit | Exit tftp . An end-of-file also exits. |
| rexmt<br>*retransmission-timeout* | Set the per-packet retransmission time-out, in seconds. |
| status | Show current status. |
| timeout<br>*total-transmission-timeout* | Set the total transmission time-out, in seconds. |
| trace | Toggle packet tracing. |
| verbose | Toggle verbose mode. |

## BUGS

Because there is no user-login or validation within the TFTP protocol, the remote site will probably have some sort of file-access restrictions in place. The exact methods are specific to each site and therefore difficult to document here.

## HISTORY

The `tftp` command appeared in BSD 4.3.

*BSD 4.3, 22 April 1991*

# tgatoppm

`tgatoppm`—Convert TrueVision Targa file into a portable pixmap

## SYNOPSIS

`tgatoppm [-debug][`*tgafile*`]`

## DESCRIPTION

Reads a TrueVision Targa file as input. Produces a portable pixmap as output.

## OPTIONS

`-debug`     Causes the header information to be dumped to `stderr`

All flags can be abbreviated to their shortest unique prefix.

## BUGS

Should really be in `pnm`, not `ppm`.

## SEE ALSO

`ppmtotga`(1), `ppm`(5)

## AUTHOR

Partially based on `tga2rast`, version 1.0, by Ian J. MacPhedran

Copyright© 1989 by Jef Poskanzer.

*26 August 1989*

# tifftopnm

`tifftopnm`—Convert a TIFF file into a portable anymap

## SYNOPSIS

`tifftopnm [-headerdump] `*tifffile*

## DESCRIPTION

`tifftopnm` reads a TIFF file as input and produces a portable anymap as output. The type of the output file depends on the input file; if it's black and white, a `pbm` file is written;, if it's grayscale, a `pgm` file; otherwise, a `ppm` file. The program tells you which type it is writing.

## OPTIONS

`-headerdump`     Dump TIFF file information to `stderr`. This information may be useful in debugging TIFF file conversion problems.

All flags can be abbreviated to their shortest unique prefix.

## SEE ALSO

pnmtotiff(1), pnm(5)

## BUGS

This program is not self-contained. To use it you must fetch the TIFF Software package listed in the OTHER.SYSTEMS file and configure pbmplus to use libtiff. See the pbmplus Makefile for details on this configuration.

## AUTHOR

Derived by Jef Poskanzer from tif2ras.c, which is copyright© 1990 by Sun Microsystems, Inc. Author Patrick J. Naughton (naughton@wind.sun.com).

*13 January 1991*

# tin, rtin, cdtin, tind

tin, rtin, cdtin, tind—A Netnews reader

## SYNOPSIS

tin/rtin/cdtin/tind [ *options* ][*newsgroups* ]

## DESCRIPTION

tin is a full-screen easy-to-use Netnews reader. It can read news locally (/usr/spool/news) or remotely (rtin or tin -r option) via an NNTP (Network News Transport Protocol) server. cdtin can read news locally and news archived on CD-ROM. It will automatically utilize nov (news overview)-style index files if available locally or via the nntp xover command.

tin has five separate levels of operation: group selection level, spooldir selection level, group level, thread level and article level. Use the h (help) command to view a list of the commands available at a particular level.

On startup, tin will show a list of the newsgroups found in $HOME/.newsrc. An arrow -> or highlighted bar will point to the first newsgroup. Move to a group by using the terminal arrow keys (terminal-dependent) or j and k. Use PgUp/PgDn (terminal-dependent) or Ctrl-U and Ctrl-D to page up/down. Enter a newsgroup by pressing Return.

The Tab key advances to the next newsgroup with unread articles and enters it.

## OPTIONS

| | |
|---|---|
| -c | Create/update index files for every group in $HOME/.newsrc or file specified by -f option and mark all articles as read. |
| -f *file* | Use the specified file of subscribed to newsgroups in place of $HOME/.newsrc. |
| -h | Help listing all command-line options. |
| -H | Brief introduction to tin that is also shown the first time it is started. |
| -I *dir* | Directory in which to store newsgroup index files. Default is $HOME/.tin/.index. |
| -m *dir* | Mailbox directory to use. Default is $HOME/Mail. |
| -M *user* | Mail unread articles to specified user for later reading. For more information read the "Automatic Mailing and Saving New News" section later in this manual page. |
| -n | Only load groups from the active file that are also subscribed to in the users .newsrc. This allows a noticeable speedup when connecting via a slow line. |
| -p *program* | Print program with options. |
| -q | Quick start without checking for new newsgroups. |
| -P | Purge group index files of articles that no longer exist. Care should be taken when using this command as it starts each and every article in each group that is accessed. On a low-speed connection, this can have an undesirable effect and it also knocks the hell out of your file system. |

| | |
|---|---|
| -r | Read news remotely from the default NNTP server specified in the environment variable NNTPSERVER or contained in the file /etc/nntpserver. |
| -R | Read news saved by -S option (not yet implemented). |
| -s *dir* | Save articles to directory. Default is $HOME/News. |
| -S | Save unread articles for later reading by -R option. For more information, see "Automatic Mailing and Saving New News." |
| -u | Create/update index files for every group in $HOME/.newsrc or file specified by -f option. This option is disabled if tin retrieves its index files via an NNTP server. |
| -U | Start tin in the background to update index files while reading news in the foreground. This option is disabled if tin retrieves its index files via an NNTP server. |
| -v | Verbose mode for -c, -M, -S, -u, and -Z options. |
| -w | Quick mode to post an article and then exit. |
| -z | Only start tin if there is any new/unread news. If there is news, tin will position cursor at first group with unread news. Useful for putting in login file. |
| -Z | Check if there is any new/unread news and exit with appropriate status. If -v option is specified, the number of unread articles in each group is printed. An exit code 0 indicates no news, 1 that an error occurred, and 2 that new/unread news exists. Useful for writing scripts. |

tin can also dynamically change its options by the M menu command. Any changes are written to $HOME/.tin/tinrc.

The index daemon version, tind, only supports the -f, -h, -I, and -v options.

## INDEX FILES

In order to keep track of threads, tin maintains an index for each newsgroup. There are a number of methods in which index files can be created and updated.

The simplest method is that each user creates/updates his or her own index files that are stored in $HOME/.tin/.index. This has the advantage that any user can compile and install tin, but the disadvantage is that each user is going to be creating duplicate files and using precious disk space. A good way to keep index files updated is by doing a tin -U that will update index files in the background while you are reading news in the foreground. You can also update index files via the system batcher cron with the -u option: 30 6 ***/usr/local/bin/tin -u.

A slightly better method is to set tin setuid news and have all index files created and updated in the news spool directory (that is, /usr/spool/news/.index). This has the advantage that there will only be one copy of the index files on each machine on your network, but the disadvantage is that you will have tin running setuid news.

A better method is to install the tind index file updating daemon and have it create and update index files for all groups in your active file at regular intervals in the news spool directory (/usr/spool/news/.index). This has the advantage that there will only be one copy of the index files on each machine on your network, and tin must not be setuid news, but the disadvantage is that you will have to have news permissions to install tind and root permissions to install an entry in the cron batcher system to have tind regularly update index files.

The best method is to install the tind index file updating daemon on your NNTP server and have it create and update index files for all groups in your active file at regular intervals in the news spool directory (/usr/spool/news/.index). This has the advantage that there will only be one copy of the index files on the NNTP server for the whole of your network, but the disadvantage is that you will have to install my NNTP server patches to allow tin to retrieve index file from your NNTP server and you must install an entry in the cron batcher system to have tind regularly update index files. (This is the method we use on our network of 40 to 50 machines and we have not had any problems.)

Entering a group the first time tends to be slow because the index file must be built from scratch unless the tind update daemon is being used. To alleviate the slowness, start tin to create all index files for the groups you subscribe to with tin -u -v and go for a coffee. Subsequent readings of a group will cause incremental updating of the index file.

If reading news remotely and locally updating index files operation will be somewhat slower because the articles must be retrieved from the NNTP server.

## NEWS ADMINISTRATION

Maintaining Netnews on large networks of machines can be a pretty time-consuming job, as I discovered when I was given the job of maintaining our news system and news users.

`tin` is a News User Agent and so most of the users were always asking questions or doing things that could be frowned upon by their departments. To relieve news administrators (and especially me) of this, features have been added to make life easier for them.

When a user starts `tin`, it is possible to inform them of any important changes or information concerning the news system by displaying a message of the day (`motd`) file. The `motd` file should be created in your news lib directory (`/usr/lib/news/motd`) and should have file permissions set to `0644`. The `motd` file will only be displayed if its contents is newer than the last time the user started `tin`. If reading news via NNTP, my `XMOTD` patch will have to have been applied to your NNTP server.

A user starting `tin` for the first time can be automatically subscribed to a list of newsgroups that are deemed appropriate by the news administrator. At our site the subscriptions file has 125 groups (our active file contains more than 400 groups with many only being marginally interesting to most people). The subscriptions file should be created in your news lib directory (`/usr/lib/news/subscriptions`) and should have file permissions set to `0644`. If reading news via NNTP, my `LIST SUBSCRIPTIONS` patch will have to have been applied to your NNTP server.

If my NNTP `XUSER` patch has been applied to your NNTP server, you will be able to log the username and machine to your NNTP logfile for usage statistics.

## SCREEN FORMAT

`tin` has five separate levels of operation: group selection level, `spooldir` selection level, group level, thread level, and article level.

At the group selection level, the title displays the number of subscribed groups. The newsgroups are displayed on the left of the screen with the number of unread articles displayed on the same line in the middle of the screen, like this:

```
<Selection Num><Newsgroup><Num of unread articles>
i.e.,
  1    alt.sources              10
  2    comp.sources.misc         3
  3    news.software.readers    12
```

At the group level, the title contains the name of the group, the number of conversation threads, and total number of articles, for example, `alt.sources (7 23)`. If the group has been set up not to thread articles (for example, `alt.sources` is in `$(HOME)/.tin/unthread`), the title will be `alt.sources (U 23)`. There are two possible display formats:

```
<Selection Num><Unread><Responses><Subject><Author>
e.g.,
  1  +   3    Bnews sources?            iain@anl433.uucp
  2      1    This question has         ether@net
```

or

```
<Selection Num><Unread><Responses><Subject (longer)>
e.g.,
  1  +   3    Bnews sources?
  2      1    This question has a longer subject line
```

At the article level, the page header has the following format:

```
<Date posted><Newsgroup>
<Thread 1 of n>
<Article Num><Subject><Num of responses in thread>
```

```
<Author><Organization>
<Article body>
i.e.,
  24 Jul 15:20:03 GMT      alt.sources          Thread 1 of 2
  Article 452             Bnews sources?       3 responses
  iain@anl433.uucp        Organization name
```

## COMMON MOVING KEYS

The following table shows the common keys/commands for moving at all five levels within tin:

| | |
|---|---|
| Beginning of list/article | Home 1 (^R or g at article level) |
| End of list/article | End $ (also G at article level) |
| Page up | PgUp ^U or ^B or b |
| Page down | PgDn ^D or ^F or <SPACE> |
| Line up | Up arrow k (not at article level) |
| Line down | Down arrow j (not at article level) |

## COMMON EDITING COMMANDS

An emacs-style editing package allows the easy editing of input strings. A history list allows the easy reuse of previously entered strings. The following commands are available when editing a string:

| | |
|---|---|
| ^A, ^E | Move to beginning or end of line, respectively. |
| ^F, ^B | Nondestructive move forward or back one location, respectively. |
| ^D | Delete the character currently under the cursor, or send EOF if no characters are in the buffer. |
| ^H, <DEL> | Delete character left of the cursor. |
| ^K | Delete from cursor to end of line. |
| ^P, ^N | Move through history, previous and next, respectively. |
| ^L, ^R | Redraw the current line. |
| <CR> | Places line on history list if nonblank, appends newline, and returns to the caller. |
| <ESC> | Aborts the present editing operation. |

## NEWSGROUP SELECTION COMMANDS

| | |
|---|---|
| 4 | Select group 4. |
| ^K | Delete current group from $HOME/.newsrc file. |
| ^L | Redraw page. |
| ^R | Reset $HOME/.newsrc file. |
| <CR> | Read current group. |
| <TAB> | View next group with unread news. Will wrap around to the beginning of the group selection list looking for unread groups. |
| B | Mail a bug report or comment to the author. This is the best way to get bugs fixed and features added/changed. |
| c | Mark current group as all read with confirmation and go to next group in group selection list. |
| C | Mark current group as all read and go to next unread group in group selection list. |
| d | Toggle display to show just the group name or the group name and the group's description. |
| g | Choose a new group by name. The position of the group within the group list will also be asked for. When 1 is entered, the new group will be the first group in the displayed list; when 8 is entered, the group will be the eighth group in the list; and so on. When $ is entered, the group will be the last group displayed. |

| | |
|---|---|
| h | Help screen of newsgroup selection commands. |
| H | Toggle the display of help mini-menu at the bottom of the screen. |
| I | Toggle inverse video. |
| l | List and allow selection of the available spool directories. This feature requires a special library to be linked with tin to create cdtin, which can then read news from an active news feed and also from multiple CD-ROMs. |
| m | Move the current group within the group selection list. When 1 is entered, the group will become the first displayed group in the list; when 8 is entered, the eighth group in the list; and so on. When $ is entered, the group will be the last group displayed. |
| M | User-configurable Options menu (for more information, see the "Global Options Menu" section later in this manual page). |
| q | Quit tin. |
| Q | Quit tin. |
| r | Toggle display of all subscribed-to groups and just the subscribed-to groups containing unread articles. Command has no effect if groups were read from the command line when tin was started. |
| s | Subscribe to current group. |
| S | Subscribe to groups matching user-specified pattern. |
| u | Unsubscribe to current group. |
| U | Unsubscribe to groups matching user-specified pattern. |
| v | Print tin version information. |
| w | Post an article to current group. |
| W | List articles posted by user. The date posted, the newsgroup, and the subject are listed. |
| y | The first time this command is called, it will yank in all groups from $LIB-DIR/active that are not in $HOME/.newsrc. |
| | After any groups have been subscribed/unsubscribed to, this command, if pressed again, will reread $HOME/.newsrc and display only the subscribed groups. |
| Y | Reread the active file to see if any new news has arrived since starting tin. |
| z | Mark all articles in the current group as unread. |
| Z | Undelete previously deleted group by ^K command from $HOME/.newsrc. |
| / | Group forward search. |
| ? | Group backward search. |

## SPOOL DIRECTORY SELECTION COMMANDS

| | |
|---|---|
| 4 | Select spool directory 4. |
| ^L | Redraw page. |
| <CR> | Read news from selected spool directory. |
| B | Mail a bug report or comment to the author. This is the best way to get bugs fixed and features added/changed. |
| h | Help screen of spool directory selection commands. |
| H | Toggle the display of help mini-menu at the bottom of the screen. |
| I | Toggle inverse video. |
| q | Return to previous level. |
| Q | Quit tin. |
| v | Print tin version information. |

## GROUP INDEX COMMANDS

| | |
|---|---|
| 4 | Select article 4. |
| ^K | Kill current article (for more information, see the "Automatic Kill and Selection" section later in this manual page). |
| ^L | Redraw page. |
| <CR> | Read current article. |
| <TAB> | View next unread article or group. |
| a | Author forward search. |
| A | Author backward search. |
| c | Mark all articles as read with confirmation. |
| C | Mark all articles as read and go to next group with unread news. |
| d | Toggle display to show just the subject or the subject and author. |
| g | Choose a new group by name. |
| h | Help screen of group index commands. |
| H | Toggle the display of help mini-menu at the bottom of the screen. |
| I | Toggle inverse video. |
| K | Mark article/thread as read and advance to next unread article/thread. |
| l | List the author of each response in current thread and enter thread selection level. |
| m | Mail current article/thread/auto-selected (hot) articles/articles matching pattern/tagged articles to someone. |
| M | User-configurable Options menu (for more information see "Global Options Menu" section). |
| n | Go to next group. |
| N | Go to next unread article. |
| o | Output current article/thread/autoselected (hot) articles/articles matching pattern/tagged articles to printer. |
| p | Go to previous group. |
| P | Go to previous unread article. |
| q | Return to previous level. |
| Q | Quit tin. |
| s | Save current article/thread/autoselected (hot) articles/articles matching pattern/tagged articles to file/files/mailbox. To save to a mailbox, enter = or =mailbox when asked for filename to save to. To save in <newsgroup name>/<filename> format, enter +filename. Environment variables are allowed within a filename (for example, $SOURCES/dir/filename). |
| t | Tag current article/thread for mailing (m)/piping (l)/printing (o)/saving (s)/crossposting (x). |
| u | Toggle display to show all articles as unthreaded or threaded. |
| U | Untag all articles that were tagged. |
| v | Print tin version information. |
| w | Post an article to current group. |
| W | List articles posted by user. The date posted, the newsgroup, and the subject are listed. |
| x | Crosspost already posted current article/thread/autoselected (hot) articles/articles matching pattern/tagged articles to another newsgroup(s). Useful for reposting from global to local newsgroups. |
| X | Mark all unread articles that have not been selected as read, redo screen to reflect changes, and put index at the first thread to begin reading. Pressing X again will toggle back to the way it was before. See ~ command for clearing the toggle effect. |
| z | Mark current article as unread. |
| Z | Mark current thread as unread. |

| | |
|---|---|
| / | Search forward for specified subject. |
| ? | Search backward for specified subject. |
| - | Show last message. |
| ¦ | Pipe current article/thread/autoselected (hot) articles/articles matching pattern/tagged articles into command. |
| * | Select current thread for later processing. |
| * | Toggle selection of current thread. If at least one unread art in thread (but not all unread arts) is selected, then all unread arts become selected. |
| @ | Reverse all selections on all articles. |
| ~ | Undo all selections on all articles. It clears the toggle effect of X command. Thus, after first doing an X, you can then do ~ to reset articles. Thus, you can iteratively whittle down uninteresting threads. |
| + | Perform autoselection on current group. |
| ; | For each thread in current group, if it at least one unread art is selected, all unread arts become selected. This is useful for autoselection on author when the reader wants to see the entire thread. |
| = | Prompts for a pattern with which to match on. All threads whose subjects match the pattern will be selected. A pattern of * will match all subjects. Entering just <CR> will cause the previous pattern to be used. |

## THREAD LISTING COMMANDS

| | |
|---|---|
| 4 | Select article 4 within thread. |
| ^L | Redraw page. |
| <CR> | Read current article within thread. |
| <TAB> | View next unread article within thread. |
| B | Mail a bug report or comment to the author. This is the best way of getting bugs fixed and features added/changed. |
| c | Mark thread as read after confirmation and return to previous level. |
| d | Toggle display to show just the subject or the subject and author. |
| h | Help screen of thread listing commands. |
| H | Toggle the display of help mini-menu at the bottom of the screen. |
| I | Toggle inverse video. |
| K | Mark thread as read and return to previous level. |
| q | Return to previous level. |
| Q | Quit tin. |
| r | Toggle display to show all articles or only unread articles. |
| B | Mail a bug report or comment to the author. This is the best way of getting bugs fixed and features added/changed. |
| t | Tag current article for mailing (m)/piping (l)/printing (o)/saving (s)/crossposting (x). |
| T | Return to group index level. |
| v | Print tin version information. |
| z | Mark current article in thread as unread. |
| Z | Mark all articles in thread as unread. |

## ARTICLE VIEWER COMMANDS

| | |
|---|---|
| 0 | Read the base article in this thread. |
| 4 | Read response 4 in this thread. |
| ^H | Show all of the article's mail header. |

| | |
|---|---|
| ^K | Kill current article (for more information, see the "Automatic Kill and Selection" section) |
| ^L | Redraw page. |
| <CR> | Go to next base article. |
| <TAB> | Go to next unread article. |
| a | Author forward search. |
| A | Author backward search. |
| c | Mark all articles as read with confirmation and return to group selection level. |
| C | Mark current group as all read and go to next unread group in group selection list. |
| d | Toggle rot-13 decoding for this article. |
| D | Delete current article. It must have been posted by the same user. The cancel message can be seen in the newsgroup control. |
| f | Post a follow-up to the current article with a copy of the article included. |
| F | Post a follow-up to the current article. |
| h | Help screen of article page commands. |
| H | Toggle the display of help mini-menu at the bottom of the screen. |
| I | Toggle inverse video. |
| k | Mark article as read and advance to next unread article. |
| K | Mark thread as read and advance to next unread thread. |
| m | Mail current article/thread/autoselected (hot) articles/articles matching pattern/tagged articles to someone. |
| M | User-configurable Options menu (for more information, see the "Global Options Menu" section later in this manual page). |
| n | Go to the next article. |
| N | Go to the next unread article. |
| o | Output current article/thread/autoselected (hot) articles/articles matching pattern/tagged articles to printer. |
| o | Output article/thread/tagged articles to printer. |
| p | Go to the previous article. |
| P | Go to the previous unread article. |
| q | Return to previous level. |
| Q | Quit `tin`. |
| r | Reply through mail to the author of the current article with a copy of the article included. |
| R | Reply through mail to the author of the current article. |
| s | Save current article/thread/autoselected (hot) articles/articles matching pattern/tagged articles to file/files/mailbox. To save to a mailbox enter = or =mailbox when asked for filename to save to. To save in <newsgroup name>/<filename> format, enter +filename. Environment variables are allowed within a filename (such as $SOURCES/dir/filename). |
| t | Return to group selection level. |
| T | Tag current article for mailing (m)/piping (¦)/printing (o)/saving (s)/crossposting (x). |
| v | Print `tin` version information. |
| w | Post an article to current group. |
| W | List articles posted by user. The date posted, the newsgroup and the subject are listed. |
| x | Crosspost already posted current article/thread/autoselected (hot) articles/articles matching pattern/tagged articles to another newsgroup(s). Useful for reposting from global to local newsgroups. |
| z | Mark article as unread. |
| / | Article forward search. |
| ? | Article backward search |

| ¦ | Pipe current article/thread/autoselected (hot) articles/articles matching pattern/tagged articles into command. |
| < | Go to the first article in the current thread. |
| > | Go to the last article in the current thread. |
| * | Select current thread for later processing. |
| * | Toggle selection of current article. |
| @ | Reverse article selections. |
| ~ | Undo all selections on current thread. |

## GLOBAL OPTIONS MENU

This menu is accessed by pressing M at all levels. It allows the user to customize the behavior of tin. The options are saved to the file $HOME/.tin/tinrc. Use <SPACE> to toggle the required option and <CR> to set.

| Auto save | Automatically save articles/threads by "Archive-name:" line in article header and post process them if process type is not set to None. |
| Editor offset | Set ON if the editor used for posting, follow-ups and bug reports has the capability of starting and positioning the cursor at a specified line within a file. |
| Mark saved read | Allows saved articles/threads to be automatically marked as read. |
| Confirm Command | Allows certain commands (such as c catchup) that require user confirmation to be executed immediately if set OFF. |
| Draw arrow | Allows groups/articles to be selected by an arrow -> if set ON or by a highlighted bar if set OFF. |
| Print header | This allows the complete mail header or only the "Subject:" and "From:" fields to be output when printing articles. |
| Go to 1st unread | This allows the cursor to be placed at the first/last unread article upon entering a newsgroup with unread news. |
| Scroll full page | If set ON, scrolling of groups/articles will be a full page at a time; otherwise, half a page at a time. |
| Catch up on quit | If set ON, the user is asked when quitting if all groups read during the current session should be marked read. |
| Thread articles | If set ON, articles will be threaded in all groups (default); otherwise, articles will be shown unthreaded. Threading or unthreading is possible on a per-group basis by setting the group attribute variable thread_arts to ON/OFF in the file $HOME/.tin/attributes. |
| Show only unread | If set ON, show only new/unread articles; otherwise, show all articles. |
| Show description | If set ON, show a short descriptive text for each displayed newsgroup. The text used is taken from the $LIBDIR/newsgroups file. |
| Show Author | If set None, only the "Subject:" line will be displayed. If set Addr, "Subject:" line and the address part of the "From:" are displayed. If set Name, "Subject:" line and the author's full name part of the "From:" line are displayed. If set Both, "Subject:" line and all of the "From:" line are displayed. |
| Process type | This specifies the default type of post processing to perform on saved articles. The following types of processing are allowed: |

- ■ None
- ■ Unpacking of multipart shell archives
- ■ Unpacking of multipart uuencoded files
- ■ Unpacking of multipart uuencoded files, which produce a *.zoo archive whose contents are listed
- ■ Unpacking of multipart uuencoded files, which produce a *.zoo archive whose contents are extracted
- ■ Unpacking of multipart uuencoded files, which produce a *.zip archive whose contents are listed

- Unpacking of multipart uuencoded files, which produce a `*.zip` archive whose contents are extracted
- Unpacking of multipart uuencoded files, which produce an `*.lha` archive whose contents are listed (AmigaDOS version only)
- Unpacking of multipart uuencoded files, which produce an `*.lha` archive whose contents is extracted (AmigaDOS version only)

| | |
|---|---|
| Sort articles by | This specifies how articles should be sorted. The following sort types are allowed: |
| | ■ Don't sort articles (default). |
| | ■ Sort articles by "Subject:" field (ascending and descending). |
| | ■ Sort articles by "From:" field (ascending and descending). |
| | ■ Sort articles by "Date:" field (ascending and descending). |
| Save directory | The directory where articles/threads are to be saved. Default is `$HOME/News`. |
| Mail directory | The directory where articles/threads are to be saved in mailbox format. This feature is mainly for use with the `elm` mail program. It allows the user to save articles, threads, or groups simply by giving = as the filename to save to. |
| Printer | The printer program with options that is to be used to print articles. Default is `lpr` for BSD machines and `lp` for SysV machines. |

## `tinrc` CONFIGURABLE VARIABLES

The following variables are user-configurable by editing `$HOME/.tin/tinrc` directly. It is hoped to eventually provide a menu to allow the setting of the most common variables.

| | |
|---|---|
| `batch_save` | If set `ON`, articles/threads will be saved in batch mode when save `-S` or mail `-M` is specified on the command line. Default is `OFF`. |
| `beginner_level` | If set `ON`, a mini-menu of the most useful commands will be displayed at the bottom of the screen for each level. Default is `ON`. |
| `display_reading_prompt` | The prompt `Reading...` will be displayed when reading an article from an NNTP server to provide feedback to the user. Default is `ON`. |
| `force_screen_redraw` | Specifies whether a screen redraw should always be done after certain external commands. Default is `OFF`. |
| `groupname_max_length` | Maximum length of the names of newsgroups to be displayed so that more of the newsgroup description can be displayed. Default is `132`. |
| `default_sigfile` | The path that specifies the signature file to use when posting, following up to, or replying to an article. If the path is a directory, then the signature will be randomly generated from files that are in the specified directory. Default is `$HOME/.Sig`. |
| `editor_format` | The format string used to create the editor start command with parameters. Default is `%E +%N %F` (for example, `/bin/vi +7 .article`). |
| `hot_art_mark` | The character used to show that an article/thread is autoselected (hot). Default is `*`. |
| `quote_chars` | The character used in quoting included text to article follow-ups and mail replies. The `' '` character represents a blank character and is replaced with `' '` when read. Default is `': '`. |
| `reread_active_file_secs` | The news active file is reread at regular intervals to show if any new news has arrived. Default is `300` seconds. |
| `return_art_mark` | The character used to show that an article will return. Default is `-`. |
| `save_to_mmdf_mailbox` | Allows articles to be saved to an `mmdf`-style mailbox instead of `mbox` format. Default is `OFF` unless reading news on SCO UNIX, which uses `MMDF` by default. |
| `show_last_line_prev_page` | The last line of the previous page will be displayed as the first line of next page. Default is `OFF`. |

| slow_speed_terminal | Strips the blanks from the end of each line, thereby speeding up the display when reading on a slow terminal or via modem. Default is OFF. |
| tab_after_X_selection | If enabled, will automatically go to the first unread article after having selected all hot articles and threads with the X command at group index level. Default is OFF. |
| tab_goto_next_unread | If enabled, pressing Tab at the article viewer level will go to the next unread article immediately instead of first paging through the current one. Default is ON. |
| unread_art_mark | The character used to show that an article has not been read. Default is +. |
| use_builtin_inews | Allows the built-in NNTP inews to be enabled/disabled. Default is ON (enabled). |
| use_keypad | Allows the scroll keys on the keypad to be enabled/disabled on supported terminals. Default is OFF. |

## GROUP ATTRIBUTES

tin allows certain attributes to be set on a per-group basis. These group attributes are read from the file $HOME/.tin/ attributes. A later version will provide a menu interface to set all the attributes. At present, you will have to edit the file with your editor :-(. The following group attributes are available:

```
newsgroup=alt.sources
maildir=/usr/iain/Mail/sources
savedir=/usr/iain/News/alt.sources
sigfile=/usr/iain/.funny sig
organization=Wacky Bits Inc.
followup to=alt.sources.d
printer=/usr/local/bin/a2ps -nn ¦ /bin/lpr
auto save=ON
batch save=OFF
delete tmp files=ON
show only unread=OFF
thread arts=ON
show author=1
sort art type=5
post proc type=1
```

Note that the newsgroup=<groupname> line has to be specified before the attributes are specified for that group.

All attributes are set to a reasonable default so you only have to specify the attribute that you want to change (for example, savedir).

All toggle attributes are set by specifying ON/OFF.

The show_author attribute is specified by a number from the following range: 0=none, 1=username, 2=network address, 3=both.

The sort_art_type attribute is specified by a number from the following range: 0=none, 1=subject descending, 2=subject ascending, 3=from descending, 4=from ascending, 5=date descending, 6=date ascending.

The post_proc_type attribute is specified by a number from the following range: 0=none, 1=unshar, 2=uudecode, 3=uudecode & list zoo archive, 4=uudecode & extract zoo archive, 5=uudecode & list zip archive, 6=uudecode & extract zip archive. (If running on AmigaDOS, the zoo options are replaced by their corresponding lha archiver options.)

## AUTOMATIC KILL AND SELECTION

When there is a subject or an author that you are either very interested in, or find completely uninteresting, you can easily instruct tin to autoselect or autokill articles with specific subjects or from specific authors. These instructions are stored in a kill file.

This menu is accessed by pressing ^K at the group and page levels. It allows the user to kill or select an article that matches the current "Subject:" line, "From:" line, or a string entered by the user. The user-entered string can be applied to the "Subject:" or "From:" lines of an article. The kill description can be limited to the current newsgroup or it can apply to all newsgroups. Once entered, the user can abort the command and not save the kill description, edit the kill file, or save the kill description.

On starting tin, the user's kill file $HOME/.tin/kill is read and on entering a newsgroup any kill or select descriptions are applied.

Articles that match a kill description are marked killed and are not displayed. Articles that match an autoselect description are marked with an * when displayed.

## POSTING ARTICLES

tin allows posting of articles, follow-up to already posted articles, and replying direct through mail to the author of an article.

Use the w command to post an article to a newsgroup. After entering the post subject, the default editor (such as vi) or the editor specified by the $VISUAL environment variable will be started and the article can be entered. To crosspost articles, simply add a comma and the name of the newsgroup(s) to the end of the "Newsgroups:" line at the beginning of the article. After saving and exiting the editor, you are asked if you wish to abort posting the article, edit the article again or post the article to the specified newsgroup(s).

Use the W command to display a history of the articles you have posted. The date the article was posted, which newsgroups the article was posted to, and the article's subject line are displayed.

Use the f/F command to post a follow-up article to an already posted article. The f command will copy the text of the original article into the editor. The editing procedure is the same as when posting an article with the w command.

Use the r/R command to reply direct through mail to the author of an already posted article. The r command will copy the text of the original article into the editor. The editing procedure is the same as when posting an article with the w command. After saving and exiting the editor, you are asked if you wish to abort sending the article, edit the article again, or send the article to the author.

## CUSTOMIZING THE ARTICLE QUOTE STRING

When posting a follow-up to an article or replying direct to the author of an article via e-mail, the text of the article can be quoted. The beginning of the quoted text can contain information about the quoted article (for example, the Name and the Message ID of the article). To allow for different situations, certain information from the article can be used in the quoted string. The following variables are expanded if found in the tinrc variables mail_quote_format= or news_quote_format=:

| | |
|---|---|
| %A | Address (e-mail) |
| %D | Date |
| %F | Full address (%N (%A)) |
| %G | Groupname |
| %M | Message ID |
| %N | Name of user |

For example,

```
mail_quote_format=On %D in %G you wrote:
news_quote_format=In %M, %F wrote:
```

would expand when used to:

```
On 21 Jul 1992 09:45:51 -0400 in alt.sources you wrote:
In <abcINN123@anl433.uucp>, Iain Lea (iain@erlm.siemens.de) wrote:
```

## MAILING, PIPING, PRINTING, REPOSTING, AND SAVING ARTICLES

The command interface to mail (m), pipe (|), print (o), crosspost (x) and save (s) articles is the same for ease of use.

The initial command will ask you to select which article, thread, hot (autoselected) regex pattern, tagged articles you wish to mail, pipe, and so on.

Tagged articles must have already been tagged with the T command. All tagged articles can be untagged by the U untag command.

If regex pattern matching is selected, you are asked to enter a regular expression (for example, to match all article subject lines containing net News, you must enter *net News*). Any articles that match the entered expression will be mailed, piped, and so on.

To save articles to a mailbox with the name of the current newsgroup (for example, Alt.sources) enter = or =<mailbox name> when asked for the save filename.

To save articles in <newsgroup name>/<filename> format, enter +<filename>.

When saving articles, you can specify whether the saved files should be post processed (such as unshar shell archive, uudecode multiple parts, and so on). A default process type can be set by the Process type: in the M Options menu.

## AUTOMATIC MAILING AND SAVING NEW NEWS

tin allows new/unread news articles to be mailed (-M option)/saved (-S option) in batch mode for later reading—useful when going on holiday and you don't want to return and find that expire has removed a whole load of unread articles. It's best to run from crontab every day while away, after which you will be mailed a report of which articles were mailed/saved from which newsgroups and the total number of articles mailed/saved. Articles are saved in a private news structure under your <savedir> directory (default is $HOME/News).

Be careful of using this option if you read a lot of groups because you could overflow your filesystem. If you only want to save a few groups, it would be best to back up your full $HOME/.newsrc and create a new one that only contains the newsgroups you want to mail/save. Saved news can be read later by tin -R.

| | |
|---|---|
| tin -M iain -c -f newsrc.mail | Mail any unread articles in newsgroups specified in file newsrc.mail |
| tin -S -c -f newsrc.save | Save any unread articles in newsgroups specified in file newsrc.save |
| tin -R | Read any articles saved by tin -S |

## SIGNATURES

tin will recognize a signature in either $HOME/.signature or $HOME/.Sig. If $HOME/.signature exists, then the signature will be pulled into the editor for mail commands. A signature in $HOME/.signature will not be pulled into the editor for posting commands because inews will append the signature itself.

A signature in $HOME/.Sig will be pulled into the editor for both posting and mailing commands.

The following is an example of a $HOME/.Sig file:

```
NAMES Iain Lea iain.lea@erlm.siemens.de
SNAIL Bruecken Strasse 12, 8500 Nuernberg 90, Germany
PHONE +49-911-331963 (home) +49-911-3089-407 (work)
```

tin also has the capability to generate random signatures on a per-newsgroup basis if so desired. The way to accomplish this is to specify the default signature or the group attribute sigfile as a directory. If, for example, the sigfile path is /usr/iain/.sigs and .sigs is a directory, then tin will select a random signature from any file that is in the directory .sigs (note: one signature per numbered file). A random signature can also consist of a fixed part signature that can contain your name, address, and so on, followed by the random sig. The fixed part of the random sig is read from the file $HOME/.sigfixed.

## ENVIRONMENT VARIABLES

| | |
|---|---|
| TINRC | Define this variable if you want to specify command-line options that tin should be started with to save typing them each time it is started. The contents of the environment variable are added to the front of the command-line options before it is parsed, therefore allowing an option specified on the command line to override the same option specified in the environment. |
| TIN_HOMEDIR | Define this variable if you do not want the .tin directory in $HOME/.tin. For example, if you want all tin's private files in /tmp/.tin, you would set TINDIR to /tmp. |

| | |
|---|---|
| TIN_INDEXDIR | Define this variable if you do not want the `.index` directory in `$HOME/.tin/.index`. For example, if you want all `tin`'s index files in `/tmp/.index`, you would set `TIN_INDEXDIR` to `/tmp`. |
| TIN_LIBDIR | Define this variable if you want to override the `LIBDIR` path that was compiled into the `tin` binary via the `Makefile`. |
| TIN_SPOOLDIR | Define this variable if you want to override the `SPOOLDIR` path that was compiled into the `tin` binary via the `Makefile`. |
| TIN_NOVROOTDIR | Define this variable if you want to override the `NOVROOTDIR` path that was compiled into the `tin` binary via the `Makefile`. |
| TIN_ACTIVEFILE | Define this variable if you want to override the `LIBDIR/active` path that was compiled into the `tin` binary via the `Makefile`. |
| NNTPSERVER | The default NNTP server to remotely read news from. This variable only needs to be set if the `-r` command-line option is specified and the file `/etc/nntpserver` does not exist. |
| DISTRIBUTION | Set the article header field "Distribution:" to the contents of the variable instead of the system default. |
| ORGANIZATION | Set the article header field "Organization:" to the contents of the variable instead of the system default. This variable has precedence over the file `$HOME/.tin/organization` that may also contain an organization string. If you are reading news on an Apollo DomainOS machine, the environment variable `NEWSORG` has to be used instead of `ORGANIZATION`. |
| REPLYTO | Set the article header field "Reply-To:" to the return address specified by the variable. This is useful if the machine is not registered in the UUCP mail maps or if you wish to receive replies at a different machine. This variable has precedence over the file `$HOME/.tin/replyto` that may also contain a return address. |
| ADD_ADDRESS | This can contain an address to append to the return address when replying directly through mail to somebody whose mail address is not directly recognized by the local host. For example say the return address is `user@bigvax`, but `bigvax` is not recognized by your host, so therefore the mail will not reach `user`. But the host `littevax` is known to recognize your host and `bigvax`, so if `ADDADDRESS` is set (for example, `setenv ADD_ADDRESS @littevax` for `csh` or `set ADD_ADDRESS @littevax`<br>and `export ADD_ADDRESS` for `sh`), the address `user@bigvax@littlevax` will be used and the mail will reach `user@bigvax`. This variable has precedence over the file `$HOME/.tin/add_address`<br>that may also contain an address. |
| BUG_ADDRESS | If the `B` command bug report mail address is not correct, this variable should be set to the correct mail address. This variable has precedence over the file `$HOME/.tin/bug_address`<br>that may also contain a mail address. |
| MAILER | This variable has precedence over the default mailer that is used in all mailing operations within `tin` (for example, replying `rR`, and bug reports `B`). |
| VISUAL | This variable has precedence over the default editor (for example, `vi`) that is used in all editing operations within `tin` (for example, posting `w`, replying `rR`, follow-ups `fF`, and bug reports `B`). |
| AUTOSUBSCRIBE | `tin` interprets this variable similarly to `rn`. It contains a list of patterns, separated by commas and possibly prefixed with exclamation points. A new group is checked against the list of patterns; if it matches, `tin` subscribes the user to the group without further query. An exclamation point negates the meaning of a match on this pattern and can be used to cancel certain matches. For example, setting `AUTOSUBSCRIBE=comp.os.unix.*,talk.*,!talk.politics.*` will automatically subscribe the user to all newsgroups in the `comp.os.unix` hierarchy, and all talk groups other than `talk.politics` groups (which will be queried for as usual). |

AUTOUNSUBSCRIBE    tin interprets this variable similarly to rn. It is handled like the AUTOSUBSCRIBE variable, but groups matching the list are unsubscribed from without further query. For example, setting AUTOUNSUBSCRIBE=alt.flame.*,u*,!uk.* will automatically unsubscribe the user from all new alt.flame groups and all groups starting with u (university groups) other than UK groups (which will be queried for as usual).

## TIPS AND TRICKS

tin can pretty much be navigated by using the four cursor keys. The left-arrow key goes up a level, the right-arrow key goes down a level, the up-arrow key goes up a line (or page, at article viewer level) and the down-arrow key goes down a line (or page, at article viewer level).

The following newsgroups provide useful information concerning news software:

--news.software.readers    Information about news user agents tin, rn, nn, vn, and so on

--news.software.nntp    Information about NNTP

--news.software.b    Information about news transport agents Bnews, Cnews, and INN

--news.answers    Frequently asked questions (FAQs) about many different themes

Many prompts (for example, Mark everything as read? (y/n):) within tin offer a default choice that the cursor is positioned on. When you press <CR>, the default value is taken.

Many prompts (for example, Post subject []>) within tin can be aborted by pressing <ESC>.

When tin is run in an xterm window, it will resize itself each time the xterm is resized.

tin will reread the active file at set intervals to show any newly arrived news.

## xterm BUTTONS

If the environment variable TERM is set to xterm, then button pressing can be used to select groups and articles.

In the Group Selection menu, if the mouse is pointing before the group's listing region, the previous page is selected (just like b). If the mouse is pointing after the group's listing region, the next page is selected (just like space). If the mouse is pointing at a group, then

Left button    Moves to the group pointed at

Other buttons    Move to and select the group pointed at, just like <CR>

In the Article menu, if the mouse is pointing before the article listing region, the previous page is selected (just like b). If the mouse is pointing after the article listing region, the next page is selected (just like space). If the mouse is pointing at an article, then

Left button    Moves to the article pointed at

Center button    Reads next unread article from that pointed at, just like <TAB>

Right button    Reads article pointed at, just like <CR>

In the Thread menu, if the mouse is pointing before the article listing region, the previous page is selected (just like b). If the mouse is pointing after the article listing region, the next page is selected (just like space). If the mouse is pointing at an article, then

Left button    Moves to the article pointed at

Center button    Reads next unread article from that pointed at, just like <TAB>

Right button    Reads article pointed at, just like <CR>

In the Spool Selection menu, if the mouse is pointing before the spool listing region, the previous page is selected (just like b). If the mouse is pointing after the spool listing region, the next page is selected (just like space). If the mouse is pointing at a spool selection, then

| | |
|---|---|
| Left button | Moves to the spool pointed at |
| Other buttons | Move to and select the spool pointed at, just like `<CR>` |

In other menus and areas, button pressing reverts back to usual cut and paste of `xterm`, but after one click of any button.

## FILES

| | |
|---|---|
| `$HOME/.newsrc` | Subscribed to newsgroups |
| `$HOME/.newsauth` | nntpserver password pairs for NNTP servers that require authorization |
| `$HOME/.tin/tinrc` | Options |
| `$HOME/.tin/attributes` | Contains user-specified group attributes |
| `$HOME/.tin/.index` | Newsgroups index files directory |
| `$HOME/.tin/.mailidx` | Mailgroups index files directory |
| `$HOME/.tin/.saveidx` | Saved newsgroups index files directory |
| `$HOME/.tin/active.mail` | Active file of users mailgroups |
| `$HOME/.tin/active.save` | Active file of users saved newsgroups |
| `$HOME/.tin/add_address` | Address to add to when replying through mail |
| `$HOME/.tin/bug address` | Address to send bug reports to |
| `$HOME/.tin/kill` | Article kill and autoselection file |
| `$HOME/.tin/organization` | String to replace default organization |
| `$HOME/.tin/posted` | History of articles posted by user |
| `$HOME/.tin/replyto` | Host address to use in "Reply-To:" mail header |
| `$HOME/.signature` | Signature |
| `$HOME/.Sig` | Signature |
| `$HOME/.sigfixed` | Fixed part of a randomly generated signature |
| `/usr/lib/news/motd` | News message-of-the-day file |
| `/usr/lib/news/newsgroups` | Short description of all newsgroups |
| `/usr/lib/news/subscriptions` | List of newsgroups to subscribe first-time user to |

## BUGS

There are bugs somewhere among the creeping featurism. Any bugs found should be reported by the B (bug report) command.

Coredumps when setting certain toggle options from the Options menu at article viewer level.

Coredumps when killing last article in a thread at article viewer level.

## HISTORY

Based on the `tass` newsreader that was developed by Rich Skrenta and posted to `alt.sources` in March 1991. `tass` was itself heavily influenced by NOTES, which was developed at the University of Illinois by Ray Essick and Rob Kolstad in 1982.

`v1.0` PL0 (full) was posted in eight parts to `alt.sources` on 23 Aug 1991. `v1.0` PL1 (full) was posted in eight parts to `alt.sources` on 03 Sep 1991. `v1.0` PL2 (full) was posted in nine parts to `alt.sources` on 24 Sep 1991. `v1.0` PL3 (patch) was posted in four parts to `alt.sources` on 30 Sep 1991. `v1.0` PL4 (patch) was posted in two parts to `alt.sources` on 02 Oct 1991. `v1.0` PL5 (patch) was posted in four parts to `alt.sources` on 17 Oct 1991. `v1.0` PL6 (patch) was posted in five parts to `alt.sources` on 27 Nov 1991. `v1.0` PL7 (patch) was posted in two parts to `alt.sources` on 27 Nov 1991. `v1.1` PL0 (full) was posted in eleven parts to `alt.sources` on 13 Feb 1992. `v1.1` PL1 (full) was posted in twelve parts to `alt.sources` on 24 Mar 1992. `v1.1` PL2 (patch) was posted in four parts to `alt.sources` on 30 Mar 1992. `v1.1` PL3 (full) was posted in fifteen parts to `alt.sources` on 13 May 1992. `v1.1` PL4 (full) was posted in fifteen parts to `alt.sources` on 22 Jun 1992. `v1.1` PL5 (patch) was posted in seven parts to `alt.sources` on 11 Aug 1992. `v1.1` PL6 (full) was posted in fifteen parts to `alt.sources` on 14 Sep 1992. `v1.1` `PL7` (patch) was posted in ten parts to `alt.sources` on 15 Nov 1992. `v1.1` `PL8` (patch) was posted in six parts to `alt.sources` on 06 Dec 1992. `v1.1` `PL9` (patch) was posted in three parts to `alt.sources` on 20 Mar 1993. `v1.2` `PL0` (full) was posted in fourteen parts to `alt.sources` on 25 May 1993. `v1.2` `PL1` (patch) was posted in eight parts to `alt.sources` on 14 Jul 1993. `v1.2` `PL2` (patch) was posted in parts to `alt.sources` in September 1993.

## CREDITS

| | |
|---|---|
| Rich Skrenta | Author of `tass` v3.2, which this newsreader used as its base |
| Bill Davidsen | Author of `envarg.c` environment variable reading routine |
| Mike Gleason | Author of `sigfile.c` random signature generation routines |
| Arnold Robbins | Author of `strftime.c` date formatting routine |
| Jim Robinson | Coauthor of `kill.c` article kill and autoselection routines |
| Rich Salz | Author of `wildmat.c` pattern matching and `parsedate.y` date parsing routines |
| Dave Taylor | Author of `curses.c` from the `elm` mailreader |
| Chris Thewalt | Author of `getline.c` emacs-style editing routine |
| Mark Tomlinson | For porting `tin` to the AmigaDOS operating system |
| Andreas Wrede | For porting `tin` to the OS/2 operating system |
| Dieter Becker | For generously posting certain releases for me when my net connection was removed by a group of very short-sighted people |

I wish to thank the following people for supplying patches:

David Abbott, Earle Ake, Joachim Astel, Anton Aylward, George Baltz, Paul Bauwens, Dieter Becker, Dan Berry, David Binderman, Fokke de Boer, Mark Boucher, Herman ten Brugge, Leila Burrell-Davis, Peter Castro, Robert Claeson, Steven Cogswell, Don Costello, Bryan Curnutt, Ned Danieley, Chris Davies, John Davis, Tom Dickey, Bryan Dongray, Craig Durland, Kirk Edson, Stefan Elf, Rob Engle, Brent Ermlick, Olle Eriksson, Michael Faurot, Werner Fleck, Callum Gibson, Mike Glendinning, Philippe Goujard, Carl Hage, Paul Halsema, Ed Hanway, Scott Hauck, Per Headland, Daniel Hermans, Jose Herrero, Tom Hite, Torsten Homeyer, Tommy Hsieh, Steve Hunt, Pieter Immelman, Robbin John-son, Nelson Kading, Fritz Kleeman, Dwarven Knight, Karl-Koenig Koenigsson, Martin Kraemer, Kris Kugel, Geoff Lane, Alex Lange, Alain Lasserre, Marty Leisner, Hakan Lennestal, Otto Lind, Richard Lloyd, Clifford Luke, David MacKenzie, Hugh Mahon, Kazushi Marukawa, Owen Medd, Soren Moller, Sergio Morales, Michael Morrell, Klaus Mueller, Udo Munk, James Nugen, Jeb Palmer, Neil Parker, Tom Parry, Jim Patterson, Walter Pelissero, Colin Perkins, Eric Peterson, Tim Pierce, Bill Poitras, Wolfgang Prediger, Ted Richards, Ollivier Robert, Jim Robinson, Stephen Roseman, Clifton Royston, Nicko-lay Saukh, Rich Salz, Gary Sanders, John Sauter, Christopher Sawtell, John Schmitz, Bart Sears, Karl Olav Serrander, Doug Sewell, Philip Shearer, Mark Smith, Steve Spearman, Cliff Stanford, Steve Starck, Jason Steiner, Ed Sznyter, Derek Terveer, Julian Thompson, Andry Timonin, Mark Tomlin, Michael Traub, Adri Verhoef, Paul Vickers, Cary Whitney, Greg Woods, Lloyd Wright

I wish to thank the following people for bug reports/comments:

Jack Applin, Klaus Arzig, Scott Babb, Reiner Balling, Preston Bannister, Bill de Beabien, Volker Beyer, Etienne Bido, Roger Binns, Georg Biehler, Jean-Marc Bonnaudet, Eric Bowles, Sean Brady, Ian Brown, Andreas Brosig, Craig Bruce, Brett Carver,Tom Czarnik, Dave Datta, Mat Davis, Karl Denninger, Klaus Dimmler, David Donovan, Peter Dressler, Gerhard Ermer, Hugh Fader, Miguel Farah, Joachim Feld, Paul Fox, Jay Geertsen, Herschel Gelman, Bernhard Gmelch, Jason Haar, Viet Hoang, Andy Jackson, Joe Johnson, Ralph Jud, Cyrill Jung, Kuo-Chein Kai, Tonis Kelder, Hans-Juergen Knopp, Sridhar Komandur, Tom Kovar, Bernhard Kroenung, Murray Laing, Per Lindqvist, Eric Litman, Bob Lukas, Michael Marshall, Kazushi Marukawa, Olaf Mittelstaedt, Phillip Molloy, Phil Molyneux, Toni Metz, Greg Miller, Deeptendu Majumder, Klaus Neuberger, Otto Niesser, Reiner Oelhaf, Alex Pakter, John Palkovic, Dave Pascoe, Wolf Paul, Andrew Phillips, Stefan Rathmann, Jon Robinson, David Ross, Jonas Rwgmyr, Malkani Sanjay, Daemon Schae-fer, Dean Schrimpf, Klamer Schutte, Fredy Schwatz, Dave Schweisguth, Bernd Schwerin, Don Sheythe, Chris Smith, Daniel Smith, Richard Stanton, Ralf Stephan, Hironobu Taka-hashi, Ken Taylor, Tony Travis, Paul Verket, Sven Werner, Dick Wexelblat, Paul Wood, Gregory Woodbury, Norm Yamane, Blair Zajac, Orest Zboroski, Thomas Ziegler

## AUTHOR

Iain Lea (`iain.lea@erlm.siemens.de`)

*Version 1.2 PL2*

# tload

`tload`—Graphic representation of system load average

## SYNOPSIS

`tload [-s scale] [-d delay] [tty]`

## DESCRIPTION

`tload` prints a graph of the current system load average to the specified `tty` (or the `tty` of the `tload` process if none is specified).

## OPTIONS

The `-s scale` option allows a vertical scale to be specified for the display (in characters between graph ticks); thus, a smaller value represents a larger scale, and vice versa.

The `-d delay` sets the delay between graph updates in seconds.

## FILES

`/proc/loadavg`          Load average information

## SEE ALSO

ps(1), top(1), uptime(1), w(1)

## BUGS

The `-d delay` option sets the time argument for an `alarm(2)`; if `-d 0` is specified, the alarm is set to `0`, which will never send the `SIGALRM` and update the display.

## AUTHORS

Branko Lankester, David Engel (`david@ods.com`), and Michael K. Johnson (`johnsonm@sunsite.unc.edu`)

*Cohesive Systems, 20 March 1993*

# top

`top`—Display top CPU processes

## SYNOPSIS

`top [-][ddelay][q][S][s][i]`

## DESCRIPTION

`top` provides an ongoing look at processor activity in real time. It displays a listing of the most CPU-intensive tasks on the system, and can provide an interactive interface for manipulating processes.

## COMMAND-LINE OPTIONS

d           Specifies the delay between screen updates. You can change this with the s interactive command.

q           This causes top to refresh without any delay. If the caller has superuser privileges, top runs with the highest possible priority.

S           Specifies cumulative mode, where each process is listed with the CPU time that it as well as its dead children has spent. This is like the -S flag to ps(1). See the discussion of the S interactive command later in this manual page.

s           Tells top to run in secure mode. This disables the potentially dangers of the interactive commands. (See "Interactive Commands," later in this manual page.) A secure top is a nifty thing to leave running on a spare terminal.

i           Start top, ignoring any idle or zombie processes. (See the interactive command i.)

## FIELD DESCRIPTIONS

top displays a variety of information about the processor state. The display is updated every five seconds by default, but you can change that with the d command-line option or the s interactive command.

uptime      This line displays the time the system has been up, and the three load averages for the system. The load averages are the average number of process ready to run during the last 1, 5, and 15 minutes. This line is just like the output of uptime(1).

processes   The total number of processes running at the time of the last update. This is also broken down into the number of tasks that are running, sleeping, stopped, or undead.

CPU states  Shows the percentage of CPU time in user mode, system mode, niced tasks, and idle. (Niced tasks are only those whose nice value is negative.) Time spent in niced tasks will also be counted in system and user time, so the total will be more than 100 percent.

Mem         Statistics on memory usage, including total available memory, free memory, used memory, shared memory, and memory used for buffers.

Swap        Statistics on swap space, including total swap space, available swap space, and used swap space. This and Mem are just like the output of free(1).

PID         The process ID of each task.

USER        The username of the task's owner.

PRI         The priority of the task.

NI          The nice value of the task. Negative nice values are lower priority.

SIZE        The size of the task's code plus data plus stack space, in kilobytes, is shown here.

RSS         The total amount of physical memory used by the task, in kilobytes, is shown here.

SHRD        The amount of shared memory used by the task is shown in this column.

ST          The state of the task is shown here. The state is either S for sleeping, D for uninterruptible sleep, R for running, Z for zombies, or T for stopped or traced.

TIME        Total CPU time the task has used since it started. If cumulative mode is on, this also includes the CPU time used by the process's children that have died. You can set cumulative mode with the S command-line option or toggle it with the interactive command S.

%CPU        The task's share of the CPU time since the last screen update, expressed as a percentage of total CPU time.

%MEM        The task's share of the physical memory.

COMMAND     The task's command name, which will be truncated if it is too long to be displayed on one line. Tasks in memory will have a full command line, but swapped-out tasks will only have the name of the program in parentheses, for example, (getty).

## INTERACTIVE COMMANDS

Several single-key commands are recognized while top is running. Some are disabled if the s option has been given on the command line.

^L            Erases and redraws the screen.

h or ?        Displays a help screen giving a brief summary of commands, and the status of secure and cumulative modes.

k             Kill a process. You will be prompted for the PID of the task, and the signal to send to it. For a normal kill, send signal 15. For a sure, but rather abrupt, kill, send signal 9. The default signal, as with kill(1), is 15, SIGTERM. This command is not available in secure mode.

i             Ignore idle and zombie processes. This is a toggle switch.

n or #        Change the number of processes to show. You will be prompted to enter the number. This overrides automatic determination of the number of processes to show, which is based on window size measurement. If 0 is specified, then top will show as many processes as will fit on the screen; this is the default.

q             Quit.

r             Renice a process. You will be prompted for the PID of the task, and the value to nice it to. Entering a positive value will cause a process to be niced to negative values, and lose priority. If root is running top, a negative value can be entered, causing a process to get a higher than normal priority. The default renice value is 10. This command is not available in secure mode.

S             This toggles cumulative mode, the equivalent of ps -S, in other words, that CPU times will include a process's defunct children. For some programs, such as compilers, which work by forking into many separate tasks, normal mode will make them appear less demanding than they actually are. For others, however, such as shells and init, this behavior is correct. In any case, try cumulative mode for an alternative view of CPU use.

s             Change the delay between updates. You will be prompted to enter the delay time, in seconds, between updates. Fractional values are recognized down to microseconds. Entering 0 causes continuous updates. The default value is 5 seconds. Note that low values cause nearly unreadably fast displays, and greatly raise the load. This command is not available in secure mode.

## NOTES

This proc-based top works by reading the files in the proc filesystem, mounted on /proc. If /proc is not mounted, top will not work.

%CPU shows the cputime/realtime percentage in the period of time between updates. For the first update, a short delay is used, and top itself dominates the CPU usage. After that, top will drop back, and a more reliable estimate of CPU usage is available.

The SIZE and RSS fields don't count the page tables and the task struct of a process; this is at least 12K of memory that is always resident. SIZE is the virtual size of the process (code+data+stack).

Keep in mind that a process must die for its time to be recorded on its parent by cumulative mode. Perhaps more useful behavior would be to follow each process upwards, adding time, but that would be more expensive, possibly prohibitively so. In any case, that would make top's behavior incompatible with ps.

## SEE ALSO

ps(1), free(1), uptime(1), kill(1), renice(1).

## BUGS

If the window is less than about 70×7, top will not format information correctly.

## AUTHOR

top was originally written by Roger Binns, based on Branko Lankester's (lankeste@fwi.uva.nl) ps program. Robert Nation (nation@rocket.sanders.lockheed.com) rewrote it significantly to use the proc filesystem, based on Michael K. Johnson's (johnsonm@sunsite.unc.edu) proc-based ps program. Many changes were made, including secure and cumulative modes and a general cleanup, by Michael Shields (mjshield@nyx.cs.du.edu).

# touch

touch—Change file timestamps

## SYNOPSIS

touch [-acfm] [-r *reference-file*] [-t MMDDhhmm[[CC]YY][.ss]] [-d *time*]
[--time={*atime, access, use, mtime, modify*}] [--date=*time*] [--file=*reference-file*]
[--no-create] [--help] [--version] *file*...

## DESCRIPTION

This manual page documents the GNU version of touch. touch changes the access and modification times of each given file to the current time. Files that do not exist are created empty. If the first filename given would be a valid argument to the -t option and no timestamp is given with any of the -d, -r, or -t options and the -- argument is not given, that argument is interpreted as the time for the other files instead of as a filename.

If changing both the access and modification times to the current time, touch can change the timestamps for files that the user running it does not own but has write permission for. Otherwise, the user must own the files.

## OPTIONS

| | |
|---|---|
| -a, --time=*atime*, <br> --time=*access*, <br> --time=*use* | Change the access time only. |
| -c, --no-create | Do not create files that do not exist. |
| -d, --date *time* | Use *time* (which can be in various common formats) instead of the current time. It can contain month names, time zones, am and pm, and so on. |
| -f | Ignored; for compatibility with BSD versions of touch. |
| -m, --time=*mtime*, <br> --time=*modify* | Change the modification time only. |
| -r, --file *reference-file* | Use the times of *reference-file* instead of the current time. |
| -t *MMDDhhmm[[CC]YY][.ss]* | Use the argument (months, days, hours, minutes, optional century and years, optional seconds) instead of the current time. |
| --help | Print a usage message on standard output and exit successfully. |
| --version | Print version information on standard output, then exit successfully. |

*GNU File Utilities*

# tr

tr—Translate or delete characters

## SYNOPSIS

tr [-cst] [--complement] [--squeeze-repeats] [--truncate-set1] *string1 string2*

tr f-s,--squeeze-repeatsg [-c] [--complement] *string1*

tr f-d,--deleteg [-c] *string1*

tr f-d,--deleteg f-s,--squeeze-repeatsg [-c] [--complement] *string1 string2*

GNU tr also accepts the --help and --version options.

## DESCRIPTION

This manual page documents the GNU version of tr. tr copies the standard input to the standard output, performing one of the following operations:

- Translate and optionally squeeze repeated characters in the result
- Squeeze repeated characters
- Delete characters
- Delete characters, then squeeze repeated characters from the result.

The *string1* and (if given) *string2* arguments define ordered sets of characters, referred to below as *set1* and *set2*. These sets are the characters of the input that tr operates on. The --complement (-c) option replaces *set1* with its complement (all of the characters that are not in *set1*).

## SPECIFYING SETS OF CHARACTERS

The format of the *string1* and *string2* arguments resembles the format of regular expressions; however, they are not regular expressions, only lists of characters. Most characters simply represent themselves in these strings, but the strings can contain the shorthands in the following list, for convenience. Some of them can be used only in *string1* or *string2*, as noted.

**Backslash escapes**. A backslash followed by a character not listed causes an error message.

| | |
|---|---|
| \a | Control-G |
| \b | Control-H |
| \f | Control-L |
| \n | Control-J |
| \r | Control-M |
| \t | Control-I |
| \v | Control-K |
| \ooo | The character with the value given by ooo, which is 1 to 3 octal digits |
| \n | A backslash |

**Ranges**. The notation m-n expands to all of the characters from m through n, in ascending order. m should collate before n; if it doesn't, an error results. As an example, 0–9 is the same as 0123456789. Although GNU tr does not support the System V syntax that uses square brackets to enclose ranges, translations specified in that format will still work as long as the brackets in *string1* correspond to identical brackets in *string2*.

**Repeated characters**. The notation [c*n] in *string2* expands to n copies of character c. Thus, [y*6] is the same as yyyyyy. The notation [c*] in *string2* expands to as many copies of c as are needed to make *set2* as long as *set1*. If n begins with a 0, it is interpreted in octal, otherwise in decimal.

**Character classes**. The notation [:class-name:] expands to all of the characters in the (predefined) class named class-name. The characters expand in no particular order, except for the upper and lower classes, which expand in ascending order. When the --delete (-d) and --squeeze-repeats (-s) options are both given, any character class can be used in *string2*. Otherwise, only the character classes lower and upper are accepted in *string2*, and then only if the corresponding character class (upper and lower, respectively) is specified in the same relative position in *string1*. Doing this specifies case conversion. The class names are given in the following list; an error results when an invalid class name is given.

| | |
|---|---|
| alnum | Letters and digits |
| alpha | Letters |
| blank | Horizontal whitespace |
| cntrl | Control characters |
| digit | Digits |
| graph | Printable characters, not including space |
| lower | Lowercase letters |

| print | Printable characters, including space |
|-------|---------------------------------------|
| punct | Punctuation characters |
| space | Horizontal or vertical whitespace |
| upper | Uppercase letters |
| xdigit | Hexadecimal digits |

Equivalence classes. The syntax [=c=] expands to all of the characters that are equivalent to c, in no particular order. Equivalence classes are a recent invention intended to support non-English alphabets. But there seems to be no standard way to define them or determine their contents. Therefore, they are not fully implemented in GNU tr; each character's equivalence class consists only of that character, which makes this a useless construction currently.

## TRANSLATING

tr performs translation when *string1* and *string2* are both given and the --delete (-d) option is not given. tr translates each character of its input that is in *set1* to the corresponding character in *set2*. Characters not in *set1* are passed through unchanged. When a character appears more than once in *set1* and the corresponding characters in *set2* are not all the same, only the final one is used. For example, these two commands are equivalent:

```
tr aaa xyz
```

```
tr a z
```

A common use of tr is to convert lowercase characters to uppercase. This can be done in many ways. Here are three of them:

```
tr abcdefghijklmnopqrstuvwxyz ABCDEFGHIJKLMNOPQRSTUVWXYZ
```

```
tr a-z A-Z
```

```
tr '[:lower:]' '[:upper:]'
```

When tr is performing translation, *set1* and *set2* should normally have the same length. If *set1* is shorter than *set2*, the extra characters at the end of *set2* are ignored.

On the other hand, making *set1* longer than *set2* is not portable; POSIX.2 says that the result is undefined. In this situation, the BSD tr pads *set2* to the length of *set1* by repeating the last character of *set2* as many times as necessary. The System V tr truncates *set1* to the length of *set2*.

By default, GNU tr handles this case like the BSD tr does. When the --truncate-set1 (-t) option is given, GNU tr handles this case like the System V tr instead. This option is ignored for operations other than translation.

Acting like the System V tr in this case breaks the relatively common BSD idiom:

```
tr -cs A-Za-z0-9 'n012'
```

because it converts only zero bytes (the first element in the complement of *set1*), rather than all nonalphanumerics, to newlines.

## SQUEEZING REPEATS AND DELETING

When given just the --delete (-d) option, tr removes any input characters that are in *set1*.

When given just the --squeeze-repeats (-s) option, tr replaces each input sequence of a repeated character that is in *set1* with a single occurrence of that character.

When given both the --delete and the --squeeze-repeats options, tr first performs any deletions using *set1*, then squeezes repeats from any remaining characters using *set2*.

The --squeeze-repeats option may also be used when translating, in which case tr first performs translation, then squeezes repeats from any remaining characters using *set2*.

Here are some examples to illustrate various combinations of options.

Remove all zero bytes:

```
tr -d 'n000'
```

Put all words on lines by themselves. This converts all nonalphanumeric characters to newlines, then squeezes each string of repeated newlines into a single newline:

```
tr -cs '[a-zA-Z0-9]' '[nn*]'
```

Convert each sequence of repeated newlines to a single newline:

```
tr -s 'nn'
```

GNU tr also accepts the following options in any combination with the others.

| | |
|---|---|
| --help | Print a usage message and exit with a non-zero status. |
| --version | Print version information on standard output, then exit. |

## WARNING MESSAGES

Setting the environment variable POSIXLY_CORRECT turns off several warning and error messages, for strict compliance with POSIX.2. The messages normally occur in the following circumstances:

1. When the --delete option is given but --squeeze-repeats is not, and *string2* is given, GNU tr by default prints a usage message and exits, because *string2* would not be used. The POSIX specification says that *string2* must be ignored in this case. Silently ignoring arguments is a bad idea.
2. When an ambiguous octal escape is given. For example, n400 is actually n40 followed by the digit 0, because the value 400 octal does not fit into a single byte.

Note that GNU tr does not provide complete BSD or System V compatibility. For example, there is no option to disable interpretation of the POSIX constructs [:alpha:], [=c=], and [c*10]. Also, GNU tr does not delete zero bytes automatically, unlike traditional UNIX versions, which provide no way to preserve zero bytes.

*GNU Text Utilities*

# tset, reset

tset, reset—Terminal initialization

## SYNOPSIS

```
tset [-IQrs] [-t] [-e ch] [-i ch] [-k ch] [-m mapping] [terminal]

tset -h

tset -V

reset [-IQrs] [-t] [-e ch] [-i ch] [-k ch] [-m mapping] [terminal]

reset -h

reset -V
```

## DESCRIPTION

tset initializes terminals. tset first determines the type of terminal that you are using. This determination is done as follows, using the first terminal type found:

- The terminal argument specified on the command line
- The value of the TERM environmental variable
- The terminal type associated with the standard error output device in the /etc/ttytype file
- The default terminal type, unknown

If the terminal type was not specified on the command line, the -m option mappings are then applied (see the following section, "Options," for more information). Then, if the terminal type begins with a question mark (?), the user is prompted for confirmation of the terminal type. An empty response confirms the type, or, another type can be entered to specify a new type. After the terminal type has been determined, the termcap entry for the terminal is retrieved. If no termcap entry is found for the type, the user is prompted for another terminal type.

After the termcap entry is retrieved, the window size, backspace, interrupt, and line kill characters (among many other things) are set and the terminal and tab initialization strings are sent to the standard error output. Finally, if the erase, interrupt, and line kill characters have changed, or are not set to their default values, their values are displayed to the standard error output.

When invoked as reset, tset sets cooked and echo modes, turns off cbreak and raw modes, turns on newline translation and resets any unset special characters to their default values before doing the terminal initialization described above. This is useful after a program dies leaving a terminal in an abnormal state. Note, you may have to type <LF>reset<LF> (the line-feed character is normally control-J) to get the terminal to work, as carriage-return may no longer work in the abnormal state. Also, the terminal will often not echo the command.

## OPTIONS

The options are as follows:

-t  The terminal type is displayed to the standard output, and the terminal is not initialized in any way.

-e  Set the erase character to ch.

-I  Do not send the terminal or tab initialization strings to the terminal.

-i  Set the interrupt character to ch.

-k  Set the line kill character to ch.

-m  Specify a mapping from a port type to a terminal. See the following section, "Setting the Environment," for more information.

-r  Print the terminal type to the standard error output.

-s  Print the sequence of shell commands to initialize the environment variables COLUMNS, LINES, TERM, and TERMCAP to the standard output.

Q  Don't display any values for the erase, interrupt, and line kill characters.

-w  Force setting of display size as defined in /etc/termcap file.

-h  Print short usage message.

-V  Print version number.

The arguments for the -e, -i, and -k options may either be entered as actual characters or by using the hat notation, for example, control-h may be specified as ^ H or ^ h.

## SETTING THE ENVIRONMENT

It is often desirable to set the terminal type and information about the terminal's capabilities and display size in the shell's environment. This is done with the -s option; when this option is specified, the commands to enter the information into the shell's environment are output to the standard output. If the SHELL environmental variable ends in csh, the output commands are for the csh(1); otherwise, they are for sh(1). Note, the output commands for the csh set and unset the shell variable noglob. The following line in the .login or .profile files will initialize the environment correctly:

```
eval 'tset -s options ... '
```

## TERMINAL TYPE MAPPING

When the terminal is not hardwired into the system (or the current system information is incorrect), the terminal type derived from the /etc/ttytype file or the TERM environmental variable is often something generic like network, dialup, or unknown. When tset is used in a startup script .profile for sh(1) users or .login for csh(1) users), it is often desirable to provide information about the type of terminal used on such ports. The purpose of the -m option is to map from some set of conditions to a terminal type; that is, to tell tset, "If I'm on this port at a particular speed, guess that I'm on that kind of terminal."

The argument to the -m option consists of an optional port type, an optional operator, an optional baud rate specification, an optional colon (:) character, and a terminal type. The port type is a string (delimited by either the operator or the colon character). The operator may be any combination of: &>, &<, &@, and &!; &> means greater than, &< means less than, &@ means equal to, and &! inverts the sense of the test. The baud rate is specified as a number and is compared with the speed of the standard error output (which should be the control terminal). The terminal type is a string.

If the terminal type is not specified on the command line, the -m mappings are applied to the terminal type. If the port type and baud rate match the mapping, the terminal type specified in the mapping replaces the current type. If more than one mapping is specified, the first applicable mapping is used.

For example, consider the following:

```
dialup>9600:vt100
```

The port type is dialup, the operator is >, the baud rate specification is 9600, and the terminal type is vt100 . The result of this mapping is to specify that if the terminal type is dialup, and the baud rate is greater than 9600 baud, a terminal type of vt100 will be used.

If no port type is specified, the terminal type will match any port type; for example,

```
-m dialup:vt100 -m :?xterm
```

will cause any dialup port, regardless of baud rate, to match the terminal type:

```
vt100,
```

and any nondialup port type to match the terminal type:

```
?xterm.
```

Note, because of the leading question mark, the user will be queried on a default port as to whether they are actually using an xterm terminal.

No whitespace characters are permitted in the -m option argument. Also, to avoid problems with metacharacters, it is suggested that the entire -m option argument be placed within single quote characters, and that csh users insert a backslash character (\) before any exclamation marks (!).

## ENVIRONMENT

The tset command utilizes the SHELL and TERM environment variables.

tset can set COLUMNS, LINES, TERM, and TERMCAP environmental variables.

## FILES

/etc/ttytype system     Port name to terminal type mapping database

/etc/termcap               Terminal capability database

## SEE ALSO

csh(1), tcsh(1), sh(1),bash(1),stty(1), tty(4), termcap(5), ttytype(5), environ(7)

## HISTORY

The tset command appeared in BSD 3.0.

## COMPATIBILITY

The -A, -E, -h, -S, -u, and -v options have been deleted from the tset utility. None of them were documented in 4.3BSD and all are of limited utility at best. The -a, -d, and -p options are similarly not documented or useful, but were retained as they appear to be in widespread use. It is strongly recommended that any usage of these three options be changed to use the -m option instead. The -n option remains, but has no effect. It is still permissible to specify the -e, -i, and -k options without arguments, although it is strongly recommended that such usage be fixed to explicitly specify the character.

Executing tset as reset no longer implies the -Q option. Also, the interaction between the - option and the terminal argument in some historic implementations of tset has been removed and has been replaced with -t option.

Finally, the tset implementation has been completely redone as part of the addition to the system of a IEEE Std1003.1-1988 (POSIX) -compliant terminal interface and will no longer compile on systems with older terminal interfaces.

*Linux, 12 January 1995*

# tsort

tsort—Topological sort of a directed graph

## SYNOPSIS

tsort [*file*]

## DESCRIPTION

tsort takes a list of pairs of node names representing directed arcs in a graph and prints the nodes in topological order on standard output. Input is taken from the named file, or from standard input if no file is given.

Node names in the input are separated by whitespace, and there must be an even number of nodes.

Presence of a node in a graph can be represented by an arc from the node to itself. This is useful when a node is not connected to any other nodes.

If the graph contains a cycle (and therefore cannot be properly sorted), one of the arcs in the cycle is ignored and the sort continues. Cycles are reported on standard error.

## SEE ALSO

ar(1)

## HISTORY

A tsort command appeared in AT&T v7. This tsort command and manual page are derived from sources contributed to Berkeley by Michael Rendell of Memorial University of Newfoundland.

*23 April 1991*

# twm

twm—Tab Window Manager for the X Window System

## SYNTAX

twm [ -display *dpy* ][ -s ][ -f *initfile* ][ -v ]

## DESCRIPTION

twm is a window manager for the X Window System. It provides titlebars, shaped windows, several forms of icon management, user-defined macro functions, click-to-type and pointer-driven keyboard focus, and user-specified key and pointer button bindings.

This program is usually started by the user's session manager or startup script. When used from xdm(1) or xinit(1) without a session manager, twm is frequently executed in the foreground as the last client. When run this way, exiting twm causes the session to be terminated (logged out).

By default, application windows are surrounded by a "frame" with a titlebar at the top and a special border around the window. The titlebar contains the window's name, a rectangle that is lit when the window is receiving keyboard input, and function boxes known as *titlebuttons* at the left and right edges of the titlebar.

Pressing pointer Button1 (usually the leftmost button unless it has been changed with xmodmap) on a titlebutton will invoke the function associated with the button. In the default interface, windows are iconified by clicking (pressing and then immediately releasing) the left titlebutton (which looks like a dot). Conversely, windows are deiconified by clicking in the associated icon or entry in the icon manager. (See description of the variable Show-IconManager and of the function f.showiconmgr.)

Windows are resized by pressing the right titlebutton (which resembles a group of nested squares), dragging the pointer over the edge that is to be moved, and releasing the pointer when the outline of the window is the desired size. Similarly, windows are moved by pressing in the title or highlight region, dragging a window outline to the new location, and then releasing when the outline is in the desired position. Just clicking in the title or highlight region raises the window without moving it.

When new windows are created, twm will honor any size and location information requested by the user (usually through -geometry command-line argument or resources for the individual applications). Otherwise, an outline of the window's default size, its titlebar, and lines dividing the window into a 3×3 grid that track the pointer are displayed. Clicking pointer Button1 will position the window at the current position and give it the default size. Pressing pointer Button2 (usually the middle pointer button) and dragging the outline will give the window its current position but allow the sides to be resized as described above. Clicking pointer Button3 (usually the right pointer button) will give the window its current position but attempt to make it long enough to touch the bottom of the screen.

## OPTIONS

twm accepts the following command-line options:

| | |
|---|---|
| -display *dpy* | This option specifies the X server to use. |
| -s | This option indicates that only the default screen (as specified by -display or by the DISPLAY environment variable) should be managed. By default, twm will attempt to manage all screens on the display. |
| -f *filename* | This option specifies the name of the startup file to use. By default, twm will look in the user's home directory for files named .twmrc.num (where num is a screen number) or .twmrc. |
| -v | This option indicates that twm should print error messages whenever an unexpected X Error event is received. This can be useful when debugging applications but can be distracting in regular use. |

## CUSTOMIZATION

Much of twm's appearance and behavior can be controlled by providing a startup file in one of the following locations (searched in order for each screen being managed when twm begins):

| | |
|---|---|
| $HOME/.twmrc.*screennumber* | The *screennumber* is a small positive number (for example, 0, 1, and so on) representing the screen number (for example, the last number in the DISPLAY environment variable host:displaynum.screennum) that would be used to contact that screen of the display. This is intended for displays with multiple screens of differing visual types. |
| $HOME/.twmrc | This is the usual name for an individual user's startup file. |
| <XRoot>/lib/X11/twm/system.twmrc | If neither of the preceding files are found, twm will look in this file for a default configuration. This is often tailored by the site administrator to provide convenient menus or familiar bindings for novice users. <XRoot> refers to the root of the X11 install tree. |

If no startup files are found, twm will use the built-in defaults described. The only resource used by twm is bitmapFilePath for a colon-separated list of directories to search when looking for bitmap files. For more information, see the Athena Widgets manual and xrdb(1).

twm startup files are logically broken up into three types of specifications: Variables, Bindings, and Menus. The Variables section must come first and is used to describe the fonts, colors, cursors, border widths, icon and window placement, highlighting, autoraising, layout of titles, warping, and use of the icon manager. The Bindings section usually comes second and is used to specify the functions that should be invoked when keyboard and pointer buttons are pressed in windows, icons, titles, and frames. The Menus section gives any user-defined menus (containing functions to be invoked or commands to be executed).

Variable names and keywords are case-insensitive. Strings must be surrounded by double quote characters (for example, "blue") and are case-sensitive. A pound sign (#) outside of a string causes the remainder of the line in which the character appears to be treated as a comment.

## VARIABLES

Many of the aspects of twm's user interface are controlled by variables that may be set in the user's startup file. Some of the options are enabled or disabled simply by the presence of a particular keyword. Other options require keywords, numbers, strings, or lists of all of these.

Lists are surrounded by braces and are usually separated by whitespace or a newline. For example,

```
AutoRaise { "emacs" "XTerm" "Xmh" }
```

or

```
AutoRaise
{
    "emacs"
    "XTerm"
    "Xmh"
}
```

When a variable containing a list of strings representing windows is searched (for example, to determine whether or not to enable autoraise, as shown in the preceding example), a string must be an exact, case-sensitive match to the window's name (given by the WM_NAME window property), resource name, or class name (both given by the WM_CLASS window property). The preceding example would enable autoraise on windows named emacs as well as any xterm (because they are of class XTerm) or xmh windows (which are of class Xmh).

String arguments that are interpreted as filenames (see Pixmaps, Cursors, and IconDirectory in the following list of variables) will prepend the user's directory (specified by the HOME environment variable) if the first character is a tilde (˜). If, instead, the first character is a colon (:), the name is assumed to refer to one of the internal bitmaps that are used to create the default titlebars symbols: :xlogo or :delete (both refer to the X logo), :dot or :iconify (both refer to the dot), :resize (the nested squares used by the resize button), :menu (a page with lines), and :question (the question mark used for nonexistent bitmap files).

The following variables may be specified at the top of a twm startup file. Lists of Window name prefix strings are indicated by *win-list*. Optional arguments are shown in square brackets:

| | |
|---|---|
| AutoRaise { *win-list* ] | This variable specifies a list of windows that should automatically be raised whenever the pointer enters the window. This action can be interactively enabled or disabled on individual windows using the function f.autoraise. |
| AutoRelativeResize | This variable indicates that dragging out a window size (either when initially sizing the window with pointer Button2 or when resizing it) should not wait until the pointer has crossed the window edges. Instead, moving the pointer automatically causes the nearest edge or edges to move by the same amount. This allows the resizing of windows that extend off the edge of the screen. If the pointer is in the center of the window, or if the resize is begun |

by pressing a titlebutton, twm will still wait for the pointer to cross a window edge (to prevent accidents). This option is particularly useful for people who like the press-drag-release method of sweeping out window sizes.

| | |
|---|---|
| BorderColor *string* windows, [{ *wincolorlist* }] | This variable specifies the default color of the border to be placed around all noniconified and may only be given within a Color, Grayscale, or Monochrome list. The optional wincolorlist specifies a list of window and color name pairs for specifying particular border colors for different types of windows. For example: |

```
BorderColor
"gray50"
{
"XTerm" "red"
"xmh" "green"
}
```

The default is black.

| | |
|---|---|
| BorderTileBackground *wincolorlist* }] | This variable specifies the default background color in the gray pattern used in *string* [{ unhighlighted borders (only if NoHighlight hasn't been set), and may only be given within a Color, Grayscale, or Monochrome list. The optional wincolorlist allows per-window colors to be specified. The default is white. |
| BorderTileForeground *string* [{ *wincolorlist* }] | This variable specifies the default foreground color in the gray pattern used in unhighlighted borders (only if NoHighlight hasn't been set), and may only be given within a Color, Grayscale, or Monochrome list. The optional wincolorlist allows per-window colors to be specified. The default is black. |
| BorderWidth *pixels* | This variable specifies the width in pixels of the border surrounding all client window frames if ClientBorderWidth has not been specified. This value is also used to set the border size of windows created by twm (such as the icon manager). The default is 2. |
| ButtonIndent *pixels* | This variable specifies the amount by which titlebuttons should be indented on all sides. Positive values cause the buttons to be smaller than the window text and highlight area so that they stand out. Setting this and the TitleButtonBorderWidth variables to 0 makes titlebuttons as tall and wide as possible. The default is 1. |
| ClientBorderWidth | This variable indicates that border width of a window's frame should be set to the initial border width of the window, rather than to the value of BorderWidth. |
| Color { *colors-list* } | This variable specifies a list of color assignments to be made if the default display is capable of displaying more than simple black and white. The *colors-list* is made up of the following color variables and their values: |

```
DefaultBackground
DefaultForeground
MenuBackground
MenuForeground
MenuTitleBackground
MenuTitleForeground
MenuShadowColor
PointerForeground
PointerBackground
```

The following color variables may also be given a list of window and color name pairs to allow per-window colors to be specified (see BorderColor for details):

```
BorderColor
IconManagerHighlight
BorderTitleBackground
BorderTitleForeground
TitleBackground
```

```
                              TitleForeground
                              IconBackground
                              IconForeground
                              IconBorderColor
                              IconManagerBackground
                              IconManagerForeground
```

For example:

```
Color
{
MenuBackground "gray50"
MenuForeground "blue"
BorderColor "red" { "XTerm" "yellow" }
TitleForeground "yellow"
TitleBackground "blue"
}
```

All of these color variables may also be specified for the Monochrome variable, allowing the same initialization file to be used on both color and monochrome displays.

**ConstrainedMoveTime**
***milliseconds***

This variable specifies the length of time between button clicks needed to begin a constrained move peration. Double-clicking within this amount of time when invoking f.move will cause the window to be moved only in a horizontal or vertical direction. Setting this value to 0 will disable constrained moves. The default is 400 milliseconds.

**Cursors { *cursor-list* }**

This variable specifies the glyphs that twm should use for various pointer cursors. Each cursor may be defined either from the cursor font or from two bitmap files. Shapes from the cursor font may be specified directly as

`0 cursorname "string"`

where *cursorname* is one of the cursor names listed below, and *string* is the name of a glyph as found in the file:

`<XRoot>/include/X11/cursorfont.h`

(without the XC prefix). If the cursor is to be defined from bitmap files, the following syntax is used instead:

`0 cursorname "image" "mask"`

The *image* and *mask* strings specify the names of files containing the glyph image and mask in bitmap(1) form. The bitmap files are located in the same manner as icon bitmap files. The following example shows the default cursor definitions:

```
Cursors
{
Frame        "top_left_arrow"
Title        "top_left_arrow"
Icon         "top_left_arrow"
IconMgr      "top_left_arrow"
Move         "fleur"
Resize       "fleur"
Menu         "sb_left_arrow"
Button       "hand2"
Wait         "watch"
Select       "dot"
Destroy      "pirate"
}
```

**DecorateTransients**

This variable indicates that transient windows (those containing a WM_TRANSIENT_FOR property) should have titlebars. By default, transients are not reparented.

**DefaultBackground *string***

This variable specifies the background color to be used for sizing and information windows. The default is white.

| | |
|---|---|
| DefaultForeground *string* | This variable specifies the foreground color to be used for sizing and information windows. The default is black. |
| DontIconifyByUnmapping { *win-list* } | This variable specifies a list of windows that should not be iconified window (as would be the case if IconifyByUnmapping had been set). This is frequently used to force some windows to be treated as icons while other windows are handled by the icon manager. |
| DontMoveOff | This variable indicates that windows should not be allowed to be moved off the screen. It can be overridden by the f.forcemove function. |
| DontSqueezeTitle [{ *win-list* }] | This variable indicates that titlebars should not be squeezed to their minimum size as described under SqueezeTitle below. If the optional window list is supplied, only those windows will be prevented from being squeezed. |
| ForceIcons | This variable indicates that icon pixmaps specified in the Icons variable should override any client-supplied pixmaps. |
| FramePadding *pixels* | This variable specifies the distance between the titlebar decorations (the button and text) and the window frame. The default is 2 pixels. |
| Grayscale { *colors* } | This variable specifies a list of color assignments that should be made if the screen has a GrayScale default visual. See the description of Colors. |
| IconBackground *string* [{ *win-list* }] | This variable specifies the background color of icons, and may only be specified inside of a Color, Grayscale, or Monochrome list. The optional *win-list* is a list of window names and colors so that per-window colors may be specified. See the Border-Color variable for a complete description of the *win-list*. The default is white. |
| IconBorderColor *string* [{ *win-list* }] | This variable specifies the color of the border used for icon windows, and may only be specified inside of a Color, Grayscale, or Monochrome list. The optional *win-list* is a list of window names and colors so that per-window colors may be specified. See the BorderColor variable for a complete description of the *win-list*. The default is black. |
| IconBorderWidth *pixels* | This variable specifies the width in pixels of the border surrounding icon windows. The default is 2. |
| IconDirectory *string* | This variable specifies the directory that should be searched if a bitmap file cannot be found in any of the directories in the bitmapFilePath resource. |
| IconFont *string* | This variable specifies the font to be used to display icon names within icons. The default is variable. |
| IconForeground string [{ *win-list* }] | This variable specifies the foreground color to be used when displaying icons, and may only be specified inside of a Color, Grayscale, or Monochrome list. The optional win-list is a list of window names and colors so that per-window colors may be specified. See the BorderColor variable for a complete description of the *win-list*. The default is black. |
| IconifyByUnmapping [{ *win-list* }] | This variable indicates that windows should be iconified by being unmapped without trying to map any icons. This assumes that the user will remap the window through the icon manager, the f.warpto function, or the TwmWindows menu. If the optional *win-list* is provided, only those windows will be iconified by simply unmapping. Windows that have both this and the IconManager DontShow options set may not be accessible if no binding to the TwmWindows menu is set in the user's startup file. |
| IconManagerBackground string [{ *win-list* }] | This variable specifies the background color to use for icon manager entries, and may only be specified inside of a Color, Grayscale, or Monochrome list. The optional *win-list* is a list of window names and colors so that per-window colors may be specified. See the BorderColor variable for a complete description of the *win-list*. The default is white. |
| IconManagerDontShow [{ *win-list* }] | This variable indicates that the icon manager should not display any windows. If the optional *win-list* is given, only those windows will not be displayed. This variable is used to prevent windows that are rarely iconified (such as xclock or xload) from taking up space in the icon manager. |

IconManagerFont *string*  This variable specifies the font to be used when displaying icon manager entries. The default is `variable`.

IconManagerForeground *string* [{ *win-list* }]  This variable specifies the foreground color to be used when displaying icon manager entries, and may be specified only inside of a `Color`, `Grayscale`, or `Monochrome` list. The optional *win-list* is a list of window names and colors so that per-window colors may be specified. See the `BorderColor` variable for a complete description of the *win-list*. The default is `black`.

IconManagerGeometry *string* [ *columns* ]  This variable specifies the geometry of the icon manager window. The *string* argument is standard geometry specification that indicates the initial full size of the icon manager. The icon manager window is then broken into *columns* pieces and scaled according to the number of entries in the icon manager. Extra entries are wrapped to form additional rows. The default number of columns is 1.

IconManagerHighlight *string* [{ *win-list* }]  This variable specifies the border color to be used when highlighting the icon manager entry that currently has the focus, and can only be specified inside of a `Color`, `Grayscale`, or `Monochrome` list. The optional *win-list* is a list of window names and colors so that per-window colors may be specified. See the `Border-Color` variable for a complete description of the *win-list*. The default is `black`.

IconManagers { *iconmgr-list* }  This variable specifies a list of icon managers to create. Each item in the *iconmgr-list* has the following format:

```
0 "win-name"["iconname"]
"geometry" columns
```

where *winname* is the name of the windows that should be put into this icon manager, *iconname* is the name of that icon manager window's icon, *geometry* is a standard geometry specification, and *columns* is the number of columns in this icon manager as described in `Icon-ManagerGeometry`. For example:

```
IconManagers
{
"XTerm" "=300x5+800+5" 5
"myhost" "=400x5+100+5" 2
}
```

Clients whose name or class is `XTerm` will have an entry created in the `XTerm` icon manager. Clients whose name was `myhost` would be put into the `myhost` icon manager.

IconManagerShow{ *win-list* }  This variable specifies a list of windows that should appear in the icon manager. When used in conjunction with the `IconManagerDontShow` variable, only the windows in this list will be shown in the icon manager.

IconRegion *geomstring vgrav hgrav gridwidth gridheight*  This variable specifies an area on the root window in which icons are placed if no specific icon location is provided by the client. The *geomstring* is a quoted string containing a standard geometry specification. If more than one `IconRegion` line is given, icons will be put into the succeeding icon regions when the first is full. The *vgrav* argument should be either `North` or `South` and is used to control whether icons are first filled in from the top or bottom of the icon region. Similarly, the *hgrav* argument should be either `East` or `West` and is used to control whether icons should be filled in from the left or from the right. Icons are laid out within the region in a grid with cells *gridwidth* pixels wide and *gridheight* pixels high.

Icons { *win-list* }  This variable specifies a list of window names and the `bitmap` filenames that should be used as their icons. For example,

```
Icons
{
"XTerm" "xterm.icon"
"xfd" "xfd_icon"
}
```

Windows that match "XTerm" and would not be iconified by unmapping would try to use the icon bitmap in the file xterm.icon. If ForceIcons is specified, this bitmap will be used even if the client has requested its own icon pixmap.

| | |
|---|---|
| InterpolateMenuColors | This variable indicates that menu entry colors should be interpolated between entry specified colors. In this example, |

```
Menu "mymenu"
{
"Title" ("black":"red") f.title
"entry1" f.nop
"entry2" f.nop
"entry3" ("white":"green") f.nop
"entry4" f.nop
"entry5" ("red":"white") f.nop
}
```

the foreground colors for "entry1" and "entry2" will be interpolated between black and white, and the background colors between red and green. Similarly, the foreground for "entry4" will be halfway between white and red, and the background will be halfway between green and white.

| | |
|---|---|
| MakeTitle { *win-list* } | This variable specifies a list of windows on which a title-bar should be placed and is used to request titles on specific windows when NoTitle has been set. |
| MaxWindowSize *string* | This variable specifies a geometry in which the width and height give the maximum size for a given window. This is typically used to restrict windows to the size of the screen. The default width is 32767—screen width. The default height is 32767—screen height. |
| MenuBackground *string* | This variable specifies the background color used for menus, and can only be specified inside of a Color or Monochrome list. The default is white. |
| MenuFont *string* | This variable specifies the font to use when displaying menus. The default is variable. |
| MenuForeground *string* | This variable specifies the foreground color used for menus and can only be specified inside of a Color, Grayscale, or Monochrome list. The default is black. |
| MenuShadowColor *string* | This variable specifies the color of the shadow behind pull-down menus and can only be specified inside of a Color, Grayscale, or Monochrome list. The default is black. |
| MenuTitleBackground *string* | This variable specifies the background color for f.title entries in menus, and can only be specified inside of a Color, Grayscale, or Monochrome list. The default is white. |
| MenuTitleForeground *string* | This variable specifies the foreground color for f.title entries in menus and can only be specified inside of a Color or Monochrome list. The default is black. |
| Monochrome { *colors* } | This variable specifies a list of color assignments that should be made if the screen has a depth of 1. See the description of Colors. |
| MoveDelta *pixels* | This variable specifies the number of pixels the pointer must move before the f.move function starts working. Also see the f.deltastop function. The default is zero pixels. |
| NoBackingStore | This variable indicates that twm's menus should not request backing store to minimize repainting of menus. This is typically used with servers that can repaint faster than they can handle backing store. |
| NoCaseSensitive | This variable indicates that case should be ignored when sorting icon names in an icon manager. This option is typically used with applications that capitalize the first letter of their icon name. |
| NoDefaults | This variable indicates that twm should not supply the default titlebuttons and bindings. This option should only be used if the startup file contains a completely new set of bindings and definitions. |
| NoGrabServer | This variable indicates that twm should not grab the server when popping up menus and moving opaque windows. |

| | |
|---|---|
| NoHighlight [{ *win-list* }] | This variable indicates that borders should not be highlighted to track the location of the pointer. If the optional *win-list* is given, highlighting will only be disabled for those windows. When the border is highlighted, it will be drawn in the current BorderColor. When the border is not highlighted, it will be stippled with a gray pattern using the current BorderTileForeground and BorderTileBack-ground colors. |
| NoIconManagers | This variable indicates that no icon manager should be created. |
| NoMenuShadows | This variable indicates that menus should not have drop shadows drawn behind them. This is typically used with slower servers because it speeds up menu drawing at the expense of making the menu slightly harder to read. |
| NoRaiseOnDeiconify | This variable indicates that windows that are deiconified should not be raised. |
| NoRaiseOnMove | This variable indicates that windows should not be raised when moved. This is typically used to allow windows to slide underneath each other. |
| NoRaiseOnResize | This variable indicates that windows should not be raised when resized. This is typically used to allow windows to be resized underneath each other. |
| NoRaiseOnWarp | This variable indicates that windows should not be raised when the pointer is warped into them with the f.warpto function. If this option is set, warping to an occluded window may result in the pointer ending up in the occluding window instead the desired window, which causes unexpected behavior with f.warpring. |
| NoSaveUnders | This variable indicates that menus should not request save-unders to minimize window repainting following menu selection. It is typically used with displays that can repaint faster than they can handle save-unders. |
| NoStackMode [{ *win-list* }] | This variable indicates that client window requests to change stacking order should be ignored. If the optional *win-list* is given, only requests on those windows will be ignored. This is typically used to prevent applications from relentlessly popping themselves to the front of the window stack. |
| NoTitle [{ *win-list* }] | This variable indicates that windows should not have title-bars. If the optional *win-list* is given, only those windows will not have titlebars. MakeTitle may be used with this option to force titlebars to be put on specific windows. |
| NoTitleFocus | This variable indicates that twm should not set keyboard input focus to each window as it is entered. Normally, twm sets the focus so that focus and key events from the titlebar and icon managers are delivered to the application. If the pointer is moved quickly and twm is slow to respond, input can be directed to the old window instead of the new. This option is typically used to prevent this input lag and to work around bugs in older applications that have problems with focus events. |
| NoTitleHighlight [{ *win-list* }] | This variable indicates that the highlight area of the titlebar, which is used to indicate the window that currently has the input focus, should not be displayed. If the optional *win-list* is given, only those windows will not have highlight areas. This and the SqueezeTitle options can be set to substantially reduce the amount of screen space required by titlebars. |
| OpaqueMove | This variable indicates that the f.move function should actually move the window instead of just an outline so that the user can immediately see what the window will look like in the new position. This option is typically used on fast displays (particularly if NoGrabServer is set). |
| Pixmaps { *pixmaps* } | This variable specifies a list of pixmaps that define the appearance of various images. Each entry is a keyword indicating the pixmap to set, followed by a string giving the name of the bitmap file. The following pixmaps may be specified: 0 Pixmaps { TitleHighlight "gray1" }<br><br>The default for TitleHighlight is to use an even stipple pattern. |
| Priority *priority* | This variable sets twm's priority. priority should be an unquoted, signed number (for example, 999). This variable has an effect only if the server supports the SYNC extension. |
| RandomPlacement | This variable indicates that windows with no specified geometry should be placed in a pseudorandom location instead of having the user drag out an outline. |

| | |
|---|---|
| ResizeFont string | This variable specifies the font to be used for in the dimensions window when resizing windows. The default is fixed. |
| RestartPreviousState | This variable indicates that twm should attempt to use the WM_STATE property on client windows to tell which windows should be iconified and which should be left visible. This is typically used to try to regenerate the state that the screen was in before the previous window manager was shutdown. |
| SaveColor { colors-list } | This variable indicates a list of color assignments to be stored as pixel values in the root window property _MIT_PRIORITY_COLORS. Clients may elect to preserve these values when installing their own colormaps. Note that use of this mechanism is a way for an application to avoid the "technicolor" problem, whereby useful screen objects such as window borders and titlebars disappear when a program's custom colors are installed by the window manager. For example: |

```
SaveColor
{
BorderColor
TitleBackground
TitleForeground
"red"
"green"
"blue"
}
```

| | |
|---|---|
| | This would place on the root window three pixel values for borders and titlebars, as well as the three color strings, all taken from the default colormap. |
| ShowIconManager | This variable indicates that the icon manager window should be displayed when twm is started. It can always be brought up using the f.showiconmgr function. |
| SortIconManager | This variable indicates that entries in the icon manager should be sorted alphabetically rather than by simply appending new windows to the end. |
| SqueezeTitle [{ squeeze-list }] | This variable indicates that twm should attempt to use the SHAPE extension to make titlebars occupy only as much screen space as they need, rather than extending all the way across the top of the window. The optional squeeze-list may be used to control the location of the squeezed titlebar along the top of the window. It contains entries of the form: 0 "name" justification num denom where name is a window name, justification is either left, center, or right, and num and denom are numbers specifying a ratio giving the relative position about which the titlebar is justified. The ratio is measured from left to right if the numerator is positive, and right to left if negative. A denominator of 0 indicates that the numerator should be measured in pixels. For convenience, the ratio 0/0 is the same as 1/2 for center and -1/1 for right. For example, |

```
SqueezeTitle { "XTerm" left 0 0 "xterm1" left 1 3 "xterm2" left 2 3
"oclock" center 0 0 "emacs" right 0 0 }
```

| | |
|---|---|
| | The DontSqueezeTitle list can be used to turn off squeezing on certain titles. |
| StartIconified [{ win-list }] | This variable indicates that client windows should initially be left as icons until explicitly deiconified by the user. If the optional win-list is given, only those windows will be started iconic. This is useful for programs that do not support an -iconic command-line option or resource. |
| TitleBackground string [{ win-list }] | This variable specifies the background color used in titlebars, and may only be specified inside of a Color, Grayscale, or Monochrome list. The optional win-list is a list of window names and colors so that per-window colors may be specified. The default is white. |
| TitleButtonBorderWidth pixels | This variable specifies the width in pixels of the border surrounding titlebuttons. This is typically set to 0 to allow titlebuttons to take up as much space as possible and to not have a border. The default is 1. |

| | |
|---|---|
| TitleFont *string* | This variable specifies the font to be used for displaying window names in titlebars. The default is `variable`. |
| TitleForeground *string* [{ *win-list* }] | This variable specifies the foreground color used in titlebars, and may only be specified inside of a `Color`, `Grayscale`, or `Monochrome` list. The optional *win-list* is a list of window names and colors so that per-window colors may be specified. The default is `black`. |
| TitlePadding *pixels* | This variable specifies the distance between the various buttons, text, and highlight areas in the titlebar. The default is 8 pixels. |
| UnknownIcon *string* | This variable specifies the filename of a bitmap file to be used as the default icon. This bitmap will be used as the icon of all clients that do not provide an icon bitmap and are not listed in the `Icons` list. |
| UsePPosition *string* | This variable specifies whether or not `twm` should honor program-requested locations (given by the `PPosition` flag in the `WM_NORMAL_HINTS` property) in the absence of a user-specified position. The argument *string* may have one of three values: `off` (the default), indicating that `twm` should ignore the program-supplied position; `on`, indicating that the position should be used; and `non-zero`, indicating that the position should used if it is other than (`0,0`). The latter option is for working around a bug in older toolkits. |
| WarpCursor [{ *win-list* }] | This variable indicates that the pointer should be warped into windows when they are deiconified. If the optional *win-list* is given, the pointer will only be warped when those windows are deiconified. |
| WindowRing { *win-list* } | This variable specifies a list of windows along which the `f.warpring` function cycles. |
| WarpUnmapped | This variable indicates that the `f.warpto` function should deiconify any iconified windows it encounters. This is typically used to make a key binding that will pop up a particular window (such as `xmh`) no matter where it is. The default is for `f.warpto` to ignore iconified windows. |
| XorValue *number* | This variable specifies the value to use when drawing window outlines for moving and resizing. This should be set to a value that will result in a variety of distinguishable colors when exclusive `OR` is used with the contents of the user's typical screen. Setting this variable to 1 often gives nice results if adjacent colors in the default colormap are distinct. By default, `twm` will attempt to cause temporary lines to appear at the opposite end of the colormap from the graphics. |
| Zoom [ *count* ] | This variable indicates that outlines suggesting movement of a window to and from its iconified state should be displayed whenever a window is iconified or deiconified. The optional `count` argument specifies the number of outlines to be drawn. The default count is 8. |

The following variables must be set after the fonts have been assigned, so it is usually best to put them at the end of the variables or at the beginning of the bindings sections:

| | |
|---|---|
| DefaultFunction *function* | This variable specifies the function to be executed when a key or button event is received for which no binding is provided. This is typically bound to `f.nop`, `f.beep`, or a menu containing window operations. |
| WindowFunction *function* | This variable specifies the function to execute when a window is selected from the `TwmWindows` menu. If this variable is not set, the window will be deiconified and raised. |

## BINDINGS

After the desired variables have been set, functions may be attached titlebuttons and key and pointer buttons. Titlebuttons may be added from the left or right side and appear in the titlebar from left to right according to the order in which they are specified. Key and pointer button bindings may be given in any order.

Titlebuttons' specifications must include the name of the pixmap to use in the button box and the function to be invoked when a pointer button is pressed within them:

```
0 LeftTitleButton "bitmapname"=function
```

or

```
0 RightTitleButton "bitmapname"=function
```

The *bitmapname* may refer to one of the built-in bitmaps (which are scaled to match Title-Font) by using the appropriate colon-prefixed name described earlier.

Key and pointer button specifications must give the modifiers that must be pressed, over which parts of the screen the pointer must be, and what function is to be invoked. Keys are given as strings containing the appropriate keysym name; buttons are given as the keywords Button1-Button5: 0 "FP1" = *modlist* : *context* : *function* Button1 = *modlist* : *context* : *function*

The *modlist* is any combination of the modifier names shift, control, lock, meta, mod1, mod2, mod3, mod4, or mod5 (which may be abbreviated as s, c, l, m, m1, m2, m3, m4, m5, respectively) separated by a vertical bar (|). Similarly, the *context* is any combination of window, title, icon, root, frame, iconmgr, their first letters (iconmgr abbreviation is m), or all, separated by a vertical bar. The function is any of the f keywords described in the following list. For example, the default startup file contains the following bindings:

```
Button1 = : root : f.menu "TwmWindows"

Button1 = m : window ¦ icon : f.function "move-or-lower"

Button2 = m : window ¦ icon : f.iconify

Button3 = m : window ¦ icon : f.function "move-or-raise"

Button1 = : title : f.function "move-or-raise"

Button2 = : title : f.raiselower

Button1 = : icon : f.function "move-or-iconify"

Button2 = : icon : f.iconify

Button1 = : iconmgr : f.iconify

Button2 = : iconmgr : f.iconify
```

A user who wanted to be able to manipulate windows from the keyboard could use the following bindings:

```
"F1" = : all : f.iconify

"F2" = : all : f.raiselower

"F3" = : all : f.warpring "next"

"F4" = : all : f.warpto "xmh"

"F5" = : all : f.warpto "emacs"

"F6" = : all : f.colormap "next"

"F7" = : all : f.colormap "default"

"F20" = : all : f.warptoscreen "next"

"Left" = m : all : f.backiconmgr

"Right" = m ¦ s : all : f.forwiconmgr

"Up" = m : all : f.upiconmgr

"Down" = m ¦ s : all : f.downiconmgr
```

twm provides many more window manipulation primitives than can be conveniently stored in a titlebar, menu, or set of key bindings. Although a small set of defaults is supplied (unless the NoDefaults is specified), most users will want to have their most common operations bound to key and button strokes. To do this, twm associates names with each of the primitives and provides user-defined functions for building higher level primitives and menus for interactively selecting among groups of functions.

User-defined functions contain the name by which they are referenced in calls to f.function and a list of other functions to execute. For example,

```
Function "move-or-lower" { f.move f.deltastop f.lower }
Function "move-or-raise" { f.move f.deltastop f.raise }
Function "move-or-iconify" { f.move f.deltastop f.iconify }
Function "restore-colormap" { f.colormap "default" f.lower }
```

The function name must be used in f.function exactly as it appears in the function specification.

In the following descriptions, if the function is said to operate on the selected window, but is invoked from a root menu, the cursor will be changed to the Select cursor and the next window to receive a button press will be chosen:

| | |
|---|---|
| ! *string* | This is an abbreviation for f.exec string. |
| f.autoraise | This function toggles whether or not the selected window is raised whenever entered by the pointer. See the description of the variable AutoRaise. |
| f.backiconmgr | This function warps the pointer to the previous column in the current icon manager, wrapping back to the previous row if necessary. |
| f.beep | This function sounds the keyboard bell. |
| f.bottomzoom | This function is similar to the f.fullzoom function, but resizes the window to fill only the bottom half of the screen. |
| f.circledown | This function lowers the topmost window that occludes another window. |
| f.circleup | This function raises the bottommost window that is occluded by another window. |
| f.colormap *string* | This function rotates the colormaps (obtained from the WM_COLORMAP_WINDOWS property on the window) that twm will display when the pointer is in this window. The argument *string* may have one of the following values: next, prev, and default. It should be noted here that in general, the installed colormap is determined by keyboard focus. A pointer-driven keyboard focus will install a private colormap upon entry of the window owning the colormap. Using the click-to-type model, private colormaps will not be installed until the user clicks on the target window. |
| f.deiconify | This function deiconifies the selected window. If the window is not an icon, this function does nothing. |
| f.delete | This function sends the WM_DELETE_WINDOW message to the selected window if the client application has requested it through the WM_PROTOCOLS window property. The application is supposed to respond to the message by removing the indicated window. If the window has not requested WM_DELETE_WINDOW messages, the keyboard bell will be rung, indicating that the user should choose an alternative method. Note this is very different from f.destroy. The intent here is to delete a single window, not necessarily the entire application. |
| f.deltastop | This function allows a user-defined function to be aborted if the pointer has been moved more than MoveDelta pixels. See the example definition given for Function "move-or-raise" at the beginning of the section. |
| f.destroy | This function instructs the X server to close the display connection of the client that created the selected window. This should only be used as a last resort for shutting down runaway clients. See also f.delete. |
| f.downiconmgr | This function warps the pointer to the next row in the current icon manger, wrapping to the beginning of the next column if necessary. |
| f.exec *string* | This function passes the argument string to /bin/sh for execution. In multiscreen mode, if *string* starts a new X client without giving a display argument, the client will appear on the screen from which this function was invoked. |
| f.focus | This function toggles the keyboard focus of the server to the selected window, changing the focus rule from pointer-driven if necessary. If the selected window already was focused, this function executes an f.unfocus. |

| | |
|---|---|
| `f.forcemove` | This function is like `f.move` except that it ignores the `DontMoveOff` variable. |
| `f.forwiconmgr` | This function warps the pointer to the next column in the current icon manager, wrapping to the beginning of the next row if necessary. |
| `f.fullzoom` | This function resizes the selected window to the full size of the display or else restores the original size if the window was already zoomed. |
| `f.function string` | This function executes the user-defined function whose name is specified by the argument *string*. |
| `f.hbzoom` | This function is a synonym for `f.bottomzoom`. |
| `f.hideiconmgr` | This function unmaps the current icon manager. |
| `f.horizoom` | This variable is similar to the `f.zoom` function except that the selected window is resized to the full width of the display. |
| `f.htzoom` | This function is a synonym for `f.topzoom`. |
| `f.hzoom` | This function is a synonym for `f.horizoom`. |
| `f.iconify` | This function iconifies or deiconifies the selected window or icon, respectively. |
| `f.identify` | This function displays a summary of the name and geometry of the selected window. If the server supports the `SYNC` extension, the priority of the client owning the window is also displayed. Clicking the pointer or pressing a key in the window will dismiss it. |
| `f.lefticonmgr` | This function is similar to `f.backiconmgr` except that wrapping does not change rows. |
| `f.leftzoom` | This variable is similar to the `f.bottomzoom` function but causes the selected window to be resized only on the left half of the display. |
| `f.lower` | This function lowers the selected window. |
| `f.menu string` | This function invokes the menu specified by the argument *string*. Cascaded menus may be built by nesting calls to `f.menu`. |
| `f.move` | This function drags an outline of the selected window (or the window itself if the `OpaqueMove` variable is set) until the invoking pointer button is released. Double-clicking within the number of milliseconds given by `ConstrainedMoveTime` warps the pointer to the center of the window and constrains the move to be either horizontal or vertical, depending on which grid line is crossed. To abort a move, press another button before releasing the first button. |
| `f.nexticonmgr` | This function warps the pointer to the next icon manager containing any windows on the current or any succeeding screen. |
| `f.nop` | This function does nothing and is typically used with the `Default-Function` or `WindowFunction` variables or to introduce blank lines in menus. |
| `f.previconmgr` | This function warps the pointer to the previous icon manager containing any windows on the current or preceding screens. |
| `f.priority string` | This function sets the priority of the client owning the selected window to the numeric value of the argument *string*, which should be a signed integer in double quotes (for example, "999"). This function has an effect only if the server supports the `SYNC` extension. |
| `f.quit` | This function causes twm to restore the window's borders and exit. If twm is the first client invoked from xdm, this will result in a server reset. |
| `f.raise` | This function raises the selected window. |
| `f.raiselower` | This function raises the selected window to the top of the stacking order if it is occluded by any windows; otherwise, the window is lowered. |
| `f.refresh` | This function causes all windows to be refreshed. |
| `f.resize` | This function displays an outline of the selected window. Crossing a border (or setting `AutoRelativeResize`) will cause the outline to begin to rubber band until the invoking button is released. To abort a resize, press another button before releasing the first button. |
| `f.restart` | This function kills and restarts twm. |
| `f.righticonmgr` | This function is similar to `f.nexticonmgr` except that wrapping does not change rows. |

| | |
|---|---|
| `f.rightzoom` | This variable is similar to the `f.bottomzoom` function except that the selected window is only resized to the right half of the display. |
| `f.saveyourself` | This function sends a `WM_SAVEYOURSELF` message to the selected window if it has requested the message in its `WM_PROTOCOLS` window property. Clients that accept this message are supposed to checkpoint all states associated with the window and update the `WM_COMMAND` property as specified in the `ICCCM`. If the selected window has not been selected for this message, the keyboard bell will be rung. |
| `f.showiconmgr` | This function maps the current icon manager. |
| `f.sorticonmgr` | This function sorts the entries in the current icon manager alphabetically. See the variable `SortIconManager`. |
| `f.title` | This function provides a centered, unselectable item in a menu definition. It should not be used in any other context. |
| `f.topzoom` | This variable is similar to the `f.bottomzoom` function except that the selected window is only resized to the top half of the display. |
| `f.unfocus` | This function resets the focus back to pointer-driven. This should be used when a focused window is no longer desired. |
| `f.upiconmgr` | This function warps the pointer to the previous row in the current icon manager, wrapping to the last row in the same column if necessary. |
| `f.vlzoom` | This function is a synonym for `f.leftzoom`. |
| `f.vrzoom` | This function is a synonym for `f.rightzoom`. |
| `f.warpring` *string* | This function warps the pointer to the next or previous window (as indicated by the argument *string*, which may be `"next"` or `"prev"`) specified in the `WindowRing` variable. |
| `f.warpto` *string* | This function warps the pointer to the window that has a name or class that matches *string*. If the window is iconified, it will be deiconified if the variable `WarpUnmapped` is set or else ignored. |
| `f.warptoiconmgr` *string* | This function warps the pointer to the icon manager entry associated with the window containing the pointer in the icon manager specified by the argument *string*. If *string* is empty (that is, `""`), the current icon manager is chosen. |
| `f.warptoscreen` *string* | This function warps the pointer to the screen specified by the argument *string*. *string* may be a number (such as "`0`" or "`1`"), the word `"next"` (indicating the current screen plus 1, skipping over any unmanaged screens), the word "`back`" (indicating the current screen minus 1, skipping over any unmanaged screens), or the word `"prev"` (indicating the last screen visited). |
| `f.winrefresh` | This function is similar to the `f.refresh` function except that only the selected window is refreshed. |
| `f.zoom` | This function is similar to the `f.fullzoom` function, except that only the height of the selected window is changed. |

## MENUS

Functions may be grouped and interactively selected using pop-up (when bound to a pointer button) or pull-down (when associated with a titlebutton) menus. Each menu specification contains the name of the menu as it will be referred to by `f.menu`, optional default foreground and background colors, the list of item names and the functions they should invoke, and optional foreground and background colors for individual items:

```
Menu "menuname"[("deffore":"defback") ] { string1 [("fore1":"backn")] function1 string2
[("fore2":"backn")] function2 ...stringN [("foreN":"backN")] functionN }
```

The menuname is case-sensitive. The optional `deffore` and `defback` arguments specify the foreground and background colors used on a color display to highlight menu entries. The `string` portion of each menu entry will be the text that will appear in the menu. The optional `fore` and `back` arguments specify the foreground and background colors of the menu entry when the pointer is not in the entry. These colors will only be used on a color display. The default is to use the colors specified by the `MenuForeground` and `MenuBackground` variables. The `function` portion of the menu entry is one of the functions, including any user-defined functions, or additional menus.

There is a special menu named `TwmWindows` that contains the names of all of the client and `twm`-supplied windows. Selecting an entry will cause the `WindowFunction` to be executed on that window. If `WindowFunction` hasn't been set, the window will be deiconified and raised.

## ICONS

`twm` supports several different ways of manipulating iconified windows. The common pixmap-and-text style may be laid out by hand or automatically arranged as described by the `IconRegion` variable. In addition, a terse grid of icon names, called an icon manager, provides a more efficient use of screen space as well as the ability to navigate among windows from the keyboard.

An icon manager is a window that contains names of selected windows or all windows currently on the display. In addition to the window name, a small button using the default iconify symbol will be displayed to the left of the name when the window is iconified. By default, clicking on an entry in the icon manager performs `f.iconify`. To change the actions taken in the icon manager, use the `iconmgr` context when specifying button and keyboard bindings.

If you move the pointer into the icon manager, the keyboard focus is also directed to the indicated window (setting the focus explicitly or else sending synthetic events `NoTitleFocus` is set). Using the `f.upiconmgr`, `f.downiconmgr`, `f.lefticonmgr`, and `f.righticonmgr` functions, the input focus can be changed between windows directly from the keyboard.

## BUGS

The resource manager should have been used instead of all of the window lists.

The `IconRegion` variable should take a list.

Double-clicking very fast to get the constrained move function will sometimes cause the window to move, even though the pointer is not moved.

If `IconifyByUnmapping` is on and windows are listed in `IconManagerDontShow` but not in `DontIconifyByUnmapping`, they may be lost if they are iconified and no bindings to `f.menu "TwmWindows"` or `f.warpto` are setup.

## FILES

```
$HOME/.twmrc.<screen number>
$HOME/.twmrc
<XRoot>/lib/X11/twm/system.twmrc
```

## ENVIRONMENT VARIABLES

DISPLAY  This variable is used to determine which X server to use. It is also set during `f.exec` so that programs come up on the proper screen.

HOME  This variable is used as the prefix for files that begin with a tilde and for locating the `twm` startup file.

## SEE ALSO

X(1), Xserver(1), xdm(1), xrdb(1)

## AUTHORS

Tom LaStrange, Solbourne Computer; Jim Fulton, MIT X Consortium; Steve Pitschke, Stardent Computer; Keith Packard, MIT X Consortium; Dave Payne, Apple Computer.

## SEE ALSO

X(1), Xserver(1), x

# txt2gcal

txt2gcal—Creates a verbatim gcal resource file from a text file

## SYNOPSIS

txt2gcal [ --help ¦ --version ] ¦ [ *Text-file* ¦ - ][*Date-part* ]

## DESCRIPTION

txt2gcal is a program that creates a verbatim gcal resource file from a text file. If no *text-file* or - argument is given, the program reads and processes all input received from the standard input channel. If no *date-part* argument is given, txt2gcal creates a 0 for the date part. All results are always shown on the standard output channel. An exit status of 0 means all processing is successfully done; any other value means an error has occurred.

## OPTIONS

--help        Print a usage message listing all available options, then exit successfully.

--version     Print the version number, then exit successfully.

## COPYRIGHT

Copyright© 1996 Thomas Esken. This software doesn't claim completeness, correctness, or usability. On principle, I will not be liable for any damages or losses (implicit or explicit), which result from using or handling my software. If you use this software, you agree without any exception to this agreement, which binds you legally.

txt2cal is free software and distributed under the terms of the GNU General Public License; published by the Free Software Foundation; version 2 or (at your option) any later version.

Any suggestions, improvements, extensions, bug reports, donations, proposals for contract work, and so forth are welcome. If you like this tool, I'd appreciate a postcard from you!

Enjoy it =8^)

## AUTHOR

Thomas Esken (esken@uni-muenster.de)
m Hagenfeld 84
D-48147 Muenster; Germany
Phone : +49 251 232585

## SEE ALSO

gcal(1), tcal(1)

*16 July 1996*

# ul

ul—Do underlining

## SYNOPSIS

ul [-i] [-t terminal] [*name* ...]

## DESCRIPTION

Ul reads the named files (or standard input if none are given) and translates occurrences of underscores to the sequence that indicates underlining for the terminal in use, as specified by the environment variable TERM . The file /etc/termcap is read to determine the appropriate sequences for underlining. If the terminal is incapable of underlining but is capable of a standout mode, then that is used instead. If the terminal can overstrike, or handles underlining automatically, ul degenerates to cat(1). If the terminal cannot underline, underlining is ignored.

The following options are available:

| | |
|---|---|
| -i | Underlining is indicated by a separate line containing appropriate dashes -; this is useful when you want to look at the underlining which is present in an nroff output stream on a CRT terminal. |
| -t terminal | Overrides the terminal type specified in the environment with terminal. |

## ENVIRONMENT

The following environment variable is used

| | |
|---|---|
| TERM | Relates a tty device with its device capability description; see termcap(5). TERM is set at login time, either by the default terminal type specified in /etc/ttys or as set during the login process by the user in the login file; see setenv(1). |

## SEE ALSO

man(1), nroff(1), colcrt(1)

## BUGS

nroff usually outputs a series of backspaces and underlines intermixed with the text to indicate underlining. No attempt is made to optimize the backward motion.

## HISTORY

The ul command appeared in BSD 3.0.

*BSD 4, 6 June 1993*

# unexpand

unexpand—Convert spaces to tabs

## SYNOPSIS

unexpand [-*tab1*[,*tab2*[,...]]] [-t *tab1*[,*tab2*[,...]]] [-a][--tabs=*tab1*[,*tab2*[,...]]]
[--all] [--help] [--version] [*file*...]

## DESCRIPTION

This manual page documents the GNU version of unexpand. unexpand writes the contents of each given file, or the standard input if none are given or when a file named - is given, to the standard output, with strings of two or more space or tab characters converted to as many tabs as possible followed by as many spaces as are needed. By default, unexpand converts only initial spaces and tabs (those that precede all characters that aren't spaces or tabs) on each line. It preserves backspace characters in the output; they decrement the column count for tab calculations. By default, tabs are set at every 8th column.

## OPTIONS

| | |
|---|---|
| -, -t, --tabs *tab1*[,*tab2*[,...]] | If only one tab stop is given, set the tabs *tab1* spaces apart instead of the default 8. Otherwise, set the tabs at columns *tab1*, *tab2*, and so on (numbered from 0) and leave spaces and tabs beyond the tab stops given unchanged. If the tab stops are specified with the -t or --tabs option, they can be separated by blanks as well as by commas. This option implies the -a option. |
| -a, --all | Convert all strings of two or more spaces or tabs, not just initial ones, to tabs. |
| --help | Print a usage message and exit with a non-zero status. |
| --version | Print version information on standard output, then exit. |

*GNU Text Utilities*

# uniq

uniq—Remove duplicate lines from a sorted file

## SYNOPSIS

```
uniq [-cdu] [-f skip-fields] [-s skip-chars] [-w check-chars] [-#skip-fields]
[+#skip-chars] [--count] [--repeated] [--unique] [--skip-fields=skip-fields]
[--skip-chars=skip-chars] [--check-chars=check-chars] [--help] [--version]
[infile] [outfile]
```

## DESCRIPTION

This manual page documents the GNU version of uniq. uniq prints the unique lines in a sorted file, discarding all but one of a run of matching lines. It can optionally show only lines that appear exactly once, or lines that appear more than once. uniq requires sorted input because it compares only consecutive lines.

If the output file is not specified, uniq writes to the standard output. If the input file is not specified, it reads from the standard input.

## OPTIONS

| | |
|---|---|
| -u, --unique | Only print unique lines |
| -d, --repeated | Only print duplicate lines |
| -c, --count | Print the number of times each line occurred along with the line |
| *-number*, -f, --skip-fields=*number* | In this option, *number* is an integer representing the number of fields to skip over before checking for uniqueness. The first *number* fields, along with any blanks found before *number* fields is reached, are skipped over and not counted. Fields are defined as a strings of nonspace, nontab characters that are separated from each other by spaces and tabs. |
| *+number*, -s, --skip-chars=number | In this option, *number* is an integer representing the number of characters to skip over before checking for uniqueness. The first *number* characters, along with any blanks found before *number* characters is reached, are skipped over and not counted. If you use both the field and character skipping options, fields are skipped over first. |
| -w, --check-chars=number | Specify the number of characters to compare in the lines, after skipping any specified fields and characters. Normally, the entire remainder of the lines are compared. |
| --help | Print a usage message and exit with a non-zero status. |
| --version | Print version information on standard output, then exit. |

*GNU Text Utilities*

# unshar

unshar—Unpack a shar file

## SYNOPSIS

```
unshar [ -d directory ] [ -c ][-e ¦ -E exit_line ] [ file ... ]
```

## DESCRIPTION

unshar scans mail messages looking for the start of a shell archive. It then passes the archive through a copy of the shell to unpack it. It will accept multiple files. If no files are given, standard input is used. This manual page reflects unshar version 4.0.

## OPTIONS

Options have a one-letter version starting with `-` or a long version starting with `--`. The exceptions are `--help` and `--version`, which don't have a short version.

| | |
|---|---|
| `--version` | Print the version number of the program on standard output, then immediately exit. |
| `--help` | Print a help summary on standard output, then immediately exit. |
| `-d DIRECTORY`<br>`--directory=DIRECTORY` | Change `directory` to `DIRECTORY` before unpacking any files. |
| `-c --overwrite` | Passed as an option to the `shar` file. Many shell archive scripts (including those produced by `shar` 3.40 and newer) accept a `-c` argument to indicate that existing files should be overwritten. |
| `-e --exit-0` | This option exists mainly for people who collect many shell archives into a single mail folder. With this option, `unshar` isolates each different shell archive from the others that have been put in the same file, unpacking each in turn, from the beginning of the file towards its end. Its proper operation relies on the fact that many `shar` files are terminated by an `exit 0` at the beginning of a line.<br><br>Option `-e` is internally equivalent to `-E "exit 0"`. |
| `-E STRING`<br>`--split-at=STRING` | This option works like `-e`, but it allows you to specify the string that separates archives if `exit 0` isn't appropriate. For example, noticing that most `.signatures` have a `--` on a line right before them, one can sometimes use `-- split-at=--` for splitting shell archives that lack the `exit 0` line at end. The signature will then be skipped altogether with the headers of the following message. |

## SEE ALSO

shar(1)

## DIAGNOSTICS

Any message from the shell may be displayed.

## AUTHORS

Michael Mauldin at Carnegie-Mellon University, Guido van Rossum at CWI, Amsterdam (`guido@mcvax`), Bill Davidsen (`davidsen@sixhub.uuxp`), Warren Tucker (`wht%n4hgf@gatech.edu`)
Richard H. Gumpertz (`rhg@CPS.COM`), and Colas Nahaboo (`colas@avahi.inria.fr`). Man pages by Jan Djfrv (`jhd@irfu.se`).

*12 August 1990*

# updatedb

updatedb—Update a filename database

## SYNOPSIS

updatedb [*options*]

## DESCRIPTION

This manual page documents the GNU version of `updatedb`, which updates filename databases used by GNU `locate`. The filename databases contain lists of files that were in particular directory trees when the databases were last updated. The filename of the default database is determined when `locate` and `updatedb` are configured and installed. The frequency with which the databases and the directories for which they contain entries are updated depends on how often `updatedb` is run, and with which arguments. In networked environments, it often makes sense to build a database at the root of each filesystem, containing the entries for that filesystem. To prevent thrashing the network, updatedb is then run for each filesystem on the fileserver where that filesystem is on a local disk. Users can select which databases locate searches using an environment variable or command-line option; see locate(1L). Databases can not be concatenated together. The filename database format changed starting with GNU find and locate version 4.0 to allow machines with different byte orderings to share the databases. The new GNU locate can read both the old and new database formats. However, old versions of locate and find produce incorrect results if given a new-format database.

## OPTIONS

| | |
|---|---|
| --localpaths='*path1 path2*...' | Nonnetwork directories to put in the database. Default is /. |
| --netpaths='*path1 path2*...' | Network (NFS, AFS, RFS, and so on) directories to put in the database. Default is none. |
| --prunepaths='*path1 path2*...' | Directories to not put in the database, which would otherwise be put there. Default is /tmp /usr/tmp /var/tmp /afs. |
| --output=*dbfile* | The database file to build. Default is system-dependent, but typically /usr/local/var/locatedb. |
| --netuser=*user* | The user to search network directories as, using su(1). Default is daemon. |
| --old-format | Create the database in the old format instead of the new one. |
| --version | Print the version number of updatedb and exit. |
| --help | Print a summary of the options to updatedb and exit. |

## SEE ALSO

find(1L), locate(1L), locatedb(5L), xargs(1L) *Finding Files* (online in info, or printed)

# uptime

uptime—Tell how long the system has been running

## SYNOPSIS

uptime

## DESCRIPTION

uptime gives a one-line display of the information that follows it: the current time, how long the system has been running, how many users are currently logged on, and the system load averages for the past 1, 5, and 15 minutes.

This is the same information contained in the header line displayed by w(1).

## FILES

| | |
|---|---|
| /var/run/utmp | Information about who is currently logged on |
| /proc | Process information |

## AUTHORS

uptime was written by Larry Greenfield (greenfie@gauss.rutgers.edu) and Michael K. Johnson (johnsonm@sunsite.unc.edu).

## SEE ALSO

ps(1), top(1), utmp(5), w(1)

# userlist

userlist—User listing of who's on your system

## SYNOPSIS

userlist

## DESCRIPTION

This program simply gives you a listing of who is connected to your system. It is used primarily in the sorted listing that utilitizes the same method of display for a more uniform output between systems. It also made more sense to do it this way instead of having jumbled up display listings in sorted finger displays. Besides, it made more sense to do this than use finger. :)

This program functions with the same types of things in mind that cfingerd does. If the user has a .nofinger file, his or her username will not be displayed in the user listing.

Example output is shown as

Username Real Name Idletime TTY Remote console username I'm real ... 9d 23:59 0
(remote.site.com)

where it would display the user's login name, the user's real name, the user's idle time given in the format "*dd hh:mm*", the TTY, and the remote location (or where the user is telnetting from).

If the username is more than a certain number of characters, the program will not search for their information in the passwd file because it may be too long. Besides, it checks getpwnam, anyway.

## CONTACTING

If you like this program, have any suggestions on how it could be modified, or have bug reports, please write to khollis@bitgate.com.

Your continued public domain support is appreciated! Thanks.

## SEE ALSO

cfingerd.conf(5), cfingerd(8), finger(1)

*Userlist 0.0.1, 26 August 1995*

# uucp

uucp—UNIX-to-UNIX copy

## SYNOPSIS

uucp [ options ] *source-file destination-file*

uucp [ options ] *source-file... destination-directory*

## DESCRIPTION

The uucp command copies files between systems. Each file argument is either a pathname on the local machine or is of the form

*system!path*

which is interpreted as being on a remote system. In the first form, the contents of the first file are copied to the second. In the second form, each source file is copied into the destination directory.

A file be transferred to or from *system2* via *system1* by using

`system1!system2!path`

Any pathname that does not begin with / or ˜ will be appended to the current directory (unless the -W or --noexpand option is used); this resulting path will not necessarily exist on a remote system. A pathname beginning with a simple ˜ starts at the uucp public directory; a pathname beginning with ˜name starts at the home directory of the named user. The ˜ is interpreted on the appropriate system. Note that some shells will interpret a simple ˜ to the local home directory before uucp sees it; to avoid this, the ˜ must be quoted.

Shell metacharacters ? * [ ] are interpreted on the appropriate system, assuming they are quoted to prevent the shell from interpreting them first.

The copy does not take place immediately, but is queued up for the uucico(8) daemon; the daemon is started immediately unless the -r or --nouucico switch is given. In any case, the next time the remote system is called, the file(s) will be copied.

## OPTIONS

The following options may be given to uucp.

| | |
|---|---|
| -c, --nocopy | Do not copy local source files to the spool directory. If they are removed before being processed by the uucico(8) daemon, the copy will fail. The files must be readable by the uucico(8) daemon, and by the invoking user. |
| -C, --copy | Copy local source files to the spool directory. This is the default. |
| -d, --directories | Create all necessary directories when doing the copy. This is the default. |
| -f, --nodirectories | If any necessary directories do not exist for the destination path, abort the copy. |
| -g *grade*, --grade *grade* | Set the grade of the file transfer command. Jobs of a higher grade are executed first. Grades run 0 ... 9 A ... Z a ... z from high to low. |
| -m, --mail | Report completion or failure of the file transfer by mail(1). |
| -n *user*, --notify *user* | Report completion or failure of the file transfer by mail(1) to the named user on the remote system. |
| -r, --nouucico | Do not start uucico(8) daemon immediately; merely queue up the file transfer for later execution. |
| -j, --*jobid* | Print *jobid* on standard output. The job may be later canceled by passing the *jobid* to the -k switch of uustat(1). It is possible for some complex operations to produce more than one *jobid*, in which case, each will be printed on a separate line. For example, `uucp sys1!˜user1/file1 sys2!˜user2/file2 ˜user3` will generate two separate jobs, one for the system *sys1* and one for the system *sys2*. |
| -W, --noexpand | Do not prepend remote relative pathnames with the current directory. |
| -x *type*, --debug *type* | Turn on particular debugging types. The following types are recognized: abnormal, chat, handshake, uucp-proto, proto, port, config, spooldir, execute, incoming, outgoing. Only abnormal, config, spooldir, and execute are meaningful for uucp. Multiple types may be given, separated by commas, and the --debug option may appear multiple times. A number may also be given, which will turn on that many types from the foregoing list; for example, --debug 2 is equivalent to --debug abnormal,chat. |
| -I *file*, --config *file* | Set configuration file to use. This option may not be available, depending upon how uucp was compiled. |
| -v, --version | Report version information and exit. |
| --help | Print a help message and exit. |

## FILES

The filenames may be changed at compilation time or by the configuration file, so these are only approximations.

| | |
|---|---|
| /usr/lib/uucp/config | Configuration file |
| /usr/spool/uucp uucp | Spool directory |
| /usr/spool/uucp/Log | uucp log file |
| /usr/spool/uucppublic | Default uucp public directory |

## SEE ALSO

mail(1), uux(1), uustat(1), uucico(8)

## BUGS

Some of the options are dependent on the capabilities of the uucico(8) daemon on the remote system.

The -n and -m switches do not work when transferring a file from one remote system to another.

File modes are not preserved, except for the execute bit. The resulting file is owned by the uucp user.

## AUTHOR

Ian Lance Taylor (ian@airs.com)

*Taylor UUCP 1.05*

# uuencode

uuencode—Encode a binary file

uudecode—Decode a file created by uuencode

## SYNOPSIS

uuencode [-m] [ *file* ] *name*

uudecode [-o outfile] [ *file* ]...

## DESCRIPTION

uuencode and uudecode are used to transmit binary files over transmission mediums that do not support other than simple ASCII data.

uuencode reads *file* (or by default the standard input) and writes an encoded version to the standard output. The encoding uses only printing ASCII characters and includes the mode of the file and the operand *name* for use by uudecode. If *name* is /dev/stdout, the result will be written to standard output. By default, the standard UU encoding format will be used. If the option -m is given on the command line, base64 encoding is used instead.

uudecode transforms uuencoded files (or by default, the standard input) into the original form. The resulting file is named *name* (or outfile if the -o option is given) and will have the mode of the original file except that setuid and execute bits are not retained. If outfile or *name* is /dev/stdout, the result will be written to standard output. uudecode ignores any leading and trailing lines. The program can automatically decide which of the supported encoding schemes are used.

## EXAMPLES

The following example packages up a source tree, compresses it, uuencodes it, and mails it to a user on another system. When uudecode is run on the target system, the file src_tree.tar.Z will be created, which may then be uncompressed and extracted into the original tree.

```
tar cf - src_tree ¦ compress ¦ uuencode src_tree.tar.Z ¦ mail sys1!sys2!user
```

## SEE ALSO

compress(1), mail(1), uucp(1), uuencode(5)

## STANDARDS

This implementation is compliant with P1003.2b/D11.

## BUGS

If more than one file is given to uudecode and the -o option is given or more than one *name* in the encoded files is the same, the result is probably not what is expected.

The encoded form of the file is expanded by 37 percent for UU encoding and by 35 percent for base64 encoding (3 bytes become 4 plus control information).

## HISTORY

The uuencode command appeared in BSD 4.0.

# uustat

uustat—uucp status inquiry and control

## SYNOPSIS

```
uustat -a

uustat --all

uustat [ -eKRiMNQ ][-sS system ] [ -uU user ] [ -cC command ] [ -oy hours ]
[ -B lines ] [ --executions ][--kill-all ][--rejuvenate-all ][--prompt ][--mail ]
[--notify ][--no-list ][--system system ] [ --not-system system ] [ --user user ]
[--not-user user ] [ --command command ] [ --not-command command ]
[ --older-than hours ] [ --younger-than hours ] [ --mail-lines lines ]
uustat [ -kr jobid ] [ --kill jobid ] [ --rejuvenate jobid ]

uustat -q [ -sS system ] [ -oy hours ] [ --system system ] [ --not-system system ]
[--older-than hours ] [ --younger-than hours ]

uustat --list [ -sS system ] [ -oy hours ] [ --system system ]
[ --not-system system ] [ --older-than hours ] [ --younger-than hours ]

uustat -m

uustat --status

uustat -p

uustat --ps
```

## DESCRIPTION

The uustat command can display various types of status information about the UUCP system. It can also be used to cancel or rejuvenate requests made by uucp(1) or uux(1).

By default uustat displays all jobs queued up for the invoking user, as if given the --user option with the appropriate argument.

If any of the -a, --all, -e, --executions, -s, --system, -S, --not-system, -u, --user, -U, --not-user, -c, --command, -C, --not-command, -o, --older-than, -y, --younger-than options are given, then all jobs that match the combined specifications are displayed.

The -K or --kill-all option may be used to kill off a selected group of jobs, such as all jobs more than seven days old.

## OPTIONS

The following options may be given to uustat.

| | |
|---|---|
| -a, --all | List all queued file transfer requests. |
| -e, --executions | List queued execution requests rather than queued file transfer requests. Queued execution requests are processed by uuxqt(8) rather than uucico(8). Queued execution requests may be waiting for some file to be transferred from a remote system. They are created by an invocation of uux(1). |
| -s *system*, --system *system* | List all jobs queued up for the named system. These options may be specified multiple times, in which case all jobs for all the systems will be listed. If used with --list, only the systems named will be listed. |
| -S *system*, --not-system *system* | List all jobs queued for systems other than the one named. These options may be specified multiple times, in which case no jobs from any of the specified systems will be listed. If used with --list, only the systems not named will be listed. These options may not be used with -s or --system. |
| -u *user*, --user *user* | List all jobs queued up for the named user. These options may be specified multiple times, in which case all jobs for all the users will be listed. |
| -U *user*, --not-user *user* | List all jobs queued up for users other than the one named. These options may be specified multiple times, in which case no jobs from any of the specified users will be listed. These options may not be used with -u or --user. |
| -c *command*, --command *command* | List all jobs requesting the execution of the named command. If *command* is ALL this will list all jobs requesting the execution of some command (as opposed to simply requesting a file transfer). These options may be specified multiple times, in which case all jobs requesting any of the commands will be listed. |
| -C *command*, --not-command *command* | List all jobs requesting execution of some command other than the named command, or, if command is ALL, list all jobs that simply request a file transfer (as opposed to requesting the execution of some command). These options may be specified multiple times, in which case, no job requesting one of the specified commands will be listed. These options may not be used with -c or --command. |
| -o *hours*, --older-than *hours* | List all queued jobs older than the given number of hours. If used with --list, only systems whose oldest job is older than the given number of hours will be listed. |
| -y *hours*, --younger-than *hours* | List all queued jobs younger than the given number of hours. If used with --list, only systems whose oldest job is younger than the given number of hours will be listed. |
| -k *jobid*, --kill *jobid* | Kill the named job. The job ID is shown by the default output format, as well as by the -j or --jobid option to uucp(1) or uux(1). A job may only be killed by the user who created the job, or by the UUCP administrator or the superuser. The -k or --kill options may be used multiple times on the command line to kill several jobs. |
| -r *jobid*, --rejuvenate *jobid* | Rejuvenate the named job. This will mark it as having been invoked at the current time, affecting the output of the -o, --older-than, -y, or --younger-than options and preserving it from any automated cleanup daemon. The job ID is shown by the default output format, as well as by the -j or --jobid options to uucp(1) or uu(1). A job may only be rejuvenated by the user who created the job, or by the UUCP administrator or the superuser. The -r or --rejuvenate options may be used multiple times on the command line to rejuvenate several jobs. |

| | |
|---|---|
| -q, --list | Display the status of commands, executions, and conversations for all remote systems for which commands or executions are queued. The -s, --system, -S, --not-system, -o, --older-than, -y, and --younger-than options may be used to restrict the systems that are listed. Systems for which no commands or executions are queued will never be listed. |
| -m, --status | Display the status of conversations for all remote systems. |
| -p, --ps | Display the status of all processes holding uucp locks on systems or ports. |
| -i, --prompt | For each listed job, prompt whether to kill the job or not. If the first character of the input line is y or Y, the job will be killed. |
| -K, --kill-all | Automatically kill each listed job. This can be useful for automatic cleanup scripts, in conjunction with the --mail and --notify options. |
| -R, --rejuvenate-all | Automatically rejuvenate each listed job. This may not be used with --kill-all. |
| -M, --mail | For each listed job, send mail to the UUCP administrator. If the job is killed (due to --kill-all or --prompt with an affirmative response), the mail will indicate that. A comment specified by the --comment option may be included. If the job is an execution, the initial portion of its standard input will be included in the mail message; the number of lines to include may be set with the --mail-lines option (the default is 100). If the standard input contains null characters, it is assumed to be a binary file and is not included. |
| -N, --notify | For each listed job, send mail to the user who requested the job. The mail is identical to that sent by the -M or --mail options. |
| -W, --comment | Specify a comment to be included in mail sent with the -M, --mail, -N, or --notify options. |
| -Q, --no-list | Do not actually list the job, but only take any actions indicated by the -i, --prompt, -K, --kill-all, -M, --mail, -N, or --notify options. |
| -x type, --debug type | Turn on particular debugging types. The following types are recognized: abnormal, chat, handshake, uucp-proto, proto, port, config, spooldir, execute, incoming, outgoing. Only abnormal, config, spooldir, and execute are meaningful for uustat. |
| | Multiple types may be given, separated by commas, and the --debug option may appear multiple times. A number may also be given, which will turn on that many types from the foregoing list; for example, --debug 2 is equivalent to --debug abnormal,chat. |
| -I file, --config file | Set configuration file to use. This option may not be available, depending upon how uustat was compiled. |
| -v, --version | Report version information and exit. |
| --help | Print a help message and exit. |

## EXAMPLES

| | |
|---|---|
| uustat -all | Display status of all jobs. A sample output line is as follows: |

```
bugsA027h bugs ian 04-01 13:50 Executing rmail ian@airs.com (sending 1283
bytes)
```

The format is

*jobid system user queue-date command (size)*

The jobid may be passed to the --kill or --rejuvenate options. The size indicates how much data is to be transferred to the remote system, and is absent for a file receive request. The --system, --not-system, --user, --not-user, --command, --not-command, --older-than, and --younger-than options may be used to control which jobs are listed.

| | |
|---|---|
| uustat -executions | Display status of queued up execution requests. A sample output line is as follows: |

```
bugs bugs!ian 05-20 12:51 rmail ian
```

The format is

*system requestor queue-date command*

The --system, --not-system, --user, --not-user, --command, --not-command, --older-than, and --younger-than options may be used to control which requests are listed.

| | |
|---|---|
| uustat -list | Display status for all systems with queued-up commands. A sample output line is as follows:<br><br>`bugs 4C (1 hour) 0X (0 secs) 04-01 14:45 Dial failed`<br><br>This indicates the system, the number of queued commands, the age of the oldest queued command, the number of queued local executions, the age of the oldest queued execution, the date of the last conversation, and the status of that conversation. |
| uustat -status | Display conversation status for all remote systems. A sample output line is as follows:<br><br>`bugs 04-01 15:51 Conversation complete`<br><br>This indicates the system, the date of the last conversation, and the status of that conversation. If the last conversation failed, uustat will indicate how many attempts have been made to call the system. If the retry period is currently preventing calls to that system, uustat also displays the time when the next call will be permitted. |
| uustat -ps | Display the status of all processes holding uucp locks. The output format is system-dependent, as uustat simply invokes ps(1) on each process holding a lock. A sample output line is as follows:<br><br>`uustat -command rmail -older-than 168 -kill-all -no-list -mail -notify -comment "Queued for over 1 week"`<br><br>This will kill all rmail commands that have been queued up waiting for delivery for over one week (168 hours). For each such command, mail will be sent both to the UUCP administrator and to the user who requested the rmail execution. The mail message sent will include the string given by the --comment option. The --no-list option prevents any of the jobs from being listed on the terminal, so any output from the program will be error messages. |

## FILES

The filenames may be changed at compilation time or by the configuration file, so these are only approximations.

`/usr/lib/uucp/config` Configuration file

`/usr/spool/uucp` uucp spool directory

## SEE ALSO

ps(1), rmail(1), uucp(1), uux(1), uucico(8), uuxqt(8)

## AUTHOR

Ian Lance Taylor (ian@airs.com)

*Taylor UUCP 1.05*

# UUX

uux—Remote command execution over uucp

## SYNOPSIS

uux [ *options* ] *command*

## DESCRIPTION

The uux command is used to execute a command on a remote system, or to execute a command on the local system using files from remote systems. The command is not executed immediately; the request is queued until the uucico(8) daemon calls the system and executes it. The daemon is started automatically unless one of the -r or --nouucico options is given.

The actual command execution is done by the uuxqt(8) daemon.

File arguments can be gathered from remote systems to the execution system, as can standard input. Standard output may be directed to a file on a remote system.

The command name may be preceded by a system name followed by an exclamation point if it is to be executed on a remote system. An empty system name is taken as the local system.

Each argument that contains an exclamation point is treated as naming a file. The system that the file is on is before the exclamation point, and the pathname on that system follows it. An empty system name is taken as the local system; this must be used to transfer a file to a command being executed on a remote system. If the path is not absolute, it will be appended to the current working directory on the local system; the result may not be meaningful on the remote system. A pathname may begin with ˜/, in which case it is relative to the uucp public directory (usually /usr/spool/uucppublic) on the appropriate system. A pathname may begin with ˜name/, in which case it is relative to the home directory of the named user on the appropriate system.

Standard input and output may be redirected as usual; the pathnames used may contain exclamation points to indicate that they are on remote systems. Note that the redirection characters must be quoted so that they are passed to uux rather than interpreted by the shell. Append redirection (>>) does not work.

All specified files are gathered together into a single directory before execution of the command begins. This means that each file must have a distinct base name. For example,

```
uux 'sys1!diff sys2!˜user1/foo sys3!˜user2/foo >!foo.diff'
```

will fail because both files will be copied to sys1 and stored under the name foo.

Arguments may be quoted by parentheses to avoid interpretation of exclamation points. This is useful when executing the uucp command on a remote system.

## OPTIONS

The following options may be given to uux.

| | |
|---|---|
| -, -p, --stdin | Read standard input and use it as the standard input for the command to be executed. |
| -c, --nocopy | Do not copy local files to the spool directory. This is the default. If they are removed before being processed by the uucico(8) daemon, the copy will fail. The files must be readable by the uucico(8) daemon, as well as by the invoker of uux. |
| -C, --copy | Copy local files to the spool directory. |
| -l, --link | Link local files into the spool directory. If a file can not be linked because it is on a different device, it will be copied unless one of the -c or --nocopy options also appears (in other words, use of --link switches the default from --nocopy to --copy). If the files are changed before being processed by the uucico(8) daemon, the changed versions will be used. The files must be readable by the uucico(8) daemon, as well as by the invoker of uux. |
| -g *grade*, --grade *grade* | Set the grade of the file transfer command. Jobs of a higher grade are executed first. Grades run 0 ... 9 A ... Z a ... z from high to low. |
| -n, --notification=no | Do not send mail about the status of the job, even if it fails. |
| -z, --notification=*error* | Send mail about the status of the job if an error occurs. For many uuxqt daemons, including the Taylor uucp uuxqt, this is the default action; for those, --notification=*error* will have no effect. However, some uuxqt daemons will send mail if the job succeeds unless the --notification=error option is used, and some other uuxqt daemons will not send mail if the job fails unless the --notification=error option is used. |
| -r, --nouucico | Do not start the uucico(8) daemon immediately; merely queue up the execution request for later processing. |

| | |
|---|---|
| -j, --jobid | Print jobids on standard output. A jobid will be generated for each file copy operation required to perform the operation. These file copies may be canceled by passing the jobid to the --kill switch of uustat(1), which will make the execution impossible to complete. |
| -a address, --requestor address | Report job status to the specified e-mail address. |
| -x type, --debug type | Turn on particular debugging types. The following types are recognized: abnormal, chat, handshake, uucp-proto, proto, port, config, spooldir, execute, incoming, outgoing. Only abnormal, config, spooldir, and execute are meaningful for *uux*. Multiple types may be given, separated by commas, and the --debug option may appear multiple times. A number may also be given, which will turn on that many types from the foregoing list; for example, --debug 2 is equivalent to --debug abnormal,chat. |
| -I file, --config file | Set configuration file to use. This option may not be available, depending upon how uux was compiled. |
| -v, --version | Report version information and exit. |
| --help | Print a help message and exit. |

## EXAMPLES

uux -z - sys1!rmail user1—Execute the command rmail user1 on the system sys1, giving it as standard input whatever is given to uux as standard input. If a failure occurs, send a message using mail(1).

uux 'diff -c sys1!~user1/file1 sys2!~user2/file2 >!file.diff'—Fetch the two named files from system sys1 and system sys2 and execute diff, putting the result in file.diff in the current directory. The current directory must be writable by the uuxqt(8) daemon for this to work.

uux 'sys1!uucp ~user1/file1 (sys2!~user2/file2)'—Execute uucp on the system sys1 copying file1 (on system sys1) to sys2. This illustrates the use of parentheses for quoting.

## RESTRICTIONS

The remote system may not permit you to execute certain commands. Many remote systems only permit the execution of rmail and rnews.

Some of the options are dependent on the capabilities of the uuxqt(8) daemon on the remote system.

## FILES

The filenames may be changed at compilation time or by the configuration file, so these are only approximations.

| | |
|---|---|
| /usr/lib/uucp/config | Configuration file |
| /usr/spool/uucp uucp | spool directory |
| /usr/spool/uucp/Log | uucp log file |
| /usr/spool/uucppublic | Default uucp public directory |

## SEE ALSO

mail(1), uustat(1), uucp(1), uucico(8), uuxqt(8)

## BUGS

Files can not be referenced across multiple systems.

Too many jobids are output by --jobid, and there is no good way to cancel a local execution requiring remote files.

## AUTHOR

Ian Lance Taylor (ian@airs.com)

# uuxqt

uuxqt—uucp execution daemon

## SYNOPSIS

uuxqt [ *options* ]

## DESCRIPTION

The uuxqt daemon executes commands requested by uux(1) from either the local system or from remote systems. It is started automatically by the uucico(8) daemon (unless uucico(8) is given the -q or --nouuxqt option).

There is normally no need to run this command because it will be invoked by uucico(8). However, it can be used to provide greater control over the processing of the work queue.

Multiple invocations of uuxqt may be run at once, as controlled by the max-uuxqts configuration command.

## OPTIONS

The following options may be given to uuxqt:

| | |
|---|---|
| -c *command*, --command *command* | Only execute requests for the specified command. For example, uuxqt -command rmail |
| -s *system*, --system *system* | Only execute requests originating from the specified system. |
| -x *type*, --debug *type* | Turn on particular debugging types. The following types are recognized: abnormal, chat, handshake, uucp-proto, proto, port, config, spooldir, execute, incoming, outgoing. Only abnormal, config, spooldir and execute are meaningful for uuxqt. Multiple types may be given, separated by commas, and the --debug option may appear multiple times. A number may also be given, which will turn on that many types from the foregoing list; for example, --debug 2 is equivalent to --debug abnormal,chat. |
| | The debugging output is sent to the debugging file, usually /usr/spool/uucp/ Debug, /usr/spool/uucp/DEBUG, or /usr/spool/uucp/.Admin/audit.local. |
| -I *file*, --config | Set configuration file to use. This option may not be available, depending upon how uuxqt was compiled. |
| -v, --version | Report version information and exit. |
| --help | Print a help message and exit. |

## FILES

The filenames may be changed at compilation time or by the configuration file, so these are only approximations.

| | |
|---|---|
| /usr/lib/uucp/config | Configuration file |
| /usr/spool/uucp uucp | spool directory |
| /usr/spool/uucp/Log | uucp log file |
| /usr/spool/uucppublic | Default uucp public directory |
| /usr/spool/uucp/Debug | Debugging file |

## SEE ALSO

uucp(1), uux(1), uucico(8)

## AUTHOR

Ian Lance Taylor (ian@airs.com)

# W

w—Present who users are and what they are doing

## SYNOPSIS

w [-hin] [-*user*]

## DESCRIPTION

The w utility prints a summary of the current activity on the system, including what each user is doing. The first line displays the current time of day, how long the system has been running, the number of users logged into the system, and the load averages. The load average numbers give the number of jobs in the run queue averaged over 1, 5, and 15 minutes.

The fields output are the user's login name, the name of the terminal the user is on, the host from which the user is logged in, the time the user logged on, the time since the user last typed anything, and the name and arguments of the current process.

The options are as follows:

-h          Suppress the heading
-i          Output is sorted by idle time
-n          Show network addresses as numbers
-w          Interpret addresses and attempt to display them symbolically

If a username is specified, the output is restricted to that user.

## FILES

/var/run/utmp    List of users on the system

## SEE ALSO

who(1), finger(1), ps(1), uptime(1),

## BUGS

The notion of the current process is muddy. The current algorithm is "the highest numbered process on the terminal that is not ignoring interrupts, or, if there is none, the highest numbered process on the terminal." This fails, for example, in critical sections of programs like the shell and editor, or when faulty programs running in the background fork and fail to ignore interrupts. (In cases where no process can be found, w prints a period.)

The CPU time is only an estimate; in particular, if someone leaves a background process running after logging out, the person currently on that terminal is charged with the time.

Background processes are not shown, even though they account for much of the load on the system.

Sometimes processes, typically those in the background, are printed with null or garbaged arguments. In these cases, the name of the command is printed in parentheses.

The w utility does not know about the new conventions for detection of background jobs. It will sometimes find a background job instead of the right one.

## COMPATIBILITY

The -f, -l, -s, and -w flags are no longer supported.

## HISTORY

The w command appeared in BSD 3.0.

# wall

wall—Write a message to users

## SYNOPSIS

wall [*file*]

## DESCRIPTION

wall displays the contents of file or, by default, its standard input, on the terminals of all currently logged in users.

Only the superuser can write on the terminals of users who have chosen to deny messages or are using a program that automatically denies messages.

## SEE ALSO

mesg(1), talk(1), write(1), shutdown(8)

## HISTORY

A wall command appeared in AT&T v7.

*Linux 0.99, 8 March 1993*

# WC

wc—Print the number of bytes, words, and lines in files

## SYNOPSIS

wc [-clw] [--bytes] [--chars] [--lines] [--words] [--help] [--version] [*file...*]

## DESCRIPTION

This manual page documents the GNU version of wc. wc counts the number of bytes, whitespace-separated words, and newlines in each given file, or the standard input if none are given or when a file named - is given. It prints one line of counts for each file, and if the file was given as an argument, it prints the filename following the counts. If more than one filename is given, wc prints a final line containing the cumulative counts, with the filename total. The counts are printed in the order lines, words, bytes.

By default, wc prints all three counts. Options can specify that only certain counts be printed. Options do not undo others previously given, so wc --bytes --words prints both the byte counts and the word counts.

## OPTIONS

| | |
|---|---|
| -c, --bytes, --chars | Print only the byte counts. |
| -w, --words | Print only the word counts. |
| -l, --lines | Print only the newline counts. |
| --help | Print a usage message and exit with a non-zero status. |
| --version | Print version information on standard output, then exit. |

*GNU Text Utilities*

# whereis

whereis—Locate the binary, source, and manual page files for a command

## SYNOPSIS

whereis [ -bmsu ][-BMS *directory...* -f ] *filename* ...

## DESCRIPTION

whereis locates source/binary and manuals sections for specified files. The supplied names are first stripped of leading pathname components and any (single) trailing extension of the form `.ext`, for example, `.c`. Prefixes of `s.` resulting from use of source code control are also dealt with. whereis then attempts to locate the desired program in a list of standard Linux places:

```
/bin
/usr/bin
/etc
/usr/etc
/sbin
/usr/sbin
/usr/games
/usr/games/bin
/usr/emacs/etc
/usr/lib/emacs/19.22/etc
/usr/lib/emacs/19.23/etc
/usr/lib/emacs/19.24/etc
/usr/lib/emacs/19.25/etc
/usr/lib/emacs/19.26/etc
/usr/lib/emacs/19.27/etc
/usr/lib/emacs/19.28/etc
/usr/lib/emacs/19.29/etc
/usr/lib/emacs/19.30/etc
/usr/TeX/bin
/usr/tex/bin
/usr/interviews/bin/LINUX
/usr/bin/X11
/usr/X11/bin
/usr/X11R5/bin
/usr/X11R6/bin
/usr/X386/bin
/usr/local/bin
/usr/local/etc
/usr/local/sbin
/usr/local/games
/usr/local/games/bin
/usr/local/emacs/etc
/usr/local/TeX/bin
/usr/local/tex/bin
/usr/local/bin/X11
/usr/contrib
/usr/hosts
/usr/include
/usr/g++-include
```

## OPTIONS

-b       Search only for binaries.

-m      Search only for manual sections.

-s       Search only for sources.

-u      Search for unusual entries. A file is said to be unusual if it does not have one entry of each requested type. Thus whereisnn-mm-unn* asks for those files in the current directory which have no documentation.

-B      Change or otherwise limit the places where whereis searches for binaries.

-M      Change or otherwise limit the places where whereis searches for manual sections.

-S      Change or otherwise limit the places where whereis searches for sources.

-f       Terminate the last directory list and signals the start of filenames; *must* be used when any of the -B, -M, or -S options are used.

## EXAMPLE

Find all files in /usr/bin that are not documented in /usr/man/man1 with source in /usr/src:

```
example% cd /usr/bin
example% whereis -u -M /usr/man/man1 -S /usr/src -f *
```

## FILES

```
/{bin,sbin,etc}
/usr/{lib,bin,old,new,local,games,include,etc,src,man,sbin,
X386, TeX, g++-include}
/usr/local/{X386,TeX,X11,include,lib,man,etc,bin,games,emacs}
```

## SEE ALSO

chdir(2V)

## BUGS

Since whereis uses chdir(2V) to run faster, pathnames given with the -M, -S, or -B must be full; that is, they must begin with a /.

*8 May 1994*

# write

write—Send a message to another user

## SYNOPSIS

write *user* [*ttyname*]

## DESCRIPTION

write allows you to communicate with other users by copying lines from your terminal to theirs.

When you run the write command, the user you are writing to gets a message of the form:

Message from yourname@yourhost on yourtty at hh:mm ...

Any further lines you enter will be copied to the specified user's terminal. If the other user wants to reply, he or she must run write as well.

When you are done, type an end-of-file or interrupt character. The other user will see the message EOF, indicating that the conversation is over.

You can prevent people (other than the superuser) from writing to you with the mesg(1) command. Some commands, for example, nroff(1) and pr(1), may disallow writing automatically, so that your output isn't overwritten.

If the user you want to write to is logged in on more than one terminal, you can specify which terminal to write to by specifying the terminal name as the second oper and to the write command. Alternatively, you can let write select one of the terminals—it will pick the one with the shortest idle time. Thus, if the user is logged in at work and also dialed up from home, the message will go to the right place.

The traditional protocol for writing to someone is that the string -o, either at the end of a line or on a line by itself, means that it's the other person's turn to talk. The string oo means that the person believes the conversation to be over.

## SEE ALSO

mesg(1), talk(1), who(1)

## HISTORY

A write command appeared in Version 6 AT&T UNIX.

*12 March 1995*

# x11perf

x11perf—X11 server performance test program

## SYNTAX

x11perf [ -option ... ]

## DESCRIPTION

The x11perf program runs one or more performance tests and reports how fast an X server can execute the tests.

Many graphics benchmarks assume that the graphics device is used to display the output of a single fancy graphics application, and that the user gets his work done on some other device, like a terminal. Such benchmarks usually measure drawing speed for lines, polygons, text, and so on.

Because workstations are not used as standalone graphics engines, but as super-terminals, x11perf measures window management performance as well as traditional graphics performance. x11perf includes benchmarks for the time it takes to create and map windows (as when you start up an application); to map a preexisting set of windows onto the screen (as when you deiconify an application or pop up a menu); and to rearrange windows (as when you slosh windows to and fro trying to find the one you want).

x11perf also measures graphics performance for operations not normally used in standalone graphics displays, but are nonetheless used frequently by X applications. Such operations include CopyPlane (used to map bitmaps into pixels), scrolling (used in text windows), and various stipples and tiles (used for CAD and color halftoning, respectively).

x11perf should be used to analyze particular strengths and weaknesses of servers, and is most useful to a server writer who wants to analyze and improve a server. x11perf is meant to comprehensively exercise just about every X11 operation you can perform; it does not purport to be a representative sample of the operations that X11 applications actually use. Although it can be used as a benchmark, it was written and is intended as a performance testing tool.

As such, x11perf does not whittle down measurements to a single HeXStones or MeXops number. We consider such numbers to be uninformative at best and misleading at worst. Some servers that are very fast for certain applications can be very slow for others. No single number or small set of numbers is sufficient to characterize how an X implementation will perform on all applications. However, by knowledge of your favorite application, you may be able to use the numbers x11perf reports to predict its performance on a given X implementation.

That said, you might also want to look at x11perfcomp(1), a program to compare the outputs of different x11perf runs. You provide a list of files containing results from x11perf, and it lays them out in a nice tabular format.

For repeatable results, x11perf should be run using a local connection on a freshly started server. The default configuration runs each test five times in order to see if each trial takes approximately the same amount of time. Strange glitches should be examined; if nonrepeatable, you might chalk them up to daemons and network traffic. Each trial is run for five seconds, in order to reduce random time differences. The number of objects processed per second is displayed to three significant digits, but you'll be lucky on most UNIX systems if the numbers are actually consistent to two digits. x11perf moves the cursor out of the test window; you should be careful not to bump the mouse and move it back into the window. (A prize to people who correctly explain why!)

Before running a test, x11perf determines what the round trip time to the server is, and factors this out of the final timing reported. It ensures that the server has actually performed the work requested by fetching a pixel back from the test window, which means that servers talking to graphics accelerators can't claim that they are done, while in the meantime the accelerator is painting madly.

By default, x11perf automatically calibrates the number of repetitions of each test, so that each should take approximately the same length of time to run across servers of widely differing speeds. However, because each test must be run to completion at least once, some slow servers may take a very long time, particularly on the window moving and resizing tests, and on the arc drawing tests.

All timing reports are for the smallest object involved. For example, the line tests use a PolyLine request to paint several lines at once, but report how many lines per second the server can paint, not how many PolyLine requests per second. Text tests paint a line of characters, but report on the number of characters per second. Some window tests map, unmap, or move a single parent window, but report on how many children windows per second the server can map, unmap, or move.

The current program is mostly the responsibility of Joel McCormack. It is based upon the x11perf developed by Phil Karlton, Susan Angebranndt, Chris Kent, Mary Walker, and Todd Newman, who wanted to assess performance differences between various servers. Several tests were added in order to write and tune the PMAX (DECStation 3100) servers. For a general release to the world, x11perf was rewritten to ease making comparisons between widely varying machines, to cover most important (and unimportant) X functionality, and to exercise graphics operations in as many different orientations and alignments as possible.

## OPTIONS

x11perf is solely Xlib based, and accepts the following options:

| | |
|---|---|
| -display *host:dpy* | Specifies which display to use. |
| -sync | Runs the tests in synchronous mode. Normally only useful for debugging x11perf. |
| -pack | Runs rectangle tests so that they pack rectangles right next to each other. This makes it easy to debug server code for stipples and tiles; if the pattern looks ugly, you've got alignment problems. |
| -repeat *<n>* | Repeats each test *n* times (by default each test is run fivetimes). |
| -time *<s>* | Specifies how long in seconds each test should be run (default 5 seconds). |
| -all | Runs all tests. This may take a while. |
| -range *<test1>*[,*<test2>*] | Runs all the tests starting from the specified name *test1* until the name *test2*, tests. The testnames should be one of the options starting from -dot. For example, -range line100 will perform the tests from the 100 pixel line test, and go on till the last test; -range line100,dline10 will do the tests from line100 to dline10. |
| -labels | Generates just the descriptive labels for each test specified. See x11perfcomp for more details. |
| -fg *color-or-pixel* | Specifies the foreground color or pixel value to use. |
| -bg *color-or-pixel* | Specifies the background color or pixel value to use. |
| -clips *default* | Default number of clip windows. |

| | |
|---|---|
| -ddbg *color-or-pixel* | Specifies the color or pixel value to use for drawing the odd segments of a DoubleDashed line or arc. This will default to the bg color. |
| -rop <rop0 rop1 ...> | Use specified raster ops (default is GXcopy). This option only affects graphics benchmarks in which the graphics function is actually used. |
| -pm <*pm0 pm1* ...> | Use specified planemasks (default is ˜0). This option only affects graphics benchmarks in which the planemask is actually used. |
| -depth <*depth*> | Use a visual with <depth> planes per pixel. (Default is the default visual.) |
| -vclass <*vclass*> | Use a visual with of class <*vclass*>. <*vclass*> can be StaticGray, GrayScale, StaticColor, PseudoColor, TrueColor, or DirectColor. (Default is the default visual). |
| -reps <*n*> | Specify the repetition count. (Default is number that takes approximately five seconds.) |
| -subs <*s0 s1* ...> | Specify the number of sub windows to use in the Window tests. Default is 4, 16, 25, 50, 75, 100, and 200. |
| -v1.2 | Perform only x11perf version 1.2 tests using version 1.2 semantics. |
| -v1.3 | Perform only x11perf version 1.3 tests using version 1.3 semantics. |
| -su | Set the save_under window attribute to True on all windows created by x11perf. Default is False. |
| -bs <backing_store_hint> | Set the backing_store window attribute to the given value on all windows created by x11perf. <backing_store_hint> can be WhenMapped or Always. Default is NotUseful. |
| -dot | Dot. |
| -rect1 | 1×1 solid-filled rectangle. |
| -rect10 | 10×10 solid-filled rectangle. |
| -rect100 | 100×100 solid-filled rectangle. |
| -rect500 | 500×500 solid-filled rectangle. |
| -srect1 | 1×1 transparent stippled rectangle, 8×8 stipple pattern. |
| -srect10 | 10×10 transparent stippled rectangle, 8×8 stipple pattern. |
| -srect100 | 100×100 transparent stippled rectangle, 8×8 stipple pattern. |
| -srect500 | 500×500 transparent stippled rectangle, 8×8 stipple pattern. |
| -osrect1 | 1×1 opaque stippled rectangle, 8×8 stipple pattern. |
| -osrect10 | 10×10 opaque stippled rectangle, 8×8 stipple pattern. |
| -osrect100 | 100×100 opaque stippled rectangle, 8×8 stipple pattern. |
| -osrect500 | 500×500 opaque stippled rectangle, 8×8 stipple pattern. |
| -tilerect1 | 1×1 tiled rectangle, 4×4 tile pattern. |
| -tilerect10 | 10×10 tiled rectangle, 4×4 tile pattern. |
| -tilerect100 | 100×100 tiled rectangle, 4×4 tile pattern. |
| -tilerect500 | 500×500 tiled rectangle, 4×4 tile pattern. |
| -oddsrect1 | 1×1 transparent stippled rectangle, 17×15 stipple pattern. |
| -oddsrect10 | 10×10 transparent stippled rectangle, 17×15 stipple pattern. |
| -oddsrect100 | 100×100 transparent stippled rectangle, 17×15 stipple pattern. |
| -oddsrect500 | 500×500 transparent stippled rectangle, 17×15 stipple pattern. |
| -oddosrect1 | 1×1 opaque stippled rectangle, 17×15 stipple pattern. |
| -oddosrect10 | 10×10 opaque stippled rectangle, 17×15 stipple pattern. |
| -oddosrect100 | 100×100 opaque stippled rectangle, 17×15 stipple pattern. |
| -oddosrect500 | 500×500 opaque stippled rectangle, 17×15 stipple pattern. |
| -oddtilerect1 | 1×1 tiled rectangle, 17×15 tile pattern. |
| -oddtilerect10 | 10×10 tiled rectangle, 17×15 tile pattern. |

| | |
|---|---|
| `-oddtilerect100` | 100×100 tiled rectangle, 17×15 tile pattern. |
| `-oddtilerect500` | 500×500 tiled rectangle, 17×15 tile pattern. |
| `-bigsrect1` | 1×1 stippled rectangle, 161×145 stipple pattern. |
| `-bigsrect10` | 10×10 stippled rectangle, 161×145 stipple pattern. |
| `-bigsrect100` | 100×100 stippled rectangle, 161×145 stipple pattern. |
| `-bigsrect500` | 500×500 stippled rectangle, 161×145 stipple pattern. |
| `-bigosrect1` | 1×1 opaque stippled rectangle, 161×145 stipple pattern. |
| `-bigosrect10` | 10×10 opaque stippled rectangle, 161×145 stipple pattern. |
| `-bigosrect100` | 100×100 opaque stippled rectangle, 161×145 stipple pattern. |
| `-bigosrect500` | 500×500 opaque stippled rectangle, 161×145 stipple pattern. |
| `-bigtilerect1` | 1×1 tiled rectangle, 161×145 tile pattern. |
| `-bigtilerect10` | 10×10 tiled rectangle, 161×145 tile pattern. |
| `-bigtilerect100` | 100×100 tiled rectangle, 161×145 tile pattern. |
| `-bigtilerect500` | 500×500 tiled rectangle, 161×145 tile pattern. |
| `-eschertilerect1` | 1×1 tiled rectangle, 215×208 tile pattern. |
| `-eschertilerect10` | 10×10 tiled rectangle, 215×208 tile pattern. |
| `-eschertilerect100` | 100×100 tiled rectangle, 215×208 tile pattern. |
| `-eschertilerect500` | 500×500 tiled rectangle, 215×208 tile pattern. |
| `-seg1` | 1-pixel thin line segment. |
| `-seg10` | 10-pixel thin line segment. |
| `-seg100` | 100-pixel thin line segment. |
| `-seg500` | 500-pixel thin line segment. |
| `-seg100c1` | 100-pixel thin line segment (1 obscuring rectangle). |
| `-seg100c2` | 100-pixel thin line segment (2 obscuring rectangles). |
| `-seg100c3` | 100-pixel thin line segment (3 obscuring rectangles). |
| `-dseg10` | 10-pixel thin dashed segment (3 on, 2 off). |
| `-dseg100` | 100-pixel thin dashed segment (3 on, 2 off). |
| `-ddseg100` | 100-pixel thin double-dashed segment (3 fg, 2 bg). |
| `-hseg10` | 10-pixel thin horizontal line segment. |
| `-hseg100` | 100-pixel thin horizontal line segment. |
| `-hseg500` | 500-pixel thin horizontal line segment. |
| `-vseg10` | 10-pixel thin vertical line segment. |
| `-vseg100` | 100-pixel thin vertical line segment. |
| `-vseg500` | 500-pixel thin vertical line segment. |
| `-whseg10` | 10-pixel wide horizontal line segment. |
| `-whseg100` | 100-pixel wide horizontal line segment. |
| `-whseg500` | 500-pixel wide horizontal line segment. |
| `-wvseg10` | 10-pixel wide vertical line segment. |
| `-wvseg100` | 100-pixel wide vertical line segment. |
| `-wvseg500` | 500-pixel wide vertical line segment. |
| `-line1` | 1-pixel thin (width 0) line. |
| `-line10` | 10-pixel thin line. |
| `-line100` | 100-pixel thin line. |
| `-line500` | 500-pixel thin line. |

| | |
|---|---|
| -dline10 | 10-pixel thin dashed line (3 on, 2 off). |
| -dline100 | 100-pixel thin dashed line (3 on, 2 off). |
| -ddline100 | 100-pixel thin double-dashed line (3 fg, 2 bg). |
| -wline10 | 10-pixel line, line width 1. |
| -wline100 | 100-pixel line, line width 10. |
| -wline500 | 500-pixel line, line width 50. |
| -wdline100 | 100-pixel dashed line, line width 10 (30 on, 20 off). |
| -wddline100 | 100-pixel double-dashed line, line width 10 (30 fg, 20 bg). |
| -orect10 | 10x10 thin rectangle outline. |
| -orect100 | 100-pixel thin vertical line segment. |
| -orect500 | 500-pixel thin vertical line segment. |
| -worect10 | 10×10 wide rectangle outline. |
| -worect100 | 100-pixel wide vertical line segment. |
| -worect500 | 500-pixel wide vertical line segment. |
| -circle1 | 1-pixel diameter thin (line-width 0) circle. |
| -circle10 | 10-pixel diameter thin circle. |
| -circle100 | 100-pixel diameter thin circle. |
| -circle500 | 500-pixel diameter thin circle. |
| -dcircle100 | 100-pixel diameter thin dashed circle (3 on, 2 off). |
| -ddcircle100 | 100-pixel diameter thin double-dashed circle (3 fg, 2 bg). |
| -wcircle10 | 10-pixel diameter circle, line width 1. |
| -wcircle100 | 100-pixel diameter circle, line width 10. |
| -wcircle500 | 500-pixel diameter circle, line width 50. |
| -wdcircle100 | 100-pixel diameter dashed circle, line width 10 (30 on, 20 off). |
| -wddcircle100 | 100-pixel diameter double-dashed circle, line width 10 (30 fg, 20 bg). |
| -pcircle10 | 10-pixel diameter thin partial circle, orientation and arc angle evenly distributed. |
| -pcircle100 | 100-pixel diameter thin partial circle. |
| -wpcircle10 | 10-pixel diameter wide partial circle. |
| -wpcircle100 | 100-pixel diameter wide partial circle. |
| -fcircle1 | 1-pixel diameter filled circle. |
| -fcircle10 | 10-pixel diameter filled circle. |
| -fcircle100 | 100-pixel diameter filled circle. |
| -fcircle500 | 500-pixel diameter filled circle. |
| -fcpcircle10 | 10-pixel diameter partial-filled circle, chord fill, orientation and arc angle evenly distributed. |
| -fcpcircle100 | 100-pixel diameter partial-filled circle, chord fill. |
| -fspcircle10 | 10-pixel diameter partial-filled circle, pie slice fill, orientation and arc angle evenly distributed. |
| -fspcircle100 | 100-pixel diameter partial-filled circle, pie slice fill. |
| -ellipse10 | 10-pixel diameter thin (line width 0) ellipse, major and minor axis sizes evenly distributed. |
| -ellipse100 | 100-pixel diameter thin ellipse. |
| -ellipse500 | 500-pixel diameter thin ellipse. |
| -dellipse100 | 100-pixel diameter thin dashed ellipse (3 on, 2 off). |
| -ddellipse100 | 100-pixel diameter thin double-dashed ellipse (3 fg, 2 bg). |
| -wellipse10 | 10-pixel diameter ellipse, line width 1. |

| | |
|---|---|
| `-wellipse100` | 100-pixel diameter ellipse, line width 10. |
| `-wellipse500` | 500-pixel diameter ellipse, line width 50. |
| `-wdellipse100` | 100-pixel diameter dashed ellipse, line width 10 (30 on, 20 off). |
| `-wddellipse100` | 100-pixel diameter double-dashed ellipse, line width 10 (30 `fg`, 20 `bg`). |
| `-pellipse10` | 10-pixel diameter thin partial ellipse. |
| `-pellipse100` | 100 pixel diameter thin partial ellipse. |
| `-wpellipse10` | 10-pixel diameter wide partial ellipse. |
| `-wpellipse100` | 100-pixel diameter wide partial ellipse. |
| `-fellipse10` | 10-pixel diameter filled ellipse. |
| `-fellipse100` | 100-pixel diameter filled ellipse. |
| `-fellipse500` | 500-pixel diameter filled ellipse. |
| `-fcpellipse10` | 10-pixel diameter partial-filled ellipse, chord fill. |
| `-fcpellipse100` | 100-pixel diameter partial-filled ellipse, chord fill. |
| `-fspellipse10` | 10-pixel diameter partial-filled ellipse, pie slice fill. |
| `-fspellipse100` | 100-pixel diameter partial-filled ellipse, pie slice fill. |
| `-triangle1` | Fill 1-pixel/side triangle. |
| `-triangle10` | Fill 10-pixel/side triangle. |
| `-triangle100` | Fill 100-pixel/side triangle. |
| `-trap1` | Fill 1×1 trapezoid. |
| `-trap10` | Fill 10×10 trapezoid. |
| `-trap100` | Fill 100×100 trapezoid. |
| `-trap300` | Fill 300×300 trapezoid. |
| `-strap1` | Fill 1×1 transparent stippled trapezoid, 8×8 stipple pattern. |
| `-strap10` | Fill 10×10 transparent stippled trapezoid, 8×8 stipple pattern. |
| `-strap100` | Fill 100×100 transparent stippled trapezoid, 8×8 stipple pattern. |
| `-strap300` | Fill 300×300 transparent stippled trapezoid, 8×8 stipple pattern. |
| `-ostrap1` | Fill 10×10 opaque stippled trapezoid, 8×8 stipple pattern. |
| `-ostrap10` | Fill 10×10 opaque stippled trapezoid, 8×8 stipple pattern. |
| `-ostrap100` | Fill 100×100 opaque stippled trapezoid, 8×8 stipple pattern. |
| `-ostrap300` | Fill 300×300 opaque stippled trapezoid, 8×8 stipple pattern. |
| `-tiletrap1` | Fill 10×10 tiled trapezoid, 4×4 tile pattern. |
| `-tiletrap10` | Fill 10×10 tiled trapezoid, 4×4 tile pattern. |
| `-tiletrap100` | Fill 100×100 tiled trapezoid, 4×4 tile pattern. |
| `-tiletrap300` | Fill 300×300 tiled trapezoid, 4×4 tile pattern. |
| `-oddstrap1` | Fill 1×1 transparent stippled trapezoid, 17×15 stipple pattern. |
| `-oddstrap10` | Fill 10×10 transparent stippled trapezoid, 17×15 stipple pattern. |
| `-oddstrap100` | Fill 100×100 transparent stippled trapezoid, 17×15 stipple pattern. |
| `-oddstrap300` | Fill 300×300 transparent stippled trapezoid, 17×15 stipple pattern. |
| `-oddostrap1` | Fill 10×10 opaque stippled trapezoid, 17×15 stipple pattern. |
| `-oddostrap10` | Fill 10×10 opaque stippled trapezoid, 17×15 stipple pattern. |
| `-oddostrap100` | Fill 100×100 opaque stippled trapezoid, 17×15 stipple pattern. |
| `-oddostrap300` | Fill 300×300 opaque stippled trapezoid, 17×15 stipple pat-tern. |
| `-oddtiletrap1` | Fill 10×10 tiled trapezoid, 17×15 tile pattern. |
| `-oddtiletrap10` | Fill 10×10 tiled trapezoid, 17×15 tile pattern. |

| | |
|---|---|
| `-oddtiletrap100` | Fill 100×100 tiled trapezoid, 17×15 tile pattern. |
| `-oddtiletrap300` | Fill 300×300 tiled trapezoid, 17×15 tile pattern. |
| `-bigstrap1` | Fill 1×1 transparent stippled trapezoid, 161×145 stipple pattern. |
| `-bigstrap10` | Fill 10×10 transparent stippled trapezoid, 161×145 stipple pattern. |
| `-bigstrap100` | Fill 100×100 transparent stippled trapezoid, 161×145 stipple pattern. |
| `-bigstrap300` | Fill 300×300 transparent stippled trapezoid, 161×145 stipple pattern. |
| `-bigostrap1` | Fill 10×10 opaque stippled trapezoid, 161×145 stipple pattern. |
| `-bigostrap10` | Fill 10×10 opaque stippled trapezoid, 161×145 stipple pattern. |
| `-bigostrap100` | Fill 100×100 opaque stippled trapezoid, 161×145 stipple pattern. |
| `-bigostrap300` | Fill 300×300 opaque stippled trapezoid, 161×145 stipple pattern. |
| `-bigtiletrap1` | Fill 10×10 tiled trapezoid, 161×145 tile pattern. |
| `-bigtiletrap10` | Fill 10×10 tiled trapezoid, 161×145 tile pattern. |
| `-bigtiletrap100` | Fill 100×100 tiled trapezoid, 161×145 tile pattern. |
| `-bigtiletrap300` | Fill 300×300 tiled trapezoid, 161×145 tile pattern. |
| `-eschertiletrap1` | Fill 1×1 tiled trapezoid, 216×208 tile pattern. |
| `-eschertiletrap10` | Fill 10×10 tiled trapezoid, 216×208 tile pattern. |
| `-eschertiletrap100` | Fill 100×100 tiled trapezoid, 216×208 tile pattern. |
| `-eschertiletrap300` | Fill 300×300 tiled trapezoid, 216×208 tile pattern. |
| `-complex10` | Fill 10-pixel/side complex polygon. |
| `-complex100` | Fill 100-pixel/side complex polygon. |
| `-64poly10convex` | Fill 10×10 convex 64-gon. |
| `-64poly100convex` | Fill 100×100 convex 64-gon. |
| `-64poly10complex` | Fill 10×10 complex 64-gon. |
| `-64poly100complex` | Fill 100×100 complex 64-gon. |
| `-ftext` | Character in 80-char line (6×13). |
| `-f8text` | Character in 70-char line (8×13). |
| `-f9text` | Character in 60-char line (9×15). |
| `-f14text16` | 2-byte character in 40-char line (k14). |
| `-tr10text` | Character in 80-char line (Times-Roman 10). |
| `-tr24text` | Character in 30-char line (Times-Roman 24). |
| `-polytext` | Character in 20/40/20 line (6×13, Times-Roman 10, 6×13). |
| `-polytext16` | 2-byte character in 7/14/7 line (k14, k24). |
| `-fitext` | Character in 80-char image line (6×13). |
| `-f8itext` | Character in 70-char image line (8×13). |
| `-f9itext` | Character in 60-char image line (9×15). |
| `-f14itext16` | 2-byte character in 40-char image line (k14). |
| `-f24itext16` | 2-byte character in 23-char image line (k24). |
| `-tr10itext` | Character in 80-char image line (Times-Roman 10). |
| `-tr24itext` | Character in 30-char image line (Times-Roman 24). |
| `-scroll10` | Scroll 10×10 pixels vertically. |
| `-scroll100` | Scroll 100×100 pixels vertically. |
| `-scroll500` | Scroll 500×500 pixels vertically. |

| | |
|---|---|
| -copywinwin10 | Copy 10×10 square from window to window. |
| -copywinwin100 | Copy 100×100 square from window to window. |
| -copywinwin500 | Copy 500×500 square from window to window. |
| -copypixwin10 | Copy 10×10 square from pixmap to window. |
| -copypixwin100 | Copy 100×100 square from pixmap to window. |
| -copypixwin500 | Copy 500×500 square from pixmap to window. |
| -copywinpix10 | Copy 10×10 square from window to pixmap. |
| -copywinpix100 | Copy 100×100 square from window to pixmap. |
| -copywinpix500 | Copy 500×500 square from window to pixmap. |
| -copypixpix10 | Copy 10×10 square from pixmap to pixmap. |
| -copypixpix100 | Copy 100×100 square from pixmap to pixmap. |
| -copypixpix500 | Copy 500×500 square from pixmap to pixmap. |
| -copyplane10 | Copy 10×10 1-bit deep plane. |
| -copyplane100 | Copy 100×100 1-bit deep plane. |
| -copyplane500 | Copy 500×500 1-bit deep plane. |
| -putimage10 | PutImage 10×10 square. |
| -putimage100 | PutImage 100×100 square. |
| -putimage500 | PutImage 500×500 square. |
| -putimagexy10 | PutImage XY format 10×10 square. |
| -putimagexy100 | PutImage XY format 100×100 square. |
| -putimagexy500 | PutImage XY format 500×500 square. |
| -shmput10 | PutImage 10×10 square, MIT-shared memory extension. |
| -shmput100 | PutImage 100×100 square, MIT-shared memory extension. |
| -shmput500 | PutImage 500×500 square, MIT-shared memory extension. |
| -shmputxy10 | PutImage XY format 10×10 square, MIT-shared memory extension. |
| -shmputxy100 | PutImage XY format 100×100 square, MIT-shared memory extension. |
| -shmputxy500 | PutImage XY format 500×500 square, MIT-shared memory extension. |
| -getimage10 | GetImage 10×10 square. |
| -getimage100 | GetImage 100×100 square. |
| -getimage500 | GetImage 500×500 square. |
| -getimagexy10 | GetImage XY format 10×10 square. |
| -getimagexy100 | GetImage XY format 100×100 square. |
| -getimagexy500 | GetImage XY format 500×500 square. |
| -noop | X protocol NoOperation. |
| -atom | GetAtomName. |
| -pointer | QueryPointer. |
| -prop | GetProperty. |
| -gc | Change graphics context. |
| -create | Create child window and map using MapSubwindows. |
| -ucreate | Create unmapped window. |
| -map | Map child window via MapWindow on parent. |
| -unmap | Unmap child window via UnmapWindow on parent. |
| -destroy | Destroy child window via DestroyWindow parent. |
| -popup | Hide/expose window via Map/Unmap pop-up window. |

| -move | Move window. |
|---|---|
| -umove | Moved unmapped window. |
| -movetree | Move window via MoveWindow on parent. |
| -resize | Resize window. |
| -uresize | Resize unmapped window. |
| -circulate | Circulate lowest window to top. |
| -ucirculate | Circulate unmapped window to top. |

## X DEFAULTS

There are no X defaults used by this program.

## SEE ALSO

X(1), xbench(1), x11perfcomp(1)

## AUTHORS

Joel McCormack
Phil Karlton
Susan Angebranndt
Chris Kent
Keith Packard
Graeme Gill

*X Version 11 Release 6*

# x11perfcomp

x11perfcomp—X11 server performance comparison program

## SYNTAX

x11perfcomp [-rj -ro ] [ -l label_file ] *files*

## DESCRIPTION

The x11perfcomp program merges the output of several x11perf(1) runs into a nice tabular format. It takes the results in each file, fills in any missing test results if necessary, and for each test shows the objects/second rate of each server. If invoked with the -r or -ro options, it shows the relative performance of each server to the first server.

Normally, x11perfcomp uses the first file specified to determine which specific tests it should report on. Some (non-DEC:) servers may fail to perform all tests. In this case, x11perfcomp automatically substitutes in a rate of 0.0 objects/second. Since the first file determines which tests to report on, this file must contain a superset of the tests reported in the other files, else x11perfcomp will fail.

You can provide an explicit list of tests to report on by using the -l switch to specify a file of labels. You can create a label file by using the -label option in x11perf.

## OPTIONS

x11perfcomp accepts the following options:

| -r | Specifies that the output should also include relative server performance. |
|---|---|
| -ro | Specifies that the output should include only relative server performance. |
| -l_label_file | Specifies a label file to use. |

## X DEFAULTS

There are no X defaults used by this program.

## SEE ALSO

X(1), x11perf(1)

## AUTHORS

Mark Moraes wrote the original scripts to compare servers. Joel McCormack just munged them together a bit.

*X Version 11 Release 6*

# xargs

xargs—Build and execute command lines from standard input

## SYNOPSIS

**xargs** [-0prtx] [-e[eof-str]] [-i[replace-str]] [-l[max-lines]] [-n max-args]
[-s max-chars] [-P max-procs] [--null] [--eof[=eof-str]] [--replace[=replace-str]]
[--max-lines[=max-lines]] [--interactive] [--max-chars=max-chars] [--verbose]
[--exit] [--max-procs=max-procs] [--max-args=max-args] [--no-run-if-empty]
[--version] [--help] [command [initial-arguments]]

## DESCRIPTION

This manual page documents the GNU version of xargs. xargs reads arguments from the standard input, delimited by blanks (which can be protected with double or single quotes or a backslash) or newlines, and executes the command (default is /bin/echo) one or more times with any initial-arguments followed by arguments read from standard input. Blank lines on the standard input are ignored.

xargs exits with the following status:

   0 if it succeeds

   123 if any invocation of the command exited with status 1-125

   124 if the command exited with status 255

   125 if the command is killed by a signal

   126 if the command cannot be run

   127 if the command is not found

   1 if some other error occurred.

## OPTIONS

| | |
|---|---|
| --null, -0 | Input filenames are terminated by a null character instead of by whitespace, and the quotes and backslash are not special (every character is taken literally). Disables the end-of-file string, which is treated like any other argument. Useful when arguments might contain whitespace, quote marks, or backslashes. The GNU find -print0 option produces input suitable for this mode. |
| --eof[=eof-str], -e[eof-str] | Set the end-of-file string to eof-str. If the end-of-file string occurs as a line of input, the rest of the input is ignored. If eof-str is omitted, there is no end of file string. If this option is not given, the end-of-file string defaults to an underscore. |
| --help | Print a summary of the options to xargs and exit. |
| --replace[=replace-str], -i[replace-str] | Replace occurrences of *replace-str* in the initial arguments with names read from standard input. Also, unquoted blanks do not terminate arguments. If replace-str is omitted, it defaults to {} (like for find -exec). Implies -x and -l 1. |

| | |
|---|---|
| --max-lines[=*max-lines*], -l[*max-lines*] | Use at most *max-lines* nonblank input lines per command line; *max-lines* defaults to 1 if omitted. Trailing blanks cause an input line to be logically continued on the next input line. Implies -x. |
| --max-args=*max-args*, -n *max-args* | Use at most *max-args* arguments per command line. Fewer than *max-args* arguments will be used if the size (see the -s option) is exceeded, unless the -x option is given, in which case xargs will exit. |
| --interactive, -p | Prompt the user about whether to run each command line and read a line from the terminal. Only run the command line if the response starts with y or Y. Implies -t. |
| --no-run-if-empty, -r | If the standard input does not contain any nonblanks, do not run the command. Normally, the command is run once even if there is no input. |
| --max-chars=*max-chars*, -s *max-chars* | Use at most *max-chars* characters per command line, including the command and initial arguments and the terminating nulls at the ends of the argument strings. The default is as large as possible, up to 20k characters. |
| --verbose, -t | Print the command line on the standard error output before executing it. |
| --version | Print the version number of xargs and exit. |
| --exit, -x | Exit if the size (see the -s option) is exceeded. |
| --max-procs=*max-procs*, -P *max-procs* | Run up to *max-procs* processes at a time; the default is 1. If *max-procs* is 0, xargs will run as many processes as possible at a time. Use the -n option with -P; otherwise, chances are that only one exec will be done. |

## SEE ALSO

find(1L), locate(1L), locatedb(5L), updatedb(1) *Finding Files* (online in info, or printed)

# xauth

xauth—X authority file utility

## SYNOPSIS

xauth [ -f *authfile* ][-vqib ][command *arg* ... ]

## DESCRIPTION

The xauth program is used to edit and display the authorization information used in connecting to the X server. This program is usually used to extract authorization records from one machine and merge them in on another (as is the case when using remote logins or granting access to other users). Commands (described below) may be entered interactively, on the xauth command line, or in scripts. Note that this program does not contact the X server. Normally xauth is not used to create the authority file entry in the first place; xdm does that.

## OPTIONS

The following options may be used with xauth. They may be given individually (for example, -q -i ) or may combined (for example, -qi).

| | |
|---|---|
| -f *authfile* | This option specifies the name of the authority file to use. By default, xauth will use the file specified by the XAUTHORITY environment variable or Xauthority in the user's home directory. |
| -q | This option indicates that xauth should operate quietly and not print unsolicited status messages. This is the default if an xauth command is given on the command line or if the standard output is not directed to a terminal. |
| -v | This option indicates that xauth should operate verbosely and print status messages indicating the results of various operations (such as how many records have been read in or written out). This is the default if xauth is reading commands from its standard input and its standard output is directed to a terminal. |

-i    This option indicates that xauth should ignore any authority file locks. Normally, xauth will refuse to read or edit any authority files that have been locked by other programs (usually xdm or another xauth).

-b    This option indicates that xauth should attempt to break any authority file locks before proceeding. Use this option only to clean up stale locks.

## COMMANDS

The following commands may be used to manipulate authority files:

add *displayname* *protocolname hexkey*    An authorization entry for the indicated display using the given protocol and key data is added to the authorization file. The data is specified as an even-lengthed string   of hexadecimal digits, each pair representing one octet. The first digit of each pair gives the most significant 4 bits of the octet, and the second digit of the pair gives the least significant 4 bits. For example, a 32-character hexkey would represent a 128-bit value. A protocol name consisting of just a single period is treated as an abbreviation for MIT-MAGIC-COOKIE-1.

[n]extract *filename* *displayname...*    Authorization entries for each of the specified displays are written to the indicated file. If the nextract command is used, the entries are written in a numeric format suitable for nonbinary transmission (such as secure electronic mail). The extracted entries can be read back in using the merge and nmerge commands.

If the filename consists of just a single dash, the entries will be written to the standard output.

[n]list [*displayname...*]    Authorization entries for each of the specified displays (or all if no displays are named) are printed on the standard output. If the nlist command is used, entries will be shown in the numeric format used by the nextract command; otherwise, they are shown in a textual format. Key data is always displayed in the hexadecimal format given in the description of the add command.

[n]merge [*filename...*]    Authorization entries are read from the specified files and are merged into the authorization database, superceding any matching existing entries. If the nmerge command is used, the numeric format given in the description of the extract command is used. If a filename consists of just a single dash, the standard input will be read if it hasn't been read before.

remove *displayname...*    Authorization entries matching the specified displays are removed from the authority file.

source *filename*    The specified file is treated as a script containing xauth commands to execute. Blank lines and lines beginning with a pound sign (#) are ignored. A single hyphen may be used to indicate the standard input, if it hasn't already been read.

info    Information describing the authorization file, whether or not any changes have been made, and from where xauth commands are being read is printed on the standard output.

exit    If any modifications have been made, the authority file is written out (if allowed), and the program exits. An end-of-file is treated as an implicit exit command.

quit    The program exits, ignoring any modifications. This may also be accomplished by pressing the interrupt character.

help [*string*]    A description of all commands that begin with the given string (or all commands if no string is given) is printed on the standard output.

?    A short list of the valid commands is printed on the standard output.

## DISPLAY NAMES

Display names for the add, [n]extract, [n]list, [n]merge,and remove commands use the same format as the DISPLAY environment variable and the common -display command-line argument. Display-specific information (such as the screen number) is unnecessary and will be ignored. Same-machine connections (such as local-host sockets, shared memory, and the Internet Protocol hostname localhost) are referred to as hostname/unix:displaynumber so that local entries for different machines may be stored in one authority file.

## EXAMPLE

The most common use for xauth is to extract the entry for the current display, copy it to another machine, and merge it into the user's authority file on the remote machine:

```
% xauth extract
  - $DISPLAY ¦ rsh otherhost xauth merge -
```

## ENVIRONMENT

This xauth program uses the following environment variables:

XAUTHORITY    To get the name of the authority file to use if the -f option isn't used.

HOME          To get the user's home directory if XAUTHORITY isn't defined.

## FILES

$HOME/.Xauthority is the default authority file if XAUTHORITY isn't defined.

*X Version 11 Release 6*

| | |
|---|---|
| [n]list [*displayname*...] | Authorization entries for each of the specified displays (or all if no displays are named) are printed on the standard output. If the nlist command is used, entries will be shown in the numeric format used by the nextract command; otherwise, they are shown in a textual format. Key data is always displayed in the hexadecimal format given in the description of the add command. |
| [n]merge [*filename*...] | Authorization entries are read from the specified files and are merged into the authorization database, superseding any matching existing entries. If the nmerge command is used, the numeric format given in the description of the extract command is used. If a filename consists of just a single dash, the standard input will be read if it hasn't been read before. |
| remove *displayname*... | Authorization entries matching the specified displays are removed from the authority file. |
| source *filename* | The specified file is treated as a script containing xauth commands to execute. Blank lines and lines beginning with a # are ignored. A single dash may be used to indicate the standard input, if it hasn't already been read. |
| info | Information describing the authorization file, whether or not any changes have been made, and from where xauth commands are being read is printed on the standard output. |
| exit | If any modifications have been made, the authority file is written out (if allowed), and the program exits. An end of file is treated as an implicit exit command. |
| quit | The program exits, ignoring any modifications. This may also be accomplished by pressing the interrupt character. |
| help [*string*] | A description of all commands that begin with the given string (or all commands if no string is given) is printed on the standard output. |
| ? | A short list of the valid commands is printed on the standard output. |

## DISPLAY NAMES

Display names for the add, [n]extract, [n]list, [n]merge, and remove commands use the same format as the DISPLAY environment variable and the common -display command-line argument. Display-specific information (such as the screen number) is unnecessary and will be ignored. Same-machine connections (such as local-host sockets, shared memory, and the Internet Protocol hostname*localhost*) are referred to as hostname/unix:displaynumber so that local entries for different machines may be stored in one authority file.

## EXAMPLE

The most common use for xauth is to extract the entry for the current display, copy it to another machine, and merge it into the user's authority file on the remote machine:

```
% xauth extract
- $DISPLAY rsh otherhost xauth merge -
```

## ENVIRONMENT

This xauth program uses the following environment variables:

| | |
|---|---|
| XAUTHORITY | To get the name of the authority file to use if the -f option isn't used |
| HOME | To get the user's home directory if XAUTHORITY isn't defined |

## FILES

| | |
|---|---|
| $HOME/.Xauthority | Default authority file if XAUTHORITY isn't defined |

## BUGS

Users that have unsecured networks should take care to use encrypted file transfer mechanisms to copy authorization entries between machines. Similarly, the MIT-MAGIC-COOKIE-1 protocol is not very useful in unsecured environments. Sites that are interested in additional security may need to use encrypted authorization mechanisms such as Kerberos.

Spaces are currently not allowed in the protocol name. Quoting could be added for the truly perverse.

## AUTHOR

Jim Fulton, MIT X Consortium

*X Version 11 Release 6*

# xbmtopbm

xbmtopbm—Convert an X11 or X10 bitmap into a portable bitmap

## SYNOPSIS

xbmtopbm [*bitmapfile*]

## DESCRIPTION

Reads an X11 or X10 bitmap as input. Produces a portable bitmap as output.

## SEE ALSO

pbmtoxbm(1), pbmtox10bm(1), pbm(5)

## AUTHOR

Copyright (c) 1988 by Jef Poskanzer.

*31 August 1988*

# xcmsdb

xcmsdb—Device Color Characterization utility for X Color Management System

## SYNOPSIS

xcmsdb [ -query ][-remove ][-format 32j16j8 ][*filename* ]

## DESCRIPTION

xcmsdb is used to load, query, or remove device color characterization data stored in properties on the root window of the screen as specified in section 7, Device Color Characterization, of the ICCCM. Device color characterization data (also called the Device Profile) is an integral part of Xlib's X Color Management System (xcms), necessary for proper conversion of color specification between device-independent and device-dependent forms. xcms uses 3×3 matrices stored in the XDCCC_LINEAR_RGB_MATRICES property to convert color specifications between CIEXYZ and RGB Intensity (XcmsRGBi, also referred to as linear RGB). xcms then uses display gamma information stored in the XDCCC_LINEAR_RGB_CORRECTION property to convert color specifications between RGBi and RGB device (XcmsRGB, also referred to as device RGB).

Note that xcms allows clients to register function sets in addition to its built-in function set for CRT color monitors. Additional function sets may store their device profile information in other properties in function set specific format. This utility is unaware of these nonstandard properties.

The ASCII readable contents of filename (or the standard input if no input file is given) are appropriately transformed for storage in properties, provided the -query or -remove options are not specified.

## OPTIONS

xcmsdb program accepts the following options:

| | |
|---|---|
| -query | This option attempts to read the XDCCC properties off the screen's root window. If successful, it transforms the data into a more readable format, then sends the data to standard out. |
| -remove | This option attempts to remove the XDCCC properties on the screen's root window. |
| -format 32j16j8 | Specifies the property format (32, 16, or 8 bits per entry) for the XDCCC_LINEAR_RGB_CORRECTION property. Precision of encoded floating-point values increases with the increase in bits per entry. The default is 32 bits per entry. |

## SEE ALSO

xprop(1), Xlib documentation

## ENVIRONMENT

| | |
|---|---|
| DISPLAY | To figure out which display and screen to use |

## AUTHOR

Chuck Adams, Tektronix, Inc., and Al Tabayoyon, SynChromatics, Inc. (added multivisual support)

*X Version 11 Release 6*

# xclock

xclock—Analog/digital clock for X

## SYNOPSIS

xclock [ -help ][-analog ][-digital ][-chime ][-hd *color* ][-hl *color* ]
      [-update *seconds* ][-padding *number* ]

## DESCRIPTION

The xclock program displays the time in analog or digital form. The time is continuously updated at a frequency which may be specified by the user.

## OPTIONS

`xclock` accepts all of the standard X Toolkit command-line options along with the additional options listed here:

| | |
|---|---|
| -help | This option indicates that a brief summary of the allowed options should be printed on the standard error. |
| -analog | This option indicates that a conventional 12-hour clock face with tick marks and hands should be used. This is the default. |
| -digital or -d | This option indicates that a 24-hour digital clock should be used. |
| -chime | This option indicates that the clock should chime once on the half hour and twice on the hour. |
| -hands *color* (or -hd *color*) | This option specifies the color of the hands on an analog clock. The default is `black`. |
| -highlight *color* (or -hl *color*) | This option specifies the color of the edges of the hands on an analog clock, and is only useful on color displays. The default is `black`. |
| -update *seconds* | This option specifies the frequency in seconds at which `xclock` should update its display. If the clock is obscured and then exposed, it will be updated immediately. A value of 30 seconds or less will enable a second hand on an analog clock. The default is `60` seconds. |
| -padding *number* | This option specifies the width in pixels of the padding between the window border and clock text or picture. The default is `10` on a digital clock and `8` on an analog clock. |

## X DEFAULTS

This program uses the Clock widget. It understands all of the core resource names and classes as well as:

| | |
|---|---|
| width (class Width) | Specifies the width of the clock. The default for analog clocks is `164` pixels; the default for digital clocks is whatever is needed to hold the clock when displayed in the chosen font. |
| height (class Height) | Specifies the height of the clock. The default for analog clocks is `164` pixels; the default for digital clocks is whatever is needed to hold the clock when displayed in the chosen font. |
| update (class Interval) | Specifies the frequency in seconds at which the time should be redisplayed. |
| foreground (class Foreground) | Specifies the color for the tick marks. The default is depends on whether `reverseVideo` is specified. If `reverseVideo` is specified, the default is `lwhite`; otherwise, the default is `black`. |
| hands (class Foreground) | Specifies the color of the insides of the clock's hands. The default depends on whether `reverseVideo` is specified. If `reverseVideo` is specified, the default is `lwhite`; otherwise, the default is `black`. |
| highlight (class Foreground) | Specifies the color used to highlight the clock's hands. The default depends on whether `reverseVideo` is specified. If `reverseVideo` is specified, the default is `lwhite`; otherwise, the default is `black`. |
| analog (class Boolean) | Specifies whether or not an analog clock should be used instead of a digital one. The default is `True`. |
| chime (class Boolean) | Specifies whether or not a bell should be rung on the hour and half hour. |

padding (class Margin)                    Specifies the amount of internal padding in pixels to be used.
                                          The default is 8.

font (class Font)                         Specifies the font to be used for the digital clock. Note that
                                          variable width fonts currently will not always display correctly.

## WIDGETS

In order to specify resources, it is useful to know the hierarchy of the widgets which compose xclock. In the following
notation, indentation indicates hierarchical structure. The widget class name is given first, followed by the widget instance
name:

```
XClock xclock
     Clock clock
```

## ENVIRONMENT

DISPLAY                                   To get the default host and display number

XENVIRONMENT                              To get the name of a resource file that overrides the global
                                          resources stored in the RESOURCE_MANAGER property

## FILES

<XRoott/lib/X11/app-defaults/XClock       Specifies required resources

## SEE ALSO

X(1), xrdb(1), time(3C)

## BUGS

xclock believes the system clock.

When in digital mode, the string should be centered automatically.

## AUTHORS

Tony Della Fera (MIT-Athena, DEC), Dave Mankins (MIT-Athena, BBN), and Ed Moy (UC Berkeley)

*X Version 11 Release 6*

# xclipboard

xclipboard—X clipboard client

## SYNOPSIS

xclipboard [ -toolkitoption ... ] [ -w ][-nw ]

## DESCRIPTION

The xclipboard program is used to collect and display text selections that are sent to the Clipboard by other clients. It is
typically used to save Clipboard selections for later use. It stores each Clipboard selection as a separate string, each of which
can be selected. Each time Clipboard is asserted by another application, xclipboard transfers the contents of that selection to
a new buffer and displays it in the text window. Buffers are never automatically deleted, so you'll want to use the delete
button to get rid of useless items.

Since xclipboard uses a Text Widget to display the contents of the clipboard, text sent to the Clipboard may be reselected for
use in other applications. xclipboard also responds to requests for the Clipboard selection from other clients by sending the
entire contents of the currently displayed buffer.

An xclipboard window has the following buttons across the top:

| | |
|---|---|
| quit | When this button is pressed, xclipboard exits. |
| delete | When this button is pressed, the current buffer is deleted and the next one displayed. |
| new | Creates a new buffer with no contents. Useful in constructing a new Clipboard selection by hand. |
| save | Displays a File Save dialog box. Pressing the Accept button saves the currently displayed buffer to the file specified in the text field. |
| next | Displays the next buffer in the list. |
| previous | Displays the previous buffer. |

## OPTIONS

The xclipboard program accepts all of the standard X Toolkit command-line options as well as the following:

| | |
|---|---|
| -w | This option indicates that lines of text that are too long to be displayed on one line in the clipboard should wrap around to the following lines. |
| -nw | This option indicates that long lines of text should not wrap around. This is the default behavior. |

## WIDGETS

In order to specify resources, it is useful to know the hierarchy of the widgets which compose xclipboard. In the following notation, indentation indicates hierarchical structure. The widget class name is given first, followed by the widget instance name.

```
XClipboard xclipboard
    Form form
        Command Quit
        Command delete
        Command new
        Command Save
        Command next
        Command prev
        Label index
        Text text
    TransientShell fileDialogShell
        Dialog fileDialog
        Label label
        Command accept
        Command cancel
        Text value
    TransientShell failDialogShell
        Dialog failDialog
        Label label
        Command continue
```

## SENDING/RETRIEVING CLIPBOARD CONTENTS

Text is copied to the Clipboard whenever a client asserts ownership of the Clipboard selection. Text is copied from the Clipboard whenever a client requests the contents of the Clipboard selection. Examples of event bindings that a user may wish to include in a resource configuration file to use the Clipboard are

```
*VT100.Translations: #override \
<Btn3Up>: select-end(CLIPBOARD) \n\
```

```
<Btn2Up>: insert-selection(PRIMARY,CLIPBOARD) \n\
<Btn2Down>: ignore ()
```

## SEE ALSO

X(1), xcutsel(1), xterm(1), individual client documentation for how to make a selection and send it to the Clipboard.

## ENVIRONMENT

DISPLAY                                To get the default host and display number

XENVIRONMENT                           To get the name of a resource file that overrides the global
                                       resources stored in the RESOURCE_MANAGER property

## FILES

<XRoot>/lib/X11/app-defaults/XClipboard        Specifies required resources

## AUTHOR

Ralph R. Swick (DEC/MIT Project Athena), Chris D. Peterson (MIT X Consortium), Keith Packard (MIT X Consortium)

*X Version 11 Release 6*

# xconsole

xconsole—Monitor system console messages with X

## SYNOPSIS

xconsole [-*toolkitoption* ...] [-file *file-name*] [-notify] [-stripNonprint] [-daemon] [-verbose]
    [-exitOnFail]

## DESCRIPTION

The xconsole program displays messages that are usually sent to /dev/console.

## OPTIONS

xconsole accepts all of the standard X Toolkit command-line options along with the additional options listed here:

-file *file-name*                      To monitor some other device, use this option to specify the
                                       device name. This does not work on regular files as they are
                                       always ready to be read from.

-notify, -nonotify                     When new data are received from the console and the notify
                                       option is set, the icon name of the application has * appended,
                                       so that it is evident even when the application is iconified. -
                                       notify is the default.

-daemon                                This option causes Xconsole to place itself in the background,
                                       using fork/exit.

-verbose                               When set, this option directs xconsole to display an informa-
                                       tive message in the first line of the text buffer.

—exitOnFail                            When set, this option directs xconsole to exit when it is unable
                                       to redirect the console output.

## X DEFAULTS

This program uses the Athena Text widget, look in the Athena Widget Set documentation for controlling it.

## WIDGETS

In order to specify resources, it is useful to know the hierarchy of the widgets that compose xconsole. In the following notation, indentation indicates hierarchical structure. The widget class name is given first, followed by the widget instance name.

```
XConsole xconsole
    XConsole text
```

## ENVIRONMENT

DISPLAY                                        To get the default host and display number.

XENVIRONMENT                                    To get the name of a resource file that overrides the global resources stored in the RESOURCE_MANAGER property.

## FILES

<XRoot>/lib/X11/app-defaults/XConsole            Specifies required resources

## SEE ALSO

X(1), xrdb(1), Athena Text widget

## AUTHOR

Keith Packard (MIT X Consortium)

*X Version 11 Release 6*

# xcutsel

xcutsel—Interchange between cut buffer and selection

## SYNOPSIS

xcutsel [ *-toolkitoption* ...] [-selection *selection*] [-cutbuffer *number*]

## DESCRIPTION

The xcutsel program is used to copy the current selection into a cut buffer and to make a selection that contains the current contents of the cut buffer. It acts as a bridge between applications that don't support selections and those that do.

By default, xcutsel will use the selection named PRIMARY and the cut buffer CUT_BUFFER0. Either or both of these can be overridden by command-line arguments or by resources.

An xcutsel window has the following buttons:

quit                                            When this button is pressed, xcutsel exits. Any selections held by xcutsel are automatically released.

copy PRIMARY to 0                               When this button is pressed, xcutsel copies the current selection into the cut buffer.

copy 0 to PRIMARY                               When this button is pressed, xcutsel converts the current contents of the cut buffer into the selection.

The button labels reflect the selection and cut buffer selected by command-line options or through the resource database.

When the copy 0 to PRIMARY button is activated, the button will remain inverted as long as xcutsel remains the owner of the selection. This serves to remind you which client owns the current selection. Note that the value of the selection remains constant; if the cut buffer is changed, you must again activate the copy button to retrieve the new value when desired.

## OPTIONS

Xcutsel accepts all of the standard X Toolkit command-line options as well as the following:

| | |
|---|---|
| -selection *name* | This option specifies the name of the selection to use. The default is PRIMARY. The only supported abbreviations for this option are -select, -sel, and -s, as the standard toolkit option -selectionTimeout has a similar name. |
| -cutbuffer *number* | This option specifies the cut buffer to use. The default is cutbuffer 0. |

## X DEFAULTS

This program accepts all of the standard X Toolkit resource names and classes as well as the following:

| | |
|---|---|
| selection (class Selection) | This resource specifies the name of the selection to use. The default is PRIMARY. |
| cutBuffer (class CutBuffer) | This resource specifies the number of the cutbuffer to use. The default is 0. |

## WIDGET NAMES

The following instance names may be used when user configuration of the labels in them is desired:

| | |
|---|---|
| sel-cut (class Command) | This is the "copy SELECTION to BUFFER" button. |
| cut-sel (class Command) | This is the "copy BUFFER to SELECTION" button. |
| quit (class Command) | This is the "quit" button. |

## SEE ALSO

X(1), xclipboard(1), xterm(1), text widget documentation, individual client documentation for how to make a selection.

## BUGS

There is no way to change the name of the selection or the number of the cut buffer while the program is running.

## AUTHOR

Ralph R. Swick (DEC/MIT Project Athena)

*X Version 11 Release 6*

# xdm

xdm—X Display Manager with support for XDMCP, host chooser

## SYNOPSIS

xdm [ -config *configuration_file* ][-nodaemon ][-debug *debug_level* ]
[-error *error_log_file* ][-resources *resource_file* ][-server *server_entry* ]
[-sessionsession_program]

## DESCRIPTION

xdm manages a collection of X displays, which may be on the local host or remote servers. The design of xdm was guided by the needs of X terminals as well as the X Consortium standard XDMCP, the X Display Manager Control Protocol. Xdm provides services similar to those provided by init, getty, and login on character terminals: prompting for login name and password, authenticating the user, and running a session.

A *session* is defined by the lifetime of a particular process; in the traditional character-based terminal world, it is the user's login shell. In the xdm context, it is an arbitrary session manager. This is because in a windowing environment, a user's login shell process does not necessarily have any terminal-like interface with which to connect. When a real session manager is not available, a window manager or terminal emulator is typically used as the *session manager*, meaning that termination of this process terminates the user's session.

When the session is terminated, xdm resets the X server and (optionally) restarts the whole process.

When xdm receives an Indirect query via XDMCP, it can run a chooser process to perform an XDMCP BroadcastQuery (or an XDMCP Query to specified hosts) on behalf of the display and offer a menu of possible hosts that offer XDMCP display management. This feature is useful with X terminals that do not offer a host menu themselves.

Because xdm provides the first interface that users will see, it is designed to be simple to use and easy to customize to the needs of a particular site. xdm has many options, most of which have reasonable defaults. Browse through the various sections of this manual, picking and choosing the things you want to change. Pay particular attention to the "Session Program" subsection, which will describe how to set up the style of session desired.

## OVERVIEW

xdm is highly configurable, and most of its behavior can be controlled by resource files and shell scripts. The names of these files themselves are resources read from the file xdm-config or the file named by the -config option.

xdm offers display management two different ways. It can manage X servers running on the local machine and specified in Xservers, and it can manage remote X servers (typically X terminals) using XDMCP (the XDM Control Protocol) as specified in the Xaccess file.

The resources of the X clients run by xdm outside the user's session, including xdm's own login window, can be affected by setting resources in the Xresources file.

For X terminals that do not offer a menu of hosts to get display management from, xdm can collect willing hosts and run the chooser program to offer the user a menu. For X displays attached to a host, this step is typically not used, as the local host does the display management.

After resetting the X server, xdm runs the Xsetup script to assist in setting up the screen the user sees along with the xlogin widget.

When the user logs in, xdm runs the Xstartup script as root.

Then xdm runs the Xsession script as the user. This system session file may do some additional startup and typically runs a script in the user's home directory. When the Xsession script exits, the session is over.

At the end of the session, the Xreset script is run to clean up, the X server is reset, and the cycle starts over.

The file /usr/X11R6/lib/X11/xdm/xdm-errors will contain error messages from xdm and anything output to stderr by Xsetup, Xstartup, Xsession, or Xreset. When you have trouble getting xdm working, check this file to see if xdm has any clues to the trouble.

## OPTIONS

All of these options, except -config itself, specify values that can also be specified in the configuration file as resources.

| | |
|---|---|
| -config *configuration_file* | Names the configuration file, which specifies resources to control the behavior of xdm. <XRoot>/lib/X11/xdm/xdm-config is the default. See the subsection called "Configuration File." |
| -nodaemon | Specifies false as the value for the DisplayManager.daemonMode resource. This suppresses the normal daemon behavior, which is for xdm to close all file descriptors, disassociate itself from the controlling terminal, and put itself in the background when it first starts up. |

| | |
|---|---|
| -debug *debug_level* | Specifies the numeric value for the `DisplayManager.debugLevel` resource. A non-zero value causes xdm to print lots of debugging statements to the terminal; it also disables the `DisplayManager.daemonMode` resource, forcing xdm to run synchronously. To interpret these debugging messages, a copy of the source code for xdm is almost a necessity. No attempt has been made to rationalize or standardize the output. |
| -error *error_log_file* | Specifies the value for the `DisplayManager.errorLogFile` resource. This file contains errors from xdm as well as anything written to stderr by the various scripts and programs run during the progress of the session. |
| -resources *resource_file* | Specifies the value for the `DisplayManager*resources` resource. This file is loaded using xrdb to specify configuration parameters for the authentication widget. |
| -server *server_entry* | Specifies the value for the `DisplayManager.servers` resource. See the subsection "Local Server Specification" for a description of this resource. |
| -udpPort *port_number* | Specifies the value for the `DisplayManager.requestPort` resource. This sets the port number, which xdm will monitor for XDMCP requests. As XDMCP uses the registered well-known UDP port 177, this resource should not be changed except for debugging. |
| -session *session_program* | Specifies the value for the `DisplayManager*session` resource. This indicates the program to run as the session after the user has logged in. |
| -xrm *resource_specification* | Allows an arbitrary resource to be specified, as in most X Toolkit applications. |

## RESOURCES

At many stages the actions of xdm can be controlled through the use of its configuration file, which is in the X resource format. Some resources modify the behavior of xdm on all displays, while others modify its behavior on a single display. Where actions relate to a specific display, the display name is inserted into the resource name between `Display-Manager` and the final resource name segment.

For local displays, the resource name and class are as read from the Xservers file.

For remote displays, the resource name is what the network address of the display resolves to. See the `removeDomain` resource. The name must match exactly; xdm is not aware of all the network aliases that might reach a given display. If the name resolve fails, the address is used. The resource class is as sent by the display in the XDMCP Manage request.

Because the resource manager uses colons to separate the name of the resource from its value and dots to separate resource name parts, xdm substitutes underscores for both dots and colons when generating the resource name. For example, `DisplayManager.expo x org 0.startup` is the name of the resource that defines the startup shell file for the expo.x.org:0 display.

| | |
|---|---|
| `DisplayManager.servers` | This resource either specifies a filename full of server entries, one per line (if the value starts with a slash), or a single server entry. See the subsection "Local Server Specification" for the details. |
| `DisplayManager.requestPort` | This indicates the UDP port number that xdm uses to listen for incoming XDMCP requests. Unless you need to debug the system, leave this with its default value of 177. |

DisplayManager.errorLogFile

Error output is normally directed at the system console. To redirect it, set this resource to a filename. A method to send these messages to syslog should be developed for systems that support it; however, the wide variety of interfaces precludes any system-independent implementation. This file also contains any output directed to stderr by the Xsetup, Xstartup, Xsession, and Xreset files, so it will contain descriptions of problems in those scripts as well.

DisplayManager.debugLevel

If the integer value of this resource is greater than zero, reams of debugging information will be printed. It also disables daemon mode, which would redirect the information into the bit-bucket, and allows nonroot users to run xdm, which would normally not be useful.

DisplayManager.daemonMode

Normally, xdm attempts to make itself into a daemon process unassociated with any terminal. This is accomplished by forking and leaving the parent process to exit, then closing file descriptors and releasing the controlling terminal. In some environments this is not desired (in particular, when debugging). Setting this resource to false will disable this feature.

DisplayManager.pidFile

The filename specified will be created to contain an ASCII representation of the process-id of the main xdm process. xdm also uses file locking on this file to attempt to eliminate multiple daemons running on the same machine, which would cause quite a bit of havoc.

DisplayManager.lockPidFile

This is the resource which controls whether xdm uses file locking to keep multiple display managers from running amok. On System V, this uses the lockf library call, while on BSD it uses flock.

DisplayManager.authDir

This names a directory in which xdm stores authorization files while initializing the session. The default value is y.

DisplayManager.autoRescan

This Boolean controls whether xdm rescans the configuration, servers, access control and authentication keys files after a session terminates and the files have changed. By default it is true. You can force xdm to reread these files by sending a SIGHUP to the main process.

DisplayManager.removeDomainname

When computing the display name for XDMCP clients, the name resolver will typically create a fully qualified hostname for the terminal. As this is sometimes confusing, xdm will remove the domain name portion of the hostname if it is the same as the domain name of the local host when this variable is set. By default the value is true.

DisplayManager.keyFile

XDM-AUTHENTICATION-1 style XDMCP authentication requires that a private key be shared between xdm and the terminal. This resource specifies the file containing those values. Each entry in the file consists of a display name and the shared key. By default, xdm does not include support for XDM-AUTHENTICATION-1, as it requires DES, which is not generally distributable because of United States export restrictions.

| | |
|---|---|
| DisplayManager.accessFile | To prevent unauthorized XDMCP service and to allow forwarding of XDMCP IndirectQuery requests, this file contains a database of hostnames that are either allowed direct access to this machine, or have a list of hosts to which queries should be forwarded to. The format of this file is described in the subsection "XDMCP Access Control." |
| DisplayManager.exportList | A list of additional environment variables, separated by whitespace, to pass on to the Xsetup, Xstartup, Xsession,and Xreset programs. |
| DisplayManager.randomFile | A file to checksum to generate the seed of authorization keys. This should be a file that changes frequently. The default is /dev/mem. |
| DisplayManager.greeterLib | On systems that support a dynamically loadable greeter library, the name of the library. Default is <XRoot>/lib/X11/xdm/ libXdmGreet.so. |
| DisplayManager.choiceTimeout | Number of seconds to wait for display to respond after user has selected a host from the chooser. If the display sends an XDMCP IndirectQuery within this time, the request is forwarded to the chosen host. Otherwise, it is assumed to be from a new session and the chooser is offered again. Default is 15. |
| DisplayManager.*DISPLAY*.resources | This resource specifies the name of the file to be loaded by xrdb as the resource database onto the root window of screen 0 of the display. The Xsetup program, the Login widget, and chooser will use the resources set in this file. This resource database is loaded just before the authentication procedure is started, so it can control the appearance of the login window. See the subsection "Authentication Widget," which describes the various resources that are appropriate to place in this file. There is no default value for this resource, but <XRoot>/lib/ X11/xdm/Xresources is the conventional name. |
| DisplayManager.*DISPLAY*.chooser | Specifies the program run to offer a host menu for Indirect queries redirected to the special hostname CHOOSER. <XRoot> /lib/X11/xdm/chooser is the default. See the subsections "XDMCP Access Control" and "chooser." |
| DisplayManager.*DISPLAY*.xrdb | Specifies the program used to load the resources. By default, xdm uses <XRoot>/bin/xrdb. |
| DisplayManager.*DISPLAY*.cpp | This specifies the name of the C preprocessor that is used by xrdb. |
| DisplayManager.*DISPLAY*.setup | This specifies a program that is run (as root) before offering the Login window. This may be used to change the appearance of the screen around the Login window or to put up other windows (for example, you may want to run xconsole here). By default, no program is run. The conventional name for a file used here is Xsetup. See the subsection "Setup Program." |
| DisplayManager.*DISPLAY*.startup | This specifies a program that is run (as root) after the authentication process succeeds. By default, no program is run. The conventional name for a file used here is Xstartup. See the subsection "Startup Program." |
| DisplayManager.*DISPLAY*.session | This specifies the session to be executed (not running as root). By default, <XRoot>/bin/xterm is run. The conventional name is Xsession. See the subsection "Session Program." |

DisplayManager.*DISPLAY*.reset

This specifies a program which is run (as root) after the session terminates. Again, by default, no program is run. The conventional name is Xreset. See the subsection "Reset Program."

DisplayManager.*DISPLAY*.openDelay,
DisplayManager.*DISPLAY*.openRepeat,
DisplayManager.*DISPLAY*.openTimeout,
DisplayManager.*DISPLAY*.startAttempts

These numeric resources control the behavior of xdm when attempting to open intransigent servers. openDelay is the length of the pause (in seconds) between successive attempts, openRepeat is the number of attempts to make, openTimeout is the amount of time to wait while actually attempting the open (that is, the maximum time spent in the connect(2) system call) and startAttempts is the number of times this entire process is done before giving up on the server. After openRepeat attempts have been made, or if openTimeout seconds elapse in any particular attempt, xdm terminates and restarts the server, attempting to connect again. This process is repeated startAttempts times, at which point the display is declared dead and disabled. Although this behavior may seem arbitrary, it has been empirically developed and works quite well on most systems. The default values are 5 for openDelay, 5 for openRepeat, 30 for openTimeout and 4 for startAttempts.

DisplayManager.*DISPLAY*.pingInterval,
DisplayManager.*DISPLAY*.pingTimeout

To discover when remote displays disappear, xdm occasionally pings them, using an X connection and XSync calls. pingInterval specifies the time (in minutes) between each ping attempt, pingTimeout specifies the maximum amount of time (in minutes) to wait for the terminal to respond to the request. If the terminal does not respond, the session is declared dead and terminated. By default, both are set to 5 minutes. If you frequently use X terminals that can become isolated from the managing host, you might want to increase this value. The only worry is that sessions will continue to exist after the terminal has been accidentally disabled. xdm will not ping local displays. Although it would seem harmless, it is unpleasant when the workstation session is terminated as a result of the server hanging for NFS service and not responding to the ping.

DisplayManager.*DISPLAY*.
terminateServer

This Boolean resource specifies whether the X server should be terminated when a session terminates (instead of resetting it). This option can be used when the server tends to grow without bound over time, in order to limit the amount of time the server is run. The default value is false.

DisplayManager.*DISPLAY*.userPath

xdm sets the PATH environment variable for the session to this value. It should be a colon separated list of directories; see sh(1) for a full description. :/bin:/usr/bin:/usr/X11R6/bin :/usr/ucb is a common setting. The default value can be specified at build time in the X system configuration file with DefaultUserPath.

DisplayManager.*DISPLAY*.
systemPath

Xdm sets the PATH environment variable for the startup and reset scripts to the value of this resource. The default for this resource is specified at build time by the DefaultSystem-Path entry in the system configuration file; /etc:/bin:/usr/bin

: /usr/X11R6/bin:/usr/ ucb is a common choice. Note the absence of (.) from this entry. This is a good practice to follow for root; it avoids many common Trojan Horse system penetration schemes.

DisplayManager.*DISPLAY*.systemShell

Xdm sets the SHELL environment variable for the startup and reset scripts to the value of this resource. It is /bin/sh by default.

DisplayManager.*DISPLAY* failsafeClient

If the default session fails to execute, xdm will fall back to this program. This program is executed with no arguments, but executes using the same environment variables as the session would have had. (See the subsection "Session Program.") By default, <XRoot>/bin/xterm is used.

DisplayManager.*DISPLAY*.grabServer,
DisplayManager.*DISPLAY*. grabTimeout xdm

To improve security, this grabs the server and keyboard while reading the login name and password. The grabServer resource specifies if the server should be held for the duration of the name/password reading. When false, the server is ungrabbed after the keyboard grab succeeds; otherwise, the server is grabbed until just before the session begins. The default is false. The grabTimeout resource specifies the maximum time xdm will wait for the grab to succeed. The grab may fail if some other client has the server grabbed, or possibly if the network latencies are very high. This resource has a default value of 3 seconds; you should be cautious when raising it, as a user can be spoofed by a look-alike window on the display. If the grab fails, xdm kills and restarts the server (if possible) and the session.

DisplayManager.*DISPLAY*.authorize,
DisplayManager.*DISPLAY*.authName

authorize is a Boolean resource that controls whether xdm generates and uses authorization for the local server connections. If authorization is used, authName is a list of authorization mechanisms to use, separated by whitespace. XDMCP connections dynamically specify which authorization mechanisms are supported, so authName is ignored in this case. When authorize is set for a display and authorization is not available, the user is informed by having a different message displayed in the Login widget. By default, authorize is true. authName is MIT-MAGIC-COOKIE-1, or, if XDM-AUTHORIZATION-1 is available, XDM-AUTHORIZATION-1 MIT-MAGIC-COOKIE-1.

DisplayManager.*DISPLAY*.authFile

This file is used to communicate the authorization data from xdm to the server, using the -auth server command-line option. It should be kept in a directory that is not world-writable as it could easily be removed, disabling the authorization mechanism in the server.

DisplayManager.*DISPLAY*.authComplain

If set to false, disables the use of the unsecureGreeting in the login window. See the subsection "Authentication Widget." The default is true.

DisplayManager.*DISPLAY*.resetSignal

The number of the signal xdm sends to reset the server. See the subsection "Controlling the Server." The default is 1 (SIGHUP).

DisplayManager.*DISPLAY*.termSignal

The number of the signal xdm sends to terminate the server. See the subsection "Controlling the Server." The default is 15 (SIGTERM).

| DisplayManager.*DISPLAY.* resetForAuth | The original implementation of authorization in the sample server reread the authorization file at server reset time, instead of when checking the initial connection. As xdm generates the authorization information just before connecting to the display, an old server would not get up-to-date authorization information. This resource causes xdm to send SIGHUP to the server after setting up the file, causing an additional server reset to occur, during which time the new authorization information will be read. The default is false, which will work for all MIT servers. |
|---|---|
| DisplayManager.*DISPLAY.* userAuthDir | When xdm is unable to write to the usual user authorization file ($HOME/.Xauthority), it creates a unique filename in this directory and points the environment variable XAUTHORITY at the created file. It uses /tmp by default. |

## CONFIGURATION FILE

First, the xdm configuration file should be set up. Make a directory (usually <XRoot>/lib/X11/xdm, where <XRoot> refers to the root of the X11 install tree) to contain all of the relevant files. In the examples that follow, /usr/X11R6 is used as the value of <XRoot>.

Here is a reasonable configuration file, which could be named xdm-config:

```
DisplayManager.servers: /usr/X11R6/lib/X11/xdm/Xservers
DisplayManager.errorLogFile: /usr/X11R6/lib/X11/xdm/xdm-errors
DisplayManager*resources: /usr/X11R6/lib/X11/xdm/Xresources
DisplayManager*startup: /usr/X11R6/lib/X11/xdm/Xstartup
DisplayManager*session: /usr/X11R6/lib/X11/xdm/Xsession
DisplayManager.pidFile: /usr/X11R6/lib/X11/xdm/xdm-pid
DisplayManager. 0.authorize: true
DisplayManager*authorize: false
```

Note that this file mostly contains references to other files. Note also that some of the resources are specified with * separating the components. These resources can be made unique for each different display, by replacing the * with the display name, but normally this is not very useful. See the "Resources" section for a complete discussion.

## XDMCP ACCESS CONTROL

The database file specified by the DisplayManager.accessFile provides information which xdm uses to control access from displays requesting XDMCP service. This file contains three types of entries: entries that control the response to Direct and Broadcast queries, entries that control the response to Indirect queries, and macro definitions.

The format of the Direct entries is simple, either a hostname or a pattern, which is distinguished from a hostname by the inclusion of one or more metacharacters (* matches any sequence of 0 or more characters, and ? matches any single character) which are compared against the hostname of the display device. If the entry is a hostname, all comparisons are done using network addresses, so any name which converts to the correct network address may be used. For patterns, only canonical hostnames are used in the comparison, so ensure that you do not attempt to match aliases. Preceding either a hostname or a pattern with a ! character causes hosts that match that entry to be excluded.

An Indirect entry also contains a hostname or pattern, but follows it with a list of hostnames or macros to which indirect queries should be sent.

A macro definition contains a macro name and a list of hostnames and other macros that the macro expands to. To distinguish macros from hostnames, macro names start with a % character. Macros may be nested.

Indirect entries may also specify to have xdm run chooser to offer a menu of hosts to connect to. See the subsection "chooser."

When checking access for a particular display host, each entry is scanned in turn and the first matching entry determines the response. `Direct` and `Broadcast` entries are ignored when scanning for an `Indirect` entry and vice versa.

Blank lines are ignored, `#` is treated as a comment delimiter causing the rest of that line to be ignored, and `\newline` causes the newline to be ignored, allowing indirect host lists to span multiple lines. Here is a sample `Xaccess` file:

```
#
# Xaccess - XDMCP access control file
#
#
# Direct/Broadcast query entries
#
!xtra.lcs.mit.edu # disallow direct/broadcast service for xtra
bambi.ogi.edu # allow access from this particular display
.lcs.mit.edu # allow access from any display in LCS
#
# Indirect query entries
#
%HOSTS expo.lcs.mit.edu xenon.lcs.mit.edu \
excess.lcs.mit.edu kanga.lcs.mit.edu extract.lcs.mit.edu xenon.lcs.mit.edu #force extract to contact xenon
!xtra.lcs.mit.edu dummy #disallow indirect access
.lcs.mit.edu %HOSTS #all others get to choose
```

## chooser

For X terminals that do not offer a host menu for use with `Broadcast` or `Indirect` queries, the `chooser` program can do this for them. In the `Xaccess` file, specify `CHOOSER` as the first entry in the `Indirect` host list. `chooser` will send a Query request to each of the remaining hostnames in the list and offer a menu of all the hosts that respond.

The list may consist of the word `BROADCAST`, in which case `chooser` will send a `Broadcast` instead, again offering a menu of all hosts that respond. Note that on some operating systems, UDP packets cannot be broadcast, so this feature will not work.

Example `Xaccess` file using `chooser`:

```
extract.lcs.mit.edu CHOOSER %HOSTS #offer a menu of these hosts
xtra.lcs.mit.edu CHOOSER BROADCAST #offer a menu of all hosts
```

The program to use for `chooser` is specified by the `DisplayManager.DISPLAY.chooser` resource. For more flexibility at this step, the `chooser` could be a shell script. `chooser` is the session manager here; it is run instead of a child `xdm` to manage the display.

Resources for this program can be put into the file named by `DisplayManager.DISPLAY.resources`.

When the user selects a host, `chooser` prints the host chosen, which is read by the parent `xdm`, and exits. `xdm` closes its connection to the X server, and the server resets and sends another `Indirect` XDMCP request. `xdm` remembers the user's choice (for `DisplayManager.choiceTimeout` seconds) and forwards the request to the chosen host, which starts a session on that display.

## LOCAL SERVER SPECIFICATION

The resource `DisplayManager.servers` gives a server specification or, if the values starts with a slash (`/`), the name of a file containing server specifications, one per line.

Each specification indicates a display which should constantly be managed and which is not using XDMCP. This method is used typically for local servers only. If the resource or the file named by the resource is empty, `xdm` will offer XDMCP service only.

Each specification consists of at least three parts: a display name, a display class, a display type, and (for local servers) a command line to start the server. A typical entry for local display number 0 would be

```
:0 Digital-QV local /usr/X11R6/bin/X :0
```

The display types are

Local local display: xdm must run the server

Foreign remote display: xdm opens an X connection to a running server

The display name must be something that can be passed in the -display option to an X program. This string is used to generate the display-specific resource names, so be careful to match the names (for example, use :0 Sun-CG3 local /usr /X11R6/bin/X :0 instead of localhost:0 Sun CG3 local /usr/X11R6/bin/X :0 if your other resources are specified as DisplayManager._0.session). The display class portion is also used in the display-specific resources, as the class of the resource. This is useful if you have a large collection of similar displays (such as a corral of X terminals) and would like to set resources for groups of them. When using XDMCP, the display is required to specify the display class, so the manual for your particular X terminal should document the display class string for your device. If it doesn't, you can run xdm in debug mode and look at the resource strings that it generates for that device, which will include the class string.

When xdm starts a session, it sets up authorization data for the server. For local servers, xdm passes -auth filename on the server's command line to point it at its authorization data. For XDMCP servers, xdm passes the authorization data to the server via the Accept XDMCP request.

## RESOURCES FILE

The Xresources file is loaded onto the display as a resource database using xrdb. As the authentication widget reads this database before starting up, it usually contains parameters for that widget:

```
xlogin*login.translations: #override\
Ctrl<Key>R: abort-display()\n\
<Key>F1: set-session-argument(failsafe) finish-field()\n\
<Key>Return: set-session-argument() finish-field()
xlogin*borderWidth: 3
xlogin*greeting: CLIENTHOST
#ifdef COLOR
xlogin*greetColor: CadetBlue
xlogin*failColor: red
#endif
```

Please note the translations entry; it specifies a few new translations for the widget that allow users to escape from the default session (and avoid troubles that may occur in it). Note that if #override is not specified, the default translations are removed and replaced by the new value, not a very useful result as some of the default translations are quite useful (such as <Key>: insert-char (), which responds to normal typing).

This file may also contain resources for the setup program and chooser.

## SETUP PROGRAM

The Xsetup file is run after the server is reset, but before the Login window is offered. The file is typically a shell script. It is run as root, so you should be careful about security. This is the place to change the root background or bring up other windows that should appear on the screen along with the Login widget.

In addition to any specified by DisplayManager.exportList, the following environment variables are passed:

| | |
|---|---|
| DISPLAY | The associated display name |
| PATH | The value of DisplayManager.*DISPLAY*.systemPath |
| SHELL | The value of DisplayManager.*DISPLAY*.systemShell |
| XAUTHORITY | May be set to an authority file |

Note that since xdm grabs the keyboard, any other windows will not be able to receive keyboard input. They will be able to interact with the mouse, however; beware of potential security holes here. If DisplayManager.*DISPLAY*.grabServer is set, Xsetup will not be able to connect to the display at all. Resources for this program can be put into the file named by DisplayManager.*DISPLAY*.resources.

Here is a sample Xsetup script:

```
#!/bin/sh
# Xsetup 0 - setup script for one workstation
xcmsdb </usr/X11R6/lib/monitors/alex.0
xconsole -geometry 480x130-0-0 -notify -verbose -exitOnFail &
```

## AUTHENTICATION WIDGET

The authentication widget reads a name/password pair from the keyboard. Nearly every imaginable parameter can be controlled with a resource. Resources for this widget should be put into the file named by DisplayManager.*DISPLAY*.resources. All of these have reasonable default values, so it is not necessary to specify any of them.

| | |
|---|---|
| xlogin.Login.width,<br>xlogin.Login.height,<br>xlogin.Login.x,<br>xlogin.Login.y | The geometry of the Login widget is normally computed automatically. If you wish to position it elsewhere, specify each of these resources. |
| xlogin.Login.foreground | The color used to display the typed-in username. |
| xlogin.Login.font | The font used to display the typed-in username. |
| xlogin.Login.greeting | A string which identifies this window. The default is X Window System. |
| xlogin.Login.unsecureGreeting | When X authorization is requested in the configuration file for this display and none is in use, this greeting replaces the standard greeting. The default is This is an unsecure session. |
| xlogin.Login.greetFont | The font used to display the greeting. |
| xlogin.Login.greetColor | The color used to display the greeting. |
| xlogin.Login.namePrompt | The string displayed to prompt for a username. Xrdb strips trailing whitespace from resource values, so to add spaces at the end of the prompt (usually a nice thing), add spaces escaped with backslashes. The default is Login:. |
| xlogin.Login.passwdPrompt | The string displayed to prompt for a password. The default is Password:. |
| xlogin.Login.promptFont | The font used to display both prompts. |
| xlogin.Login.promptColor | The color used to display both prompts. |
| xlogin.Login.fail | A message that is displayed when the authentication fails. The default is Login incorrect. |
| xlogin.Login.failFont | The font used to display the failure message. |
| xlogin.Login.failColor | The color used to display the failure message. |
| xlogin.Login.failTimeout | The number of seconds that the failure message is displayed. The default is 30. |
| xlogin.Login.translations | This specifies the translations used for the login widget. Refer to the X Toolkit documentation for a complete discussion on translations. The default translation table is |

| | |
|---|---|
| Ctrl<Key>H | delete-previous-character() \n\ |
| Ctrl<Key>D | delete-character() \n\ |
| Ctrl<Key>B | move-backward-character() \n\ |
| Ctrl<Key>F | move-forward-character() \n\ |
| Ctrl<Key>A | move-to-begining() \n\ |
| Ctrl<Key>E | move-to-end() \n\ |

```
Ctrl<Key>K          erase-to-end-of-line() \n\
Ctrl<Key>U          erase-line() \n\
Ctrl<Key>X          erase-line() \n\
Ctrl<Key>C          restart-session() \n\
Ctrl<Key>nn         abort-session() \n\
<Key>BackSpace      delete-previous-character() \n\
<Key>Delete         delete-previous-character() \n\
<Key>Return         finish-field() \n\
<Key>               insert-char() \
```

The actions that are supported by the widget are

| | |
|---|---|
| `delete-previous-character` | Erases the character before the cursor. |
| `delete-character` | Erases the character after the cursor. |
| `move-backward-character` | Moves the cursor backward. |
| `move-forward-character` | Moves the cursor forward. |
| `move-to-begining` | (Apologies about the spelling error.) Moves the cursor to the beginning of the editable text. |
| `move-to-end` | Moves the cursor to the end of the editable text. |
| `erase-to-end-of-line` | Erases all text after the cursor. |
| `erase-line` | Erases the entire text. |
| `finish-field` | If the cursor is in the name field, proceeds to the password field; if the cursor is in the password field, checks the current name/password pair. If the name/password pair is valid, xdm starts the session. Otherwise, the failure message is displayed and the user is prompted again. |
| `abort-session` | Terminates and restarts the server. |
| `abort-display` | Terminates the server, disabling it. This action is not accessible in the default configuration. There are various reasons to stop xdm on a system console, such as when shutting the system down, when using xdmshell, to start another type of server, or to generally access the console. Sending xdm a SIGHUP will restart the display. See the subsection "Controlling XDM." |
| `restart-session` | Resets the X server and starts a new session. This can be used when the resources have been changed and you want to test them or when the screen has been overwritten with system messages. |
| `insert-char` | Inserts the character typed. |
| `set-session-argument` | Specifies a single word argument that is passed to the session at startup. See the subsection "Session Program." |
| `allow-all-access` | Disables access control in the server. This can be used when the .Xauthority file cannot be created by xdm. Be very careful using this; it might be better to disconnect the machine from the network before doing this. |

## STARTUP PROGRAM

The Xstartup file is typically a shell script. It is run as root and should be very careful about security. This is the place to put commands that add entries to /etc/utmp (the sessreg program may be useful here), mount users' home directories from file servers, display the message of the day, or abort the session if logins are not allowed.

In addition to any specified by `DisplayManager.exportList`, the following environment variables are passed:

| | |
|---|---|
| DISPLAY | The associated display name |
| HOME | The initial working directory of the user |
| USER | The username |
| PATH | The value of `DisplayManager.DISPLAY.systemPath` |
| SHELL | The value of `DisplayManager.DISPLAY.systemShell` |
| XAUTHORITY | May be set to an authority file |

No arguments are passed to the script. xdm waits until this script exits before starting the user session. If the exit value of this script is non-zero, xdm discontinues the session and starts another authentication cycle.

The sample Xstartup file shown here prevents login while the file /etc/nologin exists. Thus, this is not a complete example, but simply a demonstration of the available functionality.

Here is a sample Xstartup script:

```
#!/bin/sh
#
# Xstartup
#
# This program is run as root after the user is verified
#
if [ -f /etc/nologin ]; then
  xmessage -file /etc/nologin
  exit 1
fi
sessreg -a -l $DISPLAY -x /usr/X11R6/lib/xdm/Xservers $USER
/usr/X11R6/lib/xdm/GiveConsole
exit 0
```

## SESSION PROGRAM

The Xsession program is the command that is run as the user's session. It is run with the permissions of the authorized user.

In addition to any specified by `DisplayManager.exportList`, the following environment variables are passed:

| | |
|---|---|
| DISPLAY | The associated display name |
| HOME | The initial working directory of the user |
| USER | The username |
| PATH | The value of `DisplayManager.DISPLAY.userPath` |
| SHELL | The user's default shell (from `getpwnam`) |
| AUTHORITY | May be set to a nonstandard authority file |
| KRB5CCNAME | May be set to a Kerberos credentials cache file |

At most installations, Xsession should look in $HOME for a file xsession, which contains commands that each user would like to use as a session. Xsession should also implement a system default session if no user-specified session exists. See the subsection "Typical Usage."

An argument may be passed to this program from the authentication widget using the `set-session-argument` action. This can be used to select different styles of session. One good use of this feature is to allow the user to escape from the ordinary session when it fails. This allows users to repair their own .xsession if it fails, without requiring administrative intervention. The example following demonstrates this feature.

This example recognizes the special failsafe mode, specified in the translations in the Xresources file, to provide an escape from the ordinary session. It also requires that the .xsession file be executable so you don't have to guess what shell it wants to use.

```
#!/bin/sh
#
# Xsession
#
# This is the program that is run as the client
# for the display manager.
case $# in
  1)
   case $1 in
     failsafe)
     exec xterm -geometry 80x24-0-0
     ;;
   esac
esac
startup=$HOME/.xsession
resources=$HOME/.Xresources
if [ -f "$startup" ]; then
  exec "$startup"
else
if [ -f "$resources" ]; then
  xrdb -load "$resources"
fi
twm &
xman -geometry +10-10 &
exec xterm -geometry 80x24+10+10 -ls
fi
```

The user's .xsession file might look something like the following example. Don't forget that the file must have execute permission.

```
#!/bin/csh
# no -f in the previous line so .cshrc gets run to set $PATH
twm &
xrdb -merge "$HOME/.Xresources"
emacs -geometry +0+50 &
xbiff -geometry -430+5 &
xterm -geometry -0+50 -ls
```

## RESET PROGRAM

Symmetrical with Xstartup, the Xreset script is run after the user session has terminated. Run as root, it should contain commands that undo the effects of commands in Xstartup, removing entries from /etc/utmp or unmounting directories from file servers. The environment variables that were passed to Xstartup are also passed to Xreset.

A sample Xreset script:

```
#!/bin/sh
#
# Xreset
#
# This program is run as root after the session ends
#
sessreg -d -l $DISPLAY -x /usr/X11R6/lib/xdm/Xservers $USER
/usr/X11R6/lib/xdm/TakeConsole
exit 0
```

## CONTROLLING THE SERVER

xdm controls local servers using POSIX signals. SIGHUP is expected to reset the server, closing all client connections and performing other cleanup duties. SIGTERM is expected to terminate the server. If these signals do not perform the expected actions, the resources DisplayManager.DISPLAY.resetSignal and DisplayManager.DISPLAY.termSignal can specify alternate signals.

To control remote terminals not using XDMCP, xdm searches the window hierarchy on the display and uses the protocol request KillClient in an attempt to clean up the terminal for the next session. This may not actually kill all of the clients, as only those which have created windows will be noticed. XDMCP provides a more sure mechanism; when xdm closes its initial connection, the session is over and the terminal is required to close all other connections.

## CONTROLLING xdm

xdm responds to two signals: SIGHUP and SIGTERM. When sent a SIGHUP, xdm rereads the configuration file, the access control file, and the servers file. For the servers file, it notices if entries have been added or removed. If a new entry has been added, xdm starts a session on the associated display. Entries that have been removed are disabled immediately, meaning that any session in progress will be terminated without notice and no new session will be started.

When sent a SIGTERM, xdm terminates all sessions in progress and exits. This can be used when shutting down the system.

xdm attempts to mark its various subprocesses for ps(1) by editing the command-line argument list in place. Because xdm can't allocate additional space for this task, it is useful to start xdm with a reasonably long command line (using the full pathname should be enough). Each process which is servicing a display is marked -display.

## OTHER POSSIBILITIES

You can use xdm to run a single session at a time, using the 4.3 init options or other suitable daemon by specifying the server on the command line:

```
xdm -server ":0 SUN-3/60CG4 local /usr/X11R6/bin/X :0"
```

Or you might have a file server and a collection of X terminals. The configuration for this is identical to that of the preceding sample, except the Xservers file would look like this:

```
extol:0 VISUAL-19 foreign
exalt:0 NCD-19 foreign
explode:0 NCR-TOWERVIEW3000 foreign
```

This directs xdm to manage sessions on all three of these terminals. See the subsection "Controlling xdm" for a description of using signals to enable and disable these terminals in a manner reminiscent of init(8).

## LIMITATIONS

One thing that xdm isn't very good at doing is coexisting with other window systems. To use multiple window systems on the same hardware, you'll probably be more interested in xinit.

## FILES

| | |
|---|---|
| <XRoot>/lib/X11/xdm/xdm-config | The default configuration file |
| $HOME/.Xauthority | User authorization file where xdm stores keys for clients to read |
| <XRoot>/lib/X11/xdm/chooser | The default chooser |
| <XRoot>/bin/X11/xrdb | The default resource database loader |
| <XRoot>/bin/X11/X | The default server |
| <XRoot>/bin/X11/xterm | The default session program and failsafe client |
| <XRoot>/lib/X11/xdm/A<display>-<suffix> | The default place for authorization files |
| /tmp/K5C<display> Kerberos | Credentials cache |

Note: <XRoot> refers to the root of the X11 install tree.

## See Also

X(1), xinit(1), xauth(1), Xsecurity(1), sessreg(1), Xserver(1)

X Display Manager Control Protocol

## AUTHOR

Keith Packard (MIT X Consortium)

X Version 11 Release 6

# xdpyinfo

xdpyinfo—Display information utility for X

## SYNOPSIS

xdpyinfo [-display *displayname*] [-queryExtensions] [-ext *extension-name*]

## DESCRIPTION

xdpyinfo is a utility for displaying information about an X server. It is used to examine the capabilities of a server, the predefined values for various parameters used in communicating between clients and the server, and the different types of screens and visuals that are available.

By default, numeric information (opcode, base event, base error) about protocol extensions is not displayed. This information can be obtained with the -queryExtensions option. Use of this option on servers that dynamically load extensions will likely cause all possible extensions to be loaded, which can be slow and can consume significant server resources.

Detailed information about a particular extension is displayed with the -ext extensionName option. If extensionName is all, information about all extensions supported by both xdpy-info and the server is displayed.

## ENVIRONMENT

DISPLAY                                                    To get the default host, display number, and screen

## SEE ALSO

X(1), xwininfo(1), xprop(1), xrdb(1)

## AUTHOR

Jim Fulton (MIT X Consortium)

X Version 11 Release 6

# Xf86_Accel

XF86_Accel—Accelerated X Window System servers for UNIX on x86 platforms with an S3, Mach8, Mach32, Mach64, P9000, AGX, ET4000/W32, or 8514/A accelerator board

## SYNOPSIS

```
XF86_S3 [:displaynumber] [ option ] ...
XF86_Mach8 [:displaynumber] [ option ] ...
XF86_Mach32 [:displaynumber] [ option ] ...
XF86_Mach64 [:displaynumber] [ option ] ...
XF86_P9000 [:displaynumber] [ option ] ...
XF86_AGX [:displaynumber] [ option ] ...
XF86_W32 [:displaynumber] [ option ] ...
XF86_8514 [:displaynumber] [ option ] ...
```

## DESCRIPTION

XF86_S3 is an 8-bit PseudoColor, 16-bit TrueColor and 24-bit TrueColor server for S3 graphic accelerator boards. Note, 16-bit and 24-bit operation is not supported on all S3 accelerator boards. Refer to README.S3 for details of which boards are supported at which depths.

XF86_Mach8 is an 8-bit PseudoColor server for ATI Mach8 graphic accelerator boards.

XF86_Mach32 is an 8-bit PseudoColor and 16-bit TrueColor server for ATI Mach32 graphic accelerator boards. Note, 16-bit operation is not supported on all Mach32 accelerator boards.

XF86_Mach64 is an 8-bit PseudoColor, 16-bit TrueColor, and 24-bit TrueColor server for ATI Mach64 graphic accelerator boards. Note, 16-bit and 24-bit operation is not supported for all RAMDACs. Refer to README.Mach64 for details of which RAMDACs are supported at which depths.

XF86_P9000 is an 8-bit PseudoColor, 16-bit TrueColor, and 24-bit TrueColor server for Weitek Power 9000 (P9000) graphic accelerator boards.

XF86_AGX is an 8-bit PseudoColor and 16-bit TrueColor server for AGX/XGA graphic accelerator boards.

XF86_W32 is an 8-bit PseudoColor server for ET4000/W32, ET4000/W32i, and ET4000/W32p graphic accelerator boards.

XF86_8514 is an 8-bit PseudoColor server for 8514/A graphic accelerator boards.

These are derived from the X386 server provided with X11R5, and from the X8514 server developed by Kevin Martin (<martin@cs.unc.edu>).

## CONFIGURATIONS

The servers support the following chipsets:

| | |
|---|---|
| XF86_S3 | 86C911, 86C924, 86C801, 86C805, 86C805i, 86C928, 86C928- P, 86C732 (Trio32), 86C764 (Trio64), 86C864, 86C868, 86C964, 86C968 |
| XF86_Mach8 | ATI Mach8, ATI Mach32 |
| XF86_Mach32 | ATI Mach32 |
| XF86_Mach64 | ATI Mach64 |
| XF86_P9000 | Diamond Viper VLB, Diamond Viper PCI, Orchid P9000, and some clones (Weitek P9000) |
| XF86_AGX | AGX-010, AGX-014, AGX-015, AGX-016, XGA-1, XGA-2 |
| XF86_W32 | ET4000/W32, ET4000/W32i, ET3000/W32p |
| XF86_8514 | IBM 8514/A and true clones |

For S3, virtual resolutions up to (approximately) 1,152×800 are supported, using (up to) 1MB of display memory (the S3 uses an internal width of 1,280 except for new revisions of some of the chips, hence 1MB can't support 1,152×900). Physical resolutions up to 1,280×1,024 (1,600×1,280 on some cards) are possible using 2MB or more of display memory. (Virtual resolution is dependent solely on the amount of memory installed, with the maximum virtual width being 2,048, and maximum virtual height is 4,096.)

Similar resolutions are supported on the Mach64. Refer to README.Mach64 for configuration details.

Similar resolutions are supported on the Mach32. For the Mach32, the maximum virtual width is 1,536, and the maximum virtual height is 1,280.

For Mach8, the maximum virtual width is 1,024.

For 8514, the maximum resolution is 1,024×768.

For the AGX chips, maximum resolution depends upon the chip revision and amount of available display memory. Refer to README.agx for configuration details.

For the P9000, the virtual and physical resolutions must be the same. With sufficient memory, resolutions up to 1,280×1,024 are supported.

All the servers that support 24-bit visuals do so using a 32-bit per pixel configuration where 8 bits in every 32 bits is unused. This needs to be taken into account when calculating the maximum virtual display size that can be supported at this depth.

## OPTIONS

In addition to the normal server options described in the Xserver(1) manual page, these servers accept some more command-line switches, as described in the XFree86(1) man page.

The Mach64, Mach32, S3, P9000, and AGX servers now support more than 8-bit color. The Mach32 and AGX servers support 16-bit TrueColor and the Mach64, S3, and P9000 servers support 16-and 32-bit TrueColor. The 32-bit TrueColor mode only uses 24 bits per pixel for color information (giving you 16 million colors). These modes may be used by specifying the -bpp option as specified in the XFree86(1) man page.

## SETUP

XFree86 uses a configuration file called XF86Config for its initial setup.

See the XF86Config(4/5) man page for general details. Here only the parts specific to the XF86_S3, XF86_Mach8, XF86_Mach32, XF86_Mach64, XF86_P9000, XF86_AGX, XF86_W32, and XF86_8514 servers are explained.

Entries for the Device section in the XF86Config file include the following:

Chipset "name"
  Specifies a chipset so the correct driver can be used. Possible chipsets are

  XF86_S3

  S3_generic: (for a standard IO-driven server)

  Mmio_928: (for a memory-mapped IO-driven server on 86C928, 86C732, 86C764, 86C864, 86C868, 86C964, and 86C968 boards)

  XF86_Mach8, Mach8 (to force the Mach8 server to run on Mach32 boards)

  XF86_Mach32, Mach32

  XF86_Mach64, Mach64

  XF86_P9000

    Vipervlb (for the Diamond Viper VLB)

    Viperpci (for the Diamond Viper PCI)

    Orchidp9000 (for the Orchid P9000 and many generic P9000-based boards)

  XF86_AGX

    Agx-016

    Agx-015

    Agx-014

    Agx-010

    Xga-2

    Xga-1

## NOTE

Only the agx-016, agx-015, agx-014, and XGA-2 have been tested. Refer to the XGA and AGX-010 section of README.agx before attempting to use the other chipsets.

XF86 W32

        Et4000w32

        Et4000w32i

        Et4000w32i_rev_b

        Et4000w32i_rev_c

        Et4000w32p_rev_a

        Et4000w32p_rev_b

        Et4000w32p_rev_c

        Et4000w32p_rev_d

XF86_8514

        Ibm8514

**Clocks *clock* ...**
For boards with nonprogrammable clock chips, the clocks can be specified here (see XF86Config(4/5)). The P9000 server now no longer requires a Clocks line. It will now work the same way as other servers with a programmable clock chip (that is, use the clocks as specified in the Modes). Note, clocks over 110 MHz are not recommended or supported by the P9000 server. The Mach64 server also does not require a Clocks line because the clocks are normally read directly from the video card's BIOS. For the Mach64 server, the clocks given in the XF86Config file are ignored unless the no_bios_clocks option is given (see below).

**ClockChip *"clockchip-type"***
For boards with programmable clock chips (except with the P9000 and AGX servers), the name of the clock chip is given. Possible values for the S3 server include "icd2061a", "ics9161a", "dcs2834", "sc11412", "s3gendac", "s3 sdac", "ti3025", "ti3026", "ics2595", "ics5300", "ics5342", "ch8391", "stg1703", and "ibm_rgb5xx".

**Ramdac *"ramdac-type"***
This specifies the type of RAMDAC used on the board. Only the S3, AGX, and W32 servers use this.

Normal—(S3, AGX) Card does not have one of the other RAMDACs mentioned here. This option is only required for the S3 server if the server incorrectly detects one of those other RAMDACs. The AGX server does not yet auto-detect RAMDACs, this is the default if no RAMDAC is specified.

Generic—(W32) This forces the W32 server to treat the RAMDAC as a generic VGA RAMDAC.

Att20c490—(S3, AGX) Card has an AT&T 20C490 or AT&T 20C491 RAMDAC. When the dac_8_bit option is specified, these RAMDACs may be operated in 8-bit per RGB mode. It also allows 16bpp operation with 801/805/928 boards. True AT&T 20C490 RAMDACs should be autodetected by the S3 server. This RAMDAC must be specified explicitly in other cases. Note that 8-bit per RGB mode does not appear to work with the Winbond 82C490 RAMDACs (which SuperProbe identifies as AT&T 20C492). 16bpp works fine with the Winbond 82C490. The Diamond SS2410 RAMDAC is reported to be compatible when operating in 15bpp mode (not 16bpp). The Chrontel 8391 appears to be compatible in all modes.

Sc15025—(S3, AGX) Card has a Sierra SC15025 or SC15026 RAMDAC. The S3 server has code to autodetect this RAMDAC.

Sc11482—(S3) Card has a Sierra SC11482, SC11483, or SC11484 RAMDAC. The S3 server has code to autodetect this RAMDAC.

Sc11485—(S3) Card has a Sierra SC11485, SC11487 or SC11489 RAMDAC. The S3 server will detect these RAMDACs as an sc11482, so this option must be specified to take advantage of extra features (they support 16bpp, 15bpp, and 8bpp, while the others only support 15bpp and 8bpp).

Bt485—(S3) Card has a BrookTree Bt485 or Bt9485 RAMDAC. This must be specified if the server fails to detect it.

Att20c505—(S3) Card has an AT&T 20C505 RAMDAC. This must be specified either if the server fails to detect the 20C505, or if the card has a Bt485 RAMDAC and there are problems using clocks higher than 67.5MHz.

Att20c498—(S3) Card has an AT&T 20C498 or 21C498 RAMDAC. This must be specified if the server fails to detect it.

Att22c498—(S3) Card has an AT&T 22C498 RAMDAC. This must be specified if the server fails to detect it.

Ibm_rgb514—(S3) Card has an IBM RGB514 RAMDAC. This must be specified if the server fails to detect it.

Ibm_rgb524—(S3) Card has an IBM RGB524 RAMDAC. This must be specified if the server fails to detect it.

Ibm_rgb525—(S3) Card has an IBM RGB525 RAMDAC. This must be specified if the server fails to detect it.

Ibm_rgb528—(S3) Card has an IBM RGB528 RAMDAC. This must be specified if the server fails to detect it.

Stg1700—(S3) Card has an STG1700 RAMDAC. This must be specified if the server fails to detect it.

Stg1703—(S3) Card has an STG1703 RAMDAC. This must be specified if the server fails to detect it.

S3gendac—(S3) Card has an S3 86C708 GENDAC. This RAMDAC does not support 8-bit per RGB mode (don't specify the dac_8_bit option). It allows 16bpp operation with 801/805 boards. There is currently no autodetection for this RAMDAC.

S3_sdac—(S3) Card has an S3 86C716 SDAC RAMDAC. This must be specified if the server fails to detect it.

Ics5300—(S3) Card has an ICS5300 RAMDAC. This must be specified if the server fails to detect it (the server will recognize this as an S3 GENDAC which is OK).

Ics5342—(S3) Card has an ICS5342 RAMDAC. This must be specified if the server fails to detect it (the server will recognize this as an S3 SDAC which is OK).

Ti3020—(S3) Card has a TI ViewPoint Ti3020 RAMDAC. This must be specified if the server fails to detect the Ti3020. Note that pixel multiplexing will be used for this RAMDAC if any mode requires a dot clock higher than 70MHz.

`Ti3025`—(S3) Card has a TI ViewPoint Ti3025 RAMDAC. This must be specified if the server fails to detect the Ti3025.

`Ti3026`—(S3) Card has a TI ViewPoint Ti3026 RAMDAC. This must be specified if the server fails to detect the Ti3026.

`Bt481`—(AGX) Card has a BrookTree Bt481 RAMDAC.

`Bt482`—(AGX) Card has a BrookTree Bt482 RAMDAC.

`Herc_dual_dac`—(AGX) Card (Hercules Graphite Pro) has both the 84-pin (Bt485 or AT&T20C505) and 44-pin (Bt481 or Bt482) RAMDACs installed.

`Herc_small_dac`—(AGX) Card (Hercules Graphite Pro) has only the 44-pin (Bt481 or Bt482) RAMDAC installed.

`IOBase` *ioaddress*

Specifies the base address for extended IO registers. This is only used by the AGX server, and by the P9000 server for the Viper PCI. For details of how to use it, refer to `README.agx` and `README.P9000`.

`MemBase` *memaddress*

Specifies the hard-wired part of the linear framebuffer base address. This option is only used by the P9000, S3, Mach64, and Mach32 servers (and only when using a linear framebuffer). For the S3 server, the hard-wired part is the high 10 bits of the 32-bit address (that is, *memaddress* is masked with `0xFFC00000`). Note: This should not be required for the 864 and 964 chips where the entire framebuffer address is software-selectable. Also, note that in versions prior to 3.1.1, the S3 server used only the top 6 bits of *memaddress*, and `ORed` it with `0x3C00000`. To get the same behavior, `OR 0x3C00000` with the value given previously. For the Mach32 server, the mask is `0xF8000000` (except for PCI cards, where the membase setting is ignored).

This option must be specified with the P9000 server. With local bus Diamond Vipers the value of *memaddress* can be either `0x80000000`, `0x20000000`, or `0xA0000000`. The default is `0x80000000`. Any value should work as long as it does not conflict with another device already at that address. For the Viper PCI, refer to `README.P9000`. For the Orchid P9000, the base address may be `0xC0000000`, `0xD0000000`, or `0xE0000000`, and must correspond the board's jumper setting. Note: The `S3` server will normally probe for this address automatically. Setting this option overrides that probe. This is not normally recommended because the failure of the server's probe usually indicates problems in using the linear framebuffer.

## NOTE

The Mach64 server requires the memory aperture. For ISA bus video cards, this means that the aperture must be enabled and the aperture address must be set to a value less than 16MB (which means that, on ISA systems only, to use the Mach64 server you must have 12MB of main memory or less). Normally the Mach64 server will use predefined values for this address, but setting this option will override the predefined address.

The Mach32 server should not require the use of this option under normal circumstances.

| | |
|---|---|
| COPBase *baseaddress* | This sets the coprocessor base address for the AGX server. Refer to README.agx for details. |
| Instance *instance* | This sets the XGA instance number for the AGX server. Refer to README.agx for details. |
| S3MClk *memclk* | This allows the video card's memory clock value to be specified. This is only used for 805i, 864 and Trio32/64 cards, and the value should not normally be given here for cards with an S3 Gendac or Trio64. This entry doesn't change the card's memory clock, but it is used to calculate the DRAM timing parameters. For further details refer to README.S3. |
| S3MNAdjust *M N* | This allows some memory timing parameters to be adjusted for DRAM cards. For further details refer to README.S3. |
| S3RefClk *refclk* | This allows the PLL reference clock to be specified. This may be required for some cards that use the IBM RGB5xx RAMDACs. The value is in MHz. For further details refer to README.S3. |

Option flags may be specified in either the Device section or the Display subsection of the XF86Config file.

| | |
|---|---|
| Option "*optionstring*" | Allows the user to select certain options provided by the drivers. Currently the following strings are recognized: |
| | Nomemaccess—(S3) Disable direct access to video memory. This option is ignored for the 864 and 964 chips. |
| | Noaccel—(AGX, P9000) Disable hardware acceleration for the P9000, and disables the font cache with the AGX. |
| | Vram_128—(AGX, P9000) When memory probe fails, use if you have 128Kx8 VRAMs. |
| | Vram_256—(AGX, P9000) When memory probe fails, use if you don't have 128Kx8 VRAMs. |
| | Nolinear—(S3 and Mach32) Disable use of a linear-mapped framebuffer. |
| | Ti3020_curs—(S3) Enables the Ti3020's internal HW cursor. (Default) |
| | No_ti3020_curs—(S3) Disables the Ti3020's internal HW cursor. |
| | Sw_cursor—(S3, Mach32, Mach64, P9000, AGX) Disable the hardware cursor. |
| | Dac_8_bit—(S3, Mach32, Mach64, AGX) Enables 8-bit per RGB. Currently only supported with the Ti3020/5/6, Bt485, AT&T20C505, AT&T20C490/1, Sierra SC15025/6, AT&T20C498 and STG1700/3, IBM RGB5xx (S3 server), Bt481 and Bt482 (AGX server), ATI68875/TLC34075/Bt885 (Mach32 server), ATI68875, TLC34075, ATI68860, ATI68880, STG1702, and STG1703 (Mach64 server) RAMDACs. This is now set by default in the S3 server when one of the preceding RAMDACs other than the AT&T20C490/1 is used. |
| | Dac_6_bit—(S3) Force 6-bit per RGB in cases where 8-bit mode would automatically be enabled. |
| | Sync_on_green—(S3, P9000) Enables generation of sync on the green signal on cards with Bt485, AT&T20C505, Ti3020/5/6 or IBMRGB5xx RAMDACs. Note: Although these RAMDACs support sync_on_green, it won't work on many cards because of the way they are designed. |

Power_saver—(S3 and Mach64) This option enables the server to use the power-saving features of VESA DPMS-compatible monitors. The suspend level is currently only supported for the Mach64 and for the 732, 764, 864, 868, 964, 968 S3 chips. Refer to the XF86Config(4/5) manual page for details of how to set the time-outs for the different levels of operation. This option is experimental.

intel_gx—(Mach32) Sets the hard-wired offset for the linear framebuffer correctly for the Intel GX Pro cards. This option is equivalent to setting the membase to 0x78000000.

spea_mercury—(S3) Enables pixel multiplex support for SPEA Mercury cards (928 + Bt485 RAMDAC). For these cards, pixel multiplexing is required in order to use dot clocks higher than 67.5 MHz and to access more than 1MB of video memory. Pixel multiplexing is currently supported only for noninterlaced modes, and modes with a physical width no smaller than 1,024.

stb_pegasus—(S3) Enables pixel multiplex support for STB Pegasus cards (928 + Bt485 RAMDAC). For these cards, pixel multiplexing is required in order to use dot clocks higher than 67.5 MHz. Pixel multiplexing is currently supported only for noninterlaced modes, and modes with a physical width no smaller than 1,024.

number_nine—(S3) Enables pixel multiplex support for Number Nine GXe level 10, 11, 12 cards (928 + Bt485 RAMDAC). For these cards, pixel multiplexing is required in order to use dot clocks higher than 85MHz. Pixel multiplexing is currently supported only for noninterlaced modes, and modes with a physical width no smaller than 800. This option is also required for some other Number Nine cards (for example, GXE64 and GXE64pro).

diamond—(S3) This option may be required for some Diamond cards (in particular, the 964/968 VRAM cards).

elsa_w1000pro—(S3) Enables support for the ELSA Winner 1000 PRO. This option is not usually required because the board can be autodetected.

elsa_w1000isa—(S3) Enables support for the ELSA Winner 1000 ISA. This option is not usually required because the board can be autodetected.

elsa_w2000pro—(S3) Enables support for the ELSA Winner 2000 PRO. This option is not usually required because the board can be autodetected.

pci_hack—(S3) Enables a workaround for problems seen with some PCI 928 cards on machines with a buggy SMC UART.

s3_964_bt485_vclk—(S3) Enables a workaround for possible problems on cards using the 964 and Bt485.

genoa, stb, hercules, or number_nine,—(S3) These options may be used to select different defaults for the blank delay settings for untested cards with IBM RGB5xx RAMDACs to avoid pixel-wrapping problems.

slow_vram—(S3) Adjusts the VRAM timings for cards using slow VRAM. This is required for some Diamond Stealth 64 VRAM and Hercules Terminator 64 cards.

Fast_vram—(S3) Adjusts the VRAM timings for faster VRAM access. There will be display errors and pixel garbage if your card can't support it.

Slow_dram_refresh—(S3) Adjusts the DRAM refresh for cards with slow DRAM to avoid lines of corrupted pixels when switching modes.

No_block_write—(Mach64) Disables the block write mode on certain types of VRAM Mach64 cards. If noise or shadows appear on the screen, this option should remove them.

Block_write—(Mach64) Enables the block write mode on certain types of VRAM Mach64 cards. Normally the Mach64 server will automatically determine if the card can handle block write mode, but this option will override the probe result.

No_bios_clocks—(Mach64) The Mach64 server normally reads the clocks from the bios. This option overrides the bios clocks and forces the server to use the clocks given in the XF86Config file.

There are also numerous tuning options for the AGX server. Refer to README.agx for details.

Note that XFree86 has some internal capabilities to determine what hardware it is running on. Thus, normally the keywords chipset, clocks, and videoram don't have to be specified. But there may be occasions when this autodetection mechanism fails, (for example, too high a load on the machine when you start the server). For cases like this, one should first run the server on an unloaded machine, look at the results of the autodetection (that are printed out during server startup), and then explicitly specify these parameters in the configuration file. It is recommended that all parameters, especially Clock values, be specified in the XF86Config file.

## FILES

| | |
|---|---|
| `<XRoot>/bin/XF86 S3` | The 8-, 16-, and 24-bit color X server for S3 |
| `<XRoot>/bin/XF86 Mach8` | The 8-bit color X server for Mach8 |
| `<XRoot>/bin/XF86 Mach32` | The 8- and 16-bit color X server for Mach32 |
| `<XRoot>/bin/XF86 Mach64` | The 8-, 16-, and 24-bit color X server for Mach64 |
| `<XRoot>/bin/XF86 P9000` | The 8-, 16-, and 24-bit color X server for the P9000 |
| `<XRoot>/bin/XF86 AGX` | The 8- and 16-bit color X server for AGX and XGA |
| `<XRoot>/bin/XF86 W32` | The 8-bit color X server for ET4000/W32 |
| `<XRoot>/bin/XF86 8514` | The 8-bit color X server for IBM 8514 and true compatibles |
| `/etc/XF86Config` | Server configuration file |
| `<XRoot>/lib/X11/XF86Config` | Server configuration file (secondary location) |
| `<XRoot>/lib/X11/doc/README.agx` | Extra documentation for the AGX server |
| `<XRoot>/lib/X11/doc/README.P9000` | Extra documentation for the P9000 server |
| `<XRoot>/lib/X11/doc/README.S3` | Extra documentation for the S3 server |
| `<XRoot>/lib/X11/doc/README.W32` | Extra documentation for the W32 server |

Note: `<XRoot>` refers to the root of the X11 install tree.

## SEE ALSO

X(1), Xserver(1), XFree86(1), XF86Config(4/5), xvidtune(1), xdm(1), xf86config(1), xinit(1)

## AUTHORS

In addition to the authors of XFree86 the following people contributed major work to this server: Kevin Martin (martin@cs.unc.edu), Jon Tombs (tombs@XFree86.org), Rik Faith (faith@cs.unc.edu). (Did the overall work on the base accelerated servers.)

David Dawes (dawes@XFree86.org), Dirk Hohndel (hohndel@XFree86.org), David Wexelblat (dwex@XFree86.org). (Merged their work into XFree86.)

Jon Tombs (tombs@XFree86.org), David Wexelblat (dwex@XFree86.org), David Dawes (dawes@XFree86.org), Amancio Hasty (hasty@netcom.com), Robin Cutshaw (robin@XFree86.org), Norbert Distler (Norbert.Distler@physik.tu-muenchen.de), Leonard N. Zubkoff (lnz@dandelion.com), Harald Koenig (koenig@tat.physik.uni-tuebingen.de), Bernhard Bender (br@elsa.mhs.compuserve.com), Hans Nasten (nasten@everyware.se). (Development and improvement of the S3-specific code.)

Kevin Martin (martin@cs.unc.edu), Rik Faith (faith@cs.unc.edu), Tiago Gons (tiago@comosjn.hobby.nl), Hans Nasten (nasten@everyware.se), Scott Laird (lair@midway.uchicago.edu). (Development and improvement of the Mach8- and 8514/A-specific code.)

Kevin Martin (martin@cs.unc.edu), Rik Faith (faith@cs.unc.edu), Mike Bernson (mike@mbsun.mlb.org), Mark Weaver (MarkWeaver@brown.edu), Craig Groeschel (craig@metrolink.com). (Development and improvement of the Mach32-specific code.)

Kevin Martin, (martin@cs.unc.edu). (Development of the Mach64-specific code.)

Erik Nygren (nygren@mit.edu), Harry Langenbacher (harry@brain.jpl.nasa.gov), Chris Mason (clmtch@osfmail.isc.rit.edu), Henrik Harmsen (harmsen@eritel.se). (Development and improvement of the P9000-specific code.)

Henry Worth (henry.worth@amail.amdahl.com). (Development of the AGX specific code.)

Glenn Lai (glenn@cs.utexas.edu). (Development of the ET4000/W32-specific code.)

See also the XFree86(1) manual page.

## BUGS

Some S3 cards with Bt485 RAMDACs are currently restricted to dot-clocks less than 85MHz.

The P9000 server may still have problems with cards other than the Diamond Viper VLB. There may still be problems with VGA mode restoration, but these should almost never occur. Using physical resolutions different from the virtual resolution is not supported and is not possible with the P9000. Use at dot-clocks greater than 110MHz is not recommended and not supported. Diamond claims that 135MHz is the maximum clock speed, but some of its bt485s are not rated that high. If you do not have a 135MHz bt485 on your Viper, contact Diamond tech support and they will send you an RMA number to replace the board. Acceleration is being added in slowly. At the present, only CopyArea, MoveWindow, and DrawLine are implemented. Other accelerated features are being tested and may be available in the next release. There seems to be a problem with olvwm when used with xdm and VT switching. The cursor will be messed up when you return to a VT if the cursor changed while you were in the VT.

## CONTACT INFO

XFree86 source is available from the FTP server ftp.XFree86.Org and mirrors. Send e-mail to XFree86@XFree86.Org for details.

# XF86_Mono

XF86_Mono—1-bit nonaccelerated X Window System servers for UNIX on x86 platforms

## SYNOPSIS

XFR6 Mono [:displaynumber] [ option ] ...

## DESCRIPTION

XF86_Mono is a 1-bit StaticGrey server for VGA and Super VGA cards and for some other monochrome cards.

## CONFIGURATIONS

The XF86_Mono server supports the following popular Super VGA chipsets in monochrome mode:

| | |
|---|---|
| ATI | 18800, 18800-1, 28800-2, 28800-4, 28800-5, 28800-6, 68800-3, 68800-6, 68800AX, 68800LX, 88800CX, 88800GX |
| Tseng | ET3000, ET4000, ET4000/W32 |
| Western Digital | PVGA1, WD90C00, WD90C10, WD90C11, WD90C30, WD90C31, WD90C33 |
| Genoa | GVGA |
| Trident | TVGA8800CS, TVGA8900B, TVGA8900C, TVGA8900CL, TVGA9000 |
| NCR | 77C22, 77C22E |
| Compaq | AVGA |
| Oak | OTI067, OTI077, OTI087 |
| Cirrus | CLGD5420, CLGD5422, CLGD5424, CLGD5426, CLGD5428, CLGD5429, CLGD5430, CLGD5434, CLGD5436, CLGD6205, CLGD6215, CLGD6225, CLGD6235, CL6410, CL6412, CL6420, CL6440 |

The XF86_Mono server supports the following monochrome cards and resolutions:

| | |
|---|---|
| Sigma | L-View, LaserView PLUS (in 1bpp mode): 1,664×1,280 |
| Hyundai | HGC-1280: 1,280[1,472]×1,024 |
| Apollo | Monochrome card (with ID 9) from Apollo workstations: 1,280×1,024 |
| Hercules and compatibles cards | 720×348 |

Additionally, it supports generic VGA cards with a maximum virtual resolution of (approximately) 800×650.

On supported SVGA chipsets, XF86_Mono will use up to $1/4$ of display memory, which yields a maximum virtual resolution of (approximately) 1,664×1,260 with 1MB of display memory. XF86_Mono does not support the accelerated functions of the supported chipsets.

## OPTIONS

In addition to the normal server options described in the Xserver(1) manual page, XF86_Mono accepts some more command-line switches, as described in the XFree86(1) man page.

## SETUP

XFree86 uses a configuration file called XF86Config for its initial setup.

See the XF86Config(4/5) man page for general details. Here only the XF86_Mono specific parts are explained.

The Driver entry in Screen section of the XF86Config file should be set to vga2 for VGA and SVGA boards, and mono for non-VGA mono boards. If Screen sections are present for both of these, the server will start in a dual-headed configuration.

Entries for the Device section in the XF86Config file include the following:

| | |
|---|---|
| chipset "name" | Specifies a chipset so the correct driver can be used. Possible chipsets for VGA2: |

| | |
|---|---|
| ATI | Vgawonder |
| Tseng | Et3000, et4000, et4000w32, et4000w32i, et4000w32p |
| Western Digital | Pvga1, wd90c00, wd90c10, wd90c30, wd90c31, wd90c33 |
| Genoa | Gvga |
| Trident | Tvga8800cs, tvga8900b, tvga8900c, tvga8900cl, tvga9000 |
| NCR | Ncr77c22, ncr77c22e Compaq: cpq avga OAK: oti067, oti077, oti087 |
| Cirrus | Clgd5420, clgd5422, clgd5424, clgd5426, clgd5428, clgd5429, clgd5430, clgd5434, clgd5436, clgd6205, clgd6215, clgd6225, clgd6235, cl6410, cl6412, cl6420, cl6440 |
| Generic VGA | generic |

Possible chipsets for mono:

| | |
|---|---|
| Hyundai | hgc1280 |
| Sigma | sigmalview |
| Apollo | apollo9 |
| Hercules | hercules |

| | |
|---|---|
| MemBase *memaddress* | Specifies the base address of the video memory. This option is only used for the Sigma LaserViewcards. Valid addresses for these cards are 0xA0000, 0xB0000, 0xC0000, 0xD0000, 0xE0000. The default is 0xE0000. |
| Black *red green blue* | Sets the black color to the RGB values specified. These values must be given as integers in the range 0–63. The default is 0 0 0. This option is only valid for the vga2 screen type. |
| White *red green blue* | Sets the white color to the RGB values specified. These values must be given as integers in the range 0–63. The default is 63 63 63. This option is only valid for the vga2 screen type. |
| Option "*optionstring*" | Allows the user to select certain options provided by the drivers. Currently the following strings are recognized: |

legend—For Sigma Legend ET4000-based boards. This option enables a special clock-selection algorithm used on Legend boards, and MUST be specified for these boards to function correctly.

swap_hibit—For Western Digital/PVGA1 chipsets. Some Western Digital-based boards require the high-order clock-select lead to be inverted. It is not possible for the server to determine this information at run-time. If the 9th clock in the list of clocks detected by the server is less than 30Mhz, this option likely needs to be set.

Hibit_low, hibit_high—For Tseng ET4000 chipsets. With some ET4000 cards, the server has difficulty getting the state of the high-order clocks select bit right when started from a high-resolution text mode. These options allow the correct initial state of that bit to be specified. To find out what the correct initial state is, start the server from an 80×25 text mode. This option is only needed if the clocks reported by the server when started from a high-resolution text mode differ from those reported when it is started from an 80×25 text mode.

8clocks—For the PVGA1 chipset, the default is 4 clocks. Some cards with this chipset may support 8 clocks. Specifying this option will allow the driver to detect and use the extra clocks.

16clocks—For Trident TVGA8900B and 8900C chipsets. Some newer boards using 8900B and 8900C chipsets actually support 16 clocks rather than the standard 8 clocks. Such boards will have a TCK9002 or TCK9004 chip on them. Specifying this option will allow the driver to detect and use the extra 8 clocks.

Power_saver—This option enables the server to use the power saving features of VESA DPMS-compatible monitors. The suspend level is currently not supported. Refer to the XF86Config(4/5) manual page for details of how to set the time-outs for the different levels of operation. This option is experimental.

secondary—For the hgc1280 and apollo9 chipsets. This option allows the use of these cards jumpered to the secondary I/O/ memory address. These addresses are

hgc1280:    I/O 0x3B0-0x3BF, mem 0xB0000-0xBFFFF (prim.)

            I/O 0x390-0x39F, mem 0xC8000-0xCFFFF (sec.)

apollo9:    I/O 0x3B0-0x3BF, mem 0xFA0000-0xFDFFFF (prim.)

            I/O 0x3D0-0x3DF, mem 0xA0000-0xDFFFF (sec.)

XFree86 can detect the HGC-1280 on both primary and secondary address; for the apollo card the primary address is used by default.

Note that XFree86 has some internal capabilities to determine what hardware it is running on. Thus, normally the keywords chipset, clocks, and videoram don't have to be specified. But there may be occasions when this autodetection mechanism fails, (for example, too high a load on the machine when you start the server). For cases like this, one should first run XF86_Mono on an unloaded machine, look at the results of the autodetection (that are printed out during server startup) and then explicitly specify these parameters in the configuration file. It is recommended that all parameters, especially Clock values, be specified in the XF86Config file.

## FILES

| | |
|---|---|
| <XRoot>/bin/XF86 Mono | The monochrome X server for VGA, SVGA and other monochrome cards |
| /etc/XF86Config | Server configuration file |
| <XRoot>/lib/X11/XF86Config | Server configuration file |

Note: <XRoot refers to the root of the X11 install tree.

## SEE ALSO

X(1), Xserver(1), XFree86(1), XF86Config(4/5), xf86config(1), xvidtune(1), xdm(1), xinit(1)

## BUGS

There are no known bugs at this time, although we welcome reports e-mailed to the address listed below.

## CONTACT INFO

XFree86 source is available from the FTP server ftp.XFree86.org.

Send e-mail to XFree86@XFree86.org for details.

## AUTHORS

Refer to the XFree86(1) manual page.

*XFree86 Version 3.1.2*

# XF86_SVGA

XF86_SVGA—Nonaccelerated SVGA X Window System servers for UNIX on x86 platforms

## SYNOPSIS

XF86 SVGA [:displaynumber] [ option ] ...

## DESCRIPTION

XF86_SVGA is an 8-bit PseudoColor, 16-bit TrueColor and 24-bit TrueColor server for Super VGA cards. It is derived from the X386 server provided with X11R5. Note: 16-bit TrueColor is currently only supported for some Cirrus and ARK chips, and 24-bit TrueColor is only supported for some Cirrus chips.

## CONFIGURATIONS

The XF86_SVGA server supports the following popular Super VGA chipsets in 256-color mode. Virtual resolutions up to (approximately) 1152×900 are supported, using (up to) 1MB of display memory. The Western Digital WD90C33 and some of the Cirrus chipsets support up to 2MB of display memory and virtual resolutions of 1,280×1,024 and higher. Some of the Cirrus chipsets also support 16bpp and 32bpp (truecolor) modes on certain configurations. Some of the ARK chipsets support 16bpp modes on certain configurations. Generic VGA cards are also supported at 8bpp 320×200 only.

| | |
|---|---|
| ATI | 18800, 18800-1, 28800-2, 28800-4, 28800-5, 28800-6, 68800-3, 68800-6, 68800AX, 68800LX, 88800CX, 88800GX |
| Tseng | ET3000, ET4000, ET4000/W32 |
| Western Digital | PVGA1, WD90C00, WD90C10, WD90C11, WD90C24A, WD90C30, WD90C31, WD90C33 |
| Genoa | GVGA |
| Trident | TVGA8800CS, TVGA8900B, TVGA8900C, TVGA8900CL, TVGA9000 |
| NCR | 77C22, 77C22E |
| Cirrus Logic | CLGD5420, CLGD5422, CLGD5424, CLGD5426, CLGD5428, CLGD5429,CLGD5430, CLGD5434, CLGD5436, CLGD6205, CLGD6215, CLGD6225, CLGD6235, CL6410, CL6412, CL6420, CL6440 |
| ARK | ARK1000PV, ARK1000VL, ARK2000PV |
| RealTek | RTG3106 |
| Compaq | AVGA |
| Oak | OTI067, OTI077, OTI087 |

| Avance Logic | AL2101, ALI2301, ALI2302, ALI2308, ALI2401 |
| Chips & Technology | 65520, 65530, 65540, 65545 |
| MX | MX68000, MX68010 |
| Video7 | HT216-32 |

Accelerated support is included for most of the Cirrus chipsets, and for the Western Digital WD90C31 and WD90C33 chipsets. Accelerated support for the ET4000/W32 is implemented in a separate server (see XF86_W32(1)). Users of boards based on ATI's Mach8, Mach32, and Mach64 chipsets should refer to the XF86_Mach8(1), XF86_Mach32(1) and XF86_Mach64(1) manual pages, respectively.

## OPTIONS

In addition to the normal server options described in the Xserver(1) manual page, XF86_SVGA accepts some more command-line switches, as described in the XFree86(1) man page.

## SETUP

XFree86 uses a configuration file called XF86Config for its initial setup.

See the XF86Config(4/5) man page for general details. Here only the XF86_SVGA specific parts are explained.

This server requires a Screen section in the XF86Config file with the Driver entry set to svga.

Entries for the Device section in the XF86Config file include

chipset "*name*"

Specifies a chipset so the correct driver can be used. Possible chipsets are

| ATI | vgawonder |
| Tseng | et3000, et4000, et4000w32, et4000w32i, et4000w32p |
| Western Digital | pvga1, wd90c00, wd90c10, wd90c24, wd90c30, wd90c31, wd90c33 |
| Genoa | gvga |
| Trident | tvga8800cs, tvga8900b, tvga8900c, tvga8900cl, tvga9000 |
| NCR | ncr77c22, ncr77c22e |
| Cirrus Logic | clgd5420, clgd5422, clgd5424, clgd5426, clgd5428, clgd5429, clgd5430, clgd5434, clgd5436, clgd6205, clgd6215, clgd6225, clgd6235, cl6410, cl6412, cl6420, cl6440 |
| RealTek | realtek |
| ARK | ark1000pv, ark1000vl, ark2000pv |
| Compaq | cpq_avga |
| Oak | oti067, oti077, oti087 |
| Avance Logic | al2101, ali2301, ali2302, ali2308, ali2401 |
| Chips & Technology | ct65520, ct65530, ct65540, ct65545 |
| MX | mx |
| Video7 | video7 |
| Generic | generic |

Option `"optionstring"`

Allows the user to select certain options provided by the drivers. Currently the following strings are recognized:

`legend`—For Sigma Legend `ET4000`-based boards. This option enables a special clock-selection algorithm used on Legend boards, and MUST be specified for these boards to function correctly.

`swap_hibit`—For Western Digital/PVGA1 chipsets. Some Western Digital-based boards require the high-order clock-select lead to be inverted. It is not possible for the server to determine this information at run-time. If the 9th clock in the list of clocks detected by the server is less than 30Mhz, this option likely needs to be set.

`Hibit_low, hibit_high`—For Tseng `ET4000` chipsets. With some `ET4000` cards, the server has difficulty getting the state of the high-order clocks select bit right when started from a high-resolution text mode. These options allow the correct initial state of that bit to be specified. To find out what the correct initial state is, start the server from an 80×25 text mode. This option is only needed if the clocks reported by the server when started from a high-resolution text mode differ from those reported when it is started from an 80×25 text mode.

`8clocks`—For the PVGA1 chipset, the default is 4 clocks. Some cards with this chipset may support 8 clocks. Specifying this option will allow the driver to detect and use the extra clocks.

`16clocks`—For Trident `TVGA8900B` and `8900C` chipsets. Some newer boards using `8900B` and `8900C` chipsets actually support 16 clocks rather than the standard 8 clocks. Such boards will have a `TCK9002` or `TCK9004` chip on them. Specifying this option will allow the driver to detect and use the extra 8 clocks.

`probe_clocks`—For Cirrus chipsets. The Cirrus driver has a fixed set of clocks that are normally used. Specifying this option will force the driver to probe for clocks instead of reporting the built-in defaults. This option is for debugging purposes only.

`power_saver`—This option enables the server to use the power-saving features of VESA DPMS-compatible monitors. The suspend level is currently not supported. Refer to the `XF86Config(4/5)` manual page for details of how to set the time-outs for the different levels of operation. This option is experimental.

`noaccel`—For Cirrus and WD chipsets. This option disables the accelerated features for the `clgd5426`, `clgd5428`, `wd90c24`, `wd90c31`, and `wd90c33` chipsets.

`fifo_conservative`—For Cirrus chipsets. This option sets the `CRT_FIFO` threshold to a conservative value for dot clocks above 65MHz. This reduces performance, but may help in eliminating problems with "streaks" on the screen during `BitBLT` operations.

`fifo_aggressive`—For Cirrus chipsets. This option sets the `CRT_FIFO` threshold to an aggressive value for dot clocks above 65MHz. This may increase performance.

slow_dram—For Cirrus chipsets. This option sets the DRAM timings for slow DRAM chips.

fast_dram—For ET4000 and Cirrus chipsets. This option sets the DRAM timings for fast DRAM chips.

no_2mb_banksel—For Cirrus chipsets. This option is required for Cirrus cards with 2MB of videoram, which is in the form of 512kx8 DRAMs (4 chips) rather than 256kx4 DRAMs (16 chips).

no_bitblt—For Cirrus chipsets. This option disables use of hardware BitBLT.

linear—Attempt a linear mapping of the framebuffer into high memory. Currently only supported for some Cirrus configurations.

med_dram, favour_bitblt, sw_cursor, clgd6225_lcd, mmio—More Cirrus-specific options. Refer to /usr/X11R6/lib/X11/doc/README.cirrus for a detailed description of Cirrus options.

| | |
|---|---|
| speedup "*selection*" | Sets the selection of SpeedUps to use. The optional selection string can take the following values: |

all

If the selection string is omitted, or if the speedup option is omitted, the selection defaults to all. Some of the SpeedUps can only be used with the ET4000, WD90C31, and WD90C33 chipsets and others require a virtual resolution with a xdim of 1024. SpeedUps that won't work with a given configuration are automatically disabled.

| | |
|---|---|
| nospeedup | Disables the SpeedUp code. This is equivalent to speedup none. |
| Ramdac *ramdac-type* | This specifies the type of RAMDAC used on the board. Only the ARK driver currently uses this. RAMDAC types recognized include |

Att20c490—AT&T 20C490 or compatible 8-bit RAMDAC.

Att20c498—AT&T 20C498 or compatible 16-bit RAMDAC.

Zoomdac—RAMDAC used by the Hercules Stingray Pro/V and 64/V.

Stg1700—STG1700 or compatible RAMDAC.

Note that XFree86 has some internal capabilities to determine what hardware it is running on. Thus, normally the keywords chipset, clocks, and videoram don't have to be specified. But there may be occasions when this autodetection mechanism fails, (for example, too high a load on the machine when you start the server). For cases like this, you should first run XF86_SVGA on an unloaded machine, look at the results of the autodetection (that are printed out during server startup), and then explicitly specify these parameters in the configuration file. It is recommended that all parameters, especially Clock values, be specified in the XF86Config file.

## FILES

| | |
|---|---|
| <XRoot>/bin/XF86 SVGA | The SVGA color X server |
| /etc/XF86Config | Server configuration file |
| <XRoot>/lib/X11/XF86Config | Server configuration file |
| <XRoot>/lib/X11/doc/README.ark | Extra documentation for the ARK driver |
| <XRoot>/lib/X11/doc/README.ati | Extra documentation for the ATI vgawon-der driver |

| <XRoot>/lib/X11/doc/README.cirrus | Extra documentation for the Cirrus driver |
| <XRoot>/lib/X11/doc/README.trident | Extra documentation for the Trident driver |
| <XRoot>/lib/X11/doc/README.tseng | Extra documentation for the ET4000 and ET3000 drivers |
| <XRoot>/lib/X11/doc/README.Oak | Extra documentation for the Oak driver |
| <XRoot>/lib/X11/doc/README.Video7 | Extra documentation for the Video7 driver |
| <XRoot>/lib/X11/doc/README.WstDig | Extra documentation for the WD/PVGA driver |

Note: <XRoot> refers to the root of the X11 install tree.

## SEE ALSO

X(1), Xserver(1), XFree86(1), XF86Config(4/5), xf86config(1), xvidtune(1), xdm(1), xinit(1)

## BUGS

Bug reports are welcome, and should be e-mailed to the address listed below.

## CONTACT INFO

XFree86 source is available from the FTP server ftp.XFree86.org.

Send e-mail to XFree86@XFree86.org for details.

## AUTHORS

Refer to the XFree86(1) manual page.

XFree86 *Version 3.1.2*

# XF86_VGA16

XF86 VGA16—4-bit nonaccelerated X Window System server for UNIX on x86 platforms

## SYNOPSIS

XF86 VGA16 [:displaynumber] [ option ] ...

## DESCRIPTION

XF86_VGA16 is a 4-bit color server for VGA cards. The default root visual for this server is StaticColor. It also includes support for the non-VGA monochrome cards described in the XF86_Mono(1) manual page. It may be run in a dual-headed configuration.

## CONFIGURATIONS

The XF86_VGA16 server supports the following popular SVGA chipsets in 16-color mode.

| ATI | 18800, 18800-1, 28800-2, 28800-4, 28800-5, 28800-6, 68800-3, 68800-6, 68800AX, 68800LX, 88800CX, 88800GX |
| Tseng | ET4000 |
| Trident | TVGA8800CS, TVGA8900B, TVGA8900C, TVGA8900CL, TVGA9000 |
| Cirrus | CL6410, CL6412, CL6420, CL6440 |
| Oak | OTI067, OTI077, OTI087 |

Additionally, it supports generic VGA cards.

XF86_VGA16 does not support the accelerated functions of the supported chipsets.

## OPTIONS

In addition to the normal server options described in the Xserver(1) manual page, XF86_VGA16 accepts some more command-line switches, as described in the XFree86(1) man page.

## SETUP

XFree86 uses a configuration file called XF86Config for its initial setup.

See the XF86Config(4/5) man page for general details. Here, only the XF86_VGA16 specific parts are explained.

The Driver entry in the Screen section of the XF86Config file should be set to vga16. To run in dual-headed configuration, there should also be a Screen section with the Driver entry set to mono.

Entries for the Device section in the XF86Config file include the following:

chipset "*name*"

Specifies a chipset so the correct driver can be used. Possible chipsets are

| | |
|---|---|
| ATI | vgawonder |
| Tseng | et4000, et4000w32, et4000w32i, et4000w32p |
| Trident | tvga8800cs, tvga8900b, tvga8900c, tvga8900cl, tvga9000 |
| Cirrus | cl6410, cl6412, cl6420, cl6440 |
| Oak | oti067, oti077, oti087 |
| Generic VGA | generic |

Option "*optionstring*"

Allows the user to select certain options provided by the drivers. Currently, the following strings are recognized:

legend—For Sigma Legend ET4000-based boards. This option enables a special clock-selection algorithm used on Legend boards, and MUST be specified for these boards to function correctly.

hibit_low, hibit_high—For Tseng ET4000 chipsets. With some ET4000 cards, the server has difficulty getting the state of the high-order clocks select bit right when started from a high-resolution text mode. These options allow the correct initial state of that bit to be specified. To find out what the correct initial state is, start the server from an 80×25 text mode. This option is only needed if the clocks reported by the server when started from a high-resolution text mode differ from those reported when it is started from an 80×25 text mode.

power_saver—This option enables the server to use the power saving features of VESA DPMS-compatible monitors. The suspend level is currently not supported.

Refer to the XF86Config(4/5) manual page for details of how to set the time-outs for the different levels of operation. This option is experimental.

Note that XFree86 has some internal capabilities to determine what hardware it is running on. Thus normally the keywords chipset, clocks, and videoram don't have to be specified. But there may be occasions when this autodetection mechanism fails, (for example, too high a load on the machine when you start the server). For cases like this, you should first run XF86 VGA16 on an unloaded machine, look at the results of the autodetection (that are printed out during server startup), and then explicitly specify these parameters in the configuration file. It is recommended that all parameters, especially Clock values, be specified in the XF86Config file.

## FILES

| | |
|---|---|
| `<XRoot>/bin/XF86 VGA16` | The 16-color X server |
| `/etc/XF86Config` | Server configuration file |
| `<XRoot>/lib/X11/XF86Config` | Server configuration file |

Note: `<XRoot>` refers to the root of the X11 install tree.

## SEE ALSO

`X`(1), `Xserver`(1), `XFree86`(1), `XF86Config`(4/5), `XF86 Mono`(1), `xf86config`(1), `xvidtune`(1), `xdm`(1), `xinit`(1)

## CONTACT INFO

XFree86 source is available from the FTP server `ftp.XFree86.org`.

Send e-mail to `XFree86@XFree86.org` for details.

## AUTHORS

The primary developer of this server is Gertjan Akkerman (`akkerman@dutiba.twi.tudelft.nl`).

See also the `XFree86`(1) manual page.

XFree86 *Version 3.1.2*

# xf86config

`xf86config`—Generate an `XF86Config` file

## SYNOPSIS

`xf86config`

## DESCRIPTION

`xf86config` is an interactive program for generating an `XF86Config file` for use with `XFree86` X servers.

## FILES

| | |
|---|---|
| `<xroot>/lib/X11/Cards` | Video cards database |

## SEE ALSO

`XFree86`(1), `XF86Config`(4/5), `reconfig`(1)

## AUTHOR

Harm Hanemaayer

XFree86 *Version 3.1.1*

# xfd

`xfd`—Display all the characters in an X font

## SYNOPSIS

`xfd [-options ...] -fn fontname`

## DESCRIPTION

The xfd utility creates a window containing the name of the font being displayed, a row of command buttons, several lines of text for displaying character metrics, and a grid containing one glyph per cell. The characters are shown in increasing order from left to right, top to bottom. The first character displayed at the top left will be character number 0 unless the -start option has been supplied, in which case the character with the number given in the -start option will be used.

The characters are displayed in a grid of boxes, each large enough to hold any single character in the font. Each character glyph is drawn using the PolyText16 request (used by the Xlib routine XDrawString16). If the -box option is given, a rectangle will be drawn around each character, showing where an ImageText16 request (used by the Xlib routine XDrawImageString16) would cause background color to be displayed.

The origin of each glyph is normally set so that the character is drawn in the upper left corner of the grid cell. However, if a glyph has a negative left bearing or an unusually large ascent, descent, or right bearing (as is the case with cursor font), some characters may not appear in their own grid cells. The -center option may be used to force all glyphs to be centered in their respective cells.

All the characters in the font may not fit in the window at once. To see the next page of glyphs, press the Next button at the top of the window. To see the previous page, press Prev. To exit xfd, press Quit.

Individual character metrics (index, width, bearings, ascent, and descent) can be displayed at the top of the window by clicking on the desired character.

The font name displayed at the top of the window is the full name of the font, as determined by the server. See xlsfonts for ways to generate lists of fonts, as well as more detailed summaries of their metrics and properties.

## OPTIONS

xfd accepts all of the standard toolkit command-line options along with the following additional options:

| | |
|---|---|
| -fn *font* | This option specifies the font to be displayed. This can also be set with the FontGrid font resource. A font must be specified. |
| -box | This option indicates that a box should be displayed outlining the area that would be filled with background color by an ImageText request. This can also be set with the FontGrid boxChars resource. The default is False. |
| -center | This option indicates that each glyph should be centered in its grid. This can also be set with the FontGrid centerChars resource. The default is False. |
| -start *number* | This option specifies the glyph index of the upper left corner of the grid. This is used to view characters at arbitrary locations in the font. This can also be set with the FontGrid startChar resource. The default is 0. |
| -bc *color* | This option specifies the color to be used if ImageText boxes are drawn. This can also be set with the FontGrid boxColor resource. |
| -rows *numrows* | This option specifies the number of rows in the grid. This can also be set with the FontGrid cellRows resource. |
| -columns *numcols* | This option specifies the number of columns in the grid. This can also be set with the FontGrid cellColumns resource. |

## WIDGETS

In order to specify resources, it is useful to know the widgets that compose xfd. In the notation below, indentation indicates hierarchical structure. The widget class name is given first, followed by the widget instance name. The application class name is Xfd.

```
Xfd xfd
     Paned pane
          Label fontname
               Box box
                    Command quit
                    Command prev
                    Command next
          Label select
          Label metrics
          Label range
          Label start
Form form
FontGrid grid
```

## FONTGRID RESOURCES

The FontGrid widget is an application-specific widget, and a subclass of the Simple widget in the Athena widget set. The effects and instance names of this widget's resources are given in the "Options" subsection. Capitalize the first letter of the resource instance name to get the corresponding class name.

## APPLICATION SPECIFIC RESOURCES

The instance names of the application-specific resources are given in the following list. Capitalize the first letter of the resource instance name to get the corresponding class name. These resources are unlikely to be interesting unless you are localizing xfd for a different language.

| | |
|---|---|
| selectFormat | Specifies a printf-style format string used to display information about the selected character. The default is character 0x%02x%02x (%u,%u) (%#o,%#o). The arguments that will come after the format string are |
| | char.byte1, char.byte2, char.byte1, char.byte2, char.byte1, char.byte2. char.byte1 is byte 1 of the selected character. char.byte2 is byte 2 of the selected character. |
| metricsFormat | Specifies a printf-style format string used to display character metrics. The default is width %d; left %d, right %d; ascent %d, descent %d (font %d, %d). The arguments that will come after the format string are the character metrics width, lbearing, rbearing, character ascent, character descent, font ascent, and font descent. |
| rangeFormat | Specifies a printf-style format string used to display the range of characters currently being displayed. The default is range: 0x%02x%02x (%u,%u) thru 0x%02x%02x (%u,%u). The arguments that will come after the format string are the following fields from the XFontStruct that is returned from opening the font: |
| | min_byte1, min_char_or_byte2, min_byte1, min_char_or_byte2, max_byte1, max_char_or_byte2, max_byte1, max_char_or_byte2. |
| startFormat | Specifies a printf-style format string used to display information about the character at the upper left corner of the font grid. The default is upper left: 0x%04x (%d,%d). The arguments that will come after the format string are the new character, the high byte of the new character, and the low byte of the new character. |
| nocharFormat | Specifies a printf-style format string to display when the selected character does not exist. The default is no such character 0x%02x%02x (%u,%u) (%#o,%#o. The arguments that will come after the format string are the same as for the select-Format resource. |

## SEE ALSO

X(1), xlsfonts(1), xrdb(1), xfontsel(1), X Logical Font Description Conventions

## BUGS

The program should skip over pages full of nonexistent characters.

## AUTHOR

Jim Fulton (MIT X Consortium); previous program of the same name by Mark Lillibridge (MIT Project Athena)

*X Version 11 Release 6*

# XFree86

XFree86—X11R6 for UNIX on x86 platforms

## DESCRIPTION

XFree86 is a collection of X servers for UNIX-like OSs on Intel x86 platforms. This work is derived from X386n1.2, which was contributed to X11R5 by Snitily Graphics Consulting Service.

## CONFIGURATIONS

XFree86 operates under the following operating systems:

- SVR3.2: SCO 3.2.2, 3.2.4, ISC 3.x, 4.x
- SVR4.0: ESIX, Microport, Dell, UHC, Consensys, MST, ISC, AT&T, NCR
- SVR4.2: Consensys, Univel (UNIXWare)
- Solaris (x86) 2.1, 2.4
- FreeBSD 1.1.5, 2.0, 2.0.5, NetBSD 1.0 (i386 port only)
- BSD/386 version 1.1 and BSD/OS 2.0
- Mach (from CMU)
- Linux
- Amoeba version 5.1
- Minix-386vm version 1.6.25.1
- LynxOS AT versions 2.2.1 and 2.3

## NETWORK CONNECTIONS

XFree86 supports connections made using the following reliable byte-streams:

Local

XFree86 supports local connections via Streams pipe via various mechanisms, using the following paths (n represents the display number):

/dev/X/server.n (SVR3 and SVR4)

/dev/X/Nserver.n (SVR4)

/dev/XnS and /dev/XnR (SCO SVR3)

In SVR4.0.4, if the Advanced Compatibility Package is installed, and in SVR4.2, XFree86 supports local connections from clients for SCO XSight/ODT, and (with modifications to the binary) clients for ISC SVR3.

UNIX Domain

XFree86 uses /tmp/.X11-unix/Xn as the filename for the socket, where n is the display number.

| | |
|---|---|
| TCPIP | XFree86 listens on port htons (6000+*n*), where *n* is the display number. |
| Amoeba RPC | This is the default communication medium used under native Amoeba. Note that under Amoeba, the server should be started with a *hostname:displaynumber* argument. |

## ENVIRONMENT VARIABLES

For operating systems that support local connections other than UNIX Domain sockets (SVR3 and SVR4), there is a compiled-in list specifying the order in which local connections should be attempted. This list can be overridden by the XLOCAL environment variable described next. If the display name indicates a best-choice connection should be made (for example, :0.0), each connection mechanism is tried until a connection succeeds or no more mechanisms are available. Note: For these OSs, the UNIX Domain socket connection is treated differently from the other local connection types. To use it the connection must be made to unix:0.0.

The XLOCAL environment variable should contain a list of one more of the following:

NAMED

PTS

SCO

ISC

which represent SVR4 Named Streams pipe, Old-style USL Streams pipe, SCO XSight Streams pipe, and ISC Streams pipe, respectively. You can select a single mechanism (for example, XLOCAL=NAMED), or an ordered list, for example,

XLOCAL="NAMED:PTS:SCO"

This variable overrides the compiled-in defaults. For SVR4 it is recommended that NAMED be the first preference connection. The default setting is

PTS:NAMED:ISC:SCO.

To globally override the compiled-in defaults, you should define (and export if using sh or ksh) XLOCAL globally. If you use startx/xinit, the definition should be at the top of your .xinitrc file. If you use xdm, the definitions should be early on in the <XRoot>/lib/X11/xdm/Xsession script.

## OPTIONS

In addition to the normal server options described in the Xserver(1) manual page, XFree86 accepts the following command-line switches:

| | |
|---|---|
| vt*XX* | *XX* specifies the Virtual Terminal device number that XFree86 will use. Without this option, XFree86 will pick the first available Virtual Terminal that it can locate. This option applies only to SVR3, SVR4, Linux, and BSD OSs with the syscons or pcvt driver. |
| -probeonly | Causes the server to exit after the device probing stage. The XF86Config file is still used when this option is given, so information that can be auto detected should be commented out. |
| -quiet | Suppresses most informational messages at startup. |
| -bpp n | Set number of bits per pixel. The default is 8. Legal values are 8, 15, 16, 24, 32. Not all servers support all values. |
| -weight *nnn* | Sets RGB weighting at 16 bpp. The default is 565. This applies only to those servers that support 16 bpp. |
| -gamma *value* | Sets the gamma correction. *value* must be between 0.1 and 10. The default is 1.0. This value is applied equally to the R, G, and B values. Not all servers support this. |

| | |
|---|---|
| -rgamma value | Sets the red gamma correction. value must be between 0.1 and 10. The default is 1.0. Not all servers support this. |
| -ggamma value | Sets the green gamma correction. value must be between 0.1 and 1.0. The default is 1.0. Not all servers support this. |
| -bgamma value | Sets the blue gamma correction. value must be between 0.1 and 1.0. The default is 1.0. Not all servers support this. |
| -showconfig | Prints out a list of screen drivers configured in the server. |
| -verbose | Maximizes information printed at startup (more than the default). |
| -xf86config file | Reads the server configuration from file. This option is only available when the server is run as root (that is, with real-UID 0). |
| -keeptty | Prevents the server from detaching its initial controlling terminal. This option is only useful when debugging the server. |

## KEYBOARD

Multiple key presses recognized directly by XFree86 are

| | |
|---|---|
| Ctrl+Alt+Backspace | Immediately kills the server—no questions asked. (Can be disabled by specifying "DontZap" in the Server-Flags section of the XF86Config file.) |
| Ctrl+Alt+Keypad-Plus | Changes video mode to next one specified in the configuration file, (increasing video resolution order). |
| Ctrl+Alt+Keypad-Minus | Changes video mode to previous one specified in the configuration file, (decreasing video resolution order). |
| Ctrl+Alt+F1...F12 | For BSD systems using the syscons driver and Linux, these keystroke combinations are used to switch to Virtual Console 1 through 12. |

## SETUP

XFree86 uses a configuration file called XF86Config for its initial setup. Refer to the XF86Config(4/5) manual page for more information.

## FILES

| | |
|---|---|
| <XRoot>/bin/XF86 SVGA | The color SVGA X server |
| <XRoot>/bin/XF86 Mono | The monochrome X server for VGA and other mono cards |
| <XRoot>/bin/XF86 S3 | The accelerated S3 X server |
| <XRoot>/bin/XF86 Mach8 | The accelerated Mach8 X server |
| <XRoot>/bin/XF86 Mach32 | The accelerated Mach32 X server |
| <XRoot>/bin/XF86 Mach64 | The accelerated Mach64 X server |
| <XRoot>/bin/XF86 P9000 | The accelerated P9000 X server |
| <XRoot>/bin/XF86 AGX | The accelerated AGX X server |
| <XRoot>/bin/XF86 W32 | The accelerated ET4000/W32 X server |
| <XRoot>/bin/XF86 8514 | The accelerated 8514/A X server |
| /etc/XF86Config | Server configuration file |
| <XRoot>/lib/X11/XF86Config.hostname | Server configuration file |
| <XRoot>/lib/X11/XF86Config | Server configuration file |
| <XRoot>/bin/ | Client binaries |

| | |
|---|---|
| `<XRoot>/include/` | Header files |
| `<XRoot>/lib/` | Libraries |
| `<XRoot>/lib/X11/fonts/` | Fonts |
| `<XRoot>/lib/X11/rgb.txt` | Color names to RGB mapping |
| `<XRoot>/lib/X11/XErrorDB` | Client error message database |
| `<XRoot>/lib/X11/app-defaults/` | Client resource specifications |
| `<XRoot>/man/man?/` | Manual pages |
| `/etc/Xn.hosts` | Initial access control list for display n |

Note: `<XRoot>` refers to the root of the X11 install tree.

## SEE ALSO

X(1), Xserver(1), xdm(1), xinit(1), XF86Config(4/5), xf86config(1), XF86 SVGA(1), XF86 VGA16(1), XF86 Mono(1), XF86 Accel(1), xvidtune(1)

## AUTHORS

For X11R5, XF86 1.2 was provided by the following:

Thomas Roell (roell@informatik.tu-muenchen.de; server and SVR4 stuff), Mark W. Snitily (mark@sgcs.com SGCS; SVR3 support, X Consortium Sponsor), and many more people out there on the Net who helped with ideas and bug fixes.

XFree86 was integrated into X11R6 by the following team:

Stuart Anderson (anderson@metrolink.com), Doug Anson (danson@lgc.com), Gertjan Akkerman (akkerman@dutiba.twi.tudelft.nl), Mike Bernson (mike@mbsun.mlb.org), Robin Cutshaw (robin@XFree86.org), David Dawes (dawes@XFree86.org), Marc Evans (marc@XFree86.org), Pascal Haible (haible@izfm.uni-stuttgart.de), Matthieu Herrb (Matthieu.Herrb@laas.fr), Dirk Hohndel (hohndel@XFree86.org), David Holland (davidh@use.com), Alan Hourihane (alanh@fairlite.demon.co.uk), Jeffrey Hsu (hsu@soda.berkeley.edu), Glenn Lai (glenn@cs.utexas.edu), Ted Lemon (mellon@ncd.com), Rich Murphey (rich@XFree86.org), Hans Nasten (nasten@everyware.se), Mark Snitily (mark@sgcs.com), Randy Terbush (randyt@cse.unl.edu), Jon Tombs (tombs@XFree86.org), Kees Verstoep (versto@cs.vu.nl), Paul Vixie (paul@vix.com), Mark Weaver (Mark Weaver@brown.edu), David Wexelblat (dwex@XFree86.org), Philip Wheatley (Philip.Wheatley@ColumbiaSC.NCR.COM), Thomas Wolfram (wolf@prz.tu-berlin.de), and Orest Zborowski (orestz@eskimo.com).

The XFree86 enhancement package was provided by

| | |
|---|---|
| David Dawes, dawes@XFree86.org | Release coordination, administration of FTP repository and mailing lists. Source tree management and integration, accelerated server integration, fixing, and coding. |
| Glenn Lai, glenn@cs.utexas.edu | The SpeedUp code for ET4000-based SVGA cards, and ET4000/W32 accelerated server. |
| Jim Tsillas, jtsilla@ccs.neu.edu | Many server speedups from the fX386 series of enhancements. |
| David Wexelblat, dwex@XFree86.org | Integration of the fX386 code into the default server, many driver fixes, and driver documentation, assembly of the VGA card/monitor database, development of the generic video mode listing. Accelerated server integration, fixing, and coding. |
| Dirk Hohndel, hohndel@XFree86.org | Linux-shared libraries and release coordination. Accelerated server integration and fixing. Generic administrivia and documentation. |
| Amancio Hasty Jr., hasty@netcom.com | Porting to 386BSD version 0.1 and XS3 development. |
| Rich Murphey, rich@XFree86.org | Ported to 386BSD version 0.1 based on the original port by Pace Willison. Support for 386BSD, FreeBSD, and NetBSD. |

| | |
|---|---|
| Robert Baron, Robert.Baron@ernst.mach.cs.cmu.edu | Ported to Mach. |
| Orest Zborowski, orestz@eskimo.com | Ported to Linux. |
| Doug Anson, danson@lgc.com | Ported to Solaris x86. |
| David Holland, davidh@use.com | Ported to Solaris x86. |
| David McCullough, davidm@stallion.oz.au | Ported to SCO SVR3. |
| Michael Rohleder, michael.rohleder@stadt-frankfurt.de | Ported to ISC SVR3. |
| Kees Verstoep, versto@cs.vu.nl | Ported to Amoeba based on Leendert van Doorn's original Amoeba port of X11R5. |
| | |
| Marc Evans, Marc@XFree86.org | Ported to OSF/1. |
| Philip Homburg, philip@cs.vu.nl | Ported to Minix-386vm. |
| Thomas Mueller, tm@systrix.de | Ported to LynxOS. |
| Jon Tombs, tombs@XFree86.org | S3 server and accelerated server coordination. |
| Harald Koenig, koenig@tat.physik.uni-tuebingen.de | S3 server development. |
| Bernhard Bender, br@elsa.mhs.compuserve.com | S3 server development. |
| Kevin Martin, martin@cs.unc.edu | Overall work on the base accelerated servers (ATI and 8514/A), and Mach64 server. |
| | |
| Rik Faith, faith@cs.unc.edu | Overall work on the base accelerated servers (ATI and 8514/A). |
| Tiago Gons, tiago@comosjn.hobby.nl | Mach8 and 8514/A server development. |
| Hans Nasten, nasten@everyware.se | Mach8, 8514/A, and S3 server development and BSD/386 support. |
| | |
| Mike Bernson, mike@mbsun.mlb.org | Mach32 server development. |
| Mark Weaver, Mark_Weaver@brown.edu | Mach32 server development. |
| Craig Groeschel, craig@metrolink.com | Mach32 server development. |
| Henry Worth, Henry.Worth@amail.amdahl.com | AGX server. |
| Erik Nygren, nygren@mit.edu | P9000 server. |
| Harry Langenbacher, harry@brain.jpl.nasa.gov | P9000 server. |
| Chris Mason, mason@mail.csh.rit.edu | P9000 server. |
| Henrik Harmsen, harmsen@eritel.se | P9000 server. |
| Simon Cooper, scooper@vizlab.rutgers.edu | Cirrus accelerated code (based on work by Bill Reynolds). |
| Harm Hanemaayer, hhanemaa@cs.ruu.nl | Cirrus accelerated code and ARK driver. |
| Mike Tierney, floyd@eng.umd.edu | WD accelerated code. |
| Bill Conn, conn@bnr.ca | WD accelerated code. |
| Brad Bosch, brad@lachman.com | WD 90C24A support. |
| Alan Hourihane, alanh@fairlite.demon.co.uk | Trident SVGA driver |
| Marc La France, Marc.La-France@ualberta.ca | ATI vgawonder SVGA driver |
| Steve Goldman, sgoldman@encore.com Oak | 067/077 SVGA driver. |
| Jorge Delgado, ernar@dit.upm.es | Oak SVGA driver, and 087 accelerated code. |
| Bill Conn, conn@bnr.ca | WD accelerated code. |
| Paolo Severini, lendl@dist.dist.unige.it | AL2101 SVGA driver. |
| Ching-Tai Chiu, cchiu@netcom.com | Avance Logic ALI SVGA driver. |
| Manfred Brands, mb@oceonics.nl | Cirrus 64xx SVGA driver. |
| Randy Hendry, randy@sgi.com | Cirrus 6440 support in the cl64xx SVGA driver. |
| Frank Dikker, dikker@cs.utwente.nl | MX SVGA driver. |
| Regis Cridlig, cridlig@dmi.ens.fr | Chips & Technology driver. |
| Jon Block, block@frc.com | Chips & Technology driver. |

| | |
|---|---|
| Mike Hollick, `hollick@graphics.cis.upenn.edu` | Chips & Technology driver |
| Peter Trattler, `peter@sbox.tu-graz.ac.at` | RealTek SVGA driver. |
| Craig Struble, `cstruble@acm.vt.edu` | Video7 SVGA driver. |
| Gertjan Akkerman, `akkerman@dutiba.twi.tudelft.nl` | 16-color VGA server, and XF86Config parser. |
| Davor Matic, `dmatic@Athena.MIT.EDU` | Hercules driver. |
| Pascal Haible, `haible@izfm.uni-stuttgart.de` | Banked monochrome VGA support, Hercules support, and mono frame buffer support for dumb monochrome devices. |

and many more people out there on the Net who helped with beta-testing this enhancement.

XFree86 source is available from the FTP server `ftp.XFree86.org`, among others. Send e-mail to `XFree86@XFree86.org` for details.

XFree86 *Version 3.1.2*

# xfs

xfs—X font server

## SYNOPSIS

xfs [-config *configuration_file*] [-port *tcp_port*]

## DESCRIPTION

xfs is the X Window System font server. It supplies fonts to X Window System display servers.

## STARTING THE SERVER

The server is usually run by a system administrator, and started via boot files like `/etc/rc.local`. Users may also wish to start private font servers for specific sets of fonts.

## OPTIONS

| | |
|---|---|
| -config configuration_file | Specifies the configuration file the font server will use. |
| -ls listen-socket | Specifies a file descriptor that is already set up to be used as the listen socket. This option is only intended to be used by the font server itself when automatically spawning another copy of itself to handle additional connections. |
| -port tcp_port | Specifies the TCP port number on which the server will listen for connections. |

## SIGNALS

| | |
|---|---|
| SIGTERM | This causes the font server to exit cleanly. |
| SIGUSR1 | This signal is used to cause the server to reread its configuration file. |
| SIGUSR2 | This signal is used to cause the server to flush any cached data it may have. |
| SIGHUP | This signal is used to cause the server to reset, closing all active connections and rereading the configuration file. |

## CONFIGURATION

The configuration language is a list of keyword and value pairs. Each keyword is followed by an = and then the desired value.

Recognized keywords include the following:

catalogue (list of string)

Ordered list of font path element names. Use of the key-word "catalogue" is very misleading at present; the current implementation only supports a single catalogue (all), containing all of the specified fonts.

alternate-servers (list of string)

List of alternate servers for this font server.

client-limit (cardinal)

Number of clients this font server will support before refusing service. This is useful for tuning the load on each individual font server.

clone-self (Boolean)

Whether this font server should attempt to clone itself when it reaches the client-limit.

default-point-size (cardinal)

The default pointsize (in decipoints) for fonts that don't specify. The default is 120.

default-resolutions (list of resolutions)

Resolutions the server supports by default. This information may be used as a hint for prerendering, and substituted for scaled fonts that do not specify a resolution. A resolution is a comma-separated pair of x and y resolutions in pixels per inch. Multiple resolutions are separated by commas.

error-file (string)

Filename of the error file. All warnings and errors will be logged here.

port (cardinal)

TCP port on which the server will listen for connections.

use-syslog (Boolean)

Whether syslog(3) (on supported systems) is to be used for errors.

deferglyphs (string)

Set the mode for delayed fetching and caching of glyphs. Value is none, meaning deferred glyphs is disabled, all, meaning it is enabled for all fonts, and 16, meaning it is enabled only for 16-bits fonts.

## EXAMPLE

```
#
# sample font server configuration file
#
# allow a max of 10 clients to connect to this font server client-limit = 10
# when a font server reaches its limit, start up a new one clone-self = on
# alternate font servers for clients to use alternate-servers = hansen:7101,hansen:7102
# where to look for fonts
# the first is a set of Speedo outlines, the second is a set of
# misc bitmaps and the last is a set of 100dpi bitmaps
#
catalogue = /usr/X11R6/lib/X11/fonts/speedo,
/usr/X11R6/lib/X11/fonts/misc,
/usr/X11R6/lib/X11/fonts/100dpi/
# in 12 points, decipoints
default-point-size = 120
# 100 x 100 and 75 x 75
default-resolutions = 100,100,75,75
use-syslog = off
```

## FONT SERVER NAMES

One of the following forms can be used to name a font server that accepts TCP connections:

`tcp/hostname:port tcp/hostname:port/cataloguelist`

The *hostname* specifies the name (or decimal numeric address) of the machine on which the font server is running. The *port* is the decimal TCP port on which the font server is listening for connections. The *cataloguelist* specifies a list of catalogue names, with + as a separator.

Examples: `tcp/fs.x.org:7100`, `tcp/18.30.0.212:7101/all`.

One of the following forms can be used to name a font server that accepts DECnet connections:

`decnet/nodename::font$objname decnet/nodename::font$objname/cataloguelist`

The *nodename* specifies the name (or decimal numeric address) of the machine on which the font server is running. The *objname* is a normal, case-insensitive DECnet object name. The *cataloguelist* specifies a list of catalogue names, with + as a separator.

Examples: `DECnet/SRVNOD::FONT$DEFAULT`, `decnet/44.70::font$special/symbols`.

## SEE ALSO

X(1), font server implementation overview

## BUGS

Multiple catalogues should be supported.

## AUTHORS

Dave Lemke (Network Computing Devices, Inc.), Keith Packard (Massachusetts Institute of Technology)

*X Version 11 Release 6*

# xhost

xhost—Server access control program for X

## SYNOPSIS

`xhost [[+-]name ...]`

## DESCRIPTION

The `xhost` program is used to add and delete hostnames or usernames to the list allowed to make connections to the X server. In the case of hosts, this provides a rudimentary form of privacy control and security. It is only sufficient for a workstation (single user) environment, although it does limit the worst abuses. Environments that require more sophisticated measures should implement the user-based mechanism or use the hooks in the protocol for passing other authentication data to the server.

## OPTIONS

Xhost accepts the following command-line options. For security, the options that effect access control may only be run from the "controlling host." For workstations, this is the same machine as the server. For X terminals, it is the login host.

| | |
|---|---|
| `-help` | Prints a usage message. |
| `[+]name` | The given *name* (the plus sign is optional) is added to the list allowed to connect to the X server. The name can be a hostname or a username. |

| | |
|---|---|
| *-name* | The given *name* is removed from the list allowed to connect to the server. The name can be a hostname or a username. Existing connections are not broken, but new connection attempts will be denied. Note that the current machine is allowed to be removed; however, further connections (including attempts to add it back) will not be permitted. Resetting the server (thereby breaking all connections) is the only way to allow local connections again. |
| + | Access is granted to everyone, even if they aren't on the list (in other words, access control is turned off). |
| - | Access is restricted to only those on the list (that is, access control is turned on). |
| *nothing* | If no command-line arguments are given, a message indicating whether or not access control is currently enabled is printed, followed by the list of those allowed to connect. This is the only option that may be used from machines other than the controlling host. |

## NAMES

A complete name has the syntax *family*:*name* where the families are as follows:

| | |
|---|---|
| inet | Internet host |
| dne | DECnet host |
| nis | Secure RPC network name |
| krb | Kerberos V5 principal |
| local | Contains only one name, the empty string |

The family is case insensitive. The format of the name varies with the family.

When Secure RPC is being used, the network-independent netname (for example, nis:unix.uid@domainname) can be specified, or a local user can be specified with just the username and a trailing at sign (@) (for example, nis:pat@).

For backward compatibility with pre-R6 xhost, names that contain an at sign are assumed to be in the nis family. Otherwise, the inet family is assumed.

## DIAGNOSTICS

For each name added to the access control list, a line of the form name being added to access control list is printed. For each name removed from the access control list, a line of the form name being removed from access control list is printed.

## FILES

/etc/X*.hosts

## SEE ALSO

X(1), Xsecurity(1), Xserver(1), xdm(1)

## ENVIRONMENT

| | |
|---|---|
| DISPLAY | To get the default host and display to use |

## BUGS

You can't specify a display on the command line because -display is a valid command-line argument (indicating that you want to remove the machine named display from the access list).

The X server stores network addresses, not hostnames. This is not really a bug. If somehow you change a host's network address while the server is still running, xhost must be used to add the new address and/or remove the old address.

## AUTHORS

Bob Scheifler (MIT Laboratory for Computer Science) and Jim Gettys (MIT Project Athena/DEC)

*X Version 11 Release 6*

# xieperf

xieperf—XIE server extension test and demo program

## SYNTAX

xieperf [-option ...]

## DESCRIPTION

The xieperf program is based upon R5 x11perf(1) , and while not entirely comprehensive in its coverage of the XIE protocol (see the "Bugs" subsection), it is intended to be useful in the evaluation of XIE implementations in the areas of protocol adherence and performance. The xieperf program includes tests that execute each of the protocol requests and photoflo elements specified by revision 5.0 of the XIE protocol. In addition, xieperf provides a set of tests that can be used to validate the detection and transmission of XIE protocol request errors, such as FloMatch, FloValue, and so forth. Finally, xieperf provides a customizable demonstration program for XIE.

A test is made up of three components executed in sequence: an initialization function, a test function, and an end function. The initialization function is responsible for allocating and populating test resources, such as photomaps and LUTs, and for creating a stored photoflo that will be executed by the test function. The test function, in most cases, simply executes the stored photoflo for a specified number of repetitions. The end function, which is called following the test function, is used primarily to destroy any noncacheable server resources used by the test, and to free any memory that was dynamically allocated by the client. Some tests, such as -modify1, -await, -abort, and -redefine, perform additional steps within the test function inner loop, as required by the element being tested, or in an attempt to make the test more visually appealing.

Evaluating the performance of individual XIE elements is not as simple as measuring Core X drawing times. The XIE protocol requires elements to be embedded within photoflos in order to be exercised, and the minimum possible photoflo size is two. This implies that it is impossible to measure performance of a single element in isolation—the time it takes to run the flo depends on what other elements exist in the flo. Extrapolating performance of a single element (or technique) in a flo must be done carefully, on a case-by-case basis, because in general, measured element performance depends on input image size, data type, and other factors, all of which can be influenced by upstream flo elements. Note further that the number and type of elements in a flo can be influenced by the visuals available on the display, so even flo-flo comparisons on machines with different visuals must be done with caution.

Many test labels contain an abbreviated pipeline description. For instance, IP/IL/P/ED indicates ImportPhotomap, ImportLUT, Point, and ExportDrawable. Pipelines ending in ED (ExportDrawable) often include hidden elements such as BandExtract, ConvertToIndex, Dither, or Point to match the flo output to the screen visual. Pipelines ending in EP (ExportPhotomap) will result in a blank window.

xieperf is compatible with x11perfcomp(1), which is used to compare the outputs of different xieperf and x11perf runs in a nice, tabular format. In xieperf you will need to use the -labels option (see the "Options" subsection), and provide the resulting labels file to x11perfcomp(1) to obtain correct output. See the x11perfcomp(1) man pages for more details on this.

## OPTIONS

xieperf accepts the following options:

-display host:dpy

Specifies which display to use.

-images *<path>*

Normally, xieperf references image files located in the directory images, which xieperf assumes is located in your current directory. If the images directory is not in your current directory, or the file has been renamed, use this option to specify its location.

-timeout*<s>*

Some tests require the reception of an event such as FloNotify to continue, and may cause xieperf to hang should these events not be received. This option allows the user to specify a time-out value which, if exceeded, will cause xieperf to give up waiting for an event, and continue on with the next test in sequence. Should an event time-out, a warning message will be printed to stderr. The default time-out value is 60 seconds.

-sync

Runs the tests in synchronous mode.

-script *<file>*

Using this option gives the user the ability to run a subset of the available tests and control the number of times the tests are executed on an individual basis. This is thought to be especially useful for those running xieperf for demonstration purposes. Using this option causes xieperf to read commands specified in a script file, or from stdin if *<file>* is -. Tests are specified by newline-terminated input lines of the form command [ -reps n ] [ -repeat m ]. Characters following and including # are treated as comments. See the -mkscript option.

-repeat *<n>*

Repeats each test *n* times (by default each test is run two times). This option may be used in script files also, in which case the script file -repeat overrides the command-line option.

-time *<s>*

Specifies how long in seconds each test should be run (default 5 seconds).

-depth *<depth>*

Use a visual with *<depth>* planes per pixel (default is the default visual).

-GrayScale

Use a GrayScale visual (default is the default visual).

-PseudoColor

Use a PseudoColor visual (default is the default visual).

-StaticGray

Use a StaticGray visual (default is the default visual).

-StaticColor

Use a StaticColor visual (default is the default visual).

-TrueColor

Use a TrueColor visual (default is the default visual).

-DirectColor

Use a DirectColor visual (default is the default visual).

-WMSafe

If xieperf must be run in a window manager environment, use this flag to make xieperf aware of this. If specified, xieperf will create a window, identical to the size of the root window, and all further windows created by xieperf will be transient pop-up children of this window. If this flag is omitted, xieperf will set the override_redirect attribute of all windows to True and will also do evil things such as calling XInstallColormap. Using this option will cause the window manager to (hopefully) obey window geometry hints specified by xieperf.

| | |
|---|---|
| -showtechs | Display a comprehensive list of techniques, by category, indicating which of the techniques are supported by the XIE server. |
| -showlabels | Print test label to screen prior to calling any of the test code. This allows the user to know which test is executing in case the test hangs for some reason. |
| -showevents | Be verbose when running event and error tests. Also, can be used to catch and display information on any signals received during execution of xieperf. Note that this flag is best used in a debugging situation, or to validate that the error events received by xieperf are valid the first time the tests are executed on a new platform. |
| -events | Run tests that test for event generation. |
| -errors | Run tests that test for error event generation. |
| -loCal | Skip test calibration. This may be used when running xieperf in situations where execution timing is not important. Execution times will not be reported by xieperf when this option is enabled. The inner loop repeat count, additionally, is set to a value of 5 (but can be overridden by the -reps option). |
| -all | Runs all tests. This may take a while, depending on the speed of your machine, and its floating-point capabilities. This option is ignored if a script file is used. |
| -tests | Generate a list of the available tests for the xieperf program. In x11perf, this list is normally displayed in the usage statement. It was yanked from the usage of xieperf because it was too lengthy. |
| -mkscript | Generate a script file suitable for use with the script option. If -repeat or -reps are also specified, they will be automatically placed at the end of each command in the script. The script is generated to stderr. See the -script command, above. |
| -cache <n> | Most test flos utilize a photomap resource for a source. A photomap cache of up to n entries is controlled by xieperf to avoid having to constantly reload these images during test initialization. The default cache size is 4. If a value less than the default is specified, the cache size will be set to the default. |
| -labels | Generates just the descriptive labels for each test specified. Use -all or -range to specify which tests are included. See x11perfcomp(1) for more details. |
| -DIS | Pretend we are running xieperf while connected to a DIS-only capable implementation of XIE. This will cause xieperf to execute those tests that only use protocol requests found in the DIS subset of XIE, and bypass those which are not DIS-compatible. If xieperf detects a DIS server, it will do this automatically, and this option is ignored. Use -all or -range to specify the initial range of tests. |
| -range <test1>[,<test2>] | Runs all the tests starting from the specified name *test1* until the name *test2*, including both the specified tests. Some tests, like the event and error tests, also require the -errors or -events options to specified. This option is ignored if a script is used. |

| | |
|---|---|
| -reps <n> | Fix the inner loop repetitions to *n*. This indicates how many times the photoflo will be executed each time the test is run. This option is overridden on a per test basis if specified in a script. Typically, xieperf determines the ideal number of reps during each test's calibration period. |
| -ImportObscuredEvent through -ExportAvailable | Test generation of events. Requires -events flag. |
| -BadValue through -FloValueError | Test generation of errors. Requires -errors flag. |
| -ColorList | Create anddestroy ColorList resource test. |
| -LUT | Create and destroy LUT resource test. |
| -Photomap | Create and destroy Photomap resource test. |
| -ROI | Create and destroy ROI resource test. |
| -Photospace | Create and destroy Photospace test. |
| -Photoflo | Create and destroy Photoflo test. |
| -QueryPhotomap | Query Photomap resource test. |
| -QueryColorList | Query ColorList resource test. |
| -QueryTechniquesDefault through -QueryTechniques WhiteAdjust | Query techniques as specified by test name. |
| -QueryPhotoflo | Query Photoflo test. |
| -PurgeColorList | Purge ColorList test. |
| -Abort | This test creates a photoflo that is started and blocks for data provided by PutClientData(). Instead of sending the data, the test uses XieAbort() to stop the photoflo, and then waits for the PhotofloDone event to be sent by the server. If the test times out waiting for the event, an error message is sent to stderr. |
| -Await | This test creates a flo of the form ImportClientLUT -> ExportLUT, and starts the flo executing. xieperf then forks, and the child process streams the LUT data to the flo using PutClientData, while the parent blocks in XieAwait. If the flo successfully finishes, XieAwait will return and the flo state, after query, will indicate that it has completed. If XieAwait does not complete naturally, or after return from XieAwait the flo is still active, an error is reported to stderr. Note, on a really slow machine, it is possible that XieAwait will return before the flo has a chance to finish. In this case, use the -timeout option to increase the time-out for this test. |
| -importclientlut1 | ImportClientLUT -> ExportLUT test. |
| -importclientphoto1 through -importclientphoto9 | Flos of the form ImportClient-Photo -> ExportPhotomap using various decode techniques, for example, G32D, TIFF2, UncompressedTriple. |
| -importclientroi1 | ImportClientROI with 10 rectangles. |
| -importclientroi2 | ImportClientROI with 100 rectangles. |
| -encodephoto1 through -encodephoto14 | Flos of the form ImportPhotomap - ExportPhotomap using various encode techniques, for example G32D, TIFF2, UncompressedTriple. Original encoding is shown in left window; image after encoding is shown in right window. |

| | |
|---|---|
| -encodeclientphoto1 through<br>-encodeclientphoto11 | Two flos, one of the form `ImportPhotomap` -> `ExportClientPhoto`, and the other of the form `ImportClientPhoto` -> `ExportPhotomap`, where `ExportClientPhoto` in the first flo uses various encode techniques, for example `G32D`, `TIFF2`, `UncompressedTriple`. The image before encoding is displayed in the left window, while the right window shows the image that was encoded in the first flo and read back in the second flo. |
| -exportclientlut1 | `ExportClientLUT` test. LUT is displayed in a histogram window. |
| -exportclientroi1 | `ExportClientROI` test, 10 ROIs. The ROIs that are sent to the server are represented by the filled rectangles. The ROIs that are received back from the server by the client are drawn as white-bordered, nonfilled rectangles. The resulting output illustrates how the server combined the rectangles sent to it. |
| -exportclientroi2 | Same as exportclientroi1, except using 100 rectangles. |
| -exportclienthistogram1 through<br>-exportclienthistogram4 | `ExportClientHistogram` tests using various images. The histogram is displayed in a window that overlaps the image. |
| -exportclienthistogramroi1 through<br>-exportclienthistogramroi4 | Same as the `ExportClientHistogram` test, but using a ROI to identify the area of interest. |
| -exportclienthistogramcplane1 through<br>-exportclienthistogramcplane4 | Same as the `ExportClientHistogram` test, but using a control plane to identify the area of interest. |
| -importlut1 | Test `ImportLUT` element; LUT size is 256. |
| -importphoto1 | `ImportPhotomap` -> `ExportPhotomap`, with source and destination equal. |
| -importphoto2 | `ImportPhotomap` -> `ExportDrawable`, window destination. |
| -importroi1 | `ImportROI` -> `ExportROI`, 10 rectangles, source and destination ROIs equal. |
| -importroi2 | `ImportROI` -> `ExportROI`, 100 rectangles, source and destination ROIs equal. |
| -importdrawable1 | `ImportDrawable` -> `ExportDrawable`, source is pixmap, destination is window. |
| -importdrawable2 | `ImportDrawable` -> `ExportDrawable`, source and destination are both window. |
| -importdrawable3 | `ImportDrawable` -> `ExportDrawable`, destination window obscured by source window. |
| -importdrawable4 | `ImportDrawable` -> `ExportDrawable`, source window obscured by destination window. |
| -importdrawable5 | `ImportDrawablePlane` -> `ExportDrawablePlane`, pixmap, source = destination. |
| -importdrawable6 | `ImportDrawablePlane` -> `ExportDrawablePlane`, window, source = destination. |
| -importdrawable7 | `ImportDrawablePlane` -> `ExportDrawablePlane`, window, source obscures destination. |
| -importdrawable8 | `ImportDrawablePlane` -> `ExportDrawablePlane`, window, destination obscures source. |
| -constrain1 | Constrain `HardClip` technique test, drawable destination. |

| | |
|---|---|
| -constrain2 | Constrain `ClipScale` technique test, drawable destination. |
| -constrainphoto1 | Constrain `HardClip` technique test, photomap destination. |
| -constrainphoto2 | Constrain `ClipScale` technique test, photomap destination. |
| -convolve1 | Boxcar 3×3 convolution test. Smoothing or lowpass filter. |
| -convolve2 | Boxcar 5×5 convolution test. Smoothing or lowpass filter. |
| —convolve3 | LaPlacian 3×3 convolution test. Edge or highpass filter. |
| -convolve4 | LaPlacian 5×5 convolution test. Edge or highpass filter. |
| -convolveroi1 | LaPlacian 3×3 convolution test, with ROI. |
| -convolveroi2 | LaPlacian 5×5 convolution test, with ROI. |
| -convolvecplane1 | LaPlacian 3×3 convolution test, with control plane. |
| -convolvecplane2 | LaPlacian 5×5 convolution test, with control plane. |
| -math1 through –mathcplane7 | Various tests that exercise the math element, some tests using ROIs and control planes. |
| -arithmeticdyadic1 through -arithmeticdyadic5 | Arithmetic element tests, using photomaps as the operands. |
| -arithmeticmonadic1 through -arithmeticmonadic9 | Arithmetic element tests, photomap and constant operands. |
| -arithmeticdyadicroi1 through arithmeticdyadicroi5 | Arithmetic element tests, using - photomaps as the operands, with ROIs. |
| -arithmeticmonadicroi1 through -arithmeticmonadicroi9 | Arithmetic element tests, photomap and constant operands, with ROIs. |
| -arithmeticdyadiccplane1 through -arithmeticdyadiccplane5 | Arithmetic element tests, using photomaps as the operands, with control planes. |
| -arithmeticmonadiccplane1 through -arithmeticmonadiccplane9 | Arithmetic element tests, photomap and constant operands, with control planes. |
| -arithmeticfloatdyadic1 though -arithmeticfloatdyadic5 | Arithmetic element tests, using photomaps as the operands, unconstrained. |
| -arithmeticfloatmonadic1 though -arithmeticfloatmonadic9 | Arithmetic element tests, photomap and constant operands, unconstrained. |
| -arithmeticroifloatdyadic1 to -arithmeticroifloatdyadic5 | Arithmetic element tests, photomaps as the operands, ROIs, unconstrained. |
| -arithmeticroifloatmonadic1 to -rithmeticroifloatmonadic9 | Arithmetic element tests, photomap and constant operands, ROIs, unconstrained. |
| -band1 | BandSelect element test. Image input is triple band. If visual of xieperf window is a color visual, then three Band-Select elements are used to extract the individual bands; they are combined once again using BandCombine, and displayed using ConvertToIndex. If the visual is not color, for example, GrayScale or StaticGray, then the flo simply uses one BandSelect element to extract a single band for display. |

| | |
|---|---|
| -band2 | BandCombine test. Input bands are made of three separate single band photomaps. These are combined using a BandCombine element, which is followed by a BandExtract and ExportDrawable. CCIR 601-1 coefficients. |
| -band3 | BandExtract test. Input is a triple band photomap. CCIR 601-1 coefficients. Destination window colormap is gray ramp. |
| -band4 | BandExtract test. Input is a triple band photomap. CCIR 601-1 coefficients. Destination window colormap is RGB BEST MAP standard colormap. |
| -band5 | BandExtract test. Input is a triple band photomap. CCIR 601-1 coefficients. Destination window colormap is RGB_DEFAULT_MAP standard colormap. |
| -comparedyadic1 through -comparedyadic6 | Test various compare operators with dyadic photomap operands. |
| -comparemonadic1 through -comparemonadic6 | Test various compare operators with photomap, constant operands. |
| -compareroidyadic1 through -compareroidyadic6 | Test various compare operators with dyadic photomap operands, using ROIs. |
| -compareroimonadic1 through compare compareroimonadic6 | Test various operators with photomap, constant operands, using ROIs. |
| -comparecplanedyadic1 through -comparecplanedyadic6 | Test various compare operators with dyadic photomap operands, control planes. |
| -comparecplanemonadic1 through —comparecplanemonadic6 | Test various compare operators with photomap, constant operands, control planes. |
| -matchhistogram1 through -matchhistogram18 | MatchHistogram element tests, using various images and histogram matching techniques. |
| -matchhistogramroi1 through -matchhistogramroi6 | A selection of MatchHistogram element tests, with ROIs. |
| -matchhistogramcplane1 through -matchhistogramcplane6 | A selection of MatchHistogram element tests, with control planes. |
| -unconstrain1 | ImportPhotomap, Unconstrain, Constrain(ClipScale), ExportDrawable test. |
| -pasteup1 through -pasteup2 | PasteUp element tests. |
| -geometry1 through -geometry14 | Geometry element tests, including rotations, scales, and mirroring. NearestNeighbor technique. |
| -geometry15 through -geometry28 | Geometry element tests, including rotations, scales, and mirroring. AntiAlias technique. |
| -geometry29 through -geometry42 | Geometry element tests, including rotations, scales, and mirroring. BilinearInterpolation technique. |
| -geomg31dscale1 through -geometryfaxradio1 | Tests to exercise the various FAX decoders and the Geometry element. |
| -dither1 | Dither test, ErrorDiffusion dither technique, ExportDrawable. |
| -dither2 | Dither test, ErrorDiffusion dither technique, ExportDrawablePlane. |

| | |
|---|---|
| -dither3 | Dither test, Ordered(4) dither technique, ExportDrawable. |
| -dither4 | Dither·test, Ordered(4) dither technique, ExportDrawablePlane. |
| -dither5 | Dither test, Ordered(8) dither technique, ExportDrawable. |
| -dither6 | Dither test, Ordered(8) dither technique, ExportDrawablePlane. |
| -dither7 | Dither test, Default dither technique, ExportDrawable. |
| -dither8 | Dither test, Default dither technique, ExportDrawablePlane. |
| -logicalmonadic1 through -logicalmonadic16 | Logical element, photomap and a constant of 0 as operands, various operators. |
| -logicaldyadic1 through -logicaldyadic16 | Logical element tests, dyadic photomaps as operands, various operators. |
| -logicalmonadicroi1 through -logicalmonadicroi16 | Logical element, photomap and constant of 0 operands, various operators, ROIs. |
| -logicaldyadicroi1 through -logicaldyadicroi16 | Logical element, dyadic photomaps as operands, various operators, ROIs. |
| -logicalmonadiccplane1 through -logicalmonadiccplane16 | Logical element, photomap and constant of 0 operands, various operators, Control Planes. |
| -logicaldyadiccplane1 through -logicaldyadiccplane16 | Logical element, dyadic photomaps as operands, various operators, control planes. |
| -blend1 | Blend element test. Monadic source, 0.1 source constant. Alpha constant of 0.5. |
| -blend2 | Blend element test. Dyadic sources. Alpha constant of 0.5. |
| -blendroi1 | Blend test. Monadic source, 0.1 source constant. Alpha constant of 0.5. ROIs. |
| -blendroi2 | Blend element test. Dyadic sources. Alpha constant of 0.5. Uses ROIs. |
| -blendcplane1 | Blend test. Monadic source, 0.1 source constant. Alpha constant of 0.5. control plane. |
| -blendcplane2 | Blend element test. Dyadic sources. Alpha constant of 0.5. control plane. |
| -blendalpha1 | Blend test. Monadic source, 220 source constant. Alpha plane is a photomap. |
| -blendalpha2 | Blend test. Dyadic sources. Alpha plane is a constant 220. |
| -blendalpharoi1 | Blend test. Monadic source, 220 source constant. Alpha plane photomap. ROIs. |
| -blendalpharoi2 | Blend test. Dyadic sources. Alpha plane is a constant 220. ROIs. |
| -triplepoint1 through -triplepoint2 | Illustrate use of point and standard colormaps for rendering triple band images. |
| -funnyencode1 through -funnyencode8 | These tests are designed to perform limited exercising of XIE's capability of dealing with various encodings of flo source data. The test init function obtains a photomap using ICP -> EP. A series of independent permanent flo pairs, one of the form IP -> EP, and the other of the basic form IP -> ED, are constructed. The encoding parameters for the ExportPhotomap (EP) element in the first flo are derived from test configuration. The number of flo pairs created is also dependent upon test |

configuration. The tests can be configured so that the test `init` function will constrain the input `photomap` to a specified number of levels, on a per band basis, so that word-sized and quad-sized pixels are passed through the flos. Some tests below take advantage of this. See `tests.c` for test configuration, and hints on how to add similar tests.

| | |
|---|---|
| `-point1 through -point3` | Simple `Point` element tests. Drawable destination. |
| `-pointroi1` | Simple `Point` element test that uses ROIs. Drawable destination. |
| `-pointcplane1` | Simple `Point` element test that uses a control plane. Drawable destination. |
| `-pointphoto1` | Simple `Point` element test. Photomap destination. |
| `-pointroiphoto1` | Simple `Point` element test that uses ROIs. Photomap destination. |
| `-pointcplanephoto1` | Simple `Point` element test that uses a control plane. Photomap destination. |
| `-redefine` | Two flographs are created that are the same in structure, except for the x and y offsets specified for the `ExportDrawable` flo elements. The test `init` function creates a photoflo based upon one of the two flographs. The inner loop of the test function uses `XieRedefinePhotoflo()` to alternate between each of the flographs. Make sure that your inner loop reps are 2 or greater in order to exercise this test fully (see `-reps`). |
| `-modify1` | Test `XieModifyPhotoflo()` by adjusting ROI offsets and size. |
| `-modify2` | Test `XieModifyPhotoflo()` by changing the LUT input to a `Point` element. |
| `-modify3` | Test `XieModifyPhotoflo()` by changing `ExportDrawable` x and y offsets. |
| `-modify4` | This test creates a rather long flo of arithmetic elements, each of which does nothing more than add 1 to a small image. The test `init` function scales the input photomap. The `ExportDrawable` x and y offset is modified randomly during each iteration of the test function inner loop. |
| `-modify5` | This test creates a rather long flo of arithmetic elements, each of which does nothing more than add 1 to a large image. Each rep, the `Geometry` and `ExportDrawable` elements at the end of the flo are modified to crop a small piece of the input into its appropriate place in the larger image. |
| `-rgb1 through -rgb16` | These tests all basically take an `UncompressedTriple` image as input, send it to `ConvertFromRGB`, which converts the image to some configured colorspace, and then send the converted image on to `ConvertToRGB` prior to display. The original image is displayed in the left-hand window, and the image that has passed through the flo is shown in the right-hand window. The goal of these test is to show that `ConvertFromRGB` -> `ConvertToRGB` is lossless. |
| `-converttoindexpixel` | `ConvertToIndex` test, TripleBand BandByPixel. |
| `-converttoindexplane` | `ConvertToIndex` test, TripleBand BandByPlane. |

-convertfromindex                    The test init function uses a flo containing ConvertToIndex to
                                     display an image in the left window. The test function uses
                                     this drawable as input to a flo that does ConvertFromIndex ->
                                     ConvertToIndex and sends the resulting image to the right
                                     window. The result should be lossless.

-complcx                             A somewhat large flo that uses control planes, LUTs, Point,
                                     PasteUp, Logical, Constrain, Dither, Geometry, MatchHistogram,
                                     BandCombine, and BandSelect elements. See the Postscript file
                                     complex.ps for a rendition of the photoflo that is executed.

## X DEFAULTS

There are no X defaults used by this program.

## SEE ALSO

X(1), x11perf(1), x11perfcomp(1)

## BUGS

There should be an IMAGES environment variable to augment the -images option.

Many tests only scratch the surface of possible test cases. Some of the options available for certain flo elements are either inadequately tested, or ignored altogether. There are insufficient tests for bitonal, large pixel, or triple band tests.

Some of the test names are inconsistently cased, for example, -Abort and -dither1.

Some tests are hopelessly slow when run against machines with slow FPUs.

Bitonal images are, for the most part, displayed using the ExportDrawable flo element; however, ExportDrawablePlane would be a better choice.

## AUTHOR

Syd Logan (AGE Logic, Inc.)

*X Version 11 Release 6*

# ximtoppm

ximtoppm—Convert an XIM file into a portable pixmap

## SYNOPSIS

ximtoppm [*ximfile*]

## DESCRIPTION

Reads an Xim file as input. Produces a portable pixmap as output. The Xim toolkit is included in the contrib tree of the X.V11R4 release.

## SEE ALSO

ppm(5)

## AUTHOR

Copyright (c) 1991 by Jef Poskanzer.

*25 March 1990*

# xinetd

xinetd—The extended Internet services daemon

## SYNOPSIS

xinetd [*options*]

## DESCRIPTION

xinetd performs the same function as inetd: it starts programs that provide Internet services. Instead of having such servers started at system initialization time, and be dormant until a connection request arrives, xinetd is the only daemon process started and it listens on all service ports for the services listed in its configuration file. When a request comes in, xinetd starts the appropriate server. Because of the way it operates, xinetd (as well as inetd) is also referred to as a super-server.

The services listed in xinetd's configuration file can be separated into two groups. Services in the first group are called multithreaded and they require the forking of a new server process for each new connection request. The new server then handles that connection. For such services, xinetd keeps listening for new requests so that it can spawn new servers. On the other hand, the second group includes services for which the service daemon is responsible for handling all new connection requests. Such services are called single-threaded and xinetd will stop handling new requests for them until the server dies. Services in this group are usually datagram based.

So far, the only reason for the existence of a super-server was to conserve system resources by avoiding to fork a lot of processes who might be dormant for most of their lifetime. While fulfilling this function, xinetd takes advantage of the idea of a super-server to provide features such as access control and logging. Furthermore, xinetd is not limited to services listed in /etc/services. Therefore, anybody can use xinetd to start special-purpose servers.

## OPTIONS

| | |
|---|---|
| -d | Enables debug mode. This produces a lot of debugging output, and it makes it possible to use a debugger on xinetd. |
| -syslog *syslog_facility* | This option enables syslog logging of xinetd-produced messages using the specified syslog facility. The following facility names are supported: daemon, auth, user, local[0-7] (check syslog.conf(5) for their meanings). This option is ineffective in debug mode because all relevant messages are sent to the terminal. |
| -filelog *logfile* | xinetd-produced messages will be placed in the specified file. Messages are always appended to the file. If the file does not exist, it will be created. This option is ineffective in debug mode because all relevant messages are sent to the terminal. |
| -f config_file | Determines the file that xinetd uses for configuration. The default is /etc/xinetd.conf. |
| -pid | The process pid is written to standard error. This option is ineffective in debug mode. |
| -loop *rate* | This option sets the loop rate beyond which a service is considered in error and is deactivated. The loop rate is specified in terms of the number of servers per second that can be forked for a process. The speed of your machine determines the correct value for this option. The default rate is 10. |
| -reuse | If this option is used, xinetd will set the socket option SO_REUSEADDR before binding the service socket to an Internet address. This allows binding of the address even if there are programs that use it, which happens when a previous instance of xinetd has started some servers that are still running. This option has no effect on RPC services. |

| | |
|---|---|
| -limit *proc_limit* | This option places a limit on the number of concurrently running processes that can be started by xinetd. Its purpose is to prevent process table overflows. |
| -logprocs *limit* | This option places a limit on the number of concurrently running servers for remote user ID acquisition. |
| -shutdownprocs *limit* | This option places a limit on the number of concurrently running servers for service shutdown (forked when the RECORD option is used). |

The syslog and filelog options are mutually exclusive. If none is specified, the default is syslog using the daemon facility. You should not confuse xinetd messages with messages related to service logging. The latter are logged only if this is specified via the configuration file.

## CONFIGURATION FILE

The configuration file determines the services provided by xinetd. Any line whose first nonwhitespace character is a # is considered a comment line. Empty lines are ignored.

The file contains entries of the form:

```
service <service_name>
{
<attribute> <assign_op><value><value> ...
...
}
```

The assignment operator, assign_op, can be one of =, +=, -=. The majority of attributes support only the simple assignment operator, =. Attributes whose value is a set of values support all assignment operators. For such attributes, += means adding a value to the set and -= means removing a value from the set. A list of these attributes is given after all the attributes are described.

Each entry defines a service identified by the service_name. The following is a list of available attributes:

| | | |
|---|---|---|
| id | | This attribute is used to uniquely identify a service. This is useful because there exist services that can use different protocols and need to be described with different entries in the configuration file. By default, the service id is the same as the service name. |
| type | | Possible values are the following: |
| | RPC | If this is an RPC service |
| | INTERNAL | If this is a service provided by xinetd. |
| | UNLISTED | If this is a service not listed in /etc/services. |
| flags | | Possible flag values are |
| | REUSE | Set the SO_REUSEADDR flag on the service socket. |
| | INTERCEPT | Intercept packets or accepted connections in order to verify that they are coming from acceptable locations (internal or multithreaded services cannot be intercepted). |
| | NORETRY | Avoid retry attempts in case of fork failure. |
| socket type | | Possible values are |
| | stream | Stream-based service |
| | dgram | Datagram-based service |
| | raw | Service that requires direct access to IP |
| | seqpacket | Service that requires reliable sequential datagram transmission |

| | |
|---|---|
| protocol | Determines the protocol that is employed by the service. The protocol must exist in /etc/protocols. If this attribute is not defined, the default protocol employed by the service will be used. |
| wait | This attribute determines if the service is single-threaded or multithreaded. If its value is yes, the service is single-threaded; this means that xinetd will start the server and then it will stop handling requests for the service until the server dies. If the attribute value is no, the service is multithreaded and xinetd will keep handling new service requests. |
| user | Determines the uid for the server process. The username must exist in /etc/passwd. This attribute is ineffective if the effective user ID of xinetd is not super-user. |
| group | Determines the gid for the server process. The group name must exist in /etc/group. If a group is not specified, the group of user will be used (from /etc/passwd). This attribute is ineffective if the effective user ID of xinetd is not super-user. |
| instances | Determines the number of servers that can be simultaneously active for a service. By default, there is no limit. The value of this attribute can be either a number or UNLIMITED, which means that there is no limit. |
| server | Determines the program to execute for this service. |
| server_args | Determines the arguments passed to the server. In contrast to inetd, the server name should not be included in server_args. |
| only_from | Determines the remote hosts to which the particular service is available. Its value is a list of IP addresses that can be specified in any combination of the following ways: |

only_from:

a) A numeric address in the form of %d.%d.%d.%d. If the rightmost components are 0, they are treated as wildcards (for example, 128.138.12.0 matches all hosts on the 128.138.12 subnet). 0.0.0.0 matches all Internet addresses.

b) A factorized address in the form of %d.%d.%d.{%d,%d,...}. There is no need for all four components (%d.%d.{%d,%d,...%d} is also OK). However, the factorized part must be at the end of the address.

c) A network name (from /etc/networks).

d) A hostname. All IP addresses of the specified hostname will be used.

| | |
|---|---|
| " " | Specifying this attribute without a value makes the service available to nobody. |
| no_access | Determines the remote hosts to which the particular service is unavailable. Its value can be specified in the same way as the value of the only_from attribute. These two attributes determine the location access control enforced by xinetd. If none of the two is specified for a service, the service is available to anyone. If both are specified for a service, the one that is the better match for the address of the remote host determines if the service is available to that host (for example, if the only from list contains 128.138.209.0 and the no access list contains 128.138.209.10, then the host with the address 128.138.209.10 can not access the service). |

access_times

Determines the time intervals when the service is available. An interval has the form *hour:min-hour:min* (connections will be accepted at the bounds of an interval). Hours can range from 0 to 23 and minutes from 0 to 59.

log_type

Determines where the service log output is sent. There are two formats:

SYSLOG syslog facility [syslog level]

The log output is sent to syslog at the specified facility. If a level is present, the messages will be recorded at that level instead of LOG_INFO (which is the default level).

FILE *file* [soft_limit [hard_limit]]

The log output is appended to *file*, which will be created if it does not exist. Two limits on the size of the log file can be optionally specified. The first limit is a soft one; xinetd will log a message the first time this limit is exceeded (if xinetd logs to syslog, the message will be sent at the LOG_ALERT priority level). The second limit is a hard limit; xinetd will stop logging for the affected service (if the log file is a common log file, then more than one service may be affected) and will log a message about this (if xinetd logs to syslog, the message will be sent at the LOG_ALERT priority level). If a hard limit is not specified, it defaults to the soft limit increased by 1 percent but the extra size must be within the parameters LOG_EXTRA_MIN and LOG_EXTRA_MAX (defined in config.h).

log_on_success

Determines what information is logged when a server is started and when that server exits (the service ID is always included in the log entry). Any combination of the following values may be specified:

PID

Logs the server process ID. (If the service is implemented by xinetd without forking another process, the logged process ID will be 0.)

HOST

Logs the remote host address

TIME

Logs the time when the server was started.

USERID

Logs the user ID of the remote user using the RFC 931 identification protocol. This option is available only for multithreaded stream services.

EXIT

Logs the fact that a server exited along with the exit status or the termination signal (the process ID is also logged if the PID option is used).

DURATION

Logs the duration of a service session.

log_on_failure

Determines what information is logged when a server cannot be started (either because of a lack of resources or because of access control restrictions). The service ID is always included in the log entry along with the reason for failure. Any combination of the following values may be specified:

HOST

Logs the remote host address.

| | |
|---|---|
| TIME | Logs the time when the server was started. |
| USERID | Logs the user ID of the remote user using the RFC 931 identification protocol. This option is available only for multithreaded stream services. |
| ATTEMPT | Logs the fact that a failed attempt was made. |
| RECORD | Records information from the remote end in case the server could not be started. This allows monitoring of attempts to use the service. For example, the login service logs the local user, remote user, and terminal type. Currently, the services that support this option are logiun, shell, exec, finger. |

| | |
|---|---|
| rpc_version | Determines the RPC version for an RPC service. The version can be a single number or a range in the form number-number. |
| env | The value of this attribute is a list of strings of the form name=value. These strings will be added to the environment before starting a server (therefore the server's environment will include xinetd's environment plus the specified strings). |
| passenv | The value of this attribute is a list of environment variables from xinetd's environment that will be passed to the server. |
| port | Determines the service port. If this attribute is specified for a service listed in /etc/services, it must be equal to the port number listed in that file. |

You don't need to specify all of the preceding attributes for each service. The necessary attributes for a service are the following:

| | |
|---|---|
| socket type | |
| user | (non-unlisted services only) |
| server | (non-internal services only) |
| wait | |
| protocol | (RPC and unlisted services only) |
| rpc_version | (RPC services only) |
| port | (unlisted services only) |

The following attributes support all assignment operators, except as indicated:

| | |
|---|---|
| only_from | |
| no_access | |
| log_on_success | |
| log_on_failure | |
| passenv | |
| env | (does not support the -= operator) |

These attributes can also appear more than once in a service entry. The remaining attributes support only the = operator and can appear at most once in a service entry.

The configuration file may also contain a single defaults entry that has the form:

```
defaults
{
<attribute> = <value><value> ...
...
}
```

This entry provides default attribute values for service entries that don't specify those attributes. Possible default attributes:

| | |
|---|---|
| `log_type` | |
| `log_on_success` | (cumulative effect) |
| `log_on_failure` | (cumulative effect) |
| `only_from` | (cumulative effect) |
| `no_access` | (cumulative effect) |
| `passenv` | (cumulative effect) |
| `instances` | |
| `disabled` | (cumulative effect) |

Attributes with a cumulative effect can be specified multiple times with the values specified each time accumulating (in other words, = does the same thing as +=). With the exception of `disabled` they all have the same meaning as if they were specified in a service entry. `disabled` determines services that are disabled even if they have entries in the configuration file. This allows for quick reconfiguration by specifying disabled services with the `disabled` attribute instead of commenting them out. The value of this attribute is a list of space-separated service IDs.

## INTERNAL SERVICES

xinetd provides the following services internally (both stream- and datagram-based): `echo`, `time`, `daytime`, `chargen`, and `discard`. These services are under the same access restrictions as all other services except for the ones that don't require xinetd to fork another process for them. Those ones (`time`, `daytime`, and the datagram-based `echo`, `chargen`, and `discard`) have no limitation in the number of instances.

## CONTROLLING `xinetd`

xinetd performs certain actions when it receives certain signals. The actions associated with the specific signals can be redefined by editing `config.h` and recompiling.

| | |
|---|---|
| SIGUSR1 | Causes a soft reconfiguration, which means that xinetd rereads the configuration file and adjusts accordingly. |
| SIGUSR2 | Causes a hard reconfiguration, which is the same as a soft reconfiguration except that servers for services that are no longer available are terminated. Access control is performed again on running servers by checking the remote location, access times and server instances. If the number of server instances is lowered, some arbitrarily picked servers will be killed to satisfy the limit; this will happen after any servers are terminated because of failing the remote location or access time checks. Also, if the INTERCEPT flag was clear and is set, any running servers for that service will be terminated; the purpose of this is to ensure that after a hard reconfiguration there will be no running servers that can accept packets from addresses that do not meet the access control criteria. |
| SIGQUIT | Causes program termination. |
| SIGTERM | Terminates all running servers before terminating xinetd. |
| SIGHUP | Causes an internal state dump (the default dump file is `/tmp/xinetd.dump`; to change the filename, edit `config.h` and recompile). |
| SIGIOT | Causes an internal consistency check to verify that the data structures used by the program have not been corrupted. When the check is completed xinetd will generate a message that says if the check was successful or not. |

On reconfiguration, the log files are closed and reopened. This allows removal of old log files. Also, the following attributes cannot be changed on reconfiguration: `socket_type`, `wait`, `protocol`, `type`.

## `xinetd` LOG FORMAT

Log entries are lines with the following format:

`entry: service-id data`

The data depends on the entry. Possible entry types:

| | |
|---|---|
| START | Generated when a server is started |
| EXIT | Generated when a server exits |
| FAIL | Generated when it is not possible to start a server |
| DATA | Generated when an attempt to start a server fails and the service supports the RECORD log option. |
| USERID | Generated if the USERID log option is used. |

In the following formats, the information enclosed in brackets appears if the appropriate log option is used.

A START entry has the format

`START: service-id [pid=%d] [from=%d.%d.%d.%d] [time=time]`

Time is given as `year/month/day@hour:minutes:seconds`.

An EXIT entry has the format

`EXIT: service-id [type=%d] [pid=%d] [duration=%d(sec)]`

*type* can be either status or signal. The number is either the exit status or the signal that caused process termination.

A FAIL entry has the format:

`FAIL: service-id reason [from=%d.%d.%d.%d] [time=time]`

Possible reasons are

| | |
|---|---|
| fork | A certain number of consecutive fork attempts failed (this number is a configurable parameter). |
| time | The time check failed. |
| address | The address check failed. |
| service_limit | The allowed number of server instances for this service would be exceeded. |
| process_limit | A limit on the number of forked processes was specified and it would be exceeded. |

A DATA entry has the format

`DATA: service-id data`

The *data* logged depends on the service.

| | |
|---|---|
| login | remote_user=%s local_user=%s tty=%s |
| exec | remote_user=%s verify=status command=%s Possible status values: |

| | |
|---|---|
| ok | The password was correct |
| failed | The password was incorrect |
| baduser | No such user |
| shell | remote_user=%s local_user=%s command=%s |
| finger | received string or EMPTY-LINE |

A USERID entry has the format

```
USERID: text
```

The *text* is the response of the RFC 931 daemon at the remote end excluding the port numbers (which are included in the response). Here's an example:

```
#
# Sample configuration file for xinetd
#
defaults
{
        log_type = FILE /var/log/servicelog
        log_on_success = PID
        log_on_failure = HOST TIME RECORD
        only_from = 128.138.193.0 128.138.204.0 128.138.209.0
        only_from = 128.138.252.1
        instances = 10
        disabled = rstatd
}
#
# Note 1: the protocol attribute is not required
# Note 2: the instances attribute overrides the default
#
service login
{
        socket_type = stream
        protocol = tcp
        wait = no
        user = root
        server = /usr/etc/in.rlogind
        instances = UNLIMITED
}
#
# Note 1: the instances attribute overrides the default
# Note 2: the log on success flags are augmented
#
service shell
{
        socket_type = stream
        wait = no
        user = root
        instances = UNLIMITED
        server = /usr/etc/in.rshd
        log_on_success += HOST TIME RECORD
}
service ftp
{
        socket_type = stream
        wait = no
        user = root
        server = /usr/etc/in.ftpd
        server_args = -l
        instances = 4
        log_on_success += DURATION HOST USERID
        access_times = 2:00-9:00 12:00-24:00
}
#
# This entry and the next one specify internal services. Since this
# is the same service using a different socket type, the id attribute
# is used to uniquely identify each entry
#
```

```
service echo
{
        id = echo-stream
        type = INTERNAL
        socket_type = stream
        user = root
        wait = no
}
service echo
{
        id = echo-dgram
        type = INTERNAL
        socket_type = dgram
        user = root
        wait = no
}
#
# Sample RPC service
#
service rstatd

        type = RPC
        socket_type = dgram
        protocol = udp
        server = /usr/etc/rpc.rstatd
        wait = yes
        user = root
        rpc_version = 2-4
        env = LD_LIBRARY_PATH=/etc/securelib
}
#
# Sample unlisted service
#.
service unlisted
{
        type = UNLISTED
        socket_type = stream
        protocol = tcp
        wait = no
        server = /home/user/some server
        port = 20020
}
```

## FILES

| | |
|---|---|
| /etc/xinetd.conf | Default configuration file |
| /tmp/xinetd.dump | Default dump file |

## SEE ALSO

inetd(8)

Postel J., *Echo Protocol*, RFC 862, May 1983.

Postel J., *Discard Protocol*, RFC 863, May 1983.

Postel J., *Character Generator Protocol*, RFC 864, May 1983.

Postel J., *Daytime Protocol*, RFC 867, May 1983.

Postel J., Harrenstien K., *Time Protocol*, RFC 868, May 1983.

St. Johns M., *Authentication Server*, RFC 931, January 1985.

## AUTHOR

Panos Tsirigotis (CS Department, University of Colorado, Boulder)

## NOTES

When the attributes only_from and no_access are not specified for a service (either directly or via defaults), the address check is considered successful (that is, access will not be denied).

If the USERID log option is specified and the remote RFC 931 server sends back an ERROR reply, access will not be denied.

If the USERID log option is specified and the remote host does not run an RFC 931 server, there will be no indication in the log of that fact (other than the missing USERID log entry).

## BUGS

Supplementary group IDs are not supported.

If the INTERCEPT flag is not used, access control on the address of the remote host is not performed when wait is yes and socket_type is stream.

If the INTERCEPT flag is not used, access control on the address of the remote host for services where wait is yes and socket_type is dgram is performed only on the first packet. The server may then accept packets from hosts not in the access control list. This can happen with RPC services.

Unlisted RPC services are not supported; that is, all RPC services must be registered in /etc/rpc. Specifying an RPC service by its RPC program number is not (yet) possible.

There is no way to put a SPACE in an environment variable.

When wait is yes and socket_type is stream, the socket passed to the server can only accept connections.

The INTERCEPT flag is not supported for internal services or multithreaded services.

Interception works by forking a process that acts as a filter between the remote host(s) and the local server. This obviously has a performance impact which depends on the volume of information exchanged. It is up to you to make the compromise between security and performance for each service.

## PRONUNCIATION

xinetd is pronounced "zy-net-d."

*10 May 1992*

# xinit

xinit—X Window System initializer

## SYNOPSIS

xinit [[*client* ] *options* ][-- [ *server* ][*display* ] *options* ]

## DESCRIPTION

The xinit program is used to start the X Window System server and a first client program on systems that cannot start X directly from /etc/init or in environments that use multiple window systems. When this first client exits, xinit will kill the X server and then terminate.

If no specific client program is given on the command line, xinit will look for a file in the user's home directory called .xinitrc to run as a shell script to start up client programs. If no such file exists, xinit will use the following as a default:

```
xterm -geometry +1+1 -n login -display :0
```

If no specific server program is given on the command line, xinit will look for a file in the user's home directory called .xserverrc to run as a shell script to start up the server. If no such file exists, xinit will use the following as a default:

```
X :0
```

Note that this assumes that there is a program named X in the current search path. However, servers are usually named Xdisplaytype where displaytype is the type of graphics display that is driven by this server. The site administrator should, therefore, make a link to the appropriate type of server on the machine, or create a shell script that runs xinit with the appropriate server.

Note, when using a .xserverrc script be sure to mark the real X server as exec. Failing to do this can make the X server slow to start and exit. For example

```
exec Xdisplaytype
```

An important point is that programs which are run by xinitrc should be run in the background if they do not exit right away, so that they don't prevent other programs from starting up. However, the last long-lived program started (usually a window manager or terminal emulator) should be left in the foreground so that the script won't exit (which indicates that the user is done and that xinit should exit).

An alternate client and/or server may be specified on the command line. The desired client program and its arguments should be given as the first command-line arguments to xinit.To specify a particular server command line, append two dashes (--) to the xinit command line (after any client and arguments) followed by the desired server command.

Both the client program name and the server program name must begin with a slash (/) or a period (.). Otherwise, they are treated as arguments to be appended to their respective startup lines. This makes it possible to add arguments (for example, foreground and background colors) without having to retype the whole command line.

If an explicit server name is not given and the first argument following the double dash (--) is a colon followed by a digit, xinit will use that number as the display number instead of zero. All remaining arguments are appended to the server command line.

## EXAMPLES

Following are several examples of how command-line arguments in xinit are used:

This will start up a server named X and run the user's xinitrc, if it exists, or else start an xterm:

```
xinit
```

This is how one could start a specific type of server on an alternate display:

```
xinit -- /usr/X11R6/bin/Xqdss :1
```

This will start up a server named X, and will append the given arguments to the default xterm command (it will ignore xinitrc):

```
xinit -geometry =80x65+10+10 -fn 8x13 -j -fg white -bg navy
```

This will use the command Xsun -l -c to start the server and will append the arguments -e widgets to the default xterm command:

```
xinit -e widgets -- ./Xsun -l -c
```

This will start a server named X on display 1 with the arguments -a 2 -t5:

```
xinit /usr/ucb/rsh fasthost cpupig -display ws:1 -- :1 -a 2 -t 5
```

It will then start a remote shell on the machine fasthost in which it will run the command cpupig, telling it to display back on the local workstation.

Following is a sample xinitrc that starts a clock, starts several terminals, and leaves the window manager running as the "last" application. Assuming that the window manager has been configured properly, the user then chooses the Exit menu item to shut down X.

```
xrdb -load $HOME/.Xresources
xsetroot -solid gray &
```

```
xclock -g 50x50-0+0 -bw 0 &
xload -g 50x50-50+0 -bw 0 &
xterm -g 80x24+0+0 &
xterm -g 80x24+0-0 &
twm
```

Sites that want to create a common startup environment could simply create a default xinitrc that references a site-wide startup file:

```
#!/bin/sh
. /usr/local/lib/site.xinitrc
```

Another approach is to write a script that starts xinit with a specific shell script. Such scripts are usually named x11, xstart, or startx, and are a convenient way to provide a simple interface for novice users:

```
#!/bin/sh
xinit /usr/local/lib/site.xinitrc -- /usr/X11R6/bin/X bc
```

## ENVIRONMENT VARIABLES

DISPLAY                              This variable gets set to the name of the display to which clients should connect.

XINITRC                             This variable specifies an init file containing shell commands to start up the initial windows. By default, xinitrc in the home directory will be used.

## FILES

.xinitrc                            Default client script
xterm                               Client to run if .xinitrc does not exist
.xserverrc                          Default server script
X                                   Server to run if .xserverrc does not exist

## SEE ALSO

X(1), startx(1), Xserver(1), xterm(1)

## AUTHOR

Bob Scheifler (MIT Laboratory for Computer Science)

*X Version 11 Release 6*

# xkill

xkill—Kill a client by its X resource

## SYNOPSIS

xkill [-display *displayname*] [-id *resource*] [-button number] [-frame] [-all]

## DESCRIPTION

xkill is a utility for forcing the X server to close connections to clients. This program is very dangerous, but is useful for aborting programs that have displayed undesired windows on a user's screen. If no resource identifier is given with -id, xkill will display a special cursor as a prompt for the user to select a window to be killed. If a pointer button is pressed over a nonroot window, the server will close its connection to the client that created the window.

## OPTIONS

| | |
|---|---|
| `-display` *displayname* | This option specifies the name of the X server to contact. |
| `-id` *resource* | This option specifies the X identifier for the resource whose creator is to be aborted. If no resource is specified, xkill will display a special cursor with which you should select a window to be kill. |
| `-button` *number* | This option specifies the number of pointer button that should be used in selecting a window to kill. If the word "any" is specified, any button on the pointer may be used. By default, the first button in the pointer map (which is usually the leftmost button) is used. |
| `-all` | This option indicates that all clients with top-level windows on the screen should be killed. xkill will ask you to select the root window with each of the currently defined buttons to give you several chances to abort. Use of this option is highly discouraged. |
| `-frame` | This option indicates that xkill should ignore the standard conventions for finding top-level client windows (which are typically nested inside a window manager window), and simply believe that you want to kill direct children of the root. |

## XDEFAULTS

| | |
|---|---|
| Button | Specifies a specific pointer button number or the word "any" to use when selecting windows. |

## SEE ALSO

X(1), xwininfo(1), XKillClient and XGetPointerMapping in the *Xlib Programmers Manual*, KillClient in the *X Protocol Specification*

## AUTHOR

Jim Fulton (MIT X Consortium) and Dana Chee (Bellcore)

*X Version 11 Release 6*

# xlogo

xlogo—X Window System logo

## SYNOPSIS

xlogo [ *-toolkitoption* ... ]

## DESCRIPTION

The xlogo program displays the X Window System logo.

## OPTIONS

Xlogo accepts all of the standard X Toolkit command-line options, as well as the following:

| | |
|---|---|
| -shape | This option indicates that the logo window should be shaped rather than rectangular. |

## RESOURCES

The default width and the default height are each 100 pixels. This program uses the Logo widget in the Athena widget set. It understands all of the Simple widget resource names and classes as well as:

| | |
|---|---|
| foreground (class Foreground) | Specifies the color for the logo. The default depends on whether reverseVideo is specified. If reverseVideo is specified, the default is XtDefaultForeground, otherwise the default is XtDefaultBackground. |
| shapeWindow (class ShapeWindow) | Specifies that the window is shaped to the X logo. The default is False. |

## WIDGETS

In order to specify resources, it is useful to know the hierarchy of the widgets that compose xlogo.In the following notation, indentation indicates hierarchical structure. The widget class name is given first, followed by the widget instance name.

```
XLogo xlogo
    Logo xlogo
```

## ENVIRONMENT

| | |
|---|---|
| DISPLAY | To get the default host and display number. |
| XENVIRONMENT | To get the name of a resource file that overrides the global resources stored in the RESOURCE_MANAGER property. |

## FILES

<XRoot>/lib/X11/app-defaults/XLogo     Specifies required resources

## SEE ALSO

X(1), xrdb(1)

## AUTHORS

Ollie Jones of Apollo Computer and Jim Fulton of the MIT X Consortium wrote the logo graphics routine, based on a graphic design by Danny Chong and Ross Chapman of Apollo Computer.

*X Version 11 Release 6*

# xlsatoms

xlsatoms—List interned atoms defined on server

## SYNOPSIS

xlsatoms [-options ...]

## DESCRIPTION

xlsatoms lists the interned atoms. By default, all atoms starting from 1 (the lowest atom value defined by the protocol) are listed until unknown atom is found. If an explicit range is given, xlsatoms will try all atoms in the range, regardless of whether or not any are undefined.

## OPTIONS

-display *dpy*                     This option specifies the X server to which to connect.

-format *string*                   This option specifies a `printf`-style string used to list each
                                  atom <value,name> pair, printed in that order (value is an
                                  unsigned long and name is a char *). xlsatoms will supply a
                                  newline at the end of each line. The default is %ld\t%s.

-range [*low*]-[*high*]             This option specifies the range of atom values to check. If *low*
                                  is not given, a value of 1 is assumed. If *high* is not given,
                                  xlsatoms will stop at the first undefined atom at or above *low*.

-name *string*                     This option specifies the name of an atom to list. If the atom
                                  does not exist, a message will be printed on the standard error.

## SEE ALSO

X(1), Xserver(1), xprop(1)

## ENVIRONMENT

DISPLAY                            To get the default host and display to use

## AUTHOR

Jim Fulton (MIT X Consortium)

*X Version 11 Release 6*

# xlsclients

xlsclients—List client applications running on a display

## SYNOPSIS

xlsclients [-display *displayname*] [-a] [-l] [-m maxcmdlen]

## DESCRIPTION

xlsclients is a utility for listing information about the client applications running on a display. It may be used to generate
scripts representing a snapshot of the user's current session.

## OPTIONS

-display *displayname*             This option specifies the X server to contact.

-a                                This option indicates that clients on all screens should be
                                  listed. By default, only those clients on the default screen are
                                  listed.

-l                                List in long format, giving the window name, icon name, and
                                  class hints in addition to the machine name and command
                                  string shown in the default format.

-m maxcmdlen                      This option specifies the maximum number of characters in a
                                  command to print out. The default is 10000.

## ENVIRONMENT

DISPLAY                            To get the default host, display number, and screen.

## SEE ALSO

X(1), xwininfo(1), xprop(1)

## AUTHOR

Jim Fulton (MIT X Consortium)

*X Version 11 Release 6*

# xlsfonts

xlsfonts—Server font list displayer for X

## SYNOPSIS

xlsfonts [-options ...] [-fn pattern]

## DESCRIPTION

xlsfonts lists the fonts that match the given pattern. The wildcard character * may be used to match any sequence of characters (including none), and ? to match any single character. If no pattern is given, * is assumed.

The * and ? characters must be quoted to prevent them from being expanded by the shell.

## OPTIONS

| | |
|---|---|
| -display *host:dpy* | This option specifies the X server to contact. |
| -l | Lists some attributes of the font on one line in addition to its name. |
| -ll | Lists font properties in addition to -l output. |
| -lll | Lists character metrics in addition to -ll output. |
| -m | This option indicates that long listings should also print the minimum and maximum bounds of each font. |
| -C | This option indicates that listings should use multiple columns. This is the same as -n 0. |
| -1 | This option indicates that listings should use a single column. This is the same as -n 1. |
| -w *width* | This option specifies the width in characters that should be used in figuring out how many columns to print. The default is 79. |
| -n *columns* | This option specifies the number of columns to use in displaying the output. By default, it will attempt to fit as many columns of font names into the number of character specified by -w *width*. |
| -u | This option indicates that the output should be left unsorted. |
| -o | This option indicates that xlsfonts should do an OpenFont (and QueryFont, if appropriate) rather than a ListFonts. This is useful if ListFonts or ListFontsWithInfo fail to list a known font (as is the case with some scaled font systems). |
| -fn *pattern* | This option specifies the font name pattern to match. |

## SEE ALSO

X(1), Xserver(1), xset(1), xfd(1), X Logical Font Description Conventions

## ENVIRONMENT

DISPLAY                                              To get the default host and display to use

## BUGS

Doing xlsfonts -l can tie up your server for a very long time. This is really a bug with single-threaded nonpreemptable servers, not with this program.

## AUTHOR

Mark Lillibridge (MIT Project Athena), Jim Fulton (MIT X Consortium), and Phil Karlton (SGI)

*X Version 11 Release 6*

# xmag

xmag—Magnify parts of the screen

## SYNOPSIS

xmag [ -mag *magfactor* ][-source *geom* ][-*toolkitoption* ...]

## DESCRIPTION

The xmag program allows you to magnify portions of an X screen. If no explicit region is specified, a square with the pointer in the upper-left corner is displayed indicating the area to be enlarged. The area can be dragged out to the desired size by pressing Button 2. After a region has been selected, a window is popped up showing a blown-up version of the region in which each pixel in the source image is represented by a small square of the same color. Pressing Button 1 in the enlargement window shows the position and RGB value of the pixel under the pointer until the button is released. Typing **Q** or **^C** in the enlargement window exits the program. The application has five buttons across its top. Close deletes this particular magnification instance. Replace brings up the rubber band selector again to select another region for this magnification instance. New brings up the rubber band selector to create a new magnification instance. Cut puts the magnification image into the primary selection. Paste copies the primary selection buffer into xmag. Note that you can cut and paste between xmag and the bitmap program. Resizing xmag resizes the magnification area. xmag preserves the colormap, visual, and window depth of the source.

## WIDGETS

xmag uses the X Toolkit and the Athena Widget Set. The magnified image is displayed in the Scale widget. For more information, see the Athena Widget Set documentation. Following is the widget structure of the xmag application. Indentation indicates hierarchical structure. The widget class name is given first, followed by the widget instance name.

```
Xmag xmag
    RootWindow root
    TopLevelShell xmag
        Paned pane1
            Paned pane2
                Command close
                Command replace
                Command new
                Command select
                Command paste
                Label xmag label
            Paned pane2
                Scale scale
OverrideShell pixShell
    Label pixLabel
```

## OPTIONS

-source geom

This option specifies the size and/or location of the source region on the screen. By default, a 64×64 square is provided for the user to select an area of the screen.

-mag integer

This option indicates the magnification to be used. The default is 5.

## AUTHORS

Dave Sternlicht and Davor Matic (MIT X Consortium)

*X Version 11 Release 6*

# xmkmf

xmkmf—Create a Makefile from an Imakefile

## SYNOPSIS

xmkmf [-a][topdir [ curdir ]]

## DESCRIPTION

The xmkmf command is the normal way to create a Makefile from an Imakefile shipped with third-party software.

When invoked with no arguments in a directory containing an Imakefile, the imake program is run with arguments appropriate for your system (configured into xmkmf when X was built) and generates a Makefile.

When invoked with the -a option, xmkmf builds the Makefile in the current directory, and then automatically executes make Makefiles (in case there are subdirectories), make includes, and make depend for you. This is the normal way to configure software that is outside the X Consortium build tree.

If working inside the X Consortium build tree (unlikely unless you are an X developer, and even then this option is never really used), the topdir argument should be specified as the relative pathname from the current directory to the top of the build tree. Optionally, curdir may be specified as a relative pathname from the top of the build tree to the current directory. It is necessary to supply curdir if the current directory has subdirectories, or the Makefile will not be able to build the subdirectories. If a topdir is given, xmkmf assumes nothing is installed on your system and looks for files in the build tree instead of using the installed versions.

## SEE ALSO

imake(1)

*X Version 11 Release 6*

# xmodmap

xmodmap—Utility for modifying keymaps in X

## SYNOPSIS

xmodmap [-options ...] [filename]

## DESCRIPTION

The xmodmap program is used to edit and display the keyboard modifier map and keymap table that are used by client applications to convert event keycodes into keysyms. It is usually run from the user's session startup script to configure the keyboard according to personal tastes.

## OPTIONS

The following options may be used with xmodmap:

| | |
|---|---|
| `-display display` | This option specifies the host and display to use. |
| `-help` | This option indicates that a brief description of the command-line arguments should be printed on the standard error channel. This will be done whenever an unhandled argument is given to xmodmap. |
| `-grammar` | This option indicates that a help message describing the expression grammar used in files and with -e expressions should be printed on the standard error. |
| `-verbose` | This option indicates that xmodmap should print logging information as it parses its input. |
| `-quiet` | This option turns off the verbose logging. This is the default. |
| `-n` | This option indicates that xmodmap should not change the mappings, but should display what it would do, like make(1) does when given this option. |
| `-e expression` | This option specifies an expression to be executed. Any number of expressions may be specified from the command line. |
| `-pm` | This option indicates that the current modifier map should be printed on the standard output. |
| `-pk` | This option indicates that the current keymap table should be printed on the standard output. |
| `-pke` | This option indicates that the current keymap table should be printed on the standard output in the form of expressions that can be fed back to xmodmap. |
| `-pp` | This option indicates that the current pointer map should be printed on the standard output. |
| `-` | A lone dash means that the standard input should be used as the input file. |

The filename specifies a file containing xmodmap expressions to be executed. This file is usually kept in the user's home directory with a name like `.xmodmaprc`.

## EXPRESSION GRAMMAR

The xmodmap program reads a list of expressions and parses them all before attempting to execute any of them. This makes it possible to refer to keysyms that are being redefined in a natural way without having to worry as much about name conflicts.

| | |
|---|---|
| `keycode NUMBER = KEYSYMNAME ...` | The list of keysyms is assigned to the indicated keycode (which may be specified in decimal, hex, or octal and can be determined by running the xev program. |
| `keycode any = KEYSYMNAME ...` | If no existing key has the specified list of keysyms assigned to it, a spare key on the keyboard is selected and the keysyms are assigned to it. The list of keysyms may be specified in decimal, hex, or octal. |
| `keysym KEYSYMNAME = KEYSYMNAME ...` | The KEYSYMNAME on the left side is translated into matching keycodes used to perform the corresponding set of keycode expressions. The list of keysym names may be found in the |

|                                | header file `<X11/keysymdef.h` (without the `XK_prefix`) or the keysym database `<XRoot>/lib/X11/XKeysymDB`, where `<XRoot>` refers to the root of the X11 install tree. Note that if the same keysym is bound to multiple keys, the expression is executed for each matching keycode. |
|--------------------------------|---|
| clear *MODIFIERNAME*           | This removes all entries in the modifier map for the given modifier, where valid names are `Shift`, `Lock`, `Control`, `Mod1`, `Mod2`, `Mod3`, `Mod4`, and `Mod5` (case does not matter in modifier names, although it does matter for all other names). For example, `clear Lock` will remove any keys that were bound to the shift lock modifier. |
| add *MODIFIERNAME* = *KEYSYMNAME* ... | This adds all keys containing the given keysyms to the indicated modifier map. The keysym names are evaluated after all input expressions are read to make it easy to write expressions to swap keys. (See the "Examples" subsection). |
| remove *MODIFIERNAME* = *KEYSYMNAME* ... | This removes all keys containing the given keysyms from the indicated modifier map. Unlike `add`, the keysym names are evaluated as the line is read in. This allows you to remove keys from a modifier without having to worry about whether or not they have been reassigned. |
| pointer =default              | This sets the pointer map back to its default settings (button 1 generates a code of 1, button 2 generates a 2, and so on). |
| pointer = *NUMBER* ...         | This sets to pointer map to contain the indicated button codes. The list always starts with the first physical button. |

Lines that begin with an exclamation point (!) are taken as comments.

If you want to change the binding of a modifier key, you must also remove it from the appropriate modifier map.

## EXAMPLES

Many pointers are designed such that the first button is pressed using the index finger of the right hand. People who are left-handed frequently find that it is more comfortable to reverse the button codes that are generated so that the primary button is pressed using the index finger of the left hand. This could be done on a 3 button pointer as follows: `% xmodmap -e "pointer =3 2 1"`.

Many applications support the notion of Meta keys (similar to Control keys except that Meta is held down instead of Control). However, some servers do not have a Meta keysym in the default keymap table, so one needs to be added by hand. The following command will attach Meta to the Multilanguage key (sometimes labeled Compose Character). It also takes advantage of the fact that applications that need a Meta key simply need to get the keycode and don't require the keysym to be in the first column of the keymap table. This means that applications that are looking for a Multi key (including the default modifier map) won't notice any change. Example:

```
% xmodmap -e "keysym Multi_key = Multi_key Meta_L"
```

Similarly, some keyboards have an Alt key but no Meta key. In that case the following may be useful:

```
% xmodmap -e "keysym Alt L = Meta L Alt L"
```

One of the more simple, yet convenient, uses of xmodmap is to set the keyboard's "rubout" key to generate an alternate keysym. This frequently involves exchanging Backspace with Delete to be more comfortable to the user. If the `ttyModes` resource in xterm is set as well, all terminal emulator windows will use the same key for erasing characters:

```
% xmodmap -e "keysym BackSpace = Delete"
% echo "XTerm*ttyModes: erase ^?" ¦ xrdb -merge
```

Some keyboards do not automatically generate less than and greater than characters when the comma and period keys are shifted. This can be remedied with xmodmap by resetting the bindings for the comma and period with the following scripts:

```
!
! make shift-, be $<$ and shift-. be $>$
!
keysym comma = comma less
keysym period = period greater
```

One of the more irritating differences between keyboards is the location of the Control and Shift Lock keys. A common use of xmodmap is to swap these two keys as follows:

```
!
! Swap Caps_Lock and Control_L
!
remove Lock = Caps_Lock
remove Control = Control_L
keysym Control_L = Caps_Lock
keysym Caps_Lock = Control_L
add Lock = Caps_Lock
add Control = Control_L
```

The keycode command is useful for assigning the same keysym to multiple keycodes. Although unportable, it also makes it possible to write scripts that can reset the keyboard to a known state. The following script sets the Backspace key to generate Delete (as shown earlier), flushes all existing caps lock bindings, makes the Caps Lock key be a control key, make F5 generate Escape, and makes Break/Reset be a shift lock.

```
!
! On the HP, the following keycodes have key caps as listed:
!
!       101 Backspace
!        55 Caps
!        14 Ctrl
!        15 Break/Reset
!        86 Stop
!        89 F5
!
keycode 101 = Delete
keycode 55 = Control_R
clear Lock
add Control = Control_R
keycode 89 = Escape
keycode 15 = Caps_Lock
add Lock = Caps_Lock
```

## ENVIRONMENT

DISPLAY                                To get default host and display number

## SEE ALSO

X(1), xev(1), Xlib documentation on key and pointer events

## BUGS

Every time a keycode expression is evaluated, the server generates a MappingNotify event on every client. This can cause some thrashing. All of the changes should be batched together and done at once. Clients that receive keyboard input and ignore MappingNotify events will not notice any changes made to keyboard mappings.

xmodmap should generate add and remove expressions automatically whenever a keycode that is already bound to a modifier is changed.

There should be a way to have the remove expression accept keycodes as well as keysyms for those times when you really mess up your mappings.

## AUTHOR

Jim Fulton (MIT X Consortium), rewritten from an earlier version by David Rosenthal (Sun Microsystems)

*X Version 11 Release 6*

# xon

xon—Start an X program on a remote machine

## SYNOPSIS

xon remote-host [-access] [-debug] [-name window-name] [-nols] [-screen screen-no] [-user user-name] [command ...]

## DESCRIPTION

xon runs the specified command (default xterm -ls) on the remote machine using rsh, remsh, or rcmd. xon passes the DISPLAY, XAUTHORITY, and XUSERFILESEARCHPATH environment variables to the remote command.

When no command is specified, xon runs xterm -ls. It additionally specifies the application name to be xterm-*remote-host* and the window title to be -fl*remote-host*.

xon can only work when the remote host will allow you to log in without a password, by having an entry in the .rhosts file permitting access.

## OPTIONS

Note that the options follow the remote hostname (as they do with rlogin).

-access
: Runs xhost locally to add the remote host to the host access list in the X server. This won't work unless xhost is given permission to modify the access list.

-debug
: Normally, xon disconnects the remote process from stdin, stdout, and stderr to eliminate the daemon processes that usually connect them across the network. Specifying the -debug option leaves them connected so that error messages from the remote execution are sent back to the originating host.

-name window-name
: This specifies a different application name and window title for the default command (xterm).

-nols
: Normally xon passes the -ls option to the remote xterm; this option suspends that behavior.

-screen screen-no
: This changes the screen number of the DISPLAY variable passed to the remote command.

-user user-name
: By default, xon simply uses rsh/remsh/rcmd to connect to the remote machine using the same username as on the local machine. This option causes xon to specify an alternative username. This will not work unless you have authorization to access the remote account, by placing an appropriate entry in the remote user's .rhosts file.

## BUGS

xon can get easily confused when the remote host, username, or various environment variable values contain whitespace.

xon has no way to send the appropriate X authorization information to the remote host.

*X Version 11 Release 6*

# xpmtoppm

xpmtoppm—Convert an X11 pixmap into a portable pixmap

## SYNOPSIS

xpmtoppm [*xpmfile*]

## DESCRIPTION

Reads an X11 pixmap (XPM version 1 or 3) as input. Produces a portable pixmap as output.

## KNOWN BUGS

The support to XPM version 3 is limited. Comments can only be single lines and there must be for every pixel a default color name for a color type visual.

## SEE ALSO

ppmtoxpm(1), ppm(5)

XPM Manual by Arnaud Le Hors (lehors@mirsa.inria.fr)

## AUTHOR

Copyright (c) 1991 by Jef Poskanzer.

Upgraded to support XPM version 3 by Arnaud Le Hors (lehors@mirsa.inria.fr) 9 April 1991

*16 August 1990*

# xprop

xprop—Property displayer for X

## SYNOPSIS

xprop [-help] [-grammar] [-id *id*] [-root] [-name *name*] [-frame] [-font *font*]
[-display *display*] [-len *n*] [-notype] [-fs *file*] [-remove *property-name*]
[-spy] [-f atom format [dformat]]* [format [dformat] atom]*

## SUMMARY

The xprop utility is for displaying window and font properties in an X server. One window or font is selected using the command-line arguments or possibly in the case of a window, by clicking on the desired window. A list of properties is then given, possibly with formatting information.

## OPTIONS

| | |
|---|---|
| -help | Print out a summary of command-line options. |
| -grammar | Print out a detailed grammar for all command-line options. |
| -id *id* | This argument allows the user to select window id on the command line rather than using the pointer to select the target window. This is very useful in debugging X applications where the target window is not mapped to the screen or where the use of the pointer might be impossible or interfere with the application. |
| -name *name* | This argument allows the user to specify that the window named name is the target window on the command line rather than using the pointer to select the target window. |

| | |
|---|---|
| `-font` *font* | This argument allows the user to specify that the properties of font *font* should be displayed. |
| `-root` | This argument specifies that X's root window is the target window. This is useful in situations where the root window is completely obscured. |
| `display` *display* | This argument allows you to specify the server to connect to; see X(1). |
| `-len` *n* | Specifies that at most, *n* bytes of any property should be read or displayed. |
| `-notype` | Specifies that the type of each property should not be displayed. |
| `-fs` *file* | Specifies that file *file* should be used as a source of more formats for properties. |
| `-frame` | Specifies that when selecting a window by hand (that is, if neither `-name`, `-root`, nor `-id` is given), look at the window manager frame (if any) instead of looking for the client window. |
| `-remove` *property-name* | Specifies the name of a property to be removed from the indicated window. |
| `-spy` | Examine window properties forever, looking for property change events. |
| `-f` *name format [dformat]* | Specifies that the format for *name* should be *format* and that the dformat for *name* should be *dformat*. If *dformat* is missing, `"= $0+\n"` is assumed. |

## DESCRIPTION

For each of these properties, its value on the selected window or font is printed using the supplied formatting information, if any. If no formatting information is supplied, internal defaults are used. If a property is not defined on the selected window or font, not defined is printed as the value for that property. If no property list is given, all the properties possessed by the selected window or font are printed.

A window may be selected in one of four ways. First, if the desired window is the root window, the `-root` argument may be used. If the desired window is not the root window, it may be selected in two ways on the command line, either by id number, such as might be obtained from xwininfo, or by name if the window possesses a name. The `-id` argument selects a window by id number in either decimal or hex (must start with `0x`) while the `-name` argument selects a window by name.

The last way to select a window does not involve the command line at all. If none of `-font`, `-id`, `-name`, and `-root` are specified, a crosshairs cursor is displayed and the user is allowed to choose any visible window by pressing any pointer button in the desired window. If it is desired to display properties of a font as opposed to a window, the `-font` argument must be used.

Other than the preceding four arguments and the `-help` argument for obtaining help, and the `-grammar` argument for listing the full grammar for the command line, all the other command-line arguments are used in specifying both the format of the properties to be displayed and how to display them. The `-len` *n* argument specifies that at most, *n* bytes of any given property will be read and displayed. This is useful, for example, when displaying the cut buffer on the root window, which could run to several pages if displayed in full.

Normally, each property name is displayed by printing first the property name then its type (if it has one) in parentheses, followed by its value. The `-notype` argument specifies that property types should not be displayed. The `-fs` argument is used to specify a file containing a list of formats for properties, while the `-f` argument is used to specify the format for one property.

The formatting information for a property actually consists of two parts, a format and a dformat. The *format* specifies the actual formatting of the property (that is, is it made up of words, bytes, or longs?, and so on) while the *dformat* specifies how the property should be displayed.

The following paragraphs describe how to construct formats and dformats. However, for the vast majority of users and uses, this should not be necessary as the built-in defaults contain the formats and dformats necessary to display all the standard properties. It should only be necessary to specify formats and dformats if a new property is being dealt with or the user dislikes the standard display format. New users especially are encouraged to skip this part.

A format consists of a 0, 8, 16, or 32 followed by a sequence of one or more format characters. The 0, 8, 16, or 32 specifies how many bits per field there are in the property.

Zero is a special case that means use the field size information associated with the property itself. (This is only needed for special cases like type INTEGER, which is actually three different types, depending on the size of the fields of the property.)

A value of 8 means that the property is a sequence of bytes, while a value of 16 means that the property is a sequence of words. The difference between these two lies in the fact that the sequence of words will be byte swapped while the sequence of bytes will not be when read by a machine of the opposite byte order of the machine that originally wrote the property. For more information on how properties are formatted and stored, consult the Xlib manual.

After the size of the fields has been specified, it is necessary to specify the type of each field (is it an integer, a string, an atom, or what?) This is done using one format character per field. If there are more fields in the property than format characters supplied, the last character will be repeated as many times as necessary for the extra fields. The format characters and their meaning are as follows:

| | |
|---|---|
| a | The field holds an atom number. A field of this type should be of size 32. |
| b | The field is a Boolean. A 0 means false while anything else means true. |
| c | The field is an unsigned number, a cardinal. |
| i | The field is a signed integer. |
| m | The field is a set of bit flags, 1 meaning on. |
| s | This field and the next ones—until either a 0 or the end of the property—represent a sequence of bytes. This format character is only usable with a field size of 8 and is most often used to represent a string. |
| x | The field is a hex number (like c but displayed in hex—most useful for displaying window ids and the like). |

An example format is 32ica, which is the format for a property of three fields of 32 bits each—the first holding a signed integer, the second an unsigned integer, and the third an atom.

The format of a dformat, unlike that of a format, is not so rigid. The only limitations on a dformat is that one may not start with a letter or a dash. This is so that it can be distinguished from a property name or an argument. A dformat is a text string containing special characters instructing that various fields be printed at various points in a manner similar to the formatting string used by printf. For example, the dformat is ( $0, $1 \)\n would render the POINT 3, -4, which has a format of 32ii as is ( 3, -4 )\n.

Any character other than a $, ?, \, or a ( in a dformat prints as itself. To print out a $, ?, \, or (, precede it with a \. For example, to print out a $, use \$. Several special backslash sequences are provided as shortcuts. \n will cause a newline to be displayed, while \t will cause a tab to be displayed. \o, where o is an octal number, will display character number o.

A $ followed by a number n causes field number n to be displayed. The format of the displayed field depends on the formatting character used to describe it in the corresponding format. In other words, if a cardinal is described by c, it will print in decimal, while if it is described by an x, it is displayed in hex.

If the field is not present in the property (this is possible with some properties), `<field not available>` is displayed instead. `$n+` will display field number *n*, then a comma, then field number *n*+1, then another comma, then ... until the last field defined. If field *n* is not defined, nothing is displayed. This is useful for a property that is a list of values.

A `?` is used to start a conditional expression, a kind of if-then statement. `?exp(text)` will display text if and only if *exp* evaluates to non-zero. This is useful for two things. First, it allows fields to be displayed if and only if a flag is set. And second, it allows a value such as a state number to be displayed as a name rather than as just a number. The syntax of *exp* is as follows:

```
exp ::= term | term=exp | !exp
term ::= n | $n | mn
```

The `!` operator is a logical NOT, changing 0 to 1 and any non-zero value to 0. `=` is an equality operator. Note that internally, all expressions are evaluated as 32-bit numbers, so -1 is not equal to 65535. `=` returns 1 if the two values are equal and 0 if not. *n* represents the constant value *n* while `$n` represents the value of field number *n*. `mn` is 1 if flag number *n* in the first field having format character `m` in the corresponding format is 1; 0 otherwise.

Examples: `?m3(count: $3\n)` displays field 3 with a label of `count` if and only if flag number 3 (count starts at 0!) is on. `?$2=0(True)?!$2=0(False)` displays the inverted value of field 2 as a Boolean.

In order to display a property, xprop needs both a `format` and a `dformat`. Before xprop uses its default values of a `format` of `32x` and a `dformat` of `" = { $0+ }\n"`, it searches several places in an attempt to find more specific formats. First, a search is made using the name of the property. If this fails, a search is made using the type of the property. This allows type `STRING` to be defined with one set of formats while allowing property `WM_NAME`, which is of type `STRING` to be defined with a different format. In this way, the display formats for a given type can be overridden for specific properties.

The locations searched are in order: the format, if any, specified with the property name (as in `8x WM_NAME`), the formats defined by `-f` options in last to first order, the contents of the file specified by the `-fs` option if any, the contents of the file specified by the environmental variable `XPROPFORMATS` if any, and finally xprop's built-in file of formats.

The format of the files referred to by the `-fs` argument and the `XPROPFORMATS` variable is one or more lines of the following form:

```
name format [dformat]
```

Where *name* is either the name of a property or the name of a type, *format* is the format to be used with name, and *dformat* is the dformat to be used with *name*. If *dformat* is not present, `"=$0+\n"` is assumed.

## EXAMPLES

To display the name of the root window: xprop `-root WM_NAME`

To display the window manager hints for the clock: xprop `-name xclock WM_HINTS`

To display the start of the cut buffer: xprop `-root -len 100 CUT_BUFFER0`

To display the point size of the fixed font: xprop `-font fixed POINT_SIZE`

To display all the properties of window # 0x200007: xprop `-id 0x200007`

## ENVIRONMENT

| | |
|---|---|
| DISPLAY | To get default display. |
| XPROPFORMATS | Specifies the name of a file from which additional formats are to be obtained. |

## SEE ALSO

X(1), xwininfo(1)

## AUTHOR

Mark Lillibridge (MIT Project Athena)

# xrdb

xrdb—X server resource database utility

## SYNOPSIS

xrdb [-option ...] [*filename*]

## DESCRIPTION

xrdb is used to get or set the contents of the RESOURCE_MANAGER property on the root window of screen 0, or the SCREEN_RESOURCES property on the root window of any or all screens, or everything combined. You would normally run this program from your X startup file.

Most X clients use the RESOURCE_MANAGER and SCREEN_RESOURCES properties to get user preferences about color, fonts, and so on for applications. Having this information in the server (where it is available to all clients) instead of on disk solves the problem in previous versions of X that required you to maintain defaults files on every machine that you might use. It also allows for dynamic changing of defaults without editing files.

The RESOURCE_MANAGER property is used for resources that apply to all screens of the display. The SCREEN_RESOURCES property on each screen specifies additional (or overriding) resources to be used for that screen. (When there is only one screen, SCREEN_RESOURCES is normally not used; all resources are just placed in the RESOURCE_MANAGER property.)

The file specified by filename (or the contents from standard input if - or no filename is given) is optionally passed through the C preprocessor with the following symbols defined, based on the capabilities of the server being used:

| | |
|---|---|
| SERVERHOST=*hostname* | The *hostname* portion of the display to which you are connected. |
| SRVR_*name* | The SERVERHOSThostnamestring turned into a legal identifier. For example, my-dpy.lcs.mit.edu becomes SRVR my dpy lcs mit edu. |
| HOST=*hostname* | The same as SERVERHOST. |
| DISPLAY_NUM=*num* | The number of the display on the server host. |
| CLIENTHOST=*hostname* | The name of the host on which xrdb is running. |
| CLNT_*name* | The CLIENTHOST hostname string turned into a legal identifier. For example, "expo.lcs.mit.edu" becomes CLNT expo lcs mit edu. |
| RELEASE=*num* | The vendor release number for the server. The interpretation of this number will vary depending on VENDOR. |
| REVISION=*num* | The X protocol minor version supported by this server (currently 0). |
| VERSION=*num* | The X protocol major version supported by this server (should always be 11). |
| VENDOR="*vendor*" | A string literal specifying the vendor of the server. |
| VNDR_*name* | The VENDOR name string turned into a legal identifier. For example, "MIT X Consortium" becomes VNDR_MIT_X Consortium. |
| EXT_*name* | A symbol is defined for each protocol extension supported by the server. Each extension string name is turned into a legal identifier. For example, "X3D-PEX" becomes EXT_X3D_PEX. |

| | |
|---|---|
| NUM_SCREENS=*num* | The total number of screens. |
| SCREEN_NUM=*num* | The number of the current screen (from zero). |
| BITS_PER_RGB=*num* | The number of significant bits in an RGB color specification. This is the log base 2 of the number of distinct shades of each primary that the hardware can generate. Note that it usually is not related to PLANES. |
| CLASS=*visualclass* | One of StaticGray, GrayScale, StaticColor, PseudoColor, TrueColor, DirectColor. This is the visual class of the root window. |
| CLASS_*visualclass*=*visualid* | The visual class of the root window in a form you can #ifdef on. The value is the numeric id of the visual. |
| COLOR | Defined only if CLASS is one of StaticColor, PseudoColor, TrueColor, or DirectColor. |
| CLASS_visualclass_depth=num | A symbol is defined for each visual supported for the screen. The symbol includes the class of the visual and its depth; the value is the numeric id of the visual. (If more than one visual has the same class and depth, the numeric id of the first one reported by the server is used.) |
| HEIGHT=num | The height of the root window in pixels. |
| WIDTH=num | The width of the root window in pixels. |
| PLANES=num | The number of bit planes (the depth) of the root window. |
| X_RESOLUTION=num | The x resolution of the screen in pixels per meter. |
| Y_RESOLUTION=num | The y resolution of the screen in pixels per meter. |

SRVR_name, CLNT_name, VNDR_name, and EXT_name identifiers are formed by changing all characters other than letters and digits into underscores.

Lines that begin with an exclamation mark (!) are ignored and may be used as comments.

Note that since xrdb can read from standard input, it can be used to change the contents of properties directly from a terminal or from a shell script.

## OPTIONS

xrdb program accepts the following options:

| | |
|---|---|
| –help | This option (or any unsupported option) will cause a brief description of the allowable options and parameters to be printed. |
| -display *display* | This option specifies the X server to be used; see X(1). It also specifies the screen to use for the -screen option, and it specifies the screen from which preprocessor symbols are derived for the -global option. |
| -all | This option indicates that operation should be performed on the screen-independent resource property (RESOURCE_MANAGER), as well as the screen-specific property (SCREEN_RESOURCES) on every screen of the display. For example, when used in conjunction with -query, the contents of all properties are output. For -load, -override, and -merge, the input file is processed once for each screen. The resources that occur in common in the output for every screen are collected, and these are applied as the screen-independent resources. The remaining resources are applied for each individual per-screen property. This the default mode of operation. |

-global

This option indicates that the operation should only be performed on the screen-independent RESOURCE_MANAGER property.

-screen

This option indicates that the operation should only be performed on the SCREEN_RESOURCES property of the default screen of the display.

-screens

This option indicates that the operation should be performed on the SCREEN_RESOURCES property of each screen of the display. For -load, -override, and -merge, the input file is processed for each screen.

-n

This option indicates that changes to the specified properties (when used with -load, -override, or -merge) or to the resource file (when used with -edit) should be shown on the standard output, but should not be performed.

-quiet

This option indicates that warning about duplicate entries should not be displayed.

-cpp filename

This option specifies the pathname of the C preprocessor program to be used. Although xrdb was designed to use CPP, any program that acts as a filter and accepts the -D, -I, and -U options may be used.

-nocpp

This option indicates that xrdb should not run the input file through a preprocessor before loading it into properties.

-symbols

This option indicates that the symbols that are defined for the preprocessor should be printed onto the standard output.

-query

This option indicates that the current contents of the specified properties should be printed onto the standard output. Note that since preprocessor commands in the input resource file are part of the input file, not part of the property, they won't appear in the output from this option. The -edit option can be used to merge the contents of properties back into the input resource file without damaging preprocessor commands.

-load

This option indicates that the input should be loaded as the new value of the specified properties, replacing whatever was there; that is, the old contents are removed. This is the default action.

-override

This option indicates that the input should be added to, instead of replacing, the current contents of the specified properties. New entries override previous entries.

-merge

This option indicates that the input should be merged and lexicographically sorted with, instead of replacing, the current contents of the specified properties.

-remove

This option indicates that the specified properties should be removed from the server.

-retain

This option indicates that the server should be instructed not to reset if xrdb is the first client. This should never be necessary under normal conditions, since xdm and xinit always act as the first client.

-edit filename

This option indicates that the contents of the specified properties should be edited into the given file, replacing any values already listed there. This allows you to put changes that you have made to your defaults back into your resource file, preserving any comments or preprocessor lines.

| | |
|---|---|
| `-backup` *string* | This option specifies a suffix to be appended to the filename used with `-edit` to generate a backup file. |
| `-Dname[=value]` | This option is passed through to the preprocessor and is used to define symbols for use with conditionals such as `#ifdef`. |
| `-Uname` | This option is passed through to the preprocessor and is used to remove any definitions of this symbol. |
| `-Idirectory` | This option is passed through to the preprocessor and is used to specify a directory to search for files that are referenced with `#include`. |

## FILES

Generalizes ~/.Xdefaults files

## SEE ALSO

X(1), Xlib Resource Manager documentation, Xt resource documentation

## ENVIRONMENT

| | |
|---|---|
| `DISPLAY` | To figure out which display to use. |

## BUGS

The default for no arguments should be to query, not to overwrite, so that it is consistent with other programs.

## AUTHORS

Bob Scheifler and Phil Karlton, rewritten from the original by Jim Gettys

*X Version 11 Release 6*

# xrefresh

xrefresh—Refresh all or part of an X screen

## SYNOPSIS

`xrefresh [-option ...]`

## DESCRIPTION

xrefresh is a simple X program that causes all or part of your screen to be repainted. This is useful when system messages have messed up your screen. xrefresh maps a window on top of the desired area of the screen and then immediately unmaps it, causing refresh events to be sent to all applications. By default, a window with no background is used, causing all applications to repaint smoothly. However, the various options can be used to indicate that a solid background (of any color) or the root window background should be used instead.

## ARGUMENTS

| | |
|---|---|
| `-white` | Use a white background. The screen just appears to flash quickly, and then repaint. |
| `-black` | Use a black background (in effect, turning off all of the electron guns to the tube). This can be somewhat disorienting as everything goes black for a moment. |
| `-solid` *color* | Use a solid background of the specified color. Try green. |
| `-root` | Use the root window background. |

| | |
|---|---|
| `-none` | This is the default. All of the windows simply repaint. |
| `-geometry WxH+X+Y` | Specifies the portion of the screen to be repainted; see X(1). |
| `-display display` | This argument allows you to specify the server and screen to refresh; see X(1). |

## X DEFAULTS

The xrefresh program uses the routine `XGetDefault(3X)` to read defaults, so its resource names are all capitalized.

| | |
|---|---|
| `Black, White, Solid, None, Root` | Determines what sort of window background to use |
| `Geometry` | Determines the area to refresh. Not very useful. |

## ENVIRONMENT

| | |
|---|---|
| `DISPLAY` | To get default host and display number. |

## SEE ALSO

X(1)

## BUGS

It should have just one default type for the background.

## AUTHORS

Jim Gettys (Digital Equipment Corporation, MIT Project Athena)

*X Version 11 Release 6*

# Xserver

Xserver—X Window System display server

## SYNOPSIS

X [option ...]

## DESCRIPTION

X is the generic name for the X Window System display server. It is frequently a link or a copy of the appropriate server binary for driving the most frequently used server on a given machine.

## STARTING THE SERVER

The X server is usually started from the X Display Manager program xdm(1). This utility is run from the system boot files and takes care of keeping the server running, prompting for usernames and passwords, and starting up the user sessions.

Installations that run more than one window system may need to use the xinit(1) utility instead of xdm. However, xinit is to be considered a tool for building startup scripts and is not intended for use by end users. Site administrators are strongly urged to use xdm, or build other interfaces for novice users.

The X server may also be started directly by the user, though this method is usually reserved for testing and is not recommended for normal operation. On some platforms, the user must have special permission to start the X server, often because access to certain devices. (For example, /dev/mouse is restricted.)

When the X server starts up, it typically takes over the display. If you are running on a workstation whose console is the display, you may not be able to log into the console while the server is running.

## OPTIONS

All of the X servers accept the following command-line options:

| | |
|---|---|
| `:displaynumber` | The X server runs as the given *displaynumber*, which by default is 0. If multiple X servers are to run simultaneously on a host, each must have a unique display number. See the "Display Names" subsection of the X(1) manual page to learn how to specify which display number clients should try to use. |
| `-a number` | Sets pointer acceleration (that is, the ratio of how much is reported to how much the user actually moved the pointer). |
| `-ac` | Disables host-based access control mechanisms. Enables access by any host, and permits any host to modify the access control list. Use with extreme caution. This option exists primarily for running test suites remotely. |
| `-audit level` | Sets the audit trail level. The default level is 1, meaning only connection rejections are reported. Level 2 additionally reports all successful connections and disconnects. Level 0 turns off the audit trail. Audit lines are sent as standard error output. |
| `-auth authorization-file` | Specifies a file which contains a collection of authorization records used to authenticate access. See also the xdm and Xsecurity manual pages. |
| `bc` | Disables certain kinds of error checking, for bug compatibility with previous releases (for example, to work around bugs in R2 and R3 xterms and toolkits). Deprecated. |
| `-bs` | Disables backing store support on all screens. |
| `-c` | Turns off key-click. |
| `c volume` | Sets key-click volume (allowable range: 0–100). |
| `-cc class` | Sets the visual class for the root window of color screens. The class numbers are as specified in the X protocol. Not obeyed by all servers. |
| `-co filename` | Sets name of RGB color database. The default is <XRoot>/lib/X11/rgb, where <Xroot> refers to the root of the X11 install tree. |
| `-config filename` | Reads more options from the given file. Options in the file may be separated by newlines if desired. If a # character appears on a line, all characters between it and the next newline are ignored, providing a simple commenting facility. The -config option itself may appear in the file. |
| `-core` | Causes the server to generate a core dump on fatal errors. |
| `-dpi resolution` | Sets the resolution of the screen, in dots per inch. To be used when the server cannot determine the screen size from the hardware. |
| `-deferglyphs whichfonts` | Specifies the types of fonts for which the server should attempt to use deferred glyph loading. *whichfonts* can be all (all fonts), none (no fonts), or 16 (16-bit fonts only). |
| `-f volume` | Sets feep (bell) volume (allowable range: 0–100). |
| `-fc cursorFont` | Sets default cursor font. |
| `-fn font` | Sets the default font. |

| | |
|---|---|
| `-fp fontPath` | Sets the search path for fonts. This path is a comma-separated list of directories that the X server searches for font databases. `-help` prints a usage message. |
| `-I` | Causes all remaining command-line arguments to be ignored. |
| `-kb` | Disables the XKEYBOARD extension if present. |
| `-p minutes` | Sets screen saver pattern cycle time in minutes. |
| `-pn` | Permits the server to continue running if it fails to establish all of its well-known sockets (connection points for clients), but establishes at least one. |
| `-r` | Turns off auto-repeat. |
| `r` | Turns on auto-repeat. |
| `-s minutes` | Sets screen saver time-out time in minutes. |
| `-su` | Disables save under support on all screens. |
| `-t number` | Sets pointer acceleration threshold in pixels (that is, sets after how many pixels pointer acceleration should take effect). |
| `-terminate` | Causes the server to terminate at server reset, instead of continuing to run. |
| `-to seconds` | Sets default connection time-out in seconds. |
| `-tst` | Disables all testing extensions (for example, XTEST, XTrap, XTestExtension1). |
| `ttyxx` | Ignored, for servers started the ancient way (from init). |
| `v` | Sets video-off screen saver preference. |
| `-v` | Sets video-on screen saver preference. |
| `-wm` | Forces the default backing-store of all windows to be When-Mapped. This is a backdoor way of getting backing-store to apply to all windows. Although all mapped windows will have backing-store, the backing-store attribute value reported by the server for a window will be the last value established by a client. If it has never been set by a client, the server will report the default value, NotUseful. This behavior is required by the X protocol, which allows the server to exceed the client's backing-store expectations but does not provide a way to tell the client that it is doing so. |
| `-x extension` | Loads the specified extension at init. This is a no-op for most implementations. |

## SERVER DEPENDENT OPTIONS

Some X servers accept the following options:

| | |
|---|---|
| `-ld kilobytes` | Sets the data space limit of the server to the specified number of kilobytes. A value of zero makes the data size as large as possible. The default value of -1 leaves the data space limit unchanged. |
| `-lf files` | Sets the number-of-open-files limit of the server to the specified number. A value of zero makes the limit as large as possible. The default value of -1 leaves the limit unchanged. |
| `-ls kilobytes` | Sets the stack space limit of the server to the specified number of kilobytes. A value of zero makes the stack size as large as possible. The default value of -1 leaves the stack space limit unchanged. |

| | |
|---|---|
| -logo | Turns on the X Window System logo display in the screen saver. There is currently no way to change this from a client. |
| nologo | Turns off the X Window System logo display in the screen saver. There is currently no way to change this from a client. |

## XDMCP OPTIONS

X servers that support XDMCP have the following options. (See the *X Display Manager Control Protocol* specification for more information.)

| | |
|---|---|
| -query *host-name* | Enable XDMCP and send Query packets to the specified host. |
| -broadcast | Enable XDMCP and broadcast BroadcastQuery packets to the network. The first responding display manager will be chosen for the session. |
| -indirect *host-name* | Enable XDMCP and send IndirectQuery packets to the specified host. |
| -port *port-num* | Use an alternate port number for XDMCP packets. Must be specified before any -query, -broadcast, or -indirect options. |
| -class *display-class* | XDMCP has an additional display qualifier used in resource lookup for display-specific options. This option sets that value; by default it is MIT-Unspecified (not a very useful value). |
| -cookie xdm-auth-bits | When testing XDM-AUTHENTICATION-1, a private key is shared between the server and the manager. This option sets the value of that private data (not that it is very private, being on the command line!). |
| -displayID display-id | Yet another XDMCP-specific value, this one allows the display manager to identify each display so that it can locate the shared key. |

## XKEYBOARD OPTIONS

X servers that support the XKEYBOARD extension accept the following options:

| | |
|---|---|
| -xkbdir *directory* | Base directory for keyboard layout files |
| -xkbmap *filename* | Keyboard description to load on startup |
| [+-]accessx | Enable(+) or disable(-) AccessX key sequences |
| -ar1 *milliseconds* | Sets the length of time in milliseconds that a key must be depressed before auto-repeat starts |
| -ar2 *milliseconds* | Sets the length of time in milliseconds that should elapse between auto-repeat–generated keystrokes |

Many servers also have device-specific command-line options. See the manual pages for the individual servers for more details.

## NETWORK CONNECTIONS

The X server supports client connections via a platform-dependent subset of the following transport types: TCPIP, UNIX Domain sockets, DECnet, and several varieties of SVR4 local connections. See the "Display Names" subsection of the X(1) manual page to learn how to specify which transport type clients should try to use.

## SECURITY

The X server implements a platform-dependent subset of the following authorization protocols: -MIT-MAGICCOOKIE-1, XDM-AUTHORIZATION-1, SUN-DES-1, and MIT-KERBEROS-5. See the Xsecurity(1) manual page for information on the operation of these protocols.

Authorization data required by the preceding protocols is passed to the server in a private file named with the -auth command-line option. Each time the server is about to accept the first connection after a reset (or when the server is starting), it reads this file. If this file contains any authorization records, the local host is not automatically allowed access to the server, and only clients that send one of the authorization records contained in the file in the connection setup information will be allowed access. See the xau manual page for a description of the binary format of this file. See xauth(1) for maintenance of this file, and distribution of its contents to remote hosts.

The X server also uses a host-based access control list for deciding whether or not to accept connections from clients on a particular machine. If no other authorization mechanism is being used, this list initially consists of the host on which the server is running as well as any machines listed in the file /etc/Xn.hosts, where n is the display number of the server. Each line of the file should contain either an Internet hostname (for example expo.lcs.mit.edu) or a DECnet hostname in double colon format (for example, hydra::). There should be no leading or trailing spaces on any lines. For example,

```
joesworkstation
corporate.company.com
star::
bigcpu::
```

Users can add or remove hosts from this list and enable or disable access control using the xhost command from the same machine as the server.

The X protocol intrinsically does not have any notion of window operation permissions or place any restrictions on what a client can do; if a program can connect to a display, it has full run of the screen. Sites that have better authentication and authorization systems might wish to make use of the hooks in the libraries and the server to provide additional security models.

## SIGNALS

The X server attaches special meaning to the following signals:

| | |
|---|---|
| SIGHUP | This signal causes the server to close all existing connections, free all resources, and restore all defaults. It is sent by the display manager whenever the main user's main application (usually an xterm or window manager) exits to force the server to clean up and prepare for the next user. |
| SIGTERM | This signal causes the server to exit cleanly. |
| SIGUSR1 | This signal is used quite differently from either of the above. When the server starts, it checks to see if it has inherited SIGUSR1 as SIG_IGN instead of the usual SIG_DFL. In this case, the server sends a SIGUSR1 to its parent process after it has set up the various connection schemes. xdm uses this feature to recognize when connecting to the server is possible. |

## FONTS

The X server can obtain fonts from directories or from font servers. The list of directories and font servers the X server uses when trying to open a font is controlled by the font path.

The default font path is

```
<XRoot>/lib/X11/fonts/misc/,
<XRoot>/lib/X11/fonts/Speedo/,
<XRoot>/lib/X11/fonts/Type1/,
<XRoot>/lib/X11/fonts/75dpi/,
<XRoot>/lib/X11/fonts/100dpi/
```

where <XRoot> refers to the root of the X11 install tree.

The font path can be set with the -fp option or by xset(1) after the server has started.

## FILES

| | |
|---|---|
| `/etc/X`*n*`.hosts` | Initial access control list for display number *n* |
| `<XRoot>/lib/X11/fonts/misc` | |
| `<XRoot>/lib/X11/fonts/75dpi` | |
| `<XRoot>/lib/X11/fonts/100dpi` | Bitmap font directories |
| `<XRoot>/lib/X11/fonts/Speedo` | |
| `<XRoot>/lib/X11/fonts/Type1` | Outline font directories |
| `<XRoot>/lib/X11/fonts/PEX` | PEX font directories |
| `<XRoot>/lib/X11/rgb.txt` | Color database |
| `/tmp/.X11-unix/X`*n* | UNIX domain socket for display number *n* |
| `/tmp/rcX`*n* | Kerberos 5 replay cache for display number *n* |
| `/usr/adm/Xnmsgs` | Error log file for display number *n* if run from `init`(8) |
| `<XRoot>/lib/X11/xdm/xdm-errors` | Default error log file if the server is run from `xdm`(1) |

Note: `<XRoot>` refers to the root of the X11 install tree.

## SEE ALSO

General information: X(1)

Protocols: X Window System Protocol, The X Font Service Protocol, X Display Manager Control Protocol

Fonts: bdftopcf(1), mkfontdir(1), xfs(1), xlsfonts(1), xfontsel(1), xfd(1), X Logical Font Description Conventions

Security: Xsecurity(1), xauth(1), xau(1), xdm(1), xhost(1)

Starting the server: xdm(1), xinit(1)

Controlling the server once started: xset(1), xsetroot(1), xhost(1)

Server-specific man pages: Xdec(1), XmacII(1), Xsun(1), Xnest(1), Xvfb(1), XF86 Accel(1), XF86 Mono(1), XF86 SVGA(1), XF86 VGA16(1), XFree86(1)

Server internal documentation: "Definition of the Porting Layer for the X v11 Sample Server," "Strategies for Porting the X v11 Sample Server," "Godzilla's Guide to Porting the X v11 Sample Server"

## AUTHORS

The sample server was originally written by Susan Angebranndt, Raymond Drewry, Philip Karlton, and Todd Newman, from Digital Equipment Corporation, with support from a large cast. It has since been extensively rewritten by Keith Packard and Bob Scheifler, from MIT.

*X Version 11 Release 6*

# xset

xset—User preference utility for X

## SYNOPSIS

```
xset [-display display] [-b] [b on/off] [b [volume [pitch [duration]]]] [[-]bc]
[-c] [c on/off] [c [volume]] [[-+]fp[-+=] path[,path[,...]]] [fp default]
[fp rehash] [[-]led [integer]] [led on/off] [m[ouse] [accel_mult[/accel_div]
[threshold]]] [m[ouse] default] [p pixel color] [[-]r [keycode]] [r on/off]
[s [length [period]]] [s blank/noblank] [s expose/noexpose] [s on/off]
[s default] [s activate] [s reset] [q]
```

## DESCRIPTION

This program is used to set various user preference options of the display.

## OPTIONS

`-display` *display*

This option specifies the server to use; see X(1).

`b`

The b option controls bell volume, pitch, and duration. This option accepts up to three numerical parameters, a preceding dash (-), or an on/off flag. If no parameters are given, or the on flag is used, the system defaults will be used. If the dash or off is given, the bell will be turned off. If only one numerical parameter is given, the bell volume will be set to that value, as a percentage of its maximum. Likewise, the second numerical parameter specifies the bell pitch, in hertz, and the third numerical parameter specifies the duration in milliseconds. Note that not all hardware can vary the bell characteristics. The X server will set the characteristics of the bell as closely as it can to the user's specifications.

`bc`

The bc option controls bug compatibility mode in the server, if possible; a preceding dash (-) disables the mode; otherwise, the mode is enabled. Various pre-R4 clients pass illegal values in some protocol requests, and pre-R4 servers did not correctly generate errors in these cases. Such clients, when run against an R4 server, will terminate abnormally or otherwise fail to operate correctly. Bug compatibility mode explicitly reintroduces certain bugs into the X server, so that many such clients can still be run. This mode should be used with care; new application development should be done with this mode disabled. The server must support the MIT-SUNDRY-NONSTANDARD protocol extension in order for this option to work.

`c`

The c option controls key click. This option can take an optional value, a preceding dash (-), or an on/off flag. If no parameter or the on flag is given, the system defaults will be used. If the dash or off flag is used, key click will be disabled. If a value from 0 to 100 is given, it is used to indicate volume, as a percentage of the maximum. The X server will set the volume to the nearest value that the hardware can support.

`fp=` *path,...*

The fp= sets the font path to the entries given in the path argument. The entries are interpreted by the server, not by the client. Typically, they are directory names or font server names, but the interpretation is server-dependent.

`fp default`

The default argument causes the font path to be reset to the server's default.

`fp rehash`

The rehash argument resets the font path to its current value, causing the server to reread the font databases in the current font path. This is generally only used when adding new fonts to a font directory (after running mkfontdir to re-create the font database).

`-fp or fp-`

The -fp and fp- options remove elements from the current font path. They must be followed by a comma-separated list of entries.

fp or fp

This fp and fp options prepend and append elements to the current font path, respectively. They must be followed by a comma-separated list of entries.

led

The led option controls the keyboard LEDs. This controls the turning on or off of one or all of the LEDs. It accepts an optional integer, a preceding dash (-) or an on/off flag. If no parameter or the on flag is given, all LEDs are turned on. If a preceding dash or the flag off is given, all LEDs are turned off. If a value between 1 and 32 is given, that LED will be turned on or off depending on the existence of a preceding dash. A common LED that can be controlled is the Caps Lock LED. xset led 3 would turn led #3 on. xset -led 3 would turn it off. The particular LED values may refer to different LEDs on different hardware.

m

The m option controls the mouse parameters. The parameters for the mouse are acceleration and threshold. The acceleration can be specified as an integer, or as a simple fraction. The mouse, or whatever pointer the machine is connected to, will go acceleration times as fast when it travels more than threshold pixels in a short time. This way, the mouse can be used for precise alignment when it is moved slowly, yet it can be set to travel across the screen in a flick of the wrist when desired. One or both parameters for the m option can be omitted, but if only one is given, it will be interpreted as the acceleration. If no parameters or the flag default is used, the system defaults will be set.

p

The p option controls pixel color values. The parameters are the color map entry number in decimal, and a color specification. The root background colors may be changed on some servers by altering the entries for BlackPixel and WhitePixel. Although these are often 0 and 1, they need not be. Also, a server may choose to allocate those colors privately, in which case an error will be generated. The map entry must not be a read-only color, or an error will result.

r

The r option controls the auto-repeat. If a preceding dash or the off flag is used, auto-repeat will be disabled. If no parameters or the on flag is used, auto-repeat will be enabled. If a specific keycode is specified as a parameter, auto-repeat for that keycode is enabled or disabled.

s

The s option lets you set the screen saver parameters. This option accepts up to two numerical parameters, a blank/noblank flag, an expose/noexpose flag, an on/off flag, an activate/reset flag, or the default flag. If no parameters or the default flag is used, the system will be set to its default screen saver characteristics. The on/off flags simply turn the screen saver functions on or off. The activate flag forces activation of screen saver even if the screen saver had been turned off. The reset flag forces deactivation of screen saver if it is active. The blank flag sets the preference to blank the video (if the hardware can do so) rather than display a background pattern, while noblank sets the preference to display a pattern rather than blank the video. The expose flag sets the preference to allow window exposures (the server can freely discard window contents), while noexpose sets the preference to disable screen saver unless the server can regenerate the screens without causing exposure events. The length and period parameters for the screen saver function determines how long the server must be inactive for screen saving to activate, and the period to change the background pattern to avoid burn in. The arguments are specified in seconds. If only one numerical parameter is given, it will be used for the length.

q                                               The q option gives you information on the current settings.

These settings will be reset to default values when you log out.

Note that not all X implementations are guaranteed to honor all of these options.

## SEE ALSO

X(1), Xserver(1), xmodmap(1), xrdb(1), xsetroot(1)

## AUTHOR

Bob Scheifler (MIT Laboratory for Computer Science), David Krikorian (MIT Project Athena; X11 version)

*X Version 11 Release 6*

# xsetroot

xsetroot—Root window parameter setting utility for X

## SYNOPSIS

xsetroot [-help] [-def] [-display *display*] [-cursor *cursorfile maskfile*]
[-cursor_name *cursorname*] [-bitmap *filename*] [-mod x y] [-gray] [-grey]
[-fg *color*] [-bg *color*] [-rv] [-solid *color*] [-name *string*]

## DESCRIPTION

The setroot program allows you to tailor the appearance of the background (root) window on a workstation display running X. Normally, you experiment with xsetroot until you find a personalized look that you like, then put the xsetroot command that produces it into your X startup file. If no options are specified, or if -def is specified, the window is reset to its default state. The -def option can be specified along with other options and only the nonspecified characteristics will be reset to the default state.

Only one of the background color/tiling changing options (-solid, -gray, -grey, -bitmap, and -mod) may be specified at a time.

## OPTIONS

The various options are as follows:

-help                                           Print a usage message and exit.

-def                                            Reset unspecified attributes to the default values. (Restores the background to the familiar gray mesh and the cursor to the hollow x shape.)

-cursor *cursorfile maskfile*                   This lets you change the pointer cursor to whatever you want when the pointer cursor is outside of any window. Cursor and mask files are bitmaps (little pictures), and can be made with the bitmap(1) program. You probably want the mask file to be all black until you get used to the way masks work.

| | |
|---|---|
| -cursor_name *cursorname* | This lets you change the pointer cursor to one of the standard cursors from the cursor font. Refer to Appendix B of the X protocol for the names (except that the XC prefix is elided for this option). |
| -bitmap *filename* | Use the bitmap specified in the file to set the window pattern. You can make your own bitmap files (little pictures) using the bitmap(1) program. The entire background will be made up of repeated "tiles" of the bitmap. |
| -mod *x y* | This is used if you want a plaid-like grid pattern on your screen. *x* and *y* are integers ranging from 1 to 16. Try the different combinations. Zero and negative numbers are taken as 1. |
| -gray | Make the entire background gray. (Easier on the eyes.) |
| -grey | Make the entire background grey. |
| -fg *color* | Use *color* as the foreground color. Foreground and background colors are meaningful only in combination with -cursor, -bitmap, or -mod. |
| -bg *color* | Use *color* as the background color. |
| -rv | This exchanges the foreground and background colors. Normally the foreground color is black and the background color is white. |
| -solid *color* | This sets the background of the root window to the specified color. This option is only useful on color servers. |
| -name *string* | Set the name of the root window to *string*. There is no default value. Usually a name is assigned to a window so that the window manager can use a text representation when the window is iconified. This option is unused because you can't iconify the background. |
| -display *display* | Specifies the server to connect to; see X(1). |

## SEE ALSO

X(1), xset(1), xrdb(1)

## AUTHOR

Mark Lillibridge (MIT Project Athena)

*X Version 11 Release 6*

# XSM

xsm—X Session Manager

## SYNOPSIS

xsm [-display *display*] [-session *sessionName*] [-verbose]

## DESCRIPTION

xsm is a session manager. A session is a group of applications, each of which has a particular state. xsm allows you to create arbitrary sessions. For example, you might have a light session, a development session, or an xterminal session. Each session can have its own set of applications. Within a session, you can perform a checkpoint to save application state, or a shutdown to save state and exit the session. When you log back in to the system, you can load a specific session, and you can delete sessions you no longer want to keep.

Some session managers simply allow you to manually specify a list of applications to be started in a session. xsm is more powerful because it lets you run applications and have them automatically become part of the session. On a simple level, xsm is useful because it gives you this ability to easily define which applications are in a session. The true power of xsm, however, can be taken advantage of when more and more applications learn to save and restore their state.

## OPTIONS

| | |
|---|---|
| -display *display* | Causes xsm to connect to the specified X display. |
| -session *sessionName* | Causes xsm to load the specified session, bypassing the session menu. |
| -verbose | Turns on debugging information. |

## SETUP

### .xsession FILE

Using xsm requires a change to your .xsession file:

The last program executed by your .xsession file should be xsm. With this configuration, when the user chooses to shut down the session using xsm, the session will truly be over.

Because the goal of the session manager is to restart clients when logging into a session, your .xsession file, in general, should not directly start up applications. Rather, the applications should be started within a session. When xsm shuts down the session, xsm will know to restart these applications. Note, however, that there are some types of applications that are not "session aware". xsm enables you to manually add these applications to your session. (See the subsection titled "Client List.")

### SM_SAVE_DIR ENVIRONMENT VARIABLE

If the SM_SAVE_DIR environment variable is defined, xsm will save all configuration files in this directory. Otherwise, they will be stored in the user's home directory. Session-aware applications are also encouraged to save their checkpoint files in the SM_SAVE_DIR directory, although the user should not depend on this convention.

### DEFAULT STARTUP APPLICATIONS

The first time xsm is started, it will need to locate a list of applications to start up. For example, this list might include a window manager, a session management proxy, and an xterm. xsm will first look for the file .xsmstartup in the user's home directory. If that file does not exist, it will look for the system.xsm file that was set up at installation time. Note that xsm provides a failsafe option when the user chooses a session to start up. The failsafe option simply loads the default applications described above.

Each line in the startup file should contain a command to start an application. A sample startup file might look this:

```
<start of file>
twm
smproxy
xterm
<end of file>
```

## STARTING A SESSION

When xsm starts up, it first checks to see if the user previously saved any sessions. If no saved sessions exist, xsm starts up a set of default applications (as described above in the subsection titled "Default Startup Applications"). If at least one session exists, a Session menu is presented. The [-session sessionName] option forces the specified session to be loaded, bypassing the session menu.

### THE SESSION MENU

The Session menu presents the user with a list of sessions to choose from. The user can change the currently selected session with the mouse, or by using the up and down arrows on the keyboard. Note that sessions that are locked (that is, running on a different display) cannot be loaded or deleted.

The following operations can be performed from the Session menu:

| | |
|---|---|
| Load Session | Pressing this button will load the currently selected session. Alternatively, hitting the Return key will also load the currently selected session, or the user can double-click a session from the list. |
| Delete Session | This operation will delete the currently selected session, along with all of the application checkpoint files associated with the session. After pressing this button, the user will be asked to press the button a second time in order to confirm the operation. |
| Default/Fail Safe | xsm will start up a set of default applications (as described earlier in the section titled "Default Startup Applications"). This is useful when the user wants to start a fresh session, or if the session configuration files were corrupted and the user wants a failsafe session. |
| Cancel | Pressing this button will cause xsm to exit. It can also be used to cancel a Delete Session operation. |

## CONTROLLING A SESSION

After xsm determines which session to load, it brings up its main window, then starts up all applications that are part of the session. The title bar for the session manager's main window will contain the name of the session that was loaded.

The following options are available from xsm's main window:

| | |
|---|---|
| Client List | Pressing this button brings up a window containing a list of all clients that are in the current session. For each client, the host machine that the client is running on is presented. As clients are added and removed from the session, this list is updated to reflect the changes. The user is able to control how these clients are restarted. |
| | By pressing the View Properties button, the user can view the session management properties associated with the currently selected client. |
| | By pressing the Clone button, the user can start a copy of the selected application. |
| | By pressing the Kill Client button, the user can remove a client from the session. By selecting a restart hint from the Restart Hint menu, the user can control the restarting of a client. The following hints are available: |

- The Restart If Running hint indicates that the client should be restarted in the next session if it is connected to the session manager at the end of the current session.
- The Restart Anyway hint indicates that the client should be restarted in the next session even if it exits before the current session is terminated.
- The Restart Immediately hint is similar to the Restart Anyway hint, but in addition, the client is meant to run continuously. If the client exits, the session manager will try to restart it in the current session.
- The Restart Never hint indicates that the client should not be restarted in the next session.

Note that all X applications may not be session aware. Applications that are not session aware are ones that do not support the X Session Management Protocol or they cannot be detected by the Session Management Proxy. (See the subsection titled "The Proxy."). xsm allows the user to manually add such applications to the session. The bottom of the Client List window contains a text entry field into which application commands can be typed. Each command should go on its own line. This information will be saved with the session at checkpoint or shutdown time. When the session is restarted, xsm will restart these applications in addition to the regular session aware applications. Pressing the Done button removes the Client List window.

Session Log…

The Session Log window presents useful information about the session. For example, when a session is restarted, all of the restart commands will be displayed in the log window.

Checkpoint

By performing a checkpoint, all applications that are in the session are asked to save their state. Not every application will save its complete state, but at a minimum, the session manager is guaranteed that it will receive the command required to restart the application (along with all command-line options). A window manager participating in the session should guarantee that the applications will come back up with the same window configurations.

If the session being checkpointed was never assigned a name, the user will be required to specify a session name. Otherwise, the user can perform the checkpoint using the current session name, or a new session name can be specified. If the session name specified already exists, the user will be given the opportunity to specify a different name or to overwrite the already existing session. Note that a session that is locked can not be overwritten.

When performing a checkpoint, the user must specify a Save Type that informs the applications in the session how much state they should save.

The Local type indicates that the application should save enough information to restore the state as seen by the user. It should not affect the state as seen by other users. For example, an editor would create a temporary file containing the contents of its editing buffer, the location of the cursor, and so on.

The Global type indicates that the application should commit all of its data to permanent, globally accessible storage. For example, the editor would simply save the edited file.

The Both type indicates that the application should do both of these. For example, the editor would save the edited file, then create a temporary file with information such as the location of the cursor, and so on.

In addition to the Save Type, the user must specify an Interact Style.

The None type indicates that the application should not interact with the user while saving state.

The Errors type indicates that the application may interact with the user only if an error condition arises.

The Any type indicates that the application may interact with the user for any purpose. Note that xsm will only allow one application to interact with the user at a time.

After the checkpoint is completed, xsm will, if necessary, display a window containing the list of applications that did not report a successful save of state.

Shutdown     A shutdown provides all of the options found in a checkpoint, but, in addition, can cause the session to exit. Note that if the interaction style is Errors or Any, the user may cancel the shutdown. The user may also cancel the shutdown if any of the applications report an unsuccessful save of state. The user may choose to shut down the session with or without performing a checkpoint.

## THE PROXY

Because not all applications have been ported to support the X Session Management Protocol, a proxy service exists to enable "old" clients to work with the session manager. In order for the proxy to detect an application joining a session, one of the following must be true:

■ The application maps a top-level window containing the WM_CLIENT_LEADER property. This property provides a pointer to the client leader window that contains the WM_CLASS, WM_NAME, WM_COMMAND, and WM_CLIENT_MACHINE properties.
or

■ The application maps a top-level window that does not contain the WM_CLIENT_LEADER property. However, this top-level window contains the WM_CLASS, WM_NAME, WM_COMMAND, and WM_CLIENT_MACHINE properties.

An application that supports the WM_SAVE_YOURSELF protocol will receive a WM_SAVE_YOURSELF client message each time the session manager issues a checkpoint or shutdown. This allows the application to save state. If an application does not support the WM_SAVE_YOURSELF protocol, then the proxy will provide enough information to the session manager to restart the application (using WM_COMMAND), but no state will be restored.

## REMOTE APPLICATIONS

xsm requires a remote execution protocol in order to restart applications on remote machines. Currently, xsm supports the rstart protocol. In order to restart an application on remote machine X, machine X must have rstart installed. In the future, additional remote execution protocols may be supported.

## SEE ALSO

smproxy(1), rstart(1)

## AUTHORS

Ralph Mor (X Consortium), Jordan Brown (Quarterdeck Office Systems)

*X Version 11 Release 6*

# xsmclient

xsmclient—X session manager tester

## SYNOPSIS

xsmclient [ TBD ]

## DESCRIPTION

The xsmclient program is used to test the session manager

## AUTHOR

Ralph Mor (X Consortium)

*X Version 11 Release 6*

# xstdcmap

xstdcmap—X standard colormap utility

## SYNOPSIS

xstdcmap [-all] [-best] [-blue] [-default] [-delete *map*] [-display *display*]
[-gray] [-green] [-help] [-red] [-verbose]

## DESCRIPTION

The xstdcmap utility can be used to selectively define standard colormap properties. It is intended to be run from a user's X startup script to create standard colormap definitions in order to facilitate sharing of scarce colormap resources among clients. Where at all possible, colormaps are created with read-only allocations.

## OPTIONS

The following options may be used with xstdcmap:

| | |
|---|---|
| -all | This option indicates that all six standard colormap properties should be defined on each screen of the display. Not all screens will support visuals under which all six standard colormap properties are meaningful. xst-dcmap will determine the best allocations and visuals for the colormap properties of a screen. Any previously existing standard colormap properties will be replaced. |
| -best | This option indicates that the RGB_BEST_MAP should be defined. |
| -blue | This option indicates that the RGB_BLUE_MAP should be defined. |
| -default | This option indicates that the RGB_DEFAULT_MAP should be defined. |
| -delete *map* | This option specifies that a specific standard colormap property, or all such properties, should be removed. *map* may be one of: default, best, red, green, blue, gray, or all. |
| -display *display* | This option specifies the host and display to use; see X(1). |
| -gray | This option indicates that the RGB_GRAY_MAP should be defined. |
| -green | This option indicates that the RGB_GREEN_MAP should be defined. |
| -help | This option indicates that a brief description of the command-line arguments should be printed on the standard error. This will be done whenever an unhandled argument is given to xstdcmap. |
| -red | This option indicates that the RGB_RED_MAP should be defined. |
| -verbose | This option indicates that xstdcmap should print logging information as it parses its input and defines the standard colormap properties. |

## ENVIRONMENT

DISPLAY                                      To get default host and display number

## SEE ALSO

X(1)

## AUTHOR

Donna Converse (MIT X Consortium)

*X Version 11 Release 6*

# xterm

xterm—Terminal emulator for X

## SYNOPSIS

xterm [-*toolkitoption* ...] [-option ...]

## DESCRIPTION

The xterm program is a terminal emulator for the X Window System. It provides DEC VT102- and Tektronix 4014-compatible terminals for programs that can't use the window system directly. If the underlying operating system supports terminal resizing capabilities (for example, the SIGWINCH signal in systems derived from 4.3bsd), xterm will use the facilities to notify programs running in the window whenever it is resized.

The VT102 and Tektronix 4014 terminals all have their own windows so that you can edit text in one and look at graphics in the other at the same time. To maintain the correct aspect ratio (height/width), Tektronix graphics will be restricted to the largest box with a 4014's aspect ratio that will fit in the window. This box is located in the upper-left area of the window.

Although both windows may be displayed at the same time, one of them is considered the active window for receiving keyboard input and terminal output. This is the window that contains the text cursor. The active window can be chosen through escape sequences, the VT Options menu in the VT102 window, and the Tek Options menu in the 4014 window.

## EMULATIONS

The VT102 emulation is fairly complete, but does not support smooth scrolling, VT52 mode, the blinking character attribute nor the double-wide and double-size character sets. termcap(5) entries that work with xterm include xterm, vt102, vt100, and ansi, and xterm automatically searches the termcap file in this order for these entries and then sets the TERM and the TERMCAP environment variables.

Many of the special xterm features may be modified under program control through a set of escape sequences different from the standard VT102 escape sequences. (See the "Xterm Control Sequences" document.)

The Tektronix 4014 emulation is also fairly good. It supports 12-bit graphics addressing, scaled to the window size. Four different font sizes and five different lines types are supported. There is no write-through or defocused mode support. The Tektronix text and graphics commands are recorded internally by xterm and may be written to a file by sending the COPY escape sequence (or through the Tektronix menu, discussed later in this section). The name of the file will be COPY*yy-MM-dd.hh:mm:ss*, where *yy, MM, dd, hh, mm,* and *ss* are the year, month, day, hour, minute, and second when the COPY was performed (the file is created in the directory xterm is started in, or the home directory for a login xterm).

## OTHER FEATURES

xterm automatically highlights the text cursor when the pointer enters the window (selected) and unhighlights it when the pointer leaves the window (unselected). If the window is the focus window, then the text cursor is highlighted no matter where the pointer is. In VT102 mode, there are escape sequences to activate and deactivate an alternate screen buffer, which is the same size as the display area of the window. When activated, the current screen is saved and replaced with the alternate screen. Saving of lines scrolled off the top of the window is disabled until the normal screen is restored. The termcap(5) entry for xterm allows the visual editor vi(1) to switch to the alternate screen for editing and to restore the screen on exit.

In either VT102 or Tektronix mode, there are escape sequences to change the name of the windows. See xterm Control Sequences for details.

## OPTIONS

The xterm terminal emulator accepts all of the standard X Toolkit command line options as well as the following (if the option begins with a + instead of a -, the option is restored to its default value):

| | |
|---|---|
| -help | This causes xterm to print out a verbose message describing its options. |
| -132 | Normally, the VT102 DECCOLM escape sequence that switches between 80 and 132 column mode is ignored. This option causes the DECCOLM escape sequence to be recognized, and the xterm window will resize appropriately. |
| -ah | This option indicates that xterm should always highlight the text cursor. By default, xterm will display a hollow text cursor whenever the focus is lost or the pointer leaves the window. |
| ah | This option indicates that xterm should do text cursor highlighting based on focus. |
| -b *number* | This option specifies the size of the inner border (the distance between the outer edge of the characters and the window border) in pixels. The default is 2. |
| -cb | Set the vt100 resource cutToBeginningOfLine to False. |
| cb | Set the vt100 resource cutToBeginningOfLine to True. |
| -cc *characterclassrange:* *value*[,...] | This sets classes indicated by the given ranges to use in selecting by words. See the subsection "Character Classes." |
| -cn | This option indicates that newlines should not be cut in line-mode selections. |
| cn | This option indicates that newlines should be cut in line-mode selections. |
| -cr *color* | This option specifies the color to use for text cursor. The default is to use the same foreground color that is used for text. |
| -cu | This option indicates that xterm should work around a bug in the more(1) program that causes it to incorrectly display lines that are exactly the width of the window and are followed by a line beginning with a tab (the leading tabs are not displayed). This option is so named because it was originally thought to be a bug in the curses(3x) cursor motion package. |
| cu | This option indicates that xterm should not work around the more(3x) bug mentioned in the preceding paragraph. |
| -e *program* [ *arguments* . . . ] | This option specifies the program (and its command-line arguments) to be run in the xterm window. It also sets the window title and icon name to be the basename of the program being executed if neither -T nor -n are given on the command line. This must be the last option on the command line. |
| -fb *font* | This option specifies a font to be used when displaying bold text. This font must be the same height and width as the normal font. If only one of the normal or bold fonts is |

specified, it will be used as the normal font and the bold font will be produced by overstriking this font. The default is to do overstriking of the normal font.

|  |  |
|---|---|
| -im | Turn on the useInsertMode resource. |
| +im | Turn off the useInsertMode resource. |
| -j | This option indicates that xterm should do jump scrolling. Normally, text is scrolled one line at a time; this option allows xterm to move multiple lines at a time so that it doesn't fall as far behind. Its use is strongly recommended because it makes xterm much faster when scanning through large amounts of text. The VT100 escape sequences for enabling and disabling smooth scroll as well as the VT Options menu can be used to turn this feature on or off. |
| j | This option indicates that xterm should not do jump scrolling. |
| -ls | This option indicates that the shell that is started in the xterm window will be a login shell (that is, the first character of argv[0] will be a dash, indicating to the shell that it should read the user's .login or .profile). |
| ls | This option indicates that the shell that is started should not be a login shell (that is, it will be a normal subshell). |
| -mb | This option indicates that xterm should ring a margin bell when the user types near the right end of a line. This option can be turned on and off from the VT Options menu. |
| mb | This option indicates that margin bell should not be rung. |
| -mc*milliseconds* | This option specifies the maximum time between multiclick selections. |
| -ms *color* | This option specifies the color to be used for the pointer cursor. The default is to use the foreground color. |
| -nb *number* | This option specifies the number of characters from the right end of a line at which the margin bell, if enabled, will ring. The default is 10. |
| -rw | This option indicates that reverse-wraparound should be allowed. This allows the cursor to back up from the leftmost column of one line to the rightmost column of the previous line. This is very useful for editing long shell command lines and is encouraged. This option can be turned on and off from the VT Options menu. |
| rw | This option indicates that reverse-wraparound should not be allowed. |
| -aw | This option indicates that auto-wraparound should be allowed. This allows the cursor to automatically wrap to the beginning of the next line when it is at the rightmost position of a line and text is output. |
| aw | This option indicates that auto-wraparound should not be allowed. |
| -s | This option indicates that xterm may scroll asynchronously, meaning that the screen does not have to be kept completely up to date while scrolling. This allows xterm to run faster when network latencies are very high and is typically useful when running across a very large Internet or many gateways. |

| | |
|---|---|
| s | This option indicates that xterm should scroll synchronously. |
| -sb | This option indicates that some number of lines that are scrolled off the top of the window should be saved and that a scrollbar should be displayed so that those lines can be viewed. This option may be turned on and off from the VT Options menu. |
| sb | This option indicates that a scrollbar should not be displayed. |
| -sf | This option indicates that Sun Function Key escape codes should be generated for function keys. |
| sf | This option indicates that the standard escape codes should be generated for function keys. |
| -si | This option indicates that output to a window should not automatically reposition the screen to the bottom of the scrolling region. This option can be turned on and off from the VT Options menu. |
| si | This option indicates that output to a window should cause it to scroll to the bottom. |
| -sk | This option indicates that pressing a key while using the scrollbar to review previous lines of text should cause the window to be repositioned automatically in the normal position at the bottom of the scroll region. |
| sk | This option indicates that pressing a key while using the scrollbar should not cause the window to be repositioned. |
| -sl *number* | This option specifies the number of lines to save that have been scrolled off the top of the screen. The default is 64. |
| -t | This option indicates that xterm should start in Tektronix mode, rather than in VT102 mode. Switching between the two windows is done using the Options menus. |
| t | This option indicates that xterm should start in VT102 mode. |
| -tm *string* | This option specifies a series of terminal setting keywords followed by the characters that should be bound to those functions, similar to the stty program. Allowable keywords include: intr, quit, erase, kill, eof, eol, swtch, start, stop, brk, susp, dsusp, rprnt, flush, weras, and lnext. Control characters may be specified as ^char (for example, ^c or ^u) and ^? may be used to indicate delete. |
| -tn *name* | This option specifies the name of the terminal type to be set in the TERM environment variable. This terminal type must exist in the termcap(5) database and should have li# and co# entries. |
| -ut | This option indicates that xterm shouldn't write a record into the system log file /etc/utmp. |
| ut | This option indicates that xterm should write a record into the system log file /etc/utmp. |
| -vb | This option indicates that a visual bell is preferred over an audible one. Instead of ringing the terminal bell whenever a Ctrl+G is received, the window will be flashed. |
| vb | This option indicates that a visual bell should not be used. |
| -wf | This option indicates that xterm should wait for the window to be mapped the first time before starting the subprocess so that the initial terminal size settings and environment variables are |

correct. It is the application's responsibility to catch subsequent terminal size changes.

wf                     This option indicates that xterm show not wait before starting the subprocess.

-C                     This option indicates that this window should receive console output. This is not supported on all systems. To obtain console output, you must be the owner of the console device, and you must have read and write permission for it. If you are running X under xdm on the console screen, you may need to have the session startup and reset programs explicitly change the ownership of the console device in order to get this option to work.

-Sccn                  This option specifies the last two letters of the name of a pseudo-terminal to use in slave mode, plus the number of the inherited file descriptor. The option is parsed "%c%c%d". This allows xterm to be used as an input and output channel for an existing program and is sometimes used in specialized applications.

The following command-line arguments are provided for compatibility with older versions. They may not be supported in the next release as the X Toolkit provides standard options that accomplish the same task.

%geom                  This option specifies the preferred size and position of the Tektronix window. It is shorthand for specifying the *tekGeometry resource.

geom                   This option specifies the preferred position of the icon window. It is shorthand for specifying the *iconGeometry resource.

-T string              This option specifies the title for xterm's windows. It is equivalent to -title.

-n string              This option specifies the icon name for xterm's windows. It is shorthand for specifying the *iconName resource. Note that this is not the same as the toolkit option -name (see below). The default icon name is the application name.

-r                     This option indicates that reverse video should be simulated by swapping the foreground and background colors. It is equivalent to -rv.

-w number              This option specifies the width in pixels of the border surrounding the window. It is equivalent to -borderwidth or -bw.

The following standard X Toolkit command-line arguments are commonly used with xterm:

-bg color              This option specifies the color to use for the background of the window. The default is white.

-bd color              This option specifies the color to use for the border of the window. The default is black.

-bw number             This option specifies the width in pixels of the border surrounding the window.

-fg color              This option specifies the color to use for displaying text. The default is black.

-fn font               This option specifies the font to be used for displaying normal text. The default is fixed.

| | |
|---|---|
| `-name name` | This option specifies the application name under which resources are to be obtained, rather than the default executable filename. Name should not contain . or * characters. |
| `-title string` | This option specifies the window title string, which may be displayed by window managers if the user so chooses. The default title is the command line specified after the `-e` option, if any; otherwise, the application name. |
| `-rv` | This option indicates that reverse video should be simulated by swapping the foreground and background colors. |
| `-geometry geometry` | This option specifies the preferred size and position of the VT102 window; see X(1). |
| `-display display` | This option specifies the X server to contact; see X(1). |
| `-xrm resourcestring` | This option specifies a resource string to be used. This is especially useful for setting resources that do not have separate command-line options. |
| `-iconic` | This option indicates that xterm should ask the window manager to start it as an icon rather than as the normal window. |

## RESOURCES

The program understands all of the core X Toolkit resource names and classes as well as the following:

| | |
|---|---|
| `iconGeometry (class IconGeometry)` | Specifies the preferred size and position of the application when iconified. It is not necessarily obeyed by all window managers. |
| `iconName (class IconName)` | Specifies the icon name. The default is the application name. |
| `termName (class TermName)` | Specifies the terminal type name to be set in the TERM environment variable. |
| `title (class Title)` | Specifies a string that may be used by the window manager when displaying this application. |
| `ttyModes (class TtyModes)` | Specifies a string containing terminal setting keywords and the characters to which they may be bound. Allowable keywords include intr, quit, erase, kill, eof, eol, swtch, start, stop, brk, susp, dsusp, rprnt, flush, weras, and lnext. Control characters may be specified as ^char (for example, ^c or ^u) and ^? may be used to indicate delete. This is very useful for overriding the default terminal settings without having to do an stty every time an xterm is started. |
| `useInsertMode (class UseInsertMode)` | Force use of insert mode by adding appropriate entries to the TERMCAP environment variable. This is useful if the system termcap is broken. The default is False. |
| `utmpInhibit (class UtmpInhibit)` | Specifies whether or not xterm should try to record the user's terminal in /etc/utmp. |
| `sunFunctionKeys (class SunFunctionKeys)` | Specifies whether or not Sun Function Key escape codes should be generated for function keys instead of standard escape sequences. |
| `waitForMap (class WaitForMap)` | Specifies whether or not xterm should wait for the initial window map before starting the subprocess. The default is false. |

The following resources are specified as part of the vt100 widget (class VT100):

| | |
|---|---|
| allowSendEvents (class AllowSendEvents) | Specifies whether or not synthetic key and button events (generated using the X protocol SendEvent request) should be interpreted or discarded. The default is False, meaning they are discarded. Note that allowing such events creates a very large security hole. |
| alwaysHighlight (class AlwaysHighlight) | Specifies whether or not xterm should always display a highlighted text cursor. By default, a hollow text cursor is displayed whenever the pointer moves out of the window or the window loses the input focus. |
| appcursorDefault (class AppcursorDefault) | If true, the cursor keys are initially in application mode. The default is false. |
| appkeypadDefault (class AppkeypadDefault) | If true, the keypad keys are initially in application mode. The default is false. |
| autoWrap (class AutoWrap) | Specifies whether or not auto-wraparound should be enabled. The default is true. |
| bellSuppressTime (class BellSuppressTime) | Number of milliseconds after a bell command is sent during which additional bells will be suppressed. Default is 200. If set non-zero, additional bells will also be suppressed until the server reports that processing of the first bell has been completed; this feature is most useful with the visible bell. |
| boldFont (class BoldFont) | Specifies the name of the bold font to use instead of overstriking. |
| c132 (class C132) | Specifies whether or not the VT102 DECCOLM escape sequence should be honored. The default is false. |
| cutNewline (class CutNewline) | If false, triple-clicking to select a line does not include the Newline at the end of the line. If true, the Newline is selected. The default is true. |
| cutToBeginningOfLine (class CutToBeginningOfLine) | If false, triple-clicking to select a line selects only from the current word forward. If true, the entire line is selected. The default is true. |
| charClass (class CharClass) | Specifies comma-separated lists of character class bindings of the form [low-]high:value. These are used in determining which sets of characters should be treated the same when doing cut and paste. See the section on specifying character classes. |
| curses (class Curses) | Specifies whether or not the last column bug in more(1) should be worked around. See the -cu option for details. The default is false. |
| background (class Background) | Specifies the color to use for the background of the window. The default is white. |
| foreground (class Foreground) | Specifies the color to use for displaying text in the window. Setting the class name instead of the instance name is an easy way to have everything that would normally appear in the text color change color. The default is black. |
| cursorColor (class Foreground) | Specifies the color to use for the text cursor. The default is black. |
| eightBitInput (class EightBitInput) | If true, metacharacters input from the keyboard are presented as a single character with the eighth bit turned on. If false, metacharacters are converted into a two-character sequence with the character itself preceded by ESC. The default is true. |

`eightBitOutput`
`(class EightBitOutput)`

Specifies whether or not eight-bit characters sent from the host should be accepted as is or stripped when printed. The default is `true`.

`font (class Font)`

Specifies the name of the normal font. The default is `fixed`.

`font1 (class Font1)`

Specifies the name of the first alternative font.

`font2 (class Font2)`

Specifies the name of the second alternative font.

`font3 (class Font3)`

Specifies the name of the third alternative font.

`font4 (class Font4)`

Specifies the name of the fourth alternative font.

`font5 (class Font5)`

Specifies the name of the fifth alternative font.

`font6 (class Font6)`

Specifies the name of the sixth alternative font.

`geometry (class Geometry)`

Specifies the preferred size and position of the VT102 window.

`hpLowerleftBugCompat`
`(class HpLowerleftBugCompat)`

Specifies whether to work around a bug in HP's xdb, which ignores termcap and always sends ESC F to move to the lower-left corner. `true` causes xterm to interpret ESC F as a request to move to the lower-left corner of the screen. The default is `false`.

`internalBorder`
`(class BorderWidth)`

Specifies the number of pixels between the characters and the window border. The default is 2.

`jumpScroll`
`(class JumpScroll)`

Specifies whether or not jump scroll should be used. The default is `true`.

`loginShell`
`(class LoginShell)`

Specifies whether or not the shell to be run in the window should be started as a login shell. The default is `false`.

`marginBell`
`(class MarginBell)`

Specifies whether or not the bell should be run when the user types near the right margin. The default is `false`.

`multiClickTime`
`(class MultiClickTime)`

Specifies the maximum time in milliseconds between multiclick select events. The default is `250` milliseconds.

`multiScroll`
`(class MultiScroll)`

Specifies whether or not scrolling should be done asynchronously. The default is `false`.

`nMarginBell (class Column)`

Specifies the number of characters from the right margin at which the margin bell should be rung, when enabled.

`pointerColor`
`(class Foreground)`

Specifies the foreground color of the pointer. The default is `XtDefaultForeground`.

`pointerColorBackground`
`(class Background)`

Specifies the background color of the pointer. The default is `XtDefaultBackground`.

`pointerShape`
`(class Cursor)`

Specifies the name of the shape of the pointer. The default is `xterm`.

`resizeGravity`
`(class ResizeGravity)`

Affects the behavior when the window is resized to be taller or shorter. `NorthWest` specifies that the top line of text on the screen stay fixed. If the window is made shorter, lines are dropped from the bottom; if the window is made taller, blank lines are added at the bottom. This is compatible with the behavior in R4. `SouthWest` (the default) specifies that the bottom line of text on the screen stay fixed. If the window is made taller, additional saved lines will be scrolled down onto the screen; if the window is made shorter, lines will be scrolled off the top of the screen, and the top saved lines will be dropped.

`reverseVideo`
`(class ReverseVideo)`

Specifies whether `reverse video` should be simulated. The default is `false`.

reverseWrap
(class ReverseWrap)

Specifies whether or not reverse-wraparound should be enabled. The default is false.

saveLines
(class SaveLines)

Specifies the number of lines to save beyond the top of the screen when a scrollbar is turned on. The default is 64.

scrollBar
(class ScrollBar)

Specifies whether or not the scrollbar should be displayed. The default is false.

scrollTtyOutput
(class ScrollCond)

Specifies whether or not output to the terminal should automatically cause the scrollbar to go to the bottom of the scrolling region. The default is true.

scrollKey
(class ScrollCond)

Specifies whether or not pressing a key should automatically cause the scrollbar to go to the bottom of the scrolling region. The default is false.

scrollLines
(class ScrollLines)

Specifies the number of lines that the scroll-back and scroll-forw actions should use as a default. The default value is 1.

signalInhibit
(class SignalInhibit)

Specifies whether or not the entries in the Main Options menu for sending signals to xterm should be disallowed. The default is false.

tekGeometry
(class Geometry)

Specifies the preferred size and position of the Tektronix window.

tekInhibit
(class TekInhibit)

Specifies whether or not the escape sequence to enter Tektronix mode should be ignored. The default is false.

tekSmall (class TekSmall)

Specifies whether or not the Tektronix mode window should start in its smallest size if no explicit geometry is given. This is useful when running xterm on displays with small screens. The default is false.

tekStartup
(class TekStartup)

Specifies whether or not xterm should start up in Tektronix mode. The default is false.

titeInhibit
(class TiteInhibit)

Specifies whether or not xterm should remove ti and te termcap entries (used to switch between alternate screens on startup of many screen-oriented programs) from the TERMCAP string. If set, xterm also ignores the escape sequence to switch to the alternate screen.

translations
(class Translations)

Specifies the key and button bindings for menus, selections, "programmed strings," and so on. See the "ACTIONS" subsection, later in this section.

visualBell
(class VisualBell)

Specifies whether or not a visible bell (that is, flashing) should be used instead of an audible bell when Control-G is received. The default is false.

The following resources are specified as part of the tek4014 widget (class Tek4014):

width (class Width)

Specifies the width of the Tektronix window in pixels.

height (class Height)

Specifies the height of the Tektronix window in pixels.

fontLarge (class Font)

Specifies the large font to use in the Tektronix window.

font2 (class Font)

Specifies font number 2 to use in the Tektronix window.

font3 (class Font)

Specifies font number 3 to use in the Tektronix window.

fontSmall (class Font)

Specifies the small font to use in the Tektronix window.

initialFont (class InitialFont)

Specifies which of the four Tektronix fonts to use initially. Values are the same as for the set-tek-text action. The default is large.

ginTerminator
(class GinTerminator)

Specifies what character(s) should follow a GIN report or status report. The possibilities are none, which sends no terminating characters, CRonly, which sends CR, and CR&EOT, which sends both CR and EOT. The default is none.

The resources that may be specified for the various menus are described in the documentation for the Athena SimpleMenu widget. The name and classes of the entries in each of the menus are listed next.

The mainMenu has the following entries:

| | |
|---|---|
| securekbd (class SmeBSB) | This entry invokes the secure() action. |
| allowsends (class SmeBSB) | This entry invokes the allow-send-events(toggle) action. |
| redraw (class SmeBSB) | This entry invokes the redraw() action. |
| line1 (class SmeLine) | This is a separator. |
| suspend (class SmeBSB) | This entry invokes the send-signal(tstp) action on systems that support job control. |
| continue (class SmeBSB) | This entry invokes the send-signal(cont) action on systems that support job control. |
| interrupt (class SmeBSB) | This entry invokes the send-signal(int) action. |
| hangup (class SmeBSB) | This entry invokes the send-signal(hup) action. |
| terminate (class SmeBSB) | This entry invokes the send-signal(term) action. |
| kill (class SmeBSB) | This entry invokes the send-signal(kill) action. |
| line2 (class SmeLine) | This is a separator. |
| quit (class SmeBSB) | This entry invokes the quit() action. |

The vtMenu has the following entries:

| | |
|---|---|
| scrollbar (class SmeBSB) | This entry invokes the set-scrollbar(toggle) action. |
| jumpscroll (class SmeBSB) | This entry invokes the set-jumpscroll(toggle) action. |
| reversevideo (class SmeBSB) | This entry invokes the set-reverse-video(toggle) action. |
| autowrap (class SmeBSB) | This entry invokes the set-autowrap(toggle) action. |
| reversewrap (class SmeBSB) | This entry invokes the set-reversewrap(toggle) action. |
| autolinefeed (class SmeBSB) | This entry invokes the set-autolinefeed(toggle) action. |
| appcursor (class SmeBSB) | This entry invokes the set-appcursor(toggle) action. |
| appkeypad (class SmeBSB) | This entry invokes the set-appkeypad(toggle) action. |
| scrollkey (class SmeBSB) | This entry invokes the set-scroll-on-key(toggle) action. |
| scrollttyoutput (class SmeBSB) | This entry invokes the set-scroll-on-tty-output(toggle) action. |
| allow132 (class SmeBSB) | This entry invokes the set-allow132(toggle) action. |
| cursesemul (class SmeBSB) | This entry invokes the set-cursesemul(toggle) action. |
| visualbell (class SmeBSB) | This entry invokes the set-visualbell(toggle) action. |
| marginbell (class SmeBSB) | This entry invokes the set-marginbell(toggle) action. |
| altscreen (class SmeBSB) | This entry is currently disabled. |
| line1 (class SmeLine) | This is a separator. |
| softreset (class SmeBSB) | This entry invokes the soft-reset() action. |
| hardreset (class SmeBSB) | This entry invokes the hard-reset() action. |
| clearsavedlines (class SmeBSB)" | This entry invokes the clear-saved-lines() action. |
| line2 (class SmeLine) | This is a separator. |
| tekshow (class SmeBSB) | This entry invokes the set-visibility(tek,toggle) action. |
| tekmode (class SmeBSB) | This entry invokes the set-terminal-type(tek) action. |

vthide (class SmeBSB)                          This entry invokes the set-visibility(vt,off) action.

The fontMenu has the following entries:

fontdefault (class SmeBSB)                     This entry invokes the set-vt-font(d) action.

font1 (class SmeBSB)                           This entry invokes the set-vt-font(1) action.

font2 (class SmeBSB)                           This entry invokes the set-vt-font(2) action.

font3 (class SmeBSB)                           This entry invokes the set-vt-font(3) action.

font4 (class SmeBSB)                           This entry invokes the set-vt-font(4) action.

font5 (class SmeBSB)                           This entry invokes the set-vt-font(5) action.

font6 (class SmeBSB)                           This entry invokes the set-vt-font(6) action.

fontescape (class SmeBSB)                      This entry invokes the set-vt-font(e) action.

fontsel (class SmeBSB)                         This entry invokes the set-vt-font(s) action.

The tekMenu has the following entries:

tektextlarge (class SmeBSB)                    This entry invokes the set-tek-text(1) action.

tektext2 (class SmeBSB)                        This entry invokes the set-tek-text(2) action.

tektext3 (class SmeBSB)                        This entry invokes the set-tek-text(3) action.

tektextsmall (class SmeBSB)                    This entry invokes the set-tek-text(s) action.

line1 (class SmeLine)                          This is a separator.

tekpage (class SmeBSB)                         This entry invokes the tek-page() action.

tekreset (class SmeBSB)                        This entry invokes the tek-reset() action.

tekcopy (class SmeBSB)                         This entry invokes the tek-copy() action.

line2 (class SmeLine)                          This is a separator.

vtshow (class SmeBSB)                          This entry invokes the set-visibility(vt,toggle) action.

vtmode (class SmeBSB)                          This entry invokes the set-terminal-type(vt) action.

tekhide (class SmeBSB)                         This entry invokes the set-visibility(tek,toggle) action.

The following resources are useful when specified for the Athena Scrollbar widget:

thickness (class Thickness)                    Specifies the width in pixels of the scrollbar.

background (class Background)                   Specifies the color to use for the background of the scrollbar.

foreground (class Foreground)                  Specifies the color to use for the foreground of the scrollbar. The "thumb" of the scrollbar is a simple checkerboard pattern alternating pixels for foreground and background color.

## POINTER USAGE

Once the VT102 window is created, xterm allows you to select text and copy it within the same or other windows.

The selection functions are invoked when the pointer buttons are used with no modifiers, and when they are used with the Shift key. The assignment of the functions described in this subsection to keys and buttons may be changed through the resource database; see the "Actions" subsection later in this section.

Pointer button one (usually left) is used to save text into the cut buffer. Move the cursor to the beginning of the text, and then hold the button down while moving the cursor to the end of the region and releasing the button. The selected text is highlighted and is saved in the global cut buffer and made the PRIMARY selection when the button is released. Double-clicking selects by words. Triple-clicking selects by lines. Quadruple-clicking goes back to characters, and so on. Multiple-click is determined by the time from button up to button down, so you can change the selection unit in the middle of a selection. If the key/button bindings specify that an X selection is to be made, xterm will leave the selected text highlighted for as long as it is the selection owner.

Pointer button two (usually middle) "types" (pastes) the text from the PRIMARY selection, if any, otherwise from the cut buffer, inserting it as keyboard input.

Pointer button three (usually right) extends the current selection. (Without loss of generality, you can swap "right" and "left" everywhere in the rest of this paragraph.) If pressed while closer to the right edge of the selection than the left, it extends/contracts the right edge of the selection. If you contract the selection past the left edge of the selection, xterm assumes you really meant the left edge, restores the original selection, then extends/contracts the left edge of the selection. Extension starts in the selection unit mode that the last selection or extension was performed in; you can multiple-click to cycle through them.

By cutting and pasting pieces of text without trailing new lines, you can take text from several places in different windows and form a command to the shell, for example, or take output from a program and insert it into your favorite editor. Since the cut buffer is globally shared among different applications, you should regard it as a file whose contents you know. The terminal emulator and other text programs should be treating it as if it were a text file; that is, the text is delimited by new lines.

The scroll region displays the position and amount of text currently showing in the window (highlighted) relative to the amount of text actually saved. As more text is saved (up to the maximum), the size of the highlighted area decreases.

Clicking button one with the pointer in the scroll region moves the adjacent line to the top of the display window.

Clicking button three moves the top line of the display window down to the pointer position.

Clicking button two moves the display to a position in the saved text that corresponds to the pointer's position in the scrollbar.

Unlike the VT102 window, the Tektronix window does not allow the copying of text. It does allow Tektronix GIN mode, and in this mode the cursor will change from an arrow to a cross. Pressing any key will send that key and the current coordinate of the cross cursor. Pressing button one, two, or three will return the letters l, m, and r, respectively. If the Shift key is pressed when a pointer button is pressed, the corresponding uppercase letter is sent. To distinguish a pointer button from a key, the high bit of the character is set (but this is bit is normally stripped unless the terminal mode is RAW; see tty(4) for details).

## MENUS

Xterm has four menus: mainMenu, vtMenu, fontMenu, and tekMenu. Each menu pops up under the correct combinations of key and button presses. Most menus are divided into two sections, separated by a horizontal line. The top portion contains various modes that can be altered. A check mark appears next to a mode that is currently active. Selecting one of these modes toggles its state. The bottom portion of the menu consists of command entries; selecting one of these performs the indicated function.

The xterm menu pops up when the Control key and pointer button one are pressed in a window. The mainMenu contains items that apply to both the VT102 and Tektronix windows. The Secure Keyboard mode is used when typing in passwords or other sensitive data in an unsecured environment. (See the "SECURITY" subsection.) Notable entries in the command section of the menu are the Continue, Suspend, Interrupt, Hangup, Terminate, and Kill, which send the SIGCONT, SIGTSTP, SIGINT, SIGHUP, SIGTERM, and SIGKILL signals, respectively, to the process group of the process running under xterm (usually the shell). The Continue function is especially useful if the user has accidentally typed CTRL-Z, suspending the process.

The vtMenu sets various modes in the VT102 emulation, and is popped up when the Control key and pointer button two are pressed in the VT102 window. In the command section of this menu, the Soft Reset entry will reset scroll regions. This can be convenient when some program has left the scroll regions set incorrectly (often a problem when using VMS or TOPS-20). The Full Reset entry will clear the screen, reset tabs to every eight columns, and reset the terminal modes (such as wrap and smooth scroll) to their initial states just after xterm has finished processing the command-line options.

The fontMenu sets the font used in the VT102 window. In addition to the default font and a number of alternatives that are set with resources, the menu offers the font last specified by the Set Font escape sequence (see the document "Xterm Control Sequences") and the current selection as a font name (if the PRIMARY selection is owned).

The tekMenu sets various modes in the Tektronix emulation, and is popped up when the Control key and pointer button two are pressed in the Tektronix window. The current font size is checked in the Modes section of the menu. The PAGE entry in the Command section clears the Tektronix window.

## SECURITY

X environments differ in their security consciousness. Most servers, run under xdm, are capable of using a "magic cookie" authorization scheme that can provide a reasonable level of security for many people. If your server is only using a host-based mechanism to control access to the server (see xhost(1)), then if you enable access for a host and other users are also permitted to run clients on that same host, there is every possibility that someone can run an application that will use the basic services of the X protocol to snoop on your activities, potentially capturing a transcript of everything you type at the keyboard. This is of particular concern when you want to type in a password or other sensitive data. The best solution to this problem is to use a better authorization mechanism that host-based control, but a simple mechanism exists for protecting keyboard input in xterm.

The xterm menu (see "Menus," earlier in this section) contains a Secure Keyboard entry which, when enabled, ensures that all keyboard input is directed only to xterm (using the GrabKeyboard protocol request). When an application prompts you for a password (or other sensitive data), you can enable Secure Keyboard using the menu, type in the data, and then disable Secure Keyboard using the menu again. Only one X client at a time can secure the keyboard, so when you attempt to enable Secure Keyboard, it may fail. In this case, the bell will sound. If the Secure Keyboard succeeds, the foreground and background colors will be exchanged (as if you selected the Reverse Video entry in the Modes menu); they will be exchanged again when you exit secure mode. If the colors do not switch, then you should be very suspicious that you are being spoofed. If the application you are running displays a prompt before asking for the password, it is safest to enter secure mode before the prompt gets displayed, and to make sure that the prompt gets displayed correctly (in the new colors), to minimize the probability of spoofing. You can also bring up the menu again and make sure that a check mark appears next to the entry.

Secure Keyboard mode will be disabled automatically if your xterm window becomes iconified (or otherwise unmapped), or if you start up a reparenting window manager (that places a title bar or other decoration around the window) while in Secure Keyboard mode. (This is a feature of the X protocol that isn't easily overcome.) When this happens, the foreground and background colors will be switched back and the bell will sound in warning.

## CHARACTER CLASSES

Clicking the middle mouse button twice in rapid succession will cause all characters of the same class (for example, letters, whitespace, punctuation) to be selected. Since different people have different preferences for what should be selected (for example, should filenames be selected as a whole or only the separate subnames?), the default mapping can be overridden through the use of the charClass (class CharClass) resource.

This resource is a series of comma-separated *range:value* pairs. The range is either a single number or low-high in the range of 0 to 127, corresponding to the ASCII code for the character or characters to be set. The value is arbitrary, although the default table uses the character number of the first character occurring in the set.

The default table is

```
static int charClass[128] = {
/* NUL SOH STX ETX EOT ENQ ACK BEL */
32, 1, 1, 1, 1, 1, 1, 1,
/* BS HT NL VT NP CR SO SI */
1, 32, 1, 1, 1, 1, 1, 1,
/* DLE DC1 DC2 DC3 DC4 NAK SYN ETB */
1, 1, 1, 1, 1, 1, 1, 1,
/* CAN EM SUB ESC FS GS RS US */
1, 1, 1, 1, 1, 1, 1, 1,
/*SP!"#$%&'*/
32, 33, 34, 35, 36, 37, 38, 39,
/*()*+,-./*/
40, 41, 42, 43, 44, 45, 46, 47,
/*0 1 2 3 4 5 6 7 */
```

```
48, 48, 48, 48, 48, 48, 48, 48,
/*8 9 :;< => ?*/
48, 48, 58, 59, 60, 61, 62, 63,
/*@ABC D E F G*/
64, 48, 48, 48, 48, 48, 48, 48,
/* H I J K L M N O */
48, 48, 48, 48, 48, 48, 48, 48,
/*P QR S T UVW*/
48, 48, 48, 48, 48, 48, 48, 48,
/*XY Z [\]^ */
48, 48, 48, 91, 92, 93, 94, 48,
/*'ab c d e fg */
96, 48, 48, 48, 48, 48, 48, 48,
/*h ijklm n o */
48, 48, 48, 48, 48, 48, 48, 48,
/*p q rs tu v w */
48, 48, 48, 48, 48, 48, 48, 48,
/*x y zf jg¯ DEL */
48, 48, 48, 123, 124, 125, 126, 1};
```

For example, the string `33:48,37:48,45-47:48,64:48` indicates that the exclamation mark, percent sign, dash, period, slash, and ampersand characters should be treated the same way as characters and numbers. This is useful for cutting and pasting electronic mailing addresses and filenames.

## ACTIONS

It is possible to rebind keys (or sequences of keys) to arbitrary strings for input by changing the translations for the vt100 or tek4014 widgets. Changing the translations for events other than key and button events is not expected, and will cause unpredictable behavior. The following actions are provided for using within the vt100 or tek4014 translations resources:

| | |
|---|---|
| bell([*percent*]) | This action rings the keyboard bell at the specified percentage above or below the base volume. |
| ignore() | This action ignores the event but checks for special pointer position escape sequences. |
| insert() | This action inserts the character or string associated with the key that was pressed. |
| insert-seven-bit() | This action is a synonym for insert(). |
| insert-eight-bit() | This action inserts an eight-bit (Meta) version of the character or string associated with the key that was pressed. The exact action depends on the value of the eightBitInput resource. |
| insert-selection (*sourcename* [, ...]) | This action inserts the string found in the selection or cut buffer indicated by sourcename. Sources are checked in the order given (case is significant) until one is found. Commonly used selections include PRIMARY, SECONDARY, and CLIPBOARD. Cut buffers are typically named CUT_BUFFER0 through CUT_BUFFER7. |
| keymap(*name*) | This action dynamically defines a new translation table whose resource name is name with the suffix Keymap (case is significant). The name None restores the original translation table. |
| popup-menu(*menuname*) | This action displays the specified pop-up menu. Valid names (case is significant) include mainMenu, vtMenu, fontMenu, and tekMenu. |
| secure() | This action toggles the Secure Keyboard mode described in the "Security" subsection, and is invoked from the securekbd entry in mainMenu. |

| | |
|---|---|
| select-start() | This action begins text selection at the current pointer location. See the subsection on "Pointer Usage" for information on making selections. |
| select-extend() | This action tracks the pointer and extends the selection. It should only be bound to Motion events. |
| select-end<br>(*destname* [, ...]) | This action puts the currently selected text into all of the selections or cut buffers specified by *destname*. |
| select-cursor-start() | This action is similar to select-start except that it begins the selection at the current text cursor position. |
| select-cursor-end<br>(*destname* [, ...]) | This action is similar to select-end except that it should be used with select-cursor-start. |
| set-vt-font<br>(*d*/*1*/*2*/*3*/*4*/*5*/*6*/*e*/*s*<br>[,*normalfont* [, *boldfont*]]) | This action sets the font or fonts currently being used in the VT102 window. The first argument is a single character that specifies the font to be used: *d* or *D* indicate the default font (the font initially used when xterm was started), 1 through 6 indicate the fonts specified by the font1 through font6 resources, e or E indicate the normal and bold fonts that have been set through escape codes (or specified as the second and third action arguments, respectively), and s or S indicate the font selection (as made by programs such as xfontsel(1)) indicated by the second action argument. |
| start-extend() | This action is similar to select-start except that the selection is extended to the current pointer location. |
| start-cursor-extend() | This action is similar to select-extend except that the selection is extended to the current text cursor position. |
| string(*string*) | This action inserts the specified text string as if it had been typed. Quotation is necessary if the string contains whitespace or nonalphanumeric characters. If the string argument begins with the characters 0x, it is interpreted as a hex character constant. |
| scroll-back(count [,units]) | This action scrolls the text window backward so that text that had previously scrolled off the top of the screen is now visible. The count argument indicates the number of units (which may be page, half page, pixel, or line) by which to scroll. |
| scroll-forw(*count* [,*units*]) | This action scroll is similar to scroll-back except that it scrolls the other direction. |
| allow-send-events<br>(*on*/*off*/*toggle*) | This action set or toggles the allowSendEvents resource and is also invoked by the allowsends entry in mainMenu. |
| redraw() | This action redraws the window and is also invoked by the redraw entry in mainMenu. |
| send-signal(*signame*) | This action sends the signal named by *signame* to the xterm subprocess (the shell or program specified with the -e command-line option) and is also invoked by the suspend, continue, interrupt, hangup, terminate, and kill entries in mainMenu. Allowable signal names are (case is not significant) tstp (if supported by the operating system), suspend (same as tstp), cont (if supported by the operating system), int, hup, term, quit, alrm, alarm (same as alrm), and kill. |
| quit() | This action sends a SIGHUP to the subprogram and exits. It is also invoked by the quit entry in mainMenu. |

| | |
|---|---|
| set-scrollbar(*on*/*off*/*toggle*) | This action toggles the scrollbar resource and is also invoked by the scrollbar entry in vtMenu. |
| set-jumpscroll(*on*/*off*/*toggle*) | This action toggles the jumpscroll resource and is also invoked by the jumpscroll entry in vtMenu. |
| set-reverse-video(*on*/*off*/*toggle*) | This action toggles the reverseVideo resource and is also invoked by the reversevideo entry in vtMenu. |
| set-autowrap(*on*/*off*/*toggle*) | This action toggles automatic wrapping of long lines and is also invoked by the autowrap entry in vtMenu. |
| set-reversewrap(*on*/*off*/*toggle*) | This action toggles the reverseWrap resource and is also invoked by the reversewrap entry in vtMenu. |
| set-autolinefeed(*on*/*off*/*toggle*) | This action toggles automatic insertion of line-feeds and is also invoked by the autolinefeed entry in vtMenu. |
| set-appcursor(*on*/*off*/*toggle*) | This action toggles the handling Application Cursor Key mode and is also invoked by the appcursor entry in vtMenu. |
| set-appkeypad(*on*/*off*/*toggle*) | This action toggles the handling of Application Key-pad mode and is also invoked by the appkeypad entry in vtMenu. |
| set-scroll-on-key(*on*/*off*/*toggle*) | This action toggles the scrollKey resource and is also invoked from the scrollkey entry in vtMenu. |
| set-scroll-on-tty-output(*on*/*off*/*toggle*) | This action toggles the scrollTtyOutput resource and is also invoked from the scrolttyoutput entry in vtMenu. |
| set-allow132(*on*/*off*/*toggle*) | This action toggles the c132 resource and is also invoked from the allow132 entry in vtMenu. |
| set-cursesemul(*on*/*off*/*toggle*) | This action toggles the curses resource and is also invoked from the cursesemul entry in vtMenu. |
| set-visual-bell(*on*/*off*/*toggle*) | This action toggles the visualBell resource and is also invoked by the visualbell entry in vtMenu. |
| set-marginbell(*on*/*off*/*toggle*) | This action toggles the marginBell resource and is also invoked from the marginbell entry in vtMenu. |
| set-altscreen(*on*/*off*/*toggle*) | This action toggles between the alternate and current screens. |
| soft-reset() | This action resets the scrolling region and is also invoked from the softreset entry in vtMenu. |
| hard-reset() | This action resets the scrolling region, tabs, window size, and cursor keys, and clears the screen. It is also invoked from the hardreset entry in vtMenu. |
| clear-saved-lines() | This action does hard-reset() and also clears the history of lines saved off the top of the screen. It is also invoked from the clearsavedlines entry in vtMenu. |
| set-terminal-type(*type*) | This action directs output to either the vt or tek windows, according to the *type* string. It is also invoked by the tekmode entry in vtMenu and the vtmode entry in tekMenu. |
| set-visibility(*vt*/*tek*,*on*/*off*/*toggle*) | This action controls whether or not the vt or tek windows are visible. It is also invoked from the tekshow and vthide entries in vtMenu and the vtshow and tekhide entries in tekMenu. |
| set-tek-text(*large*/*2*/*3*/*small*) | This action sets font used in the Tektronix window to the value of the resources tektextlarge, tektext2, tektext3, and tektextsmall according to the argument. It is also by the entries of the same names as the resources in tekMenu. |
| tek-page() | This action clears the Tektronix window and is also invoked by the tekpage entry in tekMenu. |

| | |
|---|---|
| `tek-reset()` | This action resets the Tektronix window and is also invoked by the `tekreset` entry in `tekMenu`. |
| `tek-copy()` | This action copies the escape codes used to generate the current window contents to a file in the current directory beginning with the name `COPY`. It is also invoked from the `tekcopy` entry in `tekMenu`. |
| `visual-bell()` | This action flashes the window quickly. |

The Tektronix window also has the following action:

| | |
|---|---|
| `gin-press(l/L/m/M/r/R)` | This action sends the indicated graphics input code. |

The default bindings in the VT102 window are

```
Shift <KeyPress> Prior: scroll-back(1,halfpage) \n\
Shift <KeyPress> Next: scroll-forw(1,halfpage) \n\
Shift <KeyPress> Select: select-cursor-start() \
select-cursor-end(PRIMARY, CUT_BUFFER0) \n\
Shift <KeyPress> Insert: insert-selection(PRIMARY, CUT_BUFFER0) \n\
~Meta<KeyPress>: insert-seven-bit() \n\
Meta<KeyPress>: insert-eight-bit() \n\
!Ctrl <Btn1Down>: popup-menu(mainMenu) \n\
!Lock Ctrl <Btn1Down>: popup-menu(mainMenu) \n\
!Mod2 Ctrl <Btn1Down>: popup-menu(mainMenu) \n\
!Mod2 Lock Ctrl <Btn1Down>: popup-menu(mainMenu) \n\
~Meta <Btn1Down>: select-start() \n\
~Meta <Btn1Motion>: select-extend() \n\
!Ctrl <Btn2Down>: popup-menu(vtMenu) \n\
!Lock Ctrl <Btn2Down>: popup-m
```

The default bindings in the Tektronix window are

```
~Meta<KeyPress>: insert-seven-bit() \n\
Meta<KeyPress>: insert-eight-bit() \n\
!Ctrl <Btn1Down>: popup-menu(mainMenu) \n\
!Lock Ctrl <Btn1Down>: popup-menu(mainMenu) \n\
!Mod2 Ctrl <Btn1Down>: popup-menu(mainMenu) \n\
!Mod2 Lock Ctrl <Btn1Down>: popup-menu(mainMenu) \n\
!Ctrl <Btn2Down>: popup-menu(tekMenu) \n\
!Lock Ctrl <Btn2Down>: popup-menu(tekMenu) \n\
!Mod2 Ctrl <Btn2Down>: popup-menu(tekMenu) \n\
!Mod2 Lock Ctrl <Btn2Down>: popup-menu(tekMenu) \n\
Shift ~Meta<Btn1Down>: gin-press(L) \n\
~Meta<Btn1Down>: gin-press(l) \n\
Shift ~Meta<Btn2Down>: gin-press(M) \n\
~Meta<Btn2Down>: gin-press(m) \n\
Shift ~Meta<Btn3Down>: gin-press(R) \n\
~Meta<Btn3Down>: gin-press(r)
```

Below is a sample how of the `keymap()` action is used to add special keys for entering commonly typed works:

```
*VT100.Translations: #override <Key>F13: keymap(dbx)
VT100.dbxKeymap.translations: \
<Key>F14: keymap(None) \n\
<Key>F17: string("next") string(0x0d) \n\
<Key>F18: string("step") string(0x0d) \n\
<Key>F19: string("continue") string(0x0d) \n\
<Key>F20: string("print ") insert-selection(PRIMARY, CUT_BUFFER0)
```

## ENVIRONMENT

xterm sets the environment variables TERM and TERMCAP properly for the size window you have created. It also uses and sets the environment variable DISPLAY to specify which bit map display terminal to use. The environment variable WINDOWID is set to the X window id number of the xterm window.

## SEE ALSO

resize(1), X(1), pty(4), tty(4)

Xterm Control Sequences

## BUGS

Large pastes do not work on some systems. This is not a bug in xterm; it is a bug in the pseudo-terminal driver of those systems. xterm feeds large pastes to the pty only as fast as the pty will accept data, but some pty drivers do not return enough information to know if the write has succeeded.

Many of the options are not resettable after xterm starts.

Only fixed-width, character-cell fonts are supported.

This program still needs to be rewritten. It should be split into very modular sections, with the various emulators being completely separate widgets that don't know about each other. Ideally, you'd like to be able to pick and choose emulator widgets and stick them into a single control widget.

There needs to be a dialog box to allow entry of the Tek COPY filename.

## AUTHORS

Far too many people, including Loretta Guarino Reid (DEC-UEG-WSL), Joel McCormack (DEC-UEG-WSL), Terry Weissman (DEC-UEG-WSL), Edward Moy (Berkeley), Ralph R. Swick (MIT-Athena), Mark Vandevoorde (MIT-Athena), Bob McNamara (DEC-MAD), Jim Gettys (MIT-Athena), Bob Scheifler (MIT X Consortium), Doug Mink (SAO), Steve Pitschke (Stellar), Ron Newman (MIT-Athena), Jim Fulton (MIT X Consortium), Dave Serisky (HP), Jonathan Kamens (MIT-Athena)

*X Version 11 Release 6*

# Xvfb

Xvfb—Virtual framebuffer X server for X Version 11

## SYNOPSIS

Xvfb [ option ] ...

## DESCRIPTION

Xvfb is an X server that can run on machines with no display hardware and no physical input devices. It emulates a dumb framebuffer using virtual memory.

The primary use of this server is intended to be server testing. The mfb or cfb code for any depth can be exercised with this server without the need for real hardware that supports the desired depths.

A secondary use is testing clients against unusual depths and screen configurations.

## OPTIONS

In addition to the normal server options described in the Xserver(1) manual page, Xvfb accepts the following command-line switches:

-screen *screennum WxHxD*
This option creates screen *screennum* and sets its width, height, and depth to *W*, *H*, and *D*, respectively. By default, only screen 0 exists and has the dimensions 1280×1024×8.

-pixdepths *list-of-depths*
This option specifies a list of pixmap depths that the server should support in addition to the depths implied by the supported screens. list-of-depths is a space-separated list of integers that can have values from 1 to 32.

-fbdir *framebuffer-directory*
This option specifies the directory in which the memory-mapped files containing the framebuffer memory should be created. (See "Files.") This option only exists on machines that have the mmap and msync system calls.

-shmem
This option specifies that the framebuffer should be put in shared memory. The shared memory ID for each screen will be printed by the server. The shared memory is in xwd format. This option only exists on machines that support the System V shared memory interface.

If neither -shmem nor -fbdir is specified, the framebuffer memory will be allocated with malloc().

## FILES

The following file is created if the -fbdir option is given:

*framebuffer-directory*
/Xvfb_screen<n>
Memory-mapped file containing screen *n*'s framebuffer memory, one file per screen. The file is in xwd format.

## EXAMPLES

Xvfb :1 -screen 0 1600x1200x32
The server will listen for connections as server number 1, and screen 0 will be depth 32 1600×1200.

Xvfb :1 -screen 1 1600x1200x16
The server will listen for connections as server number 1, will have the default screen configuration (one screen, 1280×1024×8), and screen 1 will be depth 16 1600×1200.

Xvfb -pixdepths 3 27
-fbdir /usr/tmp
The server will listen for connections as server number 0, will have the default screen configuration (one screen, 1280×1024×8), will also support pixmap depths of 3 and 27, and will use memory-mapped files in /usr/tmp for the framebuffer.

xwud -in /usr/tmp/Xvfb screen0
Displays screen 0 of the server started by the preceding example.

## SEE ALSO

X(1), Xserver(1), xwd(1), xwud(1), XWDFile.h

## AUTHORS

David P. Wiggins (X Consortium, Inc.)

*X Version 11 Release 6*

# xvidtune

xvidtune—Video mode tuner for XFree86

## SYNOPSIS

xvidtune [ -prev j -next j -unlock j -query j -saver *suspendtime* [ *offtime* ]][*-toolkitoption* ... ]

## DESCRIPTION

Xvidtune is a client interface to the XFree86 X server video mode extension (XFree86-VidModeExtension).

When given one of the nontoolkit options, xvidtune provides a command-line interface to either switch the video mode or get/set monitor powersaver time-outs.

Without any options (or with only toolkit options) it presents the user with various buttons and sliders that can be used to interactively adjust existing video modes. It will also print the settings in a format suitable for inclusion in an XF86Config file.

## NOTE

The original mode settings can be restored by pressing the R key, and this can be used to restore a stable screen in situations where the screen becomes unreadable.

The available buttons are

Left

Right

Up

Down

Adjust the video mode so that the display will be moved in the appropriate direction:

Wider

Narrower

Shorter

Taller

Adjust the video mode so that the display size is altered appropriately:

| | |
|---|---|
| Quit | Exit the program. |
| Apply | Adjust the current video mode to match the selected settings. |
| Auto | Cause the Up/Down/Right/Left, Wider/Narrower/Shorter/Taller, Restore, and the special S3 buttons to be applied immediately. This button can be toggled. |
| Test | Temporarily switch to the selected settings. |
| Restore | Return the settings to their original values. |
| Fetch | Query the server for its current settings. |
| Show | Print the currently selected settings to stdout in XF86Config Modeline format. The primary selection is similarly set. |
| Next | Switch the Xserver to the next video mode. |
| Prev | Switch the Xserver to the previous video mode. |

For some S3-based cards (964 and 968) the following are also available:

| | |
|---|---|
| InvertVCLK | Change the VCLK invert/noninvert state. |
| EarlySC | Change the Early SC state. This affects screen wrapping. |

BlankDelay1, BlankDelay2

Set the blank delay values. This affects screen wrapping. Acceptable values are in the range 0–7. The values may be incremented or decremented with the + and - buttons, or by pressing the + or - keys in the text field.

For S3-864/868 based cards, `InvertVCLK` and `BlankDelay1` may be useful. For S3 Trio32/Trio64 cards, only `InvertVCLK` is available. At the moment there are no default settings available for these chips in the video mode extension and thus this feature is disabled in xvidtune. It can be enabled by setting any of the optional S3 commands in the screen section of XF86Config, for example, using

```
blank delay "" 0
```

## OPTIONS

xvidtune accepts the standard X Toolkit command-line options as well as the following:

-prev

Switch the Xserver to the previous video mode.

-next

Switch the Xserver to the next video mode.

-unlock

Normally, xvidtune will disable the switching of video modes via hot keys while it is running. If for some reason the program did not exit cleanly and they are still disabled, the program can be rerun with this option to reenable the mode switching key combinations.

-saver *suspendtime* [*offtime*]

Set the suspend and off screen saver inactivity time-outs. The values are in seconds.

-query

Display the monitor parameters and extended screen saver time-outs.

## SEE ALSO

XF86Config(4/5)

## AUTHORS

Kaleb S. Keithley (X Consortium), additions and modifications by Jon Tombs, David Dawes, and Joe Moss

*X Version 11 Release 6*

# xvminitoppm

xvminitoppm—Convert an XV thumbnail picture to PPM

## SYNOPSIS

xvminitoppm [*xvminipic*]

## DESCRIPTION

Reads an XV *thumbnail* picture (a miniature picture generated by the VisualSchnauzer browser) as input. Produces a portable pixmap as output.

## SEE ALSO

ppm(5), xv(1)

## AUTHOR

Copyright (c) 1993 by Ingo Wilken

*14 December 1993*

# xwd

xwd—Dump an image of an X window

## SYNOPSIS

xwd [-debug] [-help] [-nobdrs] [-out *file*] [-xy] [-frame] [-add *value*]
[-root j -id *id* j -name *name* ] [-icmap] [-screen] [-display *display*]

## DESCRIPTION

xwd is an X Window System window dumping utility. xwd allows X users to store window images in a specially formatted dump file. This file can then be read by various other X utilities for redisplay, printing, editing, formatting, archiving, image processing, and so on. The target window is selected by clicking the pointer in the desired window. The keyboard bell is rung once at the beginning of the dump and twice when the dump is completed.

## OPTIONS

| | |
|---|---|
| -display *display* | This argument allows you to specify the server to connect to; see X(1). |
| -help | Print out the Usage: command syntax summary. |
| -nobdrs | This argument specifies that the window dump should not include the pixels that compose the X window border. This is useful in situations in which you may wish to include the window contents in a document as an illustration. |
| -out *file* | This argument allows the user to explicitly specify the output file on the command line. The default is to output to standard out. |
| -xy | This option applies to color displays only. It selects XY format dumping instead of the default Z format. |
| -add *value* | This option specifies a signed value to be added to every pixel. |
| -frame | This option indicates that the window manager frame should be included when manually selecting a window. |
| -root | This option indicates that the root window should be selected for the window dump, without requiring the user to select a window with the pointer. |
| -id *id* | This option indicates that the window with the specified resource *id* should be selected for the window dump, without requiring the user to select a window with the pointer. |
| -name *name* | This option indicates that the window with the specified WM_NAME property should be selected for the window dump, without requiring the user to select a window with the pointer. |
| -icmap | Normally, the colormap of the chosen window is used to obtain RGB values. This option forces the first installed colormap of the screen to be used instead. |
| -screen | This option indicates that the GetImage request used to obtain the image should be done on the root window, rather than directly on the specified window. In this way, you can obtain pieces of other windows that overlap the specified window, and more importantly, you can capture menus or other popups that are independent windows but that appear over the specified window. |

## ENVIRONMENT

DISPLAY                                              To get default host and display number

## FILES

XWDFile.h X                                          Window dump file format definition file.

## SEE ALSO

xwud(1), xpr(1), X(1)

## AUTHORS

Tony Della Fera (Digital Equipment Corporation, MIT Project Athena) and William F. Wyatt (Smithsonian Astrophysical Observatory)

*X Version 11 Release 6*

# xwdtopnm

xwdtopnm—Convert an X11 or X10 window dump file into a portable anymap

## SYNOPSIS

xwdtopnm [*xwdfile*]

## DESCRIPTION

Reads an X11 or X10 window dump file as input. Produces a portable anymap as output. The type of the output file depends on the input file. If it's black and white, a pbm file is written; if it's grayscale, a pgm file, else a ppm file. The program tells you which type it is writing.

Using this program, you can convert anything on an X workstation's screen into an anymap. Just display whatever you're interested in, do an xwd, run it through xwdtopnm, and then use pnmcut to select the part you want.

## BUGS

I haven't tested this tool with very many configurations, so there are probably bugs. Please let me know if you find any.

## SEE ALSO

pnmtoxwd(1), pnm(5), xwd(1)

## AUTHOR

Copyright (c) 1989, 1991 by Jef Poskanzer.

*11 January 1991*

# xwininfo

xwininfo—Window information utility for X

## SYNOPSIS

xwininfo [-help] [-id *id*] [-root] [-name *name*] [-int] [-children] [-tree]
[-stats] [-bits] [-events] [-size] [-wm] [-shape] [-frame] [-all] [-english]
[-metric] [-display *display*]

## DESCRIPTION

xwininfo is a utility for displaying information about windows. Various information is displayed depending on which options are selected. If no options are chosen, -stats is assumed.

The user has the option of selecting the target window with the mouse (by clicking any mouse button in the desired window) or by specifying its window id on the command line with the -id option. Or instead of specifying the window by its id number, the -name option may be used to specify which window is desired by name. There is also a special -root option to quickly obtain information on the screen's root window.

## OPTIONS

| | |
|---|---|
| -help | Print out the Usage: command syntax summary. |
| -id id | This option allows the user to specify a target window id on the command line rather than using the mouse to select the target window. This is very useful in debugging X applications where the target window is not mapped to the screen or where the use of the mouse might be impossible or interfere with the application. |
| -name name | This option allows the user to specify that the window name is the target window on the command line rather than using the mouse to select the target window. |
| -root | This option specifies that X's root window is the target window. This is useful in situations where the root window is completely obscured. |
| -int | This option specifies that all X window ids should be displayed as integer values. The default is to display them as hexadecimal values. |
| -children | This option causes the root, parent, and children windows' ids and names of the selected window to be displayed. |
| -tree | This option is like -children but displays all children recursively. |
| -stats | This option causes the display of various attributes pertaining to the location and appearance of the selected window. Information displayed includes the location of the window, its width and height, its depth, border width, class, colormap id if any, map state, backing-store hint, and location of the corners. |
| -bits | This option causes the display of various attributes pertaining to the selected window's raw bits and how the selected window is to be stored. Displayed information includes the selected window's bit gravity, window gravity, backing-store hint, backing-planes value, backing pixel, and whether or not the window has save-under set. |
| -events | This option causes the selected window's event masks to be displayed. Both the event mask of events wanted by some client and the event mask of events not to propagate are displayed. |
| -size | This option causes the selected window's sizing hints to be displayed. Displayed information includes the following: for both the normal size hints and the zoom size hints, the user supplied location, if any; the program supplied location, if any; the user supplied size, if any; the program supplied size, if any; |

the minimum size, if any; the maximum size, if any; the resize increments, if any; and the minimum and maximum aspect ratios, if any.

-wm                         This option causes the selected window's window manager hints to be displayed. Information displayed may include whether or not the application accepts input, what the window's icon window # and name is, where the window's icon should go, and what the window's initial state should be.

-shape                      This option causes the selected window's window and border shape extents to be displayed.

-frame                      This option causes window manager frames to be considered when manually selecting windows.

-metric                     This option causes all individual height, width, and x and y positions to be displayed in millimeters as well as number of pixels, based on what the server thinks the resolution is. Geometry specifications that are in +x+y form are not changed.

-english                    This option causes all individual height, width, and x and y positions to be displayed in inches (and feet, yards, and miles if necessary) as well as number of pixels. -metric and -english may both be enabled at the same time.

-all                        This option is a quick way to ask for all information possible.

-display *display*          This option allows you to specify the server to connect to; see x(1).

## EXAMPLE

The following is a sample summary taken with no options specified:

```
xwininfo: Window id: 0x60000f "xterm" Absolute upper-left X: 2
Absolute upper-left Y: 85 Relative upper-left X: 0 Relative upper-left Y: 25
Width: 579 Height: 316 Depth: 8 Visual Class: PseudoColor Border width: 0
Class: InputOutput Colormap: 0x27 (installed) Bit Gravity State:
NorthWestGravity Window Gravity State: NorthWestGravity Backing Store State:
NotUseful Save Under State: no Map State: IsViewable Override Redirect State:
no Corners: +2+85 -699+85 -699-623 +2-623 -geometry 80x24+0+58
```

## ENVIRONMENT

DISPLAY                                  To get the default host and display number

## SEE ALSO

X(1), xprop(1)

## BUGS

Using -stats -bits shows some redundant information.

The -geometry string displayed must make assumptions about the window's border width and the behavior of the application and the window manager. As a result, the location given is not always correct.

## AUTHOR

Mark Lillibridge (MIT Project Athena)

# xwud

xwud—Image displayer for X

## SYNOPSIS

xwud [-in *file*] [-noclick] [-geometry *geom*] [-display *display*]
[-new] [-std <maptype>] [-raw] [-vis <vis-type-or-id>] [-help] [-rv]
[-plane *number*] [-fg *color*] [-bg *color*]

## DESCRIPTION

xwud is an X Window System image undumping utility. xwud allows X users to display in a window an image saved in a specially formatted dump file, such as produced by xwd(1).

## OPTIONS

| | |
|---|---|
| -bg *color* | If a bitmap image (or a single plane of an image) is displayed, this option can be used to specify the color to display for the 0 bits in the image. |
| -display *display* | This option allows you to specify the server to connect to; see x(1). |
| -fg *color* | If a bitmap image (or a single plane of an image) is displayed, this option can be used to specify the color to display for the 1 bits in the image. |
| -geometry *geom* | This option allows you to specify the size and position of the window. Typically, you will only want to specify the position, and let the size default to the actual size of the image. |
| -help | Print out a short description of the allowable options. |
| -in *file* | This option enables the user to explicitly specify the input file on the command line. If no input file is given, the standard input is assumed. |
| -new | This option forces creation of a new colormap for displaying the image. If the image characteristics happen to match those of the display, this can get the image on the screen faster, but at the cost of using a new colormap (which on most displays will cause other windows to go Technicolor). |
| -noclick | Clicking any button in the window will terminate the application, unless this option is specified. Termination can always be achieved by typing q, Q, or Ctrl+C. |
| -plane *number* | You can select a single bit plane of the image to display with this option. Planes are numbered with zero being the least significant bit. This option can be used to figure out which plane to pass to xpr(1) for printing. |
| -raw | This option forces the image to be displayed with whatever color values happen to currently exist on the screen. This option is mostly useful when undumping an image back onto the same screen that the image originally came from, while the original windows are still on the screen, and results in getting the image on the screen faster. |
| -rv | If a bitmap image (or a single plane of an image) is displayed, this option forces the foreground and background colors to be swapped. This may be needed when displaying a bitmap image that has the color sense of pixel values 0 and 1 reversed from what they are on your display. |

| | |
|---|---|
| -std *maptype* | This option causes the image to be displayed using the specified standard colormap. The property name is obtained by converting the type to uppercase, prepending RGB, and appending MAP. Typical types are best, default, and gray. See xstd-cmap(1) for one way of creating standard colormaps. |
| -vis *vis-type-or-id* | This option allows you to specify a particular visual or visual class. The default is to pick the "best" one. A particular class can be specified: StaticGray, GrayScale, StaticColor, PseudoColor, DirectColor, or TrueColor. Or Match can be specified, meaning use the same class as the source image. Alternatively, an exact visual id (specific to the server) can be specified, either as a hexadecimal number (prefixed with 0x) or as a decimal number. Finally, default can be specified, meaning to use the same class as the colormap of the root window. Case is not significant in any of these strings. |

## ENVIRONMENT

| | |
|---|---|
| DISPLAY | To get default display |

## FILES

| | |
|---|---|
| XWDFile.h | X Window dump file format definition file |

## SEE ALSO

xwd(1), xpr(1), xstdcmap(1), X(1)

## AUTHOR

Bob Scheifler (MIT X Consortium)

*X Version 11 Release 6*

# ybmtopbm

ybmtopbm—Convert a Bennet Yee "face" file into a portable bitmap

## SYNOPSIS

ybmtopbm [*facefile*]

## DESCRIPTION

Reads a file acceptable to the face and xbm programs by Bennet Yee (bsy+@cs.cmu.edu). Writes a portable bitmap as output.

## SEE ALSO

pbmtoybm(1), pbm(5), face(1), face(5), xbm(1)

## AUTHOR

Copyright (c) 1991 by Jamie Zawinski and Jef Poskanzer.

*6 March 1990*

# ytalk

ytalk—A multiuser chat program.

## SYNOPSIS

ytalk [-x] username...

## DESCRIPTION

ytalk (V3.0 Patch Level 1) is in essence a multiuser chat program. It works almost exactly like the UNIX talk program and even communicates with the same talk daemon(s), but YTalk allows for multiple connections.

The username field may be formatted in several different ways:

| | |
|---|---|
| name | Some user on your machine |
| name@host | Some user on a different machine |
| name#tty | Some user on a particular terminal |
| name#tty@host | Some user on a particular tty on a different machine |
| name@host#tty | Same as name#tty@host |

You can specify multiple usernames on the command line, for example,

ytalk george fred@hissun.edu marc@grumpy.cc

The -x option disables the X11 interface (described below).

For each user on the command line, ytalk will attempt to connect to the talk daemon on the specified user's host and determine if that user has left an invitation for you to call. If not, ytalk leaves an invitation for him and tells his talk daemon to send an announcement to his screen. There is not yet a dedicated ytalk daemon, but there will be. Right now, ytalk is able to communicate with both existing versions of UNIX talk daemons. For any particular host, ytalk will attempt to communicate with a talk daemon the caller's host also supports. If the two hosts have no daemon in common, then UNIX talk will not function at all, but a connection is possible through (and only through) ytalk.

After a connection has been established between two users, they can chat back and forth to their hearts' content. The connection is terminated when one of them hits Control-C or selects Quit from the main menu.

ytalk is perfectly compatible with UNIX talk and they can even converse with each other without any problems. However, many of the features of ytalk can only operate when you are connected to a user who is also using ytalk. For the rest of this document, it will be assumed that all connected users are using ytalk unless otherwise stated.

If you specified more than one user on the ytalk command line, then ytalk will process and add each user to the conversation as they respond to your invitation. As each new user enters the conversation, the screen is further subdivided into smaller and smaller windows, one for each connected user. Right now, the number of connected users is limited by the number of lines on your terminal (or window), for each connected user needs at least three lines.

ytalk does implement primitive support of the X11 Windowing System. If the environment variable DISPLAY is set, then ytalk attempts to connect to that X server. Further details about the X11 interface (and how to turn it off) are given later in this section.

As each new user is added to the conversation, ytalk will transmit information about that user to all other connected ytalk users so that their screens will also subdivide and incorporate the new user. If the new user is using UNIX talk, then information about him will NOT be transmitted, as his screen would be unable to accept multiple connections. I have given brief thought to allowing at least the output of UNIX talk users to be transmitted to all connected ytalk users, but I have not written any code to do so. Note that even though UNIX talk cannot handle multiple connections, it is still possible for ytalk to handle multiple UNIX "talk" connections. For example, george (using ytalk) could communicate with fred and joe (both using UNIX talk), but fred and joe would be unaware of each other. The best way to understand the limitations that UNIX "talk" places on ytalk is to test various connections between the two and see how things work.

## ESCAPE MENU

Whenever you are using ytalk, you can hit the Escape key to bring up a menu that at this moment has these options:

| | |
|---|---|
| a | Add a user |
| d | Delete a user |
| o | Options |
| s | Shell |
| u | User list |
| w | Output user to file |
| q | Quit |

By choosing option a, you are given the opportunity to type the name of any user you wish to include into the conversation. Again, YTALK will accept an invitation from that user if an invitation exists, or will leave an invitation and ring the given user.

By choosing option d, you can select the name of a connection to terminate.

By choosing option o, you can view and/or modify any of the ytalk options. (See the "Options" subsection for a list of ytalk options.)

By choosing option s, you can invoke a shell in your ytalk window. All other users will see what happens in your shell. ytalk will automatically resize your window down to the size of the smallest window you are connected to, in order to ensure that all users always see the same thing.

The u option displays a list of connected and unconnected users, as well as their window sizes and what version of talk software they are running.

By choosing option w, you can select any connected user and type the name of a file, and all further output from that user will be dumped to the specified file. The file, if it exists, will be overwritten. If you choose w and the same user again, further output to the file will be terminated.

Oh, one other thing: when user A attempts to ytalk to user B, but user B is already ytalking with user C, user A's ytalk program will realize that user B is already using ytalk, and will communicate with user B's ytalk program directly in order to initialize the conversation. User B will see a nice windowed message such as

```
Do you wish to talk with user A?
```

and he will be prompted for a yes/no answer. This, in my opinion, is much preferable to blitting the announcement message and messing up user B's screen.

## RUNTIME OPTIONS

When you select Options from the main menu, you are given the opportunity to edit the ytalk options. The current options are

| | |
|---|---|
| s | Turn scrolling [off/on] |
| w | Turn word-wrap [off/on] |
| i | Turn auto-import [off/on] |
| v | Turn auto-invite [off/on] |
| r | Turn auto-rering [off/on] |
| a | Turn asides [off/on] |

If scrolling is turned on, then a user's window will scroll when he reaches the bottom, instead of wrapping back around to the top.

If word-wrap is turned on, then any word that would overextend the right margin will be automatically moved to the next line on your screen.

If auto-import is turned on, then ytalk will assume that you wish to talk to any users that connect to other ytalk users that are connected to you. That last sentence does make sense; try again. ytalk will add these users to your session automatically, without asking you for verification.

If auto-invite is turned on, then ytalk will automatically accept any connection requested by another user and add the user to your session. You will not be asked for verification.

If auto-rering is turned on, then ytalk will automatically re-ring any user who does not respond to your invitation within 30 seconds. You will not be asked for verification.

If asides is turned on (it may not be available), then keyboard input received while the input focus is in a specific user's window will only be sent to that user. (See the "X11 Interface" subsection.)

Any of these options can be set to your preference in your .ytalkrc file, as described in the next subsection.

## YTALK STARTUP FILE

If your home directory contains a file named .ytalkrc, then ytalk will read this file while starting up. All ytalk runtime options, as well as some startup options, can be set in this file.

## SETTING BOOLEAN OPTIONS

Boolean options can be preset with the following syntax:

turn *option* [off ¦ on]

where *option* is one of scrolling, word-wrap, auto-import, auto-invite, auto-rering, asides, or X. Setting these options works just like described earlier in this section. Turning X on or off will enable or disable the X11 Interface. For example, one could enable word-wrap with the line:

turn word-wrap on

## SETTING READDRESS MODES

The purpose of readdressing is to allow ytalk connections across point-to-point network gateways where the local machines know themselves by a different address (and typically hostname) than the remote machines. The basic syntax of a readdress command is this:

readdress *from-address to-address domain*

The readdress statement simply makes a claim that the machine(s) in *domain* communicate with the machine(s) at *from address* by sending a packet to *to-address*. Because most users have no use for this whatsoever, I'll describe it only briefly.

THIS IS NOT ROUTING. For example, my machine at home is connected via PPP to the network at my office. My machine at home thinks its Ethernet address is 192.188.253.1 and its hostname is "talisman.com". The network at my office has the address 192.67.141.0. When I'm connected via PPP, my home machine is placed into the office network as address 192.67.141.9 with hostname "talisman.austin.eds.com".

ytalk needs to know that if it is running on domain 192.67.141.0 and receives packets from 192.188.253.1 that it should respond to 192.67.141.9, not 192.188.253.1. Right? Right. Okay, okay, okay. I put this line into my .ytalkrc on both ends:

readdress talisman talisman.austin.eds.com 192.67.141.0

On my home end, this translates to

readdress 192.188.253.1 192.67.141.9 192.67.141.0

which tells my home machine to advertise itself as 192.67.141.9 instead of 192.188.253.1 when ytalking to machines on the network 192.67.141.0. On the office end, the readdress command translates to

readdress 192.67.141.9 192.67.141.9 192.67.141.0

which the office machines basically ignore.

Enough. For more information on how to use this, consult the source code or send me a letter. :-)

## X11 INTERFACE

If the DISPLAY environment variable is defined when ytalk starts up, then ytalk will attempt to communicate with that X server. A window will be created for you and each user you are connected to. The X11 Interface can be disabled either by specifying -x on the command line or by putting this line into your .ytalkrc file:

turn X off

A window is created for each individual user in the conversation. If the input focus is in the main window (the one with ytalk in the title bar) then anything typed will be sent to all connected users. If the input focus is in one of the user's windows, then anything typed will be sent as an aside to only that user. If the aside option is turned off, then ytalk will beep and not accept anything typed when the input focus is not in the main window.

ytalk consults the X11 Resource Database for these user-definable configuration options:

ytalk.display: X server to connect to, defaulting to the DISPLAY environment variable.

ytalk.reverse: Reverse black/white pixels.

ytalk.font: Font to use, defaulting to 9x15.

ytalk.geometry: Window size, defaulting to 80x24.

## FUTURE WORK

Work is being done on the following ideas:

- Private conversations that do not get interrupted or transmitted to all ytalk connections
- A dedicated ytalk daemon

## FILES

| | |
|---|---|
| /usr/local/etc/ytalkrc | Systemwide defaults file. |
| $HOME/.ytalkrc | User's local configuration file. This file overrides options set in the system ytalkrc file. |

## AUTHOR

Britt Yenne (yenne@austin.eds.com)

## CONTRIBUTORS

Special thanks to Carl Edman for numerous code patches, beta testing, and comments. I think this guy spends as much time on ytalk as I do. Special thanks to Tobias Hahn and Geoff W. for beta testing and suggestions. Thanks to Sitaram Ramaswamy for the original ytalk man page. Thanks to Magnus Hammerin for Solaris 2.* support. Thanks to Jonas Yngvesson for aside messages in X. Thanks to Andreas Stolcke for fixing the X resource database calls. Thanks to John Vanderpool, Shih-Chen Huang, Andrew Myers, Duncan Sinclair, Evan McLean, and Larry Schwimmer for comments and ideas. The README file shipped with ytalk gives detailed attributions.

## BUGS

If you have any ideas, comments, or questions, I'd be happy to hear from you at ytalk@austin.eds.com.

*24 June 1993*

# yuvplittoppm

yuvplittoppm—Convert a Y-, a U-, and a V- file into a portable pixmap.

## SYNOPSIS

yuvsplittoppm *basename* width height [-ccir601]

## DESCRIPTION

Reads three files, containing the YUV components, as input. These files are basename.Y, basename.U and basename.V. Produces a portable pixmap on stdout.

Since the YUV files are raw files, the dimensions width and height must be specified on the command line.

## OPTIONS

-ccir601    Assumes that the YUV triplets are scaled into the smaller range of the CCIR 601 (MPEG) standard. Otherwise, the JFIF (JPEG) standard is assumed.

## SEE ALSO

ppmtoyuvsplit(1), yuvtoppm(1), ppm(5)

## AUTHOR

Marcel Wijkstra (<wijkstra@fwi.uva.nl>), based on ppmtoyuvsplit

*26 August 1993*

# yuvtoppm

yuvtoppm—Convert Abekas YUV bytes into a portable pixmap

## SYNOPSIS

yuvtoppm *width* height [*imagedata*]

## DESCRIPTION

Reads raw Abekas YUV bytes as input. Produces a portable pixmap as output. The input file is just YUV bytes. You have to specify the width and height on the command line, since the program obviously can't get them from the file. The maxval is assumed to be 255.

## SEE ALSO

ppmtoyuv(1), ppm(5)

## AUTHOR

Marc Boucher (<marc@PostImage.COM>)), based on Example Conversion Program, *A60/A64 Digital Video Interface Manual*, page 69. Copyright (c) 1991 by DHD PostImage, Inc. Copyright (c) 1987 by Abekas Video Systems, Inc.

*25 March 1991*

# zcmp, zdiff

zcmp, zdiff—Compare compressed files

## SYNOPSIS

zcmp [ cmp_options ] file1 [ file2 ]
zdiff [diff_options ] file1 [ file2 ]

## DESCRIPTION

Zcmp and zdiff are used to invoke the cmp or the diff program on compressed files. All options specified are passed directly to cmp or diff. If only one file is specified, then the files compared are file1 and an uncompressed file1.gz. If two files are specified, then they are uncompressed if necessary and fed to cmp or diff. The exit status from cmp or diff is preserved.

## SEE ALSO

cmp(1), diff(1), zmore(1), zgrep(1), znew(1), zforce(1), gzip(1), gzexe(1)

## BUGS

Messages from the cmp or diff programs refer to temporary filenames instead of those specified.

# zeisstopnm

zeisstopnm—Convert a Zeiss confocal file into a portable anymap

## SYNOPSIS

zeisstopnm [-pgm j -ppm][zeissfile]

## DESCRIPTION

Reads a Zeiss confocal file as input. Produces a portable anymap as output. The type of the output file depends on the input file—if it's grayscale, a pgm file will be produced; otherwise, it will be a ppm file. The program tells you which type it is writing.

## OPTIONS

| | |
|---|---|
| -pgm | Force the output to be a pgm file |
| -ppm | Force the output to be a ppm file |

## SEE ALSO

pnm(5)

## AUTHOR

Copyright (c) 1993 by Oliver Trepte.

*15 June 1993*

# zforce

zforce—Force a .gz extension on all gzip files

## SYNOPSIS

zforce [ name ... ]

## DESCRIPTION

zforce forces a .gz extension on all gzip files so that gzip will not compress them twice. This can be useful for files with names truncated after a file transfer. On systems with a 14-character limitation on filenames, the original name is truncated to make room for the .gz suffix. For example, 12345678901234 is renamed to 12345678901.gz. A filename such as foo.tgz is left intact.

## SEE ALSO

gzip(1), znew(1), zmore(1), zgrep(1), zdiff(1), gzexe(1)

# zgrep

zgrep—Search possibly compressed files for a regular expression

## SYNOPSIS

zgrep [ grep_options ] [-e] *pattern filename...*

## DESCRIPTION

zgrep is used to invoke the grep on compressed or gziped files. All options specified are passed directly to grep. If no file is specified, then the standard input is decompressed if necessary and fed to grep. Otherwise, the given files are uncompressed if necessary and fed to grep.

If zgrep is invoked as zegrep or zfgrep, then egrep or fgrep is used instead of grep. If the GREP environment variable is set, zgrep uses it as the grep program to be invoked. For example,

for sh: GREP=fgrep zgrep string files for csh: (setenv GREP fgrep; zgrep string files)

## AUTHOR

Charles Levert (charles@comm.polymtl.ca)

## SEE ALSO

grep(1), egrep(1), fgrep(1), zdiff(1), zmore(1), znew(1), zforce(1), gzip(1), gzexe(1)

# zmore

zmore—File perusal filter for crt viewing of compressed text

## SYNOPSIS

zmore [ name ... ]

## DESCRIPTION

zmore is a filter that allows examination of compressed or plain text files one screenful at a time on a soft-copy terminal. zmore works on files compressed with compress, pack, or gzip, and also on uncompressed files. If a file does not exist, zmore looks for a file of the same name with the addition of a .gz, .z, or .Z suffix.

zmore normally pauses after each screenful, printing -More- at the bottom of the screen. If the user then types a carriage return, one more line is displayed. If the user hits a space, another screenful is displayed. Other possibilities are enumerated later.

zmore looks in the file /etc/termcap to determine terminal characteristics, and to determine the default window size. On a terminal capable of displaying 24 lines, the default window size is 22 lines. To use a pager other than the default more, set environment variable PAGER to the name of the desired program, such as less.

Other sequences that may be typed when zmore pauses, and their effects, are as follows (i is an optional integer argument, defaulting to 1) :

| | |
|---|---|
| *i* <space> | Display i more lines, (or another screenful if no argument is given). |
| ^D | Display 11 more lines (a "scroll"). If i is given, then the scroll size is set to i. |
| d | Same as ^D (control-D) |

| | |
|---|---|
| i z | Same as typing a space except that i, if present, becomes the new window size. Note that the window size reverts back to the default at the end of the current file. |
| i s | Skip *i* lines and print a screenful of lines. |
| i f | Skip *i* screenfuls and print a screenful of lines. |
| q or Q | Quit reading the current file; go on to the next (if any). |
| e or q | When the prompt -More-(Next file: *file*) is printed, this command causes zmore to exit. |
| s | When the prompt -More-(Next file: *file*) is printed, this command causes zmore to skip the next file and continue. |
| = | Display the current line number. |
| i /expr | Search for the *i*th occurrence of the regular expression expr. If the pattern is not found, zmore goes on to the next file (if any). Otherwise, a screenful is displayed, starting two lines before the place where the expression was found. The user's erase and kill characters may be used to edit the regular expression. Erasing back past the first column cancels the search command. |
| i n | Search for the *i*th occurrence of the last regular expression entered. |
| !command | Invoke a shell with *command*. The character ! in *command* is replaced with the previous shell command. The sequence \! is replaced by !. |
| :q or :Q | Quit reading the current file; go on to the next (if any) (same as q or Q). |
| . | (dot) Repeat the previous command. |

The commands take effect immediately; that is, it is not necessary to type a carriage return. Up to the time when the command character itself is given, the user may hit the line kill character to cancel the numerical argument being formed. In addition, the user may hit the erase character to redisplay the -More- message.

At any time when output is being sent to the terminal, the user can hit the quit key (normally Control–n). zmore will stop sending output, and will display the usual -More- prompt. The user may then enter one of the preceding commands in the normal manner. Unfortunately, some output is lost when this is done because any characters waiting in the terminal's output queue are flushed when the quit signal occurs.

The terminal is set to noecho mode by this program so that the output can be continuous. What you type will thus not show on your terminal, except for the / and ! commands.

If the standard output is not a teletype, then zmore acts just like zcat, except that a header is printed before each file.

## FILES

/etc/termcap      Terminal database

## SEE ALSO

more(1), gzip(1), zdiff(1), zgrep(1), znew(1), zforce(1), gzexe(1)

# znew

znew—Recompress Ẑ files to GZ files

## SYNOPSIS

znew [ -ftv9PK] [ name.Z ... ]

## DESCRIPTION

znew recompresses files from Z (compress) format to GZ (gzip) format. If you want to recompress a file already in gzip format, rename the file to force a .Z extension, then apply znew.

## OPTIONS

| | |
|---|---|
| -f | Force recompression from Z to GZ format even if a GZ file already exists. |
| -t | Test the new files before deleting originals. |
| -v | Verbose. Display the name and percentage reduction for each file compressed. |
| -9 | Use the slowest compression method (optimal compression). |
| -P | Use pipes for the conversion to reduce disk space usage. |
| -K | Keep a Z file when it is smaller than the GZ file. |

## SEE ALSO

gzip(1), zmore(1), zdiff(1), zgrep(1), zforce(1), gzexe(1), compress(1)

## BUGS

znew does not maintain the timestamp with the -P option if cpmod(1) is not available and touch(1) does not support the -r option.

# Part II:
# System Calls

# intro

intro—Introduction to system calls

## DESCRIPTION

This chapter describes the Linux system calls.

## CALLING DIRECTLY

In most cases, it is unnecessary to invoke a system call directly, but there are times when the standard C library does not implement a nice function call for you.

## SYNOPSIS

```
#include <linux/unistd.h>
```

A _syscall macro

Desired system call

## SETUP

The important thing to know about a system call is its prototype. You need to know how many arguments, their types, and the function return type. Six macros make the actual call into the system easier. They have the form

```
syscallX(type,name,type1,arg1,type2,arg2,...)
```

where

| | |
|---|---|
| *X* | 0–5, which are the number of arguments taken by the system call |
| *type* | The return type of the system call |
| *name* | The name of the system call |
| *typeN* | The Nth argument's type |
| *argN* | The name of the Nth argument |

These macros create a function called *name* with the arguments you specify. Once you include _syscall() in your source file, you call the system call by *name*.

## EXAMPLE

```
{
        struct sysinfo s_info;
        int error;

        error = sysinfo(&s_info);
        printf("code error = %d\n", error);
        printf("Uptime = %ds\nLoad: 1 min %d / 5 min %d / 15 min %d\n"
                "RAM: total %d / free %d / shared %d\n"
                "Memory in buffers = %d\nSwap: total %d / free  %d\n"
                "Number of processes = %d\n",
            s_info.uptime, s_info.loads[0],
            s_info.loads[1], s_info.loads[2],
            s_info.totalram, s_info.freeram,
            s_info.sharedram, s_info.bufferram,
            s_info.totalswap, s_info.freeswap,
            s_info.procs);
        return(0);
}
```

## SAMPLE OUTPUT

```
code error = 0
uptime = 502034s
Load: 1 min 13376 / 5 min 5504 / 15 min 1152
RAM: total 15343616 / free 827392 / shared 8237056
Memory in buffers = 5066752
Swap: total 27881472 / free 24698880
Number of processes = 40
```

## NOTES

The _syscall() macros *do not* produce a prototype. You might have to create one, especially for C++ users.

System calls are not required to return only positive or negative error codes. You need to read the source to be sure how it will return errors. Usually, it is the negative of a standard error code, for example, -EPERM. The _syscall() macros will return the result *r* of the system call when *r* is nonnegative, but will return -1 and set the variable errno to -*r* when *r* is negative.

Some system calls, such as mmap, require more than five arguments. These are handled by pushing the arguments on the stack and passing a pointer to the block of arguments.

When defining a system call, the argument types *must* be passed by value or by pointer (for aggregates such as structs).

## FILES

/usr/include/linux/unistd.h

## AUTHORS

Look at the header of the manual page for the author(s) and copyright conditions. Note that these can be different from page to page.

*Linux 1.2.13, 22 May 1996*

# exit

exit—Terminate the current process

## SYNOPSIS

```
#include <unistd.h>
void exit(int status);
```

## DESCRIPTION

exit terminates the calling process immediately. Any open file descriptors belonging to the process are closed; any children of the process are inherited by process 1, init, and the process's parent is sent a SIGCHLD signal.

*status* is returned to the parent process as the process's exit status and can be collected using one of the wait family of calls.

## RETURN VALUE

exit never returns.

## CONFORMS TO

SVID, AT&T, POSIX, X/OPEN, BSD 4.3

## NOTES

exit does not call any functions registered with the ANSI C atexit function and does not flush standard I/O buffers. To do these things, use exit(3).

## SEE ALSO

fork(2), execve(2), waitpid(2), wait4(2), kill(2), wait(3), exit(3)

*Linux, 21 July 1993*

# accept

accept—Accept a connection on a socket

## SYNOPSIS

```
#include <sys/types.h>
#include <sys/socket.h>
int accept(int s, struct sockaddr *addr,int*addrlen);
```

## DESCRIPTION

The argument *s* is a socket that has been created with socket(2), bound to an address with bind(2), and is listening for connections after a listen(2). The accept function extracts the first connection request on the queue of pending connections, creates a new socket with the same properties of *s*, and allocates a new file descriptor for the socket. If no pending connections are present on the queue and the socket is not marked as nonblocking, accept blocks the caller until a connection is present. If the socket is marked nonblocking and no pending connections are present on the queue, accept returns an error as described below. The accepted socket may not be used to accept more connections. The original socket *s* remains open.

The argument *addr* is a result parameter that is filled in with the address of the connecting entity, as known to the communications layer. The exact format of the *addr* parameter is determined by the domain in which the communication is occurring. The *addrlen* is a value-result parameter; it should initially contain the amount of space pointed to by *addr*; on return it will contain the actual length (in bytes) of the address returned. This call is used with connection-based socket types, currently with SOCK_STREAM.

It is possible to select(2) a socket for the purposes of doing an accept by selecting it for read.

For certain protocols that require an explicit confirmation, such as ISO and DATAKIT, accept can be thought of as merely dequeuing the next connection request and not implying confirmation. Confirmation can be implied by a normal read or write on the new file descriptor, and rejection can be implied by closing the new socket.

One can obtain user connection request data without confirming the connection by issuing a recvmsg(2) call with a msg iovlen of 0 and a nonzero msg controllen, or by issuing a getsockopt(2) request. Similarly, one can provide user connection rejection information by issuing a sendmsg(2) call providing only the control information, or by calling setsockopt(2).

## RETURN VALUES

The call returns -1 on error. If it succeeds, it returns a nonnegative integer that is a descriptor for the accepted socket.

## ERRORS

| | |
|---|---|
| EBADF | The descriptor is invalid. |
| ENOTSOCK | The descriptor references a file, not a socket. |
| EOPNOTSUPP | The referenced socket is not of type SOCK_STREAM. |
| EFAULT | The addr parameter is not in a writable part of the user address space. |
| EWOULDBLOCK | The socket is marked nonblocking and no connections are present to be accepted. |

## HISTORY

The accept function appeared in BSD 4.2.

## SEE ALSO

bind(2), connect(2), listen(2), select(2), socket(2)

*BSD Man Page, 24 July 1993*

# access

access—Checks user's permissions for a file

## SYNOPSIS

```
#include <unistd.h>
int access(const char *pathname,intmode);
```

## DESCRIPTION

access checks whether the process would be allowed to read, write, or test for existence of the file (or other file system object) whose name is *pathname*. If *pathname* is a symbolic link, permissions of the file referred by this symbolic link are tested.

mode is a mask consisting of one or more of R_OK, W_OK, X_OK, and F_OK.

R_OK, W_OK, and X_OK request checking whether the file exists and has read, write, and execute permissions, respectively. F_OK just requests checking for the existence of the file.

The tests depend on the permissions of the directories occurring in the path to the file, as given in *pathname*, and on the permissions of directories and files referred by symbolic links encountered on the way.

The check is done with the process's real UID and GID, rather than with the effective IDs as is done when actually attempting an operation. This is to allow set-UID programs to easily determine the invoking user's authority.

Only access bits are checked, not the file type or contents. Therefore, if a directory is found to be "writable," it probably means that files can be created in the directory, and not that the directory can be written as a file. Similarly, a DOS file may be found to be "executable," but the execve(2) call will still fail.

## RETURN VALUE

On success (all requested permissions granted), 0 is returned. On error (at least 1 bit in *mode* asked for a permission that is denied, or some other error occurred), -1 is returned and errno is set appropriately.

## ERRORS

| | |
|---|---|
| EACCES | The requested access would be denied, either to the file itself or one of the directories in *pathname*. |
| EFAULT | *pathname* points outside your accessible address space. |
| EINVAL | *mode* was incorrectly specified. |
| ENAMETOOLONG | *pathname* is too long. |
| ENOENT | A directory component in *pathname* would have been accessible but does not exist or was a dangling symbolic link. |
| ENOTDIR | A component used as a directory in *pathname* is not, in fact, a directory. |
| ENOMEM | Insufficient kernel memory was available. |
| ELOOP | *pathname* contains a reference to a circular symbolic link, that is, a symbolic link containing a reference to itself. |

## RESTRICTIONS

access returns an error if any of the access types in the requested call fails, even if other types might be successful. access may not work correctly on NFS file systems with UID mapping enabled because UID mapping is done on the server and hidden from the client, which checks permissions.

## CONFORMS TO

SVID, AT&T, POSIX, X/OPEN, BSD 4.3

## SEE ALSO

stat(2), open(2), chmod(2), chown(2), setuid(2), setgid(2)

*Linux 1.2.13, 17 March 1996*

# acct

acct—Switches process accounting on or off

## SYNOPSIS

```
#include <unistd.h>
int acct(const char *filename);
```

## DESCRIPTION

Warning: Since this function is not implemented as of Linux 0.99.11, it will always return -1 and set errno to ENOSYS. If acctkit is installed, the function performs as advertised.

When called with the name of an existing file as argument, accounting is turned on and records for each terminating process are appended to *filename* as it terminates. An argument of NULL causes accounting to be turned off.

## RETURN VALUE

On success, 0 is returned. On error, -1 is returned and errno is set appropriately.

## NOTES

No accounting is produced for programs running when a crash occurs. In particular, nonterminating processes are never accounted for.

## SEE ALSO

acct(5)

*Linux 0.99.11, 10 August 1993*

# adjtimex

adjtimex—Tunes kernel clock

## SYNOPSIS

```
#include <sys/timex.h>
int adjtimex(struct timex *buf);
```

## DESCRIPTION

Linux uses David Mill's clock adjustment algorithm. adjtimex reads and optionally sets adjustment parameters for this algorithm.

adjtimex takes a pointer to a *timex* structure, updates kernel parameters from field values, and returns the same structure with current kernel values. This structure is declared as follows:

```
struct timex
        {
            int mode;              /* mode selector */
            long offset;           /* time offset (usec) */
            long frequency;        /* frequency offset (scaled ppm) */
            long maxerror;         /* maximum error (usec) */
            long esterror;         /* estimated error (usec) */
            int status;            /* clock command/status */
            long time_constant;    /* pll time constant */
            long precision;        /* clock precision (usec) (read only) */
            long tolerance;        /* clock frequency tolerance (ppm)
                                      (read only) */
            struct timeval time;   /* (read only) */
            long tick;             /* usecs between clock ticks */
        };
```

The *mode* field determines which parameters, if any, to set. It may contain a bitwise-or combination of zero or more of the following bits:

```
#define ADJ_OFFSET            0x0001 /* time offset */
        #define ADJ_FREQUENCY        0x0002 /* frequency offset */
        #define ADJ_MAXERROR         0x0004 /* maximum time error */
        #define ADJ_ESTERROR         0x0008 /* estimated time error */
        #define ADJ_STATUS           0x0010 /* clock status */
        #define ADJ_TIMECONST        0x0020 /* pll time constant */
        #define ADJ_TICK             0x4000 /* tick value */
        #define ADJ_OFFSET_SINGLESHOT 0x8001 /* old-fashioned adjtime */
```

Ordinary users are restricted to a **0** value for *mode*. Only the superuser may set any parameters.

## RETURN VALUE

On success, adjtimex returns the value of *buf.status*:

```
#define TIME OK 0 /* clock synchronized */
#define TIME INS 1 /* insert leap second */
#define TIME DEL 2 /* delete leap second */
#define TIME OOP 3 /* leap second in progress */
#define TIME BAD 4 /* clock not synchronized */
```

On failure, adjtimex returns –1 and sets errno.

## ERRORS

| | |
|---|---|
| EFAULT | *buf* does not point to writable memory. |
| EPERM | *buf.mode* is nonzero and the user is not superuser. |
| EINVAL | An attempt is made to set *buf.offset* to a value outside the range -131071 to +131071, or to set *buf.status* to a value other than those listed above, or to set *buf.tick* to a value outside the range 900000/**HZ** to 1100000/**HZ**, where **HZ** is the system timer interrupt frequency. |

## SEE ALSO

settimeofday(2)

# alarm

alarm—Sets an alarm clock for delivery of a signal

## SYNOPSIS

```
#include <unistd.h>
unsigned int alarm(unsigned int seconds);
```

## DESCRIPTION

alarm arranges for a SIGALRM signal to be delivered to the process in *seconds* seconds.

If *seconds* is 0, no new alarm is scheduled.

In any event, any previously set alarm is canceled.

## RETURN VALUE

alarm returns the number of seconds remaining until any previously scheduled alarm was due to be delivered, or 0 if there was no previously scheduled alarm.

## NOTES

alarm and setitimer share the same timer; calls to one will interfere with use of the other.

Scheduling delays can, as ever, cause the execution of the process to be delayed by an arbitrary amount of time.

## CONFORMS TO

SVID, AT&T, POSIX, X/OPEN, BSD 4.3

## SEE ALSO

setitimer(2), signal(2), sigaction(2), gettimeofday(2), select(2), pause(2), sleep(3)

*Linux, 21 July 1993*

# bdflush

bdflush—Starts, flushes, or tunes the buffer-dirty-flush daemon

## SYNOPSIS

```
int bdflush(int func, long *address);
int bdflush(int func, long data);
```

## DESCRIPTION

bdflush starts, flushes, or tunes the buffer-dirty-flush daemon. Only the superuser may call bdflush.

If *func* is negative or 0 and no daemon has been started, bdflush enters the daemon code and never returns.

If *func* is 1, some dirty buffers are written to disk.

If *func* is 2 or more and is even (low bit is 0), *address* is the address of a long word, and the tuning parameter numbered (*func*-2)/2 is returned to the caller in that address.

If *func* is 3 or more and is odd (low bit is 1), *data* is a long word and the kernel sets tuning parameter numbered (*func*-3)/2 to that value.

The set of parameters, their values, and their legal ranges are defined in the kernel source file *fs/buffer.c*.

## RETURN VALUE

If *func* is negative or 0 and the daemon successfully starts, bdflush never returns. Otherwise, the return value is 0 on success and -1 on failure, with errno set to indicate the error.

## ERRORS

| | |
|---|---|
| EPERM | Caller is not superuser. |
| EFAULT | *address* points outside your accessible address space. |
| EBUSY | An attempt was made to enter the daemon code after another process has already been entered. |
| EINVAL | An attempt was made to read or write an invalid parameter number, or to write an invalid value to a parameter. |

## SEE ALSO

fsync(2), sync(2), update(8), sync(8)

*Linux 1.2.4, 15 April 1995*

# bind

bind—Binds a name to a socket

## SYNOPSIS

```
#include <sys/types.h>
#include <sys/socket.h>
int bind(int sockfd, struct sockaddr *my_addr, intaddrlen);
```

## DESCRIPTION

bind gives the socket, *sockfd*, the local address *my_addr*. *my_addr* is *addrlen* bytes long. Traditionally, this is called assigning a name to a socket. (When a socket is created with socket(2), it exists in a name space—an address family—but has no name assigned.)

## NOTES

Binding a name in the UNIX domain creates a socket in the file system that must be deleted by the caller—using unlink(2) —when it is no longer needed.

The rules used in name binding vary between communication domains. Consult the manual entries in section 4 for detailed information.

## RETURN VALUE

On success, 0 is returned. On error, -1 is returned, and errno is set appropriately.

## ERRORS

| | |
|---|---|
| EBADF | *sockfd* is not a valid descriptor. |
| EINVAL | The socket is already bound to an address. This may change in the future. See linux/unix/sock.c for details. |
| EACCES | The address is protected and the user is not the superuser. |

The following errors are specific to UNIX domain (AF_UNIX) sockets:

| | |
|---|---|
| EINVAL | *addr len* was wrong, or the socket was not in the AF_UNIX family. |
| EROFS | The socket inode would reside on a read-only file system. |
| EFAULT | *my_addr* points outside your accessible address space. |

| ENAMETOOLONG | *my_addr* is too long. |
| ENOENT | The file does not exist. |
| ENOMEM | Insufficient kernel memory was available. |
| ENOTDIR | A component of the path prefix is not a directory. |
| EACCES | Search permission is denied on a component of the path prefix. |
| ELOOP | *my_addr* contains a circular reference (that is, via a symbolic link). |

## HISTORY

The bind function call appeared in BSD 4.2.

## SEE ALSO

accept(2), connect(2), listen(2), socket(2), getsockname(2)

*Linux 0.99.11, 23 July 1993*

# brk, sbrk

brk, sbrk—Change data segment size

## SYNOPSIS

```
#include <unistd.h>
int brk(void *end_data_segment);
void *sbrk(ptrdiff tincrement);
```

## DESCRIPTION

brk sets the end of the data segment to the value specified by *end_data_segment*.

*end_data_segment* must be greater than the end of the text segment and it must be 16KB before the end of the stack.

sbrk increments the program's data space by *increment* bytes. sbrk isn't a system call; it is just a C library wrapper.

## RETURN VALUE

On success, brk returns 0, and sbrk returns a pointer to the start of the new area. On error, -1 is returned and errno is set to ENOMEM.

## CONFORMS TO

BSD 4.3

brk and sbrk are not defined in the C standard and are deliberately excluded from the POSIX.1 standard (see paragraphs B.1.1.1.3 and B.8.3.3).

## SEE ALSO

execve(2), getrlimit(2), malloc(3), end(3)

*Linux 0.99.11, 21 July 1993*

# cacheflush

cacheflush—Flushes contents of the instruction and/or data cache

## SYNOPSIS

```
#include <asm/cachectl.h>
int cacheflush(char *addr,intnbytes,intcache);
```

## DESCRIPTION

cacheflush flushes contents of indicated cache(s) for user addresses in the range addr to (addr+nbytes-1). The cache may be one of the following:

| | |
|---|---|
| ICACHE | Flush the instruction cache. |
| DCACHE | Write back to memory and invalidate the affected valid cache lines. |
| BCACHE | Same as (ICACHE|DCACHE). |

## RETURN VALUE

cacheflush returns 0 on success or -1 on error. If errors are detected, errno will indicate the error.

## ERRORS

| | |
|---|---|
| EINVAL | The cache parameter is not one of ICACHE, DCACHE, or BCACHE. |
| EFAULT | Some or all of the address range addr to (addr+nbytes-1) is not accessible. |

## BUGS

The current implementation ignores the addr and nbytes parameters. Therefore, the whole cache is always flushed.

## NOTE

This system call is only available on MIPS-based systems.

## SEE ALSO

cachectl(2)

*Linux, 27 June 95*

# chdir, fchdir

chdir, fchdir—Changes the working directory

## SYNOPSIS

```
#include <unistd.h>
int chdir(const char *path);
int fchdir(int fd);
```

## DESCRIPTION

chdir changes the current directory to that specified in *path*.

fchdir is identical to chdir, only the directory is given as an open file descriptor.

## RETURN VALUE

On success, 0 is returned. On error, -1 is returned, and errno is set appropriately.

## ERRORS

Depending on the file system, other errors can be returned. The more general errors are listed here:

| | |
|---|---|
| EPERM | The process does not have execute permission on the directory. |
| EFAULT | *path* points outside your accessible address space. |
| ENAMETOOLONG | *path* is too long. |

| EBADF | *fd* is not a valid file descriptor. |
| ENOENT | The file does not exist. |
| ENOMEM | Insufficient kernel memory was available. |
| ENOTDIR | A component of the path prefix is not a directory. |
| EACCES | Search permission is denied on a component of the path prefix. |
| ELOOP | *path* contains a circular reference (that is, via a symbolic link) |

## SEE ALSO

getcwd(3), chroot(2)

*Linux 1.2.4, 15 April 1995*

# chmod, fchmod

chmod, fchmod—Changes permissions of a file

## SYNOPSIS

```
#include <sys/types.h>
#include <sys/stat.h>
int chmod(const char *path,modetmode);
int fchmod(int fildes,modetmode);
```

## DESCRIPTION

The mode of the file given by *path* or referenced by *filedes* is changed.

Modes are specified by oring the following:

| S_ISUID | 04000 Set user ID on execution |
| S_ISGID | 02000 Set group ID on execution |
| S_ISVTX | 01000 Sticky bit |
| S_IRUSR (S_IREAD) | 00400 Read by owner |
| S_IWUSR (S_IWRITE) | 00200 Write by owner |
| S_IXUSR (S_IEXEC) | 00100 Execute/search by owner |
| S_IRGRP | 00040 Read by group |
| S_IWGRP | 00020 Write by group |
| S_IXGRP | 00010 Execute/search by group |
| S_IROTH | 00004 Read by others |
| S_IWOTH | 00002 Write by others |
| S_IXOTH | 00001 Execute/search by others |

The effective UID of the process must be 0 or must match the owner of the file.

The effective UID or GID must be appropriate for setting execution bits.

Depending on the file system, set user ID and set group ID execution bits may be turned off if a file is written. On some file systems, only the superuser can set the sticky bit, which may have a special meaning (that is, for directories, a file can only be deleted by the owner or the superuser).

## RETURN VALUE

On success, 0 is returned. On error, -1 is returned and errno is set appropriately.

## ERRORS

Depending on the file system, other errors can be returned. The more general errors for chmod are listed here:

| | |
|---|---|
| EPERM | The effective UID does not match the owner of the file and is not 0. |
| EROFS | The named file resides on a read-only file system. |
| EFAULT | *path* points outside your accessible address space. |
| ENAMETOOLONG | *path* is too long. |
| ENOENT | The file does not exist. |
| ENOMEM | Insufficient kernel memory was available. |
| ENOTDIR | A component of the path prefix is not a directory. |
| EACCES | Search permission is denied on a component of the path prefix. |
| ELOOP | *path* contains a circular reference (that is, via a symbolic link) |

The general errors for fchmod are listed here:

| | |
|---|---|
| EBADF | The descriptor is not value. |
| ENOENT | See above. |
| EPERM | See above. |
| EROFS | See above. |

## SEE ALSO

open(2), chown(2), stat(2)

*Linux 0.99.11, 21 July 1993*

# chown, fchown

chown, fchown—Changes ownership of a file

## SYNOPSIS

```
#include <sys/types.h>
#include <unistd.h>
int chown(const char *path, uid t owner, gid_t group);
int fchown(int fd, uid t owner, gid_t group);
```

## DESCRIPTION

The owner of the file specified by *path* or by *fd* is changed. Only the superuser may change the owner of a file. The owner of a file may change the group of the file to any group of which that owner is a member. The superuser may change the group arbitrarily.

If the *owner* or *group* is specified as -1, that ID is not changed.

## RETURN VALUE

On success, 0 is returned. On error, -1 is returned and errno is set appropriately.

## ERRORS

Depending on the file system, other errors can be returned. The more general errors for chown are listed here:

| | |
|---|---|
| EPERM | The effective UID does not match the owner of the file, and is not 0; or the *owner* or *group* were specified incorrectly. |
| EROFS | The named file resides on a read-only file system. |
| EFAULT | *path* points outside your accessible address space. |

| ENAMETOOLONG | *path* is too long. |
| ENOENT | The file does not exist. |
| ENOMEM | Insufficient kernel memory was available. |
| ENOTDIR | A component of the path prefix is not a directory. |
| EACCES | Search permission is denied on a component of the path prefix. |
| ELOOP | *path* contains a circular reference (that is, via a symbolic link). |

The general errors for fchown are listed here:

| EBADF | The descriptor is not value. |
| ENOENT | See above. |
| EPERM | See above. |
| EROFS | See above. |

## NOTES

chown does not follow symbolic links. The prototype for fchown is only available if USE BSD is defined.

## SEE ALSO

chmod(2), flock(2)

*Linux 0.99.11, 21 July 1993*

# chroot

chroot—Changes root directory

## SYNOPSIS

```
#include <unistd.h>
int chroot(const char *path);
```

## DESCRIPTION

chroot changes the root directory to that specified in *path*. This directory will be used for pathnames beginning with /. The root directory is inherited by all children of the current process.

Only the superuser may change the root directory.

Note that this call does not change the current working directory, so that . can be outside the tree rooted at /.

## RETURN VALUE

On success, 0 is returned. On error, -1 is returned and errno is set appropriately.

## ERRORS

Depending on the file system, other errors can be returned. The more general errors are listed here:

| EPERM | The effective UID does not match the owner of the file, and is not 0; or the *owner* or *group* were specified incorrectly. |
| EROFS | The named file resides on a read-only file system. |
| EFAULT | *path* points outside your accessible address space. |
| ENAMETOOLONG | *path* is too long. |
| ENOENT | The file does not exist. |
| ENOMEM | Insufficient kernel memory was available. |

| ENOTDIR | A component of the path prefix is not a directory. |
| EACCES | Search permission is denied on a component of the path prefix. |
| ELOOP | *path* contains a circular reference (that is, via a symbolic link) |

## SEE ALSO

chdir(2)

*Linux 1.1.46, 21 August 1994*

# clone

clone—Creates a child process

## SYNOPSIS

```
#include <linux/sched.h>
#include <linux/unistd.h>

pid t clone(void *sp, unsigned long flags);
```

## DESCRIPTION

clone is an alternate interface to fork, with more options. fork is equivalent to clone(0, SIGCLD¦COPYVM).

If *sp* is nonzero, the child process uses *sp* as its initial stack pointer.

The low byte of *flags* contains the signal sent to the parent when the child dies. *flags* may also be bitwise ored with either or both of COPYVM and COPYFD.

If COPYVM is set, child pages are copy-on-write images of the parent pages. If COPYVM is not set, the child process shares the same pages as the parent, and both parent and child may write on the same data.

If COPYFD is set, the child's file descriptors are copies of the parent's file descriptors. If COPYFD is not set, the child's file descriptors are shared with the parent.

## RETURN VALUE

On success, the PID of the child process is returned in the parent's thread of execution, and 0 is returned in the child's thread of execution. On failure, a -1 will be returned in the parent's context, no child process will be created, and errno will be set appropriately.

## ERRORS

| ENOSYS | clone will always return this error, unless your kernel was compiled with CLONE_ACTUALLY_WORKS_OK defined. |
| EAGAIN | fork cannot allocate sufficient memory to copy the parent's page tables and allocate a task structure for the child. |

## BUGS

By default, CLONE_ACTUALLY_WORKS_OK is not defined.

There is no entry for clone in /lib/libc.so.4.5.26.

Comments in the kernel as of 1.1.46 indicate that it mishandles the case where COPYVM is not set.

## SEE ALSO

fork(2)

*Linux 1.2.9, 10 June 1995*

# close

close—Closes a file descriptor

## SYNOPSIS

```
#include <unistd.h>
int close(int fd);
```

## DESCRIPTION

close closes a file descriptor so that it no longer refers to any file and may be reused. Any locks held on the file it was associated with, and owned by the process, are removed (regardless of the file descriptor that was used to obtain the lock).

If *fd* is the last copy of a particular file descriptor, the resources associated with it are freed; if the descriptor was the last reference to a file that has been removed using unlink, the file is deleted.

## RETURN VALUE

close returns 0 on success, or -1 if an error occurred.

## ERRORS

EBADF                              *fd* isn't a valid open file descriptor.

## CONFORMS TO

SVID, AT&T, POSIX, X/OPEN, BSD 4.3

## NOTES

Not checking the return value of close is a common but nevertheless serious programming error. File system implementations that use techniques as write-behind to increase performance may lead to *write*(2) succeeding, although the data has not been written yet. The error status may be reported at a later write operation, but it is guaranteed to be reported on closing the file. Not checking the return value when closing the file may lead to silent loss of data. This can especially be observed with NFS and disk quotas.

## SEE ALSO

open(2), fcntl(2), shutdown(2), unlink(2), fclose(3)

*14 April 1996*

# connect

connect—Initiates a connection on a socket

## SYNOPSIS

```
#include <sys/types.h>
#include <sys/socket.h>
int connect(int sockfd, struct sockaddr *serv_addr,intaddrlen);
```

## DESCRIPTION

The parameter *sockfd* is a socket. If it is of type SOCK_DGRAM, this call specifies the peer with which the socket is to be associated; this address is that to which datagrams are to be sent, and the only address from which datagrams are to be received. If the socket is of type SOCK_STREAM, this call attempts to make a connection to another socket. The other socket is specified by serv_addr, which is an address in the communications space of the socket. Each communications space interprets the serv_addr, parameter in its own way. Generally, stream sockets may successfully connect only once; datagram sockets may use connect multiple times to change their association. Datagram sockets may dissolve the association by connecting to an invalid address, such as a null address.

## RETURN VALUE

If the connection or binding succeeds, 0 is returned. On error, -1 is returned and errno is set appropriately.

## ERRORS

See the Linux kernel source code for details.

## HISTORY

The connect function call first appeared in BSD 4.2.

## SEE ALSO

accept(2), bind(2), listen(2), socket(2), getsockname(2)

*Linux 0.99.11, 23 July 1993*

# dup, dup2

dup, dup2—Duplicate a file descriptor

## SYNOPSIS

```
#include <unistd.h>
int dup(int oldfd);
int dup2(int oldfd,intnewfd);
```

## DESCRIPTION

dup and dup2 create a copy of the file descriptor oldfd.

The old and new descriptors can be used interchangeably. They share locks, file position pointers and flags; for example, if the file position is modified by using lseek on one of the descriptors, the position is also changed for the other.

The two descriptors do not share the close-on-exec flag, however.

dup uses the lowest-numbered unused descriptor for the new descriptor.

dup2 makes newfd be the copy of oldfd, closing newfd first if necessary.

## RETURN VALUE

dup and dup2 return the new descriptor, or -1 if an error occurred (in which case errno is set appropriately).

## ERRORS

| EBADF | oldfd isn't an open file descriptor, or newfd is out of the allowed range for file descriptors. |
| EMFILE | The process already has the maximum number of file descriptors open and tried to open a new one. |

## WARNING

The error returned by dup2 is different from that returned by fcntl(...,F_DUPFD,...) when newfd is out of range. On some systems dup2 also sometimes returns EINVAL like F_DUPFD.

## CONFORMS TO

SVID, AT&T, POSIX, X/OPEN, BSD 4.3

## SEE ALSO

fcntl(2), open(2), close(2).

*Linux 1.1.46, 21 August 1994*

# execve

execve—Execute program

## SYNOPSIS

```
#include <unistd.h>
int execve (const char *filename, const char *argv [], const char *envp[]);
```

## DESCRIPTION

execve() executes the program pointed to by *filename*. *filename* must be either a binary executable or a shell script starting with a line in the format #! *interpreter* [arg].

execve() does not return on success, and the text, data, bss, and stack of the calling process are overwritten by that of the program loaded. The program invoked inherits the calling process's PID, and any open file descriptors that are not set to close on exec. Signals pending on the parent process are cleared.

If the current program is being ptraced, a SIGTRAP is sent to it after a successful execve().

## RETURN VALUE

On success, execve() does not return; on error -1 is returned and errno is set appropriately.

## ERRORS

| | |
|---|---|
| EACCES | The file is not a regular file. |
| EACCES | Execute permission is denied for the file. |
| EPERM | The file system is mounted *noexec*. |
| EPERM | The file system is mounted *nosuid* and the file has an SUID or SGID bit set. |
| E2BIG | The argument list is too big. |
| ENOEXEC | The magic number in the file is incorrect. |
| EFAULT | *filename* points outside your accessible address space. |
| ENAMETOOLONG | *filename* is too long. |
| ENOENT | The file does not exist. |
| ENOMEM | Insufficient kernel memory was available. |
| ENOTDIR | A component of the path prefix is not a directory. |
| EACCES | Search permission is denied on a component of the path prefix. |
| ELOOP | *filename* contains a circular reference (that is, via a symbolic link). |

## CONFORMS TO

SVID, AT&T, POSIX, X/OPEN, BSD 4.3

## NOTES

SUID and SGID processes can not be ptrace()'d SUID or SGID.

A maximum line length of 127 characters is allowed for the first line in a #! executable shell script. This may be circumvented by changing the max size of buf, in which case you will become bound by the 1024 byte size of a buffer, which is not easily worked around.

## SEE ALSO

execl(3), fork(2)

*Linux 1.1.46, 21 August 1994*

# fcntl

fcntl—Manipulate file descriptor

## SYNOPSIS

```
#include <unistd.h>
#include <fcntl.h>
int fcntl(int fd,intcmd);
int fcntl(int fd,intcmd,longarg);
```

## DESCRIPTION

fcntl performs one of various miscellaneous operations on *fd*. The operation in question is determined by *cmd*:

| | |
|---|---|
| F_DUPFD | Makes *arg* be a copy of *fd*, closing *fd* first if necessary. |
| | The same functionality can be more easily achieved by using dup2(2). |
| | The old and new descriptors may be used interchangeably. They share locks, file position pointers, and flags; for example, if the file position is modified by using lseek on one of the descriptors, the position is also changed for the other. |
| | The two descriptors do not share the close-on-exec flag, however. |
| | On success, the new descriptor is returned. |
| F_GETFD | Read the close-on-exec flag. If the low-order bit is 0, the file will remain open across exec; otherwise, it will be closed. |
| F_SETFD | Set the close-on-exec flag to the value specified by *arg* (only the least significant bit is used). |
| F_GETFL | Read the descriptor's flags (all flags—as set by open(2)—are returned). |
| F_SETFL | Set the descriptor's flags to the value specified by *arg*. |
| | Only O_APPEND and O_NONBLOCK may be set. |
| | The flags are shared between copies (made with dup and so on) of the same file descriptor. The flags and their semantics are described in open(2). |
| F_GETLK, F_SETLK, and F_SETLKW | Manage discretionary file locks. The third argument *arg* is a pointer to a struct flock (that may be overwritten by this call). |
| F_GETLK | Return the flock structure that prevents us from obtaining the lock, or set the l type field of the lock to F_UNLCK if there is no obstruction. |
| F_SETLK | The lock is set (when l type is F_RDLCK or F_WRLCK) or cleared (when it is F_UNLCK). If the lock is held by someone else, this call returns -1 and sets errno to EACCES or EAGAIN. |
| F_SETLKW | Like F_SETLK, but instead of returning an error, we wait for the lock to be released. |
| F_GETOWN | Get the process ID (or process group) of the owner of a socket. |
| | Process groups are returned as negative values. |
| F_SETOWN | Set the process or process group that owns a socket. |
| | For these commands, ownership means receiving SIGIO or SIG-URG signals. |
| | Process groups are specified using negative values. |

## RETURN VALUE

The return value depends on the operation:

| | |
|---|---|
| F_DUPFD | The new descriptor. |
| F_GETFD | Value of flag. |
| F_GFTFL | Value of flags. |
| F_GETOWN | Value of descriptor owner. |

On error, -1 is returned and errno is set appropriately.

## ERRORS

| | |
|---|---|
| EBADF | fd is not an open file descriptor. |
| EINVAL | For F_DUPFD, *arg* is negative or is greater than the maximum allowable value. |
| EMFILE | For F_DUPFD, the process already has the maximum number of file descriptors open. |

## NOTES

The errors returned by dup2 are different from those returned by F_DUPFD.

## CONFORMS TO

SVID, AT&T, POSIX, X/OPEN, BSD 4.3

## SEE ALSO

dup2(2), open(2), socket(2).

*Linux, 26 September 1995*

# fdatasync

fdatasync—Synchronizes a file's in-core data with that on disk

## SYNOPSIS

```
#include <unistd.h>
#ifdef POSIX SYNCHRONIZED IO
int fdatasync(int fd);
#endif
```

## DESCRIPTION

fdatasync flushes all data buffers of a file to disk (before the system call returns). It resembles fsync but is not required to update the metadata such as access time.

Applications that access databases or log files often write a tiny data fragment (for example, one line in a log file) and then call fsync immediately in order to ensure that the written data is physically stored on the hard disk. Unfortunately, fsync will always initiate two write operations: one for the newly written data and another one in order to update the modification time stored in the inode. If the modification time is not a part of the transaction concept fdatasync can be used to avoid unnecessary inode disk write operations.

## RETURN VALUE

On success, 0 is returned. On error, -1 is returned and errno is set appropriately.

## ERRORS

| | |
|---|---|
| EBADF | *fd* is not a valid file descriptor open for writing. |
| EROFS, EINVAL | *fd* is bound to a special file which does not support synchronization. |
| EIO | An error occurred during synchronization. |

## BUGS

Currently (Linux 1.3.86) fdatasync is equivalent to fsync.

## CONFORMS TO

POSIX.4

## SEE ALSO

fsync(2), B.O. Gallmeister, *POSIX.4*, O'Reilly, pp. 220–223, 343.

*Linux 1.3.86, 13 April 1996*

# flock

flock—Applies or removes an advisory lock on an open file

## SYNOPSIS

```
#include <sys/file.h>
int flock(int fd,intoperation);
```

## DESCRIPTION

Apply or remove an advisory lock on an open file. The file is specified by *fd*. Valid operations are given here:

| | |
|---|---|
| LOCK_SH | Shared lock. More than one process may hold a shared lock for a given file at a given time. |
| LOCK_EX | Exclusive lock. Only one process may hold an exclusive lock for a given file at a given time. |
| LOCK_UN | Unlock. |
| LOCK_NB | Don't block when locking. May be specified (by oring) along with one of the other operations. |
| | A single file may not have both shared and exclusive locks. A file is locked (that is, the inode), *not* the file descriptor. So, dup(2) and fork(2) do not create multiple instances of a lock. |

## RETURN VALUE

On success, 0 is returned. On error, -1 is returned and errno is set appropriately.

## ERRORS

| | |
|---|---|
| EWOULDBLOCK | The file is locked and the LOCK_NB flag was selected. |

## NOTES

Under Linux, flock is implemented as a call to fcntl. Please see fcntl(2) for more details on errors.

## SEE ALSO

open(2), close(2), dup(2), execve(2), fcntl(2), fork(2)

*Linux 0.99.11, 22 July 1993*

# fork, vfork

fork, vfork—Creates a child process

## SYNOPSIS

```
#include <unistd.h>
pid t fork(void);
pid t vfork(void);
```

## DESCRIPTION

fork creates a child process that differs from the parent process only in its PID and PPID, and in the fact that resource utilizations are set to 0. File locks and pending signals are not inherited.

Under Linux, fork is implemented using copy-on-write pages, so the only penalties incurred by fork are the time and memory required to duplicate the parent's page tables and to create a unique task structure for the child.

## RETURN VALUE

On success, the PID of the child process is returned in the parent's thread of execution, and a 0 is returned in the child's thread of execution. On failure, a –1 will be returned in the parent's context, no child process will be created, and errno will be set appropriately.

## ERRORS

EAGAIN                           fork cannot allocate sufficient memory to copy the parent's page tables and allocate a task structure for the child.

## BUGS

Under Linux, vfork is merely an alias for fork. fork never returns the error ENOMEM.

## CONFORMS TO

SVID, AT&T, POSIX, X/OPEN, BSD 4.3

## SEE ALSO

clone(2), execve(2), wait(2)

*Linux 1.2.9, 10 June 1995*

# fsync

fsync—Synchronizes a file's complete in-core state with that on disk

## SYNOPSIS

```
#include <unistd.h>
int fsync(int fd);
```

## DESCRIPTION

fsync copies all in-core parts of a file to disk.

In some applications, fdatasync is a more efficient alternative to fsync.

## RETURN VALUE

On success, 0 is returned. On error, –1 is returned and errno is set appropriately.

## ERRORS

| EBADF | *fd* is not a valid file descriptor open for writing. |
| EROFS, EINVAL | *fd* is bound to a special file that does not support synchronization. |
| EIO | An error occurred during synchronization. |

## CONFORMS TO

POSIX.1b

## SEE ALSO

bdflush(2), fdatasync(2), sync(2), update(8), sync(8)

*Linux 1.3.85, 13 April 1996*

# getdents

getdents—Gets directory entries

## SYNOPSIS

```
#include <unistd.h>
#include <linux/dirent.h>
#include <linux/unistd.h>
syscall3(int, getdents, uint, fd, struct dirent *, dirp, uint, count);
int getdents(unsigned int fd, struct dirent *dirp, unsigned int count);
```

## DESCRIPTION

getdents reads several *dirent* structures from the directory pointed at by *fd* into the memory area pointed to by *dirp*. The parameter *count* is the size of the memory area.

The *dirent* structure is declared as follows:

```
struct dirent
        {
            long d_ino;                  /* inode number */
            off_t d_off;                 /* offset to next dirent */
            unsigned short d_reclen;     /* length of this dirent */
            char d_name [NAME_MAX+1];    /* file name (null-terminated) */
        }
```

*d_ino* is an inode number. *d_off* is the distance from the start of the directory to the start of the next *dirent*. *d_reclen* is the size of this entire *dirent*. *d_name* is a null-terminated filename.

This call supersedes readdir(2).

## RETURN VALUE

On success, the number of bytes read is returned. On end of directory, 0 is returned. On error, -1 is returned and errno is set appropriately.

## ERRORS

| EBADF | Invalid file descriptor *fd*. |
| ENOTDIR | File descriptor does not refer to a directory. |

## SEE ALSO

readdir(2), readdir(3)

*Linux 1.3.6, 22 July 1995*

# getdomainname, setdomainname

getdomainname, setdomainname—Gets/sets domain name

## SYNOPSIS

```
#include <unistd.h>
int getdomainname(char *name, size_t len);
int setdomainname(const char *name, size_t len);
```

## DESCRIPTION

These functions are used to access or to change the domain name of the current processor.

## RETURN VALUE

On success, 0 is returned. On error, -1 is returned and errno is set appropriately.

## ERRORS

| | |
|---|---|
| EINVAL | For getdomainname, *name* points to NULL or *name* is longer than *len*. |
| EPERM | For setdomainname, the caller was not the superuser. |
| EINVAL | For setdomainname, *len* was too long. |

## CONFORMS TO

POSIX does not specify these calls.

## BUGS

getdomainname is not compliant with other implementations because they always return *len* bytes, even if *name* is longer. Linux, however, returns EINVAL in this case (as of DLL 4.4.1 libraries).

## NOTES

Under Linux, getdomainname is implemented at the library level by calling uname(2).

## SEE ALSO

gethostname(2), sethostname(2), uname(2)

*Linux 0.99.11, 22 July 1993*

# getdtablesize

getdtablesize—Gets descriptor table size

## SYNOPSIS

```
#include <unistd.h>
int getdtablesize(void);
```

## DESCRIPTION

getdtablesize returns the maximum number of files a process can have open.

## NOTES

getdtablesize is implemented as a library function in DLL 4.4.1. This function returns OPEN_MAX (set to 256 in Linux 0.99.11) if OPEN_MAX was defined when the library was compiled. Otherwise, -1 is returned and errno is set to ENOSYS.

## SEE ALSO

close(2), dup(2), open(2)

# getgid, getegid

getgid, getegid—Gets group identity

## SYNOPSIS

```
#include <unistd.h>
gid_t getgid(void);
gid_t getegid(void);
```

## DESCRIPTION

getgid returns the real group ID of the current process.

getegid returns the effective group ID of the current process.

The real ID corresponds to the ID of the calling process. The effective ID corresponds to the set ID bit on the file being executed.

## ERRORS

These functions are always successful.

## CONFORMS TO

POSIX, BSD 4.3

## SEE ALSO

setregid(2), setgid(2)

# getgroups, setgroups

getgroups, setgroups—Gets/sets group access list

## SYNOPSIS

```
#include <unistd.h>
int getgroups(int size, gid_t list[]);
#define_USE_BSD
#include <grp.h>
int setgroups(size_t size, const gid_t *list);
```

## DESCRIPTION

| | |
|---|---|
| getgroups | Up to *size* supplemental groups are returned in *list*. If *size* is 0, *list* is not modified, but the total number of supplemental groups for the process is returned. |
| setgroups | Sets the supplemental groups for the process. Only the superuser may use this function. |

## RETURN VALUE

getgroups                On success, the number of groups stored in *list* is returned (if *size* is 0, however, the number of supplemental group IDs associated with the process is returned). On error, -1 is returned and errno is set appropriately.

setgroups                On success, 0 is returned. On error, -1 is returned and errno is set appropriately.

## ERRORS

EFAULT                   *list* has an invalid address.

EPERM                    For setgroups, the user is not the superuser.

EINVAL                   For setgroups, *gidsetsize* is greater than NGROUPS (32 for Linux 0.99.11).

## CONFORMS TO

getgroups conforms to POSIX.1 (and is present in BSD 4.3). Since setgroups requires privilege, it is not covered under POSIX.1.

## BUGS

The USE BSD flag probably shouldn't be required for setgroups.

## SEE ALSO

initgroups(3)

*Linux 0.99.11, 23 July 1993*


# gethostid, sethostid

gethostid, sethostid—Gets/sets the unique identifier of the current host

## SYNOPSIS

```
#include <unistd.h>

long int gethostid(void);
int sethostid(long int hostid);
```

## DESCRIPTION

Get or set a unique 32-bit identifier for the current machine. The 32-bit identifier is intended to be unique among all UNIX systems in existence. This normally resembles the Internet address for the local machine, as returned by gethostbyname(3), and thus usually never needs to be set.

The sethostid call is restricted to the superuser.

The *hostid* argument is stored in the file /etc/hostid.

## RETURN VALUES

gethostid returns the 32-bit identifier for the current host as set by sethostid(2).

## CONFORMS TO

POSIX.1 does not define these functions, but ISO/IEC 9945-1:1990 mentions them in B.4.4.1.

## FILES

/etc/hostid

hostid(1), gethostbyname(3)

# gethostname, sethostname

gethostname, sethostname—Gets/sets hostname

## SYNOPSIS

```
#include <unistd.h>
int gethostname(char *name, size_t len);
int sethostname(const char *name, size_t len);
```

## DESCRIPTION

These functions are used to access or to change the hostname of the current processor.

## RETURN VALUE

On success, 0 is returned. On error, -1 is returned and errno is set appropriately.

## ERRORS

| | |
|---|---|
| EINVAL | *len* is negative or, for sethostname, larger than the maximum allowed size. For gethostname on Linux/i386, *len* is smaller than the actual size. |
| EPERM | For sethostname, the caller was not the superuser. |
| EFAULT | *name* is an invalid address. |

## CONFORMS TO

POSIX.1 does not define these functions, but ISO/IEC 9945-1:1990 mentions them in B.4.4.1.

## BUGS

Some other implementations of gethostname successfully return *len* bytes even if *name* is longer. Linux/Alpha complies with this behavior. Linux/i386, however, returns EINVAL in this case (as of DLL 4.6.27 libraries).

## NOTES

Under Linux/Alpha, gethostname is a system call. Under Linux/i386, gethostname is implemented at the library level by calling uname(2).

## SEE ALSO

getdomainname(2), setdomainname(2), uname(2)

# getitimer, setitimer

getitimer, setitimer—Gets/sets value of an interval timer

## SYNOPSIS

```
#include <sys/time.h>
int getitimer(int which, struct itimerval *value);
int setitimer(int which,conststruct itimer-val *value, struct itimerval *ovalue);
```

## DESCRIPTION

The system provides each process with three interval timers, each decrementing in a distinct time domain. When any timer expires, a signal is sent to the process, and the timer (potentially) restarts.

ITIMER_REAL                  Decrements in real time and delivers SIGALRM upon expiration.

ITIMER_VIRTUAL               Decrements only when the process is executing, and delivers SIGVTALRM upon expiration.

ITIMER_PROF                  Decrements both when the process executes and when the system is executing on behalf of the process. Coupled with ITIMER_VIRTUAL, this timer is usually used to profile the time spent by the application in user and kernel space. SIGPROF is delivered upon expiration.

Timer values are defined by the following structures:

```
struct itimerval {
            struct timeval it_interval; /* next value */
            struct timeval it_value;    /* current value */
        };
        struct timeval {
            long tv_sec;                /* seconds */
            long tv_usec;               /* microseconds */
        };
```

getitimer(2) fills the structure indicated by *value* with the current setting for the timer indicated by *which* (one of ITIMER_REAL, ITIMER_VIRTUAL, or ITIMER_PROF). The element it_value is set to the amount of time remaining on the timer, or 0 if the timer is disabled. Similarly, it_interval is set to the reset value. setitimer(2) sets the indicated timer to the value in *value*. If *ovalue* is nonzero, the old value of the timer is stored there.

Timers decrement from *it_value* to 0, generate a signal, and reset to *it_interval*. A timer that is set to 0 (*it_value* is 0 or the timer expires and *it_interval* is 0) stops.

Both *tv_sec* and *tv_usec* are significant in determining the duration of a timer.

Timers will never expire before the requested time, instead expiring some short, constant time afterward, dependent on the system timer resolution (currently 10ms). Upon expiration, a signal will be generated and the timer reset. If the timer expires while the process is active (always true for ITIMER_VIRT), the signal will be delivered immediately when generated. Otherwise, the delivery will be offset by a small time dependent on the system loading.

## RETURN VALUE

On success, 0 is returned. On error, -1 is returned and errno is set appropriately.

## ERRORS

EFAULT                       *value* and *ovalue* are not valid pointers.

EINVAL                       *which* is not one of ITIMER_REAL, ITIMER_VIRT, or ITIMER_PROF.

## SEE ALSO

gettimeofday(2), sigaction(2), signal(2)

## BUGS

Under Linux, the generation and delivery of a signal are distinct and there each signal is permitted only one outstanding event. It's therefore conceivable that under pathologically heavy loading, ITIMER_REAL will expire before the signal from a previous expiration has been delivered. The second signal in such an event will be lost.

*Linux 0.99.11, 5 August 1993*

# getpagesize

getpagesize—Gets system page size

## SYNOPSIS

```
#include <unistd.h>
size_t getpagesize(void);
```

## DESCRIPTION

Returns the number of bytes in a page. This is the system's page size, which is not necessarily the same as the hardware page size.

## NOTES

getpagesize is implemented as a library function in DLL 4.4.1. Depending on what is defined when the library is compiled, this function returns EXEC_PAGESIZE (set to 4096 in Linux 0.99.11), NBPG (set to 4096 in Linux 0.99.11), or NBPC (not defined in Linux 0.99.11 or DLL 4.4.1 libraries).

## SEE ALSO

sbrk(2)

*Linux 0.99.11, 23 July 1993*

# getpeername

getpeername—Gets the name of the connected peer

## SYNOPSIS

```
int getpeername(int s, struct sockaddr *name,int*namelen);
```

## DESCRIPTION

getpeername returns the name of the peer connected to socket *s*. The *namelen* parameter should be initialized to indicate the amount of space pointed to by *name*. On return it contains the actual size of the name returned (in bytes). The name is truncated if the buffer provided is too small.

## RETURN VALUE

On success, 0 is returned. On error, -1 is returned and errno is set appropriately.

## ERRORS

| | |
|---|---|
| EBADF | The argument *s* is not a valid descriptor. |
| ENOTSOCK | The argument *s* is a file, not a socket. |
| ENOTCONN | The socket is not connected. |
| ENOBUFS | Insufficient resources were available in the system to perform the operation. |
| EFAULT | The *name* parameter points to memory not in a valid part of the process address space. |

## HISTORY

The getpeername function call appeared in BSD 4.2.

## SEE ALSO

accept(2), bind(2), getsockname(2)

*BSD Man Page, 24 July 1993*

# getpid, getppid

getpid, getppid—Gets process identification

## SYNOPSIS

```
#include <unistd.h>
pid_t getpid(void);
pid_t getppid(void);
```

## DESCRIPTION

getpid returns the process ID of the current process. (This is often used by routines that generate unique temporary filenames.)

getppid returns the process ID of the parent of the current process.

## CONFORMS TO

POSIX, BSD 4.3, SVID

## SEE ALSO

exec(2), fork(2), kill(2), mkstemp(3), tmpnam(3), tempnam(3), tmpfile(3)

*Linux 0.99.11, 23 July 1993*

# getpriority, setpriority

getpriority, setpriority—Gets/sets program scheduling priority

## SYNOPSIS

```
#include <sys/time.h>
#include <sys/resource.h>
int getpriority(int which,int who);
int setpriority(int which,int who,int prio);
```

## DESCRIPTION

The scheduling priority of the process, process group, or user, as indicated by *which* and *who,* is obtained with the getpriority call and set with the setpriority call. *which* is one of PRIO_PROCESS, PRIO_PGRP,or PRIO_USER, and *who* is interpreted relative to *which* (a process identifier for PRIO_PROCESS, process group identifier for PRIO_PGRP, and a user ID for PRIO_USER). A 0 value of *who* denotes the current process, process group, or user. *prio* is a value in the range –20 to 20. The default priority is 0; lower priorities cause more favorable scheduling.

The getpriority call returns the highest priority (lowest numerical value) enjoyed by any of the specified processes. The setpriority call sets the priorities of all the specified processes to the specified value. Only the superuser may lower priorities.

## RETURN VALUES

Because getpriority can legitimately return the value -1, it is necessary to clear the external variable errno prior to the call, and then check it afterward to determine whether a -1 is an error or a legitimate value. The setpriority call returns 0 if there is no error, or -1 if there is.

## ERRORS

| | |
|---|---|
| ESRCH | No process was located using the *which* and *who* values specified. |
| EINVAL | *which* was not one of PRIO_PROCESS, PRIO_PGRP,or PRIO_USER. |

In addition to these errors, setpriority will fail with the following:

EPERM                          A process was located, but neither its effective nor real user ID matched the effective user ID
                               of the caller.

EACCES                         A nonsuperuser attempted to lower a process priority.

## HISTORY

These function calls appeared in BSD 4.2.

## SEE ALSO

nice(1), fork(2), renice(8)

*BSD Man Page, 24 July 1993*

# getrlimit, getrusage, setrlimit

getrlimit, getrusage, setrlimit—Get/set resource limits and usage

## SYNOPSIS

```
#include <sys/time.h>
#include <sys/resource.h>
#include <unistd.h>

int getrlimit (int resource, struct rlimit *rlim);
int getrusage (int who, struct rusage *usage);
int setrlimit (int resource, const struct rlimit *rlim);
```

## DESCRIPTION

getrlimit and setrlimit get and set resource limits. *resource* should be one of the following:

```
RLIMIT CPU /* CPU time in seconds */
RLIMIT FSIZE /* Maximum filesize */
RLIMIT DATA /* max data size */
RLIMIT STACK /* max stack size */
RLIMIT CORE /* max core file size */
RLIMIT RSS /* max resident set size */
RLIMIT NPROC /* max number of processes */
RLIMIT NOFILE /* max number of open files */
RLIMIT MEMLOCK /* max locked-in-memory address space*/
```

A resource may be unlimited if you set the limit to RLIM_INFINITY. RLIMIT_OFILE is the BSD name for RLIMIT_NOFILE.

The rlimit structure is defined as follows :

```
struct rlimit
        {
            int  rlim_cur;
            int  rlim_max;
        };
```

getrusage returns the current resource usages for a *who* of either RUSAGE_SELF or RUSAGE_CHILDREN:

```
struct rusage
        {
            struct timeval ru_utime; /* user time used */
            struct timeval ru_stime; /* system time used */
            long ru_maxrss;          /* maximum resident set size */
            long ru_ixrss;           /* integral shared memory size */
```

```
                long ru_idrss;           /* integral unshared data size */
                long ru_isrss;           /* integral unshared stack size */
                long ru_minflt;          /* page reclaims */
                long ru_majflt;          /* page faults */
                long ru_nswap;           /* swaps */
                long ru_inblock;         /* block input operations */
                long ru_oublock;         /* block output operations */
                long ru_msgsnd;          /* messages sent */
                long ru_msgrcv;          /* messages received */
                long ru_nsignals;        /* signals received */
                long ru_nvcsw;           /* voluntary context switches */
                long ru_nivcsw;          /* involuntary context switches */
        };
```

## RETURN VALUE

On success, 0 is returned. On error, -1 is returned and errno is set appropriately.

## ERRORS

EINVAL                 getrlimit or setrlimit is called with a bad *resource*. getrusage is called with a bad *who*.

EPERM                  A nonsuperuser tries to use setrlimit() to increase the soft or hard limit above the current hard limit, or a superuser tries to increase RLIMIT_NOFILE above the current kernel maximum.

## CONFORMS TO

BSD 4.3

## SEE ALSO

ulimit(2), quota(2)

*Linux, 23 July 1993*


# getsid

getsid—Gets session ID

## SYNOPSIS

```
#include <unistd.h>
pid_t getsid(void);
```

## DESCRIPTION

getsid(0) returns the session ID of the calling process. getsid(*p*) returns the session ID of the process with process ID *p*.

## ERRORS

On error, -1 will be returned. The only error that can happen is ESRCH, when no process with process ID *p* was found.

## CONFORMS TO

This call is Linux specific.

## SEE ALSO

setsid(2)

*Linux 1.3.85, 11 April 1996*

# getsockname

`getsockname`—Gets socket name

## SYNOPSIS

```
int getsockname(int s ", struct sockaddr *" name ", int *" namelen );
```

## DESCRIPTION

`getsockname` returns the current *name* for the specified socket. The *namelen* parameter should be initialized to indicate the amount of space pointed to by *name*. On return it contains the actual size of the name returned (in bytes).

## RETURN VALUE

On success, `0` is returned. On error, `-1` is returned and `errno` is set appropriately.

## ERRORS

| | |
|---|---|
| EBADF | The argument *s* is not a valid descriptor. |
| ENOTSOCK | The argument *s* is a file, not a socket. |
| ENOBUFS | Insufficient resources were available in the system to perform the operation. |
| EFAULT | The *name* parameter points to memory not in a valid part of the process address space. |

## HISTORY

The `getsockname` function call appeared in BSD 4.2.

## BUGS

Names bound to sockets in the UNIX domain are inaccessible; `getsockname` returns a 0-length name.

## SEE ALSO

bind(2), socket(2)

*BSD Man Page, 24 July 1993*

# getsockopt, setsockopt

`getsockopt, setsockopt`—Get and set options on sockets

## SYNOPSIS

```
#include <sys/types.h>
#include <sys/socket.h>
int getsockopt(int s,int level,int optname,void *optval,int *optlen);
int setsockopt(int s,int level,int optname, const void *optval,int optlen);
```

## DESCRIPTION

`getsockopt` and `setsockopt` manipulate the *options* associated with a socket. Options may exist at multiple protocol levels; they are always present at the uppermost socket level.

When manipulating socket options, the level at which the option resides and the name of the option must be specified. To manipulate options at the socket level, *level* is specified as `SOL_SOCKET`. To manipulate options at any other level, the protocol number of the appropriate protocol controlling the option is supplied. For example, to indicate that an option is to be interpreted by the TCP protocol, *level* should be set to the protocol number of TCP; see getprotoent(3).

The parameters *optval* and *optlen* are used to access option values for setsockopt. For getsockopt they identify a buffer in which the value for the requested option(s) is to be returned. For getsockopt, *optlen* is a value-result parameter, initially containing the size of the buffer pointed to by *optval*, and modified on return to indicate the actual size of the value returned. If no option value is to be supplied or returned, *optval* may be NULL.

*optname* and any specified options are passed uninterpreted to the appropriate protocol module for interpretation. The include file <sys/socket.h> contains definitions for socket-level options, described below. Options at other protocol levels vary in format and name; consult the appropriate entries in section 4 of the manual.

Most socket-level options utilize an *int* parameter for *optval*. For setsockopt, the parameter should be nonzero to enable a boolean option, or 0 if the option is to be disabled. SO_LINGER uses a *struct* linger parameter, defined in <linux/socket.h>, which specifies the desired state of the option and the linger interval (see below). SO_SNDTIMEO and SO_RCVTIMEO use a *struct* timeval parameter, defined in <sys/time.h>.

The following options are recognized at the socket level. Except as noted, each may be examined with getsockopt and set with setsockopt:

| | |
|---|---|
| SO_DEBUG | Enables recording of debugging information. |
| SO_REUSEADDR | Enables local address reuse. |
| SO_KEEPALIVE | Enables keep connections alive. |
| SO_DONTROUTE | Enables routing bypass for outgoing messages. |
| SO_LINGER | Linger on close if data present. |
| SO_BROADCAST | Enables permission to transmit broadcast messages. |
| SO_OOBINLINE | Enables reception of out-of-band data in band. |
| SO_SNDBUF | Sets buffer size for output. |
| SO_RCVBUF | Sets buffer size for input. |
| SO_SNDLOWAT | Sets minimum count for output. |
| SO_RCVLOWAT | Sets minimum count for input. |
| SO_SNDTIMEO | Sets time-out value for output. |
| SO_RCVTIMEO | Sets time-out value for input. |
| SO_TYPE | Gets the type of the socket (get only). |
| SO_ERROR | Gets and clears error on the socket (get only). |

SO_DEBUG enables debugging in the underlying protocol modules.

SO_REUSEADDR indicates that the rules used in validating addresses supplied in a bind(2) call should allow reuse of local addresses.

SO_KEEPALIVE enables the periodic transmission of messages on a connected socket. Should the connected party fail to respond to these messages, the connection is considered broken and processes using the socket are notified via a SIGPIPE signal when attempting to send data.

SO_DONTROUTE indicates that outgoing messages should bypass the standard routing facilities. Instead, messages are directed to the appropriate network interface according to the network portion of the destination address.

SO_LINGER controls the action taken when unsent messages are queued on socket and a close(2) is performed. If the socket promises reliable delivery of data and SO_LINGER is set, the system will block the process on the close attempt until it is able to transmit the data or until it decides it is unable to deliver the information (a time-out period, termed the linger interval, is specified in the setsockopt call when SO_LINGER is requested). If SO_LINGER is disabled and a close is issued, the system will process the close in a manner that allows the process to continue as quickly as possible.

The *linger* structure is defined in <linux/socket.h> as follows:

```
struct linger {
                int l_onoff;    /* Linger active */
                int l_linger;   /* How long to linger for */
        };
```

l_onoff indicates whether to linger. If it is set to 1, l_linger contains the time in hundredths of seconds how long the process should linger to complete the close. If l_onoff is set to 0, the process returns immediately.

The option SO_BROADCAST requests permission to send broadcast datagrams on the socket. Broadcast was a privileged operation in earlier versions of the system. With protocols that support out-of-band data, the SO_OOBINLINE option requests that out-of-band data be placed in the normal data input queue as received; it will then be accessible with recv or read calls without the MSG_OOB flag. Some protocols always behave as if this option is set.

SO_SNDBUF and SO_RCVBUF are options to adjust the normal buffer sizes allocated for output and input buffers, respectively. The buffer size may be increased for high-volume connections or may be decreased to limit the possible backlog of incoming data. The system places an absolute limit on these values.

SO_SNDLOWAT is an option to set the minimum count for output operations. Most output operations process all of the data supplied by the call, delivering data to the protocol for transmission and blocking as necessary for flow control. Nonblocking output operations will process as much data as permitted subject to flow control without blocking, but will process no data if flow control does not allow the smaller of the low water mark value or the entire request to be processed. A select(2) operation testing the ability to write to a socket will return true only if the low water mark amount could be processed. The default value for SO_SNDLOWAT is set to a convenient size for network efficiency, often 1024.

SO_RCVLOWAT is an option to set the minimum count for input operations. In general, receive calls will block until any (nonzero) amount of data is received, then return with the smaller of the amount available or the amount requested. The default value for SO_RCVLOWAT is 1. If SO_RCVLOWAT is set to a larger value, blocking receive calls normally wait until they have received the smaller of the low water mark value or the requested amount. Receive calls may still return less than the low water mark if an error occurs, a signal is caught, or the type of data next in the receive queue is different than that returned.

SO_SNDTIMEO is an option to set a time-out value for output operations. It accepts a *struct* timeval parameter with the number of seconds and microseconds used to limit waits for output operations to complete. If a send operation has blocked for this much time, it returns with a partial count or with the error EWOULDBLOCK if no data were sent. In the current implementation, this timer is restarted each time additional data are delivered to the protocol, implying that the limit applies to output portions ranging in size from the low water mark to the high water mark for output.

SO_RCVTIMEO is an option to set a time-out value for input operations. It accepts a *struct* timeval parameter with the number of seconds and microseconds used to limit waits for input operations to complete. In the current implementation, this timer is restarted each time additional data are received by the protocol, and thus the limit is in effect an inactivity timer. If a receive operation has been blocked for this much time without receiving additional data, it returns with a short count or with the error EWOULDBLOCK if no data were received.

Finally, SO_TYPE and SO_ERROR are options used only with setsockopt.

SO_TYPE returns the type of the socket, such as SOCK_STREAM; it is useful for servers that inherit sockets on startup.

SO_ERROR returns any pending error on the socket and clears the error status. It may be used to check for asynchronous errors on connected datagram sockets or for other asynchronous errors.

## RETURN VALUE

On success, 0 is returned. On error, -1 is returned and errno is set appropriately.

## ERRORS

| | |
|---|---|
| EBADF | The argument s is not a valid descriptor. |
| ENOTSOCK | The argument s is a file, not a socket. |
| ENOPROTOOPT | The option is unknown at the level indicated. |
| EFAULT | The address pointed to by *optval* is not in a valid part of the process address space. For getsockopt, this error may also be returned if *optlen* is not in a valid part of the process address space. |

## HISTORY

These system calls appeared in BSD 4.2.

## BUGS

Several of the socket options should be handled at lower levels of the system.

## SEE ALSO

ioctl(2), socket(2), getprotoent(3), protocols(5)

*BSD Man Page, 22 April 1996*

# gettimeofday, settimeofday

gettimeofday, settimeofday—Get/set time

## SYNOPSIS

```
#include <sys/time.h>
#include <unistd.h>

int gettimeofday(struct timeval *tv, struct timezone *tz);
int settimeofday(const struct timeval *tv , const struct timezone *tz);
```

## DESCRIPTION

gettimeofday and settimeofday can set the time as well as a time zone. *tv* is a timeval struct, as specified in /usr/include/sys/time.h:

```
struct timeval {
                long tv_sec;        /* seconds */
                long tv_usec;  /* microseconds */
                };

    and tz is a timezone:

    struct timezone {
                int  tz_minuteswest;
                /* minutes west of Greenwich */
                int  tz_dsttime;
                /* type of dst correction */
                };
```

with daylight savings times defined as follows:

```
DST_NONE        /* not on dst */
    DST_USA         /* USA style dst */
    DST_AUST        /* Australian style dst */
    DST_WET         /* Western European dst */
    DST_MET         /* Middle European dst */
    DST_EET         /* Eastern European dst */
    DST_CAN         /* Canada */
    DST_GB          /* Great Britain and Eire */
    DST_RUM         /* Rumania */
    DST_TUR         /* Turkey */
    DST_AUSTALT     /* Australian style with shift in 1986 */
```

And the following macros are defined to operate on this :

```
#define    timerisset(tvp)\
                ((tvp)->tv_sec ¦¦ (tvp)->tv_usec)
      #define    timercmp(tvp, uvp, cmp)\
                ((tvp)->tv_sec cmp (uvp)->tv_sec ¦¦\
                (tvp)->tv_sec == (uvp)->tv_sec &&\
                (tvp)->tv_usec cmp (uvp)->tv_usec)
      #define    timerclear(tvp)
                ((tvp)->tv_sec = (tvp)->tv_usec = 0)
```

If either *tv* or *tz* is null, the corresponding structure is not set or returned.

Only the superuser can use `settimeofday`.

## ERRORS

EPERM                          `settimeofday` is called by someone other than the superuser.

EINVAL                         Time zone (or something else) is invalid.

## CONFORMS TO

BSD 4.3

## SEE ALSO

date(1), adjtimex(2), time(2), ctime(3), ftime(3)

*Linux 1.2.4, 15 April 1995*

# getuid, geteuid

getuid, geteuid—Get user identity

## SYNOPSIS

```
#include <unistd.h>
uid_t getuid(void);
uid_t geteuid(void);
```

## DESCRIPTION

getuid returns the real user ID of the current process.

geteuid returns the effective user ID of the current process.

The real ID corresponds to the ID of the calling process. The effective ID corresponds to the set ID bit on the file being executed.

## ERRORS

These functions are always successful.

## CONFORMS TO

POSIX, BSD 4.3

## SEE ALSO

setreuid(2), setuid(2)

*Linux 0.99.11, 23 July 1993*

# idle

idle—Makes process 0 idle

## SYNOPSIS

```
#include <unistd.h>
void idle(void);
```

## DESCRIPTION

idle is an internal system call used during bootstrap. It marks the process's pages as swappable, lowers its priority, and enters the main scheduling loop. idle never returns.

Only process 0 may call idle. Any user process, even a process with superuser permission, will receive EPERM.

## RETURN VALUE

idle never returns for process 0, and always returns -1 for a user process.

## ERRORS

EPERM                        Always, for a user process.

*Linux 1.1.46, 21 August 1994*

# ioctl

ioctl—Controls devices

## SYNOPSIS

```
#include <sys/ioctl.h>
int ioctl(int d,intrequest, ...);
```

(The "third" argument is traditionally char *argp and will be so named for this discussion.)

## DESCRIPTION

The ioctl function manipulates the underlying device parameters of special files. In particular, many operating characteristics of character special files (for example, terminals) may be controlled with ioctl requests. The argument *d* must be an open file descriptor.

An ioctl *request* has encoded in it whether the argument is an *in* parameter or *out* parameter, and the size of the argument *argp* in bytes. Macros and defines used in specifying an ioctl *request* are located in the file <sys/ioctl.h>.

## RETURN VALUE

On success, 0 is returned. On error, -1 is returned and errno is set appropriately.

## ERRORS

EBADF                        *d* is not a valid descriptor.

ENOTTY                       *d* is not associated with a character special device.

ENOTTY                       The specified request does not apply to the kind of object that the descriptor *d* references.

EINVAL                       *request* or *argp* is not valid.

## HISTORY

An ioctl function call appeared in version 7 AT&T UNIX.

## SEE ALSO

execve(2), fcntl(2), mt(4), sd(4), tty(4)

## INTRODUCTION

This is ioctl List 1.3.27, a list of ioctl calls in Linux/i386 kernel 1.3.27. It contains 421 ioctls from /usr/include/ fasm,linuxg/*.h. For each ioctl, you'll find the numerical value, name, and argument type.

An argument type of const struct foo * means the argument is input to the kernel. struct foo * means the kernel outputs the argument. If the kernel uses the argument for both input and output, this is marked with // I-0.

Some ioctls take more arguments or return more values than a single structure. These are marked with // MORE and are documented further in a separate section.

This list is incomplete. It does not include

- ioctls defined internal to the kernel (scsi ioctl.h).
- ioctls defined in modules distributed separately from the kernel.

And, of course, I may have errors and omissions.

Please e-mail changes and comments to mec@duracef.shout.net. I am particularly interested in loadable modules that define their own ioctls. If you know of such a module, tell me where I can ftp it, and I'll include its ioctls in my next release.

## MAIN TABLE

*<include/asm-i386/socket.h>*

| | | |
|---|---|---|
| 0x00008901 | FIOSETOWN | const int * |
| 0x00008902 | SIOCSPGRP | const int * |
| 0x00008903 | FIOGETOWN | int * |
| 0x00008904 | SIOCGPGRP | int * |
| 0x00008905 | SIOCATMARK | int * |
| 0x00008906 | SIOCGSTAMP | timeval * |

*<include/asm-i386/termios.h>*

| | | |
|---|---|---|
| 0x00005401 | TCGETS | struct termios * |
| 0x00005402 | TCSETS | const struct termios * |
| 0x00005403 | TCSETSW | const struct termios * |
| 0x00005404 | TCSETSF | const struct termios * |
| 0x00005405 | TCGETA | struct termio * |
| 0x00005406 | TCSETA | const struct termio * |
| 0x00005407 | TCSETAW | const struct termio * |
| 0x00005408 | TCSETAF | const struct termio * |
| 0x00005409 | TCSBRK | int |
| 0x0000540A | TCXONC | int |
| 0x0000540B | TCFLSH | int |
| 0x0000540C | TIOCEXCL | void |
| 0x0000540D | TIOCNXCL | void |
| 0x0000540E | TIOCSCTTY | int |
| 0x0000540F | TIOCGPGRP | pid_t * |
| 0x00005410 | TIOCSPGRP | const pid_t * |

`<include/asm-i386/termios.h>`

| | | |
|---|---|---|
| 0x00005411 | TIOCOUTQ | int * |
| 0x00005412 | TIOCSTI | const char * |
| 0x00005413 | TIOCGWINSZ | const struct winsize * |
| 0x00005414 | TIOCSWINSZ | struct winsize * |
| 0x00005415 | TIOCMGET | int * |
| 0x00005416 | TIOCMBIS | const int * |
| 0x00005417 | TIOCMBIC | const int * |
| 0x00005418 | TIOCMSET | const int * |
| 0x00005419 | TIOCGSOFTCAR | int * |
| 0x0000541A | TIOCSSOFTCAR | const int * |
| 0x0000541B | FIONREAD | int * |
| 0x0000541B | TIOCINQ | int * |
| 0x0000541C | TIOCLINUX | const char * |
| 0x0000541D | TIOCCONS | void |
| 0x0000541E | TIOCGSERIAL | struct serial_strucct * |
| 0x0000541F | TIOCSSERIAL | const struct serial_strucct * |
| 0x00005420 | TIOCPKT | const int * |
| 0x00005421 | FIONBIO | const int * |
| 0x00005422 | TIOCNOTTY | void |
| 0x00005423 | TIOCSETD | const int * |
| 0x00005424 | TIOCGETD | int * |
| 0x00005425 | TCSBRKP | int |
| 0x00005426 | TIOCTTYGSTRUCT | struct tty_strucct * |
| 0x00005450 | FIONCLEX | void |
| 0x00005451 | FIOCLEX | void |
| 0x00005452 | FIOASYNC | const int * |
| 0x00005453 | TIOCSERCONFIG | void |
| 0x00005454 | TIOCSERGWILD | int * |
| 0x00005455 | TIOCSERSWILD | const int * |
| 0x00005456 | TIOCGLCKTRMIOS | struct termios * |
| 0x00005457 | TIOCSLCKTRMIOS | const struct temios * |
| 0x00005458 | TIOCSERGSTRUCT | struct async_strucct * |
| 0x00005459 | TIOCSERGETLSR | int * |
| 0x0000545A | TIOCSERGETMULTI | struct serial_multiport_strucct * |
| 0x0000545B | TIOCSERSETMULTI | const struct serial_multiport_strucct * |

`<include/linux/ax25.h>`

| | | |
|---|---|---|
| 0x000089E0 | SIOCAX25GETUID | const struct sockaddr_ax25 * |
| 0x000089E1 | SIOCAX25ADDUID | const struct sockaddr_ax25 * |
| 0x000089E2 | SIOCAX25DELUID | const struct sockaddr_ax25 * |
| 0x000089E3 | SIOCAX25NOUID | const int * |

<include/linux/ax25.h>

| | | |
|---|---|---|
| 0x000089E4 | SIOCAX25DIGCTL | const int * |
| 0x000089E5 | SIOCAX25GETPARMS | struct ax25_parms_strucct * // I-O |
| 0x000089E6 | SIOCAX25SETPARMS | const struct ax25_parms-struct * |

<include/linux/cdk.h>

| | | |
|---|---|---|
| 0x00007314 | STL_BINTR | void |
| 0x00007315 | STL_BSTART | void |
| 0x00007316 | STL_BSTOP | void |
| 0x00007317 | STL_BRESET | void |

<include/linux/cdrom.h>

| | | |
|---|---|---|
| 0x00005301 | CDROMPAUSE | void |
| 0x00005302 | CDROMRESUME | void |
| 0x00005303 | CDROMPLAYMSF | const struct cdrom_msf * |
| 0x00005304 | CDROMPLAYTRKIND | const struct cdrom_ti * |
| 0x00005305 | CDROMREADTOCHDR | struct cdrom_tochdr * |
| 0x00005306 | CDROMREADTOCENTRY | struct cdrom_tocentry *// I-O |
| 0x00005307 | CDROMSTOP | void |
| 0x00005308 | CDROMSTART | void |
| 0x00005309 | CDROMEJECT | void |
| 0x0000530A | CDROMVOLCTRL | const struct cdrom_volctrl * |
| 0x0000530B | CDROMSUBCHNL | struct cdrom_subchnl * // I-O |
| 0x0000530C | CDROMREADMODE2 | const struct cdrom_msf * // MORE |
| 0x0000530D | CDROMREADMODE1 | const struct cdrom_msf * // MORE |
| 0x0000530E | CDROMREADAUDIO | const struct cdrom_read_audio * |
| 0x0000530F | CDROMEJECT | SW int |
| 0x00005310 | CDROMMULTISESSION | struct cdrom_multisession * // I-O |
| 0x00005311 | CDROM_GET_UPC | struct f char [8]; g * |
| 0x00005312 | CDROMRESET | void |
| 0x00005313 | CDROMVOLREAD | struct cdrom_volctrl * |
| 0x00005314 | CDROMREADRAW | const struct cdrom_msf * // MORE |
| 0x00005315 | CDROMREADCOOKED | const struct cdrom_msf * // MORE |
| 0x00005316 | CDROMSEEK | const struct cdrom_msf * |

<include/linux/cm206.h>

| | | |
|---|---|---|
| 0x00002000 | CM206CTL_GET_STAT | int |
| 0x00002001 | CM206CTL_GET_LAST_STAT | int |

*<include/linux/cyclades.h>*

| | | |
|---|---|---|
| 0x00435901 | CYGETMON | struct cyclades_monitor * |
| 0x00435902 | CYGETTHRESH | int * |
| 0x00435903 | CYSETTHRESH | int |
| 0x00435904 | CYGETDEFTHRESH | int * |
| 0x00435905 | CYSETDEFTHRESH | int |
| 0x00435906 | CYGETTIMEOUT | int * |
| 0x00435907 | CYSETTIMEOUT | int |
| 0x00435908 | CYGETDEFTIMEOUT | int * |
| 0x00435909 | CYSETDEFTIMEOUT | int |

*<include/linux/ext2 fs.h>*

| | | |
|---|---|---|
| 0x80046601 | EXT2_IOC_GETFLAGS | int * |
| 0x40046602 | EXT2_IOC_SETFLAGS | const int * |
| 0x80047601 | EXT2_IOC_GETVERSION | int * |
| 0x40047602 | EXT2_IOC_SETVERSION | const int * |

*<include/linux/fd.h>*

| | | |
|---|---|---|
| 0x00000000 | FDCLRPRM | void |
| 0x00000001 | FDSETPRM | const struct floppy_struct * |
| 0x00000002 | FDDEFPRM | const struct floppy_struct * |
| 0x00000003 | FDGETPRM | struct floppy_struct * |
| 0x00000004 | FDMSGON | void |
| 0x00000005 | FDMSGOFF | void |
| 0x00000006 | FDFMTBEG | void |
| 0x00000007 | FDFMTTRK | const struct format_descr * |
| 0x00000008 | FDFMTEND | void |
| 0x0000000A | FDSETEMSGTRESH | int |
| 0x0000000B | FDFLUSH | void |
| 0x0000000C | FDSETMAXERRS | const struct floppy_max_errors * |
| 0x0000000E | FDGETMAXERRS | struct floppy_max_errors * |
| 0x00000010 | FDGETDRVTYP | struct f char [16]; g * |
| 0x00000014 | FDSETDRVPRM | const struct floppy_drive_params * |
| 0x00000015 | FDGETDRVPRM | struct floppy_drive_params * |
| 0x00000016 | FDGETDRVSTAT | struct floppy_drive_struct * |
| 0x00000017 | FDPOLLDRVSTAT | struct floppy_drive_struct * |
| 0x00000018 | FDRESET | int |
| 0x00000019 | FDGETFDCSTAT | struct floppy_fdc_state * |
| 0x0000001B | FDWERRORCLR | void |
| 0x0000001C | FDWERRORGET | struct floppy_write_errors * |
| 0x0000001E | FDRAWCMD | struct floppy_raw_cmd * // MORE // I-O |
| 0x00000028 | FDTWADDLE | void |

*<include/linux/fs.h>*

| | | |
|---|---|---|
| 0x0000125D | BLKROSET | const int * |
| 0x0000125E | BLKROGET | int * |
| 0x0000125F | BLKRRPART | void |
| 0x00001260 | BLKGETSIZE | int * |
| 0x00001261 | BLKFLSBUF | void |
| 0x00001262 | BLKRASET | int |
| 0x00001263 | BLKRAGET | int * |
| 0x00000001 | FIBMAP | int * // I-O |
| 0x00000002 | FIGETBSZ | int * |

*<include/linux/hdreg.h>*

| | | |
|---|---|---|
| 0x00000301 | HDIO_GETGEO | struct hd geometry * |
| 0x00000302 | HDIO_GET_UNMASKINTR | int * |
| 0x00000304 | HDIO_GET_MULTCOUNT | int * |
| 0x00000307 | HDIO_GET_IDENTITY | struct hd driveid * |
| 0x00000308 | HDIO_GET_KEEPSETTINGS | int * |
| 0x00000309 | HDIO_GET_CHIPSET | int * |
| 0x0000030A | HDIO_GET_NOWERR | int * |
| 0x0000030B | HDIO_GET_DMA | int * |
| 0x0000031F | HDIO_DRIVE_CMD | int * // I-O |
| 0x00000321 | HDIO_SET_MULTCOUNT | int |
| 0x00000322 | HDIO_SET_UNMASKINTR | int |
| 0x00000323 | HDIO_SET_KEEPSETTINGS | int |
| 0x00000324 | HDIO_SET_CHIPSET | int |
| 0x00000325 | HDIO_SET_NOWERR | int |
| 0x00000326 | HDIO_SET_DMA | int |

*<include/linux/if eql.h>*

| | | |
|---|---|---|
| 0x000089F0 | EQL_ENSLAVE | struct ifreq * // MORE // I-O |
| 0x000089F1 | EQL_EMANCIPATE | struct ifreq * // MORE // I-O |
| 0x000089F2 | EQL_GETSLAVECFG | struct ifreq * // MORE // I-O |
| 0x000089F3 | EQL_SETSLAVECFG | struct ifreq * // MORE // I-O |
| 0x000089F4 | EQL_GETMASTRCFG | struct ifreq * // MORE // I-O |
| 0x000089F5 | EQL_SETMASTRCFG | struct ifreq * // MORE // I-O |

*<include/linux/if plip.h>*

| | | |
|---|---|---|
| 0x000089F0 | SIOCDEVPLIP | struct ifreq * // I-O |

*<include/linux/if ppp.h>*

| | | |
|---|---|---|
| 0x00005490 | PPPIOCGFLAGS | int * |
| 0x00005491 | PPPIOCSFLAGS | const int * |
| 0x00005492 | PPPIOCGASYNCMAP | int * |
| 0x00005493 | PPPIOCSASYNCMAP | const int * |
| 0x00005494 | PPPIOCGUNIT | int * |
| 0x00005495 | PPPIOCSINPSIG | const int * |
| 0x00005497 | PPPIOCSDEBUG | const int * |
| 0x00005498 | PPPIOCGDEBUG | int * |
| 0x00005499 | PPPIOCGSTAT | struct ppp_stats * |
| 0x0000549A | PPPIOCGTIME | struct ppp_ddinfo * |
| 0x0000549B | PPPIOCGXASYNCMAP | struct f int [8]; g * |
| 0x0000549C | PPPIOCSXASYNCMAP | const struct f int [8]; g * |
| 0x0000549D | PPPIOCSMRU | const int * |
| 0x0000549E | PPPIOCRASYNCMAP | const int * |
| 0x0000549F | PPPIOCSMAXCID | const int * |

*<include/linux/ipx.h>*

| | | |
|---|---|---|
| 0x000089E0 | SIOCAIPXITFCRT | const char * |
| 0x000089E1 | SIOCAIPXPRISLT | const char * |
| 0x000089E2 | SIOCIPXCFGDATA | struct ipx_config_data * |

*<include/linux/kd.h>*

| | | |
|---|---|---|
| 0x00004B60 | GIO_FONT | struct f char [8192]; g * |
| 0x00004B61 | PIO_FONT | const struct f char [8192]; g * |
| 0x00004B6B | GIO_FONTX | struct console_font_desc * // MORE I-O |
| 0x00004B6C | PIO_FONTX | const struct console_font_desc * //MORE |
| 0x00004B70 | GIO_CMAP | struct f char [48]; g * |
| 0x00004B71 | PIO_CMAP | const struct f char [48]; g |
| 0x00004B2F | KIOCSOUND | int |
| 0x00004B30 | KDMKTONE | int |
| 0x00004B31 | KDGETLED | char * |
| 0x00004B32 | KDSETLED | int |
| 0x00004B33 | KDGKBTYPE | char * |
| 0x00004B34 | KDADDIO | int // MORE |
| 0x00004B35 | KDDELIO | int // MORE |
| 0x00004B36 | KDENABIO | void // MORE |
| 0x00004B37 | KDDISABIO | void // MORE |
| 0x00004B3A | KDSETMODE | int |
| 0x00004B3B | KDGETMODE | int * |
| 0x00004B3C | KDMAPDISP | void // MORE |

*<include/linux/kd.h>*

| | | |
|---|---|---|
| 0x00004B3D | KDUNMAPDISP | void // MORE |
| 0x00004B40 | GIO_SCRNMAP | struct f char [E_TABSZ]; g * |
| 0x00004B41 | PIO_SCRNMAP | const struct f char [E_TABSZ]; g * |
| 0x00004B69 | GIO_UNISCRNMAP | struct f short [E_TABSZ]; g * |
| 0x00004B6A | PIO_UNISCRNMAP | const struct f short [E_TABSZ]; g * |
| 0x00004B66 | GIO_UNIMAP | struct unimapdesc * // MORE // I-O |
| 0x00004B67 | PIO_UNIMAP | const struct unimapdesc * // MORE |
| 0x00004B68 | PIO_UNIMAPCLR | const struct unimapinit * |
| 0x00004B44 | KDGKBMODE | int * |
| 0x00004B45 | KDSKBMODE | int |
| 0x00004B62 | KDGKBMETA | int * |
| 0x00004B63 | KDSKBMETA | int |
| 0x00004B64 | KDGKBLED | int * |
| 0x00004B65 | KDSKBLED | int |
| 0x00004B46 | KDGKBENT | struct kbentry * // I-O |
| 0x00004B47 | KDSKBENT | const struct kbentry * |
| 0x00004B48 | KDGKBSENT | struct kbsentry * // I-O |
| 0x00004B49 | KDSKBSENT | const struct kbsentry * |
| 0x00004B4A | KDGKBDIACR | struct kbdiacrs * |
| 0x00004B4B | KDSKBDIACR | const struct kbdiacrs * |
| 0x00004B4C | KDGETKEYCODE | struct kbkeycode * // I-O |
| 0x00004B4D | KDSETKEYCODE | const struct kbkeycode * |
| 0x00004B4E | KDSIGACCEPT | int |

*<include/linux/lp.h>*

| | | |
|---|---|---|
| 0x00000601 | LPCHAR | int |
| 0x00000602 | LPTIME | int |
| 0x00000604 | LPABORT | int |
| 0x00000605 | LPSETIRQ | int |
| 0x00000606 | LPGETIRQ | int * |
| 0x00000608 | LPWAIT | int |
| 0x00000609 | LPCAREFUL | int |
| 0x0000060A | LPABORTOPEN | int |
| 0x0000060B | LPGETSTATUS | int * |
| 0x0000060C | LPRESET | void |
| 0x0000060D | LPGETSTATS | struct lp stats * |

*<include/linux/mroute.h>*

| | | |
|---|---|---|
| 0x000089E0 | SIOCGETVIFCNT | struct sioc_vif_req * // I-O |
| 0x000089E1 | SIOCGETSGCNT | struct sioc_sg_req * // I-O |

*<include/linux/mtio.h>*

| 0x40086D01 | MTIOCTOP | const struct mtop * |
| 0x801C6D02 | MTIOCGET | struct mtget * |
| 0x80046D03 | MTIOCPOS | struct mtpos * |
| 0x80206D04 | MTIOCGETCONFIG | struct mtconfiginfo * |
| 0x40206D05 | MTIOCSETCONFIG | const struct mtconfiginfo * |

*<include/linux/netrom.h>*

| 0x000089E0 | SIOCNRGETPARMS | struct nr_parms_struct * // I-O |
| 0x000089E1 | SIOCNRSETPARMS | const struct nr_parms_struct * |
| 0x000089E2 | SIOCNRDECOBS | void |
| 0x000089E3 | SIOCNRRTCTL | const int * |

*<include/linux/sbpcd.h>*

| 0x00009000 | DDIOCSDBG | const int * |
| 0x00005382 | CDROMAUDIOBUFSIZ | int |

*<include/linux/scc.h>*

| 0x00005470 | TIOCSCCINI | void |
| 0x00005471 | TIOCCHANINI | const struct scc_modem * |
| 0x00005472 | TIOCGKISS | struct ioctl_command * // I-O |
| 0x00005473 | TIOCSKISS | const struct ioctl_command * |
| 0x00005474 | TIOCSCCSTAT | struct scc_stat * |

*<include/linux/scsi.h>*

| 0x00005382 | SCSI_IOCTL_GET_IDLUN | struct f int [2]; g * |
| 0x00005383 | SCSI_IOCTL_TAGGED_ENABLE | void |
| 0x00005384 | SCSI_IOCTL_TAGGED_DISABLE | void |
| 0x00005385 | SCSI_IOCTL_PROBE_HOST | const int * // MORE |

*<include/linux/smb fs.h>*

| 0x80027501 | SMB_IOC_GETMOUNTUID | uid t * |

*<include/linux/sockios.h>*

| 0x0000890B | SIOCADDRT | const struct rtentry * // MORE |
| 0x0000890C | SIOCDELRT | const struct rtentry * // MORE |
| 0x00008910 | SIOCGIFNAME | char [] |
| 0x00008911 | SIOCSIFLINK | void |
| 0x00008912 | SIOCGIFCONF | struct ifconf * // MORE // I-O |
| 0x00008913 | SIOCGIFFLAGS | struct ifreq * // I-O |
| 0x00008914 | SIOCSIFFLAGS | const struct ifreq * |

<include/linux/sockios.h>

| | | |
|---|---|---|
| 0x00008915 | SIOCGIFADDR | struct ifreq * // I-O |
| 0x00008916 | SIOCSIFADDR | const struct ifreq * |
| 0x00008917 | SIOCGIFDSTADDR | struct ifreq * // I-O |
| 0x00008918 | SIOCSIFDSTADDR | const struct ifreq * |
| 0x00008919 | SIOCGIFBRDADDR | struct ifreq * // I-O |
| 0x0000891A | SIOCSIFBRDADDR | const struct ifreq * |
| 0x0000891B | SIOCGIFNETMASK | struct ifreq * // I-O |
| 0x0000891C | SIOCSIFNETMASK | const struct ifreq * |
| 0x0000891D | SIOCGIFMETRIC | struct ifreq * // I-O |
| 0x0000891E | SIOCSIFMETRIC | const struct ifreq * |
| 0x0000891F | SIOCGIFMEM | struct ifreq * // I-O |
| 0x00008920 | SIOCSIFMEM | const struct ifreq * |
| 0x00008921 | SIOCGIFMTU | struct ifreq * // I-O |
| 0x00008922 | SIOCSIFMTU | const struct ifreq * |
| 0x00008923 | OLD SIOCGIFHWADDR | struct ifreq * // I-O |
| 0x00008924 | SIOCSIFHWADDR | const struct ifreq * // MORE |
| 0x00008925 | SIOCGIFENCAP | int * |
| 0x00008926 | SIOCSIFENCAP | const int * |
| 0x00008927 | SIOCGIFHWADDR | struct ifreq * // I-O |
| 0x00008929 | SIOCGIFSLAVE | void |
| 0x00008930 | SIOCSIFSLAVE | void |
| 0x00008931 | SIOCADDMULTI | const struct ifreq * |
| 0x00008932 | SIOCDELMULTI | const struct ifreq * |
| 0x00008940 | SIOCADDRTOLD | void |
| 0x00008941 | SIOCDELRTOLD | void |
| 0x00008950 | SIOCDARP | const struct arpreq * |
| 0x00008951 | SIOCGARP | struct arpreq * // I-O |
| 0x00008952 | SIOCSARP | const struct arpreq * |
| 0x00008960 | SIOCDRARP | const struct arpreq * |
| 0x00008961 | SIOCGRARP | struct arpreq * // I-O |
| 0x00008962 | SIOCSRARP | const struct arpreq * |
| 0x00008970 | SIOCGIFMAP | struct ifreq * // I-O |
| 0x00008971 | SIOCSIFMAP | const struct ifreq * |

<include/linux/soundcard.h>

| | | |
|---|---|---|
| 0x00005100 | SNDCTL_SEQ_RESET | void |
| 0x00005101 | SNDCTL_SEQ_SYNC | void |
| 0xC08C5102 | SNDCTL_SYNTH_INFO | struct synth_info * // I-O |
| 0xC0045103 | SNDCTL_SEQ_CTRLRATE | int * // I-O |
| 0x80045104 | SNDCTL_SEQ_GETOUTCOUNT | int * |
| 0x80045105 | SNDCTL_SEQ_GETINCOUNT | int * |
| 0x40045106 | SNDCTL_SEQ_PERCMODE | void |

<include/linux/soundcard.h>

| | | |
|---|---|---|
| 0x40285107 | SNDCTL_FM_LOAD_INSTR | const struct sbi_instrument * |
| 0x40045108 | SNDCTL_SEQ_TESTMIDI | const int * |
| 0x40045109 | SNDCTL_SEQ_RESETSAMPLES | const int * |
| 0x8004510A | SNDCTL_SEQ_NRSYNTHS | int * |
| 0x8004510B | SNDCTL_SEQ_NRMIDIS | int * |
| 0xC074510C | SNDCTL_MIDI_INFO | struct midi_info * // I-O |
| 0x4004510D | SNDCTL_SEQ_THRESHOLD | const int * |
| 0xC004510E | SNDCTL_SYNTH_MEMAVL | int * // I-O |
| 0x4004510F | SNDCTL_FM_4OP_ENABLE | const int * |
| 0xCFB85110 | SNDCTL_PMGR_ACCESS | struct patmgr_info * // I-O |
| 0x00005111 | SNDCTL_SEQ_PANIC | void |
| 0x40085112 | SNDCTL_SEQ_OUTOFBAND | const struct seq_event_rec * |
| 0xC0045401 | SNDCTL_TMR_TIMEBASE | int * // I-O |
| 0x00005402 | SNDCTL_TMR_START | void |
| 0x00005403 | SNDCTL_TMR_STOP | void |
| 0x00005404 | SNDCTL_TMR_CONTINUE | void |
| 0xC0045405 | SNDCTL_TMR_TEMPO | int * // I-O |
| 0xC0045406 | SNDCTL_TMR_SOURCE | int * // I-O |
| 0x40045407 | SNDCTL_TMR_METRONOME | const int * |
| 0x40045408 | SNDCTL_TMR_SELECT | int * // I-O |
| 0xCFB85001 | SNDCTL_PMGR_IFACE | struct patmgr_info * // I-O |
| 0xC0046D00 | SNDCTL_MIDI_PRETIME | int * // I-O |
| 0xC0046D01 | SNDCTL_MIDI_MPUMODE | const int * |
| 0xC0216D02 | SNDCTL_MIDI_MPUCMD | struct mpu_command_rec * // I-O |
| 0x00005000 | SNDCTL_DSP_RESET | void |
| 0x00005001 | SNDCTL_DSP_SYNC | void |
| 0xC0045002 | SNDCTL_DSP_SPEED | int * // I-O |
| 0xC0045003 | SNDCTL_DSP_STEREO | int * // I-O |
| 0xC0045004 | SNDCTL_DSP_GETBLKSIZE | int * // I-O |
| 0xC0045006 | SOUND_PCM_WRITE_CHANNELS | int * // I-O |
| 0xC0045007 | SOUND_PCM_WRITE_FILTER | int * // I-O |
| 0x00005008 | SNDCTL_DSP_POST | void |
| 0xC0045009 | SNDCTL_DSP_SUBDIVIDE | int * // I-O |
| 0xC004500A | SNDCTL_DSP_SETFRAGMENT | int * // I-O |
| 0x8004500B | SNDCTL_DSP_GETFMTS | int * |
| 0xC0045005 | SNDCTL_DSP_SETFMT | int * // I-O |
| 0x800C500C | SNDCTL_DSP_GETOSPACE | struct audio-buf-info * |
| 0x800C500D | SNDCTL_DSP_GETISPACE | struct audio-buf-info * |
| 0x0000500E | SNDCTL_DSP_NONBLOCK | void |
| 0x80045002 | SOUND_PCM_READ_RATE | int * |
| 0x80045006 | SOUND_PCM_READ_CHANNELS | int * |
| 0x80045005 | SOUND_PCM_READ_BITS | int * |

<include/linux/soundcard.h>

| | | |
|---|---|---|
| 0x80045007 | SOUND_PCM_READ FILTER | int * |
| 0x00004300 | SNDCTL_COPR_RESET | void |
| 0xCFB04301 | SNDCTL_COPR_LOAD | const struct copr_buffer * |
| 0xC0144302 | SNDCTL_COPR_RDATA | struct copr_debug_buf * // I-O |
| 0xC0144303 | SNDCTL_COPR_RCODE | struct copr_debug_buf * // I-O |
| 0x40144304 | SNDCTL_COPR_WDATA | const struct copr_debug_buf * |
| 0x40144305 | SNDCTL_COPR_WCODE | const struct copr_debug_buf * |
| 0xC0144306 | SNDCTL_COPR_RUN | struct copr_debug_buf * // I-O |
| 0xC0144307 | SNDCTL_COPR_HALT | struct copr_debug_buf * // I-O |
| 0x4FA44308 | SNDCTL_COPR_SENDMSG | const struct copr_msg * |
| 0x8FA44309 | SNDCTL_COPR_RCVMSG | struct copr_msg * |
| 0x80044D00 | SOUND_MIXER_READ_VOLUME | int * |
| 0x80044D01 | SOUND_MIXER_READ_BASS | int * |
| 0x80044D02 | SOUND_MIXER_READ_TREBLE | int * |
| 0x80044D03 | SOUND_MIXER_READ_SYNTH | int * |
| 0x80044D04 | SOUND_MIXER_READ_PCM | int * |
| 0x80044D05 | SOUND_MIXER_READ_SPEAKER | int * |
| 0x80044D06 | SOUND_MIXER_READ_LINE | int * |
| 0x80044D07 | SOUND_MIXER_READ_MIC | int * |
| 0x80044D08 | SOUND_MIXER_READ_CD | int * |
| 0x80044D09 | SOUND_MIXER_READ_IMIX | int * |
| 0x80044D0A | SOUND_MIXER_READ_ALTPCM | int * |
| 0x80044D0B | SOUND_MIXER_READ_RECLEV | int * |
| 0x80044D0C | SOUND_MIXER_READ_IGAIN | int * |
| 0x80044D0D | SOUND_MIXER_READ_OGAIN | int * |
| 0x80044D0E | SOUND_MIXER_READ_LINE1 | int * |
| 0x80044D0F | SOUND_MIXER_READ_LINE2 | int * |
| 0x80044D10 | SOUND_MIXER_READ_LINE3 | int * |
| 0x80044D1C | SOUND_MIXER_READ_MUTE | int * |
| 0x80044D1D | SOUND_MIXER_READ_ENHANCE | int * |
| 0x80044D1E | SOUND_MIXER_READ_LOUD | int * |
| 0x80044DFF | SOUND_MIXER_READ_RECSRC | int * |
| 0x80044DFE | SOUND_MIXER_READ_DEVMASK | int * |
| 0x80044DFD | SOUND_MIXER_READ_RECMASK | int * |
| 0x80044DFB | SOUND_MIXER_READ_STEREODEVS | int * |
| 0x80044DFC | SOUND_MIXER_READ_CAPS | int * |
| 0xC0044D00 | SOUND_MIXER_WRITE_VOLUME | int * // I-O |
| 0xC0044D01 | SOUND_MIXER_WRITE_BASS | int * // I-O |
| 0xC0044D02 | SOUND_MIXER_WRITE_TREBLE | int * // I-O |
| 0xC0044D03 | SOUND_MIXER_WRITE_SYNTH | int * // I-O |
| 0xC0044D04 | SOUND_MIXER_WRITE_PCM | int * // I-O |
| 0xC0044D05 | SOUND_MIXER_WRITE_SPEAKER | int * // I-O |

*<include/linux/soundcard.h>*

| | | |
|---|---|---|
| 0xC0044D06 | SOUND_MIXER_WRITE_LINE | int * // I-O |
| 0xC0044D07 | SOUND_MIXER_WRITE_MIC | int * // I-O |
| 0xC0044D08 | SOUND_MIXER_WRITE_CD | int * // I-O |
| 0xC0044D09 | SOUND_MIXER_WRITE_IMIX | int * // I-O |
| 0xC0044D0A | SOUND_MIXER_WRITE_ALTPCM | int * // I-O |
| 0xC0044D0B | SOUND_MIXER_WRITE_RECLEV | int * // I-O |
| 0xC0044D0C | SOUND_MIXER_WRITE_IGAIN | int * // I-O |
| 0xC0044D0D | SOUND_MIXER_WRITE_OGAIN | int * // I-O |
| 0xC0044D0E | SOUND_MIXER_WRITE_LINE1 | int * // I-O |
| 0xC0044D0F | SOUND_MIXER_WRITE_LINE2 | int * // I-O |
| 0xC0044D10 | SOUND_MIXER_WRITE_LINE3 | int * // I-O |
| 0xC0044D1C | SOUND_MIXER_WRITE_MUTE | int * // I-O |
| 0xC0044D1D | SOUND_MIXER_WRITE_ENHANCE | int * // I-O |
| 0xC0044D1E | SOUND_MIXER_WRITE_LOUD | int * // I-O |
| 0xC0044DFF | SOUND_MIXER_WRITE_RECSRC | int * // I-O |

*<include/linux/umsdos fs.h>*

| | | |
|---|---|---|
| 0x000004D2 | UMSDOS_READDIR_DOS | struct umsdos_ioctl * // I-O |
| 0x000004D3 | UMSDOS_UNLINK_DOS | const struct umsdos_ioctl * |
| 0x000004D4 | UMSDOS_RMDIR_DOS | const struct umsdos_ioctl * |
| 0x000004D5 | UMSDOS_STAT_DOS | struct umsdos_ioctl * // I-O |
| 0x000004D6 | UMSDOS_CREAT_EMD | const struct umsdos_ioctl * |
| 0x000004D7 | UMSDOS_UNLINK_EMD | const struct umsdos_ioctl * |
| 0x000004D8 | UMSDOS_READDIR_EMD | struct umsdos_ioctl * // I-O |
| 0x000004D9 | UMSDOS_GETVERSION | struct umsdos_ioctl * |
| 0x000004DA | UMSDOS_INIT_EMD | void |
| 0x000004DB | UMSDOS_DOS_SETUP | const struct umsdos_ioctl * |
| 0x000004DC | UMSDOS_RENAME_DOS | const struct umsdos_ioctl * |

*<include/linux/vt.h>*

| | | |
|---|---|---|
| 0x00005600 | VT_OPENQRY | int * |
| 0x00005601 | VT_GETMODE | struct vt_mode * |
| 0x00005602 | VT_SETMODE | const struct vt_mode * |
| 0x00005603 | VT_GETSTATE | struct vt_stat * |
| 0x00005604 | VT_SENDSIG | void |
| 0x00005605 | VT_RELDISP | int |
| 0x00005606 | VT_ACTIVATE | int |
| 0x00005607 | VT_WAI TACTI VE | int |
| 0x00005608 | VT_DISALLOCATE | int |
| 0x00005609 | VT_RESIZE | const struct vt_sizes * |
| 0x0000560A | VT_RESIZEX | const struct vt_consize * |

## MORE ARGUMENTS

Some ioctls take a pointer to a structure that contains additional pointers. These are documented here in alphabetical order.

CDROMREADAUDIO takes an input pointer const struct cdrom read audio *. The buf field points to an output buffer of length nframes * CD FRAMESIZE RAW.

CDROMREADCOOKED, CDROMREADMODE1, CDROMREADMODE2, and CDROM-READRAW take an input pointer const struct cdrom msf *. They use the same pointer as an output pointer to char []. The length varies by request. For CDROMREADMODE1, most drivers use CD_FRAMESIZE, but the optics storage driver uses OPT BLOCKSIZE instead (both have the numerical value 2048).

| | |
|---|---|
| CDROMREADCOOKED | char [CD_FRAMESIZE] |
| CDROMREADMODE1 | char [CD_FRAMESIZE or OPT_BLOCKSIZE] |
| CDROMREADMODE2 | char [CD_FRAMESIZE_RAW0] |
| CDROMREADRAW | char [CD_FRAMESIZE_RAW] |

EQL_ENSLAVE, EQL_EMANCIPATE, EQL_GETSLAVECFG, EQL_SETSLAVECFG, EQL_GETMASTERCFG, and EQL_SETMASTERCFG take a struct ifreq *. The ifr data field is a pointer to another structure as follows:

| | |
|---|---|
| EQL_ENSLAVE | const struct slaving_request * |
| EQL_EMANCIPATE | const struct slaving_request * |
| EQL_GETSLAVECFG | struct slave_config * // I-O |
| EQL_SETSLAVECFG | const struct slave_config * |
| EQL_GETMASTERCFG | struct master_config * |
| EQL_SETMASTERCFG | const struct master_config * |

FDRAWCMD takes a struct floppy raw cmd *. If flags & FD RAW WRITE is nonzero, then data points to an input buffer of length length. If flags & FD RAW READ is nonzero, then data points to an output buffer of length length.

GIO_FONTX and PIO_FONTX take a struct console font desc * or a const struct console_font_desc *, respectively. chardata points to a buffer of char [charcount]. This is an output buffer for GIO_FONTX and an input buffer for PIO_FONTX.

GIO_UNIMAP and PIO_UNIMAP take a struct unimapdesc * or a const struct unimapdesc *, respectively. entries points to a buffer of struct unipair [entry ct]. This is an output buffer for GIO_UNIMAP and an input buffer for PIO_UNIMAP.

KDADDIO, KDDELIO, KDDISABIO, and KDENABIO enable or disable access to I/O ports. They are essentially alternate interfaces to ioperm.

KDMAPDISP and KDUNMAPDISP enable or disable memory mappings or I/O port access. They are not implemented in the kernel.

SCSI_IOCTL_PROBE_HOST takes an input pointer const int *, which is a length. It uses the same pointer as an output pointer to a char [] buffer of this length.

SIOCADDRT and SIOCDELRT take an input pointer whose type depends on the protocol:

| | |
|---|---|
| Most protocols | const struct rtentry * |
| AX.25 | const struct ax25_route * |
| NET/ROM | const struct nr_route_struct * |

SIOCGIFCONF takes a struct ifconf *. The ifc buf field points to a buffer of length ifc len bytes, into which the kernel writes a list of type struct ifreq [].

SIOCSIFHWADDR takes an input pointer whose type depends on the protocol:

| | |
|---|---|
| Most protocols | const struct ifreq * |
| AX.25 | const char [AX25_ADDR_LEN] |

TIOCLINUX takes a const char *. It uses this to distinguish several independent subcases. In the following table, N + foo means foo after an *N*-byte pad. struct selection is implicitly defined in drivers/char/selection.c:

```
TIOCLINUX-2          1 + const struct selection *
TIOCLINUX-3          void
TIOCLINUX-4          void
TIOCLINUX-5          4 + const struct f long [8]; g *
TIOCLINUX-6          char *
TIOCLINUX-7          char *
TIOCLINUX-10         1 + const char *
```

## DUPLICATE `ioctls`

This list does not include `ioctls` in the range `SIOCDEVPRIVATE` and `SIOCPROTOPRIVATE`:

| | | |
|---|---|---|
| 0x00000001 | FDSETPRM | FIBMAP |
| 0x00000002 | FDDEFPRM | FIGETBSZ |
| 0x00005382 | CDROMAUDIOBUFSIZ | SCSI_IOCTL_GET_IDLUN |
| 0x00005402 | SNDCTL_TMR_START | TCSETS |
| 0x00005403 | SNDCTL_TMR_STOP | TCSETSW |
| 0x00005404 | SNDCTL_TMR_CONTINUE | TCSETSF |

*Linux, 17 September 1995*

# ioperm

`ioperm`—Sets port input/output permissions

## SYNOPSIS

```
#include <unistd.h>
int ioperm(unsigned long from, unsigned long num,intturn_on);
```

## DESCRIPTION

`ioperm` sets the port access permission bits for the process for *num* bytes starting from port address from to the value *turn_on*. The use of `ioperm` requires root privileges.

Only the first 0×3ff I/O ports can be specified in this manner. For more ports, the `iopl` function must be used. Permissions are not inherited on `fork`, but on `exec` they are. This is useful for giving port access permissions to nonprivileged tasks.

## RETURN VALUE

On success, 0 is returned. On error, -1 is returned and `errno` is set appropriately.

## CONFORMS TO

`ioperm` is Linux specific.

## SEE ALSO

`iopl`(2)

*Linux, 21 January 1993*

# iopl

`iopl`—Changes I/O privilege level

## SYNOPSIS

```
#include <unistd.h>
int iopl(int level);
```

## DESCRIPTION

iopl changes the I/O privilege level of the current process, as specified in *level*.

This call is necessary to allow 8514-compatible X servers to run under Linux. Because these X servers require access to all 65536 I/O ports, the ioperm call is not sufficient.

In addition to granting unrestricted I/O port access, running at a higher I/O privilege level also allows the process to disable interrupts. This will probably crash the system and is not recommended.

The I/O privilege level for a normal process is 0.

## RETURN VALUE

On success, 0 is returned. On error, -1 is returned and errno is set appropriately.

## ERRORS

| | |
|---|---|
| EINVAL | *level* is greater than 3. |
| EPERM | The current user is not the superuser. |

## NOTES FROM THE KERNEL SOURCE

iopl has to be used when you want to access the I/O ports beyond the 0x3ff range: To get the full 65536 ports bitmapped, you'd need 8KB of bitmaps/process, which is a bit excessive.

## SEE ALSO

ioperm(2)

*Linux 0.99.11, 24 July 1993*

# ipc

ipc—System V IPC system calls

## SYNOPSIS

```
int ipc(unsigned int call, int first, int second,
int third, void *ptr, long fifth);
```

## DESCRIPTION

ipc is a common kernel entry point for the System V IPC calls for messages, semaphores, and shared memory. *call* determines which IPC function to invoke; the other arguments are passed through to the appropriate call.

User programs should call the appropriate functions by their usual names. Only standard library implementors and kernel hackers need to know about ipc.

## SEE ALSO

msgctl(2), msgget(2), msgrcv(2), msgsnd(2), semctl(2), semget(2), semop(2), shmat(2), shmctl(2), shmdt(2), shmget(2)

*Linux 1.2.4, 15 April 1995*

# kill

kill—Sends signal to a process

## SYNOPSIS

```
#include <sys/types.h>
#include <signal.h>
int kill(pid t pid,intsig);
```

## DESCRIPTION

The kill system call can be used to send any signal to any process group or process.

If *pid* is positive, then signal *sig* is sent to *pid*. In this case, 0 is returned on success and a negative value is returned on error.

If *pid* equals -1, then *sig* is sent to every process except the first one, from higher numbers in the proc table to lower. In this case, 0 is returned on success, or the error condition resulting from signaling the last process is returned.

If *pid* is less than -1, then *sig* is sent to every process in the process group -*pid*. In this case, the number of processes the signal was sent to is returned and a negative value is returned for failure.

## RETURN VALUE

On success, 0 is returned. On error, -1 is returned and errno is set appropriately.

## ERRORS

| | |
|---|---|
| EINVAL | An invalid signal is sent. |
| ESRCH | The pid or process group does not exist. Note that an existing process might be a zombie, a process that already committed termination, but has not yet been wait()ed for. |
| EPERM | The effective userID of the process calling kill() is not equal to the effective user ID of *pid*, unless the superuser called kill(). |

## BUGS

It is impossible to send a signal to task number one, the init process, for which it has not installed a signal handler. This is done to ensure that the system is not brought down accidentally.

## CONFORMS TO

SVID, AT&T, POSIX.1, X/OPEN, BSD 4.3

## SEE ALSO

exit(2), exit(2), signal(2), signal(7)

*Linux, 1 November 1995*

# killpg

killpg—Sends signal to a process group

## SYNOPSIS

```
#include <signal.h>
int killpg(int pgrp,intsig);
```

## DESCRIPTION

killpg sends the signal *sig* to the process group *pgrp*. See sigaction(2) for a list of signals. If *pgrp* is 0, killpg sends the signal to the sending process's process group.

The sending process and members of the process group must have the same effective user ID, or the sender must be the superuser. As a single special case, the continue signal `SIGCONT` may be sent to any process that is a descendant of the current process.

## RETURN VALUE

On success, `0` is returned. On error, `-1` is returned and `errno` is set appropriately.

## ERRORS

| | |
|---|---|
| EINVAL | *sig* is not a valid signal number. |
| ESRCH | No process can be found in the process group specified by *pgrp*. |
| ESRCH | The process group was given as `0`, but the sending process does not have a process group. |
| EPERM | The sending process is not the superuser and one or more of the target processes has an effective user ID different from that of the sending process. |

## HISTORY

The `killpg` function call appeared in BSD4.0.

## SEE ALSO

`kill(2)`, `getpgrp(2)`, `signal(2)`

*BSD Man Page, 23 July 1993*

# link

link—Makes a new name for a file

## SYNOPSIS

```
#include <unistd.h>
int link(const char *oldpath, const char *newpath);
```

## DESCRIPTION

`link` creates a new link (also known as a hard link) to an existing file.

If *newpath* exists, it will *not* be overwritten.

This new name may be used exactly as the old one for any operation; both names refer to the same file (and so have the same permissions and ownership) and it is impossible to tell which name was the original.

## RETURN VALUE

On success, `0` is returned. On error, `-1` is returned and `errno` is set appropriately.

## ERRORS

| | |
|---|---|
| EXDEV | *oldpath* and *newpath* are not on the same filesystem. |
| EPERM | The filesystem containing *oldpath* and *newpath* does not support the creation of hard links. |
| EFAULT | *oldpath* or *newpath* points outside your accessible address space. |
| EACCES | Write access to the directory containing *newpath* is not allowed for the process's effective UID, or one of the directories in *oldpath* or *newpath* did not allow search (execute) permission. |
| ENAMETOOLONG | *oldpath* or *newpath* was too long. |
| ENOENT | A directory component in *oldpath* or *newpath* does not exist or is a dangling symbolic link. |
| ENOTDIR | A component used as a directory in *oldpath* or *newpath* is not, in fact, a directory. |

| ENOMEM | Insufficient kernel memory was available. |
|---|---|
| EROFS | The file is on a read-only filesystem. |
| EEXIST | *newpath* already exists. |
| EMLINK | The file referred to by *oldpath* already has the maximum number of links to it. |
| ELOOP | *oldpath* or *newpath* contains a reference to a circular symbolic link, that is, a symbolic link whose expansion contains a reference to itself. |
| ENOSPC | The device containing the file has no room for the new directory entry. |
| EPERM | *oldpath* is the . or .. entry of a directory. |

## NOTES

Hard links, as created by link, cannot span filesystems. Use symlink if this is required.

## CONFORMS TO

SVID, AT&T, POSIX, BSD 4.3

## BUGS

On NFS file systems, the return code may be wrong in case the NFS server performs the link creation and dies before it can say so. Use stat(2) to find out if the link was created.

## SEE ALSO

symlink(2), unlink(2), rename(2), open(2), stat(2), ln(1), link(8)

*Linux, 17 August 1994*

# listen

listen—Listens for connections on a socket

## SYNOPSIS

```
#include <sys/socket.h>
int listen(int_s,int backlog);
```

## DESCRIPTION

To accept connections, a socket is first created with socket(2), a willingness to accept incoming connections and a queue limit for incoming connections are specified with listen, and then the connections are accepted with accept(2). The listen call applies only to sockets of type SOCK_STREAM or SOCK_SEQPACKET.

The *backlog* parameter defines the maximum length the queue of pending connections may grow to. If a connection request arrives with the queue full, the client might receive an error with an indication of ECONNREFUSED, or, if the underlying protocol supports retransmission, the request may be ignored so that retries may succeed.

## RETURN VALUE

On success, 0 is returned. On error, -1 is returned and errno is set appropriately.

## ERRORS

| EBADF | The argument *s* is not a valid descriptor. |
|---|---|
| ENOTSOCK | The argument *s* is not a socket. |
| EOPNOTSUPP | The socket is not of a type that supports the operation listen. |

## HISTORY

The listen function call appeared in BSD 4.2.

## BUGS

If the socket is of type af_inet and the backlog argument is greater than 128, it is silently truncated to 128. For portable applications, don't rely on this value since BSD (and at least some BSD-derived systems) limit the backlog to 5.

## SEE ALSO

accept(2), connect(2), socket(2)

*BSD Man Page, 23 July 1993*

# llseek

_llseek—Repositions the read/write file offset

## SYNOPSIS

```
#include <unistd.h>
#include <linux/unistd.h>
_syscall5(int, llseek, uint, fd, ulong, hi, ulong, lo, loff_t*,res,uint,wh);
int llseek(unsigned int fd, unsigned long offset_high,
unsigned long offset_low,loff_t * result , unsigned int whence);
```

## DESCRIPTION

The _llseek function repositions the offset of the file descriptor *fd* to *(offset_high<<32)* ¦ offset_low bytes relative to the beginning of the file, the current position in the file, or the end of the file, depending on whether *whence* is SEEK_SET, SEEK_CUR,or SEEK_END, respectively. It returns the resulting file position in the argument *result*.

## RETURN VALUES

Upon successful completion, _llseek returns 0. Otherwise, a value of -1 is returned and errno is set to indicate the error.

## ERRORS

EBADF                          *fd* is not an open file descriptor.

EINVAL                         *whence* is invalid.

## CONFORMS TO

This function is Linux specific.

## BUGS

There is no support for files with a size of 2GB or more.

## SEE ALSO

lseek(2)

*Linux 1.2.9, 10 June 1995*

# lseek

lseek—Repositions read/write file offset

## SYNOPSIS

```
#include <unistd.h>
off_t lseek(int fildes,off_t offset,int whence);
```

## DESCRIPTION

The lseek function repositions the offset of the file descriptor *fildes* to the argument *offset* according to the directive *whence*. The argument *fildes* must be an open file descriptor. lseek repositions the file pointer *fildes* as follows:

If *whence* is SEEK_SET, the offset is set to *offset* bytes.

If *whence* is SEEK_CUR, the offset is set to its current location plus *offset* bytes.

If *whence* is SEEK_END, the offset is set to the size of the file plus *offset* bytes.

The lseek function allows the file offset to be set beyond the end of the existing end-of-file of the file. If data is later written at this point, subsequent reads of the data in the gap return bytes of zeros (until data is actually written into the gap).

Some devices are incapable of seeking. The value of the pointer associated with such a device is undefined.

## RETURN VALUES

Upon successful completion, lseek returns the resulting offset location as measured in bytes from the beginning of the file. Otherwise, a value of -1 is returned and errno is set to indicate the error.

## ERRORS

| | |
|---|---|
| EBADF | *fildes* is not an open file descriptor. |
| ESPIPE | *fildes* is associated with a pipe, socket, or FIFO. |
| EINVAL | *whence* is not a proper value. |

## CONFORMS TO

POSIX, BSD 4.3

## BUGS

This document's use of *whence* is incorrect English, but maintained for historical reasons.

## SEE ALSO

dup(2), open(2), fseek(3)

*Linux 1.2.9, 10 June 1995*

# mkdir

mkdir—Creates a directory

## SYNOPSIS

```
#include <sys/types.h>
#include <fcntl.h>
#include <unistd.h>
int mkdir(const char *pathname, mode_t mode);
```

## DESCRIPTION

mkdir attempts to create a directory named *pathname*.

*mode* specifies the permissions to use. It is modified by the process's umask in the usual way: the permissions of the created file is (mode & ˜umask).

The newly created directory will be owned by the effective UID of the process. If the directory containing the file has the set group ID bit set, or if the filesystem is mounted with BSD group semantics, the new directory will inherit the group ownership from its parent; otherwise, it will be owned by the effective GID of the process.

If the parent directory has the set group ID bit set, so will the newly created directory.

## RETURN VALUE

mkdir returns 0 on success, or -1 if an error occurred (in which case, errno is set appropriately).

## ERRORS

| | |
|---|---|
| EEXIST | *pathname* already exists (not necessarily as a directory). |
| EFAULT | *pathname* points outside your accessible address space. |
| EACCES | The parent directory does not allow write permission to the process, or one of the directories in *pathname* did not allow search (execute) permission. |
| ENAMETOOLONG | *pathname* was too long. |
| ENOENT | A directory component in *pathname* does not exist or is a dangling symbolic link. |
| ENOTDIR | A component used as a directory in *pathname* is not, in fact, a directory. |
| ENOMEM | Insufficient kernel memory was available. |
| EROFS | *pathname* refers to a file on a read-only filesystem and write access was requested. |
| ELOOP | *pathname* contains a reference to a circular symbolic link, that is, a symbolic link whose expansion contains a reference to itself. |
| ENOSPC | The device containing *pathname* has no room for the new directory. |
| ENOSPC | The new directory cannot be created because the user's disk quota is exhausted. |

## BUGS

In some older versions of Linux (for example, 0.99pl7) all the normal filesystems sometime allow the creation of two files in the same directory with the same name. This occurs only rarely and only on a heavily loaded system. It is believed that this bug was fixed in the Minix filesystem in Linux 0.99pl8 prerelease; and it is hoped that it was fixed in the other filesystems shortly afterward.

There are many infelicities in the protocol underlying NFS.

## SEE ALSO

read(2), write(2), fcntl(2), close(2), unlink(2), open(2), mknod(2), stat(2), umask(2), mount(2), socket(2), socket(2), fopen(3)

*Linux 1.0, 29 March 1994*

# mknod

mknod—Creates a directory

## SYNOPSIS

```
#include <sys/types.h>
#include <sys/stat.h>
#include <fcntl.h>
#include <unistd.h>
int mknod(const char *pathname, mode_t mode,dev_t dev);
```

## DESCRIPTION

mknod attempts to create a filesystem node (file, device special file, or named pipe) named *pathname*, specified by *mode* and *dev*.

*mode* specifies both the permissions to use and the type of node to be created.

It should be a combination (using bitwise OR) of one of the file types listed below and the permissions for the new node.

The permissions are modified by the process's umask in the usual way: The permissions of the created node is (mode & ˜umask).

The file type should be one of S_IFREG, S_IFCHR, S_IFBLK, or S_IFIFO to specify a normal file (which will be created empty), character special file, block special file, or FIFO (named pipe), respectively, or 0, which will create a normal file.

If the file type is S_IFCHR or S_IFBLK, then *dev* specifies the major and minor numbers of the newly created device special file; otherwise, it is ignored.

The newly created node will be owned by the effective UID of the process. If the directory containing the node has the set group ID bit set, or if the filesystem is mounted with BSD group semantics, the new node will inherit the group ownership from its parent directory; otherwise it will be owned by the effective GID of the process.

## RETURN VALUE

mknod returns 0 on success, or -1 if an error occurred (in which case, errno is set appropriately).

## ERRORS

| | |
|---|---|
| EPERM | *mode* requested creation of something other than a FIFO (named pipe), and the caller is not the superuser; also returned if the filesystem containing *pathname* does not support the type of node requested. |
| EINVAL | *mode* requested creation of something other than a normal file, device special file or FIFO. |
| EEXIST | *pathname* already exists. |
| EFAULT | *pathname* points outside your accessible address space. |
| EACCES | The parent directory does not allow write permission to the process, or one of the directories in *pathname* did not allow search (execute) permission. |
| ENAMETOOLONG | *pathname* was too long. |
| ENOENT | A directory component in *pathname* does not exist or is a dangling symbolic link. |
| ENOTDIR | A component used as a directory in *pathname* is not, in fact, a directory. |
| ENOMEM | Insufficient kernel memory was available. |
| EROFS | *pathname* refers to a file on a read-only filesystem and write access was requested. |
| ELOOP | *pathname* contains a reference to a circular symbolic link, that is, a symbolic link whose expansion contains a reference to itself. |
| ENOSPC | The device containing *pathname* has no room for the new node. |

## BUGS

In some older versions of Linux (for example, 0.99pl7) all the normal filesystems sometime allow the creation of two files in the same directory with the same name. This occurs only rarely and only on a heavily loaded system. It is believed that this bug was fixed in the Minix filesystem in Linux 0.99pl8 prerelease; and it is hoped that it was fixed in the other filesystems shortly afterward.

mknod cannot be used to create directories or socket files, and cannot be used to create normal files by users other than the superuser.

There are many infelicities in the protocol underlying NFS.

## SEE ALSO

read(2), write(2), fcntl(2), close(2), unlink(2), open(2), mkdir(2), stat(2), umask(2), mount(2), socket(2), fopen(3)

*Linux 1.0, 29 March 1994*

# mlock

mlock—Disables paging for some parts of memory

## SYNOPSIS

```
#include <sys/mman.h>
int mlock(const void *addr, size_t len);
```

## DESCRIPTION

mlock disables paging for the memory in the range starting at *addr* with length *len* bytes. All pages that contain a part of the specified memory range are guaranteed to be resident in RAM when the mlock system call returns successfully and they are guaranteed to stay in RAM until the pages are unlocked again by munlock or munlockall or until the process terminates or starts another program with exec. Child processes do not inherit page locks across a fork.

Memory locking has two main applications: real-time algorithms and high-security data processing. Real-time applications require deterministic timing, and, like scheduling, paging is one major cause of unexpected program execution delays. Real-time applications will usually also switch to a real-time scheduler with sched setscheduler.

Cryptographic security software often handles critical bytes such as passwords or secret keys as data structures. As a result of paging, these secrets could be transferred onto a persistent swap store medium, where they might be accessible to the enemy long after the security software has erased the secrets in RAM and terminated.

Memory locks do not stack, that is, pages that have been locked several times by calls to mlock or mlockall will be unlocked by a single call to munlock for the corresponding range or by munlockall. Pages that are mapped to several locations or by several processes stay locked into RAM as long as they are locked at least at one location or by at least one process.

On POSIX systems on which mlock and munlock are available, _POSIX_MEMLOCK_RANGE is defined in <unistd.h> and the value PAGESIZE from <limits.h> indicates the number of bytes per page.

## RETURN VALUE

On success, mlock returns 0. On error, –1 is returned, errno is set appropriately, and no changes are made to any locks in the address space of the process.

## ERRORS

| | |
|---|---|
| ENOMEM | Some of the specified address range does not correspond to mapped pages in the address space of the process or the process tried to exceed the maximum number of allowed locked pages. |
| EPERM | The calling process does not have appropriate privileges. Only root processes are allowed to lock pages. |
| EINVAL | *len* was not a positive number. |

## STANDARDS

POSIX.1b, SVR4

## SEE ALSO

munlock(2), mlockall(2), munlockall(2).

*Linux 1.3.43, 26 November 1995*

# mlockall

mlockall—Disables paging for calling process

## SYNOPSIS

```
#include <sys/mman.h>
int mlockall(int flags);
```

## DESCRIPTION

mlockall disables paging for all pages mapped into the address space of the calling process. This includes the pages of the code, data and stack segments, shared libraries, user space kernel data, shared memory, and memory-mapped files. All mapped pages are guaranteed to be resident in RAM when the mlockall system call returns successfully and they are guaranteed to stay in RAM until the pages are unlocked again by munlock or munlockall or until the process terminates or starts another program with exec. Child processes do not inherit page locks across a fork.

Memory locking has two main applications: real-time algorithms and high-security data processing. Real-time applications require deterministic timing, and, like scheduling, paging is one major cause of unexpected program execution delays. Real-time applications will usually also switch to a real-time scheduler with sched setscheduler. Cryptographic security software often handles critical bytes such as passwords or secret keys as data structures. As a result of paging, these secrets could be transferred onto a persistent swap store medium, where they might be accessible to the enemy long after the security software has erased the secrets in RAM and terminated. For security applications, only small parts of memory have to be locked, for which mlock is available.

The *flags* parameter can be constructed from the logical OR of the following constants:

| | |
|---|---|
| MCL_CURRENT | Lock all pages that are currently mapped into the address space of the process. |
| MCL_FUTURE | Lock all pages that will become mapped into the address space of the process in the future. These could be, for instance, new pages required by a growing heap and stack as well as new memory mapped files or shared memory regions. |

If MCL_FUTURE has been specified and the number of locked pages exceeds the upper limit of allowed locked pages, the system call that caused the new mapping will fail with ENOMEM. If these new pages have been mapped by the growing stack, the kernel will deny stack expansion and send a SIGSEGV.

Real-time processes should reserve enough locked stack pages before entering the time-critical section, so no page fault can be caused by function calls. This can be achieved by calling a function that has a sufficiently large automatic variable and that writes to the memory occupied by this large array in order to touch these stack pages. This way, enough pages will be mapped for the stack and can be locked into RAM. The dummy writes ensure that not even copy-on-write page faults can occur in the critical section.

Memory locks do not stack, that is, pages that have been locked several times by calls to mlockall or mlock will be unlocked by a single call to munlockall. Pages that are mapped to several locations or by several processes stay locked into RAM as long as they are locked at least at one location or by at least one process.

On POSIX systems on which mlockall and munlockall are available, POSIX MEMLOCK is defined in <unistd.h>.

## RETURN VALUE

On success, mlockall returns 0. On error, -1 is returned and errno is set appropriately.

## ERRORS

| | |
|---|---|
| ENOMEM | The process tried to exceed the maximum number of allowed locked pages. |
| EPERM | The calling process does not have appropriate privileges. Only root processes are allowed to lock pages. |
| EINVAL | Unknown flags were specified. |

## STANDARDS

POSIX.1b, SVR4

## SEE ALSO

munlockall(2), mlock(2), munlock(2)

# mmap, munmap

mmap, munmap—Map or unmap files or devices into memory

## SYNOPSIS

```
#include <unistd.h>
#include <sys/mman.h>
#ifdef POSIX MAPPED FILES
void * mmap(void *start, size_t length,int prot ,int flags,int fd,off_t offset);
int munmap(void *start, size_t length);
#endif
```

## DESCRIPTION

The mmap function asks to map *length* bytes starting at offset *offset* from the file (or other object) specified by *fd* into memory, preferably at address *start*. This latter address is a hint only, and is usually specified as 0. The actual place where the object is mapped is returned by mmap. The *prot* argument describes the desired memory protection. It has the following bits:

| | |
|---|---|
| PROT_EXEC | Pages may be executed. |
| PROT_READ | Pages may be read. |
| PROT_WRITE | Pages may be written. |

The *flags* parameter specifies the type of the mapped object, mapping options, and whether modifications made to the mapped copy of the page are private to the process or are to be shared with other references. It has the following bits:

| | |
|---|---|
| MAP_FIXED | Do not select a different address than the one specified. If the specified address cannot be used, mmap will fail. If MAP_FIXED is specified, *start* must be a multiple of the pagesize. Use of this option is discouraged. |
| MAP_SHARED | Share this mapping with all other processes that map this object. |
| MAP_PRIVATE | Create a private copy-on-write mapping. |

These three flags are described in POSIX.4. Linux also knows about MAP_DENYWRITE, MAP_EXECUTABLE, and MAP_ANON(YMOUS).

The munmap system call deletes the mappings for the specified address range and causes further references to addresses within the range to generate invalid memory references.

## RETURN VALUE

On success, mmap returns a pointer to the mapped area. On error, MAP_FAILED (-1) is returned and errno is set appropriately. On success, munmap returns 0, and on failure it returns -1 and sets errno (probably to EINVAL).

## ERRORS

| | |
|---|---|
| EBADF | *fd* is not a valid file descriptor (and MAP_ANONYMOUS was not set). |
| EACCES | MAP_PRIVATE was asked, but *fd* is not open for reading. Or MAP_SHARED was asked and PROT_WRITE is set, *fd* is not open for writing. |
| EINVAL | *start* or *length, and offset* are too large, or not aligned on a PAGESIZE boundary. |
| ETXTBUSY | MAP_DENYWRITE was set but the object specified by *fd* is open for writing. |
| EAGAIN | The file has been locked, or too much memory has been locked. |
| ENOMEM | No memory is available. |

## CONFORMS TO

POSIX.4.

## SEE ALSO

getpagesize(2), msync(2), shm_open(2), B. O. Gallmeister, *POSIX.4*, O'Reilly, pp. 128–129, 389–391.

# modify_ldt

modify_ldt—Gets or sets ldt

## SYNOPSIS

```
#include <linux/ldt.h> #include <linux/unistd.h>

_syscall3( int, modify_ldt, int, func, void *, ptr, unsigned long, bytecount )

int modify_ldt(int func,void *ptr, unsigned long bytecount);
```

## DESCRIPTION

modify_ldt reads or writes the local descriptor table (ldt) for a process. The ldt is a per-process memory-management table used by the i386 processor. For more information on this table, see an Intel 386 processor handbook.

When *func* is 0, modify_ldt reads the ldt into the memory pointed to by *ptr*. The number of bytes read is the smaller of *bytecount* and the actual size of the ldt.

When *func* is 1, modify_ldt modifies one ldt entry. *ptr* points to a *modify_ldt_ldt_s* structure and *bytecount* must equal the size of this structure.

## RETURN VALUE

On success, modify_ldt returns either the actual number of bytes read (for reading) or 0 (for writing). On failure, modify_ldt returns –1 and sets errno.

## ERRORS

| | |
|---|---|
| ENOSYS | *func* is neither 0 nor 1. |
| EINVAL | *ptr* is 0, or *func* is 1 and *bytecount* is not equal to the size of the structure *modify_ldt_ldt_s*,or *func* is 1 and the new ldt entry has illegal values. |
| EFAULT | *ptr* points outside the address space. |

## SEE ALSO

vm86(2)

# get_kernel_syms, create_module, init_module, delete_module

get_kernel_syms, create_module, init_module, delete_module—Loadable module support

## SYNOPSIS

```
#include <linux/module.h>

    int get_kernel_syms(struct kernel_sym *table);

    int create_module(char *module_name, unsigned long size);
```

```
    int init_module(char *module_name, char *code, unsigned codesize,
        struct mod_routines *routines, struct symbol_table *symtab);

    int delete_module(char *module_name);

    struct kernel_sym {
        unsigned long value;
        char name[SYM_MAX_NAME];
    };

    struct mod_routines {
        int (*init)(void);
        void (*cleanup)(void);
    };

    struct module_ref {
        struct module *module;
        struct module_ref *next;
    };

    struct internal_symbol {
        void *addr;
        char *name;
    };

    struct symbol_table {
        int size; /* total, including string table!!! */
        int n_symbols;
        int n_refs;
        struct internal_symbol symbol[0];
        struct module_ref ref[0];
    };
```

## DESCRIPTION

These system calls have not yet been included in any library, which means that they have to be called by the syscall(_NR_function) mechanism. get_kernel_syms(table); has two uses: First, if table is NULL, this call will only return the number of symbols, including module names, that are available. This number should be used to reserve memory for that many items of struct kernel sym.

If table is not NULL, this call will copy all kernel symbols and module names (and version info) from the kernel to the space pointed to by table. The entries are ordered in module LIFO order. For each module an entry that describes the module will be followed by entries describing the symbols exported by this module.

Note that for symbols that describe a module, the value part of the structure will contain the kernel address of the structure that describes the module.

The name part of the structure is the module name prepended with #, as in #my module. The symbol that describes a module will appear before the symbols defined by this module.

Ahead of the kernel resident symbols, a module name symbol with the "dummy" name # will appear. This information can be used to build a table of module references when modules are stacked (or layered). create_module(module_name, size); will allocate size bytes of kernel space for a module and also create the necessary kernel structures— called name—for the new module. The module will now exist in kernel space, with the status MOD_UNINITIALIZED. init module(module_name, code, codesize, routines, symtab);.

This is the actual "module loader" that will load the module named name into the kernel. The parameters code and codesize refer to the relocated binary object module that is codesize bytes long. Note that the first 4 bytes will be used as a reference counter in kernel space, updated by the MOD_INC_USE_COUNT and MOD_DEC_USE_COUNT macros.

The functions described in routines will be used to start and stop the module. These pointers should therefore contain the addresses of the init_module() and cleanup_module() functions that have to be defined for all loadable modules.

If a module wants to export symbols for use by other modules, or if the module makes references to symbols defined by other modules, the parameter symtab has to point to a structure that describes these. A NULL value for symtab means that no symbols are exported and no references to other modules are made.

The symtab that will be copied into the kernel consists of a symbol table structure immediately followed by a string table, containing the names of the symbols defined by the module. The size element has to include the size of this string table as well. Special considerations follow.

The n_symbols and n_refs elements tells how many symbols and how many module references are included in the symbol table structure. Immediately after these integers, the array of symbol definitions follows. The name element in each struct internal symbol should actually not be an ordinary pointer, but instead the offset of the corresponding string table entry relative to the start of the symbol table structure.

When all defined symbols have been listed, the symbol_table structure continues with the array of module references, as described by the struct module_ref elements. Only the module field of these structures have to be initialized. The module addresses that were obtained from a previous get_kernel_syms call, for elements with names starting with # should be copied to this field.

If the module could be successfully loaded, and if the call to the module function init_module() also succeeds, the status of the module will be changed to MOD_RUNNING. Otherwise, the kernel memory occupied by module will be freed.

delete_module(module_name); should be used to unload a module. If the module reference count shows that the module is not active, and if there are no references to this module from other modules, the module function cleanup_module() will be called. If all these steps succeed, the kernel memory occupied by the module and its structures will be freed.

## DIAGNOSTICS

If there are any errors, these functions will return the value -1, and the global variable errno will contain the error number. A descriptive text will also be written on the console device.

## SEE ALSO

insmod(1), rmmod(1), lsmod(1), ksyms(1)

## HISTORY

The module support was first conceived by Anonymous.

Linux version by Bas Laarhoven (bas@vimec.nl), 0.99.14 version by Jon Tombs (jon@gtex02.us.es), extended by Bjorn Ekwall (bj0rn@blox.se).

## BUGS

Naah...

*Linux, 25 January 1995*

# mount, umount

mount, umount—Mount and unmount filesystems.

## SYNOPSIS

```
#include <sys/mount.h>
#include <linux/fs.h>
int mount(const char *specialfile, const char * dir ,
const char * filesystemtype, unsigned long rwflag , const void * data);
int umount(const char *specialfile);
int umount(const char *dir);
```

## DESCRIPTION

mount attaches the filesystem specified by *specialfile* (which is often a device name) to the directory specified by *dir*.

umount removes the attachment of the filesystem specified by *specialfile* or *dir*.

Only the superuser may mount and unmount filesystems.

The *filesystemtype* argument may take one of the values listed in /proc/filesystems (such as minix, ext2, msdos, proc, nfs, iso9660).

The *rwflag* argument has the magic number 0xC0ED in the top 16 bits, and various mount flags (as defined in <linux/fs.h>) in the low order 16 bits:

```
#define MS_RDONLY 1 /* mount read-only */
#define MS_NOSUID 2 /* ignore suid and sgid bits */
#define MS_NODEV 4 /* disallow access to device special files */
#define MS_NOEXEC 8 /* disallow program execution */
#define MS_SYNC 16 /* writes are synced at once */
#define MS_REMOUNT 32 /* alter flags of a mounted FS */
#define MS_MGC_VAL 0xC0ED0000
```

If the magic number is absent, then the last two arguments are not used.

The *data* argument is interpreted by the different filesystems.

## RETURN VALUE

On success, 0 is returned. On error, -1 is returned and errno is set appropriately.

## ERRORS

The following error values result from filesystem type independent errors. Each filesystem type may have its own special errors and its own special behavior. See the kernel source code for details.

| | |
|---|---|
| EPERM | The user is not the superuser. |
| ENODEV | *filesystemtype* not configured in the kernel. |
| ENOTBLK | *specialfile* is not a block device (if a device was required). |
| EBUSY | *specialfile* is already mounted. Or it cannot be remounted read-only because it still holds files open for writing. Or, it cannot be mounted on *dir* because *dir* is still busy (it is the working directory of some task, the mount point of another device, has open files, and so on). |
| EINVAL | *specialfile* had an invalid superblock. Or, a remount was attempted, while *specialfile* was not already mounted on *dir*. Or, an umount was attempted, while *dir* was not a mount point. |
| EFAULT | One of the pointer arguments points outside the user address space. |
| ENOMEM | The kernel could not allocate a free page to copy filenames or data into. |
| ENAMETOOLONG | A pathname was longer than MAXPATHLEN. |
| ENOENT | A pathname was empty or had a nonexistent component. |
| ENOTDIR | The second argument, or a prefix of the first argument, is not a directory. |
| EACCES | A component of a path was not searchable. |
| | Or, mounting a read-only filesystem was attempted without giving the MS_RDONLY flag. |
| | Or, the block device *specialfile* is located on a filesystem mounted with the MS_NODEV option. |
| ENXIO | The major number of the block device *specialfile* is out of range. |
| EMFILE | (In case no block device is required:) Table of dummy devices is full. |

## CONFORMS TO

These functions are rather Linux specific.

## SEE ALSO

mount(8), umount(8)

*Linux 1.1.67, 28 November 1994*

# mprotect

mprotect—Controls allowable accesses to a region of memory

## SYNOPSIS

```
#include <sys/mman.h>
int mprotect(caddr_t addr, size_t *len, int prot);
```

## DESCRIPTION

mprotect controls how a section of memory can be accessed. If an access is disallowed by the protection given it, the program receives a SIGSEGV.

*prot* is a bitwise-OR of the following values:

| | |
|---|---|
| PROT_NONE | The memory cannot be accessed at all. |
| PROT_READ | The memory can be read. |
| PROT_WRITE | The memory can be written to. |
| PROT_EXEC | The memory can contain executing code. |

The new protection replaces any existing protection. For example, if the memory had previously been marked PROT_READ, and *mprotect* is then called with *prot* PROT_WRITE, it will no longer be readable.

## RETURN VALUE

On success, mprotect returns 0. On error, -1 is returned and errno is set appropriately.

## ERRORS

| | |
|---|---|
| EINVAL | *addr* is not a valid pointer. |
| EFAULT | The memory cannot be accessed. |
| EACCES | The memory cannot be given the specified access. This can happen, for example, if you mmap(2) a file to which you have read-only access, then ask mprotect to mark it PROT_WRITE. |
| ENOMEM | Internal kernel structures could not be allocated. |

## EXAMPLE

```
#include <stdio.h>
#include <stdlib.h>
#include <errno.h>
#include <sys/mman.h>

int
main(void)
{
    char *p;
    char c;
```

```
        /* Allocate a buffer; it will have the default
           protection of PROT_READ¦PROT_WRITE. */
        p = malloc(1024);
        if (!p) {
            perror("Couldn't malloc(1024)");
            exit(errno);
        }

        c = p[666];         /* Read; ok */
        p[666] = 42;        /* Write; ok */

        /* Mark the buffer read-only. */
        if (mprotect(p, 1024, PROT_READ)) {
            perror("Couldn't mprotect");
            exit(errno);
        }

        c = p[666];         /* Read; ok */
        p[666] = 42;        /* Write; program dies on SIGSEGV */

        exit(0);
    }
```

## SEE ALSO

mmap(2)

*Linux 1.2, 23 June 1995*

# mremap

mremap—Remaps a virtual memory address

## SYNOPSIS

```
#include <unistd.h>
#include <sys/mman.h>
void * mremap(void * old_address, size_t old_size , size_t new_size, unsigned long flags)
```

## DESCRIPTION

mremap expands (or shrinks) an existing memory mapping, potentially moving it at the same time (controlled by the *flags* argument and the available virtual address space).

*old_address* is the old address of the virtual memory block that you want to expand (or shrink). Note that *old_address* has to be page aligned. *old_size* is the old size of the virtual memory block. *new_size* is the requested size of the virtual memory block after the resize.

The *flags* argument is a bitmap of flags.

In Linux the memory is divided into pages. A user process has one or linear virtual memory segments. Each virtual memory segment has one or more mappings to real memory pages (in the page table). Each virtual memory segment has its own protection (access rights), which may cause a segmentation violation if the memory is accessed incorrectly (for example, writing to a read-only segment). Accessing virtual memory outside of the segments will also cause a segmentation violation.

mremap uses the Linux page table scheme. mremap changes the mapping between virtual addresses and memory pages. This can be used to implement a very efficient realloc.

## FLAGS

MREMAP_MAYMOVE                 Indicates whether the operation should fail, or changes the virtual address if the resize cannot be done at the current virtual address.

## RETURN VALUE

On success, mremap returns a pointer to the new virtual memory area. On error, -1 is returned, and errno is set appropriately.

## ERRORS

EINVAL                         An invalid argument was given. Most likely old_address was not page aligned.

EFAULT                         Segmentation fault. Some address in the range old_address to old_address+old_size is an invalid virtual memory address for this process. You can also get EFAULT even if there exist mappings that cover the whole address space requested, but those mappings are of different types.

EAGAIN                         The memory segment is locked and cannot be remapped.

ENOMEM                         The memory area cannot be expanded at the current virtual address, and the MREMAP_MAYMOVE flag is not set in *flags*. Or there is not enough (virtual) memory available.

## SEE ALSO

getpagesize(2), realloc(3), malloc(3), brk(2), sbrk(2), mmap(2), your favorite OS text book for more information on paged memory. (*Modern Operating Systems* by Andrew S. Tannenbaum, *Inside Linux* by Randolf Bentson, *The Design of the UNIX Operating System* by Maurice J. Bach.)

*Linux 1.3.87, 12 April 1996*

# msgctl

msgctl—Handles message control operations

## SYNOPSIS

```
# include <sys/types.h>
# include <sys/ipc.h>
# include <sys/msg.h>
int msgctl ( int msqid,  int cmd ,  struct msqid_ds *buf );
int cmd, struct msqid_ds *buf;
```

## DESCRIPTION

The function performs the control operation specified by *cmd* on the message queue with identifier *msqid*. Legal values for *cmd* are

IPC_STAT                       Copies info from the message queue data structure into the structure pointed to by *buf*. The user must have read access privileges on the message queue.

IPC_SET                        Writes the values of some members of the msqid ds structure pointed to by *buf* to the message queue data structure, updating also its msg_ctime member. Considered members from the user-supplied struct msqid ds pointed to by *buf* are msg_perm.uid, msg_perm.gid, and msg_perm.mode /* only lowest 9-bits */ msg_qbytes.

The calling process effective user ID must be one among superuser, creator or owner of the message queue. Only the superuser can raise the msg_qbytes value beyond the system parameter MSGMNB.

IPC_RMID                       Remove immediately the message queue and its data structures awakening all waiting reader and writer processes (with an error return and errno set to EIDRM). The calling process effective user ID must be one among superuser, creator or owner of the message queue.

## RETURN VALUE

If successful, the return value will be 0;otherwise, the return value will be -1 with errno indicating the error.

## ERRORS

For a failing return, errno will be set to one of the following values:

| | |
|---|---|
| EACCESS | The argument *cmd* is equal to IPC_STAT, but the calling process has no read access permissions on the message queue *msqid*. |
| EFAULT | The argument *cmd* has value IPC_SET or IPC_STAT, but the address pointed to by *buf* isn't accessible. |
| EIDRM | The message queue was removed. |
| EINVAL | Invalid value for *cmd* or *msqid*. |
| EPERM | The argument *cmd* has value IPC_SET or IPC_RMID, but the calling process effective user ID has insufficient privileges to execute the command. Note that this is also the case of a nonsuperuser process trying to increase the msg_qbytes value beyond the value specified by the system parameter MSGMNB. |

## NOTES

The IPC_INFO, MSG_STAT, and MSG_INFO control calls are used by the ipcs(1) program to provide information on allocated resources. In the future these can be modified as needed or moved to a proc file system interface.

## SEE ALSO

ipc(5), msgget(2), msgsnd(2), msgrcv(2)

*Linux 0.99.13, 1 November 1993*

# msgget

msgget—Gets a message queue identifier

## SYNOPSIS

```
# include <sys/types.h>
# include <sys/ipc.h>
# include <sys/msg.h>
int msgget ( key_t key,int msgflg );
```

## DESCRIPTION

The function returns the message queue identifier associated to the value of the *key* argument. A new message queue is created if *key* has value IPC_PRIVATE or *key* isn't IPC_PRIVATE, no existing message queue is associated to *key*, and IPC_CREAT is asserted in *msgflg* (that is, *msgflg* &IPC_CREAT isn't 0). The presence in *msgflg* of the fields IPC_CREAT and IPC_EXCL plays the same role, with respect to the existence of the message queue, as the presence of O_CREAT and O_EXCL in the mode argument of the op_en(2) system call: That is, the msgget function fails if *msgflg* asserts both IPC_CREAT and IPC_EXCL and a message queue already exists for *key*.

Upon creation, the lower 9 bits of the argument *msgflg* define the access permissions (for owner, group, and others) to the message queue in the same format, and with the same meaning, as for the access permissions parameter in the open(2) or creat(2) system calls (though the execute permissions are not used by the system).

Furthermore, while creating, the system call initializes the system message queue data structure msqid ds as follows:

msg_perm.cuid and msg_perm.uid are set to the effective user ID of the calling process.

msg_perm.cgid and msg_perm.gid are set to the effective group ID of the calling process.

The lowest-order 9 bits of msg_perm.mode are set to the lowest-order 9 bit of *msgflg*.

msg_qnum, msg_lspid, msg_lrpid, msg_stime, and msg_rtime are set to 0.

msg_ctime is set to the current time.

msg_qbytes is set to the system limit MSGMNB.

If the message queue already exists, the access permissions are verified, and a check is made to see whether it is marked for destruction.

## RETURN VALUE

If successful, the return value will be the message queue identifier (a positive integer), otherwise -1 with errno indicating the error.

## ERRORS

For a failing return, errno will be set to one of the following values:

| | |
|---|---|
| EACCES | A message queue exists for *key*, but the calling process has no access permissions to the queue. |
| EEXIST | A message queue exists for key and *msgflg* was asserting both IPC_CREAT and IPC_EXCL. |
| EIDRM | The message queue is marked as to be removed. |
| ENOENT | No message queue exists for *key* and *msgflg* wasn't asserting IPC_CREAT. |
| ENOMEM | A message queue has to be created but the system has not enough memory for the new data structure. |
| ENOSPC | A message queue has to be created but the system limit for the maximum number of message queues (MSGMNI) would be exceeded. |

## NOTES

IPC_PRIVATE isn't a flag field, but a key_t type. If this special value is used for *key*, the system call ignores everything but the lowest-order 9 bits of *msgflg* and creates a new message queue (on success).

The following is a system limit on message queue resources affecting a msgget call:

| | |
|---|---|
| MSGMNI | Systemwide maximum number of message queues; policy dependent. |

## BUGS

Use of IPC_PRIVATE doesn't inhibit other processes the access to the allocated message queue.

As for the files, there is currently no intrinsic way for a process to ensure exclusive access to a message queue. Asserting both IPC_CREAT and IPC_EXCL in *msgflg* only ensures (on success) that a new message queue will be created; it doesn't imply exclusive access to the message queue.

## SEE ALSO

ftok(3), ipc(5), msgctl(2),.msgsnd(2), msgrcv(2)

*Linux 0.99.13, 1 November 1993*

# msgop

msgop—Completes message operations

## SYNOPSIS

```
# include <sys/types.h>
# include <sys/ipc.h>
# include <sys/msg.h>
```

```
int msgsnd ( int msqid, struct msgbuf *msgp",int msgsz,int msgflg );

int msgrcv ( int msqid, struct msgbuf *msgp,int msgsz,long msgtyp,int msgflg );
```

## DESCRIPTION

To send or receive a message, the calling process allocates a structure that looks like the following:

```
struct msgbuf {
  long mtype; /* message type, must be > 0 */
  char mtext[1]; /* message data */
};
```

but with an array mtext of size *msgsz*, a nonnegative integer value. The structure member mtype must have a strictly positive integer value that can be used by the receiving process for message selection (see the section about msgrcv).

The calling process must have write access permissions to send and read access permissions to receive a message on the queue.

The msgsnd system call queues a copy of the message pointed to by the *msgp* argument on the message queue whose identifier is specified by the value of the *msqid* argument.

The argument *msgflg* specifies the system call behavior if queuing the new message will require more than msg_qbytes in the queue. Asserting IPC_NOWAIT, the message will not be sent and the system call fails, returning with errno set to EAGAIN. Otherwise the process is suspended until the condition for the suspension no longer exists (in which case the message is sent and the system call succeeds), or the queue is removed (in which case the system call fails with errno set to EIDRM), or the process receives a signal that has to be caught (in which case the system call fails with errno set to EINTR).

Upon successful completion, the message queue data structure is updated as follows:

| | |
|---|---|
| msg_lspid | Set to the process D of the calling process. |
| msg_qnum | Incremented by 1. |
| msg_stime | Set to the current time. |

The system call msgrcv reads a message from the message queue specified by *msqid* into the msgbuf pointed to by the *msgp* argument, removing from the queue, on success, the read message.

The argument *msgsz* specifies the maximum size in bytes for the member mtext of the structure pointed to by the *msgp* argument. If the message text has length greater than *msgsz*, then if the *msgflg* argument asserts MSG_NOERROR, the message text will be truncated (and the truncated part will be lost); otherwise, the message isn't removed from the queue and the system call fails, returning with errno set to E2BIG.

The argument *msgtyp* specifies the type of message requested as follows:

If *msgtyp* is 0, the message on the queue's front is read.

If *msgtyp* is greater than 0, the first message on the queue of type *msgtyp* is read if MSG_EXCEPT isn't asserted by the *msgflg* argument; otherwise, the first message on the queue of type not equal to *msgtyp* will be read.

If *msgtyp* is less than 0, the first message on the queue with the lowest type less than or equal to the absolute value of *msgtyp* will be read.

The *msgflg* argument asserts none, one, or more (OR–ing them) among the following flags:

| | |
|---|---|
| IPC_NOWAIT | For immediate return if no message of the requested type is on the queue. The system call fails with errno set to ENOMSG. |
| MSG_EXCEPT | Used with *msgtyp* greater than 0 to read the first message on the queue with message type that differs from *msgtyp*. |
| MSG_NOERROR | To truncate the message text if longer than *msgsz* bytes. |

If no message of the requested type is available and IPC_NOWAIT isn't asserted in *msgflg*, the calling process is blocked until one of the following conditions occurs:

A message of the desired type is placed on the queue.

The message queue is removed from the system. In such a case the system call fails with errno set to EIDRM.

The calling process receives a signal that has to be caught. In such a case the system call fails with errno set to EINTR.

Upon successful completion, the message queue data structure is updated as follows:

| | |
|---|---|
| msg_lrpid | Set to the process D of the calling process. |
| msg_qnum | Decremented by 1. |
| msg_rtime | Set to the current time. |

## RETURN VALUE

On a failure, both functions return -1 with errno indicating the error; otherwise, msgsnd returns 0 and msgrvc returns the number of bytes actually copied into the mtext array.

## ERRORS

When msgsnd fails, at return errno will be set to one of the following values:

| | |
|---|---|
| EAGAIN | The message can't be sent due to the msg_qbytes limit for the queue, and IPC_NOWAIT was asserted in *mgsflg*. |
| EACCES | The calling process has no write access permissions on the message queue. |
| EFAULT | The address pointed to by *msgp* isn't accessible. |
| EIDRM | The message queue was removed. |
| EINTR | Sleeping on a full message queue condition, the process received a signal that had to be caught. |
| EINVAL | Invalid *msqid* value, or nonpositive *mtype* value, or invalid *msgsz* value (less than 0 or greater than the system value MSGMAX). |
| ENOMEM | The system has not enough memory to make a copy of the supplied msgbuf. |

When msgrcv fails, at return errno will be set to one of the following values:

| | |
|---|---|
| E2BIG | The message text length is greater than *msgsz* and MSG_NOERROR isn't asserted in *msgflg*. |
| EACCES | The calling process has no read access permissions on the message queue. |
| EFAULT | The address pointed to by *msgp* isn't accessible. |
| EIDRM | While the process was sleeping to receive a message, the message queue was removed. |
| EINTR | While the process was sleeping to receive a message, the process received a signal that had to be caught. |
| EINVAL | Illegal *msgqid* value, or *msgsz* less than 0. |
| ENOMSG | IPC_NOWAIT was asserted in *msgflg* and no message of the requested type existed on the message queue. |

## NOTES

The followings are system limits affecting a msgsnd system call:

| | |
|---|---|
| MSGMAX | Maximum size for a message text; the implementation set this value to 4080 bytes. |
| MSGMNB | Default maximum size in bytes of a message queue: policy dependent. The superuser can increase the size of a message queue beyond MSGMNB by a msgctl system call. |

The implementation has no intrinsic limits for the systemwide maximum number of message headers (MSGTQL) and for the systemwide maximum size in bytes of the message pool (MSGPOOL).

## SEE ALSO

ipc(5), msgctl(2), msgget(2), msgrcv(2), msgsnd(2)

*Linux 0.99.13, 1 November 1993*

# msync

msync—Synchronizes a file with a memory map

## SYNOPSIS

```
#include <unistd.h>
#include <sys/mman.h>

#ifdef _POSIX_MAPPED_FILES
#ifdef _POSIX_SYNCHRONIZED_IO

int msync(const void *start, size_t length,int flags);
#endif
#endif
```

## DESCRIPTION

msync flushes changes made to the in-core copy of a file that was mapped into memory using mmap(2) back to disk. Without use of this call, there is no guarantee that changes are written back before munmap(2) is called. To be more precise, the part of the file that corresponds to the memory area starting at *start* and having length *length* is updated. The *flags* argument may have the bits MS_ASYNC, MS_SYNC, and MS_INVALIDATE set, but not both MS_ASYNC and MS_SYNC. MS_ASYNC specifies that an update be scheduled, but the call returns immediately. MS_SYNC asks for an update and waits for it to complete. MS_INVALIDATE asks to invalidate other mappings of the same file (so that they can be updated with the fresh values just written).

## RETURN VALUE

On success, 0 is returned. On error, -1 is returned and errno is set appropriately.

## ERRORS

| | |
|---|---|
| EINVAL | *start* is not a multiple of PAGESIZE, or any bit other than MS_ASYNC ¦ MS_INVALIDATE ¦ MS_SYNC is set in *flags*. |
| EFAULT | The indicated memory (or part of it) was not mapped. |

## CONFORMS TO

POSIX.4.

## SEE ALSO

mmap(2), B.O. Gallmeister, POSIX.4, O'Reilly, pp. 128–129, 389–391.

*Linux 1.3.86, 12 April 1996*

# munlock

munlock—Reenables paging for some parts of memory

## SYNOPSIS

```
#include <sys/mman.h>
int munlock(const void *addr, size_t len);
```

## DESCRIPTION

munlock reenables paging for the memory in the range starting at *addr* with length *len* bytes. All pages that contain a part of the specified memory range can after calling munlock be moved to external swap space again by the kernel.

Memory locks do not stack, that is, pages that have been locked several times by calls to mlock or mlockall will be unlocked by a single call to munlock for the corresponding range or by munlockall. Pages that are mapped to several locations or by several processes stay locked into RAM as long as they are locked at least at one location or by at least one process.

On POSIX systems on which mlock and munlock are available, _POSIX_MEMLOCK_RANGE is defined in <unistd.h> and the value PAGESIZE from <limits.h> indicates the number of bytes per page.

## RETURN VALUE

On success, munlock returns 0. On error, -1 is returned, errno is set appropriately, and no changes are made to any locks in the address space of the process.

## ERRORS

ENOMEM              Some of the specified address range does not correspond to mapped pages in the address
                    space of the process.

EINVAL              *len* was not a positive number.

## STANDARDS

POSIX.1b, SVR4

## SEE ALSO

mlock(2), mlockall(2), munlockall(2).

*Linux 1.3.43, 26 November 1995*

# munlockall

munlockall—Reenables paging for calling process

## SYNOPSIS

```
#include <sys/mman.h>
int munlockall(void);
```

## DESCRIPTION

munlockall reenables paging for all pages mapped into the address space of the calling process.

Memory locks do not stack, that is, pages that have been locked several times by calls to mlock or mlockall will be unlocked by a single call to munlockall. Pages that are mapped to several locations or by several processes stay locked into RAM as long as they are locked at least at one location or by at least one process.

On POSIX systems on which mlockall and munlockall are available, _POSIX_MEMLOCK is defined in *<unistd.h>*.

## RETURN VALUE

On success, munlockall returns 0. On error, -1 is returned and errno is set appropriately.

## STANDARDS

POSIX.1b, SVR4

## SEE ALSO

mlockall(2), mlock(2), munlock(2)

*Linux 1.3.43, 26 November 1995*

# nanosleep

nanosleep—Pauses execution for a specified time

## SYNOPSIS

```
#include <time.h>

int nanosleep(const struct timespec *req, struct timespec *rem);
```

## DESCRIPTION

nanosleep delays the execution of the program for at least the time specified in *req.*The function can return earlier if a signal has been delivered to the process. In this case, it returns -1, sets errno to EINTR, and writes the remaining time into the structure pointed to by *rem* unless *rem* is NULL. The value of *rem* can then be used to call nanosleep again and complete the specified pause.

The structure *timespec* is used to specify intervals of time with nanosecond precision. It is specified in <*time.h*> and has the form

```
struct timespec
{
time_t tv_sec; /* seconds */
long tv_nsec; /* nanoseconds */
};
```

The value of the nanoseconds field must be in the range 0 to 999 999 999.

Compared to sleep(3) and usleep(3), nanosleep has the advantage of not affecting any signals; it is standardized by POSIX, it provides higher timing resolution, and it allows to continue a sleep that has been interrupted by a signal more easily.

## ERRORS

In case of an error or exception, the nanosleep system call returns -1 instead of 0 and sets errno to one of the following values:

| | |
|---|---|
| EINTR | The pause has been interrupted by a nonblocked signal that was delivered to the process. The remaining sleep time has been written into *rem* so that the process can easily call nanosleep again and continue with the pause. |
| EINVAL | The value in the *tv_nsec* field was not in the range 0 to 999 999 999 or *tv_sec* was negative. |

## BUGS

The current implementation of nanosleep is based on the normal kernel timer mechanism, which has a resolution of 1/*HZ* s (that is, 10ms on Linux/i386 and 1ms on Linux/Alpha). Therefore, nanosleep pauses always for at least the specified time; however, it can take up to 10ms longer than specified until the process becomes runnable again. For the same reason, the value returned in case of a delivered signal in *rem* is usually rounded to the next larger multiple of 1/*HZ* s.

Because some applications require much more precise pauses (for example, in order to control some time-critical hardware), nanosleep is also capable of short high-precision pauses. If the process is scheduled under a real-time policy such as *SCHED_FIFO* or *SCHED_RR*, then pauses of up to 2ms will be performed as busy waits with microsecond precision.

## STANDARDS

POSIX.1b

## SEE ALSO

sleep(3), usleep(3), sched_setscheduler(2), timer_create(2)

*Linux 1.3.85, 10 April 1996*

# nice

nice—Changes process priority

## SYNOPSIS

```
#include <unistd.h>
int nice(int inc);
```

## DESCRIPTION

nice adds *inc* to the priority for the calling PID. Note that only the superuser may specify a negative increment, or priority increase. Note that internally, a higher number is a higher priority. Do not confuse this with the priority scheme as used by the nice interface.

## RETURN VALUE

On success, 0 is returned. On error, -1 is returned and errno is set appropriately.

## ERRORS

EPERM                          A nonsuperuser attempts to do a priority increase, a numerical decrease, by supplying a negative *inc*.

## CONFORMS TO

SVID EXT, AT&T, X/OPEN, BSD 4.3

## SEE ALSO

nice(1), setpriority(2), fork(2), renice(8)

*Linux, 28 March 1992*

# oldfstat, oldlstat, oldstat, oldolduname, olduname

oldfstat, oldlstat, oldstat, oldolduname, olduname—Obsolete system calls

## SYNOPSIS

Obsolete system calls.

## DESCRIPTION

The Linux 1.3.6 kernel implements these calls to support old executables. These calls return structures that have grown since their first implementations, but old executables must continue to receive old smaller structures.

Current executables should be linked with current libraries and never use these calls.

## SEE ALSO

fstat(2), lstat(2), stat(2), uname(2), undocumented(2), unimplemented(2)

*Linux 1.3.6, 22 July 1995*

# open, creat

open, creat—Open and possibly create a file or device

## SYNOPSIS

```
#include <sys/types.h>
#include <sys/stat.h>
#include <fcntl.h>
int open(const char *pathname,int flags);
int open(const char *pathname,int flags,mode_t mode);
int creat(const char *pathname,mode_t mode);
```

## DESCRIPTION

open attempts to open a file and return a file descriptor (a small, nonnegative integer for use in read, write, and so on).

*flags* is one of O_RDONLY, O_WRONLY, or O_RDWR, which request opening the file read-only, write-only, or read/write, respectively.

*flags* may also be bitwise-ORed with one or more of the following:

| | |
|---|---|
| O_CREAT | If the file does not exist it will be created. |
| O_EXCL | When used with O_CREAT, if the file already exists, it is an error and the open will fail. *See* the "Bugs" section, though. |
| O_NOCTTY | If *pathname* refers to a terminal device—see tty(4)— it will not become the process's controlling terminal even if the process does not have one. |
| O_TRUNC | If the file already exists, it will be truncated. |
| O_APPEND | The file is opened in append mode. Initially, and before each write, the file pointer is positioned at the end of the file, as if with lseek. |
| O_NONBLOCK or O_NDELAY | The file is opened in nonblocking mode. Neither the open nor any subsequent operations on the file descriptor that is returned will cause the calling process to wait. |
| O_SYNC | The file is opened for synchronous I/O. Any writes on the resulting file descriptor will block the calling process until the data has been physically written to the underlying hardware. *See* the "Bugs" section, though. |

Some of these optional flags can be altered using fcntl after the file has been opened.

*mode* specifies the permissions to use if a new file is created. It is modified by the process's umask in the usual way: The permission of the created file is (mode & ~umask).

The following symbolic constants are provided for *mode*:

| | |
|---|---|
| S_IRWXU | 00700 user (file owner) has read, write, and execute permission. |
| S_IRUSR (S_IREAD) | 00400 user has read permission. |
| S_IWUSR (S_IWRITE) | 00200 user has write permission. |
| S_IXUSR (S_IEXEC) | 00100 user has execute permission. |
| S_IRWXG | 00070 group has read, write, and execute permission. |
| S_IRGRP | 00040 group has read permission. |
| S_IWGRP | 00020 group has write permission. |
| S_IXGRP | 00010 group has execute permission. |
| S_IRWXO | 00007 others have read, write, and execute permission. |
| S_IROTH | 00004 others have read permission. |
| S_IWOTH | 00002 others have write permission. |
| S_IXOTH | 00001 others have execute permission. |

*mode* should always be specified when O_CREAT is in the *flags*, and is ignored otherwise.

creat is equivalent to open with *flags* equal to O_CREAT¦O_WRONLY¦O_TRUNC.

## RETURN VALUE

open and creat return the new file descriptor, or –1 if an error occurred (in which case errno is set appropriately). Note that open can open device-special files, but creat cannot create them—use mknod(2) instead.

## ERRORS

| | |
|---|---|
| EEXIST | *pathname* already exists and O_CREAT and O_EXCL were used. |
| EISDIR | *pathname* refers to a directory and the access requested involved writing. |
| ETXTBSY | *pathname* refers to an executable image which is currently being executed and write access was requested. |
| EFAULT | *pathname* points outside your accessible address space. |
| EACCES | The requested access to the file is not allowed, or one of the directories in *pathname* did not allow search (execute) permission. |
| ENAMETOOLONG | *pathname* was too long. |
| ENOENT | A directory component in *pathname* does not exist or is a dangling symbolic link. |
| ENOTDIR | A component used as a directory in *pathname* is not, in fact, a directory. |
| EMFILE | The process already has the maximum number of files open. |
| ENFILE | The limit on the total number of files open on the system has been reached. |
| ENOMEM | Insufficient kernel memory was available. |
| EROFS | *pathname* refers to a file on a read-only filesystem and write access was requested. |
| ELOOP | *pathname* contains a reference to a circular symbolic link, that is, a symbolic link whose expansion contains a reference to itself. |
| ENOSPC | *pathname* was to be created but the device containing *pathname* has no room for the new file. |

## CONFORMS TO

SVID, AT&T, POSIX, X/OPEN, BSD 4.3

## BUGS

O_SYNC is not currently implemented (as of Linux 0.99pl7).

There are many infelicities in the protocol underlying NFS, affecting amongst others O_SYNC, O_NDELAY, and O_APPEND.

O_EXCL is broken on NFS filesystems; programs that rely on it for performing locking tasks will contain a race condition. The solution for performing atomic file locking using a lockfile is to create a unique file on the same fs (for example, incorporating hostname and PID), use link(2) to make a link to the lockfile, and use stat(2) on the unique file to check if its link count has increased to 2. Do not use the return value of the link() call.

## SEE ALSO

read(2), write(2), fcntl(2), close(2), unlink(2), mknod(2), stat(2), umask(2), mount(2), socket(2), socket(2), fopen(3), link(2)

*Linux 0.99.7, 21 July 1993*

# outb, outw, outl, outsb, outsw, outsl

outb, outw, outl, outsb, outsw, outsl—Port output

inb, inw, inl, insb, insw, insl—Port input

outb_p, outw_p, outl_p, inb_p, inw_p, inl_p—Pause I/O

## DESCRIPTION

This family of functions is used to do low-level port input and output. They are primarily designed for internal kernel use, but can be used from user space, given the following information in addition to that given in outb(9).

You compile with -0 or -02 or something similar. The functions are defined as inline macros and will not be substituted in without optimization enabled, causing unresolved references at link time.

You use `ioperm(2)` or alternatively `iopl(2)` to tell the kernel to allow the user space application to access the I/O ports in question. Failure to do this will cause the application to receive a segmentation fault.

## CONFORMS TO

`outb` and friends are hardware specific. The *port* and *value* arguments are in the opposite order from most DOS implementations.

## SEE ALSO

`outb(9)`, `ioperm(2)`, `iopl(2)`

*Linux, 29 November 1995*

# pause

pause—Waits for signal

## SYNOPSIS

```
#include <unistd.h>
int pause(void);
```

## DESCRIPTION

The `pause` system call causes the invoking process to sleep until a signal is received.

## RETURN VALUE

`pause` always returns -1, and `errno` is set to `ERESTARTNOHAND`.

## ERRORS

EINTR                     Signal was received.

## CONFORMS TO

SVID, AT&T, POSIX, X/OPEN, BSD 4.3

## SEE ALSO

`kill(2)`, `select(2)`, `signal(2)`

*Linux, 31 August 1995*

# personality

personality—Sets the process execution domain

## SYNOPSIS

```
int personality(unsigned long persona);
```

## DESCRIPTION

Linux supports different execution domains, or personalities, for each process. Among other things, execution domains tell Linux how to map signal numbers into signal actions. The execution domain system allows Linux to provide limited support for binaries compiled under other UNIX-like operating systems.

`personality` will make the execution domain referenced by *persona* the new execution domain of the current process.

## RETURN VALUE

On success, *persona* is made the new execution domain and the previous *persona* is returned. On error, -1 is returned and errno is set appropriately.

## ERRORS

EINVAL                 *persona* does not refer to a valid execution domain.

## FILE

/usr/include/linux/personality.h

## CONFORMS TO

personality is Linux specific.

*Linux 2.0, 22 July 1996*

# phys

phys—Allows a process to access physical addresses (this command is not implemented)

## SYNOPSIS

int phys(int physnum, char *virtaddr,longsize, char *physaddr);

## DESCRIPTION

Warning: Because this function is not implemented as of Linux 0.99.11, it will always return -1 and set errno to ENOSYS.

phys maps arbitrary physical memory into a process's virtual address space. physnum is a number (0–3) that specifies which of the four physical spaces to set up. Up to four phys calls can be active at any one time. virtaddr is the process's virtual address. size is the number of bytes to map in. physaddr is the physical address to map in.

Valid virtaddr and physaddr values are constrained by hardware and must be at an address multiple of the resolution of the CPU's memory management scheme. If size is nonzero, size is rounded up to the next MMU resolution boundary. If size is 0, any previous phys(2) mapping for that physnum is nullified.

## RETURN VALUE

On success, 0 is returned. On error, −1 is returned and errno is set appropriately.

## CONFORMS TO

version 7 AT&T UNIX

## BUGS

phys is very machine dependent.

## SEE ALSO

mmap(2), munmap(2)

*Linux 0.99.11, 24 July 1993*

# pipe

pipe—Creates a pipe

## SYNOPSIS

```
#include <unistd.h>
int pipe(int filedes[2]);
```

## DESCRIPTION

pipe creates a pair of file descriptors, pointing to a pipe inode, and places them in the array pointed to by filedes. filedes[0] is for reading, filedes[1] is for writing.

## RETURN VALUE

On success, 0 is returned. On error, -1 is returned and errno is set appropriately.

## ERRORS

| | |
|---|---|
| EMFILE | Too many file descriptors are in use by the process. |
| ENFILE | The system file table is full. |
| EFAULT | filedes is not valid. |

## SEE ALSO

read(2), write(2), fork(2), socketpair(2)

*Linux 0.99.11, 23 July 1993*

# profil

profil—Execution time profile

## SYNOPSIS

```
#include <unistd.h>
int profil(char *buf, int bufsiz,int offset,int scale);
```

## DESCRIPTION

Under Linux 0.99.11, profil is not implemented in the kernel. Instead, the DLL 4.4.1 libraries provide a user-space implementation.

buf points to *bufsiz* bytes of core. Every virtual 10 milliseconds, the user's program counter (PC) is examined: *offset* is subtracted and the result is multiplied by *scale*. If this address is in buf, the word pointed to is incremented.

If *scale* is less than 2 or *bufsiz* is 0, profiling is disabled.

## RETURN VALUE

0 is always returned.

## BUGS

profil cannot be used on a program that also uses ITIMER_PROF itimers.

Calling profil with an invalid buf will result in a core dump.

True kernel profiling provides more accurate results.

## SEE ALSO

gprof(1), setitimer(2), signal(2), sigaction(2)

*Linux 0.99.11, 23 July 1993*

# ptrace

ptrace—Process trace

## SYNOPSIS

```
#include <sys/ptrace.h>
int ptrace(int request,int pid,int addr,int data);
```

## DESCRIPTION

ptrace provides a means by which a parent process can control the execution of a child process and examine and change its core image. Its primary use is for the implementation of breakpoint debugging. A traced process runs until a signal occurs. Then it stops and the parent is notified with wait(2). When the process is in the stopped state, its memory can be read and written. The parent can also cause the child to continue execution, optionally ignoring the signal which caused stopping.

The value of the request argument determines the precise action of the system call:

| | |
|---|---|
| PTRACE_TRACEME | This process is to be traced by its parent. The parent should be expecting to trace the child. |
| PTRACE_PEEKTEXT, PTRACE_PEEKDATA | Read word at location *addr*. |
| PTRACE_PEEKUSR | Read word at location addr in the USER area. |
| PTRACE_POKETEXT, PTRACE_POKEDATA | Write word at location *addr*. |
| PTRACE_POKEUSR | Write word at location *addr* in the USER area. |
| PTRACE_SYSCALL, PTRACE_CONT | Restart after signal. |
| PTRACE_KILL | Send the child a SIGKILL to make it exit. |
| PTRACE_SINGLESTEP | Set the trap flag for single stepping. |
| PTRACE_ATTACH | Attach to the process specified in *pid*. |
| PTRACE_DETACH | Detach a process that was previously attached. |

## NOTES

*init*, the process with process ID *1*, may not use this function.

## RETURN VALUE

On success, 0 is returned. On error, -1 is returned and errno is set appropriately.

## ERRORS

| | |
|---|---|
| EPERM | The specified process (that is, init), cannot be traced or is already being traced. |
| ESRCH | The specified process does not exist. |
| EIO | Request is not valid. |

## CONFORMS TO

SVID EXT, AT&T, X/OPEN, BSD 4.3

## SEE ALSO

gdb(1), exec(2), signal(2), wait(2)

*Linux 0.99.11, 23 July 1993*

# quotactl

quotactl—Manipulates disk quotas

## SYNOPSIS

```
#include <sys/types.h>
#include <sys/quota.h>
int quotactl (int cmd, const char *special, intid , caddr_t addr);
#include <linux/unistd.h>
syscall4(int, quotactl, int, cmd, const char *, special ,int, id, caddr_t, addr);
```

## DESCRIPTION

The quota system defines for each user or group a soft limit and a hard limit bounding the amount of disk space that can be used on a given filesystem. The hard limit cannot be crossed. The soft limit can be crossed, but warnings will ensue. Moreover, the user cannot be above the soft limit for more than one week (by default) at a time: After this week the soft limit counts as a hard limit.

The quotactl system call manipulates these quotas. Its first argument is of the form

QCMD(subcmd,type)

where type is either USRQUOTA or GRPQUOTA (for user quota and group quota, respectively.

The second argument special is the block special device these quotas apply to. It must be mounted.

The third argument ID is the user or group ID these quotas apply to (when relevant).

The fourth argument, addr, is the address of a data structure, depending on the command.

The subcmd is one of the following:

| | |
|---|---|
| Q_QUOTAON | Enables quotas. The addr argument is the pathname of the file containing the quotas for the filesystem. |
| Q_QUOTAOFF | Disables quotas. |
| Q_GETQUOTA | Gets limits and current usage of disk space. The addr argument is a pointer to a dqblk structure (defined in <sys/quota.h>). |
| Q_SETQUOTA | Sets limits and current usage; addr is as before. |
| Q_SETQLIM | Sets limits; addr is as before. |
| Q_SETUSE | Sets usage. |
| Q_SYNC | Syncs disk copy of a filesystem's quotas. |
| Q_GETSTATS | Gets collected stats. |

## RETURN VALUE

On success, quotactl returns 0. On error, -1 is returned and errno is set appropriately.

## ERRORS

| | |
|---|---|
| ENOPKG | The kernel was compiled without quota support. |
| EFAULT | Bad addr value. |
| EINVAL | type is not a known quota type. Or special could not be found. |
| ENOTBLK | special is not a block special device. |
| ENODEV | special cannot be found in the mount table. |
| EACCES | The quota file is not an ordinary file. |
| EIO | Cannot read or write the quota file. |
| EMFILE | Too many open files: Cannot open quota file. |

| EBUSY | Q_QUOTAON was asked, but quota were enabled already. |
|---|---|
| ESRCH | Q_GETQUOTA or Q_SETQUOTA or Q_SETUSE or Q_SETQLIM was asked for a filesystem that didn't have quota enabled. |
| EPERM | The process was not root (for the filesystem), and Q_GETQUOTA was asked for another ID than that of the process itself, or anything other than Q_GETSTATS or Q_SYNC was asked. |

## CONFORMS TO

BSD

*Linux 1.3.88, 14 April 1996*

# read

read—Reads from a file descriptor

## SYNOPSIS

```
#include <unistd.h>
ssize_t read(int fd,void*buf, size_t count);
```

## DESCRIPTION

read() attempts to read up to count bytes from file descriptor fd into the buffer starting at buf.

If count is 0, read() returns 0 and has no other results. If count is greater than SSIZE_MAX, the result is unspecified.

## RETURN VALUE

On success, the number of bytes read is returned (0 indicates end of file) and the file position is advanced by this number. It is not an error if this number is smaller than the number of bytes requested; this may happen, for example, because fewer bytes are actually available right now (maybe because we were close to end-of-file or because we are reading from a pipe, or from a terminal), or because read() was interrupted by a signal. On error, -1 is returned and errno is set appropriately. In this case it is left unspecified whether the file position (if any) changes.

## ERRORS

| EINTR | The call was interrupted by a signal before any data was read. |
|---|---|
| EAGAIN | Non-blocking I/O has been selected using O_NONBLOCK and no data was immediately available for reading. |
| EIO | I/O error. This will happen, for example, when the process is in a background process group, tries to read from its controlling tty, and it is ignoring or blocking SIGTTIN or its process group is orphaned. |
| EISDIR | fd refers to a directory. |
| EBADF | fd is not a valid file descriptor or is not open for reading. |
| EINVAL | fd is attached to an object that is unsuitable for reading. |
| EFAULT | buf is outside your accessible address space. |

Other errors may occur, depending on the object connected to fd. POSIX allows a read that is interrupted after reading some data to return -1 (with errno set to EINTR) or to return the number of bytes already read.

## CONFORMS TO

SVID, AT&T, POSIX, X/OPEN, BSD 4.3

## SEE ALSO

readdir(2), write(2), write(2), fcntl(2), close(2), lseek(2), select(2), readlink(2), ioctl(2), fread(3)

*Linux, 17 January 1996*

# readdir

readdir—Reads directory entry

## SYNOPSIS

```
#include <unistd.h>
#include <linux/dirent.h>
#include <linux/unistd.h>
syscall3(int, readdir, uint, fd, struct dirent *, dirp, uint, count);
int readdir(unsigned int fd, struct dirent *dirp, unsigned int count);
```

## DESCRIPTION

This is not the function you are interested in. Look at readdir(3) for the POSIX-conforming C library interface. This page documents the bare kernel system call interface, which can change, and which is superseded by getdents(2).

readdir reads one dirent structure from the directory pointed at by fd into the memory area pointed to by *dirp*. The parameter count is ignored; at most one dirent structure is read.

The dirent structure is declared as follows:

```
struct dirent
{
    long d_ino;                 /* inode number */
    off_t d_off;                /* offset to this dirent */
    unsigned short d_reclen;    /* length of this d_name */
    char d_name [NAME_MAX+1];   /* file name (null-terminated) */
}
```

*d_ino* is an inode number. *d_off* is the distance from the start of the directory to this dirent. *d_reclen* is the size of *d_name*, not counting the null terminator. *d_name* is a null-terminated filename.

## RETURN VALUE

On success, 1 is returned. On end of directory, 0 is returned. On error, –1 is returned and errno is set appropriately.

## ERRORS

| | |
|---|---|
| EBADF | Invalid file descriptor fd. |
| ENOTDIR | File descriptor does not refer to a directory. |

## CONFORMS TO

This system call is Linux specific.

## SEE ALSO

getdents(2), readdir(3)

*Linux 1.3.6, 22 July 1995*

# readlink

readlink—Reads value of a symbolic link

## SYNOPSIS

```
#include <unistd.h>
int readlink(const char *path, char *buf, size_t bufsiz);
```

## DESCRIPTION

readlink places the contents of the symbolic link path in the buffer *buf*, which has size *bufsiz*. Readlink does not append a NUL character to *buf*.

## RETURN VALUES

The call returns the count of characters placed in the buffer if it succeeds, or a -1 if an error occurs, placing the error code in the global variable errno.

## ERRORS

| | |
|---|---|
| ENOTDIR | A component of the path prefix is not a directory. |
| EINVAL | The pathname contains a character with the high-order bit set. |
| ENAMETOOLONG | A component of a pathname exceeded 255 characters, or an entire path name exceeded 1023 characters. |
| ENOENT | The named file does not exist. |
| EACCES | Search permission is denied for a component of the path prefix. |
| ELOOP | Too many symbolic links were encountered in translating the pathname. |
| EINVAL | The named file is not a symbolic link. |
| EIO | An I/O error occurred while reading from the filesystem. |
| EFAULT | *buf* extends outside the process's allocated address space. |

## HISTORY

The readlink function call appeared in BSD 4.2.

## SEE ALSO

stat(2), lstat(2), symlink(2)

*BSD Man Page, 24 July 1993*

# readv, writev

readv, writev—Reads or writes a vector

## SYNOPSIS

```
#include <sys/uio.h>
int readv(int fd, const struct iovec * vector, size_t count);
int writev(int fd, const struct iovec * vector, size_t count);
struct iovec {
ptr_t iov_base; /* Starting address. */
size_t iov_len; /* Length in bytes. */
};
```

## DESCRIPTION

readv reads data from file descriptor *fd* and puts the result in the buffers described by *vector*. The number of buffers is specified by *count*. The buffers are filled in the order specified. Operates just like read except that data is put in vector instead of a contiguous buffer.

writev writes data to file descriptor *fd*, and from the buffers described by vector. The number of buffers is specified by *count*. The buffers are used in the order specified. Operates just like write except that data is taken from *vector* instead of a contiguous buffer.

## RETURN VALUE

On success, readv returns the number of bytes read. On success, writev returns the number of bytes written. On error, -1 is returned, and errno is set appropriately.

## ERRORS

| | |
|---|---|
| EINVAL | An invalid argument was given. For instance *count* might be greater than MAX_IOVEC, or 0. *fd* could also be attached to an object that is unsuitable for reading. |
| EFAULT | Segmentation fault. Most likely *vector* or some of the *iov_base* pointers points to memory that is not properly allocated. |
| EBADF | The file descriptor *fd* is not valid. |
| EINTR | The call was interrupted by a signal before any data was read/written. |
| EAGAIN | Non-blocking I/O has been selected using O_NONBLOCK and no data was immediately available for reading. (Or the file descriptor *fd* is for an object that is locked.) |
| EISDIR | *fd* refers to a directory. |
| EOPNOTSUP | *fd* refers to a socket or device that does not support reading/writing. |

Other errors may occur, depending on the object connected to *fd*.

## SEE ALSO

read(2), write(2), fprintf(3), fscanf(2)

*Linux 1.3.86, 12 April 1996*

# reboot

reboot—Reboots or disables Ctrl+Alt+Del

## SYNOPSIS

```
#include <unistd.h>
int reboot (int magic,int magic_too,int flag);
```

## DESCRIPTION

reboot reboots the system or enables/disables CAD.

If magic = 0xfee1dead and magic_too = 672274793, the action performed will be based on *flag*.

If flag=0x1234567, a hard reset is performed.

If flag=0x89abcdef, CAD is enabled.

If flag=0, CAD is disabled and a signal is sent to process ID 1.

Note that reboot() does *not* sync()!

Only the superuser may use this function.

## RETURN VALUE

On success, 0 is returned. On error, -1 is returned, and *errno* is set appropriately.

## ERRORS

| | |
|---|---|
| EINVAL | Bad *magic* numbers or *flag*. |
| EPERM | A non-root user has attempted to call reboot. |

## CONFORMS TO

reboot is Linux specific.

## SEE ALSO

sync(2), ctrlaltdel(8), halt(8), reboot(8)

*Linux 0.99.10, 28 March 1992*

# recv, recvfrom, recvmsg

recv, recvfrom, recvmsg—Receives a message from a socket

## SYNOPSIS

```
#include <sys/types.h>
#include <sys/socket.h>
int recv(int s, void *buf, intlen, unsigned int flags);
int recvfrom(int s, void*buf, int len, unsigned int flags,
    struct sockaddr *from, int *fromlen);
int recvmsg(int s, struct msghdr *msg, unsigned int flags);
```

## DESCRIPTION

Warning: This is a BSD man page. As of Linux 0.99.11, recvmsg was not implemented.

recvfrom and recvmsg are used to receive messages from a socket, and may be used to receive data on a socket whether or not it is connection oriented.

If from is non-nil, and the socket is not connection-oriented, the source address of the message is filled in. fromlen is a value-result parameter, initialized to the size of the buffer associated with from and modified on return to indicate the actual size of the address stored there.

The recv call is normally used only on a connected socket (see connect(2)) and is identical to recvfrom with a nil from parameter. Because it is redundant, it might not be supported in future releases.

All three routines return the length of the message on successful completion. If a message is too long to fit in the supplied buffer, excess bytes might be discarded depending on the type of socket from which the message is received (see socket(2)).

If no messages are available at the socket, the receive call waits for a message to arrive—unless the socket is nonblocking (see fcntl(2)), in which case the value –1 is returned and the external variable errno is set to EWOULDBLOCK. The receive calls normally return any data available, up to the requested amount, rather than wait for receipt of the full amount requested; this behavior is affected by the socket-level options SO_RCVLOWAT and SO_RCVTIMEO, described in getsockopt(2).

The select(2) call may be used to determine when more data arrives.

The flags argument to a recv call is formed by oring one or more of the values:

| | |
|---|---|
| MSG_OOB | Process out-of-band data |
| MSG_PEEK | Peek at incoming message |
| MSG_WAITALL | Wait for full request or error |

The MSG_OOB flag requests receipt of out-of-band data that would not be received in the normal data stream. Some protocols place expedited data at the head of the normal data queue; thus this flag cannot be used with such protocols. The MSG_PEEK flag causes the receive operation to return data from the beginning of the receive queue without removing that data from the queue; thus, a subsequent receive call will return the same data. The MSG_WAITALL flag requests that the operation block until the full request is satisfied. However, the call might still return less data than requested if a signal is caught, an error or disconnect occurs, or the next data to be received is of a different type than that returned.

The recvmsg call uses a msghdr structure to minimize the number of directly supplied parameters. This structure has the following form, as defined in sys/socket.h:

```
struct msghdr {
    caddr_t msg_name; /* optional address */
    u_int msg_namelen; /* size of address */
    struct iovec *msg_iov; /* scatter/gather array */
    u_int msg_iovlen; /* # elements in msg_iov */
    caddr_t msg_control; /* ancillary data, see below */
    u_int msg_controllen; /* ancillary data buffer len */
    int msg_flags; /* flags on received message */
};
```

Here msg_name and msg_namelen specify the destination address if the socket is unconnected; msg_name may be given as a null pointer if no names are desired or required. msg_iov and msg_iovlen describe scatter gather locations, as discussed in read(2). msg_control, which has length msg_controllen, points to a buffer for other protocol control–related messages or other miscellaneous ancillary data. The messages are of the form

```
struct cmsghdr {
    u_int cmsg_len; /* data byte count, including hdr */
    int cmsg_level; /* originating protocol */
    int cmsg_type; /* protocol-specific type */
/* followed by
    u_char cmsg_data[]; */
};
```

You could use this, for example, to learn of changes in the data stream in XNS/SPP, or in ISO, to obtain user-connection-request data by requesting a recvmsg with no data buffer provided immediately after an accept call.

Open file descriptors are now passed as ancillary data for AF_UNIX domain sockets, with cmsg_level set to SOL_SOCKET and cmsg_type set to SCM_RIGHTS.

The msg_flags field is set on return according to the message received. MSG_EOR indicates end-of-record; the data returned completed a record (generally used with sockets of type SOCK_SEQPACKET). MSG_TRUNC indicates that the trailing portion of a datagram was discarded because the datagram was larger than the buffer supplied. MSG_CTRUNC indicates that some control data was discarded due to lack of space in the buffer for ancillary data. MSG_OOB is returned to indicate that expedited or out-of-band data was received.

## RETURN VALUES

These calls return the number of bytes received, or -1 if an error occurred.

## ERRORS

| | |
|---|---|
| EBADF | The argument s is an invalid descriptor. |
| ENOTCONN | The socket is associated with a connection-oriented protocol and has not been connected (see connect(2) and accept(2)). |
| ENOTSOCK | The argument s does not refer to a socket. |
| EWOULDBLOCK | The socket is marked non-blocking, and the receive operation would block, or a receive timeout had been set, and the timeout expired before data was received. |
| EINTR | The receive was interrupted by delivery of a signal before any data was available. |
| EFAULT | The receive buffer pointer(s) point outside the process's address space. |

## HISTORY

These function calls appeared in BSD 4.2.

## SEE ALSO

fcntl(2), read(2), select(2), getsockopt(2), socket(2)

*BSD Man Page, 24 July 1993*

# rename

rename—Changes the name or location of a file

## SYNOPSIS

```
#include <unistd.h>
int rename(const char *oldpath, const char *newpath);
```

## DESCRIPTION

rename renames a file, moving it between directories if required.

Any other hard links to the file (as created using link) are unaffected.

If *newpath* already exists it will be automatically overwritten (subject to a few conditions—see the "Errors" section), so that there is no point at which another process attempting to access *newpath* will find it missing.

If *newpath* exists but the operation fails for some reason or the system crashes, rename guarantees to leave an instance of *newpath* in place.

However, when overwriting there will probably be a window in which both *oldpath* and *newpath* refer to the file being renamed.

If *oldpath* refers to a symbolic link, the link will be renamed; if *newpath* refers to a symbolic link, the link will be overwritten.

## RETURN VALUE

On success, 0 is returned. On error, -1 is returned, and errno is set appropriately.

## ERRORS

| | |
|---|---|
| EISDIR | *newpath* is an existing directory, but *oldpath* is not a directory. |
| EXDEV | *oldpath* and *newpath* are not on the same filesystem. |
| ENOTEMPTY | *newpath* is a non-empty directory. |
| EBUSY | *newpath* exists and is the current working directory or root directory of some process. |
| EINVAL | An attempt was made to make a directory a subdirectory of itself. |
| EMLINK | *oldpath* already has the maximum number of links to it, or it was a directory and the directory containing *newpath* has the maximum number of links. |
| ENOTDIR | A component used as a directory in *oldpath* or *newpath* is not, in fact, a directory. |
| EFAULT | *oldpath* or *newpath* points outside your accessible address space. |
| EACCES | Write access to the directory containing *oldpath* or *newpath* is not allowed for the process's effective UID, or one of the directories in *oldpath* or *newpath* did not allow search (execute) permission, or *oldpath* was a directory and did not allow write permission (needed to update the .. entry). |
| EPERM | The directory containing *oldpath* has the sticky bit set, and the process's effective UID is neither the UID of the file to be deleted nor that of the directory containing it, or the filesystem containing *pathname* does not support renaming of the type requested. |
| ENAMETOOLONG | *oldpath* or *newpath* was too long. |
| ENOENT | A directory component in *oldpath* or *newpath* does not exist or is a dangling symbolic link. |
| ENOMEM | Insufficient kernel memory was available. |
| EROFS | The file is on a read-only filesystem. |

| ELOOP | *oldpath* or *newpath* contains a reference to a circular symbolic link; that is, a symbolic link whose expansion contains a reference to itself. |
| ENOSPC | The device containing the file has no room for the new directory entry. |

## CONFORMS TO

POSIX, BSD 4.3, ANSI C

## BUGS

Currently (Linux 0.99pl7), most of the filesystems except Minix will not allow any overwriting renames involving directories. You get EEXIST if you try.

On NFS filesystems, you cannot assume that just because the operation failed, the file was not renamed. If the server does the rename operation and then crashes, the retransmitted RPC, which will be processed when the server is up again, causes a failure. The application is expected to deal with this. See link(2) for a similar problem.

## SEE ALSO

link(2), unlink(2), symlink(2), mv(1), link(8)

*Linux 0.99.7, 24 July 1993*

# rmdir

rmdir—Deletes a directory

## SYNOPSIS

```
#include <unistd.h>
int rmdir(const char *pathname);
```

## DESCRIPTION

rmdir deletes a directory, which must be empty.

## RETURN VALUE

On success, 0 is returned. On error, -1 is returned, and errno is set appropriately.

## ERRORS

| EPERM | The filesystem containing *pathname* does not support the removal of directories. |
| EFAULT | *pathname* points outside your accessible address space. |
| EACCES | Write access to the directory containing *pathname* was not allowed for the process's effective UID, or one of the directories in *pathname* did not allow search (execute) permission. |
| EPERM | The directory containing *pathname* has the sticky bit (S_ISVTX) set, and the process's effective UID is neither the UID of the file to be deleted nor that of the directory containing it. |
| ENAMETOOLONG | *pathname* was too long. |
| ENOENT | A directory component in *pathname* does not exist or is a dangling symbolic link. |
| ENOTDIR | *pathname*, or a component used as a directory in *pathname*, is not, in fact, a directory. |
| ENOTEMPTY | *pathname* contains entries other than . and ... |
| EBUSY | *pathname* is the current working directory or root directory of some process. |
| ENOMEM | Insufficient kernel memory was available. |
| EROFS | *pathname* refers to a file on a read-only filesystem. |
| ELOOP | *pathname* contains a reference to a circular symbolic link; that is, a symbolic link containing a reference to itself. |

## CONFORMS TO

SVID, AT&T, POSIX, BSD 4.3

## BUGS

Infelicities in the protocol underlying NFS can cause the unexpected disappearance of directories that are still being used.

## SEE ALSO

rename(2), mkdir(2), chdir(2), unlink(2), rmdir(1), rm(1)

*Linux 0.99.7, 24 July 1993*

# sched_get_priority_max, sched_get_priority_min

sched_get_priority_max, sched_get_priority_min—Gets static priority range

## SYNOPSIS

```
#include <sched.h>
int sched_get_priority_max(int policy);
int_sched_get_priority_min(int policy);
```

## DESCRIPTION

sched_get_priority_max returns the maximum priority value that can be used with the scheduling algorithm identified by *policy*. sched_get_priority_min returns the minimum priority value that can be used with the scheduling algorithm identified by *policy*. Supported *policy* values are SCHED_FIFO, SCHED_RR, and SCHED_OTHER.

Processes with numerically higher priority values are scheduled before processes with numerically lower priority values. Therefore, the value returned by sched_get_priority_max will be greater than the value returned by sched_get_priority_min.

Linux allows the static priority value range 1 to 99 for SCHED_FIFO and SCHED_RR, and the priority 0 for SCHED_OTHER. Scheduling priority ranges for the various policies are not alterable.

The range of scheduling priorities may vary on other POSIX systems, so it is a good idea for portable applications to use a virtual priority range and map it to the interval given by sched_get_priority_max and sched_get_priority_min. POSIX.1b requires a spread of at least 32 between the maximum and the minimum values for SCHED_FIFO and SCHED_RR.

POSIX systems on which sched_get_priority_max and sched_get_priority_min are available define _POSIX_PRIORITY_SCHEDULING in <unistd.h>.

## RETURN VALUE

On success, sched_get_priority_max and sched_get_priority_min return the maximum and minimum priority values for the named scheduling policy. On error, -1 is returned, and errno is set appropriately.

## ERRORS

EINVAL                    The parameter policy does not identify a defined scheduling policy.

## STANDARDS

POSIX.1b (formerly POSIX.4)

## SEE ALSO

sched_setscheduler(2), sched_getscheduler(2), sched_setparam(2), sched_getparam(2)

sched_setscheduler(2) has a description of the Linux scheduling scheme.

*Programming for the Real World—POSIX.4* by Bill O. Gallmeister, O'Reilly & Associates, Inc., ISBN 1-56592-074-0

IEEE Std 1003.1b-1003 (POSIX.1b standard)

ISO/IEC 9945-1:1996

*Linux 1.3.81, 10 April 1996*

# sched_rr_get_interval

sched_rr_get_interval—Gets the SCHED_RR interval for the named process

## SYNOPSIS

```
#include <sched.h>
int sched_rr_get_interval(pid_t pid, struct timespec *tp);
struct timespec {
    time_t tv_sec; /* seconds */
    long tv_nsec; /* nanoseconds */
};
```

## DESCRIPTION

sched_rr_get_interval writes into the *timespec* structure pointed to by *tp* the round-robin time quantum for the process identified by *pid*. If *pid* is 0, the time quantum for the calling process is written into *tp*. The identified process should be running under the SCHED_RR scheduling policy.

The round robin time quantum value is not alterable under Linux 1.3.81.

POSIX systems on which sched_rr_get_interval is available define _POSIX_PRIORITY_SCHEDULING in <unistd.h>.

## RETURN VALUE

On success, sched_rr_get_interval returns 0. On error, –1 is returned, and errno is set appropriately.

## ERRORS

| | |
|---|---|
| ESRCH | The process whose ID is *pid* could not be found. |
| ENOSYS | The system call is not yet implemented. |

## STANDARDS

POSIX.1b (formerly POSIX.4)

## BUGS

As of Linux 1.3.81, sched_rr_get_interval returns with error ENOSYS, because SCHED_RR has not yet been fully implemented or tested properly.

## SEE ALSO

sched_setscheduler(2) has a description of the Linux scheduling scheme.

*Programming for the Real World—POSIX.4* by Bill O. Gallmeister, O'Reilly & Associates, Inc., ISBN 1-56592-074-0

IEEE Std 1003.1b-1993 (POSIX.1b standard)

ISO/IEC 9945-1:1996

*Linux 1.3.81, 10 April 1996*

# sched_setparam, sched_getparam

sched_setparam, sched_getparam—Sets and get scheduling parameters

## SYNOPSIS

```
#include <sched.h>
int sched_setparam(pid_t pid, const struct sched param *p);
int sched_getparam(pid_t pid, struct sched_param *p);
struct sched_param {
...
int sched_priority;
...
};
```

## DESCRIPTION

sched_setparam sets the scheduling parameters associated with the scheduling policy for the process identified by *pid*. If *pid* is 0, the parameters of the current process are set. The interpretation of the parameter *p* depends on the selected policy. Currently, the following three scheduling policies are supported under Linux: SCHED_FIFO, SCHED_RR, and SCHED_OTHER.

sched_getparam retrieves the scheduling parameters for the process identified by *pid*. If *pid* is 0, the parameters of the current process are retrieved.

sched_setparam checks the validity of *p* for the scheduling policy of the process. The parameter p->sched_priority must lie within the range given by sched_get_priority_min and sched_get_priority_max.

POSIX systems on which sched_setparam and sched_getparam are available define _POSIX_PRIORITY_SCHEDULING in <unistd.h>.

## RETURN VALUE

On success, sched_setparam and sched_getparam return 0. On error, -1 is returned, and errno is set appropriately.

## ERRORS

| | |
|---|---|
| ESRCH | The process whose ID is *pid* could not be found. |
| EPERM | The calling process does not have appropriate privileges. The process calling sched_setparam needs an effective UID equal to the UID or UID of the process identified by *pid*, or it must be a superuser process. |
| EINVAL | The parameter *p* does not make sense for the current scheduling policy. |

## STANDARDS

POSIX.1b (formerly POSIX.4)

## SEE ALSO

sched_setscheduler(2), sched_getscheduler(2), sched_get_priority_max(2), sched_get_priority_min(2), nice(2), setpriority(2), getpriority(2)

sched_setscheduler(2) has a description of the Linux scheduling scheme.

*Programming for the Real World—POSIX.4* by Bill O. Gallmeister, O'Reilly & Associates, Inc., ISBN 1-56592-074-0

IEEE Std 1003.1b-1993 (POSIX.1b standard)

ISO/IEC 9945-1:1996

# sched_setscheduler, sched_getscheduler

sched_setscheduler, sched_getscheduler—Sets and gets scheduling algorithm/parameters

## SYNOPSIS

```
#include <sched.h>
int sched_setscheduler(pid_t pid,intpolicy, const struct sched_param *p);
int sched_getscheduler(pid_t pid);
struct sched_param {
...
int sched_priority;
...
};
```

## DESCRIPTION

sched_setscheduler sets both the scheduling policy and the associated parameters for the process identified by *pid*. If *pid* is 0, the scheduler of the calling process will be set. The interpretation of the parameter *p* depends on the selected policy. Currently, the following three scheduling policies are supported under Linux: SCHED_FIFO, SCHED_RR, and SCHED_OTHER; their respective semantics are described in the following section.

sched_getscheduler queries the scheduling policy currently applied to the process identified by *pid*. If *pid* is 0, the policy of the calling process will be retrieved.

## SCHEDULING POLICIES

The scheduler is the kernel part that decides which runnable process will be executed next by the CPU. The Linux scheduler offers three different scheduling policies, one for normal processes and two for real-time applications. A static priority value, *sched_priority*, is assigned to each process, and this value can be changed only via system calls. Conceptually, the scheduler maintains a list of runnable processes for each possible *sched_priority* value, and *sched_priority* can have a value in the range 0 to 99. To determine the process that runs next, the Linux scheduler looks for the non-empty list with the highest static priority and takes the process at the head of this list. The scheduling policy determines, for each process, where it will be inserted into the list of processes with equal static priority and how it will move inside this list.

SCHED_OTHER is the default universal time-sharing scheduler policy used by most processes; SCHED_FIFO and SCHED_RR are intended for special, time-critical applications that need precise control over the way in which runnable processes are selected for execution. Processes scheduled with SCHED_OTHER must be assigned the static priority 0; processes scheduled under SCHED_FIFO or SCHED_RR can have a static priority in the range 1 to 99. Only processes with superuser privileges can get a static priority higher than 0 and can therefore be scheduled under SCHED_FIFO or SCHED_RR. The system calls sched_get_priority_min and sched_get_priority_max can be used to find out the valid priority range for a scheduling policy in a portable way on all POSIX.1b-conforming systems.

All scheduling is preemptive: If a process with a higher static priority gets ready to run, the current process will be preempted and returned into its wait list. The scheduling policy determines the ordering within the list of runnable processes only among those with equal static priority.

## SCHED_FIFO: FIRST IN–FIRST OUT SCHEDULING

SCHED_FIFO can only be used with static priorities higher than 0, which means that when a SCHED_FIFO process becomes runnable, it will always preempt immediately any currently running normal SCHED_OTHER process. SCHED_FIFO is a simple scheduling algorithm without time slicing.

For processes scheduled under the SCHED_FIFO policy, the following rules are applied: A SCHED_FIFO process that has been preempted by another process of higher priority will stay at the head of the list for its priority and will resume execution as soon as all processes of higher priority are blocked again. When a SCHED_FIFO process becomes runnable, it will be inserted at the end of the list for its priority. A call to sched_setscheduler or sched_setparam will put the SCHED_FIFO process identified by *pid* at the end of the list if it was runnable. A process calling sched_yield will be put at the end of the list. No other events will move a process scheduled under the SCHED_FIFO policy in the wait list of runnable processes with equal static priority. A SCHED_FIFO process runs until it is blocked by an I/O request, it is preempted by a higher-priority process, or it calls sched_yield.

## SCHED_RR: ROUND-ROBIN SCHEDULING

SCHED_RR is a simple enhancement of SCHED_FIFO. Everything described in the preceding section for SCHED_FIFO also applies to SCHED_RR, except that each process is only allowed to run for a maximum time quantum. If a SCHED_RR process has been running for a time period equal to or longer than the time quantum, it will be put at the end of the list for its priority. A SCHED_RR process that has been preempted by a higher-priority process and subsequently resumes execution as a running process will complete the unexpired portion of its round-robin time quantum. The length of the time quantum can be retrieved by sched_rr_get_interval.

## SCHED_OTHER: DEFAULT LINUX TIME-SHARING SCHEDULING

SCHED_OTHER can only be used at static priority 0. SCHED_OTHER is the standard Linux time-sharing scheduler that is intended for all processes that do not require special static-priority real-time mechanisms. The process to run is chosen from the static priority 0 list based on a dynamic priority that is determined only inside this list. The dynamic priority is based on the nice level (set by the nice or setpriority system call) and is increased for each time quantum the process is ready to run but is denied to run by the scheduler. This ensures fair progress among all SCHED_OTHER processes.

## RESPONSE TIME

A blocked high-priority process waiting for the I/O has a certain response time before it is scheduled again. The device driver writer can greatly reduce this response time by using a *slow interrupt* interrupt handler, as described in request irq(9).

## MISCELLANEOUS

Child processes inherit the scheduling algorithm and parameters across a fork.

Memory locking is usually needed for real-time processes to avoid paging delays; this can be done with mlock or mlockall.

Because a non-blocking endless loop in a process scheduled under SCHED_FIFO or SCHED_RR will block all processes with lower priority forever, a software developer should always keep available on the console a shell scheduled under a higher static priority than the tested application. This will allow an emergency kill of tested real-time applications that do not block or terminate as expected. Because SCHED_FIFO and SCHED_RR processes can preempt other processes forever, only root processes are allowed to activate these policies under Linux.

POSIX systems on which sched_setscheduler and sched_getscheduler are available define _POSIX_PRIORITY_SCHEDULING in <unistd.h>.

## RETURN VALUE

On success, sched_setscheduler returns 0. On success, sched_getscheduler returns the policy for the process (a non-negative integer). On error, -1 is returned, and errno is set appropriately.

## ERRORS

| | |
|---|---|
| ESRCH | The process whose ID is *pid* could not be found. |
| EPERM | The calling process does not have appropriate privileges. Only root processes are allowed to activate the SCHED_FIFO and SCHED_RR policies. The process calling sched_setscheduler needs an effective UID equal to the EUID or UID of the process identified by *pid*, or it must be a superuser process. |
| EINVAL | The scheduling policy is not one of the recognized policies, or the parameter p does not make sense for the policy. |

## STANDARDS

POSIX.1b (formerly POSIX.4)

## BUGS

As of Linux 1.3.81, SCHED_RR has not yet been tested carefully and might not behave exactly as described or required by POSIX.1b.

## SEE ALSO

sched_setparam(2), sched_getparam(2), sched_yield(2), sched_get_priority_max(2), sched_get_priority_min(2), nice(2), setpriority(2), getpriority(2), mlockall(2), munlockall(2), mlock(2), munlock(2).

*Programming for the Real World—POSIX.4* by Bill O. Gallmeister, O'Reilly & Associates, Inc., ISBN 1-56592-074-0

IEEE Std 1003.1b-1003 (POSIX.1b standard)

ISO/IEC 9945-1:1996—This is the new 1996 revision of POSIX.1, which contains in one single standard POSIX.1(1990), POSIX.1b(1993), POSIX.1c(1995), and POSIX.1i(1995).

*Linux 1.3.81, 10 April 1996*

# sched_yield

sched_yield—Yields the processor

## SYNOPSIS

```
#include <sched.h>
int sched_yield(void);
```

## DESCRIPTION

A process can relinquish the processor voluntarily without blocking by calling sched_yield. The process will then be moved to the end of the queue for its static priority and a new process gets to run.

Note: If the current process is the only process in the highest priority list at that time, this process will continue to run after a call to sched_yield.

POSIX systems on which sched_yield is available define _POSIX_PRIORITY_SCHEDULING in <unistd.h>.

## RETURN VALUE

On success, sched_yield returns 0. On error, –1 is returned, and errno is set appropriately.

## STANDARDS

POSIX.1b (formerly POSIX.4)

## SEE ALSO

sched_setscheduler(2) for a description of Linux scheduling

*Programming for the Real World—POSIX.4* by Bill O. Gallmeister, O'Reilly & Associates, Inc., ISBN 1-56592-074-0

IEEE Std 1003.1b-1993 (POSIX.1b standard)

ISO/IEC 9945-1:1996

*Linux 1.3.81, 10 April 1996*

# select, FD_CLR, FD_ISSET, FD_SET, FD_ZERO

select, FD_CLR, FD_ISSET, FD_SET, FD_ZERO—Synchronous I/O multiplexing

## SYNOPSIS

```
#include <sys/time.h>
#include <sys/types.h>
#include <unistd.h>
int select(int n,fd_set *readfds,fd_set *writefds,fd_set *exceptfds,
    struct timeval *timeout);
FD_CLR(int fd,fd_set *set);
FD_ISSFT(int fd,fd_cot *set);
FD_SET(int fd,fd_set *set);
FD_ZERO(fd_set *set)
```

## DESCRIPTION

select waits for a number of file descriptors to change status.

Three independent sets of descriptors are watched. Those listed in *readfds* will be watched to see if characters become available for reading, those in *writefds* will be watched to see if it is okay to immediately write on them, and those in *exceptfds* will be watched for exceptions. On exit, the sets are modified in place to indicate which descriptors actually changed status.

Four macros are provided to manipulate the sets. FD_ZERO will clear a set. FD_SET and FD_CLR add or remove a given descriptor from a set. FD_ISSET tests to see if a descriptor is part of the set; this is useful after select returns.

*n* is the highest-numbered descriptor in any of the three sets, plus 1.

*timeout* is an upper bound on the amount of time elapsed before select returns. It may be 0, which causes select to return immediately. If timeout is NULL (no timeout), select can block indefinitely.

## RETURN VALUE

On success, select returns the number of descriptors contained in the descriptor sets, which may be 0 if the timeout expires before anything interesting happens. On error, -1 is returned, and errno is set appropriately; the sets and *timeout* become undefined, so do not rely on their contents after an error.

## ERRORS

| | |
|---|---|
| EBADF | An invalid file descriptor was given in one of the sets. |
| EINTR | A non-blocked signal was caught. |
| EINVAL | *n* is negative. |
| ENOMEM | select was unable to allocate memory for internal tables. |

## NOTES

Some code calls select with all three sets empty, *n*=0, and a non-null timeout; this is a fairly portable way to sleep with subsecond precision.

On Linux, *timeout* is modified to reflect the amount of time not slept; most other implementations do not do this. This causes problems both when Linux code that reads *timeout* is ported to other operating systems and when code is ported to Linux that reuses a struct timeval for multiple selects in a loop without reinitializing it. Consider *timeout* to be undefined after select returns.

## EXAMPLE

```
#include <stdio.h>
#include <sys/time.h>
#include <sys/types.h>
#include <unistd.h>
```

```
int
main(void)
{
    fd_set rfds;
    struct timeval tv;
    int retval;

    /* Watch stdin (fd 0) to see when it has input. */
    FD_ZERO(&rfds);
    FD_SET(0, &rfds);
    /* Wait up to five seconds. */
    tv.tv_sec = 5;
    tv.tv_usec = 0;

    retval = select(1, &rfds, NULL, NULL, &tv);
    /* Don't rely on the value of tv now! */

    if (retval)
        printf("Data is available now.nn");
        /* FD_ISSET(0, &rfds) will be true. */
    else
        printf("No data within five seconds.nn");
    exit(0);
}
```

## SEE ALSO

accept(2), connect(2), read(2), recv(2), send(2), write(2)

*Linux 1.2, 11 February 1996*

# semctl

semctl—Semaphore-control operations

## SYNOPSIS

```
#include <sys/types.h>
#include <sys/ipc.h>
#include <sys/sem.h>
int semctl ( int semid,int semnun,int cmd, union semun arg );
```

## DESCRIPTION

The function performs the control operation specified by *cmd* on the semaphore set (or on the *sumun*-nth semaphore of the set) identified by *semid*. The first semaphore of the set is indicated by a value of 0 for *semun*.

The type of *arg* is the union

```
union semun {
    int val; /* used for SETVAL only */
    struct semid_ds *buf; /* for IPC_STAT and IPC_SET */
    ushort *array; /* used for GETALL and SETALL */
};
```

Legal values for *cmd* are

IPC_STAT          Copies info from the semaphore set data structure into the structure pointed to by *arg*.buf. The argument *semnum* is ignored. The calling process must have read access privileges on the semaphore set.

| | |
|---|---|
| IPC_SET | Writes the values of some members of the semid_ds structure pointed to by arg.buf to the semaphore set data structure, updating also its sem_ctime member. Considered members from the user-supplied struct semid_ds pointed to by arg.buf are |

sem_perm.uid

sem_perm.gid

sem_perm.mode /* only lowest 9-bits */

The calling process's effective user ID must be super-user, creator, or owner of the semaphore set. The argument *semnum* is ignored.

| | |
|---|---|
| IPC_RMID | Removes the semaphore set and its data structures immediately, awakening all waiting processes (with an error return and errno set to EIDRM). The calling process's effective user ID must be super-user, creator, or owner of the semaphore set. The argument *semnum* is ignored. |
| GETALL | Returns semval for all semaphores of the set into arg.array. The argument *semnum* is ignored. The calling process must have read access privileges on the semaphore set. |
| GETNCNT | The system call returns the value of semncnt for the *semno*-th semaphore of the set (that is, the number of processes waiting for an increase of semval for the *semno*-th semaphore of the set). The calling process must have read access privileges on the semaphore set. |
| GETPID | The system call returns the value of sempid for the *semno*-th semaphore of the set (that is, the pid of the process that executed the last semop call for the *semno*-th semaphore of the set). The calling process must have read access privileges on the semaphore set. |
| GETVAL | The system call returns the value of semval for the *semno*-th semaphore of the set. The calling process must have read access privileges on the semaphore set. |
| GETZCNT | The system call returns the value of semzcnt for the *semno*-th semaphore of the set (that is, the number of processes waiting for the semval of the *semno*-th semaphore of the set to become 0). The calling process must have read access privileges on the semaphore set. |
| SETALL | Sets semval for all semaphores of the set using arg.array, updating also the sem_ctime member of the semid_ds structure associated with the set. Undo entries are cleared for altered semaphores in all processes. Processes sleeping on the wait queue are awakened if some semval becomes 0 or increases. The argument *semnum* is ignored. The calling process must have alter access privileges on the semaphore set. |
| SETVAL | Sets the value of semval to arg.val for the *semnum*-th semaphore of the set, updating also the sem_ctime member of the semid_ds structure associated to the set. The undo entry is cleared for the altered semaphore in all processes. Processes sleeping on the wait queue are awakened if semval becomes 0 or increases. The calling process must have alter access privileges on the semaphore set. |

## RETURN VALUE

On fail, the system call returns -1, with errno indicating the error. Otherwise the system call returns a non-negative value, depending on *cmd*, as follows:

| | |
|---|---|
| GETNCNT | The value of semncnt. |
| GETPID | The value of sempid. |
| GETVAL | The value of semval. |
| GETZCNT | The value of semzcnt. |

## ERRORS

For a failing return, errno will be set to one of the following values:

| | |
|---|---|
| EACCESS | The calling process has no access permissions needed to execute *cmd*. |
| EFAULT | The address pointed to by arg.buf or arg.array isn't accessible. |
| EIDRM | The semaphore set was removed. |
| EINVAL | Invalid value for *cmd* or *semid*. |

| EPERM | The argument *cmd* has the value IPC_SET or IPC_RMID, but the calling process's effective user ID has insufficient privileges to execute the command. |
|---|---|
| ERANGE | The argument *cmd* has the value SETALL or SETVAL, and the value to which semval has to be set (for some semaphore of the set) is less than 0 or greater than the implementation value SEMVMX. |

## NOTES

The IPC_INFO, SEM_STAT, and SEM_INFO control calls are used by the ipcs(1) program to provide information on allocated resources. In the future these can be modified as needed or moved to a proc filesystem interface.

The following system limit on semaphore sets affects a semctl call:

| SEMVMX | Maximum value for semval; implementation dependent (32767). |
|---|---|

## SEE ALSO

ipc(5), shmget(2), shmat(2), shmdt(2)

*Linux 0.99.13, 1 November 1993*

# semget

semget—Gets a semaphore set identifier

## SYNOPSIS

```
# include <sys/types.h>
# include <sys/ipc.h>
# include <sys/sem.h>
int semget ( key_t key,int nsems,int semflg );
```

## DESCRIPTION

This function returns the semaphore set identifier associated with the value of the argument key. A new set of *nsems* semaphores is created if *key* has the value IPC_PRIVATE or *key* isn't IPC_PRIVATE, if no existing message queue is associated to *key*, and if IPC_CREAT is asserted in *semflg* (that is, semflg&IPC_CREAT isn't 0). The presence in *semflg* of the fields IPC_CREAT and IPC_EXCL plays the same role, with respect to the existence of the semaphore set, as the presence of O_CREAT and O_EXCL in the mode argument of the open(2) system call—that is, the msgget function fails if *semflg* asserts both IPC_CREAT and IPC_EXCL and a semaphore set already exists for *key*.

Upon creation, the lower 9 bits of the argument *semflg* define the access permissions (for owner, group, and others) to the semaphore set in the same format, and with the same meaning, as for the access permissions parameter in the open(2) or creat(2) system call (although the execute permissions are not used by the system, and the term *write permissions*, for a semaphore set, effectively means *alter permissions*).

Furthermore, while creating, the system call initializes the system semaphore set data structure semid_ds as follows:

- sem_perm.cuid and sem_perm.uid are set to the effective user ID of the calling process.
- sem_perm.cgid and sem_perm.gid are set to the effective group ID of the calling process.
- The lowest-order 9 bits of sem_perm.mode are set to the lowest-order 9 bits of *semflg*.
- sem_nsems is set to the value of *nsems*.
- sem_otime is set to 0.
- sem_ctime is set to the current time.

The argument *nsems* can be 0 (a "don't care") when the system call isn't create(2). Otherwise, *nsems* must be greater than 0 and less or equal to the maximum number of semaphores per semid (SEMMSL).

If the semaphore set already exists, the access permissions are verified, and a check is made to see if it is marked for destruction.

## RETURN VALUE

If successful, the return value will be the semaphore set identifier (a positive integer); otherwise it will be -1, with errno indicating the error.

## ERRORS

For a failing return, errno will be set to one of the following values:

| | |
|---|---|
| EACCES | A semaphore set exists for *key*, but the calling process has no access permissions to the set. |
| EEXIST | A semaphore set exists for *key*, and *semflg* was asserting both IPC_CREAT and IPC_EXCL. |
| EIDRM | The semaphore set is marked to be deleted. |
| ENOENT | No semaphore set exists for *key*, and *semflg* wasn't asserting IPC_CREAT. |
| ENOMEM | A semaphore set has to be created, but the system does not have enough memory for the new data structure. |
| ENOSPC | A semaphore set has to be created, but the system limit for the maximum number of semaphore sets (SEMMNI) or the system-wide maximum number of semaphores (SEMMNS) would be exceeded. |

## NOTES

IPC_PRIVATE isn't a flag field but a key_t type. If this special value is used for *key*, the system call ignores everything but the lowest-order 9 bits of *semflg* and creates a new semaphore set (on success).

The followings are limits on semaphore set resources affecting a semget call:

| | |
|---|---|
| SEMMNI | System-wide maximum number of semaphore sets; policy dependent. |
| SEMMSL | Maximum number of semaphores per semid; implementation dependent (500 currently). |
| SEMMNS | System-wide maximum number of semaphores; policy dependent. A value greater than SEMMSL×SEMMNI makes it irrelevant. |

## BUGS

Use of IPC_PRIVATE doesn't inhibit other processes' access to the allocated semaphore set.

As for the files, there is currently no intrinsic way for a process to ensure exclusive access to a semaphore set. Asserting both IPC_CREAT and IPC_EXCL in *semflg* only ensures (on success) that a new semaphore set will be created; it doesn't imply exclusive access to the semaphore set.

The data structure associated with each semaphore in the set isn't initialized by the system call. In order to initialize those data structures, you have to execute a subsequent call to semctl(2) to perform a SETVAL or a SETALL command on the semaphore set.

## SEE ALSO

ftok(3), ipc(5), semctl(2), semop(2)

*Linux 0.99.13, 1 November 1993*

# semop

semop—Semaphore operations

## SYNOPSIS

```
# include <sys/types.h>
# include <sys/ipc.h>
# include <sys/sem.h>
int semop ( int semid,struct sembuf *sops, unsigned nsops );
```

## DESCRIPTION

The function performs operations on selected members of the semaphore set indicated by *semid*. Each of the *nsops* elements in the array pointed to by *sops* specifies an operation to be performed on a semaphore by a struct sembuf including the following members:

```
short sem_num; /* semaphore number: 0 = first */
short sem_op; /* semaphore operation */
short sem_flg; /* operation flags */
```

Flags recognized in sem_flg are IPC_NOWAIT and SEM_UNDO. If an operation asserts SEM_UNDO, it will be undone when the process exits.

The system call semantic assures that the operations will be performed if and only if all of them will succeed. Each operation is performed on the sem_num–th semaphore of the semaphore set, where the first semaphore of the set is semaphore 0 and is one of the following three:

■ If sem_op is a positive integer, the operation adds this value to semval. Furthermore, if SEM_UNDO is asserted for this operation, the system updates the process undo count for this semaphore. The operation always goes through, so no process sleeping can happen. The calling process must have alter permissions on the semaphore set.

■ If sem_op is 0, the process must have read access permissions on the semaphore set. If semval is 0, the operation goes through. Otherwise, if IPC_NOWAIT is asserted in sem_flg, the system call fails (undoing all previous actions performed), with errno set to EAGAIN. Otherwise, semzcnt is incremented by 1, and the process sleeps until one of the following occurs:

    ■ semval becomes 0, at which time the value of semzcnt is decremented.

    ■ The semaphore set is removed, causing the system call to fail with errno set to EIDRM.

    ■ The calling process receives a signal that has to be caught; which causes the value of semzcnt to be decremented and the system call to fail with errno set to EINTR.

■ If sem_op is less than 0, the process must have alter permissions on the semaphore set. If semval is greater than or equal to the absolute value of sem_op, the absolute value of sem_op is subtracted by semval. Furthermore, if SEM_UNDO is asserted for this operation, the system updates the process undo count for this semaphore. Then the operation goes through. Otherwise, if IPC_NOWAIT is asserted in sem_flg, the system call fails (undoing all previous actions performed), with errno set to EAGAIN. Otherwise, semncnt is incremented by 1 and the process sleeps until one of the following occurs:

    ■ semval becomes greater than or equal to the absolute value of sem_op, at which time the value of semncnt is decremented, the absolute value of sem_op is subtracted from semval and, if SEM_UNDO is asserted for this operation, the system updates the process undo count for this semaphore.

    ■ The semaphore set is removed from the system: the system call fails, with errno set to EIDRM.

    ■ The calling process receives a signal that has to be caught; the value of semncnt is decremented, and the system call fails with errno set to EINTR.

In case of success, the sempid member of the structure sem for each semaphore specified in the array pointed to by *sops* is set to the process ID of the calling process. Furthermore both sem_otime and sem_ctime are set to the current time.

## RETURN VALUE

If successful, the system call returns 0; otherwise, it returns -1, with errno indicating the error.

## ERRORS

For a failing return, errno will be set to one of the following values:

| | |
|---|---|
| E2BIG | The argument *nsops* is greater than SEMOPM, the maximum number of operations allowed per system call. |
| EACCES | The calling process has no access permissions on the semaphore set as required by one of the specified operations. |
| EAGAIN | An operation could not go through, and IPC_NOWAIT was asserted in its *sem_flg*. |
| EFAULT | The address pointed to by *sops* isn't accessible. |

| EFBIG | For some operation, the value of sem_num is less than 0 or greater than or equal to the number of semaphores in the set. |
| EIDRM | The semaphore set was removed. |
| EINTR | Sleeping on a wait queue, the process received a signal that had to be caught. |
| EINVAL | The semaphore set doesn't exist, or *semid* is less than 0, or *nsops* has a non-positive value. |
| ENOMEM | The sem_flg of some operation asserted SEM_UNDO, and the system does not have enough memory to allocate the undo structure. |
| ERANGE | For some operation, semop+semvalis is greater than SEMVMX, the implementation-dependent maximum value for semval. |

## NOTES

The sem_undo structures of a process aren't inherited by its child on execution of a fork(2) system call. They are instead inherited by the substituting process resulting from the execution of the exec(2) system call.

The following are limits on semaphore set resources affecting a semop call:

| SEMOPM | Maximum number of operations allowed for one semop call; policy dependent. |
| SEMVMX | Maximum allowable value for semval; implementation dependent (32767). |

The implementation has no intrinsic limits for the adjust on exit maximum value (SEMAEM), the system-wide maximum number of undo structures (SEMMNU), or the per-process maximum number of undo entries system parameters.

## BUGS

The system maintains a per-process sem_undo structure for each semaphore altered by the process with undo requests. Those structures are free at process exit. One major cause for unhappiness with the undo mechanism is that it does not fit in with the notion of having an atomic set of operations in an array of semaphores. The undo requests for an array and each semaphore therein might have been accumulated over many semopt calls. Should the process sleep when exiting, or should all undo operations be applied with the IPC_NOWAIT flag in effect? Currently those undo operations that go through immediately are applied, and those that require a wait are ignored silently. Therefore harmless undo usage is guaranteed with private semaphores only.

## SEE ALSO

ipc(5), semctl(2), semget(2)

*Linux 0.99.13, 1 November 1993*

# send, sendto, sendmsg

send, sendto, sendmsg—Sends a message from a socket

## SYNOPSIS

```
#include <sys/types.h>
#include <sys/socket.h>
int send(int s, const void *msg,int len, unsigned int flags);
int sendto(int s, const void *msg, int len, unsigned int flags,
  const struct sockaddr *to, int tolen);
int sendmsg(int s, const struct msghdr *msg , unsigned int flags);
```

## DESCRIPTION

Warning: This is a BSD man page. As of Linux 0.99.11, sendmsg was not implemented.

send, sendto, and sendmsg are used to transmit a message to another socket. send may be used only when the socket is in a connected state, whereas sendto and sendmsg may be used at any time.

The address of the target is given by *to*, with *tolen* specifying its size. The length of the message is given by *len*. If the message is too long to pass atomically through the underlying protocol, the error `EMSGSIZE` is returned, and the message is not transmitted.

No indication of failure to deliver is implicit in a send. Locally detected errors are indicated by a return value of –1.

If no message space is available at the socket to hold the message to be transmitted, send normally blocks, unless the socket has been placed in non-blocking I/O mode. The `select(2)` call may be used to determine when it is possible to send more data.

The *flags* parameter may include one or more of the following:

```
#define MSG_OOB 0x1 /* process out-of-band data */
#define MSG_DONTROUTE 0x4 /* bypass routing, use direct interface */
```

The flag `MSG_OOB` is used to send out-of-band data on sockets that support this notion (for example, `SOCK_STREAM`); the underlying protocol must also support out-of-band data. `MSG_DONTROUTE` is usually used only by diagnostic or routing programs.

See `recv(2)` for a description of the `msghdr` structure.

## RETURN VALUES

The call returns the number of characters sent, or –1 if an error occurred.

## ERRORS

| | |
|---|---|
| `EBADF` | An invalid descriptor was specified. |
| `ENOTSOCK` | The argument *s* is not a socket. |
| `EFAULT` | An invalid user space address was specified for a parameter. |
| `EMSGSIZE` | The socket requires that message be sent atomically, and the size of the message to be sent made this impossible. |
| `EWOULDBLOCK` | The socket is marked non-blocking, and the requested operation would block. |
| `ENOBUFS` | The system was unable to allocate an internal buffer. The operation might succeed when buffers become available. |
| `ENOBUFS` | The output queue for a network interface was full. This generally indicates that the interface has stopped sending, but it might be caused by transient congestion. |

## HISTORY

These function calls appeared in BSD 4.2.

## SEE ALSO

`fcntl(2)`, `recv(2)`, `select(2)`, `getsockopt(2)`, `socket(2)`, `write(2)`

*BSD Man Page, 24 July 1993*

# setfsgid

setfsgid—Sets group identity used for filesystem checks

## SYNOPSIS

```
int setfsgid(uid_t fsgid);
```

## DESCRIPTION

setfsgid sets the group ID that the Linux kernel uses to check for all accesses to the filesystem. Normally, the value of *fsgid* will shadow the value of the effective group ID. In fact, whenever the effective group ID is changed, *fsgid* will also be changed to the new value of the effective group ID.

An explicit call to setfsgid is usually only used by programs such as the Linux NFS server that need to change what group ID is used for file access without a corresponding change in the real and effective group IDs. A change in the normal group IDs for a program such as the NFS server is a security hole that can expose it to unwanted signals from other group IDs.

setfsgid will succeed only if the caller is the superuser or if *fsgid* matches either the real group ID, effective group ID, saved group ID, or the current value of *fsgid*.

## RETURN VALUE

On success, the previous value of *fsgid* is returned. On error, the current value of *fsgid* is returned.

## CONFORMS TO

setfsgid is Linux specific.

## BUGS

No error messages of any kind are returned to the caller. At the very least, EPERM should be returned when the call fails.

## SEE ALSO

setfsuid(2)

*Linux 1.3.15, 6 August 1995*

# setfsuid

setfsuid—Sets user identity used for filesystem checks

## SYNOPSIS

```
int setfsuid(uid_t fsuid);
```

## DESCRIPTION

setfsuid sets the user ID that the Linux kernel uses to check for all accesses to the filesystem. Normally, the value of *fsuid* will shadow the value of the effective user ID. In fact, whenever the effective user ID is changed, *fsuid* will also be changed to the new value of the effective user ID.

An explicit call to setfsuid is usually used only by programs such as the Linux NFS server that need to change what user ID is used for file access without a corresponding change in the real and effective user IDs. A change in the normal user IDs for a program such as the NFS server is a security hole that can expose it to unwanted signals from other user IDs.

setfsuid will succeed only if the caller is the superuser or if *fsuid* matches either the real user ID, effective user ID, saved user ID, or the current value of *fsuid*.

## RETURN VALUE

On success, the previous value of *fsuid* is returned. On error, the current value of *fsuid* is returned.

## CONFORMS TO

setfsuid is Linux specific.

## BUGS

No error messages of any kind are returned to the caller. At the very least, EPERM should be returned when the call fails.

## SEE ALSO

setfsgid(2)

*Linux 1.3.15, 6 August 1995*

# setgid

setgid—Sets group identity

## SYNOPSIS

```
#include <unistd.h>
int setgid(gid_t gid);
```

## DESCRIPTION

setgid sets the effective group ID of the current process. If the caller is the superuser, the real and saved group IDs are also set.

Under Linux, setgid is implemented like SYSV, with SAVED_IDS. This allows a setgid (other than root) program to drop all its group privileges, do some unprivileged work, and then re-engage the original effective group ID in a secure manner.

If the user is root or the program is setgid root, special care must be taken. The setgid function checks the effective gid of the caller and, if it is that of the superuser, all process-related group IDs are set to gid. After this has occurred, it is impossible for the program to regain root privileges.

## RETURN VALUE

On success, 0 is returned. On error, -1 is returned, and errno is set appropriately.

## ERRORS

EPERM          The user is not the superuser, and gid does not match the effective or saved group ID of the calling process.

## CONFORMS TO

System V

## SEE ALSO

getgid(2), setregid(2), setegid(2)

*Linux 1.1.36, 29 July 1994*

# setpgid, getpgid, setpgrp, getpgrp

setpgid, getpgid, setpgrp, getpgrp—Sets/gets process group

## SYNOPSIS

```
#include <unistd.h>
int setpgid(pid_t pid, pid_t pgid);
pid_t getpgid(pid_t pid);
int setpgrp(void);
pid_t getpgrp(void);
```

## DESCRIPTION

setpgid sets the process group ID of the process specified by pid to pgid. If pid is 0, the process ID of the current process is used. If pgid is 0, the process ID of the process specified by pid is used.

getpgid returns the process group ID of the process specified by pid. If pid is 0, the process ID of the current process is used.

In the Linux DLL 4.4.1 library, setpgrp simply calls setpgid(0,0).

getpgrp is equivalent to getpgid(0).

Process groups are used for distribution of signals, and by terminals to arbitrate requests for their input; processes that have the same process group as the terminal are foreground and may read, whereas others will block with a signal if they attempt to read.

These calls are thus used by programs such as csh(1) to create process groups in implementing job control. The TIOCGPGRP and TIOCSPGRP calls described in termios(4) are used to get/set the process group of the control terminal.

## RETURN VALUE

On success, setpgid and setpgrp return 0. On error, -1 is returned, and errno is set appropriately.

getpgid returns a process group on success. On error, -1 is returned, and errno is set appropriately.

getpgrp always returns the current process group.

## ERRORS

| | |
|---|---|
| EINVAL | *pgid* is less than 0. |
| EPERM | Various permission violations. |
| ESRCH | *pid* does not match any process. |

## CONFORMS TO

The functions setpgid and getpgrp conform to POSIX.1. The function setpgrp is from BSD 4.2. I have no information on the source of getpgid.

## SEE ALSO

getuid(2), setsid(2), tcsetpgrp(3), termios(4)

*Linux 1.2.4, 15 April 1995*

# setregid, setegid

setregid, setegid—Sets real and/or effective group ID

## SYNOPSIS

```
#include <unistd.h>
int setregid(gid_t rgid, gid_t egid);
int setegid(gid_t egid);
```

## DESCRIPTION

setregid sets real and effective group IDs of the current process. Unprivileged users may change the real group ID to the effective group ID, and vice versa.

Prior to Linux 1.1.38, the saved ID paradigm, when used with setregid or setegid, was broken. Starting at 1.1.38, it is also possible to set the effective group ID from the saved user ID.

Only the superuser may make other changes.

Supplying a value of -1 for either the real or effective group ID forces the system to leave that ID unchanged.

Currently (libc-4.x.x), setegid(*egid*) is functionally equivalent to setregid(-1, *egid*).

If the real group ID is changed or the effective group ID is set to a value not equal to the previous real group ID, the saved group ID will be set to the new effective group ID.

## RETURN VALUE

On success, 0 is returned. On error, -1 is returned, and errno is set appropriately.

## ERRORS

EPERM      The current process is not the superuser, and changes other than swapping the effective group ID with the real group ID, setting one to the value of the other, or setting the effective group ID to the value of the saved group ID was specified.

## HISTORY

The setregid function call appeared in BSD 4.2.

## CONFORMS TO

BSD 4.3

## SEE ALSO

getgid(2), setgid(2)

*Linux 1.1.38, 2 August 1994*

# setreuid, seteuid

setreuid, seteuid—Sets real and / or effective user ID

## SYNOPSIS

```
#include <unistd.h>
int setreuid(uid_t ruid, uid_t euid);
int seteuid(uid_t euid);
```

## DESCRIPTION

setreuid sets real and effective user IDs of the current process. Unprivileged users may change the real user ID to the effective user ID, and vice versa.

Prior to Linux 1.1.37, the saved ID paradigm, when used with setreuid or seteuid, was broken.

Starting at 1.1.37, it is also possible to set the effective user ID from the saved user ID.

Only the superuser may make other changes.

Supplying a value of –1 for either the real or effective user ID forces the system to leave that ID unchanged.

Currently (libc-4.x.x), seteuid(*euid*) is functionally equivalent to setreuid(*-1, euid*).

If the real user ID is changed or the effective user ID is set to a value not equal to the previous real user ID, the saved user ID will be set to the new effective user ID.

## RETURN VALUE

On success, 0 is returned. On error, –1 is returned, and errno is set appropriately.

## ERRORS

EPERM      The current process is not the superuser, and changes other than swapping the effective user ID with the real user ID, setting one to the value of the other, or setting the effective user ID to the value of the saved user ID was specified.

## HISTORY

The setreuid function call appeared in BSD 4.2.

## CONFORMS TO

BSD 4.3

## SEE ALSO

getuid(2), setuid(2)

*Linux 1.1.38, 2 August 1994*

# setsid

setsid—Creates a session and sets the process group ID

## SYNOPSIS

```
#include <unistd.h>
pid_t setsid(void);
```

## DESCRIPTION

setsid() creates a new session if the calling process is not a process group leader. The calling process is the leader of the new session, the process group leader of the new process group, and has no controlling tty. The process group ID and session ID of the calling process are set to the PID of the calling process. The calling process will be the only process in this new process group and in this new session.

## RETURN VALUE

It returns the session ID of the calling process.

## ERRORS

On error, -1 will be returned. The only error that can happen is EPERM, which is returned when the process group ID of any process equals the PID of the calling process. Thus, in particular, setsid fails if the calling process is already a process group leader.

## NOTES

A *process group leader* is a process with process group ID equal to its PID. In order to be sure that setsid will succeed, fork, and exit, and have the child do setsid().

## CONFORMS TO

POSIX

## SEE ALSO

setpgid(2), setpgrp(2)

*27 August 1994*

# setuid

setuid—Sets user identity

## SYNOPSIS

```
#include <unistd.h>
int setuid(uid_t uid);
```

## DESCRIPTION

setuid sets the effective user ID of the current process. If the caller is the superuser, the real and saved user IDs are also set.

Under Linux, setuid is implemented like SYSV, with SAVED_IDS. This allows a setuid (other than root) program to drop all its user privileges, do some unprivileged work, and then re-engage the original effective user ID in a secure manner.

If the user is root or the program is setuid root, special care must be taken. The setuid function checks the effective UID of the caller, and, if it is the superuser, all process-related user IDs are set to *uid*. After this has occurred, it is impossible for the program to regain root privileges.

## RETURN VALUE

On success, 0 is returned. On error, -1 is returned, and errno is set appropriately.

## ERRORS

EPERM                The user is not the superuser, and *uid* does not match the effective or saved user ID of the calling process.

## CONFORMS TO

System V

## SEE ALSO

getuid(2), setreuid(2), seteuid(2)

*Linux 1.1.36 29 July 1994*


# setup

setup—Sets up devices and filesystems, mount root filesystem

## SYNOPSIS

```
#include <unistd.h>
syscall0(int, setup);
int setup(void);
```

## DESCRIPTION

setup is called once from within linux/init/main.c. It calls initialization functions for devices and filesystems configured into the kernel and then mounts the root filesystem.

No user process may call setup. Any user process, even a process with superuser permission, will receive EPERM.

## RETURN VALUE

setup always returns -1 for a user process.

## ERRORS

EPERM                Always, for a user process.

## CONFORMS TO

This function is Linux specific.

*Linux 1.2.9, 3 May 1996*


# shmctl

shmctl—Shared memory control

## SYNOPSIS

```
#include <sys/ipc.h>
#include <sys/shm.h>
int shmctl(int shmid,int cmd, struct shmid ds *buf);
```

## DESCRIPTION

shmctl() allows the user to receive information on a shared memory segment, set the owner, group, and permissions of a shared memory segment, or destroy a segment. The information about the segment identified by *shmid* is returned in a *shmid_ds* structure:

```
struct shmid_ds {
    struct ipc_perm shm_perm; /* operation perms */
    int shm_segsz; /* size of segment (bytes) */
    time_t shm_atime; /* last attach time */
    time_t shm_dtime; /* last detach time */
    time_t shm_ctime; /* last change time */
    unsigned short shm_cpid; /* pid of creator */
    unsigned short shm_lpid; /* pid of last operator */
    short shm_nattch; /* no. of current attaches */
    /* the following are private */
    unsigned short shm_npages; /* size of segment (pages) */
    unsigned long *shm_pages;
    struct shm_desc *attaches; /* descriptors for attaches */
};
```

The fields in the member *shm_perm* can be set:

```
struct ipc_perm
{
    key_t key;
    ushort uid;/*owner euid and egid */
    ushort gid;
    ushort cuid; /* creator euid and egid */
    ushort cgid;
    ushort mode; /* lower 9 bits of access modes */
    ushort seq; /* sequence number */
};
```

The following *cmds* are available:

| | |
|---|---|
| IPC_STAT | Used to copy the information about the shared memory segment into the buffer, *buf*. The user must have read access to the shared memory segment. |
| IPC_SET | Used to apply the changes the user has made to the *uid*, *gid*, or *mode* members of the *shm_perms* field. Only the lowest 9 bits of mode are used. The *shm_ctime* member is also updated. The user must be the owner, the creator, or the superuser. |
| IPC_RMID | Used to mark the segment as destroyed. It will actually be destroyed after the last detach. (That is, when the *shm_nattch* member of the associated structure *shmid_ds* is zero.)The user must be the owner, the creator, or the superuser. |

The user must ensure that a segment is eventually destroyed; otherwise the pages that were faulted in will remain in memory or swap.

In addition, the superuser can prevent or allow swapping of a shared memory segment with the following *cmds*: (Linux only)

| | |
|---|---|
| SHM_LOCK | Prevents swapping of a shared memory segment. The user must fault in any pages that are required to be present after locking is enabled. |
| SHM_UNLOCK | Allows the shared memory segment to be swapped out. |

The IPC_INFO, SHM_STAT, and SHM_INFO control calls are used by the ipcs(1) program to provide information on allocated resources. In the future, these may be modified as needed or moved to a proc filesystem interface.

## SYSTEM CALLS

| | |
|---|---|
| fork() | After a fork(), the child inherits the attached shared memory segments. |
| exec() | After an exec(), all attached shared memory segments are detached (not destroyed). |
| exit() | On exit(), all attached shared memory segments are detached (not destroyed). |

## RETURN VALUE

0 is returned on success; -1 on error.

## ERRORS

On error, errno will be set to one of the following:

| | |
|---|---|
| EACCESS | Returned if IPC_STAT is requested and shm_perm.modes does not allow read access for msqid. |
| EFAULT | The argument cmd has the value IPC_SET or IPC_STAT, but the address pointed to by *buf* isn't accessible. |
| EINVAL | Returned if shmid is not a valid identifier, or cmd is not a valid command. |
| EIDRM | Returned if shmid points to a removed identifier. |
| EPERM | Returned if IPC_SET or IPC_RMID is attempted, if the user is not the creator, the owner, or the superuser, and if the user does not have permission granted to his group or to the world. |

## SEE ALSO

shmget(2), shmop(2)

*Linux 0.99.11, 28 November 1993*

# shmget

shmget—Allocates a shared memory segment

## SYNOPSIS

```
#include <sys/ipc.h>
#include <sys/shm.h>
int shmget(key_t key,int size, int shmflg);
```

## DESCRIPTION

shmget() returns the identifier of the shared memory segment associated with the value of the argument *key*. A new shared memory segment, with its size equal to the rounding up of *size* to a multiple of PAGE_SIZE, is created if *key* has the value IPC_PRIVATE or if *key* isn't IPC_PRIVATE, if no shared memory segment is associated to *key*, and if IPC_CREAT is asserted in shmflg (that is, shmflg&IPC_CREAT isn't 0). The presence in shmflg is composed of

| | |
|---|---|
| IPC_CREAT | Creates a new segment. If this flag is not used, shmget() will find the segment associated with *key*, check to see if the user has permission to receive the shmid associated with the segment, and ensure the segment is not marked for destruction. |
| IPC_EXCL | Used with IPC_CREAT to ensure failure if the segment exists. |
| mode_flags | (lowest 9 bits) Specifies the permissions granted to the owner, group, and world. Presently, the execute permissions are not used by the system. |

If a new segment is created, the access permissions from shmflg are copied into the shm_perm member of the shmid_ds structure that defines the segment. Following is the shmid_ds structure:

```
struct shmid_ds {
    struct ipc_perm shm_perm; /* operation perms */
    int shm_segsz; /* size of segment (bytes) */
```

```
    time_t shm_atime; /* last attach time */
    time_t shm_dtime; /* last detach time */
    time_t shm_ctime; /* last change time */
    unsigned short shm_cpid; /* pid of creator */
    unsigned short shm_lpid; /* pid of last operator */
    short shm_nattch; /* no. of current attaches */
};

struct ipc_perm
{
    key_t key;
    ushort uid; /* owner euid and egid */
    ushort gid;
    ushort cuid; /* creator euid and egid */
    ushort cgid;
    ushort mode; /* lower 9 bits of shmflg */
    ushort seq; /* sequence number */
};
```

Furthermore, while creating, the system call initializes the system shared memory segment data structure shmid_ds as follows:

- shm_perm.cuid and shm_perm.uid are set to the effective user ID of the calling process.
- shm_perm.cgid and shm_perm.gid are set to the effective group ID of the calling process.
- The lowest-order 9 bits of shm_perm.mode are set to the lowest-order 9 bit of shmflg.
- shm_segsz is set to the value of *size*.
- shm_lpid, shm_nattch, shm_atime, and shm_dtime are set to 0.
- shm_ctime is set to the current time.

If the shared memory segment already exists, the access permissions are verified, and a check is made to see if it is marked for destruction.

## SYSTEM CALLS

| | |
|---|---|
| fork() | After a fork(), the child inherits the attached shared memory segments. |
| exec() | After an exec(), all attached shared memory segments are detached (not destroyed). |
| exit() | On exit(), all attached shared memory segments are detached (not destroyed). |

## RETURN VALUE

A valid segment identifier, shmid, is returned on success, -1 on error.

## ERRORS

On failure, errno is set to one of the following:

| | |
|---|---|
| EINVAL | Returned if SHMMIN is greater than *size*, if *size* is greater than SHMMAX, or if *size* is greater than the size of the segment. |
| EEXIST | Returned if IPC_CREAT ¦ IPC_EXCL was specified and the segment exists. |
| EIDRM | Returned if the segment is marked as destroyed or was removed. |
| ENOSPC | Returned if all possible shared memory IDs have been taken (SHMMNI) or if allocating a segment of the requested size would cause the system to exceed the system-wide limit on shared memory (SHMALL). |
| ENOENT | Returned if no segment exists for the given *key*, and IPC_CREAT was not specified. |
| EACCES | Returned if the user does not have permission to access the shared memory segment. |
| ENOMEM | Returned if no memory could be allocated for segment overhead. |

## NOTES

IPC_PRIVATE isn't a flag field but a key_t type. If this special value is used for *key*, the system call ignores everything but the lowest order 9 bits of *shmflg* and creates a new shared memory segment (on success).

The following are limits on shared memory segment resources affecting a shmget call:

| | |
|---|---|
| SHMALL | System-wide maximum of shared memory pages; policy dependent. |
| SHMMAX | Maximum size, in bytes, for a shared memory segment; implementation dependent (currently 4MB). |
| SHMMIN | Minimum size, in bytes, for a shared memory segment; implementation dependent (currently 1 byte, although PAGE_SIZE is the effective minimum size). |
| SHMMNI | System-wide maximum number of shared memory segments; implementation dependent (currently 4096). |

The implementation has no specific limits for the per-process maximum number of shared memory segments (SHMSEG).

## BUGS

Use of IPC_PRIVATE does not inhibit other processes' access to the allocated shared memory segment.

As for the files, there is currently no intrinsic way for a process to ensure exclusive access to a shared memory segment. Asserting both IPC_CREAT and IPC_EXCL in *shmflg* only ensures (on success) that a new shared memory segment will be created; it doesn't imply exclusive access to the segment.

## SEE ALSO

ftok(3), ipc(5), shmctl(2), shmat(2), shmdt(2)

*Linux 0.99.11, 28 November 1993*

# shmop

shmop—Shared memory operations

## SYNOPSIS

```
#include <sys/types.h>
#include <sys/ipc.h>
#include <sys/shm.h>
char *shmat ( int shmid, char *shmaddr, int shmflg );
int shmdt ( char *shmaddr);
```

## DESCRIPTION

The function shmat attaches the shared memory segment identified by shmid to the data segment of the calling process. The attaching address is specified by shmaddr with one of the following criteria:

■ If shmaddr is 0, the system tries to find an unmapped region in the range 1–1.5GB, starting from the upper value and coming down from there.

■ If shmaddr isn't 0 and SHM_RND is asserted in shmflg, the attach occurs at the address equal to the rounding down of shmaddr to a multiple of SHMLBA. Otherwise, shmaddr must be a page-aligned address at which the attach occurs.

If SHM_RDONLY is asserted in *shmflg*, the segment is attached for reading, and the process must have read access permissions to the segment. Otherwise the segment is attached for read and write, and the process must have read and write access permissions to the segment. There is no notion of a write-only shared memory segment.

The brk value of the calling process is not altered by the attach. The segment will automatically be detached at process exit. The same segment may be attached as a read and as a read-write segment, more than once, in the process's address space.

On a successful shmat call, the system updates the members of the structure shmid_ds associated to the shared memory segment as follows:

- ■ shm_atime is set to the current time.
- ■ shm_lpid is set to the process ID of the calling process.
- ■ shm_nattch is incremented by 1.

Note that the attachment will also succeed if the shared memory segment is marked to be deleted.

The function shmdt detaches from the calling process's data segment the shared memory segment located at the address specified by shmaddr. The detaching shared memory segment must be one among the currently attached ones (to the process's address space) with shmaddr equal to the value returned by its attaching shat call.

On a successful shmdt call, the system updates the members of the structure shmid_ds associated to the shared memory segment as follows:

- ■ shm_dtime is set to the current time.
- ■ shm_lpid is set to the process ID of the calling process.
- ■ shm_nattch is decremented by 1. If it becomes 0 and the segment is marked for deletion, the segment is deleted.

The occupied region in the user space of the calling process is unmapped.

## SYSTEM CALLS

| | |
|---|---|
| fork() | After a fork(), the child inherits the attached shared memory segments. |
| exec() | After an exec(), all attached shared memory segments are detached (not destroyed). |
| exit() | On exit(), all attached shared memory segments are detached (not destroyed). |

## RETURN VALUE

On a failure, both functions return -1 with errno indicating the error; otherwise, shmat returns the address of the attached shared memory segment, and shmdt returns 0.

## ERRORS

When shmat fails, at return errno will be set to one of the following values:

| | |
|---|---|
| EACCES | The calling process has no access permissions for the requested attach type. |
| EINVAL | Invalid *shmid* value, unaligned (that is, not page-aligned and SHM_RND was not specified) or invalid *shmaddr* value, or failing attach at brk. |
| ENOMEM | Could not allocate memory for the descriptor or for the page tables. |

The function shmdt can fail only if there is no shared memory segment attached at *shmaddr*; in such a case, errno will be set to EINVAL at return.

## NOTES

On executing a fork(2) system call, the child inherits all the attached shared memory segments.

The shared memory segments attached to a process executing an exec(2) system call will not be attached to the resulting process.

The following is a system parameter affecting a shmat system call:

| | |
|---|---|
| SHMLBA | Segments low-boundary address multiple. Must be page aligned. For the current implementation, the SHMBLA value is PAGE_SIZE. |

The implementation has no intrinsic limit to the per-process maximum number of shared memory segments (SHMSEG)

## SEE ALSO

ipc(5), shmctl(2), shmget(2)

# shutdown

shutdown—Shuts down part of a full-duplex connection

## SYNOPSIS

```
#include <sys/socket.h>
int shutdown(int s,int how);
```

## DESCRIPTION

The shutdown call causes all or part of a full-duplex connection on the socket associated with *s* to be shut down. If *how* is 0, further receives will be disallowed. If *how* is 1, further sends will be disallowed. If *how* is 2, further sends and receives will be disallowed.

## RETURN VALUE

On success, 0 is returned. On error, –1 is returned, and errno is set appropriately.

## ERRORS

| | |
|---|---|
| EBADF | *s* is not a valid descriptor. |
| ENOTSOCK | *s* is a file, not a socket. |
| ENOTCONN | The specified socket is not connected. |

## HISTORY

The shutdown function call appeared in BSD 4.2.

## SEE ALSO

connect(2), socket(2)

*BSD Man Page, 24 July 1993*

# sigaction, sigprocmask, sigpending, sigsuspend

sigaction, sigprocmask, sigpending, sigsuspend—POSIX signal-handling functions.

## SYNOPSIS

```
#include <signal.h>
int sigaction(int signum, const struct sigaction *act, struct sigaction *oldact);
int sigprocmask(int how, const sigset_t *set, sigset_t *oldset);
int sigpending(sigset_t *set);
int sigsuspend(const sigset_t *mask);
```

## DESCRIPTION

The sigaction system call is used to change the action taken by a process on receipt of a specific signal.

*signum* specifies the signal and can be any valid signal except SIGKILL and SIGSTOP.

If *act* is non–null, the new action for signal signum is installed from *act*. If *oldact* is non–null, the previous action is saved in *oldact*.

The sigaction structure is defined as

```
struct sigaction {
    void (*sa_handler)(int);
    sigset_t sa_mask;
    int sa_flags;
```

```
        void (*sa_restorer)(void);
}
```

sa_handler specifies the action to be associated with *signum* and can be SIG_DFL for the default action, SIG_IGN to ignore this signal, or a pointer to a signal-handling function.

sa_mask gives a mask of signals that should be blocked during execution of the signal handler. In addition, the signal that triggered the handler will be blocked unless the SA_NODEFER or SA_NOMASK flag is used.

sa_flags specifies a set of flags that modify the behavior of the signal-handling process. It is formed by the bitwise OR of zero or more of the following:

| | |
|---|---|
| SA_NOCLDSTOP | If *signum* is SIGCHLD, do not receive notification when child processes stop (that is, when child processes receive one of SIGSTOP, SIGTSTP, SIGTTIN, or SIGTTOU). |
| SA_ONESHOT or SA_RESETHAND | Restores the signal action to the default state once the signal handler has been called. (This is the default behavior of the signal(2) system call.) |
| SA_RESTART | Provides behavior compatible with BSD signal semantics by making certain system calls restartable across signals. |
| SA_NOMASK or SA_NODEFER | Does not prevent the signal from being received from within its own signal handler. |

The sa_restorer element is obsolete and should not be used.

The sigprocmask call is used to change the list of currently blocked signals. The behavior of the call is dependent on the value of *how*, as follows:

| | |
|---|---|
| SIG_BLOCK | The set of blocked signals is the union of the current set and the *set* argument. |
| SIG_UNBLOCK | The signals in *set* are removed from the current set of blocked signals. It is legal to attempt to unblock a signal that is not blocked. |
| SIG_SETMASK | The set of blocked signals is set to the argument *set*. |

If *oldset* is non–null, the previous value of the signal mask is stored in *oldset*.

The sigpending call allows the examination of pending signals (those that have been raised while blocked). The signal mask of pending signals is stored in *set*.

The sigsuspend call temporarily replaces the signal mask for the process with that given by *mask* and then suspends the process until a signal is received.

## RETURN VALUES

sigaction, sigprocmask, sigpending, and sigsuspend return 0 on success and -1 on error.

## ERRORS

| | |
|---|---|
| EINVAL | An invalid signal was specified. This will also be generated if an attempt is made to change the action for SIGKILL or SIGSTOP, which cannot be caught. |
| EFAULT | *act*, *oldact*, *set*, or *oldset* points to memory that is not a valid part of the process address space. |
| EINTR | System call was interrupted. |

## NOTES

It is not possible to block SIGKILL or SIGSTOP with the sigprocmask call. Attempts to do so will be silently ignored.

Setting SIGCHLD to SIG_IGN provides automatic reaping of child processes.

The POSIX spec only defines SA_NOCLDSTOP. Use of other sa flags is non–portable.

The SA_RESETHAND flag is compatible with the SVR4 flag of the same name.

The SA_NODEFER flag is compatible with the SVR4 flag of the same name under kernels 1.3.9 and newer. On older kernels, the Linux implementation will allow the receipt of any signal, not just the one you are installing (effectively overriding any sa_mask settings).

The SA_RESETHAND and SA_NODEFER names for SVR4 compatibility are present only in library versions 3.0.9 and greater.

sigaction can be called with a null second argument to query the current signal handler. It can also be used to check whether a given signal is valid for the current machine by calling it with null second and third arguments.

See sigsetops(3) for details on manipulating signal sets.

## CONFORMS TO

POSIX, SVR4

## SEE ALSO

kill(1), kill(2), killpg(2), pause(2), raise(3), siginterrupt(3), signal(2), signal(7), sigse-tops(3), sigvec(2)

*Linux 1.3, 24 August 1995*

# signal

signal—ANSI C signal handling

## SYNOPSIS

```
#include <signal.h>
void (*signal(int signum,void (*handler)(int)))(int);
```

## DESCRIPTION

The signal system call installs a new signal handler for the signal with number *signum*. The signal handler is set to *handler*, which can be a user-specified function or one of the following:

SIG_IGN      Ignores the signal.

SIG_DFL      Resets the signal to its default behavior.

The integer argument that is handed over to the signal-handling routine is the signal number. This makes it possible to use one signal handler for several signals.

## RETURN VALUE

signal returns the previous value of the signal handler, or SIG_ERR on error.

## NOTES

Signal handlers cannot be set for SIGKILL or SIGSTOP.

Unlike on BSD systems, signals under Linux are reset to their default behavior when raised. However, if you include <bsd/signal.h> instead of <signal.h>, signal is redefined as _bsd_signal, and signal has the BSD semantics. Both versions of signal are library routines built on top of sigaction(2).

If you're confused by the prototype at the top of this man page, it may help to see it separated out like this:

```
typedef void (*sighandler_t)(int);
sighandler_t signal(int signum, sighandler_t handler);
```

According to POSIX, the behavior of a process is undefined after it ignores a SIGFPE, SIGILL, or SIGSEGV signal that was not generated by the kill() or raise() function. Integer division by 0 has undefined result. On some architectures it will generate a SIGFPE signal. Ignoring this signal might lead to an endless loop.

## CONFORMS TO

ANSI C

## SEE ALSO

kill(1), kill(2), killpg(2), pause(2), raise(3), sigaction(2), signal(7), sigsetops(3), sigvec(2), alarm(2)

# sigblock, siggetmask, sigsetmask, sigmask

sigblock, siggetmask, sigsetmask, sigmask—Manipulate the signal mask

## SYNOPSIS

```
#include <signal.h>
int sigblock(int mask);
int siggetmask(void);
int sigsetmask(int mask);
int sigmask(int signum);
```

## DESCRIPTION

This interface is made obsolete by sigprocmask(2).

The sigblock system call adds the signals specified in *mask* to the set of signals currently being blocked from delivery.

The sigsetmask system call replaces the set of blocked signals totally with a new set specified in *mask*. Signals are blocked if the corresponding bit in *mask* is a 1.

The current set of blocked signals can be obtained using siggetmask.

The sigmask macro is provided to construct the mask for a given *signum*.

## RETURN VALUES

siggetmask returns the current set of masked signals.

sigsetmask and sigblock return the previous set of masked signals.

## NOTES

Prototypes for these functions are only available if __USE_BSD is defined before <signal.h> is included.

It is not possible to block SIGKILL or SIGSTOP—this restriction is silently imposed by the system.

## HISTORY

These function calls appeared in BSD 4.3 and are deprecated.

## SEE ALSO

kill(2), sigprocmask(2), signal(7)

# sigpause

sigpause—Atomically releases blocked signals and waits for interrupt

## SYNOPSIS

```
#include <signal.h>
int sigpause(int sigmask);
```

## DESCRIPTION

This interface is made obsolete by sigsuspend(2).

sigpause assigns *sigmask* to the set of masked signals and then waits for a signal to arrive; on return, the set of masked signals is restored.

sigmask is usually 0 to indicate that no signals are to be blocked. sigpause always terminates by being interrupted, returning -1 with errno set to EINTR.

## HISTORY

The sigpause function call appeared in BSD 4.3 and is deprecated.

## SEE ALSO

sigsuspend(2), kill(2), sigaction(2), sigprocmask(2), sigblock(2), sigvec(2)

*Linux 1.3, 24 July 1993*

# sigreturn

sigreturn—Returns from the signal handler and cleans up the stack frame

## SYNOPSIS

```
int sigreturn(unsigned long __unused);
```

## DESCRIPTION

When the Linux kernel creates the stack frame for a signal handler, a call to sigreturn is inserted into the stack frame so that the signal handler will call sigreturn upon return. This inserted call to sigreturn cleans up the stack so that the process can restart from where it was interrupted by the signal.

## RETURN VALUE

sigreturn never returns.

## WARNING

The sigreturn call is used by the kernel to implement signal handlers. It should never be called directly. Better yet, the specific use of the unused argument varies depending on the architecture.

## CONFORMS TO

sigreturn is specific to Linux.

## FILES

```
/usr/src/linux/arch/i386/kernel/signal.c
/usr/src/linux/arch/alpha/kernel/entry.S
```

## SEE ALSO

kill(2), signal(2), signal(7)

*Linux 1.3.20, 21 August 1995*

# sigvec

`sigvec`—BSD software signal facilities

## SYNOPSIS

```
#include <bsd/signal.h>
int sigvec(int sig, struct sigvec *vec, struct sigvec *ovec);
```

## DESCRIPTION

This interface is made obsolete by `sigaction(2)`.

Under Linux, `sigvec` is `#defined` to `sigaction`, and provides at best a rough approximation of the BSD `sigvec` interface.

## SEE ALSO

`sigaction(2)`, `signal(2)`

*Linux 1.3 31 August 1995*

# socket

`socket`—Creates an endpoint for communication

## SYNOPSIS

```
#include <sys/types.h>
#include <sys/socket.h>
int socket(int domain,inttype, int protocol);
```

## DESCRIPTION

`socket` creates an endpoint for communication and returns a descriptor.

The *domain* parameter specifies a communications domain within which communication will take place; this selects the protocol family that should be used. These families are defined in the include file `sys/socket.h`. The currently understood formats are

| | |
|---|---|
| `AF_UNIX` | UNIX internal protocols |
| `AF_INET` | ARPA Internet protocols |
| `AF_ISO` | ISO protocols |
| `AF_NS` | Xerox Network Systems protocols |
| `AF_IMPLINK` | IMP host at IMP link layer |

The socket has the indicated type, which specifies the semantics of communication. The currently defined types are

`SOCK_STREAM`

`SOCK_DGRAM`

`SOCK_RAW`

`SOCK_SEQPACKET`

`SOCK_RDM`

A `SOCK_STREAM` type provides sequenced, reliable, two-way connection–based byte streams. An out-of-band data transmission mechanism may be supported. A `SOCK_DGRAM` socket supports datagrams (connectionless, unreliable messages of a fixed, typically small, maximum length). A `SOCK_SEQPACKET` socket may provide a sequenced, reliable, two-way connection–based data transmission path for datagrams of fixed maximum length; a consumer might be required to read an entire packet with each read system call. This facility is protocol specific, and presently is implemented only for `PF_NS`. `SOCK_RAW` sockets provide access to internal network protocols and interfaces. The types SOCK_RAW, which is available only to the superuser, and SOCK_RDM, which is planned but not yet implemented, are not described here.

The *protocol* specifies a particular protocol to be used with the socket. Normally only a single protocol exists to support a particular socket type within a given protocol family. However, it is possible that many protocols may exist, in which case a particular protocol must be specified in this manner. The protocol number to use is particular to the communication domain in which communication is to take place; see protocols(5).

Sockets of type SOCK_STREAM are full-duplex byte streams, similar to pipes. A stream socket must be in a connected state before any data can be sent or received on it. A connection to another socket is created with a connect(2) call. Once connected, data may be transferred using read(2) and write(2) calls or some variant of the send(2) and recv(2) calls. When a session has been completed, a close(2) may be performed. Out-of-band data can also be transmitted as described in send(2) and received as described in recv(2).

The communications protocols used to implement a SOCK_STREAM ensure that data is not lost or duplicated. If a piece of data for which the peer protocol has buffer space cannot be successfully transmitted within a reasonable length of time, the connection is considered broken, and calls will indicate an error with –1 returns and with ETIMEDOUT as the specific code in the global variable errno. The protocols optionally keep sockets warm by forcing transmissions roughly every minute in the absence of other activity. An error is then indicated if no response can be elicited on an otherwise idle connection for an extended period (for example, 5 minutes). A SIGPIPE signal is raised if a process sends on a broken stream; this causes naive processes, which do not handle the signal, to exit.

SOCK_SEQPACKET sockets employ the same system calls as SOCK_STREAM sockets. The only difference is that read(2) calls will return only the amount of data requested, and any that is remaining in the arriving packet will be discarded.

SOCK_DGRAM and SOCK_RAW sockets allow the sending of datagrams to correspondents named in send(2) calls. Datagrams are generally received with recvfrom(2), which returns the next datagram with its return address.

An fcntl(2) call can be used to specify a process group to receive a SIGURG signal when the out-of-band data arrives. It can also enable non-blocking I/O and asynchronous notification of I/O events via SIGIO.

The operation of sockets is controlled by socket-level options. These options are defined in the file sys/socket.h. setsockopt(2) and getsockopt(2) and are used to set and get options, respectively.

## RETURN VALUES

A –1 is returned if an error occurs; otherwise, the return value is a descriptor referencing the socket.

## ERRORS

| | |
|---|---|
| EPROTONOSUPPORT | The protocol type or the specified protocol is not supported within this domain. |
| EMFILE | The per-process descriptor table is full. |
| ENFILE | The system file table is full. |
| EACCESS | Permission to create a socket of the specified type and/or protocol is denied. |
| ENOBUFS | Insufficient buffer space is available. The socket cannot be created until sufficient resources are freed. |

## HISTORY

The socket function call appeared in BSD 4.2.

## SEE ALSO

accept(2), bind(2), connect(2), getprotoent(3), getsockname(2), getsockopt(2), ioctl(2), listen(2), read(2), recv(2), select(2), send(2), shutdown(2), socketpair(2), write(2)

"An Introductory 4.3 BSD Interprocess Communication Tutorial" is reprinted in UNIX Programmer's Supplementary Documents Volume 1

"BSD Interprocess Communication Tutorial" is reprinted in UNIX Programmer's Supplementary Documents Volume 1

# socketcall

socketcall—Socket system calls

## SYNOPSIS

```
int socketcall(int call, unsigned long *args);
```

## DESCRIPTION

socketcall is a common kernel entry point for the socket system calls. *call* determines which socket function to invoke. *args* points to a block containing the actual arguments, which are passed through to the appropriate call.

User programs should call the appropriate functions by their usual names. Only standard library implementors and kernel hackers need to know about socketcall.

## SEE ALSO

accept(2), bind(2), connect(2), getpeername(2), getsockname(2), getsockopt(2), listen(2), recv(2), recvfrom(2), send(2), sendto(2), setsockopt(2), shutdown(2), socket(2), socketpair(2)

*Linux 1.2.4, 15 April 1995*

# socketpair

socketpair—Creates a pair of connected sockets

## SYNOPSIS

```
#include <sys/types.h>
#include <sys/socket.h>
int socketpair(int d, int type, int protocol, int sv[2]);
```

## DESCRIPTION

The call creates an unnamed pair of connected sockets in the specified domain *d*, of the specified *type*, and using the optionally specified *protocol*. The descriptors used in referencing the new sockets are returned in *sv*[0] and *sv*[1]. The two sockets are indistinguishable.

## RETURN VALUE

On success, 0 is returned. On error, -1 is returned, and errno is set appropriately.

## ERRORS

| | |
|---|---|
| EMFILE | Too many descriptors are in use by this process. |
| EAFNOSUPPORT | The specified address family is not supported on this machine. |
| EPROTONOSUPPORT | The specified protocol is not supported on this machine. |
| EOPNOSUPPORT | The specified protocol does not support creation of socket pairs. |
| EFAULT | The address *sv* does not specify a valid part of the process's address space. |

## HISTORY

The socketpair function call appeared in BSD 4.2.

## BUGS

This call is currently implemented only for the UNIX domain.

## SEE ALSO

read(2), write(2), pipe(2)

*BSD Man Page, 24 July 1993*

# stat, fstat, lstat

stat, fstat, lstat—Get file status

## SYNOPSIS

```
#include <sys/stat.h>
#include <unistd.h>
int stat(const char *file_name,struct stat *buf);
int fstat(int filedes,struct stat *buf);
int lstat(const char *file_name, struct stat *buf);
```

## DESCRIPTION

These functions return information about the specified file. You do not need any access rights to the file to get this information, but you need search rights to all directories named in the path leading to the file.

stat stats the file pointed to by *file_name* and fills in *buf*.

lstat is identical to stat, except that the link itself is stated, not the file that is obtained by tracing the links.

fstat is identical to stat, except that the open file pointed to by *filedes* (as returned by open(2)) is stated in place of *file_name*.

They all return a stat structure, which is declared as follows:

```
struct stat
{
    dev_t          st_dev;        /* device */
    ino_t          st_ino;        /* inode */
    umode_t        st_mode;       /*protection */
    nlink_t        st_nlink;      /* number of hard links */
    uid_t          st_uid;        /* user ID of owner */
    gid_t          st_gid;        /* group ID of owner */
    dev_t          st_rdev;       /* device type (if inode device) */
    off_t          st_size;       /* total size, in bytes */
    unsigned long  st_blksize;    /* blocksize for filesystem I/O */
    unsigned long  st_blocks;     /* number of blocks allocated */
    time_t         st_atime;      /* time of last access */
    time_t         st_mtime;      /* time of last modification */
    time_t         st_ctime;      /* time of last change */
};
```

Note that *st_blocks* may not always be in terms of blocks of size *st_blksize*, and that *st_blksize* may instead provide a notion of the "preferred" block size for efficient filesystem I/O.

Not all the Linux filesystems implement all the time fields. Traditionally, *st_atime* is changed by mknod(2), utime(2), read(2), write(2), and truncate(2).

Traditionally, *st_mtime* is changed by mknod(2), utime(2), and write(2). *st_mtime* is not changed for changes in owner, group, hard link count, or mode.

Traditionally, *st_ctime* is changed by writing or by setting inode information (that is, owner, group, link count, mode, and so on).

The following macros are defined to check the file type:

| | |
|---|---|
| S_ISLNK(*m*) | Is it a symbolic link? |
| S_ISREG(*m*) | Is it a regular file? |
| S_ISDIR(*m*) | Is it a directory? |
| S_ISCHR(*m*) | Is it a character device? |
| S_ISBLK(*m*) | Is it a block device? |
| S_ISFIFO(*m*) | Is it fifo? |
| S_ISSOCK(*m*) | Is it a socket? |

The following flags are defined for the *st_mode* field:

| | |
|---|---|
| S_IFMT | 00170000 Bitmask for the file type bitfields |
| S_IFSOCK | 0140000 Socket |
| S_IFLNK | 0120000 Symbolic link |
| S_IFREG | 0100000 Regular file |
| S_IFBLK | 0060000 Block device |
| S_IFDIR | 0040000 Directory |
| S_IFCHR | 0020000 Character device |
| S_IFIFO | 0010000 Fifo |
| S_ISUID | 0004000 Set UID bit |
| S_ISGID | 0002000 Set GID bit |
| S_ISVTX | 0001000 Sticky bit |
| S_IRWXU | 00700 User (file owner) has read, write, and execute permission |
| S_IRUSR (S_IREAD) | 00400 User has read permission |
| S_IWUSR (S_IWRITE) | 00200 User has write permission |
| S_IXUSR (S_IEXEC) | 00100 User has execute permission |
| S_IRWXG | 00070 Group has read, write, and execute permission |
| S_IRGRP | 00040 Group has read permission |
| S_IWGRP | 00020 Group has write permission |
| S_IXGRP | 00010 Group has execute permission |
| S_IRWXO | 00007 others have read, write, and execute permission |
| S_IROTH | 00004 Others have read permission |
| S_IWOTH | 00002 Others have write permission |
| S_IXOTH | 00001 Others have execute permission |

## RETURN VALUE

On success, 0 is returned. On error, -1 is returned, and errno is set appropriately.

## ERRORS

| | |
|---|---|
| EBADF | *filedes* is bad. |
| ENOENT | File does not exist. |

## CONFORMS TO

SVID (not lstat()), AT&T (not lstat()), POSIX (not lstat()), X/OPEN (not lstat()), BSD 4.3

## SEE ALSO

chmod(2), chown(2), readlink(2), utime(2)

# statfs, fstatfs

statfs, fstatfs—Get filesystem statistics

## SYNOPSIS

```
#include <sys/vfs.h>
int statfs(const char *path, struct statfs *buf);
int fstatfs(int fd, struct statfs *buf);
```

## DESCRIPTION

statfs returns information about a mounted filesystem. *path* is the pathname of any file within the mounted filesystem. *buf* is a pointer to a statfs structure defined as follows:

```
struct statfs {
    long    f_type;       /* type of filesystem (see below) */
    long    f_bsize;      /* optimal transfer block size */
    long    f_blocks;     /* total data blocks in filesystem */
    long    f_bfree;      /* free blocks in fs */
    long    f_bavail;     /* free blocks avail to non-superuser */
    long    f_files;      /* total file nodes in filesystem */
    long    f_ffree;      /* free file nodes in fs */
    fsid_t  f_fsid;       /* filesystem id */
    long    f_namelen;    /* maximum length of filenames */
    long    f_spare[6];   /* spare for later */
};
```

Filesystem types:

```
linux/ext2_fs.h:    EXT2_OLD_SUPER_MAGIC   0xEF51
linux/ext2_fs.h:    EXT2_SUPER_MAGIC       0xEF53
linux/ext_fs.h:     EXT_SUPER_MAGIC        0x137D
linux/iso_fs.h:     ISOFS_SUPER_MAGIC      0x9660
linux/minix_fs.h:   MINIX_SUPER_MAGIC      0x137F /* orig. minix */
linux/minix_fs.h:   MINIX_SUPER_MAGIC2     0x138F /* 30 char minix */
linux/minix_fs.h:   NEW_MINIX_SUPER_MAGIC  0x2468 /* minix V2 */
linux/msdos_fs.h:   MSDOS_SUPER_MAGIC      0x4d44
linux/nfs_fs.h:     NFS_SUPER_MAGIC        0x6969
linux/proc_fs.h:    PROC_SUPER_MAGIC       0x9fa0
linux/xia_fs.h:     XIAFS_SUPER_MAGIC      0x012FD16D
```

Fields that are undefined for a particular filesystem are set to -1. fstatfs returns the same information about an open file referenced by descriptor *fd*.

## RETURN VALUE

On success, 0 is returned. On error, -1 is returned, and errno is set appropriately.

## ERRORS

For statfs:

| | |
|---|---|
| ENOTDIR | A component of the path prefix of *path* is not a directory. |
| EINVAL | *path* contains a character with the high-order bit set. |
| ENAMETOOLONG | The length of a component of *path* exceeds 255 characters, or the length of *path* exceeds 1,023 characters. |
| ENOENT | The file referred to by *path* does not exist. |
| EACCES | Search permission is denied for a component of the path prefix of *path*. |
| ELOOP | Too many symbolic links were encountered in translating *path*. |

| EFAULT | *buf* or *path* points to an invalid address. |
| EIO | An I/O error occurred while reading from or writing to the filesystem. |

For fstatfs:

| EBADF | *fd* is not a valid open file descriptor. |
| EFAULT | *buf* points to an invalid address. |
| EIO | An I/O error occurred while reading from or writing to the filesystem. |

## SEE ALSO

stat(2)

*Linux 0.99.11, 24 July 1993*

# stime

stime—Set time

## SYNOPSIS

```
#include <time.h>
int stime(time_t *t);
```

## DESCRIPTION

stime sets the system's idea of the time and date. time, pointed to by *t*, is measured in seconds from 00:00:00 GMT January 1, 1970. stime() may only be executed by the superuser.

## RETURN VALUE

On success, 0 is returned. On error, -1 is returned, and errno is set appropriately.

## ERRORS

| EPERM | The caller is not the superuser. |

## CONFORMS TO

SVID, AT&T, X/OPEN

## SEE ALSO

date(1)

*Linux 0.99.11, 24 July 1993*

# swapon, swapoff

swapon, swapoff—Start/stop swapping to file/device

## SYNOPSIS

```
#include <unistd.h>
#include <linux/swap.h>
int swapon(const char *path, int swapflags);
int swapoff(const char *path);
```

## DESCRIPTION

swapon sets the swap area to the file or block device specified by *path*. swapoff stops swapping to the file or block device specified by *path*.

swapon takes a *swapflags* argument. If *swapflags* has the SWAP_FLAG_PREFER bit turned on, the new swap area will have a higher priority than default. The priority is encoded as (prio << SWAP_FLAG_PRIO_SHIFT) & SWAP_FLAG_PRIO_MASK. These functions may only be used by the superuser.

## PRIORITY

Each swap area has a priority, either high or low. The default priority is low. Within the low-priority areas, newer areas are of even lower priority than older areas.

All priorities set with *swapflags* are high priority, higher than the default. They may have any non-negative value chosen by the caller. Higher numbers mean higher priority.

Swap pages are allocated from areas in priority order, highest priority first. For areas with different priorities, a higher-priority area is exhausted before using a lower-priority area. If two or more areas have the same priority, and that is the highest priority available, pages are allocated on a round-robin basis between them.

As of Linux 1.3.6, the kernel usually follows these rules, but there are exceptions.

## RETURN VALUE

On success, 0 is returned. On error, -1 is returned, and errno is set appropriately.

## ERRORS

Many other errors besides the following can occur if path is not valid:

| | |
|---|---|
| EPERM | The user is not the superuser, or more than MAX_SWAPFILES (defined to be 8 in Linux 1.3.6) are in use. |
| EINVAL | Returned if *path* exists, but is neither a regular path nor a block device. |
| ENOENT | Returned if *path* does not exist. |
| ENOMEM | Returned if there is insufficient memory to start swapping. |

## CONFORMS TO

These functions are Linux specific.

## NOTES

The partition or path must be prepared with mkswap(8).

## HISTORY

The second (swapflags) argument was introduced in Linux 1.3.2.

## SEE ALSO

mkswap(8), swapon(8), swapoff(8)

*Linux 1.3.6, 22 July 1995*

# symlink

symlink—Makes a new name for a file

## SYNOPSIS

```
#include <unistd.h>
int symlink(const char *oldpath, const char *newpath);
```

## DESCRIPTION

symlink creates a symbolic link named *oldpath* that contains *newpath*.

Symbolic links are interpreted at runtime, as if the contents of the link were substituted into the path being followed to find a file or directory.

Symbolic links may contain .. path components that (if used at the start of the link) refer to the parent directories of the one in which the link resides.

A symbolic link (also known as a *soft link*) can point to an existing file or to a nonexistent one; the latter case is known as a *dangling link*.

The permissions of a symbolic link are irrelevant; the ownership is ignored when following the link, but is checked when removal or renaming of the link is requested and the link is in a directory with the sticky bit set.

If *newpath* exists, it will not be overwritten.

## RETURN VALUE

On success, 0 is returned. On error, -1 is returned, and errno is set appropriately.

## ERRORS

| | |
|---|---|
| EPERM | The filesystem containing *pathname* does not support the creation of symbolic links. |
| EFAULT | *oldpath* or *newpath* points outside your accessible address space. |
| EACCES | Write access to the directory containing *newpath* is not allowed for the process's effective UID, or one of the directories in *newpath* did not allow search (execute) permission. |
| ENAMETOOLONG | *oldpath* or *newpath* was too long. |
| ENOENT | A directory component in *newpath* does not exist or is a dangling symbolic link, or *oldpath* is the empty string. |
| ENOTDIR | A component used as a directory in *newpath* is not, in fact, a directory. |
| ENOMEM | Insufficient kernel memory was available. |
| EROFS | The file is on a read-only filesystem. |
| EEXIST | *newpath* already exists. |
| ELOOP | *newpath* contains a reference to a circular symbolic link—that is, a symbolic link whose expansion contains a reference to itself. |
| ENOSPC | The device containing the file has no room for the new directory entry. |

## NOTES

No checking of *oldpath* is done.

Deleting the name referred to by a symlink will actually delete the file (unless it also has other hard links). If this behavior is not desired, use link.

## CONFORMS TO

SVID, AT&T, POSIX, BSD 4.3

## BUGS

See open(2) regarding multiple files with the same name, and NFS.

*Linux, 24 July 1993*

# sync

sync—Commits buffer cache to disk

## SYNOPSIS

```
#include <unistd.h>
int sync(void);
```

## DESCRIPTION

sync first commits inodes to buffers, and then buffers to disk.

## RETURN VALUE

sync always returns 0.

## CONFORMS TO

SVID, AT&T, X/OPEN, BSD 4.3

## BUGS

According to the standard specification (for example, SVID), sync() schedules the writes, but it might return before the actual writing is done. However, since version 1.3.20, Linux does actually wait. (This still does not guarantee data integrity; modern disks have large caches.)

## SEE ALSO

bdflush(2), fsync(2), fdatasync(2), update(8), sync(8)

*Linux 1.3.88, 15 April 1995*

# sysctl

sysctl—Reads/writes system parameters

## SYNOPSIS

```
#include <unistd.h>
#include <linux/unistd.h>
#include <linux/sysctl.h>
_syscall1(int_sysctl, struct __sysctl_args *args);
int sysctl(struct __sysctl_args *args);
```

## DESCRIPTION

The sysctl call reads and/or writes kernel parameters—for example, the hostname or the maximum number of open files. The argument has the form

```
struct __sysctl_args {
    int *name; /* integer vector describing variable */
    int nlen; /* length of this vector */
    void *oldval; /* 0 or address where to store old value */
    size_t *oldlenp; /* available room for old value,
```

```
         overwritten by actual size of old value */
    void *newval; /* 0 or address of new value */
    size_t newlen; /* size of new value */
};
```

This call does a search in a tree structure, possibly resembling a directory tree under /proc/sys, and, if the requested item is found, calls some appropriate routine to read or modify the value.

## EXAMPLE

```
#include <linux/unistd.h>
#include <linux/types.h>
#include <linux/sysctl.h>

_syscall1(int, _sysctl, struct __sysctl args *, args);
int sysctl(int *name, int nlen, void *oldval, size_t *oldlenp,
        void *newval, size_t newlen)
{
    struct __sysctl__args args={name,nlen,oldval,oldlenp,newval,newlen};
    return _sysctl(&args);
}

#define SIZE(x) sizeof(x)/sizeof(x[0])
#define OSNAMESZ 100

char osname[OSNAMESZ];
int osnamelth;
int name[] = { CTL_KERN, KERN_OSTYPE };

main(){
    osnamelth = SIZE(osname);
    if (sysctl(name, SIZE(name), osname, &osnamelth, 0, 0))
        perror("sysctl");
    else
        printf("This machine is running %*s\n", osnamelth, osname);
    return 0;
}
```

## RETURN VALUES

Upon successful completion, sysctl returns 0. Otherwise, a value of -1 is returned, and errno is set to indicate the error.

## ERRORS

| | |
|---|---|
| ENOTDIR | *name* was not found. |
| EPERM | No search permission for one of the encountered directories, or no read permission where *oldval* was nonzero, or no write permission where *newval* was nonzero. |
| EFAULT | The invocation asked for the previous value by setting *oldval* non-NULL, but allowed zero room in *oldlenp*. |

## CONFORMS TO

This call is Linux specific.

## HISTORY

A sysctl call has been present in Linux since version 1.3.57. It originated in BSD-4.4. Only Linux has the /proc/sys mirror, and the object-naming schemes differ between Linux and BSD 4.4, but the declaration of the sysctl(2) function is the same in both.

## BUGS

Not all available objects are properly documented.

It is not yet possible to change operating system by writing to /proc/sys/kernel/ostype.

## SEE ALSO

proc(5)

*Linux 1.3.85, 11 April 1996*

# sysfs

sysfs—Gets filesystem type information

## SYNOPSIS

```
int sysfs(int option, const char * fsname);
int sysfs(int option, unsigned int fs_index, char * buf);
int sysfs(int option);
```

## DESCRIPTION

sysfs returns information about the filesystem types currently present in the kernel. The specific form of the sysfs call and the information returned depend on the option in effect. You can

- Translate the filesystem identifier string *fsname* into a filesystem type index.
- Translate the filesystem type index *fs_index* into a null-terminated filesystem identifier string. This string will be written to the buffer pointed to by *buf*. Make sure that *buf* has enough space to accept the string.
- Return the total number of filesystem types currently present in the kernel.

The numbering of the filesystem type indexes begins with 0.

## RETURN VALUE

On success, sysfs returns the filesystem index for the first option, 0 for the second option, and the number of currently configured filesystems for the third option. On error, -1 is returned, and errno is set appropriately.

## ERRORS

| | |
|---|---|
| EINVAL | *fsname* is not a valid filesystem type identifier; *fs_index* is out of bounds; *option* is invalid. |
| EFAULT | Either *fsname* or *buf* is outside your accessible address space. |

## CONFORMS TO

System V

*Linux 1.3.16, 9 August 1995*

# sysinfo

sysinfo—Returns information on overall system statistics

## SYNOPSIS

As of Linux 0.99.10 and image release 4.4,

```
#include <linux/kernel.h>
#include <linux/sys.h>
int sysinfo(struct sysinfo *info);
```

## DESCRIPTION

sysinfo returns information in the following structure:

```
struct sysinfo {
    long uptime;              /* Seconds since boot */
    unsigned long loads[3];   /* 1, 5, and 15 minute load averages */
    unsigned long totalram;   /* Total usable main memory size */
    unsigned long freeram;    /* Available memory size */
    unsigned long sharedram;  /* Amount of shared memory */
    unsigned long bufferram;  /* Memory used by buffers */
    unsigned long totalswap;  /* Total swap space size */
    unsigned long freeswap;   /* swap space still available */
    unsigned short procs;     /* Number of current processes */
    char _f[22];              /* Pads structure to 64 bytes */
};
```

sysinfo provides a simple way of getting overall system statistics. This is more portable than reading /dev/kmem.

## RETURN VALUE

On success, 0 is returned. On error, -1 is returned, and errno is set appropriately.

## ERRORS

EFAULT                  The pointer to *struct sysinfo* is invalid.

## CONFORMS TO

This function is Linux specific.

## BUGS

The Linux DLL 4.4.1 libraries do not contain a proper prototype for this function.

*Linux 0.99.10, 24 July 1993*

# syslog

syslog—Reads and/or clears kernel message ring buffer; sets console_loglevel

## SYNOPSIS

```
#include <unistd.h>
#include <linux/unistd.h>
_syscall3(int syslog, int type, char *bufp, int len);
int syslog(int type, char *bufp, int len);
```

## DESCRIPTION

This is probably not the function you are interested in. Look at syslog(3) for the C library interface. This page only documents the bare kernel system call interface.

The *type* argument determines the action taken by syslog.

From kernel/printk.c: /*

Valid commands to syslog are

0—Close the log. Currently a NOP.

1—Open the log. Currently a NOP.

2—Read from the log.

3—Read up to the last 4KB of messages in the ring buffer.

4—Read and clear last 4KB of messages in the ring buffer.

5—Clear ring buffer.

6—Disable printks to console.

7—Enable printks to console.

8—Set level of messages printed to console.

Only function 3 is allowed to non-root processes.

## THE KERNEL LOG BUFFER

The kernel has a cyclic buffer of length LOG_BUF_LEN (4096) in which messages given as argument to the kernel function printk() are stored (regardless of their loglevel).

The call syslog (2,*buf*,*len*) waits until this kernel log buffer is nonempty, and then reads at most *len* bytes into the buffer *buf*. It returns the number of bytes read. Bytes read from the log disappear from the log buffer; the information can only be read once. This is the function executed by the kernel when a user program reads /proc/kmsg.

The call syslog (3,*buf*,*len*) will read the last *len* bytes from the log buffer (nondestructively), but will not read more than was written into the buffer since the last "clear ring buffer" command (which does not clear the buffer at all). It returns the number of bytes read.

The call syslog (4,*buf*,*len*) does precisely the same, but also executes the "clear ring buffer" command.

The call syslog (5,*dummy*,*idummy*) only executes the "clear ring buffer" command.

## THE LOGLEVEL

The kernel routine printk() will print a message on the console only if it has a loglevel less than the value of the variable *console_loglevel* (initially DEFAULT_CONSOLE_LOGLEVEL (7), but set to 10 if the kernel command line contains the word debug, and to 15 in case of a kernel fault—the 10 and 15 are just silly, and are equivalent to 8). This variable is set (to a value in the range 1–8) by the call syslog (8,*dummy*,*value*). The call syslog (type,*dummy*,*idummy*) with type equal to 6 or 7, sets it to 1 (kernel panics only) or 7 (all except debugging messages), respectively.

Every text line in a message has its own loglevel. This level is DEFAULT_MESSAGE_LOGLEVEL-1 (6) unless the line starts with <*d*> where *d* is a digit in the range 1–7, in which case the level is *d*. The conventional meaning of the loglevel is defined in <linux/kernel.h> as follows:

```
#define KERN_EMERG     "<0>"  /* system is unusable              */
#define KERN_ALERT     "<1>"  /* action must be taken immediately */
#define KERN_CRIT      "<2>"  /* critical conditions             */
#define KERN_ERR       "<3>"  /* error conditions                */
#define KERN_WARNING   "<4>"  /* warning conditions              */
#define KERN_NOTICE    "<5>"  /* normal but significant condition */
#define KERN_INFO      "<6>"  /* informational                   */
#define KERN_DEBUG     "<7>"  /* debug-level messages            */
```

## RETURN VALUE

In case of error, -1 is returned, and errno is set. On success, for *type* equal to 2, 3, or 4, syslog() returns the number of bytes read; otherwise, it returns 0.

## ERRORS

| | |
|---|---|
| EPERM | An attempt was made to change console_loglevel or clear the kernel message ring buffer by a process without root permissions. |
| EINVAL | Bad parameters. |
| ERESTARTSYS | System call was interrupted by a signal—nothing was read. |

## CONFORMS TO

This system call is Linux specific.

## SEE ALSO

syslog(3)

*Linux 1.2.9, 11 June 1995*

# termios, tcgetattr, tcsetattr, tcsendbreak, tcdrain, tcflush, tcflow, cfgetospeed, cfgetispeed, cfsetispeed, cfsetospeed, tcgetpgrp, tcsetpgrp

termios, tcgetattr, tcsetattr, tcsendbreak, tcdrain, tcflush, tcflow, cfgetospeed, cfgetispeed, cfsetispeed, cfsetospeed, tcgetpgrp, tcsetpgrp—Get and set terminal attributes, do line control, get and set baud rate, get and set terminal foreground process group ID

## SYNOPSIS

```
#include <termios.h>
#include <unistd.h>
int tcgetattr ( int fd, struct termios *termios_p );
int tcsetattr ( int fd, int optional_actions, struct termios *termios_p );
int tcsendbreak ( int fd, int duration );
int tcdrain ( int fd );
int tcflush ( int fd, int queue_selector );
int tcflow ( int fd, int action );
speed_t cfgetospeed ( struct termios *termios_p );
int cfsetospeed ( struct termios *termios_p, speed_t speed );
speed_t cfgetispeed ( struct termios *termios_p );
int cfsetispeed ( struct termios *termios_p, speed_t speed );
pid_t tcgetpgrp ( int fd );
int tcsetpgrp ( int fd, pid_t pgrpid );
```

## DESCRIPTION

The termios functions describe a general terminal interface that is provided to control asynchronous communications ports.

Many of the functions described here have a *termios_p* argument that is a pointer to a termios structure. This structure contains the following members:

```
tcflag_t c_iflag; /* input modes */
tcflag_t c_oflag; /* output modes */
tcflag_t c_cflag; /* control modes */
tcflag_t c_lflag;/*local modes*/
cc_t c_cc[NCCS]; /* control chars */
```

The following are the c_*iflag* flag constants:

| | |
|---|---|
| IGNBRK | Ignore BREAK condition on input. |
| BRKINT | If IGNBRK is not set, generate SIGINT on BREAK condition; otherwise, read BREAK as character \0. |
| IGNPAR | Ignore framing errors and parity errors. |
| PARMRK | If IGNPAR is not set, prefix a character with a parity error or framing error with \377 \0. If neither IGNPAR nor PARMRK is set, read a character with a parity error or framing error as \0. |
| INPCK | Enable input parity checking. |

*termios, tcgetattr, tcsetattr, tcsendbreak, tcdrain, tcflush, tcflow, cfgetospeed, cfgetispeed, cfsetispeed, cfsetospeed, tcgetpgrp, tcsetpgrp*

875

| | |
|---|---|
| ISTRIP | Strip off the eighth bit. |
| INLCR | Translate NL to CR on input. |
| IGNCR | Ignore carriage return on input. |
| ICRNL | Translate carriage return to newline on input (unless IGNCR is set). |
| IUCLC | Map uppercase characters to lowercase on input. |
| IXON | Enable XON/XOFF flow control on output. |
| IXANY | Enable any character to restart output. |
| IXOFF | Enable XON/XOFF flow control on input IMAXBEL ring bell when input queue is full. |

The following are the c_oflag flag constants:

| | |
|---|---|
| OPOST | Enable implementation-defined output processing. |
| OLCUC | Map lowercase characters to uppercase on output. |
| ONLCR | Map NL to CR-NL on output. |
| OCRNL | Map CR to NL on output. |
| ONOCR | Don't output CR at column 0. |
| ONLRET | Don't output CR. |
| OFILL | Send fill characters for a delay rather than use a timed delay. |
| OFDEL | Fill character is ASCII DEL. If unset, fill character is ASCII NUL. |
| NLDLY | Newline delay mask. Values are NL0 and NL1. |
| CRDLY | Carriage-return delay mask. Values are CR0, CR1, CR2, and CR3. |
| TABDLY | Horizontal-tab delay mask. Values are TAB0, TAB1, TAB2, TAB3, and XTABS. A value of XTABS expands tabs to spaces (with tab stops every eight columns). |
| BSDLY | Backspace delay mask. Values are BS0 and BS1. |
| VTDLY | Vertical-tab delay mask. Values are VT0 and VT1. |
| FFDLY | Form-feed delay mask. Values are FF0 and FF1. |

The following are the c_cflag flag constants:

| | |
|---|---|
| CSIZE | Character size mask. Values are CS5, CS6, CS7, and CS8. |
| CSTOPB | Set two stop bits rather than one. |
| CREAD | Enable receiver. |
| PARENB | Enable parity generation on output and parity checking for input. |
| PARODD | Parity for input and output is odd. |
| HUPCL | Lower modem control lines after last process closes the device (hangs up). |
| CLOCAL | Ignore modem control lines. |
| CIBAUD | Mask for input speeds (not used). |
| CRTSCTS | Flow control. |

The following are the c_lflag flag constants:

| | |
|---|---|
| ISIG | When any of the characters INTR, QUIT, SUSP, or DSUSP are received, generate the corresponding signal. |
| ICANON | Enables canonical mode. This allows the special characters EOF, EOL, EOL2, ERASE, KILL, REPRINT, STATUS, and WERASE, and also buffers by lines. |
| XCASE | If ICANON is also set, terminal is uppercase only. Input is converted to lowercase, except for characters preceded by \. On output, uppercase characters are preceded by \, and lowercase characters are converted to uppercase. |
| ECHO | Echo input characters. |

| | |
|---|---|
| ECHOE | If ICANON is also set, the ERASE character erases the preceding input character, and WERASE erases the preceding word. |
| ECHOK | If ICANON is also set, the KILL character erases the current line. |
| ECHONL | If ICANON is also set, echo the NL character even If ECHO is not set. |
| ECHOCTL | If ECHO is also set, ASCII control signals other than TAB, NL, START, and STOP are echoed as Ctrl+X, where $X$ is the character with ASCII code 0x10 greater than the control signal. For example, character 0x28 (BS) is echoed as Ctrl+H. |
| ECHOPRT | If ICANON and IECHO are also set, characters are printed as they are being erased. |
| ECHOKE | If ICANON is also set, KILL is echoed by erasing each character on the line, as specified by ECHOE and ECHOPRT. |
| FLUSHO | Output is being flushed. This flag is toggled by typing the DISCARD character. |
| NOFLSH | Disables flushing of the input and output queues when generating the SIGINT and SIGQUIT signals, and flushing of the input queue when generating the SIGSUSP signal. |
| TOSTOP | Sends the SIGTTOU signal to the process group of a background process that tries to write to its controlling terminal. |
| PENDIN | All characters in the input queue are reprinted when the next character is read. (bash handles typeahead this way.) |
| IEXTEN | Enable implementation-defined input processing. |

tcgetattr() gets the parameters associated with the object referred by *fd* and stores them in the termios structure referenced by *termios_p*. This function may be invoked from a background process; however, the terminal attributes may be subsequently changed by a foreground process.

tcsetattr() sets the parameters associated with the terminal (unless support is required from the underlying hardware that is not available) from the termios structure referred to by *termios_p*. *optional_actions* specifies when the changes take effect:

| | |
|---|---|
| TCSANOW | The change occurs immediately. |
| TCSADRAIN | The change occurs after all output written to *fd* has been transmitted. This function should be used when changing parameters that affect output. |
| TCSAFLUSH | The change occurs after all output written to the object referred to by *fd* has been transmitted, and all input that has been received but not read will be discarded before the change is made. |

tcsendbreak() transmits a continuous stream of zero-valued bits for a specific duration, if the terminal is using asynchronous serial data transmission. If *duration* is 0, it transmits zero-valued bits for at least 0.25 seconds, and not more than 0.5 seconds. If *duration* is not 0, it sends zero-valued bits for *duration* *$N$ seconds, where $N$ is at least 0.25, and not more than 0.5.

If the terminal is not using asynchronous serial data transmission, tcsendbreak() returns without taking any action.

tcdrain() waits until all output written to the object referred to by *fd* has been transmitted.

tcflush() discards data written to the object referred to by *fd* but not transmitted, or data received but not read, depending on the value of *queue_selector*:

| | |
|---|---|
| TCIFLUSH | Flushes data received but not read. |
| TCOFLUSH | Flushes data written but not transmitted. |
| TCIOFLUSH | Flushes both data received but not read and data written but not transmitted. |

tcflow() suspends transmission or reception of data on the object referred to by *fd*, depending on the value of *action*:

| | |
|---|---|
| TCOOFF | Suspends output. |
| TCOON | Restarts suspended output. |
| TCIOFF | Transmits a STOP character, which stops the terminal device from transmitting data to the system. |
| TCION | Transmits a START character, which starts the terminal device transmitting data to the system. |

*termios, tcgetattr, tcsetattr, tcsendbreak, tcdrain, tcflush, tcflow, cfgetospeed, cfgetispeed, cfsetispeed, cfsetospeed, tcgetpgrp, tcsetpgrp*

877

The default on open of a terminal file is that neither its input nor its output is suspended.

The baud rate functions are provided for getting and setting the values of the input and output baud rates in the termios structure. The new values do not take effect until tcsetattr() is successfully called.

Setting the speed to B0 instructs the modem to hang up. The actual bit rate corresponding to B38400 may be altered with setserial(8).

The input and output baud rates are stored in the termios structure.

cfgetospeed() returns the output baud rate stored in the termios structure pointed to by *termios_p*.

cfsetospeed() sets the output baud rate stored in the termios structure pointed to by *termios_p* to *speed*, which must be one of these constants:

B0
B50
B75
B110
B134
B150
B200
B300
B600
B1200
B1800
B2400
B4800
B9600
B19200
B38400
B57600
B115200
B230400

The zero baud rate, B0, is used to terminate the connection. If B0 is specified, the modem control lines will no longer be asserted. Normally, this will disconnect the line. CBAUDEX is a mask for the speeds beyond those defined in POSIX.1 (57600 and later). Thus, B57600 & CBAUDEX is nonzero.

cfgetispeed() returns the input baud rate stored in the termios structure.

cfsetispeed() sets the input baud rate stored in the termios structure to *speed*. If the input baud rate is set to 0, it will be equal to the output baud rate.

tcgetpgrp() returns the process group ID of the foreground processing group, or -1 on error.

tcsetpgrp() sets the process group ID to pgrpid. pgrpid must be the ID of a process group in the same session.

## RETURN VALUES

cfgetispeed() returns the input baud rate stored in the termios structure.

cfgetospeed() returns the output baud rate stored in the termios structure.

tcgetpgrp() returns the process group ID of foreground processing group, or -1 on error.

All other functions return

0 On success.

-1 on failure (and set errno to indicate the error).

## SEE ALSO

setserial(8)

# time

time—Gets time in seconds

## SYNOPSIS

```
#include <time.h>
time_t time(time_t *t);
```

## DESCRIPTION

time returns the time since 00:00:00 GMT, January 1, 1970, measured in seconds.

If *t* is non null, the return value is also stored in the memory pointed to by *t*.

## CONFORMS TO

SVID, AT&T, POSIX, X/OPEN, BSD 4.3

(Under BSD 4.3, this call is made obsolete by gettimeofday(2).)

## SEE ALSO

ctime(3), date(1), ftime(3), gettimeofday(2)

# times

times—Gets process times

## SYNOPSIS

```
#include <sys/times.h>
clock_t times(struct tms *buf);
```

## DESCRIPTION

times stores the current process times in *buf*.

*struct* tms is as defined in /usr/include/sys/times.h:

```
struct  tms  {
            time_t tms_utime;  /* user time */
            time_t tms_stime;  /* system time */
            time_t tms_cutime; /* user time of children */
            time_t tms_cstime; /* system time of children */
            };
```

times returns the number of clock ticks that have elapsed since the system has been up.

## CONFORMS TO

SVID, AT&T, POSIX, X/OPEN, BSD 4.3

## SEE ALSO

time(1), getrusage(2), wait(2)

*Linux 0.99.11, 24 July 1993*

# truncate, ftruncate

truncate, ftruncate—Truncate a file to a specified length

## SYNOPSIS

```
#include <unistd.h>
int truncate(const char *path, size_t length);
int ftruncate(int fd, size_t length);
```

## DESCRIPTION

truncate causes the file named by *path* or referenced by *fd* to be truncated to at most *length* bytes in size. If the file previously was larger than this size, the extra data is lost. With ftruncate, the file must be open for writing.

## RETURN VALUE

On success, 0 is returned. On error, -1 is returned, and errno is set appropriately.

## ERRORS

The errors for truncate are

| | |
|---|---|
| ENOTDIR | A component of the path prefix is not a directory. |
| EINVAL | The pathname contains a character with the high-order bit set. |
| ENAMETOOLONG | A component of a pathname exceeded 255 characters, or an entire pathname exceeded 1,023 characters. |
| ENOENT | The named file does not exist. |
| EACCES | Search permission is denied for a component of the path prefix. |
| EACCES | The named file is not writeable by the user. |
| ELOOP | Too many symbolic links were encountered in translating the pathname. |
| EISDIR | The named file is a directory. |
| EROFS | The named file resides on a read-only filesystem. |
| ETXTBSY | The file is a pure procedure (shared text) file that is being executed. |
| EIO | An I/O error occurred updating the inode. |
| EFAULT | *path* points outside the process's allocated address space. |

The errors for ftruncate are

| | |
|---|---|
| EBADF | *fd* is not a valid descriptor. |
| EINVAL | *fd* references a socket, not a file. |
| EINVAL | *fd* is not open for writing. |

## HISTORY

These function calls appeared in BSD 4.2.

## BUGS

These calls should be generalized to allow ranges of bytes in a file to be discarded.

## SEE ALSO

open(2)

*BSD Man Page, 24 July 1993*

# umask

umask—Sets a file-creation mask

## SYNOPSIS

```
#include <sys/stat.h>
int umask(int mask);
```

## DESCRIPTION

umask sets the umask to *mask* & 0777.

## RETURN VALUE

The previous value of the mask is returned.

## CONFORMS TO

SVID, AT&T, POSIX, X/OPEN, BSD 4.3

## SEE ALSO

creat(2), open(2)

*Linux 24 July 93*

# uname

uname—Gets name and information about the current kernel

## SYNOPSIS

```
#include <sys/utsname.h>
int uname(struct utsname *buf);
```

## DESCRIPTION

uname returns system information in *buf*. The *utsname* struct is as defined in /usr/include/sys/utsname.h:

```
struct utsname {
            char sysname[65];
            char nodename[65];
            char release[65];
            char version[65];
            char machine[65];
            char domainname[65];
            };
```

## RETURN VALUE

On success, 0 is returned. On error, -1 is returned, and errno is set appropriately.

## ERRORS

EFAULT                    *buf* is not valid.

## CONFORMS TO

SVID, AT&T, POSIX, X/OPEN

## SEE ALSO

uname(1), getdomainname(2), gethostname(2)

*Linux 0.99.11 24 July 93*


# none

none—Undocumented system calls

## SYNOPSIS

Undocumented system calls.

## DESCRIPTION

As of Linux 1.3.88, there are 163 system calls listed in /usr/include/asm/unistd.h. This man page mentions those calls that are implemented in the kernel but not yet documented in man pages. Some of these calls do not yet have prototypes in the libc include files.

## SOLICITATION

If you have information about these system calls, please look in the kernel source code, write a man page (using a style similar to that of the other Linux section 2 man pages), and send it to aeb@cwi.nl for inclusion in the next man page release from the Linux Documentation Project.

## STATUS

Undocumented are msync, readv, writev, getsid, fdatasync, sysctl, sched_setparam, sched_getparam, sched_setscheduler, sched_getscheduler, sched_yield, sched_get_priority_max, sched_get_priority_min, sched_rr_get_interval.

## SEE ALSO

obsolete(2), unimplemented(2)

*Linux 1.3.86 12 April 1996*


# afs_syscall, break, gtty, lock, mpx, prof, quotactl, stty, ustat

afs_syscall, break, gtty, lock, mpx, prof, quotactl, stty, ustat—Unimplemented system calls

## SYNOPSIS

Unimplemented system calls.

## DESCRIPTION

These system calls are not implemented in the Linux 1.2.4 kernel.

## RETURN VALUE

These system calls always return -1 and set errno to ENOSYS.

## SEE ALSO

obsolete(2), undocumented(2)

*Linux 1.2.4, 15 April 1995*

# unlink

unlink—Deletes a name and possibly the file it refers to

## SYNOPSIS

```
#include <unistd.h>
int unlink(const char *pathname);
```

## DESCRIPTION

unlink deletes a name from the filesystem. If that name was the last link to a file and no processes have the file open, the file is deleted, and the space it was using is made available for reuse.

If the name was the last link to a file but any processes still have the file open, the file will remain in existence until the last file descriptor referring to it is closed.

If the name referred to a symbolic link, the link is removed.

If the name referred to a socket, fifo, or device, the name for it is removed but processes that have the object open can continue to use it.

## RETURN VALUE

On success, 0 is returned. On error, -1 is returned, and errno is set appropriately.

## ERRORS

| | |
|---|---|
| EFAULT | *pathname* points outside your accessible address space. |
| EACCES | Write access to the directory containing *pathname* is not allowed for the process's effective UID, or one of the directories in *pathname* did not allow search (execute) permission. |
| EPERM | The directory containing *pathname* has the sticky bit (S_ISVTX) set, and the process's effective UID is neither the UID of the file to be deleted nor that of the directory containing it, or *pathname* is a directory. |
| ENAMETOOLONG | *pathname* was too long. |
| ENOENT | A directory component in *pathname* does not exist or is a dangling symbolic link. |
| ENOTDIR | A component used as a directory in *pathname* is not, in fact, a directory. |
| EISDIR | *pathname* refers to a directory. |
| ENOMEM | Insufficient kernel memory was available. |
| EROFS | *pathname* refers to a file on a read-only filesystem. |

## CONFORMS TO

SVID, AT&T, POSIX, X/OPEN, BSD 4.3

## BUGS

Infelicities in the protocol underlying NFS can cause the unexpected disappearance of files that are still being used.

## SEE ALSO

link(2), rename(2), open(2), rmdir(2), mknod(2), mkfifo(3), remove(3), rm(1), unlink(8).

*Linux, 24 July 1993*

# uselib

uselib—Selects shared library

## SYNOPSIS

```
#include <unistd.h>
int uselib(const char *library);
```

## DESCRIPTION

uselib selects the shared library binary that will be used by this process.

## RETURN VALUE

On success, 0 is returned. On error, -1 is returned, and errno is set appropriately.

## ERRORS

In addition to all the error codes returned by open(2) and mmap(2), the following may also be returned:

ENOEXEC             The file specified by *library* is not executable, or does not have the correct magic numbers.

EACCES              The library specified by *library* is not readable.

## CONFORMS TO

uselib() is Linux specific.

## SEE ALSO

open(2), mmap(2), ldd(1), gcc(1), ar(1), ld(1)

*Linux 0.99.11, 24 July 1993*


# ustat

ustat—Gets filesystem statistics

## SYNOPSIS

```
#include <sys/types.h>
int ustat(dev_t dev, struct ustat * ubuf);
```

## DESCRIPTION

ustat returns information about a mounted filesystem. *dev* is a device number identifying a device containing a mounted filesystem. *ubuf* is a pointer to a ustat structure that contains the following members:

```
daddr_t f_tfree; /* Total free blocks */
ino_t f_tinode; /* Number of free inodes */
char f_fname[6]; /* Filsys name */
char f_fpack[6]; /* Filsys pack name */
```

The last two fields, f_fname and f_fpack, are not implemented and will always be filled with null characters.

## RETURN VALUE

On success, 0 is returned, and the ustat structure pointed to by *ubuf* will be filled in. On error, -1 is returned, and errno is set appropriately.

## ERRORS

| | |
|---|---|
| EINVAL | *dev* does not refer to a device containing a mounted filesystem. |
| EFAULT | *ubuf* points outside of your accessible address space. |
| ENOSYS | The mounted filesystem referenced by *dev* does not support this operation, or any version of Linux before 1.3.16. |

## NOTES

ustat has been provided for compatibility only. All new programs should use statfs(2) instead.

## HISTORY

ustat was first implemented in Linux 1.3.16. All versions of Linux before 1.3.16 will return ENOSYS.

## CONFORMS TO

System V

## SEE ALSO

statfs(2), stat(2)

*Linux 1.3.16, 9 August 1995*

# utime, utimes

utime, utimes—Change access and/or modification times of an inode

## SYNOPSIS

```
#include <sys/types.h>
#include <utime.h>
int utime(const char *filename, struct utimbuf *buf);
#include <sys/time.h>
int utimes(char *filename, struct timeval *tvp);
```

## DESCRIPTION

utime changes the access and modification times of the inode specified by *filename* to the *actime* and *modtime* fields of *buf*, respectively. If *buf* is NULL, the access and modification times of the file are set to the current time. The utimbuf structure is

```
struct utimbuf {
time_t actime; /* access time */
time_t modtime; /* modification time */
};
```

In the Linux DLL 4.4.1 libraries, utimes is just a wrapper for utime, *tvp*[0].*tv_sec* is *actime*, and *tvp*[1].*tv_sec* is *modtime*. The timeval structure is

```
struct timeval {
long tv_sec; /* seconds */
long tv_usec; /* microseconds */
};
```

## RETURN VALUE

On success, 0 is returned. On error, -1 is returned, and errno is set appropriately.

## ERRORS

Other errors may occur.

| | |
|---|---|
| EACCESS | Permission to write the file is denied. |
| ENOENT | *filename* does not exist. |

## CONFORMS TO

utime: SVID, POSIX
utimes:BSD4.3

## SEE ALSO

stat(2)

*Linux, 10 June 1995*

# vhangup

vhangup—Virtually hangs up the current tty

## SYNOPSIS

```
#include <unistd.h>
int vhangup(void);
```

## DESCRIPTION

vhangup simulates a hangup on the current terminal. This call arranges for other users to have a clean tty at login time.

## RETURN VALUE

On success, 0 is returned. On error, -1 is returned, and errno is set appropriately.

## ERRORS

| | |
|---|---|
| EPERM | The user is not the superuser. |

## SEE ALSO

init(8)

*Linux 0.99.11, 24 July 1993*

# vm86

vm86—Enters virtual 8086 mode

## SYNOPSIS

```
#include <sys/vm86.h>
int vm86(struct vm86_struct * info);
```

## DESCRIPTION

Enter VM86 mode with information as specified in *info*:

```
struct vm86_struct {
        struct vm86_regs regs;
        unsigned long flags;
```

```
        unsigned long screen_bitmap;
};

struct vm86_regs {
/*
 * normal regs, with special meaning for the segment descriptors..
 */
        long ebx;
        long ecx;
        long edx;
        long esi;
        long edi;
        long ebp;
        long eax;
        long __null_ds;
        long __null_es;
        long __null_fs;
        long __null_gs;
        long orig_eax;
        long eip;
        long cs;
        long eflags;
        long esp;
        long ss;
/*
 * these are specific to v86 mode:
 */
        long es;
        long ds;
        long fs;
        long gs;
};
```

these are specific to v86 mode:

```
/
long es;
long ds;
long fs;
long gs;
};
```

## RETURN VALUE

On success, 0 is returned. On error, -1 is returned, and errno is set appropriately.

## ERRORS

EPERM                    Saved kernel stack exists.

*Linux 0.99.11, 24 July 1993*

# wait, waitpid

wait, waitpid—Wait for process termination

## SYNOPSIS

```
#include <sys/types.h>
#include <sys/wait.h>
```

```
pid_t wait(int *status)
pid_t waitpid(pid_t pid,int*status,int options);
```

## DESCRIPTION

The wait function suspends execution of the current process until a child has exited, or until a signal is delivered whose action is to terminate the current process or to call a signal-handling function. If a child has already exited by the time of the call (a so–called *zombie* process), the function returns immediately. Any system resources used by the child are freed.

The waitpid function suspends execution of the current process until a child as specified by the *pid* argument has exited, or until a signal is delivered whose action is to terminate the current process or to call a signal-handling function. Just as with wait, if a child requested by *pid* has already exited by the time of the call, the function returns immediately. Any system resources used by the child are freed.

The value of *pid* can be one of the following:

| | |
|---|---|
| < -1 | Wait for any child process whose process group ID is equal to the absolute value of *pid*. |
| -1 | Wait for any child process; this is the same behavior that wait exhibits. |
| 0 | Wait for any child process whose process group ID is equal to that of the calling process. |
| > 0 | Wait for the child whose process ID is equal to the value of *pid*. |

The value of *options* is an OR of zero or more of the following constants:

| | |
|---|---|
| WNOHANG | Return immediately if no child has exited. |
| WUNTRACED | Also return for children that are stopped and whose status has not been reported. |

If *status* is not NULL, wait or waitpid stores status information in the location pointed to by *statloc*.

This status can be evaluated with the following macros (these macros take the stat buffer as an argument—not a pointer to the buffer!):

| | |
|---|---|
| WIFEXITED(*status*) | Is nonzero if the child exited normally. |
| WEXITSTATUS(*status*) | Evaluates to the least significant eight bits of the return code of the child that terminated, which may have been set as the argument to a call to exit() or as the argument for a return statement in the main program. This macro can only be evaluated if WIFEXITED returned nonzero. |
| WIFSIGNALED(*status*) | Returns true if the child process exited because of a signal that was not caught. |
| WTERMSIG(*status*) | Returns the number of the signal that caused the child process to terminate. This macro can only be evaluated if WIFSIGNALED returned nonzero. |
| WIFSTOPPED(*status*) | Returns true if the child process that caused the return is currently stopped; this is only possible if the call was done using WUNTRACED. |
| WSTOPSIG(*status*) | Returns the number of the signal that caused the child to stop. This macro can only be evaluated if WIFSTOPPED returned nonzero. |

## RETURN VALUE

The process ID of the child that exited returns -1 on error or 0 if WNOHANG was used and no child was available (in which case errno is set to an appropriate value).

## ERRORS

| | |
|---|---|
| ECHILD | If the child process specified in *pid* does not exist. |
| EPERM | If the effective user ID of the calling process does not match that of the process being waited for, and the effective user ID of the calling process is not that of the superuser. |
| ERESTARTSYS | If WNOHANG was not set and an unblocked signal or a SIGCHLD was caught; this is an extension to the POSIX.1 standard. |

## CONFORMS TO

POSIX.1

## SEE ALSO

signal(2), wait4(2), signal(7)

*Linux, 24 July 1993*

# wait3, wait4

wait3, wait4—Wait for process termination, BSD style

## SYNOPSIS

```
#define _USE_BSD
#include <sys/types.h>
#include <sys/resource.h>
#include <sys/wait.h>
pid_t wait3(int *status,int options,
struct rusage *rusage);
pid_t wait4(pid_t pid,int*status,int options,
struct rusage *rusage);
```

## DESCRIPTION

The wait3 function suspends execution of the current process until a child has exited, or until a signal is delivered whose action is to terminate the current process or to call a signal-handling function. If a child has already exited by the time of the call (a zombie process), the function returns immediately. Any system resources used by the child are freed.

The wait4 function suspends execution of the current process until a child as specified by the *pid* argument has exited, or until a signal is delivered whose action is to terminate the current process or to call a signal-handling function. If a child as requested by *pid* has already exited by the time of the call (a zombie process), the function returns immediately. Any system resources used by the child are freed.

The value of *pid* can be one of the following:

| | |
|---|---|
| < -1 | Wait for any child process whose process group ID is equal to the absolute value of *pid*. |
| -1 | Wait for any child process; this is equivalent to calling wait3. |
| 0 | Wait for any child process whose process group ID is equal to that of the calling process. |
| > 0 | Wait for the child whose process ID is equal to the value of *pid*. |

The value of *options* is an exclusive OR of zero or more of the following constants:

| | |
|---|---|
| WNOHANG | Return immediately if no child is there to be waited for. |
| WUNTRACED | Also return for children that are stopped and whose status has not been reported. |

If *status* is not NULL, wait3 and wait4 store status information in the location pointed to by *statloc*.

This status can be evaluated with the following macros:

| | |
|---|---|
| WIFEXITED(*status) | Is nonzero if the child exited normally. |
| WEXITSTATUS(*status) | Evaluates to the least significant eight bits of the return code of the child that terminated, which may have been set as the argument to a call to exit or as the argument for a return statement in the main program. This macro can only be evaluated if WIFEXITED returned nonzero. |
| WIFSIGNALED(*status) | Returns true if the child process exited because of a signal that was not caught. |
| WTERMSIG(*status) | Returns the number of the signal that caused the child process to terminate. This macro can only be evaluated if WIFSIGNALED returned nonzero. |

| WIFSTOPPED(*status*) | Returns true if the child process that caused the return is currently stopped; this is only possible if the call was done using WUNTRACED. |
| WSTOPSIG(*status*) | Returns the number of the signal that caused the child to stop. This macro can only be evaluated if WIFSTOPPED returned nonzero. If *rusage* is not NULL, the struct rusage as defined in <sys/resource.h> it points to will be filled with accounting information. See getrusage(2) for details. |

## RETURN VALUE

These calls return the process ID of the child that exited, -1 on error, or 0 if WNOHANG was used and no child was available (in which case errno will be set appropriately).

## ERRORS

| ECHILD | If the child process specified in *pid* does not exist. |
| EPERM | If the effective user ID of the calling process does not match that of the process being waited for, and the effective user ID of the calling process is not that of the superuser. |
| ERESTARTSYS | If WNOHANG was not set and an unblocked signal or a SIGCHLD was caught; this is an extension to the POSIX.1 standard. |

## CONFORMS TO

POSIX.1

## SEE ALSO

signal(2), getrusage(2), wait(2), signal(7)

*Linux, 24 July 1993*

# write

write—Writes to a file descriptor

## SYNOPSIS

```
#include <unistd.h>
ssize_t write(int fd, const void *buf, size_t count);
```

## DESCRIPTION

write writes up to *count* bytes to the file referenced by the file descriptor *fd* from the buffer starting at *buf*. POSIX requires that a read() that can be proved to occur after a write() returned returns the new data. Note that not all filesystems are POSIX conforming.

## RETURN VALUE

On success, the number of bytes written is returned (0 indicates nothing was written). On error, -1 is returned, and errno is set appropriately. If *count* is 0 and the file descriptor refers to a regular file, 0 will be returned without causing any other effect. For a special file, the results are not portable.

## ERRORS

| EBADF | *fd* is not a valid file descriptor or is not open for writing. |
| EINVAL | *fd* is attached to an object that is unsuitable for writing. |
| EFAULT | *buf* is outside your accessible address space. |

| EPIPE | *fd* is connected to a pipe or socket whose reading end is closed. When this happens, the writing process will receive a SIGPIPE signal; if it catches, blocks, or ignores this, the error EPIPE is returned. |
| EAGAIN | Non-blocking I/O has been selected using O_NONBLOCK, and there was no room in the pipe or socket connected to *fd* to write the data immediately. |
| EINTR | The call was interrupted by a signal before any data was written. |
| ENOSPC | The device containing the file referred to by *fd* has no room for the data. |

Other errors may occur, depending on the object connected to *fd*.

## CONFORMS TO

SVID, AT&T, POSIX, X/OPEN, BSD 4.3

## SEE ALSO

open(2), read(2), fcntl(2), close(2), lseek(2), select(2), ioctl(2), fsync(2), fwrite(3)

# Part III:
# Library Functions

# Intro

## DESCRIPTION

This chapter describes all the library functions, excluding the library functions described in Part 2, which implement system calls. The various function groups are identified by a letter that is appended to the chapter number:

| | |
|---|---|
| (3C) | These functions—the functions from Chapter 2 and from Chapter 3S—are contained in the C standard library libc, which will be used by cc(1) by default. |
| (3S) | These functions are parts of the stdio(3S) library. They are contained in the standard C library libc. |
| (3M) | These functions are contained in the arithmetic library libm. They are used by the f77(1) FORTRAN compiler by default, but not by the cc(1) C compiler, which needs the option -1m. |
| (3F) | These functions are part of the FORTRAN library libF77. There are no special compiler flags needed to use these functions. |
| (3X) | Various special libraries. The manual pages documenting their functions specify the library names. |

## AUTHORS

Look at the header of the manual page for the author(s) and copyright conditions. Note that these can be different from page to page!

*Linux, 13 December 1995*

# abort

abort—Causes abnormal program termination

## SYNOPSIS

```
#include <stdlib.h>
void abort(void);
```

## DESCRIPTION

The abort() function causes abnormal program termination unless the signal SIGABORT is caught and the signal handler does not return. If the abort() function causes program termination, all open streams are closed and flushed.

If the SIGABORT function is blocked or ignored, the abort() function will still override it.

## RETURN VALUE

The abort() function never returns.

## CONFORMS TO

SVID 3, POSIX, BSD 4.3, ISO 9899

## SEE ALSO

sigaction(2), exit(3)

*GNU, 12 April 1993*

# abs

abs—Computes the absolute value of an integer

## SYNOPSIS

```
#include <stdlib.h>
int abs(int j);
```

## DESCRIPTION

The abs() function computes the absolute value of the integer argument *j*.

## RETURN VALUE

Returns the absolute value of the integer argument.

## CONFORMS TO

SVID 3, POSIX, BSD 4.3, ISO 9899

## NOTES

Trying to take the absolute value of the most negative integer is not defined.

## SEE ALSO

ceil(3), floor(3), fabs(3), labs(3), rint(3)

*GNU, 6 June 1993*

# acos

acos—Arc cosine function

## SYNOPSIS

```
#include <math.h>
double acos(double x);
```

## DESCRIPTION

The acos() function calculates the arc cosine of *x*; that is the value whose cosine is *x*. If *x* falls outside the range –1 to 1, acos() fails and errno is set.

## RETURN VALUE

The acos() function returns the arc cosine in radians; the value is mathematically defined to be between 0 and pi (inclusive).

## ERRORS

EDOM            *x* is out of range.

## CONFORMS TO

SVID 3, POSIX, BSD 4.3, ISO 9899

## SEE ALSO

asin(3), atan(3), atan2(3), cos(3), sin(3), tan(3)

*8 June 1993*

# acosh

acosh—Inverse hyperbolic cosine function

## SYNOPSIS

```
#include <math.h>
double acosh(double x);
```

## DESCRIPTION

The acosh() function calculates the inverse hyperbolic cosine of $x$; that is the value whose hyperbolic cosine is $x$. If $x$ is less than 1.0, acosh() returns not-a-number (NaN), and errno is set.

## ERRORS

EDOM            $x$ is out of range.

## CONFORMS TO

SVID 3, POSIX, BSD 4.3, ISO 9899

## SEE ALSO

asinh(3), atanh(3), cosh(3), sinh(3), tanh(3)

*13 June 1993*

# alloca

alloca—Memory allocator

## SYNOPSIS

```
#include <stdlib.h>
void *alloca( size_t size);
```

## DESCRIPTION

The alloca function allocates *size* bytes of space in the stack frame of the caller. This temporary space is automatically freed on return.

## RETURN VALUES

The alloca function returns a pointer to the beginning of the allocated space. If the allocation fails, a NULL pointer is returned.

## CONFORMS TO

There is evidence that the alloca function appeared in 32v, pwb, pwb.2, 3bsd, and 4bsd. There is a man page for it in BSD 4.3. Linux uses the GNU version.

## BUGS

The alloca function is machine dependent.

## SEE ALSO

brk(2), pagesize(2), calloc(3), malloc(3), realloc(3)

*GNU, 29 November 1993*

# asin

asin—Arc sine function

## SYNOPSIS

```
#include <math.h>
double asin(double x);
```

## DESCRIPTION

The asin() function calculates the arc sine of x, which is the value whose sine is x. If x falls outside the range −1 to 1, asin() fails and errno is set.

## RETURN VALUE

The asin() function returns the arc sine in radians, and the value is mathematically defined to be between -PI/2 and PI/2 (inclusive).

## ERRORS

EDOM            x is out of range.

## CONFORMS TO

SVID 3, POSIX, BSD 4.3, ISO 9899

## SEE ALSO

acos(3), atan(3), atan2(3), cos(3), sin(3), tan(3)

*8 June 1993*

# asinh

asinh—Inverse hyperbolic sine function

## SYNOPSIS

```
#include <math.h>
double asinh(double x);
```

## DESCRIPTION

The asinh() function calculates the inverse hyperbolic sine of x—that is, the value whose hyperbolic sine is x.

## CONFORMS TO

SVID 3, POSIX, BSD 4.3, ISO 9899

## SEE ALSO

acosh(3), atanh(3), cosh(3), sinh(3), tanh(3)

*13 June 1993*

# assert

assert—Abort the program if assertion is false

## SYNOPSIS

```
#include <assert.h>
void assert (int expression);
```

## DESCRIPTION

assert() prints an error message to standard output and terminates the program by calling abort() if *expression* is false (that is, evaluates to 0). This only happens when the macro NDEBUG is undefined.

## RETURN VALUE

No value is returned.

## CONFORMS TO

ISO9899 (ANSI C)

## BUGS

assert() is implemented as a macro; if the expression tested has side effects, program behavior will be different depending on whether NDEBUG is defined. This may create Heisenbugs, which go away when debugging is turned on.

## SEE ALSO

exit(3), abort(3)

*GNU, 4 April 1993*

# atan

atan—Arc tangent function

## SYNOPSIS

```
#include <math.h>
double atan(double x);
```

## DESCRIPTION

The atan() function calculates the arc tangent of *x*—that is, the value whose tangent is *x*.

## RETURN VALUE

The atan() function returns the arc tangent in radians, and the value is mathematically defined to be between -PI/2 and PI/2 (inclusive).

## CONFORMS TO

SVID 3, POSIX, BSD 4.3, ISO 9899

## SEE ALSO

acos(3), asin(3), atan2(3), cos(3), sin(3), tan(3)

*8 June 1993*

# atan2

atan2—Arc tangent function of two variables

## SYNOPSIS

```
#include <math.h>
double atan2(double y, double x);
```

## DESCRIPTION

The atan2() function calculates the arc tangent of the two variables, *x* and *y*. It is similar to calculating the arc tangent of *y/x*, except that the sines of both arguments are used to determine the quadrant of the result.

## RETURN VALUE

The atan2() function returns the result in radians, which is between -PI and PI (inclusive).

## CONFORMS TO

SVID 3, POSIX, BSD 4.3, ISO 9899

## SEE ALSO

acos(3), asin(3), atan(3), cos(3), sin(3), tan(3)

*8 June 1993*

# atanh

atanh—Inverse hyperbolic tangent function

## SYNOPSIS

```
#include <math.h>
double atanh(double x);
```

## DESCRIPTION

The atanh() function calculates the inverse hyperbolic tangent of *x*; that is the value whose hyperbolic tangent is *x*. If the absolute value of *x* is greater than 1.0, acosh() returns not-a-number (NaN), and errno is set.

## ERRORS

EDOM            *x* is out of range.

## CONFORMS TO

SVID 3, POSIX, BSD 4.3, ISO 9899

## SEE ALSO

asinh(3), acosh(3), cosh(3), sinh(3), tanh(3)

*13 June 1993*

# atexit

atexit—Register a function to be called at normal program termination

## SYNOPSIS

```
#include <stdlib.h>
int atexit(void *function)(void));
```

## DESCRIPTION

The atexit() function registers the given function to be called at normal program termination, whether via exit(2) or via return from the program's main. Functions so registered are called in the reverse order of their registration; no arguments are passed.

### RETURN VALUE

The atexit()function returns the value 0 if successful; otherwise, the value –1 is returned, and the global variable errno is set to indicate the error.

### ERRORS

ENOMEM            Insufficient memory available to add the function.

### CONFORMS TO

SVID 3, BSD 4.3, ISO 9899

### SEE ALSO

exit(3), on exit(3)

*GNU, 29 March 1993*

# atof

atof—Convert a string to a double

### SYNOPSIS

```
#include <stdlib.h>
double atof(const char *nptr);
```

### DESCRIPTION

The atof() function converts the initial portion of the string pointed to by *nptr* to double. The behavior is the same as

```
strtod(nptr, (char **)NULL);
```

except that atof() does not detect errors.

### RETURN VALUE

The converted value.

### CONFORMS TO

SVID 3, POSIX, BSD 4.3, ISO 9899

### SEE ALSO

atoi(3), atol(3), strtod(3), strtol(3), strtoul(3)

*GNU, 29 March 1993*

# atoi

atoi—Convert a string to an integer

### SYNOPSIS

```
#include <stdlib.h>
int atoi(const char *nptr);
```

## DESCRIPTION

The `atoi()` function converts the initial portion of the string pointed to by *nptr* to int. The behavior is the same as

```
strtol(nptr, (char **)NULL, 10);
```

except that `atoi()` does not detect errors.

## RETURN VALUE

The converted value.

## CONFORMS TO

SVID 3, POSIX, BSD 4.3, ISO 9899

## SEE ALSO

atof(3), atol(3), strtod(3), strtol(3), strtoul(3)

*GNU, 29 March 1993*

# atol

atol—Convert a string to a long integer

## SYNOPSIS

```
#include <stdlib.h>
long atol(const char *nptr);
```

## DESCRIPTION

The `atol()` function converts the initial portion of the string pointed to by *nptr* to long. The behavior is the same as

```
strtol(nptr, (char **)NULL, 10);
```

except that `atol()` does not detect errors.

## RETURN VALUE

The converted value.

## CONFORMS TO

SVID 3, POSIX, BSD 4.3, ISO 9899

## SEE ALSO

atof(3), atoi(3), strtod(3), strtol(3), strtoul(3)

*GNU, 29 March 1993*

# bcmp

bcmp—Compare byte strings

## SYNOPSIS

```
#include <string.h>
int bcmp(const void *s1, const void *s2, int n);
```

## DESCRIPTION

The bcmp() function compares the first *n* bytes of the strings *s1* and *s2*. If the two strings are equal, bcmp() returns 0; otherwise, it returns a nonzero result. If *n* is 0, the two strings are assumed to be equal.

## RETURN VALUE

The bcmp() function returns 0 if the strings are equal; otherwise, a nonzero result is returned.

## CONFORMS TO

4.3BSD. This function is deprecated—use memcmp in new programs.

## SEE ALSO

memcmp(3), strcasecmp(3), strcmp(3), strcoll(3), strncmp(3), strncasecmp(3)

*GNU, 9 April 1993*

# bcopy

bcopy—Copy byte strings

## SYNOPSIS

```
#include <string.h>
void bcopy (const void *src, void*dest, int n);
```

## DESCRIPTION

The bcopy() function copies the first *n* bytes of the source string *src* to the destination string *dest*. If *n* is 0, no bytes are copied.

## RETURN VALUE

The bcopy() function returns no value.

## CONFORMS TO

4.3BSD. This function is deprecated—use memcpy in new programs.

## SEE ALSO

memccpy(3), memcpy(3), memmove(3), strcpy(3), strncpy(3)

*GNU, 9 April 1993*

# bsearch

bsearch—Binary search of a sorted array.

## SYNOPSIS

```
#include <stdlib.h>
void *bsearch(const void *key, const void *base, size_t nmemb,
size_t size,int(*compar)(const void *, const void *));
```

## DESCRIPTION

The bsearch() function searches an array of *nmemb* objects, the initial member of which is pointed to by *base*, for a member that matches the object pointed to by *key*. The size of each member of the array is specified by *size*.

The contents of the array should be in ascending sorted order according to the comparison function referenced by *compar*.

The *compar* routine is expected to have two arguments that point to the *key* object and to an array member, in that order, and should return an integer less than, equal to, or greater than 0, respectively, if the *key* object is found to be less than, match, or be greater than the array member.

## RETURN VALUE

The bsearch() function returns a pointer to a matching member of the array, or NULL if no match is found. If there are multiple elements that match the key, the element returned is unspecified.

## CONFORMS TO

SVID 3, BSD 4.3, ISO 9899

## SEE ALSO

qsort(3)

*GNU, 29 March 1993*

# bcmp, bcopy, bzero, memccpy, memchr, memcmp, memcpy, memfrob, memmem, memmove, memset

bcmp, bcopy, bzero, memccpy, memchr, memcmp, memcpy, memfrob, memmem, memmove, memset—Byte string operations

## SYNOPSIS

```
#include <string.h>
int bcmp(const void *s1, const void *s2, int n);
void bcopy(const void *src, void *dest, int n);
void bzero(void *s, int n);
void *memccpy(void *dest, const void *src, int c, size_t n);
void *memchr(const void *s, int c, size_t n);
int memcmp(const void *s1, const void *s2, size_t n);
void *memcpy(void *dest, const void *src, size_t n);
void *memfrob(void *s, size_t n);
void *memmem(const void *needle, size_t needlelen,
const void *haystack, size_t haystacklen);
void *memmove(void *dest, const void *src, size_t n);
void *memset(void *s, int c, size_t n);
```

## DESCRIPTION

The byte string functions perform operations on strings that are not NULL terminated. See the individual man pages for descriptions of each function.

## SEE ALSO

bcmp(3), bcopy(3), bzero(3), memccpy(3), memchr(3), memcmp(3), memcpy(3), memfrob(3), memmem(3), memmove(3), memset(3)

*GNU, 12 April 1993*

# htonl, htons, ntohl, ntohs

htonl, htons, ntohl, ntohs—Convert values between host and network byte order

## SYNOPSIS

```
#include <netinet/in.h>
unsigned long int htonl(unsigned long int hostlong);
unsigned short int htons(unsigned short int hostshort);
```

```
unsigned long int ntohl(unsigned long int netlong);
unsigned short int ntohs(unsigned short int netshort);
```

## DESCRIPTION

The htonl() function converts the long integer *hostlong* from host byte order to network byte order.

The htons() function converts the short integer *hostshort* from host byte order to network byte order.

The ntohl() function converts the long integer *netlong* from network byte order to host byte order.

The ntohs() function converts the short integer *netshort* from network byte order to host byte order.

On the i80x86, the host byte order is least significant byte first, whereas the network byte order, as used on the Internet, is most significant byte first.

## CONFORMS TO

BSD 4.3

## SEE ALSO

gethostbyname(3), getservent(3)

*BSD, 15 April 1993*


# bzero

bzero—Writes 0s to a byte string

## SYNOPSIS

```
#include <string.h>
void bzero(void *s, int n);
```

## DESCRIPTION

The bzero() function sets the first *n* bytes of the byte string *s* to 0.

## RETURN VALUE

The bzero() function returns no value.

## CONFORMS TO

4.3BSD. This function is deprecated—use memset in new programs.

## SEE ALSO

memset(3), swab(3)

*GNU, 9 April 1993*


# catgets

catgets—Gets message from a message catalog

## SYNOPSIS

```
#include <features.h>
#include <nl_types.h>
char *catgets(nl_catd catalog, int set_number, int
message_number, char *message);
```

## DESCRIPTION

catgets() reads the message message_number, in set set_number, from the message catalog identified by *catalog*. (*catalog* is a catalog descriptor returned from an earlier call to catopen(3).) The fourth argument message points to a default message string that will be returned by catgets() if the identified message catalog is not currently open or is damaged. The message text is contained in an internal buffer area and should be copied by the application if it is to be saved or modified. The return string is always terminated with a null byte.

## RETURN VALUES

On success, catgets() returns a pointer to an internal buffer area containing the null-terminated message string. catgets() returns a pointer to message if it fails because the message catalog specified by catalog is not currently open. Otherwise, catgets() returns a pointer to an empty string if the message catalog is available but does not contain the specified message.

## NOTES

These functions are only available in libc.so.4.4.4c and above.

## SEE ALSO

catopen(3), setlocale(3)

*29 November 1993*

# catopen, catclose

catopen, catclose—Open/close a message catalog

## SYNOPSIS

```
#include <features.h>
#include <nl_types.h>
nl catd catopen(char *name, int flag);
void catclose(nl_catd catalog);
```

## DESCRIPTION

catopen() opens a message catalog and returns a catalog descriptor. *name* specifies the name of the message catalog to be opened. If *name* specifies an absolute path (that is, contains a /), *name* specifies a pathname for the message catalog. Otherwise, the environment variable NLSPATH is used, with *name* substituted for %N (see locale(5)). If NLSPATH does not exist in the environment, or if a message catalog cannot be opened in any of the paths specified by NLSPATH, the following paths are searched in order:

```
/etc/locale/LC_MESSAGES
/usr/lib/locale/LC_MESSAGES
/usr/lib/locale/name/LC_MESSAGES
```

In all cases, LC_MESSAGES stands for the current setting of the LC_MESSAGES category of locale from a previous call to setlocale() and defaults to the C" locale. In the last search path, name refers to the catalog name.

The *flag* argument to catopen is used to indicate the type of loading desired. This should be either MCLoadBySet or MCLoadAll. The former value indicates that only the required set from the catalog is loaded into memory when needed, whereas the latter causes the initial call to catopen() to load the entire catalog into memory.

catclose() closes the message catalog identified by *catalog*. It invalidates any subsequent references to the message catalog defined by *catalog*.

## RETURN VALUES

catopen() returns a message catalog descriptor of type nl_catd on success. On failure, it returns –1.

catclose() returns 0 on success, or -1 on failure.

## NOTES

These functions are only available in libc.so.4.4.4c and above. In the case of Linux, the catalog descriptor nl_catd is actually an area of memory assigned by mmap() and not a file descriptor, thus allowing catalogs to be shared.

## SEE ALSO

catgets(3), setlocale(3)

*30 November 1993*

# ceil

ceil—Smallest integral value not less than *x*

## SYNOPSIS

```
#include <math.h>
double ceil (double x);
```

## DESCRIPTION

The ceil() function rounds up *x* to the nearest integer, returning that value as a double.

## CONFORMS TO

SVID 3, POSIX, BSD 4.3, ISO 9899

## SEE ALSO

abs(3), fabs(3), floor(3), labs(3), rint(3)

*6 June 1993*

# clientlib

clientlib—NNTP clientlib part of InterNetNews library

## SYNOPSIS

```
extern FILE *ser_rd_fp;
extern FILE *ser_wr_fp;
extern char ser_line[];
char * getserverbyfile(file);
char *file; int server_init(host);
char *host;
int handle_server_response(response, host);
int reponse;
char *host;
void put_server(text);
char *text;
int get_server(buff, buffsize);
char *buff;
int buffsize;
void close_server();
```

## DESCRIPTION

The routines described in this manual page are part of the InterNetNews library, libinn(3). They are replacements for the clientlib part of the NNTP distribution, and are intended to be used in building programs such as rrn.

getserverbyfile calls GetConfigValue to get the name of the local NNTP server. It returns a pointer to static space. The *file* parameter is ignored.

server_init opens a connect to the NNTP server at the specified *host*. It returns the server's response code or -1 on error. If a connection was made, ser_rd_fp and ser_wr_fp can be used to read from and write to the server, respectively, and ser_line will contain the server's response. ser_line can also be used in other routines.

handle_server_response decodes the response, which comes from the server on *host*. If the client is authorized, it returns 0. A client that is only allowed to read is authorized, but handle_server_response will print a message on the standard output. If the client is not authorized to talk to the server, a message is printed, and the routine returns -1.

put_server sends the text in *buff* to the server, adding the necessary NNTP line terminators and flushing the I/O buffer.

get_server reads a line of text from the server into *buff*, reading at most *buffsize* characters. Any trailing \r\n terminators are stripped off. get_server returns -1 on error.

close_server sends a quit command to the server and closes the connection.

## HISTORY

Written by Rich $alz (rsalz@uunet.uu.net) for InterNetNews.

## SEE ALSO

libinn(3)

# clock

clock—Determine processor time

## SYNOPSIS

```
#include <time.h>
clock_t clock(void);
```

## DESCRIPTION

The clock() function returns an approximation of processor time used by the program.

## RETURN VALUE

The value returned is the CPU time used so far as a clock_t; to get the number of seconds used, divide by CLOCKS_PER_SEC.

## CONFORMS TO

ANSI C

## BUGS

The C standard allows for arbitrary values at the start of the program; take the difference between the value returned from a call to clock() at the start of the program and the value returned at the end for maximum portability.

The times() function call returns more information.

## SEE ALSO

times(2)

*GNU, 21 April 1993*

# closedir

closedir—Close a directory

## SYNOPSIS

```
#include <sys/types.h>
#include <dirent.h>
int closedir(DIR *dir);
```

## DESCRIPTION

The closedir() function closes the directory stream associated with *dir*. The directory stream descriptor *dir* is not available after this call.

## RETURN VALUE

The closedir() function returns 0 on success or -1 on failure.

## ERRORS

EBADF            Invalid directory stream descriptor *dir*.

## CONFORMS TO

SVID 3, POSIX, BSD 4.3

## SEE ALSO

close(2), opendir(3), readdir(3), rewinddir(3), seekdir(3), telldir(3), scandir(3)

*11 June 1995*


# confstr

confstr—Get configuration-dependent string variables

## SYNOPSIS

```
#define __USE_POSIX_2
#include <unistd.h>
size_t confstr(int name, char *buf, size_t len);
```

## DESCRIPTION

confstr() gets the value of configuration-dependent string variables.

The *name* argument is the system variable to be queried. The following variables are supported:

CS_PATH          A value for the PATH variable that indicates where all the POSIX.2 standard utilities can be found.

If *buf* is not NULL, and *len* is not 0, confstr() copies the value of the string to *buf* truncated to len–1 characters if necessary, with a null character as termination. This can be detected by comparing the return value of confstr() against *len*.

If *len* is 0 and *buf* is NULL, confstr() just returns the value in Return Value.

## RETURN VALUE

If *name* does not correspond to a valid configuration variable, confstr() returns 0.

## EXAMPLES

The following code fragment determines the path where you can find the POSIX.2 system utilities:

```
char *pathbuf; size_t n;
n = confstr(_CS_PATH,NULL,(size_t)0);
if ((pathbuf = malloc(n)) == NULL) abort();
confstr(_CS_PATH, pathbuf, n);
```

## ERRORS

If the value of *name* is invalid, `errno` is set to `EINVAL`.

## CONFORMS TO

Proposed POSIX.2

## BUGS

POSIX.2 is not yet an approved standard; the information in this man page is subject to change.

## SEE ALSO

sh(1), exec(2), system(3)

# copysign

copysign—Copies the sign of a number

## SYNOPSIS

```
#include <math.h>
double copysign(double x, double y);
```

## DESCRIPTION

The `copysign()` function returns a value whose absolute value matches *x*, but whose sign matches that of *y*.

## CONFORMS TO

BSD 4.3

# cos

cos—Cosine function

## SYNOPSIS

```
#include <math.h>
double cos(double x);
```

## DESCRIPTION

The `cos()` function returns the cosine of *x*, where *x* is given in radians.

## RETURN VALUE

The `cos()` function returns a value between –1 and 1.

## CONFORMS TO

SVID 3, POSIX, BSD 4.3, ISO 9899

## SEE ALSO

acos(3), asin(3), atan(3), atan2(3), sin(3), tan(3)

# cosh

cosh—Hyperbolic cosine function

## SYNOPSIS

```
#include <math.h>
double cosh(double x);
```

## DESCRIPTION

The cosh() function returns the hyperbolic cosine of *x*, which is defined mathematically as (exp(x)+exp(-x))/2.

## CONFORMS TO

SVID 3, POSIX, BSD 4.3, ISO 9899

## SEE ALSO

acosh(3), asinh(3), atanh(3), sinh(3), tanh(3)

*13 June 1993*

# crypt

crypt—Password and data encryption

## SYNOPSIS

```
#include <unistd.h>
char *crypt(const char *key, const char *salt);
```

## DESCRIPTION

crypt is the password-encryption function. It is based on the Data Encryption Standard algorithm, with variations intended (among other things) to discourage the use of hardware implementations of a key search.

*key* is a user's typed password.

*salt* is a two-character string chosen from the set [a-zA-Z0-9./]. This string is used to perturb the algorithm in one of 4,096 different ways.

By taking the lowest seven bits of each character of the key, a 56-bit key is obtained. This 56-bit key is used to repeatedly encrypt a constant string (usually a string consisting of all 0s). The returned value points to the encrypted password, a series of 13 printable ASCII characters (with the first two characters representing the salt itself). The return value points to static data whose content is overwritten by each call.

Warning: The key space consists of equal 7.2e16 possible values. Exhaustive searches of this key space are possible using massively parallel computers. Software, such as crack(1), is available to search the portion of this key space that is generally used by humans for passwords. Hence, password selection should, at minimum, avoid common words and names. Using a passwd(1) program that checks for crackable passwords during the selection process is recommended.

The DES algorithm itself has a few quirks that make using the crypt(3) interface a very poor choice for anything other than password authentication. If you are planning to use the crypt(3) interface for a cryptography project, don't do it; get a good book on encryption and one of the widely available DES libraries instead.

## CONFORMS TO

SVID, X/OPEN, BSD 4.3

## SEE ALSO

login(1), passwd(1), encrypt(3), getpass(3), passwd(5)

*3 September 1994*

# ctermid

ctermid—Gets controlling terminal name

## SYNOPSIS

```
#include <stdio.h>
char *ctermid(char *s);
```

## DESCRIPTION

ctermid() returns a string that is the pathname for the current controlling terminal for this process. If s is NULL, a static buffer is used; otherwise, s points to a buffer used to hold the terminal pathname. The symbolic constant L_ctermid is the maximum number of characters in the returned pathname.

## RETURN VALUE

This function returns the pointer to the pathname.

## CONFORMS TO

POSIX.1

## BUGS

The path returned might not uniquely identify the controlling terminal; it might, for example, be /dev/tty.

It is not assured that the program can open the terminal.

## SEE ALSO

ttyname(3)

*GNU, 6 April 1993*

# asctime, ctime, gmtime, localtime, mktime

asctime, ctime, gmtime, localtime, mktime—Transform binary date and time to ASCII

## SYNOPSIS

```
#include <time.h>
char *asctime(const struct tm *timeptr);
char *ctime(const time_t *timep);
struct tm *gmtime(const time_t *timep);
struct tm *localtime(const time_t *timep);
time_t mktime(struct tm *timeptr);
extern char *tzname[2];
long int timezone;
extern int daylight;
```

## DESCRIPTION

The ctime(), gmtime(), and localtime() functions all take an argument of data type time_t, which represents calendar time. When interpreted as an absolute time value, it represents the number of seconds elapsed since 00:00:00 on January 1, 1970, Coordinated Universal Time (UTC).

The asctime() and mktime() functions both take an argument representing broken-down time, which is a binary representation separated into year, month, day, and so on. Broken-down time is stored in the structure *tm*, which is defined in <time.h> as follows:

```
struct tm
{
int tm_sec; /* seconds */
int tm_min; /* minutes */
int tm_hour; /* hours */
int tm_mday; /* day of the month */
int tm_mon; /* month */
int tm_year; /* year */
int tm_wday; /* day of the week */
int tm_yday; /* day in the year */
int tm_isdst; /* daylight saving time */
};
```

The members of the *tm* structure are

| | |
|---|---|
| tm_sec | The number of seconds after the minute, normally in the range 0 to 59, but can be up to 61 to allow for leap seconds. |
| tm_min | The number of minutes after the hour, in the range 0 to 59. |
| tm_hour | The number of hours past midnight, in the range 0 to 23. |
| tm_mday | The day of the month, in the range 1 to 31. |
| tm_mon | The number of months since January, in the range 0 to 11. |
| tm_year | The number of years since 1900. |
| tm_wday | The number of days since Sunday, in the range 0 to 6. |
| tm_yday | The number of days since January 1, in the range 0 to 365. |
| tm_isdst | A flag that indicates whether daylight savings time is in effect at the time described. The value is positive if daylight saving time is in effect, 0 if it is not, and negative if the information is not available. |

The ctime() function converts the calendar time *timep* into a string of the form

```
"Wed Jun 30 21:49:08 1993\n"
```

The abbreviations for the days of the week are Sun, Mon , Tue, Wed, Thu, Fri, and Sat. The abbreviations for the months are Jan, Feb, Mar, Apr, May, Jun, Jul, Aug, Sep, Oct, Nov, and Dec. The return value points to a statically allocated string that might be overwritten by subsequent calls to any of the date and time functions. The function also sets the external variable tzname with information about the current time zone.

The gmtime() function converts the calendar time timep to broken-down time representation, expressed in Coordinated Universal Time (UTC).

The localtime() function converts the calendar time *timep* to broken-time representation, expressed relative to the user's specified time zone. The function sets the external variables *tzname* with information about the current time zone, *timezone* with the difference between Coordinated Universal Time and local standard time in seconds, and *daylight* to a nonzero value if standard U.S. daylight saving time rules apply.

The asctime() function converts the broken-down time value *timeptr* into a string with the same format as ctime(). The return value points to a statically allocated string that might be overwritten by subsequent calls to any of the date and time functions.

The mktime() function converts a broken-down time structure, expressed as local time, to calendar time representation. The function ignores the specified contents of the structure members tm_wday and tm_yday and recomputes them from the other information in the broken-down time structure. Calling mktime() also sets the external variable *tzname* with information about the current time zone. If the specified broken-down time cannot be represented as calendar time, mktime() returns a value of (time_t)(-1) and does not alter the *tm_wday* and *tm_yday* members of the broken-down time structure.

## CONFORMS TO

SVID 3, POSIX, BSD 4.3, ISO 9899

## SEE ALSO

date(1), gettimeofday(2), time(2), tzset(3), difftime(3), strftime(3), newctime(3)

*BSD, 26 April 1996*

# difftime

difftime—Calculates time difference

## SYNOPSIS

```
#include <time.h>
double difftime(time_t time1, time_t time0);
```

## DESCRIPTION

The difftime() function returns the number of seconds elapsed between time *time1* and time *time0*. The two times are specified in calendar time, which represents the time elapsed since 00:00:00 on January 1, 1970, Coordinated Universal Time (UTC).

## CONFORMS TO

SVID 3, BSD 4.3, ISO 9899

## SEE ALSO

date(1), gettimeofday(2), time(2), ctime(3), gmtime(3), localtime(3)

*GNU, 2 July 1993*

# div

div—Computes the quotient and remainder of integer division

## SYNOPSIS

```
#include <stdlib.h>
div_t div(int numer, int denom);
```

## DESCRIPTION

The div() function computes the value *numer/denom* and returns the quotient and remainder in a structure named div_t that contains two integer members named *quot* and *rem*.

## RETURN VALUE

The div_t structure.

## CONFORMS TO

SVID 3, BSD 4.3, ISO 9899

## SEE ALSO

ldiv(3)

*6 June 1993*

# drand48, erand48, lrand48, nrand48, mrand48, jrand48, srand48, seed48, lcong48

drand48, erand48, lrand48, nrand48, mrand48, jrand48, srand48, seed48, lcong48—Generate uniformly distributed pseudo-random numbers

## SYNOPSIS

```
#include <stdlib.h>
double drand48(void);
double erand48(unsigned short int xsubi[3]);
long int lrand48(void);
long int nrand48(unsigned short int xsubi[3]);
long int mrand48(void);
long int jrand48(unsigned short int xsubi[3]);
void srand48(long int seedval);
unsigned short int * seed48(unsigned short int seed16v [3]);
void lcong48(unsigned short int param[7]);
```

## DESCRIPTION

These functions generate pseudo-random numbers using the linear congruential algorithm and 48-bit integer arithmetic.

The drand48() and erand48() functions return non-negative double-precision floating-point values uniformly distributed between [0.0, 1.0].

The lrand48() and nrand48() functions return non-negative long integers uniformly distributed between 0 and $2^{31}$.

The mrand48() and jrand48() functions return signed long integers uniformly distributed between $-2^{31}$ and $2^{31}$.

The srand48(),seed48(), and lcong48() functions are initialization functions, one of which should be called before using drand48(), lrand48(), or mrand49(). The functions erand48(), nrand48(), and jrand48() do not require an initialization function to be called first.

All the functions work by generating a sequence of 48-bit integers, $Xi$, according to the linear congruential formula

$Xi+1=(aXi+c)$ mod $m$, where $i >=0$

The parameter $m=2^{48}$; hence 48-bit integer arithmetic is performed. Unless lcong48() is called, $a$ and $c$ are given by

```
a = 0x5DEECE66D
c = 0xB
```

The value returned by any of the functions drand48(), erand48(), lrand48(), nrand48(), mrand48(), or jrand48() is computed by first generating the next 48-bit $Xi$ in the sequence. Then the appropriate number of bits, according to the type of data item to be returned, is copied from the high-order bits of $Xi$ and transformed into the returned value.

The functions drand48(), lrand48(), and mrand48() store the last 48-bit $Xi$ generated in an internal buffer. The functions erand48(), nrand48(), and jrand48() require the calling program to provide storage for the successive $Xi$ values in the array argument $xsubi$. The functions are initialized by placing the initial value of $Xi$ into the array before calling the function for the first time.

The initializer function srand48() sets the high-order 32 bits of $Xi$ to the argument $seedval$. The low-order 16 bits are set to the arbitrary value 0x330E.

The initializer function seed48() sets the value of $Xi$ to the 48-bit value specified in the array argument seed16v. The previous value of Xi is copied into an internal buffer and a pointer to this buffer is returned by seed48().

The initialization function lcong48() allows the user to specify initial values for $Xi$, a and c. Array argument elements param[0-2] specify $Xi$, param[3-5] specify a, and param[6] specifies c. After lcong48() has been called, a subsequent call to either srand48() or seed48() will restore the standard values of a and c.

## CONFORMS TO

SVID 3

## NOTES

These functions are declared obsolete by SVID 3, which states that rand(3) should be used instead.

## SEE ALSO

rand(3), random(3)

*2 July 1993*

# drem

drem—Floating-point remainder function

## SYNOPSIS

```
#include <math.h>
double drem(double x, double y);
```

## DESCRIPTION

The drem() function computes the remainder of dividing $x$ by $y$. The return value is $x-n*y$, where $n$ is the quotient of x divided by y, rounded to the nearest integer. If the quotient is ½, it is rounded to the even number.

## RETURN VALUE

The drem() function returns the remainder unless $y$ is 0, in which case the function fails and errno is set.

## ERRORS

EDOM            The denominator y is 0.

## CONFORMS TO

BSD 4.3

## SEE ALSO

fmod(3)

*6 June 1993*

# ecvt, fcvt

ecvt, fcvt—Convert a floating-point number to a string

## SYNOPSIS

```
#include <stdlib.h>
char *ecvt(double number, size_t ndigits,int*decpt,int*sign);
char *fcvt(double number, size_t ndigits,int*decpt,int*sign);
```

## DESCRIPTION

The ecvt() function converts *number* to a NULL-terminated string of *ndigits* digits and returns a pointer to the string. The string itself does not contain a decimal point; however, the position of the decimal point relative to the start of the string is stored in *decpt*. A negative value for *decpt* means that the decimal point is to the left of the start of the string. If the sign of *number* is negative, *sign* is set to a nonzero value; otherwise, it's set to 0.

The fcvt() function is identical to ecvt(), except that *ndigits* specifies the number of digits after the decimal point.

## RETURN VALUE

Both the ecvt()and fcvt() functions return a pointer to a static string containing the ASCII representation of *number*. The static string is overwritten by each call to ecvt() or fcvt().

## SEE ALSO

gcvt(3), sprintf(3)

*28 March 1993*

# erf, erfc

erf, erfc—Error function and complementary error function

## SYNOPSIS

```
#include <math.h>
double erf(double x);
double erfc (double x);
```

## DESCRIPTION

The erf() function returns the error function of *x*, defined as

erf(x) = 2/sqrt(pi)* integral from 0 to x of exp(-t*t) dt

The erfc() function returns the complementary error function of *x*—that is, 1.0–erf(x).

## CONFORMS TO

SVID 3, BSD 4.3

## SEE ALSO

exp(3)

*BSD, 25 June 1993*

# execl, execlp, execle, exect, execv, execvp

execl, execlp, execle, exect, execv, execvp—Execute a file

## SYNOPSIS

```
#include <unistd.h>
extern char **environ;
int execl(const char *path, const char *arg, ...);
int execlp(const char *file, const char *arg, ...);
int execle(const char *path, const char *arg, ...);
int execlp(const char *file, const char *arg, ...);
int execle(const char *path, const char *arg, ...);
int execle(const char *path, const char *arg , ..., char * const envp[]);
int exect(const char *path, char *const argv[]);
int execv(const char *path, char *const argv[]);
int execvp(const char *file, char *const argv[]);
```

## DESCRIPTION

The exec family of functions replaces the current process image with a new process image. The functions described in this manual page are front ends for the function execve(2). (See the manual page for execve for detailed information about the replacement of the current process.)

The initial argument for these functions is the pathname of a file that is to be executed.

The const char *arg and subsequent ellipses in the execl, execlp, and execle functions can be thought of as arg0, arg1, ..., argn. Together they describe a list of one or more pointers to null-terminated strings that represent the argument list available to the executed program. The first argument, by convention, should point to the file name associated with the file being executed. The list of arguments must be terminated by a NULL pointer.

The exect, execv, and execvp functions provide an array of pointers to null-terminated strings that represent the argument list available to the new program. The first argument, by convention, should point to the filename associated with the file being executed. The array of pointers must be terminated by a NULL pointer.

The execle and exect functions also specify the environment of the executed process by following the NULL pointer that terminates the list of arguments in the parameter list or the pointer to the *argv* array with an additional parameter. This additional parameter is an array of pointers to null-terminated strings and must be terminated by a NULL pointer. The other functions take the environment for the new process image from the external variable *environ* in the current process.

Some of these functions have special semantics.

The functions execlp and execvp will duplicate the actions of the shell in searching for an executable file if the specified filename does not contain a slash (/) character. The search path is the path specified in the environment by the PATH variable. If this variable isn't specified, the default path /bin:/usr/bin: is used (is this true for Linux?). In addition, certain errors are treated specially.

If permission is denied for a file (the attempted execve returned EACCES), these functions will continue searching the rest of the search path. If no other file is found, however, they will return with the global variable errno set to EACCES.

If the header of a file isn't recognized (the attempted execve returned ENOEXEC), these functions will execute the shell with the path of the file as its first argument. (If this attempt fails, no further searching is done.)

If the file is currently busy (the attempted execve returned ETXTBUSY), these functions will sleep for several seconds, periodically re-attempting to execute the file. (Is this true for Linux?)

The function exect executes a file with the program-tracing facilities enabled (see ptrace(2)).

## RETURN VALUES

If any of the exec functions returns, an error will have occurred. The return value is –1, and the global variable errno will be set to indicate the error.

## FILES

/bin/sh

## ERRORS

execl, execle, execlp, and execvp may fail and set errno for any of the errors specified for the library functions execve(2) and malloc(3).

exect and execv may fail and set errno for any of the errors specified for the library function execve(2).

## SEE ALSO

sh(1), execve(2), fork(2), trace(2), environ(5), ptrace(2)

## COMPATIBILITY

Historically, the default path for the execlp and execvp functions was /bin:/usr/bin. This was changed to place the current directory last to enhance system security.

The behavior of `execlp` and `execvp` when errors occur while attempting to execute the file is historic practice, but has not traditionally been documented and is not specified by the POSIX standard.

Traditionally, the functions `execlp` and `execvp` ignored all errors except for the ones described above and `ENOMEM` and `E2BIG`, upon which they returned. They now return if any error other than the ones described in the "Errors" section occurs.

## STANDARDS

`execl`, `execv`, `execle`, `execlp`, and `execvp` conform to IEEE Std1003.1-88 (POSIX.1).

*BSD Man Page, 29 November 1993*

# errno

errno—Number of last error

## SYNOPSIS

```
#include <errno.h>
extern int errno;
```

## DESCRIPTION

The integer `errno` is set by system calls (and some library functions) to indicate what went wrong. Its value is significant only when the call returns an error (usually −1), and a library function that does succeed is allowed to change `errno`.

Sometimes, when −1 is also a legal return value, you have to set `errno` to 0 before the call in order to detect possible errors.

POSIX lists the following symbolic error names:

| | |
|---|---|
| E2BIG | Arg list too long |
| EACCES | Permission denied |
| EAGAIN | Resource temporarily unavailable |
| EBADF | Bad file descriptor |
| EBUSY | Resource busy |
| ECHILD | No child processes |
| EDEADLK | Resource deadlock avoided |
| EDOM | Domain error |
| EEXIST | File exists |
| EFAULT | Bad address |
| EFBIG | File too large |
| EINTR | Interrupted function call |
| EINVAL | Invalid argument |
| EIO | Input/output error |
| EISDIR | Is a directory |
| EMFILE | Too many open files |
| EMLINK | Too many links |
| ENAMETOOLONG | Filename too long |
| ENFILE | Too many open files in system |
| ENODEV | No such device |
| ENOENT | No such file or directory |
| ENOEXEC | Exec format error |
| ENOLCK | No locks available |
| ENOMEM | Not enough space |

| ENOSPC | No space left on device |
| ENOSYS | Function not implemented |
| ENOTDIR | Not a directory |
| ENOTEMPTY | Directory not empty |
| ENOTTY | Inappropriate I/O control operation |
| ENXIO | No such device or address |
| EPERM | Operation not permitted |
| EPIPE | Broken pipe |
| ERANGE | Result too large |
| EROFS | Read-only filesystem |
| ESPIPE | Invalid seek |
| ESRCH | No such process |
| EXDEV | Improper link |

## SEE ALSO

perror(3)

*21 July 1996*

# exit

exit—Causes normal program termination

## SYNOPSIS

```
#include <stdlib.h>
void exit(int status);
```

## DESCRIPTION

The exit() function causes normal program termination, and the value of *status* is returned to the parent. All functions registered with atexit() and on exit() are called in the reverse order of their registration, and all open streams are flushed and closed.

## RETURN VALUE

The exit() function does not return.

## CONFORMS TO

SVID 3, POSIX, BSD 4.3, ISO 9899

## SEE ALSO

_exit(2), atexit(3), on_exit(3)

*GNU, 2 April 1993*

# exp, log, log10, pow

exp, log, log10, pow—Exponential, logarithmic, and power functions

## SYNOPSIS

```
#include <math.h>
double exp(double x);
```

```
double log(double x);
double log10(double x);
double pow(double x, double y);
```

## DESCRIPTION

The exp() function returns the value of e (the base of natural logarithms) raised to the power of x.

The log() function returns the natural logarithm of x.

The log10() function returns the base-10 logarithm of x.

The pow() function returns the value of x raised to the power of y.

## ERRORS

The log() and log10() functions can return the following errors:

EDOM            The argument x is negative.

ERANGE          The argument x is 0. The log of 0 is not defined.

The pow() function can return the following error:

EDOM            The argument x is negative and y is not an integral value. This would result in a complex number.

## CONFORMS TO

SVID 3, POSIX, BSD 4.3, ISO 9899

## SEE ALSO

sqrt(3), cbrt(3)

*GNU June 16, 1993*

# expm1, log1p

expm1, log1p—Exponential minus 1, logarithm of 1 plus argument

## SYNOPSIS

```
#include <math.h>
double expm1 (double x);
double log1p (double x);
```

## DESCRIPTION

expm1(x) returns a value equivalent to exp (x)−1. It is computed in a way that is accurate even if the value of x is near 0—a case where exp (x)−1 would be inaccurate due to subtraction of two numbers that are nearly equal.

log1p(x) returns a value equivalent to log (1 + x). It is computed in a way that is accurate even if the value of x is near 0.

## CONFORMS TO

BSD

## SEE ALSO

exp(3), log(3)

*GNU, 16 September 1995*

# fabs

Fabs—Absolute value of floating-point number

## SYNOPSIS

```
#include <math.h>
double fabs(double x);
```

## DESCRIPTION

The fabs() function returns the absolute value of the floating-point number x.

## CONFORMS TO

SVID 3, POSIX, BSD 4.3, ISO 9899

## SEE ALSO

abs(3), ceil(3), floor(3), labs(3), rint(3)

*25 June 1993*

# fclose

fclose—Closes a stream

## SYNOPSIS

```
#include <stdio.h>
int fclose(FILE *stream);
```

## DESCRIPTION

The fclose function dissociates the named *stream* from its underlying file or set of functions. If the stream was being used for output, any buffered data is written first, using fflush(3).

## RETURN VALUES

Upon successful completion, 0 is returned. Otherwise, EOF is returned, and the global variable errno is set to indicate the error. In either case, no further access to the stream is possible.

## ERRORS

EBADF           The argument stream is not an open stream.

The fclose function may also fail and set errno for any of the errors specified for the routines close(2) or fflush(3).

## SEE ALSO

close(2), fflush(3), fopen(3), setbuf(3)

## STANDARDS

The fclose function conforms to ANSI C3.159-1989 ("ANSI C").

*BSD Man Page, 29 November 1993*

# clearerr, feof, ferror, fileno

clearerr, feof, ferror, fileno—Check and reset stream status

## SYNOPSIS

```
#include <stdio.h>
void clearerr( FILE *stream);
int feof(FILE *stream);
int ferror(FILE *stream);
int fileno(FILE *stream);
```

## DESCRIPTION

The function `clearerr` clears the end-of-file and error indicators for the stream pointed to by *stream*.

The function `feof` tests the end-of-file indicator for the stream pointed to by *stream*, returning nonzero if it is set. The end-of-file indicator can only be cleared by the function `clearerr`.

The function `ferror` tests the error indicator for the stream pointed to by *stream*, returning nonzero if it is set. The error indicator can only be reset by the `clearerr` function.

The function `fileno` examines the argument *stream* and returns its integer descriptor.

## ERRORS

These functions should not fail and do not set the external variable `errno`.

## SEE ALSO

open(2), stdio(3)

## STANDARDS

The functions `clearerr`, `feof`, and `ferror` conform to C3.159-1989 ("ANSI C").

*BSD Man Page, 29 November 1993*

# fflush, fpurge

fflush, fpurge—Flush a stream

## SYNOPSIS

```
#include <stdio.h>
int fflush( FILE *stream);
int fpurge( FILE *stream);
```

## DESCRIPTION

The function `fflush` forces a write of all buffered data for the given output or update stream via the stream's underlying write function. The open status of the stream is unaffected.

If the stream argument is `NULL`, `fflush` flushes all open output streams. (Does this happen under Linux?)

The function `fpurge` erases any input or output buffered in the given stream. For output streams, this discards any unwritten output. For input streams, this discards any input read from the underlying object but not yet obtained via getc(3); this includes any text pushed back via ungetc.

## RETURN VALUES

Upon successful completion, `0` is returned. Otherwise, `EOF` is returned, and the global variable `errno` is set to indicate the error.

## ERRORS

EBADF    Stream is not an open stream, or, in the case of `fflush`, not a stream open for writing.

The function `fflush` may also fail and set `errno` for any of the errors specified for the routine write(2).

## BUGS

Linux may not support fpurge.

## SEE ALSO

write(2), fopen(3), fclose(3), setbuf(3)

## STANDARDS

The fflush function conforms to ANSI C3.159-1989 ("ANSI C").

*BSD Man Page, 29 November 1993*

# ffs

ffs—Finds first bit set in a word

## SYNOPSIS

```
#include <string.h>
int ffs(int i);
```

## DESCRIPTION

The ffs() function returns the position of the first bit set in the word *i*. The least significant bit is position 1, and the most significant position 32.

## RETURN VALUE

The ffs() function returns the position of the first bit set, or NULL if no bits are set.

## CONFORMS TO

BSD 4.3

*GNU, 13 April 1993*

# fgetgrent

fgetgrent—Gets group file entry

## SYNOPSIS

```
#include <grp.h>
#include <stdio.h>
#include <sys/types.h>
struct group *fgetgrent(FILE *stream);
```

## DESCRIPTION

The fgetgrent() function returns a pointer to a structure containing the group information from the file *stream*. The first time it is called it returns the first entry; thereafter, it returns successive entries. The file *stream* must have the same format as /etc/group.

The group structure is defined in <grp.h> as follows:

```
struct group {
        char    *gr_name;       /* group name */
        char    *gr_passwd;     /* group password */
        gid_t   gr_gid;         /* group id */
        char    **gr_mem;       /* group members */
};
```

## RETURN VALUE

The `fgetgrent()` function returns the group information structure, or NULL if there are no more entries or an error occurs.

## ERRORS

ENOMEM          Insufficient memory to allocate group information structure.

## CONFORMS TO

SVID 3

## SEE ALSO

getgrnam(3), getgrgid(3), getgrent(3), setgrent(3), endgrent(3)

*GNU, 4 April 1993*

# fgetpwent

fgetpwent—Gets password file entry

## SYNOPSIS

```
#include <pwd.h>
#include <stdio.h>
#include <sys/types.h>
struct passwd *fgetpwent(FILE *stream);
```

## DESCRIPTION

The `fgetpwent()` function returns a pointer to a structure containing the broken-out fields of a line in the file *stream*. The first time it is called it returns the first entry; thereafter, it returns successive entries. The file *stream* must have the same format as /etc/passwd.

The *passwd* structure is defined in <pwd.h> as follows:

```
struct passwd {
        char    *pw_name;       /* username */
        char    *pw_passwd;     /* user password */
        uid_t   pw_uid;         /* user id */
        gid_t   pw_gid;         /* group id */
        char    *pw_gecos;      /* real name */
        char    *pw_dir;        /* home directory */
        char    *pw_shell;      /* shell program */
};
```

## RETURN VALUE

The `fgetpwent()` function returns the passwd structure, or NULL if there are no more entries or an error occurs.

## ERRORS

ENOMEM          Insufficient memory to allocate passwd structure.

## FILES

/etc/passwd          password database file

## CONFORMS TO

SVID 3

## SEE ALSO

getpwnam(3), getpwuid(3), getpwent(3), setpwent(3), endpwent(3), getpw(3), putpwent( 3), passwd(5)

*GNU, 17 May 1996*

# floor

floor—Largest integral value not greater than *x*

## SYNOPSIS

```
#include <math.h>
double floor(double x);
```

## DESCRIPTION

The floor() function rounds *x* downward to the nearest integer, returning that value as a double.

## CONFORMS TO

SVID 3, POSIX, BSD 4.3, ISO 9899

## SEE ALSO

abs(3), fabs(3), ceil(3), rint(3)

*6 June 1993*

# fmod

fmod—Floating-point remainder function

## SYNOPSIS

```
#include <math.h>
double fmod(double x, double y);
```

## DESCRIPTION

The modf() function computes the remainder of dividing *x* by *y*. The return value is x–$n$*y, where $n$ is the quotient of x/y, rounded toward 0 to an integer.

## RETURN VALUE

The fmod() function returns the remainder unless *y* is 0, in which case the function fails and errno is set.

## ERRORS

EDOM             The denominator *y* is 0.

## CONFORMS TO

SVID 3, POSIX, BSD 4.3, ISO 9899

## SEE ALSO

drem(3)

*6 June 1993*

# fnmatch

fnmatch—Matches filename or pathname

## SYNOPSIS

```
#include <fnmatch.h>
int fnmatch(const char *pattern, const char *strings,int flags);
```

## DESCRIPTION

fnmatch() checks the *strings* argument and checks whether it matches the *pattern* argument, which is a shell wildcard pattern.

The *flags* argument modifies the behavior; it is the bitwise OR of zero or more of the following flags:

| | |
|---|---|
| FNM_NOESCAPE | If this flag is set, treat backslash as an ordinary character instead of as an escape character. |
| FNM_PATHNAME | If this flag is set, match a slash in *string* only with a slash in *pattern* and not, for example, with a [] · sequence containing a slash. |
| FNM_PERIOD | If this flag is set, a leading period in *string* has to be matched exactly by a period in *pattern*. A period is considered to be leading if it is the first character in *string*, or if both FNM_PATHNAME is set and the period immediately follows a slash. |

## RETURN VALUE

Zero if *string* matches *pattern*, FNM_NOMATCH if there is no match, or another value if there is an error.

## CONFORMS TO

Proposed POSIX.2

## BUGS

POSIX.2 is not yet an approved standard; the information in this man page is subject to change.

## SEE ALSO

sh(1), glob(3), glob(7)

*GNU, 19 April 1993*

# fopen, fdopen, freopen

fopen, fdopen, freopen—Stream open functions

## SYNOPSIS

```
#include <stdio.h>
FILE *fopen( char *path, char *mode);
FILE *fdopen( int fildes, char *mode);
FILE *freopen( char *path, char *mode,FILE*stream);
```

## DESCRIPTION

The fopen function opens the file whose name is the string pointed to by *path* and associates a stream with it.

The argument *mode* points to a string beginning with one of the following sequences (additional characters may follow these sequences):

| | |
|---|---|
| r | Open text file for reading. The stream is positioned at the beginning of the file. |
| r+ | Open for reading and writing. The stream is positioned at the beginning of the file. |

| w | Truncate file to zero length or create a text file for writing. The stream is positioned at the beginning of the file. |
|---|---|
| w+ | Open for reading and writing. The file is created if it does not exist; otherwise it is truncated. The stream is positioned at the beginning of the file. |
| a | Open for writing. The file is created if it does not exist. The stream is positioned at the end of the file. |
| a+ | Open for reading and writing. The file is created if it does not exist. The stream is positioned at the end of the file. |

The *mode* string can also include the letter b either as a third character or as a character between the characters in any of the two-character strings described previously. This is strictly for compatibility with ANSI C3.159-1989 (ANSI C) and has no effect; the b is ignored.

Any created files will have mode S_IRUSR¦S_IWUSR¦S_IRGRP¦S_IWGRP¦S_IROTH¦S_IWOTH (0666), as modified by the process's umask value. (See umask(2).)

Reads and writes may be intermixed on read/write streams in any order. Note that ANSI C requires that a file positioning function intervene between output and input, unless an input operation encounters end-of-file. (If this condition is not met, then a read is allowed to return the result of writes other than the most recent.) Therefore it is good practice (and indeed sometimes necessary under Linux) to put an fseek or fgetpos operation between write and read operations on such a stream. This operation may be an apparent no-op (as in fseek(..., 0L, SEEK_CUR)) called for its synchronizing side effect.

The fdopen function associates a stream with the existing file descriptor, fildes. The *mode* of the stream must be compatible with the mode of the file descriptor. The file descriptor is not duplicated.

The freopen function opens the file whose name is the string pointed to by *path* and associates the stream pointed to by *stream* with it. The original stream (if it exists) is closed. The *mode* argument is used just as in the fopen function. The primary use of the freopen function is to change the file associated with a standard text stream (stderr, stdin, or stdout).

## RETURN VALUES

On successful completion, fopen, fdopen, and freopen return a FILE pointer. Otherwise, NULL is returned, and the global variable errno is set to indicate the error.

## ERRORS

EINVAL      The mode provided to fopen, fdopen, or freopen was invalid.

The fopen, fdopen, and freopen functions may also fail and set errno for any of the errors specified for the routine malloc(3).

The fopen function may also fail and set errno for any of the errors specified for the routine open(2).

The fdopen function may also fail and set errno for any of the errors specified for the routine fcntl(2).

The freopen function may also fail and set errno for any of the errors specified for the routines open(2), fclose(3) and fflush(3).

## SEE ALSO

open(2), fclose(3)

## STANDARDS

The fopen and freopen functions conform to ANSI C3.159-1989 (ANSI C). The fdopen function conforms to IEEE Std1003.1-1988 (POSIX.1).

*BSD Man Page, 13 December 1995*

# fpathconf, pathconf

fpathconf, pathconf—Get configuration values for files

## SYNOPSIS

```
#include <unistd.h>
long fpathconf(int filedes,intname);
long pathconf(char *path, int name);
```

## DESCRIPTION

fpathconf() gets a value for the configuration option *name* for the open file descriptor `filedes`.

pathconf() gets a value for configuration option *name* for the filename `path`.

The corresponding macros defined in <unistd.h> are the minimum values; if an application wants to take advantage of values that may change, a call to fpathconf() or pathconf() can be made, which may yield more liberal results.

Setting *name* equal to one of the following constants returns the following configuration options:

| | |
|---|---|
| _PC_LINK_MAX | Returns the maximum number of links to the file. If `filedes` or `path` refers to a directory, the value applies to the whole directory. The corresponding macro is _POSIX_LINK_MAX. |
| _PC_MAX_CANON | Returns the maximum length of a formatted input line, where `filedes` or `path` must refer to a terminal. The corresponding macro is _POSIX_MAX_CANON. |
| _PC_MAX_INPUT | Returns the maximum length of an input line, where `filedes` or `path` must refer to a terminal. The corresponding macro is _POSIX_MAX_INPUT. |
| _PC_NAME_MAX | Returns the maximum length of a filename in the directory path or `filedes` the process is allowed to create. The corresponding macro is _POSIX_MAX_. |
| _PC PATH_MAX | Returns the maximum length of a relative pathname when `path` or `filedes` is the current working directory. The corresponding macro is _POSIX_PATH_MAX. |
| _PC_PIPE_BUF | Returns the size of the pipe buffer, where `filedes` must refer to a pipe or FIFO, and `path` must refer to a FIFO. The corresponding macro is _POSIX_PIPE_BUF. |
| _PC_CHOWN_RESTRICTED | Returns nonzero if the chown(2) call may not be used on this file. If `filedes` or `path` refers to a directory, this applies to all files in that directory. The corresponding macro is _POSIX_CHOWN_RESTRICTED. |
| _PC_NO_TRUNC | Returns nonzero if accessing filenames longer than _POSIX_NAME_MAX generates an error. The corresponding macro is _POSIX_NO_TRUNC. |
| _PC_VDISABLE | Returns nonzero if special character processing can be disabled, where `filedes` or `path` must refer to a terminal. |

## RETURN VALUE

The limit is returned, if one exists. If the system does not have a limit for the requested resource, -1 is returned, and errno is unchanged. If there is an error, -1 is returned, and errno is set to reflect the nature of the error.

## CONFORMS TO

POSIX.1. Files with name lengths longer than the value returned for *name* equal to _PC_NAME_MAX may exist in the given directory.

Some returned values may be huge; they are not suitable for allocating memory.

## SEE ALSO

getconf(1), statfs(2), open(2), sysconf(3)

*GNU, 4 April 1993*

# fread, fwrite

fread, fwrite—Binary stream input/output

## SYNOPSIS

```
#include <stdio.h>
size_t fread(void *ptr, size_t size, size_t nmemb,FILE*stream);
size_t fwrite(void *ptr, size_t size, size_t nmemb,FILE*stream);
```

## DESCRIPTION

The function `fread` reads *nmemb* elements of data, each *size* bytes long, from the stream pointed to by *stream*, storing them at the location given by *ptr*.

The function `fwrite` writes *nmemb* elements of data, each *size* bytes long, to the stream pointed to by *stream*, obtaining them from the location given by *ptr*.

## RETURN VALUES

`fread` and `fwrite` return the number of items successfully read or written (that is, not the number of characters). If an error occurs, or the end-of-file is reached, the return value is a short item count (or `0`).

`fread` does not distinguish between end-of-file and error, and callers must use `feof`(3) and `ferror`(3) to determine which occurred.

## SEE ALSO

`feof`(3), `ferror`(3), `read`(2), `write`(2)

## STANDARDS

The functions `fread` and `fwrite` conform to ANSI C3.159-1989 ("ANSI C").

*BSD Man Page, 17 May 1996*

# frexp

frexp—Converts floating-point number to fractional and integral components

## SYNOPSIS

```
#include <math.h>
double frexp(double x, int *exp);
```

## DESCRIPTION

The `frexp()` function is used to split the number *x* into a normalized fraction and an exponent that is stored in *exp*.

## RETURN VALUE

The `frexp()` function returns the normalized fraction. If the argument *x* is not `0`, the normalized fraction is *x* times a power of 2, and is always in the range ½ (inclusive) to 1 (exclusive). If *x* is `0`, the normalized fraction is 0, and `0` is stored in *exp*.

## CONFORMS TO

SVID 3, POSIX, BSD 4.3, ISO 9899

## SEE ALSO

`ldexp`(3), `modf`(3)

*GNU, 6 June 1993*

# fgetpos, fseek, fsetpos, ftell, rewind

fgetpos, fseek, fsetpos, ftell, rewind—Reposition a stream

## SYNOPSIS

```
#include <stdio.h>
int fseek(FILE *stream, longo ffset, int whence);
long ftell(FILE *stream);
void rewind(FILE *stream);
int fgetpos(FILE *stream, fpos_t *pos);
int fsetpos(FILE *stream, fpos_t *pos);
```

## DESCRIPTION

The fseek function sets the file position indicator for the stream pointed to by stream. The new position, measured in bytes, is obtained by adding offset bytes to the position specified by whence. If whence is set to SEEK_SET, SEEK_CUR, or SEEK_END, the offset is relative to the start of the file, the current position indicator, or end-of-file, respectively. A successful call to the fseek function clears the end-of-file indicator for the stream and undoes any effects of the ungetc(3) function on the same stream.

The ftell function obtains the current value of the file position indicator for the stream pointed to by stream.

The rewind function sets the file position indicator for the stream pointed to by stream to the beginning of the file. It is equivalent to

```
(void)fseek(stream, 0L, SEEK_SET);
```

except that the error indicator for the stream is also cleared. (See clearerr(3).)

The fgetpos and fsetpos functions are alternate interfaces equivalent to ftell and fseek (with whence set to SEEK_SET), setting and storing the current value of the file offset into or from the object referenced by pos. On some non-UNIX systems, an fpos_t object may be a complex object, and these routines might be the only way to portably reposition a text stream.

## RETURN VALUES

The rewind function returns no value. Upon successful completion, fgetpos, fseek, and fsetpos return 0, and ftell returns the current offset. Otherwise, -1 is returned, and the global variable errno is set to indicate the error.

## ERRORS

EBADF        The stream specified is not a seekable stream.

EINVAL       The whence argument to fseek was not SEEK_SET, SEEK_END, or SEEK_CUR.

The function fgetpos, fseek, fsetpos, and ftell might also fail and set errno for any of the errors specified for the routines fflush(3), fstat(2), lseek(2), and malloc(3).

## SEE ALSO

lseek(2)

## STANDARDS

The fgetpos, fsetpos, fseek, ftell, and rewind functions conform to ANSI C3.159-1989 (ANSI C).

*BSD Man Page, 29 November 1993*

# ftime

ftime—Returns date and time

## SYNOPSIS

```
#include <sys/timeb.h>
int ftime(struct timeb *tp);
```

## DESCRIPTION

Return current date and time in *tp*, which is declared as follows:

```
struct timeb {
time_t time;
unsigned short millitm;
short timezone;
short dstflag;
};
```

## RETURN VALUE

This function always returns 0.

## NOTES

Under Linux, this function is implemented in a compatibility library instead of in the kernel.

## CONFORMS TO

Version 7, BSD 4.3

Under BSD 4.3, this call is obsoleted by gettimeofday(2).

## SEE ALSO

time(2)

*Linux, 24 July 1993*

# ftok

ftok—Converts a pathname and a project identifier to a System V IPC key

## SYNOPSIS

```
#include <sys/types.h>
#include <sys/ipc.h>
key_t ftok (char *pathname, char proj);
```

## DESCRIPTION

The function converts the pathname of an existing accessible file and a project identifier into a key_t type System V IPC key.

## RETURN VALUE

On success, the return value will be the converted key_t value; otherwise it will be –1, with errno indicating the error as for the stat(2) system call.

## BUGS

The generated key_t value is obtained by stating the disk file corresponding to *pathname* in order to get its i–node number and the minor device number of the filesystem on which the disk file resides, then by combining the 8-bit *proj* value along with the lower 16 bits of the inode number with the 8 bits of the minor device number. The algorithm does not guarantee a unique key value. In fact,

- Two different names linking to the same file produce the same key values.
- Using the lower 16 bits of the i–node number gives some chance (although usually small) to have the same key values for filenames referring to different inodes.
- Not discriminating among major device numbers gives some chance of collision (also usually small) for systems with multiple disk controllers.

## SEE ALSO

ipc(5), msgget(2), semget(2), shmget(2), stat(2)

# ftw

ftw—File tree walk

## SYNOPSIS

```
#include <ftw.h>
int ftw(const char *directory,
int(*funcptr)(const char *file, struct stat *sb, int flag), int depth);
```

## DESCRIPTION

ftw() walks through the directory tree, starting from the indicated *directory*. For each found entry in the tree, it calls *funcptr* with the full pathname of the entry relative to *directory*, a pointer to the stat(2) structure for the entry and an int whose value will be one of the following:

| | |
|---|---|
| FTW_F | Item is a normal file |
| FTW_D | Item is a directory |
| FTW_NS | The stat failed on the item |
| FTW_DNR | Item is a directory which can't be read |

Warning: Anything other than directories, such as symbolic links, gets the FTW_F tag.

ftw() recursively calls itself for traversing found directories. To avoid using up all a program's file descriptors, *depth* specifies the number of simultaneous open directories. When the depth is exceeded, ftw() will become slower because directories have to be closed and reopened.

To stop the tree walk, *funcptr* returns a nonzero value; this value will become the return value of ftp(). Otherwise, ftw() will continue until it has traversed the entire tree (in which case it will return 0), or until it hits an error such as a malloc(3) failure, in which case it will return -1.

Because ftp() uses dynamic data structures, the only safe way to exit a tree walk is to return a nonzero value. To handle interrupts, for example, mark that the interrupt occurred and return a nonzero value—don't use longjmp(3) unless the program is going to terminate.

## SEE ALSO

stat(2)

# gcvt

gcvt—Converts a floating-point number to a string

## SYNOPSIS

```
#include <stdlib.h>
char *gcvt(double number, size_t ndigit, char *buf);
```

## DESCRIPTION

The gcvt() function converts *number* to a minimal-length, NULL-terminated ASCII string and stores the result in *buf*. It produces *ndigit* significant digits in either printf() F format or E format.

## RETURN VALUE

The gcvt() function returns the address of the string pointed to by *buf*.

## SEE ALSO

ecvt(3), fcvt(3), sprintf(3)

*29 March 1993*

# getcwd, get_current_dir_name, getwd

getcwd, get_current_dir_name, getwd—Get current working directory

## SYNOPSIS

```
#include <unistd.h>
char *getcwd(char *buf, size_t size);
char *get_current_working_dir_name(void);
char *getwd(char *buf);
```

## DESCRIPTION

The getcwd() function copies the absolute pathname of the current working directory to the array pointed to by *buf*, which is of length *size*.

If the current absolute pathname would require a buffer longer than *size* elements, NULL is returned, and errno is set to ERANGE; an application should check for this error, and allocate a larger buffer if necessary.

As an extension to the POSIX.1 standard, getcwd() allocates the buffer dynamically using malloc() if buf is NULL on call. In this case, the allocated buffer has the length *size* unless *size* is less than 0, when *buf* is allocated as large as necessary. It is possible (and, indeed, advisable) to free the buffers if they have been obtained this way.

get_current_dir_name, which is only prototyped if __USE_GNU is defined, will malloc(3) an array big enough to hold the current directory name. If the environment variable PWD is set, and its value is correct, that value will be returned.

getwd, which is only prototyped if __USE_BSD is defined, will not malloc(3) any memory. The *buf* argument should be a pointer to an array at least PATH_MAX bytes long. getwd returns only the first PATH_MAX bytes of the actual pathname.

## RETURN VALUE

NULL on failure  (for example, if the current directory is not readable), with errno set accordingly, and *buf* on success.

## CONFORMS TO

POSIX.1

## SEE ALSO

chdir(2), free(3), malloc(3).

*GNU, 21 July 1993*

# getdirentries

getdirentries—Gets directory entries in a filesystem-independent format

## SYNOPSIS

```
#define __USE_BSD  or  #define __USE_MISC
#include <dirent.h>
ssize_t getdirentries(int fd, char *buf, size_t nbytes ,offt *basep);
```

## DESCRIPTION

This function reads directory entries from the directory specified by *fd* into *buf*. At most, *nbytes* are read. Reading starts at offset *\*basep*, and *\*basep* is updated with the new position after reading.

## RETURN VALUE

getdirentries returns the number of bytes read, or 0 when at the end of the directory. If an error occurs, -1 is returned, and errno is set appropriately.

## ERRORS

See the Linux library source code for details.

## SEE ALSO

open(2), lseek(2)

*BSD/MISC, 22 July 1993*


# getenv

getenv—Gets an environment variable

## SYNOPSIS

```
#include <stdlib.h>
char *getenv(const char *name);
```

## DESCRIPTION

The getenv() function searches the environment list for a string that matches the string pointed to by *name*. The strings are of the form *name=value*.

## RETURN VALUE

The getenv() function returns a pointer to the value in the environment, or NULL if there is no match.

## CONFORMS TO

SVID 3, POSIX, BSD 4.3, ISO 9899

## SEE ALSO

putenv(3), setenv(3), unsetenv(3)

*GNU, 3 April 1993*


# getgrent, setgrent, endgrent

getgrent, setgrent, endgrent—Get group file entry

## SYNOPSIS

```
#include <grp.h>
#include <sys/types.h>
struct group *getgrent(void);
void setgrent(void);
void endgrent(void);
```

## DESCRIPTION

The getgrent() function returns a pointer to a structure containing the group information from /etc/group. The first time it is called it returns the first entry; thereafter, it returns successive entries.

The setgrent() function rewinds the file pointer to the beginning of the /etc/group file.

The endgrent() function closes the /etc/group file.

The group structure is defined in <grp.h> as follows:

```
struct group {
        char    *gr_name;     /* group name */
        char    *gr_passwd;   /* group password */
        gid_t   gr_gid;       /* group id */
        char    **gr_mem;     /* group members */
};
```

## RETURN VALUE

The getgrent()function returns the group information structure, or NULL if there are no more entries or an error occurs.

## ERRORS

ENOMEM          Insufficient memory to allocate group information structure.

## FILES

/etc/group group database file

## CONFORMS TO

SVID 3, BSD 4.3

## SEE ALSO

fgetgrent(3), getgrnam(3), getgrgid(3)

*GNU, 4 April 1993*

# getgrnam, getgrgid

getgrnam, getgrgid—Get group file entry

## SYNOPSIS

```
#include <grp.h>
#include <sys/types.h>
struct group *getgrnam(const char *name);
struct group *getgrgid(gid_t gid);
```

## DESCRIPTION

The getgrnam() function returns a pointer to a structure containing the group information from /etc/group for the entry that matches the group name *name*.

The getgrgid() function returns a pointer to a structure containing the group information from /etc/group for the entry that matches the group id *gid*.

The group structure is defined in <grp.h> as follows:

```
struct group {
        char    *gr_name;     /* group name */
        char    *gr_passwd;   /* group password */
```

```
     gid_t    gr_gid;      /* group id */
     char     **gr_mem;    /* group members */
};
```

## RETURN VALUE

The getgrnam()and getgrgid() functions return the group information structure, or NULL if the matching entry is not found or an error occurs.

## ERRORS

ENOMEM                Insufficient memory to allocate group information structure.

## FILES

/etc/group group database file

## CONFORMS TO

SVID 3, POSIX, BSD 4.3

## SEE ALSO

fgetgrent(3), getgrent(3), setgrent(3), endgrent(3)

*GNU, 4 April 1993*

# getlogin, cuserid

getlogin, cuserid—Get username

## SYNOPSIS

```
#include <unistd.h>
char * getlogin ( void );
#include <stdio.h>
char * cuserid ( char *string );
```

## DESCRIPTION

getlogin returns a pointer to a string containing the name of the user logged in on the controlling terminal of the process, or a null pointer if this information cannot be determined. The string is statically allocated and might be overwritten on subsequent calls to this function or to cuserid.

cuserid returns a pointer to a string containing a username associated with the effective user ID of the process. If *string* is not a null pointer, it should be an array that can hold at least L_cuserid characters; the string is returned in this array. Otherwise, a pointer to a string in a static area is returned. This string is statically allocated and might be overwritten on subsequent calls to this function or to getlogin.

The macro L_cuserid is an integer constant that indicates how long an array you might need to store a username. L_cuserid is declared in stdio.h.

These functions let your program positively identify the user who is running (cuserid) or the user who logged in this session (getlogin). (These can differ when setuid programs are involved.) The user cannot do anything to fool these functions.

For most purposes, it is more useful to use the environment variable LOGNAME to find out who the user is. This is more flexible precisely because the user can set LOGNAME arbitrarily.

## ERRORS

ENOMEM                Insufficient memory to allocate passwd structure.

## FILES

The /etc/passwd password database file /etc/utmp (or /var/adm/utmp, or wherever your utmp file lives these days—the proper location depends on your libc version)

## CONFORMS TO

POSIX.1. System V has a cuserid function that uses the real user ID rather than the effective user ID. The cuserid function was included in the 1988 version of POSIX, but was removed from the 1990 version.

## BUGS

Unfortunately, it is often rather easy to fool getlogin(). Sometimes it does not work at all, because some program messed up the utmp file. Often, it gives only the first eight characters of the login name. The user currently logged in on the controlling tty of your program need not be the user who started it.

Nobody knows precisely what cuserid() does; so

- Avoid it in portable programs
- Avoid it altogether
- Use getpwuid (geteuid()) instead, if that is what you meant.

Simply, *do not use* cuserid().

## SEE ALSO

geteuid(2), getuid(2)

*Linux 1.2.13, 3 September 1995*

# getmntent, setmntent, addmntent, endmntent, hasmntopt

getmntent, setmntent, addmntent, endmntent, hasmntopt—Get filesystem descriptor file entry

## SYNOPSIS

```
#include <stdio.h>
#include <mntent.h>
FILE *setmntent(const char *filep, const char *type);
struct mntent *getmntent(FILE *filep);
int addmntent(FILE *filep, const struct mntent *mnt);
int endmntent(FILE *filep);
char *hasmntopt(const struct mntent *mnt, const char *opt);
```

## DESCRIPTION

These routines are used to access the filesystem description file /etc/fstab and the mounted filesystem description file /etc/mstab.

The setmntent() function opens the filesystem description file filep and returns a file pointer that can be used by getmntent(). The argument type is the type of access required and can take the same values as the mode argument of fopen(3).

The getmntent() function reads the next line from the filesystem description file filep and returns a pointer to a structure containing the broken-out fields from a line in the file. The pointer points to a static area of memory that is overwritten by subsequent calls to getmntent().

The addmntent() function adds the mntent structure mnt to the end of the open file filep.

The endmntent() function closes the filesystem description file filep.

The hasmntopt() function scans the mnt_opts field of the mntent structure mnt for a substring that matches opt. (See <mntent.h> for valid mount options.)

The mntent structure is defined in `<mntent.h>` as follows:

```
struct mntent {
        char    *mnt_fsname;    /* name of mounted filesystem */
        char    *mnt_dir;       /* filesystem path prefix */
        char    *mnt_type;      /* mount type (see mntent.h) */
        char    *mnt_opts;      /* mount options (see mntent.h) */
        int     mnt_freq;       /* dump frequency in days */
        int     mnt_passno;     /* pass number on parallel fsck */
};
```

## RETURN VALUE

The getmntent() function returns a pointer to the mntent structure or NULL on failure.

The addmntent() function returns 0 on success and 1 on failure.

The endmntent() functions always returns 1.

The hasmntopt() function returns the address of the substring if a match is found, and NULL otherwise.

## FILES

/etc/fstab filesystem description file

/etc/mtab mounted filesystem description file

## CONFORMS TO

BSD 4.3

## SEE ALSO

fopen(3), fstab(5)

*27 June 1993*

# getnetent, getnetbyaddr, getnetbyname, setnetent, endnetent

getnetent, getnetbyaddr, getnetbyname, setnetent, endnetent—Get network entry

## SYNTAX

```
#include <netdb.h>
struct netent *getnetent()
struct netent *getnetbyname(name)
char *name;
struct netent *getnetbyaddr(net, type)
long net; int type;
void setnetent(stayopen)
int stayopen;
void endnetent()
```

## DESCRIPTION

The getnetent, getnetbyname, and getnetbyaddr subroutines each return a pointer to an object with the following structure, containing the broken-out fields of a line in the network database, /etc/networks:

```
struct netent {
        char    *n_name;        /* official name of net */
        char    **n_aliases;    /* alias list */
        int     n_addrtype;     /* net number type */
        long    n_net;          /* net number */
};
```

The members of this structure are

| | |
|---|---|
| n_name | The official name of the network. |
| n_aliases | A zero-terminated list of alternate names for the network. |
| n_addrtype | The type of the network number returned: AF_INET. |
| n_net | The network number. Network numbers are returned in machine byte order. |

If the *stayopen* flag on a setnetent subroutine is NULL, the network database is opened. Otherwise the setnetent has the effect of rewinding the network database. The endnetent may be called to close the network database when processing is complete.

The getnetent subroutine simply reads the next line whereas getnetbyname and getnetbyaddr search until a matching *name* or *net* number is found (or until EOF is encountered). The *type* must be AF_INET. The getnetent subroutine keeps a pointer in the database, allowing successive calls to be used to search the entire file.

A call to setnetent must be made before a while loop using getnetent to perform initialization, and an endnetent must be used after the loop. Both getnetbyname and getnetbyaddr make calls to setnetent and endnetent.

## FILES

/etc/networks

## DIAGNOSTICS

Null pointer (0) returned on EOF or error.

## SEE ALSO

networks(5), RFC 1101

## HISTORY

The getnetent(), getnetbyaddr(), getnetbyname(), setnetent(), and endnetent() functions appeared in 4.2BSD.

## BUGS

The data space used by these functions is static; if future use requires the data, it should be copied before any subsequent calls to these functions overwrite it. Only Internet network numbers are currently understood. Expecting network numbers to fit in no more than 32 bits is probably naive.

# getopt

getopt—Parses command-line options

## SYNOPSIS

```
#include <unistd.h>
int getopt(int argc, char * const argv[],
  const char *optstring);
extern char *optarg;
extern int optind, opterr, optopt;
#include <getopt.h>
int getopt_long(int argc, char * const argv[],

  const char *optstring,
  const struct option *longopts, int *longindex);
int getopt_long_only(int argc, char * const argv[],

  const char *optstring,
  const struct option *longopts, int *longindex);
```

## DESCRIPTION

The getopt() function parses the command-line arguments. Its arguments argc and argv are the argument count and array as passed to the main() function on program invocation. An element of argv that starts with - (and is not exactly - or --) is an option element. The characters of this element (aside from the initial -) are option characters. If getopt() is called repeatedly, it returns successively each of the option characters from each of the option elements.

If getopt() finds another option character, it returns that character, updating the external variable optind and a static variable nextchar so that the next call to getopt() can resume the scan with the following option character or argv element.

If there are no more option characters, getopt() returns EOF. Then optind is the index in argv of the first argv element that is not an option.

optstring is a string containing the legitimate option characters. If such a character is followed by a colon, the option requires an argument, so getopt places a pointer to the following text in the same argv element, or the text of the following argv element, in optarg. Two colons mean an option takes an optional arg; if there is text in the current argv element, it is returned in optarg; otherwise, optarg is set to 0.

By default, getargs() permutes the contents of argv as it scans, so that eventually all the non-options are at the end. Two other modes are also implemented. If the first character of optstring is + or the environment variable POSIXLY_CORRECT is set, option processing stops as soon as a non-option argument is encountered. If the first character of optstring is -, each non-option argv element is handled as if it were the argument of an option with character code 1. (This is used by programs that were written to expect options and other argv elements in any order and that care about the ordering of the two.) The special argument - forces an end of option-scanning regardless of the scanning mode.

If getopt() does not recognize an option character, it prints an error message to stderr, stores the character in optopt, and returns?. The calling program may prevent the error message by setting opterr to 0.

The getopt_long() function works like getopt(), except that it also accepts long options, started out by two dashes. Long option names may be abbreviated if the abbreviation is unique or is an exact match for some defined option. A long option may take a parameter, of the form --arg=param or --arg param.

longopts is a pointer to the first element of an array of struct option declared in <getopt.h>:

```
as struct option {
   const char *name;
   int has_arg;
   int *flag;
   int val;
};
```

The meanings of the different fields are

| | |
|---|---|
| name | The name of the long option. |
| has_arg | no_argument (or 0) if the option does not take an argument, required_argument (or 1) if the option requires an argument, or optional_argument (or 2) if the option takes an optional argument. |
| flag | Specifies how results are returned for a long option. If flag is NULL, getopt_long() returns val. (For example, the calling program might set val to the equivalent short option character.) Otherwise, getopt_long() returns 0, and flag points to a variable that is set to val if the option is found, but left unchanged if the option is not found. |
| val | The value to return or to load into the variable pointed to by flag. |

The last element of the array has to be filled with zeroes.

If longindex is not NULL, it points to a variable that is set to the index of the long option relative to longopts.

getopt_long_only() is like getopt_long(), but - as well as -- can indicate a long option. If an option that starts with - (not --) doesn't match a long option but does match a short option, it is parsed as a short option instead.

## RETURN VALUE

The getopt()function returns the option character if the option was found successfully, : if there was a missing parameter for one of the options, ? for an unknown option character, or EOF for the end of the option list.

getopt_long() and getopt_long_only() also return the option character when a short option is recognized. For a long option, they return *val* if *flag* is NULL, and 0 otherwise. Error and EOF returns are the same as for getopt(), plus ? for an ambiguous match or an extraneous parameter.

## ENVIRONMENT VARIABLES

POSIXLY_CORRECT          If this is set, option processing stops as soon as a non-option argument is encountered.

## EXAMPLE

The following example program, from the source code, illustrates the use of getopt_long() with most of its features:

```
#include <stdio.h>
int
main (argc, argv)
   int argc;
   char **argv;
{
   int c;
   int digit_optind = 0;
   while (1)
   {
     int this_option_optind = optind ? optind : 1;
     int option_index = 0;
     static struct option long_options[] =
     {
       {"add", 1, 0, 0},
       {"append", 0, 0, 0},
       {"delete", 1, 0, 0},
       {"verbose", 0, 0, 0},
       {"create", 1, 0, 'c'},
       {"file", 1, 0, 0g, f0, 0, 0, 0}
     };
     c = getopt_long (argc, argv, "abc:d:012",
       long_options, &option_index);
     if (c == -1)
       break;
     switch(c)
     {
       case 0:
         printf ("option %s", long_options[option_index].name);
         if (optarg)
           printf (" with arg %s", optarg);
         printf ("\n");
         break;
       case '0':
       case '1':
       case '2':
         if (digit_optind != 0 && digit_optind != this_option_optind)
           printf ("digits occur in two different argv-elements.\n");
           digit_optind = this_option_optind;
         printf ("option %c\n", c);
         break;
       case 'a':
         printf ("option a\n");
         break;
       case 'b':
```

```
        printf ("option b\n");
        break;
      case 'c':
        printf ("option c with value '%s'\n", optarg);
        break;
      case 'd':
        printf ("option d with value '%s' \n", optarg);
        break;
      case '?':
        break;
      default:
        printf ("?? getopt returned character code 0%o ??\n", c);
    }
  }
  if (optind < argc)
  {
    printf ("non-option ARGV-elements: ");
    while (optind < argc)
      printf ("%s ", argv[optind++]);
    printf ("\n");
  }
  exit (0);
}
```

## BUGS

This man page is confusing.

## CONFORMS TO

getopt():          POSIX.1, provided the environment variable POSIXLY_CORRECT is set. Otherwise, the elements of *argv* aren't really const, because they get permuted. They're set const in the prototype to be compatible with other systems.

*GNU, 30 August 1995*

# getpass

getpass—Gets a password

## SYNOPSIS

```
#include <pwd.h>
#include <unistd.h>
char *getpass( const char * prompt );
```

## DESCRIPTION

The getpass function displays a prompt to, and reads in, a password from, /dev/tty. If this file is not accessible, getpass displays the prompt on the standard error output and reads from the standard input.

The password may be up to _PASSWORD_LEN (currently 128) characters in length. Any additional characters and the terminating newline character are discarded. (This might be different in Linux.)

getpass turns off character echoing while reading the password.

## RETURN VALUES

getpass returns a pointer to the null-terminated password.

## FILES

/dev/tty

## SEE ALSO

crypt(3)

## HISTORY

A getpass function appeared in Version 7 AT&T UNIX.

## BUGS

The getpass function leaves its result in an internal static object and returns a pointer to that object. Subsequent calls to getpass will modify the same object.

The calling process should zero the password as soon as possible to avoid leaving the cleartext password visible in the process's address space.

*BSD Man Page 29 November 1993*

# getprotoent, getprotobyname, getprotobynumber, setprotoent, endprotoent

getprotoent, getprotobyname, getprotobynumber, setprotoent, endprotoent—Get protocol entry

## SYNOPSIS

```
#include <netdb.h>
struct protoent *getprotoent(void);
struct protoent *getprotobyname(const char *name);
struct protoent *getprotobynumber(int proto);
void setprotoent(int stayopen);
void endprotoent(void);
```

## DESCRIPTION

The getprotoent() function reads the next line from the file /etc/protocols and returns a structure *protoent* containing the broken-out fields from the line. The /etc/protocols file is opened if necessary.

The getprotobyname() function returns a *protoent* structure for the line from /etc/protocols that matches the protocol name *name*.

The getprotobynumber() function returns a *protoent* structure for the line that matches the protocol number *number*.

The setprotoent() function opens and rewinds the /etc/protocols file. If *stayopen* is true (1), the file will not be closed between calls to getprotobyname() or getprotobynumber().

The endprotoent() function closes /etc/protocols.

The protoent structure is defined in <netdb.h> as follows:

```
struct protoent {
        char    *p_name;        /* official protocol name */
        char    **p_aliases;    /* alias list */
        int     p_proto;        /* protocol number */
}
```

The members of the protoent structure are

p_name          The official name of the protocol.

p_aliases       A zero-terminated list of alternative names for the protocol.

p_proto         The protocol number.

## RETURN VALUE

The getprotoent(), getprotobyname(), and getprotobynumber() functions return the *protoent* structure, or a NULL pointer if an error occurs or the end of the file is reached.

## FILES

/etc/protocols protocol database file

## CONFORMS TO

BSD 4.3

## SEE ALSO

getservent(3), getnetent(3), protocols(5)

*BSD, 24 April 1993*

# getpw

getpw—Reconstructs password line entry

## SYNOPSIS

```
#include <pwd.h>
#include <sys/types.h>
int getpw(uid_t uid, char *buf);
```

## DESCRIPTION

The getpw() function reconstructs the password line entry for the given user UID *uid* in the buffer *buf*. The returned buffer contains a line of format

```
name:passwd:uid:gid:gecos:dir:shell
```

The passwd structure is defined in <pwd.h> as follows:

```
struct passwd {
        char    *pw_name;       /*username*/
        char    *pw_passwd;     /* user password */
        uid_t   pw_uid;         /* user id */
        gid_t   pw_gid;         /* group id */
        char    *pw_gecos;      /* real name */
        char    *pw_dir;        /* home directory */
        char    *pw_shell;      /* shell program */
};
```

## RETURN VALUE

The getpw()function returns 0 on success, or –1 if an error occurs.

## ERRORS

ENOMEM          Insufficient memory to allocate passwd structure.

## FILES

/etc/passwd          Password database file

## SEE ALSO

fgetpwent(3), getpwent(3), setpwent(3), endpwent(3), getpwnam(3), getpwuid(3), putpwent(3), passwd(5)

# getpwent, setpwent, endpwent

getpwent, setpwent, endpwent—get password file entry

## SYNOPSIS

```
#include <pwd.h>
#include <sys/types.h>
struct passwd *getpwent(void);
void setpwent(void);
void endpwent(void);
```

## DESCRIPTION

The getpwent() function returns a pointer to a structure containing the broken-out fields of a line from /etc/passwd. The first time it is called it returns the first entry; thereafter, it returns successive entries.

The setpwent() function rewinds the file pointer to the beginning of the /etc/passwd file.

The endpwent() function closes the /etc/passwd file.

The passwd structure is defined in <pwd.h> as follows:

```
struct passwd {
        char    *pw_name;      /*username*/
        char    *pw_passwd;    /* user password */
        uid_t   pw_uid;        /* user id */
        gid_t   pw_gid;        /* group id */
        char    *pw_gecos;     /* real name */
        char    *pw_dir;       /* home directory */
        char    *pw_shell;     /* shell program */
};
```

## RETURN VALUE

The getpwent() function returns the passwd structure, or NULL if there are no more entries or an error occurs.

## ERRORS

ENOMEM          Insufficient memory to allocate passwd structure.

## FILES

/etc/passwd          Password database file

## CONFORMS TO

SVID 3, BSD 4.3

## SEE ALSO

fgetpwent(3), getpwnam(3), getpwuid(3), getpw(3), putpwent(3), passwd(5).

# getpwnam, getpwuid

getpwnam, getpwuid—Get password file entry

## SYNOPSIS

```
#include <pwd.h>
#include <sys/types.h>
struct passwd *getpwnam(const char * name);
struct passwd *getpwuid(uid_t uid);
```

## DESCRIPTION

The getpwnam() function returns a pointer to a structure containing the broken out fields of a line from /etc/passwd for the entry that matches the username *name*.

The getpwuid() function returns a pointer to a structure containing the broken-out fields of a line from /etc/passwd for the entry that matches the user UID *uid*.

The passwd structure is defined in <pwd.h> as follows:

```
struct passwd {
        char    *pw_name;       /*username*/
        char    *pw_passwd;     /* user password */
        uid_t   pw_uid;         /* user id */
        gid_t   pw_gid;         /* group id */
        char    *pw_gecos;      /* real name */
        char    *pw_dir;        /* home directory */
        char    *pw_shell;      /* shell program */
};
```

## RETURN VALUE

The getpwnam()and getpwuid() functions return the passwd structure, or NULL if the matching entry is not found or an error occurs.

## ERRORS

ENOMEM          Insufficient memory to allocate passwd structure.

## FILES

/etc/passwd     Password database file

## CONFORMS TO

SVID 3, POSIX, BSD 4.3

## SEE ALSO

fgetpwent(3), getpwent(3), setpwent(3), endpwent(3), getpw(3), putpwent(3), passwd(5)

*GNU, 27 May 1996*

# fgetc, fgets, getc, getchar, gets, ungetc

fgetc, fgets, getc, getchar, gets, ungetc—Input of characters and strings

## SYNOPSIS

```
#include <stdio.h>
int fgetc(FILE *stream);
char *fgets(char *s,int size, FILE *stream);
```

```
int getc(FILE *stream);
int getchar(void);
char *gets(char *s);
int ungetc(int c, FILE *stream);
```

## DESCRIPTION

`fgetc()` reads the next character from `stream` and returns it as an unsigned char cast to an `int`, or `EOF` on end of file or error.

`getc()` is equivalent to `fgetc()` except that it can be implemented as a macro that evaluates `stream` more than once.

`getchar()` is equivalent to `getc(stdin)`.

`gets()` reads a line from `stdin` into the buffer pointed to by `s` until either a terminating newline or EOF, which it replaces with `\0`. No check for buffer overrun is performed (see the following "Bus" section).

`fgets()` reads in at most one less than `n` characters from `stream` and stores them into the buffer pointed to by `s`. Reading stops after an `EOF` or a newline. If a newline is read, it is stored into the buffer. `\0` is stored after the last character in the buffer.

`ungetc()` pushes `c` back to `stream`, cast to unsigned char, where it is available for subsequent read operations. Pushed-back characters will be returned in reverse order; only one pushback is guaranteed.

Calls to the functions described here can be mixed with each other and with calls to other input functions from the `stdio` library for the same input stream.

## RETURN VALUES

`fgetc()`, `getc()`, and `getchar()` return the character read as an unsigned char cast to an `int`, or `EOF` on end of file or error.

`gets()` and `fgets()` return `s` on success, and `NULL` on error or when end of file occurs while no characters have been read.

`ungetc()` returns `c` on success, or `EOF` on error.

## CONFORMS TO

ANSI—C, POSIX.1

## BUGS

Because it is impossible to tell without knowing the data in advance how many characters `gets()` will read, and because `gets()` will continue to store characters past the end of the buffer, it is extremely dangerous to use. It has been used to break computer security. Use `fgets()` instead.

It is not advisable to mix calls to input functions from the stdio library with low-level calls to `read()` for the file descriptor associated with the input stream; the results will be undefined and very probably not what you want.

## SEE ALSO

`read(2)`, `write(2)`, `fopen(3)`, `fread(3)`, `scanf(3)`, `puts(3)`, `fseek(3)`, `ferror(3)`

*GNU, 4 April 1993*

# getservent, getservbyname, getservbyport, setservent, endservent

getservent, getservbyname, getservbyport, setservent, endservent—Get service entry

## SYNOPSIS

```
#include <netdb.h>
struct servent *getservent(void);
struct servent *getservbyname(const char *name, const char *proto);
struct servent *getservbyport(int port, const char *proto);
```

```
void setservent(int stayopen);
void endservent(void);
```

## DESCRIPTION

The getservent()function reads the next line from the file /etc/services and returns a structure, *servent*, containing the broken out fields from the line. The /etc/services file is opened if necessary.

The getservbyname()function returns a *servent* structure for the line from /etc/services that matches the service name using protocol *proto*.

The getservbyport()function returns a *servent* structure for the line that matches the port *port* given in network byte order using protocol *proto*.

The setservent()function opens and rewinds the /etc/services file. If stayopen is true (1), the file will not be closed between calls to getservbyname() and getservbyport().

The endservent() function closes /etc/services.

The *servent* structure is defined in <netdb.h> as follows:

```
struct servent {
char *s_name; /* official service name */
char **s_aliases; /* alias list */
int s_port; /* port number */
char *s_proto; /* protocol to use */
}
```

The members of the *servent* structure are:

| | |
|---|---|
| s_name | The official name of the service. |
| s_aliases | A zero-terminated list of alternative names for the service. |
| s_port | The port number for the service, given in network byte order. |
| s_proto | The name of the protocol to use with this service. |

## RETURN VALUE

The getservent(), getservbyname(), and getservbyport() functions return the *servent* structure, or a NULL pointer if an error occurs or the end of the file is reached.

## FILES

/etc/services    Services database file

## CONFORMS TO

BSD 4.3

## SEE ALSO

getprotoent(3), getnetent(3), services(5)

*BSD, 22 April 1996*

# getusershell, setusershell, endusershell

getusershell, setusershell, endusershell—Get legal user shells

## SYNOPSIS

```
#include <unistd.h>
char *getusershell(void);
```

```
void setusershell(void);
void endusershell(void);
```

## DESCRIPTION

The getusershell() function returns the next line from the file /etc/shells, opening the file if necessary. The line should contain the pathname of a valid user shell. If /etc/shells does not exist or is unreadable, getusershell() behaves as if /bin/sh and /bin/csh were listed in the file.

The setusershell() function rewinds /etc/shells.

The endusershell() function closes /etc/shells.

## RETURN VALUE

The getusershell() function returns a NULL pointer on end of file.

## FILES

/etc/shells

## CONFORMS TO

BSD 4.3

## SEE ALSO

shells(5)

*BSD, 4 July 1993*

# getutent, getutid, getutline, pututline, setutent, endutent, utmpname

getutent, getutid, getutline, pututline, setutent, endutent, utmpname—Access utmp file entries

## SYNOPSIS

```
#include <utmp.h>
struct utmp *getutent(void);
struct utmp *getutid(struct utmp *ut);
struct utmp *getutline(struct utmp *ut);
void pututline(struct utmp *ut);
void setutent(void);
void endutent(void);
void utmpname(const char *file);
```

## DESCRIPTION

utmpname() sets the name of the utmp-format file for the other utmp functions to access. If utmpname() is not used to set the filename before the other functions are used, they assume PATH_UTMP, as defined in <paths.h>.

setutent() rewinds the file pointer to the beginning of the utmp file. It is generally a good idea to call it before any of the other functions.

endutent()closes the utmp file. It should be called when the user code is done accessing the file with the other functions.

getutent() reads a line from the current file position in the utmp file. It returns a pointer to a structure containing the fields of the line.

getutid()searches forward from the current file position in the utmp file based on *ut*. If *ut*->ut_type is RUN_LVL, BOOT_TIME, NEW_TIME, or OLD_TIME, getutid() will find the first entry whose ut_type field matches *ut*->ut_type. If *ut*->ut_type is

INIT_PROCESS, LOGIN_PROCESS, USER_PROCESS, or DEAD_PROCESS, getutid() will find the first entry whose ut_id field matches *ut*->ut_id.

getutline() searches forward from the current file position in the utmp file. It scans entries whose *ut* type is USER_PROCESS or LOGIN_PROCESS and returns the first one whose ut_line field matches *ut*->ut_line.

pututline()writes the utmp structure *ut* into the utmp file. It uses getutid() to search for the proper place in the file to insert the new entry. If it cannot find an appropriate slot for *ut*, pututline() will append the new entry to the end of the file.

### RETURN VALUE

getutent(), getutid(), and getutline() return a pointer to a struct utmp, which is defined in <utmp.h>.

### FILES

/var/run/utmp—Database of currently logged-in users

/var/log/wtmp—Database of past user logins

### CONFORMS TO

XPG 2, SVID 2, Linux FSSTND 1.2

### SEE ALSO

utmp(5)

*Linux libc 5.0.0, 22 March 1995*


# getw, putw

getw, putw—Input and output of words (ints)

### SYNOPSIS

```
#include <stdio.h>
int getw(FILE *stream);
int putw(int w,FILE*stream);
```

### DESCRIPTION

getw reads a word (that is, an int) from *stream*. It's provided for compatibility with SVID. I recommend you use fread(3) instead. putw writes the word *w* (that is, an int) to *stream*. It is provided for compatibility with SVID, but I recommend you use fwrite(3) instead.

### RETURN VALUES

Normally, getw returns the word read, and putw returns the word written. On error, they return EOF.

### BUGS

The value returned on error is also a legitimate data value. ferror(3) can be used to distinguish between the two cases.

### CONFORMS TO

SVID

### SEE ALSO

fread(3), fwrite(3), ferror(3), getc(3), putc(3)

*GNU, 16 September 1995*

# glob, globfree

glob, globfree—Find pathnames matching a pattern; free memory from glob()

## SYNOPSIS

```
#include <glob.h>
int glob(const char *pattern, int flags,
int errfunc(const char * epath, int eerrno),
glob_t *pglob);
void globfree(glob_t *pglob);
```

## DESCRIPTION

The glob() function searches for all the pathnames matching *pattern* according to the rules used by the shell (see glob(7)). No tilde expansion or parameter substitution is done.

The globfree() function frees the dynamically allocated storage from an earlier call to glob().

The results of a glob() call are stored in the structure pointed to by pglob, which is a glob_t that is declared in <glob.h> as

```
typedef struct
{
    int gl_pathc;        /* Count of paths matched so far */
    char **gl_pathv;     /* List of matched pathnames. */
    int gl_offs;         /* Slots to reserve in 'gl pathv'. */
    int gl_flags;        /* Flags for globbing */
} glob_t;
```

Results are stored in dynamically allocated storage.

The parameter *flags* is made up of bitwise OR of zero or more the following symbolic constants, which modify the of behavior of glob():

| | |
|---|---|
| GLOB_ERR | Return on read error (because a directory does not have read permission, for example). |
| GLOB_MARK | Append a slash to each path which corresponds to a directory. |
| GLOB_NOSORT | Don't sort the returned pathnames (they are by default). |
| GLOB_DOOFS | *pglob->gl_offs* slots will be reserved at the beginning of the list of strings in *pglob->pathv*. |
| GLOB_NOCHECK | If no pattern matches, return the original pattern. |
| GLOB_APPEND | Append to the results of a previous call. Do not set this flag on the first invocation of glob(). |
| GLOB_NOESCAPE | Meta characters cannot be quoted by backslashes. |
| GLOB_PERIOD | A leading period can be matched by meta characters. |

If errfunc is not NULL, it will be called in case of an error with the arguments epath, a pointer to the path that failed, and eerrno, the value of errno as returned from one of the calls to opendir(), readdir(), or stat(). If errfunc returns nonzero, or if GLOB_ERR is set, glob() will terminate after the call to errfunc.

Upon successful return, *pglob->gl_pathc* contains the number of matched pathnames and *pglob->gl_pathv* a pointer to the list of matched pathnames. The first pointer after the last pathname is NULL.

It is possible to call glob() several times. In that case, the GLOB_APPEND flag has to be set in *flags* on the second and later invocations.

## RETURN VALUES

On successful completion, glob() returns 0. Other possible returns are

| | |
|---|---|
| GLOB_NOSPACE | For running out of memory, |
| GLOB_ABEND | For a read error, and |
| GLOB_NOMATCH | For no found matches. |

## EXAMPLES

One example of use is the following code, which simulates typing in the shell:

```
ls -l *.c ../*.c
```

```
glob_t globbuf;
globbuf.gl_offs = 2;
glob("*.c", GLOB_DOOFS, NULL, &globbuf);
glob("../*.c", GLOB_DOOFS | GLOB_APPEND, NULL, &globbuf);
globbuf.gl_pathv[0] = "ls";
globbuf.gl_pathv[1] = "-l";
execvp("ls", &globbuf.gl_pathv[0]);
```

## CONFORMS TO

Proposed POSIX.2

## BUGS

The glob()function may fail due to failure of underlying function calls, such as malloc() or opendir(). These will store their error code in errno.

POSIX.2 is not yet an approved standard; the information in this man page is subject to change.

## SEE ALSO

ls(1), sh(1), exec(2), stat(2), malloc(3), opendir(3), readdir(3), wordexp(3), glob(7)

*GNU, 13 May 1996*

# hosts_access, hosts_ctl

hosts_access, hosts_ctl—Access-control library functions

## SYNOPSIS

```
#include "log_tcp.h"
extern int allow_severity;
extern int deny_severity;
int hosts_access(daemon, client)
char *daemon;
struct client_info *client;
int hosts_ctl(daemon, client_name, client_addr, client_user)
char *daemon;
char *client_name;
char *client_addr;
char *client_user;
```

## DESCRIPTION

The routines described in this document are part of the libwrap.a library. They implement a pattern-based access-control language with optional shell commands that are executed when a pattern fires.

In all cases, the *daemon* argument should specify a daemon process name (*argv[0]* value). The client host address should be a valid address, or FROM_UNKNOWN if the address lookup failed. The client hostname and username should be empty strings if no information is available, FROM_UNKNOWN if the lookup failed, or an actual hostname or username.

hosts_access() consults the access-control tables described in the hosts_access(5) manual page. hosts_access() returns 0 if access should be denied.

hosts_ctl() is a wrapper around the hosts_access() routine with a perhaps more convenient interface (although it does not pass on enough information to support automated remote username lookups). hosts_ctl() returns 0 if access should be denied.

The `allow_severity` and `deny_severity` variables determine how accepted and rejected requests can be logged. They must be provided by the caller and can be modified by rules in the access-control tables.

## DIAGNOSTICS

Problems are reported via the `syslog` daemon.

## SEE ALSO

hosts_access(5) (format of the access control tables), hosts_options(5), optional extensions to the base language

## FILES

`/etc/hosts.access`, `/etc/hosts.deny` access-control tables

## BUGS

The functions described here do not make copies of their string-valued arguments. Beware of data from functions that overwrite their results on each call.

hosts_access() uses the `strtok()` library function. This may interfere with other code that relies on `strtok()`.

## AUTHOR

Wietse Venema (`wietse@wzv.win.tue.nl`)

Department of Mathematics and Computing Science

Eindhoven University of Technology

Den Dolech 2, P.O. Box 513, 5600 MB Eindhoven, The Netherlands

# hcreate, hdestroy, hsearch

hcreate, hdestroy, hsearch—Hash table management

## SYNOPSIS

```
#include <search.h>
ENTRY *hsearch(ENTRY item, ACTION action);
int hcreate(unsigned nel);
void hdestroy(void);
```

## DESCRIPTION

These three functions allow the user to create a hash table that associates a key with any data.

First, the table must be created with the function hcreate(). *nel* is an estimate of the number of entries in the table. hcreate() may adjust this value upward to improve the performance of the resulting hash table. The GNU implementation of hsearch() will also enlarge the table if it gets nearly full. malloc(3) is used to allocate space for the table.

The corresponding function hdestroy() frees the memory occupied by the hash table so that a new table can be constructed.

*item* is of type ENTRY, which is a typedef defined in `<search.h>` and includes these elements:

```
typedef struct entry
{
  char *key;
  char *data;
} ENTRY;
```

*key* points to the zero-terminated ASCII string that is the search key. *data* points to the data associated with that key. (A pointer to a type other than character should be cast to pointer-to-character.) hsearch()searches the hash table for an item with the same key as *item*, and if successful returns a pointer to it. *action* determines what hsearch() does after an unsuccessful search. A value of ENTER instructs it to insert the new item, whereas a value of FIND means to return NULL.

## RETURN VALUE

hcreate() returns NULL if the hash table cannot be successfully installed.

hsearch()returns NULL if *action* is ENTER and there is insufficient memory to expand the hash table, or if *action* is FIND and *item* cannot be found in the hash table.

## CONFORMS TO

SVID, except that in SysV, the hash table cannot grow.

## BUGS

The implementation can manage only one hash table at a time. Individual hash table entries can be added, but not deleted.

## EXAMPLE

The following program inserts 24 items into a hash table and then prints some of them:

```
#include <stdio.h>
#include <search.h>
char *data[]={ "alpha", "bravo", "charley", "delta",
  "echo", "foxtrot", "golf", "hotel", "india", "juliette",
  "kilo", "lima", "mike", "november", "oscar", "papa",
  "quebec", "romeo", "sierra", "tango", "uniform",
  "victor", "whiskey", "x-ray", "yankee", "zulu"
};
int main()
{
  ENTRY e, *ep;
  int i;
  /* start with small table, and let it grow */
  hcreate(3);
  for (i = 0; i < 24; i++)
  {
    e.key = data[i];
    /* data is just an integer, instead of a pointer
      to something */
    e.data = (char *)i;
    ep = hsearch(e, ENTER);
    /* there should be no failures */
    if(ep == NULL) {fprintf(stderr, "entry failed\n"); exit(1);}
  }
  for (i = 22; i < 26; i++)
    /* print two entries from the table, and show that
      two are not in the table */
  {
  e.key = data[i];
  ep = hsearch(e, FIND);
  printf("%9.9s -> %9.9s:%d\n", e.key, ep?ep->key:"NULL",
    ep?(int)(ep->data):0);
  }
  return 0;
}
```

## SEE ALSO

bsearch(3), lsearch(3), tsearch(3), malloc(3)

# hypot

hypot—Euclidean distance function

## SYNOPSIS

```
#include <math.h>
double hypot(double x, double y);
```

## DESCRIPTION

The hypot() function returns the sqrt(x*x+y*y). This is the length of the hypotenuse of a right-angle triangle with sides of length $x$ and $y$, or the distance of the point (x, y) from the origin.

## CONFORMS TO

SVID 3, BSD 4.3

## SEE ALSO

sqrt(3)

*25 June 1993*


# index, rindex

index, rindex—Locate character in string

## SYNOPSIS

```
#include <string.h>
char *index(const char *s,int c);
char *rindex(const char *s,int c);
```

## DESCRIPTION

The index() function returns a pointer to the first occurrence of the character $c$ in the string $s$.

The rindex() function returns a pointer to the last occurrence of the character $c$ in the string $s$.

The terminating NULL character is considered to be a part of the strings.

## RETURN VALUE

The index() and rindex() functions return a pointer to the matched character, or NULL if the character is not found.

## CONFORMS TO

BSD 4.3

## SEE ALSO

memchr(3), strchr(3), strpbrk(3), strrchr(3), strsep(3), strspn(3), strstr(3), strtok(3)

*GNU, 12 April 1993*


# inet_aton, inet_addr, inet_network, inet_ntoa, inet_makeaddr, inet_lnaof, inet_netof

inet_aton, inet_addr, inet_network, inet_ntoa, inet_makeaddr, inet_lnaof, inet_netof—Internet address–manipulation routines

## SYNOPSIS

```
#include <sys/socket.h>
#include <netinet/in.h>
#include <arpa/inet.h>
int inet_aton(const char *cp, struct in_addr *inp);
unsigned long int inet_addr(const char *cp);
unsigned long int inet_network(const char *cp);
char *inet_ntoa(struct in_addr in);
struct in addr inet makeaddr(int net, int host);
unsigned long int inet_lnaof(struct in_addr in);
unsigned long int inet_netof(struct in_addr in);
```

## DESCRIPTION

inet_aton() converts the Internet host address *cp* from the standard numbers-and-dots notation into binary data and stores it in the structure that inp points to. inet_aton returns nonzero if the address is valid, and 0 if it is not.

The inet_addr() function converts the Internet host address *cp* from numbers-and-dots notation into binary data in network byte order. If the input is invalid, -1 is returned. This is an obsolete interface to inet_aton; it is obsolete because -1 is a valid address (255.255.255.255), and inet_aton provides a cleaner way to indicate error return.

The inet_network() function extracts the network number in network byte order from the address *cp* in numbers-and-dots notation. If the input is invalid, -1 is returned.

The inet_ntoa() function converts the Internet host address given in network byte order to a string in standard numbers-and-dots notation. The string is returned in a statically allocated buffer, which subsequent calls will overwrite.

The inet_makeaddr() function makes an Internet host address in network byte order by combining the network number *net* with the local address *host* in network *net*, both in local host byte order.

The inet_lnaof() function returns the local host address part of the Internet address *in*. The local host address is returned in local host byte order.

The inet_netof() function returns the network number part of the Internet address *in*. The network number is returned in local host byte order.

The structure in_addr as used in inet_ntoa(), inet_makeaddr(), inet_lnoaf(), and inet_netof() is defined in netinet/in.h as

```
struct in_addr {
unsigned long int s_addr;
}
```

Note that on the i80x86 the host byte order is Least Significant Byte first, whereas the network byte order, as used on the Internet, is Most Significant Byte first.

## CONFORMS TO

BSD 4.3

## SEE ALSO

gethostbyname(3), getnetent(3), hosts(5), networks(5)

*BSD, 3 September 1995*

# infnan

infnan—Deals with infinite or not-a-number (NaN) result

## SYNOPSIS

```
#include <math.h>
double infnan(int error);
```

## DESCRIPTION

The infnan() function returns a suitable value for infinity and not-a-number (NaN) results. The value of *error* can be ERANGE to represent infinity, or anything else to represent NaN. errno is also set.

## RETURN VALUE

If *error* is ERANGE (Infinity), HUGE_VAL is returned.

If *error* is -ERANGE (-Infinity), -HUGE_VAL is returned.

If *error* is anything else, NaN is returned.

## ERRORS

| | |
|---|---|
| ERANGE | The value of *error* is positive or negative infinity. |
| EDOM | The value of *error* is not-a-number (NaN). |

## CONFORMS TO

BSD 4.3

# initgroups

initgroups—Initializes the supplementary group access list

## SYNOPSIS

```
#include <grp.h>
#include <sys/types.h>
int initgroups(const char *user, gid_t group);
```

## DESCRIPTION

The initgroups() function initializes the group access list by reading the group database /etc/group and using all groups of which *user* is a member. The additional group *group* is also added to the list.

## RETURN VALUE

The initgroups() function returns 0 on success, or –1 if an error occurs.

## ERRORS

| | |
|---|---|
| EPERM | The calling process does not have sufficient privileges. |
| ENOMEM | Insufficient memory to allocate group information structure. |

## FILES

/etc/group group database file

## CONFORMS TO

SVID 3, BSD 4.3

## SEE ALSO

getgroups(2), setgroups(2)

# inndcomm

inndcomm—INND communication part of InterNetNews library

## SYNOPSIS

```
#include "inndcomm.h"
int ICCopen()
int ICCclose()
void ICCsettimeout(i)
int i;
int ICCcommand(cmd, argv, replyp)
char cmd;
char *argv[];
char **replyp;
int ICCcancel(mesgid)
char *mesgid;
int ICCreserve(why)
char *why;
int ICCpause(why)
char *why;
int ICCgo(why)
char *why;
extern char *ICCfailure;
```

## DESCRIPTION

The routines described in this manual page are part of the InterNetNews library, libinn(3). They are used to send commands to a running innd(8) daemon on the local host. The letters *ICC* stand for Innd Control Command.

ICCopen creates a UNIX-domain datagram socket and binds it to the server's control socket. It returns -1 on failure or 0 on success. This routine must be called before any other routine.

ICCclose closes any descriptors that have been created by ICCopen. It returns -1 on failure or 0 on success.

ICCsettimeout can be called before any of the following routines to determine how long the library should wait before giving up on getting the server's reply. This is done by setting and catching a SIGALRM signal(2). If the timeout is less than 0, no reply will be waited for. The SC_SHUTDOWN, SC_XABORT, and SC_XEXEC commands do not get a reply either. The default, which can be obtained by setting the timeout to 0, is to wait until the server replies.

ICCcommand sends the command *cmd* with parameters *argv* to the server. It returns -1 on error. If the server replies, and *replyp* is not NULL, it will be filled in with an allocated buffer that contains the full text of the server's reply. This buffer is a string in the form *<digits><space><text>* where *digits* is the text value of the recommended exit code; 0 indicates success. Replies longer than 4,000 bytes will be truncated. The possible values of *cmd* are defined in the inndcomm.h header file. The parameters for each command are described in ctlinnd(8). This routine returns -1 on communication failure; on success it returns the exit status sent by the server, which will never be negative.

ICCcancel sends a cancel message to the server. *mesgid* is the message ID of the article that should be canceled. The return value is the same as for ICCcommand.

ICCpause, ICCreserve, and ICCgo send a pause, reserve, or go command to the server, respectively. If ICCreserve is used, the *why* value used in the ICCpause invocation must match; the value used in the ICCgo invocation must always match the one used in the ICCpause invocation. The return value for all three routines is the same as for ICCcommand.

If any of these routines fail, the ICCfailure variable will identify the system call that failed.

## HISTORY

Written by Rich $alz (rsalz@uunet.uu.net) for InterNetNews.

## SEE ALSO

ctlinnd(8), innd(8), libinn(3).

# insque, remque

insque, remque—Insert/Remove an item from a queue

## SYNOPSIS

```
#include <stdlib.h>
void insque(struct qelem * elem, struct qelem * prev);
void remque(struct qelem*elem);
```

## DESCRIPTION

insque() and remque() are functions for manipulating queues made from doubly linked lists. Each element in this list is of type struct qelem.

The qelem structure is defined as

```
struct qelem {
struct qelem *q_forw;
struct qelem *q_back;
char q_data[1];
};
```

insque() inserts the element pointed to by *elem* immediately after the element pointed to by *prev*, which must *not* be NULL.

remque() removes the element pointed to by *elem* from the doubly linked list.

## CONFORMS TO

SVR4

## BUGS

The q_data field is sometimes defined to be of type char *, and under Solaris 2.x, it doesn't appear to exist at all.

The location of the prototypes for these functions differs among several versions of UNIX. Some systems place them in <search.h>, others in <string.h>. Linux places them in <stdlib.h> because that seems to make the most sense.

Some versions of UNIX (such as HP-UX 10.x) do not define a struct qelem but rather have the arguments to insque() and remque() be of type void *.

*GNU, 30 October 1996*

# isalnum, isalpha, isascii, isblank, iscntrl, isdigit, isgraph, islower, isprint, ispunct, isspace, isupper, isxdigit

isalnum, isalpha, isascii, isblank, iscntrl, isdigit, isgraph, islower, isprint, ispunct, isspace, isupper, isxdigit—Character classification routines

## SYNOPSIS

```
#include <ctype.h>
int isalnum (int c);
int isalpha (int c);
int isascii (int c);
int isblank (int c);
int iscntrl (int c);
int isdigit (int c);
int isgraph (int c);
int islower (int c);
int isprint (int c);
int ispunct (int c);
```

```
int isspace (int c);
int isupper (int c);
int isxdigit (int c);
```

## DESCRIPTION

These functions check whether c, which must have the value of an unsigned char or EOF, falls into a certain character class according to the current locale:

| | |
|---|---|
| isalnum() | Checks for an alphanumeric character; it is equivalent to (isalpha(c) ¦¦ isdigit(c)). |
| isalpha() | Checks for an alphabetic character; in the standard C locale, it is equivalent to (isupper(c) ¦¦ islower(c)). In some locales, there may be additional characters for which isalpha() is true—letters that are neither uppercase nor lowercase. |
| isascii() | Checks whether c is a 7-bit unsigned char value that fits into the ASCII character set. This function is a BSD extension and is also an SVID extension. |
| isblank() | Checks for a blank character; that is, a space or a tab. This function is a GNU extension. |
| iscntrl() | Checks for a control character. |
| isdigit() | Checks for a digit (0 through 9). |
| isgraph() | Checks for any printable character except space. |
| islower() | Checks for a lowercase character. |
| isprint() | Checks for any printable character, including space. |
| ispunct() | Checks for any printable character that is not a space or an alphanumeric character. |
| isspace() | Checks for whitespace characters. They are space, form-feed ('\f'), newline ('\n'), carriage return ('\r'), horizontal tab ('\t'), and vertical tab ('\v'). |
| isupper() | Checks for an uppercase letter. |
| isxdigit() | Checks for a hexadecimal digit (that is, one of 0 1 2 3 4 5 6 7 8 9 0 a b c d e f A B C D E F). |

## RETURN VALUE

The values returned are nonzero if the character c falls into the tested class, and 0 if it does not.

## CONFORMS TO

ANSI C, BSD 4.3. isascii() is a BSD extension and is also an SVID extension. isblank() is a GNU extension.

## BUGS

The details of what characters belong in which class depend on the current locale. For example, isupper() will not recognize an A with an umlaut (Ä) as an uppercase letter in the default C locale.

## SEE ALSO

tolower(3), toupper(3), setlocale(3), ascii(7), locale(7)

*GNU, 2 September 1995*

# isatty

isatty—Tests whether this descriptor refers to a terminal

## SYNOPSIS

```
#include <unistd.h>
int isatty (int desc );
```

## DESCRIPTION

isatty returns 1 if desc is an open descriptor connected to a terminal, and 0 otherwise.

## CONFORMS TO

SVID, AT&T, X/OPEN, BSD 4.3

## SEE ALSO

fstat(2), ttyname(3)

*Linux, 20 April 1995*

# isinf, isnan, finite

isinf, isnan, finite—Test for infinity or not-a-number (NaN)

## SYNOPSIS

```
#include <math.h>
int isinf(double value);
int isnan(double value);
int finite(double value);
```

## DESCRIPTION

The isinf() function returns -1 if value represents negative infinity, 1 if value represents positive infinity, and 0 otherwise.

The isnan() function returns a nonzero value if *value* is not-a-number (NaN), and 0 otherwise.

The finite() function returns a nonzero value if *value* is finite or is not a not-a-number (NaN) value, and 0 otherwise.

## CONFORMS TO

BSD 4.3

*GNU, 2 June 1993*

# j0, j1, jn, y0, y1, yn

j0, j1, jn, y0, y1, yn—Bessel functions

## SYNOPSIS

```
#include <math.h>
double j0(double x);
double j1(double x);
double jn(int n, double x);
double y0(double x);
double y1(double x);
double yn(int n, double x);
```

## DESCRIPTION

The j0() and j1() functions return Bessel functions of x of the first kind of orders 0 and 1, respectively. The jn()function returns the Bessel function of x of the first kind of order n.

The y0() and y1() functions return Bessel functions of *x* of the second kind, orders 0 and 1, respectively. The yn()function returns the Bessel function of *x* of the second kind, order *n*.

For the functions y0(), y1() and yn(),the value of *x* must be positive. For negative values of *x*, these functions return -HUGE_VAL.

## CONFORMS TO

SVID 3, BSD 4.3

## BUGS

There are errors of up to 2e–16 in the values returned by j0(), j1(), and jn() for values of *x* between –8 and 8.

# killpg

killpg—Sends a signal to all members of a process group

## SYNOPSIS

```
#include <signal.h>
int killpg(pid_t pidgrp, int signal);
```

## DESCRIPTION

The killpg() function causes the signal *signal* to be sent to all the processes in the process group *pidgrp* or to the processes' own process group if pidgrp is equal to 0.

It is equivalent to kill(-pidgrp,signal);.

## RETURN VALUE

The value returned is -1 on error, or 0 for success.

## ERRORS

Errors are returned in errno and can be one of the following:

EINVAL          Signal is invalid.

ESRCH           Process group does not exist.

EPERM           The user ID of the calling process is not equal to that of the process the signal is sent to, and the user ID is not that of the super-user.

## SEE ALSO

kill(2), signal(2), signal(7)

# labs

labs—Computes the absolute value of a long integer

## SYNOPSIS

```
#include <stdlib.h>
long int labs(long int j);
```

## DESCRIPTION

The labs() function computes the absolute value of the long integer argument *j*.

## RETURN VALUE

Returns the absolute value of the long integer argument.

## CONFORMS TO

SVID 3, BSD 4.3, ISO 9899

## NOTES

Trying to take the absolute value of the most negative integer is not defined.

## SEE ALSO

abs(3), ceil(3), floor(3), fabs(3), rint(3)

# ldexp

ldexp—Multiplies floating-point number by integral power of 2

## SYNOPSIS

```
#include <math.h>
double ldexp(double x, int exp);
```

## DESCRIPTION

The ldexp() function returns the result of multiplying the floating-point number x by 2 raised to the power exp.

## CONFORMS TO

SVID 3, POSIX, BSD 4.3, ISO 9899

## SEE ALSO

frexp(3), modf(3)

# ldiv

ldiv—Computes the quotient and remainder of long integer division

## SYNOPSIS

```
#include <stdlib.h>
ldiv_t ldiv(long int numer, long int denom);
```

## DESCRIPTION

The ldiv() function computes the value numer/denom and returns the quotient and remainder in a structure named ldiv_t that contains two long integer members named quot and rem.

## RETURN VALUE

The ldiv_t structure.

## CONFORMS TO

SVID 3, BSD 4.3, ISO 9899

## SEE ALSO

div(3)

# lgamma

lgamma—Logs gamma function

## SYNOPSIS

```
#include <math.h>
double lgamma(double x);
```

## DESCRIPTION

The lgamma() function returns the log of the absolute value of the Gamma function. The sign of the Gamma function is returned in the external integer *signgam*.

For negative integer values of *x*, lgamma() returns HUGE_VAL, and errno is set to ERANGE.

## ERRORS

ERANGE          Invalid argument—negative integer value of *x*.

## CONFORMS TO

SVID 3, BSD 4.3

## SEE ALSO

infnan(3)

*BSD, 25 June 1993*

# libinn

libinn—InterNetNews library routines

## SYNOPSIS

```
#include "libinn.h"
typedef struct _TIMEINFO {
  time_t time;
  long usec;
  long tzone;
} TIMEINFO;

char *GenerateMessageID()

void HeaderCleanFrom(from)
char *from;

char *HeaderFind(Article, Header, size)
char *Article;
char *Header;
int size;

FILE *CAopen(FromServer, ToServer)
FILE *FromServer;
FILE *ToServer;

FILE *CAlistopen(FromServer, ToServer, request)
FILE *FromServer;
FILE *ToServer;
char *request;
```

```
void CAclose()

struct _DDHANDLE *DDstart(FromServer, ToServer)
FILE *FromServer;
FILE *ToServer;
} DDHANDLE;

void DDcheck(h, group)
DDHANDLE *h;
char *group;

char * DDend(h)
DDHANDLE *h;

void CloseOnExec(fd, flag)
int fd;
int flag;

int SetNonBlocking(fd, flag)
int fd;
int flag;

int LockFile(fd, flag)
int fd;
int flag;

char * GetConfigValue(value)
char *value;

char * GetFileConfigValue(value)
char *value;

char * GetFQDN()

char * GetModeratorAddress(group)
char *group;

int GetResourceUsage(usertime, systime)
double *usertime;
double *systime;

int GetTimeInfo(now)
TIMEINFO *now;

int NNTPlocalopen(FromServerp, ToServerp, errbuff)
FILE **FromServerp;
FILE **ToServerp;
char *errbuff;

int NNTPremoteopen(FromServerp, ToServerp, errbuff)
FILE **FromServerp;
FILE **ToServerp;
char *errbuff;

int NNTPconnect(host, FromServerp, ToServerp, errbuff)
char *host;
FILE **FromServerp;
FILE **ToServerp;
char *errbuff;

int NNTPcheckarticle(text)
```

```
char *text;

int NNTPsendarticle(text, ToServer, Terminate)
char *text;
FILE *ToServer;
int Terminate;

int NNTPsendpassword(server, FromServer, ToServer)
char *server;
FILE *FromServer;
FILE *ToServer;

void Radix32(value, p)
unsigned long value;
char *p;

char * ReadInFile(name, Sbp)
char *name;
struct stat *Sbp;

char * ReadInDescriptor(fd, Sbp)
int fd;
struct stat *Sbp;


char * INNVersion()
```

## DESCRIPTION

libinn is a library of utility routines for manipulating Usenet articles and related data. It is not necessary to use the header file libinn.h; if it is not available, it is only necessary to properly declare the TIMEINFO datatype, as shown in the preceding code.

GenerateMessageID uses the current time, process ID, and fully qualified domain name of the local host to create a Message ID header that is highly likely to be unique. The returned value points to static space that is reused on subsequent calls.

HeaderCleanFrom removes the extraneous information from the value of a From or Reply-To header and leaves just the official mailing address. In particular, the following transformations are made to the *from* parameter:

```
address -> address
address (stuff) -> address
stuff <address>-> address
```

The transformations are simple and are based on RFC 1036, which limits the format of the header.

HeaderFind searches through *Article* looking for the specified *Header*. *size* should be the length of the header name. It returns a pointer to the value of the header, skipping leading whitespace, or NULL if the header cannot be found. *Article* should be a standard C string containing the text of the article; the end of a header is indicated by a blank line: two consecutive \n characters.

CAopen and CAclose provide news clients with access to the active file; the CA stands for Client Active. CAopen opens the active(5) file for reading. It returns a pointer to an open FILE, or NULL on error. If a local or an NFS-mounted copy exists, CAopen will use that file. The *FromServer* and *ToServer* parameters should be FILEs connected to the NNTP server for input and output, respectively. (See the discussions of NNTPremoteopen and NNTPlocalopen later in this section.) If either parameter is NULL, CAopen will just return NULL if the file is not locally available. If neither is NULL, CAopen will use them to query the NNTP server using the "list" command to make a local temporary copy.

The CAlistopen sends a "list" command to the server and returns a temporary file containing the results. The *request* parameter, if not NULL, will be sent as an argument to the command. Unlike CAopen, this routine will never use a locally available copy of the active file.

CAclose closes the active file and removes any temporary file that might have been created by CAopen or CAlistopen.

CloseOnExec can make a descriptor *close-on-exec* so that it is not shared with any child processes. If the flag is nonzero, the file is so marked; if it is 0, the close-on-exec mode is cleared.

DDstart, DDcheck, and DDend are used to set the Distribution header; the DD stands for Default Distribution. The distrib.pats(5) file is consulted to determine the proper value for the Distribution header after all newsgroups have been checked. DDstart begins the parsing. It returns a pointer to an opaque handle that should be used on subsequent calls. The *FromServer* and *ToServer* parameters should be FILEs connected to the NNTP server for input and output, respectively. If either parameter is NULL, an empty default will ultimately be returned if the file is not locally available.

DDcheck should be called with the handle, *h*, returned by DDstart and a new group, *group*, to check. It can be called as often as necessary.

DDend releases any state maintained in the handle and returns an allocated copy of the text that should be used for the Distribution header.

SetNonBlocking enables (if *flag* is nonzero) or disables (if *flag* is 0) non-blocking I/O on the indicated descriptor. It returns -1 on failure and 0 on success.

LockFile tries to lock the file descriptor *fd*. If *flag* is nonzero it will block until the lock can be made; otherwise it will return -1 if the file cannot be locked. It returns -1 on failure and 0 on success.

GetConfigValue returns the value of the specified configuration parameter. (See inn.conf(5) for details on the parameters and their interpretation.) The returned value points to static space that is reused on subsequent calls.

GetFileConfigValue returns the specified configuration parameter from the inn.conf file without checking for any defaults. The returned value points to static space that is reused on subsequent calls, or NULL if the value is not present.

GetFQDN returns the fully qualified domain name of the local host. The returned value points to static space that is reused on subsequent calls, or NULL on error.

GetModeratorAddress returns the mailing address of the moderator for the specified *group* or NULL on error. (See moderators(5) for details on how the address is determined.) GetModeratorAddress does no checking to see if the specified group is actually moderated. The returned value points to static space that is reused on subsequent calls.

GetResourceUsage fills in the *usertime* and *systime* parameters with the total user and system time used by the current process and any children it may have spawned. It gets the values by doing a times(2) system call. It returns -1 on failure, or 0 on success.

GetTimeInfo fills in the *now* parameter with information about the current time and *tzone*. The *time* and *usec* fields will be filled in by a call to gettimeofday(2). The *time* field will be filled in by a call to time(2), and the *usec* field will be set to 0. The *tzone* field will be filled in with the current offset from GMT. This is done by calling localtime(3) and taking the value of the *tm_gmtoff* field, negating it, and dividing it by 60. This is done by calling localtime(3) and comparing the value with that returned by a call to gmtime(3). For efficiency, the *tzone* field is only recalculated if more than an hour has passed since the last time GetTimeInfo was called. This routine returns -1 on failure, and 0 on success.

NNTPlocalopen opens a connection to the private port of an InterNetNews server running on the local host. It returns -1 on failure, or 0 on success. *FromServerp* and *ToServerp* will be filled in with FILEs that can be used to communicate with the server. *errbuff* can either be NULL or a pointer to a buffer at least 512 bytes long. If it is not NULL, and the server refuses the connection, it will be filled in with the text of the server's reply. This routine is not for general use; it is a subroutine for compatibility with systems that have UNIX-domain stream sockets. It always returns -1.

NNTPremoteopen does the same as NNTPlocalopen, except that it calls GetConfigValue to find the name of the local server and opens a connection to the standard NNTP port. Any client program can use this routine. It returns -1 on failure, or 0 on success.

NNTPconnect is the same as NNTPremoteopen, except that the desired host is given as the *host* parameter.

NNTPcheckarticle verifies that the text meets the NNTP limitations on line length. It returns -1 on failure, or 0 if the text is valid.

NNTPsendarticle writes text on *ToServer* using NNTP conventions for line termination. The text should consist of one or more lines ending with a newline. If *Terminate* is nonzero, the routine will also write the NNTP data-termination marker on the stream. It returns -1 on failure, or 0 on success.

NNTPsendpassword sends authentication information to an NNTP server by finding the appropriate entry in the passwd.nntp(5) file. *server* contains the name of the host; GetConfigValue will be used if server is NULL. *FromServer* and *ToServer* should be FILEs that are connected to the server. No action is taken if the specified host is not listed in the password file.

Radix32 converts the number in *value* into a radix-32 string in the buffer pointed to by *p*. The number is split into five-bit pieces, and each piece is converted into a character using the alphabet 0...9a...v to represent the numbers 0–32. Only the lowest 32 bits of *value* are used, so *p* need only point to a buffer of eight bytes (seven characters and the trailing \0).

ReadInFile reads the file named *name* into allocated memory, appending a terminating \0 byte. It returns a pointer to the space, or NULL on error. If *Sbp* is not NULL, it is taken as the address of a place to store the results of a stat(2) call.

ReadInDescriptor performs the same function as ReadInFile, except that fd refers to an already-open file.

INNVersion returns a pointer to a string identifying the INN version, suitable for printing in logon banners.

## EXAMPLES

```
char *p;
char *Article;
char buff[256];
FILE *F;
FILE *ToServer;
FILE *FromServer;
if ((p = HeaderFind(Article, "From", 4)) == NULL)
  Fatal("Can't find From line");
(void)strcpy(buff, p);
HeaderCleanFrom(buff);
if ((F = CAopen(FromServer, ToServer)) == NULL)
  Fatal("Can't open active file");
/* Don't pass the file on to our children. */
CloseOnExec(fileno(F), 1);
/* Make a local copy. */
p = ReadInDescriptor(fileno(F), (struct stat *)NULL);
/* Close the file. */
CAclose();
if (NNTPremoteopen(&FromServer, &ToServer) < 0)
  Fatal("Can't connect to server");
if ((p = GetModeratorAddress("comp.sources.unix")) == NULL)
Fatal("Can't find moderator's address");
```

## HISTORY

Written by Rich $alz (rsalz@uunet.uu.net) for InterNetNews.

## SEE ALSO

active(5), dbz(3z), parsedate(3), inn.conf(5), inndcomm(3), moderators(5), passwd.nntp(5)

*GNU, 30 October 1996*

# libpbm

libpbm—Functions to support portable bitmap programs

## SYNOPSIS

```
#include <pbm.h>
cc ... libpbm.a
```

## DESCRIPTION—PACKAGEWIDE ROUTINES

The following sections describe string and file management routines available in libpbm.

## KEYWORD MATCHING

The following does a case-insensitive match of *str* against *keyword*:

```
int pm_keymatch( char* str, char* keyword, int minchars )
```

*str* can be a leading substring of *keyword*, but at least *minchars* must be present.

## LOG BASE TWO

This converts between a maxval and the minimum number of bits required to hold it:

```
int pm_maxvaltobits(int maxval)
int pm_bitstomaxval(int bits)
```

## MESSAGES AND ERRORS

This is a printf()-style routine to write an informational message:

```
void pm_message(char* fmt, ... )
```

This is a printf() style routine to write an error message and abort:

```
void pm_error(char* fmt, ... )
```

The following writes a usage message; the string should indicate what arguments are to be provided to the program:

```
void pm_usage(char* usage)
```

## GENERIC FILE MANAGEMENT

The following opens the given file for reading, with appropriate error checking:

```
FILE* pm_openr(char* name)
```

A filename of - is taken as equivalent to stdin.

The following opens the given file for writing, with appropriate error checking:

```
FILE* pm_openw(char* name)
```

The following closes the file descriptor, with appropriate error checking:

```
void pm_close(FILE* fp)
```

## ENDIAN I/O

The following are routines to read and write short and long ints in either big- or little-endian byte order:

```
int pm_readbigshort(FILE* in, short* sP)
int pm_writebigshort(FILE* out, short s)
int pm_readbiglong(FILE* in, long* lP)
int pm_writebiglong(FILE* out, long l)
int pm_readlittleshort(FILE* in, short* sP)
int pm_writelittleshort(FILE* out, short s)
int pm_readlittlelong(FILE* in, long* lP)
int pm_writelittlelong(FILE* out, long l)
```

## DESCRIPTION—PBM-SPECIFIC ROUTINES

The following sections describe file management routines available in libpbm.

## TYPES AND CONSTANTS

Each bit should contain only the values of PBM_WHITE or PBM_BLACK:

```
typedef ... bit;
#define PBM_WHITE ...
#define PBM_BLACK ...
```

These are routines for distinguishing different file formats and types:

```
#define PBM_FORMAT ...
#define RPBM_FORMAT ...
#define PBM_TYPE PBM_FORMAT
#define PBM_FORMAT TYPE(f) ...
```

## INITIALIZATION

All PBM programs must call this routine:

```
void pbm_init(int* argcP, char* argv[] )
```

## MEMORY MANAGEMENT

This allocates an array of bits:

```
bit** pbm_allocarray(int cols, int rows)
```

This allocates a row of the given number of bits:

```
bit* pbm_allocrow(int cols)
```

This frees the array allocated with pbm_allocarray() containing the given number of rows:

```
void pbm_freearray(bit** bits, int rows)
```

This frees a row of bits:

```
void pbm_freerow(bit* bitrow)
```

## READING FILES

This reads the header from a PBM file, filling in the *rows*, *cols*, and *format* variables:

```
void pbm_readpbminit(FILE* fp, int* colsP, int* rowsP, int* formatP)
```

This reads a row of bits into the *bitrow* array (*format* and *cols* are filled in by pbm_readpbminit()):

```
void pbm_readpbmrow(FILE* fp, bit* bitrow, int cols, int format)
```

This function combines pbm_readpbminit(), pbm_allocarray(), and pbm_readpbmrow():

```
bit** pbm_readpbm(FILE* fp, int* colsP, int* rowsP)
```

It reads an entire bitmap file into memory, returning the allocated array and filling in the *rows* and *cols* variables.

This reads an entire file or input stream of unknown size to a buffer and allocates more memory as needed:

```
char* pm_read unknown size(FILE* fp, long* nread)
```

The calling routine has to free the allocated buffer with free(). pm_read_unknown_size() returns a pointer to the allocated buffer; the *nread* argument returns the number of bytes read.

## WRITING FILES

This writes the header for a portable bitmap file:

```
void pbm_writepbminit(FILE* fp, int cols, int rows, int forceplain)
```

The *forceplain* flag forces a plain-format file to be written, as opposed to a raw-format one.

This writes a row from a portable bitmap:

```
void pbm_writepbmrow(FILE* fp, bit* bitrow, int cols, int forceplain)
```

This writes the header and all data for a portable bitmap:

```
void pbm_writepbm(FILE* fp, bit** bits, int cols, int rows, int forceplain)
```

This function combines pbm_writepbminit() and pbm_writepbmrow().

## SEE ALSO

libpgm(3), libppm(3), libpnm(3)

## AUTHOR

Copyright © 1989, 1991 by Tony Hansen and Jef Poskanzer

# libpgm

libpgm—Functions to support portable graymap programs

## SYNOPSIS

```
#include <pgm.h>
cc ... libpgm.a libpbm.a
```

## DESCRIPTION

The following sections describe memory and file management routines available in libpgm.

## TYPES AND CONSTANTS

Each *gray* should contain only the values between 0 and PGM_MAXMAXVAL.

pgm_pbmmaxval is the *maxval* used when a PGM program reads a PBM file. Normally it is 1, but for some programs, a larger value gives better results.

```
typedef ... gray;
#define PGM_MAXMAXVAL ...
extern gray pgm_pbmmaxval;
```

The following are for distinguishing different file formats and types:

```
#define PGM_FORMAT ...
#define RPGM_FORMAT ...
#define PGM_TYPE PGM_FORMAT
int PGM_FORMAT_TYPE(int format)
```

## INITIALIZATION

All PGM programs must call this routine:

```
void pgm_init(int* argcP, char* argv[])
```

## MEMORY MANAGEMENT

This allocates an array of grays:

```
gray** pgm_allocarray(int cols, int rows)
```

This allocates a row of the given number of grays:

```
gray* pgm_allocrow(int cols)
```

This frees the array allocated with pgm_allocarray() containing the given number of rows:

```
void pgm_freearray(gray** grays, int rows)
```

This frees a row of grays:

```
void pgm_freerow(gray* grayrow)
```

## READING FILES

This reads the header from a PGM file, filling in the *rows, cols, maxval,* and *format* variables:

```
void pgm_readpgminit(FILE* fp, int* colsP, int* rowsP, gray* maxvalP,
int* formatP)
```

This reads a row of grays into the grayrow array. *format, cols,* and *maxval* are filled in by pgm_readpgminit():

```
void pgm_readpgmrow(FILE* fp, gray* grayrow, int cols, gray maxval, int format)
```

This function combines pgm_readpgminit(), pgm_allocarray(), and pgm_readpgmrow():

```
gray** pgm_readpgm(FILE* fp, int* colsP, int* rowsP, gray* maxvalP)
```

It reads an entire graymap file into memory, returning the allocated array and filling in the *rows, cols,* and *maxval* variables.

## WRITING FILES

This writes the header for a portable graymap file:

```
void pgm_writepgminit( FILE* fp, int cols, int rows, gray  maxval,
int forceplain )
```

The *forceplain* flag forces a plain-format file to be written, as opposed to a raw-format one.

This writes a row from a portable graymap:

```
void pgm_writepgmrow(FILE* fp, gray* grayrow, int cols, gray  maxval,
int forceplain)
```

This function combines pgm_writepgminit() and pgm_writepgmrow(); it writes the header and all data for a portable graymap:

```
void pgm_writepgm( FILE* fp, gray** grays, int cols, int rows, gray  maxval, int forceplain)
```

## SEE ALSO

libpbm(3), libppm(3), libpnm(3)

## AUTHOR

Copyright © 1989, 1991 by Tony Hansen and Jef Poskanzer.

# libpnm

libpnm—Functions to support portable anymap programs

## SYNOPSIS

```
#include <pnm.h>
cc ... libpnm.a libppm.a libpgm.a libpbm.a
```

## DESCRIPTION

The following sections describe memory and file management routines available in libpnm.

## TYPES AND CONSTANTS

Each xel contains three xelvals, each of which should contain only a value between 0 and PNM_MAXMAXVAL. pnm_pbmmaxval is the maxval used when a PNM program reads a PBM file. Normally it is 1, but for some programs, a larger value gives better results.

```
typedef ... xel;
typedef ... xelval;
#define PNM_MAXMAXVAL ...
extern xelval pnm_pbmmaxval;
```

## XEL MANIPULATIONS

This macro extracts a single value from an xel when you know it's from a PBM or PGM file:

`xelval PNM_GET1( xel x )`

When the xel is from a PPM file, use `PPM_GETR()`, `PPM_GETG()`, and `PPM GETB()`.

This macro assigns a single value to an xel when you know it's from a PBM or PGM file:

`void PNM_ASSIGN1( xel x, xelval v )`

When the xel is from a PPM file, use `PPM_ASSIGN()`.

This macro checks two xels for equality:

`int PNM_EQUAL( xel x, xel y )`

This one is for distinguishing different file types:

`int PNM_FORMAT TYPE( int format )`

## INITIALIZATION

All PNM programs must call this routine:

`void pnm_init( int* argcP, char* argv[] )`

## MEMORY MANAGEMENT

This allocates an array of xels:

`xel** pnm_allocarray( int cols, int rows )`

This allocates a row of the given number of xels:

`xel* pnm_allocrow( int cols )`

This frees the array allocated with pnm_allocarray() that contains the given number of rows:

`void pnm_freearray( xel** xels, int rows )`

This frees a row of xels:

`void pnm_freerow( xel* xelrow )`

## READING FILES

This reads the header from a PNM file, filling in the rows, cols, maxval, and format variables:

`void pnm_readpnminit( FILE* fp, int* colsP, int* rowsP, xelval* maxvalP, int* formatP )`

This reads a row of xels into the xelrow array. format, cols, and maxval are filled in by pnm_readpnminit():

`void pnm_readpnmrow( FILE* fp, xel* xelrow, int cols, xelval maxval, int format )`

This reads an entire anymap file into memory, returning the allocated array and filling in the rows, cols, maxval, and format variables:

`xel** pnm_readpnm( FILE* fp, int* colsP, int* rowsP, xelval* maxvalP, int* formatP )`

This function combines pnm_readpnminit(), pnm_allocarray(), and pnm_readpnmrow(). Unlike the equivalent functions in PBM, PGM, and PPM, it returns the format so you can tell what type the file is.

## WRITING FILES

This writes the header for a portable anymap file:

`void pnm_writepnminit( FILE* fp, int cols, int rows, xelval maxval, int format, int force-plain)`

Unlike the equivalent functions in PBM, PGM, and PPM, you have to specify the output type. The `forceplain` flag forces a plain-format file to be written, as opposed to a raw-format one.

This writes a row from a portable anymap:

```
void pnm_writepnmrow( FILE* fp, xel* xelrow, int cols, xelval maxval, int format,
int forceplain )
```

This writes the header and all data for a portable anymap:

```
void pnm writepnm( FILE* fp, xel** xels, int cols, int rows, xelval maxval, int format,
int forceplain )
```

This function combines pnm_writepnminit() and pnm_writepnmrow().

## FORMAT PROMOTION

This promotes a row of xels from one maxval and format to a new set:

```
void pnm_promoteformatrow( xel* xelrow, int cols, xelval maxval, int format, xelval new-maxval,
int newformat )
```

Use this when combining multiple anymaps of different types—just take the maximum value of the maxvals and the max of the formats, and promote them all to that.

This promotes an entire anymap:

```
void pnm_promoteformat( xel** xels, int cols, int rows, xelval maxval,
int format, xelval newmaxval, int newformat )
```

## XEL MANIPULATION

These return a white or black xel, respectively, for the given maxval and format:

```
xel pnm_whitexel( xelval maxval, int format )
xel pnm_blackxel( xelval maxval, int format )
```

This inverts an xel:

```
void pnm_invertxel( xel* x, xelval maxval, int format )
```

This figures out an appropriate background xel based on this row:

```
xel pnm_backgroundxelrow( xel* xelrow, int cols, xelval maxval, int format )
```

This figures out a background xel based on an entire anymap:

```
xel pnm_backgroundxel( xel** xels, int cols, int rows, xelval maxval,
int format )
```

This can do a slightly better job than pnm_backgroundxelrow().

## SEE ALSO

pbm(3), pgm(3), ppm(3)

## AUTHOR

Copyright © 1989, 1991 by Tony Hansen and Jef Poskanzer.

# libppm

libppm—Functions to support portable pixmap programs

## SYNOPSIS

```
#include <ppm.h>
cc ... libppm.a libpgm.a libpbm.a
```

## TYPES AND CONSTANTS

```
typedef ... pixel;
typedef ... pixval;
#define PPM_MAXMAXVAL ...
extern pixval ppm_pbmmaxval;
```

Each pixel contains three pixvals, each of which should contain only the values between 0 and PPM_MAXMAXVAL. ppm_pbmmaxval is the maxval used when a PPM program reads a PBM file. Normally it is 1; however, for some programs, a larger value gives better results.

For distinguishing different file formats and types, use

```
#define PPM_FORMAT ...
#define RPPM_FORMAT ...
#define PPM_TYPE PPM_FORMAT
int PPM_FORMAT_TYPE( int format )
```

These three macros retrieve the red, green, or blue value from the given pixel:

```
pixval PPM_GETR( pixel p )
pixval PPM_GETG( pixel p )
pixval PPM_GETB( pixel p )
```

This macro assigns the given red, green, and blue values to the pixel:

```
void PPM_ASSIGN( pixel p, pixval red, pixval grn, pixval blu )
```

This macro checks two pixels for equality:

```
int PPM_EQUAL( pixel p, pixel q )
```

The following macro scales the colors of pixel p according the old and new maximum values and assigns the new values to newp. It is intended to make writing ppm to whatever easier.

```
void PPM_DEPTH( pixel newp, pixel p, pixval oldmaxval, pixval newmaxval )
```

This macro determines the luminance of the pixel p:

```
float PPM_LUMIN( pixel p )
```

## MEMORY MANAGEMENT

Allocate an array of pixels:

```
pixel** ppm_allocarray( int cols, int rows )
```

Allocate a row of the given number of pixels:

```
pixel* ppm_allocrow( int cols )
```

Free the array allocated with ppm_allocarray() containing the given number of rows:

```
void ppm_freearray( pixel** pixels, int rows )
```

Free a row of pixels:

```
void pbm_freerow( pixel* pixelrow )
```

## READING PBM FILES

```
void ppm_readppminit( FILE* fp, int* colsP, int* rowsP, pixval* maxvalP, int* formatP )
```

Read the header from a PPM file, filling in the rows, cols, maxval, and format variables.

```
void ppm_readppmrow( FILE* fp, pixel* pixelrow, int cols, pixval maxval, int format )
```

Read a row of pixels into the pixelrow array. Format, cols, and maxval were filled in by ppm readppminit().

```
pixel** ppm_readppm( FILE* fp, int* colsP, int* rowsP, pixval* maxvalP )
```

Read an entire pixmap file into memory, returning the allocated array and filling in the rows, cols, and maxval variables. This function combines ppm_readppminit(), ppm_allocarray(), and ppm_readppmrow().

## WRITING FILES

```
void ppm_writeppminit( FILE* fp, int cols, int rows, pixval maxval, int forceplain )
```

Write the header for a portable pixmap file. The forceplain flag forces a plain-format file to be written, as opposed to a raw-format one.

```
void ppm_writeppmrow( FILE* fp, pixel* pixelrow, int cols, pixval maxval, int forceplain)
```

Write a row from a portable pixmap.

```
void ppm_writeppm( FILE* fp, pixel** pixels, int cols, int rows, pixval maxval, int force-plain)
```

Write the header and all data for a portable pixmap. This function combines ppm_writeppminit() and ppm_writeppmrow().

## COLOR NAMES

This line parses an ASCII color name into a pixel:

```
pixel ppm_parsecolor( char* colorname, pixval maxval )
```

The color can be specified in three ways: as a name, assuming that a pointer to an X11-style color names file was compiled in; as an X11-style hexadecimal number (#rgb, #rrggbb, #rrrgggbbb, or #rrrrggggbbbb); or as a triplet of decimal floating point numbers separated by commas (r.r,g.g,b.b).

This line returns a pointer to a string describing the given color:

```
char* ppm_colorname( pixel* colorP, pixval maxval, int hexok )
```

If the X11 color names file is available and the color appears in it, that name is returned. Otherwise, if the hexok flag is true, then a hexadecimal colorspec is returned; if hexok is false and the X11 color names file is available, then the closest matching color is returned; otherwise, it's an error.

## SEE ALSO

pbm(3), pgm(3)

## AUTHOR

Copyright © 1989, 1991 by Tony Hansen and Jef Poskanzer

# localeconv

localeconv—Gets numeric formatting information

## SYNOPSIS

```
#include <locale.h>
struct lconv *localeconf(void);
```

## DESCRIPTION

The localeconf() function returns a string to a struct lconv for the current locale.

## CONFORMS TO

This command conforms to ANSI C and POSIX.1.

Linux supports the portable locales C and POSIX and also the European Latin-1 ISO-8859-1, and Russian KOI-8 locales.

The printf() family of functions may or may not honor the current locale.

## SEE ALSO

locale(1), localedef(1), strcoll(3), isalpha(3), setlocale(3), strftime(3), locale(7)

*GNU, 25 April 1993*

# longjmp

longjmp—Nonlocal jump to a saved stack context

## SYNOPSIS

```
#include <setjmp.h>
void longjmp(jmp_buf env,int val);
```

## DESCRIPTION

longjmp() and setjmp(3) are useful for dealing with errors and interrupts encountered in a low-level subroutine of a program. longjmp() restores the environment saved by the last call of setjmp() with the corresponding env argument. After longjmp() is completed, program execution continues as if the corresponding call of setjmp() had just returned the value val. longjmp() cannot cause 0 to be returned. If longjmp is invoked with a second argument of 0, 1 will be returned instead.

## RETURN VALUE

This function never returns.

## CONFORMS TO

POSIX

## NOTES

POSIX does not specify if the signal context will be restored or not. If you want to save restore signal masks, use siglongjmp(3). longjmp() makes programs hard to understand and maintain. If possible, an alternative should be used.

## SEE ALSO

setjmp(3), sigsetjmp(2), siglongjmp(2)

*25 November 1994*

# lfind, lsearch

lfind, lsearch—Linear search of an array

## SYNOPSIS

```
#include <stdlib.h>
void *lfind(const void *key, const void *base, size t *nmemb,
```

```
size_t size,int(*compar)(const void *, const void *));
void *lsearch(const void *key, const void *base, size_t *nmemb,
size_t size,int(*compar)(const void *, const void *));
```

## DESCRIPTION

lfind() and lsearch() perform a linear search for key in the array base, which has *nmemb elements of size bytes each. The comparison function referenced by compar is expected to have two arguments that point to the key object and to an array member, in that order, and which returns zero if the key object matches the array member, and non-zero otherwise.

If lsearch() does not find a matching element, then the key object is inserted at the end of the table, and *nmemb is incremented.

## RETURN VALUE

lfind() returns a pointer to a matching member of the array, or NULL if no match is found. lsearch() returns a pointer to a matching member of the array, or to the newly added member if no match is found.

## CONFORMS TO

SVID 3, BSD 4.3, ISO 9899

## SEE ALSO

bsearch(3), hsearch(3), tsearch(3)

*GNU, 17 September 1995*

# calloc, malloc, free, realloc

calloc, malloc, free, realloc—Allocate and free dynamic memory

## SYNOPSIS

```
#include <stdlib.h>
void *calloc(size_t nmemb, size_t size);
void *malloc(size_t size);
void free(void *ptr);
void *realloc(void *ptr, size_t size);
```

## DESCRIPTION

calloc() allocates memory for an array of nmemb elements of size bytes each and returns a pointer to the allocated memory. The memory is set to zero.

malloc() allocates size bytes and returns a pointer to the allocated memory. The memory is not cleared.

free() frees the memory space pointed to by ptr, which must have been returned by a previous call to malloc(), calloc() or realloc(). If ptr is NULL, no operation is performed.

realloc() changes the size of the memory block pointed to by ptr to size bytes. The contents will be unchanged to the minimum of the old and new sizes; newly allocated memory will be uninitialized. If ptr is NULL, the call is equivalent to malloc(size); if size is equal to zero, the call is equivalent to free(ptr). Unless ptr is NULL, it must have been returned by an earlier call to malloc(), calloc(), or realloc().

## RETURN VALUES

For calloc() and malloc(), the value returned is a pointer to the allocated memory, which is suitably aligned for any kind of variable, or NULL if the request fails.

free() returns no value.

realloc()returns a pointer to the newly allocated memory, which is suitably aligned for any kind of variable and may be different from ptr, or NULL if the request fails or if size was equal to 0. If realloc() fails, the original block is left untouched; it is not freed or moved.

## CONFORMS TO

ANSI C

## SEE ALSO

brk(2)

*GNU, 4 April 1993*

# mblen

mblen—Determines the number of bytes in a character

## SYNOPSIS

```
#include <stdlib.h>
int_mblen(const char *s, size_t n);
```

## DESCRIPTION

The mblen() function scans the first *n* bytes of the string *s* and returns the number of bytes in a character. The mblen() function is equivalent to

```
mbtowc((wchat t*)0,s,n);
```

except that the shift state of the mbtowc() function is not affected.

## RETURN VALUE

The mblen()returns the number of bytes in a character, or -1 if the character is invalid, or 0 if it is a NULL string.

## CONFORMS TO

SVID 3, ISO 9899

## SEE ALSO

mbstowcs(3), mbtowc(3), wcstombs(3), wctomb(3)

*GNU, 29 March 1993*

# mbstowcs

mbstowcs—Converts a multibyte string to a wide character string

## SYNOPSIS

```
#include <stdlib.h>
size_t mbstowcs(wchar_t *pwcs, const char *s, size_t n);
```

## DESCRIPTION

The mbstowcs() function converts a sequence of multibyte characters from the array *s* into a sequence of wide characters and stores up to *n* wide characters in the array *pwcs*.

## RETURN VALUE

mbstowcs() returns the number of wide characters stored, or -1 if s contains an invalid multibyte character.

## CONFORMS TO

SVID 3, ISO 9899

## SEE ALSO

mblen(3), mbtowc(3), wcstombs(3), wctomb(3)

*GNU, 29 March 1993*

# mbtowc

mbtowc—Converts a multibyte character to a wide character

## SYNOPSIS

```
#include <stdlib.h>
int mbtowc(wchar_t *pwc, const char *s, size_t n);
```

## DESCRIPTION

The mbtowc() function converts a multibyte character s, which is no longer than n bytes, into a wide character and, if pwc is not NULL, stores the wide character in pwc.

## RETURN VALUE

mbtowc() returns the number of bytes in the multibyte character, or -1 if the multibyte character is not valid.

## CONFORMS TO

SVID 3, ISO 9899

## SEE ALSO

mblen(3), mbstowcs(3), wcstombs(3), wctomb(3)

*GNU, 29 March 1993*

# memccpy.

memccpy—Copies memory area

## SYNOPSIS

```
#include <string.h>
void *memccpy(void *dest, const void *src,int c, size_t n);
```

## DESCRIPTION

The memccpy() function copies no more than n bytes from memory area src to memory area dest, stopping when the character c is found.

## RETURN VALUE

The memccpy() function returns a pointer to the next character in dest after c, or NULL if c was not found in the first n characters of src.

## CONFORMS TO

SVID 3, BSD 4.3

## SEE ALSO

bcopy(3), memcpy(3), memmove(3), strcpy(3), strncpy(3)

# memchr

memchr—Scans memory for a character

## SYNOPSIS

```
#include <string.h>
void *memchr(const void *s,int c, size_t n);
```

## DESCRIPTION

The memchr() function scans the first *n* bytes of the memory area pointed to by *s* for the character *c*. The first byte to match *c* (interpreted as an unsigned character) stops the operation.

## RETURN VALUE

The memchr() function returns a pointer to the matching byte or NULL if the character does not occur in the given memory area.

## CONFORMS TO

SVID 3, BSD 4.3, ISO 9899

## SEE ALSO

index(3), rindex(3), strchr(3), strpbrk(3), strrchr(3), strsep(3), strspn(3), strstr(3)

# memcmp

memcmp—Compares memory areas

## SYNOPSIS

```
#include <string.h>
int memcmp(const void *s1, const void *s2, size_t n);
```

## DESCRIPTION

The memcmp() function compares the first *n* bytes of the memory areas *s1* and *s2*. It returns an integer less than, equal to, or greater than zero if *s1* is found, respectively, to be less than, to match, or to be greater than *s2*.

## RETURN VALUE

The memcmp() function returns an integer less than, equal to, or greater than zero if the first *n* bytes of *s1* is found, respectively, to be less than, to match, or be greater than the first *n* bytes of *s2*.

## CONFORMS TO

SVID 3, BSD 4.3, ISO 9899

## SEE ALSO

bcmp(3), strcasecmp(3), strcmp(3), strcoll(3), strncmp(3), strncasecmp(3)

*10 April 1993*

# memcpy

memcpy—Copies memory area

## SYNOPSIS

```
#include <string.h>
void *memcpy(void *dest, const void *src, size_t n);
```

## DESCRIPTION

The memcpy() function copies *n* bytes from memory area *src* to memory area *dest*. The memory areas may not overlap. Use memmove(3) if the memory areas do overlap.

## RETURN VALUE

The memcpy() function returns a pointer to *dest*.

## CONFORMS TO

SVID 3, BSD 4.3, ISO 9899

## SEE ALSO

bcopy(3), memccpy(3), memmove(3), strcpy(3), strncpy(3)

*GNU, 10 April 1993*

# memfrob

memfrob—Frobnicates (encrypts) a memory area

## SYNOPSIS

```
#include <string.h>
void *memfrob(void *s, size_t n);
```

## DESCRIPTION

The memfrob() function encrypts the first *n* bytes of the memory area *s* by using exclusive OR on each character with the number 42. The effect can be reversed by using memfrob() on the encrypted memory area.

Note that this function is not a proper encryption routine as the XOR constant is fixed, and is only suitable for hiding strings.

## RETURN VALUE

The memfrob() function returns a pointer to the encrypted memory area.

## CONFORMS TO

The `memfrob()` function is unique to the Linux C Library and GNU C Library.

## SEE ALSO

`strfry(3)`

# memmem

`memmem`—Locates a substring

## SYNOPSIS

```
#include <string.h>
void *memmem(const void *needle, size_t needlelen,
const void *haystack, size_t haystacklen");"
```

## DESCRIPTION

The `memmem()` function finds the first occurrence of the substring `needle` of length `needlelen` in the memory area `haystack` of length `haystacklen`.

## RETURN VALUE

The `memmem()` function returns a pointer to the beginning of the substring, or `NULL` if the substring is not found.

## SEE ALSO

`strstr(3)`

# memmove

`memmove`—Copies memory area

## SYNOPSIS

```
#include <string.h>
void *memmove(void *dest, const void *src, size_t n);
```

## DESCRIPTION

The `memmove()` function copies *n* bytes from memory area `src` to memory area `dest`. The memory areas may overlap.

## RETURN VALUE

The `memmove()` function returns a pointer to `dest`.

## CONFORMS TO

SVID 3, BSD 4.3, ISO 9899

## SEE ALSO

`bcopy(3)`, `memccpy(3)`, `memcpy(3)`, `strcpy(3)`, `strncpy(3)`

# memset

`memset`—Fills memory with a constant byte

## SYNOPSIS

```
#include <string.h>
void *memset(void *s,int c, size_t n);
```

## DESCRIPTION

The `memset()` function fills the first *n* bytes of the memory area pointed to be *s* with the constant byte *c*.

## RETURN VALUE

The `memset()` function returns a pointer to the memory area *s*.

## CONFORMS TO

SVID 3, BSD 4.3, ISO 9899

## SEE ALSO

`bzero(3)`, `swab(3)`

*GNU, 11 April 1993*

# mkfifo

`mkfifo`—Makes a FIFO special file (a named pipe)

## SYNOPSIS

```
#include <sys/types.h>
#include <sys/stat.h>
int mkfifo ( const char *pathname,mode_t mode );
```

## DESCRIPTION

`mkfifo` makes a FIFO special file with name *pathname*. `mode` specifies the FIFO's permissions. It is modified by the process's umask in the usual way: the permissions of the created file are (mode&umask).

A FIFO special file is similar to a pipe, except that it is created in a different way. Instead of being an anonymous communications channel, a FIFO special file is entered into the filesystem by calling `mkfifo`.

After you have created a FIFO special file in this way, any process can open it for reading or writing, in the same way as an ordinary file. However, it has to be open at both ends simultaneously before you can proceed to do any input or output operations on it. Opening a FIFO for reading normally blocks until some other process opens the same FIFO for writing, and vice versa.

## RETURN VALUE

The normal, successful return value from `mkfifo` is 0. In the case of an error, -1 is returned (in which case, errno is set appropriately).

## ERRORS

| | |
|---|---|
| EACCES | One of the directories in `pathname` did not allow search (execute) permission. |
| EEXIST | `pathname` already exists. |

| | |
|---|---|
| ENAMETOOLONG | Either the total length of `pathname` is greater than `PATH_MAX`, or an individual filename component has a length greater than `NAME_MAX`. In the GNU system, there is no imposed limit on overall filename length, but some filesystems may place limits on the length of a component. |
| ENOENT | A directory component in `pathname` does not exist or is a dangling symbolic link. |
| ENOSPC | The directory or filesystem has no room for the new file. |
| ENOTDIR | A component used as a directory in `pathname` is not, in fact, a directory. |
| EROFS | `pathname` refers to a read-only filesystem. |

## CONFORMS TO

POSIX.1

## SEE ALSO

mkfifo(1), read(2), write(2), open(2), close(2), stat(2), umask(2)

*Linux 1.2.13, 3 September 1995*

# mkstemp

mkstemp—Creates a unique temporary file

## SYNOPSIS

```
#include <unistd.h>
int *mkstemp(char *template);
```

## DESCRIPTION

The mkstemp() function generates a unique temporary filename from *template*. The last six characters of *template* must be XXXXXX and these are replaced with a string that makes the filename unique. The file is then created with mode read/write and permissions 0666.

## RETURN VALUE

The mkstemp() function returns the file descriptor fd of the temporary file.

## ERRORS

| | |
|---|---|
| EINVAL | The last six characters of *template* were not XXXXXX. |
| EEXIST | The temporary file is not unique. |

## CONFORMS TO

BSD 4.3

## SEE ALSO

mktemp(3), tmpnam(3), tempnam(3), tmpfile(3)

*GNU, 3 April 1993*

# mktemp

mktemp—Makes a unique temporary filename

## SYNOPSIS

```
#include <unistd.h>
char *mktemp(char *template);
```

## DESCRIPTION

The mktemp() function generates a unique temporary filename from *template*. The last six characters of *template* must be XXXXXX and these are replaced with a string that makes the filename unique.

## RETURN VALUE

The mktemp() function returns a pointer to *template* on success, and NULL on failure.

## ERRORS

EINVAL                       The last six characters of template were not XXXXXX.

## CONFORMS TO

BSD 4.3. POSIX dictates tmpnam().

## SEE ALSO

mkstemp(3), tmpnam(3), tempnam(3), tmpfile(3)

*GNU, 3 April 1993*

# modf

modf—Extracts signed integral and fractional values from floating-point number

## SYNOPSIS

```
#include <math.h>
double modf(double x, double *iptr);
```

## DESCRIPTION

The modf() function breaks the argument *x* into an integral part and a fractional part, each of which has the same sign as *x*. The integral part is stored in *iptr*.

## RETURN VALUE

The modf() function returns the fractional part of *x*.

## CONFORMS TO

SVID 3, POSIX, BSD 4.3, ISO 9899

## SEE ALSO

frexp(3), ldexp(3)

*6 June 1993*

# asctime, ctime, difftime, gmtime, localtime, mktime

asctime, ctime, difftime, gmtime, localtime, mktime—Convert date and time to ASCII

## SYNOPSIS

```
extern char *tzname[2];

void tzset()

#include <sys/types.h>

char *ctime(clock)
const time_t *clock;

double difftime(time1, time0)
time_t time1;
time_t time0;

#include <time.h>

char *asctime(tm)
const struct tm *tm;

struct tm *localtime(clock)
const time_t *clock;

struct tm *gmtime(clock)
const time_t *clock;

time_t mktime(tm)
struct tm *tm;

cc ... -lz
```

## DESCRIPTION

ctime converts a long integer, pointed to by clock, representing the time in seconds since 00:00:00 UTC, January 1, 1970, and returns a pointer to a 26-character string of the form Thu Nov 24 18:22:48 1986. (Note: UTC is Coordinated Universal Time.) All the fields have constant width.

localtime and gmtime return pointers to tm structures, described in the following paragraphs. localtime corrects for the time zone and any time zone adjustments (such as Daylight Saving Time in the United States). Before doing so, localtime calls tzset (if tzset has not been called in the current process). After filling in the tm structure, localtime sets the tm_isdst'th element of tzname to a pointer to an ASCII string that's the time zone abbreviation to be used with localtime's return value.

gmtime converts to Coordinated Universal Time.

asctime converts a time value contained in a tm structure to a 26-character string, as shown in the preceding example, and returns a pointer to the string.

mktime converts the broken-down time, expressed as local time, in the structure pointed to by tm into a calendar time value with the same encoding as that of the values returned by the time function. The original values of the tm_wday and tm_yday components of the structure are ignored, and the original values of the other components are not restricted to their normal ranges. (A positive or zero value for tm_isdst causes mktime to presume initially that summer time (for example, Daylight Saving Time in the United States) respectively, is or is not in effect for the specified time. A negative value for tm_isdst causes the mktime function to attempt to divine whether summer time is in effect for the specified time.) On successful completion, the values of the tm_wday and tm_yday components of the structure are set appropriately, and the other components are set to represent the specified calendar time, but with their values forced to their normal ranges; the final value of tm_mday is not set until tm_mon and tm_year are determined. mktime returns the specified calendar time; if the calendar time cannot be represented, it returns -1.

`difftime` returns the difference between two calendar times, (*time1* - *time0*), expressed in seconds.

Declarations of all the functions and externals, and the tm structure, are in the `<time.h>` header file. The structure (of type) struct tm includes the following fields:

```
int tm_sec;    / seconds (0 - 60) /
int tm_min;    / minutes (0 - 59) /
int tm_hour;   / hours (0 - 23) /
int tm_mday;   / day of month (1 - 31) /
int tm_mon;    / month of year (0 - 11) /
int tm_year;   / year - 1900 /
int tm_wday;   / day of week (Sunday = 0) /
int tm_yday;   / day of year (0 - 365) /
int tm_isdst;  / is summer time in effect? /
char tm_zone;  / abbreviation of timezone name /
long tm_gmtoff; / offset from UTC in seconds /
```

The tm_zone and tm_gmtoff fields exist, and are filled in, only if arrangements to do so were made when the library containing these functions was created. There is no guarantee that these fields will continue to exist in this form in future releases of this code.

Tm_isdst is non-zero if summer time is in effect.

Tm_gmtoff is the offset (in seconds) of the time represented from UTC, with positive values indicating east of the Prime Meridian.

## FILES

| | |
|---|---|
| /usr/local/etc/zoneinfo | Time zone information directory |
| /usr/local/etc/zoneinfo/localtime | Local time zone file |
| /usr/local/etc/zoneinfo/posixrules | Used with POSIX-style TZs |
| /usr/local/etc/zoneinfo/GMT | For UTC leap seconds |

If /usr/local/etc/zoneinfo/GMT is absent, UTC leap seconds are loaded from /usr/local/etc/zoneinfo/posixrules.

## SEE ALSO

getenv(3), newtzset(3), time(2), tzfile(5)

## NOTES

The return values point to static data; the data is overwritten by each call. The tm_zone field of a returned struct tm points to a static array of characters, which will also be overwritten at the next call (and by calls to tzset).

Avoid using out-of-range values with mktime when setting up lunch with promptness sticklers in Riyadh.

# tzset

tzset—Initializes time conversion information

## SYNOPSIS

```
void tzset();
cc ... -lz
```

## DESCRIPTION

tzset uses the value of the environment variable TZ to set time conversion information used by localtime. If TZ does not appear in the environment, the best available approximation to local wall clock time, as specified by the tzfile(5)-format file localtime in the system time conversion information directory, is used by localtime. If TZ appears in the environment but its value is a null string, Coordinated Universal Time (UTC) is used (without leap second correction). If TZ appears in the environment and its value is not a null string, it is used in one of the following ways:

If the value begins with a colon, it is used as a pathname of a file from which to read the time conversion information.

If the value does not begin with a colon, it is first used as the pathname of a file from which to read the time conversion information, and, if that file cannot be read, is used directly as a specification of the time conversion information.

When TZ is used as a pathname, if it begins with a slash, it is used as an absolute pathname; otherwise, it is used as a pathname relative to a system time conversion information directory. The file must be in the format specified in tzfile(5).

When TZ is used directly as a specification of the time conversion information, it must have the following syntax (spaces inserted for clarity):

```
std offset[dst[offset][,rule]]
```

The elements are as follows:

| | |
|---|---|
| *std* and *dst* | Three or more bytes that are the designation for the standard (*std*) or summer (*dst*) time zone. Only *std* is required; if *dst* is missing, then summer time does not apply in this locale. Uppercase and lowercase letters are explicitly allowed. Any characters except a leading colon (:), digits, comma (,), minus (-), plus (+), and ASCII NUL are allowed. |
| *offset* | Indicates the value one must add to the local time to arrive at Coordinated Universal Time. The *offset* has the form: |
| | `hh[:mm[:ss]]` |
| | The minutes (*mm*) and seconds (*ss*) are optional. The hour (*hh*) is required and may be a single digit. The *offset* following *std* is required. If no *offset* follows *dst*, summer time is assumed to be one hour ahead of standard time. One or more digits may be used; the value is always interpreted as a decimal number. The hour must be between zero and 24, and the minutes (and seconds)—if present—between zero and 59. If preceded by a "+", the time zone shall be east of the Prime Meridian; otherwise, it shall be west (which may be indicated by an optional preceding "-"). |
| *rule* | Indicates when to change to and back from summer time. The *rule* has the form: |
| | `date/time,date/time` |
| | where the first *date* describes when the change from standard to summer time occurs and the second *date* describes when the change back happens. Each *time* field describes when, in current local time, the change to the other time is made. |
| | The format of *date* is one of the following: |
| | The *d*'th day (0 <= d <= 6) of week *n* of month *m* of the year (1 <= n <= 5, 1 <= m <= 12, where week 5 means "the last *d* day in month *m*" which may occur in either the fourth or the fifth week). Week 1 is the first week in which the *d*'th day occurs. Day zero is Sunday. |
| *Jn* | The Julian day *n* (1 <= n <= 365). Leap days are not counted; that is, in all years—including leap years—February 28 is day 59 and March 1 is day 60. It is impossible to explicitly refer to the occasional February 29. |

| | |
|---|---|
| *n* | The zero-based Julian day (0 <= n <= 365). Leap days are counted, and it is possible to refer to February 29. |
| M*m.n.d* | The *d*'th day (0 <= d <= 6) of week *n* of month *m* of the year (1 <= n <= 5, 1 <= m <= 12, where week 5 means "the last *d* day in month *m*," which may occur in either the fourth or the fifth week). Week 1 is the first week in which the *d*'th day occurs. Day zero is Sunday. |
| | The time has the same format as offset except that no leading sign ("+" or "-") is allowed. The default, if time is not given, is 02:00:00. |

If no rule is present in TZ, the rules specified by the tzfile(5)-format file posixrules in the system time conversion information directory are used, with the standard and summer time offsets from UTC replaced by those specified by the offset values in TZ.

For compatibility with System V Release 3.1, a semicolon (;) may be used to separate the rule from the rest of the specification.

If the TZ environment variable does not specify a tzfile(5)-format and cannot be interpreted as a direct specification, UTC is used.

## FILES

| | |
|---|---|
| /usr/local/etc/zoneinfo | Time zone information directory |
| /usr/local/etc/zoneinfo/localtime | Local time zone file |
| /usr/local/etc/zoneinfo/posixrules | Used with POSIX-style TZs |
| /usr/local/etc/zoneinfo/GMT | For UTC leap seconds |

If /usr/local/etc/zoneinfo/GMT is absent, UTC leap seconds are loaded from /usr/local/etc/zoneinfo/posixrules.

## SEE ALSO

getenv(3), newctime(3), time(2), tzfile(5)

# on_exit

on exit—Registers a function to be called at normal program termination

## SYNOPSIS

```
#include <stdlib.h>
int on_exit(void (*function)(int , void *), void *arg);
```

## DESCRIPTION

The on_exit() function registers the given function to be called at normal program termination, whether via exit(2) or via return from the program's main. The function is passed the argument to exit(3) and the arg argument from on_exit().

## RETURN VALUE

The on_exit() function returns the value 0 if successful; otherwise, the value –1 is returned.

## SEE ALSO

exit(3), atexit(3)

# opendir

opendir—Opens a directory

## SYNOPSIS

```
#include <sys/types.h>
#include <dirent.h>
DIR *opendir(const char *name);
```

## DESCRIPTION

The opendir() function opens a directory stream corresponding to the directory name, and returns a pointer to the directory stream. The stream is positioned at the first entry in the directory.

## RETURN VALUE

The opendir() function returns a pointer to the directory stream or NULL if an error occurred.

## ERRORS

| | |
|---|---|
| EACESS | Permission denied |
| EMFILE | Too many file descriptors in use by process |
| ENFILE | Too many files are currently open in the system |
| ENOENT | Directory does not exist, or *name* is an empty string |
| ENOMEM | Insufficient memory to complete the operation |
| ENOTDIR | *name* is not a directory |

## CONFORMS TO

SVID 3, POSIX, BSD 4.3

## SEE ALSO

open(2), readdir(3), closedir(3), rewinddir(3), seekdir(3), telldir(3), scandir(3)

*11 June 1995*

# parsedate

parsedate—Converts time and date string to number

## SYNOPSIS

```
#include <sys/types.h>
typedef struct_TIMEINFO f
time_t time;
long usec;
long tzone;
} TIMEINFO;
time_t
parsedate(text, now)
char *text;
TIMEINFO *now;
```

## DESCRIPTION

parsedate converts many common time specifications into the number of seconds since the epoch, that is, a time_t; see time(2).

parsedate returns the time, or –1 on error. text is a character string containing the time and date. now is a pointer to the time that should be used for calculating relative dates. If now is NULL, then GetTimeInfo in libinn(3) is used to obtain the current time and time zone.

The character string consists of zero or more specifications of the following form:

| | |
|---|---|
| time | A time of day, which is of the form hh[:mm[:ss]] [meridian][zone] or hhmm [meridian][zone]. If no meridian is specified, hh is interpreted on a 24-hour clock. |
| date | A specific month and day with optional year. The acceptable formats are mm/dd[/yy], yyyy/mm/dd, monthname dd[, yy], dd monthname [yy], and day,ddmonthnameyy, and day, dd monthname yy. The default year is the current year. If the year is less then 100, then 1900 is added to it; if it is less then 21, then 2000 is added to it. |
| relative time | A specification relative to the current time. The format is number unit; acceptable units are year, month, week, day, hour, minute (or min), and second (or sec). The unit can be specified as a singular or plural, as in 3 weeks. |

The actual date is calculated according to the following steps. First, any absolute date or time is processed and converted. Using that time as the base, day-of-week specifications are added. Next, relative specifications are used. If a date or day is specified, and no absolute or relative time is given, midnight is used. Finally, a correction is applied so that the correct hour of the day is produced after allowing for Daylight Savings Time differences.

parsedate ignores case when parsing all words; unknown words are taken to be unknown time zones, which are treated as GMT. The names of the months and days of the week can be abbreviated to their first three letters, with optional trailing period. Periods are ignored in any time zone or meridian values.

## BUGS

parsedate does not accept all desirable and unambiguous constructions. Semantically incorrect dates such as "February 31" are accepted.

· Daylight Savings Time is always taken as a one-hour change that is wrong for some places. The Daylight Savings Time correction can get confused if parsing a time within an hour of when the reckoning changes, or if given a partial date.

## HISTORY

Originally written by Steven M. Bellovin (smb@research.att.com) while at the University of North Carolina at Chapel Hill and distributed under the name getdate.

A major overhaul was done by Rich $alz (rsalz@bbn.com) and Jim Berets (jberets@bbn.com) in August, 1990.

It was further revised (primarily to remove obsolete constructs and time zone names) a year later by Rich (now rsalz@osf.org) for InterNetNews, and the name was changed.

## SEE ALSO

date(1), ctime(3), libinn(3), time(2)

# perror

perror—Prints a system error message

## SYNOPSIS

```
#include <stdio.h>

void perror(const char *s);

#include <errno.h>
```

```
const char *sys_errlist[];
int sys_nerr;
```

## DESCRIPTION

The routine perror() produces a message on the standard error output, describing the last error encountered during a call to a system or library function. The argument string s is printed first, then a colon and a blank, then the message and a newline. To be of most use, the argument string should include the name of the function that incurred the error. The error number is taken from the external variable *errno*, which is set when errors occur but not cleared when nonerroneous calls are made.

The global error list sys_errlist[] indexed by *errno* can be used to obtain the error message without the newline. The largest message number provided in the table is sys_nerr –1. Be careful when directly accessing this list because new error values may not have been added to sys_errlist[].

When a system call fails, it usually returns –1 and sets the variable *errno* to a value describing what went wrong. (These values can be found in <errno.h>.) Many library functions do likewise. The function perror() serves to translate this error code into human-readable form. Note that *errno* is undefined after a successful library call. This call may well change this variable, even though it succeeds, for example, because it internally used some other library function that failed. Thus, if a failing call is not immediately followed by a call to perror,the value of *errno* should be saved.

## CONFORMS TO

ANSI C, BSD 4.3, POSIX, X/OPEN

## SEE ALSO

strerror(3)

*16 May 1996*

# popen, pclose

popen, pclose—Process I/O

## SYNOPSIS

```
#include <stdio.h>

FILE *popen(const char *command, const char *type);

int pclose(FILE *stream);
```

## DESCRIPTION

The popen() function opens a process by creating a pipe, forking, and invoking the shell. Because a pipe is by definition unidirectional, the type argument may specify only reading or writing, not both; the resulting stream is correspondingly read-only or write-only.

The command argument is a pointer to a null-terminated string containing a shell command line. This command is passed to /bin/sh using the –c flag; interpretation, if any, is performed by the shell. The mode argument is a pointer to a null-terminated string which must be either r for reading or w for writing.

The return value from popen() is a normal standard I/O stream in all respects save that it must be closed with pclose() rather than fclose(). Writing to such a stream writes to the standard input of the command; the command's standard output is the same as that of the process that called popen(), unless this is altered by the command itself. Conversely, reading from a "popened" stream reads the command's standard output, and the command's standard input is the same as that of the process that called popen.

Note that output popen streams are fully buffered by default.

The pclose function waits for the associated process to terminate and returns the exit status of the command as returned by wait4.

## RETURN VALUE

The popen function returns NULL if the fork(2) or pipe(2) calls fail, or if it cannot allocate memory.

The pclose function returns –1 if stream is not associated with a "popened" command, if stream already "pclosed," or if wait4 returns an error.

## ERRORS

The popen function does not reliably set *errno*. (Is this true for Linux?)

## BUGS

The standard input of a command opened for reading shares its seek offset with the process that called popen(); therefore, if the original process has done a buffered read, the command's input position may not be as expected. Similarly, the output from a command opened for writing may become intermingled with that of the original process. The latter can be avoided by calling fflush(3) before popen.

Failure to execute the shell is indistinguishable from the shell's failure to execute command, or an immediate exit of the command. The only hint is an exit status of 127. (Is this true under Linux?)

The function popen() always calls sh, never calls csh.

## HISTORY

A popen() and a pclose() function appeared in Version 7 AT&T UNIX.

## SEE ALSO

fork(2), sh(1), pipe(2), wait4(2), fflush(3), fclose(3), fopen(3), stdio(3), system(3), fclose(3), fopen(3), stdio(3), system(3).

*BSD man page, 17 May 1996*

# printf, fprintf, sprintf, snprintf, vprintf, vfprintf, vsprintf, vsnprintf

printf, fprintf, sprintf, snprintf, vprintf, vfprintf, vsprintf, vsnprintf—Formatted output conversion

## SYNOPSIS

```
#include <stdio.h>

int printf( const char *format, ...);
int fprintf( FILE *stream, const char *format, ...);
int sprintf( char *str, const char *format, ...);
int snprintf( char *str, size_t size, const char *format, ...);

#include <stdarg.h>

int vprintf( const char *format,va_list ap);
ant vfprintf( FILE *stream, const char *format,va_list ap);
int vsprintf( char *str, char *format, va_list ap);
int vsnprintf( char *str, size_t size, char *format,va_list ap);
```

## DESCRIPTION

The printf family of functions produces output according to a *format,* as described in the following paragraphs. The functions printf and vprintf write output to stdout, the standard output *stream;* fprintf and vfprintf write output to the given output *stream;* sprintf, snprintf, vsprintf, and vsnprintf write to the character string *str.*

These functions write the output under the control of a *format* string that specifies how subsequent arguments (or arguments accessed via the variable-length argument facilities of stdarg(3)) are converted for output.

These functions return the number of characters printed (not including the trailing \0 used to end output to strings). snprintf and vsnprintf do not write more than *size* bytes (including the trailing \0), and return -1 if the output was truncated due to this limit.

The *format* string is composed of zero or more directives: ordinary characters (not %), which are copied unchanged to the output stream; and conversion specifications, each of which results in fetching zero or more subsequent arguments. Each conversion specification is introduced by the character %. The arguments must correspond properly (after type promotion) with the conversion specifier. After the %, zero or more of the following flags appear in sequence:

| | |
|---|---|
| # | Specifying that the value should be converted to an alternate form. For c, d, i, n, p, s, and u conversions, this option has no effect. For o conversions, the precision of the number is increased to force the first character of the output string to a zero (except if a zero value is printed with an explicit precision of zero). For x and X conversions, a non-zero result has the string 0x (or 0X for X conversions) prepended to it. For e, E, f, g, and G conversions, the result will always contain a decimal point, even if no digits follow it (normally, a decimal point appears in the results of those conversions only if a digit follows). For g and G conversions, trailing zeros are not removed from the result as they would otherwise be. |
| 0 | Specifying zero padding. For all conversions except n, the converted value is padded on the left with zeros rather than blanks. If a precision is given with a numeric conversion (d, i, o, u, i, x, and X), the 0 flag is ignored. |
| - | (a negative field width flag) Indicates the converted value is to be left adjusted on the field boundary. Except for n conversions, the converted value is padded on the right with blanks, rather than on the left with blanks or zeros. A - overrides a 0 if both are given. |
| ' ' | (a space) Specifying that a blank should be left before a positive number produced by a signed conversion (d, e, E, f, g, G, or i). |
| + | Specifying that a sign always be placed before a number produced by a signed conversion. A + overrides a space if both are used. |
| ' | Specifying that in a numerical argument the output is to be grouped if the locale information indicates any. Note that many versions of gcc cannot parse this option and will issue a warning. |
| | An optional decimal digit string specifying a minimum field width. If the converted value has fewer characters than the field width, it will be padded with spaces on the left (or right, if the left-adjustment flag has been given) to fill out the field width. |
| | An optional precision, in the form of a period (.) followed by an optional digit string. If the digit string is omitted, the precision is taken as zero. This gives the minimum number of digits to appear for d, i, o, u, x, and X conversions; the number of digits to appear after the decimal point for e, E, and f conversions; the maximum number of significant digits for g and G conversions; or the maximum number of characters to be printed from a string for s conversions. |
| | The optional character h, specifying that a following d, i, o, u, x, or X conversion corresponds to a short int or unsigned short int argument, or that a following n conversion corresponds to a pointer to a short int argument. |
| | The optional character l (ell) specifying that a following d, i, o, u, x, or X conversion applies to a pointer to a long int or unsigned long int argument, or that a following n conversion corresponds to a pointer to a long int argument. Linux provides a non-ANSI–compliant use of two l flags as a synonym to q or L. Thus, ll can be used in combination with float conversions. This usage is, however, strongly discouraged. |

The character L specifying that a following e, E, f, g, or G conversion corresponds to a `long double` argument, or a following d, i, o, u, x, or X conversion corresponds to a `long long` argument. Note that `long long` is not specified in ANSI C and therefore not portable to all architectures.

The optional character q. This is equivalent to L. See the "Standards" and "Bugs" sections for comments on the use of ll, L, and q.

A Z character specifying that the following integer (d, i, o, u, i, x, and X) conversion corresponds to a `size_t` argument.

A character that specifies the type of conversion to be applied.

A field width or precision, or both, may be indicated by an asterisk * instead of a digit string. In this case, an int argument supplies the field width or precision. A negative field width is treated as a left adjustment flag followed by a positive field width; a negative precision is treated as though it were missing.

The conversion specifiers and their meanings are as follows:

| | |
|---|---|
| diouxX | The `int` (or appropriate variant) argument is converted to signed decimal (d and i), unsigned octal (o), unsigned decimal (u), or unsigned hexadecimal (x and X) notation. The letters abcdef are used for x conversions; the letters ABCDEF are used for X conversions. The precision, if any, gives the minimum number of digits that must appear; if the converted value requires fewer digits, it is padded on the left with zeros. |
| eE | The `double` argument is rounded and converted in the style [-]d.ddde\dd where there is one digit before the decimal-point character and the number of digits after it is equal to the precision; if the precision is missing, it is taken as 6; if the precision is zero, no decimal-point character appears. An E conversion uses the letter E (rather than e) to introduce the exponent. The exponent always contains at least two digits; if the value is zero, the exponent is 00. |
| f | The `double` argument is rounded and converted to decimal notation in the style [-]*ddd.ddd*, where the number of digits after the decimal-point character is equal to the precision specification. If the precision is missing, it is taken as 6; if the precision is explicitly zero, no decimal-point character appears. If a decimal point appears, at least one digit appears before it. |
| g | The `double` argument is converted in style f or e (or E for G conversions). The precision specifies the number of significant digits. If the precision is missing, 6 digits are given; if the precision is zero, it is treated as 1. Style e is used if the exponent from its conversion is less than negative 4 or greater than or equal to the precision. Trailing zeros are removed from the fractional part of the result; a decimal point appears only if it is followed by at least one digit. |
| c | The `int` argument is converted to an unsigned char, and the resulting character is written. |
| s | The `char *` argument is expected to be a pointer to an array of character type (pointer to a string). Characters from the array are written up to (but not including) a terminating NUL character; if a precision is specified, no more than the number specified are written. If a precision is given, no null character need be present; if the precision is not specified, or is greater than the size of the array, the array must contain a terminating NUL character. |
| p | The `void *` pointer argument is printed in hexadecimal (as if by %#x or %#lx). |
| n | The number of characters written so far is stored into the integer indicated by the int * (or variant) pointer argument. No argument is converted. |
| % | A % is written. No argument is converted. The complete conversion specification is %%. |

In no case does a nonexistent or small field width cause truncation of a field; if the result of a conversion is wider than the field width, the field is expanded to contain the conversion result.

## EXAMPLES

To print a date and time in the form "Sunday, July 3, 10:02," where weekday and month are pointers to strings:

```
#include <stdio.h>
fprintf(stdout, "%s, %s %d, %.2d:%.2d\n",
weekday, month, day, hour, min);
```

To print to five decimal places:

```
#include <math.h>
#include <stdio.h>
fprintf(stdout, "pi = %.5f\n", 4 * atan(1.0));
```

To allocate a 128-byte string and print into it:

```
#include <stdio.h>
#include <stdlib.h>
#include <stdarg.h>

char *newfmt(const char *fmt, ...)
{
        char *p;
        va_list ap;
        if ((p = malloc(128)) == NULL)
                return (NULL);
        va_start(ap, fmt);
        (void) vsnprintf(p, 128, fmt, ap);
        va_end(ap);
        return (p);
}
```

## SEE ALSO

printf(1), scanf(3)

## STANDARDS

The fprintf, printf, sprintf, vprintf, vfprintf, and vsprintf functions conform to ANSI C3.159-1989 ("ANSI C").

The q flag is the BSD 4.4 notation for long long, while ll or the usage of L in integer conversions is the GNU notation.

The Linux version of these functions is based on the GNU libio library. Take a look at the info documentation of GNU libc (glibc-1.08) for a more concise description.

## BUGS

Some floating point conversions under Linux cause memory leaks.

All functions are fully ANSI C3.159-1989 conformant, but provide the additional flags q, Z, and ' as well as an additional behavior of the L and l flags. The latter may be considered to be a bug, as it changes the behavior of flags defined in ANSI C3.159-1989.

The effect of padding the %p format with zeros (either by the 0 flag or by specifying a precision), and the benign effect (that is, none) of the # flag on %n and %p conversions, as well as nonsensical combinations that are not standard; such combinations should be avoided.

Some combinations of flags defined by ANSI C are not making sense (for example, %Ld). While they may have a well-defined behavior on Linux, this need not to be so on other architectures. Therefore, it usually is better not to use flags that are not defined by ANSI C at all; in other words, that use q instead of L in combination with diouxX conversions or ll.

The usage of q is not the same as on BSD 4.4, as it may be used in float conversions equivalently to L.

Because sprintf and vsprintf assume an infinitely long string, callers must be careful not to overflow the actual space; this is often impossible to assure.

*Linux man page, 28 January 1996*

# psignal

psignal—Prints signal message

## SYNOPSIS

```
#include <signal.h>
void psignal(int sig, const char *s);
extern const char *const sys_siglist[]
```

## DESCRIPTION

The psignal() function displays a message on stderr consisting of the string s, a colon, a space, and a string describing the signal number sig. If sig is invalid, the message displayed will indicate an unknown signal.

The array sys siglist holds the signal description strings indexed by signal number.

## RETURN VALUE

The psignal() function returns no value.

## CONFORMS TO

BSD 4.3

## SEE ALSO

perror(3), strsignal(3)

*GNU, 13 April 1993*

# putenv

putenv—Changes or adds an environment variable

## SYNOPSIS

```
#include <stdlib.h>
int putenv(const char *string);
```

## DESCRIPTION

The putenv() function adds or changes the value of environment variables. The argument string is of the form *name* = *value*. If *name* does not already exist in the environment, then string is added to the environment. If *name* does exist, then the value of *name* in the environment is changed to *value*.

## RETURN VALUE

The putenv() function returns zero on success, or –1 if an error occurs.

## ERRORS

ENOMEM                                Insufficient space to allocate new environment

## CONFORMS TO

SVID 3, POSIX, BSD 4.3

## SEE ALSO

getenv(3), setenv(3), unsetenv(3)

# putpwent

putpwent—Writes a password file entry

## SYNOPSIS

```
#include <pwd.h>
#include <stdio.h>
#include <sys/types.h>
int putpwent(const struct passwd *p,FILE*stream);
```

## DESCRIPTION

The putpwent() function writes a password entry from the structure p in the file associated with *stream*.

The passwd structure is defined in <pwd.h> as follows:

```
struct passwd {
        char    *pw_name;       /* user name */
        char    *pw_passwd;     /* user password */
        uid_t   pw_uid;         /* user id */
        gid_t   pw_gid;         /* group id */
        char    *pw_gecos;      /* real name */
        char    *pw_dir;        /* home directory */
        char    *pw_shell;      /* shell program */
};
```

## RETURN VALUE

The putpwent() function returns 0 on success, or -1 if an error occurs.

## ERRORS

EINVAL                          Invalid (NULL) argument given

## CONFORMS TO

SVID 3

## SEE ALSO

fgetpwent(3), getpwent(3), setpwent(3), endpwent(3), getpwnam(3), getpwuid(3), getpw(3)

# fputc, fputs, putc, putchar, puts

fputc, fputs, putc, putchar, puts—Output of characters and strings

## SYNOPSIS

```
#include <stdio.h>
int fputc(int c,FILE*stream);
int fputs(const char *s,FILE*stream);
int putc(int c,FILE *stream);
int putchar(int c);
int puts(char *s);
int ungetc(int c,FILE *stream);
```

## DESCRIPTION

fputc() writes the character c, cast to an unsigned char, to stream.

fputs() writes the string s to stream, without its trailing \0.

putc() is equivalent to fputc() except that it may be implemented as a macro that evaluates stream more than once.

putchar(c); is equivalent to putc(c,stdout).

puts() writes the string s and a trailing newline to stdout.

Calls to the functions described here can be mixed with each other and with calls to other output functions from the stdio library for the same output stream.

## RETURN VALUES

fputc(), putc(), and putchar() return the character written as an unsigned char cast to an int or EOF on error.

puts() and fputs() return a non-negative number on success, or EOF on error.

## CONFORMS TO

ANSI C, POSIX.1

## BUGS

It is not advisable to mix calls to output functions from the stdio library with low-level calls to write() for the file descriptor associated with the same output stream; the results will be undefined and very probably not what you want.

## SEE ALSO

write(2), fopen(3), fwrite(3), scanf(3), gets(3), fseek(3), ferror(3)

*GNU, 4 April 1993*

# qio

qio—Quick I/O part of InterNetNews library

## SYNOPSIS

```
#include "qio.h"
QIOSTATE *
QIOopen(name, size)
char *name;
int size;
QIOSTATE * QIOfdopen(fd, size)
int fd;
int size;
void QIOclose(qp)
QIOSTATE *qp;
```

```
char * QIOread(qp)
QIOSTATE *qp;
int QIOlength(qp)
QIOSTATE *qp;
int QIOtoolong(qp)
QIOSTATE *qp;
int QIOerror(qp)
QIOSTATE *qp;
int QIOtell(qp)
QIOSTATE *qp;
int QIOrewind(qp)
QIOSTATE *qp;
int QIOfileno(qp)
QIOSTATE *qp;
```

## DESCRIPTION

The routines described in this manual page are part of the InterNetNews library, libinn(3). They are used to provide quick read access to files. The letters QIO stand for Quick I/O.

QIOopen opens the file *name* for reading. It uses a buffer of size bytes, which must also be larger then the longest expected line. The header file defines the constant QIO_BUFFER as a reasonable default. If size is zero, then QIOopen will call stat(2) and use the returned block size; if that fails it will use QIO_BUFFER. It returns NULL on error, or a pointer to a handle to be used in other calls. QIOfdopen performs the same function except that fd refers to an already-open descriptor.

QIOclose closes the open file and releases any resources used by it.

QIOread returns a pointer to the next line in the file. The trailing newline will be replaced with a \0. If EOF is reached, an error occurs, or if the line is longer than the buffer, QIOread returns NULL.

After a successful call to QIOread, QIOlength will return the length of the current line.

The functions QIOtoolong and QIOerror can be called after QIOread returns NULL to determine if there was an error, or if the line was too long. If QIOtoolong returns non-zero, then the current line did not fit in the buffer, and the next call to QIOread will try read the rest of the line. Long lines can only be discarded. If QIOerror returns non-zero, then a serious I/O error occurred.

QIOtell returns the lseek(2) offset at which the next line will start.

QIOrewind sets the read pointer back to the beginning of the file.

QIOfileno returns the descriptor of the open file.

QIOlength, QIOtoolong, QIOerror, QIOtell, and QIOfileno are implemented as macros defined in the header file.

## EXAMPLE

```
QIOSTATE *h;
long offset;
char *p;
h = QIOopen("/etc/motd", QIO_BUFFER);
for (offset = QIOtell(h); (p = QIOread(h)) != NULL; offset = QIOtell(h))
printf("At %ld, %s\n", offset, p);
if (QIOerror(h)) {
   perror("Read error");
   exit(1);
   }
QIOclose(h);
```

## HISTORY

Written by Rich $alz (rsalz@uunet.uu.net) for InterNetNews.

# qsort

qsort—Sorts an array

## SYNOPSIS

```
#include <stdlib.h>
void qsort(void *base, size_t nmemb, size_t size,int(*compar)
(const void *, const void *));
```

## DESCRIPTION

The qsort() function sorts an array with *nmemb* elements of size *size*. The base argument points to the start of the array.

The contents of the array are sorted in ascending order according to a comparison function pointed to by compar, which is called with two arguments that point to the objects being compared.

The comparison function must return an integer less than, equal to, or greater than zero if the first argument is considered to be respectively less than, equal to, or greater than the second. If two members compare as equal, their order in the sorted array is undefined.

## RETURN VALUE

The qsort() function returns no value.

## CONFORMS TO

SVID 3, POSIX, BSD 4.3, ISO 9899

## SEE ALSO

sort(1)

*GNU, 29 March 1993*

# raise

raise—Sends a signal to the current process

## SYNOPSIS

```
#include <signal.h>
int raise (int sig);
```

## DESCRIPTION

The raise function sends a signal to the current process. It is equivalent to

```
kill(getpid(),sig)
```

## RETURN VALUE

Zero on success, non-zero for failure.

## CONFORMS TO

ANSI C

## SEE ALSO

kill(2), signal(2), getpid(2)

*GNU, 31 August 1995*

# rand, srand

rand, srand—Random number generator

## SYNOPSIS

```
#include <stdlib.h>
int rand(void);
void srand(unsigned int seed);
```

## DESCRIPTION

The rand() function returns a pseudo-random integer between 0 and RAND_MAX.

The srand() function sets its argument as the seed for a new sequence of pseudo-random integers to be returned by rand(). These sequences are repeatable by calling srand() with the same *seed* value.

If no *seed* value is provided, the rand() function is automatically seeded with a value of 1.

## RETURN VALUE

The rand() function returns a value between 0 and RAND_MAX. The srand() returns no value.

## NOTES

The versions of rand() and srand() in the Linux C Library use the same random number generator as random() and srandom(), so the lower-order bits should be as random as the higher-order bits. However, on older rand() implementations, the lower-order bits are much less random than the higher-order bits.

In *Numerical Recipes in C: The Art of Scientific Computing* (William H. Press, Brian P. Flannery, Saul A. Teukolsky, William T. Vetterling; New York: Cambridge University Press, 1990, first ed, p. 207), the following comments are made:

"If you want to generate a random integer between 1 and 10, you should always do it by

```
j=1+(int) (10.0*rand()/(RAND+MAX+1.0));
```

and never by anything resembling

```
j=1+((int) (1000000.0*rand()) % 10);
```

(which uses lower-order bits)."

Random-number generation is a complex topic. The Numerical Recipes in C book (see preceding reference) provides an excellent discussion of practical random-number generation issues in Chapter 7, "Random Numbers."

For a more theoretical discussion that also covers many practical issues in depth, please see Chapter 3, "Random Numbers," in Donald E. Knuth's *The Art of Computer Programming, Volume 2* (Seminumerical Algorithms), 2nd ed.; Reading, Massachusetts: Addison-Wesley Publishing Company, 1981.

## CONFORMS TO

SVID 3, BSD 4.3, ISO 9899

## SEE ALSO

random(3), srandom(3), initstate(3), setstate(3)

*GNU, 18 May 1995*

# random, srandom, initstate, setstate

random, srandom, initstate, setstate—Random number generator

## SYNOPSIS

```
#include <stdlib.h>
long int random(void);
void srandom(unsigned int seed);
char *initstate(unsigned int seed, char *state,int n);
char *setstate(char *state);
```

## DESCRIPTION

The random() function uses a nonlinear additive feedback random number generator employing a default table of size 31 long integers to return successive pseudo-random numbers in the range from 0 to RAND_MAX. The period of this random number generator is very large, approximately 16*((2**31)-1).

The srandom() function sets its argument as the seed for a new sequence of pseudo-random integers to be returned by random(). These sequences are repeatable by calling srandom() with the same seed value. If no seed value is provided, the random() function is automatically seeded with a value of 1.

The initstate() function allows a state array state to be initialized for use by random().The size of the state array n is used by initstate() to decide how sophisticated a random number generator it should use—the larger the state array, the better the random numbers will be. seed is the seed for the initialization, which specifies a starting point for the random number sequence, and provides for restarting at the same point.

The setstate() function changes the state array used by the random() function. The state array state is used for random number generation until the next call to initstate() or setstate(). state must first have been initialized using initstate().

## RETURN VALUE

The random() function returns a value between 0 and RAND_MAX. The srandom() function returns no value. The initstate() and setstate() functions return a pointer to the previous state array.

## ERRORS

EINVAL          A state array of less than 8 bytes was specified to initstate().

## NOTES

Current "optimal" values for the size of the state array n are 8, 32, 64, 128, and 256 bytes; other amounts will be rounded down to the nearest known amount. Using less than 8 bytes will cause an error.

## CONFORMS TO

BSD 4.3

## SEE ALSO

rand(3), srand(3)

*GNU, 28 March 1993*

# readdir

readdir—Reads a directory

## SYNOPSIS

```
#include <sys/types.h>
#include <dirent.h>
struct dirent *readdir(DIR *dir);
```

## DESCRIPTION

The readdir() function returns a pointer to a dirent structure representing the next directory entry in the directory stream pointed to by *dir*. It returns NULL on reaching the end-of-file or if an error occurred.

The data returned by readdir() is overwritten by subsequent calls to readdir() for the same directory stream.

According to POSIX, the dirent structure contains a field char_d_name[] of unspecified size, with at most NAME_MAX characters preceding the terminating null character. Use of other fields will harm the portability of your programs.

## RETURN VALUE

The readdir() function returns a pointer to a dirent structure, or NULL if an error occurs or end-of-file is reached.

## ERRORS

EBADF                                    Invalid directory stream descriptor dir

## CONFORMS TO

SVID 3, POSIX, BSD 4.3

## SEE ALSO

read(2), opendir(3), closedir(3), rewinddir(3), seekdir(3), telldir(3), scandir(3)

*22 April 1996*

# readv, writev

readv, writev—Reads or writes data into multiple buffers

## SYNOPSIS

```
#include <sys/uio.h>
int readv(int filedes, const struct iovec *vector,
size_t count);
int writev(int filedes, const struct iovec *vector,
size_t count);
```

## DESCRIPTION

The readv() function reads *count* blocks from the file associated with the file descriptor *filedes* into the multiple buffers described by *vector*.

The writev() function writes at most *count* blocks described by *vector* to the file associated with the file descriptor *filedes*.

The pointer *vector* points to a struct iovec defined in <sys/uio.h> as

```
struct iovect
{
void *iovbase; /* Starting address */
size_t iov_len; /* Number of bytes */
} ;
```

Buffers are processed in the order vector[0], vector[1], ... vector[count].

The readv() function works just like read(2) except that multiple buffers are filled.

The writev() function works just like write(2) except that multiple buffers are written out.

## RETURN VALUES

The readv() function returns the number of bytes or –1 on error; the writev() function returns the number of bytes written.

## ERRORS

The readv() and writev() functions can fail and set errno to the following values:

| | |
|---|---|
| EBADF | fd is not a valid file descriptor. |
| EINVAL | fd is unsuitable for reading (for readv()) or writing (for writev()). |
| EFAULT | buf is outside the processes' address space. |
| EAGAIN | Nonblocking I/O had been selected in the open() call, and reading or writing could not be done immediately. |
| EINTR | Reading or writing was interrupted before any data was transferred. |

## CONFORMS TO

unknown

## BUGS

It is not advisable to mix calls to functions like readv() or writev(), which operate on file descriptors, with the functions from the stdio library; the results will be undefined and probably not what you want.

## SEE ALSO

read(2), write(2)

*GNU, 25 April 1993*

# realpath

realpath—Returns the canonicalized absolute pathname.

## SYNOPSIS

```
#include <sys/param.h>
#include <unistd.h>
char *realpath(char *path, char resolved_path[]);
```

## DESCRIPTION

realpath expands all symbolic links and resolves references to /./, /../ and extra / characters in the null-terminated string named by path and stores the canonicalized absolute pathname in the buffer of size MAXPATHLEN named by resolved_path. The resulting path will have no symbolic link, /./, or /../ components.

## RETURN VALUE

If there is no error, it returns a pointer to the resolved_path.

Otherwise, it returns a NULL pointer and places in resolved_path the absolute pathname of the path component that could not be resolved. The global variable errno is set to indicate the error.

## ERRORS

| | |
|---|---|
| ENOTDIR | A component of the path prefix is not a directory. |
| EINVAL | The pathname contains a character with the high-order bit set. |
| ENAMETOOLONG | A component of a pathname exceeded MAXNAMLEN characters, or an entire path name exceeded MAXPATHLEN characters. |
| ENOENT | The named file does not exist. |
| EACCES | Search permission is denied for a component of the path prefix. |
| ELOOP | Too many symbolic links were encountered in translating the pathname. |
| EIO | An I/O error occurred while reading from the filesystem. |

## SEE ALSO

readlink(2), getcwd(3)

*GNU, 29 July 1994*

# Re_comp, re_exec

re_comp, re_exec—BSD regex functions

## SYNOPSIS

```
#include <regex.h>
char *re comp(char *regex);
int re exec(char *string);
```

## DESCRIPTION

re_comp is used to compile the null-terminated regular expression pointed to by regex. The compiled pattern occupies a static area, the pattern buffer, which is overwritten by subsequent use of re_comp. If regex is NULL, no operation is performed and the pattern buffer's contents are not altered.

re_exec is used to assess whether the null-terminated string pointed to by string matches the previously compiled regex.

## RETURN VALUE

re_comp returns NULL on successful compilation of regex; otherwise, it returns a pointer to an appropriate error message.

re_exec returns 1 for a successful match, zero for failure.

## CONFORMS TO

BSD 4.3

## SEE ALSO

regex(7), GNU regex manual

*Linux, 14 July 1995*

# regcomp, regexec, regerror, regfree

regcomp, regexec, regerror, regfree—POSIX regex functions

## SYNOPSIS

```
#include <regex.h>
int regcomp(regex_t *preg, const char *regex,int cflags);
int regexec(const regex_t *preg, const char *string, size_t nmatch, regmatch_t pmatch[], int eflags);
size_t regerror(int errcode, const regex_t *preg, char *errbuf, size_t errbuf_size);
void regfree(regex_t *preg);
```

## POSIX REGEX COMPILING

regcomp is used to compile a regular expression into a form that is suitable for subsequent regexec searches.

regcomp is supplied with *preg*, a pointer to a pattern buffer storage area; regex, a pointer to the null-terminated string; and *cflags*, flags used to determine the type of compilation. All regular expression searching must be done via a compiled pattern buffer; thus, regexec must always be supplied with the address of a regcomp initialized pattern buffer.

*cflags* may be the bitwise or of one or more of the following:

| | |
|---|---|
| REG_EXTENDED | Use POSIX extended regular expression syntax when interpreting *regex*. If not set, POSIX basic regular expression syntax is used. |
| REG_ICASE | Do not differentiate case. Subsequent regexec searches using this pattern buffer will be case-insensitive. |
| REG_NOSUB | Support for substring addressing of matches is not required. The *nmatch* and *pmatch* parameters to regexec are ignored if the pattern buffer supplied was compiled with this flag set. |
| REG_NEWLINE | Match-any-character operators don't match a newline. A nonmatching list ([^...]) not containing a newline matches a newline. Match-beginning-of-line operator (^) matches the empty string immediately after a newline, regardless of whether *eflags*, the execution flags of regexec, contains REG_NOTBOL. Match-end-of-line operator ($) matches the empty string immediately before a newline, regardless of whether *eflags* contains REG_NOTEOL. |

## POSIX REGEX MATCHING

regexec is used to match a null-terminated string against the precompiled pattern buffer, *preg*. *nmatch* and *pmatch* are used to provide information regarding the location of any matches. *eflags* may be the bitwise or of one or both of REG_NOTBOL and REG_NOTEOL, which cause changes in matching behavior described in the following list.

| | |
|---|---|
| REG_NOTBOL | The match-beginning-of-line operator always fails to match (but see the compilation flag REG_NEWLINE, in the preceding subsection). This flag may be used when different portions of a string are passed to regexec and the beginning of the string should not be interpreted as the beginning of the line. |
| REG_NOTEOL | The match-end-of-line operator always fails to match (but see the compilation flag REG_NEWLINE, in the preceding subsection). |

## BYTE OFFSETS

Unless REG_NOSUB was set for the compilation of the pattern buffer, it is possible to obtain substring match addressing information. *pmatch* must be dimensioned to have at least *nmatch* elements. These are filled in by regexec with substring match addresses. Any unused structure elements will contain the value -1.

The regmatch_t structure that is the type of *pmatch* is defined in regex.h:

```
typedef struct
{
  regoff_t rm_so;
  regoff_t rm_eo;
} regmatch_t;
```

Each rm_so element that is not -1 indicates the start offset of the next largest substring match within the string. The relative rm_eo element indicates the end offset of the match.

## POSIX ERROR REPORTING

regerror is used to turn the error codes that can be returned by both regcomp and regexec into error message strings.

regerror is passed the error code, *errcode*; the pattern buffer, *preg*; a pointer to a character string buffer, *errbuf*; and the size of the string buffer, *errbuf_size*. It returns the size of the *errbuf* required to contain the null-terminated error message string. If both *errbuf* and *errbuf_size* are non-zero, *errbuf* is filled in with the first errbuf_size - 1 characters of the error message and a terminating null.

## POSIX PATTERN BUFFER FREEING

Supplying `regfree` with a precompiled pattern buffer, *preg* will free the memory allocated to the pattern buffer by the compiling process, `regcomp`.

## RETURN VALUE

`regcomp` returns zero for a successful compilation or an error code for failure.

`regexec` returns zero for a successful match or `REG_NOMATCH` for failure.

## ERRORS

The following errors can be returned by `regcomp`:

| | |
|---|---|
| REG_BADRPT | Invalid use of repetition operators, such as using * as the first character |
| REG_BADBR | Invalid use of back reference operator |
| REG_EBRACE | Unmatched brace interval operators |
| REG_EBRACK | Unmatched bracket list operators |
| REG_ERANGE | Invalid use of the range operator; for example, the ending point of the range occurs prior to the starting point |
| REG_ECTYPE | Unknown character class name |
| REG_EPAREN | Unmatched parenthesis group operators |
| REG_ESUBREG | Invalid back reference to a subexpression |
| REG_EEND | Non-specific error |
| REG_ESCAPE | Invalid escape sequence |
| REG_BADPAT | Invalid use of pattern operators such as group or list |
| REG_ESIZE | Compiled regular expression requires a pattern buffer larger than 64Kb |
| REG_ESPACE | The regex routines ran out of memory |

## CONFORMS TO

POSIX

## SEE ALSO

`regex`(7), GNU `regex` manual

*Linux, 13 July 1994*

# remove

remove—Deletes a name and possibly the file to which it refers

## SYNOPSIS

```
#include <stdio.h>
int remove(const char *pathname);
```

## DESCRIPTION

remove deletes a name from the filesystem. If that name was the last link to a file and no processes have the file open, the file is deleted and the space it was using is made available for reuse.

If the name was the last link to a file but any processes still have the file open, the file will remain in existence until the last file descriptor referring to it is closed.

If the name referred to a symbolic link, the link is removed.

If the name referred to a socket, fifo, or device, the name for it is removed, but processes that have the object open may continue to use it.

## RETURN VALUE

On success, zero is returned. On error, -1 is returned, and *errno* is set appropriately.

## ERRORS

| | |
|---|---|
| EFAULT | *pathname* points outside your accessible address space. |
| EACCES | Write access to the directory containing *pathname* is not allowed for the process's effective uid, or one of the directories in *pathname* did not allow search (execute) permission. |
| EPERM | The directory containing *pathname* has the sticky-bit (S_ISVTX) set and the process's effective uid is neither the uid of the file to be deleted nor that of the directory containing it. |
| ENAMETOOLONG | *pathname* was too long. |
| ENOENT | A directory component in *pathname* does not exist or is a dangling symbolic link. |
| ENOTDIR | A component used as a directory in *pathname* is not, in fact, a directory. |
| EISDIR | *pathname* refers to a directory. |
| ENOMEM | Insufficient kernel memory was available. |
| EROFS | *pathname* refers to a file on a read-only filesystem. |

## CONFORMS TO

SVID, AT&T, POSIX, X/OPEN, BSD 4.3

## BUGS

Inadequacies in the protocol underlying NFS can cause the unexpected disappearance of files that are still being used.

## SEE ALSO

unlink(2), rename(2), open(2), rmdir(2), mknod(2), mkfifo(3), link(2), rm(1), unlink(8)

*Linux, 13 July 1994*

# res_query, res_search, res_mkquery, res_send, res_init, dn_comp, dn_expand

res_query, res_search, res_mkquery, res_send, res_init, dn_comp, dn_expand—Resolver routines

## SYNOPSIS

```
#include <sys/types.h>
#include <netinet/in.h>
#include <arpa/nameser.h>
#include <resolv.h>
```

```
res_query(dname, class, type, answer, anslen)
const char *dname;
int class, type;
u_char *answer;
int anslen;
```

```
res_search(dname, class, type, answer, anslen)
const char *dname;
int class, type;
u char *answer;
int anslen;

res mkquery(op, dname, class, type, data, datalen, newrr, buf, buflen)
int op;
const char *dname;
int class, type;
const char *data;
int datalen;
struct rrec *newrr;
u_char *buf;
int buflen;

res_send(msg, msglen, answer, anslen)
const u_char *msg;
int msglen;
u_char *answer;
int anslen;

res_init()

dn_comp(exp_dn, comp_dn, length, dnptrs, lastdnptr)
const char *exp_dn;
u char *comp_dn;
int length;
u_char **dnptrs, **lastdnptr;

dn_expand(msg, eomorig, comp_dn, exp_dn, length)
const u_char *msg, *eomorig, *comp_dn;
char *exp_dn;
int length;
hstrerror(int err);
```

## DESCRIPTION

These routines are used for making, sending and interpreting query and reply messages with Internet domain name servers.

Global configuration and state information that is used by the resolver routines is kept in the structure _res. Most of the values have reasonable defaults and can be ignored. Options stored in _res.options are defined in resolv.h and are as follows. Options are stored as a simple bit mask containing the bitwise or of the options enabled.

| | |
|---|---|
| RES_INIT | True if the initial name server address and default domain name are initialized (that is, res_init has been called). |
| RES_DEBUG | Print debugging messages. |
| RES_AAONLY | Accept authoritative answers only. With this option, res_send should continue until it finds an authoritative answer or finds an error. Currently, this is not implemented. |
| RES_USEVC | Use TCP connections for queries instead of UDP datagrams. |
| RES_STAYOPEN | Used with RES_USEVC to keep the TCP connection open between queries. This is useful only in programs that regularly do many queries. UDP should be the normal mode used. |
| RES_IGNTC | Unused currently (ignore truncation errors—don't retry with TCP). |
| RES_RECURSE | Set the recursion-desired bit in queries. This is the default. (res_send does not do iterative queries and expects the name server to handle recursion.) |

| | |
|---|---|
| RES_DEFNAMES | If set, res_search will append the default domain name to single-component names (those that do not contain a dot). This option is enabled by default. |
| RES_DNSRCH | If this option is set, res_search will search for hostnames in the current domain and in parent domains; see hostname(7). This is used by the standard host lookup routine gethostbyname(3). This option is enabled by default. |
| RES_NOALIASES | This option turns off the user level aliasing feature controlled by the HOSTALIASES environment variable. Network daemons should set this option. |

The res_init routine reads the configuration file (if any; see resolver(5)) to get the default domain name, search list and the Internet address of the local name server(s). If no server is configured, the host running the resolver is tried. The current domain name is defined by the hostname if not specified in the configuration file; it can be overridden by the environment variable LOCALDOMAIN. This environment variable may contain several blank-separated tokens if you wish to override the search list on a per-process basis. This is similar to the search command in the configuration file. Another environment variable (RES_OPTIONS) can be set to override certain internal resolver options that are otherwise set by changing fields in the _res structure or are inherited from the configuration file's options command. The syntax of the RES_OPTIONS environment variable is explained in resolver(5). Initialization normally occurs on the first call to one of the other resolver routines.

The res_query function provides an interface to the server query mechanism. It constructs a query, sends it to the local server, awaits a response, and makes preliminary checks on the reply. The query requests information of the specified type and class for the specified fully-qualified domain name *dname*. The reply message is left in the answer buffer with length *anslen* supplied by the caller.

The res_search routine makes a query and awaits a response like res_query, but in addition, it implements the default and search rules controlled by the RES_DEFNAMES and RES_DNSRCH options. It returns the first successful reply.

The remaining routines are lower-level routines used by res_query. The res_mkquery function constructs a standard query message and places it in buf. It returns the size of the query, or -1 if the query is larger than buflen. The query type *op* is usually QUERY, but can be any of the query types defined in <arpa/nameser.h>. The domain name for the query is given by *dname*. Newrr is currently unused but is intended for making update messages.

The res_send routine sends a preformatted query and returns an answer. It will call res_init if RES_INIT is not set, send the query to the local name server, and handle time-outs and retries. The length of the reply message is returned, or -1 if there were errors.

The dn_comp function compresses the domain name exp_dn and stores it in comp_dn.The size of the compressed name is returned or -1 if there were errors. The size of the array pointed to by comp_dn is given by length. The compression uses an array of pointers dnptrs to previously-compressed names in the current message. The first pointer points to the beginning of the message and the list ends with NULL. The limit to the array is specified by lastdnptr. A side effect of dn_comp is to update the list of pointers for labels inserted into the message as the name is compressed. If dnptr is NULL, names are not compressed. If lastdnptr is NULL, the list of labels is not updated.

The dn_expand entry expands the compressed domain name comp_dn to a full domain name. The compressed name is contained in a query or reply message; msg is a pointer to the beginning of the message. The uncompressed name is placed in the buffer indicated by exp_dn, which is of size length. The size of compressed name is returned or -1 if there was an error.

## FILES

| | |
|---|---|
| /etc/resolv.conf | See resolver(5) |

**SEE ALSO**

gethostbyname(3), named(8), resolver(5), hostname(7),

RFC1032, RFC1033, RFC1034, RFC1035, RFC974

SMM: 11 Name Server Operations Guide for BIND

*11 December 1995*

# rewinddir

rewinddir—Resets directory stream

**SYNOPSIS**

```
#include <sys/types.h>
#include <dirent.h>
void rewinddir(DIR *dir);
```

**DESCRIPTION**

The rewinddir() function resets the position of the directory stream dir to the beginning of the directory.

**RETURN VALUE**

The readdir() function returns no value.

**CONFORMS TO**

SVID 3, POSIX, BSD 4.3

**SEE ALSO**

opendir(3), readdir(3), closedir(3), seekdir(3), telldir(3), scandir(3)

*11 June 1995*

# rint

rint—Rounds to closest integer

**SYNOPSIS**

```
#include <math.h>
double rint(double x);
```

**DESCRIPTION**

The rint() function rounds $x$ to an integer value according to the prevalent rounding mode. The default rounding mode is to round to the nearest integer.

**RETURN VALUE**

The rint() function returns the integer value as a floating-point number.

**CONFORMS TO**

BSD 4.3

## SEE ALSO

abs(3), ceil(3), fabs(3), floor(3), labs(3)

*6 June 1993*

# rquota

rquota—Implements quotas on remote machines

## SYNOPSIS

/usr/include/rpcsvc/rquota.x

## DESCRIPTION

The rquota( ) protocol inquires about quotas on remote machines. It is used in conjunction with NFS because NFS itself does not implement quotas.

## PROGRAMMING

#include <rpcsvc/rquota.h>

The following XDR routines are available in librpcsvc: xdr_getquota_arg:

xdr_getquota_rslt
xdr_rquota

## SEE ALSO

quota(1), quotactl(2)

*6 October 1987*

# scandir, alphasort

scandir, alphasort—Scan a directory for matching entries

## SYNOPSIS

```
#include <dirent.h>
int scandir(const char *dir, struct dirent ***namelist,
int (*select)(const struct dirent *),
int (*compar)(const struct dirent **, const struct dirent **));
int alphasort(const struct dirent **a, const struct dirent **b);
```

## DESCRIPTION

The scandir() function scans the directory *dir*, calling select() on each directory entry. Entries for which select() returns non-zero are stored in strings allocated via malloc(), sorted using qsort() with the comparison function compar(), and collected in array *namelist* that is allocated via malloc().If select is NULL, all entries are selected.

The alphasort() function can be used as the comparison function for the scandir() function to sort the directory entries into alphabetical order. Its parameters are the two directory entries, a and b, to compare.

## RETURN VALUE

The scandir() function returns the number of directory entries selected or –1 if an error occurs.

The alphasort() function returns an integer less than, equal to, or greater than zero if the first argument is considered to be respectively less than, equal to, or greater than the second.

## ERRORS

ENOMEM                                   Insufficient memory to complete the operation

## CONFORMS TO

BSD 4.3

## EXAMPLE

```
/* print files in current directory in reverse order */
#include <dirent.h>
main(){
    struct dirent **namelist;
    int n;

    n = scandir(".", &namelist, 0, alphasort);
    if (n < 0)
        perror("scandir");
    else
        while(n—) printf("%s\n", namelist[n]->d_name);
}
```

## SEE ALSO

opendir(3), readdir(3), closedir(3), rewinddir(3), telldir(3), seekdir(3)

*GNU, 11 April 1996*

# scanf, fscanf, sscanf, vscanf, vsscanf, vfscanf

scanf, fscanf, sscanf, vscanf, vsscanf, vfscanf—Input format conversion

## SYNOPSIS

```
#include <stdio.h>
int scanf( const char *format, ...);
int fscanf( FILE *stream, const char *format, ...);
int sscanf( const char *str, const char *format, ...);
#include <stdarg.h>
int vscanf( const char *format,valist ap);
int vsscanf( const char *str, const char *format,va_ist ap);
int vfscanf( FILE *stream, const char *format,va_list ap);
```

## DESCRIPTION

The scanf family of functions scans input according to a format as described below. This format may contain conversion specifiers ; the results from such conversions, if any, are stored through the pointer arguments. The scanf function reads input from the standard input stream stdin, fscanf reads input from the stream pointer stream, and sscanf reads its input from the character string pointed to by str.

The vfscanf function is analogous to vfprintf(3) and reads input from the stream pointer stream using a variable argument list of pointers (see stdarg(3)). The vscanf function scans a variable argument list from the standard input and the vsscanf function scans it from a string; these are analogous to the vprintf and vsprintf functions respectively.

Each successive pointer argument must correspond properly with each successive conversion specifier. All conversions are introduced by the % (percent sign) character. The format string may also contain other characters. Whitespace (such as blanks, tabs, or newlines) in the format string match any amount of whitespace, including none, in the input. Everything else matches only itself. Scanning stops when an input character does not match such a format character. Scanning also stops when an input conversion cannot be made.

## CONVERSIONS

Following the % character introducing a conversion, there may be a number of flag characters, as follows:

| | |
|---|---|
| * | Suppresses assignment. The conversion that follows occurs as usual, but no pointer is used; the result of the conversion is simply discarded. |
| a | Indicates that the conversion will be s, malloc will be applied to the needed memory space for the string, and the pointer to it will be assigned to the char pointer variable, which does not have to be initialized before. This flag does not exist in ANSI C. |
| n | Indicates that the conversion will be one of dioux or n and the next pointer is a pointer to a short int (rather than int). |
| l | Indicates either that the conversion will be one of dioux or n and the next pointer is a pointer to a long int (rather than int), or that the conversion will be one of efg and the next pointer is a pointer to double (rather than float). Specifying two l flags is equivalent to the L flag. |
| L | Indicates that the conversion will be either efg and the next pointer is a pointer to long double or the conversion will be dioux and the next pointer is a pointer to long long. (Note that long long is not an ANSI C type. Any program using this will not be portable to all architectures). |
| q | Equivalent to L. This flag does not exist in ANSI C. |

In addition to these flags, there may be an optional maximum field width, expressed as a decimal integer, between the % and the conversion. If no width is given, a default of infinity is used (with one exception, below); otherwise, at most this many characters are scanned in processing the conversion. Before conversion begins, most conversions skip whitespace; this whitespace is not counted against the field width.

The following conversions are available:

| | |
|---|---|
| % | Matches a literal %. That is, %% in the format string matches a single input % character. No conversion is done, and assignment does not occur. |
| d | Matches an optionally signed decimal integer; the next pointer must be a pointer to int. |
| D | Equivalent to ld; this exists only for backwards compatibility. |
| i | Matches an optionally signed integer; the next pointer must be a pointer to int. The integer is read in base 16 if it begins with 0x or 0X, in base 8 if it begins with 0, and in base 10 otherwise. Only characters that correspond to the base are used. |
| o | Matches an unsigned octal integer; the next pointer must be a pointer to unsigned int. |
| u | Matches an unsigned decimal integer; the next pointer must be a pointer to unsigned int. |
| x | Matches an unsigned hexadecimal integer; the next pointer must be a pointer to unsigned int. |
| X | Equivalent to x. |
| f | Matches an optionally signed floating-point number; the next pointer must be a pointer to float. |
| e | Equivalent to f. |
| g | Equivalent to f. |
| E | Equivalent to f. |
| s | Matches a sequence of nonwhitespace characters; the next pointer must be a pointer to char, and the array must be large enough to accept all the sequence and the terminating NUL character. The input string stops at whitespace or at the maximum field width, whichever occurs first. |
| c | Matches a sequence of width count characters (default 1); the next pointer must be a pointer to char, and there must be enough room for all the characters (no terminating NUL is added). The usual skip of leading whitespace is suppressed. To skip whitespace first, use an explicit space in the format. |
| [ | Matches a nonempty sequence of characters from the specified set of accepted characters; the next pointer must be a pointer to char, and there must be enough room for all the characters in the string, plus a terminating NUL character. The usual skip of leading whitespace is suppressed. The string is to be made up of characters in (or not in) a particular set; the set is defined by the characters between the open bracket [ character and a close bracket ] character. The set excludes those characters if the first |

character after the open bracket is a circumflex (^). To include a close bracket in the set, make it the first character after the open bracket or the circumflex; any other position will end the set. The hyphen character (-) is also special; when placed between two other characters, it adds all intervening characters to the set. To include a hyphen, make it the last character before the final close bracket. For instance, [^]0-9-] means the set "everything except close bracket, zero through nine, and hyphen." The string ends with the appearance of a character not in (or, with a circumflex, in) the set or when the field width runs out.

p      Matches a pointer value (as printed by %p in printf(3); the next pointer must be a pointer to void.

n      Nothing is expected; instead, the number of characters consumed thus far from the input is stored through the next pointer, which must be a pointer to int. This is not a conversion, although it can be suppressed with the * flag.

## RETURN VALUES

These functions return the number of input items assigned, which can be fewer than provided for, or even zero, in the event of a matching failure. Zero indicates that, while there was input available, no conversions were assigned; typically, this is due to an invalid input character, such as an alphabetic character for a %d conversion. The value EOF is returned if an input failure occurs before any conversion such as an end-of-file occurs. If an error or end-of-file occurs after conversion has begun, the number of conversions which were successfully completed is returned.

## SEE ALSO

strtol(3), strtoul(3), strtod(3), getc(3), printf(3)

## STANDARDS

The functions fscanf, scanf, and sscanf conform to ANSI C3.159-1989 (ANSI C).

The q flag is the BSD 4.4 notation for long long, while ll or the usage of L in integer conversions is the GNU notation.

The Linux version of these functions is based on the GNU libio library. Take a look at the info documentation of GNU libc (glibc-1.08) for a more concise description.

## BUGS

All functions are fully ANSI C3.159-1989-conformant, but provide the additional flags q and a as well as an additional behavior of the L and l flags. The latter may be considered to be a bug, as it changes the behavior of flags defined in ANSI C3.159-1989.

Some combinations of flags defined by ANSI C are not making sense in ANSI C (for example, %Ld). While they may have a well-defined behavior on Linux, this need not to be so on other architectures. Therefore, it usually is better to use flags that are not defined by ANSI C at all, that is, use q instead of L in combination with diouxX conversions or ll.

The usage of q is not the same as on BSD 4.4, as it may be used in float conversions equivalently to L.

*Linux man page, 1 November 1995*

# seekdir

seekdir—Sets the position of the next readdir() call in the directory stream.

## SYNOPSIS

```
#include <dirent.h>
void seekdir(DIR *dir,off_t offset);
```

## DESCRIPTION

The seekdir() function sets the location in the directory stream from which the next readdir() call will start. seekdir() should be used with an *offset* returned by telldir().

## RETURN VALUE

The seekdir() function returns no value.

## CONFORMS TO

BSD 4.3

## SEE ALSO

lseek(2), opendir(3), readdir(3), closedir(3), rewinddir(3), telldir(3), scandir(3)

*31 March 1993*

# setbuf, setbuffer, setlinebuf, setvbuf

setbuf, setbuffer, setlinebuf, setvbuf—Stream buffering operations

## SYNOPSIS

```
#include <stdio.h>

int setbuf( FILE *stream, char *buf);
int setbuffer( FILE *stream, char *buf, size_tsize);
int setlinebuf( FILE *stream);
int setvbuf( FILE *stream, char *buf,intmode , size_t size);
```

## DESCRIPTION

The three types of buffering available are unbuffered, block buffered, and line buffered. When an output stream is unbuffered, information appears on the destination file or terminal as soon as written; when it is block buffered, many characters are saved up and written as a block; when it is line buffered, characters are saved up until a newline is output or input is read from any stream attached to a terminal device (typically stdin). The function fflush(3) may be used to force the block out early. (See fclose(3).) Normally all files are block buffered. When the first I/O operation occurs on a file, malloc(3) is called, and a buffer is obtained. If a stream refers to a terminal (as stdout normally does), it is line buffered. The standard error stream stderr is always unbuffered.

The setvbuf function may be used at any time on any open stream to change its buffer. The mode parameter must be one of the following three macros:

| | |
|---|---|
| _IONBF | Unbuffered |
| _IOLBF | Line buffered |
| _IOFBF | Fully buffered |

Except for unbuffered files, the *buf* argument should point to a buffer at least *size* bytes long; this buffer will be used instead of the current buffer. If the argument buf is NULL, only the mode is affected; a new buffer will be allocated on the next read or write operation. The setvbuf function may be used at any time, but can only change the mode of a stream when it is not "active"; that is, before any I/O, or immediately after a call to fflush.

The other three calls are, in effect, simply aliases for calls to setvbuf. The setbuf function is exactly equivalent to the call:

setvbuf(*stream, buf, buf* ?_IOFBF :_IONBF, BUFSIZ);

The setbuffer function is the same, except that the size of the buffer is up to the caller, rather than being determined by the default BUFSIZ. The setlinebuf function is exactly equivalent to the call:

setvbuf(*stream*, (char *)NULL,_IOLBF, 0);

## SEE ALSO

fopen(3), fclose(3), fread(3), malloc(3), puts(3), printf(3)

## STANDARDS

The setbuf and setvbuf functions conform to ANSI C3.159-1989 (ANSI C).

## BUGS

The setbuffer and setlinebuf functions are not portable to versions of BSD before 4.2BSD, and may not be available under Linux. On 4.2BSD and 4.3BSD systems, setbuf always uses a suboptimal buffer size and should be avoided. You must make sure that both buf and the space it points to still exist by the time stream is closed, which also happens at program termination. For example, the following is illegal:

```
#include <stdio.h>
int main()
{
    char buf[BUFSIZ];
    setbuf(stdin, buf);
    printf("Hello, world!\n");
    return 0;
}
```

*BSD man page, 29 November 1993*

# setenv

setenv—Changes or adds an environment variable

## SYNOPSIS

```
#include <stdlib.h>
int setenv(const char *name, const char *value,int overwrite);
void unsetenv(const char *name);
```

## DESCRIPTION

The setenv() function adds the variable name to the environment with the value value, if *name* does not already exist. If *name* does exist in the environment, then its value is changed to value if overwrite is non-zero; if overwrite is zero, then the value of *name* is not changed.

The unsetenv() function deletes the variable name from the environment.

## RETURN VALUE

The setenv() function returns zero on success, or -1 if there was insufficient space in the environment.

## CONFORMS TO

BSD 4.3

## SEE ALSO

getenv(3), putenv(3)

*BSD, 4 April 1993*

# setjmp

setjmp—Saves stack context for nonlocal goto

## SYNOPSIS

```
#include <setjmp.h>
int setjmp(jmp_buf env );
```

## DESCRIPTION

setjmp and longjmp(3) are useful for dealing with errors and interrupts encountered in a low-level subroutine of a program. setjmp() saves the stack context/environment in env for later use by longjmp(). The stack context will be invalidated if the function which called setjmp() returns.

## RETURN VALUE

It returns the value 0 if returning directly and non-zero when returning from longjmp() using the saved context.

## CONFORMS TO

POSIX

## NOTES

POSIX does not specify if the signal context will be saved or not. If you want to save signal masks, use sigsetjmp(3). setjmp() makes programs hard to understand and maintain. If possible, an alternative should be used.

## SEE ALSO

longjmp(3), sigsetjmp(2), siglongjmp(2)

*25 November 1994*

# setlocale

setlocale—Sets the current locale

## SYNOPSIS

```
#include <locale.h>
char *setlocale(int category, const char * locale);
```

## DESCRIPTION

The setlocale() function is used to set or query the program's current locale. If locale is C or POSIX, the current locale is set to the portable locale.

If locale is "", the locale is set to the default locale that is selected from the environment variable LANG.

On startup of the main program, the portable locale is selected as default.

The argument category determines which functions are influenced by the new locale:

| | |
|---|---|
| LC_ALL | For all of the locale. |
| LC_COLLATE | For the functions strcoll() and strxfrm(). |
| LC_CTYPE | For the character classification and conversion routines. |
| LC_MONETARY | For localeconv(). |
| LC_NUMERIC | For the decimal character. |
| LC_TIME | For strftime(). NULL if the request can not be honored. This string may be allocated in static storage. |

A program may be made portable to all locales by calling `setlocale(LC_ALL, """""")` after program initialization, by using the values returned from a `localeconv()` call for locale–dependent information and by using `strcoll()` or `strxfrm()` to compare strings.

## CONFORMS TO

ANSI C, POSIX.1

Linux supports the portable locales C and POSIX and also the European Latin-1 and Russian locales.

The `printf()` family of functions may or may not honor the current locale.

## SEE ALSO

`locale(1)`, `localedef(1)`, `strcoll(3)`, `isalpha(3)`, `localeconv(3)`, `strftime(3)`, `locale(7)`

*GNU, 18 April 1993*

# siginterrupt

`siginterrupt`—Allows signals to interrupt system calls

## SYNOPSIS

```
#include <signal.h>
int siginterrupt(int sig,int flag);
```

## DESCRIPTION

The `siginterrupt()` function changes the restart behavior when a system call is interrupted by the signal `sig`. If the `flag` argument is false (`0`), then systems calls will be restarted if interrupted by the specified signal `sig`. This is the default behavior in Linux. However, when a new signal handler is specified with the `signal(2)` function, the system call is interrupted by default.

If the `flag` argument is true (`1`) and no data has been transferred, then a system call interrupted by the signal `sig` will return `-1` and the global variable *errno* will be set to `EINTR`.

If the `flag` argument is true (`1`) and data transfer has started, then the system call will be interrupted and will return the actual amount of data transferred.

## RETURN VALUE

The `siginterrupt()` function returns `0` on success, or `-1` if the signal number `sig` is invalid.

## ERRORS

EINVAL                                   The specified signal number is invalid.

## CONFORMS TO

BSD 4.3

## SEE ALSO

`signal(2)`

*13 April 1993*

# sigemptyset, sigfillset, sigaddset, sigdelset, sigismember

`sigemptyset`, `sigfillset`, `sigaddset`, `sigdelset`, `sigismember`—POSIX signal set operations

## SYNOPSIS

```
#include <signal.h>
int sigemptyset(sigset_t *set);
int sigfillset(sigset_t *set);
int sigaddset(sigset_t *set,int signum);
int sigdelset(sigset_t *set,int signum);
int sigismember(const sigset_t *set,int signum);
```

## DESCRIPTION

The sigsetops(3) functions allow the manipulation of POSIX signal sets.

sigemptyset initializes the signal set given by *set* to empty, with all signals excluded from the set.

sigfillset initializes *set* to full, including all signals.

sigaddset and sigdelset add and delete, respectively, signal *signum* from *set*.

sigismember tests whether *signum* is a member of *set*.

## RETURN VALUES

sigemptyset, sigfullset, sigaddset, and sigdelset return 0 on success and -1 on error.

sigismember returns 1 if signum is a member of set, 0 if signum is not a member, and -1 on error.

## ERRORS

EINVAL                              *sig* is not a valid signal.

## CONFORMS TO

POSIX

## SEE ALSO

sigaction(2), sigpending(2), sigprocmask(2), sigsuspend(2)

*Linux 1.0, 24 September 1994*

# sin

sin—Sine function

## SYNOPSIS

```
#include <math.h>
double sin(double x);
```

## DESCRIPTION

The sin() function returns the sine of *x*, where *x* is given in radians.

## RETURN VALUE

The sin() function returns a value between –1 and 1.

## CONFORMS TO

SVID 3, POSIX, BSD 4.3, ISO 9899

## SEE ALSO

acos(3), asin(3), atan(3), atan2(3), cos(3), tan(3)

*8 June 1993*


# sinh

sinh—Hyperbolic sine function

## SYNOPSIS

```
#include <math.h>
double sinh(double x);
```

## DESCRIPTION

The sinh() function returns the hyperbolic sine of *x*, which is defined mathematically as [exp(x)–exp(-x)] / 2.

## CONFORMS TO

SVID 3, POSIX, BSD 4.3, ISO 9899

## SEE ALSO

acosh(3), asinh(3), atanh(3), cosh(3), tanh(3)

*13 June 1993*


# sleep

sleep—Sleeps for the specified number of seconds

## SYNOPSIS

```
#include <unistd.h>
unsigned int sleep(unsigned int seconds);
```

## DESCRIPTION

sleep() makes the current process sleep until *seconds* seconds have elapsed or a signal arrives that is not ignored.

## RETURN VALUE

The return value is zero if the requested time has elapsed, or the number of seconds left to sleep.

## CONFORMS TO

POSIX.1

## BUGS

sleep()may be implemented using SIGALRM; mixing calls to alarm() and sleep() is a bad idea.

Using longjmp() from a signal handler or modifying the handling of SIGALRM while sleeping will cause undefined results.

## SEE ALSO

signal(2), alarm(2)

*GNU, 7 April 1993*

# snprintf, vsnprintf

snprintf, vsnprintf—Formatted output conversion

## SYNOPSIS

```
#include <stdio.h>

int snprintf ( char *str, size_t n,
const char *format, ... );

#include <stdarg.h>

int vsnprintf ( char *str, size_t n,
const char *format, va_list ap );
```

## DESCRIPTION

snprintf writes output to the string *str*, under control of the *format* string that specifies how subsequent arguments are converted for output. It is similar to sprintf(3), except that *n* specifies the maximum number of characters to produce. The trailing null character is counted towards this limit, so you should allocate at least *n* characters for the string *str*.

vsnprintf is the equivalent of snprintf with the variable argument list specified directly as for vprintf.

## RETURN VALUE

The return value is the number of characters stored, not including the terminating null. If this value equals *n*, then there was not enough space in *str* for all the output. You should try again with a bigger output string.

## EXAMPLE

Here is a sample program that dynamically enlarges its output buffer:

```
/* Construct a message describing the value of a
   variable whose name is NAME and whose value is
   VALUE. */
char *
make_message (char *name, char *value)
{
  /* Guess we need no more than 100 chars of space. */
  int size = 100;
  char *buffer = (char *) xmalloc (size);
  while (1)
    {
      /* Try to print in the allocated space. */
      int nchars = snprintf (buffer, size,
                   "value of %s is %s", name, value);
      /* If that worked, return the string. */
      if (nchars < size)
        return buffer;
      /* Else try again with twice as much space. */
      size *= 2;
      buffer = (char *) xrealloc (size, buffer);
    }
}
```

## CONFORMS TO

These are GNU extensions.

## SEE ALSO

printf(3), sprintf(3), vsprintf(3), stdarg(3)

*GNU, 16 September 1995*

# sqrt

sqrt—Square root function

## SYNOPSIS

```
#include <math.h>
double sqrt(double x);
```

## DESCRIPTION

The sqrt() function returns the non-negative square root of *x*. It fails and sets *errno* to EDOM, if *x* is negative.

## ERRORS

EDOM                          *x* is negative.

## CONFORMS TO

SVID 3, POSIX, BSD 4.3, ISO 9899

## SEE ALSO

hypot(3)

*21 June 1993*

# stdarg

stdarg—Variable argument lists

## SYNOPSIS

```
#include <stdarg.h>
void va_start( va_list ap, last);
type va_arg( va_list ap, type);
void va_end( va_list ap);
```

## DESCRIPTION

A function may be called with a varying number of arguments of varying types. The include file stdarg.h declares a type va_list and defines three macros for stepping through a list of arguments whose number and types are not known to the called function.

The called function must declare an object of type va_list that is used by the macros va_start, va_arg, and va_end.

The va_start macro initializes *ap* for subsequent use by va_arg and va_end, and must be called first.

The parameter *last* is the name of the last parameter before the variable argument list; that is, the last parameter of which the calling function knows the type.

Because the address of this parameter is used in the va_start macro, it should not be declared as a register variable, a function, or an array type.

The va_start macro returns no value.

The va_arg macro expands to an expression that has the type and value of the next argument in the call. The parameter *ap* is the va_list *ap* initialized by va_start. Each call to va_arg modifies *ap* so that the next call returns the next argument. The parameter type is a type name specified so that the type of a pointer to an object that has the specified type can be obtained simply by adding a * to type.

If there is no next argument, or if type is not compatible with the type of the actual next argument (as promoted according to the default argument promotions), random errors will occur.

The first use of the va_arg macro after that of the va_start macro returns the argument after last. Successive invocations return the values of the remaining arguments.

The va_end macro handles a normal return from the function whose variable argument list was initialized by va_start.

The va_end macro returns no value.

## EXAMPLE

The function foo takes a string of format characters and prints out the argument associated with each format character based on the type.

```
void foo(char *fmt, ...)
{
    va_list ap;
    int d;
    char c, *p, *s;

    va_start(ap, fmt);
    while (*fmt)
        switch(*fmt++) {
        case 's':              /* string */
            s = va_arg(ap, char *);
            printf("string %s\n", s);
            break;
        case 'd':              /* int */
            d = va_arg(ap, int);
            printf("int %d\n", d);
            break;
        case 'c':              /* char */
            c = va_arg(ap, char);
            printf("char %c\n", c);
            break;
        }
    va_end(ap);
}
```

## STANDARDS

The va_start, va_arg, and va_end macros conform to ANSI C3.159-1989 (ANSI C).

## COMPATIBILITY

These macros are not compatible with the historic macros they replace. A backwards-compatible version can be found in the include file varargs.h.

## BUGS

Unlike the varargs macros, the stdarg macros do not permit programmers to code a function with no fixed arguments. This problem generates work mainly when converting varargs code to stdarg code, but it also creates difficulties for variadic functions that wish to pass all of their arguments on to a function that takes a va_list argument, such as vfprintf(3).

# stdio

stdio—Standard input/output library functions

## SYNOPSIS

```
#include <stdio.h>
FILE *stdin;
FILE *stdout;
FILE *stderr;
```

## DESCRIPTION

The standard I/O library provides a simple and efficient buffered stream I/O interface. Input and output is mapped into logical data streams and the physical I/O characteristics are concealed. The functions and macros are listed in this section; more information is available from the individual man pages.

A stream is associated with an external file (which may be a physical device) by opening a file, which may involve creating a new file. Creating an existing file causes its former contents to be discarded. If a file can support positioning requests (such as a disk file, as opposed to a terminal), then a file position indicator associated with the stream is positioned at the start of the file (byte zero), unless the file is opened with append mode. If append mode is used, the position indicator will be placed the end-of-file. The position indicator is maintained by subsequent reads, writes, and positioning requests. All input occurs as if the characters were read by successive calls to the fgetc(3) function; all output takes place as if all characters were read by successive calls to the fputc(3) function.

A file is disassociated from a stream by closing the file. Output streams are flushed (any unwritten buffer contents are transferred to the host environment) before the stream is disassociated from the file. The value of a pointer to a FILE object is indeterminate after a file is closed (garbage).

A file may be subsequently reopened, by the same or another program execution, and its contents reclaimed or modified (if it can be repositioned at the start). If the main function returns to its original caller, or the exit(3) function is called, all open files are closed (hence all output streams are flushed) before program termination. Other methods of program termination, such as abort(3) do not bother about closing files properly.

At program startup, three text streams are predefined and need not be opened explicitly: standard input (for reading conventional input), standard output (for writing conventional input), and standard error (for writing diagnostic output). These streams are abbreviated stdin, stdout, and stderr. When opened, the standard error stream is not fully buffered; the standard input and output streams are fully buffered if and only if the streams do not to refer to an interactive device.

Output streams that refer to terminal devices are always line buffered by default; pending output to such streams is written automatically whenever an input stream that refers to a terminal device is read. In cases where a large amount of computation is done after printing part of a line on an output terminal, it is necessary to fflush(3) the standard output before going off and computing so that the output will appear.

The stdio library is a part of the library libc and routines are automatically loaded as needed by the compilers cc(1) and pc(1). The SYNOPSIS sections of the following manual pages indicate which include files are to be used, what the compiler declaration for the function looks like, and which external variables are of interest.

The following are defined as macros; these names may not be reused without first removing their current definitions with #undef: BUFSIZ, EOF, FILENAME_MAX, FOPEN_MAX, L_cuserid, L_ctermid, L_tmpnam, NULL, SEEK_END, SEEK_SET, SEE_CUR, TMP_MAX, clearerr, feof, ferror, fileno, fropen, fwopen, getc, getchar, putc, putchar, stderr, stdin, stdout. Function versions of the macro functions feof, ferror, clearerr, fileno, getc, getchar, putc, and putchar exist and will be used if the macros definitions are explicitly removed.

## SEE ALSO

open(2), close(2), read(2), write(2)

## BUGS

The standard buffered functions do not interact well with certain other library and system functions, especially vfork and abort. This may not be the case under Linux.

## STANDARDS

The stdio library conforms to ANSI C3.159-1989 (ANSI C).

## LIST OF FUNCTIONS

| Function | Description |
| --- | --- |
| clearerr | Check and reset stream status |
| fclose | Close a stream |
| fdopen | Stream open functions |
| feof | Check and reset stream status |
| ferror | Check and reset stream status |
| fflush | Flush a stream |
| fgetc | Get next character or word from input stream |
| fgetline | Get a line from a stream |
| fgetpos | Reposition a stream |
| fgets | Get a line from a stream |
| fileno | Check and reset stream status |
| fopen | Stream open functions |
| fprintf | Formatted output conversion |
| fpurge | Flush a stream |
| fputc | Output a character or word to a stream |
| fputs | Output a line to a stream |
| fread | Binary stream input/output |
| freopen | Stream open functions |
| fropen | Open a stream |
| fscanf | Input format conversion |
| fseek | Reposition a stream |
| fsetpos | Reposition a stream |
| ftell | Reposition a stream |
| fwrite | Binary stream input/output |
| getc | Get next character or word from input stream |
| getchar | Get next character or word from input stream |
| gets | Get a line from a stream |
| getw | Get next character or word from input stream |
| mktemp | Make temporary filename (unique) |
| perror | System error messages |
| printf | Formatted output conversion |
| putc | Output a character or word to a stream |
| putchar | Output a character or word to a stream |
| puts | Output a line to a stream |
| putw | Output a character or word to a stream |

| | |
|---|---|
| remove | Remove directory entry |
| rewind | Reposition a stream |
| scanf | Input format conversion |
| setbuf | Stream buffering operations |
| setbuffer | Stream buffering operations |
| setlinebuf | Stream buffering operations |
| setvbuf | Stream buffering operations |
| sprintf | Formatted output conversion |
| sscanf | Input format conversion |
| strerror | System error messages |
| sys_errlist | System error messages |
| sys_nerr | System error messages |
| tempnam | Temporary file routines |
| tmpfile | Temporary file routines |
| tmpnam | Temporary file routines |
| ungetc | Un-get character from input stream |
| vfprintf | Formatted output conversion |
| vfscanf | Input format conversion |
| vprintf | Formatted output conversion |
| vscanf | Input format conversion |
| vsprintf | Formatted output conversion |
| vsscanf | Input format conversion |

*BSD man page, 29 November 1993*

# stpcpy

stpcpy—Copies a string returning a pointer to its end

## SYNOPSIS

```
#include <string.h>
char *stpcpy(char *dest, const char *src);
```

## DESCRIPTION

The stpcpy() function copies the string pointed to by *src* (including the terminating \0 character) to the array pointed to by *dest*. The strings may not overlap, and the destination string *dest* must be large enough to receive the copy.

## RETURN VALUE

stpcpy() returns a pointer to the end of the string *dest* (that is, the address of the terminating null character) rather than the beginning.

## EXAMPLE

For example, this program uses stpcpy to concatenate foo and bar to produce foobar, which it then prints:

```
#include <string.h>

int
main (void)
{
```

```
        char *to = buffer;
        to = stpcpy (to, "foo");
        to = stpcpy (to, "bar");
        printf ("%s\n", buffer);
    }
```

## CONFORMS TO

This function is not part of the ANSI or POSIX standards, and is not customary on UNIX systems, but is not a GNU invention either. Perhaps it comes from MS-DOS.

## SEE ALSO

strcpy(3), bcopy(3), memccpy(3), memcpy(3), memmove(3)

*GNU, 3 September 1995*


# strcasecmp, strncasecmp

strcasecmp, strncasecmp—Compare two strings, ignoring case

## SYNOPSIS

```
#include <string.h>
int strcasecmp(const char *s1, const char *s2);
int strncasecmp(const char *s1, const char *s2, size_t n);
```

## DESCRIPTION

The strcasecmp() function compares the two strings *s1* and *s2*, ignoring the case of the characters. It returns an integer less than, equal to, or greater than zero if *s1* is found, respectively, to be less than, to match, or be greater than *s2*.

The strncasecmp() function is similar, except it only compares the first *n* characters of *s1*.

## RETURN VALUE

The strcasecmp() and strncasecmp() functions return an integer less than, equal to, or greater than zero if s1 (or the first *n* bytes thereof) is found, respectively, to be less than, to match, or be greater than s2.

## CONFORMS TO

BSD 4.3

## SEE ALSO

bcmp(3), memcmp(3), strcmp(3), strcoll(3), strncmp(3)

*11 April 1993*


# strcat, strncat

strcat, strncat—Concatenate two strings

## SYNOPSIS

```
#include <string.h>
char *strcat(char *dest, const char *src);
char *strncat(char *dest, const char *src, size_t n);
```

## DESCRIPTION

The strcat() function appends the *src* string to the *dest* string, overwriting the \0 character at the end of *dest*, and then adds a terminating \0 character. The strings may not overlap, and the *dest* string must have enough space for the result.

The strncat() function is similar, except that only the first *n* characters of *src* are appended to *dest*.

## RETURN VALUE

The strcat() and strncat() functions return a pointer to the resulting string *dest*.

## CONFORMS TO

SVID 3, POSIX, BSD 4.3, ISO 9899

## SEE ALSO

bcopy(3), memccpy(3), memcpy(3), strcpy(3), strncpy(3)

*GNU, 11 April 1993*

# strchr, strrchr

strchr, strrchr—Locate character in string

## SYNOPSIS

```
#include <string.h>
char *strchr(const char *s,int c);
char *strrchr(const char *s,int c);
```

## DESCRIPTION

The strchr() function returns a pointer to the first occurrence of the character *c* in the string *s*.

The strrchr() function returns a pointer to the last occurrence of the character *c* in the string *s*.

## RETURN VALUE

The strchr() and strrchr() functions return a pointer to the matched character or NULL if the character is not found.

## CONFORMS TO

SVID 3, POSIX, BSD 4.3, ISO 9899

## SEE ALSO

index(3), memchr(3), rindex(3), strpbrk(3), strsep(3), strspn(3), strstr(3), strtok(3)

*12 April 1993*

# strcmp, strncmp

strcmp, strncmp—Compare two strings

## SYNOPSIS

```
#include <string.h>
int strcmp(const char *s1, const char *s2);
int strncmp(const char *s1, const char *s2, size_t n);
```

## DESCRIPTION

The strcmp() function compares the two strings s1 and s2. It returns an integer less than, equal to, or greater than zero if s1 is found, respectively, to be less than, to match, or be greater than s2.

The strncmp() function is similar, except it only compares the first *n* characters of s1.

## RETURN VALUE

The strcmp() and strncmp() functions return an integer less than, equal to, or greater than zero if s1 (or the first *n* bytes thereof) is found, respectively, to be less than, to match, or be greater than s2.

## CONFORMS TO

SVID 3, POSIX, BSD 4.3, ISO 9899

## SEE ALSO

bcmp(3), memcmp(3), strcasecmp(3), strncasecmp(3), strcoll(3)

*11 April 1993*

# strcoll

strcoll—Compares two strings using the current locale

## SYNOPSIS

```
#include <string.h>
int strcoll(const char *s1, const char *s2);
```

## DESCRIPTION

The strcoll() function compares the two strings s1 and s2. It returns an integer less than, equal to, or greater than zero if s1 is found, respectively, to be less than, to match, or be greater than s2. The comparison is based on strings interpreted as appropriate for the program's current locale for category LC_COLLATE. (See setlocale(3)).

## RETURN VALUE

The strcoll() function returns an integer less than, equal to, or greater than zero if s1 is found, respectively, to be less than, to match, or be greater than s2, when both are interpreted as appropriate for the current locale.

## CONFORMS TO

SVID 3, BSD 4.3, ISO 9899

## NOTES

The Linux C Library currently hasn't implemented the complete POSIX-collating.

In the POSIX or C locales, strcoll() is equivalent to strcmp().

## SEE ALSO

bcmp(3), memcmp(3), strcasecmp(3), strcmp(3), strxfrm(3), setlocale(3)

*GNU, 12 April 1993*

# strcpy, strncpy

strcpy, strncpy—Copy a string

## SYNOPSIS

```
#include <string.h>
char *strcpy(char *dest, const char *src);
char *strncpy(char *dest, const char *src, size_t n);
```

## DESCRIPTION

The strcpy() function copies the string pointed to be *src* (including the terminating \0 character) to the array pointed to by *dest*. The strings may not overlap, and the destination string *dest* must be large enough to receive the copy.

The strncpy() function is similar, except that not more than *n* bytes of *src* are copied. Thus, if there is no null byte among the first *n* bytes of *src*, the result will not be null-terminated.

In the case where the length of *src* is less than that of *n*, the remainder of *dest* will be padded with nulls.

## RETURN VALUE

The strcpy() and strncpy() functions return a pointer to the destination string *dest*.

## CONFORMS TO

SVID 3, POSIX, BSD 4.3, ISO 9899

## SEE ALSO

bcopy(3), memccpy(3), memcpy(3), memmove(3)

*GNU, 11 April 1993*


# strdup

strdup—Duplicates a string

## SYNOPSIS

```
#include <string.h>
char *strdup(const char *s);
```

## DESCRIPTION

The strdup() function returns a pointer to a new string that is a duplicate of the string *s*. Memory for the new string is obtained with malloc(3), and can be freed with free(3).

## RETURN VALUE

The strdup() function returns a pointer to the duplicated string, or NULL if insufficient memory was available.

## ERRORS

ENOMEM               Insufficient memory available to allocate duplicate string

## CONFORMS TO

SVID 3, BSD 4.3

## SEE ALSO

calloc(3), malloc(3), realloc(3), free(3)

*GNU, 12 April 1993*

# strerror

strerror—Returns string describing error code

## SYNOPSIS

```
#include <string.h>

char *strerror(int errnum);
```

## DESCRIPTION

The strerror() function returns a string describing the error code passed in the argument *errnum*. The string can only be used until the next call to strerror().

## RETURN VALUE

The strerror() function returns the appropriate description string, or an unknown error message if the error code is unknown.

## CONFORMS TO

SVID 3, POSIX, BSD 4.3, ISO 9899

## SEE ALSO

errno(3), perror(3), strsignal(3)

*GNU, 13 April 1993*

# strfry

strfry—Randomizes a string

## SYNOPSIS

```
#include <string.h>
char *strfry(char *string);
```

## DESCRIPTION

The strfry() function randomizes the contents of *string* by using rand(3) to randomly swap characters in the string. The result is an anagram of *string*.

## RETURN VALUE

The strfry() function returns a pointer to the randomized string.

## CONFORMS TO

The strfry() function is unique to the Linux C Library and GNU C Library.

## SEE ALSO

memfrob(3)

*GNU, 12 April 1993*

# strftime

strftime—Formats date and time

## SYNOPSIS

```
#include <time.h>
size t strftime(char *s, size_t max, const char *format,
const struct tm *tm);
```

## DESCRIPTION

The strftime() function formats the broken-down time *tm* according to the format specification format and places the result in the character array *s* of size *max*.

Ordinary characters placed in the format string are copied to *s* without conversion. Conversion specifiers are introduced by a % character, and are replaced in *s* as follows:

| | |
|---|---|
| %a | The abbreviated weekday name according to the current locale |
| %A | The full weekday name according to the current locale |
| %b | The abbreviated month name according to the current locale |
| %B | The full month name according to the current locale |
| %c | The preferred date and time representation for the current locale |
| %d | The day of the month as a decimal number (range 01 to 31) |
| %H | The hour as a decimal number using a 24-hour clock (range 00 to 23) |
| %I | The hour as a decimal number using a 12-hour clock (range 01 to 12) |
| %j | The day of the year as a decimal number (range 001 to 366) |
| %m | The month as a decimal number (range 01 to 12) |
| %M | The minute as a decimal number |
| %p | Either a.m. or p.m. according to the given time value, or the corresponding strings for the current locale |
| %S | The second as a decimal number |
| %U | The week number of the current year as a decimal number, starting with the first Sunday as the first day of the first week |
| %W | The week number of the current year as a decimal number, starting with the first Monday as the first day of the first week |
| %w | The day of the week as a decimal, Sunday being 0 |
| %x | The preferred date representation for the current locale without the time |
| %X | The preferred time representation for the current locale without the date |
| %y | The year as a decimal number without a century (range 00 to 99) |
| %Y | The year as a decimal number including the century |
| %Z | The time zone or name or abbreviation |
| %% | A literal % character |

The broken-down time structure tm is defined in <time.h> as follows:

```
struct tm
{
int tm sec; /* seconds */
int tm min; /* minutes */
int tm hour; /* hours */
int tm mday; /* day of the month */
int tm mon; /* month */
int tm year; /* year */
int tm wday; /* day of the week */
int tm yday; /* day in the year */
int tm isdst; /* daylight saving time */
};
```

The members of the tm structure are

| | |
|---|---|
| tm_sec | The number of seconds after the minute, normally in the range 0 to 59, but can be up to 61 to allow for leap seconds. |
| tm_min | The number of minutes after the hour, in the range 0 to 59. |
| tm_hour | The number of hours past midnight, in the range 0 to 23. |
| tm_mday | The day of the month, in the range 1 to 31. |
| tm_mon | The number of months since January, in the range 0 to 11. |
| tm_year | The number of years since 1900. |
| tm_wday | The number of days since Sunday, in the range 0 to 6. |
| tm_yday | The number of days since January 1, in the range 0 to 365. |
| tm_isdst | A flag that indicates whether daylight saving time is in effect at the time described. The value is positive if daylight saving time is in effect, zero if it is not, and negative if the information is not available. |

## RETURN VALUE

The strftime() function returns the number of characters placed in the array s, not including the terminating NULL character. If the value equals max, it means that the array was too small.

## CONFORMS TO

SVID 3, POSIX, BSD 4.3, ISO 9899

## SEE ALSO

date(1), time(2), ctime(3), setlocale(3), sprintf(3)

## NOTES

The function supports only those locales specified in locale(7)

*GNU, 2 July 1993*

# strcasecmp, strcat, strchr, strcmp, strcoll, strcpy, strcspn, strdup, strfry, strlen, strncat, strncmp, strncpy, strncasecmp, strpbrk, strrchr, strsep, strspn, strstr, strtok, strxfrm, index, rindex

strcasecmp, strcat, strchr, strcmp, strcoll, strcpy, strcspn, strdup, strfry, strlen, strncat, strncmp, strncpy, strncasecmp, strpbrk, strrchr, strsep, strspn, strstr, strtok, strxfrm, index, rindex—String operations

## SYNOPSIS

```
#include <string.h>
int strcasecmp(const char *s1, const char *s2);
char *strcat(char *dest, const char *src);
char *strchr(const char *s,int c);
int strcmp(const char *s1, const char *s2);
int strcoll(const char *s1, const char *s2);
char *strcpy(char *dest, const char *src);
size_t strcspn(const char *s, const char *reject);
char *strdup(const char *s);
```

```
char *strfry(char *string);
size_t strlen(const char *s);
char *strncat(char *dest, const char *src, size_t n);
int strncmp(const char *s1, const char *s2, size_t n);
char *strncpy(char *dest, const char *src, size_t n);
int strncasecmp(const char *s1, const char *s2, size_t n);
char *strpbrk(const char *s, const char *accept);
char *strrchr(const char *s,int c);
char *strsep(char **stringp, const char *delim);
size_t strspn(const char *s, const char *accept);
char *strstr(const char *haystack, const char *needle);
char *strtok(char *s, const char *delim);
size_t strxfrm(char *dest, const char *src, size_t n);
char *index(constchar*"s,int c);
char *rindex(const char *s,int c);
```

## DESCRIPTION

The string functions perform string operations on NULL-terminated strings. See the individual man pages for descriptions of each function.

## SEE ALSO

index(3), rindex(3), strcasecmp(3), strcat(3), strchr(3), strcmp(3), strcoll(3), strcpy(3), strcspn(3), strdup(3), strfry(3), strlen(3), strncat(3), strncmp(3), strncpy(3), strncasecmp(3), strpbrk(3), strrchr(3), strsep(3), strspn(3), strstr(3), strtok(3), strxfrm(3)

*9 April 1993*

# strlen

strlen—Calculates the length of a string

## SYNOPSIS

```
#include <string.h>
size_t strlen(const char *s);
```

## DESCRIPTION

The strlen() function calculates the length of the string s, not including the terminating \0 character.

## RETURN VALUE

The strlen() function returns the number of characters in s.

## CONFORMS TO

SVID 3, POSIX, BSD 4.3, ISO 9899

## SEE ALSO

string(3)

*12 April 1993*

# strpbrk

strpbrk—Searches a string for any of a set of characters

## SYNOPSIS

```
#include <string.h>
char *strpbrk(const char *s, const char *accept);
```

## DESCRIPTION

The strpbrk() function locates the first occurrence in the string *s* of any of the characters in the string *accept*.

## RETURN VALUE

The strpbrk() function returns a pointer to the character in *s* that matches one of the characters in *accept*.

## CONFORMS TO

SVID 3, POSIX, BSD 4.3, ISO 9899

## SEE ALSO

index(3), memchr(3), rindex(3), strchr(3), strsep(3), strspn(3), strstr(3), strtok(3)

*12 April 1993*

# strptime

strptime—Converts a string representation of time to a time tm structure

## SYNOPSIS

```
#include <time.h>
char *strptime(char *buf, const char *format, const struct tm *tm);
```

## DESCRIPTION

strptime() is the complementary function to strftime() and converts the character string pointed to by *buf* to a time value, which is stored in the tm structure pointed to by *tm*, using the format specified by *format*. *format* is a character string that consists of field descriptors and text characters, reminiscent of scanf(3). Each field descriptor consists of a % character followed by another character that specifies the replacement for the field descriptor. All other characters are copied from *format* into the result. The following field descriptors are supported:

| | |
|---|---|
| %% | Same as %. |
| %a, %A | Day of week, using locale's weekday names; either the abbreviated or full name may be specified. |
| %b, %B, %h | Month, using locale's month names; either the abbreviated or full name may be specified. |
| %c | Date and time as %x, %X. |
| %C | Date and time, in locale's long-format date and time representation. |
| %d, %e | Day of month (1–31; leading zeroes are permitted but not required). |
| %D | Date as %m/%d/%y. |
| %H, %k | Hour (0–23; leading zeroes are permitted but not required). |
| %I, %l | Hour (0–12; leading zeroes are permitted but not required). |
| %j | Day number of year (001–366). |
| %m | Month number (1–12; leading zeroes are permitted but not required). |
| %M | Minute (0–59; leading zeroes are permitted but not required). |
| %p | Locale's equivalent of a.m. or p.m. |
| %r | Time as %I:%M:%S %p. |

| %R | Time as %H:%M. |
| %S | Seconds (0–61; leading zeroes are permitted but not required; extra second allowed for leap years). |
| %T | Time as %H:%M:%S. |
| %w | Weekday number (0–6) with Sunday as the first day of the week. |
| %x | Date, using locale's date format. |
| %X | Time, using locale's time format. |
| %y | Year within century (0–99; leading zeroes are permitted but not required. Unfortunately, this makes the assumption that we are stuck in the 20th century, as 1900 is automatically added onto this number for the tm year field.) |
| %Y | Year, including century (for example, 1988). |

Case is ignored when matching items such as month or weekday names.

The broken-down time structure tm is defined in <time.h> as follows:

```
struct tm
{
   int tm_sec; /* seconds */
   int tm_min; /* minutes */
   int tm_hour; /* hours */
   int tm_mday; /* day of the month */
   int tm_mon; /* month */
   int tm_year; /* year */
   int tm_wday; /* day of the week */
   int tm_yday; /* day in the year */
   int tm_isdst; /* daylight saving time */
};
```

## RETURN VALUE

The strptime() function returns a pointer to the character following the last character in the string pointed to by *buf*.

## SEE ALSO

strftime(3), time(2), setlocale(3), scanf(3)

## BUGS

The return values point to static data, whose contents are overwritten by each call.

## NOTES

This function is only available in libraries newer than version 4.6.5.

The function supports only those locales specified in locale(7).

*GNU, 26 September 1994*

# strsep

strsep—Extracts token from string

## SYNOPSIS

```
#include <string.h>
char *strsep(char **stringp, const char *delim);
```

## DESCRIPTION

The strsep() function returns the next token from the string *stringp* which is delimited by delim. The token is terminated with a \0 character and *stringp* is updated to point past the token.

## RETURN VALUE

The strsep() function returns a pointer to the token, or NULL if delim is not found in *stringp*.

## CONFORMS TO

BSD 4.3

## SEE ALSO

index(3), memchr(3), rindex(3), strchr(3), strpbrk(3), strspn(3), strstr(3), strtok(3)

*GNU, 12 April 1993*

# strsignal

strsignal—Returns string describing signal

## SYNOPSIS

```
#include <string.h>
char *strsignal(int sig);
extern const char * const sys_siglist[]
```

## DESCRIPTION

The strsignal() function returns a string describing the signal number passed in the argument *sig*. The string can only be used until the next call to strsignal().

The array sys_siglist holds the signal description strings indexed by signal number.

## RETURN VALUE

The strsignal() function returns the appropriate description string, or an unknown signal message if the signal number is invalid.

## SEE ALSO

psignal(3), strerror(3)

*GNU, 13 April 1993*

# strspn, strcspn

strspn, strcspn—Search a string for a set of characters

## SYNOPSIS

```
#include <string.h>
size t strspn(const char *s, const char *accept);
size t strcspn(const char *s, const char *reject);
```

## DESCRIPTION

The strspn() function calculates the length of the initial segment of *s*, which consists entirely of characters in *accept*.

The strcspn() function calculates the length of the initial segment of *s*, which consists entirely of characters not in *reject*.

## RETURN VALUE

The strspn() function returns the number of characters in the initial segment of *s*, which consist only of characters from *accept*.

The strcspn() function returns the number of characters in the initial segment of *s*, which are not in the string *reject*.

## CONFORMS TO

SVID 3, POSIX, BSD 4.3, ISO 9899

## SEE ALSO

index(3), memchr(3), rindex(3), strchr(3), strpbrk(3), strsep(3), strstr(3), strtok(3)

*12 April 1993*

# strstr

strstr—Locates a substring

## SYNOPSIS

```
#include <string.h>
char *strstr(const char *haystack, const char *needle);
```

## DESCRIPTION

The strstr() function finds the first occurrence of the substring *needle* in the string *haystack*. The terminating \0 characters are not compared.

## RETURN VALUE

The strstr() function returns a pointer to the beginning of the substring, or NULL if the substring is not found.

## SEE ALSO

index(3), memchr(3), rindex(3), strchr(3), strpbrk(3), strsep(3), strspn(3), strtok(3)

*GNU, 12 April 1993*

# strtod

strtod—Converts ASCII string to double

## SYNOPSIS

```
#include <stdlib.h>
double strtod(const char *nptr, char **endptr);
```

## DESCRIPTION

The strtod() function converts the initial portion of the string pointed to by *nptr* to double representation.

The expected form of the string is optional leading whitespace as checked by isspace(3), an optional plus (+) or minus sign (-) followed by a sequence of digits optionally containing a decimal point character, optionally followed by an exponent. An exponent consists of an E or e, followed by an optional plus or minus sign, followed by a nonempty sequence of digits. If the locale is not C or POSIX, different formats may be used.

## RETURN VALUES

The strtod function returns the converted value, if any.

If *endptr* is not NULL, a pointer to the character after the last character used in the conversion is stored in the location referenced by *endptr*.

If no conversion is performed, zero is returned and the value of *nptr* is stored in the location referenced by *endptr*.

If the correct value would cause overflow, plus or minus HUGE_VAL is returned (according to the sign of the value), and ERANGE is stored in *errno*. If the correct value would cause underflow, zero is returned and ERANGE is stored in *errno*.

## ERRORS

ERANGE                          Overflow or underflow occurred.

## CONFORMS TO

ANSI C

## SEE ALSO

atof(3), atoi(3), atol(3), strtol(3), strtoul(3)

*BSD man page, 4 March 1996*


# strtok

strtok—Extracts token from string

## SYNOPSIS

```
#include <string.h>
char *strtok(char *s, const char *delim);
```

## DESCRIPTION

A token is a nonempty string of characters not occurring in the string *delim*, followed by \0 or by a character occurring in *delim*.

The strtok() function can be used to parse the string *s* into tokens. The first call to strtok() should have *s* as its first argument. Subsequent calls should have the first argument set to NULL. Each call returns a pointer to the next token, or NULL when no more tokens are found.

If a token ends with a delimiter, this delimiting character is overwritten with a \0 and a pointer to the next character is saved for the next call to strtok. The delimiter string *delim* may be different for each call.

## BUGS

This function modifies its first argument. The identity of the delimiting character is lost.

## RETURN VALUE

The strtok() function returns a pointer to the next token, or NULL if there are no more tokens.

## CONFORMS TO

SVID 3, POSIX, BSD 4.3, ISO 9899

## SEE ALSO

index(3), memchr(3), rindex(3), strchr(3), strpbrk(3), strsep(3), strspn(3), strstr(3)

*GNU, 10 February 1996*

# strtol

strtol—Converts a string to a long integer

## SYNOPSIS

```
#include <stdlib.h>
long int strtol(const char *nptr, char '**endptr,int base);
```

## DESCRIPTION

The strtol() function converts the string in *nptr* to a long integer value according to the given *base*, which must be between 2 and 36 inclusive, or be the special value 0.

The string must begin with an arbitrary amount of whitespace (as determined by isspace(3)) followed by a single optional + or - sign. If base is zero or 16, the string may then include a 0x prefix, and the number will be read in base 16; otherwise, a zero base is taken as 10 (decimal) unless the next character is 0, in which case it is taken as 8 (octal).

The remainder of the string is converted to a long int value in the obvious manner, stopping at the first character that is not a valid digit in the given base. (In bases above 10, the letter A in either upper- or lowercase represents 10, B represents 11, and so forth, with Z representing 35.)

If endptr is not NULL, strtol() stores the address of the first invalid character in *endptr. If there were no digits at all, strtol() stores the original value of nptr in *endptr. (Thus, if *nptr is not \0 but **endptr is \0 on return, the entire string is valid.)

## RETURN VALUE

The strtol() function returns the result of the conversion, unless the value would underflow or overflow. If an underflow occurs, strtol() returns LONG_MIN. If an overflow occurs, strtol() returns LONG_MAX. In both cases, *errno* is set to ERANGE.

## ERRORS

ERANGE          The given string was out of range; the value converted has been clamped.

## CONFORMS TO

SVID 3, BSD 4.3, ISO 9899

## SEE ALSO

atof(3), atoi(3), atol(3), strtod(3), strtoul(3)

## BUGS

Ignores the current locale.

*GNU, 10 June 1995*

# strtoul

strtoul—Converts a string to an unsigned long integer.

## SYNOPSIS

```
#include <stdlib.h>
unsigned long int strtoul(const char *nptr, char **endptr,
int base);
```

## DESCRIPTION

The strtoul() function converts the string in *nptr* to an unsigned long integer value according to the given base, which must be between 2 and 36 inclusive, or be the special value 0.

The string must begin with an arbitrary amount of whitespace (as determined by isspace(3)) followed by a single optional + or - sign. If base is zero or 16, the string may then include a 0x prefix, and the number will be read in base 16; otherwise, a zero base is taken as 10 (decimal) unless the next character is 0, in which case it is taken as 8 (octal).

The remainder of the string is converted to an unsigned long int value in the obvious manner, stopping at the first character that is not a valid digit in the given base. (In bases above 10, the letter A in either upper- or lowercase represents 10, B represents 11, and so forth, with Z representing 35.)

If endptr is not NULL, strtoul() stores the address of the first invalid character in *endptr. If there were no digits at all, strtoul() stores the original value of nptr in *endptr. (Thus, if *nptr is not \0 but **endptr is \0 on return, the entire string is invalid.)

## RETURN VALUE

The strtoul() function returns either the result of the conversion or, if there was a leading minus sign, the negation of the result of the conversion, unless the original (non-negated) value would overflow; in the latter case, strtoul() returns ULONG_MAX and sets the global variable *errno* to ERANGE.

## ERRORS

ERANGE          The given string was out of range; the value converted has been clamped.

## CONFORMS TO

SVID 3, BSD 4.3, ISO 9899

## SEE ALSO

atof(3), atoi(3), atol(3), strtod(3), strtol(3)

## BUGS

strtoul ignores the current locale.

*GNU, 29 March 1993*

# strxfrm

strxfrm—String transformation

## SYNOPSIS

```
#include <string.h>

size t strxfrm(char *dest, const char *src, size_t n);
```

## DESCRIPTION

The strxfrm() function transforms the *src* string into a form such that the result of strcmp() on two strings that have been transformed with strxfrm() is the same as the result of strcoll() on the two strings before their transformation. The first *n* characters of the transformed string are placed in *dest*. The transformation is based on the program's current locale for category LC_COLLATE. (See setlocale(3).)

## RETURN VALUE

The strxfrm() function returns the number of bytes required to store the transformed string in *dest* excluding the terminating \0 character. If the value returned is *n* or more, the contents of *dest* are indeterminate.

## CONFORMS TO

SVID 3, BSD 4.3, ISO 9899

## NOTES

The Linux C Library currently hasn't implemented the complete POSIX-collating.

In the POSIX or C locales `strxfrm()` is equivalent to copying the string with `strncpy()`.

## SEE ALSO

bcmp(3), memcmp(3), strcasecmp(3), strcmp(3), strcoll(3), setlocale(3)

*GNU, 12 April 1993*

# swab

swab—Swaps adjacent bytes

## SYNOPSIS

```
#include <string.h>
void swab(const void *from, void*to, size_t n);
```

## DESCRIPTION

The swab() function copies *n* bytes from the array pointed to by from to the array pointed to by to, exchanging adjacent even and odd bytes. This function is used to exchange data between machines that have different low/high byte ordering.

## RETURN VALUE

The swab() function returns no value.

## CONFORMS TO

SVID 3, BSD 4.3

## SEE ALSO

bstring(3)

*GNU, 13 April 1993*

# sysconf

sysconf—Gets configuration information at runtime

## SYNOPSIS

```
#include <unistd.h>
long sysconf(int name);
```

## DESCRIPTION

sysconf() provides a way for the application to determine values for system limits or options at runtime.

The equivalent macros defined in <unistd.h> can only give conservative values; if an application wants to take advantage of values that may change, a call to sysconf() can be made, which may yield more liberal results.

For getting information about a particular file, see fpathconf() or pathconf().

The following values are supported for name. First, the POSIX.1_compatible values:

| | |
|---|---|
| _SC_ARG_MAX | The maximum length of the arguments to the exec() family of functions; the corresponding macro is ARG_MAX. |
| _SC_CHILD_MAX | The number of simultaneous processes per user ID; the corresponding macro is _POSIX_CHILD_MAX. |
| _SC_CLK_TCK | The number of clock ticks per second; the corresponding macro is CLK_TCK. |
| _SC_STREAM_MAX | The maximum number of streams that a process can have open at any time. The corresponding POSIX macro is STREAM_MAX, the corresponding standard C macro is FOPEN_MAX. |
| _SC_TZNAME_MAX | The maximum number of bytes in a time zone name; the corresponding macro is TZNAME_MAX. |
| _SC_OPEN_MAX | The maximum number of files that a process can have open at any time; the corresponding macro is _POSIX_OPEN_MAX. |
| _SC_JOB_CONTROL | This indicates whether POSIX–style job control is supported, the corresponding macro is _POSIX_JOB_CONTROL. |
| _SC_SAVED_IDS | This indicates whether a process has a saved set-user-ID and a saved set-group-ID; the corresponding macro is _POSIX_SAVED_IDS. |
| _SC_VERSION | Indicates the year and month the POSIX.1 standard was approved in the format YYYYMML; the value 199009L indicates the most recent revision, 1990. |

Next, the POSIX.2 values:

| | |
|---|---|
| _SC_BC_BASE_MAX | Indicates the maximum obase value accepted by the bc(1) utility; the corresponding macro is BC_BASE_MAX. |
| _SC_BC_DIM_MAX | Indicates the maximum value of elements permitted in an array by bc(1); the corresponding macro is BC_DIM_MAX. |
| _SC_BC_SCALE_MAX | Indicates the maximum scale value allowed by bc(1); the corresponding macro is BC_SCALE_MAX. |
| _SC_BC_STRING_MAX | Indicates the maximum length of a string accepted by bc(1); the corresponding macro is BC_STRING_MAX. |
| _SC_COLL_WEIGHTS_MAX | Indicates the maximum numbers of weights that can be assigned to an entry of the LC_COLLATE order keyword in the locale definition file; the corresponding macro is COLL_WEIGHTS_MAX. |
| _SC_EXPR_NEST_MAX | Is the maximum number of expressions that can be nested within parentheses by expr(1). The corresponding macro is EXPR_NEST_MAX. |
| _SC_LINE_MAX | The maximum length of a utility's input line length, either from standard input or from a file. This includes length for a trailing newline. The corresponding macro is LINE_MAX. |
| _SC_RE_DUP_MAX | The maximum number of repeated occurrences of a regular expression when the interval notation \{m,n\} is used. The value of the corresponding macro is RE_DUP_MAX. |
| _SC_2_VERSION | Indicates the version of the POSIX.2 standard in the format of YYYYMML. The corresponding macro is POSIX2_VERSION. |
| _SC_2_DEV | Indicates whether the POSIX.2 C language development facilities are supported. The corresponding macro is POSIX2_C_DEV. |
| _SC_2_FORT_DEV | Indicates whether the POSIX.2 FORTRAN development utilities are supported. The corresponding macro is POSIX2_FORT_RUN. |
| _SC_2_FORT_RUN | Indicates whether the POSIX.2 FORTRAN runtime utilities are supported. The corresponding macro is POSIX2_FORT_RUN. |

| POSIX2_LOCALEDEF | Indicates whether the POSIX.2 creation of locates via locale(1) is supported. The corresponding macro is POSIX2_LOCALEDEF. |
| _SC_2_SW_DEV | Indicates whether the POSIX.2 software development utilities option is supported. The corresponding macro is POSIX2_SW_DEV. |

## RETURN VALUE

The value returned is the value of the system resource, 1 if a queried option is available, 0 if it is not, or -1 on error. The variable *errno* is not set.

## CONFORMS TO

POSIX.1, proposed POSIX.2

## BUGS

It is difficult use ARG_MAX because it is not specified how much of the argument space for exec() is consumed by the user's environment variables.

Some returned values may be huge; they are not suitable for allocating memory.

POSIX.2 is not yet an approved standard; the information in this man page is subject to change.

## SEE ALSO

bc(1), expr(1), locale(1), fpathconf(3), pathconf(3)

*GNU, 18 April 1993*

# closelog, openlog, syslog

closelog, openlog, syslog—Send messages to the system logger

## SYNOPSIS

```
#include <syslog.h>
void openlog( char *ident,int option,int facility);
void syslog( int priority, char *format, ...);
void closelog( void );
```

## DESCRIPTION

closelog() closes the descriptor being used to write to the system logger. The use of closelog() is optional.

openlog() opens a connection to the system logger for a program. The string pointed to by *ident* is added to each message, and is typically set to the program name. Values for *option* and *facility* are given in the next subsection. The use of openlog() is optional; it will automatically be called by syslog() if necessary, in which case *ident* will default to NULL.

syslog() generates a log message, which will be distributed by syslogd(8). *priority* is a combination of the *facility* and the *level*, values for which are given in the next subsection. The remaining arguments are a *format*, as in printf(3) and any arguments required by the *format*, except that the two characters %m will be replaced by the error message string (strerror) corresponding to the present value of *errno*.

## PARAMETERS

This section lists the parameters used to set the values of *option*, *facility*, and *priority*.

## OPTION

The option argument to openlog() is an OR of any of these:

| | |
|---|---|
| LOG_CONS | Write directly to system console if there is an error while sending to system logger |
| LOG_NDELAY | Open the connection immediately (normally, the connection is opened when the first message is logged) |
| LOG_PERROR | Print to stderr as well |
| LOG_PID | Include PID with each message |

## FACILITY

The facility argument is used to specify what type of program is logging the message. This lets the configuration file specify that messages from different facilities will be handled differently.

| | |
|---|---|
| LOG_AUTH | Security/authorization messages (DEPRECATED use LOG_AUTHPRIV instead) |
| LOG_AUTHPRIV | Security/authorization messages (private) |
| LOG_CRON | Clock daemon (cron and at) |
| LOG_DAEMON | Other system daemons |
| LOG_KERN | Kernel messages |
| LOG_LOCAL0 through LOG_LOCAL7 | Reserved for local use |
| LOG_LPR | Line printer subsystem |
| LOG_MAIL | Mail subsystem |
| LOG_NEWS | Usenet news subsystem |
| LOG_SYSLOG | Messages generated internally by syslogd |
| LOG_USER (default) | Generic user-level messages |
| LOG_UUCP | UUCP subsystem |

## LEVEL

This determines the importance of the message. The levels, in order of decreasing importance, are

| | |
|---|---|
| LOG_EMERG | System is unusable |
| LOG_ALERT | Action must be taken immediately |
| LOG_CRIT | Critical conditions |
| LOG_ERR | Error conditions |
| LOG_WARNING | Warning conditions |
| LOG_NOTICE | Normal, but significant, condition |
| LOG_INFO | Informational message |
| LOG_DEBUG | Debug-level message |

## HISTORY

A syslog function call appeared in BSD 4.2.

## SEE ALSO

logger(1), syslog.conf(5), syslogd(8)

# system

system—Executes a shell command

## SYNOPSIS

```
#include <stdlib.h>
int system (const char * string);
```

## DESCRIPTION

system() executes a command specified in string by calling /bin/sh -c string, and returns after the command has been completed. During execution of the command, SIGCHLD will be blocked, and SIGINT and SIGQUIT will be ignored.

## RETURN VALUE

The value returned is 127 if the execve() call for /bin/sh fails, -1 if there was another error, and the return code of the command otherwise.

If the value of string is NULL, system() returns non-zero if the shell is available, and zero if not.

system() does not affect the wait status of any other children.

## CONFORMS TO

ANSI C, POSIX.1, proposed POSIX.2, BSD 4.3

## BUGS

Do not use system() from a program with suid or sgid privileges, because strange values for some environment variables might be used to subvert system integrity. Use the exec(2) family of functions instead, but not execlp(2) or execvp(2).

The check for the availability of /bin/sh is not actually performed; it is always assumed to be available.

It is possible for the shell command to return 127, so that code is not a sure indication that the execve() call failed; check *errno* to make sure.

## SEE ALSO

sh(1), exec(2), signal(2)

*GNU, 13 April 1993*

# tan

tan—Tangent function

## SYNOPSIS

```
#include <math.h>
double tan(double x);
```

## DESCRIPTION

The tan() function returns the tangent of x, where x is given in radians.

## CONFORMS TO

SVID 3, POSIX, BSD 4.3, ISO 9899

## SEE ALSO

acos(3), asin(3), atan(3), atan2(3), cos(3), sin(3)

*8 June 1993*

# tanh

tanh—Hyperbolic tangent function

## SYNOPSIS

```
#include <math.h>
double tanh(double x);
```

## DESCRIPTION

The tanh() function returns the hyperbolic tangent of x, which is defined mathematically as $\sinh(x) / \cosh(x)$.

## CONFORMS TO

SVID 3, POSIX, BSD 4.3, ISO 9899

## SEE ALSO

acosh(3), asinh(3), atanh(3), cosh(3), sinh(3)

*13 June 1993*

# telldir

telldir—Returns current location in directory stream

## SYNOPSIS

```
#include <dirent.h>
off t telldir(DIR *dir);
```

## DESCRIPTION

The telldir() function returns the current location associated with the directory stream *dir*.

## RETURN VALUE

The telldir() function returns the current location in the directory stream or -1 if an error occurs.

## ERRORS

EBADF                           Invalid directory stream descriptor *dir*

## CONFORMS TO

BSD 4.3

## SEE ALSO

opendir(3), readdir(3), closedir(3), rewinddir(3), seekdir(3), scandir(3)

*31 March 1993*

*termios, tcgetattr, tcsetattr, tcsendbreak, tcdrain, tcflush, tcflow, cfmakeraw, cfgetospeed, cfgetispeed, cfsetispeed, cfsetospeed, tcgetpgrp, tcsetpgrp*

1049

# tempnam

tempnam—Creates a name for a temporary file

## SYNOPSIS

```
#include <stdio.h>
char *tempnam(const char *dir, const char *pfx);
```

## DESCRIPTION

The tempnam() function generates a unique temporary filename using up to five characters of *pfx*, if it is not NULL. The directory to place the file is searched for in the following order:

1.  The directory specified by the environment variable TMPDIR, if it is writable
2.  The directory specified by the argument *dir*, if it is not NULL
3.  The directory specified by P_tmpdir
4.  The directory \tmp

The storage for the filename is allocated by malloc(), and so can be freed by the function free().

## RETURN VALUE

The tempnam() function returns a pointer to the unique temporary filename, or NULL if a unique filename cannot be generated.

## ERRORS

EEXIST                                    Unable to generate a unique filename

## CONFORMS TO

SVID 3, BSD 4.3

## SEE ALSO

mktemp(3), mkstemp(3), tmpnam(3), tmpfile(3)

*GNU, 3 April 1993*

# termios, tcgetattr, tcsetattr, tcsendbreak, tcdrain, tcflush, tcflow, cfmakeraw, cfgetospeed, cfgetispeed, cfsetispeed, cfsetospeed, tcgetpgrp, tcsetpgrp

termios, tcgetattr, tcsetattr, tcsendbreak, tcdrain, tcflush, tcflow, cfmakeraw, cfgetospeed, cfgetispeed, cfsetispeed, cfsetospeed, tcgetpgrp, tcsetpgrp—Get and set terminal attributes, line control, get and set baud rate, get and set terminal foreground process group ID

## SYNOPSIS

```
#include <termios.h>
#include <unistd.h>

int tcgetattr ( int fd, struct termios *termios_p );
int tcsetattr ( int fd,int optional_actions, struct termios *termios_p );
int tcsendbreak ( int fd,int duration );
int tcdrain ( int fd );
int tcflush ( int fd,int queue_selector );
```

```
int tcflow ( int fd,int action );
int cfmakeraw ( struct termios *termios_p );
speed_t cfgetospeed ( struct termios *termios_p );
int cfsetospeed ( struct termios *termios_p, speed_t speed );
speed_t cfgetispeed ( struct termios *termios_p );
int cfsetispeed ( struct termios *termios_p, speed_t speed );
pid_t tcgetpgrp ( int fd );
int tcsetpgrp ( int fd, pid_t pgrpid );
```

## DESCRIPTION

The termios functions describe a general terminal interface that is provided to control asynchronous communications ports.

Many of the functions described here have a *termios_p* argument that is a pointer to a termios structure. This structure contains the following members:

```
tcflag_t c_iflag; /* input modes */
tcflag_t c_oflag; /* output modes */
tcflag_t c_cflag; /* control modes */
tcflag_t c_lflag;/*localmodes*/
cc_t c_cc[NCCS]; /* control chars */
```

The c_iflag flag constants are

| | |
|---|---|
| IGNBRK | Ignore BREAK condition on input. |
| BRKINT | If IGNBRK is not set, generate SIGINT on BREAK condition, else read BREAK as character \0. |
| IGNPAR | Ignore framing errors and parity errors. |
| PARMRK | If IGNPAR is not set, prefix a character with a parity error or framing error with \377 \0. If neither IGNPAR nor PARMRK is set, read a character with a parity error or framing error as \0. |
| INPCK | Enable input parity checking. |
| ISTRIP | Strip off eighth bit. |
| INLCR | Translate NL to CR on input. |
| IGNCR | Ignore carriage return on input. |
| ICRNL | Translate carriage return to newline on input (unless IGNCR is set). |
| IUCLC | Map uppercase characters to lowercase on input. |
| IXON | Enable XON/XOFF flow control on output. |
| IXANY | Enable any character to restart output. |
| IXOFF | Enable XON/XOFF flow control on input. |
| IMAXBEL | Ring bell when input queue is full. |

The c_oflag flag constants are

| | |
|---|---|
| OPOST | Enable implementation-defined output processing. |
| OLCUC | Map lowercase characters to uppercase on output. |
| ONLCR | Map NL to CR-NL on output. |
| OCRNL | Map CR to NL on output. |
| ONOCR | Don't output CR at column 0. |
| ONLRET | Don't output CR. |
| OFILL | Send fill characters for a delay, rather than using a timed delay. |
| OFDEL | Fill character is ASCII DEL. If unset, fill character is ASCII NUL. |
| NLDLY | Newline delay mask. Values are NL0 and NL1. |
| CRDLY | Carriage return delay mask. Values are CR0, CR1, CR2,or CR3. |

*termios, tcgetattr, tcsetattr, tcsendbreak, tcdrain, tcflush, tcflow, cfmakeraw, cfgetospeed, cfgetispeed, cfsetispeed, cfsetospeed, tcgetpgrp, tcsetpgrp*

1051

| TABDLY | Horizontal tab delay mask. Values are TAB0, TAB1, TAB2, TAB3, or XTABS. A value of XTABS expands tabs to spaces (with tab stops every eight columns). |
| BSDLY | Backspace delay mask. Values are BS0 or BS1. |
| VTDLY | Vertical tab delay mask. Values are VT0 or VT1. |
| FFDLY | Form feed delay mask. Values are FF0 or FF1. |

The c_cflag flag constants are

| CSIZE | Character size mask. Values are CS5, CS6, CS7,or CS8. |
| CSTOPB | Set two stop bits, rather than one. |
| CREAD | Enable receiver. |
| PARENB | Enable parity generation on output and parity checking for input. |
| PARODD | Parity for input and output is odd. |
| HUPCL | Lower modem control lines after last process closes the device (hang up). |
| CLOCAL | Ignore modem control lines. |
| CIBAUD | Mask for input speeds (not used). |
| CRTSCTS | Flow control. |

The c_lflag flag constants are

| ISIG | When any of the characters INTR, QUIT, SUSP, or DSUSP are received, generate the corresponding signal. |
| ICANON | Enable canonical mode. This enables the special characters EOF, EOL, EOL2, ERASE, KILL, REPRINT, STATUS, and WERASE, and buffers by lines. |
| XCASE | If ICANON is also set, terminal is uppercase only. Input is converted to lowercase, except for characters preceded by \. On output, uppercase characters are preceded by \ and lowercase characters are converted to uppercase. |
| ECHO | echo input characters. |
| ECHOE | If ICANON is also set, the ERASE character erases the preceding input character, and WERASE erases the preceding word. |
| ECHOK | If ICANON is also set, the KILL character erases the current line. |
| ECHONL | If ICANON is also set, echo the NL character even if ECHO is not set. |
| ECHOCTL | If ECHO is also set, ASCII control signals other than TAB, NL, START, and STOP are echoed as ^X, where X is the character with ASCII code 0x10 greater than the control signal. For example, character 0x28 (BS) is echoed as ^H. |
| ECHOPRT | If ICANON and IECHO are also set, characters are printed as they are being erased. |
| ECHOKE | If ICANON is also set, KILL is echoed by erasing each character on the line, as specified by ECHOE and ECHOPRT. |
| FLUSHO | Output is being flushed. This flag is toggled by typing the DISCARD character. |
| NOFLSH | Disable flushing the input and output queues when generating the SIGINT and SIGQUIT signals, and flushing the input queue when generating the SIGSUSP signal. |
| TOSTOP | Send the SIGTTOU signal to the process group of a background process that tries to write to its controlling terminal. |
| PENDIN | All characters in the input queue are reprinted when the next character is read. (bash handles typeahead this way.) |
| IEXTEN | Enable implementation-defined input processing. |

tcgetattr() gets the parameters associated with the object referred by fd and stores them in the termios structure referenced by *termios_p*. This function may be invoked from a background process; however, the terminal attributes may be subsequently changed by a foreground process.

tcsetattr() sets the parameters associated with the terminal (unless support is required from the underlying hardware that is not available) from the termios structure referred to by *termios_p*. optional_actions specifies when the changes take effect:

| | |
|---|---|
| TCSANOW | The change occurs immediately. |
| TCSADRAIN | The change occurs after all output written to fd has been transmitted. This function should be used when changing parameters that affect output. |
| TCSAFLUSH | The change occurs after all output written to the object referred by fd has been transmitted, and all input that has been received but not read will be discarded before the change is made. |

tcsendbreak() transmits a continuous stream of zero-valued bits for a specific duration, if the terminal is using asynchronous serial data transmission. If duration is zero, it transmits zero-valued bits for at least 0.25 seconds, and not more that 0.5 seconds. If duration is not zero, it sends zero-valued bits for duration*N seconds, where N is at least 0.25, and not more than 0.5.

If the terminal is not using asynchronous serial data transmission, tcsendbreak() returns without taking any action.

tcdrain() waits until all output written to the object referred to by fd has been transmitted.

tcflush() discards data written to the object referred by fd but not transmitted, or data received but not read, depending on the value of queue_selector:

| | |
|---|---|
| TCIFLUSH | Flushes data received but not read |
| TCOFLUSH | Flushes data written but not transmitted |
| TCIOFLUSH | Flushes both data received but not read, and data written but not transmitted |

tcflow() suspends transmission or reception of data on the object referred to by fd, depending on the value of action:

| | |
|---|---|
| TCOOFF | Suspends output |
| TCOON | Restarts suspended output |
| TCIOFF | Transmits a STOP character, which stops the terminal device from transmitting data to the system |
| TCION | Transmits a START character, which starts the terminal device transmitting data to the system |

The default on open of a terminal file is that neither its input nor its output is suspended.

The baud rate functions are provided for getting and setting the values of the input and output baud rates in the termios structure. The new values do not take effect until tcsetattr() is successfully called.

Setting the speed to B0 instructs the modem to hang up. The actual bit rate corresponding to B38400 may be altered with setserial(8).

The input and output baud rates are stored in the termios structure.

cfmakeraw sets the terminal attributes as follows:

```
termios_p->c_iflag &= ~(IGNBRK|BRKINT|PARMRK|ISTRIP
|INLCR|IGNCR|ICRNL|IXON);
termios_p->c_oflag &= ~OPOST;
termios_p->c_lflag &= ~(ECHO|ECHONL|ICANON|ISIG|IEXTEN);
termios_p->c_cflag &= ~(CSIZE|PARENB) ;
termios_p->c_cflag |=CS8;
```

cfgetospeed() returns the output baud rate stored in the termios structure pointed to by termios_p.

cfsetospeed() sets the output baud rate stored in the termios structure pointed to by termios_p to speed, which must be one of these constants:

```
B0
B50
B75
```

```
B110
B134
B150
B200
B300
B600
B1200
B1800
B2400
B4800
B9600
B19200
B38400
B57600
B115200
B230400
```

The zero baud rate, B0, is used to terminate the connection. If B0 is specified, the modem control lines shall no longer be asserted. Normally, this will disconnect the line. CBAUDEX is a mask for the speeds beyond those defined in POSIX.1 (57600 and above). Thus, B57600 & CBAUDEX is non-zero.

cfgetispeed() returns the input baud rate stored in the termios structure.

cfsetispeed() sets the input baud rate stored in the termios structure to speed. If the input baud rate is set to zero, the input baud rate will be equal to the output baud rate.

tcgetpgrp() returns process group ID of foreground processing group, or -1 on error.

tcsetpgrp() sets process group ID to pgrpid. pgrpid must be the ID of a process group in the same session.

## RETURN VALUES

cfgetispeed() returns the input baud rate stored in the termios structure.

cfgetospeed() returns the output baud rate stored in the termios structure.

tcgetpgrp() returns process group ID of foreground processing group, or -1 on error.

All other functions return

| | |
|---|---|
| 0 | On success |
| -1 | On failure and set *errno* to indicate the error |

## SEE ALSO

setserial(8)

*Linux, 2 September 1995*

# tmpfile

tmpfile—Creates a temporary file

## SYNOPSIS

```
#include <stdio.h>
FILE *tmpfile (void);
```

## DESCRIPTION

The tmpfile() function generates a unique temporary filename using the path prefix P_tmpdir defined in <stdio.h>. The temporary file is then opened in binary read/write (w+b) mode. The file will be automatically deleted when it is closed or the program terminates.

## RETURN VALUE

The tmpfile() function returns a stream descriptor, or NULL if a unique filename cannot be generated or the unique file cannot be opened.

## ERRORS

| | |
|---|---|
| EACCES | Search permission denied for directory in file's path prefix |
| EEXIST | Unable to generate a unique filename |
| EMFILE | Too many file descriptors in use by process |
| ENFILE | Too many files open in system |
| EROFS | Read-only filesystem |

## CONFORMS TO

SVID 3, POSIX, BSD 4.3, ISO 9899

## SEE ALSO

mktemp(3), mkstemp(3), tmpnam(3), tempnam(3)

*GNU, 3 April 1993*

# tmpnam

tmpnam—Creates a name for a temporary file

## SYNOPSIS

```
#include <stdio.h>
char *tmpnam(char *s);
```

## DESCRIPTION

The tmpnam() function generates a unique temporary filename using the path prefix P_tmpdir defined in <stdio.h>. If the argument s is NULL, tmpnam() returns the address of an internal static area that holds the filename, which is overwritten by subsequent calls to tmpnam(). If s is not NULL, the filename is returned in s.

## RETURN VALUE

The tmpnam() function returns a pointer to the unique temporary filename, or NULL if a unique name cannot be generated.

## ERRORS

| | |
|---|---|
| EEXIST | Unable to generate a unique filename |

## CONFORMS TO

SVID 3, POSIX, BSD 4.3, ISO 9899

## SEE ALSO

mktemp(3), mkstemp(3), tempnam(3), tmpfile(3)

*GNU, 3 April 1993*

# toascii

toascii—Converts character to ASCII

## SYNOPSIS

```
#include <ctype.h>
int toascii (int c);
```

## DESCRIPTION

toascii() converts c to a 7-bit unsigned char value that fits into the ASCII character set, by clearing the high-order bits.

## RETURN VALUE

The value returned is that of the converted character.

## CONFORMS TO

SVID, BSD

## BUGS

Many people will be unhappy if you use this function. This function will convert accented letters into random characters.

## SEE ALSO

isascii(3), toupper(3), tolower(3)

*GNU, 16 September 1995*

# toupper, tolower

toupper, tolower—Convert letter to uppercase or lowercase

## SYNOPSIS

```
#include <ctype.h>
int toupper (int c);
int tolower (int c);
```

## DESCRIPTION

toupper() converts the letter c to uppercase, if possible.

tolower() converts the letter c to lowercase, if possible.

## RETURN VALUE

The value returned is that of the converted letter, or c if the conversion was not possible.

## CONFORMS TO

ANSI C, BSD 4.3

## BUGS

The details of what constitutes an uppercase or lowercase letter depend on the current locale. For example, the default locale does not know about umlauts, so no conversion is done for them.

In some non-English locales, there are lowercase letters with no corresponding uppercase equivalent; the German sharp *s* is one example.

## SEE ALSO

isalpha(3), setlocale(3), locale(7)

*GNU, 4 April 1993*

# tsearch, tfind, tdelete, twalk

tsearch, tfind, tdelete, twalk—Manage a binary tree

## SYNOPSIS

```
#include <search.h>
void *tsearch (const void *key,void **rootp,
int (*compar)(const void *, const void *));
void *tfind (const void *key, const void **rootp,
int (*compar)(const void *, const void *));
void *tdelete (const void *key,void**rootp,
int (*compar)(const void *, const void *));
void twalk (const void *root,void (*action)(const void*nodep,
const VISIT which,
const int depth));
```

## DESCRIPTION

tsearch, tfind, twalk, and tdelete manage a binary tree. They are generalized from Knuth (6.2.2) Algorithm T. The first field in each node of the tree is a pointer to the corresponding data item. (The calling program must store the actual data.) compar points to a comparison routine, which takes pointers to two items. It should return an integer that is negative, zero, or positive, depending on whether the first item is less than, equal to, or greater than the second.

tsearch searches the tree for an item. key points to the item to be searched for. rootp points to a variable that points to the root of the tree. If the tree is empty, then the variable that rootp points to should be set to NULL. If the item is found in the tree, then tsearch returns a pointer to it. If it is not found, then tsearch adds it, and returns a pointer to the newly added item.

tfind is like tsearch, except that if the item is not found, then tfind returns NULL.

tdelete deletes an item from the tree. Its arguments are the same as for tsearch.

twalk performs depth-first, left-to-right traversal of a binary tree. root points to the starting node for the traversal. If that node is not the root, then only part of the tree will be visited. twalk calls the user function action each time a node is visited (that is, three times for an internal node, and once for a leaf). action, in turn, takes three arguments. The first is a pointer to the node being visited. The second is an integer that takes on the values preorder, postorder, and endorder depending on whether this is the first, second, or third visit to the internal node, or leaf if it is the single visit to a leaf node. (These symbols are defined in <search.h>.) The third argument is the depth of the node, with zero being the root.

## RETURN VALUE

tsearch returns a pointer to a matching item in the tree, or to the newly added item, or NULL if there was insufficient memory to add the item. tfind returns a pointer to the item, or NULL if no match is found. If there are multiple elements that match the key, the element returned is unspecified.

tdelete returns a pointer to the parent of the item deleted, or NULL if the item was not found.

tsearch, tfind, and tdelete also return NULL if rootp was NULL on entry.

## WARNINGS

twalk takes a pointer to the root, while the other functions take a pointer to a variable that points to the root.

twalk uses postorder to mean "after the left subtree, but before the right subtree." Some authorities would call this inorder, and reserve postorder to mean "after both subtrees."

tdelete frees the memory required for the node in the tree. The user is responsible for freeing the memory for the corresponding data.

The example program depends on the fact that twalk makes no further reference to a node after calling the user function with argument endorder or leaf. This works with the GNU library implementation, but is not in the SysV documentation.

## EXAMPLE

The following program inserts twelve random numbers into a binary tree, then prints the numbers in order. The numbers are removed from the tree and their storage freed during the traversal.

```
#include <search.h>
#include <stdlib.h>
#include <stdio.h>

void *root=NULL;

void *xmalloc(unsigned n)
{
  void *p;
  p = malloc(n);
  if(p) return p;
  fprintf(stderr, "insufficient memory\n");
  exit(1);
}

int compare(const void *pa, const void *pb)
{
  if(*(int *)pa < *(int *)pb) return -1;
  if(*(int *)pa > *(int *)pb) return 1;
  return 0;
}

void action(const void *nodep, const VISIT which, const int depth)
{
  int *datap;
  void *val;

  switch(which)
    {
    case preorder:
      break;
    case postorder:
      datap = *(int **)nodep;
      printf("%6d\n", *datap);
      break;
    case endorder:
      datap = *(int **)nodep;
      (void)tdelete(datap, &root, compare);
      free(datap);
      break;
    case leaf:
      datap = *(int **)nodep;
      printf("%6d\n", *datap);
      val = tdelete(datap, &root, compare);
      free(datap);
      break;
    }
  return;
```

```
    }

    int main()
    {
      int i, *ptr;
      void *val;

      for (i = 0; i < 12; i++)
        {
          ptr = (int *)xmalloc(sizeof(int));
          *ptr = rand()&0xff;
          val = tsearch((void *)ptr, &root, compare);
          if(val == NULL) exit(1);
        }
      twalk(root, action);
      return 0;
    }
```

## CONFORMS TO

SVID

## SEE ALSO

qsort(3), bsearch(3), hsearch(3), lsearch(3)

*GNU, 24 September 1995*

# ttyname

ttyname—Returns name of a terminal

## SYNOPSIS

```
#include <unistd.h>
char *ttyname ( int desc );
```

## DESCRIPTION

Returns a pointer to the pathname of the terminal device that is open on the file descriptor *desc*, or NULL on error (for example, if *desc* is not connected to a terminal).

## CONFORMS TO

POSIX.1

## SEE ALSO

isatty(3), fstat(3)

*Linux, 20 April 1995*

# tzset

tzset—Initializes time conversion information

## SYNOPSIS

```
#include <time.h>
void tzset (void);
extern char *tzname[2];
```

## DESCRIPTION

The tzset() function initializes the *tzname* variable from the TZ environment variable. This function is automatically called by the other time conversion functions that depend on the time zone.

If the TZ variable does not appear in the environment, the *tzname* variable is initialized with the best approximation of local wall clock time, as specified by the tzfile(5)-format file /usr/lib/zoneinfo/localtime.

If the TZ variable does appear in the environment but its value is NULL or its value cannot be interpreted using any of the formats specified in the following paragraphs, Coordinated Universal Time (UTC) is used.

The value of TZ can be one of three formats. The first format is used when there is no daylight saving time in the local time zone:

std offset

The *std* string specifies the name of the time zone and must be three or more alphabetic characters. The offset string immediately follows *std* and specifies the time value to be added to the local time to get Coordinated Universal Time (UTC). The offset is positive if the local time zone is west of the Prime Meridian and negative if it is east. The hour must be between 0 and 24, and the minutes and seconds 0 and 59.

The second format is used when there is daylight saving time:

std offset dst [offset],start[/time],end[/time]

There are no spaces in the specification. The initial *std* and offset specify the standard time zone, as described. The dst string and offset specify the name and offset for the corresponding daylight savings time zone. If the offset is omitted, it defaults to one hour ahead of standard time.

The start field specifies when Daylight Savings Time goes into effect and the end field specifies when the change is made back to Standard Time. These fields may have the following formats:

| | |
|---|---|
| J*n* | This specifies the Julian day with *n* between 1 and 365. February 29 is never counted even in leap years. |
| *n* | This specifies the Julian day with *n* between 1 and 365. February 29 is counted in leap years. |
| M*m.w.d* | This specifies day *d* (0 <= d <= 6) of week *w* (1 <= w <=5) of month *m* (1 <= m <= 12). Week 1 is the first week in which day *d* occurs and week 5 is the last week in which day *d* occurs. Day 0 is a Sunday. |

The time fields specify when, in the local time currently in effect, the change to the other time occurs. If omitted, the default is 02:00:00.

The third format specifies that the time zone information should be read from a file:

:[filespec]

If the file specification filespec is omitted, the time zone information is read from /usr/lib/zoneinfo/localtime, which is in tzfile(5) format. If filespec is given, it specifies an-other tzfile(5)-format file to read the time zone information from. If filespec does not begin with a /, the file specification is relative to the system time conversion information directory /usr/lib/zoneinfo.

## FILES

| | |
|---|---|
| /usr/lib/zoneinfo | System time zone directory |
| /usr/lib/zoneinfo/localtime | Local time zone file |
| /usr/lib/zoneinfo/posixrules | Rules for POSIX-style TZs |

## CONFORMS TO

SVID 3, POSIX, BSD 4.3

## SEE ALSO

date(1), gettimeofday(2), time(2), ctime(3), getenv(3), tzfile(5)

*BSD, 2 July 1993*

# none

none—Undocumented library functions

## SYNOPSIS

Undocumented library functions

## DESCRIPTION

This man page mentions those library functions that are implemented in the standard libraries but not yet documented in man pages.

## SOLICITATION

If you have information about these functions, please look in the source code, write a man page (using a style similar to that of the other Linux section 3 man pages), and send it to aeb@cwi.nl for inclusion in the next man page release.

## THE LIST

des_setparity, dn_skipname, ecb_crypt, encrypt, endnetgrent, endrpcent, endutent, execlp, fcrypt, fp_nquery, fp_query, fp_resstat, get_myaddress, getnetgrent, getnetname, getopt_long_only, getpublickey, getrpcbyname, getrpcbynumber, getrpcent, getrpcport, getsecretkey, getutid, getutline, h_errlist, host2netname, hostalias, inet_nsap_addr, inet_nsap_ntoa_init_des, innetgr, key_decryptsession, key_encryptsession, key_gendes, key_setsecret, lfind, libc_nls_init, lockf, lsearch, mcheck, memalign, mstats, mtrace, netname2host, netname2user, nlist, obstack_free, p_cdname, p_cdnname, p_class, p_fqname, p_option, p_query, p_rr, p_time, p_type, passwd2des, pmap_getmaps, pmap_getport, pmap_rmtcall, pmap_set, pmap_unset, putlong, putshort, pututline, rcmd, re_compile_fastmap, re_compile_pattern, re_match, re_match_2, re_rx_search, re_search, re_search_2, re_set_registers, re_set_syntax, registerrpc, res_send_setqhook, res_send_setrhook, rexec, rresvport, rtime, ruserok, ruserpass, setfileno, sethostfile, setkey, setlogmask, setnetgrent, setrpcent, setutent, siglongjmp, snprintf, stpcpy, svc_exit, svc_getreq, svc_getreqset, svc_register, svc_run, svc_sendreply, svc_unregister, svcerr_auth, svcerr_decode, svcerr_noproc, svcerr_noprog, svcerr_progvers, svcerr_systemerr, svcerr_weakauth, svcfd_create, svcraw_create, svctcp_create, svcudp_bufcreate, svcudp_create, svcudp_enablecachesyscall, tdelete, tell, tfind, timegm, tr_break, tsearch, twalk, tzsetwall, ufc_dofinalperm, ufc_doit, user2netname, utmpname, valloc, vsnprintf, vsyslog, xdecrypt, xdr_accepted_reply, xdr_array, xdr_authdes_cred, xdr_authdes_verf, xdr_authunix_parms, xdr_bool, xdr_bytes, xdr_callhdr, xdr_callmsg, xdr_char, xdr_cryptkeyarg, xdr_cryptkeyres, xdr_datum, xdr_des_block, xdr_domainname, xdr_double, xdr_enum, xdr_float, xdr_free, xdr_getcredres, xdr_int, xdr_keybuf, xdr_keystatus, xdr_long, xdr_mapname, xdr_netnamestr, xdr_netobj, xdr_opaque, xdr_opaque_auth, xdr_passwd, xdr_peername, xdr_pmap, xdr_pmaplist, xdr_pointer, xdr_reference, xdr_rejected_reply, xdr_replymsg, xdr_rmtcall_args, xdr_rmtcallres, xdr_short, xdr_string, xdr_u_char, xdr_u_int, xdr_u_long, xdr_u_short, xdr_union, xdr_unixcred, xdr_vector, xdr_void, xdr_wrapstring, xdr_yp_buf, xdr_yp_inaddr, xdr_ypbind_binding, xdr_ypbind_resp, xdr_ypbind_resptype, xdr_ypbind_setdom, xdr_ypdelete_args, xdr_ypmaplist, xdr_ypmaplist_str, xdr_yppasswd, xdr_ypreq_key, xdr_ypreq_nokey, xdr_ypresp_all, xdr_ypresp_all_seq, xdr_ypresp_key_val, xdr_ypresp_maplist, xdr_ypresp_master, xdr_ypresp_order, xdr_ypresp_val, xdr_ypstat, xdr_ypupdate_args, xdrmem_create, xdrrec_create, xdrrec_endofrecord, xdrrec_eof, xdrrec_skiprecord, xdrstdio_create, xencrypt, xprt_register, xprt_unregister, yp_all, yp_bind, yp_first, yp_get_default_domain, yp_maplist, yp_master, yp_match, yp_next, yp_order, yp_unbind, yp_update, yperr_string, ypprot_err

*Linux 1.3.15, 25 August 1995*

# usleep

usleep—Suspends execution for interval of microseconds

## SYNOPSIS

```
#include <unistd.h>
void usleep(unsigned long usec);
```

## DESCRIPTION

The usleep() function suspends execution of the calling process for *usec* microseconds. The sleep may be lengthened slightly by any system activity or by the time spent processing the call.

## CONFORMS TO

BSD 4.3

## SEE ALSO

setitimer(2), getitimer(2), sleep(3), alarm(3), select(3)

*4 July 1993*

# wcstombs

wcstombs—Converts a wide character string to a multibyte character string

## SYNOPSIS

```
#include <stdlib.h>
size_t wcstombs(char *s, const wchar_t *pwcs, size_t n);
```

## DESCRIPTION

The wcstombs() function converts a sequence of wide characters from the array *pwcs* into a sequence of multibyte characters and stores up to *n* bytes of multibyte characters in the array *s*.

## RETURN VALUE

wcstombs() returns the number of bytes stored in s or –1 if s contains an invalid wide character.

## CONFORMS TO

SVID 3, ISO 9899

## SEE ALSO

mblen(3), mbtowc(3), mbstowcs(3), wctomb(3)

*GNU, 29 March 1993*

# wctomb

wctomb—Converts a wide character to a multibyte character

## SYNOPSIS

```
#include <stdlib.h>
int wctomb(char *s, wchar_t wchar);
```

## DESCRIPTION

The wctomb() function converts a wide character wchar into a multibyte character and, if *s* is not NULL, stores the multibyte character representation in *s*.

## RETURN VALUE

wctomb() returns the number of bytes in the multibyte character or –1 if the wide character is not valid.

## CONFORMS TO

SVID 3, ISO 9899

## SEE ALSO

mblen(3), mbstowcs(3), mbtowc(3), wcstombs(3)

# Part IV:
# Special Files

## INTRODUCTION

This part describes special files.

## FILES

/dev/* Device files

## AUTHORS

Look at the header of the manual page for the author(s) and copyright conditions. Note that these can be different from page to page.

*Linux, 24 July 1993*

# charsets

charsets—Programmer's view of character sets and internationalization

## DESCRIPTION

Linux is an international operating system. Several of its utilities and device drivers (including the console driver) support multilingual character sets including Latin-alphabet letters with diacritical marks, accents, ligatures, and entire non-Latin alphabets including Greek, Cyrillic, Arabic, and Hebrew.

This manual page presents a programmer's-eye view of different character-set standards and how they fit together on Linux. Standards discussed include ASCII, ISO 8859, KOI8-R, Unicode, ISO 2022, and ISO 4873.

## ASCII

ASCII (American Standard Code for Information) is the original 7-bit character set, originally designed for American English. It is currently described by the ECMA-6 standard.

An ASCII variant replacing the American crosshatch/octothorpe/hash pound symbol with the British pound-sterling symbol is used in Great Britain; when needed, the American and British variants may be distinguished as U.S. ASCII and U.K. ASCII.

As Linux was written for hardware designed in the United States, it natively supports U.S. ASCII.

## ISO 8859

ISO 8859 is a series of 10 8-bit character sets, all of which have U.S. ASCII in their low (7-bit) half, invisible control characters in positions 128 to 159, and 96 fixed-width graphics in positions 160-255.

Of these, the most important is ISO 8859-1 (Latin-1). It is natively supported in the Linux console driver, fairly well supported in X11R6, and is the base character set of HTML.

Console support for the other 8859 character sets is available under Linux through user-mode utilities (such as setfont(8)) that modify keyboard bindings and the EGA graphics table and employ the "user mapping" font table in the console driver.

Here are brief descriptions of each set:

| | |
|---|---|
| 8859-1 (Latin-1) | Latin-1 covers most Western European languages such as Albanian, Catalan, Danish, Dutch, English, Faroese, Finnish, French, German, Galician, Irish, Icelandic, Italian, Norwegian, Portuguese, Spanish, and Swedish. The lack of the ligatures Dutch *ij*, French *oe*, and old-style German quotation marks is tolerable. |
| 8859-2 (Latin-2) | Latin-2 supports most Latin-written Slavic and Central European languages: Czech, German, Hungarian, Polish, Rumanian, Croatian, Slovak, and Slovene. |
| 8859-3 (Latin-3) | Latin-3 is popular with authors of Esperanto, Galician, Maltese, and Turkish. |
| 8859-4 (Latin-4) | Latin-4 introduced letters for Estonian, Latvian, and Lithuanian. It is essentially obsolete; see 8859-10 (Latin-6). |

| 8859-5 | Cyrillic letters supporting Bulgarian, Byelorussian, Macedonian, Russian, Serbian, and Ukrainian. Ukrainians read the letter *ghe* with downstroke as *heh* and would need a *ghe* with upstroke to write a correct *ghe*. (See the discussion of KOI8-R in the next subsection.) |
|---|---|
| 8859-6 | Supports Arabic. The 8859-6 glyph table is a fixed font of separate letter forms, but a proper display engine should combine there pairwise into initial, medial, and final forms. |
| 8859-7 | Supports modern Greek. |
| 8859-8 | Supports Hebrew. |
| 8859-9 (Latin-5) | This is a variant of Latin-1 that replaces rarely used Icelandic letters with Turkish ones. |
| 8859-10 (Latin-6) | Latin-6 adds the last Inuit (Greenlandic) and Sami (Lappish) letters that were missing in Latin 4 to cover the entire Nordic area. RFC 1345 listed a preliminary and different Latin 6. Skolt Sami still needs a few more accents than these. |

## KOI8-R

KOI8-R is a non-ISO character set popular in Russia. The lower half is U.S. ASCII; the upper is a Cyrillic character set somewhat better designed than ISO 8859-5.

Console support for KOI8-R is available under Linux through user-mode utilities that modify keyboard bindings and the EGA graphics table, and that employ the "user mapping" font table in the console driver.

## UNICODE

Unicode (ISO 10646) is a standard that aims to unambiguously represent every known glyph in every human language. Unicode's native encoding is 32-bit (older versions used 16 bits). Information on Unicode is available at `http://www.unicode.com`.

Linux represents Unicode using the 8-bit Unicode Transfer Format (UTF-8). UTF-8 is a variable length encoding of Unicode. It uses 1 byte to code 7 bits, 2 bytes for 11 bits, 3 bytes for 16 bits, 4 bytes for 21 bits, 5 bytes for 26 bits, and 6 bytes for 31 bits.

Let `0`, `1`, `x` stand for a zero, one, or arbitrary bit. A byte `0xxxxxxx` stands for the Unicode `00000000 0xxxxxxx`, which codes the same symbol as the ASCII `0xxxxxxx`. Thus, ASCII goes unchanged into UTF-8, and people using only ASCII do not notice any change—not in code, and not in file size.

A byte `110xxxxx` is the start of a 2-byte code, and `110xxxxx 10yyyyyy` is assembled into `00000xxx xxyyyyyy`. A byte `1110xxxx` is the start of a 3-byte code, and `1110xxxx 10yyyyyy 10zzzzzz` is assembled into `xxxxyyyy yyzzzzzz`. (When `UTF-8` is used to code the 31-bit ISO 10646, then this progression continues up to 6-byte codes.)

For ISO-8859-1 users this means that the characters with high bit set now are coded with two bytes. This tends to expand ordinary text files by one or two percent. There are no conversion problems, however, since the Unicode value of ISO-8859-1 symbols equals their ISO-8859-1 value (extended by eight leading zero bits). For Japanese users, this means that the 16-bit codes now in common use will take three bytes, and extensive mapping tables are required. Many Japanese therefore prefer `ISO 2022`.

Note that UTF-8 is self-synchronizing: `10xxxxxx` is a tail, any other byte is the head of a code. Note that the only way ASCII bytes occur in a UTF-8 stream is as themselves. In particular, there are no embedded NULs or /s that form part of some larger code.

Because ASCII, and, in particular, NUL and /, are unchanged, the kernel does not notice that UTF-8 is being used. It does not care at all what the bytes it is handling stand for.

Rendering of Unicode data streams is typically handled through subfont tables that map a subset of Unicode to glyphs. Internally, the kernel uses Unicode to describe the subfont loaded in video RAM. This means that in UTF-8 mode one can use a character set with 512 different symbols. This is not enough for Japanese, Chinese, and Korean, but it is enough for most other purposes.

## ISO 2022 AND ISO 4873

The ISO 2022 and 4873 standards describe a font-control model based on VT100 practice. This model is (partially) supported by the Linux kernel and by xterm(1). It is popular in Japan and Korea.

There are four graphic character sets, called G0, G1, G2, and G3, and one of them is the current character set for codes with high bit zero (initially G0), and one of them is the current character set for codes with high bit one (initially G1). Each graphic character set has 94 or 96 characters, and is essentially a 7-bit character set. It uses codes either 040–0177 (041–0176) or 0240–0377 (0241–0376). G0 always has size 94 and uses codes 041–0176.

Switching between character sets is done using the shift functions ^N (S0 or LS1), ^O (SI or LS0), ESC n (LS2), ESC o (LS3), ESC N (SS2),

ESC O (SS3), ESC ˜ (LS1R), ESC } (LS2R), ESC ¦ (LS3R). The function LSn makes character set G*n* the current one for codes with high bit zero. The function LSnR makes character set G*n* the current one for codes with high bit one. The function SSn makes character set G*n* (*n*=2 or 3) the current one for the next character only (regardless of the value of its high order bit).

A 94-character set is designated as G*n* character set by an escape sequence ESC ( xx (for G0), ESC ) xx (for G1), ESC * xx (for G2), ESC + xx (for G3), where xx is a symbol or a pair of symbols found in the ISO 2375 International Register of Coded Character Sets. For example, ESC ( @ selects the ISO 646 character set as G0, ESC ( A selects the U.K. standard character set (with pound instead of number sign), ESC ( B selects ASCII (with dollar instead of currency sign), ESC ( M selects a character set for African languages, ESC ( ! A selects the Cuban character set, and so on.

A 96-character set is designated as Gn character set by an escape sequence ESC - xx (for G1), ESC . xx (for G2) or ESC / xx (for G3). For example, ESC - G selects the Hebrew alphabet as G1.

A multibyte character set is designated as G*n* character set by an escape sequence ESC $ xx or ESC $ ( xx (for G0), ESC $ ) xx (for G1), ESC $ * xx (for G2), ESC $ + xx (for G3). For example, ESC $ ( C selects the Korean character set for G0. The Japanese character set selected by ESC $ B has a more recent version selected by ESC & @ESC $ B.

ISO 4873 stipulates a narrower use of character sets, where G0 is fixed (always ASCII), so that G1, G2, and G3 can only be invoked for codes with the high order bit set. In particular, ^N and ^O are not used anymore, ESC ( xx can be used only with *xx*=B, and ESC ) xx, ESC * xx, ESC + xx are equivalent to ESC - xx, ESC . xx, and ESC / xx, respectively.

## SEE ALSO

console(4), console_ioctl(4), console_codes(4)

*Linux, 5 November 1996*

# console

console—Console terminal and virtual consoles

## DESCRIPTION

A Linux system has up to 63 *virtual consoles* (character devices with major number 4 and minor number 1 to 63), usually called /dev/ttyn with 1 n 63. The current console is also addressed by /dev/console or /dev/tty0, the character device with major number 4 and minor number 0. The device files /dev/* are usually created using the script MAKEDEV, or using mknod(1), usually with mode 0622 and owner root.tty.

Before kernel version 1.1.54, the number of virtual consoles was compiled into the kernel (in tty.h: #define NR_CONSOLES 8) and could be changed by editing and recompiling because version 1.1.54 virtual consoles are created on-the-fly, as soon as they are needed.

Common ways to start a process on a console are the following:

- Tell init(8) (in inittab(5)) to start a getty(8) on the console
- Ask open(1) to start a process on the console
- Start X; it will find the first unused console and display its output there. (There is also the ancient doshell(8).)

Common ways to switch consoles are the following:

■ Use Alt+Fn or Ctrl+Alt+Fn to switch to console n; AltGr+Fn might bring you to console n+12 [here Alt and AltGr refer to the left and right Alt keys, respectively]

■ Use Alt+RightArrow or Alt+LeftArrow to cycle through the presently allocated consoles

■ Use the program chvt(1). (The key mapping can be set by the user; see loadkeys(1); the preceding key combinations are according to the default settings.)

The command disalloc(8) will free the memory taken by the screen buffers for consoles that no longer have any associated process.

## PROPERTIES

Consoles carry a lot of state. I hope to document that some other time. The most important fact is that the consoles simulate vt100 terminals. In particular, a console is reset to the initial state by printing the two characters ESC c. All escape sequences can be found in console codes(4).

## FILES

/dev/console
/dev/tty*

## SEE ALSO

charsets(4), console_codes(4), console_ioctl(4), mknod(1), tty(4), ttys(4), getty(8), init(8), chvt(1), open(1), disalloc(8), loadkeys(1), resizecons(8), setfont(8), mapscrn(8)

*Linux, 31 October 1994*

# console_codes

console_codes—Linux console escape and control sequences

## DESCRIPTION

The Linux console implements a large subset of the VT102 and ECMA-48/ISO 6429/ANSI X3.64 terminal controls, plus certain private-mode sequences for changing the color palette, character-set mapping, and so on. In the following tabular descriptions, the second column gives ECMA-48 or DEC mnemonics (the latter if prefixed with DEC) for the given function. Sequences without a mnemonic are neither ECMA-48 nor VT102.

After all the normal output processing has been done, and a stream of characters arrives at the console driver for actual printing, the first thing that happens is a translation from the code used for processing to the code used for printing.

If the console is in UTF-8 mode, then the incoming bytes are first assembled into 16-bit Unicode codes. Otherwise, each byte is transformed according to the current mapping table (which translates it to a Unicode value). (See the "Character Sets" subsection for discussion.)

In the normal case, the Unicode value is converted to a font index, and this is stored in video memory, so that the corresponding glyph (as found in video ROM) appears on the screen. Note that the use of Unicode (and the design of the PC hardware) allows the use of 512 different glyphs simultaneously.

If the current Unicode value is a control character, or you are currently processing an escape sequence, the value will treated specially. Instead of being turned into a font index and rendered as a glyph, it may trigger cursor movement or other control functions. (See the "Linux Console Controls" subsection.)

It is generally not good practice to hardwire terminal controls into programs. Linux supports a terminfo(5) database of terminal capabilities. Rather than emitting console escape sequences by hand, you will almost always want to use a terminfo-aware screen library or utility such as ncurses(3), tput(1), or reset(1).

## LINUX CONSOLE CONTROLS

This section describes all the control characters and escape sequences that invoke special functions (that is, anything other than writing a glyph at the current cursor location) on the Linux console.

## CONTROL CHARACTERS

A character is a control character if (before transformation according to the mapping table) it has one of the 14 codes 00 (NUL), 07 (BEL), 08 (BS), 09 (HT), 0a (LF), 0b (VT), 0c (FF), 0d (CR), 0e (SO), 0f (SI), 18 (CAN), 1a (SUB), 1b (ESC), 7f (DEL). One can set a display control characters mode (see below), and allow 07, 09, 0b, 18, 1a, 7f to be displayed as glyphs. On the other hand, in UTF-8 mode all codes 00–1f are regarded as control characters, regardless of any display control characters mode.

If you have a control character, it is acted upon immediately and then discarded (even in the middle of an escape sequence) and the escape sequence continues with the next character. (However, ESC starts a new escape sequence, possibly aborting a previous unfinished one, and CAN and SUB abort any escape sequence.) The recognized control characters are BEL, BS, HT, LF, VT, FF, CR, SO, SI, CAN, SUB, ESC, DEL, CSI. They do what one would expect:

BEL (0x07, ^G) beeps.

BS (0x08, ^H) backspaces one column (but not past the beginning of the line).

HT (0x09, ^I) goes to the next tab stop or to the end of the line if there is no earlier tab stop.

LF (0x0A, ^J), VT (0x0B, ^K) and FF (0x0C, ^L) all give a linefeed.

CR (0x0D, ^M) gives a carriage return.

SO (0x0E, ^N) activates the G1 character set, and if LF/NL (new line mode) is set, also a carriage return.

SI (0x0F, ^O) activates the G0 character set.

CAN (0x18, ^X) and SUB (0x1A, ^Z) interrupt escape sequences.

ESC (0x1B, ^[) starts an escape sequence.

DEL (0x7F) is ignored.

CSI (0x9B) is equivalent to ESC [ .

## ESC SEQUENCES, NOT CSI SEQUENCES

| | | |
|---|---|---|
| ESC c | RIS | Reset. |
| ESC D | IND | Linefeed. |
| ESC E | NEL | Newline. |
| ESC H | HTS | Set tab stop at current column. |
| ESC M | RI | Reverse linefeed. |
| ESC Z | DECID | DEC private identification. The kernel returns the string ESC [ ? 6 c, claiming that it is a VT102. |
| ESC 7 | DECSC | Save current state (cursor coordinates, attributes, character sets). |
| ESC 8 | DECRC | Restore most recently saved state. |
| ESC [ | CSI | Control sequence introducer. |
| ESC % | | Start sequence selecting character set. |
| ESC % @ | | Select default (ISO 646 / ISO 8859-1). |
| ESC % G | | Select UTF-8. |
| ESC % 8 | | Select UTF-8 (obsolete). |
| ESC # 8 | DECALN | DEC screen alignment test: fill screen with Es. |
| ESC ( | | Start sequence defining G0 character set. |
| ESC ( B | | Select default (ISO 8859-1 mapping). |
| ESC ( 0 | | Select vt100 graphics mapping. |

| ESC ( U | | Select null mapping—straight to character ROM. |
| ESC ( K | | Select user mapping, the map that is loaded by the utility mapscrn(8). |
| ESC ) | | Start sequence defining G1 (followed by one of B, 0, U, K, as above). |
| ESC > | DECPNM | Set numeric keypad mode. |
| ESC = | DECPAM | Set application keypad mode. |
| ESC ] | OSC | (Should be: Operating system command) ESC ] P nrrggbb: set palette, with parameter given in 7 hexadecimal digits after the final P : - (. Here n is the color (0–16), and rrggbb indicates the red/green/blue values (0–255). ESC ] R: reset palette. |

## ECMA-48 CSI SEQUENCES

CSI (or ESC [) is followed by a sequence of parameters, at most NPAR(16), that are decimal numbers separated by semicolons. An empty or absent parameter is taken to be 0. The sequence of parameters may be preceded by a single question mark.

However, after CSI [ (or ESC [ [) a single character is read and this entire sequence is ignored. (The idea is to ignore an echoed function key.)

The action of a CSI sequence is determined by its final character.

| Character | Function | Description |
| --- | --- | --- |
| @ | ICH | Insert the indicated # of blank characters. |
| A | CUU | Move cursor up the indicated # of rows. |
| B | CUD | Move cursor down the indicated # of rows. |
| C | CUF | Move cursor right the indicated # of columns. |
| D | CUB | Move cursor left the indicated # of columns. |
| E | CNL | Move cursor down the indicated # of rows, to column 1. |
| F | CPL | Move cursor up the indicated # of rows, to column 1. |
| G | CHA | Move cursor to indicated column in current row. |
| H | CUP | Move cursor to the indicated row, column (origin at 1,1). |
| J | ED | Erase display (default: from cursor to end of display). |
| | | ESC [ 1 J: erase from start to cursor. |
| | | ESC [ 2 J: erase whole display. |
| K | EL | Erase line (default: from cursor to end of line). |
| | | ESC [ 1 K: erase from start of line to cursor. |
| | | ESC [ 2 K: erase whole line. |
| L | IL | Insert the indicated # of blank lines. |
| M | DL | Delete the indicated # of lines. |
| P | DCH | Delete the indicated # of characters on the current line. |
| X | ECH | Erase the indicated # of characters on the current line. |
| a | HPR | Move cursor right the indicated # of columns. |
| c | DA | Answer ESC [ ? 6 c: 'I am a VT102'. |
| d | VPA | Move cursor to the indicated row, current column. |
| e | VPR | Move cursor down the indicated # of rows. |
| f | HVP | Move cursor to the indicated row, column. |

*continues*

| Character | Function | Description |
|-----------|----------|-------------|
| g | TBC | Without parameter: clear tab stop at the current position. |
|   |     | ESC [ 3 g: delete all tab stops. |
| h | SM | Set mode. |
| l | RM | Reset mode. |
| m | SGR | Set attributes. |
| n | DSR | Status report. |
| q | DECLL | Set keyboard LEDs. |
|   |       | ESC [ 0 q: clear all LEDs |
|   |       | ESC [ 1 q: set Scroll Lock LED |
|   |       | ESC [ 2 q: set Num Lock LED |
|   |       | ESC [ 3 q: set Caps Lock LED |
| r | DECSTBM | Set scrolling region; parameters are top and bottom row. |
| s | ? | Save cursor location. |
| u | ? | Restore cursor location. |
| ' | HPA | Move cursor to indicated column in current row. |

## ECMA-48 SET GRAPHICS RENDITION

The ECMA-48 SGR sequence ESC [ <parameters> m sets display attributes. Several attributes can be set in the same sequence.

| Parameter | Result |
|-----------|--------|
| 0 | Reset all attributes to their defaults. |
| 1 | Set bold. |
| 2 | Set half-bright (simulated with color on a color display). |
| 4 | Set underscore (simulated with color on a color display). |
|   | (The colors used to simulate dim or underline are set using ESC ] ....) |
| 5 | Set blink. |
| 7 | Set reverse video. |
| 10 | Reset selected mapping, display control flag, and toggle meta flag. |
| 11 | Select null mapping, set display control flag, reset toggle meta flag. |
| 12 | Select null mapping, set display control flag, set toggle meta flag. (The toggle meta flag causes the high bit of a byte to be toggled before the mapping table translation is done.) |
| 21 | Set normal intensity. (This is not compatible with ECMA-48.) |
| 22 | Set normal intensity. |
| 24 | Underline off. |
| 25 | Blink off. |
| 27 | Reverse video off. |
| 30 | Set black foreground. |
| 31 | Set red foreground. |
| 32 | Set green foreground. |
| 33 | Set brown foreground. |
| 34 | Set blue foreground. |
| 35 | Set magenta foreground. |

| Parameter | Result |
|---|---|
| 36 | Set cyan foreground. |
| 37 | Set white foreground. |
| 38 | Set underscore on, set default foreground color. |
| 39 | Set underscore off, set default foreground color. |
| 40 | Set black background. |
| 41 | Set red background. |
| 42 | Set green background. |
| 43 | Set brown background. |
| 44 | Set blue background. |
| 45 | Set magenta background. |
| 46 | Set cyan background. |
| 47 | Set white background. |
| 49 | Set default background color. |

## ECMA-48 MODE SWITCHES

| | |
|---|---|
| ESC [ 3 h | DECCRM (default off): Display control chars. |
| ESC [ 4 h | DECIM (default off): Set insert mode. |
| ESC [ 20 h | LF/NL (default off): Automatically follow echo of LF, VT, or FF with CR. |

## ECMA-48 STATUS REPORT COMMANDS

| | |
|---|---|
| ESC [ 5 n | Device status report (DSR): Answer is ESC [ 0 n (Terminal OK). |
| ESC [ 6 n | Cursor position report (CPR): Answer is ESC [ y ; x R, where x, y is the cursor location. |

## DEC PRIVATE MODE(DECSET/DECRST) SEQUENCES

These are not described in ECMA-48. The Set Mode sequences are listed; the Reset Mode sequences are obtained by replacing the final h by l.

| | |
|---|---|
| ESC [ ? 1 h | DECCKM (default off): When set, the cursor keys send an ESC O prefix, rather than ESC [. |
| ESC [ ? 3 h | DECCOLM (default off = 80 columns): 80/132 col mode switch. The driver sources note that this alone does not suffice; some user-mode utility such as resizecons(8) has to change the hardware registers on the console video card. |
| ESC [ ? 5 h | DECSCNM (default off): Set reverse-video mode. |
| ESC [ ? 6 h | DECOM (default off): When set, cursor addressing is relative to the upper left corner of the scrolling region. |
| ESC [ ? 7 h | DECAWM(default on): Set autowrap on. In this mode, a graphics character emitted after column 80 (or column 132 of DECCOLM is on) forces a wrap to the beginning of the following line first. |
| ESC [ ? 8 h | DECARM (default on): Set keyboard autorepeat on. |
| ESC [ ? 9 | h X10 Mouse Reporting (default off): Set reporting mode to 1 (or reset to 0). (See "Mouse Tracking.") |
| ESC [ ? 25 h | DECCM (default on): Make cursor visible. |
| ESC [ ? 1000 h | X11 Mouse Reporting (default off): Set reporting mode to 2 (or reset to 0). (See "Mouse Tracking.") |

## LINUX CONSOLE PRIVATE CSI SEQUENCES

The following sequences are neither ECMA-48 nor native VT102. They are native to the Linux console driver. Colors are in SGR parameters: 0 = black, 1 = red, 2 = green, 3 = brown, 4 = blue, 5 = magenta, 6 = cyan, 7 = white.

| | |
|---|---|
| ESC [ 1 ; n ] | Set color *n* as the underline color |
| ESC [ 2 ; n ] | Set color *n* as the dim color |
| ESC [ 8 ] | Make the current color pair the default attributes |
| ESC [ 9 ; n ] | Set screen blank time-out to *n* minutes |
| ESC [ 10 ; n ] | Set bell frequency in Hz |
| ESC [ 11 ; n ] | Set bell duration in msec |
| ESC [ 12 ; n ] | Bring specified console to the front |
| ESC [ 13 ] | Unblank the screen |
| ESC [ 14 ] | Set the VESA powerdown interval |

## CHARACTER SETS

The kernel knows about four translations of bytes into console-screen symbols. The four tables are

- Latin1 to PC
- VT100 graphics to PC
- PC to PC
- User-defined

There are two character sets, called G0 and G1, and one of them is the current character set. (Initially G0.) Typing ^N causes G1 to become current, ^0 causes G0 to become current.

These variables G0 and G1 point to a translation table, and can be changed by the user. Initially, they point at the first two tables, Latin1 to PC and VT100 graphics to PC, respectively. The sequences ESC ( B and ESC ( 0 and ESC ( U and ESC ( K cause G0 to point at the first, second, third, and fourth translation tables in the preceding list, respectively. The sequences ESC ) B and ESC ) 0 and ESC ) U and ESC ) K cause G1 to point at the first, second, third, and fourth translation tables in the preceding list, respectively.

The sequence ESC c causes a terminal reset, which is what you want if the screen is all garbled. The oft-advised "echo ^V^O" will only make G0 current, but there is no guarantee that G0 points at the first table. In some distributions there is a program reset(1) that just does echo ^[c. If your terminfo entry for the console is correct (and has an entry rs1=c), then tput reset will also work.

The user-defined mapping table can be set using mapscrn(8). The result of the mapping is that if a symbol c is printed, the symbol s = map[c] is sent to the video memory. The bitmap that corresponds to s is found in the character ROM, and can be changed using setfont(8).

## MOUSE TRACKING

The mouse tracking facility is intended to return xterm-compatible mouse status reports. Because the console driver has no way to know the device or type of the mouse, these reports are returned in the console input stream only when the virtual terminal driver receives a mouse update ioctl. These ioctls must be generated by a mouse-aware user-mode application such as the gpm(8) daemon.

Parameters for all mouse tracking escape sequences generated by xterm encode numeric parameters in a single character as value+040. For example, ! is 1. The screen coordinate system is 1-based.

The X10 compatibility mode sends an escape sequence on button press encoding the location and the mouse button pressed. It is enabled by sending ESC [ ? 9 h and disabled with ESC [ ? 9 l. On button press, xterm sends ESC [ M bxy (six characters). Here b is button 1, and x and y are the x and y coordinates of the mouse when the button was pressed. This is the same code the kernel also produces.

Normal tracking mode (not implemented in Linux 2.0.24) sends an escape sequence on both button press and release. Modifier information is also sent. It is enabled by sending ESC [ ? 1000 h and disabled with ESC [ 1000 l. On button press or release, xterm sends ESC [ M bxy. The low two bits of b encode button information: 0=MB1 pressed, 1=MB2 pressed, 2=MB3 pressed, 3=release. The upper bits encode what modifiers were down when the button was pressed and are added together: 4=Shift, 8=Meta, 16=Control. Again, x and y are the x and y coordinates of the mouse event. The upper-left corner is (1,1).

## COMPARISONS WITH OTHER TERMINALS

Many different terminal types are described, like the Linux console, as being VT100-compatible. Here we discuss differences between the Linux console and the two most important others, the DEC VT102 and xterm(1).

### CONTROL-CHARACTER HANDLING

The vt102 also recognized the following control characters:

NUL (0x00) was ignored.

ENQ (0x05) triggered an answerback message.

DC1 (0x11, ^Q, XON) resumed transmission.

DC3 (0x13, ^S, XOFF) caused vt100 to ignore (and stop transmitting) all codes except XOFF and XON.

VT100-like DC1/DC3 processing may be enabled by the tty driver.

The xterm program (in vt100 mode) recognizes the control characters BEL, BS, HT, LF, VT, FF, CR, SO, SI, ESC.

### ESCAPE SEQUENCES

The following VT100 console sequences are not implemented on the Linux console:

| Escape Sequence | Function | Description |
|---|---|---|
| ESC N | SS2 | Single shift 2. (Select G2 character set for the next character only.) |
| ESC O | SS3 | Single shift 3. (Select G3 character set for the next character only.) |
| ESC P | DCS | Device control string (ended by ESC \). |
| ESC X | SOS | Start of string. |
| ESC ^ | PM | Privacy message (ended by ESC\). |
| ESC \ | ST | String terminator. |
| ESC * ... | | Designate G2 character set. |
| ESC + ... | | Designate G3 character set. |

The program xterm (in vt100 mode) recognizes ESC c, ESC # 8, ESC >, ESC =, ESC D, ESC E, ESC H, ESC M, ESC N, ESC O, ESC P ... ESC ESC Z (it answers ESC [ ? 1 ; 2 c, "I am a vt100 with advanced video option") and ESC ^ ... ESC with the same meanings as indicated above. It accepts ESC (, ESC ), ESC *, ESC + followed by 0, A, B for the DEC special character and line drawing set, UK, and USASCII, respectively. It accepts ESC ] for the setting of certain resources:

| | |
|---|---|
| ESC ] 0 ; txt BEL | Set icon name and window title to txt. |
| ESC ]1 ; txt BEL | Set icon name to txt. |
| ESC ] 2 ; txt BEL | Set window title to txt. |
| ESC ] 4 6 ; name BEL | Change log file to name (normally disabled by a compile-time option). |
| ESC ] 5 0 ; fn BEL | Set font to fn. |

It recognizes the following with slightly modified meaning:

| | |
|---|---|
| ESC 7 DECSC | Save cursor |
| ESC 8 DECRC | Restore cursor |

It also recognizes

| | | |
|---|---|---|
| ESC F | | Cursor to lower-left corner of screen (if enabled by the hpLowerleftBugCompat resource). |
| ESC l | | Memory lock (per HP terminals). Locks memory above the cursor. |
| ESC m | | Memory unlock (per HP terminals). |
| ESC n | LS2 | Invoke the G2 character set. |
| ESC o | L33 | Invoke the G3 character set. |
| ESC j | LS3R | Invoke the G3 character set as GR. Has no visible effect in xterm. |
| ESC g | LS2R | Invoke the G2 character set as GR. Has no visible effect in xterm. |
| ESC ˜ | LS1R | Invoke the G1 character set as GR. Has no visible effect in xterm. |

It does not recognize ESC % ...

## CSI SEQUENCES

The xterm program (as of XFree86 3.1.2G) does not recognize the blink or invisible-mode SGRs. Stock X11R6 versions do not recognize the color-setting SGRs. All other ECMA-48 CSI sequences recognized by Linux are also recognized by xterm, and vice versa.

The xterm program will recognize all of the DEC Private Mode sequences listed earlier, but none of the Linux private-mode sequences. For discussion of xterm's own private-mode sequences, refer to the *Xterm Control Sequences* document by Edward Moy and Stephen Gildea, available with the X distribution.

## BUGS

In 2.0.23, CSI is broken, and NUL is not ignored inside escape sequences.

## SEE ALSO

console(4), console_ioctl(4), charsets(4)

*Linux, 31 October 1996*

# console ioctls

console ioctls—Ioctls for console terminal and virtual consoles

## DESCRIPTION

The following Linux-peculiar ioctl() requests are supported. Each requires a third argument, assumed here to be argp.

### WARNING

If you use the following information, you are going to burn yourself. Ioctls are undocumented Linux internals, liable to be changed without warning. Use POSIX functions.

| KDGETLED | Get state of LEDs. argp points to a long int. The lower three bits of *argp are set to the state of the LEDs, as follows: |
|---|---|

| LED_CAP | 0x04 | caps lock LED |
| LEC_NUM | 0x02 | num lock LED |
| LED_SCR | 0x01 | scroll lock LED |

| KDSETLED | Set the LEDs. The LEDs are set to correspond to the lower three bits of argp. However, if a higher order bit is set, the LEDs revert to normal, displaying the state of the keyboard functions of caps lock, num lock, and scroll lock. |
|---|---|

Before 1.1.54, the LEDs just reflected the state of the corresponding keyboard flags, and KDGETLED/KDSETLED would also change the keyboard flags. Since 1.1.54 the LEDs can be made to display arbitrary information, but by default they display the keyboard flags. The following two ioctls are used to access the keyboard flags.

| KDGKBLED | Get keyboard flags CapsLock, NumLock, ScrollLock (not lights). argp points to a char that is set to the flag state. The low order three bits (mask 0x7) get the current flag state, and the low order bits of the next nibble (mask 0x70) get the default flag state (since 1.1.54). |
|---|---|
| KDSKBLED | Set keyboard flags CapsLock, NumLock, ScrollLock (not lights). argp has the desired flag state. The low order three bits (mask 0x7) have the flag state, and the low order bits of the next nibble (mask 0x70) have the default flag state (since 1.1.54). |
| KDGKBTYPE | Get keyboard type. This returns the value KB 101, defined as 0x02. |
| KDADDIO | Add I/O port as valid. Equivalent to ioperm(arg,1,1). |
| KDDELIO | Delete I/O port as valid. Equivalent to ioperm(arg,1,0). |
| KDENABIO | Enable I/O to video board. Equivalent to ioperm(0x3b4, 0x3df-0x3b4+1, 1). |
| KDDISABIO | Disable I/O to video board. Equivalent to ioperm(0x3b4, 0x3df-0x3b4+ 1, 0). |
| KDSETMODE | Set text/graphics mode. argp is one of these: |

| KD_TEXT | 0x00 |
| KD_GRAPHICS | 0x01 |

| KDGETMODE | Get text/graphics mode. argp points to a long which is set to one of the above values. |
|---|---|
| KDMKTONE | Generate tone of specified length. The lower 16 bits of argp specify the period in clock cycles, and the upper 16 bits give the duration in msec. If the duration is zero, the sound is turned off. Control returns immediately. For example, argp = (125<<16) + 0x637 would specify the beep normally associated with a ctrl-G. |
| KIOCSOUND | Start or stop sound generation. The lower 16 bits of argp specify the period in clock cycles (that is, argp = 1193180/frequency). argp = 0 turns sound off. In either case, control returns immediately. |
| GIO_CMAP | Get the current default color map from kernel. argp points to a 48-byte array. (Since 1.3.3.) |
| PIO_CMAP | Change the default text-mode color map. argp points to a 48-byte array that contains, in order, the red, green, and blue values for the 16 available screen colors: 0 is off, and 255 is full intensity. The default colors are, in order: black, dark red, dark green, brown, dark blue, dark purple, dark cyan, light grey, dark grey, bright red, bright green, yellow, bright blue, bright purple, bright cyan, and white. (Since 1.3.3.) |
| GIO_FONT | Gets 256-character screen font in expanded form. argp points to an 8192-byte array. Fails with error code EINVAL if the currently loaded font is a 512-character font, or if the console is not in text mode. |

GIO_FONTX

Gets screen font and associated information. argp points to a struct consolefontdesc (see PIO_FONTX). On call, the charcount field should be set to the maximum number of characters that would fit in the buffer pointed to by chardata. On return, the charcount and charheight are filled with the respective data for the currently loaded font, and the chardata array contains the font data if the initial value of charcount indicated enough space was available; otherwise the buffer is untouched and errno is set to ENOMEM. (Since 1.3.1.)

PIO_FONT

Sets 256-character screen font. Load font into the EGA/VGA character generator. argp points to a 8192-byte map, with 32 bytes per character. Only first N of them are used for an 8xN font (0 < N <= 32). This call also invalidates the Unicode mapping.

PIO_FONTX

Sets screen font and associated rendering information. argp points to a

```
struct consolefontdesc {
u_short charcount; /* characters in font

                        (256 or 512) */
u_short charheight; /* scan lines per

                        character (1-32) */
char *chardata; /* font data in

                        expanded form */
};
```

If necessary, the screen will be appropriately resized, and SIGWINCH sent to the appropriate processes. This call also invalidates the Unicode mapping. (Since 1.3.1.)

PIO_FONTRESET

Resets the screen font, size, and Unicode mapping to the bootup defaults. argp is unused, but should be set to NULL to ensure compatibility with future versions of Linux. (Since 1.3.28.)

GIO_SCRNMAP

Get screen mapping from kernel. argp points to an area of size E_TABSZ, which is loaded with the font positions used to display each character. This call is likely to return useless information if the currently loaded font is more than 256 characters.

GIO_UNISCRNMAP

Get full Unicode screen mapping from kernel. argp points to an area of size E_TABSZ*sizeof (unsigned short), which is loaded with the Unicodes each character represent. A special set of Unicodes, starting at U+F000, are used to represent "direct to font" mappings. (Since 1.3.1.)

PIO_SCRNMAP

Loads the user-definable (fourth) table in the kernel that maps bytes into console screen symbols. argp points to an area of size E_TABSZ.

PIO_UNISCRNMAP

Loads the user-definable (fourth) table in the kernel that maps bytes into Unicodes, which are then translated into screen symbols according to the currently loaded Unicode-to-font map. Special Unicodes starting at U+F000 can be used to map directly to the font symbols. (Since 1.3.1.)

GIO_UNIMAP

Get Unicode-to-font mapping from kernel. argp points to a

```
struct unimapdesc {
u_short entry_ct;
struct unipair *entries;
};
where entries points to an array of
struct unipair {
u_short unicode;
u_short fontpos;
};
(Since 1.1.92.)
```

PIO_UNIMAP

Put Unicode-to-font mapping in kernel. argp points to a struct unimapdesc. (Since 1.1.92.)

| | |
|---|---|
| PIO_UNIMAPCLR | Clear table, possibly advise hash algorithm. argp points to a |

```
struct unimapinit {
u short advised hashsize; /* 0 if no opinion */
u short advised hashstep; /* 0 if no opinion */
u short advised hashlevel; /* 0 if no opinion */
};
```
(Since 1.1.92.)

| | |
|---|---|
| KDGKBMODE | Gets current keyboard mode. argp points to a long, which is set to one of these: |

| | |
|---|---|
| K_RAW | 0x00 |
| K_XLATE | 0x01 |
| K_MEDIUMRAW | 0x02 |
| K_UNICODE | 0x03 |

| | |
|---|---|
| KDSKBMODE | Sets current keyboard mode. argp is a long equal to one of the above values. |
| KDGKBMETA | Gets meta key handling mode. argp points to a long which is set to one of these: |

| | | |
|---|---|---|
| K_METABIT | 0x03 | Set high order bit |
| K_ESCPREFIX | 0x04 | Escape prefix |

| | |
|---|---|
| KDSKBMETA | Sets meta key handling mode. argp is a long equal to one of the preceding values. |
| KDGKBENT | Gets one entry in key translation table (keycode to action code). argp points to a |

```
struct kbentry {
u_char kb_table;
u_char kb_index;
u_short kb_value;
};
```

with the first two members filled in: kb_table selects the key table (0 <= kb_table <MAX_NR_KEYMAPS), and kb_index is the keycode (0 <= kb index <NR_KEYS). kb_value is set to the corresponding action code, or K_HOLE if there is no such key, or K_NOSUCHMAP if kb_table is invalid.

| | |
|---|---|
| KDSKBENT | Sets one entry in translation table. argp points to a struct kbentry. |
| KDGKBSENT | Gets one function key string. argp points to a |

```
struct kbsentry {
u_char kb_func;
u_char kb_string[512];
;
```

kb_string is set to the (NULL-terminated) string corresponding to the kb_functh function key action code.

| | |
|---|---|
| KDSKBSENT | Sets one function key string entry. argp points to a struct kbsentry. |
| KDGKBDIACR | Read kernel accent table. argp points to a |

```
struct kbdiacrs {
unsigned int kb_cnt;
struct kbdiacr kbdiacr[256];
};
```

where kb_cnt is the number of entries in the array, each of which is a
struct kbdiacr { u_char diacr, base, result ;};

| | |
|---|---|
| KDGETKEYCODE | Read kernel keycode table entry (scan code to keycode). argp points to a |

struct kbkeycode { unsigned int scancode, keycode; };
keycode is set to correspond to the given scancode.(89<=scancode <= 255 only.
For 1 <= scancode <= 88, keycode==scancode.) (Since 1.1.63.)

| | |
|---|---|
| KDSETKEYCODE | Write kernel keycode table entry. argp points to struct kbkeycode. (Since 1.1.63.) |

| | |
|---|---|
| KDSIGACCEPT | The calling process indicates its willingness to accept the signal argp when it is generated by pressing an appropriate key combination. (1 <= argp <=NSIG). |
| | (See spawn_console() in linux/drivers/char/keyboard.c.) |
| VT_OPENQRY | Returns the first available (nonopened) console. argp points to an int that is set to the number of the vt (1 <= *argp <=MAX_NR_CONSOLES). |
| VT_GETMODE | Get mode of active vt. argp points to a |

```
struct vt mode {
char mode;/*vtmode*/
char waitv; /* if set, hang on writes if not active */
short relsig; /* signal to raise on release req */
short acqsig; /* signal to raise on acquisition */
short frsig; /* unused (set to 0) */
};
```

mode is set to one of these values:

| | |
|---|---|
| VT_AUTO | Auto vt switching |
| VT_PROCESS | Process controls switching |
| VT_ACKACQ | Acknowledge switch |

| | |
|---|---|
| VT_SETMODE | Set mode of active vt. argp points to a struct vt_mode. |
| VT_GETSTATE | Get global vt state info. argp points to a |

```
struct vt_stat {
ushort v_active; /* active vt */
ushort v_signal;/*signalto send*/
ushort v_state;/*vtbitmask*/
};
```

For each vt in use, the corresponding bit in the v state member is set. (Kernels 1.0 through 1.1.92.)

| | |
|---|---|
| VT_RELDISP | Release a display. |
| VT_ACTIVATE | Switch to vt argp (1 <= argp <=MAX_NR_CONSOLES). |
| VT_WAITACTIVE | Wait until vt argp has been activated. |
| VT_DISALLOCATE | Deallocate the memory associated with vt argp. (Since 1.1.54.) |
| VT_RESIZE | Set the kernel's idea of screensize. argp points to a |

```
struct vt_sizes {
ushort v_rows;/*#rows*/
ushort v_cols;/*#columns */
ushort v_scrollsize; /* no longer used */
};
```

Note that this does not change the video mode. See resizecons(8). (Since 1.1.54.)

| | |
|---|---|
| VT_RESIZEX | Set the kernel's idea of various screen parameters. argp points to a |

```
struct vt_consize {
ushort v_rows; /* number of rows */
ushort v_cols; /* number of columns */
ushort v_vlin; /* number of pixel rows on screen */
ushort v_clin; /* number of pixel rows per character */
ushort v_vcol; /* number of pixel columns on screen */
ushort v_ccol; /* number of pixel columns per character */
};
```

Any parameter may be set to zero, indicating no change, but if multiple parameters are set, they must be self-consistent. Note that this does not change the video mode. See resizecons(8). (Since 1.3.3.)

The action of the following ioctls depends on the first byte in the struct pointed to by argp, referred to here as the subcode. These are legal only for the superuser or the owner of the current tty.

| | |
|---|---|
| TIOCLINUX, subcode=0 | Dump the screen. Disappeared in 1.1.92. (With kernel 1.1.92 or later, read from /dev/vcsN or /dev/vcsaN instead.) |
| TIOCLINUX, subcode=1 | Get task information. Disappeared in 1.1.92. |
| TIOCLINUX, subcode=2 | Set selection. argp points to a |

struct{fchar subcode; short xs, ys, xe, ye; short sel_mode; }

xs and ys are the starting column and row. xe and ye are the ending column and row. (Upper-left corner is row=column=1.) sel_mode is 0 for character-by-character selection, 1 for word-by-word selection, or 2 for line-by-line selection. The indicated screen characters are highlighted and saved in the static array sel buffer in devices/char/console.c.

| | |
|---|---|
| TIOCLINUX, subcode=3 | Paste selection. The characters in the selection buffer are written to fd. |
| TIOCLINUX, subcode=4 | Unblank the screen. |
| TIOCLINUX, subcode=5 | Sets contents of a 256-bit look up table defining characters in a "word", for word-by-word selection. (Since 1.1.32.) |
| TIOCLINUX, subcode=6 | argp points to a char that is set to the value of the kernel variable shift state. (Since 1.1.32.) |
| TIOCLINUX, subcode=7 | argp points to a char that is set to the value of the kernel variable report mouse. (Since 1.1.33.) |
| TIOCLINUX, subcode=8 | Dump screen width and height, cursor position, and all the character-attribute pairs. (Kernels 1.1.67 through 1.1.91 only. With kernel 1.1.92 or later, read from /dev/vcsa* instead.) |
| TIOCLINUX, subcode=9 | Restore screen width and height, cursor position, and all the character-attribute pairs. (Kernels 1.1.67 through 1.1.91 only. With kernel 1.1.92 or later, write to /dev/vcsa* instead.) |
| TIOCLINUX, subcode=10 | Handles the power saving feature of the new generation of monitors. VESA screen blanking mode is set to argp[1], which governs what screen blanking does: |

| | |
|---|---|
| 0 | Screen blanking is disabled. |
| 1 | The current video adapter register settings are saved, then the controller is programmed to turn off the vertical synchronization pulses. This puts the monitor into standby mode. If your monitor has an Off_Mode timer, then it will eventually power down by itself. |
| 2 | The current settings are saved, then both the vertical and horizontal synchronization pulses are turned off. This puts the monitor into off mode. If your monitor has no Off_Mode timer, or if you want your monitor to power down immediately when the blank timer times out, then you choose this option. (Caution: Powering down frequently will damage the monitor.) (Since 1.1.76.) |

## RETURN VALUES

-1 for error, and errno is set.

## ERRORS

errno may take on these values:

| | |
|---|---|
| EBADF | File descriptor is invalid. |
| ENOTTY | File descriptor is not associated with a character special device, or the specified request does not apply to it. |

| | |
|---|---|
| EINVAL | File descriptor or argp is invalid. |
| EPERM | Permission violation. |

## WARNING

Do not regard this man page as documentation of the Linux console ioctls. This is provided for the curious only, as an alternative to reading the source. Ioctls are undocumented Linux internals, liable to be changed without warning. (And indeed, this page more or less describes the situation as of kernel version 1.1.94; there are many minor and not-so-minor differences with earlier versions.)

Very often, ioctls are introduced for communication between the kernel and one particular well-known program (fdisk, hdparm, setserial, tunelp, loadkeys, selection, setfont, and so on), and their behavior will be changed when required by this particular program.

Programs using these ioctls will not be portable to other versions of UNIX, will not work on older versions of Linux, and will not work on future versions of Linux.

Use POSIX functions.

## SEE ALSO

kbd_mode(1), loadkeys(1), dumpkeys(1), mknod(1), setleds(1), setmetamode(1), ioperm(2), termios(2), execve(2), fcntl(2), charsets(4), console(4), console_codes(4), mt(4), sd(4), tty(4), ttys(4), vcs(4), vcsa(4), mapscrn(8), setfont(8), resizecons(8), /usr/include/linux/kd.h, /usr/include/linux/vt.h.

*Linux, 18 September 1995*

# fd

fd—Floppy disk device

## CONFIGURATION

Floppy drives are block devices with major number 2. Typically, they are owned by root.floppy (that is, user root, group floppy) and have either mode 0660 (access checking via group membership) or mode 0666 (everybody has access). The minor numbers encode the device type, drive number, and controller number. For each device type (that is, combination of density and track count), there is a base minor number. To this base number, add the drive's number on its controller and 128 if the drive is on the secondary controller. In the following device tables, n represents the drive number.

## WARNING

If you use formats with more tracks than supported by your drive, you may cause it mechanical damage. Trying once if more tracks than the usual 40/80 are supported should not damage it, but no warranty is given for that. Don't create device entries for those formats to prevent their usage if you are not sure.

Drive-independent device files that automatically detect the media format and capacity are

| Name | Base minor # |
|------|--------------|
| fdn  | 0 |

5.25-inch double density device files:

| Name | Capac. | Cyl. | Sect. | Heads | Base minor # |
|------|--------|------|-------|-------|--------------|
| fdnd360 | 360K | 40 | 9 | 2 | 4 |

5.25-inch high density device files:

| Name | Capac. | Cyl. | Sect. | Heads | Base minor # |
|------|--------|------|-------|-------|--------------|
| fdnh360 | 360K | 40 | 9 | 2 | 20 |
| fdnh410 | 410K | 41 | 10 | 2 | 48 |
| fdnh420 | 420K | 42 | 10 | 2 | 64 |
| fdnh720 | 720K | 80 | 9 | 2 | 24 |
| fdnh880 | 880K | 80 | 11 | 2 | 80 |
| fdnh1200 | 1200K | 80 | 15 | 2 | 8 |
| fdnh1440 | 1440K | 80 | 18 | 2 | 40 |
| fdnh1476 | 1476K | 82 | 18 | 2 | 56 |
| fdnh1494 | 1494K | 83 | 18 | 2 | 72 |
| fdnh1600 | 1600K | 80 | 20 | 2 | 92 |

3.5-inch double density device files:

| Name | Capac. | Cyl. | Sect. | Heads | Base minor # |
|------|--------|------|-------|-------|--------------|
| fdnD360 | 360K | 80 | 9 | 1 | 12 |
| fdnD720 | 720K | 80 | 9 | 2 | 16 |
| fdnD800 | 800K | 80 | 10 | 2 | 120 |
| fdnD1040 | 1040K | 80 | 13 | 2 | 84 |
| fdnD1120 | 1120K | 80 | 14 | 2 | 88 |

3.5-inch high density device files:

| Name | Capac. | Cyl. | Sect. | Heads | Base minor # |
|------|--------|------|-------|-------|--------------|
| fdnH360 | 360K | 40 | 9 | 2 | 12 |
| fdnH720 | 720K | 80 | 9 | 2 | 16 |
| fdnH820 | 820K | 82 | 10 | 2 | 52 |
| fdnH830 | 830K | 83 | 10 | 2 | 68 |
| fdnH1440 | 1440K | 80 | 18 | 2 | 28 |
| fdnH1600 | 1600K | 80 | 20 | 2 | 124 |
| fdnH1680 | 1680K | 80 | 21 | 2 | 44 |
| fdnH1722 | 1722K | 82 | 21 | 2 | 60 |
| fdnH1743 | 1743K | 83 | 21 | 2 | 76 |
| fdnH1760 | 1760K | 80 | 22 | 2 | 96 |
| fdnH1840 | 1840K | 80 | 23 | 2 | 116 |
| fdnH1920 | 1920K | 80 | 24 | 2 | 100 |

3.5-inch extra density device files:

| Name | Capac. | Cyl. | Sect. | Heads | Base minor # |
|------|--------|------|-------|-------|--------------|
| fdnE2880 | 2880K | 80 | 36 | 2 | 32 |
| fdnCompaQ | 2880K | 80 | 36 | 2 | 36 |
| fdnE3200 | 3200K | 80 | 40 | 2 | 104 |
| fdnE3520 | 3520K | 80 | 44 | 2 | 108 |
| fdnE3840 | 3840K | 80 | 48 | 2 | 112 |

## DESCRIPTION

fd special files access the floppy disk drives in raw mode. The following ioctl(2) calls are supported by fd devices:

FDCLRPRM clears the media information of a drive (geometry of disk in drive).

FDSETPRM sets the media information of a drive. The media information will be lost when the media is changed.

FDDEFPRM sets the media information of a drive (geometry of disk in drive). The media information will not be lost when the media is changed. This will disable autodetection. In order to re-enable autodetection, you have to issue an FDCLRPRM.

FDGETDRVTYP displays the type of a drive (name parameter). For formats that work in several drive types, FDGETDRVTYP returns a name that is appropriate for the oldest drive type that supports this format.

FDFLUSH invalidates the buffer cache for the given drive.

FDFLUSH invalidates the buffer cache for the given drive.

FDSETMAXERRS sets the error thresholds for reporting errors, aborting the operation, recalibrating, resetting, and reading sector by sector.

FDSETMAXERRS gets the current error thresholds.

FDGETDRVTYP gets the internal name of the drive.

FDWERRORCLR clears the write error statistics.

FDWERRORGET reads the write error statistics. These include the total number of write errors, the location and disk of the first write error, and the location and disk of the last write error. Disks are identified by a generation number that is incremented at (almost) each disk change.

FDTWADDLE switches the drive motor off for a few microseconds. This might be needed in order to access a disk whose sectors are too close together.

FDSETDRVPRM sets various drive parameters.

FDGETDRVPRM reads these parameters back.

FDGETDRVSTAT gets the cached drive state (disk changed, write protected et al.)

FDPOLLDRVSTAT polls the drive and return its state.

FDGETFDCSTAT gets the floppy controller state.

FDRESET resets the floppy controller under certain conditions.

FDRAWCMD sends a raw command to the floppy controller.

For more precise information, consult also the <linux/fd.h> and <linux/fdreg.h> include files, as well as the manual page for floppy control.

## NOTES

The various formats allow you to read and write many types of disks. However, if a floppy is formatted with a too small intersector gap, performance may drop, up to needing a few seconds to access an entire track. To prevent this, use interleaved formats. It is not possible to read floppies that are formatted using GCR (group code recording), which is used by Apple II and Macintosh computers (800K disks). Reading floppies that are hard sectored (one hole per sector, with the index hole being a little skewed) is not supported. This used to be common with older 8-inch floppies.

## FILES

/dev/fd*

## AUTHORS

Alain Knaff (Alain.Knaff@imag.fr), David Niemi (niemidc@clark.net), Bill Broadhurst (bbroad@netcom.com).

## SEE ALSO

floppycontrol(1), mknod(1), chown(1), getfdprm(1), superformat(1), mount(8), setfd-prm(8)

*Linux, 29 January 1995*

# hd

hd — MFM/IDE hard disk device

## DESCRIPTION

hd* are block devices to access MFM/IDE hard disk drives in raw mode. The master drive on the primary IDE controller (major device number 3) is hda; the slave drive is hdb. The master drive of the second controller (major device number 22) is hdc and the slave hdd.

General IDE block device names have the form hdX , or hdXP, where X is a letter denoting the physical drive, and P is a number denoting the partition on that physical drive. The first form, hdX, is used to address the whole drive. Partition numbers are assigned in the order the partitions are discovered, and only nonempty, nonextended partitions get a number. However, partition numbers 1–4 are given to the four partitions described in the MBR (the primary partitions), regardless of whether they are unused or extended. Thus, the first logical partition will be hdX5. Both DOS-type partitioning and BSD-disk label partitioning are supported. You can have at most 63 partitions on an IDE disk.

For example, /dev/hda refers to all of the first IDE drive in the system; and /dev/hdb3 refers to the third DOS primary partition on the second one.

They are typically created by the following:

```
mknod -m 660 /dev/hda b 3 0
mknod -m 660 /dev/hda1 b 3 1
mknod -m 660 /dev/hda2 b 3 2


...
mknod -m 660 /dev/hda8 b 3 8
mknod -m 660 /dev/hdb b 3 64
mknod -m 660 /dev/hdb1 b 3 65
mknod -m 660 /dev/hdb2 b 3 66


...
mknod -m 660 /dev/hdb8 b 3 72
chown root.disk /dev/hd*
```

## FILES

/dev/hd*

## SEE ALSO

mknod(1), chown(1), mount(8), sd(4)

*Linux, 17 December 1992*

# ispell

ispell—Format of ispell dictionaries and affix files

## DESCRIPTION

ispell(1) requires two files to define the language that it is spell checking. The first file is a dictionary containing words for the language, and the second is an affix file that defines he meaning of special flags in the dictionary. The two files are combined by buildhash (see spell(1)) and written to a hash file that is not described here.

A raw ispell dictionary (either the main dictionary or your own personal dictionary) contains a list of words, one per line. Each word may optionally be followed by a slash (/) and one or more flags, which modify the root word as explained later. Depending on the options with which ispell was built, case may or may not be significant in either the root word or the flags, independently. Specifically, if the compile-time option CAPITALIZATION is defined, case is significant in the root word; if not, case is ignored in the root word. If the compile-time option MASKBITS is set to a value of 32, case is ignored in the flags; otherwise, case is significant in the flags. Contact your system administrator or ispell maintainer for more information (or use the -vv flag to find out). The dictionary should be sorted with the -f flag of sort(1) before the hash file is built; this is done automatically by unhlist(1), which is the normal way of building dictionaries.

If the dictionary contains words that have string characters (see the affix file documentation, following), they must be written in the format given by the defstringtype statement in the affix file. This will be the case for most non-English languages. Be careful to use this format, rather than that of your favorite formatter, when adding words to a dictionary. If you add words to your personal dictionary during an ispell session, they will automatically be converted to the correct format. This feature can be used to convert an entire dictionary if necessary:

```
echo qqqqq > dummy.dict
buildhash dummy.dict affix-file dummy.hash
awk 'fprint "*"gENDfprint "#"g' old-dict-file \
¦ ispell -a -T old-dict-string-type \
-d ./dummy.hash -p ./new-dict-file \
> /dev/null
rm dummy.*
```

The case of the root word controls the case of words accepted by ispell, as follows:

1. If the root word appears only in lowercase (for example, bob), it will be accepted in lowercase, capitalized, or all capitals.
2. If the root word appears capitalized (for example, Robert), it will not be accepted in all lowercase, but will be accepted capitalized or all in capitals.
3. If the root word appears all in capitals (for example, UNIX), it will only be accepted all in capitals.
4. If the root word appears with a "funny" capitalization (for example, ITCorp), a word will be accepted only if it follows that capitalization, or if it appears all in capitals.
5. More than one capitalization of a root word may appear in the dictionary. Flags from different capitalizations are combined using OR.

Redundant capitalizations (for example, bob and Bob) will be combined by buildhash and by ispell (for personal dictionaries), and can be removed from a raw dictionary by munchlist.

For example, the dictionary

```
bob
Robert
UNIX
ITcorp
ITCorp
```

will accept bob, Bob, BOB, Robert, ROBERT, UNIX, ITcorp, ITCorp, and ITCORP, and will reject all others. Some of the unacceptable forms are bOb, robert, Unix, and ItCorp.

As mentioned, root words in any dictionary may be extended by flags. Each flag is a single alphabetic character, which represents a prefix or suffix that may be added to the root to form a new word. For example, in an English dictionary the D flag can be added to bathe to make bathed. Because flags are represented as a single bit in the hashed dictionary, this results in significant space savings. The munchlist script will reduce an existing raw dictionary by adding flags when possible.

When a word is extended with an affix, the affix will be accepted only if it appears in the same case as the initial (prefix) or final (suffix) letter of the word. Thus, for example, the entry UNIX/M in the main dictionary (M means add an apostrophe and an *s* to make a possessive) would accept UNIX'S but would reject UNIX's. If UNIX's is legal, it must appear as a separate dictionary entry, and it will not be combined by munchlist. (In general, you don't need to worry about these things; munchlist guarantees that its output dictionary will accept the same set of words as its input, so all you have to do is add words to the dictionary and occasionally run munchlist to reduce its size.)

As mentioned, the affix definition file describes the affixes associated with particular flags. It also describes the character set used by the language.

Although the affix-definition grammar is designed for a line-oriented layout, it is actually a free-format grammar and can be laid out weirdly if you want. Comments are started by a pound (sharp) sign (#), and continue to the end of the line. Backslashes are supported in the usual fashion (\nnn, plus specials \n, \r, \t, \v, \f, \b, and the new hex format \xnn). Any character with special meaning to the parser can be changed to an uninterpreted token by backslashing it; for example, you can declare a flag named asterisk or colon with flag n* or flag n::.

The grammar will be presented in a top-down fashion, with discussion of each element. An affix-definition file must contain exactly one table:

```
table :[headers][prefixes][suffixes]
```

At least one of prefixes and suffixes is required. They can appear in either order.

```
headers :[options ] char-sets
```

The headers describe options global to this dictionary and language. These include the character sets to be used and the formatter, and the defaults for certain *ispell* flags.

```
options : { fmtr-stmt ¦ opt-stmt ¦ flag-stmt ¦ num-stmt }
```

The options statements define the defaults for certain ispell flags and for the character sets used by the formatters.

```
fmtr-stmt : { nroff-stmt ¦ tex-stmt }
```

A fmtr-stmt statement describes characters that have special meaning to a formatter. Normally, this statement is not necessary, but some languages may have preempted the usual defaults for use as language-specific characters. In this case, these statements may be used to redefine the special characters expected by the formatter.

```
nroff-stmt : { nroffchars ¦ troffchars } string
```

The nroffchars statement allows redefinition of certain nroff control characters. The string given must be exactly five characters long, and must list substitutions for the left and right parentheses, the period, the backslash, and the asterisk. (The right parenthesis is not currently used, but is included for completeness.) For example, the statement:

```
nroffchars {}.\\*
```

would replace the left and right parentheses with left and right curly braces for purposes of parsing nroff/troff strings, with no effect on the others (admittedly a contrived example). Note that the backslash is escaped with a backslash.

```
tex-stmt : { TeXchars ¦ texchars } string
```

The TeXchars statement allows redefinition of certain TeX/LaTeX control characters. The string given must be exactly thirteen characters long, and must list substitutions for the left and right parentheses, the left and right square brackets, the left and right curly braces, the left and right angle brackets, the backslash, the dollar sign, the asterisk, the period or dot, and the percent sign. For example, the statement:

```
texchars ()\[]<\><\>\\$*.%
```

would replace the functions of the left and right curly braces with the left and right angle brackets for purposes of parsing TeX/LaTeX constructs, while retaining their functions for the `tib` bibliographic preprocessor. Note that the backslash, the left square bracket, and the right angle bracket must be escaped with a backslash.

```
opt-stmt : { cmpnd-stmt | aff-stmt }
cmpnd-stmt : compoundwords compound-opt
 aff-stmt : allaffixes on-or-off
 on-or-off : { on | off }
compound-opt : { on-or-off | controlled character }
```

An opt-stmt, used in the preceding code, controls certain ispell defaults that are best made language-specific. The `allaffixes` statement controls the default for the -P and -m options to `ispell`. If `allaffixes` is turned off (the default), `ispell` will default to the behavior of the -P flag: root/affix suggestions will only be made if there are no "near misses." If `allaffixes` is turned on, `ispell` will default to the behavior of the -m flag: root/affix suggestions will always be made.

The `compoundwords` statement controls the default for the -B and -C options to `ispell`. If `compoundwords` is turned off (the default), `ispell` will default to the behavior of the -B flag: run-together words will be reported as errors. If `compoundwords` is turned on, `ispell` will default to the behavior of the -C flag: run-together words will be considered as compounds if both are in the dictionary. This is useful for languages such as German and Norwegian, which form large numbers of compound words. Finally, if `compoundwords` is set to controlled, only words marked with the flag indicated by character (which should not be otherwise used) will be allowed to participate in compound formation. Because this option requires the flags to be specified in the dictionary, it is not available from the command line.

```
flag-stmt : flagmarker character
```

The `flagmarker` statement describes the character that is used to separate affix flags from the root word in a raw dictionary file. This must be a character that is not found in any word (including in string characters; see following). The default is / because this character is not normally used to represent special characters in any language.

```
num-stmt : compoundmin digit
```

The `compoundmin` statement controls the length of the two components of a compound word. This only has an effect if `compoundwords` is turned on or if the –C flag is given to ispell. In that case, only words at least as long as the given minimum will be accepted as components of a compound. The default is 3 characters.

```
char-sets : norm-sets [ alt-sets ]
```

The character-set section describes the characters that can be part of a word, and defines their collating order. There must always be a definition of "normal" character sets; in addition, there may be one or more partial definitions of "alternate" sets that are used with various text formatters.

```
norm-sets :[deftype ] charset-group
```

A "normal" character set may optionally begin with a definition of the file suffixes that make use of this set. Following this are one or more character-set declarations.

```
deftype : defstringtype name deformatter suffix*
```

The *defstringtype* declaration gives a list of file suffixes that should make use of the default string characters defined as part of the base character set; it is only necessary if string characters are being defined. The `name` parameter is a string giving the unique name associated with these suffixes; often it is a formatter name. If the formatter is a member of the `troff` family, `nroff` should be used for the name associated with the most popular macro package; members of the TeX family should use `tex`. Other names may be chosen freely, but they should be kept simple, as they are used in `ispell`'s -T switch to specify a formatter type. The `deformatter` parameter specifies the deformatting style to use when processing files with the given suffixes. Currently, this must be either `tex` or `nroff`. The suffix parameters are a whitespace-separated list of strings which, if present at the end of a filename, indicate that the associated set of string characters should be used by default for this file. For example, the suffix list for the `troff` family typically includes suffixes such as .ms, .me, .mm, and so on.

```
charset-group : { char-stmt | string-stmt | dup-stmt}*
```

A `char-stmt` describes single characters; a `string-stmt` describes characters that must appear together as a string, and which usually represent a single character in the target language. Either may also describe conversion between uppercase and lowercase. A `dup-stmt` is used to describe alternate forms of string characters, so that a single dictionary may be used with several formatting programs that use different conventions for representing non-ASCII characters.

```
char-stmt :    wordchars character-range
          |    wordchars lowercase-range uppercase-range
          |    boundarychars character-range
          |    boundarychars lowercase-range uppercase-range
string-stmt  :    stringchar string
          |    stringchar lowercase-string uppercase-string
```

Characters described with the `boundarychars` statement are considered part of a word only if they appear singly, embedded between characters declared with the `wordchars` or `stringchar` statements. For example, if the hyphen is a boundary character (useful in French), the string `foo-bar` would be a single word, but `-foo` would be the same as `foo`, and `foo--bar` would be two words separated by nonword characters.

If two ranges or strings are given in a `char-stmt` or `string-stmt`, the first describes characters that are interpreted as lowercase and the second describes uppercase. In the case of a `stringchar` statement, the two strings must be of the same length. Also, in a `stringchar` statement, the actual strings may contain both uppercase and characters themselves without difficulty; for instance, the statement:

`stringchar "\\*(sS" "\\*(Ss"`

is legal and will not interfere with (or be interfered with by) other declarations of `"s"` and `"S"` as lowercase and uppercase, respectively.

A final note on string characters: some languages collate certain special characters as if they were strings. For example, the German "a-umlaut" is traditionally sorted as if it were *ae*. `ispell` is not capable of this; each character must be treated as an individual entity. So in certain cases, `ispell` will sort a list of words into a different order than the standard "dictionary" order for the target language.

`alt-sets : alttype [ alt-stmt*]`

Because different formatters use different notations to represent non-ASCII characters, ispell must be aware of the representations used by these formatters. These are declared as alternate sets of string characters.

`alttype : altstringtype name suffix*`

The `altstringtype` statement introduces each set by declaring the associated formatter name and filename suffix list. This name and list are interpreted exactly as in the `defstringtype` statement. Following this header are one or more `alt-stmts` that declare the alternate string characters used by this formatter.

`alt-stmt : altstringchar alt-string std-string`

The `altstringchar` statement describes alternate representations for string characters. For example, the —mm macro package of `troff` represents the German "a-umlaut" as a\*:, while TeX uses the sequence \"a. If the `troff` versions are declared as the standard versions using `stringchar`, the TeX versions may be declared as alternates by using the statement:

`altstringchar \\\"a a\\*`

When the `altstringchar` statement is used to specify alternate forms, all forms for a particular formatter must be declared together as a group. Also, each formatter or macro package must provide a complete set of characters, both uppercase and lowercase, and the character sequences used for each formatter must be completely distinct. Character sequences that describe uppercase and lowercase versions of the same printable character must also be the same length. It may be necessary to define some new macros for a given formatter to satisfy these restrictions. (The current version of `buildhash` does not enforce these restrictions, but failure to obey them may result in errors being introduced into files that are processed with `ispell`.)

An important minor point is that `ispell` assumes that all characters declared as `wordchars` or `boundarychars` will occupy exactly one position on the terminal screen.

A single character-set statement can declare either a single character or a contiguous range of characters. A range is given as in egrep and the shell: [a-z] means lowercase alphabetics; [^a-z] means all but lowercase, and so on. All character-set statements are combined (unioned) to produce the final list of characters that may be part of a word. The collating order of the characters is defined by the order of their declaration; if a range is used, the characters are considered to have been declared in ASCII order. Characters that have case are collated next to each other, with the uppercase character first.

The character-declaration statements have a rather strange behavior caused by the need to match each lowercase character with its uppercase equivalent. In any given wordchars or boundarychars statement, the characters in each range are first sorted into ASCII collating sequence, then matched one-for-one with the other range. (The two ranges must have the same number of characters). Thus, for example, the two statements:

```
wordchars [aeiou] [AEIOU]
wordchars [aeiou] [UOIEA]
```

would produce exactly the same effect. To get the vowels to match up "wrong," you would have to use separate statements:

```
wordchars a U
wordchars e O
wordchars i I
wordchars o E
wordchars u A
```

which would cause uppercase *e* to be *O*, and lowercase *0* to be *e*. This should normally be a problem only with languages that have been forced to use a strange ASCII collating sequence. If your uppercase and lowercase letters both collate in the same order, you shouldn't have to worry about this "feature."

The prefixes and suffixes sections have exactly the same syntax, except for the introductory keyword:

```
prefixes : prefixes flagdef*
suffixes : suffixes flagdef*
flagdef : flag [*jÚ] char : repl *
```

A prefix or suffix table consists of an introductory keyword and a list of flag definitions. Flags can be defined more than once, in which case the definitions are combined. Each flag controls one or more repls (replacements), which are conditionally applied to the beginnings or endings of various words.

Flags are named by a single character char. Depending on a configuration option, this character can be either any uppercase letter (the default configuration) or any 7-bit ASCII character. Most languages should be able to get along with just 26 flags.

A flag character may be prefixed with one or more option characters. (If you wish to use one of the option characters as a flag character, simply enclose it in double quotes.)

The asterisk (*) option means that this flag participates in cross-product formation. This only matters if the file contains both prefix and suffix tables. If so, all prefixes and suffixes marked with an asterisk will be applied in all cross-combinations to the root word. For example, consider the root *fix* with prefixes *pre* and *in*, and suffixes *es* and *ed*. If all flags controlling these prefixes and suffixes are marked with an asterisk, then the single root *fix* would also generate *prefix, prefixes, prefixed, infix, infixes, infixed, fix, fixes,* and *fixed.* Cross-product formation can produce a large number of words quickly, some of which may be illegal, so watch out. If cross-products produce illegal words, munchlist will not produce those flag combinations, and the flag will not be useful.

```
repl : condition* > [ - strip-string , ] append-string
```

The ~ option specifies that the associated flag is only active when a compound word is being formed. This is useful in a language like German, in which the form of a word sometimes changes inside a compound.

A repl is a conditional rule for modifying a root word. Up to eight conditions may be specified. If the conditions are satisfied, the rules on the rightside of the repl are applied, as follows:

1.  If a strip-string is given, it is first stripped from the beginning or ending (as appropriate) of the root word.
2.  The append-string is added at that point.

For example, the condition . means "any word", and the condition Y means "any word ending in Y." The following (suffix) replacements:

```
. > MENT
Y > -Y,IES
```

would change *induce* to *inducement* and *fly* to *flies*. (If they were controlled by the same flag, they would also change *fly* to *flyment*, which might not be what was wanted. munchlist can be used to protect against this sort of problem; see the command sequence given in the next paragraph.)

No matter how much you might want it, the strings on the right must be strings of specific characters, not ranges. The reasons are rooted deeply in the way ispell works, and it would be difficult or impossible to provide for more flexibility. For example, you might want to write:

```
[EY] > -[EY],IES
```

This will not work. Instead, you must use two separate rules:

```
E > -E,IES
Y > -Y,IES
```

The application of repls can be restricted to certain words with conditions:

```
condition : { . ¦ character ¦ range }
```

A condition is a restriction on the characters that adjoin, and/or are replaced by, the right-hand side of the repl. Up to eight conditions may be given, which should be enough context for anyone. The right-hand side will be applied only if the conditions in the repl are satisfied. The conditions also implicitly define a length; roots shorter than the number of conditions will not pass the test. (As a special case, a condition of a single dot defines a length of zero, so that the rule applies to all words indiscriminately.) This length is independent of the separate test that insists that all flags produce an output word length of at least four.

Conditions that are single characters should be separated by whitespace. For example, to specify words ending in *ED*, write this:

```
E D> -ED,ING # As in covered > covering
```

If you write this:

```
ED > -ED,ING
```

the effect will be the same as

```
[ED] > -ED,ING
```

As a final, minor but important point, it is sometimes useful to rebuild a dictionary file using an incompatible suffix file. For example, suppose you expand the R flag to generate "er" and "ers" (thus making the Z flag somewhat obsolete). To build a new dictionary newdict that using new affixes will accept exactly the same list of words as the old list olddict did using old affixes, the -c switch of munchlist is useful, as in the following example:

```
$ munchlist -c oldaffixes -l newaffixes olddict > newdict
```

If you use this procedure, your new dictionary will always accept the same list the original did, even if you badly screwed up the affix file. This is because munchlist compares the words generated by a flag with the original word list and refuses to use any flags that generate illegal words. (Don't forget that the munchlist step takes a long time and eats up temporary file space.)

## EXAMPLES

As an example of conditional suffixes, here is the specification of the S flag from the English affix file:

```
flag *S:
[^AEIOU]Y > -Y,IES # As in imply > implies
[AEIOU]Y > S # As in convey > conveys
[SXZH] > ES # As in fix > fixes
[^SXZHY] > S #As in bat > bats
```

The first line applies to words ending in Y but not in vowel-Y. The second takes care of the vowel-Y words. The third then handles those words that end in a sibilant or near-sibilant, and the last picks up everything else.

Note that the conditions are written very carefully so that they apply to disjoint sets of words. In particular, note that the fourth line excludes words ending in Y as well as the obvious SXZH. Otherwise, it would convert "imply" into "implys."

Although the English affix file does not do so, you can also have a flag generate more than one variation on a root word. For example, you could extend the English R flag as follows:

```
flag *R:
E > R #As in skate > skater
E > RS # As in skate > skaters
[^AEIOU]Y > -Y,IER # As in multiply > multiplier
[^AEIOU]Y > -Y,IERS # As in multiply > multipliers
[AEIOU]Y > ER # As in convey > conveyer
[AEIOU]Y > ERS # As in convey > conveyers
[^EY] > ER # As in build > builder
[^EY] > ERS # As in build > builders
```

This flag would generate both "skater" and "skaters" from "skate." This capability can be very useful in languages that make use of noun, verb, and adjective endings. For instance, one could define a single flag that generated all the German "weak" verb endings.

## SEE ALSO

ispell(1)

*Local*

# lp

lp—Line printer devices.

## SYNOPSIS

#include <linux/lp.h>

## CONFIGURATION

lp[02] are character devices for the parallel line printers; they have major number 6 and minor number 02. The minor numbers correspond to the printer port base addresses 0x03bc, 0x0378, and 0x0278. Usually, they have mode 220 and are owned by root and group lp. You can use printer ports either with polling or with interrupts. Interrupts are recommended when high traffic is expected, such as for laser printers. For usual dot matrix printers, polling will usually be enough. The default is polling.

## DESCRIPTION

The following ioctl(2) calls are supported:

| | |
|---|---|
| int ioctl(int fd, LPTIME, int arg) | Sets the amount of time that the driver sleeps before rechecking the printer when the printer's buffer appears to be filled to arg. If you have a fast printer, decrease this number; if you have a slow printer, then increase it. This is in hundredths of a second; the default 2 is 0.05 seconds. It only influences the polling driver. |
| int ioctl(int fd, LPCHAR, int arg) | Sets the maximum number of busy-wait iterations that the polling driver does while waiting for the printer to get ready for receiving a character to arg. If printing is too slow, increase this number; if the system gets too slow, decrease this number. The default is 1000. It only influences the polling driver. |

| | |
|---|---|
| `int ioctl(int fd, LPABORT, int arg)` | If arg is `0`, the printer driver will retry on errors; otherwise, it will abort. The default is `0`. |
| `int ioctl(int fd, LPABORTOPEN, int arg)` | If arg is `0`, open(2) will be aborted on error; otherwise, the error will be ignored. The default is to ignore it. |
| `int ioctl(int fd, LPCAREFUL, int arg)` | If arg is `0`, then the out-of-paper, offline, and error signals are required to be false on all writes; otherwise, they are ignored. The default is to ignore them. |
| `int ioctl(int fd, LPWAIT, int arg)` | Sets the number of busy-wait iterations to wait before strobing the printer to accept a just-written character and the number of iterations to wait before turning the strobe off again to arg. The specification says this time should be 0.5 microseconds, but experience has shown the delay caused by the code is already enough. For that reason, the default value is `0`. This is used for both the polling and the interrupt driver. |
| `int ioctl(int fd, LPSETIRQ, int arg)` | This ioctl() requires superuser privileges. It takes an `int` containing the new IRQ as argument. As a side effect, the printer is reset. When arg is `0`, the polling driver will be used, which is also default. |
| `int ioctl(int fd, LPGETIRQ, int *arg)` | Stores the currently used IRQ in arg. |
| `int ioctl(int fd, LPGETSTATUS, int *arg)` | Stores the value of the status port in arg. The bits have the following meaning: |
| `LP_PBUSY` | Inverted busy input, active high |
| `LP_PACK` | Unchanged acknowledge input, active low |
| `LP_POUTPA` | Unchanged out-of-paper input, active high |
| `LP_PSELECD` | Unchanged selected input, active high |
| `LP_PERRORP` | Unchanged error input, active low |
| | Refer to your printer manual for the meaning of the signals. Note that undocumented bits can also be set, depending on your printer. |
| `int ioctl(int fd, LPRESET)` | Resets the printer. No argument is used. |

## FILES

`/dev/lp*`

## AUTHORS

The printer driver was originally written by Jim Weigand and Linus Torvalds. It was further improved by Michael K. Johnson. The interrupt code was written by Nigel Gamble. Alan Cox modularized it. `LPCAREFUL`, `LPABORT`, `LPGETSTATUS` were added by Chris Metcalf.

## SEE ALSO

`mknod(1)`, `chown(1)`, `chmod(1)`, `tunelp(8)`, `lpcntl(8)`

*15 January 1995*

# mem, kmem, port

`mem`, `kmem`, `port`—System memory, kernel memory, and system ports

## DESCRIPTION

`mem` is a character device file that is an image of the main memory of the computer. It can be used, for example, to examine (and even patch) the system.

Byte addresses in mem are interpreted as physical memory addresses. References to non-existent locations cause errors to be returned.

Examining and patching is likely to lead to unexpected results when read-only or write-only bits are present.

It is typically created by

```
mknod -m 660 /dev/mem c 1 1
chown root.mem /dev/mem
```

The file kmem is the same as mem, except that the kernel virtual memory rather than physical memory is accessed.

It is typically created by

```
mknod -m 640 /dev/kmem c 1 2
chown root.mem /dev/kmem
```

port is similar to mem, but the IO ports are accessed.

It is typically created by

```
mknod -m 660 /dev/port c 1 4
chown root.mem /dev/port
```

## FILES

/dev/mem

/dev/kmem

/dev/port

## SEE ALSO

mknod(1), chown(1), ioperm(2)

*Linux, 21 November 1992*


# mouse

mouse—Serial mouse interface.

## CONFIG

Serial mice are connected to a serial RS232/V24 dialout line; see cua(4) for a description.

## DESCRIPTION

The pinout of the usual 9 pin plug as used for serial mice is

| Pin | Name | Used for |
|-----|------|----------|
| 2 | RX | Data |
| 3 | TX | -12 V, Imax = 10 mA |
| 4 | DTR | +12 V, Imax = 10 mA |
| 7 | RTS | +12 V, Imax = 10 mA |
| 5 | GND | Ground |

This is the specification; in fact, 9 V suffices with most mice.

The mouse driver can recognize a mouse by dropping RTS to low. About 14ms later, the mouse will send 0x4D on the data line. After a further 63ms, Microsoft-compatible mice will send 0x33. Other mice send different values.

The relative mouse movement is sent as dx (positive means right) and dy (positive means down). Various mice can operate at different speeds. To select speeds, cycle through the speeds 9600, 4800, 2400, and 1200 bits/sec, each time writing the two characters from the table below and waiting 0.1 seconds. The following table shows available speeds and the strings that select them:

| Bits/sec | String |
|----------|--------|
| 9600 | *q |
| 4800 | *p |
| 2400 | *o |
| 1200 | *n |

The first byte of a data packet can be used to synchronization purposes.

## MICROSOFT PROTOCOL

The Microsoft protocol uses 1 start bit, 7 data bits, no parity, and 1 stop bit at the speed of 1200 bits/sec. Data is sent to RxD in 3-byte packets. The dx and dy movements are sent as two's-complement, lb (rb) is set when the left (right) button is pressed:

| Byte | d6 | d5 | d4 | d3 | d2 | d1 | d0 |
|------|----|----|----|----|----|----|----|
| 1 | 1 | lb | rb | dy7 | dy6 | dx7 | dx7 |
| 2 | 0 | dx5 | dx4 | dx3 | dx2 | dx1 | dx0 |
| 3 | 0 | dy5 | dy4 | dy3 | dy2 | dy1 | dy0 |

Original Microsoft mice have only two buttons. However, there are some three-button mice that also use the Microsoft protocol. Pressing the third button is reported by sending a packet with zero movement and no buttons pressed.

## MOUSESYSTEMS PROTOCOL

The MouseSystems protocol uses 1 start bit, 8 data bits, no parity, and 2 stop bits at the speed of 1200 bits/sec. Data is sent to RxD in 5-byte packets. dx is sent as the sum of the two two's-complement values, dy is send as negated sum of the two two's-complement values. lb (mb, rb) is cleared when the left (middle, right) button is pressed:

| Byte | d7 | d6 | d5 | d4 | d3 | d2 | d1 | d0 |
|------|----|----|----|----|----|----|----|----|
| 1 | 1 | ? | ? | ? | ? | lb | mb | rb |
| 2 | 0 | dxa6 | dxa5 | dxa4 | dxa3 | dxa2 | dxa1 | dxa0 |
| 3 | 0 | dxb6 | dxb5 | dxb4 | dxb3 | dxb2 | dxb1 | dxb0 |
| 4 | 0 | dya6 | dya5 | dya4 | dya3 | dya2 | dya1 | dya0 |
| 5 | 0 | dyb6 | dyb5 | dyb4 | dyb3 | dyb2 | dyb1 | dyb0 |

## SUN PROTOCOL

The Sun protocol uses 1 start bit, 8 data bits, no parity, and 2 stop bits at the speed of 1200 bits/sec. Data is sent to RxD in 3-byte packets. dx is sent as single two's-complement value, dy as negated two's-complement value. lb (mb, rb) is cleared when the left (middle, right) button is pressed:

| Byte | d7 | d6 | d5 | d4 | d3 | d2 | d1 | d0 |
|------|----|----|----|----|----|----|----|----|
| 1 | 1 | ? | ? | ? | ? | lb | mb | rb |
| 2 | 0 | dx6 | dx5 | dx4 | dx3 | dx2 | dx1 | dx0 |
| 3 | 0 | dy6 | dy5 | dy4 | dy3 | dy2 | dy1 | dy0 |

## MM PROTOCOL

The MM protocol uses 1 start bit, 8 data bits, odd parity, and 1 stop bit at the speed of 1200 bits/sec. Data is sent to RxD in 3-byte packets. dx and dy are sent as single signed values, the sign bit indicating a negative value. lb (mb, rb) is set when the left (middle, right) button is pressed:

| Byte | d7 | d6 | d5 | d4 | d3 | d2 | d1 | d0 |
|------|----|----|----|----|----|----|----|----|
| 1 | 1 | ? | ? | dxs | dys | lb | mb | rb |
| 2 | 0 | dx6 | dx5 | dx4 | dx3 | dx2 | dx1 | dx0 |
| 3 | 0 | dy6 | dy5 | dy4 | dy3 | dy2 | dy1 | dy0 |

## FILES

/dev/mouse a commonly used symlink pointing to a mouse device

## SEE ALSO

cua(4), bm(4)

*Linux, 10 February 1996*

# null, zero

null, zero—Data sink.

## DESCRIPTION

Data written on a null or zero special file is discarded.

Reads from the null special file always return end of file, whereas reads from zero always return \0 characters.

null and zero are typically created by

```
mknod -m 666 /dev/null c 1 3
mknod -m 666 /dev/zero c 1 5
chown root.mem /dev/null /dev/zero
```

## NOTES

If these devices are not writable and readable for all users, many programs will act strangely.

## FILES

/dev/null

/dev/zero

## SEE ALSO

mknod(1), chown(1)

*Linux, 21 November 1992*

# ram

ram—Ram disk device.

## DESCRIPTION

ram is a block device to access the ram disk in raw mode.

It is typically created by

```
mknod -m 660 /dev/ram b 1 1
chown root.disk /dev/ram
```

## FILES

/dev/ram

## SEE ALSO

mknod(1), chown(1), mount(8)

*Linux, 21 November 1992*

# sd

sd—Driver for SCSI disk drives.

## SYNOPSIS

```
#include <linux/hdreg.h>
```

## CONFIG

The block device name has the following form: sd1p, where 1 is a letter denoting the physical drive, and p is a number denoting the partition on that physical drive. Often, the partition number, p, will be left off when the device corresponds to the whole drive.

SCSI disks have a major device number of 8 and a minor device number of the form (16 * drive_number) + partition_number, where drive_number is the number of the physical drive in order of detection and partition_number is as follows:

| | |
|---|---|
| Partition 0 | The whole drive |
| Partitions 1-4 | The DOS "primary" partitions |
| Partitions 5-8 | The DOS "extended" (or "logical") partitions |

For example, /dev/sda will have major 8 and minor 0 and will refer to all the first SCSI drives in the system; /dev/sdb3 will have major 8 and minor 19 and will refer to the third DOS "primary" partition on the second SCSI drive in the system.

At this time, only block devices are provided. Raw devices have not yet been implemented.

## DESCRIPTION

The following ioctls are provided:

| | |
|---|---|
| HDIO_REQ | Returns the BIOS disk parameters in the following structure: |

```
struct hd geometry {
unsigned char heads;
unsigned char sectors;
unsigned short cylinders;
unsigned long start;
};
```

A pointer to this structure is passed as the ioctl(2) parameter.

The information returned in the parameter is the disk geometry of the drive as understood by DOS! This geometry is not the physical geometry of the drive. It is used when constructing the drive's partition table, however, and is needed for convenient operation of fdisk(1), efdisk(1), and lilo(1). If the geometry information is not available, zero is returned for all the parameters.

BLKGETSIZE    Returns the device size in sectors. The ioctl(2) parameter should be a pointer to a long.

BLKRRPART    Forces a re-read of the SCSI disk partition tables. No parameter is needed.

The scsi(4) ioctls are also supported. If the ioctl(2) parameter is required and it is NULL, then ioctl(2) will return -EINVAL.

## FILES

/dev/sd[a-h]: The whole device

/dev/sd[a-h][0-8]: Individual block partitions

## SEE ALSO

scsi(4)

*17 December 1992*

# st

st—SCSI tape device.

## SYNOPSIS

```
#include <sys/mtio.h>
int ioctl(int fd, int request [, (void *)arg3])
int ioctl(int fd, MTIOCTOP, (struct mtop *)mt_cmd)
int ioctl(int fd, MTIOCGET, (struct mtget *)mt_status)
int ioctl(int fd, MTIOCPOS, (struct mtpos *)mt_pos)
```

## DESCRIPTION

The st driver provides the interface to a variety of SCSI tape devices. Currently, the driver takes control of all detected devices of type sequential-access. The st driver uses major device number 9.

Each device uses two minor device numbers: a principal minor device number, n, assigned sequentially in order of detection, and a no-rewind device number, (n + 128). Devices opened using the principal device number are sent a REWIND command when they are closed. Devices opened using the no-rewind device number are not. Options such as density or block size are not coded in the minor device number. These options must be set by explicit ioctl() calls and remain in effect when the device is closed and reopened.

Devices are typically created by

```
mknod -m 660 /dev/st0 c 9 0
mknod -m 660 /dev/st1 c 9 1
mknod -m 660 /dev/nst0 c 9 128
mknod -m 660 /dev/nst1 c 9 129
```

There is no corresponding block device. The character device provides buffering and read-ahead by default and supports reads and writes of arbitrary size (limited by the driver's internal buffer size, which defaults to 32768 bytes but can be changed either by using a kernel startup option or by changing a compile-time constant).

Device /dev/tape is usually created as a hard or soft link to the default tape device on the system.

# ioctls

The driver supports three ioctl requests. Requests not recognized by the st driver are passed to the scsi driver. The definitions below are from /usr/include/linux/mtio.h:

## MTIOCTOP: PERFORM A TAPE OPERATION

This request takes an argument of type (struct mtop *). Not all drives support all operations. The driver returns an EIO error if the drive rejects an operation.

```
/* Structure for MTIOCTOP - mag tape op command: */
struct mtop {
short mt_op; /* operations defined below */
int mt_count; /* how many of them */
};
```

Magnetic tape operations:

| | |
|---|---|
| MTBSF | Backward space over mt_count filemarks. |
| MTBSFM | Backward space over mt_count filemarks. Reposition the tape to the EOT side of the last filemark. |
| MTBSR | Backward space over mt_count records (tape blocks). |
| MTBSS | Backward space over mt_count setmarks. |
| MTEOM | Go to the end of the recorded media (for appending files). |
| MTERASE | Erase tape. |
| MTFSF | Forward space over mt_count filemarks. |
| MTFSFM | Forward space over mt_count filemarks. Reposition the tape to the BOT side of the last filemark. |
| MTFSR | Forward space over mt_count records (tape blocks). |
| MTFSS | Forward space over mt_count setmarks. |
| MTNOP | No op; flushes the driver's buffer as a side effect. Should be used before reading status with MTIOCGET. |
| MTOFFL | Rewind and put the drive off line. |
| MTRESET | Reset drive. |
| MTRETEN | Retention tape. |
| MTREW | Rewind. |
| MTSEEK | Seek to the tape block number specified in mt_count. This operation requires either a SCSI-2 drive that supports the LOCATE command (device-specific address) or a Tandberg-compatible SCSI-1 drive (Tandberg, Archive Viper, Wangtek,...). The block number should be one that was previously returned by MTIOCPOS because the number is device-specific. |
| MTSETBLK | Set the drive's block length to the value specified in mt_count. A block length of zero sets the drive to variable block size mode. |
| MTSETDENSITY | Set the tape density to the code in mt_count. Some useful density codes are<br><br>18 0x00 Implicit 0x11 QIC-525<br>0x04 QIC-11 0x12 QIC-1350<br>0x05 QIC-24 0x13 DDS<br>0x0F QIC-120 0x14 Exabyte EXB-8200<br>0x10 QIC-150 0x15 Exabyte EXB-8500 |
| MTWEOF | Write mt_count filemarks. |
| MTWSM | Write mt_count setmarks. |

MTSETDRVBUFFER

Set various drive and driver options according to bits encoded in mt_count. These consist of the drive's buffering mode, six Boolean driver options, and the buffer write threshold. These parameters are initialized only when the device is first detected. The settings persist when the device is closed and reopened. A single operation can affect just the buffering mode, just the Boolean options, or just the write threshold.

A value having zeros in the high-order 4 bits will be used to set the drive's buffering mode. The buffering modes are:

0        The drive will not report GOOD status on write commands until the data blocks are actually written to the medium.

1        The drive may report GOOD status on write commands as soon as all the data has been transferred to the drive's internal buffer.

2        The drive may report GOOD status on write commands as soon as all the data has been transferred to the drive's internal buffer and all buffered data from different initiators has been successfully written to the medium.

To control the write threshold, the value in mt_count must include the constant MT_ST_WRITE_THRESHOLD logically ORed with a block count in the low 28 bits. The block count refers to 1024-byte blocks, not the physical block size on the tape. The threshold cannot exceed the driver's internal buffer size (see the description).

To set and clear the Boolean options, the value in mt_count must include the constant MT_ST_BOOLEANS logically ORed with whatever combination of the following options is desired. Any options not specified are set false. The Boolean options are

MT_ST_BUFFER_WRITES

(Default: true) Buffer all write operations. If this option is false and the drive uses a fixed block size, then all write operations must be for a multiple of the block size. This option must be set false to write reliable multi-volume archives.

MT_ST_ASYNC_WRITES

(Default: true) When this options is true, write operations return immediately without waiting for the data to be transferred to the drive if the data fits into the driver's buffer. The write threshold determines how full the buffer must be before a new SCSI write command is issued. Any errors reported by the drive will be held until the next operation. This option must be set false to write reliable multi-volume archives.

MT_ST_READ_AHEAD

(Default: true) This option causes the driver to provide read buffering and read-ahead. If this option is false and the drive uses a fixed block size, then all read operations must be for a multiple of the block size.

MT_ST_TWO_FM

(Default: false) This option modifies the driver behavior when a file is closed. The normal action is to write a single filemark. If the option is true, the driver will write two filemarks and backspace over the second one.

Note that this option should not be set true for QIC tape drives because they are unable to overwrite a filemark. These drives detect the end of recorded data by testing for blank tape rather than two consecutive filemarks.

MT_ST_DEBUGGING

(Default: false) This option turns on various debugging messages from the driver (effective only if the driver was compiled with DEBUG defined).

MT_ST_FAST_EOM

(Default: false) This option causes the MTEOM operation to be sent directly to the drive, potentially speeding up the operation but causing the driver to lose track of the current file number normally returned by the MTIOCGET request. If MT_ST_FAST_EOM is false, the driver will respond to an MTEOM request by forward spacing over files.

Example:

```
struct mtop mt_cmd;
mt_cmd.mt_op = MTSETDRVBUFFER;
mt_cmd.mt_count =MT_ST_BOOLEANS ¦
            MT_ST_BUFFER_WRITES ¦
            MT_ST_ASYNC_WRITES;
ioctl(fd, MTIOCTOP, &mt_cmd);
```

## MTIOCGET: GET STATUS

This request takes an argument of type (struct mtget *). The driver returns an EIO error if the drive rejects an operation.

```
/* structure for MTIOCGET - mag tape get status command */
struct mtget {
    long    mt_type;
    long    mt_resid;
    /* the following registers are device dependent */
    long    mt_dsreg;
    long    mt_gstat;
    long    mt_erreg;
    /* The next two fields are not always used */
    daddr_t         mt_fileno;
    daddr_t         mt_blkno;
};
```

The header file defines many values for mt_type, but the current driver reports only the generic types MT_ISSCSI1 (Generic SCSI-1 tape) and MT_ISSCSI2 (Generic SCSI-2 tape).

mt_resid is always zero. (Not implemented for SCSI tape drives.)

mt_dsreg reports the drive's current settings for block size (in the low 24 bits) and density (in the high 8 bits). These fields are defined by MT_ST_BLKSIZE_SHIFT, MT_ST_BLKSIZE_MASK, MT_ST_DENSITY_SHIFT, and MT_ST_DENSITY_MASK.

mt_gstat reports generic (device independent) status information. The header file defines macros for testing these status bits:

| | |
|---|---|
| GMT_EOF(x) | The tape is positioned just after a filemark (always false after an MTSEEK operation). |
| GMT_BOT(x) | The tape is positioned at the beginning of the first file (always false after an MTSEEK operation). |
| GMT_EOT(x) | A tape operation has reached the physical End of Tape. |
| GMT_SM(x) | The tape is currently positioned at a setmark (always false after an MTSEEK operation). |
| GMT_EOD(x) | The tape is positioned at the end of recorded data. |
| GMT_WR_PROT(x) | The drive is write-protected. For some drives this can also mean that the drive does not support writing on the current medium type. |
| GMT_ONLINE(x) | The last open() found the drive with a tape in place and ready for operation. |
| GMT_D_6250(x), GMT_D_1600(x), GMT_D_800(x) | This generic status information reports the current density setting for 9-track tape drives only. |
| GMT_DR_OPEN(x) | The drive does not have a tape in place. |
| GMT_IM_REP_EN(x) | Immediate report mode (not supported). |
| | mt_erreg: The only field defined in mt_erreg is the recovered error count in the low 16 bits (as defined by MT_ST_SOFTERR_SHIFT and MT_ST_SOFTERR_MASK). Due to inconsistencies in the way drives report recovered errors, this count is often not maintained. |

`mt_fileno` reports the current file number (zero-based). This value is set to -1 when the file number is unknown (such as after `MTBSS` or `MTSEEK`).

`mt_blkno` reports the block number (zero-based) within the current file. This value is set to -1 when the block number is unknown (such as after `MTBSF`, `MTBSS`, or `MTSEEK`).

## MTIOCPOS: GET TAPE POSITION

This request takes an argument of type (`struct mtpos *`) and reports the drive's notion of the current tape block number, which is not the same as `mt_blkno` returned by `MTIOCGET`. This drive must be a SCSI-2 drive that supports the `READ POSITION` command (device-specific address) or a Tandberg-compatible SCSI-1 drive (Tandberg, Archive Viper, Wangtek,...).

```
/* structure for MTIOCPOS - mag tape get position command */
struct mtpos {
long mt_blkno; /* current block number */
};
```

## RETURN VALUE

| | |
|---|---|
| EIO | The requested operation could not be completed. |
| ENOSPC | A write operation could not be completed because the tape reached end-of-medium. |
| EACCES | An attempt was made to write or erase a write-protected tape. (This error is not detected during `open()`.) |
| ENXIO | During opening, the tape device does not exist. |
| EBUSY | The device is already in use or the driver was unable to allocate a buffer. |
| EOVERFLOW | An attempt was made to read or write a variable-length block that is larger than the driver's internal buffer. |
| EINVAL | An `ioctl()` had an illegal argument, or a requested block size was illegal. |
| ENOSYS | Unknown `ioctl()`. |

## COPYRIGHT

Copyright 1995, Robert K. Nichols.

Permission is granted to make and distribute verbatim copies of this manual, provided the copyright notice and this permission notice are preserved on all copies. Additional permissions are contained in the header of the source file.

## SEE ALSO

`mt(1)`

*Linux 1.1.86, 31 January 1995*

# tty

tty—Controlling terminal.

## DESCRIPTION

The file `/dev/tty` is a character file with major number 5 and minor number 0, usually of mode 0666 and owner.group root.tty. It is a synonym for the controlling terminal of a process, if any.

In addition to the `ioctl()` requests supported by the device that tty refers to, the following `ioctl()` request is supported:

TIOCNOTTY • Detach the current process from its controlling terminal and remove it from its current process group, without attaching it to a new process group (that is, set its process group ID to zero). This ioctl() call only works on file descriptors connected to /dev/tty; this is used by daemon processes when they are invoked by a user at a terminal. The process attempts to open /dev/tty; if the open succeeds, it detaches itself from the terminal by using TIOCNOTTY, but if the open fails, it is obviously not attached to a terminal and does not need to detach itself.

## FILES

/dev/tty

## SEE ALSO

mknod(1), chown(1), getty(1), termios(2), console(4), ttys(4)

*Linux, 21 January 1992*

# ttys

ttys—Serial terminal lines.

## DESCRIPTION

ttyS[0-3] are character devices for the serial terminal lines.

They are typically created by

```
mknod -m 660 /dev/ttyS0 c 4 64 # base address 0x03f8
mknod -m 660 /dev/ttyS1 c 4 65 # base address 0x02f8
mknod -m 660 /dev/ttyS2 c 4 66 # base address 0x03e8
mknod -m 660 /dev/ttyS3 c 4 67 # base address 0x02e8
chown root.tty /dev/ttyS[0-3]
```

## FILES

/dev/ttyS[0-3]

## SEE ALSO

mknod(1), chown(1), getty(1), tty(4)

*Linux, 19 December 1992*

# vcs, vcsa

vcs, vcsa—Virtual console memory.

## DESCRIPTION

/dev/vcs0 is a character device with major number 7 and minor number 0, usually of mode 0644 and owner root.tty. It refers to the memory of the currently displayed virtual console terminal.

/dev/vcs[1-63] are character devices for virtual console terminals; they have major number 7 and minor number 1 to 63, usually mode 0644 and owner root.tty. /dev/vcsa[0-63] are the same but include attributes and are prefixed with four bytes, giving the screen dimensions and cursor position: lines, columns, x, y.(x = y = 0 at the top-left corner of the screen.)

These replace the screendump ioctls of console(4), so the system administrator can control access using filesystem permissions.

The devices for the first eight virtual consoles may be created by

```
for x in 0 1 2 3 4 5 6 7 8; do
mknod -m 644 /dev/vcs$x c 7 $x;
mknod -m 644 /dev/vcsa$x c 7 $[$x+128];
done
chown root.tty /dev/vcs*
```

No ioctl() requests are supported.

## EXAMPLES

You can do a screendump on vt3 by switching to vt1 and typing cat /dev/vcs3 >foo.

This program displays the character and screen attributes under the cursor of the second virtual console and then changes the background color there:

```
#include <unistd.h>
#include <stdio.h>
#include <fcntl.h>

void main()
{ int fd;
    struct {char lines, cols, x, y;} scrn;
    char ch, attrib;

    fd = open("/dev/vcsa2", O_RDWR);
    (void)read(fd, &scrn, 4);
    (void)lseek(fd, 4 + 2*(scrn.y*scrn.cols + scrn.x), 0);
    (void)read(fd, &ch, 1);
    (void)read(fd, &attrib, 1);
    printf("ch='%c' attrib=0x%02x\n", ch, attrib);
    attrib ^= 0x10;
    (void)lseek(fd, -1, 1);
    (void)write(fd, &attrib, 1);
}
```

## FILES

/dev/vcs[0-63]

/dev/vcsa[0-63]

## AUTHOR

Andries Brouwer (aeb@cwi.nl)

## HISTORY

Introduced with version 1.1.92 of the Linux kernel.

## SEE ALSO

console(4), tty(4), ttys(4), selection(1)

# Part V:

# File Formats

# intro

intro—Introduction to file formats.

## DESCRIPTION

This chapter describes various file formats and protocols, and the used C structures, if any.

## AUTHORS

Look at the header of the manual page for the authors and copyright conditions. Note that these can be different from page to page!

*Linux, 24 July 1993*

# active, active.times

active, active.times—List of active Usenet newsgroups.

## DESCRIPTION

The file /news/lib/active lists the newsgroups that the local site receives. Each newsgroup should be listed only once. Each line specifies one group; their order in the file does not matter. Within each newsgroup, articles are assigned unique names, which are monotonically increasing numbers.

If an article is posted to newsgroups not mentioned in this file, those newsgroups are ignored. If no valid newsgroups are specified, the article is filed into the newsgroup "junk" and only propagated to sites that receive the "junk" newsgroup.

Each line consists of four fields specified by a space:

```
name himark lomark flags
```

The first field is the name of the newsgroup. Newsgroups that start with the three characters to. are treated specially; see innd(8). The second field is the highest article number that has been used in that newsgroup. The third field is the lowest article number in the group; this number is not guaranteed to be accurate and should only be taken as a hint. Note that because of article cancellations, there may be gaps in the numbering sequence. If the lowest article number is greater than the highest article number, there are no articles in the newsgroup. To make it possible to update an entry in-place without rewriting the entire file, the second and third fields are padded with leading zeros to make them a fixed width.

The fourth field can contain one of the following flags:

| | |
|---|---|
| y | Local postings are allowed |
| n | No local postings are allowed, only remote ones |
| m | The group is moderated and all postings must be approved |
| j | Articles in this group are not kept but only passed on |
| x | Articles cannot be posted to this newsgroup |
| =foo.bar | Articles are locally filed into the foo.bar group |

If a newsgroup has the j flag, then no articles will be filed into that newsgroup and local postings to that group should not be generated. If an article for such a newsgroup is received from a remote site, it will be filed into the "junk" newsgroup if it is not cross-posted. This is different from not having a newsgroup listed in the file because sites can subscribe to j newsgroups and the article will be propagated to them.

If the fourth field of a newsgroup starts with an equal sign, then the newsgroup is an alias. Articles can be posted to the group but will be treated as if they were posted to the group named after the equal sign. The second and third fields are ignored. Note that the newsgroup header is not modified (Alias groups are typically used during a transition and are typically created with ctlinnd(8)). An alias newsgroup should not point to another alias.

The file /news/lib/active.times provides a chronological record of when newsgroups are created. This file is normally updated by innd(8) whenever a ctlinnd newgroup command is done. Each line consist of three fields:

```
name time creator
```

The first field is the name of the newsgroup. The second field is the time it was created, expressed as the number of seconds since the epoch—a time_t; see gettimeofday(2). The third field is the electronic mail address of the person who created the group.

## HISTORY

Written by Rich $alz (rsalz@uunet.uu.net) for InterNetNews.

## SEE ALSO

ctlinnd(8), innd(8)

# adduser.conf

adduser.conf—Configuration file for adduser(8) and addgroup(8).

## SYNOPSIS

/etc/adduser.conf

## DESCRIPTION

The file adduser.conf contains defaults for the programs adduser(8) and addgroup(8). Each option takes the form *option = value*.

The valid configuration options are

| | |
|---|---|
| DSHELL | The login shell to be used for all new users. Defaults to /bin/bash. |
| DHOME | The directory in which new home directories should be created. Defaults to /home. |
| SKEL | The directory from which skeletal user configuration files should be copied. Defaults to /etc/skel. |
| FIRST_UID | Specifies the lowest valid UID for normal users on your system. IDs below FIRST_UID are reserved for administrative and system accounts. Defaults to 1000. |
| USERGROUPS | The USERGROUPS variable can be either yes or no. If yes, each created user will be given their own group to use as a default, and their setup will arrange to have them create files group-writable by default, thus allowing them to effectively use group-writeable filespace areas (such as /usr/local). If no, each created user will be placed in the group whose GID is USERS_GID, and they will create files not group-writeable by default. |
| USERS_GID | If USERGROUPS is no, then USERS_GID is the GID given to all newly created users. The default value is 100. |

## FILES

/etc/adduser.conf

## SEE ALSO

adduser(8)

*Debian GNU/Linux version 1.94*

# aliases

aliases—Aliases file for sendmail.

## SYNOPSIS

aliases

## DESCRIPTION

This file describes user ID aliases used by . The file resides in and is formatted as a series of lines of the form:

*name*: *name_1, name_2, name_3, ...*

The *name* is the name to alias, and the *name_n* are the aliases for that name. Lines beginning with whitespace are continuation lines. Lines beginning with # are comments.

Aliasing occurs only on local names. Loops cannot occur because no message will be sent to any person more than once.

After aliasing has been done, local and valid recipients who have a .forward file in their home directory have messages forwarded to the list of users defined in that file.

This is only the raw data file; the actual aliasing information is placed into a binary format in the files and using the program newaliases(1). A newaliases command should be executed each time the aliases file is changed for the change to take effect.

## SEE ALSO

newaliases(1), dbm(3), sendmail(8), "Sendmail Installation and Operation Guide," "Sendmail: An Internetwork Mail Router."

## BUGS

Because of restrictions in dbm(3), a single alias cannot contain more than about 1000 bytes of information. You can get longer aliases by "chaining"—that is, making the last name in the alias a dummy name that is a continuation alias.

## HISTORY

The aliases file format appeared in BSD 4.0.

*BSD 4, 10 May 1991*

# cfingerd

cfingerd—Configurable finger daemon.

## SYNOPSIS

cfingerd [-c¦-d¦-e¦-o¦-v]

| | |
|---|---|
| -c | Check configuration |
| -d | Run as daemon, not inetd |
| -e | Emulate local finger without inetd |
| -o | Turn off all finger queries |
| -v | Request version information |

-c checks your installed configuration. This makes sure there are no existing errors in the current cfingerd.conf file.

-d runs cfingerd as a daemon. Don't run cfingerd this way if you're using inetd.

-e allows you to emulate a local finger on a user that exists on your system. This makes it so that you can test cfingerd on your system before installing it. Using the -e directive is the same as installing the software, typing finger *username@* and getting the output. Using -e *username* does the same.

-o turns off all finger queries. This makes it so that no one can finger your system—no matter what they try to do.

-v requests *cfingerd* version information.

## DESCRIPTION

*cfingerd* is a totally new and totally configurable finger daemon—one of the first. It utilizes the finger port (port 79) to provide useful information on each user on your system. However, *cfingerd* provides a unique twist.

*cfingerd* was designed for the sole purpose of making output on finger queries configurable. If you want to change any text that is displayed during finger queries, you can configure the finger daemon to display just about anything you want.

*cfingerd* also takes into account any security breaches and attempts to close them. With .nofinger files, this is displayed instead of finger information, making it possible for users to keep themselves relatively anonymous from outside users.

## WHY WAS IT DONE?

The answer is simple: security. Many sites turn off finger for the reason that they don't want outside users to see who's on their system or get information about a specific user on their system. This seemed unfair to the rest of the users out there, so this program was created. Those sites were waiting for this type of program. Many sites that originally had their finger turned off turned them back on because of *cfingerd*.

Many sites complained that they wanted the capability to create a fake user or a user that doesn't exist but calls a prewritten shell script. *cfingerd* takes this into account and provides the best method possible for creating such scripts. (See cfingerd.conf(5) for more information on the configuration file.)

## FEATURES cfingerd PROVIDES AND DESCRIPTIONS OF EACH

*cfingerd* was totally rewritten. Why is this? The older version of *cfingerd* had quite a few bugs, and it didn't quite do all the things that *cfingerd* now does. This new version was totally revamped, and most of the bugs that were in the older version of *cfingerd* were removed in this one. The code is also more compact.

Header and footer displays were a big part of the original release of *cfingerd* and shall continue to remain in all versions. Headers and footers are only displays at the beginning and ending of all finger displays and are used as unique little advertisements.

The last time displayed is always a critical issue. It's covered in *cfingerd*. *cfingerd* simply shows how many times this user is connected, what their idle time is on each tty they're connected to, and whether they are accepting messages. If they're not accepting messages, a [MESG-N] display will be shown. This display also shows the last time mail was read and whether this user has mail.

Stand-alone and inetd support is compiled into the program, but only inetd support is given for the time being. The reason is that I have not yet added the option for stand-alone daemon mode.

.nofinger files are used when a user wants to remain anonymous. These files should be placed in their home directories and can display anything they want. There's just a few restrictions. These .nofinger display files cannot be character devices, directories, FIFOs, soft or hard links, or anything else of that caliber. They must only be normal files.

Fake users were supported for the simple fact that many sites want to create users who don't exist and make them execute a shell. If you want this done, install a fake user. Read cfingerd.conf(5) for more information on these useful options.

Service displays were used to show what fake users you have installed on your system. These can be formatted however you want and are explained in cfingerd.conf(5).

Searching for usernames is a powerful feature that *cfingerd* takes full advantage of. If you are looking for a specific username on the system or don't know what their name is, simply use the search.username directive with *cfingerd*, and you can search for a user on your system.

Searching for usernames is not case sensitive. If you are searching for a specific username or part of the user's name, chances are that it'll be displayed.

There's also an option to display your public PGP key if you have one. This is very useful if you want to keep your mail or other information secret to yourself and don't want "big brother" watching over your shoulder as you talk among yourselves. (Thanks to Andy Smith for this patch.) The standard plan file is `.plan`, project is `.project`, and PGP info is `.pgpkey`.

Remember, any or all of these options stated can be turned on or off at will. If you want a specific option turned off, turn it off.

## ERROR MESSAGES

Any error messages that result are fairly easy to debug if you know what to look for.

Segmentation violations don't always occur, but if they ever do, you can pretty easily figure out what's going on. Unfortunately, `cfingerd` doesn't have any compatibility with older `cfingerd.conf` files, so if you get a segmentation violation, this means (usually) that your `cfingerd.conf` file needs to be replaced.

Time-outs usually mean that a script has timed out or a connection to another site timed out.

## SYSLOGGING MESSAGES

There's no real way to describe `SYSLOG` messages because they can be changed as the system administrator chooses. Although, examples can be given based on the standard configuration that was distributed.

If any IP addresses cannot be matched to a hostname, SYSLOG will display `IP: Hostname not matched`.

If the `renice` fails (to make the program run at the highest priority), then SYSLOG will display `Fatal - Nice died: (reason)`.

If there is no buffer information is waiting in the `STDIN` buffer, SYSLOG will display `STDIN contains no data`.

If a trusted host fingers your site, a `<- Trusted` will appear.

If a rejected host fingers your site, a `<- Rejected` will appear.

If root is fingered on your site, it will display `Root`.

If a service listing was fingered on your site, SYSLOG will display `Service listing`.

If a user listing was requested, SYSLOG will display `User listing`.

If a fake user was requested, SYSLOG will display `Fake user`.

If whois data was requested, SYSLOG will display `Whois request`. (Note that whois was not implemented in this release because it wasn't RFC compliant.)

Any extra information pertaining to the incoming finger is displayed in the syslogging area. (It's also recommended that you reconfigure `syslog.conf(5)` to display to an unused VT.)

## BUGS

When data is forwarded to other sites for fingering, it shows the output of the system that it forwarded the finger request to. This has got to change.

On ELF-specific systems, services lists usually show a bit of garbage at the beginning of the finger display. This doesn't appear to be a problem on `a.out` systems, so if you have ELF, you might want to compile `cfingerd` as `a.out` if this becomes a problem.

## PLANS

Any other options or improvements will probably come from user suggestions.

Later plans will mean you can define your own display formats for the finger display. This means that you can redefine how you want your finger display to look.

## CONTACTING

If you like the software and you want to learn more about it or want to see a feature added to it that isn't already here, write to `khollis@bitgate.com`.

I've received calls at work pertaining to the software, and although I appreciate the fact that people like the software I wrote, I'd appreciate it if you leave me e–mail and be considerate.

cfingerd is now being maintained by Michael Jarvis. Any additions after cfingerd 1.2.3 should be directed toward Michael. You can reach him at mjarvis@qns.com.

If you want to see other projects that Bitgate Software is currently developing, check out the Web page at http:// www.bitgate.com/. This will contain all the update information on the software that is being developed and that is already released.

## SEE ALSO

cfingerd.conf(5), finger(1), userlist(1), syslog.conf(5)

*cfingerd 1.2.3, 24 May 1996*

# cfingerd.conf

cfingerd.conf—Configurable finger daemon configuration file.

## SYNOPSIS

/etc/cfingerd.conf

## DESCRIPTION

cfingerd.conf is the configuration file for cfingerd. This has been totally rewritten to support a more readable configuration file. This version of the new configuration file is not compatible with the older versions from 1.0.3 or earlier.

Each line in the configuration file is split into three sections: FILES, CONFIG, and HOSTS. Each one of those sections is split into subsections.

Subtext of each option is either Boolean options, string options, or switchable options, all changeable by the system administrator.

Each section is split into a series of sections that resembles C-type definition; it's not exact but close enough to be familiar. There's only one exception: These are not case sensitive. Any casing will do as long as the option is legal.

Thus, each option is formatted like this:

```
OPTION sub_option_name = {
(tab/space) string_option = "string format",
(tab/space) boolean_option = [BOOL, BOOL],
(tab/space) +/-internal_config_option
(tab/space) host.name.here
}
```

This shows that string options are strings put into quotes, Boolean options are given as TRUE and FALSE, switchable options are given with the + or - directive, and hostnames are used as substrings so that wildcards are not necessary.

You can add comments using the hash mark (#) at the beginning of the line. Please note that no comments are allowed inside of an OPTION.

## DISPLAY FILES SECTION (FILES display files)

Each option here is a string option. These are formatted as the example shows.

PLAN is the plan file that is used when displaying a plan. The standard here is .plan.

PROJECT is the project file that is used when displaying a project description. The standard here is .project.

PGP_KEY is the Pretty–Good–Privacy file that is shown when displaying a public or private key. The standard here is .pgpkey.

(The preceding three files must be world readable but should not be world writable. This makes sure that cfingerd can read the file once it becomes the "nobody" UID/GID. This is generally a good idea for protection.)

NO_FINGER is the file that is shown when a user wants to remain anonymous. This is usually the case with root users (which should be standard anyway). The standard here is .nofinger. This file can only be a standard displayable file.

LOGFILE is the file that is used to keep logs of everything that happens to both your system and the finger program. These logs are kept as backups for your finger file and can be used to guard against attacks against your system if a finger attack occurs. Remember, the cfingerd.conf file is root owned, so this file should be kept in a safe, hidden place.

HEADER_DISPLAY is the file that is displayed at the top of each finger display. The standard here is /etc/cfingerd/top_finger.txt.

FOOTER_DISPLAY is the file that is displayed at the end of each finger display. The standard here is /etc/cfingerd/bottom_finger.txt.

NO_USER_BANNER is the file that is displayed if the user doesn't exist. The standard here is /etc/cfingerd/nouser_banner.txt.

NO_NAME_BANNER is the file that is displayed if no name was specified in a finger display. This is used in conjunction with the SYSTEM_LIST option (explained later). The standard here is /etc/cfingerd/noname_banner.txt.

REJECTED_BANNER is the file that is displayed if a rejected host tries to finger your system for any reason. The standard here is /etc/cfingerd/rejected_banner.txt.

## FINGER DISPLAY CONFIGURE SECTION (CONFIG finger display)

Each option in this section is Boolean. The way this works is as follows: The first Boolean option is the setting for a remote host or a host that fingers you from the outside. The second Boolean option is the setting for the local host or trusted host. This is what people from your own system will see.

Each option has a - or + option. This is for user–overridable options, which will be in the next release of cfingerd. These will allow users to manipulate if this information is displayed when that specific user is fingered.

HEADER_FILE displays the header file at the beginning of each finger query.

FOOTER_FILE displays the footer file at the end of each finger query.

LOGIN_ID displays the login ID of that particular user.

REAL_NAME displays the real name of that particular user.

DIRECTORY displays the user's directory.

SHELL displays the user's shell.

ROOM_NUMBER displays the user's room number.

WORK_NUMBER displays the user's work phone number.

HOME_NUMBER displays the user's home phone number.

OTHER displays the user's other information.

LAST_TIME_ON displays the last time the user logged into the fingered system.

IF_ONLINE displays whether the user is currently logged into the fingered system.

TIME_MAIL_READ displays the last time that the fingered user read mail.

DAY_MAIL_READ displays the last day that the fingered user read his or her mail.

ORIGINATION displays the site from which the user logged in (if applicable).

PLAN displays the user's plan file.

PROJECT displays the user's project file.

PGP displays the user's Pretty–Good–Privacy key file.

NO_NAME_BANNER displays the banner if no username was given.

REJECTED_BANNER displays the rejected banner if the site fingering your system was in the banned–site listing.

SYSTEM_LIST displays the system list if one was requested.

NO_NAME displays the no–name display file if no user was selected.

## INTERNAL CONFIG CONFIGURE SECTION (CONFIG internal config)

Each item in this section is a switchable option. This means that a + before the item is turned on and a - before the item is turned off.

ALLOW_MULTIPLE_FINGER_DISPLAY allows you to give a sorted output of all users on more than one specific system. This is useful when you have more than one ISP machine, located in different cities or even states.

ALLOW_SEARCHABLE_FINGER allows you to let others outside your system (or within it) to search for a specific username by using the search.*username* directive.

ALLOW_NO_IP_MATCH_FINGER allows you to let sites finger your system if a hostname could not be matched to their IP address successfully.

ALLOW_USER_OVERRIDE will allow your users to override specific options in the FINGER DISPLAY section that you enable.

ALLOW_USERLIST_ONLY will allow other sites that are fingering your system for a specific compiled user list to finger your system and get a user listing of who's online. This could be a security risk, so you might want to turn this option off if you feel it's a security risk.

ALLOW_FINGER_FORWARDING will allow other sites to forward finger requests to a different machine if the user could not be located on the current machine. (In order to use this option, you must have the HOSTS finger forward option set and have other sites in there.)

ALLOW_STRICT_FORMATTING makes the finger display remove all returns between display options. This makes the finger display look horrible (as with GNU Finger or the other generic fingers) and makes your system look, well, "generic."

ALLOW_VERBOSE_TIMESTAMPING makes the timestamp that is displayed (at any place) very verbose. For instance, where it used to say

```
On since Sat Aug 12 03:43PM(PDT)
```

would now be shown as

```
On since Sat Aug 12, 1995 03:43PM(PDT)
```

(Basically, ALLOW_VERBOSE_TIMESTAMPING just takes up more room on the display field.)

ALLOW_NONIDENT_ACCESS lets you only allow connections from sites that run the ident daemon (or RFC 1413-compliant program.) This is for security sake and is a good measure against unknown users trying to finger your system. If this option is enabled, users who do not have identd running on their system (such as Windows users) will be able to finger your system. Systems not running identd will return unknown as the user ID and will not be permitted to finger a user on your system.

ALLOW_FINGER_LOGGING enables cfingerd to use the LOGFILE file to store any logs of activity that happen to your system via finger.

ALLOW_LINE_PARSING makes cfingerd parse each line of every display file (including the plan, project, and pgp files) for any cfingerd-specific $ commands. If any are found, cfingerd will parse these commands and display correct information accordingly. Otherwise, if this is turned off, the display will appear without parsed commands.

ALLOW_EXECUTION will allow users to execute scripts in place of their .plan, .project, and .pgp files. This is used to display the standard output of another program directly to the screen of the user. Keep in mind that this is a huge security risk if you choose to use it. It's normally suggested that this option remain off, but you can turn it on if necessary. Nevertheless, these programs are called as nobody.nogroup.

ALLOW_FAKEUSER_FINGER turns on or off the fake user option in cfingerd. If you want fake users to be defined and available to be fingered, you will want to enable this option. This can be a security risk in some instances if you allow for searchable fingers and your script calls an execute routine on that variable. Chances are that'll never happen.

ALLOW_USERLOG will allow users to keep track of who has fingered them and at what time. A little file called .fingerlog will appear in their directory, which they can examine to see who has fingered them. If you don't care about this, you can disable it. Otherwise, it's not a bad idea. (It also logs root fingers as well.)

## SYSTEM LIST SITES CONFIGURE SECTION (CONFIG system list sites)

This is just a series of hostnames that you want to finger when displaying your user-list display. If you have more than one system that you want to show, simply put their hostname in this list, separated on a line by itself.

For example, if I have a separate ISP system that I'm running on the side, say chatlink.com, I would change my configuration to say

```
CONFIG system_list_sites = { chatlink.com, localhost }
```

Remember, if you are listing only a couple of sites, list the sites you will want to have listed (in order) first. The ending entry must be *localhost* or the finger listing will not include your site. If you include *localhost* anywhere else in the list, it will stop once it has reached the *localhost* entry, so remember to list it last!

I want to get a user listing from my own machine and from chatlink.com's system. This would be automatically formatted nicely (sorted and parsed) and would display on the screen in sorted order. This program is usually used in tandem with the supplied userlist(1) program.

If no system list sites are specified, multiple system sites will not be specified.

## TRUSTED HOST SECTION (HOSTS trusted)

This is a listing of the sites that you allow to finger your system exclusively, giving them the same access that your local users would get. In other words, they are treated as *localhost* users.

Each site that you list in this section should be separated by using the , directive. You can include up to 80 sites in this listing.

Wildcards are supported in this section, and you can use them in the regex format as well. Any wildcards with *, ?, or any other regex wildcard matching character will work. IP addresses will also work. Hostnames are compared case insensitive.

## REJECTED HOST SECTION (HOSTS rejected)

This is a listing of the sites that you do not allow to finger your system. These sites don't get to finger anyone (or anything for that matter) on your system, regardless of what they try to do. In essence, finger is cut off to that particular system.

Each site that you list in this section should be separated by using the , directive. You can include up to 80 sites in this listing.

Wildcards are supported in this section, and you can use them in the regex format as well. Any wildcards with *, ?, or any other regex wildcard matching character will work. IP addresses will also work. Hostnames are compared case insensitive.

## FORWARDED HOST SECTION (HOSTS finger forward)

This is a listing of sites that are used to forward a finger query to when a finger request was processed but that particular user was not found on the associated system. It will step through this listing, and it will search for the user in question. If the user could not be found, then it will step through to the next host and the next, until it finds one.

Each site that you list in this section should be separated by using the , directive. You can include up to 80 sites in this listing.

Wildcards are supported in this section, and you can use them in the regex format as well. Any wildcards with *, ?, or any other regex wildcard matching character will work. Hostnames are compared case insensitive.

If you do not specify any forwarding sites in this section, finger forwarding will be disabled for your system.

## FINGER STRINGS CONFIGURE SECTION (CONFIG finger strings)

Each option in this section is a string that can be changed to fit your needs when displaying finger information. These strings are limited to about 20 characters on the display. (If you use more than 20, the finger display will end up looking strange.)

USER_NAME is the string that is displayed when the user's username is shown.

REAL_NAME is the string that is displayed when the user's real name is shown.

DIRECTORY is the string that is displayed when the user's directory is shown.

SHELL is the string that is displayed when the user's shell is shown.

ROOM_NUMBER is the string that is displayed when the user's room number is shown.

WORK_NUMBER is the string that is displayed when the user's work phone number is shown.

HOME_NUMBER is the string that is displayed when the user's home phone number is shown.

OTHER is the string that is displayed when the user's other display information is show.

PLAN is the string that is displayed when the user's plan is shown.

PROJECT is the string that is displayed when the user's project is shown.

PGPKEY is the string that is displayed when the user's PGP key is shown.

NO_PLAN is the string that is displayed when the user doesn't have a plan file to show you.

NO_PROJECT is the string that is displayed when the user doesn't have a project file to show you.

NO_PGP is the string that is displayed when the user doesn't have a PGP key file to show you.

WAIT is the string that is shown when the system gathers information from other sites for a user listing.

## INTERNAL STRINGS CONFIGURE SECTION (CONFIG internal strings)

These strings are changeable and can be any length you want (within reason). These strings are concatenated into the syslogging display when the appropriate finger has been issued. This section also includes error messages that may occur.

NO_IP_HOST is shown when there is no hostname that matches the incoming IP address. This usually indicates that either the site didn't register its IP address with the InterNIC or it is coming from a hacked site.

RENICE_FATAL is shown when the system failed to change the execution priority on the current process of cfingerd.

STDIN_EMPTY is shown when the input buffer on the cfingerd port is empty. (This should never really happen; it's here for sanity.)

TRUSTED_HOST is shown when a trusted host fingers your system. If you do not specify a trusted host, cfingerd will insert *localhost* into this field.

REJECTED_HOST is shown when a rejected host fingers your system. If you do not specify a rejected host, cfingerd will insert 0.0.0.0 into this field.

ROOT_FINGER is shown when a user fingers root.

SERVICE_FINGER is shown when a user requests fake user services from your system.

USER_LIST is shown when a user requests a user listing from your system.

FAKE_USER is shown when a user fingers a fake user from your system.

WHOIS_USER is shown when a user fingers a user with a WHOIS query. (This option is not yet available.)

FINGER_DENY is shown when a user tries to finger with a forward request such as *user@host1@host2*. This is not supported because it could result in finger loops and a lot of traffic.

## SIGNAL STRINGS CONFIGURE SECTION (CONFIG signal strings)

This section is used in changing the output that is given when a system crashes, or a signal is caught, and reported to the finger output.

The supported caught signals are as follows:

```
SIGHUP, SIGINT, SIGQUIT, SIGILL, SIGTRAP, SIGABRT, SIGFPE, SIGUSR1, SIGSEGV, SIGUSR2, SIGPIPE, SIGALRM, SIGTERM, SIGCONT,
SIGTSTP, SIGTTIN, SIGTTOU, SIGIO, SIGXCPU, SIGXFSZ, SIGVTALRM, SIGPROF, SIGWINCH
```

## FINGER PROGRAMS FILES SECTION (FILES finger programs)

These are the programs that are called when a specific action is take on the finger display.

FINGER is the file that is used when a user listing is requested from your machine. This is used in the standard user list and in the sorted user list, so it is wise to use the standard here: /usr/sbin/userlist.

WHOIS is the program that is used when a WHOIS request is done on a specific user.

## FINGER FAKE USERS FILES SECTION (FILES finger fakeusers)

These are the ever–popular fake users that you can create on your system. These users are ones that don't exist (and should not exist, for that matter). These are, instead, treated as normal scripts that can be called for your use.

The format is as follows for fake users:

```
fake_username Script_name SEARCHBOOL script
```

*fake_username* is the name of the fake user you want to request. Make sure that this is a user that does not exist on your system. Keep in mind that if you create a fake username and that user already exists, the fake username will be shown.

*Script_name* is the standard name of your script. This is used in the display of your services listing.

SEARCHBOOL specifies whether parameters can be sent to that specific fake user. If you decide to use the SEARCHBOOL option (TRUE in this case), the passed variables are

| | |
|---|---|
| $1 | First passed option |
| $2 | Second passed option |
| $3 | Third passed option |
| $4 | Fourth passed option |

(If more than four options were passed to this, the request will be ignored, and an error message will be returned to the user who requested the finger request.)

*script* is the location of your script. It should be chmod 700 and readable only by root.

If you do not specify any fake users, a fake user called None will be created. This is a fake user that does nothing and calls /dev/null for the script.

## SERVICES HEADER CONFIGURE SECTION (CONFIG services header)

This is the display that is given during a services finger. It should be formatted the same way that you want it to display on the screen.

When specifying the finger formatted options, you should specify them as C formatted strings as well, with the standard options. This should always be given last in the display.

An example of this is

```
Welcome to this system's services!
User: Service name: Searchable:
——— ———————— ————
%-8s %-20s %-s
```

Remember to keep the format string last or a SIGSEGV will result.

## SERVICES POSITIONS CONFIGURE SECTION (CONFIG services positions)

This specifies where in the preceding display string that the information from a service listing is to appear. These numbers can be anywhere between 1 and 3.

USER specifies the position of the username listing.

SERVICE specifies the position of the service full–name listing.

SEARCH specifies the position of the Boolean search display.

## CONTACTING

If you like this program and have questions or comments about the program's functionality or what–have–you, write to khollis@bitgate.com.

As always, I appreciate any suggestions or bug reports you might have, so bring them on!

## SEE ALSO

cfingerd(8), cfingerd.text(5), userlist(1), finger(1), regex(3), regexp(3)

*16 May 1996*

# cfingerd *text rules*

## EXPLANATION

cfingerd offers different commands that can be placed in text files to display corresponding information. Each command used with cfingerd in text files begins with a dollar sign ($). This usually indicates to cfingerd that when it's displaying a file, it parses the command directly after that character.

If you want to display a raw $ sign, simply put two $ signs together, or $$.

## TEXT COMMANDS

The following is a list of text commands and what they do. Each of the text commands can be in any text case; it doesn't matter.

| | |
|---|---|
| $CENTER | Displays the entire contents of the line. This command must start at the beginning of the line. This is a very common command. |
| $DATE | Displays the current system date in the format of MM/DD/YY. |
| $TIME | Displays the current system time in the format HH:MM A/PM (time zone). |
| $IDENT | Displays the identity of the current person fingering your system. |
| $COMPILE_DATETIME | Displays the date and time of which the current issue of cfingerd was compiled on your system. |
| $VERSION | Displays the current version of cfingerd. |
| $EXEC | Executes a file with x parameters after it. The $EXEC command must be on a line by itself in order to function properly. The command is executed as nobody.nogroup. |

## SEE ALSO

cfingerd(8), cfingerd.conf(5), finger(1), userlist(1), any of the included docs with the standard cfingerd distribution.

*cfingerd 1.2.1, 6 Jan 1996*

# control.ctl

control.ctl—Specify handling of Usenet control messages.

## DESCRIPTION

The file /news/lib/control.ctl is used to determine what action is taken when a control message is received. It is read by the parsecontrol script, which is called by all the control scripts. (For an explanation of how the control scripts are invoked, see innd(8).)

The file consists of a series of lines; blank lines and lines beginning with a number sign (#) are ignored. All other lines consist of four fields separated by a colon:

```
message:from:newsgroups:action
```

The first field is the name of the message for which this line is valid. It should be either the name of the control message, or the word all to mean that it is valid for all messages.

The second field is a shell-style pattern that matches the e-mail address of the person posting the message. (The poster's address is first converted to lowercase.) The matching is done using the shell's case statement; see sh(1) for details.

If the control message is newgroup or rmgroup, then the third field specifies the shell-style pattern that must match the group being created or removed. If the control message is of a different type, then this field is ignored.

The fourth field specifies what action to take if this line is selected for the message. The following actions are understood:

| | |
|---|---|
| doit | The action requested by the control message should be performed. In most cases, the control script will also send mail to Usenet. |
| doifarg | If the control message has an argument, this is treated as a doit action. If no argument was given, it is treated as a mail entry. This is used in a sendsys entries script so that a site can request its own newsfeeds(5) entry by posting a sendsys mysite article. On the other hand, sendsys bombs ask that the newsfeeds file be sent; if you use doifarg, such messages will not be processed automatically. |
| doit=file | The action is performed, but a log entry is written to the specified log file, file. If file is the word mail, then the record is mailed. A null string is equivalent to /dev/null. A pathname that starts with a slash is taken as the absolute filename to use as the log. All other pathnames are written to /var/log/news/file.log. The log is written by writelog (see newslog(8)). |
| drop | No action is taken; the message is ignored. |
| log | A one-line log notice is sent to standard error. innd normally directs this to the file /var/log/news/errlog. |
| log=file | A log entry is written to the specified log file, file, which is interpreted as described previously. |
| mail | A mail message is sent to the news administrator. |

Lines are matched in order; the last match found in the file is the one that is used. For example, with the following three lines:

```
newgroup:*:*:drop
newgroup:tale@*.uu.net:comp.*¦misc.*¦news.*¦rec.*¦sci.*¦soc.*¦talk.*:doit
newgroup:kre@munnari.oz.au:aus.*:mail
```

A newgroup coming from tale at a UUNET machine will be honored if it is in the mainstream Usenet hierarchy. If kre posts a newgroup message creating aus.foo, then mail will be sent. All other newgroup messages are ignored.

## HISTORY

Written by Rich $alz (rsalz@uunet.uu.net) for InterNetNews.

## SEE ALSO

innd(8), newsfeeds(5), scanlogs(8)

# CVS

cvs—Concurrent Versions System support files.

## SYNOPSIS

```
$CVSROOT/CVSROOT/commitinfo,v
$CVSROOT/CVSROOT/cvsignore,v
$CVSROOT/CVSROOT/cvswrappers,v
$CVSROOT/CVSROOT/editinfo,v
$CVSROOT/CVSROOT/history
$CVSROOT/CVSROOT/loginfo,v
$CVSROOT/CVSROOT/modules,v
$CVSROOT/CVSROOT/rcsinfo,v
$CVSROOT/CVSROOT/taginfo,v
```

## DESCRIPTION

cvs is a system for providing source control to hierarchical collections of source directories. Commands and procedures for using cvs are described in cvs(1). cvs manages source repositories, the directories containing master copies of the revision-controlled files, by copying particular revisions of the files to (and modifications back from) developers' private working directories. In terms of file structure, each individual source repository is an immediate subdirectory of $CVSROOT. The files described here are supporting files; they do not have to exist for cvs to operate, but they allow you to make cvs operation more flexible.

You can use the modules file to define symbolic names for collections of source maintained with cvs. If there is no modules file, developers must specify complete pathnames (absolute or relative to $CVSROOT) for the files they want to manage with cvs commands. You can use the commitinfo file to define programs to execute whenever cvs commit is about to execute. These programs are used for "precommit" checking to verify that the modified, added, and removed files are really ready to be committed. Some uses for this check might be to turn off a portion (or all) of the source repository from a particular person or group or perhaps to verify that the changed files conform to the site's standards for coding practice.

You can use the cvswrappers file to record cvs wrapper commands to be used when checking files into and out of the repository. Wrappers allow the file or directory to be processed on the way in and out of cvs. The intended uses are many; one possible use is to reformat a C file before the file is checked in so all the code in the repository looks the same. You can use the loginfo file to define programs to execute after any commit, which writes a log entry for changes in the repository. These logging programs might be used to append the log message to a file or send the log message through electronic mail to a group of developers. You can also post the log message to a particular newsgroup.

You can use the taginfo file to define programs to execute after any tag or rtag operation. These programs might be used to append a message to a file listing the new tag name and the programmer who created it, to send mail to a group of developers, or to post a message to a particular newsgroup. You can use the rcsinfo file to define forms for log messages. You can use the editinfo file to define a program to execute for editing or validating cvs commit log entries. This is most useful when used with a rcsinfo forms specification because it can verify that the proper fields of the form were filled in by the user committing the change. You can use the cvsignore file to specify the default list of files to ignore during update. You can use the history file to record the cvs commands that affect the repository. The creation of this file enables history logging.

## FILES

modules
The modules file records your definitions of names for collections of source code. cvs will use these definitions if you use cvs to check in a file with the right format to $CVSROOT/CVSROOT/modules,v. The modules file can contain blank lines and comments (lines beginning with #) as well as module definitions. Long lines can be continued on the next line by specifying a backslash (\) as the last character on the line. A module definition is a single line of the modules file in either of two formats. In both cases, *mname* represents the symbolic module name, and the remainder of the line is its definition.

*mname -a aliases ...*

This represents the simplest way of defining a module *mname*. The -a flags the definition as a simple alias: cvs will treat any use of mname (as a command argument) as if the list of names *aliases* had been specified instead. *aliases* may contain either other module names or paths. When you use paths in `aliases`, cvs checkout creates all intermediate directories in the working directory, just as if the path had been specified explicitly in the cvs arguments.

`mname [ options ] dir [ files ... ] [&module ...]`

In the simplest case, this form of module definition reduces to `mname dir`. This defines all the files in directory `dir` as module mname. `dir` is a relative path (from `$CVSROOT`) to a directory of source in one of the source repositories. In this case, on checkout, a single directory called `mname` is created as a working directory; no intermediate directory levels are used by default, even if `dir` was a path involving several directory levels. By explicitly specifying files in the module definition after `dir`, you can select particular files from directory `dir`. The sample definition for modules is an example of a module defined with a single file from a particular directory. Here is another example:

`m4test unsupported/gnu/m4 foreach.m4 forloop.m4`

With this definition, executing cvs checkout m4test will create a single working directory m4test containing the two files listed, which both come from a common directory several levels deep in the cvs source repository. A module definition can refer to other modules by including `&module` in its definition. The checkout command creates a subdirectory for each such module in your working directory. New in cvs 1.3; avoid this feature if sharing module definitions with older versions of cvs.

Finally, you can use one or more of the following options in module definitions: `-d name` names the working directory something other than the module name. This option is new in cvs 1.3; avoid this feature if sharing module definitions with older versions of cvs. `-i prog` allows you to specify a program `prog` to run whenever files in a module are committed. `prog` runs with a single argument, the full pathname of the affected directory in a source repository. The commitinfo, loginfo, and editinfo files provide other ways to call a program on commit. `-o prog` allows you to specify a program `prog` to run whenever files in a module are checked out. `prog` runs with a single argument, the module name. `-e prog` allows you to specify a program `prog` to run whenever files in a module are exported. `prog` runs with a single argument, the module name. `-t prog` allows you to specify a program `prog` to run whenever files in a module are tagged. `prog` runs with two arguments: the module name and the symbolic tag specified to rtag. `-u prog` allows you to specify a program `prog` to run whenever cvs update is executed from the top-level directory of the checked-out module. `prog` runs with a single argument, the full path to the source repository for this module.

### commitinfo, loginfo, rcsinfo, editinfo

These files all specify programs to call at different points in the cvs commit process. They have a common structure. Each line is a pair of fields: a regular expression, separated by whitespace from a filename or command-line template. Whenever one of the regular expression matches a directory name in the repository, the rest of the line is used. If the line begins with a # character, the entire line is considered a comment and is ignored. Whitespace between the fields is also ignored. For loginfo, the rest of the line is a command-line template to execute. The templates can include not only a program name, but also whatever list of arguments you want. If you write %s somewhere on the argument list, cvs supplies, at that point, the list of files affected by the commit. The first entry in the list is the relative path within the source repository where the change is being made. The remaining arguments list the files that are being modified, added, or removed by this commit invocation. For taginfo, the rest of the line is a command-line template to execute. The arguments passed to the command are, in order, the *tagname*, *operation* (add for tag, mov for tag -F, and del for tag -d), and *repository*, and any remaining are pairs of filename revision. A nonzero exit of the filter program will cause the tag to be aborted. For commitinfo, the rest of the line is a command-line template to execute. The template can include not only a program name but also whatever list of arguments you want. The full path to the current source repository is appended to the template, followed by the filenames of any files involved in the commit (added, removed, and modified files). For rcsinfo, the rest of the line is the full path to a file that should be loaded into the log message template. For editinfo, the rest of the line is a command-line template to execute. The template can include not only a program name but also whatever list of arguments you want. The full path to the current log message template file is appended to the template. You can use one of two special strings instead of a regular expression: ALL specifies a command-line template that must always be executed, and DEFAULT specifies a command-line template to use if no regular expression is a match. The commitinfo file contains commands to execute before any other commit activity, to allow you to check any conditions that must be satisfied before commit can proceed. The rest of the commit will execute only if all selected commands from this file exit with exit status 0. The rcsinfo file allows you to specify log templates for the commit logging session; you can use this to provide a form to edit when filling out the commit log. The field after the regular expression, in this file, contains filenames (of files containing the logging forms) rather than command templates. The editinfo file allows you to execute a script before the commit starts but after the log information is recorded. These "edit" scripts can verify information recorded in the log file. If the edit script exits with a nonzero exit status, the commit is aborted. The loginfo file contains commands to execute at the end of a commit. The text specified as a commit log message is piped through the command; typical uses include sending mail, filing an article in a newsgroup, or appending to a central file.

cvsignore, .cvsignore

The default list of files (or sh(1) filename patterns) to ignore during cvs update. At startup time, cvs loads the compiled default list of filename patterns (see cvs(1)). Then the per-repository list included in $CVSROOT/CVSROOT/cvsignore is loaded, if it exists.

Then the per-user list is loaded from $HOME/.cvsignore. Finally, as cvs traverses through your directories, it will load any per-directory .cvsignore files whenever it finds one. These per-directory files are only valid for exactly the directory that contains them, not for any subdirectories.

history

Create this file in $CVSROOT/CVSROOT to enable history logging (see the description of cvs history).

## SEE ALSO

cvs(1)

## COPYING

Permission is granted to copy and distribute translations of this manual into another language, under the preceding conditions for modified versions, except that this permission notice may be included in translations approved by the Free Software Foundation instead of in the original English.

*12 February 1992*

# DEVINFO

DEVINFO—Device entry database.

## DESCRIPTION

DEVINFO is a text file that describes all the possible devices for a system. It is used by MAKEDEV(8) to create special file entries in /dev. It may be named either /dev/DEVINFO or /etc/devinfo. Information about custom local devices, if any, should be placed in DEVINFO.local or /etc/devinfo.local, which has the same syntax.

The file format is free-form. C, C++, and shell comments are understood. There are basically four statements:

| | |
|---|---|
| ignore { *proc-device...* } | This causes the specified names to be ignored if found in /proc/devices. |
| batch { *device...* } | This creates a "batch"—a collection of devices that will all be created when the batch is invoked. For example, in the standard DEVINFO, "generic" is a batch. |
| block *device-spec* | This defines one or more block devices. |
| char *device-spec* | This defines one or more character devices. |

Here is a sample *device-spec*:

```
(std, 1) {
mem (kmem) : 1
null (public) : 3
core -> "/proc/kcore"
}
```

This example defines a group of devices called std, with major number 1. Running will create all the devices in the group; running, for example, would make just the one device null.

It is possible to specify, instead of just std, something like std=foo. In this case, the stuff on the right-hand side of the equals sign specifies a name from /proc/devices, and the major number will be retrieved from there if present. If an entry from /proc/devices is specified, the explicit major number may be omitted. In this case, if the number is not found in /proc/devices, attempts to create the device will be rejected.

Inside the braces is a list of specific devices. The name in parenthesis is the "class"; this is something specified in MAKEDEV.cfg that determines the ownership and permissions of the special file created. In the preceding example, the device mem was set to have the class kmem, but null was set to be public. Ordinarily, you'd define public to be mode 666 but kmem to be mode 660 and owned by group kmem. The number after the colon is the minor number for this particular device; for instance, 3 for null.

You may also specify a symbolic link with ->. For instance, core was made a link to /proc/kcore. Note that names may contain any characters, but names that contain things other than alphanumerics, dash, and underscore should be put in double quotes.

An entire range of devices can be created. You may specify a range of numbers in brackets:

```
tty[1-8] (tty) : 1
```

This creates tty1–tty8 with minor device numbers starting with 1. If you specify the range in hex (prefixed by 0x), the device names will be created numbered in hex, as is normal for ptys. The range may appear inside the name string, but there may only be one range.

There is a special syntax for creating the entire banks of devices for a hard drive:

```
hd[a-d] 8/64
```

What this means is as follows: Create `hda`, and eight partitions on `hda` (`hda1` through `hda8`), starting with minor number 0. Then create `hdb`, and eight partitions, starting with minor number 64. Then `hdc`, and so on, with minor number 64*2 = 128—and so forth. These are automatically placed in the class `disk`. The necessary groups and batches are created so you can ask `MAKEDEV` to create `hd` or `hda` or `hda1` and expect it to do the correct thing.

Note that simple arithmetic is permitted for specifying the minor device number, as this often makes things much clearer and less likely to be accidentally broken.

## SEE ALSO

`MAKEDEV(8)`, `MAKEDEV.cfg(5)`

*Version 1.4, January 1995*

# environ

`environ`—User environment.

## SYNOPSIS

`extern char **environ;`

## DESCRIPTION

An array of strings called the *environment* is made available by exec(2) when a process begins. By convention, these strings have the form *name=value*. Common examples are

| | |
|---|---|
| USER | The name of the logged-in user (used by some BSD-derived programs). |
| LOGNAME | The name of the logged-in user (used by some System-V derived programs). |
| HOME | A user's login directory, set by login(1) from the password file passwd(5). |
| LANG | The name of a locale to use for locale categories when not overridden by LC_ALL or more specific environment variables. |
| PATH | The sequence of directory prefixes that sh(1) and many other programs apply in searching for a file known by an incomplete pathname. The prefixes are separated by :. |
| SHELL | The filename of the user's login shell. |
| TERM | The terminal type for which output is to be prepared. |

Further names maybe placed in the environment by the export command and *name=value* in sh(1) or by the setenv command if you use csh(1). Arguments may also be placed in the environment at the point of an exec(2).

It is risky practice to set *name=value* pairs that conflict with well-known shell variables. Setting these could cause surprising behavior in subshells or system(3) commands.

## SEE ALSO

login(1), sh(1), bash(1), csh(1), tcsh(1), exec(2), system(3)

*Linux, 21 October 1996*

# expire.ctl

`expire.ctl`—Control file for Usenet article expiration.

## DESCRIPTION

The file /news/lib/expire.ctl is the default control file for the expire(8) program, which reads it at startup. Blank lines and lines beginning with a number sign (#) are ignored. All other lines should be in one of two formats.

The first format specifies how long to keep a record of fully expired articles. This is useful when a newsfeed intermittently offers older news that is not kept around very long. (The case of very old news is handled by the -c flag of innd(8).) There should only be one line in this format, which looks like this:

```
/remember/:days
```

Where *days* is a floating-point number that specifies the upper limit to remember a Message-ID, even if the article has already expired. (It does not affect article expirations.)

Most of the lines in the file will consist of five colon-separated fields, as follows:

```
pattern:modflag:keep:default:purge
```

The *pattern* field is comma-separated set of single wildmat(3)-style patterns that specify the newsgroups to which the rest of the line applies. Because the file is interpreted in order, the most general patterns should be specified first, and the most specific patterns should be specified last.

The *modflag* field can be used to further limit newsgroups to which the line applies and should be chosen from the following set:

| | |
|---|---|
| M | Only moderated groups |
| U | Only unmoderated groups |
| A | All groups |

The next three fields are used to determine how long an article should be kept. Each field should be either a number of days (fractions such as 8.5 are allowed) or the word never. The most common use is to specify the default value for how long an article should be kept. The first and third fields—*keep* and *purge*—specify the boundaries within which an Expires header will be honored. They are ignored if an article has no Expires header. The fields are specified in the file as "lower-bound default upper-bound," and they are explained in this order. Because most articles do not have explicit expiration dates, however, the second field tends to be the most important one.

The *keep* field specifies how many days an article should be kept before it will be removed. No article in the newsgroup will be removed if it has been filed for less than *keep* days, regardless of any expiration date. If this field is the word never, then an article cannot have been kept for enough days so it will never be expired.

The *default* field specifies how long to keep an article if no Expires header is present. If this field is the word never, then articles without explicit expiration dates will never be expired.

The *purge* field specifies the upper bound on how long an article can be kept. No article will be kept longer than the number of days specified by this field. All articles will be removed after they have been kept for *purge* days. If purge is the word never, then the article will never be deleted.

It is often useful to honor the expiration headers in articles, especially those in moderated groups. To do this, set *keep* to zero, *default* to whatever value you want, and *purge* to never. To ignore any Expires header, set all three fields to the same value.

There must be exactly one line with a *pattern* of * and a *modflags* of A; this matches all groups and is used to set the expiration default. It should be the first expiration line. For example:

```
## How long to keep expired history
/remember/:5
## Most things stay for two weeks
:A:14:14:14
## Believe expiration dates in moderated groups, up to six weeks
:M:1:30:42
## Keep local stuff for a long time
foo.*:A:30:30:30
```

## HISTORY

Written by Rich $alz (rsalz@uunet.uu.net) for InterNetNews.

## SEE ALSO

expire(8), wildmat(3)

# exports

exports—NFS filesystems being exported.

## SYNOPSIS

/etc/exports

## DESCRIPTION

The file /etc/exports serves as the access control list for filesystems that can be exported to NFS clients. It is used by both the NFS mount daemon mountd(8) and the NFS file server daemon nfsd(8).

The file format is similar to the SunOS exports file, except that several additional options are permitted. Each line contains a mount point and a list of machine or netgroup names allowed to mount the filesystem at that point. An optional parenthesized list of mount parameters may follow each machine name. Blank lines are ignored, and a # introduces a comment to the end of the line.

## GENERAL OPTIONS

| | |
|---|---|
| secure | This option requires that requests originate on an Internet port less than IPPORT_RESERVED (1024). This option is on by default. To turn it off, specify insecure. |
| ro | Allow only read-only requests on this NFS volume. The default is to allow write requests as well, which can also be made explicit by using the rw option. |
| link_relative | Convert absolute symbolic links (where the link contents start with a slash) into relative links by prepending the necessary number of ../s to get from the directory containing the link to the root on the server. This has subtle, perhaps questionable, semantics when the file hierarchy is not mounted at its root. |
| link_absolute | Leave all symbolic links as they are. This is the default operation. |

## USER ID MAPPING

nfsd bases its access control to files on the server machine on the UID and GID provided in each NFS RPC request. The normal behavior a user would expect is that she can access her files on the server just as she would on a normal filesystem. This requires that the same UIDs and GIDs are used on the client and the server machine. This is not always true, nor is it always desirable.

Very often, it is not desirable that the root user on a client machine is also treated as root when accessing files on the NFS server. To this end, UID 0 is normally mapped to a different ID: the so-called anonymous or nobody UID. This mode of operation (called root squashing) is the default and can be turned off with no_root_squash.

By default, nfsd tries to obtain the anonymous UID and GID by looking up user nobody in the password file at startup time. If it isn't found, a UID and GID of -2 (65534) is used. These values can also be overridden by the anonuid and anongid options.

In addition to this, nfsd lets you specify arbitrary UIDs and GIDs that should be mapped to user nobody as well. Finally, you can map all user requests to the anonymous UID by specifying the all_squash option.

For the benefit of installations where UIDs differ between different machines, nfsd provides a way to dynamically map server UIDs to client UIDs and vice versa. This is enabled with the map daemon option and uses the UGID RPC protocol. For this to work, you have to run the ugidd(8) mapping daemon on the client host.

Here's the complete list of mapping options:

| | |
|---|---|
| root_squash | Map requests from UID/GID 0 to the anonymous UID/GID. Note that this does not apply to any other UIDs that might be equally sensitive, such as user bin. |
| no_root_squash | Turn off root squashing. This option is mainly useful for diskless clients. |
| squash_uids and squash_gids | This option specifies a list of UIDs or GIDs that should be subject to anonymous mapping. A valid list of IDs looks like this: |

squash_uids=0-15,20,25-60

Usually, your squash lists will look a lot simpler, such as

squash_uids=0-100

| | |
|---|---|
| all_squash | Map all UIDs and GIDs to the anonymous user. Useful for NFS-exported public FTP directories, newsspool directories, and so on. The opposite option is no_all_squash, which is the default setting. |
| map_daemon | This option turns on dynamic UID/GID mapping. Each UID in an NFS request will be translated to the equivalent server UID, and each UID in an NFS reply will be mapped the other way round. This option requires that rpc.ugidd(8) runs on the client host. The default setting is map_identity, which leaves all UIDs untouched. The normal squash options apply regardless of whether dynamic mapping is requested. |
| anonuid and anongid | These options explicitly set the UID and GID of the anonymous account. This option is primarily useful for PC/NFS clients, where you might want all requests appear to be from one user. As an example, consider the export entry for /home/joe in the section "Example," which maps all requests to UID 150 (which is supposedly that of user joe). |

## EXAMPLE

```
# sample /etc/exports file
/ master(rw) trusty(rw,no_root_squash)
/projects proj*.local.domain(rw)
/usr *.local.domain(ro) @trusted(rw)
/home/joe pc001(rw,all_squash,anonuid=150,anongid=100)
/pub (ro,insecure,all_squash)
```

The first line exports the entire filesystem to machines master and trusty. In addition to write access, all UID squashing is turned off for host trusty. The second and third entry show examples for wildcard hostnames and netgroups (this is the entry @trusted). The fourth line shows the entry for the PC/NFS client discussed previously. The last line exports the public FTP directory to every host in the world, executing all requests under the nobody account. The insecure option in this entry also allows clients with NFS implementations that don't use a reserved port for NFS.

## CAVEATS

Unlike other NFS server implementations, this nfsd allows you to export both a directory and a subdirectory thereof to the same host, for instance /usr and /usr/X11R6. In this case, the mount options of the most specific entry apply. For instance, when a user on the client host accesses a file in /usr/X11R6, the mount options given in the /usr/X11R6 entry apply. This is also true when the latter is a wildcard or netgroup entry.

## FILES

| | |
|---|---|
| /etc/exports | Configuration file for nfsd(8) |
| /etc/passwd | The password file |

## DIAGNOSTICS

An error parsing the file is reported using syslogd(8) as level NOTICE from a DAEMON whenever nfsd(8) or mountd(8) is started. Any unknown host is reported at that time, but often not all hosts are not yet known to named(8) at boot time, so as hosts are found, they are reported with the same syslogd(8) parameters.

## SEE ALSO

mountd(8), nfsd(8), nfs(5), passwd(5)

*21 October 1996*

# filesystems

filesystems—Linux filesystem types: minix, ext, ext2, xia, msdos, umsdos, vfat, proc, nfs, iso9660, hpfs, sysv, smb, ncpfs.

## DESCRIPTION

In the file /proc/filesystems, you can find which filesystems your kernel currently supports. (If you need a currently unsupported one, insert the corresponding module or recompile the kernel.)

Following is a description of the various filesystems.

| | |
|---|---|
| minix | The filesystem used in the Minix operating system, the first to run under Linux. It has a number of shortcomings: a 64MB partition size limit, short filenames, a single time stamp, and so on. It remains useful for floppies and RAM disks. |
| ext | An elaborate extension of the minix filesystem. It has been completely superseded by the second version of the extended filesystem (ext2) and will eventually be removed from the kernel. |
| ext2 | The high performance disk filesystem used by Linux for fixed disks as well as removable media. |
| | The second extended filesystem was designed as an extension of the extended filesystem (ext). ext2 offers the best performance (in terms of speed and CPU usage) of the filesystems supported under Linux. |
| xiafs | Designed and implemented to be a stable, safe filesystem by extending the Minix filesystem code. It provides the basic, most requested features without undue complexity. The xia filesystem is no longer actively developed or maintained. It is used infrequently. |
| msdos | The filesystem used by DOS, Windows, and some OS/2 computers. msdos filenames can be no longer than an eight-character name followed by an optional period and three-character extension. |
| umsdos | An extended DOS filesystem used by Linux. It adds capability for long filenames, UID/GID, POSIX permissions, and special files (devices, named pipes, and so on) under the DOS filesystem, without sacrificing compatibility with DOS. |
| vfat | Extended DOS filesystem used by Microsoft Windows 95 and Windows NT. vfat adds capability for long filenames under the MS-DOS filesystem. |
| proc | A pseudo-filesystem that is used as an interface to kernel data structures rather than reading and interpreting /dev/kmem. In particular, its files do not take disk space. See proc(5). |
| iso9660 | A CD-ROM filesystem type conforming to the ISO 9660 standard. |
| High Sierra | Linux supports High Sierra, the precursor to the ISO 9660 standard for CD-ROM filesystems. It is automatically recognized within the iso9660 filesystem support under Linux. |
| Rock Ridge | Linux also supports the System Use Sharing Protocol records specified by the Rock Ridge Interchange Protocol. They are used to further describe the files in the iso9660 filesystem to a UNIX host and provides information such as long filenames, UID/GID, POSIX permissions, and devices. It is automatically recognized within the iso9660 filesystem support under Linux. |
| hpfs | The High Performance Filesystem, used in OS/2. This filesystem is read-only under Linux due to the lack of available documentation. |
| sysv | An implementation of the SystemV/Coherent filesystem for Linux. It implements all Xenix FS, SystemV/386 FS, and Coherent FS. |
| nfs | The network filesystem used to access disks located on remote computers. |

smb                          A network filesystem that supports the SMB protocol, used by Windows for Workgroups,
                             Windows NT, and LAN Manager.

                             To use smb, you need a special mount program, which can be found in the ksmbfs package at
                             ftp://sunsite.unc.edu/pub/Linux/system/Filesystems/smbfs.

ncpfs                        A network filesystem that supports the NCP protocol, used by Novell NetWare.

                             To use ncpfs, you need special programs found at ftp://linux01.gwdg.de/pub/ncpfc.

## SEE ALSO

proc(5), fsck(8), mkfs(8), mount(8)

*25 March 1996*


# fstab

fstab—Static information about the filesystems.

## SYNOPSIS

#include <fstab.h>

## DESCRIPTION

The file fstab contains descriptive information about the various filesystems. fstab is only read by programs and not written; it is the duty of the system administrator to properly create and maintain this file. Each filesystem is described on a separate line; fields on each line are separated by tabs or spaces. The order of records in fstab is important because fsck(8), mount(8), and umount(8) sequentially iterate through fstab doing their thing.

The first field (fs_spec) describes the block special device or remote filesystem to be mounted.

The second field (fs_file) describes the mount point for the filesystem. For swap partitions, this field should be specified as none.

The third field (fs_vfstype) describes the type of the filesystem. The system currently supports three types of filesystems:

minix                        A local filesystem, supporting filenames of length 14 or 30 characters.

ext                          A local filesystem with longer filenames and larger inodes. This filesystem has been replaced
                             by the ext2 filesystem and should no longer be used.

ext2                         A local filesystem with longer filenames, larger inodes, and a lot of other features.

xiafs                        A local filesystem with longer filenames, larger inodes, and a lot of other features.

msdos                        A local filesystem for MS-DOS partitions.

hpfs                         A local filesystem for HPFS partitions.

iso9660                      A local filesystem used for CD-ROM drives.

nfs                          A filesystem for mounting partitions from remote systems.

swap                         A disk partition to be used for swapping.

If vfs_fstype is specified as ignore, the entry is ignored. This is useful to show disk partitions that are currently unused.

The fourth field (fs_mntops) describes the mount options associated with the filesystem.

It is formatted as a comma-separated list of options. It contains at least the type of mount plus any additional options appropriate to the filesystem type. For documentation on the available options for non-NFS file systems, see mount(8). For documentation on all NFS-specific options, take a look at nfs(5). Common for all types of filesystems are the options noauto (do not mount when mount -a is given, such as at boot time) and user (allow a user to mount). For more details, see mount(8).

The fifth field (fs_freq) is used for these filesystems by the dump(8) command to determine which filesystems need to be dumped. If the fifth field is not present, a value of zero is returned and dump will assume that the filesystem does not need to be dumped.

The sixth field (fs_passno) is used by the fsck(8) program to determine the order in which filesystem checks are done at reboot time. The root filesystem should be specified with a fs_passno of 1, and other filesystems should have a fs_passno of 2. Filesystems within a drive will be checked sequentially, but filesystems on different drives will be checked at the same time to utilize parallelism available in the hardware. If the sixth field is not present or zero, a value of zero is returned and fsck will assume that the filesystem does not need to be checked.

The proper way to read records from fstab is to use the routine getmntent(3).

## FILES

/etc/fstab

## BUGS

The documentation in mount(8) is often more up-to-date.

## SEE ALSO

getmntent(3), mount(8), swapon(8), nfs(5)

## HISTORY

The fstab file format appeared in 4.0 BSD.

*Linux 0.99, 27 November 1993*

# groff_font

groff_font—Format of groff device and font description files.

## DESCRIPTION

The groff_font format is roughly a superset of the ditroff font format. Unlike the ditroff font format, there is no associated binary format. The font files for device *name* are stored in a directory dev*name*. There are two types of file: a device description file called DESC and for each font F, a font file called F. These are text files; there is no associated binary format.

## DESC FILE FORMAT

The DESC file can contain the following types of lines:

| | |
|---|---|
| res *n* | There are *n* machine units per inch. |
| hor *n* | The horizontal resolution is *n* machine units. |
| vert *n* | The vertical resolution is *n* machine units. |
| sizescale *n* | The scale factor for point sizes. By default, this has a value of 1. One scaled point is equal to one point/*n*. The arguments to the unitwidth and sizes commands are given in scaled points. |
| unitwidth *n* | Quantities in the font files are given in machine units for fonts whose point size is *n* scaled points. |
| tcommand | This means that the postprocessor can handle the t and u output commands. |
| sizes s1 s2 ... s*n*0 | This means that the device has fonts at s1, s2,...s*n* scaled points. The list of sizes must be terminated by a 0. Each s*i* can also be a range of sizes *m–n*. The list can extend over more than one line. |
| styles S1 S2 ... S*m* | The first *m* font positions will be associated with styles S1...S*m*. |
| fonts *n* F1 F2 F3 ... F*n* | Fonts F1...F*n* will be mounted in the font positions *m*+1,...,*m*+*n* where *m* is the number of styles. This command may extend over more than one line. A font name of 0 will cause no font to be mounted on the corresponding font position. |

| family *fam* | The default font family is *fam*. |
| charset | This line and everything following in the file are ignored. It is allowed for the sake of backwards compatibility. |

The res, unitwidth, fonts, and sizes lines are compulsory. Other commands are ignored by troff but may be used by postprocessors to store arbitrary information about the device in the DESC file.

## FONT FILE FORMAT

A font file has two sections. The first section is a sequence of lines, each containing a sequence of blank delimited words; the first word in the line is a key, and subsequent words give a value for that key.

| name *F* | The name of the font is *F*. |
| spacewidth *n* | The normal width of a space is *n*. |
| slant *n* | The characters of the font have a slant of *n* degrees. (Positive means forward.) |
| ligatures lig1 lig2 ... lig*n* [0] | Characters lig1, lig2,...,lig*n* are ligatures; possible ligatures are ff, fi, fl, and ffl. For backwards compatibility, the list of ligatures may be terminated with a 0. The list of ligatures may not extend over more than one line. |
| special | The font is special; this means that when a character is requested that is not present in the current font, it will be searched for in any special fonts that are mounted. |

Other commands are ignored by troff but may be used by postprocessors to store arbitrary information about the font in the font file.

The first section can contain comments, which start with the # character and extend to the end of a line.

The second section contains one or two subsections. It must contain a charset subsection and it may also contain a kernpairs subsection. These subsections can appear in any order. Each subsection starts with a word on a line by itself.

The word charset starts the charset subsection. The charset line is followed by a sequence of lines. Each line gives information for one character. A line comprises a number of fields separated by blanks or tabs. The format is

*name metrics type code comment*

*name* identifies the character: if *name* is a single character c, it corresponds to the groff input character c; if it is of the form \c where c is a single character, then it corresponds to the groff input character nc; otherwise, it corresponds to the groff input character \[*name*] (if it is exactly two characters *xx*, it can be entered as \(*xx*). groff supports eight-bit characters; however, some utilities have difficulties with eight-bit characters. For this reason, there is a convention that the name char*n* is equivalent to the single character whose code is *n*. For example, char163 is equivalent to the character with code 163, which is the pounds sterling sign in ISO Latin-1. The name — is special and indicates that the character is unnamed; such characters can only be used by means of the \N escape sequence in troff.

The *type* field gives the character type:

| 1 | The character has an descender, such as p. |
| 2 | The character has an ascender, such as b. |
| 3 | The character has both an ascender and a descender, such as (. |

The *code* field gives the code that the postprocessor uses to print the character. The character can also be input to groff using this code by means of the \N escape sequence. The code can be any integer. If it starts with a 0, it will be interpreted as octal; if it starts with 0x or 0X, it will be interpreted as hexadecimal.

Anything on the line after the code field will be ignored.

The *metrics* field has the form:

width[,height[,depth[,italic_correction[,left_italic_correction
➥[,subscript_correction]]]]]]

There must not be any spaces between these subfields. Missing subfields are assumed to be 0. The subfields are all decimal integers. Because there is no associated binary format, these values are not required to fit into a variable of type char as they are in ditroff. The *width* subfields gives the width of the character. The *height* subfield gives the height of the character (upwards is positive); if a character does not extend above the baseline, it should be given a zero height, rather than a negative height. The *depth* subfield gives the depth of the character, that is, the distance below the lowest point below the baseline to which the character extends (downwards is positive); if a character does not extend below above the baseline, it should be given a zero depth, rather than a negative depth. The *italic_correction* subfield gives the amount of space that should be added after the character when it is immediately to be followed by a character from a roman font. The *left_italic_correction* subfield gives the amount of space that should be added before the character when it is immediately to be preceded by a character from a roman font. The *subscript_correction* gives the amount of space that should be added after a character before adding a subscript. This should be less than the *italic_correction*.

A line in the charset section can also have the format

```
name "
```

This indicates that *name* is just another name for the character mentioned in the preceding line.

The word kernpairs starts the kernpairs section. This contains a sequence of lines of the form:

```
c1 c2 n
```

This means that when character c1 appears next to character c2, the space between them should be increased by *n*. Most entries in kernpairs section will have a negative value for *n*.

## FILES

/usr/lib/groff/font/dev name/DESC    Device description file for device name.

/usr/lib/groff/font/devname/F    Font file for font *F* of device name.

## SEE ALSO

groff_out(5), gtroff(1)

*Groff Version 1.09, 14 February 1994*

# groff_out

groff_out—groff intermediate output format.

## DESCRIPTION

This manual page describes the format output by GNU troff. The output format used by GNU troff is very similar to that used by UNIX device-independent troff. Only the differences are documented here.

The argument to the s command is in scaled points (units of points/*n*, where *n* is the argument to the sizescale command in the DESC file.) The argument to the x Height command is also in scaled points.

The first three output commands are guaranteed to be

```
x T device
x res n h v
x init
```

If the tcommand line is present in the DESC file, troff will use the following two commands:

t*xxx*    *xxx* is any sequence of characters terminated by a space or a newline; the first character should be printed at the current position, the current horizontal position should be increased by the width of the first character, and so on for each character. The width of the character is that given in the font file, appropriately scaled for the current point size and rounded so that it is a multiple of the horizontal resolution. Special characters cannot be printed using this command.

| | |
|---|---|
| *unxxx* | This is same as the t command except that after printing each character, the current horizontal position is increased by the sum of the width of that character and *n*. |

Note that single characters can have the eighth bit set, as can the names of fonts and special characters.

The names of characters and fonts can be of arbitrary length; drivers should not assume that they will be only two characters long.

When a character is to be printed, that character will always be in the current font. Unlike device-independent troff, it is not necessary for drivers to search special fonts to find a character.

The D drawing command has been extended. These extensions will not be used by GNU pic if the -n option is given.

| | |
|---|---|
| Df *n*\n | Set the shade of gray to be used for filling solid objects to *n*; *n* must be an integer between 0 and 1000, where 0 corresponds to solid white and 1000 to solid black and values in between correspond to intermediate shades of gray. This applies only to solid circles, solid ellipses, and solid polygons. By default, a level of 1000 will be used. Whatever color a solid object has, it should completely obscure everything beneath it. A value greater than 1000 or less than 0 can also be used: This means fill with the shade of gray that is currently being used for lines and text. Normally, this will be black, but some drivers may provide a way of changing this. |
| DC *d*\n | Draw a solid circle with a diameter of *d* with the leftmost point at the current position. |
| DE *dx dy*\n | Draw a solid ellipse with a horizontal diameter of *dx* and a vertical diameter of *dy* with the leftmost point at the current position. |
| Dp *dx1 dy1 dx2 dy2* ... *dxn dyn*\n | Draw a polygon with, for $i$ = 1, ..., $n$+1, the $i$th vertex at the current position + $\sum_{j=1}^{i-1}(dxj, dyj)$. At the moment, GNU pic only uses this command to generate triangles and rectangles. |
| DP *dx1 dy1 dx2 dy2* ... *dxn dyn*\n | Like Dp, but draw a solid rather than outlined polygon. |
| Dt *n*\n | Set the current line thickness to *n* machine units. Traditionally, UNIX troff drivers use a line thickness proportional to the current point size; drivers should continue to do this if no Dt command has been given or if a Dt command has been given with a negative value of *n*. A zero value of *n* selects the smallest available line thickness. |

A difficulty arises in how the current position should be changed after the execution of these commands. This is not of great importance because the code generated by GNU pic does not depend on this. Given a drawing command of the form

\Dc *x1 y1 x2 y2* ... *xn yn*

where c is not one of c, e, l, a, or ~, UNIX troff will treat each of the *xi* as a horizontal quantity and each of the *yi* as a vertical quantity and will assume that the width of the drawn object is $\sum_{i=1}^{n} xi$ and that the height is $\sum_{i=1}^{n} yi$. (The assumption about the height can be seen by examining the st and sb registers after using such a D command in a \w escape sequence.) This rule also holds for all the original drawing commands with the exception of De. For the sake of compatibility, GNU troff also follows this rule, even though it produces an ugly result in the case of the Df, Dt, and, to a lesser extent, DE commands. Thus after executing a D command of the form

Dc *x1 y1 x2 y2* ... *xn yn*\n

the current position should be increased by $(\sum_{i=1}^{n} xi; \sum_{i=1}^{n} yi)$.

A continuation convention permits the argument to the x X command to contain newlines: when outputting the argument to the x X command, GNU troff will follow each newline in the argument with a + character (as usual, it will terminate the entire argument with a newline); thus if the line after the line containing the x X command starts with +, then the newline ending the line containing the x X command should be treated as part of the argument to the x X command, the + should be ignored, and the part of the line following the + should be treated like the part of the line following the x X command.

## SEE ALSO

groff_font(5)

# group

group—User group file.

## DESCRIPTION

/etc/group is an ASCII file that defines the groups to which users belong. There is one entry per line, and each line has the format

group_name:passwd:GID:user_list

The field descriptions are

| | |
|---|---|
| group_name | The name of the group. |
| passwd | The (encrypted) group password. If this field is empty, no password is needed. |
| GID | The numerical group ID. |
| user_list | All the group member's usernames, separated by commas. |

## FILES

/etc/group

## SEE ALSO

login(1), newgrp(1), passwd(5)

# history

history—Record of current and recently expired Usenet articles.

## DESCRIPTION

The file /news/lib/history keeps a record of all articles currently stored in the news system, as well as those that have been received but since expired.

The file consists of text lines. Each line corresponds to one article. The file is normally kept sorted in the order in which articles are received, although this is not a requirement. innd(8) appends a new line each time it files an article, and expire(8) builds a new version of the file by removing old articles and purging old entries.

Each line consists of two or three fields separated by a tab, shown below as \t:

<Message-ID>\t date
<Message-ID>\t date \t files

The Message-ID field is the value of the article's Message-ID header, including the angle brackets.

The date field consists of three subfields separated by a tilde. All subfields are the text representation of the number of seconds since the epoch—a time_t; see gettimeofday(2). The first subfield is the article's arrival date. If copies of the article are still present, then the second subfield is either the value of the article's Expires header or a hyphen if no expiration date was specified. If an article has been expired, the second subfield will be a hyphen. The third subfield is the value of the article's Date header, recording when the article was posted.

The `files` field is a set of entries separated by one or more spaces. Each entry consists of the name of the newsgroup, a slash, and the article number. This field is empty if the article has been expired.

For example, an article cross-posted to `comp.sources.unix` and `comp.sources.d` that was posted on February 10, 1991, (and received three minutes later) with an expiration date of May 5, 1991, could have a history line (broken into two lines for display) like the following:

```
<312@litchi.foo.com> \t 666162000˜673329600˜666162180
\t comp.sources.unix/1104 comp.sources.d/7056
```

In addition to the text file, there is a dbz(3z) database associated with the file that uses the Message-ID field as a key to determine the offset in the text file where the associated line begins. For historical reasons, the key includes the trailing `\0` byte (which is not stored in the text file).

## HISTORY

Written by Rich $alz (`rsalz@uunet.uu.net`) for InterNetNews.

## SEE ALSO

dbz(3z), expire(8), innd(8), news-recovery(8)

# hosts.nntp, hosts.nntp.nolimit

`hosts.nntp`, `hosts.nntp.nolimit`—List of hosts that feed NNTP news.

## DESCRIPTION

The file `/news/lib/hosts.nntp` is read by innd(8) to get the list of hosts that feed the local site Usenet news using the NNTP protocol. The server reads this file at startup or when directed to by ctlinnd(8). When a hosts connects to the NNTP port of the system on which innd is running, the server will do a check to see if their Internet address is the same as one of the hosts named in this file. If the host is not mentioned, then innd will spawn an nnrpd(8) to process the connection, with the accepted connection on standard input and standard output.

Comments begin with a number sign (#) and continue through the end of the line. Blank lines and comments are also ignored. All other lines should consist of two or three fields separated by a colon.

The first field should be either an Internet address in dotted-quad format or an address that can be parsed by `gethostbyname(3)`. If a host's entry has multiple addresses, all of them will be added to the access list. The second field, which may be blank, is the password the foreign host is required to use when first connecting. The third field, which may be omitted, is a list of newsgroups to which the host may post articles. This list is parsed as a newsfeeds(5) subscription list; groups not in the list are ignored.

Because innd is usually started at system boot time, the local nameserver may not be fully operational when innd parses this file. As a work-around, a ctlinnd reload command can be performed after a delay of an hour or so. It is also possible to provide both a host's name and its dotted-quad address in the file.

For example:

```
## FOO has a password, UUNET doesn't.
## UUNET cannot post to local groups.
## These are comment lines.
news.foo.com:magic
uunet.uu.net::!foo.*
```

If the file contains passwords, it should not be world-readable. The file `/news/lib/hosts.nntp.nolimit`, if it exists, is read whenever the hosts.nntp file is read. It has the same format, although only the first field is used. Any host mentioned in this file is not subject to the incoming connections limit specified by innd's -c flag. This can be used to allow local hosts or time-sensitive peers to connect regardless of the local conditions.

## HISTORY

Written by Rich $alz (`rsalz@uunet.uu.net`) for InterNetNews.

## SEE ALSO

`ctlinnd(8)`, `innd(8)`, `nnrpd(8)`

# hosts_access

hosts_access—Format of host access control files.

## DESCRIPTION

This manual page describes a simple access control language that is based on client (hostname/address, username) and server (process name) patterns. Examples are given at the end. The impatient reader can skip to the "Examples" section for a quick introduction.

In the following text, `daemon` is the process name of a network daemon process, and client is the name or address of a host requesting service. Network daemon process names are specified in the `inetd` configuration file.

## ACCESS CONTROL FILES

The access control software consults two files. The search stops at the first match:

Access will be granted when a (*daemon,client*) pair matches an entry in the `/etc/hosts.allow` file.

Otherwise, access will be denied when a (*daemon,client*) pair matches an entry in the `/etc/hosts.deny` file.

Otherwise, access will be granted.

A non-existing access control file is treated as if it were an empty file. Thus, access control can be turned off by providing no access control files.

## ACCESS CONTROL RULES

Each access control file consists of zero or more lines of text. These lines are processed in order of appearance. The search terminates when a match is found.

A newline character is ignored when it is preceded by a backslash character.

Blank lines or lines that begin with a # character are ignored.

All other lines should satisfy the following format, things between [] being optional:

*daemon_list* : *client_list* [ : *shell_command* ]

*daemon_list* is a list of one or more daemon process names (`argv[0]` values) or wildcards.

*client_list* is a list of one or more hostnames, host addresses, patterns, or wildcards that will be matched against the remote hostname or address.

List elements should be separated by blanks or commas.

With the exception of NIS (YP) netgroup lookups, all access control checks are case insensitive.

## PATTERNS

The access control language implements the following patterns:

A string that begins with a . character: A client name or address is matched if its last components match the specified pattern. For example, the pattern `.tue.nl` matches the hostname `wzv.win.tue.nl`.

A string that ends with a . character: A client name or address is matched if its first fields match the given string. For example, the pattern `131.155.` matches the address of (almost) every host on the Eindhoven University network ($131.155.x.x$).

A string that begins with a @ character is treated as a netgroup name: Netgroups are usually supported on systems with NIS (formerly YP) databases. A client hostname is matched if it is a (host) member of the specified netgroup.

An expression of the form *n.n.n.n/m.m.m.m* is interpreted as a *net/mask* pair. A client address is matched if *net* is equal to the bitwise AND of the address and the *mask*. For example, the *net/mask* pattern 131.155.72.0/255.255.254.0 matches every address in the range 131.155.72.0 through 131.155.73.255.

## WILDCARDS

The access control language supports explicit wildcards:

| | |
|---|---|
| ALL | If this token appears in a daemon list, it matches all network daemon process names. If the ALL token appears in a client list, it matches all client names and addresses. |
| LOCAL | Matches any string that does not contain a dot character. Typical use is in client lists. |
| UNKNOWN | Matches any host whose name or address are unknown. Should be used with care: Hostnames may be unavailable due to temporary nameserver problems. A network address will be unavailable when the software cannot figure out what type of network it is talking to. |
| KNOWN | Matches any host whose name and address are known. Should be used with care: Hostnames may be unavailable due to temporary nameserver problems. A network address will be unavailable when the software cannot figure out what type of network it is talking to. |
| FAIL | Like the ALL wildcard but causes the software to pretend that the scan of the current access control table fails. FAIL is being phased out; it will become an undocumented feature. The EXCEPT operator is a much cleaner alternative. |

## OPERATORS

| | |
|---|---|
| EXCEPT | Intended use is of the form: *list_1* EXCEPT *list_2*; this construct matches anything that matches *list_1* unless it matches *list_2*. This construct can be used in daemon lists and in client lists. The EXCEPT operator can be nested: If the control language would permit the use of parentheses, a EXCEPT b EXCEPT c would parse as (a EXCEPT (b EXCEPT c)). |

## SHELL COMMANDS

If the first-matched access control rule contains a shell command, that command is subjected to the following substitutions:

| | |
|---|---|
| %a | Expands to the remote host address. |
| %c | Expands to client information: *user@host*, *user@address*, a hostname, or just an address, depending on how much information is available. |
| %h | Expands to the remote hostname (or address, if the hostname is unavailable). |
| %d | Expands to the daemon process name (argv[0] value). |
| %p | Expands to the daemon process ID. |
| %u | Expands to the remote username (or unknown). |
| %% | Expands to a single % character. |

Characters in % expansions that may confuse the shell are replaced by underscores. The result is executed by a /bin/sh child process with standard input, output, and error connected to /dev/null. Specify an & at the end of the command if you do not want to wait until it has completed.

Shell commands should not rely on the PATH setting of the inetd. Instead, they should use absolute pathnames, or they should begin with an explicit PATH=*whatever* statement.

## REMOTE USERNAME LOOKUP

When the client host supports the RFC 931 protocol or one of its descendants (TAP, IDENT) the wrapper programs can retrieve additional information about the owner of a connection. When available, remote username information is logged together with the client hostname and can be used to match patterns like

daemon_list : ... user_pattern@host_pattern ...

The daemon wrappers can be configured at compile time to perform rule-driven username lookups (default) or to always interrogate the client host. In the case of rule-driven username lookups, the preceding rule would cause username lookup only when both the *daemon_list* and the *host_pattern* match.

A user pattern has the same syntax as a daemon process name, hostname, or host address pattern, so the same wildcards and so on apply (but netgroup membership of users is not supported). One should not get carried away with username lookups, however.

The remote username information cannot be trusted when it is needed most—that is, when the remote system has been compromised. In general, ALL and (UN)KNOWN are the only username patterns that make sense.

Username lookups are possible only with TCP-based services and only when the client host runs a suitable daemon; in all other cases the result is unknown.

A well-known UNIX kernel bug may cause loss of service when username lookups are blocked by a firewall. The wrapper README document describes a procedure to find out if your kernel has this bug.

Username lookups cause noticeable delays for PC users. The default time-out for username lookups is ten seconds: too short to cope with slow networks but long enough to irritate PC users.

Selective username lookups can alleviate the last problem. For example, a rule like

*daemon_list* : @*pcnetgroup* ALL@ALL

would match members of the *pcnetgroup* without doing username lookups but would perform username lookups with all other systems.

## EXAMPLES

The language is flexible enough that different types of access control policy can be expressed with a minimum of fuss. Although the language uses two access control tables, the most common policies can be implemented with one of the tables being trivial or even empty.

When reading the following examples, it is important to realize that the allow table is scanned before the deny table, that the search terminates when a match is found, and that access is granted when no match is found at all.

The examples use host and domain names. They can be improved by including address or network/netmask information to reduce the impact of temporary nameserver lookup failures.

## MOSTLY CLOSED

In this case, access is denied by default. Only explicitly authorized hosts are permitted access.

The default policy (no access) is implemented with a trivial deny file:

/etc/hosts.deny:

ALL: ALL

This denies all service to all hosts, unless they are permitted access by entries in the allow file.

The explicitly authorized hosts are listed in the allow file:

/etc/hosts.allow:

ALL: LOCAL @*some_netgroup*
ALL: .foobar.edu EXCEPT terminalserver.foobar.edu

The first rule permits access to all services from hosts in the local domain (no . in the hostname) and from members of the *some_netgroup* netgroup. The second rule permits access to all services from all hosts in the .foobar.edu domain, with the exception of terminalserver.foobar.edu.

## MOSTLY OPEN

Here, access is granted by default; only explicitly specified hosts are refused service.

The default policy (access granted) makes the allow file redundant so that it can be omitted. The explicitly non-authorized hosts are listed in the deny file:

```
/etc/hosts.deny:
```

```
ALL: some.host.name, .some.domain
ALL EXCEPT in.fingerd: other.host.name, .other.domain
```

The first rule denies some hosts all services; the second rule still permits finger requests from other hosts.

## BOOBY TRAPS

The next example permits tftp requests from hosts in the local domain. Requests from any other hosts are denied. Instead of the requested file, a finger probe is sent to the offending host. The result is mailed to the superuser.

```
/etc/hosts.allow:
```

```
in.tftpd: LOCAL, .my.domain
/etc/hosts.deny:
in.tftpd: ALL: (/some/where/safe_finger -l @%h ¦ \
/usr/ucb/mail -s %d-%h root) &
```

The safe_finger command comes with the tcpd wrapper and should be installed in a suitable place. It limits possible damage from data sent by the remote finger server. It gives better protection than the standard finger command.

The expansion of the %h (remote host) and %d (service name) sequences is described in the section on shell commands.

Warning: Do not booby-trap your finger daemon, unless you are prepared for infinite finger loops.

On network firewall systems, this trick can be carried even further. The typical network firewall only provides a limited set of services to the outer world. All other services can be "bugged" just like the preceding tftp example. The result is an excellent early-warning system.

## DIAGNOSTICS

An error is reported when a syntax error is found in a host access control rule, when the length of an access control rule exceeds the capacity of an internal buffer, when an access control rule is not terminated by a newline character, when the result of %<*character*> expansion would overflow an internal buffer, and when a system call fails that shouldn't. All problems are reported via the syslog daemon.

## FILES

/etc/hosts.allow, (*daemon,client*) pairs that are granted access.

/etc/hosts.deny, (*daemon,client*) pairs that are denied access.

## SEE ALSO

tcpd(8), TCP/IP daemon wrapper program

## BUGS

If a nameserver lookup times out, the hostname will not be available to the access control software, even though the host is registered.

Domain nameserver lookups are case insensitive; NIS (formerly YP) netgroup lookups are case sensitive.

## AUTHOR

Wietse Venema (wietse@wzv.win.tue.nl), Department of Mathematics and Computing Science, Eindhoven University of Technology, Den Dolech 2, P.O. Box 513, 5600 MB Eindhoven, The Netherlands.

# hosts_options

hosts_options—Host access control language extensions.

## DESCRIPTION

This document describes optional extensions to the language described in the hosts_access(5) document. The extensions are enabled at program build time by editing the makefile.

The extensible language uses the following format:

*daemon_list : client_list : option : option ...*

The first two fields are described in the hosts_access(5) manual page. The remainder of the rules is a list of zero or more options. Any : characters within options should be protected with a backslash.

An option is of the form *keyword* or *keyword = value*. Options are processed in the specified order. With some options, the value is subjected to %<*character*> substitutions.

## OPTIONS

| | |
|---|---|
| severity = mail.info | Change the severity level at which the event will be logged. Facility names (such as mail) are optional and are not supported on systems with older syslog implementations. The severity option can be used to emphasize or to completely ignore specific events. |
| allow (deny) | Grant (deny) service, even when the matched rule was found in the hosts.deny (hosts.allow) file. These options must appear at the end of a rule. |

With the allow and deny keywords, it is possible to keep all access control rules within a single file—for example, in the hosts.allow file:

```
ALL: .friendly.domain: allow
ALL: ALL: deny
```

This permits access from specific hosts only. On the other hand,

```
ALL: .trouble.makers: deny
ALL: ALL: allow
```

This permits access from all hosts except a few troublemakers.

| | |
|---|---|
| twist = shell_command | Replace the current process by an instance of the specified shell command, after performing the %<*character*> expansions described in the hosts_access(5) manual page. stdin, stdout, and stderr are connected to the remote client process. This option must appear at the end of a rule. Examples: |
| in.ftpd : ... : twist = /bin/echo 421 | Some bounce message sends a customized bounce message to the remote client instead of running the real FTP daemon. |
| in.telnetd : ... : twist = PATH=/some/other; exec in.telnetd | Runs /some/other/in.telnetd without polluting its command-line array or its process environment. Warning: In case of UDP services, do not twist into commands that use the standard I/O or the read(2)/write(2) routines to communicate with the client process; UDP requires other I/O primitives. |
| spawn = shell_command | Execute the shell command in a child process, after performing the %<*character*> expansions described in the hosts_access(5) manual page. The command |

| | |
|---|---|
| | is executed with stdin, stdout, and stderr connected to the null device so that it won't mess up the conversation with the remote host. Example: |
| spawn = (/some/where/safe_finger -l @%h ¦ /usr/ucb/mail root) & | Executes, in a background child process, the shell command safe_finger -l @%h ¦ mail root after replacing %h by the name or address of the remote host. |
| | The example uses the safe_finger command instead of the regular finger command to limit possible damage from data sent by the finger server. The safe_finger command is part of the daemon wrapper package; it is a wrapper around the regular finger command that filters the data sent by the remote host. |
| umask = 022 | Like the umask command that is built into the shell. An umask of 022 prevents the creation of files with group and world write permission. The umask argument should be an octal number. |
| keepalive | Causes the server to periodically send a message to the client. The connection is considered broken when the client does not respond. The keepalive option can be useful when users turn off their machine while it is still connected to a server. The keepalive option is not useful for datagram (UDP) services. |
| linger = *number_of_seconds* | Specifies how long the kernel will try to deliver not-yet delivered data after the server process closes a connection. |
| nice = niceval<br>nice (no argument) | Change the nice value of the process (default 10). Specify a positive value to spend more CPU resources on other processes. |
| user = nobody | Assume the privileges of the nobody account. This is useful with inetd implementations that run all services with root privilege. It is good practice to run services such as finger at a reduced privilege level. |
| group = tty | Assume the privileges of the tty group. This is useful mostly in combination with the user option. In order to switch both user and group IDs, switch group ID before switching user ID. |
| setenv = *name value* | Place a (*name*, *value*) pair into the process environment. The *value* is subjected to %<*character*> expansions and may contain whitespace (but leading and trailing blanks are stripped off). |
| | Warning: Many network daemons reset their environment before spawning a login or shell process. |

rfc931 = *timeout_in_seconds*

rfc931 (no argument)

Look up the remote user name with the RFC 931 (ident and so on) protocol. This option is silently ignored in case of services based on transports other than TCP. It requires that the client system runs an RFC 931 (ident and so on) compliant daemon and may cause noticeable delays with connections from non-UNIX hosts. The time-out period is optional. If no time-out is specified, a default value is taken.

## DIAGNOSTICS

When a syntax error is found in an access control rule, the error is reported to the syslog daemon; further options will be ignored, and service is denied.

## SEE ALSO

hosts_access(5), the default access control language

## AUTHOR

Wietse Venema (wietse@wzv.win.tue.nl), Department of Mathematics and Computing Science, Eindhoven University of Technology, Den Dolech 2, P.O. Box 513, 5600 MB Eindhoven, The Netherlands.

# inittab

inittab—Format of the inittab file used by the SysV-compatible init process.

## DESCRIPTION

The inittab file describes which processes are started at bootup and during normal operation (such as /etc/rc, gettys). init distinguishes multiple run levels, of which each can have its own set of processes that are started. Valid *runlevels* are 0–6 and A, B, and C for ondemand entries. An entry in the inittab file has the following format:

*id:runlevels:action:process*

Lines beginning with # are ignored.

| | |
|---|---|
| *id* | A unique two-character-sequence which identifies an entry in inittab. |
| | Note: For gettys or other login processes, the *id* field should be the tty suffix of the corresponding tty, such as 1 for tty1. Otherwise, the login accounting will not work correctly. This is a bug in login and will be fixed. |
| *runlevels* | Describes in which run levels the specified action should be taken. |
| *action* | Describes which action should be taken. |
| *process* | Specifies the process to be executed. If the process field starts with a + character, init will not do utmp and wtmp accounting for that process. This is needed for gettys that insist on doing their own utmp/wtmp housekeeping. This is also a historic bug. |

Valid actions are

| | |
|---|---|
| respawn | The process will be restarted whenever it terminates (such as getty). |
| wait | The process will be started once when the specified run level is entered and init will wait for its termination. |
| once | The process will be executed once when the specified run level is entered. |
| boot | The process will be executed during system boot. The run level field is ignored. |

| bootwait | The process will be executed during system boot while init waits for its termination (such as /etc/rc). The *runlevel* field is ignored. |
| off | This does nothing. |
| ondemand | A process marked with ondemand will be executed whenever the specified ondemand run level is called. However, no *runlevel* change will occur. |
| initdefault | An initdefault-entry specifies the run level that should be entered after system boot. If none exists, init will ask for a *runlevel* on the console. |
| sysinit | The process will be executed during system boot. It will be executed before any boot or bootwait entries. |
| powerwait | The process will be executed when init receives the SIGPWR signal, indicating that there is something wrong with the power. init will wait for the process to finish before continuing. |
| powerfail | As powerwait but init will not wait for the processes completion. |
| powerokwait | The process will be executed when init receives the SIGPWR signal, provided there is a file called /etc/powerstatus containing the word OK. This means that the power has come back again. |
| ctrlaltdel | The process will be executed when init receives the SIGINT signal. This means that someone on the system console pressed the Ctrl+Alt+Del key combination. Typically, one wants to execute some sort of shutdown either to get into single–user level or to reboot the machine. |

The *runlevel* field may contain multiple characters for different run levels, such as 123 if the process should be started in run levels 1, 2 and 3. Ondemand entries may contain an A, B, or C. The *runlevel* field of sysinit, boot, and bootwait entries are ignored.

When the run level is changed, any running processes that are not specified for the new run level are killed, first with SIGTERM and then with SIGKILL.

## EXAMPLES

This is an example of an inittab that resembles the old Linux inittab:

```
# inittab for linux
id:1:initdefault:
rc::bootwait:/etc/rc
1:1:respawn:/etc/getty 9600 tty1
2:1:respawn:/etc/getty 9600 tty2
3:1:respawn:/etc/getty 9600 tty3
4:1:respawn:/etc/getty 9600 tty4
```

This inittab file executes /etc/rc during boot and starts gettys on tty1–tty4.

A more elaborate inittab with different run levels (see the comments inside) is

```
#Level to run in
id:4:initdefault:
ud::boot:/etc/update
rc::bootwait:/etc/rc
cr::boot:/etc/crond
#
# level 1: getty on tty1
# level 2: getty on tty1-4
# level 3: tty1-4, dialin via modem(ttys2)
# level 4: tty1-4, ttyb
#
mr:126:once:/usr/bin/nodialin
mi:345:once:/usr/bin/dialin
1:1234:respawn:/etc/getty 9600 tty1
2:234:respawn:/etc/getty 9600 tty2
3:234:respawn:/etc/getty 9600 tty3
```

```
4:234:respawn:/etc/getty 9600 tty4
s2:3:respawn:/etc/mgetty ttys2 19200
b:4:respawn:/etc/getty 19200L ttyb
ca::ctrlaltdel:/etc/shutdown -t3 -rf now
```

## FILES

/etc/inittab

## AUTHOR

init was written by Miquel van Smoorenburg (miquels@drinkel.nl.mugnet.org). The manual page was written by Sebastian Lederer (lederer@francium.informatik.uni-bonn.de) and modified by Michael Haardt (u31b3hs@pool.informatik.rwth-aachen.de).

## SEE ALSO

init(8), telinit(8)

*13 May 1993*

# inn.conf

inn.conf—Configuration data for InterNetNews programs.

## DESCRIPTION

The file /news/lib/inn.conf is used to determine various parameters. Blank lines and lines starting with a number sign (#) are ignored. All other lines specify parameters that may be read and should be of the following form:

*name* : [optional whitespace] *value*

Everything after the whitespace and up to the end of the line is taken as the *value*; multi-word values should not be put in quotes. The case of names is significant; server is not the same as Server or SERVER.

Some parameters specified in the file may be overridden by environment variables, and some file parameters may be used to mask real data, such as when hiding a cluster of hosts behind a single electronic mail hostname. The current set of parameters is as follows:

| | |
|---|---|
| fromhost | This is the name of the host to use when building the From header line. The default is the fully qualified domain name of the local host. The value of the FROMHOST environment variable, if it exists, overrides this. |
| moderatormailer | This names the default machine that contains forwarding aliases for all moderated groups. It is only used if the moderators(5) file doesn't exist or if the group is not matched by that file. The value is interpreted as a pattern match; see moderators(5). |
| organization | This specifies what to put in the Organization header if it is blank. The value of the ORGANIZATION environment variable, if it exists, overrides this. |
| pathhost | This specifies how to name the local site when building the Path header line. The default is the fully qualified domain name of the local host. |
| server | This specifies the name of the NNTP server to which an article should be posted. The value of the NNTPSERVER environment variable, if it exists, overrides this. |
| domain | This should be the domain name of the local host. It should not have a leading period, and it should not be a full host address. It is used only if the GetFQDN routine in libinn(3) cannot get the fully qualified domain name by using either the gethostname(2) or gethostbyname(3) calls. The check is very simple; if either routine returns a name with a period in it, then it is assumed to have the full domain name. |

Three parameters are used only by nnrpd when accepting postings from clients:

| | |
|---|---|
| mime-version | If this parameter is present, then nnrpd will add the necessary MIME (Multipurpose Internet Mail Extensions) headers to all any articles that do not have a Mime-Version header. This parameter specifies the MIME version and should normally be 1.0. |
| mime-contenttype | If MIME headers are being added, this parameter specifies the value of the Content-Type header. The default value is text/plain; charset=US-ASCII. |
| mime-encoding | If MIME headers are being added, this parameter specifies the value of the Content-Transfer-Encoding header. The default value is 7bit. |

Note that this file can be identical on all machines in an organization.

## EXAMPLE

| | |
|---|---|
| fromhost: | foo.com |
| moderatormailer: | %s@uunet.uu.net |
| organization: | Foo, Incorporated |
| #pathhost: | Use FQDN. |
| server: | news.foo.com |
| domain: | foo.com |

This file is intended to be fairly static; any changes made to it are typically not reflected until a program restarts.

## HISTORY

Written by Rich $alz (rsalz@uunet.uu.net) for InterNetNews.

## SEE ALSO

libinn(3), moderators(5)

# innwatch.ctl

innwatch.ctl—Control Usenet supervision by innwatch.

## DESCRIPTION

The file /news/lib/innwatch.ctl is used to determine what actions are taken during the periodic supervisions by innwatch.

The file consists of a series of lines; blank lines and lines beginning with a number sign (#) are ignored. All other lines consist of seven fields, each preceded by a delimiting character:

:label:state:condition:test:limit:command:reason

The delimiter can be any one of several non-alphanumeric characters that does not appear elsewhere in the line; there is no way to quote it to include it in any of the fields. Any of !, ,, :, @, ;, or ? is a good choice. Each line can have a different delimiter; the first character on each line is the delimiter for that line. Whitespace surrounding delimiters, except before the first, is ignored and does not form part of the fields; whitespace within fields is permitted. All delimiters must be present.

The first field is a label for the control line. It is used as an internal state indicator and in ctlinnd messages to control the server. If omitted, the line number is used.

The second field specifies when this control line should be used. It consists of a list of labels and special indicators separated by whitespace. If the current state matches against any of the labels in this field, this line will be used as described below. The values that may be used are

| | |
|---|---|
| - | This line matches if the current state is the same as the label on this line, or if the current state is run, the initial state. This is also the default state if this field is empty. |

| | |
|---|---|
| + | This line matches if the current state is run. |
| * | This line always matches. |
| label | This line matches if the current state is the specified *label*. |
| -label | This line matches if the current state is not the specified *label*. |

The third field specifies a shell command that is invoked if this line matches. Do not use any shell filename expansion characters such as *, ?, or [ (even quoted, they're not likely to work as intended). If the command succeeds, as indicated by its exit status, it is expected to have printed a single integer to standard output. This gives the value of this control line, to be used below. If the command fails, the line is ignored. The command is executed with its current directory set to the newsspool directory, /news/spool.

The fourth field specifies the operator to use to test the value returned above. It should be one of the two-letter numeric test operators defined in test(1) such as eq, lt, and the like. The leading dash (-) should not be included.

The fifth field specifies a constant with which to compare the value using the operator just defined. This is done by invoking the command

```
test value -operator constant
```

The line is said to "succeed" if it returns true.

The sixth field specifies what should be done if the line succeeds and in some cases if it fails. Any of the following words may be used:

| | |
|---|---|
| throttle | Causes innwatch to throttle the server if this line succeeds. It also sets the state to the value of the line's label. If the line fails and the state was previously equal to the label on this line (that is, this line had previously succeeded), then a go command will be sent to the server, and innwatch will return to the run state. The throttle is only performed if the current state is run or a state other than the label of this line, regardless of whether the command succeeds. |
| pause | Is identical to throttle except that the server is paused. |
| shutdown | Sends a shutdown command to the server. It is for emergency use only. |
| flush | Sends a flush command to the server. |
| go | Causes innwatch to send a go command to the server and to set the state to run. |
| exit | Causes innwatch to exit. |
| skip | The result of the control file is skipped for the current pass. |

The last field specifies the reason that is used in those ctlinnd commands that require one. More strictly, it is part of the reason; innwatch appends some information to it. In order to enable other sites to recognize the state of the local innd server, this field should usually be set to one of several standard values. Use No space if the server is rejecting articles because of a lack of filesystem resources. Use loadav if the server is rejecting articles because of a lack of CPU resources.

Once innwatch has taken some action as a consequence of its control line, it skips the rest of the control file for this pass. If the action was to restart the server (that is, issue a go command), then the next pass will commence almost immediately so that innwatch can discover any other condition that may mean that the server should be suspended again.

## EXAMPLES

```
@@@df .¦awk 'NR==2 {print $4}'@lt@10000@throttle@No space
@@@df -i .¦awk 'NR==2 {print $4}'@lt@1000@throttle@No space (inodes)
```

The first line causes the server to be throttled if the free space drops below 10000 units (using whatever units df uses) and restarted again when free space increases above the threshold.

The second line does the same for inodes.

The next three lines act as a group and should appear in the following order. It is easier to explain them, however, if they are described from the last up.

```
!load!load hiload!loadavg!lt!5!go!
:hiload:+ load:loadavg:gt:8:throttle:loadav
/load/+/loadavg/ge/6/pause/loadav
```

The final line causes the server to be paused if innwatch is in the run state and the load average rises to, or above, six. The state is set to load when this happens. The previous line causes the server to be throttled when innwatch is in the run or load state, and the load average rises above eight. The state is set to hiload when this happens. Note that innwatch can switch the server from paused to throttled if the load average rises from below six to between six and seven and then to above eight. The first line causes the server to be sent a go command if innwatch is in the load or hiload state and the load average drops below five.

Note that all three lines assume a mythical command loadavg that is assumed to print the current load average as an integer. In more practical circumstances, a pipe of uptime into awk is more likely to be useful.

## BUGS

This file must be tailored for each individual site; the sample supplied is truly no more than a sample. The file should be ordered so that the more common problems are tested first.

The run state is not actually identified by the label with that three letter name, and using it will not work as expected.

Using an "unusual" character for the delimiter such as (, *, &, " ", and the like is likely to lead to obscure and hard-to-locate bugs.

## HISTORY

Written by (kre@munnari.oz.au) for InterNetNews.

## SEE ALSO

innd*(8)*, ctlinnd*(8)*, news.daily*(8)*

# ipc

ipc—System V interprocess communication mechanisms.

## SYNOPSIS

```
# include <sys/types.h>
# include <sys/ipc.h>
# include <sys/msg.h>
# include <sys/sem.h>
# include <sys/shm.h>
```

## DESCRIPTION

The manual page refers to the Linux implementation of the System V interprocess communication mechanisms: message queues, semaphore sets, and shared memory segments. In the following, the word resource means an instantiation of one among such mechanisms.

### RESOURCE ACCESS PERMISSIONS

For each resource, the system uses a common structure of type struct ipc_perm to store information needed in determining permissions to perform an ipc operation. The ipc_perm structure, defined by the <sys/ipc.h> system header file, includes the following members:

```
ushort cuid; /* creator user id */
ushort cgid; /* creator group id */
ushort uid; /* owner user id */
ushort gid; /* owner group id */
ushort mode; /* r/w permissions */
```

The mode member of the `ipc_perm` structure defines, with its lower nine bits, the access permissions to the resource for a process executing an `ipc` system call. The permissions are interpreted as follows:

| | |
|---|---|
| `0400` | Read by user. |
| `0200` | Write by user. |
| `0040` | Read by group. |
| `0020` | Write by group. |
| `0004` | Read by others. |
| `0002` | Write by others. |

Bits 0100, 0010, and 0001 (the execute bits) are unused by the system. Furthermore "write" effectively means "alter" for a semaphore set.

The same system header file defines also the following symbolic constants:

| | |
|---|---|
| `IPC_CREAT` | Create entry if key doesn't exists. |
| `IPC_EXCL` | Fail if key exists. |
| `IPC_NOWAIT` | Error if request must wait. |
| `IPC_PRIVATE` | Private key. |
| `IPC_RMID` | Remove resource. |
| `IPC_SET` | Set resource options. |
| `IPC_STAT` | Get resource options. |

Note that `IPC_PRIVATE` is a `key_t` type, whereas all the others symbolic constants are flag fields ORable into an `int` type variable.

## MESSAGE QUEUES

A message queue is uniquely identified by a positive integer (its `msqid`) and has an associated data structure of type `struct msquid_ds`, defined in `<sys/msg.h>`, containing the following members:

```
struct ipc_perm msg_perm;
ushort msg_qnum; /* no of messages on queue */
ushort msg_qbytes; /* bytes max on a queue */
ushort msg_lspid; /* pid of last msgsnd call */
ushort msg_lrpid; /* pid of last msgrcv call */
time_t msg_stime; /* last msgsnd time */
time_t msg_rtime; /* last msgrcv time */
time_t msg_ctime; /* last change time */
```

| | |
|---|---|
| `msg_perm` | `ipc_perm` structure that specifies the access permissions on the message queue. |
| `msg_qnum` | Number of messages currently on the message queue. |
| `msg_qbytes` | Maximum number of bytes of message text allowed on the message queue. |
| `msg_lspid` | ID of the process that performed the last `msgsnd` system call. |
| `msg_lrpid` | ID of the process that performed the last `msgrcv` system call. |
| `msg_stime` | Time of the last `msgsnd` system call. |
| `msg_rtime` | Time of the last `msgcv` system call. |
| `msg_ctime` | Time of the last system call that changed a member of the `msqid_ds` structure. |

## SEMAPHORE SETS

A semaphore set is uniquely identified by a positive integer (its `semid`) and has an associated data structure of type `struct semid_ds`, defined in `<sys/sem.h>`, containing the following members:

```
struct ipc_perm sem_perm;
time_t sem_otime; /* last operation time */
```

```
time_t sem_ctime; /* last change time */
ushort sem_nsems; /* count of sems in set */
```

| | |
|---|---|
| sem_perm | ipc_perm structure that specifies the access permissions on the semaphore set. |
| sem_otime | Time of last semop system call. |
| sem_ctime | Time of last semctl system call that changed a member of the above structure or of one semaphore belonging to the set. |
| sem_nsems | Number of semaphores in the set. Each semaphore of the set is referenced by a non-negative integer ranging from 0 to sem_nsems-1. |

A semaphore is a data structure of type struct sem containing the following members:

```
ushort semval; /* semaphore value */
short sempid; /* pid for last operation */
ushort semncnt; /* no. of awaiting semval to increase */
ushort semzcnt; /* no. of awaiting semval = 0 */
```

| | |
|---|---|
| semval | Semaphore value: a non-negative integer. |
| sempid | ID of the last process that performed a semaphore operation on this semaphore. |
| semncnt | Number of processes suspended awaiting for semval to increase. |
| semznt | Number of processes suspended awaiting for semval to become zero. |

## SHARED MEMORY SEGMENTS

A shared memory segment is uniquely identified by a positive integer (its shmid) and has an associated data structure of type struct shmid_ds, defined in <sys/shm.h>, containing the following members:

```
struct ipc_perm shm_perm;
int shm_segsz; /* size of segment */
ushort shm_cpid; /* pid of creator */
ushort shm_lpid; /* pid, last operation */
short shm_nattch; /* no. of current attaches */
time_t shm_atime; /* time of last attach */
time_t shm_dtime; /* time of last detach */
time_t shm_ctime; /* time of last change */
```

| | |
|---|---|
| shm_perm | ipc_perm structure that specifies the access permissions on the shared memory segment. |
| shm_segsz | Size in bytes of the shared memory segment. |
| shm_cpid | ID of the process that created the shared memory segment. |
| shm_lpid | ID of the last process that executed a shmat or shmdt system call. |
| shm_nattch | Number of current alive attaches for this shared memory segment. |
| shm_atime | Time of the last shmat system call. |
| shm_dtime | Time of the last shmdt system call. |
| shm_ctime | Time of the last shmctl system call that changed shmid_ds. |

## SEE ALSO

ftok(3), msgctl(2), msgget(2), msgrcv(2), msgsnd(2), semctl(2), semget(2), semop(2), shmat(2), shmctl(2), shmget(2), shmdt (2)

*Linux 0.99.13, 1 November 1993*

# issue

issue—Issue identification file.

## DESCRIPTION

The file /etc/issue is a text file that contains a message or system identification to be printed before the login prompt. It may contain various @*char* and \*char* sequences if supported by getty(1).

## FILES

/etc/issue

## SEE ALSO

getty(1), motd(5)

*Linux, 24 July 1993*

# lilo.conf

lilo.conf—Configuration file for LILO.

## DESCRIPTION

This file, by default /etc/lilo.conf, is read by the boot loader installer LILO (see lilo(8)).

It might look as follows:

```
boot = /dev/hda
delay = 40
compact
vga = normal
root = /dev/hda1
read-only
image = /zImage-1.5.99
        label = try
image = /zImage-1.0.9
        label = 1.0.9
image = /tamu/vmlinuz
        label = tamu
        root = /dev/hdb2
        vga = ask
other = /dev/hda3
        label = dos
        table = /dev/hda
```

This configuration file specifies that LILO uses the Master Boot Record on /dev/hda. (For a discussion of the various ways to use LILO and the interaction with other operating systems, see user.tex from the LILO documentation.)

When booting, the boot loader will wait 4 seconds (40 deciseconds) for you to press Shift. If you don't, then the first kernel image mentioned (/zImage-1.5.99, which you probably installed just 5 minutes ago) will be booted. If you do, the boot loader will ask you which image to boot. In case you forgot the possible choices, press Tab (or ? if you have a U.S. keyboard), and you will be presented with a menu. You now have the choice of booting this brand new kernel, an old trusted kernel, or a kernel on another root file system (just in case you did something stupid on your usual root) or booting a different operating system. There can be up to 16 images mentioned in lilo.conf.

As can be seen previously, a configuration file starts with a number of global options (the top six lines in the example), followed by descriptions of the options for the various images. An option in an image description will override a global option.

## GLOBAL OPTIONS

There are many possible keywords. The description that follows is almost literally from user.tex (just slightly abbreviated):

backup=*backup-file*

Copy the original boot sector to *backup-file* (which may also be a device, such as /dev/null) instead of /boot/boot.NNNN.

boot=*boot-device*

Sets the name of the device (such as a hard disk partition) that contains the boot sector. If this keyword is omitted, the boot sector is read from (and possibly written to) the device that is currently mounted as root.

compact

Tries to merge read requests for adjacent sectors into a single read request. This drastically reduces load time and keeps the map smaller. Using compact is especially recommended when booting from a floppy disk.

default=*name*

Uses the specified image as the default boot image. If default is omitted, the image appearing first in the configuration file is used.

delay=*tsecs*

Specifies the number of tenths of a second the boot loader should wait before booting the first image. This is useful on systems that immediately boot from the hard disk after enabling the keyboard. The boot loader doesn't wait if delay is omitted or is set to zero.

disk=*device-name*

Defines non-standard parameters for the specified disk. See section "Disk Geometry" of user.tex for details.

disktab=*disktab-file*

Specifies the name of the disk parameter table. The map installer looks for /etc/disktab if disktab is omitted. The use of disktabs is discouraged.

fix-table

This allows LILO to adjust 3-D addresses in partition tables. Each partition entry contains a 3-D (sector/head/cylinder) and a linear address of the first and the last sector of the partition. If a partition is not track-aligned and if certain other operating systems (such as PC/MS-DOS or OS/2) are using the same disk, they may change the 3-D address. LILO can store its boot sector only on partitions where both address types correspond. LILO readjusts incorrect 3-D start addresses if fix-table is set.

Warning: This does not guarantee that other operating systems may not attempt to reset the address later. It is also possible that this change has other, unexpected side effects. The correct fix is to repartition the drive with a program that does align partitions to tracks. Also, with some disks (such as some large EIDE disks with address translation enabled), under some circumstances, it may even be unavoidable to have conflicting partition table entries.

force-backup=*backup-file*

Like backup but overwrite an old backup copy if it exists.

ignore-table

Tells LILO to ignore corrupt partition tables.

install=*boot-sector*

Install the specified file as the new boot sector. If install is omitted, /boot/boot.b is used as the default.

linear

Generate linear sector addresses instead of sector/head/cylinder addresses. Linear addresses are translated at runtime and do not depend on disk geometry. Note that boot disks may not be portable if linear is used because the BIOS service to determine the disk geometry does not work reliably for floppy disks. When using linear with large disks, /sbin/lilo may generate references to inaccessible disk areas because 3-D sector addresses are not known before boot time.

lock

Enables automatic recording of boot command lines as the defaults for the following boots. This way, LILO "locks" on a choice until it is manually overridden.

map=*map-file*

Specifies the location of the map file. If map is omitted, the file /boot/map is used.

message=*message-file*

Specifies a file containing a message that is displayed before the boot prompt. No message is displayed while waiting for a shifting key after printing LILO . In the message, the FF character (Ctrl+L) clears the local screen. The size of the message file is limited to 65,535 bytes. The map file has to be rebuilt if the message file is changed or moved.

nowarn

Disables warnings about possible future dangers.

| | |
|---|---|
| optional | The per-image option optional applies to all images. |
| password=*password* | The per-image option password=... applies to all images. |
| prompt | Forces entering the boot prompt without expecting any prior key presses. Unattended reboots are impossible if prompt is set and timeout isn't. |
| restricted | The per-image option restricted applies to all images. |
| serial=*parameters* | Enables control from a serial line. The specified serial port is initialized and the boot loader is accepting input from it and from the PC's keyboard. Sending a break on the serial line corresponds to pressing a Shift key on the console in order to get the boot loader's attention. All boot images should be password-protected if the serial access is less secure than access to the console, such as if the line is connected to a modem. The parameter string has the following syntax: |

*<port>*[,*<bps>*[*<parity>*[*<bits>*]]]

*<port>*: The number of the serial port, zero-based. 0 corresponds to COM1 alias /dev/ttyS0, and so on. All four ports can be used (if present). *<bps>*: The baud rate of the serial port. The following baud rates are supported: 110, 150, 300, 600, 1200, 2400, 4800, and 9600 bps. Default is 2400 bps.

*<parity>*: The parity used on the serial line. The boot loader ignores input parity and strips the eighth bit. The following (uppercase or lowercase) characters are used to describe the parity: n for no parity, e for even parity, and o for odd parity.

*<bits>*: The number of bits in a character. Only 7 and 8 bits are supported. Default is 8 if parity is none and 7 if parity is even or odd.

If serial is set, the value of delay is automatically raised to 20. For example, serial=0,2400n8 initializes COM1 with the default parameters.

| | |
|---|---|
| timeout=*tsecs* | Sets a time-out (in tenths of a second) for keyboard input. If no key is pressed for the specified time, the first image is automatically booted. Similarly, password input is aborted if the user is idle for too long. The default time-out is infinite. |
| verbose=*level* | Turns on a lot of progress reporting. Higher numbers give more verbose output. If -v is additionally specified on the LILO command line, the level is increased accordingly. The maximum verbosity level is 5. |

Additionally, the kernel configuration parameters append, ramdisk, read-only, read-write, root, and vga can be set in the global options section. They are used as defaults if they aren't specified in the configuration sections of the respective kernel images.

## PER-IMAGE SECTION

A per-image section starts with either a line

image=*pathname*

to indicate a file or device containing the boot image of a Linux kernel or a line

other=*pathname*

to indicate an arbitrary system to boot.

In the former case, if an image line specifies booting from a device, then one has to indicate the range of sectors to be mapped using

range=*start-end*

In the latter case (booting another system), there are the three options:

| | |
|---|---|
| loader=*chain-loader* | This specifies the chain loader that should be used. By default, /boot/chain.b is used. The chain loader must be specified if booting from a device other than the first hard or floppy disk. |

| | |
|---|---|
| table=*device* | This specifies the device that contains the partition table. The boot loader will not pass partition information to the booted operating system if this variable is omitted. (Some operating systems have other means to determine from which partition they have been booted. For example, MS-DOS usually stores the geometry of the boot disk or partition in its boot sector.) Note that /sbin/lilo must be rerun if a partition table mapped referenced with table is modified. |
| unsafe | Do not access the boot sector at map creation time. This disables some sanity checks, including a partition table check. If the boot sector is on a fixed-format floppy disk device, using UNSAFE avoids the need to put a readable disk into the drive when running the map installer. unsafe and table are mutually incompatible. |

In both cases, the following options apply:

| | |
|---|---|
| label=*name* | The boot loader uses the main file *name* (without its path) of each image specification to identify that image. A different name can be used by setting the variable label. |
| alias=*name* | A second name for the same entry can be used by specifying an alias. |
| lock | (See previous description.) |
| optional | Omit the image if it is not available at map creation time. This is useful to specify test kernels that are not always present. |
| password=*password* | Protect the image by a password. |
| restricted | A password is only required to boot the image if parameters are specified on the command line (such as single). |

## KERNEL OPTIONS

If the booted image is a Linux kernel, then one may pass command-line parameters to this kernel.

| | |
|---|---|
| append=*string* | Appends the options specified to the parameter line passed to the kernel. This is typically used to specify parameters of hardware that can't be entirely autodetected or for which probing may be dangerous. Example: append = "hd=64,32,202". |
| literal=*string* | Like append but removes all other options (such as setting of the root device). Because vital options can be removed unintentionally with literal, this option cannot be set in the global options section. |
| ramdisk=*size* | This specifies the size of the optional RAM disk. A value of zero indicates that no RAM disk should be created. If this variable is omitted, the RAM disk size configured into the boot image is used. |
| read-only | This specifies that the root filesystem should be mounted read-only. Typically, the system startup procedure remounts the root filesystem read-write later (such as after fscking it). |
| read-write | This specifies that the root filesystem should be mounted read-write. |
| root=*root-device* | This specifies the device that should be mounted as root. If the special name current is used, the root device is set to the device on which the root filesystem is currently mounted. If the root has been changed with -r, the respective device is used. If the variable root is omitted, the root device setting contained in the kernel image is used. (That is set at compile time using the ROOT DEV variable in the kernel makefile and can later be changed with the rdev(8) program.) |
| vga=*mode* | This specifies the VGA text mode that should be selected when booting. The following values are recognized (case is ignored): |
| | normal: Select normal 80x25 text mode. |
| | extended (or ext): Select 80x50 text mode. |
| | ask: Stop and ask for user input (at boot time). |
| | *<number>*: Use the corresponding text mode. A list of available modes can be obtained by booting with vga=ask and pressing Enter. |

If this variable is omitted, the VGA mode setting contained in the kernel image is used. (That is set at compile time using the SVGA MODE variable in the kernel makefile and can later be changed with the rdev(8) program.)

## SEE ALSO

lilo(8), rdev(8). The LILO distribution comes with very extensive documentation of which the preceding information is an extract.

*28 July 1995*

# MAKEDEV.cfg

MAKEDEV.cfg—Configuration for MAKEDEV(8).

## DESCRIPTION

MAKEDEV.cfg is a text file that tells MAKEDEV(8) what to do (and equally importantly, what not to do). Unlike DEVINFO(5), which is meant to be centrally maintained, it contains all local configuration for a particular site and all customization. There are basically two kinds of declaration in this file: a "class" declaration and an "omit" declaration.

A class declaration has the form

```
class name : owner group-owner permissions
```

This says that any devices placed in the specified class by DEVINFO should be created with this ownership and these permissions. A sample entry might be

```
class public: root system 0666
```

This says that devices marked public should be owned by root.system and have mode 666.

An omit declaration has the form

```
omit { device... }
```

This causes the specified devices to never be created, even if explicitly specified. Use caution when setting this up. The intent is to be able to run MAKEDEV update and not have it create all sorts of useless devices you'd never use.

## SEE ALSO

MAKEDEV(8), DEVINFO(5)

*Version 1.4, January 1995*

# moderators

moderators—Mail addresses for moderated Usenet newsgroups.

## DESCRIPTION

The GetModeratorAddress(3) routine reads the file /news/lib/moderators to determine how to reach the moderator of a newsgroup. This is used by inews(1) when an unapproved local posting is made to a moderated newsgroup.

The file is read until a match is found. Blank lines and lines starting with a number sign (#) are ignored. All other lines should consist of two fields separated by a colon.

The first field is a wildmat(3)-style pattern. If it matches the name of the newsgroup, then the second field is taken to be a format string for sprintf(3). This string should have at most one %s parameter, which will be given the name of the newsgroup with periods transliterated to dashes.

Here is a sample file:

```
foo.important:announce-request@foo.com
foo.*:%s@mailer.foo.com
gnu.*:%s@prep.ai.mit.edu
:%s@uunet.uu.net
```

Using this file, postings to the moderated newsgroup in the left column will be sent to the address shown in the right column:

```
foo.important announce-request@foo.com
foo.x.announce foo-x-announce@mailer.foo.com
gnu.emacs.sources gnu-emacs-sources@prep.ai.mit.edu
comp.sources.unix comp-sources-unix@uunet.uu.net
```

## HISTORY

Written by Rich $alz (`rsalz@uunet.uu.net`) for InterNetNews.

## SEE ALSO

inews(1), inn.conf(5), libinn(3), wildmat(3)

# /etc/modules

`/etc/modules`—Kernel modules to load at boot time.

## DESCRIPTION

The `/etc/modules` file contains the names of kernel modules that are to be loaded at boot time, one per line. Comments begin with a #, and everything on the line after them are ignored.

*Debian GNU/Linux version 0.93*

# motd

`motd`—Message of the day.

## DESCRIPTION

The contents of `/etc/motd` are displayed by `login`(1) after a successful login but just before it executes the login shell.

The `motd` stands for "message of the day," and this file has been traditionally been used for exactly that. (It requires much less disk space than mail to all users.)

## FILES

/etc/motd

## SEE ALSO

`login`(1) `issue`(5)

*Linux, 29 December 1992*

# mtools

`mtools`—Table of DOS devices.

## DESCRIPTION

/etc/mtools.conf and ~/.mtoolsrc are the configuration files for mtools. These configuration files describe the following items:

Global configuration flags and variables

Per-drive flags and variables

Character translation tables

/etc/mtools.conf is the system-wide configuration file, and ~/.mtoolsrc is the user's private configuration file.

### GENERAL SYNTAX

The configuration files is made up of sections. Each section starts with a keyword identifying the section followed by a colon. Then follow variable assignments and flags. Variable assignments take the following form:

*name=value*

Flags are lone keywords without an equal sign and *value* following them. A section either ends at the end of the file or where the next section begins.

Lines starting with a hash (#) are comments. Newline characters are equivalent to whitespace (except where ending a comment). The configuration file is case insensitive, except for items enclosed in quotes (such as filenames).

### DEFAULT VALUES

For most platforms, mtools contains reasonable compiled-in defaults. You usually don't need to bother with the configuration file, if all you want to do with mtools is access your floppy drives. On the other hand, the configuration file is needed if you also want to use mtools to access your hard disk partitions and dosemu image files.

## GLOBAL VARIABLES

Global variables may be set to 1 or to 0.

The following global flags are recognized:

| | |
|---|---|
| MTOOLS_SKIP_CHECK | If this is set to 1, mtools skips most of its sanity checks. This is needed to read some Atari disks that have been made with the earlier ROMs and that would not be recognized otherwise. |
| MTOOLS_FAT_COMPATIBILITY | If this is set to 1, mtools skips the FAT size checks. Some disks have a bigger FAT than they really need. These are rejected if this option is not set. |
| MTOOLS_LOWER_CASE | If this is set to 1, mtools displays all-uppercase short filenames as lowercase. This has been done to allow a behavior that is consistent with older versions of mtools, which didn't know about the case bits. |

For example, inserting the following line into your configuration file instructs mtools to skip the sanity checks:
MTOOLS_SKIP_CHECK=1.

Global variables may also be set via the environment: export MTOOLS_SKIP_CHECK=1.

## PER-DRIVE FLAGS AND VARIABLES

Per-drive flags and values may be described in a drive section. A drive section starts with drive *driveletter:*.

Then follow variable-value pairs and flags.

### GENERAL PURPOSE DRIVE VARIABLES

The following variables are available:

| | |
|---|---|
| file | The name of the file or device holding the disk image. This is mandatory. The filename should be enclosed in quotes. |

| | |
|---|---|
| use_xdf | If this is set to a nonzero value, mtools also tries to access this disk as an Xdf disk. Xdf is a high-capacity format used by OS/2. This is off by default. |
| partition | Tells mtools to treat the drive as a partitioned device and to use the given partition. Only primary partitions are accessible using this method, and they are numbered from 1 to 4. For logical partitions, use the more general offset variable. The partition variable is intended for Syquests, ZIP drives, and DOSEMU hdimages. It is not recommended for hard disks to which direct access to partitions is available. |
| offset | Describes where in the file the MS-DOS filesystem starts. This is useful for logical partitions in DOSEMU hdimages and for ATARI RAM disks. By default, this is zero, meaning that the filesystem starts right at the beginning of the device or file. |
| fat_bits | The number of FAT bits. This can be 12 or 16. This is very rarely needed because it can almost always be deduced from information in the boot sector. On the contrary, describing the number of fat bits can actually be harmful if you get it wrong. You should only use it if mtools gets the autodetected number of fat bits wrong or if you want to mformat a disk with a weird number of fat bits. |

Only the file option is mandatory. The other parameters may be left out. In that case, a default value or an autodetected value is used.

## DRIVE GEOMETRY CONFIGURATION

Geometry information describes the physical characteristics about the disk. Its has three purposes:

| | |
|---|---|
| mformat | The geometry information is written into the boot sector of the newly made disk. However, you may also describe the geometry information on the command line. See mformat(1) for details. |
| filtering | On some Unices, device nodes only support one physical geometry. The geometry is compared to the actual geometry stored on the boot sector to make sure that this device node is able to correctly read the disk. If the geometry doesn't match, this drive entry fails, and the next drive entry bearing the same drive letter is tried. See the next section "Supplying Multiple Descriptions for a Drive" for more details on supplying several descriptions for a drive letter. |
| | If no geometry information is supplied in the configuration file, all disks are accepted. On Linux (and on Sparc), there exist device nodes with configurable geometry (/dev/fd0, /dev/fd1 etc), so filtering is not needed (and ignored) for disk drives. (mtools still does do filtering on plain files (disk images) in Linux: This is mainly intended for test purposes because I don't have access to a UNIX that would actually need filtering.) |
| initial geometry | The geometry information (if available) is also used to set the initial geometry on configurable device nodes. This initial geometry is used to read the boot sector, which contains the real geometry. If no geometry information is supplied in the configuration file, no initial configuration is done. On Linux, this is not really needed either because the configurable devices are able to autodetect the disk type accurately enough (for most common formats) to read the boot sector. |

Wrong geometry information may lead to very bizarre errors. That's why I strongly recommend that you don't use geometry configuration unless you really need it.

The following geometry related variables are available:

| | |
|---|---|
| cylinders | The number of cylinders. |
| heads | The number of heads (sides). |
| sectors | The number of sectors per track. |

For example, the following drive section describes a 1.44M drive:

```
drive a:
file="/dev/fd0H1440"
fat_bits=12
tracks=80 heads=2 sectors=18
```

The following shorthand geometry descriptions are available:

| | |
|---|---|
| 1.44M | High density, 3 1/2 disk. Equivalent to `fat_bits=12 tracks=80 heads=2 sectors=18`. |
| 1.2M | High density, 5 1/4 disk. Equivalent to `fat_bits=12 tracks=80 heads=2 sectors=15`. |
| 720K | Double density, 3 1/2 disk. Equivalent to `fat_bits=12 tracks=80 heads=2 sectors=9`. |
| 360K | Double density, 5 1/4 disk. Equivalent to `fat_bits=12 tracks=40 heads=2 sectors=9`. |

The shorthand format descriptions may be amended. For example, `360K sectors=8` describes a 320K disk and is equivalent to `fat_bits=12 tracks=40 heads=2 sectors=8`.

## OPEN FLAGS

Moreover, the following flags are available:

| | |
|---|---|
| sync | All I/O operations are done synchronously. |
| nodelay | The device or file is opened with the `O_NDELAY` flag. This is needed on some non-Linux architectures. |
| exclusive | The device or file is opened with the `O_EXCL` flag. On Linux, this ensures exclusive access to the floppy drive. On most other architectures and for plain files, it has no effect at all. |

## SUPPLYING MULTIPLE DESCRIPTIONS FOR A DRIVE

It is possible to supply multiple descriptions for a drive. In that case, the descriptions are tried in order until one is found that fits. Descriptions may fail for several reasons:

- The geometry is not appropriate
- There is no disk in the drive
- Other problems

Multiple definitions are useful when using physical devices that are only able to support one single disk geometry:

```
drive a: file="/dev/fd0H1440" 1.44m
drive a: file="/dev/fd0H720" 720k
```

This instructs `mtools` to use `/dev/fd0H1440` for 1.44M (high density) disks and `/dev/fd0H720` for 720K (double density) disks. On Linux, this feature is not really needed because the `/dev/fd0` device is able to handle any geometry.

You can also use multiple drive descriptions to access both of your physical drives through one drive letter:

```
drive z: file="/dev/fd0"
drive z: file="/dev/fd1"
```

With this description, `mdir z:` accesses your first physical drive if it contains a disk. If the first drive doesn't contain a disk, `mtools` checks the second drive.

When using multiple configuration files, drive descriptions in the files parsed last override descriptions for the same drive in earlier files. In order to avoid this, use the `drive+` or `+drive` keywords instead of `drive`. The first adds a description to the end of the list (will be tried last), and the second adds it to the start of the list.

## CHARACTER TRANSLATION TABLES

If you live in the USA, in Western Europe, or in Australia, you can skip this section.

## INTRODUCTION

DOS uses a different character code mapping from UNIX. Seven-bit characters still have the same meaning; only characters with the eight-bit set are affected. To make matters worse, there are several translation tables available depending on the country where you are. The appearance of the characters is defined using code pages. These code pages aren't the same for all countries. For instance, some code pages don't contain upper -case accented characters. On the other hand, some code pages contain characters that don't exist in UNIX, such as certain line-drawing characters or accented consonants used by some Eastern European countries. This affects two things relating to filenames:

| | |
|---|---|
| Uppercase characters | In short names, only uppercase characters are allowed. This also holds for accented characters. For instance, in a code page that doesn't contain accented uppercase characters, the accented lowercase characters get transformed into their unaccented counterparts. |
| Long filenames | Microsoft has finally come to their senses and uses a more standard mapping for the long filenames. They use Unicode, which is basically a 32-bit version of ASCII. Its first 256 characters are identical to UNIX ASCII. Thus, the code page also affects the correspondence between the codes used in long names and those used in short names. |

mtools considers the filenames entered on the command line as having the UNIX mapping and translates the characters to get short names. By default, code page 850 is used with the Swiss uppercase/lowercase mapping. I chose this code page because its set of existing characters most closely matches UNIX's. Moreover, this code page covers most characters in use in the USA, Australia, and Western Europe. However, it is still possible to chose a different mapping. There are two methods: the country variable and explicit tables.

## CONFIGURATION USING COUNTRY

The COUNTRY variable is recommended for people that also have access to MS-DOS system files and documentation. If you don't have access to these, I'd suggest you use explicit tables instead.

Syntax: COUNTRY=" *country* [,[ *codepage* ], *country.sys* ]"

This tells mtools to use a UNIX-to-DOS translation table that matches *codepage* and an lowercase-to-uppercase table for *country* and to use the *country.sys* file to get the lowercase-to-uppercase table. The country code is most often the telephone prefix of the country. Refer to the DOS help page on country for more details. The *codepage* and the *country.sys* parameters are optional. Don't type in the square brackets; they are only there to indicate which parameters are optional. The *country.sys* file is supplied with MS-DOS. In most cases, you don't need it because the most common translation tables are compiled into mtools. Don't worry if you run a UNIX-only box that lacks this file.

If *codepage* is not given, a per-country default code page is used. If the *country.sys* parameter isn't given, compiled-in defaults are used for the lowercase-to-uppercase table. This is useful for other Unices than Linux, which may have no *country.sys* file available online.

The UNIX-to-DOS are not contained in the *country.sys* file, and thus mtools always uses compiled-in defaults for those. Thus, only a limited amount of code pages are supported. If your preferred code page is missing, or if you know the name of the Windows 95 file that contains this mapping, drop me a line at Alain.Knaff@inrialpes.fr.

The COUNTRY variable can also be set using the environment.

## CONFIGURATION USING EXPLICIT TRANSLATION TABLES

Translation tables may be described in lines in the configuration file. Two tables are needed: first the DOS-to-UNIX table and then the lowercase-to-uppercase table. A DOS-to-UNIX table starts with the tounix keyword, followed by a colon and 128 hexadecimal numbers. A lower-to-upper table starts with the fucase keyword, followed by a colon and 128 hexadecimal numbers.

The tables only show the translations for characters whose codes is greater than 128 because translation for lower codes is trivial. Example:

```
tounix:

0xc7 0xfc 0xe9 0xe2 0xe4 0xe0 0xe5 0xe7
0xea 0xeb 0xe8 0xef 0xee 0xec 0xc4 0xc5
0xc9 0xe6 0xc6 0xf4 0xf6 0xf2 0xfb 0xf9
0xff 0xd6 0xdc 0xf8 0xa3 0xd8 0xd7 0x5f
0xe1 0xed 0xf3 0xfa 0xf1 0xd1 0xaa 0xba
0xbf 0xae 0xac 0xbd 0xbc 0xa1 0xab 0xbb
0x5f 0x5f 0x5f 0x5f 0x5f 0xc1 0xc2 0xc0
0xa9 0x5f 0x5f 0x5f 0x5f 0xa2 0xa5 0xac
0x5f 0x5f 0x5f 0x5f 0x5f 0x5f 0xe3 0xc3
0x5f 0x5f 0x5f 0x5f 0x5f 0x5f 0x5f 0xa4
0xf0 0xd0 0xc9 0xcb 0xc8 0x69 0xcd 0xce
0xcf 0x5f 0x5f 0x5f 0x5f 0x7c 0x49 0x5f
0xd3 0xdf 0xd4 0xd2 0xf5 0xd5 0xb5 0xfe
0xde 0xda 0xd9 0xfd 0xdd 0xde 0xaf 0xb4
0xad 0xb1 0x5f 0xbe 0xb6 0xa7 0xf7 0xb8
0xb0 0xa8 0xb7 0xb9 0xb3 0xb2 0x5f 0x5f

fucase:

0x80 0x9a 0x90 0xb6 0x8e 0xb7 0x8f 0x80
0xd2 0xd3 0xd4 0xd8 0xd7 0xde 0x8e 0x8f
0x90 0x92 0x92 0xe2 0x99 0xe3 0xea 0xeb
0x59 0x99 0x9a 0x9d 0x9c 0x9d 0x9e 0x9f
0xb5 0xd6 0xe0 0xe9 0xa5 0xa5 0xa6 0xa7
0xa8 0xa9 0xaa 0xab 0xac 0xad 0xae 0xaf
0xb0 0xb1 0xb2 0xb3 0xb4 0xb5 0xb6 0xb7
0xb8 0xb9 0xba 0xbb 0xbc 0xbd 0xbe 0xbf
0xc0 0xc1 0xc2 0xc3 0xc4 0xc5 0xc7 0xc7
0xc8 0xc9 0xca 0xcb 0xcc 0xcd 0xce 0xcf
0xd1 0xd1 0xd2 0xd3 0xd4 0x49 0xd6 0xd7
0xd8 0xd9 0xda 0xdb 0xdc 0xdd 0xde 0xdf
0xe0 0xe1 0xe2 0xe3 0xe5 0xe5 0xe6 0xe8
0xe8 0xe9 0xea 0xeb 0xed 0xed 0xee 0xef
0xf0 0xf1 0xf2 0xf3 0xf4 0xf5 0xf6 0xf7
0xf8 0xf9 0xfa 0xfb 0xfc 0xfd 0xfe 0xff
```

The first table maps DOS character codes to UNIX character codes. For example, the DOS character number 129 is a u with two dots on top of it. To translate it into UNIX, we look at the character number 1 in the first table (1 = 129 - 128). This is 0xfc. (Beware; numbering starts at 0.) The second table maps lowercase DOS characters to uppercase DOS characters. The same lowercase u with dots maps to character 0x9a, which is an uppercase U with dots in DOS.

## UNICODE CHARACTERS GREATER THAN 256

If an existing MS-DOS name contains Unicode character greater than 256, these are translated to underscores or to characters that are close in visual appearance. For example, accented consonants are translated into their unaccented counterparts. This translation is used for mdir and for the UNIX filenames generated by mcopy. Linux does support Unicode too, but unfortunately, too few applications support it yet to bother with it in mtools. Most importantly, xterm can't display Unicode yet. If there is sufficient demand, I might include support for Unicode in the UNIX filenames as well.

Caution: When deleting files with mtools, the underscore matches all characters that can't be represented in UNIX. Be careful before mdel!

## LOCATION OF CONFIGURATION FILES AND PARSING ORDER

The configuration files are parsed in the following order:

Compiled-in defaults

/etc/mtools.conf

/etc/mtools. This is for backwards compatibility only and is only parsed if mtools.conf doesn't exist.

~/.mtoolsrc

Options described in the later files override those described in the earlier files. Drives defined in earlier files persist if they are not overridden in the later files. For instance, drives A and B may be defined in /etc/mtools.conf and drives C and D may be defined in ~/.mtoolsrc. However, if ~/.mtoolsrc also defines drive A, this new description would override the description of drive A in /etc/mtools.conf instead of adding to it. If you want to add a new description to a drive already described in an earlier file, you need to use either the +drive or drive+ keywords.

## BACKWARDS COMPATIBILITY

The syntax described herein is new for version mtools 2.5.4. The old line-oriented syntax is still supported. Each line beginning with a single letter is considered to be a drive description using the old syntax. Old style and new style drive sections may be mixed within the same configuration file to make upgrading easier. Support for the old syntax will be phased out eventually, and to discourage its use, I purposefully omit its description here.

## FILES

/etc/mtools.conf

~/.mtoolsrc

## SEE ALSO

mtools(1)

*5 December 1995*

# newsfeeds

newsfeeds—Determine where Usenet articles get sent.

## DESCRIPTION

The file /news/lib/newsfeeds specifies how incoming articles should be distributed to other sites. It is parsed by the InterNetNews server innd(8) when it starts up or when directed to by ctlinnd(8).

The file is interpreted as a set of lines according to the following rules. If a line ends with a backslash, then the backslash, the newline, and any whitespace at the start of the next line is deleted. This is repeated until the entire "logical" line is collected. If the logical line is blank or starts with a number sign (#), it is ignored.

All other lines are interpreted as feed entries. An entry should consist of four colon-separated fields; two of the fields may have optional subfields, marked off by a slash. Fields or subfields that take multiple parameters should be separated by a comma. Extra whitespace can cause problems. Except for the site names, case is significant. The format of an entry is

```
sitename[/exclude,exclude,...]\
:pattern,pattern...[/distrib,distrib...]\
:flag,flag...\
:param
```

Each field is described below.

The *sitename* is the name of the site to which a news article can be sent. It is used for writing log entries and for determining if an article should be forwarded to a site. If *sitename* already appears in the article's Path header, then the article will not be sent to the site. The name is usually whatever the remote site uses to identify itself in the Path line but can be almost any word that makes sense; special local entries (such as archivers or gateways) should probably end with an exclamation point to make sure that they do not have the same name as any real site. For example, gateway is an obvious name for the local entry that forwards articles out to a mailing list. If a site with the name gateway posts an article, when the local site receives the article, it will see the name in the Path and not send the article to its own gateway entry. If an entry has an exclusion subfield, then the article will not be sent to that site if any of the names specified as excludes appear in the Path header. The same sitename can be used more than once; the appropriate action will be taken for each site that should receive the article, regardless of the name, although this is recommended only for program feeds to avoid confusion. Case is not significant in site names.

The *patterns* specify which groups to send to the site and are interpreted to build a "subscription list" for the site. The default subscription is to get all groups. The patterns in the field are wildmat(3)-style patterns and are matched in order against the list of newsgroups that the local site receives. If the first character of a pattern is an exclamation mark, then any groups matching the pattern are removed from the subscription; otherwise, any matching groups are added. For example, to receive all comp groups but only comp.sources.unix within the sources newsgroups, the following set of patterns can be used:

```
comp.*,!comp.sources.*,comp.sources.unix
```

There are three things to note about this example. The first is that the trailing .* is required. The second is that, again, the result of the last match is the most important. The third is that comp.sources.* could be written as comp.sources*, but this would not have the same effect if there were a comp.sources-only group.

See innd(8) for details on the propagation of control messages.

A subscription can be further modified by specifying "distributions" that the site should or should not receive. The default is to send all articles to all sites that subscribe to any of the groups where it has been posted, but if an article has a Distribution header and any distribs are specified, then they are checked according to the following rules:

1.  If the Distribution header matches any of the values in the subfield, then the article is sent.
2.  If a distrib starts with an exclamation point and it matches the Distribution header, then the article is not sent.
3.  If Distribution header does not match any distrib in the site's entry and no negations were used, then the article is not sent.
4.  If Distribution header does not match any distrib in the site's entry and any distrib started with an exclamation point, then the article is sent.

If an article has more than one distribution specified, then each one is evaluated according to the preceding rules. If any of the specified distributions indicate that the article should be sent, it is. If none do, it is not sent: The rules are used as a "logical or." It is almost definitely a mistake to have a single feed that specifies distributions that start with an exclamation point along with some that don't.

Distributions are text words, not patterns; it is usually a mistake to have entries like * or all there.

The *flags* parameter specifies miscellaneous parameters. They may be specified in any order; flags that take values should have the value immediately after the flag letter with no whitespace. The valid flags are

| | |
|---|---|
| < *size* | An article will only be sent to the site if it is less than *size* bytes long. The default is no limit. |
| A *checks* | An article will only be sent to the site if it meets the requirements specified in the *checks*, which should be chosen from the following set: |
| | d             Distribution header required |
| | p             Do not check Path header before propagating. |
| B *high/low* | If a site is being fed by a file, channel, or exploder, the server will usually start trying to write the information as soon as possible. Providing a buffer may give better system performance and help smooth out overall load if a large batch of news comes in. The value of the this flag should be two numbers separated by a slash. The first specifies the point at which the server can start draining the feed's I/O buffer, and the second specifies when to stop writing and begin buffering again; the units are bytes. The default is to do no buffering, sending output as soon as it is possible to do so. |
| F *name* | This flag specifies the name of the file that should be used if it is necessary to begin spooling for the site. If name is not an absolute pathname, it is taken to be relative to /news/spool/out.going. Then, if the destination is a directory, the file to go in that directory will be used as filename. |

| | |
|---|---|
| G *count* | If this flag is specified, an article will only be sent to the site if it is posted to no more than *count* newsgroups. |
| H *count* | If this flag is specified, an article will only be sent to the site if it has *count* or fewer sites in its Path line. This flag should only be used as a rough guide because of the loose interpretation of the Path header; some sites put the poster's name in the header, and some sites that might logically be considered to be one hop become two because they put the posting workstation's name in the header. The default value for *count* is one. |
| I *size* | The flag specifies the size of the internal buffer for a file feed. If there are more file feeds than allowed by the system, they will be buffered internally in least recently used order. If the internal buffer grows bigger than *size* bytes, however, the data will be written out to the appropriate file. |
| N *modifiers* | The newsgroups that a site receives are modified according to the modifiers, which should be chosen from the following set: |

| | |
|---|---|
| m | Only moderated groups |
| u | Only unmoderated groups |

| | |
|---|---|
| S *size* | If the amount of data queued for the site gets to be larger than *size* bytes, then the server will switch to spooling, appending to a file specified by the F flag or /news/spool/out.going/ *sitename* if the F flag is not specified. Spooling usually happens only for channel or exploder feeds. |
| T *type* | This flag specifies the type of feed for the site. *type* should be a letter chosen from the following set: |

| | |
|---|---|
| c | Channel |
| f | File |
| l | Log entry only |
| m | Funnel (multiple entries feed into one) |
| p | Program |
| x | Exploder. Each feed is described in the section on feed types. |

The default is T*f*.

| | |
|---|---|
| W *items* | If a site is fed by file, channel, or exploder, this flag controls what information is written. If a site is fed by a program, only the asterisk (*) has any effect. The items should be chosen from the following set: |

| | |
|---|---|
| b | Size of the article in bytes. |
| f | Article's full pathname. |
| g | The newsgroup the article is in; if cross-posted, then the first of the groups this site gets. |
| m | Article's Message-ID. |
| n | Article's pathname relative to the spool directory. |
| p | The site that fed the article to the server; from the Path header. |
| s | The IP address of the site that sent the article. |
| t | Time article was received as seconds since epoch. |
| * | Names of the appropriate funnel entries; or all sites that get the article. |
| D | Value of the Distribution header; ? if none present. |
| H | All headers. |
| N | Value of the Newsgroups header. |
| O | Overview data. |
| R | Information needed for replication. More than one letter can be used; the entries will be separated by a space and written in the order in which they are specified. The default is W*n*. |

The H and O items are intended for use by programs that create news overview databases. If H is present, then the all the article's headers are written followed by a blank line. An Xref header (even if one does not appear in the filed article) and a Bytes header, specifying the article's size, will also be part of the headers. If used, this should be the only item in the list; if preceded by other items, however, a newline will be written before the headers. The O generates input to the overchan(8) program. It, too, should be the only item in the list.

The asterisk has special meaning. It expands to a space-separated list of all sites that received the current article. If the site is the target of a funnel, however (that is, it is named by other sites that have a Tm flag), then the asterisk expands to the names of the funnel feeds that received the article. If the site is fed by a program, then an asterisk in the param field will be expanded into the list of funnel feeds that received the article. A site fed by a program cannot get the site list unless it is the target of other Tm feeds.

The interpretation of the *param* field depends on the type of feed, and is explained in more detail in the section on feed types. It can be omitted.

The site named ME is special. There should only be one such entry, and it should be the first entry in the file. If the ME entry has a subscription list, then that list is automatically prepended to the subscription list of all other entries. For example, *,!control,!junk,!foo.* can be used to set up the initial subscription list for all feeds so that local postings are not propagated unless foo.* explicitly appears in the site's subscription list. Note that most subscriptions should have !junk,!control in their pattern list; see the discussion of control messages in innd(8). (Unlike other news software, it does not affect what groups are received; that is done by the active(5) file.)

If the ME entry has a distribution subfield, then only articles that match the distribution list are accepted; all other articles are rejected. A commercial news server, for example, might have /!local to reject local postings from other, misconfigured, sites.

## FEED TYPES

innd provides four basic types of feeds: log, file, program, and channel. An exploder is a special type of channel. In addition, several entries can feed into the same feed; these are funnel feeds, which refer to an entry that is one of the other types. Note that the term "feed" is technically a misnomer because the server does not transfer articles but reports that an article should be sent to the site.

The simplest feed is one that is fed by a log entry. Other than a mention in the news logfile, no data is ever written out. This is equivalent to a Tf entry writing to /dev/null except that no file is opened.

A site fed by a file is simplest type of feed. When the site should receive an article, one line is written to the file named by the *param* field. If *param* is not an absolute pathname, it is taken to be relative to /news/spool/out.going. If empty, the filename defaults to /news/spool/out.going/*sitename*. This name should be unique.

When a site fed by a file is flushed (see ctlinnd), the following steps are performed. The script doing the flush should have first renamed the file. The server tries to write out any buffered data and then closes the file. The renamed file is now available for use. The server will then reopen the original file, which will now get created.

A site fed by a program has a process spawned for every article that the site receives. The *param* field must be a sprintf(3) format string that may have a single %s parameter, which will be given a pathname for the article, relative to the news spool directory. The full pathname may be obtained by prefixing the %s in the *param* field by the news spool directory prefix. Standard input will be set to the article or /dev/null if the article cannot be opened for some reason. Standard output and error will be set to the error log. The process will run with the user and group ID of the /news/lib/innd directory. innd will try to avoid spawning a shell if the command has no shell meta-characters; this feature can be defeated by appending a semicolon to the end of the command. The full pathname of the program to be run must be specified; for security, PATH is not searched.

If the entry is the target of a funnel, and if the W* flag is used, then a single asterisk may be used in the *param* field where it will be replaced by the names of the sites that fed into the funnel. If the entry is not a funnel, or if the W* flag is not used, then the asterisk has no special meaning.

Flushing a site fed by a program does no action.

When a site is fed by a channel or exploder, the *param* field names the process to start. Again, the full pathname of the process must be given. When the site is to receive an article, the process receives a line on its standard input telling it about the article. Standard output and error and the user and group ID of the all subprocess are set as for a program feed. If the process exits, it will be restarted. If the process cannot be started, the server will spool input to a file named /news/spool/out.going/ *sitename*. It will then try to start the process some time later.

When a site fed by a channel or exploder is flushed, the server closes down its end of the pipe. Any pending data that has not been written will be spooled; see the description of the S flag. No signal is sent; it is up to the program to notice EOF on its standard input and exit. The server then starts a new process.

Exploders are a superset of channel feeds. In addition to channel behavior, exploders can be sent command lines. These lines start with an exclamation point, and their interpretation is up to the exploder. The following messages are generated automatically by the server:

```
newgroup group
rmgroup group
flush
flush site
```

These messages are sent when the ctlinnd command of the same name is received by the server. In addition, the send command can be used to send an arbitrary command line to the exploder child-process. The primary exploder is buffchan(8).

Funnel feeds provide a way of merging several site entries into a single output stream. For a site feeding into a funnel, the *param* field names the actual entry that does the feeding.

For more details on setting up different types of news feeds, see the INN installation manual.

## EXAMPLES

```
## Initial subscription list and our distributions.
ME:*,!junk,!foo.*/world,usa,ne,ne,foo,ddn,gnu,inet\
::
## Feed all moderated source postings to an archiver
source-archive!::!*,comp.sources.*\
:Tp,Nm:/usr/local/bin/archive %s
## Watch for big postings
watcher!:*\
:Tc,Wbnm\
:exec awk '$1 > 1000000 { print "BIG", $2, $3 }' >/dev/console
## A UUCP feed, where we try to keep the "batching" between 4 and 1K.
ihnp4:/world,usa,na,ddn,gnu\
:Tf,Wfb,B4096/1024:
## Usenet as mail; note ! in funnel name to avoid Path conflicts.
## Can't use ! in "fred" since it would like look a UUCP address.
fred:!*,comp.sources.unix,comp.sources.bugs\
:Tm:mailer!
barney@bar.com:!*,news.software.nntp,comp.sources.bugs\
:Tm:mailer!
mailer!:!*\
:W*,Tp:/usr/ucb/Mail -s "News article" *
## NNTP feeds fed off-line via nntpsend or equivalent.
feed1::Tf,Wnm:feed1.domain.name
peer.foo.com:foo.*:Tf,Wnm:peer.foo.com
## Real-time transmission.
mit.edu:/world,usa,na,ne,ddn,gnu,inet\
:Tc,Wnm:/nntplink -i stdin mit.edu
## Two sites feeding into a hypothetical NNTP fan-out program:
nic.near.net:\
:Tm:nntpfunnel1
```

```
uunet.uu.net/uunet:!ne.*/world,usa,na,foo,ddn,gnu,inet\
:Tm:nntpfunnel1
nntpfunnel1:!*\
:Tc,Wmn*:/nntpfanout
## A UUCP site that wants comp.* and moderated soc groups
uucpsite!comp:!*,comp.*/world,usa,na,gnu\
:Tm:uucpsite
uucpsite!soc:!*,soc.*/world,usa,na,gnu\
:Tm,Nm:uucpsite
uucpsite:!*\
:Tf,Wfb:/usr/spool/batch/uucpsite
```

The last two sets of entries show how funnel feeds can be used. For example, the `nntpfanout` program would receive lines like the following on its standard input:

```
<123@litchi.foo.com> comp/sources/unix/888 nic.near.net uunet.uu.net
<124@litchi.foo.com> ne/general/1003 nic.near.net
```

Because the UUCP funnel is only destined for one site, the asterisk is not needed and entries like the following will be written into the file:

```
<qwe#37x@snark.uu.net>comp/society/folklore/3
<123@litchi.foo.com> comp/sources/unix/888
```

## HISTORY

Written by Rich $alz (rsalz@uunet.uu.net) for InterNetNews.

## SEE ALSO

active(5), buffchan(8), ctlinnd(8), innd(8), wildmat(3)

# newslog

newslog—Description of Usenet log files.

## DESCRIPTION

Most log files created by Usenet programs reside in the `/var/log/news` directory and have a `.log` extension. Several versions are usually kept with an additional extension such as `.1`, `.2`, and so on; the higher the number, the older the log. The older versions are compressed.

The `scanlogs` script and related utilities (see `newslog(8)`) are responsible for rotating and compressing these files.

Some log files always have data, others only have data if there is a problem, and others are only created if a particular program is used or configuration parameter is set. The `innstat` script (see `newslog(8)`) monitors the size of all log files.

The following files will only accumulate data under the direction of `control.ctl(5)`:

`control.log, miscctl.log, newgroup.log, rmgroup.log, unwanted.log`

In order to create these files, the `message` and `action` fields of `control.ctl` should be chosen from the following table:

| Message | Action | Meaning |
|---------|--------|---------|
| all | log=miscctl | Log all messages by default |
| default | log=miscctl | Log unknown messages |
| newgroup | doit=newgroup | Create group and log message |
| newgroup | log=newgroup | Log message |

*continues*

| *Message* | *Action* | *Meaning* |
|-----------|----------|-----------|
| rmgroup | doit=rmgroup | Remove group and log message |
| rmgroup | log=rmgroup | Log message |
| "other" | doit=miscctl | Log and process the message |
| "other" | log=miscctl | Log message |

Here, "other" refers to any other control message such as:

checkgroups ihave sendme sendsys senduuname version

The following is a list of log files.

| | |
|---|---|
| control.log | This file maintains a count of the number of newgroup and rmgroup control messages seen for each newsgroup. The count is of the number of control messages with identical arguments, regardless of whether they were actually processed. All control arguments, including invalid ones, are counted. This file is updated by tally.control, which is invoked by scanlogs if either the newgroup or rmgroup logs exist. This file is not rotated. |
| errlog | This file contains the standard output and standard error of any program spawned by innd(8). The most common programs are the control-message handlers found in /news/bin/control. This file should be empty. Scanlogs will print the entire contents of this log file if it is non-empty. |
| expire.log | By default, when news.daily is going to expire old news articles, it writes the date to this file, followed by any output from expire(8) and the ending date. All lines but the first are indented four spaces. |
| miscctl.log | When control.ctl is configured as described above, all control messages except newgroup and rmgroup are appended to this file by writelog. There will be a summary line describing the message and the action taken, followed by the article indented by four spaces and a blank line. |
| newgroup.log | When control.ctl is configured as described above, all newgroup messages are appended to this file using the same format as for miscctl.log. |
| news | This file logs articles received by innd. scanlogs summarizes the rejected articles reported in this file. |
| news.crit | All critical error messages issued by innd are appended to this file via syslog(3). This log file should be empty. scanlogs will print the entire contents of this log file if it is non-empty. You should have the following line in your syslog.conf(5) file: |
| | news.crit /var/log/news/news.crit |
| news.err | All major error messages issued by innd are appended to this file via syslog. This log file should be empty. scanlogs will print the entire contents of this log file if it is non-empty. You should have the following line in your syslog.conf file: |
| | news.err /var/log/news/news.err |
| news.notice | All standard error messages and status messages issued by innd are appended to this file via syslog. scanlogs uses the awk(1) script innlog.awk to summarize this file. You should have the following line in your syslog.conf file: |
| | news.notice /var/log/news/news.notice |
| nntpsend.log | The nntpsend(8) programs appends all status messages to this file. |
| rmgroup.log | When control.ctl is configured as described previously, all rmgroup messages are appended to this file using the same format as for miscctl.log. |
| unwanted.log | This log maintains a count of the number of articles that were rejected because they were posted to newsgroups that do not exist at the local site. This file is updated by tally.unwanted and maintained in reverse numeric order (the most popular rejected group first). This file is not rotated. |

## HISTORY

Written by Landon Curt Noll (chongo@toad.com) and Rich $alz (rsalz@uunet.uu.net) for InterNetNews.

## SEE ALSO

control.ctl*(5)*, ctlinnd*(8)*, expire*(8)*, innd*(8)*, news.daily*(8)*, nntpsend*(8)*, newslog*(8)*

# nfs

nfs—NFS fstab format and options.

## SYNOPSIS

/etc/fstab

## DESCRIPTION

The fstab file contains information about which filesystems to mount where and with what options. For NFS mounts, it contains the server name and exported server directory to mount from, the local directory that is the mount point, and the NFS-specific options that control the way the filesystem is mounted. Here is an example from an /etc/fstab file from an NFS mount.

server:/usr/local/pub /pub nfs rsize=8192,wsize=8192,timeo=14,intr

## OPTIONS

| | |
|---|---|
| rsize=*n* | The number of bytes NFS uses when reading files from an NFS server. The default value is dependent on the kernel, currently 1024 bytes. (However, throughput is improved greatly by asking for rsize=8192.) |
| wsize=*n* | The number of bytes NFS uses when writing files to an NFS server. The default value is dependent on the kernel, currently 1024 bytes. (However, throughput is improved greatly by asking for wsize=8192.) |
| timeo=*n* | The value in tenths of a second before sending the first retransmission after an RPC time-out. The default value is 7 tenths of a second. After the first time-out, the time-out is doubled after each successive time-out until a maximum time-out of 60 seconds is reached or the enough retransmissions have occurred to cause a major time-out. Then, if the filesystem is hard mounted, each new time-out cascade restarts at twice the initial value of the previous cascade, again doubling at each retransmission. The maximum time-out is always 60 seconds. Better overall performance may be achieved by increasing the time-out when mounting on a busy network, to a slow server, or through several routers or gateways. |
| retrans=*n* | The number of minor time-outs and retransmissions that must occur before a major time-out occurs. The default is 3 time-outs. When a major time-out occurs, the file operation is either aborted or a "server not responding" message is printed on the console. |
| acregmin=*n* | The minimum time in seconds that attributes of a regular file should be cached before requesting fresh information from a server. The default is 3 seconds. |
| acregmax=*n* | The maximum time in seconds that attributes of a regular file can be cached before requesting fresh information from a server. The default is 60 seconds. |
| acdirmin=*n* | The minimum time in seconds that attributes of a directory should be cached before requesting fresh information from a server. The default is 30 seconds. |
| acdirmax=*n* | The maximum time in seconds that attributes of a directory can be cached before requesting fresh information from a server. The default is 60 seconds. |
| actimeo=*n* | Using actimeo sets all of acregmin, acregmax, acdirmin, and acdirmax to the same value. There is no default value. |

| | |
|---|---|
| retry=*n* | The number of times to retry a backgrounded NFS mount operation before giving up. The default value is 10000 times. |
| namlen=*n* | When an NFS server does not support version 2 of the RPC mount protocol, this option can be used to specify the maximum length of a filename that is supported on the remote filesystem. This is used to support the POSIX pathconf functions. The default is 255 characters. |
| port=*n* | The numeric value of the port to connect to the NFS server on. If the port number is 0 (the default) then query the remote host's port mapper for the port number to use. If the remote host's NFS daemon is not registered with its port mapper, the standard NFS port number 2049 is used instead. |
| mountport=*n* | The numeric value of the mountd port. |
| mounthost=*name* | The name of the host running mountd. |
| mountprog=*n* | Use an alternate RPC program number to contact the mount daemon on the remote host. This option is useful for hosts that can run multiple NFS servers. The default value is 100005, which is the standard RPC mount daemon program number. |
| mountvers=*n* | Use an alternate RPC version number to contact the mount daemon on the remote host. This option is useful for hosts that can run multiple NFS servers. The default value is version 1. |
| nfsprog=*n* | Use an alternate RPC program number to contact the NFS daemon on the remote host. This option is useful for hosts that can run multiple NFS servers. The default value is 100003, which is the standard RPC NFS daemon program number. |
| nfsvers=*n* | Use an alternate RPC version number to contact the NFS daemon on the remote host. This option is useful for hosts that can run multiple NFS servers. The default value is version 2. |
| bg | If the first NFS mount attempt times out, continue trying the mount in the background. The default is to not to background the mount on time-out but to fail. |
| fg | If the first NFS mount attempt times out, fail immediately. This is the default. |
| soft | If an NFS file operation has a major time-out, then report an I/O error to the calling program. The default is to continue retrying NFS file operations indefinitely. |
| hard | If an NFS file operation has a major time-out, then report "server not responding" on the console and continue retrying indefinitely. This is the default. |
| intr | If an NFS file operation has a major time-out and it is hard mounted, then allow signals to interrupt the file operation and cause it to return EINTR to the calling program. The default is to not allow file operations to be interrupted. |
| posix | Mount the NFS filesystem using POSIX semantics. This allows an NFS filesystem to properly support the POSIX pathconf command by querying the mount server for the maximum length of a filename. To do this, the remote host must support version 2 of the RPC mount protocol. Many NFS servers support only version 1. |
| nocto | Suppress the retrieval of new attributes when creating a file. |
| noac | Disable all forms of attribute caching entirely. This extracts a server performance penalty, but it allows two different NFS clients to get reasonably good results when both clients are actively writing to a common filesystem on the server. |
| tcp | Mount the NFS filesystem using the TCP protocol instead of the default UDP protocol. Many NFS severs only support UDP. |
| udp | Mount the NFS filesystem using the UDP protocol. This is the default. All the non-value options have corresponding nooption forms. For example, nointr means don't allow file operations to be interrupted. |

## FILES

/etc/fstab

## SEE ALSO

fstab(5), mount(8), umount(8), exports(5)

## AUTHOR

Rick Sladkey (jrs@world.std.com)

## BUGS

The bg, fg, retry, posix, and nocto options are parsed by mount but currently are silently ignored. The tcp and namlen options are implemented but are not currently supported by the Linux kernel. The umount command should notify the server when an NFS filesystem is unmounted.

*Linux 0.99, 20 November 1993*

# nnrp.access

nnrp.access—Access file for on-campus NNTP sites.

## DESCRIPTION

The file /news/lib/nnrp.access specifies the access control for those NNTP sites that are not handled by the main InterNetNews daemon innd(8). The nnrpd(8) server reads it when first spawned by innd.

Comments begin with a number sign (#) and continue through the end of the line. Blank lines and comments are ignored. All other lines should consist of five fields separated by colons:

*hosts:perms:username:password:patterns*

The first field is a wildmat(3)-style pattern specifying the names or Internet address of a set of hosts. Before a match is checked, the client's hostname (or its Internet address if gethostbyaddr(3) fails) is converted to lowercase. Each line is matched in turn, and the last successful match is taken as the correct one.

The second field is a set of letters specifying the permissions granted to the client. The *perms* should be chosen from the following set:

R                                  The client can retrieve articles
P                                  The client can post articles

The third and fourth fields specify the *username* and *password* that the client must use to authenticate themselves before the server will accept any articles. Note that no authentication (other than a matching entry in this file) is required for newsreading. If they are empty, then no password is required. Whitespace in these fields will result in the client being unable to properly authenticate themselves and may be used to disable access.

The fifth field is a set of patterns identifying the newsgroups that the client is allowed to access. The *patterns* are interpreted in the same manner as the newsfeeds(5) file. The default, however, denies access to all groups.

The access file is normally used to provide host-level access control for reading and posting articles. There are times, however, when this is not sufficient and user-level access control is needed. Whenever an NNTP authinfo command is used, the nnrpd server rereads this file and looks for a matching username and password. If the local newsreaders are modified to send the authinfo command, then all host entries can have no access and specific users can be granted the appropriate read and post access. For example:

```
## host:perm:user:pass:groups
## Default is no access.
:: -no- : -no- :!*
## FOO hosts have no password, can read anything.
.foo.com:Read Post:::*
## A related workstation can't access FOO newsgroups.
lenox.foo.net:RP:martha:hiatt:*,!foo.*
```

If the file contains passwords, it should not be world-readable.

## HISTORY

Written by Rich $alz (rsalz@uunet.uu.net) for InterNetNews.

## SEE ALSO

innd(8), newsfeeds(5), nnrpd(8), wildmat(3)

# nntpsend.ctl

nntpsend.ctl—List of sites to feed via nntpsend.

## DESCRIPTION

The file /news/lib/nntpsend.ctl specifies the default list of sites to be fed by nntpsend(8).

Comments begin with a number sign (#) and continue through the end of the line. Blank lines and comments are ignored. All other lines should consist of four fields separated by a colon.

The first field is the name of the site as specified in the newsfeeds(5) file.

The second field should be the hostname or IP address of the remote site.

The third field, if non-empty, specifies the default tail truncation size of site's batchfile. This is passed to shrinkfile as the -s flag. If this field is empty, no truncation is performed.

The fourth field specifies some default flags passed to innxmit(8). The flag -a is always given to innxmit and need not appear here. If no -t *timeout* flag is given in this field and on the nntpsend command line, -t 180 will be given to innxmit.

## HISTORY

Written by Landon Curt Noll (chongo@toad.com) for InterNetNews.

## SEE ALSO

innxmit(8), newsfeeds(5), nntpsend(8), trunc(1)

# nologin

nologin—Prevent usual users from logging into the system.

## DESCRIPTION

If the file /etc/nologin exists, login(1) will allow access only to root. Other users will be shown the contents of this file and their logins refused.

## FILES

/etc/nologin

## SEE ALSO

login(1), shutdown(8)

*Linux, 29 December 1992*

# overview.fmt

overview.fmt—Format of news overview database.

## DESCRIPTION

The file `/news/lib/overview.fmt` specifies the organization of the news overview database. Blank lines and lines beginning with a number sign (#) are ignored. The order of lines in this file is important; it determines the order in which the fields will appear in the database.

Most lines will consist of an article header name, optionally followed by a colon. A trailing set of lines can have the word `full` appear after the colon; this indicates that the header should appear as well as its value.

If this file is changed, it is usually necessary to rebuild the existing overview database using `expireover(8)` after removing all existing overview files.

The default file, show here, is compatible with Geoff Collyer's nov package:

```
Subject:
From:
Date:
Message-ID:
References:
Bytes:
Lines:
## Some newsreaders get better performance if Xref is present
#Xref:full
```

## HISTORY

Written by Rich $alz (`rsalz@uunet.uu.net`) for InterNetNews. Intended to be compatible with the nov package written by Geoff Collyer (`geoff@world.std.com`).

# passwd

passwd—Password file.

## DESCRIPTION

passwd is an ASCII file that contains a list of the system's users and the passwords they must use for access. The password file should have general read permission (many utilities, such as `ls(1)`, use it to map user IDs to usernames) but write access only for the superuser.

In the good old days, there was no great problem with this general read permission. Everybody could read the encrypted passwords, but the hardware was too slow to crack a well-chosen password, and moreover, the basic assumption used to be that of a friendly user community. These days, many people run some version of the shadow password suite, where `/etc/passwd` has *s instead of passwords, and the encrypted passwords are in `/etc/shadow`, which is readable by root only.

When you create a new login, leave the password field empty and use `passwd(1)` to fill it. A star (*) in the password field means that this user cannot log in via `login(1)`.

There is one entry per line, and each line has the format:

```
login_name:passwd:UID:GID:user_name:directory:shell
```

The field descriptions are

| | |
|---|---|
| *login_name* | The name of the user on the system. |
| *password* | The encrypted optional user password. |
| *UID* | The numerical user ID. |
| *GID* | The numerical group ID for this user. |
| *user_name* | The (optional) comment field (often a full username). |
| *directory* | The user's $HOME directory. |
| *shell* | The program to run at login (if empty, use `/bin/sh`). |

## NOTE

If your root file system is on /dev/ram, you must save a changed password file to your root filesystem floppy before you shut down the system and check the access rights. If you want to create user groups, their GIDs must be equal and there must be an entry in /etc/group, or no group will exist.

## FILES

/etc/passwd

## SEE ALSO

passwd(1), login(1), group(5), shadow(5)

Linux, 24 July 1993

# passwd.nntp

passwd.nntp—Passwords for connecting to remote NNTP servers.

## DESCRIPTION

The file /news/lib/passwd.nntp contains host-name-password triplets for use when authenticating client programs to NNTP servers. This file is normally interpreted by the NNTPsend-password routine in libinn(3). Blank lines and lines beginning with a number sign (#) are ignored. All other lines should consist of three or fields separated by colons:

```
host:name:password
host:name:password:style
```

The first field is the name of a host and is matched in a case-insensitive manner. The second field is a username, and the third is a password. The optional fourth field specifies the type of authentication to use. The default is authinfo, which means that NNTP authinfo commands are used to authenticate to the remote host. If either the username or password are empty, then the related command will not be sent. (The authinfo command is a common extension to RFC 977.) For example:

```
## UUNET needs a password, MIT doesn't.
mit.edu:bbn::authinfo
uunet.uu.net:bbn:yoyoma:authinfo
```

This file should not be world-readable.

## HISTORY

Written by Rich $alz (rsalz@uunet.uu.net) for InterNetNews.

## SEE ALSO

innd(8), libinn(3)

# pbm

pbm—Portable bitmap file format.

## DESCRIPTION

The portable bitmap format is a lowest common denominator monochrome file format. It was originally designed to make it reasonable to mail bitmaps between different types of machines using the typical stupid network mailers we have today. Now it serves as the common language of a large family of bitmap conversion filters. The definition is as follows:

A "magic number" for identifying the file type. A pbm file's magic number is the two characters P1.

Whitespace (blanks, Tabs, CRs, LFs).

A width, formatted as ASCII characters in decimal.

Whitespace.

A height, again in ASCII decimal.

Whitespace.

Width * height bits, each either 1 or 0, starting at the top-left corner of the bitmap, proceeding in normal English reading order.

The character 1 means black; 0 means white.

Whitespace in the bits section is ignored.

Characters from a # to the next end-of-line are ignored (comments).

No line should be longer than 70 characters.

Here is an example of a small bitmap in this format:

```
P1
# feep.pbm
24 7
0 0 0 0 0 0 0 0 0 0 0 0 0 0 0 0 0 0 0 0 0 0 0 0
0 1 1 1 1 0 0 1 1 1 1 0 0 1 1 1 1 0 0 1 1 1 1 0
0 1 0 0 0 0 1 0 0 0 0 1 0 0 0 0 1 0 0 1 0 0 1 0
0 1 1 1 0 0 0 1 1 1 0 0 0 1 1 1 0 0 0 1 1 1 1 0
0 1 0 0 0 0 1 0 0 0 0 1 0 0 0 0 1 0 0 0 1 0 0 0
0 1 0 0 0 0 1 1 1 1 0 0 1 1 1 1 0 0 1 0 0 0 0
0 0 0 0 0 0 0 0 0 0 0 0 0 0 0 0 0 0 0 0 0 0 0 0
```

Programs that read this format should be as lenient as possible, accepting anything that looks remotely like a bitmap.

There is also a variant on the format, available by setting the RAWBITS option at compile time. This variant is different in the following ways:

The "magic number" is P4 instead of P1.

The bits are stored eight per byte, high bit first and low bit last.

No whitespace is allowed in the bits section, and only a single character of whitespace (typically a newline) is allowed after the height.

The files are eight times smaller and many times faster to read and write.

## SEE ALSO

atktopbm(1), brushtopbm(1), cmuwmtopbm(1), g3topbm(1), gemtopbm(1), icontopbm(1), macptopbm(1), mgrtopbm(1), pi3topbm(1), xbmtopbm(1), ybmtopbm(1), pbmto10x(1), pnmtoascii(1), pbmtoatk(1), pbmtobbnbg(1), pbmtocmuwm(1), pbmtoepson(1), pbmtog3(1), pbmtogem(1), pbmtogo(1), pbmtoicon(1), pbmtolj(1), pbmtomacp(1), pbmtomgr(1), pbmtopi3(1), pbmtoplot(1), pbmtoptx(1), pbmtox10bm(1), pbmtoxbm(1), pbmtoybm(1), pbmtozinc(1), pbmlife(1), pbmmake(1), pbmmask(1), pbmreduce(1), pbmtext(1), pbmupc(1), pnm(5), pgm(5), ppm(5)

## AUTHOR

Copyright 1989, 1991 by Jef Poskanzer.

*27 September 1991*

# pgm

pgm—Portable graymap file format.

## DESCRIPTION

The portable graymap format is a lowest common denominator grayscale file format. The definition is as follows:

A "magic number" for identifying the file type. A pgm file's magic number is the two characters P2.

Whitespace (blanks, Tabs, CRs, LFs).

A width, formatted as ASCII characters in decimal.

Whitespace.

A height, again in ASCII decimal.

Whitespace.

The maximum gray value, again in ASCII decimal.

Whitespace.

Width * height gray values, each in ASCII decimal, between 0 and the specified maximum value, separated by whitespace, starting at the top-left corner of the graymap, proceeding in normal English reading order. A value of 0 means black, and the maximum value means white.

Characters from a # to the next end-of-line are ignored (comments).

No line should be longer than 70 characters.

Here is an example of a small graymap in this format:

```
P2
# feep.pgm
24 7
15
0  0  0  0  0  0  0  0  0  0  0  0  0  0  0  0  0  0  0  0  0  0  0  0
0  3  3  3  3  0  0  7  7  7  7  0  0  11 11 1111 0  0  15 1515 15 0
0  3  0  0  0  0  0  7  0  0  0  0  0  11 0  0  0  0  0  15 0  0  150
0  3  3  3  0  0  0  7  7  7  0  0  0  11 11 110 0  0  15 15 15 150
0  3  0  0  0  0  0  7  0  0  0  0  0  11 0  0  0  0  0  15 0  0  0
0  3  0  0  0  0  0  7  7  7  7  0  0  11 11 1111 0  0  15 0  0  0  0
0  0  0  0  0  0  0  0  0  0  0  0  0  0  0  0  0  0  0  0  0  0  0  0
```

Programs that read this format should be as lenient as possible, accepting anything that looks remotely like a graymap.

There is also a variant on the format, available by setting the RAWBITS option at compile time. This variant is different in the following ways:

The "magic number" is P5 instead of P2.

The gray values are stored as plain bytes, instead of ASCII decimal.

No whitespace is allowed in the grays section, and only a single character of whitespace (typically a newline) is allowed after the maxval.

The files are smaller and many times faster to read and write.

Note that this raw format can only be used for maxvals less than or equal to 255. If you use the pgm library and try to write a file with a larger maxval, it will automatically fall back on the slower but more general plain format.

## SEE ALSO

fitstopgm(1), fstopgm(1), hipstopgm(1), lispmtopgm(1), psidtopgm(1), rawtopgm(1), pgmbentley(1), pgmcrater(1), pgmedge(1), pgmenhance(1), pgmhist(1), pgmnorm(1), pgmoil(1), pgmramp(1), pgmtexture(1), pgmtofits(1), pgmtofs(1), pgmtolispm(1), pgmtopbm(1), pnm(5), pbm(5), ppm(5)

## AUTHOR

Copyright 1989, 1991 by Jef Poskanzer.

*12 November 1991*

# pnm

pnm—Portable anymap file format.

## DESCRIPTION

The pnm programs operate on portable bitmaps, graymaps, and pixmaps produced by the pbm, pgm, and ppm segments. There is no file format associated with pnm itself.

## SEE ALSO

anytopnm(1), rasttopnm(1), tifftopnm(1), xwdtopnm(1), pnmtops(1), pnmtorast(1), pnmtotiff(1), pnmtoxwd(1), pnmarith(1), pnmcat(1), pnmconvol(1), pnmcrop(1), pnmcut(1), pnmdepth(1), pnmenlarge(1), pnmfile(1), pnmflip(1), pnmgamma(1), pnmindex(1), pnminvert(1), pnmmargin(1), pnmnoraw(1), pnmpaste(1), pnmrotate(1), pnmscale(1), pnmshear(1), pnmsmooth(1), pnmtile(1), ppm(5), pgm(5), pbm(5)

## AUTHOR

Copyright 1989, 1991 by Jef Poskanzer.

*27 September 1991*

# ppm

ppm—Portable pixmap file format.

## DESCRIPTION

The portable pixmap format is a lowest common denominator color image file format. The definition is as follows:

A "magic number" for identifying the file type. A ppm file's magic number is the two characters P3.

Whitespace (blanks, Tabs, CRs, LFs).

A width, formatted as ASCII characters in decimal.

Whitespace.

A height, again in ASCII decimal.

Whitespace.

The maximum color-component value, again in ASCII decimal.

Whitespace.

Width * height pixels, each three ASCII decimal values between 0 and the specified maximum value, starting at the top-left corner of the pixmap, proceeding in normal English reading order. The three values for each pixel represent red, green, and blue; a value of 0 means that color is off, and the maximum value means that color is maxed out.

Characters from a # to the next end-of-line are ignored (comments).

No line should be longer than 70 characters.

Here is an example of a small pixmap in this format:

```
P3
# feep.ppm
4 4
15
0  0  0    0  0  0    0  0  0   15  0 15
0  0  0    0 15  7    0  0  0    0  0  0
0  0  0    0  0  0    0 15  7    0  0  0
15  0 150   0  0  0   0  0  0    0  0  0
```

Programs that read this format should be as lenient as possible, accepting anything that looks remotely like a pixmap.

There is also a variant on the format, available by setting the RAWBITS option at compile time. This variant is different in the following ways:

The "magic number" is P6 instead of P3.

The pixel values are stored as plain bytes, instead of ASCII decimal.

Whitespace is not allowed in the pixels area, and only a single character of whitespace (typically a newline) is allowed after the maxval.

The files are smaller and many times faster to read and write.

Note that this raw format can only be used for maxvals less than or equal to 255. If you use the ppm library and try to write a file with a larger maxval, it will automatically fall back on the slower but more general plain format.

## SEE ALSO

giftoppm(1), gouldtoppm(1), ilbmtoppm(1), imgtoppm(1), mtvtoppm(1), pcxtoppm(1), pgmtoppm(1), pi1toppm(1), picttoppm(1), pjtoppm(1), qrttoppm(1), rawtoppm(1), rgb3toppm(1), sldtoppm(1), spctoppm(1), sputoppm(1), tgatoppm(1), ximtoppm(1), xpmtoppm(1), yuvtoppm(1), ppmtoacad(1), ppmtogif(1), ppmtoicr(1), ppmtoilbm(1), ppmtopcx(1), ppmtopgm(1), ppmtopi1(1), ppmtopict(1), ppmtopj(1), ppmtopuzz(1), ppmtorgb3(1), ppmtosixel(1), ppmtotga(1), ppmtouil(1), ppmtoxpm(1), ppmtoyuv(1), ppmdither(1), ppmforge(1), ppmhist(1), ppmmake(1), ppmpat(1), ppmquant(1), ppmquantall(1), ppmrelief(1), pnm(5), pgm(5), pbm(5)

## AUTHOR

Copyright 1989, 1991 by Jef Poskanzer.

*27 September 1991*

# /proc

/proc—Process information pseudo-filesystem.

## DESCRIPTION

/proc is a pseudo-filesystem that is used as an interface to kernel data structures rather than reading and interpreting /dev/kmem. Most of it is read-only, but some files allow kernel variables to be changed.

The following outline gives a quick tour through the /proc hierarchy.

| | |
|---|---|
| [*number*] | There is a numerical subdirectory for each running process; the subdirectory is named by the process ID. Each contains the following pseudo-files and directories. |
| cmdline | This holds the complete command line for the process, unless the whole process has been swapped out or unless the process is a zombie. In either of these later cases, there is nothing in this file: That is, a read on this file will return as having read 0 characters. This file is null-terminated but not newline-terminated. |
| cwd | This is a link current working directory of the process. To find out the cwd of process 20, for instance, you can do this: cd /proc/20/cwd; /bin/pwd. Note that the pwd command is often a shell built in and might not work properly in this context. |
| environ | This file contains the environment for the process. The entries are separated by null characters, and there may be a null character at the end. Thus, to print out the environment of process 1, you would do |
| | (cat /proc/1/environ; echo) ¦ tr "\000" "\n" |
| | For a reason why one should want to do this, see lilo(8). |
| exe | A pointer to the binary that was executed and appears as a symbolic link. readlink(2) on the exe special file returns a string in the format: |
| | [*device*]:*inode* |
| | For example, [0301]:1502 is inode 1502 on device major 03 (IDE, MFM, and so on drives), minor |

01 (first partition on the first drive). Also, the symbolic link can be dereferenced normally; attempting to open exe will open the executable. You can even type /proc/[number]/exe to run another copy of the same process as [number].

find(1) with the -inum option can be used to locate the file.

**fd**

This is a subdirectory containing one entry for each file that the process has open, named by its file descriptor, and that is a symbolic link to the actual file (as the exe entry does). Thus, 0 is standard input, 1 standard output, 2 standard error, and so on.

Programs that will take a filename but will not take the standard input and that write to a file but will not send their output to standard output can be effectively foiled this way, assuming that -i is the flag designating an input file and -o is the flag designating an output file:

```
foobar -i /proc/self/fd/0 -o /proc/self/fd/1 ...
```

and you have a working filter. Note that this will not work for programs that seek on their files because the files in the fd directory are not seekable.

/proc/self/fd/N is approximately the same as /dev/fd/N in some UNIX and UNIX-like systems. Most Linux MAKEDEV scripts symbolically link /dev/fd to /proc/self/fd, in fact.

**maps**

A file containing the currently mapped memory regions and their access permissions.

The format is

| address | perms | offset | dev | inode |
|---------|-------|--------|-----|-------|
| 00000000-0002f000 | r-x- | 00000400 | 03:03 | 1401 |
| 0002f000-00032000 | rwx-p | 0002f400 | 03:03 | 1401 |
| 00032000-0005b000 | rwx-p | 00000000 | 00:00 | 0 |
| 60000000-60098000 | rwx-p | 00000400 | 03:03 | 215 |
| 60098000-600c7000 | rwx-p | 00000000 | 00:00 | 0 |
| bfffa000-c0000000 | rwx-p | 00000000 | 00:00 | 0 |

address is the address space in the process that it occupies. perms is a set of permissions: r = read, w = write, x = execute, s = shared, p = private (copy on write).

offset is the offset into the file/whatever, dev is the device (major: minor), and inode is the inode on that device. 0 indicates that no inode is associated with the memory region, as the case would be with bss.

**mem**

This is not the same as the mem (1,1) device, despite the fact that it has the same device numbers. The /dev/mem device is the physical memory before any address translation is done, but the mem file here is the memory of the process that accesses it. This cannot be mmap(2)ed currently, and will not be until a general mmap(2) is added to the kernel. (This might have happened by the time you read this.)

**mmap**

Directory of maps by mmap(2) that are symbolic links such as exe, fd/*, and so on. Note that maps includes a superset of this information, so /proc/*/mmap should be considered obsolete.

0 is usually libc.so.4.

/proc/*/mmap was removed in Linux kernel version 1.1.40. (It really was obsolete!)

**root**

UNIX and Linux support the idea of a per-process root of the filesystem, set by the chroot(2) system call. root points to the filesystem root and behaves as exe, fd/*, and so on do.

**stat**

Status information about the process. This is used by ps(1). The fields, in order, with their proper scanf(3) format specifiers, are

| pid %d | The process ID. |
|--------|-----------------|
| comm %s | The filename of the executable in parentheses. This is visible whether or not the executable is swapped out. |

| | |
|---|---|
| state %c | One character from the string RSDZT where R is running, S is sleeping in an interruptible wait, D is sleeping in an uninterruptible wait or swapping, Z is zombie, and T is traced or stopped (on a signal). |
| ppid %d | The PID of the parent. |
| pgrp %d | The process group ID of the process. |
| session %d | The session ID of the process. |
| tty %d | The tty the process uses. |
| tpgid %d | The process group ID of the process that currently owns the tty that the process is connected to. |
| flags %u | The flags of the process. Currently, every flag has the math bit set because crt0.s checks for math emulation, so this is not included in the output. This is probably a bug because not every process is a compiled C program. The math bit should be a decimal 4, and the traced bit is decimal 10. |
| minflt %u | The number of minor faults the process has made, those that have not required loading a memory page from disk. |
| cminflt %u | The number of minor faults that the process and its children have made. |
| majflt %u | The number of major faults the process has made, those that have required loading a memory page from disk. |
| cmajflt %u | The number of major faults that the process and its children have made. |
| utime %d | The number of jiffies that this process has been scheduled in user mode. |
| stime %d | The number of jiffies that this process has been scheduled in kernel mode. |
| cutime %d | The number of jiffies that this process and its children have been scheduled in user mode. |
| cstime %d | The number of jiffies that this process and its children have been scheduled in kernel mode. |
| counter %d | The current maximum size in jiffies of the process's next timeslice, or what is currently left of its current timeslice if it is the currently running process. |
| priority %d | The standard nice value, plus fifteen. The value is never negative in the kernel. |
| timeout %u | The time in jiffies of the process's next time-out. |
| itrealvalue %u | The time (in jiffies) before the next SIGALRM is sent to the process due to an interval timer. |
| starttime %d | Time the process started in jiffies after system boot. |
| vsize %u | Virtual memory size. |
| rss %u | Resident set size: Number of pages the process has in real memory, minus 3 for administrative purposes. This is just the pages that count toward text, data, or stack space. This does not include pages that have not been demand-loaded in or that are swapped out. |
| rlim %u | Current limit in bytes on the rss of the process (usually 2,147,483,647). |
| startcode %u | The address above which program text can run. |
| endcode %u | The address below which program text can run. |
| startstack %u | The address of the start of the stack. |
| kstkesp %u | The current value of esp (32-bit stack pointer), as found in the kernel stack page for the process. |
| kstkeip %u | The current EIP (32-bit instruction pointer). |
| signal %d | The bitmap of pending signals (usually 0). |
| blocked %d | The bitmap of blocked signals (usually 0, 2 for shells). |

| | | |
|---|---|---|
| sigignore %d | | The bitmap of ignored signals. |
| sigcatch %d | | The bitmap of catched signals. |
| wchan %u | | This is the "channel" in which the process is waiting. This is the address of a system call and can be looked up in a name list if you need a textual name. (If you have an up-to-date /etc/psdatabase, then try ps -l to see the WCHAN field in action.) |

| | |
|---|---|
| cpuinfo | This is a collection of CPU and system architecture dependent items; for each supported architecture is a different list. The only two common entries are cpu, which is the CPU currently in use, and BogoMIPS, a system constant that is calculated during kernel initialization. |
| devices | Text listing of major numbers and device groups. This can be used by MAKEDEV scripts for consistency with the kernel. |
| dma | This is a list of the registered ISA DMA (direct memory access) channels in use. |
| filesystems | A text listing of the filesystems that were compiled into the kernel. Incidentally, this is used by mount(1) to cycle through different filesystems when none is specified. |
| interrupts | This is used to record the number of interrupts per each IRQ on (at least) the i386 architecture. Very easy to read formatting done in ASCII. |
| ioports | This is a list of currently registered input-output port regions that are in use. |
| kcore | This file represents the physical memory of the system and is stored in the core file format. With this pseudo-file and an unstripped kernel (/usr/src/linux/tools/zSystem) binary, GDB can be used to examine the current state of any kernel data structures.<br><br>The total length of the file is the size of physical memory (RAM) plus 4KB. |
| kmsg | This file can be used instead of the syslog(2) system call to log kernel messages. A process must have superuser privileges to read this file, and only one process should read this file. This file should not be read if a syslog process is running that uses the syslog(2) system call facility to log kernel messages.<br><br>Information in this file is retrieved with the dmesg(8) program. |
| ksyms | This holds the kernel exported symbol definitions used by the modules(X) tools to dynamically link and bind loadable modules. |
| loadavg | The load average numbers give the number of jobs in the run queue averaged over 1, 5, and 15 minutes. They are the same as the load average numbers given by uptime(1) and other programs. |
| malloc | This file is only present if CONFIGDEBUGMALLOC was defined during compilation. |
| meminfo | This is used by free(1) to report the amount of free and used memory (both physical and swap) on the system as well as the shared memory and buffers used by the kernel.<br><br>It is in the same format as free(1) except in bytes rather than KB. |
| modules | A text list of the modules that have been loaded by the system. |
| net | Various net pseudo-files, all of which give the status of some part of the networking layer. These files contain ASCII structures and are therefore readable with cat. However, the standard netstat(8) suite provides much cleaner access to these files. |
| arp | This holds an ASCII readable dump of the kernel ARP table used for address resolutions. It will show both dynamically learned and pre-programmed ARP entries. The format is |

| IP address | HW type | Flags | HW address |
|---|---|---|---|
| 10.11.100.129 | 0x1 | 0x6 | 00:20:8A:00:0C:5A |
| 10.11.100.5 | 0x1 | 0x2 | 00:C0:EA:00:00:4E |
| 44.131.10.6 | 0x3 | 0x2 | GW4PTS |

*IP address* is the IPv4 address of the machine. The *HW type* is the hardware type of the address from RFC 826. The flags are the internal flags of the ARP structure (as defined in /usr/include/linux/if_arp.h) and the *HW address* is the physical layer mapping for that IP address if it is known.

| dev | The dev pseudo-file contains network device status information. This gives the number of received and sent packets, the number of errors and collisions, and other basic statistics. These are used by the ifconfig(8) program to report device status. The format is |

```
Inter-¦ Receive                    ¦ Transmit
face   ¦packets errs drop fifo frame¦packets errs drop fifo colls carrier

lo:    0       0    0    0    0      2353    0    0    0    0     0

eth0:  644324  1    0    0    1      563770  0    0    0    581   0
```

| ipx | No information. |
| ipx_route | No information. |
| rarp | This file uses the same format as the ARP file and contains the current reverse mapping database used to provide rarp(8) reverse address lookup services. If rarp is not configured into the kernel, this file will not be present. |
| raw | Holds a dump of the RAW socket table. Much of the information is not of use apart from debugging. The sl value is the kernel hash slot for the socket; the local_address is the local address and protocol number pair. St is the internal status of the socket. The tx_queue and rx_queue are the outgoing and incoming data queue in terms of kernel memory usage. The tr, tm->when, and rexmits fields are not used by RAW. The uid field holds the creator euid of the socket. |
| route | No information but looks similar to route(8). |
| snmp | This file holds the ASCII data needed for the IP, ICMP, TCP, and UDP management information bases for an snmp agent. As of writing, the TCP mib is incomplete. It should be completed by 1.2.0. |
| tcp | Holds a dump of the TCP socket table. Much of the information is not of use apart from debugging. The sl value is the kernel hash slot for the socket; the local_address is the local address and port number pair. The remote_address is the remote address and port number pair (if connected). St is the internal status of the socket. The tx_queue and rx_queue are the outgoing and incoming data queue in terms of kernel memory usage. The tr, tm->when, and rexmits fields hold internal information of the kernel socket state and are only useful for debugging. The uid field holds the creator euid of the socket. |
| udp | Holds a dump of the UDP socket table. Much of the information is not of use apart from debugging. The sl value is the kernel hash slot for the socket; the local_address is the local address and port number pair. The remote_address is the remote address and port number pair (if connected). St is the internal status of the socket. The tx_queue and rx_queue are the outgoing and incoming data queue in terms of kernel memory usage. The tr, tm->when, and rexmits fields are not used by UDP. The uid field holds the creator euid of the socket. The format is |

```
sl local_address rem_address    st tx_queue rx_queue tr rexmits tm->when uid

1: 01642C89:0201 0C642C89:03FF 01 00000000:00000001 01:000071BA 00000000 0

1: 00000000:0801 00000000:0000 0A 00000000:00000000 00:00000000 6F000100 0
1: 00000000:0201 00000000:0000 0A 00000000:00000000 00:00000000 00000000 0
```

| unix | Lists the UNIX domain sockets present within the system and their status. The format is |

```
Num RefCount Protocol Flags    Type St Path
0:  00000002 00000000 00000000 0001 03
1:  00000001 00000000 00010000 0001 01 /dev/printer
```

Num is the kernel table slot number, RefCount is the number of users of the socket, Protocol is currently always 0, and Flags represents the internal kernel flags holding the status of the socket. Type is currently always 1 (UNIX domain datagram sockets are not yet supported in the kernel). St is the internal state of the socket and Path is the bound path (if any) of the socket.

| | |
|---|---|
| pci | This is a listing of all PCI devices found during kernel initialization and their configuration. |
| scsi | A directory with the SCSI mid-level pseudo-file and various SCSI low-level driver directories, which contain a file for each SCSI host in this system, all of which give the status of some part of the SCSI IO subsystem. These files contain ASCII structures and are therefore readable with cat. |
| | You can also write to some of the files to reconfigure the subsystem or switch certain features on or off. |
| scsi/scsi | This is a listing of all SCSI devices known to the kernel. The listing is similar to the one seen during bootup. scsi currently supports only the single device command, which allows root to add a hot-plugged device to the list of known devices. |
| | An echo 'scsisingledevice1 0 5 0'> /proc/scsi/scsi will cause host scsi1 to scan on SCSI channel 0 for a device on ID 5 LUN 0. If there is already a device known on this address or the address is invalid, an error will be returned. |
| drivername | drivername can currently be NCR53c7xx, aha152x, aha1542, aha1740, aic7xxx, buslogic, eata_dma, eata_pio, fdomain, in2000, pas16, qlogic, scsi_debug, seagate, t128, u15-24f, ultrastor, or wd7000. These directories show up for all drivers that registered at least one SCSI HBA. Every directory contains one file per registered host. Every host-file is named after the number the host got assigned during initialization. |
| | Reading these files will usually show driver and host configuration, statistics, and so on. |
| | Writing to these files allows different things on different hosts. For example, with the latency and nolatency commands, root can switch on and off command latency measurement code in the eata_dma driver. With the lockup and unlock commands, root can control bus lockups simulated by the scsi_debug driver. |
| self | This directory refers to the process accessing the /proc filesystem and is identical to the /proc directory named by the process ID of the same process. |
| stat | kernel/system statistics. |
| cpu 3357 0 4313 1362393 | The number of jiffies (1/100ths of a second) that the system spent in user mode, user mode with low priority (nice), system mode, and the idle task. The last value should be 100 times the second entry in the uptime pseudo-file. |
| disk 0 0 0 0 | The four disk entries are not implemented at this time. I'm not even sure what this should be because kernel statistics on other machines usually track both transfer rate and I/Os per second and this only allows for one field per drive. |
| page 5741 1808 | The number of pages the system paged in and the number that were paged out (from disk). |
| swap 1 0 | The number of swap pages that have been brought in and out. |
| intr 1462898 | The number of interrupts received from the system boot. |
| ctxt 115315 | The number of context switches that the system underwent. |
| btime 769041601 | Boot time in seconds since the epoch (January 1, 1970). |
| sys | This directory (present since 1.3.57) contains a number of files and subdirectories corresponding to kernel variables. These variables can be read and sometimes modified using the proc filesystem and using the sysctl(2) system call. Presently, there are subdirectories kernel, net, and vm that each contain more files and subdirectories. |
| kernel | This contains the files domainname, file-max, file-nr, hostname, inode-max, inode-nr, osrelease, ostype, panic, real-root-dev, securelevel, and version, with function fairly clear from the name. |
| | The (read-only) file file-nr gives the number of files presently opened. The file file-max gives the maximum number of open files the kernel is willing to handle. If 1024 is not enough for you, try echo 4096 > /proc/sys/kernel/file-max. |
| | Similarly, the files inode-nr and inode-max indicate the present and the maximum number of inodes. |

The files ostype, osrelease, and version give substrings of /proc/version.

The file panic gives r/w access to the kernel variable panic_timeout. If this is zero, the kernel will loop on a panic; if nonzero, it indicates that the kernel should autoreboot after this number of minutes.

The file securelevel seems rather meaningless at present; root is just too powerful.

uptime    This file contains two numbers: the uptime of the system (seconds) and the amount of time spent in idle process (seconds).

version   This string identifies the kernel version that is currently running. For instance.

```
Linux version 1.0.9 (quinlan@phaze) #1 Sat May 14 01:51:54 EDT 1994
```

## SEE ALSO

cat(1), find(1), free(1), mount(1), ps(1), tr(1), uptime(1), readlink(2), mmap(2), chroot(2), syslog(2), hier(7), arp(8), dmesg(8), netstat(8), route(8), ifconfig(8), procinfo(8) and much more

## CONFORMS TO

This roughly conforms to a Linux 1.3.11 kernel. Please update this as necessary! Last updated for Linux 1.3.11.

## CAVEATS

Note that many strings (the environment and command line) are in the internal format, with subfields terminated by null bytes, so you might find that things are more readable if you use od -c or tr "\000" "\n" to read them.

This manual page is incomplete, possibly inaccurate, and is the kind of thing that needs to be updated very often.

## BUGS

The /proc filesystem may introduce security holes into processes running with chroot(2). For example, if /proc is mounted in the chroot hierarchy, a chdir(2) to /proc/1/root will return to the original root of the filesystem. This may be considered a feature instead of a bug because Linux does not yet support the fchroot(2) call.

*22 July 1996*

# protocols

protocols—The protocols definition file.

## DESCRIPTION

This file is a plain ASCII file, describing the various DARPA Internet protocols that are available from the TCP/IP subsystem. It should be consulted instead of using the numbers in the ARPA include files or, even worse, just guessing them. These numbers will occur in the protocol field of any IP header.

Keep this file untouched because changes would result in incorrect IP packages. Protocol numbers and names are specified by the DDN Network Information Center.

Each line is of the following format:

protocol number aliases ...

The fields are delimited by spaces or tabs. Empty lines and lines starting with a hash mark (#) are ignored. Remainder of lines are also ignored from the occurrence of a hash mark.

The field descriptions are

protocol    The native name for the protocol—for example, ip, tcp, or udp.

number      The official number for this protocol as it will appear within the IP header.

aliases     Optional aliases for the protocol.

This file might be distributed over a network using a network-wide naming service such as Yellow Pages/NIS or BIND/Hesoid.

## FILES

/etc/protocols                    The protocols definition file.

## SEE ALSO

getprotoent(3), *Guide to Yellow Pages Service, Guide to BIND/Hesiod Service*

*Linux, 18 October 1995*

# rcsfile

rcsfile—Format of RCS file.

## DESCRIPTION

An RCS file's contents are described by the grammar below.

The text is free format: space, backspace, tab, newline, vertical tab, form feed, and carriage return (collectively, whitespace) have no significance except in strings. However, whitespace cannot appear within an ID, num, or sym, and an RCS file must end with a newline.

Strings are enclosed by @. If a string contains a @, it must be doubled; otherwise, strings can contain arbitrary binary data.

The meta syntax uses the following conventions: ¦ (bar) separates alternatives; { and } enclose optional phrases. { and }* enclose phrases that can be repeated zero or more times. { and {+ enclose phrases that must appear at least once and can be repeated. Terminal symbols are in **boldface**; non-terminal symbols are in *italics*.

```
rcstext ::= admin {delta}* desc {deltatext}*
    admin ::= head {num};
              { branch {num}; }
              access {id}*;
              symbols {sym : num}*;
              locks {id : num}*; {strict ;}

              { comment {string}; }
              { expand {string}; }
              { newphrase }*
    delta ::= num
              date num;
              author id;
              state {id};
              branches {num}*;
              next {num};
              { new-phrase }*
    desc ::= desc string
    deltatext ::= num
                  log string
                  { newphrase }*
                  text string
    num ::= {digit ¦ .}+
    digit ::= 0 ¦ 1 ¦ 2 ¦ 3 ¦ 4 ¦ 5 ¦ 6 ¦ 7 ¦ 8 ¦ 9
    id ::= {num} idchar {idchar ¦ num}*
    sym ::= {digit}* idchar {idchar ¦ digit}*
    idchar ::= any visible graphic character except special
    special ::= $ ¦ , ¦ . ¦ : ¦ ; ¦ @
    string ::= @{any character, with @doubled}*@
```

```
newphrase ::= id word* ;
word ::= id | num | string | :
```

Identifiers are case sensitive. Keywords are in lowercase only. The sets of keywords and identifiers can overlap. In most environments, RCS uses the ISO8859/1 encoding: visible graphic characters are codes 041–176 and 240–377, and whitespace characters are codes 010–015 and 040.

Dates, which appear after the date keyword, are of the form *Y.mm.dd.hh.mm.ss*, where *Y* is the year, *mm* the month (01–12), *dd* the day (01–31), *hh* the hour (00–23), *mm* the minute (00–59), and *ss* the second (00–60). *Y* contains just the last two digits of the year for years from 1900 through 1999, and all the digits of years thereafter. Dates use the Gregorian calendar; times use UTC.

The newphrase productions in the grammar are reserved for future extensions to the format of RCS files. No newphrase will begin with any keyword already in use.

The delta nodes form a tree. All nodes whose numbers consist of a single pair (such as 2.3, 2.1, 1.3, and so on) are on the trunk and are linked through the next field in order of decreasing numbers. The head field in the admin node points to the head of that sequence (contains the highest pair). The branch node in the admin node indicates the default branch (or revision) for most RCS operations. If empty, the default branch is the highest branch on the trunk.

All delta nodes whose numbers consist of 2*n* fields (*n*2) (such as 3.1.1.1, 2.1.2.2, and so on) are linked as follows. All nodes whose first 2*n*–1 number fields are identical are linked through the next field in order of increasing numbers. For each such sequence, the delta node whose number is identical to the first 2*n*–2 number fields of the deltas on that sequence is called the branchpoint. The branches field of a node contains a list of the numbers of the first nodes of all sequences for which it is a branchpoint. This list is ordered in increasing numbers.

The following diagram shows an example of an RCS file's organization.

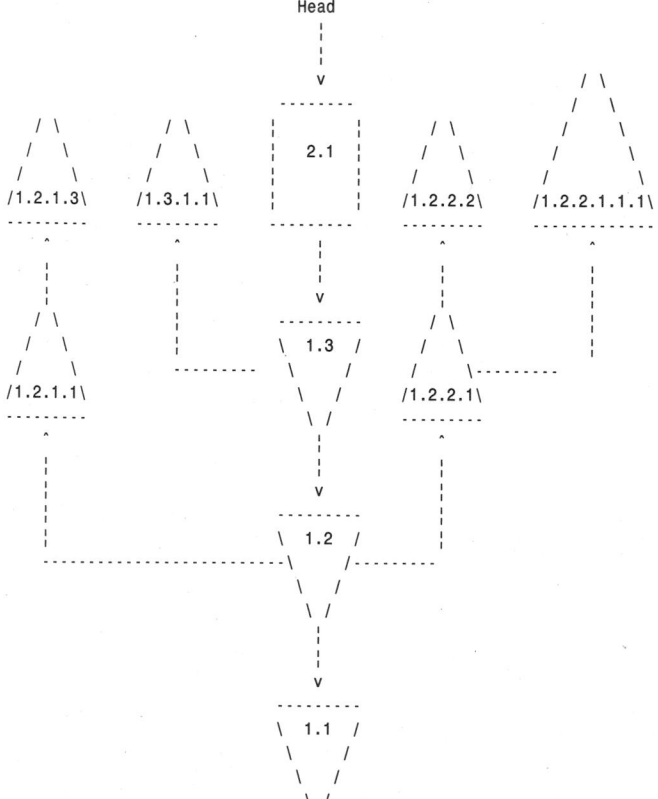

## IDENTIFICATION

Author: Walter F. Tichy, Purdue University, West Lafayette, IN, 47907. Manual Page Revision: 5.6; Release Date: 1995/06/05. Copyright 1982, 1988, 1989, Walter F. Tichy. Copyright 1990, 1991, 1992, 1993, 1994, 1995, Paul Eggert.

## SEE ALSO

rcsintro(1), ci(1), co(1), ident(1), rcs(1), rcsclean(1), rcsdiff(1), rcsmerge(1), rlog(1), Walter F. Tichy, RCS, "A System for Version Control," *Software—Practice & Experience*, 15, 7 (July 1985), 637-654.

*GNU, 5 June 1995*

# resolver

resolver—Resolver configuration file.

## SYNOPSIS

/etc/resolv.conf

## DESCRIPTION

The resolver is a set of routines in the C library (resolv(3)) that provides access to the Internet Domain Name System. The resolver configuration file contains information that is read by the resolver routines the first time they are invoked by a process. The file is designed to be human readable and contains a list of keywords with values that provide various types of resolver information.

On a normally configured system, this file should not be necessary. The only nameserver to be queried will be on the local machine, the domain name is determined from the host name, and the domain search path is constructed from the domain name.

The different configuration options are

| | |
|---|---|
| nameserver | Internet address (in dot notation) of a nameserver that the resolver should query. Up to MAXNS (currently 3) nameservers may be listed, one per keyword. If there are multiple servers, the resolver library queries them in the order listed. If no nameserver entries are present, the default is to use the nameserver on the local machine. (The algorithm used is to try a nameserver, and if the query times out, try the next until you run out of nameservers, and then repeat trying all the nameservers until a maximum number of retries are made.) |
| domain | Local domain name. Most queries for names within this domain can use short names relative to the local domain. If no domain entry is present, the domain is determined from the local hostname returned by gethostname(2); the domain part is taken to be everything after the first .. Finally, if the hostname does not contain a domain part, the root domain is assumed. |
| search | Search list for hostname lookup. The search list is normally determined from the local domain name; by default, it contains only the local domain name. This may be changed by listing the desired domain search path following the search keyword with spaces or tabs separating the names. Most resolver queries will be attempted using each component of the search path in turn until a match is found. Note that this process may be slow and will generate a lot of network traffic if the servers for the listed domains are not local and that queries will time out if no server is available for one of the domains. |
| | The search list is currently limited to six domains with a total of 256 characters. |
| sortlist | sortlist allows addresses returned by gethostbyname to be sorted. A sort list is specified by IP address netmask pairs. The netmask is optional and defaults to the natural netmask of the net. The IP address and optional network pairs are separated by slashes. Up to 10 pairs may be specified. |
| | sortlist 130.155.160.0/255.255.240.0 130.155.0.0 |

options                     `options` allows certain internal `resolver` variables to be modified. The syntax is

options *option* ...

where *option* is one of the following:

debug sets `RESDEBUG` in `res.options`.

ndots:*n* sets a threshold for the number of dots that must appear in a name given to `res_query` (see `resolver`(3)) before an initial absolute query will be made. The default for *n* is 1, meaning that if there are any dots in a name, the name will be tried first as an absolute name before any search list elements are appended to it.

The `domain` and `search` keywords are mutually exclusive. If more than one instance of these keywords is present, the last instance wins.

The `search` keyword of a system's `resolv.conf` file can be overridden on a per-process basis by setting the environment variable `LOCALDOMAIN` to a space-separated list of search domains.

The `options` keyword of a system's `resolv.conf` file can be amended on a per-process basis by setting the environment variable `RES_OPTIONS` to a space-separated list of resolver options as explained previously.

The keyword and value must appear on a single line, and the keyword (such as `nameserver`) must start the line. The value follows the keyword, separated by whitespace.

## FILES

/etc/resolv.conf

## SEE ALSO

`gethostbyname`(3), `resolver`(3), `hostname`(7), `named`(8), Name Server Operations Guide for BIND

*11 November 1993*

# securetty

securetty—File that lists `ttys` from which root can log in.

## DESCRIPTION

/etc/securetty is used by `login`(1); the file contains the device names of `tty` lines (one per line, without leading /dev/) on which root is allowed to log in.

## FILES

/etc/securetty

## SEE ALSO

login(1)

*Linux, 29 December 1992*

# services

services—Internet network services list.

## DESCRIPTION

services is a plain ASCII file providing a mapping between friendly textual names for Internet services and their underlying assigned port numbers and protocol types. Every networking program should look into this file to get the port number (and protocol) for its service. The C library routines getservent(3), getservbyname(3), getservbyport(3), setservent(3), and endservent(3) support querying this file from programs.

Port numbers are assigned by the IANA (Internet Assigned Numbers Authority), and their current policy is to assign both TCP and UDP protocols when assigning a port number. Therefore, most entries will have two entries, even for TCP-only services.

Port numbers below 1024 (so-called low-numbered ports) can only be bound to by root (see bind(2), tcp(7), and udp(7).) This is so that clients connecting to low-numbered ports can trust that the service running on the port is the standard implementation and not a rogue service run by a user of the machine. Well-known port numbers specified by the IANA are normally located in this root-only space.

The presence of an entry for a service in the services file does not necessarily mean that the service is currently running on the machine. See inetd.conf(5) for the configuration of Internet services offered. Note that not all networking services are started by inetd(8) and so won't appear in inetd.conf(5). In particular, news (NNTP) and mail (SMTP) servers are often initialized from the system boot scripts.

The location of the services file is defined by PATH SERVICES in /usr/include/netdb.h. This is usually set to /etc/services.

Each line describes one service and is of the form:

```
service-name port/protocol [aliases ...]
```

| | |
|---|---|
| *service-name* | The friendly name the service is known by and looked up under. It is case sensitive. Often, the client program is named after the *service-name*. |
| *port* | The port number (in decimal) to use for this service. |
| *protocol* | The type of protocol to be used. This field should match an entry in the protocols(5) file. Typical values include tcp and udp. |
| *aliases* | An optional space- or tab-separated list of other names for this service (see the Bugs section below). Again, the names are case sensitive. |

Either spaces or tabs may be used to separate the fields.

Comments are started by the hash sign (#) and continue until the end of the line. Blank lines are skipped.

The *service-name* should begin in the first column of the file because leading spaces are not stripped. *service-names* can be any printable characters excluding space and tab; however, a conservative choice of characters should be used to minimize inter-operability problems. For example, a–z, 0–9, and hyphen (–) would seem a sensible choice.

Lines not matching this format should not be present in the file. (Currently, they are silently skipped by getservent(3), getservbyname(3), and getservbyport(3). However, this behavior should not be relied on.)

As a backwards compatibility feature, the slash (/) between the port number and protocol name can in fact be either a slash or a comma (,). Use of the comma in modern installations is depreciated.

This file might be distributed over a network using a network-wide naming service such as Yellow Pages/NIS or BIND/Hesiod.

A sample services file might look like this:

```
netstat     15/tcp
qotd        17/tcp      quote
msp         18/tcp      # message send protocol
msp         18/udp      # message send protocol
chargen     19/tcp      ttytst source
chargen     19/udp      ttytst source
ftp         21/tcp
#           22 - unassigned
telnet      23/tcp
```

## BUGS

There is a maximum of 35 aliases, due to the way the getservent(3) code is written.

Lines longer than BUFSIZ (currently 1024) characters will be ignored by getservent(3), getservbyname(3), and getservbyport(3). However, this will also cause the next line to be misparsed.

## FILES

| | |
|---|---|
| /etc/services | The Internet network services list |
| /usr/include/netdb.h | Definition of _PATH_SERVICES |

## SEE ALSO

getservent(3), getservbyname(3), getservbyport(3), setservent(3), endservent(3), protocols(5), listen(2), inetd.conf(5), inetd(8), Assigned Numbers RFC, most recently RFC 1700 (AKA STD0002), *Guide to Yellow Pages Service*, *Guide to BIND/Hesiod Service*.

*Linux, 11 January 1996*

# shells

shells—Pathnames of valid login shells.

## DESCRIPTION

/etc/shells is a text file that contains the full pathnames of valid login shells. This file is consulted by chsh(1) and is available to be queried by other programs.

## EXAMPLES

/etc/shells may contain the following paths:

/bin/sh
/bin/csh

## FILES

/etc/shells

## SEE ALSO

chsh(1)

*21 November 1993*

# syslog.conf

syslog.conf—syslogd(8) configuration file.

## DESCRIPTION

The syslog.conf file is the configuration file for the syslogd(8) program. It consists of lines with two fields: the selector field, which specifies the types of messages and priorities to which the line applies, and an action field, which specifies the action to be taken if a message syslogd received matches the selection criteria. There cannot be any spaces in the action field. The selector field is separated from the action field by one or more tab or space characters. (This is a departure from the standard BSD way of doing things; both tabs and spaces can be used to separate the selector from the action.)

The selector functions are encoded as a facility, a period (.), and a level, with no intervening whitespace. Both the facility and the level are case insensitive.

The facility describes the part of the system generating the message and is one of the following keywords: auth, authpriv, cron, daemon, kern, lpr, mail, mark, news, syslog, user, uucp, and local0 through local7. These keywords (with the exception of mark) correspond to the similar Dv LOG_ values specified to the openlog(3) and syslog(3) library routines.

The level describes the severity of the message and is a keyword, optionally preceded by an equals (=), from the following ordered list (higher to lower): emerg, alert, crit, err, warning, notice, info, and debug. These keywords correspond to the similar Dv LOG_ values specified to the syslog library routine.

See syslog(3) for further descriptions of both the facility and level keywords and their significance.

If a received message matches the specified facility and is of the specified level (or a higher level if level was specified without =), the action specified in the action field will be taken.

Multiple selectors may be specified for a single action by separating them with semicolon (;) characters. It is important to note, however, that each selector can modify the ones preceding it.

Multiple facilities may be specified for a single level by separating them with comma (,) characters.

An asterisk (*) can be used to specify all facilities or all levels.

The special facility "mark" receives a message at priority "info" every 20 minutes (see syslogd(8)). This is not enabled by a facility field containing an asterisk.

The special level "none" disables a particular facility.

The action field of each line specifies the action to be taken when the selector field selects a message. There are four forms:

A pathname (beginning with a leading slash). Selected messages are appended to the file.

A hostname (preceded by an at (@) sign). Selected messages are forwarded to the syslogd program on the named host.

A comma-separated list of users. Selected messages are written to those users if they are logged in.

An asterisk. Selected messages are written to all logged-in users.

Blank lines and lines whose first non-blank character is a hash (#) character are ignored.

## EXAMPLES

A configuration file might appear as follows:

```
# Log all kernel messages, authentication messages of
# level notice or higher and anything of level err or
# higher to the console.
# Don't log private authentication messages!
*.err;kern.*;auth.notice;authpriv.none          /dev/console

# Log anything (except mail) of level info or higher.
# Don't log private authentication messages!
*.info;mail.none;authpriv.none                  /var/log/messages

# Log debug messages only
*.=debug                                        /var/log/debug

# The authpriv file has restricted access.
authpriv.*                                      /var/log/secure

# Log all the mail messages in one place.
mail.*                                          /var/log/maillog

# Everybody gets emergency messages, plus log them on another
# machine.
*.emerg                                         *
*.emerg                                         @arpa.berkeley.edu
```

```
# Root and Eric get alert and higher messages.
*.alert                                              root,eric

# Save mail and news errors of level err and higher in a
# special file.
uucp,news.crit                                       /var/log/spoolerr
```

## FILES

/etc/syslog.conf            The syslogd(8) configuration file.

## BUGS

The effects of multiple selectors are sometimes not intuitive. For example mail.crit,*.err will select mail facility messages at the level of err or higher, not at the level of crit or higher.

## SEE ALSO

syslog(3), syslogd(8)

*10 May 1991*

# termcap

termcap—Terminal capability database.

## DESCRIPTION

The termcap database is an obsolete facility for describing the capabilities of character-cell terminals and printers. It is retained only for capability with old programs; new ones should use the terminfo(5) database and associated libraries.

/etc/termcap is an ASCII file (the database master) that lists the capabilities of many different types of terminals. Programs can read termcap to find the particular escape codes needed to control the visual attributes of the terminal actually in use. (Other aspects of the terminal are handled by stty.) The termcap database is indexed on the TERM environment variable.

termcap entries must be defined on a single logical line, with \ used to suppress the newline. Fields are separated by :. The first field of each entry starts at the left-hand margin and contains a list of names for the terminal, separated by ¦.

The first subfield may (in BSD termcap entries from versions 4.3 and prior) contain a short name consisting of two characters. This short name may consist of capital or small letters. In 4.4 BSD termcap entries, this field is omitted.

The second subfield (first in the newer 4.4 BSD format) contains the name used by the environment variable TERM. It should be spelled in lowercase letters. Selectable hardware capabilities should be marked by appending a hyphen and a suffix to this name. Usual suffixes are w (more than 80 characters wide), am (automatic margins), nam (no automatic margins) and rv (reverse video display). The third subfield contains a long and descriptive name for this termcap entry.

Subsequent fields contain the terminal capabilities; any continued capability lines must be indented one tab from the left margin.

Although there is no defined order, it is suggested to write first Boolean, then numeric, and at last string capabilities, each sorted alphabetically without looking at lower or upper spelling. Capabilities of similar functions can be written in one line.

Example:

```
Head line: vt¦vt101¦DEC VT 101 terminal in 80 character mode:\
Head line: Vt¦vt101-w¦DEC VT 101 terminal in (wide) 132 character mode:\
Boolean: :bs:\
Numeric: :co#80:\
String: :sr=nE[H:\
```

## Boolean Capabilities

| | |
|---|---|
| 5i | Printer will not echo on screen |
| am | Automatic margins which means automatic line wrap |
| bs | Ctrl+H (8 dec.) performs a backspace |
| bw | Backspace on left margin wraps to previous line and right margin |
| da | Display retained above screen |
| db | Display retained below screen |
| eo | A space erases all characters at cursor position |
| es | Escape sequences and special characters work in status line |
| gn | Generic device |
| hc | This is a hardcopy terminal |
| HC | The cursor is hard to see when not on bottom line |
| hs | Has a status line |
| hz | Hazeltine bug; the terminal cannot print tilde characters |
| in | Terminal inserts nulls, not spaces, to fill whitespace |
| km | Terminal has a meta key |
| mi | Cursor movement works in insert mode |
| ms | Cursor movement works in standout/underline mode |
| NP | No pad character |
| NR | ti does not reverse te |
| nx | No padding; must use XON/XOFF |
| os | Terminal can overstrike |
| ul | Terminal underlines, although it cannot overstrike |
| xb | Beehive glitch; F1 sends Escape and F2 sends ^C |
| xn | Newline/wraparound glitch |
| xo | Terminal uses XON/XOFF protocol |
| xs | Text typed over standout text will be displayed in standout |
| xt | Teleray glitch; destructive tabs and odd standout mode |

## Numeric Capabilities

| | |
|---|---|
| co | Number of columns |
| dB | Delay in milliseconds for backspace on hardcopy terminals |
| dC | Delay in milliseconds for carriage return on hardcopy terminals |
| dF | Delay in milliseconds for form feed on hardcopy terminals |
| dN | Delay in milliseconds for newline on hardcopy terminals |
| dT | Delay in milliseconds for tabulator stop on hardcopy terminals |
| dV | Delay in milliseconds for vertical tabulator stop on hardcopy terminals |
| it | Difference between tab positions |
| lh | Height of soft labels |
| lm | Lines of memory |
| lw | Width of soft labels |

*continues*

## Numeric Capabilities

| | |
|---|---|
| li | Number of lines |
| Nl | Number of soft labels |
| pb | Lowest baud rate that needs padding |
| sg | Standout glitch |
| ug | Underline glitch |
| vt | Virtual terminal number |
| ws | Width of status line if different from screen width |

## String Capabilities

| | |
|---|---|
| !1 | Shifted save key |
| !2 | Shifted suspend key |
| !3 | Shifted undo key |
| #1 | Shifted help key |
| #2 | Shifted home key |
| #3 | Shifted input key |
| #4 | Shifted cursor left key |
| %0 | Redo key |
| %1 | Help key |
| %2 | Mark key |
| %3 | Message key |
| %4 | Move key |
| %5 | Next-object key |
| %6 | Open key |
| %7 | Options key |
| %8 | Previous-object key |
| %9 | Print key |
| %a | Shifted message key |
| %b | Shifted move key |
| %c | Shifted next key |
| %d | Shifted options key |
| %e | Shifted previous key |
| %f | Shifted print key |
| %g | Shifted redo key |
| %h | Shifted replace key |
| %i | Shifted cursor right key |
| %j | Shifted resume key |
| &0 | Shifted cancel key |
| &1 | Reference key |
| &2 | Refresh key |
| &3 | Replace key |
| &4 | Restart key |

*String Capabilities*

| | |
|---|---|
| &5 | Resume key |
| &6 | Save key |
| &7 | Suspend key |
| &8 | Undo key |
| &9 | Shifted begin key |
| *0 | Shifted find key |
| *1 | Shifted command key |
| *2 | Shifted copy key |
| *3 | Shifted create key |
| *4 | Shifted delete character |
| *5 | Shifted delete line |
| *6 | Select key |
| *7 | Shifted end key |
| *8 | Shifted clear line key |
| *9 | Shifted exit key |
| @0 | Find key |
| @1 | Begin key |
| @2 | Cancel key |
| @3 | Close key |
| @4 | Command key |
| @5 | Copy key |
| @6 | Create key |
| @7 | End key |
| @8 | Enter/send key |
| @9 | Exit key |
| al | Insert one line |
| AL | Insert %1 lines |
| ac | Pairs of block graphic characters to map alternate character set |
| ae | End alternative character set |
| as | Start alternative character set for block graphic characters |
| bc | Backspace if not ^H |
| bl | Audio bell |
| bt | Move to previous tab stop |
| cb | Clear from beginning of line to cursor |
| cc | Dummy command character |
| cd | Clear to end of screen |
| ce | Clear to end of line |
| ch | Move cursor horizontally only to column %1 |
| cl | Clear screen and cursor home |
| cm | Cursor move to row %1 and column %2 (on screen) |
| CM | Move cursor to row %1 and column %2 (in memory) |

*continues*

*String Capabilities*

| | |
|---|---|
| cr | Carriage return |
| cs | Scroll region from line %1 to %2 |
| ct | Clear tabs |
| cv | Move cursor vertically only to line %1 |
| dc | Delete one character |
| DC | Delete %1 characters |
| dl | Delete one line |
| DL | Delete %1 lines |
| dm | Begin delete mode |
| do | Cursor down one line |
| DO | Cursor down #1 lines |
| ds | Disable status line |
| eA | Enable alternate character set |
| ec | Erase %1 characters starting at cursor |
| ed | End delete mode |
| ei | End insert mode |
| ff | Formfeed character on hardcopy terminals |
| fs | Return character to its position before going to status line |
| F1 | The string sent by function key f11 |
| F2 | The string sent by function key f12 |
| F3 | The string sent by function key f13 |
| ... | ... |
| F9 | The string sent by function key f19 |
| FA | The string sent by function key f20 |
| FB | The string sent by function key f21 |
| ... | ... |
| FZ | The string sent by function key f45 |
| Fa | The string sent by function key f46 |
| Fb | The string sent by function key f47 |
| ... | ... |
| Fr | The string sent by function key f63 |
| hd | Move cursor a half line down |
| ho | Cursor home |
| hu | Move cursor a half line up |
| i1 | Initialization string 1 at login |
| i3 | Initialization string 3 at login |
| is | Initialization string 2 at login |
| ic | Insert one character |
| IC | Insert %1 characters |
| if | Initialization file |
| im | Begin insert mode |

## String Capabilities

| | |
|---|---|
| ip | Insert pad time and needed special characters after insert |
| iP | Initialization program |
| K1 | Upper-left key on keypad |
| K2 | Center key on keypad |
| K3 | Upper-right key on keypad |
| K4 | Bottom-left key on keypad |
| K5 | Bottom-right key on keypad |
| k0 | Function key 0 |
| k1 | Function key 1 |
| k2 | Function key 2 |
| k3 | Function key 3 |
| k4 | Function key 4 |
| k5 | Function key 5 |
| k6 | Function key 6 |
| k7 | Function key 7 |
| k8 | Function key 8 |
| k9 | Function key 9 |
| k; | Function key 10 |
| ka | Clear all tabs key |
| kA | Insert line key |
| kb | Backspace key |
| kB | Back tab stop |
| kC | Clear screen key |
| kd | Cursor down key |
| kD | Key for delete character under cursor |
| ke | Turn keypad off |
| kE | Key for clear to end of line |
| kF | Key for scrolling forward/down |
| kh | Cursor home key |
| kH | Cursor down key |
| kI | Insert character/insert mode key |
| kl | Cursor left key |
| kL | Key for delete line |
| kM | Key for exit insert mode |
| kN | Key for next page |
| kP | Key for previous page |
| kr | Cursor right key |
| kR | Key for scrolling backward/up |
| ks | Turn keypad on |
| kS | Clear to end of screen key |
| kt | Clear this tab key |

*continues*

*String Capabilities*

| | |
|---|---|
| kT | Set tab here key |
| ku | Cursor up key |
| l0 | Label of zeroth function key, if not f0 |
| l1 | Label of first function key, if not f1 |
| l2 | Label of first function key, if not f2 |
| ... | ... |
| la | Label of tenth function key, if not f10 |
| le | Cursor left one character |
| ll | Move cursor to lower-left corner |
| LE | Cursor left %1 characters |
| LF | Turn soft labels off |
| LO | Turn soft labels on |
| mb | Start blinking |
| MC | Clear soft margins |
| md | Start bold mode |
| me | End all modes such as so, us, mb, md, and mr |
| mh | Start half bright mode |
| mk | Dark mode (Characters invisible) |
| ML | Set left soft margin |
| mm | Put terminal in meta mode |
| mo | Put terminal out of meta mode |
| mp | Turn on protected attribute |
| mr | Start reverse mode |
| MR | Set right soft margin |
| nd | Cursor right one character |
| nw | Carriage return command |
| pc | Padding character |
| pf | Turn printer off |
| pk | Program key %1 to send string %2 as if typed by user |
| pl | Program key %1 to execute string %2 in local mode |
| pn | Program soft label %1 to show string %2 |
| po | Turn the printer on |
| pO | Turn the printer on for %1 (<256) bytes |
| ps | Print screen contents on printer |
| px | Program key %1 to send string %2 to computer |
| r1 | Reset string 1 to set terminal to sane modes |
| r2 | Reset string 2 to set terminal to sane modes |
| r3 | Reset string 3 to set terminal to sane modes |
| RA | Disable automatic margins |
| rc | Restore saved cursor position |
| rf | Reset string file name |

*String Capabilities*

| | |
|---|---|
| RF | Request for input from terminal |
| RI | Cursor right %1 characters |
| rp | Repeat character %1 for %2 times |
| rP | Padding after character sent in replace mode |
| rs | Reset string |
| RX | Turn off XON/XOFF flow control |
| sa | Set %1 %2 %3 %4 %5 %6%7 %8 %9 attributes |
| SA | Enable automatic margins |
| sc | Save cursor position |
| se | End standout mode |
| sf | Normal scroll one line |
| SF | Normal scroll %1 lines |
| so | Start standout mode |
| sr | Reverse scroll |
| SR | Scroll back %1 lines |
| st | Set tabulator stop in all rows at current column |
| SX | Turn on XON/XOFF flow control |
| ta | Move to next hardware tab |
| tc | Read in terminal description from another entry |
| te | End program that uses cursor motion |
| ti | Begin program that uses cursor motion |
| ts | Move cursor to column %1 of status line |
| uc | Underline character under cursor and move cursor right |
| ue | End underlining |
| up | Cursor up one line |
| UP | Cursor up %1 lines |
| us | Start underlining |
| vb | Visible bell |
| ve | Normal cursor visible |
| vi | Cursor invisible |
| vs | Standout cursor |
| wi | Set window from line %1 to %2 and column %3 to %4 |
| XF | XOFF character if not ^S |

There are several ways of defining the control codes for string capabilities:

Normal characters except ^, \, and % represent themselves.

A ^x means Ctrl+x. Ctrl+A equals 1 decimal. \x means a special code. x can be one of the following characters:

| | |
|---|---|
| E | Escape (27). |
| n | Linefeed (10). |
| r | Carriage return (13). |
| t | Tabulation (9). |

| b | Backspace (8). |
| f | Form feed (12). |
| 0 | Null character. A \\*xxx* specifies the octal character *xxx*. |
| i | Increments parameters by one. |
| r | Single parameter capability. |
| + | Add value of next character to this parameter and do binary output. |
| 2 | Do ASCII output of this parameter with a field width of 2. |
| d | Do ASCII output of this parameter with a field width of 3. |
| % | Print a % |

If you use binary output, then you should avoid the null character because it terminates the string. You should reset tabulator expansion if a tabulator can be the binary output of a parameter.

Warning: The preceding metacharacters for parameters may be wrong; they document Minix termcap, which may not be compatible with Linux termcap.

The block graphic characters can be specified by three string capabilities:

| as | Start the alternative charset. |
| ae | End it. |
| ac | Pairs of characters. The first character is the name of the block graphic symbol and the second character is its definition. |

The following names are available:

| + | Right arrow (>) |
| , | Left arrow (<) |
| . | Down arrow (v) |
| 0 | Full square (#) |
| I | Latern (#) |
| - | Upper arrow (^) |
| ' | Rhombus (+) |
| a | Chess board (:) |
| f | Degree (') |
| g | Plus-minus (#) |
| h | Square (#) |
| j | Right bottom corner (+) |
| k | Right upper corner (+) |
| l | Left upper corner (+) |
| m | Left bottom corner (+) |
| n | Cross (+) |
| o | Upper horizontal line (·) |
| q | Middle horizontal line (-) |
| s | Bottom horizontal line (_) |
| t | Left tee (+) |
| u | Right tee (+) |
| v | Bottom tee (+) |
| w | Normal tee (+) |
| x | Vertical line (_) |
| ~ | Paragraph (???) |

The values in parentheses are suggested defaults that are used by curses if the capabilities are missing.

## SEE ALSO

termcap(3), curses(3), terminfo(5)

# ttytype

ttytype—Terminal name and device list.

## DESCRIPTION

The /etc/ttytype file associates termcap/terminfo terminal type names with tty lines. Each line consists of a terminal type, followed by whitespace, followed by a tty name (a device name without the /dev/ prefix).

This association is used by the program tset(1) to set the environment variable TERM to the default terminal name for the user's current tty.

This facility was designed for a traditional time-sharing environment featuring character-cell terminals hardwired to a UNIX minicomputer. It is little used on modern workstation and personal UNIXes.

## EXAMPLE

A typical /etc/ttytype is

```
con80x25 tty1
vt320 ttys0
```

## FILES

/etc/ttytype      The tty definitions file

## SEE ALSO

getty(1), terminfo(5), termcap(5)

# tzfile

tzfile—Time zone information.

## SYNOPSIS

```
#include <tzfile.h>
```

## DESCRIPTION

The time zone information files used by tzset(3) begin with bytes reserved for future use, followed by six four-byte values of type long, written in a "standard" byte order (the high-order byte of the value is written first). These values are, in order

| | |
|---|---|
| tzh_ttisgmtcnt | The number of GMT/local indicators stored in the file. |
| tzh_ttisstdcnt | The number of standard/wall indicators stored in the file. |
| tzh_leapcnt | The number of leap seconds for which data is stored in the file. |
| tzh_timecnt | The number of "transition times" for which data is stored in the file. |
| tzh_typecnt | The number of "local time types" for which data is stored in the file (must not be zero). |
| tzh_charcnt | The number of characters of "time zone abbreviation strings" stored in the file. |

The preceding header is followed by tzh_timecnt four-byte values of type long, sorted in ascending order. These values are written in "standard" byte order. Each is used as a transition time (as returned by time(2)) at which the rules for computing local time change. Next come tzh_timecnt one-byte values of type unsigned char; each one tells which of the different types of "local time" types described in the file is associated with the same-indexed transition time. These values serve as indices into an array of ttinfo structures that appears next in the file; these structures are defined as follows:

```
struct ttinfo {
long tt_gmtoff;
int tt_isdst;
unsigned int tt_abbrind;
};
```

Each structure is written as a four-byte value for tt_gmtoff of type long, in a standard byte order, followed by a one-byte value for tt_isdst and a one-byte value for tt_abbrind. In each structure, tt_gmtoff gives the number of seconds to be added to GMT, tt_isdst tells whether tm_isdst should be set by localtime(3) and tt_abbrind serves as an index into the array of time zone abbreviation characters that follow the ttinfo structures in the file.

Then there are tzh_leapcnt pairs of four-byte values, written in standard byte order; the first value of each pair gives the time (as returned by time(2)) at which a leap second occurs; the second gives the total number of leap seconds to be applied after the given time. The pairs of values are sorted in ascending order by time.

Then there are tzh_ttisstdcnt standard/wall indicators, each stored as a one-byte value; they tell whether the transition times associated with local time types were specified as standard time or wall clock time and are used when a time zone file is used in handling POSIX-style time zone environment variables.

Finally, there are tzh_ttisgmtcnt GMT/local indicators, each stored as a one-byte value; they tell whether the transition times associated with local time types were specified as GMT or local time and are used when a time zone file is used in handling POSIX-style time zone environment variables.

Localtime uses the first standard-time ttinfo structure in the file (or simply the first ttinfo structure in the absence of a standard-time structure) if either tzh_timecnt is zero or the time argument is less than the first transition time recorded in the file.

## SEE ALSO

newctime(3)

# utmp, wtmp

utmp, wtmp—Login records.

## SYNOPSIS

```
#include <utmp.h>
```

## DESCRIPTION

The utmp file allows you to discover information about who is currently using the system. There may be more users currently using the system because not all programs use utmp logging.

Warning: utmp must not be writable because many system programs depend on its integrity. You risk faked system log files and modifications of system files if you leave utmp writable to any user.

The file is a sequence of entries with the following structure declared in the include file:

```
#define UT_UNKNOWN 0
#define RUN_LVL 1
#define BOOT_TIME 2
#define NEW_TIME 3
#define OLD_TIME 4
```

```
#define INIT_PROCESS 5
#define LOGIN_PROCESS 6
#define USER_PROCESS 7
#define DEAD_PROCESS 8

#define UT_LINESIZE 12
#define UT_NAMESIZE 8
#define UT_HOSTSIZE 16

struct utmp {
    short ut_type;                /* type of login */
    pid_t ut_pid;                 /* pid of process */
    char ut_line[UT_LINESIZE];    /* device name of tty - "/dev/" */
    char ut_id[2];                /* init id or abbrev. ttyname */
    time_t ut_time;               /* login time */
    char ut_user[UT_NAMESIZE];    /* user name */
    char ut_host[UT_HOSTSIZE];    /* host name for remote login */
    long ut_addr;                 /* IP addr of remote host */
};
```

This structure gives the name of the special file associated with the user's terminal, the user's login name, and the time of login in the form of time(2). String fields are terminated by \0 if they are shorter than the size of the field.

The first entries ever created result from init(8) processing inittab(5). Before an entry is processed, though, init(8) cleans up utmp by setting ut_type to DEAD_PROCESS, clearing ut_user, ut_host and ut_time with null bytes for each record that ut_type is not DEAD_PROCESS or RUN_LVL and where no process with PID ut_pid exists. If no empty record with the needed ut_id can be found, init creates a new one. It sets ut_id from the inittab, ut_pid and ut_time to the current values, and ut_type to INIT_PROCESS.

getty(8) locates the entry by the PID, changes ut_type to LOGIN_PROCESS, changes ut_time, sets ut_line and waits for connection to be established. login(8), after a user has been authenticated, changes ut_type to USER_PROCESS, changes ut_time, and sets ut_host and ut_addr. Depending on getty(8) and login(8), records may be located by ut_line instead of the preferable ut_pid.

When init(8) finds that a process has exited, it locates its utmp entry by ut_pid, sets ut_type to DEAD_PROCESS, and clears ut_user, ut_host, and ut_time with null bytes.

xterm(1) and other terminal emulators directly create a USER_PROCESS record and generate the ut_id by using the last two letters of /dev/ttyp%c or by using p%d for /dev/pts/%d.

If they find a DEAD_PROCESS for this ID, they recycle it; otherwise, they create a new entry. If they can, they will mark it as DEAD_PROCESS on exiting and it is advised that they null ut_line, ut_time, ut_user, and ut_host as well.

xdm(8) should not create an utmp record because there is no assigned terminal. Letting it create one will result in trouble such as finger: cannot stat /dev/machine.dom. It should create wtmp entries, though, just like ftpd(8) does.

telnetd(8) sets up a LOGIN_PROCESS entry and leaves the rest to login(8) as usual. After the Telnet session ends, telnetd(8) cleans up utmp in the described way.

The wtmp file records all logins and logouts. Its format is exactly like utmp except that a null username indicates a logout on the associated terminal. Furthermore, the terminal name ~ with username shutdown or reboot indicates a system shutdown or reboot and the pair of terminal names "¦"/"}" logs the old/new system time when date(1) changes it. wtmp is maintained by login(1) and init(1) and some variation of getty(1). Neither of these programs creates the file, so if it is removed, record-keeping is turned off.

## FILES

```
/var/run/utmp
/var/log/wtmp
```

## CONFORMING TO

Linux utmp entries conform neither to v7/BSD nor to SYSV: They are a mix of the two. v7/BSD has fewer fields; most importantly, it lacks ut_type, which causes native v7/BSD-like programs to display (for example) dead or login entries. Further there is no configuration file that allocates slots to sessions. BSD does so because it lacks ut_id fields. In Linux (as in SYSV), the ut_id field of a record will never change once it is set, which reserves that slot without needing a configuration file. Clearing ut_id may result in race conditions leading to corrupted utmp entries and potential security holes. Clearing the previously mentioned fields by filling them with null bytes is not required by SYSV semantics, but it allows you to run many programs that assume BSD semantics and that do not modify utmp. Linux uses the BSD conventions for line contents. SYSV only uses the type field to mark them and logs informative messages such as new time in the line field. SYSV has one more field to log the exit status of dead processes. UT_UNKNOWN seems to be a Linux invention. There is no type ACCOUNTING in Linux. SYSV has no ut_host or ut_addr fields. Unlike various other systems, where utmp logging can be disabled by removing the file, utmp must always exist on Linux. If you want to disable who(1), then do not make utmp world readable.

## RESTRICTIONS

The file format is machine dependent, so it is recommended that it be processed only on the machine architecture where it got created.

## SEE ALSO

ac(1), date(1), last(1), login(1), who(1), getutent(3), init(8)

*20 July 1996*

# uuencode

uuencode—Format of an encoded uuencode file.

## DESCRIPTION

Files output by uuencode(1) consist of a header line, followed by a number of body lines, and a trailer line. The uudecode(1) command will ignore any lines preceding the header or following the trailer. Lines preceding a header must not, of course, look like a header.

The header line is distinguished by having the first six characters begin. The word begin is followed by a mode (in octal) and a string that names the remote file. A space separates the three items in the header line.

The body consists of a number of lines, each at most 62 characters long (including the trailing newline). These consist of a character count, followed by encoded characters, followed by a newline. The character count is a single printing character and represents an integer, the number of bytes the rest of the line represents. Such integers are always in the range from 0 to 63 and can be determined by subtracting the character space (octal 40) from the character.

Groups of three bytes are stored in four characters, six bits per character. All are offset by a space to make the characters print. The last line may be shorter than the normal 45 bytes. If the size is not a multiple of three, this fact can be determined by the value of the count on the last line. Extra garbage will be included to make the character count a multiple of four. The body is terminated by a line with a count of zero. This line consists of one ASCII space.

The trailer line consists of end on a line by itself.

## SEE ALSO

uuencode(1), uudecode(1), uusend(1), uucp(1), mail(1)

## HISTORY

The uuencode file format appeared in BSD 4.0.

# XF86Config

XF86Config—Configuration file for XFree86.

## DESCRIPTION

XFree86 uses a configuration file called XF86Config for its initial setup. This configuration file is searched for in the following places:

```
/etc/XF86Config
<XRoot>/lib/X11/XF86Config.hostname
<XRoot>/lib/X11/XF86Config
```

*<XRoot>* refers to the root of the X11 install tree.

This file is composed of a number of sections. Each section has the form:

```
Section "SectionName"
SectionEntry ...
EndSection
```

The section names are

| | |
|---|---|
| Files | File pathnames |
| ServerFlags | Server flags |
| Keyboard | Keyboard configuration |
| Pointer | Pointer configuration |
| Monitor | Monitor description |
| Device | Graphics device description |
| Screen | Screen configuration |

The Files section is used to specify the default font path and the path to the RGB database. These paths can also be set from the command line (see Xserver(1)). The entries available for this section are

| | |
|---|---|
| FontPath "path" | Sets the search path for fonts. This path is a comma-separated list of directories that the X server searches for font databases. Multiple FontPath entries may be specified, and they will be concatenated to build up the fontpath used by the server. |
| | X11R6 allows the X server to request fonts from a font server. A font server is specified by placing a "*<trans>*/*<hostname>*:*<port_number>*" entry into the fontpath. For example, the fontpath |
| | "/usr/X11R6/lib/X11/fonts/misc/,tcp/zok:7100" |
| | tells the X server to first try to locate the font in the local directory /usr/X11R6/lib/X11/fonts/misc. If that fails, then request the font from the font server running on machine zok listening for connections on TCP port number 7100. |
| RGBPath "path" | Sets the path name for the RGB color database. |

The ServerFlags section is used to specify some miscellaneous X server options. The entries available for this section are

| | |
|---|---|
| NoTrapSignals | This prevents the X server from trapping a range of unexpected fatal signals and exiting cleanly. Instead, the X server will die and drop core where the fault occurred. The default behavior is for the X server exit cleanly but still drop a core file. In general, you never want to use this option unless you are debugging an X server problem. |
| DontZap | This disallows the use of the Ctrl+Alt+Backspace sequence. This sequence allows you to terminate the X server. Setting DontZap allows this key sequence to be passed to clients. |
| DontZoom | This disallows the use of the Ctrl+Alt+Keypad-Plus and Ctrl+Alt+Keypad-Minus sequences. These sequences allow you to switch between video modes. Setting DontZoom allows these key sequences to be passed to clients. |

The Keyboard section is used to specify the keyboard input device, parameters, and some default keyboard mapping options. The entries available for this section are

| | |
|---|---|
| Protocol "*kbd-protocol*" | *kbd-protocol* may be either Standard or Xqueue. Xqueue is specified when using the event queue driver on SVR3 or SVR4. |
| AutoRepeat *delay rate* | Changes the behavior of the autorepeat of the keyboard. This does not work on all platforms. |
| ServerNumLock | Forces the X server to handle the numlock key internally. The X server sends a different set of keycodes for the numpad when the numlock key is active. This enables applications to make use of the numpad. |

LeftAlt *mapping* RightAlt *mapping* AltGr *mapping*
ScrollLock *mapping* RightCtl *mapping*

Allows a default mapping to be set for the preceding keys (note that AltGr is a synonym for RightAlt). The values that may be specified for *mapping* are

Meta

Compose

ModeShift

ModeLock

ScrollLock

Control

The default mapping when none of these options are specified is

LeftAlt Meta

RightAlt Meta

ScrollLock Compose

RightCtl Control

| | |
|---|---|
| XLeds *led* ... | Makes *led* available for clients instead of using the traditional function (Scroll Lock, Caps Lock, and Num Lock). *led* is a list of numbers in the range 1 to 3. |
| VTSysReq | Enables the SYSV-style VT switch sequence for non-SYSV systems that support VT switching. This sequence is Alt-SysRq followed by a function key (F*n*). This prevents the X server trapping the keys used for the default VT switch sequence. |
| VTInit "*command*" | Runs *command* after the VT used by the server has been opened. The command string is passed to /bin/sh -c and is run with the real user's ID with stdin and stdout set to the VT. The purpose of this option is to allow system-dependent VT initialization commands to be run. One example is a command to disable the two-key VT switching sequence that is the default on some systems. |

The Pointer section is used to specify the pointer device and parameters. The entries available for this section are

| | |
|---|---|
| Protocol "*protocol-type*" | Specifies the pointer device protocol type. The protocol types available are |

BusMouse

Logitech

Microsoft

MMSeries

Mouseman

MouseSystems

PS/2

        MMHitTab

        Xqueue

        OSMouse

One should specify BusMouse for the Logitech bus mouse. Also, many newer Logitech serial mice use either the Microsoft or MouseMan protocol. Xqueue should be specified here if it was used in the Keyboard section. OSMouse refers to the event-driver mouse interface available on SCO's SVR3. This may optionally be followed by a number specifying the number of buttons the mouse has.

| | |
|---|---|
| Device "*pointer-dev*" | Specifies the device the server should open for pointer input (such as /dev/tty00 or /dev/mouse). A device should not be specified when using the Xqueue or OSMouse protocols. |
| BaudRate *rate* | Sets the baud rate of the serial mouse to *rate*. For mice that allow dynamic speed adjustments (such as Logitech), the baud rate is changed in the mouse. Otherwise, the rate is simply set on the computer's side to allow mice with non-standard rates (the standard rate is 1200). |
| Emulate3Buttons | Enables the emulation of the third mouse button for mice that only have two physical buttons. The third button is emulated by pressing both buttons simultaneously. |
| Emulate3Timeout *timeout* | Sets the time (in milliseconds) that the server waits before deciding if two buttons were pressed "simultaneously" when three-button emulation is enabled. The default time-out is 50ms. |
| ChordMiddle | Handles mice that send left+right events when the middle button is used (such as some Logitech Mouseman mice). |
| SampleRate *rate* | Sets the number of motion/button-events the mouse sends per second. This is currently only supported for some Logitech mice. |
| ClearDTR | This option clears the DTR line on the serial port used by the mouse. This option is only valid for a mouse using the MouseSystems protocol. Some dual-protocol mice require DTR to be cleared to operate in MouseSystems mode. Note, in versions of XFree86 prior to 2.1, this option also cleared the RTS line. A separate ClearRTS option has since been added for mice that require this. |
| ClearRTS | This option clears the RTS line on the serial port used by the mouse. This option is only valid for a mouse using the MouseSystems protocol. Some dual-protocol mice require both DTR and RTS to be cleared to operate in MouseSystems mode. Both the ClearDTR and ClearRTS options should be used for such mice. |

The Monitor sections are used to define the specifications of a monitor and a list of video modes suitable for use with a monitor. More than one Monitor section may be present in an XF86Config file. The entries available for this section are

| | |
|---|---|
| Identifier "*ID string*" | This specifies a string by which the monitor can be referred to in a later Screen section. Each Monitor section should have a unique ID string. |
| VendorName "*vendor*" | This optional entry specifies the monitor's manufacturer. |
| ModelName "*model*" | This optional entry specifies the monitor's model. |
| HorizSync *horizsync-range* | Gives the ranges of horizontal sync frequencies supported by the monitor. *horizsync-range* may be a comma-separated list of either discrete values or ranges of values. A range of values is two values separated by a dash. By default, the values are in units of kHz. They may be specified in MHz or Hz if MHz or Hz is added to the end of the line. The data given here is used by the X server to determine if video modes are within the specifications of the monitor. This information should be available in the monitor's handbook. |

| | |
|---|---|
| VertRefresh *vertrefresh-range* | Gives the ranges of vertical refresh frequencies supported by the monitor. *vertrefresh-range* may be a comma-separated list of either discrete values or ranges of values. A range of values is two values separated by a dash. By default, the values are in units of Hz. They may be specified in MHz or kHz if MHz or kHz is added to the end of the line. The data given here is used by the X server to determine if video modes are within the specifications of the monitor. This information should be available in the monitor's handbook. |
| Gamma *gamma-values* | This is an optional entry that can be used to specify the gamma correction for the monitor. It may be specified as either a single value or as three separate RGB values. Not all X servers are capable of using this information. |
| Mode "*name*" | Indicates the start of a multi-line video mode description. The mode description is terminated with an End-Mode line. The mode description consists of the following entries: |
| DotClock *clock* | The dot clock rate to be used for the mode. |
| HTimings *hdisp hsyncstart hsyncend htotal* | Specifies the horizontal timings for the mode. |
| VTimings *vdisp vsyncstart vsyncend vtotal* | Specifies the vertical timings for the mode. |
| Flags "*flag*" ... | Specifies an optional set of mode flags. Interlace indicates that the mode is interlaced. DoubleScan indicates a mode where each scanline is doubled. +HSync and -HSync can be used to select the polarity of the HSync signal. +VSync and -VSync can be used to select the polarity of the VSync signal. Composite can be used to specify composite sync on hardware where this is supported. Additionally, on some hardware, +CSync and -CSync may be used to select the composite sync polarity. |
| Modeline "*name*" *mode-description* | A single line format for specifying video modes. The *mode-description* is in four sections, the first three of which are mandatory. The first is the pixel clock. This is a single number specifying the pixel clock rate for the mode. The second section is a list of four numbers specifying the horizontal timings. These numbers are the hdisp, hsyncstart, hsyncend, htotal. The third section is a list of four numbers specifying the vertical timings. These numbers are vdisp, vsyncstart, vsyncend, vtotal. The final section is a list of flags specifying other characteristics of the mode. Interlace indicates that the mode is interlaced. DoubleScan indicates a mode where each scanline is doubled. +HSync and –HSync can be used to select the polarity of the HSync signal. +VSync and –VSync can be used to select the polarity of the VSync signal. Composite can be used to specify composite sync on hardware where this is supported. Additionally, on some hardware, +CSync and -CSync may be used to select the composite sync polarity. |

The Device sections are used to define a graphics device (video board). More than one Device section may be present in an XF86Config file. The entries available for this section are

| | |
|---|---|
| Identifier "*ID string*" | This specifies a string by which the graphics device can be referred to in a later Screen section. Each Device section should have a unique ID string. |
| VendorName "*vendor*" | This optional entry specifies the graphics device's manufacturer. |
| BoardName "*model*" | This optional entry specifies the name of the graphics device. |
| Chipset "*chipset-type*" | This optional entry specifies the chipset used on the graphics board. In most cases, this entry is not required because the X servers will probe the hardware to determine the chipset type. |

| | |
|---|---|
| Ramdac `"ramdac-type"` | This optional entry specifies the type of RAMDAC used on the graphics board. This is only used by a few of the X servers, and in most cases, it is not required because the X servers will probe the hardware to determine the RAMDAC type where possible. |
| DacSpeed *speed* | This optional entry specifies the RAMDAC speed rating (which is usually printed on the RAMDAC chip). The speed is in MHz. This is only used by a few of the X servers and only needs to be specified when the speed rating of the RAMDAC is different from the default built in to the X server. |
| Clocks *clock* ... | Specifies the dotclocks that are on your graphics board. The clocks are in MHz and may be specified as a floating-point number. The value is stored internally to the nearest kHz. The ordering of the clocks is important. It must match the order in which they are selected on the graphics board. Multiple Clocks lines may be specified. For boards with programmable clock chips, the ClockChip entry should be used instead of this. A Clocks entry is not mandatory for boards with non-programmable clock chips but is highly recommended because it prevents the clock probing phase during server startup. This clock probing phase can cause problems for some monitors. |
| ClockChip `"clockchip-type"` | This optional entry is used to specify the clock chip type on graphics boards that have a programmable clock generator. Only a few X servers support programmable clock chips. For details, see the appropriate X server manual page. |
| ClockProg *command* [*textclock*] | This optional entry runs *command* to set the clock on the graphics board instead of using the internal code. The command string must consist of the full pathname (and no flags). When using this option, a Clocks entry is required to specify which clock values are to be made available to the server (up to 128 clocks may be specified). The optional *textclock* value is to tell the server that *command* must be run to restore the text-mode clock at server exit (or when VT switching). *textclock* must match one of the values in the Clocks entry. This parameter is required when the clock used for text mode is a programmable clock. |
| | The command is run with the real user's ID with stdin and stdout set to the graphics console device. Two arguments are passed to the command. The first is the clock frequency in MHz as a floating-point number and the second is the index of the clock in the Clocks entry. The command should return an exit status of 0 when successful and something in the range 1–254 otherwise. |
| | The *command* is run when the initial graphics mode is set and when changing screen resolution with the hotkey sequences. If the program fails at initialization, the server exits. If it fails during a mode switch, the mode switch is aborted but the server keeps running. It is assumed that if the command fails, the clock has not been changed. |
| Option *optionstring* | This optional entry allows the user to select certain options provided by the drivers. Multiple Option entries may be given. The supported values for *optionstring* are given in the appropriate X server manual pages. |
| VideoRam *mem* | This optional entry specifies the amount of video RAM that is installed on the graphics board. This is measured in kilobytes. In most cases, this is not required because the X server probes the graphics board to determine this quantity. |
| BIOSBase *baseaddress* | This optional entry specifies the base address of the video BIOS for the VGA board. This address is usually 0xC0000, which is the default the X servers use. Some systems, particularly those with on-board VGA hardware, have the BIOS located at an alternate address, usually 0xE0000. If your video BIOS is at an address other than 0xC0000, you must specify the base address in the XF86Config file. Note that some X servers don't access the BIOS at all and those that do only use the BIOS when searching for information during the hardware probe phase. |

| | |
|---|---|
| MemBase *baseaddress* | This optional entry specifies the memory base address of a graphics board's linear frame buffer. This entry is only used by a few X servers, and the interpretation of this base address may be different for different X servers. Refer to the appropriate X server manual page for details. |
| IOBase *baseaddress* | This optional entry specifies the IO base address. This entry is only used for a few X servers. Refer to the appropriate X server manual page for details. |
| DACBase *baseaddress* | This optional entry specifies the DAC base address. This entry is only used for a few X servers. Refer to the appropriate X server manual page for details. |
| POSBase *baseaddress* | This optional entry specifies the POS base address. This entry is only used for a few X servers. Refer to the appropriate X server manual page for details. |
| COPBase *baseaddress* | This optional entry specifies the coprocessor base address. This entry is only used for a few X servers. Refer to the appropriate X server manual page for details. |
| VGABase *baseaddress* | This optional entry specifies the VGA memory base address. This entry is only used for a few X servers. Refer to the appropriate X server manual page for details. |
| Instance *number* | This optional entry specifies the instance (which indicates if the chip is integrated on the motherboard or on an expansion card). This entry is only used for a few X servers. Refer to the appropriate X server manual page for details. |
| Speedup *selection* | This optional entry specifies the selection of speedups to be enabled. This entry is only used for a few X servers. Refer to the appropriate X server manual page for details. |
| S3MNAdjust *MN* | This optional entry is specific to the S3 X server. For details, refer to the XF86_S3(1) manual page. |
| S3MClk *clock* | This optional entry is specific to the S3 X server. For details, refer to the XF86_S3(1) manual page. |
| S3RefClock *clock* | This optional entry is specific to the S3 X server. For details, refer to the XF86_S3(1) manual page. |

The Screen sections are used to specify which graphics boards and monitors are used with a particular X server and the configuration in which they are to be used. The entries available for this section are

| | |
|---|---|
| Driver *driver-name* | Each Screen section must begin with a Driver entry, and the *driver-name* given in each Screen section must be unique. The *driver-name* determines which X server (or driver type within an X server when an X server supports more than one head) reads and uses a particular Screen section. The driver names available are<br><br>Accel<br><br>Mono<br><br>SVGA<br><br>VGA2<br><br>VGA16<br><br>Accel is used by all the accelerated X servers (see XF86_Accel(1)). Mono is used by the non-VGA mono drivers in the 2-bit and 4-bit X servers (see XF86_Mono(1) and XF86_VGA16(1)). VGA2 and VGA16 are used by the VGA drivers in the 2-bit and 4-bit X servers. SVGA is used by the XF86_SVGA X server. |
| Device *device-id* | Specifies which graphics device description is to be used. |
| Monitor *monitor-id* | Specifies which monitor description is to be used. |
| ScreenNo *scrnum* | This optional entry overrides the default screen numbering in a multi-headed configuration. The default numbering is determined by the ordering of the Screen sections in the XF86Config file. To override this, all relevant Screen sections must have this entry specified. |

| | |
|---|---|
| BlankTime *time* | Sets the inactivity time-out for the blanking phase of the screensaver. *time* is in minutes, and the default is 10. This is equivalent to the X server's -s flag, and the value can be changed at runtime with xset(1). |
| SuspendTime *time* | Sets the inactivity time-out for the "suspend" phase of the screensaver. *time* is in minutes, the default is 15, and it can be changed at runtime with xvidtune(1). This is only suitable for VESA DPMS compatible monitors and is only supported currently by some X servers. The "power_saver" Option must be set for this to be enabled. |
| OffTime *time* | Sets the inactivity time-out for the "off" phase of the screensaver. *time* is in minutes, the default is 30, and it can be changed at runtime with xvidtune(1). This is only suitable for VESA DPMS compatible monitors and is only supported currently by some X servers. The "power_saver" Option must be set for this to be enabled. |
| SubSection Display | This entry is a subsection that is used to specify some display specific parameters. This subsection is terminated by an EndSubSection entry. For some X servers and drivers (those requiring a list of video modes), this subsection is mandatory. For X servers that support multiple display depths, more than one Display subsec-tion can be present. When multiple Display subsections are present, each must have a unique Depth entry. The entries available for the Display subsection are |
| Depth *bpp* | This entry is mandatory when more than one Display subsection is present in a Screen section. When only one Display subsection is present, it specifies the default depth where the X server will run. When more than one Display subsection is present, the depth determines which gets used by the X server. The subsection used is the one matching the depth at which the X server is run. Not all X servers (or drivers) support more than one depth. Permitted values for *bpp* are 8, 15, 16, 24, and 32. Not all X servers (or drivers) support all these values. *bpp* values of 24 and 32 are treated equivalently by those X servers that support them. |
| Weight *RGB* | This optional entry specifies the relative RGB weighting to be used for an X server running at 16bpp. This may also be specified from the command line (see XFree86(1)). Values supported by most 16bpp X servers are 555 and 565. For further details, refer to the appropriate X server manual page. |
| Virtual *xdim ydim* | This optional entry specifies the virtual screen resolution to be used. *xdim* must be a multiple of either 8 or 16 for most color X servers and a multiple of 32 for the monochrome X server. The given value is rounded down if this is not the case. For most X servers, video modes that are too large for the specified virtual size are rejected. If this entry is not present, the virtual screen resolution is set to accommo-date all the valid video modes given in the Modes entry. Some X servers do not support this entry. Refer to the appropriate X server manual pages for details. |
| ViewPort *x0 y0* | This optional entry sets the upper-left corner of the initial display. This is only relevant when the virtual screen resolution is different from the resolution of the initial video mode. If this entry is not given, then the initial display is centered in the virtual display area. |
| Modes *modename* ... | This entry is mandatory for most X servers, and it specifies the list of video modes to use. The video mode names must correspond to those specified in the appropriate Monitor section. Most X servers delete modes from this list that don't satisfy various requirements. The first valid mode in this list is the default display mode for startup. The list of valid modes is converted internally into a circular list. It is possible to switch to the next mode with Ctrl+Alt+Keypad Plus and to the previous mode with Ctrl+Alt+Keypad Minus. |
| InvertVCLK *modename* 0¦1 | This optional entry is specific to the S3 server only. It can be used to change the default VCLK invert/non-invert state for individual modes. If "*modename*" is "", the setting applies to all modes unless overridden by later entries. |

| | |
|---|---|
| EarlySC *modename* 0¦1 | This optional entry is specific to the S3 server only. It can be used to change the default EarlySC setting for individual modes. This setting can affect screen wrapping. If "*modename*" is "", the setting applies to all modes unless overridden by later entries. |
| BlankDelay *modename value1 value2* | This optional entry is specific to the S3 server only. It can be used to change the default blank delay settings for individual modes. This can affect screen wrapping. *value1* and *value2* must be integers in the range 0–7. If "*modename*" is "", the setting applies to all modes unless overridden by later entries. |
| Visual *visual-name* | This optional entry sets the default root visual type. This can also be specified from the command line (see Xserver(1)). The visual types available for 8bpp X servers are (default is PseudoColor): |

StaticGray

GrayScale

StaticColor

PseudoColor

TrueColor

DirectColor

The visual type available for the 16bpp and 32bpp X servers is TrueColor.

The visual type available for the 1bpp X server is StaticGray.

The visual types available for the 4bpp X server are (default is PseudoColor):

StaticGray

GrayScale

StaticColor

PseudoColor

| | |
|---|---|
| Option *optionstring* | This optional entry allows the user to select certain options provided by the drivers. Multiple Option entries can be given. The supported values for *option-string* are given in the appropriate X server manual pages. |
| Black *red green blue* | This optional entry allows the "black" color to be specified. This is only supported with the VGA2 driver in the XF86_Mono server (for details, see XF86_Mono(1)). |
| White *red green blue* | This optional entry allows the "white" color to be specified. This is only supported with the VGA2 driver in the XF86_Mono server (for details, see XF86_Mono(1)). |

For an example of an XF86Config file, see the file installed as <XRoot>/lib/X11/XF86Config.eg.

## FILES

/etc/XF86Config
<XRoot>/lib/X11/XF86Config. hostname <XRoot>/lib/X11/XF86Config

Note that <XRoot> refers to the root of the X11 install tree.

## SEE ALSO

X(1), Xserver(1), XFree86(1), XF86_SVGA(1), XF86_VGA16(1), XF86_Mono(1), XF86_S3(1), XF86_8514(1), XF86_Mach8(1), XF86_Mach32(1), XF86_P9000(1), XF86_AGX(1), XF86_W32(1)

## AUTHORS

Refer to the XFree86(1) manual page.

# Part VI:
# Games

# intro

intro—Introduction to games.

## DESCRIPTION

This chapter describes all the games and funny little programs available on the system.

## AUTHORS

Look at the header of the manual page for the authors and copyright conditions. Note that these can be different from page to page!

*Linux, 24 July 1993*

# banner

banner—Print large banner on printer.

## SYNOPSIS

/usr/games/banner [ -wn ] *message* ...

## DESCRIPTION

banner prints a large, high-quality banner on the standard output. If the message is omitted, it prompts for and reads one line of its standard input. If -w is given, the output is scrunched down from a width of 132 to n, suitable for a narrow terminal. If n is omitted, it defaults to 80.

The output should be printed on a hard-copy device, up to 132 columns wide, with no breaks between the pages. The volume is great enough that you might want a printer or a fast hard-copy terminal, but if you are patient, a decwriter or other 300 baud terminal will do.

## BUGS

Several ASCII characters are not defined, notably <, >, [, ], \, ^, _, {, }, ¦, and ˉ. Also, the characters ", ', and & are funny-looking (but in a useful way).

The -w option is implemented by skipping some rows and columns. The smaller it gets, the grainier the output. Sometimes it runs letters together.

## AUTHOR

Mark Horton

*6 June 1993*

# ddate

ddate—Converts boring normal dates to fun Discordian dates.

## SYNOPSIS

ddate

## DESCRIPTION

ddate prints the date in Discordian date format.

## AUTHOR

Druel the Chaotic, a.k.a. Jeremy Johnson (mpython@gnu.ai.mit.edu). Modifications for UNIX by Lee Harvey Oswald Smith, K.S.C. Five tons of flax.

*55 Confusion 3160*

# Part VII:
# Miscellaneous

# intro

intro—Introduction to miscellany section.

## DESCRIPTION

This chapter describes miscellaneous things such as nroff macro packages, tables, C header files, the file hierarchy, general concepts, and other things that don't fit anywhere else.

## AUTHORS

Look at the header of the manual page for the authors and copyright conditions. Note that these can be different from page to page!

*Linux, 23 April 1993*

# ascii

ascii—The ASCII character set encoded in octal, decimal, and hexadecimal

## DESCRIPTION

The following table contains the 128 ASCII characters.

C program '\X' escapes are noted.

| Oct | Dec | Hex | Char | Oct | Dec | Hex | Char |
|-----|-----|-----|------|-----|-----|-----|------|
| 000 | 0 | 00 | NUL '\0' | 100 | 64 | 40 | @ |
| 001 | 1 | 01 | SOH | 101 | 65 | 41 | A |
| 002 | 2 | 02 | STX | 102 | 66 | 42 | B |
| 003 | 3 | 03 | ETX | 103 | 67 | 43 | C |
| 004 | 4 | 04 | EOT | 104 | 68 | 44 | D |
| 005 | 5 | 05 | ENQ | 105 | 69 | 45 | E |
| 006 | 6 | 06 | ACK | 106 | 70 | 46 | F |
| 007 | 7 | 07 | BEL '\a' | 107 | 71 | 47 | G |
| 010 | 8 | 08 | BS '\b' | 110 | 72 | 48 | H |
| 011 | 9 | 09 | HT '\t' | 111 | 73 | 49 | I |
| 012 | 10 | 0A | LF '\n' | 112 | 74 | 4A | J |
| 013 | 11 | 0B | VT '\v' | 113 | 75 | 4B | K |
| 014 | 12 | 0C | FF '\f' | 114 | 76 | 4C | L |
| 015 | 13 | 0D | CR '\r' | 115 | 77 | 4D | M |
| 016 | 14 | 0E | SO | 116 | 78 | 4E | N |
| 017 | 15 | 0F | SI | 117 | 79 | 4F | O |
| 020 | 16 | 10 | DLE | 120 | 80 | 50 | P |
| 021 | 17 | 11 | DC1 | 121 | 81 | 51 | Q |
| 022 | 18 | 12 | DC2 | 122 | 82 | 52 | R |
| 023 | 19 | 13 | DC3 | 123 | 83 | 53 | S |
| 024 | 20 | 14 | DC4 | 124 | 84 | 54 | T |
| 025 | 21 | 15 | NAK | 125 | 85 | 55 | U |
| 026 | 22 | 16 | SYN | 126 | 86 | 56 | V |

| Oct | Dec | Hex | Char | Oct | Dec | Hex | Char |
|-----|-----|-----|------|-----|-----|-----|------|
| 027 | 23 | 17 | ETB | 127 | 87 | 57 | W |
| 030 | 24 | 18 | CAN | 130 | 88 | 58 | X |
| 031 | 25 | 19 | EM | 131 | 89 | 59 | Y |
| 032 | 26 | 1A | SUB | 132 | 90 | 5A | Z |
| 033 | 27 | 1B | ESC | 133 | 91 | 5B | [ |
| 034 | 28 | 1C | FS | 134 | 92 | 5C | \'\\\' |
| 035 | 29 | 1D | GS | 135 | 93 | 5D | ] |
| 036 | 30 | 1E | RS | 136 | 94 | 5E | ^ |
| 037 | 31 | 1F | US | 137 | 95 | 5F | _ |
| 040 | 32 | 20 | SPACE | 140 | 96 | 60 | ` |
| 041 | 33 | 21 | ! | 141 | 97 | 61 | a |
| 042 | 34 | 22 | " | 142 | 98 | 62 | b |
| 043 | 35 | 23 | # | 143 | 99 | 63 | c |
| 044 | 36 | 24 | $ | 144 | 100 | 64 | d |
| 045 | 37 | 25 | % | 145 | 101 | 65 | e |
| 046 | 38 | 26 | & | 146 | 102 | 66 | f |
| 047 | 39 | 27 | ' | 147 | 103 | 67 | g |
| 050 | 40 | 28 | ( | 150 | 104 | 68 | h |
| 051 | 41 | 29 | ) | 151 | 105 | 69 | i |
| 052 | 42 | 2A | * | 152 | 106 | 6A | j |
| 053 | 43 | 2B | + | 153 | 107 | 6B | k |
| 054 | 44 | 2C | , | 154 | 108 | 6C | l |
| 055 | 45 | 2D | – | 155 | 109 | 6D | m |
| 056 | 46 | 2E | . | 156 | 110 | 6E | n |
| 057 | 47 | 2F | / | 157 | 111 | 6F | o |
| 060 | 48 | 30 | 0 | 160 | 112 | 70 | p |
| 061 | 49 | 31 | 1 | 161 | 113 | 71 | q |
| 062 | 50 | 32 | 2 | 162 | 114 | 72 | r |
| 063 | 51 | 33 | 3 | 163 | 115 | 73 | s |
| 064 | 52 | 34 | 4 | 164 | 116 | 74 | t |
| 065 | 53 | 35 | 5 | 165 | 117 | 75 | u |
| 066 | 54 | 36 | 6 | 166 | 118 | 76 | v |
| 067 | 55 | 37 | 7 | 167 | 119 | 77 | w |
| 070 | 56 | 38 | 8 | 170 | 120 | 78 | x |
| 071 | 57 | 39 | 9 | 171 | 121 | 79 | y |
| 072 | 58 | 3A | : | 172 | 122 | 7A | z |
| 073 | 59 | 3B | ; | 173 | 123 | 7B | { |
| 074 | 60 | 3C | < | 174 | 124 | 7C | | |
| 075 | 61 | 3D | = | 175 | 125 | 7D | } |
| 076 | 62 | 3E | > | 176 | 126 | 7E | ~ |
| 077 | 63 | 3F | ? | 177 | 127 | 7F | DEL |

## HISTORY

An ascii manual page appeared in version 7 AT&T UNIX.

## SEE ALSO

iso_8859_1(7)

*Linux*

# bootparam

bootparam—Introduction to boot-time parameters of the Linux kernel.

## DESCRIPTION

The Linux kernel accepts certain command-line options or boot-time parameters at the moment it is started. In general, this is used to supply the kernel with information about hardware parameters that the kernel would not be able to determine on its own, or to avoid or override the values that the kernel would otherwise detect.

When the kernel is booted directly by the BIOS (say, from a floppy to which you copied a kernel using cp zImage /dev/fd0), you have no opportunity to specify any parameters. To take advantage of this possibility, you have to use software that is able to pass parameters, such as LILO or loadlin. For a few parameters, one can also modify the kernel image itself, using rdev; see rdev(8) for further details.

The LILO program (LInux LOader) written by Werner Almesberger is the most commonly used. It has the ability to boot various kernels and stores the configuration information in a plain text file. (See lilo(8) and lilo.conf(5).) LILO can boot DOS, OS/2, Linux, FreeBSD, and so on and is quite flexible.

The other commonly used Linux loader is loadlin, which is a DOS program that has the capability to launch a Linux kernel from the DOS prompt (with boot args) assuming that certain resources are available. This is good for people who want to launch Linux from DOS.

It is also very useful if you have certain hardware that relies on the supplied DOS driver to put the hardware into a known state. A common example is SoundBlaster-compatible sound cards that require the DOS driver to twiddle a few mystical registers to put the card into a SB-compatible mode. Booting DOS with the supplied driver and then loading Linux from the DOS prompt with loadlin avoids the reset of the card that happens if one reboots instead.

## THE ARGUMENT LIST

Most of the boot args take the form of

name[=value_1][,value_2]...[,value_11]

name is a unique keyword that is used to identify what part of the kernel the associated values (if any) are to be given to. Multiple boot args are just a space-separated list of the preceding format. Note the limit of 11 is real because the present code handles only 11 comma-separated parameters per keyword. (However, you can reuse the same keyword with up to an additional 11 parameters in unusually complicated situations, assuming the setup function supports it.)

Most of the sorting occurs in linux/init/main.c. First, the kernel checks to see if the argument is any of the special arguments root=, ro, rw, or debug. The meaning of these special arguments is described later in the document.

Then, it walks a list of setup functions (contained in the bootsetups array) to see if the specified argument string (such as foo) is associated with a setup function (foo_setup()) for a particular device or part of the kernel. If you passed the kernel the line foo=3,4,5,6, then the kernel searches the bootsetups array to see if foo is registered. If it is, it calls the setup function associated with foo (foo_setup()) and hands it the arguments 3, 4, 5, and 6 as given on the kernel command line.

Anything of the form foo=bar that is not accepted as a setup function as described is then interpreted as an environment variable to be set. A (useless?) example is to use TERM=vt100 as a boot argument.

Any remaining arguments that were not picked up by the kernel and were not interpreted as environment variables are then passed onto process one, which is usually the init program. The most common argument that is passed to the init process is the word single, which instructs init to boot the computer in single-user mode and not launch all the usual daemons. Check the manual page for the version of init installed on your system to see what arguments it accepts.

## GENERAL NON-DEVICE-SPECIFIC BOOT ARGS

### no387

Some i387 coprocessor chips have bugs that show up when used in 32-bit protected mode.

For example, some of the early ULSI-387 chips cause solid lockups while performing floating-point calculations. Using the 'no387' boot arg causes Linux to ignore the maths coprocessor even if you have one. Of course, you must then have your kernel compiled with math emulation support!

### no-hlt

Some of the early i486DX-100 chips have a problem with the hlt instruction in that they can't reliably return to operating mode after this instruction is used. Using the 'no-hlt' instruction tells Linux to just run an infinite loop when there is nothing else to do and to not halt the CPU. This allows people with these broken chips to use Linux.

### root=...

This argument tells the kernel what device is to be used as the root filesystem while booting. The default of this setting is determined at compile time and usually is the value of the root device of the system that the kernel was built on. To override this value and select the second floppy drive as the root device, one uses 'root=/dev/fd1'. (The root device can also be set using rdev(8).)

The root device can be specified symbolically or numerically. A symbolic specification has the form /dev/*XXYN*, where *XX* designates the device type (hd for ST-506-compatible hard disk with *Y* in a-h; sd for SCSI-compatible disk with *Y* in a-e; xd for XT-compatible disk with *Y* either a or b; fd for floppy disk with *Y* the floppy drive number—fd0 is the DOS A: drive and fd1 is B:), *Y* is the driver letter or number, and *N* is the number of the partition on this device (absent in the case of floppies).

Note that this has nothing to do with the designation of these devices on your filesystem. The /dev/ part is purely conventional.

The more awkward and less portable numeric specification of the previous possible root devices in major/minor format is also accepted. (For example, /dev/sda3 is major 8, minor 3, so you can use root=0x803 as an alternative.)

#### ro and rw

The ro option tells the kernel to mount the root filesystem as readonly so that filesystem consistency check programs (fsck) can do their work on a quiescent file system. No processes can write to files on the filesystem in question until it is re-mounted as read/write capable, such as by mount -w -n -o remount /. (See also mount(8).)

The rw option tells the kernel to mount the root filesystem read/write. This is the default.

The choice between read-only and read/write can also be set usingrdev(8).

#### debug

Kernel messages are handed off to the kernel log daemon klogd so that they can be logged to disk. Messages with a priority above console_loglevel are also printed on the console. (For these levels, see <linux/kernel.h>.) By default, this variable is set to log anything more important than debug messages. This boot argument causes the kernel to also print the messages of DEBUG priority. The console log level can also be set at runtime via an option to klogd. See klogd(8).

#### reserve=...

This is used to protect I/O port regions from probes. The form of the command is

reserve=*iobase,extent*[,*iobase,extent*]...

In some machines, it might be necessary to prevent device drivers from checking for devices (auto-probing) in a specific region. This may be because of hardware that reacts badly to the probing, hardware that would be mistakenly identified, or hardware you don't want the kernel to initialize.

The reserve boot-time argument specifies an I/O port region that shouldn't be probed. A device driver does not probe a reserved region unless another boot argument explicitly specifies that it do so.

For example, the boot line

`reserve=0x300,32 blah=0x300`

keeps all device drivers except the driver for `blah` from probing 0x300-0x31f.

### `ramdisk=...`

This option is obsolete since Linux 1.3.48 or so. It specifies the size in kilobytes of the optional RAM disk device. For example, if one wants to have a root filesystem on a 1.44MB floppy loaded into the RAM disk device, they use

`ramdisk=1440`

This option is set at compile time (default is no RAM disk), and can be modified using `rdev(8)`.

### `mem=...`

The BIOS call defined in the PC specification that returns the amount of installed memory was only designed to be able to report up to 64MB. Linux uses this BIOS call at boot to determine how much memory is installed. If you have more than 64MB of RAM installed, you can use this boot arg to tell Linux how much memory you have. The value is in decimal or hexadecimal (prefix 0x), and the suffixes K (times 1024) or M (times 1048576) can be used. The following quote from Linus describes the use of the `mem=` parameter:

"The kernel will accept any `mem=xx` parameter you give it, and if it turns out that you lied to it, it will crash horribly sooner or later. The parameter indicates the highest addressable RAM address, so `'mem=0x1000000'` means you have 16MB of memory, for example. For a 96MB machine this would be `mem=0x6000000`.

NOTE: Some machines might use the top of memory for BIOS caching or whatever, so you might not actually have up to the full 96MB addressable. The reverse is also true: Some chipsets will map the physical memory that is covered by the BIOS area into the area just past the top of memory, so the top-of-mem might actually be 96MB + 384KB, for example. If you tell Linux that it has more memory than it actually does have, bad things will happen: maybe not at once, but surely eventually."

### `reboot=warm`

Since 2.0.22, a reboot is by default a cold reboot. This command-line option changes back to the old default, a warm reboot.

## BOOT ARGUMENTS FOR SCSI DEVICES

General notation for this section:

`iobase`—the first I/O port that the SCSI host occupies. These are specified in hexadecimal notation and usually lie in the range from 0x200 to 0x3ff.

`irq`—the hardware interrupt that the card is configured to use. Valid values are dependent on the card in question but are usually 5, 7, 9, 10, 11, 12, and 15. The other values are usually used for common peripherals such as IDE hard disks, floppies, serial ports, and so on.

`scsi-id`—the ID that the host adapter uses to identify itself on the SCSI bus. Only some host adapters allow you to change this value because most have it permanently specified internally. The usual default value is 7, but the Seagate and Future Domain TMC-950 boards use 6.

`parity`—whether the SCSI host adapter expects the attached devices to supply a parity value with all information exchanges. Specifying a 1 indicates parity checking is enabled, and a 0 disables parity checking. Again, not all adapters support selection of parity behavior as a boot argument.

```
max_scsi_luns=...
```

A SCSI device can have a number of subdevices contained within itself. The most common example is one of the new SCSI CD-ROMs that handle more than one disk at a time. Each CD is addressed as a Logical Unit Number (LUN) of that particular device. Most devices, such as hard disks and tape drives, are only one device and are assigned to LUN 0.

Some poorly designed SCSI devices cannot handle being probed for LUNs not equal to 0. Therefore, if the compile-time flag CONFIG SCSI MULTI LUN is not set, newer kernels by default only probe LUN 0.

To specify the number of probed LUNs at boot, one enters max scsi luns=n as a boot arg, where n is a number between 1 and 8. To avoid problems as described, one uses n=1 to avoid upsetting such broken devices.

## SCSI TAPE CONFIGURATION

Some boot-time configuration of the SCSI tape driver can be achieved with the following:

```
st=buf_size[,write_threshold[,max_bufs]]
```

The first two numbers are specified in units of kilobytes. The default buf_size is 32KB, and the maximum size that can be specified is a ridiculous 16384KB. The write_threshold is the value at which the buffer is committed to tape with a default value of 30KB. The maximum number of buffers varies with the number of drives detected and has a default of two. A sample usage is

```
st=32,30,2
```

Full details can be found in the README.st file that is in the scsi directory of the kernel source tree.

## ADAPTEC AHA151X, AHA152X, AIC6260, AIC6360, SB16-SCSI CONFIGURATION

The aha numbers refer to cards and the aic numbers refer to the actual SCSI chip on these types of cards, including the SoundBlaster-16 SCSI.

The probe code for these SCSI hosts looks for an installed BIOS, and if none is present, the probe will not find your card. Then you must use a boot arg of the form:

```
aha152x=iobase[,irq[,scsi-id[,reconnect[,parity]]]]
```

If the driver was compiled with debugging enabled, a sixth value can be specified to set the debug level.

All the parameters are as described at the top of this section, and the reconnect value allows device disconnect/reconnect if a nonzero value is used. A sample usage is as follows:

```
aha152x=0x340,11,7,1
```

Note that the parameters must be specified in order, meaning that if you want to specify a parity setting, then you must specify an iobase, irq, scsi-id, and reconnect value as well.

## ADAPTEC AHA154X CONFIGURATION

The aha1542 series cards have an i82077 floppy controller on board, whereas the aha1540 series cards do not. These are bus-mastering cards and have parameters to set the "fairness" that is used to share the bus with other devices. The boot arg looks like the following:

```
aha1542=iobase[,buson,busoff[,dmaspeed]]
```

Valid iobase values are usually one of 0x130, 0x134, 0x230, 0x234, 0x330, or 0x334. Clone cards may permit other values.

The buson and busoff values refer to the number of microseconds that the card dominates the ISA bus. The defaults are 11us on and 4us off so that other cards (such as an ISA LANCE Ethernet card) have a chance to get access to the ISA bus.

The dmaspeed value refers to the rate (in MB/s) at which the DMA (Direct Memory Access) transfers proceed. The default is 5MB/s. Newer revision cards allow you to select this value as part of the soft-configuration; older cards use jumpers. You can use values up to 10MB/s, assuming that your motherboard is capable of handling it. Experiment with caution if using values over 5MB/s.

## ADAPTEC AHA274X, AHA284X, AIC7XXX CONFIGURATION

These boards can accept an argument of the form:

`aic7xxx=extended,no_reset`

The extended value, if nonzero, indicates that extended translation for large disks is enabled. The *no_reset* value, if nonzero, tells the driver not to reset the SCSI bus when setting up the host adapter at boot.

## BUSLOGIC SCSI HOSTS CONFIGURATION (`buslogic=`)

At present, the buslogic driver accepts only one parameter, the I/O base. It expects that to be one of the following valid values: 0x130, 0x134, 0x230, 0x234, 0x330, or 0x334.

## FUTURE DOMAIN TMC-8XX, TMC-950 CONFIGURATION

If your card is not detected at boot time, you must use a boot arg of the form

`tmc8xx=mem_base,irq`

The *mem_base* value is the value of the memory-mapped I/O region that the card uses. This is usually one of the following values: 0xc8000, 0xca000, 0xcc000, 0xce000, 0xdc000, or 0xde000.

## PRO AUDIO SPECTRUM CONFIGURATION

The PAS16 uses an NC5380 SCSI chip, and newer models support jumperless configuration. The boot arg is of the form

`pas16=iobase,irq`

The only difference is that you can specify an IRQ value of 255, which tells the driver to work without using interrupts, albeit at a performance loss. The *iobase* is usually 0x388.

## SEAGATE ST-0X CONFIGURATION

If your card is not detected at boot time, you must use a boot arg of the form

`st0x=mem_base,irq`

The *mem_base* value is the value of the memory-mapped I/O region that the card uses. This is usually one of the following values: 0xc8000, 0xca000, 0xcc000, 0xce000, 0xdc000, or 0xde000.

## TRANTOR T128 CONFIGURATION

These cards are also based on the NCR5380 chip and accept the following options:

`t128=mem_base,irq`

The valid values for *mem_base* are as follows: 0xcc000, 0xc8000, 0xdc000, and 0xd8000.

## CARDS THAT DON'T ACCEPT BOOT ARGS

At present, the following SCSI cards do not make use of any boot-time parameters. In some cases, you can hard-wire values by directly editing the driver itself, if required.

Always IN2000, Adaptec aha1740, EATA-DMA, EATA-PIO, Future Domain 16xx, NCR5380 (generic), NCR53c7xx to NCR53c8xx, Qlogic, Ultrastor (including u?4f), and Western Digital wd7000.

## HARD DISKS

### IDE DISK/CD-ROM DRIVER PARAMETERS

The IDE driver accepts a number of parameters, which range from disk geometry specifications to support for broken controller chips. Drive specific options are specified by using hd*X*= with *X* in a-h.

Non-drive–specific options are specified with the prefix hd=. Note that using a drive-specific prefix for a non-drive–specific option will still work, and the option will just be applied as expected.

Also note that hd= can be used to refer to the next unspecified drive in the (a, ..., h) sequence. For the following discussions, the hd= option will be cited for brevity. See the file README.ide in linux/drivers/block for more details.

## THE hd=cyls,heads,sects[,wpcom[,irq]] OPTIONS

These options are used to specify the physical geometry of the disk. Only the first three values are required. The cylinder, head, and sectors values are those used by fdisk. The write precompensation value is ignored for IDE disks. The IRQ value specified is the IRQ used for the interface that the drive resides on and is not really a drive-specific parameter.

## THE hd=serialize OPTION

The dual IDE interface CMD-640 chip is broken as designed such that when drives on the secondary interface are used at the same time as drives on the primary interface, it will corrupt your data. Using this option tells the driver to make sure that both interfaces are never used at the same time.

## THE hd=dtc2278 OPTION

This option tells the driver that you have a DTC-2278D IDE interface. The driver then tries to do DTC-specific operations to enable the second interface and to enable faster transfer modes.

## THE hd=noprobe OPTION

Do not probe for this drive. The following line

```
hdb=noprobe hdb=1166,7,17
```

disables the probe but still specifies the drive geometry so that it is registered as a valid block device and hence usable.

## THE hd=nowerr OPTION

Some drives apparently have the WRERR STAT bit stuck on permanently. This enables a work-around for these broken devices.

## THE hd=cdrom OPTION

This tells the IDE driver that there is an ATAPI compatible CD-ROM attached in place of a normal IDE hard disk. In most cases, the CD-ROM is identified automatically, but if it isn't, then this might help.

## STANDARD ST-506 DISK DRIVER OPTIONS (hd=)

The standard disk driver can accept geometry arguments for the disks similar to the IDE driver. Note however that it only expects three values (C/H/S); any more or any less and it will silently ignore you. Also, it only accepts hd= as an argument; hda= and so on are not valid here. The format is as follows:

```
hd=cyls,heads,sects
```

If there are two disks installed, the preceding line is repeated with the geometry parameters of the second disk.

## XT DISK DRIVER OPTIONS (xd=)

If you are unfortunate enough to be using one of these old 8-bit cards that move data at a whopping 125KB/s, then here is the scoop. If the card is not recognized, you must use a boot arg of the form

```
xd=type,irq,iobase,dma_chan
```

The type value specifies the particular manufacturer of the card, and you use one of the following: 0=generic, 1=DTC, 2, 3, 4=Western Digital, 5, 6, 7=Seagate, or 8=OMTI. The only difference between multiple types from the same manufacturer is the BIOS string used for detection, which is not used if the type is specified.

The xd_setup() function does no checking on the values and assumes that you entered all four values. Don't disappoint it. Here is a sample usage for a WD1002 controller with the BIOS disabled or removed, using the default XT controller parameters:

```
xd=2,5,0x320,3
```

## CD-ROMS (NON-SCSI/ATAPI/IDE)

### THE AZTECH INTERFACE

The syntax for this type of card is

`aztcd=`*iobase*`[,`*magic_number*`]`

If you set the *magic_number* to `0x79`, the driver will run anyway in the event of an unknown firmware version. All other values are ignored.

### THE CDU-31A AND CDU-33A SONY INTERFACE

This CD-ROM interface is found on some of the Pro Audio Spectrum sound cards and other Sony supplied interface cards. The syntax is as follows:

`cdu31a=`*iobase*`,[`*irq*`[,`*is_pas_card*`]]`

Specifying an IRQ value of `0` tells the driver that hardware interrupts aren't supported (as on some PAS cards). If your card supports interrupts, you should use them because they cut down on the CPU usage of the driver.

The *is_pas_card* should be entered as `PAS` if using a Pro Audio Spectrum card; otherwise, it should not be specified at all.

### THE CDU-535 SONY INTERFACE

The syntax for this CD-ROM interface is

`sonycd535=`*iobase*`[,`*irq*`]`

A `0` can be used for the I/O base as a placeholder if you want to specify an IRQ value.

### THE GOLDSTAR INTERFACE

The syntax for this CD-ROM interface is

`gscd=`*iobase*

### THE MITSUMI STANDARD INTERFACE

The syntax for this CD-ROM interface is

`mcd=`*iobase*`,[`*irq*`[,`*wait_value*`]]`

The *wait_value* is used as an internal time-out value for people who are having problems with their drive and may or may not be implemented depending on a compile-time `#define`. The Mitsumi FX400 is an IDE/ATAPI CD-ROM player and does not use the mcd driver.

### THE MITSUMI XA/MULTISESSION INTERFACE (`mcdx=`)

At present, this experimental driver has a setup function, but no parameters are implemented (as of 1.3.15). This is for the same hardware as previously described, but the driver has extended features.

### THE OPTICS STORAGE INTERFACE

The syntax for this type of card is

`optcd=`*iobase*

### THE PHILLIPS CM206 INTERFACE

The syntax for this type of card is

`cm206=[`*iobase*`][,`*irq*`]`

The driver assumes numbers between 3 and 11 are IRQ values and numbers between 0x300 and 0x370 are I/O ports, so you can specify one, or both numbers, in any order. It also accepts `cm206=auto` to enable autoprobing.

### THE SANYO INTERFACE

The syntax for this type of card is

`sjcd=iobase[,irq[,dma_channel]]`

### THE SOUNDBLASTER PRO INTERFACE

The syntax for this type of card is

`sbpcd=iobase,type`

*type* is one of the following (case-sensitive) strings: SoundBlaster, LaserMate, or SPEA. The I/O base is that of the CD-ROM interface and not that of the sound portion of the card.

## ETHERNET DEVICES

Different drivers use different parameters, but they all at least share having an IRQ, an I/O port base value, and a name. In its most generic form, it looks something like this:

`ether=irq,iobase[,param_1[,param_2,...param_8]],name`

The first non-numeric argument is taken as the name. The *param_n* values (if applicable) usually have different meanings for each different card or driver. Typical *param_n* values are used to specify things such as shared memory address, interface selection, DMA channel, and the like.

The most common use of this parameter is to force probing for a second ethercard because the default is to only probe for one. This can be accomplished with a simple

`ether=0,0,eth1`

Note that the values of 0 for the IRQ and I/O base in the example tell the drivers to autoprobe.

The Ethernet How To has extensive documentation on using multiple cards and on the card-specific or driver-specific implementation of the *param_n* values where used. Interested readers should refer to the section in that document on their particular card.

## THE FLOPPY DISK DRIVER

There are many floppy driver options, and they are all listed in README.fd in linux/drivers/block. This information is taken directly from that file.

### floppy=mask,allowed_drive_mask

Sets the bitmask of allowed drives to mask. By default, only units 0 and 1 of each floppy controller are allowed. This is done because certain non-standard hardware (ASUS PCI motherboards) mess up the keyboard when accessing units 2 or 3. This option is somewhat obsolete because of the cmos option.

### floppy=all_drives

Sets the bitmask of allowed drives to all drives. Use this if you have more than two drives connected to a floppy controller.

### floppy=asus_pci

Sets the bitmask to allow only units 0 and 1 (the default).

### floppy=daring

Tells the floppy driver that you have a well-behaved floppy controller. This allows more efficient and smoother operation but may fail on certain controllers. This can speed up certain operations.

### floppy=0,daring

Tells the floppy driver that your floppy controller should be used with caution.

`floppy=one_fdc`

Tells the floppy driver that you have only one floppy controller (default).

`floppy=two_fdc` OR `floppy=address,two_fdc`

Tells the floppy driver that you have two floppy controllers. The second floppy controller is assumed to be at address. If address is not given, `0x370` is assumed.

`floppy=thinkpad`

Tells the floppy driver that you have a Thinkpad. Thinkpads use an inverted convention for the disk change line.

`floppy=0,thinkpad`

Tells the floppy driver that you don't have a Thinkpad.

`floppy=drive,type,cmos`

Sets the cmos type of drive to type. Additionally, this drive is allowed in the bitmask. This is useful if you have more than two floppy drives (only two can be described in the physical cmos), or if your BIOS uses non-standard cmos types. Setting the cmos to 0 for the first two drives (default) makes the floppy driver read the physical cmos for those drives.

`floppy=unexpected_interrupts`

Print a warning message when an unexpected interrupt is received (default behavior)

## `floppy=no unexpected_interrupts` OR `floppy=L40SX`

Don't print a message when an unexpected interrupt is received. This is needed on IBM L40SX laptops in certain video modes. (There seems to be an interaction between video and floppy. The unexpected interrupts only affect performance and can safely be ignored.)

## THE SOUND DRIVER

The sound driver can also accept boot args to override the compiled in values. This is not recommended because it is rather complex. It is described in the `Readme.Linux` file in `linux/drivers/sound`. It accepts a boot arg of the form

`sound=device1[,device2[,device3...[,device11]]]`

Each *deviceN* value is of the format `0xTaaaId` and the bytes are used as follows:

*T*—device type: 1=FM, 2=SB, 3=PAS, 4=GUS, 5=MPU401, 6=SB16, and 7=SB16-MPU401

*aaa*—I/O address in hex

*I*—interrupt line in hex (10=a, 11=b, ...)

*d*—DMA channel

As you can see, it gets pretty messy, and you are better off to compile in your own personal values as recommended. Using a boot arg of sound=0 disables the sound driver entirely.

## THE BUS MOUSE DRIVER (bmouse=)

The busmouse driver only accepts one parameter, the hardware IRQ value to be used.

## AUTHORS

Linus Torvalds (and many others)

## SEE ALSO

`klogd(8)`, `lilo.conf(5)`, `lilo(8)`, `mount(8)`, `rdev(8)`

This man page was derived from the Boot Parameter HOWTO (version 1.0.1) written by Paul Gortmaker. More information can be found in this (or a more recent) HOWTO.

# groff_me

groff_me—troff macros for formatting papers.

## SYNOPSIS

```
groff_me [ options ] file ...
troff_me [ options ] file ...
```

## DESCRIPTION

This manual page describes the GNU version of the _me macros, which is part of the groff document formatting system. This version can be used with both GNU troff and UNIX troff. This package of troff macro definitions provides a canned formatting facility for technical papers in various formats.

The macro requests are defined as follows. Many troff requests are unsafe in conjunction with this package; however, these requests can be used with impunity after the first .pp:

| | |
|---|---|
| .bp | Begin new page |
| .br | Break output line here |
| .sp n | Insert n spacing lines |
| .ls n | Line spacing; n=1 single, n=2 double space |
| .na | No alignment of right margin |
| .ce n | Center next n lines |
| .ul n | Underline next n lines |

Output of the pic, eqn, refer, and tbl preprocessors is acceptable as input.

## FILES

/usr/lib/groff/tmac/tmac.e

## SEE ALSO

groff(1), gtroff(1), _me Reference Manual, Eric P. Allman, Writing Papers with Groff Using _me

## REQUESTS

This list is incomplete; see the _me Reference Manual for interesting details.

| Request | Initial Value | Cause Break | Explanation |
|---|---|---|---|
| .(c | - | Yes | Begin centered block. |
| .(d | - | No | Begin delayed text. |
| .(f | - | No | Begin footnote. |
| .(l | - | Yes | Begin list. |
| .(q | - | Yes | Begin major quote. |
| .(x x | - | No | Begin indexed item in index x. |
| .(z | - | No | Begin floating keep. |
| .)c | - | Yes | End centered block. |
| .)d | - | Yes | End delayed text. |
| .)f | - | Yes | End footnote. |
| .)l | - | Yes | End list. |
| .)q | - | Yes | End major quote. |

*continues*

| Request | Initial Value | Cause Break | Explanation |
|---|---|---|---|
| .)x | - | Yes | End index item. |
| .)z | - | Yes | End floating keep. |
| .++ *m H* | - | No | Define paper section. |
| | | | *m* defines the part of the paper and can be C (chapter), A (appendix), P (preliminary, such as abstract, table of contents, and so on), B (bibliography), RC (chapters renumbered from page one each chapter), or RA (appendix renumbered from page one). |
| .+c *T* | - | Yes | Begin chapter (or appendix and so on as set by .++). *T* is the chapter title. |
| .1c | 1 | Yes | One column format on a new page. |
| .2c | 1 | Yes | Two column format. Equation number is y. |
| .EN | - | Yes | Space after equation produced by eqn or neqn. |
| .EQ *x y* | - | Yes | Precede equation; break out and add space. |
| | | | The optional argument *x* may be I to indent equation (default), L to left-adjust the equation, or C to center the equation. |
| .GE | - | Yes | End gremlin picture. |
| .GS | - | Yes | Begin gremlin picture. |
| .PE | - | Yes | End pic picture. |
| .PS | - | Yes | Begin pic picture. |
| .TE | - | Yes | End table. |
| .TH | - | Yes | End heading section of table. |
| .TS *x* | - | Yes | Begin table; if *x* is H, table has repeated heading. |
| .b *x* | No | No | Print *x* in boldface; if no argument switch to boldface. |
| .ba +n | 0 | Yes | Augments the base indent by n. |
| | | | This indent is used to set the indent on regular text (like paragraphs). |
| .bc | No | Yes | Begin new column. |
| .bi *x* | No | No | Print *x* in bold italics (no fill only). |
| .bu | - | Yes | Begin bulleted paragraph. |
| .bx *x* | No | No | Print *x* in a box (no fill only). |
| .ef 'x'y'z' | " " | No | Set even footer to *x y z*. |
| .eh 'x'y'z' | " " | No | Set even header to *x y z*. |
| .fo 'x'y'z' | " " | No | Set footer to *x y z*. |
| .hx | - | No | Suppress headers and footers on next page. |
| .he 'x'y'z' | " " | No | Set header to *x y z*. |
| .hl | - | Yes | Draw a horizontal line. |
| .i *x* | No | No | Italicize *x*; if *x* is missing, italic text follows. |
| .ip *x y* | No | Yes | Start indented paragraph with hanging tag *x*. Indentation is *y* ens (default is 5). |

| Request | Initial Value | Cause Break | Explanation |
|---------|---------------|-------------|-------------|
| .lp | Yes | Yes | Start left-blocked paragraph. |
| .np | 1 | Yes | Start numbered paragraph. |
| .of 'x'y'z' | "" | No | Set odd footer to x y z. |
| .oh 'x'y'z' | "" | No | Set odd header to x y z. |
| .pd | - | Yes | Print delayed text. |
| .pp | No | Yes | Begin paragraph. First line indented. |
| .r | Yes | No | Roman text follows. |
| .re | - | No | Reset tabs to default values. |
| .sh n x | - | Yes | Section head follows; font is automatically bold. n is level of section. x is title of section. |
| .sk | No | No | Leave the next page blank. Only one page is remembered ahead. |
| .sm x | - | No | Set x in a smaller point size. |
| .sz +n | 10p | No | Augment the point size by n points. |
| .tp | No | Yes | Begin title page. |
| .u x | - | No | Underline argument (even in troff) (nofill only). |
| .uh | - | Yes | Like .sh but unnumbered. |
| .xp x | - | No | Print index x. |

*Groff Version 1.09, 6 August 1992*

# groff_mm

groff_mm—groff mm macros.

## SYNOPSIS

groff_mgm [ *options...* ] [*files...* ]

## DESCRIPTION

The groff mm macros are intended to be compatible with the DWB mm macros with the following limitations:

No letter macros are implemented (yet).

No Bell Labs localisms are implemented.

The macros OK and PM are not implemented.

groff mm does not support cut marks.

mgm is intended to be international. Therefore, it is possible to write short national macro-files that change all English text to the preferred language. Use mgmse as an example.

groff mm has several extensions:

| | |
|---|---|
| 1C [1] | Begin one column processing. A 1 as argument disables the page break. |
| APP *name text* | Begin an appendix with the name *name*. Automatic naming occurs if name is "". The appendixes starts with A if auto is used. A new page is ejected, and a header is also produced if the number variable Aph is non-zero. This is the default. The appendix always appear in the list of contents with the correct page number. The name APPENDIX can be changed by setting the string App to the desired text. |

| | |
|---|---|
| APPSK *name pages text* | Same as .APP, but the page number is incremented with *pages*. This is used when diagrams or other non-formatted documents are included as appendixes. |
| B1 | Begin box (as the ms macro) Draws a box around the text. |
| B2 | End box. Finish the box. |
| BVL | Start of broken variable-item list. Like VL but text begins always at the next line. |
| COVER [*arg*] | COVER begins a coversheet definition. It is important that .COVER appears before any normal text. .COVER uses *arg* to build the filename /usr/lib/groff/ tmac/mm/arg.cov. Therefore, it is possible to create unlimited types of coversheets. ms.cov is supposed to look like the ms coversheet. .COVER requires a .COVEND at the end of the cover definition. Always use this order of the cover macros: |

.COVER

.TL

.AF

.AU

.AT

.AS

.AE

.COVEND

However, only .TL and .AU are required.

| | |
|---|---|
| COVEND | This finishes the cover description and prints the cover page. It is defined in the cover file. |
| GETHN *refname* [*varname*] | Includes the header number where the corresponding SETR *refname* was placed. Will be X.X.X. in pass 1. See INITR. If *varname* is used, GETHN sets the string variable *varname* to the header number. |
| GETPN *refname* [*varname*] | Includes the page number where the corresponding SETR *refname* was placed. Will be 9999 in pass 1. See INITR. If *varname* is used, GETPN sets the string variable *varname* to the page number. |
| GETR *refname* | Combines GETHN and GETPN with the text 'chapter' and ', page'. The string *Qrf* contains the text for reference: .ds Qrf See chapter \\*[Qrfh], page \\*[Qrfp]. *Qrf* may be changed to support other languages. Strings *Qrfh* and *Qrfp* are set by GETR and contain the page and header number. |
| GETST *refname* [*varname*] | Includes the string saved with the second argument to .SETR. Will be dummy string in pass 1. If *varname* is used, GETST sets the string variable *varname* to the saved string. See INITR. |
| INITR *filename* | Initialize the reference macros. References will be written to *filename.* tmp and *filename*.qrf. Requires two passes with groff. The first looks for references and the second includes them. INITR can be used several times, but it is only the first occurrence of INITR that is active. See also SETR, GETPN, and GETHN. |
| MC *column-size* [*column-separation*] | Begin multiple columns. Return to normal with 1C. |
| MT [*arg* [*addressee*]] | Memorandum type. The *arg* is part of a filename in /usr/lib/groff/tmac/mm/ *.MT. Memorandum type 0 through 5 are supported, including *string*. *addressee* just sets a variable, used in the AT&T macros. |
| MOVE *y-pos* [*x-pos*[*line-length*]] | Move to a position, page offset set to *x-pos*. If *line-length* is not given, the difference between the current and new page offset is used. Use PGFORM without arguments to return to normal. |

| MULB *cw1 space1*[*cw2 space2* [*cw3* ...]] | Begin a special multi-column mode. Every column's width must be specified. Also, the space between the columns must be specified. The last column does not need any space definition. MULB starts a diversion and MULE ends the diversion and prints the columns. The unit for width and space is *n*, but MULB accepts all normal unit specifications such as c and i. MULB operates in a separate environment. |

| MULN | Begin the next column. This is the only way to switch columns. |

| MULE | End the multi-column mode and print the columns. |

| PGFORM [*linelength*[*pagelength*[*pageoffset* [1]]]] *linelength*, *pagelength* and/or *pageoffset*. | This macro can be used for special formatting, such as PGFORM letterheads. Sets can be used without arguments to reset everything after a MOVE. A line break is done unless the fourth argument is given. This can be used to avoid the page number on the first page while setting new width and length. |

| PGNH | No header is printed on the next page. Used to get rid of the header in letters or other special texts. This macro must be used before any text to inhibit the page header on the first page. |

| SETR *refname* [*string*] | Remember the current header and page number as *refname*. Saves *string* if *string* is defined. *string* is retrieved with .GETST. See INITR. |

| TAB | Reset tabs to every 5*n*. Usually used to reset any previous tab positions. |

| VERBON [*flag* [*pointsize*[*font*]]] | Begin verbatim output using Courier font. Usually for printing programs. All characters have equal width. The point size can be changed with the second argument. By specifying the font argument, it is possible to use another font instead of Courier. *flag* controls several special features. It contains the sum of all wanted features: |

| Value | Description |
| --- | --- |
| 1 | Disable the escape-character (*n*). This is usually turned on during verbose output. |
| 2 | Add an empty line before the verbose text. |
| 4 | Add an empty line after the verbose text. |
| 8 | Print the verbose text with numbered lines. This adds four digit-sized spaces in the beginning of each line. Finer control is available with the string-variable Verbnm. It contains all arguments to the troff-command .nm, usually 1. |
| 16 | Indent the verbose text with five ns. This is controlled by the number-variable Verbin (in units). |

| VERBOFF | End verbatim output. |

New variables in mgm:

| App | A string containing the word APPENDIX. |
| Aph | Print an appendix page for every new appendix if this number variable is nonzero. No output will occur if Aph is zero, but there |

|         | will always be an appendix entry in the list of contents. |
|---------|-----------------------------------------------------------|
| Hps | Number variable with the heading pre-space level. If the heading level is less than or equal to Hps, then two lines precede the section heading instead of one. Default is first level only. The real amount of lines is controlled by the variables Hps1 and Hps2. |
| Hps1 | This is the number of lines preceding .H when the heading level is greater than Hps. Value is in units, usually 0.5v. |
| Hps2 | This is the number of lines preceding .H when the heading level is less than or equal to Hps. Value is in units, usually 1v. |
| Lifg | String containing figure. |
| Litb | String containing table. |
| Liex | String containing exhibit. |
| Liec | String containing equation. |
| Licon | String containing contents. |
| Lsp | The size of an empty line. Usually 0.5v, but it is 1v if n is set (.nroff). |
| MO1 - MO12 | Strings containing January to December. |
| Qrf | String containing "See chapter \\*[Qrfh], page \\n[Qrfp].". |
| Pgps | Controls whether header and footer point size should follow the current setting or just change when the header and footer is defined. |

| Value | Description |
|-------|-------------|
| 0 | Point size will only change to the current setting when .PH, .PF, .OH, .EH, .OF, or .OE is executed. |
| 1 | Point size will change after every .S. This is the default. |

|         |                                                          |
|---------|----------------------------------------------------------|
| Sectf | Flag controlling section figures. A nonzero value enables this. See also register N. |
| Sectp | Flag controlling section page numbers. A nonzero value enables this. See also register N. |
| .mgm | Always 1. |

A file called locale or lang_locale is read after the initiation of the global variables. It is therefore possible to localize the macros with a company name and so on.

The following standard macros are implemented:

|         |                                                          |
|---------|----------------------------------------------------------|
| 2C | Begin two column processing. |
| AE | Abstract end. |
| AF [*name of firm*] | Author's firm. |
| AL [*type*[*text-indent* [1]]]] | Start autoincrement list. |
| AS [*arg* [*indent*]] | Abstract start. Indent is specified in ens, but scaling is allowed. |
| AST [*title*] | Abstract title. Default is 'ABSTRACT'. |
| AT *title1* [*title2* ...] | Author's title. |
| AU *name* [*initials* [*loc* [*dept* | |
|  | [*ext* [*room* [*arg* [*arg* [*arg*]]]]]]]]  Author information. |
| B [*bold-text*[*prev-font-text* [...]]] | Begin boldface. No limit on the number of arguments. |

| | |
|---|---|
| BE | End bottom block. |
| BI[*bold-text* [*italic-text* [*bold-text* [...]]]] | Bold italic. No limit on the number of arguments. |
| BL [*text-indent* [1]] | Start bullet list. |
| BR [*bold-text* [*roman-text*[*bold-text* [...]]]] | Bold roman. No limit on the number of arguments. |
| BS | Bottom block start. |
| DE | Display end. |
| DF[*format* [*fill* [*rindent*]]] | Begin floating display (no nesting allowed). |
| DL [*text-indent* [1]] | Dash list start. |
| DS [*format*[*fill* [*rindent*]]] | Static display start. Can now have unlimited nesting. Also, right-adjusted text and block may be used (R or RB as format). |
| EC [*title* [*override*[*flag* [*refname*]]]] | Equation title. If *refname* is used, then the equation number is saved with .SETR and can be retrieved with .GETST *refname*. |
| EF [*arg*] | Even page footer. |
| EH [*arg*] | Even page header. |
| EN | Equation end. |
| EQ [*label*] | Equation start. |
| EX [*title* [*override*[*flag* [*refname*]]]] | Exhibit title. If *refname* is used, then the exhibit number is saved with .SETR and can be retrieved with .GETST *refname*. |
| FD [*arg* [1]] | Footnote default format. |
| FE | Footnote end. |
| FG [*title* [*override*[*flag* [*refname*]]]] | Figure title. If *refname* is used, then the figure number is saved with .SETR and can be retrieved with .GETST *refname*. |
| FS | Footnote start. Footnotes in displays is now possible. |
| H *level* [*heading-text*[*heading-suffix*]] | Numbered heading. |
| HC [*hyphenation-character*] | Set hyphenation character. |
| HM [*arg1* [*arg2*[... [*arg7*]]]] | Heading mark style. |
| HU *heading-text* | Unnumbered header. |
| HX *dlevel rlevel heading-text* | User-defined heading exit. Called just before printing the header. |
| HY *dlevel rlevel heading-text* | User-defined heading exit. Called just before printing the header. |
| HZ *dlevel rlevel heading-text* | User-defined heading exit. Called just after printing the header. |
| I [*italic-text*. [*prev-font-text* [*italic-text* [...]]] | Italic. |
| IB [*italic-text* [*bold-text* [*italic-text* [...]]] | Italic bold. |
| IR [*italic-text* [*roman-text* [*italic-text* [...]]] | Italic roman. |
| LB *text-indentmark-indent* *pad type*[*mark* [*LI-space* [*LB-space*]]] | List begin macro. |
| LC [*list level*] | List status clear. |
| LE | List end. |
| LI [*mark* [1]] | List item. |
| ML *mark* [*text-indent*] | Marked list start. |
| MT [*arg* [*addressee*]] | Memorandum type. See above note about MT. |

| | |
|---|---|
| ND *new-date* | New date. |
| OF *[arg]* | Odd page footer. |
| OH *[arg]* | Odd page header. |
| OP | Skip to odd page. |
| P *[type]* | Begin new paragraph. |
| PE | Picture end. |
| PF *[arg]* | Page footer. |
| PH *[arg]* | Page header. |
| PS | Picture start (from pic). |
| PX | Page header user-defined exit. |
| R | Roman. |
| RB *[roman-text [bold-text* | |
| | *[roman-text [...]]]*    Roman-bold. |
| RD *[prompt[diversion [string]]]* | Read to *diversion* and/or *string*. |
| RF | Reference end. |
| RI *[roman-text* | |
| | *[italic-text* |
| | *[roman-text [...]]]*    Roman italic. |
| RL *[text-indent [1]]* | Reference list start. |
| RP *[arg [arg]]* | Produce reference page. |
| RS *[string-name]* | Reference start. |
| S *[size [spacing]]* | Set point size and vertical spacing. If any argument equals P, then the previous value is used. A C means current value, and D means default value. If + or - is used before the value, an increment or decrement of the current value is done. |
| SA *[arg]* | Set adjustment. |
| SK *[pages]* | Skip pages. |
| SM *string1[string2 [string3]]* | Make a string smaller. |
| SP *[lines]* | Space vertically. *lines* can have any scaling factor, such as 3i or 8v. |
| TB *[title [override[flag [refname]]]]* | Table title. If *refname* is used, then the table number is saved with .SETR and can be retrieved with .GETST *refname*. |
| TC *[slevel [spacing* | |
| | *[tlevel [tab [h1 [h2* |
| | *[h3 [h4 [h5]]]]]]]]]* |
| | Table of contents. All texts can be redefined. new string variables Lifg, Litb, Liex, Liec, and Licon contain "Figure", "TABLE", "Exhibit", "Equation", and "CONTENTS". These can be redefined to other languages. |
| TE | Table end. |
| TH *[N]* | Table header. |
| TL | Begin title of memorandum. |
| TM *[num1 [num2 [...]]]* | Technical memorandum numbers used in .MT. Unlimited number of arguments may be given. |
| TP | Top of page user-defined macro. Note that header and footer is printed in a separate environment. Line length is preserved. |
| TS *[H]* | Table start. |
| TX | User-defined table of contents exit. |
| TY | User-defined table of contents exit (no "CONTENTS"). |

| | |
|---|---|
| VL [*text-indent* [*mark-indent* [1]]] | Variable-item list start. |
| VM [*top* [*bottom*]] | Vertical margin. |
| WC [*format*] | Footnote and display width control. |

Strings used in mgm:

| | |
|---|---|
| EM | Em dash string. |
| HF | Font list for headings, usually "2 2 2 2 2 2". Nonnumeric font names may also be used. |
| HP | Point size list for headings. Usually "0 0 0 0 0 0 0", which is the same as "10 10 10 10 10 10 10". |
| Lf | Contains "LIST OF FIGURES". |
| Lt | Contains "LIST OF TABLES". |
| Lx | Contains "LIST OF EXHIBITS". |
| Le | Contains "LIST OF EQUATIONS". |
| Rp | Contains "REFERENCES". |
| Tm | Contains \(tm, trademark. |

Number variables used in mgm:

| | |
|---|---|
| Cl=2 | Contents level [0:7]; contents saved if heading level <=Cl. |
| Cp=0 | Eject page between LIST OF XXXX if Cp == 0. |
| D=0 | Debug flag, values greater than 0 produce varying degree of debug. A value of 1 gives information about the progress of formatting. |
| De=0 | Eject after floating display is output [0:1]. |
| Df=5 | Floating keep output [0:5]. |
| Ds=1 | Space before and after display if == 1 [0:1]. |
| Ej=0 | Eject page. |
| Eq=0 | Equation label adjust 0=left, 1=right. |
| Fs=1 | Footnote spacing. |
| H1 - H7 | Heading counters. |
| Hb=2 | Heading break level [0:7]. |
| Hc=0 | Heading centering level [0:7]. |
| Hi=1 | Heading temporary indent [0:2]. 0 is no indent, left margin. 1 is indent to right, like .P 1. 2 is indent to line up with text part of preceding heading. |
| Hs=2 | Heading space level [0:7] |
| Ht=0 | Heading numbering type 0 is multiple (1.1.1...). 1 is single. |
| Hu=2 | Unnumbered heading level. |
| Hy=1 | Hyphenation in body. 0 is no hyphenation. 1 is hyphenation 14 on. |
| Lf=1, Lt=1, Lx=1, Le=0 | Enables (1) or disables (0) the printing of a list of figures, list of tables, list of exhibits, and list of equations. |
| Li=6 | List indent, used by .AL. |
| Ls=99 | List space, if current list level is greater than Ls, then no spacing occurs around lists. |
| N=0 | Numbering style [0:5]:<br>0 == (Default) Normal header for all pages.<br>1 == Header replaces footer on first page; header is empty.<br>2 == Page header is removed on the first page. |

|  |  |
|---|---|
|  | 3 == Section page numbering enabled. |
|  | 4 == Page header is removed on the first page. |
|  | 5 == Section page and section figure numbering enabled. See also the number register Sectf and Sectp. |
| Np=0 | Numbered paragraphs. 0 is not numbered. 1 is numbered in first-level headings. |
| Of=0 | Format of figure, table, exhibit, and equation titles. 0 is ". ". 1 is "-". |
| P | Current page number, usually the same as % unless section-page numbering is enabled. |
| Pi=5 | Paragraph indent. |
| Ps=1 | Paragraph spacing. |
| Pt=0 | Paragraph type. 0 is left-justified. 1 is indented .P. 2 is indented .P except after .H, .DE, or .LE. |
| Si=5 | Display indent. |

## AUTHOR

Jorgen Hagg, Lund Institute of Technology, Sweden (jh@efd.lth.se).

## FILES

```
/usr/lib/groff/tmac/tmac.gm
/usr/lib/groff/tmac/mm/*.cov
/usr/lib/groff/tmac/mm/*.MT
/usr/lib/groff/tmac/mm/locale
```

## SEE ALSO

groff(1), gtroff(1), gtbl(1), gpic(1), geqn(1), mm(7), mgmse(7)

*Groff Version 1.09, 14 February 1994*

# groff_ms

groff_ms—groff ms macros.

## SYNOPSIS

groff_mgs [ *options*... ] [*files*... ]

## DESCRIPTION

This manual page describes the GNU version of the ms macros, which is part of the groff document formatting system. The groff ms macros are intended to be compatible with the documented behavior of the 4.3 BSD UNIX ms macros, subject to the following limitations:

The internals of groff ms are not similar to the internals of UNIX ms, so documents that depend upon implementation details of UNIX ms might not work with groff ms.

There is no support for typewriter-like devices.

Berkeley localisms, in particular the TM and CT macros, are not implemented.

groff ms does not provide cut marks.

Multiple line spacing is not allowed. (Use a larger vertical spacing instead.)

groff ms does not work in compatibility mode (such as with the -C option).

The error-handling policy of groff ms is to detect and report errors, rather than silently ignore them.

The groff ms macros use many features of GNU troff and therefore cannot be used with any other troff.

Bell Labs localisms are not implemented in either the BSD ms macros or in the groff ms macros.

Some UNIX ms documentation says that the CW and GW number registers can be used to control the column width and gutter width. This is not the case. These number registers are not used in groff ms.

Macros that cause a reset set the indent. Macros that change the indent do not increment or decrement the indent, but rather set it absolutely. This can cause problems for documents that define additional macros of their own. The solution is to not use the in request but instead to use the RS and RE macros.

The number register GS is set to 1 by the groff ms macros but is not used by the UNIX ms macros. It is intended that documents that need to determine whether they are being formatted with UNIX ms or groff ms use this number register.

Footnotes are implemented so that they can safely be used within keeps and displays. Automatically numbered footnotes within floating keeps are not recommended. It is safe to have another \** between a \** and the corresponding .FS; it is required only that each .FS occur after the corresponding \** and that the occurrences of .FS are in the same order as the corresponding occurrences of \**.

The strings \*{ and \*} can be used to begin and end a superscript.

Some UNIX V10 ms features are implemented. The B, I, and BI macros can have an optional third argument that is printed in the current font before the first argument. There is a macro CW like B that changes to a constant-width font.

The following strings can be redefined to adapt the groff ms macros to languages other than English:

| String | Default Value |
| --- | --- |
| REFERENCES | References |
| ABSTRACT | ABSTRACT |
| TOC | Table of Contents |
| MONTH1 | January |
| MONTH2 | February |
| MONTH3 | March |
| MONTH4 | April |
| MONTH5 | May |
| MONTH6 | June |
| MONTH7 | July |
| MONTH8 | August |
| MONTH9 | September |
| MONTH10 | October |
| MONTH11 | November |
| MONTH12 | December |

The font family is reset from the string FAM; at initialization if this string is undefined, it is set to the current font family. The point size, vertical spacing, and inter-paragraph spacing for footnotes are taken from the number registers FPS, FVS, and FPD; at initialization, these are set to \n(PS-2, \n[FPS]+2, and \n(PD/2; however, if any of these registers was defined before initialization, it is not set. The hyphenation flags (as set by the .hy request) are set from the HY register; if this was not defined at initialization, it is set to 14.

Right-aligned displays are available with .DS R and .RD.

The following conventions are used for names of macros, strings, and number registers. External names available to documents that use the groff ms macros contain only uppercase letters and digits. Internally, the macros are divided into modules. Names used only within one module are of the form *module*name*. Names used outside the module in which they are defined are of the form *module@name*. Names associated with a particular environment are of the form *environment:name*; these are used only within the par module, and *name* does not have a module prefix. Constructed names used to implement arrays are of the form *array!index*. Thus, the groff ms macros reserve the following names:

Names containing *

Names containing @

Names containing :

Names containing only uppercase letters and digits

## FILES

/usr/lib/groff/tmac/tmac.gs

## SEE ALSO

groff(1), gtroff(1), gtbl(1), gpic(1), geqn(1), ms(7)

*Groff Version 1.09, 9 January 1994*

# hier

hier—Description of the filesystem hierarchy.

## DESCRIPTION

A typical Linux system has, among others, the following directories:

| | |
|---|---|
| / | This is the root directory. This is where the whole tree starts. |
| /bin | This directory contains executable programs that are needed in single-user mode and to bring the system up or repair it. |
| /boot | Contains static files for the boot loader. This directory only holds the files that are needed during the boot process. The map installer and configuration files should go to /sbin and /etc. |
| /dev | Special or device files that refer to physical devices. See mknod(1). |
| /dos | If both MS–DOS and Linux are run on one computer, this is a typical place to mount a DOS filesystem. |
| /etc | Contains configuration files that are local to the machine. Some larger software packages, such as X11, can have their own subdirectories below /etc. Site-wide configuration files may be placed here or in /usr/etc. Nevertheless, programs should always look for these files in /etc and you may have links for these files to /usr/etc. |
| /etc/skel | When a new user account is created, files from this directory are usually copied into the user's home directory. |
| /etc/X11 | Configuration files for the X11 window system. |
| /home | On machines with home directories for users, these are usually beneath this directory, directly or not. The structure of this directory depends on local administration decisions. |
| /lib | This directory should hold those shared libraries that are necessary to boot the system and to run the commands in the root filesystem. |
| /mnt | This is a mount point for temporarily mounted filesystems. |
| /proc | This is a mount point for the proc filesystem, which provides information about running processes and the kernel. This pseudo-filesystem is described in more detail in proc(5). |

| | |
|---|---|
| /sbin | Like /bin, this directory holds commands needed to boot the system but usually not executed by normal users. |
| /tmp | This directory contains temporary files that may be deleted with no notice, such as by a regular job or at system bootup. |
| /usr | This directory is usually mounted from a separate partition. It should hold only sharable, read-only data so that it can be mounted by various machines running Linux. |
| /usr/X11R6 | The X window system, version 11, release 6. |
| /usr/X11R6/bin | Binaries that belong to the X window system; often, there is a symbolic link from the more traditional /usr/bin/X11 to here. |
| /usr/X11R6/lib | Data files associated with the X window system. |
| /usr/X11R6/lib/X11 | These contain miscellaneous files needed to run X; Often, there is a symbolic link from /usr/lib/X11 to this directory. |
| /usr/X11R6/include/X11 | Contains include files needed for compiling programs using the X11 window system. Often, there is a symbolic link from /usr/include/X11 to this directory. |
| /usr/bin | This is the primary directory for executable programs. Most programs executed by normal users that are not needed for booting or for repairing the system and that are not installed locally should be placed in this directory. |
| /usr/bin/X11 | This is the traditional place to look for X11 executables; on Linux, it usually is a symbolic link to /usr/X11R6/bin. |
| /usr/dict | This directory holds files containing word lists for spell-checkers. |
| /usr/etc | Site-wide configuration files to be shared between several machines may be stored in this directory. However, commands should always reference those files using the /etc directory. Links from files in /etc should point to the appropriate files in /usr/etc. |
| /usr/include | Include files for the C compiler. |
| /usr/include/X11 | Include files for the C compiler and the X window system. This is usually a symbolic link to /usr/X11R6/include/X11. |
| /usr/include/asm | Include files that declare some assembler functions. This should be a symbolic link to /usr/src/linux/include/asm. |
| /usr/include/linux | This contains information that may change from system release to system release and should be a symbolic link to /usr/src/linux/include/linux to get at operating-system–specific information. |
| /usr/include/g++ | Include files to use with the GNU C++ compiler. |
| /usr/lib | Object libraries, including dynamic libraries, plus some executables that usually are not invoked directly. More complicated programs may have whole subdirectories there. |
| /usr/lib/X11 | The usual place for data files associated with X programs and configuration files for the X system itself. On Linux, it usually is a symbolic link to /usr/X11R6/lib/X11. |
| /usr/lib/gcc-lib | Contains executables and include files for the GNU C compiler, gcc(1). |
| /usr/lib/groff | Files for the GNU groff document formatting system. |
| /usr/lib/uucp | Files for uucp(1). |
| /usr/lib/zoneinfo | Files for time zone information. |
| /usr/local | This is where programs that are local to the site typically go. |
| /usr/local/bin | Binaries for programs local to the site go there. |
| /usr/local/doc | Local documentation. |
| /usr/local/etc | Configuration files associated with locally installed programs go there. |
| /usr/local/lib | Files associated with locally installed programs go there. |
| /usr/local/info | Info pages associated with locally installed programs go there. |
| /usr/local/man | Man pages associated with locally installed programs go there. |
| /usr/local/sbin | Locally installed programs for system administration. |

| | |
|---|---|
| /usr/local/src | Source code for locally installed software. |
| /usr/man | Man pages go in there into their subdirectories. |
| /usr/man/cat[1-9] | These directories contain preformatted manual pages according to their man page section. |
| /usr/man/*locale*/man[1-9] | These directories contain manual pages that are in source code form. Systems that use a unique language and code set for all manual pages may omit the *locale* substring. |
| /usr/sbin | This directory contains program binaries for system administration that are not essential for the boot process, for mounting /usr, or for system repair. |
| /usr/src | Source files for different parts of the system. |
| /usr/src/linux | This contains the sources for the kernel of the operating system itself. |
| /usr/tmp | An alternative place to store temporary files; This should be a link to /var/tmp. |
| /var | This directory contains files that may change in size, such as spool and log files. |
| /var/adm | This directory is superseded by /var/log and should be a symbolic link to /var/log. |
| /var/lock | Lock files are placed in this directory. The naming convention for device lock files is LCK..*device* where *device* is the device's name in the filesystem. The format used is that of HDU UUCP lock files—that is, lock files contain a PID as a 10-byte ASCII decimal number, followed by a newline character. |
| /var/log | Miscellaneous log files. |
| /var/preserve | This is where vi(1) saves edit sessions so they can be restored later. |
| /var/run | Runtime variable files, such as files holding process identifiers (PIDs) and logged user information (utmp). Files in this directory are usually cleared when the system boots. |
| /var/spool | Spooled (or queued) files for various programs. |
| /var/spool/at | Spooled jobs for at(1). |
| /var/spool/cron | Spooled jobs for cron(1). |
| /var/spool/lpd | Spooled files for printing. |
| /var/spool/mail | Users' mailboxes. |
| /var/spool/smail | Spooled files for the smail(1) mail delivery program. |
| /var/spool/news | Spool directory for the news subsystem. |
| /var/spool/uucp | Spooled files for uucp(1). |
| /var/tmp | Like /tmp, this directory holds temporary files stored for an unspecified duration. |

## CONFORMS TO

The Linux filesystem standard, release 1.2.

## BUGS

This list is not exhaustive; different systems may be configured differently.

## SEE ALSO

find(1), ln(1), mount(1), proc(5), The Linux Filesystem Standard

*Linux, 10 February 1996*

# hostname

hostname—Hostname resolution description.

## DESCRIPTION

Hostnames are domains. A domain is a hierarchical, dot-separated list of subdomains. For example, the machine monet in the Berkeley subdomain of the EDU subdomain of the Internet Domain Name System is represented as monet.Berkeley.EDU (with no trailing dot).

Hostnames are often used with network client and server programs, which must generally translate the name to an address for use. (This task is usually performed by the library routine gethostbyname(3).) The default method for resolving hostnames by the Internet name resolver is to follow RFC 1535's security recommendations. Actions can be taken by the administrator to override these recommendations and to have the resolver behave the same as earlier, non-RFC 1535 resolvers.

The default method (using RFC 1535 guidelines) follows.

If the name consists of a single component (that is, contains no dot) and if the environment variable HOSTALIASES is set to the name of a file, that file is searched for a string matching the input hostname. The file should consist of lines made up of two strings separated by whitespace, the first of which is the hostname alias and the second of which is the complete hostname to be substituted for that alias. If a case-insensitive match is found between the hostname to be resolved and the first field of a line in the file, the substituted name is looked up with no further processing.

If there is at least one dot in the name, then the name is first tried as is. The number of dots to cause this action is configurable by setting the threshold using the ndots option in /etc/resolv.conf (default is 1). If the name ends with a dot, the trailing dot is removed, and the remaining name is looked up (regardless of the setting of the ndots option) and no further processing is done.

If the input name does not end with a trailing dot, it is looked up by searching through a list of domains until a match is found. If neither the search option in the /etc/resolv.conf file or the LOCALDOMAIN environment variable is used, then the search list of domains contains only the full domain specified by the domain option (in /etc/resolv.conf) or the domain used in the local hostname (see hostname(1) and resolver(5)). For example, if the domain option is set to CS.Berkeley.EDU, then only CS.Berkeley.EDU is in the search list and is the only domain appended to the partial hostname. For example, a setting of lithium makes lithium.CS.Berkeley.EDU the only name to be tried using the search list.

If the search option is used in /etc/resolv.conf or the environment variable, LOCALDOMAIN is set by the user, then the search list includes what is set by these methods. For example, if the search option contained CS.Berkeley.EDU CChem.Berkeley.EDU Berkeley.EDU, then the partial hostname (such as lithium) is tried with each domain name appended (in the same order specified). The resulting hostnames that are tried include

```
lithium.CS.Berkeley.EDU
lithium.CChem.Berkeley.EDU
lithium.Berkeley.EDU
```

The environment variable LOCALDOMAIN overrides the search and domain options, and if both search and domain options are present in the resolver configuration file, then only the last one listed is used (see resolver(5)).

If the name was not previously tried "as is" (that is, it fell below the ndots threshold or did not contain a dot), then the name as originally provided is attempted.

## SEE ALSO

gethostbyname(3), resolver(5), mailaddr(7), named(8)

*16 February 1994*

# iso_8859_1

iso_8859_1—The ISO 8859-1 character set encoded in octal, decimal, and hexadecimal.

## DESCRIPTION

The ISO 8859 standard includes several 8-bit extensions to the ASCII character set (also known as ISO 646-IRV). Especially important is ISO 8859-1, the Latin Alphabet No. 1, which has become widely implemented and may already be seen as the *de facto* standard ASCII replacement. ISO 8859-1 supports the following languages: Afrikaans, Basque, Catalan, Danish, Dutch, English, Faeroes, Finnish, French, Galician, German, Icelandic, Irish, Italian, Norwegian, Portuguese, Scottish, Spanish, and Swedish. Note that the ISO 8859-1 characters are also the first 256 characters of ISO 10646 (Unicode).

## ISO 8859 ALPHABETS

The full set of ISO 8859 alphabets includes

| | |
|---|---|
| ISO 8859-1 | West European languages (Latin-1) |
| ISO 8859-2 | East European languages (Latin-2) |
| ISO 8859-3 | Southeast European and miscellaneous languages (Latin-3) |
| ISO 8859-4 | Scandinavian/Baltic languages (Latin-4) |
| ISO 8859-5 | Latin/Cyrillic |
| ISO 8859-6 | Latin/Arabic |
| ISO 8859-7 | Latin/Greek |
| ISO 8859-8 | Latin/Hebrew |
| ISO 8859-9 | Latin-1 modification for Turkish (Latin-5) |
| ISO 8859-10 | Lappish/Nordic/Eskimo languages (Latin-6) |

## ISO 8859-1 CHARACTERS

The following table displays the characters in ISO 8859 Latin-1, which are printable and unlisted in the `ascii`(7) manual page.

| *Oct* | *Dec* | *Hex* | *Char* | *Description* |
|---|---|---|---|---|
| 240 | 160 | A0 | | No-break space |
| 241 | 161 | A1 | ¡ | Inverted exclamation mark |
| 242 | 162 | A2 | ¢ | Cent sign |
| 243 | 163 | A3 | £ | Pound sign |
| 244 | 164 | A4 | $ | Currency sign |
| 245 | 165 | A5 | ¥ | Yen sign |
| 246 | 166 | A6 | ¦ | Broken bar |
| 247 | 167 | A7 | § | Section sign |
| 250 | 168 | A8 | ¨ | Diaeresis |
| 251 | 169 | A9 | © | Copyright sign |
| 252 | 170 | AA | ª | Feminine ordinal indicator |
| 253 | 171 | AB | << | Left-pointing double angle quotation mark |
| 254 | 172 | AC | ¬ | Not sign |
| 255 | 173 | AD | - | Soft hyphen |
| 256 | 174 | AE | ® | Registered sign |
| 257 | 175 | AF | ¯ | Macron |
| 260 | 176 | B0 | ° | Degree sign |
| 261 | 177 | B1 | ± | Plus-minus sign |
| 262 | 178 | B2 | $^2$ | Superscript two |
| 263 | 179 | B3 | $^3$ | Superscript three |

| *Oct* | *Dec* | *Hex* | *Char* | *Description* |
|-------|-------|-------|--------|---------------|
| 264 | 180 | B4 | ´ | Acute accent |
| 265 | 181 | B5 | | Micro sign |
| 266 | 182 | B6 | ¶ | Pilcrow sign |
| 267 | 183 | B7 | · | Middle dot |
| 270 | 184 | B8 | ¸ | Cedilla |
| 271 | 185 | B9 | ¹ | Superscript one |
| 272 | 186 | BA | º | Masculine ordinal indicator |
| 273 | 187 | BB | >> | Right-pointing double angle quotation mark |
| 274 | 188 | BC | 1/4 | Vulgar fraction one quarter |
| 275 | 189 | BD | 1/2 | Vulgar fraction one half |
| 276 | 190 | BE | 3/4 | Vulgar fraction three quarters |
| 277 | 191 | BF | ¿ | Inverted question mark |
| 300 | 192 | C0 | À | Latin capital letter A with grave |
| 301 | 193 | C1 | Á | Latin capital letter A with acute |
| 302 | 194 | C2 | Â | Latin capital letter A with circumflex |
| 303 | 195 | C3 | Ã | Latin capital letter A with tilde |
| 304 | 196 | C4 | Ä | Latin capital letter A with diaeresis |
| 305 | 197 | C5 | Å | Latin capital letter A with ring above |
| 306 | 198 | C6 | Æ | Latin capital ligature AE |
| 307 | 199 | C7 | Ç | Latin capital letter C with cedilla |
| 310 | 200 | C8 | È | Latin capital letter E with grave |
| 311 | 201 | C9 | É | Latin capital letter E with acute |
| 312 | 202 | CA | Ê | Latin capital letter E with circumflex |
| 313 | 203 | CB | Ë | Latin capital letter E with diaeresis |
| 314 | 204 | CC | Ì | Latin capital letter I with grave |
| 315 | 205 | CD | Í | Latin capital letter I with acute |
| 316 | 206 | CE | Î | Latin capital letter I with circumflex |
| 317 | 207 | CF | Ï | Latin capital letter I with diaeresis |
| 320 | 208 | D0 | Ð | Latin capital letter eth |
| 321 | 209 | D1 | Ñ | Latin capital letter N with tilde |
| 322 | 210 | D2 | O | Latin capital letter O with grave |
| 323 | 211 | D3 | Ó | Latin capital letter O with acute |
| 324 | 212 | D4 | Ô | Latin capital letter O with circumflex |
| 325 | 213 | D5 | Õ | Latin capital letter O with tilde |
| 326 | 214 | D6 | Ö | Latin capital letter O with diaeresis |
| 327 | 215 | D7 | × | Multiplication sign |
| 330 | 216 | D8 | Ø | Latin capital letter O with stroke |
| 331 | 217 | D9 | Ù | Latin capital letter U with grave |
| 332 | 218 | DA | Ú | Latin capital letter U with acute |
| 333 | 219 | DB | Û | Latin capital letter U with circumflex |

*continues*

| *Oct* | *Dec* | *Hex* | *Char* | *Description* |
|-------|-------|-------|--------|---------------|
| 334 | 220 | DC | Ü | Latin capital letter U with diaeresis |
| 335 | 221 | DD | Ý | Latin capital letter Y with acute |
| 336 | 222 | DE | þ | Latin capital letter thorn |
| 337 | 223 | DF | ß | Latin small letter sharp s |
| 340 | 224 | E0 | à | Latin small letter a with grave |
| 341 | 225 | E1 | á | Latin small letter a with acute |
| 342 | 226 | E2 | â | Latin small letter a with circumflex |
| 343 | 227 | E3 | ã | Latin small letter a with tilde |
| 344 | 228 | E4 | ä | Latin small letter a with diaeresis |
| 345 | 229 | E5 | å | Latin small letter a with ring above |
| 346 | 230 | E6 | æ | Latin small ligature ae |
| 347 | 231 | E7 | ç | Latin small letter c with cedilla |
| 350 | 232 | E8 | è | Latin small letter e with grave |
| 351 | 233 | E9 | é | Latin small letter e with acute |
| 352 | 234 | EA | ê | Latin small letter e with circumflex |
| 353 | 235 | EB | ë | Latin small letter e with diaeresis |
| 354 | 236 | EC | ì | Latin small letter i with grave |
| 355 | 237 | ED | í | Latin small letter i with acute |
| 356 | 238 | EE | î | Latin small letter i with circumflex |
| 357 | 239 | EF | ï | Latin small letter i with diaeresis |
| 360 | 240 | F0 |   | Latin small letter eth |
| 361 | 241 | F1 | ñ | Latin small letter n with tilde |
| 362 | 242 | F2 | ò | Latin small letter o with grave |
| 363 | 243 | F3 | ó | Latin small letter o with acute |
| 364 | 244 | F4 | ô | Latin small letter o with circumflex |
| 365 | 245 | F5 | õ | Latin small letter o with tilde |
| 366 | 246 | F6 | ö | Latin small letter o with diaeresis |
| 367 | 247 | F7 | ÷ | Division sign |
| 370 | 248 | F8 | ø | Latin small letter o with stroke |
| 371 | 249 | F9 | ù | Latin small letter u with grave |
| 372 | 250 | FA | ú | Latin small letter u with acute |
| 373 | 251 | FB | û | Latin small letter u with circumflex |
| 374 | 252 | FC | ü | Latin small letter u with diaeresis |
| 375 | 253 | FD | ý | Latin small letter y with acute |
| 376 | 254 | FE | þ | Latin small letter thorn |
| 377 | 255 | FF | ÿ | Latin small letter y with diaeresis |

## SEE ALSO

ascii(7)

*11 July 1995*

# locale

Locale—Description of multi-language support.

## SYNOPSIS

```
#include <locale.h>
```

## DESCRIPTION

A locale is a set of language and cultural rules. These cover aspects such as language for messages, different character sets, lexigraphic conventions, and so on. A program needs to be able to determine its locale and act accordingly to be portable to different cultures.

The header `<locale.h>` declares data types, functions and macros that are useful in this task.

The functions it declares are `setlocale()` to set the current locale and `localeconv()` to get information about number formatting.

There are different categories for local information a program might need; they are declared as macros. Using them as the first argument to the `setlocale()` function, it is possible to set one of these to the desired locale:

| | |
|---|---|
| LC_COLLATE | This is used to change the behavior of the functions `strcoll()` and `strxfrm()`, which are used to compare strings in the local alphabet. For example, the German sharp s is sorted as "ss." |
| LC_TYPE | This changes the behavior of the character handling and classification functions, such as `isupper()` and `toupper()` and the multi–byte character functions such as `mblen()` or `wctomb()`. |
| LC_MONETARY | Changes the behavior of the information returned by `localeconv()`, which describes the way numbers are usually printed, with details such as decimal point versus decimal comma. |
| LC_MESSAGES | Changes the language messages are displayed in. |
| LC_TIME | Changes the behavior of the `strftime()` function to display the current time in a locally acceptable form; for example, most of Europe uses a 24–hour clock versus the U.S. 12–hour clock. |
| LC_ALL | All of the above. |

If the second argument to `setlocale()` is empty string for the default locale, it is determined using the following steps:

1. If there is a non-null environment variable LC_ALL, the value of LC_ALL is used.
2. If an environment variable with the same name as one of the preceding categories exists and is non-null, its value is used for that category.
3. If there is a non-null environment variable LANG, the value of LANG is used.

Values about local numeric formatting are made available in a `struct lconv` returned by the `localeconv()` function, which has the following declaration:

```
struct lconv
{
/* Numeric (non-monetary) information. */
char *decimal_point; /* Decimal point character. */
char *thousands_sep; /* Thousands separator. */
/* Each element is the number of digits in each group;
elements with higher indices are farther left.
An element with value CHAR_MAX means that no further grouping is done.
An element with value 0 means that the previous element is used for all
groups farther left. */
char *grouping;
/* Monetary information. */
```

```
/* First three chars are a currency symbol from ISO 4217.
Fourth char is the separator. Fifth char is ' '. */
char *int_curr_symbol;
char *currency_symbol; /* Local currency symbol. */
char *mon_decimal_point; /* Decimal point character. */
char *mon_thousands_sep; /* Thousands separator. */
char *mon_grouping; /* Like 'grouping' element (above). */
char *positive_sign; /* Sign for positive values. */
char *negative_sign; /* Sign for negative values. */
char int_frac_digits; /* Int'l fractional digits. */
char frac_digits; /* Local fractional digits. */
/* 1 if currency_symbol precedes a positive value, 0 if succeeds. */
char_p_cs_precedes;
/* 1 if a space separates currency_symbol from a positive value. */
char_p_sep_by_space;
/* 1 if currency_symbol precedes a negative value, 0 if succeeds. */
char_n_cs_precedes;
/* 1 if a space separates currency_symbol from a negative value. */
char_n_sep_by_space;
/* Positive and negative sign positions:
0 Parentheses surround the quantity and currency_symbol.
1 The sign string precedes the quantity and currency_symbol.
2 The sign string succeeds the quantity and currency_symbol.
3 The sign string immediately precedes the currency_symbol.
4 The sign string immediately succeeds the currency_symbol. */
char_p_sign_posn;
char_n_sign_posn;
};
```

## CONFORMS TO

POSIX.1

At the moment, the only locales supported by Linux are the portable C, POSIX (identical to the C locale), ISO-8859-1 (European Latin-1), and KOI-8 (Russian) locales.

## SEE ALSO

setlocale(3), localeconf(3), locale(1), localedef(1)

*Linux, 24 April 1993*

# mailaddr

mailaddr—Mail addressing description.

## DESCRIPTION

Mail addresses are based on the ARPANET protocol listed at the end of this manual page. These addresses are in the general format

*user@domain*

A *domain* is a hierarchical dot separated list of subdomains. For example, the address

eric@monet.berkeley.edu

is usually interpreted from right to left. The message should go to the ARPA name tables (which do not correspond exactly to the physical ARPANET) and then to the Berkeley gateway, after which it should go to the local host monet. When the message reaches monet, it is delivered to the user eric.

Unlike some other forms of addressing, this does not imply any routing. Thus, although this address is specified as an ARPA address, it might travel by an alternate route if that were more convenient or efficient. For example, at Berkeley, the associated message would probably go directly to monet over the Ethernet rather than go via the Berkeley ARPANET gateway.

## ABBREVIATION

Under certain circumstances, it might not be necessary to type the entire domain name. In general, anything following the first dot may be omitted if it is the same as the domain from which you are sending the message. For example, a user on `calder.berkeley.edu` could send to `eric@monet` without adding the `berkeley.edu` because it is the same on both sending and receiving hosts.

Certain other abbreviations may be permitted as special cases. For example, at Berkeley, ARPANET hosts may be referenced without adding the `berkeley.edu` as long as their names do not conflict with a local host name.

## COMPATIBILITY

Certain old address formats are converted to the new format to provide compatibility with the previous mail system. In particular,

*user@host*`.ARPA`

is allowed and

*host:user*

is converted to

*user@host*

to be consistent with the rcp(1) command.

Also, the syntax

*host!user*

is converted to

*user@host*`.UUCP`

This is usually converted back to the *host!user* form before being sent on for compatibility with older UUCP hosts.

The current implementation is not able to route messages automatically through the UUCP network. Until that time, you must explicitly tell the mail system which hosts to send your message through to get to your final destination.

## CASE DISTINCTIONS

Domain names (anything after the @ sign) may be given in any mixture of uppercase and lowercase with the exception of UUCP hostnames. Most hosts accept any combination of case in usernames, with the notable exception of MULTICS sites.

## ROUTE-ADDRS

Under some circumstances, it might be necessary to route a message through several hosts to get it to the final destination. Usually, this routing is done automatically, but sometimes it is desirable to route the message manually. Addresses that show these relays are termed "route-addrs." These use the syntax

*<@hosta,@hostb:user@hostc>*

This specifies that the message should be sent to *hosta*, from there to *hostb*, and finally to *hostc*. This path is forced even if there is a more efficient path to *hostc*.

Route-addrs occur frequently on return addresses because these are generally augmented by the software at each host. It is generally possible to ignore all but the *user@domain* part of the address to determine the actual sender.

## POSTMASTER

Every site is required to have a user or user alias designated "postmaster" to which problems with the mail system may be addressed.

## OTHER NETWORKS

Some other networks can be reached by giving the name of the network as the last component of the domain. This is not a standard feature and might not be supported at all sites. For example, messages to CSNET or BITNET sites can often be sent to `user@host.CSNET` or `user@host.BITNET`.

## BUGS

The RFC 822 group syntax (`group:user1,user2,user3;`) is not supported except in the special case of `group:;` because of a conflict with old berknet-style addresses.

Route-Address syntax is `grotty`.

UUCP- and ARPANET-style addresses do not coexist politely.

## SEE ALSO

`mail`(1), `sendmail`(8); Crocker, D. H., Standard for the Format of Arpa Internet Text Messages, RFC822.

*14 February 1989*

# man

man—Macros to format man pages.

## SYNOPSIS

```
groff -Tascii -man file ...
groff -Tps -man file ...
man [section] title
```

## DESCRIPTION

This manual page explains the `groff tmac.an` macro package. This macro package should be used by developers when writing or porting man pages for Linux. It is fairly compatible with other versions of this macro package, so porting man pages should not be a major problem (exceptions include the NET-2 BSD release, which uses a totally different macro package).

Note that NET-2 BSD man pages can be used with `groff` simply by specifying the `-mdoc` option instead of the `-man` option. Using the `-mandoc` option is, however, recommended because this automatically detects which macro package is in use.

## PREAMBLE

The first command in a man page should be

`.TH title section date source manual,`

| | |
|---|---|
| `title` | The title of the man page (such as `MAN`). |
| `section` | The section number the man page should be placed in (such as 7). |
| `date` | The date of the last revision; remember to change this every time a change is made to the man page because this is the most general way of doing version control. |
| `source` | The source of the command. |
| | For binaries, use something such as GNU, NET-2, SLS Distribution, MCC Distribution. |
| | For system calls, use the version of the kernel that you are currently looking at: |

Linux 0.99.11.

For library calls, use the source of the function: GNU, BSD 4.3, Linux DLL 4.4.1.

*manual*    The title of the manual (such as *Linux Programmer's Manual*).

The manual sections are traditionally defined as follows:

1 Commands    Those commands that can be executed by the user from within a shell.

2 System calls    Those functions that must be performed by the kernel.

3 Library calls    Most of the `libc` functions, such as `sort`(3).

4 Special files    Files found in `/dev`.

5 File formats and conventions    The format for `/etc/passwd` and other human-readable files.

6 Games

7 Macro packages and conventions    A description of the standard file system layout, this man page, and other things.

8 System management commands    Commands such as `mount`(8), which only root can execute.

9 Kernel routines    This is a non-standard manual section and is included because the source code to the Linux kernel is freely available under the GNU Public License and many people are working on changes to the kernel.

## FONTS

Although there are many arbitrary conventions for man pages in the UNIX world, the existence of several hundred Linux-specific man pages defines the standards:

For functions, the arguments are always specified using italics, even in the SYNOPSIS section, where the rest of the function is specified in bold:

`int myfunction(int argc, char **argv);`

Filenames are always in italics (such as `/usr/include/stdio.h`), except in the SYNOPSIS section, where included files are in bold (such as `#include <stdio.h>`).

Special macros, which are usually in uppercase, are in bold (such as MAXINT).

When enumerating a list of error codes, the codes are in bold (this list usually uses the `.TP` macro).

Any reference to another man page (or to the subject of the current man page) is in bold. If the manual section number is given, it is given in roman, without any spaces (such as `man`(7)).

The commands to select the typeface are given below:

| | |
|---|---|
| `.B` | Bold |
| `.BI` | Bold alternating with italics |
| `.BR` | Bold alternating with Roman |
| `.I` | Italics |
| `.IB` | Italics alternating with bold |
| `.IR` | Italics alternating with Roman |
| `.RB` | Roman alternating with bold |
| `.RI` | Roman alternating with italics |
| `.SB` | Small alternating with bold |
| `.SM` | Small |

Traditionally, each command can have up to six arguments, but the GNU version seems to remove this limitation. Arguments are delimited by spaces. Double quotes can be used to specify an argument that contains spaces. All the arguments will be printed next to each other without intervening spaces, so that the `.BR` command can be used to specify a word in bold followed by a mark of punctuation in Roman.

## SECTIONS

Sections are started with `.SH` followed by the heading name. If the name contains spaces and appears on the same line as `.SH`, then place the heading in double quotes. Traditional headings include NAME, SYNOPSIS, DESCRIPTION, OPTIONS, FILES, SEE ALSO, DIAGNOSTICS, BUGS, and AUTHOR. The only required heading is NAME, which should be followed on the next line by a one line description of the program:

```
.SH NAME
chess \- the game of chess
```

It is extremely important that this format is followed and that there is a backslash before the single dash that follows the command name. This syntax is used by the makewhatis(8) program to create a database of short command descriptions for the whatis(1) and apropos(1) commands.

## OTHER MACROS

Other macros include the following:

| | |
|---|---|
| `.DT` | Default tabs. |
| `.HP` | Begin hanging indent. |
| `.IP` | Begin paragraph with hanging tag. This is the same as `.TP`, except the tag is given on the same line, not on the following line. |
| `.LP` | Same as `.PP`. |
| `.PD` | Set interparagraph distance to argument. |
| `.PP` | Begin a new paragraph. |
| `.RE` | End relative indent (indented paragraph). |
| `.RS` | Start relative indent (indented paragraph). |
| `.SS` | Subheading (like `.SH` but used for a subsection). |
| `.TP` | Begin paragraph with hanging tag. The tag is given on the next line. This command is similar to `.IP`. |

## FILES

```
/usr/local/lib/groff/tmac/tmac.an
/usr/man/whatis
```

## SEE ALSO

groff(1), man(1), whatis(1), apropos(1), makewhatis(8)

*Linux, 25 July 1993*

# signal

signal—List of available signals.

## DESCRIPTION

Linux supports the signals listed in this section. Several signal numbers are architecture dependent. First are the signals described in POSIX.1:

abort(3) alarm(1) Next various other signals.

(Here, – denotes that a signal is absent; there, where three values are given, the first one is usually valid for alpha and sparc, the middle one for i386 and ppc, the last one for mips. Signal 29 is SIGINFO/SIGPWR on an alpha but SIGLOST on a sparc.)

The letters in the Action column have the following meanings:

| A | Default action is to terminate the process. |
| B | Default action is to ignore the signal. |
| C | Default action is to dump core. |
| D | Default action is to stop the process. |
| E | Signal cannot be caught. |
| F | Signal cannot be ignored. |
| G | Not a POSIX.1 conformant signal. |

## CONFORMING TO

POSIX.1

## BUGS

SIGIO and SIGLOST have the same value. The latter is commented out in the kernel source, but the build process of some software still thinks that Signal 29 is SIGLOST.

## SEE ALSO

kill(1), kill(2), setitimer(2)

*Linux 1.3.88, 14 April 1996*

# suffixes

suffixes—List of file suffixes.

## DESCRIPTION

It is customary to indicate the contents of a file with the file suffix, which consists of a period followed by one or more letters. Many standard utilities, such as compilers, use this to recognize the type of file they are dealing with. The make(1) utility is driven by rules based on file suffixes.

Following is a list of suffixes that are likely to be found on a Linux system:

| Suffix | File Type |
| --- | --- |
| ,v | Files for RCS (Revision Control System) |
| - | Backup file |
| .C | C++ source code |
| .F | FORTRAN source with cpp(1) directives |
| .S | Assembler source with cpp(1) directives |
| .Z | File compressed using compress(1) |
| .[0-9]+pk | TeX font files |
| .[1-9] | Manual page for the corresponding section |
| .[1-9][a-z] | Manual page for section plus subsection |
| .a | Static object code library |
| .afm | PostScript font metrics |
| .arc | ARC archive |
| .arj | ARJ archive |
| .asc | PGP ASCII-armored data |

*continues*

| *Suffix* | *File Type* |
| --- | --- |
| .awk | AWK language program |
| .bak | Backup file |
| .bm | Bitmap source |
| .c | C source |
| .cat | Message catalog files |
| .cc | C++ source |
| .cf | Configuration file |
| .conf | Configuration file |
| .config | Configuration file |
| .cweb | Donald Knuth's WEB for C |
| .dat | Data file |
| .def | Modula-2 source for definition modules |
| .def | Other definition files |
| .diff | ASCII File differences |
| .doc | Documentation file |
| .dvi | TeX device independent output |
| .el | EMACS lisp source |
| .elc | Compiled EMACS lisp |
| .eps | Encapsulated PostScript |
| .f | FORTRAN source |
| .fas | Precompiled common lisp |
| .fi | FORTRAN include files |
| .gif | Graphics Interchange Format |
| .gsf | Ghostscript fonts |
| .gz | File compressed using `gzip(1)` |
| .h | C or C++ header files |
| .hlp | Help file |
| .htm | HTML file imported without renaming from a brain-damaged OS |
| .html | HTML document used with the World Wide Web |
| .i | C source after preprocessing |
| .idx | Reference or datum-index file for hypertext or database system |
| .icon | Bitmap source |
| .image | Bitmap source |
| .in | Configuration template, especially for GNU `autoconf` |
| .info | Files for the EMACS info browser |
| .java | A Java source file |
| .jpg | JPEG compressed picture format |
| .l | `lex(1)` or `flex(1)` files |
| .lib | Common lisp library |
| .ln | Files for use with `lint(1)` |
| .lsp | Common lisp source |
| .m4 | `M4(1)` source |
| .mac | Macro files for various programs |

| Suffix | File Type |
|---|---|
| .man | Manual page (usually source rather than formatted) |
| .me | nroff source using the me macro package |
| .mf | Metafont (font generator for TeX) source |
| .mm | Sources for groff(1) in mm format |
| .mod | Modula-2 source for implementation modules |
| .o | Object file |
| .old | Old or backup file |
| .orig | Backup (original) version of a file from patch(1) |
| .out | Output file, often an executable program (a.out) |
| .p | Pascal source |
| .patch | File differences from patch(1) |
| .pcf | X11 font files |
| .pfa | PostScript font definition files, ASCII format |
| .pfb | PostScript font definition files, binary format |
| .pgp | PGP binary data |
| .pid | File to store daemon PID (such as crond.pid) |
| .png | Portable Network Graphics file |
| .pl | Perl script |
| .pr | Bitmap source |
| .ps | PostScript file |
| .r | RATFOR source (obsolete) |
| .rej | Patches that patch(1) couldn't apply |
| .rules | Rules for something |
| .s | Assembler source |
| .sa | Stub libraries for a.out shared libraries |
| .sc | sc(1) spreadsheet commands |
| .sh | sh(1) scripts |
| .shar | Archive created by the shar(1) utility |
| .so | DLL dynamic library |
| .sqml | SQML schema or query program |
| .sty | LaTeX style files |
| .sym | Modula-2 compiled definition modules |
| .tar | Archive created by the tar(1) utility |
| .tar.Z | tar archive compressed with compress(1) |
| .tar.gz | tar archive compressed with gzip(1) |
| .taz | tar archive compressed with compress(1) |
| .tex | TeX or LaTeX source |
| .texi | Equivalent to .texinfo |
| .texinfo | TeXinfo documentation source |
| .tfm | TeX font metrics |
| .tgz | tar archive compressed with gzip(1) |
| .tmpl | Template files |

*continues*

| *Suffix* | *File Type* |
|---|---|
| .txt | Text file |
| .uue | Binary file encoded with uuencode(1) |
| .web | Donald Knuth's WEB |
| .y | yacc(1) or bison(1) (parser generator) files |
| .z | File compressed using pack(1) (or an old gzip(1)) |
| .zoo | ZOO archive |
| ~ | EMACS or patch backup file |
| rc | Startup (run control) file, such as .newsrc |

## CONFORMS TO

General UNIX conventions.

## BUGS

This list is not exhaustive.

## SEE ALSO

file(1), make(1)

*Linux, 4 April 1996*

# tr2tex

tr2tex—Convert a document from troff to LaTeX

## SYNOPSIS

tr2tex [ -m ] *filename*

## DESCRIPTION

tr2tex converts a document typeset in troff to a LaTeX format. It is intended to do the first pass of the conversion. The user should then finish up the rest of the conversion and customize the converted manuscript to his or her liking. It can also serve as a tutor for those who want to convert from troff to LaTeX.

Most of the converted document will be in LaTeX, but some of it may be in plain TeX. It will also use some macros in troffms.sty or troffman.sty, which are included in the package and must be available to the document when processed with LaTeX.

If there is more than one input file, they will all be converted into one LaTeX document.

tr2tex understands most of the -ms and -man macros and eqn preprocessor symbols. It also understands several plain troff commands. Few tbl preprocessor commands are understood to help convert very simple tables.

When converting manuals, use the -m flag.

If a troff command cannot be converted, the line that contain that command will be commented out.

Note that if you have eqn symbols, you must have the inline mathematics delimiter defined by delim in the file you are converting. If it is defined in another setup file, that setup file must be concatenated with the file to be converted; otherwise, tr2tex regards the inline math as ordinary text.

## BUGS

Many of these bugs are harmless. Most of them cause local errors that can be fixed in the converted manuscript.

- Some macros and macro arguments are not recognized.
- Commands that are not separated from their argument by a space are not properly parsed (such as .sp3i).
- When some operators (notably over, sub, and sup) are renamed (via define) and then they are encountered in the text, tr2tex treats them as ordinary macros and does not apply their rules.
- rpile, lpile, and cpile are treated the same as cpile.
- rcol and lcol are treated the same as ccol.
- Math-mode size, gsize, fat, and gfont are ignored.
- lineup and mark are ignored. The rules are so different.
- Some troff commands are translated to commands that require delimiters that have to be explicitly put. Because they are sometimes not put in troff, they can create problems. Example: .nf is not closed by .fi.
- When local motions are converted to nraise or nlower, an nhbox is needed, which must be put manually after the conversion.
- a sub i sub j is converted to a_i_j, which TeX parses as a_i{}_j} with a complaint that it is vague. a sub {i subj} is parsed correctly and converted to a_{i_j}.
- Line spacing is not changed within a paragraph in TeX (which is a bad practice anyway). TeX uses the last line spacing in effect in that paragraph.

## TO DO

Access registers via the .nr command.

## SEE ALSO

texmatch(9), trmatch(9)

## AUTHOR

Kamal Al-Yahya, Stanford University

*1 January 1987*


# Unicode

Unicode—The unified 16-bit super character set.

## DESCRIPTION

The international standard ISO 10646 defines the Universal Character Set (UCS). UCS contains all the characters of all other character-set standards. It also guarantees round-trip compatibility; conversion tables can be built such that no information is lost when a string is converted from any other encoding to UCS and back.

UCS contains the characters required to represent almost all known languages. This includes apart from the many languages that use extensions of the Latin script also the following scripts and languages: Greek, Cyrillic, Hebrew, Arabic, Armenian, Gregorian, Japanese, Chinese, Hiragana, Katakana, Korean, Hangul, Devangari, Bengali, Gurmukhi, Gujarati, Oriya, Tamil, Telugu, Kannada, Malayam, Thai, Lao, Bopomofo, and a number of others. Work is going on to include further scripts such as Tibetan, Khmer, Runic, Ethiopian, Hieroglyphics, various Indo-European languages, and many others. For most of these latter scripts, it was not yet clear how they can be encoded best when the standard was published in 1993. In addition to the characters required by these scripts, also a large number of graphical, typographical, mathematical, and scientific symbols such as those provided by TeX, PostScript, MS-DOS, Macintosh, Videotext, OCR, and many word processing systems have been included, as well as special codes that guarantee round-trip compatibility to all other existing character-set standards.

The UCS standard (ISO 10646) describes a 31-bit character-set architecture; however, today only the first 65534 code positions (0x0000 to 0xfffd), which are called the Basic Multilingual Plane (BMP), have been assigned characters, and it is expected that only very exotic characters (such as Hieroglyphics) for special scientific purposes will ever get a place outside this 16-bit BMP.

The UCS characters 0x0000 to 0x007f are identical to those of the classic US-ASCII character set and the characters in the range 0x0000 to 0x00ff are identical to those in the ISO 8859-1 Latin-1 character set.

## COMBINING CHARACTERS

Some code points in UCS have been assigned to combining characters. These are similar to the non-spacing accent keys on a typewriter. A combining character just adds an accent to the previous character. The most important accented characters have codes of their own in UCS; however, the combining character mechanism allows you to add accents and other diacritical marks to any character. The combining characters always follow the character that they modify. For example, the German character Umlaut-A ("Latin capital letter A with diaeresis") can either be represented by the precomposed UCS code 0x00c4 or alternately as the combination of a normal "Latin capital letter A" followed by a "combining diaeresis": 0x0041 0x0308.

## IMPLEMENTATION LEVELS

As not all systems are expected to support advanced mechanisms such as combining characters, ISO 10646 specifies the following three implementation levels of UCS:

| | |
|---|---|
| Level 1 | Combining characters and Hangul Jamo characters (a special, more complicated encoding of the Korean script, where Hangul syllables are coded as two or three subcharacters) are not supported. |
| Level 2 | Like level 1, except in some scripts, some combining characters are now allowed (such as Hebrew, Arabic, Devangari, Bengali, Gurmukhi, Gujarati, Oriya, Tamil, Telugo, Kannada, Malayalam, Thai, and Lao). |
| Level 3 | All UCS characters are supported. |

The Unicode 1.1 standard published by the Unicode Consortium contains exactly the UCS Basic Multilingual Plane at implementation Level 3, as described in ISO 10646. Unicode 1.1 also adds some semantical definitions for some characters to the definitions of ISO 10646.

## UNICODE UNDER LINUX

Under Linux, only the BMP at implementation Level 1 should be used at the moment to keep the implementation complexity of combining characters low. The higher implementation levels are more suitable for special word processing formats but not as a generic system character set. The C type wchar_t is on Linux an unsigned 16-bit integer type and its values are interpreted as UCS Level 1 BMP codes.

The locale setting specifies whether the system character encoding is UTF-8 or ISO 8859-1, for example. Library functions such as wctomb, mbtowc, or wprintf can be used to transform the internal wchar_t characters and strings into the system character encoding and back.

## PRIVATE AREA

In the BMP, the range 0xe000 to 0xf8ff will never be assigned any characters by the standard and is reserved for private usage. For the Linux community, this private area is subdivided further into the range 0xe000 to 0xefff, which can be used individually by any end user and the Linux zone in the range 0xf000 to 0xf8ff where extensions are coordinated among all Linux users. The registry of the characters assigned to the Linux zone is currently maintained by H. Peter Anvin (Peter.Anvin@linux.org), Yggdrasil Computing, Inc. It contains some DEC VT100 graphics characters missing in Unicode, gives direct access to the characters in the console font buffer, and contains the characters used by a few advanced scripts such as Klingon.

## LITERATURE

*Information technology—Universal Multiple-Octet Coded Character Set (UCS).* Part 1: Architecture and Basic Multilingual Plane. International Standard ISO 10646-1, International Organization for Standardization, Geneva, 1993.

This is the official specification of UCS. Pretty official, pretty thick, and pretty expensive. For ordering information, check www.iso.ch.

*The Unicode Standard—Worldwide Character Encoding Version 1.0.* The Unicode Consortium, Addison-Wesley, Reading, MA, 1991.

There is already Unicode 1.1.4 available. The changes to the 1.0 book are available from ftp.unicode.org. Unicode 2.0 will be published again as a book in 1996.

S. Harbison, G. Steele. C, *A Reference Manual.* Fourth edition, Prentice Hall, Englewood Cliffs, 1995, ISBN 0-13-326224-3.

A good reference book about the C programming language. The fourth edition now covers also the 1994 Amendment 1 to the ISO C standard (ISO/IEC 9899:1990), which adds a large number of new C library functions for handling wide character sets.

## BUGS

At the time when this man page was written, the Linux libc support for UCS was far from complete.

## AUTHOR

Markus Kuhn (mskuhn@cip.informatik.uni-erlangen.de)

## SEE ALSO

utf-8(7)

*Linux, 27 December 1995*

# UTF-8

UTF-8—An ASCII-compatible multibyte Unicode encoding.

## DESCRIPTION

The Unicode character set occupies a 16-bit code space. The most obvious Unicode encoding (known as UCS-2) consists of a sequence of 16-bit words. Such strings can contain as parts of many 16-bit characters bytes such as \0 or /, which have a special meaning in filenames and other C library function parameters. In addition, the majority of UNIX tools expects ASCII files and can't read 16-bit words as characters without major modifications. For these reasons, UCS-2 is not a suitable external encoding of Unicode in filenames, text files, environment variables, and so on. The ISO 10646 Universal Character Set (UCS), a superset of Unicode, occupies even a 31-bit code space, and the obvious UCS-4 encoding for it (a sequence of 32-bit words) has the same problems.

The UTF-8 encoding of Unicode and UCS does not have these problems and is the way to go for using the Unicode character set under UNIX-style operating systems.

## PROPERTIES

The UTF-8 encoding has the following nice properties:

UCS characters 0x00000000 to 0x0000007f (the classical U.S. ASCII characters) are encoded simply as bytes 0x00 to 0x7f (ASCII compatibility). This means that files and strings that contain only 7-bit ASCII characters have the same encoding under both ASCII and UTF-8.

All UCS characters greater than 0x7f are encoded as a multibyte sequence consisting only of bytes in the range 0x80 to 0xfd, so no ASCII byte can appear as part of another character and there are no problems with \0 or /.

The lexicographic sorting order of UCS-4 strings is preserved.

All possible 2^31 UCS codes can be encoded using UTF-8.

The bytes 0xfe and 0xff are never used in the UTF-8 encoding.

The first byte of a multibyte sequence that represents a single non-ASCII UCS character is always in the range 0xc0 to 0xfd and indicates how long this multibyte sequence is. All further bytes in a multibyte sequence are in the range 0x80 to 0xbf. This allows easy resynchronization and makes the encoding stateless and robust against missing bytes.

UTF-8–encoded UCS characters may be up to six bytes long; however, Unicode characters can only be up to three bytes long. Because Linux uses only the 16-bit Unicode subset of UCS, under Linux, UTF-8 multibyte sequences can only be one, two, or three bytes long.

## ENCODING

The following byte sequences are used to represent a character. The sequence to be used depends on the UCS code number of the character:

```
0x00000000 - 0x0000007F: 0xxxxxxx
0x00000080 - 0x000007FF: 110xxxxx 10xxxxxx
0x00000800 - 0x0000FFFF: 1110xxxx 10xxxxxx 10xxxxxx
0x00010000 - 0x001FFFFF: 11110xxx 10xxxxxx 10xxxxxx 10xxxxxx
0x00200000 - 0x03FFFFFF: 111110xx 10xxxxxx 10xxxxxx 10xxxxxx 10xxxxxx
0x04000000 - 0x7FFFFFFF: 1111110x 10xxxxxx 10xxxxxx 10xxxxxx 10xxxxxx
10xxxxxx
```

The *xxx*-bit positions are filled with the bits of the character code number in binary representation. Only the shortest possible multibyte sequence that can represent the code number of the character can be used.

## EXAMPLES

The Unicode character 0xa9 = 1010 1001 (the copyright sign) is encoded in UTF-8 as

```
11000010 10101001 = 0xc2 0xa9
```

and character 0x2260 = 0010 0010 0110 0000 (the "not equal" symbol) is encoded as

```
11100010 10001001 10100000 = 0xe2 0x89 0xa0
```

## STANDARDS

ISO 10646, Unicode 1.1, XPG4, Plan 9.

## AUTHOR

Markus Kuhn (`mskuhn@cip.informatik.uni-erlangen.de`)

## SEE ALSO

`unicode(7)`

# Part VIII:

# Administration and Privileged Commands

# intro

intro—Introduction to administration and privileged commands.

## DESCRIPTION

This chapter describes commands that either can be or are only used by the superuser, such as daemons and machine or hardware-related commands.

## AUTHORS

Look at the header of the manual page for the authors and copyright conditions. Note that these can be different from page to page.

*Linux, 24 July 1993*

# adduser, addgroup

adduser, addgroup—Add a user or group to the system.

## SYNOPSIS

```
adduser [--system [--home directory] [--group]] [--quiet]
 [--force-badname] [--help] [--version] [--debug] username
adduser [--quiet] [--force-badname] [--help] [--version]
[--debug] username group
adduser [--group] [--quiet] [--force-badname] [--help]
[--version] [--debug] group
```

## DESCRIPTION

adduser and addgroup add users and groups to the system according to information provided in the configuration file /etc/ adduser.conf. adduser and addgroup automatically determine the UID or GID and place the entity in the password or group file as appropriate.

If necessary, adduser creates a home directory for the new user, copies "skeletal" user files to it from /etc/skel, and allows the system administrator to set an initial password and finger information for the user.

Because it needs to be able to write to such files as /etc/passwd, adduser can only be run as root.

Generally, there are two types of users and groups on a system: those users that log into the system and those "non-user" accounts and groups that exist for various system tasks and projects. Henceforth, user will refer to the login type and system user or group will refer to the type used for system maintenance and projects.

By default, each user in Debian GNU/Linux is given a corresponding group with the same name and ID, allowing people easily to give access to their home directories to others. This option can be turned off in the configuration file, in which case each user is, by default, added to a group called users.

Under Debian GNU/Linux, IDs less than or equal to 100 are allocated by the base system maintainer for various purposes. IDs from 101 to the value specified in the configuration file (1000, by default) are used for system users and groups. IDs greater than 1000 are reserved for users and their corresponding groups.

When invoked with a single name, adduser creates a user with that name. When given two names, adduser assumes that the first name represents an existing user and that the second name represents an existing group. In this case, the user is added to the group.

## OPTIONS

| | |
|---|---|
| --system | Create a system user. This user will be assigned the shell /bin/false and have an asterisk in the password field. Unless otherwise specified, the user will be placed in the group nogroup. Skeletal configuration files will not be copied into the user's home directory. |
| --home *directory* | When used with --system, this uses *directory* as the user's home directory, rather than the default specified in the configuration file. If the directory does not exist, it is created. |
| --group | When combined with −system, a group with the same name and ID as the system user is created. If not combined with --system, a group with the given name is created. This is the default action if the program is invoked as addgroup. |
| --quiet | Suppress progress messages. |
| --force-badname | By default, user and group names are required to consist of a lowercase letter followed by one or more lowercase letters or numbers. This option forces adduser or addgroup to be more lenient. |
| --help | Display brief instructions. |
| --version | Display version and copyright information. |
| --debug | Display a large quantity of debugging information. |

## SEE ALSO

adduser.conf(5)

## COPYRIGHT

Copyright(c) 1995, Ted Hajek, with a great deal borrowed from the original Debian adduser, copyright(c) 1994, Ian Murdock. adduser is free software; see the GNU General Public License version two or later for copying conditions. There is no warranty.

*Debian GNU/Linux version 1.94*

# agetty

agetty—Alternative Linux getty.

## SYNOPSIS

agetty [-ihL] [-l *login_program*] [-m] [-t *timeout*] *port baud_rate*,... [*term*]
agetty [-ihL] [-l *login_program*] [-m] [-t *timeout*] *baud_rate*,... *port* [*term*]

## DESCRIPTION

agetty opens a tty port, prompts for a login name, and invokes the /bin/login command. It is usually invoked by init(8).

agetty has several non-standard features that are useful for hard-wired and for dial-in lines:

Adapts the tty settings to parity bits and to erase, kill, end-of-line, and uppercase characters when it reads a login name. The program can handle 7-bit characters with even, odd, none, or space parity and 8-bit characters with no parity. The following special characters are recognized: @ and Control+U (kill); #, Del and Backspace (erase); carriage return and line feed (end of line).

Optionally deduces the baud rate from the CONNECT messages produced by Hayes-compatible modems.

Optionally does not hang up when it is given an already opened line (useful for call-back applications).

Optionally does not display the contents of the /etc/issue file (System V only).

Optionally invokes a non-standard login program instead of /bin/login.

Optionally turns on hardware flow control.

Optionally forces the line to be local with no need for carrier detect.

This program does not use the /etc/gettydefs (System V) or /etc/gettytab (SunOS 4) files.

## ARGUMENTS

port

A path name relative to the /dev directory. If a - is specified, agetty assumes that its standard input is already connected to a tty port and that a connection to a remote user has already been established. Under System V, a - port argument should be preceded by a -.

baud rate,...

A comma-separated list of one or more baud rates. Each time agetty receives a break character, it advances through the list, which is treated as if it were circular. Baud rates should be specified in descending order, so that the null character (Ctrl+@) can also be used for baud rate switching.

term

The value to be used for the TERM environment variable. This overrides whatever init(8) may have set and is inherited by login and the shell.

## OPTIONS

-h

Enable hardware (RTS/CTS) flow control. It is left up to the application to disable software (XON/XOFF) flow protocol where appropriate.

-i

Do not display the contents of /etc/issue before writing the login prompt. Terminals or communications hardware might become confused when receiving lots of text at the wrong baud rate; dial-up scripts might fail if the login prompt is preceded by too much text.

-l login_program

Invoke the specified login program instead of /bin/login. This allows the use of a non-standard login program (for example, one that asks for a dial-up password or that uses a different password file).

-m

Try to extract the baud rate the connect status message produced by some Hayes-compatible modems. These status messages are of the form: "<junk><speed><junk>". agetty assumes that the modem emits its status message at the same speed as specified with (the first) baud rate value on the command line.

Because the -m feature might fail on heavily loaded systems, you still should enable break processing by enumerating all expected baud rates on the command line.

-t timeout

Terminate if no username could be read within timeout seconds. This option should probably not be used with hard-wired lines.

-L

Force the line to be a local line with no need for carrier detect. This can be useful when you have a locally attached terminal where the serial line does not set the carrier detect signal.

## EXAMPLES

This section shows sample entries for the /etc/inittab file.

For a hard-wired line:

```
tty1:con80x60:/sbin/agetty 9600 tty1
```

For a dial-in line with a 9600/2400/1200 baud modem:

```
ttyS1:dumb:/sbin/agetty -mt60 ttyS1 9600,2400,1200
```

These examples assume you use the `simpleinit(8)` init program for Linux. If you use a SysV-like init (does `/etc/inittab` mention "respawn"?), refer to the appropriate manual page.

## ISSUE ESCAPES

The `/etc/issue` file might contain certain escape codes to display the system name, date and time, and so on. All escape codes consist of a backslash (\) immediately followed by one of the following letters:

| | |
|---|---|
| b | Insert the baudrate of the current line. |
| d | Insert the current date. |
| s | Insert the system name, the name of the operating system. |
| l | Insert the name of the current `tty` line. |
| m | Insert the architecture identifier of the machine, such as `i486`. |
| n | Insert the nodename of the machine, also known as the hostname. |
| o | Insert the domain name of the machine. |
| r | Insert the release number of the OS, such as 1.1.9. |
| t | Insert the current time. |
| u | Insert the number of current users logged in. |
| U | Insert the string 1 user or *n* users where *n* is the number of current users logged in. |
| v | Insert the version of the OS, such as the build date and so on. |

For example, on my system, the following `/etc/issue` file

```
This is \n.\o (\s\m\r) \t
```

displays as

```
This is thingol.orcan.dk (Linux i386 1.1.9) 18:29:30
```

## FILES

`/var/run/utmp`, the system status file

`/etc/issue`, printed before the login prompt (System V only)

`/dev/console`, problem reports (if `syslog(3)` is not used)

`/etc/inittab` (Linux `simpleinit(8)` configuration file)

## BUGS

The baud-rate detection feature (the `-m` option) requires that `agetty` be scheduled soon enough after completion of a dial-in call (within 30ms with modems that talk at 2400 baud). For robustness, always use the `-m` option in combination with a multiple baud rate command-line argument so that break processing is enabled.

The text in the `/etc/issue` file and the login prompt are always output with 7-bit characters and space parity.

The baud-rate detection feature (the `-m` option) requires that the modem emits its status message after raising the DCD line.

## DIAGNOSTICS

Depending on how the program was configured, all diagnostics are written to the console device or reported via the `syslog(3)` facility. Error messages are produced if the port argument does not specify a terminal device, if there is no `utmp` entry for the current process (System V only), and so on.

## AUTHORS

W.Z. Venema (`wietse@wzv.win.tue.nl`) Eindhoven University of Technology, Department of Mathematics and Computer Science, Den Dolech 2, P.O. Box 513, 5600 MB Eindhoven, The Netherlands.

Peter Orbaek (`poe@daimi.aau.dk`), Linux port.

## CREATION DATE

Sat Nov 25 22:51:05 MET 1989

## LAST MODIFICATION

91/09/01 23:22:00

## VERSION/RELEASE

1.29

# archive

archive—Usenet article archiver.

## SYNOPSIS

archive [ -a *archive* ][-f ][-i *index* ][-m ][-r ][*input* ]

## DESCRIPTION

archive makes copies of files specified on its standard input. It is usually run either as a channel feed under innd(8) or by a script before expire(8) is run.

archive reads the named input file or standard input if no file is given. The input is taken as a set of lines. Blank lines and lines starting with a number sign (#) are ignored. All other lines should specify the name of a file to archive. If a filename is not an absolute pathname, it is taken to be relative to /news/spool.

Files are copied to a directory within the archive directory, /news/spool/news.archive. The default is to create a hierarchy that mimics the input files; intermediate directories are created as needed. For example, the input file comp/sources/unix/ 2211 (article 2211 in the newsgroup comp.sources.unix) is copied to /news/spool/news.archive/comp/sources/unix/ 2211. If the -f flag is used, then all directory names are flattened out, replacing the slashes with periods. In this case, the file is copied to /news/spool/news.archive/comp.sources.unix/2211.

If the -i flag is used, then archive appends one line to the specified index file for each article that it copies. This line contains the destination name and the Message-ID and Subject headers.

For example, a typical newsfeeds(5) entry to archive most source newsgroups is as follows:

```
source-archive\
:!*,*sources*,!*wanted*,!*.d\
:Tc,Wn\
:/archive -f -i \
/usr/spool/news/news.archive/INDEX
```

Files are copied by making a link. If that fails, a new file is created. If the -m flag is used, then the file is copied to the destination, and the input file is replaced with a symbolic link pointing to the new file. The -m flag is ignored.

By default, archive sets its standard error to /var/log/news/errlog. To suppress this redirection, use the -r flag.

If the input is exhausted, archive exits with a zero status. If an I/O error occurs, it tries to spool its input, copying it to a file. If there was no input filename, the standard input is copied to /news/spool/out.going/archive and the program exits. If an input filename was given, a temporary file named input.bch (if input is an absolute pathname) or /news/spool/ out.going/input.bch (if the filename does not begin with a slash) is created. Once the input is copied, archive tries to rename this temporary file to be the name of the input file and then exits.

## HISTORY

Written by Rich $alz (rsalz@uunet.uu.net) for InterNetNews.

## SEE ALSO

newsfeeds(5)

# arp

arp—Manipulate the system ARP cache.

## SYNOPSIS

```
arp [-v] [-t type] -a [hostname]
arp [-v] -d hostname ...
arp [-v] [-t type] -s hostname hw_addr
arp [-v] -f filename
```

## DESCRIPTION

arp manipulates the kernel's ARP cache in various ways. The primary options are clearing an address mapping entry and manually setting up one. For debugging purposes, the arp program also allows a complete dump of the ARP cache.

## OPTIONS

| | |
|---|---|
| -v | Tell the user what is going on by being verbose. |
| -t *type* | When setting or reading the ARP cache, this optional parameter tells arp which class of entries it should check for. The default value of this parameter is ether (hardware code 0x01 for IEEE 802.3 10Mbps Ethernet). Other values might include network technologies such as ARCnet (arcnet), PROnet (pronet), and AX.25 (ax25). |
| -a [*hostname*] | Shows the entries of the specified hosts. If the *hostname* parameter is not used, all entries are displayed. |
| -d *hostname* | Remove the entries of the specified host. This can be used if the indicated host is brought down, for example. |
| -s *hostname hw_addr* | Manually create an ARP address mapping entry for host *hostname* with hardware address set to *hw_addr*. The format of the hardware address is dependent on the hardware class, but for most classes, you can assume that the usual presentation can be used. For the Ethernet class, this is six bytes in hexadecimal, separated by colons. |
| -f *filename* | Similar to the -s option, only this time the address info is taken from file *filename*. This can be used if ARP entries for a lot of hosts have to be set up. The name of the data file is often /etc/ethers, but this is not official. |
| | The format of the file is simple; it only contains ASCII text lines with a hostname and a hardware address separated by whitespace. |

In all places where a hostname is expected, you can also enter an IP address in dotted-decimal notation.

## FILES

/proc/net/arp

/etc/ethers

## AUTHOR

Fred N. van Kempen (waltje@uwalt.nl.mugnet.org)

09 June 1994

# badblocks

badblocks—Search a device for bad blocks.

## SYNOPSIS

badblocks [ -b *block-size* ] [ -o *output_file* ] [ -v ][-w ] *device blocks-count*

## DESCRIPTION

badblocks is used to search for bad blocks on a device (usually a disk partition). device is the special file corresponding to the device (such as /dev/hdXX). blocks-count is the number of blocks on the device.

## OPTIONS

| | |
|---|---|
| -b *block-size* | Specify the size of blocks in bytes. |
| -o *output_file* | Write the list of bad blocks to the specified file. Without this option, badblocks displays the list on its standard output. |
| -v | Verbose mode. |
| -w | Use write-mode test. With this option, badblocks scans for bad blocks by writing some patterns (0xaa, 0x55, 0xff, and 0x00) on every block of the device, reading every block and comparing the contents. |

## WARNING

Never use the -w option on a device containing an existing filesystem. This option erases data!

## AUTHOR

badblocks was written by Remy Card (card@masi.ibp.fr), the developer and maintainer of the ext2 fs.

## BUGS

I had no chance to make real tests of this program because I use IDE drives, which remap bad blocks. I only made some tests on floppies.

## AVAILABILITY

badblocks is available for anonymous FTP from ftp.ibp.fr and tsx-11.mit.edu in /pub/linux/packages/ext2fs.

## SEE ALSO

e2fsck(8), mke2fs(8)

*Version 0.5b, November 1994*

# buffchan

buffchan—Buffered file-writing back end for InterNetNews.

## SYNOPSIS

buffchan [ -b ][-c *lines* ][-C *seconds* ][-d *directory* ]
[-f *fields* ][-m *map* ][-p *pidfile* ][-l *lines* ][-L *seconds* ]
[-r ][-s *file_format* ][-u ]

## DESCRIPTION

buffchan reads lines from standard input and copies certain fields in each line into files named by other fields within the line. buffchan is intended to be called by innd(8) as an exploder feed.

buffchan input is interpreted as a set of lines. Each line contains a fixed number of initial fields, followed by a variable number of filename fields. All fields in a line are separated by whitespace. The default number of initial fields is one; the -f flag may be used to specify a different number of fields. See filechan(8) for an example.

After the initial fields, each remaining field names a file to write. The -s flag may be used to specify a format string that maps the field to a filename. This is a sprintf(3) format string, which should have a single %s parameter that is given the field. The default value is /news/spool/out.going/%s. See the description of this flag in filechan(8). The -d flag may be used to specify a directory the program should change to before starting. If this flag is used, then the default for the -s flag is changed to be a simple %s.

Once buffchan opens a file, it keeps it open. The input must therefore never specify more files than the number of available descriptors can keep open. If the -b flag is used, the program will allocate a buffer and attach it to the file using setbuf(3). If the -u flag is used, the program will request unbuffered output.

If the -l flag is used with a number n, then buffchan will call fflush(3) after every n lines are written to a file. If the -c flag is used with a number n, then buffchan will close, and reopen, a file after every n lines are written to a file.

If the -L flag is used with a number n, then all files will be flushed every n seconds. Similarly, the -C flag may be used to specify that all files should be closed and reopened every n seconds.

By default, the program sets its standard error to /var/log/news/errlog. To suppress this redirection, use the -r flag.

If the -p flag is used, the program will write a line containing its process ID (in text) to the specified file.

buffchan can be invoked as an exploder feed (see newsfeeds(5)). As such, if a line starts with an exclamation point, it is treated as a command. There are three commands:

| | |
|---|---|
| flush | The flush command closes and reopens all open files; flush *xxx* flushes only the specified site. These are analogous to the ctlinnd(8) flush command and can be achieved by doing a send flush *xxx* command. Applications can tell that the flush has completed by renaming the file before issuing the command; buffchan has completed the command when the original filename reappears. |
| | buffchan also changes the access permissions of the file from read-only for everyone to read-write for owner and group as it flushes or closes each output file. It changes the modes back to read-only if it reopens the same file. |
| drop | The drop command is similar to the flush command except that any files are not reopened. If given an argument, then the specified site is dropped; otherwise, all sites are dropped. (Note that the site will be restarted if the input stream mentions the site.) When a ctlinnd "drop site" command is sent, innd will automatically forward the command to buffchan if the site is a funnel that feeds into this exploder. To drop all sites, use the ctlinnd send buffchan-site drop command. |
| readmap | The map file (specified with the -m flag) is reloaded. |

## HISTORY

Written by Rich $alz (rsalz@uunet.uu.net) for InterNetNews.

## SEE ALSO

ctlinnd(8), filechan(8), innd(8), newsfeeds(5).

# cfdisk

cfdisk—Curses-based disk partition table manipulator for Linux.

## SYNOPSIS

cfdisk [ -avz ] [ -c *cylinders* ][ -h *heads* ][ -s *sectors-per-track* ][ -P *opt* ]
[*device* ]

## DESCRIPTION

cfdisk is a curses-based program for partitioning a hard disk drive. The device can be any one of the following:

```
/dev/hda [default]
/dev/hdb
/dev/sda
/dev/sdb
/dev/sdc
/dev/sdd
```

cfdisk first tries to read the geometry of the hard disk. If it fails, an error message is displayed and cfdisk exits. This should only happen when partitioning a SCSI drive on an adapter without a BIOS. To correct this problem, you can set the cylinders, heads, and sectors-per-track on the command line. Next, cfdisk tries to read the current partition table from the disk drive. If it is unable to figure out the partition table, an error is displayed and the program exits. This might also be caused by incorrect geometry information and can be overridden on the command line. Another way around this problem is with the -z option. This will ignore the partition table on the disk.

The main display is composed of four sections, from top to bottom: the header, the partitions, the command line, and a warning line. The header contains the program name and version number followed by the disk drive and its geometry. The partitions section always displays the current partition table. The command line is the place where commands and text are entered. The available commands are usually displayed in brackets. The warning line is usually empty except when there is important information to be displayed. The current partition is highlighted with reverse video (or an arrow if the -a option is given). All partition-specific commands apply to the current partition.

The format of the partition table in the partition's section is, from left to right: Name, Flags, Partition Type, Filesystem Type, and Size. The name is the partition device name. The flags can be Boot, which designates a bootable partition or NC, which stands for "Not Compatible with DOS or OS/2." DOS, OS/2, and possibly other operating systems require the first sector of the first partition on the disk and all logical partitions to begin on the second head. This wastes the second through the last sector of the first track of the first head (the first sector is taken by the partition table itself). cfdisk allows you to recover these "lost" sectors with the maximize command (m). Note that fdisk(8) and some early versions of DOS create all partitions with the number of sectors already maximized. For more information, see the maximize command later in this chapter. The partition type can be Primary or Logical. For unallocated space on the drive, the partition type can also be Pri/Log or empty (if the space is unusable). The filesystem type section displays the name of the filesystem used on the partition, if known. If it is unknown, then Unknown and the hex value of the filesystem type are displayed. A special case occurs when there are sections of the disk drive that cannot be used (because all the primary partitions are used). When this is detected, the filesystem type is displayed as Unusable. The size field displays the size of the partition in megabytes (by default). It can also display the size in sectors and cylinders (see the change units command later in this chapter). If an asterisks (*) appears after the size, this means that the partition is not aligned on cylinder boundaries.

## DOS 6.*x* WARNING

The DOS 6.*x* FORMAT command looks for some information in the first sector of the data area of the partition and treats this information as more reliable than the information in the partition table. DOS FORMAT expects DOS FDISK to clear the first 512 bytes of the data area of a partition whenever a size change occurs. DOS FORMAT looks at this extra information even if the /U flag is given; we consider this a bug in DOS FORMAT and DOS FDISK.

The bottom line is that if you use cfdisk or fdisk to change the size of a DOS partition table entry and then you must also use dd to zero the first 512 bytes of that partition before using DOS FORMAT to format the partition. For example, if you were using cfdisk to make a DOS partition table entry for /dev/hda1, then (after exiting fdisk or cfdisk and rebooting Linux so that the partition table information is valid), you use the command dd if=/dev/zero of=/dev/hda1 bs=512 count=1 to zero the first 512 bytes of the partition.

Be extremely careful if you use the dd command because a small typo can make all of the data on your disk useless.

For best results, you should always use an OS-specific partition table program. For example, you should make DOS partitions with the DOS FDISK program and Linux partitions with the Linux fdisk or Linux cfdisk program.

# COMMANDS

cfdisk commands can be entered by pressing the desired key (pressing Enter after the command is not necessary). Here is a list of the available commands:

b        Toggle bootable flag of the current partition. This allows you to select which primary partition is bootable on the drive.

d        Delete the current partition. This will convert the current partition into free space and merge it with any free space immediately surrounding the current partition. A partition already marked as free space or marked as unusable cannot be deleted.

g        Change the disk geometry (cylinders, heads, or sectors-per-track). Warning: This option should only be used by people who know what they are doing. A command-line option is also available to change the disk geometry. While at the change disk geometry command line, you can choose to change cylinders (d), heads (h), and sectors per track (s). The default value will be printed at the prompt, which you can accept by simply pressing the Enter key or you can exit without changes by pressing the Esc key. If you want to change the default value, simply enter the desired value and press Enter. The altered disk parameter values do not take effect until you return to the main menu (by pressing Enter or Esc at the change disk geometry command line. If you change the geometry such that the disk appears larger, the extra sectors are added at the end of the disk as free space. If the disk appears smaller, the partitions that are beyond the new last sector are deleted and the last partition on the drive (or the free space at the end of the drive) is made to end at the new last sector.

h        Print the help screen.

m        Maximize disk usage of the current partition. This command will recover the the unused space between the partition table and the beginning of the partition, at the cost of making the partition incompatible with DOS, OS/2, and possibly other operating systems. This option will toggle between maximal disk usage and DOS, OS/2, and so on compatible disk usage. The default when creating a partition is to create DOS, OS/2, and so on compatible partitions.

n        Create new partitions from free space. If the partition type is Primary or Logical, a partition of that type will be created, but if the partition type is Pri/Log, you will be prompted for the type you want to create. Be aware that there are only four slots available for primary partitions and because there can be only one extended partition that contains all of the logical drives, all of the logical drives must be contiguous (with no intervening primary partition). cfdisk next prompts you for the size of the partition you want to create. The default size, equal to the entire free space of the current partition, is displayed in megabytes. You can either press the Enter key to accept the default size or enter a different size at the prompt. cfdisk accepts size entries in megabytes (M) (default), kilobytes (K), cylinders (d), and sectors (S) when you enter the number immediately followed by M, K, C, or S. If the partition fills the free space available, the partition is created and you are returned to the main command line. Otherwise, the partition can be created at the beginning or the end of the free space, and cfdisk will ask you to choose where to place the partition. After the partition is created, cfdisk automatically adjusts the other partition's partition types if all of the primary partitions are used.

p        Print the partition table to the screen or to a file. There are several different formats for the partition that you can choose from:

r        Raw data format (exactly what would be written to disk).

s        Partition table in sector order format.

t        Partition table in raw format. The raw data format will print the sectors that would be written to disk if a write command is selected. First, the primary partition table is printed, followed by the partition tables associated with each logical partition. The data is printed in hex byte-by-byte with 16 bytes per line. The partition table in sector order format will print the partition table ordered by sector number. The fields, from left to right, are the number of the partition, the partition type, the first sector, the last sector, the offset from the first sector of the partition to the start of the data, the length of the partition, the filesystem type (with the hex value in parentheses), and the flags (with the hex value in parentheses). In addition to the primary and logical partitions, free and unusable space is printed and the extended partition is printed before the first logical partition.

If a partition does not start or end on a cylinder boundary or if the partition length is not divisible by the cylinder size, an asterisk (*) is printed after the non-aligned sector number/count. This usually indicates that a partition was created by an operating system that either does not align partitions to cylinder boundaries or that used different disk geometry information. If you know the disk geometry of the other operating system, you can enter the geometry information with the change geometry command (g).

For the first partition on the disk and for all logical partitions, if the offset from the beginning of the partition is not equal to the number of sectors per track (that is, the data does not start on the first head), a number sign (#) is printed after the offset. For the remaining partitions, if the offset is not zero, a number sign is printed after the offset. This corresponds to the NC flag in the partitions section of the main display.

The partition table in raw format will print the partition table ordered by partition number. It will leave out all free and unusable space. The fields, from left to right, are the number of the partition, the flags (in hex), the starting head, sector, and cylinder, the filesystem ID (in hex), the ending head, sector, and cylinder, the starting sector in the partition, and the number of sectors in the partition. The information in this table can be directly translated to the raw data format. The partition table entries only have 10 bits available to represent the starting and ending cylinders. Thus, when the absolute starting (ending) sector number is on a cylinder greater than 1023, the maximal values for starting (ending) head, sector, and cylinder are printed. This is the method used by OS/2, and it fixes the problems associated with OS/2's fdisk rewriting the partition table when it is not in this format. Because Linux and OS/2 use absolute sector counts, the values in the starting and ending head, sector, and cylinder are not used.

| | |
|---|---|
| q | Quit program. This will exit the program without writing any data to disk. |
| t | Change the filesystem type. By default, new partitions are created as Linux partitions, but because cfdisk can create partitions for other operating systems, changing the partition type allows you to enter the hex value of the filesystem you desire. A list of the known filesystem types is displayed. You can type the filesystem type at the prompt or accept the default filesystem type (Linux). |
| u | Change units of the partition size display. It will rotate through megabytes, sectors, and cylinders. |
| W | Write partition table to disk (you must enter an uppercase W). Because this might destroy data on the disk, you must either confirm or deny the write by entering yes or no. If you enter yes, cfdisk will write the partition table to disk and the tell the kernel to re-read the partition table from the disk. The re-reading of the partition table works in most cases, but I have seen it fail. Don't panic. It will be correct after you reboot the system. In all cases, I still recommend rebooting the system just to be safe. |
| Up arrow, Down arrow | Move cursor to the previous or next partition. If there are more partitions than can be displayed on a screen, you can display the next (previous) set of partitions by moving down (up) at the last (first) partition displayed on the screen. |
| Ctrl+L | Redraws the screen. In case something goes wrong and you cannot read anything, you can refresh the screen from the main command line. |
| ? | Print the help screen. |

All the commands can be entered with either uppercase or lowercase letters (except for writes). When in a submenu or at a prompt to enter a filename, you can hit the Esc key to return to the main command line.

## OPTIONS

| | |
|---|---|
| -a | Use an arrow cursor instead of reverse video for highlighting the current partition. |
| -v | Print the version number and copyright. |

| -z | Start with zeroed partition table. This option is useful when you want to repartition your entire disk. Note that this option does not zero the partition table on the disk; rather, it simply starts the program without reading the existing partition table. |
|---|---|
| -c *cylinders* | |
| -h *heads* | |
| -s *sectors-per-track* | Override the number of cylinders, heads, and sectors-per-track read from the BIOS. If your BIOS or adapter does not supply this information or if it supplies incorrect information, use these options to set the disk geometry values. |
| -P *opt* | Prints the partition table in specified formats. *opt* can be one or more of r, s, or t. See the print command for more information on the print formats. |

## SEE ALSO

fdisk(8)

## BUGS

The current version does not support multiple disks (future addition).

## AUTHOR

Kevin E. Martin (martin@cs.unc.edu)

*The BOGUS Linux Release, 3 June 1995*

# chat

chat—Automated conversational script with a modem.

## SYNOPSIS

chat [ *options* ] *script*

## DESCRIPTION

The chat program defines a conversational exchange between the computer and the modem. Its primary purpose is to establish the connection between the Point-to-Point protocol daemon (pppd) and the remote's pppd process.

## OPTIONS

| -f *<chat file>* | Read the chat script from the chat file. The use of this option is mutually exclusive with the chat script parameters. The user must have read access to the file. Multiple lines are permitted in the file. Space or horizontal tab characters should be used to separate the strings. |
|---|---|
| -t *<timeout>* | Set the time-out for the expected string to be received. If the string is not received within the time limit, then the reply string is not sent. An alternate reply may be sent or the script will fail if there is no alternate reply string. A failed script will cause the chat program to terminate with a nonzero error code. |
| -r *<report file>* | Set the file for output of the report strings. If you use the keyword REPORT, the resulting strings are written to this file. If this option is not used and you still use REPORT keywords, the stderr file is used for the report strings. |
| -v | Request that the chat script be executed in a verbose mode. The chat program will then log all text received from the modem and the output strings that it sends to the SYSLOG. |

-v                          Request that the chat script be executed in a stderr verbose mode. The chat program
                            will then log all text received from the modem and the output strings that it sends to the
                            stderr device. This device is usually the local console at the station running the chat or
                            pppd program. This option does not work properly if the stderr is redirected to the /
                            dev/null location because in that case pppd should run in the detached mode. In that
                            case, use the -v option to record the session on the SYSLOG device.

script                      If the script is not specified in a file with the -f option, then the script is included as
                            parameters to the chat program.

## CHAT SCRIPT

The chat script defines the communications.

A script consists of one or more "expect-send" pairs of strings, separated by spaces, with an optional "subexpect-subsend"
string pair, separated by a dash as in the following example:

```
ogin:-BREAK-ogin: ppp ssword: hello2u2
```

This line indicates that the chat program should expect the string ogin:. If it fails to receive a login prompt within the time
interval allotted, it is to send a break sequence to the remote and then expect the string ogin:. If the first ogin: is received,
then the break sequence is not generated.

Once it receives the login prompt, the chat program will send the string ppp and then expect the prompt ssword:. When it
receives the prompt for the password, it will send the password hello2u2.

A carriage return is usually sent following the reply string. It is not expected in the "expect" string unless it is specifically
requested by using the nr character sequence.

The expect sequence should contain only what is needed to identify the string. Because it is usually stored on a disk file, it
should not contain variable information. It is generally not acceptable to look for time strings, network identification strings,
or other variable pieces of data such as an expect string.

To help correct for characters that may be corrupted during the initial sequence, look for the string ogin: rather than
login:. It is possible that the leading l character might be received in error and you might never find the string even though
it was sent by the system. For this reason, scripts look for ogin: rather than login: and ssword: rather than password:.

A very simple script might look like this:

```
ogin: ppp ssword: hello2u2
```

In other words, expect ....ogin:, send ppp, expect ...ssword:, send hello2u2.

In actual practice, simple scripts are rare. At the vary least, you should include subexpect sequences in case the original string
is not received. For example, consider the following script:

```
ogin:-ogin: ppp ssword: hello2u2
```

This is a better script than the simple one used earlier. This looks for the same login: prompt; however, if one was not
received, a single return sequence is sent and then it will look for login: again. Should line noise obscure the first login
prompt then sending the empty line will usually generate a login prompt again.

## ABORT STRINGS

Many modems will report the status of the call as a string. These strings may be CONNECTED or NO CARRIER or BUSY. It is
often desirable to terminate the script if the modem fails to connect to the remote. The difficulty is that a script does not
know exactly which modem string it might receive. On one attempt, it might receive BUSY, but the next time, it might
receive NO CARRIER.

These "abort" strings can be specified in the script using the ABORT sequence. It is written in the script as in the following
example:

```
ABORT BUSY ABORT 'NO CARRIER' " ATZ OK ATDT5551212 CONNECT
```

This sequence will expect nothing and then send the string ATZ. The expected response to this is the string OK. When it receives OK, the string ATDT5551212 dials the telephone. The expected string is CONNECT. If the string CONNECT is received, the remainder of the script is executed. However, if the modem finds a busy telephone, it sends the string BUSY. This causes the string to match the abort character sequence. The script then fails because it found a match to the abort string. If it received the string NO CARRIER, it aborts for the same reason. Either string may be received. Either string will terminate the chat script.

## REPORT STRINGS

A report string is similar to the ABORT string. The difference is that the strings and all characters to the next control character such as a carriage return, are written to the report file.

The report strings may be used to isolate the transmission rate of the modem's connect string and return the value to the chat user. The analysis of the report string logic occurs in conjunction with the other string processing such as looking for the expect string. The use of the same string for a report and abort sequence is probably not very useful; however, it is possible.

The report strings do not change the completion code of the program.

These "report" strings may be specified in the script using the REPORT sequence. It is written in the script as in the following example:

```
REPORT CONNECT ABORT BUSY " ATDT5551212 CONNECT " ogin: account
```

This sequence expects nothing and then sends the string ATDT5551212 to dial the telephone. The expected string is CONNECT. If the string CONNECT is received, the remainder of the script is executed. In addition, the program writes to the expect-file the string CONNECT plus any characters that follow it such as the connection rate.

## TIME-OUT

The initial time-out value is 45 seconds. This may be changed using the -t parameter.

To change the time-out value for the next expect string, the following example may be used:

```
ATZ OK ATDT5551212 CONNECT TIMEOUT 10 ogin:-ogin: TIMEOUT 5 password:: hello2u2
```

This changes the time-out to 10 seconds when it expects the login: prompt. The time-out is then changed to 5 seconds when it looks for the password prompt.

The time-out, once changed, remains in effect until it is changed again.

## SENDING EOT

The special reply string of EOT indicates that the chat program should send an EOT character to the remote. This is usually the End-of-file character sequence. A return character is not sent following the EOT. The EOT sequence may be embedded into the send string using the sequence ^D.

## GENERATING BREAK

The special reply string of BREAK causes a break condition to be sent. The break is a special signal on the transmitter. The normal processing on the receiver is to change the transmission rate. It may be used to cycle through the available transmission rates on the remote until you are able to receive a valid login prompt. The break sequence may be embedded into the send string using the \K sequence.

## ESCAPE SEQUENCES

The expect and reply strings may contain escape sequences. All the sequences are legal in the reply string. Many are legal in the expect. Those that are not valid in the expect sequence are so indicated.

| | |
|---|---|
| ' ' | Expects or sends a null string. If you send a null string, it will still send the return character. This sequence may either be a pair of apostrophe or quote characters. |
| \\b | Represents a backspace character. |

| | |
|---|---|
| \\c | Suppresses the newline at the end of the reply string. This is the only method to send a string without a trailing return character. It must be at the end of the send string. For example, the sequence hello\c will simply send the characters h, e, 1, 1, o. (Not valid in expect.) |
| \\d | Delay for one second. The program uses sleep(1), which will delay to a maximum of one second. (Not valid in expect.) |
| \\K | Insert a BREAK. (Not valid in expect.) |
| \\n | Send a newline or linefeed character. |
| \\N | Send a null character. The same sequence may be represented by \0. (Not valid in expect.) |
| \\p | Pause for a fraction of a second. The delay is one tenth of a second. (Not valid in expect.) |
| \\q | Suppress writing the string to the SYSLOG file. The string ?????? is written to the log in its place. (Not valid in expect.) |
| \\r | Send or expect a carriage return. |
| \\s | Represents a space character in the string. This may be used when it is not desirable to quote the strings that contains spaces. The sequence HI TIM and HI\sTIM are the same. |
| \\t | Send or expect a tab character. |
| \\\\ | Send or expect a backslash character. |
| \\*ddd* | Collapse the octal digits (*ddd*) into a single ASCII character and send that character. (Some characters are not valid in expect.) |
| ^*C* | Substitute the sequence with the control character represented by *C*. For example, the character DC1 (17) is shown as ^Q. (Some characters are not valid in expect.) |

## TERMINATION CODES

The chat program will terminate with the following completion codes:

| | |
|---|---|
| 0 | The normal termination of the program. This indicates that the script was executed without error to the normal conclusion. |
| 1 | One or more of the parameters are invalid or an expect string was too large for the internal buffers. This indicates that the program as not properly executed. |
| 2 | An error occurred during the execution of the program. This may be due to a read or write operation failing for some reason or chat receiving a signal such as SIGINT. |
| 3 | A time-out event occurred when there was an expect string without having a -subsend string. This may mean that you did not program the script correctly for the condition or that some unexpected event occurred and the expected string could not be found. |
| 4 | The first string marked as an ABORT condition occurred. |
| 5 | The second string marked as an ABORT condition occurred. |
| 6 | The third string marked as an ABORT condition occurred. |
| 7 | The fourth string marked as an ABORT condition occurred. |
| ... | The other termination codes are also strings marked as an ABORT condition. |

Using the termination code, it is possible to determine which event terminated the script. It is possible to decide if the string BUSY was received from the modem as opposed to NO DIAL TONE. Although the first event may be retried, the second will probably have little chance of succeeding during a retry.

## SEE ALSO

Additional information about chat scripts may be found with UUCP documentation. The chat script was taken from the ideas proposed by the scripts used by the uucico program.

uucico(1), uucp(1)

## COPYRIGHT

The chat program is in public domain. This is not the GNU public license. If it breaks, then you get to keep both pieces.

*Chat Version 1.9, 5 May 1995*

# chroot

chroot—Change root directory and execute a program there.

## SYNOPSIS

```
chroot directory program [ arg ... ]
```

## DESCRIPTION

chroot changes the root directory for a process to a new directory executes a program there.

## SEE ALSO

chroot(2)

## AUTHOR

Rick Sladkey (jrs@world.std.com)

*Linux 0.99, 20 November 1993*

# clock

clock—Manipulate the CMOS clock.

## SYNOPSIS

```
/sbin/clock [ -u ] -r
/sbin/clock [ -u ] -w
/sbin/clock [ -u ] -s
/sbin/clock [ -u ] -a
```

## DESCRIPTION

clock manipulates the CMOS clock in various ways, allowing it to be read or written and allowing synchronization between the CMOS clock and the kernel's version of the system time.

## OPTIONS

| | |
|---|---|
| -u | Indicates that the CMOS clock is set to Universal Time. |
| -r | Read CMOS clock and print the result to stdout. |
| -w | Write the system time into the CMOS clock. |
| -s | Set the system time from the CMOS clock. |
| -a | Set the system time from the CMOS clock, adjusting the time to correct for systematic error and writing it back into the CMOS clock. This option uses the file /etc/adjtime to determine how the clock changes. It contains three numbers. |
| | The first number is the correction in seconds per day. (For example, if your clock runs 5 seconds fast each day, the first number should read -5.0.) |
| | The second number tells when clock was last used in seconds since 1/1/1970. |
| | The third number is the remaining part of a second that was leftover after the last adjustment. |

The following instructions are from the source code:

1. Create a file /etc/adjtime containing as the first and only line 0.0 0 0.0.
2. Run clock -au or clock -a, depending on whether your CMOS is in Universal or Local Time. This updates the second number.
3. Set your system time using the date command.
4. Update your CMOS time using clock -wu or clock -w.
5. Replace the first number in /otc/adjtime by your correction.
6. Put the command clock -au or clock -a in your /etc/rc.local or let cron(8) start it regularly.

## FILES

/etc/adjtime

/etc/rc.local

## AUTHORS

| V1.0 | Charles Hedrick (hedrick@cs.rutgers.edu) Apr 1992 |
| V1.1 | Modified for clock adjustments, Rob Hooft (hooft@chem.ruu.nl) Nov 1992 |
| V1.2 | Patches by Harald Koenig (koenig@nova.tat.physik.uni-tuebingen.de) applied by Rob Hooft (hooft@EMBL-Heidelberg.DE) Oct 1993 |

*Linux 0.99, 24 December 1992*

# comsat

comsat—Biff server

## SYNOPSIS

comsat

## DESCRIPTION

comsat is the server process that receives reports of incoming mail and notifies users if they requested this service. comsat receives messages on a datagram port associated with the biff service specification (see services(5) and inetd(8)). The one-line messages are of the form

*user@mailbox-offset*

If the user specified is logged in to the system and the associated terminal has the owner execute bit turned on (by a biff y), the offset is used as a seek offset into the appropriate mailbox file and the first 7 lines or 560 characters of the message are printed on the user's terminal. Lines that appear to be part of the message header other than the From, To, Date, or Subject lines are not included in the displayed message.

## FILES

/var/run/utmp to find out who's logged on and on what terminals

## SEE ALSO

biff(1), inetd(8)

## BUGS

The message header filtering is prone to error. The density of the information presented is near the theoretical minimum.

Users should be notified of mail that arrives on other machines than the one to which they are currently logged in.

The notification should appear in a separate window so it does not mess up the screen.

## HISTORY

The command appeared in BSD 4.2.

*BSD 4.2, 16 March 1991*

# crond

crond—crond daemon (Dillon's Cron).

## SYNOPSIS

crond [-l#] [-d[#]] [-f] [-b] [-c *directory*]

## OPTIONS

crond is a background daemon that parses individual crontab files and executes commands on behalf of the users in question.

| | |
|---|---|
| -l*loglevel* | Set logging level; default is 8. |
| -d[*debuglevel*] | Set debugging level; default is 0. If no level is specified with the -d option, the default is 1. This option also sets the logging level to 0 and causes crond to run in the foreground. |
| -f | Run crond in the foreground. |
| -b | Run crond in the background (the default unless -d is specified). |
| -c *directory* | Specify directory containing crontab files. |

## DESCRIPTION

crond is responsible for scanning the crontab files and running their commands at the appropriate time. The crontab program communicates with crond through the cron.update file, which resides in the crontabs directory, usually /var/spool/cron/crontabs. This is accomplished by appending the filename of the modified or deleted crontab file to cron.update, which crond then picks up to resynchronize or remove its internal representation of the file.

crond has a number of built-in limitations to reduce the chance of it being ill-used. Potentially infinite loops during parsing are dealt with via a failsafe counter, and user crontabs are generally limited to 256 crontab entries. crontab lines may not be longer than 1024 characters, including the newline.

Whenever crond must run a job, it first creates a daemon-owned temporary file O_EXCL and O_APPEND to store any output, and then it fork()s and changes its user and group permissions to match that of the user the job is being run for. Then, it executes /bin/sh -c to run the job. The temporary file remains under the ownership of the daemon to prevent the user from tampering with it. Upon job completion, crond verifies the secureness of the mail file and, if it has been appended to, mails to the file to user. The sendmail program is run under the user's UID to prevent mail-related security holes. Unlike crontab, the crond program does not leave an open descriptor to the file for the duration of the job's execution because this might cause crond to run out of descriptors. When the crontab program allows a user to edit his crontab, it copies the crontab to a user-owned file before running the user's preferred editor. The suid crontab program keeps an open descriptor to the file, which it later uses to copy the file back, thereby ensuring the user has not tampered with the file type.

crond always synchronizes to the top of the minute, checking the current time against the list of possible jobs. The list is stored such that the scan goes very quickly, and crond can deal with several thousand entries without taking any noticeable amount of CPU.

## AUTHOR

Matthew Dillon (dillon@apollo.west.oic.com)

*1 May 1994*

# ctlinnd

ctlinnd—Control the InterNetNews daemon.

## SYNOPSIS

ctlinnd [ -h ][ -s ][ -t *timeout* ] *command* [ *argument...* ]

## DESCRIPTION

ctlinnd sends a message to the control channel of innd(8), the InterNetNews server.

In the normal mode of behavior, the message is sent to the server, which then performs the requested action and sends back a reply with a text message and the exit code for ctlinnd. If the server successfully performed the command, ctlinnd will exit with a status of zero and print the reply on standard output. If the server could not perform the command (for example, it was told to remove a newsgroup that does not exist), it will direct ctlinnd to exit with a status of one. The shutdown, xabort, and xexec commands do not generate a reply; ctlinnd will always exit silently with a status of zero. If the -s flag is used, then no message will be printed if the command was successful.

The -t flag can be used to specify how long to wait for the reply from the server. The timeout value specifies the number of seconds to wait. A value of zero waits forever, and a value less than zero indicates that no reply is needed. When waiting for a reply, ctlinnd will try every two minutes to see if the server is still running, so it is unlikely that -t0 will hang. The default is -t0.

To see a command summary, use the -h flag. If a command is included when ctlinnd is invoked with the -h flag, then only the usage for that command will be given.

If a large number of groups are going to be created or deleted at once, it may be more efficient to pause or throttle the server and edit the active file directly.

The complete list of commands follows. Note that all commands have a fixed number of arguments. If a parameter can be an empty string, then it is necessary to specify it as two adjacent quotes (" ").

| | |
|---|---|
| addhist*Message-IDarr exp post paths* | Add an entry to the history database. This directs the server to create a history line for Message-ID. The angle brackets are optional. *arr*, *exp*, and *post* specify when the article arrived, what its expiration date is, and when it was posted. All three values are a number indicating the number of seconds since the epoch. If the article does not have an Expires header, then *exp* should be zero. *paths* is the pathname within the newsspool directory where the article is filed. If the article is cross-posted, then the names should be separated by whitespace and the *paths* argument should be inside double quotes. If the server is paused or throttled, this command causes it to briefly open the history database. |
| allow *reason* | Remote connections are allowed. The reason must be the same text given with an earlier reject command or an empty string. |
| begin *site* | Begin feeding *site*. This will cause the server to rescan the newsfeeds(5) file to find the specified site and set up a newsfeed for it. If the site already exists, a "drop" is done first. This command is forwarded; see below. |
| cancel <*Message-ID*> | Remove the article with the specified Message-ID from the local system. This does not generate a cancel message. The angle brackets are optional. If the server is paused or throttled, this command causes it to briefly open the history database. |
| changegroup *group rest* | The newsgroup group is changed so that its fourth field in the active file becomes the value specified by the rest parameter. This may be used to make an existing group moderated or unmoderated, for example. |
| checkfile | Check the syntax of the newsfeeds file, and display a message if any errors are found. The details of the errors are reported to syslog(3). |

drop *site*

Flush and drop *site* from the server's list of active feeds. This command is forwarded; see below.

flush *site*

Flush the buffer for the specified *site*. The actions taken depend on the type of feed the site receives; see newsfeeds(5). This is useful when the site is fed by a file and batching is going to start. If site is an empty string, then all sites are flushed and the active file and history databases are also written out. This command is forwarded; see below.

flushlogs

Close the log and error log files and rename them to have a .old extension. The history database and active file are also written out.

go *reason*

Reopen the history database and start accepting articles after a pause or throttle command. The *reason* must either be an empty string or match the text that was given in the earlier pause or throttle command. If a reject command was done, this will also do an allow command if the reason matches the text that was given in the reject. If a reserve command was done, this will also clear the reservation if the reason matches the text that was given in the reserve. Note that if only the history database has changed while the server is paused or throttled, it is not necessary to send it a reload command before sending it a go command. If the server throttled itself because it accumulated too many I/O errors, this command will reset the error count. If the server was not started with the –ny flag, then this command also does a readers command with yes as the flag and *reason* as the text.

hangup *channel*

Close the socket on the specified incoming *channel*. This is useful when an incoming connection appears to be hung.

help [*command*]

Print a command summary for all commands, or just *command* if specified.

mode

Print the server's operating mode as a multiline summary of the parameters and operating state.

name *nnn*

Print the name of channel number *nnn* or of all channels if it is an empty string.

newgroup *group rest creator*

Create the specified newsgroup. The *rest* parameter should be the fourth field as described in active(5); if it is not an equal sign, only the first letter is used. The *creator* should be the name of the person creating the group. If the newsgroup already exists, this is equivalent to the changegroup command. This is the only command that has defaults. The creator can be omitted and will default to the empty string, and the *rest* parameter can be omitted and will default to y. This command can be done while the server is paused or throttled; it will update its internal state when a go command is sent. This command updates the active.times (see active(5)) file.

param *letter value*

Change the command-line parameters of the server. The combination of defaults makes it possible to use the text of the Control header directly. *letter* is the innd command-line option to set, and *value* is the new value. For example, i 5 directs the server to allow only five incoming connections. To enable or disable the action of the –n flag, use the letter y or n for the *value*.

pause *reason*

Pause the server so that no incoming articles are accepted. No existing connections are closed, but the history database is closed. This command should be used for short-term locks, such as when replacing the history files. If the server was not started with the –ny flag, then this command also does a readers command with no as the flag and *reason* as the text.

readers *flag text*

Allow or disallow newsreaders. If *flag* starts with the letter n, then newsreading is disallowed by causing the server to pass the text as the value of the nnrpd(8) –r flag. If *flag* starts with the letter y and text is either an empty string, or the same string that was used when newsreading was disallowed, then newsreading will be allowed.

reject *reason*
: Remote connections (those that would not be handed off to nnrpd) are rejected, with *reason* given as the explanation.

reload *what reason*
: The server updates its in-memory copies of various configuration files. *what* identifies what should be reloaded. If it is an empty string or the word all, then everything is reloaded; if it is the word history, then the history database is closed and opened; if it is the word hosts.nntp, then the hosts.nntp(5) file is reloaded; if it is the word active or newsfeeds, then both the active and newsfeeds files are reloaded; if it is the word overview.fmt, then the overview.fmt(5) file is reloaded. The *reason* is reported to syslog. There is no way to reload the data inn.conf(5) file; the server currently only uses the pathhost parameter, so this restriction should not be a problem.

renumber *group*
: Scan the spool directory for the specified newsgroup and update the low-water mark in the active file. If group is an empty string, then all newsgroups are scanned.

reserve *reason*
: The next pause or throttle command must use *reason* as its text. This reservation is cleared by giving an empty string for the *reason*. This command is used by programs such as expire(8) that want to avoid running into other instances of each other.

rmgroup *group*
: Remove the specified newsgroup. This is done by editing the active file. The spool directory is not touched, and any articles in the group will be expired using the default expiration parameters. Unlike the newgroup command, this command does not update the active.times file.

send *feed text...*
: The specified *text* is sent as a control line to the exploder feed.

shutdown *reason*
: The server is shut down, with the specified *reason* recorded in the log and sent to all open connections. It is a good idea to send a throttle command first.

signal *sig site*
: Signal *sig* is sent to the specified *site*, which must be a channel or exploder feed. *sig* can be a numeric signal number or the word hup, int, or term; case is not significant.

throttle *reason*
: Input is throttled so that all existing connections are closed and new connections are rejected. The history database is closed. This should be used for long-term locks, such as when expire is being run. If the server was not started with the -ny flag, then this command also does a readers command with no as the flag and *reason* as the text.

trace *item flag*
: Tracing is turned on or off for the specified item. *flag* should start with the letter y or n to turn tracing on or off. If *item* starts as a number, then tracing is set for the specified innd channel, which must be for an incoming NNTP feed. If it starts with the letter I, then general innd tracing is turned on or off. If it starts with the letter n, then future nnrpd's will or will not have the -t flag enabled, as appropriate.

xabort *reason*
: The server logs the specified *reason* and then invokes the abort(3) routine.

xexec *path*
: The server gets ready to shut itself down, but instead of exiting, it executes the specified *path* with all of its original arguments. If path is innd, then /news/bin/innd is invoked; if it is inndstart, then /news/bin/inndstart is invoked; if it is an empty string, it will invoke the appropriate program depending on whether it was started with the -p flag; any other value is an error.

In addition to being acted upon within the server, certain commands can be forwarded to the appropriate child process. If the site receiving the command is an exploder (such as `buffchan`(8)) or it is a funnel that feeds into an exploder, then the command can be forwarded. In this case, the server will send a command line to the exploder that consists of the `ctlinnd` command name. If the site funnels into an exploder that has an asterisk (*) in its W flag (see `newsfeed`(5)), then the site name is appended to the command; otherwise, no argument is appended.

## BUGS

`ctlinnd` uses the `inndcomm`(3) library and is therefore limited to server replies no larger than 4KB.

## HISTORY

Written by Rich $alz (`rsalz@uunet.uu.net`) for InterNetNews.

## SEE ALSO

`active`(5), `expire`(8), `innd`(8), `inndcomm`(3), `inn.conf`(5), `newsfeeds`(5), `overview.fmt`(5)

# ctrlaltdel

`ctrlaltdel`—Set the function of the Ctrl+Alt+Del combination.

## SYNOPSIS

`ctrlaltdel hard¦soft`

## DESCRIPTION

Based on examination of the `linux/kernel/sys.c` code, it is clear that there are two supported functions that the Ctrl+Alt+Del sequence can perform: a hard reset, which immediately reboots the computer without calling `sync`(2) and without any other preparation, and a soft reset, which sends the `SIGINT` (interrupt) signal to the `init` process (this is always the process with PID 1). If this option is used, the `init`(8) program must support this feature. Because there are now several `init`(8) programs in the Linux community, consult the documentation for the version that you are currently using.

`ctrlaltdel` is usually used in the `/etc/rc.local` file.

## FILES

`/etc/rc.local`

## SEE ALSO

`simpleinit`(8), `init`(8)

## AUTHOR

Peter Orbaek (`poe@daimi.aau.dk`)

*Linux 0.99, 25 October 1993*

# cvsbug

`cvsbug`—Send problem report (PR) about CVS to a central support site.

## SYNOPSIS

`cvsbug [ site ][-f problem-report ][-t mail-address ][-P ][-L ]`
`[--request-id ][-v ]`

## DESCRIPTION

cvsbug is a tool used to submit problem reports (PRs) to a central support site. In most cases, the correct site will be the default. This argument indicates the support site that is responsible for the category of problem involved. Some sites may use a local address as a default. Site values are defined by using the aliases(5).

cvsbug invokes an editor on a problem report template (after trying to fill in some fields with reasonable default values). When you exit the editor, cvsbug sends the completed form to the Problem Report Management System (GNATS) at a central support site. At the support site, the PR is assigned a unique number and is stored in the GNATS database according to its category and submitter ID. GNATS automatically replies with an acknowledgment, citing the category and the PR number.

To ensure that a PR is handled promptly, it should contain your (unique) submitter ID and one of the available categories to identify the problem area. (Use cvsbug -L to see a list of categories.)

The cvsbug template at your site should already be customized with your submitter ID (running install-sid submitter-id to accomplish this is part of the installation procedures for cvsbug). If this hasn't been done, see your system administrator for your submitter ID, or request one from your support site by invoking cvsbug —-request-id. If your site does not distinguish between different user sites, or if you are not affiliated with the support site, use net for this field.

The more precise your problem description and the more complete your information, the faster your support team can solve your problems.

## OPTIONS

| | |
|---|---|
| -f *problem-report* | Specify a file (*problem-report*) that already contains a complete problem report. cvsbug sends the contents of the file without invoking the editor. If the value for *problem-report* is -, then cvsbug reads from standard input. |
| -t *mail-address* | Change mail address at the support site for problem reports. The default *mail-address* is the address used for the default site. Use the site argument rather than this option in nearly all cases. |
| -P | Print the form specified by the environment variable PR FORM on standard output. If PR FORM is not set, print the standard blank PR template. No mail is sent. |
| -L | Print the list of available categories. No mail is sent. |
| --request-id | Sends mail to the default support site, or *site* if specified, with a request for your submitter ID. If you are not affiliated with *site*, use a submitter ID of net. |
| -v | Display the cvsbug version number. |

Note: Use cvsbug to submit problem reports rather than mail them directly. Using both the template and cvsbug itself will help ensure all necessary information will reach the support site.

## ENVIRONMENT

The environment variable EDITOR specifies the editor to invoke on the template. The default is vi.

If the environment variable PR FORM is set, then its value is used as the filename of the template for your problem-report editing session. You can use this to start with a partially completed form (for example, a form with the identification fields already completed).

## HOW TO FILL OUT A PROBLEM REPORT

Problem reports have to be in a particular form so that a program can easily manage them. Please remember the following guidelines:

Describe only one problem with each problem report.

For follow-up mail, use the same subject line as the one in the automatic acknowledgment. It consists of category, PR number, and the original synopsis line. This allows the support site to relate several mail messages to a particular PR and to record them automatically.

Please try to be as accurate as possible in the subject or synopsis line.

The subject and the synopsis line are not confidential. This is because open-bugs lists are compiled from them. Avoid putting confidential information there.

See the GNU Info file cvsbug.info or the document *Reporting Problems With* cvsbug for detailed information on reporting problems

## HOW TO SUBMIT TEST CASES, CODE, AND SO ON

Submit small code samples with the PR. Contact the support site for instructions on submitting larger test cases and problematic source code.

## FILES

/tmp/p$$ copy of PR used in editing session

/tmp/pf$$ copy of empty PR form, for testing purposes

/tmp/pbad$$ file for rejected PRs

## EMACS USER INTERFACE

An EMACS user interface for cvsbug with completion of field values is part of the cvsbug distribution (invoked with M-x cvsbug). See the file cvsbug.info or the ASCII file INSTALL in the top-level directory of the distribution for configuration and installation information. The EMACS LISP template file is cvsbug-el.in and is installed as cvsbug.el.

## INSTALLATION AND CONFIGURATION

See cvsbug.info or INSTALL for installation instructions.

## SEE ALSO

*Reporting Problems Using* cvsbug (also installed as the GNU Info file cvsbug.info).

gnats(l), query-pr(1), edit-pr(1), gnats(8), queue-pr(8), at-pr(8), mkcat(8), mkdist(8)

## AUTHORS

Jeffrey Osier, Brendan Kehoe, Jason Merrill, Heinz G. Seidl (Cygnus Support).

## COPYING

*xVERSIONx, February 1993*

# cvtbatch

cvtbatch—Convert Usenet batch file to INN format.

## SYNOPSIS

cvtbatch [ -w *items* ]

## DESCRIPTION

cvtbatch reads standard input as a series of lines, converts each line, and writes it to standard output. It is used to convert simple batchfiles that contain just the article name to INN batchfiles that contain additional information about each article.

Each line is taken as the pathname to a Usenet article. If it is not an absolute pathname, it is taken relative to the spool directory, /news/spool. (Only the first word of each line is parsed; anything following whitespace is ignored.)

The -w flag specifies how each output line should be written. The items for this flag should be chosen from the W flag items as specified in newsfeeds(5). They may be chosen from the following set:

| | |
|---|---|
| b | Size of article in bytes |
| f | Full pathname of article |
| m | Article Message-ID |
| n | Relative pathname of article |

If the input file consists of a series of Message-IDs, then use grephistory(1) with the -s flag piped into cvtbatch.

## HISTORY

Written by Rich $alz (rsalz@uunet.uu.net) for InterNetNews.

## SEE ALSO

grephistory(1) newsfeeds(5)

# cytune

cytune—Tune Cyclades driver parameters.

## SYNOPSIS

```
cytune [-q [-i interval]] ([-s value]¦[-S value])
[-g¦G] ([-t timeout]¦[-T timeout]) tty [tty ...]
```

## DESCRIPTION

cytune queries and modifies the interruption threshold for the Cyclades driver. Each serial line on a Cyclades card has a 12-byte FIFO for input (and another 12-byte FIFO for output). The "threshold" specifies how many input characters must be present in the FIFO before an interruption is raised. When a Cyclades tty is opened, this threshold is set to a default value based on baud rate:

| Baud | Threshold |
|---|---|
| 50-4800 | 10 |
| 9600 | 8 |
| 19200 | 4 |
| 38400 | 2 |
| 57600-150000 | 1 |

If the threshold is set too low, the large number of interruptions can load the machine and decrease overall system throughput. If the threshold is set too high, the FIFO buffer can overflow, and characters will be lost. Slower machines, however, may not be able to deal with the interrupt load and will require that the threshold be adjusted upwards.

If the Cyclades driver was compiled with ENABLE MONITORING defined, the cytune command can be used with the -q option to report interrupts over the monitoring interval and characters transferred over the monitoring interval. It will also report the state of the FIFO. The maximum number of characters in the FIFO when an interrupt occurred, the instantaneous count of characters in the FIFO, and how many characters are now in the FIFO are reported. This output might look like this:

```
/dev/cubC0: 830 ints, 9130 chars; fifo: 11 threshold, 11 max, 11 now
166.259866 interrupts/second, 1828.858521 characters/second
```

This output indicates that for this monitoring period, the interrupts were always being handled within one character time because max never rose above threshold. This is good, and you can probably run this way, provided that a large number of samples come out this way. You will lose characters if you overrun the FIFO because the Cyclades hardware does not seem to support the RTS RS-232 signal line for hardware flow control from the DCE to the DTE.

cytune will in query mode produce a summary report when ended with a SIGINT or when the threshold or time-out is changed.

There may be a responsiveness versus throughput tradeoff. The Cyclades card, at the higher speeds, is capable of putting a very high interrupt load on the system. This will reduce the amount of CPU time available for other tasks on your system. However, the time it takes to respond to a single character may be increased if you increase the threshold. This might be noticed by monitoring ping(8) times on a SLIP link controlled by a Cyclades card. If your SLIP link is generally used for interactive work such as telnet(1), you might want to leave the threshold low so that characters are responded to as quickly as possible. If your SLIP link is generally used for file transfer, WWW, and the like, setting the FIFO to a high value is likely to reduce the load on your system while not significantly affecting throughput. Alternatively, see the -t or -T options to adjust the time that the Cyclades waits before flushing its buffer. Units are 5ms.

If you are running a mouse on a Cyclades port, it is likely that you want to maintain the threshold and time-out at a low value.

## OPTIONS

| | |
|---|---|
| -s *value* | Set the current threshold to *value* characters. Note that if the tty is not being held open by another process, the threshold will be reset on the next open. Only values between 1 and 12, inclusive, are permitted. |
| -t *value* | Set the current flush time-out to *value* units. Note that if the tty is not being held open by another process, the threshold will be reset on the next open. Only values between 0 and 255, inclusive, are permitted. Setting value to 0 forces the default, currently 0x20 (160ms) but soon to be 0x02 (10ms). Units are 5ms. |
| -g | Get the current threshold and time-out. |
| -T *value* | Set the default flush time-out to *value* units. When the tty is next opened, this value is used instead of the default. If value is 0, then the value defaults to 0x20 (160ms), soon to be 0x02 (10ms). |
| -G | Get the default threshold and flush time-out values. |
| -q | Gather statistics about the tty. The results are only valid if the Cyclades driver has been compiled with ENABLE MONITORING defined. This is probably not the default. |
| -i *interval* | Statistics will be gathered every *interval* seconds. |

## BUGS

If you run two copies of cytune at the same time to report statistics about the same port, the ints, chars, and max values will be reset and not reported correctly. cytune(8) should prevent this but does not.

## AUTHOR

Nick Simicich (njs@scifi.emi.net), with modifications by Rik Faith (faith@cs.unc.edu)

## FILES

/dev/ttyC[0-8]

/dev/cubC[0-8]

## SEE ALSO

setserial(8)

*4 March 1995*

# debugfs

debugfs—ext2 filesystem debugger.

## SYNOPSIS

debugfs [[-w ]*device*]

## DESCRIPTION

debugfs is a filesystem debugger. It can be used to examine and change the state of an ext2 filesystem. device is the special file corresponding to the device containing the ext2 filesystem (such as /dev/hdXX).

## OPTIONS

-w                          Specify that the filesystem should be open in read-write mode. Without this option, the filesystem is open in read-only mode.

## COMMANDS

debugfs is an interactive debugger. It understands a number of commands:

cd *file*

chroot *file*

close                       Close the currently open filesystem.

clri *file*                 Clear the contents of the inode corresponding to *file*.

expand_dir, *file*          Expand a directory.

find_free_block [*goal*]    Find the first free block, starting from *goal*, and allocate it.

find_free_inode [*dir* [*mode*]]  Find a free inode and allocate it.

freeb *block*               Mark the block as not allocated.

freei *file*                Free the inode corresponding to *file*.

help

iname *inode*               Print the filename corresponding to *inode* (currently not implemented).

initialize *device blocksize*  Create an ext2 file system on *device*.

kill_file *file*            Remove a file and deallocate its blocks.

ln *source_file dest_file*  Create a link.

ls [*pathname*]             Emulate the ls(1) command.

Modify_inode file           Modify the contents of the inode corresponding to *file*.

mkdir *file*                Make a directory.

open [-w] *device*          Open a filesystem.

pwd

quit                        Quit debugfs.

| | |
|---|---|
| rm *file* | Remove a file. |
| rmdir *file* | Remove a directory. |
| setb *block* | Mark the block as allocated. |
| seti *file* | Mark in use the inode corresponding to file |
| show_super_stats | List the contents of the super block. |
| stat *file* | Dump the contents of the inode corresponding to *file*. |
| testb *block* | Test if the block is marked as allocated. |
| testi *file* | Test if the inode corresponding to *file* is marked as allocated. |
| unlink *file* | Remove a link. |

## AUTHOR

debugfs was written by Theodore T'so (tytso@mit.edu).

## SEE ALSO

dumpe2fs(8), e2fsck(8), mke2fs(8)

*Version 0.5b, November 1994*

# dip

dip—Dialup IP connection handler.

## SYNOPSIS

```
dip [-t]
dip [-ktv] [-m mtu] scriptfile
dip [-iv] [user_name]
```

## DESCRIPTION

dip handles the connections needed for dialup IP links, such as SLIP or PPP. It can handle both incoming and outgoing connections, using password security for incoming connections. The outgoing connections use the system's dial(3) library if available.

## COMMAND MODE

The first possible use of dip is as a stand-alone program to set up an outgoing IP connection. This can be done by invoking dip with the -t option, which means enter TEST mode and, more precisely, dump you in the COMMAND-MODE of the dip program. You are reminded of this by the DIP> prompt, or, if you also specified the -v debugging flag, the DIP [NNNN]> prompt. The latter prompt also displays the current value of the global errlvl variable, which is used mostly when dip runs in script mode. For the interactive mode, it can be used to determine if the result of the previous command was okay.

The following is a sample taken from a live session:

```
$dip-t
DIP: Dialup IP Protocol Driver version 3.3.7 (12/13/93)
Written by Fred N. van Kempen, MicroWalt Corporation.

DIP>_
```

The most helpful command in this mode is, of course, the help command, which should produce an output similar to this:

```
DIP> help
DIP knows about the following commands:
```

```
databits default dial echo flush
get goto help if init
mode modem parity print port
reset send sleep speed stopbits
term wait

DIP>_
```

All commands display how they should be used when invoking them with no or invalid arguments. Just experiment a little to get the feel of it, and have a look at the sample script files, which also use this command language.

## DIALIN MODE

The second possible way of using dip is as a login shell for incoming IP connections, as in dialup SLIP and PPP connections. To make integration into the existing UNIX system as easy as possible, dip can be installed as simply as using it as a login shell in the system's password file. A sample entry looks like

```
suunet:ij/SMxiTlGVCo:1004:10:UUNET:/tmp:/usr/bin/dip -i
```

When user suunet logs in, the login(1) program sets the home directory to /tmp and execute the dip program with the -i option, which means that dip must run in input mode. dip then tries to locate the name of the logged-in user (the name corresponding to its current user ID, as returned by the getuid(2) system call) in its database file. An optional single argument to the dip program in this mode can be the username that must be used in this lookup, regardless of the current user ID.

dip now scans the /etc/net/diphosts file for an entry for the given username. This file contains lines of text (much like the standard password file). The format looks like

```
#
# diphosts This file describes a number of name to
# address mappings for the DIP program. It
# is used to determine which IP address to
# use for in incoming call of some user.
#
# Version: @(#)diphosts 1.00 12/10/92 FvK
#
# Author: Fred N. van Kempen,
# <waltje@uwalt.nl.mugnet.org>
#
suunet::uunet.uu.net:UUNET SLIP:SLIP,296

# End of diphosts.
```

The first field of a line identifies the username, which you must match. The second field can contain an encrypted password. If this field is non-null, the dip program asks for an external security password, which must match the password in this field. The third field contains the name (or raw IP address) of the host that is connecting to the system with this link. If a hostname is given, the usual address resolving process is started, using either a nameserver or a local hosts file.

The fourth field can contain any text; it is not (yet) used by the dip program. In future releases, this info may be used in the system log files. Finally, the fifth field of a line contains a mixture of comma-separated flags. Possible flags are

SLIP to indicate you must use the SLIP protocol.

PPP to indicate you must use the PPP protocol.

*number*, which gives the MTU parameter of this connection.

After finding the correct line, dip puts the terminal line into RAW mode and asks the system networking layer to allocate a channel of the desired protocol. Finally, if the channel is activated, it adds an entry to the system's routing table to make the connection work.

dip now goes into an endless loop of sleeping, which continues until the connection is physically aborted (the line is dropped). At that time, dip removes the entry it made in the system's routing table and releases the protocol channel for reuse. It then exits, making room for another session.

## DIALOUT MODE

The last way of using dip is as a program that initiates outgoing connections. To make life easier for the people who have to manage links of this type, dip uses a chat script to set up a link to a remote system. This gives the user an enormous amount of flexibility when making the connection, which otherwise could require many command-line options. The pathname of the script to be run is then given as the single argument to dip; the program will automatically check if the file has a filename ending in a .dip part. This is not mandatory—just a tool to group scripts together in a single directory. A script should look something like this:

```
#
# sample.dip Dialup IP connection support program.
# This file (should show) shows how to use the DIP
# scripting commands to establish a link to a host.
# This host runs the 386bsd operating system, and
# thus can only be used for the "static" addresses.
#
# NOTE: We also need an examnple of a script used to
# connect to a "dynamic" SLIP server, like an Annex
# terminal server...
#
# Version: @(#)sample.dip 1.30 07/05/93
#
# Author: Fred N. van Kempen, <waltje@uWalt.NL.Mugnet.ORG>
#
main:
# First of all, set up our name for this connection.
# I am called "uwalt.hacktic.nl" (== 193.78.33.238)
get $local uwalt.hacktic.nl
# Next, set up the other side's name and address.
# My dialin machine is called 'xs4all.hacktic.nl' (== 193.78.33.42)
get $remote xs4all.hacktic.nl
# Set the desired serial port and speed.
port cua0
speed 38400
# Reset the modem and terminal line.
# This seems to cause trouble for some people!
reset
# Prepare for dialing.
send ATQ0V1E1X1
wait OK 2
if $errlvl != 0 goto error
dial 555-1234567
if $errlvl != 0 goto error
wait CONNECT 60
if $errlvl != 0 goto error
# We are connected. Login to the system.
login:
sleep 3
send \r\n\r\n
wait ogin: 10
if $errlvl != 0 goto error
send NO-WAY\n
wait ord: 5
if $errlvl != 0 goto error
send HA-HA\n
```

```
wait $ 30
if $errlvl != 0 goto error
loggedin:
# We are now logged in. Start the 'sliplogin' program,
# as this is not automatically done for me.
send sliplogin\n
wait SOME-STRING 15
# Set up the SLIP operating parameters.
get $mtu 1500
# Set Destination net/address as type 'default' (vice an address).
# This is used by the 'route' command to set the kernel routing table.
# Some machines seem to require this be done for SLIP to work properly.
default
# Say hello and fire up!
done:
print CONNECTED to $remote with address $rmtip
mode SLIP
goto exit
error:
print SLIP to $remote failed.
exit:
```

This script causes dip to dial up a host, log in, and get a SLIP interface channel going (in the same manner as with incoming connections). When all is set up, it simply goes into the background and waits for a hangup (or just a lethal signal), at which it hangs up and exits.

## FILES

/etc/passwd

/etc/diphosts

## AUTHORS

Fred N. van Kempen (waltje@uwalt.nl.mugnet.org), Paul Mossip (mossip@vizlab.rutgers.edu), Jeff Uphoff (juphoff@aoc.nrao.edu), Jim Seagrave (jes@grendel.demon.co.uk), Olaf Kirch (okir@monad.sub.de).

*Version 3.3.7, 13 December 1993*

# dmesg

dmesg—Print or control the kernel ring buffer.

## SYNOPSIS

dmesg [ -c ] [ -n *level* ]

## DESCRIPTION

dmesg is used to examine or control the kernel ring buffer.

The program helps users to print their bootup messages. Instead of copying the messages by hand, the user need only

dmesg > boot.messages

and mail the boot.messages file to whoever can debug their problem.

## OPTIONS

-c                                                  Clear the ring buffer contents after printing.

-n *level*                                          Set the level at which logging of messages is done to the console. For example, -n 1 prevents all messages, except panic messages, from appearing on the console. All levels of messages are still written to /proc/kmsg, so syslogd(8) can still be used to control exactly where kernel messages appear. When the -n option is used, dmesg will not print or clear the kernel ring buffer.

When both options are used, only the last option on the command line will have an effect.

## SEE ALSO

syslogd(8)

## AUTHOR

Theodore Ts'o (tytso@athena.mit.edu)

*Linux 0.99, 28 October 1993*


# dumpe2fs

dumpe2fs—Dump filesystem information.

## SYNOPSIS

dumpe2fs *device*

## DESCRIPTION

dumpe2fs prints the super block and blocks group information for the filesystem present on device.

dumpe2fs is similar to Berkeley's dumpfs program for the BSD Fast File System.

## BUGS

You need to know the physical filesystem structure to understand the output.

## AUTHOR

dumpe2fs was written by Remy Card (card@masi.ibp.fr), the developer and maintainer of the ext2 fs.

## AVAILABILITY

dumpe2fs is available for anonymous FTP from ftp.ibp.fr and tsx-11.mit.edu in /pub/linux/packages/ext2fs.

## SEE ALSO

e2fsck(8), mke2fs(8), tune2fs(8)

*Version 0.5b, November 1994*


# e2fsck

e2fsck—Check a Linux second extended filesystem.

## SYNOPSIS

e2fsck [ -panyrdfvtFV ][-b *superblock* ][-B *blocksize* ]
[-l¦-L *bad_blocks_file* ] *device*

## DESCRIPTION

e2fsck is used to check a Linux second extended file system.

| | |
|---|---|
| *device* | The special file corresponding to the device (such as /dev/hd*XX*). |

## OPTIONS

| | |
|---|---|
| -a | This option does the same thing as the -p option. It is provided for backwards compatibility only; it is suggested that people use -p option whenever possible. |
| -b *superblock* | Instead of using the normal superblock, use the alternative superblock specified by *superblock*. |
| -B *blocksize* | Usually, e2fsck will search for the superblock at various different block sizes in an attempt to find the appropriate block size. This search can be fooled in some cases. This option forces e2fsck to only try locating the superblock at a particular *blocksize*. If the superblock is not found, e2fsck will terminate with a fatal error. |
| -d | Print debugging output (useless unless you are debugging e2fsck ). |
| -f | Force checking even if the filesystem seems clean. |
| -F | Flush the filesystem device's buffer caches before beginning. Only really useful for doing e2fsck time trials. |
| -l *filename* | Add the blocks listed in the file specified by filename to the list of bad blocks. |
| -L *filename* | Set the bad blocks list to be the list of blocks specified by *filename*. (This option is the same as the -l option except the bad blocks list is cleared before the blocks listed in the file are added to the bad blocks list.) |
| -n | Open the filesystem read-only, and assume an answer of "no" to all questions. Allows e2fsck to be used non-interactively. (Note: if the -l or -L options are specified in addition to the -n option, then the filesystem will be opened read-write to permit the bad-blocks list to be updated. However, no other changes will be made to the filesystem.) |
| -p | Automatically repair ("preen") the filesystem without any questions. |
| -r | This option does nothing at all; it is provided only for backwards compatibility. |
| -t | Print timing statistics for e2fsck. If this option is used twice, additional timing statistics are printed on a pass-by-pass basis. |
| -v | Verbose mode. |
| -V | Print version information and exit. |
| -y | Assume an answer of "yes" to all questions; allows e2fsck to be used non-interactively. |

## EXIT CODE

The exit code returned by e2fsck is the sum of the following conditions:

| | |
|---|---|
| 0 | No errors |
| 1 | Filesystem errors corrected |
| 2 | Filesystem errors corrected; system should be rebooted if filesystem was mounted |
| 4 | Filesystem errors left uncorrected |
| 8 | Operational error |
| 16 | Usage or syntax error |
| 128 | Shared library error |

## BUGS

Almost any piece of software will have bugs. If you manage to find a filesystem that causes e2fsck to crash, or that e2fsck is unable to repair, please report it to the author.

Please include as much information as possible in your bug report. Ideally, include a complete transcript of the e2fsck run, so I can see exactly what error messages are displayed. If you have a writeable filesystem where the transcript can be stored, the script(1) program is a handy way to save the output of e2fsck to a file.

It is also useful to send the output of dumpe2fs(8). If a specific inode or inodes seems to be giving e2fsck trouble, try running the debugfs(8) command and send the output of the stat command run on the relevant inodes. If the inode is a directory, the debugfs dump command will allow you to extract the contents of the directory inode, which can sent to me after being first run through uuencode(1).

Always include the full version string that e2fsck displays when it is run so I know which version you are running.

## AUTHOR

This version of e2fsck is written by Theodore Ts'o (tytso@mit.edu).

## SEE ALSO

mke2fs(8), tune2fs(8), dumpe2fs(8), debugfs(8)

*Version 0.5b, November 1994*

# edquota

edquota—Edit user quotas.

## SYNOPSIS

/usr/etc/edquota [ -p *proto-user* ][ -ug ] *name*...
/usr/etc/edquota [ -ug ] -t

## DESCRIPTION

edquota is a quota editor. One or more users or groups may be specified on the command line. For each user or group, a temporary file is created with an ASCII representation of the current disk quotas for that user or group and an editor is then invoked on the file. The quotas may then be modified, new quotas added, and so on. Upon leaving the editor, edquota reads the temporary file and modifies the binary quota files to reflect the changes made.

The editor invoked is vi(1) unless the environment variable specifies otherwise.

Only the superuser may edit quotas. (For quotas to be established on a filesystem, the root directory of the filesystem must contain a file, owned by root, called quota.user or quota.group. See quotaon(8) for details.)

## OPTIONS

| | |
|---|---|
| -u | Edit the userquota. This is the default. |
| -g | Edit the groupquota. |
| -p | Duplicate the quotas of the prototypical user specified for each user specified. This is the normal mechanism used to initialize quotas for groups of users. |
| -t | Edit the soft time limits for each filesystem. If the time limits are zero, the default time limits in <linux/quota.h> are used. Time units of sec(onds), min(utes), hour(s), day(s), week(s), and month(s) are understood. Time limits are printed in the greatest possible time unit such that the value is greater than or equal to one. |

## FILES

quota.user or quota.group        Quota file at the filesystem root

/etc/mtab        Mounted filesystems

## SEE ALSO

quota(1), vi(1), quotactl(2), quotacheck(8), quotaon(8), repquota(8)

## BUGS

The format of the temporary file is inscrutable.

*8 June 1993*

# expire

expire—Usenet article and history expiration program.

## SYNOPSIS

```
expire [ -d dir ][-f file ][-g file ][-h file ]
[-i ][-l ][-n ][-p ][-q ][-r reason ][-s ][-t ]
[-v level ][-w number ][-x ][-z file ][expire.ctl]
```

## DESCRIPTION

expire scans the history(5) text file /news/lib/history and uses the information recorded in it to purge old news articles. To specify an alternate history file, use the -f flag. To specify an alternate input text history file, use the -h flag. expire uses the old dbz(3z) database to determine the size of the new one. To ignore the old database, use the -i flag.

expire usually just unlinks each file if it should be expired. If the -l flag is used, then all articles after the first one are treated as if they could be symbolic links to the first one. In this case, the first article will not be removed as long as any other cross-posts of the article remain.

expire usually sends a pause command to the local innd(8) daemon when it needs exclusive access to the history file, using the string Expiring as the reason. To give a different reason, use the -r flag. The process ID will be appended to the reason. When expire is finished and the new history file is ready, it sends a go command. If innd is not running, use the -n flag and expire will not send the pause or go commands. (For more details on the commands, see ctlinnd(8).) Note that expire only needs exclusive access for a very short time—long enough to see if any new articles arrived since it first hit the end of the file and to rename the new files to the working files.

If the -s flag is used, then expire will print a summary when it exits, showing the approximate number of kilobytes used by all deleted articles.

If the -t flag is used, then expire will generate a list of the files that should be removed on its standard output, and the new history file will be left in history.n, history.n.dir, and history.n.pag. This flag is useful for debugging when used with the -n and -s flags. Note that if the -f flag is used, then the name specified with that flag will be used instead of history.

If the -x flag is used, then expire will not create any new history files. This is most useful when combined with the -n, -s, and -t flags to see how different expiration policies would change the amount of disk space used.

If the -z flag is used, then articles are not removed, but their names are written to the specified file. See the description of expirerm in news.daily(8).

expire makes its decisions on the time the article arrived, as found in the history file. This means articles are often kept a little longer than with other expiration programs that base their decisions on the article's posting date. To use the article's posting date, use the -p flag. Use the -w flag to "warp" time so that expire thinks it is running at some time other then the current time. The value should be a signed floating-point number of the number of days to use as the offset.

If the -d flag is used, then the new history file and database is created in the specified directory, dir. This is useful when the filesystem does not have sufficient space to hold both the old and new history files. When this flag is used, expire leaves the server paused and creates a zero-length file named after the new history file, with an extension of .done to indicate that it has successfully completed the expiration. The calling script should install the new history file and unpause the server. The -r flag should be used with this flag.

If a filename is specified, it is taken as the control file and parsed according to the rules in expire.ctl(5). A single dash (–) may be used to read the file from standard input. If no file is specified, the file /news/lib/expire.ctl is read.

expire usually complains about articles that are posted to newsgroups not mentioned in the active file. To suppress this action, use the -q flag.

The -v flag is used to increase the verbosity of the program, generating messages to standard output. The level should be a number, where higher numbers result in more output. Level one will print totals of the various actions done (not valid if a new history file is not written), level two will print report on each individual file, and level five results in more than one line of output for every line processed. If the -g flag is given, then a one-line summary equivalent to the output of –v1 and preceded by the current time will be appended to the specified file.

## HISTORY

Written by Rich $alz (rsalz@uunet.uu.net) for InterNetNews.

## SEE ALSO

ctlinnd(8), dbz(3z), expire.ctl(5), history(5), innd(8), inndcomm(3)

# expireover

expireover—Expire entries from the news overview database.

## SYNOPSIS

```
expireover [ -a ][-D overviewdir ][-f file ][-n ]
[-O overview.fmt ][-s ][-v ][-z ][file... ]
```

## DESCRIPTION

expireover expires entries from the news overview database. It reads a list of pathnames (relative to the spool directory, /news/spool) from the specified files or standard input if none are specified. (A filename of - may be used to specify the standard input.) It then removes any mention of those articles from the appropriate overview database. If the -z flag is used, then the input is assumed to be sorted such that all entries for a newsgroup appear together so that it can be purged at once. This flag can be useful when used with the sorted output of expire(8)'s -z flag.

If the -s flag is used, then expireover will read the spool directory for all groups mentioned in the active(5) file and remove the overview entries for any articles that do not appear. To specify an alternate file, use the -f flag; a name of - is taken to mean the standard input.

The -a flag reads the spool directory and adds any missing overview entries. It will create files if necessary. This can be used to initialize a database or to sync up a overview database that may be lacking articles due to a crash. overchan should be running, to ensure that any incoming articles get included. Using this flag implies the -s flag; the -f flag may be used to add only a subset of the newsgroups.

To see a list of the entries that would be added or deleted, use the -v flag. To perform no real updates, use the -n flag.

The -D flag can be used to specify where the databases are stored. The default directory is /news/spool.

The -O flag may be used to specify an alternate location for the overview.fmt(5) file; this is usually only useful for debugging.

## HISTORY

Written by Rob Robertson (rob@violet.berkeley.edu) and Rich $alz (rsalz@uunet.uu.net) with help from Dave Laurence (tale@uunet.uu.net) for InterNetNews.

## SEE ALSO

expire(8), overview.fmt(5)

# fastrm

fastrm—Quickly remove a set of files.

## SYNOPSIS

fastrm [ -d ][ -e ][ -u*N* ][ -s*M* ][ -c*I* ] *base_directory*

## DESCRIPTION

fastrm reads a list of files, one per line, from its standard input and removes them. If a file is not an absolute pathname, it is taken relative to the directory specified on the command line. The base directory parameter must be a simple absolute pathname—that is, it must not contain any /./ or /../ references.

fastrm is designed to be faster than the typical ¦ xargs rm pipeline. For example, fastrm will usually chdir(2) into a directory before removing files from it. If the input is sorted, this means that most files to be removed will be simple names.

fastrm assumes that its input is valid and that it is safe to just do an unlink(2) call for each item to be removed. As a safety measure, if fastrm is run by root, it will first stat(2) the item to make sure that it is not a directory before unlinking it.

If the -d flag is used, then no files are removed. Instead, a list of the files to be removed, in debug form, is printed on the standard output. Each line contains either the current directory of fastrm at the time it would do the unlink and then the pathname it would pass to unlink(2) as two fields separated by white space and a / or the absolute pathname (a single field) of files it would unlink using the absolute pathname.

If the -e flag is used, fastrm will treat an empty input file (stdin) as an error. This is most useful when fastrm is last in a pipeline after a preceding sort(1) because if the sort fails, there will usually be no output to become input of fastrm.

If the -u flag is used, then fastrm makes further assumptions about its work environment—in particular, that there are no symbolic links in the target tree. This flag also suggests that it is probably faster to reference the path ../../../ rather than start from the root and come down (note that this probably isn't true on systems that have a namei cache, which usually holds everything except ..). The optional *N* is an integer that specifies the maximum number of .. segments to use—paths that would use more than this use the absolute pathname (from the root) instead. If the -u flag is given without a value, -u1 is assumed.

If the -s flag is used, then fastrm will perform the unlinks from one directory—that is, when a group of files in one directory appear in the input consecutively—in the order that the files appear in the directory from which they are to be removed. The intent of this flag is that on systems that have a per-process directory cache, finding files in the directory should be faster. It can have smaller benefits on other systems. The optional *M* is an integer that specifies the number of files that must be going to be removed from one directory before the files will be ordered. If the -s flag is given without a value, -s5 is assumed. When the directory reordering is in use, fastrm will avoid attempting to unlink files that it can't see in the directory, which can speed it appreciably when many of the filenames have already been removed.

The -c flag may be given to instruct fastrm when it should chdir(2). If the number of files to be unlinked from a directory is at least *I*, then fastrm will chdir and unlink the files from in the directory. Otherwise, it will build a path relative to its current directory. If -c is given without the optional integer *I*, then -c1 is assumed, which will cause fastrm to always use chdir. If -c is not used at all, then -c3 is assumed. Use -c0 to prevent fastrm from ever using chdir(2).

There are also -a and -r options, which do nothing at all except allow you to say `fastrm -usa`, `fastrm -ussr`, or `fastrm -user`. These happen to often be convenient sets of options to use.

`fastrm` exits with a status of 0 if there were no problems or 1 if something went wrong. Attempting to remove a file that does not exist is not considered a problem. If the program exits with a nonzero status, it is probably a good idea to feed the list of files into an `xargs rm` pipeline.

# fdformat

`fdformat`—Low-level formats a floppy disk.

## SYNOPSIS

`fdformat [ -n ] device`

## DESCRIPTION

`fdformat` does a low-level format on a floppy disk. `device` is usually one of the following (for floppy devices, the major is 2, and the minor is shown for informational purposes only):

`/dev/fd0d360` (minor = 4)

`/dev/fd0h1200` (minor = 8)

`/dev/fd0D360` (minor = 12)

`/dev/fd0H360` (minor = 12)

`/dev/fd0D720` (minor = 16)

`/dev/fd0H720` (minor = 16)

`/dev/fd0h360` (minor = 20)

`/dev/fd0h720` (minor = 24)

`/dev/fd0H1440` (minor = 28)

`/dev/fd1d360` (minor = 5)

`/dev/fd1h1200` (minor = 9)

`/dev/fd1D360` (minor = 13)

`/dev/fd1H360` (minor = 13)

`/dev/fd1D720` (minor = 17)

`/dev/fd1H720` (minor = 17)

`/dev/fd1h360` (minor = 21)

`/dev/fd1h720` (minor = 25)

`/dev/fd1H1440` (minor = 29)

The generic floppy devices, `/dev/fd0` and `/dev/fd1`, will fail to work with `fdformat` when a non-standard format is being used or if the format has not been autodetected earlier. In this case, use `setfdprm(8)` to load the disk parameters.

## OPTIONS

-n                                                        No verify. This option will disable the verification that is performed after the format.

## SEE ALSO

`fd(4)`, `setfdprm(8)`, `mkfs(8)`, `emkfs(8)`

## AUTHOR

Werner Almesberger (`almesber@nessie.cs.id.ethz.ch`)

*Linux 0.99, 1 February 1993*

# fdisk

`fdisk`—Partition table manipulator for Linux.

## SYNOPSIS

`fdisk [ -l ] [ -v ] [ -s partition] [ device ]`

## DESCRIPTION

`fdisk` is a menu-driven program for manipulation of the hard disk partition table. The device is usually one of the following:

```
/dev/hda
/dev/hdb
/dev/sda
/dev/sdb
```

The partition is a device name followed by a partition number. For example, `/dev/hda1` is the first partition on the first hard disk in the system.

If possible, `fdisk` will obtain the disk geometry automatically. This is not necessarily the physical disk geometry but is the disk geometry that MS-DOS uses for the partition table. If `fdisk` warns you that you need to set the disk geometry, please believe this statement and set the geometry. This should only be necessary with certain SCSI host adapters (the drivers for which are rapidly being modified to provide geometry information automatically).

Whenever a partition table is printed, a consistency check is performed on the partition table entries. This check verifies that the physical and logical start and end points are identical and that the partition starts and ends on a cylinder boundary (except for the first partition).

Old versions of `fdisk` (all versions prior to 1.1r including 0.93) incorrectly mapped the `cylinder/head/sector` specification onto absolute sectors. This might result in the first partition on a drive failing the consistency check. If you use LILO to boot, this situation can be ignored. However, there are reports that the OS/2 boot manager will not boot a partition with inconsistent data.

Some versions of MS-DOS create a first partition that does not begin on a cylinder boundary but on sector 2 of the first cylinder. Partitions beginning in cylinder 1 cannot begin on a cylinder boundary, but this is unlikely to cause difficulty unless you have OS/2 on your machine.

In version 1.1r, a `BLKRRPART ioctl()` is performed before exiting when the partition table is updated. This is primarily to ensure that removable SCSI disks have their partition table information updated. If the kernel does not update its partition table information, `fdisk` warns you to reboot. If you do not reboot your system after receiving such a warning, you might lose or corrupt the data on the disk. Sometimes `BLKRRPART` fails silently; when installing Linux, you should always reboot after editing the partition table.

## DOS 6.*X* WARNING

The DOS 6.*x* `FORMAT` command looks for some information in the first sector of the data area of the partition and treats this information as more reliable than the information in the partition table. `DOS FORMAT` expects DOS `FDISK` to clear the first 512 bytes of the data area of a partition whenever a size change occurs. `DOS FORMAT` will look at this extra information even if the `/U` flag is given

We consider this a bug in DOS FORMAT and DOS FDISK.

The bottom line is that if you use cfdisk or fdisk to change the size of a DOS partition table entry, then you must also use dd to zero the first 512 bytes of that partition before using DOS FORMAT to format the partition. For example, if you were using cfdisk to make a DOS partition table entry for /dev/hda1, then (after exiting fdisk or cfdisk and rebooting Linux so that the partition table information is valid) you would use the command dd if=/dev/zero of=/dev/hda1 bs=512 count=1 to zero the first 512 bytes of the partition.

Be extremely careful if you use the dd command because a small typo can make all of the data on your disk useless.

For best results, you should always use an OS-specific partition table program. For example, you should make DOS partitions with the DOS FDISK program and Linux partitions with the Linux fdisk or Linux cfdisk program.

## OPTIONS

| | |
|---|---|
| -v | Prints version number of fdisk program. |
| -l | Lists the partition tables for /dev/hda, /dev/hdb, /dev/sda, /dev/sdb, /dev/sdc, /dev/sdd, /dev/sde, /dev/sdf, /dev/sdg, and /dev/sdh and then exits. |
| -s *partition* | If the *partition* is not a DOS partition (the partition ID is greater than 10), then the size of that partition is printed on the standard output. This value is usually used as an argument to the mkfs(8) program to specify the size of the partition that will be formatted. |

## BUGS

Although this man page (written by faith@cs.unc.edu) is poor, there is excellent documentation in the README.fdisk file (written by LeBlanc@mcc.ac.uk) that should always be with the fdisk distribution. If you cannot find this file in the util-linux-* directory or with the fdisk.c source file, then you should write to the distributor of your version of fdisk and complain that you do not have all of the available documentation.

## AUTHOR

A.V. LeBlanc (LeBlanc@mcc.ac.uk). v1.0r: SCSI and extfs support added by Rik Faith (faith@cs.unc.edu). v1.1r: Bug fixes and enhancements by Rik Faith (faith@cs.unc.edu), with special thanks to Michael Bischoff (i1041905@ws.rz.tu-bs.de or mbi@mo.math.nat.tu-bs.de). v1.3: Latest enhancements and bug fixes by A.V. LeBlanc, including the addition of the -s option. v2.0: Disks larger than 2GB are now fully supported, thanks to Remy Card's llseek support.

*Linux 1.0, 3 June 1995*

# filechan

filechan—File-writing back end for InterNetNews.

## SYNOPSIS

filechan [ -d *directory* ][-f *fields* ][-m *mapfile* ][-p *pidfile* ]

## DESCRIPTION

filechan reads lines from standard input and copies certain fields in each line into files named by other fields within the line. filechan is intended to be called by innd(8) as a channel feed. (It is not a full exploder and does not accept commands; see newsfeeds(5) for a description of the difference and buffchan(8) for an exploder program.)

filechan input is interpreted as a set of lines. Each line contains a fixed number of initial fields, followed by a variable number of filename fields. All fields in a line are separated by whitespace. The default number of initial fields is one; the -f flag may be used to specify a different number of fields.

For each line of input, filechan writes the initial fields, separated by whitespace and followed by a newline, to each of the files named in the filename fields. When writing to a file, filechan opens it in append mode and tries to lock it and change the ownership to the user and group who owns the directory where the file is being written.

By default, filechan writes its arguments into the directory /news/spool/out.going. The -d flag may be used to specify a directory the program should change to before starting.

If the -p flag is used, the program will write a line containing its process ID (in text) to the specified file.

If filechan is invoked with -f 2 and given the following input:

```
news/software/b/132 <1643@munnari.oz.au>foo uunet
news/software/b/133 <102060@litchi.foo.com> uunet munnari
comp/sources/unix/2002 <999@news.foo.com>foo uunet munnari
```

Then the file foo will have these lines:

```
news/software/b/132 <1643@munnari.oz.au>
comp/sources/unix/2002 <999@news.foo.com>
```

The file munnari will have these lines:

```
news/software/b/133 <102060@litchi.foo.com>
comp/sources/unix/2002 <999@news.foo.com>
```

The file uunet will have these lines:

```
news/software/b/132 <1643@munnari.oz.au>
news/software/b/133 <102060@litchi.foo.com>
comp/sources/unix/2002 <999@news.foo.com>
```

Because the time window in which a file is open is very small, complicated flushing and locking protocols are not needed; a mv(1) followed by a sleep(1) for a couple of seconds is sufficient.

A map file may be specified by using the -m flag. Blank lines and lines starting with a number sign (#) are ignored. All other lines should have two hostnames separated by a colon. The first field is the name that may appear in the input stream; the second field names the file to be used when the name in the first field appears. For example, the following map file may be used to map the short names to the full domain names:

```
# This is a comment uunet:news.uu.net foo:foo.com munnari:munnari.oz.au
```

## HISTORY

Written by Robert Elz (kre@munnari.oz.au); flags added by Rich $alz (rsalz@uunet.uu.net).

## SEE ALSO

buffchan(8), innd(8), newsfeeds(5)

# fsck

fsck—Check and repair a Linux filesystem.

## SYNOPSIS

fsck [ -AVRTN ][-s ][-t fstype ][fs-options ] filesys [ ... ]

## DESCRIPTION

fsck is used to check and optionally repair a Linux filesystem. filesys is either the device name (such as /dev/hda1 or /dev/sdb2) or the mount point (such as /, /usr, or /home) for the filesystem. If this fsck has several filesystems on different physical disk drives to check, this fsck will try to run them in parallel. This reduces the total amount time it takes to check all of the filesystems because fsck takes advantage of the parallelism of multiple disk spindles.

The exit code returned by fsck is the sum of the following conditions:

| | |
|---|---|
| 0 | No errors |
| 1 | Filesystem errors corrected |
| 2 | System should be rebooted |
| 4 | Filesystem errors left uncorrected |
| 8 | Operational error |
| 16 | Usage or syntax error |
| 128 | Shared library error |

The exit code returned when all filesystems are checked using the -A option is the bitwise OR of the exit codes for each file system that is checked.

In actuality, fsck is simply a front end for the various filesystem checkers (fsck.fstype) available under Linux. The filesystem-specific checker is searched for in /sbin first, then in /etc/fs and /etc, and finally in the directories listed in the PATH environment variable. Please see the filesystem-specific checker manual pages for further details.

## OPTIONS

| | |
|---|---|
| -A | Walk through the /etc/fstab file and try to check all filesystems in one run. This option is typically used from the /etc/rc system initialization file, instead of multiple commands for checking a single file system. |
| -R | When checking all filesystems with the -A flag, skip the root file system (in case it's already mounted read-write). |
| -T | Don't show the title on startup. |
| -N | Don't execute; just show what would be done. |
| -s | Serialize fsck operations. This is a good idea if you checking multiple filesystems in and the checkers are in an interactive mode. (Note: e2fsck runs in an interactive mode by default. To make e2fsck run in a non-interactive mode, you must either specify the -p or -a option, if you want errors to be corrected automatically, or the -n option if you do not.) |
| -V | Produce verbose output, including all filesystem-specific commands that are executed. |
| -tfstype | Specifies the type of filesystem to be checked. When the -A flag is specified, only filesystems that match fstype are checked. If fstype is prefixed with no, only filesystems whose filesystem do not match fstype are checked. |
| | Usually, the filesystem type is deduced by searching for *filesys* in the /etc/fstab file and using the corresponding entry. If the type can not be deduced, fsck will use the type specified by the -t option if it specifies a unique filesystem type. If this type is not available, the the default filesystem type (currently ext2) is used. |
| fs-options | Any options that are not understood by fsck, or that follow the - option are treated as filesystem-specific options to be passed to the filesystem-specific checker. |

Currently, standardized filesystem-specific options are somewhat in flux. Although not guaranteed, the following options are supported by most filesystem checkers:

-a                   Automatically repair the filesystem without any questions. (Use this option with caution.) Note that e2fsck supports -a for backwards compatibility only. This option is mapped to e2fsck's -p option, which is safe to use, unlike the -a option that most filesystem checkers support.

-r                   Interactively repair the filesystem (ask for confirmations). Note: It is generally a bad idea to use this option if multiple fsck's are run in parallel. Also note that this is e2fsck default behavior; it supports this option for backwards compatibility reasons only.

## AUTHOR

Theodore Ts'o (tytso@mit.edu)

The manual page was shamelessly adapted from David Engel and Fred van Kempen's generic fsck front-end program, which in turn was shamelessly adapted from Remy Card's version for the ext2 filesystem.

## FILES

/etc/fstab

## SEE ALSO

fstab(5), mkfs(8), fsck.minix(8), fsck.ext2(8) or e2fsck(8), fsck.xiafs(8)

*Version 0.5b, November 1994*

# fsck.minix

fsck.minix—A filesystem consistency checker for Linux.

## SYNOPSIS

fsck.minix [ -larvsmf ] *device*

## DESCRIPTION

fsck.minix performs a consistency check for the Linux MINIX filesystem. The current version supports the 14 character and 30 character filename options.

The program assumes the filesystem is quiescent. fsck.minix should not be used on a mounted device unless you can be sure nobody is writing to it (and remember that the kernel can write to it when it searches for files).

The device will usually have the following form:

/dev/hda[1-8]
/dev/hdb[1-8]
/dev/sda[1-8]
/dev/sdb[1-8]

If the filesystem was changed (that is, repaired), then fsck.minix will print File system has changed and will sync(2) three times before exiting. Because Linux does not currently have raw devices, there is no need to reboot at this time (versus a system that does have raw devices).

## WARNING

fsck.minix should not be used on a mounted filesystem. Using fsck.minix on a mounted filesystem is very dangerous due to the possibility that deleted files are still in use and can seriously damage a perfectly good filesystem! If you absolutely have to run fsck.minix on a mounted filesystem (that is, the root filesystem), make sure nothing is writing to the disk and that no files are "zombies" waiting for deletion.

## OPTIONS

| | |
|---|---|
| -l | Lists all filenames. |
| -r | Performs interactive repairs. |
| -a | Performs automatic repairs (this option implies -r) and serves to answer all of the questions asked with the default. Note that this can be extremely dangerous in the case of extensive filesystem damage. |
| -v | Verbose. |
| -s | Outputs super-block information. |
| -m | Activates MINIX-like "mode not cleared" warnings. |
| -f | Force filesystem check even if the filesystem was marked as valid. (This marking is done by the kernel when the filesystem is unmounted.) |

## SEE ALSO

fsck(8), fsck.ext(8), fsck.ext2(8), fsck.xiafs(8), mkfs(8), mkfs.minix(8), mkfs.ext(8), mkfs.ext2(8), mkfs.xiafs(8), reboot(8)

## DIAGNOSTICS

There are numerous diagnostic messages. The ones mentioned here are the most commonly seen in normal usage.

If the device does not exist, fsck.minix will print Unable to read super block. If the device exists but is not a MINIX filesystem, fsck.minix will print Bad magic number in super-block.

## EXIT CODES

The exit code returned by fsck.minix is the sum of the following:

| | |
|---|---|
| 0 | No errors. |
| 3 | Filesystem errors corrected; system should be rebooted if filesystem was mounted. |
| 4 | Filesystem errors left uncorrected. |
| 8 | Operational error. |
| 16 | Usage or syntax error. |

In point of fact, only 0, 3, 4, 7, 8, and 16 can ever be returned.

## AUTHOR

Linus Torvalds (torvalds@cs.helsinki.fi). Error code values by Rik Faith (faith@cs.unc.edu). Added support for filesystem valid flag: Dr. Wettstein (greg%wind.uucp@plains.nodak.edu). Check to prevent fsck of mounted filesystem added by Daniel Quinlan (quinlan@yggdrasil.com).

*Linux 0.99, 10 January 1994*

# ftpd

ftpd—DARPA Internet File Transfer Protocol server.

## SYNOPSIS

ftpd [-d] [-l] [-t *timeout*] [-T *maxtimeout*]

## DESCRIPTION

ftpd is the DARPA Internet File Transfer Protocol server process. The server uses the TCP protocol and listens at the port specified in the FTP service specification; see services(5).

Available options:

| | |
|---|---|
| -d | Debugging information is written to the syslog. |
| -l | Each FTP 1 session is logged in the syslog. |
| -t | The inactivity timeout period is set to timeout seconds. (The default is 15 minutes.) |
| -T | A client can also request a different timeout period; the maximum period allowed can be set to timeout seconds with the -T option. The default limit is 2 hours. |

The FTP server currently supports the following FTP requests; case is not distinguished.

| Request | Description |
|---|---|
| ABOR | Abort previous command |
| ACCT | Specify account (ignored) |
| ALLO | Allocate storage (vacuously) |
| APPE | Append to a file |
| CDUP | Change to parent of current working directory |
| CWD | Change working directory |
| DELE | Delete a file |
| HELP | Give help information |
| LIST | Give list files in a directory ('' ls -lgA '') |
| MKD | Make a directory |
| MDTM | Show last modification time of file |
| MODE | Specify data transfer mode |
| NLST | Give name list of files in directory |
| NOOP | Do nothing |
| PASS | Specify password |
| PASV | Prepare for server-to-server transfer |
| PORT | Specify data connection port |
| PWD | Print the current working directory |
| QUIT | Terminate session |
| REST | Restart incomplete transfer |
| RETR | Retrieve a file |
| RMD | Remove a directory |
| RNFR | Specify rename-from filename |
| RNTO | Specify rename-to filename |
| SITE | Nonstandard commands (see next section) |
| SIZE | Return size of file |
| STAT | Return status of server |
| STOR | Store a file |
| STOU | Store a file with a unique name |
| STRU | Specify data transfer structure |
| SYST | show operating system type of server system |
| TYPE | specify data transfer type |
| USER | specify username |
| XCUP | change to parent of current working directory (deprecated) |

| Request | Description |
|---------|-------------|
| XCWD | change working directory (deprecated) |
| XMKD | make a directory (deprecated) |
| XPWD | print the current working directory (deprecated) |
| XRMD | remove a directory (deprecated) |

The following non-standard or UNIX-specific commands are supported by the SITE request:

| Request | Description | Example |
|---------|-------------|---------|
| UMASK | Change umask | SITE UMASK 002 |
| IDLE | Set idle timer | SITE IDLE 60 |
| CHMOD | Change mode of a file | SITE CHMOD 755 |
| HELP | Give help information | SITE HELP |

The remaining FTP requests specified in Internet RFC 959 are recognized but not implemented. MDTM and SIZE are not specified in RFC 959 but will appear in the next updated FTP RFC.

The FTP server will abort an active file transfer only when the ABOR command is preceded by a Telnet "Interrupt Process" (IP) signal and a Telnet "Synch" signal in the command Telnet stream, as described in Internet RFC 959. If a STAT command is received during a data transfer, preceded by a Telnet IP and Synch, transfer status will be returned.

ftpd interprets filenames according to the globbing conventions used by csh(1). This allows users to utilize the metacharacters Li &*?[].

ftpd authenticates users according to four rules:

The username must be in the password database and not have a null password. In this case, a password must be provided by the client before any file operations may be performed.

The username must not appear in the file (see ftpusers(5)).

The user must have a standard shell returned by getusershell(3).

If the username is anonymous or FTP, an anonymous FTP account must be present in the password file (user FTP). In this case, the user is allowed to log in by specifying any password. (By convention, this is given as the client host's name.)

In the last case, ftpd takes special measures to restrict the client's access privileges. The server performs a chroot(2) command to the home directory of the FTP user. So that system security is not breached, it is recommended that the FTP subtree be constructed with care; the following rules are recommended:

| | |
|---|---|
| ~ftp | Make the home directory owned by root and unwritable by anyone. |
| ~ftp/bin | Make this directory owned by root and unwritable by anyone. The program ls(1) must be present to support the list command. This program should have mode 111. |
| ~ftp/etc | Make this directory owned by root and unwritable by anyone. The files passwd(5) and group(5) must be present for the ls command to be able to produce owner names rather than numbers. The password field in passwd is not used and should not contain real encrypted passwords. These files should be mode 444 and owned by root. Don't use the system's /etc/passwd file as the password file or the system's /etc/group file as the group file in the ~ftp/etc directory. |
| Pa ~ftp/pub | Make this directory mode 755 and owned by root. Create a subdirectory in ~ftp/pub with the appropriate mode (777 or 733) if you want to allow normal users to upload files. |

## SEE ALSO

ftp(1), getusershell(3), ftpusers(5), syslogd(8)

## BUGS

The anonymous account is inherently dangerous and should avoided when possible.

The server must run as the super-user to create sockets with privileged port numbers. It maintains an effective user ID of the logged-in user, reverting to the super-user only when binding addresses to sockets. The possible security holes have been extensively scrutinized but are possibly incomplete.

## HISTORY

The command appeared in BSD 4.2.

*BSD 4.2, 16 March 1991*

# ifconfig

ifconfig—Configure a network interface.

## SYNOPSIS

```
ifconfig [interface]
ifconfig interface [aftype] options ¦ address ...
```

## DESCRIPTION

ifconfig is used to set up (and maintain thereafter) the kernel-resident network interfaces. It is used at boot time to configure most of them to a running state. After that, it is usually only needed when debugging or when system tuning is needed.

If no arguments are given, ifconfig just displays the status of the currently defined interfaces. If the single interface argument is given, it displays the status of the given interface only. Otherwise, it assumes that things have to be set up.

## ADDRESS FAMILIES

If the first argument after the interface name is recognized as the name of a supported address family, that address family is used for decoding and displaying all protocol addresses. Currently supported address families include inet (TCP/IP, default) and ax25 (AMPR Packet Radio.)

## OPTIONS

| | |
|---|---|
| interface | The name of the NET interface. This usually is a name such as wd0, sl3, or something like that: a device driver name followed by a unit number. |
| up | This flag causes the interface to be activated. It is implicitly specified if the interface is given a new address (see below). |
| down | This flag causes the driver for this interface to be shut down and is useful when things start going wrong. |
| [-]arp | Enable or disable the use of the ARP protocol on this interface. If the minus (–) sign is present, the flag is turned OFF. |
| [-]trailers | Enable or disable the use of trailers on Ethernet frames. This is not used in the current implementation of NET. |
| [-]allmulti | Enable or disable the promiscuous mode of the interface. This means that all incoming frames get sent to the network layer of the system kernel, allowing for networking monitoring. |
| metric N | This parameter sets the interface metric. It is not used at present, but we implement it for the future. |
| mtu N | This parameter sets the Maximum Transfer Unit (MTU) of an interface. For Ethernet, this is a number in the range of 1000-2000 (default is 1500). For SLIP, use something between 200 and 4096. Note that the current implementation does not handle IP fragmentation yet, so you'd better make the MTU large enough! |
| dstaddr addr | Set the "other end's" IP address in case of a point-to-point link, such as PPP. This keyword is obsoleted by the new pointopoint keyword. |

| netmask addr | Set the IP network mask for this interface. This value defaults to the usual class A, B, or C network mask (as deducted from the interface IP address), but it can be set to any value for the use of subnetting. |
|---|---|
| [-]broadcast [addr] | If the address argument is also given, set the protocol broadcast address for this interface. Otherwise, it only sets the IFF_BROADCAST flag of the interface. If the keyword was preceded by a minus (-) sign, then the flag is cleared instead. |
| [-]pointopoint [addr] | This keyword enables the point-to-point mode of an interface, meaning that it is a direct link between two machines with nobody else listening on it. (At least we hope that this is the case, grin :-).) |
| | If the address argument is also given, set the protocol address of the other side of the link, just like the obsolete dstaddr keyword does. Otherwise, it only sets the IFF_POINTOPOINT flag of the interface. If the keyword was preceded by a minus (-) sign, then the flag is cleared instead. |
| hw | Set the hardware address of this interface if the device driver supports this operation. The keyword must be followed by the name of the hardware class and the printable ASCII equivalent of the hardware address. Hardware classes currently supported include ether (Ethernet), ax25 (AMPR AX.25), and ppp, although the latter is not really supported yet. |
| address | The hostname or IP address (a hostname will be resolved into an IP address) of that interface. This parameter is required, although the syntax doesn't currently require it. |

## FILES

/dev/net/socket

## BUGS

None so far, although the syntax checking could be better.

## AUTHOR

Fred N. van Kempen (waltje@uwalt.nl.mugnet.org)

*6 October 1993*

# inetd

inetd—Internet superserver.

## SYNOPSIS

inetd [-d] [*configuration file*]

## DESCRIPTION

inetd should be run at boot time by /etc/rc.local (see rc(8)). It then listens for connections on certain Internet sockets. When a connection is found on one of its sockets, it decides what service the socket corresponds to and invokes a program to service the request. After the program is finished, it continues to listen on the socket (except in some cases, which are described later). Essentially, inetd allows running one daemon to invoke several others, reducing load on the system.

The option available for inetd:

-d                Turns on debugging.

Upon execution, inetd reads its configuration information from a configuration file, which, by default, is /etc/inetd.conf. There must be an entry for each field of the configuration file, with entries for each field separated by a tab or a space. Comments are denoted by a # at the beginning of a line. There must be an entry for each field. The fields of the configuration file are as follows:

```
service name
socket type
protocol
wait/nowait[.max]
user[.group]
server program
server program arguments
```

To specify an Sun-RPC based service, the entry would contain these fields:

```
service name/version
socket type
rpc/protocol
wait/nowait[.max]
user[.group]
server program
server program arguments
```

The service-name entry is the name of a valid service in the file /etc/services . For internal services, the service name must be the official name of the service (that is, the first entry in /etc/services). When used to specify a Sun-RPC based service, this field is a valid RPC service name in the file /etc/rpc. The part on the right of the / is the RPC version number. This can simply be a single numeric argument or a range of versions. A range is bounded by the low version to the high version - rusers/1-3.

The socket type should be one of stream, dgram, raw, rdm, or seqpacket, depending on whether the socket is a stream, datagram, raw, reliably delivered message, or sequenced packet socket.

The protocol must be a valid protocol as given in /etc/protocols. Examples might be tcp or udp. Rpc-based services are specified with the rpc/tcp or rpc/udp service type.

The wait/nowait entry is applicable to datagram sockets only. (Other sockets should have a nowait entry in this space.) If a datagram server connects to its peer, freeing the socket so inetd can receive further messages on the socket, it is said to be a multithreaded server and should use the nowait entry. For datagram servers that process all incoming datagrams on a socket and eventually time out, the server is said to be single-threaded and should use a wait entry. Comsat(8), biff(1), and talkd(8) are examples of the latter type of datagram server. Tftpd(8) is an exception; it is a datagram server that establishes pseudo-connections.

It must be listed as wait in order to avoid a race; the server reads the first packet, creates a new socket, and then forks and exits to allow inetd to check for new service requests to spawn new servers. The optional max suffix (separated from wait or nowait by a dot) specifies the maximum number of server instances that may be spawned from inetd within an interval of 60 seconds. When omitted, max defaults to 40.

The user entry should contain the username of the user as whom the server should run. This allows for servers to be given less permission than root. An optional group name can be specified by appending a dot to the username followed by the group name. This allows for servers to run with a different (primary) group ID than specified in the password file. If a group is specified and the user is not root, the supplementary groups associated with that user will still be set.

The server-program entry should contain the pathname of the program that is to be executed by inetd when a request is found on its socket. If inetd provides this service internally, this entry should be internal.

The server program arguments should appear just as arguments normally do, starting with argv[0], which is the name of the program. If the service is provided internally, the word internal should take the place of this entry.

inetd provides several trivial services internally by use of routines within itself. These services are echo, discard, chargen (character generator), daytime (human readable time), and time (machine readable time in the form of the number of seconds since midnight, January 1, 1900). All of these services are TCP based. For details of these services, consult the appropriate RFC from the Network Information Center.

inetd rereads its configuration file when it receives a hangup signal, SIGHUP. Services may be added, deleted, or modified when the configuration file is reread. inetd creates a file /etc/inetd.*pid* that contains its process identifier.

## SEE ALSO

comsat(8), fingerd(8), ftpd(8), rexecd(8), rlogind(8), rshd(8), telnetd(8), tftpd(8)

## HISTORY

The command appeared in BSD 4.3. Support for Sun-RPC based services is modeled after that provided by Sun-OS 4.1.

*BSD 4.3, 16 March 1991*


# init, telinit

init, telinit—Process control initialization.

## SYNOPSIS

```
/sbin/init [ -t sec ][0123456SsQq ]
/sbin/telinit [ -t sec ][0123456sSQqabc ]
```

## DESCRIPTION

init

init is the father of all processes. Its primary role is to create processes from a script stored in the file /etc/inittab (see inittab(5)). This file usually has entries that cause init to spawn gettys on each line that users can log in. It also controls autonomous processes required by any particular system.

A run level is a software configuration of the system that allows only a selected group of processes to exist. The processes spawned by init for each of these run levels are defined in the /etc/inittab file. init can be in one of eight run levels, 06 and S or s. The run level is changed by having a privileged user run /sbin/telinit, which sends appropriate signals to init, telling it which run level to change to.

After init is invoked as the last step of the kernel booting, it looks for the file /etc/inittab to see if there is an entry of the type initdefault (see inittab(5)). initdefault determines the initial run level of the system. If there is no such entry or no /etc/inittab at all, a run level must be entered at the system console.

Run level S or s brings the system to single-user mode and does not require an /etc/initttab file. In single-user mode, /bin/sh is invoked on /dev/console.

/dev/console need not necessarily be the physical system console. When init is told to enter single-user mode or run level 1 (either directly, by init S, or by telling shutdown to enter maintenance mode), it will link the terminal line the command was executed from to /dev/console. The device /dev/systty is called the physical system console and the device /dev/console is called the logical system console. If the logical system console is not the physical system console, pressing the combination Ctrl+Alt+Del on the physical system console will force a relink of /dev/console to /dev/systty. A terminal line can only become the logical console if it's listed in the file /etc/securetty. All this is in preparation of the day that the Linux kernel will support serial consoles.

Beware: If you want to run X or anything else that is aware of Virtual Consoles, the logical system console (/dev/console) needs to be the same as the physical system console (/dev/systty).

When entering single-user mode, init reads the console's ioctl(2) states from /etc/ioctl.save. If this file does not exist, init initializes the line at 9600 baud and with CLOCAL settings. When init leaves single-user mode, it stores the console's ioctl settings in this file so it can re-use them for the next single-user session. If the logical system console is changed to another terminal line, the settings of the line from which the init or telinit command was given are stored in /etc/ioctl.save too, so that the terminal line will be initialized correctly in single-user mode.

When entering a multi-user mode the first time, init performs the boot and bootwait entries to allow filesystems to be mounted before users can log in. Then all entries matching the run level are processed.

Each time a child terminates, init records the fact and the reason it died in /etc/utmp and /var/adm/wtmp if these files exist.

After it has spawned all the processes specified, init waits for one of its descendant processes to die, a powerfail signal, or a signal by /sbin/telinit to change the system's run level. When one of these three conditions occurs, it re-examines the /etc/inittab file. New entries can be added to this file at any time. However, init still waits for one of the three conditions to occur. To provide for an instantaneous response, the Q or q command can wake up init to re-examine the /etc/inittab file.

If init is not in single-user mode and receives a powerfail signal, special powerfail entries are invoked.

When init is requested to change the run level, it sends the warning signal SIGTERM to all processes that are undefined in the new run level. It then waits 20 seconds before forcibly terminating these processes via the kill signal SIGKILL.

Note that init assumes that all these processes (and their descendants) remain in the same process group that init originally created for them. If any process changes its process group affiliation, it will not receive these signals. Such processes need to be terminated separately.

## telinit

/sbin/telinit is linked to /sbin/init. It takes a one-character argument and signals init to perform the appropriate action. The following arguments serve as directives to /sbin/telinit:

| | |
|---|---|
| 0, 1, 2, 3, 4, 5, or 6 | Tell /sbin/init to switch to the specified run level. |
| a, b, c | Tell /sbin/init to process only those /etc/inittab file entries having run level a, b, or c. |
| Q or q | Tell /sbin/init to re-examine the /etc/inittab file. |
| S or s | Tell /sbin/init to switch to single-user mode. |

/sbin/telinit can also tell init how much time it should wait between sending processes the TERM and the KILL signal; the default is 20 seconds, but it can be changed by the -t sec option.

/sbin/telinit can be invoked only by users with appropriate privileges.

## RUN LEVELS

Run levels 0, 1, and 6 are reserved. Run level 0 is used to halt the system, run level 6 is used to reboot the system, and run level 1 is used to get the system down into single-user mode. Run level S is not really meant to be used directly but should be used by scripts that are executed when entering run level 1. For more information on this, see the man pages for shutdown(1) and inittab(5).

## FILES

```
/etc/inittab
/dev/console
/dev/systty
/etc/ioctl.save
/etc/utmp
/var/adm/wtmp
```

## CONFORMING TO

init is compatible with the System V init. The scripts that are used with it, however, are mostly modeled after the BSD startup scripts. There are startup scripts available that let Linux boot more like a System V system, but most people find them too complex.

## WARNINGS

init assumes that processes and descendants of processes remain in the same process group that was originally created for them. If the processes change their group, init can't kill them and you might end up with two processes reading from one terminal line.

## DIAGNOSTICS

If /sbin/init finds that it is continuously respawning an entry more than ten times in two minutes, it will assume that there is an error in the command string, generate an error message on the system console, and refuse to respawn this entry until either five minutes has elapsed or it receives a signal. This prevents it from eating up system resources when someone makes a typographical error in the /etc/inittab file or the program for the entry is removed.

## AUTHOR

Miquel van Smoorenburg (miquels@drinkel.nl.mugnet.org); initial manual page by Michael Haardt (u31b3hs@pool.informatik.rwth-aachen.de).

## SEE ALSO

getty(1), login(1), sh(1), who(1), shutdown(1), kill(2), inittab(5), utmp(5)

*19 January 1994*

# innd, inndstart

innd, inndstart—InterNetNews daemon.

## SYNOPSIS

```
innd [ -a ][-c days ][-d ][-f ][-i count ][-o count ][-l size ]
[-m mode ][-n flag ] [ -p port ][-r ][-s ][-S host ][-t timeout ][-u ][-x ]
inndstart [ flags ]
```

## DESCRIPTION

innd, the InterNetNews daemon, handles all incoming NNTP feeds. It reads the active(5), newsfeeds(5), and hosts.nntp(5) files into memory. It then opens the NNTP port to receive articles from remote sites, a UNIX-domain stream socket to receive articles from local processes such as nnrpd(8) and rnews(1), and a UNIX-domain datagram socket for use by ctlinnd(8) to direct the server to perform certain actions. It also opens the history(5) database and two log files to replace its standard output and standard error. If the -p flag is used, then the NNTP port is assumed to be open on the specified descriptor. (If this flag is used, then innd assumes it is running with the proper permissions and it does not call chown(2) on any files or directories it creates.)

Once the files and sockets have been opened, innd waits for connections and data to be ready on its ports by using select(2) and non-blocking I/O. If no data is available, then it flushes its in-core data structures. The default number of seconds to time out before flushing is 300. This timeout may be changed by using the -t flag.

To limit the number of incoming NNTP connections, use the -i flag. A value of 0 suppresses this check.

To limit the number of files that are kept open for outgoing file feeds, use the -o flag. The default is the number of available descriptors minus some reserved for internal use.

To limit the size of an article, use the -l flag. If this flag is used, then any article bigger than *size* bytes is rejected. The default is no checking, which can also be obtained by using a value of 0.

innd rejects articles that are too old. Although this behavior can be controlled by the history database, occasionally a site dumps a batch of very old news back onto the network. Use the -c flag to specify a cutoff. For example, -c21 rejects any articles that were posted more than 21 days ago. A value of 0 suppresses this check.

innd usually puts itself into the background, sets its standard output and error to log files, and disassociates itself from the terminal. Using the -d flag instructs the server to not do this, whereas using the -f flag just leaves the server running the foreground. The logs are usually buffered; use the -u flag to have them unbuffered.

To start the server in a paused or throttled state (see ctlinnd(8)) use the -m flag to set the initial running mode. The argument should start with a single letter g, p, or t to emulate the go, pause, or throttle commands.

If the -r flag is used, the server renumbers the active file as if a renumber command were sent.

If the -s flag is used, then innd does not do any work but instead just checks the syntax of the news-feeds file. It exits with an error status if there are any errors; the actual errors are reported in syslog(3).

If innd gets an NOSPC error (see intro(2)) while trying to write the active file, an article file, or the history database, it sends itself a throttle command. This also happens if it gets too many I/O errors while writing to any files.

Any subprocesses spawned by the server get a nice(2) value of 10.

The -n flag specifies whether pausing or throttling the server should also disable future news-reading processes. A value of y makes news readers act as the server, a value of n allows news reading even when the server is not running.

If the -S flag is used, then innd runs in slave mode. When running as a slave, the server only accepts articles from the specified host, which must use the xreplic protocol extension. Note that either the host must appear in the hosts.nntp file or the server must be started with the -a flag.

By default, if a host is not mentioned in the hosts.nntp file, then the connection is handed off to nnrpd. If the -a flag is used, then any host can connect and transfer articles.

If the -x flag is used, then a Xref header is added to all articles even if they are not cross-posted.

inndstart is a small front-end program that opens the NNTP port, sets its user ID and group ID to the news maintainer, and then executes innd with the -p flag and a minimal secure environment. This is a small, easily understood front-end program that can be used if a site does not want to run innd with root privileges.

## CONTROL MESSAGES

Arriving articles that have a Control header or have a Subject header that starts with the five characters cmsg are called control messages. Except for the cancel message, these messages are implemented by external programs in the /news/bin/control directory. (Cancel messages update the history database, so they must be handled internally; the cost of synching, locking, and then unlocking is too high, given the number of cancel messages that are received.)

When a control message arrives, the first word of the text is converted to lowercase and used as the name of the program to execute; if the named program does not exist, then a program named default is executed.

All control programs are invoked with four parameters. The first is the address of the person who posted the message; this is taken from the Sender header. If that header is empty, then it is taken from the From header. The second parameter is the address to send replies to; this is taken from the Reply-To header. If that header is empty, then the poster's address is used. The third parameter is a name under which the article is filed, relative to the news spool directory. The fourth parameter is the host that sent the article, as specified on the Path line.

The distribution of control message is also different from those of standard articles.

Control messages are usually filed in the newsgroup named control. They can be filed in subgroups, however, based on the control message command. For example, a newgroup message is filed in control.newgroup if that group exists, otherwise it will be filed in control.

Sites may explicitly have the "control" newsgroup in their subscription list, although it is usually best to exclude it. If a control message is posted to a group whose name ends with the four characters .ctl, then the suffix is stripped off and what is left is used as the group name. For example, a cancel message posted to news.admin.ctl will be sent to all sites that subscribe to control or news.admin. newgroup and rmgroup messages receive additional special treatment. If the message is approved and posted to the name of the group being created or removed, then the message is sent to all sites whose subscription patterns would cause them to receive articles posted in that group.

If an article is posted to a newsgroup that starts with the three letters to., it gets special treatment if the newsgroup does not exist in the active file. The article is filed into the newsgroup to and it is sent to the first site named after the prefix. For example, a posting to to.uunet is filed in to and sent to the site uunet.

## PROTOCOL DIFFERENCES

innd implements the NNTP commands defined in RFC 977 with the following differences:

- The list may be followed by an optional active, active.times, or newsgroups argument. This common extension is not fully supported; see nnrpd(8).
- The authinfo user and authinfo pass commands are implemented. These are based on the reference UNIX implementation; no other documentation is available.
- A new command, mode reader, is provided. This command causes the server to pass the connection on to nnrpd. The command mode query is intended for future use and is currently treated the same way.
- A new command, xreplic news.group:art[,news.group:art], is provided. This is similar to the ihave command (the same reply codes are used) except for the data that follows the command word. The data consists of entries separated by a single comma. Each entry consists of a newsgroup name, a colon, and an article number. Once processed, the article is filed in the newsgroup and article numbers specified in the command.
- A new command, xpath messageid, is provided. The server responds with a 223 response and a space-separated list of filenames where the article was filed.
- The only other commands implemented are head, help, ihave, quit, and stat.

## HEADER MODIFICATIONS

innd modifies as few article headers as possible, although it could be better in this area.

The following headers, if present, are removed:

Date-Received
Posted
Posting-Version
Received
Relay-Version

Empty headers and headers that consist of nothing but whitespace are also dropped.

The local site's name and an exclamation point are prepended to the Path header.

The Xref header is removed. If the article is cross-posted, a new header is generated.

The Lines header is added if it is missing.

innd does not rewrite incorrect headers. For example, it does not replace an incorrect Lines header but rejects the article.

## LOGGING

innd reports all incoming articles in its log file. This is a text file with a variable number of space-separated fields in one of the following formats:

```
mon dd hh:mm:ss.mmm + feed <Message-ID>site...
mon dd hh:mm:ss.mmm j feed <Message-ID> site...
mon dd hh:mm:ss.mmm c feed <Message-ID> site...
mon dd hh:mm:ss.mmm - feed <Message-ID> reason...
```

The first three fields are the date and time to millisecond resolution. The fifth field is the site that sent the article (based on the Path header), and the sixth field is the article's Message-ID; they will contain a question mark if the information is not available.

The fourth field indicates whether the article was accepted. If it is a plus sign, the article was accepted. If it is the letter j, the article was accepted, but all of newsgroups have a j in their active field, so the article was filed into the "junk" newsgroup. If the fourth field is the letter c, a cancel message was accepted before the original article arrived. In all three cases, the article has been accepted and the site... field contains the space-separated list of sites to which the article is sent.

If the fourth field is a minus sign, the article was rejected. The reasons for rejection include

%s header too long
%s wants to cancel <%s> by %s
Article exceeds local limit of %s bytes
Article posted in the future—%s

Bad %s header

Can't write history

Duplicate

Duplicate %s header

EOF in headers

Linecount %s != %s +- %s

Missing %s header

No body

No colon-space in %s header

No space

Space before colon in %s header

Too old—%s

Unapproved for %s

Unwanted newsgroup %s

Unwanted distribution %s

Whitespace in "Newsgroups" header—%s

Where %s, above, is replaced by more specific information.

Note that if an article is accepted and none of the newsgroups are valid, it is logged with both two lines, a j line and a minus sign line.

innd also makes extensive reports through syslog. The first word of the log message is the name of the site if the entry is site-specific (such as a connected message). The first word is ME if the message relates to the server itself, such as when a read error occurs.

If the second word is the four letters cant, an error is being reported. In this case, the next two words generally name the system call or library routine that failed and the object upon which the action was performed. The rest of the line might contain other information.

In other cases, the second word attempts to summarize what change has been made, and the rest of the line gives more specific information. The word internal generally indicates an internal logic error.

## HISTORY

Written by Rich $alz (rsalz@uunet.uu.net) for InterNetNews.

## SEE ALSO

active(5), ctlinnd(8), dbz(3z), history(5), hosts.nntp(5), inn.conf(5), newsfeeds(5), nnrpd(8), rnews(1), syslog(8)

# innxmit

innxmit—Send Usenet articles to a remote NNTP server.

## SYNOPSIS

```
innxmit [ -A alt_spool ][-a ][-d ][-M ][-r ][-t timeout ]
[-T timeout ][-p ][-S ] host file
```

## DESCRIPTION

innxmit connects to the NNTP server at the specified host and sends it the articles specified in the batchfile named file. It is usually invoked by a script run out of cron(8) that uses shlock(1) to lock the hostname, followed by actlinnd(8) command to flush the batchfile.

innxmit usually blocks until the connection is made. To specify a timeout on how long to try to make the connection, use the -t flag. To specify the total amount of time that should be allowed for article transfers, use the -T flag. The default is to wait until an I/O error occurs or all the articles have been transferred. If the -T flag is used, the time is checked just before an article is started; it does not abort a transfer that is in progress. Both values are measured in seconds.

If the file is not an absolute pathname, it is taken relative to the /news/spool/out.going directory. It is usually written by specifying the Wnm flags in the newsfeeds(5) file. Each line in the batchfile should be in one of the following formats:

```
filename Message-ID
filename
```

The filename field names the article to be sent. If it is not an absolute pathname, it is taken relative to the news spool directory, /news/spool. If the Message-ID field is not specified, it is obtained by scanning the article. The filename and Message-Id fields are separated by a space.

If a communication error such as a write(2) failure occurs, innxmit stops sending and rewrites the batchfile to contain the current article and any other unsent articles.

If the remote server sends an unexpected reply code, innxmit requeues the article and proceeds. Use the -r flag if the article should not be requeued.

Upon exit, innxmit reports transfer and CPU usage statistics via syslog(3). If the -v flag is used, they are also printed on the standard output. If all articles were sent successfully, innxmit removes the batchfile; otherwise, it rewrites it to contain the list of unsent articles. If no articles were sent or rejected, the file is left untouched. This can cause the batchfile to grow excessively large if many articles have been expired and there are communication problems. To always rewrite the batchfile, use the -a flag. If the -p flag is given, then no connection is made and the batchfile is purged of entries that refer to files that no longer exist. This implies the -a flag.

If the -S flag is given, then innxmit offers articles to the specified host using the xreplic protocol extension described in innd(8). To use this flag, the input file must contain the history data (commas are transliterated to spaces by the server). For this flag to be used, the input must contain the necessary history entries. This is usually done by setting up a WnR entry in the newsfeeds file.

Use the -d flag to print debugging information on standard error. This shows the protocol transactions between innxmit and the NNTP server on the remote host.

If the -M flag is used, innxmit scans an article's headers before sending it. If the article appears to be a MIME article that is not in seven-bit format, the article is sent in "quoted-printable" form.

The -A flag may be used to specify an alternate spool directory to use if the article is not found; this is usually an NFS-mounted spool directory of a master server with longer expiration times.

## HISTORY

Written by Rich $alz (rsalz@uunet.uu.net) for InterNetNews.

## SEE ALSO

ctlinnd(8), innd(8), newsfeeds(5), shlock(1)

# ipcrm

ipcrm—Remove ipc facilities.

## SYNOPSIS

ipcrm [ shm ¦ msg ¦ sem ] id

## DESCRIPTION

ipcrm removes the resource specified by id.

## SEE ALSO

ipcs(8)

## AUTHOR

Krishna Balasubramanian (balasub@cis.ohio-state.edu)

*Linux 0.99, 9 October 1993*

# ipcs

ipcs—Provide information on ipc facilities.

## SYNOPSIS

```
ipcs [ -asmq ] [ -tclup ]
ipcs [ -smq ] -i id
ipcs -h
```

## DESCRIPTION

ipcs provides information on the ipc facilities for which the calling process has read access.

The -i option allows a specific resource *id* to be specified. Only information on this *id* is printed.

Resources may be specified as follows:

| | |
|---|---|
| -m | Shared memory segments |
| -q | Message queues |
| -s | Semaphore arrays |
| -a | All (this is the default) |

The output format may be specified as follows:

| | |
|---|---|
| -t | Time |
| -p | PID |
| -c | Creator |
| -l | Limits |
| -u | Summary |

## SEE ALSO

ipcrm(8)

## AUTHOR

Krishna Balasubramanian (balasub@cis.ohio-state.edu)

*Linux 0.99, 9 October 1993*

# kbdrate

kbdrate—Reset the keyboard repeat rate and delay time.

## SYNOPSIS

```
kbdrate [ -s ] [ -r rate ][-d delay ]
```

## DESCRIPTION

kbdrate is used to change the IBM keyboard repeat rate and delay time. The delay is the amount of time that a key must be pressed before it starts to repeat. Using kbdrate without any options resets the rate to 10.9 characters per second (cps) and the delay to 250 milliseconds (ms). These are the IBM defaults.

## OPTIONS

-s              Silent. No messages are printed.

-r *rate*       Change the keyboard repeat rate to *rate* cps. The allowable range is from 2.0 to 30.0 cps. Only certain specific values are possible, and the program selects the nearest possible value to the one specified. The possible values are given, in characters per second, as follows: 2.0, 2.1, 2.3, 2.5, 2.7, 3.0, 3.3, 3.7, 4.0, 4.3, 4.6, 5.0, 5.5, 6.0, 6.7, 7.5, 8.0, 8.6, 9.2, 10.0, 10.9, 12.0, 13.3, 15.0, 16.0, 17.1, 18.5, 20.0, 21.8, 24.0, 26.7, 30.0.

-d *delay*      Change the delay to *delay* milliseconds. The allowable range is from 250 to 1000 ms, but the only possible values (based on hardware restrictions) are 250 ms, 500 ms, 750 ms, and 1000 ms.

## BUGS

Not all keyboards support all rates.

Not all keyboards have the rates mapped in the same way.

Setting the repeat rate on the Gateway AnyKey keyboard does not work. If someone with a Gateway figures out how to program the keyboard, please send mail to faith@cs.unc.edu.

## FILES

/etc/rc.local
/dev/port

## AUTHOR

Rik Faith (faith@cs.unc.edu)

*Linux 1.1.19, 22 June 1994*


# klogd

klogd—Kernel log daemon.

## SYNOPSIS

klogd -c [*n*] -d -f [*fname*] -os

## DESCRIPTION

klogd is a system daemon that intercepts and logs Linux kernel messages.

## OPTIONS

-c              Sets the default log level of console messages to [*n*].

-d              Enables debugging mode. This will generate a lot of output to stderr.

-f              Logs messages to the specified filename rather than to the syslog facility.

-o              Execute in one–shot mode. This causes klogd to read and log all the messages that are found in the kernel message buffers. After a single read and log cycle, the daemon exits.

-s              Force klogd to use the system call interface to the kernel message buffers.

## OVERVIEW

The functionality of klogd has been typically incorporated into other versions of syslogd, but this seems to be a poor place for it. In the modern Linux kernel, a number of kernel messaging issues such as sourcing and prioritization must be addressed. Incorporating kernel logging into a separate process appears to offer a cleaner separation of services.

In Linux, there are two potential sources of kernel log information: the /proc filesystem and the syscall (sys_syslog) interface, although ultimately they are one and the same. klogd is designed to choose whichever source of information is the most appropriate. It does this by first checking for the presence of a mounted /proc filesystem. If this is found, the /proc/kmsg file is used as the source of kernel log information. If the proc filesystem is not mounted, klogd uses a system call to obtain kernel messages. The command-line switch (-s) can be used to force klogd to use the system call interface as its messaging source.

If kernel messages are directed through the syslogd daemon, the klogd daemon, as of version 1.1, has the ability to properly prioritize kernel messages. Prioritization of the kernel messages was added at approximately the p113 level of the kernel. The raw kernel messages are of the form:

```
<[0-7]>Something said by the kernel.
```

The priority of the kernel message is encoded as a single numeric digit enclosed inside the <> pair. The definitions of these values is given in the kernel include file kernel.h. When a message is received from the kernel, the klogd daemon reads this priority level and assigns the appropriate priority level to the syslog message. If file output (-f) is used, the prioritization sequence is left prepended to the kernel message.

The klogd daemon also allows the ability to alter the presentation of kernel messages to the system console. Consequent with the prioritization of kernel messages was the inclusion of default messaging levels for the kernel. In a stock kernel, the default console log level is set to 7. Any messages with a priority level numerically lower than 7 (higher priority) appear on the console.

Messages of priority level 7 are considered to be debug messages and do not appear on the console. Many administrators, particularly in a multi–user environment, prefer that all kernel messages be handled by klogd and either directed to a file or to the syslogd daemon. This prevents nuisance messages such as line printer out of paper or disk change detected from cluttering the console.

By default, the klogd daemon executes a system call to inhibit all kernel messages (except for panics) from being displayed on the console. The -c switch can be used to alter this behavior. The argument given to the -c switch specifies the priority level of messages that are directed to the console. Note that messages of a priority value lower than the indicated number are directed to the console.

For example, to have the kernel display all messages with a priority level of 3 (KERN ERR) or more severe, the following command is executed:

```
klogd -c 4
```

The definitions of the numeric values for kernel messages are given in the file kernel.h, which can be found in the /usr/include/linux directory if the kernel sources are installed. These values parallel the syslog priority values, which are defined in the file syslog.h, found in the /usr/include/sys subdirectory.

The klogd daemon can also be used in a one–shot mode for reading the kernel message buffers. One-shot mode is selected by specifying the -o switch on the command line. Output is directed to either the syslogd daemon or to an alternate file specified by the -f switch.

For example, to read all the kernel messages after a system boot and record them in a file called krnl.msg, the following command is given:

```
klogd -o -f ./krnl.msg
```

## SIGNAL HANDLING

The klogd daemon responds to six signals: SIGHUP, SIGINT, SIGKILL, SIGTERM, SIGTSTP, and SIGCONT. The SIGINT, SIGKILL, SIGTERM, and SIGHUP signals cause the daemon to close its kernel log sources and terminate gracefully.

The `SIGTSTP` and `SIGCONT` signals are used to start and stop kernel logging. Upon receipt of a `SIGTSTP` signal, the daemon closes its log sources and spins in an idle loop. Subsequent receipt of a `SIGCONT` signal causes the daemon to go through its initialization sequence and rechoose an input source. Using `SIGSTOP` and `SIGCONT` in combination, the kernel log input can be rechosen without stopping and restarting the daemon. For example, if the `/proc` filesystem is to be unmounted, the following command sequence should be used:

```
# kill -TSTP pid
# umount /proc
# kill -CONT pid
```

Notations will be made in the system logs with `LOG INFO` priority documenting the start/stop of logging.

## FILES

`/proc/kmsg`

## BUGS

Probably numerous. Well-formed context diffs appreciated.

## AUTHOR

Dr. Greg Wettstein (`greg%wind.uucp@plains.nodak.edu`), Enjellic Systems Development, Oncology Research Division Computing Facility, Roger Maris Cancer Center, Fargo, ND 58122.

*Version 1.1, 28 January 1994*

# lpc

lpc—Line printer control program.

## SYNOPSIS

`lpc [command [argument ...]]`

## DESCRIPTION

lpc is used by the system administrator to control the operation of the line printer system. For each line printer configured in `/etc/printcap`, lpc may be used to

- Disable or enable a printer
- Disable or enable a printer's spooling queue
- Rearrange the order of jobs in a spooling queue
- Find the status of printers and their associated spooling queues and printer daemons

Without any arguments, lpc prompts for commands from the standard input. If arguments are supplied, lpc interprets the first argument as a command and the remaining arguments as parameters to the command. The standard input may be redirected, causing lpc to read commands from file. Commands may be abbreviated; the following is the list of recognized commands:

| | |
|---|---|
| `? [ command ... ]help [ command ... ]` | Print a short description of each command specified in the argument list or, if no arguments are given, a list of the recognized commands. |
| `Ic abort No all - printer` | Terminate an active spooling daemon on the local host immediately and then disable printing (preventing new daemons from being started by lpr) for the specified printers. |
| `clean No all - printer` | Remove any temporary files, data files, and control files that cannot be printed (that is, they do not form a complete printer job) from the specified printer queues on the local machine. |
| `disable No all - printer` | Turn the specified printer queues off. This prevents new printer jobs from being entered into the queue by lpr. |

| | |
|---|---|
| lc down No all · *printer message* ... | Turn the specified printer queue off, disable printing, and put *message* in the printer status file. The message doesn't need to be quoted; the remaining arguments are treated like echo(1). This is usually used to take a printer down and let others know why lpq(1) indicates the printer is down and print the status message. |
| enable No all -- *printer* | Enable spooling on the local queue for the listed printers. This allows lpr(1) to put new jobs in the spool queue. |
| exit, quit | Exit from lpc. |
| restart all · *printer* | Attempt to start a new printer daemon. This is useful when some abnormal condition causes the daemon to die unexpectedly leaving jobs in the queue. lpq reports that there is no daemon present when this condition occurs. If the user is the super-user, try to abort the current daemon first (that is, kill and restart a stuck daemon). |
| start all · *printer* | Enable printing and start a spooling daemon for the listed printers. |
| status No all · *printer* | Display the status of daemons and queues on the local machine. |
| stop all · *printer* | Stop a spooling daemon after the current job completes and disable printing. |
| topq *printer* [ *jobnum* ... ] [ *user* ... ] | Place the jobs in the order listed at the top of the printer queue. |
| up all · *printer* | Enable everything and start a new printer daemon. Undoes the effects of down. |

## FILES

| | |
|---|---|
| /etc/printcap | printer description file |
| /var/spool/* | spool directories |
| /var/spool/*/lock | lock file for queue control |

## SEE ALSO

lpd(8), lpr(1), lpq(1), lprm(1), printcap(5)

## DIAGNOSTICS

| | |
|---|---|
| ?Ambiguous command | Abbreviation matches more than one command. |
| ?Invalid command | No match was found. |
| ?Privileged command | Command can be executed by root only. |

## HISTORY

The lpc command appeared in BSD 4.2.

*BSD 4.2, 16 March 1991*

# lpd

lpd—Line printer spooler daemon.

## SYNOPSIS

lpd [-l] [*port#*]

## DESCRIPTION

lpd is the line printer daemon (spool area handler) and is usually invoked at boot time from the rc(8) file. It makes a single pass through the printcap(5) file to find out about the existing printers and prints any files left after a crash. It then uses the system calls listen(2) and accept(2) to receive requests to print files in the queue, transfer files to the spooling area, display the queue, or remove jobs from the queue. In each case, it forks a child to handle the request so the parent can continue to listen for more requests.

Available options:

| | |
|---|---|
| -l | The -l flag causes lpd to log valid requests received from the network. This can be useful for debugging purposes. |
| port# | The Internet port number used to rendezvous with other processes is usually obtained with getservbyname(3) but can be changed with the port# argument. |

Access control is provided by two means. First, all requests must come from one of the machines listed in the file /etc/hosts.equiv or /etc/hosts.lpd. Second, if the rs capability is specified in the printcap entry for the printer being accessed, lpr requests are only honored for those users with accounts on the machine with the printer.

The file minfree in each spool directory contains the number of disk blocks to leave free so that the line printer queue won't completely fill the disk. The minfree file can be edited with your favorite text editor.

The daemon begins processing files after it has successfully set the lock for exclusive access (described later) and scans the spool directory for files beginning with cf. Lines in each cf file specify files to be printed or non-printing actions to be performed. Each such line begins with a key character to specify what to do with the remainder of the line:

| | |
|---|---|
| J | Job name. String to be used for the job name on the burst page. |
| C | Classification. String to be used for the classification line on the burst page. |
| L | Literal. The line contains identification info from the password file and causes the banner page to be printed. |
| T | Title. String to be used as the title for pr(1). |
| H | Host name. Name of the machine where lpr was invoked. |
| P | Person. Login name of the person who invoked lpr. This is used to verify ownership by lprm. |
| M | Send mail to the specified user when the current print job completes. |
| f | Formatted file. Name of a file to print which is already formatted. |
| l | Like f but passes control characters and does not make page breaks. |
| p | Name of a file to print using pr(1) as a filter. |
| t | Troff file. The file contains troff(1) output (cat phototypesetter commands). |
| n | Ditroff file. The file contains device independent troff output. |
| r | DVI file. The file contains Tex l output DVI format from Standford. |
| g | Graph file. The file contains data produced by plot(3). |
| c | Cifplot file. The file contains data produced by cifplot. |
| v | The file contains a raster image. |
| r | The file contains text data with FORTRAN carriage control characters. |
| 1 | Troff font R. Name of the font file to use instead of the default. |
| 2 | Troff font I. Name of the font file to use instead of the default. |
| 3 | Troff font B. Name of the font file to use instead of the default. |
| 4 | Troff font S. Name of the font file to use instead of the default. |
| W | Width. Changes the page width (in characters) used by pr(1) and the text filters. |
| I | Indent. The number of characters to indent the output by (in ASCII). |
| U | Unlink. Name of file to remove upon completion of printing. |
| N | Filename. The name of the file that is being printed or a blank for the standard input (when lpr is invoked in a pipeline). |

If a file cannot be opened, a message is logged via syslog(3) using the LOG LPR facility. lpd tries up to 20 times to reopen a file it expects to be there, after which it skips the file to be printed.

lpd uses flock(2) to provide exclusive access to the lock file and to prevent multiple daemons from becoming active simultaneously. If the daemon should be killed or die unexpectedly, the lock file need not be removed. The lock file is kept in a readable ASCII form and contains two lines. The first is the process ID of the daemon and the second is the control filename of the current job being printed. The second line is updated to reflect the current status of lpd for the programs lpq(1) and lprm(1).

## FILES

| | |
|---|---|
| /etc/printcap | Printer description file |
| /var/spool/* | Spool directories |
| /var/spool/*/minfree | Minimum free space to leave |
| /dev/lp* | Line printer devices |
| /dev/printer | Socket for local requests |
| /etc/hosts.equiv | Lists machine names allowed printer access |
| /etc/hosts.lpd | Lists machine names allowed printer access but not under same administrative control |

## SEE ALSO

lpc(8), pac(1), lpr(1), lpq(1), lprm(1), syslog(3), printcap(5)

4.2 BSD Line Printer Spooler Manual

## HISTORY

An lpd daemon appeared in Version 6, AT&T UNIX.

*BSD 4.2, 16 March 1991*

# MAKEDEV

MAKEDEV—Creates and maintains filesystem device entries.

## SYNOPSIS

MAKEDEV [ -vcdnhV ] *device or device-group names*

## DESCRIPTION

MAKEDEV is used to maintain the special filesystem entries found in /dev. It creates, or optionally removes, one or more device entries. The names and device numbers are defined in the devinfo file (q.v.); site-specific configuration is found in the file MAKEDEV.cfg. MAKEDEV itself has no knowledge of device information.

## OPTIONS

| | |
|---|---|
| -v | Verbose mode; print out exactly what's being done. |
| -c | Create; create the specified devices (default). |
| -d | Delete; remove the specified devices instead of creating them. |
| -n | Do nothing; only print what would be done. Implies -v as well. |
| -h | Print a usage message. |
| -V | Print the version string. |

The following targets are special:

| | |
|---|---|
| update | Run MAKEDEV in update mode. This reads the list of devices currently available from /proc/devices and updates all entries in /dev to match the device numbers found there. |

local                       Run MAKEDEV to create local devices. This option is obsolete and just prints a warning message.
                            Use devinfo.local and makedev.cfg to achieve the same results.

## FILES

| | |
|---|---|
| /etc/devinfo | Device information |
| /usr/local/etc/devinfo.local | Local device information |
| /etc/devinfo.local | Alternate location for local device information |
| /etc/makedev.cfg | Configuration file |
| MAKEDEV.cache | Cached data for update |
| /proc/devices | The kernel's list of current devices |

## AUTHOR

David A. Holland (dholland@husc.harvard.edu). Based on the older MAKEDEV shell script written by Nick Holloway. Additional ideas were contributed by Rik Faith.

## NOTES

The LALR(1) parser generator used to build makedev.c from makedev.syn is a commercial product. You won't be able to do a complete rebuild unless you have it.

## SEE ALSO

devinfo(5), makedev.cfg(5)

*Version 1.5, March 1995*

# MAKEDEV

MAKEDEV—Creates devices.

## SYNOPSIS

```
cd dev; ./MAKEDEV -V
cd dev; ./MAKEDEV [ -n ] [ -v ] update
cd dev; ./MAKEDEV [ -n ] [ -v ] [ -d ] device ...
```

## DESCRIPTION

MAKEDEV is a script that creates the devices in /dev used to interface with drivers in the kernel.

Note that programs giving the error ENOENT: No such file or directory usually means that the device file is missing, whereas ENODEV: No such device usually means the kernel does not have the driver configured or loaded.

## OPTIONS

-V                          Print out version (actually RCS version information) and exit.

-n                          Do not actually update the devices; just print the actions that would be performed.

-d                          Delete the devices. The main use for this flag is by MAKEDEV itself.

-v                          Be verbose. Print out the actions as they are performed. This is the same output as produced by -n.

## CUSTOMIZATION

Because there is currently no standardization in what names are used for system users and groups, it is possible that you might need to modify MAKEDEV to reflect your site's settings. Near the top of the file is a mapping from device type to user, group, and permissions. (For example, all CD-ROM devices are set from the $cdrom variable.) If you want to change the defaults, this is the section to edit.

# DEVICES

*General Options*

| | |
|---|---|
| update | This only works on kernels that have /proc/interrupts (introduced during 1.1.x). This file is scanned to see what devices are currently configured into the kernel, and this is compared with the previous settings stored in the file called DEVICES. Devices that are new since then or have a different major number are created, and those that are no longer configured are deleted. |
| generic | Create a generic subset of devices. This is the standard devices, plus floppy drives, various hard drives, pseudo-terminals, console devices, basic serial devices, busmice, and printer ports. |
| %std | Standard devices. These are mem, access to physical memory; kmem, access to kernel virtual memory; null, null device (infinite sink); port, access to I/O ports; zero, null byte source (infinite source); core, symlink to /proc/kcore (for kernel debugging); full, always returns ENOSPACE on write; ram, ramdisk; tty, to access the controlling tty of a process. |
| local | This simply runs MAKEDEV.local. This is a script that can create any local devices. |

*Virtual Terminals*

| | |
|---|---|
| console | This creates the devices associated with the console. This is the virtual terminals ttyx, where x can be from 0 though 63. The device tty0 is the currently active vt and is also known as console. For each vt, there are two devices, vcsx and vcsax, which are used to generate screen-dumps of the vt (the vcsx is just the text and vcsax includes the attributes). |

*Serial Devices*

| | |
|---|---|
| ttyS{0..63} | Serial ports and corresponding dial-out device. For device ttySx, there is also the device cuax, which is used to dial out with. This can avoid the need for cooperative locks in simple situations. |
| cyclades | Dial-in and dial-out devices for the cyclades intelligent I/O serial card. The dial in device is ttyCx and the corresponding dial-out device is cubx. By default, devices for 7 lines are created, but this can be changed to 15 by removing the comment. |

*Pseudo Terminals*

| | |
|---|---|
| pty[p-s] | Each possible argument will create a bank of 16 master and slave pairs. The current kernel (1.2) is limited to 64 such pairs. The master pseudo-terminals are pty[p-s][0-9a-f] and the slaves are tty[p-s][0-9a-f]. |

*Parallel Ports*

| | |
|---|---|
| lp | Standard parallel ports. The devices are created lp0, lp1, and lp2. These correspond to ports at 0x3bc, 0x378, and 0x278. Hence, on some machines, the first printer port may actually be lp1. |
| par | Alternative to lp. Ports are named parx instead of lpx. |

*Bus Mice*

| | |
|---|---|
| busmice | The various bus mice devices. This creates the following devices: logimouse (Logitech bus mouse), psmouse (PS/2-style mouse), msmouse (Microsoft Inport bus mouse), atimouse (ATI XL bus mouse) and jmouse (J-mouse). |

*Joystick Devices*

| | |
|---|---|
| js | Joystick. Creates js0 and js1. |

*Disk Devices*

| | |
|---|---|
| fd[0-7] | Floppy disk devices. The device fdx is the device that autodetects the format, and the additional devices are fixed format (whose size is indicated in the name). The other devices are named as |

fdx*Ln*. The single letter L identifies the type of floppy disk (d = 5.25" DD, h = 5.25" HD, D =3.5" DD, H = 3.5" HD, E = 3.5" ED). The number *n* represents the capacity of that format in KB. Thus the standard formats are fdxd360, fdxh1200, fdxD720, fdxH1440, and fdxE2880.

For more information, see Alain Knaff's fdutils pack-age.

Devices fd0* through fd3* are floppy disks on the first controller, and devices fd4* through fd7* are floppy disks on the second controller.

| | |
|---|---|
| hd[a-d] | AT hard disks. The device hd*x* provides access to the whole disk, with the partitions being hd*x*[0-20]. The four primary partitions are hd*x*1 through hd*x*4, with the logical partitions being numbered from hd*x*5 though hd*x*20. (A primary partition can be made into an extended partition, which can hold four logical partitions). By default, only the devices for four logical partitions are made. The others can be made by uncommenting them.<br><br>Drives hda and hdb are the two on the first controller. If using the new IDE driver (rather than the old HD driver), then hdc and hdd are the two drives on the secondary controller. These devices can also be used to access IDE CD-ROMs if using the new IDE driver. |
| xd[a-d] | XT hard disks. Partitions are the same as IDE disks. |
| sd[a-h] | SCSI hard disks. The partitions are similar to the IDE disks, but there is a limit of 11 logical partitions (sd*x*5 through sd*x*15). This is to allow 8 SCSI disks. |
| loop | Loopback disk devices. These allow you to use a regular file as a block device. This means that images of filesystems can be mounted and used as normal. This creates 8 devices loop0 through loop7. |

### Tape Devices

| | |
|---|---|
| st[0-7] | SCSI tapes. This creates the rewinding tape device st*x* and the non-rewinding tape device nst*x*. |
| qic | QIC-80 tapes. The devices created are rmt8, rmt16, tape-d, and tape-reset. |
| ftape | Floppy driver tapes (QIC-117). There are four methods of access depending on the floppy tape drive. For each of the access methods 0, 1, 2, and 3, the devices rft*x* (rewinding) and nrft*x* (non-rewinding) are created. For compatibility, devices ftape and nftape are symlinks to rft0 and nrft0. |

### CD-ROM Devices

| | |
|---|---|
| scd[0-7] | SCSI CD players. |
| sonycd | Sony CDU-31A CD player. |
| mcd | Mitsumi CD player. |
| cdu535 | Sony CDU-535 CD player. |
| lmscd | LMS/Philips CD player. |
| sbpcd{,1,2,3} | SoundBlaster CD player. The kernel is capable of supporting 16 CD-ROMs, each of which is accessed as sbpcd[0-9a-f]. These are assigned in groups of four to each controller. sbpcd is a symlink to sbpcd0. |

### Scanner

| | |
|---|---|
| logiscan | Logitech ScanMan32 and ScanMan 256. |
| m105scan | Mustek M105 Handscanner. |
| ac4096 | A4Tek Color Handscanner. |

### Audio

| | |
|---|---|
| audio | This creates the audio devices used by the sound driver. These include mixer, sequencer, dsp, and audio. |
| pcaudio | Devices for the PC Speaker sound driver. These are pcmixer, pxsp, and pcaudio. |

*Miscellaneous*

| | |
|---|---|
| sg | Generic SCSI devices. The devices created aresg0 through sg7. These allow arbitrary commands to be sent to any SCSI device. This allows for querying information about the device or controlling SCSI devices that are not one of disk, tape, or CD-ROM (for example, a scanner or writable CD-ROM). |
| fd | To allow an arbitrary program to be fed input from file descriptor *x*, use /dev/fd/*x* as the filename. This also creates BR/dev/stdin, BR/dev/stdout, and BR/dev/stdorr. (Note that these are just symlinks into /proc/self/fd.) |
| ibcs2 | Devices (and symlinks) needed by the IBCS2 emulation. |
| apm | Devices for power management. |
| dcf | Driver for DCF-77 radio clock. |
| helloworld | Kernel modules demonstration device. See the modules source. |
| Network devices | Linux used to have devices in /dev for controlling network devices, but that is no longer the case. To see what network devices are known by the kernel, look at /proc/net/dev. |

## SEE ALSO

Linux Allocated Devices, maintained by H. Peter Anvin (Peter.Anvin@linux.org)

## AUTHOR

Nick Holloway

*Linux, 14 August 1994*

# mke2fs

mke2fs—Create a Linux second extended filesystem.

## SYNOPSIS

```
mke2fs [ -c ¦ -l filename ] [ -b block-size ] [ -f fragment-size ]
 [ -i bytes-per-inode ] [ -m reserved-blocks-percentage ] [ -q ][-v ][-S ]
 device [ blocks-count ]
```

## DESCRIPTION

mke2fs is used to create a Linux second extended filesystem on a device (usually a disk partition). *device* is the special file corresponding to the device (such as /dev/hd*XX*). *blocks-count* is the number of blocks on the device. If omitted, mke2fs automatically figures the filesystem size.

## OPTIONS

| | |
|---|---|
| -b *block-size* | Specify the size of blocks in bytes. |
| -c | Check the device for bad blocks before creating the filesystem using a fast read-only test. |
| -f *fragment-size* | Specify the size of fragments in bytes. |
| -i *bytes-per-inode* | Specify the bytes/inode ratio. mke2fs creates an inode for every *bytes-per-inode* bytes of space on the disk. This value defaults to 4096 bytes. *bytes-per-inode* must be at least 1024. |
| -l *filename* | Read the bad blocks list from *filename*. |
| -m *reserved- blocks-percentage* | Specify the percentage of reserved blocks for the super-user. This value defaults to 5 percent. |
| -q | Quiet execution. Useful if mke2fs is run in a script. |
| -v | Verbose execution. |

-S         Write superblock and group descriptors only. This is useful if all the superblock and backup superblocks are corrupted and a last-ditch recovery method is desired. It causes mke2fs to reinitialize the superblock and group descriptors while not touching the inode table and the block and inode bitmaps. The e2fsck program should be run immediately after this option is used, and there is no guarantee that any data will be salvageable.

## AUTHOR

This version of mke2fs has been written by Theodore T'so (tytso@mit.edu).

## BUGS

mke2fs accepts the -f option but currently ignores it because the second extended filesystem does not support fragments yet. There may be some other bugs. Please report them to the author.

## AVAILABILITY

mke2fs is available for anonymous FTP from ftp.ibp.fr and tsx-11.mit.edu in /pub/linux/packages/ext2fs.

## SEE ALSO

badblocks(8), dumpe2fs(8), e2fsck(8), tune2fs(8)

*Version 0.5b, November 1994*

# mkfs

mkfs—Build a Linux filesystem.

## SYNOPSIS

mkfs [ -V ][-t *fstype* ][fs-*options* ] filesys [ *blocks* ]

## DESCRIPTION

mkfs is used to build a Linux filesystem on a device, usually a hard disk partition. *filesys* is either the device name (such as /dev/hda1, /dev/sdb2) or the mount point (such as /, /usr, /home) for the filesystem. *blocks* is the number of blocks to be used for the filesystem.

The exit code returned by mkfs is 0 on success and 1 on failure.

In actuality, mkfs is simply a front end for the various filesystem builders (mkfs.fstype) available under Linux. The filesystem-specific builder is searched for in /etc/fs first, then in /etc, and finally in the directories listed in the PATH environment variable. Please see the filesystem-specific builder manual pages for further details.

## OPTIONS

-V         Produce verbose output, including all filesystem-specific commands that are executed. Specifying this option more than once inhibits execution of any filesystem-specific commands. This is really only useful for testing.

-t*fstype*         Specifies the type of filesystem to be built. If not specified, the type is deduced by searching for *filesys* in /etc/fstab and using the corresponding entry. If the type cannot be deduced, the default filesystem type (currently minix) is used.

fs-options         Filesystem-specific options to be passed to the real filesystem builder. Although not guaranteed, the following options are supported by most filesystem builders.

-c         Check the device for bad blocks before building the filesystem.

-l*filename*         Read the bad blocks list from *filename*.

-v         Produce verbose output.

## BUGS

All generic options must precede and not be combined with filesystem-specific options. Some filesystem-specific programs do not support the -v (verbose) option nor return meaningful exit codes. Also, some filesystem-specific programs do not automatically detect the device size and require the blocks parameter to be specified.

## AUTHORS

David Engel (david@ods.com), Fred N. van Kempen (waltje@uwalt.nl.mugnet.org), and Ron Sommeling (oommol@sci.kun.nl). The manual page was shamelessly adapted from Remy Card's version for the ext2 filesystem.

## SEE ALSO

fsck(8), mkfs.minix(8), mkfs.ext(8), mkfs.ext2(8), mkfs.xiafs(8)

*Version 1.9, June 1995*

# mkfs

mkfs—Make a Linux MINIX filesystem.

## SYNOPSIS

```
mkfs [ -c ] [ -nnamelength ] [ -i inodecount ] device size-in-blocks
mkfs [ -l filename ] device size-in-blocks
```

## DESCRIPTION

mkfs creates a Linux MINIX filesystem on a device (usually a disk partition).

The device is usually of the following form:

```
/dev/hda[1-8]
/dev/hdb[1-8]
/dev/sda[1-8]
/dev/sdb[1-8]
```

The *size-in-blocks* parameter is the desired size of the filesystem in blocks. This information can be determined from the fdisk(8) program. Only block counts strictly greater than 10 and strictly less than 65,536 are allowed.

## OPTIONS

| | |
|---|---|
| -c | Check the device for bad blocks before creating the filesystem. If any are found, the count is printed. |
| -nnamelength | Specify the maximum length of filenames. No space is allowed between the -n and the *namelength*. Currently, the only allowable values are 14 and 30. 30 is the default. |
| -i inodecount | Specify the number of inodes for the filesystem. |
| -l filename | Read the bad blocks list from *filename*. The file has one bad block number per line. The count of bad blocks read is printed. |

## EXIT CODES

The exit code returned by mkfs.minix is one of the following:

| | |
|---|---|
| 0 | No errors |
| 8 | Operational error |
| 16 | Usage or syntax error |

## SEE ALSO

fsck(8), mkefs(8), efsck(8), reboot(8)

## AUTHOR

Linus Torvalds (`torvalds@cs.helsinki.fi`). Error code values by Rik Faith (`faith@cs.unc.edu`). Inode request feature by Scott Heavner (`sdh@po.cwru.edu`). Support for the filesystem valid flag by Dr. Wettstein (`greg%wind.uucp@plains.nodak.edu`).

Check to prevent `mkfs` of mounted filesystem and boot sector clearing by Daniel Quinlan (`quinlan@yggdrasil.com`).

*Linux 0.99, 10 January 1994*

# mklost+found

`mklost+found`—Create a lost+found directory on a mounted Linux second extended filesystem.

## SYNOPSIS

`mklost+found`

## DESCRIPTION

`mklost+found` is used to create a lost+found directory in the current working directory on a Linux second extended filesystem. `mklost+found` pre-allocates disk blocks to the directory to make it usable by `e2fsck`.

## OPTIONS

There are none.

## AUTHOR

`mklost+found` was written by Remy Card (`card@masi.ibp.fr`), the developer and maintainer of the `ext2 fs`.

## BUGS

There are none. :-)

## AVAILABILITY

`mklost+found` is available for anonymous FTP from `ftp.ibp.fr` and `tsx-11.mit.edu` in `/pub/linux/packages/ext2fs`.

## SEE ALSO

`e2fsck`(8), `mke2fs`(8)

*Version 0.5b, November 1994*

# mkswap

`mkswap`—Set up a Linux swap area.

## SYNOPSIS

`mkswap [ -c ] device [size-in-blocks]`

## DESCRIPTION

`mkswap` sets up a Linux swap area on a device or in a file.

The device is usually of the following form:

```
/dev/hda[1-8]
/dev/hdb[1-8]
/dev/sda[1-8]
/dev/sdb[1-8]
```

The *size-in-blocks* parameter is the desired size of the filesystem in blocks. This information is determined automatically by mkswap if it is omitted. Block counts are rounded down so that the total size is an integer multiple of the machine's page size. Only block counts in the range MINCOUNT..MAXCOUNT are allowed. If the block count exceeds the MAXCOUNT, it is truncated to that value and a warning message is issued.

The MINCOUNT and MAXCOUNT values for a swap area are

    MINCOUNT = 10 * PAGE_SIZE / 1024
    MAXCOUNT = (PAGE_SIZE-10)*8 *PAGE_SIZE / 1024

For example, on a machine with 4KB pages (such as *x86*), we get

    MINCOUNT = 10 * 4096 / 1024 = 40
    MAXCOUNT = (4096 - 10) * 8 * 4096 / 1024 = 130752

As each block is 1KB, the swap area in this example could have a size that is anywhere in the range from 40KB to 127.6875MB.

If you don't know the page size that your machine uses, you may be able to look it up with cat /proc/cpuinfo.

The reason for the limit on MAXCOUNT is that a single page is used to hold the swap bitmap at the start of the swap area, where each bit represents a single page. The reason for the -10, is that the signature is SWAP-SPACE – 10 characters.

To set up a swap file, it is necessary to create that file before running mkswap. A sequence of commands similar to the following is reasonable for this purpose:

```
# dd if=/dev/zero of=swapfile bs=1024 count=8192
# mkswap swapfile 8192
# sync
# swapon swapfile
```

Note that a swap file must not contain any holes (so using cp(1) to create the file is not acceptable).

## OPTIONS

-c                          Check the device for bad blocks before creating the filesystem. If any are found, the count is printed. This option is meant to be used for swap partitions only and should not be used for regular files! To make sure that regular files do not contain bad blocks, the partition that contains the regular file should have been created with mkfs -c.

## SEE ALSO

fsck(8), mkfs(8), fdisk(8)

## AUTHOR

Linus Torvalds (torvalds@cs.helsinki.fi)

*Linux 1.0, 8 February 1995*

# mount, umount

mount, umount—Mount and dismount filesystems.

## SYNOPSIS

```
mount [-afrwuvn] [-t vfstype]
mount [-frwuvn] [-o remount [,...]] special ¦ node
mount [-frwun] [-t vfstype] [-o options] special ¦ node
umount [-an] [-t vfstype]
umount special ¦ node
```

# DESCRIPTION

The mount command calls the mount(2) system call to prepare and graft a special device onto the filesystem tree at the point node. If either *special* or *node* are not provided, the appropriate information is taken from the fstab(5) file. The special keyword none can be used instead of a path or node specification. This is useful when mounting the proc filesystem.

The system maintains a list of currently mounted filesystems. If no arguments are given to mount, this list is printed.

Options available for the mount command:

| | |
|---|---|
| -f | Causes everything to be done except for the actual system call; if it's not obvious, this "fakes" mounting the filesystem. This option is useful in conjunction with the -v flag to determine what the mount command is trying to do. |
| -o | Options are specified with a -o flag followed by a comma-separated string of options. Note that many of these options are only useful when they appear in the /etc/fstab file. The following options apply to any filesystem that is being mounted: |
| async | All I/O to the filesystem should be done asynchronously. |
| auto | Can be mounted with the -a option. |
| defaults | Use default options: rw, suid, dev, exec, auto, nouser, and async. |
| dev | Interpret character or block special devices on the filesystem. |
| exec | Permit execution of binaries. |
| noauto | Can only be mounted explicitly (that is, the -a option does not cause the filesystem to be mounted). |
| nodev | Do not interpret character or block special devices on the filesystem. This option is useful for a server that has filesystems containing special devices for architectures other than its own. |
| noexec | Do not allow execution of any binaries on the mounted filesystem. This option is useful for a server that has filesystems containing binaries for architectures other than its own. |
| nosuid | Do not allow set-user-identifier or set-group-identifier bits to take effect. |
| nouser | Forbid an ordinary (that is, non-root) user to mount the filesystem. |
| remount | Attempt to remount an already-mounted filesystem. This is commonly used to change the mount flags for a filesystem, especially to make a read-only filesystem writable. |
| ro | Mount the filesystem read-only. |
| rw | Mount the filesystem read-write. |
| suid | Allow set-user-identifier or set-group-identifier bits to take effect. |
| sync | All I/O to the filesystem should be done synchronously. |
| user | Allow an ordinary user to mount the filesystem. Ordinary users always have the following options activated: noexec, nosuid, and nodev (unless overridden by the super-user by using, for example, the following option line: user,exec,dev,suid. |

The following options apply only to certain filesystems:

| | |
|---|---|
| case=*value* | For the hpfs filesystem, specify case as lower or asis. |
| check=*value* | Tells the ext2 filesystem kernel code to do some more checks while the filesystem is mounted. Currently (0.99.15), the following values can be specified with this option: |
| none | No extra check is performed by the kernel code. |
| normal | The inodes and blocks bitmaps are checked when the filesystem is mounted (this is the default). |
| strict | In addition to the normal checks, block deallocation checks that the block to free is in the data zone. |
| check=*value* | For the msdos filesystem, three different levels of specificity can be chosen: |

| | |
|---|---|
| relaxed | Uppercase and lowercase are accepted and equivalent, long name parts are truncated (for example, verlongname.foobar becomes verylong.foo), leading and embedded spaces are accepted in each name part (name and extension). |
| normal | Like relaxed but many special characters (*, ?, <, spaces, and so on) are rejected. This is the default. |
| strict | Like normal, but names may not contain long parts and special characters that are sometimes used on Linux but are not accepted by MS-DOS are rejected (+, =, spaces, and so on). |
| conv=*value* | For the msdos, hpfs, and iso9660 filesystems, specify file conversion as binary, text, or auto. The iso9660 filesystem also allows value to be mtext. |
| | The msdos filesystem can perform CRLF<->NL (MS-DOS text format to UNIX text format) conversion in the kernel. The following conversion modes are available: |
| binary | No translation is performed. This is the default. |
| text | CRLF<->NL translation is performed on all files. |
| auto | CRLF<->NL translation is performed on all files that don't have a well-known binary extension. The list of known extensions can be found at the beginning of fs/msdos/misc.c (as of 09913r, the list is exe, com, bin, app, sys, drv, ovl, oyr, obj, lib, dll, pif, arc, zip, lha, lzh, zoo, tar, z, arj, tz, taz, tzp, tpz, gif, bmp, tif, gl, jpg, pcx, tfm, vf, gf, pk, pxl, and dvi). |

Programs that do computed lseeks won't like in-kernel text conversion.

For filesystems mounted in binary mode, a conversion tool (fromdos/todos) is available.

| | |
|---|---|
| block=*value* | For the iso9660 filesystem, set the block size. |
| bsdgroups | See grpid. |
| cruft | For the iso9660 filesystem, set the cruft flag to y. This option is available because there are buggy premastering programs out there that leave junk in the top byte of the file size. This option clears the top byte but restricts files to 16MB maximum in the process. |
| debug | For the msdos filesystem, turn on the debug flag. A version string and a list of filesystem parameters is printed. (These data are also printed if the parameters appear to be inconsistent.) |
| debug | For the ext2fs filesystem, cause the kernel code to display the filesystem parameters when the filesystem is mounted. |
| errors=*value* | For the ext2fs filesystem, specify the error behavior: |
| continue | No special action is taken on errors (except marking the filesystem as erroneous). This is the default. |
| remount, ro | The filesystem is remounted read only, and subsequent writes are refused. |
| panic | When an error is detected, the system panics. |
| fat=*value* | For the msdos filesystem, specify either a 12-bit fat or a 16-bit fat. This overrides the automatic FAT type detection routine. Use with caution! |
| gid=*value* | For the msdos and hpfs filesystems, give every file a gid equal to *value*. |
| B grpid | Causes the ext2fs to use the BSD behavior when creating files: Files are created with the group ID of their parent directory. |
| map=*value* | For the iso9660 filesystem, specify mapping as off or normal. In general, non-Rock Ridge discs have all the filenames in uppercase, and all the filenames have a ;1 appended. The map option strips the ;1 and makes the name lowercase. (See also norock.) |
| nocheck | For the ext2fs, turns off checking (see check=none). |
| nogrpid | Causes the ext2fs to use the System V behavior when creating files. Files are created with the group ID of the creating process, unless the setgid bit is set on the parent directory. This is the default for all Linux filesystems. |

| | |
|---|---|
| norock | Normal iso9600 filenames appear in a 8.3 format (that is, DOS-like restrictions on filename length), and in addition, all characters are in uppercase. Also there is no field for file ownership, protection, number of links, provision for block/character devices, and so on. |
| | Rock Ridge is an extension to iso9660 that provides all of these UNIX-like features. Basically, there are extensions to each directory record that supply all of the additional information, and when Rock Ridge is in use, the filesystem is indistinguishable from a normal UNIX filesystem (except that it is read only, of course). |
| | The norock switch disables the use of Rock Ridge extensions, even if available. (See also map.) |
| quiet | For the msdos filesystem, turn on the quiet flag. Attempts to chown or chmod files do not yield errors, although they fail. Use with caution! |
| sb=*value* | For the ext2 filesystem, use an alternate superblock located at block *value*. *value* is numbered in 1024-byte blocks. An ext2 filesystem usually has backups of the superblock at blocks 1, 8193, 16385, and so on. |
| sysvgroups | See nogrpid. |
| uid=*value* | For the msdos and hpfs filesystems, give every file a uid equal to *value*. |
| umask=*value* | For the msdos and hpfs filesystems, give every file a umask of *value*. The radix defaults to octal. |

The full set of options applied is determined by first extracting the options for the filesystem from the fstab table, then applying any options specified by the -o argument, and finally applying the -r or -w option.

If the msdos filesystem detects an inconsistency, it reports an error and sets the filesystem to read only. The filesystem can be made writable again by remounting it.

| | |
|---|---|
| -r | The filesystem object is to be mounted read only. |
| -t *vfstype* | The argument following the -t is used to indicate the filesystem type. The filesystem types that are currently supported are listed in linux/fs/filesystems.c: minux, ext, ext2, xiafs, msdos, hpfs, proc, nfs, iso9660, sysv, xenix, coherent. Note that that last three are equivalent and that xenix and coherent will be removed at some point in the future; use sysv instead. |
| | The type minix is the default. If no -t option is given, or if the auto type is specified, the superblock is probed for the filesystem type (minix, ext, ext2, and xia are supported). If this probe fails and /proc/filesystems exists, then all the filesystems listed are tried, except for those labeled nodev (such as proc and nfs). |
| | Note that the auto type may be useful for user-mounted floppies. For example, the mount command mounts all filesystems except those of type msdos and ext: |
| | `mount -a -t nomsdos,ext` |
| -v | Verbose mode. |
| -w | The filesystem object is to be read and write. |
| -n | Mount without writing in /etc/mtab. |

umount removes the *special* device grafted at point *node* from the filesystem tree.

Options for the umount command:

| | |
|---|---|
| -a | All of the filesystems described in /etc/mtab are unmounted. |
| -t *vfstype* | Is used to indicate the actions should only be taken on filesystems of the specified type. More than one type may be specified in a comma-separated list. The list of filesystem types can be prefixed with no to specify the filesystem types on which no action should be taken. (See example for the mount command.) |

## FILES

| /etc/fstab | Filesystem table |
|---|---|
| /etc/mtab~ | Lock file |
| /etc/mtab.tmp | Temporary file |

## SEE ALSO

mount(2), umount(2), fstab(5), swapon(8)

## BUGS

It is possible for a corrupted filesystem to cause a crash.

Some Linux filesystems don't support -o synchronous (the ext2fs does support synchronous updates (a la BSD) when mounted with the sync option).

The -o remount may not be able to change mount parameters (all ext2fs parameters, except sb, are changeable with a remount, for example, but you can't change gid or umask for the dosfs).

## HISTORY

A mount command appeared in Version 6, AT&T UNIX.

## AUTHORS AND CONTRIBUTORS

The Linux mount command has a long and continuing history. The following major releases are noted with the name of the primary modifier:

0.97.3: Doug Quale (quale@saavik.cs.wisc.edu)

0.98.5: H.J. Lu (hlu@eecs.wsu.edu)

0.99.2: Rick Sladkey (jrs@world.std.com)

0.99.6: Rick Sladkey (jrs@world.std.com)

0.99.10: Stephen Tweedie (sct@dcs.ed.ac.uk)

0.99.14: Rick Sladkey (jrs@world.std.com)

(Filesystem-specific information added to man page on 27 November 1993 by Rik Faith with a lot of information and text from the following filesystem authors: Werner Almesberger, Eric Youngdale, and Remy Card.)

*Linux 1.1, 8 February 1995*

# mountd

mountd—NFS mount daemon.

## SYNOPSIS

```
/usr/etc/rpc.mountd [\-f\--exports-file\][\-dhnprv\]
[\--debug\][\--exports-file=file\] [\--help\]
[\--allow-non-root\][\--re-export\][\--version\]
```

## DESCRIPTION

The mountd program is an NFS mount daemon.

## OPTIONS

-f or --exports-file          This option specifies the exports file, listing the clients that this server is prepared to serve and parameters to apply to each such mount (see exports(5)). By default, exports are read from /etc/exports.

| -d or --debug | Log each transaction verbosely to the syslog. |
|---|---|
| -h or --help | Provide a short help summary. |
| -n or --allow-non-root | Allow incoming mount requests to be honored even if they do not originate from reserved IP ports. Some older NFS client implementations require this. Some newer NFS client implementations don't believe in reserved port checking. |
| -p or --promiscuous | Put the server into promiscuous mode where it will serve any host on the network. |
| -r or --re-export | Allow imported NFS filesystems to be exported. This can be used to turn a machine into an NFS multiplier. Caution should be used when reexporting loopback NFS mounts because reentering the mount point results in deadlock between the NFS client and the NFS server. |
| -v or --version | Report the current version number of the program. |

## SEE ALSO

exports(5), nfsd(8), ugidd(8C)

## BUGS

The current implementation (still) does not keep track of remote mounts.

*13 October 1993*

# named-xfer

named-xfer—Ancillary agent for inbound zone transfers.

## SYNOPSIS

named-xfer -z *zone_to_transfer* -f *db_file* -s *serial_no* [ -d *debuglevel* ]
[ -l *debug_log_file* ][ -t *trace_file* ][ -p *port#* ][ -S ] *nameserver*

## DESCRIPTION

named-xfer is an ancillary program executed by named(8) to perform an inbound zone transfer. It is rarely executed directly and only by system administrators who are trying to debug a zone transfer problem. See RFCs 1033, 1034, and 1035 for more information on the Internet name-domain system.

Options are

| -z | Specifies the name of the zone to be transferred. |
|---|---|
| -f | Specifies the name of the file into which the zone should be dumped when it is received from the primary server. |
| -s | Specifies the serial number of the current copy of this zone. If the SOA RR you get from the primary server does not have a serial number higher than this, the transfer is aborted. |
| -d | Print debugging information. A number after the d determines the level of messages printed. |
| -l | Specifies a log file for debugging messages. The default is system-dependent but is usually in /var/tmp or /usr/tmp. Note that this only applies if -d is also specified. |
| -t | Specifies a trace file that contains a protocol trace of the zone transfer. This is probably only of interest to people debugging the nameserver itself. |
| -p | Use a different port number. The default is the standard port number as returned by getservbyname(3) for service "domain". |
| -S | Perform a restricted transfer of only the SOA, NS records, and glue A records for the zone. The SOA record is not loaded by named but is used to determine when to verify the NS records. See the stubs directive in named(8) for more information. |

Additional arguments are taken as nameserver addresses in so-called "dotted-quad" syntax only; no hostnames are allowed here. At least one address must be specified. Any additional addresses are tried in order if the first one fails to transfer successfully.

## SEE ALSO

named(8), resolver(3), resolver(5), hostname(7), RFC 882, RFC 883, RFC 973, RFC 974, RFC 1033, RFC 1034, RFC 1035, RFC 1123, *Name Server Operations Guide for BIND*

*26 June 1993*

# named

named—Internet domain nameserver.

## SYNOPSIS

```
named [ -d debuglevel ][-p port#[/localport#]][{-b} bootfile ][-q ][-r ]
```

## DESCRIPTION

named is the Internet domain nameserver. See RFCs 1033, 1034, and 1035 for more information on the Internet name-domain system. Without any arguments, named reads the default boot file /etc/named.boot, reads any initial data, and listens for queries.

Options are

| | |
|---|---|
| -d | Print debugging information. A number after the d determines the level of messages printed. |
| -p | Use nonstandard port numbers. The default is the standard port number as returned by getservbyname(3) for service "domain". The argument can specify two port numbers separated by a slash (/), in which case the first port is that used when contacting remote servers and the second one is the service port bound by the local instance of named. This is used mostly for debugging purposes. |
| -b | Use an alternate boot file. This is optional and allows you to specify a file with a leading dash. |
| -q | Trace all incoming queries if named has been compiled with QRYLOG defined. Note that this option is deprecated in favor of the boot file directive options query-log. |
| -r | Turns recursion off in the server. Answers can come only from local (primary or secondary) zones. This can be used on root servers. Note that this option is deprecated in favor of the boot file directive options no-recursion. |

Any additional argument is taken as the name of the boot file. If multiple boot files are specified, only the last is used.

The boot file contains information about where the nameserver is to get its initial data. Lines in the boot file cannot be continued on subsequent lines. The following is a small example:

```
;
; boot file for name server
;
directory /usr/local/adm/named
; type domain source host/file backup file
cache . root.cache
primary Berkeley.EDU berkeley.edu.zone
primary 32.128.IN-ADDR.ARPA ucbhosts.rev
secondary CC.Berkeley.EDU 128.32.137.8 128.32.137.3 cc.zone.bak
secondary 6.32.128.IN-ADDR.ARPA 128.32.137.8 128.32.137.3 cc.rev.bak
primary 0.0.127.IN-ADDR.ARPA localhost.rev
```

```
forwarders 10.0.0.78 10.2.0.78
limit transfers-in 10
limit datasize 64M
options forward-only query-log fake-iquery
```

The `directory` line causes the server to change its working directory to the directory specified. This can be important for the correct processing of $INCLUDE files in primary zone files.

The `cache` line specifies that data in `root.cache` is to be placed in the backup cache.

Its main use is to specify data such as locations of root domain servers. This cache is not used during normal operation, but is used as "hints" to find the current root servers. The file `root.cache` is in the same format as `berkeley.edu.zone`. There can be more than one cache file specified. The `root.cache` file should be retrieved periodically from `FTP.RS.INTERNIC.NET` because it contains a list of root servers, and this list changes periodically.

The first sample `primary` line states that the file `berkeley.edu.zone` contains authoritative data for the `Berkeley.EDU` zone. The file `berkeley.edu.zone` contains data in the master file format described in RFC 883. All domain names are relative to the origin, in this case, `Berkeley.EDU` (see below for a more detailed description). The second `primary` line states that the file `ucbhosts.rev` contains authoritative data for the domain `32.128.IN-ADDR.ARPA`, which is used to translate addresses in network 128.32 to hostnames. Each master file should begin with an SOA record for the zone (see below).

The first sample `secondary` line specifies that all authoritative data under `CC.Berkeley.EDU` is to be transferred from the nameserver at `128.32.137.8`. If the transfer fails, it tries `128.32.137.3` and continues trying the addresses, up to ten, listed on this line. The secondary copy is also authoritative for the specified domain. The first non-dotted-quad address on this line is taken as a filename in which to back up the transferred zone. The nameserver loads the zone from this backup file if it exists when it boots, providing a complete copy even if the master servers are unreachable. Whenever a new copy of the domain is received by automatic zone transfer from one of the master servers, this file is updated. If no filename is given, a temporary file is used and deleted after each successful zone transfer. This is not recommended because it is a needless waste of bandwidth. The second sample `secondary` line states that the address-to-hostname mapping for the subnet `128.32.136` should be obtained from the same list of master servers as the previous zone.

The `forwarders` line specifies the addresses of sitewide servers that will accept recursive queries from other servers. If the boot file specifies one or more forwarders, then the server sends all queries for data not in the cache to the forwarders first. Each forwarder is asked in turn until an answer is returned or the list is exhausted. If no answer is forthcoming from a forwarder, the server continues as it would have without the `forwarders` line unless it is in `forward-only` mode. The forwarding facility is useful to cause a large sitewide cache to be generated on a master and to reduce traffic over links to outside servers. It can also be used to allow servers to run that do not have direct access to the Internet but want to look up exterior names anyway.

The `slave` line (deprecated) is allowed for backward compatibility. Its meaning is identical to `options forward-only`.

The `sortlist` line can be used to indicate networks that are to be preferred over other networks. Queries for host addresses from hosts on the same network as the server receive responses with local network addresses listed first, then addresses on the sort list, and then other addresses.

The `xfrnets` directive (not shown) can be used to implement primitive access control. If this directive is given, your nameserver only answers zone transfer requests from hosts that are on networks listed in your `xfrnets` directives. This directive may also be given as `tcplist` for compatibility with older, interim servers.

The `include` directive (not shown) can be used to process the contents of some other file as though they appeared in place of the `include` directive. This is useful if you have a lot of zones or if you have logical groupings of zones that are maintained by different people. The `include` directive takes one argument, the name of the file whose contents are to be included. No quotes are necessary around the filename.

The `bogusns` directive (not shown) tells BIND that no queries are to be sent to the specified nameserver addresses (which are specified as dotted quads, not as domain names). This is useful when you know that some popular server has bad data in a zone or cache, and you want to avoid contamination while the problem is being fixed.

The `limit` directive can be used to change BIND's internal limits, some of which (`datasize`, for example) are implemented by the system and others (such as `transfers-in`) by BIND itself. The number following the limit name can be scaled by postfixing a k, m, or g for kilobytes, megabytes, and gigabytes respectively. datasize's argument sets the process data size enforced by the kernel. Note that not all systems provide a call to implement this; on such systems, the use of the datasize parameter of limit results in a warning message. transfers-in's argument is the number of named-xfer subprocesses that BIND will spawn at any one time. transfers-per-ns's argument is the maximum number of zone transfers to be simultaneously initiated to any given remote nameserver.

The options directive introduces a Boolean specifier that changes the behavior of BIND. More than one option can be specified in a single directive. The currently defined options are as follows: no-recursion, which causes BIND to answer with a referral rather than actual data whenever it receives a query for a name it is not authoritative for. Don't set this on a server that is listed in any host's resolv.conf file. no-fetch-glue keeps BIND from fetching missing glue when constructing the "additional data" section of a response; this can be used in conjunction with no-recursion to prevent BIND's cache from ever growing in size or becoming corrupted. query-log causes all queries to be logged via syslog(3). This is a lot of data; don't turn it on lightly. forward-only causes the server to query only its forwarders. This option is usually used on a machine that wants to run a server but for physical or administrative reasons cannot be given access to the Internet. fake-iquery tells BIND to send back a useless and bogus reply to "inverse queries" rather than respond with an error. This is helpful if you have a lot of microcomputers or SunOS hosts or both.

The max-fetch directive (not shown) is allowed for backward compatibility; its meaning is identical to limit transfers-in.

The master file consists of control information and a list of resource records for objects in the zone of the forms:

```
$INCLUDE <filename><opt_domain>
$ORIGIN <domain>
<domain><opt_ttl> <opt_class><type><resource_record_data>
```

domain is . for root, @ for the current origin, or a standard domain name. If domain is a standard domain name that does not end with ., the current origin is appended to the domain. Domain names ending with . are unmodified. The opt_domain field is used to define an origin for the data in an included file. It is equivalent to placing a $ORIGIN statement before the first line of the included file. The field is optional. Neither the opt_domain field nor $ORIGIN statements in the included file modify the current origin for this file. The opt_ttl field is an optional integer number for the time-to-live field. It defaults to 0, meaning the minimum value specified in the SOA record for the zone. The opt_class field is the object address type; currently only one type is supported, IN, for objects connected to the DARPA Internet. The type field contains one of the following tokens; the data expected in the resource_record_data field is in parentheses:

| | |
|---|---|
| A | A host address (dotted quad). |
| NS | An authoritative nameserver (domain). |
| MX | A mail exchanger (domain), preceded by a preference value (0..32767) with lower numeric values representing higher logical preferences. |
| CNAME | The canonical name for an alias (domain). |
| SOA | Marks the start of a zone of authority (domain of originating host, domain address of maintainer, a serial number and the following parameters in seconds: refresh, retry, expire, and minimum TTL (see RFC 883)). |
| NULL | A null resource record (no format or data). |
| RP | A responsible person for some domain name (mailbox, TXT-referral). |
| PTR | A domain name pointer (domain). |
| HINFO | Host information (cpu_type, OS_type). |

Resource records usually end at the end of a line but may be continued across lines between opening and closing parentheses. Comments are introduced by semicolons and continue to the end of the line.

Note that there are other resource record types, not shown here. You should consult the BIND Operations GUIDe (BOG) for the complete list. Some resource record types may have been standardized in newer RFCs but not yet implemented in this version of BIND.

Each master zone file should begin with an SOA record for the zone. A sample SOA record follows:

```
@ IN SOA ucbvax.Berkeley.EDU. rwh.ucbvax.Berkeley.EDU. (
1989020501 ; serial
10800 ; refresh
3600 ; retry
3600000 ; expire
86400 ) ; minimum
```

The SOA specifies a serial number, which should be changed each time the master file is changed. Note that the serial number can be given as a dotted number, but this is a very unwise thing to do because the translation to normal integers is via concatenation rather than multiplication and addition. You can spell out the year, month, day of month, and 0..99 version number and still fit inside the unsigned 32-bit size of this field. It's true that we will have to rethink this strategy in the year 4294, but we're not worried about it. Secondary servers check the serial number at intervals specified by the refresh time in seconds; if the serial number changes, a zone transfer is done to load the new data. If a master server cannot be contacted when a refresh is due, the retry time specifies the interval at which refreshes should be attempted. If a master server cannot be contacted within the interval given by the expire time, all data from the zone is discarded by secondary servers. The minimum value is the time-to-live (TTL) used by records in the file with no explicit time-to-live value.

## NOTES

The boot file directives domain and suffixes have been obsoleted by a more useful resolver-based implementation of suffixing for partially qualified domain names. The prior mechanisms could fail under a number of situations, especially when then local nameserver did not have complete information.

The following signals have the specified effect when sent to the server process using the kill(1) command:

| | |
|---|---|
| SIGHUP | Causes server to read named.boot and reload the database. If the server is built with the FORCED RELOAD compile-time option, then SIGHUP also causes the server to check the serial number on all secondary zones. Usually, the serial numbers are only checked at the SOA-specified intervals. |
| SIGINT | Dumps the current database and cache to /var/tmp/named_dump.db. |
| SIGIOT | Dumps statistics data into /var/tmp/named.stats if the server is compiled with -DSTATS. Statistics data is appended to the file. Some systems use SIGABRT rather than SIGIOT for this. |
| SIGSYS | Dumps the profiling data in /var/tmp if the server is compiled with profiling (the server forks, changes directories, and exits). |
| SIGTERM | Dumps the primary and secondary database files. Used to save modified data on shutdown if the server is compiled with dynamic updating enabled. |
| SIGUSR1 | Turns on debugging; each SIGUSR1 increments debug level (SIGEMT on older systems without SIGUSR1). |
| SIGUSR2 | Turns off debugging completely (SIGFPE on older systems without SIGUSR2). |
| SIGWINCH | Toggles logging of all incoming queries via syslog(3) (requires server to have been built with the QRYLOG option). |

## FILES

| | |
|---|---|
| /etc/named.boot | Nameserver configuration boot file |
| /etc/named.pid | The process ID (on older systems) |
| /var/run/named.pid | The process ID (on newer systems) |
| /var/tmp/named_dump.db | Dump of the nameserver database |
| /var/tmp/named.run | Debug output |
| /var/tmp/named.stats | Nameserver statistics data |

## SEE ALSO

kill(1), gethostbyname(3), signal(2), resolver(3), resolver(5), hostname(7), RFC 882, RFC 883, RFC 973, RFC 974, RFC 1033, RFC 1034, RFC 1035, RFC 1123, *Name Server Operations GUIDe for BIND*

*20 June 1995*

# named.reload

named.reload—Cause the nameserver to synchronize its database.

## DESCRIPTION

This command sends a SIGHUP to the running nameserver. This signal is documented in named(8).

## BUGS

It does not check to see if the nameserver is actually running and could use a stale pid cache file, which may result in the death of an unrelated process.

## SEE ALSO

named(8), named.restart(8)

*26 June 1993*

# named.restart

named.restart—Stop and restart the nameserver.

## DESCRIPTION

This command sends a SIGKILL to the running nameserver and then starts a new one.

## BUGS

It does not check to see if the nameserver is actually running and could use a stale pid cache file, which may result in the death of an unrelated process.

It does not wait after killing the old server before starting a new one. Because the server could take some time to die and the new one experiences a fatal error if the old one isn't gone by the time it starts, you can be left in a situation where you have no nameserver at all.

## SEE ALSO

named(8), named.reload(8)

*26 June 1993*

# ndc

ndc—Name daemon control interface.

## SYNOPSIS

ndc *directive* [ ... ]

## DESCRIPTION

This command allows the nameserver administrator to send various signals to the nameserver or to restart it. Zero or more directives may be given from the following list:

| | |
|---|---|
| status | Displays the current status of named as shown by ps(1). |
| dumpdb | Causes named to dump its database and cache to /var/tmp/named_dump.db (uses the INT signal.) |
| reload | Causes named to check the serial numbers of all primary and secondary zones and to reload those that have changed (uses the HUP signal.) |
| stats | Causes named to dump its statistics to /var/tmp/named.stats (uses the IOT or ABRT signal.) |
| trace | Causes named to increment its "tracing level" by one. Whenever the tracing level is nonzero, trace information is written to /var/tmp/named.run. Higher tracing levels result in more detailed information (uses the USR1 signal). |
| notrace | Causes named to set its "tracing level" to zero, closing /var/tmp/named.run if it is open (uses the USR2 signal). |
| querylog | Causes named to toggle the "query logging" feature, which results in a syslog(3) of each incoming query (uses the WINCH signal). Note that query logging consumes quite a lot of log file space. This directive may also be given as qrylog. |
| start | Causes named to be started as long as it isn't already running. |
| stop | Causes named to be stopped if it is running. |
| restart | Causes named to be killed and restarted. |

## BUGS

Arguments to named are not preserved by restart or known by start. Some mechanism for controlling the parameters and environment should exist.

Implemented as a sh(1) script.

## AUTHOR

Paul Vixie (Internet Software Consortium)

## SEE ALSO

named(8), namcd.reload(8), named.restart(8)

*27 November 1994*

# netstat

netstat—Display active network connections

## SYNOPSIS

```
netstat [[-a ¦ [-t ¦ -u ¦ -w]] [-n ¦ -o] ¦ -x] [-c]
netstat -r [-c] [-n]
netstat -v
```

## DESCRIPTION

netstat displays the status of network connections on either TCP, UDP, or RAW sockets to the system. By default, netstat only displays status on those TCP sockets that are not in the LISTEN state (that is, connections to active processes). To obtain information about the kernel routing table, netstat may be invoked with the option -r. A listing of internal UNIX connections can be obtained by invoking netstat with the option -x.

netstat's display includes the following information for each socket:

| | |
|---|---|
| Proto | The protocol (either TCP or UDP) used by the socket. |
| Recv-Q | The count of bytes not copied by the user program connected to this socket. |
| Send-Q | The count of bytes not acknowledged by the remote host. |
| Local Address | The local address (local hostname) and port number of the socket. Unless the -n switch is given, the socket address is resolved to its canonical hostname, and the port number is translated into the corresponding service name. |
| Foreign Address | The remote address (remote hostname) and port number of the socket. As with the local address:port, the -n switch turns off hostname and service name resolution. |
| (State) | The state of the socket. Because there are no states in RAW and usually no states used in UDP, this row may be left blank. Usually, this can be one of several values: |
| ESTABLISHED | The socket has an established connection. |
| SYN SENT | The socket is actively attempting to establish a connection. |
| SYN RECV | The connection is being initialized. |
| FIN WAIT1 | The socket is closed, and the connection is shutting down. |
| FIN WAIT2 | Connection is closed, and the socket is waiting for a shutdown from the remote end. |
| TIME WAIT | The socket is waiting after close for remote shutdown re-transmission. |
| CLOSED | The socket is not being used. |
| CLOSE WAIT | The remote end has shut down, waiting for the socket to close. |
| LAST ACK | The remote end shut down, and the socket is closed. Waiting for acknowledgment. |
| LISTEN | The socket is listening for incoming connections. |
| UNKNOWN | The state of the socket is unknown. |

If netstat is invoked with the option -o, additional information is displayed after the state info. This information is shown like this: keyword (time/backoff) and an optional asterisk. The keyword shows the state of the timer belonging to the socket, the time displayed (in seconds) is how long it will take the timer to expire, the backoff value indicates the current retry count for data transmission, and the asterisk indicates that this timer is in the expiration queue. The latter might be removed in future but is helpful for debugging the TCP-Code for now.

Invoked with the option -x, netstat displays a list of all active UNIX internal communication sockets.

netstat's display includes the following information for each socket:

| | |
|---|---|
| Proto | The protocol (usually UNIX) used by the socket. |
| RefCnt | The reference count (attached processes via this socket). |
| Flags | The only known flag to me is SO ACCEPTON (displayed as ACC); otherwise, left blank. SO ACCEPTON is used on unconnected sockets if their corresponding processes are waiting for a connect request. |
| Type | There are several types of socket access: |
| SOCK DGRAM | The socket is used in Datagram (connectionless) mode. |
| SOCK STREAM | This is a stream (connection) socket. |
| SOCK RAW | The socket is used as a raw socket. |
| SOCK RDM | This one serves reliably delivered messages. |
| SOCK SEQPACKET | This is a sequential packet socket. |
| SOCK PACKET | This socket type is used as a Linux-specific way to get packets at the dev (kernel) level. It is assumed to be used to write things such as RARP (Reverse Address Resolution Protocol) and similar things on the user level. |
| UNKNOWN | Who ever knows, what future will bring; just fill in here. :-) |
| State | This field will contain one of the following keywords: |
| FREE | The socket is not allocated. |

| | |
|---|---|
| LISTENING | The socket is listening for a connection request. |
| UNCONNECTED | The socket is not connected to another one. |
| CONNECTING | The socket is about to establish a connection. |
| CONNECTED | The socket is connected. |
| DISCONNECTING | The socket is disconnecting. |
| UNKNOWN | This state should never happen. |
| Path | This displays the pathname that the corresponding processes attached to the socket. |

The network routing table (invoked with netstat -r) shows up the following information:

| | |
|---|---|
| Destination net/address | The destination address of a resolved host or hand-entered network is displayed. Unless the option -n is given, the hosts or nets are resolved. An entry named default shows up the default route for the kernel. |
| Gateway address | If there is no asterisk (*) displayed, any data is routed to the dedicated gateway. |
| Flags | Possible routing flags are |

| | |
|---|---|
| U | This route is usable. |
| G | Destination is a gateway. |
| H | Destination is a host entry. |
| N | Destination is a Net entry. |
| R | Route will be reinstated after timeout. |
| D | This one is created dynamically (by redirection). |
| M | This one is modified dynamically (by redirection). |

| | |
|---|---|
| RefCnt | Reference count for this route. |
| Use | How many times this route was used yet. |
| Iface | This is the name of the interface where this route belongs. |

## OPTIONS

| | |
|---|---|
| -a | Display information about all Internet sockets, such as TCP, UDP, and RAW, including those sockets that are listening only. |
| -c | Generate a continuous listing of network status: network status is displayed every second until the program is interrupted. |
| -n | Causes netstat not to resolve hostnames and service names when displaying remote and local address and port information. |
| -o | Display timer states, expiration times, and backoff state. |
| -r | Display kernel routing table. |
| -t | Display information about TCP sockets only, including those that are listening. |
| -u | Display information about UDP sockets only. |
| -v | Print version information. |
| -w | Display information about raw sockets. |
| -x | Display information about UNIX domain sockets. |

## FILES

| | |
|---|---|
| /proc/net/tcp | TCP socket information |
| /proc/net/udp | UDP socket information |
| /proc/net/raw | RAW socket information |
| /proc/net/unix | UNIX domain socket information |

| | |
|---|---|
| `/proc/net/route` | Kernel routing information |
| `/etc/services` | The services translation |

## BUGS

None reported yet (5/20/93).

## AUTHORS

The `netstat` user interface was written by Fred Baumgarten (`dc6iq@insu1.etec.uni-karlsruhe.de`). The man page is basically by Matt Welsh (`mdw@tc.cornell.edu`).

*Cohesive Systems, 20 May 1993*

# makeactive, makehistory, newsrequeue

makeactive, makehistory, newsrequeue—Tools to recover Usenet databases

## SYNOPSIS

```
makeactive [ -m ][-o ]
makehistory [ -b ][-f filename ][-i ][-n ][-o ][-r ][-s size ]
[-T tmpdir ][-u [ -v]]
newsrequeue [ -a active ][-h history ][-d days ][-l ][-n newsfeeds ][input ]
```

## DESCRIPTION

makeactive invokes find(1) to get a list of all directories in the news spool tree, /news/spool. It discards directories named lost+found as well as those that have a period in them. It scans all other directories for all-numeric filenames and determines the highest and lowest number. The program's output is a set of active(5) file lines. Because there is no way to know if a group is moderated or disabled, the fourth field of all entries is y. Also, mid-level directories that aren't newsgroups are also created as newsgroups with no entries. (For example, there is a comp.sources.unix group, but no comp.sources.)

If the -o flag is used, makeactive reads an existing active file for the list of group names and just renumber all groups. It preserves the fourth field of the active file if one is present. This is analogous to the ctlinnd(8) renumber command, except that innd(8) should be throttled or not running. Do not use this flag with output redirected to the standard active file!

If the -m flag is given, then makeactive attempts to adjust the highest and lowest article numbers wherever possible. If articles are found in a newsgroup, the numbers reflect what was found. If no articles are found in a newsgroup, the high number from the old file is kept, and the low number is set to one more than the high number. This flag may only be used if the -o flag is used.

makeactive exits with nonzero status if any problems occur. A typical way to use the program is with the following /bin/sh commands:

```
ctlinnd throttle "Rebuilding active file"
TEMP=${TMPDIR-/tmp}/act$$
if [ -f /var/lib/news/active ] ; then
    if makeactive -o >${TEMP} ; then
        mv ${TEMP} /var/lib/news/active
    fi
else
    if makeactive >${TEMP} ; then
        # Edit to restore moderated
        # and aliased groups.
        ...
        mv ${TEMP} /var/lib/news/active
    fi
fi
ctlinnd reload active "New active file"
```

makehistory rebuilds the history(5) text file and the associated dbz(3) database. The default name of the text file is /news/lib/history; to specify a different name, use the -f flag. makehistory scans the active(5) file to determine which newsgroup directories within the spool directory, /news/spool, should be scanned. (If a group is removed, but its spool directory still exists, makehistory ignores it.) The program reads each file found and writes a history line for it. If the -b flag is used, then makehistory removes any articles that do not have valid Message-ID headers in them.

After the text file is written, makehistory builds the dbz database. If the -f flag is used, then the database files are named file.dir and file.pag. If the -f flag is not used, then a temporary link to the name history.n is made and the database files are written as history.n.pag and history.n.dir. If the -o flag is used, then the link is not made and any existing history files are overwritten. If the old database exists, makehistory uses it to determine the size of the new database. To ignore the old database, use the -i flag. Using the -o flag implies the -i flag. The program also ignores any old database if the -s flag is used to specify the approximate number of entries in the new database. Accurately specifying the size is an optimization that creates a more efficient database. (The size should be the estimated eventual size of the file, typically the size of the old file.) For more information, see the discussion of dbzfresh and dbzsize in dbz(3).

If the -u flag is given, then makehistory assumes that innd is running. It pauses the server while scanning and then sends addhist commands (see ctlinnd(8)) to the server for any article that is not found in the dbz database. The command makehistory -bu is useful after a system crash to delete any mangled articles and bring the article database back into a more consistent state. If the -v flag is used with the -u flag, then makehistory puts a copy of all added lines on its standard output.

To scan the spool directory without rebuilding the dbz files, use the -n flag. If used with -u, the server is not paused while scanning. To just build the dbz files from an existing text file, use the -r flag. The -i or -s flags can be useful if there are no valid dbz files to use. A typical way to use this program is with the following /bin/sh commands:

```
ctlinnd throttle "Rebuilding history file"
cd /news/lib
if makehistory -n -f history.n ; then
:
else
echo Error creating history file!
exit 1
fi
# The following line can be used to retain expired history.
# It is not necessary for the history file to be sorted.
# awk 'NF==2 { print; }' <history >>history.n
# View history file for mistakes.
if makehistory -r -s 'wc -l <history' -f history.n; then
mv history.n history
mv history.n.dir history.dir
mv history.n.pag history.pag
fi
ctlinnd go "
```

makehistory needs to create a temporary file that contains one line for each article it finds, which can become very large. This file is created in the /tmp directory. The TMPDIR environment variable may be used to specify a different directory. Alternatively, the -T flag may be used to specify a temporary directory. In addition, the sort(1) that is invoked during the build writes large temporary files (often to /var/tmp, but see your system man pages). If the -T flag is used, then the flag and its value are passed to sort. On most systems, this changes the temporary directory that sort uses. If used, this flag and its value are passed on to the sort(1) command that is invoked during the build.

makehistory does not handle symbolic links. If the news spool area is split across multiple partitions, the following commands should probably be run before the database is regenerated:

```
cd /news/spool
find . -type l -name '[1-9]*' -print ¦ xargs -t rm
```

Make sure to run the command on all the appropriate partitions!

newsrequeue can be used to rewrite batchfiles after a system crash. It operates in two modes. In the first mode, it first reads the *active* and *newsfeeds*(5) files to determine where the different newsgroups are to be distributed. To specify alternate locations for these files, use the -a or -n flags. It then opens the *history* database. To specify a different file, use the -h flag.

Once the files are opened, newsrequeue reads from the specified *input* file or standard input if no file is specified. Each line should have a single Message-ID, surrounded in angle brackets; any other text on the line is ignored. For example, the *history* file (or a trailing subset of it) is acceptable input to the program operating in this mode. If the -d flag is used, then only articles that were received within the specified number of days are processed.

newsrequeue uses the first two fields of the newsfeed entry—the sitename and the excludes field and the patterns and distribs field. It ignores all flags in the third field except for the N field and also ignores the fourth field altogether.

The second mode is used if the -l flag is used. In this mode, it reads from the specified *input* file or standard input if no file is specified. Each line should look like an innd log entry. It parses entries for accepted articles, looks up the Message-ID in the history database to get the filename, and then scans the list of sites.

In either mode, the output of newsrequeue consists of one line for each article that should be forwarded. Each such line contains the Message-ID, the filename, and the list of sites that should receive the article. The output is suitable for piping into filechan(8).

## HISTORY

Written by Rich $alz (rsalz@uunet.uu.net) for InterNetNews.

## SEE ALSO

active(5), ctlinnd(8), dbz(3), filechan(8), history(5), innd(8), newsfeeds(5)

# news.daily

news.daily—Do regular Usenet system administration

## SYNOPSIS

```
news.daily [ keyword... ]
innwatch [ -t sleeptime ][ -f controlfile ][ -l logfile ]
expirerm file
inncheck [ -v ][ -pedantic ][ -perms [ -fix ]][ -noperms ][ file... ]
```

## DESCRIPTION

news.daily performs a number of important Usenet administrative functions. This includes producing a status report, removing old news articles, processing log files, rotating the archived log files, renumbering the active file, removing any old socket files found in the firewall directory, and collecting the output. This program should be run under the news administrator's ID, not as root.

By default, news.daily performs all its functions and mails the output to the news administrator, usenet. By specifying keywords on the command line, it is possible to modify the functions performed, as well as change the arguments given to expire(8) and expireover(8).

news.daily should be run once a day, typically out of cron(8). It may be run more often, but such invocations should at least use the norotate keyword to prevent the log files from being processed and rotated too fast.

The shlock(1) program is used to prevent simultaneous executions.

The following keywords may be used:

delayrm                              This uses the -z flag when invoking expire and expireover. The names of articles to be removed are written to a temporary file and then removed after expiration by calling expirerm.

| | |
|---|---|
| nostat | This keyword disables the status report generated by innstat (see newslog(8)). Without this keyword, the status report is the first function performed, just prior to obtaining the news.daily lock. |
| noexpire | By default, expire is invoked to remove old news articles. Using this keyword disables this function. |
| noexplog | expire usually appends information to /var/log/news/expire.log (see newslog(5)). Using this keyword causes the expire output to be handled as part of news.daily's output. It has no effect if the noexpire keyword is used. |
| flags='expire\args' | By default, expire is invoked with the an argument of -v1. Using this keyword changes the arguments to those specified. Be careful to use quotes if multiple arguments are needed. This keyword has no effect if the noexpire keyword is used. |
| nologs | After expiration, scanlogs(8) is invoked to process the log files. Using this keyword disables all log processing functions. |
| norotate | By default, log processing includes rotating and cleaning out log files. Using this keyword disables the rotating and cleaning aspect of the log processing. The log files are only scanned for information and no contents are altered. This keyword has no effect if the nologs keyword is used. |
| norenumber | This keyword disables the ctlinnd(8) renumber operation. Usually, the low watermark for all newsgroups (see active(5)) is reset. |
| norm | By default, any socket ctlinnd socket that has not been modified for two days is removed. Using this keyword disables this function. |
| nomail | news.daily usually sends a mail message containing the results to the administrator. Using this keyword causes this message to be sent to stdout and stderr instead. Usually, all utilities invoked by the script have their stdout and stderr redirected into a file. If the file is empty, no message is sent. |
| expireover | The expireover program is called after expiration to purge the overview databases. |
| expireoverflags='expireovernargs' | If the expireover keyword is used, this keyword may be used to specify the flags to be passed to expireover. If the delayrm keyword is used, then the default value is -z and the list of deleted files; otherwise, the default value is -s. |
| /full/path | The program specified by the given path is executed just before any expiration is done. A typical use is to specify an alternate expiration program and use the noexpire keyword. Multiple programs may be specified; they are invoked in order. |

The norotate keyword is passed on to scanlogs if it is invoked. expirerm is a script that removes a list of files. The specified file lists the files. It is sorted and then fed into a pipeline responsible for doing the removal, usually fastrm(8). If there seemed to be a problem removing the files, then mail is sent to the news administrator. If there were no problems, then file is renamed to /var/log/news/expire.list where it is kept (for safety) until the next day's expiration.

innwatch is a script that can be started at news boot time. It periodically—every *sleeptime* seconds— examines the load average and the number of free blocks and inodes on the spool partition, as described by its control file, innwatch.ctl(5). If the load gets too high or the disk gets too full, it throttles the server. When the condition restores, it unblocks the server. In addition, on each pass through the loop, it checks the specified log file to see if it has been modified and sends mail to the news administrator if so. It is usually a good idea to set this to the syslog(3) file that receives critical news messages. Upon receipt of an interrupt signal, innwatch reports its status in the file /news/lib/innwatch.status.

inncheck is a perl(1) script that verifies the syntax and permissions of all InterNetNews configuration files. If no files are specified, it checks all files. A filename may be followed by an equal sign and a path to indicate the pathname to use for the file. For example, newsfeeds=/tmp/nf checks the syntax of a new newsfeeds(5) without requiring it to be installed. If the -v flag is used, it prints status information as it checks each file. If the -pedantic flag is used, it checks the files for omissions that are not strictly errors but might indicate a configuration error.

If any file is specified, only the permissions on those files are checked. The -noperms flag suppresses this check. If the -perms flag is used, the script verifies the ownership and permissions of all files. The -fix flag can also be used so that the output can be executed as a shell script.

## HISTORY

news.daily and this manual page were written by Landon Curt Noll (chongo@toad.com) and Rich $alz (rsalz@uunet.uu.net).

inncheck was written by Brendan Kehoe (brendan@cs.widener.edu) and Rich.

innwatch was written by Mike Cooper (mcooper@usc.edu) and (kre@munnari.oz.au).

## SEE ALSO

active(5), ctlinnd(8), expire(8), fastrm(8), newslog(5), newslog(8), innwatch.ctl(5), shlock(1)

# newslog

newslog—Maintenance of Usenet log files

## SYNOPSIS

```
scanlogs [ norotate ][nonn ]
writelog name text...
innstat
tally.unwanted
tally.control
innlog.awk
```

## DESCRIPTION

scanlogs summarizes the information recorded in the INN log files (see newslog(5)). By default, it also rotates and cleans out the logs. It is usually invoked by the news.daily(8) script.

The following keywords are accepted:

| | |
|---|---|
| norotate | Using this keyword disables the rotating and cleaning aspect of the log processing: The logs files are only scanned for information and no contents are altered. |
| nonn | Usually, the nn log file is scanned and rotated. Using this keyword disables this function. |

If scanlogs is invoked more than once a day, the norotate keyword should be used to prevent premature log cleaning.

The writelog script is used to write a log entry or send it as mail. The name parameter specifies the name of the log file where the entry should be written. If it is the word mail, then the entry is mailed to the news administrator, Usenet. The data that is written or sent consists of the text given on the command line, followed by standard input indented by four spaces. shlock(1) is used to avoid simultaneous updates to a single log file.

The innstat script prints a snapshot of the INN system. It displays the operating mode of the server, as well as disk usage and the status of all log and lock files.

The rest of the scripts described here are usually invoked by scanlogs. They parse log files that are described in newslog(5) and the server's article log file described in innd(8).

tally.unwanted script parses the article log file to update the cumulative list of articles posted to unwanted newsgroups, unwanted.log.

tally.control reads its standard input, which should be the newgroup.log and rmgroup.log log files. It updates the cumulative list of newsgroup creations and deletions, control.log.

innlog.awk is an awk(1) script that summarizes the activity that innd and nnrpd(8) report to syslog.

## HISTORY

Written by Landon Curt Noll (chongo@toad.com) and Rich $alz (rsalz@uunet.uu.net) for InterNetNews.

## SEE ALSO

innd(8) newslog(5), news.daily(8), nnrpd(8)

# nfsd

nfsd—NFS service daemon.

## SYNOPSIS

/usr/etc/rpc.nfsd [\-f\exports-file\][\-dhnprv\]
[\--debug\][\--exports-file=*file*\] [\--help\]
[\--allow-non-root\][\--re-export\][\--version\]

## DESCRIPTION

The nfsd program is an NFS service daemon that handles client filesystem requests. Unlike nfsd on some other systems, nfsd operates as a normal user-level process. The server also differs from other NFS server implementations in that it mounts an entire file hierarchy not limited by the boundaries of physical filesystems. The implementation allows the clients read-only or read-write access to the file hierarchy of the server machine.

The mountd program starts an ancillary user-level mount daemon.

## OPTIONS

| | |
|---|---|
| -f or --exports-file | This option specifies the exports file, listing the clients that this server is prepared to serve and parameters to apply to each such mount (see exports(5)). By default, exports are read from /etc/exports. |
| -d or --debug | Log each transaction verbosely to the syslog. |
| -h or --help | Provide a short help summary. |
| -n or --allow-non-root | Allow incoming NFS requests to be honored even if they do not originate from reserved IP ports. Some older NFS client implementations require this. Some newer NFS client implementations don't believe in reserved port checking. |
| -p or --promiscuous | Put the server into promiscuous mode where it serves any host on the network. |
| -r or --re-export | Allow imported NFS filesystems to be exported. This can be used to turn a machine into an NFS multiplier. Caution should be used when re-exporting loopback NFS mounts because re-entering the mount point results in deadlock between the NFS client and the NFS server. |
| -v or --version | Report the current version number of the program. |

## SEE ALSO

exports(5), mountd(8), ugidd(8C)

## AUTHORS

Mark Shand wrote the original unfsd. Don Becker extended unfsd to support authentication and allow read-write access and called it hnfs. Rick Sladkey added host matching, showmount -e support, mountd authentication, inetd support, and all the portability and configuration code.

*13 October 1993*

# nnrpd

nnrpd—NNTP server for on-campus hosts.

## SYNOPSIS

nnrpd [ -r *reason* ][-s *title padding* ][-S *host* ][-t ]

## DESCRIPTION

nnrpd is an NNTP server for newsreaders. It accepts commands on its standard input and responds on its standard output. It is usually invoked by innd(8) with those descriptors attached to a remote client connection.

If the -r flag is used, then nnrpd rejects the incoming connection giving reason as the text. This flag is used by innd when it is paused or throttled.

Unlike innd, nnrpd supports all NNTP commands for user-oriented reading and posting.

nnrpd uses the nnrp.access(5) file to control who is authorized to access the Usenet database. It also rejects connections if the load average is greater than 16.

As each command is received, nnrpd tries to change its argv array so that ps(1) prints the command being executed. To get a full display, the -s flag may be used with a long string as its argument, which is overwritten when the program changes its title.

On exit, nnrpd reports usage statistics through syslog(3).

If the -t flag is used, all client commands and initial responses are traced by reporting them in syslog. This flag is set by innd under the control of the ctlinnd(8) trace command and is toggled upon receipt of a SIGHUP; see signal(2).

If the -S flag is used, all postings are forwarded to the specified host, which should be the master NNTP server. This flag is set by innd if it is started with the -S flag.

nnrpd can accept multimedia postings that follow the MIME standard as long as such postings are also acceptable as SMTP messages. See the discussion of the MIME headers in inn.conf(5).

## PROTOCOL DIFFERENCES

nnrpd implements the NNTP commands defined in RFC 977 with the following differences:

- The ihave command is not implemented. Users should be using the post command to post articles.
- The slave command is not implemented. This command has never been fully defined.
- The list command may be followed by the optional word active.times, distributions, distrib.pats, newsgroups, or overview.fmt to get a list of when newsgroups where created, a list of valid distributions, a file specifying default distribution patterns, a one-per-line description of the current set of newsgroups, or a listing of the overview.fmt(5) file. The command list active is equivalent to the list command. This is a common extension.
- The xhdr, authinfo user, and authinfo pass commands are implemented. These are based on the reference UNIX implementation; no other documentation is available.
- A new command, xpat header range¦MessageID pat [morepat...], is provided. The first argument is the case-insensitive name of the header to be searched. The second argument is either an article range or a single Message-ID as specified in RFC 977. The third argument is a wildmat(3)-style pattern; if there are additional arguments, they are joined together separated by a single space to form the complete pattern. This command is similar to the xhdr command. It returns a 221 response code, followed by the text response of all article numbers that match the pattern.
- The listgroup group command is provided. This is a comment extension. It is equivalent to the group command, except that the reply is a multi-line response containing the list of all article numbers in the group.
- The xgtitle [group] command is provided. This extension is used by ANU-News. It returns a 282 reply code, followed by a one-line description of all newsgroups that match the pattern. The default is the current group.
- The xover [range] command is provided. It returns a 224 reply code, followed by the overview data for the specified range; the default is to return the data for the current article.
- The xpath MessageID command is provided; see innd(8).
- The date command is provided; this is based on the draft NNTP protocol revision. It returns a one-line response code of 111 followed by the GMT date and time on the server in the form *YYYYMMDDhhmmss*.

## HISTORY

Written by Rich $alz (rsalz@uunet.uu.net) for InterNetNews. Overview support added by Rob Robertston (rob@violet.berkeley.edu) and Rich in January 1993.

## SEE ALSO

ctlinnd(8), innd(8), inn.conf(5), nnrp.access(5), signal(2), wildmat(3)

# nntpsend

nntpsend—Send Usenet articles to remote site.

## SYNOPSIS

nntpsend [ -d ][-p ][-r ][-S ][-s size ][-t timeout ]
[-T timelimit ][sitename fqdn ] ...

## DESCRIPTION

nntpsend is a front end that invokes innxmit(1) to send Usenet articles to a remote NNTP site.

The sites to be fed may be specified by giving *sitename fqdn* pairs on the command line. If no such pairs are given, nntpsend defaults to the information given in the nntpsend.ctl(5) config file.

The *sitename* should be the name of the site as specified in the newsfeeds(5) file. The *fqdn* should be the hostname or IP address of the remote site. An innxmit is launched for sites with queued news. All innxmit processes are spawned in the background and the script waits for them all to finish before returning. Output is sent to the file /var/log/news/nntpsend.log. To avoid overwhelming the local system, nntpsend waits five seconds before spawning each child. The flag -a is always given as a flag to innxmit.

nntpsend expects that the batchfile for a site is named /news/spool/out.going/*sitename*. To prevent batchfile corruption, shlock(1) is used to "lock" these files.

The -p, -r, -S, -t, and -T flags are passed on to the child innxmit program. Note that if the -p flag is used then no connection is made and no articles are fed to the remote site. It is useful to have cron(8) invoke nntpsend with this flag in case a site cannot be reached for an extended period of time.

If the -s flag is used, then shrinkfile(1) is invoked to perform a tail truncation on the batchfile and the flag is passed to it.

When *sitename fqdn* pairs are given on the command line, any flags given on the command completely describe how innxmit and shrinkfile operate. When no such pairs are given on the command line, then the information found in nntpsend.ctl becomes the default flags for that site. Any flags given on the command line override the default flags for the site.

For example, with the following control file:

```
nsavax:erehwon.nsavax.gov::-S -t60
group70:group70.org::
walldrug:walldrug.com:1m:-T1800 -t300
```

The command

```
nntpsend
```

will result in the following:

```
Sitename   Truncation    Innxmit flags
nsavax     (none)        -a -S -t60
group70    (none)        -a -t180
walldrug   1m            -a -T1800 -t300
```

The command

```
nntpsend -d -T1200
```

will result in the following:

```
Sitename   Truncation   Innxmit flags
nsavax     (none)       -a -d -S -T1200 -t60
group70    (nonc)        a  d  T1200 -t180
walldrug   1m           -a -d -T1200 -t300
```

The command

```
nntpsend -s 5m -T1200 nsavax erehwon.nsavax.gov group70 group70.org
```

will result in the following:

```
Sitename   Truncation   Innxmit flags
nsavax     5m           -a -T1200 -t180
group70    5m           -a -T1200 -t180
```

Remember that –a is always given, and –t defaults to 180.

## HISTORY

Written by Landon Curt Noll (chongo@toad.com) and Rich $alz (rsalz@uunet.uu.net) for InterNetNews.

## SEE ALSO

innxmit(1), newsfeeds(5), nntpsend.ctl(5), shrinkfile(1)

# nslookup

nslookup—Query Internet nameservers interactively.

## SYNOPSIS

nslookup [ -option ... ] [ host-to-find ¦ -[server ]]

## DESCRIPTION

nslookup is a program to query Internet domain nameservers. nslookup has two modes: interactive and non-interactive. Interactive mode allows the user to query nameservers for information about various hosts and domains or to print a list of hosts in a domain. Non-interactive mode is used to print just the name and requested information for a host or domain.

## ARGUMENTS

Interactive mode is entered in the following cases:

- When no arguments are given (the default nameserver is used)
- When the first argument is a hyphen (–) and the second argument is the hostname or Internet address of a nameserver

Non-interactive mode is used when the name or Internet address of the host to be looked up is given as the first argument. The optional second argument specifies the host name or address of a nameserver.

The options listed under the set command can be specified in the .nslookuprc file in the user's home directory if they are listed one per line. Options can also be specified on the command line if they precede the arguments and are prefixed with a hyphen. For example, to change the default query type to host information, and the initial timeout to 10 seconds, type:

```
nslookup -query=hinfo -timeout=10
```

# INTERACTIVE COMMANDS

Commands may be interrupted at any time by typing Ctrl+C. To exit, type Ctrl+D (EOF) or type exit. The command-line length must be less than 256 characters. To treat a built-in command as a hostname, precede it with an escape character (n). Note that an unrecognized command is interpreted as a hostname.

| | |
|---|---|
| host [server] | Look up information for host using the current default server or using *server* if specified. If *host* is an Internet address and the query type is A or PTR, the name of the host is returned. If *host* is a name and does not have a trailing period, the default domain name is appended to the name. (This behavior depends on the state of the set options domain, srchlist, defname, and search). To look up a host not in the current domain, append a period to the name. |
| server domain, lserver domain | Change the default server to *domain*. lserver uses the initial server to look up information about *domain*, whereas server uses the current default server. If an authoritative answer can't be found, the names of servers that might have the answer are returned. |
| root | Changes the default server to the server for the root of the domain name space. Currently, the host ns.internic.net is used. (This command is a synonym for lserver ns.internic.net.) The name of the root server can be changed with the set root command. |
| finger [name][> filename], finger [name][>> filename] | Connects with the finger server on the current host. The current host is defined when a previous lookup for a host was successful and returned address information (see the set query-type= A command). *name* is optional. > and >> can be used to redirect output in the usual manner. |
| ls [option] domain [> filename], ls [option] domain [>> filename] | List the information available for domain, optionally creating or appending to *filename*. The default output contains hostnames and their Internet addresses. *option* can be one of the following: |

| | | |
|---|---|---|
| | -t querytype | Lists all records of the specified type (see querytype). |
| | -a | Lists aliases of hosts in the domain. Synonym for -t CNAME. |
| | -d | Lists all records for the domain. Synonym for -t ANY. |
| | -h | Lists CPU and operating system information for the domain. Synonym for -t HINFO. |
| | -s | Lists well-known services of hosts in the domain. Synonym for -t WKS. When output is directed to a file, hash marks are printed for every 50 records received from the server. |
| | view filename | Sorts and lists the output of previous ls commands with more(1). |
| | help, ? | Prints a brief summary of commands. |
| | exit | Exits the program. |
| | set keyword[=value] | This command is used to change state information that affects the lookups. Valid keywords are: |
| | all | Prints the current values of the frequently used options to set. Information about the current default server and host is also printed. |

| | | |
|---|---|---|
| class=value | Change the query class to one of the following: | |
| | IN | The Internet class. |
| | CHAOS | The Chaos class. |

|  | HESIOD | The MIT Athena Hesiod class. |
|  | ANY | Wildcard (any of the above). |
|  | The class specifies the protocol group of the information. (Default = IN, abbreviation = cl.) | |
| [no]debug | Turn debugging mode on. A lot more information is printed about the packet sent to the server and the resulting answer. (Default = nodebug, abbreviation = [no]deb.) | |
| [no]d2 | Turn exhaustive debugging mode on. Essentially, all fields of every packet are printed. (Default = nod2.) | |
| domain=*name* | Change the default domain name to *name*. The default domain name is appended to a lookup request depending on the state of the defname and search options. The domain search list contains the parents of the default domain if it has at least two components in its name. For example, if the default domain is CC.Berkeley.EDU, the search list is CC.Berkeley.EDU and Berkeley.EDU. Use the set srchlist command to specify a different list. Use the set all command to display the list. (Default = value from hostname, /etc/resolv.conf, or LOCALDO-MAIN, abbreviation = do.) | |
| srchlist=*name1/name2/...* | Change the default domain name to *name1* and the domain search list to *name1*, *name2*, and so on. A maximum of six names separated by slashes (/) can be specified. For example, set srchlist=lcs.MIT.EDU/ai.MIT.EDU/MIT.EDU sets the domain to lcs.MIT.EDU and the search list to the three names. This command overrides the default domain name and search list of the set domain command. Use the set all command to display the list. (Default = value based on hostname, /etc/resolv.conf, or LOCAL-DOMAIN, abbreviation = srchl.) | |
| [no]defname | If set, append the default domain name to a single-component lookup request (that is, one that does not contain a period). (Default = defname, abbreviation = [no]def.) | |
| [no]search | If the lookup request contains at least one period but doesn't end with a trailing period, append the domain names in the domain search list to the request until an answer is received. (Default = search, abbreviation = [no]sea.) | |
| port=*value* | Change the default TCP/UDP nameserver port to *value*. (Default = 53, abbreviation = po.) | |
| querytype=*value*, type=*value* | Change the type of information query to one of the following: | |
|  | A | The host's Internet address. |
|  | CNAME | The canonical name for an alias. |
|  | HINFO | The host CPU and operating system type. |
|  | MINFO | The mailbox or mail list information. |
|  | MX | The mail exchanger. |
|  | NS | The nameserver for the named zone. |
|  | PTR | The host name if the query is an Internet address; otherwise, the pointer to other information. |
|  | SOA | The domain's "start-of-authority" information. |
|  | TXT | The text information. |
|  | UINFO | The user information. |
|  | WKS | The supported well-known services. |
|  | Other types (ANY, AXFR, MB, MD, MF, NULL) are described in the RFC-1035 document. (Default = A, abbreviations = q, ty.) | |
| [no]recurse | Tell the nameserver to query other servers if it does not have the information. (Default = recurse, abbreviation = [no]rec.) | |
| retry=*number* | Set the number of retries to *number*. When a reply to a request is not received within a certain amount of time (changed with set timeout), the timeout period is doubled and the request is resent. The retry value controls how many times a request is resent before giving up. (Default = 4, abbreviation = ret.) | |

| | |
|---|---|
| `root=`*host* | Change the name of the root server to *host*. This affects the `root` command. (Default = `ns.internic.net`, abbreviation = `ro`.) |
| `timeout=`*number* | Change the initial timeout interval for waiting for a reply to *number* seconds. Each retry doubles the timeout period. (Default = 5 seconds, abbreviation = `ti`.) |
| `[no]vc` | Always use a virtual circuit when sending requests to the server. (Default = `novc`, abbreviation = `[no]v`.) |
| `[no]ignoretc` | Ignore packet truncation errors. (Default = `noignoretc`, abbreviation = `[no]ig`.) |

## DIAGNOSTICS

If the lookup request was not successful, an error message is printed. Possible errors are

| | |
|---|---|
| `Timed out` | The server did not respond to a request after a certain amount of time (changed with `set timeout=`*value*) and a certain number of retries (changed with `set retry=`*value*). |
| `No response from server` | No nameserver is running on the server machine. |
| `No records` | The server does not have resource records of the current query type for the host, although the hostname is valid. The query type is specified with the `set querytype` command. |
| `Non-existent domain` | The host or domain name does not exist. |
| `Connection refused,` `Network is unreachable` | The connection to the name or finger server could not be made at the current time. This error commonly occurs with `ls` and finger requests. |
| `Server failure` | The nameserver found an internal inconsistency in its database and could not return a valid answer. |
| `Refused` | The nameserver refused to service the request. |
| `Format error` | The nameserver found that the request packet was not in the proper format. It may indicate an error in `nslookup`. |

## FILES

| | |
|---|---|
| `/Etc/Resolv.Conf` | Initial domain name and nameserver addresses. |
| `$HOME/.nslookuprc` | User's initial options. |
| `/usr/share/misc/nslookup.help` | Summary of commands. |

## ENVIRONMENT

| | |
|---|---|
| `HOSTALIASES` | File containing host aliases. |
| `LOCALDOMAIN` | Overrides default domain. |

## SEE ALSO

`resolver`(3), `resolver`(5), `named`(8), RFC 1034 "Domain Names – Concepts and Facilities," RFC 1035 "Domain Names – Implementation and Specification"

## AUTHOR

Andrew Cherenson

*24 June 1990*

# overchan

overchan—Update the news overview database.

## SYNOPSIS

    overchan [ -D *dir* ][-c ][*file...* ]

## DESCRIPTION

overchan reads article data from files or standard input if none are specified. (A single dash in the file list means to read standard input.) It uses this information to update the news overview database. overchan is designed to be used by InterNetNews or the C News mkov packages to update the database as the articles come in. The database for each newsgroup is stored in a file named .overview in a newsgroup directory within the overview database tree.

overchan locks the database file (by locking an auxiliary file) before appending the new data. To purge data after articles have been expired, see expireover(8).

By default, overchan processes its input as an INN overview stream written as a WO entry in the newsfeeds(5) file:

    overview:*:Tc,WO:/news/bin/overchan

This data consists of a line of text separated into two parts by a tab. The first part is a list of all relative pathnames where the article has been written with a single space between entries. The second part is the data to be written into the overview file, except that the initial article number is omitted.

To process the output of the mkov(8) program, use the -c flag. This format is described in the nov distribution.

The -D flag can be used to specify where the databases are stored. The default directory is /news/spool.

## HISTORY

Written by Rob Robertson (rob@violet.berkeley.edu) and Rich $alz (rsalz@uunet.uu.net) for InterNetNews.

## SEE ALSO

newsfeeds(5), newsoverview(5), newsoverview(8)

# pac

pac—Printer/plotter accounting information.

## SYNOPSIS

    pac [-P *printer*] [-c] [-m] [-p *price*] [-s] [-r] [*name* ...]

## DESCRIPTION

pac reads the printer/plotter accounting files, accumulating the number of pages (the usual case) or feet (for raster devices) of paper consumed by each user and printing how much each user consumed in pages or feet and dollars.

Options and operands available:

| | |
|---|---|
| -P *printer* | Accounting is done for the named printer. Usually, accounting is done for the default printer (site dependent), or the value of the environment variable PRINTER is used. |
| -c • | Flag causes the output to be sorted by cost; usually, the output is sorted alphabetically by name. |
| -m | Flag causes the hostname to be ignored in the accounting file. This allows for a user on multiple machines to have all his printing charges grouped together. |
| -p *price* | The value price is used for the cost in dollars instead of the default value of 0.02 or the price specified in /etc/printcap. |
| -r | Reverse the sorting order. |
| -s | Accounting information is summarized on the summary accounting file; this summarization is necessary because on a busy system, the accounting file can grow by several lines per day. |

names                                  Statistics are only printed for users named; usually, statistics are printed for every user
                                       who has used any paper.

## FILES

/var/account/?acct                     Raw accounting files
/var/account/?_sum                     Summary accounting files
/etc/printcap                          Printer capability database

## SEE ALSO

printcap(5)

## BUGS

The relationship between the computed price and reality is as yet unknown.

## HISTORY

The pac command appeared in BSD 4.0.

*BSD 4.2, 16 March 1991*

# pcnfsd

pcnfsd—(PC)NFS authentication and print request server

## SYNOPSIS

/usr/etc/rpc.pcnfsd

## AVAILABILITY

This program is freely redistributable.

## DESCRIPTION

pcnfsd is an RPC server that supports ONC clients on PC (DOS, OS/2, Macintosh, and other) systems. This page describes
version 2 of the pcnfsd server.

rpc.pcnfsd may be started from /etc/rc.local or by the inetd(8) superdaemon. It reads the configuration file
/etc/pcnfsd.conf if present and then services RPC requests directed to program number 150001. This release of the pcnfsd
daemon supports both version 1 and version 2 of the pcnfsd protocol. Consult the rpcgen source file pcnfsd.x for details of
the protocols.

The requests serviced by pcnfsd fall into three categories: authentication, printing, and other. Only the authentication and
printing services have administrative significance.

## AUTHENTICATION

When pcnfsd receives a PCNFSD AUTH or PCNFSD2 AUTH request, it "logs in" the user by validating the username and password
and returning the corresponding UID, GIDs, home directory, and umask. If pcnfsd was built with the WTMP compile-time
option, it also appends a record to the wtmp(5) database. If you do not want to record PC logins in this way, you should add a
line of the form

wtmp off

to the /etc/pcnfsd.conf file.

By default, pcnfsd only allows authentication or print requests for users with UIDs in the range 101 to 60002. (This
corresponds in SVR4 to the range for non-system accounts.) To override this, you may add a line of the form

```
uidrange range[,range]...
```

to the /etc/pcnfsd.conf file. Here, each *range* is of the form *uid* or *uid-uid*, indicating an inclusive range.

## PRINTING

pcnfsd supports a printing model based on the use of NFS to transfer the actual print data from the client to the server. The client system issues a PCNFSD PR INIT or PCN-FSD2 PR INIT request, and the server returns the path to a spool directory that the client may use and which is exported by NFS. pcnfsd creates a subdirectory for each of its clients: The parent directory is usually /usr/spool/pcnfs and the subdirectory is the hostname of the client system. If you want to use a different parent directory, you should add a line of the form

```
spooldir path
```

to the /etc/pcnfsd.conf file.

Once a client has mounted the spool directory using NFS and has transferred print data to a file in this directory, it issues a PCNFSD_PR_START or PCNFSD2_PR_START request. pcnfsd handles this, and most other print-related requests, by constructing a command based on the printing services of the server operating system and executing the command using the identity of the PC user. Because this involves set-user-ID privileges, pcnfsd must be run as root.

Every print request from the client includes the name of the printer that is to be used. In Linux, this name corresponds to a printer definition in the /etc/printcap(5) database. If you want to define a non-standard way of processing print data, you should define a new printer and arrange for the client to print to this printer. There are two ways of setting up a new printer. The first involves the addition of an entry to /etc/printcap(5) and the creation of filters to perform the required processing. This is outside the scope of this discussion. In addition, pcnfsd includes a mechanism by which you can define virtual printers known only to pcnfsd clients. Each printer is defined by a line in the /etc/pcnfsd.conf file of the following form:

```
printer name alias-for command
```

*name* is the name of the printer you want to define. *alias-for* is the name of a "real" printer that corresponds to this printer. For example, a request to display the queue for name is translated into the corresponding request for the printer *alias-for*. If you have defined a printer in such a way that there is no "real" printer to which it corresponds, use a single - for this field. (See the definition of the printer test for an example.) *command* is a command that will be executed whenever a file is printed on *name*. This command is executed by the shell at /bin/sh using the -c option. For complex operations, you should construct an executable shell program and invoke that in *command*.

Consider the following sample /etc/pcnfsd.conf file:

```
printer rotated lw /usr/local/bin/enscript -2r $FILE
printer test - /usr/bin/cp $FILE/usr/tmp/$HOST$USER
```

If a client system prints a job on the printer rotated, the utility enscript is invoked to pre-process the file $FILE. In this case, the -2r option causes the file to be printed in two-column rotated format on the default PostScript printer. If the client requests a list of the print queue for the printer rotated, the pcnfsd daemon translates this into a request for a listing for the printer lw.

The printer test is used only for testing. Any file sent to this printer is copied into /usr/tmp. Any request to list the queue, check the status, and so on of printer test is rejected because the *alias-for* is specified as -.

## RECONFIGURATION

pcnfsd detects when printers are added or deleted and rebuilds its list of valid printers. To do this, it checks the modification time of /etc/printcap. However, it does not monitor the file /etc/pcnfsd.conf for updates; if you change this file, it is still necessary to kill and restart pcnfsd so the changes can take effect.

## FILE

/etc/pcnfsd.conf

## SEE ALSO

lpr(1), lprm(1), lpc(8), lpq(1)

*25 June 1995*


# plipconfig

plipconfig—Fine-tune PLIP device parameters.

## SYNOPSIS

plipconfig *interface*
plipconfig *interface* [nibble *NN*] [trigger *NN*] [unit *NN*]

## DESCRIPTION

plipconfig is used to improve PLIP performance by changing the default timing parameters used by the PLIP protocol. Results are dependent on the parallel port hardware, cable, and the CPU speed of each machine on each end of the PLIP link.

If the single *interface* argument is given, plipconfig displays the status of the given interface only. Otherwise, it tries to set the options.

## OPTIONS

| | |
|---|---|
| nibble *NN* | Sets the nibble wait value in microseconds. Default is 3000. |
| trigger *NN* | Sets the trigger wait value in microseconds. Default is 500. |
| unit *NN* | Sets the number of units of delay. Default is 1. |

In some cases, PLIP speed can be improved by lowering the default values. Values that are too low might cause excess use of CPU, poor interrupt response time resulting in serial ports dropping characters, or in dropping PLIP packets. Changing the plip MTU can also affect PLIP speed.

## SEE ALSO

ifconfig(8)

## BUGS

None so far.

## AUTHOR

John Paul Morrison (jmorriso@bogomips.ee.ubc.ca, ve7jpm@ve7jpm.ampr.org)

*1 July 1994*

# ping

ping—Send ICMP `ECHO_REQUEST` packets to network hosts.

## SYNOPSIS

`/etc/ping [ -r ][-v ] host [ packetsize ][count ]`

## DESCRIPTION

The DARPA Internet is a large and complex aggregation of network hardware, connected together by gateways. Tracking a single-point hardware or software failure can often be difficult. Ping utilizes the ICMP protocol's mandatory `ECHO_REQUEST` datagram to elicit an ICMP `ECHO_RESPONSE` from a host or gateway. `ECHO_REQUEST` datagrams ("pings") have an IP and ICMP header, followed by a `struct timeval` and then an arbitrary number of "pad" bytes used to fill out the packet. Default datagram length is `64` bytes, but this may be changed using the command-line option. Other options are

-r                              Bypass the normal routing tables and send directly to a host on an attached network. If the host is not on a directly attached network, an error is returned. This option can be used to ping a local host through an interface that has no route through it (for example, after the interface was dropped by `routed(8C)`).

-v                              Verbose output. ICMP packets other than `ECHO_RESPONSE` that are received are listed.

When using ping for fault isolation, it should first be run on the local host to verify that the local network interface is up and running. Then, hosts and gateways further away should be pinged. Ping sends one datagram per second and prints one line of output for every `ECHO_RESPONSE` returned. No output is produced if there is no response. If an optional count is given, only that number of requests is sent. Round-trip times and packet-loss statistics are computed. When all responses have been received or the program times out (with a count specified), or if the program is terminated with a `SIGINT`, a brief summary is displayed.

This program is intended for use in network testing, measurement, and management. It should be used primarily for manual fault isolation. Because of the load it could impose on the network, it is unwise to use ping during normal operations or from automated scripts.

## AUTHOR

Mike Muuss

## SEE ALSO

netstat(1), ifconfig(8)

*19 September 1988*


# portmap

portmap—DARPA port to RPC program number mapper.

## SYNOPSIS

`portmap [-d]`

## DESCRIPTION

`portmap` is a server that converts RPC program numbers into DARPA protocol port numbers. It must be running in order to make RPC calls.

When an RPC server is started, it tells `portmap` what port number it is listening to and what RPC program numbers it is prepared to serve. When a client wants to make an RPC call to a given program number, it first contacts `portmap` on the server machine to determine the port number where RPC packets should be sent.

portmap must be started before any RPC servers are invoked.

Usually, portmap forks and dissociates itself from the terminal like any other daemon. Portmap then logs errors using syslog(3).

Option available:

-d (debug) prevents portmap from running as a daemon and causes errors and debugging information to be printed to the standard error output.

## SEE ALSO

inetd.conf(5), rpcinfo(8), inetd(8)

## BUGS

If portmap crashes, all servers must be restarted.

## HISTORY

The portmap command appeared in BSD 4.3.

*BSD 4.3, 16 March 1991*

# powerd

powerd—Monitor a serial line connected to a UPS.

## SYNOPSIS

/etc/powerd *serial-device*

## DESCRIPTION

powerd is a daemon process that sits in the background and monitors the state of the DCD line of the serial device. It is meant that this line is connected to a UPS (Uninterruptible Power Supply) so that it knows about the state of the UPS. As soon as powerd senses that the power is failing (it sees that DCD goes low) it notifies init(8) and init executes the powerwait and powerfail entries. If powerd senses that the power has been restored, it notifies init again and init executes the powerokwait entries.

## ARGUMENTS

*serial-device*          Some serial port that is not being used by some other device and does not share an interrupt with any other serial port.

## DIAGNOSTICS

powerd regularly checks the DSR line to see if it's high. DSR should be directly connected to DTR and powerd keeps that line high, so if DSR is low, something is wrong with the connection. powerd notifies you about this fact every two minutes. When it sees that the connection is restored, it will say so.

## IMPLEMENTATION

It's pretty simple to connect your UPS to the Linux machine. The steps are easy:

1. Make sure you have an UPS with a simple relais output: it should close its connections (make) if the power is gone, and it should open its connections (break) if the power is good.
2. Buy a serial plug. Connect the DTR line to the DSR line directly. Connect the DTR line and the DCD line with a 10 kilo ohm resistor. Connect the relais-output of the UPS to GROUND and the DCD line. If you don't know what pins DSR, DTR, DCD and GROUND are, you can always ask at the store where you bought the plug.
3. You're all set.

## BUGS

Well, it's not a real bug but powerd should be able to do a broadcast or something on the Ethernet in case more Linux-boxes are connected to the same UPS and only one of them is connected to the UPS status line.

## SEE ALSO

shutdown(8), init(8), inittab(5)

## AUTHOR

Miquel van Smoorenburg (miquels@drinkel.nl.mugnet.org)

*14 February 1994*

# pppd

pppd—Point-to-Point Protocol daemon.

## SYNOPSIS

pppd [ *tty_name* ][*speed* ][*options* ]

## DESCRIPTION

The Point-to-Point Protocol (PPP) provides a method for transmitting datagrams over serial point-to-point links. PPP is composed of three parts: a method for encapsulating datagrams over serial links, an extensible Link Control Protocol (LCP), and a family of Network Control Protocols (NCP) for establishing and configuring different network-layer protocols.

The encapsulation scheme is provided by driver code in the kernel. pppd provides the basic LCP, authentication support, and an NCP for establishing and configuring the Internet Protocol (IP) (called the IP Control Protocol, IPCP).

## FREQUENTLY USED OPTIONS

| | |
|---|---|
| *tty_name* | Communicate over the named device. The string /dev/ is prepended if necessary. If no device name is given, or if the name of the controlling terminal is given, pppd uses the controlling terminal and does not fork to put itself in the background. |
| *speed* | Set the baud rate to *speed* (a decimal number). On systems such as 4.4BSD and NetBSD, any speed can be specified. Other systems (such as SunOS) allow only a limited set of speeds. |
| asyncmap *map* | Set the async character map to *map*. This map describes which control characters cannot be successfully received over the serial line. pppd asks the peer to send these characters as a 2-byte escape sequence. The argument is a 32-bit hex number with each bit representing a character to escape. Bit 0 (00000001) represents the character 0x00; bit 31 (80000000) represents the character 0x1f or ^. If multiple asyncmap options are given, the values are ORed together. If no asyncmap option is given, no async character map is negotiated for the receive direction; the peer should then escape all control characters. |
| auth | Require the peer to authenticate itself before allowing network packets to be sent or received. |
| connect *p* | Use the executable or shell command specified by *p* to set up the serial line. This script typically uses the chat(8) program to dial the modem and start the remote PPP session. |
| crtscts | Use hardware flow control (that is, RTS/CTS) to control the flow of data on the serial port. If neither the crtscts nor the -crtscts option is given, the hardware flow control setting for the serial port is left unchanged. |
| defaultroute | Add a default route to the system routing tables, using the peer as the gateway, when IPCP negotiation is successfully completed. This entry is removed when the PPP connection is broken. |

| | |
|---|---|
| disconnect *p* | Run the executable or shell command specified by *p* after pppd has terminated the link. This script could, for example, issue commands to the modem to cause it to hang up if hardware modem control signals were not available. |
| escape *xx,yy,...* | Specifies that certain characters should be escaped on transmission (regardless of whether the peer requests them to be escaped with its async control character map). The characters to be escaped are specified as a list of hex numbers separated by commas. Note that almost any character can be specified for the escape option, unlike the asyncmap option, which only allows control characters to be specified. The characters that cannot be escaped are those with hex values 0x20 - 0x3f or 0x5e. |
| file *f* | Read options from file *f* (the format is described later). |
| lock | Specifies that pppd should create a UUCP-style lock file for the serial device to ensure exclusive access to the device. |
| mru *n* | Set the MRU (Maximum Receive Unit) value to *n* for negotiation. pppd asks the peer to send packets of no more than *n* bytes. The minimum MRU value is 128. The default MRU value is 1500. A value of 296 is recommended for slow links (40 bytes for TCP/IP header plus 256 bytes of data). |
| mtu *n* | Set the MTU (Maximum Transmit Unit) value to *n*. Unless the peer requests a smaller value via MRU negotiation, pppd requests that the kernel networking code send data packets of no more than *n* bytes through the PPP network interface. |
| netmask *n* | Set the interface netmask to *n*, a 32-bit netmask in decimal dot notation (such as 255.255.255.0). If this option is given, the value specified is ORed with the default netmask. The default netmask is chosen based on the negotiated remote IP address; it is the appropriate network mask for the class of the remote IP address ORed with the netmasks for any non–point-to-point network interfaces in the system that are on the same network. |
| passive | Enables the passive option in the LCP. With this option, pppd attempts to initiate a connection; if no reply is received from the peer, pppd then waits passively for a valid LCP packet from the peer (instead of exiting as it does without this option). |
| silent | With this option, pppd does not transmit LCP packets to initiate a connection until a valid LCP packet is received from the peer (as for the passive option with ancient versions of pppd). |

## OPTIONS

| | |
|---|---|
| *local IP address:remote IP address* | Set the local and/or remote interface IP addresses. Either one may be omitted. The IP addresses can be specified with a host name or in decimal dot notation (such as 150.234.56.78). The default local address is the (first) IP address of the system (unless the noipdefault option is given). The remote address is obtained from the peer if not specified in any option. Thus, in simple cases, this option is not required. If a local and/or remote IP address is specified with this option, pppd does not accept a different value from the peer in the IPCP negotiation, unless the ipcp-accept-local and/or ipcp-accept-remote options are given. |
| -ac | Disable Address/Control compression negotiation (use default, address/control field compression disabled). |
| -all | Don't request or allow negotiation of any options for LCP and IPCP (use default values). |
| -am | Disable asyncmap negotiation (use the default asyncmap; that is, escape all control characters). |
| -as *n* | Same as asyncmap *n*. |

| | |
|---|---|
| bsdcomp *nr,nt* | Request that the peer compress packets that it sends, using the BSD-Compress scheme, with a maximum code size of *nr* bits and agree to compress packets sent to the peer with a maximum code size of *nt* bits. If *nt* is not specified, it defaults to the value given for *nr*. Values in the range 9 to 15 may be used for *nr* and *nt*; larger values give better compression but consume more kernel memory for compression dictionaries. Alternatively, a value of 0 for *nr* or *nt* disables compression in the corresponding direction. |
| -bsdcomp | Disables compression; pppd does not request or agree to compress packets using the BSD-Compress scheme. |
| +chap | Require the peer to authenticate itself using CHAP (Cryptographic Handshake Authentication Protocol) authentication. |
| -chap | Don't agree to authenticate using CHAP. |
| chap-interval *n* | If this option is given, pppd rechallenges the peer every *n* seconds. |
| chap-max-challenge *n* | Set the maximum number of CHAP challenge transmissions to *u* (default is 10). |
| chap-restart *n* | Set the CHAP restart interval (retransmission timeout for challenges) to *n* seconds (default is 3). |
| -crtscts | Disable hardware flow control (RTS/CTS) on the serial port. If neither the crtscts nor the -crtscts option is given, the hardware flow control setting for the serial port is left unchanged. |
| -d | Increase debugging level (same as the debug option). |
| debug | Increase debugging level (same as -d). If this option is given, pppd logs the contents of all control packets sent or received in a readable form. The packets are logged through syslog with facility daemon and level debug. This information can be directed to a file by setting up /etc/syslog.conf appropriately (see syslog.conf(5)). |
| -defaultroute | Disable the defaultroute option. The system administrator who wants to prevent users from creating default routes with pppd can do so by placing this option in the /etc/ppp/options file. |
| -detach | Don't fork to become a background process (otherwise, pppd will do so if a serial device other than its controlling terminal is specified). |
| dns-addr *n* | This option sets the IP address or addresses for the Domain Name Server. It is used by Microsoft Windows clients. The primary DNS address is specified by the first instance of the dns-addr option. The secondary is specified by the second instance. |
| domain *d* | Append the domain name *d* to the local hostname for authentication purposes. For example, if gethost-name() returns the name porsche, but the fully qualified domain name is porsche.Quotron.COM, you use the domain option to set the domain name to Quotron.COM. |
| -ip | Disable IP address negotiation. If this option is used, the remote IP address must be specified with an option on the command line or in an options file. |
| +ip-protocol | Enable the IPCP and IP protocols. This is the default condition. This option is only needed if the default setting is -ip-protocol. |
| -ip-protocol | Disable the IPCP and IP protocols. This should only be used if you know you are using a client that only understands IPX and you don't want to confuse the client with the IPCP protocol. |
| +ipx-protocol | Enable the IPXCP and IPX protocols. This is the default condition if your kernel supports IPX. This option is only needed if the default setting is -ipx-protocol. If your kernel does not support IPX, this option has no effect. |

| | |
|---|---|
| -ipx-protocol | Disable the IPXCP and IPX protocols. This should only be used if you know you are using a client that only understands IP and you don't want to confuse the client with the IPXCP protocol. |
| ipcp-accept-local | With this option, pppd accepts the peer's idea of a local IP address, even if the local IP address was specified in an option. |
| ipcp-accept-remote | With this option, pppd accepts the peer's idea of its (remote) IP address, even if the remote IP address was specified in an option. |
| ipcp-max-configure *n* | Set the maximum number of IPCP configure-request transmissions to *n* (default is 10). |
| ipcp-max-failure *n* | Set the maximum number of IPCP configure-NAKs returned before starting to send configure-Rejects instead to *n* (default is 10). |
| ipcp-max-terminate *n* | Set the maximum number of IPCP terminate-request transmissions to *n* (default is 3). |
| ipcp-restart *n* | Set the IPCP restart interval (retransmission timeout) to *n* seconds (default is 3). |
| ipparam *string* | Provides an extra parameter to the ip-up and ip-down scripts. If this option is given, the *string* supplied is given as the sixth parameter to those scripts. |
| ipx-network *n* | Set the IPX network number in the IPXCP configure request frame to *n*. There is no valid default. If this option is not specified, the network number is obtained from the peer. If the peer does not have the network number, the IPX protocol is not started. This is a hexadecimal number and is entered without any leading sequence such as 0x. It is related to the ipxcp-accept-network option. |
| ipx-node *n:m* | Set the IPX node numbers. The two node numbers are separated from each other with a colon character. The first number *n* is the local node number. The second number *m* is the peer's node number. Each node number is a hexadecimal number to the maximum of ten significant digits. The node numbers on the ipx-network must be unique. There is no valid default. If this option is not specified, the node number is obtained from the peer. This option is a related to the ipxcp-accept-local and ipxcp-accept-remote options. |
| ipx-router-name *string* | Set the name of the router. This is a string and is sent to the peer as information data. |
| ipx-routing *n* | Set the routing protocol to be received by this option. More than one instance of ipx-routing may be specified. The none option (0) may be specified as the only instance of ipx-routing. The values are 0 for none, 2 for RIP/SAP, and 4 for NLSP. |
| ipxcp-accept-local | Accept the peer's NAK for the node number specified in the ipx-node option. If a node number was specified and it is nonzero, the default is to insist that the value be used. If you include this option, you permit the peer to override the entry of the node number. |
| ipxcp-accept-network | Accept the peer's NAK for the network number specified in the ipx-network option. If a network number was specified and it is nonzero, the default is to insist that the value be used. If you include this option, you permit the peer to override the entry of the node number. |
| ipxcp-accept-remote | Use the peer's network number specified in the configure request frame. If a node number was specified for the peer and this option was not specified, the peer is forced to use the value that you specified. |
| ipxcp-max-configure *n* | Set the maximum number of IPXCP configure request frames that the system sends to *n*. The default is 10. |

| | |
|---|---|
| ipxcp-max-failure *n* | Set the maximum number of IPXCP NAK frames that the local system sends before it rejects the options. The default value is 3. |
| ipxcp-max-terminate *n* | Set the maximum number of IPXCP terminate request frames before the local system considers that the peer is not listening to them. The default value is 3. |
| kdebug *n* | Enable debugging code in the kernel-level PPP driver. The argument *n* is a number that is the sum of the following values: 1 to enable general debug messages, 2 to request that the contents of received packets be printed, and 4 to request that the contents of transmitted packets be printed. |
| lcp-echo-failure *n* | If this option is given, pppd presumes the peer is dead if *n* LCP echo-requests are sent without receiving a valid LCP echo-reply. If this happens, pppd terminates the connection. Use of this option requires a nonzero value for the lcp-echo-interval parameter. This option can be used to enable pppd to terminate after the physical connection has been broken (for example, the modem has hung up) in situations where no hardware modem control lines are available. |
| lcp-echo-interval *n* | If this option is given, pppd sends an LCP echo-request frame to the peer every *n* seconds. Under Linux, the echo-request is sent when no packets are received from the peer for *n* seconds. Usually, the peer should respond to the echo-request by sending an echo-reply. This option can be used with the lcp-echo-failure option to detect that the peer is no longer connected. |
| lcp-max-configure *n* | Set the maximum number of LCP configure-request transmissions to *n* (default is 10). |
| lcp-max-failure *n* | Set the maximum number of LCP configure-NAKs returned before starting to send configure-Rejects instead to *n* (default is 10). |
| lcp-max-terminate *n* | Set the maximum number of LCP terminate-request transmissions to *n* (default is 3). |
| lcp-restart *n* | Set the LCP restart interval (retransmission timeout) to *n* seconds (default is 3). |
| local | Don't use the modem control lines. With this option, pppd ignores the state of the CD (Carrier Detect) signal from the modem and does not change the state of the DTR (Data Terminal Ready) signal. |
| login | Use the system password database for authenticating the peer using PAP, and record the user in the system wtmp file. |
| modem | Use the modem control lines. This option is the default. With this option, pppd waits for the CD (Carrier Detect) signal from the modem to be asserted when opening the serial device (unless a connect script is specified), and it drops the DTR (Data Terminal Ready) signal briefly when the connection is terminated and before executing the connect script. On Ultrix, this option implies hardware flow control, as for the crtscts option. |
| -mn | Disable magic number negotiation. With this option, pppd cannot detect a looped-back line. |
| -mru | Disable MRU (MaximumReceive Unit) negotiation. With this option, pppd uses the default MRU value of 1500 bytes. |
| name *n* | Set the name of the local system for authentication purposes to *n*. |
| noipdefault | Disables the default behavior when no local IP address is specified, which is to determine (if possible) the local IP address from the hostname. With this option, the peer must supply the local IP address during IPCP |

negotiation (unless it specified explicitly on the command line or in an options file).

| | |
|---|---|
| -p | Same as the passive option. |
| +pap | Require the peer to authenticate itself using PAP. |
| -pap | Don't agree to authenticate using PAP. |
| papcrypt | Indicates that all secrets in the /etc/ppp/pap-secrets file, which are used for checking the identity of the peer, are encrypted, and thus pppd should not accept a password (before encryption) that is identical to the secret from the /etc/ppp/pap-secrets file. |
| pap-max-authreq *n* | Set the maximum number of PAP authenticate-request transmissions to *n* (default is 10). |
| pap-restart *n* | Set the PAP restart interval (retransmission timeout) to *n* seconds (default is 3). |
| pap-timeout *n* | Set the maximum time that pppd waits for the peer to authenticate itself with PAP to *n* seconds (0 means no limit). |
| -pc | Disable protocol field compression negotiation (use default, protocol field compression disabled). |
| persist | Do not exit after a connection is terminated; instead, try to reopen the connection. |
| pred1comp | Attempt to request that the peer send the local system frames, which have been compressed by the Predictor-1 compression. The compression protocols must be loaded or this option is ignored. |
| -pred1comp | Do not accept Predictor-1 compression, even if the peer wants to send this type of compression and support has been defined in the kernel. |
| proxyarp | Add an entry to this system's ARP (Address Resolution Protocol) table with the IP address of the peer and the Ethernet address of this system. |
| -proxyarp | Disable the proxyarp option. The system administrator who wants to prevent users from creating proxy ARP entries with pppd can do so by placing this option in the /etc/ppp/options file. |
| remotename *n* | Set the assumed name of the remote system for authentication purposes to *n*. |
| +ua *p* | Agree to authenticate using PAP (Password Authentication Protocol) if requested by the peer and use the data in file *p* for the user and password to send to the peer. The file contains the remote username, followed by a newline, followed by the remote password, followed by a newline. This option is obsolescent. |
| usehostname | Enforce the use of the hostname as the name of the local system for authentication purposes (overrides the name option). |
| user *u* | Set the username to use for authenticating this machine with the peer using PAP to *u*. |
| -vj | Disable negotiation of Van Jacobson-style TCP/IP header compression (use default, no compression). |
| -vjccomp | Disable the connection-ID compression option in Van Jacobson style TCP/IP header compression. With this option, pppd does not omit the connection-ID byte from Van Jacobson compressed TCP/IP headers or ask the peer to do so. |
| vj-max-slots *n* | Sets the number of connection slots to be used by the Van Jacobson TCP/IP header compression and decompression code to *n*, which must be between 2 and 16 (inclusive). |

xonxoff
Use software flow control (XON/XOFF) to control the flow of data on the serial port. This option is only implemented on Linux systems at present.

## OPTIONS FILES

Options can be taken from files as well as the command line. pppd reads options from the files /etc/ppp/options and ~/.ppprc before looking at the command line. An options file is parsed into a series of words, delimited by whitespace. Whitespace can be included in a word by enclosing the word in quotes ("). A backslash (\) quotes the following character. A hash (#) starts a comment, which continues until the end of the line.

## AUTHENTICATION

pppd provides system administrators with sufficient access control so that PPP access to a server machine can be provided to legitimate users without fear of compromising the security of the server or the network it's on. In part, this is provided by the /etc/ppp/options file, where the administrator can place options to require authentication whenever pppd is run, and in part by the PAP and CHAP secrets files, where the administrator can restrict the set of IP addresses that individual users can use.

The default behavior of pppd is to agree to authenticate if requested and to not require authentication from the peer. However, pppd does not agree to authenticate itself with a particular protocol if it has no secrets that can be used to do so.

Authentication is based on secrets, which are selected from secrets files (/etc/ppp/pap-secrets for PAP, /etc/ppp/chap-secrets for CHAP). Both secrets files have the same format, and both can store secrets for several combinations of server (authenticating peer) and client (peer being authenticated). Note that pppd can be both a server and client and that different protocols can be used in the two directions if desired.

A secrets file is parsed into words as for an options file. A secret is specified by a line containing at least three words, in the order client name, server name, and secret. Any following words on the same line are taken to be a list of acceptable IP addresses for that client. If there are only three words on the line, it is assumed that any IP address is okay; to disallow all IP addresses, use -. If the secret starts with an @, what follows is assumed to be the name of a file from which to read the secret. A * as the client or server name matches any name. When selecting a secret, pppd takes the best match—that is, the match with the fewest wildcards.

A secrets file contains both secrets for use in authenticating other hosts and secrets that you use for authenticating yourself to others. Which secret to use is chosen based on the names of the host (the local name) and its peer (the remote name). The local name is set as follows:

| | |
|---|---|
| If the usehostname option is given, | The local name is the hostname of this machine (with the domain appended, if given). |
| If the name option is given | Use the argument of the first name option seen. |
| If the local IP address is specified with a hostname | Use that name. Otherwise, use the hostname of this machine (with the domain appended, if given). |

When authenticating yourself using PAP, there is also a username, which is the local name by default, but can be set with the user option or the +ua option.

The remote name is set as follows:

| | |
|---|---|
| If the remotename option is given | Use the argument of the last remote-name option seen. |
| If the remote IP address is specified with a hostname | Use that host name. Otherwise, the remote name is the null string "". |

Secrets are selected from the PAP secrets file as follows:

- For authenticating the peer, look for a secret with client == username specified in the PAP authenticate-request and server == local name.
- For authenticating yourself to the peer, look for a secret with client == your username and server == remote name.

When authenticating the peer with PAP, a secret of `""` matches any password supplied by the peer. If the password doesn't match the secret, the password is encrypted using `crypt( )` and checked against the secret again; thus secrets for authenticating the peer can be stored in encrypted form. If the `papcrypt` option is given, the first (unencrypted) comparison is omitted for better security.

If the login option was specified, the username and password are also checked against the system password database. Thus, the system administrator can set up the `pap-secrets` file to allow PPP access only to certain users and to restrict the set of IP addresses that each user can use. Typically, when using the login option, the secret in `/etc/ppp/pap-secrets` is `""` to avoid the need to have the same secret in two places.

Secrets are selected from the CHAP secrets file as follows:

- For authenticating the peer, look for a secret with client == name specified in the CHAP-Response message and server == local name.
- For authenticating yourself to the peer, look for a secret with client == local name and server == name specified in the CHAP-Challenge message.

Authentication must be satisfactorily completed before IPCP (or any other Network Control Protocol) can be started. If authentication fails, pppd terminates the link (by closing LCP). If IPCP negotiates an unacceptable IP address for the remote host, IPCP is closed. IP packets can only be sent or received when IPCP is open.

In some cases, it is desirable to allow some hosts that can't authenticate themselves to connect and use one of a restricted set of IP addresses, even when the local host generally requires authentication. If the peer refuses to authenticate itself when requested, pppd takes that as equivalent to authenticating with PAP using the empty string for the username and password. Thus, by adding a line to the `pap-secrets` file, which specifies the empty string for the client and password, it is possible to allow restricted access to hosts that refuse to authenticate themselves.

## ROUTING

When IPCP negotiation is completed successfully, pppd informs the kernel of the local and remote IP addresses for the PPP interface. This is sufficient to create a host route to the remote end of the link, which enables the peers to exchange IP packets. Communication with other machines generally requires further modification to routing tables and/or ARP (Address Resolution Protocol) tables. In some cases, this is done automatically through the actions of the routed or gated daemons, but in most cases, some further intervention is required.

Sometimes it is desirable to add a default route through the remote host, as in the case of a machine whose only connection to the Internet is through the PPP interface. The `defaultroute` option causes pppd to create such a default route when IPCP comes up and delete it when the link is terminated.

In some cases, it is desirable to use proxy ARP—for example, on a server machine connected to a LAN—to allow other hosts to communicate with the remote host. The `proxyarp` option causes pppd to look for a network interface on the same subnet as the remote host (an interface supporting broadcast and ARP, which is up and not a point-to-point or loopback interface). If found, pppd creates a permanent, published ARP entry with the IP address of the remote host and the hardware address of the network interface found.

## EXAMPLES

In the simplest case, you can connect the serial ports of two machines and issue a command like

```
pppd /dev/ttya 9600 passive
```

to each machine, assuming there is no `getty` running on the serial ports. If one machine has a `getty` running, you can use `kermit` or `tip` on the other machine to log in to the first machine and issue a command like

```
pppd passive
```

Then exit from the communications program (making sure the connection isn't dropped) and issue a command like

```
pppd /dev/ttya 9600
```

The process of logging in to the other machine and starting pppd can be automated by using the connect option to run chat:

```
pppd /dev/ttya 38400 connect 'chat "" "" "login:" "username"
 "Password:" "pass-word" "% " "exec pppd passive"'
```

(Note, however, that running chat like this leaves the password visible in the parameter list of pppd and chat.)

If your serial connection is any more complicated than a piece of wire, you might need to arrange for some control characters to be escaped. In particular, it is often useful to escape XON (^Q) and XOFF (^S), using asyncmap a0000. If the path includes a telnet, you probably should escape ^] as well (asyncmap 200a0000). If the path includes an rlogin, you need to use the escape ff option on the end that is running the rlogin client because many rlogin implementations are not transparent; they remove the sequence (0xff, 0xff, 0x73, 0x73, followed by any 8 bytes) from the stream.

## DIAGNOSTICS

Messages are sent to the syslog daemon using the facility LOG_DAEMON. (This can be overridden by recompiling pppd with the macro LOG_PPP defined as the desired facility.) To see the error and debug messages, you need to edit your /etc/syslog.conf file to direct the messages to the desired output device or file.

The debug option causes the contents of all control packets sent or received to be logged—that is, all LCP, PAP, CHAP, or IPCP packets. This can be useful if the PPP negotiation does not succeed. If debugging is enabled at compile time, the debug option also causes other debugging messages to be logged.

Debugging can also be enabled or disabled by sending a SIGUSR1 to the pppd process. This signal acts as a toggle.

## FILES

| | |
|---|---|
| /var/run/pppn.pid (BSD or Linux) /etc/ppp/pppn.pid (others) | Process-ID for pppd process on PPP interface unit *n*. |
| /etc/ppp/ip-up | A program or script that is executed when the link is available for sending and receiving IP packets (that is, IPCP has come up). It is executed with the parameters *interface-name tty-device speed local-IP-address remote-IP-address* and with its standard input, output and error streams redirected to /dev/null. |
| | This program or script is executed with the same real and effective user-ID as pppd—that is, at least the effective user-ID and possibly the real user-ID will be root. This is so that it can be used to manipulate routes, run privileged daemons (such as send-mail), and so on. Be careful that the contents of the /etc/ppp/ip-up and /etc/ppp/ip-down scripts do not compromise your system's security. |
| /etc/ppp/ip-down | A program or script that is executed when the link is no longer available for sending and receiving IP packets. This script can be used for undoing the effects of the /etc/ppp/ip-up script. It is invoked with the same parameters as the ip-up script, and the same security considerations apply because it is executed with the same effective and real user-IDs as pppd. |
| /etc/ppp/ipx-up | A program or script that is executed when the link is available for sending and receiving IPX packets (that is, IPXCP has come up). It is executed with the parameters *interface-name tty-device speed network-number local-IPX-node-address remote-IPX-node-address local-IPX-routing-protocol remote-IPX-routing-protocol local-IPX-router-name remote-IPX-router-name ipparam pppd-pid* and with its standard input, output, and error streams redirected to /dev/null. |
| | The *local-IPX-routing*-protocol and *remote-IPX-routing-protocol* field may be one of the following: |

NONE to indicate that there is no routing protocol. RIP to indicate that RIP/SAP should be used. NLSP to indicate that Novell NLSP should be used. RIP NLSP to indicate that both RIP/SAP and NLSP should be used.

This program or script is executed with the same real and effective user-ID as pppd—that is, at least the effective user-ID and possibly the real user-ID will be root. This is so that it can be used to manipulate routes, run privileged daemons (such as ripd), and so on. Be careful that the contents of the /etc/ppp/ipx-up and /etc/ppp/ipx-down scripts do not compromise your system's security.

| | |
|---|---|
| /etc/ppp/ipx-down | A program or script that is executed when the link is no longer available for sending and receiving IPX packets. This script can be used for undoing the effects of the /etc/ppp/ipx-up script. It is invoked with the same parameters as the ipx-up script, and the same security considerations apply because it is executed with the same effective and real user-IDs as pppd. |
| /etc/ppp/pap-secrets | Usernames, passwords, and IP addresses for PAP authentication. |
| /etc/ppp/chap-secrets | Names, secrets, and IP addresses for CHAP authentication. |
| /etc/ppp/options | System default options for pppd, read before user default options or command-line options. |
| ~/.ppprc | User default options, read before command-line options. |
| /etc/ppp/options.ttyname | System default options for the serial port being used, read after command-line options. |

## SEE ALSO

| | |
|---|---|
| RFC 1144 | Jacobson, V. Compressing TCP/IP headers for low-speed serial links. February 1990. |
| RFC 1321 | Rivest, R. The MD5 Message-Digest Algorithm. April 1992. |
| RFC 1332 | McGregor, G. PPP Internet Protocol Control Protocol (IPCP). May 1992. |
| RFC 1334 | Lloyd, B.; Simpson, W.A. PPP authentication protocols. 1992 October. |
| RFC 1548 | Simpson, W.A. The Point–to–Point Protocol (PPP). December 1993. |
| RFC 1549 | Simpson, W.A. PPP in HDLC Framing. December 1993. |

## NOTES

The following signals have the specified effect when sent to the pppd process:

| | |
|---|---|
| SIGINT, SIGTERM | These signals cause pppd to terminate the link (by closing LCP), restore the serial device settings, and exit. |
| SIGHUP | This signal causes pppd to terminate the link, restore the serial device settings, and close the serial device. If the persist option has been specified, pppd tries to reopen the serial device and start another connection. Otherwise, pppd exits. |
| SIGUSR2 | This signal causes pppd to renegotiate compression. This can be useful to re-enable compression after it has been disabled as a result of a fatal decompression error. With the BSD Compress scheme, fatal decompression errors generally indicate a bug in one or another implementation. |

## AUTHORS

Drew Perkins, Brad Clements, Karl Fox, Greg Christy, Brad Parker, and Paul Mackerras (paulus@cs.anu.edu.au)

# pppstats

pppstats—Print PPP statistics.

## SYNOPSIS

```
pppstats [ -v ][-r ][-c ][-i secs][unit# ]
```

## DESCRIPTION

pppstats prints PPP-related statistics.

The -v flag causes pppstats to display additional statistics, such as the number of packets tossed (that is, which the VJ TCP header decompression code rejected).

The -r flag causes pppstats to display the overall packet compression rate. The rate value is between 0 and 1, with 0 meaning that the data is incompressible.

The -c flag is used to specify an alternate display mode that shows packet compression statistics: the number of packets and bytes uncompressed (that is, before compression or after decompression), compressed, and incompressible (packets that did not shrink on compression and were transmitted uncompressed), and the recent compression rate. This rate reflects the recent performance of the compression code rather than the overall rate the code compression was enabled.

The -i flag is used to specify the interval between printouts. The default is 5 seconds.

*unit#* specifies which interface to use for gathering statistics.

*2 May 1995*


# prunehistory

prunehistory—Remove filenames from Usenet history file.

## SYNOPSIS

```
prunehistory [ -f filename ][-p ][input ]
```

## DESCRIPTION

prunehistory modifies the history(5) text file to remove a set of filenames from it. The filenames are removed by overwriting them with spaces so that the size and position of any following entries do not change.

prunehistory reads the named input file or standard input if no file is given. The input is taken as a set of lines. Blank lines and lines starting with a number sign (#) are ignored. All other lines should consist of a Message-ID followed by zero or more filenames. prunehistory usually complains about lines that do not follow this format. If the -p flag is used, then the program silently prints any invalid lines on its standard output. (Blank lines and comment lines are also passed through.) This can be useful when prunehistory is used as a filter for other programs such as reap.

The Message-ID is used as the dbz(3) key to get an offset into the text file. If no filenames are mentioned on the input line, then all filenames in the text are removed. If any filenames are mentioned, they are converted into the history file notation. If they appear in the line for the specified Message-ID, they are removed.

The default name of the history file is /news/lib/history; to specify a different name, use the -f flag.

Because innd(8) only appends to the text file, prunehistory does not need to have any interaction with it.

It is a good idea to delete purged entries and rebuild the dbz database every so often by using a script such as the following:

```
ctlinnd throttle "Rebuilding history database"
cd /news/lib
awk 'NF > 2 {
printf "%s\t%s\t%s",$1,$2,$3;
for (i = 4; i <= NF; i++)
printf " %s", $i;
print "\n";
}' <history >history.n
if makehistory -r -f history.n ; then
```

```
mv history.n history
mv history.n.pag history.pag
mv history.n.dir history.dir
else
echo 'Problem rebuilding history; old file not replaced'
fi
ctlinnd go "Rebuilding history database"
```

Note that this keeps no record of expired articles.

## HISTORY

Written by Rich $alz (rsalz@uunet.uu.net) for InterNetNews.

## SEE ALSO

dbz(3), history(5), innd(8)

# quotacheck

quotacheck—Scan a filesystem for disk usages.

## SYNOPSIS

```
quotacheck [-g] [-u] [-v] -a
quotacheck [-g] [-u] [-v] filesys ...
```

## DESCRIPTION

quotacheck performs a filesystem scan for usage of files and directories, used by either user or group. The output is the quota file for the corresponding filesystem. By default, the names for these files are

| A user scan | quota.user |
| A group scan | quota.group |

The resulting file consists of a struct dqblk for each possible ID up to the highest existing UID or GID and contains the values for the disk file and block usage and possibly excess time for these values. (For definitions of struct dqblk, see linux/quota.h.)

quotacheck should be run each time the system boots and mounts non-valid filesystems. This is most likely to happen after a system crash.

The speed of the scan decreases with the amount of directories increasing. The time needed doubles when disk usage is doubled as well. A 100MB partition used for 94 percent is scanned in one minute; the same partition used for 50 percent is done in 25 seconds.

## OPTIONS

| | |
|---|---|
| -v | This way, the program will give some useful information about what it is doing, plus some fancy stuff. |
| -d | This means debug. It will result in a lot of information that can be used in debugging the program. The output is very verbose and the scan will not be fast. |
| -u | This flag tells the program to scan the disk and to count the files and directories used by a certain UID. This is the default action. |
| -g | This flag forces the program to count the files and directories used by a certain GID. |

## NOTE

checkquota should only be run as superuser. Non-privileged users are presumably not allowed to read all the directories on the given filesystem.

## SEE ALSO

quota(1), quotactl(2), fstab(5), quotaon(8), quotaoff(8), edquota(8), repquota(8), fsck(8), efsck(8), e2fsck(8), xfsck(8)

## FILES

`quota.user`

`quota.group`

`/etc/fstab`

## AUTHOR

Edvard Tuinder (v892231@si.hhs.nl, etuinder@delirium.nl.mugnet.org), Marco van Wieringen (v892273@si.hhs.nl, mvw@mcs.nl.mugnet.org).

*21 August 1993*

# quotaon, quotaoff

quotaon, quotaoff—Turn filesystem quotas on and off.

## SYNOPSIS

```
/usr/etc/quotaon  [ -vug ] filesystem...
/usr/etc/quotaon  [ -avug ]

/usr/etc/quotaoff [ -vug ] filesystem...
/usr/etc/quotaoff [ -avug ]
```

## DESCRIPTION

quotaon announces to the system that disk quotas should be enabled on one or more filesystems. The filesystem quota files must be present in the root directory of the specified filesystem and be named `quota.user` for user quota or `quota.group` for group quota.

quotaoff announces to the system that filesystems specified should have any disk quotas turned off.

## OPTIONS

### quotaon

| | |
|---|---|
| -a | All filesystems in `/etc/fstab` marked read-write with quotas will have their quotas turned on. This is usually used at boot time to enable quotas. |
| -v | Display a message for each filesystem where quotas are turned on. |
| -u | Manipulate user quotas. This is the default. |
| -g | Manipulate group quotas. |

### quotaoff

| | |
|---|---|
| -a | Force all filesystems in `/etc/fstab` to have their quotas disabled. |
| -v | Display a message for each filesystem affected. |
| -u | Manipulate user quotas. This is the default. |
| -g | Manipulate group quotas. |

## FILES

| | |
|---|---|
| `quota.user` | User quota file at the filesystem root |
| `quota.group` | Group quota file at the filesystem root |
| `/etc/fstab` | Default filesystems |

## SEE ALSO

quotactl(2), fstab(5)

*8 June 1993*

# rarp

rarp—Manipulate the system RARP table.

## SYNOPSIS

```
rarp [-v] [-t type] -a [hostname]
rarp [-v] -d hostname ...
rarp [-v] [-t type] -s hostname hw_addr
```

## DESCRIPTION

rarp manipulates the kernel's RARP table in various ways. The primary options are clearing an address mapping entry and manually setting up one. For debugging purposes, the rarp program also allows a complete dump of the RARP table.

## OPTIONS

| | |
|---|---|
| -v | Tell the user what is going on by being verbose. |
| -t type | When setting or reading the RARP table, this optional parameter tells rarp which class of entries it should check for. The default value of this parameter is ether (hardware code 0x01 for IEEE 802.3 10Mbps Ethernet). Other values might include network technologies such as AX.25 (ax25). |
| -a [hostname] | Shows the entries of the specified hosts. If the hostname parameter is not used, all entries are displayed. |
| -d hostname | Remove the entries of the specified host. This can be used if the indicated host is brought down, for example. |
| -s hostname hw_addr | Create an RARP address mapping entry for host hostname with hardware address set to hw_addr class, but for most classes, you can assume that the usual presentation can be used. For the Ethernet class, this is 6 bytes in hexadecimal, separated by colons. |

## FILES

/proc/net/rarp

## AUTHORS

Ross D. Martin (martin@trcsun3.eas.asu.edu), Fred N. van Kempen (waltje@uwalt.nl.mugnet.org).

*11 June 1994*

# rdev

rdev—Query/set image root device, swap device, RAM disk size, or video mode.

## SYNOPSIS

```
rdev [ -rsvh ] [ -o offset ][image [ value [ offset ]]]
rdev [ -o offset ][image [ root_device [ offset ]]]
swapdev [ -o offset ][image [ swap_device [ offset ]]]
ramsize [ -o offset ][image [ size [ offset ]]]
vidmode [ -o offset ][image [ mode [ offset ]]]
rootflags [ -o offset ][image [ flags [ offset ]]]
```

## DESCRIPTION

With no arguments, rdev outputs an /etc/mtab line for the current root filesystem. With no arguments, swapdev, ramsize, vidmode, and rootflags print usage information.

In a bootable image for the Linux kernel, there are several pairs of bytes that specify the root device, the video mode, the size of the RAM disk, and the swap device. These pairs of bytes, by default, begin at offset 504 (decimal) in the kernel image:

    498 Root flags
    (500 and 502 Reserved)
    504 RAM Disk Size
    506 VGA Mode
    508 Root Device
    (510 Boot Signature)

rdev changes these values.

Typical values for the image parameter, which is a bootable Linux kernel image, are as follows:

```
/vmlinux
/vmlinux.test
/vmunix
/vmunix.test
/dev/fd0
/dev/fd1
```

When using the rdev or swapdev commands, the root device or swap device parameter are as follows:

```
/dev/hda[1-8]
/dev/hdb[1-8]
/dev/sda[1-8]
/dev/sdb[1-8]
```

For the ramsize command, the size parameter specifies the size of the RAM disk in kilobytes.

For the rootflags command, the *flags* parameter contains extra information used when mounting root. Currently, the only effect of these flags is to force the kernel to mount the root filesystem in read-only mode if *flags* is nonzero.

For the vidmode command, the *mode* parameter specifies the video mode:

| | |
|---|---|
| -3 | Prompt |
| -2 | Extended VGA |
| -1 | Normal VGA |
| 0 | As if 0 was pressed at the prompt |
| 1 | As if 1 was pressed at the prompt |
| 2 | As if 2 was pressed at the prompt |
| n | As if n was pressed at the prompt |

If the value is not specified, the image is examined to determine the current settings.

## OPTIONS

| | |
|---|---|
| -s | Causes rdev to act like swapdev. |
| -r | Causes rdev to act like ramsize. |
| -R | Causes rdev to act like rootflags. |
| -v | Causes rdev to act like vidmode. |
| -h | Provides help. |

## BUGS

For historical reasons, there are two methods for specifying alternative values for the offset.

The user interface is cumbersome, non-intuitive, and should probably be rewritten from scratch, allowing multiple kernel image parameters to be changed or examined with a single command.

If LILO is used, rdev is no longer needed for setting the root device and the VGA mode because the parameters that rdev modifies can be set from the LILO prompt during a boot. However, rdev is still needed at this time for setting the RAM disk size. Users are encouraged to find the LILO documentation for more information and to use LILO when booting their systems.

## AUTHORS

Originally by Werner Almesberger (almesber@nessie.cs.id.ethz.ch). Modified by Peter MacDonald (pmacdona@sanjuan.UVic.CA). rootflags support added by Stephen Tweedie (sct@dcs.ed.ac.uk).

*Linux 0.99, 20 November 1993*

# renice

renice—Alter priority of running processes.

## SYNOPSIS

renice *priority* [[-p] *pid* ...] [[ -g] *pgrp* ...] [[-u] *user* ...]

## DESCRIPTION

renice alters the scheduling priority of one or more running processes. The following "who" parameters are interpreted as process IDs, process group IDs, or user names. reniceing a process group causes all processes in the process group to have their scheduling priority altered. reniceing a user causes all processes owned by the user to have their scheduling priority altered. By default, the processes to be affected are specified by their process IDs.

Options supported by renice:

| | |
|---|---|
| -g | Force who parameters to be interpreted as process group IDs. |
| -u | Force the who parameters to be interpreted as usernames. |
| -p | Reset the who interpretation to be (the default) process IDs. |

The following example changes the priority of process IDs 987 and 32 and all processes owned by users daemon and root:

renice +1 987 -u daemon root -p 32

Users other than the superuser can only alter the priority of processes they own and can only monotonically increase their "nice value" within the range 0 to PRIO_MAX (20). (This prevents overriding administrative fiats.) The superuser can alter the priority of any process and set the priority to any value in the range PRIO_MIN (-20) to PRIO_MAX. Useful priorities are: 20 (the affected processes run only when nothing else in the system wants to), 0 (the "base" scheduling priority), and anything negative (to make things go very fast).

## FILES

/etc/passwd to map usernames to user IDs

## SEE ALSO

getpriority(2), setpriority(2)

## BUGS

Non-superusers cannot increase scheduling priorities of their own processes, even if they were the ones that decreased the priorities in the first place.

## HISTORY

The renice command appeared in BSD 4.0.

*BSD 4, 9 June 1993*

# repquota

repquota—Summarize quotas for a filesystem.

## SYNOPSIS

/usr/etc/repquota [ -vug ] *filesystem...*
/usr/etc/repquota [ -avug ]

## DESCRIPTION

repquota prints a summary of the disk usage and quotas for the specified filesystems. For each user, the current number of files and amount of space (in kilobytes) is printed, along with any quotas created with edquota(8).

## OPTIONS

| | |
|---|---|
| -a | Report on all filesystems indicated in /etc/fstab to be read-write with quotas. |
| -v | Report all quotas even if there is no usage. |
| -g | Report quotas for groups. |
| -u | Report quotas for users. This is the default. |

Only the superuser can view quotas that are not their own.

## FILES

| | |
|---|---|
| quotas | Quota file at the filesystem root |
| /etc/fstab | Default filesystems |

## SEE ALSO

quota(1), quotactl(2), edquota(8), quotacheck(8), quotaon(8)

*8 June 1993*

# rexecd

rexecd—Remote execution server.

## SYNOPSIS

rexecd

## DESCRIPTION

rexecd is the server for the rexec(3) routine. The server provides remote execution facilities with authentication based on usernames and passwords.

rexecd listens for service requests at the port indicated in the exec service specification; see services(5). When a service request is received, the following protocol is initiated:

1.  The server reads characters from the socket up to a null \0 byte. The resultant string is interpreted as an ASCII number, base 10.

2.  If the number received in Step 1 is nonzero, it is interpreted as the port number of a secondary stream to be used for the `stderr`. A second connection is then created to the specified port on the client's machine.
3.  A null-terminated username of at most 16 characters is retrieved on the initial socket.
4.  A null-terminated, unencrypted password of at most 16 characters is retrieved on the initial socket.
5.  A null-terminated command to be passed to a shell is retrieved on the initial socket. The length of the command is limited by the upper bound on the size of the system's argument list.
6.  `rexecd` then validates the user as is done at login time and, if the authentication was successful, changes to the user's home directory and establishes the user and group protections of the user. If any of these steps fail, the connection is aborted with a diagnostic message returned.
7.  A null byte is returned on the initial socket and the command line is passed to the normal login shell of the user. The shell inherits the network connections established by `rexecd`.

## DIAGNOSTICS

Except for the last one listed, all diagnostic messages are returned on the initial socket, after which any network connections are closed. An error is indicated by a leading byte with a value of 1 (0 is returned in Step 7 upon successful completion of all the steps prior to the command execution).

| | |
|---|---|
| `username too long` | The name is longer than 16 characters. |
| `password too long` | The password is longer than 16 characters. |
| `command too long` | The command line passed exceeds the size of the argument list (as configured into the system). |
| `Login incorrect.` | No password file entry for the username existed or the wrong password was supplied. |
| `No remote directory.` | The `chdir` command to the home directory failed. |
| `Try again.` | A fork by the server failed. |
| `<shellname>: ...` | The user's login shell could not be started. This message is returned on the connection associated with the `stderr` and is not preceded by a flag byte. |

## SEE ALSO

`rexec(3)`

## BUGS

A facility to allow all data and password exchanges to be encrypted should be present.

## HISTORY

The `rexecd` command appeared in BSD 4.2.

*BSD 4.2, 16 March 1991*

# rlogind

`rlogind`—Remote login server.

## SYNOPSIS

`rlogind [-aln]`

## DESCRIPTION

`rlogind` is the server for the `rlogin(1)` program. The server provides a remote login facility with authentication based on privileged port numbers from trusted hosts.

Options supported by rlogind:

| | |
|---|---|
| -a | Ask hostname for verification. |
| -l | Prevent any authentication based on the user's .rhosts file unless the user is logging in as the superuser. |
| -n | Disable keep-alive messages. |

rlogind listens for service requests at the port indicated in the "login" service specification; see services(5). When a service request is received, the following protocol is initiated:

1. The server checks the client's source port. If the port is not in the range 512-1023, the server aborts the connection.
2. The server checks the client's source address and requests the corresponding hostname (see gethostbyaddr(3), hosts(5), and named(8)). If the hostname cannot be determined, the dot-notation representation of the host address is used. If the hostname is in the same domain as the server (according to the last two components of the domain name), or if the -a option is given, the addresses for the hostname are requested, verifying that the name and address correspond. Normal authentication is bypassed if the address verification fails.

Once the source port and address have been checked, rlogind proceeds with the authentication process described in rshd(8). It then allocates a pseudo terminal (see pty(4)) and manipulates file descriptors so that the slave half of the pseudo terminal becomes the stdin, stdout, and stderr for a login process. The login process is an instance of the login(1) program, invoked with the -f option if authentication has succeeded. If automatic authentication fails, the user is prompted to log in as if on a standard terminal line.

The parent of the login process manipulates the master side of the pseudo terminal, operating as an intermediary between the login process and the client instance of the rlogin program. In normal operation, the packet protocol described in pty(4) is invoked to provide $\hat{S}/\hat{Q}$ type facilities and propagate interrupt signals to the remote programs. The login process propagates the client terminal's baud rate and terminal type, as found in the environment variable, TERM; see environ(7). The screen or window size of the terminal is requested from the client, and window size changes from the client are propagated to the pseudo terminal.

Transport-level keep-alive messages are enabled unless the -n option is present. The use of keep-alive messages allows sessions to be timed out if the client crashes or becomes unreachable.

## DIAGNOSTICS

All initial diagnostic messages are indicated by a leading byte with a value of 1, after which any network connections are closed. If there are no errors before login is invoked, a null byte is returned as in indication of success.

Try again.                    A fork by the server failed.

## SEE ALSO

login(1), ruserok(3), rshd(8)

## BUGS

The authentication procedure used here assumes the integrity of each client machine and the connecting medium. This is insecure but is useful in an "open" environment.

A facility to allow all data exchanges to be encrypted should be present.

A more extensible protocol should be used.

## HISTORY

The rlogind command appeared in BSD 4.2.

*BSD 4.2, 16 March 1991*

# route

route—Show/manipulate the IP routing table.

## SYNOPSIS

```
route [ -vn ]
route [ -v ] add [ -net ¦ -host ] XXXX [gw GGGG] [metric MMMM] [netmask NNNN]
[mss NNNN] [window NNNN] [dev DDDD]
route [ -v ] del XXXX
```

## DESCRIPTION

route manipulates the kernel's IP routing table. Its primary use is to set up static routes to specific hosts or networks via an interface after it has been configured with the ifconfig(8) program. This version of route is intended solely for use with kernel versions 0.99pl14n and newer kernels.

## OPTIONS

| | |
|---|---|
| (none) | Prints out the kernel routing table, listing destination address, gateway, netmask for route ("Genmask"), flags (U = Up, H = Host, G = Gateway, D = dynamic, M = Modified), Metric (currently not supported), Ref, Use, and Iface (which device the route maps to). |
| -n | Same as previous but shows numerical addresses instead of trying to determine symbolic host names. |
| -v | A flag for verbose (not actually used). |
| del XXXX | Deletes the route associated with the destination address XXXX. |
| add[-net ¦ -host ] XXXX [gw GGGG] [metric MMMM] [netmask NNNN] [dev DDDD] | Adds a route to the IP address XXXX. The route is a network route if the -net modifier is used or XXXX is found in /etc/networks by the getnetbyname() library function and no -host modifier is used. |

The gw GGGG argument means that any IP packets sent to this address will be routed through the specified gateway. Note: The specified gateway must be reachable first. This usually means that you have to set up a static route to the gateway beforehand.

The metric MMMM modifier is not yet implemented (and with the -v option will actually print a warning).

The netmask NNNN modifier specifies the netmask of the route to be added. This only makes sense for a network route and when the address XXXX actually makes sense with the specified netmask. If no netmask is given, route guesses it instead, so for most normal setups, you won't need to specify a netmask.

The mss NNNN modifier specifies the TCP mss for the route to be added. This is usually used only for fine optimization of routing setups.

The window NNNN modifier specifies the TCP window for the route to be added. This is typically only used on AX.25 networks and with drivers unable to handle back-to-back frames—such as the 3c501 or DE600.

The dev DDDD modifier forces the route to be associated with the specified device because the kernel will otherwise try to determine the device on its own (by checking already existing routes and device specifications and where the route is added to). In most normal networks, you won't need this.

If dev DDDD is the last option on the command line, the word dev may be omitted because it's the default. Otherwise, the order of the route modifiers (metric, netmask, gw, and dev) doesn't matter.

## EXAMPLES

| | |
|---|---|
| `route add -net 127.0.0.0` | Adds the normal loopback entry, using netmask 255.0.0.0 (Class A net determined from the destination address) and associated with the lo device (assuming this device was previously set up correctly with ifconfig(8)). |
| `route add -net 192.56.76.0`<br>`netmask 255.255.255.0 dev eth0` | Adds a route to the network 192.56.76.x via eth0. The Class C netmask modifier is not really necessary here because 192.* is a Class C IP address. The word dev can be omitted here. |
| `route add default gw mango-gw` | Adds a default route (which will be used if no other route matches). All packets using this route will be gatewayed through mango-gw. The device that will actually be used for that route depends on how you can reach mango-gw; the static route to mango-gw will have to be set up before. |
| `route add ipx4 sl0 route add -net`<br>`192.57.66.0 netmask 255.255.255.0`<br>`gw ipx4` | This command sequence adds the route to the ipx4 host via the SLIP interface (assuming that ipx4 is the SLIP host) and then adds the net 192.57.66.0 to be gatewayed through that host. |

## FILES

`/proc/net/route`

`/etc/networks`

`/etc/hosts`

## SEE ALSO

`ifconfig(8)`

## HISTORY

route for Linux was originally written by Fred N. van Kempen (`waltje@uwalt.nl.mugnet.org`) and then modified by Johannes Stille and Linus Torvalds for pl15. Alan Cox added the `mss` and `window` options for Linux 1.1.22.

*14 June 1994*

# routed

routed—Network routing daemon.

## SYNOPSIS

`routed [-d] [-g] [-q] [-s] [-t] [logfile]`

## DESCRIPTION

routed is invoked at boot time to manage the network routing tables. The routing daemon uses a variant of the Xerox NS Routing Information Protocol in maintaining up-to-date kernel routing table entries. It used a generalized protocol capable of use with multiple address types but is currently used only for Internet routing within a cluster of networks.

In normal operation, routed listens on the udp(4) socket for the route(8) service (see services(5)) for routing information packets. If the host is an internetwork router, it periodically supplies copies of its routing tables to any directly connected hosts and networks.

When routed is started, it uses the SIOCGIFCONF ioctl(2) to find those directly connected interfaces configured into the system and marked "up" (the software loopback interface is ignored). If multiple interfaces are present, it is assumed that the host will forward packets between networks. routed then transmits a request packet on each interface (using a broadcast packet if the interface supports it) and enters a loop, listening for request and response packets from other hosts.

When a request packet is received, routed formulates a reply based on the information maintained in its internal tables. The response packet generated contains a list of known routes, each marked with a "hop count" metric (a count of 16, or greater, is considered "infinite"). The metric associated with each route returned provides a metric relative to the sender.

Response packets received by routed are used to update the routing tables if one of the following conditions is satisfied:

> No routing table entry exists for the destination network or host, and the metric indicates the destination is "reachable" (the hop count is not infinite).

> The source host of the packet is the same as the router in the existing routing table entry. That is, updated information is being received from the very internetwork router through which packets for the destination are being routed.

> The existing entry in the routing table has not been updated for some time (defined to be 90 seconds) and the route is at least as cost effective as the current route.

> The new route describes a shorter route to the destination than the one currently stored in the routing tables; the metric of the new route is compared against the one stored in the table to decide this.

When an update is applied, routed records the change in its internal tables and updates the kernel routing table. The change is reflected in the next response packet sent.

In addition to processing incoming packets, routed also periodically checks the routing table entries. If an entry has not been updated for three minutes, the entry's metric is set to infinity and marked for deletion. Deletions are delayed an additional 60 seconds to ensure the invalidation is propagated throughout the local Internet.

Hosts acting as internetwork routers gratuitously supply their routing tables every 30 seconds to all directly connected hosts and networks. The response is sent to the broadcast address on nets capable of that function, to the destination address on point-to-point links, and to the router's own address on other networks. The normal routing tables are bypassed when sending gratuitous responses. The reception of responses on each network is used to determine that the network and interface are functioning correctly. If no response is received on an interface, another route may be chosen to route around the interface, or the route may be dropped if no alternative is available.

Options supported by routed:

| | |
|---|---|
| -d | Enable additional debugging information to be logged, such as bad packets received. |
| -g | This flag is used on internetwork routers to offer a route to the "default" destination. This is typically used on a gateway to the Internet or on a gateway that uses another routing protocol whose routes are not reported to other local routers. |
| -s | Supplying this option forces routed to supply routing information whether it is acting as an internetwork router or not. This is the default if multiple network interfaces are present or if a point-to-point link is in use. |
| -q | This is the opposite of the -s option. |
| -t | If the -t option is specified, all packets sent or received are printed on the standard output. In addition, routed will not divorce itself from the controlling terminal so that interrupts from the keyboard will kill the process. |

Any other argument supplied is interpreted as the name of file in which routed's actions should be logged. This log contains information about any changes to the routing tables and, if not tracing all packets, a history of recent messages sent and received that are related to the changed route.

In addition to the facilities described previously, routed supports the notion of "distant" passive and active gateways. When routed is started, it reads the file to find gateways that might not be located using only information from the SIOGIFCONFioctl (2). Gateways specified in this manner should be marked passive if they are not expected to exchange routing information, whereas gateways marked active should be willing to exchange routing information (that is, they should have a routed process running on the machine). Routes through passive gateways are installed in the kernel's routing tables once upon startup. Such routes are not included in any routing information transmitted. Active gateways are treated equally to network interfaces. Routing information is distributed to the gateway, and if no routing information is received for a period of the time, the associated route is deleted. Gateways marked external are also passive but are not placed in the kernel routing table nor are they included in routing updates. The function of external entries is to inform `routed` that another routing process will install such a route and that alternate routes to that destination should not be installed. Such entries are only required when both routers might learn of routes to the same destination.

The /etc/gateways is comprised of a series of lines, each in the following format:

```
<net¦host> name1 gateway name2 metric value <passive¦active¦external>
```

The net or host keyword indicates if the route is to a network or specific host.

*name1* is the name of the destination network or host. This can be a symbolic name located in or known to the name server if started after named(8) or an Internet address specified in "dot" notation; see inet(3).

*name2* is the name or address of the gateway to which messages should be forwarded.

*value* is a metric indicating the hop count to the destination host or network.

One of the keywords passive, active, or external indicates if the gateway should be treated as passive or active (as described previously) or whether the gateway is external to the scope of the routed protocol.

Internetwork routers that are directly attached to the ARPAnet or Milnet should use the Exterior Gateway Protocol (EGP) to gather routing information rather than use a static routing table of passive gateways. EGP is required in order to provide routes for local networks to the rest of the Internet system. Sites needing assistance with such configurations should contact the Computer Systems Research Group at Berkeley.

## FILES

/etc/gateways for distant gateways

## SEE ALSO

udp(4), icmp(4), XNSrouted(8), htable(8)

Internet Transport Protocols, XSIS 028112, Xerox System Integration Standard

## BUGS

The kernel's routing tables may not correspond to those of routed when redirects change or add routes. routed should note any redirects received by reading the ICMP packets received via a raw socket.

routed should incorporate other routing protocols, such as Xerox NS, XNSrouted(8), and EGP . Using separate processes for each requires configuration options to avoid redundant or competing routes.

routed should listen to intelligent interfaces, such as an IMP, to gather more information. It does not always detect unidirectional failures in network interfaces (such as when the output side fails).

## HISTORY

The routed command appeared in BSD 4.2.

*BSD 4.2, 16 March 1991*

# rpc.rusersd

rpc.rusersd—Logged-in users server.

## SYNOPSIS

/usr/libexec/rpc.rusersd

## DESCRIPTION

rpc.rusersd is a server that returns information about users currently logged in to the system.

The currently logged-in users are queried using the rusers(1) command. The rpc.rusersd daemon is usually invoked by inetd(8).

rpc.rusersd uses an RPC protocol defined in /usr/include/rpcsvc.

## SEE ALSO

rusers(1), who(1), w(1), inetd(8)

*BSD 4.3, 7 June 1993*

# rpc.rwalld

rpc.rwalld—Write messages to users currently logged in to the server.

## SYNOPSIS

/usr/libexec/rpc.rwalld

## DESCRIPTION

rpc.rwalld is a server that will send a message to users currently logged in to the system. This server invokes the wall(1) command to actually write the messages to the system.

Messages are sent to this server by the rwall(1) command. The rpc.rwalld daemon is usually invoked by inetd(8).

rpc.rwalld uses an RPC protocol defined in /usr/include/rpcsvc/rwall.x.

## SEE ALSO

rwall(1), wall(1), inetd(8)

*BSD 4.3, 7 June 1993*

# rpcinfo

rpcinfo—Report RPC information.

## SYNOPSIS

rpcinfo -p [*host*]
rpcinfo [-n *portnum*] -u *host program* [*version*]
rpcinfo [-n *portnum*] -t *host program* [*version*]
rpcinfo -b *program version*
rpcinfo -d *program version*

## DESCRIPTION

rpcinfo makes an RPC call to an RPC server and reports what it finds.

## OPTIONS

| | |
|---|---|
| -p | Probe the port mapper on host and print a list of all registered RPC programs. If host is not specified, it defaults to the value returned by hostname(1). |
| -u | Make an RPC call to procedure 0 of *program* on the specified *host* using UDP and report whether a response was received. |
| -t | Make an RPC call to procedure 0 of *program* on the specified *host* using TCP and report whether a response was received. |
| -n | Use *portnum* as the port number for the -t and -u options instead of the port number given by the port mapper. |

-b                        Make an RPC broadcast to procedure 0 of the specified *program* and *version* using UDP
                          and report all hosts that respond.

-d                        Delete registration for the RPC service of the specified *program* and *version*. This option
                          can be exercised only by the superuser.

The program argument can be either a name or a number. If a version is specified, rpcinfo attempts to call that version of the specified program. Otherwise, rpcinfo attempts to find all the registered version numbers for the specified program by calling version 0 (which is presumed not to exist; if it does exist, rpcinfo attempts to obtain this information by calling an extremely high version number instead) and attempts to call each registered version. Note that the version number is required for -b and -d options.

## EXAMPLES

To show all the RPC services registered on the local machine, use

rpcinfo -p

To show all of the RPC services registered on the machine named klaxon, use

rpcinfo -p klaxon

To show all machines on the local net that are running the Yellow Pages service, use

rpcinfo -b ypserv 'version' -- uniq

'version' is the current Yellow Pages version obtained from the results of the -p switch above.

To delete the registration for version 1 of the walld service, use

rpcinfo -d walld 1

## SEE ALSO

rpc(5), portmap(8), *RPC Programming Guide*

## BUGS

In releases prior to SunOS 3.0, the Network File System (NFS) did not register itself with the port mapper; rpcinfo cannot be used to make RPC calls to the NFS server on hosts running such releases.

*17 December 1987*

# rquotad, rpc.rquotad

rquotad, rpc.rquotad—Remote quota server.

## SYNOPSIS

/usr/etc/rpc.rquotad

## DESCRIPTION

rquotad is an rpc(3N) server that returns quotas for a user of a local filesystem that is mounted by a remote machine over the NFS. The results are used by quota(1) to display user quotas for remote filesystems. The rquotad daemon is usually started at boot time from the rc.net script.

## FILES

quotas                    Quota file at the filesystem root

## SEE ALSO

quota(1), rpc(3N), nfs(4P), services(5) inetd(8C)

*17 December 1987*

# rshd

rshd—Remote shell server.

## SYNOPSIS

rshd [-alnL]

## DESCRIPTION

The rshd server is the server for the rcmd(3) routine and, consequently, for the rsh(1) program. The server provides remote execution facilities with authentication based on privileged port numbers from trusted hosts.

The rshd server listens for service requests at the port indicated in the cmd service specification; see services(5). When a service request is received, the following protocol is initiated:

1. The server checks the client's source port. If the port is not in the range 512-1023, the server aborts the connection.
2. The server reads characters from the socket up to a null (\0) byte. The resultant string is interpreted as an ASCII number, base 10.
3. If the number received in Step 2 is nonzero, it is interpreted as the port number of a secondary stream to be used for the stderr. A second connection is then created to the specified port on the client's machine. The source port of this second connection is also in the range 512-1023.
4. The server checks the client's source address and requests the corresponding hostname (see gethostbyaddr(3), hosts(5), and named(8)). If the hostname cannot be determined, the dot-notation representation of the host address is used. If the hostname is in the same domain as the server (according to the last two components of the domain name), or if the -a option is given, the addresses for the hostname are requested, verifying that the name and address correspond. If address verification fails, the connection is aborted with the message, Host address mismatch.
5. A null-terminated username of at most 16 characters is retrieved on the initial socket. This username is interpreted as the user identity on the client's machine.
6. A null-terminated username of at most 16 characters is retrieved on the initial socket. This username is interpreted as a user identity to use on the server's machine.
7. A null-terminated command to be passed to a shell is retrieved on the initial socket. The length of the command is limited by the upper bound on the size of the system's argument list.
8. rshd then validates the user using ruserok(3), which uses the file and the file found in the user's home directory. The -l option prevents ruserok(3) from doing any validation based on the user's .rhosts file, unless the user is the superuser.
9. A null byte is returned on the initial socket and the command line is passed to the normal login shell of the user. The shell inherits the network connections established by rshd.

Transport-level keep-alive messages are enabled unless the -n option is present. The use of keep-alive messages allows sessions to be timed out if the client crashes or becomes unreachable.

The -L option causes all successful accesses to be logged to syslogd(8) as auth.info messages and all failed accesses to be logged as auth.notice.

## DIAGNOSTICS

Except for the last one listed, all diagnostic messages are returned on the initial socket, after which any network connections are closed. An error is indicated by a leading byte with a value of 1 (0 is returned in Step 9 upon successful completion of all the steps prior to the execution of the login shell).

| | |
|---|---|
| Locuser too long. | The name of the user on the client's machine is longer than 16 characters. |
| Ruser too long. | The name of the user on the remote machine is longer than 16 characters. |
| Command too long. | The command line passed exceeds the size of the argument list (as configured into the system). |
| Login incorrect. | No password file entry for the username existed. |
| Remote directory. | The chdir command to the home directory failed. |

| | |
|---|---|
| `Permission denied.` | The authentication procedure described previously failed. |
| `Can't make pipe.` | The pipe needed for the `stderr` wasn't created. |
| `Can't fork; try again.` | A fork by the server failed. |
| `<shellname>: ...` | The user's login shell could not be started. This message is returned on the connection associated with the `stderr` and is not preceded by a flag byte. |

## SEE ALSO

`rsh`(1), `rcmd`(3), `ruserok`(3)

## BUGS

The authentication procedure used here assumes the integrity of each client machine and the connecting medium. This is insecure but is useful in an "open" environment.

A facility to allow all data exchanges to be encrypted should be present.

A more extensible protocol (such as Telnet) should be used.

*BSD 4.2, 30 April 1991*

# rwhod

`rwhod`—System status server.

## SYNOPSIS

`rwhod`

## DESCRIPTION

`rwhod` is the server that maintains the database used by the `rwho`(1) and `ruptime`(1) programs. Its operation is predicated on the ability to broadcast messages on a network.

`rwhod` operates as both a producer and consumer of status information. As a producer of information, it periodically queries the state of the system and constructs status messages that are broadcast on a network. As a consumer of information, it listens for other `rwhod` servers' status messages, validating them and then recording them in a collection of files located in the directory.

The server transmits and receives messages at the port indicated in the `rwho` service specification; see `services`(5). The messages sent and received are of the form:

```
struct outmp {
char out_line[8]; /* tty name */
char out_name[8]; /* user id */
long out_time; /* time on */
};

struct whod {
      char    wd_vers;
      char    wd_type;
      char    wd_fill[2];
      int     wd_sendtime;
      int     wd_recvtime;
      char    wd_hostname[32];
      int     wd_loadav[3];
      int     wd_boottime;
      struct whoent {
              struct outmp we_utmp;
```

```
        int    we_idle;
    } wd_we[1024 / sizeof (struct whoent)];
};
```

All fields are converted to network byte order prior to transmission. The load averages are as calculated by the w(1) program and represent load averages over the 5-, 10-, and 15-minute intervals prior to a server's transmission; they are multiplied by 100 for representation in an integer. The hostname included is that returned by the gethostname(2) system call, with any trailing domain name omitted. The array at the end of the message contains information about the users logged in to the sending machine. This information includes the contents of the utmp(5) entry for each non-idle terminal line and a value indicating the time in seconds since a character was last received on the terminal line.

Messages received by the rwho server are discarded unless they originated at an rwho server's port. In addition, if the host's name, as specified in the message, contains any unprintable ASCII characters, the message is discarded. Valid messages received by rwhod are placed in files named in the directory. These files contain only the most recent message, in the format described previously.

Status messages are generated approximately once every three minutes. rwhod performs an nlist(3) every 30 minutes to guard against the possibility that this file is not the system image currently operating.

## SEE ALSO

rwho(1), ruptime(1)

## BUGS

There should be a way to relay status information between networks. Status information should be sent only upon request rather than continuously. People often interpret the server dying or network communication failures as a machine going down.

## HISTORY

The rwhod command appeared in BSD 4.2.

*BSD 4.2, 16 March 1991*

# sendmail

sendmail—Send mail over the Internet.

## SYNOPSIS

```
sendmail [flags] [address ...]
newaliases
mailq [-v]
smtpd
bsmtp
runq
```

## DESCRIPTION

sendmail sends a message to one or more recipients, routing the message over whatever networks are necessary. sendmail does internetwork forwarding as necessary to deliver the message to the correct place.

sendmail is not intended as a user interface routine. Other programs provide user-friendly front ends. sendmail is used only to deliver preformatted messages.

With no flags, sendmail reads its standard input up to an end-of-file or a line consisting only of a single dot and sends a copy of the message found there to all the addresses listed. It determines the networks to use based on the syntax and contents of the addresses.

Local addresses are looked up in a file and aliased appropriately. Aliasing can be prevented by preceding the address with a backslash. Usually, the sender is not included in any alias expansions; for example, if john sends to group and group includes john in the expansion, then the letter will not be delivered to john.

Flags are

| | |
|---|---|
| -ba | Go into ARPANET mode. All input lines must end with a CR-LF, and all messages will be generated with a CR-LF at the end. Also, the From: and Sender: fields are examined for the name of the sender. |
| -bd | Run as a daemon. This requires Berkeley IPC. sendmail will fork and run in the background, listening on socket 25 for incoming SMTP connections. This is usually run from /etc/rc. |
| -bi | Initialize the alias database. |
| -bm | Deliver mail in the usual way (default). |
| -bp | Print a listing of the queue. |
| -bs | Use the SMTP protocol as described in RFC 821 on standard input and output. This flag implies all the operations of the -ba flag that are compatible with SMTP. |
| -bb | Read batched SMTP (BSMTP) commands from standard input. |
| -bt | Run in address test mode. This mode reads addresses and shows the steps in parsing; it is used for debugging configuration tables. |
| -bv | Verify names only; do not try to collect or deliver a message. Verify mode is usually used for validating users or mailing lists. |
| -bz | Create the configuration freeze file. |
| -C file | Use alternate configuration file. sendmail refuses to run as root if an alternate configuration file is specified. The frozen configuration file is bypassed. |
| -d X | Set debugging value to X. |
| -F fullname | Set the full name of the sender. |
| -f name | Sets the name of the "from" person (the sender of the mail). -f can only be used by trusted users (usually root, daemon, and network) or if the person you are trying to become is the same as the person you are. |
| -h N | Set the hop count to N. The hop count is incremented every time the mail is processed. When it reaches a limit, the mail is returned with an error message, the victim of an aliasing loop. If not specified, Received: lines in the message are counted. |
| -n | Don't do aliasing. |
| -o x value | Set option x to the specified value. Options are described later in this section. |
| -q time | Processed saved messages in the queue at given intervals. If time is omitted, process the queue once. time is given as a tagged number, with s being seconds, m being minutes, h being hours, d being days, and w being weeks. For example, -q1h30m or -q90m both set the time-out to 1 hour, 30 minutes. If time is specified, sendmail runs in background. This option can be used safely with -bd. |
| -M ident | Process the queued message with the queue ID ident. |
| -R addr | Process the queued messages that have the string addr in one of the recipient addresses. |
| -S addr | Process the queued messages that have the string addr in the sender address. |
| -r name | An alternate and obsolete form of the -f flag. |
| -t | Read message for recipients. To:, Cc:, and Bcc: lines are scanned for recipient addresses. The Bcc: line is deleted before transmission. Any addresses in the argument list are suppressed; that is, they do not receive copies even if listed in the message header. |
| -v | Go into verbose mode. Alias expansions are announced and so on. |

There are also a number of processing options that can be set. Usually, these will only be used by a system administrator. Options can be set either on the command line using the -o flag or in the configuration file. These are described in detail in the *Sendmail Installation and Operation Guide.* The options are

| | |
|---|---|
| A file | Use alternate alias file. |
| c | On mailers that are considered "expensive" to connect to, don't initiate immediate connection. This requires queuing. |
| d x | Set the delivery mode to x. Delivery modes are i for interactive (synchronous) delivery, b for background (asynchronous) delivery, and q for queue only (actual delivery is done the next time the queue is run). |
| D | Try to automatically rebuild the alias database if necessary. |
| e x | Set error processing to mode x. Valid modes are m to mail back the error message, w to "write" back the error message (or mail it back if the sender is not logged in), p to print the errors on the terminal (default), q to throw away error messages (only exit status is returned), and e to do special processing for the BerkNet. If the text of the message is not mailed back by modes m or w and if the sender is local to this machine, a copy of the message is appended to the file in the sender's home directory. |
| F mode | The mode to use when creating temporary files. |
| f | Save UNIX–style From: lines at the front of messages. |
| g N | The default group ID to use when calling mailers. |
| H file | The SMTP help file. |
| i | Do not take dots on a line by themselves as a message terminator. |
| k N | Checkpoint the queue file after every N successful deliveries (default is 10). This avoids excessive duplicate deliveries when sending to long mailing lists interrupted by system crashes. |
| L n | The log level. |
| m | Send also to "me" (the sender) if I am in an alias expansion. |
| o | If set, this message may have old style headers. If not set, this message is guaranteed to have new style headers (commas instead of spaces between addresses). If set, an adaptive algorithm is used that will correctly determine the header format in most cases. |
| Q queuedir | Select the directory in which to queue messages. |
| r timeout | The time-out on reads; if none is set, sendmail will wait forever for a mailer. This option violates the word (if not the intent) of the SMTP specification, so the timeout should probably be fairly large. |
| S file | Save statistics in the named file. |
| s | Always instantiate the queue file, even under circumstances where it is not strictly necessary. This provides safety against system crashes during delivery. |
| T time | Set the time-out on undelivered messages in the queue to the specified time. After delivery has failed (for example, because of a host being down) for this amount of time, failed messages will be returned to the sender. The default is three days. |
| t stz, dtz | Set the name of the time zone. |
| U userdatabase | If set, a user database is consulted to get forwarding information. You can consider this an adjunct to the aliasing mechanism, except that the database is intended to be distributed; aliases are local to a particular host. This might not be available if your sendmail does not have the USERDB option compiled in. |
| u N | Set the default user ID for mailers. |
| w | If not set, name server lookups will use a query type of ANY to find types CNAME, A, and MX and will cause all existing records to be cached by the local server. If there is (or might be) a wildcard MX in the local domain or its parents that are searched, you must set this |

option, which uses a query type of CNAME only; otherwise, it causes all fully qualified names to match as names in the local domain.

In aliases, the first character of a name can be a vertical bar to cause interpretation of the rest of the name as a command to pipe the mail to. It might be necessary to quote the name to keep sendmail from suppressing the blanks between arguments. For example, a common alias is

msgs: "|/ucr/bin/msgs -s"

Aliases can also have the syntax to ask sendmail to read the named file for a list of recipients. For example, an alias such as

poets: ":include:/usr/local/lib/poets.list"

would read for the list of addresses making up the group.

sendmail returns an exit status describing what it did. The codes are defined in sysexits.h:

| | |
|---|---|
| EX_OK | Successful completion on all addresses. |
| EX_NOUSER | Username not recognized. |
| EX_UNAVAILABLE | Catchall meaning necessary resources were not available. |
| EX_SYNTAX | Syntax error in address. |
| EX_SOFTWARE | Internal software error, including bad arguments. |
| EX_OSERR | Temporary operating system error, such as cannot fork. |
| EX_NOHOST | Hostname not recognized. |
| EX_TEMPFAIL | Message could not be sent immediately but was queued. |

If invoked as newaliases, sendmail rebuilds the alias database. If invoked as mailq, sendmail prints the contents of the mail queue. If invoked as smtpd, sendmail forks and runs as a daemon. If invoked as bsmtp, sendmail processes batched SMTP on standard input. If invoked as runq, sendmail runs through the mail queue and makes what deliveries are possible.

## FILES

Except for the file /etc/sendmail.cf itself, the following pathnames are all specified in /etc/sendmail.cf. Thus, these values are only approximations.

/etc/aliases raw data for alias names

/etc/aliases.pag

/etc/aliases.dir database of alias names

/etc/sendmail.cf configuration file

/etc/sendmail.fc frozen configuration

/etc/sendmail.hf help file

/var/log/sendmail.st collected statistics

/var/spool/mqueue/* temp files

## SEE ALSO

binmail(1), mail(1), rmail(1), syslog(3), aliases(5), mailaddr(7), rc(8); DARPA Internet Request for Comments RFC 819, RFC 821, RFC 822; "Sendmail: An Internetwork Mail Router," SMM and No.16, "Sendmail Installation and Operation Guide," SMM and No.7.

## HISTORY

The sendmail command appeared in BSD 4.2.

# setfdprm

setfdprm—Sets user-provided floppy disk parameters.

## SYNOPSIS

```
setfdprm [ -p ] device name
setfdprm [ -p ] device size sectors heads tracks stretch gap rate spec1 fmt_gap
setfdprm [ -c ] device
setfdprm [ -y ] device
setfdprm [ -n ] device
```

## DESCRIPTION

setfdprm is a utility that can be used to load disk parameters into the auto-detecting floppy devices, to clear old parameter sets, and to disable or enable diagnostic messages.

Without any options, setfdprm loads the device (usually /dev/fd0 or /dev/fd1) with a new parameter set with the name entry found in /etc/fdprm (usually named 360/360 and so on). These parameters stay in effect until the media is changed.

## OPTIONS

| | |
|---|---|
| -p device name | Permanently loads a new parameter set for the specified auto-configuring floppy device for the configuration with *name* in /etc/fdprm. Alternatively, the parameters can be given directly from the command line. |
| -c device | Clears the parameter set of the specified auto-configuring floppy device. |
| -y device | Enables format detection messages for the specified auto-configuring floppy device. |
| -n device | Disables format detection messages for the specified auto-configuring floppy device. |

## BUGS

This documentation is grossly incomplete.

## FILES

/etc/fdprm

## AUTHOR

Werner Almesberger (almesber@nessie.cs.id.eth7.ch)

*Linux 0.99, 20 November 1993*

# setserial

setserial—Get/set Linux serial port information.

## SYNOPSIS

```
setserial [ -abqvVW ] device [ parameter1 [ arg ] ] ...
setserial -g [ -abv ] device1 ...
```

## DESCRIPTION

setserial is a program designed to set or report the configuration information associated with a serial port. This information includes what I/O port and IRQ a particular serial port is using, whether the break key should be interpreted as the Secure Attention Key, and so on.

During the normal bootup process, only COM ports 1-4 are initialized, using the default I/O ports and IRQ values, as listed. To initialize any additional serial ports, or to change the COM 1-4 ports to a nonstandard configuration, the setserial program should be used. Typically, it is called from an rc.serial script, which is usually run out of /etc/rc.local.

The device argument or arguments specify the serial device that should be configured or interrogated. It will usually have the following form: /dev/cua[0-3].

If no parameters are specified, setserial prints the port type (such as 8250, 16450, 16550, 16550A), the hardware I/O port, the hardware IRQ line, its "baud base," and some of its operational flags.

If the -g option is given, the arguments to setserial are interpreted as a list of devices for which the characteristics of those devices should be printed.

Without the -g option, the first argument to setserial is interpreted as the device to be modified or characteristics to be printed, and any additional arguments are interpreted as parameters that should be assigned to that serial device.

For the most part, superuser privilege is required to set the configuration parameters of a serial port. A few serial port parameters can be set by normal users, however, and these are noted as exceptions in this manual page.

## OPTIONS

setserial accepts the following options:

| | |
|---|---|
| -a | When reporting the configuration of a serial device, print all available information. |
| -b | When reporting the configuration of a serial device, print a summary of the device's configuration, which might be suitable for printing during the bootup process during the /etc/rc script. |
| -q | Be quiet. setserial will print fewer lines of output. |
| -v | Be verbose. setserial will print additional status output. |
| -V | Display version and exit. |
| -W | Do wild interrupt initialization and exit. |

## PARAMETERS

The following parameters can be assigned to a serial port.

All argument values are assumed to be in decimal unless preceded by 0x.

| | |
|---|---|
| port *port_number* | The port option sets the I/O port as described previously. |
| irq *irq_number* | The irq option sets the hardware IRQ as described previously. |
| uart *uart_type* | This option is used to set the UART type. The permitted types are none, 8250, 16450, 16550, and 16550A. Because the 8250 and 16450 UARTs do not have FIFOs, and because the original 16550 have bugs that make the FIFOs unusable, the FIFO will only be used on chips identified as 16550A UARTs. Setting the UART type to 8250, 16450, or 16550 will enable the serial port without trying to use the FIFO. Using the UART type none will disable the port. Some internal modems are billed as having a "16550A UART with a 1KB buffer." This is a lie. They do not really have a 16550A-compatible UART; instead, what they have is a 16450-compatible UART with a 1KB receive buffer to prevent receiver overruns. This is important because they do not have a transmit FIFO. Hence, they are not compatible with a 16550A UART, and the autoconfiguration process will correctly identify them as 16450s. If you attempt to override this using the uart parameter, you see dropped characters during file transmissions. These UARTs usually have other problems: The skip test parameter also often must be specified. |
| autoconfig | When this parameter is given, setserial asks the kernel to attempt to automatically configure the serial port. The I/O port must be correctly set; the kernel will attempt to determine the UART type, and if the auto_irq parameter is set, Linux will attempt to automatically determine the IRQ. The autoconfigure parameter should be given after the port, auto_irq, and skip_test parameters have been specified. |

| | |
|---|---|
| auto_irq | During autoconfiguration, try to determine the IRQ. This feature is not guaranteed to always produce the correct result; some hardware configurations will fool the Linux kernel. It is generally safer not to use the auto_irq feature but rather to specify the IRQ to be used explicitly, using the irq parameter. |
| ^auto_irq | During autoconfiguration, do not try to determine the IRQ. |
| skip_test | During autoconfiguration, skip the UART test. Some internal modems do not have National Semiconductor compatible UARTs but have cheap imitations instead. Some of these cheesy imitation UARTs do not fully support the loopback detection mode, which is used by the kernel to make sure there really is a UART at a particular address before attempting to configure it. For certain internal modems, you will need to specify this parameter so Linux can initialize the UART correctly. |
| ^skip_test | During autoconfiguration, do not skip the UART test. |
| baud_base *baud_base* | This option sets the base baud rate, which is the clock frequency divided by 16. Usually, this value is 115200, which is also the fastest baud rate, which the UART can support. |
| spd_hi | Use 57.6KB when the application requests 38.4KB. This parameter can be specified by a non-privileged user. |
| spd_vhi | Use 115KB when the application requests 38.4KB. This parameter can be specified by a non-privileged user. |
| spd_cust | Use the custom divisor to set the speed when the application requests 38.4KB. In this case, the baud rate is the baud_base divided by the divisor. This parameter can be specified by a non-privileged user. |
| spd_normal | Use 38.4KB when the application requests 38.4KB. This parameter can be specified by a non-privileged user. |
| divisor *divisor* | This option sets the custom divisor. This divisor will be used when the spd_cust option is selected and the serial port is set to 38.4KB by the application. This parameter can be specified by a non-privileged user. |
| sak | Set the break key at the Secure Attention Key. |
| ^sak | Disable the Secure Attention Key. |
| fourport | Configure the port as an AST Fourport card. |
| ^fourport | Disable AST Fourport configuration. |
| close_delay *delay* | Specify the amount of time, in hundredths of a second, that DTR should remain low on a serial line after the callout device is closed before the blocked dial-in device raises DTR again. The default value of this option is 50, or a half-second delay. |
| Session_lockout | Lock out callout port (/dev/cua*XX*) accesses across different sessions. That is, once a process has opened a port, do not allow a process with a different session ID to open that port until the first process has closed it. |
| ^session_lockout | Do not lock out callout port accesses across different sessions. |
| pgrp_lockout | Lock out callout port (/dev/cua*XX*) accesses across different process groups. That is, once a process has opened a port, do not allow a process in a different process group to open that port until the first process has closed it. |
| ^pgrp_lockout | Do not lock out callout port accesses across different process groups. |
| hup_notify | Notify a process blocked on opening a dial-in line when a process has finished using a callout line (either by closing it or by the serial line being hung up) by returning EAGAIN to the open.<br><br>The application of this parameter is for gettys that are blocked on a serial port's dial-in line. This allows the getty to reset the modem (which may have had its configuration modified by the application using the callout device) before blocking on the open again. |
| ^hup_notify | Do not notify a process blocked on opening a dial-in line when the callout device is hung up. |

| | |
|---|---|
| split_termios | Treat the termios settings used by the callout device and the termios settings used by the dial-in devices as separate. |
| ^split_termios | Use the same termios structure to store both the dial-in and callout ports. This is the default option. |
| callout_nohup | If this particular serial port is opened as a callout device, do not hang up the tty when carrier detect is dropped. |
| ^callout_nohup | Do not skip hanging up the tty when a serial port is opened as a callout device. Of course, the HUPCL termios flag must be enabled if the hangup is to occur. |

## CONSIDERATIONS OF CONFIGURING SERIAL PORTS

It is important to note that setserial merely tells the Linux kernel where it should expect to find the I/O port and IRQ lines of a particular serial port. It does not configure the hardware, the actual serial board, to use a particular I/O port. To do that, you need to physically program the serial board, usually by setting some jumpers or by switching some DIP switches.

This section provides some pointers in helping you decide how you want to configure your serial ports.

The "standard MS-DOS" port associations are

| | |
|---|---|
| /dev/ttyS0 (COM1), port 0x3f8 | IRQ 4 |
| /dev/ttyS1 (COM2), port 0x2f8 | IRQ 3 |
| /dev/ttyS2 (COM3), port 0x3e8 | IRQ 4 |
| /dev/ttyS3 (COM4), port 0x2e8 | IRQ 3 |

Due to the limitations in the design of the AT/ISA bus architecture, an IRQ line usually cannot be shared between two or more serial ports. If you attempt to do this, one or both serial ports will become unreliable if you try to use both simultaneously. This limitation can be overcome by special multiport serial port boards, which are designed to share multiple serial ports over a single IRQ line. Multiport serial cards supported by Linux include the AST FourPort, the Accent Async board, the Usenet Serial II board, the Bocaboard BB-1004, BB-1008, and BB-2016 boards, and the HUB-6 serial board.

The selection of an alternative IRQ line is difficult because most of them are already used. The following table lists the "standard MS-DOS" assignments of available IRQ lines:

| | |
|---|---|
| IRQ 3 | COM2 |
| IRQ 4 | COM1 |
| IRQ 5 | LPT2 |
| IRQ 7 | LPT1 |

Most people find that IRQ 5 is a good choice, assuming that there is only one parallel port active in the computer. Another good choice is IRQ 2 (a.k.a. IRQ 9), although this IRQ is sometimes used by network cards, and very rarely will VGA cards be configured to use IRQ 2 as a vertical retrace interrupt. If your VGA card is configured this way, try to disable it so you can reclaim that IRQ line for some other card. It's not necessary for Linux and most other operating systems.

The only other available IRQ lines are 3, 4, and 7, and these are probably used by the other serial and parallel ports. (If your serial card has a 16-bit card edge connector and supports higher interrupt numbers, then IRQ 10, 11, 12, and 15 are also available.)

On AT class machines, IRQ 2 is seen as IRQ 9, and Linux will interpret it in this manner.

IRQs other than 2 (9), 3, 4, 5, 7, 10, 11, 12, and 15 should not be used because they are assigned to other hardware and cannot, in general, be changed. Here are the "standard" assignments:

| | |
|---|---|
| IRQ 0 | Timer channel 0 |
| IRQ 1 | Keyboard |
| IRQ 2 | Cascade for controller 2 |
| IRQ 3 | Serial port 2 |
| IRQ 4 | Serial port 1 |

| IRQ 5 | Parallel port 2 (Reserved in PS/2) |
|-------|-------------------------------------|
| IRQ 6 | Floppy diskette |
| IRQ 7 | Parallel port 1 |
| IRQ 8 | Real-time clock |
| IRQ 9 | Redirected to IRQ2 |
| IRQ 10 | Reserved |
| IRQ 11 | Reserved |
| IRQ 12 | Reserved (Auxiliary device in PS/2) |
| IRQ 13 | Math coprocessor |
| IRQ 14 | Hard disk controller |
| IRQ 15 | Reserved |

## CAUTION

Using an invalid port can lock up your machine.

## FILES

`/etc/rc.local`

`/etc/rc.serial`

## SEE ALSO

`tty`(4), `ttys`(4), `kernel/chr_drv/serial.c`

## AUTHOR

The original version of `setserial` was written by Rick Sladkey (`jrs@world.std.com`) and was modified by Michael K. Johnson (`johnsonm@stolaf.edu`).

This version has since been rewritten from scratch by Theodore Ts'o (`tytso@mit.edu`) on 1/1/93. Any bugs or problems are solely his responsibility.

*setserial 2.10, 27 August 1994*

# setsid

`setsid`—Run a program in a new session.

## SYNOPSIS

`setsid` *program* [ *arg* ... ]

## DESCRIPTION

`setsid` runs a program in a new session.

## SEE ALSO

`setsid`(2)

## AUTHOR

Rick Sladkey (`jrs@world.std.com`)

*Linux 0.99, 20 November 1993*

# showmount

showmount—Show mount information for an NFS server.

## SYNOPSIS

```
/usr/etc/showmount [\-adehv\][\--all\][\--directories\]
[\--exports\][\--help\] [\ -version\][\host\]
```

## DESCRIPTION

showmount queries the mount daemon on a remote host for information about the state of the NFS server on that machine. With no options, showmount lists the set of clients who are mounting from that host. The output from showmount is designed to appear as though it were processed through sort -u.

## OPTIONS

| | |
|---|---|
| -a or --all | List both the client hostname and mounted directory in *host*:*dir* format. |
| -d or --directories | List only the directories mounted by some client. |
| -e or --exports | Show the NFS server's export list. |
| -h or --help | Provide a short help summary. |
| -v or --version | Report the current version number of the program. |
| --no-headers | Suppress the descriptive headings from the output. |

## SEE ALSO

rpc.mountd(8), rpc.nfsd(8)

## BUGS

The completeness and accuracy of the information that showmount displays varies according to the NFS server's implementation. Because showmount sorts and uniques the output, it is impossible to determine from the output whether a client is mounting the same directory more than once.

## AUTHOR

Rick Sladkey (jrs@world.std.com)

*6 October 1993*

# shutdown

shutdown—Close down the system.

## SYNOPSIS

```
shutdown [ -h ¦ -r ] [ -fqs ] [ now ¦ hh:ss ¦ +mins ]
reboot [ -h ¦ -r ] [ -fqs ] [ now ¦ hh:ss ¦ +mins ]
fastboot [ -h ¦ -r ] [ -fqs ] [ now ¦ hh:ss ¦ +mins ]
halt [ -h ¦ -r ] [ -fqs ] [ now ¦ hh:ss ¦ +mins ]
fasthalt [ -h ¦ -r ] [ -fqs ] [ now ¦ hh:ss ¦ +mins ]
```

## DESCRIPTION

In general, shutdown prepares the system for a power down or reboot. An absolute or delta time can be given, and periodic messages will be sent to all users warning of the shutdown.

halt is the same as shutdown -h -q now.

fasthalt is the same as shutdown -h -q -f now.

reboot is the same as `shutdown -r -q now`.

fastboot is the same as `shutdown -r -q -f now`.

The default delta time, if none is specified, is two minutes.

Five minutes before shutdown (or immediately, if shutdown is less than five minutes away), the `/etc/nologin` file is created with a message stating that the system is going down and that logins are no longer permitted. The `login`(1) program will not allow non-superusers to log in during this period. A message will be sent to all users at this time.

When the shutdown time arrives, `shutdown` notifies all users, tells `init`(8) not to spawn more `getty`(8)s, writes the shutdown time into the `/var/log/wtmp` file, kills all other processes on the system, `sync`(2)s, unmounts all the disks, `sync`(2)s again, waits for a second, and then either terminates or reboots the system.

## OPTIONS

| | |
|---|---|
| `-h` | Halt the system. Do not reboot. This option is used when powering down the system. |
| `-r` | Reboot the system. |
| `-f` | Fast. When the system is rebooted, the filesystems will not be checked. This is arranged by creating `/fastboot`, which `/etc/rc` must detect (and delete). |
| `-q` | Quiet. This uses a default broadcast message and does not prompt the user for one. |
| `-s` | Reboot in single-user mode. This is arranged by creating `/etc/singleboot`, which `simpleinit`(8) detects (and deletes). |

## FILES

`/etc/rc`

`/fastboot`

`/etc/singleboot`

`/etc/nologin`

`/var/log/wtmp`

## SEE ALSO

`umount`(8), `login`(1), `reboot`(2), `simpleinit`(8), `init`(8)

## BUGS

Unlike the BSD shutdown, users are notified of shutdown only once or twice, instead of many times, and at shorter and shorter intervals as "apocalypse approaches."

## AUTHOR

`poe@daimi.aau.dk`. Modified by `jrs@world.std.com`.

*Linux 0.99, 20 November 1993*

# simpleinit

simpleinit—Process control initialization.

## SYNOPSIS

`init [ single ]`

## DESCRIPTION

init is invoked as the last step in the Linux boot sequence. If the single option is used, or if the file /etc/singleboot exists, then single-user mode will be entered, by starting /bin/sh. If the file /etc/securesingle exists, then the root password will be required to start single-user mode. If the root password does not exist; or if /etc/passwd does not exist, the checking of the password will be skipped.

If the file /cto/TZ exists, then the contents of that file will be read and used to set the TZ environment variable for each process started by simpleinit. This "feature" is only available if it's configured at compile time. It's not usually needed.

After single-user mode is terminated, the /etc/rc file is executed, and the information in /etc/inittab will be used to start processes.

While init is running, several signals are trapped with special action taken. Because init has PID 1, sending signals to the init process is easy with the kill(1) command.

If init catches a SIGHUP (hangup) signal, the /etc/inittab will be read again. If init catches a SIGTSTP (terminal stop) signal, no more processes will be spawned. This is a toggle, which is reset if init catches another SIGTSTP signal.

If init catches a SIGINT (interrupt) signal, init will sync a few times and try to start reboot. Failing this, init will execute the system reboot(2) call. Under Linux, it is possible to configure the Ctrl+Alt+Del sequence to send a signal to init instead of rebooting the system.

## THE inittab FILE

Because of the number of init programs that are appearing in the Linux community, the documentation for the /etc/inittab file, which is usually found with the inittab(5) man page, is presented here:

The format is

```
ttyline:termcap-entry:getty-command
```

An example follows:

```
tty1:console:/sbin/getty 9600 tty1
tty2:console:/sbin/getty 9600 tty2
tty3:console:/sbin/getty 9600 tty3
tty4:console:/sbin/getty 9600 tty4
# tty5:console:/sbin/getty 9600 tty5
# ttyS1:dumb:/sbin/getty 9600 ttyS1
# ttyS2:dumb:/sbin/getty -m -t60 2400 ttyS2
```

Lines beginning with the # character are treated as comments. Please see documentation for the getty(8) command that you are using because there are several of these in the Linux community at this time.

## FILES

/etc/inittab

/etc/singleboot

/etc/securesingle

/etc/TZ

/etc/passwd

/etc/rc

## SEE ALSO

inittab(5), ctrlaltdel(8) reboot(8), termcap(5), getty(8), agetty(8), shutdown(8)

## BUGS

This program is called `simpleinit` to distinguish it from the System V compatible versions of `init` that are starting to appear in the Linux community. `simpleinit` should be linked to, or made identical with, `init` for correct functionality.

## AUTHOR

Peter Orbaek (`poe@daimi.aau.dk`), version 1.20, with patches for single-user mode by Werner Almesberger.

*Linux 0.99, 20 November 1993*

# slattach

`slattach`—Attach a network interface to a serial line.

## SYNOPSIS

`slattach [-v] [-p proto] [-s speed] [tty]`

## DESCRIPTION

`slattach` is a little program that can be used to put a normal terminal ("serial") line into one of several "network" modes, thus allowing you to use it for point-to-point links to other computers.

## OPTIONS

| | |
|---|---|
| `[-v]` | Enable debugging output. Useful when determining why a given setup doesn't work. |
| `[-p proto]` | Set a specific kind of protocol to use on the line. The default is set to `cslip`, compressed SLIP. Other possible values are `slip` (normal SLIP), `ppp` (Point-to-Point Protocol), and `kiss` (AX.25 TNC protocol). |
| `[-s speed]` | Set a specific line speed other than the default. |
| | If no arguments are given, the current terminal line (usually the login device) is used. Otherwise, an attempt is made to claim the indicated terminal port, lock it, and open it. |

## FILES

`/dev/cua*`

## BUGS

None so far.

## AUTHOR

Fred N. van Kempen (`waltje@uwalt.nl.mugnet.org`)

*20 September 1993*

# sliplogin

`sliplogin`—Attach a serial line network interface.

## SYNOPSIS

`sliplogin [loginname]`

## DESCRIPTION

`sliplogin` is used to turn the terminal line on standard input into a serial line IP SLIP link to a remote host. To do this, the program searches the file for an entry matching *loginname* (which defaults to the current login name if omitted). If a matching entry is found, the line is configured appropriately for slip (8-bit transparent I/O) and converted to slip line discipline. Then a shell script is invoked to initialize the slip interface with the appropriate local and remote IP address, netmask, and so on.

The usual initialization script is /etc/slip/slip.lgin, but if particular hosts need special initialization, the file /etc/slip/slip.login.loginname will be executed instead if it exists. The script is invoked with the parameters

| | |
|---|---|
| slipunit | The unit number of the slip interface assigned to this line, such as 0 for sl0. |
| speed | The speed of the line. |
| args | The arguments from the entry, in order starting with *loginname*. |

Only the superuser can attach a network interface. The interface is automatically detached when the other end hangs up or the sliplogin process dies. If the kernel slip module has been configured for it, all routes through that interface will also disappear at the same time. If there is other processing a site wants done upon hangup, the file /etc/slip/slip.logout or /etc/slip/slip.logout.loginname is executed if it exists. It is given the same arguments as the login script.

## FORMAT OF /etc/slip.hosts

Comments (lines starting with a #) and blank lines are ignored. Other lines must start with a *loginname*, but the remaining arguments can be whatever is appropriate for the file that will be executed for that name. Arguments are separated by whitespace and follow normal sh(1) quoting conventions (however, *loginname* cannot be quoted). Usually, lines have the form *loginname local-address remote-address netmask opt-args*. *local-address* and *remote-address* are the IP hostnames or addresses of the local and remote ends of the slip line, and *netmask* is the appropriate IP netmask. These arguments are passed directly to ifconfig(8). *opt-args* are optional arguments used to configure the line.

## EXAMPLE

The normal use of sliplogin is to create a entry for each legal, remote slip site with sliplogin as the shell for that entry, such as

Sfoo:ikhuy6:2010:1:slip line to foo:/tmp:/usr/sbin/sliplogin.

(Our convention is to name the account used by remote host hostname as Shostname.) Then an entry is added that looks like

Sfoo 'hostname' foo netmask

'hostname' will be evaluated by sh to the local hostname and *netmask* is the local host IP netmask.

Note that sliplogin must be setuid to root, and although it's not a security hole, moral defectives can use it to place terminal lines in an unusable state or deny access to legitimate users of a remote slip line. To prevent this, a site can create a group, say slip, that only the slip login accounts are put in and then make sure that /sbin/sliplogin is in group slip and mode 4550 (setuid root, only group slip can execute binary).

## DIAGNOSTICS

sliplogin logs various information to the system log daemon, syslogd(8), with a facility code of daemon. The messages are listed here, grouped by severity level.

*Error Severity*

| | |
|---|---|
| ioctl (TCGETS): *reason* | A TCGETS ioctl to get the line parameters failed. |
| ioctl (TCSETS): *reason* | A TCSETS ioctl to set the line parameters failed. |
| /etc/slip.hosts: *reason* | The file could not be opened. |
| access denied for user | No entry for user was found in /etc/slip/slip.hosts |

*Notice Severity*

| | |
|---|---|
| "attaching slip unit" *unit for* *loginname SLIP unit* | Unit was successfully attached. |

## SEE ALSO

slattach(8), syslogd(8)

## HISTORY

The sliplogin command is currently in beta test.

*5 August 1991*

# swapon, swapoff

swapon, swapoff—Enable/disable devices and files for paging and swapping.

## SYNOPSIS

```
/sbin/swapon -a
/sbin/swapon specialfile ...
/sbin/swapoff -a
/sbin/swapoff specialfile ...
```

## DESCRIPTION

swapon is used to specify devices on which paging and swapping are to take place. Calls to swapon usually occur in the system multiuser initialization file /etc/rc making all swap devices available, so that the paging and swapping activity is interleaved across several devices and files.

Usually, the first form is used:

-a                                      All devices marked as sw swap devices in /etc/fstab are made available.

swapoff disables swapping on the specified devices and files or on all swap entries in /etc/fstab when the -a flag is given.

## SEE ALSO

swapon(2), swapoff(2), fstab(5), init(8), mkswap(8), rc(8), mount(8)

## FILES

| | |
|---|---|
| /dev/hd[ab]? | Standard paging devices |
| /dev/sd[ab]? | Standard (SCSI) paging devices |
| /etc/fstab | ASCII filesystem description table |

## HISTORY

The swapon command appeared in 4.0 BSD.

## AUTHORS

See the Linux mount(8) man page for a complete author list. Primary contributors include Doug Quale, H.J. Lu, Rick Sladkey, and Stephen Tweedie.

*Linux 0.99, 27 November 1993*

# sync

sync—Flush Linux filesystem buffers.

## SYNOPSIS

sync

## DESCRIPTION

sync executes sync(2), which flushes the filesystem buffers to disk. sync should be called before the processor is halted in an unusual manner (before causing a kernel panic when debugging new kernel code). In general, the processor should be halted using the reboot(8) or halt(8) commands, which attempt to put the system in a quiescent state before calling sync(2).

From Linus: "Note that sync is only guaranteed to schedule the dirty blocks for writing: It can actually take a short time before all the blocks are finally written. If you are doing the sync with the expectation of killing the machine soon after, please take this into account and sleep for a few seconds. (The reboot(8) command takes these precautions.)"

## SEE ALSO

sync(2), update(8), reboot(8), halt(8)

## AUTHOR

Linus Torvalds (torvalds@cs.helsinki.fi)

*Linux 0.99, 20 November 1993*

# sysklogd

sysklogd—Linux system logging utilities.

## DESCRIPTION

sysklogd provides two system utilities, which provide support for system logging and kernel message trapping. Support of both inetd and UNIX domain sockets enables this utility package to support both local and remote logging.

System logging is provided by a version of syslogd derived from the stock BSD sources. Support for kernel logging is provided by the klogd utility, which allows kernel logging to be conducted in either a stand-alone fashion or as a client of syslogd.

Although the syslogd sources have been heavily modified, a couple of notes are in order. First of all, there has been a systematic attempt to ensure that syslogd follows standard BSD behavior as its default. The second important concept to note is that this version of syslogd interacts transparently with the version of syslog found in the standard libraries. If a binary linked to the standard shared libraries fails to function correctly, we want an example of the anomalous behavior.

## CONFIGURATION FILE SYNTAX DIFFERENCES

syslogd uses a slightly different syntax for its configuration file from that of the original BSD sources. Originally, all messages of a specific priority and above were forwarded to the log file.

For example, the following line caused all output from the daemon facilities to go into /usr/adm/daemons:

```
# Sample syslog.conf
daemon.debug /usr/adm/daemons
```

Under the new scheme, this behavior remains the same. The difference is the addition of two new wildcard specifiers: the asterisk (*) and the equals sign (=). The * specifies that all messages for the indicated facility are to be directed to the destination. Note that this behavior is degenerate with specifying a priority level of debug. Users have indicated that the asterisk notation is more intuitive.

The = wildcard is used to restrict logging to the specified priority class. This allows, for example, routing only debug messages to a particular logging source.

For example, the following line in syslog.conf directs debug messages from all sources to the /usr/adm/debug file:

```
# Sample syslog.conf
daemon.=debug /usr/adm/debug
```

This may take some acclimatization for those individuals used to the pure BSD behavior, but testers have indicated that this syntax is somewhat more flexible than the BSD behavior. Note that these changes should not affect standard `syslog.conf` files. You must specifically modify the configuration files to obtain the enhanced behavior.

## SUPPORT FOR REMOTE LOGGING

These modifications provide network support to the `syslogd` facility. Network support means that messages can be forwarded from one node running `syslogd` to another node running `syslogd` where they will be actually logged to a disk file.

The strategy is to have `syslogd` listen on a UNIX domain socket for locally generated log messages. This behavior will allow `syslogd` to interoperate with the `syslog` found in the standard C library. At the same time, `syslogd` listens on the standard `syslog` port for messages forwarded from other hosts. To have this work correctly, the services files (typically found in `/usr/etc/inet`) must have the following entry:

```
syslog 514/udp
```

To cause messages to be forwarded to another host, replace the normal file line in the `syslog.conf` file with the name of the host to which the messages is to be sent prepended with an @.

For example, to forward all messages to a remote host, use the following `syslog.conf` entry:

```
# Sample syslogd configuration file to
# messages to a remote host forward all.
.*  @hostname
```

To forward all kernel messages to a remote host, the configuration file is

```
# Sample configuration file to forward all kernel
# messages to a remote host.
kern.*  @hostname
```

## OUTPUT TO NAMED PIPES (FIFOS)

This version of `syslogd` has support for logging output to named pipes (FIFOs). A FIFO or named pipe can be used as a destination for log messages by prepending a | to the name of the file. This is handy for debugging. Note that the FIFO must be created with the `mkfifo` command before `syslogd` is started.

The following configuration file routes debug messages from the kernel to a FIFO:

```
# Sample configuration to route kernel debugging
# messages ONLY to /usr/adm/debug which is a
# named pipe.
kern.=debug  |/usr/adm/debug
```

## INSTALLATION CONCERNS

There is probably one important consideration when installing this version of `syslogd`. This version of `syslogd` is dependent on proper formatting of messages by the `syslog` function. The functioning of the `syslog` function in the shared libraries changed somewhere in the region of `libc.so.4.[2-4].n`. The specific change was to null-terminate the message before transmitting it to the `/dev/log` socket. Proper functioning of this version of `syslogd` is dependent on null-termination of the message.

This problem will typically manifest itself if old statically linked binaries are being used on the system. Binaries using old versions of the `syslog` function will cause empty lines to be logged, followed by the message with the first character in the message removed. Relinking these binaries to newer versions of the shared libraries will correct this problem.

## SECURITY THREATS

There is the potential for the `syslogd` daemon to be used as a conduit for a denial of service attack. Thanks go to John Morrison (`jmorriso@rflab.ee.ubc.ca`) for alerting me to this potential. A rogue programmer could very easily flood the `syslogd` daemon with `syslog` messages resulting in the log files consuming all the remaining space on the filesystem.

Activating logging over the inet domain sockets will of course expose a system to risks outside of programs or individuals on the local machine.

Version 1.2 of the utility set will address this problem. In the meantime, there are a number of methods for protecting a machine:

1. Logging can be directed to an isolated or non-root filesystem, which, if filled, will not impair the machine.
2. The ext2 filesystem can be used, which can be configured to limit a certain percentage of a filesystem to usage by root only. Note that this will require syslogd to be run as a non-root process. Also note that this will prevent usage of remote logging because syslogd will be unable to bind to the 514/UDP socket.
3. Disabling inet domain sockets will limit risk to the local machine.
4. Use Step 3 and if the problem persists and is not secondary to a rogue program or daemon, get a 3.5 foot (approximately 1 meter) length of sucker rod and have a chat with the user in question. A sucker rod is 3/4-, 7/8-, or 1-inch hardened steel rod, male threaded on each end. Its primary use in the oil industry in Western North Dakota and other locations is to pump-suck oil from oil wells. Secondary uses are for the construction of cattle feed lots and for dealing with the occasional recalcitrant or belligerent individual.

## FILES

/etc/syslog.conf

## BUGS

Primarily, security concerns will be addressed in version 1.2.

## SEE ALSO

klogd(1)

## COLLABORATORS

Dr. Greg Wettstein (greg%wind.uucp@plains.nodak.edu)
Enjellic Systems Development
Oncology Research Division Computing Facility
Roger Maris Cancer Center
Fargo, ND

Stephen Tweedie
Department of Computer Science
Edinburgh University, Scotland

Juha Virtanen
(jiivee@hut.fi)

Shane Alderton
(shane@scs.apana.org.au)

*Version 1.1, 28 January 1994*

# syslogd

syslogd—Log systems messages.

## SYNOPSIS

syslogd [-f *config_file*] [-m *mark_interval*] [-p *log_socket*]

## DESCRIPTION

syslogd reads and logs messages to the system console, log files, and other machines or users as specified by its configuration file. The options are as follows:

| | |
|---|---|
| -f | Specify the pathname of an alternate configuration file; the default is /etc/syslog.conf. |
| -m | Select the number of minutes between "mark" messages; the default is 20 minutes. |
| -p | Specify the pathname of an alternate log socket; the default is /dev/log. |

syslogd reads its configuration file when it starts up and whenever it receives a hangup signal. For information on the format of the configuration file, see syslog.conf(5).

syslogd reads messages from the UNIX domain socket /dev/log, from an Internet domain socket specified in /etc/services, and from the special device /dev/klog (to read kernel messages).

syslogd creates the file /var/run/syslog.pid and stores its process ID there. This can be used to kill or reconfigure syslogd.

The message sent to syslogd should consist of a single line. The message can contain a priority code, which should be a preceding decimal number in angle braces, such as <5>. This priority code should map into the priorities defined in the include file <sys/syslog.h>.

## FILES

| | |
|---|---|
| /etc/syslog.conf | The configuration file |
| /var/run/syslog.pid | The process ID of current syslogd |
| /dev/log | Name of the UNIX domain datagram log socket |
| /dev/klog | The kernel log device |

## SEE ALSO

logger(1), syslog(3), services(5), syslog.conf(5)

## HISTORY

The syslogd command appeared in BSD 4.3.

*BSD 4.2, 16 March 1991*

# talkd

talkd—Remote user communication server.

## SYNOPSIS

talkd

## DESCRIPTION

talkd is the server that notifies a user that someone else wants to initiate a conversation. It acts a repository of invitations, responding to requests by clients who want to rendezvous to hold a conversation. In normal operation, a client, the caller, initiates a rendezvous by sending a CTL MSG to the server of type LOOK UP (see protocols/talkd.h). This causes the server to search its invitation tables to check if an invitation currently exists for the caller (to speak to the callee specified in the message). If the lookup fails, the caller then sends an ANNOUNCE message, causing the server to broadcast an announcement on the callee's login ports requesting contact. When the callee responds, the local server uses the recorded invitation to respond with the appropriate rendezvous address and the caller and callee client programs establish a stream connection through which the conversation takes place.

## SEE ALSO

talk(1), write(1)

## HISTORY

The `talkd` command appeared in BSD 4.3.

*BSD 4.3, 16 March 1991*

# telnetd

`telnetd`—DARPA Telnet protocol server.

## SYNOPSIS

`/etc/telnetd [-debug [port]] [-l][-D options][-D report]`
`[-D exercise][-D netdata] [-D ptydata]`

## DESCRIPTION

`telnetd` is a server that supports the DARPA standard Telnet virtual terminal protocol. `telnetd` is invoked by the Internet server (see inetd(8)), usually for requests to connect to the Telnet port as indicated by the /etc/services file (see services(5)). If desired the `-debug` can be used, to start up `telnetd` manually, instead of through inetd(8). If started up this way, *port* may be specified to run `telnetd` on an alternate TCP port number.

The `-D` option can be used for debugging purposes. This allows Telnet to print debugging information to the connection, allowing the user to see what `telnetd` is doing. There are several modifiers: *options* prints information about the negotiation of Telnet options, *report* prints the options information, plus some additional information about what processing is going on, *netdata* displays the data stream received by `telnetd`, *ptydata* displays data written to the pty, and *exercise* has not been implemented yet.

`telnetd` operates by allocating a pseudo-terminal device (see pty(4)) for a client) and then creating a login process that has the slave side of the pseudo-terminal as stdin, stdout, and stderr. `telnetd` manipulates the master side of the pseudo-terminal, implementing the Telnet protocol and passing characters between the remote client and the login process.

When a Telnet session is started, `telnetd` sends Telnet options to the client side, indicating a willingness to do a remote echo of characters, to suppress go ahead, to do remote flow control, and to receive terminal type information, terminal speed information, and window size information from the remote client. If the remote client is willing, the remote terminal type is propagated in the environment of the created login process. The pseudo-terminal allocated to the client is configured to operate in cooked mode and with XTABS and CRMOD enabled (see tty(4)).

`telnetd` is willing to do echo, binary, suppress go ahead, and timing mark. `telnetd` is willing to have the remote client do linemode, binary, terminal type, terminal speed, window size, toggle flow control, environment, X display location, and suppress go ahead.

If the file /etc/issue.net is present, `telnetd` will show its contents before the login prompt of a Telnet session (see issue.net(5)).

## SEE ALSO

telnet(1), issue.net(5)

## BUGS

Some Telnet commands are only partially implemented.

Because of bugs in the original 4.2 BSD telnet(1), `telnetd` performs some dubious protocol exchanges to try to discover if the remote client is, in fact, a 4.2 BSD telnet(1).

Binary mode has no common interpretation except between similar operating systems (UNIX, in this case).

The terminal type name received from the remote client is converted to lowercase. `telnetd` never sends Telnet go ahead commands.

*20 April 1991*

# tftpd

`tftpd`—DARPA Trivial File Transfer Protocol server.

## SYNOPSIS

`tftpd [`*directory* `...]`

## DESCRIPTION

`tftpd` is a server that supports the DARPA Trivial File Transfer Protocol. The TFTP server operates at the port indicated in the `tftp` service description; see `services(5)`. The server is usually started by `inetd(8)`.

The use of `tftp(1)` does not require an account or password on the remote system. Due to the lack of authentication information, `tftpd` will allow only publicly readable files to be accessed. Files may be written only if they already exist and are publicly writable. Note that this extends the concept of public to include all users on all hosts that can be reached through the network; this may not be appropriate on all systems, and its implications should be considered before enabling the `tftp` service. The server should have the user ID with the lowest possible privilege.

## SEE ALSO

`tftp(1)`, `inetd(8)`

## HISTORY

The `tftpd` command appeared in BSD 4.2.

*BSD 4.2, 13 May 1991*

# timed

`timed`—Time server daemon.

## SYNOPSIS

`timed [-M] [-t] [-d] [-i` *network*`] [-n` *network*`] [-F` *host1 host2* `...]`

## DESCRIPTION

`timed` is a time server daemon and is usually invoked at boot time from the `rc(8)` file. It synchronizes the host's time with the time of other machines in a local area network running `timed(8)`. These time servers will slow down the clocks of some machines and speed up the clocks of others to bring them to the average network time. The average network time is computed from measurements of clock differences using the ICMP timestamp request message.

The service provided by `timed` is based on a master-slave scheme. When `timed(8)` is started on a machine, it asks the master for the network time and sets the host's clock to that time. After that, it accepts synchronization messages periodically sent by the master and calls `adjtime(2)` to perform the needed corrections on the host's clock.

It also communicates with `date(1)` to set the date globally and with `timedc(8)`, a timed control program. If the machine running the master crashes, then the slaves elect a new master from among slaves running with the `-M` flag. A `timed` running without the `-M` or `-F` flags remains a slave. The `-t` flag enables `timed` to trace the messages it receives in the file `/var/log/timed.log`. Tracing can be turned on or off by the program `timedc(8)`. The `-d` flag is for debugging the daemon. It causes the program to not put itself into the background. Usually, `timed` checks for a master time server on each network to which it is connected, except as modified by the options. It requests synchronization service from the first master server located. If permitted by the -M flag, it provides synchronization service on any attached networks on which no current master server is detected. Such a server propagates the time computed by the top-level master. The -n flag, followed by the name of a network that the host is connected to (see networks(5)), overrides the default choice of the network addresses made by the program. Each time the -n flag appears, that network name is added to a list of valid networks. All other networks are ignored. The -i flag, followed by the name of a network to which the host is connected (see networks(5)), overrides the default choice of the network addresses made by the program. Each time the -i flag appears, that network name is added to a list of networks to ignore. All other networks are used by the time daemon. The -n and -i flags are meaningless if used together.

timed checks for a master time server on each network to which it is connected, except as modified by the -n and -i options. If it finds masters on more than one network, it chooses one network on which to be a "slave" and then periodically checks the other networks to see if the masters there have disappeared.

One way to synchronize a group of machines is to use an NTP daemon to synchronize the clock of one machine to a distant standard or a radio receiver and -F hostname to tell its timed daemon to trust only itself.

Messages printed by the kernel on the system console occur with interrupts disabled. This means that the clock stops while they are printing. A machine with many disk or network hardware problems and consequent messages cannot keep good time by itself. Each message typically causes the clock to lose a dozen milliseconds. A time daemon can correct the result.

Messages in the system log about machines that failed to respond usually indicate machines that crashed or were turned off. Complaints about machines that failed to respond to initial time settings are often associated with "multi-homed" machines that looked for time masters on more than one network and eventually chose to become a slave on the other network.

## WARNING

If two or more time daemons, whether timed, NTP, try to adjust the same clock, temporal chaos will result. If both this and another time daemon are run on the same machine, ensure that the -F flag is used, so that timed never attempts to adjust the local clock.

The protocol is based on UDP/IP broadcasts. All machines within the range of a broadcast that are using the TSP protocol must cooperate. There cannot be more than a single administrative domain using the -F flag among all machines reached by a broadcast packet. Failure to follow this rule is usually indicated by complaints concerning "untrusted" machines in the system log.

## FILES

/var/log/timed.log tracing file for timed

/var/log/timed.masterlog log file for master timed

## SEE ALSO

date(1), adjtime(2), gettimeofday(2), icmp(4), timedc(8), "TSP: The Time Synchronization Protocol for UNIX 4.3 BSD," R. Gusella, S. Zatti.

## HISTORY

The timed daemon appeared in BSD 4.3.

*BSD 4.3, 11 May 1993*

# timedc

timedc—Timed control program.

## SYNOPSIS

timedc [*command*] [*argument ...*]

## DESCRIPTION

timedc is used to control the operation of the timed(8) program. It may be used to

> Measure the differences between machines' clocks
>
> Find the location where the master time server is running
>
> Enable or disable tracing of messages received by timed
>
> Perform various debugging actions

Without any arguments, timedc will prompt for commands from the standard input. If arguments are supplied, timedc interprets the first argument as a command and the remaining arguments as parameters to the command. The standard input may be redirected, causing timedc to read commands from a file. Commands may be abbreviated; recognized commands are

| | |
|---|---|
| ? [*command* ...] | |
| help [*command* ...] | Print a short description of each command specified in the argument list or, if no arguments are given, a list of the recognized commands. |
| clockdiff *host* ... | Compute the differences between the clock of the host machine and the clocks of the machines given as arguments. |
| msite [*host* ...] | Show the master time server for specified hosts. |
| trace {on ¦ off} | Enable or disable the tracing of incoming messages to timed in the file. |
| election host | Asks the daemon on the target host to reset its "election" timers and to ensure that a time master has been elected. |

quit Exit from timedc

Other commands may be included for use in testing and debugging timed; the help command and the program source may be consulted for details.

## FILES

/var/log/timed.log tracing file for timed

/var/log/timed.masterlog log file for master timed

## SEE ALSO

date(1), adjtime(2), icmp(4), timed(8), "TSP: The Time Synchronization Protocol for UNIX 4.3 BSD," R. Gusella, S. Zatti.

## DIAGNOSTICS

| | |
|---|---|
| ?Ambiguous command | Abbreviation matches more than one command |
| ?Invalid command | No match found |
| ?Privileged command | Command can be executed by root only |

## HISTORY

The timedc command appeared in BSD 4.3.

*BSD 4.3, 11 May 1993*

# traceroute

traceroute—Print the route that packets take to the network host.

## SYNOPSIS

traceroute [-m *max_ttl*] [-n] [-p *port*] [-q *nqueries*]
[-r] [-s *src_addr*] [-t *tos*] [-w *waittime*] host [*packetsize*]

## DESCRIPTION

The Internet is a large and complex aggregation of network hardware, connected together by gateways. Tracking the route one's packets follow (or finding the miscreant gateway that's discarding your packets) can be difficult. traceroute utilizes the IP protocol time-to-live field and attempts to elicit an ICMP TIME_EXCEEDED response from each gateway along the path to some host.

The only mandatory parameter is the destination hostname or IP number. The default probe datagram length is 38 bytes, but this can be increased by specifying a packet size (in bytes) after the destination hostname.

Other options are

| | |
|---|---|
| -m *maxttl* | Set the max time-to-live (max number of hops) used in outgoing probe packets. The default is 30 hops (the same default used for TCP connections). |
| -n | Print hop addresses numerically rather than symbolically and numerically (saves a nameserver address-to-name lookup for each gateway found on the path). |
| -p *port* | Set the base UDP port number used in probes (default is 33434). traceroute hopes that nothing is listening on UDP ports base to base + nhops -1 at the destination host (so an ICMP PORT_UNREACHABLE message will be returned to terminate the route tracing). If something is listening on a port in the default range, this option can be used to pick an unused port range. |
| -q *nqueries* | Set the number of probes per ttl to *nqueries* (default is three probes). |
| -r | Bypass the normal routing tables and send directly to a host on an attached network. If the host is not on a directly attached network, an error is returned. This option can be used to ping a local host through an interface that has no route through it (for example, after the interface was dropped by routed(8)). |
| -s *src_addr* | Use the following IP address (which must be given as an IP number, not a hostname) as the source address in outgoing probe packets. On hosts with more than one IP address, this option can be used to force the source address to be something other than the IP address of the interface the probe packet is sent on. If the IP address is not one of this machine's interface addresses, an error is returned and nothing is sent. |
| -t *tos* | Set the type-of-service in probe packets to the following value (default zero). The value must be a decimal integer in the range 0 to 255. This option can be used to see if different types of service result in different paths. (If you are not running a BSD 4.3 tahoe or later system, this may be academic because the normal network services such as Telnet and FTP don't let you control the TOS). Not all values of TOS are legal or meaningful; see the IP spec for definitions. Useful values are probably (low delay) and (high throughput). |
| -v | Verbose output. Received ICMP packets other than TIME_EXCEEDED and UNREACHABLEs are listed. |
| -w | Set the time (in seconds) to wait for a response to a probe (default is 3 seconds). |

This program attempts to trace the route an IP packet would follow to some Internet host by launching UDP probe packets with a small ttl (time to live) and then listening for an ICMP "time exceeded" reply from a gateway. We start our probes with a ttl of one and increase by one until we get an ICMP "port unreachable" (which means we got to "host") or hit a max (which defaults to 30 hops and can be changed with the -m flag). Three probes (changed with the -q flag) are sent at each ttl setting and a line is printed showing the ttl, address of the gateway, and round-trip time of each probe. If the probe answers come from different gateways, the address of each responding system will be printed. If there is no response within a three second time-out interval (changed with the -w flag), a * is printed for that probe.

We don't want the destination host to process the UDP probe packets, so the destination port is set to an unlikely value (if some clod on the destination is using that value, it can be changed with the -p flag).

A sample use and output might be

```
[yak 71]% traceroute nis.nsf.net.
traceroute to nis.nsf.net (35.1.1.48), 30 hops max,
        56 byte packet
 1  helios.ee.lbl.gov (128.3.112.1)  19 ms  19 ms  0 ms
 2  lilac-dmc.Berkeley.EDU (128.32.216.1)  39 ms  39 ms  19 ms
 3  lilac-dmc.Berkeley.EDU (128.32.216.1)  39 ms  39 ms  19 ms
 4  ccngw-ner-cc.Berkeley.EDU (128.32.136.23)  39 ms  40 ms  39 ms
 5  ccn-nerif22.Berkeley.EDU (128.32.168.22)  39 ms  39 ms  39 ms
 6  128.32.197.4 (128.32.197.4)  40 ms  59 ms  59 ms
 7  131.119.2.5 (131.119.2.5)  59 ms  59 ms  59 ms
 8  129.140.70.13 (129.140.70.13)  99 ms  99 ms  80 ms
 9  129.140.71.6 (129.140.71.6)  139 ms  239 ms  319 ms
10  129.140.81.7 (129.140.81.7)  220 ms  199 ms  199 ms
11  nic.merit.edu (35.1.1.48)  239 ms  239 ms  239 ms
```

Note that Lines 2 and 3 are the same. This is due to a buggy kernel on the second hop system—lbl-csam.arpa—that forwards packets with a zero ttl (a bug in the distributed version of 4.3 BSD). Note that you have to guess what path the packets are taking cross-country because the NSFNet (129.140) doesn't supply address-to-name translations for its NSSs.

A more interesting example is

```
[yak 72]% traceroute allspice.lcs.mit.edu.
traceroute to allspice.lcs.mit.edu (18.26.0.115), 30 hops max
 1  helios.ee.lbl.gov (128.3.112.1)  0 ms  0 ms  0 ms
 2  lilac-dmc.Berkeley.EDU (128.32.216.1)  19 ms  19 ms  19 ms
 3  lilac-dmc.Berkeley.EDU (128.32.216.1)  39 ms  19 ms  19 ms
 4  ccngw-ner-cc.Berkeley.EDU (128.32.136.23)  19 ms  39 ms  39 ms
 5  ccn-nerif22.Berkeley.EDU (128.32.168.22)  20 ms  39 ms  39 ms
 6  128.32.197.4 (128.32.197.4)  59 ms  119 ms  39 ms
 7  131.119.2.5 (131.119.2.5)  59 ms  59 ms  39 ms
 8  129.140.70.13 (129.140.70.13)  80 ms  79 ms  99 ms
 9  129.140.71.6 (129.140.71.6)  139 ms  139 ms  159 ms
10  129.140.81.7 (129.140.81.7)  199 ms  180 ms  300 ms
11  129.140.72.17 (129.140.72.17)  300 ms  239 ms  239 ms
12  * * *
13  128.121.54.72 (128.121.54.72)  259 ms  499 ms  279 ms
14  * * *
15  * * *
16  * * *
17  * * *
18  ALLSPICE.LCS.MIT.EDU (18.26.0.115)  339 ms  279 ms  279 ms
```

Note that the gateways 12, 14, 15, 16, and 17 hop away. Either don't send ICMP "time exceeded" messages or send them with a ttl too small to reach us. Lines 14–17 are running the MIT C Gateway code that doesn't send "time exceeded"s. God only knows what's going on with 12.

The silent gateway 12 may be the result of a bug in the 4.[23] BSD network code (and its derivatives): 4.x (x <= 3) sends an unreachable message using whatever ttl remains in the original datagram. Because for gateways the remaining ttl is zero, the ICMP "time exceeded" is guaranteed to not make it back to us. The behavior of this bug is slightly more interesting when it appears on the destination system:

```
 1  helios.ee.lbl.gov (128.3.112.1)  0 ms  0 ms  0 ms
 2  lilac-dmc.Berkeley.EDU (128.32.216.1)  39 ms  19 ms  39 ms
 3  lilac-dmc.Berkeley.EDU (128.32.216.1)  19 ms  39 ms  19 ms
 4  ccngw-ner-cc.Berkeley.EDU (128.32.136.23)  39 ms  40 ms  19 ms
 5  ccn-nerif35.Berkeley.EDU (128.32.168.35)  39 ms  39 ms  39 ms
 6  csgw.Berkeley.EDU (128.32.133.254)  39 ms  59 ms  39 ms
 7  ***
 8  ***
```

```
9  ***
10  * * *
11  * * *
12  * * *
13  rip.Berkeley.EDU (128.32.131.22)  59 ms !  39 ms !  39 ms
!
```

Notice that there are 12 "gateways" (13 is the final destination) and exactly the last half of them are "missing." What's really happening is that rip (a Sun-3 running Sun OS3.5) is using the ttl from our arriving datagram as the ttl in its ICMP reply. The reply will time out on the return path (with no notice sent to anyone because ICMPs aren't sent for ICMPs) until we probe with a ttl that's at least twice the path length. That is, rip is really only seven hops away. A reply that returns with a ttl of 1 is a clue this problem exists. traceroute prints a ! after the time if the ttl is less than or equal to 1. Because vendors ship a lot of obsolete (DEC Ultrix, Sun 3.*x*) or non-standard HPUX software, expect to see this problem frequently or take care picking the target host of your probes. Other possible annotations after the time are !H, !N, !P (got a host, network, or protocol unreachable), !S, or !F (source route failed or fragmentation needed—neither of these should ever occur and the associated gateway is busted if you see one). If almost all the probes result in some kind of unreachable, traceroute will give up and exit.

This program is intended for use in network testing, measurement, and management. It should be used primarily for manual fault isolation. Because of the load it could impose on the network, it is unwise to use traceroute during normal operations or from automated scripts.

## AUTHOR

Implemented by Van Jacobson from a suggestion by Steve Deering. Debugged by a cast of thousands with particularly cogent suggestions or fixes from C. Philip Wood, Tim Seaver, and Ken Adelman.

## SEE ALSO

netstat(1), ping(8)

*BSD 4.3, 6 June 1993*

# tune2fs

tune2fs—Adjust tunable filesystem parameters on second extended filesystems.

## SYNOPSIS

```
tune2fs [ -l ][-c max-mount-counts ][-e errors-behavior ]
[-i interval-between-checks ][ -m reserved-blocks-percentage ]
[-r reserved-blocks-count ][-u user ][-g group ]device
```

## DESCRIPTION

tune2fs adjusts tunable filesystem parameters on a Linux second extended filesystem.

Never use tune2fs on a read/write mounted filesystem to change parameters!

## OPTIONS

| | |
|---|---|
| -c *max-mount-counts* | Adjust the maximal mounts count between two filesystem checks. |
| -e *errors-behavior* | Change the behavior of the kernel code when errors are detected. *errors-behavior* can be one of the following: |

| | |
|---|---|
| continue | Continue normal execution. |
| remount-ro | Remount the filesystem read-only. |
| panic | Causes a kernel panic. |

| | |
|---|---|
| -g *group* | Set the user group that can benefit from the reserved blocks. *group* can be a numerical GID or a group name. |
| -i *interval-between-checks*[d¦m¦w] | Adjust the maximal time between two filesystem checks. No postfix or d results in days, m in months, and w in weeks. A value of 0 will disable the time-dependent checking. |
| -l | List the contents of the filesystem superblock. |
| -m *reserved-blocks-percentage* | Adjust the reserved blocks percentage on the given device. |
| -r *reserved-blocks-count* | Adjust the reserved blocks count on the given device. |
| -u *user* | Set the user who can benefit from the reserved blocks. *user* can be a numerical UID or a username. |

## BUGS

We didn't find any bugs. Perhaps there are bugs, but it's unlikely.

## WARNING

Use this utility at your own risk. You're modifying filesystems.

## AUTHOR

tune2fs was written by Remy Card (card@masi.ibp.fr), the developer and maintainer of the ext2 filesystem. tune2fs uses the ext2fs library written by Theodore T'so (tytso@mit.edu). This manual page was written by Christian Kuhtz (chk@data-hh.Hanse.DE). Time-dependent checking was added by Uwe Ohse (uwe@tirka.gun.de).

## AVAILABILITY

tune2fs is available for anonymous FTP from ftp.ibp.fr and tsx-11.mit.edu in /pub/linux/packages/ext2fs.

## SEE ALSO

dumpe2fs(8), e2fsck(8), mke2fs(8)

*Version 0.5b, November 1994*

# tunelp

tunelp—Set various parameters for the lp device.

## SYNOPSIS

```
tunelp device [-i IRQ ¦ -t TIME ¦ -c CHARS
¦ -w WAIT ¦ -a [on¦off] ¦ -o [on¦off] ¦ -C [on¦off]
¦ -r ¦ -s ¦ -q [on¦off] ]
```

## DESCRIPTION

tunelp sets several parameters for the /dev/lp? devices, for better performance (or for any performance at all, if your printer won't work without it…). Without parameters, tunelp tells whether the device is using interrupts, and if so, which one. With parameters, tunelp sets the device characteristics accordingly. The parameters are as follows:

| | |
|---|---|
| -i <*IRQ*> | The IRQ to use for the parallel port in question. If this is set to something nonzero, -t and -c have no effect. If your port does not use interrupts, this option will make printing stop. tunelp -i 0 restores non-interrupt driven (polling) action, and your printer should work again. If your parallel port does support interrupts, interrupt-driven printing should be somewhat faster and efficient and will probably be desirable. |
| -t <*TIME*> | The amount of time in jiffies that the driver waits if the printer doesn't take a character for the number of tries dictated by the -c parameter. 10 is the default value. If you want the fastest possible printing and don't care about system load, you can set this to 0. If |

you don't care how fast your printer goes or are printing text on a slow printer with a buffer, then 500 (5 seconds) should be fine and will give you very low system load. This value generally should be lower for printing graphics than text, by a factor of approximately 10, for best performance.

-c <CHARS>    The number of times to try to output a character to the printer before sleeping for -t <TIME>. It is the number of times around a loop that tries to send a character to the printer. 120 appears to be a good value for most printers. 250 is the default because there are some printers that require a wait this long, but feel free to change this. If you have a very fast printer like an HP Laserjet 4, a value of 10 might make more sense. If you have a really old printer, you can increase this.

Setting -t <TIME> to 0 is equivalent to setting -c <CHARS> to infinity.

-w <WAIT>    The busy loop counter for the strobe signal. Although most printers appear to be able to deal with an extremely short strobe, some printers demand a longer one. Increasing this from the default 0 might make it possible to print with those printers. This can also make it possible to use longer cables.

-a [on¦off]    This is whether to abort on printer error; the default is not to. If you are sitting at your computer, you probably want to be able to see an error and fix it and have the printer go on printing. On the other hand, if you aren't, you might rather that your printer spooler find out that the printer isn't ready, quit trying, and send you mail about it. The choice is yours.

-o [on¦off]    This option is much like -a. It makes any open() of this device check to see that the device is online and not reporting any out-of-paper or other errors. This is the correct setting for most versions of lpd.

-C [on¦off]    This option adds extra ("careful") error checking. When this option is on, the printer driver will ensure that the printer is online and not reporting any out-of-paper or other errors before sending data. This is particularly useful for printers that usually appear to accept data when turned off.

-s    This option returns the current printer status, both as a decimal number from 0 to 255 and as a list of active flags. When this option is specified, -q off, turning off the display of the current IRQ, is implied.

-o, -C, and -s all require a Linux kernel version of 1.1.76 or later.

-r    This option resets the port. It requires a Linux kernel version of 1.1.80 or later.

-q [on¦off]    This option sets printing the display of the current IRQ setting.

*Cohesive Systems, 26 August 1992*

# update_state

update_state—Update system state.

## SYNOPSIS

update_state

## DESCRIPTION

update_state updates a bunch of system states. It takes a long time to execute and would be suitable for execution in a cron job.

Currently, update_state performs the following functions: updates the locate database (in /usr/lib/locate), updates the whatis database(in /usr/man, /usr/local/man, /usr/X386/man, and /usr/interviews/man), and updates the TeX 1s-R cache file (in /usr/lib/texmf).

## BUGS

The script expects things to be where the FSSTND says they are. For example, if you have makewhatis(8) in /usr/lib, where it is traditionally, then you lose, because it should be in /usr/bin.

## SEE ALSO

cron(8), find(1), locate(1)

## AUTHOR

Rik Faith (faith@cs.unc.edu)

*Linux 1.0 8, July 1994*

# uucico

uucico—UUCP file transfer daemon.

## SYNOPSIS

uucico [ *options* ]

## DESCRIPTION

The uucico daemon processes file transfer requests queued by uucp(1) and uux(1). It is started when uucp or uux is run (unless they are given the -r option). It is also typically started periodically using entries in the crontab tables.

When invoked with -r1, --master, -s, --system, or -S, the daemon will place a call to a remote system, running in master mode. Otherwise, the daemon will start in slave mode, accepting a call from a remote system. Typically, a special login name will be set up for UUCP, which automatically invokes uucico when a call is made.

When uucico terminates, it invokes the uuxqt(8) daemon, unless the -q or --nouuxqt option is given; uuxqt(8) executes any work orders created by uux(1) on a remote system and any work orders created locally that have received remote files for which they were waiting.

If a call fails, uucico will usually refuse to retry the call until a certain (configurable) amount of time has passed. This may be overridden by the -f, -force, or -S option.

The -1, --prompt, -e, or --loop options may be used to force uucico to produce its own prompts of login: and Password:. When another daemon calls in, it will see these prompts and log in as usual. The login name and password are usually checked against a separate list kept specially for uucico rather than the /etc/passwd file; it is possible on some systems to direct uucico to use the /etc/passwd file. The -1 or -prompt option will prompt once and then exit; in this mode, the UUCP administrator or the superuser may use the -u or -login option to force a login name, in which case uucico will not prompt for one. The -e or -loop option will prompt again after the first session is over; in this mode, uucico will permanently control a port.

If uucico receives a SIGQUIT, SIGTERM, or SIGPIPE signal, it will cleanly abort any current conversation with a remote system and exit. If it receives a SIGHUP signal, it will abort any current conversation, but will continue to place calls to (if invoked with -r1 or --master) and accept calls from (if invoked with -e or --loop) other systems. If it receives a SIGINT signal, it will finish the current conversation but will not place or accept any more calls.

## OPTIONS

The following options may be given to uucico:

| | |
|---|---|
| -r1, ---master | Start in master mode (call out to a system); implied by -s, --system, or -S. If no system is specified, call any system for which work is waiting to be done. |
| -r0, ---slave | Start in slave mode. This is the default. |
| -s *system*, ---system *system* | Call the named system. |

| | |
|---|---|
| -S system | Call the named system, ignoring any required wait. This is equivalent to -s system -f. |
| -f, ---force | Ignore any required wait for any systems to be called. |
| -l, ---prompt | Prompt for login name and password using login: and Password:. This allows uucico to be easily run from inetd(8). The login name and password are checked against the UUCP password file, which probably has no connection to the file /etc/passwd. The --login option may be used to force a login name, in which case uucico will only prompt for a password. |
| -p port, ---port port | Specify a port to call out on or to listen to. |
| -e, ---loop | Enter endless loop of login/password prompts and slave mode daemon execution. The program will not stop by itself; you must use kill(1) to shut it down. |
| -w, ---wait | After calling out (to a particular system when -s, --system, or -S is specified or to all systems that have work when just -r1 or --master is specified), begin an endless loop as with --loop. |
| -q, ---nouuxqt | Do not start the uuxqt(8) daemon when finished. |
| -c, ---quiet | If no calls are permitted at this time, then don't make the call, but also do not put an error message in the log file and do not update the system status (as reported by uustat(1)). This can be convenient for automated polling scripts, which may want to simply attempt to call every system rather than worry about which particular systems may be called at the moment. This option also suppresses the log message indicating that there is no work to be done. |
| -C, ---ifwork | Only call the system named by -s, --system, or -S if there is work for that system. |
| -D, ---nodetach | Do not detach from the controlling terminal. Normally, uucico detaches from the terminal before each call out to another system and before invoking uuxqt. This option prevents this. |
| -u name, ---login name | Set the login name to use instead of that of the invoking user. This option may only be used by the UUCP administrator or the superuser. If used with --prompt, this will cause uucico to prompt only for the password, not the login name. |
| -z, ---try-next | If a call fails after the remote system is reached, try the next alternate rather than simply exiting. |
| -i type, ---stdin type | Set the type of port to use when using standard input. The only support port type is TLI, and this is only available on machines that support the TLI networking interface. Specifying -iTLI causes uucico to use TLI calls to perform I/O. |
| -x type, -X type, ---debug type | Turn on particular debugging types. The following types are recognized: abnormal, chat, handshake, uucp-proto, proto, port, config, spooldir, execute, incoming, outgoing. |
| | Multiple types may be given, separated by commas, and the --debug option may appear multiple times. A number may also be given, which will turn on that many types from the foregoing list; for example, --debug 2 is equivalent to --debug abnormal,chat. |
| | The debugging output is sent to the debugging file, usually one of /usr/spool/uucp/Debug, /usr/spool/uucp/DEBUG, or /usr/spool/uucp/.Admin/audit.local. |
| -I file, ---config file | Set configuration file to use. This option may not be available, depending on how uucico was compiled. |
| -v, ---version | Report version information and exit. |
| --help | Print a help message and exit. |
| -u login | This option is ignored. It is only included because some versions of uucpd invoke uucico with it. |

## FILES

The filenames may be changed at compilation time or by the configuration file, so these are only approximations:

| | |
|---|---|
| /usr/lib/uucp/config | Configuration file. |
| /usr/lib/uucp/passwd | Default UUCP password file. |

| | |
|---|---|
| /usr/spool/uucp | UUCP spool directory. |
| /usr/spool/uucp/Log | UUCP log file. |
| /usr/spool/uucppublic | Default UUCP public directory. |
| /usr/spool/uucp/Debug | Debugging file. |

## SEE ALSO

kill(1), uucp(1), uux(1), uustat(1), uuxqt(8)

## AUTHOR

Ian Lance Taylor (ian@airs.com)

*Taylor UUCP 1.05*

# vmstat

vmstat—Report virtual memory statistics.

## SYNOPSIS

vmstat [ -n ] [ *delay* [ *count* ] ]

## DESCRIPTION

vmstat reports information about processes, memory, paging, block IO, traps, and CPU activity.

The first report produced gives averages since the last reboot. Additional reports give information on a sampling period of length delay. The process and memory reports are instantaneous in either case.

## OPTIONS

The -n switch causes the header to be displayed only once rather than periodically.

*delay* is the delay between updates in seconds. If no delay is specified, only one report is printed with the average values since boot.

*count* is the number of updates. If no count is specified and *delay* is defined, *count* defaults to infinity.

## FIELD DESCRIPTIONS

*Procs*

| | |
|---|---|
| r | The number of processes waiting for runtime. |
| b | The number of processes in uninterruptible sleep. |
| w | The number of processes swapped out but otherwise runnable. This field is calculated, but Linux never desperation swaps. |

*Memory*

| | |
|---|---|
| swpd | The amount of virtual memory used (KB). |
| free | The amount of idle memory (KB). |
| buff | The amount of memory used as buffers (KB). |

*Swap*

| | |
|---|---|
| si | Amount of memory swapped in from disk (KB/s). |
| so | Amount of memory swapped to disk (KB/s). |

*IO*

| | |
|---|---|
| bi | Blocks sent to a block device (blocks/s). |
| bo | Blocks received from a block device (blocks/s). |

*System*

| | |
|---|---|
| in | The number of interrupts per second, including the clock. |
| cs | The number of context switches per second. |

*CPU (These are percentages of total CPU time.)*

| | |
|---|---|
| us | User time. |
| sy | System time. |
| id | Idle time. |

## NOTES

vmstat does not require special permissions.

These reports are intended to help identify system bottlenecks. Linux vmstat does not count itself as a running process.

All Linux blocks are currently 1KB, except for CD-ROM blocks, which are 2KB.

## FILES

```
/proc/meminfo
/proc/stat
/proc/*/stat
```

## SEE ALSO

ps(1), top(1), free(1)

## BUGS

vmstat does not tabulate the block IO per device or count the number of system calls.

## AUTHOR

Written by Henry Ware (al172@yfn.ysu.edu)

*Throatwobbler Ginkgo Labs, 27 July 1994*

# vipw

vipw—Edit the password file.

## SYNOPSIS

vipw

## DESCRIPTION

vipw edits the password file after setting the appropriate locks and does any necessary processing after the password file is unlocked. If the password file is already locked for editing by another user, vipw will ask you to try again later. The default editor for vipw is vi(1).

## ENVIRONMENT

If the following environment variable exists, it will be utilized by vipw:

EDITOR                          The editor specified by the string. EDITOR will be invoked instead of the default editor
                                vi(1).

## SEE ALSO

passwd(1), vi(1), passwd(5)

## HISTORY

The vipw command appeared in BSD 4.0.

BSD 4, 16 March 1991

# zdump

zdump—Time zone dumper.

## SYNOPSIS

zdump [ -v ][-c *cutoffyear* ] [ *zonename* ... ]

## DESCRIPTION

zdump prints the current time in each *zonename* named on the command line.

These options are available:

-v                              For each *zonename* on the command line, print the current time, the time at the lowest
                                possible time value, the time one day after the lowest possible time value, the times both
                                one second before and exactly at each detected time discontinuity, the time at one day
                                less than the highest possible time value, and the time at the highest possible time value.
                                Each line ends with isdst=1 if the given time is Daylight Saving Time or isdst=0
                                otherwise.

-c *cutoffyear*                 Cut off the verbose output near the start of the given year.

## SEE ALSO

newctime(3), tzfile(5), zic(8)

# zic

zic—Time zone compiler.

## SYNOPSIS

zic [ -v ][-d *directory* ][-l *localtime* ][-p *posixrules* ]
[-L *leapsecondfilename* ][-s ] [ -y *command* ][*filename* ... ]

## DESCRIPTION

zic reads text from the files named on the command line and creates the time conversion information files specified in this
input. If a filename is -, the standard input is read.

These options are available:

-d *directory*                  Create time conversion information files in the named directory rather than in the
                                standard directory named below.

| | |
|---|---|
| `-l timezone` | Use the given time zone as local time. `zic` will act as if the input contained a link line of the form. |
| | `Link timezone localtime.` |
| `-p timezone` | Use the given time zone's rules when handling POSIX-format time zone environment variables. `zic` will act as if the input contained a link line of the form. |
| | `Link timezone posixrules.` |
| `-L leapsecondfilename` | Read leap second information from the file with the given name. If this option is not used, no leap second information appears in output files. |
| `-v` | Complain if a year that appears in a data file is outside the range of years representable by `time(2)` values. |
| `-s` | Limit time values stored in output files to values that are the same whether they're taken to be signed or unsigned. You can use this option to generate SVVS-compatible files. |
| `-y command` | Use the given command rather than `yearistype` when checking year types. |

Input lines are made up of fields. Fields are separated from one another by any number of whitespace characters. Leading and trailing whitespace on input lines is ignored. An unquoted sharp character (#) in the input introduces a comment that extends to the end of the line the sharp character appears on. Whitespace characters and sharp characters may be enclosed in double quotes (") if they're to be used as part of a field. Any line that is blank (after comment stripping) is ignored. Non-blank lines are expected to be of one of three types: rule lines, zone lines, and link lines.

A rule line has the form

```
Rule NAME FROM TO TYPE IN ON AT SAVE LETTER/S
```

For example:

```
Rule US 1967 1973 - Apr lastSun 2:00 1:00 D
```

The fields that make up a rule line are

| | |
|---|---|
| `NAME` | Gives the (arbitrary) name of the set of rules this rule is part of. |
| `FROM` | Gives the first year in which the rule applies. Any integer year can be supplied; the Gregorian calendar is assumed. The word `minimum` (or an abbreviation) means the minimum year representable as an integer. The word `maximum` (or an abbreviation) means the maximum year representable as an integer. Rules can describe times that are not representable as time values, with the unrepresentable times ignored; this allows rules to be portable among hosts with differing time value types. |
| `TO` | Gives the final year in which the rule applies. In addition to minimum and maximum, the word `only` (or an abbreviation) may be used to repeat the value of the `FROM` field. |
| `TYPE` | Gives the type of year in which the rule applies. If `TYPE` is -, the rule applies in all years between `FROM` and `TO` inclusive. If `TYPE` is something else, then `zic` executes the command |
| | `yearistype year type` |
| | to check the type of a year. An exit status of zero is taken to mean that the year is of the given type; an exit status of one is taken to mean that the year is not of the given type. |
| `IN` | Names the month in which the rule takes effect. Month names may be abbreviated. |
| `ON` | Gives the day on which the rule takes effect. Recognized forms include |

| | |
|---|---|
| `5` | The fifth of the month |
| `lastSun` | The last Sunday in the month |
| `lastMon` | The last Monday in the month |
| `Sun>=8` | First Sunday on or after the eighth |
| `Sun<=25` | Last Sunday on or before the 25th |
| | Names of days of the week may be abbreviated or spelled out in full. Note that there must be no spaces within the `ON` field. |

| | |
|---|---|
| AT | Gives the time of day at which the rule takes effect. Recognized forms include |

| | |
|---|---|
| 2 | Time in hours |
| 2:00 | Time in hours and minutes |
| 15:00 | 24-hour format time (for times after noon) |
| 1:28:14 | Time in hours, minutes, and seconds |

Any of these forms may be followed by the letter w if the given time is local wall clock time, s if the given time is local standard time, or u (or g or z) if the given time is universal time; in the absence of an indicator, wall clock time is assumed.

| | |
|---|---|
| SAVE | Gives the amount of time to be added to local standard time when the rule is in effect. This field has the same format as the AT field (although, of course, the w and s suffixes are not used). |
| LETTER/S | Gives the variable part (for example, the S or D in EST or EDT) of time-zone abbreviations to be used when this rule is in effect. If this field is -, the variable part is null. |

A zone line has the form

```
Zone NAME GMTOFF RULES/SAVE FORMAT [UNTIL]
```

For example:

```
Zone Australia/Adelaide 9:30 Aus CST 1971 Oct 31 2:00
```

The fields that make up a zone line are

| | |
|---|---|
| NAME | The name of the time zone. This is the name used in creating the time conversion information file for the zone. |
| GMTOFF | The amount of time to add to GMT to get standard time in this zone. This field has the same format as the AT and SAVE fields of rule lines; begin the field with a minus sign if time must be subtracted from GMT. |
| RULES/SAVE | The name of the rules that apply in the time zone or, alternately, an amount of time to add to local standard time. If this field is -, standard time always applies in the time zone. |
| FORMAT | The format for time zone abbreviations in this time zone. The pair of characters %s is used to show where the variable part of the time-zone abbreviation goes. Alternately, a slash (/) separates standard and daylight abbreviations. |
| UNTIL | The time at which the GMT offset or the rules change for a location. It is specified as a year, a month, a day, and a time of day. If this is specified, the time-zone information is generated from the given GMT offset and rule change until the time specified. |
| | The next line must be a continuation line; this has the same form as a zone line except that the string Zone and the name are omitted because the continuation line will place information starting at the time specified as the UNTIL field in the previous line in the file used by the previous line. Continuation lines may contain an UNTIL field, just as zone lines do, indicating that the next line is a further continuation. |

A link line has the form

```
Link LINK-FROM LINK-TO
```

For example:

```
Link US/Eastern EST5EDT
```

The LINK-FROM field should appear as the NAME field in some zone line; the LINK-TO field is used as an alternate name for that zone.

Except for continuation lines, lines may appear in any order in the input.

Lines in the file that describe leap seconds have the following form:

```
Leap YEAR MONTH DAY HH:MM:SS CORR R/S
```

For example:

```
Leap 1974 Dec 31 23:59:60 + S
```

The YEAR, MONTH, DAY, and HH:MM:SS fields tell when the leap second happened. The CORR field should be + if a second was added or - if a second was skipped. The R/S field should be (an abbreviation of) Stationary if the leap second time given by the other fields should be interpreted as GMT or (an abbreviation of) Rolling if the leap second time given by the other fields should be interpreted as local wall clock time.

## NOTE

For areas with more than two types of local time, you may need to use local standard time in the AT field of the earliest transition time's rule to ensure that the earliest transition time recorded in the compiled file is correct.

## FILE

/usr/local/etc/zoneinfo standard directory used for created files.

## SEE ALSO

newctime(3), tzfile(5), zdump(8)

# Part IX:

# Kernel Reference Guide

# add_timer, del_timer, init_timer

add_timer, del_timer, init_timer—Manage event timers.

## SYNOPSIS

```
#include <asm/param.h>
#include <linux/timer.h>
extern void add_timer(struct timer_list * timer);
extern int del_timer(struct timer_list * timer);
extern inline void init_timer(struct timer_list * timer);
```

## DESCRIPTION

add_timer schedules an event, adding it to a linked list of events maintained by the kernel. del_timer deletes a scheduled event. *timer* points to a

```
struct timer_list {
struct timer_list *next;
struct timer_list *prev;
unsigned long expires;
unsigned long data;
void (*function)(unsigned long);
};
```

init_timer sets *next* and *prev* to NULL. This is required for the argument of add_timer. *expires* is the desired duration of the timer in jiffies, where there are HZ (typically 100) jiffies per second. When the timer expires, *function* is called with *data* as its argument. It is the responsibility of function to delete the event. If the same function is managing several timers, the argument can be used to distinguish which one expired.

## RETURN VALUE

del_timer returns zero on error—if *next* or *prev* are not NULL, but the timer was not found. del_timer also sets *expires* to the time remaining before the timer expires and sets *next* and *prev* to NULL. Thus, calling del_timer followed immediately by add_timer is a no-op provided a kernel tick does not occur between the two calls.

## AUTHOR

Linus Torvalds

*Linux 1.2.8, 31 May 1995*

# adjust_clock

adjust_clock—Adjusts startup time counter to tick in GMT.

## SYNOPSIS

```
linux/kernel/sys.c
void adjust_clock();
```

## DESCRIPTION

This routine adjusts the startup time by adding the time zone information to it. The goal is to get the startup time ticking in GMT time.

## NOTES

This routine is called from settimeofday(2) when the time-zone information is first set.

## AUTHOR

Theodore T'so (tytso@mit.edu)

## SEE ALSO

settimeofday(2)

*Linux 0.99.10, 7 July 1993*

# ctrl_alt_del

ctrl_alt_del—Routes the keyboard interrupt Ctrl+Alt+Del key sequence.

## SYNOPSIS

```
linux/kernel/sys.c
void ctrl_alt_del(void);
```

## DESCRIPTION

This simple routine tests the variable C_A_D for a true/false condition. If it is true, a hard reset is done by the system. Otherwise, a signal SIGINT is sent to the process with the process ID 1, usually a program called init.

## WARNINGS

This routine is in interrupt mode. It cannot sync() your system. Data loss may occur. It is recommended that you configure your system to send a signal to init, where you can control the shutdown.

## NOTES

The default of this function is to do hard resets immediately.

## AUTHOR

Linus Torvalds

## SEE ALSO

reboot(2), reset_hard_now(9), sync(2)

*Linux 0.99.10, 6 July 1993*

# file_table

file_table—Detailed description of the table and table entry.

## SYNOPSIS

From #include <linux/fs.h>

```
struct file {
mode_t f_mode;
dev_t f_rdev; /* needed for /dev/tty */
off_t f_pos;
unsigned short f_flags;
unsigned short f_count;
unsigned short f_reada;
struct file *f_next, *f_prev;
struct inode *f_inode;
```

```
struct file_operations *f_op;
};
```

From linux/fs/file_table.c

```
struct file *first_file;
int nr_files = 0;
```

## DESCRIPTION

The file table is fundamentally important to any UNIX system. It is where all open files (Linux includes closed files as well) are stored and managed by the kernel. For Linux, you can hardly do anything without referencing it in some way.

Linux stores its file table as a double circular linked list. The root pointer to the "head" of this list is first_file. Also, a count of how many entries are in the file table is maintained, called nr_files. Under this scheme, the file table for Linux could be as large as memory could hold. Unfortunately, this would be unmanageable in most cases. Your computer would be in the kernel most of the time when processes are more important. To keep this from happening, nr_files is tested against NR_FILE to limit the number of file table entries.

### UNDERSTANDING THE STRUCTURE OF THE FILE TABLE

The file table is organized as a double circular linked list. Imagine a circle of people with everyone facing the same direction. Each person is facing so that one arm is in the circle and the other arm is outside the circle. Now, if each person put his or her right hand on the shoulder of the person in front of him or her and if each person touched the person behind him or her with his or her left hand. You have formed two circles of arms, one inside and the other outside. The right arms represent pointers to the next entry (or person). The left arms represent pointers to the previous entry (or person).

### THE FILE STRUCTURE, A FILE TABLE ENTRY

At first glance, a table entry looks quite simple. An entry contains how a file was opened, what tty device, a reference count, pointers to other entries, pointer to v-node (the vfs i-node) filesystem-specific i-node information, and so on.

| | |
|---|---|
| f_mode | After ANDing with 0 ACCMODE, this is what bits 0 and 1 mean: |
| 00 | No permissions needed |
| 01 | Read-permission |
| 10 | Write-permission |
| 11 | Read-write |
| f_rdev | It is used only with tty lines. It contains the major and minor numbers of the tty device. |
| f_pos | The current position in a file, if meaningful. |
| f_flags | Storage for the flags from open() and fcntl() |
| f_count | Reference counter |
| f_reada | This is a Boolean variable where True means that an actual read is needed. |
| f_next, f_prev | Pointers to other entries |
| f_inode | Pointer to v-node and filesystem-specific i-node information |
| f_op | Pointer to a file's operations |

## AUTHOR

Linus Torvalds

## SEE ALSO

insert_file_free(9), remove_file_free(9), put_last_free(9) grow_files(9), file_table_init(9), get_empty_filp(9)

*Linux 0.99.10, 11 July 1993*

# file_table_init

file_table_init—Initializes the file table in the kernel.

## SYNOPSIS

```
linux/fs/file_table.c unsigned long file_table_init(
unsigned long start, unsigned long end);
```

## DESCRIPTION

This routine is called from kernel_start() in linux/init/main.c. It sets first_file, a struct file pointer, to NULL. This is the head of the linked list of open files maintained in the kernel, the infamous file table in all UNIXs.

## RETURN VALUE

Returns start.

## NOTES

Because this is part of the kernel's startup routine, it has the option to allocate memory, in kernel space, for itself. It does not need to do this and returns the new start of memory for the next initializing section. In this case, start is returned unmodified.

## AUTHOR

Linus Torvalds

*Linux 0.99.10, 9 July 1993*

# filesystems

filesystems—Details the table of configured filesystems.

## SYNOPSIS

```
linux/fs/filesystems.c
```

From #include <linux/fs.h>

```
struct file system type {
struct super_block *(*read_super) (struct super_block *, void *, int);
char *name;
int requires dev;
};
```

## DESCRIPTION

This source code makes a data structure call file_systems[], which contains all the configured filesystems for the kernel. It is used primarily in linux/fs/super.c for many of the mounting of filesystems functions.

## THE MEANINGS

This first member, in struct file_system_type, is a function pointer to a routine that will read in the super_block. A super_block generically means an i-node or special place on the device where information about the overall filesystem is stored.

The name is just the string representation of the name of a specific filesystem, such as ext2 or minix.

The final member, int_requires_dev, is a Boolean value. If it is True, then the filesystem requires a block device. For False, it is unclear what happens, but an unnamed device is used, such as proc and nfs.

## AUTHOR

Linus Torvalds

# get_empty_filp

get_empty_filp—Fetches an unreferenced entry from the file table.

## SYNOPSIS

```
linux/fs/file table.c
struct file *get_empty_filp(void);
```

## DESCRIPTION

This routine will seek out an entry that is not being referenced by any processes. If none are found, then it will add new entries to the file table, minimum of NR_FILE entries.

## NOTES

Due to grow_files(), a whole page of entries is created at one time. This may make more than NR_FILE entries. Also when an unreferenced entry is found, it is moved to the "end" of the file table. This heuristic is used to speed up finding unreferenced entries.

## RETURN VALUE

NULL—No entries were found and the file table is full.

Returns a pointer to the entry in the file table.

## AUTHOR

Linus Torvalds

## SEE ALSO

grow_files(9)

# grow_files

grow_files—Adds entries to the file table.

## SYNOPSIS

```
linux/fs/file table.c
void grow_files(void);
```

## DESCRIPTION

This function adds entries to the file table. First, it allocates a page of memory. It fills the entire page with entries, adding each to the file table.

## AUTHOR

Linus Torvalds

## SEE ALSO

insert_file_free(9), remove_file_free(9), put_last_free(9)

*Linux 0.99.10, 12 July 1993*

# in_group_p

in_group_p—Searches group IDs for a match.

## SYNOPSIS

```
linux/kernel/sys.c
int in_group_p(gid_t grp);
```

## DESCRIPTION

Searches supplementary group IDs and the effective group ID for a match with `grp`.

## RETURN VALUE

Returns True (1) if found; otherwise, false (0).

## AUTHOR

Linus Torvalds

## SEE ALSO

getgroups(2), getgid(2), getregid(2), setgid(2), setregid(2), setgroups(2)

*Linux 0.99.10, 7 July 1993*

# insert_file_free

insert_file_free—Adds a file entry into the file table.

## SYNOPSIS

```
linux/fs/file_table.c
static void insert_file_free(struct file *file);
```

## DESCRIPTION

This nightmare of pointers adds `file` into the file table with the root pointer at `file`. This is a building block of the file table management.

## AUTHOR

Linus Torvalds

## SEE ALSO

file_table_init(9), remove_file_free(9), put_last_free(9)

See file_table(9) for details on the file table structure.

*Linux 0.99.10*

# kernel_mktime

kernel_mktime—Convert startup struct mktime into the number of seconds since 00:00:00 January 1, 1970.

## SYNOPSIS

```
linux/kernel/mktime.c
long kernel_mktime(struct mktime * time);
```

## DESCRIPTION

This routine is called from time_init(void), linux/init/main.c. kernel_mktime() converts struct mktime (initialized from CMOS) into an encoded long.

## CONVERSION METHOD

First an array, month[12], is created, holding how many seconds have passed to reach a peculiar month for a leap year. Next, it subtracts 70 from the current year, making 1970 the beginning year. It is math magic after this point; please look yourself. If you know why it does this, then send e-mail (see nroff source).

## RETURN VALUE

Returns the encoded time in a long.

## FILES

linux/kernel/mktime.c home of routine

## NOTES

This routine is called only during startup of the kernel.

Historically, the value (encoded long) counts the number of seconds since the Epoch, which occurred at 00:00:00 January 1, 1970, and is called Coordinated Universal Time (UTC). In older manuals, this event is called Greenwich Mean Time (GMT).

## WARNINGS

kernel_mktime() doesn't check to see if the year is greater than 1969. Be sure your CMOS is set correctly. It is customary to set on-board clocks to GMT and let processes who ask for the time to convert it to local time, if necessary.

## RESTRICTIONS

For kernel use only.

## AUTHOR

Linus Torvalds

*Linux 0.99.10, 5 July 1993*

# proc_sel

proc_sel—Select a process by a criterion.

## SYNOPSIS

```
linux/kernel/sys.c
#include <linux/resource.h>
static int proc_sel(struct task_struct *p, int which, int who);
```

## DESCRIPTION

Compares a task *p* to supplied information or the current task in some aspect of priority. If *who* is zero, the comparison is task *p* and the current task. Otherwise, *who* and *\*p* are the supplied information for the comparison.

## OPTIONS

Valid values of *which*:

| | |
|---|---|
| PRIO_PROCESS | Compares process ID numbers. There is an exception here. If *who* is not zero and task *p* is the current task, then True is always returned. |
| PRIO_PGRP | Compares process group leader numbers. |
| PRIO_USER | Compares user ID numbers. |

## RETURN VALUE

Returns truth values (0, 1).

## AUTHOR

Linus Torvalds

## SEE ALSO

sys_setpriority(2), sys_getpriority(2)

*Linux 0.99.10, 7 July 1993*

# put_file_last

put_file_last—Moves a file to the "end" of the file table.

## SYNOPSIS

```
linux/fs/file table.c
static void put_last_free(struct file *file);
```

## DESCRIPTION

This function will remove *file* from the file table and insert it again at the end. You can access by

first_file->prev

## AUTHOR

Linus Torvalds

## SEE ALSO

insert_file_free(9), remove_file_free(9)

*Linux 0.99.10, 11 July 1993*

# remove_file_free

remove_file_free—Remove a file table entry from the linked list.

## SYNOPSIS

```
linux/fs/file table.c
static void remove_file_free(struct file *file);
```

## DESCRIPTION

This routine removes the file from the table. This is used mostly for moving a file to the "end" of the list.

## AUTHOR

Linus Torvalds

## SEE ALSO

insert_file_free(9), put_file_last(9)

# Index

# Slackware Linux Unleashed, Third Edition

*Kamran Hussain, Timothy Parker, et al.*

Slackware Linux is a 32-bit version of the popular UNIX operating system. In many ways, it enhances the performance of UNIX and UNIX-based applications. Slackware is a free operating system that can be downloaded from the Internet. Because it is free, there is very little existing documentation for the product. This book fills that void and provides Slackware Linux users with the information they need to effectively run the software on their computers or networks.

*Price: $49.99 USA/$70.95 CAN*     *User level: Accomplished–Expert*
*ISBN: 0-672-31012-0*     *1,300 pages*

# Linux Unleashed, Second Edition

*Kamran Hussain, Timothy Parker, et al.*

Readers will turn to this second edition for even more in-depth coverage of hot Linux topics, such as PPPs, networking, and site setup and administration. Programmers, users, and system administrators will rely on this as their most complete reference.

*Price: $49.99 USA/$67.99 CAN*     *User level: Beginning–Intermediate*
*ISBN: 0-672-30908-4*     *1,224 pages*

# Maximum RPM

*Edward C. Bailey*

This is the complete reference for the Red Hat Package Manager (RPM) software package that is the heart of the Red Hat Linux distribution. Designed for both the novice and advanced user, *Maximum RPM* enables anyone to take full advantage of the benefits of building software packages with the package-management tools to ensure that they install simply and accurately each time. Although created by Red Hat, RPM works with all flavors of Linux.

*Price: $39.99 USA/$56.95 CAN*     *User level: Beginning–Advanced*
*ISBN: 0-672-31105-4*     *500 pages*

# TCP/IP Blueprints

*Martin Bligh, Dennis Short, Thomas Lee, et al.*

TCP/IP is the predominant network protocol in use today. *TCP/IP Blueprints* is a comprehensive, indispensable tutorial and reference for anyone working with TCP/IP using the new IP V6 standard. Using real-world, easy-to-understand examples, users will learn how to operate, maintain, debug, and troubleshoot TCP/IP.

*Price: $39.99 USA/$56.95 CAN*     *User level: Accomplished–Expert*
*ISBN: 0-672-31055-4*     *500 pages*

# Add to Your Sams Library Today with the Best Books for Programming, Operating Systems, and New Technologies

## The easiest way to order is to pick up the phone and call

# 1-800-428-5331

### between 9:00 a.m. and 5:00 p.m. EST.

## For faster service please have your credit card available.

| ISBN | Quantity | Description of Item | Unit Cost | Total Cost |
|------|----------|---------------------|-----------|------------|
| 0-672-31012-0 | | Slackware Linux Command Reference | $49.99 | |
| 0-672-30908-4 | | Linux Unleashed, Second Edition | $49.99 | |
| 0-672-31105-4 | | Maximum RPM | $39.99 | |
| 0-672-31055-4 | | TCP/IP Blueprints | $39.99 | |
| | | Shipping and Handling: See information below. | | |
| | | TOTAL | | |

Shipping and Handling: $4.00 for the first book, and $1.75 for each additional book. If you need to have it NOW, we can ship product to you in 24 hours for an additional charge of approximately $18.00, and you will receive your item overnight or in two days. Overseas shipping and handling add $2.00 per book. Prices subject to change. Call for availability and pricing information on latest editions.

**201 W. 103rd Street, Indianapolis, Indiana 46290**

**1-800-428-5331 — Orders    1-800-835-3202 — FAX    1-800-858-7674 — Customer Service**

Book ISBN 0-672-31104-6

# What's on the Disc

The companion CD-ROM for *Linux Complete Command Reference* contains the complete electronic version of this book in .PDF format. We have also included the Adobe Acrobat reader software for your convenience.

# Technical Support

If you need assistance with the information in this book or with the CD-ROM accompanying this book, please access the Knowledge Base on our Web site at http://www.mcp.com/feedback. Our most frequently asked questions are answered there. If you do not find the answers to your questions on our Web site, you can contact Macmillan Technical Support at 317-581-3833 or e-mail us at support@mcp.com.

## NOTE

If you are having difficulties reading our CD-ROM, try to clean the data side of the CD-ROM with a clean, soft cloth. One cause of this problem is dirt disrupting the access of the data on the disc. If the problem still exists, whenever possible, insert this CD-ROM into another computer to determine whether the problem is with the disc or with your CD-ROM drive.

Another common cause of this problem may be that you have outdated CD-ROM drivers. In order to update your drivers, first verify the manufacturer of your CD-ROM drive from your system's documentation. Or, under Windows 95/NT 4.0, you can also check your CD-ROM manufacturer by going to \Settings\Control Panel\System and selecting the Device Manager. Double-click on the CD-ROM option, and you will see the information on the manufacturer of your drive.

You can download the latest drivers from your manufacturer's Web site or from http://www.windows95.com.